GW00598942

PEUGEOT GOLF GUIDE

2002•2003

PEUGEOT

Une sélection du meilleur, pour que le golf soit toujours un plaisir.

Sharing our passion for golf through the Peugeot Challenge Cup, an amateur tournament played in more than 25 countries, giving the best amateur golfers the chance to excel at the Peugeot Classic, sponsoring the prestigious Trophée Lancôme and publishing a guide to the best courses in Europe... these are commitments which all add up to the contribution made by Automobiles Peugeot to the playing of golf worldwide and to the bonding of ties with golfers everywhere.

You will see inside that this guide is a reference work for every golfer and we hope it will help you to enjoy some fantastic courses. Happy reading.

Visit us on www.peugeot-avenue.com and find the latest news about Peugeot and the world of sport.

Faire partager sa passion du golf à travers la Peugeot Challenge Cup, tournoi amateur joué dans plus de 25 pays, donner une chance aux amateurs de haut niveau d'aller plus loin avec le Peugeot Classic, être partenaire du prestigieux Trophée Lancôme et éditer un guide sur les meilleurs golfs d'Europe, sont autant d'actions menées par Automobiles Peugeot pour contribuer au rayonnement du golf dans le monde et se rapprocher de ses amis golfeurs !

Vous trouverez dans ce guide la référence en terme de parcours golfiques et nous espérons qu'il vous permettra de fouler de fabuleux greens ! Bonne lecture.

Rejoignez-nous sur www.peugeot-avenue.com et retrouvez l'actualité de Peugeot dans l'univers du sport !

Peugeot hat eine Leindenschaft für Golf. Sie manifestiert sich im Peugeot Challenge Cup, einem Amateur-Turnier, das in mehr als 25 Ländern gespielt wird, das den besten Amateuren die Chance gibt, ihr Können bei dem Peugeot Classic zu reigen, in der Sponsorship der Trophée Lancôme, einem der Höhepunkte der European PGA Tour, und nicht zuletzt in der Herausgabe dieses Führers zu den besten Plätzen in Europa. Die Aktivitätan von Automobiles Peugeot sollen weltweit den Golfsport fördern und Golfem aus Teilen der Welt zusammen bringen.

Der Führer ist ein Referenzwerk für alle Golfer. Wir hoffen, dass dieser Führer hilft, einige fantastische Golfplätze zu genießen. Viel Spaß beim Lesen.

Besuchen Sie uns im Internet unter www.peugeot-avenue.com Dort finden Sie die neuesten Infos über Peugeot und seine sportlichen Aktivitäten.

A selection of the best for a great round of golf every time.

Peugeot Automobiles delar vår passion för golf, inte minst genom Peugeot Challenge Cup, en amatörtävling som spelas i över 25 länder, för att inte tala om Peugeot Classic, en tävling som ger amatörer chansen att mäta sina krafter med varandra. Dessutom sponsrar Peugeot den prestigetyngda proffstävlingen Trophée Lancôme och sist men inte minst publicerar man denna guide till Europas bästa golfbanor... Detta är åtaganden som Peugeot gör till spelet golf och som får golfare världen över att komma närmare varandra.

När du väl börjar bläddra kommer du snart märka att detta är en bok som alla golfare har stor nytta av och som hjälper dig att njuta av några fantastika golfbanor. Trevlig läsning !

Besök oss på www.peugeot-avenue.com och ta reda på de senaste nyheterna om Peugeot och sportens värld.

Comparte su pasión por el golf con la Peugeot Challenge Cup, torneo amateur que se juega en más de 25 paises; brinda una oportunidad de oro a los amateurs de élite con el Peugeot Classic; apoya el famoso Trofeo Lancôme y edita una guiá de los mejores campos de golf por el mundo así como al encuentro de tantos amigos golfistas.

Esta guía es un instrumento de referencia que, probablemente, le llevará a jugar los greenes más extraordinarios. Esperamos que su lectura le sea muy útil.

Contacten con nosotros en www.peugeot-avenue.com donde encontrarán toda la actualidad de Peugeot relacionada con el universo del deporte.

Condividere la passione del golf attraverso la Peugeot Challenge Cup, un torneo per dilettanti che si gioca in oltre 25 paesi, dare la possibilità ai migliori di andare oltre e distinguersi nel Peugeot Classic, sponsorizzare il presigioso Trofeo Lancôme e pubblicare la guida del migliori golf in Europa. Sono queste le azioni che Peugeot Automobili promuove per diffondere il gioco del golf nel mondo e per avvicinarsi agli amici golfisti !

Siamo certi che questa guida sarà un importante punti di riferimento per ognuno di voi e ci auguriamo che vi conduca a giocare su perscorsi fantastici ! Buona lettura.

Visitate il nostro sito www.peugeot-avenue.com e troverete le ultime notizie su Peugeot nel mondo dello sport !

LACOSTE

LACOSTE
DEVIENS CE QUE TU ES

TIGER'S BALL.

On this side lies the exact same technology played by Tiger Woods: The Tour Accuracy TW. Oh, it's virtually identical to the Tour Accuracy. But Tiger swings faster than the vast majority of humans. So his core

Look around. Wound balls are dying by the dozen. May we suggest an injection-molded, three-piece solid-core ball?

and cover are each 5% firmer, for a lower, flatter ball flight with slightly less spin. Results? Mr. Woods has added a plump 16 yards to his drives, and last year his putting rank leapt from 33rd to second. Find out what it does for your game. Tiger's happy to share.

This package holds both the Tour Accurac
Feel like a comparison test? For

NIKE GOLF

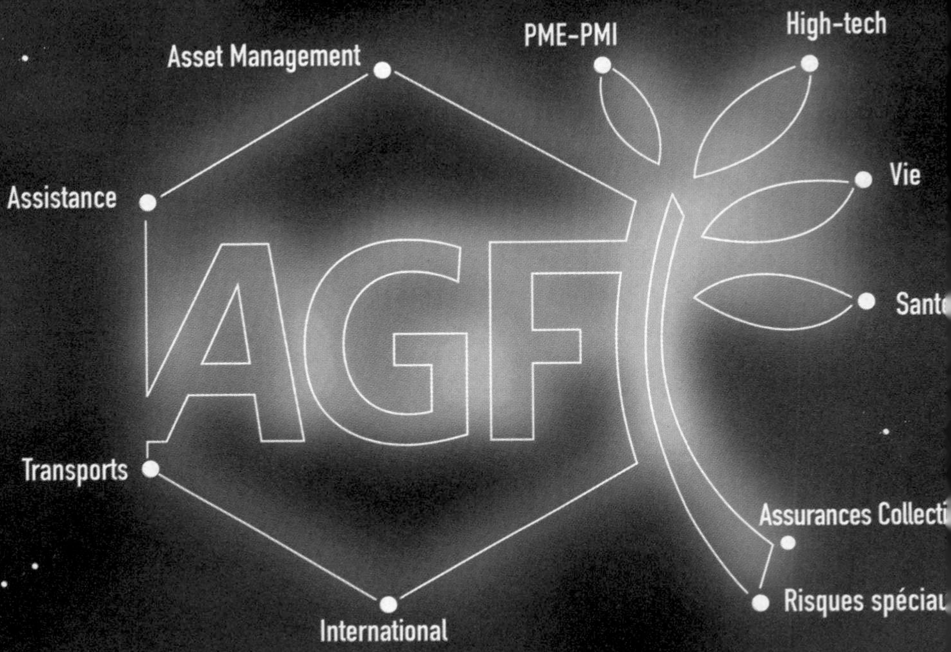

HOW TO USE YOUR PEUGEOT GOLF GUIDE

COMMENT UTILISER LE PEUGEOT GOLF GUIDE
WIE DER PEUGEOT GOLF GUIDE BENUTZT WIRD
SÅ HÄR ANVÄNDER DU PEUGEOT GOLF GUIDE
COMO UTILIZAR SU PEUGEOT GOLF GUIDE
COME USARE LA VOSTRA GOLF GUIDE

RECOMMENDED GOLFING STAY

Séjour de golf recommandé
Estancia de golf recomendada
Estadia de golf recomendada
Rekommenderad golfvistelse
Suositellaan golfin pelaamisen
Empfohlener Golf Aufenthalt
Aanbevolen golf vacantie
Soggiorno golfitistico raccomandato
Anbefalet til golfophold
Anbefalt golfopphold

RECOMMENDED HOLIDAYS

Vacances recommandées
Empfohlener Ferienort
Sitio de vacaciones recomendado
Aanbevolen vacantie-oord
Local de férias recomendado
Località di vacanze raccomandata
Rekommenderad semesterort
Anbefalet som feriested
Suositellaan lomanviettopaikkana
Anbefalt feriested

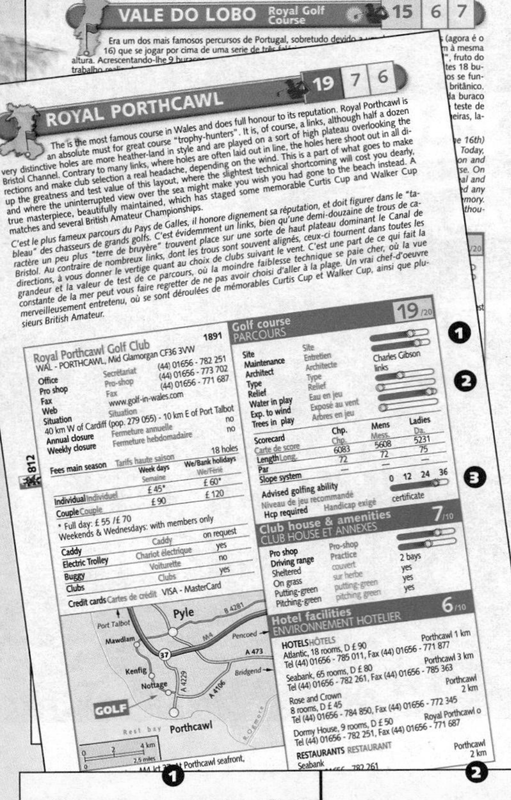

VALE DO LOBO Royal Golf Course 15 | 6 | 7

ROYAL PORTHCAWL 19 | 7 | 6

This is the most famous course in Wales and does full honour to its reputation. Royal Porthcawl is an absolute must for great course "trophy-hunters". It is, of course, a links, although half a dozen very distinctive holes are more heather-land in style and are played on a sort of high plateau overlooking the Bristol Channel. Contrary to many links, where holes are often laid out in line, the holes here shoot out in all directions and make club selection a real headache, depending on the wind. This is a part of what goes to make up the greatness and test value of this layout, where the slightest technical shortcoming will cost you dearly, and where the uninterrupted view over the sea might make you wish you had gone to the beach instead. A true masterpiece, beautifully maintained, which has staged some memorable Curtis Cup and Walker Cup matches and several British Amateur Championships.

C'est le plus fameux parcours du Pays de Galles, il honore dignement sa réputation, et doit figurer dans le "tableau" des chasseurs de grands golfs. C'est évidemment un links, bien qu'une demi-douzaine de trous de caractère un peu plus "terre de bruyère" trouvent place sur une sorte de haut plateau dominant le Canal de Bristol. Au contraire de nombreux links, dont les trous sont souvent alignés, ceux-ci tournent dans toutes les directions, à vous donner le vertige quant au choix de clubs suivant le vent. C'est une part de ce qui fait la grandeur et la valeur de test de ce parcours, où la moindre faiblesse technique se paie cher, où la vue constante de la mer peut vous faire regretter de ne pas avoir choisi d'aller à la plage. Un vrai chef-d'oeuvre merveilleusement entretenu, où se sont déroulées de mémorables Curtis Cup et Walker Cup, ainsi que plusieurs British Amateur.

Royal Porthcawl Golf Club 1891
WAL - PORTHCAWL, Mid Glamorgan CF36 3VW

Office	Secrétariat	(44) 01656 - 782 251
Pro shop	Pro-shop	(44) 01656 - 773 702
Fax	Fax	(44) 01656 - 771 687
Web	www.golf-in-wales.com	
Situation	Situation	40 km W of Cardiff (pop. 279 055) - 10 km E of Port Talbot
Annual closure	Fermeture annuelle	no
Weekly closure	Fermeture hebdomadaire	no

Fees main season / Tarifs haute saison	Week days / Semaine	We/Bank holidays / We/Férié
18 holes		
Individual / Individuel	£ 45*	£ 60*
Couple / Couple	£ 90	£ 120

* Full day: £ 55 /£ 70
Weekends & Wednesdays: with members only

Caddy	Caddy	on request
Electric Trolley	Chariot électrique	yes
Buggy	Voiturette	no
Clubs	Clubs	yes
Credit cards	Cartes de crédit	VISA - MasterCard

Golf course / PARCOURS 19/20

Site	Site	
Maintenance	Entretien	
Architect	Architecte	Charles Gibson
Type	Type	links
Relief	Relief	
Water in play	Eau en jeu	
Exp. to wind	Exposé au vent	
Trees in play	Arbres en jeu	

Scorecard / Carte de score	Chp. / Chp.	Mens / Mess.	Ladies / Da.
Length / Long.	6083	5608	5231
Par	72	72	75
Slope system	—	—	—

Advised golfing ability / Niveau de jeu recommandé: 0 12 24 36
Hcp required / Handicap exigé: certificate

Club house & amenities / CLUB HOUSE ET ANNEXES 7/10

Pro shop	Pro-shop	
Driving range	Practice	
Sheltered	couvert	2 bays
On grass	sur herbe	yes
Putting-green	putting-green	yes
Pitching-green	pitching green	yes

Hotel facilities / ENVIRONNEMENT HOTELIER 6/10

HOTELS HÔTELS
Atlantic, 18 rooms, D £ 90 — Porthcawl 1 km
Tel (44) 01656 - 785 011, Fax (44) 01656 - 771 877
Seabank, 65 rooms, D £ 80 — Porthcawl 3 km
Tel (44) 01656 - 782 261, Fax (44) 01656 - 785 363
Rose and Crown — Porthcawl 2 km
8 rooms, D £ 45
Tel (44) 01656 - 784 850, Fax (44) 01656 - 772 345
Dormy House, 9 rooms, D £ 50 — Royal Porthcawl 0 km
Tel (44) 01656 - 782 251, Fax (44) 01656 - 771 687
RESTAURANTS RESTAURANT
Seabank — Porthcawl 2 km

SCORE FOR THE COURSE (1 TO 20)

Note du parcours (1 à 20)
Benotung des Golfplatzes (1 bis 20)
Nota del campo (1 a 20)
Waardering van de baan (1 tot 20)
Nota do percurso (1 a 20)
Giudizio sul percorso (1 a 20)
Banans betyg (1 till 20)
Klassificering af banen (1 til 20)
Kentän laatuluokitus (1 to 20)
Rangering av golfbanen (1-20)

19

SCORE FOR THE CLUB HOUSE AND ANNEXES (1 TO 10)

Note du Club House et annexes (1 à 10)
Benotung des Klubhauses (1 bis 10)
Nota del Club House (1 a 10)
Waardering van het Club House (1 tot 10)
Nota do Club House (1 a 10)
Giudizio sul Club House (1 a 10)
Klubhus betyg (1 till 10)
Klassificering af Klubhuset (1 til 10)
Klubitalon laatuluokitus (1 to 10)
Rangering av Klubhus (1-10)

7

SCORE FOR HOTEL FACILITIES (1 TO 10)

Note de l'environnement hôtelier (1 à 10)
Benotung des Hotelangebots (1 bis 10)
Nota del complejo hotelero (1 a 10)
Waardering van het Hotel and ongeving (1 tot 10)
Nota das infraestructuras hoteleiras (1 a 10)
Giudizio su offerta alberghiera (1 a 10)
Hotellomgivningens betyg (1 till 10)
Klassificering af hotelfaciliteterne (1 til 10)
Hotellin laatuluokitus (1 to 10)
Rangering av Hotel (1-10)

6

❶ FAIR	EXCELLENT	❷ LITTLE	MUCH	❸ 0 12 24 36 ADVISED GOLFING ABILITY (HCP)
Passable	Excellent	Peu	Beaucoup	Niveau de jeu recommandé
Mittelmässig	Hervorragend	Wenig	Viel	Empfohlene Spielstärke
Mediana	Excelente	Poco	Mucho	Nivel de juego aconselado
Aanvaardboar	Uitstekend	Weinig	Veel	Aanbevolen golfvaardigheid
Suficiente	Excelente	Pouco	Muito	Nivel de jogo recomendado
Passabile	Eccellente	Poco	Molto	Livello di gioco consigliato
Godkänd	Förträfflig	Få	Många	Rekommenderad spelnivå
Rimelig	Fantastik	Lille	Meget	Anbefalet golfkunnen
Hyvä	Erinomainen	Vähän	Paljon	Tasoitusvaatimus
Godbra	Utmerket	Lite	Mye	Anbefalt golfnivå

CONTENTS

	Page
HOW TO USE YOUR GUIDE	13
FOREWORD	21
CLASSIFICATIONS	35
• Classification of golf courses	35
• Architects and courses	52
• Recommended seasons	67
AUSTRIA	75
Selected golf courses	80
BELGIUM AND LUXEMBOURG	91
Selected golf courses	97
DENMARK	119
Selected golf courses	126
FINLAND	141
Selected golf courses	147
FRANCE	157
Selected golf courses	207
GERMANY	351
Selected golf courses	376
GREAT BRITAIN & IRELAND	478
ENGLAND	510
SCOTLAND	687
WALES	790
IRELAND AND NORTHERN IRELAND	817
Selected golf courses	828
ITALY	929
Selected golf courses	943
THE NETHERLANDS	993
Selected golf courses	999
NORWAY	1031
Selected golf courses	1037
PORTUGAL	1047
Selected golf courses	1059
SPAIN	1085
Selected golf courses	1108
SWEDEN	1201
Selected golf courses	1211
SWITZERLAND	1267
Selected golf courses	1273
CZECH REPUBLIC	1297
SLOVENIA	1301
RUSSIA	1302
TURKEY	1303
COURSES IN ALPHABETICAL ORDER WITH CLOSEST INTERNATIONAL AIRPORTS	1307
CURRENCY EXCHANGE TABLE	1342

SOMMAIRE

	Page
COMMENT UTILISER LE GUIDE	13
INTRODUCTION	21
CLASSEMENTS	35
• Classement des parcours	35
• Architectes et parcours	52
• Saisons recommandées	67
AUTRICHE	75
Parcours sélectionnés	80
BELGIQUE ET LUXEMBOURG	91
Parcours sélectionnés	97
DANEMARK	119
Parcours sélectionnés	126
FINLANDE	141
Parcours sélectionnés	147
FRANCE	157
Parcours sélectionnés	207
ALLEMAGNE	351
Parcours sélectionnés	376
GRANDE-BRETAGNE & IRLANDE	478
ANGLETERRE	510
ECOSSE	687
PAYS DE GALLES	790
IRLANDE ET IRLANDE DU NORD	817
Parcours sélectionnés	828
ITALIE	929
Parcours sélectionnés	943
PAYS-BAS	993
Parcours sélectionnés	999
NORVEGE	1031
Parcours sélectionnés	1037
PORTUGAL	1047
Parcours sélectionnés	1059
ESPAGNE	1085
Parcours sélectionnés	1108
SUEDE	1201
Parcours sélectionnés	1211
SUISSE	1267
Parcours sélectionnés	1273
REPUBLIQUE TCHEQUE	1297
SLOVÉNIE	1301
RUSSIE	1302
TURQUIE	1303
CLASSEMENT ALPHABÉTIQUE AVEC LES AEROPORTS INTERNATIONAUX LES PLUS PROCHES	1307
CHANGE DES MONNAIES	1342

INHALT / INNEHÅLL

HOTELS CONSTANCE

Belle Mare Plage
The Resort
MAURITIUS - ILE MAURICE

SUMARIO

SOMMARIO

PEUGEOT GOLF GUIDE
FOREWORD

A TRUE GUIDE

Before the Peugeot Golf Guide came into being there was no such thing as a qualitative guide to golf courses on a full European scale, the way there has always been for hotels or restaurants. Yet as all golf-lovers know, every course is different and standards of excellence vary. Besides the championship courses that owe their fame and reputation to today's wider television coverage, there are a number of unknown courses that are true "gems", public courses that are simpler layouts with ambitions to match, pretentiously labelled but often disappointing "international" courses, and low-budget courses where the architect has worked wonders... Eight years ago, we began to take a long, hard look at golf courses in Europe, putting ourselves very firmly in the shoes of the golfer who pays to play and who expects standards of service to match his or her expectations. Over the past two years we have completed our task because now all European countries have been given consideration whenever, naturally, their courses come up to expectations. This new edition has been completely revised with references to Web sites or with e-mail addresses, the slope system ratings whenever available, even though we do sometimes have misgivings over the results of these assessments, and prices in euros for those countries joining the European single currency.

PRICES IN EUROS

Given our printing deadlines, we have of course been unable to secure final prices in euros, although we have attempted to stay as realistic as possible. Whatever, given the changes in green-fees from one year to the next, you will at least have some idea of current rates for both green fees and hotels.

1,000 SELECTED PUBLIC AND PRIVATE COURSES

Over the past eight years, we have visited and played 1,500 18-hole golf courses. We did so anonymously so we could see them like an ordinary golfer. Of all the courses we played, we selected 1,000 which are the most often open to the public, at least during weekdays. About forty or so of these appear for the first time in this new edition, in which we have also included a few very private courses further to many requests to see how they would fare in our ranking system.

THREE SCORES FOR EACH COURSE

In our ranking system, the score for the course is explicitly given out of 20, while the score for the club-house and facilities and local hotel accommodation are clearly marked out of 10. So to our mind, the actual course score has greater significance while the other marks allows us to tone down the considerable differences seen in golfing and hotel accommodation from one country to the next. On each page you will find the three scores in the top right-hand corner. The first concerns the actual course, the second is for the Club House and facilities, and the third is for surrounding hotel accommodation. A little golfer indicates a recommendation for a few days golfing while a sun recommends a full holiday stay, even though you might not always get much sun. The score given to the Club House and related services is geared to the attractiveness and comfort of the actual buildings and also to practice and additional facilities. Lastly, we assessed the region's hotel facilities. Some highly reputed restaurants were thus selected, as were hotels from different categories. The score expresses not only our opinion of hotels, it also and importantly denotes the extent and range of hotel accommodations within the immediate vicinity of the course.

THE PHILOSOPHY BEHIND THE PEUGEOT GOLF GUIDE

One last word to stress the fact that inaccuracies or errors are bound to creep in when working with such a mass of information. Our goal is to help golfers and also golf courses to raise standards in order to provide ever better service and the best possible course to play on. Their prosperity depends on their reputation and the high standards they maintain. We would like them to think that every green-fee golfer was sent by our Guide.

PEUGEOT GOLF GUIDE
AVANT-PROPOS

UN VÉRITABLE "GUIDE"

Avant le Peugeot Golf Guide, il n'existait aucun guide qualitatif des parcours à l'échelle européenne, contrairement aux guides des hôtels ou des restaurants. Pourtant, comme le savent les amateurs de golf le savent, les parcours sont aussi différents que leur qualité est variable. A côté des parcours de championnat célèbres par la télévision, il est des parcours ignorés qui sont de petits joyaux, des golfs publics au dessin très simple et aux ambitions réduites, des parcours prétentieux mais décevants, des parcours à petit budget où les architectes ont fait des prodiges... Il y a huit ans, nous avons entrepris un travail de fond sur les golfs d'Europe, en se situant résolument du côté de ceux qui paient pour jouer et attendent un service à hauteur de leurs attentes. Depuis deux ans, nous avons "bouclé" notre démarche car tous les pays d'Europe y sont pris en compte, lorsque leurs parcours sont à la hauteur des attentes, bien sûr. Cette nouvelle édition est entièrement révisée, avec les références aux sites Web ou aux adresses E-mail, et les Slope System lorsqu'il étaient disponibles, bien que l'on puisse parfois émettre des réserves sur les résultats des évaluations... et les tarifs en Euro dans les pays qui y ont adhéré.

LES PRIX EN EUROS

Etant donnés les délais d'impression, nous n'avons pas eu bien sûr les tarifs définitifs en Euros, mais nous avons cherché à coller au plus près de la réalité. En tout état de cause, étant donnée la variation des tarifs d'une année sur l'autre, vous disposerez au moins d'un ordre d'idée des tarifs, qu'il s'agisse des green-fees ou des hôtels.

1000 PARCOURS PUBLICS ET PRIVÉS

Nous avons visité et joué 1.500 parcours de 18 trous au cours des huit dernières années de manière anonyme, comme n'importe quel golfeur. Parmi tous ces parcours , nous en avons retenu 1000, le plus souvent ouverts au public, au moins en semaine. Une quarantaine font leur entrée dans cette édition, dans laquelle nous avons aussi inclus quelques parcours très privés, car on nous a beaucoup demandé de les évaluer aussi.

UNE "TRIPLE NOTE"

La note du parcours est exprimée sur 20, les notes relatives au Club-house et à ses équipements, et à l'environnement hôtelier sont clairement indiquées sur 10. Pour nous, la note du parcours est ainsi prépondérante, les autres permettent d'atténuer les fortes différences des installations et de l'hôtellerie d'un pays à l'autre. Sur chaque page, vous trouverez en haut et à droite les trois notes. La première concerne le parcours, la seconde le Club-House et ses équipements, la troisième l'environnement hôtelier. Un petit golfeur indique un séjour de golf recommandé, un soleil un séjour de vacances recommandé, pas forcément au soleil d'ailleurs. La note attribuée au Club-House et à ses équipements est fonction de l'esthétique et du confort du club house lui même, mais aussi de la qualité des installations d'entraînement, etc... Enfin, nous avons étudié l'environnement hôtelier dans la région. Certains restaurants de bonne réputation sont sélectionnés, de même que des hôtels de différentes catégories. La note attribuée n'exprime pas seulement un jugement sur les hôtels, mais elle signale surtout la quantité des équipements hôteliers et leur diversité à proximité du parcours.

LA PHILOSOPHIE DU PEUGEOT GOLF GUIDE

Un dernier mot pour souligner qu'il est impossible d'échapper à certaines imprécisions ou erreurs, avec une telle masse d'informations. Notre but est d'aider les golfeurs, et aussi les Clubs à progresser pour proposer toujours de meilleurs services et un parcours aussi bon que possible. Leur prospérité dépend de leur réputation et de leur exigence. Comme si chaque visiteur était envoyé par le Guide...

Découvrez l'Europe
avec les Cartes et Guides
Michelin

Discover Europe
with
Michelin maps & guides

PEUGEOT GOLF GUIDE
VORWORT

EIN ECHTER GOLFFUHRER

Im Gegensatz zu den zahlreichen Hotel- und Restaurantführern gab es bisher noch keinen Golfplatzführer, der alle europäischen Plätze kritisch und objektiv bewertet. Denn alle Golffreunde wissen, dass nicht nur jeder Platz ein Unikat ist, sondern auch in der Qualität der Anlagen große Unterschiede vorhanden sind. Neben den begehrten und allseits bekannten Plätzen sowie den grossen Meisterschaftsplätzen, die ihren Ruhm vor allem den Fernsehübertragungen verdanken, gibt es auch einige unentdeckte Juwele, unbekannte Plätze, öffentliche Plätze mit einfachem, aber reizvollem Design, Plätze, die mit einem kleinen Budget entstanden sind, bei denen aber der Architekt Wunder vollbrachte. Vor acht Jahren haben wir begonnen, uns die Golfplätze in Europa genau und kritisch anzusehen. Wir haben uns in die Lage von Golfer versetzt, die Greenfee zahlen und einen Platz und einen Service erwarten, der ihren Ansprüchen entspricht. In den letzten beiden Jahren haben wir unser ursprünglich gesetztes Ziel erreicht, nämlich Golfplätze in ganz Europa zu beschreiben und zu bewerten - allerdings nur sofern die Plätze den hohen Ansprüchen dieses Golfführers genügen.

PREISE IN EURO

Auf Grund unseres Redaktionsschlusses war es uns natürlich unmöglich alle Preise in Euro anzugeben, da weder Plätze noch Hotels zu diesem Zeitpunkt ihre Preise in Euro festgesetzt hatten. Auch wenn sich die Greenfees ändern, so geben die Preise in diesem Führer doch einen Anhaltspunkt.

1000 GOLFPLÄTZE AUSGEWÄHLT

Wir haben in den vergangenen acht Jahren 1500 18-Loch-Plätze besucht und darauf gespielt. Und zwar immer anonym, so dass wir einen Platz in seinem üblichen Zustand beurteilen konnten, wie ihn jeder Spieler antreffen kann. Von allen Plätzen haben wir öffentlich zugängliche ausgewählt, darunter sind jedoch auch viele private Golfplätze, die nur beschränkt oder nur wochentags zugänglich sind. Ungefähr vierzig Plätze sind erstmals aufgenommen worden. Zudem haben wir in dieser Ausgabe einige sehr private Clubs aufgenommen, um den vielen Nachfragen zu entsprechen, die wissen wollten wie diese Plätze in unserer Bewertung abschneiden.

EINE DREIFACHE NOTE

In unserem Bewertungssystem ist die höchste Bewertungszahl für den Platz 20 Punkte, während für das Clubhaus, die sonstigen Einrichtungen und die regionale Hotellerie bereits 10 Punkte die Höchstnote ist. Die Bewertung des Platzes ist für uns ausschlaggebend; die anderen Noten ermöglichen eine differenzierte Beurteilung der von Land zu Land recht unterschiedlichen Anlagen und Unterkunftsmöglichkeiten. Auf jeder Seite finden Sie oben rechts drei Noten. Die erste für den Platz, die zweite für das Clubhaus und seine Einrichtungen, die dritte für das Hotelangebot der Umgebung. Ein kleiner Golfspieler zeigt an, dass man hier gut ein paar Tage verbringen kann, eine Sonne, dass auch allgemein ein Ferienaufenthalt empfehlenswert ist, auch wenn nicht immer Sonnenschein zu erwarten ist. Die Note für das Clubhaus und den damit verbundenen Serviceleistungen beschreibt die Attraktivität und den Komfort des Gebäudes, aber ebenso die Übungsmöglichkeiten und weitere Einrichtungen. Zu guter Letzt haben wir das Hotelangebot der Gegend bewertet. Einige berühmte, von Gastronomie-führern hoch eingestufte Restaurants sind ebenso darunter wie Hotels verschiedener Kategorien. Die Note drückt nicht nur unsere Einschätzung der Qualität der Hotels, sondern — vielleicht noch wichtiger — die Vielfältigkeit des Hotelangebots in den unmittelbaren Umgebung des Platzes aus.

DIE PHILOSOPHIE DES GUIDES

Es ist uns sehr wohl bewusst, dass bei einer solchen Fülle von Informationen gewisse Ungenauigkeiten oder Fehler möglich sind. Unser Ziel ist es, Golfer bei der Auswahl lohnenswerte Plätze zu helfen, aber auch die Golfanlagen dazu anzuspornen, Greenfee-Spielern den Platz in bestmöglichem Zustand anzubieten und den Standard ihres Service zu verbessern. Der finanzielle Erfolg vieler Golfanlagen hängt auch davon ab, wie zufrieden Greenfeespieler nach ihrer Runde sind. Golfspieler sind anspruchsvoll - und jede Golfanlage sollte Gastspieler so behandeln, als seien Tester für unseren Golfführer.

Eau
Dynamisante
fraîcheur
fermeté
vitalité
Eau de Soins
CLARINS
PARIS
Eau
Dynamisante
Sentir bon
Se sentir bien.
Eau de Toilette et de beauté exceptionnelle
l'Eau Dynamisante réunit
toutes les vertus de l'AromaPhytoSoin :
plantes traitantes et délicieux
parfum vivifiant. En plus de son extrême
fraîcheur, elle tonifie, raffermit
et adoucit la peau. Un plaisir, un parfum,
un bien-être incomparables.
C'est prouvé. Clarins rend
la vie plus belle.
CLARINS
PARIS
www.clarins.com

PEUGEOT GOLF GUIDE
INLEDNING

EN ÄKTA GUIDE
Hotell- och restaurangguider har alltid funnits, men innan Peugeot Golf Guide kom i bokhandeln existerade ingen heltäckande kvalitetsguide över golfbanor i Europa. Ändå vet varje passionerad golfare att förhållandena från bana till bana kan variera stort. Vid sidan av mästerskapsbanorna, som vi ofta känner igen från olika tevesändningar, finns en mängd fantastiska banor som bara väntar på att upptäckas. Det kan vara en liten, oansenlig kommunal bana där arkitekten har gjort underverk, och sedan finns det givetvis också motsatsen: banor som lovar vitt och brett i marknadsföringen men som sedan blir en besvikelse. För åtta år sedan började vi kartlägga alla banor i Europa. Vi föreställde oss den vanlige golfarens behov, vilken service och kvalitet han eller hon har rätt att kräva. De senaste två åren har vi nått hela vägen fram: Vi har kartlagt banor i alla Europas länder, och i de fall de har levt upp till våra krav har de inkluderats i guiden. Den här nya och uppgraderade guiden innehåller web - och e-mail-adresser, priser i euro och slopevärden, när så finns.

PRISER I EURO
Med tanke på den långa trycktiden för en bok som denna är det naturligtvis omöjligt att vara säker på att priserna som är angivna i euro stämmer till punkt och pricka. I de flesta fall är de korrekta, men de kan förstås avvika en aning. Greenfees ändras från år till år, men du kommer i varje fall ha en utomordentlig vägledning över kostnadsläget.

1 000 UTVALDA BANOR, PRIVATA OCH KOMMUNALA
Under de senaste åtta åren har vi besökt och spelat fler än 1 500 banor. Vi gjorde det anonymt för att få en så rättvisande bild som möjligt av verkligheten. Av banorna valde vi ut 1 000 stycken, varav de flesta är öppna för allmänheten. Ungefär 40 av banorna presenteras för första gången i Peugeot Golf Guide, några av dem är mycket privata, men de har varit intresserade av att medverka för att se hur de klarar vårt bedömningssystem.

TRE RANKINGAR FÖR VARJE BANA
Vårt poängberäkningssystem för banorna går från 1-20 poäng. Poängberäkningssystemet för hotellen och klubbhusen går från 1-10. Naturligtvis ligger tonvikten i vår ranking på själva banorna, dessa är också enklare att poängsätta än hotellen. Hotellens kvalitet varierar mycket från land till land och detta gör det svårare att gradera dem. På varje sida kommer du uppe i högra hörnet se våra tre poäng som vi utfärdar per respektive bana. Den första poängen rör banan, den andra poängen gäller klubbhuset och den tredje poängen hotellen i närheten av banan.

ANLÄGGNINGENS STANDARD
När vi har satt poäng på banan har vi även tagit hänsyn till anläggningens standard: klubbhusets kvalitet †och design, övningsfält och andra faciliteter.

HOTELL
Vi har även †bedömt hotellen i respektive region, och dessutom har vi valt ut några högklassiga restauranger. När vi har valt hotell har vi även tagit med hotell som passar alla slags plånböcker. Hotellens geografiska närhet till golfbanan har varit av största betydelse.

SIST MEN INTE MINST
Ett sista ord på vägen: I en sådan här omfattande produktion kan felaktigheter och inaktuell information krypa in. Vårt mål är att hjälpa golfare men också uppmuntra golfbanor till att höja standarden. Vi vill tipsa om de bästa banorna du kan spela och den service du kan få där. Hur klubbarna lyckas på detta område beror på vilka krav som ställs på dem.

CHROME
Tant qu'il y aura des hommes
AZZARO
CHROME
www.parfums-azzaro.com

PEUGEOT GOLF GUIDE
INTRODUZIONE

UNA GUIDA AFFIDABILE

Contrariamente all'offerta che esiste per alberghi e ristoranti, non c'era nessuna guida dei campi da golf su scala europea prima dell'uscita della Peugeot Golf Guide. Essendo la qualità dei percorsi estremamente varia, era difficile orientarsi tra percorsi ormai famosi grazie alla televisione, campi poco conosciuti che in realtà sono dei piccoli gioielli, golf pubblici dal disegno molto semplice piuttosto che percorsi con grandi pretese ma alla fine deludenti o ancora campi realizzati in economia dove l'architetto ha fatto miracoli... Da otto anni abbiamo intrapreso un lavoro meticoloso su tutti i golf in Europa cercando di essere sempre dalla parte di coloro che pagano per giocare e desiderano quindi ricevere un servizio all'altezza delle loro aspettative. Da due anni siamo all'opera in tutti i paesi d'Europa che sono rappresentati nella guida per segnalare i percorsi che meritano. Questa nuova edizione è stata interamente rinnovata, ci sono i riferimenti per i siti Web e gli indirizzi E-mail così come i risultati dello Slope System nei paesi dove è stato già introdotto. Inoltre le tariffe saranno in Euro nei paesi che hanno adottato la moneta.

LE TARIFFE IN EURO

Avendo dovuto rispettare una scadenza precisa per andare in stampa con la guida non abbiamo potuto aspettare le tariffe definitive in Euro, ma abbiamo cercato di renderle più precise possibile. In ogni caso, le tariffe sono suscettibili di una leggera variazione da un anno all'altro e in questo modo avrete comunque un riferimento attendibile sia per quanto riguarda i green-fees che gli alberghi.

1000 PERCORSI SELEZIONATI PUBBLICI E PRIVATI

Abbiamo visitato e giocato in 1500 percorsi di 18 buche nel corso degli ultimi otto anni sempre in maniera anonima, come un golfista qualsiasi. Tra tutti questi campi ne abbiamo scelti 1000, quasi sempre aperti al pubblico, almeno durante i giorni feriali. In questa edizione entrano a far parte una quarantina di nuovi campi e tra questi abbiamo inserito anche qualche circolo estremamente esclusivo, perché ci è stato richiesto in più occasioni di non escluderli a priori.

UN "VOTO TRIPLO"

Il voto sul percorso è espresso in ventesimi, mentre i voti relativi sia al club-house ed alle sue attrezzature sia agli alberghi è indicato in decimi. Per noi il voto attribuito ai percorsi è assolutamente preponderante, gli altri voti permettono di attenuare le grandi differenze che si incontrano nei servizi e nel settore alberghiero da un paese all'altro. In ogni pagina troverete in alto a destra i tre voti: il primo riguarda il percorso, il secondo il club-house e le sue attrezzature, il terzo i servizi alberghieri. Il simbolo di un piccolo golfista indica che la sosta è assolutamente raccomandata per giocare a golf, un piccolo sole indica che il posto è ideale per una vacanza, non necessariamente sotto il sole. Il voto attribuito al club-house è in funzione dell'estetica e della comodità ma anche della qualità dei servizi a disposizione. Infine abbiamo studiato l'offerta alberghiera nei dintorni. Sono stati selezionati ristoranti già ben conosciuti così come alberghi di categorie estremamente diverse tra loro. Il voto attribuito non esprime soltanto un giudizio sugli hotel ma segnala soprattutto la quantità e la varietà delle attrezzature vicino al campo di golf.

LA FILOSOFIA DELLA PEUGEOT GOLF GUIDE

Vorremmo inoltre precisare che è praticamente impossibile non incappare in qualche errore quando si ha a che fare con una massa enorme di informazioni. Il nostro scopo fondamentale è comunque quello di essere un valido aiuto per i golfisti e anche quello di essere uno sprone per i circoli perchè continuino a progredire, proponendo servizi sempre più gradevoli e un percorso al meglio delle possibilità. La prosperità di un circolo dipende dalla sua reputazione e dalle sue pretese. Come se ogni ospite fosse stato mandato dalla Guida...

PEUGEOT GOLF GUIDE
INTRODUCCION

UNA AUTÉNTICA GUIA

Hasta que ha aparecido la Guía de golf Peugeot no se disponía de una orientación sobre la calidad de los campos de golf de Europa semejante a las guías de hoteles y restaurantes. Y sin embargo, como saben todos los aficionados al golf, los campos son tan diversos como diferente es su calidad. Junto a los recorridos de campeonato que la televisión ha hecho famosos, hay campos poco conocidos que son una joya, hay campos públicos sencillos de trazado y muy poco ambiciosos, unos campos tienen muchas pretensiones pero resultan decepcionantes, y otros, en cambio, se han hecho con un exiguo presupuesto con el cual el constructor ha hecho maravillas... Hace ocho años emprendimos un trabajo de hondo calado sobre los campos de golf de Europa, colocándonos decididamente del lado de los que pagan para jugar y esperan recibir un servicio a la altura de sus expectativas. En estos dos últimos años hemos cumplido nuestro objetivo al haber conseguido incluir en la guía a todos los países de Europa que tienen campos a la altura de ciertas exigencias, por supuesto. Esta nueva edición ha sido revisada totalmente, incorporando las referencias de los sitios de Internet y de las direcciones de e-mail, así como las valoraciones Slope disponibles, aunque se puedan tener reservas sobre estas mismas valoraciones... y los precios en euros en los países que operarán con la nueva moneda.

LOS PRECIOS EN EUROS

Esta guía se ha editado precisamente durante el cambio operativo de la moneda única, por lo que algunos precios en euros han tenido que ser necesariamente orientativos. En cualquier caso, se brindan aquí los valores que dan una idea cabal de las tarifas de hoteles y green-fees que están en vigor.

MIL CAMPOS ELEGIDOS, PUBLICOS Y PRIVADOS

De forma anónima, como cualquier otro jugador, durante estos últimos ocho años hemos visitado y jugado mil quinientos campos de 18 hoyos. De ellos hemos escogido 1.000, generalmente abiertos al público, al menos entre semana. Una cuarentena se incorporan a esta edición, en la cual hemos incluído ciertos clubs muy privados atendiendo su petición de ser valorados dentro de esta élite.

TRIPLE NOTA

En el sistema de puntuación que hemos empleado, la nota del campo se valora sobre 20, mientras las notas de la casa-club y sus instalaciones, y la de los recursos hoteleros próximos, se puntúan sobre 10. Por lo tanto, nuestro criterio da preponderancia a la nota del campo, mientras con las otras dos salvamos las evidentes diferencias en cuanto a instalaciones, servicios y hostelería que existen de un país a otro. Tres notas se encuentran en la parte superior derecha de cada página. La primera se refiere al recorrido, la segunda a la casa-club y sus instalaciones y la tercera, a la estructura hotelera de la zona.

CALIDAD DE LAS INSTALACIONES

Concedemos una nota general al campo pero también queremos dejar constancia de la calidad y servicios de la casa-club: para ello se tienen en consideración la estética y la comodidad del conjunto, el estado de campo de prácticas y las instalaciones complementarias.

INFRAESTRUCTURA HOTELERA

Finalmente, consideramos la infraestructura hotelera de la zona. Se han seleccionado buenos restaurantes y hoteles de varias categorías para diferentes presupuestos. La calificación hotelera se fija, sobre todo, en la cantidad de servicios que se ofrecen y en su proximidad al campo de golf.

FILOSOFIA DE LA GUIA PEUGEOT

Por último, somos muy conscientes de que cuando se maneja tal cantidad de datos siempre pueden escaparse ciertas imprecisiones o algún error. Pretendemos ser una referencia para los jugadores y un incentivo para que los campos mejoren sus servicios y tengan el recorrido de juego en las mejores condiciones posibles. Su prosperidad depende de que los jugadores aprecien sus cualidades. Esta guía prepara al golfista a comprender el nivel de calidad que puede exigirse en cada uno de los campos que visite pagando un green-fee.

1973

Johnny Miller (USA), surnommé l'ange blond, signe sa victoire avec un panache extraordinaire et une amplitude de swing exceptionnelle. Il rééditera l'exploit en 1979.

Presse Sport

1977

Arnold Palmer revient pour la 8e année consécutive et assure le spectacle. Du deuxième étage de la Tour Eiffel, il drive sur le champs de Mars. Alors qu'au deuxième essai sa balle est tombée sur le toit d'un autobus, le troisième fut un succès avec une distance de 366 mètres.

P. Colacicco

plus grands joue

les plus grands joueurs TROPHÉE

TROPHÉE

Didier Chicot

1997

Retour des américains au Lancôme. Pour sa première participation au Trophée, **Mark O'Meara (USA),** 40 ans, l'emporte devant le suédois Jarmo Sandelin. Il s'imposera l'année suivante au Masters et à l'Open britannique.

Didier Chicot

1998

Miguel Angel Jimenez (ESP) explose de joie. Son approche directe dans le trou du 18 devient légendaire. Il bat les meilleurs joueurs du monde : David Duval (USA), Colin Montgomerie (ECO), Mark O'Meara (USA), Fred Couples (USA).

1971

Presse Sports

Arnold Palmer (USA) marque de son empreinte le Lancôme. Il lui donne ses lettres de noblesse. Son caddie Michel Schilling reçoit 1 000 $ qu'il partage aussitôt avec ses pairs. Catherine Lacoste et Gaëtan Mourgue d'Algue sont en admiration.

1983

Arrêt de jeu de quinze minutes. La balle de **Severiano Ballesteros (ESP)** est perchée dans l'un des arbres du parcours. Un spectateur l'a fait tomber par inadvertance. Le champion espagnol remporte magistralement le Trophée pour la deuxième fois.

Didier Chicot

rs du

du

LANCÔME

LANCÔME

2001

Sergio Garcia.
Le prodige du golf espagnol s'est offert une belle victoire au 32è Trophée Lancôme. A seulement 21 ans, le favori du public de Saint-Nom-la-Bretèche a encore su démontrer son talent et sa maturité.

Gianni Caccia

TROPHÉE LANCÔME
PARIS

CLASSIFICATION OF COURSES
CLASSEMENT DES PARCOURS
EINTEILUNG DER GOLFPLÄTZE
VI RANKAR BANORNA
CLASIFICACION DE LOS RECORRIDOS
CLASSIFICA DEI PERCORSI

Within each score, the ranking is purely alphabetical

Course score					Page
19	7	6	Ballybunion *Old Course*	Ireland	831
19	8	6	Bordes (Les)	France	232
19	5	6	Carnoustie *Championship*	Scotland	708
19	8	5	Ganton	England	562
19	8	6	Kingsbarns	Scotland	738
19	7	6	Muirfield	Scotland	754
19	7	8	Nairn	Scotland	757
19	7	8	Portmarnock	Ireland	887
19	8	7	Prince de Provence (Vidauban)	France	267
19	9	7	Royal Birkdale (The)	England	618
19	6	7	Royal County Down	N.Ireland	925
19	7	7	Royal Dornoch *Championship*	Scotland	770
19	7	8	Royal Lytham & St Anne's	England	624
19	7	6	Royal Porthcawl	Wales	812
19	7	7	Royal Portrush *Dunluce Links*	N.Ireland	926
19	7	5	Royal St George's	England	627
19	7	7	Royal Troon *Old Course*	Scotland	772
19	9	8	Turnberry *Ailsa Course*	Scotland	784
19	8	6	Valderrama	Spain	1198

CLASSIFICATION OF GOLF COURSES

A: Austria **B:** Belgium **CH:** Switzerland
Cz: Czech Republic **Da:** Denmark
E: Spain **Eng:** England **F:** France
Fi: Finland **G:** Germany **I:** Italy
IRL: Republic of Ireland
L: Luxembourg **N:** Nederland
NIR: Northern Ireland **Nw:** Norway
P: Portugal **R:** Russia **S:** Sweden
Sc: Scotland **T:** Turkey **W:** Wales

18	7	7	Alwoodley (The)	Eng	513
18	7	6	Barsebäck	S	1215
18	7	8	Biella - Le Betulle	I	950
18	8	6	Blairgowrie *Rosemount*	Sc	698
18	7	6	Burnham & Berrow	Eng	532
18	8	8	Castelconturbia *Giallo + Azzurro*	I	954
18	6	8	Castletown	Eng	538
18	9	7	Celtic Manor *Roman Road*	W	797
18	7	6	Chantilly *Vineuil*	F	247
18	8	6	Chart Hills	Eng	539
18	6	5	Club zur Vahr	D	393
18	5	6	County Louth	IRL	847
18	7	6	Cruden Bay	Sc	711
18	8	6	Domaine Impérial	CH	1277
18	8	6	Eindhoven	N	1006
18	7	6	El Saler	E	1128
18	5	6	European (The)	IRL	860
18	6	7	Falkenstein	D	399
18	7	5	Falsterbo	S	1227
18	7	7	Formby	Eng	557
18	9	7	Gleneagles *King's*	Sc	728
18	7	8	Haagsche	N	1012
18	8	7	Halmstad	S	1236
18	7	7	Hillside	Eng	574
18	7	6	Ilkley	Eng	579
18	8	6	Kempferhof (Le)	F	240
18	8	8	Kennemer	N	1017
18	8	7	Las Brisas	E	1154
18	7	7	Ljunghusen	S	1245
18	8	6	Loch Lomond	Sc	744
18	6	4	Machrihanish	Sc	750
18	7	5	Médoc *Les Châteaux*	F	249
18	7	7	Moortown	Eng	599
18	6	6	Morfontaine	F	254
18	9	8	Mount Juliet	IRL	883
18	6	6	National *L'Albatros*	F	255
18	7	8	Noordwijk	N	1020
18	7	8	North Berwick	Sc	760
18	6	6	Notts (Hollinwell)	Eng	604
18	7	5	Örebro	S	1248
18	6	6	Pennard	W	809
18	7	7	PGA de Catalunya	E	1179
18	6	7	Prestwick	Sc	765
18	8	9	Puerta de Hierro *Abajo*	E	1181
18	7	6	Real Sociedad Club de Campo	E	1184
18	7	8	Royal Aberdeen *Balgownie Links*	Sc	768
18	8	7	Royal Liverpool (Hoylake)	Eng	623
18	6	6	Royal North Devon (Westward Ho!)	Eng	626
18	6	5	Royal St David's	W	813
18	7	7	Royal Zoute	B	111
18	6	6	Rye	Eng	632
18	7	6	Saunton *East Course*	Eng	635
18	8	7	Scharmützelsee Nick Faldo	D	451
18	5	4	Seascale	Eng	637
18	9	7	Seddiner See *Südplatz*	D	461
18	7	4	Silloth-on-Solway	Eng	643
18	8	7	Sotogrande	E	1194
18	6	5	Southerness	Sc	775
18	8	8	St Andrews *Old Course*	Sc	779
18	7	4	St Enodoc *Church Course*	Eng	646
18	8	8	Sunningdale *New Course*	Eng	651
18	8	8	Sunningdale *Old Course*	Eng	652
18	7	6	Tenby	W	815
18	7	6	Tralee	IRL	902
18	7	7	Walton Heath *Old Course*	Eng	664
18	8	7	Wentworth *West Course*	Eng	667
18	7	6	West Sussex	Eng	674
18	7	8	Woodhall Spa	Eng	684

CLASSIFICATION OF GOLF COURSES

Within each score, the ranking is purely alphabetical

17	7	7	Aberdovey	W	792
17	7	8	Aloha	E	1113
17	6	5	Ashburnham	W	793
17	9	9	Bad Griesbach *Brunnwies*	D	380
17	6	5	Ballyliffin *Glashedy Links*	IRL	833
17	7	6	Barbaroux	F	222
17	8	7	Berkshire (The) *Blue Course*	Eng	519
17	8	7	Berkshire (The) *Red Course*	Eng	520
17	7	6	Beuerberg	D	387
17	6	5	Blackmoor	Eng	522
17	8	7	Bogogno *Bonora*	I	951
17	8	7	Bogogno *Del Conte*	I	952
17	6	6	Bowood G&CC	Eng	525
17	7	6	Brampton	Eng	526
17	7	6	Bro-Bålsta	S	1220
17	7	7	Broadstone	Eng	528
17	8	7	Buckinghamshire (The)	Eng	530
17	7	7	Caldy	Eng	533
17	8	8	Carden Park *Nicklaus Course*	Eng	536
17	7	7	Carlisle	Eng	537
17	7	7	Castillo de Gorraiz	E	1120
17	7	7	Clitheroe	Eng	541
17	7	8	Conwy	W	798
17	4	4	County Sligo	IRL	848
17	7	7	Cumberwell Park	Eng	544
17	8	8	Dalmahoy *East Course*	Sc	712
17	6	7	Downfield	Sc	713
17	8	7	East Sussex National *East Course*	Eng	549
17	8	8	Eichenheim	A	82
17	5	8	El Cortijo	E	1126
17	7	6	El Prat *Verde*	E	1127
17	7	6	Emporda	E	1129
17	8	6	Enniscrone	IRL	858
17	7	6	European Tour Club (Kungsängen)	S	1224
17	7	8	Fairhaven	Eng	550
17	7	7	Ferndown *Old Course*	Eng	553
17	8	8	Fleesensee	D	401
17	7	7	Fontainebleau	F	221
17	6	5	Fontanals	E	1132
17	6	7	Forest Pines *Forest + Pines*	Eng	556
17	7	8	Frankfurter GC	D	402
17	7	8	Fulford	Eng	560
17	7	8	Fürstlicher GC Bad Waldsee	D	404
17	7	8	Genève	CH	1280
17	9	7	Gleneagles *PGA Centenary*	Sc	729
17	7	6	Grenoble Bresson	F	231
17	8	7	Gullane *No 1*	Sc	733
17	7	6	Gut Altentann	A	85
17	9	7	Gut Lärchenhof	D	409
17	7	7	Gütersloh (Westfälischer GC)	D	412
17	8	6	Hubbelrath	D	420
17	7	6	Hunstanton	Eng	577
17	7	7	I Roveri	I	963
17	2	6	Is Arenas	I	964
17	7	8	Is Molas	I	965
17	8	8	K Club	IRL	871
17	6	8	Kilmarnock (Barassie)	Sc	737
17	6	8	Klagenfurt-Seltenheim	A	86
17	6	7	Köln	D	425
17	7	7	Krefelder	D	426
17	7	7	Kristianstad	S	1242
17	8	6	La Cala *Norte*	E	1140
17	7	8	La Moye	Eng	583
17	7	5	Ladybank	Sc	740
17	7	7	Lage Vuursche	N	1018
17	6	6	Lahinch	IRL	877
17	8	6	Larvik	Nw	1040
17	8	7	Le Querce	I	968
17	7	4	Lerma	E	1157
17	6	5	Limère	F	245
17	8	6	Linden Hall	Eng	584
17	6	6	Lindrick	Eng	585
17	7	8	Little Aston	Eng	587
17	8	8	Lübeck-Travemünder	D	430
17	7	7	Machrie	Sc	749
17	7	7	Mittelrheinischer	D	435
17	6	5	Moliets	F	251
17	7	7	Monifieth	Sc	751

CLASSIFICATION OF GOLF COURSES

17	8	8	Montecastillo	E	1168
17	5	6	Montrose	Sc	752
17	8	7	Moor Park *High Course*	Eng	598
17	5	5	Moray	Sc	753
17	7	6	Moscow	Ru	1302
17	8	6	Motzener See	D	436
17	7	7	Neguri	E	1170
17	7	6	Nîmes-Campagne	F	257
17	8	6	Nobilis	T	1305
17	7	6	North Hants	Eng	603
17	6	8	North Wales (Llandudno)	W	807
17	6	5	Oberfranken	D	441
17	6	5	Panmure	Sc	761
17	8	8	Pevero	I	981
17	7	5	Pléneuf-Val-André	F	262
17	7	8	Portmarnock Links	IRL	888
17	6	5	Praia d'El Rey	P	1069
17	8	7	Prestbury	Eng	614
17	7	5	Pyle & Kenfig	W	810
17	8	7	Ravenstein	B	107
17	8	7	Rethmar	D	447
17	6	5	Royal Cinque Ports	Eng	619
17	8	8	Royal Mougins	F	274
17	7	6	Royal West Norfolk (Brancaster)	Eng	628
17	7	7	Rungsted	Da	136
17	6	8	S. Lourenço	P	1075
17	7	7	Saint-Germain	F	279
17	8	8	Saint-Nom-la-Bretèche *Rouge*	F	283
17	8	8	San Roque	E	1185
17	5	7	Sandiway	Eng	634
17	8	7	Scharmützelsee Arnold Palmer	D	450
17	8	6	Schloss Nippenburg	D	458
17	7	5	Schloss Wilkendorf	D	459
17	8	6	Schwanhof	D	460
17	6	4	Seacroft	Eng	636
17	7	5	Seaton Carew	Eng	638
17	7	7	Seignosse	F	288
17	7	8	Sevilla	E	1189
17	7	6	Sherwood Forest	Eng	642
17	5	5	Shiskine (Blackwaterfoot)	Sc	774
17	5	7	Skövde	S	1253
17	8	7	Slaley Hall	Eng	644
17	7	7	Southport & Ainsdale	Eng	645
17	7	7	Spa (Les Fagnes)	B	113
17	7	5	Spérone	F	291
17	8	8	St Andrews *New Course*	Sc	778
17	7	7	St George's Hill	Eng	647
17	9	7	St Mellion *Nicklaus Course*	Eng	648
17	7	6	St. Dionys	D	464
17	7	8	Stenungsund	S	1255
17	8	8	Stoke Poges	Eng	649
17	5	5	Stuttgarter Solitude	D	469
17	6	6	Tain	Sc	781
17	7	7	Trevose *Championship*	Eng	661
17	8	6	Ullna	S	1260
17	7	5	Villette d'Anthon *Les Sangliers*	F	300
17	7	7	Wallasey	Eng	662
17	6	7	Waterville	IRL	908
17	7	7	West Lancashire	Eng	672
17	5	7	Western Gailes	Sc	787
17	6	7	Whittington Heath	Eng	677
17	7	6	Wittelsbacher	D	477
17	7	7	Woburn *Dukes*	Eng	679
17	7	7	Woburn *Marquess*	Eng	680

16

Within each score, the ranking is purely alphabetical

16	5	4	Aisses (Les) *Rouge/Blanc*	F	209
16	7	7	Am Mondsee	A	80
16	7	6	Ängsö	S	1213
16	7	7	Antwerp	B	97
16	7	6	Ashridge	Eng	514
16	6	5	Åtvidaberg	S	1214
16	5	7	Ayr (Belleisle)	Sc	693
16	7	6	Ballybunion *Cashen (New Course)*	IRL	830
16	7	7	Båstad *Old Course*	S	1216
16	6	9	Bath	Eng	516
16	7	7	Beau Desert	Eng	517

CLASSIFICATION OF GOLF COURSES

16	6	5	Belle-Dune	F	225
16	7	7	Bergamo - L'Albenza		
			Blu + Giallo	I	949
16	7	7	Bergisch Land		
			Wuppertal	D	385
16	7	6	Berkhamsted	Eng	518
16	8	9	Berlin-Wannsee	D	386
16	7	7	Bodensee-		
			Weissensberg	D	390
16	6	7	Bokskogen	S	1217
16	7	6	Bondues *Blanc*	F	230
16	8	7	Bonmont	E	1116
16	6	5	Borre	Nw	1038
16	7	6	Bowood (Cornwall)	Eng	524
16	7	7	Bråviken	S	1219
16	7	5	Bresse (La)	F	234
16	7	6	Buxtehude	D	392
16	6	6	Camberley Heath	Eng	534
16	6	7	Carlow	IRL	840
16	6	6	Castlerock	NIR	916
16	6	6	Charmeil	F	248
16	6	8	Chiberta	F	252
16	8	8	Club de Campo	E	1122
16	7	3	Courson *Vert/Noir*	F	209
16	8	5	Cromstrijen	N	1003
16	9	6	Dartmouth	Eng	545
16	8	7	De Pan	N	1004
16	7	8	Disneyland Paris		
			Peter + Alice	F	212
16	6	6	Donegal (Murvagh)	IRL	852
16	9	7	Druids Glen	IRL	855
16	7	8	Duke's St Andrews	Sc	716
16	5	6	Dunbar	Sc	718
16	6	7	East Devon	Eng	548
16	8	5	Efteling	N	1005
16	7	4	El Bosque	E	1125
16	7	6	Espoo	Fi	148
16	6	7	Estérel Latitudes	F	216
16	9	5	Fågelbro	S	1225
16	7	6	Feldafing	D	400
16	7	7	Flommen	S	1229
16	8	7	Fontana	A	83
16	7	4	Forsbacka	S	1230
16	6	5	Fortrose & Rosemarkie	Sc	726
16	7	6	Fota Island	IRL	862
16	7	5	Frösåker	S	1232
16	7	7	Glasson	IRL	865
16	7	8	Golf del Sur	E	1134
16	8	6	Golfresort Haugschlag-		
			Waldviertel	A	84
16	6	6	Gouverneur (Le)		
			Le Breuil	F	226
16	6	6	Grande Bastide (La)	F	228
16	6	4	Grande-Motte (La)		
			Les Flamants Roses	F	229
16	5	8	Grange	IRL	867
16	7	6	Gut Grambek	D	407
16	7	5	Gut Thailing	D	411
16	7	7	Hadley Wood	Eng	564
16	8	7	Hamburg-Ahrensburg	D	413
16	6	6	Hanau-Wilhelmsbad	D	414
16	8	6	Haninge	S	1237
16	6	6	Hankley Common	Eng	566
16	7	7	Hannover	D	415
16	6	6	Hardelot *Les Pins*	F	233
16	7	7	Hayling	Eng	569
16	7	8	Helsinki	Fi	149
16	7	6	Herkenbosch	N	1013
16	7	7	Hilversum	N	1014
16	8	6	Himmerland		
			New Course	Da	129
16	7	6	Hindhead	Eng	575
16	6	5	Holstebro	Da	130
16	7	5	Holyhead	W	800
16	6	6	Hossegor	F	235
16	8	8	Houtrak	N	1016
16	6	7	Huddersfield (Fixby)	Eng	576
16	7	6	Iffeldorf	D	421
16	7	8	Inverness	Sc	736
16	7	7	Ipswich (Purdis Heath)	Eng	580
16	8	8	Islantilla	E	1138
16	7	4	Isle Adam (L')	F	237
16	7	6	Isle of Purbeck	Eng	581
16	7	6	John O'Gaunt	Eng	582
16	7	7	Jönköping	S	1238
16	8	7	Joyenval *Marly*	F	238
16	7	7	Kikuoka	L	118
16	7	8	Killarney *Killeen Course*	I	874
16	7	7	København		
			Eremitagen	Da	131
16	8	6	La Cala *Sur*	E	1141
16	7	8	La Moraleja		
			La Moraleja 2	E	1149
16	7	7	La Zagaleta	E	1152
16	6	5	Lanark	Sc	741
16	7	8	Las Américas	E	1153

CLASSIFICATION OF GOLF COURSES

16	7	7	Lausanne	CH	1283
16	6	6	Leven	Sc	743
16	7	4	Limburg	B	102
16	7	6	Liphook	Eng	586
16	7	7	Los Naranjos	E	1159
16	8	6	Losby	Nw	1041
16	5	6	Luffness New	Sc	747
16	6	7	Lundin	Sc	748
16	7	5	Lunds Akademiska	S	1246
16	7	5	Lüneburger Heide	D	431
16	7	7	Manchester	Eng	591
16	8	7	Marriott St Pierre *Old Course*	W	804
16	7	8	Maspalomas	E	1163
16	7	6	Mediterraneo	E	1164
16	7	4	Meland	Nw	1042
16	6	7	Mijas *Los Lagos*	E	1165
16	9	8	Milano	I	973
16	8	7	Monteenmedio	E	1169
16	7	5	Montpellier-Massane	F	253
16	7	7	München-Riedhof	D	437
16	7	5	Nefyn & District	W	805
16	9	6	Northop Country Park	W	808
16	7	7	Novo Sancti Petri	E	1171
16	7	7	Old Head	IRL	886
16	8	6	Olgiata	I	978
16	7	7	Orchardleigh	Eng	605
16	6	6	Österåker	S	1249
16	7	6	Pals	E	1175
16	7	5	Paris International	F	260
16	7	8	Parkstone	Eng	608
16	6	8	Penha Longa	P	1066
16	6	6	Perranporth	Eng	610
16	8	6	Pleasington	Eng	611
16	6	5	Pont Royal	F	264
16	5	5	Portsalon	IRL	889
16	7	7	Portstewart *Strand Course*	NIR	923
16	6	4	Powfoot	Sc	764
16	6	7	Prestwick St Nicholas	Sc	766
16	8	9	Puerta de Hierro *Arriba*	E	1182
16	7	8	Quinta do Lago *B/C*	P	1072
16	6	4	Rebetz	F	269
16	7	7	Reichswald-Nürnberg	D	446
16	8	7	Rheine/Mesum	D	448
16	8	9	Roma - Acquasanta	I	987
16	7	6	Rosapenna	IRL	893
16	7	9	Royal Burgess	Sc	769
16	8	7	Royal Dublin	IRL	895
16	7	7	Royal Guernsey	Eng	621
16	7	8	Royal Jersey	Eng	622
16	8	7	Royal Musselburgh	Sc	771
16	7	8	Royal Wimbledon	Eng	629
16	7	4	Sablé-Solesmes *La Forêt/La Rivière*	F	275
16	7	8	Saint Donat	F	276
16	6	5	Saint-Jean-de-Monts	F	280
16	8	8	Saint-Nom-la-Bretèche *Bleu*	F	282
16	7	5	Santo da Serra	P	1077
16	8	7	Sarfvik *New Course*	Fi	153
16	7	7	Sart-Tilman	B	112
16	7	7	Schloss Braunfels	D	452
16	8	6	Schloss Ebreichsdorf	A	87
16	8	7	Schloss Langenstein	D	455
16	7	7	Schloss Myllendonk	D	457
16	6	6	Scotscraig	Sc	773
16	8	7	Semlin am See	D	462
16	8	7	Sempachersee	CH	1291
16	8	7	Senne	D	463
16	8	8	Son Antem *Oeste*	E	1191
16	8	9	Son Muntaner	E	1192
16	7	4	Soufflenheim	F	290
16	7	7	Southerndown	W	814
16	8	8	St Andrews *Jubilee Course*	Sc	777
16	7	7	St Margaret's	IRL	900
16	7	6	St. Eurach	D	465
16	9	7	St. Leon-Rot *"St Leon" Course*	D	467
16	6	7	Stavanger	Nw	1045
16	8	7	Steiermärkischer Murhof	A	88
16	8	9	Stockholm	S	1256
16	7	5	Stolper Heide	D	468
16	6	8	Swinley Forest	Eng	653
16	7	7	Täby	S	1257
16	9	8	The Belfry *Brabazon*	Eng	655
16	6	4	Thurlestone	Eng	660
16	8	7	Torino - La Mandria *Percorso Blu*	I	988
16	6	7	Touquet (Le) *La Mer*	F	296
16	6	5	Troia	P	1078
16	9	8	Turnberry *Kintyre Course*	Sc	785
16	6	6	Ulzama	E	1197

CLASSIFICATION OF GOLF COURSES

16	8	7	Vale of Glamorgan	W	816
16	7	7	Vasatorp	S	1263
16	7	9	Venezia	I	990
16	7	7	Vilamoura		
			Vilamoura I (Old)	P	1082
16	9	8	Villa D'Este	I	992
16	7	6	Villamartin	E	1199
16	7	5	Visby	S	1265
16	7	6	Walddörfer	D	474
16	7	6	Walton Heath		
			New Course	Eng	663
16	6	6	Wantzenau (La)	F	302
16	8	7	Waterloo *La Marache*	B	115
16	8	7	Waterloo Le Lion	B	116
16	7	6	Wendlohe		
			A-Kurs + B-Kurs	D	476
16	8	7	Wentworth		
			East Course	Eng	666
16	7	6	West Cornwall	Eng	670
16	6	6	West Hill	Eng	671
16	7	5	West Kilbride	Sc	786
16	6	7	Weston-Super-Mare	Eng	675
16	7	6	Wilmslow	Eng	678
16	6	6	Woking	Eng	681
16	7	6	Woodenbridge	IRL	911
16	7	6	Worplesdon	Eng	685
16	7	6	Zaudin	E	1200
16	7	6	Zell am See Kaprun	A	90

15

Within each score, the ranking is purely alphabetical

15	6	4	Ableiges *Les Etangs*	F	207
15	6	7	Adare	IRL	828
15	6	5	Ailette (L')	F	208
15	6	6	Albi	F	211
15	8	8	Alicante	E	1110
15	7	6	Alloa	Sc	691
15	7	7	Amarilla	E	1114
15	7	7	Amsterdam	N	999
15	6	6	Ängelholm	S	1212
15	8	7	Antognolla	I	945
15	8	6	Apremont	F	215
15	7	5	Arendal	Nw	1037
15	9	8	Arzaga	I	946
15	7	6	Asserbo	Da	126
15	7	7	Augsburg	D	377
15	7	7	Bad Abbach-Deutenhof	D	378
15	5	7	Bad Bevensen	D	379
15	9	9	Bad Griesbach		
			Sagmühle	D	381
15	6	5	Baden	F	220
15	7	7	Bâle-Hagenthal	F	221
15	6	7	Ballater	Sc	695
15	6	5	Ballyliffin *Old Course*	IRL	834
15	7	7	Bamberg	D	384
15	7	3	Batouwe	N	1001
15	7	8	Baule (La) *Rouge*	F	223
15	5	3	Belmullet	IRL	837
15	5	6	Belvoir Park	NIR	914
15	6	5	Berwick-upon-Tweed	Eng	521
15	6	7	Biblis Wattenheim		
			A + B	D	388
15	7	8	Bitburger Land	D	389
15	8	6	Blairgowrie		
			Lansdowne	Sc	697
15	7	8	Bled *King's Course*		1301
15	7	6	Blumisberg	CH	1274
15	5	7	Bolton Old Links	Eng	523
15	7	6	Bondues Jaune	F	231
15	7	6	Bosjökloster	S	1218
15	7	8	Boulie (La) *La Vallée*	F	233
15	7	7	Bretesche (La)	F	236
15	7	6	Broekpolder	N	1002
15	6	6	Brokenhurst Manor	Eng	529
15	7	7	Brora	Sc	700
15	8	9	Bruntsfield	Sc	701
15	6	5	Bude & North Cornwall	Eng	531
15	5	6	Came Down	Eng	535
15	7	8	Cannes-Mougins	F	239
15	6	6	Canyamel	E	1118
15	6	5	Cap d'Agde	F	240
15	7	6	Capdepera	E	1119
15	6	5	Cardigan	W	795
15	7	4	Carmarthen	W	796
15	9	7	Carnegie Club		
			(Skibo Castle)	Sc	706
15	7	7	Castelgandolfo	I	955
15	7	6	Cély	F	241
15	6	7	Chamonix	F	244
15	7	6	Château de Preisch	F	249

CLASSIFICATION OF GOLF COURSES

15	6	6	Clandeboye		
			Dufferin Course	NIR	917
15	6	6	Connemara	IRL	845
15	3	5	Cork GC	IRL	846
15	7	5	County Tipperary	IRL	849
15	7	3	Courson *Lilas/Orange*	F	208
15	6	6	Coxmoor	Eng	543
15	6	6	Crail *Balcomie Links*	Sc	709
15	7	7	Crieff *Ferntower Course*	Sc	710
15	6	7	Delamere Forest	Eng	546
15	7	7	Dellach	A	81
15	7	7	Denham	Eng	547
15	5	4	Dingle Links		
			(Ceann Sibeal)	IRL	851
15	5	5	Dooks	IRL	853
15	7	9	Duddingston	Sc	714
15	6	6	Duff House Royal	Sc	715
15	7	5	Dumfries & County	Sc	717
15	6	6	Dundalk	IRL	856
15	7	7	Dunfermline	Sc	719
15	7	7	Düsseldorfer	D	395
15	6	8	East Renfrewshire	Sc	720
15	7	6	Elgin	Sc	722
15	6	6	Elie	Sc	723
15	6	6	Engadin	CH	1278
15	6	5	Esbjerg	Da	127
15	7	5	Esery	F	215
15	8	7	Essener Oefte	D	398
15	7	6	Etiolles *Les Cerfs*	F	217
15	7	9	Evian	F	219
15	4	7	Fanø	Da	128
15	6	6	Felixstowe Ferry		
			Martello Course	Eng	552
15	7	5	Feucherolles	F	220
15	6	3	Fjällbacka	S	1228
15	8	8	Forest of Arden		
			Arden Course	Eng	555
15	7	7	Frégate	F	225
15	8	8	Gardagolf	I	961
15	7	7	Gendersteyn	N	1008
15	9	7	Gleneagles *Queen's*	Sc	730
15	7	7	Gloria Golf Resort	T	1303
15	7	6	Goes	N	1009
15	7	8	Gog Magog		
			Old Course	Eng	563
15	3	7	Golf d'Aro (Mas Nou)	E	1133
15	6	7	Göteborg	S	1234
15	7	6	Graafschap	N	1010
15	7	5	Gränna	S	1235
15	7	6	Gujan-Mestras	F	232
15	7	6	Gut Kaden	D	408
15	6	6	Gut Ludwigsberg	D	410
15	7	9	Haggs Castle	Sc	734
15	7	5	Hainaut		
			Bruyere-Quesnoy-Etangs	B	100
15	6	8	Hallamshire	Eng	565
15	7	7	Harrogate	Eng	567
15	8	7	Hawkstone Park		
			Hawkstone	Eng	568
15	6	6	Headfort *New Course*	IRL	869
15	6	8	Hermitage	IRL	870
15	7	7	Hertfordshire (The)	Eng	571
15	6	7	High Post	Eng	573
15	7	5	Hof Trages	D	418
15	6	7	Hoge Kleij	N	1015
15	7	6	Hohenpähl	D	419
15	7	6	Im Chiemgau	D	422
15	7	7	International Club du Lys		
			Les Chênes	F	236
15	7	6	Isernhagen	D	423
15	7	6	Jakobsberg	D	424
15	8	7	Joyenval *Retz*	F	239
15	5	8	Kalmar	S	1239
15	7	6	Karlovy Vary	Cz	1297
15	6	6	Karlstad	S	1241
15	6	6	Kilkea Castle	IRL	872
15	7	8	Killarney		
			Mahony's Point	IRL	875
15	4	5	Kingussie	Sc	739
15	6	5	Kirkistown Castle	NIR	918
15	7	6	Knock	NIR	919
15	6	6	Kungsbacka	S	1243
15	6	6	La Herreria	E	1144
15	7	7	La Manga *Norte*	E	1145
15	7	7	La Manga *Sur*	E	1147
15	7	8	La Moraleja		
			La Moraleja 1	E	1148
15	6	5	La Sella	E	1151
15	9	7	Landskrona *Gul Bana*	S	1244
15	7	7	Langland Bay	W	801
15	7	4	Largue (La)	F	242
15	7	5	Læsø *Seaside*	Da	133
15	8	8	Le Robinie	I	969
15	7	6	Les Bois	CH	1284
15	7	5	Letham Grange		
			Old Course	Sc	742

CLASSIFICATION OF GOLF COURSES

15	7	6	Lichtenau-Weickershof	D	427
15	7	6	Limerick County	IRL	879
15	7	8	Lindau-Bad Schachen	D	428
15	7	6	Lisburn	NIR	920
15	5	8	Llandudno (Maesdu)	W	802
15	9	7	London Golf Club *International*	Eng	589
15	7	8	Lugano	CH	1285
15	7	7	Luttrellstown	IRL	880
15	7	8	Lytham Green Drive	Eng	590
15	6	8	Makila Golf Club	F	247
15	8	7	Manor House (Castle Combe)	Eng	593
15	7	8	Marbella	E	1161
15	8	8	Marco Simone	I	971
15	7	6	Masia Bach	E	1162
15	7	7	Master Master	Fi	150
15	7	5	Médoc *Les Vignes*	F	250
15	5	7	Mendip	Eng	594
15	8	7	Meon Valley *Meon Course*	Eng	595
15	7	7	Mere	Eng	596
15	7	5	Mölle	S	1247
15	7	7	Møn	Da	134
15	6	7	Monkstown	IRL	882
15	6	7	Moor Allerton	Eng	597
15	5	5	Mullingar	IRL	885
15	5	5	Mullion	Eng	600
15	6	7	Münchner-Strasslach	D	438
15	6	6	Murcar	Sc	755
15	7	7	Nairn Dunbar	Sc	758
15	7	7	National GC	T	1304
15	7	7	Neuhof	D	440
15	6	7	Newbury & Crookham	Eng	601
15	6	7	Newport	W	806
15	7	5	Nordcenter *Benz Course*	Fi	151
15	5	6	Nunspeet *North/East*	N	1021
15	6	6	Oberschwaben Bad Waldsee	D	442
15	7	7	Oitavos	P	1064
15	7	7	Oostende	B	104
15	7	7	Oosterhout	N	1022
15	7	7	Öschberghof	D	443
15	7	9	Oslo	Nw	1043
15	6	7	Pannal	Eng	607
15	7	7	Patriziale Ascona	CH	9999
15	6	5	Pedreña	E	1177
15	7	8	Peralada	E	1178
15	8	5	Pickala *Seaside Course*	Fi	152
15	7	9	Pineda	E	1180
15	7	6	Ploemeur Océan	F	263
15	7	7	Poggio dei Medici	I	982
15	6	6	Pornic	F	266
15	8	7	Portal *Championship*	Eng	612
15	7	7	Porters Park	Eng	613
15	6	7	Portpatrick (Dunskey)	Sc	763
15	7	7	Powerscourt	IRL	890
15	6	7	Praha Karlstejn	Cz	1299
15	7	7	Ring of Kerry	IRL	892
15	6	6	Rolls of Monmouth	W	811
15	7	7	Roncemay	F	273
15	7	7	Rosendael	N	1024
15	5	6	Ross-on-Wye	Eng	616
15	7	7	Roxburghe (The)	Sc	767
15	7	7	Royal Belfast	NIR	924
15	7	6	Royal Cromer	Eng	620
15	8	6	Royal Latem	B	110
15	7	5	Royal Oak	Da	135
15	6	8	Royal Winchester	Eng	630
15	8	8	Rudding Park	Eng	631
15	7	8	Rya	S	1251
15	7	4	Saint-Endréol	F	278
15	4	7	Samsø	Da	137
15	7	7	Schloss Egmating	D	453
15	6	6	Schloss Klingenburg	D	454
15	7	6	Schloss Lüdersburg *Old/New*	D	456
15	6	6	Seapoint	IRL	896
15	7	6	Shanklin & Sandown	Eng	639
15	6	7	Sherborne	Eng	640
15	7	6	Sheringham	Eng	641
15	7	5	Sint Nicolaasga	N	1025
15	8	6	Slieve Russell	IRL	898
15	7	5	Söderåsen	S	1254
15	8	8	Son Antem *Este*	E	1190
15	6	4	Sorknes	Nw	1044
15	9	7	St. Leon-Rot *"Rot" Course*	D	466
15	7	8	Stoneham	Eng	650
15	7	6	Strathaven	Sc	780
15	6	6	Sybrook	N	1026
15	6	8	Sylt	D	470
15	7	4	Taulane	F	293
15	9	8	The Belfry *PGA National*	Eng	656

CLASSIFICATION OF GOLF COURSES

15	7	7	The Island	IRL	901
15	6	5	Thornhill	Sc	783
15	7	4	Toulouse Palmola	F	294
15	7	6	Toulouse-Seilh *Rouge*	F	295
15	7	6	Tulfarris	IRL	904
15	6	5	Tullamore	IRL	905
15	7	6	Tutzing	D	473
15	7	6	Twente	N	1028
15	7	7	Urslautal	A	89
15	6	5	Val Queven	F	298
15	6	7	Vale do Lobo *Royal Golf Course*	P	1080
15	7	5	Värnamo	S	1262
15	7	4	Vaucouleurs (La) Les Vallons	F	299
15	6	7	Växjö	S	1264
15	7	7	Vejle *Blå/Rød*	Da	140
15	7	8	Warwickshire (The)	Eng	665
15	7	7	Wasserburg Anholt	D	475
15	7	7	West Berkshire	Eng	668
15	7	7	West Surrey	Eng	673
15	7	7	Westport	IRL	909
15	7	7	Whitekirk	Sc	789
15	7	6	Woodbrook	IRL	910
15	9	6	Woodbury Park *The Oaks*	Eng	683
15	7	6	Wouwse Plantage	N	1029
15	7	6	Zumikon	CH	1293

14

Within each score, the ranking is purely alphabetical

14	7	6	A 6	S	1211
14	7	6	Abenberg	D	376
14	6	6	Aboyne	Sc	690
14	8	8	Albarella	I	943
14	6	7	Alcaidesa	E	1108
14	7	5	Alhaurin	E	1109
14	7	7	Almerimar	E	1112
14	6	6	Alyth	Sc	692
14	7	8	Amirauté (L')	F	212
14	7	6	Anderstein	N	1000
14	7	8	Arcangues	F	217
14	6	4	Ardglass	NIR	912
14	6	6	Aroeira *Aroeira I*	P	1059
14	6	6	Aroeira *Aroeira II*	P	1060
14	6	6	Arras	F	218
14	6	8	Baberton	Sc	694
14	7	7	Bad Liebenzell	D	382
14	6	6	Bad Wörishofen	D	383
14	7	7	Badgemore Park	Eng	515
14	7	6	Ballykisteen	IRL	832
14	7	7	Banchory	Sc	696
14	6	6	Bangor	NIR	913
14	8	7	Barlassina	I	948
14	7	7	Bearna	IRL	835
14	8	5	Belas	P	1061
14	7	7	Bélesbat	F	224
14	6	8	Biarritz-le-Phare	F	228
14	6	5	Bitche	F	229
14	6	7	Boat of Garten	Sc	699
14	6	6	Bonalba	E	1115
14	6	5	Brancepeth Castle	Eng	527
14	6	7	Braunschweig	D	391
14	7	6	Brest Iroise	F	235
14	7	6	Brigode	F	237
14	6	6	Buchanan Castle	Sc	702
14	6	6	Burntisland	Sc	703
14	6	6	Campoamor	E	1117
14	7	8	Cannes Mandelieu *Old Course*	F	238
14	6	8	Cardiff	W	794
14	6	5	Cardross	Sc	705
14	5	6	Carnoustie *Burnside*	Sc	707
14	8	7	Castello di Tolcinasco	I	956
14	7	7	Cerdaña	E	1121
14	8	6	Chailly (Château de)	F	242
14	5	7	Chambon-sur-Lignon (Le)	F	243
14	6	3	Champ de Bataille	F	245
14	7	7	Chantaco	F	246
14	6	4	Chaumont-en-Vexin	F	250
14	7	6	Cheverny	F	251
14	8	7	Collingtree Park	Eng	542
14	6	7	Cosmopolitan	I	958
14	7	7	Costa Brava	E	1123
14	5	5	Courtown	IRL	850
14	7	8	Crans-sur-Sierre	CH	1276
14	6	5	Dieppe-Pourville	F	210
14	6	7	Divonne	F	213

CLASSIFICATION OF GOLF COURSES

14	7	7	Domtal-Mommenheim	D	394
14	7	8	Dromoland Castle	IRL	854
14	9	6	Drottningholm	S	1221
14	6	3	Edzell	Sc	721
14	7	7	Ekerum	S	1222
14	7	7	Elfrather Mühle	D	396
14	7	7	Eschenried	D	397
14	6	6	Esker Hills	IRL	859
14	7	5	Eslöv	S	1223
14	7	6	Estepona	E	1131
14	7	6	Etretat	F	218
14	7	7	Falkenberg	S	1226
14	6	7	Falmouth	Eng	551
14	7	4	Falnuée	B	99
14	6	6	Fontcaude	F	222
14	7	6	Fontenailles *Blanc*	F	223
14	6	4	Fontenelles (Les)	F	224
14	6	6	Forfar	Sc	725
14	8	6	Formby Hall	Eng	558
14	6	7	Forsgården	S	1231
14	7	8	Franciacorta	I	960
14	7	6	Fränkische Schweiz	D	403
14	7	7	Frilford Heath *Red Course*	Eng	559
14	7	6	Fürstliches Hofgut Kolnhausen	D	405
14	8	6	Gainsborough-Karsten Lakes	Eng	561
14	7	6	Galway Bay	IRL	863
14	7	8	Garlenda	I	962
14	6	7	Garmisch-Partenkirchen	D	406
14	6	6	Gävle	S	1233
14	4	5	Gelpenberg	N	1007
14	7	8	Glamorganshire	W	799
14	7	7	Glen	Sc	727
14	5	4	Golden Eagle	P	1062
14	5	4	Golspie	Sc	731
14	6	6	Gouverneur (Le) *Montaplan*	F	227
14	6	5	Granada	E	1135
14	6	7	Grantown on Spey	Sc	732
14	4	4	Granville *Les Dunes*	F	230
14	6	5	Greenore	IRL	868
14	7	4	Grevelingenhout	N	1011
14	7	6	Gruyère (La)	CH	1281
14	7	6	Guadalhorce	E	1136
14	7	7	Guadalmina *Sur*	E	1137
14	6	4	Haut-Poitou	F	234
14	6	6	Hechingen-Hohenzollern	D	416
14	7	8	Heilbronn-Hohenlohe	D	417
14	6	7	Henley	Eng	570
14	8	8	Hever	Eng	572
14	6	7	Huntercombe	Eng	578
14	6	6	Huntly	Sc	735
14	6	6	Interlaken	CH	1282
14	6	6	Karlshamn	S	1240
14	7	6	Keerbergen	B	101
14	6	5	Killorglin	IRL	876
14	4	6	Korsør	Da	132
14	7	4	La Dehesa	E	1142
14	7	7	La Manga *Oeste*	E	1146
14	8	8	La Quinta	E	1150
14	6	7	Lacanau	F	241
14	8	8	Las Palmas	E	1155
14	7	7	Lauro	E	1156
14	6	7	Lauswolt	N	1019
14	7	5	Laval-Changé *La Chabossière*	F	243
14	8	8	Le Pavoniere	I	967
14	7	5	Le Prieuré *Ouest*	F	244
14	7	7	Lignano	I	970
14	8	8	Lindenhof	D	429
14	6	5	Littlestone	Eng	588
14	6	4	Llanymynech	W	803
14	7	6	Longniddry	Sc	745
14	6	7	Los Arqueros	E	1158
14	6	8	Lothianburn	Sc	746
14	7	6	Main-Taunus	D	432
14	8	5	Maison Blanche	F	246
14	8	6	Mannings Heath *Waterfall Course*	Eng	592
14	7	6	Mariánské Lázne	Cz	1298
14	7	6	Märkischer Potsdam	D	433
14	5	6	Massereene	NIR	922
14	6	6	Memmingen Gut Westerhart	D	434
14	6	7	Monte Carlo (Mont Agel)	F	252
14	8	7	Monticello	I	977
14	7	8	Murrayshall	Sc	756
14	8	6	Nahetal	D	439
14	7	7	Neuchâtel	CH	1288
14	7	8	New Golf Deauville *Rouge/Blanc*	F	256
14	5	5	Newtonmore	Sc	759

CLASSIFICATION OF GOLF COURSES — **CLASSEMENT DES PARCOURS**

14	6	7	Oliva Nova	E	1172
14	7	5	Omaha Beach *La Mer/Le Bocage*	F	258
14	6	4	Ormskirk	Eng	606
14	7	4	Osona Montanya	E	1174
14	6	6	Oudenaarde	B	105
14	8	8	Padova	I	979
14	6	4	Panoramica	E	1176
14	7	8	Penina	P	1067
14	7	5	Perstorp	S	1250
14	7	7	Pinheiros Altos	P	1068
14	6	6	Pinnau	D	444
14	6	7	Pitlochry	Sc	762
14	6	4	Porcelaine (La)	F	265
14	6	4	Prince's *Himalayas-Shore*	Eng	615
14	6	8	Punta Ala	I	983
14	8	7	Quinta da Beloura	P	1070
14	7	7	Quinta da Marinha	P	1071
14	7	8	Quinta do Lago *Ria Formosa*	P	1073
14	7	5	Quinta do Peru	P	1074
14	7	4	Raray (Château de) *La Licorne*	F	268
14	7	6	Rathsallagh	IRL	891
14	6	7	Reichsstadt Bad Windsheim	D	445
14	8	7	Rheinhessen	D	449
14	7	6	Rigenée	B	108
14	6	5	Rijk van Nijmegen *Nijmeegse Baan*	N	1023
14	6	5	Rinkven Red - White	B	109
14	6	4	Rochefort-Chisan	F	272
14	7	6	Royal Ashdown Forest	Eng	617
14	3	8	Royal Mid-Surrey *Outer*	Eng	625
14	8	7	Saint-Cloud Vert	F	277
14	7	5	Saint-Laurent	F	281
14	7	5	Saint-Thomas	F	284
14	7	6	Sainte-Baume (La)	F	285
14	6	6	San Sebastián	E	1186
14	7	7	Sand Moor	Eng	633
14	5	4	Savenay	F	287
14	7	6	Schönenberg	CH	1290
14	5	6	Sct. Knuds	Da	138
14	7	7	Simon's	Da	139
14	6	5	Skellefteå	S	1252
14	6	7	Son Vida	E	1193
14	7	8	Spiegelven	B	114
14	8	8	St Andrews *Eden Course*	Sc	776
14	6	6	St Helen's Bay	IRL	899
14	5	4	St Laurence	Fi	154
14	8	6	Talma	Fi	155
14	7	6	Tandridge	Eng	654
14	7	7	TAT Golf Belek	T	1306
14	7	5	Tawast	Fi	156
14	7	8	Tegernseer Bad Wiessee	D	471
14	7	5	Thetford	Eng	657
14	7	6	Thorndon Park	Eng	658
14	7	7	Thorpeness	Eng	659
14	7	7	Torekov	S	1258
14	7	7	Torrequebrada	E	1196
14	7	6	Toxandria	N	1027
14	6	7	Tranås	S	1259
14	6	6	Tyrifjord	Nw	1046
14	7	5	Val de Sorne	F	297
14	6	6	Vale da Pinta	P	1079
14	8	7	Varese	I	989
14	7	7	Vila Sol	P	1081
14	7	7	Vilamoura *Vilamoura III (Laguna)*	P	1083
14	7	7	Vilamoura *Millenium*	P	1084
14	6	5	Volcans (Les)	F	301
14	6	6	Waterford	IRL	906
14	5	6	Waterford Castle	IRL	907
14	6	8	West Byfleet	Eng	669
14	8	6	Westerwood	Sc	788
14	6	6	Wheatley	Eng	676
14	4	5	Wimereux	F	303
14	7	7	Woodbridge	Eng	682
14	7	8	Zuid Limburgse	N	1030

13

Within each score, the ranking is purely alphabetical

13	5	7	Aix-les-Bains	F	210
13	6	7	Aldeburgh	Eng	512
13	8	8	Almenara	E	1111
13	7	7	Ambrosiano	I	944

CLASSIFICATION OF GOLF COURSES

CLASSEMENT DES PARCOURS

13	6	5	Amnéville	F	213
13	6	5	Annonay-Gourdan	F	214
13	6	6	Arcachon	F	216
13	7	7	Asolo	I	947
13	6	6	Athlone	IRL	829
13	6	4	Augerville	F	219
13	5	5	Aura	Fi	147
13	7	6	Bad Ragaz	CH	1273
13	6	7	Beaufort	IRL	836
13	7	7	Bercuit	B	98
13	7	5	Besançon	F	226
13	6	5	Béthemont	F	227
13	6	6	Blainroe	IRL	838
13	7	7	Bologna	I	953
13	7	6	Breitenloo	CH	1275
13	6	7	Bundoran	IRL	839
13	6	5	Cairndhu	NIR	915
13	6	7	Callander	Sc	704
13	6	8	Castle	IRL	841
13	6	6	Castletroy	IIRL	842
13	6	9	Cervia	I	957
13	4	6	Charleville	IRL	843
13	6	7	Chesterfield	Eng	540
13	6	8	Citywest	IRL	844
13	7	5	Cognac	F	207
13	6	6	Costa Dorada	E	1124
13	6	7	Dinard	F	211
13	7	4	Domont-Montmorency	F	214
13	7	8	Elm Park	IRL	857
13	7	6	Ennetsee-Holzhäusern	CH	1279
13	8	4	Escorpion	E	1130
13	7	7	Faithlegg	IRL	861
13	6	6	Falkirk Tryst	Sc	724
13	5	5	Filey	Eng	554
13	8	9	Firenze - Ugolino	I	959
13	6	6	Galway GC	IRL	864
13	6	7	Glen of the Downs	IRL	866
13	6	7	Grand Ducal de Luxembourg	L	117
13	7	7	Grasse	F	9999
13	7	6	Hauger	Nw	1039
13	7	6	Jarama R.A.C.E.	E	1139
13	7	6	Kilkenny	IRL	873
13	7	6	La Duquesa	E	1143
13	7	8	La Pinetina	I	966
13	7	6	Lee Valley	IRL	878
13	6	7	Luzern	CH	1286
13	4	6	Málaga	E	1160
13	7	8	Malahide *Red + Blue + Yellow*	IRL	881
13	6	6	Malone	NIR	921
13	7	7	Margara	I	972
13	5	4	Mazamet-La Barouge	F	248
13	6	7	Mijas *Los Olivos*	E	1166
13	7	7	Modena	I	974
13	8	8	Molinetto	I	975
13	7	6	Mont-Garni	B	103
13	5	5	Monte Mayor	E	1167
13	5	5	Montebelo	P	1063
13	8	8	Montecchia	I	976
13	6	5	Montreux	Ch	1287
13	6	5	Mount Wolseley	IRL	884
13	7	7	Niederbüren	Ch	1289
13	7	7	North Foreland	Eng	602
13	7	8	Olivar de la Hinojosa	E	1173
13	7	5	Ozoir-la-Ferrière *Château/Monthéty*	F	259
13	6	6	Palingbeek	B	106
13	7	5	Palmares	P	1065
13	6	9	Parco de' Medici	I	980
13	8	8	Patshull Park Hotel	Eng	609
13	6	8	Pau	F	261
13	6	5	Pula	E	1183
13	8	8	Rapallo	I	984
13	7	6	Reims-Champagne	F	270
13	6	8	Rimini	I	985
13	7	7	Riva dei Tessali	I	986
13	7	8	Riviéra Golf Club	F	271
13	5	6	Rosslare	IRL	894
13	7	7	Royal Portrush *Valley*	NIR	927
13	7	8	Sainte-Maxime	F	286
13	6	6	Salgados	P	1076
13	6	5	Sant Cugat	E	1187
13	6	7	Santa Ponsa	E	1188
13	5	7	Servanes	F	289
13	6	6	Shannon	IRL	897
13	7	6	Strasbourg Illkirch *Jaune + Rouge*	F	292
13	4	6	Taymouth Castle	Sc	782
13	7	7	Torremirona	E	1195
13	7	6	Tramore	IRL	903
13	8	7	Treudelberg	D	472
13	6	6	Upsala	S	1261
13	7	8	Verona	I	991
13	6	5	Warrenpoint	NIR	928
13	6	6	Wylihof	CH	1292

ARCHITECTS

AND COURSES

ARCHITECTS AND COURSES
ARCHITECTES ET PARCOURS
ARCHITEKTEN UND GOLFPLÄTZE
ARKITEKTER OCH GOLFBANOR
ARQUITECTOS Y RECORRIDOS
ARCHITETTI E PERCORSI

James Braid
Brampton 526, Clitheroe 541, Dalmahoy *East Course* 712, La Moye 583, North Hants 603, Southport & Ainsdale 645, Ayr (Belleisle) 693, Fortrose & Rosemarkie 726, Golspie 731, Grange 867, Holyhead 800, Ipswich (Purdis Heath) 580, Lundin 748, Perranporth 610, Powfoot 764, Alloa 691, Ballater 695, Brora 700, East Renfrewshire 720, Hawkstone Park *Hawkstone* 568, Kirkistown Castle 918, Langland Bay 801, Mullingar 885, Bangor 913, Boat of Garten 699, Buchanan Castle 702, Henley 570, Lothianburn 746, Newtonmore 759, Sherborne 640, Thorpeness 659, Taymouth Castle 782, Scotscraig 773

James Braid, M. Cowper
Shanklin & Sandown 639

James Braid, C.K. Cotton
Pennard 809

James Braid, George Duncan
Mere 596

James Braid, George Fernie
Hunstanton 577

James Braid, Fowler, Colt
Aberdovey 792

James Braid, Paddy Merrigan
Tullamore 905

James Braid, F. Pennink, D. Steel
Berwick-upon-Tweed 521

James Braid, J.H. Taylor
Nefyn & District 805

James Braid, Jim Steer
Fairhaven 550

James Braid, Mungo Park
Royal Musselburgh 771

Declan Branigan
Ballykisteen 832, Seapoint 896, Waterford Castle 907

Douglas Brasier
Ljunghusen 1245, Bosjökloster 1218, Växjö 1264.

Douglas Brasier, Peter Nordwall
Åtvidaberg 1214

Douglas Brasier, R. Victorsson
Karlshamn 1240

Douglas Brasier, Tommy Nordström
Kristianstad 1242

Olivier Brizon, Groupe Taiyo
Aisses (Les) *Rouge/Blanc* 209

A.C. Brown/W. Park, James Braid
Grantown on Spey 732

R.J. Browne
Bearna 835

Ture Bruce, Åke Persson
Landskrona Gul Bana 1244

Ture Bruce
Barsebäck 1215, Vasatorp 1263, Mölle 1247, Söderåsen 1254, Eslöv 1223

G. Bruns
Isernhagen 423

Mr Buchanan
West Byfleet 669

Yves Bureau
Saint-Jean-de-Monts 280, Baden 220, Val Queven 298, Fontenelles (Les) 224, Omaha Beach *La Mer/Le Bocage* 258.

Burrows, Del C. van Krimpen
Hilversum 1014

CS Butchark, J.H. Taylor
Porters Park 613

Sir Guy Campbell
Killarney Mahony's Point 875

Sir Guy Campbell, C.K. Hutchinson
West Sussex 676, Wimereux 303

Sir Guy Campbell, Hutchinson, Hotchkin
Ashridge 514

Sir Guy Campbell, John Morrison
Prince's Himalayas-Shore 615

Willie Campbell
Seascale 637

Willie Campbell, Donald Steel
Machrie 749

Enrique Canales, Luis Recasens
Islantilla 1138

S. Carrera, L. Rota Caremoli
Molinetto 975

Doug Carrick,Hans Erhard
Fontana 83

Giulio Cavalsani
Punta Ala 983

M. Chantepie
Etretat 218

Hubert Chesneau, Robert von Hagge (consult.ant)
National *L'Albatros* 255

Neil Coles
Gainsborough-Karsten 561

Neil Coles, Angel Gallardo
PGA de Catalunya 1179.

Harry S. Colt
Bath 516, Cannes Mandelieu *Old Course* 238, Chantaco 246, Royal Dublin 895, Royal Portrush *Dunluce Links* 926, Eindhoven 1006, Kennemer 1017, Rye 632, Sunningdale *New Course* 651, Wentworth *East Course* 666, Wentworth *West Course* 667, Blackmoor 522, Frankfurter GC 402, Moor Park *High Course* 598, Pyle & Kenfig 810, Saint-Germain 279, St George's Hill 647, Stoke Poges 649, Trevose *Championship* 661, Whittington Heath 677, Camberley Heath 534, De Pan 1004, Sherwood Forest 642, Isle of Purbeck 581, Manchester 591,Royal Wimbledon 629, Swinley Forest 653, Thurlestone 660, Belvoir Park 914, Brokenhurst Manor 529, Denham 547, Pedreña 1177, Royal Belfast 924, Brancepeth Castle 527, Saint-Cloud *Vert* 277, St Andrews *Eden Course* 776, Tandridge 654, Thorndon Park 658, Castle 841, Chesterfield 540.

Harry S. Colt, T. Simpson
Málaga 1160

Harry S. Colt, Alison
County Sligo 848, Haagsche 1012

Harry S. Colt, Alison, J. Morrison
Falkenstein 399

Harry S. Colt, Alister MacKenzie
Alwoodley (The) 513, Ilkley 579

Harry S. Colt, McKenzie, Alison
Knock 919

Harry S. Colt, J. Morrison
Prestbury 614

Harry S. Colt, Ross / Braid
Longniddry 745

Harry S. Colt, Alison, M. Hawtree (1992)
Granville Les Dunes 230

E. Connaughton
Charleville 843

Bill Coore
Médoc *Les Châteaux* 249

Jean-Claude Cornillot
Arras 218

Cornish & Silva
Ambrosiano 944

C.K. Cotton
Downfield 713, Marriott St Pierre *Old Course* 804, Ross-on-Wye 616 West Lancashire 672

CK Cotton, Cruikshank, Marco Croze
Venezia 990

Henry Cotton
Penina 1067

Cotton & Harris
Bologna 953

Cotton & Sutton
Bergamo - L'Albenza *Blu + Giallo* 949

Cotton, Penninck, Lawree
Keerbergen 101

Cotton, Pennink, Piero Mancinelli
Is Molas 965

Cotton, Pennink, Steel & Partners
Gardagolf 961

Cotton/Dreyer
Sct. Knuds 138

Henry Cotton, Piero Mancinelli
Olgiata 978

Henry Cotton, Rocky Roquemore
Vale do Lobo *Royal Golf Course* 1080

Arthur Croome
Liphook 586

Marco Croze
Lignano 970, Cervia 957, Riva dei Tessali 986

Juan de la Cuadra, J.M. Olazabal
La Sella 1151

Robert E. Cupp
East Sussex National *East Course* 549

Baldovino Dassù, A. Rossi Fioravanti
Poggio dei Medici 982

DeutscheGolf Consult
Öschberghof 443

F. Deyer
Jönköping 1238

José Gancedo
Canyamel 1118, Torrequebrada 1196, Lerma 1157, Golf del Sur 1134.

José Gancedo, V. Sardá Saenger
Costa Dorada 1124

P. Gancedo
Monte Mayor 1167

Peter Gannon
Villa D'Este 992

Jean Garaïalde
Porcelaine (La) 265, Cognac 207

Jonathan Gaunt
Linden Hall 584

Michel Gayon
Sablé-Solesmes *La Forêt/La Rivière* 275, Ailette (L') 208, Esery 215, Etiolles *Les Cerfs* 217, Gloria Golf Resort 1303, Saint-Endréol 278, Vaucouleurs (La) *Les Vallons* 299, Chambon-sur-Lignon (Le) 243, Fontenailles *Blanc* 223, Savenay 287.

Michel Gayon, Jacques Lebreton
Pornic 266

Charles Gibson
Royal Porthcawl 812

Andrew Gilbert, Jim Cassidy
Kilkea Castle 872

Golden Bear Design,Associates
La Moraleja *La Moraleja* 2 1149

Antonio Lucena Gomez
La Herreria 1144

G.H. Gowring
Berkhamsted 518

I.E. Grant, Hawtree & Son
Cardigan 795

Gratenau
St. Dionys 464

Karl F. Grohs
Bitburger Land 389

Eddie Hackett
Enniscrone 858, Donegal (Murvagh) 852, Belmullet 837, Connemara 845, Dooks 853, Ring of Kerry 892, Greenore 868, Killorglin 876, Castletroy 842, Malahide *Red* + *Blue* + *Yellow* 881

Eddie Hackett, Billy O'Sullivan
Killarney *Killeen Course* 874

Eddie Hackett, Christy O'Connor Jr
Dingle Links (Ceann Sibeal) 851

Eddie Hackett, John A. Mulcahy
Waterville 908

J. Hamilton Stutt
Woodbury Park *The Oaks* 683

Donald Harradine
Beuerberg 387, Schloss Myllendonk 457, Düsseldorfer 395, Schloss Klingenburg 454, Sylt 470, Zumikon 1293, Bad Wörishofen 383, Chaumont-en-Vexin 250, Grevelingenhout 1011, Neuchâtel 1288, Schönenberg 1290, Tegernseer Bad Wiessee 471,

Donald Harradine
Bad Ragaz 1273, Breitenloo 1275, Niederbüren 1289, Strasbourg Illkirch *Jaune* + *Rouge*, Bled *King's Course* 1301

Donald Harradine, Cabell B. Robinson
Lugano 1285

D. Harradine, H. Schauer
Zell am See Kaprun 90

Donald Harradine, Peter Harradine
Sainte-Maxime 286

Peter Harradine, Olivier Dongradi
Maison Blanche 246

Harris & Associates
Courtown 850

FA Harris
Berlin-Wannsee 386

John D. Harris
Shannon 897

John Harris
Garlenda 962, Lacanau 241, Padova 979, Verona 991.

John Harris, G. Albertini
La Pinetina 966

John Harris, Marco Croze
Albarella 943

Hauser, Patrick Merrigan
Neuhof 440

Fred Hawtree
Saint-Nom-la-Bretèche *Rouge* 283, John O'Gaunt 582, Limburg 102, Saint-Nom-la-Bretèche *Bleu* 282, Lisburn 920, Royal Latem 110, Westport 909,

Fred Hawtree
Le Prieuré *Ouest* 244, Massereene 922, Rochefort-Chisan 272, Domont-Montmorency 214, Malone 921, Waterloo *La Marache* 115, Pals 1175, Bondues *Jaune* 231

F. Hawtree, E. Hackett
The Island 901

Fred Hawtree
Hillside (1962) 574

Hawtree & Taylor
Båstad *Old Course* 1216, High Post 573

F.W. Hawtree
Gog Magog *Old Course* 563, Son Vida 1193, Woodbridge 682

F.W. Hawtree, J.H. Taylor
Royal Birkdale (The) 618

FW Hawtree, Rolin/Snelders
Zuid Limburgse 1030

Hawtree & Sons
Blainroe 838

Martin Hawtree
Rudding Park 631, Simon's 139, TAT Golf Belek 1306, Vilamoura *Millenium* 1084

Siegfried Heinz
Domtal-Mommenheim 394

Rolf Henning-Jensen
Møn 134

Rubens Henriquez
Las Américas 1153

S. Herd, J. Braid, T. Simpson, G.Duncan
Wilmslow 678

Sandy Herd
Harrogate 567

Sandy Herd, Charles MacKenzie
Pannal 607

Sandy Herd, Jim Steer
Lytham Green Drive 590

E.D. Hess
Wendlohe A+ B 476

L. Hewson, T. Simpson
Ballybunion *Old Course* 831

Reijo Hillberg
Pickala *Seaside Course* 152, Tawast 156

Arthur Hills
Oitavos 1064

Harold Hilton
Ferndown *Old Course* 553, Ormskirk 606

Thomas Himmel, Carlo Knauss
Fürstlicher GC Bad Waldsee 404

Pierre Hirigoyen
San Sebastián 1186

Karl-Heinz Hoffmann
Mittelrheinischer 435

Col. S.V. Hotchkin
Woodhall Spa 684

Brian Huggett
Orchardleigh 605

Brian Huggett, Knott/Bridge
Bowood (Cornwall) 524

Åke Hultström
Ängsö 1213

Bob Hunt PGA Management
Meland 1042

C.W. Hunter
Portpatrick (Dunskey) 763

Charles Hunter, J. Allan
Prestwick St Nicholas 766

Ibergolf
Granada 1135

Holcombe Ingleby
Royal West Norfolk (Brancaster) 628

Tony Jacklin
San Roque 1185

John Jacobs
The Buckinghamshire 530, Northop Country Park 808, Apremont 215, Patshull Park Hotel 609

Henrik Jacobsen
Samsø 137

Wolfgang Jersombek
Jakobsberg 424

Peter Johnson
Vale of Glamorgan 816

Gerard Jol
Houtrak 1016

Tom Jones
Llandudno (Maesdu) 802

Jean Jottrand
Falnuée 99

Armin Keller
Nahetal 439, Rheinhessen 449

Ron Kirby
Spiegelven 114, Escorpion 1130

Ron Kirby, Fritz Beindorf
Elfrather Mühle 396

Ron Kirby, Joe Carr, P. Merrigan.
Old Head 886

Ron Kirby/Golden Bear
London Golf Club International 589

C. Kramer
Tutzing 473

Kosti Kuronen
Master *Master* 150, Guadalhorce 1136, St Laurence 154

Kothe
Hanau-Wilhelmsbad 414

Max Graf Lamberg
Am Mondsee 80

Hugues Lambert
Villette d'Anthon *Les Sangliers* 300, Val de Sorne 297

Patrice Lambert
Saint-Thomas 284

Bernhard Langer
Bad Griesbach Brunnwies 380, Portmarnock Links 888, Schloss Nippenburg 458, Soufflenheim 290, Panoramica 1176, Béthemont 227, Modena 974

Bernhard Langer, Kurt Rossknecht
Stolper Heide 468

Charles Lawrie
Woburn *Dukes* 679, Hankley Common 566

Joseph Lee
S. Lourenço 1075

Joseph Lee, Rocky Roquemore
Vilamoura *Laguna* 1083

Patrice Léglise
Raray (Château de) 268

Sune Linde
Frösåker 1232, Forsgården 1231

Karl Litten
Warwickshire (The) 665

José Luis Lopez
Estepona 1131

George Low, Sandy Herd
Pleasington 611

Sandy Lyle
Schloss Wilkendorf 459

Tom MacAuley
Cromstrijen 1003, Twente 1028, Mont-Garni 103, Montecchia 976

Peter McEvoy
Powerscourt 890, Glen of the Downs 866, Woodbrook 910

Peter McEvoy, Ch. O'Connor Jr
Rathsallagh 891

M. McKenna
Hermitage 870

Charles MacKenzie
Fulford 560

Alister MacKenzie
Cork GC 846, Galway GC 864, Moortown 599, Rungsted 136, Hadley Wood 564, Bolton Old Links 523, Duff House Royal 715, Sand Moor 633.

Alister MacKenzie, James Braid
Blairgowrie *Rosemount* 698

John MacPherson
Elgin 722

Dr McCuaig , Alister McKenzie
Seaton Carew 638

Brian Magnusson
Bråviken 1219

Alejandro Maldonado
Monteenmedio 1169

Malling Petersen
Vejle *Blå/Rød* 140

Malling/Gundtoft
Royal Oak 135

C.H. Mayo, Donald Steel
Thetford 657

Dan Maples
Capdepera 1119

J. McAllister, Fred Hawtree
Athlone 829

Paddy Merrigan
Slieve Russell 898, Tulfarris 904 Woodenbridge 911

Patrick Merrigan
Faithlegg 861

Johnny Miller
Collingtree Park 542

William Mitchell
Quinta do Lago B/C 1072

William Mitchell, Rocky Roquemore
Quinta do Lago *Ria Formosa* 1073

Léonard Morandi, Donald Harradine
Nîmes-Campagne 257

Theodore Moon
Kilmarnock (Barassie) 737

John Morgan
Forest Pines
Forest + Pines 556

John Morris, D. Steel
Caldy 533

Old Tom Morris
Machrihanish 750, Ladybank 740, Moray 753, Tain 781, Dunbar 718, Luffness New 747, Crail *Balcomie Links* 709, Callander 704, Royal County Down 925, Royal North Devon (Westward Ho!) 626

Old Tom Morris, Donald Ross
Royal Dornoch *Championship* 770

Old Tom Morris, Harry S. Colt
Muirfield 754

Old Tom Morris, James Braid
Carnoustie *Championship* 708, Nairn 757, Lanark 741, Royal Burgess 769, West Kilbride 786, Alyth 692, Forfar 725

Old Tom Morris/J. Braid,Taylor/Hawtree...
Wallasey 662

Old Tom Morris, Alister MacKenzie
Lahinch 877

Old Tom Morris, Auchterlonie/Steel
St Andrews *Jubilee* 777

Old Tom Morris, Braid, Vardon
Rosapenna 893

John Morrison
Biella - Le Betulle 950, Barlassina 948,

John Morrison
Toxandria 1027.

John Morrison, Cooke/Harris/Croze
Torino - La Mandria *Percorso Blu* 988

John Morrison, M. Nicholson
Stockholm 1256

J. Morrison, S. Böstrom
Lunds Akademiska 1246

Morrison, Gärtner
Lüneburger Heide 431

Tim Morisson
Cairndhu 915, Hossegor 235.

Jack Morris
Royal Liverpool (Hoylake) 623

M. Nakowsky, Donald Harradine
Divonne 213

Narbel, Jeremy Pern
Lausanne 1283

Falco Nardi
Lauro 1156, Santa Ponsa 1188

Robin Nelson, Thierry Huau
Champ de Bataille 245

M. Nicholson, Seve Ballesteros
Crans-sur-Sierre 1276

Peter Nicholson
Hever 572

Jack Nicklaus
Mount Juliet 883, Gleneagles *PGA Centenary* 729, Gut Altentann 85, Gut Lärchenhof 409, Montecastillo 1168,

Jack Nicklaus
St Mellion *Nicklaus Course* 648, Paris International 260, Le Robinie 969

Jack Nicklaus, Desmond Muirhead
La Moraleja
La Moraleja 1 1148

Jack Nicklaus, Steve Nicklaus
Carden Park
Nicklaus Course 536

Jack Nicklaus Jr
Arzaga 946

Nicklaus Design
Hertfordshire (The) 571

Tommy Nordström
Borre 1038

Peter Nordwall
Bro-Bålsta 1220, Skövde 1253, Stenungsund 1255, Losby 1041, Gränna 1235, A 6 1211, Ekerum 1222

C. Noskowski
Karlovy Vary 1297

Christy O'Connor Jr
Glasson 865, Headfort *New Course* 869, Esker Hills 859, Galway Bay 863, Citywest 844, Lee Valley 878, Mount Wolseley 884

Christy O'Connor Jr, P. McEvoy / F. Howes
Fota Island 862

Peter O'Hare, T. Carey, B. Murphy
Monkstown 882

José Maria Olazábal
Sevilla 1189, Masia Bach 1162

Arnold Palmer
Tralee 902, K Club 871, Scharmützelsee *Arnold Palmer* 450, Castello di Tolcinasco 956, Le Pavoniere 967

Arnold Palmer, Ed Seay
Rethmar 447

Willie Park Jr
Silloth-on-Solway 643, Sunningdale *Old Course* 652, Duddingston 714, Stoneham 650, Baberton 694, Burntisland 703, Huntercombe 578, Notts (Hollinwell) 604, Montrose 752, Dieppe-Pourville 210

Willie Park Jr, Alister MacKenzie
Bruntsfield 701

Willie Park Jr, Jack White
West Hill 671

Willie Park Jr, James Braid
Parkstone 608, Portstewart *Strand Course* 923, Waterford 906

Willie Park Jr, Tom Simpson
Antwerp 97

W. Park, Harry S. Colt, Frank Pennink, Donald Steel
Formby 557

Jerry Pate, Reinhold Weishaupt
Schwanhof 460

Greger Paulsson
Upsala 1261

Frank Pennink
Noordwijk 1020, Vilamoura I *(Old Course)* 1082, Kungsbacka 1243, Aroeira *Aroeira I* 1059, Palmares 1065

Frank Pennink, Donald Steel
Gelpenberg 1007, Lauswolt 1019

Frank Pennink, Gerard Jol
Broekpolder 1002

Frank Pennink, Karl F. Grohs
Gut Kaden 408

Jeremy Pern
Bresse (La) 234, Dartmouth 545, Les Bois 1284, Roncemay 273, Gruyère (La) 1281

Jeremy Pern, Jean Garaïalde
Charmeil 248, Wantzenau (La) 302, Ableiges *Les Etangs* 207, Albi 211, Largue (La) 242, Toulouse-Seilh *Rouge* 295

Andrew Person
Göteborg 1234

PGA Projects
Formby Hall 558

Kyle Philips, Robert Trent Jones
Lage Vuursche 1018

Kyle Phillips
Eichenheim 82

Kyle Phillips, Mark Parsinen
Kingsbarns 738

WG Pikeman, George Ross
Portmarnock 887

Manuel Piñero
La Dehesa 1142

Manuel Piñero, Antonio Garrido
La Quinta 1150

Chris Pittman
Fontcaude 222

Gary Player
Zaudin 1200, Taulane 293

Gary Player, Ron Kirby
Almerimar 1112

Jean-Marie Poellot
Feucherolles 220

P. Postel
Iffeldorf 421

Alain Prat
Pléneuf-Val-André 262, Gujan-Mestras 232

Rainer Preismann, DeutscheGolfConsult
Bad Abbach-Deutenhof 378

Keith Preston
Schloss Ebreichsdorf 87

Dr W. Laidlaw Purves
Royal St George's 627

W. Laidlaw Purves, Alister Mackenzie
Littlestone 588

P. Puttman
Villamartin 1199

Quenouille & MacAuley
Ploemeur Océan 263

Ted Ray
Sandiway 634

Ruzzo Reuss
Luzern 1286, Wylihof 1292

Alan Rijks
Batouwe 1001, Gendersteyn 1008

Alan Rijks, Paul Rolin
Sybrook 1026

José Rivero
Olivar de la Hinojosa 1173

Cabell Robinson
Castillo de Gorraiz 1120, La Cala *Norte* 1140, Limère 245, Praia d'El Rey 1069, Grande Bastide (La) 228, La Cala *Sur* 1141, Evian 219

W.R. Robinson
Clandeboye *Dufferin Course* 917

Paul Rolin
Nunspeet *North/East* 1021, Rijk van Nijmegen 1023, Rinkven *Red - White* 109

Paul Rolin, Alan Rijks
Sint Nicolaasga 1025

Paul Rolin, Christophe Descampe
Rigenée 108

Paul Rolin, European Tour Design
Waterloo *Le Lion* 116

Paul Rolin, Gerard Jol
Amsterdam 999

Erik Röös
Fjällbacka 1228

Rocky Roquemore
Makila Golf Club 247, Belas 1061, Golden Eagle 1062, Quinta do Peru 1074

Mackenzie Ross
Castletown 538, Southerness 775, Maspalomas 1163, Glen 727

James Ross, Peter Samuelsen
Asserbo 126

Mackenzie Ross, Fred Hawtree
Mazamet-La Barouge 248

Mackenzie Ross, Juan Dominguez
Las Palmas 1155

Mackenzie Ross, 1945
Turnberry *Ailsa Course* 784

Mackenzie Ross, 1945, Donald Steel, 1999
Turnberry *Kintyre Course* 785

Jean-Manuel Rossi
Belle-Dune 225, Amnéville 213

Kurt Rossknecht
Bad Griesbach-Sagmühle *Sagmühle* 381, Motzener See 436, Gut Thailing 411, Sempachersee 1291, Son Muntaner 1192, Gut Ludwigsberg 410, Hof Trages 418, Hohenpähl 419, Schloss Egmating 453

Lucien Roux
Volcans (Les) 301

Pat Ruddy
European (The) 860

Pat Ruddy, M. Craddock
Druids Glen 855, Ballyliffin *Glashedy Links* 833, St Margaret's 900

Bob Sandow
Badgemore Park 515

Gregorio Sanz, C. Garcia
Campoamor 1117

Ben Sayers
Castlerock 916

Ulrich Schmidt
Bad Bevensen 379

Erik Schnack
Holstebro 130

Hannes Schreiner
St. Leon-Rot *"Rot"* 466

Archdeacon Scott
Royal Ashdown Forest 617

Jan Sederholm
Larvik 1040, Espoo 148, Haninge 1237, Himmerland *New Course* 129, Sarfvik *New Course* 153, Ängelholm 1212.

Jan Sederholm, Tor Eia
Tyrifjord 1046

F. López Segales
Son Antem *Oeste* 1191, Son Antem *Este* 1190, Pula 1183

T. Shannon, Alliss & Thomas
Dundalk 856

William Side
Mullion 600

W. Siegmann
Buxtehude 392, Lindenhof 429

W. Siegmann, Jack Nicklaus
Schloss Lüdersburg *Old/New* 456

Brian Silva
Rimini 985

Archie Simpson
Aboyne 690

A. Simpson, J. Braid
Murcar 755

Bob Simpson
Edzell 721

Bob Simpson,James Braid
Royal Aberdeen *Balgownie Links* 768, Crieff *Ferntower Course* 710

Tom Simpson
Chantilly *Vineuil* 247, County Louth 847, Cruden Bay 711, Morfontaine 254, Fontainebleau 221, Ravenstein 107, Carlow 840, Chiberta 252, Sart-Tilman 112, Hardelot *Les Pins* 233, Hainaut *Bruyere-Quesnoy-Etangs* 100, International Club du Lys *Les Chênes* 236, Spa (Les Fagnes) 113.

Tom Simpson, Henry Cotton
New Golf Deauville *Rouge/Blanc* 256

Tom Simpson, J. Harris
Puerta de Hierro *Arriba* 1182

Tom Simpson, Mackenzie Ross
Carlisle 537

Tom Simpson, Martin Hawtree
Oostende 104

Cameron Sinclair
Whitekirk 789

Nils Sköld
Forsbacka 1230, Täby 1257, Värnamo 1262, Torekov 1258

Nils Sköld, Peter Nordwall
Visby 1265

Nils Sköld, Sune Linde
Karlstad 1241, Kalmar 1239

Nils Sköld, Karlsson, Nordwall, Larsson
Skellefteå 1252

Sköld, Sederholm, Eriksson
Gävle 1233

Fred Smith
Stavanger 1045

Des Smyth
Limerick County 879

Junl Søgaard
Sorknes 1044

Jorge Soler
Peralada 1178

Duarte Sotto Mayor
Quinta da Beloura 1070

Thierry Sprecher, Géry Watine
Chailly (Château de) 242, Annonay-Gourdan 214, Servanes 289

Arthur Spring
Beaufort 836

Christoph Staedler
Semlin am See 462, Senne 463, Märkischer Potsdam 433

Christoph Staedler, Euro Golf Projekt
Rheine/Mesum 448

Donald Steel
Efteling 1005, Amarilla 1114, Forest of Arden *Arden Course* 555, Portal *Championship* 612, Aroeira *Aroeira II* 1060, Vila Sol 1081, Treudelberg 472

Donald Steel, Frank Pennink
Hoge Kleij 1015

Donald Steel, H. Hertzberger
Goes 1009

Donald Steel, Paul Rolin
Wouwse Plantage 1029

Donald Steel, Tom Mackenzie
Carnegie Club (Skibo Castle) 706

D. Steel/GK. Smith
Letham Grange *Old Course* 742

Blake Sterling, Marco Martin
El Cortijo 1126

Adrian Stiff
Cumberwell Park 544

Mark Stilwell, Malcolm Kenyon
Montebelo 1063

Hamilton Stutt
Meon Valley *Meon Course* 595, Murrayshall 756

Hamilton Stutt & Co
Costa Brava 1123, Dunfermline 719

Rafael Sundblom
Halmstad 1236, Rya 1251

Rafael Sundblom, Nils Sköld
Drottningholm 1221

Sundblom/Gierdsjö
Tranås 1259

J.H. Taylor
Hindhead 575, Carmarthen 796, Royal Winchester 630, Frilford Heath *Red Course* 559, Royal Mid-Surrey Outer 625.

J.H. Taylor, Harry S. Colt
Touquet (Le) *La Mer* 296, Royal Cromer 620

J.H. Taylor,Tom Simpson
Hayling 569

Tecnoa, Eugenio Aguado
Torremirona 1195

Dave Thomas
Nobilis 1305, St. Leon-Rot "*St Leon*" *Course* 467, Roxburghe (The) 767, The Belfry *PGA National* 656, La Manga *Oeste* 1146, Almenara 1111, Bowood G&CC 525, Slaley Hall 644, Osona Montanya 1174

Dave Thomas, P. Alliss
Blairgowrie *Lansdowne* 697

Dave Thomas, David Mezzacane
Cosmopolitan 958, Parco de' Medici 980.

Thomas/Puttman, Arnold Palmer
La Manga *Norte* 1145, La Manga *Sur* 1147

Mr Thompson
Portsalon 889

John Thompson, Willie Fernie
Aldeburgh 512

Peter Thomson
Duke's Course St Andrews 716

Capt. Tippett
Tramore 903

R. Trent Jones Jr
Puerta de Hierro *Abajo* 1181, Seddiner See *Südplatz* 461, Grenoble Bresson 231, Moscow 1302, Bonmont 1116, Penha Longa 1066, Saint Donat 276, Antognolla 945.

R. Trent Jones Sr
Castelconturbia *Giallo* + *Azzurro* 954, Celtic Manor *Roman Road* 797, I Roveri 963, Pevero 981, Spérone 291, Ballybunion *Cashen (New Course)* 830, Bodensee-Weissensberg 390, Estérel Latitudes 216, Grande-Motte (La) *Les Flamants Roses* 229, Joyenval *Marly* 238, Joyenval *Retz* 239, Adare 828, Castelgandolfo 955, Moor Allerton 597, Dromoland Castle 854, Riviéra Golf Club 271, Valderrama 1198, Las Brisas 1154, Sotogrande 1194, Genève 1280, Moliets 251, El Bosque 1125, Los Naranjos 1159, Mijas *Los Lagos* 1165, Mijas *Los Olivos* 1166, Santo da Serra 1077, Troia 1078, Chamonix 244, Marbella 1161, Quinta da Marinha 1071, Bercuit 98, La Duquesa 1143,

R. Trent Jones Sr, R. Trent Jones Jr
Bondues *Blanc* 230, Prince de Provence (Vidauban) 267

Sven Tumba
Ullna 1260

Sven Tumba, Jan Sederholm
Österåker 1249

J.H. Turner
Newbury & Crookham 601

Jeremy Turner
Hauger 1039

Reverend Tyack,
West Cornwall 670

Iwao Uematsu
Kikuoka 118

Urbis Planning
Rolls of Monmouth (The) 811

Olivier van der Vynckt
Cheverny 251

Joan Dudok van Heel
Wittelsbacher 477, Im Chiemgau 422 Oosterhout 1022

Joan Dudok van Heel, B. Steensels
Herkenbosch 1013

Joan Dudok van Heel, Gerard Jol
Anderstein 1000

D.C. van Krimpen, F. Pennink
Rosendael 1024

Harry Vardon
Little Aston 587, Kingussie 739, Bundoran 839

Harry Vardon, F. Pennink
Mendip 594

Pedro Vasconcelos
Salgados 1076

Marco Verdieri
Ennetsee-Holzhäusern 1279
Mario Verdieri Engadin 1278

Robert von Hagge
Bordes (Les) 232, Kempferhof (Le) 240, Real Sociedad Club de Campo 1184, Bogogno *Del Conte* 952, Bogogno *Bonora* 951, Emporda 1129, Royal Mougins 274, Seignosse 288, Courson Vert/Noir 209, Courson Lilas/Orange 208

Robert von Hagge (consultant) / Hubert Chesneau
National *L'Albatros* 255

Robert Von Hagge, Smelek, Barril
Is Arenas 964

B. von Limburger
Club zur Vahr (Garlstedt) 393, Gütersloh (Westfälischer GC) 412, Hubbelrath 420, Köln 425, Krefelder 426, Stuttgarter Solitude 469, Feldafing 400, Hamburg-Ahrensburg 413, Hannover 415, Schloss Braunfels 452, Steiermärkischer Murhof 88, Walddörfer 474, Bâle-Hagenthal 221, Blumisberg 1274, Essener Oefte 398, Wasserburg Anholt 475, Main-Taunus 432.

B. von Limburger, D. Harradine
Oberfranken 441, Augsburg 377

Robert Walker
Cardiff 794

Philip Walton
County Tipperary 849, St Helen's Bay 899

Henrik Wartiainen
Talma 155

Hermann Weiland
Biblis Wattenheim *A + B* 388

Tom Weiskopf, Jay Morrish
Loch Lomond 744

John Stagg West
West Berkshire 668

Rod Whitman
Médoc *Les Vignes* 250

Unknown
Burnham & Berrow 532, North Berwick 760, Prestwick 765, Royal St David's 813, St Andrews *Old Course* 779, Ashburnham 793, Conwy 798, Gullane *No 1* 733, Monifieth 751, North Wales (Llandudno) 807, Panmure 761, Bergisch Land Wuppertal 385, East Devon 548, Gut Grambek 407, Huddersfield (Fixby) 576, Inverness 736, København *Eremitagen* 131, Leven 743, Roma - Acquasanta 987, Royal Guernsey 621, Royal Jersey 622, Arendal 1037, Coxmoor 543, Dellach 81, Elie 723, Fanø 128, Haggs Castle 734, Hallamshire 565, Nairn Dunbar 758, Newport 806, Oslo 1043, Urslautal 89, Carnoustie *Burnside* 707, Falkenberg 1226, Falmouth 551, Glamorganshire 799, Huntly 735, Korsør 132, Llanymynech 803, Mannings Heath *Waterfall Course* 592, Mariánské Lázne 1298, Monte Carlo (Mont Agel) 252, Wheatley 676, Elm Park 857, Falkirk Tryst 724, Filey 554. Lübeck-Travemünder 430 Reichswald-Nürnberg 446, Schloss Langenstein 455, St. Eurach 465, Walton Heath *New Course* 663, Ballyliffin *Old Course* 834, Bamberg 384, Boulie (La) *La Vallée* 233, Lichtenau-Weickershof 427, Lindau-Bad Schachen 428, Münchner-Strasslach 438, Oberschwaben Bad Waldsee 442, Abenberg 376, Ardglass 912, Bad Liebenzell 382, Braunschweig 391, Eschenried 397, Fränkische Schweiz 403, Garmisch-Partenkirchen 406, Hechingen-Hohenzollern 416, Heilbronn-Hohenlohe 417, Interlaken 1282, Memmingen Gut Westerhart 434, Pinnau 444, Reichsstadt Bad Windsheim 445, Aix-les-Bains 210, Grand Ducal de Luxembourg 117, Kilkenny 873, Margara 972, Montreux 1287, Ozoir-la-Ferrière *Château/Monthéty* 259, Rapallo 984, Rosslare 894, Royal Portrush *Valley* 927, Sant Cugat 1187, Warrenpoint 928, Western Gailes 787, Banchory 696

RECOMMENDED SEASONS
SAISONS RECOMMANDÉES
EMPFOHLENE JAHRESZEITEN
REKOMMANDERADE MÅNADER
EPOCA DEL AÑO ACONSEJADA
MESI CONSIGLIATI

1 | 2 | 3 | 4 | 5 | 6 | 7 | 8 | 9 | 10 | 11 | 12

Course		Page
Albi	F	211
Alicante	F	1110
Amarilla	E	1114
Arcachon	F	216
Aroeira I	P	1059
Aroeira II	P	1060
Baule (La)	F	223
Belas	P	1061
Biarritz-le-Phare	F	228
Bonalba	E	1115
Bretesche (La)	F	236
Campoamor	E	1117
Cannes Mandelieu		
Old Course	F	238
Cannes-Mougins	F	239
Canyamel	E	1118
Cap d'Agde	F	240
Capdepera	E	1119
Chiberta	F	252
Cosmopolitan	I	958
Costa Dorada	E	1124
Dieppe-Pourville	F	210
El Bosque	E	1125
El Cortijo	E	1126
El Saler	E	1128
Escorpion	E	1130
Estérel Latitudes	F	216
Etretat	F	218
Garlenda	I	962
Golden Eagle	P	1062
Golf d'Aro		
(Mas Nou)	E	1133
Golf del Sur	E	1134
Grande Bastide (La)	F	228
Granville *Les Dunes*	F	230
Hardelot *Les Pins*	F	233
Hossegor	F	235
Is Arenas	I	964
Is Molas	I	965

1 | 2 | 3 | 4 | 5 | 6 | 7 | 8 | 9 | 10 | 11 | 12

Course		Page
La Manga *Norte*	E	1145
Oeste /Sur		1146/1147
La Sella	E	1151
Lacanau	F	241
Las Américas	E	1153
Las Palmas	E	1155
Maspalomas	E	1163
Mediterraneo	E	1164
Médoc		
Les Châteaux	F	249
Les Vignes	F	250
Moliets	F	251,
Monteenmedio	E	1169
Montpellier-		
Massane	F	253
Oitavos	P	1064
Oliva Nova	E	1172
Palmares	P	1065
Pals	E	1175
Penha Longa	P	1066
Penina	P	1067
Peralada	E	1178
Pevero	I	981
PGA de Catalunya	E	1179
Pineda	E	1180
Pinheiros Altos	P	1068
Ploemeur Océan	F	263
Praia d'El Rey	P	1069
Prince de Provence		
(Vidauban)	F	267
Pula	E	1183
Punta Ala	I	983
Quinta da Beloura	P	1070
Quinta da Marinha	P	1071
Quinta do Lago		
Quinta do Lago	P	1072
Ria Formosa	P	1073
Quinta do Peru	P	1074
Rapallo	I	984

1 | 2 | 3 | 4 | 5 | 6 | 7 | 8 | 9 | 10 | 11 | 12

Course		Page
Riva dei Tessali	I	986
Riviéra Golf Club	F	271
Roma - Acquasanta	I	987
Royal Mougins	F	274
S. Lourenço	P	1075
Saint Donat	F	276
Saint-Jean-de-Monts	F	280
Saint-Laurent	F	281
Saint-Thomas	F	284
Salgados	P	1076
San Roque	E	1185
Santa Ponsa	E	1188
Santo da Serra	P	1077
Savenay	F	287
Seignosse	F	288
Son Antem *Este*	E	1190
Oeste	E	1191
Son Muntaner	E	1192
Son Vida	E	1193
Sotogrande	E	1194
Torremirona	E	1195
Touquet (Le)		
La Mer	F	296
Troia	P	1078
Val Queven	F	298
Valderrama	E	1198
Vale da Pinta	P	1079
Vale do Lobo		
Royal Golf Course	P	1080
Vila Sol	P	1081
Vilamoura		
Old Course,	P	1082
Laguna,	P	1083
Millenium	P	1084
Villamartin	E	1199
Wimereux	F	303

1 | 2 | 3 | 4 | 5 | 6 | 7 | 8 | 9 | 10 | 11 | 12

Course		Page
Alhaurin	E	1109

Recommended seasons

1 | 2 | 3 | 4 | 5 | 6 | 7 | 8 | 9 | 10 | 11 | 12

Almenara	E	1111
Almerimar	E	1112
Aloha	E	1113
Estepona	E	1131
Guadalmina *Sur*	E	1137
La Cala *Norte*	E	1140
La Cala *Sur*	E	1141
Málaga	E	1160
Marbella	E	1161
Mijas *Los Lagos*	E	1165
Mijas *Los Olivos*	E	1166
Olgiata	I	978

1 | 2 | 3 | 4 | 5 | 6 | 7 | 8 | 9 | 10 | 11 | 12

Costa Brava	E	1123
El Prat *Verde*	E	1127
Nîmes-Campagne	F	257
Novo Sancti Petri	E	1171
Sant Cugat	E	1187

1 | 2 | 3 | 4 | 5 | 6 | 7 | 8 | 9 | 10 | 11 | 12

Alcaidesa	E	1108
Castelgandolfo	I	955
Guadalhorce	E	1136
Islantilla	E	1138
La Duquesa	E	1143
La Quinta	E	1150
La Zagaleta	E	1152
Las Brisas	E	1154
Lauro	E	1156
Los Arqueros	E	1158
Los Naranjos	E	1159
Marco Simone	I	971
Monte Mayor	E	1167
Montecastillo	E	1168
Panoramica	E	1176
Parco de' Medici	I	980
Sevilla	E	1189
Torrequebrada	E	1196
Zaudin	E	1200

1 | 2 | 3 | 4 | 5 | 6 | 7 | 8 | 9 | 10 | 11 | 12

Albarella	I	943
Arzaga	I	946
Franciacorta	I	960
Gardagolf	I	961
Le Querce	I	968
Lignano	I	970
Pornic	I	266
Venezia	I	990

1 | 2 | 3 | 4 | 5 | 6 | 7 | 8 | 9 | 10 | 11 | 12

Aisses (Les)		
Rouge/Blanc	F	209
Barbaroux	F	222
Belle-Dune	F	225
Bonmont	E	1116
Chantaco	F	246
Club de Campo	E	1122
Emporda	E	1129
Gujan-Mestras	F	232
Hayling	ENG	569
Mazamet-La Barouge	F	248
Montebelo	P	1063
Royal Zoute	B	111
Saint-Endréol	F	278
Sainte-Maxime	F	286
San Sebastián	E	1186
Spérone	F	291

1 | 2 | 3 | 4 | 5 | 6 | 7 | 8 | 9 | 10 | 11 | 12

Gloria Golf Resort	T	1303
National GC	T	1304
Nobilis	T	1305
TAT Golf Belek	T	1306

1 | 2 | 3 | 4 | 5 | 6 | 7 | 8 | 9 | 10 | 11 | 12

Arcangues	F	217
Asolo	I	947
Baden	F	220
Bergamo - L'Albenza		
Blu + Giallo	I	949
Berkshire (The)		
Blue Course	ENG	519
Red Course	ENG	520
Bordes (Les)	F	232
Buckinghamshire (The)	ENG	530
Castello di Tolcinasco	I	956
Castillo de Gorraiz	E	1120
Cély	F	241
Cervia	I	957
Champ de Bataille	F	245
Chantilly Vineuil	F	247
Charleville	IRL	843
Chart Hills	ENG	539
Cork GC	IRL	846
County Louth	IRL	847
County Sligo	IRL	848
Denham	ENG	547
Dinard	F	211
East Sussex National		
East Course	ENG	549
Etiolles Les Cerfs	F	217
European (The)	IRL	860
Ferndown		
Old Course	ENG	553
Firenze - Ugolino	I	959
Fontainebleau	F	221
Frégate	F	225
Gog Magog		
Old Course	ENG	563
Gouverneur (Le)		
Le Breuil	F	226
Montaplan	F	227
Grande-Motte (La)		
Les Flamants Roses	F	229
Henley	ENG	570
Hermitage	IRL	870
Hubbelrath	D	420
International Club du Lys		
Les Chênes	F	236
Jarama R.A.C.E.	E	1139
La Dehesa	E	1142
La Moraleja		
La Moraleja 1	E	1148
La Moraleja 2	E	1149
La Pinetina	I	966
Le Pavoniere	I	967
Le Robinie	I	969
Limère	F	245
Littlestone	ENG	588
Makila Golf Club	F	247
Milano	I	973
Modena	I	974
Molinetto	I	975
Monte Carlo (Mt Agel)	F	252
Montecchia	I	976
Monticello	I	977
Morfontaine	F	254
National *L'Albatros*	F	255
Neguri	E	1170
Newbury & Crookham	ENG	601
North Foreland	ENG	602
Olivar de la Hinojosa	E	1173
Oostende	B	104
Osona Montanya	E	1174
Parkstone	ENG	608
Pau	F	261
Pedreña	E	1177
Perranporth	ENG	610
Poggio dei Medici	I	982
Pont Royal	F	264
Portmarnock	IRL	887

Recommended seasons

1 | 2 | 3 | 4 | 5 | 6 | 7 | 8 | 9 | 10 | 11 | 12

Portmarnock Links IRL 888
Prince's ENG 615
Puerta de Hierro
Abajo E 1181
Arriba E 1182
Ravenstein B 107
Rebetz F 269
Rimini I 985
Rochefort-Chisan F 272
Rosslare IRL 894
Royal County Down NIR 925
Royal Dublin IRL 895
Royal St George's ENG 627
Royal Wimbledon ENG 629
Sainte-Baume (La) F 285
Servanes F 289
Stoke Poges ENG 649
Sunningdale
New Course ENG 651
Old Course ENG 652
Swinley Forest ENG 653
The Island IRL 901
Thorndon Park ENG 658
Thorpeness ENG 659
Toulouse Palmola F 294
Varese I 989
Verona I 991
Villa D'Este I 992
Walton Heath
New Course ENG 663
Old Course ENG 664
West Berkshire ENG 668
West Hill ENG 671
Woking ENG 681
Woodbridge ENG 682
Worplesdon ENG 685

1 | 2 | 3 | 4 | 5 | 6 | 7 | 8 | 9 | 10 | 11 | 12

Granada E 1135

1 | 2 | 3 | 4 | 5 | 6 | 7 | 8 | 9 | 10 | 11 | 12

Annonay-Gourdan F 214
Antognolla I 945
Barlassina I 948
Brigode F 237
Bude & North Cornwall ENG 531
Caldy ENG 533
Castlerock NIR 916
Cognac F 207
Dartmouth ENG 545

1 | 2 | 3 | 4 | 5 | 6 | 7 | 8 | 9 | 10 | 11 | 12

Dingle Links (Ceann Sibeal) IRL 851
East Devon ENG 548
Elie SC 723
Falmouth ENG 551
Goes N 1009
Greenore IRL 868
Gullane SC 733
Haagsche N 1012
Hainaut B 100
Huddersfield (Fixby) ENG 576
Isle of Purbeck ENG 581
Lisburn NIR 920
Luttrellstown IRL 880
Masia Bach E 1162
Mullion ENG 600
New Golf Deauville
Rouge/Blanc F 256
Noordwijk N 1020
Nunspeet *North/East* N 1021
Orchardleigh ENG 605
Portstewart
Strand Course NIR 923
Royal Guernsey ENG 621
Royal Portrush
Dunluce Links NIR 926
Valley NIR 927
Saunton *East Course* ENG 635
Shannon IRL 897
Thurlestone ENG 660
Tullamore IRL 905
Turnberry
Ailsa Course SC 784
Kintyre Course SC 785
Waterford Castle IRL 907
West Byfleet ENG 669
Woodbury Park
The Oaks ENG 683

1 | 2 | 3 | 4 | 5 | 6 | 7 | 8 | 9 | 10 | 11 | 12

Ambrosiano I 944
Badgemore Park ENG 515
Ballybunion *Cashen*
New Course IRL 830
Old Course IRL 831
Ballyliffin
Glashedy Links IRL 833
Old Course IRL 834
Beaufort IRL 836
Blainroe IRL 838

1 | 2 | 3 | 4 | 5 | 6 | 7 | 8 | 9 | 10 | 11 | 12

Bogogno *Bonora* I 951
Del Conte I 952
Bologna I 953
Burnham & Berrow ENG 532
Camberley Heath ENG 534
Delamere Forest ENG 546
Domtal-Mommenheim D 394
Dooks IRL 853
Dromoland Castle IRL 854
Druids Glen IRL 855
Elfrather Mühle D 396
Enniscrone IRL 858
Fontanals E 1132
Frankfurter GC D 402
Galway Bay IRL 863
Galway GC IRL 864
Hamburg-Ahrensburg D 413
Hanau-Wilhelmsbad D 414
Hankley Common ENG 566
Hertfordshire (The) ENG 571
Hever ENG 572
Hindhead ENG 575
Hof Trages D 418
Huntercombe ENG 578
I Roveri I 963
Ipswich (Purdis Heath) ENG 580
Isle Adam (L') F 237
Jakobsberg D 424
La Herreria E 1144
La Moye ENG 583
Lahinch IRL 877
Lausanne CH 1283
Lerma E 1157
Little Aston ENG 587
Lugano CH1285
Margara I 972
Mere ENG 596
Moor Park
High Course ENG 598
Muirfield SC 754
München-Riedhof D 437
Münchner-Strasslach D 438
Neuhof D 440
Ormskir ENG 606
Padova I 979
Portsalon IRL 889
Rathsallagh IRL 891
Roxburghe (The) SC 767

Recommended seasons

1 | 2 | 3 | 4 | 5 | 6 | 7 | 8 | 9 | 10 | 11 | 12

Course	Country	Page
Royal Ashdown Forest	ENG	617
Royal Cinque Ports	ENG	619
Royal Latem	B	110
Royal Mid-Surrey		
Outer	ENG	625
Saint-Germain	F	279
Seacroft	ENG	636
Seapoint	IRL	896
Sherborne	ENG	640
Southerness	SC	775
St George's Hill	ENG	647
St Helen's Bay	IRL	899
Stuttgarter Solitude	D	469
Tandridge	ENG	654
Torino - La Mandria		
Percorso Blu	I	988
Toulouse-Seilh	F	295
Tralee	IRL	902
Tramore	IRL	903
Ulzama	E	1197
Villette d'Anthon		
Les Sangliers	F	300
Walddörfer	D	474
Waterloo		
La Marache	B	115
Le Lion	B	116
Waterville	IRL	908
West Surrey	ENG	673
West Sussex	ENG	674
Weston-Super-Mare	ENG	675
Woburn		
Duke's	ENG	679
Marquess	ENG	680

1 | 2 | 3 | 4 | 5 | 6 | 7 | 8 | 9 | 10 | 11 | 12

Course	Country	Page
Aberdovey	W	792
Ailette (L')	F	208
Aix-les-Bains	F	210
Alloa	SC	691
Alwoodley (The)	ENG	513
Alyth	SC	692
Amirauté (L')	F	212
Anderstein	N	1000
Antwerp	B	97
Apremont	F	215
Ardglass	NIR	912
Ashburnham	W	793
Ashridge	ENG	514
Asserbo	DA	126
Athlone	IRL	829

1 | 2 | 3 | 4 | 5 | 6 | 7 | 8 | 9 | 10 | 11 | 12

Course	Country	Page
Augerville	F	219
Augsburg	D	377
Ayr (Belleisle)	SC	693
Bad Abbach-Deutenhof	D	378
Bad Ragaz	CH	1273
Ballykisteen	IRL	832
Bamberg	D	384
Bangor	NIR	913
Bath	ENG	516
Batouwe	N	1001
Beau Desert	ENG	517
Bélesbat	F	224
Belmullet	IRL	837
Bercuit	B	98
Bergisch Land Wuppertal	D	385
Berkhamsted	ENG	518
Berlin-Wannsee	D	386
Béthemont	F	227
Beuerberg	D	387
Biblis Wattenheim		
A + B	D	388
Biella - Le Betulle	I	950
Bitburger Land	D	389
Bitche	F	229
Blackmoor	ENG	522
Blairgowrie		
Lansdowne	SC	697
Rosemount	SC	698
Bodensee-Weissensberg	D	390
Bolton *Old Links*	ENG	523
Bondues *Blanc*	F	230
Jaune	F	231
Boulie (La) La Vallée	F	233
Bowood (Cornwall)	ENG	524
Bowood G&CC	ENG	525
Brampton	ENG	526
Brancepeth Castle	ENG	527
Brest Iroise	F	235
Broadstone	ENG	528
Broekpolder	N	1002
Brokenhurst Manor	ENG	529
Bruntsfield	SC	701
Buchanan Castle	SC	702
Bundoran	IRL	839
Burntisland	SC	703
Buxtehude	D	392
Cairndhu	NIR	915
Came Down	ENG	535

1 | 2 | 3 | 4 | 5 | 6 | 7 | 8 | 9 | 10 | 11 | 12

Course	Country	Page
Carden Park		
Nicklaus Course	ENG	536
Cardiff	W	794
Cardiga	W	795
Cardross	SC	705
Carlow	IRL	840
Carmarthen	W	796
Carnoustie *Burnside*	SC	707
Championship	SC	708
Castelconturbia		
Giallo + Azzurro	I	954
Celtic Manor		
Roman Road	W	797
Charmeil	F	248
Château de Preisch	F	249
Clandeboye		
Dufferin Course	NIR	917
Clitheroe	ENG	541
Club zur Vahr (Garlstedt)	D	393
Collingtree Park	ENG	542
Connemara	IRL	845
Conwy	W	798
County Tipperary	IRL	849
Courson		
Lilas/Orange	F	208
Vert/Noir	F	209
Crail *Balcomie Links*	SC	709
Crieff		
Ferntower Course	SC	710
Cromstrijen	N	1003
Cruden Bay	SC	711
Cumberwell Park	ENG	544
Dalmahoy		
East Course	SC	712
De Pan	N	1004
Disneyland Paris		
Peter + Alice	F	212
Domaine Impérial	CH	1277
Domont-Montmorency	F	214
Donegal (Murvagh)	IRL	852
Duff House Royal	SC	715
Duke's Course St Andrews	SC	716
Dumfries & County	SC	717
Dunbar	SC	718
Dundalk	IRL	856
Düsseldorfer	D	395
Efteling	N	1005
Eindhoven	N	1006

Recommended seasons

1	2	3	4	5	6	7	8	9	10	11	12

Course		
Elm Park	IRL	857
Ennetsee-Holzhäusern	CH	1279
Eschenried	D	397
Esery	F	215
Esker Hills	IRL	859
Essener Oefte	D	398
Fairhaven	ENG	550
Faithlegg	IRL	861
Falkenstein	D	399
Falkirk Tryst	SC	724
Falnuée	B	99
Falsterbo	S	1227
Fanø	DA	128
Felixstowe Ferry *Martello Course*	ENG	552
Feucherolles	F	220
Filey	ENG	554
Flees	D	401
Fontana	A	83
Fontcaude	F	222
Fontenailles	F	223
Fontenelles (Les)	F	224
Forest of Arden *Arden Course*	ENG	555
Formby	ENG	557
Formby Hall	ENG	558
Fortrose & Rosemarkie	SC	726
Fota Island	IRL	862
Frilford Heath *Red Course*	ENG	559
Fürstlicher GC Bad Waldsee	D	404
Fürstliches Hofgut Kolnhausen	D	405
Ganton	ENG	562
Gelpenberg	N	1007
Gendersteyn	N	1008
Genève	CH	1280
Glamorganshire	W	799
Glasson	IRL	865
Glen	SC	727
Glen of the Downs	IRL	866
Gleneagles *King's*	SC	728
Gleneagles *PGA Centenary*	SC	729
Queen's	SC	730
Golspie	SC	731
Göteborg	S	1234
Graafschap	N	1010

1	2	3	4	5	6	7	8	9	10	11	12

Course		
Grenoble Bresson	F	231
Grevelingenhout	N	1011
Gut Kaden	D	408
Gut Lärchenhof	D	409
Gut Thailing	D	411
Gütersloh (Westfälischer GC)	D	412
Hadley Wood	ENG	564
Hallamshire	ENG	565
Hannover	D	415
Haut-Poitou	F	234
Hawkstone Park *Hawkstone*	ENG	568
Headfort *New Course*	IRL	869
Hechingen-Hohenzollern	D	416
Heilbronn-Hohenlohe	D	417
High Post	ENG	573
Hillside	ENG	574
Hilversum	N	1014
Himmerland *New Course*	DA	129
Hoge Kleij	N	1015
Holyhead	W	800
Hunstanton	ENG	577
Ilkley	ENG	579
John O'Gaunt	ENG	582
K Club	IRL	871
Keerbergen	B	101
Kempferhof (Le)	F	240
Kennemer	N	1017
Kikuoka	L	118
Kilkea Castle	IRL	872
Kilkenny	IRL	873
Killorglin	IRL	876
Kilmarnock (Barassie)	SC	737
Kingsbarns	SC	738
Kirkistown Castle	NIR	918
Knock	NIR	919
København *Eremitagen*	DA	131
Köln	D	425
Krefelder	D	426
Ladybank	SC	740
Lage Vuursche	N	1018
Lanark	SC	741
Langland Bay	W	801
Lauswolt	N	1019
Le Prieuré	F	244
Lee Valley	IRL	878

1	2	3	4	5	6	7	8	9	10	11	12

Course		
Letham Grange *Old Course*	SC	742
Leven	SC	743
Lichtenau-Weickershof	D	427
Limburg	B	102
Limerick County	IRL	879
Lindau-Bad Schachen	D	428
Lindenhof	D	429
Lindrick	ENG	585
Liphook	ENG	586
Llandudno (Maesdu)	W	802
Llanymynech	W	803
Loch Lomond	SC	744
London Golf Club *International*	ENG	589
Longniddry	SC	745
Lübeck-Travemünder	D	430
Luffness New	SC	747
Lundin	SC	748
Lytham Green Drive	ENG	590
Machrie	SC	749
Machrihanish	SC	750
Main-Taunus	D	432
Malahide	IRL	881
Malone	NIR	921
Manchester	ENG	591
Mannings Heath *Waterfall Course*	ENG	592
Manor House (Castle Combe)	ENG	593
Marriott St Pierre *Old Course*	W	804
Mendip	ENG	594
Mittelrheinischer	D	435
Monifieth	SC	751
Monkstown	IRL	882
Mont-Garni	B	103
Montreux	CH	1287
Montrose	SC	752
Moor Allerton	ENG	597
Moray	SC	753
Motzener See	D	436
Mount Juliet	IRL	883
Mount Wolseley	IRL	884l
Mullingar	IRL	885
Murcar	SC	755
Murrayshall	SC	756
Nahetal	D	439
Nairn	SC	757
Nairn Dunbar	SC	758

Recommended seasons

1 2 3 4 5 6 7 8 9 10 11 12

1 2 3 4 5 6 7 8 9 10 11 12

1 2 3 4 5 6 7 8 9 10 11 12

Recommended seasons

1 | 2 | 3 | **4** | **5** | **6** | **7** | **8** | **9** | **10** | 11 | 12

Course	Country	Page
Wantzenau (La)	F	302
Warrenpoint	NIR	928
Warwickshire (The)	ENG	665
Wasserburg Anholt	D	475
Waterford	IRL	906
Wendlohe *A-Kurs + B-Kurs*	D	476
Wentworth *East Course*	ENG	666
Wentworth *West Course*	ENG	667
West Cornwall	ENG	670
West Kilbride	SC	786
West Lancashire	ENG	672
Western Gailes	SC	787
Westport	IRL	909
Wheatley	ENG	676
Whitekirk	SC	789
Whittington Heath	ENG	677
Wilmslow	ENG	678
Wittelsbacher	D	477
Woodbrook	IRL	910
Woodenbridge	IRL	911
Woodhall Spa	ENG	684
Wouwse Plantage	N	1029
Zuid Limburgse	N	1030

1 | 2 | 3 | **4** | **5** | **6** | **7** | **8** | **9** | 10 | 11 | 12

Course	Country	Page
Barsebäck	S	1215
Båstad *Old Course*	S	1216
Blumisberg	CH	1274
Bosjökloster	S	1218
Breitenloo	CH	1275
Carnegie Club (Skibo Castle)	SC	706
Castle	IRL	841
Chesterfield	ENG	540
Ekerum	S	1222
Elgin	SC	722
Eslöv	S	1223
Flommen	S	1229
Forest Pines *Forest + Pines*	ENG	556
Fulford	ENG	560
Gainsborough-Karsten Lakes	ENG	561
Gruyère (La)	CH	1281
Haggs Castle	SC	734
Kristianstad	S	1242
Landskrona *Gul Bana*	S	1244
Ljunghusen	S	1245
Mölle	S	1247
Moortown	ENG	599
Neuchâtel	CH	1288
Newtonmore	SC	759
Pannal	ENG	607
Raray (Château de) *La Licorne*	F	268
Ross-on-Wye	ENG	616
Rudding Park	ENG	631
Sherwood Forest	ENG	642
Söderåsen	S	1254
Torekov	S	1258
Vasatorp	S	1263
Visby	S	1265
Westerwood	SC	788
Zumikon	CH	1293

1 | 2 | 3 | 4 | **5** | **6** | **7** | **8** | **9** | **10** | 11 | 12

Course	Country	Page
Abenberg	D	376
Ableiges Les Etangs	F	207
Aboyne	SC	690
Adare	IRL	828
Am Mondsee	A	80
Amnéville	F	213
Amsterdam	N	999
Bad Griesbach Brunnwies	D	380
Bad Griesbach-Sagmühle *Sagmühle*	D	381
Bad Liebenzell	D	382
Bad Wörishofen	D	383
Banchory	SC	696
Bearna	IRL	835
Belvoir Park	NIR	914
Bled *King's Course*	SL	1301
Bresse (La)	F	234
Brora	SC	700
Castletroy	IRL	842
Cerdaña	E	1121
Chailly (Château de)	F	242
Chambon-sur-Lignon (Le)	F	243
Chaumont-en-Vexin	F	250
Cheverny	F	251
Citywest	IRL	844
Courtown	IRL	850
Dellach	A	81
Divonne	F	213
Duddingston	SC	714
East Renfrewshire	SC	720
Edzell	SC	721
Eichenheim	A	82
Esbjerg	DA	127
Evian	F	219
Falkenberg	S	1226
Forfar	SC	725
Garmisch-Partenkirchen	D	406
Golfresort Haugschlag-Waldviertel	A	84
Grand Ducal de Luxembourg	L	117
Grange	IRL	867
Gut Grambek	D	407
Gut Ludwigsberg	D	410
Herkenbosch	N	1013
Hohenpähl	D	419
Holstebro	DA	130
Houtrak	N	1016
Huntly	SC	735
Iffeldorf	D	421
Im Chiemgau	D	422
Inverness	SC	736
Isernhagen	D	423
Joyenval *Marly*	F	238
Joyenval *Retz*	F	239
Killarney *Killeen Course*	IRL	874
Mahony's Point	IRL	875
Klagenfurt-Seltenheim	A	86
Korsør	DA	132
Læsø *Seaside*	DA	133
Les Bois	CH	1284
Linden Hall	ENG	584
Losby	NW	1041
Maison Blanche	F	246
Märkischer Potsdam	D	433
Meland	NW	1042
Memmingen Gut Westerhart	D	434
Meon Valley *Meon Course*	ENG	595
Møn	DA	134
Oberfranken	D	441
Powerscourt	IRL	890
Reichsstadt Bad Windsheim	D	445
Royal Aberdeen *Balgownie Links*	SC	768
Royal Oak	DA	135

Recommended seasons

1 2 3 4 **5 6 7 8 9** 10 11 12

Schloss Ebreichsdorf A 87
Schloss Langenstein D 455
Schloss Nippenburg D 458
Schloss Myllendonk D 457
Semlin am See D 462
Sempachersee CH 1291
Shanklin & Sandown ENG 639
Sint Nicolaasga N 1025
Slaley Hall ENG 644
St. Eurach D 465
Steiermärkischer
Murhof A 88
Taulane F 293
Taymouth Castle SC 782
Upsala S 1261
Urslautal A 89
Val de Sorne F 297
Wylihof CH 1292
Zell am See Kaprun
Schmittenhöhe A 90

1 2 3 4 **5 6 7 8 9** 10 11 12

A 6 S 1211
Ängelholm S 1212
Arendal NW 1037
Arras F 218
Åtvidaberg S 1214
Aura FI 147
Baberton SC 694
Bad Bevensen D 379
Bâle-Hagenthal F 221
Berwick-upon-
Tweed ENG 521
Besançon F 226
Boat of Garten SC 699
Bokskogen S 1217
Borre NW 1038
Braunschweig D 391
Bråviken S 1219
Bro-Bålsta S 1220
Callander SC 704
Carlisle ENG 537
Castletown ENG 538
Coxmoor ENG 543
Downfield SC 713
Drottningholm S 1221
Dunfermline SC 719
Espoo FI 148
European Tour Club
(Kungsängen) S 1224
Fågelbro S 1225

1 2 3 4 **5 6 7 8 9** 10 11 12

Feldafing D 400
Fjällbacka S 1228
Forsgården S 1231
Fränkische Schweiz D 403
Frösåker S 1232
Gränna S 1235
Grantown on Spey SC 732
Gut Altentann A 85
Halmstad S 1236
Haninge S 1237
Harrogate ENG 567
Hauger NW 1039
Helsinki FI 149
Jönköping S 1238
Karlovy Vary CZ 1297
Karlshamn S 1240
Kungsbacka S 1243
Largue (La) F 242
Larvik NW 1040
Laval-Changé
La Chabossière F 243
Lothianburn SC 746
Lunds Akademiska S 1246
Lüneburger Heide D 431
Luzern CH 1286
Mariánské Lázne CZ 1298
Massereene NIR 922
Master *Master* FI 150
Niederbüren CH1289
Nordcenter
Benz Course FI 151
Old Head I 886
Örebro S 1248
Oslo NW1043
Österåker S 1249
Panmure SC 761
`Perstorp S 1250
Pickala
Seaside Course FI 152
Praha Karlstejn CZ1299
Sarfvik *New Course* FI 153
Schönenberg CH 1290
Shiskine
(Blackwaterfoot) SC 774
Silloth-on-Solway ENG 643
Sorknes NW 1044
St Laurence FI 154
Stavanger NW1045
Stenungsund S 1255
Stockholm S 1256
Strathaven SC 780

1 2 3 4 **5 6 7 8 9** 10 11 12

Talma FI 155
Tawast FI 156
Tegernseer
Bad Wiessee D 471
Tranås S 1259
Tutzing D 473
Tyrifjord NW1046
Ullna S 1260
Värnamo SU 1262

1 2 3 4 5 **6 7 8 9 10** 11 12

Chamonix F 244
Schloss Lüdersburg
Old/New D 456

1 2 3 **4 5 6 7 8** 9 10 11 12

Interlaken CH1282

1 2 3 4 5 **6 7 8 9** 10 11 12

Ballater SC 695
Crans-sur-Sierre CH 1276
Engadin CH 1278
Gävle S 1241
Kingussie SC 739
Moscow Ru 1302
Skellefteå S 1252

1 2 3 4 **5 6 7 8** 9 10 11 12

Ängsö S 1213
Forsbacka S 1230
Kalmar S 1239
Skövde S 1253
Täby S 1257
Växjö S 1264

1 2 3 4 5 **6 7 8** 9 10 11 12

Karlstad S 1241

EUROPE'S TOP 1000 GOLF COURSES

Austria

Gut Altentann

Austria
Österreich

Austria, a land of mountains, has quickly built up a number of golf courses which are the ideal complement to the country's many skiing resorts. There are now more than 75 courses for almost 50,000 golfers. Naturally, golf here is a real sport and walking a tradition; and despite the harsh winters, producing a course in good shape is a question of honour. Often located in idyllic natural settings, the picture postcard appearance of most courses is a joy to behold for foreign visitors. Whether here for a golfing holiday or for a quick round in between other delightful holiday activities, you are in for some great surprises and hospitality typical of a country unlike any other.

In Österreich, dem Land der Berge, sind in den letzten Jahren viele Golfplätze enststanden. So sind viele Wintersportorte auch beliebte Sommerreiseziele. In Österreich findet man derzeit fast hundert Plätze, auf denen 60.000 einheimische Golfer die Schläger schwingen. Golf in Österreich ist ein Sport, auf den meisten Plätzen geht man zu Fuß. Obwohl die Winter in der Alpenrepublik streng sind, setzen die Greenkeeper allen Ehrgeiz daran, einen perfekt gepflegten Platz zu präsentieren. Die meisten Plätze liegen idyllisch, das herrliche Alpenpanorama wird Besucher beeindrucken. Ob Sie in Österreich einen Golfurlaub verbringen oder nur mal eben zwischendurch eine Runde Golf spielen: Es wird ein angenehme Überraschung werden, zumal die österreichische Gastfreundschaft und das einzigartige Land sie faszienieren wird.

Classification

CLASSIFICATION OF COURSES
EINTEILUNG DER GOLFPLÄTZE

This classification gives priority consideration to the actual course.

Diese Einteilung berücksichtigt in erster Linie die dem Golfplatz erteilte Note

Course score Note für den Golfplatz				Page Seite
17	8	8	Eichenheim	82
17	7	6	Gut Altentann	85
17	6	8	Klagenfurt-Seltenheim	86
16	7	7	Am Mondsee	80
16	8	7	Fontana	83
16	8	6	Golfresort Haugschlag-Waldviertel	84
16	8	6	Schloss Ebreichsdorf	87
16	8	7	Steiermärkischer Murhof	88
16	7	6	Zell am See Kaprun Schmittenhöhe	90
15	7	7	Dellach	81
15	7	7	Urslautal	89

Map No 1
Karte 1
km
0 10 20
78
Bad-Griesbach (D)
Bad-Griesbach-
Sagmühle (D)
Im Chiemgau (D)
Gut Altentann
Am Mondsee
Urslautal
Kitzbühel
Seltenheim
Zell am See
Kaprun
SALZBURG
LINZ
České Budějovice
Passau
Straubing
Deggendorf
Vilshofen
Dingolfing
Landau
Pfarrkirchen
Eggenfelden
Simbach
Braunau
Burghausen
Altötting
Traunstein
Ried
Schärding
Wels
Steyr
Vöcklabruck
Gmunden
Bad Ischl
Ebensee
Mondsee
St. Wolfgang
St. Gilgen
Hallein
Bad Reichenhall
Berchtesgaden
Bad Aussee
Liezen
Hallstatt
Schladming
Radstadt
Bischofshofen
Saalfelden
Kitzbühel
Zell am See
Badgastein
Bad Hofgastein
Mittersill
Lienz
Spittal
Villach
Millstatt
Feldkirchen
Velden
St. Veit
Jesenice
Bled
Tarvisio
Cortina d'Ampezzo
Český Krumlov
Prachatice
Vimperk
Freistadt
Kremsmünster
Ruhpolding
Inzell
O B E R Ö S T E R R E I C
Ö S T E
S A L Z B U R G
K Ä R N T E
O S T T I R O L
H O H E T A U E R N
DONAU
Großglockner
Großvenediger
Dachsteingruppe
Katschberg
Radstädter Tauernpaß
Pyhrnpaß
MICHELIN

Haugschlag-Waldviertel
Schloss Ebreichsdorf
Fontana
Steiermarkischer
Klagenfurt Seltenheim
Kärtner Dellach
Bled (Slovenia)
WIEN
GRAZ
Klagenfurt
Maribor
České Budějovice
Znojmo
Břeclav
St. Pölten
Krems
Wiener Neustadt
Eisenstadt
Sopron
Baden
Leoben
Bruck an der Mur
Mariazell
Villach
Jesenice
N I E D E R Ö S T E R R E I C H
S T E I E R M A R K
B U R G E N L A N D
DONAU
79
MICHELIN
d'après carte n° 987 - 28ème édition - 2002.
Autorisation n° 0102062.

AM MONDSEE

15 | 7 | 7

Mit dem weissen, flachen Clubhaus wirkt der Platz von der Strasse aus auf den ersten Blick nicht besonders beeindruckend. Aber nach einer Runde hat man den Reiz des Platzes mit dem See in der Mitte, um den sich zahlreiche Löcher winden, schnell erkannt. Der Platz liegt über dem Mondsee, auf den das 18. Loch direkt zuführt. Dieser See gilt als einer der schönsten des Salzkammerguts. Zudem verdankt ein vorzüglicher Käse dem See seinen Namen. Die schönsten Aussichten geniesst man vom Schafberg. Nach zehn Jahr zeigt das Aufforstungsprogramm auf dem Platz erste Früchte, unter den Bäumen kann man an heissen Sommertagen den Schatten geniessen. Die Sommermonate sind die beste Jahreszeit für eine Runde, da der Platz Regen nicht gut verträgt. Der Platz ist relativ flach und gut begehbar. Da der Platz einige Doplegs aufweist, wird man wohl bei der zweiten Runde etwas besser spielen. Falls die schönen Aussichten noch nicht mit dem Score versöhnt haben, kann man sich immer noch einen angenehmen Abend in Salzburg gönnen.

With its white, flat club-house, this course does not look up to much when first seen from the road. But after a round here, nobody could really deny the charm of the place and the large lake right in the middle around which many of the holes are laid out. The course also overlooks the magnificent Mondsee, to which the 18th hole runs almost directly. This has to be one of the most soothing lakes in Salzkammergut and has also given its name to a famous cheese. You get the best view of it from the uplands of Schafberg, which have probably also inspired many a golfer. After ten years, the plantation programmes are beginning to grow, or at least the leaves are because their shade is most welcome in the hot summer months. Summer is definitely the best time to play here as the course does not take too kindly to heavy rain. Having said that, it is rather flat and so not too tiring, and also very open. Only a few doglegs might deserve a little reconnaissance work beforehand. If the splendid views are not enough for you, you can always try a nice little evening in Salzburg.

Golfclub Am Mondsee — 1988

A - 5310 ST. LORENZ

Office	Sekretariat	(43) 6232 383 50
Pro shop	Pro shop	(43) 6232 4414
Fax	Fax	(43) 6232 383 583
Web	www.golf.et/clubs/	
Situation	Lage	Salzburg, 30 km
Annual closure	Jährliche Schliessung	9/11→31/3
Weekly closure	Wöchentliche Schliessung	no

Fees main season Preisliste hochsaison	Week days Woche	We/Bank holidays We/Feiertag
	18 holes	
Individual Individuell	47 €	55 €
Couple Ehepaar	94 €	109 €

Softspikes only

Caddy	Caddy	no
Electric Trolley	Elektrokarren	yes
Buggy	Elektrischer Wagen	yes
Clubs	Leihschläger	yes

Credit cards Kreditkarten
VISA - Eurocard - MasterCard

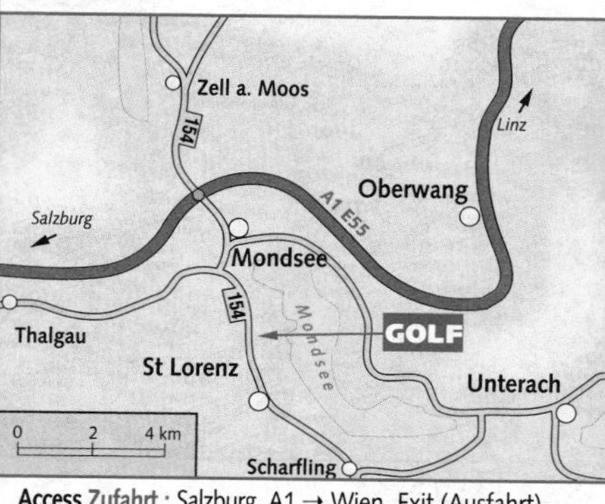

Access Zufahrt : Salzburg, A1 → Wien. Exit (Ausfahrt) Mondsee. B154 → Bad Ischl. 2 km → golf on left hand side. **Map 13 on page 107** Karte 13 Seite 107

Golf course PLATZ — 15/20

Site	Lage	
Maintenance	Instandhaltung	
Architect	Architekt	Max Graf Lamberg
Type	Typ	lakeside, parkland
Relief	Begehbarkeit	
Water in play	Platz mit Wasser	
Exp. to wind	Wind ausgesetzt	
Trees in play	Platz mit Bäumen	

Scorecard Scorekarte	Chp. Chp.	Mens Herren	Ladies Damen
Length Länge	6125	5795	5104
Par	72	72	72
Slope system	—	—	—

Advised golfing ability Empfohlene Spielstärke — 0 12 24 36

Hcp required Min. Handicap 36

Club house & amenities KLUBHAUS UND NEBENGEBÄUDE — 7/10

Pro shop	Pro shop	
Driving range	Übungsplatz	
Sheltered	überdacht	no
On grass	auf Rasen	yes
Putting-green	Putting-grün	yes
Pitching-green	Pitching-grün	yes

Hotel facilities HOTEL BESCHREIBUNG — 7/10

HOTELS HOTELS

Seehof — Loibichl 12 km
30 rooms, D 270 €
Tel (43) 06232 503 10, Fax (43) 06232 503 151

Königshof — Mondsee 5 km
25 rooms, D 160 €
Tel (43) 06232 325 627, Fax (43) 06232 3256 2755

Villa Wunderlich, 7 rooms, D 60 € — St. Lorenz 5 km
Tel (43) 06232 273 72, Fax (43) 06232 273 7299

RESTAURANTS RESTAURANT

Seehof , Tel (43) 06232 503 10 — Loibichl, 12 km

Königshof, Tel (43) 06232 325 627 — Mondsee, 5 km

DELLACH

15 | 7 | 7

Die Natur hat rund um den Wörthersee eine wunderschöne Urlaubsregion geschaffen. Klagenfurt, die Hauptstadt von Kärnten, liegt im Westen Velden im Osten. Maria Wörth findet man die Kirche mit dem Zwillingstürmen und Spuren der Römer. Wenn man ein wenig weiter durch den Karawankenturnnel fährt, kommt man nach Slowenien, wo man vorzüglich in Bled spielen kann (am Ende dieses Golfführers beschrieben). Der Platz von Dellach ist mehr als 60 Jahre alt, aber erst in den fünfziger Jahren wurde er auf 18 Löcher erweitert. Das Layout erinnert an Hamburg-Falkenstein,allerdings ist das Gelände weitaus hügeliger (ein Golfcart oder E-Trolley wird empfohlen) mit einigen steilen Anstiegen. Die Topografie und etliche blinde Löcher machen die Schlägerwahl schwierig. Die Grüns sind klein und besonders für hohe Hondicaps nicht leicht zu treffen. Trotzdem werden auch schwächere Spieler den Spaziergang und die Blicke über den Wörthersee geniessen – vielleicht die schönsten Aussichten eines Golfplatzes in Österreich.

Only Mother Nature could have created a site as beautiful as Wörthersee in this superb region of Carinthia. Klagenfurt lies to the west, the resort of Velden to the east and here you are at Maria Wörth with a twin-towered church and Roman vestiges where Gothic style mixes with later influences. If you drive on a little further you end up in Slovenia where you can play Bled for example (cf. end of this volume). This Dellach course is more than 60 years old but the full 18 holes were opened only in the 1950s. The layout is reminiscent of Falkenstein although the terrain is much hillier (buggy recommended) with some sometimes steep slopes to climb. Whence a few blind holes and trickier-than-usual club selection. In addition, the greens are small and may be more than a handful for high-handicappers. Having said that, they will still enjoy the walk and vista over the lake, and views on a golf course don't get much better than this.

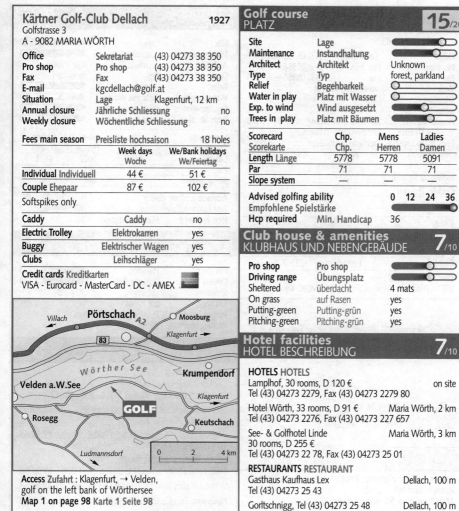

Kärtner Golf-Club Dellach — 1927

Golfstrasse 3
A - 9082 MARIA WÖRTH

Office	Sekretariat	(43) 04273 38 350
Pro shop	Pro shop	(43) 04273 38 350
Fax	Fax	(43) 04273 38 350
E-mail	kgcdellach@golf.at	
Situation	Lage	Klagenfurt, 12 km
Annual closure	Jährliche Schliessung	no
Weekly closure	Wöchentliche Schliessung	no

Fees main season Preisliste hochsaison	Week days Woche	We/Bank holidays We/Feiertag
	18 holes	
Individual Individuell	44 €	51 €
Couple Ehepaar	87 €	102 €

Softspikes only

Caddy	Caddy	no
Electric Trolley	Elektrokarren	yes
Buggy	Elektrischer Wagen	yes
Clubs	Leihschläger	yes

Credit cards Kreditkarten
VISA - Eurocard - MasterCard - DC - AMEX

Access Zufahrt : Klagenfurt, → Velden, golf on the left bank of Wörthersee
Map 1 on page 98 Karte 1 Seite 98

Golf course PLATZ — 15/20

Site	Lage	
Maintenance	Instandhaltung	
Architect	Architekt	Unknown
Type	Typ	forest, parkland
Relief	Begehbarkeit	
Water in play	Platz mit Wasser	
Exp. to wind	Wind ausgesetzt	
Trees in play	Platz mit Bäumen	

Scorecard Scorekarte	Chp. Chp.	Mens Herren	Ladies Damen
Length Länge	5778	5778	5091
Par	71	71	71
Slope system	—	—	—

Advised golfing ability Empfohlene Spielstärke — 0 12 24 36
Hcp required Min. Handicap 36

Club house & amenities KLUBHAUS UND NEBENGEBÄUDE — 7/10

Pro shop	Pro shop	
Driving range	Übungsplatz	
Sheltered	überdacht	4 mats
On grass	auf Rasen	yes
Putting-green	Putting-grün	yes
Pitching-green	Pitching-grün	yes

Hotel facilities HOTEL BESCHREIBUNG — 7/10

HOTELS HOTELS
Lamplhof, 30 rooms, D 120 € — on site
Tel (43) 04273 2279, Fax (43) 04273 2279 80

Hotel Wörth, 33 rooms, D 91 € — Maria Wörth, 2 km
Tel (43) 04273 2276, Fax (43) 04273 227 657

See- & Golfhotel Linde — Maria Wörth, 3 km
30 rooms, D 255 €
Tel (43) 04273 22 78, Fax (43) 04273 25 01

RESTAURANTS RESTAURANT
Gasthaus Kaufhaus Lex — Dellach, 100 m
Tel (43) 04273 25 43

Gorltschnigg, Tel (43) 04273 25 48 — Dellach, 100 m

EICHENHEIM

17 | 8 | 8

Mit dem neuesten Platz in Tirol ist Kitzbühel auch zu einem der Golfzentren des Landes geworden. Wie auch im Winter präsentiert sich Kitzbühel als eleganter Ferienort. Das Greenfee mag hoch erscheinen, aber dafür spielt man auf einem der vielversprechendsten Plätze Österreichs. Man sollte sich vor der Runde die Zeit nehmen den Wilden Kaiser, rauhe Berge und tiefe Schluchten zu bewundern. Der Platz fordert spielerisch und körperlich alles ab, so dass man sich den Luxus eines Golfcarts gönnen sollte. Der Pflegezustand wie auch das Design von Kyle Phillips, eine der grossen Entdeckungen der Golfplatz-Architektur der letzten Jahre, sind vorzüglich. Der Amerikaner intergrierte geschickt die Steigungen und Abhänge ins Spiel, so dass man bei der ersten Runde nie weiss, welchen Schläger man wählen sollte. Es gibt viele Bäume und einige riesige Bunker, trotzdem hat man den Eindruck eines weit offenen Platzes. Der Platz ist nicht sehr lang, aber unbedingt zu empfehlen.

With this course, one of the most recent in the region of Tyrolia, Kitzbühel has become one of the country's major golfing centres in sporting terms and for the same slightly worldly elegance it enjoys as a skiing resort. The green fee may certainly seem a little high but this is the price you pay for playing one of Austria's most promising golf courses. Take time out to admire the Wilder Kaiser, a rugged mountain with deep gorges, before setting out on a what is a physically rather demanding course where a buggy is anything but a luxury. Maintenance is on a par with the architecture of Kyle Phillips, who is decidedly one of great revelations for course design in recent years. He cleverly brings slopes and topography well into play and this implies some rather awkward club selection. There are also a lot of trees and some huge bunkers, but the overall impression is one of wide open space. Not very long but very open, this is a highly recommendable course.

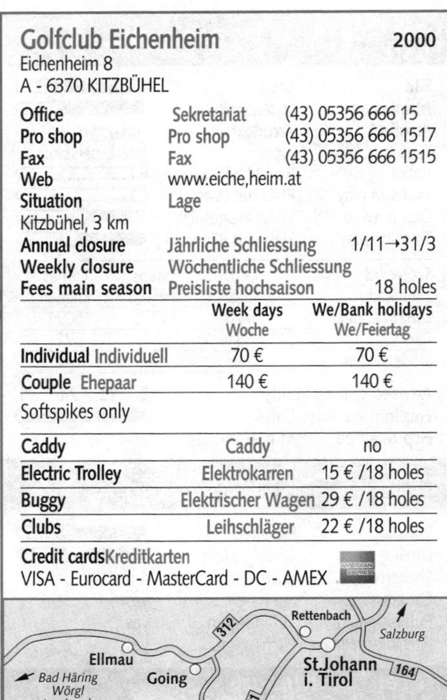

Golfclub Eichenheim — 2000

Eichenheim 8
A - 6370 KITZBÜHEL

Office	Sekretariat	(43) 05356 666 15
Pro shop	Pro shop	(43) 05356 666 1517
Fax	Fax	(43) 05356 666 1515
Web	www.eiche,heim.at	
Situation	Lage	
Kitzbühel, 3 km		
Annual closure	Jährliche Schliessung	1/11→31/3
Weekly closure	Wöchentliche Schliessung	
Fees main season	Preisliste hochsaison	18 holes

	Week days / Woche	We/Bank holidays / We/Feiertag
Individual Individuell	70 €	70 €
Couple Ehepaar	140 €	140 €

Softspikes only

Caddy	Caddy	no
Electric Trolley	Elektrokarren	15 € /18 holes
Buggy	Elektrischer Wagen	29 € /18 holes
Clubs	Leihschläger	22 € /18 holes

Credit cards Kreditkarten
VISA - Eurocard - MasterCard - DC - AMEX

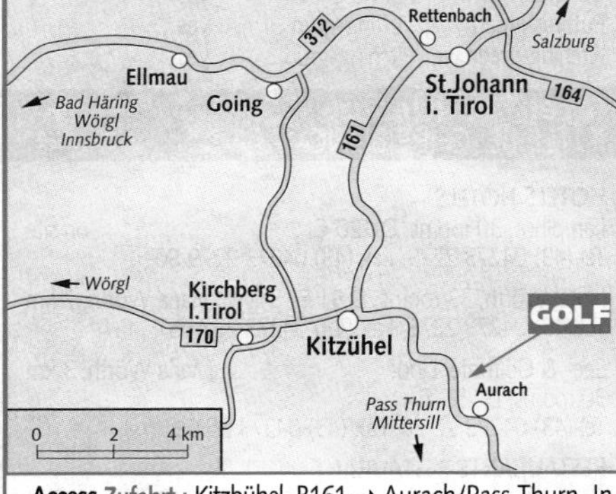

Access Zufahrt : Kitzbühel, B161 → Aurach/Pass Thurn. In Aurach, turn left → golf.

Map 1 on page 98 Karte 1 Seite 98

Golf course PLATZ — 17/20

Site	Lage	
Maintenance	Instandhaltung	
Architect	Architekt	Kyle Phillips
Type	Typ	mountain
Relief	Begehbarkeit	
Water in play	Platz mit Wasser	
Exp. to wind	Wind ausgesetzt	
Trees in play	Platz mit Bäumen	

Scorecard Scorekarte	Chp. Chp.	Mens Herren	Ladies Damen
Length Länge	6057	5622	4628
Par	71	71	71
Slope system	—	—	—

Advised golfing ability Empfohlene Spielstärke — 0 12 24 36

Hcp required Min. Handicap 36

Club house & amenities KLUBHAUS UND NEBENGEBÄUDE — 8/10

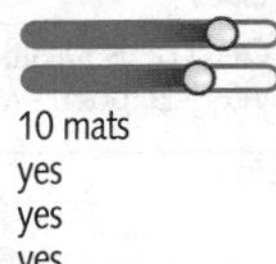

Pro shop	Pro shop	
Driving range	Übungsplatz	
Sheltered	überdacht	10 mats
On grass	auf Rasen	yes
Putting-green	Putting-grün	yes
Pitching-green	Pitching-grün	yes

Hotel facilities HOTEL BESCHREIBUNG — 8/10

HOTELS HOTELS

Golfhotel Rasmushof D 193 € — Kitzbühel, 3 km
Tel (43) 05356 - 652 52, Fax (43) 05356 - 65252-49

Sporthotel Bichlhof, 33 rooms, D from 95 € — Kitzbühel
Tel (43) 05356 - 640 220

Weisses Rössl, 68 rooms, D from 300 € — Kitzbühel
Tel (43) 05356 - 625 410

RESTAURANTS RESTAURANT

Unterberger Stuben, Tel (43) 05356 - 661 270 — Kitzbühel

Wirtshaus zum Rehkitz, Tel (43) 05356 - 661 22 — Kitzbühel

Hallerwirt, Tel (43) 05356 - 645 02 — Aurach, 1 km

FONTANA

16	8	7

Dieser Platz in dem reizvollen Städtchen Baden bei Wien gehört dem österreichisch-kanadischen Milliadär Frank Stronach. Beim Bau wurde zunächst ein zwanzig Hektar grosser künstlicher See mit einem Sandstrand angelegt. Fast alle Löcher werden durch Wasser und die an Kalifornien erinnernden Felsen verteidigt. Das verlangt nach präzisem Spiel, denn wenn man Wasser oder Felsen trifft, kann man seinen Golfball meist abschreiben. Oder anders ausgedrück: Dieser Platz wirkt künstlich – eben typisch amerikanisch und nicht österreichisch. Das Anspielen der Grüns ist voller Gefahren, man benötigt sauber getroffene, hohe Eisenschläge, eine Aufgabe, die durch den oft über das Gelände pfeifenden Wind erschwert wird. "Schutz" findet man in den bis zu fünf Meter tiefen Bundern.

This course was created by the Austrian Canadian billionaire Frank Stronach on the uplands of the delightful town of Baden bei Wien. They firstly dug an artificial lake of some 20 hectares, then an artificial sandy beach, rocks and a luxury club-house. All this water is used not only for swimming in but also for playing havoc with miscued golf balls. Virtually all the holes here are more or less protected by water and the rocks are re-creations of similar formations in California. In other words you can expect a course that is more American than Austrian in style, the downside of which is its slightly artificial nature. Playing to the greens is a somewhat hazardous occupation and calls for cleanly hit high iron shots, a feat made more complicated by the frequent wind that sweeps across this wide open space. One form of shelter is to make a visit to one of the dozen or so bunkers, some of which are up to 15 feet deep!

Golf & Sportclub Fontana — 1997

Fontana Allee 1
A - 2522 OBERWALTERSDORF

Office	Sekretariat	(43) 02253 606 401
Pro shop	Pro shop	(43) 02253 606 412
Fax	Fax	(43) 02253 606 403
Web	www.fontana.at	
Situation	Lage	Wien (pop. 1 640 000), 35 km
Annual closure	Jährliche Schliessung	no
Weekly closure	Wöchentliche Schliessung	no
Fees main season	Preisliste hochsaison	18 holes

	Week days Woche	We/Bank holidays We/Feiertag
Individual Individuell	73 €	94 €
Couple Ehepaar	145 €	189 €

Caddy	Caddy	on request
Electric Trolley	Elektrokarren	22 €
Buggy	Elektrischer Wagen	22 €
Clubs	Leihschläger	25 €

Credit cards Kreditkarten
VISA - Eurocard - MasterCard - AMEX

Access Zufahrt : Wien A2 → Graz. Exit (Ausfahrt) Baden. 210 to Oberwatersdorf.
Map 1 on page 91 Karte 1 Seite 91

Golf course PLATZ — 16/20

Site	Lage	
Maintenance	Instandhaltung	
Architect	Architekt	Doug Carrick Hans Erhard
Type	Typ	inland, residential
Relief	Begehbarkeit	
Water in play	Platz mit Wasser	
Exp. to wind	Wind ausgesetzt	
Trees in play	Platz mit Bäumen	

Scorecard Scorekarte	Chp. Chp.	Mens Herren	Ladies Damen
Length Länge	6088	5643	5012
Par	72	72	72
Slope system	—	—	—

Advised golfing ability 0 12 24 36
Empfohlene Spielstärke
Hcp required Min. Handicap 36

Club house & amenities KLUBHAUS UND NEBENGEBÄUDE — 8/10

Pro shop	Pro shop	
Driving range	Übungsplatz	
Sheltered	überdacht	no
On grass	auf Rasen	yes
Putting-green	Putting-grün	yes
Pitching-green	Pitching-grün	yes

Hotel facilities HOTEL BESCHREIBUNG — 7/10

HOTELS HOTELS

Grand Hotel Sauerhof, 200 rooms, D 182 € — Baden bei Wien
Tel (43) 02252 - 412 51 — 5 km

Dorint Biedermeier, 216 rooms, D 178 € — Wien
Tel (43) 0171 - 6710, Fax (43) 0171 - 6715 03 — 35 km

Das Triest, 73 rooms, D 203 € — Wien 35 km
Tel (43) 0158 - 9180, Fax (43) 0158 - 91818

RESTAURANTS RESTAURANT

Academie, Tel (43) 0171 - 382 56 — Wien 35 km

Selina, Tel (43) 0140 - 564 04 — Wien 35 km

Steirer Stub'n, Tel (43) 0154 443 - 49 — Wien 35 km

GOLFRESORT HAUGSCHLAG - WALDVIERTEL 16 8 6

Dieser Platz liegt nahe der tschechischen Grenze und die Landschaft dieser Gegend erinnert schon an Böhmen, einem Land mit romatischen Wälder, Seen und Bauernhöfen. Der Platz wurde auf leicht hügeligem Gelände zwischen Wäldern und Sümpfen angelegt. Trotzdem kommen Bäume nur an einem halben Dutzend Löcher gefährlich ins Spiel, ganz besonders am trickreichen Loch 4. Die Architekten meinten es gut mit hohen Handicaps, aber wiederum auch nicht gut genug, um den Spitznamen "Heimat der Birdies" zu rechtfertigen. Die Austrian Open wurde hier einige Male ausgetragen und die Pros lieferten reihenweise niedrige Ergebnisse ab. Auch Damen fühlen sich auf diesem Platz wohl. Ein zweiter Platz wurde gerade eröffnet im Waldviertel-Resort. Aber darüber mehr in der nächsten Ausgabe des Peugeot Golf Guides.

This course, lying very close to the Czech frontier, is even closer to the landscapes of nearby Bohemia, a land of romantic forests, lakes and farms which mark the whole of northern Austria. It was laid out over just slightly hilly landscape in a setting of woods and marshland, but trees are only really dangerous on half a dozen holes or so (including the very tricky hole N° 4). In fact the architects have been rather kind to high-handicappers, but perhaps not kind enough to fully warrant the nickname of "Home of Birdies". Having said that, the Austrian Open has been held here on several occasions and players have produced an array of low scores. The ladies also willingly admit to feeling rather comfortable on this course, and you do not always hear them say that. A second course has recently been opened in this very pleasant "Waldviertel" resort and we will certainly have something to say about that in our next edition.

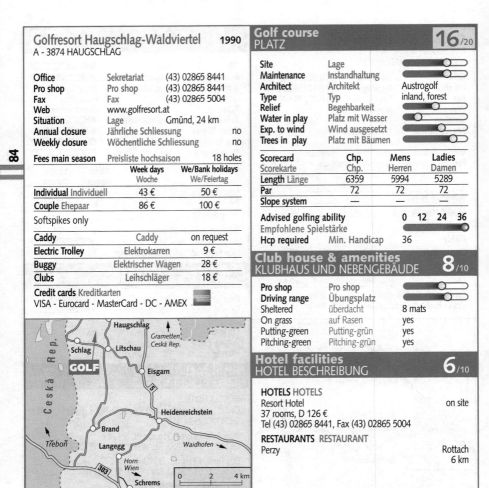

Golfresort Haugschlag-Waldviertel 1990

A - 3874 HAUGSCHLAG

Office	Sekretariat	(43) 02865 8441
Pro shop	Pro shop	(43) 02865 8441
Fax	Fax	(43) 02865 5004
Web	www.golfresort.at	
Situation	Lage	Gmünd, 24 km
Annual closure	Jährliche Schliessung	no
Weekly closure	Wöchentliche Schliessung	no

Fees main season Preisliste hochsaison	18 holes	
	Week days Woche	**We/Bank holidays** We/Feiertag
Individual Individuell	43 €	50 €
Couple Ehepaar	86 €	100 €

Softspikes only

Caddy	Caddy	on request
Electric Trolley	Elektrokarren	9 €
Buggy	Elektrischer Wagen	28 €
Clubs	Leihschläger	18 €

Credit cards Kreditkarten
VISA - Eurocard - MasterCard - DC - AMEX

Access Zufahrt : • Wien, A22, E49 → Horn, Schrems, Gmünd • Linz, E14 B38, B41 to Gmünd.
• Then, B30, B5 to Einsgarn, → Litschau, Haugschlag.
Map 1 on page 91 Karte 1 Seite 91

Golf course PLATZ 16/20

Site	Lage	
Maintenance	Instandhaltung	
Architect	Architekt	Austrogolf
Type	Typ	inland, forest
Relief	Begehbarkeit	
Water in play	Platz mit Wasser	
Exp. to wind	Wind ausgesetzt	
Trees in play	Platz mit Bäumen	

Scorecard Scorekarte	**Chp.** Chp.	**Mens** Herren	**Ladies** Damen
Length Länge	6359	5994	5289
Par	72	72	72
Slope system	—	—	—

Advised golfing ability Empfohlene Spielstärke: 0 12 24 36
Hcp required Min. Handicap 36

Club house & amenities KLUBHAUS UND NEBENGEBÄUDE 8/10

Pro shop	Pro shop	
Driving range	Übungsplatz	
Sheltered	überdacht	8 mats
On grass	auf Rasen	yes
Putting-green	Putting-grün	yes
Pitching-green	Pitching-grün	yes

Hotel facilities HOTEL BESCHREIBUNG 6/10

HOTELS HOTELS
Resort Hotel — on site
37 rooms, D 126 €
Tel (43) 02865 8441, Fax (43) 02865 5004

RESTAURANTS RESTAURANT
Perzy — Rottach 6 km

GUT ALTENTANN

17	7	6

Salzburg ist die Heimatstadt von Mozart und eine Touristenattraktion. Die Architektur von Jack Nicklaus erinnert – um einen musikalischen Vergleich zu bemühen – eher an Wagner als an die subtile Inspiration von Mozart. Gut Altentann war der erste Platz, den Nicklaus in Europa entwarf. Es ist ein schwerer Platz mit vielen Hindernissen. Das Gelände wurde für Golf modelliert, man findet Bäume, aber auch weit offene Spielbahnen mit sanften Anstiegen und Gefällen und exzellente Grüns. Natürlich hat Nicklaus auch hier seine Vorlieben ausgelebt: Wie es die Golflegende als Spieler tat, ist es auch in Altentann von Vorteil, wenn man die Grüns mit einem Fade anspielen kann. Die Schwierigkeiten des Platzes bestehen aus zwei Seen, weiteren Wasserhindernissen, Sümpfen und bestens konturierten Bunkern. Leider entspricht die Drainage auf dem Platz nicht dem hohen Design-Standard, so dass man den Platz nach heftigen Regenfällen meiden sollte.

Salzburg is Mozart's home town and an historical landmark bathed in light. The architectural style of Jack Nicklaus, though, is closer to Wagner than the brilliant inspiration and sprightliness of Mozart. Gut Altentann was the very first course designed by Nicklaus in Europe, a tough layout with spectacular continuity in terms of holes and hazards. The terrain was made for golf, sometimes full of trees, other times very open but always perfectly landscaped with gentle slopes and well-designed greens. Nicklaus has laid emphasis on the need to play intelligently and to think through each shot, and here again you will find some of his distinctive preferences, like having to fade approach shots into the greens. Hazards are basically two lakes, other water hazards and marshes, together with well-contoured bunkers, one of the hallmarks of the great man's architectural style. A class course but a little more in the way of the Baroque would have been more than welcome in Salzburg. Unfortunately the drainage is not up to the standard of the design. So beware of the condition after heavy rain.

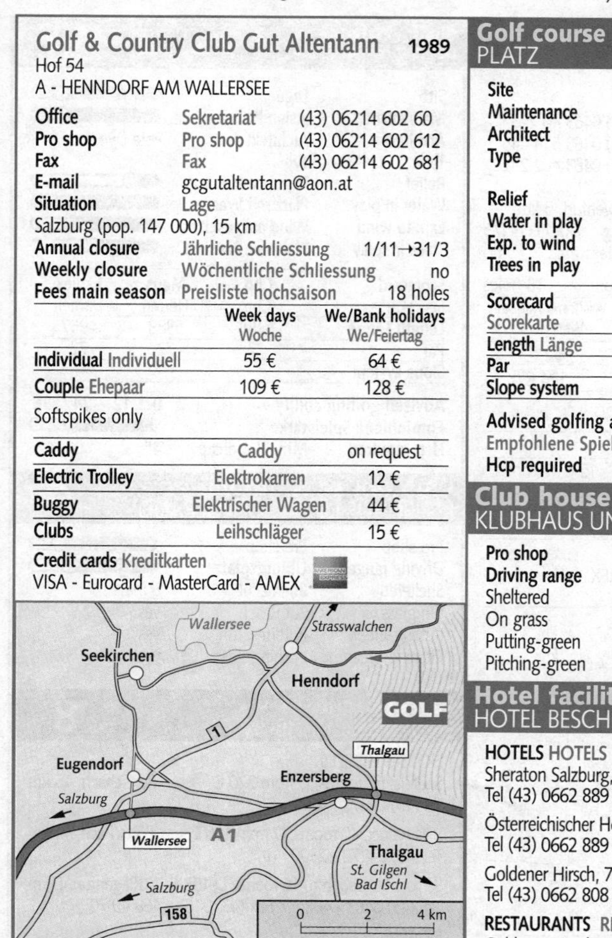

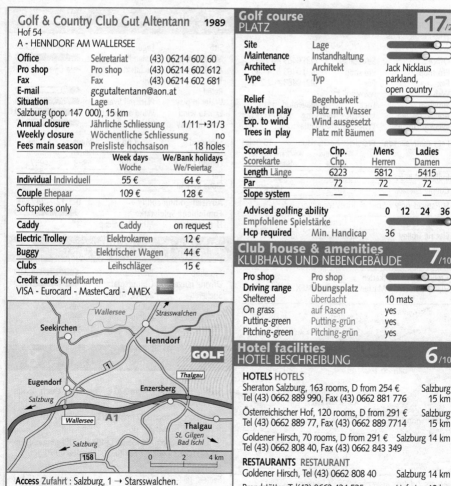

Golf & Country Club Gut Altentann 1989

Hof 54
A - HENNDORF AM WALLERSEE

Office	Sekretariat	(43) 06214 602 60
Pro shop	Pro shop	(43) 06214 602 612
Fax	Fax	(43) 06214 602 681
E-mail	gcgutaltentann@aon.at	
Situation	Lage	
Salzburg (pop. 147 000), 15 km		
Annual closure	Jährliche Schliessung	1/11→31/3
Weekly closure	Wöchentliche Schliessung	no
Fees main season	Preisliste hochsaison	18 holes

	Week days Woche	We/Bank holidays We/Feiertag
Individual Individuell	55 €	64 €
Couple Ehepaar	109 €	128 €

Softspikes only

Caddy	Caddy	on request
Electric Trolley	Elektrokarren	12 €
Buggy	Elektrischer Wagen	44 €
Clubs	Leihschläger	15 €

Credit cards Kreditkarten
VISA - Eurocard - MasterCard - AMEX

Access Zufahrt : Salzburg, 1 → Starsswalchen.
In Henndorf, turn right → Altentann, → Golfplatz.
Map 1 on page 90 Karte 1 Seite 90

Golf course
PLATZ **17/20**

Site	Lage	
Maintenance	Instandhaltung	
Architect	Architekt	Jack Nicklaus
Type	Typ	parkland, open country
Relief	Begehbarkeit	
Water in play	Platz mit Wasser	
Exp. to wind	Wind ausgesetzt	
Trees in play	Platz mit Bäumen	

Scorecard Scorekarte	Chp. Chp.	Mens Herren	Ladies Damen
Length Länge	6223	5812	5415
Par	72	72	72
Slope system	—	—	—

Advised golfing ability 0 12 24 36
Empfohlene Spielstärke
Hcp required Min. Handicap 36

Club house & amenities
KLUBHAUS UND NEBENGEBÄUDE **7/10**

Pro shop	Pro shop	
Driving range	Übungsplatz	
Sheltered	überdacht	10 mats
On grass	auf Rasen	yes
Putting-green	Putting-grün	yes
Pitching-green	Pitching-grün	yes

Hotel facilities
HOTEL BESCHREIBUNG **6/10**

HOTELS HOTELS

Sheraton Salzburg, 163 rooms, D from 254 € — Salzburg 15 km
Tel (43) 0662 889 990, Fax (43) 0662 881 776

Österreichischer Hof, 120 rooms, D from 291 € — Salzburg 15 km
Tel (43) 0662 889 77, Fax (43) 0662 889 7714

Goldener Hirsch, 70 rooms, D from 291 € — Salzburg 14 km
Tel (43) 0662 808 40, Fax (43) 0662 843 349

RESTAURANTS RESTAURANT

Goldener Hirsch, Tel (43) 0662 808 40 — Salzburg 14 km

Brandstätter, Tel(43) 0662 434 535 — Liefering 18 km

Pfefferschiff — Hallwang-Söllheim 10 km
Tel (43) 0662 661 242

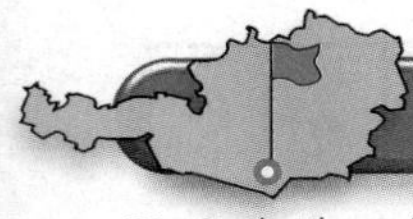

KLAGENFURT-SELTENHEIM 17 6 8

Die Stadt Klagenfurt blickt auf über 800 Jahre Geschichte zurück. In der pulsierenden Landeshauptstadt von Kärnten lässt es sich leben, zumal sie direkt am Ufer des Wörthersees liegt, einem der Lieblingsplätze von Brahms und Mahler. Auch wenn Golfplatz-Architektur eine Kunstform ist, fühlt man auf diesem klassischen Pete-Dye-Platz eine ganz andere Art von Inspiration. In dieses relativ flache Gelände legte Dye visuell reizvolle Hindernisse – immer genau an die richtige Stelle. Mit den vielen Wasserhindernissen wirkt der Platz amerikanisch, aber das nimmt man gerne in Kauf. Da der Platz insgesamt nicht weniger als sechs Abschläge findet hier jeder Golfer eine seiner Spielstärke angemessene Herausforderung, vom sehr hohen bis zum einstelligen Handicapper. Das 18. Loch fordert beide gleichermassen, zumal die Nerven aufreibende Aufgabe durch die vielen Zuschauer auf der Clubhaus-Terrasse noch erschwert wird.

The town of Klagenfurt bears the traces of 800 years of history and you can spend many a pleasant moment in the bustling old town, not to mention the banks of the Wörthersee, a favourite spot for both Brahms and Mahler. But even though golf course architecture is also an art form, the inspiration you feel on this classy Pete Dye course is of a different nature. Starting off with rather flat terrain, he has developed an array of well-designed and visually attractive hazards, particularly the contours of the many water hazards. Naturally this gives the layout a very American look, but no matter. The course is intelligent with no fewer than six tee-boxes per hole to give yardage ranging from less than 5,000 to almost 6,300 metres. If you cannot find the course to match your game, then you must be desperate, because even very high handicappers can enjoy this almost as much as their single-figure counterparts, at least as far as the 18th hole, a nerve-wracking ordeal when the club-house terrace is crowded with onlookers.

Golfclub Klagenfurt-Seltenheim — 1996

Seltenheimerstrasse 137
A - 9061 KLAGENFURT- WÖLFNITZ

Office	Sekretariat	(43) 0463 40 223
Pro shop	Pro shop	(43) 0463 514 445
Fax	Fax	(43) 0463 402 2320
Web	www.golf.at	
Situation	Lage	Klagenfurt, 5 km
Annual closure	Jährliche Schliessung	30/11→31/3
Weekly closure	Wöchentliche Schliessung	no

Fees main season Preisliste hochsaison	Week days Woche	We/Bank holidays We/Feiertag
	18 holes	
Individual Individuell	51 €	62 €
Couple Ehepaar	102 €	124 €

Softspikes only / Special prices for juniors

Caddy	Caddy	no
Electric Trolley	Elektrokarren	15 € /18 holes
Buggy	Elektrischer Wagen	25 € /18 holes
Clubs	Leihschläger	15 € /18 holes

Credit cards Kreditkarten
VISA - Eurocard - MasterCard - DC - AMEX

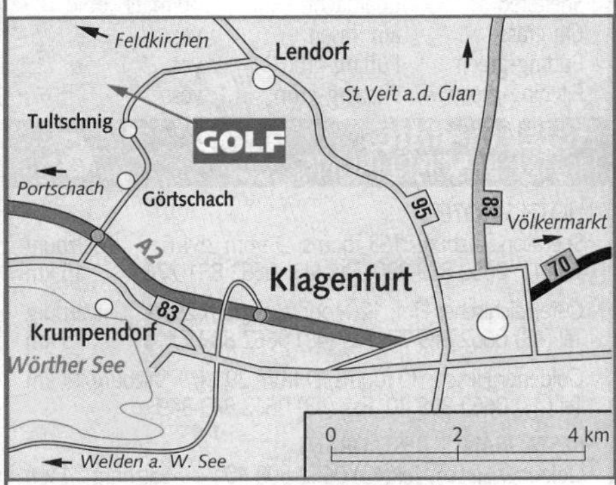

Access Zufahrt: Klagenfurt B95 → Feldkirchen. Exit (Ausfahrt) Lendorf, then turn left in Seltenheimerstrasse
Map 6 on page 173 Karte 6 Seite 173

Golf course PLATZ — 17/20

Site	Lage	
Maintenance	Instandhaltung	
Architect	Architekt	Pete Dye
Type	Typ	
Relief	Begehbarkeit	
Water in play	Platz mit Wasser	
Exp. to wind	Wind ausgesetzt	
Trees in play	Platz mit Bäumen	

Scorecard Scorekarte	Chp. Chp.	Mens Herren	Ladies Damen
Length Länge	6286	5888	4957
Par	72	72	72
Slope system	—	—	—

Advised golfing ability Empfohlene Spielstärke: 0 12 24 36
Hcp required Min. Handicap: 45

Club house & amenities KLUBHAUS UND NEBENGEBÄUDE — 6/10

Pro shop	Pro shop	
Driving range	Übungsplatz	
Sheltered	überdacht	8 mats
On grass	auf Rasen	yes
Putting-green	Putting-grün	yes
Pitching-green	Pitching-grün	yes

Hotel facilities HOTEL BESCHREIBUNG — 8/10

HOTELS HOTELS

Seefels, 57 rooms, D from 220 € — Pörtschach, 15 km
Tel (43) 04272 - 2377

Villa Rainer, 40 rooms, D from 185 € — Pörtschach, 11 km
Tel (43) 04272 - 2300

Schloss St. Georgen, 16 rooms, D 153 € — Klagenfurt, 5 km
Tel. (43) 0463 - 468 49, Fax (43) 0463 - 468 49 70

HOTELS HOTELS

Seefels, Tel (43) 04272 - 2377 — Pörtschach, 15 km
Restaurant Knes, Tel (43) 0463 - 553 39 — Lendorf, 5 km
Gasthaus Stopper, Tel (43) 0463 - 405 01 — Wölfnitz, 1 km

SCHLOSS EBREICHSDORF | 16 | 8 | 6

Egal, wo immer man in Österreich hinkommt, überall findet man Spuren von Komponisten. Unweit des Platzes findet man Eisenstadt, wo Haydn am Hof der Esterhazys musizierte. Ganz in der Nähe liegt auch Baden, das Tor zum Wienerwald mit seinen herrlichen Wälder, die bis nach Wien führen. Beethoven lebte hier, Mozart, Schubert und später die Walzerkönige waren hier oft zu Besuch. Kurstädte und Golf passen gut zuammen, wie der 15 Kilometer entfernte Platz belegt. Keith Preston auf Sandboden einen angenehmen Parkland-Course entworfen, ohne grosse Eingriffe in die Naturlandschaft. Er baute einige Doglegs ein, an denen man den Ball mit Fade oder Draw spielen muss. Wenn jedoch der Fade zum Slice und der Draw zum Hook ausartet, kann man sein Handicap nicht spielen können. Die hohen Bäume machen etliche der Fairways relativ eng. Die Platz muss man einige Male spielen, bevor man mit ihm vertraut ist.

Wherever you go in Austria, you always find the mark of at least one musician. Not far from here, there is firstly Eisenstadt, where Haydn entertained the Court of the Esterhazy (see their castle). Then there is Baden, the gateway to the Wienerwald, a magnificent forest which leads to Vienna. Beethoven used to live in this pretty spa town, also often visited by Mozart, Schubert and later on the kings of Waltz. Spas and golf go well together and this course was laid out about fifteen kilometres down the road. It is parkland with very pleasant sandy soil where Keith Preston has designed a fine layout without too much disruption to the natural site. He has designed in a few dog-legs where you will need to gently flight the ball, but overdo it and you are in trouble. If can keep that hook or slice under control, you can probably play to your handicap here, even though the now "mature" trees make some of the fairways a little tight. A course that is well worth getting to know, to be played several times if you want to make any real impression.

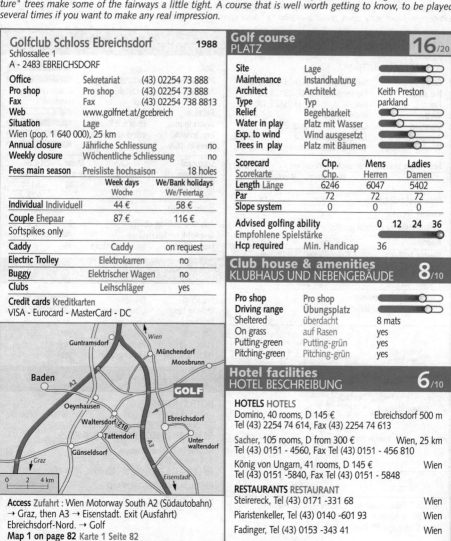

Golfclub Schloss Ebreichsdorf — 1988

Schlossallee 1
A - 2483 EBREICHSDORF

Office	Sekretariat	(43) 02254 73 888
Pro shop	Pro shop	(43) 02254 73 888
Fax	Fax	(43) 02254 738 8813
Web	www.golfnet.at/gcebreich	
Situation	Lage	
Wien (pop. 1 640 000), 25 km		
Annual closure	Jährliche Schliessung	no
Weekly closure	Wöchentliche Schliessung	no

Fees main season Preisliste hochsaison	18 holes	
	Week days Woche	**We/Bank holidays** We/Feiertag
Individual Individuell	44 €	58 €
Couple Ehepaar	87 €	116 €
Softspikes only		
Caddy	Caddy	on request
Electric Trolley	Elektrokarren	no
Buggy	Elektrischer Wagen	no
Clubs	Leihschläger	yes

Credit cards Kreditkarten
VISA - Eurocard - MasterCard - DC

Access Zufahrt : Wien Motorway South A2 (Südautobahn) → Graz, then A3 → Eisenstadt. Exit (Ausfahrt) Ebreichsdorf-Nord. → Golf
Map 1 on page 82 Karte 1 Seite 82

Golf course PLATZ — 16/20

Site	Lage	
Maintenance	Instandhaltung	
Architect	Architekt	Keith Preston
Type	Typ	parkland
Relief	Begehbarkeit	
Water in play	Platz mit Wasser	
Exp. to wind	Wind ausgesetzt	
Trees in play	Platz mit Bäumen	

Scorecard Scorekarte	Chp. Chp.	Mens Herren	Ladies Damen
Length Länge	6246	6047	5402
Par	72	72	72
Slope system	0	0	0

Advised golfing ability Empfohlene Spielstärke — 0 12 24 36
Hcp required Min. Handicap 36

Club house & amenities KLUBHAUS UND NEBENGEBÄUDE — 8/10

Pro shop	Pro shop	
Driving range	Übungsplatz	
Sheltered	überdacht	8 mats
On grass	auf Rasen	yes
Putting-green	Putting-grün	yes
Pitching-green	Pitching-grün	yes

Hotel facilities HOTEL BESCHREIBUNG — 6/10

HOTELS HOTELS
Domino, 40 rooms, D 145 € — Ebreichsdorf 500 m
Tel (43) 2254 74 614, Fax (43) 2254 74 613

Sacher, 105 rooms, D from 300 € — Wien, 25 km
Tel (43) 0151 - 4560, Fax Tel (43) 0151 - 456 810

König von Ungarn, 41 rooms, D 145 € — Wien
Tel (43) 0151 -5840, Fax Tel (43) 0151 - 5848

RESTAURANTS RESTAURANT
Steirereck, Tel (43) 0171 -331 68 — Wien
Piaristenkeller, Tel (43) 0140 -601 93 — Wien
Fadinger, Tel (43) 0153 -343 41 — Wien

STEIERMÄRKISCHER MURHOF 16 | 8 | 7

Für die meisten ausländischen Besucher besteht Österreich aus Wien und Salzburg. Dabei hat Graz, ein Weltkulturerbe der Unesco, viel zu bieten. Der Platz des Steiermärkischen Golf Clubs wurde 1993 erbaut und liegt im Norden der Stadt. Damals gehörte zum Golfplatzbau in der Steiermark Pioniergeist, heute ist der Platz einer der Topplätze des Landes. Die alten Stallungen wurde zum Clubhaus mit Restaurant und einem Hotel im steirischen Stil umgebaut. Diese Platz sollte man am besten vom Frühling bis in den Herbst spielen, allerdings werden die Fairways nach langen Trockenperioden sehr hart. Im Sommer sind die Abschlagzeiten oft lange im Voraus gebucht, deshalb sollte man rechtzeitig buchen. Im Gegensatz zu vielen anderen österreichischen Plätzen ist der Murhof, der von einem Fluss begrenzt wird, vollkommen flach. Viele Bäume sorgen für eine angenehme Umgebung, sind aber Gift für verzogene Schläge. Das Design von Limburger verlangt trotz des offenen Eindrucks genaue Drives, um einen guten Score zu erzielen.

For most foreign visitors, Austria is Vienna and Salzburg, but it would be a pity to overlook Graz, whose old town enjoys world heritage listing by Unesco. The present course was built in 1963 to the north of the town, a rather bold venture at the time as no-one in Styria was really interested in golf back then. Today it is one of the country's most prestigious courses where former stables have been transformed into a club-house with restaurant and hotel resort in traditional Austrian style. This mid-altitude course plays at its best between the end of spring and autumn, but without a watering system for the fairways the course gets extremely hard after long dry spells. Some tee-off times are even booked one year ahead of time. You might expect some steep topography, as found elsewhere on many Austrian courses, but in fact Steiermarkischer is virtually flat, flanked by a river and home to very many trees which provide at once a pleasant setting and real threat for wayward drives. The design, by von Limburger, is perfectly open, another reason to "drive carefully". A good score is anything but guaranteed.

Steiermärkischer Golf-Club Murhof 1963

Adriach 53
A - 8130 FROHNLEITEN-MURHOF

Office	Sekretariat	(43) 03126 3010
Pro shop	Pro shop	(43) 03126 3010
Fax	Fax	(43) 03126 300 029
Web	www.murhof.at	
Situation	Lage	Graz, 20 km
Annual closure	Jährliche Schliessung	1/11→31/3
Weekly closure	Wöchentliche Schliessung	no

Fees main season Preisliste hochsaison	18 holes	
	Week days Woche	**We/Bank holidays** We/Feiertag
Individual Individuell	49 €	62 €
Couple Ehepaar	99 €	125 €

Softspikes only / Hotel guests: – 50%

Caddy	Caddy	no
Electric Trolley	Elektrokarren	yes
Buggy	Elektrischer Wagen	no
Clubs	Leihschläger yes	

Credit cards Kreditkarten
VISA - Eurocard - Mastercard

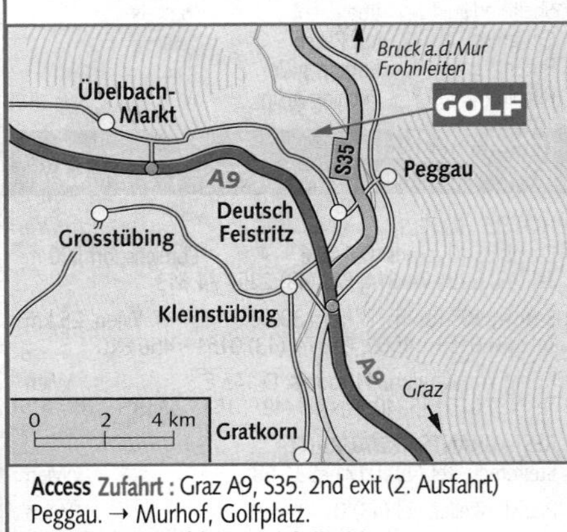

Access Zufahrt : Graz A9, S35. 2nd exit (2. Ausfahrt) Peggau. → Murhof, Golfplatz.
Map 1 on page 91 Karte 1 Seite 91

Golf course PLATZ 16/20

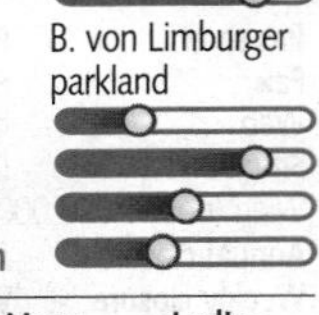

Site	Lage	
Maintenance	Instandhaltung	
Architect	Architekt	B. von Limburger
Type	Typ	parkland
Relief	Begehbarkeit	
Water in play	Platz mit Wasser	
Exp. to wind	Wind ausgesetzt	
Trees in play	Platz mit Bäumen	

Scorecard Scorekarte	**Chp.** Chp.	**Mens** Herren	**Ladies** Damen
Length Länge	6381	6198	5414
Par	72	72	72
Slope system	—	—	—

Advised golfing ability Empfohlene Spielstärke 0 12 24 36
Hcp required Min. Handicap 36

Club house & amenities KLUBHAUS UND NEBENGEBÄUDE 8/10

Pro shop	Pro shop	
Driving range	Übungsplatz	
Sheltered	überdacht	no
On grass	auf Rasen	yes
Putting-green	Putting-grün	yes
Pitching-green	Pitching-grün	yes

Hotel facilities HOTEL BESCHREIBUNG 7/10

HOTELS HOTELS

Golfhotel Murhof — on site
20 rooms, D 137 €
Tel (43) 03126 3000, Fax (43) 03126 30029

Austria Trend Hotel Europa — Graz 24 km
114 rooms, D 87 €
Tel (43) 0316 7076-0, Fax (43) 0316 7076-606

RESTAURANTS RESTAURANT

Der Pichlmaier — Graz 22 km
Tel (43) 0316 471 597

URSLAUTAL

15 | 7 | 7

Neulinge werden sich hier schnell zurecht finden, da der Grossteil des Platzes von der Clubhaus-Terrasse zu überblicken ist. Der Platz wurde von Keith Preston entworfen, der auch die österreichische Damen-Nationalmannschaft betreut. Deshalb überrascht es nicht, dass er einen Platz in die Landschaft legte, der für Golfer aller Spielstärken geeignet ist. Der Platz ist nicht übermässig lang, weist dafür aber einige enge Fairways auf. Die Hindernisse sind alle gut vom Abschlag sichtbar und wirken nicht allzu einschüchternd, obwohl das Rough oft hoch und dicht ist. Manche der Löcher liegen etwas eng beieinander. Alles in allem ein Platz ohne versteckte Tücken. Der Platz ist leicht begehbar, trotzdem sollte man sich ab und an die Zeit nehmen, die umliegende Berglandschaft zu geniessen.

New-comers can easily find their bearings here as a good part of the course is visible from the club-house terrace. It was designed by Keith Preston, who also happens to coach the Austrian Ladies team, so you will not be surprised to see that he has carefully adapted the course to suit players of all levels. It is very reasonable in length but this is balanced by some tight fairways. The main hazards are there to be seen but never terrifying, even though the rough tends to get very thick and is often in play and the holes are sometimes a little close to each other. All in all, this is a very honest course with hazards clearly in view, a laudable achievement which dispels any fear of hidden traps. The course is easily walkable, but take a break from time to time to enjoy the mountain landscape.

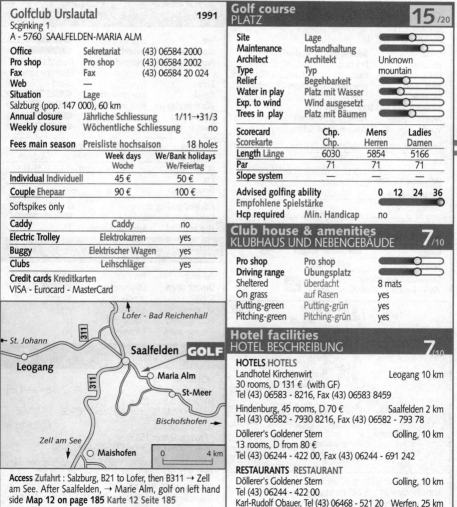

Golfclub Urslautal — 1991

Scginking 1
A - 5760 SAALFELDEN-MARIA ALM

Office	Sekretariat	(43) 06584 2000
Pro shop	Pro shop	(43) 06584 2002
Fax	Fax	(43) 06584 20 024
Web	—	
Situation	Lage	

Salzburg (pop. 147 000), 60 km

Annual closure	Jährliche Schliessung	1/11→31/3
Weekly closure	Wöchentliche Schliessung	no

Fees main season Preisliste hochsaison	Week days Woche	18 holes We/Bank holidays We/Feiertag
Individual Individuell	45 €	50 €
Couple Ehepaar	90 €	100 €

Softspikes only

Caddy	Caddy	no
Electric Trolley	Elektrokarren	yes
Buggy	Elektrischer Wagen	yes
Clubs	Leihschläger	yes

Credit cards Kreditkarten
VISA - Eurocard - MasterCard

Lofer - Bad Reichenhall
St. Johann
311
Saalfelden
GOLF
Leogang
Maria Alm
St-Meer
Bischofshofen
Zell am See
Maishofen
0 4 km

Access Zufahrt : Salzburg, B21 to Lofer, then B311 → Zell am See. After Saalfelden, → Marie Alm, golf on left hand side **Map 12 on page 185** Karte 12 Seite 185

Golf course PLATZ — 15/20

Site	Lage	
Maintenance	Instandhaltung	
Architect	Architekt	Unknown
Type	Typ	mountain
Relief	Begehbarkeit	
Water in play	Platz mit Wasser	
Exp. to wind	Wind ausgesetzt	
Trees in play	Platz mit Bäumen	

Scorecard Scorekarte	Chp. Chp.	Mens Herren	Ladies Damen
Length Länge	6030	5854	5166
Par	71	71	71
Slope system	—	—	—

Advised golfing ability Empfohlene Spielstärke: 0 12 24 36
Hcp required Min. Handicap: no

Club house & amenities KLUBHAUS UND NEBENGEBÄUDE — 7/10

Pro shop	Pro shop	
Driving range	Übungsplatz	
Sheltered	überdacht	8 mats
On grass	auf Rasen	yes
Putting-green	Putting-grün	yes
Pitching-green	Pitching-grün	yes

Hotel facilities HOTEL BESCHREIBUNG — 7/10

HOTELS HOTELS

Landhotel Kirchenwirt — Leogang 10 km
30 rooms, D 131 € (with GF)
Tel (43) 06583 - 8216, Fax (43) 06583 8459

Hindenburg, 45 rooms, D 70 € — Saalfelden 2 km
Tel (43) 06582 - 7930 8216, Fax (43) 06582 - 793 78

Döllerer's Goldener Stern — Golling, 10 km
13 rooms, D from 80 €
Tel (43) 06244 - 422 00, Fax (43) 06244 - 691 242

RESTAURANTS RESTAURANT

Döllerer's Goldener Stern — Golling, 10 km
Tel (43) 06244 - 422 00
Karl-Rudolf Obauer, Tel (43) 06468 - 521 20 — Werfen, 25 km

ZELL AM SEE KAPRUN Schmittenhöhe

16	7	6

Zell am See und Kaprun sind der Ausgangspunkt der wunderbaren Grossglockner-Hochalpenstrasse, eine herrliche 75 km lange Fahrt durch den Naturpark der Hohen Tauern. Inmitten dieser herrlichen Alpenlandschaft liegt der Zeller See, ein idyllisches Plätzchen, in dem man auf flachem Gelände mittlerweile gleich zwei Plätze findet. "Kitzsteinhorn", ein trickreiches Layout mit viel Wasser und einem Inselgrün am Ende des ersten Spielbahn, einem Par 5. Der Platz "Schmittenhöhe" weist weniger Teiche auf, trotzdem ist das Design gelungener. Longhitter werden sich auf diesem Platz wohlfühlen, denn einige der Par-5-Löcher sind mit zwei guten Schlägen zu erreichen, obwohl genug Gräben und Bäume zur Vorsicht mahnen. Auch wer den Ball nicht sonderlich weit schlägt, wird diesen Platz geniessen, wenn auch aus anderen Gründen. Folgen Sie unserem Rat, verbringen Sie ein paar Tage hier, spielen sie Golf und machen Sie einige Bergwanderungen.

Zell am See and Kaprun are the starting points for the wonderful Grossglockner-Hochalpenstrasse, an itinerary of some 75 km through the national park of Hohe Tauern. Add to this the mountainous setting and the Zell lake and you get some idea of what this idyllic site is all about. You feel privileged to play here, especially that there are now two courses: the "Kitzsteinhorn", a rather tricky layout with a lot of water (hole N°1 is a par-5 with an island green), and the "Schmittenhohe", where water is less frequent but the design more incisive. The course is not very hilly, which makes for a pleasant round, and long-hitters will enjoy playing it and taking up the few challenges that are well within their reach. There are enough ditches and trees to keep them on their toes. The rest of us will enjoy it as well but for other reasons. If you want our advice, spend a few days here playing golf and hiking in the mountains.

Golfclub Zell am See Kaprun 1984

Golfstrasse 25
A - 5700 ZELL AM SEE

Office	**Sekretariat**	(43) 06542 561 61
Pro shop	**Pro shop**	(43) 06542 564 82
Fax	**Fax**	(43) 06542 561 61-16
Web	www.europasportregion.at/golfclub	
Situation	**Lage**	
Salzburg (pop. 147 000), 100 km		
Annual closure	**Jährliche Schliessung**	1/11→31/3
Weekly closure	**Wöchentliche Schliessung**	no

Fees main season Preisliste hochsaison	18 holes	
	Week days Woche	**We/Bank holidays** We/Feiertag
Individual Individuell	50 €	57 €
Couple Ehepaar	100 €	115 €

Softspikes only

Caddy	Caddy	on request
Electric Trolley	Elektrokarren	yes
Buggy	Elektrischer Wagen	yes
Clubs	Leihschläger	yes

Credit cards Kreditkarten
VISA - Eurocard - MasterCard - AMEX

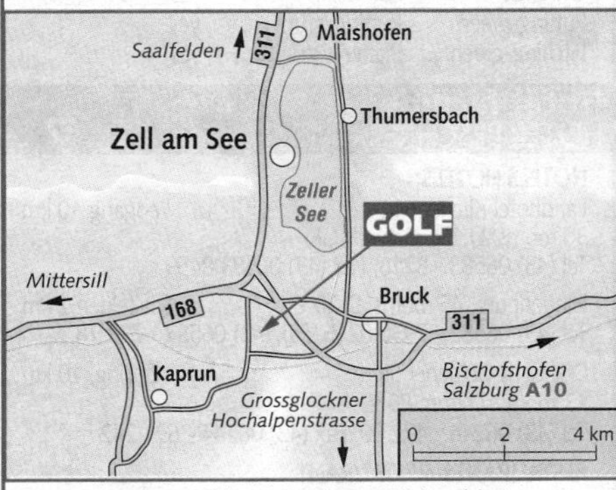

Access Zufahrt : Salzburg, A10/E55. Exit (Ausfahrt) Bischofshofen, 311 → Zell am See, → Kaprun.
Map 1 on page 90 Karte 1 Seite 90

Golf course PLATZ 16/20

Site	Lage	
Maintenance	Instandhaltung	
Architect	Architekt	Donald Harradine Hermann Schauer
Type	Typ	inland
Relief	Begehbarkeit	
Water in play	Platz mit Wasser	
Exp. to wind	Wind ausgesetzt	
Trees in play	Platz mit Bäumen	

Scorecard Scorekarte	**Chp.** Chp.	**Mens** Herren	**Ladies** Damen
Length Länge	6218	6146	5421
Par	72	72	72
Slope system	—	—	—

Advised golfing ability Empfohlene Spielstärke 0 12 24 36
Hcp required Min. Handicap 45

Club house & amenities KLUBHAUS UND NEBENGEBÄUDE 7/10

Pro shop	Pro shop	
Driving range	Übungsplatz	
Sheltered	überdacht	10 mats
On grass	auf Rasen	yes
Putting-green	Putting-grün	yes
Pitching-green	Pitching-grün	yes

Hotel facilities HOTEL BESCHREIBUNG 6/10

HOTELS HOTELS

Hotel Salzburger Hof — Zell am See 4 km
50 rooms, D from 205 €
Tel (43) 06542 765, Fax (43) 06542 765-66

Burgruine Kaprun — Kaprun 9 km
37 rooms, D from 150 €
Tel (43) 06547 8306, Fax (43) 06542 8306-60

Schloss Prielau, 8 rooms, D 190 € — Zell am See 6 km
Tel (43) 06542 72069, Fax (43) 06542 720609-55

RESTAURANTS RESTAURANT

Schloss Prielau, Tel (43) 06542 72609 — Zell am See 6 km

Belgium
Luxemburg

Royal Zoute

Belgique
België
Luxemburg
Luxembourg

La Belgique compte plus de 38.000 joueurs de golf pour 50 parcours de 18 trous environ. Les golfs présentés ici sont ouverts au public. Certes, une partie d'entre eux peut être difficile d'accès en week-end, en raison de leur grand nombre de membres, mais les voyageurs ont souvent la possibilité d'y jouer en semaine. Pour les joueurs belges comme pour les étrangers, le fait d'être muni d'une lettre d'introduction de leur propre club peut cependant faciliter les choses.

België heeft meer dan 38.000 spelers op ongeveer 50 banen 18-holesbanen. De meeste golf-clubs in Peugeot Golf Guide zijn vrij toegankelijk voor het publiek. In sommige raakt men wel moeilijker binnen tijdens het week-end, wegens hun groot aantal leden, maar 'reizigers' bevinden zich meestal gemakkelijker in de mogelijkheid om tijdens de week te spelen. Voor Belgische en buitenlandse spelers is een introductiebrief van de eigen club vaak een goed idee, om de zaken eenvoudiger te maken.

Belgium has more than 38,000 golfers playing on around 50 eighteen-hole courses. All golf courses presented in this Guide are open to the public. Some may be difficult to play on week-ends owing to the number of members, but travelling green-feers should often be able to play during the week. Carrying a letter of introduction from your club may be a help, both for Belgian and foreign players.

Map No 1
Carte 1
Auto Kaart blz 1
km
0 10 20
Kingston upon Hull
Dover
Goes (NL)
Wouwse Plantage (NL)
Royal Zoute
Oostende
Royal Latem
Royal Antwerp
Ravenstein
Oudenaarde
Bondues (F)
Hainaut
Mont-Garni
Waterloo
Rigenée
Brigode (F)
Arras (F)
Ailette (L') (F)
Zierikzee
Steenbergen
Stavenisse
N^d Beveland
Domburg
Walcheren
Veere
ZEELAND
Goes
Middelburg
Bergen op Zoom
Vlissingen
Z^d Beveland
Kruiningen
Hoedekenskerke
Breskens
Woensdrecht
Heist
Knokke-Heist
Zeebrugge
Blankenberge
Oostburg
Sluis
IJzendijke
Terneuzen
Hulst
(ANVERS)
ANTWERPEN
Brasschaat
De Haan
Oostende
(BRUGES)
BRUGGE
Maldegem
Zelzate
Middelkerke-Bad
Nieuwpoort
Jabbeke
Oostkamp
Eeklo
Stekene
Beveren
St. Niklaas
Temse
Koksijde-Bad
De Panne
Gistel
Aalter
Evergem
Lokeren
Boom
Torhout
GENT
(GAND)
Waasmunster
Willebroek
Zele
Veurne
Diksmuide
Tielt
Deinze
Dendermonde
Wetteren
(Alost)
Aalst
Hondschoote
WEST-VLAANDEREN
Roeselare
(Roulers)
Ingelmunster
Izegem
Harelbeke
Waregem
OOST-VLAANDEREN
Asse
BRUXELLES
BRUSSEL
Poperinge
Kortrijk
(Courtrai)
Ieper
(Ypres)
Menen
Wervik
Oudenaarde
Ninove
Steenvoorde
Halluin
Comines
Geraardsbergen
Bailleul
Tourcoing
Mouscron
Lessines
Halle
Enghien
Hazebrouck
Armentières
Roubaix
Merville
Estaires
LILLE
V. d'Ascq
(Doornik)
Tournai
Ath
Braine-le-Comte
Leuze
Beloeil
Haubourdin
Lillers
la Bassée
Seclin
Carvin
Pont-à-Marcq
Péruwelz
HAINAUT
St. Amand-les-Eaux
Orchies
Condé
Mons
(Bergen)
la Louvière
Gosselies
Noeux
Bully
Hénin-Beaumont
Houdain
Liévin
Lens
Douai
Marchiennes
Bruay-s-l'E.
NORD
Quiévrain
Binche
Anderlues
Aubigny
Denain
Valenciennes
Thuin
Maubeuge
Aniche
Jeumont
Avesnes-le-Cte
Arras
Bouchain
le Quesnoy
Bavay
Hautmont
Beaumetz-lès-L.
Berlaimont
Aulnoye-Aymeries
Beaumont
Marquion
Cambrai
Solesmes
Pas-en-Artois
Landrecies
Sars-Poteries
Solre-le-Château
Sains-du-N.
Caudry
Avesnes
Bapaume
le Cateau
Trélon
Chimay
Acheux
le Nouvion-en-T.
Wassigny
Fourmies
le Catelet
Bohain-en-V.
la Capelle
Albert
Roisel
Hirson
St. Michel
Mon Idée
Bray
Péronne
Villers-Bretonneux
Guise
St. Quentin
Vermand
Origny-Ste Benoite
Aubenton
Vervins
Rumigny
Rosières
Chaulnes
Sains-Richaumont
Ribemont
Moreuil
Ham
Marle
Rozoy
Nesle
Crécy
Signy-l'Abbaye
Montcornet
Roye
Guiscard
Tergnier
la Fère
AISNE
Montdidier
Chauny
Novion-Porcien
Laon
Noyon
Lassigny
St. Gobain
Sissonne
Château-Porcien
Maignelay-Montigny
Ressons
Blérancourt
Anizy-le-Château
Rethel
Ribécourt
Coucy-le-Château-Auffrique
Craonne
Asfeld
St. Just-en-Chaussée
Neufchâtel
Compiègne
Vic
Vailly
Juniville
Clermont
Arsy
Soissons
Aisne
Braine
Pierrefonds
Pontfaverger
MICHELIN
94

Toxandria (NL)
Gendersteyn (NL)
Rinkven
Eindhoven (NL)
Elfrather Mühle (D)
Schloss Myllendonk (D)
Krefelder (D)
Herkenbosch (NL)
Limburg
Zuid Limburgse (NL)
Spiegelven
Bercuit
Falnuée
Sart-Tilman
Spa (Les Fagnes)
Bitburger Land
Grand Ducal de Luxembourg
Kikuoka
EINDHOVEN
Tilburg
Helmond
Turnhout
Mönchengladbach
DUISBURG
Moers
Neuss
Roermond
Maastricht
AACHEN
Heerlen
Hasselt
Genk
Leuven (Louvain)
LIÈGE (LUIK)
Verviers
Namur
Dinant
Charleville-Mézières
Sedan
Bouillon
Bastogne
Arlon (Aarlen)
LUXEMBOURG
Düren
Eupen
Malmédy
Huy
Spa
MICHELIN
d'après carte n° 987 - 28ème édition - 2002.
Autorisation n° 0102062.

95

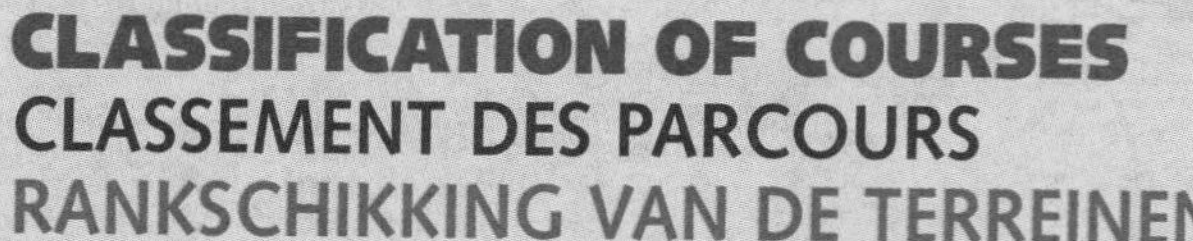

CLASSIFICATION OF COURSES
CLASSEMENT DES PARCOURS
RANKSCHIKKING VAN DE TERREINEN

This classification gives priority consideration to the score awarded to the actual course.

Course score / Note du parcours / Cijfer van het terrein — Page / Blz

Score			Course		Page
18	7	7	Royal Zoute	B	121
17	8	7	Ravenstein	B	117
17	7	7	Spa (Les Fagnes)	B	123
16	7	7	Antwerp	B	107
16	7	7	Kikuoka	L	128
16	7	4	Limburg	B	112
16	7	7	Sart-Tilman	B	122
16	8	7	Waterloo *La Marache*	B	125
16	8	7	Waterloo *Le Lion*	B	126
15	7	5	Hainaut *Bruyère-Quesnoy-Etangs*	B	110
15	7	7	Oostende	B	114
15	8	6	Royal Latem	B	120
14	7	4	Falnuée	B	109
14	7	6	Keerbergen	B	111
14	6	6	Oudenaarde	B	115
14	7	6	Rigenée	B	118
14	6	5	Rinkven *Red - White*	B	119
14	7	8	Spiegelven	B	124
13	7	7	Bercuit	B	108
13	6	7	Grand Ducal de Luxembourg	L	127
13	7	6	Mont-Garni	B	113
13	6	6	Palingbeek	B	116

TYPE OF COURSE
TYPE DE PARCOURS - TYPE BAAN

Country Falnuée 109, Waterloo *La Marache* 125

Forest Bercuit 108, Falnuée 109
Hainaut *Bruyère-Quesnoy-Etangs* 110
Limburg BF 112, Mont-Garni 113
Ravenstein 117, Rinkven *Red - White* 119
Royal Latem 120, Sart-Tilman 122
Spa (Les Fagnes) 123, Spiegelven 124

Heathland Limburg 112

Hilly Hainaut *Bruyère-Quesnoy-Etangs* 110
Sart-Tilman 122, Spa (Les Fagnes) 123

Links Oostende 114, Royal Zoute 121

Open Country
Kikuoka 128, Mont-Garni 113, Palingbeek 116
Rigenée 118

Parkland Antwerp 107, Grand Ducal de Luxembourg 127, Keerbergen 111, Oudenaarde 115, Ravenstein 117, Waterloo *La Marache* 125, Waterloo *Le Lion* 126

Residential Keerbergen 111, Royal Latem 120

Seaside course Oostende 114

ANTWERP

16	7	7

Créé en 1888, remodelé par Willie Park en 1913 et Tom Simpson en 1930, c'est l'un des plus anciens golfs d'Europe Continentale et le plus ancien golf de Belgique, mais il ne fait vraiment pas son âge. Comme il a conservé son caractère "old-style", il n'est pas utile de driver comme John Daly, ni d'avoir le toucher au putting d'un Corey Pavin. Mais il ne faut surtout pas sous-estimer les difficultés du tracé, ce parcours a une main de fer dans un gant de velours. Tous les architectes de golf pourraient d'ailleurs s'inspirer de l'intelligence du tracé, du placement très stratégique des bunkers, de la mise en jeu des arbres et de la bruyère. Ici, les principales difficultés concernent surtout les meilleurs joueurs, mais le parcours est une inspiration pour tous. Jouer ici est un vrai bonheur, et plus encore avec la pression d'une compétition. Et le charme visuel du lieu ajoute encore au plaisir.

Created in 1888 then redesigned by Willie Park in 1913 and Tom Simpson in 1930, this is Belgium's oldest club, although it looks as young as ever. Having the privilege of being an old-style course, its length doesn't mean having to drive à la John Daly and the subtle greens hardly require the putting touch of a Corey Pavin. But the trouble in store should never be under-estimated, as this is an iron hand in a velvet glove. The remarkably intelligent layout, highly strategic bunkering and the presence and use of trees and heather are an example for all modern designers. Here, the main difficulties have cleverly been reserved for the better players, but the general layout is an inspiration for us all. Playing here is a real pleasure, and playing with the pressure of a tournament even more so. The site adds visual charm to the enjoyment of golfing.

Royal Antwerp Golf Club — 1888

G. Capiaulei, 2 - B - 2950 KAPELLEN

Office	Secrétariat	(32) 03 - 666 84 56
Pro shop	Pro-shop	(32) 03 - 666 46 87
Fax	Fax	(32) 03 - 666 44 37
Web	www.golf.be/antwerp	
Situation	Situation	

Antwerpen / Anvers (pop. 403 072), 15 km

Annual closure	Fermeture annuelle	no
Weekly closure	Fermeture hebdomadaire	no

Monday (lundi), pro shop closed

Fees main season Tarifs haute saison	18 holes	
	Week days Semaine	**We/Bank holidays** We/Férié
Individual Individuel	74 €	*
Couple Couple	148 €	*

GF: 56 € if member of Belgian Golf Federation -
* W/E: members & guests only

Caddy	Caddy	no
Electric Trolley	Chariot électrique	no
Buggy	Voiturette	30 €
Clubs	Clubs	no

Credit cards Cartes de crédit VISA - Eurocard

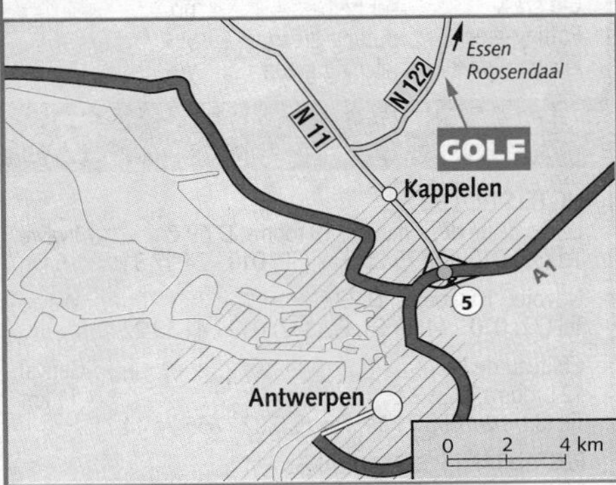

Access Accès : E19 Anvers → Breda, Exit 5 → N11
Map 1 on page 94 Carte 1 Page 94

Golf course — PARCOURS — 16/20

Site	Site	
Maintenance	Entretien	
Architect	Architecte	Willie Park Jr Tom Simpson
Type	Type	parkland
Relief	Relief	
Water in play	Eau en jeu	
Exp. to wind	Exposé au vent	
Trees in play	Arbres en jeu	

Scorecard Carte de score	**Chp.** Chp.	**Mens** Mess.	**Ladies** Da.
Length Long.	6187	5861	5252
Par	73	73	73
Slope system	135	130	131

Advised golfing ability Niveau de jeu recommandé — 0 12 24 36
Hcp required Handicap exigé 28

Club house & amenities — CLUB HOUSE ET ANNEXES — 7/10

Pro shop	Pro-shop	
Driving range	Practice	
Sheltered	couvert	4 mats
On grass	sur herbe	yes
Putting-green	putting-green	yes
Pitching-green	pitching green	yes

Hotel facilities — ENVIRONNEMENT HOTELIER — 7/10

HOTELS HÔTELS

Hilton, 199 rooms, D 337 € — Antwerpen 15 km
Tel (32) 03 - 204 12 12, Fax (32) 03 - 204 12 13

Alfa Theater, 122 rooms, D 161 € — Antwerpen
Tel (32) 03 - 203 54 10, Fax (32) 03 - 233 88 58

Rubens, 36 rooms, D 176 € — Antwerpen
Tel (32) 03 - 222 48 48, Fax (32) 03 - 225 19 40

RESTAURANTS RESTAURANT

De Bellefleur — Kapellen 1 km
Tel (32) 03 - 664 67 19

't Fornuis, Tel (32) 03 - 233 62 70 — Antwerpen

BERCUIT

13 | 7 | 7

De son propre aveu, Robert Trent Jones n'a pas donné son meilleur, et on ne retrouve notamment pas ici son dessin de bunkers. Certains trous sont assez fatigants et "tricky", mais d'autres valent le déplacement. Le relief très mouvementé interdit de quitter les fairways, et les frappeurs se sentiront souvent privés de leur liberté d'expression, du moins s'ils souhaitent absolument jouer leur driver. L'arrosage des fairways a néanmoins rendu plus facile le choix des zones de réception des balles. Les greens bien défendus, pas toujours très accueillants aux balles et souvent rapides proposent un sérieux challenge au putting. Après avoir joué plusieurs fois ce parcours, on en comprend mieux les pièges, mais il ne perdra pas complètement son caractère hasardeux. Un conseil : jouer au soleil et en voiturette, pour mieux profiter du décor arboré et des superbes panoramas sur le Brabant wallon.

You won't find here the bunkers that have come to typify Robert Trent Jones, and he readily admits that this is not one of his best courses. A number of holes are tiring and tricky but others are probably good enough to make you feel it was all worthwhile. The hilly terrain means you are best advised to keep it in the fairway, so big-hitters, if they insist on using the driver, might easily run into trouble. More optimistically, fairway sprinklers have made the choice of landing area a little easier. The greens, well-guarded, often slick but not always as receptive as they might be, are a stiff challenge to the best putter. After several rounds here you will begin to understand the traps a little better but the course is never completely risk-free. One piece of advice: play in sunny weather and with a buggy to make the most of the tree-covered landscape and wonderful views over the Walloon Brabant.

Golf de Bercuit — 1965

Domaine de Bercuit, Les Gottes, 3
B - 1390 GREZ-DOICEAU

Office	Secrétariat	(32) 010 - 84 15 01
Pro shop	Pro-shop	(32) 010 - 84 15 01
Fax	Fax	(32) 010 - 84 55 95
Web	www.golf.be/bercuit	
Situation	Situation	

Wavre (pop. 27 162), 5 km - Bruxelles / Brussel, 30 km

Annual closure	Fermeture annuelle	no
Weekly closure	Fermeture hebdomadaire	no

Monday (lundi), Pro-shop & Secretariat closed

Fees main season Tarifs haute saison — 18 holes

	Week days Semaine	We/Bank holidays We/Férié
Individual Individuel	37 € *	74 €
Couple Couple	74 € *	148 €

* Friday (vendredi) : 50 €

Caddy	Caddy	no
Electric Trolley	Chariot électrique	12 €
Buggy	Voiturette	30 €
Clubs	Clubs	12 €

Credit cards Cartes de crédit VISA - Eurocard - MasterCard

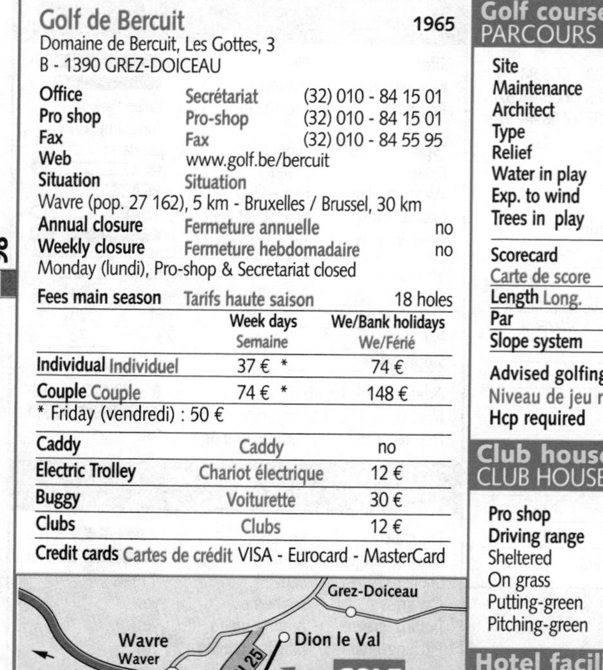

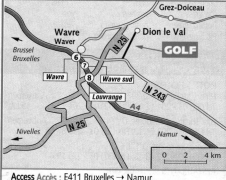

Access Accès : E411 Bruxelles → Namur,
Exit (Sortie) 8 → Grez Doiceau, turn right on N243,
2 km on left hand side → Dion

Map 1 on page 95 Carte 1 Page 95

Golf course PARCOURS — 13/20

Site	Site	
Maintenance	Entretien	
Architect	Architecte	Robert Trent Jones
Type	Type	forest
Relief	Relief	
Water in play	Eau en jeu	
Exp. to wind	Exposé au vent	
Trees in play	Arbres en jeu	

Scorecard Carte de score	Chp. Chp.	Mens Mess.	Ladies Da.
Length Long.	5961	5573	5208
Par	72	72	72
Slope system	136	129	128

Advised golfing ability Niveau de jeu recommandé — 0 12 24 36

Hcp required Handicap exigé — 32 Men, 36 Ladies

Club house & amenities CLUB HOUSE ET ANNEXES — 7/10

Pro shop	Pro-shop	
Driving range	Practice	
Sheltered	couvert	10 mats
On grass	sur herbe	no
Putting-green	putting-green	yes
Pitching-green	pitching green	yes

Hotel facilities ENVIRONNEMENT HOTELIER — 7/10

HOTELS HÔTELS

Le Domaine des Champs, 19 rooms, D 69 € — Wavre
Tel (32) 010 - 22 75 25, Fax (32) 010 - 24 17 31 — 5 km

Novotel, 102 rooms, D 99 € — Wavre
Tel (32) 010 - 41 13 63, Fax (32) 010 - 41 19 22

Château du Lac — Genval
121 rooms, D 392 € — 11 km
Tel (32) 02 - 655 71 11, Fax (32) 02 - 655 74 44

RESTAURANTS RESTAURANT

Château du Lac, Tel (32) 02 - 655 71 11 — Genval 11 km

Carte Blanche, Tel (32) 010 - 24 23 63 — Wavre

Le Bateau Ivre, Tel (32) 010 - 24 37 64 — Wavre

FALNUÉE

14 | 7 | 4

Un joli Club, avec son Club house dans les anciennes écuries voûtées remontant au Moyen-Age, le charme d'un paysage vallonné, la présence de deux rivières. Les puristes pourront relever une rupture avec la tradition, avec cinq par 3 (dont quatre au retour) et trois par 5, pour un par 70 et une longueur réduite. La grande difficulté consiste à tenir compte des dénivellations pour choisir les clubs, et aussi pour placer les drives : il suffit d'un peu d'inattention pour voir les obstacles très en jeu, et manquer quelques greens surélevés qu'il vaut mieux toucher directement. Jean Jottrand a produit un dessin agréable, bien qu'un peu rustique, mais si l'on regrette son imagination un peu timide, ce parcours reste accessible à tous niveaux. On conseillera plutôt de jouer ici entre amis, pour le plaisir, sans vouloir chercher d'émotions visuelles et golfiques très violentes.

A pretty golf club, with a club-house in former vaulted stables dating from the middle ages, rolling landscape and two rivers. The purists will point to the break from tradition, as this short course is a par 70 with five par 3s (four of which are on the back 9) and three par 5s. The major difficulty is assessing the slopes and hills before choosing your club, and positioning the tee-shot. A momentary lapse of concentration can take you straight into the hazards and result in missing some of the elevated greens, which you are well advised to pitch directly. Jean Jottrand has produced a pleasant layout, perhaps a little on the rustic side, but despite the regrettable lack of imagination, the course is playable by golfers of all levels. Your best bet here is a round with friends, just for fun, without looking for true visual or golfing excitement.

Golf de Falnuée — 1987

55, rue E. Pirson
B - 5032 MAZY

Office	Secrétariat	(32) 081 - 63 30 90
Pro shop	Pro-shop	(32) 081 - 63 30 90
Fax	Fax	(32) 081 - 63 37 64
Web	www.falnuee.be	
Situation	Situation	
Namur (pop. 97 845), 15 km		
Annual closure	Fermeture annuelle	no
Weekly closure	Fermeture hebdomadaire	monday(lundi)

Fees main season / Tarifs haute saison		18 holes
	Week days / Semaine	We/Bank holidays / We/Férié
Individual Individuel	25 €	37 €
Couple Couple	50 €	74 €
Caddy	Caddy	no
Electric Trolley	Chariot électrique	7,5 € /18 holes
Buggy	Voiturette	25 € /18 holes
Clubs	Clubs	10 € /18 holes

Credit cards Cartes de crédit
VISA - Eurocard

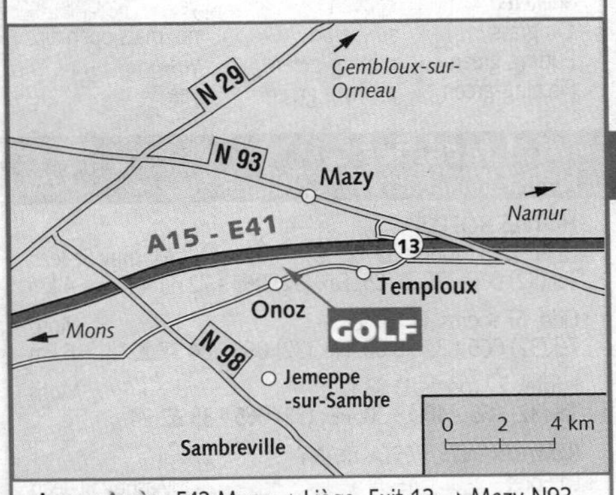

Access Accès : E42 Mons → Liège, Exit 13 → Mazy N93
Map 1 on page 95 Carte 1 Page 95

Golf course PARCOURS — 14/20

Site	Site	
Maintenance	Entretien	
Architect	Architecte	Jean Jottrand
Type	Type	country, forest
Relief	Relief	
Water in play	Eau en jeu	
Exp. to wind	Exposé au vent	
Trees in play	Arbres en jeu	

Scorecard / Carte de score	Chp. / Chp.	Mens / Mess.	Ladies / Da.
Length Long.	5590	5590	4750
Par	70	70	70
Slope system	123	119	120

Advised golfing ability / Niveau de jeu recommandé: 0 12 24 36
Hcp required / Handicap exigé: 36

Club house & amenities CLUB HOUSE ET ANNEXES — 7/10

Pro shop	Pro-shop	
Driving range	Practice	
Sheltered	couvert	6 mats
On grass	sur herbe	no, 14 mats oên air
Putting-green	putting-green	yes
Pitching-green	pitching green	yes

Hotel facilities ENVIRONNEMENT HOTELIER — 4/10

HOTELS HÔTELS

Beauregard, 47 rooms, D 99 € — Namur 15 km
Tel (32) 081 - 23 00 28, Fax (32) 081 - 24 12 09

Château de Namur, 30 rooms, D 115 € — Namur
Tel (32) 081 - 72 99 00, Fax (32) 081 - 72 99 99

L'Espièglerie, 30 rooms, D 87 € — Namur
Tel (32) 081 - 24 00 24, Fax (32) 081 - 24 00 25

RESTAURANTS RESTAURANT

La Bergerie, Tel (32) 081 - 58 06 13 Lives-sur-Meuse 20 km

Biétrumé Picar — Namur
Tel (32) 081 - 23 07 39

HAINAUT Bruyere-Quesnoy-Etangs 15 | 7 | 5

Pour le 18 trous traditionnel (Bruyères et Quesnoy), une architecture très classique de Tom Simpson, sur un terrain sablonneux jouable toute l'année. Les obstacles sont bien visibles, stratégiquement bien placés, notamment les bunkers de fairway, s'ajoutant aux nombreux arbres du parcours (certains bois devraient être aujourd'hui éclaircis), qui donnent un sentiment de calme et de charme tout à fait plaisants. Mais c'est un aspect trompeur, car les greens bien défendus sont accessibles après des drives bien placés et de bons coups de fers. Pour bien scorer, il faut maîtriser les balles levées, avec assez d'effet quand les greens sont rapides. Ce parcours au caractère britannique réserve de grandes satisfactions, avec un petit parfum d'autrefois très agréable. "Les Etangs" (9 trous) complètent cet équipement, avec beaucoup de trous en dog-leg. Très scénique et plus "moderne", il exige un jeu très long et précis, au milieu des pins.

The traditional 18-hole course is a very classic design by Tom Simpson on sandy soil that is playable all year. The hazards are clearly visible and strategically well located, especially the fairway bunkers, adding to the many trees on the course which give a pleasing impression of tranquillity and charm (some woods should be thined). But appearances can be deceptive, and here the well-defended greens, always perfectly in line with well-placed drives, call for some pretty sharp ironwork. Good scores need tight pitch and lob shots, and backspin too, when the greens are fast. The course has a pleasant British flavour and can give immense satisfaction with its very pleasant olde worlde charm. The 9-hole course ("Les Etangs") completes the picture and includes a lot of dog-legs. Now mature, very scenic and more "modern" (i.e. lots of water), it demands both length and precision through the pine-trees.

Royal Golf Club du Hainaut — 1933

2, rue de la Verrerie
B - 7050 ERBISOEUL

Office	Secrétariat	(32) 065 - 22 94 74
Pro shop	Pro-shop	(32) 065 - 22 79 29
Fax	Fax	(32) 065 - 22 51 54
Web	www.golf.be/hainaut	
Situation	Situation	

Mons (pop. 77 021), 5 km - Bruxelles / Brussel, 60 km

Annual closure	Fermeture annuelle	no
Weekly closure	Fermeture hebdomadaire	no

Fees main season Tarifs haute saison — 18 holes

	Week days / Semaine	We/Bank holidays / We/Férié
Individual Individuel	37 €	50 €
Couple Couple	74 €	100 €
Caddy Caddy		no
Electric Trolley Chariot électrique		no
Buggy Voiturette		25 €
Clubs Clubs		no

Credit cards Cartes de crédit
VISA - Eurocard - Mastercard

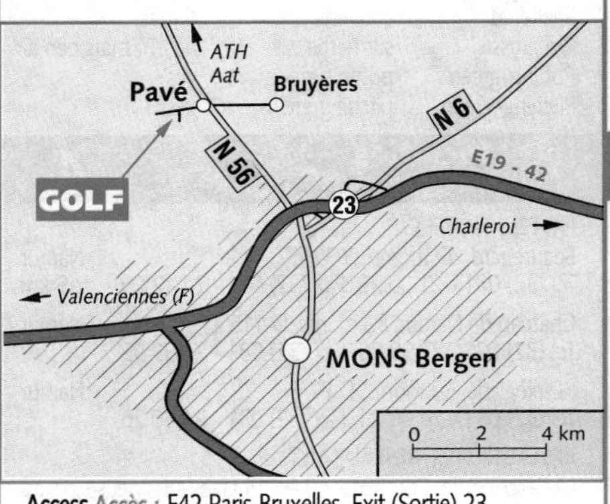

Access Accès : E42 Paris-Bruxelles, Exit (Sortie) 23, N6 → Mons, N56 → Ath
Map 1 on page 94 Carte 1 Page 94

Golf course PARCOURS — 15/20

Site	Site	
Maintenance	Entretien	
Architect	Architecte	Tom Simpson
Type	Type	forest, hilly
Relief	Relief	
Water in play	Eau en jeu	
Exp. to wind	Exposé au vent	
Trees in play	Arbres en jeu	

Scorecard / Carte de score	Chp. / Chp.	Mens / Mess.	Ladies / Da.
Length Long.	6042	6042	5364
Par	72	72	72
Slope system	123	120	124

Advised golfing ability Niveau de jeu recommandé — 0 12 24 36
Hcp required Handicap exigé — 36

Club house & amenities CLUB HOUSE ET ANNEXES — 7/10

Pro shop	Pro-shop	
Driving range	Practice	
Sheltered	couvert	yes
On grass	sur herbe	no, mats open air
Putting-green	putting-green	yes
Pitching-green	pitching green	yes

Hotel facilities ENVIRONNEMENT HOTELIER — 5/10

HOTELS HÔTELS

La Forêt, 51 rooms, D 112 € — Masnuy St-Jean
Tel (32) 065 - 72 36 85, Fax (32) 065 - 72 41 44 — 4 km

Lido, 67 rooms, D 107 € — Mons
Tel (32) 065 - 32 78 00, Fax (32) 065 - 84 37 22 — 6 km

Infotel, 22 rooms, D 88 € — Mons
Tel (32) 065 - 40 18 30, Fax (32) 065 - 35 62 24

RESTAURANTS RESTAURANT

La Forêt — Masnuy St-Jean
Tel (32) 065 - 72 36 85 — 4 km

Devos — Mons
Tel (32) 065 - 35 13 35 — 6 km

KEERBERGEN

14 | 7 | 6

De namen van de architecten alleen al zijn een aanduiding voor een grondige kennis van de golfsport. Op 38 hectare zijn ze erin geslaagd een par 70 met 6 zeer afwisselende par 3 te herbergen. Dit is een klassiek parcours, zeer kort en vlak (het kan zeer vlug gespeeld worden), maar het is een echte "challenge" qua precisie en intelligent spel. Het is geschikt voor alle handicaps, en speciaal op prijs gesteld door de dames, waarvan de besten tee-offs hebben die quasi gelijk zijn aan die van de heren. Goed onderhouden met netjes opgeruimd onderhout : dit is de perfecte golf om zichzelf een pleziertje te gunnen, maar ook om het spel met de kleinere "irons" wat bij te schaven, dankzij zeer interessante approaches van de greens naargelang de positie van de vlaggen. Talrijke "out of bounds" zetten de slordige spelers wat onder druk, en verschillende strategisch aangelegde vijvers zorgen voor wat subtiliteit, vooral op de 2, 15 en 18, een par 4 langs de rand van een vijver, waarboven het Club-House uittorent.

The names of the architects obviously denote in-depth knowledge of the game of golf. They have successfully squeezed a par 70 into 38 hectares (95 acres), with 6 very different par 3s. This is a classical, very short and flat course (ideal for fast play), but also a challenge of precision and intelligence. Suitable for all levels, it is particularly popular with the ladies, the best of whom tee off very close to the men's tees. Well upkept with the rough and undergrowth also neatly cleared, this is a perfect course for enjoying yourself and honing your short irons; some of the approach shots are a real treat, depending on the pin positions. Wayward golfers will feel the pressure of a lot of out-of-bounds, and several strategic lakes call for subtle strategy, especially holes 2, 15 and 18, a par 4 edged by a lake and overlooked by the club-house.

Keerbergen Golf Club — 1968

Vlieghavenlaan, 50
B - 3140 KEERBERGEN

Office	Secretariaat	(32) 015 - 23 49 61
Pro shop	Pro shop	(32) 015 - 23 49 63
Fax	Fax	(32) 015 - 23 57 37
Web	www.golf.be/keerbergen	
Situation	Locatie	

Mechelen / Malines (pop. 69 430), 10 km
Brussel / Bruxelles, 25 km

Annual closure	Jaarlijkse sluiting	no
Weekly closure	Wekelijkse sluitingsdag	no

Monday (maandag), restaurant closed

·Fees main season — Hoogseizoen tarieven	Week days Weekdagen	We/Bank holidays We/Feestdagen
		18 holes
Individual Individueel	32 €	50 €
Couple Paar	64 €	100 €
Caddy Caddy		no
Electric Trolley Electrische trolley		no
Buggy Buggy		25 € /18 holes
Clubs Clubs		15 € /18 holes

Credit cards Creditcards VISA - Mastercard - DC

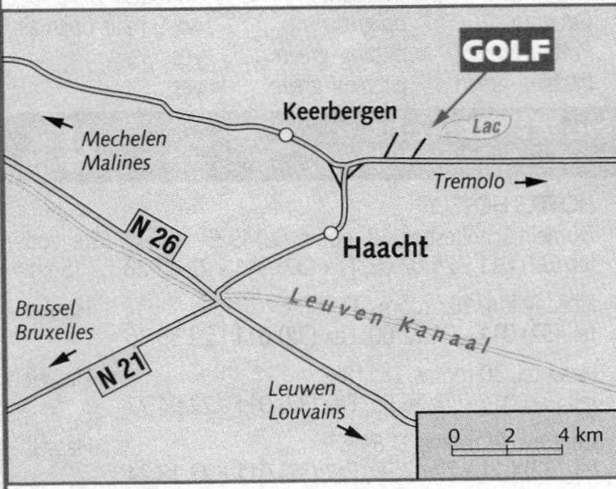

Access Toegang : N21 Bruxelles → Haacht, → Keerbergen, → Tremelo, Golf
Map 1 on page 95 Auto kaart 1 Blz 95

Golf course — BAAN — 14/20

Site	Terrein	
Maintenance	Onderhoud	
Architect	Architect	Cotton, Penninck Lawree
Type	Type baan	parkland, residential
Relief	Reliëf	
Water in play	Waterhazards	
Exp. to wind	Windgevoelig	
Trees in play	Bomen	

Scorecard Scorekaart	Chp. Back tees	Mens Heren	Ladies Damen
Length Lengte	5600	5503	4867
Par	70	70	70
Slope system	123	123	125

Advised golfing ability Aanbevolen golfvaardigheid — 0 12 24 36
Hcp required Vereiste hcp — 36

Club house & amenities — CLUB HOUSE EN ANNEXEN — 7/10

Pro shop	Pro shop	
Driving range	Oefenbaan	
Sheltered	overdekt	3 mats
On grass	op gras	no, 10 mats open air
Putting-green	putting-green	yes
Pitching-green	pitching-green	yes

Hotel facilities — HOTELS IN OMGEVING — 6/10

HOTELS HOTELS

Alfa Alba, 43 rooms, D 124 € — Mechelen
tel. (32) 015 - 42 03 03, Fax (32) 015 - 42 37 88 — 10 km

Berkenhof, 10 rooms, D 149 € — Keerbergen
tel. (32) 015 - 73 01 01, Fax (32) 015 - 73 02 02 — 1 km

Gulden Anker, 34 rooms, D 99 € — Mechelen
tel. (32) 015 - 42 25 35, Fax (32) 015 - 42 34 99 — 10 km

RESTAURANTS RESTAURANT

The Paddock, Tel (32) 015 - 51 19 34 — Keerbergen 1 km
D'Hoogh, Tel (32) 015 - 21 75 53 — Mechelen 10 km
Berkenhof, Tel (32) 015 - 73 01 01 — Kerbergen 1 km

LIMBURG

16 | 7 | 4

Midden in een natuurreservaat en een landschap van sparren en berken, typerend voor de Kempen, wordt dit licht golvend terrein een ware streling voor het oog als de heide in bloei staat, op het einde van de zomer en in de herfst. Het is het stroke-play parcours bij uitstek, met een harmonisch speelritme, enkele moeilijke pieken die gespreksstof vormen voor achteraf (sommige par 4 zijn hardnekkig), zeer mooie par 5 en een juweeltje, de 8, een kleine technische par 4 zoals men er geen meer durft ontwerpen. Het design van FW Hawtree is van een op en top Brits classicisme, het ontwerp ziet eruit alsof de natuur zelf het zo gewild heeft, mooi gelegen tussen de heide en het bos, en het heeft een zeer "intelligente" bunkering (recent gerestaureerde bunkers rond vijf greens). Daar het terrein zeer goed uitgebalanceerd is, met werkelijke verschillen tussen de champion tees en de andere, is het er zeer aangenaam spelen op elk niveau, en keert men met plezier nog eens terug. Onderhoud is nu zeer goed.

Set in a nature reserve of pine and birch that are typical of the Campine region, this slightly rolling course is a beautiful sight when the heather is in full bloom in late summer and in autumn. This is an excellent course for stroke-play, neatly balanced with a few memorable tough moments on the back nine (some par 4s are really hard going), some fabulous par 5s and a gem of a hole, the 8th, which is a short but very technical 4-par, the likes of which are hardly ever found these days. F.W. Hawtree's layout is a pure British classic, winding its way almost naturally between heather and wood with particularly intelligent bunkering (newly restored bunkers around five greens). Because it is so well balanced, with real differences between the tournament and hacker tees, it is pleasant to play, again and again, whatever your level. Upkeep is very good now.

Limburg Golf & Country Club — 1967

Golfstraat 1
B - 3530 HOUTHALEN

Office	Secretariaat	(32) 089 - 38 35 43
Pro shop	Pro shop	(32) 089 - 84 32 04
Fax	Fax	(32) 089 - 84 12 08
Web	www.golf.be/limburg	
Situation	Locatie	

Hasselt (pop. 64 722), 15 km

Annual closure	Jaarlijkse sluiting	no
Weekly closure	Wekelijkse sluitingsdag	no

Monday (maandag), Pro-shop & Restaurant closed (bar open)

Fees main season Hoogseizoen tarieven	Week days Weekdagen	We/Bank holidays We/Feestdagen
Individual Individueel	42 €	52 €
Couple Paar	84 €	104 €
Caddy Caddy	no	
Electric Trolley Electrische trolley	no	
Buggy Buggy	30 € /18 holes	
Clubs Clubs	no	

(18 holes)

Credit cards Creditcards
VISA - Eurocard - Mastercard

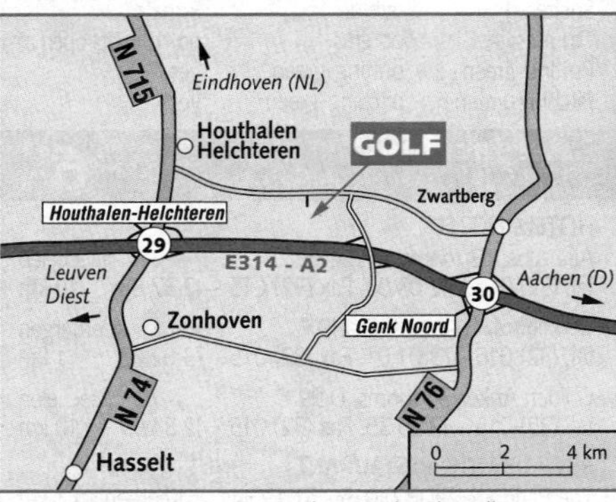

Access Toegang : E314 Brussel → Aix-la-Chapelle, Exit 29, N715 → Eindhoven, Houthalen, → Golf
Map 1 on page 95 Auto kaart 1 Blz 95

Golf course — BAAN — 16/20

Site	Terrein	
Maintenance	Onderhoud	
Architect	Architect	Fred Hawtree
Type	Type baan	forest, heathland
Relief	Reliëf	
Water in play	Waterhazards	
Exp. to wind	Windgevoelig	
Trees in play	Bomen	

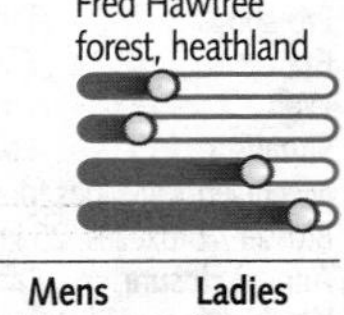

Scorecard Scorekaart	Chp. Back tees	Mens Heren	Ladies Damen
Length Lengte	6128	5750	5156
Par	72	72	72
Slope system	132	129	132

Advised golfing ability Aanbevolen golfvaardigheid: 0 12 24 36

Hcp required Vereiste hcp: W/E: 32 Men, 36 Ladies

Club house & amenities — CLUB HOUSE EN ANNEXEN — 7/10

Pro shop	Pro shop	
Driving range	Oefenbaan	
Sheltered	overdekt	14 mats
On grass	op gras	no, 9 mats open air
Putting-green	putting-green	yes
Pitching-green	pitching-green	yes

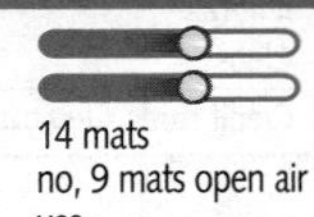

Hotel facilities — HOTELS IN OMGEVING — 4/10

HOTELS HOTELS

Domein Scholteshof, 18 rooms, D 149 € — Steevort
tel. (32) 011 - 25 02 02, Fax (32) 011 - 25 43 28 — 15 km

Holiday Inn, 107 rooms, D 198 € — Hasselt
tel. (32) 011 - 24 22 00, Fax (32) 011 - 22 39 35

Hassotel, 30 rooms, D 118 € — Hasselt
tel. (32) 011 - 23 06 55, Fax (32) 011 - 22 94 77

Century, 14 rooms, D 69 € — Hasselt
tel. (32) 011 - 22 47 99, Fax (32) 011 - 23 18 24

RESTAURANTS RESTAURANT

Domein Scholteshof, Tel (32) 011 - 25 02 02 — Steevort

De Barrier, Tel (32) 011 - 52 55 25 — Houthalen 3 km

MONT-GARNI

13 | 7 | 6

Avec quelques arbres en moins (2, 13, 14, 17) qui empiètent sur la bonne ligne de jeu, l'élagage de certaines branches et un plus large nettoyage des sous-bois, Mont-Garni donnerait plus encore de plaisir aux golfeurs, rendrait plus évidente la stratégie de jeu et ne punirait vraiment que les coups lâchés. En revanche, le challenge est réel, beaucoup de trous sont intéressants, même si les pars 3 sont plus longs que vraiment subtils (leurs départs sont mal orientés). Il faut constamment se méfier des arbres et des étangs, qui rendent cependant le site assez séduisant : sur ce parcours demandant de la précision, on ne conseillera les départs arrière qu'aux joueurs de très bon niveau, les autres s'y amuseront beaucoup en match-play, en famille ou entre amis de niveau équivalent. On suivra avec intérêt l'évolution de ce parcours, et les non-golfeurs peuvent préférer le centre équestre sur place que porter les sacs...

With fewer trees right in the line of fire (on the 2nd, 13th, 14 th and 17th holes), the trimming of a few branches and more extensive clearing of undergrowth, Mont-Garni would be even more enjoyable to play, would make game strategy more obvious and would punish only the really wayward shot. However, the challenge here hits you in the eye, with a lot of interesting holes, even though the par 3s are longer than they are subtle. You have to be constantly on the outlook to avoid the trees and lakes, which at the same time add to the course's appeal. On a course like this, which demands precision play, we would recommend the back-tees only for the better players ; the others can move forward and have fun with the family or friends with a round of match-play. It will be interesting to see how this course evolves. Rather than lug golf bags around, non-golfers may prefer the riding stables next door.

Golf du Mont-Garni — 1990

Rue du Mont-Garni, 3
B - 7331 BAUDOUR

Office	Secrétariat	(32) 065 - 62 27 19
Pro shop	Pro-shop	(32) 065 - 62 27 19
Fax	Fax	(32) 065 - 62 34 10
Web	www.golfmontgarni.be	
Situation	Situation	

Mons / Bergen (pop. 77 021), 7 km

Annual closure	Fermeture annuelle	no
Weekly closure	Fermeture hebdomadaire	no

Fees main season Tarifs haute saison	18 holes	
	Week days Semaine	**We/Bank holidays** We/Férié
Individual Individuel	25 €	37 €
Couple Couple	50 €	74 €
Caddy Caddy	no	
Electric Trolley Chariot électrique	no	
Buggy Voiturette	25 €	
Clubs Clubs	yes	

Credit cards Cartes de crédit
VISA - Eurocard - Mastercard

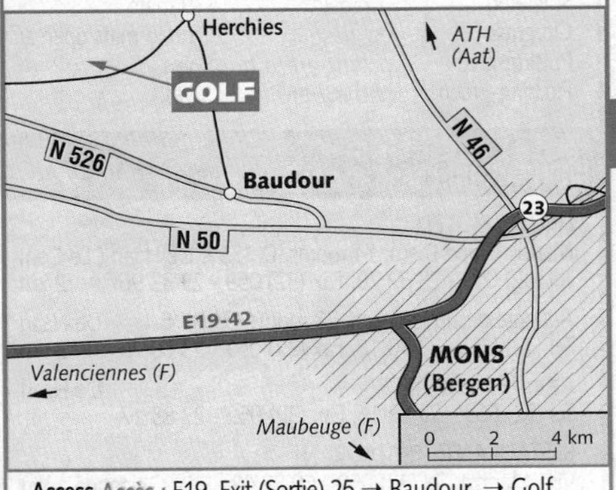

Access Accès : E19, Exit (Sortie) 25 → Baudour, → Golf
Map 1 on page 94 Carte 1 Page 94

Golf course PARCOURS — 13/20

Site	Site	
Maintenance	Entretien	
Architect	Architecte	Tom MacAuley
Type	Type	forest, open country
Relief	Relief	
Water in play	Eau en jeu	
Exp. to wind	Exposé au vent	
Trees in play	Arbres en jeu	

Scorecard Carte de score	**Chp.** Chp.	**Mens** Mess.	**Ladies** Da.
Length Long.	6353	6041	5615
Par	74	74	74
Slope system	128	124	128

Advised golfing ability Niveau de jeu recommandé — 0 12 24 36
Hcp required Handicap exigé — 28

Club house & amenities CLUB HOUSE ET ANNEXES — 7/10

Pro shop	Pro-shop	
Driving range	Practice	
Sheltered	couvert	8 mats
On grass	sur herbe	yes
Putting-green	putting-green	yes
Pitching-green	pitching green	yes

Hotel facilities ENVIRONNEMENT HOTELIER — 6/10

HOTELS HÔTELS

Lido — Mons 7 km
67 rooms, D 107 €
Tel (32) 065 - 32 78 00, Fax (32) 065 - 84 37 22

Hôtel de la Forêt — Masnuy St Jean 10 km
51 rooms, D 112 €
Tel (32) 065 - 72 36 85, Fax (32) 065 - 72 41 44

RESTAURANTS RESTAURANT

Fernez, Tel (32) 065 - 64 44 67 — Baudour 1 km
Devos, Tel (32) 065 - 35 13 35 — Mons 7 km
Le Vannes, Tel (32) 065 - 35 14 43 — Mons
Alter Ego, Tel (32) 065 - 35 52 60 — Mons

OOSTENDE

15 | 7 | 7

Het is nu bekend dat de originele design van de hand van Tom Simpson is. Het is een feit dat moderne aanpassingen niet steeds even succesvol zijn; daarom heft Martin Hawtree het effect van de links willen respecteren en waren zijn hervormingen slechts miniem. Toch is de design van hole 3, een par 3 van 200 meter, niet echt overtuigend binnen de stijl van het geheel. The holes langs de zee (van 5 tot 10) blijven indrukwekkend met hun zeer nadrukkelijk links-design. Eigenlijk ontbreken we daar 20 hectaren duinen! Het parcours blijft een serieuze fysieke inspanning vergen, vooral als er wind staat, en het is zeker een goede test voor spelers, die het lage balspel willen oefenen. Maar bij mooi weer is Oostende een parcours voor alle niveaus. De waterhindernissen die op het parcoursplan getekend staan, vormen niet echt een moeilijkheid, want de voornaamste problemen schuilen in de bunkers, het struikgewas en de rough. Eenmaal op de green aanbeland, bent u veilig: ze zijn mooi vlak en gemakkelijk bespeelbaar.

We now know that the original architect was Tom Simpson, and even though modern restyling operations are not always as successful as they are supposed to be, Martin Hawtree set out to respect the feel of this links course and made only slight changes. Having said that, his work on hole N°3, a 200-metre par 3, has raised more than a few disapproving eyebrows as far as unity of style is concerned. The seaside holes (5 to 10) are as remarkable as ever with a very distinct links flavour. In fact, what is missing here is about 50 acres of sand-dunes, although the course that crosses the dunes is a good physical exercise when the wind blows and a stiff test as to a player's ability to hit low shots. In fine weather, Oostende is a course for all golfers: the few water hazards shown on the course map are not really in play and the main problems are the very many bunkers, bushes and the rough. Once on the greens, you are almost home and dry, as the putting surfaces are flat and easy to read.

Koninklijke Golf Club Oostende — 1903

Koninklijke baan 2
B - 8420 DE HAAN

Office	Secretariaat	(32) 059 - 23 32 83
Pro shop	Pro shop	(32) 059 - 23 32 83
Fax	Fax	(32) 059 - 23 37 49
Web	www.golfoostende.be	
Situation	Locatie	

close to Oostende (pop. 67 257)

Annual closure	Jaarlijkse sluiting	no
Weekly closure	Wekelijkse sluitingsdag	no

Tuesday (diensdag): restaurant closed

Fees main season Hoogseizoen tarieven	Week days Weekdagen	We/Bank holidays We/Feestdagen
18 holes		
Individual Individueel	45 €	62 €
Couple Paar	90 €	124 €

Caddy	Caddy	no
Electric Trolley	Electrische trolley	no
Buggy	Buggy	32 €
Clubs	Clubs	no

Credit cards Creditcards
VISA - Eurocard - DC

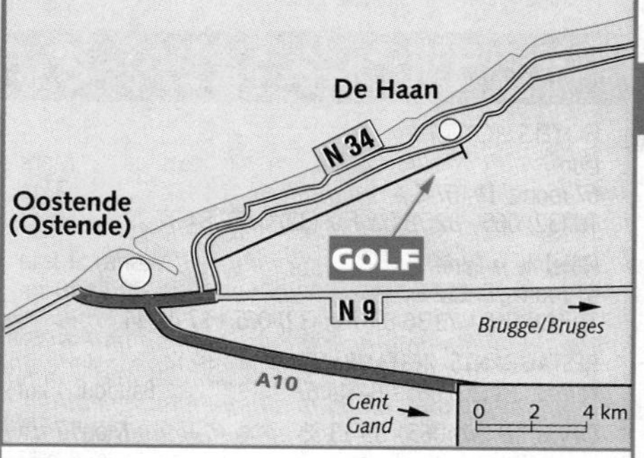

Access Toegang : N34 De Haan-Oostende
Map 1 on page 94 Auto kaart 1 Blz 94

Golf course / BAAN — 15/20

Site	Terrein	
Maintenance	Onderhoud	
Architect	Architect	Tom Simpson, Martin Hawtree,1990
Type	Type baan	seaside course, links
Relief	Reliëf	
Water in play	Waterhazards	
Exp. to wind	Windgevoelig	
Trees in play	Bomen	

Scorecard Scorekaart	Chp. Back tees	Mens Heren	Ladies Damen
Length Lengte	5618	5265	4922
Par	70	70	70
Slope system	123	118	121

Advised golfing ability Aanbevolen golfvaardigheid — 0 12 24 36
Hcp required Vereiste hcp — 34

Club house & amenities / CLUB HOUSE EN ANNEXEN — 7/10

Pro shop	Pro shop	
Driving range	Oefenbaan	
Sheltered	overdekt	9 mats
On grass	op gras	no, 5 mats open air
Putting-green	putting-green	yes
Pitching-green	pitching-green	yes

Hotel facilities / HOTELS IN OMGEVING — 7/10

HOTELS HOTELS

Manoir Carpe Diem, 14 rooms, D 136 € De Haan (Le Coq)
Tel (32) 059 - 23 32 20, Fax (32) 059 - 23 33 96 — 2 km

Auberge des Rois-Beach, 28 rooms, D 121 € — De Haan
Tel (32) 059 - 23 30 18, Fax (32) 059 - 23 60 78 — 2 km

Azur, 16 rooms, D 73 € — De Haan
Tel (32) 059 - 23 83 16, Fax (32) 059 - 23 83 17

RESTAURANTS RESTAURANT

Villa Maritza, Tel (32) 059 - 50 88 08 — Oostende 1 km

't Vistrapje, Tel (32) 059 - 80 23 82 — Oostende

Le Manoir, Tel (32) 059 - 23 32 20 — De Haan 2 km

OUDENAARDE

14	6	6

Om een mooie wandeling te maken in een uitgestrekt park (prachtige beuken!) met nadien een drankje in een club-house, dat ingericht is in een kasteel van de XIXe eeuw, is men in Oudenaarde aan het juiste adres. Als men echter een golfparcours "van sterke emoties" zoekt, dat een grote sportieve uitdaging vormt, kan men al beter van de back tees vertrekken. Hier heeft men vooral aan het genoegen van de leden gedacht! Het parcours van Oudenaarde heeft onlangs enkele wijzigingen ondergaan, die niet al te gelukkig zijn uitgevallen, omdat er enkele "goeie ouwe holes" werden geïntegreerd in een nieuw circuit van 9 holes. De nieuwe holes, die de oude verdwenen holes op het bestaande parcours vervangen, vergen wel enige athletische vastberadenheid, maar missen de charme van echt leuke golf. Het oude parcours, als het vanaf de back tees wordt gespeeld, biedt mede dankzij de talrijke hindernissen een niet te onderschatten uitdaging, zowel qua lengte als qua precisie. De greens zijn goed zichtbaar en niet te erg door bunkers omzoomd. De 9 holes die in 1991 werd aangelegd is korter. Naast de grote "monumenten" in de golfwereld, moeten er ook terreinen zoals dit zijn...

Personal assessment here depends on what you expect from a golf course. If you are looking primarily for a pleasant stroll through a large estate (with some beautiful beech trees) between Escaut and Vieil Escaut, before returning and relaxing in a club house converted from a mid-19th century castle, then Oudenaarde is for you. But if you are looking for exciting golf and a real sporting challenge, then drive on. Emphasis here is on pleasing members, most of whom are only average golfers. The main course (18 holes since 1976) is not very long and offers no great originality. The hazards are of no great danger and the greens are clearly in view with few bunkers. The 9-hole course built in 1991 is even shorter. But alongside the giant courses of this world, we also need courses like this...

Golf & Country-Club Oudenaarde — 1976

Kortrukstraat 52
B - 9790 WORTEGEM-PETEGEM

Office	Secretariaat	(32) 055 - 33 41 61
Pro shop	Pro shop	(32) 055 - 33 41 63
Fax	Fax	(32) 055 - 31 98 49
Web	www.golf.be/oudenaarde	
Situation	Locatie	

Oudenaarde, 3 km - Gent / Gand (pop. 210 704), 25 km

Annual closure	Jaarlijkse sluiting	no
Weekly closure	Wekelijkse sluitingsdag	no

Wednesday (woensdag): restaurant closed (bar open)

Fees main season Hoogseizoen tarieven	Week days Weekdagen	We/Bank holidays We/Feestdagen
	18 holes	
Individual Individueel	37 €	50 €
Couple Paar	74 €	100 €
Caddy Caddy	no	
Electric Trolley Electrische trolley	2 €	
Buggy Buggy	35 €	
Clubs Clubs	no	

Credit cards Creditcards
VISA - Eurocard - Mastercard - DC - AMEX

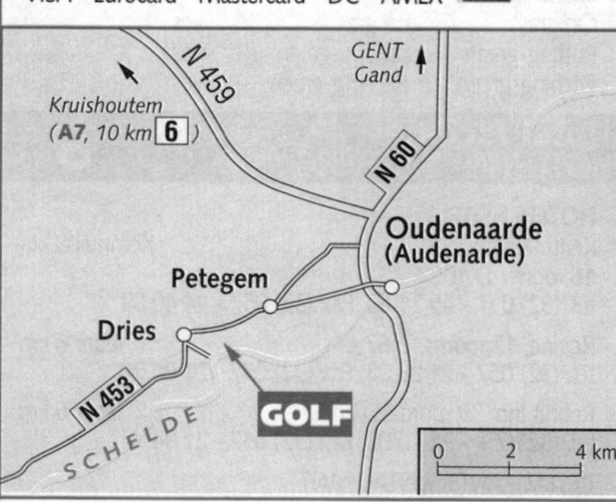

Access Toegang : E17 Kortrijk-Gent, Exit 8 De Pinte, N60 → Ronse, N453 → Kortrijk
Map 1 on page 94 Auto kaart 1 Blz 94

Golf course — BAAN — 14/20

Site	Terrein	
Maintenance	Onderhoud	
Architect	Architect	Harold Baker
Type	Type baan	parkland
Relief	Reliëf	
Water in play	Waterhazards	
Exp. to wind	Windgevoelig	
Trees in play	Bomen	

Scorecard Scorekaart	**Chp.** Back tees	**Mens** Heren	**Ladies** Damen
Length Lengte	6172	5774	5337
Par	72	72	72
Slope system	132	128	130

Advised golfing ability Aanbevolen golfvaardigheid: 0 12 24 36
Hcp required Vereiste hcp: 36

Club house & amenities — CLUB HOUSE EN ANNEXEN — 6/10

Pro shop	Pro shop	
Driving range	Oefenbaan	
Sheltered	overdekt	12 mats
On grass	op gras	no, 6 mats open air
Putting-green	putting-green	yes
Pitching-green	pitching-green	yes

Hotel facilities — HOTELS IN OMGEVING — 6/10

HOTELS HOTELS

Le Shamrock, 5 rooms, D 186 € — Ronse
Tel (32) 055 - 21 55 29, Fax (32) 055 - 21 56 83 — 12 km

La Pomme d'Or, 8 rooms, D 97 € — Oudenaarde
Tel (32) 055 - 31 19 00, Fax (32) 055 - 30 08 44 — 3 km

De Rantere, 27 rooms, D 52 € — Oudenaarde
Tel (32) 055 - 31 89 88, Fax (32) 055 - 33 01 11 — 3 km

RESTAURANTS RESTAURANT

't Craeneveldt, Tel (32) 055 - 31 72 91 — Oudenaarde 5 km
Le Shamrock, Tel (32) 055 - 21 55 29 — Ronse 12 km
La Pomme d'Or, Tel (32) 055 - 31 19 00 — Oudenaarde

PALINGBEEK

13 | 6 | 6

Gelegen langs de rand van het natuurdomein Palingbeek, doet dit parcours denken aan de esthetiek van de golf op z'n Amerikaans uit de jaren '70. Het betreft een terrein met weinig reliëf (helemaal niet vermoeiend), met enkele nogal ongevaarlijke waterhindernissen, waar de architect geen risico's heeft genomen om de stempel van zijn persoonlijkheid op het parcours te drukken (behalve op de 18). Zelfs de eerste keer staat de speler nooit voor verrassingen en verliest hij geen ballen. Deze ongedwongenheid kan veel spelers geruststellen, en indien ze al moeite hebben op de lange par 4, spelen ze toch meestal hun handicap. De greens zijn mooi ontworpen, en in goede staat, zoals trouwens het hele terrein. Er ontbreekt enkel wat beweging in het terrein zelf om het technisch gezien wat interessanter, en uit visueel oogpunt wat aangenamer te maken.

On the edge of the Palingbeek nature park, this course has all the look and appeal of american style courses at the beginning of the 1970s, and in particular the cachet of Trent Jones, minus his strategic genius. Over flattish terrain (easy on the legs), dotted with a few not too hostile water hazards, the architect backed away from the risks involved in asserting his personality on the course (except on the 18th). Players will meet with few surprises and lose few or no balls, even the first time out. In contrast, many will find such limpidity reassuring and probably play to their handicap, despite a few problems perhaps on the long par 4s. The greens are well shaped and in good condition, as is the course as a whole. The only thing missing is a little shifting of earth to make the course technically more appealing and visually more attractive.

Golf & Country Club de Palingbeek 1992

Eekhofstraat 14
B - 8902 HOLLEBEKE

Office	Secretariaat	(32) 057 - 20 04 36
Pro shop	Pro shop	(32) 057 - 20 04 36
Fax	Fax	(32) 057 - 21 89 58
Web	www.golfpalingbeek.com	
Situation	Locatie	

Ieper / Ypres (pop. 34 874), 6 km
Kortrijk / Courtrai (pop. 74 044), 30 km

Annual closure	Jaarlijkse sluiting	27/1→18/2
Weekly closure	Wekelijkse sluitingsdag	no

Fees main season Hoogseizoen tarieven	18 holes	
	Week days Weekdagen	**We/Bank holidays** We/Feestdagen
Individual Individueel	32 €	40 €
Couple Paar	64 €	80 €
Caddy	Caddy	no
Electric Trolley	Electrische trolley	no
Buggy	Buggy	30 € /18 holes
Clubs	Clubs	yes

Credit cards Creditcards
VISA - Eurocard - Mastercard

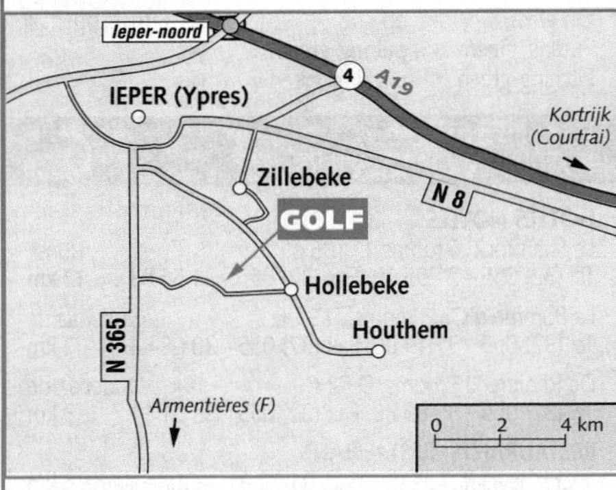

Access Toegang : A 19 Kortrijk-Veurne, N8 → Ieper-Zuid, Zillebeke, Hollebeke, Palingbeek
Map 1 on page 94 Auto kaart 1 Blz 94

Golf course BAAN — 13/20

Site	Terrein	
Maintenance	Onderhoud	
Architect	Architect	Harold Baker
Type	Type baan	open country
Relief	Reliëf	
Water in play	Waterhazards	
Exp. to wind	Windgevoelig	
Trees in play	Bomen	

Scorecard Scorekaart	**Chp.** Back tees	**Mens** Heren	**Ladies** Damen
Length Lengte	6159	5704	5278
Par	72	72	72
Slope system	127	123	126

Advised golfing ability Aanbevolen golfvaardigheid — 0 12 24 36
Hcp required Vereiste hcp — 36

Club house & amenities CLUB HOUSE EN ANNEXEN — 6/10

Pro shop	Pro shop	
Driving range	Oefenbaan	
Sheltered	overdekt	8 mats
On grass	op gras	yes
Putting-green	putting-green	yes
Pitching-green	pitching-green	yes

Hotel facilities HOTELS IN OMGEVING — 6/10

HOTELS HOTELS

Kemmelberg — Kemmel 8 km
16 rooms, D 109 €
tel. (32) 057 - 45 21 60, Fax (32) 057 - 44 40 89

Regina, 17 rooms, D 67 € — Ieper 6 km
tel. (32) 057 - 21 88 88, Fax (32) 057 - 21 90 20

Rabbit Inn, 39 rooms, D 74 € — Ieper 6 km
tel. (32) 057 - 21 70 00, Fax (32) 057 - 21 94 74

RESTAURANTS RESTAURANT

Kemmelberg, Tel (32) 057 - 44 41 45 — Kemmel 8 km

Host. St Nicolas — Ieper 6 km
Tel (32) 057 - 20 06 22

RAVENSTEIN

17	8	7

Passionné par le golf, le Roi Léopold II a été notamment à l'origine d'Oostende et du Ravenstein. Il fit appel à un architecte "royal", le grand Tom Simpson, dont le dessin a été largement préservé, de même que la végétation, d'une beauté impressionnante. Chênes, bouleaux, cèdres bleus, ormes et saules offrent un spectacle qui ferait oublier le parcours, si celui-ci n'était d'une si évidente qualité. Il offre des drives sans gros problèmes (sauf aux 2, 4, 11 et 17), mais les attaques de green sont d'autant plus passionnantes que le putting ne sera pas ensuite évident. Les greens ne sont pas très ondulés, mais leurs surfaces sont plus difficiles à lire qu'il n'y paraît. Le Ravenstein peut être joué à tous les niveaux, mais les meilleurs y trouveront quelques défis de premier ordre, alors que sa longueur reste modérée, selon les exigences modernes en tout cas. Un "must". Plusieurs trous ont été "modernisés" par Martin Hawtree, en reculant les greens aux 14 et 18, et aussi (c'est moins convaincant) avec des buttes et des bunkers aux 9 et 18.

A golf enthusiast, King Léopold II was the instigator of the courses at Oostende and Ravenstein. He called in a "royal" architect, the great Tom Simpson, whose design has remained largely unscathed. The same goes for the extremely beautiful vegetation. The impressive oak, birch, blue cedar, elm and willow trees could almost make you forget the course if it wasn't such an excellent layout. The tee shot is never too much of a problem (except on 2nd, 4th, 11th and 17th holes), but the approach shots are all the more exciting in that putting here is an equally challenging proposition. These are hardly what you would call undulating greens, but the putting surface is harder to read than you might think. Ravenstein can be played by golfers of all abilities, but the most proficient will find a number of challenges of the highest order, even though by modern standards the course posts only moderate yardage. Essential visiting. Several holes have been "modernized" by Martin Hawtree, holes 14 and 18 have been lengthened (the greens pushed back) but the sandhills on the 8th and the bunkers on the 9th and 18th holes fail to impress.

Royal Golf Club de Belgique — 1905

Château de Ravenstein
B - 3080 TERVUREN

Office	Secrétariat	(32) 02 - 767 58 01
Pro shop	Pro-shop	(32) 02 - 767 55 60
Fax	Fax	(32) 02 - 767 28 41
Web	www.golf.be/ravenstein	
Situation	Situation	Bruxelles / Brussel, 6 km
Annual closure	Fermeture annuelle	no
Weekly closure	Fermeture hebdomadaire	no

Fees main season / Tarifs haute saison	Week days / Semaine	We/Bank holidays / We/Férié
	18 holes	
Individual Individuel	62 €	*
Couple Couple	124 €	*

* Members guests only

Caddy	Caddy	on request
Electric Trolley	Chariot électrique	no
Buggy	Voiturette	no
Clubs	Clubs	no

Credit cards Cartes de crédit
(Pro shop & restaurant only) VISA - Eurocard - AMEX

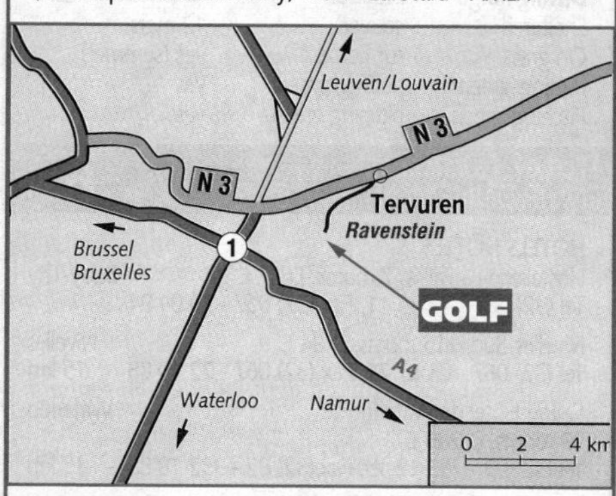

Access Accès : In Bruxelles, Avenue de Tervuren → Tervuren, go through Les Quatre Bras, → Golf
Map 1 on page 94 Carte 1 Page 94

Golf course — PARCOURS — 17/20

Site	Site	
Maintenance	Entretien	
Architect	Architecte	Tom Simpson
Type	Type	parkland, forest
Relief	Relief	
Water in play	Eau en jeu	
Exp. to wind	Exposé au vent	
Trees in play	Arbres en jeu	

Scorecard / Carte de score	Chp. / Chp.	Mens / Mess.	Ladies / Da.
Length Long.	6033	5775	5324
Par	72	72	72
Slope system	130	127	126

Advised golfing ability / Niveau de jeu recommandé: 0 12 24 36
Hcp required — Handicap exigé: 20 Men, 24 Ladies

Club house & amenities — CLUB HOUSE ET ANNEXES — 8/10

Pro shop	Pro-shop	
Driving range	Practice	
Sheltered	couvert	10 mats
On grass	sur herbe	no, 12 mats open air
Putting-green	putting-green	yes
Pitching-green	pitching green	yes

Hotel facilities — ENVIRONNEMENT HOTELIER — 7/10

HOTELS HÔTELS

Montgomery, 63 rooms, D 297 € — Woluwé-Saint-Pierre
Tel (32) 02 - 741 85 11, Fax (32) 02 - 741 85 00 — 5 km

Château du Lac, 121 rooms, D 392 € — Genval
Tel (32) 02 - 655 71 11, Fax (32) 02 - 655 74 44 — 10 km

Lambeau, 24 rooms, D 74 € — Woluwé-Saint-Lambert
Tel (32) 02 - 732 51 70, Fax (32) 02 - 732 54 90 — 6 km

RESTAURANTS RESTAURANT

Des Trois Couleurs — Woluwé-Saint-Pierre 5 km
Tel (32) 02 - 770 33 21

Le Vignoble de Margot — Woluwé-Saint-Pierre
Tel (32) 02 - 779 23 23

Les Deux Maisons, Tel (32) 02 - 771 14 47 — Woluwé-St-Pierre

RIGENÉE

14 | 7 | 6

Très ouvert et peu arboré, c'est un parcours délicat quand le vent souffle. Les défauts originels du dessin ont été peu à peu gommés par Christophe Descampe, frère de la grande joueuse belge. De nouveaux plans d'eau et des plantations devraient faire progresser cette réalisation dont l'entretien est de très bonne qualité. Les trous sont assez bien équilibrés et imposent un rythme de jeu agréable, mais on notera surtout la qualité technique des par 5. Les roughs sont bien en jeu, les greens assez vastes et moyennement modelés sont bien défendus, ce qui impose un jeu précis. Assez naturel au départ, et sans prétendre au titre de chef-d'oeuvre, Rigenée progresse dans le bon sens. L'ambiance y est très familiale et sportive, c'est un point à souligner.

This very open and almost treeless course is a tricky proposition when the wind gets up. The original flaws have been gradually designed out by Christophe Descampe, the brother of the great Belgian player. New stretches of water and plantation programmes should keep the course moving in the right direction, helped by excellent upkeep. The holes are well balanced for a pleasant playing rhythm, but most notable is the technical excellence of the par 5s. The rough is very much in play, and the rather large and averagely contoured greens are well defended, thus calling for some precision play. A natural layout at the outset and with no pretence to the masterpiece label, Rigenée is improving all the time. The atmosphere is one of family entertainment and sport, an important point that deserves a special mention.

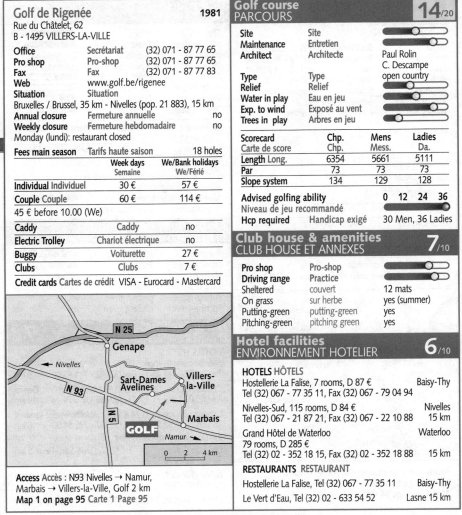

Golf de Rigenée — 1981

Rue du Châtelet, 62
B - 1495 VILLERS-LA-VILLE

Office	Secrétariat	(32) 071 - 87 77 65
Pro shop	Pro-shop	(32) 071 - 87 77 65
Fax	Fax	(32) 071 - 87 77 83
Web	www.golf.be/rigenee	
Situation	Situation	

Bruxelles / Brussel, 35 km - Nivelles (pop. 21 883), 15 km

Annual closure	Fermeture annuelle	no
Weekly closure	Fermeture hebdomadaire	no

Monday (lundi): restaurant closed

Fees main season Tarifs haute saison	Week days Semaine	We/Bank holidays We/Férié
		18 holes
Individual Individuel	30 €	57 €
Couple Couple	60 €	114 €

45 € before 10.00 (We)

Caddy	Caddy	no
Electric Trolley	Chariot électrique	no
Buggy	Voiturette	27 €
Clubs	Clubs	7 €

Credit cards Cartes de crédit VISA - Eurocard - Mastercard

Access Accès : N93 Nivelles → Namur, Marbais → Villers-la-Ville, Golf 2 km
Map 1 on page 95 Carte 1 Page 95

Golf course PARCOURS — 14/20

Site	Site	
Maintenance	Entretien	
Architect	Architecte	Paul Rolin, C. Descampe
Type	Type	open country
Relief	Relief	
Water in play	Eau en jeu	
Exp. to wind	Exposé au vent	
Trees in play	Arbres en jeu	

Scorecard Carte de score	Chp. Chp.	Mens Mess.	Ladies Da.
Length Long.	6354	5661	5111
Par	73	73	73
Slope system	134	129	128

Advised golfing ability Niveau de jeu recommandé: 0 12 24 36
Hcp required Handicap exigé: 30 Men, 36 Ladies

Club house & amenities CLUB HOUSE ET ANNEXES — 7/10

Pro shop	Pro-shop	
Driving range	Practice	
Sheltered	couvert	12 mats
On grass	sur herbe	yes (summer)
Putting-green	putting-green	yes
Pitching-green	pitching green	yes

Hotel facilities ENVIRONNEMENT HOTELIER — 6/10

HOTELS HÔTELS

Hostellerie La Falise, 7 rooms, D 87 € — Baisy-Thy
Tel (32) 067 - 77 35 11, Fax (32) 067 - 79 04 94

Nivelles-Sud, 115 rooms, D 84 € — Nivelles 15 km
Tel (32) 067 - 21 87 21, Fax (32) 067 - 22 10 88

Grand Hôtel de Waterloo — Waterloo 15 km
79 rooms, D 285 €
Tel (32) 02 - 352 18 15, Fax (32) 02 - 352 18 88

RESTAURANTS RESTAURANT

Hostellerie La Falise, Tel (32) 067 - 77 35 11 — Baisy-Thy

Le Vert d'Eau, Tel (32) 02 - 633 54 52 — Lasne 15 km

RINKVEN Red - White

14	6	5

Na een mooie toegangsweg door de bossen, valt direct het professionalisme van de club op, door de kwaliteit van de installaties en het onderhoud van het terrein. Dit laatste bestaat uit 3 combineerbare 9-holes, van gelijke moeilijkheidsgraad (vooral de bomen en water) en met greens zonder enige variatie qua esthetiek, vaak verhoogd en smal. Men mist persoonlijkheid en stijl in de architectuur van dit parcours, en krijgt veeleer een indruk van eentonigheid, dermate dat men om het even welke combinatie van 18 holes kan spelen en toch een tamelijk duidelijk beeld van het geheel krijgt. Een voordeel is dat de moeilijkheidsgraad voor elk spelniveau min of meer gelijk is, maar de betere handicaps zullen zich wel ietwat gefrustreerd voelen wegens het gebrek aan grotere uitdagingen. Ze kunnen echter wel genieten van een mooie wandeling in een aangename omgeving van berken en sparren, met een rijke fauna.

After a pleasant drive through the woods, you can tell the club's professionalism by the standard of facilities and the upkeep of the course. There are three combinable 9-hole courses offering the same level of difficulty (basically trees and water) and similar-looking greens that are often narrow and elevated. It is a pity about the lack of personality and style, which creates a slight feeling of monotony, to the point where you can play any 18-hole combination and get exactly the same impression of the site. On the upside, we noticed the average difficulty for all players, although very low handicappers might feel frustrated at the lack of real challenge. At least they will enjoy a pretty stroll over a pleasant estate of birch and pine trees, and the extensive wildlife to keep them company.

Rinkven Golf Club — 1981

Sint-Jobsteenweg, 120
B - 2970 SCHILDE

Office	Secretariaat	(32) 03 - 380 12 80
Pro shop	Pro shop	(32) 03 - 385 82 13
Fax	Fax	(32) 03 - 384 29 33
Web	www.golf.be/rinkven	
Situation	Locatie	
Antwerpen / Anvers (pop. 403 072), 15 km		
Annual closure	Jaarlijkse sluiting	no
Weekly closure	Wekelijkse sluitingsdag	no

Fees main season / Hoogseizoen tarieven	18 holes	
	Week days Weekdagen	We/Bank holidays We/Feestdagen
Individual Individueel	42 €	64 €
Couple Paar	84 €	128 €

Caddy	Caddy	no
Electric Trolley	Electrische trolley	10 € /18 holes
Buggy	Buggy	22 € /18 holes
Clubs	Clubs	no
Credit cards	Creditcards	no

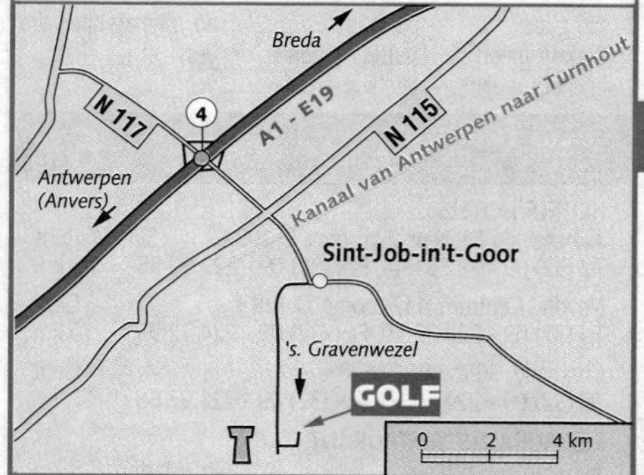

Access Toegang : E19 Anvers → Breda,
Exit (Sortie) St-Job-in-'t Goor → 's Gravenwesel → Golf
Map 1 on page 95 Auto kaart 1 Blz 95

Golf course — BAAN 14/20

Site	Terrein	
Maintenance	Onderhoud	
Architect	Architect	Paul Rolin
Type	Type baan	forest
Relief	Reliëf	
Water in play	Waterhazards	
Exp. to wind	Windgevoelig	
Trees in play	Bomen	

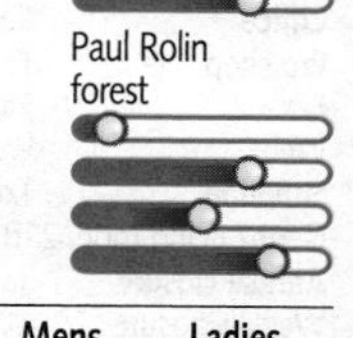

Scorecard Scorekaart	Chp. Back tees	Mens Heren	Ladies Damen
Length Lengte	6177	6000	5467
Par	72	72	72
Slope system	139	137	134

Advised golfing ability / Aanbevolen golfvaardigheid: 0 12 24 36
Hcp required / Vereiste hcp: 28

Club house & amenities — CLUB HOUSE EN ANNEXEN 6/10

Pro shop	Pro shop	
Driving range	Oefenbaan	
Sheltered	overdekt	6 mats
On grass	op gras	no, 9 mats open air
Putting-green	putting-green	yes
Pitching-green	pitching-green	yes

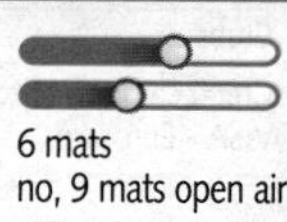

Hotel facilities — HOTELS IN OMGEVING 5/10

HOTELS HOTELS

Alfa De Keyser, 123 rooms, D 156 € — Antwerpen
Tel (32) 03 - 206 74 60, Fax (32) 03 - 232 39 70 — 15 km

Hilton — Antwerpen
199 rooms, D 337 €
Tel (32) 03 - 204 12 12, Fax (32) 03 - 204 12 13

Rubens, 36 rooms, D 176 € — Antwerpen
Tel (32) 03 - 222 48 48, Fax (32) 03 - 225 19 40

RESTAURANTS RESTAURANT

De Bellefleur — Kapellen 12 km
Tel (32) 03 - 664 67 19

't Fornuis, Tel (32) 03 - 233 62 70 — Antwerpen 15 km

ROYAL LATEM

15 | 8 | 6

Deze golfclub werd in 1909 geopend en was bekend onder de naam "les Buttes Blanches". Greens en bunkers werden in de jaren '50 hertekend door Hawtree. Het gebrek aan ruimte brengt ook een beperking in afstand met zich mee, en "out of bounds" op de helft van de holes. Het grote park is aangeplant met prachtige bomen, eiken, dennen, en beuken van meer dan 200 jaar oud, wat voor een zeer aantrekkelijke omgeving zorgt. De hindernissen zijn hoofdzakelijk bunkers, maar ook enkele vijvers en grachten, niet echt moeilijk. Het design is tamelijk eenvoudig, en de strategie voor de hand liggend, behalve op de 6 en de 18, met blinde drives. De strategie om de greens te bereiken, is niet ingewikkeld te noemen, zelfs niet de keuze van de club, behalve voor de approach van vijf ervan, die verhoogd zijn. Dankzij een afwisselend design, een matig reliëf en een opvallende charme en volkomenheid, kan Latem een parcours bieden, dat voor elk spelersniveau een plezier betekent. De zanderige bodem en de volledige irrigatie maken het mogelijk in alle seizoenen te spelen.

Opened back in 1909, this Golf Club was known under the name of "Les Buttes Blanches". The greens and bunkers were redesigned by Hawtree in the 1950s. Lack of space has resulted in a shortish course and out-of-bounds on at least half of the holes. The estate is covered with some beautiful trees - oak, pine and beech - often more than 200 years old, and makes for a very attractive setting. The main hazards are the bunkers, but there are a number of ponds and ditches awaiting the mis-hit shot. The layout is clear and strategy obvious, except on the 6 and 18th holes, where the drive is blind. Approach shots are not too complex, either, and choice of club is more or less straightforward, except for the five elevated greens. A varied layout and averagely hilly, the course is not made for the very best players, but the rest will have fun. Sandy soil and comprehensive irrigation facilities make this a course that is playable virtually all year.

Royal Latem Golf Club — 1909

B - 9380 ST-MARTENS-LATEM

Office	Secretariaat	(32) 09 - 282 54 11
Pro shop	Pro shop	(32) 09 - 282 57 65
Fax	Fax	(32) 09 - 282 90 19
Web	www.golf.be/latem	
Situation	Locatie	

Gent / Gand (pop. 210 704), 10 km

Annual closure	Jaarlijkse sluiting	no
Weekly closure	Wekelijkse sluitingsdag	no

Monday (maandag): restaurant closed

Fees main season Hoogseizoen tarieven	Week days Weekdagen	We/Bank holidays We/Feestdagen
		Full day
Individual Individueel	45 €	57 €
Couple Paar	90 €	114 €

Caddy	Caddy	no
Electric Trolley	Electrische trolley	no
Buggy	Buggy	30 € /18 holes
Clubs	Clubs	no

Credit cards Creditcards
VISA - Eurocard

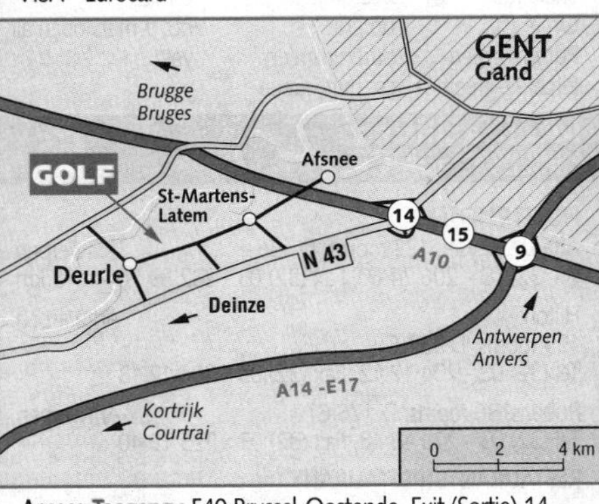

Access Toegang : E40 Brussel-Oostende, Exit (Sortie) 14, N43 → Kortrijk, → Golf
Map 1 on page 95 Auto kaart 1 Blz 95

Golf course BAAN — 15/20

Site	Terrein	
Maintenance	Onderhoud	
Architect	Architect	Fred Hawtree
Type	Type baan	forest, residential
Relief	Reliëf	
Water in play	Waterhazards	
Exp. to wind	Windgevoelig	
Trees in play	Bomen	

Scorecard Scorekaart	Chp. Back tees	Mens Heren	Ladies Damen
Length Lengte	5767	5767	5143
Par	72	72	72
Slope system	123	123	123

Advised golfing ability Aanbevolen golfvaardigheid: 0 12 24 36
Hcp required Vereiste hcp: 36 weekdays, 28 W/E

Club house & amenities CLUB HOUSE EN ANNEXEN — 8/10

Pro shop	Pro shop	
Driving range	Oefenbaan	
Sheltered	overdekt	3 mats
On grass	op gras	no, 13 mats open air
Putting-green	putting-green	yes
Pitching-green	pitching-green	yes

Hotel facilities HOTELS IN OMGEVING — 6/10

HOTELS HOTELS

Auberge du Pêcheur, 27 rooms, D 109 € — Sint-Martens 1,5 km
Tel (32) 09 - 282 31 44, Fax (32) 09 - 282 90 58

Novotel Centrum, 117 rooms, D 128 € — Gent 10 km
Tel (32) 09 - 224 22 30, Fax (32) 09 - 224 32 95

Chamade, 36 rooms, D 128 € — Gent
Tel (32) 09 - 220 15 15, Fax (32) 09 - 221 97 66

RESTAURANTS RESTAURANT

Auberge du Pêcheur — Sint-Martens 1,5 km
Tel (32) 09 - 282 31 44

Jan van den Bon, Tel (32) 09 - 221 90 85 — Gent

Waterzooi, Tel (32) 09 - 225 05 63 — Gent

ROYAL ZOUTE

18 | 7 | 7

Un parcours centenaire qui ne paraît pas trop difficile, en tout cas lorsque le haut rough n'est pas trop proche, mais c'est un formidable défi quand le vent se met à souffler. Pour juger de sa qualité, on peut faire confiance au témoignage de joueurs aussi connaisseurs d'architecture de golf que Nick Faldo, et à la signature de Harry Colt, l'un des plus grands créateurs de parcours de l'histoire du golf. Malgré tout, Le Zoute ne dissimule jamais ses difficultés, ce qui permet de savoir où placer son départ pour mieux préparer le coup suivant vers des greens rapides et bien modelés, défendus avec intelligence et subtilité. Le chemin le plus direct est clairement défini entre les dunes et les arbres, mais ne prenez pas trop vite confiance en vous, les fairways roulants peuvent réserver quelques positions de balle inconfortables et inattendues. Un parcours très classique que tous les golfeurs doivent jouer un jour ou l'autre. Un des meilleurs links du continent.

A hundred-year old course which does not look too tough, or at least not when you stay well away from the tall grass in the rough. When the winds blows, though, it is a terrific challenge for anyone. Its reputation has long been established, tributes from players such as Nick Faldo are a reference indeed, as is the label of H.S. Colt, one of greatest golf course designers in the history of golf. Anyway, Le Zoute never tries to hide any of its difficulties, notably placing the tee-shot for an easier approach shot to fast and well-contoured greens, that are cleverly and subtly defended. The "straight and narrow" is clearly laid out betwen dunes and trees, but don't feel too confident too soon. Some of the rolling fairways can provide unusual and unexpected positions. A very classic course and one that all golfers should know sooner or later. One of the best links courses in continental Europe.

Royal Zoute Golf Club — 1945

Caddiespad 14
B - 8300 KNOKKE-HEIST

Office	Secrétariat	(32) 050 - 60 12 27
Pro shop	Pro-shop	(32) 050 - 60 19 60
Fax	Fax	(32) 050 - 62 30 29
Web	www.zoute.be/golfnl.htm	
Situation	Situation	

close to Knokke-Heist (pop. 31 237)

Annual closure	Fermeture annuelle	no
Weekly closure	Fermeture hebdomadaire	no

Fees main season Tarifs haute saison	18 holes	
	Week days Semaine	**We/Bank holidays** We/Férié
Individual Individuel	87 €	87 €
Couple Couple	174 €	174 €

Caddy	Caddy	25 €
Electric Trolley	Chariot électrique	yes
Buggy	Voiturette	yes
Clubs	Clubs	yes
Credit cards	Cartes de crédit	no

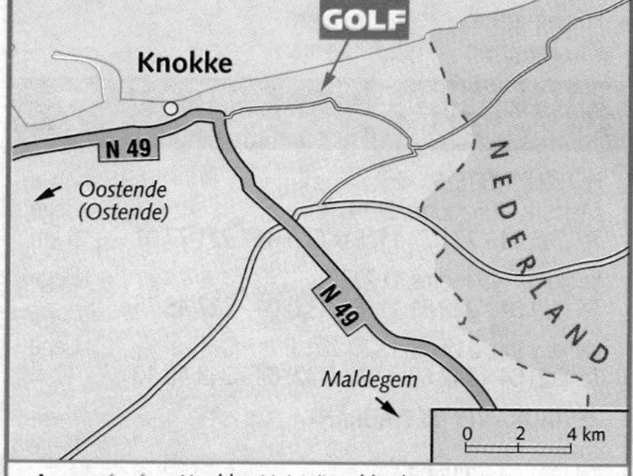

Access Accès : Knokke-Heist (Knokke-le-Zoute)
Map 1 on page 95 Carte 1 Page 95

Golf course — BAAN — 18/20

Site	Site	
Maintenance	Entretien	
Architect	Architecte	Seymour Dunn Harry S. Colt
Type	Type	links
Relief	Relief	
Water in play	Eau en jeu	
Exp. to wind	Exposé au vent	
Trees in play	Arbres en jeu	

Scorecard Carte de score	**Chp.** Chp.	**Mens** Mess.	**Ladies** Da.
Length Long.	6172	6172	5416
Par	72	72	72
Slope system	132	132	130

Advised golfing ability Niveau de jeu recommandé — 0 12 24 36

Hcp required Handicap exigé — 20 Men, 24 Ladies

Club house & amenities — CLUB HOUSE EN ANNEXEN — 7/10

Pro shop	Pro-shop	
Driving range	Practice	
Sheltered	couvert	20 mats
On grass	sur herbe	no, 6 mats open air
Putting-green	putting-green	yes
Pitching-green	pitching green	yes

Hotel facilities — HOTELS IN OMGEVING — 7/10

HOTELS HÔTELS

Royal Zoute Golf Club, 7 rooms, D 161 € — on site
Tel (32) 050 - 60 16 17, Fax (32) 050 - 62 24 26

Manoir du Dragon, 17 rooms, D 248 € — Het Zoute 1 km
Tel (32) 050 - 63 05 80, Fax (32) 050 - 6305 90

Approach, 31 rooms, D 300 € — Het Zoute
Tel (32) 050 - 61 11 30, Fax (32) 050 - 61 16 28

RESTAURANTS RESTAURANT

De Oosthoek, Tel (32) 050 - 62 23 33 — Het Zoute 1 km

De Savoye, Tel (32) 050 - 62 23 61 — Knokke 2 km

Bartholomeus, Tel (32) 050 - 51 75 76 — Heist, 5 km

SART-TILMAN

16 | 7 | 7

C'est l'un des meilleurs parcours de match-play de Belgique. La longueur de certains trous (dont quelques terribles par 4), leur relief raisonnable et naturel, la présence insistante des arbres, et des greens diaboliques le rendent difficile à scorer, notamment pour les joueurs de moins de 12 de handicap, qui pourront vraiment y tester leur jeu. Il faut établir sa stratégie dès le départ en fonction des positions de drapeau. Son relief mesuré, son excellent rythme, son honnêteté et la beauté du site traduisent bien le génie de son architecte Tom Simpson. Le lac du 14, qui cassait l'harmonie du dessin a été heureusement supprimé. La qualité de l'entretien ajoute encore au plaisir : Le Royal Sart-Tilman mérite un large détour pour sa franchise, son intérêt, son absence de "vices cachés", son confort général et son ambiance chaleureuse.

This is one of Belgium's finest match-play courses. The length of some holes(some pretty hard par 4s), the measured, natural relief, the looming presence of trees and devilishly tricky greens make scoring a tough business, especially for players with a handicap under 12, who will find this a real test. Game strategy must be set before starting out, and be geared to the pin positions. The measured relief and excellent balance, plus the course's honesty and the beauty of the site are a good reflection on the genius of architect Tom Simpson. The lake on the 14th, which broke the harmony of the layout has been filled in. The standard of upkeep only enhances the enjoyment of playing here. Royal Sart Tilman is well worth the time and journey for its openness, appeal, absence of hidden vices, general pleasantness and warm atmosphere.

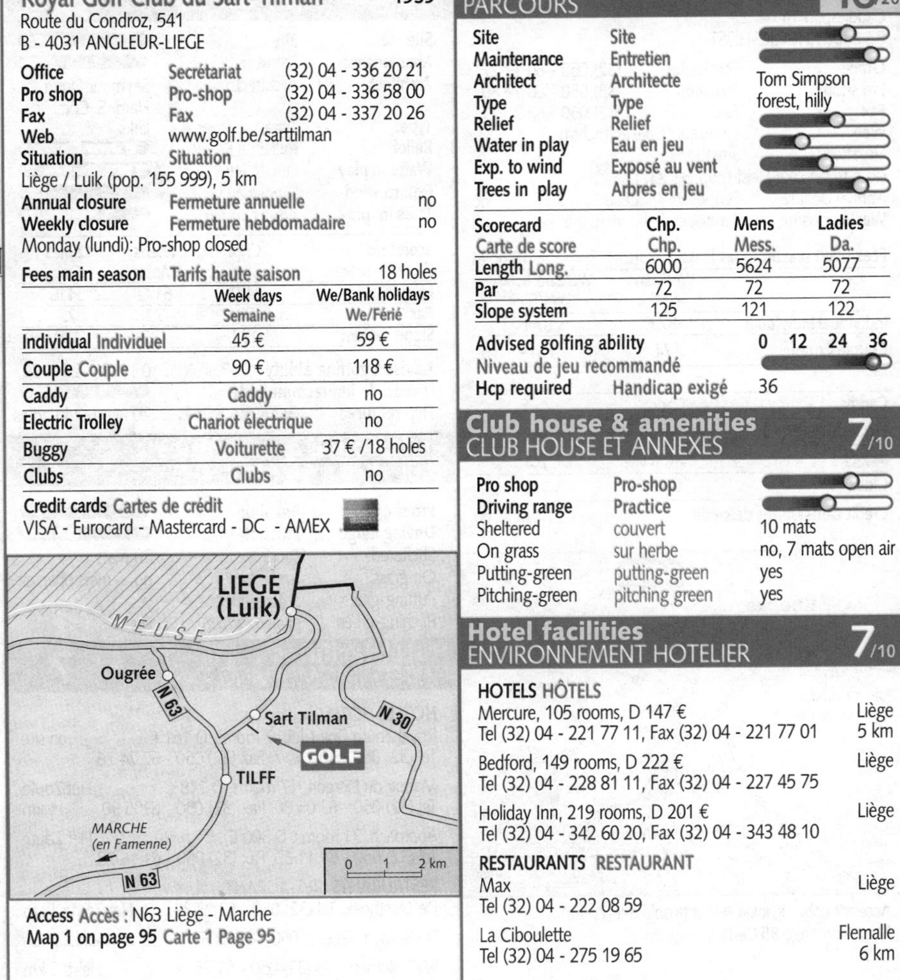

Royal Golf Club du Sart-Tilman 1939
Route du Condroz, 541
B - 4031 ANGLEUR-LIEGE

Office	Secrétariat	(32) 04 - 336 20 21
Pro shop	Pro-shop	(32) 04 - 336 58 00
Fax	Fax	(32) 04 - 337 20 26
Web	www.golf.be/sarttilman	
Situation	Situation	

Liège / Luik (pop. 155 999), 5 km

Annual closure	Fermeture annuelle	no
Weekly closure	Fermeture hebdomadaire	no

Monday (lundi): Pro-shop closed

Fees main season Tarifs haute saison	18 holes	
	Week days Semaine	**We/Bank holidays** We/Férié
Individual Individuel	45 €	59 €
Couple Couple	90 €	118 €
Caddy Caddy		no
Electric Trolley Chariot électrique		no
Buggy Voiturette		37 € /18 holes
Clubs Clubs		no

Credit cards Cartes de crédit
VISA - Eurocard - Mastercard - DC - AMEX

Access Accès : N63 Liège - Marche
Map 1 on page 95 Carte 1 Page 95

Golf course PARCOURS 16/20

Site	Site	
Maintenance	Entretien	
Architect	Architecte	Tom Simpson
Type	Type	forest, hilly
Relief	Relief	
Water in play	Eau en jeu	
Exp. to wind	Exposé au vent	
Trees in play	Arbres en jeu	

Scorecard Carte de score	**Chp.** Chp.	**Mens** Mess.	**Ladies** Da.
Length Long.	6000	5624	5077
Par	72	72	72
Slope system	125	121	122

Advised golfing ability 0 12 24 36
Niveau de jeu recommandé
Hcp required Handicap exigé 36

Club house & amenities CLUB HOUSE ET ANNEXES 7/10

Pro shop	Pro-shop	
Driving range	Practice	
Sheltered	couvert	10 mats
On grass	sur herbe	no, 7 mats open air
Putting-green	putting-green	yes
Pitching-green	pitching green	yes

Hotel facilities ENVIRONNEMENT HOTELIER 7/10

HOTELS HÔTELS

Mercure, 105 rooms, D 147 € — Liège 5 km
Tel (32) 04 - 221 77 11, Fax (32) 04 - 221 77 01

Bedford, 149 rooms, D 222 € — Liège
Tel (32) 04 - 228 81 11, Fax (32) 04 - 227 45 75

Holiday Inn, 219 rooms, D 201 € — Liège
Tel (32) 04 - 342 60 20, Fax (32) 04 - 343 48 10

RESTAURANTS RESTAURANT

Max — Liège
Tel (32) 04 - 222 08 59

La Ciboulette — Flemalle 6 km
Tel (32) 04 - 275 19 65

SPA (LES FAGNES) 17 7 7

La signature de Tom Simpson est une garantie de parcours technique et stratégique. De relief modéré, c'est un des bons exemples d'architecture classique "inland", où il faut maîtriser l'ensemble de son jeu pour éviter les bois, les roughs et autres bunkers, admirablement disposés. Le placement du drive est essentiel, notamment sur quatre longs par 4, mais le travail ne s'arrête pas là, car les greens sont bien défendus, leurs surfaces assez subtiles à lire. Dans un site d'une parfaite tranquillité, on a l'impression de prendre une retraite pour méditer non seulement sur le golf, mais aussi sur l'intelligente sobriété de l'architecture, révélant une connaissance parfaite des joueurs de tous niveaux, mais sans jamais dissimuler les pièges. Exigeant, ce parcours donne un plaisir que l'on souhaite retrouver très souvent. Les 12 (par 5), 7 et 15 (par 4) sont de pures merveilles. Et l'arrosage automatique a amélioré l'ensemble.

The Tom Simpson label is the guarantee of a technical and strategic course. This moderately hilly layout is one of the classic examples of inland architecture, where every part of your game has to be in shape to avoid the woods, rough and admirably located bunkers. Placing the tee-shot is essential, especially on the four long par 4s, but the job doesn't stop there, because the greens are well defended and the putting surfaces tricky to read. On a site of perfect tranquillity, you get the impression of being in a sanctuary from where to meditate not only about the course, but also about the smart discretion of a layout, which reveals good insight into every golfing ability but never conceals the traps. It is a demanding course but an enjoyable one, too. The type you like to come back and play again and again. 7th, 12th and 15th are architectural masterpieces. And the automatic watering system has made the course still better.

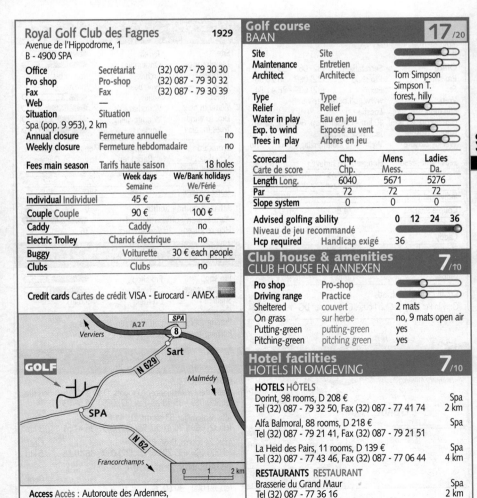

Royal Golf Club des Fagnes — 1929

Avenue de l'Hippodrome, 1
B - 4900 SPA

Office	Secrétariat	(32) 087 - 79 30 30
Pro shop	Pro-shop	(32) 087 - 79 30 32
Fax	Fax	(32) 087 - 79 30 39
Web	—	
Situation	Situation	
Spa (pop. 9 953), 2 km		
Annual closure	Fermeture annuelle	no
Weekly closure	Fermeture hebdomadaire	no

Fees main season Tarifs haute saison		18 holes
	Week days Semaine	**We/Bank holidays** We/Férié
Individual Individuel	45 €	50 €
Couple Couple	90 €	100 €
Caddy	Caddy	no
Electric Trolley	Chariot électrique	no
Buggy	Voiturette	30 € each people
Clubs	Clubs	no

Credit cards Cartes de crédit VISA - Eurocard - AMEX

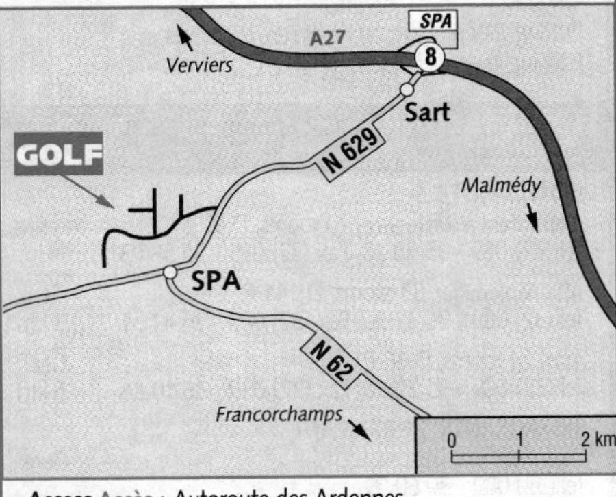

Access Accès : Autoroute des Ardennes,
Exit (Sortie) Spa → Golf
Map 2 on page 95 Carte 2 Page 95

Golf course — BAAN — 17/20

Site	Site	
Maintenance	Entretien	
Architect	Architecte	Tom Simpson Simpson T.
Type	Type	forest, hilly
Relief	Relief	
Water in play	Eau en jeu	
Exp. to wind	Exposé au vent	
Trees in play	Arbres en jeu	

Scorecard Carte de score	**Chp.** Chp.	**Mens** Mess.	**Ladies** Da.
Length Long.	6040	5671	5276
Par	72	72	72
Slope system	0	0	0

Advised golfing ability Niveau de jeu recommandé: 0 12 24 36
Hcp required Handicap exigé 36

Club house & amenities — CLUB HOUSE EN ANNEXEN — 7/10

Pro shop	Pro-shop	
Driving range	Practice	
Sheltered	couvert	2 mats
On grass	sur herbe	no, 9 mats open air
Putting-green	putting-green	yes
Pitching-green	pitching green	yes

Hotel facilities — HOTELS IN OMGEVING — 7/10

HOTELS HÔTELS

Dorint, 98 rooms, D 208 € — Spa
Tel (32) 087 - 79 32 50, Fax (32) 087 - 77 41 74 — 2 km

Alfa Balmoral, 88 rooms, D 218 € — Spa
Tel (32) 087 - 79 21 41, Fax (32) 087 - 79 21 51

La Heid des Pairs, 11 rooms, D 139 € — Spa
Tel (32) 087 - 77 43 46, Fax (32) 087 - 77 06 44 — 4 km

RESTAURANTS RESTAURANT

Brasserie du Grand Maur — Spa
Tel (32) 087 - 77 36 16 — 2 km

Château Peltzer — Verviers
Tel (32) 087 - 23 09 70 — 16 km

SPIEGELVEN

14 | 7 | 8

Een terrein dat een juist uitgebalanceerd spel vraagt. De eerste 9 holes, in de bossen, eisen veel nauwkeurigheid en aandacht bij het plaatsen van de drives. De laatste 9 liggen temidden van de heide, en zijn ook langer, meer bepaald drie van de par 4. De moeilijkheden, fairway bunkers en waterhindernissen, zijn goed zichtbaar en op een slimme manier gesitueerd; de architect, Ron Kirby, had een goed inzicht in de mogelijkheden van de spelers, en dit op verschillende niveaus. Hij heeft tegelijk echter ook zoveel mogelijk het natuurlijke uitzicht van het terrein proberen te bewaren, en het prachtig geintegreerd. De perfecte uitdunning van het onderhout is opmerkelijk. De greens zijn mooi ontworpen, niet te golvend, maar de speler moet, bij het bepalen van zijn strategie, rekening houden met de plaatsing van de vlaggen. Het terrein is tamelijk heuvelachtig, maar kan gemakkelijk te voet worden gespeeld. Geplaatst op een voormalige stortplaats, heeft dit terrein zeer vlug een plaats verworven onder de goede, recente realisaties, die waar men herinneringen aan overhoudt, behalve van de 7 de hole.

A course that demands a solid all-round game. The front nine, in the woods, call for precision in the extreme and a lot of care when placing the tee-shot. The back nine are in the heather and are longer, notably three of the par 4s. The difficulties, fairway bunkers and water hazards are clear to see and astutely located, revealing designer Ron Kirby's insight when it comes to understanding golfers of differing abilities. At the same time, he has preserved the course's natural look as far as possible, and the way it fits into the surroundings is exemplary. The undergrowth has been conveniently cleared to avoid penalising players too heavily, the greens are well designed and slope quite a bit, but the pin positions must be watched carefully if you want to establish an effective game strategy. The site is hilly but easily walkable.

Spiegelven Golf Club Genk — 1988

Wiemesmeerstraat 109
B - 3600 GENK

Office	Secretariaat	(32) 089 - 35 96 16
Pro shop	Pro shop	(32) 089 - 36 20 60
Fax	Fax	(32) 089 - 36 41 84
Web	www.golf.be/spiegelven	
Situation	Locatie	

Genk (pop. 45 906), 10 km - Hasselt (pop. 64 722), 20 km

Annual closure	Jaarlijkse sluiting	no
Weekly closure	Wekelijkse sluitingsdag	no

Fees main season Hoogseizoen tarieven	18 holes	
	Week days Weekdagen	**We/Bank holidays** We/Feestdagen
Individual Individueel	37 €	50 €
Couple Paar	74 €	100 €

Caddy	Caddy	no
Electric Trolley	Electrische trolley	no
Buggy	Buggy	30 €
Clubs	Clubs	25 €

Credit cards Creditcards
Only in Pro shop & Club house. Club house : DC - AMEX

Access Toegang : E314, Exit 32, N744 → Zutendal, Golf
Map 2 on page 95 Auto kaart 2 Blz 95

Golf course — BAAN — 14/20

Site	Terrein	
Maintenance	Onderhoud	
Architect	Architect	Ron Kirby
Type	Type baan	forest
Relief	Reliëf	
Water in play	Waterhazards	
Exp. to wind	Windgevoelig	
Trees in play	Bomen	

Scorecard Scorekaart	**Chp.** Back tees	**Mens** Heren	**Ladies** Damen
Length Lengte	6098	5732	5293
Par	72	72	72
Slope system	133	130	128

Advised golfing ability 0 12 24 36
Aanbevolen golfvaardigheid
Hcp required Vereiste hcp 36

Club house & amenities — CLUB HOUSE EN ANNEXEN — 7/10

Pro shop	Pro shop	
Driving range	Oefenbaan	
Sheltered	overdekt	9 mats
On grass	op gras	yes
Putting-green	putting-green	yes
Pitching-green	pitching-green	yes

Hotel facilities — HOTELS IN OMGEVING — 8/10

HOTELS HOTELS

Golfhotel La Résidence, 70 rooms, D 97 € — on site
Tel (32) 089 - 35 58 28, Fax (32) 089 - 35 58 03

Alfa Molenvijer, 83 rooms, D 141 € — Genk 3 km
Tel (32) 089 - 36 41 50, Fax (32) 089 - 36 41 51

Arte, 24 rooms, D 66 € — Genk 5 km
Tel (32) 089 - 35 20 06, Fax (32) 089 - 36 10 36

RESTAURANTS RESTAURANT

Da Vinci, — Genk
Tel (32) 089 - 30 60 59

't Konijtje — Genk
Tel (32) 089 - 35 26 45

WATERLOO La Marache

16 | 8 | 7

Les Français ne trouveront guère que Waterloo soit une "morne plaine" (le retour est assez vallonné), et le parcours de "La Marache", plus ancien parcours du "Lion" voisin, doit être abordé avec prudence et sagesse. Très bon exemple de l'architecture de Hawtree, il se déroule dans un environnement boisé plaisant, et souvent dangereux. Les seconds coups sont ici très intéressants, même si beaucoup des très grands greens sont assez ouverts pour y parvenir en roulant. Il est important d'être droit, même si la longueur de ce parcours est appréciable, mais chacun, selon son niveau, pourra y prendre plaisir. Les bons et longs drivers pourront cependant s'exprimer, sans trop de souci des tragédies bien plus graves dont Waterloo a été le cadre autrefois ! Ce complexe s'étend au total sur 150 hectares, et ses équipements sont dignes de ces dimensions.

Even the French could hardly describe Waterloo as the "cheerless plain" it was once said to be (the back 9 are over rolling terrain), and "La Marache", older than the neighbouring "Lion" course, should be approached with caution and good sense. An excellent example of Hawtree architecture, the course unwinds in a pleasant but often hazardous woodland environment. The second shots are interesting propositions here, even though many of the very large greens have no frontal hazard and so can be reached with chipped or low approach shots. It is important to play straight at Waterloo, the course is pretty long but every one can enjoy playing here. However, wild-hitters will be at ease, and in the past Waterloo has seen worst disasters than wayward tee-shots! The full complex stretches over 150 hectares (370 acres) and facilities are of an equally high standard.

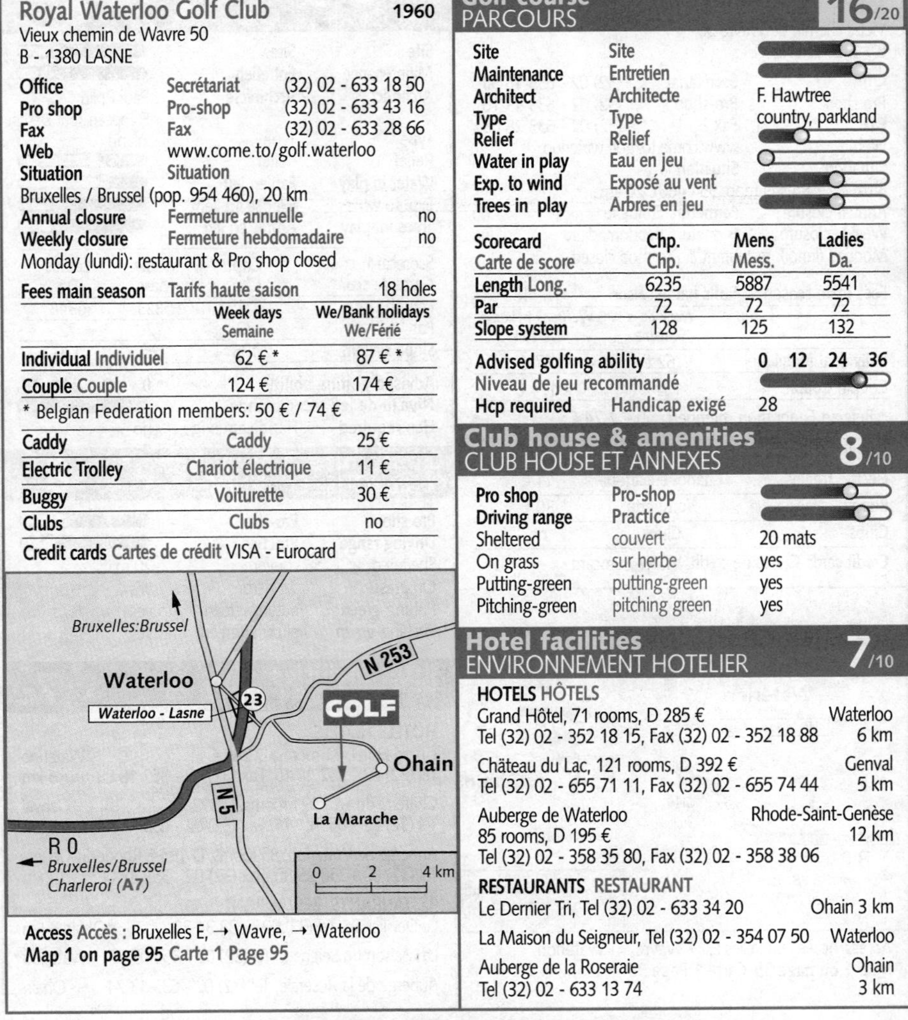

Royal Waterloo Golf Club — 1960

Vieux chemin de Wavre 50
B - 1380 LASNE

Office	Secrétariat	(32) 02 - 633 18 50
Pro shop	Pro-shop	(32) 02 - 633 43 16
Fax	Fax	(32) 02 - 633 28 66
Web	www.come.to/golf.waterloo	
Situation	Situation	

Bruxelles / Brussel (pop. 954 460), 20 km

Annual closure	Fermeture annuelle	no
Weekly closure	Fermeture hebdomadaire	no

Monday (lundi): restaurant & Pro shop closed

Fees main season Tarifs haute saison	Week days Semaine	We/Bank holidays We/Férié
		18 holes
Individual Individuel	62 € *	87 € *
Couple Couple	124 €	174 €

* Belgian Federation members: 50 € / 74 €

Caddy	Caddy	25 €
Electric Trolley	Chariot électrique	11 €
Buggy	Voiturette	30 €
Clubs	Clubs	no

Credit cards Cartes de crédit VISA - Eurocard

Access Accès : Bruxelles E, → Wavre, → Waterloo
Map 1 on page 95 Carte 1 Page 95

Golf course PARCOURS — 16/20

Site	Site	
Maintenance	Entretien	
Architect	Architecte	F. Hawtree
Type	Type	country, parkland
Relief	Relief	
Water in play	Eau en jeu	
Exp. to wind	Exposé au vent	
Trees in play	Arbres en jeu	

Scorecard Carte de score	Chp. Chp.	Mens Mess.	Ladies Da.
Length Long.	6235	5887	5541
Par	72	72	72
Slope system	128	125	132

Advised golfing ability Niveau de jeu recommandé — 0 12 24 36
Hcp required Handicap exigé — 28

Club house & amenities CLUB HOUSE ET ANNEXES — 8/10

Pro shop	Pro-shop	
Driving range	Practice	
Sheltered	couvert	20 mats
On grass	sur herbe	yes
Putting-green	putting-green	yes
Pitching-green	pitching green	yes

Hotel facilities ENVIRONNEMENT HOTELIER — 7/10

HOTELS HÔTELS

Grand Hôtel, 71 rooms, D 285 € — Waterloo
Tel (32) 02 - 352 18 15, Fax (32) 02 - 352 18 88 — 6 km

Château du Lac, 121 rooms, D 392 € — Genval
Tel (32) 02 - 655 71 11, Fax (32) 02 - 655 74 44 — 5 km

Auberge de Waterloo — Rhode-Saint-Genèse
85 rooms, D 195 € — 12 km
Tel (32) 02 - 358 35 80, Fax (32) 02 - 358 38 06

RESTAURANTS RESTAURANT

Le Dernier Tri, Tel (32) 02 - 633 34 20 — Ohain 3 km

La Maison du Seigneur, Tel (32) 02 - 354 07 50 — Waterloo

Auberge de la Roseraie — Ohain
Tel (32) 02 - 633 13 74 — 3 km

WATERLOO Le Lion

16	8	7

Le Royal Waterloo est l'un des grands clubs du continent, avec un joli site naturel, un sol bien drainant, et un fameux nom ! Son parcours du "Lion" manquait passablement de mordant, mais les interventions décisives d'European Tour Design en ont rehaussé considérablement la qualité. On peut souhaiter une refonte des départs et une révision du 14, mais ce sont des détails par rapport au plaisir éprouvé à jouer ici. Joliment paysagé, très bien équilibré dans son déroulement comme dans la répartition des obstacles, exigeant techniquement pour qui cherche à scorer,en particulier depuis les départs arrière, c'est aussi un parcours tout à fait jouable pour les moins ambitieux. La qualité de l'entretien ajoute encore à l'agrément du site. Si le visiteur est assez pressé pour ne passer qu'une journée ici, on lui conseillera le début de l'été, en mettant les deux parcours de Waterloo à son programme.

Royal Waterloo is one of the great continental golf courses stretching over a pretty and natural site which drains well and sports a famous name. This "Lion" course had become a little tame, but a number of decisive measures taken by European Tour Design have considerably enhanced overall standards. We would perhaps like to see some of the tee areas re-designed and maybe a re-styling of the 14th hole, but these are mere details when compared to the pleasure of playing here. The course is prettily landscaped and very well balanced in lay-out and for the placing of hazards. Although technically challenging for golfers looking to card a good score, especially when playing from the back tees, it is still perfectly playable for the less skilled golfer. The excellence of maintenance also does much to enhance the course's overall appeal. If you are passing through and have just one day to spare, come here in early summer and plan on playing both courses at Waterloo.

Royal Waterloo Golf Club — 1988

Vieux chemin de Wavre 50
B - 1380 LASNE

Office	Secrétariat	(32) 02 - 633 18 50
Pro shop	Pro-shop	(32) 02 - 633 43 16
Fax	Fax	(32) 02 - 633 28 66
Web	www.come.to/golf.waterloo	
Situation	Situation	

Bruxelles / Brussel (pop. 954 460), 20 km

Annual closure	Fermeture annuelle	no
Weekly closure	Fermeture hebdomadaire	no

Monday (lundi): restaurant & Pro shop closed

Fees main season Tarifs haute saison	18 holes	
	Week days Semaine	**We/Bank holidays** We/Férié
Individual Individuel	62 € *	87 € *
Couple Couple	124 €	174 €

* Belgian Federation members: 50 € / 74 €

Caddy	Caddy	25 €
Electric Trolley	Chariot électrique	11 €
Buggy	Voiturette	30 €
Clubs	Clubs	no

Credit cards Cartes de crédit VISA - Eurocard

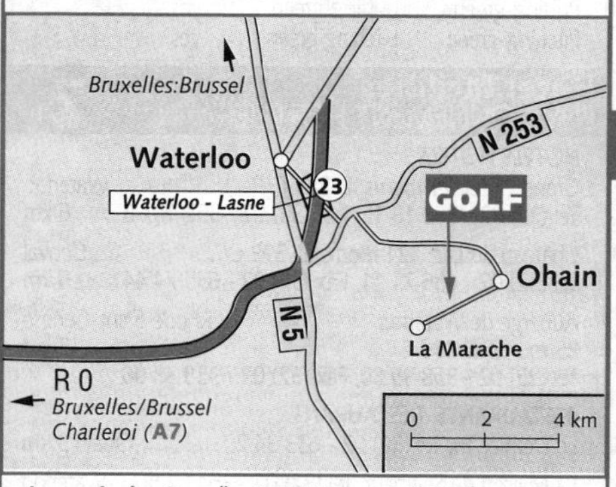

Access Accès : Bruxelles E, → Wavre, → Waterloo
Map 1 on page 95 Carte 1 Page 95

Map 1 on page 95

Golf course PARCOURS 16/20

Site	Site	
Maintenance	Entretien	
Architect	Architecte	Paul Rolin, European Tour Design
Type	Type	inland
Relief	Relief	
Water in play	Eau en jeu	
Exp. to wind	Exposé au vent	
Trees in play	Arbres en jeu	

Scorecard Carte de score	**Chp.** Chp.	**Mens** Mess.	**Ladies** Da.
Length Long.	6215	5823	5348
Par	72	72	72
Slope system	128	125	130

Advised golfing ability Niveau de jeu recommandé — 0 12 24 36
Hcp required Handicap exigé — no

Club house & amenities CLUB HOUSE ET ANNEXES 8/10

Pro shop	Pro-shop	
Driving range	Practice	
Sheltered	couvert	20 mats
On grass	sur herbe	yes
Putting-green	putting-green	yes
Pitching-green	pitching green	yes

Hotel facilities ENVIRONNEMENT HOTELIER 7/10

HOTELS HÔTELS

Grand Hôtel, 71 rooms, D 285 € — Waterloo
Tel (32) 02 - 352 18 15, Fax (32) 02 - 352 18 88 — 6 km

Château du Lac, 121 rooms, D 392 € — Genval
Tel (32) 02 - 655 71 11, Fax (32) 02 - 655 74 44 — 5 km

Auberge de Waterloo, 85 rooms, D 195 € — Rhode-St-Genèse
Tel (32) 02 - 358 35 80, Fax (32) 02 - 358 38 06 — 12 km

RESTAURANTS RESTAURANT

Le Dernier Tri, Tel (32) 02 - 633 34 20 — Ohain 3 km

La Maison du Seigneur, Tel (32) 02 - 354 07 50 — Waterloo

Auberge de la Roseraie, Tel (32) 02 - 633 13 74 — Ohain

GRAND DUCAL DE LUXEMBOURG | 13 | 6 | 7

La faible longueur du "Grand Ducal" plaira à la grande majorité des joueurs de tous niveaux. Mais que les bons frappeurs se méfient, les arbres sont très beaux, mais les éviter constitue la difficulté essentielle d'un parcours dont l'esthétique très britannique (quelques "cross-bunkers") coïncide bien avec les traditions golfiques cultivées ici. Les bunkers sont assez nombreux, mais défendent les greens sans méchanceté aucune. Ceux-ci sont de dimensions très raisonnables, mais leurs pentes exigent de l'attention avant de jouer. Le vallonnement du terrain reste modéré, il intervient surtout au 6, un long par 4 en montée, et seul trou vraiment difficile. En revanche, le 18, un par 5, laissera une bonne impression, car il présente une bonne occasion de birdie. En résumé, un parcours où le driver n'est pas indispensable, généralement en bon état, et très agréable quand on visite le pays. Cependant, les avions de l'aéroport tout proche manquent parfois de respect au golf...

The short yardage of the "Grand Ducal" will appeal to the vast majority of golfers of all levels. Yet the big-hitters should beware, the trees might look a pretty picture, but avoiding them is one of the main difficulties on a course, whose very attractive and very British style (with a few cross-bunkers to boot) perfectly reflects the golfing traditions nurtured in this part of the world. There are a lot of bunkers, which defends the greens but are never unduly spiteful. The greens themselves are very reasonably sized, but their slopes call for careful reading at all times. This is a moderately hilly course, but is especially steep on the 6th, a long uphill 4-par and the only really tough hole. In contrast, the 18th, a par 5, should leave you liking the course because the birdie here is a definite possibility. In a word or two, this is a course where the driver can easily stay in the bag. It is in good condition and very pleasant to play when you visit the "Grand Duché". Unfortunately, the planes from the neighbouring airport don't always respect the game of golf...

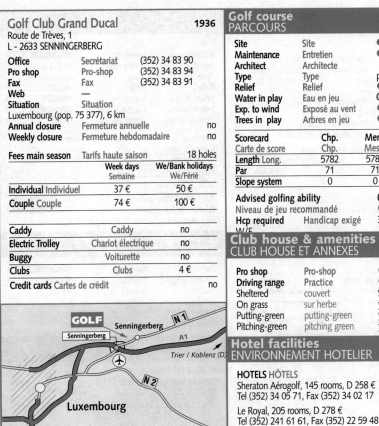

Golf Club Grand Ducal — 1936

Route de Trèves, 1
L - 2633 SENNINGERBERG

Office	Secrétariat	(352) 34 83 90
Pro shop	Pro-shop	(352) 34 83 94
Fax	Fax	(352) 34 83 91
Web	—	
Situation	Situation	

Luxembourg (pop. 75 377), 6 km

Annual closure	Fermeture annuelle	no
Weekly closure	Fermeture hebdomadaire	no

Fees main season Tarifs haute saison	**Week days** Semaine	**We/Bank holidays** We/Férié
		18 holes
Individual Individuel	37 €	50 €
Couple Couple	74 €	100 €

Caddy	Caddy	no
Electric Trolley	Chariot électrique	no
Buggy	Voiturette	no
Clubs	Clubs	4 €
Credit cards	Cartes de crédit	no

Access Accès : N1 Luxembourg → Airport (Aéroport)
Map 1 on page 73 Carte 1 Page 73

Golf course PARCOURS — 13/20

Site	Site	
Maintenance	Entretien	
Architect	Architecte	
Type	Type	parkland
Relief	Relief	
Water in play	Eau en jeu	
Exp. to wind	Exposé au vent	
Trees in play	Arbres en jeu	

Scorecard Carte de score	**Chp.** Chp.	**Mens** Mess.	**Ladies** Da.
Length Long.	5782	5782	5179
Par	71	71	71
Slope system	0	0	0

Advised golfing ability Niveau de jeu recommandé — 0 12 24 36

Hcp required Handicap exigé — 36 weekdays, 28 W/E

Club house & amenities CLUB HOUSE ET ANNEXES — 6/10

Pro shop	Pro-shop	
Driving range	Practice	
Sheltered	couvert	9 mats
On grass	sur herbe	yes
Putting-green	putting-green	yes
Pitching-green	pitching green	yes

Hotel facilities ENVIRONNEMENT HOTELIER — 7/10

HOTELS HÔTELS

Sheraton Aérogolf, 145 rooms, D 258 € — Aéroport 1 km
Tel (352) 34 05 71, Fax (352) 34 02 17

Le Royal, 205 rooms, D 278 € — Luxembourg 6 km
Tel (352) 241 61 61, Fax (352) 22 59 48

Cravat, 58 rooms, D 212 € — Luxembourg
Tel (352) 22 19 75, Fax (352) 22 67 11

RESTAURANTS RESTAURANT

Clairefontaine — Luxembourg
Tel (352) 46 22 11

Le Grimpereau — Senningerberg 1 km
Tel (352) 43 67 87

KIKUOKA

16 | 7 | 7

Sans atteindre des sommets, ce parcours créé en 1991 ne déçoit jamais. D'ailleurs, les joueurs professionnels du "Challenge Tour" en ont apprécié à la fois le "challenge" et la franchise. Sur chaque départ, on sait exactement où jouer, et les différences visuelles d'un trou à l'autre renouvellent constamment l'intérêt du jeu. Sans être sublime, le site est agréablement boisé et vallonné (facile à jouer à pied), souvent à flanc de côteau, et l'architecte en a utilisé habilement les contours. En l'absence d'arbres, quelques mouvements de terrain ont été créés, mais sans le côté spectaculaire qu'un von Hagge aurait pu donner à cet espace très ouvert. Les principaux obstacles sont les bunkers, qui sont près d'une centaine, certains de grande taille, et placés autant pour capter les balles égarées que pour définir les trous. De fait, le crayon d'Iwao Uematsu a subi des influences américaines, en particulier pour la forte défense des greens et les formes de ceux-ci. L'ouverture d'un hôtel sur place ne peut que faire mieux connaître ce parcours.

Although not what you would call a top-flight course, this 1991 layout is great golfing every time. The pros on the Challenge Tour appreciated both the challenge and the openness of the course, as from each tee-box you know exactly where to play and the visual differences from one hole to the next keep it constantly interesting. The site is pleasantly wooded over lightly rolling terrain (easily walkable) often on the side of a hill, and the architect very cleverly used the natural topology. Where there are no trees, he shifted a little earth, but without going to the lengths you might have found if someone like von Hagge had been let loose here. The main hazards are bunkers, almost a hundred in all, some of which are huge and placed to both snap up mis-hit shots and define the holes. As a result, the design of Iwao Uematsu has undergone a definite American influence, particularly concerning the well-guarded greens and the shape of the putting surfaces. The opening of an hotel should help to make this a better known course.

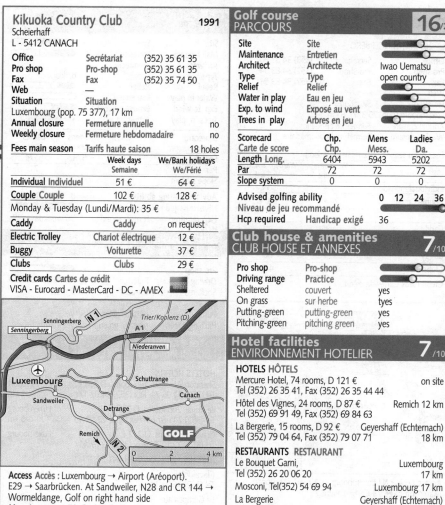

Kikuoka Country Club **1991**
Scheierhaff
L - 5412 CANACH

Office	Secrétariat	(352) 35 61 35
Pro shop	Pro-shop	(352) 35 61 35
Fax	Fax	(352) 35 74 50
Web	—	
Situation	Situation	

Luxembourg (pop. 75 377), 17 km

Annual closure	Fermeture annuelle	no
Weekly closure	Fermeture hebdomadaire	no

Fees main season Tarifs haute saison	18 holes	
	Week days Semaine	We/Bank holidays We/Férié
Individual Individuel	51 €	64 €
Couple Couple	102 €	128 €

Monday & Tuesday (Lundi/Mardi): 35 €

Caddy	Caddy	on request
Electric Trolley	Chariot électrique	12 €
Buggy	Voiturette	37 €
Clubs	Clubs	29 €

Credit cards Cartes de crédit
VISA - Eurocard - MasterCard - DC - AMEX

Access Accès : Luxembourg → Airport (Aréoport). E29 → Saarbrücken. At Sandweiler, N28 and CR 144 → Wormeldange, Golf on right hand side
Map 1 on page 73 Carte 1 Page 73

Golf course PARCOURS — 16/20

Site	Site	
Maintenance	Entretien	
Architect	Architecte	Iwao Uematsu
Type	Type	open country
Relief	Relief	
Water in play	Eau en jeu	
Exp. to wind	Exposé au vent	
Trees in play	Arbres en jeu	

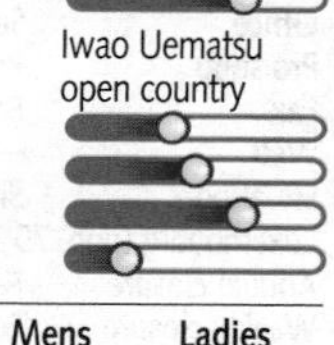

Scorecard Carte de score	Chp. Chp.	Mens Mess.	Ladies Da.
Length Long.	6404	5943	5202
Par	72	72	72
Slope system	0	0	0

Advised golfing ability Niveau de jeu recommandé — 0 12 24 36
Hcp required Handicap exigé 36

Club house & amenities CLUB HOUSE ET ANNEXES — 7/10

Pro shop	Pro-shop	
Driving range	Practice	
Sheltered	couvert	yes
On grass	sur herbe	tyes
Putting-green	putting-green	yes
Pitching-green	pitching green	yes

Hotel facilities ENVIRONNEMENT HOTELIER — 7/10

HOTELS HÔTELS
Mercure Hotel, 74 rooms, D 121 € — on site
Tel (352) 26 35 41, Fax (352) 26 35 44 44
Hôtel des Vignes, 24 rooms, D 87 € — Remich 12 km
Tel (352) 69 91 49, Fax (352) 69 84 63
La Bergerie, 15 rooms, D 92 € — Geyershaff (Echternach) 18 km
Tel (352) 79 04 64, Fax (352) 79 07 71

RESTAURANTS RESTAURANT
Le Bouquet Garni, Tel (352) 26 20 06 20 — Luxembourg 17 km
Mosconi, Tel(352) 54 69 94 — Luxembourg 17 km
La Bergerie, Tel (352) 79 04 64 — Geyershaff (Echternach) 18 km

EUROPE'S TOP 1000 GOLF COURSES

Denmark

Rungsted

Denmark
Danmark

Denmark is the southernmost Scandinavian country and climate-wise is also the mildest. Having said that, the North and Baltic Seas are never far away and it can sometimes be very wet in this part of the world, with enough rain to ensure lush landscapes and thick grass. This is, if course, ideal for golf, a sport played by 90,000 Danes on almost one hundred 18-hole courses. Denmark boasts both inland and coastal courses, sometimes nestling on the country's many islands, or again close to seaside resorts. Anyone from southern Europe would need a lot of prompting to bathe in these cold waters, but the Danes are a hardy bunch and have produced some top world golfers, the best known of whom is, of course, Thomas Bjorn.

Danmark er det sydligste af de Skandisnaviske lande og kilmaet er det mildeste. Man skal imidlertid ikke ignorere at Vesterhavet og Østersøen aldrig er langt væk og vejret kan i denne del af verden tit være meget fugtig. Her falder nok regn til at landskabeter grønt og græsset er tæt og frodigt. Det er naturligtvis ideelt for golf, en sport som har 90,000 danske udøvere og her er ca. 100 18 huls golfbaner. Danmark har både inland og kyst golfbaner, links, og til tider er banen kreeret på en af de mange øer eller tæt på et af badestæderne.
I Danmark er man aldrig mere end 30 km fra havet. Det kan være svært at få en sydeuropæer til at bade på disse kanter, men danskerne er robuste og flere top spillere i verdensklasse kommer herfra. Den bedst kendte er naturligtvis Thomas Bjørn.

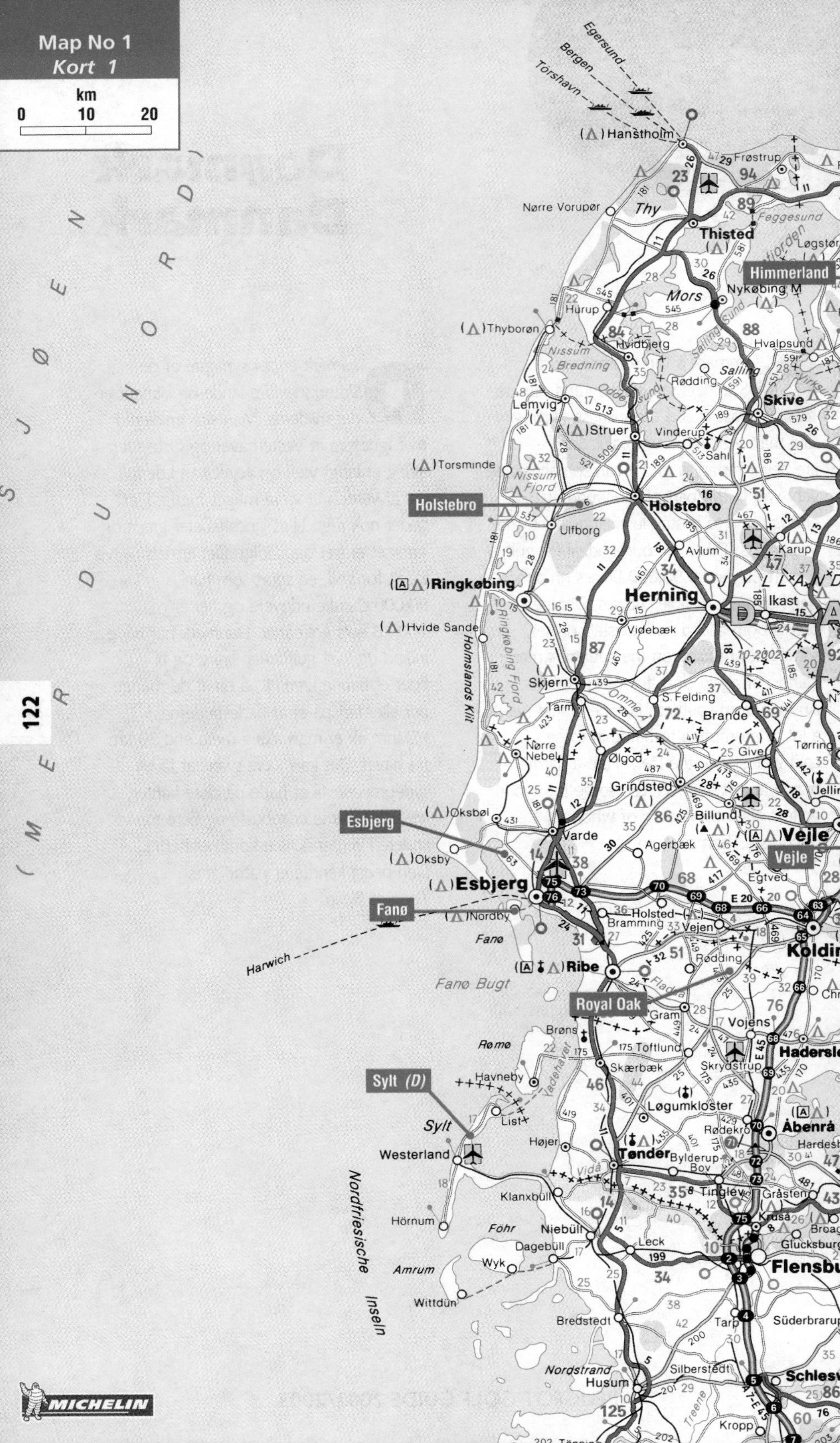

Map No 1
Kort 1
km
0
10
20
Egersund
Bergen
Tórshavn
Hanstholm
Frøstrup
Nørre Vorupør
Thy
Thisted
Feggesund
Løgstør
Himmerland
Mors
Nykøbing M
Hurup
Thyborøn
Hvidbjerg
Hvalpsund
Nissum Bredning
Rødding
Salling
Skive
Lemvig
Struer
Vinderup
Sahl
Torsminde
Nissum Fjord
Holstebro
Ulfborg
Avlum
Karup
Ringkøbing
Herning
Ikast
Hvide Sande
Videbæk
Ringkøbing Fjord
Holmslands Klit
Skjern
Tarm
S. Felding
Brande
Nørre Nebel
Ølgod
Give
Tørring
Grindsted
Jelling
Oksbøl
Billund
Esbjerg
Varde
Vejle
Oksby
Agerbæk
Egtved
Esbjerg
Fanø
Nordby
Holsted
Bramming
Vejen
Kolding
Harwich
Fanø
Ribe
Rødding
Fanø Bugt
Royal Oak
Gram
Brøns
Vojens
Rømø
Toftlund
Haderslev
Havneby
Skærbæk
Skrydstrup
Sylt (D)
List
Løgumkloster
Sylt
Højer
Rødekro
Åbenrå
Westerland
Tønder
Bylderup-Bov
Klanxbüll
Tinglev
Gråsten
Nordfriesische Inseln
Hörnum
Kruså
Föhr
Niebüll
Glücksburg
Dagebüll
Leck
Flensburg
Amrum
Wyk
Wittdün
Bredstedt
Tarp
Süderbrarup
Nordstrand
Silberstedt
Husum
Schleswig
Treene
Kropp
Tönning
MICHELIN

d'après carte n° 985 - 10ème édition - 2002.
Autorisation n° 0102062.

CLASSIFICATION OF COURSES
KLASSIFIKATION AF GOLFBANER

This classification gives priority consideration to the score awarded to the actual course.

Denne Klassifikation giver prioritet til bedømmelsen af banens standard.

Courses score / Klassifikation af golfbaner — Page / Side

Courses score			Course	Page
17	7	7	Rungsted	136
16	8	6	Himmerland *New Course*	129
16	6	5	Holstebro	130
16	7	7	København *Eremitagen*	131
15	7	6	Asserbo	126
15	6	5	Esbjerg	127
15	4	7	Fanø	128
15	7	5	Læsø *Seaside*	133
15	7	7	Møn	134
15	7	5	Royal Oak	135
15	4	7	Samsø	137
15	7	7	Vejle *Blå/Rød*	140
14	4	6	Korsør	132
14	5	6	Sct. Knuds	138
14	7	7	Simon's	139

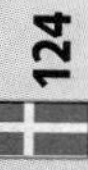

Classification

HOTEL FACILITIES
HOTEL KLASSIFIKATION

This classification gives priority consideration to the score awarded to the actual course.

Denne klassifikation giver prioritet til bedømmelsen af hotellets faciliteter.

Courses score / Hotel klassifikation — Page / Side

		Hotel	Course	Page
15	4	**7**	Fanø	128
16	7	**7**	København *Eremitagen*	131
15	7	**7**	Møn	134
17	7	**7**	Rungsted	136
15	4	**7**	Samsø	137
14	7	**7**	Simon's	139
15	7	**7**	Vejle *Blå/Rød*	140
15	7	**6**	Asserbo	126
16	8	**6**	Himmerland *New Course*	129
14	4	**6**	Korsør	132
14	5	**6**	Sct. Knuds	138
15	6	**5**	Esbjerg	127
16	6	**5**	Holstebro	130
15	7	**5**	Læsø Seaside	133
15	7	**5**	Royal Oak	135

RECOMMENDED GOLFING STAY
ANBEFALET TIL GOLFOPHOLD

Himmerland *New Course*	16 8 6	129
Holstebro	16 6 5	130
Rungsted	17 7 7	136

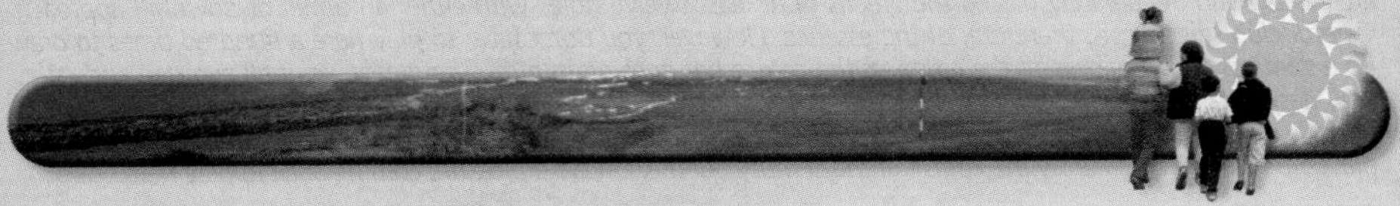

RECOMMENDED HOLIDAYS
ANBEFALET SOM FERIESTED

Esbjerg	15 6 5	127
Fanø	15 4 7	128
Læsø *Seaside*	15 7 5	133
Rungsted	17 7 7	136

TYPE OF COURSE
TYPE

Country
Møn 134, Korsør 132, Samsø 137, Simon's 139.

Forest
Holstebro 130, Læsø *Seaside* 133, Rungsted 136, Sct. Knuds 138, Vejle *Blå/Rød* 140.

Hilly
Asserbo 126, Møn 134, Vejle *Blå/Rød* 140.

Inland
København Eremitagen 131, Simon's 139.

Links
Fanø 128.

Open country
Himmerland *New Course* 129 København Eremitagen 131, Sct. Knuds 138.

Parkland
Asserbo 126, Holstebro 130, Royal Oak 135, Rungsted 136.

Seaside course
Esbjerg 127, Korsør 132
Læsø *Seaside* 133, Samsø 137.

ASSERBO

15 | 7 | 6

Nordsjælland er behagelig langt fra den københavnske golf-alfarvej. Her ligger Asserbo, ikke så langt fra Hillerød og fra Frederiksborg Slot, der står på tre små øer, og hvis park for nylig er blevet beriget med landets smukkeste haveanlæg i romantisk stil. Banen er temmelig kuperet (el-vogn tilrådes), og skråninger er på to tredjedele af hullerne udnyttet, så ens approach-slag skal spilles enten op eller ned for at komme på green. Derfor er det vigtigt, at man er omhyggelig med sit valg af jern. Det er nu ikke nødvendigt at spille her 20 gange for at vide, hvad du skal, for trods højdeforskellene byder banen ikke på særlig mange blinde slag. Den er tværtimod åben og ærlig. Greens er fornuftigt designede og ligger godt beskyttet. Flere steder er såvel enkeltstående som klynger af træer i allerhøjeste grad i spil, og der er vand-hazarder med i billedet især på de sidste ni huller. En meget smukt og dejlig afsides beliggende bane, der ikke er sværere, end at alle kan være med. Ikke Sjællands bedste, men altid en fornøjelse at vende tilbage til.

To the north of Copenhagen but a little removed from the destinations most frequented by the Danish capital's city folk, this course is close to the royal castle of Frederiksborg in Hillerød, curiously built on three islands and now the Museum of Danish History. The terrain is hilly (buggy recommended) and the slopes have been cleverly used by the architects, who deliberately placed the greens of at least twelve holes with either an uphill or downhill approach. Careful club selection is, therefore, of the essence. However, you don't have to play here a hundred times to draw up a game strategy, as despite the contours the course has nothing to hide. The greens are well guarded and rather well designed, there are a few very dangerous trees to negotiate and water hazards are also a part of the scene, especially on the back 9, although they are seldom really dangerous. A pretty course in a calm, isolated setting, playable by all. This is hardly the course of the century but it is always a pleasure coming back to play here...

Asserbo Golf Club — 1946

Bødkergaardsvej
DK - 3300 FREDERIKSVÆRK

Office	Sekretariat	(45) 47 72 14 90	
Pro shop	Pro-shop	(45) 47 72 12 84	
Fax	Fax	(45) 47 72 14 26	
Web	www.agc.dk		
Situation	Sted	Hillerød, 20 km	
Annual closure	Årlig lukkeperiode		no
Weekly closure	Ugentlig lukketid		no

Fees main season Priser i højsæson	18 holes	
	Week days Hverdage	**We/Bank holidays** Helligdage
Individual Individuelt	DKr 300	DKr 350
Couple Par	DKr 600	DKr 700

Junior: – 50%

Caddy	Caddie	no
Electric Trolley	Bagvogn	no
Buggy	Golf car	DKr 150 /18 holes
Clubs	Koller	DKr 150 /18 holes

Credit cards Kreditkord VISA - Eurocard - DC

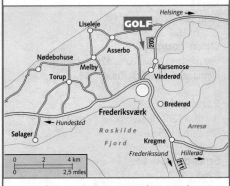

Access Adgang : København E4 → Helsingør. 50 km, 19 → Hillerød, 16 → Frederiksværk. → Liseleje. 1 km → Golf **Map 1 on page 123** Kort 1 på side 123

Golf course BAN — 15/20

Site	Sted	
Maintenance	Vedligeholdelse	
Architect	Arkitekt	James Ross Peter Samuelsen
Type	Type	parkland, hilly
Relief	Lettelse	
Water in play	Vand i spil	
Exp. to wind	Udsat for vind	
Trees in play	Træer i spil	

Scorecard Scorekort	**Chp.** Back tee	**Mens** Herre tee	**Ladies** Dame tee
Length Længde	5861	5861	4915
Par	72	72	72
Slope system	—	—	—

Advised golfing ability Anbefalet golfkunnen — 0 12 24 36

Hcp required Maks. handicap 30

Club house & amenities KLUBHUSET OG FACILITETER — 7/10

Pro shop	Pro-shop	
Driving range	Driving range	
Sheltered	Ly	no
On grass	På græs	12 mats open air
Putting-green	Putting-green	yes
Pitching-green	Indspilsgreen	yes

Hotel facilities HOTEL FACILITETERNE — 6/10

HOTELS HOTELLER

Sankt Helene Centret — Tisvildeleje 5 km
12 rooms, D DKr 660
Tel (45) 48 70 98 50, Fax (45) 48 70 98 97

Hotel Hillerød — Hillerød 20 km
32 rooms, D DKr 480
Tel (45) 48 24 08 00, Fax (45) 48 24 08 74

RESTAURANTS RESTAURANTER

Le Provençal — Hornbæk 40 km
Tel (45) 49 76 11 77

Søstjernen — Raageleje 20 km
Tel (45) 48 71 53 27

ESBJERG

15 | 6 | 5

Vestjyllands marsk, sandklitter og strande langs Vesterhavet er ikke Danmarks golfmekka. Synd, for de baner, området byder på, er temmelig gode. Som nu for eksempel Esbjergs fine gamle mesterskabsbane, der som den altid er det, især når det blæser – ved DM i 1999 var en skrap test for de bedste spillere. Her bliver ikke lavet stribevis af 5 under par-runder! Banen er uden egentlige vand-hazarder, og der er heller ikke mange træer. Dens hovedforhindringer er en række meget velplacerede bunkers, især på de sidste ni huller, og så den altid tilstedeværende vind. Læg dertil, at hullerne er meget flade, og man kunne få det indtryk, at de er meget ens. Javist, men mere naturlig bane i så barske omgivelser skal man lede længe efter, i hvert fald i Danmark. Den er indbegrebet af underspillet charme, og man føler sig virkelig i pagt med naturen på runden. Ni relativt nye huller er med til at gøre et besøg mere varieret.

The west coast of Jutland is not the most popular area of Denmark for tourists, but it certainly has its share of romance with infinite stretches of moor-land which seem to merge with the sand dunes alongside the North Sea. The first good reason for coming here is the pretty medieval town of Ribe, a major trading centre and port from the Viking era. Another reason is this golf course, the only real seaside course in a country where you are never far from the sea. Strangely enough, there are no water hazards on this pretty layout. There are not many trees, either, and the main difficulties lie with some excellent bunkering, particularly in the fairways on the back 9, and the ever present wind. Should we add that the holes are very flat, you might get the impression that they are all much the same. In actual fact, what is a very natural course in a rather rough setting is a picture of subtlety and charm, helped by the impression of isolation you get when playing here. An extra 9 holes enhance these qualities still further.

Esbjerg Golfklub — 1964

Sønderhedevej 11
DK - 6710 ESBJERG V

Office	Sekretariat	(45) 75 26 92 19
Pro shop	Pro-shop	(45) 75 26 92 72
Fax	Fax	(45) 75 26 94 19
Web	info	
Situation	Sted	Esbjerg, 15 km
Annual closure	Årlig lukkeperiodee	no
Weekly closure	Ugentlig lukketid	no

Fees main season / Priser i højsæson	Week days / Hverdage	We/Bank holidays / Helligdage
	Full day	
Individual Individuelt	DKr 200	DKr 200
Couple Par	DKr 400	DKr 400

Junior: – 50%

Caddy	Caddie	no
Electric Trolley	Bagvogn	DKr 15 /18 holes
Buggy	Golf car	DKr 200 /18 holes
Clubs	Koller	DKr 150 /18 holes

Credit cards Kreditkord VISA - Eurocard - DC

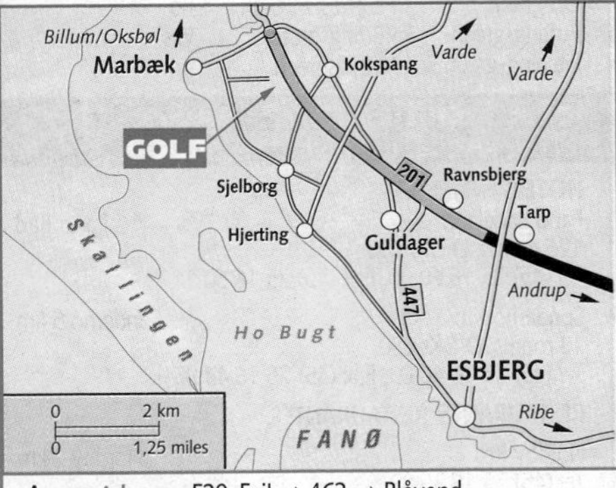

Access Adgang : E20, Exit → 463 → Blåvand. → Marbæk/Golf
Map 1 on page 122 Kort 1 på side 122

Golf course — BAN — 15/20

Site	Sted	
Maintenance	Vedligeholdelse	
Architect	Arkitekt	Frederik Dreyer
Type	Type	seaside course
Relief	Lettelse	
Water in play	Vand i spil	
Exp. to wind	Udsat for vind	
Trees in play	Træer i spil	

Scorecard / Scorekort	Chp. / Back tee	Mens / Herre tee	Ladies / Dame tee
Length Længde	5728	5728	4977
Par	71	71	71
Slope system	—	—	—

Advised golfing ability / Anbefalet golfkunnen: 0 12 24 36
Hcp required / Maks. handicap: 36

Club house & amenities — KLUBHUSET OG FACILITETER — 6/10

Pro shop	Pro-shop	
Driving range	Driving range	
Sheltered	Ly	5 mats
On grass	På græs	yes (04 → 10)
Putting-green	Putting-green	yes
Pitching-green	Indspilsgreen	yes

Hotel facilities — HOTEL FACILITETERNE — 5/10

HOTELS HOTELLER

Britannia — Esbjerg 15 km
85 rooms, D DKr 700
Tel (45) 75 13 01 11, Fax (45) 75 45 20 85

Hjerting, 55 rooms, D DKr 750 — Esbjerg 15 km
Tel (45) 75 11 52 44

RESTAURANTS RESTAURANTER

Pakhuset, Tel (45) 75 12 74 55 — Esbjerg 15 km

Henne Kirkeby Kro, Tel (45) 75 25 54 00 — Henne 30 km

Schackenborg Slotskro — Møgeltønder 70 km
Tel (45) 74 83 83 83

FANØ

15 | 4 | 7

Ti minutter med færgen fra Esbjerg – og man er i helt andre omgivelser på Fanø. Et kig indenfor i banens "kontor" med efterfølgende spil på banen, og man kunne tilføje: I en helt anden tidsalder. Fanø er Danmarks ældste bane, fra før verden gik af lave. Den åbnede i 1901, og tre af hullerne samt én green, den 16., fra det originale hulforløb eksisterer den dag i dag. Hullerne løber ikke helt ud til vandet, men der er ikke desto mindre tale om Danmarks eneste links-bane udlagt blandt de for links-baner karakteristiske sandklitter. Disse er banens fornemste forhindringer. Dels fordi de ikke er rare at stifte bekendtskab med for éns bold, dels fordi de resulterer i mange mere eller mindre blinde slag, både fra tee og ind til green. Det kræver adskillige runder at finde ud af, hvordan banens spidsfindigheder skal tackles. I banens jubilæumsår har man bygget et regulært klubhus, og banen er blevet forlænget. Den har fået to nye par 5-huller og færre par 3-huller, så par nu er 70.

This course, located on the island of Fanø, is just opposite the town of Esbjerg, which is also well worth a visit via a 10-minute boat-trip. The crossing only adds to the change of surroundings. Only a few houses here and there are able to counter the sensation of travelling through time on a course opened in 1901 and doubtless designed by a Brit, judging by the style (the green on hole N° 16 is most original). Although not exactly by the sea, this is a real links course where the dunes, and of course the wind, are the main obstacles. The tall rough is omnipresent but the dunes carefully conceal a number of greens and fairways, resulting in a number of blind shots and blind greens. You will need several rounds to size up the layout and understand its more subtle features. For the golf's centenary year, a club house has been built, and the course lengthened. It now has two new par 5s and fewer par 3s. The overall par is now of 70.

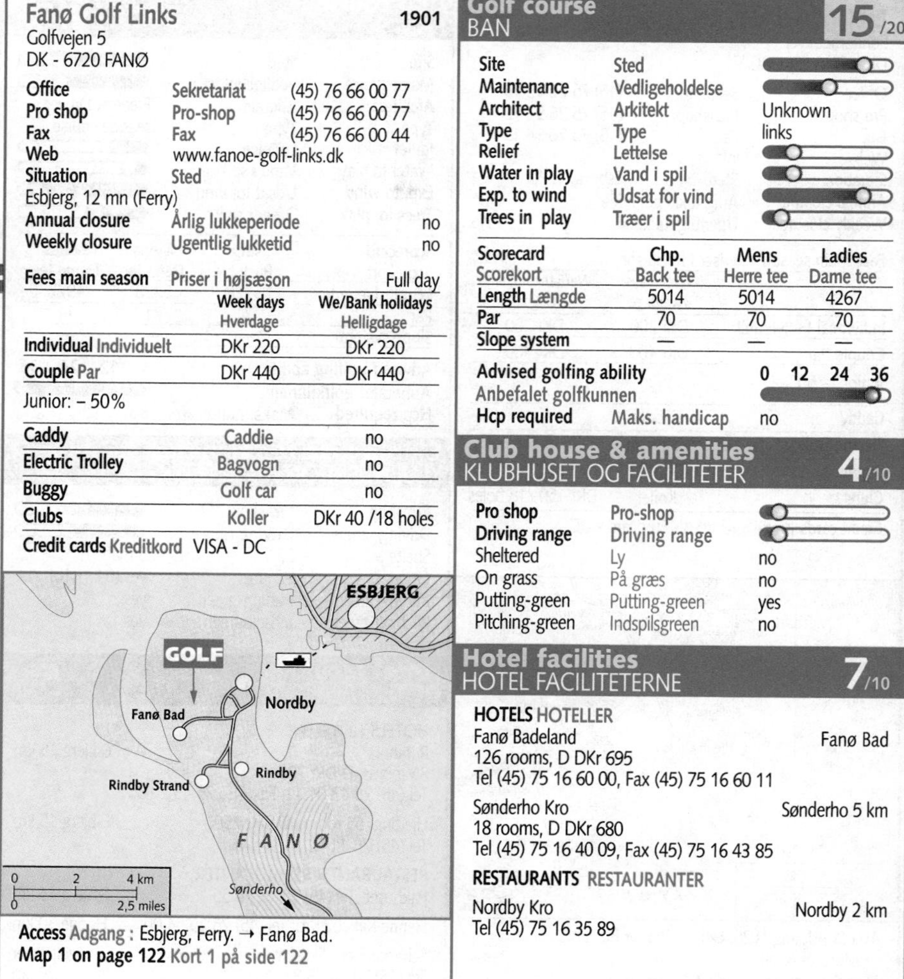

Fanø Golf Links — 1901

Golfvejen 5
DK - 6720 FANØ

Office	Sekretariat	(45) 76 66 00 77
Pro shop	Pro-shop	(45) 76 66 00 77
Fax	Fax	(45) 76 66 00 44
Web	www.fanoe-golf-links.dk	
Situation	Sted	

Esbjerg, 12 mn (Ferry)

Annual closure	Årlig lukkeperiode	no
Weekly closure	Ugentlig lukketid	no

Fees main season Priser i højsæson	Full day	
	Week days Hverdage	**We/Bank holidays** Helligdage
Individual Individuelt	DKr 220	DKr 220
Couple Par	DKr 440	DKr 440

Junior: – 50%

Caddy	Caddie	no
Electric Trolley	Bagvogn	no
Buggy	Golf car	no
Clubs	Koller	DKr 40 /18 holes

Credit cards Kreditkord VISA - DC

Access Adgang : Esbjerg, Ferry. → Fanø Bad.
Map 1 on page 122 Kort 1 på side 122

Golf course BAN — 15/20

Site	Sted	
Maintenance	Vedligeholdelse	
Architect	Arkitekt	Unknown
Type	Type	links
Relief	Lettelse	
Water in play	Vand i spil	
Exp. to wind	Udsat for vind	
Trees in play	Træer i spil	

Scorecard Scorekort	**Chp.** Back tee	**Mens** Herre tee	**Ladies** Dame tee
Length Længde	5014	5014	4267
Par	70	70	70
Slope system	—	—	—

Advised golfing ability Anbefalet golfkunnen — 0 12 24 36

Hcp required Maks. handicap — no

Club house & amenities KLUBHUSET OG FACILITETER — 4/10

Pro shop	Pro-shop	
Driving range	Driving range	
Sheltered	Ly	no
On grass	På græs	no
Putting-green	Putting-green	yes
Pitching-green	Indspilsgreen	no

Hotel facilities HOTEL FACILITETERNE — 7/10

HOTELS HOTELLER

Fanø Badeland — Fanø Bad
126 rooms, D DKr 695
Tel (45) 75 16 60 00, Fax (45) 75 16 60 11

Sønderho Kro — Sønderho 5 km
18 rooms, D DKr 680
Tel (45) 75 16 40 09, Fax (45) 75 16 43 85

RESTAURANTS RESTAURANTER

Nordby Kro — Nordby 2 km
Tel (45) 75 16 35 89

HIMMERLAND New Course 16 | 8 | 6

Den gamle vikingebegravelsesplads Lindholm samt Rold Skov, Danmarks største, er blandt seværdighederne i nærheden af Himmerland. Selv på dette 36-hullers anlæg er der andet at tage sig til end at spille golf, stå på vandski på Gatten sø, fx. Banerne kaldes Old Course og New Course. Den sidste er tegnet Jan Sederholm, og det bærer greens som altid præg af: De er udlagt, så greenkeeperen har mulighed for meget forskellige flagplaceringer. Området er relativt fladt og åbent. Vand-hazarder her og der giver nærmest indtryk af amerikansk parkbane, og det samme gør de i visse tilfælde meget store fairwaybunkers. 18. hul er en glimrende afslutning – lige op til klubhuset, hvor man kan sidde og følge dristige spilleres forsøg på at skære hjørnet af den sø, der æder sig ind i fairway på det kun godt 300 m lange hul. New Course er en krævende bane, også fordi den er temmelig lang, og det skyldes blandt andet et af golfverdenens meget sjældne par 6-huller – i dette tilfalede det 10., som er hele 610 m. Bedre egnet til spillere på alle niveauer er den 700 m kortere Old Course, og Himmerland byder også på en par 3-bane.

Travelling from one side of Denmark to the other never involves any more than a few hours of driving, but the eastern region of Jutland is more protected from oceanic influences than the west coast and the landscapes are more lush with alternating meadows and forests. After a visit to Ålborg, Europe's cleanest city, don't miss Lindholm Høje, an age-old Viking cemetery kept in perfect condition. The same goes for Rold Skov, the country's largest forest, before reaching Himmerland. This 36-hole resort comprises the New Course, designed by Jan Sederholm, whose greens most connoisseurs would recognize, always laid out in the true spirit of the game. In relatively flat and clear open space, the scattering of a few hazards gives a slightly American flavour, and the same goes for the fairway bunkers, some of which are very large. Well designed and demanding, this layout is probably difficult for inexperienced players, but they will find a welcome on the other course here (very pleasant golfing). A curiosity is the par-6 10th hole... reachable in 3 by the longer hitters.

Himmerland Golf Klub — 1993

Centervej 1 - Gatten
DK - 9640 FARSØ

Office	Sekretariat	(45) 96 49 61 00
Pro shop	Pro-shop	(45) 96 49 61 09
Fax	Fax	(45) 98 66 14 56
Web	www.himmerlandgolf.dk	
Situation	Sted	
Aalborg, 50 km		
Annual closure	Årlig lukkeperiode	no
Weekly closure	Ugentlig lukketid	no

Fees main season Priser i højsæson		Full day
	Week days Hverdage	We/Bank holidays Helligdage
Individual Individuelt	DKr 230	DKr 320
Couple Par	DKr 460	DKr 640

Junior: – 50%

Caddy	Caddie	no
Electric Trolley	Bagvogn	no
Buggy	Golf car	DKr 320 /18 holes
Clubs	Koller	DKr 100 /18 holes

Credit cards Kreditkord VISA - Eurocard - DC

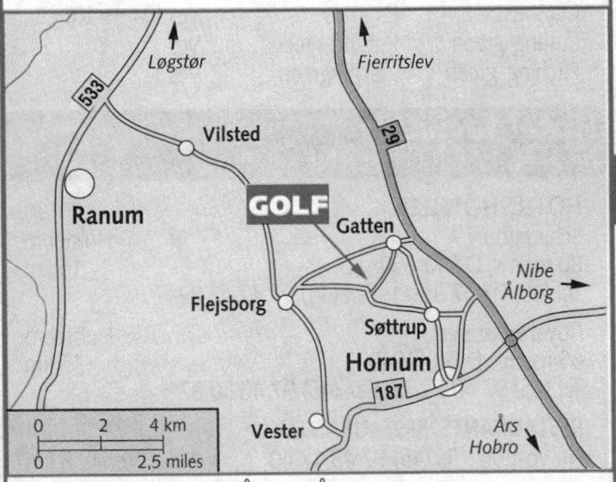

Access Adgang : E 45 Århus - Ålborg.
Exit (Frakørsel) 33, 535 → Aars. 29 → Løgstør.
Map 1 on page 122 Kort 1 på side 122

Golf course BAN — 16/20

Site	Sted	
Maintenance	Vedligeholdelse	
Architect	Arkitekt	Jan Sederholm
Type	Type	open country
Relief	Lettelse	
Water in play	Vand i spil	
Exp. to wind	Udsat for vind	
Trees in play	Træer i spil	

Scorecard Scorekort	Chp. Back tee	Mens Herre tee	Ladies Dame tee
Length Længde	6102	6102	5347
Par	73	73	73
Slope system	—	—	—

Advised golfing ability Anbefalet golfkunnen: 0 12 24 36
Hcp required Maks. handicap 36

Club house & amenities KLUBHUSET OG FACILITETER — 8/10

Pro shop	Pro-shop	
Driving range	Driving range	
Sheltered	Ly	no
On grass	På græs	yes
Putting-green	Putting-green	yes
Pitching-green	Indspilsgreen	yes

Hotel facilities HOTEL FACILITETERNE — 6/10

HOTELS HOTELLER
Golfagergård Motel — Gatten 1
24 rooms, D DKr 250
Tel (45) 98 66 30 98Himmerland Golf Hotel — Farsø 2 km
48 rooms, D DKr 610
Tel (45) 96 49 61 00, Fax (45) 98 66 14 66

RESTAURANTS RESTAURANTER
Himmerland Golf Hotel — Farsø 2 km
Tel (45) 96 49 61 00

129

HOLSTEBRO

16 | 6 | 5

Denne bane er næsten altid at finde på danske golferes top 3. Den ligger i et tidligere plantageområde og må om nogen betegnes som en skovbane. Fairways er forholdsvis brede, men kommer du først uden for fairway, kan der være problemer med overhovedet at finde den igen. Det er ingen overdrivelse, men forholdet mellem brede fairways og straffende skov er helt rigtigt, og det forklarer, hvorfor banen kun har ganske få bunkers. Træerne – mellem hvilke man går i storladen isolation – er sammen med en række vandhazarder alt rigeligt til at holde selv den bedste spiller i ørerne. Men Holstebro er også en åben og ærlig bane. Spilleplanen for hvert hul er klar. Kun på dogleg-huller kan man ikke se green fra teestedet. Greens er veldesignede uden de store ondulationer. Banen ER svær – men så byder Holstebros anlæg også på en ni-hullers bane for de lidt mindre skrappe.

This course is regularly ranked amongst the country's top three, even by those people who have never played here. That's what reputation can do for you. It is located in a former plantation, which explains the very many trees. The fairways are wide, but if you spray the ball left or right you might end up not actually knowing how to get back onto the "short stuff". That's no exaggeration. It all gives a marvellous sensation of isolation and explains why there are few green-side bunkers and just a single fairway bunker; the trees and water hazards are enough to keep most players on their toes. With this said, Holstebro is a very forthright course: game strategy is immediately clear, there are no blind greens (except on the dog-legs) and greens are well designed without any excessively steep slopes. Spectacular for its forest setting, very pleasant for its peace and quiet but a little tough for high-handicappers, Holstebro is worth a visit. What's more, there is another shortish 9 hole course, which is perfect for all the family.

Holstebro Golfklub — 1970

Brandsbjergvej 4
DK - 7570 VEMB

Office	Sekretariat	(45) 97 48 51 55
Pro shop	Pro-shop	(45) 97 48 52 93
Fax	Fax	(45) 97 48 51 11
Web	—	
Situation	Sted	Århus, 100 km Holstebro, 15 km
Annual closure	Årlig lukkeperiode	no
Weekly closure	Ugentlig lukketid	no

Fees main season Priser i højsæson	Week days Hverdage	We/Bank holidays Helligdage
		Full day
Individual Individuelt	DKr 200	DKr 220
Couple Par	DKr 400	DKr 440
Junior : – 50%		

Caddy	Caddie	no
Electric Trolley	Bagvogn	no
Buggy	Golf car	DKr 180 /18 holes
Clubs	Koller	DKr 100 /18 holes

Credit cards Kreditkord VISA - Eurocard - DC

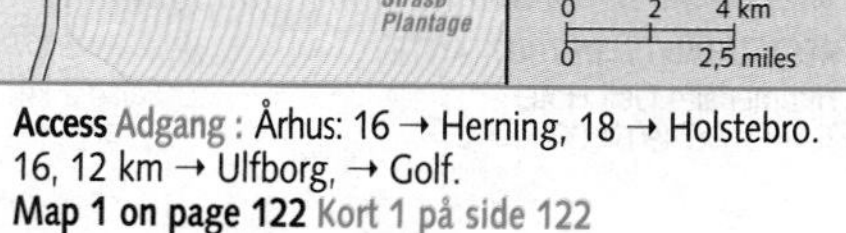

Access Adgang : Århus: 16 → Herning, 18 → Holstebro. 16, 12 km → Ulfborg, → Golf.
Map 1 on page 122 Kort 1 på side 122

Golf course BAN — 16/20

Site	Sted	
Maintenance	Vedligeholdelse	
Architect	Arkitekt	Erik Schnack
Type	Type	forest, parkland
Relief	Lettelse	
Water in play	Vand i spil	
Exp. to wind	Udsat for vind	
Trees in play	Træer i spil	

Scorecard Scorekort	Chp. Back tee	Mens Herre tee	Ladies Dame tee
Length Længde	5853	5853	4705
Par	72	72	72
Slope system	—	—	—

Advised golfing ability Anbefalet golfkunnen — 0 12 24 36

Hcp required Maks. handicap — no

Club house & amenities KLUBHUSET OG FACILITETER — 6/10

Pro shop	Pro-shop	
Driving range	Driving range	
Sheltered	Ly	no
On grass	På græs	yes (04 → 10)
Putting-green	Putting-green	yes
Pitching-green	Indspilsgreen	yes

Hotel facilities HOTEL FACILITETERNE — 5/10

HOTELS HOTELLER

Schaumburg — Holstebro 15 km
80 rooms, D DKr 650
Tel (45) 97 42 31 11, Fax (45) 97 42 72 82

Royal Holstebro — Holstebro 15 km
65 rooms, D DKr 1040
Tel (45) 97 40 23 33, Fax (45) 97 40 30 87

RESTAURANTS RESTAURANTER

Nr. Vosborg, Tel (45) 97 48 17 40 — Vemb, 8 km

Teaterrestauranten — Herning 40 km
Tel (45) 97 12 20 77

Sevel Kro, Tel (45) 97 44 80 11 — Sevel, 20 km

KØBENHAVN Eremitagen

16	7	7

Det er ikke kun vindens susen, man mærker på de åbne vidder, når man spiller Københavns Golf Klubs bane kun 20 km nord for Københavns centrum. Også historiens vingesus presser sig på: Klubben er Skandinaviens ældste, fra 1899, der har været spillet golf i området siden 1901, og den nuværende bane er fra 1928. Dansk golfs grand old man, Frederik Dreyer, har siden bidraget til flere af hullernes nuværende udformning. Banens oprindelige arkitekt kendes ikke. Dreyer har prøvet at finde ham, men det er (endnu) ikke lykkes. Førnævnte vind kan sammen med sensommerens meget høje rough gøre banen til en ordentlig mundfuld. Men man går også på en bane af stor skønhed. Man kan ikke undgå at se nogle af de flere tusind rådyr, der går frit i området. Det flere kilometer lange skovparti, som løber i højre side af fem, seks huller og afgrænser banen mod nord, er uendelig smukt, især om efteråret. Og i tilgift kommer man på 16. hul helt tæt på et ægte barokslot, Eremitage-slottet, som har givet banen dens daglige tilnavn, "Eremitagen".

While you are playing at Københavns Golf Klubs, 20 kilometers north of the Danish capital, you will instantly notice two things: 1. The sizzling wind that playfully runs through the landscape. 2. The great impact that the history has on this place: the golf club, founded in 1899, is the oldest in Scandinavia, and the first balls were hit two years later. The existing course of today is from 1928. Mr Golf in Denmark, Frederik Dreyer, has thereafter contributed with a few new layout solutions. The original architect is unknown, despite some intensive research. The wind in combination with the thick rough makes the course a rather difficult test. But don't bother, the great beauty of the landscape will soon make you forget a lost ball or two. You will also notice the roe deers, there are thousands of them. Six of the holes runs through a deep forrest, but the most memorable hole is the 16th, close to an old barock castle, Eremitage-slottet, that also has given the course it's kickname, "Eremitagen".

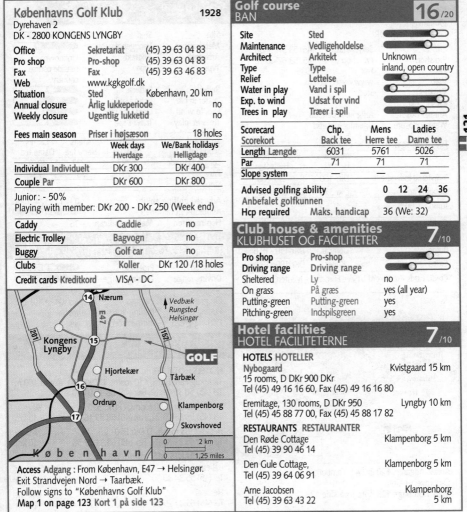

Københavns Golf Klub — 1928

Dyrehaven 2
DK - 2800 KONGENS LYNGBY

Office	Sekretariat	(45) 39 63 04 83
Pro shop	Pro-shop	(45) 39 63 04 83
Fax	Fax	(45) 39 63 46 83
Web	www.kgkgolf.dk	
Situation	Sted	København, 20 km
Annual closure	Årlig lukkeperiode	no
Weekly closure	Ugentlig lukketid	no

Fees main season / Priser i højsæson		18 holes
	Week days / Hverdage	We/Bank holidays / Helligdage
Individual Individuelt	DKr 300	DKr 400
Couple Par	DKr 600	DKr 800

Junior : - 50%
Playing with member: DKr 200 - DKr 250 (Week end)

Caddy	Caddie	no
Electric Trolley	Bagvogn	no
Buggy	Golf car	no
Clubs	Koller	DKr 120 /18 holes
Credit cards Kreditkord	VISA - DC	

Access Adgang : From København, E47 → Helsingør.
Exit Strandvejen Nord → Taarbæk.
Follow signs to "Københavns Golf Klub"
Map 1 on page 123 Kort 1 på side 123

Golf course BAN — 16/20

Site	Sted	
Maintenance	Vedligeholdelse	
Architect	Arkitekt	Unknown
Type	Type	inland, open country
Relief	Lettelse	
Water in play	Vand i spil	
Exp. to wind	Udsat for vind	
Trees in play	Træer i spil	

Scorecard / Scorekort	Chp. / Back tee	Mens / Herre tee	Ladies / Dame tee
Length Længde	6031	5761	5026
Par	71	71	71
Slope system	—	—	—

Advised golfing ability / Anbefalet golfkunnen: 0 12 24 36
Hcp required / Maks. handicap: 36 (We: 32)

Club house & amenities KLUBHUSET OG FACILITETER — 7/10

Pro shop	Pro-shop	
Driving range	Driving range	
Sheltered	Ly	no
On grass	På græs	yes (all year)
Putting-green	Putting-green	yes
Pitching-green	Indspilsgreen	yes

Hotel facilities HOTEL FACILITETERNE — 7/10

HOTELS HOTELLER

Nybogaard — Kvistgaard 15 km
15 rooms, D DKr 900 DKr
Tel (45) 49 16 16 60, Fax (45) 49 16 16 80

Eremitage, 130 rooms, D DKr 950 — Lyngby 10 km
Tel (45) 45 88 77 00, Fax (45) 45 88 17 82

RESTAURANTS RESTAURANTER

Den Røde Cottage — Klampenborg 5 km
Tel (45) 39 90 46 14

Den Gule Cottage, — Klampenborg 5 km
Tel (45) 39 64 06 91

Arne Jacobsen — Klampenborg 5 km
Tel (45) 39 63 43 22

KORSØR

14 | 4 | 6

Denne glimrende bane har hidtil ligget langt fra såvel København som Vestdanmark, men med Storebæltsbroen er den pludselig kommet tidsmæssigt meget tættere på Fyn og Jylland. Banen er designet af medlemmerne, og det forklarer måske lidt af dens af og til særprægede layout. Som fx 7. hul, der er et zigzaggende par 5, hvor man virkelig skal tænke sig om, før man slår. Det skal man faktisk på de fleste huller, og man gør klogt i at lade driveren blive i bagen det meste af tiden. Selv om banen er relativt flad, er approach-slagene til et par greens blinde. Især 5. green kan være svær at ramme. Ellers er hullernes layout gennemgående præget af opfindsomhed, og efterhånden som runden skrider frem, bygges der op til belønning: 15. og 16. hul byder på fænomenal udsigt over vandet, som de begge løber langs med. Det er værd at lægge mærke til, at 9. hul ikke fører ind til klubhuset.

The new bridge over the Storebælt, linking the islands of Sjælland and Fyn, has made it easier to drive to this latter province, described by Andersen as the garden of Denmark, and he should know. From Korsør, it is now quick and convenient to go and visit the provincial capital of Odense, the old district of which looks like a collection of theatrical props. The Korsør course was designed by club members, which explains some of the layout's more original features such as hole N° 7, a zigzagging par 5 where you really do need to think before you shoot. In fact the same can be said for nearly all the holes. One of the best ideas here is to leave the driver in the bag and stick to long irons. A few greens are blind, despite the flattish terrain, and none more so than the contentious hole N° 5. Otherwise you'll find holes that are full of imagination, some splendid views over the arm of the sea splitting the two islands, and a number of holes at the end of the course which bring the Storebælt river into play. A point to remember is that hole N° 9 does not return to the club-house.

Korsør Golf Klub — 1964

Ørnumvej 8
DK - 4220 KORSØR

Office	Sekretariat	(45) 53 57 18 36
Pro shop	Pro-shop	(45) 53 57 40 18
Fax	Fax	3936
Web	www.korsoergolf.dk	
Situation	Sted	
Korsør, 2 km		
Annual closure	Årlig lukkeperiode	no
Weekly closure	Ugentlig lukketid	no

Fees main season Priser i højsæson		Full day
	Week days Hverdage	**We/Bank holidays** Helligdage
Individual Individuelt	DKr 160	DKr 200
Couple Par	DKr 320	DKr 400

Junior: – 50%

Caddy	Caddie	no
Electric Trolley	Bagvogn	DKr 25 /18 holes
Buggy	Golf car	DKr 150 /18 holes
Clubs	Koller	DKr 100 /18 holes

Credit cards Kreditkord VISA - Eurocard - MasterCard

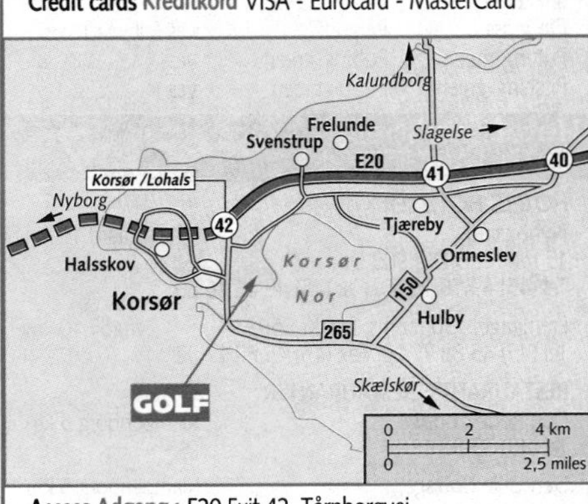

Access Adgang : E20 Exit 42. Tårnborgvej, Ørnumvej → Golf.
Map 1 on page 123 Kort 1 på side 123

Golf course — BAN — 14/20

Site	Sted	
Maintenance	Vedligeholdelse	
Architect	Arkitekt	Unknown
Type	Type	seaside course, country
Relief	Lettelse	
Water in play	Vand i spil	
Exp. to wind	Udsat for vind	
Trees in play	Træer i spil	

Scorecard Scorekort	**Chp.** Back tee	**Mens** Herre tee	**Ladies** Dame tee
Length Længde	5773	5773	4969
Par	73	73	73
Slope system	—	—	—

Advised golfing ability Anbefalet golfkunnen — 0 12 24 36

Hcp required Maks. handicap — 36

Club house & amenities — KLUBHUSET OG FACILITETER — 4/10

Pro shop	Pro-shop	
Driving range	Driving range	
Sheltered	Ly	no
On grass	På græs	yes (04 → 10)
Putting-green	Putting-green	yes
Pitching-green	Indspilsgreen	yes

Hotel facilities — HOTEL FACILITETERNE — 6/10

HOTELS HOTELLER

Tårnborg Park Hotel, 110 rooms, D DKr 650 — Korsør 100 m
Tel (45) 58 35 01 10, Fax (45) 58 35 01 20

Hotel Frederik II, 50 rooms, D DKr 520 — Slagelse 15 km
Tel (45) 58 53 03 22, Fax (45) 58 53 16 22

Hesselet, 85 rooms, D DKr 850 — Nyborg 10 km
Tel (45) 65 31 30 29, Fax (45) 65 31 29 58

RESTAURANTS RESTAURANTER

Babette — Vordingborg 45 km
Tel (45) 55 34 30 30

Hesselet — Nyborg 10 km
Tel (45) 65 31 29 58

LÆSØ SEASIDE

15 | 7 | 5

Med 90 minutters sejltur fra Frederikshavn eller en lille times taxi-flyning fra Roskilde er saltsydningens, krebsenes og biernes ø Læsø ikke et sted, man sådan lige lægger vejen forbi. Men er du allerede i Nordjylland for at spille golf, bør du gøre turen ud til øens naturskønne, varierede og svære bane. Svær, fordi man på kun ét af dens 15 lange huller hiver driveren op af bagen uden at betænke sig. På de resterende 14 er landingsområderne enten meget smalle, eller også er hullet dogleg, så der kræves den helt rigtige længde på slaget, for at bolden kommer til at ligge rigtigt. Slår man skævt, straffes man hårdt af træer med dertil hørende tyk underskov. Eller af høj rough som den, der på det prægtige par 5 afslutningshul klemmer fairway til maks. 25 meter. Vand-hazarder, der ikke alle er lige tydelige, gør ikke banen nemmere. Til gengæld er der ikke mange bunkers – men det havde næsten også været for meget. Læsø er banen for folk, der har mange slag i bagen, og har du ikke det, første gang du besøger banen, så glem din score, og nyd i stedet, hvor naturligt det kan lade sig gøre at udlægge en golbane.

With a 90 minute ferry trip leaving from Frederikshavn, you don't come here without a purpose. You can also hit your wayward shots without too many people watching in a tranquil setting made to feel even more isolated by the thick trees and rough. By contrast, you won't have much opportunity to use the driver, either because the fairways are narrow or because the turn of the dog-legs are too close, or because the water hazards lurk dangerously close to the most adventurous way forward. Fortunately, there are few bunkers, which would only have compounded the issue. In fact, this is a course designed for seasoned golfers who can quickly adjust their game The first time out, you might be put off by the demands of the course; in this case, forget your handicap and focus on discovering the course. You will understand and appreciate the course better the next time out. This layout was designed in two phases, something you notice only because the nine "old" greens are good while the nine newer ones still need a little more time. Over an area naturally suited to golf, the architect didn't have to move much earth, and this is noticeable in the already "mature" feel to the whole complex.

Læsø Seaside Golfklub — 1995

Prof. Johansens Vej 2
DK - 9940 Læsø

Office	Sekretariat	(45) 98 49 84 00
Pro shop	Pro-shop	(45) 98 49 84 00
Fax	Fax	(45) 98 49 84 02
Web	www.laesoe-golfklub.dk	
Situation	Sted	

Frederikshavn, 90 min. (Ferry)

Annual closure	Årlig lukkeperiode	no
Weekly closure	Ugentlig lukketid	no

Fees main ·season Priser i højsæson	Full day	
	Week days Hverdage	**We/Bank holidays** Helligdage
Individual Individuelt	DKr 200	DKr 200
Couple Par	DKr 400	DKr 400

Junior: - 50%

Caddy	Caddie	no
Electric Trolley	Bagvogn	yes
Buggy	Golf car	yes
Clubs	Koller	DKr 100 /18 holes

Credit cards Kreditkort
VISA - Mastercard - Eurocard

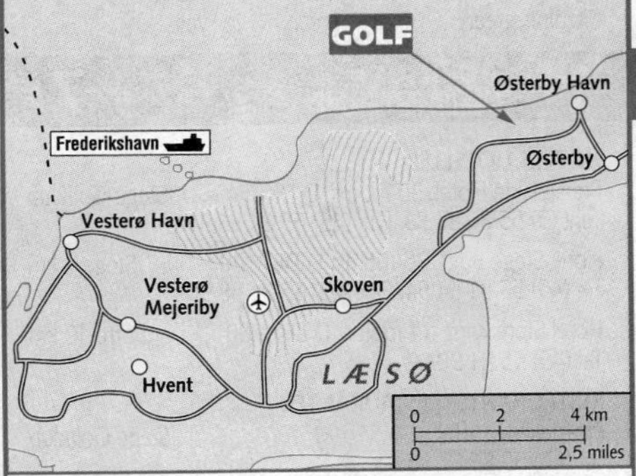

Access Adgang : Frederikshavn, 90 min. Ferry.
Vesterø → Østerby
Map 1 on page 122 Kort 1 på side 122

Golf course BAN — 15/20

Site	Sted	
Maintenance	Vedligeholdelse	
Architect	Arkitekt	Lars Andreasson Henrik Jacobsen
Type	Type	seaside course, forest
Relief	Lettelse	
Water in play	Vand i spil	
Exp. to wind	Udsat for vind	
Trees in play	Træer i spil	

Scorecard Scorekort	**Chp.** Back tee	**Mens** Herre tee	**Ladies** Dame tee
Length Længde	6068	6068	5250
Par	74	74	74
Slope system	138	129	118

Advised golfing ability Anbefalet golfkunnen — 0 12 24 36

Club house & amenities KLUBHUSET OG FACILITETER — 7/10

Pro shop	Pro-shop	
Driving range	Driving range	
Sheltered	Ly	—
On grass	På græs	no, 8 mats open air
Putting-green	Putting-green	yes
Pitching-green	Indspilsgreen	no

Hotel facilities HOTEL FACILITETERNE — 5/10

HOTELS HOTELLER

Læsø Seaside Hotel — Læsø 1 km
16 rooms, D DKr 700
Tel (45) 48 99 88 90, Fax (45) 98 49 88 00

Hotel Nygaard — Østerby 5 km
18 rooms, D DKr 510
Tel (45) 98 49 16 66, Fax (45) 98 49 88 00

RESTAURANTS RESTAURANTER

Hotel Nygaard — Østerby 5 km
Tel (45) 98 49 16 66

Delikaten — Vesterø 10 km
Tel (45) 98 49 99 01

MØN

15 | 7 | 7

Begynd gerne en udflugt til golfbanen på Møn med at køre for langt. Fortsætter du forbi banen, der ligger umiddelbart øst for Stege, ender du nemlig helt ude på øens østkyst, og her er det et helt fantastisk syn at opleve morgensolens stråler ramme de majestætiske hvide klinter. En anden af øens attraktioner er de fine middelalderlige kalkmalerier, der kan ses i flere kirker ikke langt fra banen. Den forholdsvis nye bane, der i hesteskoform strækker sig rundt om inderste del af Stege Nor, er i glimrende stand, og man lægger straks mærke til de fine fairways. Det begynder blødt med forholdsvis åbne huller, men strammer til på de sidste ni, hvor vand-hazarder og især rough straffer den, der slår skævt. 14. hul, et langt par 4, er strålende i al sin enkelhed: Lidt op ad bakke zigzagger fairwayen sig mellem den bølgende rough op til greenen, hvor en enkel bunker står vagt. Alt i alt en ærlig og ikke alt for kuperet bane, hvor golfere på alle niveauer kan være med. Som på Korsør leder 9. hul ikke ind til det i øvrigt perfekt placerede klubhus, fra hvis terrasse man har udsigt ned over Stege Nor.

Møn is hardly the best known of the many islands in Denmark, and as a result has retained unspoiled many of its natural treasures, including the huge white beaches, dunes, forests and amazing white chalk cliffs. The Møn golf course is two kilometres from the little town of Stege, surrounded by ramparts. Art-loving golfers will not want to miss visiting the three churches here, decorated with Middle Age frescos. On the course, these same golfers will want to know how to sometimes bend the ball when they stray off the excellent fairways on holes lined with trees, although there are enough more open holes to make up for poor accuracy. Caution is required however, as the tall rough is a very dangerous proposition on about half a dozen holes (particularly the 14th) and often more so than water, which only really comes into play on 3 holes. After reconnoitring, you'll find this an honest course, relatively playable by golfers of all abilities and sufficiently steep in places to recommend a buggy for unfit golfers. If you didn't know already, not all of Denmark is flat.

Møn Golfklub — 1995

Klintevej 118
DK - 4780 STEGE

Office	Sekretariat	(45) 55 81 32 60
Pro shop	Pro-shop	(45) 55 81 39 69
Fax	Fax	(45) 55 81 32 60
Web	www.golfin.dk/mgc/index.html	
Situation	Sted	Vordingborg, 20 km
Annual closure	Årlig lukkeperiode	no
Weekly closure	Ugentlig lukketid	no

Fees main season Priser i højsæson — 18 holes

	Week days Hverdage	We/Bank holidays Helligdage
Individual Individuelt	DKr 210	DKr 260
Couple Par	DKr 420	DKr 520

Junior: – 50%

Caddy	Caddie	no
Electric Trolley	Bagvogn	no
Buggy	Golf car	DKr 250 /18 holes
Clubs	Koller	DKr 80 /18 holes

Credit cards Kreditkord
VISA - Eurocard - DC

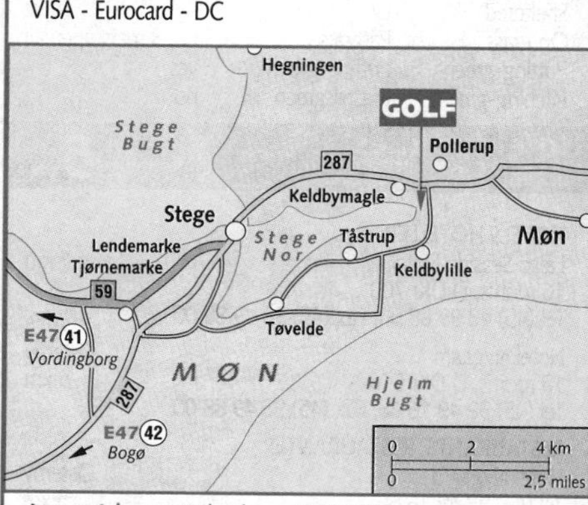

Access Adgang : København, E47/E55 → Vordingborg. → Stege.
Map 1 on page 123 Kort 1 på side 123

Golf course / BAN — 15/20

Site	Sted	
Maintenance	Vedligeholdelse	
Architect	Arkitekt	Rolf Henning-Jensen
Type	Type	country, hilly
Relief	Lettelse	
Water in play	Vand i spil	
Exp. to wind	Udsat for vind	
Trees in play	Træer i spil	

Scorecard Scorekort	Chp. Back tee	Mens Herre tee	Ladies Dame tee
Length Længde	5917	5917	4974
Par	72	72	72
Slope system	—	—	—

Advised golfing ability Anbefalet golfkunnen — 0 12 24 36
Hcp required Maks. handicap — no

Club house & amenities / KLUBHUSET OG FACILITETER — 7/10

Pro shop	Pro-shop	
Driving range	Driving range	
Sheltered	Ly	no
On grass	På græs	yes
Putting-green	Putting-green	yes
Pitching-green	Indspilsgreen	yes

Hotel facilities / HOTEL FACILITETERNE — 7/10

HOTELS HOTELLER

Præstekilde Hotel, 30 rooms, D DKr 740 — Stege Golfklub
Tel (45) 55 86 87 88, Fax (45) 55 81 36 34

Hotel Stege Bugt, 35 rooms, D DKr 620 — Stege 2 km
Tel (45) 55 81 54 54, Fax (45) 55 81 58 90

Hotel Store Klint, 14 rooms, D DKr 780 — Borre 10 km
Tel (45) 55 81 90 08

RESTAURANTS RESTAURANTER

Præstekilde Hotel — Stege Golfklub
Tel (45) 55 86 87 88

Babette, Tel (45) 55 34 30 30 — Vordingborg 20 km

Skipperkroen, Tel (45) 55 99 22 00 — Præstø 30 km

ROYAL OAK

15 | 7 | 5

Ved bredden af Jels Sø ligger Royal Oak, opkaldt efter det egetræ, hvor kongen engang gjorde holdt, og som stadig står. Træer af mere moderat størrelse er i spil flere steder på denne fine bane, der åbnede i 1992, og med bunkers og vand-hazarder spredt tilsvarende ud er problemerne ligeligt fordelt og samtidig tydelige for enhver. Den mest imponerende vand-hazard er dog selve Jels Sø, der gør flere af hullerne på de første ni ualmindelig smukke. Trods sin ærlige karakter kan banen være svær at score på, især hvis størrelsen på de veldesignede, hurtige greens udnyttes til at stille flagene svært. Banen har sammen med Simon's ry for at være den mest velplejede i Danmark, og det gør den altid til en fornøjelse at spille.

On the shores of lake Jels, the Royal Oak takes its name from the oak tree under which the king and his son rested when on the road to Vejen. It is not, however, the only tree on this course, first opened in 1992 on an estate located in the middle of Jutland. Many others are clearly in play, giving this course the look of a fabulous park, especially beautiful for the holes along the lake. With bunkers and water hazards, difficulties are evenly spread around the course and are clearly visible to allow the golfer to immediately feel at ease. Despite the visual simplicity, you need several rounds here to collect any sort of score, which will also particularly depend on the pin positions on rather large, well designed and often very fast greens. Generally speaking, green-keeping and maintenance here are first rate, resulting as always in more enjoyable golf. Rather spectacular while retaining its naturalness, this is a quality course, which is obviously much appreciated for its peaceful location and impressive landscape.

Royal Oak Golf Club — 1992

Golfvej, Jels
DK - 6630 RØDDING

Office	Sekretariat	(45) 74 55 32 94
Pro shop	Pro-shop	(45) 74 55 32 94
Fax	Fax	(45) 74 55 32 95
Web	www.royal-oak.dk	
Situation	Sted	Vejen, 15 km
Annual closure	Årlig lukkeperiode	no
Weekly closure	Ugentlig lukketid	no

Fees main season / Priser i højsæson	Full day	
	Week days / Hverdage	We/Bank holidays / Helligdage
Individual Individuelt	DKr 300	DKr 350
Couple Par	DKr 600	DKr 700

Junior: – 50%

Caddy	Caddie	no
Electric Trolley	Bagvogn	DKr 30 /18 holes
Buggy	Golf car	DKr 250 /18 holes
Clubs	Koller	DKr 140 /18 holes

Credit cards Kreditkord
VISA - Eurocard - DC

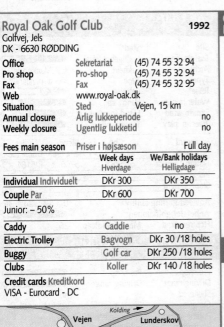

Access Adgang : E45. Exit → Kolding Syd. 403. → Jels, → Golf.
Map 1 on page 122 Kort 1 på side 122

Golf course BAN — 15/20

Site	Sted	
Maintenance	Vedligeholdelse	
Architect	Arkitekt	Malling/Gundtoft
Type	Type	parkland
Relief	Lettelse	
Water in play	Vand i spil	
Exp. to wind	Udsat for vind	
Trees in play	Træer i spil	

Scorecard / Scorekort	Chp. / Back tee	Mens / Herre tee	Ladies / Dame tee
Length Længde	6374	5967	5243
Par	72	72	72
Slope system	—	—	—

Advised golfing ability / Anbefalet golfkunnen: 0 12 24 36
Hcp required / Maks. handicap: 30

Club house & amenities KLUBHUSET OG FACILITETER — 7/10

Pro shop	Pro-shop	
Driving range	Driving range	
Sheltered	Ly	no
On grass	På græs	yes (04 → 10)
Putting-green	Putting-green	yes
Pitching-green	Indspilsgreen	yes

Hotel facilities HOTEL FACILITETERNE — 5/10

HOTELS HOTELLER

Skibelund Krat, 45 rooms, D DKr 670 — Vejen 15 km
Tel (45) 75 36 07 21, Fax (45) 75 36 62 70

SAS Radisson Koldingford — Kolding 45 km
140 rooms, D DKr 850
Tel (45) 75 51 00 00, Fax (45) 75 51 00 51

Danhotel, 80 rooms, D DKr 700 — Rødding 10 km
Tel (45) 74 55 28 69, Fax (45) 74 55 31 07

RESTAURANTS RESTAURANTER

Schackenborg Slotskro — Møgeltønder 60 km
Tel (45) 74 83 83 83

Holdbi Kro — Kruså 60 km
Tel (45) 74 67 30 00

RUNGSTED

17 | 7 | 7

En meget berømt bane – ikke kun fordi den er fra 1936 og således en af landets ældste, men fordi dens originale layout skyldes C.A. MacKenzie, bror til ingen ringere end Augusta-skaberen Alister MacKenzie. I det nordsjællandske Strandvejsområde, der domineres af marinaer og millionvillaer – og ikke langt fra Karen Blixens fødested, Rungstedlund, der i dag fungerer som Blixen-museum – ligger en af Danmarks bedste baner. Den er udlagt blandt masser af store træer, der taler deres tydelige sprog om banens alder. Få, men velplacerede bunkers og ikke mindst et vandløb, der krydser ikke færre end syv huller, sørger for, at den ikke specielt lange bane alligevel er svær at score på. Banen er ikke særlig kuperet. Der står en aura af diskret afmålthed omkring banen. Alting er i balance. Og så har banen flere karakteristisk smukke og egenartede huller: Det ubrudte skovparti langs højre side af det lange 4. hul. Den grydeagtige green nede mellem træerne på det korte 6. hul. De store rododendronbuske bag 15. green. Rungsted er en bane, man husker.

This is one of Denmark's more famous courses... because it dates back to 1936 and was one of the country's first layouts, because it was designed by C.A. Mackenzie (brother of Alister, designer of Augusta) and because it is situated in a magnificent region. Starting out from the capital Copenhagen and heading north towards Sjælland, the coast road reveals some superb villas, a number of small harbours with marinas, and a view of Sweden on the other side of the Øresund straits. Rungsted is also the birthplace of the writer Karen Blixen (Out of Africa). The golf course was laid out in a huge park, only slightly scarred by a railway line, where huge trees and very well designed bunkers testify to the art of a designer in a class of his own. Water hazards are cleverly used and well in play without ever looking artificial, and greens are well-guarded without the need for massive protection. There is a sense of measure to everything about this discreet and well-balanced course, which fairly rewards good and well shaped shots.

Rungsted Golf Klub — 1936

Vester Stationsvej 16
DK - 2960 RUNGSTED KYST

Office	Sekretariat	(45) 45 86 34 44
Pro shop	Pro-shop	(45) 45 86 34 14
Fax	Fax	(45) 45 86 57 70
Web	www.rungstedgolfklub.dk	
Situation	Sted	København, 25 km
Annual closure	Årlig lukkeperiode	no
Weekly closure	Ugentlig lukketid	no

Fees main season Priser i højsæson	18 holes	
	Week days Hverdage	We/Bank holidays Helligdage
Individual Individuelt	DKr 400	DKr 450
Couple Par	DKr 800	DKr 900

Junior: – 50%

Caddy	Caddie	no
Electric Trolley	Bagvogn	no
Buggy	Golf car	no
Clubs	Koller	DKr 250 /18 holes

Credit cards Kreditkord
VISA - Eurocard - MasterCard - DC

Access Adgang : E47, Exit Hørsholm C. → Rungsted, → Golf.
Map 1 on page 123 Kort 1 på side 123

Golf course BAN — 17/20

Site	Sted	
Maintenance	Vedligeholdelse	
Architect	Arkitekt	C.A.MacKenzie
Type	Type	forest, parkland
Relief	Lettelse	
Water in play	Vand i spil	
Exp. to wind	Udsat for vind	
Trees in play	Træer i spil	

Scorecard Scorekort	Chp. Back tee	Mens Herre tee	Ladies Dame tee
Length Længde	5761	5760	5164
Par	71	71	71
Slope system	—	—	—

Advised golfing ability Anbefalet golfkunnen: 0 12 24 36
Hcp required Maks. handicap 26

Club house & amenities KLUBHUSET OG FACILITETER — 7/10

Pro shop	Pro-shop	
Driving range	Driving range	
Sheltered	Ly	no
On grass	På græs	yes (04 → 10)
Putting-green	Putting-green	yes
Pitching-green	Indspilsgreen	yes

Hotel facilities HOTEL FACILITETERNE — 7/10

HOTELS HOTELLER

Store Kro, 40 rooms, D DKr 650 — Fredensborg 10 km
Tel (45) 48 48 00 47, Fax (45) 48 48 45 61

Nybogaard, 15 rooms, D DKr 900 — Kvistgaard 5 km
Tel (45) 49 16 16 60, Fax (45) 49 16 16 80

Scanticon Borupgaard — Snekkersten
45 rooms, D DKr 780
Tel (45) 49 22 03 33, Fax (45) 49 22 03 99

RESTAURANTS RESTAURANTER

Nokken, Tel (45) 45 57 13 14 — Rungsted 5 km
Søllerød Kro, Tel (45) 45 80 25 05 — Søllerød 10 km
Taarbæk Kro, Tel (45) 39 63 00 96 — Taarbæk 15 km

SAMSØ

15 | 4 | 7

Nogle af Danmarks bedste baner synes at spille kostbare i den forstand, at de ikke er sådan lige at komme til. Det gælder Læsø Seaside, og det gælder banen på Samsø, Strisserens ø midt i Danmark. Det tager mindst en time at sejle med færge fra Jylland eller Sjælland, men tiden er godt givet ud, for Samsøbanen er måske den smukkest beliggende i Danmark. På to tredjedele af de 18 huller går man med udsigt over Kattegat. Som helhed er banen nænsomt og stort set uden planering af jord udlagt i terræn, der for det meste skråner ned mod havet. Lidt bunkers, lidt vand-hazarder, lidt træer – alt er i balance. Og som altid, når Henrik Jacobsen har designet en bane, ligger forhindringerne, hvor de skal. Helt ned til vandet kommer man på 8. hul, et par 3, der har Kattegat som uendeligt bagtæppe, og på 16. hul, der løber langs med og kun en lille meter oven for selve stranden. Eneste anke ved banen er, at den er relativt kort.

Some of the best courses in Denmark seem to enjoy playing hard-to-get, or rather hard-to-get-to, being situated on islands and involving a few hours of travel. Samsø can be reached by ferry from Kalundborg (Sjælland) or Hov (Jutland) but it really is worth the trouble and the wait. The terrain made available to Henryk Jacobsen was ideal. Laudable concern for blending the course into the landscape, a few cleverly placed bunkers and a number of water hazards have produced a great layout. The successful outcome also required a lot of good taste and insight into the game, and there are often several solutions for reaching the medium-sized but well designed greens. From the many holes that stick in the mind, the signature hole is the most memorable, the par-3 8th hole whose green is backed by the ocean. A very pleasant course for all golfing abilities, where the only criticism might be lack of yardage (except when the wind blows) and hilly contours for senior players, but the latter is simply an excuse to stop, catch your breath and admire the scenery.

Samsø Golf Club — 1992

Besser Kirkevej 24
DK - 8305 Samsø

Office	Sekretariat	(45) 86 59 22 18
Pro shop	Pro-shop	(45) 86 59 22 18
Fax	Fax	(45) 86 59 22 21
Web	www.samsoegolfklub.dk	
Situation	Sted	on Samsø Island
Annual closure	Årlig lukkeperiode	no
Weekly closure	Ugentlig lukketid	no

Fees main season / Priser i højsæson	Week days / Hverdage	We/Bank holidays / Helligdage
	Full day	
Individual Individuelt	DKr 185	DKr 220
Couple Par	DKr 370	DKr 440

Junior: – 50%

Caddy	Caddie	no
Electric Trolley	Bagvogn	no
Buggy	Golf car	DKr 150 /18 holes
Clubs	Koller	DKr 125 /18 holes

Credit cards Kreditkord
VISA - Eurocard - DC

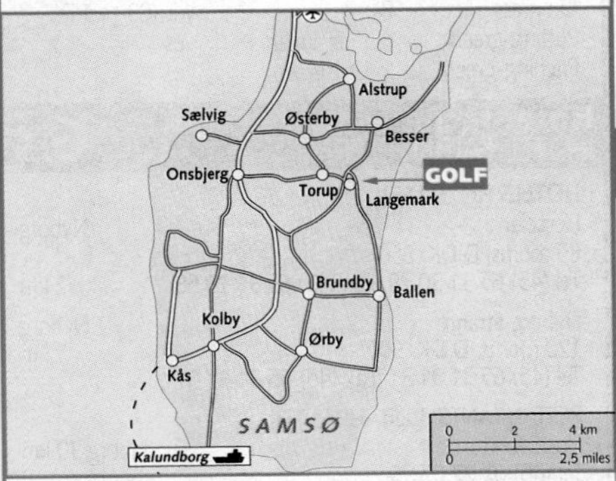

Access Adgang : Kalundborg, Ferry → Samsø → Hov (Jutland), Ferry → Sælvig
Map 1 on page 123 Kort 1 på side 123

Golf course — BAN — 15/20

Site	Sted	
Maintenance	Vedligeholdelse	
Architect	Arkitekt	Henrik Jacobsen
Type	Type	seaside course, country
Relief	Lettelse	
Water in play	Vand i spil	
Exp. to wind	Udsat for vind	
Trees in play	Træer i spil	

Scorecard / Scorekort	Chp. / Back tee	Mens / Herre tee	Ladies / Dame tee
Length Længde	5600	5600	4865
Par	72	72	72
Slope system	—	—	—

Advised golfing ability / Anbefalet golfkunnen: 0 12 24 36
Hcp required Maks. handicap: 36

Club house & amenities — KLUBHUSET OG FACILITETER — 4/10

Pro shop	Pro-shop	
Driving range	Driving range	
Sheltered	Ly	no
On grass	På græs	yes (04 → 10)
Putting-green	Putting-green	yes
Pitching-green	Indspilsgreen	yes

Hotel facilities — HOTEL FACILITETERNE — 7/10

HOTELS HOTELLER

Flinch's Hotel, 25 rooms, D DKr 475 — Tranebjerg
Tel (45) 86 59 17 22, Fax (45) 86 59 35 50 — 5 km

Ballen Badehotel, 30 rooms, D DKr 600 — Ballen
Tel (45) 86 59 17 99, Fax (45) 86 59 06 595 km

Motel Sølyst, 20 rooms, D DKr 520 — Vesterløkken 5 km
Tel (45) 86 59 16 59, Fax (45) 86 59 16 99

RESTAURANTS RESTAURANTER

Ved Kæret, Tel (45) 86 59 61 22 — Nordby 20 km
Skipperly, Tel (45) 86 59 10 18 — Ballen 5 km
Ballen Badehotel, Tel (45) 86 59 17 99 — Ballen 5 km

SCT. KNUDS

14 | 5 | 6

Måske den nemmeste bane at finde i hele Danmark, fordi man ser ned på den fra motorvejen mellem Nyborg og Storebæltsbroen. Alligevel virker støjen kun generende på et par huller. Resten af runden går man dybt inde blandt træerne eller nede ved vandet. Egentlige vand-hazarder er der kun ganske få af. Dén på det 450 meter lange 16. hul er til gengæld imponerende: Det er selve Storebælt, man kan forsøge at skære så meget af i sit drive, som man tør. Ellers sørger især de tydeligvis gamle træer og også bunkers for problemerne på den næsten helt flade bane. Sct. Knuds mangler de tekniske raffinementer, der skal til for at udfordre den dygtige spiller, men kan så til gengæld spilles uden problemer af folk med højt handicap.

Here is an easy-to-find course: the motorway that crosses the three major regions of Denmark (Sjælland, Fyn and Jutland) runs along about 6 or 7 holes but is only really a nuisance on holes 10 and 11. If you can forget it is there, this well-wooded and very varied site is most pleasant. On the clearer sections of the course, the trees give way to the Storebælt, particularly on the 16th, a magnificent short par 5. This belt of sea is moreover the only water hazard on the course, the other hazards being more classical and typically British in the form of trees (sometimes very much in play) and the standard bunkers. All this gives a very open course, which hides none of its difficulties. For the more demanding player, though, it probably lacks a little technical subtlety to be played too often. With that said, you will have fun golfing here with all the family or with friends, even with widely differing abilities.

Sct. Knuds Golfklub — 1954

Sliphavnsvej 16
DK - 5800 Nyborg

Office	Sekretariat	(45) 65 37 12 12
Pro shop	Pro-shop	(45) 65 30 02 04
Fax	Fax	(45) 65 30 28 04
E-mail	mail@sct-knuds.dk	
Situation	Sted	Nyborg, 2 km
Annual closure	Årlig lukkeperiode	no
Weekly closure	Ugentlig lukketid	no

Fees main season Priser i højsæson	Full day	
	Week days Hverdage	**We/Bank holidays** Helligdage
Individual Individuelt	DKr 200	DKr 250
Couple Par	DKr 400	DKr 500

Junior: – 50%

Caddy	Caddie	no
Electric Trolley	Bagvogn	DKr 30 /18 holes
Buggy	Golf car	DKr 200 /18 holes
Clubs	Koller	DKr 150 /18 holes

Credit cards Kreditkord
VISA - Eurocard - DC

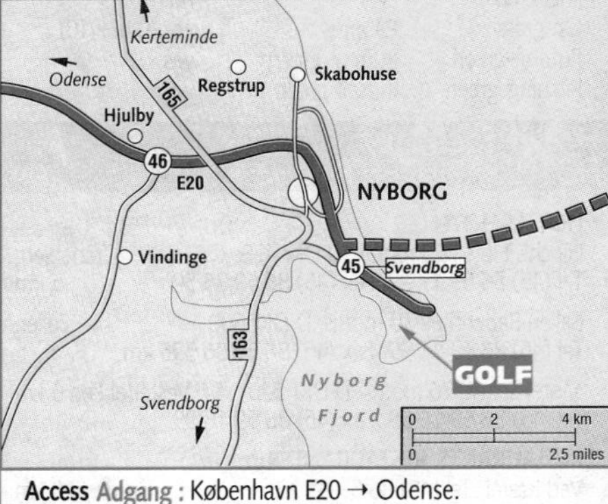

Access Adgang : København E20 → Odense. Nyborg, → Golf.
Map 1 on page 123 Kort 1 på side 123

Golf course BAN — 14/20

Site	Sted	
Maintenance	Vedligeholdelse	
Architect	Arkitekt	Cotton/Dreyer
Type	Type	forest, open country
Relief	Lettelse	
Water in play	Vand i spil	
Exp. to wind	Udsat for vind	
Trees in play	Træer i spil	

Scorecard Scorekort	**Chp.** Back tee	**Mens** Herre tee	**Ladies** Dame tee
Length Længde	5810	5810	4880
Par	72	72	72
Slope system	—	—	—

Advised golfing ability Anbefalet golfkunnen — 0 12 24 36
Hcp required Maks. handicap — 32

Club house & amenities KLUBHUSET OG FACILITETER — 5/10

Pro shop	Pro-shop	
Driving range	Driving range	
Sheltered	Ly	no
On grass	På græs	yes (03 → 11)
Putting-green	Putting-green	yes
Pitching-green	Indspilsgreen	yes

Hotel facilities HOTEL FACILITETERNE — 6/10

HOTELS HOTELLER

Hesselet — Nyborg
85 rooms, D DKr 850
Tel (45) 65 31 30 29, Fax (45) 65 31 29 58 — 2 km

Nyborg Strand — Nyborg 3 km
120 rooms, D DKr 900
Tel (45) 65 31 31 31, Fax (45) 65 31 37 01

RESTAURANTS RESTAURANTER

Hos Svend — Svendborg 30 km
Tel (45) 62 22 07 95

Hesselet, Tel(45) 65 31 29 58 — Nyborg 2 km

Sognegården, Tel (45) 62 68 11 11 — Millinge 40 km

SIMON'S

14 | 7 | 7

Med sin placering kun få kilometer ned ad motorvejen fra Helsingør er Simon's en bane, svenskere gerne betaler de temmelig mange penge, det koster at spille den. For de ved, at de – ligesom alle andre – får noget for pengene. Fremragende stand, først og fremmest – banen regnes sammen med Royal Oak for Danmarks bedst holdte. Og en bane, der er sværere, end den ser ud til – ikke mindst på grund af dens meget store, ondulerede og efter danske forhold lynhurtige greens samt de små græstuer, der flankerer mange af dem på tre sider. Banen har været vært for adskillige turneringer på Challenge-touren, og det ses på fairways, de er ikke specielt brede. En stor sø dominerer det korte 10. hul, hvor man skal slå over for at komme på green, og det 18., hvis 460 meter lange venstre side ER søen. Banen er ikke specielt kuperet, men byder alligevel på en del blinde slag og skjulte forhindringer. Især approach-slaget til den højtliggende 3. green er svært.

A few miles from here, don't miss Helsingør and make sure you visit the castle of Kronborg on a foggy night; this is the castle of Elsenor, the setting for Shakespeare's Hamlet. The old houses in town are worth visiting as much as the castle, which in fact is more Renaissance than medieval in style. The course was opened only very recently on a pleasant site, despite the closeness of the motorway. A large lake is in play on the 10th and the 18th, a now classic par 5 edged by water up the whole of the left side. The course is not hilly but five of the greens and several hazards are almost blind, which does not help things first time out on the course. Likewise, you will need to concentrate over the whole round, not necessarily a good thing for pace of play and relaxation. Simon's is well worth a visit, even though we might have imagined a more "dramatic" course in this part of the world...

Simon's Golf Klub — 1993

Nybovej 5
DK - 3490 KVISTGAARD

Office	Sekretariat	(45) 49 19 13 28
Pro shop	Pro-shop	(45) 49 19 48 76
Fax	Fax	(45) 49 19 14 70
Web	www.simonsgolf.dk	
Situation	Sted	København, 30 km
Annual closure	Årlig lukkeperiode	no
Weekly closure	Ugentlig lukketid	no

Fees main season / Priser i højsæson	18 holes	
	Week days / Hverdage	We/Bank holidays / Helligdage
Individual Individuelt	DKr 275	DKr 375
Couple Par	DKr 550	DKr 750

Junior: – 50%

Caddy	Caddie	no
Electric Trolley	Bagvogn	no
Buggy	Golf car	DKr 75 /18 holes
Clubs	Koller	DKr 200 /18 holes

Credit cards Kreditkord
VISA - Eurocard - DC

Access Adgang : E47 Exit 5 → Humlebæk. Hørsholmvej, → Golf.
Map 1 on page 123 Kort 1 på side 123

Golf course BAN — 14/20

Site	Sted	
Maintenance	Vedligeholdelse	
Architect	Arkitekt	Martin Hawtree
Type	Type	inland, country
Relief	Lettelse	
Water in play	Vand i spil	
Exp. to wind	Udsat for vind	
Trees in play	Træer i spil	

Scorecard / Scorekort	Chp. / Back tee	Mens / Herre tee	Ladies / Dame tee
Length Længde	5787	5787	5064
Par	72	72	72
Slope system	—	—	—

Advised golfing ability / Anbefalet golfkunnen: 0 12 24 36
Hcp required / Maks. handicap: 30

Club house & amenities KLUBHUSET OG FACILITETER — 7/10

Pro shop	Pro-shop	
Driving range	Driving range	
Sheltered	Ly	no
On grass	På græs	no, 10 mats open air
Putting-green	Putting-green	yes
Pitching-green	Indspilsgreen	yes

Hotel facilities HOTEL FACILITETERNE — 7/10

HOTELS HOTELLER

Nybogaard — Kvistgaard Golf
15 rooms, D DKr 900
Tel (45) 49 16 16 60, Fax (45) 49 16 16 80

Store Kro, 40 rooms, D DKr 650 — Fredensborg 10 km
Tel (45) 48 48 00 47, Fax (45) 48 48 45 61

Scanticon Borupgaard, 45 rooms, D DKr 780 — Snekkersten
Tel (45) 49 22 03 33, Fax (45) 49 22 03 99

RESTAURANTS RESTAURANTER

Nokken, Tel (45) 45 57 13 14 — Rungsted 10 km
Jan Hurtigkarl, Tel (45) 49 70 90 03 — Ålsgårde 5 km
Taarbæk Kro, Tel (45) 39 63 00 96 — Taarbæk 20 km

VEJLE Blå / Rød

15 | 7 | 7

Legoland ligger lige i nærheden, i Billund, dér er alt i miniatureformat. På Vejle-banen er der ikke miniature over hverken banens niveau eller dens træer. Tværtimod. Storladen er det ord, der bedst beskriver træerne, højdeforskellene og isolationen på den såkaldte blå banes ni huller. Det 4. hul er helt fantastisk. Når man står på teestedet og ser de store træer og de høje klippesider, skulle man ikke tro, at man befinder sig i en dansk skov. Vejles anlæg består også af en rød og en gul bane, i alt 27 huller, der byder på meget stor variation. Anlægget har flere gange lagt huller til Danish Open på damernes Europa-tour. Kombinationen blå/rød bane hører med en course slope på 139 til blandt de allersværeste 18 huller i Danmark. Ikke specielt lang, men smal og med svære dogleg-huller. De ni gule huller kom til i 1994. De er længere og af mere åben karakter. Kombinationen rød-gul bane er banen for den mindre øvede spiller.

When you are in this region, you simply have to drive a few miles west towards Billund... a little town of no special interest except Legoland, an incredible miniature world built with the famous plastic cubes that are a favourite toy for children all over the world. And since there is a child in every golfer, find a little inspiration to get to grips with the 27 holes at Vejle, of which the "Blue" 9-hole course (Blå) is without a doubt the hardest test of golf in Denmark. What it lacks in yardage it makes up for with some devilish dog-legs, the tremendous challenge of the forest and some disconcerting, sometimes even excessive, differences in level and altitude. The "Red" course (Rød), a 9-holer which originally completed the Blue course, is hardly any easier for wayward hitters, whereas the Yellow course, opened in 1994, is both more open and forthright, despite the number of small water hazards. For mid-handicappers and inexperienced players, we would recommend a "Red/Yellow" mix. At once spectacular, tricky and very natural, Vejle will leave some sort of mark on every golfer....

Vejle Golf Club — 1972

Ibækvej 46
DK - 7100 VEJLE

Office	Sekretariat	(45) 75 85 81 85
Pro shop	Pro-shop	(45) 75 85 81 43
Fax	Fax	(45) 75 85 83 01
Web	www.vejlegolfclub.dk	
Situation	Sted	Vejle, 5 km
Annual closure	Årlig lukkeperiode	no
Weekly closure	Ugentlig lukketid	no

Fees main season Priser i højsæson		Full day
	Week days Hverdage	We/Bank holidays Helligdage
Individual Individuelt	DKr 250	DKr 250
Couple Par	DKr 500	DKr 500

Junior: – 50%

Caddy	Caddie	no
Electric Trolley	Bagvogn	no
Buggy	Golf car	DKr 200 /18 holes
Clubs	Koller	DKr 100 /18 holes

Credit cards Kreditkord
VISA - Eurocard - DC

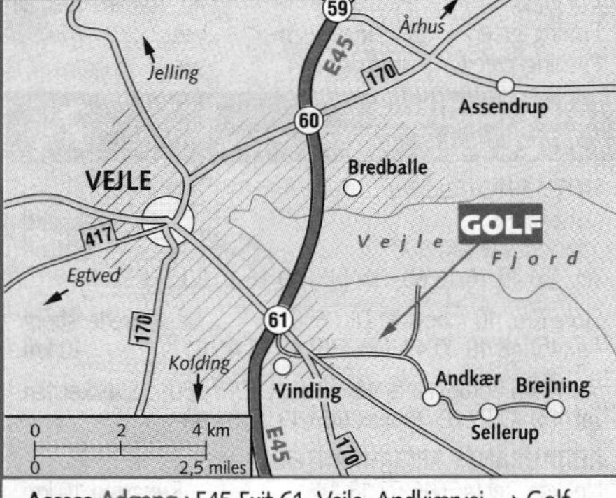

Access Adgang : E45 Exit 61. Vejle, Andkjærvej, → Golf.
Map 1 on page 122 Kort 1 på side 122

Golf course — BAN — 15/20

Site	Sted	
Maintenance	Vedligeholdelse	
Architect	Arkitekt	Malling Petersen
Type	Type	forest, hilly
Relief	Lettelse	
Water in play	Vand i spil	
Exp. to wind	Udsat for vind	
Trees in play	Træer i spil	

Scorecard Scorekort	Chp. Back tee	Mens Herre tee	Ladies Dame tee
Length Længde	5532	5532	4646
Par	72	72	72
Slope system	—	—	—

Advised golfing ability Anbefalet golfkunnen: 0 12 24 36
Hcp required Maks. handicap: 36

Club house & amenities — KLUBHUSET OG FACILITETER — 7/10

Pro shop	Pro-shop	
Driving range	Driving range	
Sheltered	Ly	no
On grass	På græs	yes (04 → 10)
Putting-green	Putting-green	yes
Pitching-green	Indspilsgreen	yes

Hotel facilities — HOTEL FACILITETERNE — 7/10

HOTELS HOTELLER
Munkebjerg, 150 rooms, D DKr 850 — Vejle 3 km
Tel (45) 76 42 85 00, Fax (45) 75 72 08 86

Vejle Center — Vejle 5 km
65 rooms, D DKr 600
Tel (45) 75 72 45 00, Fax (45) 75 72 46 60

RESTAURANTS RESTAURANER
Munkjeberg Hotel Restaurant — Vejle 3 km
Tel (45) 76 42 85 00

Merlot, Tel (45) 75 83 88 44 — Vejle 5 km

Da Franco — Vejle 5 km
Tel (45) 75 82 57 67

EUROPE'S TOP 1000 GOLF COURSES

Finland

Espoo

Finland
Suomi

This is a land of two seasons. Winter, which lasts from six to eight months, from north to south, and summer, equally intense and spectacular. Between the two, Spring and Autumn are as wonderful as they are short. Golf in Finland is played from May to late September, but you can play for twice as long as anywhere else. In the summer, night-time is just a brief period of dusk. As inveterate nature-lovers, the Finns have naturally taken to golf, which is played as soon as the ice has thawed until the first winter snowfall.

Today, there are 96 courses open (more than 55 eighteen-holers) catering to 68,000 golfers. And as here golf is a real sport, there are already enough good players for Finland to have produced many a good performance in the world team championships.

Suomi on kahden vuodenajan maa. Kuusi, jopa kahdeksankin kuukautta pitkä talvi, pohjoisesta etelään asti, ja kesä, yhtä intensiivinen ja loistelias. Niiden väliin jäävät kesä ja syksy ovat yhtä ihmeelliset kuin lyhyetkin. Golfia Suomessa pelataan toukokuusta syyskuun loppupuolelle, mutta täällä voi silti pelata kaksin verroin kauemmin kuin missään muualla, sillä Suomen kesäyö on vain lyhyt hämärän hetki. Parantumattomina luonnonystävinä suomalaiset ovat tietenkin ryhtyneet harrastamaan golfia, jota he pelaavat lumenlähdöstä ensi lumeen saakka.

Suomessa on nykyisin avoinna 96 golfkenttää (joista yli 55 on 18-reikäisiä), jotka huolehtivat 68 000:sta golfin pelaajasta. Ja koska golfia pidetään Suomessa oikeana urheilulajina, on täällä jo riittävästi hyviä pelaajia,jotka ovat antaneet monta hyvää näytöstä joukkueiden maailmanmestaruuskisoissa.

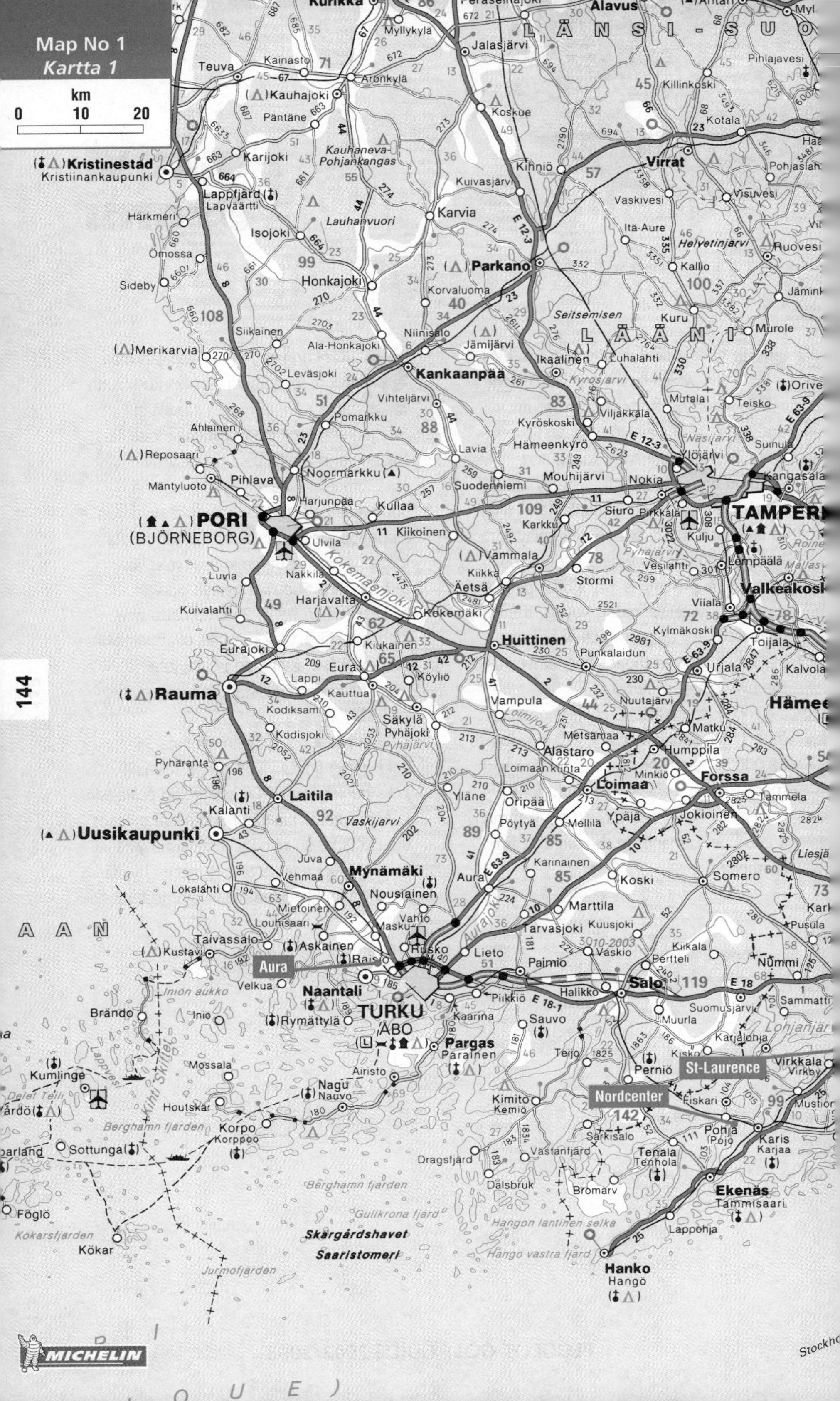

Map No 1
Kartta 1
km
0 10 20
Kristinestad
Kristiinankaupunki
Teuva
Kauhajoki
Karijoki
Lappfjärd
Lapväärtti
Härkmeri
Isojoki
Ömossa
Sideby
Honkajoki
Karvia
Parkano
Kihniö
Virrat
Jalasjärvi
Alavus
Myllykylä
Kainasto
Aronkylä
Päntäne
Kauhaneva-Pohjankangas
Lauhanvuori
Koskue
Kuivasjärvi
Vaskivesi
Visuvesi
Pohjaslahti
Kotala
Killinkoski
Pihlajavesi
Ruovesi
Helvetinjärvi
Itä-Aure
Kallio
Jämijärvi
Korvaluoma
Niinisalo
Kankaanpää
Ala-Honkajoki
Siikainen
Merikarvia
Leväsjoki
Seitsemisen
Ikaalinen
Luhalahti
Kuru
Murole
Orivesi
Teisko
Mutala
Kyrösjärvi
Viljakkala
Kyröskoski
Hämeenkyrö
Ylöjärvi
Näsijärvi
Vihteljärvi
Pomarkku
Ahlainen
Reposaari
Mäntyluoto
Pihlava
Noormarkku
Lavia
Suodenniemi
Mouhijärvi
Nokia
Siuro
Pirkkala
Kangasala
TAMPERE
PORI
(BJÖRNEBORG)
Harjunpää
Kullaa
Ulvila
Kiikoinen
Karkku
Vammala
Kiikka
Äetsä
Stormi
Kulju
Lempäälä
Vesilahti
Pyhäjärvi
Valkeakoski
Viiala
Kylmäkoski
Toijala
Kalvola
Luvia
Nakkila
Kokemäenjoki
Harjavalta
Kokemäki
Kuivalahti
Eurajoki
Kiukainen
Huittinen
Punkalaidun
Eura
Lappi
Köyliö
Rauma
Kauttua
Kodiksami
Kodisjoki
Säkylä
Pyhäjoki
Pyhäjärvi
Vampula
Loimijoki
Nuutajärvi
Urjala
Matku
Hämeenlinna
Metsämaa
Alastaro
Humppila
Minkiö
Forssa
Loimaan kunta
Loimaa
Pyhäranta
Laitila
Kalanti
Uusikaupunki
Vaskijärvi
Yläne
Oripää
Pöytyä
Mellilä
Ypäjä
Jokioinen
Tammela
Liesjärvi
Juva
Vehmaa
Mynämäki
Nousiainen
Aura
Karinainen
Koski
Somero
Lokalahti
Mietoinen
Lounaissaari
Masku
Vahto
Marttila
Kuusjoki
Karkkila
Pusula
Taivassalo
Askainen
Rusko
Lieto
Tarvasjoki
Vaskio
Kiikala
Pertteli
Nummi
Kustavi
Raisio
Velkua
Naantali
TURKU
ÅBO
Piikkiö
Paimio
Halikko
Salo
Sammatti
Iniön aukko
Iniö
Brändö
Rymättylä
Kaarina
Sauvo
Suomusjärvi
Muurla
Lohjanjärvi
Karjalohja
Kisko
Pargas
Parainen
Teijo
Perniö
St-Laurence
Virkkala
Virkby
Kumlinge
Lappveisi
Kihti Skiftet
Mossala
Airisto
Nagu
Nauvo
Kimito
Kemiö
Fiskari
Mustio
Nordcenter
Vårdö
Delet Teili
Houtskär
Berghamn fjarden
Korpo
Korppoo
Särkisalo
Pohja
Pojo
Karis
Karjaa
Sottunga
Lemland
Dragsfjärd
Västanfjärd
Tenala
Tenhola
Dalsbruk
Bromarv
Ekenäs
Tammisaari
Föglö
Kokarsfjärden
Gullkrona fjärd
Hangon läntinen selkä
Lappohja
Kökar
Skärgårdshavet
Saaristomeri
Hangö västra fjärd
Hanko
Hangö
Jurmofjärden
LÄNSI-SUOMEN LÄÄNI
AAN
MICHELIN
Stockholm

Jyväskylä
Jämsä
Mänttä
Multia
Uurainen
Laukaa
Hankasalmi
Vihtavuori
Tikkakoski
Kintaus
Vaajakoski
Petäjävesi
Huttula
Muuratjärvi
Säynätsalo
Toivakka
Sahloinen
Muurame
Koskenpää
Korpilahti
Jamsänkoski
Kaipola
Luhanka
Joutsa
Leivonmäki
Lievestuore
Hankasalmen as
Naarajärvi
Pieksämäki
Varkaus
Kangaslampi
Könönpelto
Joroinen
Virtasalmi
Hurskaala
Rantasalmi
Haukivuori
Narila
Juva
Kangasniemi
Kyyvesi
Mikkeli
Puula
Otava
Anttola
Luonteri
Hirvensalmi
Heimari
Ristiina
Hartola
Jääsjärvi
Pertunmaa
Mäntyharju
Saimaa
Suomenniemi
Kuolimo
Savitaipale
Kuortti
Sysmä
Suopelto
Päijänne
Kuhmoinen
Rauhamäki
Längelmäki
Eräjärvi
Kuhmalahti
Isojärvi
Padasjoki
Kalkkinen
Lusi
Heinolan mlk
Heinola
Voikoski
Vuohijärvi
Lemi
Kivijärvi
Tuohikotti
Luopioinen
Kukkia
Sappee
Auttoinen
Asikkala
Iso-Evo
Tuulos
Hauho
Vesivehmaa
Vierumäki
Vesijärvi
Jaala
Lammi
Hattula
Aulanko
Hollola
LAHTI
Nastola
Kuusankoski
Voikkaa
Valkeala
Luumäki
Koski
Tawast
Turenki
Kärkölä
Herrala
Salpausselkä
Litti
Koria
Kouvola
Enäjärvi
ETELÄ-SUOMEN LÄÄNI
Janakkala
Ryttylä
Järvelä
Orimattila
Artjärvi
Myllykoski
Anjalankoski
Sippola
Pyhälto
Kannusjärvi
Miehikkälä
Oitti
Hausjärvi
Riihimäki
Sälinkää
Elimäki
Muhniemi
Metsäkylä
Vehkalahti
Virolahti
Hyvinkää
Pukkila
Myrskylä
Porvoonjoki
Lapinjärvi
Lappträsk
Tavastila
Hamina
Mäntsälä
Liljendal
Siltakylä
Karhula
Mäntlahti
Kotka
Jokela
Rajamäki
Kellokoski
Askola
Ruotsinpyhtää
Strömfors
Pyhtää
Pyttis
Mussalo
Järvenpää
Pornainen
Golf Talma
Pernå
Pernaja
Loviisa
Lovisa
Valko
Kerava
Sibbo
Sipoo
Sannainen
Isnäs
Nurmijärvi
Tuusula
Porvoo
Borgå
Kirkonmaanselkä
Klaukkala
Master
Vantaa
Vanda
Valax
Itäinen Suomenlahti
Nummela
Östersundom
Sibbofjärden
Sipoonselkä
Espoo
Esbo
HELSINKI
HELSINGFORS
Suomenlinna
Kirkkonummi
Kyrkslätt
Helsinki
Upinniemi
Sarfvick
Suomenlahti
Finskij Zaliv
Naissaar
TALLINN
Loksa
M 11-E 20
145
MICHELIN
d'après carte n° 985 - 10ème édition - 2002.
Autorisation n° 0102062.

Classification

CLASSIFICATION OF COURSES
GOLFIKENTTIEN LUOKITUS

This classification gives priority consideration to the score awarded to the actual course.

Courses score / Golfikenttien luokitus — Page / Sivulla

			Course	Page
16	7	6	Espoo	148
16	7	8	Helsinki	149
16	8	7	Sarfvik *New Course*	153
15	7	7	Master Master	150
15	7	5	Nordcenter *Benz Course*	151
15	8	5	Pickala *Seaside Course*	152
14	5	4	St Laurence	154
14	8	6	Talma	155
14	7	5	Tawast	156
13	5	5	Aura	147

Classification

HOTELS FACILITIES
HOTELLIEN LUOKITUS

			Course	Page
16	7	**8**	Helsinki	149
15	7	**7**	Master *Master*	150
16	8	**7**	Sarfvik *New Course*	153
16	7	**6**	Espoo	148
14	8	**6**	Talma	155
13	5	**5**	Aura	147
15	7	**5**	Nordcenter *Benz Course*	151
15	8	**5**	Pickala *Seaside Course*	152
14	7	**5**	Tawast	156
14	5	**4**	St Laurence	154

TYPE OF COURSE
KENTÄN OMINAISUUS

Forest
Nordcenter *Benz Course* 151, Sarfvik *New Course* 153, St Laurence 154 Talma 155, Tawast 156

Inland Tawast 156.

Links Pickala *Seaside Course* 152

Open country Espoo 148

Parkland
Aura 147, Helsinki 149, Master *Master* 150, St Laurence 154, Talma 155

Seaside course
Pickala *Seaside Course* 152

AURA

13 | 5 | 5

Turku (ruotsiksi Åbo) oli kauan Suomen pääkaupunki, ja se on edelleenkin hyvin vilkas kaupunki niin kulttuurillisesti kuin taloudellisestikin. Tiiviillä meriyhteyksillä Ruotsiin ja Baltian maihin on ollut huomattava merkitys. Turun palo v. 1827 jätti jälkensä, ja tämän päivän Turku onkin hyvin nykyaikainen kaupunki, jossa matkailija viihtyy erinomaisesti, samoin kuin tuhansista saarista muodostuvassa Turun saaristossakin. Aura Golfin kenttä on rakennettu yhdelle näistä saarista, Ruissaloon, ja kuten useimmilla Suomen kentillä on täälläkin kesä- ja heinäkuussa käytännössä mahdollista pelata golfia ympäri vuorokauden. Tämä vanhaan linnanpuistoon rakennettu puistokenttä on ihastuttava suurine metsineen, joissa kasvaa jopa yli 400 vuotta vanhoja tammia. Kenttä avattiin v. 1958. Kokonaisuus on hyvä ja pitkät ja lyhyet reiät vuorottelevat hienosti. Kaksi par 4 -reikää on pituudeltaan yli 400 metriä, mutta jos pelaaja lyö kauas, on hänellä mahdollisuus siirtyä par 5 -rei'ille kahdella lyönnillä. Lisäksi kentällä on kaksi todella lyhyttä par 4 -reikää.

Turku (or Abo in Swedish, the country's second most widely-spoken language), was the capital of Finland for many a year and is still today a busy city both culturally and commercially, particularly through the frequent sea-links with Sweden and the Baltic ports. After the great fire of 1827, this is now a very modern city and still as attractive as ever with the thousands of islands making up the Turku archipelago. The Aura golf course is laid out on one such isle, the island of Ruissalo, and like most other courses in Finland is playable almost 24 hours a day in June and July. It is a superb park thick with woods, in a former castle estate where some of the oak trees are over 400 years old. The course was opened in 1958 and is a great layout with holes of reasonable length; two of the par 4s are over 400 metres long and big-hitters can expect to reach the par 5s in two and make light work of some short par 4s. A wonderful site and very enjoyable course.

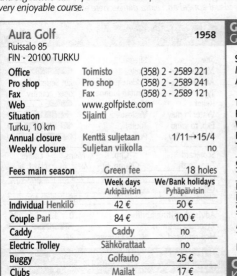

Aura Golf — 1958

Ruissalo 85
FIN - 20100 TURKU

Office	Toimisto	(358) 2 - 2589 221
Pro shop	Pro shop	(358) 2 - 2589 241
Fax	Fax	(358) 2 - 2589 121
Web	www.golfpiste.com	
Situation	Sijainti	
Turku, 10 km		
Annual closure	Kenttä suljetaan	1/11→15/4
Weekly closure	Suljetan viikolla	no

Fees main season	Green fee	18 holes
	Week days / Arkipäivisin	We/Bank holidays / Pyhäpäivisin
Individual Henkilö	42 €	50 €
Couple Pari	84 €	100 €
Caddy	Caddy	no
Electric Trolley	Sähkörattaat	no
Buggy	Golfauto	25 €
Clubs	Mailat	17 €

Credit cards Luottokortit
VISA - Eurocard - MasterCard - DC - AMEX

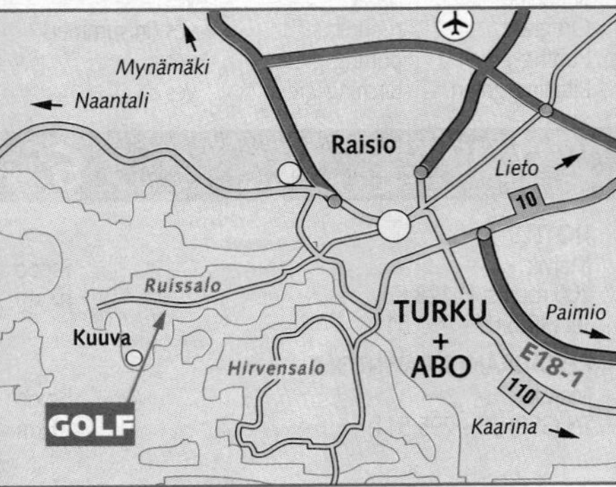

Access Pääsy : On Ruissalo island, W. of Turku.
Map 1 on page 144 Kartta 1 sivulla : 144

Golf course GOLFBANEN — 13/20

Site	Sijainti	
Maintenance	Hoito	
Architect	Arkkitehti	Lauri Arkkola, Pekka Sivula
Type	Kentän luonne	parkland
Relief	Vapautuminen	
Water in play	Vesiesteitä	
Exp. to wind	Tuulta	
Trees in play	Puita	

Scorecard / Tuloskortti	Chp. / Champ. tii	Mens / Miest. tii	Ladies / Naist. tii
Length Pituus	5858	5629	4856
Par	71	71	71
Slope system	131	135	125

Advised golfing ability Tasoitusvaatimus — 0 12 24 36
Hcp required Hcp-vaatimus — 24 Men, 30 Ladies

Club house & amenities KLUBHUS OG OMGIVELSER — 5/10

Pro shop	Pro shop	
Driving range	Driving range	
Sheltered	suoja	yes
On grass	ruoholla	yes (Summer)
Putting-green	putting-green	yes
Pitching-green	pitching-green	yes

Hotel facilities HOTELFASILITETER — 5/10

HOTELS
Scandic Marina Palace — Turku 8 km
183 rooms, D 101 €
Tel (358) 02 - 336 300

RESTAURANTS RAVINTOLA
Marina Palace — Turku 8 km
Tel (358) 02 - 336 300

Hermanni — Turku 8 km
Tel (358) 02 - 220 3333

Harald — Turku 8 km
Tel (358) 02 - 276 5050

ESPOO

16 | 7 | 6

Espoon (ruotsiksi Esbo) ympäristössä on joitakin Suomen tunnetuimmista rakennuksista. Espoon kirkossa voi katsella keskiaikaisia seinämaalauksia.Vähän kauempana, Tapiolassa, voi käydä kävelyllä puistoissa ja puutarhoissa (kaupunki rakennettiin 1950-luvulla). Arkkitehti Saarisen kotina olleessa Hvitträskin huvilassa, joka on nykyisin museona, on yöpynyt monia kuuluisuuksia,kuten esimerkiksi Gorki, Sibelius ja Edvard Munch. Espoon golfkenttä puolestaan edustaa ruotsalaista arkkitehtuuria. Sen on piirtänyt kenttäarkkitehtinä tunnettu Jan Sederholm. Pituudeltaan ja vaikeusasteeltaan Espoon kenttää voidaan pitää oikeana mestaruuskilpailukenttänä. Kenttä sijaitsee melko avoimessa maastossa, joten vaarana voi olla, että kentällä tuulee. Kokonaisuus on nerokkaasti rakennettu, ja tasoerojen vuoksi voi mailan valinta osoittautua pulmalliseksi. Niin alemmissa kuin ylemmissäkin tasoitusryhmissä pelaavilla voi olla vaikeuksia päästä kunnon pistemääriin. Griinit ovat pieniä ja niiden sijainti on suojainen.

From the church of Espoo (Esbo in Swedish), housing medieval mural frescoes, to the garden city of Tapiloa, a model in mid-20th century town-planning, to Hvitträsk, a sort of romantic style national castle where the most illustrious guests have included Gorki, Sibelius, Edvard Munch and the architect Saarinen, you have some of the finest examples of the Finnish art of building all within a few miles of each other. The Espoo golf course, for its part, is an example of well-known Swedish art by course architect Jan Sederholm. It has the length and the hazards to rightfully claim the title of championship course in wide open space that is so exposed that the wind is almost always a constant threat to your ball. Both natural and cleverly laid out, this is a difficult course to score well on, whatever your golfing ability, particularly on account of subtle and sometimes steep terrain, which makes the choice of club a little more complicated. In addition, the greens are on the small side and very well guarded. A stream comes into play on several holes, adding a little visual appeal and extra danger here and there.

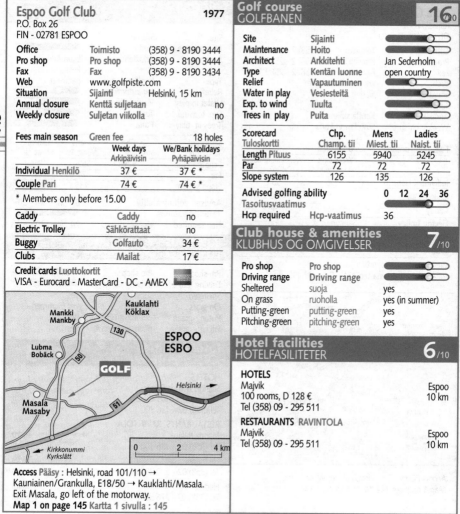

Espoo Golf Club — 1977

P.O. Box 26
FIN - 02781 ESPOO

Office	Toimisto	(358) 9 - 8190 3444
Pro shop	Pro shop	(358) 9 - 8190 3444
Fax	Fax	(358) 9 - 8190 3434
Web	www.golfpiste.com	
Situation	Sijainti	Helsinki, 15 km
Annual closure	Kenttä suljetaan	no
Weekly closure	Suljetan viikolla	no

Fees main season Green fee	18 holes	
	Week days Arkipäivisin	We/Bank holidays Pyhäpäivisin
Individual Henkilö	37 €	37 € *
Couple Pari	74 €	74 € *

* Members only before 15.00

Caddy	Caddy	no
Electric Trolley	Sähkörattaat	no
Buggy	Golfauto	34 €
Clubs	Mailat	17 €

Credit cards Luottokortit
VISA - Eurocard - MasterCard - DC - AMEX

Access Pääsy : Helsinki, road 101/110 → Kauniainen/Grankulla, E18/50 → Kauklahti/Masala. Exit Masala, go left of the motorway.
Map 1 on page 145 Kartta 1 sivulla : 145

Golf course GOLFBANEN — 16/20

Site	Sijainti	
Maintenance	Hoito	
Architect	Arkkitehti	Jan Sederholm
Type	Kentän luonne	open country
Relief	Vapautuminen	
Water in play	Vesiesteitä	
Exp. to wind	Tuulta	
Trees in play	Puita	

Scorecard Tuloskortti	Chp. Champ. tii	Mens Miest. tii	Ladies Naist. tii
Length Pituus	6155	5940	5245
Par	72	72	72
Slope system	126	135	126

Advised golfing ability Tasoitusvaatimus — 0 12 24 36
Hcp required Hcp-vaatimus 36

Club house & amenities KLUBHUS OG OMGIVELSER — 7/10

Pro shop	Pro shop	
Driving range	Driving range	
Sheltered	suoja	yes
On grass	ruoholla	yes (in summer)
Putting-green	putting-green	yes
Pitching-green	pitching-green	yes

Hotel facilities HOTELFASILITETER — 6/10

HOTELS
Majvik — Espoo 10 km
100 rooms, D 128 €
Tel (358) 09 - 295 511

RESTAURANTS RAVINTOLA
Majvik — Espoo 10 km
Tel (358) 09 - 295 511

HELSINKI

16 | 7 | 8

Helsingissä (ruotsiksi Helsingfors) tuntuu voimakkaasti 1900 luvun suurien arkkitehtien Eliel Saarisen ja Alvar Aallon vaikutus. Jos haluaa nähdä vanhoja, perinteisiä rakennuksia, on Seurasaaren ulkomuseo, joka sijaitsee vain lyhyen bussimatkan päässä kaupungista, käymisen arvoinen. Kaupunkia on kutsuttu Itämeren tyttäreksi, ja Seurasaari (Fölisön) on vain yksi sitä ympäröivistä saarista. Vaikka Suomen ilmasto asettaakin rajoituksensa on golf saanut nopeasti jalansijaa urheilulajina. Helsingin Golfklubin kenttä on Suomen vanhin ja se sijaitsee lähellä keskustaa. Kerho on järjestänyt monia suuria amatöörikilpailuja. Lauri Arkkolan kauniiseen lehtomaisemaan suunnittelemalla kentällä on ilmiselviä brittiläisiä esikuvia. Kenttää kehystävät jättimäiset puut, maasto on tasaista ja väylät erinomaiset. Vesiesteitä on vain muutama, kolmen reiän kohdalla on kuitenkin otettava huomioon joki. Kenttä on houkuttelevan avoin ja liikkuminen on helppoa, mutta täällä on kuitenkin vaikea päästä hyviin pistelukemiin. Reikien pituus vaihtelee, joten on viisasta pitää mukanaan kaikki 14 mailaa.

Helsinki has been marked by successive trends in architecture and by the great designers of the 20th century like Saarinen or Alvar Aalto. To find old traditional buildings, the open-air Seurasaari Ulkomuseo museum is a short bus ride on one of the many isles and peninsulas spread around Helsinki, known as "the daughter of the Baltic". In a country where nature commands so much respect, the game of golf has quickly gained a foothold despite the sometimes harsh climate. The Helsinki golf club is the oldest of them all and the course, virtually within the city limits, has hosted a number of top amateur events. Designed by Lauri Arkkola with a very definite British influence, this is a magnificent park with some wonderful trees, virtually flat terrain and great fairways. There are not many water hazards, just a stream that only really comes into play on three holes, on a course which is very forthright, easy to play on foot but much harder to come to terms with and card a good score. Holes come in all lengths so pack the full 14 clubs.

Helsinki Golf Club — 1932

Talin Kartano
FIN - 00350 HELSINKI

Office	Toimisto	(358) 09 - 225 2370
Pro shop	Pro shop	(358) 09 - 2252 3714
Fax	Fax	(358) 09 - 2252 3737
Web	—	
Situation	Sijainti	
within Helsinki (pop. 492 000)		
Annual closure	Kenttä suljetaan	no
Weekly closure	Suljetan viikolla	no

Fees main season Green fee		18 holes
	Week days Arkipäivisin	**We/Bank holidays** Pyhäpäivisin
Individual Henkilö	42 €	47 €
Couple Pari	84 €	94 €

Caddy	Caddy	no
Electric Trolley	Sähkörattaat	no
Buggy	Golfauto	no
Clubs	Mailat	17 €
Credit cards	Luottokortit	no

Access Pääsy : In Helsinki, → Haaga then Pajamäki

Map 1 on page 145 Kartta 1 sivulla : 145

Golf course — GOLFBANEN — 16/20

Site	Sijainti	
Maintenance	Hoito	
Architect	Arkkitehti	Lauri Arkkola
Type	Kentän luonne	parkland, skogsdungar
Relief	Vapautuminen	
Water in play	Vesiesteitä	
Exp. to wind	Tuulta	
Trees in play	Puita	

Scorecard Tuloskortti	**Chp.** Champ. tii	**Mens** Miest. tii	**Ladies** Naist. tii
Length Pituus	5788	5465	4783
Par	71	71	71
Slope system	123	130	122

Advised golfing ability Tasoitusvaatimus — 0 12 24 36

Hcp required Hcp-vaatimus — 36

Club house & amenities — KLUBHUS OG OMGIVELSER — 7/10

Pro shop	Pro shop	
Driving range	Driving range	
Sheltered	suoja	yes
On grass	ruoholla	yes (Summer)
Putting-green	putting-green	yes
Pitching-green	pitching-green	yes

Hotel facilities — HOTELFASILITETER — 8/10

HOTELS

Scandic Hotel Kalastajatorrpa 235 rooms, D 101 € Tel (358) 09 - 45 811	Helsinki 3 km
Rivoli Jardin 53 rooms, D 156 € Tel (358) 09 - 177 880	Helsinki 5 km

RESTAURANTS RAVINTOLA

Kalastajorrpa, Tel (358) 09 - 45 811	Helsinki 3 km
Havis Amanda, Tel (358) 09 - 666 882	Helsinki 5 km
Savoy, Tel (358) 09 -4684 40020	Helsinki 5 km

MASTER Master

15 | 7 | 7

Espoo (ruotsiksi Esbo) on Helsingin rajanaapuri ja yksi Suomen suurimmista kaupungeista. Lähes 90 prosenttia rakennuksista on rakennettu vuoden 1960 jälkeen, mutta alue oli aikaisemmin tunnettu monista kartanoistaan, jotka sijaitsivat vanhan rantatien tuntumassa. Master Golf klubin kaksi 18-reikäistä kenttää on rakennettu tähän näyttävään ympäristöön. Forest-kenttä kaikkine puineen on saanut varsin osuvan nimen. Laajassa puistomaisemassa sijaitseva Master-kenttä on vielä parempi. Ensimmäiset seitsemän reikää ovat avoimia, mutta kierroksen loppuosassa on paljon vettä, mukaan luettuna lampi, joka on otettava huomioon etenkin viimeisten yhdeksän reiän kohdalla. Kenttä on erittäin tasapainoinen ja soveltuu kaikenlaisille pelaajille. Master-kenttä onkin suomalaisten golfinpelaajien suosiossa ammattitaitoisen palvelun ja kenttien erinomaisen kunnon ansiosta.

Espoo/Esbo is one of the largest cities in Finland and today virtually adjoins Helsinki. While almost 90% of the housing dates from the 1960s and thereafter, this used to be a region of a extensive properties not far from the old coast road. This grand golf club, with two 18-hole courses, is laid out on one such former estate. The first course, "the Forest", has the name it deserves and boasts any number of age-old trees. The second, "the Master", is even better and sprawls over a huge park. While the first seven holes are laid out over wide open space, the rest of the course features a lot of water, including a lake which spectacularly comes into play on half the holes, especially on the back nine. Well-balanced overall, open and adapting to players of all abilities, the "Master" is a very popular course with Finnish golfers, a fact equally explained to some extent by very professional administration and excellent maintenance.

Master Golf Club — 1988

Bodomintie 4
FIN - 02940 ESPOO

Office	Toimisto	(358) 09 - 849 2300
Pro shop	Pro shop	(358) 09 - 8492 3060
Fax	Fax	(358) 09 - 8492 3011
Web	www.golfpiste.com	
Situation	Sijainti	Helsinki, 15 km
Annual closure	Kenttä suljetaan	no
Weekly closure	Suljetan viikolla	no

Fees main season Green fee	18 holes	
	Week days Arkipäivisin	**We/Bank holidays** Pyhäpäivisin
Individual Henkilö	39 €	45 € *
Couple Pari	78 €	90 € *

* With members only

Caddy	Caddy	no
Electric Trolley	Sähkörattaat	no
Buggy	Golfauto	25 €
Clubs	Mailat	17 €

Credit cards Luottokortit
VISA - Eurocard - MasterCard - DC - AMEX

Access Pääsy : Helsinki, take 50/E18,
Exit Bodominjärvi/Bodom, go left towards the lake.
Map 1 on page 145 Kartta 1 sivulla : 145

Golf course GOLFBANEN — 15/20

Site	Sijainti	
Maintenance	Hoito	
Architect	Arkkitehti	Kosti Kuronen
Type	Kentän luonne	parkland
Relief	Vapautuminen	
Water in play	Vesiesteitä	
Exp. to wind	Tuulta	
Trees in play	Puita	

Scorecard Tuloskortti	**Chp.** Champ. tii	**Mens** Miest. tii	**Ladies** Naist. tii
Length Pituus	6083	5708	4799
Par	72	72	72
Slope system	131	136	125

Advised golfing ability Tasoitusvaatimus — 0 12 24 36

Hcp required Hcp-vaatimus — no

Club house & amenities KLUBHUS OG OMGIVELSER — 7/10

Pro shop	Pro shop	
Driving range	Driving range	
Sheltered	suoja	yes
On grass	ruoholla	yes (Summer)
Putting-green	putting-green	yes
Pitching-green	pitching-green	yes

Hotel facilities HOTELFASILITETER — 7/10

HOTELS
Kaisankoti — Espoo 3 km
80 rooms, D 94 €
Tel (358) 09 - 887 191

RESTAURANTS RAVINTOLA
Kaisankoti — Espoo 3 km
Tel (358) 09 - 887 191

NORDCENTER Benz Course

15 | 7 | 5

Vain 75 kilometrin päässä Helsingistä sijaitsee Nordcenter, joka on 36-reikäinen kenttä kuten lähellä olevat Pickalan ja Sarfvikin kentätkin. Lohjanjärven rannalle rakennettu Nordcenter on kahden amerikkalaisen suunnittelema, varsin eksklusiivinen kenttä, joka ei varmaankaan oudoksuta niitä, jotka ovat pelanneet golfia USA:ssa. Ronald Freamin suunnittelema kenttä on avoin ja maaston korkeuserot ovat suuret (suosittelemme golfauton käyttöä). Neljä reikää pelataan vedenrajassa. Nordcenterissä suosittelemme korkeuseroiltaan helpompaa Benz kenttää, jolla liikkuminen ei ole yhtä rasittavaa kuin Fream kentällä. Tämän kentän on piirtänyt Bradford Benz, ja metsineen ja vesistöineen se tuntuu paljon "suomalaisemmalta". Vesi ja puut tulevat mukaan peliin kymmenen reiän kohdalla. Väylät ovat leveitä ja pieleen menneistä lyönneistä voi täällä pelastautua: varomattomuudesta ei sakoteta. Takatiiltä ei kuitenkaan kannata pelata, vaikka kenttä onkin avoin eikä sisällä salattuja vaikeuksia. Riittää kun lyö klubitiiltä. Nordcenter on täydellinen "resort"-kenttä.

Like the Master Golf Club, Pickala or Sarfvik, here is another 36-hole resort just 75 km from Helsinki in a setting that overlooks the lake of Lohjanjarvi. This also happens to be a very exclusive club, which called on the services of two American architects to design the courses on which any American would feel very much at home. The course designed by Ronald Fream is very open and very hilly (buggy recommended) where four holes run along the shores of the lake. We would recommend the less hilly and so more easily walkable course designed by Bradford Benz, which is more specifically Finnish in its landscape of wood and water, both of which are very much in play on about ten holes. The fairways are wide, so the less accurate or less cautious golfers should get by without too much damage to their card. Don't think twice about opting for the front tees (men and ladies), at least to get to know the layout, even though the course is very open and hides nothing. A great golfing resort.

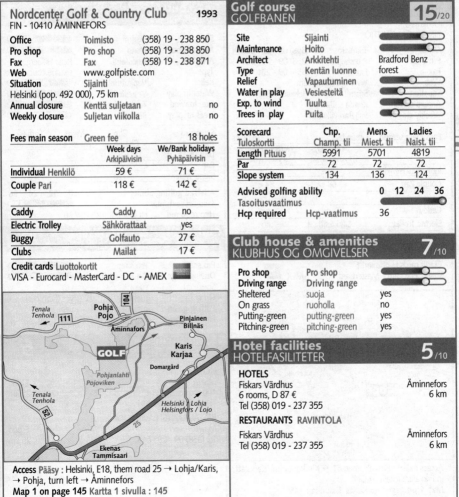

Nordcenter Golf & Country Club — 1993

FIN - 10410 ÅMINNEFORS

Office	Toimisto	(358) 19 - 238 850
Pro shop	Pro shop	(358) 19 - 238 850
Fax	Fax	(358) 19 - 238 871
Web	www.golfpiste.com	
Situation	Sijainti	
Helsinki (pop. 492 000), 75 km		
Annual closure	Kenttä suljetaan	no
Weekly closure	Suljetan viikolla	no

Fees main season Green fee	18 holes	
	Week days Arkipäivisin	**We/Bank holidays** Pyhäpäivisin
Individual Henkilö	59 €	71 €
Couple Pari	118 €	142 €

Caddy	Caddy	no
Electric Trolley	Sähkörattaat	yes
Buggy	Golfauto	27 €
Clubs	Mailat	17 €

Credit cards Luottokortit
VISA - Eurocard - MasterCard - DC - AMEX

Access Pääsy : Helsinki, E18, them road 25 → Lohja/Karis, → Pohja, turn left → Åminnefors
Map 1 on page 145 Kartta 1 sivulla : 145

Golf course GOLFBANEN — 15/20

Site	Sijainti	
Maintenance	Hoito	
Architect	Arkkitehti	Bradford Benz
Type	Kentän luonne	forest
Relief	Vapautuminen	
Water in play	Vesiesteitä	
Exp. to wind	Tuulta	
Trees in play	Puita	

Scorecard Tuloskortti	**Chp.** Champ. tii	**Mens** Miest. tii	**Ladies** Naist. tii
Length Pituus	5991	5701	4819
Par	72	72	72
Slope system	134	136	124

Advised golfing ability Tasoitusvaatimus — 0 12 24 36
Hcp required Hcp-vaatimus 36

Club house & amenities KLUBHUS OG OMGIVELSER — 7/10

Pro shop	Pro shop	
Driving range	Driving range	
Sheltered	suoja	yes
On grass	ruoholla	no
Putting-green	putting-green	yes
Pitching-green	pitching-green	yes

Hotel facilities HOTELFASILITETER — 5/10

HOTELS
Fiskars Värdhus — Åminnefors 6 km
6 rooms, D 87 €
Tel (358) 019 - 237 355

RESTAURANTS RAVINTOLA
Fiskars Värdhus — Åminnefors 6 km
Tel (358) 019 - 237 355

PICKALA Seaside Course

15 | 8 | 5

Pickalan Golfclubiin kuuluu suuri urheilulaitos tenniskenttineen ja hevostalleineen, ja täällä voi purjehtia sekä pelata golfia kahdella kentällä. Sijainti Itämeren rannalla on upea, ja toinen, kentistä kapeampi, onkin saanut nimekseen Seaside. Leveämpi kenttä on nimeltään Park. Seaside-kenttään kuuluu vähemmän puita, mutta sitäkin enemmän vesiesteitä, patoja ja lammikoita, joita yhdistää pieni joki. Vesi on mukana pelissä kahdentoista reiän kohdalla, mikä asettaa suuria vaatimuksia aloituslyönnille ja rankaisee epäonnistuneista jatkolyönneistä. Griinien ympärillä on bunkkerointeja, harvemmin vettä. Jos kyseessä on vain harjoituskierros, sopii kenttä hyvin kaikenlaisille pelaajille: ensiksi vaaratekijöiden arviointi, seuraavaksi aloituslyönti, ja sitten voikin vain toivoa parasta. Hyvänä uutisena mainittakoon, että Seaside ei sisällä todella pitkiä reikiä. Tuuli sen sijaan on aina otettava huomioon. Park-kenttä on myös erittäin hyvä ja kerhotalo, ravintola ja alueen vuokramökit ovat erinomaiset.

The Pickala golf club is a huge sporting complex which features tennis courts, horse-riding, sailing and two golf courses. The location is quite magnificent, on the Baltic coastline, which, as the name suggests, serves as a backdrop for the "Seaside" course. Tighter than the "Park Course", "Seaside" has very few trees but a lot of water in the shape of ponds and small lakes, linked by a small river. Water actually comes into play on about a dozen holes as frontal or lateral hazards and is more dangerous for the drive or wayward second shot than when really attacking the greens, where the bunkers take over. In practice, players of all abilities can play here, calculate the risks they are willing to take and hope for the best. Last but not least, there are no excessively long holes here, good news for big-hitters, who will nonetheless have to reckon with the wind. The second course has much to be said for it, as do the club-house, restaurant and chalets for rent on site.

Pickala Golf Club — 1986

Golfkuja 5
FIN - 02580 SIUNTIO

Office	Toimisto	(358) 09 - 221 90844
Pro shop	Pro shop	(358) 09 - 221 90844
Fax	Fax	(358) 09 - 221 90899
Web	www.golfpiste.com	
Situation	Sijainti	Helsinki , 45 km
Annual closure	Kenttä suljetaan	no
Weekly closure	Suljetaan viikolla	no

152

Fees main season Green fee	18 holes	
	Week days Arkipäivisin	**We/Bank holidays** Pyhäpäivisin
Individual Henkilö	34 €	42 €
Couple Pari	68 €	84 €

Caddy	Caddy	no
Electric Trolley	Sähkörattaat	no
Buggy	Golfauto	34 €
Clubs	Mailat	25 €

Credit cards Luottokortit
VISA - Eurocard - MasterCard - DC - AMEX

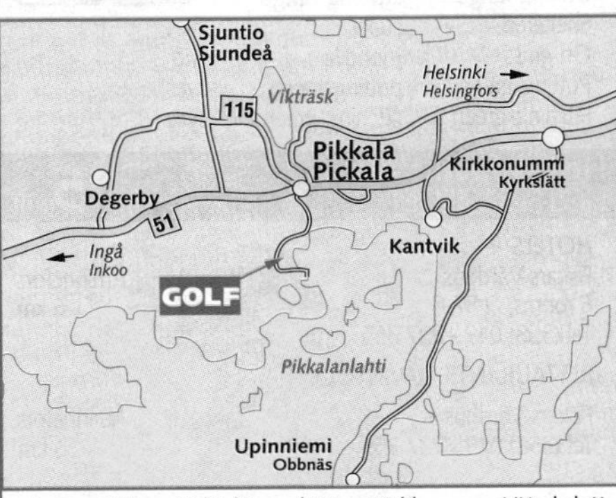

Access Pääsy : Helsinki, road 51 → Kirkkonummi/Kyrkslatt, in Pikkala/Pickala → Golf
Map 1 on page 145 Kartta 1 sivulla : 145

Golf course — GOLFBANEN — 15/20

Site	Sijainti	
Maintenance	Hoito	
Architect	Arkkitehti	Reijo Hillberg
Type	Kentän luonne	seaside course, links
Relief	Vapautuminen	
Water in play	Vesiesteitä	
Exp. to wind	Tuulta	
Trees in play	Puita	

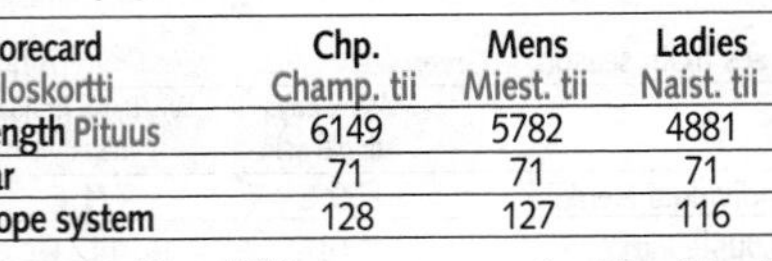

Scorecard Tuloskortti	**Chp.** Champ. tii	**Mens** Miest. tii	**Ladies** Naist. tii
Length Pituus	6149	5782	4881
Par	71	71	71
Slope system	128	127	116

Advised golfing ability 0 12 24 36
Tasoitusvaatimus
Hcp required Hcp-vaatimus 36

Club house & amenities — KLUBHUS OG OMGIVELSER — 8/10

Pro shop	Pro shop	
Driving range	Driving range	
Sheltered	suoja	yes
On grass	ruoholla	yes (Summer)
Putting-green	putting-green	yes
Pitching-green	pitching-green	yes

Hotel facilities — HOTELFASILITETER — 5/10

HOTELS
Majvik — Espoo 25 km
100 rooms, D 128 €
Tel (358) 09 - 295 511

RESTAURANTS RAVINTOLA
Majvik — Espoo 25 km
Tel (358) 09 - 295 511

SARFVIK New Course

16 | 8 | 7

Sarfvik Golfklubista on kehittynyt kaikkien tavoittelema, Suomen eksklusiivisin ja kallein kerho. Vaikka kenttiä on kaksi, voi täällä pelata greenfee-vieraana ainoastaan viikonloppuisin ja silloinkin vain jonkun kerhonjäsenen seurassa. Molempien kenttien suunnittelusta vastaa Jan Sederholm, joka on yksi Ruotsin tuotteliaimpia arkkitehtejä. Pelaaminen on nautinnollista molemmilla kentillä, vaikkakin eri syistä: Old Course on tasainen, avoin puistokenttä kun taas New Course on mäkinen ja kiemurtelee metsän läpi. Jälkimmäinen on kentistä haastavampi, koska tasoerot vaikeuttavat oikean mailan valintaa. Tämän lisäksi on palloa välillä taivutettava, ellei halua päätyä puiden sekaan. Samanaikaisesti metsä luo miellyttävän erillisyyden ja rauhan tunteen. Muutama vesieste luo elävyyttä kaiken vihreyden keskellä, ja griinibunkkerit, joita ei ole kovin monta, on erittäin hyvin sijoitettu. New Course on erittäin hyvä kenttä, joka vaatii pelaajaltaan keskittäytymistä, jos haluaa pelata taitoaan vastaavasti. Täällä pelaamiseen voi varata pitkän kesäpäivän ja pelata molemmat kentät.

It is Finland's most highly coveted, most exclusive and most expensive golf club. And even though there are two courses, you can only play here on week-ends if accompanied by a member. Both courses were laid out by Jan Sederholm, one of Sweden's most prolific architects, and both are very enjoyable in their very different ways. The "Old Course" is flat like a park with wide open space, while the "New Course" is hilly and runs through a forest. The latter is the most challenging of the two, as the steep topography adds to the difficulty of club selection and players need to be able to bend the ball to keep out of the trees. At the same time, the forest landscape gives a great feeling of isolation and tranquillity, while a few water hazards give visual variety to all the shades of green around you, not forgetting the few but well located sand traps by the greens. A very fine complex where you need to concentrate long and hard to play to your handicap. Play both courses on one long summer's day.

Sarfvik Golf Club — 1984

Finnbyntie 30
FIN - 02430 MASALA

Office	Toimisto	(358) 09 - 221 9000
Pro shop	Pro shop	(358) 09 - 221 9000
Fax	Fax	(358) 09 - 297 7134
Web	www.golfpiste.com	
Situation	Sijainti	Helsinki, 15 km
Annual closure	Kenttä suljetaan	no
Weekly closure	Suljetan viikolla	no

Fees main season — Green fee	Week days / Arkipäivisin	We/Bank holidays / Pyhäpäivisin
	18 holes	
Individual Henkilö	84 €	*
Couple Pari	168 €	*

* Members only

Caddy	Caddy	no
Electric Trolley	Sähköratta at	no
Buggy	Golfauto	25 €
Clubs	Mailat	25 €

Credit cards Luottokortit
VISA - Eurocard - MasterCard - DC - AMEX

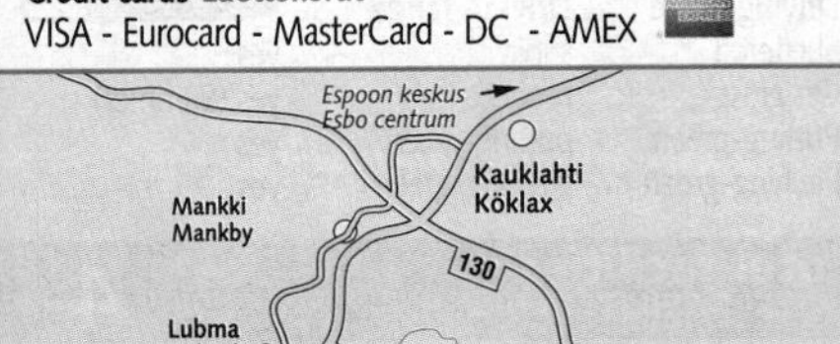

Access Pääsy : Helsinki, 51 → Kirkkonummi/Kyrkslatt.
After Espoonlahti and bridge, turn left → Sarfvik
Map 1 on page 145 Kartta 1 sivulla : 145

Golf course GOLFBANEN — 16/20

Site	Sijainti	
Maintenance	Hoito	
Architect	Arkkitehti	Jan Sederholm
Type	Kentän luonne	forest
Relief	Vapautuminen	
Water in play	Vesiesteitä	
Exp. to wind	Tuulta	
Trees in play	Puita	

Scorecard Tuloskortti	Chp. Champ. tii	Mens Miest. tii	Ladies Naist. tii
Length Pituus	5854	5688	4696
Par	72	72	72
Slope system	135	137	125

Advised golfing ability Tasoitusvaatimus: 0 12 24 36
Hcp required Hcp-vaatimus: no

Club house & amenities KLUBHUS OG OMGIVELSER — 8/10

Pro shop	Pro shop	
Driving range	Driving range	
Sheltered	suoja	yes
On grass	ruoholla	yes (Summer)
Putting-green	putting-green	yes
Pitching-green	pitching-green	yes

Hotel facilities HOTELFASILITETER — 7/10

HOTELS
Majvik — Espoo 9 km
100 rooms, D 128 €
Tel (358) 09 - 295 511

RESTAURANTS RAVINTOLA
Majvik — Espoo 9 km
Tel (358) 09 - 295 511

ST LAURENCE

14 | 5 | 4

Kenttä sijaitsee aivan Lohjan kaupungin ja Lohjanjärven tuntumassa. Kymmenen prosenttia Etelä-Suomen pinta-alasta on vettä ja Lohjanjärvi on alueen toiseksi suurin järvi. Arkkitehti Kosti Kuronen, joka on yksi Suomen parhaista amatöörigolfareista, on epäilemättä tuntenut houkutusta vesiesteiden käyttöön. Vesi on tietenkin mukana kuvassa, mutta Kurosen perus- ratkaisu on varovaisempi ja kenttä sulautuu hyvin metsä- ja peltomaisemaansa. Vaikka Suomen golfkausi on lyhyt on St. Laurence aina erinomaisessa kunnossa. Väylät ja griinibunkkeristo on suunniteltu hyvin, samoin kuin suuret viheriöt, joilla kannattaa pysytellä lipun tuntumassa, muuten seuraa "three put". Griinit ovat melko kumpuilevia, suhteellisen kovia, nopeudeltaan sopivia ja hyvin suojattuja. St. Laurence on erittäin miellyttävä kenttä, pelaajan valmiuksista riippumatta.

The course is located within the immediate vicinity of the town of Lohja and lake Lohjanjärvi, the largest in southern Finland, where ten percent of surface area is made up of lakes. Kosti Kuronen, one of the top Finnish golfers, was obviously tempted to pepper the course with water hazards, but while paying an obvious tribute to the very strategic style of American architecture, he resisted the easy option of excess water and preserved a more typical setting of forest and fields. Although the golfing season is short in Finland, this very neatly landscaped course is always in very satisfactory condition, a compliment that is valid for the well-located fairway and green-side bunkers, the fairways and very large greens, where you need to keep it near the pin if you want avoid three putts. The putting surfaces are slightly undulating, rather firm, not too slick and well guarded. A very pleasant course, regardless of playing ability.

St Laurence Golf — 1989

Kaivurinkatu 133
FIN - 08 200 LOHJA

Office	Toimisto	(358) 019 - 386 603
Pro shop	Pro shop	(358) 019 - 386 603
Fax	Fax	(358) 019 - 386 666
Web	www.golfpiste.com	
Situation	Sijainti	Lohja, 5 km
Annual closure	Kenttä suljetaan	no
Weekly closure	Suljetan viikolla	no

Fees main season Green fee	18 holes	
	Week days Arkipäivisin	We/Bank holidays Pyhäpäivisin
Individual Henkilö	42 €	50 €
Couple Pari	84 €	100 €

Caddy	Caddy	no
Electric Trolley	Sähkörattaat	no
Buggy	Golfauto	no
Clubs	Mailat	8 €

Credit cards Luottokortit
VISA - Eurocard - MasterCard - DC - AMEX

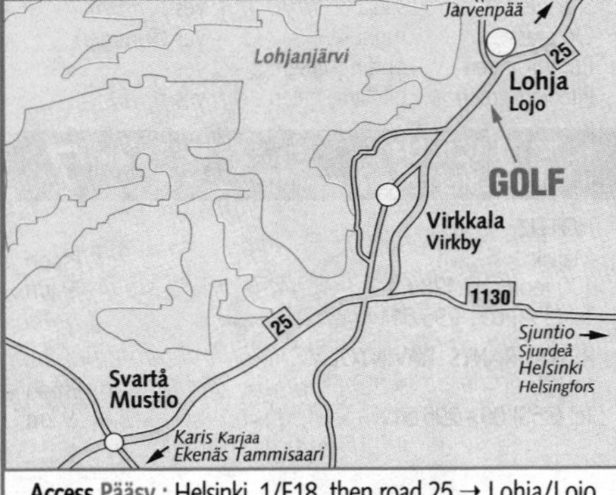

Access Pääsy : Helsinki, 1/E18, then road 25 → Lohja/Lojo
Map 1 on page 145 Kartta 1 sivulla : 145

Golf course GOLFBANEN — 14/20

Site	Sijainti	
Maintenance	Hoito	
Architect	Arkkitehti	Kosti Kuronen
Type	Kentän luonne	forest, parkland
Relief	Vapautuminen	
Water in play	Vesiesteitä	
Exp. to wind	Tuulta	
Trees in play	Puita	

Scorecard Tuloskortti	Chp. Champ. tii	Mens Miest. tii	Ladies Naist. tii
Length Pituus	6247	5769	5018
Par	72	72	72
Slope system	125	129	121

Advised golfing ability Tasoitusvaatimus: 0 12 24 36
Hcp required Hcp-vaatimus 36

Club house & amenities KLUBHUS OG OMGIVELSER — 5/10

Pro shop	Pro shop	
Driving range	Driving range	
Sheltered	suoja	yes
On grass	ruoholla	yes (Summer)
Putting-green	putting-green	yes
Pitching-green	pitching-green	yes

Hotel facilities HOTELFASILITETER — 4/10

HOTELS
Mustio Castle — Lohja 30 km
30 rooms, D 148 € (w. GF)
Tel (358) 019 - 362 31

RESTAURANTS RAVINTOLA
Mustio Castle — Lohja 30 km
Tel (358) 019 - 362 31

TALMA

14 | 8 | 6

Musiikista kiinnostunut pelaaja jatkaa kentältä Tuusulanjärven rannalla sijaitsevaan Ainolaan, missä säveltäjä Jean Sibelius asui suurimman osan elämästään. Lähistöllä on myös Gauguinin oppilaana olleen taidemaalari Pekka Halosen talo. Niin Halosen kuin Sibeliuksenkin inspiraation lähteitä olivat Suomen kansa, luonto ja legendat. Golf Talman klubitalo on rakennettu suomalaisten taide- ja suunnitteluperinteiden hengessä. 27-reikäisen kentänkin luulisi silloin olevan erikoisemman, mutta kokonaisuus on varsin hillitty, ja maisema sisältää niin metsäosuuksia kuin puistomaisempiakin alueita. Jos pelaa vain 18 reikää, ovat A- ja B-väylä golfteknisesti vaikein osuus. Muutoin erot eivät ole suuria. Erityistä kiitosta ansaitsevat erinomaiset harjoitusmahdollisuudet, jotka kohottavat kokonaisvaikutelmaa.

Music-lovers will want to push a little further north-west from this course as far as Ainola on the shores of lake Tuusula. This is where the composer Jean Sibelius spent most of his life. A little further still and you can visit the house and studio of the painter Pekka Halonen, a student with Gauguin. The two men were inspired by the Finnish people, their legends and nature. The club-house here follows the country's tradition of art and design, and as such might leave you expecting a more exceptional and stylish course than is actually the case. As it happens, the 27 holes here are rather more sedate in a calm setting between parkland and forest. If you play only 18 holes, the combination of the two nine-hole A and B courses is perhaps the most difficult golf-wise, but there is little difference between the three. The whole complex is enhanced by the excellence of the practice facilities.

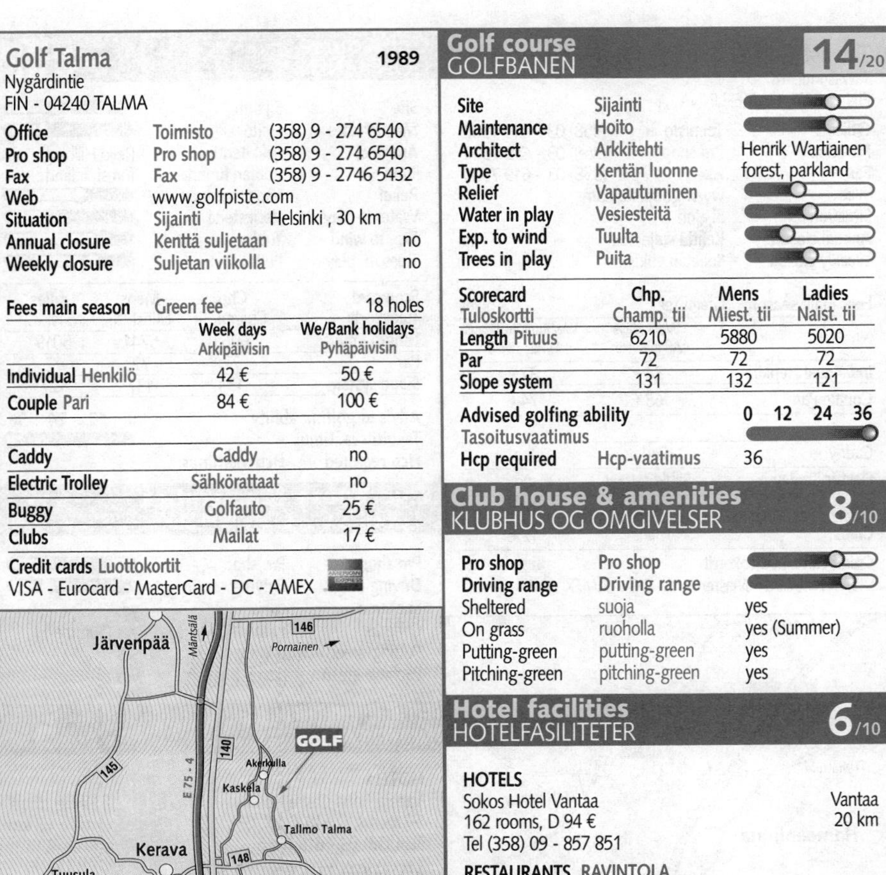

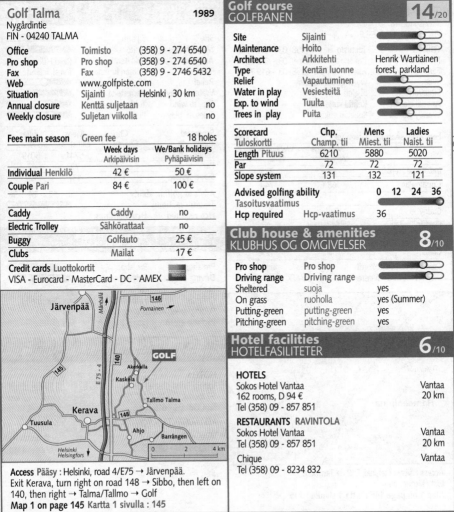

Golf Talma — 1989

Nygårdintie
FIN - 04240 TALMA

Office	Toimisto	(358) 9 - 274 6540
Pro shop	Pro shop	(358) 9 - 274 6540
Fax	Fax	(358) 9 - 2746 5432
Web	www.golfpiste.com	
Situation	Sijainti	Helsinki , 30 km
Annual closure	Kenttä suljetaan	no
Weekly closure	Suljetan viikolla	no

Fees main season Green fee	18 holes	
	Week days Arkipäivisin	**We/Bank holidays** Pyhäpäivisin
Individual Henkilö	42 €	50 €
Couple Pari	84 €	100 €

Caddy	Caddy	no
Electric Trolley	Sähkörattaat	no
Buggy	Golfauto	25 €
Clubs	Mailat	17 €

Credit cards Luottokortit
VISA - Eurocard - MasterCard - DC - AMEX

Access Pääsy : Helsinki, road 4/E75 → Järvenpää. Exit Kerava, turn right on road 148 → Sibbo, then left on 140, then right → Talma/Tallmo → Golf
Map 1 on page 145 Kartta 1 sivulla : 145

Golf course — GOLFBANEN — 14/20

Site	Sijainti	
Maintenance	Hoito	
Architect	Arkkitehti	Henrik Wartiainen
Type	Kentän luonne	forest, parkland
Relief	Vapautuminen	
Water in play	Vesiesteitä	
Exp. to wind	Tuulta	
Trees in play	Puita	

Scorecard Tuloskortti	**Chp.** Champ. tii	**Mens** Miest. tii	**Ladies** Naist. tii
Length Pituus	6210	5880	5020
Par	72	72	72
Slope system	131	132	121

Advised golfing ability Tasoitusvaatimus — 0 12 24 36

Hcp required Hcp-vaatimus 36

Club house & amenities — KLUBHUS OG OMGIVELSER — 8/10

Pro shop	Pro shop	
Driving range	Driving range	
Sheltered	suoja	yes
On grass	ruoholla	yes (Summer)
Putting-green	putting-green	yes
Pitching-green	pitching-green	yes

Hotel facilities — HOTELFASILITETER — 6/10

HOTELS

Sokos Hotel Vantaa — Vantaa 20 km
162 rooms, D 94 €
Tel (358) 09 - 857 851

RESTAURANTS RAVINTOLA

Sokos Hotel Vantaa — Vantaa 20 km
Tel (358) 09 - 857 851

Chique — Vantaa
Tel (358) 09 - 8234 832

155

TAWAST

14	7	5

Hämeenlinnan (ruotsiksi Tavastehus) Tawast-kenttä sijaitsee upeassa rantamaisemassa. Metsät rikkovat vain harvakseltaan alueen rikkaita vesistöjä, joilla voi tehdä laivamatkoja järveltä toiselle. Alue on yksi Suomen suurimmista turistikeskuksista, ja suurimmat kaupungit ovat nimeltään Tampere (Tammerfors) ja Savonlinna (Nyslott). Tawastin kenttä sijaitsee Katumajärven rannalla, puistomaisemassa, ja arkkitehdillä on ollut siinä määrin mieltymys dog leg -välien käyttöön, että pelaaja yllättyy, kun par 3 -reiät ovatkin suoria. Tawastin kokonaisuus on kuitenkin erittäin mielenkiintoinen, joskin kenttä on lyhyenlainen monien Suomen kenttien tapaan. Arkkitehdit hemmottelevat kuntoilijagolfareita! Tawast vaatii keskittymistä monien esteiden selvittämiseksi. Pelaajalta vaaditaan erilaisten lyöntien hallintaa tasoerojen aiheuttamien tilanteiden hallitsemiseksi. Vanhan kartanon talliin rakennettu kerhotalo on erittäin viihtyisä ja tyylikäs.

Hämeenlinna (Tavastehus) is one of the gateways to the wonderful region of lakes, interrupted only occasionally by forests, where you can set out on almost endless water cruises across lakes that are often inter-linked by stretches of water. This is one of the country's major tourist areas, around the two centres of Tempere and Savonlinna. The Tawast course lies along one of these superb lakes in a wood-covered parkland landscape where the architect seems to have been hell-bent on producing nothing but dog-legs. It's a wonder he did not curve the par 3s as well. Having said that, this is an interesting layout, albeit not very long (like most courses in Finland), where the designers had a lot of thought for mid-handicappers. Every golfer here will have to negotiate all types of hazard, try every shot in the book and cope with a number of different situations owing to the topology. Facilities are good, including a very pleasant and stylish club-house in the old stables of a former lordly estate.

Tawast Golf & Country Club — 1987

Tawastintie 48
FIN - 13270 HÄMESLINNA

Office	Toimisto	(358) 03 - 619 7502
Pro shop	Pro shop	(358) 03 - 619 7502
Fax	Fax	(358) 03 - 619 7503
Web	www.golfpiste.com	
Situation	Sijainti	
Annual closure	Kenttä suljetaan	no
Weekly closure	Suljetan viikolla	no

Fees main season Green fee	Week days Arkipäivisin	We/Bank holidays Pyhäpäivisin
	18 holes	
Individual Henkilö	34 €	37 €
Couple Pari	68 €	74 €

Caddy	Caddy	no
Electric Trolley	Sähkörattaat	no
Buggy	Golfauto	34 €
Clubs	Mailat	17 €

Credit cards Luottokortit
VISA - Eurocard - MasterCard - DC - AMEX

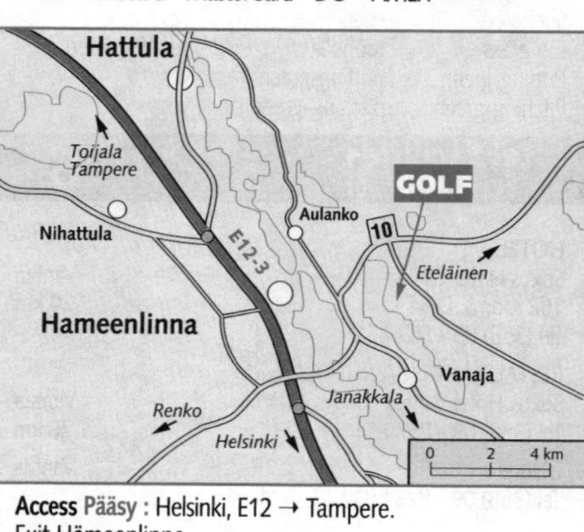

Access Pääsy : Helsinki, E12 → Tampere.
Exit Hämeenlinna.
Map 1 on page 145 Kartta 1 sivulla : 145

Golf course GOLFBANEN — 14/20

Site	Sijainti	
Maintenance	Hoito	
Architect	Arkkitehti	Reijo Hillberg
Type	Kentän luonne	forest, inland
Relief	Vapautuminen	
Water in play	Vesiesteitä	
Exp. to wind	Tuulta	
Trees in play	Puita	

Scorecard Tuloskortti	**Chp.** Champ. tii	**Mens** Miest. tii	**Ladies** Naist. tii
Length Pituus	6063	5741	5019
Par	72	72	72
Slope system	134	137	127

Advised golfing ability Tasoitusvaatimus — 0 12 24 36
Hcp required Hcp-vaatimus 36

Club house & amenities KLUBHUS OG OMGIVELSER — 7/10

Pro shop	Pro shop	
Driving range	Driving range	
Sheltered	suoja	yes
On grass	ruoholla	yes (Summer)
Putting-green	putting-green	yes
Pitching-green	pitching-green	yes

Hotel facilities HOTELFASILITETER — 5/10

HOTELS
Vanajanlinna Castle Hotel — Hämesnlinna
50 rooms, D 118 € (w. GF) — 3 km
Tel (358) 03 - 619 6565

RESTAURANTS RAVINTOLA
Vanajanlinna — Hämesnlinna
Tel (358) 03 - 619 6565 — 3 km

EUROPE'S TOP 1000 GOLF COURSES

France

Les Bordes

LA PEUGEOT 607 EST MUNIE D'UN DÉTECTEUR D'OBSTACLE ARRIÈRE*.
CE SERAIT DOMMAGE D'ABÎMER LE PARE-CHOCS.

www.607.peugeot.fr

POUR VOUS GARER EN TOUTE SÉCURITÉ, LA PEUGEOT 607 DISPOSE* DE CAPTEURS INTÉGRÉS AU PARE-CHOCS ARRIÈRE. À L'AIDE D'ULTRASONS, CES CAPTEURS DÉTECTERONT LES OBSTACLES HORS DE VOTRE CHAMP DE VISION ET UN SIGNAL SONORE, DONT L'INTENSITÉ VARIE SELON LEUR PROXIMITÉ, VOUS PERMETTRA DE VOUS GARER LES YEUX FERMÉS. LA PEUGEOT 607 NE POUVANT SE CONTENTER QUE DE LA PERFECTION, AU PASSAGE DE LA MARCHE ARRIÈRE, LES MIROIRS DES RÉTROVISEURS EXTÉRIEURS PEUVENT, SI VOUS LE DÉSIREZ, PIVOTER VERS LE BAS ET AINSI FACILITER VOS CRÉNEAUX*.
POUR QUE L'AUTOMOBILE SOIT TOUJOURS UN PLAISIR.

*En option ou sur version Pack.

France

Bien que son histoire soit longue, et que le premier golf du continent y ait été construit (à Pau), le golf en France ne s'est vraiment développé qu'à partir des années 80, et compte aujourd'hui plus de 320.000 golfeurs pour environ 500 parcours, dont plus de 350 de 18 trous. Il reste encore beaucoup de place pour les visiteurs, en tout cas en semaine ! Premier pays du monde pour le tourisme, la France commence seulement à être considérée comme une destination golfique, et ses arguments en la matière ne manquent pas.

Vous trouverez essentiellement ici les meilleurs parcours ouverts au public. Les grands golfs privés traditionnels acceptent parfois les visiteurs, en semaine notamment, et en été, mais sans faire vraiment de publicité à ce sujet. Avec une lettre d'introduction de votre club, vous pouvez tenter votre chance auprès des plus réputés: par exemple Chantilly, Saint-Germain, Fontainebleau, Saint-Nom-la-Bretèche, le Paris International, Joyenval, La Boulie.

Tous figuraient déjà dans ce Guide... Nous y avons ajouté deux golfs très exclusifs, Morfontaine, et le Prince de Provence à Vidauban, parce que vous avez peut-être pensé, ou parce que vous aimeriez en devenir membre, parce qu'un membre peut vous y inviter, ou tout simplement pour connaître notre évaluation dans la hiérarchie.

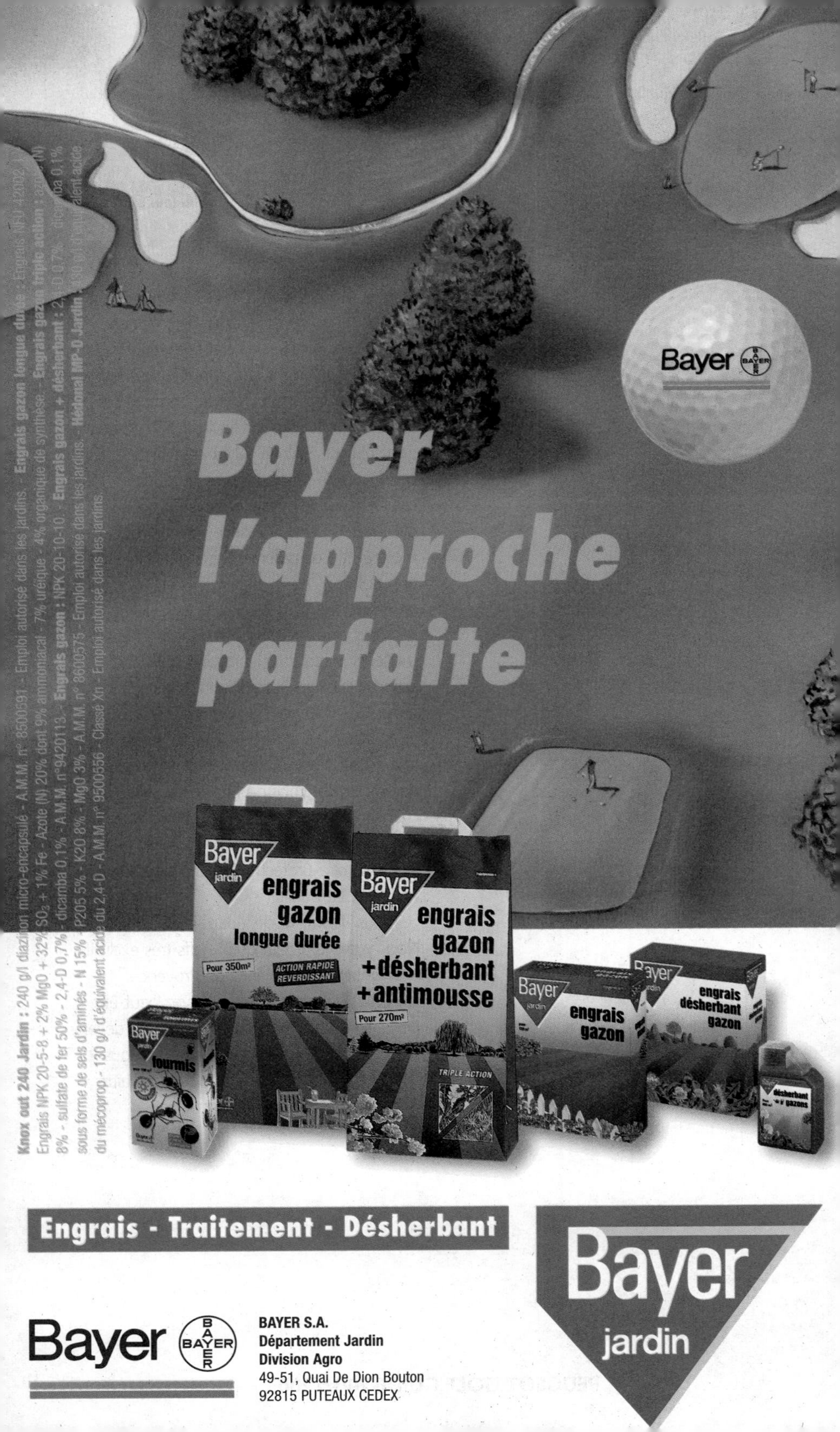

Bayer l'approche parfaite

Knox out 240 Jardin : 240 g/l diazinon micro-encapsulé - A.M.M. n° 8500891 - Emploi autorisé dans les jardins. - **Engrais gazon longue durée** : Engrais NFU 42002 ... Engrais NPK 20-5-8 + 2% MgO + 32% SO_3 + 1% Fe - Azote (N) 20% dont 9% ammoniacal - 7% uréique - 4% organique de synthèse. - **Engrais gazon triple action** : azote (N) 8% - sulfate de fer 50% - 2,4-D 0,7% - dicamba 0,1% - A.M.M. n°9420113 - **Engrais gazon** : NPK 20-10-10. - **Engrais gazon + désherbant** : 2,4-D 0,7% - dicamba 0,1% sous forme de sels d'aminés - N 15% - P205 5% - K20 8% - MgO 3% - A.M.M. n° 8600575 - Emploi autorisé dans les jardins. - **Hédonal MP-D Jardin** : 330 g/l d'équivalent acide du mécoprop - 130 g/l d'équivalent acide du 2,4-D - A.M.M. n° 9500556 - Classé Xn - Emploi autorisé dans les jardins.

Engrais - Traitement - Désherbant

BAYER S.A.
Département Jardin
Division Agro
49-51, Quai De Dion Bouton
92815 PUTEAUX CEDEX

France

The first golf course on the continent was built in France (Pau), but the game only really took off in this country in the 1980s.Today there are more than 320,000 golfers for about 500 courses, of which more than 350 are eighteen-hole layouts. So there is room enough for visitors, at least during the weekdays. A world leader for tourism, France is now only starting to be considered as a golfing destination and it has a lot going for it.

We have included here the best courses open to the public. The great traditional private courses sometimes admit visitors, especially during the week and summer, but they never really promote the idea. With a letter of introduction from your club you can try your luck at some of the more highly-reputed courses such as Chantilly, Joyenval, Saint-Germain, Fontainebleau, Saint-Nom-la-Bretèche, Paris International and La Boulie in the greater Paris area.

All are featured in this edition and we have also added two highly exclusive courses in Morfontaine, to the north of Paris, and the Prince de Provence in Vidauban. Maybe because you are thinking about becoming a member yourself, or because a member might invite you for a round, or quite simply to see how they figure in our ranking system.

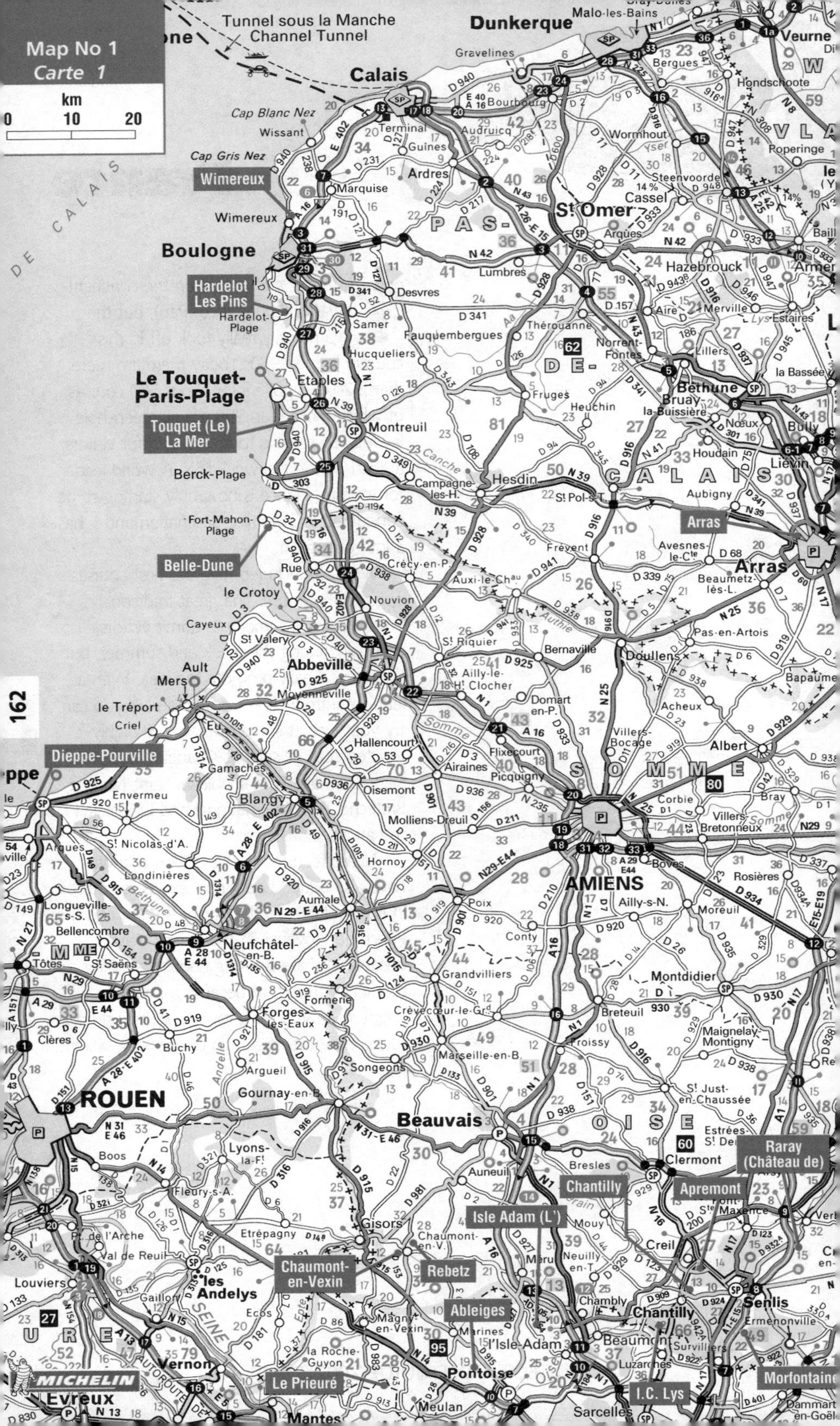

Map No 1
Carte 1
km
0 10 20
Tunnel sous la Manche
Channel Tunnel
Dunkerque
Malo-les-Bains
Calais
Gravelines
Bergues
Hondschoote
Veurne
Cap Blanc Nez
Wissant
Cap Gris Nez
Wimereux
Boulogne
Hardelot Les Pins
Hardelot-Plage
Le Touquet-Paris-Plage
Touquet (Le) La Mer
Berck-Plage
Fort-Mahon-Plage
Belle-Dune
Rue
le Crotoy
Cayeux
St Valery
Ault
Mers
le Tréport
Criel
Dieppe-Pourville
Marquise
Guînes
Ardres
Audruicq
Bourbourg
Wormhout
Steenvoorde
Poperinge
Cassel
St Omer
Arques
Hazebrouck
Lumbres
Desvres
Samer
Hucqueliers
Fauquembergues
Thérouanne
Aire
Merville
Estaires
Lillers
Norrent-Fontes
Béthune
Bruay-la-Buissière
Noeux
Bully
Liévin
la Bassée
Houdain
Heuchin
Fruges
Etaples
Montreuil
Campagne-les-H.
Hesdin
St Pol-s-T.
Aubigny
Arras
Frévent
Avesnes-le-Cte
Beaumetz-lès-L.
Auxi-le-Château
Crécy-en-P.
Nouvion
Abbeville
St Riquier
Bernaville
Doullens
Pas-en-Artois
Bapaume
Acheux
Albert
Aillly-le-Ht Clocher
Domart-en-P.
Moyenneville
Eu
Gamaches
Blangy
Hallencourt
Airaines
Oisemont
Flixecourt
Picquigny
Villers-Bocage
Corbie
Bray
Villers-Bretonneux
AMIENS
Boves
Molliens-Dreuil
Hornoy
Aumale
Poix
Conty
Ailly-s-N.
Moreuil
Rosières
Envermeu
Arques
St Nicolas-d'A.
Londinières
Longueville-s-S.
Bellencombre
Neufchâtel-en-B.
Tôtes
St Saëns
Clères
Buchy
Forges-les-Eaux
Formerie
Grandvilliers
Crèvecoeur-le-Gd
Breteuil
Montdidier
Maignelay-Montigny
Froissy
Marseille-en-B.
Songeons
Argueil
Gournay-en-B.
ROUEN
Beauvais
St Just-en-Chaussée
Estrées-St Denis
Clermont
Raray (Château de)
Boos
Lyons-la-F.
Fleury-s-A.
Auneuil
Bresles
Chantilly
Apremont
Isle Adam (L')
Mouy
Creil
Pont-Ste Maxence
Verberie
Pt de l'Arche
Val de Reuil
Etrépagny
Gisors
Chaumont-en-V.
Chaumont-en-Vexin
Rebetz
Méru
Neuilly-en-T.
Louviers
les Andelys
Gaillon
Ecos
Magny-en-Vexin
Marines
Ableiges
l'Isle-Adam
Chambly
Beaumont
Luzarches
Senlis
Ermenonville
Survilliers
Vernon
la Roche-Guyon
Pontoise
Le Prieuré
I.C. Lys
Morfontaine
Evreux
Mantes
Meulan
Sarcelles
Dammartin-en-Goële
PAS-DE-CALAIS
SOMME
OISE
EURE
SEINE
MICHELIN

d'après cartes n° 237 - 22ème édition et n° 989 - 30ème édition - 2002. Autorisation n° 0102062.

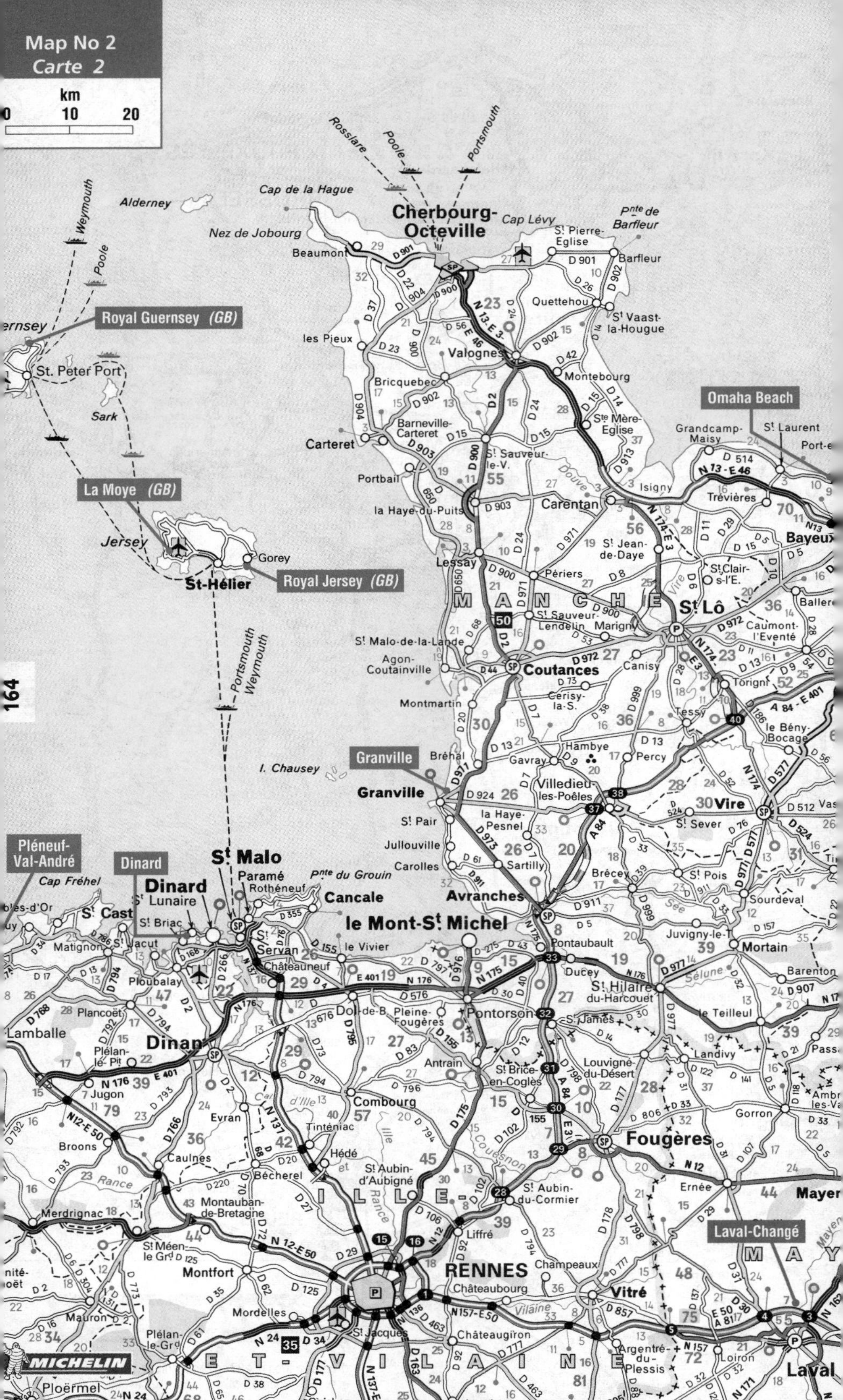

Map No 2
Carte 2
km
0
10
20
Rosslare
Poole
Portsmouth
Weymouth
Poole
Alderney
Cap de la Hague
Nez de Jobourg
Cherbourg-Octeville
Cap Lévy
Pnte de Barfleur
St Pierre-Eglise
Barfleur
Beaumont
Quettehou
St Vaast-la-Hougue
Royal Guernsey (GB)
St. Peter Port
Sark
les Pieux
Valognes
Bricquebec
Montebourg
Barneville-Carteret
Carteret
Ste Mère-Eglise
Omaha Beach
Grandcamp-Maisy
St Laurent
Port-e
Portbail
St Sauveur-le-V.
Isigny
Trévières
Carentan
La Moye (GB)
la Haye-du-Puits
Bayeux
Jersey
Gorey
St-Hélier
Royal Jersey (GB)
Lessay
St Jean-de-Daye
St Clair-s-l'E.
Périers
MANCHE
St Lô
St Sauveur-Lendelin
Marigny
Caumont-l'Eventé
St Malo-de-la-Lande
Agon-Coutainville
Coutances
Canisy
Torigni
Cerisy-la-S.
Montmartin
Tessy
le Bény-Bocage
Portsmouth
Weymouth
Hambye
Percy
Gavray
Bréhal
I. Chausey
Granville
Granville
Villedieu-les-Poêles
Vire
St Pair
la Haye-Pesnel
St Sever
Jullouville
Carolles
Sartilly
Brécey
St Pois
Pléneuf-Val-André
Dinard
Cap Fréhel
St Malo
Paramé
Rothéneuf
Pnte du Grouin
Cancale
Avranches
Sourdeval
Dinard
St Lunaire
St Cast
St Briac
le Mont-St Michel
Juvigny-le-T.
St Servan
Pontaubault
Mortain
Matignon
St Jacut
le Vivier
Châteauneuf
Ducey
Barenton
Ploubalay
St Hilaire-du-Harcouët
Plancoët
Dol-de-B.
Pleine-Fougères
Pontorson
le Teilleul
Lamballe
St James
Dinan
Plélan-le-Pt
Antrain
Landivy
Louvigné-du-Désert
St Brice-en-Coglès
Jugon
Combourg
Evran
Tinténiac
Gorron
Broons
Caulnes
Hédé
Fougères
Bécherel
St Aubin-d'Aubigné
Ernée
Mayer
St Aubin-du-Cormier
Merdrignac
Montauban-de-Bretagne
ILLE-
Liffré
Laval-Changé
St Méen-le Grd
Montfort
RENNES
Champeaux
Châteaubourg
Vitré
Mordelles
Mauron
St Jacques
Châteaugiron
Plélan-le-Gd
Argentré-du-Plessis
Loiron
ET-VILAINE
Laval
Ploërmel
MICHELIN

Dieppe-Pourville
Dieppe
Varengeville
Veules-les-Roses
St Valery-en-Caux
Veulettes
Offranville
Fontaine-le-Dun
Cany-Barville
Bacqueville
Etretat
Fécamp
Yport
Valmont
Ourville
Doudeville
Yerville
Etretat
Criquetot-l'Esneval
Goderville
Fauville
Yvetot
Pavilly
Bolbec
Caudebec
Barentin
Montivilliers
Ste Adresse
St Romain-de-C.
Lillebonne
St Wandrille
LE HAVRE
Duclair
Portsmouth
P. de Tancarville
Quillebeuf
New Golf de Deauville
Villerville
Honfleur
Jumièges
Trouville
Deauville
Blonville
Villers
Houlgate
Beuzeville
Grd Couronne
Arromanches
Courseulles
St Aubin
Langrune
Luc
Ouistreham
Lion
Cabourg
Dives
Pont-Audemer
Bourg-Achard
Bourgtheroulde
Creully
Douvres-la-D.
Merville
Pont-l'Evêque
Cormeilles
Montfort s. R.
Elbeuf
Le Bec-Hellouin
Champ de Bataille
Amirauté (L')
Blangy-le-Châu
Lieurey
Brionne
Louviers
Tilly-s-S.
Troarn
Cambremer
Thiberville
le Neubourg
CAEN
Evrecy
Moult
Mézidon
Lisieux
Bernay
la Rivière-Thibouville
CALVADOS
Aunay-s-O
Thury-Harcourt
St Pierre-s-D.
Orbec
Beaumont-le-Roger
Broglie
Beaumesnil
Livarot
Conches
Potigny
Clécy
Vimoutiers
Falaise
Condé-s-Noireau
Pont-d'Ouilly
la Neuve-Lyre
Damville
Trun
la Ferté-Frênel
Rugles
Breteuil
Flers
Gacé
Exmes
l'Aigle
Tillières
Putanges
Ecouché
Argentan
Verneuil
Messei
Nonant-le-Pin
le Merlerault
Brezolles
Briouze
Moulins-la-Marche
ORNE
Mortrée
Courtomer
la Ferté-Vidame
Domfront
la Ferté-Macé
Sées
Tourouvre
Bagnoles-de-l Orne
Carrouges
Senonches
Juvigny-s/s-A.
Couptrain
Bazoches-s-H.
Longny
Mortagne-au-Perche
le Mêle
Lassay
Pré-en-Pail
Mt des Avaloirs
Alençon
la Loupe
Rémalard
Javron
Pervenchères
Villaines-la-Juhel
Mamers
Bellême
Nogent-le-Rotrou
Thiron-Gardais
Fresnay-s-S.
le Theil
Bais
Beaumont-s-S.
Marolles-les-Braults
Bonnétable
Montsûrs
Sillé-le-Guillaume
Evron
la Ferté-Bernard
Authon
Ballon
Ste Suzanne
Conlie
Tuffé
Montmirail
St Denis-d'Orques
Vaiges
Connerré
Vibraye
MANS
MICHELIN

165

Map No 3
Carte 3
km
0 10 20
Beauvais
Raray (Château de)
Apremont
Isle Adam (L')
Chantilly
Morfontaine
Rebetz
Chaumont-en Vexin
Ableiges
Le Prieuré
I.C. Lys
Voir carte 15
Vaucouleurs (La) Les Vallons
Guerville
Yvelines Les Chênes
Rochefort-Chisan
Courson
Belesbat
Cély
Fontainebleau
Augerville
Bordes (Les)
Limère
Aisses (Les)
Cheverny
Gisors
Louviers
les Andelys
Vernon
Evreux
Mantes
Pacy
Dreux
Houdan
Rambouillet
Chartres
Châteaudun
Vendôme
Blois
Orléans
Etampes
Pithiviers
Nemours
Gien
Sully
Meulan
Nanterre
St Germain
VERSAILLES
PARIS
75
St Denis
Bobigny
Torcy
Créteil
Evry
Corbeil-Essonnes
Sarcelles
Beaumont
Senlis
Creil
Clermont
Montfort-l'A.
Chevreuse
Palaiseau
Maintenon
Nogent-le-Roi
Châteauneuf-en-Th.
Brou
Bonneval
Voves
Cloyes
Beaugency
Meung
Olivet
Châteauneuf-s-L.
Malesherbes
Milly-la-Forêt
Angerville
Dourdan
Toury
Artenay
Patay
Lamotte-Beuvron
Nouan-le-Fuzelier
Salbris
Aubigny
Argent
Romorantin
Chambord
Bracieux
Cour-Cheverny
Contres
Amboise
Mer
Marchenoir
Ouzouer-le-Marché
Lorris
Bellegarde
Beaune-la-Rolande
Puiseaux
Montargis
Briare
EURE
OISE
EURE-ET-LOIR
LOIRET
LOIR-ET-CHER
SEINE
LOIRE
166
MICHELIN

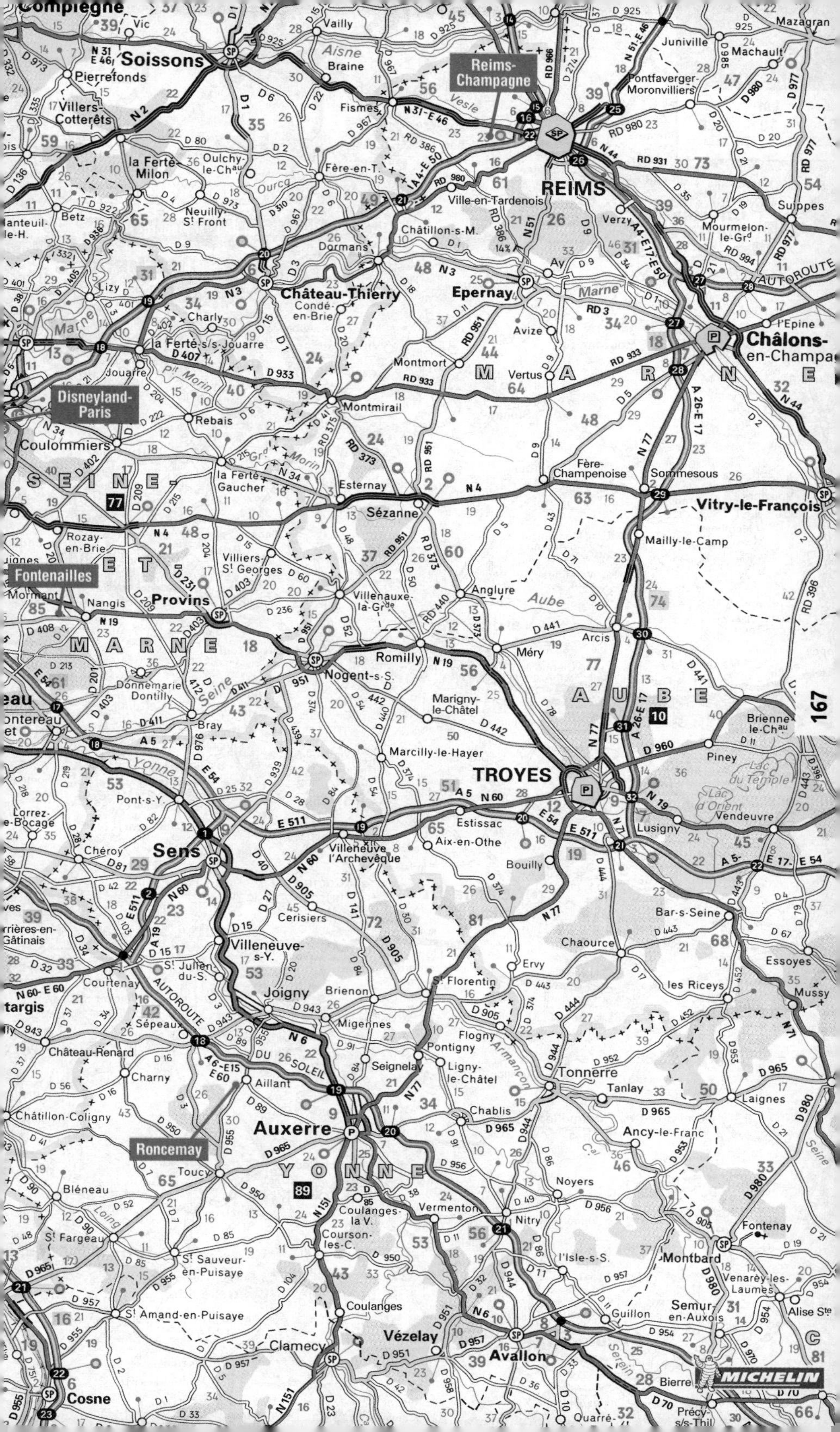

Compiègne
Vic
Soissons
Pierrefonds
Villers-Cotterêts
Vailly
Aisne
Braine
Fismes
Vesle
Reims-Champagne
Juniville
Mazagran
Machault
Pontfaverger-Moronvilliers
REIMS
Ville-en-Tardenois
Châtillon-s-M.
Dormans
Verzy
Mourmelon-le-Gd
Suippes
la Ferté-Milon
Oulchy-le-Chau
Ourcq
Fère-en-T.
Neuilly-St Front
Betz
Nanteuil-le-H.
Lizy
Château-Thierry
Condé-en-Brie
Epernay
Ay
Marne
Avize
Vertus
l'Epine
Châlons-en-Champa
Charly
la Ferté-s/s-Jouarre
Jouarre
Pt Morin
Montmort
Montmirail
Disneyland-Paris
Rebais
Coulommiers
Gd Morin
la Ferté-Gaucher
Esternay
Sézanne
Fère-Champenoise
Sommesous
Vitry-le-François
SEINE-ET-MARNE
MARNE
77
Rozay-en-Brie
Mailly-le-Camp
Villiers-St Georges
Fontenailles
Mormant
Nangis
Provins
Villenauxe-la-Gde
Anglure
Aube
Arcis
Méry
Romilly
Nogent-s-S.
Donnemarie-Dontilly
Marigny-le-Châtel
AUBE
10
Brienne-le-Chau
Montereau
Bray
Seine
Yonne
Marcilly-le-Hayer
TROYES
Piney
Lac du Temple
Lac d'Orient
Lorrez-le-Bocage
Pont-s-Y.
Estissac
Aix-en-Othe
Lusigny
Vendeuvre
Chéroy
Sens
Villeneuve-l'Archevêque
Bouilly
Cerisiers
Bar-s-Seine
Ferrières-en-Gâtinais
Villeneuve-s-Y.
Chaource
St Julien-du-S.
Courtenay
Ervy
Essoyes
St Florentin
les Riceys
Mussy
Montargis
Joigny
Brienon
Sépeaux
Migennes
Flogny
Armançon
Château-Renard
Pontigny
Charny
Seignelay
Ligny-le-Châtel
Tonnerre
Tanlay
Laignes
Aillant
Châtillon-Coligny
AUTOROUTE DU SOLEIL
Chablis
Auxerre
Roncemay
Ancy-le-Franc
YONNE
89
Bléneau
Toucy
Loing
Noyers
Coulanges-la V.
Vermenton
Nitry
Fontenay
St Fargeau
Courson-les-C.
St Sauveur-en-Puisaye
l'Isle-s-S.
Montbard
Venarey-les-Laumes
St Amand-en-Puisaye
Coulanges
Guillon
Semur-en-Auxois
Alise Ste
Clamecy
Vézelay
Avallon
Serein
Cosne
Bierre
Quarré-
Précy-s/s-Thil
MICHELIN

167

Map No 4
Carte 4
km
0 10 20
Charleville-Mézières
Sedan
Bouillon
Neufchâteau
Bastogne
Wiltz
Vianden
Diekirch
Ettelbruck
Echternach
LUXEMBOURG
Grand Ducal de Luxembourg (L)
Kikuoka (L)
Preisch
Arlon (Aarlen)
Florenville
Carignan
Virton
Longwy
Differdange
Esch-s-A.
Dudelange
Montmédy
Stenay
Longuyon
Thionville
Hayange
Amnéville
Briey
Metz
Vouziers
Buzancy
Dun
Damvillers
Spincourt
Etain
Verdun
Ste Menehould
Clermont-en-Argonne
Souilly
Fresnes-en-W.
Mars-la-Tour
Pont-à-Mousson
St Mihiel
Commercy
Bar-le-Duc
Toul
Nancy
Ligny-en-Barrois
Vaucouleurs
St Dizier
Joinville
Gondrecourt
Domrémy
Neufchâteau
Mirecourt
Vittel
Contrexéville
Chaumont
Bar-s-Aube
Montier-en-Der
Wassy
Andelot
Bologne
Darney
Lamarche
Monthureux
Bains-les-Bains
Nogent
Châteauvillain
LUXEMBOURG
ARDENNES
MEUSE
MEURTHE-ET-MOSELLE
HAUTE-MARNE
VOSGES
MICHELIN
168

Wittlich
Bitburg
Traben-Trarbach
Kirchberg (Hunsrück)
Simmern
Stromberg
MAINZ
Nierstein
Bernkastel-Kues
Gemünden
Bad Kreuznach
Wörrstadt
Köngernheim
Trittenheim
Schweich
Ehrang
P F A L Z
Morbach
Kirn
Nahe
Bad Münster am Stein-Ebernburg
Nahetal (D)
Westhofen
Trier
Ruwer
Thalfang
Idar-Oberstein
Meisenheim
Kirchheimbolanden
Flörsheim-Dalsheim
Konz
Hermeskeil
Birkenfeld
Lauterecken
Rockenhausen
Grünstadt
Saarburg
Zerf
Baumholder
Winnweiler
Trassem
Nohfelden
Kusel
Glan-Münchenweiler
Bad Dürkheim
Ludwigshafen
Primstal
Losheim
Mettlach
Tholey
St. Wendel
Ramstein
Frankenstein
Deidesheim
Hochspeyer
S A A R L A N D
Kaiserslautern
Lambrecht
Merzig
Lebach
Ottweiler
Landstuhl
Neustadt-a-d-W
Kalmit
Neunkirchen
Dillingen
Homburg
Edenkoben
Saarlouis
Friedrichsthal
Sulzbach
St. Ingbert
Zweibrücken
Waldfischbach-Burgalben
Völklingen
Dudweiler
Annweiler
Hinterweidenthal
Trifels
Landau
Blieskastel
SAARBRÜCKEN
Pirmasens
Creutzwald
Freyming-Merlebach
Forbach
Bad Bergzabern
Dahn
Carling
Volmunster
Kandel
Sarreguemines
Bitche
Fleckenstein
Wissembourg
St. Avold
Rohrbach
Lembach
Seebach
Faulquemont
Puttelange
Niederbronn
Woerth
Soultz-s/s-Forêts
Hunspach
169
Grostenquin
Sarralbe
Soufflenheim
Reichshoffen
Albestroff
Sarre-Union
Rastatt
Morhange
Drulingen
la Pte Pierre
Ingwiller
Haguenau
Château-Salins
Fénétrange
Bouxwiller
Drusenheim
Dieuze
Phalsbourg
Bischwiller
Sarrebourg
Saverne
Wantzenau (La)
Lutzelbourg
Hochfelden
Truchtersheim
Arracourt
Marmoutier
Lorquin
Wasselonne
Achern
Dabo
STRASBOURG
Kehl
Abreschviller
Wangenbourg
Marlenheim
Renchen
Lunéville
Blâmont
Molsheim
Appenweier
Cirey
Strasbourg Illkirch
Oberhaslach
Offenburg
Col du Donon
Badonviller
Schirmeck
Rosheim
Obernai
Mt Ste Odile
Erstein
Kempferhof (Le)
Gerbeviller
Baccarat
le Hohwald
Barr
Lahr/Schwarzwald
Raon-l'Etape
Senones
Benfeld
Rambervillers
Saales
Villé
Rhinau
Haslach
Provenchères
Châtel-s M.
St Dié-des-Vosges
Ste Marie-aux-Mines
Sélestat
Ettenheim
Herbolzheim
Oberprechtal
Ht-Kœnigsbourg
Kenzingen
C. du Bonhomme
Ribeauvillé
Illhæusern
Elzach
Bruyères
Corcieux
Fraize
Riquewihr
Kaysersberg
Marckolsheim
Riegel
Emmendingen
Waldkirch
Lapoutroie
Orbey
3 Epis
COLMAR
Granges-s-Vologne
C. de la Schlucht
Turckheim
Kandel
Epinal
Eloyes
Wintzenheim
Breisach
FREIBURG
St. Märgen
Gérardmer
Hohneck
Munster
Neuf-Brisach
Xertigny
Grosse Pierre
St Amé
Remiremont
la Bresse
Rouffach
Bad Krozingen
Schauinsland
MICHELIN

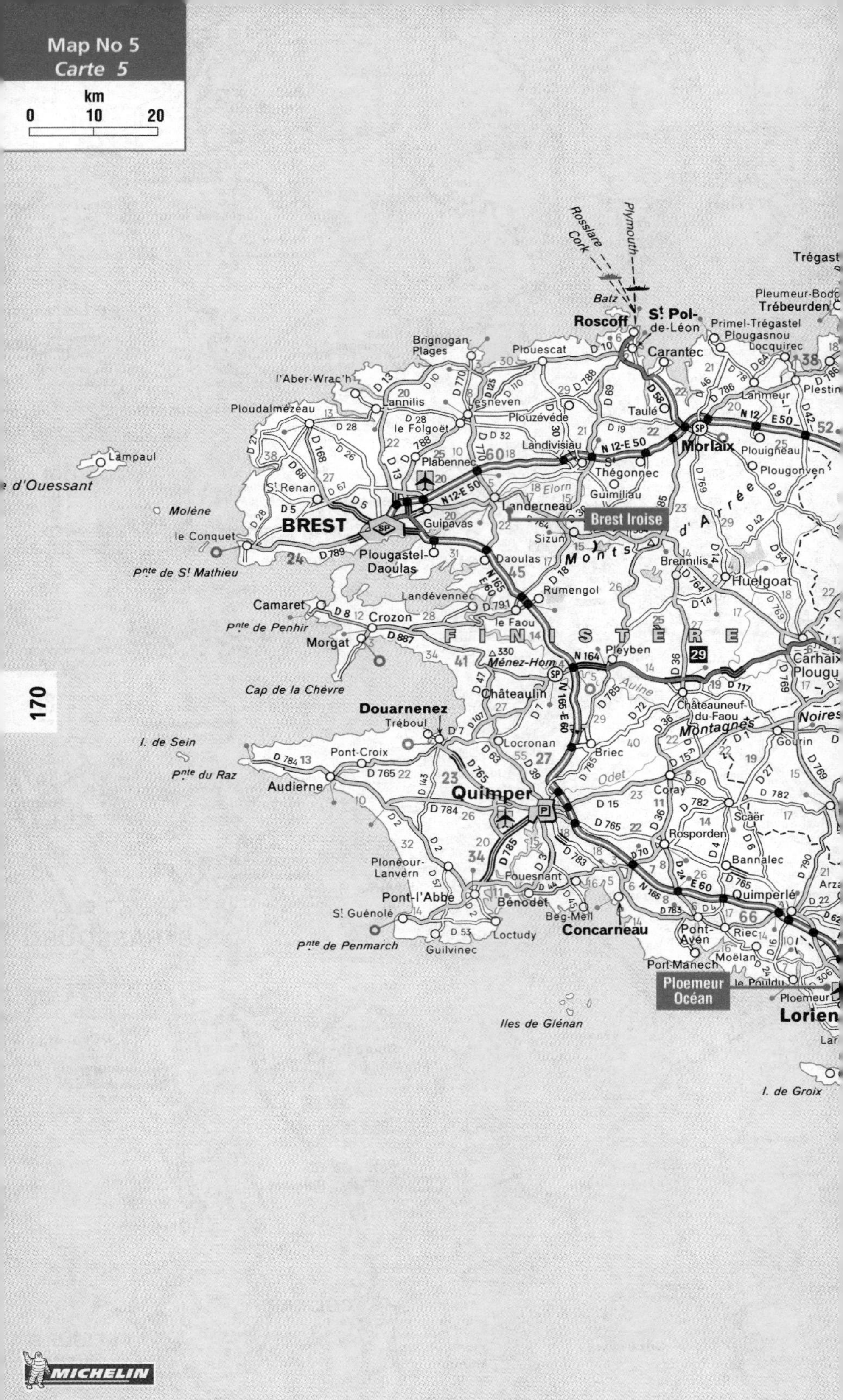

Map No 5
Carte 5

km
0 10 20

Plymouth
Rosslare
Cork
Trégast
Batz
Roscoff
St Pol-de-Léon
Pleumeur-Bod
Trébeurden
Primel-Trégastel
Plougasnou
Locquirec
Carantec
Brignogan-Plages
Plouescat
l'Aber-Wrac'h
Lannilis
Lesneven
Taulé
Lanmeur
Plestin
Ploudalmézeau
Plouzévédé
le Folgoët
Morlaix
Lampaul
Landivisiau
Plabennec
St Thégonnec
Plouigneau
Plougonven
d'Ouessant
St Renan
Guimiliau
Landerneau
Elorn
Molène
BREST
Guipavas
Brest Iroise
le Conquet
Sizun
Monts d'Arrée
Plougastel-Daoulas
Daoulas
Brennilis
Pnte de St Mathieu
Huelgoat
Rumengol
Camaret
Landévennec
Crozon
le Faou
Pnte de Penhir
Morgat
FINISTÈRE
Pleyben
Ménez-Hom
Carhaix-Plougu
Châteaulin
Aulne
Cap de la Chèvre
Châteauneuf-du-Faou
Montagnes Noires
Douarnenez
Tréboul
Gourin
I. de Sein
Locronan
Pont-Croix
Briec
Pnte du Raz
Audierne
Odet
Coray
Quimper
Scaër
Rosporden
Bannalec
Plonéour-Lanvern
Fouesnant
Quimperlé
Pont-l'Abbé
Bénodet
Arz
St Guénolé
Beg-Meil
Concarneau
Pont-Aven
Riec
Pnte de Penmarch
Guilvinec
Loctudy
Moëlan
Port-Manech
Ploemeur Océan
le Pouldu
Ploemeur
Lorien
Iles de Glénan
I. de Groix

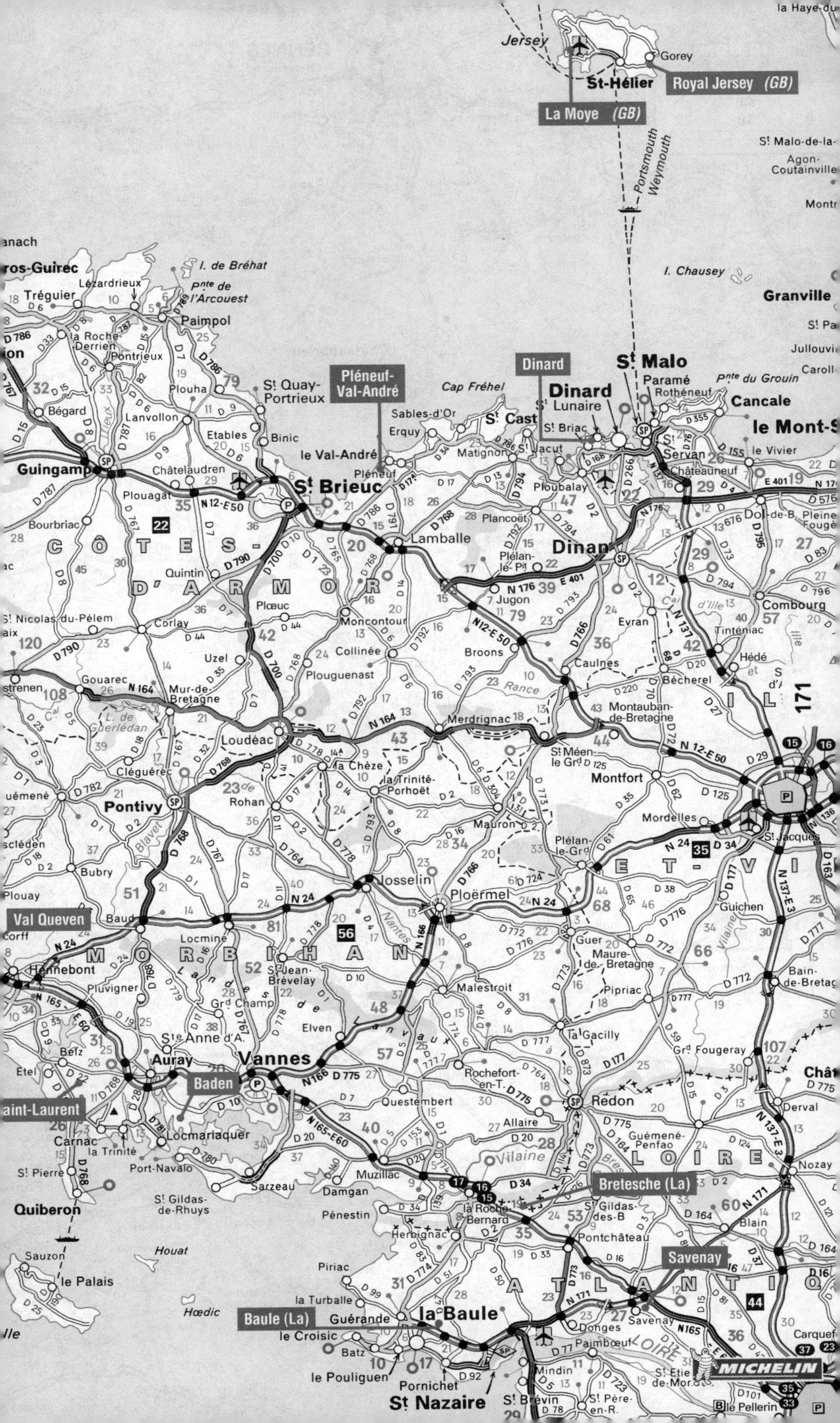

Jersey
St-Hélier
Gorey
Royal Jersey (GB)
La Moye (GB)
Portsmouth
Weymouth
la Haye-du
St Malo-de-la-
Agon-Coutainville
Montr
I. Chausey
Granville
I. de Bréhat
Pnte de l'Arcouest
Lézardrieux
Tréguier
Paimpol
la Roche-Derrien
Pontrieux
Plouha
St Quay-Portrieux
Pléneuf-Val-André
Cap Fréhel
Dinard
St Malo
Paramé
Rothéneuf
Pnte du Grouin
Cancale
le Mont-S
Bégard
Lanvollon
Etables
Binic
Sables-d'Or
Erquy
St Cast
St Lunaire
St Briac
St Jacut
Matignon
le Val-André
Pléneuf
St Servan
Châteauneuf
le Vivier
Guingamp
Châtelaudren
St Brieuc
Plouagat
Ploubalay
Dol-de-B.
Pleine-Fougè
Bourbriac
22
CÔTES-D'ARMOR
Lamballe
Plancoët
Dinan
Plélan-le-Pt
Quintin
Jugon
Combourg
St Nicolas-du-Pélem
Corlay
Ploeuc
Moncontour
Evran
Tinténiac
Hédé
Uzel
Collinée
Broons
Caulnes
Bécherel
Gouarec
Plouguenast
Rance
Montauban-de-Bretagne
Mur-de-Bretagne
L. de Guerlédan
Loudéac
Merdrignac
St Méen-le Grd
La Chèze
La Trinité-Porhoët
Montfort
Cléguérec
Pontivy
Rohan
Mauron
Mordelles
St Jacques
Plélan-le-Grd
Bubry
Josselin
Ploërmel
35
Plouay
Baud
Val Queven
Locminé
56
MORBIHAN
Guer
Guichen
Maure-de-Bretagne
Hennebont
St Jean-Brévelay
Malestroit
Pipriac
Bain-de-Bretag
Pluvigner
Grd Champ
Elven
Landes de Lanvaux
Ste Anne d'A.
Belz
Auray
Vannes
La Gacilly
Grd Fougeray
Etel
Baden
Rochefort-en-T.
Redon
Derval
Saint-Laurent
Questembert
Allaire
Carnac
la Trinité
Locmariaquer
Guémené-Penfao
LOIRE
Port-Navalo
Vilaine
Nozay
St Pierre
Quiberon
Sarzeau
Muzillac
Damgan
Bretesche (La)
St Gildas-de-Rhuys
Pénestin
la Roche-Bernard
St Gildas-des-B
Blain
Herbignac
Pontchâteau
Houat
Sauzon
le Palais
Piriac
Savenay
ATLANTIQUE
44
la Turballe
Hoedic
Baule (La)
Guérande
la Baule
Donges
le Croisic
Batz
Paimboeuf
le Pouliguen
Pornichet
St Nazaire
St Brévin
Mindin
St Etie de-Mor.
St Père-en-R.
le Pellerin
Carquef
MICHELIN

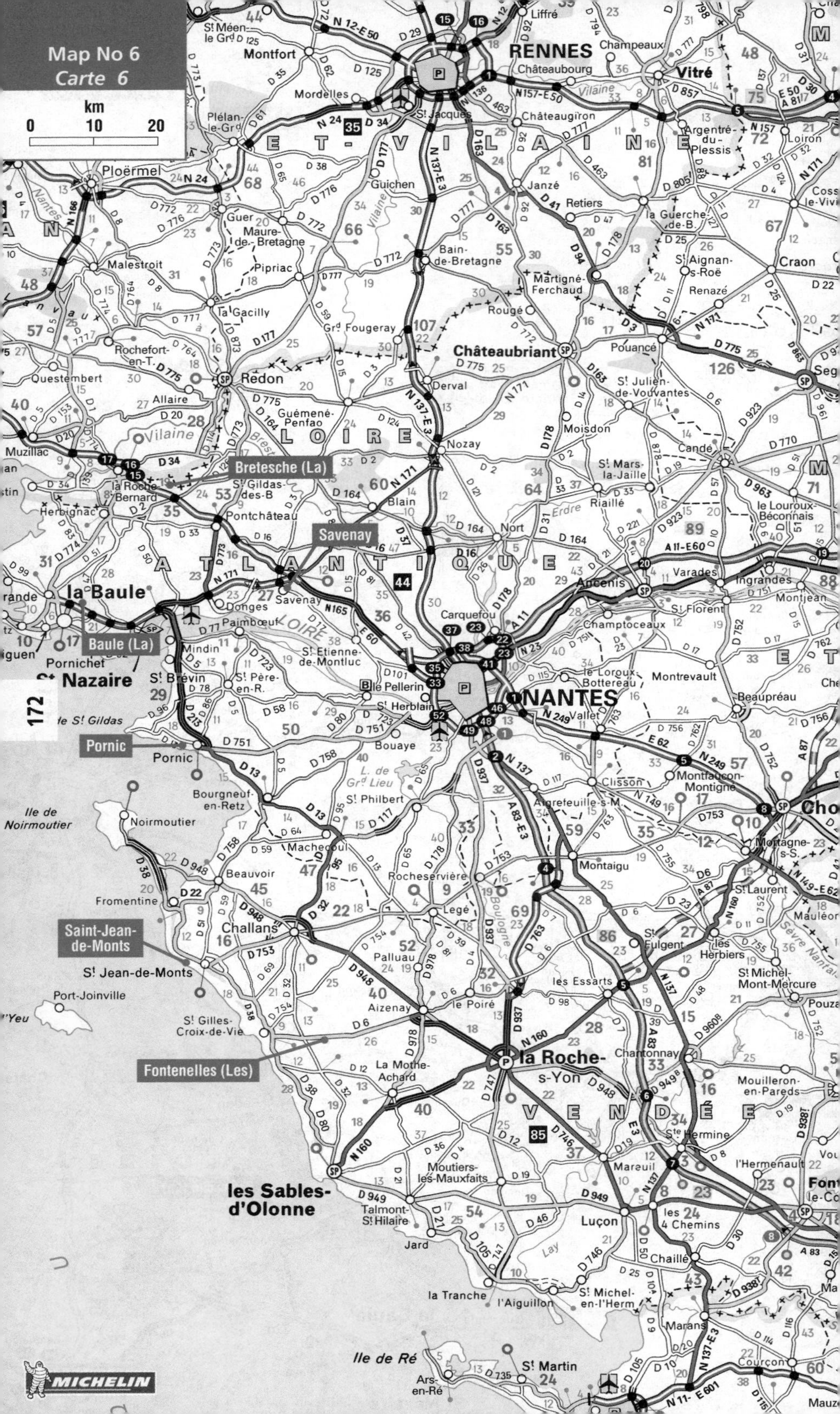
Map No 6
Carte 6
km
0 10 20
RENNES
Montfort
Mordelles
St Jacques
Liffré
Châteaubourg
Vitré
Châteaugiron
Argentré-du-Plessis
Janzé
Retiers
la Guerche-de-B.
Ploërmel
Malestroit
Guer
Maure-de-Bretagne
Pipriac
Guichen
Bain-de-Bretagne
Martigné-Ferchaud
Craon
Rougé
Grd Fougeray
Châteaubriant
Pouancé
Redon
Rochefort-en-T.
Questembert
Allaire
Derval
Guémené-Penfao
Nozay
Moisdon
St Julien-de-Vouvantes
Candé
Muzillac
Bretesche (La)
la Roche-Bernard
Herbignac
St Gildas-des-B
Pontchâteau
Blain
Savenay
Nort
Riaillé
St Mars-la-Jaille
le Louroux-Béconnais
la Baule
Baule (La)
Pornichet
St Nazaire
Donges
Paimboeuf
Mindin
St Brévin
St Père-en-R.
St Etienne-de-Montluc
le Pellerin
St Herblain
NANTES
Carquefou
Ancenis
Varades
Ingrandes
Champtoceaux
St Florent
le Loroux-Bottereau
Montrevault
Beaupréau
Vallet
Bouaye
Pornic
Bourgneuf-en-Retz
Ile de Noirmoutier
Noirmoutier
L. de Grd Lieu
St Philbert
Machecoul
Clisson
Aigrefeuille-s-M.
Montfaucon-Montigné
Montaigu
Mortagne-s-S.
Rocheservière
Beauvoir
Fromentine
Challans
Legé
Palluau
St Fulgent
les Herbiers
St Laurent
Mauléon
Saint-Jean-de-Monts
St Jean-de-Monts
Port-Joinville
les Essarts
St Michel-Mont-Mercure
Aizenay
le Poiré
St Gilles-Croix-de-Vie
Fontenelles (Les)
la Roche-s-Yon
Chantonnay
La Mothe-Achard
Mouilleron-en-Pareds
V E N D É E
Ste Hermine
l'Hermenault
les Sables-d'Olonne
Moutiers-les-Mauxfaits
Mareuil
Talmont-St Hilaire
Jard
Luçon
les 4 Chemins
Chaillé
la Tranche
l'Aiguillon
St Michel-en-l'Herm
Marans
Ile de Ré
St Martin
Ars-en-Ré
Courçon
Mauzé
I L L E - E T - V I L A I N E
L O I R E - A T L A N T I Q U E
MICHELIN

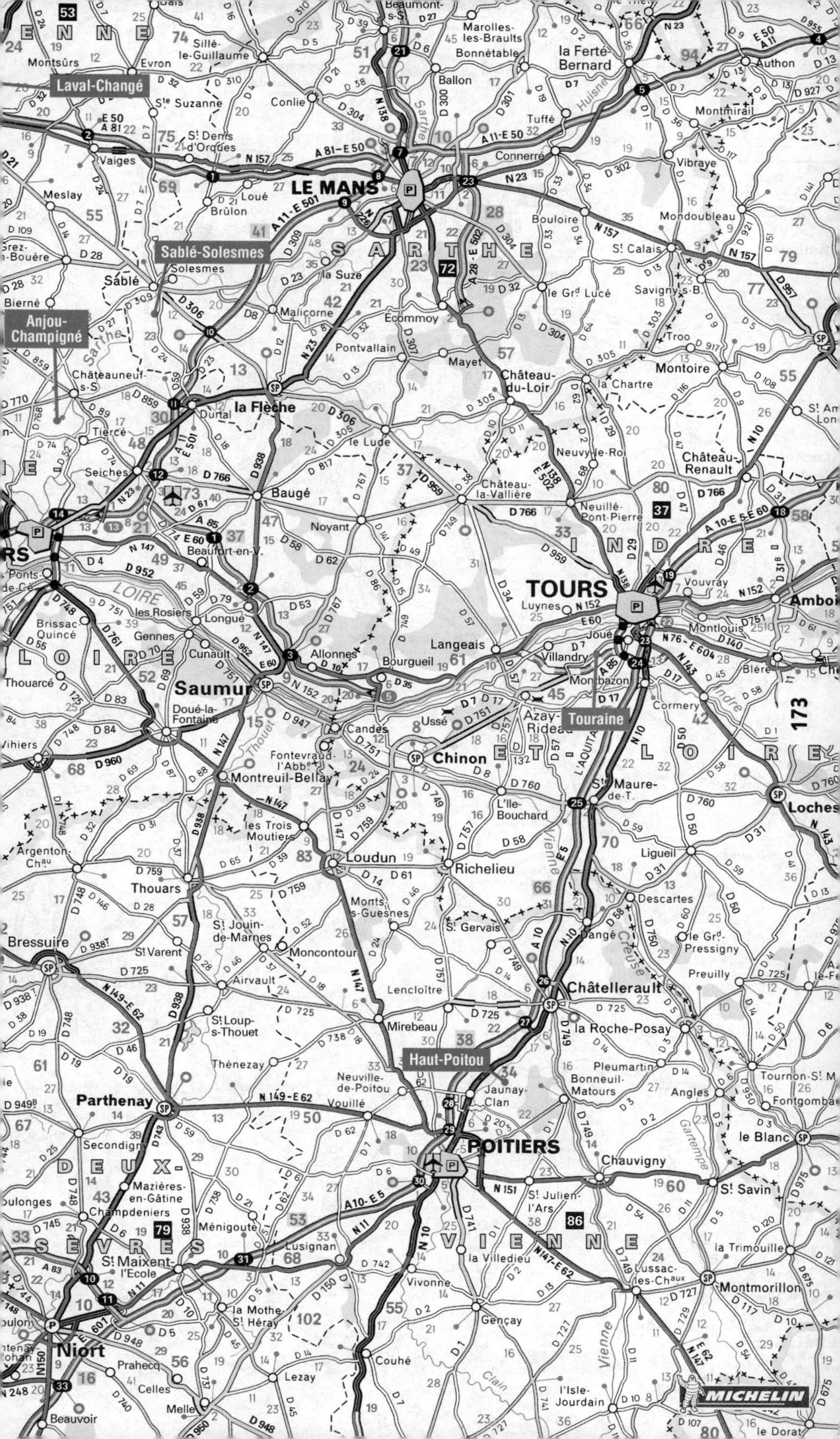

53
Montsûrs
Evron
Sillé-le-Guillaume
Beaumont-s-S.
Marolles-les-Braults
Bonnétable
la Ferté-Bernard
Authon
Laval-Changé
Ste Suzanne
Conlie
Ballon
Tuffé
Montmirail
St Denis-d'Orques
Vaiges
Connerré
Vibraye
Meslay
Loué
Brûlon
LE MANS
Bouloire
Mondoubleau
Grez-en-Bouère
Sablé-Solesmes
Solesmes
Sablé
St Calais
SARTHE
72
La Suze
le Grd Lucé
Savigny-s-B.
Bierné
Anjou-Champigné
Malicorne
Écommoy
Troo
Pontvallain
Mayet
Montoire
Châteauneuf-s-S.
Château-du-Loir
la Chartre
la Flèche
Durtal
Tiercé
le Lude
Neuvy-le-Roi
St Am
Château-Renault
Seiches
Baugé
Château-la-Vallière
Noyant
Neuillé-Pont-Pierre
37
Beaufort-en-V.
INDRE
Ponts-de-Cé
LOIRE
Longué
les Rosiers
Brissac-Quincé
Gennes
Cunault
TOURS
Luynes
Vouvray
Amboi
Montlouis
Langeais
Joué
Villandry
Allonnes
Bourgueil
Bléré
Thouarcé
Saumur
Montbazon
Doué-la-Fontaine
Candes
Ussé
Azay-Rideau
Touraine
Cormery
Vihiers
Fontevraud-l'Abbe
Chinon
173
ET LOIRE
Montreuil-Bellay
Ste Maure-de-T.
Loches
L'Ile-Bouchard
les Trois Moutiers
Argenton-Chau
Loudun
Richelieu
Ligueil
Thouars
Descartes
Monts-s-Guesnes
St Jouin-de-Marnes
St Gervais
Dangé
le Grd-Pressigny
Bressuire
St Varent
Moncontour
Preuilly
Airvault
Lencloître
Châtellerault
St Loup-s-Thouet
Mirebeau
la Roche-Posay
Haut-Poitou
Thénezay
Pleumartin
Neuville-de-Poitou
Bonneuil-Matours
Tournon-St M
Jaunay-Clan
Angles
Fontgomba
Parthenay
Vouillé
Secondigny
POITIERS
le Blanc
DEUX-SÈVRES
Chauvigny
Mazières-en-Gâtine
St Savin
Champdeniers
St Julien-l'Ars
86
Ménigoute
VIENNE
la Trimouille
79
Lusignan
St Maixent-l'Ecole
la Villedieu
Lussac-les-Chaux
Montmorillon
la Mothe-St Héray
Vivonne
Gençay
Niort
Prahecq
Couhé
Celles
Lezay
Melle
l'Isle-Jourdain
Beauvoir
le Dorat
MICHELIN

Map No 7
Carte 7
km
0 10 20
Beaugency
Bordes (Les)
Aisses (Les)
la Ferté-St Aubin
Sully
Gien
Briare
Châtillon-s-L.
Chambord
Lamotte-Beuvron
Neung
Bracieux
Nouan-le-Fuzelier
Argent
Aubigny
Onzain
Cheverny
Chaumont
Souesmes
Vailly
Amboise
Contres
Salbris
Pontlevoy
Romorantin-Lanthenay
la Chlle d'Angillon
Montrichard
Henrichemont
Chenonceaux
St Aignan
Selles
Villefranche-s-Cher
Neuvy-s-B
Mennetou
Chabris
Vierzon
St Martin-d'Auxigny
les Aix-d'An
Montrésor
Valençay
Graçay
Méhun
Lury
Loches
BOURGES
Ecueillé
Vatan
Reuilly
Avord
Châtillon-s-I.
Levroux
Chârost
St Florent
Issoudun
Levet
Azay-le-Ferron
Buzançais
Châteauneuf-s-C.
Dun-s-Auron
Châteauroux
Mézières-en-Brenne
INDRE
Meillant
St Amand-Montrond
Ardentes
Lignières
St Gaultier
le Châtelet
Argenton-s-C.
la Châtre
Neuvy-St Sépulchre
Châteaumeillant
Culan
Vallon-en-Sully
Bélâbre
Gargilesse-Dampierre
Ste Sévère
St Benoit-du-Sault
Eguzon
Aigurande
Crozant
Huriel
Montluçon
Dun-le-Palestel
Bonnat
Boussac
Châtelus-Malvaleix
St Sulpice-les-Feuilles
Néris-les-Bs
la Souterraine
St Vaury
Magnac-Laval
Chambon-s-V.
Marcillat-en-C
le Grand-Bourg
Guéret
Jarnages
Gouzon
Châteauponsac
Evaux-les-Bs
Bessines
Bénévent-l'Abbaye
Chénérailles
Laurière
Ahun
CREUSE
Nantiat
Pontarion
Bellegarde-en-Marche
Auzances
Ambazac
Bourganeuf
Aubusson
Oradour-s-Glane
Nieul
Felletin
HAUTE-VIENNE
St Léonard-de-Noblat
Royère-de-Vassivière
Crocq
LIMOGES
Porcelaine (La)
Peyrat-le-Château
Gentioux
Giat
Aixe
Millevaches
Lac de Vassivière
Eymoutiers
Plateau de
Herment
Châteauneuf-la-Forêt
la Courtine
Nexon
MICHELIN
174

Y O N N E
89
Roncemay
Toucy
Bléneau
St Fargeau
St Sauveur-en-Puisaye
St Amand-en-Puisaye
Coulanges-la V.
Courson-les-C.
Vermenton
Noyers
Nitry
Montbard
Fontenay
Venarey-les-Laumes
Alise Ste Reine
l'Isle-s-S.
Guillon
Semur-en-Auxois
Coulanges
Vézelay
Avallon
Clamecy
Bierre
Vitteaux
Précy-s/s-Thil
Quarré-les-Tombes
Cosne
Donzy
Varzy
Lormes
Saulieu
Pouilly-en-Auxois
Pouilly
Brinon
Corbigny
Montsauche
les Settons
Chailly (Château de)
21
C Ô
la Charité-s-Loire
Prémery
58
N I È V R E
Arnay-le-Duc
Lucenay-l'Evêque
Pougues-les-Eaux
Guérigny
St Saulge
Château-Chinon
Fourchambault
Châtillon-en-Bazois
Moulins-Engilbert
Epinac
Nevers
St Benin-d'Azy
St Léger
Autun
Imphy
Mont Beuvray
St Honoré
la Machine
Etang-s-Arroux
Mesvres
Decize
Fours
le Creusot
St Pierre-le-Moûtier
Luzy
Montcenis
Montchanin
175
Dornes
Toulon
Montceau-les-Mines
Blanzy
Issy-l'Evêque
S A Ô N E - E T
Mont-St Vincent
Chevagnes
Bourbon-Lancy
Bourbon-l'Archambault
Gueugnon
Moulins
Yzeure
Palinges
Souvigny
Dompierre
Digoin
Neuilly-le-Réal
St Bonnet-de-Joux
Paray-le-Monial
Charolles
le Montet
03
A L L I E R
Jaligny
le Donjon
Varennes-s-A.
Anzy-le-Duc
la Clayette
Matour
St Pourçain
Marcigny
Lapalisse
Semur-en-B.
Chantelle
Chauffailles
St Germain-des-Fossés
la Pacaudière
Charlieu
Belmont
les Echarmeaux
VICHY
Ebreuil
Cusset
Châtel-Mgne
Ambierle
Pouilly
Cours
69
R H Ô
Gannat
Bellerive
le Mayet-de-Mgne
St Haon-le-Châtel
Roanne
Lamure
Thizy
Perreux
St Yorre
Châteauneuf-les-Bs
Aigueperse
Randan
Châteldon
Amplepuis
Villefranche-s-Saône
Combronde
Puy-Guillaume
Maringues
St Symphorien-de-Lay
Tarare
Châtelguyon
Tournoël
Ennezat
St Rémy-s-D.
St Just-en-Chevalet
Volcans (Les)
Riom
Thiers
St Germain-Laval
Néronde
l'Arbresle
Lezoux
Pont-de-Dore
Balbigny
Pont-du-Château
Noirétable
St Laurent-de-Ch.
CLERMONT-FERRAND
Courpière
Boën
Feurs
Royat
Ceyrat
Cournon-d'Auvergne
Billom
St Dier-d'A.
Olliergues
St Georges-en-Couzan
St Amant-Tallende
Ste Foy
L O I R E
MICHELIN

Map No 8
Carte 8
km
0 10 20
HAUTE-MARNE
CÔTE-D'OR
SAÔNE-ET-LOIRE
Chaumont
Langres
Contrexéville
Bourbonne-les-Bains
Châtillon-s-S.
Montbard
Semur-en-Auxois
Saulieu
Dijon
Beaune
Nuits-St Georges
Gray
Dole
Auxonne
Autun
le Creusot
Montceau-les-Mines
Chalon-s-S.
Tournus
Mâcon
Cluny
Charolles
Paray-le-Monial
Louhans
Lons-le-Saunier
Bourg
Oyonnax
Arbois
Poligny
Chailly (Château de)
Val de Sorne
176
MICHELIN

Epinal
VOSGES
Remiremont
Plombières
Gérardmer
C. du Bonhomme
C. de la Schlucht
Hohneck
Munster
Ribeauvillé
Riquewihr
Kaysersberg
COLMAR
Breisach
Neuf-Brisach
HT-RHIN
Guebwiller
Bussang
Ballon d'Alsace
Thann
MULHOUSE
Luxeuil
Vesoul
HAUTE-SAÔNE
Lure
Belfort
Montbéliard
Sochaux
Audincourt
Delle
Porrentruy
Altkirch
Bâle-Hagenthal
St Louis
BASEL
Lörrach
Largue (La)
Laufen
Liestal
Delémont
JURA
Moutier
Wylihof (S)
Solothurn
Grenchen
Les Bois Golf Club (S)
Biel/Bienne
Baume-les-Dames
BESANÇON
Besançon
DOUBS
Maîche
St Hippolyte
la Chaux-de-Fonds
le Locle
Morteau
Neuchâtel (S)
Neuchâtel
Pontarlier
BERN
Burgdorf
Blumisberg (S)
Fribourg
Murten
Payerne
Yverdon-les-Bains
Estavayer
Pont-la-Ville (S)
Bulle
Gruyères
Lausanne (S)
VAUD
SUISSE
LAUSANNE
Domaine Impérial (S)
Morges
Vevey
Montreux
Montreux (S)
Crans-sur-Sierre (S)
Crans
Montana
Sierre
Sion
Gstaad
Zweisimmen
Adelboden
Frutigen
Évian
Evian
Thonon
Divonne
Maison Blanche
Genève (S)
GENÈVE
Annemasse
Aigle
Villars
Bex
Monthey
Champéry
Avoriaz
les Gets
MICHELIN
177

Map No 9
Carte 9

km
0 10 20

LA ROCHELLE

Ile de Ré
Ars-en-Ré
St Martin
la Pallice
la Tranche
l'Aiguillon
St Michel-en-l'Herm
Maillezais
Marans
Coulon
Sèvre Niortaise
Frontenay-Rohan-Rohan
Niort
Courçon
Mauzé
Beauvoir
Aigrefeuille-d'Aunis
Surgères
Châtelaillon-Plage
Loulay
St Denis
I. d'Aix
Fouras
St Pierre
Ile d'Oléron
Rochefort
le Château
Tonnay-Boutonne
Tonnay-Charente
St Jean-d'Angély
St Agnant
Brouage
St Savinien
St Hilaire-de-Villefranche
St Trojan
Pont-d'Oléron
Ronce
Marennes
St Porchaire
la Tremblade
Burie
Saintes
Saujon
Pnte de la Coubre
Charente
Cognac
St Palais
Royan
St Georges-de-Didonne
Pnte de Grave
le Verdon
Meschers
Cozes
Gémozac
Pons
Archiac
Soulac
Seudre
Mortagne
St Genis-de-Saintonge
St Vivien-de-Médoc
Jonzac
Montalivet
Mirambeau
Lesparre-Médoc
St Ciers
Montendre
Pauillac
Hourtin
Blaye
St Laurent-Médoc
Lamarque
St Savin
Carcans-Plage
Carcans
Maubuisson
Bourg
Castelnau-de-Médoc
Lacanau-Océan
Lacanau
Médoc
Ambès
St André-de-Cubzac
Ste Hélène
Ambares-et-Lagrave
Blanquefort
Libourne
St Médard-en-Jalles
Bassens
Carbon Blanc
Mérignac
BORDEAUX
Arès
Andernos
Créon
Arcachon
Audenge
Cap Ferret
Gujan-Mestras
Facture
la Brède
Podensac
Pyla
Pilat-Plage
la Teste
Langon
Cazaux
Sanguinet
Belin-Béliet
Biscarrosse-Plage
Villandraut
Biscarrosse
St Symphorien
Parentis-en-Born
Pissos
Sore

CHARENTE-MARITIME
GIRONDE
AUTOROUTE

Lacanau
Arcachon
Gujan-Mestras

la Mothe-St Héray
Gençay
Couhé
Lezay
l'Isle-Jourdain
St Sulpice-les-Feuilles
Magnac-Laval
le Dorat
Civray
Sauzé-Vaussais
Charroux
Availles-Limouzine
Châteauponsac
Bessines
Chef-Boutonne
Mézières
Bellac
Ruffec
Confolens
Villefagnan
Nantiat
Ambazac
Champagne-Mouton
Oradour-s-Glane
Nieul
Porcelaine (La)
Aigre
Mansle
St Claud
St Junien
HAUTE-VIENNE
Chasseneuil
Chabanais
Rochechouart
LIMOGES
Rouillac
CHARENTE
St Laurent
Aixe
la Rochefoucauld
Oradour-s-Vayres
Solignac
Jarnac
Ruelle
Montbron
St Mathieu
Nexon
Hiersac
Bussière-Badil
Châlus
Pierre-Buffière
Angoulême
Châteauneuf
Marthon
la Couronne
Nontron
St Yrieix-la-Perche
St Pardoux-la-Rivière
Jumilhac-le-Grd
Blanzac
Villebois-Lavalette
Mareuil
Lubersac
Montmoreau
Thiviers
Champagnac-de-Belair
Lanouaille
Brantôme
Brossac
Verteillac
Bourdeilles
Excideuil
Aubeterre
Montagrier
Juillac
Chalais
Ribérac
Savignac-les-Eglises
Hautefort
Objat
Montguyon
St Aulaye
St Astier
Terrasson-Lavilledieu
la Roche-Chalais
Périgueux
Thenon
Neuvic
St Pierre-de-Chignac
Larche
Coutras
Montignac
Montpon-Ménestérol
Mussidan
DORDOGNE
Grotte de Lascaux
Vergt
Salignac-Eyvigues
Lussac
Villefranche-de-Lonchat
les Eyzies de T.
Emilion
Sarlat-la-Canéda
Souillac
Castillon-la-Bataille
le Bugue
St Cyprien
Vélines
Bergerac
le Buisson-de-Cadouin
Beynac-et-Cazenac
Ste-Foy-la-Grande
Lalinde
la Roque-Gageac
Pujols
Monbazillac
Cadouin
Belvès
Payrac
Domme
Beaumont-du-Périgord
Pellegrue
Issigeac
Gourdon
Sauveterre-de-Guyenne
Duras
Salviac
Eymet
Castillonnès
Monpazier
Monségur
Villeréal
Villefranche-du-Périgord
Cazals
Lauzun
la Réole
Miramont-de-Guyenne
Seyches
Cancon
Monflanquin
Chau de Bonaguil
Catus
Fumel
Puy-l'Evêque
Tombebœuf
Auros
Marmande
LOT-ET-GARONNE
Luzech
le Mas-d'Agenais
Villeneuve-s-Lot
Tournon-d'Agenais
Cahors
Castelmoron
Ste Livrade
Grignols
Tonneins
Penne-d'A.
Montaigu-de-Quercy
Casteljaloux
Montcuq
Vienne
Clain
Charente
Gartempe
Couze
Isle
Dronne
Auvézère
Vézère
Dordogne
Lot
MICHELIN
179

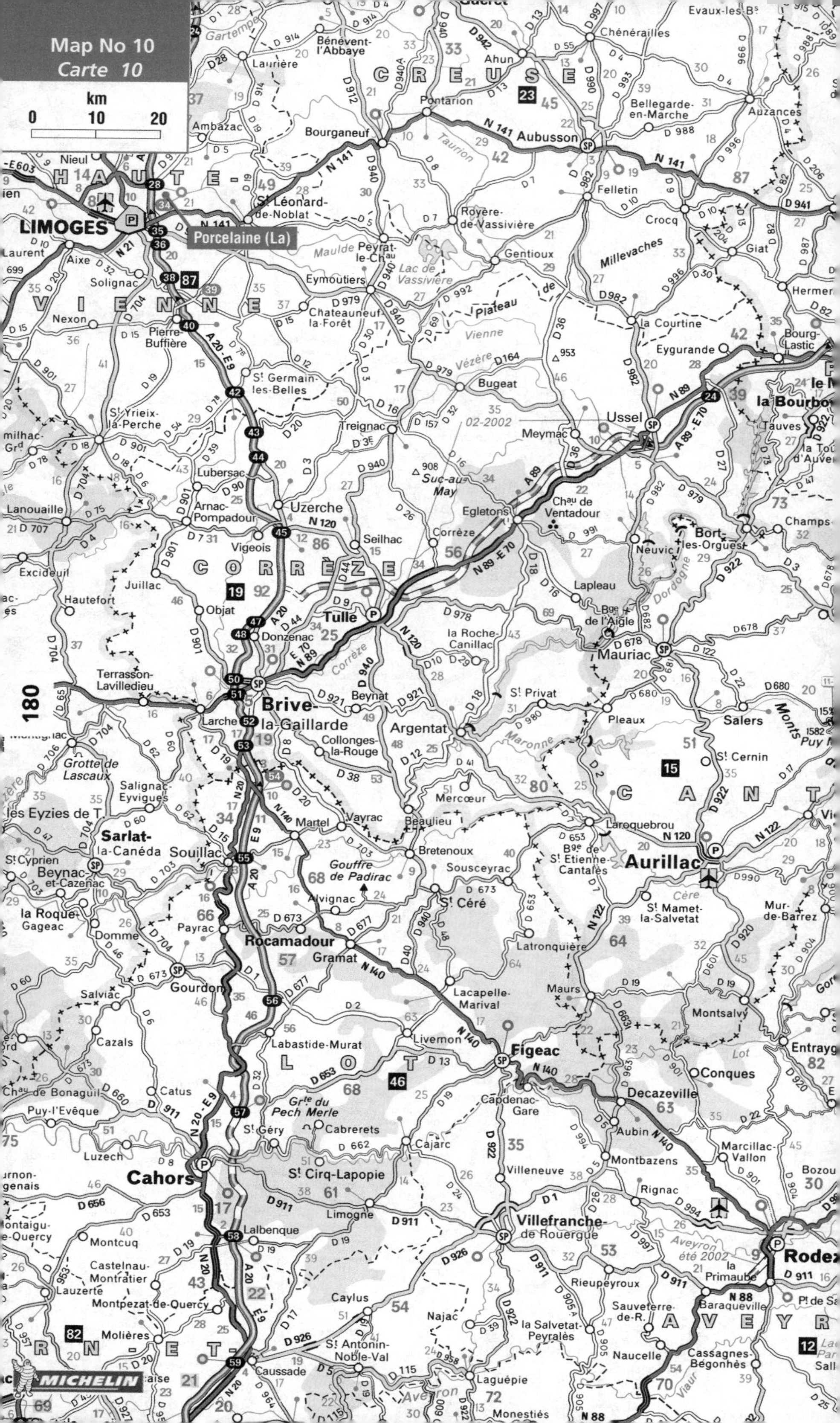

Map No 10
Carte 10
km
0
10
20
180
MICHELIN
HAUTE-VIENNE
CREUSE
CORRÈZE
CANTAL
LOT
AVEYRON
Limoges
Porcelaine (La)
Guéret
Évaux-les-Bains
Chénérailles
Bénévent-l'Abbaye
Laurière
Ahun
Pontarion
Bourganeuf
Aubusson
Bellegarde-en-Marche
Auzances
Ambazac
Nieul
St Léonard-de-Noblat
Royère-de-Vassivière
Felletin
Crocq
Giat
Aixe
Solignac
Laurent
Peyrat-le-Château
Lac de Vassivière
Gentioux
Millevaches
Eymoutiers
Plateau de Millevaches
Hermen
Nexon
Pierre-Buffière
Châteauneuf-la-Forêt
La Courtine
Bourg-Lastic
Eygurande
St Germain-les-Belles
Bugeat
Vienne
Vézère
St Yrieix-la-Perche
Treignac
Ussel
Meymac
la Bourboule
Tauves
La Tour-d'Auvergne
Suc-au-May
Lubersac
Uzerche
Arnac-Pompadour
Egletons
Châu de Ventadour
Lanouaille
Vigeois
Seilhac
Corrèze
Neuvic
Bort-les-Orgues
Champs-
Excideuil
Juillac
Lapleau
Dordogne
Hautefort
Objat
Tulle
Bge de l'Aigle
Donzenac
la Roche-Canillac
Mauriac
Terrasson-Lavilledieu
Brive-la-Gaillarde
Beynat
St Privat
Pleaux
Salers
Monts du Cantal
Puy Mary
Larche
Argentat
Maronne
Grotte de Lascaux
Collonges-la-Rouge
St Cernin
Salignac-Eyvigues
Mercœur
Les Eyzies de T.
Martel
Vayrac
Beaulieu
Laroquebrou
Sarlat-la-Canéda
Souillac
Bretenoux
Bge de St Étienne-Cantalès
Aurillac
St Cyprien
Beynac-et-Cazenac
Gouffre de Padirac
Sousceyrac
St Céré
Cère
La Roque-Gageac
Alvignac
St Mamet-la-Salvetat
Mur-de-Barrez
Domme
Payrac
Rocamadour
Gramat
Latronquière
Gourdon
Lacapelle-Marival
Maurs
Salviac
Montsalvy
Cazals
Labastide-Murat
Livernon
Figeac
Entraygues
Lot
Conques
Châu de Bonaguil
Catus
Capdenac-Gare
Decazeville
Puy-l'Évêque
Grte du Pech Merle
Cabrerets
Aubin
St Géry
Luzech
Cajarc
Marcillac-Vallon
Montbazens
Cahors
St Cirq-Lapopie
Villeneuve
Bozouls
Limogne
Rignac
Villefranche-de-Rouergue
Rodez
Montcuq
Lalbenque
Aveyron été 2002
La Primaube
Castelnau-Montratier
Rieupeyroux
Pt de Salars
Lauzerte
Caylus
Sauveterre-de-R.
Montpezat-de-Quercy
Najac
Baraqueville
Molières
La Salvetat-Peyralès
St Antonin-Noble-Val
Naucelle
Cassagnes-Bégonhès
Caussade
Laguépie
Viaur
Monestiés
A 20 - E 9
N 141
N 89
N 120
N 140
N 88
A 89 - E 70
N 122
D 911
D 922

181
VICHY
Cusset
Châtel-Mgne
Ambierle
Pouilly
Roanne
Ebreuil
Bellerive
Gannat
St Yorre
le Mayet-de-Mgne
St Haon-le-Châtel
Perreux
Thizy
Lamure
Cours
Menat
Châteauneuf-les-Bs
Aigueperse
Randan
Châteldon
Amplepuis
Manzat
Combronde
Puy-Guillaume
St Just-en-Chevalet
St Symphorien-de-Lay
Tarare
Châtelguyon
Volcans (Les)
Maringues
Ennezat
St Rémy-s-D
Riom
Volvic
Thiers
Lezoux
Pont-de-Dore
St Germain-Laval
Néronde
Balbigny
Noirétable
Pont-du-Chau
St Laurent-de-Ch.
Feurs
de Dôme
Royat
CLERMONT-FERRAND
Ceyrat
Courpière
St Georges-en-Couzan
Boën
Cournon d'Auvergne
Billom
Olliergues
Monts du Forez
St Amant-Tallende
Veyre
Randanne
Orcival
St Dier-d'A.
Cunlhat
Vic-le-Comte
Chazelles
LOIRE
Montbrison
Montrond-les-Bs
St Symphorien
St Galmier
PUY-DE-DÔME
St Nectaire
Champeix
Chambon-s-L.
Murol
St Amant-Roche-Savine
Ambert
St Anthème
Andrézieux-Bouthéon
St Etienne
Issoire
Besse
Super-Besse
Sauxillanges
St Just-St Rambert
St Germain-l'Herm
St Germain-Lembron
Jumeaux
Viverols
St Bonnet-le-Chau
Firminy
Ardes
Brassac-les-Mines
Arlanc
Lempdes
Auzon
le Chambon-Feugerolles
Aurec-s-Loire
St Genest-Malifaux
Craponne
Bas-en-Basset
Blesle
Brioude
la Chaise-Dieu
St Didier-en-V.
Monistrol-s-L.
Massiac
Paulhaguet
Allanche
Allègre
Retournac
Montfaucon-en-Velay
Vorey
HTE-LOIRE
Yssingeaux
Murat
Lavoûte-Chilhac
St Paulien
Tence
Langeac
Loudes
le Chambon-s-Lignon
Plomb du Cantal
St Flour
Pinols
le Puy-en-Velay
St Julien-Chapteuil
Fay-s-L.
Ruynes-en-Margeride
Vduc de Garabit
Rochebonne
Saugues
Monistrol-d'A.
Solignac
le Monastier
St Martin-de-Valamas
Alleuze
Cayres
Mt Mézenc
Bge de Grandval
Arlempdes
Gerbier de Jonc
Cheylard
Truyère
Chaudes-Aigues
le Malzieu-Ville
Col des 4 Vios
Fournels
St Chély-d'Apcher
St Alban
Grandrieu
Pradelles
ARDÈCHE
Bge de Naussac
Langogne
Montpezat-s/s-Bauzon
Antraigue
Aumont-Aubrac
Laguiole
St Amans
St Etienne-de-Lugdarès
Thueyts
Vals-les-Bains
Nasbinals
St Laurent-les-Bains
C. de Meyrand
Aubenas
Monts d'Aubrac
Aubrac
Châteauneuf-de-Randon
Valgorge
St Chély-d'A.
Marvejols
LOZÈRE
Largentière
Espalion
Bagnols-les-Bs
St Germain-du-Teil
Mende
Joyeuse
St Geniez-d'Olt
le Bleymard
la Canourgue
Chanac
Mt Lozère
Villefort
Ruoms
les Vans
Vallon-Pont-d'arc
Parc National
le Pont-de-Montvert
Ste Enimie
Sévérac-le-Chau
Génolhac
Aven d'Orgnac
Barjac
le Massegrós
Florac
Bessèges
Vézins-de-L.
la Malène
Barre-des-C.
St Germain-de-Calberte
St Ambroix
Gorges du Tarn
les Vignes
Aven Armand
le Rozier
Corniche des Cévennes
la Grd Combe
Salindres
St Beauzély
Grte de Dargilan
Chaos de Montpellier le Vx
Meyrueis
St André-de-V.
St Jean-du-Gard
Lussan
Millau
Trèves
Mt Aigoual
MICHELIN

Map No 11
Carte 11
km
0 10 20
Mâcon
Bourg-en-Bresse
Bresse (La)
Oyonnax
Nantua
Bellegarde-s-
Villefranche-s-Saône
Gouverneur (Le)
Breuil - Montaplan
Villette d'Anthon
Les Sangliers
LYON
Pérouges
Ambérieu-en-Bugey
Belley
Tarare
Feurs
St Etienne
Vienne
Bourgoin-Jallieu
la Tour-du-Pin
Voiron
Annonay
Annonay-Gourdan
Charmeil
Grenoble
Bresson
Le Chambon-sur-Lignon
Tournon-s-R.
Romans
Valence
Villard-de-Lans
Privas
Crest
Die
Aubenas
Montélimar
Nyons
Pierrelatte
182
RHÔNE
AIN
ISÈRE
ARDÈCHE
DRÔME
MICHELIN

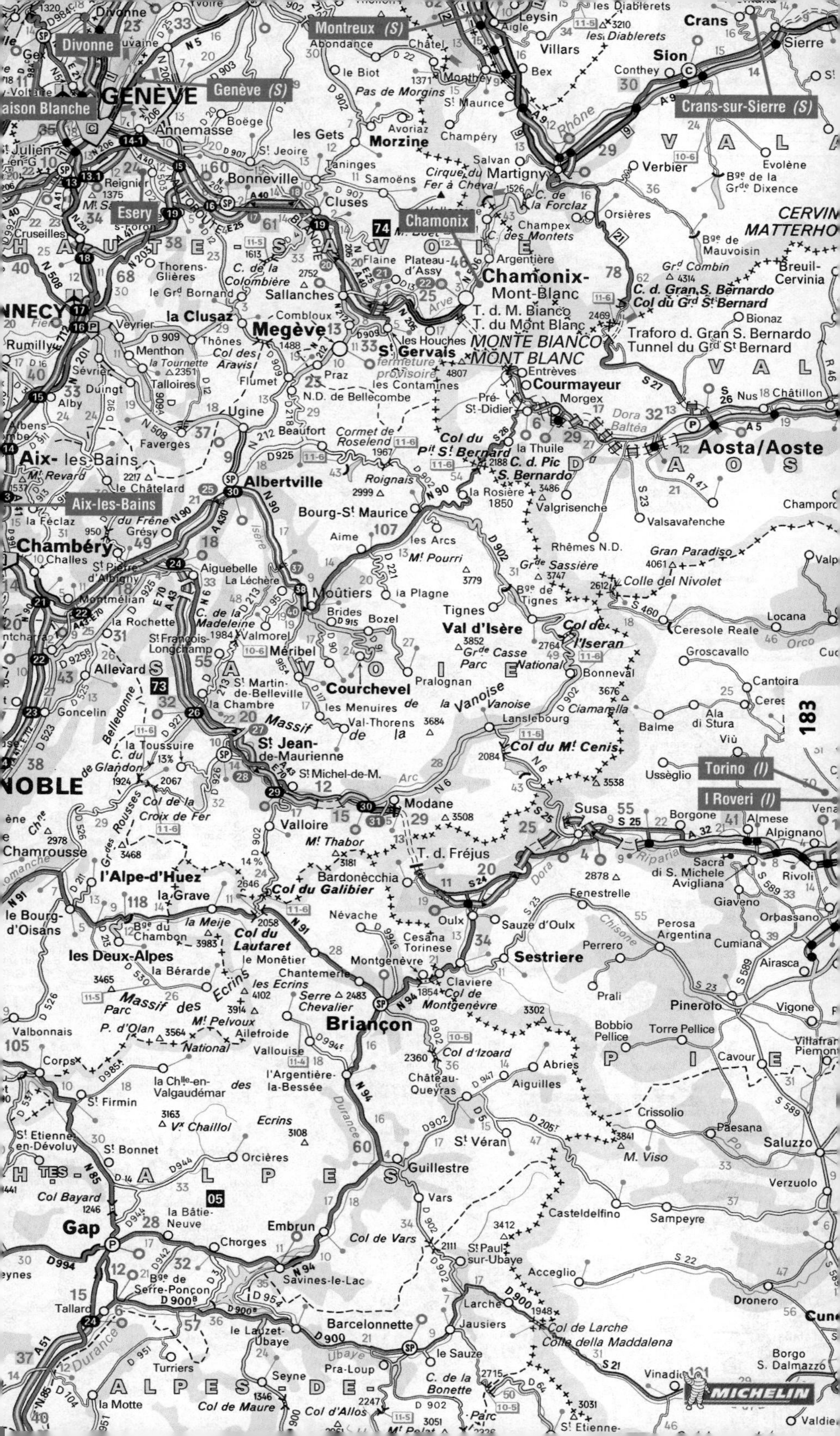

Divonne
Gex
GENÈVE
Genève (S)
Montreux (S)
Abondance
Châtel
le Biot
Monthey
Aigle
Leysin
les Diablerets
Villars
Bex
Crans
Sion
Sierre
Conthey
Crans-sur-Sierre (S)
Annemasse
Boëge
St Jeoire
les Gets
Morzine
Avoriaz
Pas de Morgins
St Maurice
Champéry
Salvan
Martigny
Verbier
Evolène
Bge de la Grde Dixence
St Julien-en-G
Reignier
Bonneville
Taninges
Samoëns
Cirque du Fer à Cheval
C. de la Forclaz
Orsières
Cluses
Esery
Cruseilles
Chamonix
Champex
C. des Montets
Bge de Mauvoisin
CERVIN
MATTERHORN
Thorens-Glières
C. de la Colombière
le Grd Bornand
Flaine
Plateau-d'Assy
Argentière
Chamonix-Mont-Blanc
Grd Combin
Breuil-Cervinia
Sallanches
C. d. Gran S. Bernardo
Col du Grd St Bernard
ANNECY
la Clusaz
Combloux
Megève
T. d. M. Bianco
T. du Mont Blanc
Bionaz
Traforo d. Gran S. Bernardo
Tunnel du Grd St Bernard
Veyrier
Thônes
Rumilly
Menthon
Col des Aravis
St Gervais
les Houches
MONTE BIANCO
MONT BLANC
Sévrier
la Tournette
Talloires
Flumet
Praz
fermeture provisoire
les Contamines
Entrèves
Courmayeur
Nus
Châtillon
Duingt
Alby
N.D. de Bellecombe
Pré-St-Didier
Morgex
Ugine
Faverges
Beaufort
Cormet de Roselend
Col du Pt St Bernard
la Thuile
Dora Baltea
Aosta/Aoste
Aix-les-Bains
Mt Revard
le Châtelard
Albertville
Roignais
C. d. Pic S. Bernardo
la Rosière
Valgrisenche
Champorcher
Aix-les-Bains
la Féclaz
du Frêne
Grésy
Bourg-St Maurice
Valsavarenche
Chambéry
Challes
Aime
les Arcs
Mt Pourri
Rhêmes N.D.
Gran Paradiso
St Pierre-d'Albigny
Aiguebelle
La Léchère
Grde Sassière
Colle del Nivolet
Montmélian
Moûtiers
la Plagne
Bge de Tignes
Tignes
C. de la Madeleine
la Rochette
Valmorel
Brides
Bozel
Val d'Isère
Col de l'Iseran
Locana
Ceresole Reale
St François-Longchamp
Méribel
Grde Casse
Parc National
Groscavallo
Allevard
Courchevel
Pralognan
Bonneval
Cantoira
St Martin-de-Belleville
les Menuires
de la Vanoise
Vanoise
Ciamarella
Ceres
Goncelin
la Chambre
Val-Thorens
Massif de la
Lanslebourg
Balme
Ala di Stura
Belledonne
la Toussuire
St Jean-de-Maurienne
Col du Mt Cenis
Viù
C. du Glandon
St Michel-de-M.
Usseglio
Torino (I)
I Roveri (I)
GRENOBLE
Col de la Croix de Fer
Arc
Modane
Susa
Almese
Alpignano
Chamrousse
Grdes Rousses
Valloire
Mt Thabor
T. d. Fréjus
Sacra di S. Michele
Avigliana
Rivoli
l'Alpe-d'Huez
Bardonècchia
Col du Galibier
Fenestrelle
Giaveno
la Grave
le Bourg-d'Oisans
Bge du Chambon
la Meije
Col du Lautaret
Névache
Oulx
Sauze d'Oulx
Perosa Argentina
Orbassano
Cumiana
les Deux-Alpes
le Monêtier
Cesana Torinese
Sestriere
Perrero
Chisone
la Bérarde
Chantemerle
Montgenèvre
Airasca
les Ecrins
Claviere
Col de Montgenèvre
Prali
Pinerolo
Massif des Ecrins
Serre Chevalier
Briançon
Vigone
Parc
Mt Pelvoux
Bobbio Pellice
Torre Pellice
P. d'Olan
Ailefroide
National
Vallouise
Col d'Izoard
Villafranca Piemonte
Valbonnais
Corps
l'Argentière-la-Bessée
Abries
Cavour
la Chlle-en-Valgaudémar
des
Château-Queyras
Aiguilles
St Firmin
Ecrins
Crissolio
Vx Chaillol
Durance
Paesana
St Etienne-en-Dévoluy
St Véran
St Bonnet
Orcières
M. Viso
Saluzzo
Guillestre
HAUTES-ALPES
Verzuolo
Col Bayard
Vars
la Bâtie-Neuve
Casteldelfino
Sampeyre
Gap
Embrun
Chorges
Col de Vars
St Paul-sur-Ubaye
Bge de Serre-Ponçon
Savines-le-Lac
Acceglio
Tallard
Larche
Dronero
Jausiers
Col de Larche
Colle della Maddalena
Barcelonnette
le Lauzet-Ubaye
Cuneo
Ubaye
le Sauze
Borgo S. Dalmazzo
Turriers
Pra-Loup
C. de la Bonette
Vinadio
Seyne
ALPES-DE-
la Motte
Col de Maure
Col d'Allos
Parc
St Etienne-
Valdieri
MICHELIN

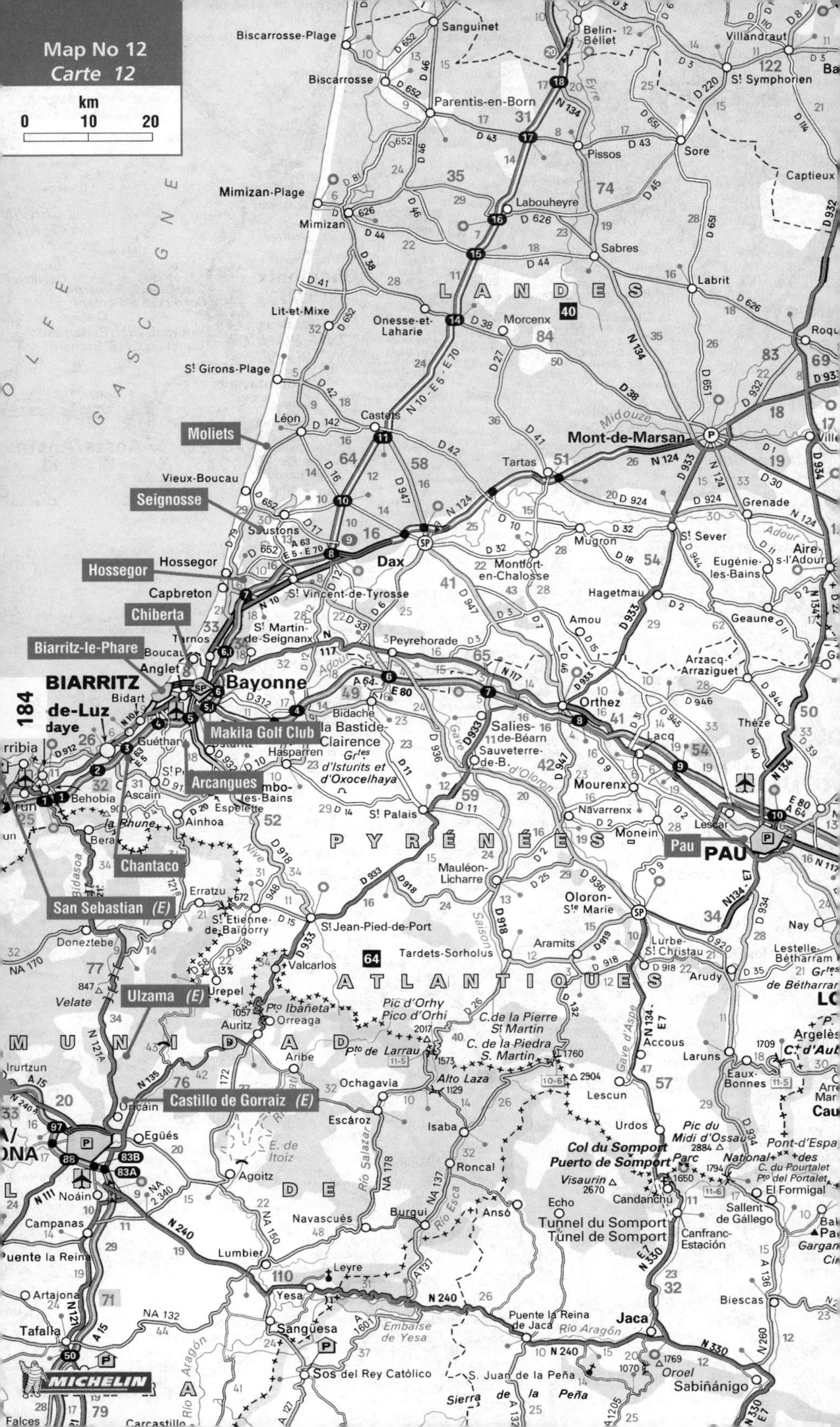

Map No 12
Carte 12
km
0 10 20
Biscarrosse-Plage
Sanguinet
Belin-Béliet
Villandraut
Biscarrosse
St Symphorien
Parentis-en-Born
Pissos
Sore
Captieux
Mimizan-Plage
Mimizan
Labouheyre
Sabres
Labrit
Lit-et-Mixe
Onesse-et-Laharie
Morcenx
LANDES
St Girons-Plage
Léon
Castets
Mont-de-Marsan
Midouze
Moliets
Vieux-Boucau
Tartas
Seignosse
Soustons
Dax
Grenade
Mugron
St Sever
Adour
Aire-s-l'Adour
Hossegor
Capbreton
St Vincent-de-Tyrosse
Montfort-en-Chalosse
Eugénie-les-Bains
Hagetmau
Chiberta
Tarnos
St Martin-de-Seignanx
Amou
Geaune
Biarritz-le-Phare
Boucau
Peyrehorade
Arzacq-Arraziguet
Anglet
BIARRITZ
Bayonne
Orthez
Bidart
Bidache
Salies-de-Béarn
de-Luz
daye
Makila Golf Club
La Bastide-Clairence
Sauveterre-de-B.
Lacq
Thèze
Guéthary
Hasparren
Grtes d'Isturits et d'Oxocelhaya
Gave d'Oloron
Mourenx
Arcangues
Cambo-les-Bains
Ascain
Espelette
Navarrenx
Monein
Lescar
Behobia
Ainhoa
St Palais
Pau
PAU
la Rhune
Bera
PYRÉNÉES
Bidasoa
Chantaco
Nive
Mauléon-Licharre
Oloron-Ste Marie
Erratzu
San Sebastian (E)
St Etienne-de-Baïgorry
St Jean-Pied-de-Port
Lurbe-St Christau
Nay
Saison
Doneztebe
Tardets-Sorholus
Aramits
Lestelle-Bétharram
Arudy
Grtes de Bétharram
Valcarlos
ATLANTIQUES
Velate
Urepel
Ulzama (E)
Pto Ibañeta
Pic d'Orhy
Pico d'Orhi
C. de la Pierre St Martin
Argelès
Orreaga
Auritz
C. de la Piedra S. Martin
Accous
Laruns
MUNIDAD
Pto de Larrau
Aribe
Alto Laza
Lescun
Eaux-Bonnes
Irurtzun
Ochagavia
Gave d'Aspe
Castillo de Gorraiz (E)
Oricáin
Escároz
Isaba
Urdos
Egüés
E. de Itoiz
Col du Somport
Puerto de Somport
Pic du Midi d'Ossau
Pont-d'Espagne
Parc National des
C. du Pourtalet
Pto del Portalet
Roncal
Visaurin
Agoitz
Candanchú
El Formigal
Noáin
Río Salazar
Echo
Ansó
Tunnel du Somport
Túnel de Somport
Sallent de Gállego
Campanas
Navascués
Burgui
Río Esca
Canfranc-Estación
Puente la Reina
Lumbier
Leyre
Artajona
Yesa
Biescas
Tafalla
Sangüesa
Embalse de Yesa
Puente la Reina de Jaca
Río Aragón
Jaca
Oroel
Sos del Rey Católico
S. Juan de la Peña
Sabiñánigo
Sierra de la Peña
Falces
Carcastillo
Río Aragón
MICHELIN
184

Marmande
Tombebœuf
Fumel
Puy-l'Evêque
Luzech
Cahors
le Mas-d'Agenais
Castelmoron
Ste Livrade
Villeneuve-s-Lot
Tournon-d'Agenais
Grignols
Tonneins
Penne-d'A.
Casteljaloux
Damazan
Aiguillon
Montaigu-de-Quercy
Montcuq
Laroque-Timbaut
Castelnau-Montratier
Port-Ste Marie
Bourg-de-Visa
Lauzerte
Montpezat-de-Quercy
Houeillès
Agen
Molières
Lavardac
Puymirol
Valence-d'A.
Moissac
Lafrançaise
Nérac
Laplume
Astaffort
Auvillar
Castelsarrasin
Mézin
St Nicolas-de-la-Grave
Gabarret
Barbotan
Montréal
Condom
Lavit
Montech
Lectoure
St Clar
Beaumont-de-Lomagne
Eauze
Valence
Fleurance
Verdun
Fronton
Grisolles
Nogaro
Vic-Fézensac
Jegun
Mauvezin
Grenade
Cologne
Aignan
Auch
Toulouse-Seilh
Riscle
Gimont
l'Isle-Jourdain
Blagnac
Plaisance
Montesquiou
l'Isle-de-Noé
Léguevin
Marciac
Mirande
Saramon
St Lys
Maubourguet
Seissan
Lombez
Samatan
Muret
Miélan
Masseube
Vic-en-Bigorre
Rieumes
Rabastens-de-Bigorre
l'Isle-en-Dodon
Auterive
Trie
Castelnau-Magnoac
Boulogne
le Fousseret
Carbonne
Lézat
Pouyastruc
Rieux
Tarbes
Galan
Aurignac
Montesquieu-Volvestre
Ossun
Tournay
Boussens
Cazères
Capvern
Lannemezan
St Martory
Ste Croix-Volvestre
le Fossat
Bagnères-de-Bigorre
la Barthe-de-Neste
Montréjeau
Encausse
St Gaudens
Salies-du-Salat
le Mas-d'Azil
Campan
St Bertrand-de-Comminges
Barbazan
Aspet
la Bastide-de-Sérou
Grte de Médous
Col de Portet d'Aspet
St Girons
Pierrefitte-Nestalas
P. du Midi de Bigorre
Col d'Aspin
C. des Ares
Barèges
Arreau
St Béat
Castillon-en-Couserans
la Mongie
C. du Tourmalet
Bordères-Louron
Oust
Massat
Col de Port
Luz-St Sauveur
Vielle Aure
Fos
Pic de Néouvielle
St Lary-Soulan
C. de Peyresourde
Les Bossòst
Aulus-les-Bains
Héas
Tunnel de Bielsa
Bagnères-de-Luchon
Vall d'Aran
Guzet-Neige
Gavarnie
Vielha
Salardú
Beret
Baqueira
Monte Perdido
Pico Posets
Arties
Port de la Bonaigua
Parque nacional de Ordesa
Bielsa
Pico de Aneto
Esterri d'Àneu
Benasque
MALADETA
Cerler
Caldes de Boí
Parc national d'Aigüestortes
Espot
Ribera de Cardós
Castejón de Sos
Vilaller
Llavorsí
la Vella
LOT-ET-GARONNE
TARN-ET-GARONNE
GERS
HTES-PYRÉNÉES
HTE-GARONNE
ARIÈGE
MICHELIN
185

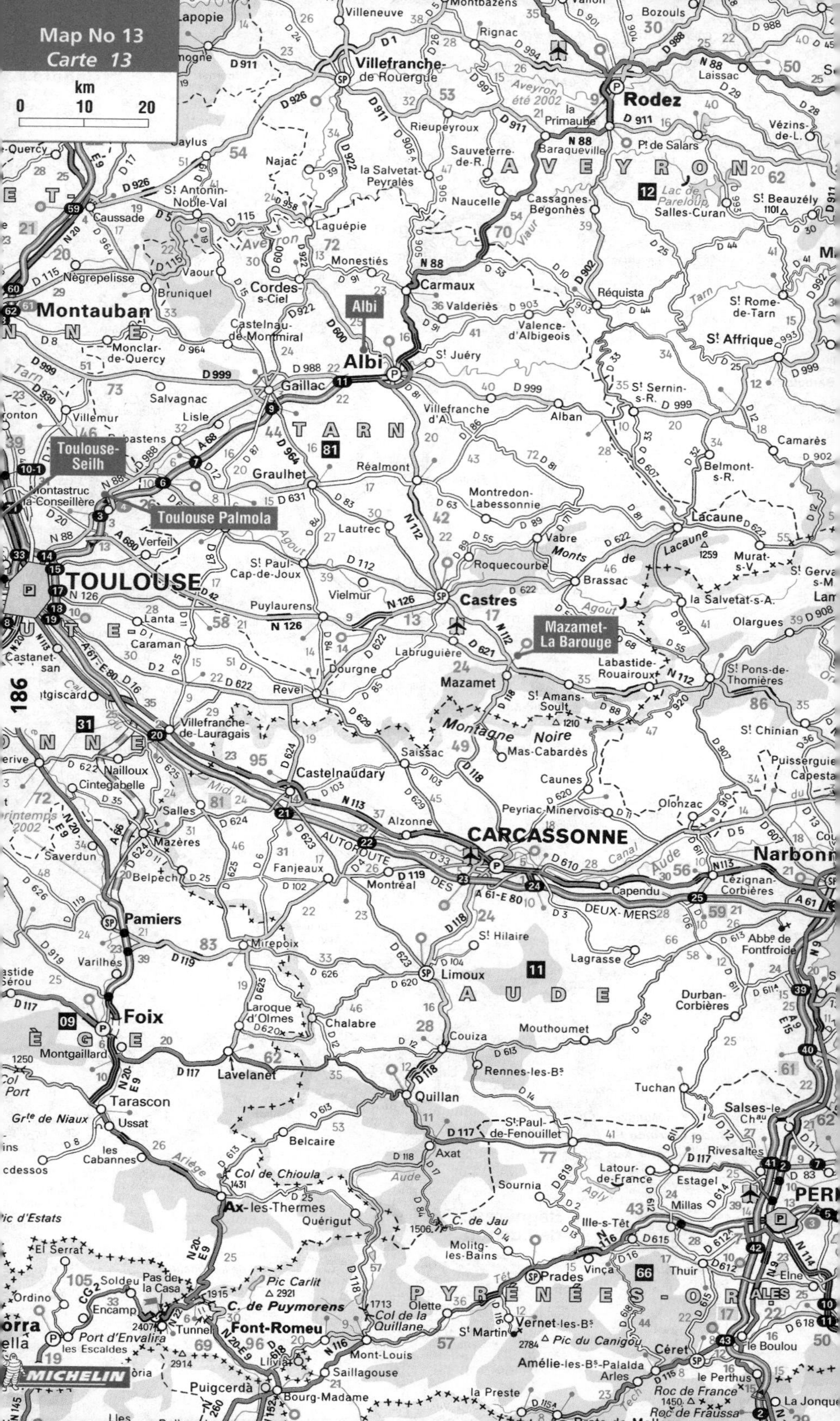

Map No 13
Carte 13
km
0 10 20
Villefranche-de Rouergue
Rodez
Aveyron été 2002
Rignac
Bozouls
Laissac
la Primaube
Baraqueville
Pt de Salars
Vézins-de-L.
Rieupeyroux
Sauveterre-de-R.
Naucelle
Cassagnes-Begonhès
Salles-Curan
Lac de Pareloup
St Beauzély
AVEYRON
Najac
la Salvetat-Peyralès
Caylus
St Antonin-Noble-Val
Caussade
Laguépie
Monestiés
Carmaux
Valderiès
Valence-d'Albigeois
Réquista
St Rome-de-Tarn
St Affrique
Nègrepelisse
Bruniquel
Vaour
Cordes-s-Ciel
Montauban
Castelnau-de-Montmiral
Monclar-de-Quercy
Albi
St Juéry
Gaillac
Salvagnac
Villemur
Lisle
Rabastens
Toulouse-Seilh
Montastruc-la-Conseillère
Toulouse Palmola
TARN
Graulhet
Réalmont
Villefranche d'A.
Alban
St Sernin-s-R.
Belmont-s-R.
Camarès
Montredon-Labessonnie
Lacaune
Murat-s-V.
Lautrec
Vabre
Monts de Lacaune
Verfeil
TOULOUSE
St Paul-Cap-de-Joux
Vielmur
Roquecourbe
Brassac
Castres
Puylaurens
Lanta
Caraman
Labruguière
Mazamet-La Barouge
la Salvetat-s-A.
Olargues
Castanet-san
Dourgne
Revel
Mazamet
Labastide-Rouairoux
St Pons-de-Thomières
St Amans-Soult
Villefranche-de-Lauragais
Montagne Noire
Mas-Cabardès
St Chinian
Nailloux
Saissac
Castelnaudary
Cintegabelle
Caunes
Puisserguier
Capestang
Salles
Alzonne
Peyriac-Minervois
Olonzac
Mazères
Saverdun
CARCASSONNE
Narbonne
Belpech
Fanjeaux
Montréal
Capendu
Lézignan-Corbières
Pamiers
AUTOROUTE DES DEUX-MERS
Canal du Midi
Mirepoix
St Hilaire
Lagrasse
Abbe de Fontfroide
Varilhes
Limoux
AUDE
Foix
Laroque d'Olmes
Chalabre
Durban-Corbières
Mouthoumet
Montgaillard
Lavelanet
Couiza
Rennes-les-Bs
Tarascon
Ussat
Quillan
Tuchan
Salses-le-Chau
Gr te de Niaux
les Cabannes
Belcaire
St Paul-de-Fenouillet
Axat
Rivesaltes
Col de Chioula
Latour-de-France
Estagel
Ax-les-Thermes
Sournia
Millas
Quérigut
C. de Jau
Ille-s-Têt
Pic d'Estats
Molitg-les-Bains
El Serrat
Pic Carlit
Pas de la Casa
Soldeu
Prades
Vinça
Thuir
Elne
Ordino
Encamp
C. de Puymorens
Olette
Col de la Quillane
PYRÉNÉES-ORIENTALES
Tunnel
Font-Romeu
Vernet-les-Bs
St Martin
Pic du Canigou
Port d'Envalira
les Escaldes
Mont-Louis
Céret
le Boulou
Llivia
Saillagouse
Amélie-les-Bs-Palalda
Arles
le Perthus
Puigcerdà
Bourg-Madame
la Preste
Roc de France
Roc de Frausa
La Jonquera
MICHELIN

Montpellier-Massane
Fontcaude
Nîmes-Campagne
Saint-Thomas
Grande Motte (La)
Cap d'Agde
MONTPELLIER
NÎMES
HÉRAULT
GARD
BOUCHES
Alès
Florac
Uzès
Lodève
Ganges
le Vigan
Anduze
Sommières
Lunel
Mauguio
Gignac
Aniane
Clermont-l'Hérault
Bédarieux
Pézenas
Mèze
Sète
Frontignan
Agde
le Cap d'Agde
Palavas
Carnon
la Grde Motte
le Grau-du-Roi
Aigues-Mortes
Stes Maries-de-la-Mer
St Gilles
Beaucaire
Bagnols-s-C.
Pont-St Esprit
Remoulins
Pont du Gard
Valras-Plage
Narbonne-Plage
Gruissan
Port-Vendres
Banyuls
Cerbère
Portbou
Collioure
GOLFE DU LION
MÉDI
MICHELIN

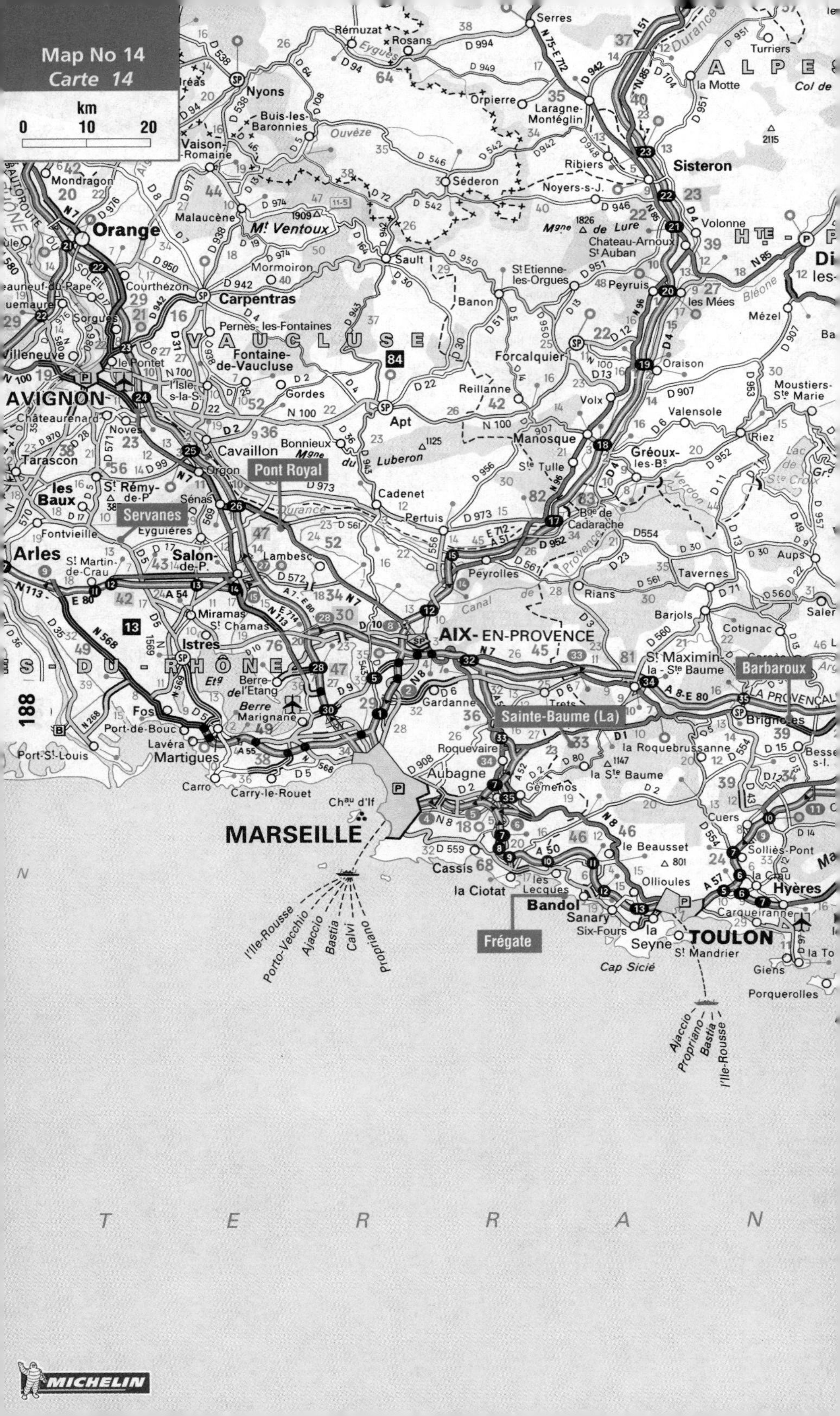

Map No 14
Carte 14
km
0 10 20
Orange
Mondragon
Vaison-la-Romaine
Nyons
Buis-les-Baronnies
Rémuzat
Rosans
Serres
Orpierre
Laragne-Montéglin
Ribiers
Sisteron
Turriers
la Motte
ALPES
Séderon
Noyers-s-J.
Volonne
Malaucène
Mt Ventoux
Mgne de Lure
Chateau-Arnoux
St Auban
Sault
Mormoiron
Carpentras
Courthézon
Sorgues
St Etienne-les-Orgues
Peyruis
les Mées
Mézel
Banon
Pernes-les-Fontaines
VAUCLUSE
Forcalquier
Oraison
Villeneuve
le Pontet
AVIGNON
l'Isle-s-la-S.
Fontaine-de-Vaucluse
Gordes
Reillanne
Volx
Moustiers-Ste Marie
Châteaurenard
Noves
Apt
Valensole
Manosque
Riez
Tarascon
Cavaillon
Bonnieux
Mgne du Luberon
Gréoux-les-Bs
les Baux
St Rémy-de-P
Orgon
Pont Royal
Ste Tulle
Sénas
Cadenet
Servanes
Eyguières
Fontvieille
Pertuis
Bge de Cadarache
Arles
St Martin-de-Crau
Salon-de-P.
Lambesc
Peyrolles
Rians
Tavernes
Aups
Miramas
St Chamas
Istres
Barjols
Cotignac
AIX-EN-PROVENCE
Canal de Provence
St Maximin-la-Ste Baume
Barbaroux
LA PROVENÇALE
Brignoles
Berre-l'Etang
Etg de Berre
Marignane
Gardanne
Trets
Sainte-Baume (La)
la Roquebrussanne
Fos
Port-de-Bouc
Lavéra
Martigues
Port-St-Louis
Roquevaire
Aubagne
Gémenos
la Ste Baume
Carro
Carry-le-Rouet
Chau d'If
MARSEILLE
Cuers
Solliès-Pont
le Beausset
Cassis
la Ciotat
les Lecques
Bandol
Ollioules
Hyères
Carqueiranne
Sanary
Six-Fours
la Seyne
TOULON
Frégate
St Mandrier
Cap Sicié
Giens
Porquerolles
l'Ile-Rousse
Porto-Vecchio
Ajaccio
Bastia
Calvi
Propriano
Ajaccio
Propriano
Bastia
l'Ile-Rousse
T E R R A N
MICHELIN

188

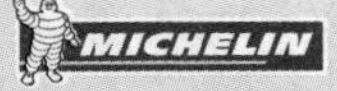

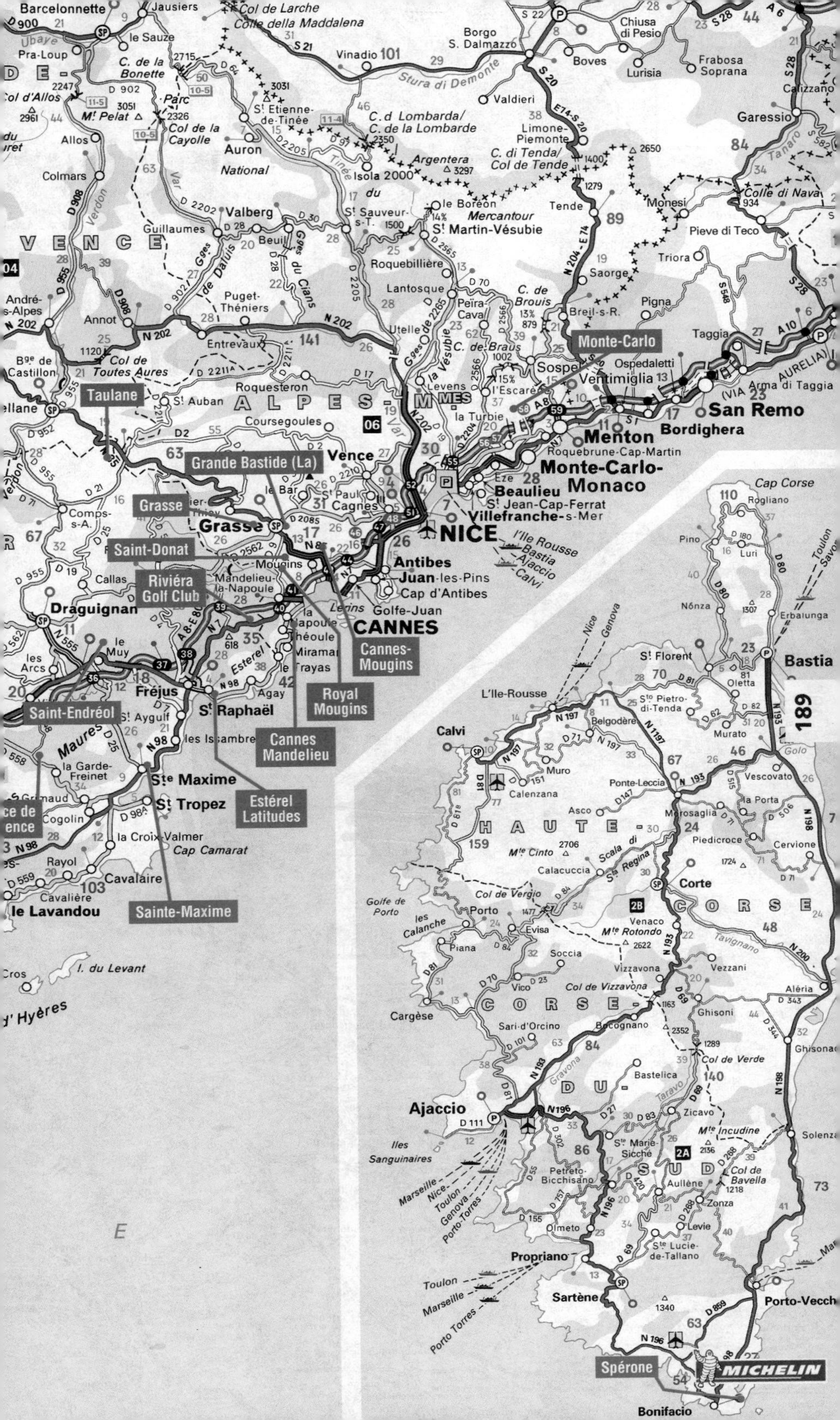

Barcelonnette
Jausiers
Col de Larche
Colle della Maddalena
Borgo S. Dalmazzo
Chiusa di Pesio
Vinadio
Boves
Lurisia
Frabosa Soprana
Pra-Loup
le Sauze
C. de la Bonette
Stura di Demonte
Valdieri
Calizzano
Col d'Allos
Mt Pelat
Parc
Col de la Cayolle
St Etienne-de-Tinée
C.d Lombarda/ C. de la Lombarde
Limone-Piemonte
Garessio
Allos
Auron
National
Argentera
C. di Tenda/ Col de Tende
Colmars
Isola 2000
du
Mercantour
le Boréon
Tende
Colle di Nava
Monesi
Valberg
St Sauveur-s-T.
St Martin-Vésubie
Pieve di Teco
Guillaumes
Beuil
Gges de Daluis
Gges du Cians
Roquebillière
Triora
Saorge
Lantosque
Peïra-Cava
C. de Brouis
Puget-Théniers
André-les-Alpes
Annot
Breil-s-R.
Pigna
Entrevaux
Utelle
Gges de la Vésubie
C. de Braus
Taggia
Monte-Carlo
Col de Toutes Aures
Castillon
Sospel
Ospedaletti
Ventimiglia
Levens
l'Escarène
Roquesteron
Arma di Taggia
Taulane
St Auban
ALPES-MARITIMES
la Turbie
San Remo
Bordighera
Coursegoules
Menton
Roquebrune-Cap-Martin
Vence
Monte-Carlo-Monaco
Grande Bastide (La)
Eze
Beaulieu
St Jean-Cap-Ferrat
Villefranche-s-Mer
le Bar
St Paul
Cagnes
Grasse
NICE
Comps-s-A.
l'Ile Rousse
Bastia
Ajaccio
Calvi
Saint-Donat
Antibes
Juan-les-Pins
Mougins
Callas
Mandelieu-la-Napoule
Cap d'Antibes
Riviéra Golf Club
Draguignan
Golfe-Juan
Lérins
CANNES
la Napoule
Théoule
Miramar
le Trayas
Cannes-Mougins
Cap Corse
Rogliano
le Muy
les Arcs
Esterel
Fréjus
Agay
Royal Mougins
St Raphaël
Saint-Endréol
St Aygulf
Maures
les Issambres
Cannes Mandelieu
la Garde-Freinet
Ste Maxime
St Tropez
Estérel Latitudes
Grimaud
Cogolin
la Croix-Valmer
Cap Camarat
Rayol
Cavalaire
Cavalière
le Lavandou
Sainte-Maxime
I. du Levant
d'Hyères
E
Pino
Luri
Nonza
Erbalunga
St Florent
Oletta
L'Ile-Rousse
Sto Pietro-di-Tenda
Belgodère
Murato
Muro
Calenzana
Golo
Vescovato
Ponte-Leccia
Asco
Morosaglia
la Porta
Piedicroce
HAUTE-CORSE
Mte Cinto
Scala di Sta Regina
Calacuccia
Cervione
Corte
Golfe de Porto
Col de Vergio
Porto
les Calanche
Evisa
Venaco
Mte Rotondo
Piana
Soccia
Tavignano
Vezzani
Vizzavona
Col de Vizzavona
Vico
Aléria
Cargèse
CORSE-DU-SUD
Ghisoni
Sari-d'Orcino
Bocognano
Ghisonaccia
Col de Verde
Bastelica
Gravona
Taravo
Ajaccio
Zicavo
Mte Incudine
Solenzara
Iles Sanguinaires
Ste Marie-Sicché
Col de Bavella
Petreto-Bicchisano
Aullène
Zonza
Marseille
Nice
Toulon
Genova
Porto-Torres
Olmeto
Levie
Ste Lucie-de-Tallano
Propriano
Sartène
Porto-Vecchio
Porto Torres
Spérone
MICHELIN
Bonifacio
189

Map No 15
Carte 15
km
0
2
4
Paris International
Domont-Montmorency
Saint-Germain
Béthemont
Joyenval
Feucherolles
Saint-Nom-La-Bretèche
Saint-Cloud
RCF La Boulie
Golf National
Courson
Rochefort-Chisan
190
Pontoise
Cergy
Cergy-Pontoise
L'Isle-Adam
Meulan
Poissy
St-GERMAIN-EN-LAYE
Maisons-Laffitte
Argenteuil
Nanterre
Neuilly-s-Seine
Boulogne-Billancourt
VERSAILLES
Sèvres
Meudon
Clamart
Montrouge
Antony
Massy
Palaiseau
Orsay
Chevreuse
Limours en-Hurepoix
Trappes
Montigny-le-Bretonneux
St Quentin-en-Yvelines
PARC RÉGIONAL
HAUTE VALLÉE DE CHEVREUSE
MICHELIN

Goussainville
Roissy-en-France
AÉROPORT DE PARIS-CHARLES-DE-GAULLE
Dammartin-en-Goële
Sarcelles
Gonesse
Villiers-le-Bel
Ecouen
Mitry-Mory
Tremblay-en-France
Villepinte
Sevran
Aulnay-s/s-Bois
Le Bourget
Drancy
Bobigny
Aubervilliers
Pantin
Stains
Pierrefitte
Dugny
Garges-lès-G.
Livry-Gargan
Le Raincy
Montfermeil
Chelles
Claye-Souilly
Villeparisis
Bondy
Noisy-le-Sec
Romainville
Les Lilas
Bagnolet
Montreuil
Vincennes
Rosny-s/s-Bois
Neuilly-Plaisance
Noisy-le-Grand
Champs-s-M.
Noisiel
Torcy
Lagny-s-M.
Disneyland-Paris
Bussy-St-Georges
Ferrières-en-Brie
Nogent-s-M.
Le Perreux
Joinville
Champigny-s-M.
Villiers-s-M.
Charenton
Ivry-s-Seine
Alfortville
Maisons-Alfort
St Maur
CRETEIL
Vitry-s-Seine
Choisy-le-Roi
Thiais
Orly
Villeneuve-le-Roi
Athis-Mons
Bonneuil-s-M.
Sucy-en-Brie
Boissy-St-Léger
Chennevières-s-M.
Ormesson
Pontault-Combault
Ozoir-la-Ferrière
Roissy-en-Brie
Émerainville
Forêt d'Armainvilliers
Valenton
Villeneuve-St-Georges
Yerres
Villecresnes
Montgeron
Brunoy
Draveil
Forêt de Sénart
Etiolles
EVRY
Corbeil-Essonnes
Brie-Comte-Robert
Combs-la-Ville
Sénart (Ville Nlle)
Moissy-Cramayel
Lieusaint
Melun-Sénart
Ris-Orangis
Courcouronnes
Lisses
191
MICHELIN

CLASSIFICATION OF FRENCH COURSES
CLASSEMENT DES PARCOURS FRANÇAIS

This classification gives priority consideration to the score awarded to the actual course.

Ce classement donne priorité à la note attribuée au parcours .

Course score / Note du parcours				Page
19	8	6	Bordes (Les)	232
19	8	7	Prince de Provence (Vidauban)	267
18	7	6	Chantilly *Vineuil*	247
18	8	6	Kempferhof (Le)	240
18	7	5	Médoc *Les Châteaux*	249
18	6	6	Morfontaine	254
18	6	6	National *L'Albatros*	255
17	7	6	Barbaroux	222
17	7	7	Fontainebleau	221
17	7	6	Grenoble Bresson	231
17	6	5	Limère	245
17	6	5	Moliets	251
17	7	6	Nîmes-Campagne	257
17	7	5	Pléneuf-Val-André	262
17	8	8	Royal Mougins	274
17	7	7	Saint-Germain	279
17	8	8	Saint-Nom-la-Bretèche *Rouge*	283
17	7	7	Seignosse	288
17	7	5	Spérone	291
17	7	5	Villette d'Anthon *Les Sangliers*	300
16	5	4	Aisses (Les) *Rouge/Blanc*	209
16	6	5	Belle-Dune	225
16	7	6	Bondues *Blanc*	230
16	7	5	Bresse (La)	234
16	6	6	Charmeil	248
16	6	8	Chiberta	252
16	7	3	Courson *Vert/Noir*	209
16	7	8	Disneyland Paris *Peter + Alice*	212
16	6	7	Estérel Latitudes	216
16	6	6	Gouverneur (Le) *Le Breuil*	226
16	6	6	Grande Bastide (La)	228
16	6	4	Grande-Motte (La) *Les Flamants Roses*	229
16	6	6	Hardelot *Les Pins*	233
16	6	6	Hossegor	235
16	7	4	Isle Adam (L')	237
16	8	7	Joyenval *Marly*	238
16	7	5	Montpellier-Massane	253
16	7	5	Paris International	260
16	6	5	Pont Royal	264
16	6	4	Rebetz	269
16	7	4	Sablé-Solesmes *La Forêt/La Rivière*	275
16	7	8	Saint Donat	276
16	6	5	Saint-Jean-de-Monts	280
16	8	8	Saint-Nom-la-Bretèche *Bleu*	282
16	7	4	Soufflenheim	290
16	6	7	Touquet (Le) *La Mer*	296
16	6	6	Wantzenau (La)	302
15	6	4	Ableiges *Les Etangs*	207
15	6	5	Ailette (L')	208
15	6	6	Albi	211
15	8	6	Apremont	215
15	6	5	Baden	220
15	7	7	Bâle-Hagenthal	221
15	7	8	Baule (La) *Rouge*	223
15	7	6	Bondues *Jaune*	231
15	7	8	Boulie (La) *La Vallée*	233
15	7	7	Bretesche (La)	236
15	7	8	Cannes-Mougins	239
15	6	5	Cap d'Agde	240
15	7	6	Cély	241
15	6	7	Chamonix	244
15	7	6	Château de Preisch	249
15	7	3	Courson *Lilas/Orange*	208
15	7	5	Esery	215
15	7	6	Etiolles *Les Cerfs*	217
15	7	9	Evian	219
15	7	5	Feucherolles	220
15	7	7	Frégate	225
15	7	6	Gujan-Mestras	232

Chopard
BOUTIQUE
XII
Chopard
GENÈVE
III
VI
IX
Chopard
72, Faubourg St-Honoré - 75008 Pa
Tél. 01 42 66 67 30
www.chopard.com

CLASSIFICATION OF GOLF COURSES

CLASSEMENT DES PARCOURS

15	7	7	International Club du Lys *Les Chênes*	236
15	8	7	Joyenval *Retz*	239
15	7	4	Largue (La)	242
15	6	8	Makila Golf Club	247
15	7	5	Médoc *Les Vignes*	250
15	7	6	Ploemeur Océan	263
15	6	6	Pornic	266
15	7	7	Roncemay	273
15	7	4	Saint-Endréol	278
15	7	4	Taulane	293
15	7	4	Toulouse Palmola	294
15	7	6	Toulouse-Seilh *Rouge*	295
15	6	5	Val Queven	298
15	7	4	Vaucouleurs (La) *Les Vallons*	299
14	7	8	Amirauté (L')	212
14	7	8	Arcangues	217
14	6	6	Arras	218
14	7	7	Bélesbat	224
14	6	8	Biarritz-le-Phare	228
14	6	5	Bitche	229
14	7	6	Brest Iroise	235
14	7	6	Brigode	237
14	7	8	Cannes Mandelieu *Old Course*	238
14	8	6	Chailly (Château de)	242
14	5	7	Chambon-sur-Lignon (Le)	243
14	6	3	Champ de Bataille	245
14	7	7	Chantaco	246
14	6	4	Chaumont-en-Vexin	250
14	7	6	Cheverny	251
14	6	5	Dieppe-Pourville	210
14	6	7	Divonne	213
14	7	6	Etretat	218
14	6	6	Fontcaude	222
14	7	6	Fontenailles *Blanc*	223
14	6	4	Fontenelles (Les)	224
14	6	6	Gouverneur (Le) *Montaplan*	227
14	4	4	Granville *Les Dunes*	230
14	6	4	Haut-Poitou	234
14	6	7	Lacanau	241
14	7	5	Laval-Changé *La Chabossière*	243
14	7	5	Le Prieuré *Ouest*	244
14	8	5	Maison *Blanc*he	246
14	6	7	Monte Carlo (Mont Agel)	252
14	7	8	New Golf Deauville *Rouge/Blanc*	256
14	7	5	Omaha Beach *La Mer/Le Bocage*	258
14	6	4	Porcelaine (La)	265
14	7	4	Raray (Château de) *La Licorne*	268
14	6	4	Rochefort-Chisan	272
14	8	7	Saint-Cloud *Vert*	277
14	7	5	Saint-Laurent	281
14	7	5	Saint-Thomas	284
14	7	6	Sainte-Baume (La)	285
14	5	4	Savenay	287
14	7	5	Val de Sorne	297
14	6	5	Volcans (Les)	301
14	4	5	Wimereux	303
13	5	7	Aix-les-Bains	210
13	6	5	Amnéville	213
13	6	5	Annonay-Gourdan	214
13	6	6	Arcachon	216
13	6	4	Augerville	219
13	7	5	Besançon	226
13	6	5	Béthemont	227
13	7	5	Cognac	207
13	6	7	Dinard	211
13	7	4	Domont-Montmorency	214
13	7	7	Grasse	9999
13	5	4	Mazamet-La Ba*Rouge*	248
13	7	5	Ozoir-la-Ferrière *Château/Monthéty*	259
13	6	8	Pau	261
13	7	6	Reims-Champagne	270
13	7	8	Riviéra Golf Club	271
13	7	8	Sainte-Maxime	286
13	5	7	Servanes	289
13	7	6	Strasbourg Illkirch *Jaune + Rouge*	292

HOTELS FACILITIES
ENVIRONNEMENT HOTELIER

This classification gives priority consideration to the score awarded to the hotel facilities.

Ce classement donne priorité à la note attribuée à l'environnement hôtelier .

HOTEL FACILITY SCORE
Note de l'environnement hotelier

				Page
15	7	**9**	Evian	219
14	7	**8**	Amirauté (L')	212
14	7	**8**	Arcangues 217	
15	7	**8**	Baule (La) *Rouge*	223
14	6	**8**	Biarritz-le-Phare	228
15	7	**8**	Boulie (La) *La Vallée*	233
14	7	**8**	Cannes Mandelieu *Old Course*	238
15	7	**8**	Cannes-Mougins	239
16	6	**8**	Chiberta	252
16	7	**8**	Disneyland Paris *Peter + Alice*	212
15	6	**8**	Makila Golf Club	247
14	7	**8**	New Golf Deauville *Rouge/Blanc*	256
13	6	**8**	Pau	261
13	7	**8**	Riviéra Golf Club	271
17	8	**8**	Royal Mougins	274
16	7	**8**	Saint Donat	276
16	8	**8**	Saint-Nom-la-Bretèche *Bleu*	282
17	8	**8**	Saint-Nom-la-Bretèche *Rouge*	283
13	7	**8**	Sainte-Maxime	286
13	5	**7**	Aix-les-Bains	210
15	7	**7**	Bâle-Hagenthal	221
14	7	**7**	Bélesbat	224
15	7	**7**	Bretesche (La)	236
14	5	**7**	Chambon-sur-Lignon (Le)	243
15	6	**7**	Chamonix	244
14	7	**7**	Chantaco	246
13	6	**7**	Dinard	211
14	6	**7**	Divonne	213
16	6	**7**	Estérel Latitudes	216
17	7	**7**	Fontainebleau	221
15	7	**7**	Frégate	225
15	7	**7**	International Club du Lys *Les Chênes*	236
16	8	**7**	Joyenval *Marly*	238
15	8	**7**	Joyenval *Retz*	239
14	6	**7**	Lacanau	241
14	6	**7**	Monte Carlo (Mont Agel)	252
19	8	**7**	Prince de Provence (Vidauban)	267
15	7	**7**	Roncemay	273
14	8	**7**	Saint-Cloud *Vert*	277
17	7	**7**	Saint-Germain	279
17	7	**7**	Seignosse	288
13	5	**7**	Servanes	289
16	6	**7**	Touquet (Le) *La Mer*	296
15	6	**6**	Albi	211
15	8	**6**	Apremont	215
13	6	**6**	Arcachon	216
14	6	**6**	Arras	218
17	7	**6**	Barbaroux	222
16	7	**6**	Bondues *Blanc*	230
15	7	**6**	Bondues *Jaune*	231
19	8	**6**	Bordes (Les)	232
14	7	**6**	Brest Iroise	235
14	7	**6**	Brigode	237
15	7	**6**	Cély	241
14	8	**6**	Chailly (Château de)	242
18	7	**6**	Chantilly *Vineuil*	247
16	6	**6**	Charmeil	248
15	7	**6**	Château de Preisch	249
14	7	**6**	Cheverny	251
15	7	**6**	Etiolles *Les Cerfs*	217
14	7	**6**	Etretat	218
14	6	**6**	Fontcaude	222
14	7	**6**	Fontenailles *Blanc*	223
16	6	**6**	Gouverneur (Le) *Le Breuil*	226
14	6	**6**	Gouverneur (Le) *Montaplan*	227
16	6	**6**	Grande Bastide (La)	228
17	7	**6**	Grenoble Bresson	231
15	7	**6**	Gujan-Mestras	232
16	6	**6**	Hardelot *Les Pins*	233
16	6	**6**	Hossegor	235

HOTEL FACILITIES

ENVIRONNEMENT HOTELIER

18	8	**6**	Kempferhof (Le)	240
18	6	**6**	Morfontaine	254
18	6	**6**	National *L'Albatros*	255
17	7	**6**	Nîmes-Campagne	257
15	7	**6**	Ploemeur Océan	263
15	6	**6**	Pornic	266
13	7	**6**	Reims-Champagne	270
14	7	**6**	Sainte-Baume (La)	285
13	7	**6**	Strasbourg Illkirch *Jaune + Rouge*	292
15	7	**6**	Toulouse-Seilh *Rouge*	295
16	6	**6**	Wantzenau (La)	302
15	6	**5**	Ailette (L')	208
13	6	**5**	Amnéville	213
13	6	**5**	Annonay-Gourdan	214
15	6	**5**	Baden	220
16	6	**5**	Belle-Dune	225
13	7	**5**	Besançon	226
13	6	**5**	Béthemont	227
14	6	**5**	Bitche	229
16	7	**5**	Bresse (La)	234
15	6	**5**	Cap d'Agde	240
13	7	**5**	Cognac	207
14	6	**5**	Dieppe-Pourville	210
15	7	**5**	Esery	215
15	7	**5**	Feucherolles	220
14	7	**5**	Laval-Changé *La Chabossière*	243
14	7	**5**	Le Prieuré *Ouest*	244
17	6	**5**	Limère	245
14	8	**5**	Maison *Blanc*he	246
18	7	**5**	Médoc *Les Châteaux*	249
15	7	**5**	Médoc *Les Vignes*	250
17	6	**5**	Moliets	251
16	7	**5**	Montpellier-Massane	253
14	7	**5**	Omaha Beach *La Mer/Le Bocage*	258
13	7	**5**	Ozoir-la-Ferrière *Château/Monthéty*	259
16	7	**5**	Paris International	260
17	7	**5**	Pléneuf-Val-André	262
16	6	**5**	Pont Royal	264
16	6	**5**	Saint-Jean-de-Monts	280
14	7	**5**	Saint-Laurent	281
14	7	**5**	Saint-Thomas	284
17	7	**5**	Spérone	291
14	7	**5**	Val de Sorne	297
15	6	**5**	Val Queven	298
17	7	**5**	Villette d'Anthon *Les Sangliers*	300
14	6	**5**	Volcans (Les)	301
14	4	**5**	Wimereux	303
15	6	**4**	Ableiges *Les Etangs*	207
16	5	**4**	Aisses (Les) *Rouge/Blanc*	209
13	6	**4**	Augerville	219
14	6	**4**	Chaumont-en-Vexin	250
13	7	**4**	Domont-Montmorency	214
14	6	**4**	Fontenelles (Les)	224
16	6	**4**	Grande-Motte (La) *Les Flamants Roses*	229
14	4	**4**	Granville *Les Dunes*	230
14	6	**4**	Haut-Poitou	234
16	7	**4**	Isle Adam (L')	237
15	7	**4**	Largue (La)	242
13	5	**4**	Mazamet-La Ba*Rouge*	248
14	6	**4**	Porcelaine (La)	265
14	7	**4**	Raray (Château de) *La Licorne*	268
16	6	**4**	Rebetz	269
14	6	**4**	Rochefort-Chisan	272
16	7	**4**	Sablé-Solesmes *La Forêt/La Rivière*	275
15	7	**4**	Saint-Endréol	278
14	5	**4**	Savenay	287
16	7	**4**	Soufflenheim	290
15	7	**4**	Taulane	293
15	7	**4**	Toulouse Palmola	294
15	7	**4**	Vaucouleurs (La) *Les Vallons*	299
14	6	**3**	Champ de Bataille	245
15	7	**3**	Courson *Lilas/Orange*	208
16	7	**3**	Courson *Vert/Noir*	209

RECOMMENDED GOLFING STAY
SEJOUR DE GOLF RECOMMANDÉ

Barbaroux	17 7 6	222
Belle-Dune	16 6 5	225
Bondues *Blanc*	16 7 6	230
Bondues *Jaune*	15 7 6	231
Bordes (Les)	19 8 6	232
Bretesche (La)	15 7 7	236
Courson *Lilas/Orange*	15 7 3	208
Courso *Vert/Noir*	16 7 3	209
Gouverneur (Le) *Le Breuil*	16 6 6	226
Gouverneur (Le) *Montaplan*	14 6 6	227
Grande Bastide (La)	16 6 6	228
Grande-Motte (La)		
Les Flamants Roses	16 6 4	229
Gujan-Mestras	15 7 6	232
Hardelot *Les Pins*	16 6 6	233
Limère	17 6 5	245
Médoc *Les Châteaux*	18 7 5	249
Médoc *Les Vignes*	15 7 5	250
Moliets	17 6 5	251
Montpellier-Massane	16 7 5	253
National *L'Albatros*	18 6 6	255
Pléneuf-Val-André	17 7 5	262
Sablé-Solesmes		
La Forêt/La Rivière	16 7 4	275
Spérone	17 7 5	291
Taulane	15 7 4	293
Toulouse-Seilh *Rouge*	15 7 6	295
Touquet (Le) La Mer	16 6 7	296
Villette d'Anthon *Les Sangliers*	17 7 5	300

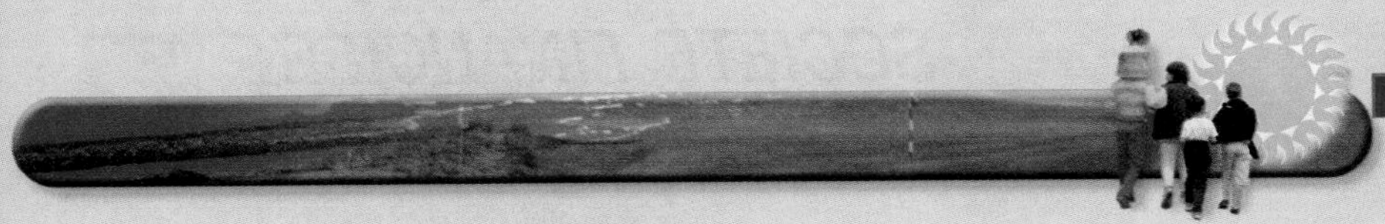

RECOMMENDED GOLFING HOLIDAYS
VACANCES RECOMMANDÉES

Aix-les-Bains	13 5 7	210
Amirauté (L')	14 7 8	212
Arcachon	13 6 6	216
Arcangues	14 7 8	217
Baule (La) *Rouge*	15 7 8	223
Biarritz-le-Phare	14 6 8	228
Cannes Mandelieu *Old Course*	14 7 8	238
Cannes-Mougins	15 7 8	239
Cap d'Agde	15 6 5	240
Chamonix	15 6 7	244
Chantaco	14 7 7	246
Chiberta	16 6 8	252
Dinard	13 6 7	211
Disneyland Paris *Peter + Alice*	16 7 8	212
Estérel Latitudes	16 6 7	216
Frégate	15 7 7	225
Grande Bastide (La)	16 6 6	228
Grande-Motte (La)		
Les Flamants Roses	16 6 4	229
Gujan-Mestras	15 7 6	232
Hardelot *Les Pins*	16 6 6	233
Hossegor	16 6 6	235
Lacanau	14 6 7	241
Makila Golf Club	15 6 8	247
Moliets	17 6 5	251
Monte Carlo (Mont Agel)	14 6 7	252
New Golf Deauville *Rouge/Blanc*	14 7 8	256
Pornic	15 6 6	266
Riviéra Golf Club	13 7 8	271
Royal Mougins	17 8 8	274
Saint Donat	16 7 8	276
Saint-Laurent	14 7 5	281
Sainte-Maxime	13 7 8	286
Spérone	17 7 5	291

GÉOGRAPHICAL RELIEF
RELIEF DES PARCOURS

Aisses (Les) *Rouge/Blanc*	16	5	4	209
Médoc *Les Châteaux*	18	7	5	249
Médoc *Les Vignes*	15	7	5	250

Amirauté (L')	14	7	8	212
Apremont	15	8	6	215
Bélesbat	14	7	7	224
Biarritz-le-Phare	14	6	8	228
Bordes (Les)	19	8	6	232
Bresse (La)	16	7	5	234
Bretesche (La)	15	7	7	236
Brigode	14	7	6	237
Cannes Mandelieu *Old Course*	14	7	8	238
Cap d'Agde	15	6	5	240
Chailly (Château de)	14	8	6	242
Cheverny	14	7	6	251
Dieppe-Pourville	14	6	5	210
Disneyland Paris *Peter + Alice*	16	7	8	212
Etiolles *Les Cerfs*	15	7	6	217
Etretat	14	7	6	218
Fontenailles *Blanc*	14	7	6	223
Gouverneur (Le) *Le Breuil*	16	6	6	226
Grande Bastide (La)	16	6	6	228
Grande-Motte (La) *Les Flamants Roses*	16	6	4	229
Granville *Les Dunes*	14	4	4	230
Gujan-Mestras	15	7	6	232
Hossegor	16	6	6	235
International Club du Lys *Les Chênes*	15	7	7	236
Limère	17	6	5	245
Montpellier-Massane	16	7	5	253
Ozoir-la-Ferrière Château/Monthéty	13	7	5	259
Pau	13	6	8	261
Raray (Château de) *La Licorne*	14	7	4	268
Roncemay	15	7	7	273
Sablé-Solesmes *La Forêt/La Rivière*	16	7	4	275
Saint-Germain	17	7	7	279
Saint-Thomas	14	7	5	284
Sainte-Baume (La)	14	7	6	285
Soufflenheim	16	7	4	290
Strasbourg Illkirch *Jaune + Rouge*	13	7	6	292
Touquet (Le) La Mer	16	6	7	296
Wimereux	14	4	5	303

Ailette (L')	15	6	5	208
Aix-les-Bains	13	5	7	210
Baule (La) *Rouge*	15	7	8	223
Bondues *Blanc*	16	7	6	230
Bondues *Jaune*	15	7	6	231
Cannes-Mougins	15	7	8	239
Charmeil	16	6	6	248
Chiberta	16	6	8	252
Cognac	13	7	5	207
Dinard	13	6	7	211
Fontainebleau	17	7	7	221
Fontenelles (Les)	14	6	4	224
Gouverneur (Le) *Montaplan*	14	6	6	227
Kempferhof (Le)	18	8	6	240
Morfontaine	18	6	6	254
National *L'Albatros*	18	6	6	255
New Golf Deauville *Rouge/Blanc*	14	7	8	256
Nîmes-Campagne	17	7	6	257
Ploemeur Océan	15	7	6	263
Porcelaine (La)	14	6	4	265
Saint-Jean-de-Monts	16	6	5	280
Servanes	13	5	7	289
Toulouse-Seilh *Rouge*	15	7	6	295
Villette d'Anthon *Les Sangliers*	17	7	5	300
Wantzenau (La)	16	6	6	302

Belle-Dune	16	6	5	225
Besançon	13	7	5	226
Béthemont	13	6	5	227
Brest Iroise	14	7	6	235
Cély	15	7	6	241
Chamonix	15	6	7	244
Chantaco	14	7	7	246
Chantilly *Vineuil*	18	7	6	247
Château de Preisch	15	7	6	249
Courson *Lilas/Orange*	15	7	3	208
Courson *Vert/Noir*	16	7	3	209
Estérel Latitudes	16	6	7	216
Hardelot *Les Pins*	16	6	6	233
Le Prieuré *Ouest*	14	7	5	244
Mazamet-La Ba*rouge*	13	5	4	248
Rebetz	16	6	4	269
Reims-Champagne	13	7	6	270
Riviéra Golf Club	13	7	8	271
Saint-Laurent	14	7	5	281
Saint-Nom-la-Bretèche *Bleu*	16	8	8	282
Taulane	15	7	4	293
Toulouse Palmola	15	7	4	294
Val Queven	15	6	5	298
Vaucouleurs (La) *Les Vallons*	15	7	4	299
Volcans (Les)	14	6	5	301

Albi	15	6	6	211
Annonay-Gourdan	13	6	5	214
Arcachon	13	6	6	216
Augerville	13	6	4	219
Bâle-Hagenthal	15	7	7	221
Champ de Bataille	14	6	3	245
Divonne	14	6	7	213
Haut-Poitou	14	6	4	234
Isle Adam (L')	16	7	4	237
Joyenval *Marly*	16	8	7	238
Joyenval *Retz*	15	8	7	239
Lacanau	14	6	7	241
Laval-Changé *La Chabossière*	14	7	5	243
Moliets	17	6	5	251
Omaha Beach La Mer/Le Bocage	14	7	5	258
Pornic	15	6	6	266
Prince de Provence (Vidauban)	19	8	7	267
Royal Mougins	17	8	8	274
Saint Donat	16	7	8	276
Saint-Cloud *Vert*	14	8	7	277
Saint-Nom-la-Bretèche *Rouge*	17	8	8	283
Savenay	14	5	4	287
Seignosse	17	7	7	288
Spérone	17	7	5	291
Val de Sorne	14	7	5	297

Ableiges *Les Etangs*	15	6	4	207
Arras	14	6	6	218
Baden	15	6	5	220
Barbaroux	17	7	6	222
Boulie (La) *La Vallée*	15	7	8	233
Feucherolles	15	7	5	220
Fontcaude	14	6	6	222
Grasse	13	7	7	9999
Largue (La)	15	7	4	242
Maison *Blanc*he	14	8	5	246
Monte Carlo (Mont Agel)	14	6	7	252
Pléneuf-Val-André	17	7	5	262
Pont Royal	16	6	5	264
Rochefort-Chisan	14	6	4	272

Amnéville	13	6	5	213
Arcangues	14	7	8	217
Chaumont-en-Vexin	14	6	4	250
Domont-Montmorency	13	7	4	214
Esery	15	7	5	215
Evian	15	7	9	219
Frégate	15	7	7	225
Grenoble Bresson	17	7	6	231
Makila Golf Club	15	6	8	247
Paris International	16	7	5	260
Sainte-Maxime	13	7	8	286

Bitche	14	6	5	229
Chambon-sur-Lignon (Le)	14	5	7	243
Saint-Endréol	15	7	4	278

TYPE OF COURSE
TYPE DE PARCOURS

Roncemay 273, Sablé-Solesmes *La Forêt/La Rivière* 275, Savenay 287, Soufflenheim 290, Toulouse-Seilh *Rouge* 295, Wantzenau (La) 302.

Mountain

Chamonix 244, Esery 215, Grenoble Bresson 231, Volcans (Les) 301.

Parkland

Ailette (L') 208, Aisses (Les) *Rouge/Blanc* 209, Apremont 215, Aix-les-Bains 210, Albi 211, Annonay-Gourdan 214, Arras 218, Bélesbat 224, Bondues *Blanc* 230, Bondues *Jaune* 231, Bretesche (La) 236, Brigode 237, Cély 241, Chamonix 244, Cannes-Mougins 239, Chantaco 246, Chaumont-en-Vexin 250, Divonne 213, Evian 219, Feucherolles 220, Fontenailles *Blanc* 223, Hardelot *Les Pins* 233, International Club du Lys *Les Chênes* 236, Joyenval *Marly* 238, Joyenval *Retz* 239, Kempferhof (Le) 240, Largue (La) 242, Le Prieuré *Ouest* 244, Limère 245, Makila Golf Club 247, Mazamet-La Ba*Rouge* 248, Monte Carlo (Mont Agel) 252, New Golf Deauville *Rouge/Blanc* 256, Nîmes-Campagne 257, Ozoir-la-Ferrière *Château/Monthéty* 259, Paris International 260, Pau 261, Rebetz 269, Reims-Champagne 270, Riviéra Golf Club 271, Saint-Cloud *Vert* 277, Saint Donat 276, Saint-Nom-la-Bretèche *Bleu* 282, Saint-Nom-la-Bretèche *Rouge* 283, Savenay 287, Val de Sorne 297.

Seaside course

Arcachon 216, Baden 220, Belle-Dune 225, Cannes Mandelieu *Old Course* 238, Cap d'Agde 240, Dieppe-Pourville 210, Dinard 211, Etretat 218, Frégate 225, Grande-Motte (La) *Les Flamants Roses* 229, Omaha Beach *La Mer/Le Bocage* 258, Pléneuf-Val-André 262, Ploemeur Océan 263, Spérone 291.

Country

Baden 220, Bâle-Hagenthal 221, Besançon 226, Cognac 207, Kempferhof (Le) 240, Vaucouleurs (La) *Les Vallons* 299, Villette d'Anthon *Les Sangliers* 300.

Hilly

Ableiges *Les Etangs* 207, Arcachon 216, Arcangues 217, Augerville 219, Barbaroux 222, Béthemont 227, Bitche 229, Chambon-sur-Lignon (Le) 243, Chaumont-en-Vexin 250, Divonne 213, Domont-Montmorency 214, Esery 215, Evian 219, Fontcaude 222, Frégate 225, Lacanau 241, Laval-Changé *La Chabossière* 243, Maison *Blanc*he 246, Makila Golf Club 247, Monte Carlo (Mont Agel) 252, Paris International 260, Pont Royal 264, Royal Mougins 274, Saint Donat 276, Saint-Endréol 278, Sainte-Maxime 286, Seignosse 288, Spérone 291.

Residential

Biarritz-le-Phare 228, Bondues *Blanc* 230, Bondues *Jaune* 231, Estérel Latitudes 216, Fontcaude 222, Grande-Motte (La) *Les Flamants Roses* 229, Montpellier-Massane 253, Riviéra Golf Club 271, Saint-Nom-la-Bretèche *Bleu* 282, Saint-Nom-la-Bretèche *Rouge* 283, Sainte-Maxime 286, Toulouse Palmola 294, Toulouse-Seilh *Rouge* 295, Wantzenau (La) 302.

ABLEIGES Les Etangs

15 | 6 | 4

En plaine et dans les vallons du Vexin, l'architecture du 18 trous des "Etangs" présente des styles différents, mais sans rupture de style trop marquée. Le haut du domaine s'apparente aux links, avec de jolis mouvements de terrain, alors que la partie basse est plus "américaine". La plupart des drives, tout comme les approches, exigent une bonne technique et un placement attentif, en raison des nombreux obstacles très en jeu, qu'il s'agisse des bunkers, du rough ou de l'eau. L'architecte Jeremy Pern a généreusement modelé et défendu les greens (deux ont été refaits), où les positions de drapeau peuvent changer radicalement le jeu. Les reliefs du terrain rendent ce parcours assez physique (à jouer en voiturette), et imposent de choisir les départs adaptés à son niveau. C'est un bon test, mais certains trous peuvent être très humides et un sérieux drainage reste nécessaire.

On the plain and through the vales of Vexin, the architecture of the 18 hole "Etangs" course features a number of different styles stitched together in almost seamless fashion. The upper section is links territory, with attractive sandhills and dips, while the lower section is more American in its layout. Most tee-shots and approach-shots demand good technique and careful placing of the ball owing to the numerous hazards in play, ranging from unforgiving rough to water. Architect Jeremy Pern has generously contoured and defended the greens (two of them have been remodeled), where the pin-positions can radically change the course. Ableiges can be a tiring course on foot (it is worth taking a buggy) and you should choose those tees that best suit your golfing ability. A good test of golf, but some of the holes tend to be very wet and are still in need of some serious drainage work.

Golf Club d'Ableiges — 1989

Chaussée Jules César
F - 95450 ABLEIGES

Office	Secrétariat	(33) 01 30 27 97 00
Pro shop	Pro-shop	(33) 01 34 27 97 00
Fax	Fax	(33) 01 30 27 97 10
Web	—	
Situation	Situation	Paris, 40 km

Pontoise (pop. 27 150), 9 km

Annual closure	Fermeture annuelle	no
Weekly closure	Fermeture hebdomadaire	no

Fees main season Tarifs haute saison	18 holes	
	Week days Semaine	**We/Bank holidays** We/Férié
Individual Individuel	23 €	44 €
Couple Couple	46 €	88 €

Tuesday (Mardi): GF + lunch, 29 €

Caddy	Caddy	no
Electric Trolley	Chariot électrique	no
Buggy	Voiturette	23 € /18 holes
Clubs	Clubs	no
Credit cards	Cartes de crédit	CB

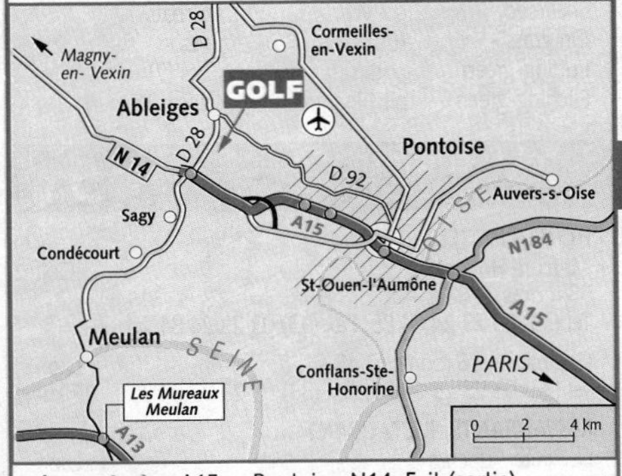

Access Accès : A15 → Pontoise, N14. Exit (sortie) Ableiges, → Golf
Map 3 on page 166 Carte 3 Page 166

Golf course PARCOURS — 15/20

Site	Site	
Maintenance	Entretien	
Architect	Architecte	Jeremy Pern, Jean Garaïalde
Type	Type	open country, hilly
Relief	Relief	
Water in play	Eau en jeu	
Exp. to wind	Exposé au vent	
Trees in play	Arbres en jeu	

Scorecard Carte de score	**Chp.** Chp.	**Mens** Mess.	**Ladies** Da.
Length Long.	6261	5634	5274
Par	72	72	72
Slope system	133	125	121

Advised golfing ability Niveau de jeu recommandé: 0 12 24 36

Hcp required Handicap exigé: 30 Mens, 32 Ladies

Club house & amenities CLUB-HOUSE ET ANNEXES — 6/10

Pro shop	Pro-shop	
Driving range	Practice	
Sheltered	couvert	15 mats
On grass	sur herbe	yes
Putting-green	putting-green	yes
Pitching-green	pitching green	yes

Hotel facilities ENVIRONNEMENT HOTELIER — 4/10

HOTELS HÔTELS

Astrée, 55 rooms, D 93 € — Pontoise 10 km
Tel (33) 01 34 24 94 94, Fax (33) 01 34 24 95 15

Campanile — Pontoise 10 km
81 rooms, D 55 €
Tel (33) 01 30 38 55 44, Fax (33) 01 30 30 48 87

RESTAURANTS RESTAURANT

Relais Sainte-Jeanne — Cormeilles-en-Vexin 4 km
Tel (33) 03 34 66 61 56

Le Chiquito — La Bonneville 5 km
Tel (33) 01 30 36 40 23

AILETTE (L') 15 | 6 | 5

L'Ailette représente une sorte de modèle de golf public et sportif, avec un club-house bien amélioré. Bien que vallonné, il n'est pas difficile à marcher, mais quelques greens très surélevés peuvent déconcerter au premier abord, accentuant le côté technique et tactique du parcours. Ses difficultés augmentent à mesure que l'on joue les départs reculés, mais il reste à la portée des joueurs moyens, nombreux ici. On remarquera l'alternance de trous assez reposants et de trous plus difficiles, ce qui donne un bon rythme au jeu, et des possibilités de reprendre des forces quand il le faut. Les greens sont vastes et francs, et bien défendus par des bunkers dessinés avec soin, mais avec parfois peu de positions de drapeau. Certains trous sont tracés dans les bois, généralement assez éloignés du jeu, et les obstacles d'eau sont dangereux sans être trop préoccupants. C'était le site du Chemin des Dames, témoin de la première Guerre Mondiale, il n'est plus le théâtre que de pacifiques batailles...

Ailette is a sort of a model public and sporting golf course now with a much improved club-house. Although far from flat, the course is not too tiring to walk around. A number of elevated greens are a little disconcerting at first and emphasise the course's technical and tactical sides. The difficulties of playing here increase as you tee-off further back, but Ailette is playable by mid-to-high handicappers, of whom there are many here. This is a nicely balanced course, with pleasant alternation between tough and easier holes allowing players breathing space and the chance to recuperate. The greens are huge, forthright and well-protected by well-designed bunkers, but sometimes a little short on good pin positions. Some holes run through woodland, although the trees are usually not too close, and the water hazards are dangerous but never over-bearing. The site of Chemin des Dames, a testimony to World War I, is now simply the theatre of more peaceful conflict with a little white ball...

Golf de l'Ailette — 1988

F - 02860 CERNY-EN LAONNOIS

Office Secrétariat (33) 03 23 24 83 99
Pro shop Pro-shop (33) 03 23 24 81 24
Fax Fax (33) 03 23 24 84 66
E-mail golfdelailette@wanadoo.fr
Situation Situation
Laon (pop. 26 490), 17 km
Annual closure Fermeture annuelle — no
Weekly closure Fermeture hebdomadaire — no

Fees main season Tarifs haute saison	Full day	
	Week days Semaine	We/Bank holidays We/Férié
Individual Individuel	32 €	41 €
Couple Couple	64 €	82 €

Caddy	Caddy	no
Electric Trolley	Chariot électrique	no
Buggy	Voiturette	30 € /18 holes
Clubs	Clubs	8 € /full day

Credit cards Cartes de crédit
VISA - CB - Eurocard - MasterCard

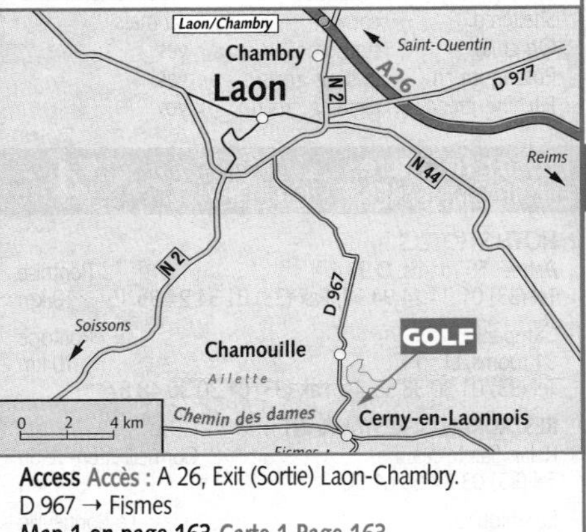

Access Accès : A 26, Exit (Sortie) Laon-Chambry.
D 967 → Fismes
Map 1 on page 163 Carte 1 Page 163

Golf course PARCOURS — 15/20

Site	Site	
Maintenance	Entretien	
Architect	Architecte	Michel Gayon
Type	Type	forest, parkland
Relief	Relief	
Water in play	Eau en jeu	
Exp. to wind	Exposé au vent	
Trees in play	Arbres en jeu	

Scorecard Carte de score	Chp. Chp.	Mens Mess.	Ladies Da.
Length Long.	6115	5727	4860
Par	72	72	72
Slope system	138	141	132

Advised golfing ability Niveau de jeu recommandé — 0 12 24 36
Hcp required Handicap exigé — 35

Club house & amenities CLUB-HOUSE ET ANNEXES — 6/10

Pro shop	Pro-shop	
Driving range	Practice	
Sheltered	couvert	5 mats
On grass	sur herbe	yes
Putting-green	putting-green	yes (2)
Pitching-green	pitching green	yes

Hotel facilities ENVIRONNEMENT HOTELIER — 5/10

HOTELS HÔTELS

Mercure Holigolf — Golf
58 rooms, D 88 €
Tel (33) 03 23 24 84 85, Fax (33) 03 23 24 81 20

Campanile, 46 rooms, D 48 € — Laon
Tel (33) 03 23 23 15 05, Fax (33) 03 23 23 04 25 — 17 km

RESTAURANTS RESTAURANT

La Petite Auberge — Laon
Tel (33) 03 23 23 02 38 — 17 km

Bannière de France — Laon
Tel (33) 03 23 23 21 44 — 17 km

AISSES (LES) Rouge/Blanc

16 | 5 | 4

Cet ensemble est composé de trois neuf trous combinables, le Rouge, le Blanc et le Bleu, dans un domaine de 250 hectares. Sur les deux premiers parcours, d'immenses bunkers sont à la fois des obstacles (ceux de fairway sont très plats) et des éléments d'architecture pour mieux préciser les trous dans l'espace. Le paysage de Sologne est calme et séduisant, mais le relief est absent, et les architectes n'ont pas voulu modeler beaucoup le terrain. Sur le dernier 9 trous, les obstacles d'eau prennent le relais des bunkers. La végétation est assez naturelle, avec les bouleaux, hêtres, sapins et chênes de la région. Un ensemble plaisant, mais le Club-House reste spartiate, et si le parcours ne mérite pas à lui seul un long voyage, il complète bien l'équipement golfique remarquable de la région (Les Bordes, Limère).

This is a complex of three combinable 9-hole courses - Red, White and Blue - over an estate of some 250 hectares. The first two are marked by huge bunkers (fairway bunkers are absolutely flat!) which are at once the layout's main hazards and the principal features. The Sologne landscape is calm and appealing, but the area is flat and the architects visibly avoided shaping the course. On the Blue course, bunkers are largely replaced by water. Vegetation is mostly natural, with birch, beech, pine and oak trees, typical of this area. A pleasant venue, but the club-house is still inadequate, and while the course itself is hardly worth a long trip out of your way, it completes some remarkable golfing facilities in this region (Les Bordes and Limère).

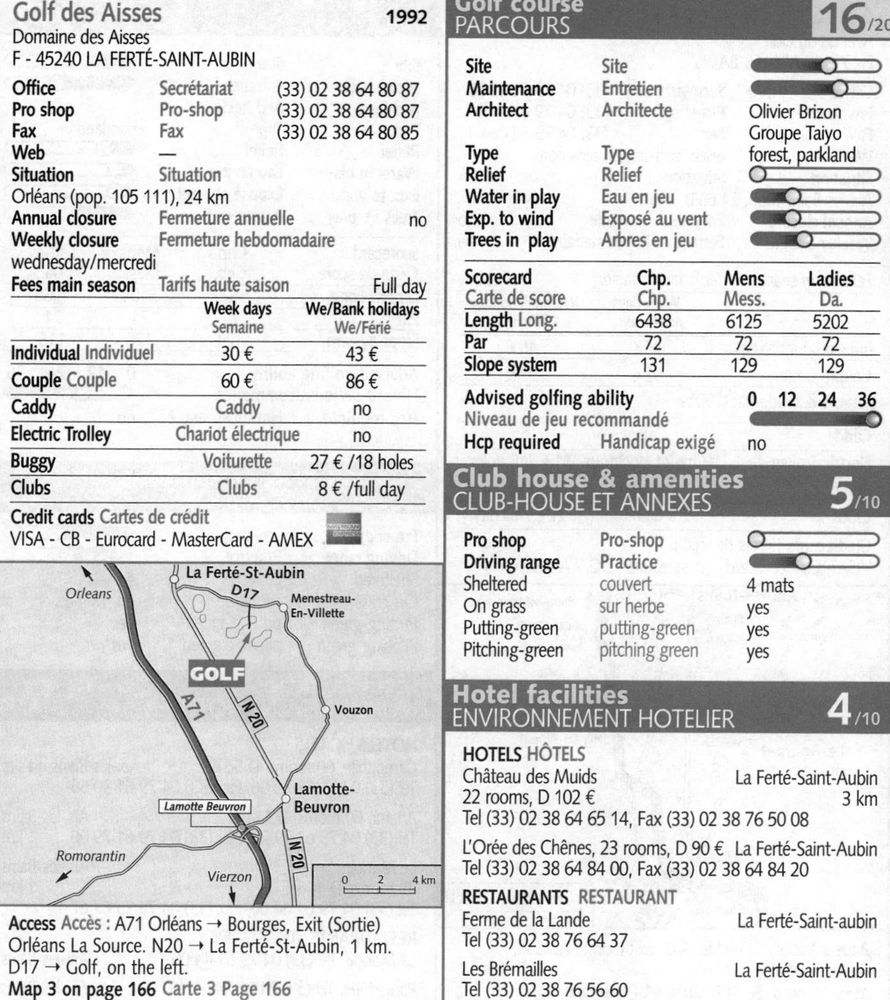

Golf des Aisses — 1992

Domaine des Aisses
F - 45240 LA FERTÉ-SAINT-AUBIN

Office	Secrétariat	(33) 02 38 64 80 87
Pro shop	Pro-shop	(33) 02 38 64 80 87
Fax	Fax	(33) 02 38 64 80 85
Web	—	
Situation	Situation	

Orléans (pop. 105 111), 24 km

Annual closure	Fermeture annuelle	no
Weekly closure	Fermeture hebdomadaire	

wednesday/mercredi

Fees main season Tarifs haute saison — Full day

	Week days Semaine	We/Bank holidays We/Férié
Individual Individuel	30 €	43 €
Couple Couple	60 €	86 €

Caddy	Caddy	no
Electric Trolley	Chariot électrique	no
Buggy	Voiturette	27 € /18 holes
Clubs	Clubs	8 € /full day

Credit cards Cartes de crédit
VISA - CB - Eurocard - MasterCard - AMEX

Access Accès : A71 Orléans → Bourges, Exit (Sortie) Orléans La Source. N20 → La Ferté-St-Aubin, 1 km. D17 → Golf, on the left.
Map 3 on page 166 Carte 3 Page 166

Golf course PARCOURS — 16/20

Site	Site	
Maintenance	Entretien	
Architect	Architecte	Olivier Brizon, Groupe Taiyo
Type	Type	forest, parkland
Relief	Relief	
Water in play	Eau en jeu	
Exp. to wind	Exposé au vent	
Trees in play	Arbres en jeu	

Scorecard Carte de score	**Chp.** Chp.	**Mens** Mess.	**Ladies** Da.
Length Long.	6438	6125	5202
Par	72	72	72
Slope system	131	129	129

Advised golfing ability Niveau de jeu recommandé — 0 12 24 36

Hcp required Handicap exigé — no

Club house & amenities CLUB-HOUSE ET ANNEXES — 5/10

Pro shop	Pro-shop	
Driving range	Practice	
Sheltered	couvert	4 mats
On grass	sur herbe	yes
Putting-green	putting-green	yes
Pitching-green	pitching green	yes

Hotel facilities ENVIRONNEMENT HOTELIER — 4/10

HOTELS HÔTELS

Château des Muids — La Ferté-Saint-Aubin 3 km
22 rooms, D 102 €
Tel (33) 02 38 64 65 14, Fax (33) 02 38 76 50 08

L'Orée des Chênes, 23 rooms, D 90 € — La Ferté-Saint-Aubin
Tel (33) 02 38 64 84 00, Fax (33) 02 38 64 84 20

RESTAURANTS RESTAURANT

Ferme de la Lande — La Ferté-Saint-aubin
Tel (33) 02 38 76 64 37

Les Brémailles — La Ferté-Saint-Aubin
Tel (33) 02 38 76 56 60

AIX-LES-BAINS

13 | 5 | 7

Ce parcours a été créé en 1936 pour répondre aux demandes de la clientèle étrangère de cette jolie ville d'eaux. Le terrain ne manque pas de charme, mais le rythme des trous est saccadé, donnant une sensation d'assemblage désordonné : du 6 au 12, on trouve cinq par 3 ! Avec des par 4 en général très courts et trois des cinq par 5 prenables en deux, un bon score est à la portée de tous les joueurs, par rapport à leur niveau bien sûr. S'ils évitent quelques hors-limites dangereux, les joueurs du meilleur niveau seront vite frustrés par le manque de difficultés et de longueur de ce parcours, mais ils prendront du plaisir à jouer en famille ou avec des amis de plus faible niveau. Bien boisé, mais assez humide, surtout au retour, Aix-les-Bains est l'occasion d'une agréable promenade. L'amélioration est en cours, avec deux greens refaits, quelques bunkers, et une zone d'entraînement bienvenue dans un club qui a toujours une bonne activité sportive.

This course was opened in 1936 to cater to the numerous foreign visitors heading to this pretty spa town. It is a charming site, sure enough, but the general layout lacks any sort of pattern, rather as if the holes were just thrown together. For example, there are five par 3s between the 6th and 12th holes. With the par 4s generally pretty short and three of the five par 5s reachable in two, a good score is within the capability of most players. If they avoid the few dangerous out-of-bounds, the better players will quickly feel a little frustrated at the lack of difficulty and yardage, but should have fun playing with the family or with friends of lesser ability. There are a lot of trees and the course is damp, especially on the back nine, but Aix-les-Bains is the opportunity for a pleasant round of golf. Improvements are ongoing, with two greens already restyled, a few bunkers and a driving range that is most welcome in a very active club.

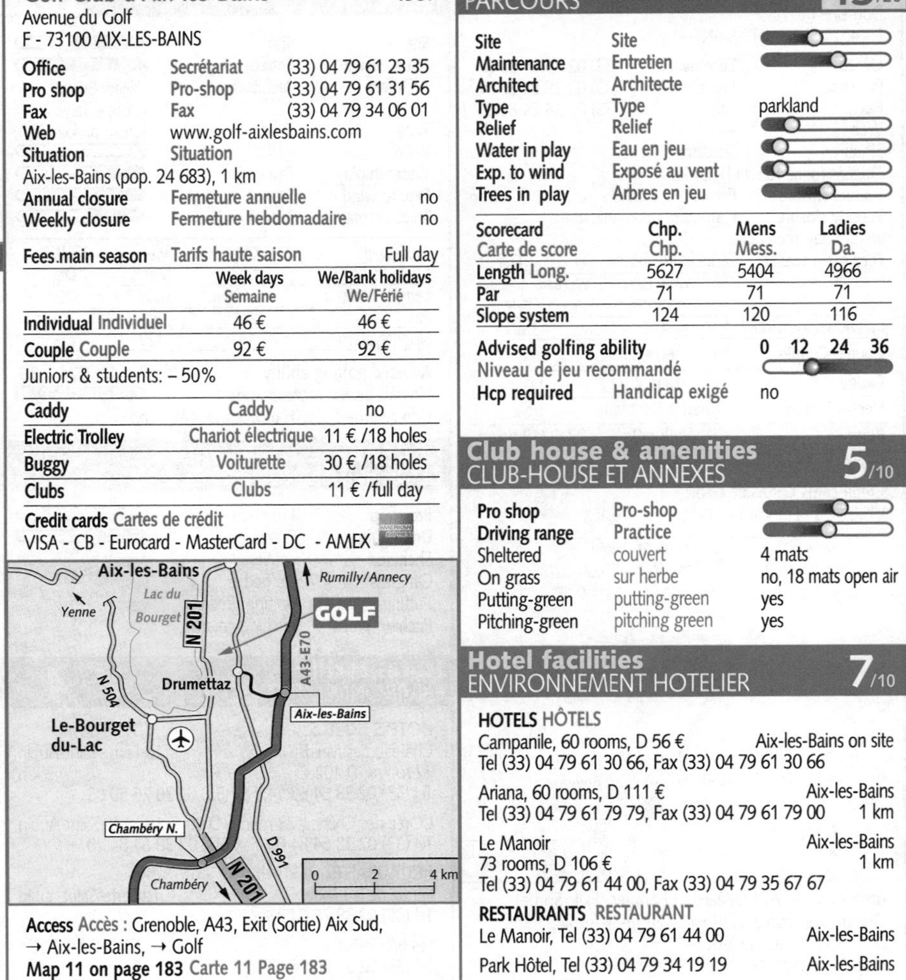

Golf Club d'Aix-les-Bains — 1937

Avenue du Golf
F - 73100 AIX-LES-BAINS

Office	Secrétariat	(33) 04 79 61 23 35
Pro shop	Pro-shop	(33) 04 79 61 31 56
Fax	Fax	(33) 04 79 34 06 01
Web	www.golf-aixlesbains.com	
Situation	Situation	

Aix-les-Bains (pop. 24 683), 1 km

Annual closure	Fermeture annuelle	no
Weekly closure	Fermeture hebdomadaire	no

Fees main season Tarifs haute saison	Week days Semaine	We/Bank holidays We/Férié (Full day)
Individual Individuel	46 €	46 €
Couple Couple	92 €	92 €

Juniors & students: – 50%

Caddy	Caddy	no
Electric Trolley	Chariot électrique	11 € /18 holes
Buggy	Voiturette	30 € /18 holes
Clubs	Clubs	11 € /full day

Credit cards Cartes de crédit
VISA - CB - Eurocard - MasterCard - DC - AMEX

Access Accès : Grenoble, A43, Exit (Sortie) Aix Sud, → Aix-les-Bains, → Golf
Map 11 on page 183 Carte 11 Page 183

Golf course PARCOURS — 13/20

Site	Site	
Maintenance	Entretien	
Architect	Architecte	
Type	Type	parkland
Relief	Relief	
Water in play	Eau en jeu	
Exp. to wind	Exposé au vent	
Trees in play	Arbres en jeu	

Scorecard Carte de score	Chp. Chp.	Mens Mess.	Ladies Da.
Length Long.	5627	5404	4966
Par	71	71	71
Slope system	124	120	116

Advised golfing ability Niveau de jeu recommandé — 0 12 24 36
Hcp required Handicap exigé — no

Club house & amenities CLUB-HOUSE ET ANNEXES — 5/10

Pro shop	Pro-shop	
Driving range	Practice	
Sheltered	couvert	4 mats
On grass	sur herbe	no, 18 mats open air
Putting-green	putting-green	yes
Pitching-green	pitching green	yes

Hotel facilities ENVIRONNEMENT HOTELIER — 7/10

HOTELS HÔTELS

Campanile, 60 rooms, D 56 € — Aix-les-Bains on site
Tel (33) 04 79 61 30 66, Fax (33) 04 79 61 30 66

Ariana, 60 rooms, D 111 € — Aix-les-Bains 1 km
Tel (33) 04 79 61 79 79, Fax (33) 04 79 61 79 00

Le Manoir — Aix-les-Bains 1 km
73 rooms, D 106 €
Tel (33) 04 79 61 44 00, Fax (33) 04 79 35 67 67

RESTAURANTS RESTAURANT

Le Manoir, Tel (33) 04 79 61 44 00 — Aix-les-Bains
Park Hôtel, Tel (33) 04 79 34 19 19 — Aix-les-Bains

ALBI

15 | 6 | 6

Dans un très joli environnement à proximité du Tarn, ce parcours a été modelé dans un paysage de campagne par Jeremy Pern, architecte de nombreux parcours en France. On y retrouve sa mise en jeu traditionnelle de nombreux bunkers et d'obstacles d'eau, ici en jeu sur une demi-douzaine de trous, mais sans trop pénaliser les joueurs peu expérimentés. Une bonne alternance de trous techniques et de trous plus faciles offre un bon rythme de jeu, sans pression excessive., L'entretien y est toujours honnête, mais un peu irrégulier, et toujours meilleur sur les trous en bordure du Tarn. Quand les roughs sont laissés à l'état naturel, il arrive d'y perdre des balles, mais il faut beaucoup s'écarter, ils ont aussi l'avantage de mieux dessiner l'espace de jeu. Les fairways sont assez larges, le tracé en général très agréable. Un parcours utile dans une région où l'on sait bien vivre.

Architect Jeremy Pern has designed many courses in France, including this one located in beautiful surroundings near the River Tarn. His traditional use of countless bunkers and water hazards is very much to the fore, coming into play on half a dozen holes but without penalising the less experienced players. The more difficult holes alternate agreeably with the easier ones to give a good playing pattern without too much pressure. Maintenance is still decent but a little inconsistent and always better on the holes running alongside the Tarn river. When the rough is left untended, you can lose a ball or two, but if you do you are miles off track. The fairways are on the wide side in what is a very pleasant layout, which the rough, tended or untended, helps to shape. A nice course to play in a great region for food and wine.

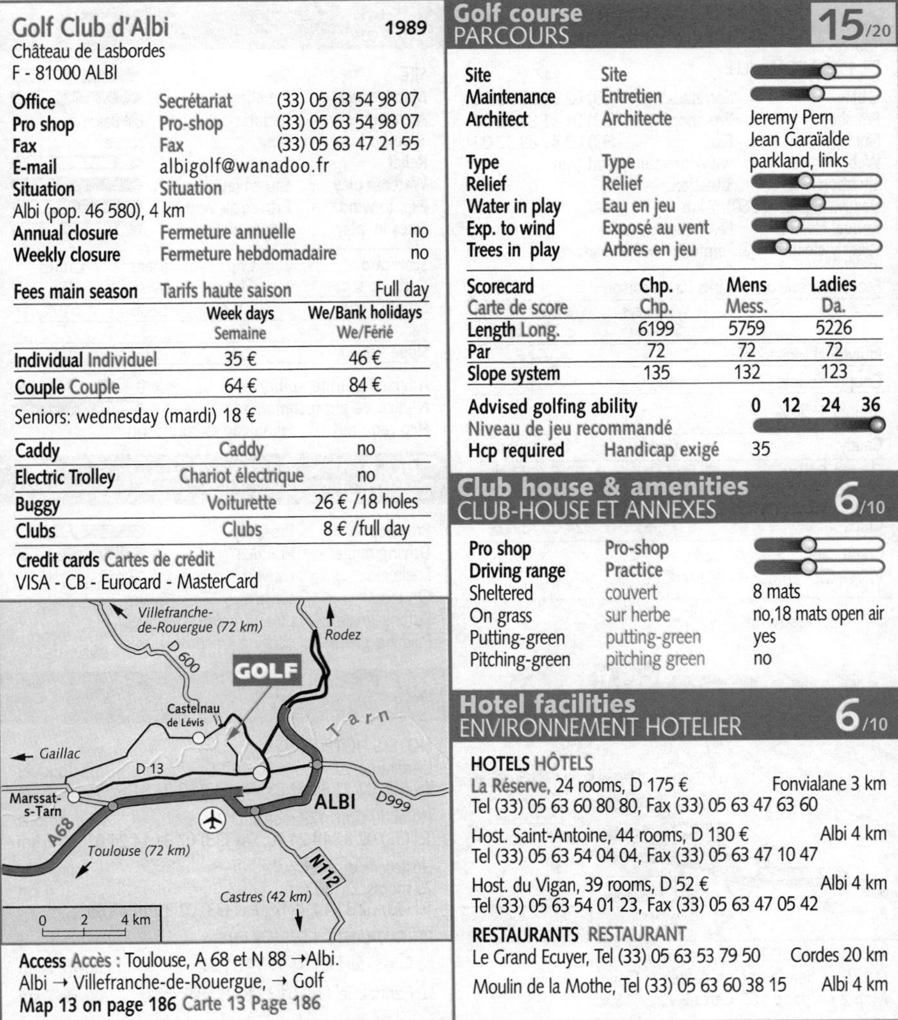

Golf Club d'Albi — 1989

Château de Lasbordes
F - 81000 ALBI

Office	Secrétariat	(33) 05 63 54 98 07
Pro shop	Pro-shop	(33) 05 63 54 98 07
Fax	Fax	(33) 05 63 47 21 55
E-mail	albigolf@wanadoo.fr	
Situation	Situation	
Albi (pop. 46 580), 4 km		
Annual closure	Fermeture annuelle	no
Weekly closure	Fermeture hebdomadaire	no

Fees main season Tarifs haute saison	Full day	
	Week days Semaine	**We/Bank holidays** We/Férié
Individual Individuel	35 €	46 €
Couple Couple	64 €	84 €
Seniors: wednesday (mardi) 18 €		

Caddy	Caddy	no
Electric Trolley	Chariot électrique	no
Buggy	Voiturette	26 € /18 holes
Clubs	Clubs	8 € /full day

Credit cards Cartes de crédit
VISA - CB - Eurocard - MasterCard

Access Accès : Toulouse, A 68 et N 88 →Albi.
Albi → Villefranche-de-Rouergue, → Golf
Map 13 on page 186 Carte 13 Page 186

Golf course — PARCOURS — 15/20

Site	Site	
Maintenance	Entretien	
Architect	Architecte	Jeremy Pern Jean Garaïalde
Type	Type	parkland, links
Relief	Relief	
Water in play	Eau en jeu	
Exp. to wind	Exposé au vent	
Trees in play	Arbres en jeu	

Scorecard Carte de score	**Chp.** Chp.	**Mens** Mess.	**Ladies** Da.
Length Long.	6199	5759	5226
Par	72	72	72
Slope system	135	132	123

Advised golfing ability Niveau de jeu recommandé — 0 12 24 36
Hcp required Handicap exigé — 35

Club house & amenities — CLUB-HOUSE ET ANNEXES — 6/10

Pro shop	Pro-shop	
Driving range	Practice	
Sheltered	couvert	8 mats
On grass	sur herbe	no,18 mats open air
Putting-green	putting-green	yes
Pitching-green	pitching green	no

Hotel facilities — ENVIRONNEMENT HOTELIER — 6/10

HOTELS HÔTELS

La Réserve, 24 rooms, D 175 € — Fonvialane 3 km
Tel (33) 05 63 60 80 80, Fax (33) 05 63 47 63 60

Host. Saint-Antoine, 44 rooms, D 130 € — Albi 4 km
Tel (33) 05 63 54 04 04, Fax (33) 05 63 47 10 47

Host. du Vigan, 39 rooms, D 52 € — Albi 4 km
Tel (33) 05 63 54 01 23, Fax (33) 05 63 47 05 42

RESTAURANTS RESTAURANT

Le Grand Ecuyer, Tel (33) 05 63 53 79 50 — Cordes 20 km

Moulin de la Mothe, Tel (33) 05 63 60 38 15 — Albi 4 km

AMIRAUTÉ (L')

14	7	8

Dominant un paysage normand de bocage et de marais, le Club house luxueux paraît annoncer un parcours exceptionnel, de même que les installations d'entraînement de bonne qualité, et l'éclairage de sept trous (trois du 18 trous et quatre du parcours d'initiation). Ce n'est pas vraiment le cas. Avec ses larges boulevards, des obstacles de fairway peu dangereux, des greens sans grande personnalité et très peu défendus, la stratégie de jeu est évidente, et la motivation peut s'estomper si on joue souvent ici. Les obstacles d'eau constituent les seules véritables difficultés, les bunkers étant généralement peu profonds et éloignés des limites des greens. Si les joueurs expérimentés regretteront le manque de "souffle" du parcours, généralement bien entretenu, mais les joueurs de tous niveaux peuvent y évoluer facilement, ce qui est bien la fonction de ce club "de vacances" et de week-end.

Overlooking a Norman landscape of farmsteads and marshland, the luxurious club-house seems to suggest an exceptional course, as do the excellent practice facilities and lighting on seven holes (three on the 18-hole course and four on the beginner's course). But this is not really so. With wide open fairways, a few benign fairway hazards, and greens with little character and even fewer bunkers to guard them, the course has no hidden dangers and can border on the monotonous if played often. The only real difficulties are the water hazards, as the bunkers are shallow and generally well away from the greens. While the better player may regret the course's lack of gusto (despite excellent maintenance), players of all levels will find this an easy way to improve their game, which is exactly what this "holiday" and week-end course sets out to do.

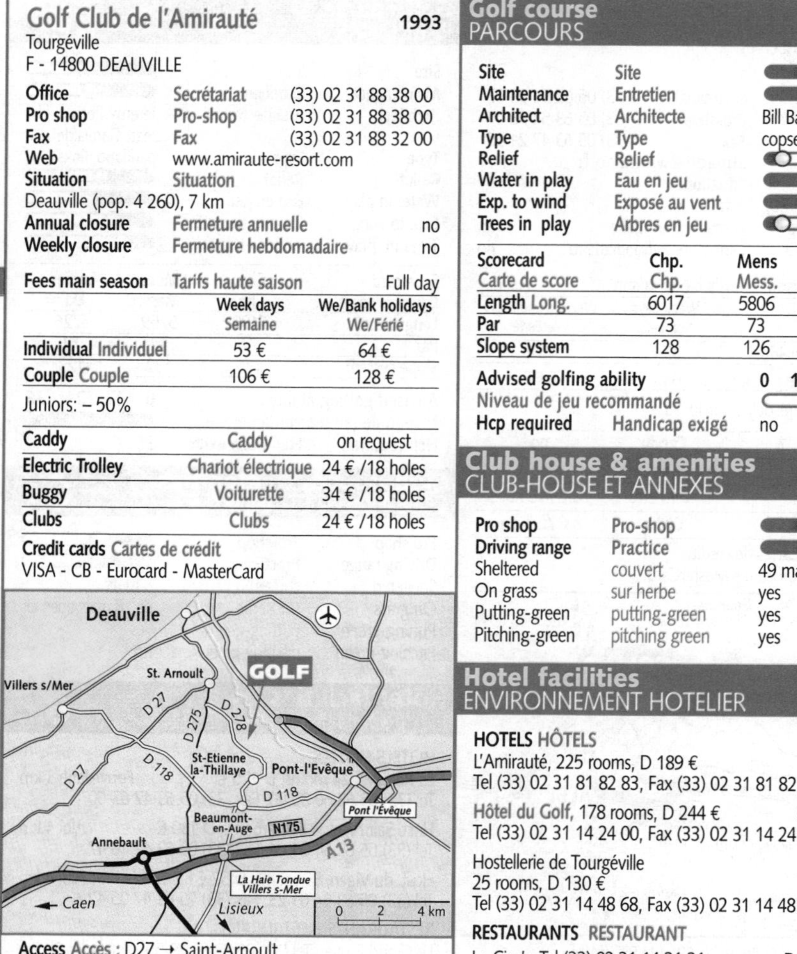

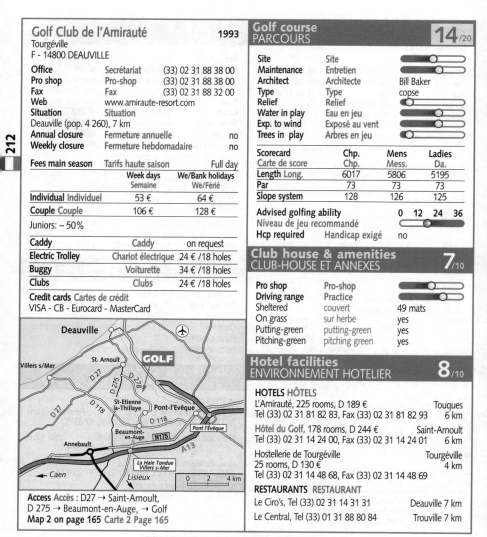

Golf Club de l'Amirauté — 1993

Tourgéville
F - 14800 DEAUVILLE

Office	Secrétariat	(33) 02 31 88 38 00
Pro shop	Pro-shop	(33) 02 31 88 38 00
Fax	Fax	(33) 02 31 88 32 00
Web	www.amiraute-resort.com	
Situation	Situation	

Deauville (pop. 4 260), 7 km

Annual closure	Fermeture annuelle	no
Weekly closure	Fermeture hebdomadaire	no

Fees main season Tarifs haute saison	Week days Semaine	We/Bank holidays We/Férié
		Full day
Individual Individuel	53 €	64 €
Couple Couple	106 €	128 €

Juniors: – 50%

Caddy	Caddy	on request
Electric Trolley	Chariot électrique	24 € /18 holes
Buggy	Voiturette	34 € /18 holes
Clubs	Clubs	24 € /18 holes

Credit cards Cartes de crédit
VISA - CB - Eurocard - MasterCard

Access Accès : D27 → Saint-Arnoult, D 275 → Beaumont-en-Auge, → Golf
Map 2 on page 165 Carte 2 Page 165

Golf course PARCOURS — 14/20

Site	Site	
Maintenance	Entretien	
Architect	Architecte	Bill Baker
Type	Type	copse
Relief	Relief	
Water in play	Eau en jeu	
Exp. to wind	Exposé au vent	
Trees in play	Arbres en jeu	

Scorecard Carte de score	Chp. Chp.	Mens Mess.	Ladies Da.
Length Long.	6017	5806	5195
Par	73	73	73
Slope system	128	126	125

Advised golfing ability Niveau de jeu recommandé — 0 12 24 36
Hcp required Handicap exigé — no

Club house & amenities CLUB-HOUSE ET ANNEXES — 7/10

Pro shop	Pro-shop	
Driving range	Practice	
Sheltered	couvert	49 mats
On grass	sur herbe	yes
Putting-green	putting-green	yes
Pitching-green	pitching green	yes

Hotel facilities ENVIRONNEMENT HOTELIER — 8/10

HOTELS HÔTELS

L'Amirauté, 225 rooms, D 189 € — Touques
Tel (33) 02 31 81 82 83, Fax (33) 02 31 81 82 93 — 6 km

Hôtel du Golf, 178 rooms, D 244 € — Saint-Arnoult
Tel (33) 02 31 14 24 00, Fax (33) 02 31 14 24 01 — 6 km

Hostellerie de Tourgéville — Tourgéville
25 rooms, D 130 € — 4 km
Tel (33) 02 31 14 48 68, Fax (33) 02 31 14 48 69

RESTAURANTS RESTAURANT

Le Ciro's, Tel (33) 02 31 14 31 31 — Deauville 7 km

Le Central, Tel (33) 01 31 88 80 84 — Trouville 7 km

AMNÉVILLE

13 | 6 | 5

Situé au coeur du centre touristique thermal d'Amnéville, ce parcours est accidenté et physique, mais bénéficie d'un environnement boisé très tranquille (chênes, hêtres, bouleaux) qui constitue l'essentiel des difficultés. Dans son dessin, l'architecte Jean-Manuel Rossi a conservé et suivi le caractère naturel du terrain. En revanche, il a beaucoup travaillé les greens, généralement de bonne taille. Les obstacles sont bien visibles, mais certains trous comme le 2, le 5, le 11 et le 17 sont délicats à négocier, et obligent à savoir jouer tous les coups. Amusant à jouer en famille, notamment en match-play, Amnéville est difficile à scorer pour tous les niveaux de jeu, mais plus encore pour les néophytes. En revanche, les situations de jeu sont assez variées pour que l'on revienne volontiers jouer ici. Dans une région pauvre en parcours de qualité, celui-ci s'impose comme le plus intéressant. A noter que l'aller et le retour ont été inversés, et que des travaux sont en projet. A suivre.

Located at the heart of the spa and tourist town of Amnéville, this is a hilly and physically testing course, laid out in a peaceful, woodland setting where the oak, beech and birch trees are the main hazards. In this lay-out, architect Jean-Manuel Rossi has preserved and espoused the natural features of the terrain. By contrast, he has done a lot of switchback work on the greens, which are generally big. The hazards are visible, but a number of holes, like the 2nd, 5th, 11th and 17th, are tricky little numbers and require the full range of shots. Fun to play with the family, particularly in match-play, Amnéville is a tough course for anyone to card low scores, especially beginners. Yet there so many different playing situations that can arise here that you always want to come back for more. In a region where golf courses are few and far between, this has to be the best. One final point: the front and back 9s have been reversed and there are plans for improvement work. Watch this space.

Amnéville Cité Thermale — 1993

Boulevard de l'Europe
F - 57360 AMNEVILLE

Office	Secrétariat	(33) 03 87 71 30 13
Pro shop	Pro-shop	(33) 03 87 71 30 13
Fax	Fax	(33) 03 87 70 26 96
E-mail	golf.amneville@wanadoo.fr	
Situation	Situation	

Metz (pop. 119 590), 15 km - Thionville (pop. 39 712), 15 km

Annual closure	Fermeture annuelle	no
Weekly closure	Fermeture hebdomadaire	no

Fees main season Tarifs haute saison	Full day	
	Week days Semaine	**We/Bank holidays** We/Férié
Individual Individuel	26 €	35 €
Couple Couple	52 €	70 €

Week days, GF + lunch, 30 € / We 38 €

Caddy	Caddy	no
Electric Trolley	Chariot électrique	12 € /18 holes
Buggy	Voiturette	18 € /18 holes
Clubs	Clubs	6 € /full day

Credit cards Cartes de crédit
VISA - CB - Eurocard - MasterCard

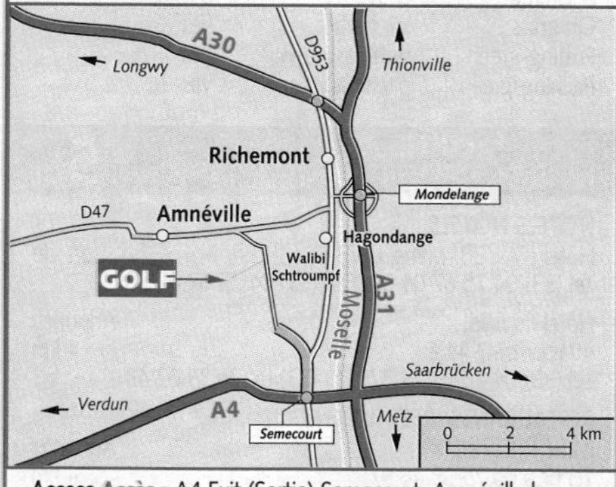

Access Accès : A4 Exit (Sortie) Semecourt, Amnéville les Thermes → "Centre touristique et thermal", → Golf
Map 4 on page 169 Carte 4 Page 169

Golf course PARCOURS — 13/20

Site	Site	
Maintenance	Entretien	
Architect	Architecte	Jean-Manuel Rossi
Type	Type	forest
Relief	Relief	
Water in play	Eau en jeu	
Exp. to wind	Exposé au vent	
Trees in play	Arbres en jeu	

Scorecard Carte de score	**Chp.** Chp.	**Mens** Mess.	**Ladies** Da.
Length Long.	5985	5985	5618
Par	71	71	71
Slope system	131	128	122

Advised golfing ability Niveau de jeu recommandé — 0 12 24 36
Hcp required Handicap exigé — 35

Club house & amenities CLUB-HOUSE ET ANNEXES — 6/10

Pro shop	Pro-shop	
Driving range	Practice	
Sheltered	couvert	10 mats
On grass	sur herbe	yes
Putting-green	putting-green	yes
Pitching-green	pitching green	yes

Hotel facilities ENVIRONNEMENT HOTELIER — 5/10

HOTELS HÔTELS

Diane, 50 rooms, D 56 € — Amnéville
Tel (33) 03 87 70 16 33, Fax (33) 03 87 72 36 72 — 1 km

Orion, 44 rooms, D 46 € — Amnéville
Tel (33) 03 87 70 20 20, Fax (33) 03 87 72 36 21

Saint-Eloi, 47 rooms, D 53 € — Amnéville
Tel (33) 03 87 70 32 62, Fax (33) 03 87 71 71 59

RESTAURANTS RESTAURANT

La Forêt (Hôtel Diane) — Amnéville
Tel (33) 03 87 70 34 34

Orion, Tel (33) 03 87 70 20 20 — Amnéville

ANNONAY-GOURDAN

13 | 6 | 5

A l'exception des trois premiers trous, ce parcours ouvert en 1988 est situé dans le parc d'un petit château, clos de hauts murs, ce qui garantit une atmosphère très calme. Sa longueur reste raisonnable mais son relief peut paraître parfois important, ce qui oblige à une bonne condition physique, ou à la voiturette. L'eau vient en jeu sur une demi-douzaine de trous (étangs, ruisseau, fossés), mais essentiellement sur le 11 et le 15. Les greens ne sont pas très grands, ce qui exige un jeu de fers assez exact, mais permet de ne pas craindre les 3-putts toujours vexants, une fois que l'on y est en sécurité bien sûr. Quelques beaux arbres (notamment des cyprès bleus) et un bon placement des bunkers amènent à recommander de faire attention pour préserver un bon score : les longs frappeurs se feront souvent dominer par les bons joueurs de fers. Mais tous les niveaux de jeu peuvent cohabiter ici. Les tempêtes de Noël 1999 ont abattu quelques arbres, on connaît des joueurs qui ne s'en plaindront pas.

With the exception of the first three holes, this 1988 course is laid out in the grounds of a small castle surrounded by high walls, so you couldn't hope for a more tranquil atmosphere. Length is reasonable but the course's topography can take its toll, so you either get in shape or hire a buggy. Water comes into play on half a dozen holes (lakes, a stream and ditches), but is basically dangerous on the 11th and 15th. The greens are not large, so accurate ironwork is a must. But once home on the green, you have less chance of recording those irksome 3-putts. A few beautiful trees (notably some fine blue cypress) and astutely-placed bunkers keep golfers on their toes if they want to keep their score down. Long-hitters will probably be outplayed here by good iron players, but all in all, this is a course for all types of player. The storms of December 1999 flattened a few trees, but we know quite a few players who will not be complaining.

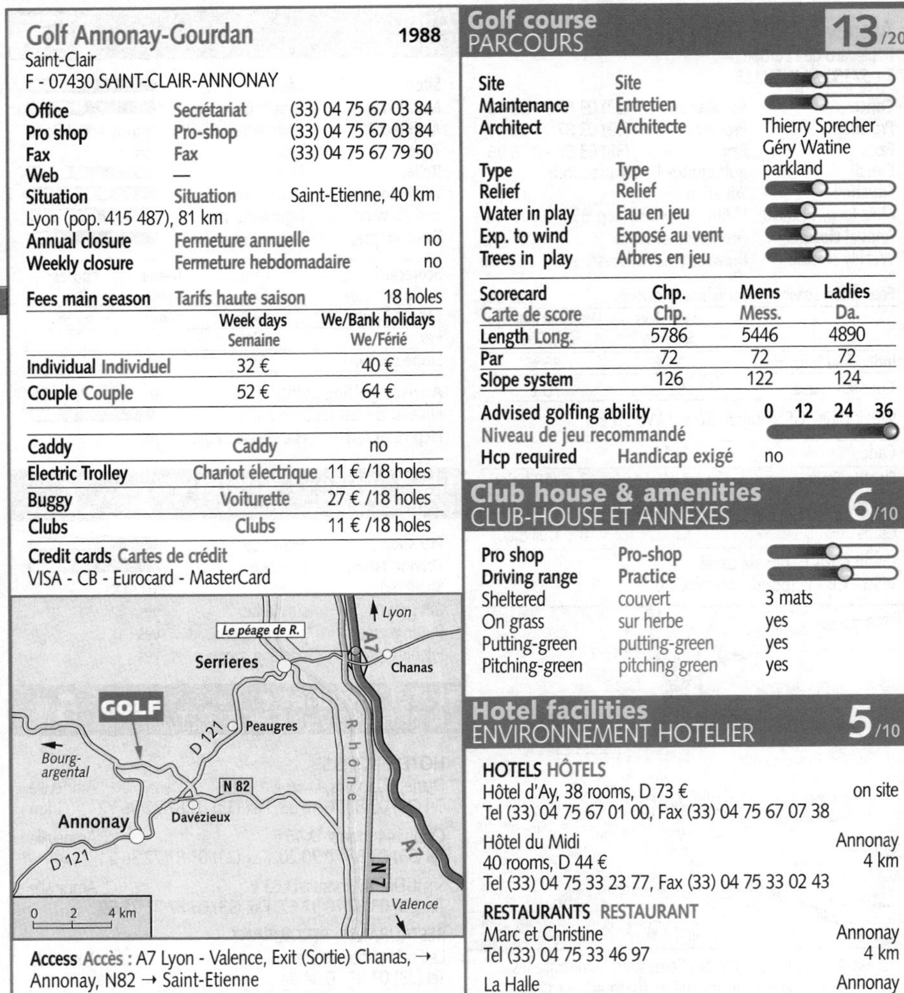

Golf Annonay-Gourdan — 1988

Saint-Clair
F - 07430 SAINT-CLAIR-ANNONAY

Office	Secrétariat	(33) 04 75 67 03 84
Pro shop	Pro-shop	(33) 04 75 67 03 84
Fax	Fax	(33) 04 75 67 79 50
Web	—	
Situation	Situation	Saint-Etienne, 40 km

Lyon (pop. 415 487), 81 km

Annual closure	Fermeture annuelle	no
Weekly closure	Fermeture hebdomadaire	no

Fees main season Tarifs haute saison	Week days Semaine	We/Bank holidays We/Férié
18 holes		
Individual Individuel	32 €	40 €
Couple Couple	52 €	64 €

Caddy	Caddy	no
Electric Trolley	Chariot électrique	11 € /18 holes
Buggy	Voiturette	27 € /18 holes
Clubs	Clubs	11 € /18 holes

Credit cards Cartes de crédit
VISA - CB - Eurocard - MasterCard

Access Accès : A7 Lyon - Valence, Exit (Sortie) Chanas, → Annonay, N82 → Saint-Etienne
Map 11 on page 182 Carte 11 Page 182

Golf course PARCOURS — 13/20

Site	Site	
Maintenance	Entretien	
Architect	Architecte	Thierry Sprecher, Géry Watine
Type	Type	parkland
Relief	Relief	
Water in play	Eau en jeu	
Exp. to wind	Exposé au vent	
Trees in play	Arbres en jeu	

Scorecard Carte de score	Chp. Chp.	Mens Mess.	Ladies Da.
Length Long.	5786	5446	4890
Par	72	72	72
Slope system	126	122	124

Advised golfing ability Niveau de jeu recommandé — 0 12 24 36
Hcp required Handicap exigé — no

Club house & amenities CLUB-HOUSE ET ANNEXES — 6/10

Pro shop	Pro-shop	
Driving range	Practice	
Sheltered	couvert	3 mats
On grass	sur herbe	yes
Putting-green	putting-green	yes
Pitching-green	pitching green	yes

Hotel facilities ENVIRONNEMENT HOTELIER — 5/10

HOTELS HÔTELS

Hôtel d'Ay, 38 rooms, D 73 € — on site
Tel (33) 04 75 67 01 00, Fax (33) 04 75 67 07 38

Hôtel du Midi — Annonay 4 km
40 rooms, D 44 €
Tel (33) 04 75 33 23 77, Fax (33) 04 75 33 02 43

RESTAURANTS RESTAURANT

Marc et Christine — Annonay 4 km
Tel (33) 04 75 33 46 97

La Halle — Annonay 4 km
Tel (33) 04 75 32 04 62

APREMONT

15 | 8 | 6

Nous continuons à penser que le parcours aurait bénéficié d'un investissement aussi important que le luxueux Club house, mais son entretien reste excellent, bien que la situation économique ne soit plus aussi "royale" qu'autrefois. Conçu par John Jacobs, le parcours reste très agréable à parcourir, avec 14 trous en forêt d'Halatte et les autres organisés autour de pièces d'eau. L'ensemble est plat, facile à marcher avec les départs très proches des greens. Certes, le dessin de John Jacobs ne propose pas de grandes émotions, visuelles ou tactiques, et la stratégie de jeu est assez évidente, mais faute d'affrontements épiques avec le parcours, on appréciera le silence des lieux et la majesté du cadre. Apremont n'a sans doute pas droit à l'appellation de chef-d'oeuvre, dans la mesure où les meilleurs golfeurs trouveront ses défis techniques un peu modestes, mais la majorité des joueurs y passeront une bonne journée, et pourront espérer évoluer à hauteur de leur handicap.

We still feel that the course could have benefited from the same investment that was obviously given to the luxurious club-house, but maintenance is still excellent despite the club having fallen on economically harder times. Designed by John Jacobs, this is a very pleasant course to play, with 14 holes in the forest of Halatte and the others laid out around lakes. The whole course is flat, with very little distance between green and next tee. There is nothing truly exciting about this layout, whether visually or from a tactical viewpoint, and game strategy is pretty obvious, but in the absence of epic confrontation with the course, players will enjoy the silence and the majestic setting. Apremont could never really claim the label of golfing masterpiece in that the better player will find the technical challenge within easy reach, but most players spend a good day's golfing here and can hold out hopes of playing to their handicap.

Apremont Golf-Club — 1992

F - 60300 APREMONT

Office	Secrétariat	(33) 03 44 25 61 11
Pro shop	Pro-shop	(33) 03 44 25 61 11
Fax	Fax	(33) 03 44 25 11 72
E-mail	golfapremont@free.fr	
Situation	Situation	

Chantilly (pop. 11 340), 6 km - Senlis (pop. 14 439), 7 km

Annual closure	Fermeture annuelle	no
Weekly closure	Fermeture hebdomadaire	

monday/1/10 → 31/3

Fees main season Tarifs haute saison	Week days Semaine	We/Bank holidays We/Férié
	full day	
Individual Individuel	38 €	73 €
Couple Couple	73 €	110 €

Special fees after 2 pm

Caddy	Caddy	no
Electric Trolley	Chariot électrique	11 € /full day
Buggy	Voiturette	27 € /18 holes
Clubs	Clubs	18 € /full day

Credit cards Cartes de crédit
VISA - CB - Eurocard - MasterCard - JCB - AMEX

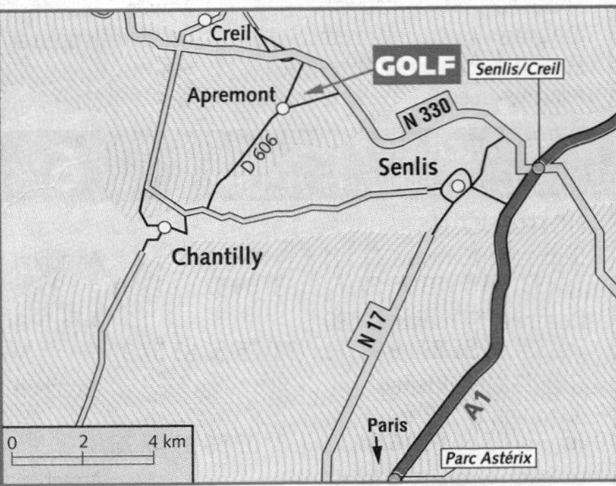

Access Accès : A1 Paris → Lille, Exit (Sortie) 8 Senlis/Creil. N 330 → Creil. 7 km. after Senlis, → Apremont on the left
Map 1 on page 162 Carte 1 Page 162

Golf course PARCOURS — 15/20

Site	Site	
Maintenance	Entretien	
Architect	Architecte	John Jacobs
Type	Type	forest, parkland
Relief	Relief	
Water in play	Eau en jeu	
Exp. to wind	Exposé au vent	
Trees in play	Arbres en jeu	

Scorecard Carte de score	Chp. Chp.	Mens Mess.	Ladies Da.
Length Long.	6436	5843	5395
Par	72	72	72
Slope system	124	134	117

Advised golfing ability Niveau de jeu recommandé: 0 12 24 36
Hcp required Handicap exigé: no

Club house & amenities CLUB-HOUSE ET ANNEXES — 8/10

Pro shop	Pro-shop	
Driving range	Practice	
Sheltered	couvert	3 mats
On grass	sur herbe	no, 7 mats open air
Putting-green	putting-green	yes
Pitching-green	pitching green	yes

Hotel facilities ENVIRONNEMENT HOTELIER — 6/10

HOTELS HÔTELS

Golf Hôtel, 202 rooms, D 305 € — Domaine de Chantilly 4 km
Tel (33) 03 44 58 47 77, Fax (33) 03 44 58 50 11

Château Hôtel Mont-Royal — La Chapelle-en-Serval 15 km
100 rooms, D 244 €
Tel (33) 03 44 54 50 50, Fax (33) 03 44 54 50 20

Château de la Tour, 41 rooms, D 136 € — Gouvieux 8 km
Tel (33) 03 44 62 38 38, Fax (33) 03 44 57 31 97

RESTAURANTS RESTAURANT

Restaurant du golf, Tel (33) 03 44 25 61 11 — Apremont
Verbois, Tel (33) 03 44 24 06 22 — Saint-Maximin 4 km

ARCACHON

13 | 6 | 6

C'est depuis longtemps le golf des Bordelais en week-end, et des vacanciers du Pyla tout proche. Il n'était pas question pour eux d'un parcours trop difficile ni audacieux. En pays de vieille tradition britannique, les architectes Blandford et Pierre Hirigoyen en ont dessiné un sans grandes aspérités, épousant sans trop le bousculer un terrain accidenté à l'aller, et plus plat au retour. Avec le relief, l'approche de certains greens surélevés n'est pas toujours simple ; les fairways souvent étroits, bien défendus par les arbres, imposent de bien placer les coups de départ, quitte à laisser le driver dans le sac. Mais le parcours est assez court, et la précision plus souvent récompensée que la longueur. Avec les travaux de drainage sur la partie basse du parcours, il est jouable toute l'année. Les non-golfeurs de la famille trouveront de multiples activités dans la station balnéaire d'Arcachon, en haute saison. Le Club-House est placé au sommet de cet ensemble, l'ambiance y est toujours aussi familiale et amicale.

This has long been the traditional week-end course for the good folk of Bordeaux and holiday-makers at Pylat, so don't expect an overly difficult or bold layout here. In a region of British tradition, architects Blandford and Pierre Hirigoyen laid out a subdued course which embraces but never disrupts the hilly terrain on the front nine and the flatter holes around the back. The broken relief means that the second shot to a number of elevated greens is not always easy. And a few tight fairways, well-defended by trees, require a well-placed tee-shot, even if that means leaving the driver in the bag. But the course is short, and precision is more often better rewarded than length off the tee. With the lower section of the course now fitted with a drainage system, Arcachon is playable all year. Non-golfers in the family will find lots to do in the seaside resort of Arcachon in summer, while the friendly family atmosphere in club-house overlooking the course is as warm as ever.

Golf d'Arcachon — 1952

35, boulevard d'Arcachon
F - 33260 LA TESTE

Office	Secrétariat	(33) 05 56 54 44 00
Pro shop	Pro-shop	(33) 05 57 15 26 57
Fax	Fax	(33) 05 56 66 86 32
E-mail	golfarcach@aol.com	
Situation	Situation	
Arcachon (pop. 11 770), 3 km		
Annual closure	Fermeture annuelle	no
Weekly closure	Fermeture hebdomadaire	no

Fees main season Tarifs haute saison	18 holes	
	Week days Semaine	**We/Bank holidays** We/Férié
Individual Individuel	41 €	41 €
Couple Couple	70 €	70 €

Caddy	Caddy	no
Electric Trolley	Chariot électrique	no
Buggy	Voiturette	23 € /18 holes
Clubs	Clubs	12 € /full day

Credit cards Cartes de crédit
VISA - CB- Eurocard - MasterCard - AMEX

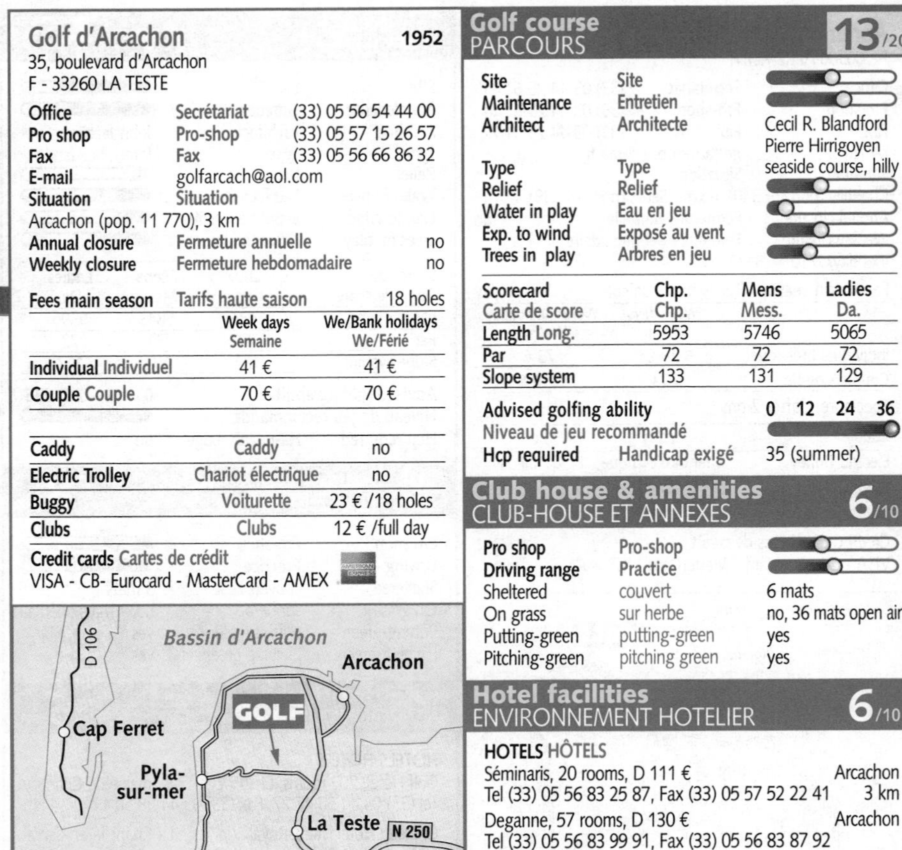

Access Accès : N250 → La Teste → Pyla-sur-Mer
Map 9 on page 179 Carte 9 Page 179

Golf course — PARCOURS — 13/20

Site	Site	
Maintenance	Entretien	
Architect	Architecte	Cecil R. Blandford Pierre Hirrigoyen
Type	Type	seaside course, hilly
Relief	Relief	
Water in play	Eau en jeu	
Exp. to wind	Exposé au vent	
Trees in play	Arbres en jeu	

Scorecard Carte de score	**Chp.** Chp.	**Mens** Mess.	**Ladies** Da.
Length Long.	5953	5746	5065
Par	72	72	72
Slope system	133	131	129

Advised golfing ability Niveau de jeu recommandé — 0 12 24 36
Hcp required Handicap exigé — 35 (summer)

Club house & amenities — CLUB-HOUSE ET ANNEXES — 6/10

Pro shop	Pro-shop	
Driving range	Practice	
Sheltered	couvert	6 mats
On grass	sur herbe	no, 36 mats open air
Putting-green	putting-green	yes
Pitching-green	pitching green	yes

Hotel facilities — ENVIRONNEMENT HOTELIER — 6/10

HOTELS HÔTELS

Séminaris, 20 rooms, D 111 € — Arcachon
Tel (33) 05 56 83 25 87, Fax (33) 05 57 52 22 41 — 3 km

Deganne, 57 rooms, D 130 € — Arcachon
Tel (33) 05 56 83 99 91, Fax (33) 05 56 83 87 92

Grand Hôtel Richelieu — Arcachon
43 rooms, D 119 €
Tel (33) 05 56 83 16 50, Fax (33) 05 56 83 47 78

Le Parc, 30 rooms, D 87 € — Arcachon
Tel (33) 05 56 83 10 58, Fax (33) 05 56 54 05 30

RESTAURANTS RESTAURANT

L'Ombrière, Tel (33) 05 56 83 86 20 — Arcachon

ARCANGUES

14 | 7 | 8

Le site offre de jolies vues sur la campagne basque et les Pyrénées, avec un bon rythme entre les trous dégagés et les trous boisés. Il a fallu beaucoup modifier le terrain accidenté pour le rendre jouable, mais de nombreux dévers et pentes étaient inévitables, et peuvent entraîner des coups délicats : il faut savoir jouer des balles à effets. Pour cela, on ne le conseillera pas aux débutants, ni aux seniors, à moins de jouer en voiturette. Comme souvent avec l'architecte Ronald Fream, les bunkers et les greens sont très travaillés et bien en jeu, mais c'est logique pour un parcours assez court des départs normaux : vive la précision... Et aussi un peu la chance, car la franchise n'est pas le point fort de ce dessin. Ce golf très technique doit être reconnu avant d'espérer un bon score, il offre des caractéristiques bien différentes des autres parcours de la région. Certains travaux d'amélioration permettent de faciliter le jeu et l'entretien du lieu.

The setting provides beautiful views over the Basque countryside and the Pyrenees, and there is a nice balance between woodland holes and holes through open country. A lot of earth was moved to make this once rugged landscape into a playable course, but inevitably slopes and hills still remain and can lead to some tricky shots. Being able to flight the ball is more of an advantage than usual. For this reason we would not recommend Arcangues to beginners or to seniors, unless on wheels. As is often the case with Ronald Fream, the bunkers and greens have been given a lot of careful thought, which is only logical for a course as short as this. The watchword here is precision play... with perhaps a bit of luck thrown in, as the layout is not as forthright as it might be. Arcangues is a very technical course that needs a little reconnaissance work before hoping to card a good score. And its features are very different from the other courses in the region. A certain amount of improvement work is ongoing to ease the course and site maintenance.

Golf d'Arcangues — 1991

Club House
F - 64200 ARCANGUES

Office	Secrétariat	(33) 05 59 43 10 56
Pro shop	Pro-shop	(33) 05 59 43 10 56
Fax	Fax	(33) 05 59 43 12 60
Web	www.golfpass.fr	
Situation	Situation	

Biarritz (pop. 28 740), 6 km - Bayonne (pop. 40 050), 10 km

Annual closure Fermeture annuelle — no

Weekly closure Fermeture hebdomadaire
monday/30/10 → 1/3

Fees main season Tarifs haute saison	18 holes	
	Week days Semaine	We/Bank holidays We/Férié
Individual Individuel	49 €	49 €
Couple Couple	91 €	91 €
Juniors: 27 €		

Caddy	Caddy	no
Electric Trolley	Chariot électrique	no
Buggy	Voiturette	23 € /18 holes
Clubs	Clubs	9 € /18 holes

Credit cards Cartes de crédit
VISA - CB - Eurocard - MasterCard - AMEX

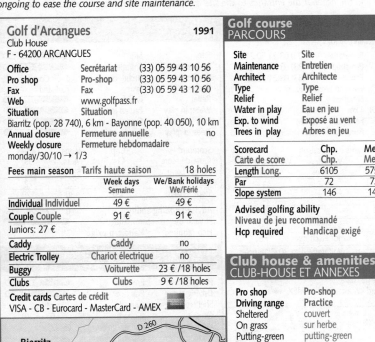

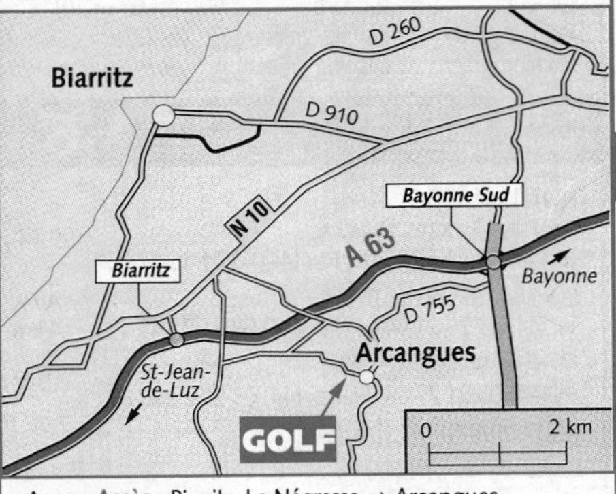

Access Accès : Biarritz, La Négresse → Arcangues
Map 12 on page 184 Carte 12 Page 184

Golf course — PARCOURS — 14/20

Site	Site	
Maintenance	Entretien	
Architect	Architecte	Ronald Fream
Type	Type	hilly
Relief	Relief	
Water in play	Eau en jeu	
Exp. to wind	Exposé au vent	
Trees in play	Arbres en jeu	

Scorecard Carte de score	Chp. Chp.	Mens Mess.	Ladies Da.
Length Long.	6105	5758	4655
Par	72	72	72
Slope system	146	142	130

Advised golfing ability — 0 12 24 36
Niveau de jeu recommandé

Hcp required Handicap exigé — 35

Club house & amenities — CLUB-HOUSE ET ANNEXES — 7/10

Pro shop	Pro-shop	
Driving range	Practice	
Sheltered	couvert	6 mats
On grass	sur herbe	yes
Putting-green	putting-green	yes
Pitching-green	pitching green	yes

Hotel facilities — ENVIRONNEMENT HOTELIER — 8/10

HOTELS HÔTELS

Le Palais, 156 rooms, D 335 € — Biarritz
Tel (33) 05 59 41 64 00, Fax (33) 05 59 41 67 99 — 6 km

Château de Brindos — Anglet
12 rooms, D 198 € — 8 km
Tel (33) 05 59 23 17 68, Fax (33) 05 59 23 48 47

Hôtel Laminak, 12 rooms, D 85 € — Arbonne
Tel (33) 05 59 41 95 40, Fax (33) 05 59 41 87 65 — 4 km

RESTAURANTS RESTAURANT

Auberge d'Achtal, Tel (33) 05 59 43 05 56 — Arcangues

Les Platanes, Tel (33) 05 59 23 13 68 — Biarritz 6 km

ARRAS

14 | 6 | 6

En dehors des routes touristiques, mais profitant d'une grosse promotion grâce à son Président Gervais Martel, patron de l'équipe de football de Lens, ce parcours mérite le détour, surtout quand il est préparé pour les compétitions. Amusant et très varié quand il est joué des départs avancés, il devient beaucoup plus technique des départs arrière (hommes ou dames). Il faut alors pas mal d'intelligence stratégique et de lucidité, un bon sens du placement de la balle. Assez vallonné, il cache parfois ses dangers, avec quelques trous aveugles, péché mignon de l'architecte. Il faut donc bien le repérer avant d'espérer faire un score : il y a tout de même 12 trous avec de l'eau. Le site est agréable, avec une esthétique de parc à l'anglaise, quelques dénivellées mais pas insurmontables. Le seul gros défaut reste que le parcours absorbe assez lentement les pluies. Un 9 trous supplémentaire et l'hôtel construit à l'entrée du site complètent bien ce parcours sympathique.

Off the tourist track but heavily promoted by chairman Gervais Martel, boss of First Division Lens FC, this course is worth going out of your way for, especially when set up for tournaments. A bag of fun and variety when played from the front tees, the layout is much more technical when played from the tips (men's and ladies), calling for strategic intelligence, clear-thinking and good sense for placing the ball. This rather hilly course sometimes hides its hazards with a few blind holes that the architect couldn't resist. So you will need to check these out before hoping to card any sort of score, talking of which we might also add that there are 12 holes with water. The site is pleasant, a sort of English-style park with a few climbs and slopes, but nothing too insurmountable. The only real flaw here is that the terrain takes a while to soak up the rain. An additional 9-hole course and the hotel at the entrance to the site complete the picture for this pleasant course.

Golf Club d'Arras — 1990

F - 62223 ANZIN- SAINT-AUBIN

Office	Secrétariat	(33) 03 21 50 24 24
Pro shop	Pro-shop	(33) 03 21 50 24 24
Fax	Fax	(33) 03 21 50 29 71
Web	www.arras-golfclub.com	
Situation	Situation	
Arras (pop. 39 000), 4 km		
Annual closure	Fermeture annuelle	no
Weekly closure	Fermeture hebdomadaire	no

Fees main season Tarifs haute saison	**Week days** Semaine	**We/Bank holidays** We/Férié
		Full day
Individual Individuel	29 €	43 €
Couple Couple	58 €	86 €

Caddy	Caddy	no
Electric Trolley	Chariot électrique	no
Buggy	Voiturette	30 €/18 holes
Clubs	Clubs	9 €/full day

Credit cards Cartes de crédit
VISA - CB - Eurocard - MasterCard - AMEX

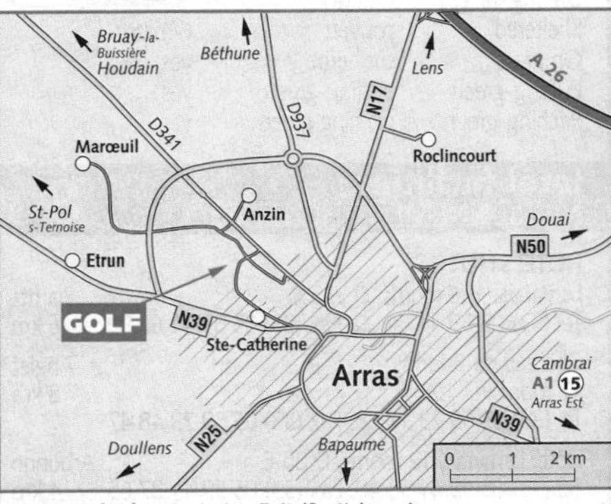

Access Accès : Paris A1. Exit (Sortie) → Arras. N39 → Le Touquet, D64 → Golf.

Map 1 on page 162 Carte 1 Page 162

Golf course PARCOURS — 14/20

Site	Site	
Maintenance	Entretien	
Architect	Architecte	J.-Cl. Cornillot
Type	Type	parkland
Relief	Relief	
Water in play	Eau en jeu	
Exp. to wind	Exposé au vent	
Trees in play	Arbres en jeu	

Scorecard Carte de score	**Chp.** Chp.	**Mens** Mess.	**Ladies** Da.
Length Long.	5846	5846	4830
Par	72	72	72
Slope system	137	130	129

Advised golfing ability Niveau de jeu recommandé: 0 12 24 36

Hcp required Handicap exigé: 35

Club house & amenities CLUB-HOUSE ET ANNEXES — 6/10

Pro shop	Pro-shop	
Driving range	Practice	
Sheltered	couvert	20 mats
On grass	sur herbe	yes (05 → 10)
Putting-green	putting-green	yes (2)
Pitching-green	pitching green	yes

Hotel facilities ENVIRONNEMENT HOTELIER — 6/10

HOTELS HÔTELS

Le Golf, 43 rooms, D 149 € — on site
Tel (44) 03 21 50 45 04, Fax (44) 03 21 15 07 00

L'Univers, 37 rooms, D 114 € — Arras 4 km
Tel (44) 03 21 71 34 01, Fax (44) 03 21 71 41 42

Mercure, 80 rooms, D 82 € — Arras
Tel (44) 03 21 23 88 88, Fax (44) 03 21 23 88 89

RESTAURANTS RESTAURANT

La Faisanderie, Tel (44) 03 21 48 20 76 — Arras

Le Régent, Tel (44) 03 21 71 51 09 — Arras

La Coupole d'Arras, Tel (44) 03 21 71 88 44 — Arras

AUGERVILLE

13	6	4

Pas très long, et bien accidenté, ce nouveau parcours bénéficie d'un bel environnement forestier, et de la présence d'un château du XVIIème siècle, qui constitue à présent un Club house très agréable. Un nouveau système d'arrosage du parcours a lui aussi nettement rehaussé l'ensemble, autrefois un peu rudimentaire. A côté de très jolis trous, certains autres restent fort contestables, notamment un par 5 et quelques par 3 où des arbres empiètent fortement sur la ligne de jeu. On doit aussi signaler la présence de quelques greens aveugles, ce que les visiteurs n'aiment généralement pas beaucoup, ils obligent non seulement à bien connaître le parcours mais aussi la position des drapeaux. Un dernier regret : la difficulté excessive du 18, qui laisse sur une impression mitigée. La beauté du cadre et les promesses du lieu incitent à conseiller une visite, mais on aimerait quelques travaux pour rendre le parcours plus franc, et son entretien constant pendant toute l'année.

Not very long and rather hilly, this new course lies in a beautiful setting of forest enhanced by a 17th century castle, which now forms a most pleasant club-house. A new course watering system has also worked wonders for the whole site, whose facilities were once pretty basic. Alongside some very pretty holes, others are very questionable, notably one par 5 and a few par 3s, where trees come right into the firing line. There are also a few blind greens, which visitors generally find rather distasteful and which require prior knowledge of the course and the pin-position. Our last little regret is the excessively difficult 18th hole, which leaves the golfer with a mixed impression of the course as a whole. The beauty and promise of the setting and site make this a visit we would recommend, but we would like to see a little more work done to make the course a fairer challenge and ensure consistent maintenance all year.

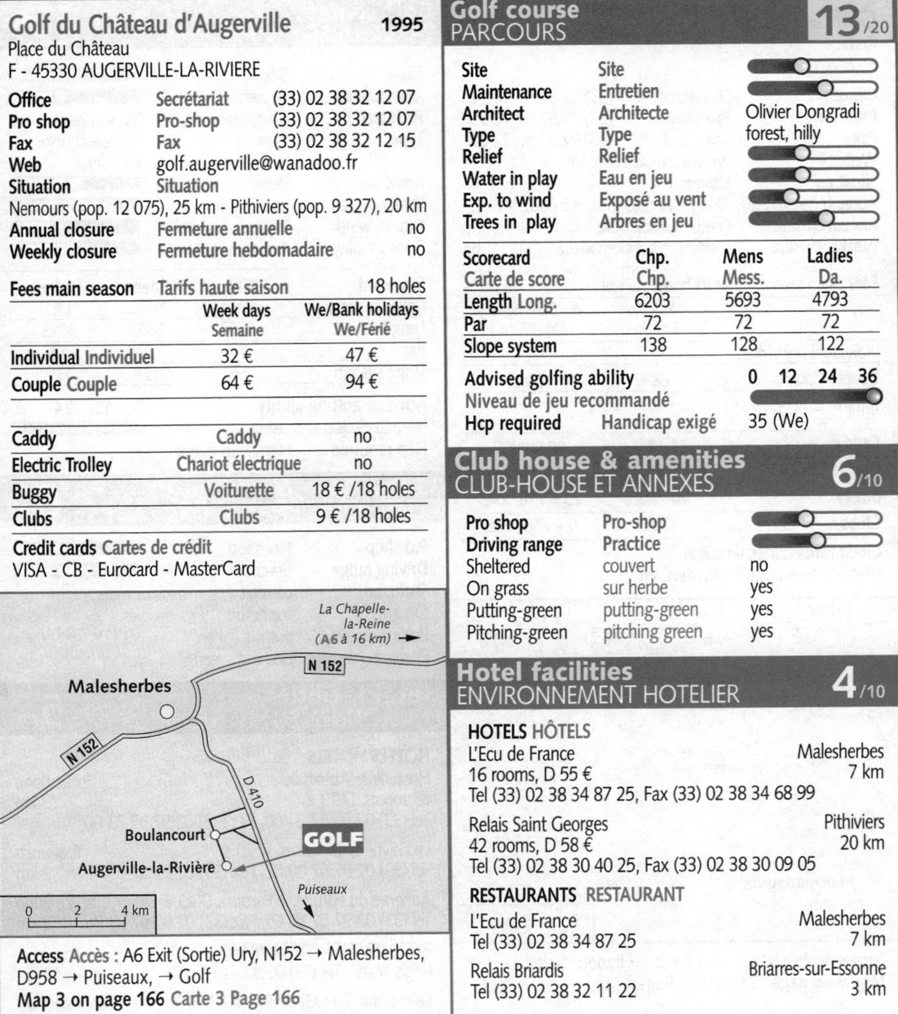

Golf du Château d'Augerville — 1995

Place du Château
F - 45330 AUGERVILLE-LA-RIVIERE

Office	Secrétariat	(33) 02 38 32 12 07
Pro shop	Pro-shop	(33) 02 38 32 12 07
Fax	Fax	(33) 02 38 32 12 15
Web	golf.augerville@wanadoo.fr	
Situation	Situation	

Nemours (pop. 12 075), 25 km - Pithiviers (pop. 9 327), 20 km

Annual closure	Fermeture annuelle	no
Weekly closure	Fermeture hebdomadaire	no

Fees main season Tarifs haute saison	18 holes	
	Week days Semaine	We/Bank holidays We/Férié
Individual Individuel	32 €	47 €
Couple Couple	64 €	94 €

Caddy	Caddy	no
Electric Trolley	Chariot électrique	no
Buggy	Voiturette	18 € /18 holes
Clubs	Clubs	9 € /18 holes

Credit cards Cartes de crédit
VISA - CB - Eurocard - MasterCard

Access Accès : A6 Exit (Sortie) Ury, N152 → Malesherbes, D958 → Puiseaux, → Golf
Map 3 on page 166 Carte 3 Page 166

Golf course PARCOURS — 13/20

Site	Site	
Maintenance	Entretien	
Architect	Architecte	Olivier Dongradi
Type	Type	forest, hilly
Relief	Relief	
Water in play	Eau en jeu	
Exp. to wind	Exposé au vent	
Trees in play	Arbres en jeu	

Scorecard Carte de score	Chp. Chp.	Mens Mess.	Ladies Da.
Length Long.	6203	5693	4793
Par	72	72	72
Slope system	138	128	122

Advised golfing ability Niveau de jeu recommandé — 0 12 24 36
Hcp required Handicap exigé — 35 (We)

Club house & amenities CLUB-HOUSE ET ANNEXES — 6/10

Pro shop	Pro-shop	
Driving range	Practice	
Sheltered	couvert	no
On grass	sur herbe	yes
Putting-green	putting-green	yes
Pitching-green	pitching green	yes

Hotel facilities ENVIRONNEMENT HOTELIER — 4/10

HOTELS HÔTELS

L'Ecu de France — Malesherbes 7 km
16 rooms, D 55 €
Tel (33) 02 38 34 87 25, Fax (33) 02 38 34 68 99

Relais Saint Georges — Pithiviers 20 km
42 rooms, D 58 €
Tel (33) 02 38 30 40 25, Fax (33) 02 38 30 09 05

RESTAURANTS RESTAURANT

L'Ecu de France — Malesherbes 7 km
Tel (33) 02 38 34 87 25

Relais Briardis — Briarres-sur-Essonne 3 km
Tel (33) 02 38 32 11 22

BADEN

15 | 6 | 5

Sans être un véritable links, Baden est un excellent parcours de bord de mer, dominant l'estuaire de la rivière d'Auray. Seuls quelques trous sont vraiment tracés dans les pins, mais on n'a jamais l'impression de monotonie, étant donnée la variété du tracé. Les reliefs du terrain, les arbustes, une végétation assez sauvage, quelques arbres isolés, et le dessin d'Yves Bureau en font un lieu de charme pour les yeux, et pour le jeu. Sans être d'une difficulté extrême, il offre aux meilleurs joueurs un défi constant, parfois rehaussé par le vent, tout en permettant aux joueurs moyens et même aux novices de passer une journée agréable. Un morceau de choix dans une région bien équipée en golfs. Le Club house n'est toujours pas vraiment à la hauteur, mais l'entretien devrait s'améliorer avec les bénéfices d'un arrosage automatique très bienvenu. Certes, il crachine parfois en Bretagne, mais les périodes sèchent rendaient le sol très dur.

While not a real links, Baden is an excellent seaside course overlooking the estuary of the river Auray. Only a few holes are laid out really amongst the pine-trees, but given the variety, the course is never tedious. The sloping terrain, bushes, wild-growing vegetation, a few isolated trees and the layout of Yves Bureau make this a charming course both to look at and play. Although not over-difficult, the challenge to the better player never eases and is sometimes made tougher in windy weather. At the same time, high-handicappers and even beginners can enjoy a good day out. A choice venue in a region well-endowed with golf courses. The club-house is still not quite up to scratch, but maintenance should improve with a new and most welcome automatic watering system. We know it often drizzles in Brittany, but long dry spells leave the fairways rock-hard.

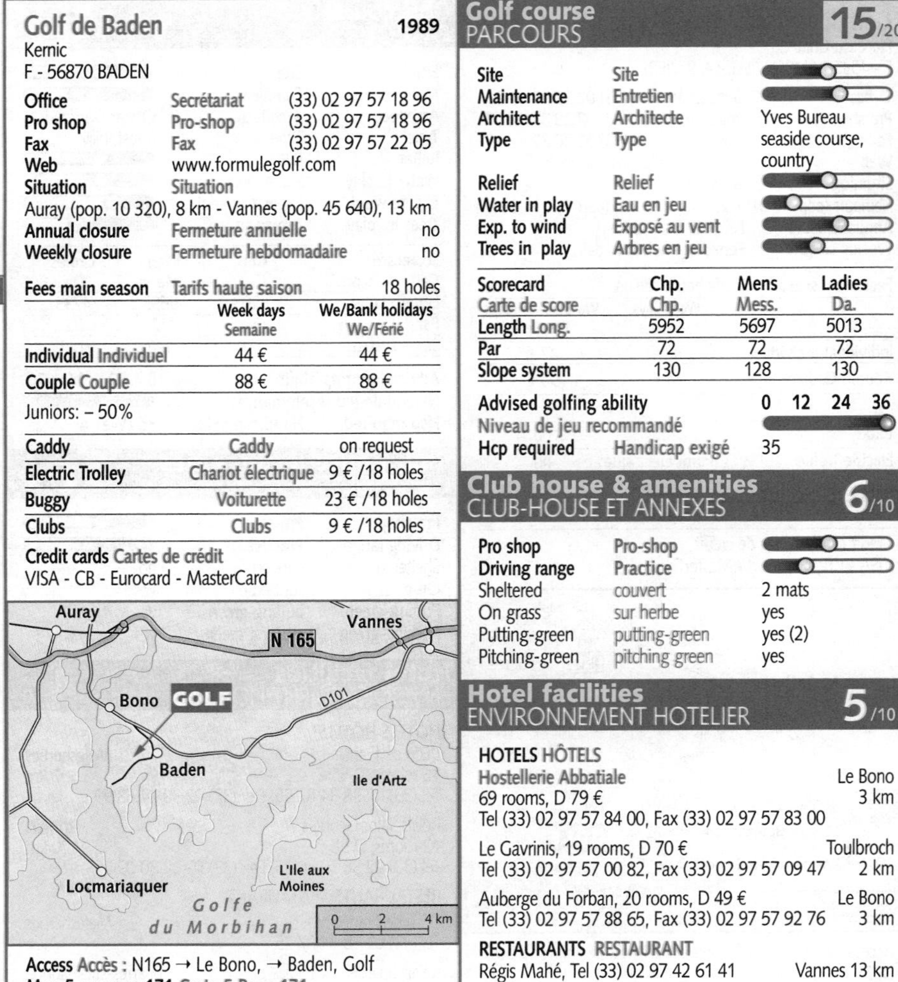

Golf de Baden — 1989

Kernic
F - 56870 BADEN

Office	Secrétariat	(33) 02 97 57 18 96
Pro shop	Pro-shop	(33) 02 97 57 18 96
Fax	Fax	(33) 02 97 57 22 05
Web	www.formulegolf.com	
Situation	Situation	

Auray (pop. 10 320), 8 km - Vannes (pop. 45 640), 13 km

Annual closure	Fermeture annuelle	no
Weekly closure	Fermeture hebdomadaire	no

Fees main season Tarifs haute saison	18 holes	
	Week days Semaine	**We/Bank holidays** We/Férié
Individual Individuel	44 €	44 €
Couple Couple	88 €	88 €

Juniors: – 50%

Caddy	Caddy	on request
Electric Trolley	Chariot électrique	9 € /18 holes
Buggy	Voiturette	23 € /18 holes
Clubs	Clubs	9 € /18 holes

Credit cards Cartes de crédit
VISA - CB - Eurocard - MasterCard

Access Accès : N165 → Le Bono, → Baden, Golf
Map 5 on page 171 Carte 5 Page 171

Golf course PARCOURS — 15/20

Site	Site	
Maintenance	Entretien	
Architect	Architecte	Yves Bureau
Type	Type	seaside course, country
Relief	Relief	
Water in play	Eau en jeu	
Exp. to wind	Exposé au vent	
Trees in play	Arbres en jeu	

Scorecard Carte de score	**Chp.** Chp.	**Mens** Mess.	**Ladies** Da.
Length Long.	5952	5697	5013
Par	72	72	72
Slope system	130	128	130

Advised golfing ability Niveau de jeu recommandé — 0 12 24 36

Hcp required Handicap exigé 35

Club house & amenities CLUB-HOUSE ET ANNEXES — 6/10

Pro shop	Pro-shop	
Driving range	Practice	
Sheltered	couvert	2 mats
On grass	sur herbe	yes
Putting-green	putting-green	yes (2)
Pitching-green	pitching green	yes

Hotel facilities ENVIRONNEMENT HOTELIER — 5/10

HOTELS HÔTELS

Hostellerie Abbatiale — Le Bono
69 rooms, D 79 € — 3 km
Tel (33) 02 97 57 84 00, Fax (33) 02 97 57 83 00

Le Gavrinis, 19 rooms, D 70 € — Toulbroch
Tel (33) 02 97 57 00 82, Fax (33) 02 97 57 09 47 — 2 km

Auberge du Forban, 20 rooms, D 49 € — Le Bono
Tel (33) 02 97 57 88 65, Fax (33) 02 97 57 92 76 — 3 km

RESTAURANTS RESTAURANT

Régis Mahé, Tel (33) 02 97 42 61 41 — Vannes 13 km

Le Pressoir, Tel (33) 02 97 60 87 63 — Vannes 13 km

BÂLE-HAGENTHAL 15 | 7 | 7

Dans un très beau site de campagne et de bois, ce parcours est une sorte d'enclave suisse en France. Dessiné par l'architecte allemand Bernhard von Limburger, quelques reliefs accentués obligent à réfléchir sur les choix de club, et sa longueur est encore accentuée par un terrain assez lourd quand il pleut. Sans présenter de caractère très original sur le plan visuel, c'est un parcours stratégique intelligent, avec des obstacles bien visibles, mais pas excessivement dangereux (sauf les arbres), seules deux petites mares constituant des obstacles d'eau. Ces difficultés raisonnables amènent à le conseiller à tous les niveaux de joueurs classés, dans la mesure où ils pourront attaquer les greens, largement ouverts, en faisant rouler la balle (deux de ces greens ont été bien refaits). Mais pour jouer son handicap, il vaut mieux savoir faire des balles à effet. La deuxième partie du parcours, la plus boisée, est techniquement la plus intéressante. A connaître.

In a beautiful setting of countryside and woodland, this course is a sort of a Swiss enclave in France. Laid out by German architect Bernhard von Limburger, the course's topography calls for careful thought when choosing which club to play and yardage feels even longer when the ground gets heavy in rainy weather. Although visually speaking the course is nothing to write home about, it is a strategically intelligent layout, with clearly visible but not excessively dangerous hazards (except the trees). The only water hazards are two little ponds. We would therefore recommend it to high-handicappers and better, especially since the greens are wide open and reachable with easier chip shots (two of the greens have been re-laid). Being able to move the ball both ways (deliberately) will definitely be helpful for players looking to play to their handicap. The second part of the course, where the woods are thicker, is technically speaking the most interesting. Well worth a round.

Golf & Country Club de Bâle — 1968

Route de Wentzwiller
F - 68220 HAGENTHAL-LE-BAS

Office	Secrétariat	(33) 03 89 68 50 91
Pro shop	Pro-shop	(33) 03 89 68 51 61
Fax	Fax	(33) 03 89 68 57 36
E-mail	gccbasel@wanadoo.fr	
Situation	Situation	Bâle/Basel, 9 km
Annual closure	Fermeture annuelle	1/1 → 31/1
Weekly closure	Fermeture hebdomadaire	no

Fees main season Tarifs haute saison	Week days Semaine	We/Bank holidays We/Férié
		full day
Individual Individuel	55 €	*
Couple Couple	110 €	*

* We: members only

Caddy	Caddy	no
Electric Trolley	Chariot électrique	12 € /18 holes
Buggy	Voiturette	no
Clubs	Clubs	12 € /full day

Credit cards Cartes de crédit
VISA - Eurocard - MasterCard

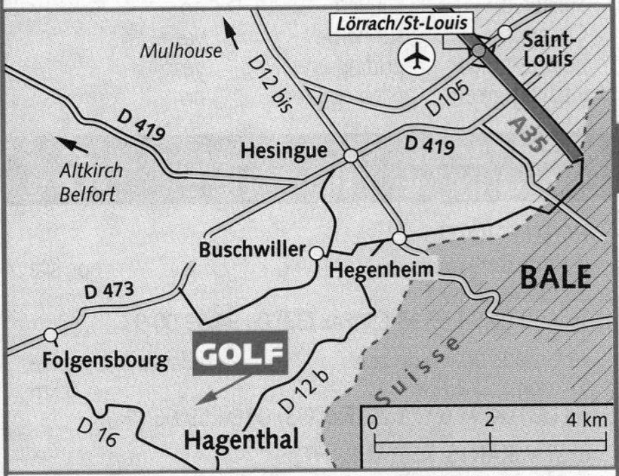

Access Accès : • Mulhouse A35 Exit (Sortie) Saint-Louis, → Aéroport, D473 → Hesingue, → Folgensbourg, D16 → Hagenthal. • Bâle → Hegenheim. • Belfort D419 → Bâle
Map 8 on page 177 Carte 8 Page 177

Golf course PARCOURS — 15/20

Site	Site	
Maintenance	Entretien	
Architect	Architecte	B. von Limburger
Type	Type	forest, country
Relief	Relief	
Water in play	Eau en jeu	
Exp. to wind	Exposé au vent	
Trees in play	Arbres en jeu	

Scorecard Carte de score	Chp. Chp.	Mens Mess.	Ladies Da.
Length Long.	6255	5938	5497
Par	72	72	72
Slope system	131	127	126

Advised golfing ability Niveau de jeu recommandé — 0 12 24 36
Hcp required Handicap exigé — 32

Club house & amenities CLUB-HOUSE ET ANNEXES — 7/10

Pro shop	Pro-shop	
Driving range	Practice	
Sheltered	couvert	5 mats
On grass	sur herbe	no, 25 mats open air
Putting-green	putting-green	yes
Pitching-green	pitching green	yes

Hotel facilities ENVIRONNEMENT HOTELIER — 7/10

HOTELS HÔTELS

Jenny, 26 rooms, D CHF 475 — Hagenthal
Tel (33) 03 89 68 50 09, Fax (33) 03 89 68 58 64 — 1 km

Trois Rois, 88 rooms, D CHF 500 — Bâle
Tel (41) 061 - 260 50 50, Fax (41) 061 - 260 50 60 — 9 km

Merian, 65 rooms, D CHF 300 — Bâle
Tel (41) 061 - 681 00 00, Fax (41) 061 - 681 11 01 — 9 km

RESTAURANTS RESTAURANT

Jenny, Tel (33) 03 89 68 50 09 — Hagenthal-le-Bas 1 km

Ancienne Forge ,Tel (33) 03 89 68 56 10 — Hagenthal-le-Haut

Stucki, Tel (41) 061 - 361 82 22 — Bâle 9 km

BARBAROUX

17 | 7 | 6

Un parcours toujours aussi controversé que passionnant, notamment par son style composite, un véritable exercice de styles : on a l'impression de se trouver successivement en Irlande, en Ecosse, aux Etats-Unis. Le paysage sauvage de Provence modère cependant ce manque d'unité. Barbaroux est une succession de tests techniques dont il serait vain de décrire tous les détails. Les mouvements de terrain créés par Pete et P.B. Dye, le dessin des bunkers et des greens (quelques-uns aveugles) constituent non seulement un spectacle permanent, mais aussi une série de difficultés que bien peu sauront maîtriser. Ici, il faut d'abord accepter que l'on ne fait pas toujours un bon score avec du bon jeu, bref, savoir accepter d'être battu par un grand parcours. L'inversion de l'aller et du retour a facilité le jeu mais un peu diminué l'impact du final originel. Ce parcours pas trop encombré est une expérience à vivre, et l'on peut souhaiter que les nouveaux maîtres des lieux en maintiennent la qualité en permanence.

A course that is still as controversial as it is exciting to play, primarily because of its contrasting styles. The impression you get here is one of a catalogue for world golf-courses; one minute you could be in Ireland, the next in Scotland and the next in the United States. Yet the wild Provence landscape tempers any lack of unity, making Barbaroux a succession of technical ordeals, all the details of which can hardly be described here. The contoured fairways, created by Pete and P.B. Dye, and the design of the greens (some are blind) and bunkers make for not only a never-ending spectacle but also a series of difficulties that few golfers will find easy to master. Here, lesson number one is admitting that good play does not always end up as a good score, in other words accepting defeat at the hands of a great and seldom busy course. The reversal of the front and back nine has made things a little easier but also diminished somewhat the impact of the course's original "grand finale". This is an essential golfing experience and we can only hope that the new owners permanently keep the course up to its present excellent standard.

Golf Club de Barbaroux — 1989

Route de Cabasse
F - 83170 BRIGNOLES

Office	Secrétariat	(33) 04 94 69 63 63
Pro shop	Pro-shop	(33) 04 94 69 63 63
Fax	Fax	(33) 04 94 59 00 93
Web	www.barbaroux.com	
Situation	Situation	Brignoles, 9 km
Annual closure	Fermeture annuelle	no
Weekly closure	Fermeture hebdomadaire	no

222

Fees main season Tarifs haute saison	Week days Semaine	We/Bank holidays We/Férié
	18 holes	
Individual Individuel	46 €	46 €
Couple Couple	92 €	92 €

GF full day: 58 €

Caddy	Caddy	no
Electric Trolley	Chariot électrique	no
Buggy	Voiturette	27 € /18 holes
Clubs	Clubs	9 € /full day

Credit cards Cartes de crédit
VISA - CB - Eurocard - MasterCard - AMEX

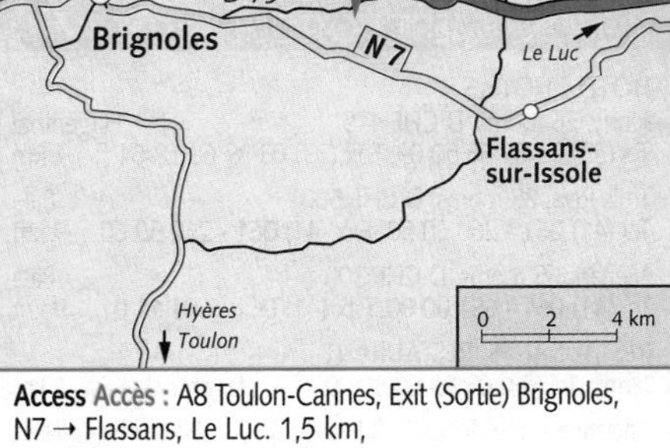

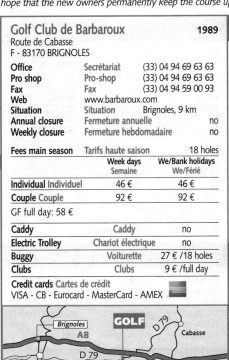

Access Accès : A8 Toulon-Cannes, Exit (Sortie) Brignoles, N7 → Flassans, Le Luc. 1,5 km, turn left on D79 → La Cabane
Map 14 on page 188 Carte 14 Page 188

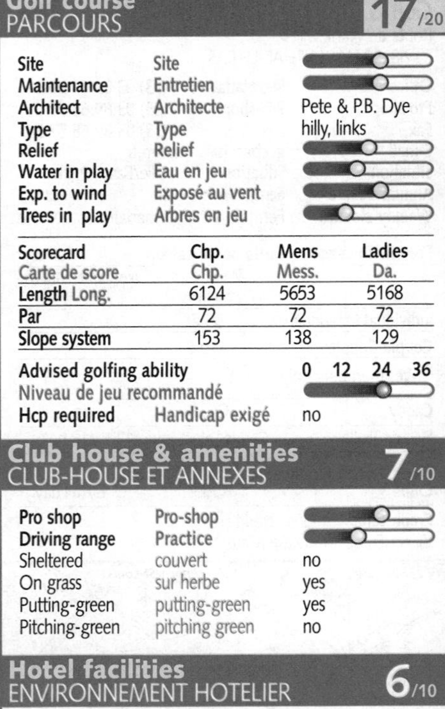

Golf course PARCOURS — 17/20

Site	Site	
Maintenance	Entretien	
Architect	Architecte	Pete & P.B. Dye
Type	Type	hilly, links
Relief	Relief	
Water in play	Eau en jeu	
Exp. to wind	Exposé au vent	
Trees in play	Arbres en jeu	

Scorecard Carte de score	Chp. Chp.	Mens Mess.	Ladies Da.
Length Long.	6124	5653	5168
Par	72	72	72
Slope system	153	138	129

Advised golfing ability 0 12 24 36
Niveau de jeu recommandé
Hcp required Handicap exigé no

Club house & amenities CLUB-HOUSE ET ANNEXES — 7/10

Pro shop	Pro-shop	
Driving range	Practice	
Sheltered	couvert	no
On grass	sur herbe	yes
Putting-green	putting-green	yes
Pitching-green	pitching green	no

Hotel facilities ENVIRONNEMENT HOTELIER — 6/10

HOTELS HÔTELS

Golf de Barbaroux — on site
24 rooms, D 64 €
Tel (33) 04 94 69 63 63, Fax (33) 04 94 59 00 93

La Grillade au feu de bois — Flassans-sur-Issole 8 km
17 rooms, D 137 €
Tel (33) 04 94 69 71 20, Fax (33) 04 94 59 66 11

RESTAURANTS RESTAURANT

Le Lingousto — Cuers 25 km
Tel (33) 04 94 28 69 10

BAULE (LA) Rouge

15 | 7 | 8

Neuf des 18 trous originaux dessinés par Alliss et Thomas en 1978 ont été conservés, les neuf autres primitifs ayant été séparés pour constituer un parcours de par 35. Neuf trous supplémentaires ont été tracés par Michel Gayon, plus proches de la campagne que d'un parc, quant au paysage et même au jeu. Ces trous ont intercalés entre le 4 et le 14, ce qui rompt la monotonie des allers et retours d'autrefois (les anciens 10 à 16). Bien sûr, le manque d'unité de style est flagrant, mais le plaisir d'évoluer dans la campagne de La Baule reste intact. Tout aussi stratégiques que les autres, les "greens et bunkers Gayon" sont dessinés avec plus d'attention et de relief (à remarquer le double green des 5 et 12), Un nouveau 18 trous a été dessiné par Michel Gayon et Jacques Lebreton, qui modifie et élargit le paysage du golf de la Baule, devenu avec 45 trous un ensemble impressionnant. Les premières visites ayant été assez mitigées, nous attendrons que ce nouveau parcours mûrisse un peu afin d'en juger plus objectivement.

Nine of the original 18 holes designed by Alliss and Thomas in 1978 have been retained, while the other nine now form a separate par 35 course. Michel Gayon designed nine additional holes, which are more country than parkland in terms of landscape and the way they play. The new holes have been inserted between the 4th and the 14th, and so break up the monotony of the earlier up and down holes (formerly holes 10 to 16). Obviously, there is a clear lack of unity in style, but the pleasure of walking La Baule countryside is as great as ever. As strategic as on the other holes, the "Gayon" greens and bunkers have been more carefully designed, with sharper relief (note the double green shared by the 5th and 12th holes). A new 18-hole course has been designed by Michel Gayon and Jacques Lebreton, which has changed and broadened the golfing landscape of La Baule, now an impressive 45-hole complex. As we came away from our first visit with mixed feelings, we will wait for the new course to mature a little so as to form a more objective opinion.

Golf de La Baule — 1994

Domaine de Saint-Denac
F - 44117 SAINT-ANDRE-DES-EAUX

Office	Secrétariat	(33) 02 40 60 46 18
Pro shop	Pro-shop	(33) 02 40 60 46 18
Fax	Fax	(33) 02 40 60 41 41
Web	www.lucienbarriere.com	
Situation	Situation	

St-Nazaire (pop. 64 810), 12 km - La Baule, 7 km

Annual closure Fermeture annuelle — no
Weekly closure Fermeture hebdomadaire
tuesday/1/11→31/3

Fees main season Tarifs haute saison		full day
	Week days Semaine	**We/Bank holidays** We/Férié
Individual Individuel	53 €	53 €
Couple Couple	106 €	106 €
Juniors: – 50%		

Caddy	Caddy	no
Electric Trolley	Chariot électrique	no
Buggy	Voiturette	30 € /18 holes
Clubs	Clubs	15 € /18 holes

Credit cards Cartes de crédit
VISA - CB - Eurocard - MasterCard - AMEX

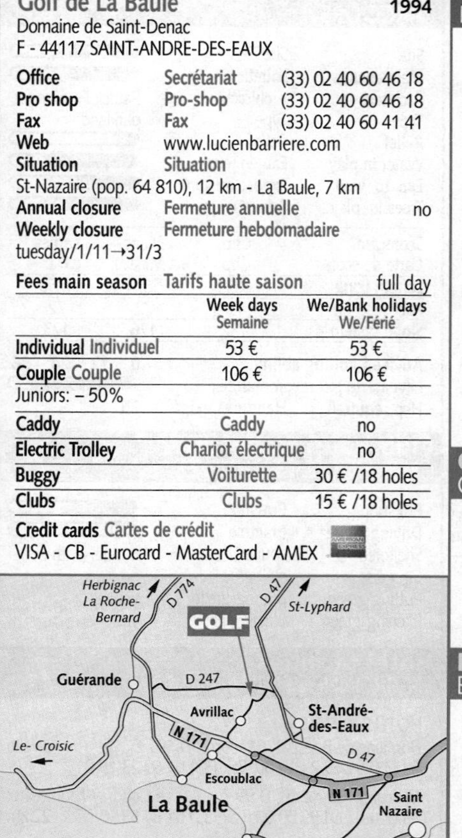

Access Accès : La Baule → La Baule-Escoublac, cross the road N171. → Golf
Map 5 on page 171 Carte 5 Page 171

Golf course PARCOURS — 15/20

Site	Site	
Maintenance	Entretien	
Architect	Architecte	Alliss & Thomas Michel Gayon
Type	Type	forest, open country
Relief	Relief	
Water in play	Eau en jeu	
Exp. to wind	Exposé au vent	
Trees in play	Arbres en jeu	

Scorecard Carte de score	**Chp.** Chp.	**Mens** Mess.	**Ladies** Da.
Length Long.	6055	5700	4776
Par	72	72	72
Slope system	134	130	121

Advised golfing ability Niveau de jeu recommandé — 0 12 24 36
Hcp required Handicap exigé — 30 (main season)

Club house & amenities CLUB-HOUSE ET ANNEXES — 7/10

Pro shop	Pro-shop	
Driving range	Practice	
Sheltered	couvert	10 mats
On grass	sur herbe	yes
Putting-green	putting-green	yes
Pitching-green	pitching green	yes

Hotel facilities ENVIRONNEMENT HOTELIER — 8/10

HOTELS HÔTELS

Castel Marie-Louise, 31 rooms, D 297 € — La Baule
Tel (33) 02 40 11 48 38, Fax (33) 02 40 11 48 35 — 7 km

Hermitage, 215 rooms, D 335 € — La Baule
Tel (33) 02 40 11 46 46, Fax (33) 02 40 11 46 45

Saint-Christophe, 32 rooms, D 120 € — La Baule
Tel (33) 02 40 60 35 35, Fax (33) 02 40 60 11 74

Hotel du Golf, 31 rooms, Studio 163 € — St André des Eaux
Tel (33) 02 40 17 57 57, Fax (33) 02 40 17 57 58

RESTAURANTS RESTAURANT

Maréchal, Tel (33) 02 40 24 51 14 — La Baule

L'Hermitage, Tel (33) 02 40 11 46 46 — La Baule

BÉLESBAT

14 | 7 | 7

Avec dix hectares de plus et davantage de génie architectural, on aurait pu avoir là un grand parcours. Mais Bélesbat est tout de même un parcours très correct et visuellement plaisant, qu'une refonte du bunkering pourrait facilement améliorer. La plupart des 60 et quelque bunkers sont trop étendus et surtout sans grand relief. De même, on peut trouver les greens beaucoup trop vastes, même s'ils ont été réduits depuis les origines : ils sont souvent disproportionnés avec le coup à jouer. On peut également penser que les obstacles d'eau sont trop regroupés sur la fin, et pas toujours bien placés (les joueurs peu expérimentés auront du mal à finir), mais les architectes avaient il est vrai un cahier des charges très contraignant sur ce secteur. Reste que malgré ces observations, l'ensemble ne manque ni de beauté, ni de qualités ni de grandeur, que l'hôtellerie sur place est de bonne qualité, et que les plus charmantes des femmes ont parfois des défauts, à bien regarder. Longtemps fermé, Bélesbat est sur la bonne voie.

With another 25 acres and little more imagination, this could have been a masterpiece. As it stands, it is a good and visually attractive course that could be easily improved upon with some changes made to the bunkering. Most of the 60 or something bunkers are too expansive and especially too flat. Likewise, you might find the greens much too large and disproportionate to the shot you need to play, even though they have been cut back since the course was first opened. You might also find that there is too much poorly positioned water hogging the back nine (inexperienced players will find the last few holes something of an ordeal) but it is true to say that the architects were given highly restrictive specifications in this respect. Despite everything, the whole course has much to be said for it in terms of beauty and quality and the on-site hotel is excellent. Let's face it, even the most beautiful face can have flaws when taking a really close look. Belesbat remained closed for long periods but is now definitely on the way back.

Golf de Bélesbat — 1990

F - 91820 BOUTIGNY-SUR-ESSONNE

Office	Secrétariat	(33) 01 69 23 19 10
Pro shop	Pro-shop	(33) 01 69 23 19 10
Fax	Fax	(33) 01 69 23 19 01
Web	www.belesbat.com	
Situation	Situation	

Fontainebleau (pop. 15 714), 25 km

Annual closure	Fermeture annuelle	no
Weekly closure	Fermeture hebdomadaire	no

Fees main season Tarifs haute saison — 18 holes

	Week days / Semaine	We/Bank holidays / We/Férié
Individual Individuel	34 €	67 €
Couple Couple	68 €	134 €

Tuesday: 2 players for 1 green fee (mardi, 1 GF pour 2 joueurs)

Caddy	Caddy	no
Electric Trolley	Chariot électrique	no
Buggy	Voiturette	no
Clubs	Clubs	18 € /18 holes

Credit cards Cartes de crédit
VISA - CB - Eurocard - MasterCard - DC - JCB - AMEX

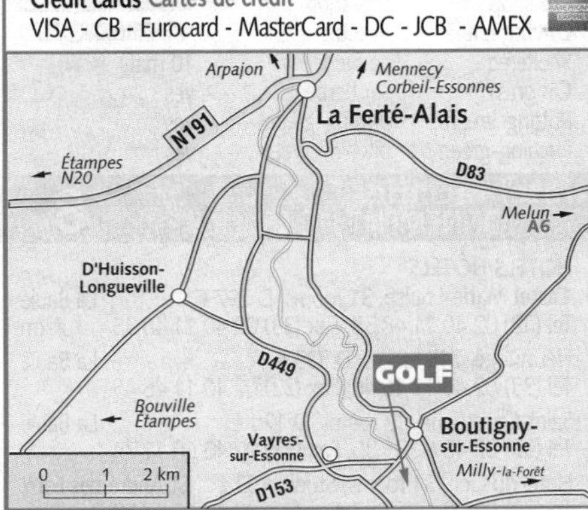

Access Accès : Paris A6 Exit (sortie) 11 → Le Coudray. D948 → Milly-la-Forêt. 9 km turn right on D83 → La Ferté-Alais. 4 km turn left on D153 to Boutigny. → Golf

Map 3 on page 166 Carte 3 Page 166

Golf course PARCOURS — 14/20

Site	Site	
Maintenance	Entretien	
Architect	Architecte	Patrick Fromanger
Type	Type	parkland
Relief	Relief	
Water in play	Eau en jeu	
Exp. to wind	Exposé au vent	
Trees in play	Arbres en jeu	

Scorecard Carte de score	Chp. Chp.	Mens Mess.	Ladies Da.
Length Long.	6033	5674	4750
Par	72	72	72
Slope system	132	126	123

Advised golfing ability Niveau de jeu recommandé — 0 12 24 36

Hcp required Handicap exigé 35

Club house & amenities CLUB-HOUSE ET ANNEXES — 7/10

Pro shop	Pro-shop	
Driving range	Practice	
Sheltered	couvert	4 mats (with net)
On grass	sur herbe	no
Putting-green	putting-green	yes
Pitching-green	pitching green	yes

Hotel facilities ENVIRONNEMENT HOTELIER — 7/10

HOTELS HÔTELS

Domaine de Belesbat, 61 rooms, D 191 € — on site
Tel (33) 01 69 23 19 00, Fax (33) 01 69 23 19 01

Mercure, 125 rooms, D 99 € — Le Coudray-Montceaux
Tel (33) 01 64 99 00 00, Fax (33) 01 64 93 95 55 — 22 km

Bas Bréau, 21 rooms, D 229 € — Barbizon
Tel (33) 01 60 66 40 05, Fax (33) 01 60 69 22 89 — 25 km

RESTAURANTS RESTAURANT

Le Pavillon, Tel (33) 01 69 23 19 00 — on site

Auberge d'Auvers Galant, Tel (33) 01 64 24 51 02 — Auvers

Auberge du Grand Veneur, Tel (33) 01 60 66 40 44 — Barbizon

BELLE-DUNE

16 | 6 | 5

Ce golf public est devenu l'un des classiques de la région. On regrette toujours que la plupart des bunkers n'aient toujours pas été"ensablés", car ils apporteraient des contrastes visuels dans tout ce vert, et accentueraient le caractère dunaire du lieu, même si l'environnement est boisé sur un grand nombre de trous. Plusieurs greens sont presque aveugles, avec des contours peuvent parfois excessifs, mais on retrouve ces caractéristiques sur de nombreux links britanniques. Epousant les contours de dunes tourmentées (parfois de façon exagérée), ce golf est assez physique pour les golfeurs rouillés mais reste jouable à pied. Alors que les arbres protègent certains trous, d'autres plus dénudés deviennent très difficiles quand le vent est violent : il faudra alors davantage "limiter les dégâts" que rechercher les exploits. Un Club-House dans le style local complète cet équipement de bonne qualité, où l'accueil peut être cependant très "fonctionnaire": c'est là qu'il nous a été dit que le sable dans les bunkers serait "trop difficile pour les amateurs".

This public course has become one of the region's "must play" layouts. Sadly, though, most of the bunkers are still awaiting their sand, which would add a little visual contrast to a sea of green and emphasise the sand-dune features of the whole site, even though a number of holes are more reminiscent of a woodland course. Several greens are almost blind and some of the slopes are a little excessive, but that is often the way it is on many British links. The course hugs the sometimes excessively twisting dunes, and although hilly, even the rustier golfers can play it without a buggy. While trees protect some of the holes, others are exposed and become a very tricky proposition in windy conditions. The result is often an exercise in damage limitation rather than a quest for a good card. A Club-house in local style completes the good quality facilities at a course where the reception might sometimes seem off-hand. This is where we were told that sand in the bunkers would be "too difficult for the average amateur golfer".

Golf de Belle-Dune — 1993

Promenade du Marquenterre
F - 80790 FORT-MAHON-PLAGE

Office	Secrétariat	(33) 03 22 23 45 50
Pro shop	Pro-shop	(33) 03 22 23 45 50
Fax	Fax	(33) 03 22 23 93 41
Web	—	
Situation	Situation	

Le Touquet, 25 km - Berck-Plage (pop. 14 160), 20 km

Annual closure	Fermeture annuelle	no
Weekly closure	Fermeture hebdomadaire	no

only Fridays in winter (vendredi en hiver)

Fees main season Tarifs haute saison	Week days Semaine	We/Bank holidays We/Férié
Individual Individuel	34 €	42 €
Couple Couple	59 €	69 €

Juniors: 27 € (weekdays) - 33 € (We)

18 holes

Caddy	Caddy	no
Electric Trolley	Chariot électrique	11 € /18 holes
Buggy	Voiturette	34 € /18 holes
Clubs	Clubs	9 € /full day

Credit cards Cartes de crédit VISA - CB - Eurocard

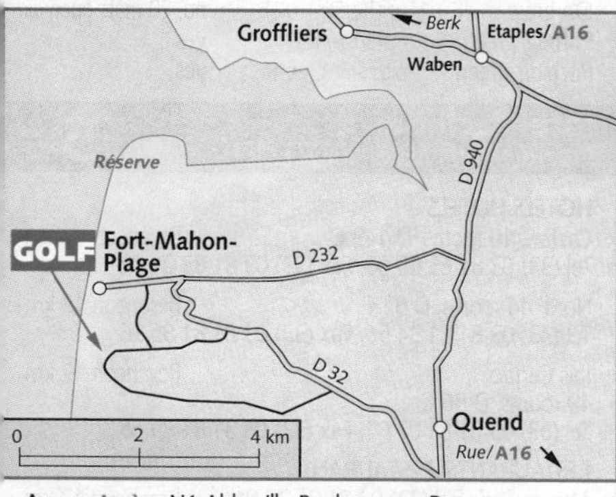

Access Accès : N1 Abbeville-Boulogne, → Rue, → Quend-Plage, D32 → Fort-Mahon-Plage, → Golf

Map 1 on page 162 Carte 1 Page 162

Golf course — PARCOURS — 16/20

Site	Site	
Maintenance	Entretien	
Architect	Architecte	Jean-Manuel Rossi
Type	Type	seaside course, forest
Relief	Relief	
Water in play	Eau en jeu	
Exp. to wind	Exposé au vent	
Trees in play	Arbres en jeu	

Scorecard Carte de score	Chp. Chp.	Mens Mess.	Ladies Da.
Length Long.	5952	5562	5008
Par	72	72	72
Slope system	147	138	131

Advised golfing ability Niveau de jeu recommandé: 0 12 24 36

Hcp required Handicap exigé: 35

Club house & amenities — CLUB-HOUSE ET ANNEXES — 6/10

Pro shop	Pro-shop	
Driving range	Practice	
Sheltered	couvert	5 mats
On grass	sur herbe	no,15 mats open air
Putting-green	putting-green	yes
Pitching-green	pitching green	yes

Hotel facilities — ENVIRONNEMENT HOTELIER — 5/10

HOTELS HÔTELS

La Terrasse, 56 rooms, D 60 € — Fort-Mahon-Plage 1 km
Tel (33) 03 22 23 37 77, Fax (33) 03 22 23 36 74

Le Lion d'Or, 16 rooms, D 52 € — Rue 12 km
Tel (33) 03 22 25 74 18, Fax (33) 03 22 25 66 63

La Chipodière, 18 rooms, D 46 € — Fort-Mahon-Plage 1 km
Tel (33) 03 22 27 70 36, Fax (33) 03 22 23 38 16

RESTAURANTS RESTAURANT

La Grenouillère — La Madelaine sous Montreuil 12 km
Tel (33) 03 21 06 07 22

La Terrasse, Tel (33) 03 22 23 37 77 — Fort-Mahon-Plage1 km

Auberge Le Fiacre ,Tel (33) 03 22 23 47 30 — Routhiauville 2 km

BESANÇON

13 | 7 | 5

Un golf très équilibré : le parcours se déroule dans un site agréable, entre plaine et forêt, il n'est pas trop plat, ni trop mouvementé, pas trop facile, ni trop difficile, avec très peu d'eau. Il offre ainsi un bon dosage des obstacles, une bonne alternance de trous faciles et plus délicats : de quoi satisfaire les débutants et les joueurs moyens, sans les effrayer par des difficultés hors de leurs compétences. Certes, les joueurs de haut niveau n'y trouveront alors pas leur compte, mais ce n'est pas la vocation de ce golf de les satisfaire exclusivement, il est essentiellement fréquenté par les joueurs de la région. Dessiné par Michael Fenn, il représente un style de parcours bien adapté à un usage "local", mais sans mériter vraiment le détour. Mais, d'avril à octobre, si vous êtes dans la région, vous y passerez une journée détendue.

A nicely balanced course, pleasantly located between plain and forest, not too flat and not too hilly, not too easy yet none too difficult, with little in the way of water. Hazards are astutely dispensed here and there, with easier holes alternating pleasantly with harder numbers, giving enough to satisfy beginners and twenty-plus handicappers without scaring them off with hazards that might be beyond them. Better players will certainly feel a touch of frustration, but there again the course was not designed with only them in mind. It is basically played by local players. Designed by Michael Fenn, the course's style is well suited to local golfing but not really worth any long trip out of your way. But if you are in the region between April and October, drop by and enjoy a good day out.

Golf Club de Besançon — 1972

La Chevillotte
F - 25620 MAMIROLLE

Office	Secrétariat	(33) 03 81 55 73 54
Pro shop	Pro-shop	(33) 03 81 55 86 13
Fax	Fax	(33) 03 81 55 88 64
E-mail	golfbesancon@wanadoo.fr	
Situation	Situation	

Besançon (pop. 113 820), 12 km

Annual closure	Fermeture annuelle	no
Weekly closure	Fermeture hebdomadaire	no

restaurant open 01/03 → 31/12

Fees main season Tarifs haute saison	Week days Semaine	We/Bank holidays We/Férié
		18 holes
Individual Individuel	34 €	40 €
Couple Couple	68 €	80 €
Caddy Caddy		no
Electric Trolley Chariot électrique		15 € /18 holes
Buggy Voiturette		24 € /18 holes
Clubs Clubs		8 € /full day

Credit cards Cartes de crédit
VISA - CB - Eurocard - MasterCard - AMEX

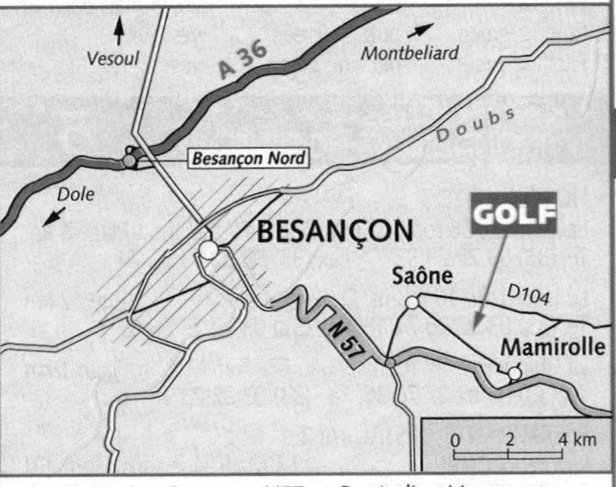

Access Accès : Besançon N57 → Pontarlier / Lausanne, → Saône, → Golf
Map 8 on page 177 Carte 8 Page 177

Golf course — PARCOURS — 13/20

Site	Site	
Maintenance	Entretien	
Architect	Architecte	Michael Fenn
Type	Type	forest, country
Relief	Relief	
Water in play	Eau en jeu	
Exp. to wind	Exposé au vent	
Trees in play	Arbres en jeu	

Scorecard Carte de score	Chp. Chp.	Mens Mess.	Ladies Da.
Length Long.	6071	5705	5117
Par	72	72	72
Slope system	134	131	122

Advised golfing ability Niveau de jeu recommandé — 0 12 24 36
Hcp required Handicap exigé — 35

Club house & amenities — CLUB-HOUSE ET ANNEXES — 7/10

Pro shop	Pro-shop	
Driving range	Practice	
Sheltered	couvert	7 mats
On grass	sur herbe	no, 20 mats open air
Putting-green	putting-green	yes
Pitching-green	pitching green	yes

Hotel facilities — ENVIRONNEMENT HOTELIER — 5/10

HOTELS HÔTELS

Castan, 10 rooms, D 149 € — Besançon 12 km
Tel (33) 03 81 65 02 00, Fax (33) 03 81 83 01 02

Nord, 44 rooms, D 52 € — Besançon 12 km
Tel (33) 03 81 81 34 56, Fax (33) 03 81 81 85 96

Ibis Centre — Besançon 12 km
49 rooms, D 56 €
Tel (33) 03 81 81 02 02, Fax (33) 03 81 81 89 65

RESTAURANTS RESTAURANT

Mungo Park, Tel (33) 03 81 81 28 01 — Besançon 12 km

Le Chaland, Tel(33) 03 81 80 61 61 — Besançon 12 km

BÉTHEMONT

13 | 6 | 5

Les premiers et derniers trous donnent l'impression d'un parcours physique, mais la plupart des trous sont situés sur un plateau. Il est assez court, mais bordé d'arbres souvent bien en jeu, avec un grand nombre de bunkers, de beaux obstacles d'eau, et quelques doglegs assez diaboliques. La signature de Bernhard Langer est évidente en ce qu'elle réclame beaucoup de précision avec les fers, pas mal de réflexion avant de jouer, plus que de la longueur. Dans ces conditions, une seule visite ne suffit pas pour prétendre le maîtriser, et les joueurs moyens risquent de le trouver trop exigeant pour eux au premier abord, d'autant que les greens sont souvent très modelés. On ne saurait placer Béthemont parmi les grands parcours de la région parisienne, mais on peut y passer une bonne journée quand il fait beau. Assez humide, il aurait besoin de sérieux travaux de drainage, et ce n'est pas à l'ordre du jour car l'avenir du club est incertain à date de parution, avec un service minimum au club house…

The 1st and 18th at Béthemont give the impression of a physically demanding course, but in fact the majority of holes are laid out on a plateau. Rather short by today's standards, the course is edged by what sometimes seem to be unmissable trees and is generously dotted with bunkers, attractive water hazards and a few devilish dog-legs. This is a Bernhard Langer design, and it shows, calling for precision ironwork and a lot of thought before each stroke. Length off the tee is secondary. Under these conditions, a single round is hardly enough to make any impression on the course and the less experienced player may well find it too demanding first time out, especially with the undulating greens. Although perhaps not one of the greatest courses around Paris, Béthemont does however make for an excellent day's golfing in fine weather. The problem is that this rather damp course is in need of some serious drainage work which unfortunately is not on the agenda. The club's future was uncertain at the time of going to press and club-house facilities stripped to a bare minimum.

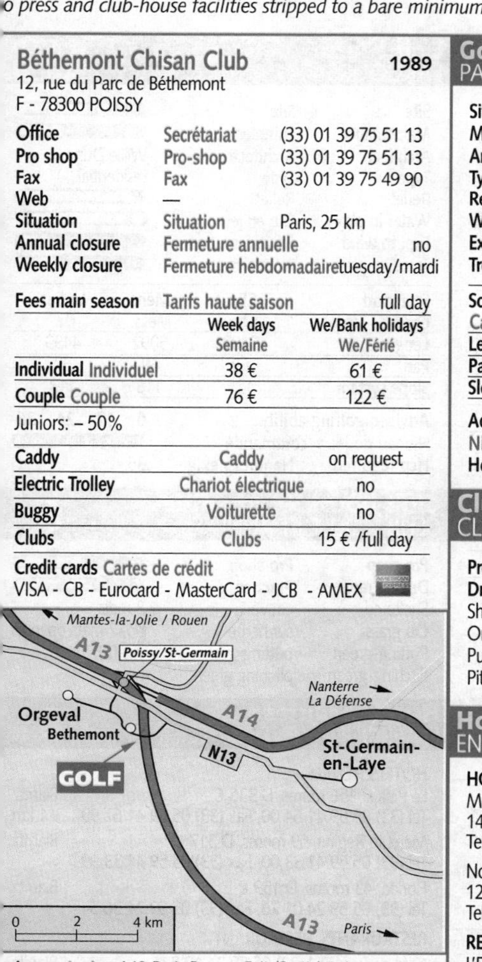

Béthemont Chisan Club 1989
12, rue du Parc de Béthemont
F - 78300 POISSY

Office	Secrétariat	(33) 01 39 75 51 13
Pro shop	Pro-shop	(33) 01 39 75 51 13
Fax	Fax	(33) 01 39 75 49 90
Web	—	
Situation	Situation	Paris, 25 km
Annual closure	Fermeture annuelle	no
Weekly closure	Fermeture hebdomadaire	tuesday/mardi

Fees main season Tarifs haute saison	full day	
	Week days Semaine	**We/Bank holidays** We/Férié
Individual Individuel	38 €	61 €
Couple Couple	76 €	122 €
Juniors: – 50%		

Caddy	Caddy	on request
Electric Trolley	Chariot électrique	no
Buggy	Voiturette	no
Clubs	Clubs	15 € /full day

Credit cards Cartes de crédit
VISA - CB - Eurocard - MasterCard - JCB - AMEX

Access Accès : A13 Paris-Rouen, Exit (Sortie) Poissy → Chambourcy, roundabout → Saint-Germain, 1st road on the right.
Map 15 on page 190 Carte 15 Page 190

Golf course PARCOURS — 13/20

Site	Site	
Maintenance	Entretien	
Architect	Architecte	Bernhard Langer
Type	Type	forest, hilly
Relief	Relief	
Water in play	Eau en jeu	
Exp. to wind	Exposé au vent	
Trees in play	Arbres en jeu	

Scorecard Carte de score	**Chp.** Chp.	**Mens** Mess.	**Ladies** Da.
Length Long.	6035	5550	5128
Par	72	72	72
Slope system	140	122	121

Advised golfing ability 0 12 24 36
Niveau de jeu recommandé
Hcp required Handicap exigé 35

Club house & amenities CLUB-HOUSE ET ANNEXES — 6/10

Pro shop	Pro-shop	
Driving range	Practice	
Sheltered	couvert	5 mats
On grass	sur herbe	no, 9 mats open air
Putting-green	putting-green	yes
Pitching-green	pitching green	no

Hotel facilities ENVIRONNEMENT HOTELIER — 5/10

HOTELS HÔTELS
Moulin d'Orgeval — Orgeval 5 km
14 rooms, D 130 €
Tel (33) 01 39 75 85 74, Fax (33) 01 39 75 48 52

Novotel — Orgeval 5 km
120 rooms, D 93 €
Tel (33) 01 39 22 35 11, Fax (33) 01 39 75 48 93

RESTAURANTS RESTAURANT
L'Esturgeon, — Poissy; 4 km
Tel (33) 01 39 65 00 04

Le Bon Vivant — Poissy
Tel (44) 01 39 65 02 14

BIARRITZ-LE-PHARE

14 | 6 | 8

Dessiné il y a plus de 100 ans par Willie Dunn, ce parcours a été tellement modifié qu'il n'a plus rien du quasi "links" des origines. Ayant perdu ses trous de bord de mer, c'est devenu un joli golf de parc, très court, ce qui ne veut pas dire facile à scorer, car les greens peuvent être rendus fermes, rapides et alors démoniaques, et même une attaque avec un petit fer peut alors s'avérer redoutable. Les fairways sont séparés par de minces rideaux d'arbres et arbustes, et si l'on n'est pas précis, il vaut mieux s'en écarter franchement que de rester entre deux fairways. Mais, sauf aux 1, 15 et 16, il est inutile de jouer le driver au départ, un bois 3 ou un long fer suffit largement. On peut considérer "Le Phare" comme un peu désuet, mais il porte la tradition irremplaçable du golf des origines en Pays Basque, et peut être joué à tous les niveaux. Souvent injouable en cas de fortes pluies, ce qui n'est pas si rare dans la région, le parcours a fait l'objet de travaux de drainage bienvenus.

Laid out more than 100 years ago by Willie Dunn, this course has seen so much change that there is virtually nothing left of the original links. Having lost its sea-side holes, it has become a pretty parkland course, very short but by no means easy. The greens can be hard, fast and so devilishly tricky, and even short iron approach shots can prove to be a formidable ordeal. The fairways are separated by thin rows of trees and bushes, so if you are going to stray left or right, go the whole way to avoid being stuck in the middle ground. The 3-wood or a long iron will suffice here, except on the 1st, 15th and 16th holes where you can go for your driver. "Le Phare" could be considered a little antiquated, but it bears the irreplaceable tradition of the origins of golf in the Basque country and can be played by golfers of all levels. Since the course is often unplayable after heavy rain, which is not so rare in these parts, the club has recently carried out some welcome drainage work.

Golf de Biarritz-Le-Phare — 1888

2, avenue Edith-Cavell
F - 64200 BIARRITZ

Office	Secrétariat	(33) 05 59 03 71 80
Pro shop	Pro-shop	(33) 05 59 03 71 80
Fax	Fax	(33) 05 59 03 26 74
Web	www.golf-biarritz.com	
Situation	Situation	Biarritz (pop. 28 740), 1 km
Annual closure	Fermeture annuelle	no
Weekly closure	Fermeture hebdomadaire	tuesday

out of main season (mardi basse saison)

Fees main season Tarifs haute saison	18 holes	
	Week days Semaine	**We/Bank holidays** We/Férié
Individual Individuel	53 €	53 €
Couple Couple	97 €	97 €

Juniors: – 50%

Caddy	Caddy	on request
Electric Trolley	Chariot électrique	11 € /18 holes
Buggy	Voiturette	30 € /18 holes
Clubs	Clubs	8 € /full day

Credit cards Cartes de crédit
VISA - CB - Eurocard - MasterCard - AMEX

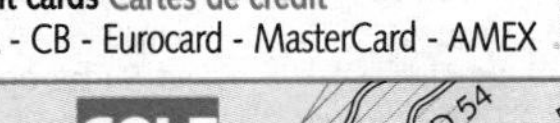

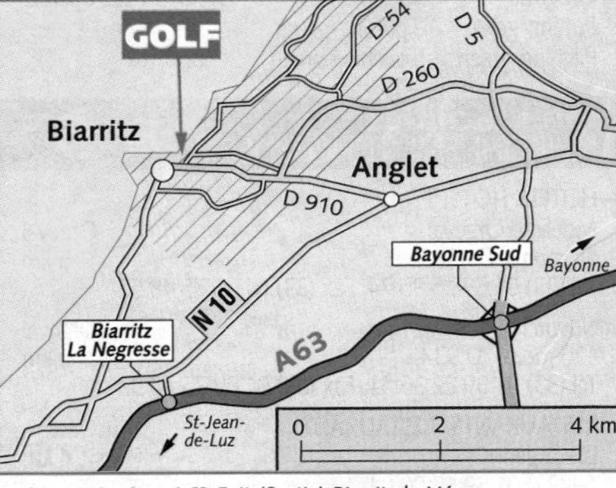

Access Accès : A63 Exit (Sortie) Biarritz la Négresse, → Biarritz, → Anglet
Map 12 on page 184 Carte 12 Page 184

Golf course PARCOURS — 14/20

Site	Site	
Maintenance	Entretien	
Architect	Architecte	Willie Dunn
Type	Type	residential
Relief	Relief	
Water in play	Eau en jeu	
Exp. to wind	Exposé au vent	
Trees in play	Arbres en jeu	

Scorecard Carte de score	**Chp.** Chp.	**Mens** Mess.	**Ladies** Da.
Length Long.	5402	5092	4499
Par	69	69	69
Slope system	121	118	113

Advised golfing ability 0 12 24 36
Niveau de jeu recommandé
Hcp required Handicap exigé 35

Club house & amenities CLUB-HOUSE ET ANNEXES — 6/10

Pro shop	Pro-shop	
Driving range	Practice	
Sheltered	couvert	8 mats
On grass	sur herbe	no, 7 mats open air
Putting-green	putting-green	yes (2)
Pitching-green	pitching green	no

Hotel facilities ENVIRONNEMENT HOTELIER — 8/10

HOTELS HÔTELS

Le Palais, 156 rooms, D 335 € — Biarritz 1 km
Tel (33) 05 59 41 64 00, Fax (33) 05 59 41 67 99

Mercure Regina, 59 rooms, D 317 € — Biarritz
Tel (33) 05 59 41 33 00, Fax (33) 05 59 41 33 99

Florida, 43 rooms, D 159 € — Biarritz
Tel (33) 05 59 24 01 76, Fax (33) 05 59 24 36 54

RESTAURANTS RESTAURANT

Café de Paris, Tel (33) 05 59 24 19 53 — Biarritz

Les Platanes, Tel (33) 05 59 23 13 68 — Biarritz 2 km

La Table des Frères Ibarboure, Tel (33) 05 59 54 81 64 — Bidart 10 km

BITCHE

14 | 6 | 5

Son excellent entretien distingue ce parcours, ainsi que son site pittoresque, entouré de forêt. Assez accidenté pour offrir de beaux points de vue sur la région, mais aussi demander une bonne forme physique, ses difficultés sont assez visibles pour être abordé sans complexes dès la première fois. L'architecture de Fromanger et Adam a conservé le caractère naturel du lieu, elle manque un peu de grandeur et d'inspiration, mais la franchise de leur dessin est à souligner. Il n'a pas été possible d'éviter un green aveugle (le 14), mais s'il reste le seul, les autres sont assez bien défendus pour exiger souvent de porter la balle. Quelques obstacles d'eau ponctuent le paysage, mais ils sont assez peu en jeu. Assez facile des départs avancés, le parcours progresse en difficultés à mesure que l'on recule, et sa longueur est plus effective qu'au vu de la carte, en raison des importantes dénivellations. A noter enfin, quelques travaux de bunkering.

A course that stands out for its excellent maintenance, plus a picturesque setting surrounded by a forest. Hilly enough to provide some fine views over the region and to require a good pair of legs, the course's difficulties are visible enough for players to cope first time out. The architecture, by Fromanger and Adam, has preserved the site's natural character, and although sometimes lacking ambition and inspiration, the course is open and fair, a point we would like to emphasise. They were unable to avoid one blind green (the 14th), while the others are guarded enough to require lofted shots almost every time. Elsewhere, the landscape is dotted with water hazards which don't really come into play. Easy enough from the front tees, it logically gets harder as you move back, and the overall yardage plays longer than you might guess from the card, owing to some steep slopes. The club has recently undertaken a little bunkering work.

Golf de Bitche — 1988

Rue des Prés
F - 57230 BITCHE

Office	Secrétariat	(33) 03 87 96 15 30
Pro shop	Pro-shop	no Pro Shop
Fax	Fax	(33) 03 87 96 08 04
Web	—	
Situation	Situation	

Sarreguemines, 33 km Haguenau (pop. 27 675), 43 km

Annual closure	Fermeture annuelle	25/12→1/1
Weekly closure	Fermeture hebdomadaire	no

Fees main season Tarifs haute saison — Full day

	Week days Semaine	We/Bank holidays We/Férié
Individual Individuel	34 €	53 €
Couple Couple	68 €	106 €

Under 18: – 50%

Caddy	Caddy	no
Electric Trolley	Chariot électrique	no
Buggy	Voiturette	30 € /18 holes
Clubs	Clubs	11 € /full day

Credit cards Cartes de crédit
VISA - CB - Eurocard - MasterCard

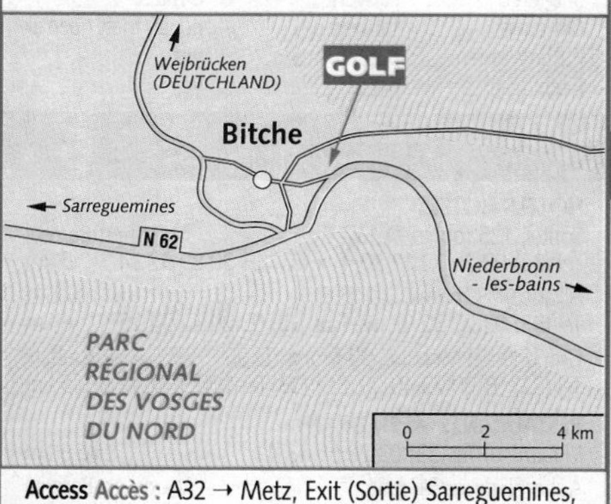

Access Accès : A32 → Metz, Exit (Sortie) Sarreguemines, N62 → Bitche
Map 4 on page 169 Carte 4 Page 169

Golf course PARCOURS — 14/20

Site	Site	
Maintenance	Entretien	
Architect	Architecte	Marc Adam Patrick Fromanger
Type	Type	forest, hilly
Relief	Relief	
Water in play	Eau en jeu	
Exp. to wind	Exposé au vent	
Trees in play	Arbres en jeu	

Scorecard Carte de score	**Chp.** Chp.	**Mens** Mess.	**Ladies** Da.
Length Long.	6060	5850	4950
Par	72	72	72
Slope system	126	126	118

Advised golfing ability Niveau de jeu recommandé — 0 12 24 36
Hcp required Handicap exigé — 35 (We)

Club house & amenities CLUB-HOUSE ET ANNEXES — 6/10

Pro shop	Pro-shop	
Driving range	Practice	
Sheltered	couvert	6 mats
On grass	sur herbe	yes
Putting-green	putting-green	yes
Pitching-green	pitching green	yes

Hotel facilities ENVIRONNEMENT HOTELIER — 5/10

HOTELS HÔTELS

Relais des Châteaux-Forts — Bitche 800 m
30 rooms, D 60 €
Tel (33) 03 87 96 14 14, Fax (33) 03 87 96 07 36

Auberge de Strasbourg — Bitche 1 km
7 rooms, D 44 €
Tel (33) 03 87 96 00 44, Fax (33) 03 87 06 10 60

RESTAURANTS RESTAURANT

Relais des Châteaux-Forts, Tel (33) 03 87 96 14 14 — Bitche
Auberge de la Tour, Tel(33) 03 87 96 29 25 — Bitche 1 km
Auberge de Strasbourg, Tel (33) 03 87 96 00 44 — Bitche 1 km

BONDUES Blanc

16 | 7 | 6

Le "Blanc" offre la particularité d'offrir neuf trous de Robert Trent Jones père et neuf trous du fils. L'architecture est évidemment très américaine, avec de multiples obstacles d'eau, en jeu sur près d'une douzaine de trous. Quand ils le peuvent, les membres se réfugient sur le "Jaune", moins pénalisant de ce point de vue. Comme les arbres sont peu menaçants, marquant simplement les limites des trous, la panoplie des obstacles est complétée par de nombreux bunkers, protégeant à la fois les arrivées de drive et les greens. Cependant, le parcours n'est pas très long, et, une fois familiarisé avec l'eau, il n'est pas impossible de jouer son handicap. Certes, les joueurs de niveau moyen auront du mal à scorer, mais ce 18 trous amène une rupture des habitudes tout à fait bienvenue. Les greens sont de bonne dimension, assez profonds pour poser des problèmes de choix de club.

The "Blanc" course has the peculiarity of featuring nine holes designed by Robert Trent Jones Sr. et nine by his son Robert Trent Jones Jr. This is evidently a very American style course with countless water hazards in play on almost a dozen holes. Whenever they can, members seek solace on the "Jaune" course, a little easier a far as water is concerned. Since the trees offer very little threat and are there simply to demarcate the holes, the panoply of hazards is completed by numerous bunkers, protecting both the tee-shot landing site and the greens. Having said that, the course is not too long and once you have become acquainted with the water, playing to your handicap is not impossible. High handicappers might be hard put to card a good score, but this 18-hole layout makes a welcome break from your everyday course. The greens are nicely sized and deep enough to pose a few problems of club selection.

Golf de Bondues — 1967

Château de la Vigne
F - 59910 BONDUES

Office	Secrétariat	(33) 03 20 23 20 62
Pro shop	Pro-shop	no Pro shop
Fax	Fax	(33) 03 20 23 24 11
E-mail	golfdebondues@nordnet.fr	
Situation	Situation	

Lille (pop. 172 142), 6 km -Tourcoing (pop. 93 760), 4 km

Annual closure	Fermeture annuelle	no
Weekly closure	Fermeture hebdomadaire	

tuesday/mardi

Fees main season Tarifs haute saison	Full day	
	Week days Semaine	**We/Bank holidays** We/Férié
Individual Individuel	30 €	46 €
Couple Couple	46 €	69 €

Caddy	Caddy	no
Electric Trolley	Chariot électrique	no
Buggy	Voiturette	23 € /18 holes
Clubs	Clubs	no

Credit cards Cartes de crédit VISA - CB

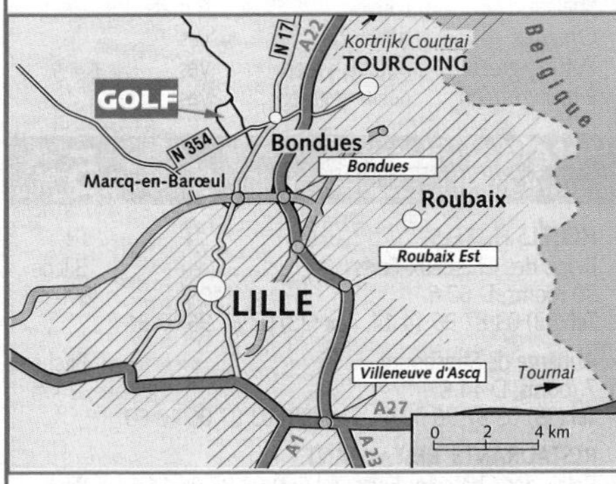

Access Accès : Lille N17, N354, → Golf
Map 1 on page 163 Carte 1 Page 163

Golf course — PARCOURS — 16/20

Site	Site	
Maintenance	Entretien	
Architect	Architecte	R. Trent Jones Sr R. Trent Jones Jr
Type	Type	parkland, residential
Relief	Relief	
Water in play	Eau en jeu	
Exp. to wind	Exposé au vent	
Trees in play	Arbres en jeu	

Scorecard Carte de score	**Chp.** Chp.	**Mens** Mess.	**Ladies** Da.
Length Long.	6009	5470	4551
Par	72	72	72
Slope system	130	125	125

Advised golfing ability Niveau de jeu recommandé — 0 12 24 36

Hcp required Handicap exigé 34

Club house & amenities — CLUB-HOUSE ET ANNEXES — 7/10

Pro shop	Pro-shop	
Driving range	Practice	
Sheltered	couvert	8 mats
On grass	sur herbe	no, 20 mats open air
Putting-green	putting-green	yes
Pitching-green	pitching green	yes

Hotel facilities — ENVIRONNEMENT HOTELIER — 6/10

HOTELS HÔTELS

Sofitel, 125 rooms, D 137 € — Marcq-en-Barœul
Tel (33) 03 20 72 17 30, Fax (33) 03 20 89 92 34 — 5 km

Alliance, 83 rooms, D 145 € — Lille
Tel (33) 03 20 30 62 62, Fax (33) 03 20 42 94 25 — 6 km

Grand Hotel Mercure, 93 rooms, D 90 € — Roubaix
Tel (33) 03 20 73 40 00, Fax (33) 03 20 73 42 42 — 5 km

RESTAURANTS RESTAURANT

L'Huitrière, Tel (33) 03 20 55 43 41 — Lille 6 km

Auberge de la Garenne — Marcq-en-Baroeul
Tel(33) 03 20 46 20 20 — 4 km

Château Blanc, Tel (33) 03 20 21 81 41 — Verlinghem 6 km

BONDUES Jaune

15 | 7 | 6

Bondues est l'un des grands clubs traditionnels de la région lilloise, et d'un accès parfois difficile en week-end. Le parcours "Jaune" est signé Fred Hawtree, dans la pure tradition britannique, avec assez peu d'obstacles d'eau, mais des arbres bien en jeu et des bunkers de dessin sans originalité particulière de forme, mais toujours bien placés. En revanche, il n'est pas très facile de mémoriser le parcours, sans grande personnalité ni recherche esthétique très affirmée. Il n'en est pas plus facile pour autant d'y scorer. Bondues "Jaune" fait partie de ces parcours classiques parfaitement adaptés à leur destination : il a été essentiellement conçu pour ses membres (qui trouvent facilement leurs marques et leurs habitudes) et non pour des voyageurs de passage. Certains le préfèrent d'ailleurs à son voisin. Certes, la région n'est pas vraiment une destination de vacances, mais c'est une halte très intéressante, avec deux parcours complémentaires.

Bondues is one of the great traditional clubs from the Lille region and is sometimes difficult to play on week-ends. The "Jaune" course was designed by Fred Hawtree in the pure British tradition, i.e. few water hazards but trees very much in play and bunkers that, although hardly original in shape and design, are always shrewdly placed. This is not a course that sticks in the memory; it has no clear-cut personality or elaborate style, although that doesn't mean it is any easier to score on. Bondues "Jaune" is one of those classic courses that is perfectly suited to the people it was designed for, i.e. basically club members (who can easily find their landmarks and habits) and not for green-feers passing through. Some people, though, prefer this layout to its neighbour, and while the region is not really a holiday destination, it makes a very interesting stop-off with two complementary layouts.

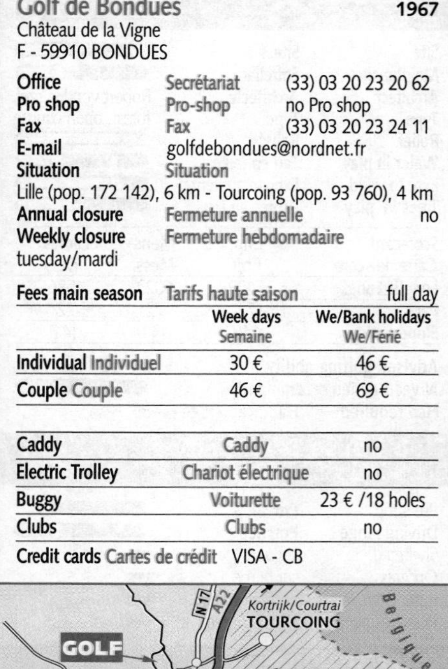

Golf de Bondues — 1967

Château de la Vigne
F - 59910 BONDUES

Office	Secrétariat	(33) 03 20 23 20 62
Pro shop	Pro-shop	no Pro shop
Fax	Fax	(33) 03 20 23 24 11
E-mail	golfdebondues@nordnet.fr	
Situation	Situation	

Lille (pop. 172 142), 6 km - Tourcoing (pop. 93 760), 4 km

Annual closure Fermeture annuelle — no

Weekly closure Fermeture hebdomadaire
tuesday/mardi

Fees main season Tarifs haute saison	full day	
	Week days Semaine	**We/Bank holidays** We/Férié
Individual Individuel	30 €	46 €
Couple Couple	46 €	69 €

Caddy	Caddy	no
Electric Trolley	Chariot électrique	no
Buggy	Voiturette	23 € /18 holes
Clubs	Clubs	no
Credit cards	Cartes de crédit	VISA - CB

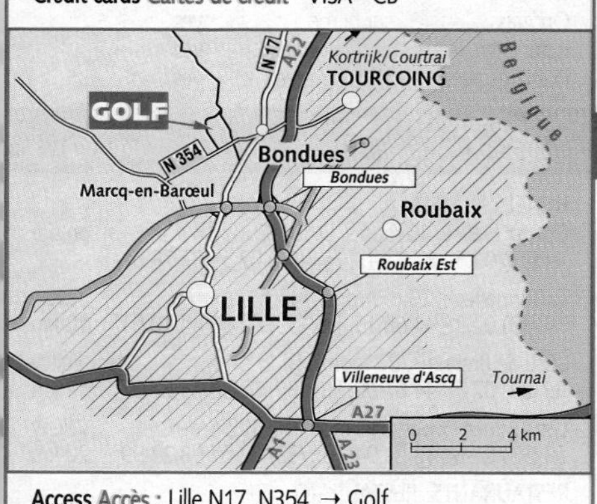

Access Accès : Lille N17, N354, → Golf
Map 1 on page 163 Carte 1 Page 163

Golf course PARCOURS — 15/20

Site	Site	
Maintenance	Entretien	
Architect	Architecte	Frederic Hawtree
Type	Type	parkland, residential
Relief	Relief	
Water in play	Eau en jeu	
Exp. to wind	Exposé au vent	
Trees in play	Arbres en jeu	

Scorecard Carte de score	**Chp.** Chp.	**Mens** Mess.	**Ladies** Da.
Length Long.	6163	5764	4913
Par	73	73	73
Slope system	130	127	125

Advised golfing ability Niveau de jeu recommandé — 0 12 24 36

Hcp required Handicap exigé — 34

Club house & amenities CLUB-HOUSE ET ANNEXES — 7/10

Pro shop	Pro-shop	
Driving range	Practice	
Sheltered	couvert	8 mats
On grass	sur herbe	no, 20 mats open air
Putting-green	putting-green	yes
Pitching-green	pitching green	yes

Hotel facilities ENVIRONNEMENT HOTELIER — 6/10

HOTELS HÔTELS

Sofitel, 125 rooms, D 137 € — Marcq-en-Barœul
Tel (33) 03 20 72 17 30, Fax (33) 03 20 89 92 34 — 5 km

Alliance, 83 rooms, D 145 € — Lille
Tel (33) 03 20 30 62 62, Fax (33) 03 20 42 94 25 — 6 km

Grand Hotel Mercure, 93 rooms, D 90 € — Roubaix
Tel (33) 03 20 73 40 00, Fax (33) 03 20 73 42 42 — 5 km

RESTAURANTS RESTAURANT

L'Huitrière, Tel (33) 03 20 55 43 41 — Lille 6 km

Auberge de la Garenne — Marcq-en-Baroeul
Tel(33) 03 20 46 20 20 — 4 km

Château Blanc, Tel (33) 03 20 21 81 41 — Verlinghem 6 km

BORDES (LES)

19 | 8 | 6

Ce parcours reste incontestablement au premier rang français, et son entretien est revenu au niveau où il était du temps de son fondateur Marcel Bich. Les Bordes fait toujours partie de ces parcours impossibles à ignorer, pour son tracé d'une grande variété de jeu et de stratégie, et pour son environnement : Les Bordes est une initiation à la Sologne, le parcours un lieu de méditation sur la vérité de son propre jeu, où il est impossible de maquiller ses faiblesses. Nos jugements précédents n'ont pas changé : si vous abordez ce parcours avec simplicité, intelligence et surtout humilité, il pourra se montrer généreux, car il ne cache rien de ses difficultés. Le practice, le Club-House, les chambres d'hôtes (il y en a maintenant 40) sont exemplaires. Ici, l'argent investi ne s'étale pas, comme si cet ensemble récent avait des siècles d'existence. Désormais largement ouvert aux membres extérieurs, c'est un "incontournable" du golf, comme une grande adresse gastronomique où le prix du plaisir n'a pas d'importance.

This is still unquestionably one of France's top-rate courses, even more so now that maintenance is back up to the standards set by the course founder, Marcel Bich. Les Bordes is one of those courses you simply have to play for its variety in layout, its ever-changing game strategy and its setting. Les Bordes is an introduction to the Sologne and the course an arena of meditation for the truth about your golfing ability. Any chinks in your game are ruthlessly exposed. Our previous judgments are still valid. If you approach the course with simplicity, intelligence and humility, it can be rewarding because all of its difficulties are there to see. The driving range, club-house and guestrooms (there are now 40 of them) are first-rate. And there are no flashy signs of new money and investment, rather as if this recently-designed course had been around for centuries. Now wide-open to green-feers, Les Bordes is an absolute must and a great address for excellent food. Here, the price you pay for sheer pleasure matters little.

Golf International des Bordes — 1987

F - 41220 SAINT-LAURENT-NOUAN

Office	Secrétariat	(33) 02 54 87 72 13
Pro shop	Pro-shop	(33) 02 54 87 72 13
Fax	Fax	(33) 02 54 87 78 61
Web	www.les.bordes.fr	
Situation	Situation	

Beaugency, 11 km - Orléans (pop. 105 110), 30 km

Annual closure	Fermeture annuelle	no
Weekly closure	Fermeture hebdomadaire	no

Fees main season Tarifs haute saison	18 holes	
	Week days Semaine	**We/Bank holidays** We/Férié
Individual Individuel	69 €	91 €
Couple Couple	122 €	182 €

Seniors: 46 € (Monday-Tuesday/Lundi-Mardi))

Caddy	Caddy	no
Electric Trolley	Chariot électrique	no
Buggy	Voiturette	46 € /18 holes
Clubs	Clubs	30 € /full day

Credit cards Cartes de crédit
VISA - CB - Eurocard - MasterCard - AMEX

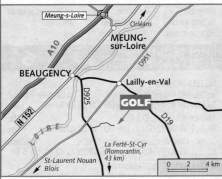

Access Accès : A10 Paris/Blois, Exit (Sortie) Meung-sur-Loire, N152 → Beaugency. In Beaugency → Lailly-en-Val. Cross over the Loire, → La Ferté Saint- Cyr (D925)
Map 3 on page 166 Carte 3 Page 166

Golf course PARCOURS — 19/20

Site	Site	
Maintenance	Entretien	
Architect	Architecte	Robert von Hagge
Type	Type	forest, open country
Relief	Relief	
Water in play	Eau en jeu	
Exp. to wind	Exposé au vent	
Trees in play	Arbres en jeu	

Scorecard Carte de score	**Chp.** Chp.	**Mens** Mess.	**Ladies** Da.
Length Long.	6409	6023	4586
Par	72	72	72
Slope system	148	141	141

Advised golfing ability Niveau de jeu recommandé — 0 12 24 36
Hcp required Handicap exigé — 35

Club house & amenities CLUB-HOUSE ET ANNEXES — 8/10

Pro shop	Pro-shop	
Driving range	Practice	
Sheltered	couvert	no
On grass	sur herbe	yes
Putting-green	putting-green	yes
Pitching-green	pitching green	yes

Hotel facilities ENVIRONNEMENT HOTELIER — 6/10

HOTELS HÔTELS

Dormy House, 40 rooms, D 191 € — on site
Tel (33) 02 54 87 72 13, Fax (33) 02 54 87 78 61

La Tonnellerie, 20 rooms, D 145 € — Tavers 10 km
Tel (33) 02 38 44 68 15, Fax (33) 02 38 44 10 01

L'Ecu de Bretagne, 27 rooms, D 75 € — Beaugency 7 km
Tel (33) 02 38 44 67 60, Fax (33) 02 38 44 68 07

Les Chênes Rouges, 10 rooms, D 122 € — Villeny 20 km
Tel (33) 02 54 98 23 94, Fax (33) 02 54 98 23 99

RESTAURANTS RESTAURANT

P'tit Bateau, Tel (33) 02 38 44 56 38 — Beaugency 11 km
Auberge Gourmande, Tel (33) 02 38 45 01 02 — Baule 16 km

BOULIE (LA) La Vallée

15 | 7 | 8

Le seul véritable reproche que l'on puisse faire à ce parcours, c'est que les arbres ont pris une telle densité depuis les origines que s'ils constituent un bon écran contre l'autoroute voisine, on peut éprouver sinon une sensation de claustrophobie, du moins se trouver à l'étroit. Et les tempêtes de 1999 n'en ont pas abattu assez ! Ce n'est pas fait pour ceux qui aiment les grands espaces, comme ce parcours en présentait au moment de sa construction. Parcours original du Golf de Paris, devenu Golf du Racing-Club de France (le plus grand club omnisports français), "La Vallée" réclame un jeu très complet, des drives puissants et droits, des fers très précis pour des greens souvent assez animés, et une grande maîtrise des coups de rattrapage (balles basses sous les arbres !). Sans oublier les sorties de bunker car ils protègent solidement les greens. Quelques coups aveugles sont ici inévitables en raison du relief général assez prononcé mais sans fatigue excessive (sauf au 9). A connaître, d'autant que l'arrosage a été très amélioré.

The only real reproach you can level at this course is that the trees have grown so thick since its inception that, while now they form an effective sound barrier from the neighbouring motorway, they also create a feeling if not of claustrophobia then at least of having very little space to play in. The storms of December 1999 left too many of them standing! This is not a course for golfers who love wide open expanses, although when first opened this course was full of them. "La Vallée", the original Golf de Paris course and now one of the two courses at the Racing-Club de France (France's biggest all sports club), requires a good all-round game, powerful and straight driving, accurate ironwork for greens that are often bouncy, and mastery in the art of recovery (particularly low shots from under the trees). Not to mention sand shots from bunkers that offer a solid line of defence around the greens. A few blind shots were unavoidable here owing to the sloping terrain, which is hilly but not too tiring (except the 9th). Well worth knowing, especially now that the watering system has been improved.

Golf de La Boulie - Racing Club de France 1901

F - 78000 VERSAILLES

Office	Secrétariat	(33) 01 39 50 59 41
Pro shop	Pro-shop	(33) 01 39 49 92 77
Fax	Fax	(33) 01 39 49 04 16
Web	—	
Situation	Situation	Paris, 22 km
Annual closure	Fermeture annuelle	no
Weekly closure	Fermeture hebdomadaire	

tuesday/mardi

Fees main season Tarifs haute saison		18 holes
	Week days Semaine	**We/Bank holidays** We/Férié
Individual Individuel	61 €	76 € *
Couple Couple	122 €	152 € *

* members' guests (sur invitation d'un membre)

Caddy	Caddy	no
Electric Trolley	Chariot électrique	15 € /18 holes
Buggy	Voiturette	no
Clubs	Clubs	27 € /18 holes

Credit cards Cartes de crédit
VISA - Eurocard - Mastercard - AMEX

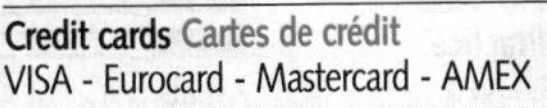

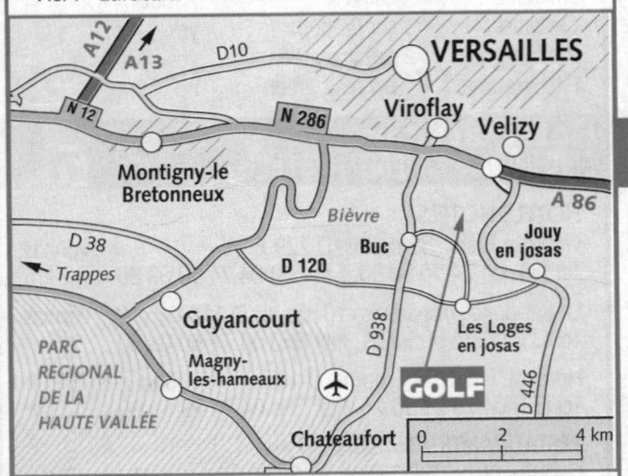

Access Accès : Paris A13 → Rouen, Exit (Sortie) Versailles-Vaucresson. D182 → Versailles, D185 → Château, → Versailles-Chantiers. N186 → Golf.
Map 15 on page 190 Carte 15 Page 190

Golf course PARCOURS 15/20

Site	Site	
Maintenance	Entretien	
Architect	Architecte	unknown
Type	Type	forest
Relief	Relief	
Water in play	Eau en jeu	
Exp. to wind	Exposé au vent	
Trees in play	Arbres en jeu	

Scorecard Carte de score	**Chp.** Chp.	**Mens** Mess.	**Ladies** Da.
Length Long.	5995	5698	5062
Par	72	72	72
Slope system	138	135	138

Advised golfing ability Niveau de jeu recommandé — 0 12 24 36
Hcp required Handicap exigé — 24 Men, 28 Ladies

Club house & amenities CLUB-HOUSE ET ANNEXES 7/10

Pro shop	Pro-shop	
Driving range	Practice	
Sheltered	couvert	15 mats
On grass	sur herbe	no, 5 mats open air
Putting-green	putting-green	yes
Pitching-green	pitching green	yes

Hotel facilities ENVIRONNEMENT HOTELIER 8/10

HOTELS HÔTELS

Trianon Palace, 188 rooms, D 457 € — Versailles 3 km
Tel (33) 01 30 84 38 00, Fax (33) 01 30 84 50 01

Pavillon Trianon, 98 rooms, D 305 € — Versailles
Tel (33) 01 30 84 38 00, Fax (33) 01 30 89 50 01

Résidence du Berry, 38 rooms, D 93 € — Versailles
Tel (33) 01 39 49 07 07, Fax (33) 01 39 50 59 40

RESTAURANTS RESTAURANT

Les Trois Marches — Versailles 3 km
Tel (33) 01 39 50 13 21

La Marée de Versailles, Tel (33) 01 30 21 73 73 — Versailles

Le Potager du Roy, Tel (33) 01 39 50 35 34 — Versailles

BRESSE (LA)

16 | 7 | 5

Au calme et sur un terrain peu fatigant, Jeremy Pern a dessiné un parcours faisant appel à toutes les qualités : puissance, précision du grand jeu, subtilité du petit jeu, finesse du putting. Un peu long quand il est mouillé, il prend toute sa dimension aux beaux jours. Le rythme de jeu est excellent, avec une bonne alternance de trous de plaine et de trous dans les bois, permettant à tous les goûts de trouver leur plaisir. Les golfeurs expérimentés affronteront des défis intéressants, notamment pour leur choix de clubs, mais les joueurs de tous niveaux ne sont jamais vraiment découragés. Les greens, parfois modelés à l'excès, avec peu de positions différentes de drapeaux sont délicats à interpréter, et peuvent "charger la carte" quand on ne parvient pas à les lire. Le Club-House est sympathique, la restauration de bonne qualité est typique d'une région où l'on sait bien manger. L'entretien a été très amélioré, en particulier par le drainage très important. Attention en week-end, les membres n'ont aucune discipline.

In a calm region on flattish terrain, Jeremy Pern has designed a course which requires just about every golfing skill: power and precision off the tee, a sharp and clever short game and slick putting. It might be hard to play in damp conditions, but when the sun shines the course comes into its own. The tempo of play is good here, with pleasantly alternating open-field and woodland holes. In fact, there's something for all tastes. The better golfer will enjoy the opportunity to get to grips with a number of interesting challenges, especially for club selection, but the lesser player will never really feel too despondent, either. The sometimes excessively undulating greens are not always easy to read and can add a few unwelcome strokes to the card when mis-read. Some also have too few different pin positions. The club-house is very pleasant and the food is good... typical, you might suppose, of a region where they know what good food is all about. Maintenance has been much improved, particularly after some extensive drainage work. But watch out for some sloppy etiquette from members on weekends.

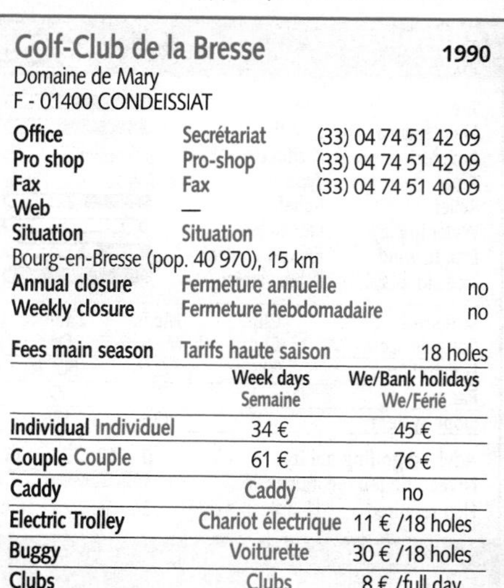

Golf-Club de la Bresse — 1990

Domaine de Mary
F - 01400 CONDEISSIAT

Office	Secrétariat	(33) 04 74 51 42 09
Pro shop	Pro-shop	(33) 04 74 51 42 09
Fax	Fax	(33) 04 74 51 40 09
Web	—	
Situation	Situation	

Bourg-en-Bresse (pop. 40 970), 15 km

Annual closure	Fermeture annuelle	no
Weekly closure	Fermeture hebdomadaire	no

234

Fees main season Tarifs haute saison	18 holes	
	Week days Semaine	**We/Bank holidays** We/Férié
Individual Individuel	34 €	45 €
Couple Couple	61 €	76 €
Caddy	Caddy	no
Electric Trolley	Chariot électrique	11 € /18 holes
Buggy	Voiturette	30 € /18 holes
Clubs	Clubs	8 € /full day

Credit cards Cartes de crédit
VISA - CB - Eurocard - MasterCard - AMEX

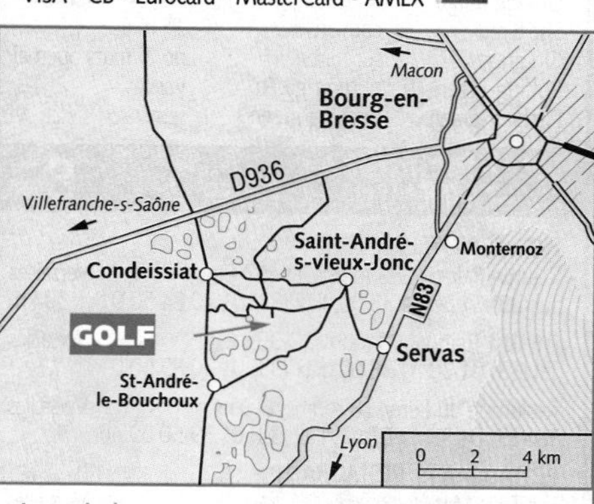

Access Accès : • Lyon, N83 → Bourg-en-Bresse. Servas, → Condeissiat • Mâcon A40, Exit (Sortie) Bourg-en-Bresse Nord, D936 → Châtillon-sur-Chalaronne, on the left, Condeissiat → Servas **Map 11 on page 182** Carte 11 Page 182

Golf course PARCOURS — 16/20

Site	Site	
Maintenance	Entretien	
Architect	Architecte	Jeremy Pern
Type	Type	open country, forest
Relief	Relief	
Water in play	Eau en jeu	
Exp. to wind	Exposé au vent	
Trees in play	Arbres en jeu	

Scorecard Carte de score	**Chp.** Chp.	**Mens** Mess.	**Ladies** Da.
Length Long.	6177	5707	4825
Par	72	72	72
Slope system	128	123	124

Advised golfing ability 0 12 24 36
Niveau de jeu recommandé

Hcp required Handicap exigé no

Club house & amenities CLUB-HOUSE ET ANNEXES — 7/10

Pro shop	Pro-shop	
Driving range	Practice	
Sheltered	couvert	7 mats
On grass	sur herbe	yes
Putting-green	putting-green	yes
Pitching-green	pitching green	no

Hotel facilities ENVIRONNEMENT HOTELIER — 5/10

HOTELS HÔTELS

Georges Blanc, 59 rooms, D 229 € — Vonnas
Tel (33) 04 74 50 90 90, Fax (33) 04 74 50 08 80 — 7 km

La Résidence des Saules, 10 rooms, D 114 € — Vonnas
Tel (33) 04 74 50 90 51, Fax (33) 04 74 50 08 80

Hôtel de France, 44 rooms, D 105 € — Bourg-en-Bresse
Tel (33) 04 74 23 30 24, Fax (33) 04 74 23 69 90 — 12 km

RESTAURANTS RESTAURANT

Georges Blanc, Tel (33) 04 74 50 90 90 — Vonnas 7 km

Chez Rolande, Tel (33) 04 74 51 43 08 — Condeissiat 3 km

Auberge Bressane — Bourg-en-Bresse
Tel (33) 04 74 22 22 68 — 15 km

BREST IROISE

14 | 7 | 6

Tracé en paysage de landes, ce golf est le plus occidental de France. Michael Fenn y a dessiné un parcours épousant un terrain qui se prêtait bien à la construction d'un golf, avec un certain nombre de dénivellations pour rompre la monotonie. Elles permettent d'offrir de beaux points de vue sur la campagne et les Monts d'Arée. Le paysage - sinon le jeu - est agrémenté d'une végétation rustique et dense, de genêts et de gros rochers. De longueur raisonnable, il est accessible à tous les niveaux, avec des greens généralement très fermes, et bien défendus par des bunkers au dessin cependant sans grande subtilité. L'entretien a progressé, grâce à d'importants travaux de drainage, mais reste assez inégal tout au long de l'année, et quelques modifications ont fait perdre un peu de caractère au parcours. Le Club-House fait partie de l'hôtel, bien rafraîchi, Brest Iroise devient une bonne destination de week-end, avec la réouverture d'un 9 trous.

Laid out amidst heath and moor-land, this is France's western-most course. Michael Fenn has designed a layout that hugs terrain which was almost made for golf, with a number of slopes to break the monotony. This gives some fine views over the country and the Monts d'Arée. The landscape, and the round, are enhanced with some thick country bush, gorse-bushes and rocks. Reasonable in length, this is a course for golfers of all standards who will enjoy greens that are generally hard and well defended by some pretty ordinary bunkers. Maintenance has improved thanks to some extensive drainage work but is inconsistent throughout the year. Also, a few changes made have detracted from the course's character. The club-house is now part of the totally refurbished Golf hotel, and with the re-opening of a 9-hole course, Brest Iroise is now a good week-end destination.

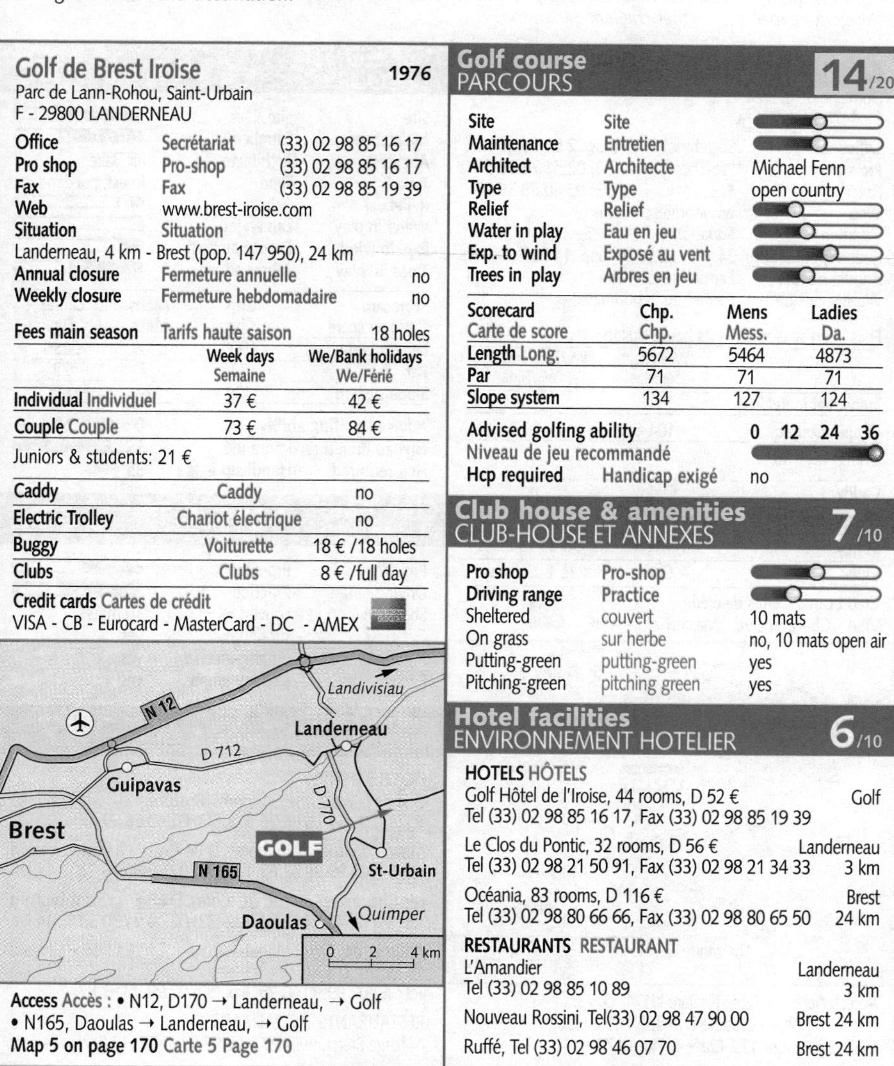

Golf de Brest Iroise — 1976

Parc de Lann-Rohou, Saint-Urbain
F - 29800 LANDERNEAU

Office	Secrétariat	(33) 02 98 85 16 17
Pro shop	Pro-shop	(33) 02 98 85 16 17
Fax	Fax	(33) 02 98 85 19 39
Web	www.brest-iroise.com	
Situation	Situation	

Landerneau, 4 km - Brest (pop. 147 950), 24 km

Annual closure	Fermeture annuelle	no
Weekly closure	Fermeture hebdomadaire	no

Fees main season Tarifs haute saison	18 holes	
	Week days Semaine	**We/Bank holidays** We/Férié
Individual Individuel	37 €	42 €
Couple Couple	73 €	84 €

Juniors & students: 21 €

Caddy	Caddy	no
Electric Trolley	Chariot électrique	no
Buggy	Voiturette	18 € /18 holes
Clubs	Clubs	8 € /full day

Credit cards Cartes de crédit
VISA - CB - Eurocard - MasterCard - DC - AMEX

Access Accès : • N12, D170 → Landerneau, → Golf
• N165, Daoulas → Landerneau, → Golf
Map 5 on page 170 Carte 5 Page 170

Golf course PARCOURS — 14/20

Site	Site	
Maintenance	Entretien	
Architect	Architecte	Michael Fenn
Type	Type	open country
Relief	Relief	
Water in play	Eau en jeu	
Exp. to wind	Exposé au vent	
Trees in play	Arbres en jeu	

Scorecard Carte de score	**Chp.** Chp.	**Mens** Mess.	**Ladies** Da.
Length Long.	5672	5464	4873
Par	71	71	71
Slope system	134	127	124

Advised golfing ability 0 12 24 36
Niveau de jeu recommandé

Hcp required Handicap exigé no

Club house & amenities CLUB-HOUSE ET ANNEXES — 7/10

Pro shop	Pro-shop	
Driving range	Practice	
Sheltered	couvert	10 mats
On grass	sur herbe	no, 10 mats open air
Putting-green	putting-green	yes
Pitching-green	pitching green	yes

Hotel facilities ENVIRONNEMENT HOTELIER — 6/10

HOTELS HÔTELS

Golf Hôtel de l'Iroise, 44 rooms, D 52 € — Golf
Tel (33) 02 98 85 16 17, Fax (33) 02 98 85 19 39

Le Clos du Pontic, 32 rooms, D 56 € — Landerneau 3 km
Tel (33) 02 98 21 50 91, Fax (33) 02 98 21 34 33

Océania, 83 rooms, D 116 € — Brest 24 km
Tel (33) 02 98 80 66 66, Fax (33) 02 98 80 65 50

RESTAURANTS RESTAURANT

L'Amandier — Landerneau 3 km
Tel (33) 02 98 85 10 89

Nouveau Rossini, Tel(33) 02 98 47 90 00 — Brest 24 km

Ruffé, Tel (33) 02 98 46 07 70 — Brest 24 km

BRETESCHE (LA)

15 | 7 | 7

On aimerait un restyling complet du parcours car le site est de grande qualité. L'environnement de parc est très joli, le château séduisant pour les français, mais aussi les étrangers : ce lieu typique d'une certaine idée de la France plaît beaucoup. Le parcours manquant un peu de longueur, on souhaiterait des greens mieux travaillés et défendus, dont l'approche soit un peu plus exigeante quand on les attaque avec des petits fers. Car ce n'est pas la difficulté technique qui inspirera pour sublimer son jeu. S'il est difficile de souligner un quelconque aspect surprenant du parcours, sinon l'habituel trou en boomerang (le 16 ici) de l'architecte Bill Baker, le plaisir d'évoluer sur ce parcours bien entretenu est certain. Le dessin des trous est honorable, les greens et bunkers sans grosses difficultés, leurs défenses raisonnables. Cela fait donc un parcours sans danger et très plaisant pour y évoluer en famille, et pour la majorité des joueurs, d'autant l'ensemble est très soigné. Les meilleurs attendent des défis plus décisifs.

We would like to see this course completely restyled, because the site is a beauty. The park's surroundings are pretty and the castle appealing to both the French and foreigners, who see this as representing a typical picture of France. Since this is a shortish course, we would like to see better designed and better-guarded greens, calling for a more demanding approach shot when hitting short irons into the green. Here, it is definitely not the technical difficulty that will inspire golfers to better things. While it is difficult to underline any one surprising aspect of the course, excepting the usual boomerang hole by architect Bill Baker (the 16th), the pleasure of playing here on a well-manicured course is obvious. The holes are pleasantly laid out, and the greens and bunkers are none too difficult and reasonably well-protected. All in all, this gives a course without too much danger which is fun to play with all the family and players of almost every ability, especially since the whole complex is a very slick affair. The better golfer expects a tougher challenge than this.

Golf de la Bretesche — 1967

Domaine de la Bretesche
F - 44780 MISSILLAC

Office	Secrétariat	(33) 02 51 76 86 86
Pro shop	Pro-shop	(33) 02 51 76 86 86
Fax	Fax	(33) 02 40 88 36 28
Web	www.bretesche.com	
Situation	Situation	

Redon (pop. 9 260), 24 km - La Baule (pop. 14 850), 30 km

Annual closure	Fermeture annuelle	no
Weekly closure	Fermeture hebdomadaire	no

236

Fees main season Tarifs haute saison	18 holes	
	Week days Semaine	**We/Bank holidays** We/Férié
Individual Individuel	52 €	52 €
Couple Couple	104 €	104 €
Under 18: 180		

Caddy	Caddy	no
Electric Trolley	Chariot électrique	no
Buggy	Voiturette	38 € /18 holes
Clubs	Clubs	15 € /full day

Credit cards Cartes de crédit
VISA - CB - Eurocard - MasterCard - AMEX

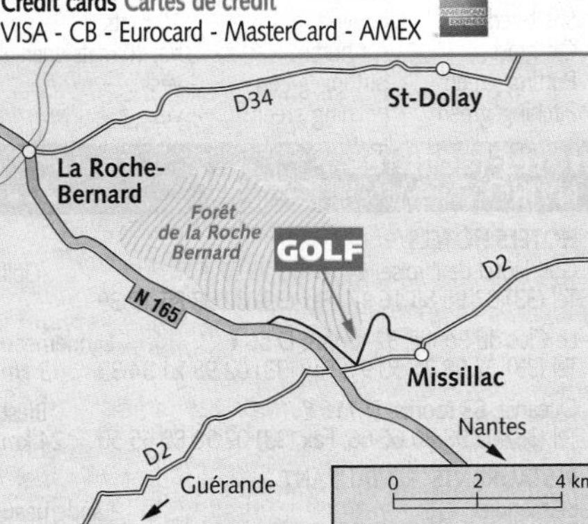

Access Accès : • Saint-Nazaire N171, D773, N165 → Golf • La Baule D774, N165 → Golf
Map 6 on page 172 Carte 6 Page 172

Golf course PARCOURS — 15/20

Site	Site	
Maintenance	Entretien	
Architect	Architecte	Bill Baker
Type	Type	forest, parkland
Relief	Relief	
Water in play	Eau en jeu	
Exp. to wind	Exposé au vent	
Trees in play	Arbres en jeu	

Scorecard Carte de score	**Chp.** Chp.	**Mens** Mess.	**Ladies** Da.
Length Long.	6080	5809	5136
Par	72	72	72
Slope system	129	124	125

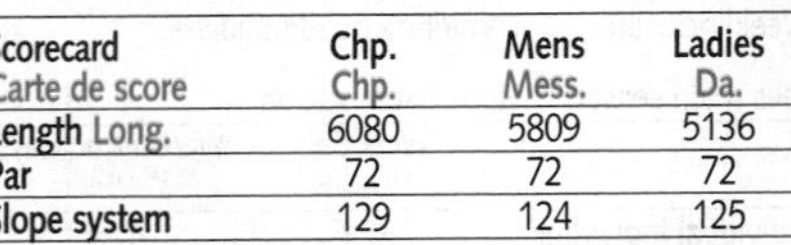

Advised golfing ability Niveau de jeu recommandé — 0 12 24 36
Hcp required Handicap exigé — 35

Club house & amenities CLUB-HOUSE ET ANNEXES — 7/10

Pro shop	Pro-shop	
Driving range	Practice	
Sheltered	couvert	10 mats
On grass	sur herbe	yes
Putting-green	putting-green	yes
Pitching-green	pitching green	yes

Hotel facilities ENVIRONNEMENT HOTELIER — 7/10

HOTELS HÔTELS

Golf de la Bretesche, 31 rooms, D 183 € — on site
Tel (33) 02 51 76 86 96, Fax (33) 02 40 66 99 47

Manoir du Rodoir, 26 rooms, D 84 € — La Roche Bernard 11 km
Tel (33) 02 99 90 82 68, Fax (33) 02 99 90 76 22

Les Chaumières du Lac, 20 rooms, D 88 € — Saint-Lyphard 14 km
Tel (33) 02 40 91 32 32, Fax (33) 02 40 91 30 33

Auberge des Deux Magots — La Roche Bernard 11 km
15 rooms, D 73 €
Tel (33) 02 99 90 60 75, Fax (33) 02 99 90 87 87

RESTAURANTS RESTAURANT

Auberge Bretonne, Tel (33) 02 99 90 60 28 — La Roche-Bernard

BRIGODE

14 | 7 | 6

Ce parcours signé Harold Baker est l'un des grands clubs traditionnels des Lillois, dont beaucoup y ont élu résidence, mais l'impression d'un golf immobilier n'est pas trop pesante car les maisons sont de bonne qualité. Assez plat, quelques obstacles d'eau, un bon nombre de bunkers, et les arbres lui donnent des allures de grand parc à la britannique, d'allure assez harmonieuse et séduisante, avec assez de maturité pour ne plus vraiment bouger. Dans cet environnement, c'est un parcours aussi agréable pour les joueurs de bon niveau que pour les joueurs moyens. Certes, ce n'est pas un test d'une énorme difficulté, l'architecture est restée sobre, peut-être même un peu timide, mais on a visiblement recherché à favoriser le plaisir du jeu en famille. Un vrai "golf de membres" où les golfeurs de passage seront mieux accueillis en semaine, les week-ends étant souvent chargés.

This Harold Baker course is one of the great traditional clubs of Lille and many people have bought homes here, although the quality standard of houses fortunately rules out any great impression of this being a property development course. Being rather flat, with a few water hazards and a good number of bunkers, Brigode looks like a British park, at once harmonious and attractive, and mature enough to stay the way it is for ever. In this setting, the course is pleasant for skilled and less skilful golfers alike. It is certainly not too tough a test for the better golfer, as the architecture is unobtrusive and even a little on the shy side, but the designers visibly were looking to promote the pleasure of family golfing. This is a real "members' club" where green-feers get a warmer welcome during the week. Week-ends are often heavily booked.

Golf de Brigode — 1967

36, avenue du Golf
F - 59650 VILLENEUVE-D'ASCQ

Office	Secrétariat	(33) 03 20 91 17 86
Pro shop	Pro-shop	no Pro shop
Fax	Fax	(33) 03 20 05 96 36
E-mail	brigode@free.fr	
Situation	Situation	Lille (pop. 172 142), 11 km
Annual closure	Fermeture annuelle	no
Weekly closure	Fermeture hebdomadaire	tuesday (mardi)

Fees main season Tarifs haute saison	**Week days** Semaine	**We/Bank holidays** We/Férié
	Full day	
Individual Individuel	30 €	46 €
Couple Couple	60 €	92 €
Caddy Caddy	no	
Electric Trolley Chariot électrique	no	
Buggy Voiturette	30 € /18 holes	
Clubs Clubs	8 € /18 holes	

Credit cards Cartes de crédit
VISA - CB - Eurocard - MasterCard

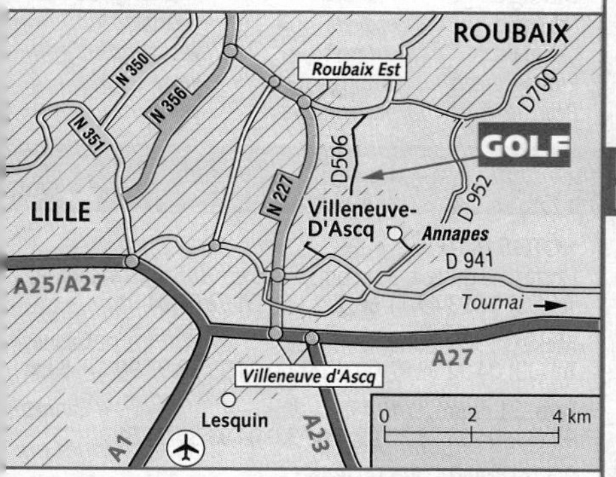

Access Accès : "Rocade" Paris-Gand • Paris/Lille, Exit (Sortie) Pont de Bois → Annappes-cousinerie • Gand-Tourcoing, Exit (Sortie) Roubaix-Est, 1 km on the right → Annappes. 2 km, in front of Stadium → Golf **Map 1 on page 163** Carte 1 Page 163

Golf course — PARCOURS — 14/20

Site	Site	
Maintenance	Entretien	
Architect	Architecte	Bill Baker
Type	Type	parkland
Relief	Relief	
Water in play	Eau en jeu	
Exp. to wind	Exposé au vent	
Trees in play	Arbres en jeu	

Scorecard Carte de score	**Chp.** Chp.	**Mens** Mess.	**Ladies** Da.
Length Long.	6010	5628	4780
Par	72	72	72
Slope system	134	132	124

Advised golfing ability Niveau de jeu recommandé: 0 12 24 36
Hcp required Handicap exigé: 30

Club house & amenities — CLUB-HOUSE ET ANNEXES — 7/10

Pro shop	Pro-shop	
Driving range	Practice	
Sheltered	couvert	6 mats
On grass	sur herbe	no, 34 mats open air
Putting-green	putting-green	yes
Pitching-green	pitching green	no

Hotel facilities — ENVIRONNEMENT HOTELIER — 6/10

HOTELS HÔTELS

Alliance, 83 rooms, D 145 € — Lille
Tel (33) 03 20 30 62 62, Fax (33) 03 20 42 94 25 — 11 km

Mercure Lille-Centre, 99 rooms, D 107 € — Lille
Tel (33) 03 20 14 71 47, Fax (33) 03 20 14 71 48 — 11 km

Campanile, 46 rooms, D 52 € — Villeneuve-d'Ascq
Tel (33) 03 20 91 83 10, Fax (33) 03 20 67 21 18 — 1 km

RESTAURANTS RESTAURANT

L'Huitrière, Tel (33) 03 20 55 43 41 — Lille 11 km

La Cour des Grands, Tel (33) 03 20 06 83 61 — Lille 11 km

Champlain, Tel (33) 03 20 54 01 38 — Lille 11 km

CANNES MANDELIEU Old Course 14 | 7 | 8

Si personne ne sait qui a dessiné le 18 trous original de Mandelieu, on sait que le grand architecte Harry Colt a participé à son remaniement, comme en témoigne la forme des bunkers, parfois assez profonds pour poser problème aux joueurs moyens. Pourtant, ce sont les pins parasols qui constituent les principaux obstacles, leur envergure impressionnante rendant bien étroits les fairways. Les techniciens adorent ce parcours, car la plupart des coups de départ demandent des effets de fade ou de draw, un contrôle précis des trajectoires, un choix de club très subtil pour se retrouver en bonne position et signer les birdies que l'on peut espérer. Si sa longueur ne répond plus tout à fait aux exigences du jeu moderne, Cannes-Mandelieu reste un parcours de charme, où les par 3 (il y en a cinq) y sont d'une remarquable diversité. Le rajeunissement paraît porter ses fruits, mais n'est pas encore achevé, et il reste à faire pour stabiliser l'entretien au meilleur niveau, en permanence.

While no-one knows exactly who laid out the original 18 holes at Mandelieu, we do know that the great Harry Colt had a hand in re-designing the course, as seen in the shape of the bunkers that are sometimes deep enough to cause high-handicappers real problems. Yet the main hazards here are the huge parasol pines, which stretch majestically upward and outward and make a number of fairways a little on the tight side. The more technically-minded golfers love this course, because the majority of tee-shots require draws or fades, precise flight control and very careful club selection to get into the right position to line up the birdies we all hope and pray for. While not as long as the modern game might require, Cannes-Mandelieu remains a charming course, where the five par 3s are all remarkably different. Restyling work seems to be having the right effect but is ongoing, and work is still needed to keep course maintenance consistently at the highest level.

Cannes Mandelieu Old Course — 1891

Route du Golf
F - 06210 MANDELIEU

Office	Secrétariat	(33) 04 92 97 32 00
Pro shop	Pro-shop	(33) 04 92 97 32 00
Fax	Fax	(33) 04 93 49 92 90
Web	www.golfoldcourse.com	
Situation	Situation	

Cannes (pop. 68 670), 5 km

Annual closure	Fermeture annuelle	no
Weekly closure	Fermeture hebdomadaire	no

Fees main season Tarifs haute saison		full day
	Week days Semaine	**We/Bank holidays** We/Férié
Individual Individuel	59 €	59 €
Couple Couple	118 €	118 €
Caddy	Caddy	no
Electric Trolley	Chariot électrique	no
Buggy	Voiturette	34 € /18 holes
Clubs	Clubs	23 € /18 holes

Credit cards Cartes de crédit
VISA - CB - Eurocard - MasterCard - AMEX

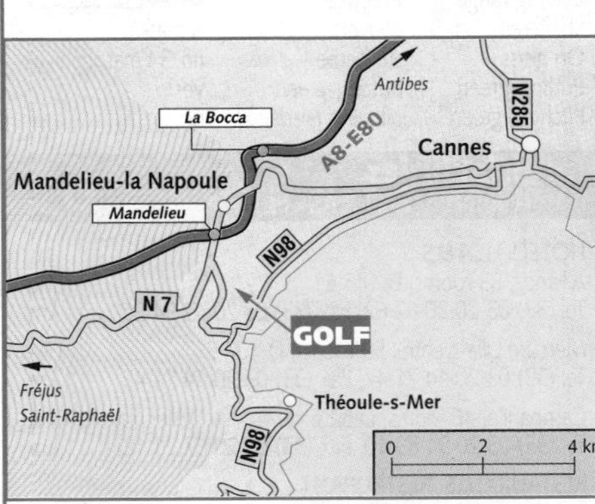

Access Accès : A8 Exit (Sortie) Mandelieu-La Napoule, → Mandelieu, → "Old Course"
Map 14 on page 189 Carte 14 Page 189

Golf course PARCOURS — 14/20

Site	Site	
Maintenance	Entretien	
Architect	Architecte	Harry Colt
Type	Type	seaside course, forest
Relief	Relief	
Water in play	Eau en jeu	
Exp. to wind	Exposé au vent	
Trees in play	Arbres en jeu	

Scorecard Carte de score	**Chp.** Chp.	**Mens** Mess.	**Ladies** Da.
Length Long.	5745	5520	4999
Par	71	71	71
Slope system	121	122	122

Advised golfing ability Niveau de jeu recommandé — 0 12 24 36
Hcp required Handicap exigé 28

Club house & amenities CLUB-HOUSE ET ANNEXES — 7/10

Pro shop	Pro-shop	
Driving range	Practice	
Sheltered	couvert	10 mats
On grass	sur herbe	yes
Putting-green	putting-green	yes
Pitching-green	pitching green	yes

Hotel facilities ENVIRONNEMENT HOTELIER — 8/10

HOTELS HÔTELS

Hostellerie du golf, 39 rooms, D 85 € — Mandelieu
Tel (33) 04 93 49 11 66, Fax (33) 04 92 97 04 01

Majestic, 305 rooms, D 457 € — Cannes 5 km
Tel (33) 04 92 98 77 00, Fax (33) 04 93 38 97 90

Paris, 51 rooms, D 103 € — Cannes
Tel (33) 04 93 38 30 89, Fax (33) 04 93 39 04 61

RESTAURANTS RESTAURANT

La Palme d'Or, Tel (33) 04 92 98 74 14 — Cannes 5 km
Arcimboldo, Tel (33) 04 93 94 14 15 — Cannes
Villa des Lys (Majestic), Tel (33) 04 92 98 77 00 — Cannes

CANNES-MOUGINS

15 | 7 | 8

Longtemps le club le plus prestigieux et le mieux entretenu de la région, il s'est un peu endormi face à la concurrence, mais paraît vouloir retrouver son prestige. Sa séduction apparente dissimule ses réelles difficultés. Les obstacles d'eau ne sont pas nombreux, mais ils sont placés de manière très stratégique. Si on peut avoir l'impression de pouvoir signer un bon score, le parcours résiste bien, notamment parce qu'il est difficile de récupérer le par quand on a manqué un green. Très divers dans son tracé, très bien paysagé, il ne récompense que les meilleurs, et surtout les techniciens du golf, les manieurs de balles. Pendant plus de dix ans, Cannes-Mougins a servi de cadre à un Open européen, ce qui a contribué à améliorer la qualité du terrain et à imposer des transformations. La grandeur passée de Cannes-Mougins revit parfois ici mais l'accueil est rarement chaleureux, et certains travaux fait par des locaux sur le parcours sont d'un intérêt très discutable.

For many a year the region's most prestigious and best-maintained golf course, Cannes-Mougins has of late been caught napping by its rivals and only now seems to be striving to recover its prestige. The course's outer appeal tends to hide the real difficulties. There are not many water hazards, but they are strategically placed. And while signing for a good score might look a possibility, the course always fights back, especially since saving par can be so hard when you miss a green. Full of variety and nicely landscaped, this course rewards only the best, and especially skilled flighters of the ball. Cannes-Mougins has hosted a European Open event for more than 10 years, which has helped to improve the quality of the course and led to necessary changes. You sometimes get glimpses of the past greatness of Cannes-Mougins, but there is rarely a warm welcome to be had here. In addition, some of the work carried out by the locals on the course seems highly questionable.

Golf Country Club de Cannes Mougins 1978

175, Avenue du Golf
F - 06250 MOUGINS

Office	Secrétariat	(33) 04 93 75 79 13
Pro shop	Pro-shop	(33) 04 93 75 53 32
Fax	Fax	(33) 04 93 75 27 60
Web	—	
Situation	Situation	
Cannes (pop. 68 670), 9 km		
Annual closure	Fermeture annuelle	no
Weekly closure	Fermeture hebdomadaire	no

Fees main season Tarifs haute saison		18 holes
	Week days Semaine	**We/Bank holidays** We/Férié
Individual Individuel	69 €	76 €
Couple Couple	138 €	152 €
Juniors: 37 €		
Caddy	Caddy	no
Electric Trolley	Chariot électrique	no
Buggy	Voiturette	43 € /18 holes
Clubs	Clubs	23 € /18 holes

Credit cards Cartes de crédit
VISA - CB - Eurocard - MasterCard - AMEX

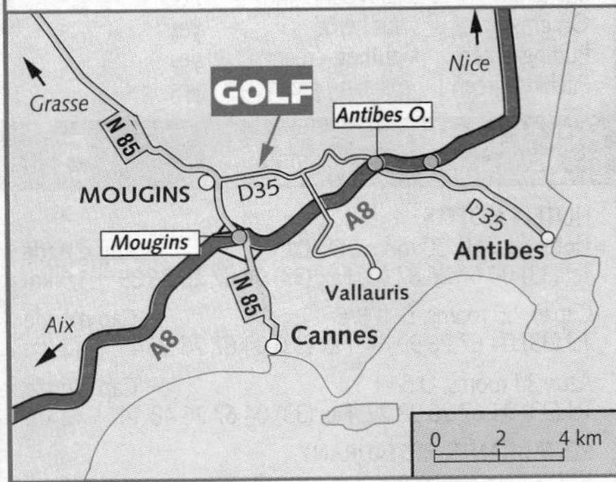

Access Accès : A8. Exit (Sortie) Mougins, → Grasse, Exit (Sortie) Antibes, → Golf
Map 14 on page 189 Carte 14 Page 189

Golf course PARCOURS 15/20

Site	Site	
Maintenance	Entretien	
Architect	Architecte	Peter Alliss Dave Thomas
Type	Type	forest, parkland
Relief	Relief	
Water in play	Eau en jeu	
Exp. to wind	Exposé au vent	
Trees in play	Arbres en jeu	

Scorecard Carte de score	**Chp.** Chp.	**Mens** Mess.	**Ladies** Da.
Length Long.	6207	5823	5017
Par	72	72	72
Slope system	135	129	125

Advised golfing ability Niveau de jeu recommandé — 0 12 24 36
Hcp required Handicap exigé — 24 Men, 28 Ladies

Club house & amenities CLUB-HOUSE ET ANNEXES 7/10

Pro shop	Pro-shop	
Driving range	Practice	
Sheltered	couvert	5 mats
On grass	sur herbe	no, 20 mats open air
Putting-green	putting-green	yes
Pitching-green	pitching green	yes

Hotel facilities ENVIRONNEMENT HOTELIER 8/10

HOTELS HÔTELS

Hôtel de Mougins, 51 rooms, D 221 € — Mougins
Tel (33) 04 92 92 17 07, Fax (33) 04 92 92 17 08

Les Muscadins, 11 rooms, D 213 € — Mougins 5 km
Tel (33) 04 92 28 28 28, Fax (33) 04 92 92 88 23

Le Manoir de l'Etang, 15 rooms, D 122 € — Mougins 5 km
Tel (33) 04 92 28 36 00, Fax (33) 04 92 28 36 10

RESTAURANTS RESTAURANT

Les Muscadins, Tel (33) 04 92 28 28 28 — Mougins 5 km
Le Moulin de Mougins, Tel (33) 04 93 75 78 24 — Mougins
L'Amandier de Mougins, Tel (33) 04 93 90 00 91 — Mougins

CAP D'AGDE

15 | 6 | 5

Le dessin de Ronald Fream reste de grande qualité, mais les abords immédiats des fairways sont toujours trop rocailleux, ce qui pose quelques problèmes quand on y envoie sa balle. Tous les trous demandent une bonne dose de réflexion avant de prendre les risques nécessaires pour espérer un bon score. Même si les obstacles sont bien visibles, leur nombre et leur placement stratégique poseront des problèmes aux débutants. Les joueurs moyens s'en sortiront mieux, et les frappeurs devront être d'une grande précision, surtout quand le vent souffle, ce qui arrive assez souvent ici. Une belle réussite architecturale, mais qui exigerait un entretien parfait et des travaux d'aménagement à proximité des fairways. La station balnéaire de Cap d'Agde est très proche et pas bien belle, mais sa présence n'est pas trop envahissante, grâce aux modelages du parcours, et à une certaine végétation.

This layout, designed by Ronald Fream, is excellent, but the areas immediately skirting the fairways are still too rocky and so pose a few problems for wayward shots. All the holes here require careful thought before taking the risks required if you hope to card a good score. Even though most hazards are there to be seen, their number and strategic placement might be a little too much for beginners. Mid-handicappers should get by a little easier, although big-hitters should aim for precision, especially when the wind blows as it does fairly often. In architectural terms this is an impressive site, but one which requires perfect maintenance and development work close to the fairways. The seaside resort of Cap d'Agde is close by and hardly the most beautiful sight on earth, but the way the course is contoured and the vegetation keep most of it out of view.

Golf du Cap d'Agde — 1989

4, avenue des Alizés
F - 34300 CAP D'AGDE

Office	Secrétariat	(33) 04 67 26 54 40
Pro shop	Pro-shop	(33) 04 67 26 54 40
Fax	Fax	(33) 04 67 26 97 00
Web	www.surfrance.com/golf/capdagde.asp	
Situation	Situation	

Béziers (pop. 71 000), 22 km

Annual closure	Fermeture annuelle	no
Weekly closure	Fermeture hebdomadaire	no

Fees main season Tarifs haute saison	Week days Semaine	We/Bank holidays We/Férié (18 holes)
Individual Individuel	41 €	41 €
Couple Couple	82 €	82 €

Caddy	Caddy	no
Electric Trolley	Chariot électrique	no
Buggy	Voiturette	21 € /18 holes
Clubs	Clubs	9 € /full day

Credit cards Cartes de crédit
VISA - CB - Eurocard - MasterCard

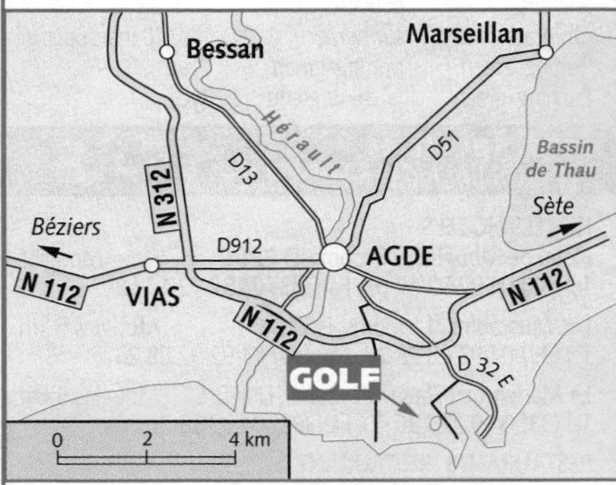

Access Accès : A9 Exit (Sortie) 34 → Agde, → "Ile des Loisirs", golf in front of "Aqualand"
Map 13 on page 187 Carte 13 Page 187

Golf course PARCOURS — 15/20

Site	Site	
Maintenance	Entretien	
Architect	Architecte	Ronald Fream
Type	Type	seaside course, open country
Relief	Relief	
Water in play	Eau en jeu	
Exp. to wind	Exposé au vent	
Trees in play	Arbres en jeu	

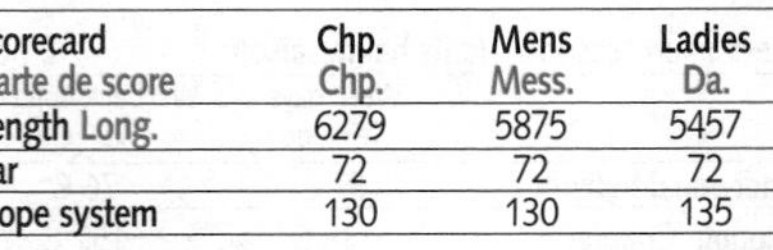

Scorecard Carte de score	Chp. Chp.	Mens Mess.	Ladies Da.
Length Long.	6279	5875	5457
Par	72	72	72
Slope system	130	130	135

Advised golfing ability 0 12 24 36
Niveau de jeu recommandé
Hcp required Handicap exigé no

Club house & amenities CLUB-HOUSE ET ANNEXES — 6/10

Pro shop	Pro-shop	
Driving range	Practice	
Sheltered	couvert	no
On grass	sur herbe	yes
Putting-green	putting-green	yes
Pitching-green	pitching green	yes

Hotel facilities ENVIRONNEMENT HOTELIER — 5/10

HOTELS HÔTELS

Hôtel du Golf, 50 rooms, D 101 € — Cap d'Agde
Tel (33) 04 67 26 87 03, Fax (33) 04 67 26 26 89 — 1,5 km

Capaô, 55 rooms, D 103 € — Cap d'Agde
Tel (33) 04 67 26 99 44, Fax (33) 04 67 26 55 41 — 2 km

Azur, 34 rooms, D 54 € — Cap d'Agde
Tel (33) 04 67 26 98 22, Fax (33) 04 67 26 48 14 — 2 km

RESTAURANTS RESTAURANT

La Tamarissière, Tel (33) 04 67 94 20 87 — Agde 2 km
La Table d'Emilie, — Marseillan 6 km
Tel (33) 04 67 77 63 59

CÉLY

15 | 7 | 6

Dessiné par Fromanger et Adam, ce parcours a été remodelé à la suite de son achat par un groupe japonais, il est alors devenu un véritable jardin, très paysagé, où le moindre détail était autrefois très soigné, un peu moins aujourd'hui. Longtemps célèbre par un Club house luxueux et un entretien éblouissant, digne de véritables manucures, il a subi quelques revers financiers et ces avantages se sont aujourd'hui estompés, révélant les insuffisances du tracé. C'est un très agréable parcours, mais il manque de longueur et de difficultés stratégiques pour passionner les joueurs de bon niveau. Son tracé est plaisant, les attaques de green sont très intéressantes, les trous sont de profils variés, mais il manque sans doute un zeste de génie et de "souffle" pour en faire un "grand" parcours. Jouer Cély est à recommander, le jouer souvent est une autre question. Un regret, le bruit de l'autoroute toute proche.

Originally designed by Fromanger and Adam, Cély has been restyled further to a buy-out by a Japanese group. It is now very much a landscaped garden in style, once perfectly manicured, now a little less so. Famous for its luxurious club-house and beautifully kept fairways and greens, the club has met with a few financial difficulties and these features have lost some of their shine, revealing in the process some of the layout's shortcomings. This is a very pleasant course, but it lacks the length and strategic complexity to excite the best players. The layout is pleasing with some interesting approach shots to the greens, and the holes offer variety enough, but it is almost certainly lacks that touch of genius and the staying power to be a truly great course. A round of golf at Cély is to be recommended, but playing it often is another matter. The one drawback is the noise from the adjacent A6 motorway.

Cély Golf Club — 1990

Château de Cély, route de Saint-Germain
F - 77930 CELY-EN-BIERE

Office	Secrétariat	(33) 01 64 38 03 07
Pro shop	Pro-shop	(33) 01 64 38 03 07
Fax	Fax	(33) 01 64 38 08 78
E-mail	cely.golf.club@wanadoo.fr	
Situation	Situation	Fontainebleau, 14 km
Annual closure	Fermeture annuelle	no
Weekly closure	Fermeture hebdomadaire	no

Fees main season Tarifs haute saison		full day
	Week days Semaine	**We/Bank holidays** We/Férié
Individual Individuel	34 €	53 €
Couple Couple	55 €	90 €

Under 25: 100 (Weekdays), 23 € (We) - Seniors 41 € (GF + lunch, Weekdays)

Caddy	Caddy	no
Electric Trolley	Chariot électrique	15 € /18 holes
Buggy	Voiturette	no
Clubs	Clubs	15 € /full day

Credit cards Cartes de crédit
VISA - CB - Eurocard - MasterCard - DC - JCB - AMEX

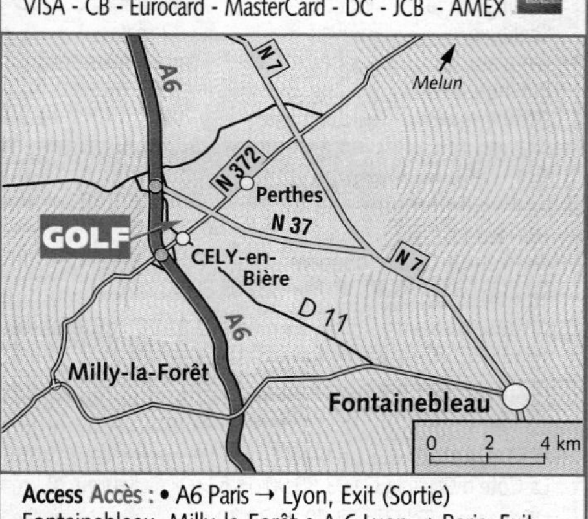

Access Accès : • A6 Paris → Lyon, Exit (Sortie) Fontainebleau, Milly-la-Forêt • A 6 Lyon → Paris, Exit (Sortie) Cély
Map 3 on page 166 Carte 3 Page 166

Golf course — PARCOURS — 15/20

Site	Site	
Maintenance	Entretien	
Architect	Architecte	Marc Adam Patrick Fromanger
Type	Type	parkland
Relief	Relief	
Water in play	Eau en jeu	
Exp. to wind	Exposé au vent	
Trees in play	Arbres en jeu	

Scorecard Carte de score	**Chp.** Chp.	**Mens** Mess.	**Ladies** Da.
Length Long.	5874	5424	4686
Par	72	72	72
Slope system	130	128	120

Advised golfing ability 0 12 24 36
Niveau de jeu recommandé
Hcp required Handicap exigé 30

Club house & amenities — CLUB-HOUSE ET ANNEXES — 7/10

Pro shop	Pro-shop	
Driving range	Practice	
Sheltered	couvert	no
On grass	sur herbe	yes
Putting-green	putting-green	yes
Pitching-green	pitching green	yes

Hotel facilities — ENVIRONNEMENT HOTELIER — 6/10

HOTELS HÔTELS

Bas Bréau, 21 rooms, D 229 € — Barbizon
Tel (33) 01 60 66 40 05, Fax (33) 01 60 69 22 89 — 7 km

Les Alouettes, 22 rooms, D 59 € — Barbizon
Tel (33) 01 60 66 41 98, Fax (33) 01 60 66 20 69 — 7 km

Aigle Noir, 56 rooms, D 191 € — Fontainebleau
Tel (33) 01 60 74 60 00, Fax (33) 01 60 74 60 01 — 14 km

RESTAURANTS RESTAURANT

Le Bas Bréau, Tel (33) 01 60 66 40 05 — Barbizon 7 km

L'Angelus, Tel (33) 01 60 66 40 30 — Barbizon

CHAILLY (CHÂTEAU DE) 14 | 8 | 6

Avec ce golf à proximité de Dijon et de l'autoroute A6 (sans bruits), le propriétaire souhaitait faire un "links" à l'intérieur des terres. On peut le regretter pour l'animation du paysage, il n'a pas voulu faire de plantations dans cet espace d'origine agricole parcouru par un ruisseau, et parsemé de quelques grandes pièces d'eau. L'architecture de Thierry Sprecher et Géry Watine est de bonne qualité et de bon goût, mais reste un peu timide et sans originalité frappante. Alors que les intentions de départ auraient dû imposer quelques modelages et davantage de violence visuelle, ils sont peu importants. Ce qui peut laisser une impression de platitude, avec en contrepartie l'avantage de permettre aux joueurs de tous niveaux de ne pas connaître trop de problèmes. Le château du domaine a été aménagé avec des chambres d'hôtel et un restaurant gastronomique, qui ont beaucoup contribué à la réputation du parcours.

The owner of this course close to Dijon and the A6 motorway (no noise), set out to create an inland links. He had no intention of planting trees or bushes on a site which was originally farming land crossed by a stream and dotted with a few stretches of water, and seeing the landscape today, we wonder whether this was the right option. The design by Thierry Sprecher and Géry Watine is high class and tasteful but lacks boldness and originality. While original designs would have required a little shaping of ground and greater visual impact, neither one nor the other is very much in evidence. This gives an impression of flatness and a round of golf where players of all levels should stay out of trouble. The estate's castle has been refurbished with hotel rooms and a gourmet restaurant, which have done much to enhance the course's reputation.

Golf Club du Château de Chailly — 1990

F - 21320 CHAILLY-SUR-ARMENCON

Office	Secrétariat	(33) 03 80 90 30 40
Pro shop	Pro-shop	(33) 03 80 90 30 40
Fax	Fax	(33) 03 80 90 30 05
Web	www.chailly.com	
Situation	Situation	

Dijon (pop. 146 700), 55 km - Pouilly-en-Auxois, 5 km

Annual closure	Fermeture annuelle	1/1 → 31/1
Weekly closure	Fermeture hebdomadaire	no

Fees main season / Tarifs haute saison	Week days / Semaine	We/Bank holidays / We/Férié
18 holes		
Individual Individuel	34 €	46 €
Couple Couple	68 €	92 €

Caddy	Caddy	no
Electric Trolley	Chariot électrique	9 € /18 holes
Buggy	Voiturette	38 € /18 holes
Clubs	Clubs	15 € /full day

Credit cards Cartes de crédit
VISA - CB - Eurocard - MasterCard - DC - JCB - AMEX

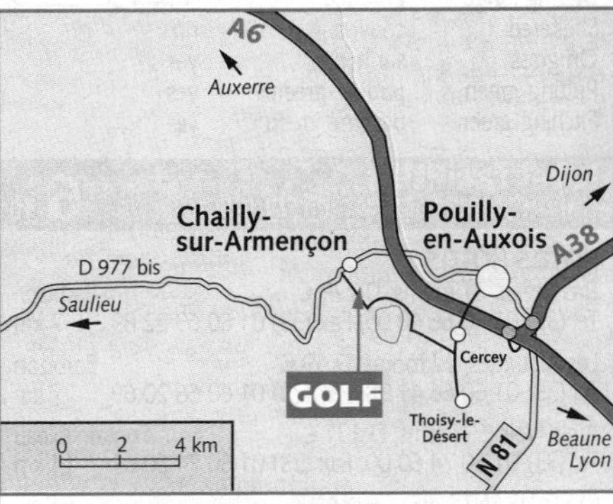

Access Accès : A6 Exit (Sortie) Pouilly-en-Auxois, D977 bis → Saulieu
Map 7 on page 175 Carte 7 Page 175

Golf course PARCOURS — 14/20

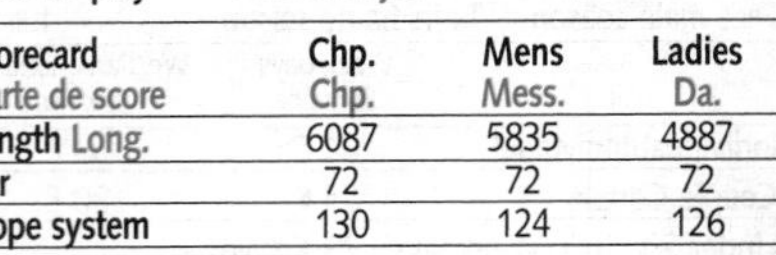

Site	Site	
Maintenance	Entretien	
Architect	Architecte	Thierry Sprecher Géry Watine
Type	Type	open country
Relief	Relief	
Water in play	Eau en jeu	
Exp. to wind	Exposé au vent	
Trees in play	Arbres en jeu	

Scorecard / Carte de score	Chp. / Chp.	Mens / Mess.	Ladies / Da.
Length Long.	6087	5835	4887
Par	72	72	72
Slope system	130	124	126

Advised golfing ability / Niveau de jeu recommandé: 0 12 24 36
Hcp required / Handicap exigé: no

Club house & amenities CLUB-HOUSE ET ANNEXES — 8/10

Pro shop	Pro-shop	
Driving range	Practice	
Sheltered	couvert	12 mats
On grass	sur herbe	no, 8 mats open air
Putting-green	putting-green	yes
Pitching-green	pitching green	yes

Hotel facilities ENVIRONNEMENT HOTELIER — 6/10

HOTELS HÔTELS

Château de Chailly, 45 rooms, D 381 € — Chailly on site
Tel (33) 03 80 90 30 30, Fax (33) 03 80 90 30 00

Château de Sainte-Sabine, 23 rooms, D 114 € — Ste-Sabine 14 km
Tel (33) 03 80 49 22 01, Fax (33) 03 80 49 20 01

Hostellerie du Château, 17 rooms, D 57 € — Châteauneuf 15 km
Tel (33) 03 80 49 22 00, Fax (33) 03 80 49 21 27

RESTAURANTS RESTAURANT

La Côte d'Or, Tel (33) 03 80 90 53 53 — Saulieu 20 km

L'Armançon, Tel (33) 03 80 90 30 30 — on site

L'Auxois — Vandenesse-en-Auxois 8 km
Tel (33) 03 80 49 22 36

CHAMBON-SUR-LIGNON (LE) 14 | 5 | 7

Dans les montagnes au sud de Saint-Etienne, tout près de la vieille cité épiscopale du Puy-en-Velay, la petite ville de Chambon sur Lignon est au départ de randonnées superbes du printemps à l'automne car les hivers sont parfois rigoureux à mille mètres d'altitude. Il fallait pas mal de foi pour y construire un golf. Mais il vaut largement le déplacement. Visuellement, et par le caractère de son architecture insinuée dans le relief, il rappelle parfois les parcours des Highlands écossais, avec en prime quelques panoramas somptueux, depuis les départs du 6 et du 13 en particulier. Nul ici ne prétend au luxe d'un entretien à l'américaine, mais l'atmosphère est sympathique, l'entretien très correct, avec généralement de bons greens, bien dessinés. Quelques coups aveugles réservent des émotions (au 14), inévitables avec les dénivellées. Elles sont assez importantes pour conseiller la voiturette si l'on veut faire les 18 trous sans arrêt. Le charme et la variété de ce parcours méconnu, la beauté de son décor en surprendront plus d'un.

In the mountains to the south of Saint Etienne, close to the old Episcopal city of Puy-en-Velay, the small town of Chambon sur Lignon is the starting point for some wonderful hikes. From spring to autumn that is, because at an altitude of 1,000 metres, the winters are sometimes harsh. It took a lot of faith to build a golf course here, but this unpretentious layout is well worth a visit. Visually, and through architecture which winds it way through some marked topology, it is sometimes reminiscent of the Scottish highland courses with a few splendid vistas to boot, particularly from the 6th and 13th tees. Nobody should expect US-style standards of green-keeping here, but the atmosphere is jovial and maintenance pretty fair, with good and well-designed greens by and large. A few blind shots will set the pulse racing (on the 14th hole), but this was hardly to be avoided on a rather hilly course where a buggy is recommended if you want to play 18 holes without stopping off for lunch. More than a few golfers have been surprised by the charm, the variety and the beautiful setting of this little known course.

Golf du Chambon-sur-Lignon — 1994

Riondet, La Pierre de la Lune, BP 12
F - 43400 LE CHAMBON-SUR-LIGNON

Office	Secrétariat	(33) 04 71 59 28 10
Pro shop	Pro-shop	(33) 04 71 59 28 10
Fax	Fax	(33) 04 71 65 87 14
Web	www.golf-chambon.com	
Situation	Situation	Valence, 70 km

Saint-Etienne (pop. 199 396), 68 km

Annual closure	Fermeture annuelle	11/11→1/4
Weekly closure	Fermeture hebdomadaire	no

Fees main season Tarifs haute saison	18 holes	
	Week days Semaine	We/Bank holidays We/Férié
Individual Individuel	34 €	34 €
Couple Couple	68 €	68 €
Caddy Caddy	no	
Electric Trolley Chariot électrique	12 € /18 holes	
Buggy Voiturette	23 € /18 holes	
Clubs Clubs	8 € /full day	

Credit cards Cartes de crédit VISA - Eurocard - MasterCard

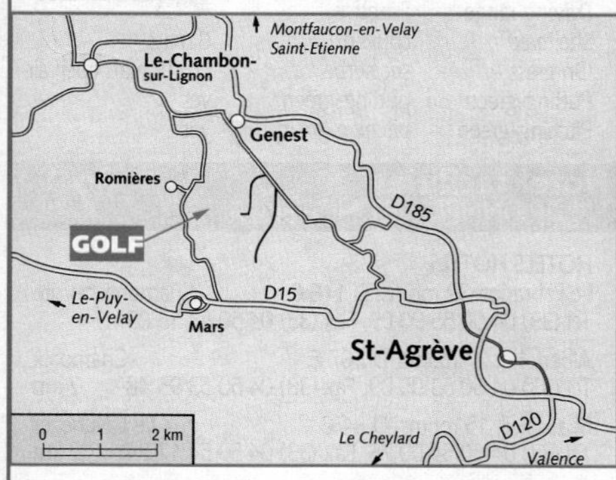

Access Accès : • Saint-Etienne, N88 → Le-Puy-en-Velay. Yssingeaux, D103 → Tence, D151 → Le Chambon-sur-Lignon. SE, D103, D155 → Golf. • Valence, D533 → Lamastre, St Agrève. D185, D151 → Chambon-sur-Lignon. **Map 10 on page 181** Carte 10 Page 181

Golf course PARCOURS — 14/20

Site	Site	
Maintenance	Entretien	
Architect	Architecte	Michel Gayon
Type	Type	hilly, forest
Relief	Relief	
Water in play	Eau en jeu	
Exp. to wind	Exposé au vent	
Trees in play	Arbres en jeu	

Scorecard Carte de score	Chp. Chp.	Mens Mess.	Ladies Da.
Length Long.	5872	5511	4639
Par	72	72	72
Slope system	149	140	140

Advised golfing ability Niveau de jeu recommandé — 0 12 24 36

Hcp required Handicap exigé 35

Club house & amenities CLUB-HOUSE ET ANNEXES — 5/10

Pro shop	Pro-shop	
Driving range	Practice	
Sheltered	couvert	4 mats
On grass	sur herbe	no, 11 mats open air
Putting-green	putting-green	yes
Pitching-green	pitching green	yes

Hotel facilities ENVIRONNEMENT HOTELIER — 7/10

HOTELS HÔTELS

Bel Horizon, 20 rooms, D 99 € — Le Chambon-sur-Lignon
Tel (33) 04 71 59 74 39, Fax (33) 04 71 59 79 81 — 5 km

Bois Vialotte, 17 rooms, D 47 € — Le Chambon-sur-Lignon
Tel (33) 04 71 59 74 03, Fax (33) 04 71 65 86 32 — 3 km

Domaine de Rilhac, 8 rooms, D 69 € — Saint-Agrève
Tel (33) 04 75 30 20 20, Fax (33) 04 75 30 20 00 — 8 km

Château d'Urbilhac, 12 rooms, D 107 € — Lamastre 3 km
Tel (33) 04 75 06 42 11, Fax (33) 04 75 06 52 75

RESTAURANTS RESTAURANT

Domaine de Rilhac, Tel (33) 04 75 30 20 20 — Saint-Agrève 8 km

Vidal, Tel (33) 04 71 08 70 50 — Saint-Julien-Chapteuil 25 km

CHAMONIX

15 | 6 | 7

Dessiné par Robert Trent Jones, ce parcours souffrait parfois d'un entretien en deçà de son architecture, mais les travaux récents de drainage ont été efficaces et l'état du parcours peut être remarquable quand la saison est favorable : les greens demandent une attention permanente à cette altitude. Dans ce site exceptionnel de la vallée de Chamonix, orné de sapins et de bouleaux, il n'a de golf de montagne que son paysage, car son relief est très modéré. Parcouru par de petits ruisseaux et par l'Arve, ses difficultés ne sont pas insurmontables pour un joueur de bon niveau capable de réfléchir sur la stratégie mais il peut être délicat pour un débutant, en raison de l'étroitesse de ses fairways. Conçu comme un golf de vacances, il peut être joué plusieurs fois sans ennui, mais ses difficultés assez subtiles apparaissent vite quand on chasse un bon score... C'est néanmoins l'un des tout meilleurs parcours de montagne, et le point de départ de balades magnifiques au pied du Mont Blanc.

Designed by Robert Trent Jones, this course has suffered from a standard of maintenance well below that of the actual layout, but the recent drainage work has had effective results and the condition of the course can be quite remarkable in season. At this altitude, the greens require constant maintenance. Laid out over an exceptional site in the valley of Chamonix, lined with fir and birch trees, the only thing mountainous about this course is the landscape because the actual terrain is flat. Crossed by a number of streams and the gushing Arve river, the difficulties here are not impossible for a player with good ability and a strategic brain, but the course can pose a problem or two for beginners owing to a number of tight fairways. Designed as a holiday course, you can play it several times with the same fun and enthusiasm, although the subtle difficulties tend to emerge pretty quickly when you are after a good score. In the final reckoning, this is one of Europe's best Alpine golf courses and a great base-camp for some magnificent hikes at the foot of Mont Blanc.

Golf Club de Chamonix — 1934

35, route du Golf
F - 74400 CHAMONIX

Office	Secrétariat	(33) 04 50 53 06 28
Pro shop	Pro-shop	(33) 04 50 53 45 23
Fax	Fax	(33) 04 50 53 38 69
Web	www.golfdechamonix.com	
Situation	Situation	

Chamonix, 3 km - Genève (pop. 167 200), 85 km

Annual closure	Fermeture annuelle	1/12→15/3
Weekly closure	Fermeture hebdomadaire	no

Fees main season Tarifs haute saison — full day

	Week days / Semaine	We/Bank holidays / We/Férié
Individual Individuel	53 €	53 €
Couple Couple	106 €	106 €

Caddy	Caddy	no
Electric Trolley	Chariot électrique	no
Buggy	Voiturette	30 € /18 holes
Clubs	Clubs	15 € /full day

Credit cards Cartes de crédit
VISA - CB - Eurocard - MasterCard

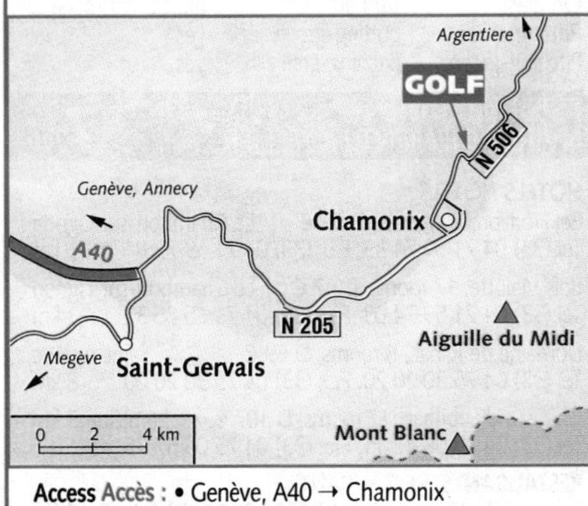

Access Accès : • Genève, A40 → Chamonix
• Megève, N212, D909, N205
Map 11 on page 183 Carte 11 Page 183

Golf course PARCOURS — 15/20

Site	Site	
Maintenance	Entretien	
Architect	Architecte	Robert Trent Jones
Type	Type	parkland, mountain
Relief	Relief	
Water in play	Eau en jeu	
Exp. to wind	Exposé au vent	
Trees in play	Arbres en jeu	

Scorecard / Carte de score	Chp. / Chp.	Mens / Mess.	Ladies / Da.
Length Long.	6076	5855	5056
Par	72	72	72
Slope system	127	125	124

Advised golfing ability Niveau de jeu recommandé — 0 12 24 36
Hcp required Handicap exigé — 35

Club house & amenities CLUB-HOUSE ET ANNEXES — 6/10

Pro shop	Pro-shop	
Driving range	Practice	
Sheltered	couvert	6 mats
On grass	sur herbe	no, 18 mats open air
Putting-green	putting-green	yes
Pitching-green	pitching green	yes

Hotel facilities ENVIRONNEMENT HOTELIER — 7/10

HOTELS HÔTELS

Le Labrador, 32 rooms, D 146 € — Chamonix on site
Tel (33) 04 50 55 90 09, Fax (33) 04 50 53 15 85

Albert 1er, 27 rooms, D 267 € — Chamonix
Tel (33) 04 50 53 05 09, Fax (33) 04 50 53 95 48 — 2 km

Beausoleil, 15 rooms, D 84 € — Le Lavancher
Tel (33) 04 50 54 00 78, Fax (33) 04 50 54 17 34 — 2 km

RESTAURANTS RESTAURANT

Albert 1er, Tel (33) 04 50 53 05 09 — Chamonix 2 km
Atmosphère, Tel (33) 04 50 55 97 97 — Chamonix
Maison Carrier, Tel (33) 04 50 53 00 03 — Chamonix

CHAMP DE BATAILLE

14 | 6 | 3

En dehors du premier et du dernier trou, directement inspirés de l'architecture à la française, et assez insipides (il est sérieusement question de les refaire), ce parcours accidenté, dessiné par Nelson et Huau, est une jolie promenade dans les bois, avec quelques spécimens d'arbres magnifiques, mais des fairways généralement de bonne taille. De nombreux sapins font parfois imaginer être en montagne, alors que nous sommes au coeur de la Normandie. Chez les architectes, on sent les paysagistes sans doute plus que les golfeurs, mais si l'on peut regretter un certain manque de souffle, il n'y a pas de fautes graves, ce qui incite à le recommander davantage aux amoureux de belles balades en famille (ou avec des amis) qu'aux joueurs de haut niveau à la recherche de grands défis. Les écuries du château ont été aménagées pour recevoir le Club House, autrefois situé dans le château.

Excepting the first and last holes, directly inspired by French style architecture but otherwise totally tasteless (they are seriously thinking of redesigning both), this hilly course, designed by Nelson and Huau, is a beautiful stroll through the woods, where some magnificent trees leave enough room for some decently sized fairways. With some of the pine-trees, you'd think you were in the Alps, rather than in the heart of Normandy. Architecturally speaking, the course is the work of landscapers rather than golfers, but if we overlook a little lack of punch, there is nothing at all wrong with this course, which is to be recommended more for family outings (or rounds with friends) rather than for skilful players looking for a tough challenge. The castle's stables have been refurbished and converted into a club-house, which used to be in the castle.

Golf du Champ de Bataille — 1988

Château du Champ-de-Bataille
F - 27110 LE NEUBOURG

Office	Secrétariat	(33) 02 32 35 03 72
Pro shop	Pro-shop	(33) 02 32 35 03 72
Fax	Fax	(33) 02 32 35 83 10
E-mail	golf.champ.bataille@free.fr	
Situation	Situation	Evreux (pop. 49 100), 27 km
Annual closure	Fermeture annuelle	no
Weekly closure	Fermeture hebdomadaire	no

Fees main season Tarifs haute saison		18 holes
	Week days Semaine	**We/Bank holidays** We/Férié
Individual Individuel	34 €	53 €
Couple Couple	61 €	96 €

Juniors: – 50%

Caddy	Caddy	on request
Electric Trolley	Chariot électrique	no
Buggy	Voiturette	34 € /18 holes
Clubs	Clubs	no

Credit cards Cartes de crédit
VISA - CB - Eurocard - MasterCard

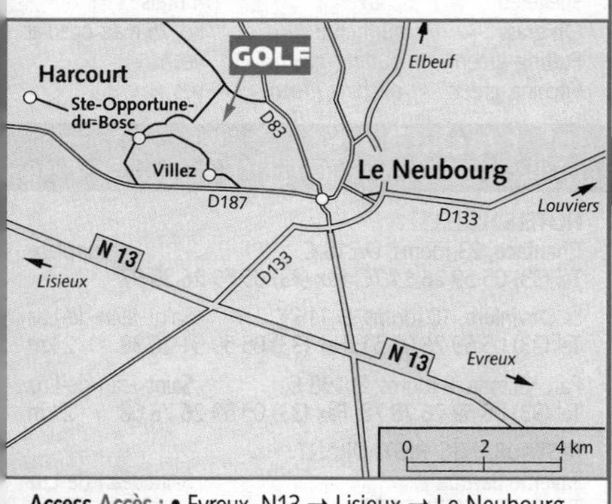

Access Accès : • Evreux, N13 → Lisieux → Le Neubourg
• Caen or Lisieux, N13 → Evreux → Le Neubourg
Map 2 on page 165 Carte 2 Page 165

Golf course — PARCOURS — 14/20

Site	Site	
Maintenance	Entretien	
Architect	Architecte	Robin Nelson Thierry Huau
Type	Type	forest
Relief	Relief	
Water in play	Eau en jeu	
Exp. to wind	Exposé au vent	
Trees in play	Arbres en jeu	

Scorecard Carte de score	**Chp.** Chp.	**Mens** Mess.	**Ladies** Da.
Length Long.	5950	5593	4471
Par	72	72	72
Slope system	137	135	131

Advised golfing ability — 0 12 24 36
Niveau de jeu recommandé
Hcp required Handicap exigé — no

Club house & amenities — CLUB-HOUSE ET ANNEXES — 6/10

Pro shop	Pro-shop	
Driving range	Practice	
Sheltered	couvert	no
On grass	sur herbe	yes (Summer)
Putting-green	putting-green	yes
Pitching-green	pitching green	yes

Hotel facilities — ENVIRONNEMENT HOTELIER — 3/10

HOTELS HÔTELS

Le Logis de Brionne, 13 rooms, D 73 € — Brionne 5 km
Tel (33) 02 32 44 81 73, Fax (33) 02 32 45 10 92

Pré Saint-Germain, 30 rooms, D 75 € — Louviers 20 km
Tel (33) 02 32 40 48 48, Fax (33) 02 32 50 75 60

Auberge du Vieux-Donjon — Brionne 5 km
8 rooms, D 47 €
Tel (33) 02 32 44 80 62, Fax (33) 02 32 45 83 23

RESTAURANTS RESTAURANT

Les Saisons, Tel (33) 02 32 40 02 56 — Vironvay 25 km
Le Logis de Brionne, Tel (33) 02 32 44 81 73 — Brionne 5 km

CHANTACO

14 | 7 | 7

Ce parcours, l'un des plus célèbres de la Côte Basque, reste incontournable par son charme, son ambiance et sa tradition sportive, cultivée par la famille Lacoste. Mais son manque de longueur ou l'espace commun au practice et au trou n°16 ne pouvaient lui accorder le titre de grand golf. Heureusement, le déplacement du practice et la refonte de deux trous du retour constituent un progrès réel. Relativement accidenté, il est cependant plus fatigant d'en déjouer les pièges que d'y marcher. Il donne l'impression de promettre une journée tranquille, mais résiste bien aux ambitieux : souvent étroit, avec quelques dévers redoutables et de petits greens, il demande plus de précision que de longueur. Si l'on ne cherche pas à défier un monstre pendant ses vacances, Chantaco reste par beau temps (il peut être humide) un parcours plaisant. L'architecte originel était Harry Colt, mais la diversité des styles rencontrés laisse à penser que son travail a été modifié, moins sans doute à l'aller, qui reste d'un niveau supérieur au reste du parcours. Mais attendons le résultat des travaux…

Chantaco, one of the Basque Coast's most celebrated golf courses, is a must for its charm, atmosphere and sporting tradition, nurtured by the Lacoste family. But its lack of length and driving range infringing on the 16th hole kept it from being ranked as one of the greats. Happily, the shifting of the driving range and the restyling of two holes on the back nine are a real step in the right direction. Although rather hilly, the most tiring thing about Chantaco is not so much the walking but trying to avoid the traps. It gives the impression of a quiet day's golfing, but even the most ambitious golfer will find it more than a handful. Often tight, with a few formidably sloping fairways and small greens, the course demands precision more than length off the tee. Avoid trying to defy this monster during your holidays and you will find Chantaco a very pleasant course when the weather is fine (it can get very wet). The original architect was Harry Colt, but with the variety of styles around the course, we suspect his design might have been altered here and there, perhaps less so on the front 9, which are of a higher standard than the rest of the course. We will wait and see what the ongoing work produces…

Golf de Chantaco — 1928

Route d'Ascain
F - 64500 SAINT-JEAN-DE-LUZ

Office	Secrétariat	(33) 05 59 26 14 22
Pro shop	Pro-shop	(33) 05 59 26 21 45
Fax	Fax	(33) 05 59 26 48 37
Web	www.golfdechantaco.com	
Situation	Situation	St-Jean-de-Luz, 2 km
Annual closure	Fermeture annuelle	no
Weekly closure	Fermeture hebdomadaire	

tuesday except during holidays (mardi sauf vacances)

Fees main season Tarifs haute saison — 18 holes

	Week days Semaine	We/Bank holidays We/Férié
Individual Individuel	53 €	53 €
Couple Couple	90 €	90 €

Juniors: 27 €

Caddy	Caddy	on request
Electric Trolley	Chariot électrique	12 € /18 holes
Buggy	Voiturette	30 € /18 holes
Clubs	Clubs	12 € /full day

Credit cards Cartes de crédit
VISA - CB - Eurocard - MasterCard

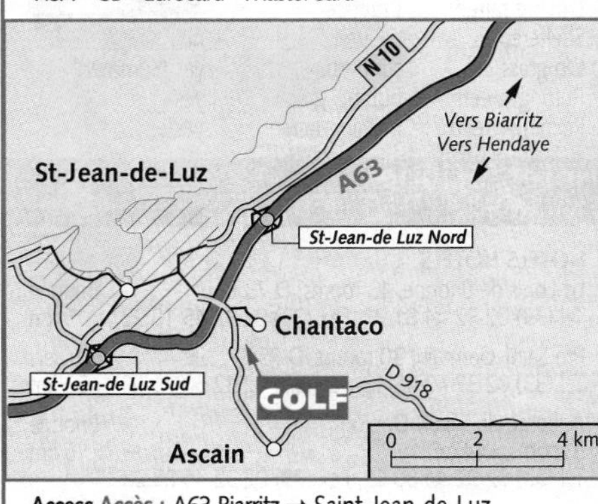

Access Accès : A63 Biarritz → Saint-Jean-de-Luz, Exit (Sortie) Saint-Jean-de-Luz Nord, D918 → Chantaco, Ascain
Map 12 on page 184 Carte 12 Page 184

Golf course PARCOURS — 14/20

Site	Site	
Maintenance	Entretien	
Architect	Architecte	Harry Colt
Type	Type	forest, parkland
Relief	Relief	
Water in play	Eau en jeu	
Exp. to wind	Exposé au vent	
Trees in play	Arbres en jeu	

Scorecard Carte de score	Chp. Chp.	Mens Mess.	Ladies Da.
Length Long.	5724	5305	4905
Par	70	70	70
Slope system	126	122	119

Advised golfing ability Niveau de jeu recommandé — 0 12 24 36
Hcp required Handicap exigé — no

Club house & amenities CLUB-HOUSE ET ANNEXES — 7/10

Pro shop	Pro-shop	
Driving range	Practice	
Sheltered	couvert	4 mats
On grass	sur herbe	no, 25 mats open air
Putting-green	putting-green	yes
Pitching-green	pitching green	yes

Hotel facilities ENVIRONNEMENT HOTELIER — 7/10

HOTELS HÔTELS

Chantaco, 23 rooms, D 218 € — sur place
Tel (33) 05 59 26 14 76, Fax (33) 05 59 26 35 97

La Devinière, 10 rooms, D 116 € — Saint-Jean-de-Luz 2 km
Tel (33) 05 59 26 05 51, Fax (33) 05 59 51 26 38

Parc Victoria, 8 rooms, D 198 € — Saint-Jean-de-Luz 2 km
Tel (33) 05 59 26 78 78, Fax (33) 05 59 26 78 08

RESTAURANTS RESTAURANT

Taverne Basque — Saint-Jean-de-Luz 2 km
Tel (33) 05 59 26 01 26

Chez Dominique — Ciboure 3 km
Tel (33) 05 59 47 29 16

CHANTILLY Vineuil

18 | 7 | 6

"Vineuil" reste l'incontournable grand classique en France, et si le passage du golf à 36 trous en a modifié le déroulement, notamment le finale de ce 18 trous, aucune blessure n'a été infligée aux trous "Simpson", une marque de respect dont bien des golfs auraient dû s'inspirer. Et bien des architectes aussi, qui devraient faire des stages prolongés ici, tant s'y exprime la grandeur dans la sobriété et la franchise, la subtilité technique dans la beauté esthétique. Hautement stratégique, diaboliquement intelligent, Vineuil exige une stratégie exactement adaptée à ses limites du moment, et se révèle un sérieux examen de passage des capacités à jouer au golf. Très difficile des départs les plus reculés, plus aimable des départs normaux, parfois un peu injuste pour les dames de très bon niveau (de leurs départs), c'est simplement un très grand parcours. L'entretien est nettement amélioré et devrait progressivement rendre à Chantilly son prestige et l'exigence d'un grand challenge.

The "Vineuil" course is still France's great classic contribution to golf, and while the upgrading to 36 holes has changed the way the course unwinds, particularly the finish of the former 18 holes, no harm has been done to Simpson's original layout, a mark of respect that many golf clubs might have done well to ponder. And many designers, as well, who should come here for extended training to see just how well greatness can spring from discretion and honesty, and technical subtlety from sheer beauty. Highly strategic and devilishly intelligent, Vineuil requires strategy tailored to your limitations on the day and can prove to be a very serious examination of your golfing ability. Very tough indeed from the back tees and sometimes a little unfair for the best lady players (from their own tees), this is simply a really great course. Maintenance has improved a great deal and should gradually restore the club's prestige and status as a most exacting challenge.

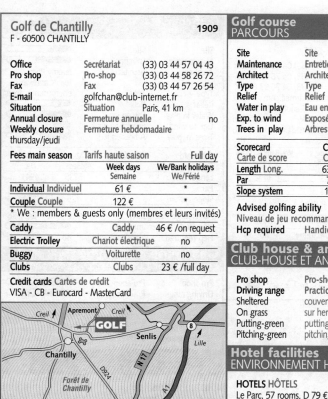

Golf de Chantilly — 1909

F - 60500 CHANTILLY

Office	Secrétariat	(33) 03 44 57 04 43
Pro shop	Pro-shop	(33) 03 44 58 26 72
Fax	Fax	(33) 03 44 57 26 54
E-mail	golfchan@club-internet.fr	
Situation	Situation	Paris, 41 km
Annual closure	Fermeture annuelle	no
Weekly closure	Fermeture hebdomadaire	

thursday/jeudi

Fees main season Tarifs haute saison	Week days Semaine	We/Bank holidays We/Férié
		Full day
Individual Individuel	61 €	*
Couple Couple	122 €	*

* We : members & guests only (membres et leurs invités)

Caddy	Caddy	46 € /on request
Electric Trolley	Chariot électrique	no
Buggy	Voiturette	no
Clubs	Clubs	23 € /full day

Credit cards Cartes de crédit
VISA - CB - Eurocard - MasterCard

Access Accès : A1 Exit (Sortie) Survilliers, D922 → Fosses. N17 → La Chapelle en Serval. In La Chapelle, go left D924 → Chantilly. Après le Château, à droite → Vineuil, Golf. **Map 3 on page 166** Carte 3 Page 166

Golf course PARCOURS — 18/20

Site	Site	
Maintenance	Entretien	
Architect	Architecte	Tom Simpson
Type	Type	forest, inland
Relief	Relief	
Water in play	Eau en jeu	
Exp. to wind	Exposé au vent	
Trees in play	Arbres en jeu	

Scorecard Carte de score	**Chp.** Chp.	**Mens** Mess.	**Ladies** Da.
Length Long.	6396	5664	4809
Par	71	71	74
Slope system	134	130	132

Advised golfing ability 0 12 24 36
Niveau de jeu recommandé

Hcp required Handicap exigé 35

Club house & amenities CLUB-HOUSE ET ANNEXES — 7/10

Pro shop	Pro-shop	
Driving range	Practice	
Sheltered	couvert	5 mats
On grass	sur herbe	yes
Putting-green	putting-green	yes
Pitching-green	pitching green	yes

Hotel facilities ENVIRONNEMENT HOTELIER — 6/10

HOTELS HÔTELS

Le Parc, 57 rooms, D 79 € — Chantilly 3 km
Tel (33) 03 44 58 20 00, Fax (33) 03 44 57 31 10

Château de la Tour, 41 rooms, D 136 € — Gouvieux 6 km
Tel (33) 03 44 62 38 38, Fax (33) 03 44 57 31 97

Relais d'Aumale, 22 rooms, D 125 € — Montgrésin 8 km
Tel (33) 03 44 54 61 31, Fax (33) 03 44 54 69 15

RESTAURANTS RESTAURANT

La Renardière — Gouvieux 6 km
Tel (33) 03 44 57 08 23

Le Verbois — St Maximin 5 km
Tel (33) 03 44 24 06 22

CHARMEIL

16 | 6 | 6

Avec une moitié de trous en forêt et l'autre en plaine, ce parcours est assez plat, mais jamais monotone. Jeremy Pern aime l'architecture de links, et le montre par son modelage de buttes et une grande utilisation de bunkers de toutes tailles, y compris des "pot-bunkers". Les obstacles d'eau sont pratiquement tous naturels, y compris un étang de trois hectares, ce qui apporte de jolis éléments paysagers. Un joueur réfléchi peut toujours jouer la sécurité, ce qui rend le parcours amusant pour tous les niveaux, les difficultés étant visibles. Franc et plaisant, il peut cependant être un peu long pour les joueurs de plus de 24 de handicap. Les greens sont assez faciles à lire, mais certaines attaques sont délicates à apprécier. Ce beau tracé bénéficie d'un entretien correct, mais il vaut mieux jouer pendant les périodes sèches, car il supporte toujours mal l'humidité. L'hôtel sur place est bien pratique.

With half the holes in the woods and the other half in open country, this is a fairly flat but never tedious course. Architect Jeremy Pern is fond of links layouts and shows it here, with carefully shaped mounds and the widespread use of bunkers in all shapes and sizes, including a number of pot-bunkers. Nearly all the water is natural, including a lake of some 7 acres or more, which adds to the pretty landscape. A thoughtful player, as always, can play safe, thus making this an amusing course for all golfers of all abilities, as the difficulties are there to be seen. Open and pleasant to play, it can however be a little long for high-handicappers. The greens are easy to read but some approach shots tend to be a little tricky to assess. The standard of green-keeping for this fine layout is average. And as it doesn't like rain, this is a course for the drier days. The on-site hotel is most convenient..

Golf du Charmeil — 1987

Saint-Quentin-sur-Isère
F - 38210 SAINT-QUENTIN-SUR-ISERE

Office	Secrétariat	(33) 04 76 93 67 28
Pro shop	Pro-shop	(33) 04 76 93 67 28
Fax	Fax	(33) 04 76 93 62 04
Web	www.golfhotelcharmeil.com	
Situation	Situation	Grenoble, 24 km
Annual closure	Fermeture annuelle	no
Weekly closure	Fermeture hebdomadaire	no
Fees main season	Tarifs haute saison	full day

	Week days Semaine	We/Bank holidays We/Férié
Individual Individuel	32 €	43 €
Couple Couple	64 €	86 €

Juniors: 15 € (Weekdays) - 21 € (We) -

Caddy	Caddy	no
Electric Trolley	Chariot électrique	no
Buggy	Voiturette	23 € /18 holes
Clubs	Clubs	8 € /full day

Credit cards Cartes de crédit
VISA - CB - Eurocard - MasterCard - DC - AMEX

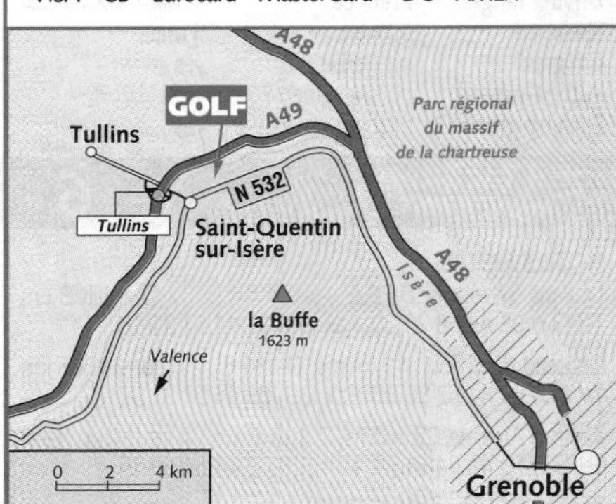

Access Accès : • Grenoble A49 → Valence
• Lyon A48 → Grenoble → A49 Valence, Exit (Sortie) Tullins → Saint-Quentin-sur-Isère
Map 11 on page 182 Carte 11 Page 182

Golf course PARCOURS — 16/20

Site	Site	
Maintenance	Entretien	
Architect	Architecte	Jeremy Pern, Jean Garaïalde
Type	Type	open country, forest
Relief	Relief	
Water in play	Eau en jeu	
Exp. to wind	Exposé au vent	
Trees in play	Arbres en jeu	

Scorecard Carte de score	Chp. Chp.	Mens Mess.	Ladies Da.
Length Long.	6114	5735	4941
Par	73	73	73
Slope system	127	125	124

Advised golfing ability / Niveau de jeu recommandé: 0 12 24 36
Hcp required / Handicap exigé: no

Club house & amenities CLUB-HOUSE ET ANNEXES — 6/10

Pro shop	Pro-shop	
Driving range	Practice	
Sheltered	couvert	8 mats
On grass	sur herbe	no, 19 mats open air
Putting-green	putting-green	yes (2)
Pitching-green	pitching green	yes

Hotel facilities ENVIRONNEMENT HOTELIER — 6/10

HOTELS HÔTELS

Golf Hôtel du Charmeil, 50 rooms, D 79 € — on site
Tel (33) 04 76 93 67 28, Fax (33) 04 76 93 62 04

Auberge de Malatras, 18 rooms, D 39 € — Tullins 6 km
Tel (33) 04 76 07 02 30, Fax (33) 04 76 07 76 48

Campanile, 39 rooms, D 48 € — Saint-Egrène 10 km
Tel (33) 04 76 75 57 88, Fax (33) 04 76 75 06 49

RESTAURANTS RESTAURANT

Philippe Serratrice, Tel (33) 04 76 05 29 88 — Voiron 16 km

La Table d'Ernest, Tel (33) 04 76 43 19 56 — Grenoble 24 km

Auberge de Malatras, Tel (33) 04 76 07 02 30 — Tullins 6 km

CHÂTEAU DE PREISCH

15 | 7 | 6

Trois 9 trous sont ici combinables, mais le parcours de référence semble être l'ensemble France et Luxembourg. Logique, car il est situé exactement à la frontière. Trois trous sont en forêt, une demi-douzaine d'autres mettent pas mal d'eau en jeu (on ne la voit pas toujours), les autres sont assez classiques, avec des buttes pour paysager l'espace, et peu d'arbres. Le vent peut y jouer un rôle d'autant plus important que l'ensemble est assez long, et plus encore quand le temps est hostile. L'attaque des greens n'en sera pas facilitée, car leur pente générale est souvent très marquée. Il est difficile d'espérer le maîtriser sans l'avoir joué plusieurs fois, car il ne faut pas se fier à l'apparente franchise qu'offrent des fairways un peu "boulevards", qui mériteraient un tracé plus imaginatif. Au moins, les frappeurs pourront s'y déchaîner. En résumé, un ensemble très honorable,bien construit, et sans doute un peu difficile pour les débutants.

There are three combinable 9-hole courses here but the main course seems to be the "Luxembourg" and "France" combination, which is only logical since the course is located exactly on the frontier between the two countries. Three holes run through a forest, half a dozen others bring water into play (not always visibly so) and the rest is classical in style, with sand-hills and few trees. The wind can be an important factor, especially since the whole course is long and plays even longer in rough weather. Attacking the pins is never easy because of the very marked slopes on the greens. It would be hard to imagine getting the better of this course without at least a few practice rounds, and you should be wary of the apparent openness of the wide fairways, which might have deserved a more imaginative layout. At least the big-hitters can enjoy themselves. All in all, a very respectful, well-designed course, but perhaps a little difficult for beginners.

Château de Preisch — 1997

1, rue du Vieux Moulin
F - 57570 BASSE RENTGEN

Office	Secrétariat	(33) 03 82 83 00 00
Pro shop	Pro-shop	(33) 03 82 83 00 00
Fax	Fax	(33) 03 82 83 00 09
Web	—	
Situation	Situation	

Luxembourg (pop. 75 377), 13 km

Annual closure	Fermeture annuelle	24/12→2/1
Weekly closure	Fermeture hebdomadaire	no

Fees main season Tarifs haute saison	18 holes	
	Week days Semaine	**We/Bank holidays** We/Férié
Individual Individuel	46 €	53 €
Couple Couple	92 €	106 €
Caddy	Caddy	no
Electric Trolley	Chariot électrique	yes
Buggy	Voiturette	yes
Clubs	Clubs	yes

Credit cards Cartes de crédit
VISA - Eurocard - MasterCard

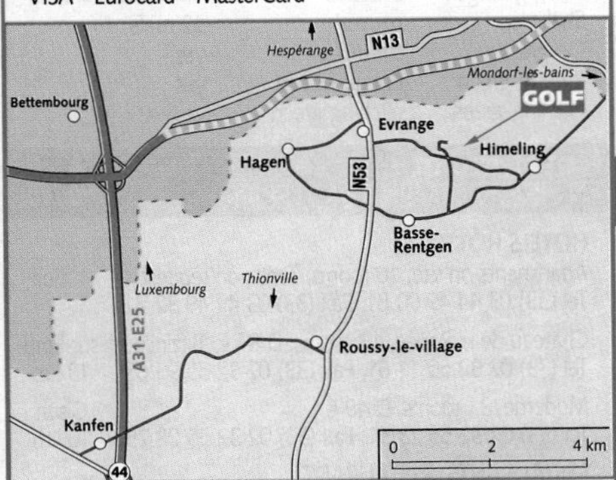

Access Accès : In Thionville, N53 → Luxembourg. Just before Evrange, turn right → Himeling. Golf on left hand side.
Map 4 on page 168 Carte 4 Page 168

Golf course — PARCOURS — 15/20

Site	Site	
Maintenance	Entretien	
Architect	Architecte	William Amick
Type	Type	inland, forest
Relief	Relief	
Water in play	Eau en jeu	
Exp. to wind	Exposé au vent	
Trees in play	Arbres en jeu	

Scorecard Carte de score	**Chp.** Chp.	**Mens** Mess.	**Ladies** Da.
Length Long.	6448	6081	5101
Par	72	72	72
Slope system	133	133	127

Advised golfing ability Niveau de jeu recommandé — 0 12 24 36
Hcp required Handicap exigé — 36

Club house & amenities — CLUB-HOUSE ET ANNEXES — 7/10

Pro shop	Pro-shop	
Driving range	Practice	
Sheltered	couvert	25 mats
On grass	sur herbe	no
Putting-green	putting-green	yes
Pitching-green	pitching green	yes

Hotel facilities — ENVIRONNEMENT HOTELIER — 6/10

HOTELS HÔTELS

Le Parc, 134 rooms, D 149 € — Mondorf-les-Bains (Lux.)
Tel (352) 661 212 555, Fax (352) 661 093 — 7 km

Hôtel de la Frontière — Frisange (Luxembourg)
18 rooms, D 67 € — 3 km
Tel (352) 668 405, Fax (352) 661 753

RESTAURANTS RESTAURANT

L'Agath, Tel (352) 488 687 Hesperange (Luxembourg) 14 km

Léa Linster, Tel (352) 668 411 Frisange (Luxembourg) 3 km

La Rameaudière — Ellange Gare (Mondorf)
Tel (352) 661 063 — 9 km

CHAUMONT-EN-VEXIN

14 | 6 | 4

C'est à la fois l'aîné et le voisin de Rebetz, dans un site constitué de deux plateaux de niveaux très différents (un peu physique pour les seniors). L'entrée comme le château font un lieu assez prestigieux, mais pas si luxueux qu'on pourrait le croire. En fait, c'est une belle "campagne". Dessiné par Donald Harradine, le parcours est plutôt franc, même si certaines dénivellées, quelques greens élevés, ou à plateaux obligent à réfléchir. Très divers de décor comme de tracé, les 18 trous constituent pourtant un ensemble cohérent. Si les difficultés dépendent pour beaucoup de la vitesse des greens, il faut être constamment attentif, car quelques ruisseaux et de puissants arbres menacent constamment. Pour la beauté du cadre, pour l'intérêt d'un parcours amusant à tous niveaux, Chaumont-en-Vexin (ou Bertichère comme on le nomme aussi) mérite une visite, même si ce n'est pas tout à fait un "grand" parcours. Le drainage a amélioré la partie basse du lieu, et on en a profité pour rétablir les obstacles d'eau du 6 et du 11.

This is the older neighbour of Rebetz on a site of two plateaux of very different heights (tough on the legs, especially for seniors). The driveway and the castle make this a very prestigious location but it is not as luxurious as you might imagine. In fact there is a beautiful "country" style to the whole site. The course, designed by Donald Harradine, is candid enough, although a few slopes, elevated greens and plateaux call for some serious thought before putting club to ball. Although different in setting and layout, the 18 holes form a rather consistent whole, and while the difficulty here depends for a large part on the speed of the greens, you have to be constantly on your toes owing to the threat of streams and some sturdy trees. Chaumont-en-Vexin (or Bertichère as it is often called) is fun for golfers of all abilities owing to the beauty of the setting and appeal of the course. Even though nobody would call this a "great" course, it is well worth a visit. Lastly, drainage has significantly improved the lower area of the course and they also took the opportunity to restore the water hazards on holes 6 and 11.

Golf de Chaumont-en-Vexin — 1968

Château de Bertichère
F - 60240 CHAUMONT-EN-VEXIN

Office	Secrétariat	(33) 03 44 49 00 81
Pro shop	Pro-shop	(33) 03 44 49 00 81
Fax	Fax	(33) 03 44 49 32 71
Web	www.golf-paris.net	
Situation	Situation	Pontoise, 25 km
Annual closure	Fermeture annuelle	no
Weekly closure	Fermeture hebdomadaire	no

Fees main season Tarifs haute saison	18 holes	
	Week days Semaine	**We/Bank holidays** We/Férié
Individual Individuel	23 €	46 €
Couple Couple	46 €	92 €

Juniors: 30 € (We) - Special fees for seniors (Tuesdays) & Ladies (Wednesdays)

Caddy	Caddy	on request
Electric Trolley	Chariot électrique	no
Buggy	Voiturette	30 € /18 holes
Clubs	Clubs	15 € /18 holes

Credit cards Cartes de crédit
VISA - CB - Eurocard - MasterCard

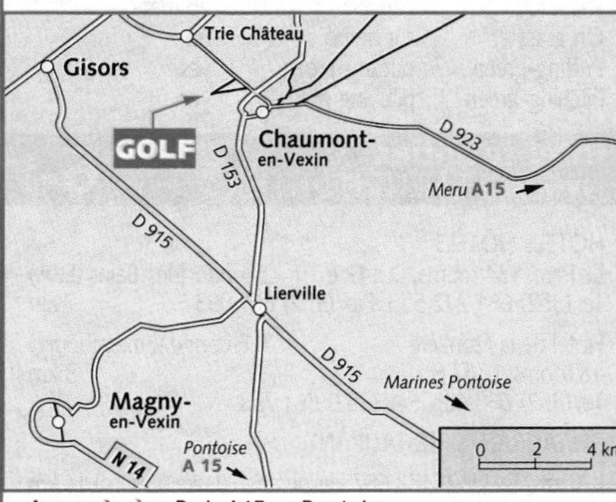

Access Accès : Paris A15 → Pontoise, N14 → Magny-en-Vexin, D153 → Chaumont-en-Vexin. Chaumont → Golf Bertichère.
Map 1 on page 162 Carte 1 Page 162

Golf course PARCOURS — 14/20

Site	Site	
Maintenance	Entretien	
Architect	Architecte	Donald Harradine
Type	Type	parkland, hilly
Relief	Relief	
Water in play	Eau en jeu	
Exp. to wind	Exposé au vent	
Trees in play	Arbres en jeu	

Scorecard Carte de score	**Chp.** Chp.	**Mens** Mess.	**Ladies** Da.
Length Long.	6197	6197	5266
Par	72	72	72
Slope system	144	140	130

Advised golfing ability Niveau de jeu recommandé: 0 12 24 36
Hcp required Handicap exigé: no

Club house & amenities CLUB-HOUSE ET ANNEXES — 6/10

Pro shop	Pro-shop	
Driving range	Practice	
Sheltered	couvert	12 mats
On grass	sur herbe	yes
Putting-green	putting-green	yes
Pitching-green	pitching green	yes

Hotel facilities ENVIRONNEMENT HOTELIER — 4/10

HOTELS HÔTELS

Apartments on site, 10 rooms, Tariffs on request — Golf
Tel (33) 03 44 49 00 81, Fax (33) 03 44 49 32 71

Château de la Rapée, 13 rooms, D 84 € — Bazincourt-sur-Epte
Tel (33) 02 32 55 11 61, Fax (33) 02 32 55 95 65 — 13 km

Moderne, 31 rooms, D 49 € — Gisors
Tel (33) 02 32 55 23 51, Fax (33) 02 32 55 08 75 — 10 km

RESTAURANTS RESTAURANT

Relais Sainte-Jeanne — Cormeilles-en-Vexin
Tel (33) 03 34 66 61 56 — 14 km

Le Cappeville, Tel (33) 03 32 55 11 08 — Gisors10 km

Chiquito, Tel (33) 03 30 36 40 23 — Méry-sur-Oise 27 km

CHEVERNY

14	7	6

A proximité immédiate du château historique de Cheverny, ce parcours contribue favorablement au "parcours golfique" des Châteaux de la Loire. Il se déroule largement en forêt, mais aussi autour de l'étang de la Rousselière. De nombreux petits obstacles d'eau apportent des éléments de jeu bienvenus dans cet espace très plat, mais toujours humide en saison pluvieuse. L'architecte Olivier van der Vynckt a très peu bougé le terrain, recherché la subtilité des formes, notamment au niveau des alentours de green, mais on aurait souhaité que le terrain soit davantage modelé, ne serait-ce que pour mieux définir les trous dans cet espace, et donner de meilleurs points de repère : on se trompe facilement de club quand on ne connaît pas bien le parcours. Le rythme de jeu est plaisant, les différents départs permettent de l'adapter à tous les niveaux. Une réalisation de bonne facture, avec un Club-House sympathique.

In the immediate vicinity of the historic Château de Cheverny, the course of the same name is one of a trail of golfing venues amidst the castles of the Loire valley. It is laid out mostly through a forest but also around a lake. Numerous minor water hazards add welcome spice to a very flat setting, which is always wet in autumn and winter. Architect Olivier van der Vinckt moved very little earth and preferred a more subtle touch, particularly around the greens. However, a little more shaping of terrain would have been welcome, if only to create greater definition for individual holes and clearer points of reference. You can easily choose the wrong club when you don't know the course well enough. Overall, the balance is pleasing and the difference in tee-off areas makes this a course for all abilities. A good quality course with a friendly club-house.

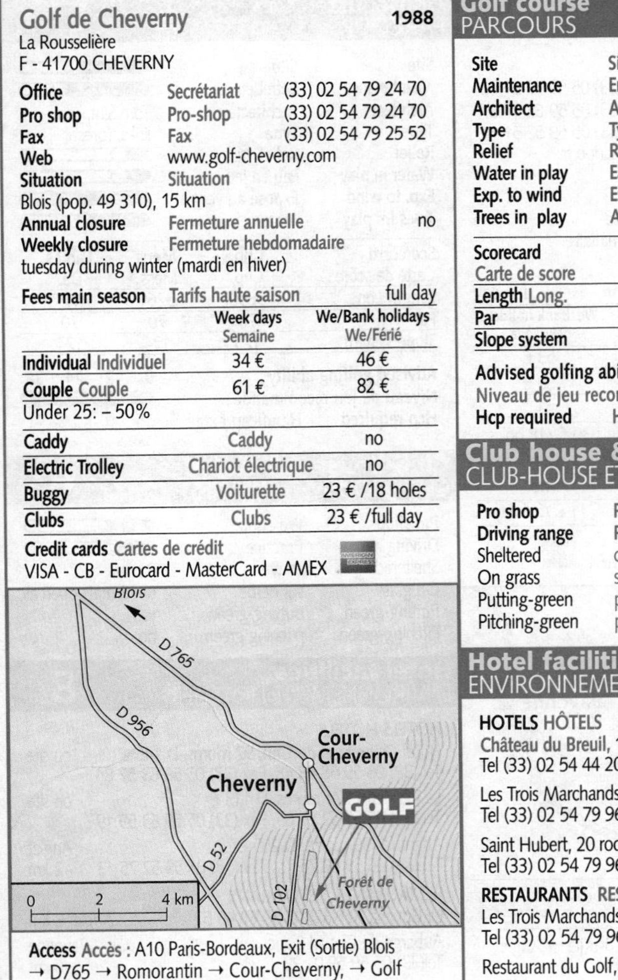

Golf de Cheverny — 1988

La Rousselière
F - 41700 CHEVERNY

Office	Secrétariat	(33) 02 54 79 24 70
Pro shop	Pro-shop	(33) 02 54 79 24 70
Fax	Fax	(33) 02 54 79 25 52
Web	www.golf-cheverny.com	
Situation	Situation	

Blois (pop. 49 310), 15 km

Annual closure Fermeture annuelle — no

Weekly closure Fermeture hebdomadaire

tuesday during winter (mardi en hiver)

Fees main season Tarifs haute saison		full day
	Week days Semaine	**We/Bank holidays** We/Férié
Individual Individuel	34 €	46 €
Couple Couple	61 €	82 €

Under 25: – 50%

Caddy	Caddy	no
Electric Trolley	Chariot électrique	no
Buggy	Voiturette	23 € /18 holes
Clubs	Clubs	23 € /full day

Credit cards Cartes de crédit

VISA - CB - Eurocard - MasterCard - AMEX

Access Accès : A10 Paris-Bordeaux, Exit (Sortie) Blois → D765 → Romorantin → Cour-Cheverny, → Golf

Map 3 on page 166 Carte 3 Page 166

Golf course PARCOURS — 14/20

Site	Site	
Maintenance	Entretien	
Architect	Architecte	O. van der Vynckt
Type	Type	forest, open country
Relief	Relief	
Water in play	Eau en jeu	
Exp. to wind	Exposé au vent	
Trees in play	Arbres en jeu	

Scorecard Carte de score	**Chp.** Chp.	**Mens** Mess.	**Ladies** Da.
Length Long.	6279	5832	4780
Par	71	71	71
Slope system	124	124	116

Advised golfing ability Niveau de jeu recommandé — 0 12 24 36

Hcp required Handicap exigé — no

Club house & amenities CLUB-HOUSE ET ANNEXES — 7/10

Pro shop	Pro-shop	
Driving range	Practice	
Sheltered	couvert	5 mats
On grass	sur herbe	no, 15 mats open air
Putting-green	putting-green	yes
Pitching-green	pitching green	yes

Hotel facilities ENVIRONNEMENT HOTELIER — 6/10

HOTELS HÔTELS

Château du Breuil, 16 rooms, D 128 € — Cour-Cheverny
Tel (33) 02 54 44 20 20, Fax (33) 02 54 44 30 40 — 2 km

Les Trois Marchands, 24 rooms, D 49 € — Cour-Cheverny
Tel (33) 02 54 79 96 44, Fax (33) 02 54 79 25 60 — 2 km

Saint Hubert, 20 rooms, D 43 € — Cour-Cheverny
Tel (33) 02 54 79 96 60, Fax (33) 02 54 79 21 17 — 2 km

RESTAURANTS RESTAURANT

Les Trois Marchands — Cour-Cheverny 2 km
Tel (33) 02 54 79 96 44

Restaurant du Golf, Tel (33) 02 54 79 23 02 — on site

CHIBERTA

16 | 6 | 8

Un des grands exemples français de links, signé par le légendaire Tom Simpson. L'essentiel de son dessin a été préservé, même si les aspects les plus sauvages ont été gommés par l'arrosage automatique et certaines "améliorations" pas forcément aussi inspirées qu'on pouvait l'espérer. La disparition de quelques difficultés a rendu le parcours plus accessible à tous les niveaux, surtout par beau temps comme sur tous ces types de golfs en bord de mer. Les greens sont de bonne qualité, les obstacles bien visibles, la stratégie assez évidente, l'absence de relief et le confort d'un sol sablonneux rendent la marche plaisante. Mais, quand le vent souffle, Chiberta devient un test où la maîtrise des trajectoires de balles est essentielle et les spécialistes du petit jeu s'en donneront à coeur joie. L'entretien a été très amélioré. A jouer sans réserve, y compris par mauvais temps. On pourrait presque dire surtout par mauvais temps !

One of the great French examples of a links course, designed by the legendary Tom Simpson. The original basic design has been preserved, although the wilder features have been smoothed away by automatic sprinklers and a number of "improvements" which are not quite as inspired as we might have hoped. With fewer difficulties, the course is more accessible to all golfers, especially in fine weather (as always). The greens are good, the hazards clearly visible, strategy is pretty obvious, and the absence of any real relief with the comfort of sandy soil make for a pleasant walk. But once the wind gets up, Chiberta becomes a test where ball-control is essential and where players with a tight short game will come into their own. Maintenance has been much improved. A must, even, or might we say especially, in bad weather.

Golf de Chiberta — 1927

104, bd des Plages
F - 64600 ANGLET

Office	Secrétariat	(33) 05 59 52 51 10
Pro shop	Pro-shop	(33) 05 59 63 17 87
Fax	Fax	(33) 05 59 52 51 11
E-mail	golf.chiberta@wanadoo.fr	
Situation	Situation	

3 km Biarritz (pop. 28 740), 3 km

Annual closure Fermeture annuelle — no
Weekly closure Fermeture hebdomadaire
thursday (jeudi)16/9→30/4

Fees main season Tarifs haute saison — full day

	Week days Semaine	We/Bank holidays We/Férié
Individual Individuel	53 €	53 €
Couple Couple	88 €	88 €

Under 21: 26 € - under 25: 36 €

Caddy	Caddy	30 € /18 holes
Electric Trolley	Chariot électrique	no
Buggy	Voiturette	no
Clubs	Clubs	11 € /full day

Credit cards Cartes de crédit
VISA - CB - Eurocard - MasterCard - AMEX

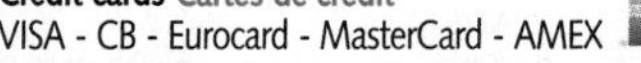

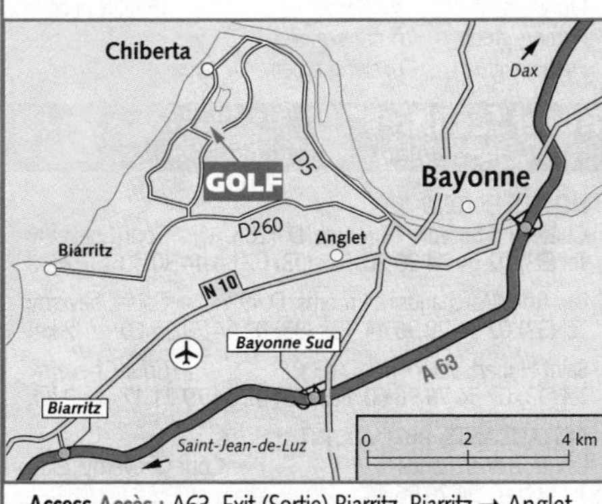

Access Accès : A63, Exit (Sortie) Biarritz. Biarritz → Anglet
Map 12 on page 184 Carte 12 Page 184

Golf course PARCOURS — 16/20

Site	Site	
Maintenance	Entretien	
Architect	Architecte	Tom Simpson
Type	Type	links, forest
Relief	Relief	
Water in play	Eau en jeu	
Exp. to wind	Exposé au vent	
Trees in play	Arbres en jeu	

Scorecard Carte de score	**Chp.** Chp.	**Mens** Mess.	**Ladies** Da.
Length Long.	5650	5261	4727
Par	70	70	70
Slope system	125	124	124

Advised golfing ability Niveau de jeu recommandé — 0 12 24 36
Hcp required Handicap exigé — 35

Club house & amenities CLUB-HOUSE ET ANNEXES — 6/10

Pro shop	Pro-shop	
Driving range	Practice	
Sheltered	couvert	8 mats
On grass	sur herbe	no, 8 mats open air
Putting-green	putting-green	yes
Pitching-green	pitching green	no

Hotel facilities ENVIRONNEMENT HOTELIER — 8/10

HOTELS HÔTELS

Hôtel Chiberta et du Golf, 92 rooms, D 145 € — on site
Tel (33) 05 59 58 48 48, Fax (33) 05 59 63 57 84

La Résidence, 71 rooms, D 113 € — on site
Tel (33) 05 59 52 87 65, Fax (33) 05 59 63 59 19

Atlanthal, 99 rooms, D 255 € — Anglet 2 km
Tel (33) 05 59 52 75 75, Fax (33) 05 59 52 75 13

RESTAURANTS RESTAURANT

La Concha, Tel (33) 05 59 63 49 52 — Anglet 3 km

Auberge du Cheval Blanc — Bayonne 6 km
Tel(33) 05 59 59 01 33

Le Bayonnais, Tel (33) 05 59 25 61 19 — Bayonne

CLAUX AMIC (GRASSE)

13 | 7 | 7

A côté de très jolis trous (le 2 ou le 7), d'autres paraissent d'une étonnante banalité, certains greens dépourvus de défenses, et on sent que ce parcours dessiné par Jean-Pascal Fourès n'a pas été achevé par le même architecte, tant le style est inégal.. La forêt de chênes est belle, mais réserve peu d'espace au parcours. Les fairways étroits sont bordés de roughs autrefois très caillouteux,mais très améliorés par le nouveau propriétaire. Ils obligent néanmoins à la prudence, ou à la précision si l'on veut bien scorer. A 600 mètres d'altitude, les points de vue sur la région de Cannes et la mer sont magnifiques, et le climat contraste en été avec les chaleurs du littoral. Les joueurs assez droits prendront cependant du plaisir à faire une belle balade en moyenne montagne, plutôt que de vouloir batailler contre le parcours. Comme il est plutôt accidenté, on leur conseille la voiturette. On signalera enfin la réfection du lac du 1, la création de nouveaux départs, et l'agrandissement de l'hôtel. De gros progrès, à suivre de près.

This layout, designed by Jean-Pascal Fourès, is so inconsistent in style as to leave the impression of a course that was not completed by the same architect. Next to some very pretty holes (N° 2 or N° 7), others seem amazingly ordinary while some of the greens are devoid of any protection whatsoever. The oak-forest is a real beauty but leaves little space for the course. The tight fairways are edged with rough that used to be stony but which has been much improved by the new owner. For a good card, they call for great care or extreme precision (or both). But at 600 m above-sea level, the views over the Mediterranean and the region of Cannes are magnificent and the climate in summer is a pleasant contrast to the heat on the Riviera. Straight-hitters will have more fun roaming through this upland terrain than they will trying to take on the course. Being rather hilly, we recommend a buggy every time. We can now also report the re-designing of the lake on hole N°1, the building of new tee-boxes and an extension to the hotel. Real progress which calls for close monitoring.

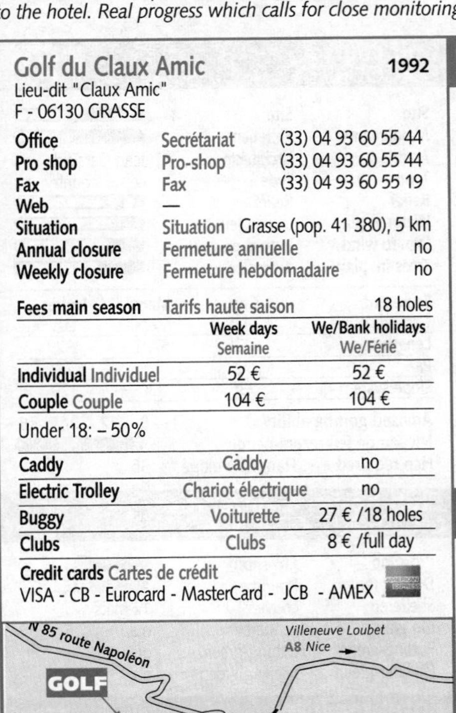

Golf du Claux Amic 1992
Lieu-dit "Claux Amic"
F - 06130 GRASSE

Office	Secrétariat	(33) 04 93 60 55 44
Pro shop	Pro-shop	(33) 04 93 60 55 44
Fax	Fax	(33) 04 93 60 55 19
Web	—	
Situation	Situation	Grasse (pop. 41 380), 5 km
Annual closure	Fermeture annuelle	no
Weekly closure	Fermeture hebdomadaire	no

Fees main season Tarifs haute saison	**Week days** Semaine	**We/Bank holidays** We/Férié
	18 holes	
Individual Individuel	52 €	52 €
Couple Couple	104 €	104 €

Under 18: – 50%

Caddy	Caddy	no
Electric Trolley	Chariot électrique	no
Buggy	Voiturette	27 € /18 holes
Clubs	Clubs	8 € /full day

Credit cards Cartes de crédit
VISA - CB - Eurocard - MasterCard - JCB - AMEX

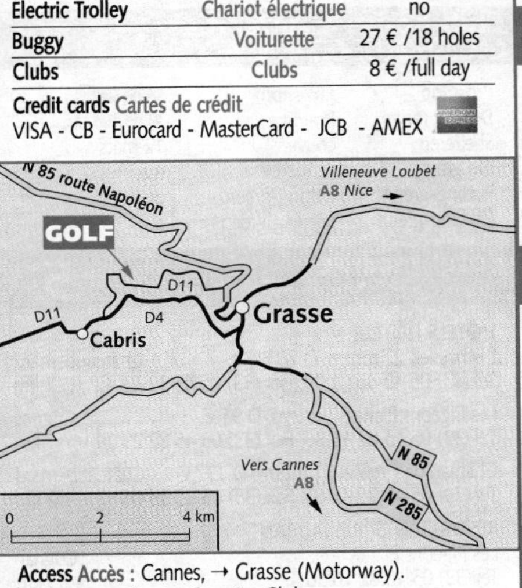

Access Accès : Cannes, → Grasse (Motorway). In Grasse → Grasse Country Club
Map 14 on page 189 Carte 14 Page 189

Golf course PARCOURS — 13/20

Site	Site	
Maintenance	Entretien	
Architect	Architecte	Jean-Pascal Fourès
Type	Type	forest, hilly
Relief	Relief	
Water in play	Eau en jeu	
Exp. to wind	Exposé au vent	
Trees in play	Arbres en jeu	

Scorecard Carte de score	**Chp.** Chp.	**Mens** Mess.	**Ladies** Da.
Length Long.	5896	5334	4332
Par	72	72	72
Slope system	133	122	114

Advised golfing ability 0 12 24 36
Niveau de jeu recommandé
Hcp required Handicap exigé no

Club house & amenities CLUB-HOUSE ET ANNEXES — 7/10

Pro shop	Pro-shop	
Driving range	Practice	
Sheltered	couvert	no
On grass	sur herbe	yes
Putting-green	putting-green	yes
Pitching-green	pitching green	no

Hotel facilities ENVIRONNEMENT HOTELIER — 7/10

HOTELS HÔTELS

Hotel du golf — Claux-Amic on site
15 rooms, D 183 €
Tel (33) 04 93 60 55 44, Fax (33) 04 93 60 55 19

L'Horizon, 22 rooms, D 102 € — Cabris 3 km
Tel (33) 04 93 60 51 69, Fax (33) 04 93 60 56 29

Bastide Saint Antoine, 11 rooms, D 236 € — Grasse 5 km
Tel (33) 04 93 70 94 94, Fax (33) 04 93 70 94 95

RESTAURANTS RESTAURANT

Bastide Saint Antoine, Tel (33) 04 93 70 94 94 — Grasse 5 km
Vieux Château, Tel (33) 04 93 60 50 12 — Cabris 3 km
Arnaud, Tel (33) 04 93 36 44 88 — Grasse 5 km

COGNAC

13 | 7 | 5

Dans une région très touristique en raison de ses vignobles (... et fameux alcools), la création de ce golf public était bienvenue, et on remarquera d'abord son Club-House sympathique, construit dans une ancienne ferme. Le paysage est un mélange plaisant de campagne et de bocages et le relief assez modéré. L'architecture du parcours est agréable visuellement et très honnête sur le plan du jeu, sans recherche excessive d'originalité. Les coups imprécis ne sont rarement pénalisés sévèrement car les fairways sont assez larges, les greens peu complexes et les bunkers rarement très dangereux. Seuls deux trous comportent des obstacles d'eau. Visiblement, ce parcours a été conçu pour les joueurs moyens, ce qui en fait un "produit" utile et de qualité estimable pour la majorité des golfeurs, de la région ou de passage. Les meilleurs joueurs ne s'y ennuieront pas. Une ombre au tableau, la fragilité du parcours quand il pleut, les drainages devraient y mettre bon ordre.

The opening of a public course was most welcome in a region where vineyards (and the famous spirits they produce) attract tourists in their droves. Just as welcoming is the club-house built in an old farmhouse. The landscape is a pleasing "blend" (this is cognac country, after all) of open country and green pastures, and the course tends to be rather hilly in places. The design is visually attractive and very forthright in golfing terms, albeit not excessively original. Wayward shots are only rarely heavily penalised, as the fairways are wide, the greens comparatively straightforward and the bunkers seldom too dangerous. There are water hazards on two holes only. The course was visibly designed for the average golfer, thus making it a "useful" product of considerable class for the majority of golfers, whether local or passing through, but even the best players will enjoy their golf here. The one flaw is the state of the course after heavy rain, but this should be remedied by drainage systems.

Golf du Cognac — 1988

Saint-Brice
F - 16100 COGNAC

Office	Secrétariat	(33) 05 45 32 18 17
Pro shop	Pro-shop	(33) 05 45 32 37 60
Fax	Fax	(33) 05 45 35 10 76
E-mail	golfducognac@wanadoo.fr	
Situation	Situation	

Cognac (pop. 19 520), 5 km - Angoulême (pop. 42 880), 32 km

Annual closure Fermeture annuelle — no

Weekly closure Fermeture hebdomadaire

tuesday (mardi) 30/9→30/4

Fees main season Tarifs haute saison	Week days Semaine	We/Bank holidays We/Férié
		full day
Individual Individuel	37 €	37 €
Couple Couple	64 €	64 €
Caddy Caddy		no
Electric Trolley Chariot électrique		12 € /18 holes
Buggy Voiturette		23 € /18 holes
Clubs Clubs		8 € /full day

Credit cards Cartes de crédit
VISA - CB - Eurocard - MasterCard

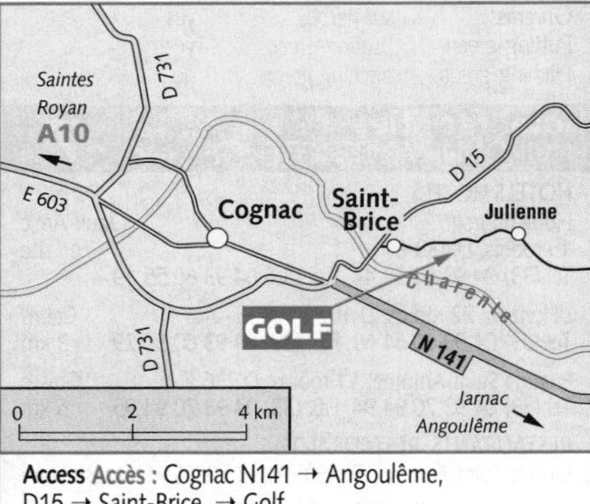

Access Accès : Cognac N141 → Angoulême, D15 → Saint-Brice, → Golf

Map 9 on page 179 Carte 9 Page 179

Golf course PARCOURS — 13/20

Site	Site	
Maintenance	Entretien	
Architect	Architecte	Jean Garaïalde
Type	Type	copse, country
Relief	Relief	
Water in play	Eau en jeu	
Exp. to wind	Exposé au vent	
Trees in play	Arbres en jeu	

Scorecard Carte de score	Chp. Chp.	Mens Mess.	Ladies Da.
Length Long.	6125	5701	4929
Par	72	72	72
Slope system	135	130	129

Advised golfing ability Niveau de jeu recommandé — 0 12 24 36

Hcp required Handicap exigé — 35

Club house & amenities CLUB-HOUSE ET ANNEXES — 7/10

Pro shop	Pro-shop	
Driving range	Practice	
Sheltered	couvert	12 mats
On grass	sur herbe	oui
Putting-green	putting-green	oui
Pitching-green	pitching green	oui

Hotel facilities ENVIRONNEMENT HOTELIER — 5/10

HOTELS HÔTELS

L'Echassier, 22 rooms, D 78 € — Châteaubernard
Tel (33) 05 45 35 01 09, Fax (33) 05 45 32 22 43 — 2 km

Les Pigeons Blancs, 7 rooms, D 91 € — Cognac
Tel (33) 05 45 82 16 36, Fax (33) 05 45 82 29 29 — 5 km

Château de l'Yeuse, 21 rooms, D 137 € — Châteaubernard
Tel (33) 05 45 36 82 60, Fax (33) 05 45 35 06 32 — 2 km

RESTAURANTS RESTAURANT

Les Pigeons Blancs — Cognac
Tel (33) 05 45 82 16 36 — 5 km

L'Echassier — Châteaubernard
Tel(33) 05 45 35 01 09 — 2 km

COURSON Lilas/Orange

15 | 7 | 3

Grand club omnisports, le Stade Français a créé un complexe golfique composé de quatre neuf trous combinables, dont la configuration idéale. est Vert-Noir et Lilas-Orange. Ce dernier 18 trous est un peu moins long, mais aussi exigeant techniquement. Dans un immense espace, Bob von Hagge a beaucoup modelé le terrain pour isoler les fairways, lui donnant un aspect un peu lunaire. L'esthétique est assez américaine, sans refuser pour autant certaines références aux links. Le "Orange" est assez accidenté, sans être vraiment fatigant : après quatre trous assez tranquilles, il en offre cinq de toute beauté, où les scores peuvent s'alourdir. Plus classique, le "Lilas" met en jeu quelques redoutables obstacles d'eau, généralement plus intimidants visuellement que dangereux. Ici, l'important est d'être précis, et de bien maîtriser le petit jeu quand on manque les greens. L'entretien n'est pas toujours à la hauteur du dessin.

Le Stade Français, one of the country's leading multi-sports clubs, has created a golf complex formed from four combinable 9-hole courses. The ideal combinations are Green and Black (see after) and Lilac and Orange (see here). The latter is a little less long but technically just as demanding. Over a huge area of land, Bob van Hagge has shifted a lot of earth to isolate the fairways and form a sort of lunar landscape. Although rather American in style, there is something of the links about all four courses. The "Orange" course is hilly but not too tiring. After four average holes, the next five are simply beautiful... and can ruin your card. The "Lilac" course, a little more classical if you will, involves some formidable water hazards, which are generally more intimidating to the eye than dangerous to the score. What matters here is straight-hitting and a sharp short game when you miss the greens. Maintenance is not always up to the design.

Golf Courson-Monteloup — 1991

Stade Français
F - 91680 COURSON-MONTELOUP

Office	Secrétariat	(33) 01 64 58 80 80
Pro shop	Pro-shop	(33) 01 64 58 80 80
Fax	Fax	(33) 01 64 58 83 06
Web	—	
Situation	Situation	

Les Ulis (pop. 27 160), 15 km - Paris (pop. 2 152 333), 34 km

Annual closure Fermeture annuelle 25/12→1/1

Weekly closure Fermeture hebdomadaire
wednesday/mercredi

Fees main season Tarifs haute saison		full day
	Week days Semaine	**We/Bank holidays** We/Férié
Individual Individuel	38 €	61 €
Couple Couple	76 €	122 €

Tuesday: 23 € - under 24 after 16.00: 28 €(Weekdays)

Caddy	Caddy	no
Electric Trolley	Chariot électrique	12 € /18 holes
Buggy	Voiturette	30 € /18 holes
Clubs	Clubs	15 € /full day

Credit cards Cartes de crédit
VISA - CB - Eurocard - MasterCard

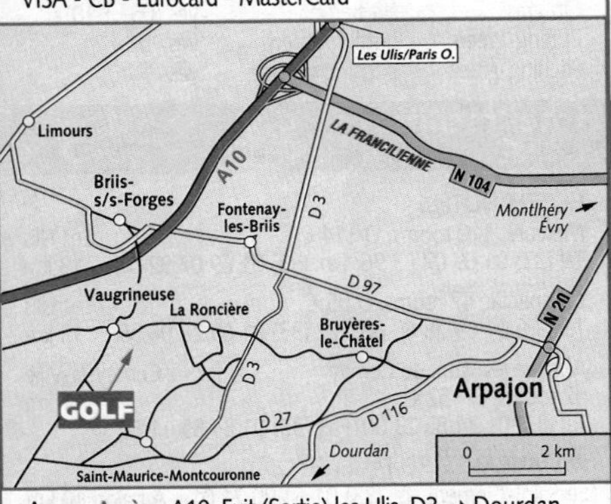

Access Accès : A10, Exit (Sortie) les Ulis, D3 → Dourdan, Château de Courson, La Roncière, → Golf
Map 15 on page 190 Carte 15 Page 190

Golf course PARCOURS — 15/20

Site	Site	
Maintenance	Entretien	
Architect	Architecte	Robert von Hagge
Type	Type	open country
Relief	Relief	
Water in play	Eau en jeu	
Exp. to wind	Exposé au vent	
Trees in play	Arbres en jeu	

Scorecard Carte de score	**Chp.** Chp.	**Mens** Mess.	**Ladies** Da.
Length Long.	6184	5753	4557
Par	72	72	72
Slope system	135	126	120

Advised golfing ability Niveau de jeu recommandé — 0 12 24 36

Hcp required Handicap exigé — 35 / 24-28 We

Club house & amenities CLUB-HOUSE ET ANNEXES — 7/10

Pro shop	Pro-shop	
Driving range	Practice	
Sheltered	couvert	15 mats
On grass	sur herbe	yes (05 → 10)
Putting-green	putting-green	yes
Pitching-green	pitching green	yes

Hotel facilities ENVIRONNEMENT HOTELIER — 3/10

HOTELS HÔTELS

Mercure, 110 rooms, D 114 € — Les Ulis
Tel (33) 01 69 07 63 96, Fax (33) 01 69 07 92 00 — 13 km

Campanile, 47 rooms, D 55 € — Les Ulis
Tel (33) 01 69 28 60 60, Fax (33) 01 69 28 06 35 — 13 km

Abbaye les Vaux de Cernay — Cernay-la-Ville
57 rooms, D 152 € — 11 km
Tel (33) 01 34 85 23 00, Fax (33) 01 34 85 11 60

RESTAURANTS RESTAURANT

Le Saint-Clément, Tel (33) 01 64 90 21 01 — Arpajon 10 km

Auberge de la Cressonière — Saint-Chéron
Tel (33) 05 64 56 60 55 — 9 km

COURSON Vert/Noir

16 | 7 | 3

Les quatre 9 trous de Courson constituent une véritable création en trois dimensions à partir d'un terrain sans grand relief naturel. Sur le "Vert", il vaut mieux partir des départs avancés, car sa longueur peut décourager les joueurs moyens (les pars 4 sont redoutables). Le "Noir" est moins brutal, parfois accidenté, mais les derniers trous mettent beaucoup d'eau en jeu. Le paysage ne manque pas de majesté, et les trous ont été bien isolés par la création de buttes spectaculaires, dont l'aspect visuel ne plaît pas à tous ! Très protégés par de beaux bunkers, les greens sont très vastes et souvent à multiples plateaux : il faut choisir celui où est le drapeau pour ne pas craindre les "trois-putts". Comme les par 5 sont difficilement prenables en deux coups, il est difficile d'y scorer très bien. Un parcours où il faut utiliser la tête autant que les clubs. L'entretien n'est pas toujours au niveau du green-fee...

The four 9-hole courses at Courson form a genuine 3-dimensional creation built out of terrain with no great natural relief. On the "Green" course, swallow your pride and play from the forward tees; it is long enough to discourage any mid-handicapper (the par 4s are quite formidable). The "Black" course is a little kinder and sometimes hilly, and the last few holes involve a lot of water. There is something very majestic about the landscape here, and the holes are clearly separated by spectacular sand-hills and hillocks, which from a visual point of view are not to everyone's liking. The greens are huge, often multi-tiered and defended by magnificent bunkers, so wayward approach shots are often greeted with 3 putts. And as the par 5s are tough to reach in two, a good score is not always easy. A typical course where brains are almost as important as your clubs. Maintenance is not always on a par with the size of the green-fee.

Golf Courson-Monteloup — 1991

Stade Français
F - 91680 COURSON-MONTELOUP

Office	Secrétariat	(33) 01 64 58 80 80
Pro shop	Pro-shop	(33) 01 64 58 80 80
Fax	Fax	(33) 01 64 58 83 06
Web	—	
Situation	Situation	

Les Ulis (pop. 27 160), 15 km - Paris (pop. 2 152 333), 34 km

Annual closure Fermeture annuelle 25/12→1/1
Weekly closure Fermeture hebdomadaire
wednesday/mercredi

Fees main season Tarifs haute saison — full day

	Week days / Semaine	We/Bank holidays / We/Férié
Individual Individuel	38 €	61 €
Couple Couple	76 €	122 €

Tuesday: 23 € - under 24 after 16.00: 28 € (Weekdays)

Caddy	Caddy	no
Electric Trolley	Chariot électrique	12 € /18 holes
Buggy	Voiturette	30 € /18 holes
Clubs	Clubs	15 € /full day

Credit cards Cartes de crédit
VISA - CB - Eurocard - MasterCard

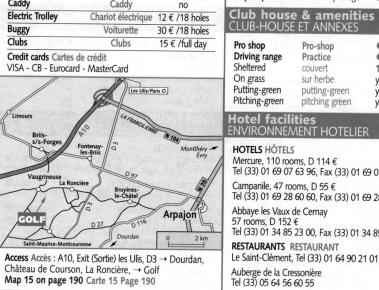

Access Accès : A10, Exit (Sortie) les Ulis, D3 → Dourdan, Château de Courson, La Roncière, → Golf
Map 15 on page 190 Carte 15 Page 190

Golf course PARCOURS — 16/20

Site	Site	
Maintenance	Entretien	
Architect	Architecte	Robert von Hagge
Type	Type	open country
Relief	Relief	
Water in play	Eau en jeu	
Exp. to wind	Exposé au vent	
Trees in play	Arbres en jeu	

Scorecard / Carte de score	Chp. / Chp.	Mens / Mess.	Ladies / Da.
Length Long.	6557	6039	4803
Par	72	72	72
Slope system	134	129	135

Advised golfing ability Niveau de jeu recommandé — 0 12 24 36
Hcp required Handicap exigé 35

Club house & amenities CLUB-HOUSE ET ANNEXES — 7/10

Pro shop	Pro-shop	
Driving range	Practice	
Sheltered	couvert	15 mats
On grass	sur herbe	yes (05 → 10)
Putting-green	putting-green	yes
Pitching-green	pitching green	yes

Hotel facilities ENVIRONNEMENT HOTELIER — 3/10

HOTELS HÔTELS

Mercure, 110 rooms, D 114 € — Les Ulis
Tel (33) 01 69 07 63 96, Fax (33) 01 69 07 92 00 — 13 km

Campanile, 47 rooms, D 55 € — Les Ulis
Tel (33) 01 69 28 60 60, Fax (33) 01 69 28 06 35 — 13 km

Abbaye les Vaux de Cernay — Cernay-la-Ville
57 rooms, D 152 € — 11 km
Tel (33) 01 34 85 23 00, Fax (33) 01 34 85 11 60

RESTAURANTS RESTAURANT

Le Saint-Clément, Tel (33) 01 64 90 21 01 — Arpajon 10 km

Auberge de la Cressonière — Saint-Chéron
Tel (33) 05 64 56 60 55 — 9 km

DIEPPE-POURVILLE

14 | 6 | 5

Un golf familial, dont le parcours tracé par le grand Willie Park en 1897, a été notablement modifié depuis, notamment après la dernière guerre et l'occupation. 9 des 27 trous d'avant-guerre n'ont alors pas été réouverts. Situé en bord de mer, ce n'est pas exactement un links, étant donné la nature du terrain mais les conditions de jeu en sont souvent proches (attention au vent !). Pour accentuer cet aspect "maritime, quatre nouveaux trous ont été tracés sur la falaise, avec une vue imprenable. Le style du parcours reste très britannique, avec des greens bien protégés., mais souvent accessibles avec des "pitch and run". Sa longueur est raisonnable, mais les scores ne sont pas toujours tels qu'on pourrait les espérer au vu de la carte. Le relief est modéré, ce qui convient bien aux joueurs de tous âges comme de tous niveaux. L'ambiance, sans prétention, est très plaisante, comme la simplicité des équipements. On ne perd certes pas sa journée à jouer ici, entre amis et en famille, un golf décontracté et sportif.

A family course designed by the great Willie Park in 1897 but considerably restyled, particularly since the end of last war and the occupation. Nine of the 27 pre-war holes have not been re-opened. Laid out along the sea-shore, this is not exactly a links course, given the nature of the terrain, but conditions of play are often very similar (watch out for the wind). To emphasise this "seaside" impression, four new holes have been laid out along the cliff-top and provide a breath-taking view. Dieppe is still a very British style course with well protected greens that can often be reached with bump and run shots. It is a reasonable length, but scores are not always as low as you might have hoped for when looking at the card. It is rather hilly but suitable for players of all ages and abilities. The atmosphere is unpretentious and pleasant, as is the simplicity of facilities. You certainly will not waste your time spending a day's golfing here, with friends or the family, in a relaxed and very sporting atmosphere.

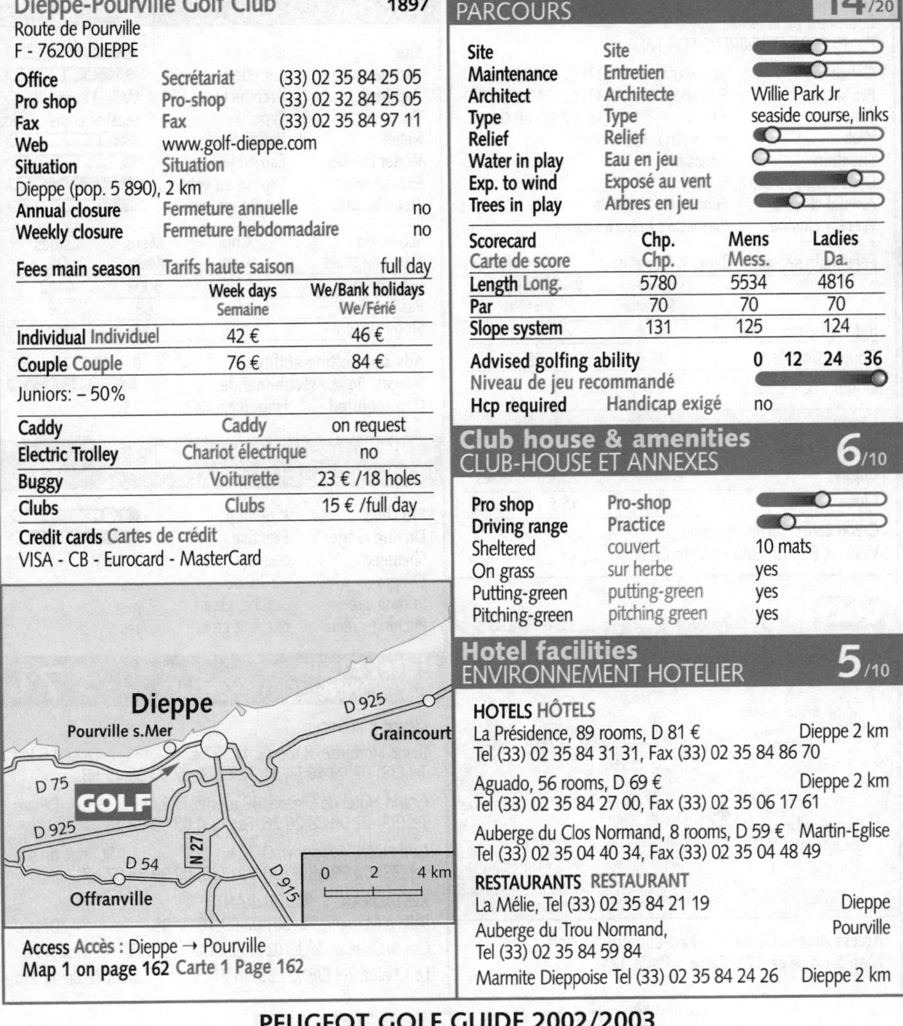

Dieppe-Pourville Golf Club — 1897

Route de Pourville
F - 76200 DIEPPE

Office	Secrétariat	(33) 02 35 84 25 05
Pro shop	Pro-shop	(33) 02 32 84 25 05
Fax	Fax	(33) 02 35 84 97 11
Web	www.golf-dieppe.com	
Situation	Situation	

Dieppe (pop. 5 890), 2 km

Annual closure	Fermeture annuelle	no
Weekly closure	Fermeture hebdomadaire	no

Fees main season Tarifs haute saison		full day
	Week days Semaine	We/Bank holidays We/Férié
Individual Individuel	42 €	46 €
Couple Couple	76 €	84 €

Juniors: – 50%

Caddy	Caddy	on request
Electric Trolley	Chariot électrique	no
Buggy	Voiturette	23 € /18 holes
Clubs	Clubs	15 € /full day

Credit cards Cartes de crédit
VISA - CB - Eurocard - MasterCard

Access Accès : Dieppe → Pourville
Map 1 on page 162 Carte 1 Page 162

Golf course PARCOURS — 14/20

Site	Site	
Maintenance	Entretien	
Architect	Architecte	Willie Park Jr
Type	Type	seaside course, links
Relief	Relief	
Water in play	Eau en jeu	
Exp. to wind	Exposé au vent	
Trees in play	Arbres en jeu	

Scorecard Carte de score	Chp. Chp.	Mens Mess.	Ladies Da.
Length Long.	5780	5534	4816
Par	70	70	70
Slope system	131	125	124

Advised golfing ability / Niveau de jeu recommandé: 0 12 24 36

Hcp required Handicap exigé: no

Club house & amenities CLUB-HOUSE ET ANNEXES — 6/10

Pro shop	Pro-shop	
Driving range	Practice	
Sheltered	couvert	10 mats
On grass	sur herbe	yes
Putting-green	putting-green	yes
Pitching-green	pitching green	yes

Hotel facilities ENVIRONNEMENT HOTELIER — 5/10

HOTELS HÔTELS

La Présidence, 89 rooms, D 81 € — Dieppe 2 km
Tel (33) 02 35 84 31 31, Fax (33) 02 35 84 86 70

Aguado, 56 rooms, D 69 € — Dieppe 2 km
Tel (33) 02 35 84 27 00, Fax (33) 02 35 06 17 61

Auberge du Clos Normand, 8 rooms, D 59 € — Martin-Eglise
Tel (33) 02 35 04 40 34, Fax (33) 02 35 04 48 49

RESTAURANTS RESTAURANT

La Mélie, Tel (33) 02 35 84 21 19 — Dieppe
Auberge du Trou Normand, Tel (33) 02 35 84 59 84 — Pourville
Marmite Dieppoise Tel (33) 02 35 84 24 26 — Dieppe 2 km

DINARD

13 | 6 | 7

Ouvert en 1887, ce parcours a été, comme Biarritz, originellement dessiné par Willie Dunn, mais remanié depuis à tel point qu'il ne reste qu'une dizaine de trous d'une esthétique spécifiquement écossaise. Ils suffisent à faire de Dinard un golf à connaître. Sa longueur peut paraître dérisoire, même avec un par 68, mais attendez que le vent souffle un peu... il faut être alors spécialiste en balistique pour calculer les dérives ! Et un seul par 5 offre une franche occasion de birdie. Ici, le choix de club est difficile, et l'on se retrouve sans cesse "entre deux clubs" pour attaquer les drapeaux. Les greens sont bien défendus, et souvent de petite taille, ce qui oblige à une extrême précision. Un golf surtout amusant, à jouer avec les golfeurs de tous niveaux , et dont l'ambiance est très sportive : beaucoup de familles de grands golfeurs parisiens viennent ici depuis des lustres. L'arrosage des fairways a amélioré l'entretien en été, et la vue sur la mer reste splendide par tous les temps.

Opened in 1887, this course was originally designed, like Biarritz, by Willie Dunn, but it has been restyled so many times over the years that only about ten holes have preserved their special Scottish flavour. And they alone are enough to make Dinard a course worth knowing. The length may appear derisory by today's standards, even as a par 68, but when the wind howls, it feels and plays much longer. Specialising in ballistics can be a handy asset here to calculate flight and deviation! Only one par 5 provides a real birdie chance. Elsewhere, difficulties arise from club selection, and players are often stuck "between two clubs" for their approach shots. The greens are often small and well defended, thus calling for extreme precision. An entertaining course with a great sporting atmosphere, to be played with golfers of all levels. Many families of great Parisian golfers have been coming here for years. The watering of fairways has improved maintenance during summer months. The view over the sea is splendid whatever the weather.

Golf de Dinard — 1887

Boulevard de la Houle
F - 35 800 SAINT-BRIAC-SUR-MER

Office	Secrétariat	(33) 02 99 88 32 07
Pro shop	Pro-shop	(33) 02 99 88 30 55
Fax	Fax	(33) 02 99 88 04 53
Web	www.dinardgolf.com	
Situation	Situation	
Dinard (pop. 9 920), 5 km		
Annual closure	Fermeture annuelle	no
Weekly closure	Fermeture hebdomadaire	no

Fees main season Tarifs haute saison	full day	
	Week days Semaine	**We/Bank holidays** We/Férié
Individual Individuel	49 €	49 €
Couple Couple	98 €	98 €
Under 18: – 50%		

Caddy	Caddy	no
Electric Trolley	Chariot électrique	no
Buggy	Voiturette	23 € /18 holes
Clubs	Clubs	15 € /18 holes

Credit cards Cartes de crédit
VISA - CB - Eurocard - MasterCard

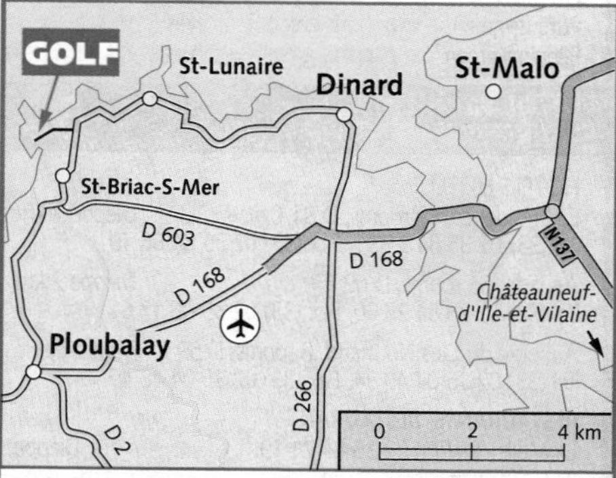

Access Accès : Dinard → Saint-Lunaire, → Golf
Map 5 on page 171 Carte 5 Page 171

Golf course PARCOURS — 13/20

Site	Site	
Maintenance	Entretien	
Architect	Architecte	Willie Dunn
Type	Type	seaside course, links
Relief	Relief	
Water in play	Eau en jeu	
Exp. to wind	Exposé au vent	
Trees in play	Arbres en jeu	

Scorecard Carte de score	**Chp.** Chp.	**Mens** Mess.	**Ladies** Da.
Length Long.	5227	5003	4442
Par	68	68	68
Slope system	113	110	111

Advised golfing ability Niveau de jeu recommandé — 0 12 24 36

Hcp required Handicap exigé — 35

Club house & amenities CLUB-HOUSE ET ANNEXES — 6/10

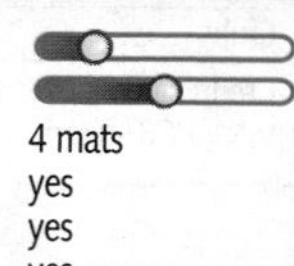

Pro shop	Pro-shop	
Driving range	Practice	
Sheltered	couvert	4 mats
On grass	sur herbe	yes
Putting-green	putting-green	yes
Pitching-green	pitching green	yes

Hotel facilities ENVIRONNEMENT HOTELIER — 7/10

HOTELS HÔTELS

Reine Hortense, 8 rooms, D 157 € — Dinard 5 km
Tel (33) 02 99 46 54 31, Fax (33) 02 99 88 15 88

Grand Hôtel de Dinard, 87 rooms, D 277 € — Dinard
Tel (33) 02 99 88 26 26, Fax (33) 02 99 88 26 27

Golf Hôtel, 40 rooms, D 72 € — St Briac on site
Tel (33) 02 99 88 30 30, Fax (33) 02 99 88 07 87

RESTAURANTS RESTAURANT

Salle à Manger, Tel (33) 02 99 16 07 95 — Dinard
Clos du Chanoine Tel(33) 02 99 82 84 57 — St Malo (→ Cancale)18 km
Le Chalut, Tel (33) 02 99 56 71 58 — Saint-Malo 12 km

DISNEYLAND PARIS Peter + Alice

16 | 7 | 8

Ce n'est pas encore un énorme complexe golfique comme Disneyworld à Orlando, mais Disneyland Paris offre un 18 trous et un 9 trous de bonne valeur, construits par Ronald Fream sur un terrain plat, mais fortement modelé. Cet ensemble n'est pas d'une trop grande complexité technique, les pièges sont immédiatement visibles et les grands espaces favorisent les longs frappeurs. Cependant, les contours assez tourmentés des greens et quelques difficultés stratégiques permettent aux techniciens d'y exprimer leur virtuosité. L'ensemble présente un visage très américain, il ne faudra pas s'en étonner, avec bon nombre d'obstacles d'eau. Si les trois parcours de 9 trous affirment peu à peu leur personnalité, le Club House et les équipements sont fonctionnels, mais manquent toujours de chaleur. C'est un complexe évidemment commercial, sans véritable vie de Club... mais évidemment destiné aux joueurs de passage. On aime ou pas.

This is not yet your actual outsized golfing complex as in Disneyworld Orlando, but Disneyland Paris presently provides an 18-hole and a 9-hole course built by Ronald Fream over flat terrain bulldozed into shape. Technically speaking, the course is not too complex, as traps are immediately visible and wide open space is a gift for long-hitters. However, the twisting greens and a number of strategic difficulties also give the technicians a chance to practice their skills. Not surprisingly, the whole layout has a very American look to it with a good number of water hazards. While the three courses gradually forge a personality, the Club House and facilities are functional, but lack warmth or soul. This is obviously a business venture without any real club life, but is obviously intended for people passing through Paris. Not to everyone's liking.

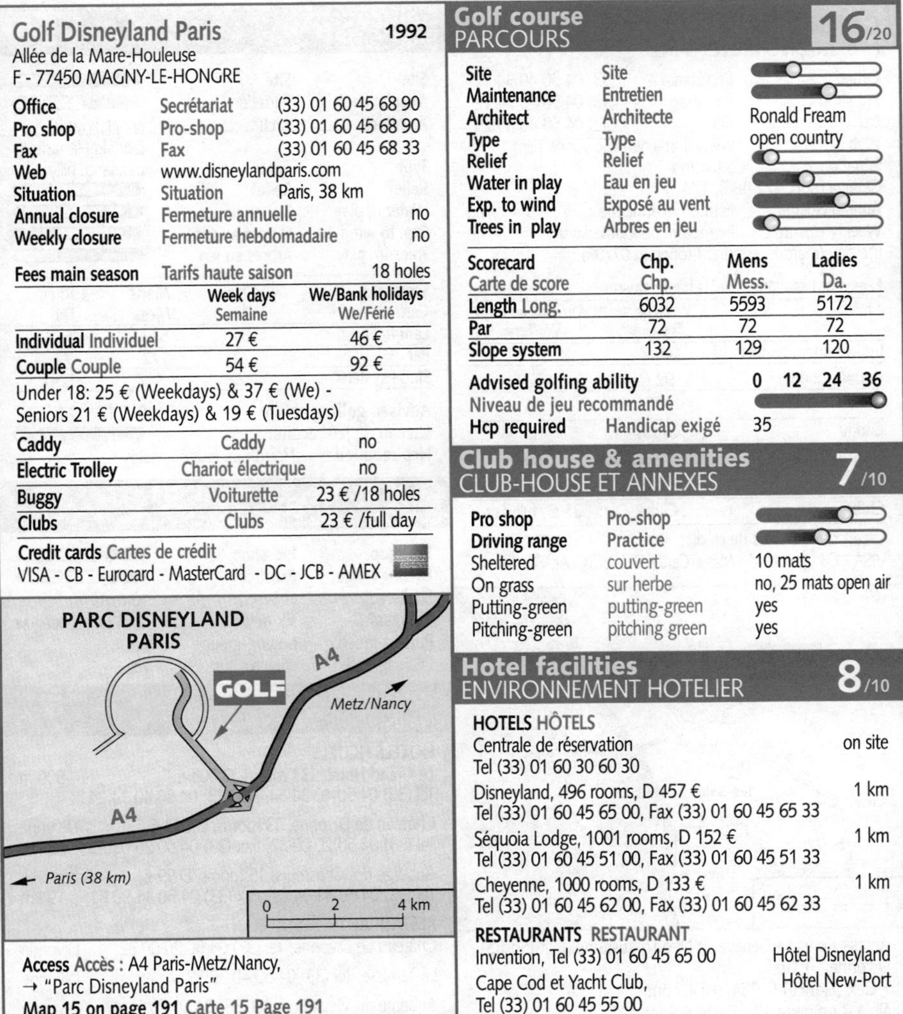

Golf Disneyland Paris — 1992

Allée de la Mare-Houleuse
F - 77450 MAGNY-LE-HONGRE

Office	Secrétariat	(33) 01 60 45 68 90
Pro shop	Pro-shop	(33) 01 60 45 68 90
Fax	Fax	(33) 01 60 45 68 33
Web	www.disneylandparis.com	
Situation	Situation	Paris, 38 km
Annual closure	Fermeture annuelle	no
Weekly closure	Fermeture hebdomadaire	no

Fees main season Tarifs haute saison	18 holes	
	Week days Semaine	**We/Bank holidays** We/Férié
Individual Individuel	27 €	46 €
Couple Couple	54 €	92 €

Under 18: 25 € (Weekdays) & 37 € (We) - Seniors 21 € (Weekdays) & 19 € (Tuesdays)

Caddy	Caddy	no
Electric Trolley	Chariot électrique	no
Buggy	Voiturette	23 € /18 holes
Clubs	Clubs	23 € /full day

Credit cards Cartes de crédit
VISA - CB - Eurocard - MasterCard - DC - JCB - AMEX

Access Accès : A4 Paris-Metz/Nancy, → "Parc Disneyland Paris"
Map 15 on page 191 Carte 15 Page 191

Golf course PARCOURS — 16/20

Site	Site	
Maintenance	Entretien	
Architect	Architecte	Ronald Fream
Type	Type	open country
Relief	Relief	
Water in play	Eau en jeu	
Exp. to wind	Exposé au vent	
Trees in play	Arbres en jeu	

Scorecard Carte de score	**Chp.** Chp.	**Mens** Mess.	**Ladies** Da.
Length Long.	6032	5593	5172
Par	72	72	72
Slope system	132	129	120

Advised golfing ability Niveau de jeu recommandé — 0 12 24 36
Hcp required Handicap exigé — 35

Club house & amenities CLUB-HOUSE ET ANNEXES — 7/10

Pro shop	Pro-shop	
Driving range	Practice	
Sheltered	couvert	10 mats
On grass	sur herbe	no, 25 mats open air
Putting-green	putting-green	yes
Pitching-green	pitching green	yes

Hotel facilities ENVIRONNEMENT HOTELIER — 8/10

HOTELS HÔTELS

Centrale de réservation — on site
Tel (33) 01 60 30 60 30

Disneyland, 496 rooms, D 457 € — 1 km
Tel (33) 01 60 45 65 00, Fax (33) 01 60 45 65 33

Séquoia Lodge, 1001 rooms, D 152 € — 1 km
Tel (33) 01 60 45 51 00, Fax (33) 01 60 45 51 33

Cheyenne, 1000 rooms, D 133 € — 1 km
Tel (33) 01 60 45 62 00, Fax (33) 01 60 45 62 33

RESTAURANTS RESTAURANT

Invention, Tel (33) 01 60 45 65 00 — Hôtel Disneyland
Cape Cod et Yacht Club, Tel (33) 01 60 45 55 00 — Hôtel New-Port

DIVONNE

14 | 6 | 7

Avec six par 4, six par 5 et six par 3, le parcours de Divonne est original, mais le fait de commencer et de terminer par des par 3 n'est pas son point fort. Dominant le Lac Léman, ce parcours de moyenne montagne est assez bien rythmé pour ne pas être épuisant, quand il n'est pas trop humide. L'environnement boisé est très plaisant (en automne notamment), et permet au minimum de transformer une mauvaise partie en jolie promenade. Peut-être un peu difficile pour les joueurs non classés, Divonne permet cependant aux golfeurs de tous niveaux de jouer ensemble, et constitue un challenge appréciable pour les meilleurs frappeurs : ils auront de multiples occasions de prendre des risques, même si l'absence de subtilités stratégiques empêche de renouveler constamment le plaisir. C'est en tout cas une halte de qualité pendant un séjour à la belle saison, mais on pourrait souhaiter un lifting de certains des trous les plus faibles, on ne manque pas trop de moyens ici.

With six par 4s, six par 5s and six par 3s, Divonne is an original course, but starting and finishing with par 3s is hardly its strong point. Overlooking lake Geneva, Divonne is a mid-mountain course which is not too tiring, when the weather is not too damp. The woody surroundings are very pleasant (especially in autumn) and at the very least can help change a rotten round into a pleasant walk. Divonne might be a little too tough for very high handicappers but it does allow golfers of all abilities to play together. It is certainly quite some challenge for the longer-hitters, who have countless opportunities to take risks, even though the course lacks strategic subtlety. At all events, this is a great stop-off over the summer months, although we could hope for the re-styling of some of the lesser holes. The resources are certainly there.

Golf de Divonne — 1931

F - 01220 DIVONNE-LES-BAINS

Office	Secrétariat	(33) 04 50 40 34 11
Pro shop	Pro-shop	(33) 04 50 40 34 11
Fax	Fax	(33) 04 50 40 34 25
Web	www.domaine-de-divonne.com	
Situation	Situation	

Genève (pop. 172 486), 17 km

Annual closure	Fermeture annuelle	no
Weekly closure	Fermeture hebdomadaire	no

tuesday (mardi): restaurant (open in 07/08)

Fees main season Tarifs haute saison	Week days Semaine	We/Bank holidays We/Férié
18 holes		
Individual Individuel	46 €	76 €
Couple Couple	92 €	152 €

Juniors: –50%

Caddy	Caddy	no
Electric Trolley	Chariot électrique	no
Buggy	Voiturette	38 € /18 holes
Clubs	Clubs	21 € /full day

Credit cards Cartes de crédit
VISA - CB - Eurocard - MasterCard - DC - JCB - AMEX

Nyon
GOLF
D 984 C
Divonne-les-Bains
Divonne Coppet
GEX
N1
LAC LÉMAN
Genève
0 2 4 km

Access Accès : • Genève → Nyon/Lausanne, Exit (Sortie) Divonne, → Golf
• Gex (France) D 984 → Divonne

Map 8 on page 177 Carte 8 Page 177

Golf course PARCOURS — 14/20

Site	Site	
Maintenance	Entretien	
Architect	Architecte	M. Nakowsky, Donald Harradine
Type	Type	parkland, hilly
Relief	Relief	
Water in play	Eau en jeu	
Exp. to wind	Exposé au vent	
Trees in play	Arbres en jeu	

Scorecard Carte de score	Chp. Chp.	Mens Mess.	Ladies Da.
Length Long.	5858	5433	4614
Par	72	72	72
Slope system	122	117	124

Advised golfing ability Niveau de jeu recommandé — 0 12 24 36

Hcp required Handicap exigé 35

Club house & amenities CLUB-HOUSE ET ANNEXES — 6/10

Pro shop	Pro-shop	
Driving range	Practice	
Sheltered	couvert	10 mats
On grass	sur herbe	no, 12 mats open air
Putting-green	putting-green	yes
Pitching-green	pitching green	yes

Hotel facilities ENVIRONNEMENT HOTELIER — 7/10

HOTELS HÔTELS

Le Grand Hôtel, 133 rooms, D 305 € — 500 m
Tel (33) 04 50 40 34 34, Fax (33) 04 50 40 34 24

Château de Divonne, 33 rooms, D 213 € — Divonne
Tel (33) 04 50 20 00 32, Fax (33) 04 50 20 03 73 — 2 km

Auberge des Chasseurs, 15 rooms, D 99 € — Echenevex
Tel (33) 04 50 41 54 07, Fax (33) 04 50 41 90 61 — 9 km

RESTAURANTS RESTAURANT

Château de Divonne, Tel (33) 04 50 20 00 32 — Divonne

La Terrasse, Tel (33) 04 50 40 35 39 — Divonne

Auberge du Vieux Bois, Tel (33) 04 50 20 01 43 — Divonne

DOMONT-MONTMORENCY | 13 | 7 | 4

Depuis 1966, Domont a conquis une réputation de club très familial, où l'accueil est toujours agréable. L'architecture manque un peu de style, mais l'architecte n'a visiblement pas souhaité bouleverser le terrain. Comme l'eau n'est en jeu que sur un seul trou, que les nombreux bunkers sont bien placés, mais rarement très profonds, les difficultés tiennent essentiellement à la présence imposante de beaux arbres souvent serrés les uns contre les autres. Ils donnent une impression trompeuse de parcours étroit, ce qui oblige à une prudence excessive : en fait, les arrivées de drive sont assez larges. Les accidents du terrain compliquent le choix de club, mais aussi l'exécution des coups quand on se trouve dans un dévers. Cependant, le parcours étant assez court, rien n'oblige à prendre des risques avec le driver, et les joueurs précis réussissent mieux ici que les frappeurs. Un parcours très plaisant, revenu à son déroulement d'origine.

Since 1966, Domont has built up a reputation as a very family club where visitors are always warmly welcomed. The layout lacks a wee bit of style, but the architect was clearly keen not to disrupt the natural terrain. With water in play on one hole only, and with numerous bunkers that, although cleverly placed, are never too deep, the main problems here come essentially from the beautiful trees that closely line nearly every fairway. They give the false impression of narrow fairways, calling for excessive caution, but in fact the drive landing areas are wide enough. The undulating terrain makes club selection a little more difficult than usual, and stroke-making is never easy on some of the sloping fairways. On the upside, the course is comparatively short, so there's no need to risk the driver. All in all, a very pleasant golf course where the straight player will almost certainly card a better score than the long-hitters. A very pleasant course now back to its original layout.

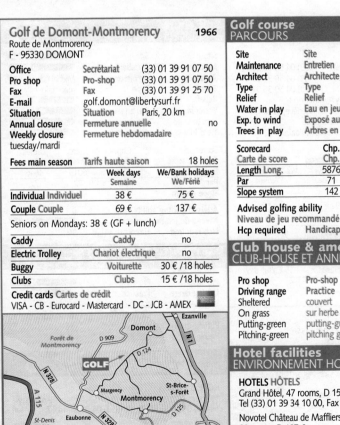

Golf de Domont-Montmorency — 1966

Route de Montmorency
F - 95330 DOMONT

Office	Secrétariat	(33) 01 39 91 07 50
Pro shop	Pro-shop	(33) 01 39 91 07 50
Fax	Fax	(33) 01 39 91 25 70
E-mail	golf.domont@libertysurf.fr	
Situation	Situation	Paris, 20 km
Annual closure	Fermeture annuelle	no
Weekly closure	Fermeture hebdomadaire	

tuesday/mardi

Fees main season / Tarifs haute saison	18 holes	
	Week days / Semaine	We/Bank holidays / We/Férié
Individual Individuel	38 €	75 €
Couple Couple	69 €	137 €

Seniors on Mondays: 38 € (GF + lunch)

Caddy	Caddy	no
Electric Trolley	Chariot électrique	no
Buggy	Voiturette	30 € /18 holes
Clubs	Clubs	15 € /18 holes

Credit cards Cartes de crédit
VISA - CB - Eurocard - Mastercard - DC - JCB - AMEX

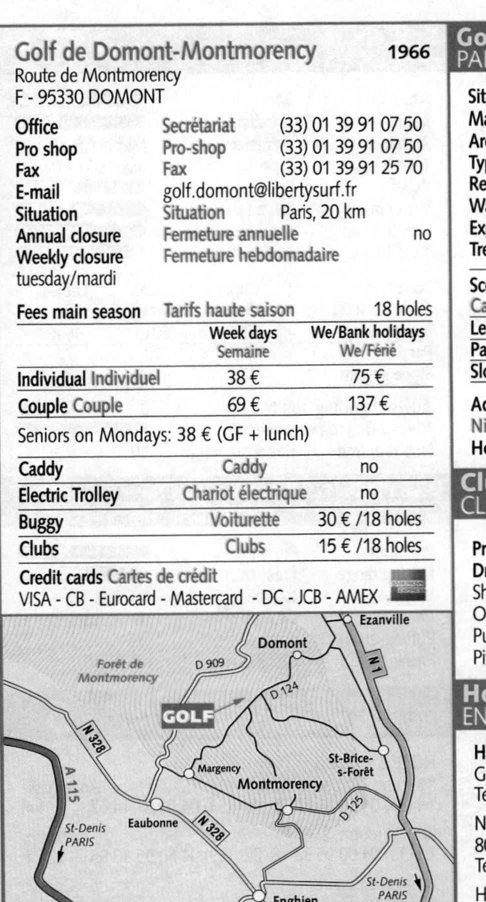

Access Accès : Paris, A1 then N1 → Beauvais, Exit (Sortie) Domont-Ezanville → Montmorency
Map 15 on page 190 Carte 15 Page 190

Golf course / PARCOURS — 13/20

Site	Site	
Maintenance	Entretien	
Architect	Architecte	Fred Hawtree
Type	Type	forest, hilly
Relief	Relief	
Water in play	Eau en jeu	
Exp. to wind	Exposé au vent	
Trees in play	Arbres en jeu	

Scorecard / Carte de score	Chp. / Chp.	Mens / Mess.	Ladies / Da.
Length Long.	5876	5570	4856
Par	71	71	71
Slope system	142	137	130

Advised golfing ability / Niveau de jeu recommandé: 0 12 24 36
Hcp required / Handicap exigé: 35

Club house & amenities / CLUB-HOUSE ET ANNEXES — 7/10

Pro shop	Pro-shop	
Driving range	Practice	
Sheltered	couvert	15 mats
On grass	sur herbe	no
Putting-green	putting-green	yes
Pitching-green	pitching green	no

Hotel facilities / ENVIRONNEMENT HOTELIER — 4/10

HOTELS HÔTELS

Grand Hôtel, 47 rooms, D 157 € — Enghien 10 km
Tel (33) 01 39 34 10 00, Fax (33) 01 39 34 10 01

Novotel Château de Mafffliers, 80 rooms, D 107 € — Maffliers 7 km
Tel (33) 01 34 08 35 35, Fax (33) 01 34 08 35 00

Hôtel du Lac, 106 rooms, D 164 € — Enghien 10 km
Tel (33) 01 39 34 11 00, Fax (33) 01 39 34 11 01

RESTAURANTS RESTAURANT

Au Cœur de la Forêt — Montmorency 5 km
Tel (33) 01 39 64 99 19

Auberge Landaise, Tel (33) 02 34 12 78 36 — Enghien 10 km

ESERY

15 | 7 | 5

Très fréquenté par les Suisses, ce parcours a été dessiné par Michel Gayon sur un terrain accidenté, avec très peu d'arbres, dans un site classé offrant des vues magnifiques. Ses difficultés viennent essentiellement des dévers, du relief, des rivières traversant les fairways et de quelques mares. Il serait sans doute plus délicat à négocier avec des roughs plus épais. Les greens sont dessinés avec beaucoup de soin, protégés par le relief naturel du terrain et par un grand nombre de bunkers, tout comme les arrivées de drive. Pour les joueurs à partir de 15 de handicap, il peut être très long, mais de nombreux départs différents permettent de se faire un parcours "à sa main", si l'on ne veut pas trop forcer son talent. Le rythme général est assez saccadé, avec des trous difficiles en succession, puis des moments de relâchement, mais la fin de parcours est technique, montant en puissance à partir du 13. L'entretien est généralement très bon.

Very popular with Swiss golfers, Esery was designed by Michel Gayon over a hilly terrain with very few trees on a listed site which provides some wonderful views. The major difficulty comes from the sloping fairways, the topography, the rivers crossing the fairways and a few ponds. It would certainly be a tougher test with thicker rough. The greens have been very carefully designed and are very well defended, not only by the naturally hilly terrain but also by well-placed bunkers. The same goes for the fairways at driving distance. For players with handicaps in the upper teens, this could prove to be a very long course, but the large number of tees lets you tailor the course to your own ability if you don't feel up to the test. The overall balance is a little disjointed with a series of difficult holes followed by a number of easier ones. The run-in is more technical, getting harder from the 13th hole onwards.

Golf Club d'Esery — 1990

Esery
F - 74930 REIGNIER

Office	Secrétariat	(33) 04 50 36 58 70
Pro shop	Pro-shop	(33) 04 50 31 20 15
Fax	Fax	(33) 04 50 36 57 62
E-mail	golf.esery@wanadoo.fr	
Situation	Situation	Genève, 12 km
Annual closure	Fermeture annuelle	no
Weekly closure	Fermeture hebdomadaire	no

monday (lundi): club-house

Fees main season Tarifs haute saison — Full day

	Week days / Semaine	We/Bank holidays / We/Férié
Individual Individuel	46 €	*
Couple Couple	92 €	*

Week-ends: members only

Caddy	Caddy	on request
Electric Trolley	Chariot électrique	15 € /18 holes
Buggy	Voiturette	30 € /18 holes
Clubs	Clubs	15 € /full day

Credit cards Cartes de crédit
VISA - CB - Eurocard - MasterCard

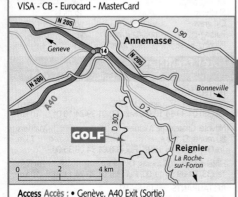

N 205
Geneve
Annemasse
D 90
14
N 205
N 206
Bonneville
A40
D 2
D 302
GOLF
Reignier
La Roche-sur-Foron
0 2 4 km

Access Accès : • Genève, A40 Exit (Sortie) Annemasse → Reignier
• Annecy, A41 Exit (Sortie) 14, → Reignier
Map 11 on page 183 Carte 11 Page 183

Golf course — PARCOURS — 15/20

Site	Site	
Maintenance	Entretien	
Architect	Architecte	Michel Gayon
Type	Type	mountain, hilly
Relief	Relief	
Water in play	Eau en jeu	
Exp. to wind	Exposé au vent	
Trees in play	Arbres en jeu	

Scorecard / Carte de score	Chp. / Chp.	Mens / Mess.	Ladies / Da.
Length Long.	6350	6019	4646
Par	72	72	72
Slope system	132	132	116

Advised golfing ability Niveau de jeu recommandé — 0 12 24 36
Hcp required Handicap exigé — 30

Club house & amenities — CLUB-HOUSE ET ANNEXES — 7/10

Pro shop	Pro-shop	
Driving range	Practice	
Sheltered	couvert	10 mats
On grass	sur herbe	no, 10 mats open air
Putting-green	putting-green	yes
Pitching-green	pitching green	no

Hotel facilities — ENVIRONNEMENT HOTELIER — 5/10

HOTELS HÔTELS

Mercure, 78 rooms, D 93 € — Annemasse
Tel (33) 04 50 92 05 25, Fax (33) 04 50 87 14 57 — 7 km

Ibis, 84 rooms, D 49 € — Archamps
Tel (33) 04 50 95 38 18, Fax (33) 04 50 95 38 95 — 12 km

Hôtel des Bergues — Genève
107 rooms, D CHF 850 — 15 km
Tel (41) 022 - 908 70 00, Fax (41) 022 - 908 70 90

RESTAURANTS RESTAURANT

Le Béarn, Tel (41) 022 - 321 00 28 — Genève 12 km

Le Chat Botté, Tel (41) 022 - 731 02 21 — Genève

ESTÉREL LATITUDES

16	6	7

A proximité immédiate du "vieux" Valescure, un peu daté mais toujours sympathique, l'Estérel constitue un ensemble touristique dans un environnement de pins, et sur un terrain modérément accidenté. Robert Trent Jones y a tracé un parcours techniquement très intéressant, d'une grande diversité de difficultés et souvent spectaculaire : notamment le 6, petit par 3 où il faut franchir un véritable gouffre. Il faut savoir bien travailler la balle pour y scorer convenablement, et choisir soigneusement son club à chaque coup, le driver n'étant certes pas obligatoire sur chaque départ. Des dizaines de bunkers et quelques obstacles d'eau très en jeu imposent de définir soigneusement sa stratégie. Les greens sont le point faible de ce parcours tactique, non par leur entretien, mais par leurs ondulations excessives (sur une demi-douzaine) qui laissent trop de place à la chance... Un parcours à connaître, malgré la présence des maisons qui enserrent parfois de trop près ce golf de style "resort".

Esterel, which lies within the immediate vicinity of the "old" Valescure course, a litte dated but as agreeable as ever, is a tourist resort in a setting of pine forest and pretty hilly countryside. Robert Trent Jones has laid out what is technically a very interesting course with a number of varied and often spectacular hazards. This is particularly so on the 6th, a short 3-par, where a sort of chasm separates tee from green. Careful club selection and ball-control are the key to a goodish score at Esterel, and the driver can certainly be banished on several holes. Dozens of bunkers and a few water hazards call for deliberate strategy. The weak point on this tactical course comes from the greens, not through their maintenance but because of excessive slope and undulation (on half a dozen holes), which leave too much to chance. A course worth knowing, despite the presence of condos now all around this resort style complex.

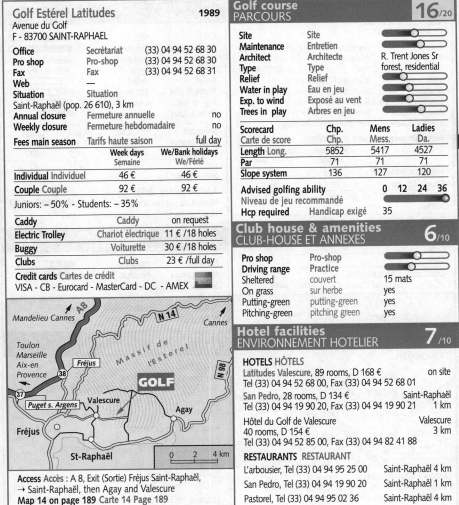

Golf Estérel Latitudes — 1989

Avenue du Golf
F - 83700 SAINT-RAPHAEL

Office	Secrétariat	(33) 04 94 52 68 30
Pro shop	Pro-shop	(33) 04 94 52 68 30
Fax	Fax	(33) 04 94 52 68 31
Web	—	
Situation	Situation	

Saint-Raphaël (pop. 26 610), 3 km

Annual closure	Fermeture annuelle	no
Weekly closure	Fermeture hebdomadaire	no
Fees main season	Tarifs haute saison	full day

	Week days Semaine	We/Bank holidays We/Férié
Individual Individuel	46 €	46 €
Couple Couple	92 €	92 €

Juniors: – 50% - Students: – 35%

Caddy	Caddy	on request
Electric Trolley	Chariot électrique	11 € /18 holes
Buggy	Voiturette	30 € /18 holes
Clubs	Clubs	23 € /full day

Credit cards Cartes de crédit
VISA - CB - Eurocard - MasterCard - DC - AMEX

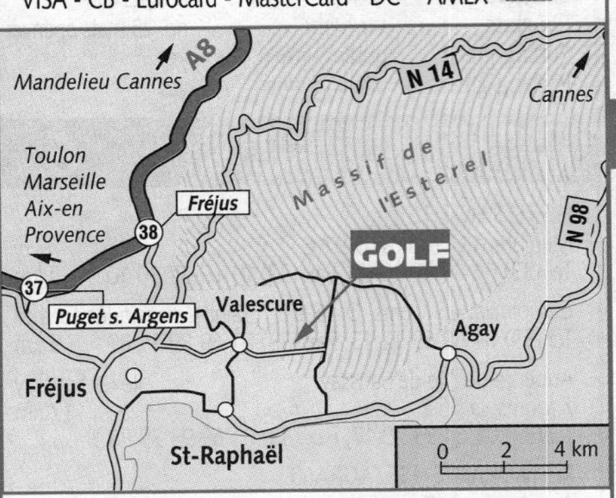

Access Accès : A 8, Exit (Sortie) Fréjus Saint-Raphaël, → Saint-Raphaël, then Agay and Valescure
Map 14 on page 189 Carte 14 Page 189

Golf course PARCOURS — 16/20

Site	Site	
Maintenance	Entretien	
Architect	Architecte	R. Trent Jones Sr
Type	Type	forest, residential
Relief	Relief	
Water in play	Eau en jeu	
Exp. to wind	Exposé au vent	
Trees in play	Arbres en jeu	

Scorecard Carte de score	Chp. Chp.	Mens Mess.	Ladies Da.
Length Long.	5852	5417	4527
Par	71	71	71
Slope system	136	127	120

Advised golfing ability 0 12 24 36
Niveau de jeu recommandé
Hcp required Handicap exigé 35

Club house & amenities CLUB-HOUSE ET ANNEXES — 6/10

Pro shop	Pro-shop	
Driving range	Practice	
Sheltered	couvert	15 mats
On grass	sur herbe	yes
Putting-green	putting-green	yes
Pitching-green	pitching green	yes

Hotel facilities ENVIRONNEMENT HOTELIER — 7/10

HOTELS HÔTELS

Latitudes Valescure, 89 rooms, D 168 € — on site
Tel (33) 04 94 52 68 00, Fax (33) 04 94 52 68 01

San Pedro, 28 rooms, D 134 € — Saint-Raphaël 1 km
Tel (33) 04 94 19 90 20, Fax (33) 04 94 19 90 21

Hôtel du Golf de Valescure — Valescure 3 km
40 rooms, D 154 €
Tel (33) 04 94 52 85 00, Fax (33) 04 94 82 41 88

RESTAURANTS RESTAURANT

L'arbousier, Tel (33) 04 94 95 25 00 — Saint-Raphaël 4 km
San Pedro, Tel (33) 04 94 19 90 20 — Saint-Raphaël 1 km
Pastorel, Tel (33) 04 94 95 02 36 — Saint-Raphaël 4 km

ETIOLLES Les Cerfs

15 | 7 | 6

Construit dans une très vaste clairière (on souhaiterait plus d'arbres), avec quelques maisons assez séduisantes, Etiolles est un exemple de bon parcours commercial, indulgent aux coups décentrés, et donc accessible à tous. Dessiné par Michel Gayon, il permet à chacun de trouver son bonheur. Les fairways (de bonne dimension) sont bien isolés par des buttes importantes, qui non seulement ajoutent du relief à un terrain assez plat, mais ramènent volontiers les balles en jeu. Les greens sont vastes, mais pas trop difficiles à lire. Logiquement, ils ne sont pas trop défendus quand l'approche se fait avec un long fer ou un bois. Parmi les trous remarquables, on distinguera le 18, de physionomie très américaine dans son dessin, ramenant vers le Club House de style colonial. On notera la construction de quelques nouveaux départs surélevés, qui donnent une meilleure appréciation de la façon d'aborder certains trous. L'entretien est très correct, et le neuf trous adjacent de bonne qualité.

Laid out over a huge clearing (a few more trees would be welcome), with some very attractive houses, Etiolles is a good example of a successful business golfing venture. Designed by Michel Gayon, there is something for everyone here. The wide fairways are neatly isolated by mounds, which not only add a little relief to a flat terrain but also obligingly bring the ball back into play. The greens are large but not too difficult to read, and so logically they are not over-protected when hitting into them with a long iron or fairway wood. One of the most remarkable holes is the very American style 18th, leading the player back to the colonial style club-house. We noted the building of some new, elevated tee-boxes, which give a clearer appreciation of how to play certain holes. Maintenance is very good, and the same goes for the adjacent 9-hole course.

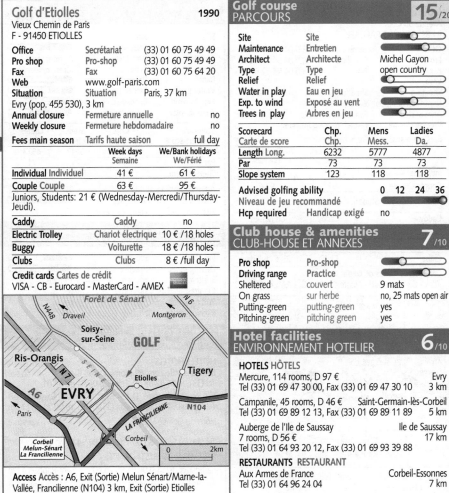

Golf d'Etiolles — 1990

Vieux Chemin de Paris
F - 91450 ETIOLLES

Office	Secrétariat	(33) 01 60 75 49 49
Pro shop	Pro-shop	(33) 01 60 75 49 49
Fax	Fax	(33) 01 60 75 64 20
Web	www.golf-paris.com	
Situation	Situation	Paris, 37 km

Evry (pop. 455 530), 3 km

Annual closure	Fermeture annuelle	no
Weekly closure	Fermeture hebdomadaire	no

Fees main season Tarifs haute saison	Week days Semaine	We/Bank holidays We/Férié
Individual Individuel	41 €	61 €
Couple Couple	63 €	95 €

Juniors, Students: 21 € (Wednesday-Mercredi/Thursday-Jeudi).

full day

Caddy	Caddy	no
Electric Trolley	Chariot électrique	10 € /18 holes
Buggy	Voiturette	18 € /18 holes
Clubs	Clubs	8 € /full day

Credit cards Cartes de crédit
VISA - CB - Eurocard - MasterCard - AMEX

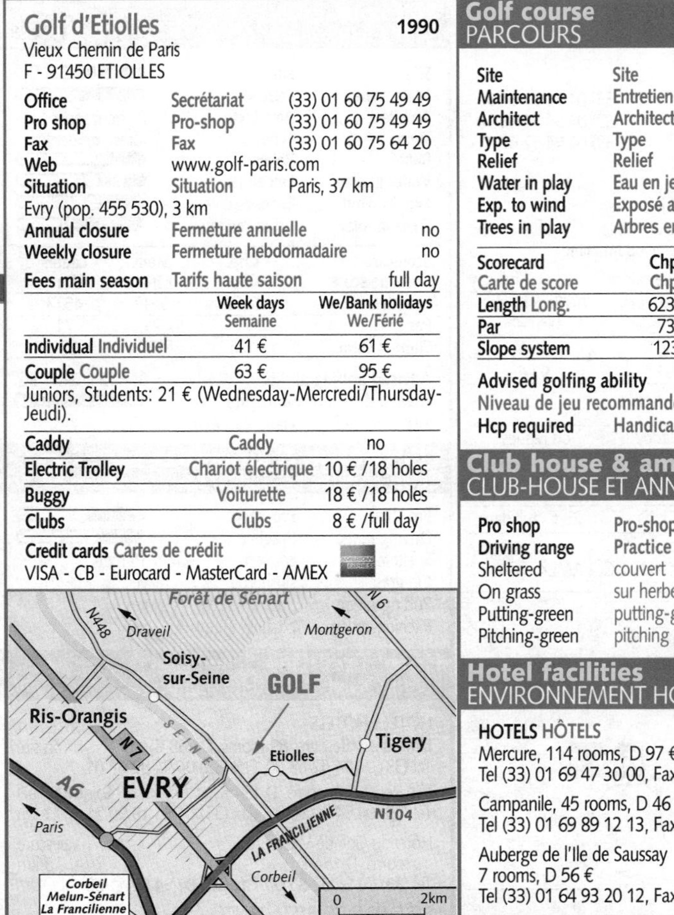

Access Accès : A6, Exit (Sortie) Melun Sénart/Marne-la-Vallée, Francilienne (N104) 3 km, Exit (Sortie) Etiolles
Map 15 on page 191 Carte 15 Page 191

Golf course PARCOURS — 15/20

Site	Site	
Maintenance	Entretien	
Architect	Architecte	Michel Gayon
Type	Type	open country
Relief	Relief	
Water in play	Eau en jeu	
Exp. to wind	Exposé au vent	
Trees in play	Arbres en jeu	

Scorecard Carte de score	Chp. Chp.	Mens Mess.	Ladies Da.
Length Long.	6232	5777	4877
Par	73	73	73
Slope system	123	118	118

Advised golfing ability Niveau de jeu recommandé — 0 12 24 36

Hcp required Handicap exigé — no

Club house & amenities CLUB-HOUSE ET ANNEXES — 7/10

Pro shop	Pro-shop	
Driving range	Practice	
Sheltered	couvert	9 mats
On grass	sur herbe	no, 25 mats open air
Putting-green	putting-green	yes
Pitching-green	pitching green	yes

Hotel facilities ENVIRONNEMENT HOTELIER — 6/10

HOTELS HÔTELS

Mercure, 114 rooms, D 97 € — Evry 3 km
Tel (33) 01 69 47 30 00, Fax (33) 01 69 47 30 10

Campanile, 45 rooms, D 46 € — Saint-Germain-lès-Corbeil 5 km
Tel (33) 01 69 89 12 13, Fax (33) 01 69 89 11 89

Auberge de l'Ile de Saussay — Ile de Saussay 17 km
7 rooms, D 56 €
Tel (33) 01 64 93 20 12, Fax (33) 01 69 93 39 88

RESTAURANTS RESTAURANT

Aux Armes de France — Corbeil-Essonnes 7 km
Tel (33) 01 64 96 24 04

Le Canal, Tel(33) 01 60 78 34 72 Evry-Courcouronnes 7 km

ETRETAT

14	7	6

La vue sur la mer, les falaises et la ville est splendide. On ne se lassera pas du 10, plongeant au drive en bord de mer, pour remonter ensuite vers le green sur un plateau. Ouvert à tous les vents, ce parcours a fait l'objet de modifications depuis sa création en 1908. Pour le classer parmi les grands links, il faudrait reprendre pas mal de bunkers, quelques greens aux surfaces souvent sans intérêt, et déplacer plusieurs départs, mais ce golf familial ne dispose pas des moyens des clubs prestigieux et les améliorations ne peuvent être que progressives. Cela dit, on peut jouer ici plusieurs jours avec beaucoup de plaisir, par beau temps au moins. Quand le vent souffle, c'est une bataille contre le parcours, et il vaut mieux jouer en match-play ! Le profil général du parcours en fait un "challenge" attachant, ne serait ce que pour travailler les balles basses. L'atmosphère du club est sympathique, avec un club house agrandi et modernisé.

The view over the sea, cliffs and the town is magnificent, and the 10th hole, with a drive plunging seaward from the cliffs before sweeping back up to an elevated green, is a moment to cherish. Exposed to all winds, the course has been altered several times since its creation in 1908, but to be ranked among the truly great links, some tees need moving and a number of bunkers require attention, as do the putting surfaces on several greens. But this is a family club that lacks the resources of the more prestigious courses, and improvements can only come gradually. Having said that, you can play here time and time again and enjoy every minute, at least if the weather holds. When the wind blows, it is a tough battle with the course and match-play is the obvious resort. The club has a friendly atmosphere in a now enlarged and modernised and the general layout of the course makes it a pleasing challenge, if only for the opportunity to practice those knock-down shots.

Golf d'Etretat — 1908

Route du Havre
F - 76790 ETRETAT

Office	Secrétariat	(33) 02 35 27 04 89
Pro shop	Pro-shop	(33) 02 35 28 56 67
Fax	Fax	(33) 02 35 29 49 02
Web	www.golfetretat.com	
Situation	Situation	

Fécamp, 16 km - Le Havre (pop. 197 210), 30 km

Annual closure	Fermeture annuelle	no
Weekly closure	Fermeture hebdomadaire	

tuesday (mardi) restaurant closed

Fees main season Tarifs haute saison	Week days Semaine	We/Bank holidays We/Férié
		full day
Individual Individuel	34 €	53 €
Couple Couple	58 €	96 €

Juniors & Students: 20 € (Weekends) - 24 € (We)

Caddy	Caddy	no
Electric Trolley	Chariot électrique	no
Buggy	Voiturette	30 € /18 holes
Clubs	Clubs	no

Credit cards Cartes de crédit
VISA - CB - Eurocard - MasterCard

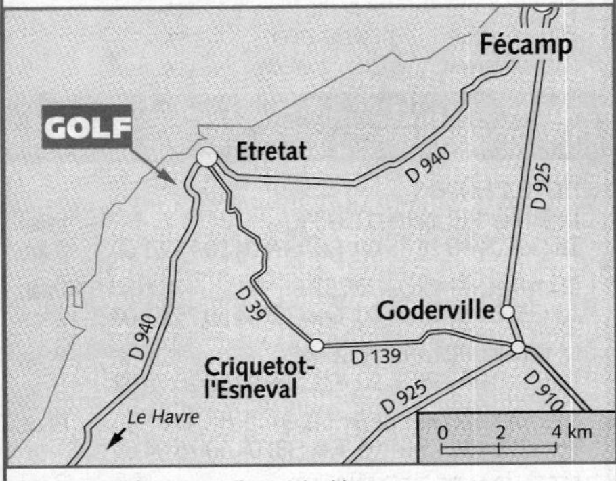

Access Accès : D940 Etretat-Le Havre
Map 2 on page 165 Carte 2 Page 165

Golf course PARCOURS — 14/20

Site	Site	
Maintenance	Entretien	
Architect	Architecte	M. Chantepie, D. Fruchet (4 trous)
Type	Type	seaside course, open country
Relief	Relief	
Water in play	Eau en jeu	
Exp. to wind	Exposé au vent	
Trees in play	Arbres en jeu	

Scorecard Carte de score	Chp. Chp.	Mens Mess.	Ladies Da.
Length Long.	6073	5679	4786
Par	72	72	72
Slope system	126	119	119

Advised golfing ability Niveau de jeu recommandé: 0 12 24 36
Hcp required Handicap exigé: 35 - 28 We

Club house & amenities CLUB-HOUSE ET ANNEXES — 7/10

Pro shop	Pro-shop	
Driving range	Practice	
Sheltered	couvert	2 mats
On grass	sur herbe	yes (in Summer)
Putting-green	putting-green	yes
Pitching-green	pitching green	yes

Hotel facilities ENVIRONNEMENT HOTELIER — 6/10

HOTELS HÔTELS

Dormy House Golf Hôtel, 49 rooms, D 95 € — 500 m
Tel (33) 02 35 27 07 88, Fax (33) 02 35 29 86 19

Le Donjon, 11 rooms, D 152 € — Etretat 2 km
Tel (33) 02 35 27 08 23, Fax (33) 02 35 29 92 24

Les Falaises, 24 rooms, D 56 € — Etretat
Tel (33) 02 35 27 02 77

RESTAURANTS RESTAURANT

Le Belvédère, Tel (33) 02 35 20 13 76 — Etretat 2 km
Le Galion, Tel(33) 02 35 29 48 74 — Etretat
Auberge de la Rouge, Tel (33) 02 35 28 07 59 — Fécamp

EVIAN

15 | 7 | 9

Le remodelage effectué par Cabell Robinson en 1990 a "réveillé" et beaucoup amélioré ce parcours. Les greens sont maintenant très protégés, avec des jeux de buttes et de nombreux bunkers très en jeu, mettant beaucoup plus l'accent sur les aspects techniques du jeu. Si les joueurs très moyens ont parfois regretté ces nouvelles difficultés, le parcours a repris son rang parmi les meilleurs de la région lémanique. Assez accidenté (voiturette conseillée pour les seniors), quasiment comme un golf de montagne, Evian n'est pas très long, mais les dénivellations peuvent être trompeuses, notamment au 15, petit par 3 très spectaculaire dominant le lac Léman. Le plus joli point de vue du parcours, couronnant l'impression très agréable d'évoluer dans un beau parc. L'entretien est généralement assez remarquable, dans la continuité de l'Evian Masters qui s'y joue chaque année. On peut trouver aussi qu'il y a une certaine indigestion de petites fleurs.

The restyling carried out by Cabell Robinson in 1990 has revamped and much improved this course. The greens are now particularly well guarded, with a series of sand-hills and easy-to-hit bunkers, thus placing much more emphasis on the technical side of the game. While high-handicappers may often come to regret these new difficulties, the course has recovered its status as one of the best courses in the region. Hilly enough to be virtually a mountain course (buggy recommended for seniors), Evian is not very long, but the steep slopes can be deceiving, especially on the 15th, a highly spectacular short par 3 overlooking Lake Geneva. This is the prettiest spot on the course and crowns the very pleasant impression of playing golf in a beautiful park. Maintenance is by and large quite remarkable, as befits a course which hosts the Evian Masters each year. You might also find that there are a little too many flowers...

Royal Golf Club Evian — 1904

B.P. No 8
F - 74502 EVIAN

Office	Secrétariat	(33) 04 50 75 46 66
Pro shop	Pro-shop	(33) 04 50 75 51 96
Fax	Fax	(33) 04 50 75 65 54
Web	www.evianmasters.com	
Situation	Situation	

Evian (pop. 8 900), 2.5 km - Genève (pop. 172 486), 46 km

Annual closure	Fermeture annuelle	15/12→31/1
Weekly closure	Fermeture hebdomadaire	no

Fees main season Tarifs haute saison — 18 holes

	Week days Semaine	We/Bank holidays We/Férié
Individual Individuel	53 €	61 €
Couple Couple	106 €	122 €

Juniors: – 50%

Caddy	Caddy	on request
Electric Trolley	Chariot électrique	21 € /18 holes
Buggy	Voiturette	43 € /18 holes
Clubs	Clubs	23 € /18 holes

Credit cards Cartes de crédit
VISA - CB - Eurocard - MasterCard - DC - JCB - AMEX

LAC LÉMAN
Amphion les-Bains
Évian-les-Bains
N 5
vers St-Gingolph
GOLF
Thonon les-Bains
vers Genève
0 2 4 km

Access Accès : Genève → Evian, take right → Golf
Map 8 on page 177 Carte 8 Page 177

Golf course PARCOURS — 15/20

Site	Site	
Maintenance	Entretien	
Architect	Architecte	Cabell Robinson
Type	Type	parkland, hilly
Relief	Relief	
Water in play	Eau en jeu	
Exp. to wind	Exposé au vent	
Trees in play	Arbres en jeu	

Scorecard Carte de score	Chp. Chp.	Mens Mess.	Ladies Da.
Length Long.	6006	5651	5094
Par	72	72	72
Slope system	128	123	125

Advised golfing ability Niveau de jeu recommandé — 0 12 24 36
Hcp required Handicap exigé — 35

Club house & amenities CLUB-HOUSE ET ANNEXES — 7/10

Pro shop	Pro-shop	
Driving range	Practice	
Sheltered	couvert	20 mats
On grass	sur herbe	yes
Putting-green	putting-green	yes
Pitching-green	pitching green	yes

Hotel facilities ENVIRONNEMENT HOTELIER — 9/10

HOTELS HÔTELS

Le Royal, 155 rooms, D 335 € — Evian 3 km
Tel (33) 04 50 26 85 00, Fax (33) 04 50 75 61 00

L'Ermitage, 91 rooms, D 259 € — Evian 2 km
Tel (33) 04 50 26 85 00, Fax (33) 04 50 75 61 00

La Verniaz, 30 rooms, D 229 € — Evian
Tel (33) 04 50 75 04 90, Fax (33) 04 50 70 78 92

Bourgogne et Ducs de Savoie, 31 rooms, D 82 € — Evian
Tel (33) 04 50 75 01 05, Fax (33) 04 50 75 04 05

RESTAURANTS RESTAURANT

Café Royal, Tel (33) 04 50 26 85 00 — Evian 3 km

FEUCHEROLLES

15 | 7 | 5

Un parcours assez vallonné, mais où la mise en oeuvre des reliefs a été faite avec intelligence, et le souci d'éviter les coups aveugles. Cette franchise a beaucoup contribué à sa réputation. Très varié, le dessin de l'américain Jean-Marie Poellot met en jeu tous les types d'obstacles et exige tous les coups de golf; il propose fréquemment des choix stratégiques intéressants, et des situations de petit jeu excitantes. Les trous sont de bonne longueur, à l'exception du 13, un par 3 démesuré, mais on ne recommandera les départs arrière qu'aux handicaps à un chiffre. Très travaillés, les greens demandent beaucoup de finesse et d'attention pour ne pas perdre trop de points au putting. Le fonctionnement du club est complètement commercial, mais l'ensemble reste accueillant. Le drainage a bien amélioré certains trous volontiers humides. Et le Club-House est à la hauteur, sinon très chaleureux.

A comparatively hilly course where relief has been employed intelligently to carefully avoid blind shots. This straight and honest side to the layout has done much to help the course's reputation. The very varied design of American architect Jean-Marie Poellot brings all types of hazard into play and demands every shot in the book. Interestingly, the layout often gives a choice of strategy and some exciting situations for short-play around the greens. All the holes are of a good length, except the outsized 13th hole, a par-3 of over 200 metres, but generally the back-tees are to be recommended for single-figure handicappers. A lot of work has gone into the greens, which require more than a touch of finesse if you want to avoid too many 3-putts (and who doesn't?). The club is a totally commercial affair, but the whole complex extends a warm welcome. A drainage system has improved some of the very wet holes and the very hospitable club-house is worthy of the rest.

Golf de Feucherolles — 1993

Sainte-Gemme
F -78810 FEUCHEROLLES

Office	Secrétariat	(33) 01 30 54 94 94
Pro shop	Pro-shop	(33) 01 30 54 94 94
Fax	Fax	(33) 01 30 54 92 37
Web	www.golf-de-feucherolles.com	
Situation	Situation	Paris, 39 km

St-Germain-en-Laye (pop. 39 920), 12 km

Annual closure	Fermeture annuelle	no
Weekly closure	Fermeture hebdomadaire	

tuesday (mardi) 1/11→28/2

Fees main season Tarifs haute saison	**Week days** Semaine	**We/Bank holidays** We/Férié
	18 holes	
Individual Individuel	46 €	61 €
Couple Couple	92 €	122 €

Caddy	Caddy	on request
Electric Trolley	Chariot électrique	no
Buggy	Voiturette	18 € /18 holes
Clubs	Clubs	23 € /full day

Credit cards Cartes de crédit
VISA - CB - Eurocard - MasterCard - DC - JCB - AMEX

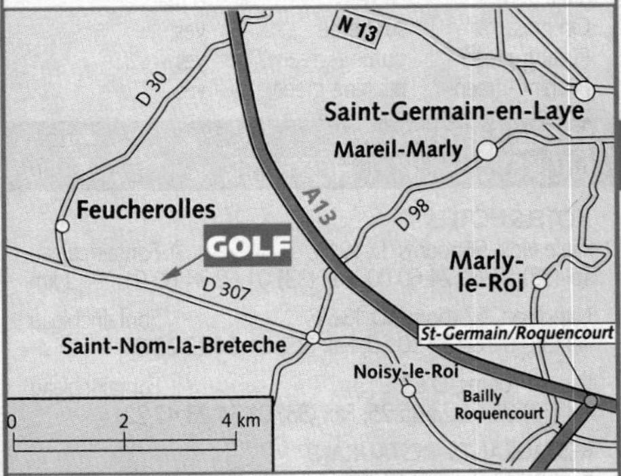

Access Accès : Paris A13 → Versailles, Exit (Sortie) Saint-Germain-en-Laye → Saint-Nom-la- Bretèche, → Feucherolles
Map 15 on page 191 Carte 15 Page 191

Golf course — PARCOURS — 15/20

Site	Site	
Maintenance	Entretien	
Architect	Architecte	Jean-Marie Poellot
Type	Type	parkland, open country
Relief	Relief	
Water in play	Eau en jeu	
Exp. to wind	Exposé au vent	
Trees in play	Arbres en jeu	

Scorecard Carte de score	**Chp.** Chp.	**Mens** Mess.	**Ladies** Da.
Length Long.	6358	5887	4970
Par	72	72	72
Slope system	141	138	137

Advised golfing ability Niveau de jeu recommandé — 0 12 24 36

Hcp required Handicap exigé — no

Club house & amenities — CLUB-HOUSE ET ANNEXES — 7/10

Pro shop	Pro-shop	
Driving range	Practice	
Sheltered	couvert	4 mats
On grass	sur herbe	no, 8 mats open air
Putting-green	putting-green	yes
Pitching-green	pitching green	no

Hotel facilities — ENVIRONNEMENT HOTELIER — 5/10

HOTELS HÔTELS

La Forestière, 30 rooms, D 213 € — Saint-Germain 12 km
Tel (33) 01 30 61 64 64, Fax (33) 01 39 73 88 88

Le Pavillon Henri IV, 42 rooms, D 172 € — Saint-Germain 12 km
Tel (33) 01 39 10 15 15, Fax (33) 01 39 93 73 93

Ermitage des Loges — Saint-Germain 12 km
56 rooms, D 108 €
Tel (33) 01 39 21 50 90, Fax (33) 01 39 21 50 91

RESTAURANTS RESTAURANT

Les Trois Marches — Versailles 10 km
Tel (33) 01 39 50 13 21

Le Potager du Roy, Tel (33) 01 39 50 35 34 Versailles 10 km

FONTAINEBLEAU

17 | 7 | 7

Situé à l'orée de la superbe forêt de Fontainebleau, ce parcours est l'un des plus tranquilles de la région parisienne. Il fait partie de ces grands refuges d'une certaine tradition britannique, bien que l'on puisse regretter que certaines retouches aient été apportées au dessin de Simpson au cours des années, notamment sur quelques greens, et par exemple une restauration du 14 (bêtement aveugle) ne serait pas du luxe. Un regret mineur en regard des satisfactions visuelles et golfiques que l'on peut éprouver ici, au milieu des chênes, des pins et des hêtres, où l'on devine parfois les ombres des biches, où l'on dérange souvent lièvres et lapins. Grâce au terrain très sablonneux et au gazon très souple, on peut découvrir ici toute l'année un parcours plus que plaisant, pas trop difficile, bien que les greens soient souvent petits et parfois très torturés, mais où un bon score n'est jamais le fait du hasard. Un parcours complet, où l'aspect visuel a été encore amélioré.

This course, lying on the edge of the magnificent forest of Fontainebleau, is one of the quietest around Paris. It is one of those great bastions of British tradition, although some might regret the way Simpson's layout has been retouched here and there over the years, particularly on some of the greens. For example, restoring the original green on the 14th, presently an inanely blind hole, would be most welcome. This is only a minor gripe given the visual and golfing pleasure to be had here amidst the oak, pine and beech trees, where you can sometimes make out the shape of deer or disturb hares and rabbits. With very sandy terrain and plush grass, you can play this more than pleasant and not too difficult course all year, although the greens are often small and very torturous. Here, a good score is never down to chance on a course that has everything and where visual appeal has been improved.

Golf de Fontainebleau — 1909

Route d'Orléans
F - 77300 FONTAINEBLEAU

Office	Secrétariat	(33) 01 64 22 22 95
Pro shop	Pro-shop	(33) 01 64 22 74 19
Fax	Fax	(33) 01 64 22 63 76
E-mail	golf.fontainebleau@wanadoo.fr	
Situation	Situation	Fontainebleau , 1 km
Annual closure	Fermeture annuelle	no
Weekly closure	Fermeture hebdomadaire	tuesday mardi

268

Fees main season Tarifs haute saison		full day
	Week days Semaine	**We/Bank holidays** We/Férié
Individual Individuel	53 €	*
Couple Couple	106 €	*

* We : members only (réservé aux membres)

Caddy	Caddy	30 € /on request
Electric Trolley	Chariot électrique	no
Buggy	Voiturette	no
Clubs	Clubs	15 € /full day

Credit cards Cartes de crédit
VISA - CB - MasterCard - Eurocard

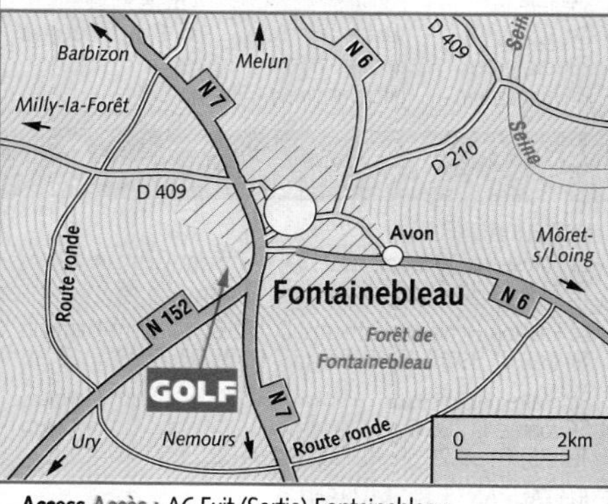

Access Accès : A6 Exit (Sortie) Fontainebleau.
N7 → Fontainebleau. "Carrefour de l'Obélisque",
N152 → Malesherbes. Golf 500 m on right hand side.
Map 3 on page 166 Carte 3 Page 166

Golf course — PARCOURS — 17/20

Site	Site	
Maintenance	Entretien	
Architect	Architecte	Tom Simpson
Type	Type	forest
Relief	Relief	
Water in play	Eau en jeu	
Exp. to wind	Exposé au vent	
Trees in play	Arbres en jeu	

Scorecard Carte de score	**Chp.** Chp.	**Mens** Mess.	**Ladies** Da.
Length Long.	6074	5711	5168
Par	72	72	72
Slope system	130	124	126

Advised golfing ability Niveau de jeu recommandé — 0 12 24 36
Hcp required Handicap exigé — 24 Men, 28 Ladies

Club house & amenities — CLUB-HOUSE ET ANNEXES — 7/10

Pro shop	Pro-shop	
Driving range	Practice	
Sheltered	couvert	6 mats
On grass	sur herbe	yes
Putting-green	putting-green	yes
Pitching-green	pitching green	yes

Hotel facilities — ENVIRONNEMENT HOTELIER — 7/10

HOTELS HÔTELS

Aigle Noir, 56 rooms, D 191 € — Fontainebleau
Tel (33) 01 60 74 60 00, Fax (33) 01 60 74 60 01 — 2 km

Napoléon, 57 rooms, D 136 € — Fontainebleau
Tel (33) 01 60 39 50 50, Fax (33) 01 64 22 20 87

Ibis, 81 rooms, D 62 € — Fontainebleau
Tel (33) 01 64 23 45 25, Fax (33) 01 64 23 42 22

RESTAURANTS RESTAURANT

Bas- Bréau, Tel (33) 01 60 66 40 05 — Barbizon 10 km

Table des Maréchaux — Fontainebleau 2 km
Tel (33) 01 60 39 50 50

Croquembouche, Tel (33) 01 64 22 01 57 — Fontainebleau

FONTCAUDE

14 | 6 | 6

Dans un environnement immobilier manquant singulièrement de beauté, ce parcours a été dessiné par Chris Pittman sur un terrain relativement accidenté. Quelques accidents de terrain (ravin au 11), de petits arbustes, la garrigue et quelques grands arbres interviennent pour compliquer le jeu, ainsi que des dénivellations et dévers parfois préoccupants. Si l'on ajoute quelques trous en bordure de rivière, des greens bien modelés et des bunkers assez profonds pour inciter à s'entraîner avant de les affronter, les joueurs trouveront là un parcours varié et amusant, mais les meilleurs estimeront sans doute qu'il manque "un petit quelque chose" pour en faire un grand parcours. Néammoins, c'est un bon complément dans une région de bonne qualité golfique, notamment avec La Grande Motte, Massane, Cap d'Agde et Nîmes-Campagne.

Laid out in an environment of property development singularly lacking in appeal, this course was designed by Chris Pittman over comparatively hilly terrain. A few drastic features (a ravine on the 11th), small bushes, the "garrigue" and a few big trees actively complicate the course, as do some of the steep slopes and inclines, which can cause considerable concern. Add to this a few holes alongside a river, well-contoured greens and bunkers that are deep enough to prompt some sand practice before the round, and you have here a varied and amusing course, but one where the best players will doubtless feel that there is something missing for it to become a great course. Nevertheless, this is a good addition in a great region for golf, with in particular La Grande Motte, Massane, Cap d'Agde and Nîmes-Campagne in the neighbourhood.

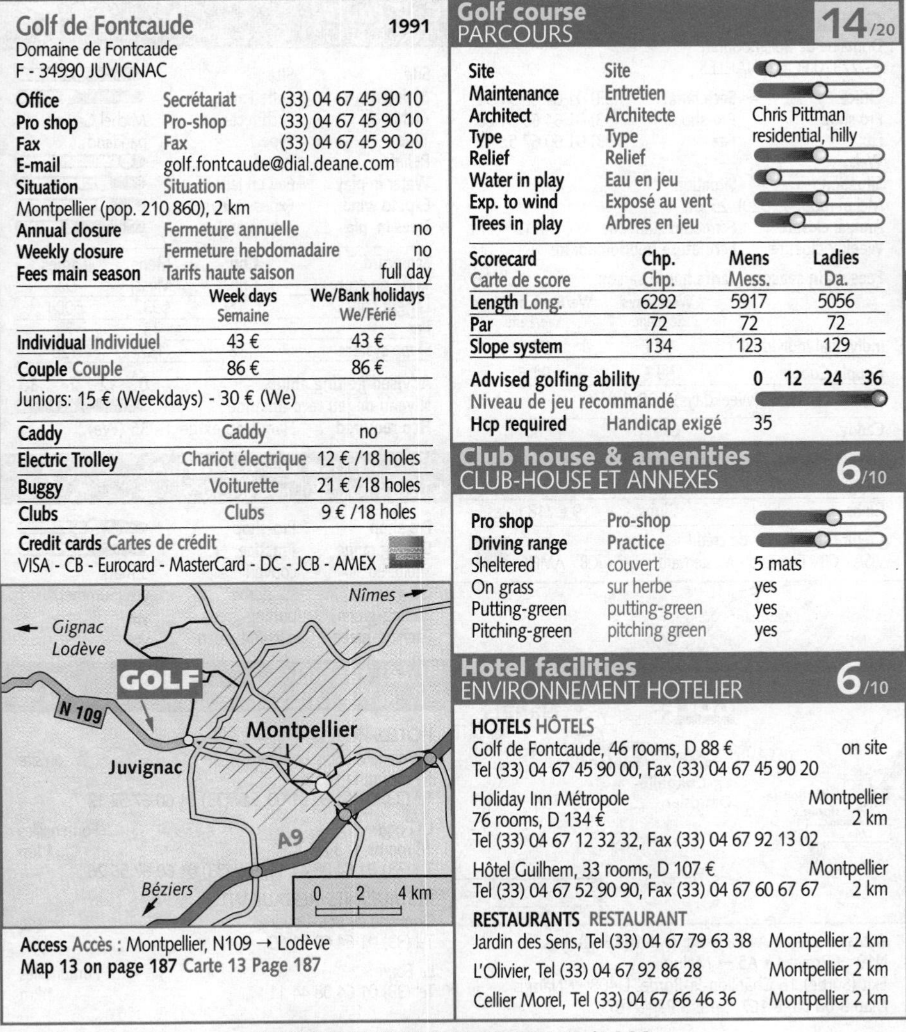

Golf de Fontcaude **1991**
Domaine de Fontcaude
F - 34990 JUVIGNAC

Office	Secrétariat	(33) 04 67 45 90 10
Pro shop	Pro-shop	(33) 04 67 45 90 10
Fax	Fax	(33) 04 67 45 90 20
E-mail	golf.fontcaude@dial.deane.com	
Situation	Situation	

Montpellier (pop. 210 860), 2 km

Annual closure	Fermeture annuelle	no
Weekly closure	Fermeture hebdomadaire	no
Fees main season	Tarifs haute saison	full day

	Week days Semaine	We/Bank holidays We/Férié
Individual Individuel	43 €	43 €
Couple Couple	86 €	86 €

Juniors: 15 € (Weekdays) - 30 € (We)

Caddy	Caddy	no
Electric Trolley	Chariot électrique	12 € /18 holes
Buggy	Voiturette	21 € /18 holes
Clubs	Clubs	9 € /18 holes

Credit cards Cartes de crédit
VISA - CB - Eurocard - MasterCard - DC - JCB - AMEX

Access Accès : Montpellier, N109 → Lodève
Map 13 on page 187 Carte 13 Page 187

Golf course PARCOURS 14/20

Site	Site	
Maintenance	Entretien	
Architect	Architecte	Chris Pittman
Type	Type	residential, hilly
Relief	Relief	
Water in play	Eau en jeu	
Exp. to wind	Exposé au vent	
Trees in play	Arbres en jeu	

Scorecard Carte de score	Chp. Chp.	Mens Mess.	Ladies Da.
Length Long.	6292	5917	5056
Par	72	72	72
Slope system	134	123	129

Advised golfing ability 0 12 24 36
Niveau de jeu recommandé
Hcp required Handicap exigé 35

Club house & amenities CLUB-HOUSE ET ANNEXES 6/10

Pro shop	Pro-shop	
Driving range	Practice	
Sheltered	couvert	5 mats
On grass	sur herbe	yes
Putting-green	putting-green	yes
Pitching-green	pitching green	yes

Hotel facilities ENVIRONNEMENT HOTELIER 6/10

HOTELS HÔTELS

Golf de Fontcaude, 46 rooms, D 88 € — on site
Tel (33) 04 67 45 90 00, Fax (33) 04 67 45 90 20

Holiday Inn Métropole — Montpellier 2 km
76 rooms, D 134 €
Tel (33) 04 67 12 32 32, Fax (33) 04 67 92 13 02

Hôtel Guilhem, 33 rooms, D 107 € — Montpellier 2 km
Tel (33) 04 67 52 90 90, Fax (33) 04 67 60 67 67

RESTAURANTS RESTAURANT

Jardin des Sens, Tel (33) 04 67 79 63 38 — Montpellier 2 km
L'Olivier, Tel (33) 04 67 92 86 28 — Montpellier 2 km
Cellier Morel, Tel (33) 04 67 66 46 36 — Montpellier 2 km

FONTENAILLES Blanc

14 | 7 | 6

Dans cet ensemble de 27 trous, le 18 trous "Blanc" est considéré comme le pacours principal, même si le "Rouge" propose aussi quelques bons trous. L'architecte Michel Gayon a travaillé avec dextérité et imagination ce vaste espace plat et joliment boisé. Il faut profiter de quelques trous assez courts pour ne pas trop gâter une carte de score forcément mise à mal sur d'autres trous, exigeant beaucoup de puissance au drive. C'est en général un parcours mieux adapté aux frappeurs qu'aux techniciens. En tout cas, certains obstacles cachés impliquent de le jouer plusieurs fois pour bien le connaître avant d'espérer bien y scorer. L'entretien du parcours est généralement de bonne qualité, mais il reste un peu humide en hiver, notamment dans les zones les plus boisées. Le complexe Club house-Hôtel est assez confortable et plaisant pour que l'on s'y attarde.

In this 27-hole complex, the 18-hole "White" course is considered to be the main layout, although the 9-hole "Red" alternative also features a few interesting holes. Architect Michel Gayon has employed a lot of skill and imagination in developing this enormous flat space, which has more than its fair share of woodland. Here, you take advantage of a few short holes in order to protect a card that will definitely be hard pushed to survive some of the others, which require power-play and length off the tee. Generally speaking, this is a course for long-hitters rather than for technicians. In any case, a number of hidden hazards call for several outings before hoping to card a good score. Maintenance is generally good, but the course is bit damp in winter, especially in the woodier areas. The club-house/hotel complex is comfortable and pleasant enough to warrant spending some time here.

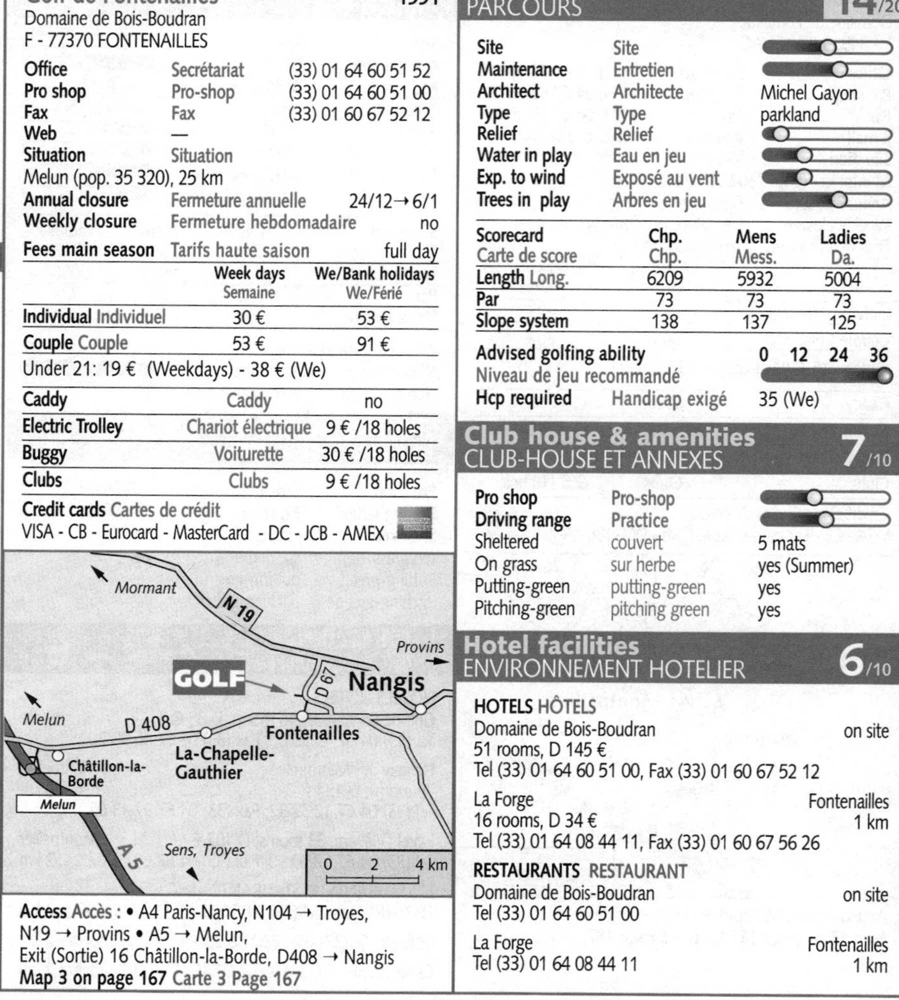

Golf de Fontenailles — 1991

Domaine de Bois-Boudran
F - 77370 FONTENAILLES

Office	Secrétariat	(33) 01 64 60 51 52
Pro shop	Pro-shop	(33) 01 64 60 51 00
Fax	Fax	(33) 01 60 67 52 12
Web	—	
Situation	Situation	

Melun (pop. 35 320), 25 km

Annual closure	Fermeture annuelle	24/12→6/1
Weekly closure	Fermeture hebdomadaire	no
Fees main season	Tarifs haute saison	full day

	Week days Semaine	We/Bank holidays We/Férié
Individual Individuel	30 €	53 €
Couple Couple	53 €	91 €

Under 21: 19 € (Weekdays) - 38 € (We)

Caddy	Caddy	no
Electric Trolley	Chariot électrique	9 € /18 holes
Buggy	Voiturette	30 € /18 holes
Clubs	Clubs	9 € /18 holes

Credit cards Cartes de crédit
VISA - CB - Eurocard - MasterCard - DC - JCB - AMEX

Access Accès : • A4 Paris-Nancy, N104 → Troyes, N19 → Provins • A5 → Melun, Exit (Sortie) 16 Châtillon-la-Borde, D408 → Nangis
Map 3 on page 167 Carte 3 Page 167

Golf course PARCOURS — 14/20

Site	Site	
Maintenance	Entretien	
Architect	Architecte	Michel Gayon
Type	Type	parkland
Relief	Relief	
Water in play	Eau en jeu	
Exp. to wind	Exposé au vent	
Trees in play	Arbres en jeu	

Scorecard Carte de score	Chp. Chp.	Mens Mess.	Ladies Da.
Length Long.	6209	5932	5004
Par	73	73	73
Slope system	138	137	125

Advised golfing ability Niveau de jeu recommandé — 0 12 24 36
Hcp required Handicap exigé — 35 (We)

Club house & amenities CLUB-HOUSE ET ANNEXES — 7/10

Pro shop	Pro-shop	
Driving range	Practice	
Sheltered	couvert	5 mats
On grass	sur herbe	yes (Summer)
Putting-green	putting-green	yes
Pitching-green	pitching green	yes

Hotel facilities ENVIRONNEMENT HOTELIER — 6/10

HOTELS HÔTELS

Domaine de Bois-Boudran — on site
51 rooms, D 145 €
Tel (33) 01 64 60 51 00, Fax (33) 01 60 67 52 12

La Forge — Fontenailles 1 km
16 rooms, D 34 €
Tel (33) 01 64 08 44 11, Fax (33) 01 60 67 56 26

RESTAURANTS RESTAURANT

Domaine de Bois-Boudran — on site
Tel (33) 01 64 60 51 00

La Forge — Fontenailles 1 km
Tel (33) 01 64 08 44 11

FONTENELLES (LES)

14	6	4

A proximité de Saint-Jean-de-Monts, ce golf complète un bel itinéraire dans la province historique de Vendée. A proximité de la station balnéaire de Saint-Gilles-Croix-de-Vie, l'architecte Yves Bureau a conçu un parcours très propre (comme à son habitude) et pour tous niveaux, dans un site de campagne aux reliefs très doux, dans un paysage de chênes verts et de pins maritimes. Des plans d'eau pas trop en jeu agrémentent un dessin sans pièges, adapté à tous les types de joueurs, en harmonie visuelle avec les marais de la région. Ce parcours est de bonne longueur des départs arrière, ce qui permettra aux meilleurs de s'exprimer avec plaisir mais sans trop de soucis. Cependant, la construction de trois nouveaux plans d'eau va leur compliquer un peu les choses. Un joli golf de vacances, où le vent peut apporter un piment, et quelques surprises supplémentaires.

Close to Saint-Jean-de-Monts, this course is a fine addition to a great golfing itinerary through the historical province of La Vendée. Not far from the seaside resort of Saint-Gilles-Croix-de-Vie, architect Yves Bureau has, as usual, designed a very neat golf course for all golfers in gently undulating countryside, lined with oak trees and maritime pines. Stretches of water enhance a layout that is free of hidden traps and tailored to all types of golfer. Visually, the course also blends in well with the region's marshlands. This is a good length course from the back tees, thus giving the better players the chance to show their mettle without too much to worry about. However, the addition of three new stretches of water will make life a little more complicated. All in all, a pretty holiday course where the wind can add a little spice and a few extra surprises.

Golf des Fontenelles — 1990

F - 85220 L'AIGUILLON-SUR-VIE

Office	Secrétariat	(33) 02 51 54 13 94
Pro shop	Pro-shop	(33) 02 51 54 13 94
Fax	Fax	(33) 02 51 55 45 77
Web	www.formule-golf.com	
Situation	Situation	

St-Gilles-Croix-de-Vie, 10 km - Nantes (pop. 252 030), 65 km

Annual closure Fermeture annuelle — no

Weekly closure Fermeture hebdomadaire

monday (lundi) 15/10 → 31/03

Fees main season Tarifs haute saison		18 holes
	Week days Semaine	**We/Bank holidays** We/Férié
Individual Individuel	40 €	40 €
Couple Couple	80 €	80 €

Juniors: – 50%

Caddy	Caddy	no
Electric Trolley	Chariot électrique	no
Buggy	Voiturette	23 € /18 holes
Clubs	Clubs	9 € /full day

Credit cards Cartes de crédit

VISA - CB - Eurocard - MasterCard

Challans
D38
Saint-Gilles-Croix-de-Vie
D 32
Aizenay →
Coëx
D 6
GOLF
D 32
L'Aiguillon-s-vie
Les Sables-d'Olonne
Bretignolles
0 2 4 km

Access Accès : • Sables d'Olonne D32 → Challans • La Roche-sur-Yon → Aizenay/Saint-Gilles-Croix-de-Vie D6. Go through Coëx, Golf 2 km.

Map 6 on page 172 Carte 6 Page 172

Golf course PARCOURS — 14/20

Site	Site	
Maintenance	Entretien	
Architect	Architecte	Yves Bureau
Type	Type	copse
Relief	Relief	
Water in play	Eau en jeu	
Exp. to wind	Exposé au vent	
Trees in play	Arbres en jeu	

Scorecard Carte de score	**Chp.** Chp.	**Mens** Mess.	**Ladies** Da.
Length Long.	6195	5747	4780
Par	72	72	72
Slope system	131	126	120

Advised golfing ability Niveau de jeu recommandé — 0 12 24 36

Hcp required Handicap exigé — no

Club house & amenities CLUB-HOUSE ET ANNEXES — 6/10

Pro shop	Pro-shop	
Driving range	Practice	
Sheltered	couvert	10 mats
On grass	sur herbe	yes
Putting-green	putting-green	yes
Pitching-green	pitching green	yes

Hotel facilities ENVIRONNEMENT HOTELIER — 4/10

HOTELS HÔTELS

Le Château de la Vérie, 23 rooms, D 123 € — Challans
Tel (33) 02 51 35 33 44, Fax (33) 02 51 35 14 84 — 20 km

Le Lion d'Or, 52 rooms, D 58 € — St-Gilles-Croix-de-Vie
Tel (33) 02 51 55 50 39, Fax (33) 02 51 55 22 84 — 10 km

Embruns, 21 rooms, D 44 € — St-Gilles-Croix-de-Vie
Tel (33) 02 51 95 25 99, Fax (33) 02 51 95 84 48 — 10 km

RESTAURANTS RESTAURANT

Les Embruns — St-Gilles-Croix-de-Vie 10 km
Tel (33) 02 51 55 11 40

La Grand Roche, Tel (33) 02 51 90 15 21 Bretignolles-s-Mer

Gîte du Tourne-Pierre — Challans (D 69
Tel (33) 02 51 68 14 78 —)20 km

FRÉGATE

15 | 7 | 7

L'architecte Ronald Fream a tiré le meilleur parti d'un site très accidenté (en voie d'urbanisation), mais qui propose de belles vues sur la mer et des trous spectaculaires. Il faut payer le prix de ce décor tourmenté, dans une région où les reliefs sont très accentués : de nombreux dévers peuvent compliquer les trajectoires de balle, quelques coups sont aveugles (moins qu'on pourrait le croire), le rough est souvent très pénalisant, les fairways parfois étroits, et quelques rochers viennent dangereusement en jeu. Fort heureusement, beaucoup de zones en bordure de fairway ont été très bien aménagées, et l'ensemble est en progrès constants. Très bien paysagé, très technique, c'est un parcours que l'on prendra du plaisir à jouer en voiturette, ou au minimum avec un chariot électrique, pour conserver des forces physiques et mentales, non seulement pour choisir les bons clubs, mais aussi pour les utiliser. Si l'on connaît mal le parcours, il ne faut pas trop penser au score, mais commencer en match-play.

Ronald Fream has made good use of a very hilly site (now being built upon more and more) which features fine views of the sea and some spectacular holes. But this twisted and winding scenery comes at a cost in a region of rolling hills and dales. A lot of slanting fairways make life a little difficult at times, a few shots are blind (but less so than you might imagine), the rough gives no quarter, the fairways are sometimes very tight indeed and a few rocks loom dangerously at strategic areas. Fortunately, many of the areas bordering the fairways have been cleaned up and further improvements are constantly being made to the whole layout. Beautifully landscaped and a technically demanding course, Frégate is good fun to play in a buggy in order to preserve mental and physical strength, not only for choosing the right club but also for using them in the right way. If you don't know the course, don't worry too much about the score and go around in match-play.

Golf de Frégate 1992

Route de Bandol RD 559
F - 83270 SAINT-CYR-SUR-MER

Office	Secrétariat	(33) 04 94 29 38 00
Pro shop	Pro-shop	(33) 04 94 29 38 00
Fax	Fax	(33) 04 94 29 96 94
Web	www.fregate.fr	
Situation	Situation	

Bandol (pop. 7 430), 3 km - Toulon (pop. 167 620), 25 km

Annual closure	Fermeture annuelle	no
Weekly closure	Fermeture hebdomadaire	no

Fees main season Tarifs haute saison	18 holes	
	Week days Semaine	We/Bank holidays We/Férié
Individual Individuel	52 €	52 €
Couple Couple	104 €	104 €

Caddy	Caddy	on request
Electric Trolley	Chariot électrique	17 € /18 holes
Buggy	Voiturette	30 € /18 holes
Clubs	Clubs	26 € /18 holes

Credit cards Cartes de crédit

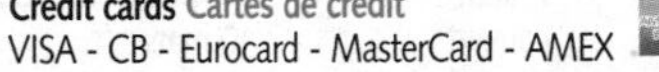
VISA - CB - Eurocard - MasterCard - AMEX

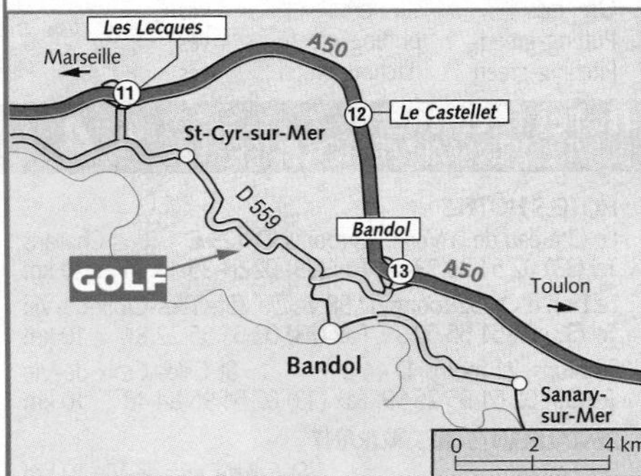

Access Accès : • A50 Marseille → Toulon, Exit (Sortie) Saint-Cyr-sur-Mer
• A50 Toulon → Marseille, Exit Bandol, D559
Map 14 on page 188 Carte 14 Page 188

Golf course PARCOURS 15/20

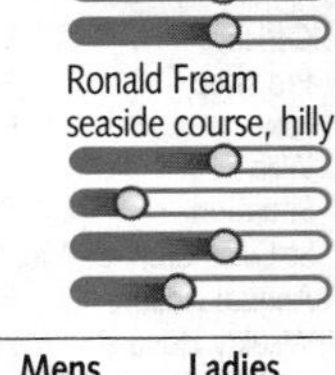

Site	Site	
Maintenance	Entretien	
Architect	Architecte	Ronald Fream
Type	Type	seaside course, hilly
Relief	Relief	
Water in play	Eau en jeu	
Exp. to wind	Exposé au vent	
Trees in play	Arbres en jeu	

Scorecard Carte de score	Chp. Chp.	Mens Mess.	Ladies Da.
Length Long.	6209	5850	4965
Par	72	72	72
Slope system	136	134	134

Advised golfing ability Niveau de jeu recommandé: 0 12 24 36
Hcp required Handicap exigé 35

Club house & amenities CLUB-HOUSE ET ANNEXES 7/10

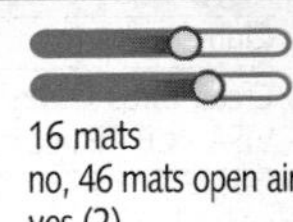

Pro shop	Pro-shop	
Driving range	Practice	
Sheltered	couvert	16 mats
On grass	sur herbe	no, 46 mats open air
Putting-green	putting-green	yes (2)
Pitching-green	pitching green	yes

Hotel facilities ENVIRONNEMENT HOTELIER 7/10

HOTELS HÔTELS

Frégate, 130 rooms, D 223 € — on site
Tel (33) 04 94 29 39 39, Fax (33) 04 94 29 39 40

L'Ile Rousse, 54 rooms, D 305 € — Bandol 4 km
Tel (33) 04 94 29 33 00, Fax (33) 04 94 29 49 49

Bérard, 40 rooms, D 152 € — La Cadière-d'Azur 7 km
Tel (33) 04 94 90 11 43, Fax (33) 04 94 90 01 94

RESTAURANTS RESTAURANT

L'Ile Rousse, Tel (33) 04 94 29 33 00 — Bandol 4 km
Le Mas des Vignes, Tel (33) 04 94 29 39 39 — on site
Le Clocher, Tel (33) 04 94 32 47 65 — Bandol 4 km

GOUVERNEUR (LE) Le Breuil 16 6 6

Des deux 18 trous de ce complexe ambitieux, Le Breuil est le plus "héroïque" dans son déroulement, notamment avec neuf trous insinués entre les superbes étangs de la Dombe, dont l'aspect sauvage a été préservé. Il reste en bon état en toutes saisons. Plat et long, c'est l'un des parcours les plus techniques et exigeants de la région lyonnaise, mais il affiche clairement ses difficultés stratégiques. On pourra seulement lui reprocher la longueur excessive et uniforme de ses par 3, un manque de modelage des alentours de green et des bunkers. Délicat pour les joueurs peu expérimentés, il doit absolument être joué des départs normaux par les golfeurs moyens. Les greens sont peu complexes à lire, mais les difficultés étaient suffisantes pour ne pas en rajouter à ce niveau. Le Club-House a été établi dans de magnifiques bâtiments anciens, mais les murs valent beaucoup mieux que l'intérieur, vraiment pas à la hauteur du standing du lieu. A revoir sérieusement.

"Le Breuil" is the boldest of the two 18-hole courses in this ambitious golfing resort, with nine holes winding their way through the superb lakes of La Dombes, which have lost nothing of their wild natural character. The course is in good condition whatever the season. Flat and long, it is one of the most technical and most demanding courses in the Lyons region, but the strategic difficulties are clearly visible. The few criticisms that might be levelled are the very long and samey par 3s and the lack of relief around the greens and bunkers. A tricky proposition for inexperienced players, this is a course that should be played from the normal tees for mid-handicappers. The greens are straightforward to read, but the course is already difficult enough without adding any more around the pin. The club-house has been laid out in magnificent old buildings, but the outer walls hold greater appeal than the inside, which falls well below the standard of the courses. A serious overhaul would not go amiss.

Golf du Gouverneur — 1992

Château du Breuil
F - 01390 MONTHIEUX

Office	Secrétariat	(33) 04 72 26 40 34
Pro shop	Pro-shop	(33) 04 72 26 40 34
Fax	Fax	(33) 04 72 26 41 61
Web	www.golfgouverneur.fr	
Situation	Situation	

Lyon (pop. 413 090), 28 km - Bourg-en-Bresse, 38 km

Annual closure	Fermeture annuelle	no
Weekly closure	Fermeture hebdomadaire	no

Fees main season Tarifs haute saison	18 holes	
	Week days Semaine	We/Bank holidays We/Férié
Individual Individuel	34 €	45 €
Couple Couple	61 €	76 €

Caddy	Caddy	no
Electric Trolley	Chariot électrique	9 € /18 holes
Buggy	Voiturette	30 € /18 holes
Clubs	Clubs	9 € /18 holes

Credit cards Cartes de crédit
VISA - CB - Eurocard - MasterCard - AMEX

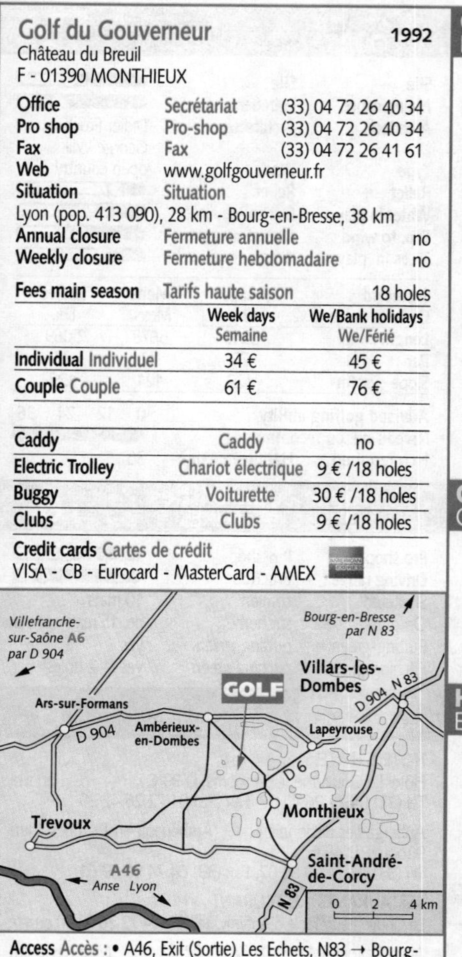

Access Accès : • A46, Exit (Sortie) Les Echets, N83 → Bourg-en-Bresse. In St-André de Corcy → Monthieux • A6, Exit Villefranche, → Bourg, Ars, Ambérieux-en-Dombes → Monthieux Map 11 on page 182 Carte 11 Page 182

Golf course PARCOURS 16/20

Site	Site	
Maintenance	Entretien	
Architect	Architecte	Didier Fruchet George Will
Type	Type	open country
Relief	Relief	
Water in play	Eau en jeu	
Exp. to wind	Exposé au vent	
Trees in play	Arbres en jeu	

Scorecard Carte de score	Chp. Chp.	Mens Mess.	Ladies Da.
Length Long.	6162	5657	4914
Par	72	72	72
Slope system	130	123	120

Advised golfing ability Niveau de jeu recommandé: 0 12 24 36
Hcp required Handicap exigé: 35

Club house & amenities CLUB-HOUSE ET ANNEXES 6/10

Pro shop	Pro-shop	
Driving range	Practice	
Sheltered	couvert	10 mats
On grass	sur herbe	no, 15 mats open air
Putting-green	putting-green	yes
Pitching-green	pitching green	yes (+ 2 holes)

Hotel facilities ENVIRONNEMENT HOTELIER 6/10

HOTELS HÔTELS

Hôtel Le Gouverneur, 53 rooms, D 90 € — on site
Tel (33) 04 72 26 42 00, Fax (33) 04 72 26 42 20

Auberge Les Bichonnières — Ambérieux-en-Dombes
9 rooms, D 49 € — 4 km
Tel (33) 04 74 00 82 07, Fax (33) 04 74 00 89 61

RESTAURANTS RESTAURANT

Le Gouverneur, Tel (33) 04 72 26 42 00 — on site
Alain Chapel, Tel (33) 04 78 91 82 02 — Mionnay 8 km
Auberge des Chasseurs — Bouligneux
Tel (33) 04 74 98 10 02 — 8 km

GOUVERNEUR (LE) Montaplan 14 6 6

Ce parcours considéré comme plus "humain" que Le Breuil est accessible à tous les niveaux, même si quelques trous du retour sont puissamment protégés par des obstacles d'eau. A peine plus accidenté, il n'est jamais fatigant, sa technicité comme sa franchise le rendent très plaisant, et si les bons joueurs auront plus d'émotions sur le parcours voisin, ils ne doivent pas se laisser abuser par l'apparente amabilité de Montaplan. Quelques trous boisés (surtout à l'aller) apportent une certaine variété à ce paysage typique de la Dombes, et les plantations sur d'autres trous commence à mieux encore le "dessiner" visuellement. On remarquera aussi la qualité et les reliefs subtils des greens, et les progrès de son entretien après les drainages. Les joueurs non classés auront ici l'occasion d'aborder un parcours de golf présentant pratiquement toutes les difficultés possibles sans se faire trop peur. Les autres n'auront pas peur, mais on demande à voir leurs scores à l'arrivée.

Slightly more "human" than "Breuil", the Montaplan course is within the reach of golfers of all levels, even though some holes are heavily protected by water hazards. Only slightly more hilly, the course's technical challenge and openness make it a very pleasant golfing experience. And while the better player will probably find its neighbour more exciting, no-one should be fooled by the apparent friendliness of Montaplan. A few holes amidst the trees (especially on the front nine) add a little variety to this typical landscape of La Dombes, and a plantation programme on other holes is now starting to enhance the whole layout from a visual angle. We noted the excellence and subtle contours of the greens, and the progress achieved in maintenance further to drainage work. Here, beginners and high-handicappers have the opportunity to tackle a course which features just about every difficulty you can find on a golf course, without ever being too fearsome. It won't scare the rest of you but we would still like to see your scorecards at the end of the round...

Golf du Gouverneur — 1992

Château du Breuil
F - 01390 MONTHIEUX

Office	Secrétariat	(33) 04 72 26 40 34
Pro shop	Pro-shop	(33) 04 72 26 40 34
Fax	Fax	(33) 04 72 26 41 61
Web	www.golfgouverneur.fr	
Situation	Situation	

Lyon (pop. 413 090), 28 km - Bourg-en-Bresse, 38 km

Annual closure	Fermeture annuelle	no
Weekly closure	Fermeture hebdomadaire	no

Fees main season Tarifs haute saison	Week days Semaine	We/Bank holidays We/Férié
18 holes		
Individual Individuel	30 €	41 €
Couple Couple	55 €	73 €
Caddy Caddy	no	
Electric Trolley Chariot électrique	9 € /18 holes	
Buggy Voiturette	30 € /18 holes	
Clubs Clubs	9 € /18 holes	

Credit cards Cartes de crédit
VISA - CB - Eurocard - MasterCard - AMEX

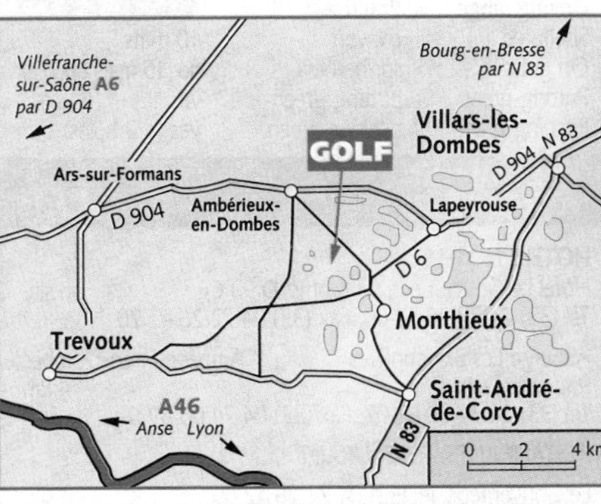

Access Accès : • A46, Exit (Sortie) Les Echets, N83 → Bourg-en-Bresse. In St-André de Corcy → Monthieux • A6, Exit Villefranche, → Bourg, Ars, Ambérieux-en-Dombes → Monthieux **Map 11 on page 182** Carte 11 Page 182

Golf course PARCOURS — 14/20

Site	Site	
Maintenance	Entretien	
Architect	Architecte	Didier Fruchet, George Will
Type	Type	open country
Relief	Relief	
Water in play	Eau en jeu	
Exp. to wind	Exposé au vent	
Trees in play	Arbres en jeu	

Scorecard Carte de score	Chp. Chp.	Mens Mess.	Ladies Da.
Length Long.	5959	5678	5069
Par	72	72	72
Slope system	129	121	123

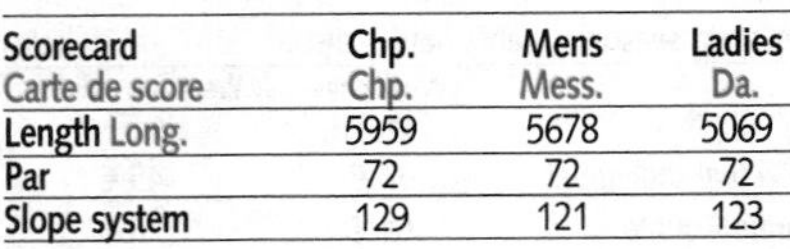

Advised golfing ability — Niveau de jeu recommandé: 0 12 24 36
Hcp required — Handicap exigé: 35

Club house & amenities CLUB-HOUSE ET ANNEXES — 6/10

Pro shop	Pro-shop	
Driving range	Practice	
Sheltered	couvert	10 mats
On grass	sur herbe	no, 15 mats open air
Putting-green	putting-green	yes
Pitching-green	pitching green	yes (+ 2 holes)

Hotel facilities ENVIRONNEMENT HOTELIER — 6/10

HOTELS HÔTELS

Hôtel Le Gouverneur, 53 rooms, D 90 € — on site
Tel (33) 04 72 26 42 00, Fax (33) 04 72 26 42 20

Auberge Les Bichonnières — Ambérieux-en-Dombes 4 km
9 rooms, D 49 €
Tel (33) 04 74 00 82 07, Fax (33) 04 74 00 89 61

RESTAURANTS RESTAURANT

Le Gouverneur/Table d'Antigny, Tel (33) 04 72 26 42 00 on site

Alain Chapel, Tel (33) 04 78 91 82 02 — Mionnay 8 km

Auberge de Rancé — Rancé 5 km
Tel (33) 04 74 00 87 08

GRANDE BASTIDE (LA) 16 6 6

Ce 18 trous créé par le Club Med a pris une place de choix parmi les bons parcours de la région. L'architecte Cabell Robinson a voulu faire un parcours "tous usages", jouable par tous, même si quelques obstacles d'eau peuvent effrayer les débutants. Les arrivées de drive sont assez larges, mais la densité des roughs incite à taper droit. Les obstacles tiennent essentiellement des mouvements de terrain et des vastes bunkers, souvent très en jeu, qui délimitent bien les fairways. Le programme de plantations commence à atténuer une certaine imprécision des trous, dans un si vaste espace. Les greens sont assez modelés pour imposer une grande maîtrise du petit jeu et du putting, et le plus contestable (celui du 11) a été refait. Amusant à jouer et très divers, ce parcours est facile à jouer à pied, ce n'est pas si fréquent sur la Côte d'Azur. Seul inconvénient : les joueurs sont nombreux ici, et pas toujours très rapides... Jouez tôt le matin.

This 18-hole course ranks among the best in the region. Architect Cabell Robinson set out to build an "all-purpose" course for all golfers, even though a number of water hazards might well scare the true beginner. At driving distance, the fairways are wide enough, but the thick rough is a good reason for hitting in the fairway. The basic hazards here are the graded fairways and huge bunkers, which are often fully in play and clearly demarcate the playing area. The new plantation programme is beginning to give greater definition to some holes laid out over such a wide area. The well-contoured greens require a sharp short game and good putting, and the most controversial surface (the 11th green) has been re-laid. Fun to play with variety all round, this is an easily walkable course, which is seldom the case on courses on the French Riviera. The only drawback is the number of players and frequent slow play... Play here early in the morning.

Golf de la Grande Bastide — 1990

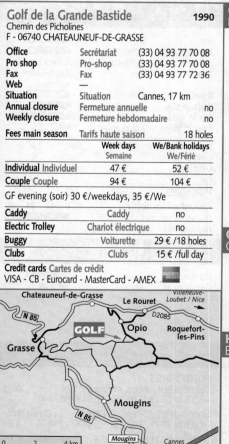

Chemin des Picholines
F - 06740 CHATEAUNEUF-DE-GRASSE

Office	Secrétariat	(33) 04 93 77 70 08
Pro shop	Pro-shop	(33) 04 93 77 70 08
Fax	Fax	(33) 04 93 77 72 36
Web	—	
Situation	Situation	Cannes, 17 km
Annual closure	Fermeture annuelle	no
Weekly closure	Fermeture hebdomadaire	no

Fees main season Tarifs haute saison	18 holes	
	Week days Semaine	**We/Bank holidays** We/Férié
Individual Individuel	47 €	52 €
Couple Couple	94 €	104 €

GF evening (soir) 30 €/weekdays, 35 €/We

Caddy	Caddy	no
Electric Trolley	Chariot électrique	no
Buggy	Voiturette	29 € /18 holes
Clubs	Clubs	15 € /full day

Credit cards Cartes de crédit
VISA - CB - Eurocard - MasterCard - AMEX

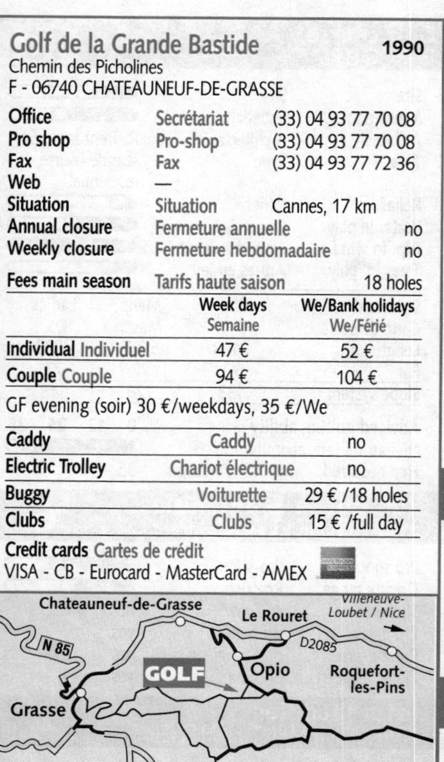

Access Accès : • Cannes, N85 → Valbonne
• Nice, A8 Exit (Sortie) Villeneuve-Loubet → Grasse, Roquefort-les-Pins, → Opio
Map 14 on page 189 Carte 14 Page 189

Golf course PARCOURS — 16/20

Site	Site	
Maintenance	Entretien	
Architect	Architecte	Cabell Robinson
Type	Type	open country
Relief	Relief	
Water in play	Eau en jeu	
Exp. to wind	Exposé au vent	
Trees in play	Arbres en jeu	

Scorecard Carte de score	**Chp.** Chp.	**Mens** Mess.	**Ladies** Da.
Length Long.	6105	5610	5175
Par	72	72	72
Slope system	128	116	111

Advised golfing ability 0 12 24 36
Niveau de jeu recommandé
Hcp required Handicap exigé 35

Club house & amenities CLUB-HOUSE ET ANNEXES — 6/10

Pro shop	Pro-shop	
Driving range	Practice	
Sheltered	couvert	no
On grass	sur herbe	no, mats with nets
Putting-green	putting-green	yes
Pitching-green	pitching green	yes

Hotel facilities ENVIRONNEMENT HOTELIER — 6/10

HOTELS HÔTELS

Club Méditerranée, 443 rooms, D 229 € — Opio 2 km
Tel (33) 04 93 09 71 00, Fax (33) 04 93 09 71 70

Bastide Saint Antoine, 11 rooms, D 236 € — Grasse 4 km
Tel (33) 04 93 70 94 94, Fax (33) 04 93 70 94 95

Hôtel du Patti — Grasse 4 km
73 rooms, D 73 €
Tel (33) 04 93 36 01 00, Fax (33) 04 93 36 36 40

RESTAURANTS RESTAURANT

Bastide Saint Antoine, Tel (33) 04 93 70 94 94 Grasse 5 km
L'Auberge Fleurie, Tel (33) 04 93 12 02 80 Valbonne 5 km
Lou Cigalon, Tel (33) 04 93 12 27 07 Valbonne 5 km

GRANDE-MOTTE (LA) Les Flamants Roses

16 | 6 | 4

En paysage d'étangs, à partir d'un terrain sans relief naturel, et très peu boisé Robert Trent Jones a signé un parcours de grande qualité, modelé avec une grande intelligence, sans jamais donner l'impression de monotonie. Certes, les longs frappeurs peuvent s'y déchaîner, mais les seconds coups, le petit jeu et le putting demandent beaucoup d'inspiration., et les joueurs précis pourront y réussir. L'eau joue un rôle important, mais sans sévérité excessive. Avec une bonne connaissance de ce parcours bien défini dans l'espace (lorsque la tonte du fairway et du petit rough est bien faite) et un peu de réflexion, tous les joueurs peuvent y prendre plaisir, à l'exception des débutants, qui trouveront avec un joli parcours de 6 trous et un 18 trous de par 58 de quoi largement s'occuper et s'aguerrir. La Grande Motte est un golf commercial, son club house manque de chaleur... et de distinction, tout comme certaines constructions adjacentes.

Set in a landscape of lakes with no natural relief and very few trees, Robert Trent Jones has cleverly shaped a high class course which never seems monotonous. Long-hitters can definitely open their shoulders, but approach shots, short play and putting call for a lot of inspiration which should suit the more accurate players. Water is a significant part of the course but is never too severe a test. When you get to know this neatly laid-out course (and when the fairways and short rough are properly mown) and with a little careful thought, every golfer will enjoy playing here, except beginners, who can learn the ropes and get to grips with the compact 6-holer and the par-58 18 hole course. La Grande Motte is a business venture course but the club-house lacks both warmth... and distinction, in the same way as some of adjoining buildings.

Golf de La Grande-Motte — 1987

BP 16
F - 34280 LA GRANDE-MOTTE

Office	Secrétariat	(33) 04 67 56 05 00
Pro shop	Pro-shop	(33) 04 67 29 93 02
Fax	Fax	(33) 04 67 29 18 84
Web	—	
Situation	Situation	

Montpellier (pop. 210 860), 22 km - La Grande-Motte, 1 km

Annual closure	Fermeture annuelle	no
Weekly closure	Fermeture hebdomadaire	no

Fees main season Tarifs haute saison		full day
	Week days Semaine	**We/Bank holidays** We/Férié
Individual Individuel	43 €	43 €
Couple Couple	86 €	86 €

Under 16: – 50% - Under 25: – 30%

Caddy	Caddy	no
Electric Trolley	Chariot électrique	no
Buggy	Voiturette	24 € /18 holes
Clubs	Clubs	12 € /18 holes

Credit cards Cartes de crédit
VISA - CB - Eurocard - MasterCard - DC - JCB - AMEX

Nîmes
A9
Sortie **A9** Gallargues-le-Montueux › LUNEL
D 61
Montpellier
Montpellier Est Fréjorgues
D66
Béziers
D21
D 62
D 62
La Grande-Motte
0 2 4 km

Access Accès : • Nîmes, A9, Exit (Sortie) 26 Gallargues, N113 → Lunel, D61 → La Grande-Motte • Montpellier A9 Exit Fréjorgues, D21 et D62 → La Grande-Motte
Map 13 on page 187 Carte 13 Page 187

Golf course PARCOURS — 16/20

Site	Site	
Maintenance	Entretien	
Architect	Architecte	R. Trent Jones Sr
Type	Type	seaside course, residential
Relief	Relief	
Water in play	Eau en jeu	
Exp. to wind	Exposé au vent	
Trees in play	Arbres en jeu	

Scorecard Carte de score	**Chp.** Chp.	**Mens** Mess.	**Ladies** Da.
Length Long.	6128	5647	4828
Par	72	72	72
Slope system	133	126	118

Advised golfing ability 0 12 24 36
Niveau de jeu recommandé
Hcp required Handicap exigé 35

Club house & amenities CLUB-HOUSE ET ANNEXES — 6/10

Pro shop	Pro-shop	
Driving range	Practice	
Sheltered	couvert	no
On grass	sur herbe	yes
Putting-green	putting-green	yes
Pitching-green	pitching green	yes

Hotel facilities ENVIRONNEMENT HOTELIER — 4/10

HOTELS HÔTELS

Golf Hôtel Best Western, 45 rooms, D 85 € — 300 m
Tel (33) 04 67 29 72 00, Fax (33) 04 67 56 12 44

Grand M Hôtel, 33 rooms, D 139 € — La Grande Motte 1 km
Tel (33) 04 67 29 13 13, Fax (33) 04 67 29 14 74

Les Templiers, 11 rooms, D 122 € — Aigues-Mortes 11 km
Tel (33) 04 66 53 66 56, Fax (33) 04 66 53 69 61

RESTAURANTS RESTAURANT

Alexandre — La Grande Motte 1 km
Tel (33) 04 67 56 63 63

Arcades, Tel (33) 04 66 53 81 13 — Aigues-Mortes 11 km

GRANVILLE Les Dunes

14	4	4

Originellement dessiné par Colt et Allison, Granville était un chef-d'oeuvre à l'écart des sentiers battus. Ce grand links était malheureusement traversé par une petite route, qui a obligé à modifier beaucoup de trous, alors qu'elle aurait sans doute pu être déviée. Hélas, ces trous n'ont pas été les seuls altérés, et une bonne partie du caractère a été perdue (les nouveaux bunkers n'ont rien à voir avec l'esthétique originelle). Il s'agissait là d'un véritable trésor caché, au niveau du Touquet et de Chiberta, mais il a suffi de quelques décisions iconoclastes pour détruire cinquante ans de tradition. S'il reste néammoins une bonne douzaine de bons trous, qui justifient à eux seuls une visite, on est bien obligé de passer par les autres. Granville est par l'absurde , une leçon d'architecture, et une bonne leçon de prudence et de respect pour les golfs qui veulent s'engager dans un remodelage. La réfection du club house n'est qu'une bien faible consolation.

Originally designed by Colt and Allison, Granville used to be a masterpiece off the beaten track. Unfortunately, this great links course has been crossed by a small road, which could have been re-routed, and a number of holes have had to be altered. Worse, other features of the course have also been tampered with and a lot of its character has evaporated (the new bunkers have nothing common with the original style). This used to be a real gem of a course, pleasantly remote and on a par with Le Touquet or Chiberta, but a few hasty decisions were enough to destroy fifty years of tradition. While there are still a dozen excellent holes, which are worth the visit in themselves, there is no avoiding the others. Through an absurd course of events, Granville has proven to be a lesson in architecture, underlining the caution and respect that should be shown by any golf course that might be considering a change in style. The re-designed club-house is scant consolation.

Golf de Granville — 1928

Pavillon du Golf
F - 50290 BREVILLE

Office	Secrétariat	(33) 02 33 50 23 06
Pro shop	Pro-shop	(33) 02 33 50 23 06
Fax	Fax	(33) 02 33 61 91 87
Web	www.best-golfs.com/granville	
Situation	Situation	
Granville (pop. 12 410), 6 km		
Annual closure	Fermeture annuelle	no
Weekly closure	Fermeture hebdomadaire	no

Fees main season Tarifs haute saison	full day	
	Week days Semaine	**We/Bank holidays** We/Férié
Individual Individuel	38 €	38 €
Couple Couple	64 €	64 €
Under 21: 20 €		

Caddy	Caddy	no
Electric Trolley	Chariot électrique	no
Buggy	Voiturette	18 € /18 holes
Clubs	Clubs	9 € /full day

Credit cards Cartes de crédit
VISA - CB - Eurocard - MasterCard

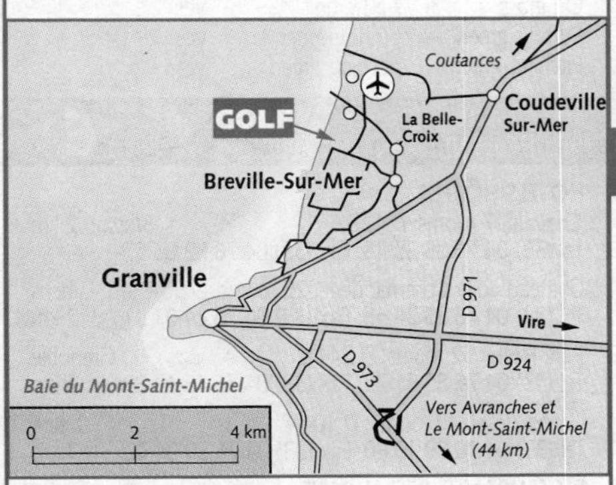

Access Accès : Avranches D973 → Granville, Bréville s/Mer
Map 2 on page 164 Carte 2 Page 164

Golf course PARCOURS — 14/20

Site	Site	
Maintenance	Entretien	
Architect	Architecte	Colt, Alison M. Hawtree (1992)
Type	Type	links
Relief	Relief	
Water in play	Eau en jeu	
Exp. to wind	Exposé au vent	
Trees in play	Arbres en jeu	

Scorecard Carte de score	**Chp.** Chp.	**Mens** Mess.	**Ladies** Da.
Length Long.	5834	5513	4949
Par	71	71	71
Slope system	125	124	125

Advised golfing ability Niveau de jeu recommandé — 0 12 24 36
Hcp required Handicap exigé — 35

Club house & amenities CLUB-HOUSE ET ANNEXES — 4/10

Pro shop	Pro-shop	
Driving range	Practice	
Sheltered	couvert	10 mats
On grass	sur herbe	yes
Putting-green	putting-green	yes
Pitching-green	pitching green	yes

Hotel facilities ENVIRONNEMENT HOTELIER — 4/10

HOTELS HÔTELS

La Beaumonderie — Bréville-sur-Mer 1 km
13 rooms, D 91 €
Tel (33) 02 33 50 36 36, Fax (33) 02 33 50 36 45

Hôtel des Bains — Granville 6 km
47 rooms, D 136 €
Tel (33) 02 33 50 17 31, Fax (33) 02 33 50 89 22

RESTAURANTS RESTAURANT

L'Orangerie, Tel (33) 02 33 50 36 36 — Bréville-sur-Mer 1 km
La Citadelle, Tel (33) 02 33 50 34 10 — Granville
La Gentilhommière, Tel (33) 02 33 50 17 99 — Granville

GRENOBLE BRESSON

17 | 7 | 6

Ce terrain reste très accidenté, parfois même épuisant (voiturette conseillée), mais Robert Trent Jones Jr a réussi l'exploit de ne pas imposer de coups aveugles. Cependant, il n'a pu éviter de faire trois ou quatre trous assez indifférents dans un ensemble autrement de belle qualité, et même excitant à parcourir. Souvent spectaculaire, ce parcours ne livre pas facilement ses secrets, et mérite d'être joué plusieurs fois, ne serait-ce que pour négocier les greens. Dans un paysage quasiment montagnard, des hêtres, des chênes et des genêts apportent des touches de végétation au modelage des fairways, à la sculpture des nombreux bunkers. Quelle que soit la beauté de la balade, la maîtrise du jeu que réclame Bresson incite à ne pas le recommander aux joueurs à haut handicap. Ce parcours exige un dessin précis des fairways et un entretien attentif à la hauteur du tracé, ce qui n'est pas toujours le cas.

This is a very hilly and sometimes exhausting course (buggy recommended) but Robert Trent Jones Jr has achieved the virtually impossible by avoiding blind shots. In contrast, there was no other way around three or four rather ordinary holes in an otherwise excellent setting, which makes for exciting golf. This sometimes spectacular course does not give up its secrets easily and deserves a number of rounds, if only to get to grips with the greens. In virtually mountainous landscape, oak-trees, beech and gorse add a touch of vegetation to the contoured fairways and numerous bunkers. But however beautiful the scenery, the skill required to play Bresson is perhaps beyond your average high-handicapper. The course requires tightly-mown fairways and proper maintenance, which is not always the case at the present time.

Golf International de Grenoble — 1990

Route de Montavie
F - 38320 BRESSON

Office	Secrétariat	(33) 04 76 73 65 00
Pro shop	Pro-shop	(33) 04 76 73 65 00
Fax	Fax	(33) 04 76 73 65 51
Web	www.golf-club-privilege.com	
Situation	Situation	

Grenoble (pop. 150 750), 5 km - Vizille (pop. 7 100), 8 km

Annual closure	Fermeture annuelle	21/12 → 23/1
Weekly closure	Fermeture hebdomadaire	no

Fees main season Tarifs haute saison	Week days Semaine	We/Bank holidays We/Férié
		Full day
Individual Individuel	43 €	43 €
Couple Couple	86 €	86 €

Juniors: 23 € (Weekdays) - 21 € (We)

Caddy	Caddy	no
Electric Trolley	Chariot électrique	11 € /18 holes
Buggy	Voiturette	26 € /18 holes
Clubs	Clubs	11 € /full day

Credit cards Cartes de crédit
VISA - CB - Eurocard - MasterCard

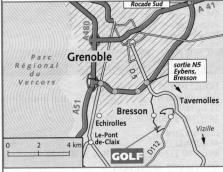

Rocade Sud
A 41
A480
Parc Régional du Vercors
Grenoble
D 5
sortie N5 Eybens, Bresson
Tavernolles
A51
Bresson
Echirolles
Le-Pont de-Claix
Vizille
0 2 4 km
GOLF
D112

Access Accès : Lyon A48 → Chambéry.
At toll (Péage) go to the "Rocade", Exit 5, Eybens, Bresson → Tavernolles, → Golf
Map 11 on page 182 Carte 11 Page 182

Golf course PARCOURS — 17/20

Site	Site	
Maintenance	Entretien	
Architect	Architecte	R. Trent Jones Jr
Type	Type	montagne
Relief	Relief	
Water in play	Eau en jeu	
Exp. to wind	Exposé au vent	
Trees in play	Arbres en jeu	

Scorecard Carte de score	Chp. Chp.	Mens Mess.	Ladies Da.
Length Long.	6201	5876	4750
Par	73	73	73
Slope system	145	139	128

Advised golfing ability Niveau de jeu recommandé — 0 12 24 36
Hcp required Handicap exigé — no

Club house & amenities CLUB-HOUSE ET ANNEXES — 7/10

Pro shop	Pro-shop	
Driving range	Practice	
Sheltered	couvert	20 mats
On grass	sur herbe	yes
Putting-green	putting-green	yes
Pitching-green	pitching green	yes

Hotel facilities ENVIRONNEMENT HOTELIER — 6/10

HOTELS HÔTELS

Chavant, 7 rooms, D 128 € — Bresson 2 km
Tel (33) 04 76 25 25 38, Fax (33) 04 76 62 06 55

Château de la Commanderie, 25 rooms, D 98 € — Eybens 2 km
Tel (33) 04 76 25 34 58, Fax (33) 04 76 24 07 31

Park Hôtel, 52 rooms, D 244 € — Grenoble 5 km
Tel (33) 04 76 85 81 23, Fax (33) 04 76 46 49 88

Grand Hôtel, 42 rooms, D 104 € — Uriage 7 km
Tel (33) 04 76 89 10 80, Fax (33) 04 76 89 04 62

RESTAURANTS RESTAURANT

Chavant, Tel (33) 04 76 25 25 38 — Bresson 2 km

Auberge Napoléon, Tel (33) 04 76 87 53 64 — Grenoble 5 km

GUJAN-MESTRAS

15	7	6

Entre Arcachon et Bordeaux, ce 18 trous (complété par un petit 9 trous) a été dessiné par Alain Prat avec beaucoup de bon sens : il n'a pas voulu exagérer les difficultés et son tracé ne pénalise que ceux qui prennent des risques excessifs. Le terrain plat a été légèrement modelé pour les besoins de la cause, et le sol sablonneux est idéal pour le golf. Le déroulement dans les pins et la bruyère est agréable, avec des difficultés mesurées pour ne rebuter personne, les principaux dangers (en dehors de quelques obstacles d'eau) étant constitués par les bunkers et les arbres, qui laissent souvent libres les accès aux vastes greens. Mais les débutants auront sans doute du mal quand ils sont très défendus. On peut jouer facilement ici toute l'année : les hivers sont plutôt doux, le parcours supporte bien les intempéries et son entretien s'est considérablement amélioré. Un regret, la perte de nombreux arbres après les tempêtes de Noël 1999.

Located between Arcachon and Bordeaux, this 18-hole course was designed by Alain Prat (with an adjoining 9 hole course). Using a lot of good sense, he has avoided any excessive difficulties and the layout only penalises the players who take one risk too many. The flat terrain has been slightly graded for greater relief and the sandy sub-soil is ideal for a golf course. It winds its way pleasantly through pine-trees and heather, with playing difficulties carefully gauged to avoid scaring the lesser player. Aside from the few water hazards, the main problems are the bunkers and trees, which generally speaking afford easy access to the greens. Beginners will probably find the going a little harder when dealing with some of the better-protected holes. You can easily play here all year, as the winters are mild, the ground withstands all weathers and maintenance has been considerably improved. Our sole regret is the loss of so many trees after the storms around Xmas 1999.

Golf de Gujan-Mestras — 1990

Route de Sanguinet
F - 33470 GUJAN-MESTRAS

Office	Secrétariat	(33) 05 57 52 73 73
Pro shop	Pro-shop	(33) 05 57 52 73 73
Fax	Fax	(33) 05 56 66 10 93
E-mail	gujan@bluegreen.com	
Situation	Situation	Gujan-Mestras, 6 km

Arcachon (pop. 11 770), 12 km

Annual closure	Fermeture annuelle	no
Weekly closure	Fermeture hebdomadaire	no

Fees main season Tarifs haute saison	full day	
	Week days Semaine	**We/Bank holidays** We/Férié
Individual Individuel	41 €	41 €
Couple Couple	82 €	82 €

Under 18: 23 € - Students 30 €

Caddy	Caddy	no
Electric Trolley	Chariot électrique	no
Buggy	Voiturette	21 € /18 holes
Clubs	Clubs	9 € /full day

Credit cards Cartes de crédit
VISA - CB - Eurocard - MasterCard - DC - AMEX

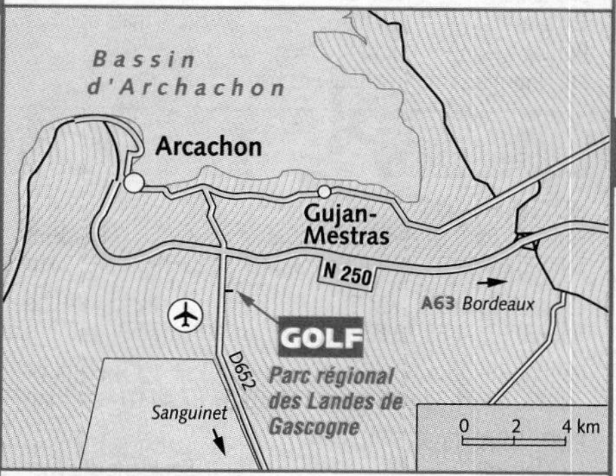

Access Accès : Bordeaux, A63, Exit (Sortie) Arcachon, at Aqua City, → Golf
Map 9 on page 179 Carte 9 Page 179

Golf course PARCOURS — 15/20

Site	Site	
Maintenance	Entretien	
Architect	Architecte	Alain Prat
Type	Type	forest
Relief	Relief	
Water in play	Eau en jeu	
Exp. to wind	Exposé au vent	
Trees in play	Arbres en jeu	

Scorecard Carte de score	**Chp.** Chp.	**Mens** Mess.	**Ladies** Da.
Length Long.	6225	6005	5185
Par	72	72	72
Slope system	129	127	125

Advised golfing ability Niveau de jeu recommandé: 0 12 24 36
Hcp required Handicap exigé: 35

Club house & amenities CLUB-HOUSE ET ANNEXES — 7/10

Pro shop	Pro-shop	
Driving range	Practice	
Sheltered	couvert	8 mats
On grass	sur herbe	yes
Putting-green	putting-green	yes
Pitching-green	pitching green	yes

Hotel facilities ENVIRONNEMENT HOTELIER — 6/10

HOTELS HÔTELS

La Guérinière — Gujan-Mestras 6 km
25 rooms, D 111 €
Tel (33) 05 56 66 08 78, Fax (33) 05 56 66 13 39

Séminaris — Arcachon 12 km
20 rooms, D 111 €
Tel (33) 05 56 83 25 87, Fax (33) 05 57 52 22 41

Deganne, 57 rooms, D 130 € — Arcachon
Tel (33) 05 56 83 99 91, Fax (33) 05 56 83 87 92 — 12 km

RESTAURANTS RESTAURANT

Les Deux Eglises, Tel (33) 05 56 66 77 12 — La Hume 8 km
Le Patio, Tel (33) 05 56 83 02 72 — Arcachon12 km

HARDELOT Les Pins

16 | 6 | 6

Depuis sa création, "Les Pins" est un des excellents exemples du style de Tom Simson et reste un parcours plus passionnant que le récent parcours des "Dunes". C'est un témoignage de l'architecture classique britannique. Quelques coups sont aveugles, mais faussement trompeurs et sans véritable gêne pour le jeu. Avec des greens subtils, des reliefs bien utilisés, des bunkers diaboliquement placés, le parcours impose d'être précis, et de savoir quand attaquer. On doit simplement suivre les pas de l'architecte pour le négocier correctement, tant le dessin est empreint de bon sens. "Les Pins" est de ces parcours polis par le temps que l'on doit connaître si l'on joue surtout des golfs "modernes". Tout ici est empreint de tradition. Les Anglais ne s'y trompent pas, ils y viennent nombreux. Mais les visites en périodes sèches montrent que ce parcours peut parfois être d'un entretien problématique... Dommage, car c'est l'un des grands tracés classiques en France.

On the same site, "Les Pins" is still a more exciting and forthright course than the more recent "Les Dunes". One of Simpson's finest works, "Les Pins" is testimony to classic British architecture. Some shots are blind but never really deceive the player or affect play. With subtle greens and devilishly well-placed bunkers, this course cries out for precision stroke-making and the ability to utilise opportunities for attacking play. The impression is one of simply following in the footsteps of the architect in order to play the course correctly. That is how sensible the layout is. "Les Pins" is one of those courses that becomes more polished with time and is a must for anyone raised exclusively on "modern" courses. Everything here smacks of tradition. The British know a good golf course when they see one, and a lot of Brits come and play here. But our visits during the summer months have shown that maintenance is sometimes a problem. That's a pity, because this is one of the great classic layouts in France.

Golf d'Hardelot-les-Pins — 1931

3, avenue du Golf
F - 62152 HARDELOT

Office	Secrétariat	(33) 03 21 83 73 10
Pro shop	Pro-shop	(33) 03 21 83 73 10
Fax	Fax	(33) 03 21 83 24 33
Web	www.opengolf.com	
Situation	Situation	Boulogne s/Mer, 15 km
Annual closure	Fermeture annuelle	no
Weekly closure	Fermeture hebdomadaire	no

Fees main season Tarifs haute saison — 18 holes

	Week days Semaine	We/Bank holidays We/Férié
Individual Individuel	46 €	55 €
Couple Couple	92 €	110 €

Juniors & students: 24 € - GF full day: 46 € (Weekdays) - 84 € (We)

Caddy	Caddy	no
Electric Trolley	Chariot électrique	no
Buggy	Voiturette	38 € /18 holes
Clubs	Clubs	15 € /full day

Credit cards Cartes de crédit
VISA - CB - Eurocard - MasterCard - AMEX

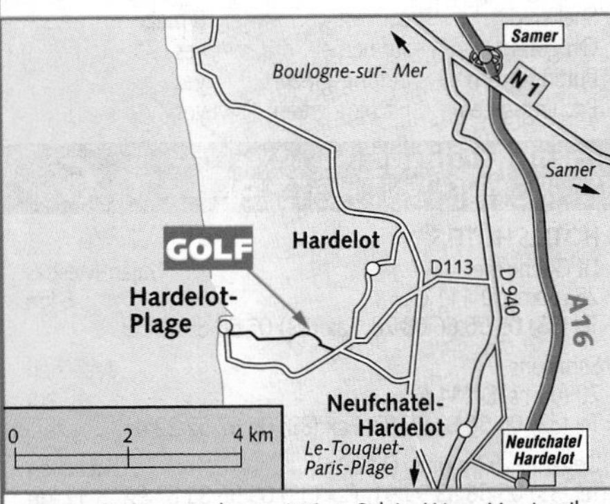

Access Accès : • Boulogne, A16 → Calais, N1 → Montreuil, through Pont-de-Briques, turn right on D940 → Hardelot • Montreuil, N1 → Boulogne-sur-Mer, or D940 coming from Le Touquet **Map 1 on page 162** Carte 1 Page 162

Golf course PARCOURS — 16/20

Site	Site	
Maintenance	Entretien	
Architect	Architecte	Tom Simpson
Type	Type	forest, parkland
Relief	Relief	
Water in play	Eau en jeu	
Exp. to wind	Exposé au vent	
Trees in play	Arbres en jeu	

Scorecard Carte de score	Chp. Chp.	Mens Mess.	Ladies Da.
Length Long.	5926	5605	5212
Par	73	73	73
Slope system	132	127	130

Advised golfing ability 0 12 24 36
Niveau de jeu recommandé
Hcp required Handicap exigé 35

Club house & amenities CLUB-HOUSE ET ANNEXES — 6/10

Pro shop	Pro-shop	
Driving range	Practice	
Sheltered	couvert	6 mats
On grass	sur herbe	no, 6 mats open air
Putting-green	putting-green	yes
Pitching-green	pitching green	yes

Hotel facilities ENVIRONNEMENT HOTELIER — 6/10

HOTELS HÔTELS

Hôtel du Parc, 81 rooms, D 106 € — Hardelot
Tel (33) 03 21 33 22 11, Fax (33) 03 21 83 29 71 — 1 km

Cléry, 22 rooms, D 107 € — Hesdin-l'Abbé
Tel (33) 03 21 83 19 83, Fax (33) 03 21 87 52 59 — 7 km

Régina, 38 rooms, D 55 € — Hardelot
Tel (33) 03 21 83 81 88, Fax (33) 03 21 87 44 01 — 1 km

RESTAURANTS RESTAURANT

La Matelote — Boulogne-sur-Mer
Tel (33) 03 21 30 17 97 — 15 km

Host. de la Rivière — Pont-de-Briques
Tel (33) 03 21 32 22 81 — 7 km

HAUT-POITOU

14	6	4

Un parcours paradoxalement difficile pour une région où les néophytes sont nombreux, avec un relief qui rend assez fatigants les neuf derniers trous, tracés dans une zone agréable de pins et de bouleaux. A cause de sa longueur (même avec un par 73), on conseillera à tous de ne pas partir des départs les plus reculés, s'ils espèrent jouer leur handicap. Les neuf premiers trous sont plus plats, avec des obstacles d'eau pas trop pénalisants. L'architecture du parcours manque certes de charme et d'originalité (le 13 est joli), mais les greens sont en majorité bien dessinés, et quelques bunkers ont été refaits pour le bonheur du jeu. En résumé, un golf à jouer si l'on se trouve dans la région, notamment pour compléter un séjour en famille, un petit parcours de 9 trous permettant de loger les débutants. Une base de loisirs est toute proche, ainsi que le Futuroscope de Poitiers.

A paradoxically tough course in region where beginners abound. The sloping terrain makes the back 9 a tiring but pleasant walk through pines and birch trees. Haut Poitou is a long course, and even at a par 73 we would not recommend the back tees to anyone wishing to play to his handicap. The front 9 are flatter with water hazards that could be rated as avoidable and so not too heavy on the score. The overall architecture probably lacks originality and charm (although the 13th is a pretty hole), but the majority of greens are well-designed and a few bunkers have been reshaped for the better. In short, a course worth playing if you are in the region, especially if you are with the family, as a neighbouring 9 hole pitch 'n putt is ideal for beginners. The course is also close to a leisure centre and to the Futuroscope.

Golf Club du Haut-Poitou — 1987

F - 86130 SAINT-CYR

Office	Secrétariat	(33) 05 49 62 53 62
Pro shop	Pro-shop	(33) 05 49 62 53 62
Fax	Fax	(33) 05 49 88 77 14
Web	www.golfduhautpoitou.com	
Situation	Situation	

Châtellerault, 15 km - Poitiers (pop. 78 890), 20 km

Annual closure	Fermeture annuelle	no
Weekly closure	Fermeture hebdomadaire	no

Fees main season / Tarifs haute saison	full day	
	Week days / Semaine	We/Bank holidays / We/Férié
Individual Individuel	29 €	34 €
Couple Couple	50 €	59 €

Under 25: – 30%

Caddy	Caddy	no
Electric Trolley	Chariot électrique	no
Buggy	Voiturette	20 € /18 holes
Clubs	Clubs	8 € /full day

Credit cards Cartes de crédit
VISA - CB - Eurocard - MasterCard

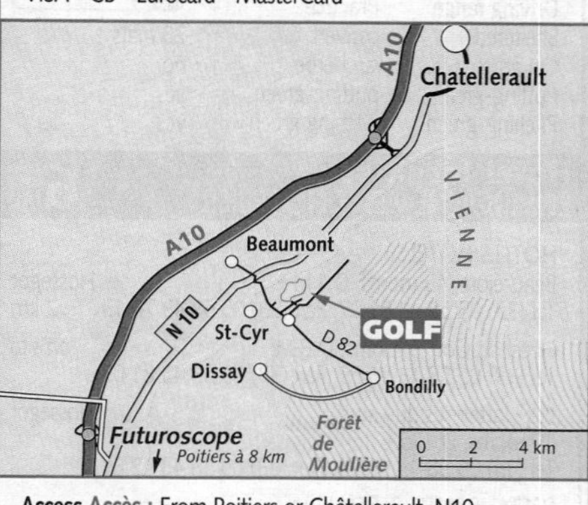

Access Accès : From Poitiers or Châtellerault, N10, Exit (Sortie) Beaumont, → Golf
Map 6 on page 173 Carte 6 Page 173

Golf course / PARCOURS — 14/20

Site	Site	
Maintenance	Entretien	
Architect	Architecte	Bill Baker
Type	Type	open country, forest
Relief	Relief	
Water in play	Eau en jeu	
Exp. to wind	Exposé au vent	
Trees in play	Arbres en jeu	

Scorecard / Carte de score	Chp. / Chp.	Mens / Mess.	Ladies / Da.
Length Long.	6590	6124	5171
Par	73	73	73
Slope system	143	141	131

Advised golfing ability / Niveau de jeu recommandé: 0 12 24 36
Hcp required / Handicap exigé: no

Club house & amenities / CLUB-HOUSE ET ANNEXES — 6/10

Pro shop	Pro-shop	
Driving range	Practice	
Sheltered	couvert	18 mats
On grass	sur herbe	yes
Putting-green	putting-green	yes
Pitching-green	pitching green	yes

Hotel facilities / ENVIRONNEMENT HOTELIER — 4/10

HOTELS HÔTELS

Château de la Ribaudière — Chasseneuil 12 km
41 rooms, D 102 €
Tel (33) 05 49 52 86 66, Fax (33) 05 49 52 86 32

Mercure Poitiers Nord, 89 rooms, D 90 € — Chasseneuil 12 km
Tel (33) 05 49 52 90 41, Fax (33) 05 49 52 51 72

Park Plaza, 279 rooms, D 178 € — Chasseneuil (Futuroscope) 12 km
Tel (33) 05 49 49 07 07, Fax (33) 05 49 49 55 49

RESTAURANTS RESTAURANT

Maxime, Tel (33) 05 49 41 09 55 — Poitiers 20 km
Benjamin, Tel (33) 05 49 52 42 37 — Dissay 2 km
Les Trois Piliers, Tel (33) 05 49 55 07 03 — Poitiers 20 km

HOSSEGOR

16 | 6 | 6

Un des grands classiques de la "Côte Basque", dont l'architecture rappelle les parcours intérieurs traditionnels de Grande-Bretagne, où les obstacles sont surtout les arbres et les bunkers. Dans un espace aussi propice au golf, il n'était guère utile de beaucoup modeler le terrain (pas de bulldozers à l'époque). Depuis les années 30, le dessin n'a pas pris une ride, mais on fera encore les mêmes observations, en suggérant une plus grande adaptation au jeu actuel, en déplaçant (sans modifier leur forme) les bunkers de fairway des par 4, qui pénalisent surtout les joueurs moyens. Le parcours est plat, et de bonne qualité toute l'année, grâce au sol sablonneux. Les obstacles bien visibles, la variété des trous et le profil des greens en font un test de stratégie et de jeu, qui masque ses réelles difficultés sous un visage souriant. Un excellent parcours, qu'il s'agisse de jouer en compétition, ou en famille, où l'on a toujours plaisir à retrouver des détails que l'on avait négligés.

One of the great classics on the Basque coast with a layout reminiscent of traditional British inland courses, where the hazards are primarily trees and bunkers. On a site so obviously made for golf, there was hardly any need to shape the terrain (anyway there were no bulldozers around at the time). Since the 1930s, the course looks and feels as young as ever, but we reiterate our original observations by suggesting more adjustment to the needs of modern play by shifting (without any change in shape) the fairway bunkers on the par 4s, which tend nowadays to penalise mid-handicappers more than anyone else. The course is flat and plays beautifully all year thanks to the sandy sub-soil. Clearly visible hazards, variety and the neat greens make this a fine test of golfing ability and strategy, and one that conceals its real difficulties beneath a cheerful exterior. An excellent course for tournaments or for all the family, where it is always fun to get back to long-neglected details of golf.

Golf Club d'Hossegor — 1930

Avenue du Golf
F - 40150 HOSSEGOR

Office	Secrétariat	(33) 05 58 43 56 99
Pro shop	Pro-shop	(33) 05 58 43 56 99
Fax	Fax	(33) 05 58 43 98 52
E-mail	golfhos@aol.com	
Situation	Situation	Bayonne, 20 km
Annual closure	Fermeture annuelle	no
Weekly closure	Fermeture hebdomadaire	

tuesday (mardi) except holidays

Fees main season Tarifs haute saison	Week days Semaine	We/Bank holidays We/Férié
		full day
Individual Individuel	55 €	55 €
Couple Couple	110 €	110 €

Under 25: – 50%

Caddy	Caddy	on request
Electric Trolley	Chariot électrique	15 € /18 holes
Buggy	Voiturette	15 € /18 holes
Clubs	Clubs	23 € /18 holes

Credit cards Cartes de crédit
VISA - CB - Eurocard - MasterCard

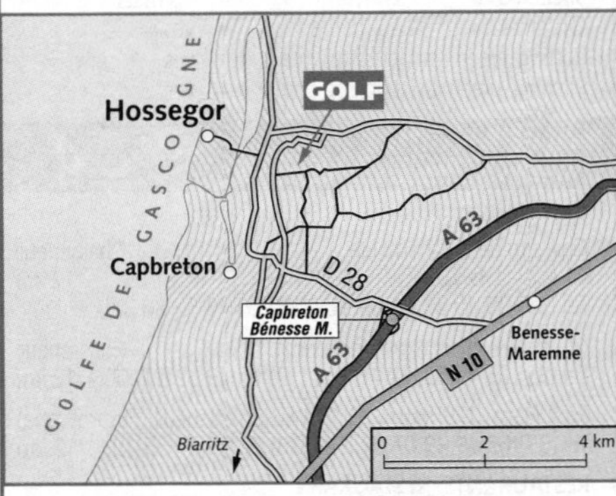

Access Accès : A63 Exit (Sortie) Capbreton/Benesse-Marenne → "Hossegor Centre Ville"
Map 12 on page 184 Carte 12 Page 184

Golf course PARCOURS — 16/20

Site	Site	
Maintenance	Entretien	
Architect	Architecte	Tim Morisson
Type	Type	forest
Relief	Relief	
Water in play	Eau en jeu	
Exp. to wind	Exposé au vent	
Trees in play	Arbres en jeu	

Scorecard Carte de score	Chp. Chp.	Mens Mess.	Ladies Da.
Length Long.	6006	5704	4881
Par	71	71	71
Slope system	134	129	124

Advised golfing ability 0 12 24 36
Niveau de jeu recommandé
Hcp required Handicap exigé 24 Men, 28 Ladies (main season)

Club house & amenities CLUB-HOUSE ET ANNEXES — 6/10

Pro shop	Pro-shop	
Driving range	Practice	
Sheltered	couvert	20 mats
On grass	sur herbe	no
Putting-green	putting-green	yes
Pitching-green	pitching green	yes

Hotel facilities ENVIRONNEMENT HOTELIER — 6/10

HOTELS HÔTELS

Beauséjour, 45 rooms, D 114 € — Hossegor 2 km
Tel (33) 05 58 43 51 07, Fax (33) 05 58 43 70 13

Hôtel du Golf, 9 rooms, D 63 € — on site
Tel (33) 05 58 43 50 59, Fax (33) 05 58 43 81 08

Les Hortensias du Lac — Hossegor
19 rooms, D 125 €
Tel (33) 05 58 43 99 00, Fax (33) 05 58 43 42 81

RESTAURANTS RESTAURANT

Café Bellevue, Tel (33) 05 58 72 10 30 — Capbreton 3 km

Regalty, Tel (33) 05 58 72 22 80 — Capbreton

INTERNATIONAL CLUB DU LYS Les Chênes

15	7	7

Le Lys est un grand club omnisports, magnifiquement logé au milieu des bois à côté de Chantilly, au royaume du pur-sang. Deux parcours font partie de cet ensemble prestigieux, dont celui-ci est le fleuron. Dans un site à la fois plat et très boisé, ce n'est pas un parcours difficile ni très pénalisant quand on sait rester droit, l'essentiel des obstacles étant constitué par les arbres et certains bunkers de fairway. On pourrait d'ailleurs imaginer une préparation plus subtile du terrain, avec des fairways plus étroits et des zones de haut rough pour pimenter le jeu. Mais cela permet aussi, dans un club très "famille" de faire jouer tout le monde, tous les obstacles étant visibles, et les greens peu protégés. Le parcours est signé Tom Simpson, mais on peut soupçonner que des modifications ont été apportées à son dessin, car il avait l'habitude d'être bien plus exigeant avec les golfeurs. Un peu frustrant pour les meilleurs, mais très agréable néanmoins.

Le Lys is a top multi-sports club magnificently sited amidst a forest next to Chantilly in the land of yearlings and thoroughbreds. This prestigious complex comprises two courses, of which "Les Chênes" holds pride of place. Laid out over a flat site strewn with trees, this course is neither too difficult nor too penalising as long as you keep the ball in the fairway, as the hazards are basically trees and a number of fairway bunkers. We suppose they could easily have made this layout a good deal trickier with tighter fairways and tall rough to add a little spice to your round, but this is a very "family" type club where everyone can play and enjoy the course the way it is. As all hazards are clearly visible with little protection around the greens, there are days when you can card a flattering score. The course was originally designed by Tom Simpson, but we suspect that a number of changes have been made over the years, as the Simpson style is usually a little more challenging than this. A wee bit frustrating for the better players but very enjoyable nonetheless.

International Club du Lys — 1929

Rond-Point du Grand Cerf
F - 60260 LAMORLAYE

Office	Secrétariat	(33) 03 44 21 26 00
Pro shop	Pro-shop	(33) 03 44 21 36 73
Fax	Fax	(33) 03 44 21 35 52
E-mail	internationalclub.du.Lys@wanadoo.fr	
Situation	Situation	Paris, 40 km
Annual closure	Fermeture annuelle	no
Weekly closure	Fermeture hebdomadaire	Tuesday(mardi)

Fees main season Tarifs haute saison	18 holes	
	Week days Semaine	**We/Bank holidays** We/Férié
Individual Individuel	46 €	76 € *
Couple Couple	92 €	152 € *

* Restrictions for visitors at weekends

Caddy	Caddy	no
Electric Trolley	Chariot électrique	no
Buggy	Voiturette	38 € /18 holes
Clubs	Clubs	15 € /18 holes

Credit cards Cartes de crédit
VISA - Eurocard - MasterCard

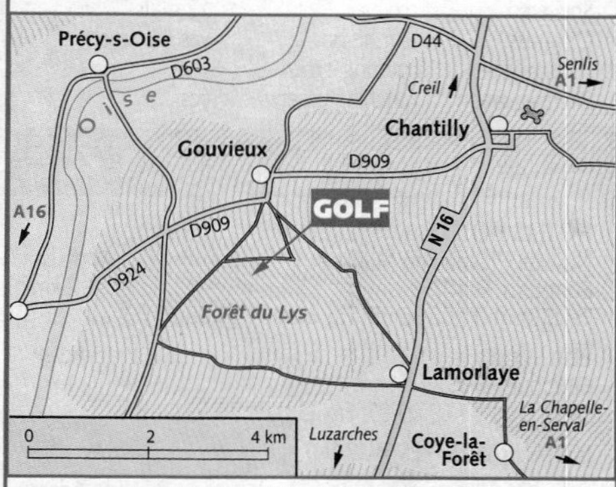

Access Accès : Paris A1 → Lille. Exit Survilliers. D922 → Fosses. N17 → La-Chapelle-en-Serval, then D924 to Chantilly. In Chantilly N16 → Paris, International Club du Lys on right hand side. **Map 3 on page 166** Carte 3 Page 166

Golf course PARCOURS — 15/20

Site	Site	
Maintenance	Entretien	
Architect	Architecte	Tom Simpson
Type	Type	Inland, parkland
Relief	Relief	
Water in play	Eau en jeu	
Exp. to wind	Exposé au vent	
Trees in play	Arbres en jeu	

Scorecard Carte de score	**Chp.** Chp.	**Mens** Mess.	**Ladies** Da.
Length Long.	5863	5517	5151
Par	70	70	70
Slope system	112	110	117

Advised golfing ability 0 12 24 36
Niveau de jeu recommandé
Hcp required Handicap exigé 36

Club house & amenities CLUB-HOUSE ET ANNEXES — 7/10

Pro shop	Pro-shop
Driving range	Practice
Sheltered	couvert
On grass	sur herbe
Putting-green	putting-green
Pitching-green	pitching green

Hotel facilities ENVIRONNEMENT HOTELIER — 7/10

HOTELS HÔTELS

Château de la Tour, 41 rooms, D 136 € — Gouvieux
Tel (33) 03 44 62 38 38, Fax (33) 03 44 57 31 97 — 3 km

Pavillon Saint-Hubert, 19 rooms, D 64 € — Toutevoie
Tel (33) 03 44 57 07 04, Fax (33) 03 44 57 75 42 — 5 km

Relais d'Aumale, 22 rooms, D 125 € — Montgrésin
Tel (33) 03 44 54 61 31, Fax (33) 03 44 54 69 15 — 11 km

RESTAURANTS RESTAURANT

La Renardière — Gouvieux
Tel (33) 03 44 57 08 23 — 3 km

Verbois — St Maximin (RN 16)
Tel (33) 03 44 24 06 22 — 12 km

ISLE ADAM (L')

16 | 7 | 4

Ce parcours a vite conquis une belle réputation. Par sa franchise, par la très grande variété de dessin et d'environnement des trous, tracés en partie dans une forêt, en partie sur un beau plateau. Le seul inconvénient, c'est de passer de l'une à l'autre et les montées sont épuisantes. La stratégie de jeu est évidente dès la première visite, les fairways sont larges, mais le placement de la balle est crucial pour pouvoir ensuite approcher les greens en bonne position, car leurs modelages et leurs dimensions exigent beaucoup d'attention. L'architecte Ronald Fream a beaucoup modelé le terrain, dans une synthèse heureuse des tendances britannique et américaine, permettant à tous les niveaux et tous les styles de jeu de s'exprimer. Les arbres et bunkers sont bien en jeu, et l'eau présente sur trois trous seulement. Une bonne réussite, d'autant plus que d'importants travaux de drainage ont permis de mieux amortir les conséquences des pluies.

This course has rapidly gained a fine reputation for its fairness and for the great variety in the design and setting of holes, some of which are laid out through a forest, others on a pretty plateau. The only drawback is walking from one part of the course to the other. The climb is so exhausting that a shuttle service might be in order. Game strategy is clear from the very first visit; the fairways are wide, but it is essential to position the tee-shot accurately in order to get a good look at greens whose slopes and size require great care. Architect Ronald Fream has shaped the terrain a great deal and created a happy combination of British and American trends. The course is fun for golfers of all abilities and styles. The trees and bunkers are clearly in play and water threatens on just three holes. A great accomplishment, especially now that significant drainage work helps to offset the effects of heavy rain.

Golf de l'Isle-Adam — 1995

1, ch. des Vanneaux
F - 95290 L'ISLE-ADAM

Office	Secrétariat	(33) 01 34 08 11 11
Pro shop	Pro-shop	(33) 01 34 08 11 11
Fax	Fax	(33) 01 34 08 11 19
Web	www.golfisleadam.com	
Situation	Situation	

Paris, 35 km - Chantilly (pop. 11 340), 21 km

Annual closure Fermeture annuelle 24/12→1/1
Weekly closure Fermeture hebdomadaire
tuesday (mardi)

Fees main season Tarifs haute saison		Full day
	Week days Semaine	**We/Bank holidays** We/Férié
Individual Individuel	38 €	57 €
Couple Couple	76 €	114 €
Caddy	Caddy	no
Electric Trolley	Chariot électrique	8 € /18 holes
Buggy	Voiturette	no
Clubs	Clubs	23 € /full day

Credit cards Cartes de crédit
VISA - CB - Eurocard - MasterCard - DC - AMEX

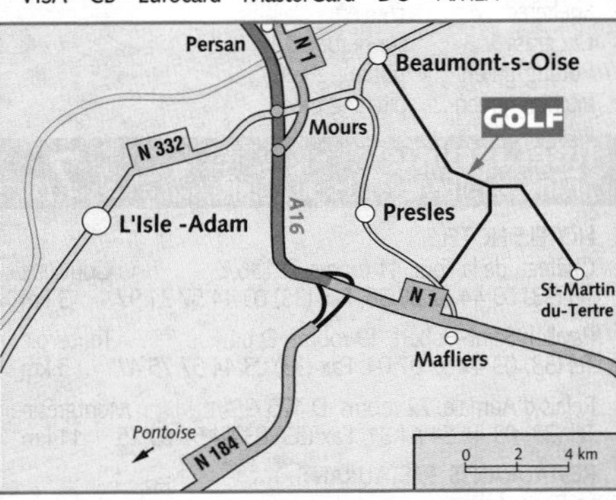

Access Accès : • A1 Paris (Porte de la Chapelle), Exit (Sortie) Beauvais, N1, Exit Beaumont-sur-Oise • A15 Paris (Porte de Clignancourt), → Pontoise, → N184, Exit Beaumont-sur-Oise **Map 1 on page 163** Carte 1 Page 163

Golf course PARCOURS — 16/20

Site	Site	
Maintenance	Entretien	
Architect	Architecte	Ronald Fream
Type	Type	forest, open country
Relief	Relief	
Water in play	Eau en jeu	
Exp. to wind	Exposé au vent	
Trees in play	Arbres en jeu	

Scorecard Carte de score	**Chp.** Chp.	**Mens** Mess.	**Ladies** Da.
Length Long.	6188	5696	4612
Par	72	72	72
Slope system	131	128	121

Advised golfing ability 0 12 24 36
Niveau de jeu recommandé
Hcp required Handicap exigé 35

Club house & amenities CLUB-HOUSE ET ANNEXES — 7/10

Pro shop	Pro-shop	
Driving range	Practice	
Sheltered	couvert	12 mats
On grass	sur herbe	yes (summer)
Putting-green	putting-green	yes
Pitching-green	pitching green	yes

Hotel facilities ENVIRONNEMENT HOTELIER — 4/10

HOTELS HÔTELS

Novotel Château de Maffliers — Maffliers 7 km
80 rooms, D 107 €
Tel (33) 01 34 08 35 35, Fax (33) 01 34 08 35 00

Etap Hôtel — L'Isle-Adam 1 km
68 rooms, D 32 €
Tel (33) 01 34 69 09 85, Fax (33) 01 34 69 11 85

RESTAURANTS RESTAURANT

Relais Fleuri — L'Isle-Adam 2 km
Tel (33) 01 34 69 01 85

Gai Rivage — L'Isle Adam 2 km
Tel (33) 01 34 69 01 09

JOYENVAL Marly

16	8	7

Après bien des péripéties, le Golf de Joyenval semble avoir trouvé sa vitesse de croisière, et sait parfois entr'ouvrir ses portes, bien qu'il soit très privé. L'avantage d'une fréquentation réduite, c'est que son entretien, notamment au niveau des greens, était généralement bon. Après une période de flottement, les choses vont bien mieux de ce côté, avec l'arrivée d'un greenkeeper américain. Des deux parcours, Marly est celui qui a le moins souffert des contraintes administratives, souvent abusives, liées à la proximité du Désert de Retz (monument historique), mais on aimerait voir les trous souvent mieux définis par des plantations. Ne désespérons pas, mais dans ces conditions, on ne voit souvent plus que les bunkers, aussi impressionnants à voir qu'à visiter. Très varié de paysage et de style, ce parcours est d'autant plus technique que les greens sont très difficiles à lire.

After a lot of starting and stopping, the Joyenval club now looks to be up and running and sometimes even opens its gate to outsiders, despite being a very private club. The upside of being under-played is that greenkeeping and the greens in particular were generally good. After a period of indecision, things have much improved in this respect with the arrival of an American green-keeper. Of the two courses, Marly is the one that suffered the least from often excessive administrative requirements related to the closeness of the Désert de Retz (an historical landmark), although we would like to see the holes better defined with a tree planting program. We still hold out hope, but under these conditions you often see only the bunkers, which are as impressive to see as they are to be in. Very varied in style and landscape, the course is made all the more technical by greens that are very difficult to read.

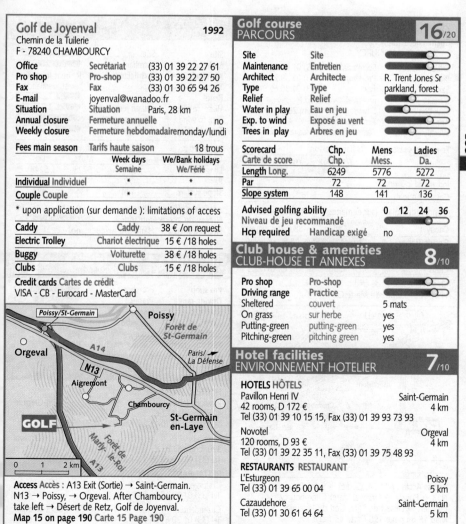

Golf de Joyenval — 1992

Chemin de la Tuilerie
F - 78240 CHAMBOURCY

Office	Secrétariat	(33) 01 39 22 27 61
Pro shop	Pro-shop	(33) 01 39 22 27 50
Fax	Fax	(33) 01 30 65 94 26
E-mail	joyenval@wanadoo.fr	
Situation	Situation	Paris, 28 km
Annual closure	Fermeture annuelle	no
Weekly closure	Fermeture hebdomadaire	monday/lundi

Fees main season Tarifs haute saison	18 trous	
	Week days Semaine	**We/Bank holidays** We/Férié
Individual Individuel	*	*
Couple Couple	*	*

* upon application (sur demande): limitations of access

Caddy	Caddy	38 € /on request
Electric Trolley	Chariot électrique	15 € /18 holes
Buggy	Voiturette	38 € /18 holes
Clubs	Clubs	15 € /18 holes

Credit cards Cartes de crédit
VISA - CB - Eurocard - MasterCard

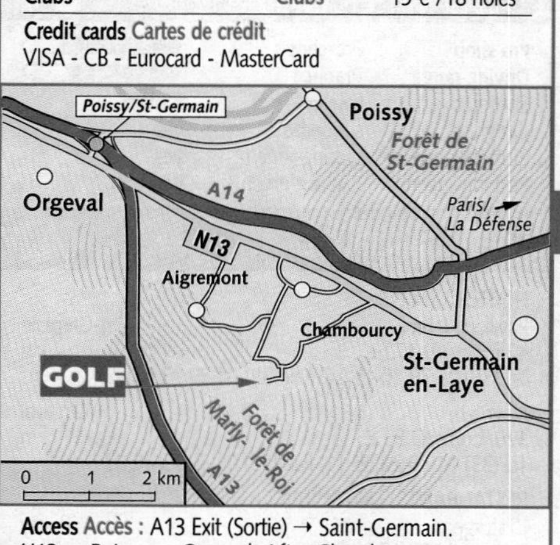

Access Accès : A13 Exit (Sortie) → Saint-Germain. N13 → Poissy, → Orgeval. After Chambourcy, take left → Désert de Retz, Golf de Joyenval.
Map 15 on page 190 Carte 15 Page 190

Golf course PARCOURS — 16/20

Site	Site	
Maintenance	Entretien	
Architect	Architecte	R. Trent Jones Sr
Type	Type	parkland, forest
Relief	Relief	
Water in play	Eau en jeu	
Exp. to wind	Exposé au vent	
Trees in play	Arbres en jeu	

Scorecard Carte de score	**Chp.** Chp.	**Mens** Mess.	**Ladies** Da.
Length Long.	6249	5776	5272
Par	72	72	72
Slope system	148	141	136

Advised golfing ability 0 12 24 36
Niveau de jeu recommandé

Hcp required Handicap exigé no

Club house & amenities CLUB-HOUSE ET ANNEXES — 8/10

Pro shop	Pro-shop	
Driving range	Practice	
Sheltered	couvert	5 mats
On grass	sur herbe	yes
Putting-green	putting-green	yes
Pitching-green	pitching green	yes

Hotel facilities ENVIRONNEMENT HOTELIER — 7/10

HOTELS HÔTELS

Pavillon Henri IV — Saint-Germain 4 km
42 rooms, D 172 €
Tel (33) 01 39 10 15 15, Fax (33) 01 39 93 73 93

Novotel — Orgeval 4 km
120 rooms, D 93 €
Tel (33) 01 39 22 35 11, Fax (33) 01 39 75 48 93

RESTAURANTS RESTAURANT

L'Esturgeon — Poissy 5 km
Tel (33) 01 39 65 00 04

Cazaudehore — Saint-Germain 5 km
Tel (33) 01 30 61 64 64

JOYENVAL Retz

15 | 8 | 7

Le site est exceptionnel, entre la forêt de Marly et une vallée que les poètes n'aurait pas reniée, à proximité immédiate du Désert de Retz, folie architecturale dûe à l'imagination d'un gentilhomme du XVIII ème siècle. On aurait d'ailleurs aimé que le parcours soit vraiment une réponse moderne à cet esprit baroque, mais le crayon parfois austère de Trent Jones a permis de limiter au minimum les contraintes. Il reste quelques trous de haute volée, entre forêt et plaine, entre parc et jardin, avec des aspects évidemment américains dans leur franchise et leur brutalité, mais aussi britanniques quand les contours deviennent plus flous, plus subtils. Très scénique, moins stratégique que "Marly", ce parcours est aussi moins exigeant pour les joueurs moyens.

The site is outstanding, between the forest of Marly and a valley to make any poet wax lyrical, within the immediate vicinity of the Désert de Retz, a piece of architectural folly born from the imagination of an 18th century gentleman. We would have liked this course really to be a modern response to this baroque spirit, but the often austere design of Trent Jones helped keep restrictions to a minimum. There are a few top-notch holes between forest and plain, park-land and garden, obviously looking very American in their openness and toughness, but also British when contours grow a little less sharp and more subtle. Very scenic and less strategic than Marly, Retz is also less demanding for the average golfer.

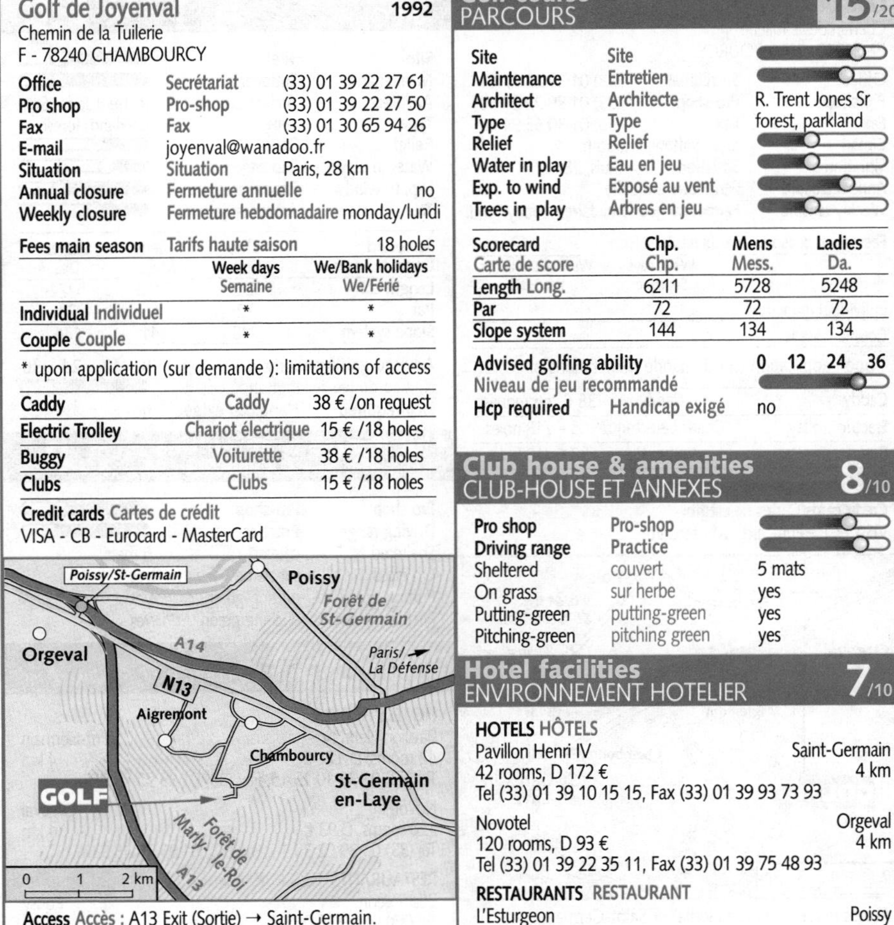

Golf de Joyenval — 1992

Chemin de la Tuilerie
F - 78240 CHAMBOURCY

Office	Secrétariat	(33) 01 39 22 27 61
Pro shop	Pro-shop	(33) 01 39 22 27 50
Fax	Fax	(33) 01 30 65 94 26
E-mail	joyenval@wanadoo.fr	
Situation	Situation	Paris, 28 km
Annual closure	Fermeture annuelle	no
Weekly closure	Fermeture hebdomadaire	monday/lundi

Fees main season Tarifs haute saison	18 holes	
	Week days Semaine	**We/Bank holidays** We/Férié
Individual Individuel	*	*
Couple Couple	*	*

* upon application (sur demande): limitations of access

Caddy	Caddy	38 € /on request
Electric Trolley	Chariot électrique	15 € /18 holes
Buggy	Voiturette	38 € /18 holes
Clubs	Clubs	15 € /18 holes

Credit cards Cartes de crédit
VISA - CB - Eurocard - MasterCard

Access Accès : A13 Exit (Sortie) → Saint-Germain. N13 → Poissy, → Orgeval. After Chambourcy, take left → Désert de Retz, Golf de Joyenval.
Map 15 on page 190 Carte 15 Page 190

Golf course — PARCOURS — 15/20

Site	Site	
Maintenance	Entretien	
Architect	Architecte	R. Trent Jones Sr
Type	Type	forest, parkland
Relief	Relief	
Water in play	Eau en jeu	
Exp. to wind	Exposé au vent	
Trees in play	Arbres en jeu	

Scorecard Carte de score	**Chp.** Chp.	**Mens** Mess.	**Ladies** Da.
Length Long.	6211	5728	5248
Par	72	72	72
Slope system	144	134	134

Advised golfing ability Niveau de jeu recommandé — 0 12 24 36
Hcp required Handicap exigé — no

Club house & amenities — CLUB-HOUSE ET ANNEXES — 8/10

Pro shop	Pro-shop	
Driving range	Practice	
Sheltered	couvert	5 mats
On grass	sur herbe	yes
Putting-green	putting-green	yes
Pitching-green	pitching green	yes

Hotel facilities — ENVIRONNEMENT HOTELIER — 7/10

HOTELS HÔTELS

Pavillon Henri IV — Saint-Germain 4 km
42 rooms, D 172 €
Tel (33) 01 39 10 15 15, Fax (33) 01 39 93 73 93

Novotel — Orgeval 4 km
120 rooms, D 93 €
Tel (33) 01 39 22 35 11, Fax (33) 01 39 75 48 93

RESTAURANTS RESTAURANT

L'Esturgeon — Poissy 5 km
Tel (33) 01 39 65 00 04

Cazaudehore — Saint-Germain 5 km
Tel (33) 01 30 61 64 64

KEMPFERHOF (LE)

18	8	6

Le plaisir des yeux commence dès l'arrivée : l'impression de finition et de soin du détail se confirme sur le parcours, signé von Hagge. Dans un environnement de campagne, avec des sapins, des hêtres et des bouleaux, il est difficile de jouer son handicap mais ce parcours sans reliefs prononcés est jouable à tous les niveaux. Les néophytes seront cependant intimidés par quelques obstacles d'eau dangereux, mais ce genre de parcours n'est guère favorable à ce type de joueurs. Très sélectif, il demande souvent de travailler la balle et de démontrer sa maîtrise de tous les clubs, avec un accent aigu sur la précision, notamment pour approcher les vastes greens, très travaillés. Tous les obstacles étant visibles, ce parcours ne cache rien de ses exigences. Le terrain a été beaucoup modelé, mais la nature a repris ses droits, donnant au lieu une belle impression de calme. Pas de changement d'appréciation ici, c'est une incontestable réussite, dans une région magnifique à découvrir, du printemps à la mi-automne.

The initial impression of careful grooming and attention to detail is confirmed when out playing this course. In a country setting of pine-trees, beech and birch, playing to your handicap might be too much to ask, but this flattish course can be played by all. Beginners may be unsettled by a few dangerous water hazards, but there again this is hardly their type of course. We found this very selective, calling for skill in ball-control and stroke-making and great emphasis on precision-play, especially for approaching the huge and carefully designed greens. As all the hazards are there to be seen, the course hides nothing of what it demands from golfers. The terrain has been contoured to a considerable extent, but mother nature has regained the upper hand to give an overall impression of tranquillity. No change of appreciation here; an unquestionably great course in a magnificent part of the country, best played from Sprint to mid-Autumn.

Kempferhof Golf Club — 1990

351, rue du Moulin
F - 67115 PLOBSHEIM

Office	Secrétariat	(33) 03 88 98 72 72
Pro shop	Pro-shop	(33) 03 88 98 72 72
Fax	Fax	(33) 03 88 98 74 76
Web	—	
Situation	Situation	

Strasbourg (pop. 252 260), 15 km

Annual closure	Fermeture annuelle	21/12→12/1
Weekly closure	Fermeture hebdomadaire	

tuesday/mardi (01/11 → 01/04)

Fees main season Tarifs haute saison	Week days Semaine	We/Bank holidays We/Férié
18 holes		
Individual Individuel	61 €	91 €
Couple Couple	122 €	182 €

Under 25: – 50%

Caddy	Caddy	no
Electric Trolley	Chariot électrique	no
Buggy	Voiturette	30 € /18 holes
Clubs	Clubs	no

Credit cards Cartes de crédit
VISA - CB - Eurocard - MasterCard - AMEX

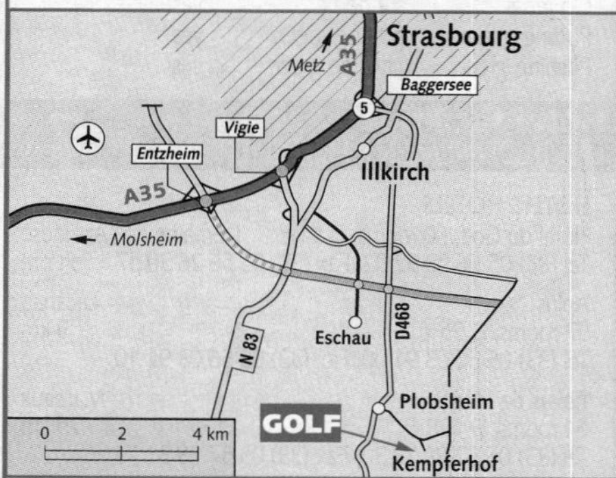

Access Accès : Strasbourg A35, Exit (Sortie) N°5 Baggersee → Eschau, → Plobsheim, → Golf

Map 4 on page 169 Carte 4 Page 169

Golf course — PARCOURS — 18/20

Site	Site	
Maintenance	Entretien	
Architect	Architecte	Robert von Hagge
Type	Type	parkland, country
Relief	Relief	
Water in play	Eau en jeu	
Exp. to wind	Exposé au vent	
Trees in play	Arbres en jeu	

Scorecard Carte de score	Chp. Chp.	Mens Mess.	Ladies Da.
Length Long.	6024	5613	4493
Par	72	72	72
Slope system	142	134	124

Advised golfing ability Niveau de jeu recommandé: 0 12 24 36
Hcp required Handicap exigé: 35, We

Club house & amenities — CLUB-HOUSE ET ANNEXES — 8/10

Pro shop	Pro-shop	
Driving range	Practice	
Sheltered	couvert	10 mats
On grass	sur herbe	yes
Putting-green	putting-green	yes
Pitching-green	pitching green	yes

Hotel facilities — ENVIRONNEMENT HOTELIER — 6/10

HOTELS HÔTELS

Kempferhof Hotel, 13 rooms, D 152 € — Golf on site
Tel (33) 03 88 98 72 72, Fax (33) 03 88 98 74 76

Holiday Inn Garden Court, 68 rooms, D 107 € — Illkirch 5 km
Tel (33) 03 88 40 84 84, Fax (33) 03 88 66 22 83

Alizés, 49 rooms, D 58 € — Lipsheim 3 km
Tel (33) 03 88 59 02 00, Fax (33) 03 88 64 21 61

RESTAURANTS RESTAURANT

Buerehiesel, Tel (33) 03 88 45 56 65 — Strasbourg 13 km

Le Crocodile, Tel (33) 03 88 32 13 02 — Strasbourg

L'Arsenal, Tel (33) 03 88 35 03 69 — Strasbourg

LACANAU

14 | 6 | 7

Dans ce site magnifique et tranquille, modérément vallonné, et au milieu d'une forêt de pins, ce parcours aurait pu être un chef d'oeuvre. Mais le dessin de John Harris est simplement de bonne qualité, avec une demi-douzaine de trous sortant de l'ordinaire. Des obstacles d'eau apportent un élément paysager intéressant, et quelques interrogations avant de jouer, sans être effrayants. Certes, il faut jouer plusieurs fois pour bien comprendre la stratégie idéale en fonction des différents départs, mais seuls les mauvais coups sont vraiment punis. Même si les débutants auront des difficultés sur certains trous étroits, les golfeurs de tous niveaux peuvent passer un séjour vivifiant au grand air et à proximité de l'Atlantique, pratiquement toute l'année car le sol sablonneux du parcours absorbe bien la pluie. L'entretien est de très bon niveau. Et si les tempêtes ont abattu pas mal d'arbres, les plus dangereux sont restés imperturbablement en place. Hélas ?

Gently rolling through a pine forest in a balmy and magnificent setting, this course could have been a true masterpiece. As it is, the layout designed by John Harris is simply a good course, although half a dozen holes clearly emerge as out of the ordinary. Water hazards are an attractive addition to the general landscape and call for a little thought before shaping the shot, but they are less than awesome. Naturally, you need to play the course several times to grasp the ideal strategy depending on the tees you choose, but here, only the really bad shots are penalised. Although beginners (and even more proficient players) will find a number of holes very tight, golfers of all abilities can spend an invigorating holiday in the sea-air close to the Atlantic Ocean. And they can play virtually all year, as the sandy soil quickly soaks up the rain. The green-keeper has worked wonders in keeping the course in prime condition, and while the storms of Xmas 1999 brought down quite a few trees, the most dangerous are still standing and, alas, often in your way.

Golf de Lacanau — 1980

Domaine de l'Ardilouse
F - 33680 LACANAU

Office	Secrétariat	(33) 05 56 03 92 98
Pro shop	Pro-shop	(33) 05 56 03 92 98
Fax	Fax	(33) 05 56 26 30 57
Web	www.golf-lacanau.com	
Situation	Situation	

Bordeaux (pop. 211 200), 50 km

Annual closure	Fermeture annuelle	no
Weekly closure	Fermeture hebdomadaire	no

Fees main season Tarifs haute saison — full day

	Week days / Semaine	We/Bank holidays / We/Férié
Individual Individuel	44 €	44 €
Couple Couple	88 €	88 €

Juniors: 18 € - 24 € during July and August (en juillet-août)

Caddy	Caddy	no
Electric Trolley	Chariot électrique	no
Buggy	Voiturette	23 € /18 holes
Clubs	Clubs	7 € /full day

Credit cards Cartes de crédit
VISA - CB - Eurocard - MasterCard - DC - AMEX

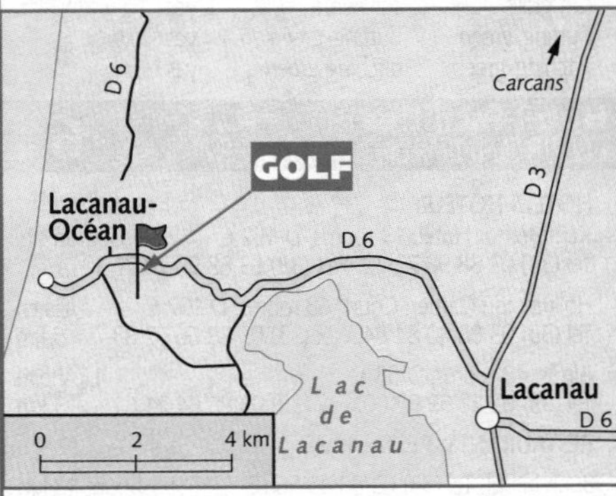

Access Accès : Ring Road ("Rocade Ouest") of Bordeaux, Exit (Sortie) No 7, N 215, D6 → Lacanau Océan
Map 9 on page 178 Carte 9 Page 178

Golf course PARCOURS — 14/20

Site	Site	
Maintenance	Entretien	
Architect	Architecte	John Harris
Type	Type	forest, hilly
Relief	Relief	
Water in play	Eau en jeu	
Exp. to wind	Exposé au vent	
Trees in play	Arbres en jeu	

Scorecard Carte de score	Chp. Chp.	Mens Mess.	Ladies Da.
Length Long.	5926	5394	4871
Par	72	72	72
Slope system	137	134	138

Advised golfing ability Niveau de jeu recommandé — 0 12 24 36
Hcp required Handicap exigé — 35 (summer/été)

Club house & amenities CLUB-HOUSE ET ANNEXES — 6/10

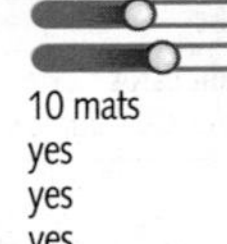

Pro shop	Pro-shop	
Driving range	Practice	
Sheltered	couvert	10 mats
On grass	sur herbe	yes
Putting-green	putting-green	yes
Pitching-green	pitching green	yes

Hotel facilities ENVIRONNEMENT HOTELIER — 7/10

HOTELS HÔTELS

Hôtel du Golf, 50 rooms, D 91 € — Domaine de l'Ardilouse
Tel (33) 05 56 03 92 92, Fax (33) 05 56 26 30 57 — on site

Aplus — Lacanau
57 rooms, D 95 € — 5 km
Tel (33) 05 56 03 91 00, Fax (33) 05 56 03 91 10

Relais de Margaux — Margaux
64 rooms, D 198 € — 25 km
Tel (33) 05 57 88 38 30, Fax (33) 05 57 88 31 73

RESTAURANTS RESTAURANT

Savoie, Tel (33) 05 57 88 31 76 — Margaux 25 km

La Vieille Auberge ,Tel (33) 05 56 26 50 40 — Lacanau 3 km

LARGUE (LA)

15	7	4

Dans une jolie propriété, traversée par la ligne Maginot, offrant alternativement un environnement de forêt et des trous de style links, ce parcours est accidenté mais plaisant, avec quelques pièces d'eau, en jeu sur cinq trous. Plus impressionnant visuellement que réellement, ses obstacles principaux sont les arbres et les nombreux bunkers. Les bunkers de green sont bien travaillés, mais parfois peu visibles. Ils constituent les principales difficultés, avec les arbres, mais La Largue est surtout délicat à négocier par le choix de clubs, étant donné sa topographie très vallonnée (voiturette recommandée pour les seniors). Les départs et fairways sont bien entretenus, les greens sont de bonne qualité, bien conçus et assez rapides : certains sont surélevés et demandent de porter la balle. Un parcours d'entraînement de 9 trous permet de faire tranquillement progresser les enfants ou amis peu expérimentés encore.

This is a hilly but pleasant course with a few stretches of water coming into play on five holes, located on a pretty estate crossed by the Maginot line. Part woodland and part links, this is a visually impressive layout where the main hazards are the trees and numerous bunkers. The green-side bunkers in particular are well-designed, but sometimes hard to spot. The course is perhaps less impressive once you are on it, with the main difficulty coming from the trees, bunkers and club selection owing to the hilly terrain (a buggy is recommended for senior players). The tees and fairways are in good condition and the greens are well laid-out and pretty fast. A number of elevated greens call for long high approaches. A 9-hole practice course is good news for children and friends still learning the game.

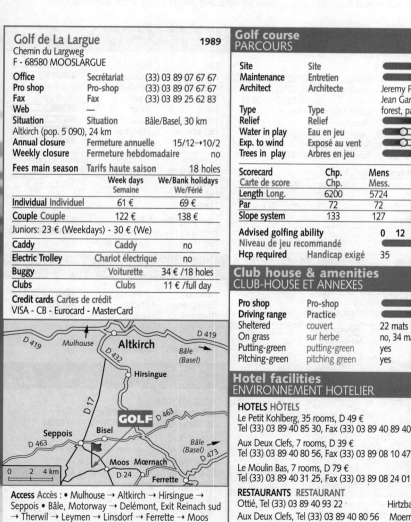

Golf de La Largue — 1989

Chemin du Largweg
F - 68580 MOOSLARGUE

Office	Secrétariat	(33) 03 89 07 67 67
Pro shop	Pro-shop	(33) 03 89 07 67 67
Fax	Fax	(33) 03 89 25 62 83
Web	—	
Situation	Situation	Bâle/Basel, 30 km

Altkirch (pop. 5 090), 24 km

Annual closure	Fermeture annuelle	15/12→10/2
Weekly closure	Fermeture hebdomadaire	no

Fees main season Tarifs haute saison	18 holes	
	Week days Semaine	**We/Bank holidays** We/Férié
Individual Individuel	61 €	69 €
Couple Couple	122 €	138 €

Juniors: 23 € (Weekdays) - 30 € (We)

Caddy	Caddy	no
Electric Trolley	Chariot électrique	no
Buggy	Voiturette	34 € /18 holes
Clubs	Clubs	11 € /full day

Credit cards Cartes de crédit
VISA - CB - Eurocard - MasterCard

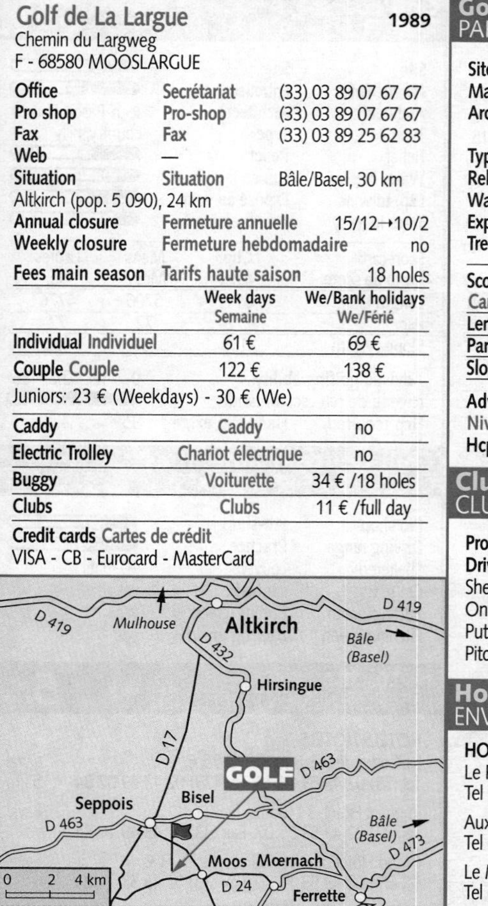

Access Accès : • Mulhouse → Altkirch → Hirsingue → Seppois • Bâle, Motorway → Delémont, Exit Reinach sud → Therwil → Leymen → Linsdorf → Ferrette → Moos

Map 8 on page 177 Carte 8 Page 177

Golf course — PARCOURS — 15/20

Site	Site	
Maintenance	Entretien	
Architect	Architecte	Jeremy Pern, Jean Garaïalde
Type	Type	forest, parkland
Relief	Relief	
Water in play	Eau en jeu	
Exp. to wind	Exposé au vent	
Trees in play	Arbres en jeu	

Scorecard Carte de score	**Chp.** Chp.	**Mens** Mess.	**Ladies** Da.
Length Long.	6200	5724	5415
Par	72	72	72
Slope system	133	127	128

Advised golfing ability — 0 12 24 36
Niveau de jeu recommandé
Hcp required Handicap exigé 35

Club house & amenities — CLUB-HOUSE ET ANNEXES — 7/10

Pro shop	Pro-shop	
Driving range	Practice	
Sheltered	couvert	22 mats
On grass	sur herbe	no, 34 mats open air
Putting-green	putting-green	yes
Pitching-green	pitching green	yes

Hotel facilities — ENVIRONNEMENT HOTELIER — 4/10

HOTELS HÔTELS

Le Petit Kohlberg, 35 rooms, D 49 € — Lucelle
Tel (33) 03 89 40 85 30, Fax (33) 03 89 40 89 40 — 12 km

Aux Deux Clefs, 7 rooms, D 39 € — Ferrette
Tel (33) 03 89 40 80 56, Fax (33) 03 89 08 10 47 — 9 km

Le Moulin Bas, 7 rooms, D 79 € — Ligsdorf
Tel (33) 03 89 40 31 25, Fax (33) 03 89 08 24 01 — 13 km

RESTAURANTS RESTAURANT

Ottié, Tel (33) 03 89 40 93 22 — Hirtzbach 15 km
Aux Deux Clefs, Tel (33) 03 89 40 80 56 — Moernach 5 km
Moulin Bas, Tel (33) 03 89 40 31 25 — Ligsdorf 13 km

LAVAL-CHANGÉ La Chabossière 14 | 7 | 5

Malheureusement situé près de l'autoroute, ce parcours a été dessiné par Jean-Pascal Fourès dans un site dégagé et de relief assez prononcé. On souhaite toujours une meilleure délimitation des fairways et des roughs (surtout entre le 1, le 9 et le 18) afin de mieux orienter le jeu du visiteur, même si des progrès ont été faits, quand le manque d'arbres ne permet pas facilement de se repérer. De longueur raisonnable, le tracé général est de bonne qualité, avec quelques coups aveugles, mais inévitables en raison du terrain. Les greens sont raisonnablement modelés, de bonnes dimensions et de très bonne qualité. Ce golf n'est pas vraiment un lieu traditionnel de vacances, ou sur un itinéraire golfique particulier, mais il a visiblement été pensé pour des membres permanents, et pour tous les niveaux de jeu. Ses jolis points de vue sur la Mayenne et son ambiance plairont aux visiteurs de passage dans la région, ils seront bien accueillis...

Unhappily located within the immediate vicinity of a motorway, this course was designed by Jean-Pascal Fourès in an open and rather hilly site. We would still like to see clearer demarcation between fairway and rough (especially between the 1st, 9th and 18th holes) for the visitor to get a clearer picture of the course, even though considerable progress has been made when the absence of trees may cause a little confusion. The general layout is of reasonable length and good standard, although there are the few unavoidable blind holes on such sloping terrain. The greens are reasonably well contoured and excellent to play. This course is not really in traditional holiday country or on any special golfing route, but it has visibly been designed for permanent members and golfers of all playing skills. Pretty panoramas over the Mayenne river and the club's atmosphere will appeal to visitors passing through, who will always find a warm welcome here.

Golf de Laval-Changé — 1992

«La Chabossière»
F - 53810 CHANGE

Office	Secrétariat	(33) 02 43 53 16 03
Pro shop	Pro-shop	(33) 02 43 53 16 03
Fax	Fax	(33) 02 43 49 35 15
E-mail	golf53.laval@wanadoo.fr	
Situation	Situation	
Laval (pop. 50 470), 5 km		
Annual closure	Fermeture annuelle	24/12→3/1
Weekly closure	Fermeture hebdomadaire	no

Fees main season Tarifs haute saison		Full day
	Week days Semaine	**We/Bank holidays** We/Férié
Individual Individuel	27 €	34 €
Couple Couple	44 €	53 €

Caddy	Caddy	no
Electric Trolley	Chariot électrique	9 € /18 holes
Buggy	Voiturette	23 € /18 holes
Clubs	Clubs	8 € /full day

Credit cards Cartes de crédit
VISA - CB - Eurocard - MasterCard - DC - AMEX

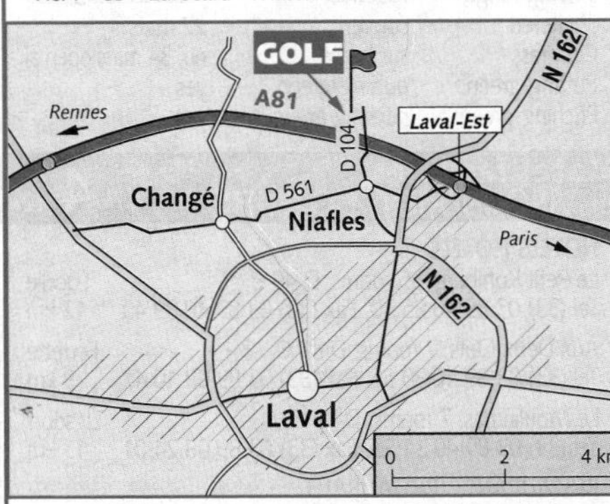

Access Accès : A81 Paris-Rennes, Exit (Sortie) Laval-Est
Map 2 on page 164 Carte 2 Page 164

Golf course PARCOURS — 14/20

Site	Site	
Maintenance	Entretien	
Architect	Architecte	Jean-Pascal Fourès
Type	Type	country, hilly
Relief	Relief	
Water in play	Eau en jeu	
Exp. to wind	Exposé au vent	
Trees in play	Arbres en jeu	

Scorecard Carte de score	**Chp.** Chp.	**Mens** Mess.	**Ladies** Da.
Length Long.	6111	5706	4776
Par	72	72	72
Slope system	138	130	125

Advised golfing ability Niveau de jeu recommandé — 0 12 24 36
Hcp required Handicap exigé 35

Club house & amenities CLUB-HOUSE ET ANNEXES — 7/10

Pro shop	Pro-shop	
Driving range	Practice	
Sheltered	couvert	10 mats
On grass	sur herbe	yes
Putting-green	putting-green	yes
Pitching-green	pitching green	yes

Hotel facilities ENVIRONNEMENT HOTELIER — 5/10

HOTELS HÔTELS

La Gerbe de Blé, 8 rooms, D 75 € — Laval 5 km
Tel (33) 02 43 53 14 10, Fax (33) 02 43 49 02 84

Impérial Hôtel, 34 rooms, D 50 € — Laval
Tel (33) 02 43 53 55 02, Fax (33) 02 43 49 16 74

Grand Hôtel de Paris, 39 rooms, D 73 € — Laval
Tel (33) 02 43 53 76 20, Fax (33) 02 43 53 91 83

RESTAURANTS RESTAURANT

Bistro de Paris, Tel (33) 02 43 56 98 29 — Laval 5 km

Table Ronde, Tel (33) 02 43 53 43 33 — Changé 2 km

Le Capucin Gourmand, Tel (33) 02 43 66 02 02 — Laval

LE PRIEURÉ Ouest

14	7	5

Ceux qui connaissent le style Hawtree ne seront guère surpris par ce tracé très honnête mais sans grandes surprises. Le parcours "Est" est sans doute plus varié et amusant, mais moins bien équilibré : le parcours "Ouest" constitue à l'évidence la référence de ce golf. Dans grand parc orné de quelques très beaux specimens d'arbres, le parcours se déroule de manière assez conventionnelle avec des défenses de green le plus souvent latérales, quelques mouvements sur les surfaces de putting, un bon équilibre des difficultés, une longueur très respectable, mais peu de chocs visuels ou de très grands défis techniques. Peu d'autres options que de taper loin et droit, de bien frapper ses fers et de putter correctement ! On est certes heureux d'avoir joué ce classique, à tous les sens du terme, mais pas forcément ému. Hawtree n'a guère pris de risques ici. L'arrosage automatique a bien arrangé cet ensemble autrefois sec en été, mais il reste très humide en hiver.

Golfers acquainted with the Hawtree style will not be surprised by this more than fair layout where there is little to raise any golfer's eyebrows. The "East" course is certainly the most varied and fun to play, although it lacks balance. The "West" course is evidently the club's "flagship". On a site of expansive parkland and a few fine trees, the course unwinds in a very classical style with greens often guarded by lateral bunkers, a few contours on the greens, well-balanced difficulties, very respectable yardage but few visual thrills or tough technical challenges. There is nothing else for it but to hit the ball long and straight, strike some clean iron shots and putt decently. Golf should be so simple. In other words, you are glad to have played this classic layout, in every sense of the term, but not necessarily too excited about it. This is perhaps one of Hawtree's more conservative designs. The automatic sprinklers have done much to help a course that often used to get very dry in summer, but stays wet in winter.

Golf du Prieuré — 1965

F - 78440 SAILLY

Office	Secrétariat	(44) 01 34 76 65 65
Pro shop	Pro-shop	(44) 01 34 76 78 29
Fax	Fax	(44) 01 34 76 65 50
E-mail	golfduprieure@wanadoo.fr	
Situation	Situation	Paris, 55 km
Annual closure	Fermeture annuelle	no
Weekly closure	Fermeture hebdomadaire	tuesday mardi

Fees main season Tarifs haute saison	18 holes	
	Week days Semaine	**We/Bank holidays** We/Férié
Individual Individuel	40 €	52 €
Couple Couple	80 €	104 €

We: members' guests only (invitation d'un membre) - Under 18 : 20 € (Weekdays)

Caddy	Caddy	on request
Electric Trolley	Chariot électrique	12 € /18 holes
Buggy	Voiturette	40 € /18 holes
Clubs	Clubs	no

Credit cards Cartes de crédit
VISA - CB - Eurocard - MasterCard

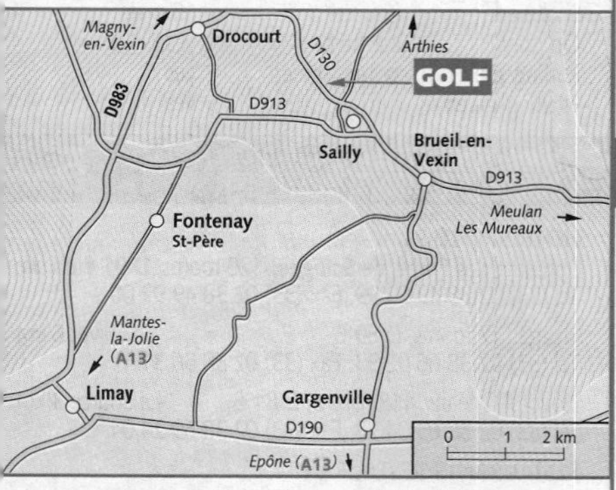

Access Accès : Paris, A13 → Rouen. Exit (Sortie) Meulan/Les Mureaux. After bridge over river Seine, take D913 to Oinville, Brueil-en-Vexin. 1 km after, turn right into Sailly, Golf 2 km **Map 3 on page 166** Carte 3 Page 166

Golf course PARCOURS — 14/20

Site	Site	
Maintenance	Entretien	
Architect	Architecte	Fred Hawtree
Type	Type	parkland
Relief	Relief	
Water in play	Eau en jeu	
Exp. to wind	Exposé au vent	
Trees in play	Arbres en jeu	

Scorecard Carte de score	**Chp.** Chp.	**Mens** Mess.	**Ladies** Da.
Length Long.	6301	5716	5346
Par	72	72	72
Slope system	125	119	127

Advised golfing ability 0 12 24 36
Niveau de jeu recommandé
Hcp required Handicap exigé 35

Club house & amenities CLUB-HOUSE ET ANNEXES — 7/10

Pro shop	Pro-shop	
Driving range	Practice	
Sheltered	couvert	7 mats
On grass	sur herbe	no, 43 mats open air
Putting-green	putting-green	yes
Pitching-green	pitching green	yes

Hotel facilities ENVIRONNEMENT HOTELIER — 5/10

HOTELS HÔTELS

Mercure — Meulan 12 km
56 rooms, D 107 €
Tel (33) 01 34 74 63 63, Fax (33) 01 34 74 00 98

Moulin d'Orgeval — Orgeval 27 km
14 rooms, D 130 €
Tel (33) 01 39 75 85 74, Fax (33) 01 39 75 48 52

RESTAURANTS RESTAURANT

Galiote, Tel (44) 01 34 77 03 02 — Mantes-la-Jolie 12 km

Auberge de la Truite, Tel (33) 01 34 76 30 52 — Rosay 22 km

Le Bon Vivant, Tel (44) 01 39 65 02 14 — Poissy 30 km

LIMÈRE

17 | 6 | 5

C'est décidément l'un des meilleurs parcours français de la dernière décennie, et un quasi sans fautes sur le plan de l'architecture. Cabell Robinson a réussi à faire un parcours réellement accessible à tous les niveaux, et passionnant pour tous les joueurs. Plat et peu fatigant, il est modérément modelé, mais toujours dans l'intérêt du jeu. Beaucoup d'arbres, de bunkers et quelques obstacles d'eau viennent menacer ceux qui manquent les fairways pourtant assez larges, les approches de green peuvent être délicates, et les placements de drapeau rendent plus intéressants encore les greens subtils et intelligemment construits. Sans excès esthétiques inutiles, le parcours se déroule avec un excellent rythme de difficultés. Dans un environnement agréable et absorbant bien l'eau, Limère mérite le détour, et un séjour, même si le Club house n'est toujours pas vraiment digne de l'ensemble. Limère est un des rares parcours à faire l'unanimité.

This is definitely one of the finest recent courses built in France over the past ten years and is virtually faultless in terms of architecture. Cabell Robinson has succeeded in producing a course that can be played by, and will excite, golfers of all levels. Flat and relaxing, the terrain has been given quite a bit of shape, but always in the right way. A lot of trees, bunkers and a few water hazards threaten balls that miss the fairways (although these are pleasantly wide), approach-shots to the greens can be tricky and pin-positions make the subtle and cleverly built greens even more enticing. Without any needless visual effects, the course unwinds with a nice balance of hazards and difficulties. In a pleasant setting which soaks up the rain as fast as it falls, Limère is well worth the trip and a few days stay, even though the club-house does not quite meet the standard of the actual course. Limère is one of those rare golfing venues that wins everyone's vote.

Golf de Limère — 1992

Allée de la Pomme-de-Pin
F - 45160 ARDON

Office	Secrétariat	(33) 02 38 63 89 40
Pro shop	Pro-shop	(33) 02 38 63 89 40
Fax	Fax	(33) 02 38 63 05 20
Web	www.bluegreen.com	
Situation	Situation	

Orléans (pop. 105 110), 13 km

Annual closure	Fermeture annuelle	no
Weekly closure	Fermeture hebdomadaire	no

Fees main season — Tarifs haute saison — 18 holes

	Week days Semaine	We/Bank holidays We/Férié
Individual Individuel	35 €	52 €
Couple Couple	70 €	104 €

Under 25: 16 € (Weekdays) - 30 € (We) - Seniors 23 € (Weekdays)

Caddy	Caddy	no
Electric Trolley	Chariot électrique	no
Buggy	Voiturette	18 € /18 holes
Clubs	Clubs	5 € /full day

Credit cards Cartes de crédit
VISA - CB - Eurocard - MasterCard - DC - AMEX

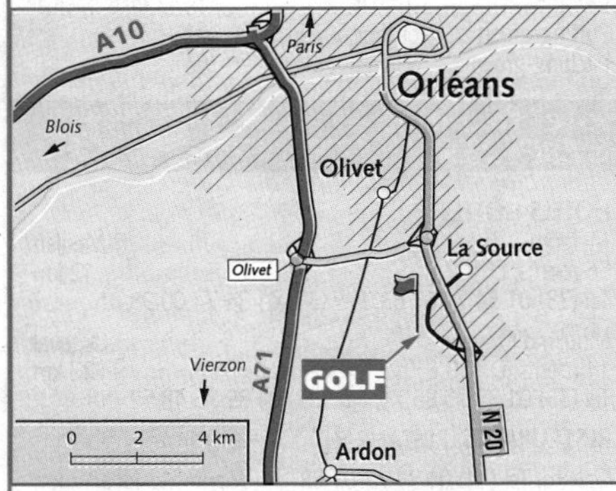

Access Accès : → Orléans La Source, sortie Olivet, RN20 → La Source, → Golf
Map 3 on page 166 Carte 3 Page 166

Golf course PARCOURS — 17/20

Site	Site	
Maintenance	Entretien	
Architect	Architecte	Cabell Robinson
Type	Type	forest, parkland
Relief	Relief	
Water in play	Eau en jeu	
Exp. to wind	Exposé au vent	
Trees in play	Arbres en jeu	

Scorecard Carte de score	Chp. Chp.	Mens Mess.	Ladies Da.
Length Long.	6221	5749	4854
Par	72	72	72
Slope system	136	128	119

Advised golfing ability — Niveau de jeu recommandé: 0 12 24 36
Hcp required — Handicap exigé: 35

Club house & amenities CLUB-HOUSE ET ANNEXES — 6/10

Pro shop	Pro-shop	
Driving range	Practice	
Sheltered	couvert	15 mats
On grass	sur herbe	yes
Putting-green	putting-green	yes
Pitching-green	pitching green	yes

Hotel facilities ENVIRONNEMENT HOTELIER — 5/10

HOTELS HÔTELS

Domaine des Portes de Sologne, 120 rooms, D 91 € on site
Tel (33) 02 38 49 99 99, Fax (33) 02 38 49 99 00

Rivage, 17 rooms, D 69 € — Olivet 6 km
Tel (33) 02 38 66 02 93, Fax (33) 02 38 56 31 11

Novotel Orléans, 113 rooms, D 81 € — La Source 3 km
Tel (33) 02 38 63 04 28, Fax (33) 02 38 69 24 04

RESTAURANTS RESTAURANT

Rivage, Tel (33) 02 38 66 02 93 — Olivet 6 km

Les Antiquaires, Tel (33) 02 38 53 52 35 — Orléans 13 km

La Chancellerie, Tel (33) 02 38 53 57 54 — Orléans 13 km

MAISON BLANCHE

14 | 8 | 5

Avec des vues magnifiques sur les Alpes et un Club house luxueux, on attendait un parcours d'un entretien constant en dehors des mois d'été : il faut être impeccable face à la concurrence des autres golfs de la région lémanique, devenue une destination de golf du printemps à l'automne. Mais le terrain est sensible à l'humidité. En dépit du standing et des ambitions de Maison Blanche, on sort d'ici avec une légère impression, comme à l'école, que l'on "pouvait encore mieux faire". Ce parcours comprend de nombreux obstacles d'eau, des arbres très en jeu et des reliefs assez prononcés (surtout au retour). Ils peuvent poser des problèmes aux débutants, mais les autres joueurs prendront plaisir à un tracé intéressant, sinon inoubliable, et garderont au minimum l'impression d'avoir effectué une belle balade en montagne. On regrettera que les bunkers n'aient pas été davantage pensés, ils ne gênent que les joueurs peu expérimentés.

With magnificent views over the Alps and a luxurious club-house, we were expecting a course with consistent standards of maintenance outside the summer months. Green-keeping has to be immaculate in the face of competition from other courses in the region of Geneva, which is nowadays a spring and autumn golf destination. All the more so in that the terrain here does not take too kindly to wet weather. Despite the status and ambitions of Maison Blanche, you go away with that niggling, school-report impression of "fair only". Designed by Peter Harradine and Olivier Dongradi, the course features a number of water hazards and trees, both very much in play, plus some undulating fairways (especially on the back 9). These may pose a few problems for beginners, but other players will have fun on this interesting if not unforgettable layout, and at the very least will feel like having enjoyed a beautiful mountain stroll. The bunkering might have been given a little more thought, as at present the sand bothers only the inexperienced player.

Golf de Maison Blanche — 1992

Naz-Dessous
F - 01170 ECHENEVEX

Office	Secrétariat	(33) 04 50 42 44 42
Pro shop	Pro-shop	(33) 04 50 42 47 27
Fax	Fax	(33) 04 50 42 44 43
E-mail	gmb2@wanadoo.fr	
Situation	Situation	

Genève (pop. 172 486), 15 km - Gex (pop. 6 620), 2 km

Annual closure	Fermeture annuelle	15/12→1/2
Weekly closure	Fermeture hebdomadaire	no

Fees main season Tarifs haute saison	18 holes	
	Week days Semaine	**We/Bank holidays** We/Férié
Individual Individuel	61 €	*
Couple Couple	122 €	*

* We: members only (membres seulement)

Caddy	Caddy	on request
Electric Trolley	Chariot électrique	20 € /on request
Buggy	Voiturette	30 € /18 holes
Clubs	Clubs	11 € /full day

Credit cards Cartes de crédit
VISA - CB - Eurocard - MasterCard

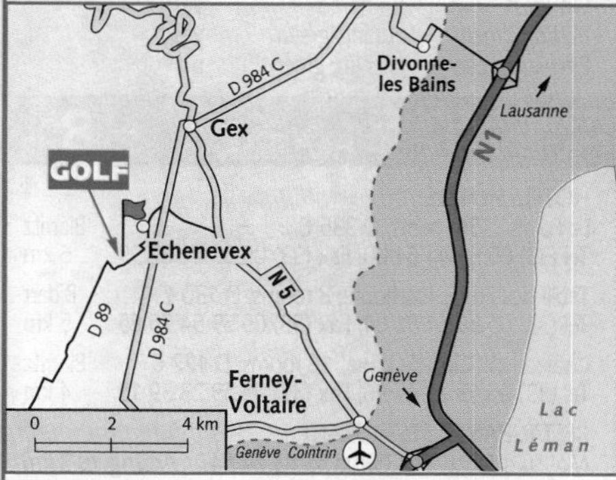

Access Accès : → Airport Genève-Cointrin → Ferney-Voltaire, → Gex, → Golf, on left hand side
Map 8 on page 177 Carte 8 Page 177

Golf course PARCOURS — 14/20

Site	Site	
Maintenance	Entretien	
Architect	Architecte	Peter Harradine Olivier Dongradi
Type	Type	country, hilly
Relief	Relief	
Water in play	Eau en jeu	
Exp. to wind	Exposé au vent	
Trees in play	Arbres en jeu	

Scorecard Carte de score	**Chp.** Chp.	**Mens** Mess.	**Ladies** Da.
Length Long.	6163	5782	4824
Par	72	72	72
Slope system	126	121	111

Advised golfing ability Niveau de jeu recommandé — 0 12 24 36
Hcp required Handicap exigé — 30

Club house & amenities CLUB-HOUSE ET ANNEXES — 8/10

Pro shop	Pro-shop	
Driving range	Practice	
Sheltered	couvert	10 mats
On grass	sur herbe	no, 20 mats open air
Putting-green	putting-green	yes
Pitching-green	pitching green	yes

Hotel facilities ENVIRONNEMENT HOTELIER — 5/10

HOTELS HÔTELS

Auberge des Chasseurs, 15 rooms, D 99 € — Echenevex
Tel (33) 04 50 41 54 07, Fax (33) 04 50 41 90 61 — 2 km

La Mainaz, 22 rooms, D 67 € — Mijoux
Tel (33) 04 50 41 31 10, Fax (33) 04 50 41 31 77 — 8 km

Le Parc, 15 rooms, D 55 € — Gex
Tel (33) 04 50 41 50 18, Fax (33) 04 50 42 37 29 — 2 km

RESTAURANTS RESTAURANT

La Champagne, Tel (33) 04 50 20 13 13 — Divonne 8 km
La Marée, Tel (33) 04 50 20 01 87 — Divonne
La Cravache, Tel (33) 04 50 41 69 61 — Gex 2 km

MAKILA GOLF CLUB

15 | 6 | 8

Peuplé de très beaux chênes, cet espace très vaste a permis de créer de larges fairways et de préserver l'isolement d'un trou à l'autre. Rocky Roquemore a dessiné un parcours de style américain sur fond de Pyrénées, avec des trous très variés, où l'on passe de la montagne aux plaines bordées d'obstacles d'eau. Les reliefs sont assez prononcés (sur trois trous), mais il était difficile de faire autrement dans cette superbe région et seuls les golfeurs en bonne condition physique pourront y évoluer sans voiturette. Avec près de 6200 mètres du fond, c'est un parcours solide pour les bons joueurs, mais les départs normaux permettent aux golfeurs de niveau moyen d'être à l'aise : les obstacles sont bien visibles, la stratégie assez évidente, les difficultés bien réparties. L'entretien est bon, le terrain est fragile par temps humide, mais un programme de drainage devrait permettre d'y remédier.

Lined with beautiful age-old oaks, this huge site gave the designer the possibility to lay out wide fairways and keep holes well apart. Rocky Roquemore has produced an American style layout set beneath the Pyrenees. Variety is the key word, ranging from mountain-side holes to lower-level holes edged with water hazards. It is pretty hilly (3 holes in particular) but it would have been difficult to do otherwise in this superb region. If you are not in top shape, take a buggy. This course plays 6,200 metres from the back tees and so is a good test for the better player, but the middle tees are perfect for the mid-handicapper. The hazards are visible, the strategy pretty obvious and difficulties are evenly spread around the course. Maintenance is good and the terrain often suffers in wet weather, but a drainage programme should solve that one.

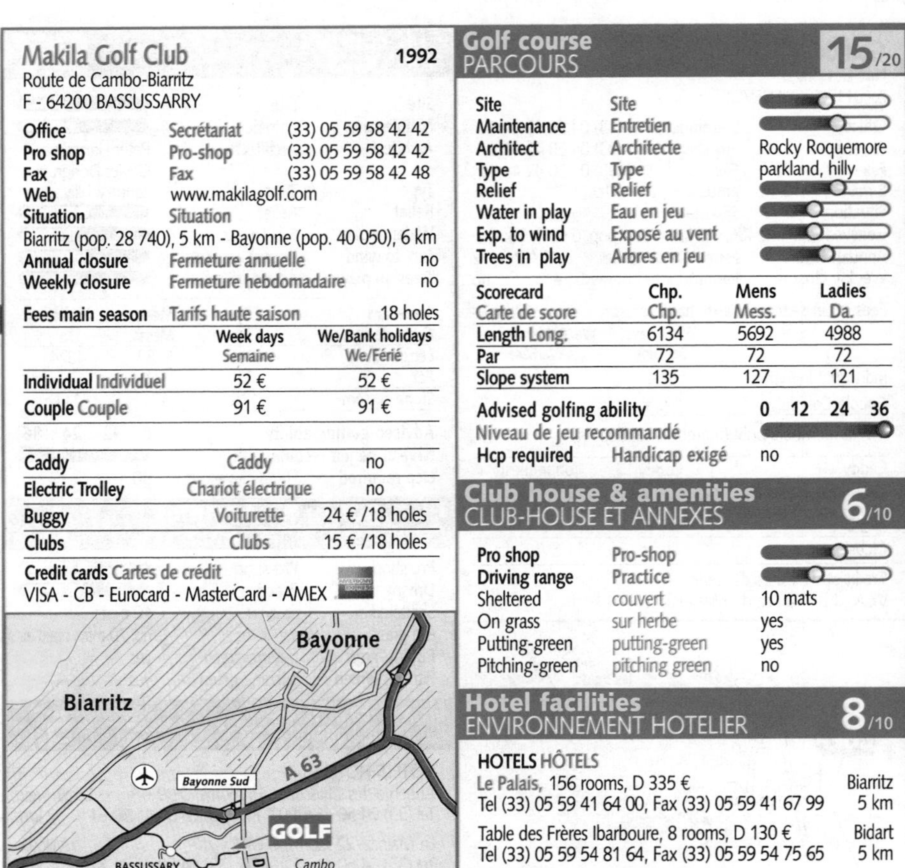

Makila Golf Club 1992

Route de Cambo-Biarritz
F - 64200 BASSUSSARRY

Office	Secrétariat	(33) 05 59 58 42 42
Pro shop	Pro-shop	(33) 05 59 58 42 42
Fax	Fax	(33) 05 59 58 42 48
Web	www.makilagolf.com	
Situation	Situation	

Biarritz (pop. 28 740), 5 km - Bayonne (pop. 40 050), 6 km

Annual closure	Fermeture annuelle	no
Weekly closure	Fermeture hebdomadaire	no

Fees main season Tarifs haute saison		18 holes
	Week days Semaine	**We/Bank holidays** We/Férié
Individual Individuel	52 €	52 €
Couple Couple	91 €	91 €

Caddy	Caddy	no
Electric Trolley	Chariot électrique	no
Buggy	Voiturette	24 € /18 holes
Clubs	Clubs	15 € /18 holes

Credit cards Cartes de crédit
VISA - CB - Eurocard - MasterCard - AMEX

Access Accès : A63, Exit (Sortie) N° 5 Bayonne Sud → Cambo D932. Golf 800 m. after roundabout
Map 12 on page 184 Carte 12 Page 184

Golf course PARCOURS 15/20

Site	Site	
Maintenance	Entretien	
Architect	Architecte	Rocky Roquemore
Type	Type	parkland, hilly
Relief	Relief	
Water in play	Eau en jeu	
Exp. to wind	Exposé au vent	
Trees in play	Arbres en jeu	

Scorecard Carte de score	**Chp.** Chp.	**Mens** Mess.	**Ladies** Da.
Length Long.	6134	5692	4988
Par	72	72	72
Slope system	135	127	121

Advised golfing ability 0 12 24 36
Niveau de jeu recommandé
Hcp required Handicap exigé no

Club house & amenities CLUB-HOUSE ET ANNEXES 6/10

Pro shop	Pro-shop	
Driving range	Practice	
Sheltered	couvert	10 mats
On grass	sur herbe	yes
Putting-green	putting-green	yes
Pitching-green	pitching green	no

Hotel facilities ENVIRONNEMENT HOTELIER 8/10

HOTELS HÔTELS

Le Palais, 156 rooms, D 335 € — Biarritz
Tel (33) 05 59 41 64 00, Fax (33) 05 59 41 67 99 — 5 km

Table des Frères Ibarboure, 8 rooms, D 130 € — Bidart
Tel (33) 05 59 54 81 64, Fax (33) 05 59 54 75 65 — 5 km

Château du Clair de Lune, 16 rooms, D 122 € — Biarritz
Tel (33) 05 59 23 45 96, Fax (33) 05 59 23 39 13 — 4 km

RESTAURANTS RESTAURANT

Moulin d'Alotz, Tel (33) 05 59 43 04 54 — Arcangues 3 km

Auberge d'Achtal, Tel (33) 05 59 43 05 56 — Arcangues2 km

Table des Frères Ibarboure, Tel (33) 05 59 54 81 64 — Bidart

MAZAMET-LA BAROUGE

13	5	4

Les neuf premiers trous ont été conçus par Mackenzie Ross, puis remodelés et complétés par le cabinet Hawtree. Avec 5600 mètres, il peut paraître court, mais c'est un par 70. Les longs frappeurs pourront s'y déchaîner, sans trop craindre les arbres de ce grand parc (beaucoup de pins). Les joueurs moyens s'amuseront aussi, car les obstacles sont bien visibles, certains trous très courts, les roughs sont propres et les sous-bois bien nettoyés. Le terrain est assez plat pour être facilement marché, ce qui accentue la sensation générale de tranquillité et de golf reposant (à conseiller aux seniors). Les difficultés existent pourtant, mais elles sont aisément négociables si l'on possède un bon jeu de petits fers : les greens ne sont pas bien grands. L'environnement, l'ambiance amicale et l'utilisation rationnelle d'une surface réduite en font une halte agréable. Soulignons enfin que quatre trous ont été refaits après les inondations de début 2001.

The first nine holes were designed by Mackenzie Ross, then completed and redesigned by Hawtree. It might appear short at just 5600 metres, but it is a par 70 where long hitters will be able to open their shoulders without worrying too much about the trees (there are a lot of pines). The average golfer can also have fun, because the hazards are clearly visible, a number of holes are short, the rough is trimmed and the undergrowth kept clear. The terrain is flat enough to make this an easily walkable course and add to the overall impression of a peaceful, relaxing golf course (recommended for seniors). But it is no push-over, and the difficulties are there to be negotiated - an easier proposition if your short irons are in good shape. Accuracy is at a premium because the greens are anything but enormous. The general setting, friendly atmosphere and rational utilisation of limited space make this a very pleasant stop-off. We should also add that four holes have been redesigned after the floods at the beginning of 2001.

Golf Club de Mazamet-La Barouge — 1956

F - 81660 PONT-DE-LARN

Office	Secrétariat	(33) 05 63 61 06 72
Pro shop	Pro-shop	(33) 05 63 61 06 72
Fax	Fax	(33) 05 63 61 13 03
Web	—	
Situation	Situation	

Castres (pop. 44 810), 16 km - Toulouse (pop. 358 690), 84 km

Annual closure	Fermeture annuelle	no
Weekly closure	Fermeture hebdomadaire	no

Fees main season Tarifs haute saison		18 holes
	Week days Semaine	**We/Bank holidays** We/Férié
Individual Individuel	27 €	36 €
Couple Couple	46 €	61 €

Seniors: 17 € (Fridays)

Caddy	Caddy	no
Electric Trolley	Chariot électrique	no
Buggy	Voiturette	30 € /18 holes
Clubs	Clubs	15 € /full day

Credit cards Cartes de crédit
VISA - CB - Eurocard - MasterCard - DC - JCB - AMEX

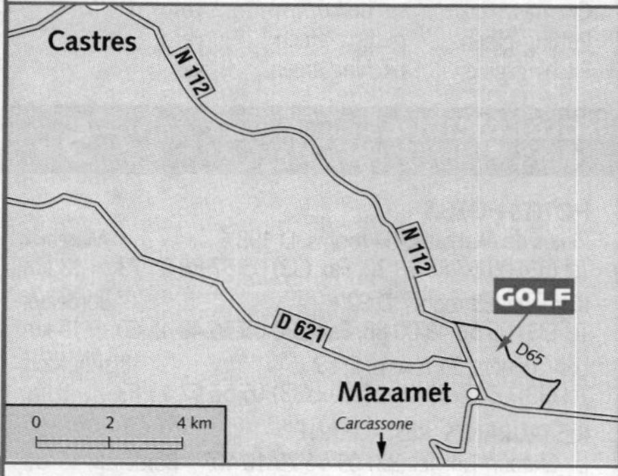

Access Accès : Mazamet, N 112 → Castres, → Golf
Map 13 on page 186 Carte 13 Page 186

Golf course PARCOURS — 13/20

Site	Site	
Maintenance	Entretien	
Architect	Architecte	Mackenzie Ross Fred Hawtree
Type	Type	parkland, forest
Relief	Relief	
Water in play	Eau en jeu	
Exp. to wind	Exposé au vent	
Trees in play	Arbres en jeu	

Scorecard Carte de score	**Chp.** Chp.	**Mens** Mess.	**Ladies** Da.
Length Long.	5635	5427	4898
Par	70	70	70
Slope system	126	124	121

Advised golfing ability Niveau de jeu recommandé — 0 12 24 36
Hcp required Handicap exigé — no

Club house & amenities CLUB-HOUSE ET ANNEXES — 5/10

Pro shop	Pro-shop	
Driving range	Practice	
Sheltered	couvert	10 mats
On grass	sur herbe	no, 9 mats open air
Putting-green	putting-green	yes
Pitching-green	pitching green	no

Hotel facilities ENVIRONNEMENT HOTELIER — 4/10

HOTELS HÔTELS

La Métairie Neuve, 14 rooms, D 73 € — Bout-du-Pont-de-Larn
Tel (33) 05 63 97 73 50, Fax (33) 05 63 61 94 75 — 1 km

H. Jourdon, 11 rooms, D 44 € — Mazamet
Tel (33) 05 63 61 56 93, Fax (33) 05 63 61 83 38 — 1 km

Demeure de Flore, 10 rooms, D 75 € — Lacabarède
Tel (33) 05 63 98 32 32, Fax (33) 05 63 98 47 56 — 16 km

Occitan, 40 rooms, D 63 € — Castres
Tel (33) 05 63 35 34 20, Fax (33) 05 63 35 70 32 — 14 km

RESTAURANTS RESTAURANT

H. Jourdon, Tel (33) 05 63 61 56 93 — Mazamet 1 km
Victoria, Tel (33) 05 63 59 14 68 — Castres 14 km

MÉDOC Les Châteaux

18 | 7 | 5

Si le parcours des "Vignes" est une agréable promenade en plaine et dans une pinède, le parcours des "Châteaux" est de meilleur cru encore (nous sommes en plein Bordelais), et sa réputation est largement méritée. Dû au crayon habile de l'Américain Bill Coore, il se déroule dans un paysage de plaine dénudé, modelé comme un links, mais sans les dunes. Des obstacles d'eau et des "ditchs" viennent parfois perturber la quiétude du golfeur, mais les ondulations du fairway, le dessin des bunkers, la bonne densité des roughs et le profil des vastes greens en font l'un des parcours les plus remarquables de la région. Les amateurs de paysages boisés peuvent sans doute lui reprocher une légère monotonie visuelle, mais il s'avère de plus en plus intéressant, à mesure qu'on le joue. C'est le parcours le plus technique de la région, et très facile à jouer à pied. Plus il prend de la maturité, plus il s'impose parmi les grands parcours français. Bref, rien de changé depuis deux ans, sinon qu'il se bonifie encore en vieillissant, comme un bon Médoc.

While "Les Vignes" course (The Vines) is a pleasant stroll through open country and a pine forest, the "Châteaux" course is an even finer vintage (we are to the west of Bordeaux) and well worth its reputation. Designed by the American Bill Coore, the course unfolds over flat open country and is designed to play like a links course, but without the dunes. Some water hazards and ditches can be a little trying, but the rolling fairways, well-designed bunkers, thick rough and the profile of the huge greens make this one of the region's finest courses. People who prefer woodland courses will probably knock "Les Châteaux" as being visually boring, but it gets better and better the more you play it. It is the most technical course in the region and easily walkable. The more it matures, the more Le Médoc has to be ranked amongst the best courses in France. In a word, nothing has changed over the past two years, except that like a good Médoc wine, it goes on getting better with age.

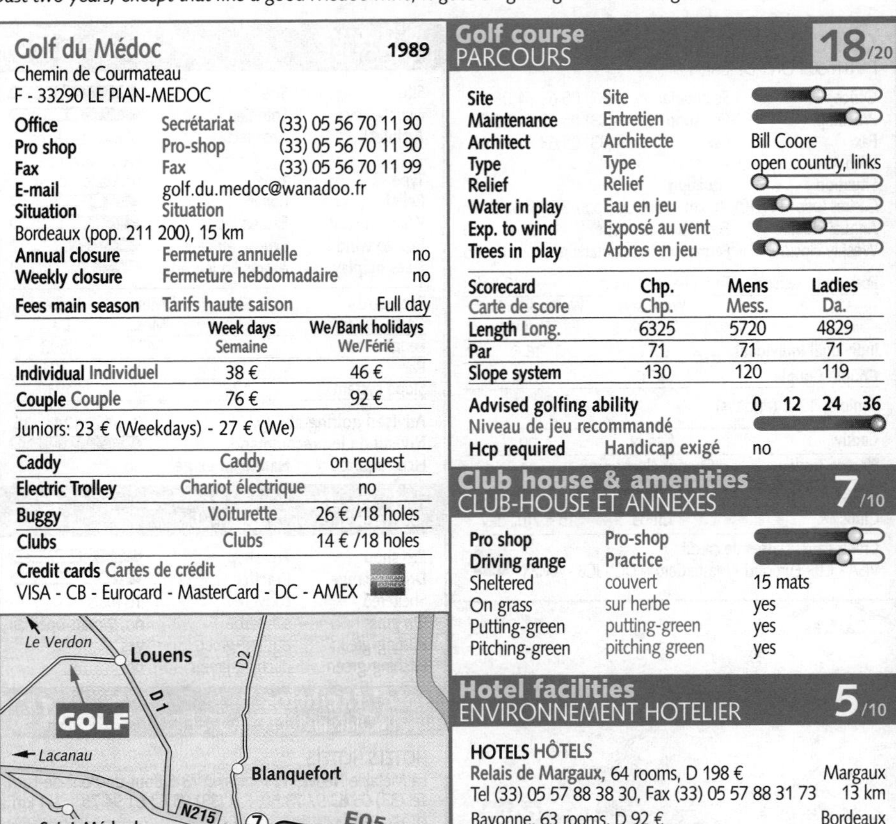

Golf du Médoc — 1989

Chemin de Courmateau
F - 33290 LE PIAN-MEDOC

Office	Secrétariat	(33) 05 56 70 11 90
Pro shop	Pro-shop	(33) 05 56 70 11 90
Fax	Fax	(33) 05 56 70 11 99
E-mail	golf.du.medoc@wanadoo.fr	
Situation	Situation	

Bordeaux (pop. 211 200), 15 km

Annual closure	Fermeture annuelle	no
Weekly closure	Fermeture hebdomadaire	no

Fees main season Tarifs haute saison		Full day
	Week days Semaine	**We/Bank holidays** We/Férié
Individual Individuel	38 €	46 €
Couple Couple	76 €	92 €

Juniors: 23 € (Weekdays) - 27 € (We)

Caddy	Caddy	on request
Electric Trolley	Chariot électrique	no
Buggy	Voiturette	26 € /18 holes
Clubs	Clubs	14 € /18 holes

Credit cards Cartes de crédit
VISA - CB - Eurocard - MasterCard - DC - AMEX

Access Accès : Bordeaux, Ring road (Rocade), Exit (Sortie) N° 7 → Lacanau, go right on D1 → Le Verdon
Map 9 on page 178 Carte 9 Page 178

Golf course PARCOURS — 18/20

Site	Site	
Maintenance	Entretien	
Architect	Architecte	Bill Coore
Type	Type	open country, links
Relief	Relief	
Water in play	Eau en jeu	
Exp. to wind	Exposé au vent	
Trees in play	Arbres en jeu	

Scorecard Carte de score	**Chp.** Chp.	**Mens** Mess.	**Ladies** Da.
Length Long.	6325	5720	4829
Par	71	71	71
Slope system	130	120	119

Advised golfing ability Niveau de jeu recommandé — 0 12 24 36
Hcp required Handicap exigé — no

Club house & amenities CLUB-HOUSE ET ANNEXES — 7/10

Pro shop	Pro-shop	
Driving range	Practice	
Sheltered	couvert	15 mats
On grass	sur herbe	yes
Putting-green	putting-green	yes
Pitching-green	pitching green	yes

Hotel facilities ENVIRONNEMENT HOTELIER — 5/10

HOTELS HÔTELS

Relais de Margaux, 64 rooms, D 198 € — Margaux
Tel (33) 05 57 88 38 30, Fax (33) 05 57 88 31 73 — 13 km

Bayonne, 63 rooms, D 92 € — Bordeaux
Tel (33) 05 56 48 00 88, Fax (33) 05 56 48 41 60 — 15 km

Les Criquets, 21 rooms, D 69 € — Blanquefort
Tel (33) 05 56 35 09 24, Fax (33) 05 56 57 13 83 — 8 km

RESTAURANTS RESTAURANT

Le Chapon Fin, Tel (33) 05 56 79 10 10 — Bordeaux 15 km
Le Vieux Bordeaux, Tel (33) 05 56 52 94 36 — Bordeaux
Jean Ramet, Tel (33) 05 56 44 12 51 — Bordeaux
Savoie, Tel (33) 05 57 88 31 76 — Margaux 13 km

MÉDOC Les Vignes

15 | 7 | 5

Sur un terrain généralement plat, l'ensemble des 36 trous du golf du Médoc peut être facilement joué dans la journée. Après le paysage très peu arboré du parcours des "Châteaux", le parcours des "Vignes" offre un contraste bienvenu, et des difficultés moins affirmées. Les amoureux des parcours dans les arbres seront comblés car un certain nombre de trous se situent dans les ombrages plaisants d'une petite pinède, qui a malheureusement été très endommagée par les tempêtes, mais le jeu n'en est pas facilité pour autant. Les autres trous offrent une végétation plus légère, mais néammoins souvent en jeu. Tout comme sur l'autre parcours, les greens sont de bonne qualité, et sans reliefs excessifs. Certes, "Les Châteaux" représente un défi plus constant, mais cet ensemble s'est incontestablement imposé comme l'un des tout meilleurs dans une région très touristique, et comme l'ensemble le plus intéressant à proximité immédiate de Bordeaux.

Laid out over what is generally flat terrain, the 36 holes at Le Pian Médoc can easily be played in one day. After the tree-less landscape of "Les Châteaux", "Les Vignes" provides a welcome contrast and plays a little more easily. Golfers who love playing woodland courses will be spoilt here, as a number of holes wind their way through a pretty and shady pine forest, which unfortunately was badly damaged by the storms. However fewer trees have not made the course any easier. The others provide a little lighter vegetation which nonetheless is very much in play. As with "Les Châteaux", the greens are excellent and not too undulating. Although a little less challenging, "Les Vignes" is still one of the best courses in a very busy tourist region, and the two courses together are easily the most attractive golfing proposition within the immediate vicinity of Bordeaux.

Golf du Médoc — 1991

Chemin de Courmateau
F - 33290 LE PIAN-MEDOC

Office	Secrétariat	(33) 05 56 70 11 90
Pro shop	Pro-shop	(33) 05 56 70 11 90
Fax	Fax	(33) 05 56 70 11 99
E-mail		golf.du.medoc@wanadoo.fr
Situation	Situation	

Bordeaux (pop. 211 200), 15 km

Annual closure	Fermeture annuelle	no
Weekly closure	Fermeture hebdomadaire	no

Fees main season Tarifs haute saison — full day

	Week days / Semaine	We/Bank holidays / We/Férié
Individual Individuel	38 €	46 €
Couple Couple	76 €	92 €

Juniors: 23 € (Weekdays) - 27 € (We)

Caddy	Caddy	on request
Electric Trolley	Chariot électrique	no
Buggy	Voiturette	26 € /18 holes
Clubs	Clubs	14 € /18 holes

Credit cards Cartes de crédit
VISA - CB - Eurocard - MasterCard - DC - AMEX

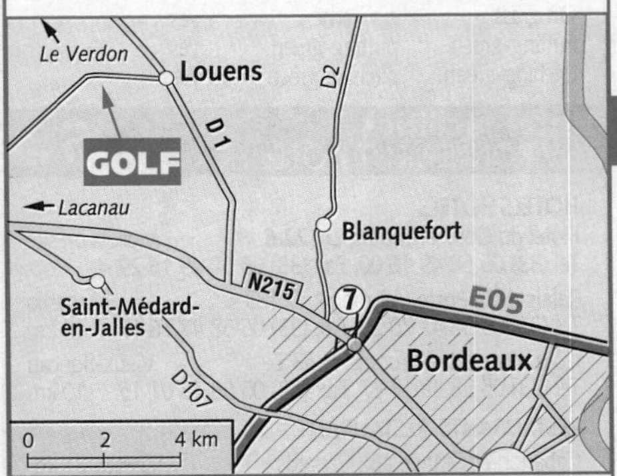

Access Accès : Bordeaux, Ring road (Rocade), Exit (Sortie) N° 7 → Lacanau, go right on D1 → Le Verdon
Map 9 on page 178 Carte 9 Page 178

Golf course — PARCOURS — 15/20

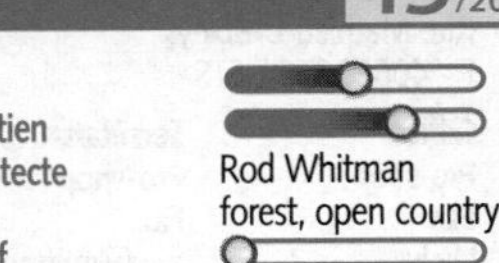

Site	Site	
Maintenance	Entretien	
Architect	Architecte	Rod Whitman
Type	Type	forest, open country
Relief	Relief	
Water in play	Eau en jeu	
Exp. to wind	Exposé au vent	
Trees in play	Arbres en jeu	

Scorecard Carte de score	Chp. Chp.	Mens Mess.	Ladies Da.
Length Long.	6237	5704	4672
Par	71	71	71
Slope system	130	128	119

Advised golfing ability Niveau de jeu recommandé — 0 12 24 36
Hcp required Handicap exigé — no

Club house & amenities — CLUB-HOUSE ET ANNEXES — 7/10

Pro shop	Pro-shop	
Driving range	Practice	
Sheltered	couvert	15 mats
On grass	sur herbe	yes
Putting-green	putting-green	yes
Pitching-green	pitching green	yes

Hotel facilities — ENVIRONNEMENT HOTELIER — 5/10

HOTELS HÔTELS

Relais de Margaux, 64 rooms, D 198 € — Margaux
Tel (33) 05 57 88 38 30, Fax (33) 05 57 88 31 73 — 13 km

Bayonne, 63 rooms, D 92 € — Bordeaux
Tel (33) 05 56 48 00 88, Fax (33) 05 56 48 41 60 — 15 km

Les Criquets, 21 rooms, D 69 € — Blanquefort
Tel (33) 05 56 35 09 24, Fax (33) 05 56 57 13 83 — 8 km

RESTAURANTS RESTAURANT

Le Chapon Fin, Tel (33) 05 56 79 10 10 — Bordeaux 15 km
Le Vieux Bordeaux, Tel (33) 05 56 52 94 36 — Bordeaux
Jean Ramet, Tel (33) 05 56 44 12 51 — Bordeaux15 km
Savoie, Tel (33) 05 57 88 31 76 — Margaux 13 km

MOLIETS

17 | 6 | 5

Ce parcours remarquable a été réalisé dans la forêt de pins des Landes (treize trous), et en bord de mer (cinq trous). L'architecte Robert Trent Jones l'a incontestablement signé, par des détails esthétiques, mais aussi avec des enjeux techniques et stratégiques dénotant une connaissance profonde du golf : si les joueurs de haut niveau y trouveront un "challenge" difficile, partir des départs avancés permet davantage d'erreurs. Visuellement, ses fameux bunkers dentelés défendent remarquablement les greens, dont trois sont pratiquement aveugles ; leurs surfaces sont modelées sans excès. Les fairways largement tondus favorisent le rythme de jeu, et la nature sablonneuse du sol permet de jouer facilement toute l'année. Il n'est pas trop fatigant, mais les distances entre greens et départs sont parfois importantes. Un bon 9 trous annexe permet d'occuper les débutants de la famille, et un centre d'entraînement très complet permet de se perfectionner, à condition d'amener son courage !

This remarkable course was laid out in the pine forests of Les Landes (for 13 holes) and along the coast (five holes). Welcome to a typical Robert Trent Jones design, where detail to style and the technical and strategic challenges reflect an in-depth knowledge of golf. While the more proficient golfer will find this a tough challenge, playing from the forward tees is, funnily enough, often more conducive to error. The famous jagged bunkers are a remarkable form of defence for the greens, three of which are virtually blind, and the putting surfaces are neatly but never excessively contoured. The closely-cropped fairways help speed up the game and the sandy sub-soil keeps the course easily playable all year. This is not a tiring course, but distances between holes are sometimes a little on the long side. A good adjoining 9 hole course is ideal for beginners in the family and a very comprehensive training centre is just the job for getting that handicap down.

Golf de Moliets — 1989

Rue Mathieu Desbieys
F - 40660 MOLIETS

Office	Secrétariat	(33) 05 58 48 54 65
Pro shop	Pro-shop	(33) 05 58 48 54 65
Fax	Fax	(33) 05 58 48 54 88
Web	www.golfmoliets.com	
Situation	Situation	Dax (pop. 19 310), 35 km
Annual closure	Fermeture annuelle	no
Weekly closure	Fermeture hebdomadaire	no

Fees main season Tarifs haute saison	18 holes	
	Week days Semaine	**We/Bank holidays** We/Férié
Individual Individuel	53 €	53 €
Couple Couple	106 €	106 €

Juniors & students: 27 €

Caddy	Caddy	no
Electric Trolley	Chariot électrique	no
Buggy	Voiturette	24 € /18 holes
Clubs	Clubs	9 € /full day

Credit cards Cartes de crédit
VISA - CB - Eurocard - MasterCard

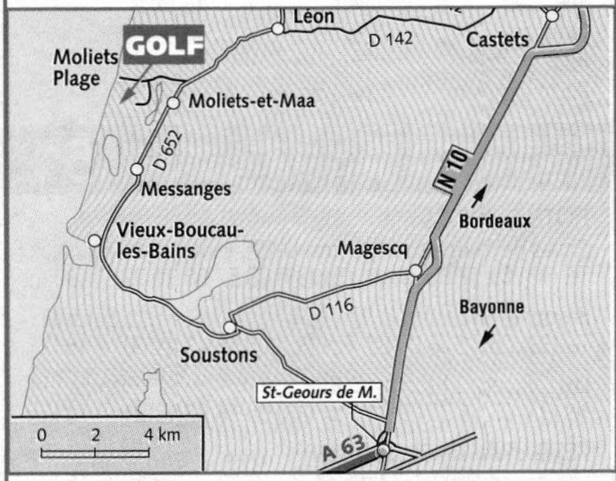

Access Accès : • Bordeaux, N10 → Castets. D142 → Léon, Moliets • Bayonne, N10 → Magescq, D116 → Soustons, D652 → Vieux-Boucau-les-Bains, Moliets

Map 12 on page 184 Carte 12 Page 184

Golf course PARCOURS — 17/20

Site	Site	
Maintenance	Entretien	
Architect	Architecte	Robert Trent Jones
Type	Type	forest, links
Relief	Relief	
Water in play	Eau en jeu	
Exp. to wind	Exposé au vent	
Trees in play	Arbres en jeu	

Scorecard Carte de score	**Chp.** Chp.	**Mens** Mess.	**Ladies** Da.
Length Long.	6173	5824	4653
Par	72	72	72
Slope system	127	127	113

Advised golfing ability Niveau de jeu recommandé: 0 12 24 36
Hcp required Handicap exigé 30

Club house & amenities CLUB-HOUSE ET ANNEXES — 6/10

Pro shop	Pro-shop	
Driving range	Practice	
Sheltered	couvert	10 mats
On grass	sur herbe	yes
Putting-green	putting-green	yes
Pitching-green	pitching green	yes

Hotel facilities ENVIRONNEMENT HOTELIER — 5/10

HOTELS HÔTELS

Hôtel du Golf, 41 rooms, D 122 € — Moliets on site
Tel (33) 05 58 49 16 00, Fax (33) 05 58 49 16 29

Relais de la Poste, 13 rooms, D 183 € — Magescq 20 km
Tel (33) 05 58 47 70 25, Fax (33) 05 58 47 76 17

Côte d'Argent, 40 rooms, D 53 € — Vieux-Boucau 10 km
Tel (33) 05 58 48 13 17, Fax (33) 05 58 48 01 15

RESTAURANTS RESTAURANT

Cabanon et Grange aux Canards — Magescq 21 km
Tel (33) 05 58 47 71 51

Relais de la Poste, Tel (33) 05 58 47 70 25 — Magescq 20 km

Marinero, Tel (33) 05 58 48 14 15 — Vieux-Boucau 10 km

MONTE CARLO (MONT AGEL) 14 | 6 | 7

Quand on évoque le golf de Monte Carlo, on pourrait s'attendre à une sorte de somptueux produit à l'américaine, très "people". En fait, le plus "flashy", c'est le panorama. A plus de 800 mètres, Monaco apparaît en contrebas comme un village de poupée, et la vue s'étend à l'infini sur la Méditerranée et la Riviera, parfois même la Corse. Quand au golf, il est d'une surprenante sobriété, la marque du vrai luxe. On vient jouer dans une atmosphère presque familiale, pas pour se faire voir. Le parcours a fait l'objet, depuis plusieurs années, de travaux en tous genres, du plus minuscule au plus impressionnant pour lui donner un peu de longueur et de largeur, mais le tracé est resté peu ou prou celui de Willie Park il y a presque un siècle. Très britannique de style, il n'est certes pas d'une grande difficulté, à priori, mais les greens sont assez petits, les pieds pas toujours à plat, et comme les idées golfiques des amateurs ne sont pas toujours claires, le score risque de surprendre. La précision et la finesse l'emporteront toujours sur la force. Ici, on vous demande de l'élégance... princière bien sûr.

When talking about golf in Monte Carlo, you might expect a sort of flashy style product. In fact the flashiest thing here is the view. Monaco lies 800 metres below you like a doll's village and the vista stretches over the Mediterranean right across the French and Italian Rivieras. Sometimes you can even see Corsica. The actual course is a picture of sobriety, but isn't that the sign of real luxury? You play here in an almost family atmosphere, not just to be seen. In recent years the course has undergone all sorts of refurbishing work to make it longer and wider, but the layout remains very much the same as that built by Willie Park almost a century ago. Very British in style, it is certainly not the hardest course around, but the greens are smallish, flat lies are rare to come by, and as clear-thinking is not always the forte of amateur golfers, your score can sometimes come as a surprise. Accuracy and finesse are more valuable assets than brute strength on a course where you are asked for a little golfing elegance, in princely style, of course.

Monte Carlo Golf Club — 1911

Route du Mont Agel
06320 LA TURBIE

Office	Secrétariat	(33) 04 92 41 50 70
Pro shop	Pro-shop	(33) 04 93 41 04 46
Fax	Fax	(33) 04 93 41 09 55
E-mail	monte_carlo_golf_club@wanadoo.fr	
Situation	Situation	

Monaco (pop. 29 972), 15 km - Nice (pop. 342 439), 16 km

Annual closure	Fermeture annuelle	no
Weekly closure	Fermeture hebdomadaire	no

Fees main season Tarifs haute saison	Week days Semaine	We/Bank holidays We/Férié
		Full day
Individual Individuel	76 €	91 €
Couple Couple	152 €	182 €

Juniors: – 50%

Caddy	Caddy	38 €
Electric Trolley	Chariot électrique	22 € /18 holes
Buggy	Voiturette	no
Clubs	Clubs	15 € /full day

Credit cards Cartes de crédit
VISA - Eurocard - MasterCard

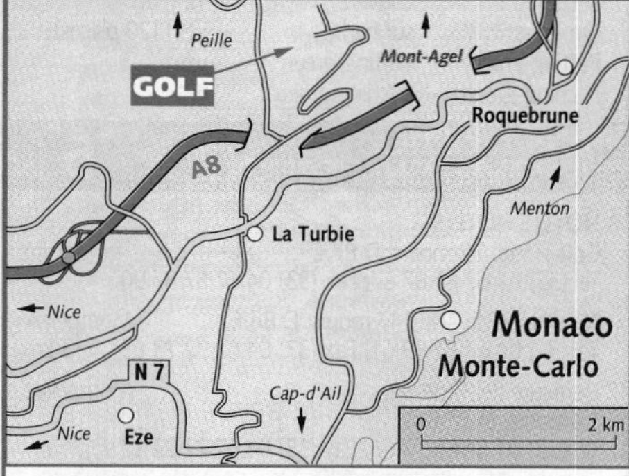

Access Accès : 10 km N. of Monaco. → La Turbie, → Mont Agel, Monte Carlo Golf Club.
Map 14 on page 189 Carte 14 Page 189

Golf course — PARCOURS — 14/20

Site	Site	
Maintenance	Entretien	
Architect	Architecte	Unknown
Type	Type	hilly, parkland
Relief	Relief	
Water in play	Eau en jeu	
Exp. to wind	Exposé au vent	
Trees in play	Arbres en jeu	

Scorecard Carte de score	Chp. Chp.	Mens Mess.	Ladies Da.
Length Long.	5683	5683	4938
Par	71	71	71
Slope system	129	129	129

Advised golfing ability Niveau de jeu recommandé — 0 12 24 36
Hcp required Handicap exigé — 32

Club house & amenities — CLUB-HOUSE ET ANNEXES — 6/10

Pro shop	Pro-shop	
Driving range	Practice	
Sheltered	couvert	4 mats
On grass	sur herbe	no
Putting-green	putting-green	yes
Pitching-green	pitching green	yes

Hotel facilities — ENVIRONNEMENT HOTELIER — 7/10

HOTELS HÔTELS

Hotel de Paris, 154 rooms, D 419 € — Monaco 15 km
Tel (377) 92 16 30 00, Fax (377) 92 16 38 50

Hotel Hermitage, 229 rooms, D 401 € — Monaco
Tel (377) 92 16 40 00, Fax (377) 92 16 38 52

Balmoral, 66 rooms, D 137 € — Monaco
Tel (377) 93 50 62 37, Fax (377) 93 15 08 69

RESTAURANTS RESTAURANT

Café de Paris, Tel (377) 92 16 20 20 — Monaco 15 km
Louis XV, Tel (377) 92 16 30 01 — Monaco
Chez Gianni, Tel (377) 93 30 46 33 — Monaco

MONTPELLIER-MASSANE 16 7 5

Dessiné par Ronald Fream, le golf de Massane n'est certes pas à conseiller aux débutants. Et, pour vraiment s'amuser, les joueurs simplement moyens devront absolument choisir les départs avancés. En revanche, les golfeurs confirmés y trouveront de quoi tester l'ensemble de leur jeu. De nombreux obstacles d'eau, des bunkers frontaux, différentes alternatives d'attaque des trous obligent à savoir précisément quand décider de rester court ou de passer les obstacles, quelle tactique choisir : il faut parfois se résigner à la prudence pour ramener un bon score. Ce parcours se joue avec ses clubs, et vraiment avec sa tête. Les bunkers et les greens sont remarquablement dessinés, ce qui accentue encore la nécessité d'un petit jeu complet et bien aiguisé. Un parcours parfois controversé, surprenant parfois, agaçant aussi dans ses détours, mais vraiment à connaître.

Designed by Ronald Fream, the Massane course is definitely not for beginners, but if the average hacker wants to enjoy a good round of golf he should make straight for the front tees. By contrast, skilled golfers will find this an excellent test for every aspect of their game. Numerous water hazards, front bunkers and different lines of approach to the green force players into tactical decisions and into choosing exactly when to lay up short or when to carry the hazard. A good score sometimes comes more from caution than from daring. This is another course where you really do play with your clubs and your brains. The bunkers and greens are remarkably well designed and only emphasise the need for an all-round and well-honed short game. A sometimes controversial course, often surprising, occasionally irritating too as it twists and turns, but also one well worth knowing.

Golf de Montpellier-Massane — 1988

Mas de Massane
F - 34670 BAILLARGUES

Office	Secrétariat	(33) 04 67 87 87 89
Pro shop	Pro-shop	(33) 04 67 87 87 89
Fax	Fax	(33) 04 67 87 87 90
Web	www.softel.fr/massane	
Situation	Situation	

Montpellier (pop. 210 860), 13 km - Nîmes (pop. 128 470), 34 km

Annual closure	Fermeture annuelle	no
Weekly closure	Fermeture hebdomadaire	no

Fees main season Tarifs haute saison	Week days Semaine	We/Bank holidays We/Férié
		Full day
Individual Individuel	44 €	44 €
Couple Couple	88 €	88 €

Juniors: 30 € (peak season/haute saison)

Caddy	Caddy	no
Electric Trolley	Chariot électrique	11 € /18 holes
Buggy	Voiturette	27 € /18 holes
Clubs	Clubs	9 € /full day

Credit cards Cartes de crédit
VISA - CB - Eurocard - MasterCard - DC - AMEX

Vendargues
N 113
Baillargues
D 65
N 113
D 112
D 260
GOLF
A9-E 15
MONTPELLIER
D 24
Mauguio
D 172
Étang de Maugio
0 2 4 km

Access Accès : A9, Exit (Sortie) Vendargues- Baillargues, N113 → Baillargues
Map 13 on page 187 Carte 13 Page 187

Golf course PARCOURS — 16/20

Site	Site	
Maintenance	Entretien	
Architect	Architecte	Ronald Fream
Type	Type	open country, residential
Relief	Relief	
Water in play	Eau en jeu	
Exp. to wind	Exposé au vent	
Trees in play	Arbres en jeu	

Scorecard Carte de score	Chp. Chp.	Mens Mess.	Ladies Da.
Length Long.	6081	5692	4972
Par	72	72	72
Slope system	141	135	130

Advised golfing ability 0 12 24 36
Niveau de jeu recommandé
Hcp required Handicap exigé no

Club house & amenities CLUB-HOUSE ET ANNEXES — 7/10

Pro shop	Pro-shop	
Driving range	Practice	
Sheltered	couvert	12 mats
On grass	sur herbe	yes (120 places)
Putting-green	putting-green	yes
Pitching-green	pitching green	yes

Hotel facilities ENVIRONNEMENT HOTELIER — 5/10

HOTELS HÔTELS

Golf-Hôtel, 32 rooms, D 87 € — on site
Tel (33) 04 67 87 87 87, Fax (33) 04 67 87 87 90

New Hôtel du Midi, 47 rooms, D 88 € — Montpellier 13 km
Tel (33) 04 67 92 69 61, Fax (33) 04 67 92 73 63

Demeure des Brousses — Montpellier
17 rooms, D 77 €
Tel (33) 04 67 65 77 66, Fax (33) 04 67 22 22 17

RESTAURANTS RESTAURANT

Jardin des Sens, Tel (33) 04 67 79 63 38 — Montpellier

Le Chandelier, Tel (33) 04 67 15 34 38 — Montpellier

MORFONTAINE

18 | 6 | 6

Il est des lieux où le monde paraît s'être arrêté au meilleur moment. Morfontaine est de ceux-là. 27 trous y constituent un paradis pour ses membres, qui n'y acceptent que leurs invités, et on les comprend. Beaucoup aimeraient en être, tant Morfontaine s'est construit une réputation de belle au bois dormant que l'on se doit de séduire un jour. Ici, on respecte assez le golf et ses traditions pour que le dessin du parcours par Tom Simpson n'ait jamais été retouché. Certes, les longs frappeurs iconoclastes pourront le juger un peu court, mais il n'en est guère plus facile si l'on peine à éviter les arbres splendides, la bruyère, des bunkers pas si nombreux, mais diablement bien placés. Et après tout, ne serait-il pas mal élevé de taper ici très fort, tout comme d'élever la voix ? A Morfontaine, on ne cherche pas à épater la galerie, on joue au golf, dans une atmosphère plutôt familiale, loin des foules. Le 18 trous est harmonieux, technique, noble. Et le 9 trous de Vallières constitue un dessert savoureux. Un modèle de club de golf.

There are places where the world seems to have stood still just at the right moment. Morfontaine is one of them. The 27 holes here are paradise on earth for members and their guests and understandably so. A lot of people would like to be amongst their ranks and play a course which has forged the reputation of a sleeping beauty waiting to be awoken and seduced one fine day. The traditions of golf are respected here to the extent that the original layout by Tom Simpson has never been tinkered with. Today's iconoclastic long hitters will certainly find it on the short side but that does not make it any easier to keep clear of the splendid trees, heather and reasonable number of wickedly located bunkers. Thinking about it, it might even seem a little rude hitting the ball too hard here, rather like raising your voice in a hallowed sanctuary. At Morfontaine you don' t set out to wow the gallery, you just play golf in a mum and dad and the family atmosphere far from the madding crowd. The 18-hole course is a picture of nobility, wonderfully well-balanced and technically challenging. The 9-hole Vallières course is the icing on the cake. A model golf club.

Golf de Morfontaine — 1907

F - 60128 MORTEFONTAINE

Office	Secrétariat	(33) 03 44 54 68 27
Pro shop	Pro-shop	(33) 03 44 54 68 27
Fax	Fax	(33) 03 44 54 60 57
Web	—	
Situation	Situation	

Paris (pop. 2 152 333), 45 km - Senlis (pop. 14 439), 15 km

Annual closure	Fermeture annuelle	no
Weekly closure	Fermeture hebdomadaire	no

Fees main season / Tarifs haute saison	Week days / Semaine	We/Bank holidays / We/Férié
	18 holes	
Individual Individuel	—	—
Couple Couple	—	—

* Members and their guests only

Caddy	Caddy	on request
Electric Trolley	Chariot électrique	no
Buggy	Voiturette	no
Clubs	Clubs	no
Credit cards	Cartes de crédit	no

Pontarmé
Thiers-s-Thève
GOLF
N 17
Senlis
La Chapelle-en-Serval
Parc Astérix
A1
Mortefontaine
Ermenonville
Plailly
D922
Survilliers
Survilliers
Paris
7
St-Witz
0 2 4 km

Access Accès : A1 Paris → Lille, Exit Survilliers, turn right on D126 → Plailly. In the middle of Mortefontaine village, turn left on D607 → Golf.
Map 3 on page 166 Carte 3 Page 166

Golf course / PARCOURS — 18/20

Site	Site	
Maintenance	Entretien	
Architect	Architecte	Tom Simpson
Type	Type	inland, forest
Relief	Relief	
Water in play	Eau en jeu	
Exp. to wind	Exposé au vent	
Trees in play	Arbres en jeu	

Scorecard / Carte de score	Chp. / Chp.	Mens / Mess.	Ladies / Da.
Length Long.	5803	5593	5246
Par	70	70	72
Slope system	131	130	132

Advised golfing ability / Niveau de jeu recommandé: 0 12 24 36

Hcp required / Handicap exigé: 36

Club house & amenities / CLUB-HOUSE ET ANNEXES — 6/10

Pro shop	Pro-shop	
Driving range	Practice	
Sheltered	couvert	4 mats
On grass	sur herbe	yes
Putting-green	putting-green	yes
Pitching-green	pitching green	yes

Hotel facilities / ENVIRONNEMENT HOTELIER — 6/10

HOTELS HÔTELS

Mont-Royal — La-Chapelle-en-Serval 7 km
100 rooms, D 229 €
Tel (33) 03 44 54 50 50, Fax (33) 03 44 54 50 21

Château d'Ermenonville — Ermenonville 10 km
49 rooms, D 137 €
Tel (33) 03 44 54 00 26, Fax (33) 03 44 54 01 00

RESTAURANTS RESTAURANT

Rabelais, Tel (33) 03 44 54 01 70 — Ver-sur-Launette 10 km
La Gentilhommière, Tel (33) 03 44 54 30 20 — Plailly 7 km
Scaramouche, Tel (33) 03 44 53 01 26 — Senlis 15 km

301

NATIONAL L'Albatros

18 | 6 | 6

L'Albatros (site de l'Open de France) est un parcours de championnat, réservé aux moins de 24 de handicap. Dessiné à partir d'un terrain totalement plat par H. Chesneau et R. von Hagge, il s'insinue entre d'énormes dunes artificielles prévues pour accueillir les spectateurs, en alternant des trous à l'américaine et des trous typiques de bord de mer. En contrebas sur le parcours, le dépaysement est total. La moindre erreur stratégique ou technique peut s'avérer catastrophique sur chacun des 18 trous, défendus par toutes sortes d'obstacles, mais aux difficultés bien réparties, où les quatre derniers trous sont toujours décisifs. Il vaut mieux jouer en match-play si l'on n'est pas dans sa meilleure forme, et choisir des départs à son niveau. Pour atténuer cette exigence, le parcours est d'une parfaite franchise, et le résultat est à hauteur de la performance du joueur. A connaître absolument... même si l'environnement du parcours et l'entretien ne sont pas forcément à la hauteur du tracé.

The "Albatros" (the venue for the French Open) is a championship course reserved for players with a minimum handicap of 24. Designed by Hubert Chesneau and Robert Von Hagge over a once totally flat plot of land, it winds its way through towering artificial sand-hills designed to cater to spectators and provides an alternating sequence of US style and typical links holes. Down in the playing arena, you are in another world. The slightest strategic or technical slip can lead to disaster on any one of the 18 holes, all of which are defended by every sort of hazard. And although difficulties are finely balanced over the whole course, the last 4 holes are decisive. If you are not on top of your game, try match-play and play further forward! Although demanding, the course shows its hand and the score on your card reflects how well you played! An absolute must... even though the course's surroundings and maintenance do not always achieve the same standard of excellence as the actual layout.

Le Golf National — 1990

2, avenue du Golf - F - 78280 GUYANCOURT

Office	Secrétariat	(33) 01 30 43 36 00
Pro shop	Pro-shop	(33) 01 30 43 36 00
Fax	Fax	(33) 01 30 43 85 58
Web	www.golf-national.com	
Situation	Situation	Paris, 30 km
Annual closure	Fermeture annuelle	no
Weekly closure	Fermeture hebdomadaire	

wednesday/mercredi (01/11 → 30/06)

Fees main season Tarifs haute saison	Week days Semaine	We/Bank holidays We/Férié
		Full day
Individual Individuel	40 €	59 €
Couple Couple	79 €	119 €

Under 21: 23 € /30 € (We) - Seniors (tuesday/mar) and Ladies (wednesday/mercredi): special offers

Caddy	Caddy	on request
Electric Trolley	Chariot électrique	no
Buggy	Voiturette	no
Clubs	Clubs	15 € /full day

Credit cards Cartes de crédit
VISA - CB - Eurocard - MasterCard

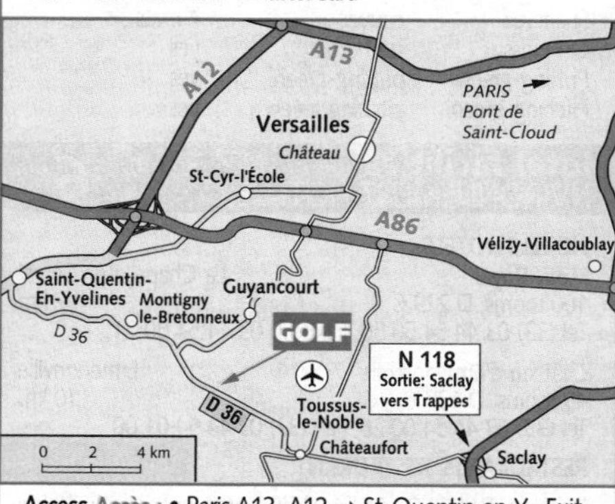

Access Accès : • Paris A13, A12 → St-Quentin en Y., Exit (Sortie) Montigny-le-Bretonneux • Paris N118 → Chartres (A10), Exit Saclay, D36 → Châteaufort, Trappes
Map 15 on page 190 Carte 15 Page 190

Golf course PARCOURS — 18/20

Site	Site	
Maintenance	Entretien	
Architect	Architecte	Hubert Chesneau
	Robert von Hagge	(consultant)
Type	Type	links
Relief	Relief	
Water in play	Eau en jeu	
Exp. to wind	Exposé au vent	
Trees in play	Arbres en jeu	

Scorecard Carte de score	Chp. Chp.	Mens Mess.	Ladies Da.
Length Long.	6495	5790	4885
Par	72	72	72
Slope system	145	133	132

Advised golfing ability — 0 12 24 36
Niveau de jeu recommandé
Hcp required Handicap exigé — 24 Men. 28 Ladies (We)

Club house & amenities CLUB-HOUSE ET ANNEXES — 6/10

Pro shop	Pro-shop	
Driving range	Practice	
Sheltered	couvert	30 mats
On grass	sur herbe	yes
Putting-green	putting-green	yes
Pitching-green	pitching green	yes

Hotel facilities ENVIRONNEMENT HOTELIER — 6/10

HOTELS HÔTELS

Novotel, 130 rooms, D 110 € — Guyancourt on site
Tel (33) 01 30 57 65 65, Fax (33) 01 30 57 65 00

Abbaye les Vaux de Cernay — Cernay-la-Ville
57 rooms, D 152 € — 17 km
Tel (33) 01 34 85 23 00, Fax (33) 01 34 85 11 60

Le Relais de Voisins — Voisin-le-Bretonneux
54 rooms, D 50 € — 2 km
Tel (33) 01 30 44 11 55, Fax (33) 01 30 44 02 04

RESTAURANTS RESTAURANT

Les Trois Marches, Tel (33) 01 39 50 13 21 Versailles 14 km

La Belle Epoque, Tel (33) 01 39 56 95 48 Châteaufort 4 km

NEW GOLF DEAUVILLE Rouge/Blanc

14	7	8

Un ensemble de 27 trous avec un bon 9 trous et un 18 trous de bon niveau, de style très britannique, assez vallonné sans être trop fatigant. Dessiné en 1929 par Tom Simpson, il a été agrandi et beaucoup remanié par Henry Cotton en 1964. Dans un agréable paysage normand, ce parcours avait tendance à se banaliser mais un dessin plus précis des limites de fairways et des roughs, la modification de certains bunkers, la décoration même lui ont donné une nouvelle jeunesse, et imposent maintenant de réfléchir sur la stratégie : les joueurs de bon niveau devraient y revenir. Il s'agit certes d'un golf commercial, pour les golfeurs en week-end et en vacances, et il convient d'assurer leur plaisir, mais les progrès réalisés incitent à le remonter notablement dans la hiérarchie. C'est le meilleur parcours de la région, mais on souhaite toujours que l'accueil y soit agréable en permanence, et la qualité d'entretien plus constante. Un espoir en ce sens, avec des travaux de drainage.

A 27-hole complex with a good 9-hole course and an excellent British style 18-hole layout over rolling countryside. Designed in 1929 by Tom Simpson, it was enlarged and very much restyled by Henry Cotton in 1964. Set in pleasant Norman countryside, the course was beginning to look a bit ordinary, but clearer demarcation of the fairways and rough, plus changes to certain bunkers and to the general decor have given Deauville a new lease of life. Good players should and almost certainly do return for more of the same. This is a business venture, of course, for week-enders and holiday-makers, and their enjoyment is naturally important, but with what has been achieved here, we can only review the course's ranking upwards. This is once again the best course in the region, and we would like to see the hospitality a little warmer still plus more consistent standards of maintenance. With ongoing drainage works, this will hopefully soon be the case.

New Golf de Deauville — 1929

Saint-Arnoult
F - 14800 DEAUVILLE

Office	Secrétariat	(33) 02 31 14 24 24
Pro shop	Pro-shop	(33) 02 31 14 24 24
Fax	Fax	(33) 02 31 14 24 25
Web	www.lucienbarriere.com	
Situation	Situation	Deauville (pop. 4 260), 3 km
Annual closure	Fermeture annuelle	no
Weekly closure	Fermeture hebdomadaire	

tuesday (mardi) except holidays

Fees main season Tarifs haute saison	18 holes	
	Week days Semaine	**We/Bank holidays** We/Férié
Individual Individuel	46 €	76 €
Couple Couple	91 €	152 €

After 16.00: GF 30 € (weekdays), 46 € (We) - Under 18: 16 € (Weekdays)

Caddy	Caddy	27 € /18 holes
Electric Trolley	Chariot électrique	no
Buggy	Voiturette	30 € /18 holes
Clubs	Clubs	complimentary

Credit cards Cartes de crédit
VISA - CB - Eurocard - MasterCard - DC - AMEX

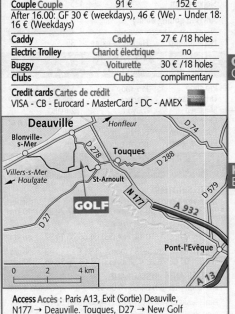

Access Accès : Paris A13, Exit (Sortie) Deauville, N177 → Deauville. Touques, D27 → New Golf
Map 2 on page 165 Carte 2 Page 165

Golf course PARCOURS — 14/20

Site	Site	
Maintenance	Entretien	
Architect	Architecte	Tom Simpson Henry Cotton
Type	Type	parkland, copse
Relief	Relief	
Water in play	Eau en jeu	
Exp. to wind	Exposé au vent	
Trees in play	Arbres en jeu	

Scorecard Carte de score	**Chp.** Chp.	**Mens** Mess.	**Ladies** Da.
Length Long.	5951	5705	5035
Par	71	71	71
Slope system	130	127	126

Advised golfing ability — 0 12 24 36
Niveau de jeu recommandé
Hcp required Handicap exigé — 24 Men, 28 Ladies

Club house & amenities CLUB-HOUSE ET ANNEXES — 7/10

Pro shop	Pro-shop	
Driving range	Practice	
Sheltered	couvert	22 mats
On grass	sur herbe	yes (summer)
Putting-green	putting-green	yes
Pitching-green	pitching green	yes

Hotel facilities ENVIRONNEMENT HOTELIER — 8/10

HOTELS HÔTELS

Hôtel du Golf, 178 rooms, D 274 € — Deauville on site
Tel (33) 02 31 14 24 00, Fax (33) 02 31 14 24 01

Normandy, 257 rooms, D 305 € — Deauville
Tel (33) 02 31 98 66 22, Fax (33) 02 31 98 66 23 — 3 km

Ferme St-Siméon, 34 rooms, D 305 € — Honfleur
Tel (33) 02 31 81 78 00, Fax (33) 02 31 89 48 48 — 15 km

RESTAURANTS RESTAURANT

Le Spinnaker, Tel (33) 02 31 88 24 40 — Deauville
Le Ciro's, Tel (33) 02 31 14 31 31 — Deauville
L'Assiette Gourmande, Tel (33) 02 31 89 24 88 — Honfleur

NÎMES-CAMPAGNE

17	7	6

D'une année sur l'autre, et pour nous tous les deux ans, on a plaisir à retrouver ce "classique" de la région, et de tradition sportive bien établie. Comme un ami d'enfance, il ne change pas. Dessiné par Morandi et Donald Harradine, il s'impose toujours comme un vrai parcours de championnat, surtout quand souffle le vent. Alors, les chênes et cyprès bleus deviennent redoutables, et la maîtrise des balles basses obligatoire, d'autant que quelques obstacles d'eau stratégiques viennent perturber le jugement comme la confiance. Les greens sont généralement bien dessinés, pas toujours très vastes, et souvent rapides. Pour les bons joueurs, la précision devra s'allier alors à la puissance, car les trous sont rarement courts des départs arrière : les joueurs lucides ne devront pas hésiter à choisir les départs normaux. Ce golf toujours bien entretenu est très fréquenté par ses nombreux membres, il est conseillé de réserver en toute saison.

Year in year out, and for us every two years, it's always a pleasure to play this "classic" course which enjoys a well established sporting tradition. Like a life-long friend, Nîmes Campagne never changes. Designed by Morandi and Donald Harradine, this is a real championship course, especially when the wind blows. Then the oaks and the blue cypress trees are formidable foes and make knock-down shots a must, especially since a few strategic water hazards can affect both judgment and confidence. The greens are generally well-designed, not always that large and often fast. For the better player, the course demands both power and precision, as holes are seldom short from the back tees. Clear-headed average golfers should use the normal tees. The course is very well maintained and played by a large number of members, so whatever the season, always book a tee-off time.

Golf de Nîmes-Campagne — 1968

Route de Saint-Gilles
F - 30900 NIMES

Office	Secrétariat	(33) 04 66 70 17 37
Pro shop	Pro-shop	(33) 04 66 70 17 37
Fax	Fax	(33) 04 66 70 03 14
E-mail		golf.nimes.campagne@wanadoo.fr
Situation	Situation	

Nîmes (pop. 128 470), 10 km

Annual closure	Fermeture annuelle	no
Weekly closure	Fermeture hebdomadaire	no

Fees main season / Tarifs haute saison	Week days / Semaine	We/Bank holidays / We/Férié
	Full day	
Individual Individuel	46 €	46 €
Couple Couple	84 €	84 €

Juniors & Students: 18 €

Caddy	Caddy	no
Electric Trolley	Chariot électrique	12 € /18 holes
Buggy	Voiturette	30 € /18 holes
Clubs	Clubs	12 € /full day

Credit cards Cartes de crédit
VISA - CB - Eurocard - MasterCard

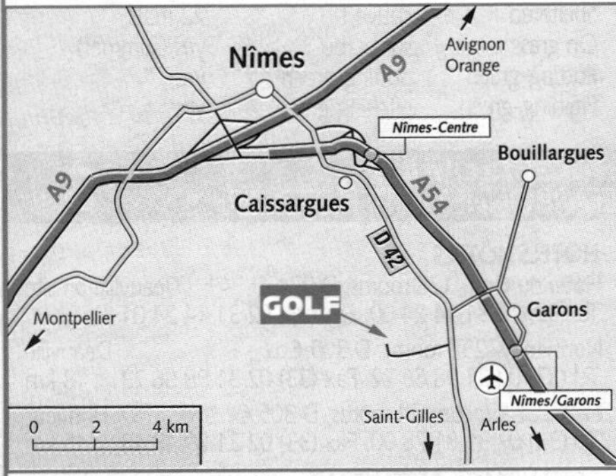

Access Accès : Montpellier or Avignon, A9, Exit (Sortie) Nîmes Centre, D42 → Saint-Gilles, take on the right of the airport, → Golf
Map 13 on page 187 Carte 13 Page 187

Golf course PARCOURS — 17/20

Site	Site	
Maintenance	Entretien	
Architect	Architecte	Léonard Morandi, Donald Harradine
Type	Type	country, parkland
Relief	Relief	
Water in play	Eau en jeu	
Exp. to wind	Exposé au vent	
Trees in play	Arbres en jeu	

Scorecard / Carte de score	Chp. / Chp.	Mens / Mess.	Ladies / Da.
Length Long.	6135	5599	5045
Par	72	72	72
Slope system	139	135	130

Advised golfing ability / Niveau de jeu recommandé: 0 12 24 36
Hcp required / Handicap exigé: 35

Club house & amenities CLUB-HOUSE ET ANNEXES — 7/10

Pro shop	Pro-shop	
Driving range	Practice	
Sheltered	couvert	2 mats
On grass	sur herbe	no, 20 mats open air
Putting-green	putting-green	yes
Pitching-green	pitching green	yes

Hotel facilities ENVIRONNEMENT HOTELIER — 6/10

HOTELS HÔTELS

Imperator Concorde, 62 rooms, D 122 € — Nîmes
Tel (33) 04 66 21 90 30, Fax (33) 04 66 67 70 25 — 10 km

Les Aubuns, 25 rooms, D 76 € — Caissargues
Tel (33) 04 66 70 10 44, Fax (33) 04 66 70 14 97 — 6 km

New Hôtel La Baume, 34 rooms, D 91 € — Nîmes
Tel (33) 04 66 76 28 42, Fax (33) 04 66 76 28 45 — 10 km

RESTAURANTS RESTAURANT

Alexandre, Tel (33) 04 66 70 08 99 — Garons 4 km

Aux Plaisirs des Halles, Tel (33) 04 66 36 01 02 — Nîmes

Lisita, Tel (33) 04 66 67 29 15 — Nîmes

OMAHA BEACH La Mer/Le Bocage | 14 | 7 | 5

Les trois 9 trous sont combinables, mais "L'Etang", assez dénudé et accidenté, n'est pas aussi caractéristique que "Le Bocage" (dans un paysage typiquement normand) et "La Mer". Ces deux derniers parcours forment la combinaison la plus cohérente au plan du jeu et de l'unité esthétique, où l'architecte Yves Bureau a utilisé les reliefs naturels sans trop bouleverser le terrain, ponctuant la route des greens de quelques grands bunkers. "La Mer", assez vallonné, propose quelques trous sur un plateau dominant l'une des plages du Débarquement, avec de magnifiques points de vue sur la côte et la mer. Ces trous sur la mer n'ont pas vraiment le caractère de links, étant donné la nature du sol et l'absence de dunes (ils se rapprochent du style d'Etretat), mais le vent peut les rendre redoutables pour le jeu et surtout pour les scores. Une réalisation sympathique et de qualité, où le souci des améliorations est permanent.

The three nine hole courses can be played in any combination, but "L'Etang", a barren and hilly layout, does not have the character of "Le Bocage" (in typically Norman countryside) or "La Mer". The latter two form the most consistent combination in terms of golfing and visual unity, where architect Yves Bureau has employed the natural relief without too much excavation work, dotting the fairways with a few large bunkers. "La Mer", which unwinds over rolling landscape, includes a few holes on a plateau overlooking one of the D-Day beaches and providing magnificent views over the coastline and English channel. The seaboard holes are hardly your typical links holes, given the nature of the soil and the absence of dunes (they are more in the Etretat style), but the wind can play havoc with your game and your card. A very pleasant golf course of excellent standard, where concern for improvements is a constant factor.

Omaha Beach Golf Club — 1987

La Ferme Saint-Sauveur
F - 14520 PORT-EN-BESSIN

Office	Secrétariat	(33) 02 31 22 12 12
Pro shop	Pro-shop	(33) 02 31 22 76 45
Fax	Fax	(33) 02 31 22 12 13
Web	www.best-channel-golfs.com	
Situation	Situation	

Bayeux (pop. 14 700), 10 km

Annual closure	Fermeture annuelle	no
Weekly closure	Fermeture hebdomadaire	no
Fees main season	Tarifs haute saison	18 holes

	Week days Semaine	We/Bank holidays We/Férié
Individual Individuel	43 €	43 €
Couple Couple	81 €	81 €

Juniors & Students: 29 €

Caddy	Caddy	on request
Electric Trolley	Chariot électrique	11 € /18 holes
Buggy	Voiturette	27 € /18 holes
Clubs	Clubs	9 € /18 holes

Credit cards Cartes de crédit
VISA - CB - Eurocard - MasterCard

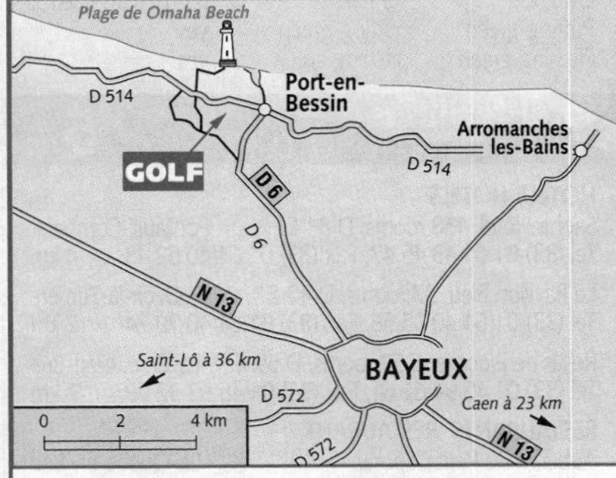

Access Accès : Bayeux, D6 → Port-en-Bessin
Map 2 on page 164 Carte 2 Page 164

Golf course PARCOURS — 14/20

Site	Site	
Maintenance	Entretien	
Architect	Architecte	Yves Bureau
Type	Type	seaside course, copse
Relief	Relief	
Water in play	Eau en jeu	
Exp. to wind	Exposé au vent	
Trees in play	Arbres en jeu	

Scorecard Carte de score	Chp. Chp.	Mens Mess.	Ladies Da.
Length Long.	6216	5647	4810
Par	72	72	72
Slope system	132	123	126

Advised golfing ability 0 12 24 36
Niveau de jeu recommandé
Hcp required Handicap exigé no

Club house & amenities CLUB-HOUSE ET ANNEXES — 7/10

Pro shop	Pro-shop	
Driving range	Practice	
Sheltered	couvert	16 mats
On grass	sur herbe	no, 35 mats open air
Putting-green	putting-green	yes
Pitching-green	pitching green	yes

Hotel facilities ENVIRONNEMENT HOTELIER — 5/10

HOTELS HÔTELS

Mercure Omaha Beach, 39 rooms, D 91 € — on site
Tel (33) 02 31 22 44 44, Fax (33) 02 31 22 36 77

La Chenevière, 21 rooms, D 201 € — Commes 2 km
Tel (33) 02 31 51 25 25, Fax (33) 02 31 51 25 20

Château de Sully, 22 rooms, D 122 € — Bayeux 8 km
Tel (33) 02 31 22 29 48, Fax (33) 02 31 22 64 77

RESTAURANTS RESTAURANT

Marine, Tel (33) 02 31 21 70 08 — Port-en-Bessin 2 km
Château de Sully, Tel (33) 02 31 22 29 48 — Bayeux 6 km
Bistrot de Paris, Tel (33) 02 31 92 00 82 — Bayeux 8 km

OZOIR-LA-FERRIÈRE Château/Monthéty

13	7	5

Dans un superbe parc plat, mais avec un sol parfois humide, de larges avenues bordées de grands arbres offrent le sentiment d'espace que l'on attend d'un golf. Même si certains trous restent assez étroits pour exiger un jeu précis, les longs frappeurs trouveront aussi de quoi s'exprimer. On peut regretter que les fairways ne soient guère modelés, ce qui facilite le jeu, il est vrai, mais les meilleurs joueurs n'y trouveront pas tout à fait un test complet de leur jeu. Les bunkers sont avec les arbres les principaux obstacles, l'eau ne venant en jeu que sur deux trous. Les greens sont de qualité, assez classiques. Celui du 10 a été refait, comme d'autres mériteraient de l'être, après des années de loyeux services. Golf de membres, c'est le parcours le plus "parisien" à l'est de Paris, comme en témoigne le très bourgeois Club-House, une vénérable maison de maître. Un très décent parcours de 9 trous, avec beaucoup d'obstacles d'eau, complète cet équipement de bon niveau, sinon exceptionnel.

In a beautiful, flat park which is sometimes a little damp underfoot, wide fairways lined by tall trees give the feeling of space you expect from a golf course. Although some holes are rather tight and demand precision play, long-hitters can let fly at Ozoir. We thought it a shame that no contouring has been done to the fairways. True, they are easier to play as they are, but they could be made more challenging for the better players. Bunkers and trees are the main hazards, as water enters the fray on only two holes. The greens are generally good and classically styled, while the 10th green has been re-laid the way a number of others deserve to be after years of devoted service. Very much a "members' club", Ozoir is the most "Parisian" course to the east of Paris, as seen with the classy club-house, a fine mansion. A very decent 9-holer with a lot of water hazards completes this excellent, if not to say exceptional, golfing complex.

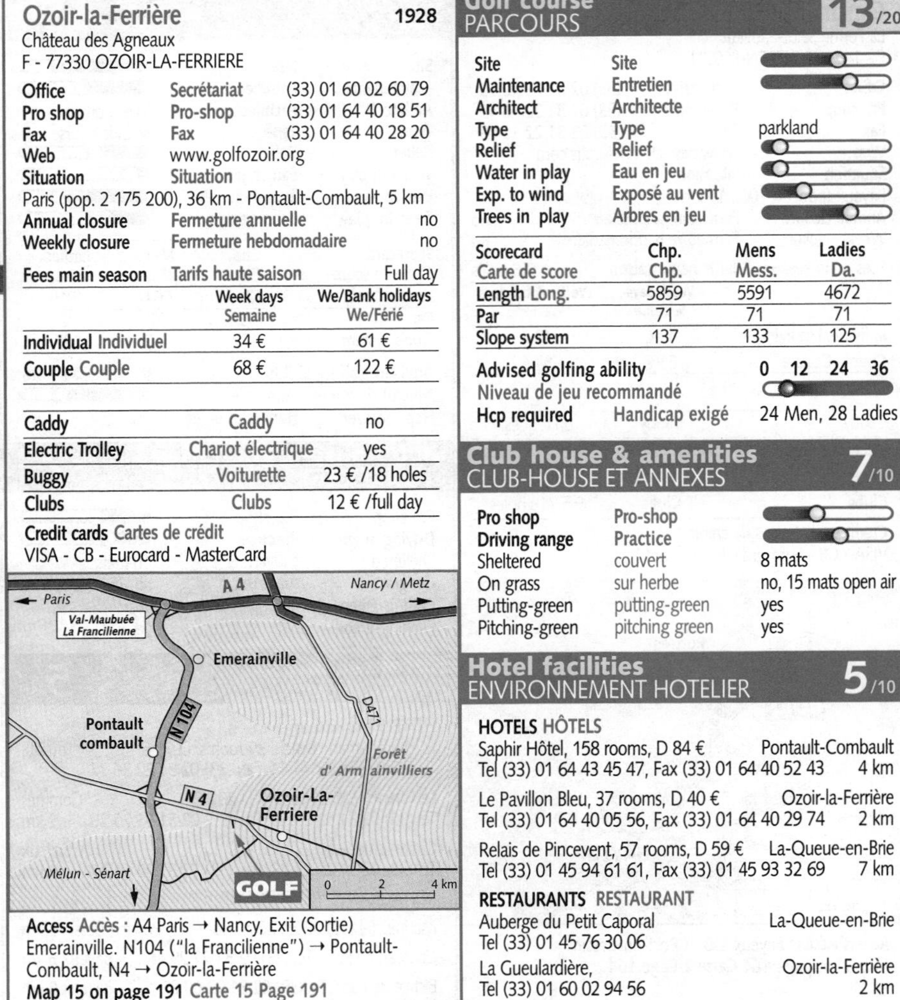

Ozoir-la-Ferrière **1928**
Château des Agneaux
F - 77330 OZOIR-LA-FERRIERE

Office	Secrétariat	(33) 01 60 02 60 79
Pro shop	Pro-shop	(33) 01 64 40 18 51
Fax	Fax	(33) 01 64 40 28 20
Web	www.golfozoir.org	
Situation	Situation	

Paris (pop. 2 175 200), 36 km - Pontault-Combault, 5 km

Annual closure	Fermeture annuelle	no
Weekly closure	Fermeture hebdomadaire	no

Fees main season Tarifs haute saison	Week days Semaine	We/Bank holidays We/Férié
Individual Individuel	34 €	61 €
Couple Couple	68 €	122 €

Full day

Caddy	Caddy	no
Electric Trolley	Chariot électrique	yes
Buggy	Voiturette	23 € /18 holes
Clubs	Clubs	12 € /full day

Credit cards Cartes de crédit
VISA - CB - Eurocard - MasterCard

Access Accès : A4 Paris → Nancy, Exit (Sortie) Emerainville. N104 ("la Francilienne") → Pontault-Combault, N4 → Ozoir-la-Ferrière
Map 15 on page 191 Carte 15 Page 191

Golf course PARCOURS 13/20

Site	Site	
Maintenance	Entretien	
Architect	Architecte	
Type	Type	parkland
Relief	Relief	
Water in play	Eau en jeu	
Exp. to wind	Exposé au vent	
Trees in play	Arbres en jeu	

Scorecard Carte de score	Chp. Chp.	Mens Mess.	Ladies Da.
Length Long.	5859	5591	4672
Par	71	71	71
Slope system	137	133	125

Advised golfing ability Niveau de jeu recommandé 0 12 24 36
Hcp required Handicap exigé 24 Men, 28 Ladies

Club house & amenities CLUB-HOUSE ET ANNEXES 7/10

Pro shop	Pro-shop	
Driving range	Practice	
Sheltered	couvert	8 mats
On grass	sur herbe	no, 15 mats open air
Putting-green	putting-green	yes
Pitching-green	pitching green	yes

Hotel facilities ENVIRONNEMENT HOTELIER 5/10

HOTELS HÔTELS

Saphir Hôtel, 158 rooms, D 84 € — Pontault-Combault
Tel (33) 01 64 43 45 47, Fax (33) 01 64 40 52 43 — 4 km

Le Pavillon Bleu, 37 rooms, D 40 € — Ozoir-la-Ferrière
Tel (33) 01 64 40 05 56, Fax (33) 01 64 40 29 74 — 2 km

Relais de Pincevent, 57 rooms, D 59 € — La-Queue-en-Brie
Tel (33) 01 45 94 61 61, Fax (33) 01 45 93 32 69 — 7 km

RESTAURANTS RESTAURANT

Auberge du Petit Caporal — La-Queue-en-Brie
Tel (33) 01 45 76 30 06

La Gueulardière, — Ozoir-la-Ferrière
Tel (33) 01 60 02 94 56 — 2 km

PARIS INTERNATIONAL

16 | 7 | 5

Avec sa situation très favorable au nord de Paris et à proximité de l'aéroport Charles-de-Gaulle, ce parcours était d'autant plus espéré que son dessin a été confié à Jack Nicklaus. Mais autant on peut reconnaître sa patte sur une douzaine de trous, où un espace très ouvert lui permettait de donner sa pleine mesure, autant on a l'impression qu'il s'est trouvé moins à l'aise et à l'étroit dans les trous en forêt, où l'on a du mal à identifier sa signature, et où les très bons joueurs auront plus de mal à s'exprimer. Ces réserves viennent surtout du fait que l'on attendait beaucoup de Nicklaus, et pour garder le meilleur souvenir du parcours, on conseillera de commencer par le retour et de finir par ce superbe aller. De plus, c'est moins fatigant dans ce sens. A connaître néanmoins, mais on évitera les journées humides, que le terrain supporte mal, même d'importants travaux de drainage ont nettement amélioré les choses.

Neatly located to the north of Paris close to Charles-de-Gaulle airport, this course was long awaited in that the designer was a one Jack Nicklaus. But as easily as you will recognize his style on a dozen or so holes, where wide open space gave him full scope for expression, as easily you will feel that the great man was not quite comfortable and even a little cramped on the holes through the forest. Here, his style is not nearly as evident and even good players will have problems coming to terms with the course. These reservations are of course voiced because so much was expected of Nicklaus. To get the best impression of this course, we would advise you to start from the 10th and leave the superb outward 9 for the end. And anyway the course is less tiring played this way. Worth playing nonetheless, but avoid the wet days as the terrain does not take too well to water, even though significant new drainage work has made a big improvement here.

Paris International Golf Club **1990**

18, route du Golf
F - 95560 BAILLET-en-FRANCE

Office	Secrétariat	(33) 01 34 69 90 00
Pro shop	Pro-shop	(33) 01 34 69 90 00
Fax	Fax	(33) 01 34 69 97 15
Web	www.paris-golf.com	
Situation	Situation	Paris, 30 km
Annual closure	Fermeture annuelle	no
Weekly closure	Fermeture hebdomadaire	monday/lundi

Fees main season Tarifs haute saison	18 holes	
	Week days Semaine	**We/Bank holidays** We/Férié
Individual Individuel	53 €	76 €
Couple Couple	106 €	152 €

Members have priority rights

Caddy	Caddy	on request
Electric Trolley	Chariot électrique	12 € /18 holes
Buggy	Voiturette	34 € /18 holes
Clubs	Clubs	23 € /full day

Credit cards Cartes de crédit
VISA - CB - Eurocard - MasterCard - DC - JCB - AMEX

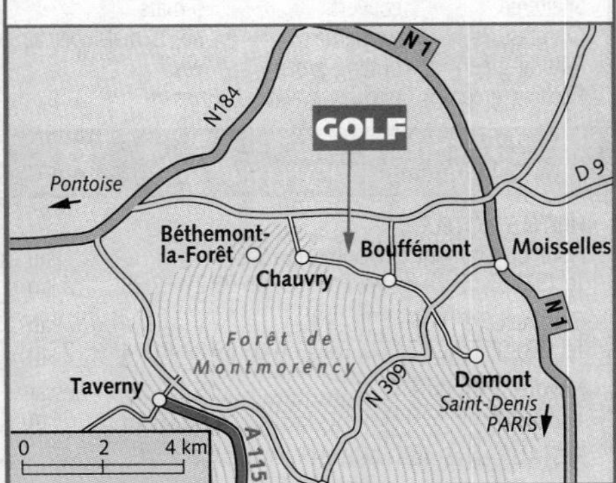

Access Accès : Paris, A1, N1.
Turn left on D3 → Baillet-en-France
Map 15 on page 190 Carte 15 Page 190

Golf course PARCOURS 16/20

Site	Site	
Maintenance	Entretien	
Architect	Architecte	Jack Nicklaus
Type	Type	parkland, hilly
Relief	Relief	
Water in play	Eau en jeu	
Exp. to wind	Exposé au vent	
Trees in play	Arbres en jeu	

Scorecard Carte de score	**Chp.** Chp.	**Mens** Mess.	**Ladies** Da.
Length Long.	6319	5740	4885
Par	72	72	72
Slope system	140	138	138

Advised golfing ability Niveau de jeu recommandé — 0 12 24 36
Hcp required Handicap exigé — no

Club house & amenities CLUB-HOUSE ET ANNEXES 7/10

Pro shop	Pro-shop	
Driving range	Practice	
Sheltered	couvert	6 mats
On grass	sur herbe	yes (summer)
Putting-green	putting-green	yes
Pitching-green	pitching green	yes

Hotel facilities ENVIRONNEMENT HOTELIER 5/10

HOTELS HÔTELS

Le Grand Hôtel, 47 rooms, D 198 € — Enghien
Tel (33) 01 39 34 10 00, Fax (33) 01 39 34 10 01 — 14 km

Campanile, 76 rooms, D 50 € — Taverny
Tel (33) 01 30 40 10 85, Fax (33) 01 30 40 10 87 — 10 km

Median, 49 rooms, D 90 € — Goussainville
Tel (33) 01 39 88 93 93, Fax (33) 01 39 88 75 65 — 10 km

RESTAURANTS RESTAURANT

Gai Rivage — L'Isle Adam
Tel (33) 01 34 69 01 09 — 9 km

Au Coeur de la Forêt — Montmorency
Tel (33) 01 39 64 99 19 — 11 km

PAU

13 | 6 | 8

Le plus ancien parcours d'Europe continentale pourrait être uniquement un lieu de pélerinage. Mais si ce n'est pas un chef-d'oeuvre, il est fort amusant et relaxant à jouer même s'il n'a plus grand chose des origines. Il a au moins gardé le goût de la décoration florale et les arbres ont grandi, tout en laissant des vues séduisantes sur les Pyrénées. La présence du Gave de Pau apporte un intérêt au jeu, dont les seules difficultés consistent à apprécier les distances : le parcours est plat et étroit (avec pas mal de hors-limites). Sa longueur réduite peut décevoir les vedettes du driver, mais c'est parfait pour affûter ses petits fers. Le putting et le petit jeu jouent évidemment un rôle essentiel, les progrès de l'entretien et du drainage ont augmenté encore le plaisir des amateurs. La chaleur de l'accueil dans le Sud-Ouest, le charme des lieux, la situation pratiquement en ville et le culte de l'esprit des origines en font un lieu de promenade agréable, on peut toujours imaginer apercevoir les fantômes des golfeurs du siècle dernier !

This is the oldest course on the continent of Europe and could get by simply as a place of pilgrimage. But while the course is hardly a masterpiece, it is great fun and relaxing to play even though there is little left of its original features. At least it has retained the tasteful floral decoration and the trees have grown, leaving some eye-catching sights over the Pyrenees. The "Gave du Pau" (a mountain stream) adds a little spice to your round, the only real difficulty of which is appreciating the distances: the course is flat and tight (with a lot of out-of-bounds to cope with). The short yardage might disappoint long-drivers, but it is perfect for honing your short irons. Putting and a good short game obviously play a key role and improved maintenance and drainage work has done much to enhance the pleasure of playing here. The warm welcome of the South-West of France, the charming site, a virtually town-centre course and the course's long-standing origins make this a lovely walk, perhaps accompanied by the old golfing spirits of the 19th century...

Pau Golf-Club — 1856

Rue du Golf
F - 64140 BILLERE

Office	Secrétariat	(33) 05 59 13 18 56
Pro shop	Pro-shop	(33) 05 59 13 18 56
Fax	Fax	(33) 05 59 13 18 57
E-mail	pau.golf.club@wanadoo.fr	
Situation	Situation	Pau (pop. 82 150), 2 km
Annual closure	Fermeture annuelle	no
Weekly closure	Fermeture hebdomadaire	

monday (lundi) restaurant closed

Fees main season Tarifs haute saison	Week days Semaine	We/Bank holidays We/Férié
		full day
Individual Individuel	43 €	43 €
Couple Couple	76 €	76 €

Under 25 & Students: 21 €

Caddy	Caddy	no
Electric Trolley	Chariot électrique	no
Buggy	Voiturette	no
Clubs	Clubs	15 € /18 holes

Credit cards Cartes de crédit
VISA - CB - Eurocard - MasterCard

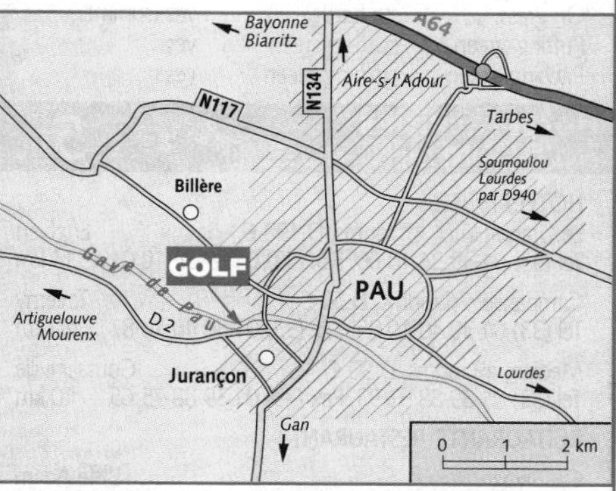

Access Accès : next to the Gave de Pau and "Parc National"
Map 12 on page 184 Carte 12 Page 184

Golf course — PARCOURS — 13/20

Site	Site	
Maintenance	Entretien	
Architect	Architecte	B. Ducwing
Type	Type	parkland
Relief	Relief	
Water in play	Eau en jeu	
Exp. to wind	Exposé au vent	
Trees in play	Arbres en jeu	

Scorecard Carte de score	Chp. Chp.	Mens Mess.	Ladies Da.
Length Long.	5314	5314	4623
Par	69	69	69
Slope system	124	124	116

Advised golfing ability Niveau de jeu recommandé — 0 12 24 36
Hcp required Handicap exigé — 35

Club house & amenities — CLUB-HOUSE ET ANNEXES — 6/10

Pro shop	Pro-shop	
Driving range	Practice	
Sheltered	couvert	5 mats
On grass	sur herbe	no, 15 mats open air
Putting-green	putting-green	yes
Pitching-green	pitching green	yes

Hotel facilities — ENVIRONNEMENT HOTELIER — 8/10

HOTELS HÔTELS

Hôtel de Gramont, 36 rooms, D 75 € — Pau 2 km
Tel (33) 05 59 27 84 04, Fax (33) 05 59 27 62 23

Commerce, 51 rooms, D 48 € — Pau 2 km
Tel (33) 05 59 27 24 40, Fax (33) 05 59 83 81 74

Novotel, 89 rooms, D 87 € — Lescar 6 km
Tel (33) 05 59 13 04 04, Fax (33) 05 59 13 04 13

RESTAURANTS RESTAURANT

Chez Ruffet, Tel (33) 05 59 06 25 13 — Jurançon 2 km
Chez Pierre, Tel (33) 05 59 27 76 86 — Pau 2 km
La Michodière, Tel (33) 05 59 27 53 85 — Pau 2 km

PLÉNEUF-VAL-ANDRÉ

17	7	5

Une jolie réussite signée par Alain Prat, en bordure de mer, sans pour autant se rattacher tout à fait au style de links traditionnels. On remarquera une bonne montée en puissance des difficultés du parcours. De même que sur chacun des trous : les fairways sont généralement assez larges, ce qui facilite la plupart des tee-shots, mais les greens sont particulièrement défendus par de nombreux bunkers de sable et d'herbe, stratégiquement placés. Le trou le plus spectaculaire est le 11, un par 5 au départ arrière situé sur un éperon rocheux, dans la partie la plus accidentée du parcours. Mais ce n'est pas un golf trop fatiguant. On notera aussi la qualité particulière des installations d'entraînement, et de jolis points de vue, mais le Club house ne mérite sans doute pas les mêmes compliments. L'entretien n'est pas toujours le point fort du lieu, mais les greens et départs autrefois très moyens sont devenus meilleurs.

A pretty layout by Alain Prat along the sea-shore, but without the traditional links style. Difficulties gradually increase as the day wears on, a good thing, and each hole has generally pretty wide fairways for easier tee-shots. However, the greens are well defended by numerous bunkers and dips, all of which are strategically located. The signature hole has to be the 11th, a par 5 whose back-tee is placed on a rocky spur on the hilliest part of the course, but there is nothing too tiring about Pleneuf. Practice facilities are very good and there are also some pretty viewpoints, but unfortunately there is not too much that can be said in favour of the club-house. Maintenance is still not this course's forte, but the once very patchy greens and tee-boxes are now better than they were.

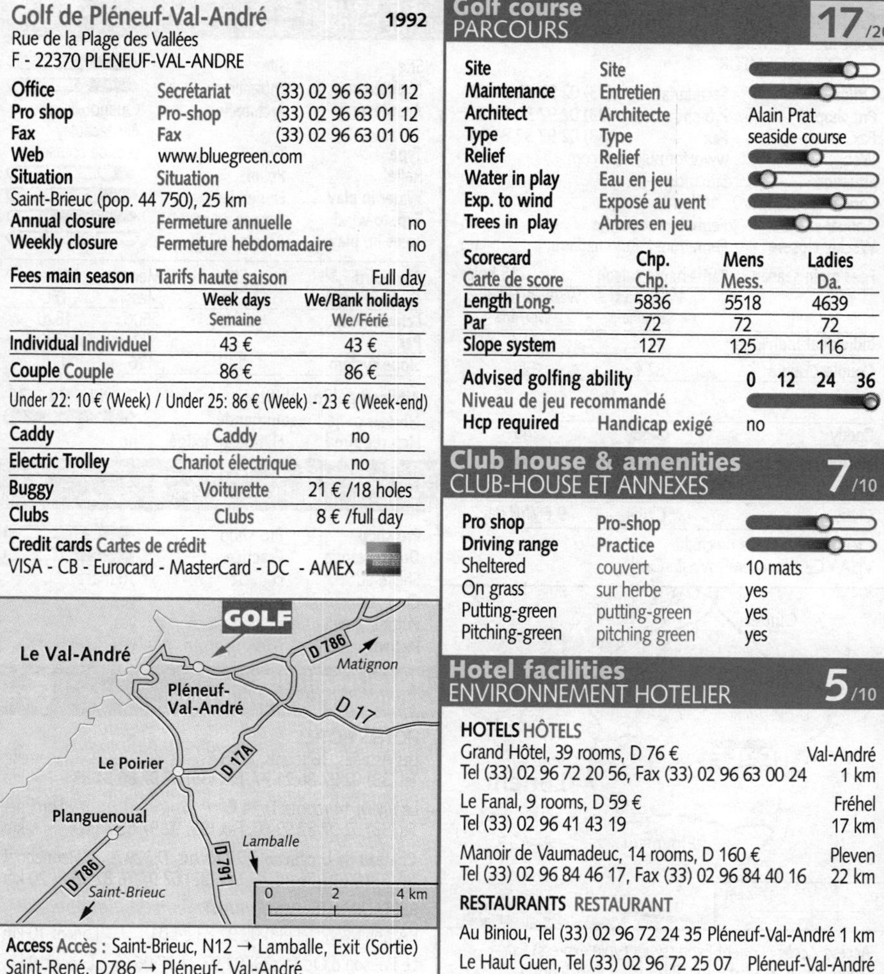

Golf de Pléneuf-Val-André — 1992

Rue de la Plage des Vallées
F - 22370 PLENEUF-VAL-ANDRE

Office	Secrétariat	(33) 02 96 63 01 12
Pro shop	Pro-shop	(33) 02 96 63 01 12
Fax	Fax	(33) 02 96 63 01 06
Web	www.bluegreen.com	
Situation	Situation	

Saint-Brieuc (pop. 44 750), 25 km

Annual closure	Fermeture annuelle	no
Weekly closure	Fermeture hebdomadaire	no

Fees main season Tarifs haute saison		Full day
	Week days Semaine	**We/Bank holidays** We/Férié
Individual Individuel	43 €	43 €
Couple Couple	86 €	86 €

Under 22: 10 € (Week) / Under 25: 86 € (Week) - 23 € (Week-end)

Caddy	Caddy	no
Electric Trolley	Chariot électrique	no
Buggy	Voiturette	21 € /18 holes
Clubs	Clubs	8 € /full day

Credit cards Cartes de crédit
VISA - CB - Eurocard - MasterCard - DC - AMEX

Access Accès : Saint-Brieuc, N12 → Lamballe, Exit (Sortie) Saint-René. D786 → Pléneuf- Val-André
Map 5 on page 171 Carte 5 Page 171

Golf course — PARCOURS — 17/20

Site	Site	
Maintenance	Entretien	
Architect	Architecte	Alain Prat
Type	Type	seaside course
Relief	Relief	
Water in play	Eau en jeu	
Exp. to wind	Exposé au vent	
Trees in play	Arbres en jeu	

Scorecard Carte de score	**Chp.** Chp.	**Mens** Mess.	**Ladies** Da.
Length Long.	5836	5518	4639
Par	72	72	72
Slope system	127	125	116

Advised golfing ability Niveau de jeu recommandé — 0 12 24 36
Hcp required Handicap exigé — no

Club house & amenities — CLUB-HOUSE ET ANNEXES — 7/10

Pro shop	Pro-shop	
Driving range	Practice	
Sheltered	couvert	10 mats
On grass	sur herbe	yes
Putting-green	putting-green	yes
Pitching-green	pitching green	yes

Hotel facilities — ENVIRONNEMENT HOTELIER — 5/10

HOTELS HÔTELS

Grand Hôtel, 39 rooms, D 76 € — Val-André
Tel (33) 02 96 72 20 56, Fax (33) 02 96 63 00 24 — 1 km

Le Fanal, 9 rooms, D 59 € — Fréhel
Tel (33) 02 96 41 43 19 — 17 km

Manoir de Vaumadeuc, 14 rooms, D 160 € — Pleven
Tel (33) 02 96 84 46 17, Fax (33) 02 96 84 40 16 — 22 km

RESTAURANTS RESTAURANT

Au Biniou, Tel (33) 02 96 72 24 35 Pléneuf-Val-André 1 km
Le Haut Guen, Tel (33) 02 96 72 25 07 Pléneuf-Val-André
La Mer, Tel (33) 02 96 72 20 44 Val-André 1 km

PLOEMEUR OCÉAN

15 | 7 | 6

A proximité de Lorient, un vaste espace de bord de mer et de campagne, sans guère plus de végétation que de bas buissons de lichens, mais dans le voisinage peu gracieux d'une grande carrière de sable et de gravier. Dommage, car ce parcours ouvert en 1990 et signé Quenouille est agréable, avec quelques jolis trous, des fairways bien fournis, des greens très corrects et de bons bunkers. Certains coups et approches sont assez techniques, mais les difficultés ne sont pas très accentuées, ce qui permet à tous les niveaux d'y évoluer simultanément. Quelques trous longent la mer, mais sans rendre vraiment un hommage évident aux parcours britanniques de situation analogue. Un plaisant parcours dans une région aujourd'hui bien fournie en golfs. L'entretien reste toujours à surveiller, mais il faut bien comprendre que si ce genre de golfs n'a pas un entretien digne d'Augusta, les tarifs d'accès ne sont pas non plus les mêmes !

This is a wide open area close to Lorient, along the seaboard with hardly any more vegetation than a few low-cut lichen bushes, but set in a rather unsightly neighbourhood of a large sand and gravel quarry. This is a pity, because Ploemeur, designed by Quenouille and opened in 1990, is a pleasant course with a few pretty holes, well-grassed fairways, very decent greens and some good bunkers to boot. Some shots require a lot of technique but the difficulties are never excessive, so that players of all aspirations can enjoy a round together. A few holes run along the sea-shore, but there is nothing to obviously compare with British courses in a similar setting. A pleasant course in a region that today has more than its fair share of golfing facilities. Maintenance still needs watching, but anyone will understand that if this type of course does not actually come up to Augusta standards maintenance-wise, it is also because the admission fee is not quite in the same class either.

Golf de Ploemeur Océan — 1990

Saint-Jude - Kerham
F - 56270 PLOEMEUR

Office	Secrétariat	(33) 02 97 32 81 82
Pro shop	Pro-shop	(33) 02 97 32 81 82
Fax	Fax	(33) 02 97 32 80 90
Web	www.formule-golf.com	
Situation	Situation	

Lorient (pop. 59 270), 10 km

Annual closure	Fermeture annuelle	no
Weekly closure	Fermeture hebdomadaire	no

Fees main season Tarifs haute saison	18 holes	
	Week days Semaine	**We/Bank holidays** We/Férié
Individual Individuel	41 €	41 €
Couple Couple	82 €	82 €

Under 18: – 50%

Caddy	Caddy	no
Electric Trolley	Chariot électrique	no
Buggy	Voiturette	23 € /18 holes
Clubs	Clubs	9 € /full day

Credit cards Cartes de crédit
VISA - CB - Eurocard - MasterCard

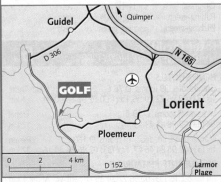

Access Accès : Lorient Expressway (Voie express) Exit Ploemeur → Airport Lann-Bihoué → Fort Bloqué
Map 5 on page 170 Carte 5 Page 170

Golf course PARCOURS — 15/20

Site	Site	
Maintenance	Entretien	
Architect	Architecte	Quenouille & Macauley
Type	Type	seaside course
Relief	Relief	
Water in play	Eau en jeu	
Exp. to wind	Exposé au vent	
Trees in play	Arbres en jeu	

Scorecard Carte de score	**Chp.** Chp.	**Mens** Mess.	**Ladies** Da.
Length Long.	5819	5606	4820
Par	72	72	72
Slope system	128	126	126

Advised golfing ability Niveau de jeu recommandé — 0 12 24 36
Hcp required Handicap exigé — no

Club house & amenities CLUB-HOUSE ET ANNEXES — 7/10

Pro shop	Pro-shop	
Driving range	Practice	
Sheltered	couvert	16 mats
On grass	sur herbe	yes
Putting-green	putting-green	yes
Pitching-green	pitching green	yes

Hotel facilities ENVIRONNEMENT HOTELIER — 6/10

HOTELS HÔTELS

Les Astéries, 36 rooms, D 63 € — Ploemeur
Tel (33) 02 97 86 21 97, Fax (33) 02 97 86 34 33 — 4 km

Le Vivier, 14 rooms, D 74 € — Lomener
Tel (33) 02 97 82 99 60, Fax (33) 02 97 82 88 89 — 6 km

Château de Locguénolé, 22 rooms, D 229 € — Hennebont
Tel (33) 02 97 76 76 76, Fax (33) 02 97 76 82 35 — 20 km

RESTAURANTS RESTAURANT

L'Amphitryon, Tel (33) 02 97 83 34 04 — Lorient 10 km
Le Poisson d'Or, Tel (33) 02 97 21 57 06 — Lorient10 km
Château de Locguénolé, Tel (33) 02 97 76 76 76 — Hennebont

PONT ROYAL

16 | 6 | 5

Premier parcours français signé par Ballesteros, Pont Royal bénéficie d'un très bon entretien. La dimension généreuse des bunkers peut réserver de longues sorties, spécialité du champion espagnol, et cauchemar des amateurs comme des professionnels. Avec de grands arbres, divers obstacles d'eau (rivière, étangs), quelques dangereux ravins, un relief assez accidenté (voiturette conseillée), Pont Royal réclame pas mal de technique, de sens tactique et une grande habileté dans le choix de clubs, ce qui le rendra difficile aux joueurs peu expérimentés. Les frappeurs auront de belles occasions de prendre des risques, avec émotions garanties. Plusieurs trous au dessin quelque peu torturé (parfois inutilement) exigent d'être reconnus avant d'être négociés correctement, surtout quand souffle le mistral ! En ce cas, rangez la carte de scores. On attendait aussi depuis longtemps un vrai club house, il est théoriquement ouvert au printemps 2002.

The first French course designed by Seve Ballesteros, Pont Royal is kept in very good condition. The very large bunkers can lead to some very long escape shots from sand, one of the Spanish champion's specialities but often a nightmare for amateurs and pros alike. With large trees, various water hazards (a river and ponds), a few dangerous ravines and a hilly landscape (buggy recommended), Pont Royal requires a lot of technique, a good tactical mind and skill in choosing the right club. This makes it a difficult proposition for inexperienced players. Long-hitters have exciting opportunities to take risks, but several holes with a sometimes needlessly twisted layout need a little reconnaissance before hoping to make any impression, especially when the Mistral is blowing. In this case, forget the scorecard. The course has long been promised a real club-house as well, and from what we heard this is due in the Spring of 2002.

Pont Royal Golf Club — 1992

F - 13370 MALLEMORT

Office	Secrétariat	(33) 04 90 57 40 79
Pro shop	Pro-shop	(33) 04 90 57 40 79
Fax	Fax	(33) 04 90 59 45 83
Web	golf.pontroyal.free.fr	
Situation	Situation	
Salon-de-Provence (pop. 34 050), 20 km		
Annual closure	Fermeture annuelle	no
Weekly closure	Fermeture hebdomadaire	no

Fees main season Tarifs haute saison	18 holes	
	Week days Semaine	**We/Bank holidays** We/Férié
Individual Individuel	53 €	53 €
Couple Couple	106 €	106 €
Under 25: 29 €		

Caddy	Caddy	no
Electric Trolley	Chariot électrique	no
Buggy	Voiturette	30 € /18 holes
Clubs	Clubs	11 € /full day

Credit cards Cartes de crédit
VISA - CB - Eurocard - MasterCard

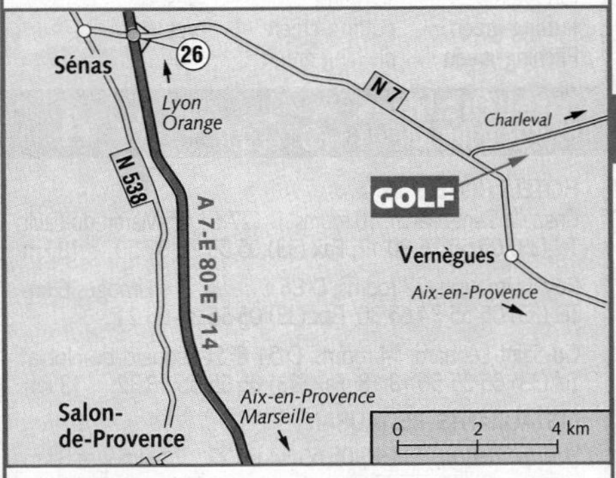

Access Accès : A7, Exit (Sortie) Sénas,
N7 → Aix-en-Provence, Golf 10 km
Map 14 on page 188 Carte 14 Page 188

Golf course PARCOURS — 16/20

Site	Site	
Maintenance	Entretien	
Architect	Architecte	Seve Ballesteros
Type	Type	country, hilly
Relief	Relief	
Water in play	Eau en jeu	
Exp. to wind	Exposé au vent	
Trees in play	Arbres en jeu	

Scorecard Carte de score	**Chp.** Chp.	**Mens** Mess.	**Ladies** Da.
Length Long.	6303	5778	4847
Par	72	72	72
Slope system	142	140	130

Advised golfing ability Niveau de jeu recommandé — 0 12 24 36

Hcp required Handicap exigé 35

Club house & amenities CLUB-HOUSE ET ANNEXES — 6/10

Pro shop	Pro-shop	
Driving range	Practice	
Sheltered	couvert	no
On grass	sur herbe	yes
Putting-green	putting-green	yes
Pitching-green	pitching green	no

Hotel facilities ENVIRONNEMENT HOTELIER — 5/10

HOTELS HÔTELS

Moulin de Vernègues, 36 rooms, D 141 € — Vernègues 1 km
Tel (33) 04 90 59 12 00, Fax (33) 04 90 59 15 90

Abbaye de Sainte-Croix, 21 rooms, D 198 € — Salon-de-Provence
Tel (33) 04 90 56 24 55, Fax (33) 04 90 56 31 12 — 12 km

Bastide de Capelongue, 17 rooms, D 366 € — Bonnieux
Tel (33) 04 90 75 89 78, Fax (33) 04 90 75 93 03 — 20 km

RESTAURANTS RESTAURANT

Abbaye de Sainte-Croix — Salon-de-Provence
Tel (33) 04 90 56 24 55 — 12 km

Le Mas du Soleil, Tel(33) 04 90 56 06 53 — Salon-de-Provence

Bastide de Capelongue, Tel (33) 04 90 75 89 78 — Bonnieux

PORCELAINE (LA)

14 | 6 | 4

Avec son relief accidenté et son sol, La Porcelaine reste toujours agréable à jouer aux beaux jours, du printemps à l'automne, quand la végétation prend des couleurs fort séduisantes. Ce parcours signé Jean Garaialde a été conçu comme une alternative privée au golf de Limoges, le premier golf public en France. Des obstacles d'eau entrent en jeu sur la moitié des trous, et constituent, avec quelques arbres stratégiquement utilisés, les principales entraves à de bons scores. Ce parcours très "campagnard" a été destiné essentiellement à satisfaire l'ensemble des membres, résidents dans la région de Limoges, et reste jouable effectivement à tous niveaux. Cependant, les grands voyageurs de golf se livrent fatalement au jeu des comparaisons, et trouveront sans doute son architecture sans éclat, et sans grandes surprises, mais l'ambiance est ici très plaisante.

With its steep slopes and soil, La Porcelaine is always pleasant to play when the weather is at its best, from spring to autumn, and when the vegetation blooms into colour. This course, designed by French champion Jean Garaialde, was designed as a private alternative to Limoges, France's first public course. Water hazards are in play on one half of the course and, along with some strategically located trees, are the main stumbling blocks to a good score. This is a very "country" style course, designed first and foremost to satisfy local members, and is effectively playable by golfers of all levels. However, hardened golf-trotters will make their usual and unavoidable comparisons and will certainly find that this design lacks both sparkle and surprise. Nonetheless, this is a club with a very pleasant atmosphere.

Golf de la Porcelaine — 1988

Célicroux
F - 87350 PANAZOL

Office	Secrétariat	(33) 05 55 31 10 69
Pro shop	Pro-shop	(33) 05 55 31 10 69
Fax	Fax	(33) 05 55 31 10 69
Web	—	
Situation	Situation	

Limoges (pop. 133 460), 6 km

Annual closure	Fermeture annuelle	no
Weekly closure	Fermeture hebdomadaire	

tuesday (mardi) 01/10 → 31/03

Fees main season Tarifs haute saison	Week days Semaine	We/Bank holidays We/Férié
		Full day
Individual Individuel	35 €	38 €
Couple Couple	70 €	76 €
Caddy Caddy		no
Electric Trolley Chariot électrique		no
Buggy Voiturette		23 € /18 holes
Clubs Clubs		8 € /full day

Credit cards Cartes de crédit
VISA - CB - Eurocard - MasterCard

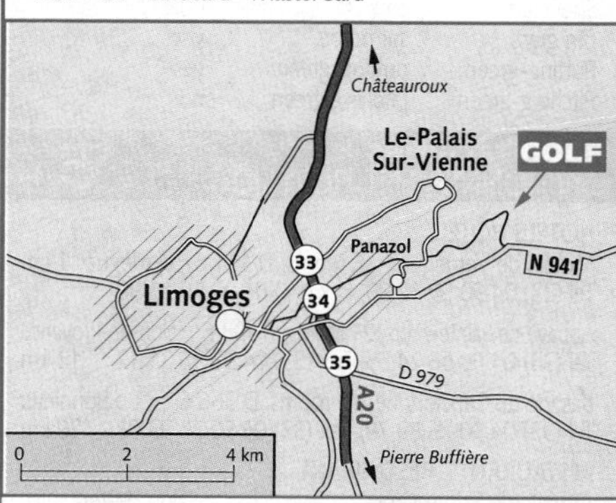

Access Accès : Limoges, D941 → Clermont-Ferrand, → Golf
Map 7 on page 174 Carte 7 Page 174

Golf course PARCOURS — 14/20

Site	Site	
Maintenance	Entretien	
Architect	Architecte	Jean Garaïalde
Type	Type	country
Relief	Relief	
Water in play	Eau en jeu	
Exp. to wind	Exposé au vent	
Trees in play	Arbres en jeu	

Scorecard Carte de score	Chp. Chp.	Mens Mess.	Ladies Da.
Length Long.	6035	5562	5218
Par	72	72	72
Slope system	135	127	131

Advised golfing ability Niveau de jeu recommandé: 0 12 24 36
Hcp required Handicap exigé: 35

Club house & amenities CLUB-HOUSE ET ANNEXES — 6/10

Pro shop	Pro-shop	
Driving range	Practice	
Sheltered	couvert	4 mats
On grass	sur herbe	yes
Putting-green	putting-green	yes
Pitching-green	pitching green	no

Hotel facilities ENVIRONNEMENT HOTELIER — 4/10

HOTELS HÔTELS

Chapelle Saint-Martin, 10 rooms, D 127 € — St-Martin-du-Fault
Tel (33) 05 55 75 80 17, Fax (33) 05 55 75 89 50 — 18 km

Royal Limousin, 77 rooms, D 86 € — Limoges 6 km
Tel (33) 05 55 34 65 30, Fax (33) 05 55 34 55 21

Gd-Saint-Léonard, 14 rooms, D 51 € — St-Léonard-de-Noblat
Tel (33) 05 55 56 18 18, Fax (33) 05 55 56 98 32 — 13 km

RESTAURANTS RESTAURANT

Philippe Redon, Tel (33) 05 55 34 66 22 — Limoges 6 km
Amphytrion, Tel (33) 05 55 33 36 39 — Limoges6 km
Chapelle Saint-Martin — Saint-Martin-du Fault
Tel (33) 05 55 75 80 17 — 18 km

PORNIC

15 | 6 | 6

A partir du neuf trous existant depuis 1929, Michel Gayon a reconstruit un 18 trous très intéressant en 1991, dans un espace assez accidenté. C'est une région traditionnelle de vacances, au sud de Nantes, mais il n'est jamais vraiment difficile d'y trouver un départ. De plus, le sol sablonneux permet de le recommander toute l'année. Cinq trous sont agrémentés de pins, les treize autres se trouvent dans une zone de bord de mer, où les fairways sont séparés par des buttes, créant ainsi un peu d'intimité. On regrettera qu'ils soient à peu près tous parallèles, mais cela permet aux frappeurs sauvages de s'écarter du droit chemin sans être trop pénalisés, ni menacer les joueurs de tous niveaux pouvant évoluer ici. Assez long des départs arrière, la disposition des départs permet cependant de se faire un parcours "à sa main". On soulignera enfin la réfection du green du 18, et un drainage conséquent sur la partie originale du parcours.

Starting out with a 9-holer opened in 1929, Michel Gayon rebuilt a very interesting 18-hole course in 1991 over very hilly terrain. This is traditional holiday territory, to the south of Nantes, but getting a tee-off time poses no real problem. In addition, the sandy sub-soil makes it playable all year. Five holes are enhanced with pine-trees, the thirteen others run along the sea-shore, where the fairways are separated by sand-hills and are sometimes a little too close together. It is a shame they all run more or less parallel, up and down, although this allows wild-hitters to wander off the straight and narrow without too much penalty and encourages players of all abilities to play here together. Rather long from the back, the number of different tees allows golfers to choose a course to suit their game. Lastly, we can report on a newly re-laid green on the 18th and extensive new drainage over the original section of the course.

Golf de Pornic — 1929

Avenue Sacalby-Newby
F - 44210 SAINTE-MARIE-SUR-MER

Office	Secrétariat	(33) 02 40 82 06 69
Pro shop	Pro-shop	(33) 02 40 82 06 69
Fax	Fax	(33) 02 40 82 80 65
Web	—	
Situation	Situation	

Pornic (pop. 9 810), 2 km - Nantes (pop. 252 030), 52 km

Annual closure Fermeture annuelle — no

Weekly closure Fermeture hebdomadaire

wednesday in winter (Mercredi en hiver)

Fees main season Tarifs haute saison — 18 holes

	Week days Semaine	We/Bank holidays We/Férié
Individual Individuel	43 €	43 €
Couple Couple	86 €	86 €

Under 21 & Students: – 50%

Caddy	Caddy	no
Electric Trolley	Chariot électrique	no
Buggy	Voiturette	23 €/18 holes
Clubs	Clubs	8 €/full day

Credit cards Cartes de crédit
VISA - CB - Eurocard - MasterCard

D 96
La Plaine-sur-Mer
D 213
D 86
D 13
PORNIC
D 751
GOLF
0 2 4 km

Access Accès : Nantes D751, Exit (Sortie) Pornic Ouest → Sainte-Marie-sur-Mer

Map 6 on page 172 Carte 6 Page 172

Golf course PARCOURS — 15/20

Site	Site	
Maintenance	Entretien	
Architect	Architecte	Michel Gayon, Jacques Lebreton
Type	Type	links, forest
Relief	Relief	
Water in play	Eau en jeu	
Exp. to wind	Exposé au vent	
Trees in play	Arbres en jeu	

Scorecard Carte de score	Chp. Chp.	Mens Mess.	Ladies Da.
Length Long.	6112	5545	5017
Par	72	72	72
Slope system	144	133	128

Advised golfing ability Niveau de jeu recommandé — 0 12 24 36

Hcp required Handicap exigé — no

Club house & amenities CLUB-HOUSE ET ANNEXES — 6/10

Pro shop	Pro-shop	
Driving range	Practice	
Sheltered	couvert	6 mats
On grass	sur herbe	yes
Putting-green	putting-green	yes
Pitching-green	pitching green	no

Hotel facilities ENVIRONNEMENT HOTELIER — 6/10

HOTELS HÔTELS

Alliance, 88 rooms, D 143 € — Pornic
Tel (33) 02 40 82 21 21, Fax (33) 02 40 82 80 89 — 2 km

Relais Saint-Giles, 24 rooms, D 61 € — Pornic
Tel (33) 02 40 82 02 25 — 2 km

Les Sablons, 30 rooms, D 65 € — Sainte-Marie
Tel (33) 02 40 82 09 14, Fax (33) 02 40 82 04 26 — 1 km

RESTAURANTS RESTAURANT

Le Beau Rivage, Tel (33) 02 40 82 03 08 — Pornic 2 km

Anne de Bretagne — La Plaine-sur-Mer
Tel (33) 02 40 21 54 72 — 10 km

PRINCE DE PROVENCE (VIDAUBAN) 19 | 8 | 7

Ce chef-d'œuvre de Trent Jones est totalement réservé à ses membres, mais nous ne pouvions l'ignorer tant sont flagrantes sa qualité et sa beauté. Le terrain est aimablement animé, bien boisé sans être oppressant, le paysage provençal calme et magnifique. En une sorte de synthèse de l'architecture et du jeu, c'est un golf où l'emplacement du drapeau détermine ce qu'il faut jouer au départ, où la stratégie est aussi importante que la puissance ou la précision : aucun drive n'y est impossible, mais chacun doit être réfléchi en vue du coup suivant. L'esthétique du lieu comme du tracé sont d'une exemplaire sobriété : ni trop ni trop peu. Quelques pins solitaires empiètent comme des sentinelles sur les fairways, aussi rares que menaçants. Un seul obstacle d'eau, aussi nécessaire que suffisant. Il faut ici contrôler ses trajectoires et ses effets, maîtriser tous les clubs et tous les coups. Et comme les alentours des greens,très travaillés, exigent un petit jeu d'une rare finesse, on aura compris la sensation de privilège que l'on peut éprouver à jouer ici. Unique et splendide, bref princier.

This Trent Jones masterpiece is totally private but its excellence and beauty meant we could not ignore it. The site is pleasantly sloping terrain, calm and magnificent Provence countryside with a lot of trees that are never too obtrusive. Architecture and golf combine here in such a way that pin positions decide which club you use off the tee, as strategy is just as important as power or precision. No drive is impossible but the tee-shot does have to be carefully considered with a view to what you do next. The beauty of the site and the course are wonderfully discreet, neither too much nor too little. A few solitary pine-trees jut onto the fairways like lone sentinels but they are as threatening as they rare, while the single water hazard is perhaps as necessary as it is sufficient. Control is the key-word here, of flight, spin, clubs and every shot you make. And as the cleverly designed areas around the greens call for a very sharp short game, you can understand the privilege of being able to play here. A unique, splendid and indeed a princely course.

Le Prince de Provence — 1999

Route Départementale 72
F - 83550 VIDAUBAN

Office	Secrétariat	(33) 04 94 73 55 87
Pro shop	Pro-shop	(33) 04 94 73 55 87
Fax	Fax	(33) 04 94 73 57 24
Web	—	
Situation	Situation	

Cannes (pop. 68 676), 68 km - St Tropez (pop. 5 754), 25 km

Annual closure	Fermeture annuelle	no
Weekly closure	Fermeture hebdomadaire	no

Fees main season Tarifs haute saison	Week days Semaine	We/Bank holidays We/Férié
18 holes		
Individual Individuel	—	—
Couple Couple	—	—

* Only with members

Caddy	Caddy	no
Electric Trolley	Chariot électrique	yes
Buggy	Voiturette	yes
Clubs	Clubs	yes

Credit cards Cartes de crédit
VISA - Eurocard - MasterCard - DC - AMEX

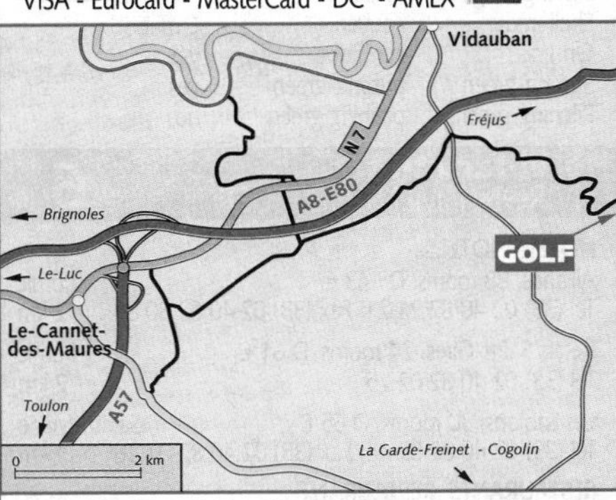

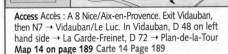

Access Accès : A 8 Nice/Aix-en-Provence. Exit Vidauban, then N7 → Vidauban/Le Luc. In Vidauban, D 48 on left hand side → La Garde-Freinet, D 72 → Plan-de-la-Tour
Map 14 on page 189 Carte 14 Page 189

Golf course PARCOURS 19/20

Site	Site	
Maintenance	Entretien	
Architect	Architecte	Robert Trent Jones, R. Trent Jones Jr
Type	Type	inland, open country
Relief	Relief	
Water in play	Eau en jeu	
Exp. to wind	Exposé au vent	
Trees in play	Arbres en jeu	

Scorecard Carte de score	Chp. Chp.	Mens Mess.	Ladies Da.
Length Long.	6640	6180	5229
Par	72	72	72
Slope system	—	—	—

Advised golfing ability Niveau de jeu recommandé: 0 12 24 36
Hcp required Handicap exigé: no

Club house & amenities CLUB-HOUSE ET ANNEXES 8/10

Pro shop	Pro-shop	
Driving range	Practice	
Sheltered	couvert	no
On grass	sur herbe	yes
Putting-green	putting-green	yes
Pitching-green	pitching green	yes

Hotel facilities ENVIRONNEMENT HOTELIER 7/10

HOTELS HÔTELS

Le Logis du Guetteur, 12 rooms, D 104 € — Les Arcs 15 km
Tel (33) 04 94 99 51 10, Fax (33) 04 94 99 51 29

Mas des Brugassières, 11 rooms, D 99 € — Plan-de-la-Tour 14 km
Tel (33) 04 94 55 50 55, Fax (33) 04 94 55 50 51

RESTAURANTS RESTAURANT

Bruno, Tel (33) 04 94 85 93 93 — Lorgues 10 km

La Bastide des Magnans, Tel (33) 04 94 99 43 91 — Vidauban 2 km

Concorde, Tel (33) 04 94 73 01 19 — Vidauban 4 km

RARAY (CHÂTEAU DE) La Licorne | 14 | 7 | 4

Ce parcours d'inspiration très britannique a été tracé par le professionnel français Patrice Léglise, head pro à Chantilly. Plusieurs trous inspirés à la fois du style de Simpson et de l'architecture de links ont été tracés en plaine, et les autres dans un même esprit ont été insinués dans une belle forêt, au terrain parfois humide. L'ensemble est d'une grande franchise, les difficultés techniques sont réelles mais raisonnables, avec quelques fossés d'apparence naturelle venant en jeu. Le dessin des bunkers est aussi sobre qu'esthétiquement réussi, de même que leur placement très stratégique. Le 18, dans une allée bordée de grands arbres, est d'une esthétique "à la française" très adéquate pour un retour vers le château, autrefois utilisé comme décor du film "La Belle et la Bête" de Jean Cocteau, et que l'on aimerait voir intégralement restauré. Le parcours étant plat, il permet aux joueurs de tous âges d'y évoluer. Autrefois fragile par temps de pluie, le plaisir d'y jouer a été nettement amélioré par des drainages, mais aussi par un nettoyage attentif des sous-bois et des roughs.

This very British style course was laid out by the French professional Patrice Léglise. There are several holes in open countryside that are reminiscent of the best links courses, while the others, equally attractive, run through a beautiful forest over rather damp terrain. The whole course is an honest test of golf with real but reasonable technical difficulties and a few natural-looking ditches which come into play. The bunkers are as discreet in design as they are pleasant to look at and strategically located. The18th hole, laid out along a wide alley edged by large trees is very French in style and a suitable way to return to the castle which, may it be said, was used for filming "The Beauty and the Beast" by Jean Cocteau. We would like to see it wholly restored one day. A flat course for golfers of all ages, but preferably in dry weather. Although once very prone to wet weather, it is much more fun playing here now that the drainage has been significant and the undergrowth and rough have been carefully trimmed back.

Château de Raray — 1988

4, rue Nicolas Lancy
F - 60810 RARAY

Office	Secrétariat	(33) 03 44 54 70 61
Pro shop	Pro-shop	(33) 03 44 54 70 61
Fax	Fax	(33) 03 44 54 72 57
E-mail	golfpari@club-internet.fr	
Situation	Situation	

Senlis (pop. 14 430), 6 km - Paris (pop. 2 152 333), 54 km

Annual closure	Fermeture annuelle	no
Weekly closure	Fermeture hebdomadaire	tuesday/mardi

Fees main season Tarifs haute saison	18 holes	
	Week days Semaine	**We/Bank holidays** We/Férié
Individual Individuel	38 €	66 €
Couple Couple	76 €	132 €

Week ends: GF 46 € after 13.30 / Seniors: 23 € (Fridays)

Caddy	Caddy	no
Electric Trolley	Chariot électrique	no
Buggy	Voiturette	23 € /18 holes
Clubs	Clubs	8 € /full day

Credit cards Cartes de crédit
VISA - CB - Eurocard - MasterCard

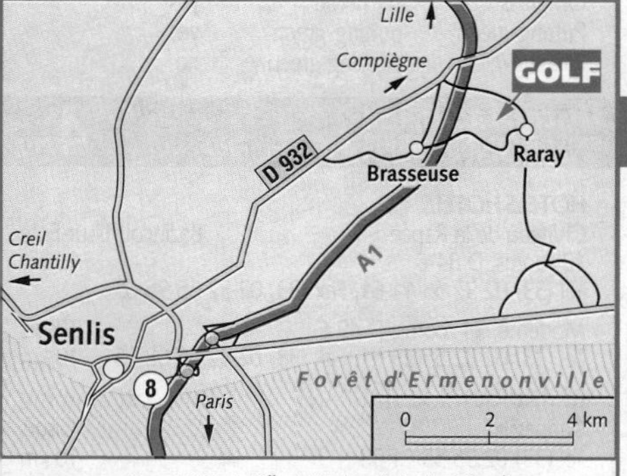

Access Accès : A1 Paris Lille, Exit (Sortie) No 8 Senlis → Creil/Chantilly, D932 → Compiègne, → Château de Raray
Map 1 on page 162 Carte 1 Page 162

Golf course PARCOURS — 14/20

Site	Site	
Maintenance	Entretien	
Architect	Architecte	Patrice Léglise
Type	Type	forest, open country
Relief	Relief	
Water in play	Eau en jeu	
Exp. to wind	Exposé au vent	
Trees in play	Arbres en jeu	

Scorecard Carte de score	**Chp.** Chp.	**Mens** Mess.	**Ladies** Da.
Length Long.	6459	5918	5184
Par	72	72	72
Slope system	133	126	127

Advised golfing ability — 0 12 24 36
Niveau de jeu recommandé
Hcp required Handicap exigé — 35 (We)

Club house & amenities CLUB-HOUSE ET ANNEXES — 7/10

Pro shop	Pro-shop	
Driving range	Practice	
Sheltered	couvert	9 mats
On grass	sur herbe	yes
Putting-green	putting-green	yes
Pitching-green	pitching green	yes

Hotel facilities ENVIRONNEMENT HOTELIER — 4/10

HOTELS HÔTELS

Château de Raray, — on site
10 rooms, D 114 €
Tel (33) 03 44 54 59 30, Fax (33) 03 44 54 74 97

Auberge de Fontaine — Fontaine-Chaalis 11 km
8 rooms, D 44 €
Tel (33) 03 44 54 20 22, Fax (33) 03 44 60 25 38

RESTAURANTS RESTAURANT

Scaramouche — Senlis 6 km
Tel (33) 03 44 53 01 26

La Maison du Gourmet — Le Meux 12 km
Tel (33) 03 44 91 10 10

REBETZ

16 | 6 | 4

Ce parcours reconnu pour la qualité et la variété de son architecture (Jean-Pascal Fourès), a beaucoup évolué avec la maturité de nombreuses plantations. Les zones de plaine constituant la majorité du terrain sont ainsi bien mieux paysagées, et les différents trous mieux délimités. Relativement aisé par beau temps, il devient plus complexe avec le vent, souvent fréquent ici, comme sur un links, auxquels certains trous font référence. L'eau vient en jeu sur huit trous, complétant bien la diversité des obstacles rencontrés. Les greens sont souvent très modelés, et les placements de drapeau (parfois peu nombreux) peuvent en modifier considérablement l'attaque, mais leur qualité reste constamment élevée (notamment en hiver). Sans être absolument exceptionnel, ce parcours a magnifiquement utilisé un budget réduit. Le Club-House est une véritable maison de campagne où l'accueil est chaleureux. Et les autres bâtiments d'une vaste cour intérieure (une ancienne ferme) sont peu à peu aménagés.

This course, acknowledged for the excellence and variety of layout (courtesy of Jean-Pascal Fourès), has developed enormously now that extensive plantation programme is starting to show signs of maturity. The areas of open countryside which form the largest part of the course are much better landscaped and the holes have gained in individuality. Relatively easy in fine weather, the frequent wind makes playing golf a trickier business, rather as if playing a links course. Water is in play on eight holes and completes the diversity of the course's hazards. The greens are often well-contoured and pin-positions can considerably change the configuration of approach shots, but they remain consistently excellent putting surfaces (particularly in winter). Without being truly exceptional, the course has put restricted resources to magnificent use. The club-house is a genuine country-style manor which extends a warm welcome to all. The other buildings around a huge inner courtyard (old farm buildings) are gradually being refurbished.

Golf Club de Rebetz — 1988

Route de Noailles
F - 60240 CHAUMONT-EN-VEXIN

Office	Secrétariat	(33) 03 44 49 15 54
Pro shop	Pro-shop	(33) 03 44 49 15 54
Fax	Fax	(33) 03 44 49 14 26
Web	www.rebetz.com	
Situation	Situation	Paris, 67 km
Annual closure	Fermeture annuelle	no
Weekly closure	Fermeture hebdomadaire	no

Fees main season Tarifs haute saison	Week days Semaine	We/Bank holidays We/Férié
18 holes		
Individual Individuel	23 €	53 €
Couple Couple	46 €	106 €

Under 21: 15 € (Weekdays) - 30 € (We) / Seniors: 15 € (Tuesdays)

Caddy	Caddy	no
Electric Trolley	Chariot électrique	9 € /18 holes
Buggy	Voiturette	30 € /18 holes
Clubs	Clubs	9 € /full day

Credit cards Cartes de crédit
VISA - CB - Eurocard - MasterCard - AMEX

Access Accès : A15 Pontoise, N14 → Magny-en-Vexin, turn right on D153 → Chaumont-en-Vexin, turn right in Chaumont-en-Vexin → Golf
Map 1 on page 162 Carte 1 Page 162

Golf course PARCOURS — 16/20

Site	Site	
Maintenance	Entretien	
Architect	Architecte	Jean-Pascal Fourès
Type	Type	parkland, open country
Relief	Relief	
Water in play	Eau en jeu	
Exp. to wind	Exposé au vent	
Trees in play	Arbres en jeu	

Scorecard Carte de score	Chp. Chp.	Mens Mess.	Ladies Da.
Length Long.	6409	5885	5317
Par	73	73	73
Slope system	127	120	122

Advised golfing ability Niveau de jeu recommandé — 0 12 24 36
Hcp required Handicap exigé — 35 (We)

Club house & amenities CLUB-HOUSE ET ANNEXES — 6/10

Pro shop	Pro-shop	
Driving range	Practice	
Sheltered	couvert	14 mats
On grass	sur herbe	yes
Putting-green	putting-green	yes
Pitching-green	pitching green	no

Hotel facilities ENVIRONNEMENT HOTELIER — 4/10

HOTELS HÔTELS

Château de la Rapée — Bazincourt-sur-Epte
13 rooms, D 84 € — 13 km
Tel (33) 02 32 55 11 61, Fax (33) 02 32 55 95 65

Moderne, 31 rooms, D 49 € — Gisors
Tel (33) 02 32 55 23 51, Fax (33) 02 32 55 08 75 — 10 km

RESTAURANTS RESTAURANT

Cappeville, — Gisors
Tel (33) 02 35 55 11 08 — 10 km

La Pommeraie — Gisors
Tel (33) 02 32 55 11 61 — 13 km

REIMS-CHAMPAGNE

13 | 7 | 6

Relativement plat et dans un espace très agréablement boisé, c'est une sorte de grand domaine avec un joli château où tous les grands noms du Champagne ont laissé leur marque. Les 9 trous construits en 1927 ont été remodelés et portés à 18 trous par Michael Fenn en 1977. Leur dessin suit les contours du terrain sans imagination particulière et seuls les par 5 sortent un peu de l'ordinaire. Les arbres constituent les principaux obstacles, mais ils font plus de peur que de mal. En dépit d'un assez bon rythme de jeu, on ne fera certainement pas de long détour pour venir jouer ici, mais si l'on passe dans la région, la visite sera sympathique et amusante. Nous sommes peut-être difficiles, mais on imagine toujours qu'il serait possible de remodeler le parcours sans lui retirer son caractère familial. Disons qu'on peut vraiment imaginer un parcours bien plus pétillant…

Relatively flat but in a pleasant woodland setting, this is a sort of large estate around a pretty castle where all the great names in champagne have left their mark. Originally a nine-hole course opened in 1927, it was upgraded to 18 holes by Michael Fenn in 1977. The layout follows the contours of the terrain without too much imagination, and only the par 5s really stand out. The main hazards here are the trees, but their bark (no pun intended) is worse than their bite. Despite a good playing tempo, it is hard to envisage making any long detour to come and play here, but if you are in the region, Reims-Champagne is a pleasant and amusing visit. Perhaps we are being a little too finicky, but we believe this course could be redesigned for the better without detracting from its family-style character. Let's just say that it is easy to imagine a slightly more "sparkling" course.

Reims-Champagne **1977**
Château des Dames de France
F - 51390 GUEUX

Office	Secrétariat	(33) 03 26 05 46 10
Pro shop	Pro-shop	(33) 03 26 05 46 10
Fax	Fax	(33) 03 26 05 46 19
Web	www.golf-reims.com	
Situation	Situation	Reims (pop. 180 620), 5 km
Annual closure	Fermeture annuelle	no
Weekly closure	Fermeture hebdomadaire	

monday (lundi): restaurant closed (11 → 03)

Fees main season Tarifs haute saison		full day
	Week days Semaine	**We/Bank holidays** We/Férié
Individual Individuel	34 €	46 €
Couple Couple	68 €	92 €

Under 22: 19 € (Weekdays) - 23 € (We)

Caddy	Caddy	no
Electric Trolley	Chariot électrique	no
Buggy	Voiturette	23 € /18 holes
Clubs	Clubs	14 € /full day

Credit cards Cartes de crédit
VISA - CB - Eurocard - Mastercard

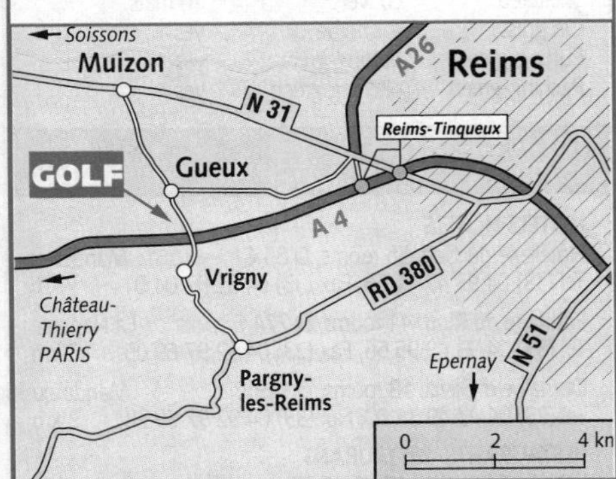

Access Accès : A4 Exit (Sortie) Reims Tinqueux → Soissons, → Gueux
Map 3 on page 167 Carte 3 Page 167

Golf course PARCOURS 13/20

Site	Site	
Maintenance	Entretien	
Architect	Architecte	Michael Fenn
Type	Type	parkland, forest
Relief	Relief	
Water in play	Eau en jeu	
Exp. to wind	Exposé au vent	
Trees in play	Arbres en jeu	

Scorecard Carte de score	**Chp.** Chp.	**Mens** Mess.	**Ladies** Da.
Length Long.	5850	5712	4815
Par	72	72	72
Slope system	123	125	118

Advised golfing ability 0 12 24 36
Niveau de jeu recommandé
Hcp required Handicap exigé 35

Club house & amenities CLUB-HOUSE ET ANNEXES 7/10

Pro shop	Pro-shop	
Driving range	Practice	
Sheltered	couvert	4 mats
On grass	sur herbe	no, 20 mats open air
Putting-green	putting-green	yes
Pitching-green	pitching green	yes

Hotel facilities ENVIRONNEMENT HOTELIER 6/10

HOTELS HÔTELS
Les Crayères, 19 rooms, D 305 € — Reims 5 km
Tel (33) 03 26 82 80 80, Fax (33) 03 26 82 65 52

Grand Hôtel des Templiers, 17 rooms, D 183 € — Reims
Tel (33) 03 26 88 55 08, Fax (33) 03 26 47 80 60

La Paix, 106 rooms, D 91 € — Reims
Tel (33) 03 26 40 04 08, Fax (33) 03 26 47 75 04

RESTAURANTS RESTAURANT
Les Crayères, Tel (33) 03 26 82 80 80 — Reims
Vigneraie, Tel (33) 03 26 88 67 27 — Reims
Chardonnay, Tel (33) 03 26 06 08 60 — Reims

RIVIÉRA GOLF CLUB

13 | 7 | 8

Le Riviera s'inscrit dans un paysage totalement différent de son voisin de Mandelieu, démontrant la diversité des paysages français de la Côte. Quelques trous plats et larges contrastent avec des trous "de montagne" souvent étroits par leur dessin. Les arbres, de nombreux bunkers et quelques obstacles d'eau créent de nombreuses difficultés, accentuées par des greens surélevés et un relief qui amène à conseiller la voiturette. Avec quatre par 3, parcours est passé à un par 71 conforme à sa longueur, réduite en raison de l'espace limité. Certains trous qui manquaient un peu de franchise ont été modifiés, et les visiteurs ont plus de facilité à l'apprécier immédiatement. Un golf parfois surprenant, au rythme heurté, où il faut garder la tête froide. Les puristes regretteront la disparition de quelques bunkers très stratégiques, qui n'a pas forcément rendu les scores meilleurs. Cependant les améliorations récentes du tracé et les progrès de l'entretien en général ont bien fait progresser ce parcours un instant mal en point.

Not far from the centenary course of Cannes-Mandelieu, the Riviera course is located in a totally different setting, as if to demonstrate the variety of French landscapes over a relatively limited surface area. A few flat and wide holes are in stark contrast with the often tightly laid out mountain-style holes. The trees, countless bunkers and a few water hazards create a lot of problems, compounded by elevated greens and steep slopes (buggy please!). With four par 3s, the course has been shortened to a par 71 in line with overall yardage, which is restricted owing to lack of space. Some holes, which had a sneaky feel to them, have been altered and visitors will feel the difference right away. A sometimes surprising and slightly inconsistent course, but a cool head will see you home safely. Purists will rue the removal of some very strategic bunkers, although scoring is still not really any easier. However, the recent improvements to the layout and much improved maintenance in general have worked wonders for this course which not so long ago was feeling a little sorry for itself.

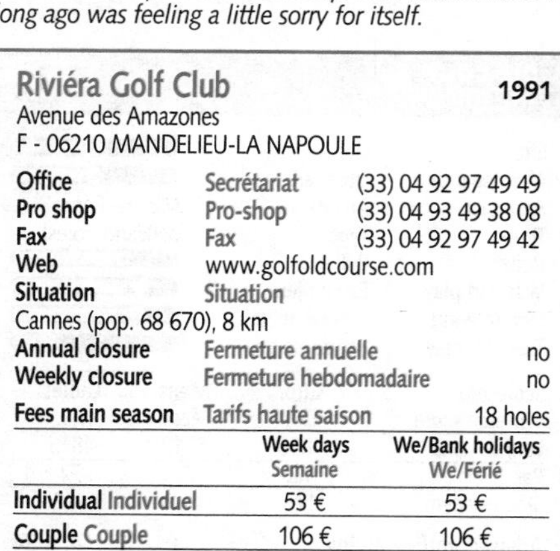

Riviéra Golf Club — 1991

Avenue des Amazones
F - 06210 MANDELIEU-LA NAPOULE

Office	Secrétariat	(33) 04 92 97 49 49
Pro shop	Pro-shop	(33) 04 93 49 38 08
Fax	Fax	(33) 04 92 97 49 42
Web	www.golfoldcourse.com	
Situation	Situation	

Cannes (pop. 68 670), 8 km

Annual closure	Fermeture annuelle	no
Weekly closure	Fermeture hebdomadaire	no

Fees main season Tarifs haute saison	18 holes	
	Week days Semaine	**We/Bank holidays** We/Férié
Individual Individuel	53 €	53 €
Couple Couple	106 €	106 €

Under 18: 23 €(Weekdays & We)

Caddy	Caddy	no
Electric Trolley	Chariot électrique	15 € /18 holes
Buggy	Voiturette	30 € /18 holes
Clubs	Clubs	15 € /full day

Credit cards Cartes de crédit
VISA - CB - Eurocard - MasterCard - AMEX

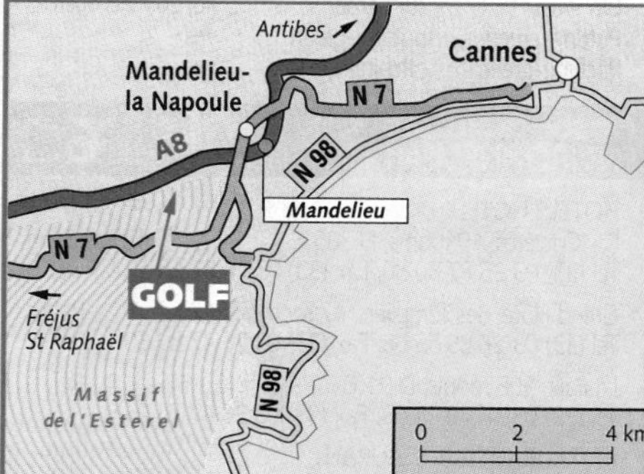

Access Accès : A8 Exit (Sortie Mandelieu-La Napoule), In Mandelieu, turn right on RN7 → Fréjus

Map 14 on page 189 Carte 14 Page 189

Golf course PARCOURS — 13/20

Site	Site	
Maintenance	Entretien	
Architect	Architecte	R. Trent Jones Sr
Type	Type	parkland, residential
Relief	Relief	
Water in play	Eau en jeu	
Exp. to wind	Exposé au vent	
Trees in play	Arbres en jeu	

Scorecard Carte de score	**Chp.** Chp.	**Mens** Mess.	**Ladies** Da.
Length Long.	5513	4984	4307
Par	71	71	71
Slope system	125	122	118

Advised golfing ability Niveau de jeu recommandé — 0 12 24 36

Hcp required Handicap exigé — 30 (morning)

Club house & amenities CLUB-HOUSE ET ANNEXES — 7/10

Pro shop	Pro-shop	
Driving range	Practice	
Sheltered	couvert	10 mats
On grass	sur herbe	yes
Putting-green	putting-green	yes
Pitching-green	pitching green	yes

Hotel facilities ENVIRONNEMENT HOTELIER — 8/10

HOTELS HÔTELS

Hôtellerie du Golf, 55 rooms, D 85 € — Mandelieu
Tel (33) 04 93 49 11 66, Fax (33) 04 92 97 04 01 — 2 km

Ermitage du Riou, 41 rooms, D 274 € — La Napoule
Tel (33) 04 93 49 95 56, Fax (33) 04 92 97 69 05 — 3 km

Domaine d'Olival, 18 rooms, D 149 € — Mandelieu
Tel (33) 04 43 49 31 00, Fax (33) 04 92 97 69 28 — 3 km

RESTAURANTS RESTAURANT

L'Oasis, Tel (33) 04 93 49 95 52 — La Napoule 4 km

L'Armorial, Tel (33) 04 93 49 91 80 — La Napoule

Le Riou, Tel (33) 04 93 49 95 56 — La Napoule 3 km

ROCHEFORT-CHISAN

14 | 6 | 4

C'est toujours un plaisir de retrouver ce type de parcours en forêt, tel que l'on ne peut plus guère en construire aujourd'hui. Ce parcours classique, dessiné par Fred Hawtree, et ouvert en 1964, a été ensuite acquis par le groupe japonais Chisan. Ce parcours offre de magnifiques lumières au printemps et en automne, ajoutant à l'agrément du jeu sur un sol de sable et de terre de bruyère. On peut ainsi l'apparenter à des parcours " inland " tel que The Berkshire. Ce n'est sans doute pas un chef-d'œuvre absolu, mais il reste très plaisant à jouer, offrant une grande variété de coups, et nécessitant un bon travail des trajectoires de balle. Les obstacles sont essentiellement les arbres, souvent très dangereux car le parcours est assez étroit, mais aussi les bunkers de fairway et de green, et le relief, parfois assez accidenté pour troubler dans le choix de clubs. Rochefort n'a pas beaucoup changé depuis quelques années, et la seule construction d'une pièce d'eau au 2 n'était pas forcément indipensable au jeu.

It is always a pleasure to play this type of woodland course, which nowadays is virtually impossible to build. This classic layout designed by Fred Hawtree was opened in 1964 and subsequently purchased by the Japanese group Chisan. The light and reflections in spring and autumn are a joy to behold, adding to the pleasure of playing on sandy sub-soil and moor-land. This gives it much in common with inland courses such as The Berkshire. Rochefort is probably not a complete masterpiece but it is a very pleasant course to play, requiring a whole variety of shots and ball-control. The hazards are basically the trees, often dangerous as they lean over some pretty tight fairways. But don't forget the fairway and green-side bunkers, either, or the sharp relief which makes club selection harder than usual. Rochefort has hardly changed at all in recent years and the addition of water on hole N°2 was hardly a necessity.

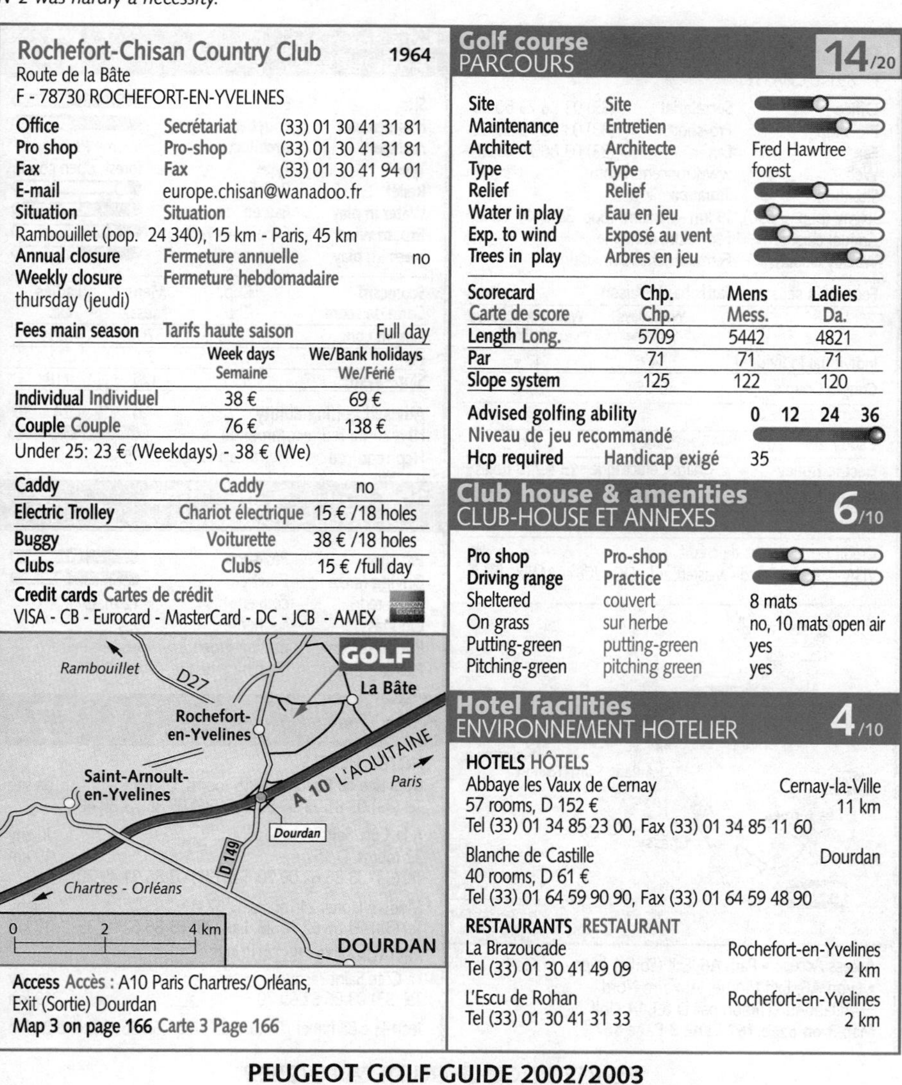

Rochefort-Chisan Country Club 1964
Route de la Bâte
F - 78730 ROCHEFORT-EN-YVELINES

Office	Secrétariat	(33) 01 30 41 31 81
Pro shop	Pro-shop	(33) 01 30 41 31 81
Fax	Fax	(33) 01 30 41 94 01
E-mail	europe.chisan@wanadoo.fr	
Situation	Situation	

Rambouillet (pop. 24 340), 15 km - Paris, 45 km

Annual closure	Fermeture annuelle	no
Weekly closure	Fermeture hebdomadaire	

thursday (jeudi)

Fees main season Tarifs haute saison — Full day

	Week days Semaine	We/Bank holidays We/Férié
Individual Individuel	38 €	69 €
Couple Couple	76 €	138 €

Under 25: 23 € (Weekdays) - 38 € (We)

Caddy	Caddy	no
Electric Trolley	Chariot électrique	15 € /18 holes
Buggy	Voiturette	38 € /18 holes
Clubs	Clubs	15 € /full day

Credit cards Cartes de crédit
VISA - CB - Eurocard - MasterCard - DC - JCB - AMEX

Access Accès : A10 Paris Chartres/Orléans, Exit (Sortie) Dourdan
Map 3 on page 166 Carte 3 Page 166

Golf course PARCOURS 14/20

Site	Site	
Maintenance	Entretien	
Architect	Architecte	Fred Hawtree
Type	Type	forest
Relief	Relief	
Water in play	Eau en jeu	
Exp. to wind	Exposé au vent	
Trees in play	Arbres en jeu	

Scorecard Carte de score	Chp. Chp.	Mens Mess.	Ladies Da.
Length Long.	5709	5442	4821
Par	71	71	71
Slope system	125	122	120

Advised golfing ability Niveau de jeu recommandé — 0 12 24 36
Hcp required Handicap exigé 35

Club house & amenities CLUB-HOUSE ET ANNEXES 6/10

Pro shop	Pro-shop	
Driving range	Practice	
Sheltered	couvert	8 mats
On grass	sur herbe	no, 10 mats open air
Putting-green	putting-green	yes
Pitching-green	pitching green	yes

Hotel facilities ENVIRONNEMENT HOTELIER 4/10

HOTELS HÔTELS
Abbaye les Vaux de Cernay — Cernay-la-Ville 11 km
57 rooms, D 152 €
Tel (33) 01 34 85 23 00, Fax (33) 01 34 85 11 60

Blanche de Castille — Dourdan
40 rooms, D 61 €
Tel (33) 01 64 59 90 90, Fax (33) 01 64 59 48 90

RESTAURANTS RESTAURANT
La Brazoucade — Rochefort-en-Yvelines 2 km
Tel (33) 01 30 41 49 09

L'Escu de Rohan — Rochefort-en-Yvelines 2 km
Tel (33) 01 30 41 31 33

RONCEMAY

15 | 7 | 7

Tracé principalement en forêt de chênes, hêtres et bouleaux (avec une demi-douzaine de trous de style links), et sur un terrain peu accidenté, ce parcours porte sans aucun doute la signature de Jeremy Pern, pour le nombre et le dessin des bunkers, de fairways comme de défense des greens. Le dessin est assez varié pour exiger tous les types de coups, ou même offrir un choix entre les approches roulées à la britannique et le "jeu de cible" à l'américaine. Les obstacles d'eau sont peu nombreux et pas trop dangereux, tous les niveaux de jeu peuvent donc cohabiter sur ce golf plaisant, dans un décor très agréable. Les greens sont de bonne dimension, et généralement très modelés : attention aux trois putts... Avec un très joli hôtel sur place, confortable et pourvu d'une bonne table, ce golf constitue un ensemble plein de charme, et une plaisante destination de week-end au calme.

This course is basically laid out through a forest of oak, beech and birch trees (plus half a dozen links holes) over flattish terrain. Looking at the number and design of bunkers, the fairways and greens, there is no doubt that this is a Jeremy Pern creation. The layout is varied enough to demand every shot in the book or even offer a choice between British "bump and run" shots and American-style target golf. Water hazards are few and far between and not too dangerous, so players of all abilities can play this pleasant course in a very attractive setting. The greens are large and undulating so watch out for the 3 putts. The very pretty hotel on site serving excellent food makes this a very charming course and a pleasant destination for a peaceful weekend.

Domaine de Roncemay — 1991

F - 89110 CHASSY

Office	Secrétariat	(33) 03 86 73 50 50
Pro shop	Pro-shop	(33) 03 86 73 50 62
Fax	Fax	(33) 03 86 73 69 46
Web	www.roncemay.com	
Situation	Situation	

Joigny (pop. 9 690), 19 km - Auxerre (pop. 38 810), 20 km

Annual closure	Fermeture annuelle	no
Weekly closure	Fermeture hebdomadaire	no

Fees main season Tarifs haute saison	Week days Semaine	We/Bank holidays We/Férié
		Full day
Individual Individuel	34 €	47 €
Couple Couple	58 €	87 €

Caddy	Caddy	no
Electric Trolley	Chariot électrique	13 € /18 holes
Buggy	Voiturette	30 € /18 holes
Clubs	Clubs	8 € /18 holes

Credit cards Cartes de crédit
VISA - CB - Eurocard - MasterCard - DC - JCB - AMEX

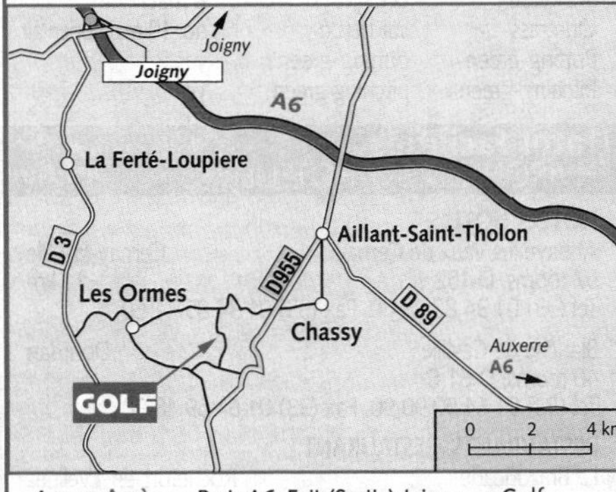

Access Accès : • Paris A6, Exit (Sortie) Joigny, → Golf
• Lyon A6, Exit (Sortie) Auxerre Nord
→ Aillant-sur-Tholon par D 89, → Golf

Map 3 on page 167 Carte 3 Page 167

Golf course PARCOURS — 15/20

Site	Site	
Maintenance	Entretien	
Architect	Architecte	Jeremy Pern
Type	Type	forest, open country
Relief	Relief	
Water in play	Eau en jeu	
Exp. to wind	Exposé au vent	
Trees in play	Arbres en jeu	

Scorecard Carte de score	Chp. Chp.	Mens Mess.	Ladies Da.
Length Long.	6270	5702	4864
Par	72	72	72
Slope system	133	125	118

Advised golfing ability Niveau de jeu recommandé: 0 12 24 36

Hcp required Handicap exigé: 35

Club house & amenities CLUB-HOUSE ET ANNEXES — 7/10

Pro shop	Pro-shop	
Driving range	Practice	
Sheltered	couvert	12 mats
On grass	sur herbe	yes
Putting-green	putting-green	yes
Pitching-green	pitching green	yes

Hotel facilities ENVIRONNEMENT HOTELIER — 7/10

HOTELS HÔTELS

Domaine de Roncemay, 15 rooms, D 168 € — on site
Tel (33) 03 86 73 50 50, Fax (33) 03 86 73 69 46

A la Côte Saint-Jacques — Joigny 19 km
32 rooms, D 152 €
Tel (33) 03 86 62 09 70, Fax (33) 03 86 91 49 70

Modern'Hôtel, 21 rooms, D 57 € — Joigny 19 km
Tel (33) 03 86 62 16 28, Fax (33) 03 86 62 44 33

RESTAURANTS RESTAURANT

La Côte Saint-Jacques, — Joigny 19 km
Tel (33) 03 86 62 09 70

Jean-Luc Barnabet, Tel (33) 03 86 51 68 88 — Auxerre 20 km

ROYAL MOUGINS

17 | 8 | 8

Ce parcours excitant et spectaculaire ne laisse pas indifférent, mais ne plaît pas à tous. Au moins pour en juger, Royal Mougins mérite une visite attentive. Certains joueurs discutent le "modernisme" du parcours comme son étroitesse, mais celle-ci est plus visuelle que réelle : certes, de nombreux mouvements de terrain animent de manière spectaculaire les limites de fairway, mais ils ramènent la balle en jeu. Ici, il faut jouer avec sa tête, faire des choix de clubs réfléchis, et jouer précis, ne serait-ce que pour éviter les obstacles d'eau menaçants qui ponctuent le parcours. Mais comme sa longueur est raisonnable, les frappeurs peuvent jouer leurs coups de départ avec un bois 3 ou un long fer. La plupart du temps, les seconds coups seront joués avec des petits et moyens fers... Le club house a été joliment refait, et on annonce l'ouverture d'un vrai practice. Le prix de la journée n'est pas vraiment à la portée d'une famille, mais Royal Mougins est avant tout un golf de membres, et le nombre de visiteurs est limité.

Bob von Hagge has made very intelligent use of limited space and created an exciting and spectacular course, with no room for indifference. Royal Mougins is well worth a close visit if only to judge for yourself. Some players question the course's modernism and tightness, but the latter is visual rather than real. We agree that the slanting terrain can sometimes result in the ball doing weird things at the edges of the fairway, but it also helps bring the thing back into play. This is a course where you play with your brains, you think before choosing your club and you hit it straight, if only to avoid the water hazards dotted around the 18 holes. But being of reasonable length, big-hitters can easily tee off with a 3-wood or long iron to stay in the fairway. Approach shots are played mostly with short or mid-irons, so there should not be too many problems there. The club-house has been prettily refurbished and they say that a real driving range is due to open soon. The price you pay for a full day's golfing is not what you might call affordable for a family of four, but Royal Mougins is primarily a members' course and the number of visitors is restricted.

Royal Mougins Golf Club — **1993**
424, avenue du Roi
F - 06250 MOUGINS

Office	Secrétariat	(33) 04 92 92 49 69
Pro shop	Pro-shop	(33) 04 92 92 49 79
Fax	Fax	(33) 04 92 92 49 70
Web	www.royalmougins.com	
Situation	Situation	

Cannes (pop. 68 670), 10 km - Grasse (pop. 41 390), 20 km

Annual closure	Fermeture annuelle	no
Weekly closure	Fermeture hebdomadaire	no

Fees main season Tarifs haute saison	Full day	
	Week days Semaine	**We/Bank holidays** We/Férié
Individual Individuel	152 € *	152 € *
Couple Couple	304 € *	304 € *

* GF full-day + practice + lunch

Caddy	Caddy	no
Electric Trolley	Chariot électrique	11 € /18 holes
Buggy	Voiturette	30 € /18 holes
Clubs	Clubs	46 € /full day

Credit cards Cartes de crédit
VISA - CB - Eurocard - MasterCard - AMEX

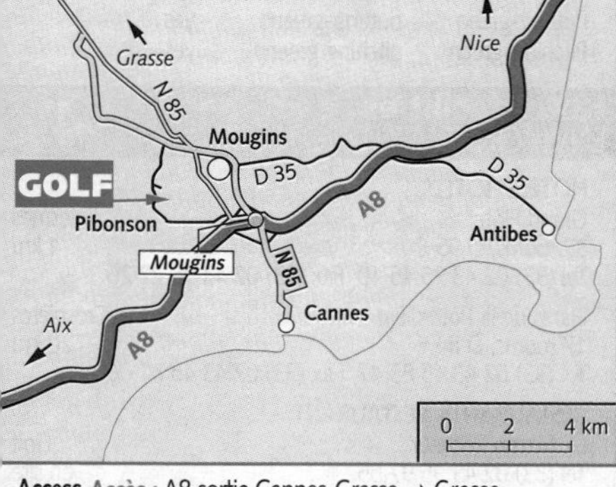

Access Accès : A8 sortie Cannes-Grasse → Grasse, 3e sortie Mougins Pibonson, Saint-Martin
Map 14 on page 189 Carte 14 Page 189

Golf course PARCOURS — 17/20

Site	Site	
Maintenance	Entretien	
Architect	Architecte	Robert von Hagge
Type	Type	forest, hilly
Relief	Relief	
Water in play	Eau en jeu	
Exp. to wind	Exposé au vent	
Trees in play	Arbres en jeu	

Scorecard Carte de score	**Chp.** Chp.	**Mens** Mess.	**Ladies** Da.
Length Long.	6004	5697	4926
Par	71	71	71
Slope system	141	130	123

Advised golfing ability Niveau de jeu recommandé — 0 12 24 36
Hcp required Handicap exigé — 30

Club house & amenities CLUB-HOUSE ET ANNEXES — 8/10

Pro shop	Pro-shop	
Driving range	Practice	
Sheltered	couvert	under construction
On grass	sur herbe	yes
Putting-green	putting-green	yes
Pitching-green	pitching green	yes

Hotel facilities ENVIRONNEMENT HOTELIER — 8/10

HOTELS HÔTELS

Mas Candille, 40 rooms, D 381 € — Mougins 3 km
Tel (33) 04 92 28 43 43, Fax (33) 04 92 28 43 40

Hôtel de Mougins, 51 rooms, D 221 € — Mougins
Tel (33) 04 92 92 17 07, Fax (33) 04 92 92 17 08

Le Manoir de l'Etang, 15 rooms, D 122 € — Mougins
Tel (33) 04 92 28 36 00, Fax (33) 04 92 28 36 10

RESTAURANTS RESTAURANT

Les Muscadins, Tel (33) 04 92 28 28 28 — Mougins
Le Feu Follet, Tel (33) 04 93 90 15 78 — Mougins
La Ferme de Mougins, Tel (33) 04 93 90 03 74 — Mougins

SABLÉ-SOLESMES La Forêt La Rivière

16 | 7 | 4

Entre les villes d'Angers et du Mans, cet ensemble de 27 trous s'est s'imposé dans le groupe de tête des parcours français, alors que l'on ne s'attendait pas à trouver des tracés d'une telle qualité en pleine campagne, ou tellement en dehors des routes traditionnelles du golf. Entre la Sarthe et la Forêt de Pincé, Michel Gayon a dessiné trois 9 trous combinables de longueur raisonnable et le terrain moyennement accidenté permet de les jouer tous en une seule journée. Sur la combinaison "La Forêt-La Rivière", l'eau intervient sur une dizaine de trous, sans être trop effrayante pour autant. "La Cascade" revendique un caractère plus écossais, avec beaucoup de bosses, de bunkers d'herbe et de sable, mais aussi un peu d'eau, comme au 8. On éprouve ici une très bonne impression d'espace et de calme, propice à la concentration que réclame ce golf à connaître. Cet ensemble désor mais bien élaboré se consacre désormais à la finition, avec des plantations notamment.

Between Angers and Le Mans, this 27-hole resort has edged its way into the group of leading French courses at a time when no-one was expecting such a great layout right out in the country or so far off the traditional golfing path. Michel Gayon has designed three combinable 9-hole courses of reasonable length, stretching between the river Sarthe and a large forest. On flattish terrain, all three can be played in one day. On the "Forêt-Rivière" combination, water is present on ten holes but never too intimidating. "La Cascade" is more Scottish in nature, with an array of sand-hills, grass- and sand-bunkers and also a little water, like on the 8th. Here you get a great feeling of space and of tranquillity conducive to the concentration required when playing a course like this. A club that is well worth discovering and an elaborate complex which is now focusing more on completion work with, in particular, an extensive plantation programme.

Golf de Sablé-Solesmes — 1991

Domaine de l'Outinière, route de Pincé
F - 72300 SABLE-SUR-SARTHE

Office	Secrétariat	(33) 02 43 95 28 78
Pro shop	Pro-shop	(33) 02 43 95 28 78
Fax	Fax	(33) 02 43 92 39 05
Web	www.golfsablesolesmes.com	
Situation	Situation	

La Flèche, 26 km - Le Mans (pop. 145 500), 59 km

Annual closure	Fermeture annuelle	no
Weekly closure	Fermeture hebdomadaire	no

Fees main season Tarifs haute saison	Week days Semaine	We/Bank holidays We/Férié
		Full day
Individual Individuel	38 €	49 €
Couple Couple	69 €	88 €

Under 18: 23€ (Weekdays) - 29 € (We)

Caddy	Caddy	no
Electric Trolley	Chariot électrique	9 € /18 holes
Buggy	Voiturette	30 € /18 holes
Clubs	Clubs	9 € /full day

Credit cards Cartes de crédit
VISA - CB - Eurocard - MasterCard

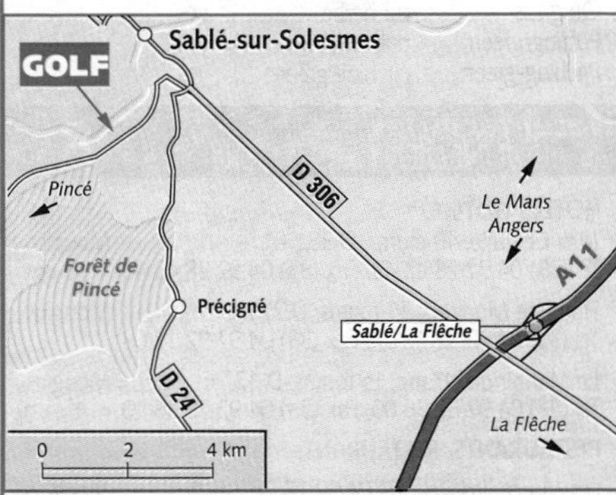

Access Accès : Le Mans-Angers, A11 Exit (Sortie) La Flèche, turn right on D306 → Sablé-sur-Sarthe
Map 6 on page 173 Carte 6 Page 173

Golf course PARCOURS — 16/20

Site	Site	
Maintenance	Entretien	
Architect	Architecte	Michel Gayon
Type	Type	open country
Relief	Relief	
Water in play	Eau en jeu	
Exp. to wind	Exposé au vent	
Trees in play	Arbres en jeu	

Scorecard Carte de score	Chp. Chp.	Mens Mess.	Ladies Da.
Length Long.	6189	5737	5217
Par	72	72	72
Slope system	137	133	137

Advised golfing ability Niveau de jeu recommandé — 0 12 24 36
Hcp required Handicap exigé 35

Club house & amenities CLUB-HOUSE ET ANNEXES — 7/10

Pro shop	Pro-shop	
Driving range	Practice	
Sheltered	couvert	7 mats
On grass	sur herbe	yes
Putting-green	putting-green	yes
Pitching-green	pitching green	yes

Hotel facilities ENVIRONNEMENT HOTELIER — 4/10

HOTELS HÔTELS

Grand Hôtel — Solesmes 4 km
32 rooms, D 95 €
Tel (33) 02 43 95 45 10, Fax (33) 02 43 95 22 26

Haras de la Potardière — Crosnières 20 km
17 rooms, D 84 €
Tel (33) 02 43 45 83 47, Fax (33) 02 43 45 81 06

RESTAURANTS RESTAURANT

Le Martin Pêcheur — Golf on site
Tel (33) 02 43 95 97 55

Hostellerie Saint-Martin — Sablé 6 km
Tel (33) 02 43 95 00 03

SAINT DONAT

16 | 7 | 8

Saint Donat a été un des premiers parcours de la région à présenter une architecture "moderne". Robert Trent Jones Jr lui a donné des contours très variés, utilisant avec intelligence la végétation existante, les reliefs (surtout au retour) et modelant sans excès les espaces plus plats. Ce qui donne un dessin très précis, où les méandres d'une petite rivière viennent en jeu sur une bonne demi-douzaine de trous. De nombreux bunkers et des bouquets d'arbres (notamment de très beaux vieux chênes) constituent des obstacles parfois préoccupants, souvent à proximité de greens intéressants et variés. Ici, il faut s'appuyer sur la technique, la sagesse dans le choix de club et pas sur la longueur, mais les joueurs de tous niveaux peuvent y évoluer, après une petite période d'adaptation et s'ils ne sont pas trop ambitieux. Alors que les dix premiers trous sont assez plats, le retour est accidenté, avec quelques trous très spectaculaires, mais assez facile à marcher en condition physique normale.

Saint Donat was one of the first courses in this region with so-called "modern" architecture. Robert Trent Jones Jr moulded the course into a variety of shapes, making intelligent use of existing vegetation and topography (especially on the back nine) and contouring the flatter areas without ever overdoing things. The result is a very precise layout, where the meanders of a small river come into play on half a dozen or so holes. A good number of bunkers and groups of trees (including some beautiful oaks) form some distinctly worrying hazards often placed close to some interesting and varied greens. Emphasis should be on technique and caution in the choice of club, not on length, although after a period of adjustment all players can enjoy a round of golf here as long as they are not over-ambitious. While the first ten holes are rather flat, the last eight are hilly encounters with a few very spectacular holes, all of which are easily walkable for the average able-bodied golfer.

Golf de Saint Donat — 1993

270, route de Cannes
F - 06130 PLAN-DE-GRASSE

Office	Secrétariat	(33) 04 93 09 76 60
Pro shop	Pro-shop	(33) 04 93 09 76 60
Fax	Fax	(33) 04 93 09 76 63
Web	—	
Situation	Situation	

Grasse (pop. 41 390), 2 km - Cannes (pop. 68 670), 18 km

Annual closure	Fermeture annuelle	no
Weekly closure	Fermeture hebdomadaire	no

Fees main season Tarifs haute saison	**Week days** Semaine	**We/Bank holidays** We/Férié
		18 holes
Individual Individuel	53 €	53 €
Couple Couple	106 €	106 €

Juniors: 27 € / Students: 38 €

Caddy	Caddy	no
Electric Trolley	Chariot électrique	15 € /18 holes
Buggy	Voiturette	30 € /18 holes
Clubs	Clubs	15 € /18 holes

Credit cards Cartes de crédit
VISA - CB - Eurocard - MasterCard - DC - AMEX

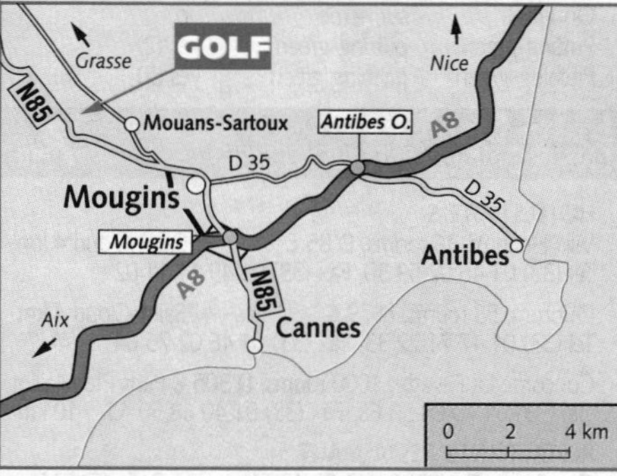

Access Accès : • Grasse N85 → Plan-de-Grasse • Cannes, Motorway → N85 Grasse, Mouans-Sartoux, → Golf de Saint Donat
Map 14 on page 189 Carte 14 Page 189

Golf course — PARCOURS — 16/20

Site	Site	
Maintenance	Entretien	
Architect	Architecte	R. Trent Jones Jr
Type	Type	hilly, parkland
Relief	Relief	
Water in play	Eau en jeu	
Exp. to wind	Exposé au vent	
Trees in play	Arbres en jeu	

Scorecard Carte de score	**Chp.** Chp.	**Mens** Mess.	**Ladies** Da.
Length Long.	6031	5558	5082
Par	71	71	71
Slope system	129	124	121

Advised golfing ability — Niveau de jeu recommandé: 0 12 24 36
Hcp required — Handicap exigé: 30

Club house & amenities — CLUB-HOUSE ET ANNEXES — 7/10

Pro shop	Pro-shop	
Driving range	Practice	
Sheltered	couvert	8 mats
On grass	sur herbe	no, 20 mats open air
Putting-green	putting-green	yes
Pitching-green	pitching green	yes

Hotel facilities — ENVIRONNEMENT HOTELIER — 8/10

HOTELS HÔTELS

Hôtel de Mougins, 51 rooms, D 221 € — Mougins
Tel (33) 04 92 92 17 07, Fax (33) 04 92 92 17 08 — 6 km

Le Manoir de l'Etang, 15 rooms, D 122 € — Mougins
Tel (33) 04 92 28 36 00, Fax (33) 04 92 28 36 10 — 6 km

Domaine de l'Albatros, 33 rooms, D 76 € — Mouans-Sartoux
Tel (33) 04 79 68 26 26, Fax (33) 04 79 68 26 29

RESTAURANTS RESTAURANT

Bastide Saint Antoine, Tel (33) 04 93 70 94 94 — Grasse 2 km

Les Muscadins, Tel (33) 04 92 28 28 28 — Mougins 6 km

La Toque Blanche, Tel (33) 04 93 36 20 64 — Magagnosc 8 km

SAINT-CLOUD Vert

15	8	7

Etre aussi proche de Paris a beaucoup contribué à la réputation de Saint-Cloud, mais aussi à la difficulté d'y jouer. A côté du petit parcours "Jaune," dont une bonne moitié des trous ne manque pas d'intérêt, le "Vert" a reçu de nombreuses compétitions internationales, même si sa longueur peut paraître aujourd'hui insuffisante. Sa technicité en fait la relative difficulté. Il a été dessiné par Harry S. Colt, mais il a fait l'objet de divers aménagements qui ont souvent fait perdre de vue l'original et donnent parfois l'impression de styles différents, en particulier pour le dessin des bunkers : ne parlons que du 8, où le green vient d'être déguisé avec sortes de pot-bunkers plus à leur place sur un links d'Ecosse qu'ici. Très agréable dans son déroulement, avec des vues superbes sur Paris, pas trop accidenté, ornementé d'une végétation somptueuse (à voir en automne !), Saint-Cloud résiste à ces traitements, et reste l'une des jolies oasis de la région, à déguster pendant les soirées d'été quand les membres sont en vacances.

Being the closest club to Paris has done much for its reputation and the difficulty encountered in being able to play here. Alongside the smaller "Jaune" course, which has a number of interesting holes, the "Vert" course has hosted any number of international tournaments even though its length, by today's standards, may appear a little on the short side. The difficulty here has always been the technical side to the layout. It was designed by Harry Colt but has been restyled in a variety of ways which often mask the original layout and sometimes give the impression of different styles lumped together, especially as far as the bunkering is concerned. One example is the 8th hole, where the green has recently been disguised with pot-bunkers, which would be better off on a Scottish links. The course unwinds very pleasantly with some superb views over Paris, is not too hilly and abounds with lush vegetation (wonderful in autumn). This is one of the region's prettiest "watering holes" and a great place to enjoy on summer evenings when the members are away on holiday.

Golf de Saint-Cloud — 1912

60, rue du 19 Janvier
F - 92380 GARCHES

Office	Secrétariat	(33) 01 47 01 01 85
Pro shop	Pro-shop	(33) 01 47 41 01 45
Fax	Fax	(33) 01 47 01 19 57
Web	www.golfsaintcloud.free.fr	
Situation	Situation	Paris, 15 km
Annual closure	Fermeture annuelle	no
Weekly closure	Fermeture hebdomadaire	

monday (lundi)

Fees main season Tarifs haute saison	18 holes	
	Week days Semaine	**We/Bank holidays** We/Férié
Individual Individuel	76 € *	76 € *
Couple Couple	152 € *	152 € *

* with a member (avec un membre)

Caddy	Caddy	on request
Electric Trolley	Chariot électrique	12 € /18 holes
Buggy	Voiturette	no
Clubs	Clubs	yes

Credit cards Cartes de crédit
VISA - CB - Eurocard - MasterCard

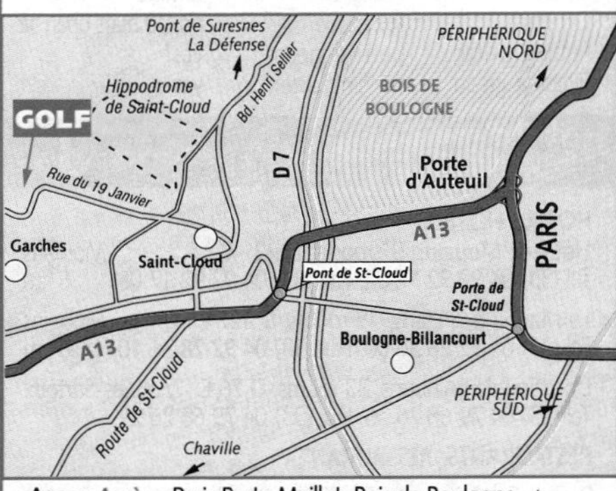

Access Accès : Paris Porte Maillot, Bois de Boulogne → Suresnes. Pont de Suresnes, Bld H. Sellier, → Hippodrome St Cloud. Turn right into Rue du 19 janvier. → Golf St Cucufa. **Map 15 on page 190** Carte 15 Page 190

Golf course PARCOURS — 15/20

Site	Site	
Maintenance	Entretien	
Architect	Architecte	Harry S. Colt
Type	Type	parkland
Relief	Relief	
Water in play	Eau en jeu	
Exp. to wind	Exposé au vent	
Trees in play	Arbres en jeu	

Scorecard Carte de score	**Chp.** Chp.	**Mens** Mess.	**Ladies** Da.
Length Long.	5939	5708	4967
Par	72	72	72
Slope system	138	131	123

Advised golfing ability Niveau de jeu recommandé — 0 12 24 36

Hcp required Handicap exigé — 24 Men, 28 Ladies

Club house & amenities CLUB-HOUSE ET ANNEXES — 8/10

Pro shop	Pro-shop	
Driving range	Practice	
Sheltered	couvert	46 mats
On grass	sur herbe	no
Putting-green	putting-green	yes (2)
Pitching-green	pitching green	yes (2)

Hotel facilities ENVIRONNEMENT HOTELIER — 7/10

HOTELS HÔTELS

Villa Henri IV, 36 rooms, D 85 € — Saint-Cloud 4 km
Tel (33) 01 46 02 59 30, Fax (33) 01 49 11 11 02

Quorum, 58 rooms, D 79 € — Saint-Cloud 4 km
Tel (33) 01 47 71 22 33, Fax (33) 01 46 02 75 64

Concorde La Fayette, 1000 rooms, D 305 € — Paris Pte Maillot 10 km
Tel (33) 01 40 68 50 68, Fax (33) 01 40 68 50 43

RESTAURANTS RESTAURANT

Guy Savoy, Tel (33) 01 43 80 40 61 — Paris 17e 12 km

La Poularde, Tel (33) 01 47 41 13 47 — Vaucresson 5 km

Michel Rostang, Tel (33) 01 47 63 40 77 — Paris 17e 12 km

SAINT-ENDRÉOL

15	7	4

Dans un paysage typique de Provence, ce parcours de Michel Gayon en épouse les reliefs, d'où quelques greens aveugles, dont certains d'ailleurs auraient pu être évités. Certains coups forcément hasardeux atténuent un peu le plaisir que l'on éprouve sur ce golf en pleine nature, dont le relief accentué invite à jouer en voiturette. Parce que la tactique de jeu n'est pas évidente à assimiler, parce qu'il faut connaître le parcours pour bien évaluer les distances, parce que que la chance joue ici un rôle important, on s'amusera beaucoup plus en match-play (où tout peut arriver) qu'en stroke play. Avec plusieurs trous spectaculaires et pour la beauté de son environnement, Saint-Endreol vaut incontestablement le détour. Le 17 a été longtemps considéré comme par 4, alors qu'il était conçu en par 5. il semble que la raison l'emporte, et que l'on revienne à ce qu'il est vraiment. Si l'on ajoute le développement de l'hôtel sur place ou la réfection des départs, on voit que Saint-Endreol bouge dans le bon sens.

Laid out in typical Provence style countryside, Michel Gayon's course hugs the contours of the landscape and in the process provides a number of blind greens, some of which could have been avoided. Certain hazardous shots tend to dampen the enjoyment of this course right out in the country where hilly terrain make a buggy a wise decision. This is a match-play course (where anything can happen) rather than a course for stroke-play, simply because the tactics needed here are not always obvious, because you need to know the course to evaluate distances, and because luck plays perhaps a bigger role than usual. With several spectacular holes and a beautiful setting, Saint Endréol is most certainly well worth the visit. The 17th was long considered a par 4, even though it was designed as a par 5. Today, reason seems to have gotten the upper hand and the hole is back to being a par 5. Add to this the development of an on-site hotel or the re-laying of tee-boxes and you will start seeing Saint-Endreol in a much better light.

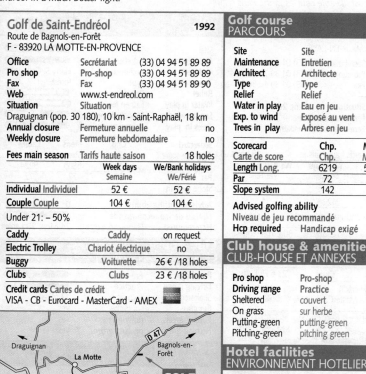

Golf de Saint-Endréol — 1992

Route de Bagnols-en-Forêt
F - 83920 LA MOTTE-EN-PROVENCE

Office	Secrétariat	(33) 04 94 51 89 89
Pro shop	Pro-shop	(33) 04 94 51 89 89
Fax	Fax	(33) 04 94 51 89 90
Web	www.st-endreol.com	
Situation	Situation	

Draguignan (pop. 30 180), 10 km - Saint-Raphaël, 18 km

Annual closure	Fermeture annuelle	no
Weekly closure	Fermeture hebdomadaire	no

Fees main season Tarifs haute saison		18 holes
	Week days Semaine	**We/Bank holidays** We/Férié
Individual Individuel	52 €	52 €
Couple Couple	104 €	104 €

Under 21: – 50%

Caddy	Caddy	on request
Electric Trolley	Chariot électrique	no
Buggy	Voiturette	26 € /18 holes
Clubs	Clubs	23 € /18 holes

Credit cards Cartes de crédit
VISA - CB - Eurocard - MasterCard - AMEX

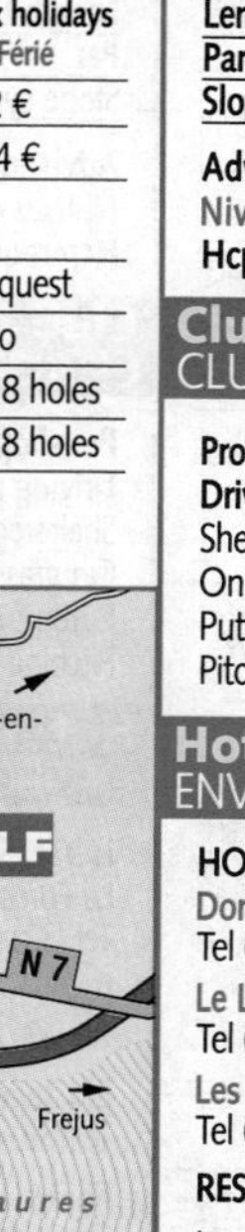

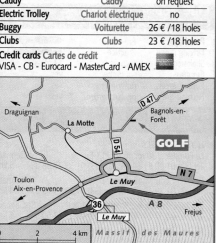

Access Accès : Saint-Raphaël, N7, Exit (Sortie) Le Muy, D54 → La Motte-en- Provence, → Golf
Map 14 on page 189 Carte 14 Page 189

Golf course PARCOURS — 15/20

Site	Site	
Maintenance	Entretien	
Architect	Architecte	Michel Gayon
Type	Type	hilly, forest
Relief	Relief	
Water in play	Eau en jeu	
Exp. to wind	Exposé au vent	
Trees in play	Arbres en jeu	

Scorecard Carte de score	**Chp.** Chp.	**Mens** Mess.	**Ladies** Da.
Length Long.	6219	5940	5011
Par	72	72	72
Slope system	142	134	135

Advised golfing ability Niveau de jeu recommandé — 0 12 24 36

Hcp required Handicap exigé — 30 (morning)

Club house & amenities CLUB-HOUSE ET ANNEXES — 7/10

Pro shop	Pro-shop	
Driving range	Practice	
Sheltered	couvert	7 mats
On grass	sur herbe	no, 15 mats open air
Putting-green	putting-green	yes
Pitching-green	pitching green	yes

Hotel facilities ENVIRONNEMENT HOTELIER — 4/10

HOTELS HÔTELS

Domaine de Saint-Endréol, 35 rooms, D 156 € — on site
Tel (33) 04 94 51 89 80, Fax (33) 04 94 51 89 81

Le Logis du Guetteur, 12 rooms, D 104 € — Les Arcs 6 km
Tel (33) 04 94 99 51 10, Fax (33) 04 94 99 51 29

Les Gorges de Pennafort, 16 rooms, D 149 € — Callas 11 km
Tel (33) 04 94 76 66 51, Fax (33) 04 94 76 67 23

RESTAURANTS RESTAURANT

Les Pignatelles, Tel (33) 04 94 70 25 70 — La Motte 5 km
Le Logis du Guetteur, Tel (33) 04 94 99 51 10 — Les Arcs 6 km
Les Gorges de Pennafort, Tel (33) 04 94 76 66 51 — Callas 11 km

SAINT-GERMAIN

17 | 7 | 7

On le considère parfois comme trop court, c'est peut-être vrai pour les meilleurs professionnels, mais bien suffisant pour 99,99 % des golfeurs, qui ont souvent du mal à y jouer leur handicap ! On y verra plutôt la quintessence de l'architecture britannique sur un terrain très plat et très ramassé, avec un très bon rythme d'enchaînement des trous et des difficultés, quelques reliefs subtils, notamment en approche des greens et sur les greens, généralement très vastes. Les obstacles essentiels sont les arbres, majestueux mais pas oppressants, et surtout les bunkers, typiques des idées stratégiques de Colt, et souvent de formes très belles. Scorer ici demande un jeu très complet, et d'abord de ne pas se laisser endormir par la tranquille séduction du lieu. Au chapitre des améliorations, une zone d'entraînement au petit jeu très réussie, la disparition de certaines haies assez disgracieuses, et en projet, la réfection du récent green du 2, dont nous avions souligné le style anachronique. Saint-Germain reste l'un des golfs les plus attachants de la région parisienne.

Saint-Germain may well sometimes be considered too short for the top pros but it certainly is long enough for 99,99% of golfers who often find playing to their handicap here something of an exploit. We see it rather as the quintessence of British-style design over very flat and very squat landscape. There is a remarkable flow of continuity between holes and difficulties and some subtly-shaped terrain, particularly when approaching or actually on the generally very large greens. The basic hazards are trees, majestic enough but not too obtrusive, and especially bunkers, typical of designer Colt's ideas of strategy and often beautifully shaped. You need an all-round game to score well here and don't let the balmy appeal of the site distract you from the task at hand. In terms of improvements, we liked the practice green for your short game, the removal of certain unsightly hedges and the planned restyling of the new green on the 2nd hole, for which we had a few unkind words last time. Saint Germain remains one of the most likeable courses in the Paris region.

Golf de Saint-Germain — 1922

Route de Poissy
F - 78100 SAINT-GERMAIN-EN-LAYE

Office	Secrétariat	(33) 01 39 10 30 30
Pro shop	Pro-shop	(33) 01 39 73 87 48
Fax	Fax	(33) 01 39 10 30 31
Web	—	
Situation	Situation	Paris, 26 km
Annual closure	Fermeture annuelle	no
Weekly closure	Fermeture hebdomadaire	

monday (lundi)

Fees main season Tarifs haute saison — 18 holes

	Week days / Semaine	We/Bank holidays / We/Férié
Individual Individuel	61 €	*
Couple Couple	122 €	*

* We : only member and guests (membres et invités)

Caddy	Caddy	30 € /on request
Electric Trolley	Chariot électrique	no
Buggy	Voiturette	no
Clubs	Clubs	23 € /full day

Credit cards Cartes de crédit
VISA - CB - Eurocard - MasterCard - AMEX

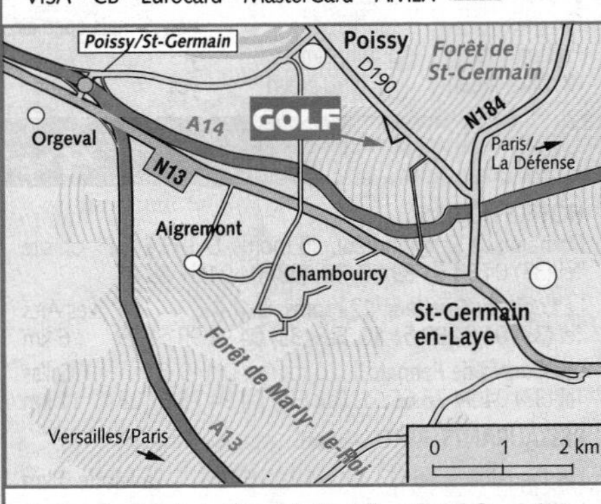

Access Accès : Paris A13, Exit (Sortie) → Saint-Germain. N13 → Poissy, N184 then D190 → Poissy. Golf on left hand side. **Map 15 on page 190** Carte 15 Page 190

Golf course — PARCOURS — 17/20

Site	Site	
Maintenance	Entretien	
Architect	Architecte	Harry S. Colt
Type	Type	forest
Relief	Relief	
Water in play	Eau en jeu	
Exp. to wind	Exposé au vent	
Trees in play	Arbres en jeu	

Scorecard / Carte de score	Chp. / Chp.	Mens / Mess.	Ladies / Da.
Length Long.	6117	5805	5224
Par	72	72	72
Slope system	136	128	131

Advised golfing ability 0 12 24 36
Niveau de jeu recommandé
Hcp required Handicap exigé — 24 Men, 28 Ladies

Club house & amenities — CLUB-HOUSE ET ANNEXES — 7/10

Pro shop	Pro-shop	
Driving range	Practice	
Sheltered	couvert	17 mats
On grass	sur herbe	yes
Putting-green	putting-green	yes
Pitching-green	pitching green	yes

Hotel facilities — ENVIRONNEMENT HOTELIER — 7/10

HOTELS HÔTELS

La Forestière, 30 rooms, D 213 € — St-Germain
Tel (33) 01 30 61 64 64, Fax (33) 01 39 73 88 88 — 5 km

Pavillon Henri IV, 42 rooms, D 172 € — St-Germain
Tel (33) 01 39 10 15 15, Fax (33) 01 39 93 73 93 — 4 km

Ermitage des Loges, 56 rooms, D 108 € — St-Germain
Tel (33) 01 39 21 50 90, Fax (33) 01 39 21 50 91 — 5 km

RESTAURANTS RESTAURANT

Cazaudehore (La Forestière) — St-Germain 5 km
Tel (33) 01 30 61 64 64

La Feuillantine, Tel (33) 01 34 51 04 24 — St-Germain 4 km

Clémentine, Tel (33) 01 34 51 77 78 — St-Germain 5 km

SAINT-JEAN-DE-MONTS

16 | 6 | 5

Ce parcours s'est vite imposé parmi les meilleurs parcours de la dernière décennie, et il maintient son standing. Il prouve que l'on peut faire de bons parcours même avec de petits budgets... Situé en bord de mer, son dessin est un hommage à l'architecture de links, même dans la dizaine de trous (parfois très étroits) situés dans une forêt de pins maritimes et de chênes verts. Les fairways très modelés, les greens souvent à double ou même triple plateau suivent les reliefs des dunes, dans un souci évident de préserver la nature. L'architecte Yves Bureau a joué davantage sur la nécessité de précision que sur la longueur, mais le vent peut rendre ce parcours démoniaque, même dans les passages boisés, où il tourbillonne volontiers. Les Britanniques n'y seront pas dépaysés ! Le parcours est jouable sans problème toute l'année, et ses tarifs raisonnables en font toujours l'un des meilleurs rapports qualité/prix de France.

This course quickly became established as one of the best new layouts of the past decade and today has preserved its status. It also proves that good courses are possible even on low budgets. Laid out along the sea, this is a homage to links golf, even though ten or so holes (sometimes very tight indeed) wind their way through a forest of maritime pines and oak trees. The highly contoured fairways and two- or even three-tiered greens hug the relief of the dunes with obvious emphasis on preserving the natural landscape. Architect Yves Bureau has played more on the need for precision rather than length, but the wind can make this a devilishly hard course even in the woods, where it seems to swirl in all directions. The British will certainly feel at home here. Saint Jean de Monts is easily playable all year and green fees are very reasonable and so continue to make this one of the best values for money in France..

Golf de Saint-Jean-de-Monts — 1988

Avenue des Pays-de-la-Loire
F - 85160 SAINT-JEAN-DE-MONTS

Office	Secrétariat	(33) 02 51 58 82 73
Pro shop	Pro-shop	(33) 02 51 58 82 73
Fax	Fax	(33) 02 51 59 18 32
Web	—	
Situation	Situation	

Challans, 17 km - Nantes (pop. 252 030), 70 km

Annual closure	Fermeture annuelle	no
Weekly closure	Fermeture hebdomadaire	no

tuesday (mardi), club-house closed from 01/11 to 31/03

Fees main season Tarifs haute saison	**Week days** Semaine	**We/Bank holidays** We/Férié
18 holes		
Individual Individuel	44 €	44 €
Couple Couple	88 €	88 €

Juniors & Students: – 50%

Caddy	Caddy	no
Electric Trolley	Chariot électrique	no
Buggy	Voiturette	27 € /18 holes
Clubs	Clubs	11 € /full day

Credit cards Cartes de crédit
VISA - CB - Eurocard - MasterCard - AMEX

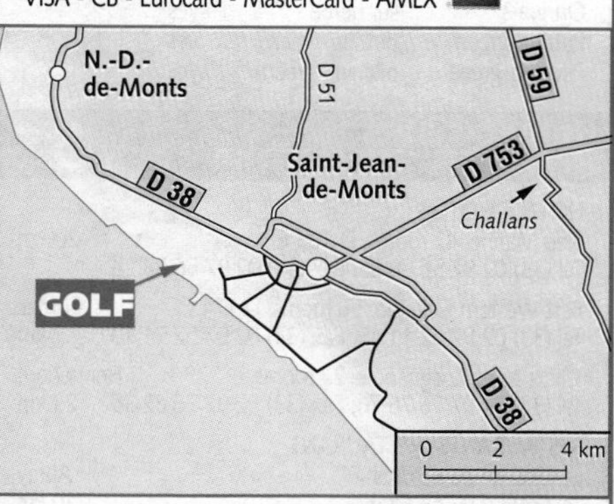

Access Accès : Challans → Saint-Jean-de-Monts, → Golf
Map 6 on page 172 Carte 6 Page 172

Golf course — PARCOURS — 16/20

Site	Site	
Maintenance	Entretien	
Architect	Architecte	Yves Bureau
Type	Type	forest, links
Relief	Relief	
Water in play	Eau en jeu	
Exp. to wind	Exposé au vent	
Trees in play	Arbres en jeu	

Scorecard Carte de score	**Chp.** Chp.	**Mens** Mess.	**Ladies** Da.
Length Long.	5937	5623	4754
Par	72	72	72
Slope system	145	140	132

Advised golfing ability Niveau de jeu recommandé — 0 12 24 36
Hcp required Handicap exigé — no

Club house & amenities — CLUB-HOUSE ET ANNEXES — 6/10

Pro shop	Pro-shop	
Driving range	Practice	
Sheltered	couvert	10 mats
On grass	sur herbe	no, 20 mats open air
Putting-green	putting-green	yes
Pitching-green	pitching green	yes

Hotel facilities — ENVIRONNEMENT HOTELIER — 5/10

HOTELS HÔTELS

Mercure, 44 rooms, D 114 € — 100 m
Tel (33) 02 51 59 15 15, Fax (33) 02 51 59 91 03

Hôtel de la Plage, 44 rooms, D 57 € — N.-D.-de-Monts 5 km
Tel (33) 02 51 58 83 09, Fax (33) 02 51 58 97 12

Château de la Vérie, 23 rooms, D 123 € — Challans 15 km
Tel (33) 02 51 35 33 44, Fax (33) 02 51 35 14 84

RESTAURANTS RESTAURANT

Hôtel de la Plage, — N.-D.-de-Monts 5 km
Tel (33) 02 51 58 83 09

Petit St-Jean, Tel (33) 02 51 59 78 50 — St-Jean-de-Monts 1 km

Quich'Notte, Tel (33) 02 51 58 62 64 — Saint-Jean-de-Monts

SAINT-LAURENT

14 | 7 | 5

Beaucoup de golfs prétendent convenir à tout le monde, mais ce n'est pas toujours vrai. Ici, oui : Saint-Laurent est un parcours réellement praticable par les joueurs de tous niveaux, même les joueurs de haut handicap, qui y perdront moins de balles que de points. Situé dans un bel espace vallonné et planté de pins ou de chênes, le 18 trous signé par Michael Fenn se déroule sans imagination particulière, mais il a été conçu et réalisé très sérieusement. Les 600 arbres plantés vont en accentuer l'exigence comme l'agrément visuel. Son entretien de bonne qualité incite à en recommander la visite, d'autant que cette belle région est une destination traditionnelle de vacances. Avec la mer et les activités balnéaires à proximité, un golfeur pourra sans trop mauvaise conscience abandonner sa famille quelques heures. Le 9 trous signé Yves Bureau est un idéal pour initier les aspirants golfeurs.

A lot of courses claim to be suitable for all golfers but are not. Saint Laurent is one of the exceptions, being a course that really is playable by golfers of all abilities, even high-handicappers, who will probably lose fewer balls than they drop strokes. Located in rolling landscape planted with pines and oak-trees, the 18-hole course, designed by Michael Fenn, unfolds with no great imagination, but it was designed and built with the most serious intentions. The 600 newly planted trees will make it both more challenging and more aesthetically pleasing. Excellent maintenance makes it well worth a visit, especially in this beautiful holiday region. With the sea and holiday resorts nearby, golfers can abandon the family for a few hours without remorse. The 9-hole course designed by Yves Bureau is the ideal venue for beginners and new-comers to the game.

Golf de Saint-Laurent — 1976

Ploemel
F - 56400 AURAY

Office	Secrétariat	(33) 02 97 56 85 18
Pro shop	Pro-shop	(33) 02 97 56 85 18
Fax	Fax	(33) 02 97 56 89 99
Web	www.formule-golf.com	
Situation	Situation	

Auray (pop. 10 320), 11 km - Vannes (pop. 45 640), 44 km

Annual closure	Fermeture annuelle	no
Weekly closure	Fermeture hebdomadaire	no

Restaurant closed tuesday (mardi), from 11 → 02

Fees main season Tarifs haute saison	18 holes	
	Week days Semaine	**We/Bank holidays** We/Férié
Individual Individuel	44 €	44 €
Couple Couple	88 €	88 €

Under 21 & Students: – 50%

Caddy	Caddy	no
Electric Trolley	Chariot électrique	no
Buggy	Voiturette	23 € /18 holes
Clubs	Clubs	9 € /full day

Credit cards Cartes de crédit
VISA - CB - Eurocard - MasterCard

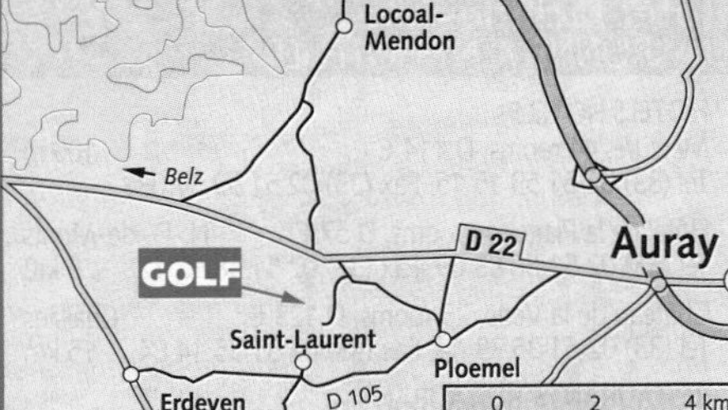

Access Accès : N165 ("Voie Express"), Exit (Sortie) Carnac-Quiberon, D22 → Belz-Etel. 6 km → Golf
Map 5 on page 170 Carte 5 Page 170

Golf course PARCOURS — 14/20

Site	Site	
Maintenance	Entretien	
Architect	Architecte	Michael Fenn
Type	Type	forest
Relief	Relief	
Water in play	Eau en jeu	
Exp. to wind	Exposé au vent	
Trees in play	Arbres en jeu	

Scorecard Carte de score	**Chp.** Chp.	**Mens** Mess.	**Ladies** Da.
Length Long.	6112	6112	5247
Par	72	72	72
Slope system	132	124	124

Advised golfing ability Niveau de jeu recommandé — 0 12 24 36
Hcp required Handicap exigé 53

Club house & amenities CLUB-HOUSE ET ANNEXES — 7/10

Pro shop	Pro-shop	
Driving range	Practice	
Sheltered	couvert	10 mats
On grass	sur herbe	yes
Putting-green	putting-green	yes
Pitching-green	pitching green	yes

Hotel facilities ENVIRONNEMENT HOTELIER — 5/10

HOTELS HÔTELS

Bleu Marine, 42 rooms, D 105 € — 200 m
Tel (33) 02 97 56 88 88, Fax (33) 02 97 56 88 28

Best Western Celtique, 56 rooms, D 174 € — Carnac 7 km
Tel (33) 02 97 52 11 49, Fax (33) 02 97 52 71 10

Château de Locguénolé, 22 rooms, D 229 € — Hennebont 23 km
Tel (33) 02 97 76 76 76, Fax (33) 02 97 76 82 35

RESTAURANTS RESTAURANT

La Closerie de Kerdrain — Auray 10 km
Tel (33) 02 97 56 61 27

Chebaudière, Tel (33) 02 97 24 09 84 — Auray 10 km

SAINT-NOM-LA-BRETÈCHE Bleu

16	8	8

Saint-Nom fut à son ouverture un événement, un exemple aussi de golf résidentiel prestigieux, qui, après des efforts patients, a acquis aujourd'hui beaucoup de maturité, en même temps que les arbres en prenaient. Comme le "Rouge", celui-ci a été dessiné par Fred Hawtree, mais beaucoup de changements ont été effectués, souvent avec bonheur, et de nombreux arbres plantés, ce qui constitue un bienfait visuel et technique. Un léger vallonnement le rend agréable à jouer, et ajoute de l'intérêt au choix de clubs. Mieux qu'un parent pauvre d'un parent prestigieux, ce parcours offre quelques parcs 4 très musclés, et peu de vraies occasions de birdies. L'utilisation de sept de ses trous pour le parcours composite du Trophée Lancôme a été l'occasion d'y apporter récemment des modifications importantes, rehaussant l'ensemble. Avec un entretien de très bon niveau, le "Bleu" devient le digne compagnon du "Rouge", au pied d'un Club-house toujours superbe.

When first opened, Saint Nom was a huge event and fine example of a prestigious residential golf club which after much patient work has today grown to maturity in pace with the trees. Like the "Rouge" course, the "Bleu" layout was designed by Fred Hawtree, although a lot of changes have been made to it, often to the better, with many new trees planted to add visual and technical appeal. The slightly rolling landscape makes it a pleasant course to play and underlines the importance of choosing the right club. Better than a poor relation to a prestigious neighbour, this layout contains a number of very demanding par 4s and few real birdie chances. The use of seven of these holes to form the composite course for the "Lancôme" has also been the opportunity to recently introduce some significant changes and enhance the layout as a whole. With excellent maintenance, the "Blue" course is now the worthy companion of its Red sister. The club-house is as superb as ever.

Golf de Saint-Nom-la-Bretèche — 1959

Hameau de la Tuilerie Bignon
F - 78860 SAINT-NOM-LA-BRETECHE

Office	Secrétariat	(33) 01 30 80 04 40
Pro shop	Pro-shop	(33) 01 30 80 04 40
Fax	Fax	(33) 01 30 80 04 50
E-mail	direction@golfsaintnom.com	
Situation	Situation	Paris, 22 km
Annual closure	Fermeture annuelle	no
Weekly closure	Fermeture hebdomadaire	tuesday/mardi

Fees main season Tarifs haute saison		Full day
	Week days Semaine	**We/Bank holidays** We/Férié
Individual Individuel	76 € *	91 € *
Couple Couple	152 € *	182 € *

* with a member (accompagné d'un membre)

Caddy	Caddy	on request
Electric Trolley	Chariot électrique	15 € /18 holes
Buggy	Voiturette	medical reasons
Clubs	Clubs	yes

Credit cards Cartes de crédit
VISA - CB - Eurocard

Access Accès : Paris A13 → Rouen. Exit (Sortie) Versailles-Ouest. → Versailles. 500 m turn right on D307 → Noisy-le-Roy, Saint-Nom-la-Bretèche
Map 15 on page 190 Carte 15 Page 190

Golf course — PARCOURS — 16/20

Site	Site	
Maintenance	Entretien	
Architect	Architecte	Fred Hawtree
Type	Type	parkland, residential
Relief	Relief	
Water in play	Eau en jeu	
Exp. to wind	Exposé au vent	
Trees in play	Arbres en jeu	

Scorecard Carte de score	**Chp.** Chp.	**Mens** Mess.	**Ladies** Da.
Length Long.	6167	5807	4971
Par	72	72	72
Slope system	142	138	131

Advised golfing ability 0 12 24 36
Niveau de jeu recommandé

Hcp required Handicap exigé 24 Men, 28 Ladies

Club house & amenities — CLUB-HOUSE ET ANNEXES — 8/10

Pro shop	Pro-shop	
Driving range	Practice	
Sheltered	couvert	5 mats
On grass	sur herbe	no, 19 mats open air
Putting-green	putting-green	yes
Pitching-green	pitching green	yes

Hotel facilities — ENVIRONNEMENT HOTELIER — 8/10

HOTELS HÔTELS

Trianon Palace, 188 rooms, D 457 € — Versailles 9 km
Tel (33) 01 30 84 38 00, Fax (33) 01 30 84 50 01

Résidence du Berry, 38 rooms, D 93 € — Versailles
Tel (33) 01 39 49 07 07, Fax (33) 01 39 50 59 40

Versailles, 46 rooms, D 101 € — Versailles
Tel (33) 01 39 50 64 65, Fax (33) 01 39 02 37 85

RESTAURANTS RESTAURANT

La Marée de Versailles — Versailles
Tel (33) 01 30 21 73 73

Les Trois Marches — Versailles
Tel (33) 01 39 50 13 21

SAINT-NOM-LA-BRETÈCHE Rouge

17	8	8

Ce parcours a été rendu célèbre par le Trophée Lancôme, qui se dispute maintenant sur un composite des deux parcours. On ne joue plus sept des derniers trous, venir ici est donc l'occasion de les redécouvrir. Le "Rouge" nécessite un driving très précis si l'on veut espérer scorer, et attaquer les greens en bonne posture. La stratégie de jeu est assez claire, la seule chose que l'on ne maîtrise pas immédiatement, c'est le putting, car les contours des greens sont peu visibles, mais souvent déconcertants. Assez vallonné, mais sans être trop fatiguant à marcher, ce parcours réclame de savoir faire (et bien faire) tous les coups de golf. La variété du dessin, la progression des difficultés permet de renouveler l'intérêt : jouer ici pour le plaisir ou en compétition n'est pas du tout la même chose ! L'entretien y est d'excellente qualité tout au long de l'année, à l'exception des mois d'hiver les plus durs, mais faut-il le dire tant c'est évident.

This course owes its fame to the Trophée Lancôme, which these days is played on a combination of the two courses. Seven of the last "Rouge" holes are not used, so playing here yourself is the opportunity to get to know them. The "Rouge" course requires very straight driving if you want to card a good score and attack the greens from the ideal position. Game strategy is clear enough and the only thing you will immediately find anything but easy is putting. The contours of these greens are not all that visible and often disconcerting. Rather hilly but not too tiring on the legs, this course demands every shot in the book (and as the book tells you). The variety of the layout and the way difficulties slowly pile up make this an interesting course every time. But here, playing for fun and playing in a tournament are two very different propositions. Maintenance is excellent all year except in really hard winters, but there again that really goes without saying.

Golf de Saint-Nom-la-Bretèche 1959

Hameau de la Tuilerie Bignon
F - 78860 SAINT-NOM-LA-BRETECHE

Office	Secrétariat	(33) 01 30 80 04 40
Pro shop	Pro-shop	(33) 01 30 80 04 40
Fax	Fax	(33) 01 30 80 04 50
E-mail	direction@golfsaintnom.com	
Situation	Situation	Versailles, 9 km
Annual closure	Fermeture annuelle	no
Weekly closure	Fermeture hebdomadaire	

tuesday/mardi

Fees main season Tarifs haute saison — Full day

	Week days / Semaine	We/Bank holidays / We/Férié
Individual Individuel	76 € *	91 € *
Couple Couple	152 € *	182 € *

* with a member (accompagné d'un membre)

Caddy	Caddy	on request
Electric Trolley	Chariot électrique	15 € /18 holes
Buggy	Voiturette	medical reasons
Clubs	Clubs	yes

Credit cards Cartes de crédit
VISA - CB - Eurocard

Access Accès : Paris A13 → Rouen. Exit (Sortie) Versailles-Ouest. → Versailles. 500 m turn right on D307 → Noisy-le-Roy, Saint-Nom-la-Bretèche
Map 15 on page 190 Carte 15 Page 190

Golf course PARCOURS 17/20

Site	Site	
Maintenance	Entretien	
Architect	Architecte	Fred Hawtree
Type	Type	parkland, residential
Relief	Relief	
Water in play	Eau en jeu	
Exp. to wind	Exposé au vent	
Trees in play	Arbres en jeu	

Scorecard / Carte de score	Chp. / Chp.	Mens / Mess.	Ladies / Da.
Length Long.	6252	5877	4920
Par	72	72	72
Slope system	145	136	131

Advised golfing ability Niveau de jeu recommandé — 0 12 24 36

Hcp required Handicap exigé — 24 Men, 28 Ladies

Club house & amenities CLUB-HOUSE ET ANNEXES 8/10

Pro shop	Pro-shop	
Driving range	Practice	
Sheltered	couvert	5 mats
On grass	sur herbe	no, 19 mats open air
Putting-green	putting-green	yes
Pitching-green	pitching green	yes

Hotel facilities ENVIRONNEMENT HOTELIER 8/10

HOTELS HÔTELS

Trianon Palace, 188 rooms, D 457 € — Versailles
Tel (33) 01 30 84 38 00, Fax (33) 01 30 84 50 01 — 9 km

Résidence du Berry, 38 rooms, D 93 € — Versailles
Tel (33) 01 39 49 07 07, Fax (33) 01 39 50 59 40

Versailles, 46 rooms, D 101 € — Versailles
Tel (33) 01 39 50 64 65, Fax (33) 01 39 02 37 85

RESTAURANTS RESTAURANT

La Marée de Versailles — Versailles
Tel (33) 01 30 21 73 73

Les Trois Marches — Versailles
Tel (33) 01 39 50 13 21

SAINT-THOMAS

14	7	5

Près de Béziers, ce parcours offre un préjugé favorable, par son arrivée dans la garrigue, par l'environnement et les couleurs de la nature, où s'épanouissent lapins, lièvres et sauvagine. Le tracé du parcours signé P. Lambert ne dément pas cette première impression. Sans apporter d'idées vraiment originales ni d'émotions de jeu exceptionnelles, les 18 trous sont généralement de bonne facture, peu fatigants à jouer, et le climat local comme la nature du sol permettent d'y jouer toute l'année, seul le vent pouvant augmenter les difficultés. L'architecte y a inclus quelques trous délicats (comme le 7 ou le 16 par exemple), mais aussi plusieurs trous assez reposants pour ne pas trop surcharger la carte, et permettre de le conseiller à tous les niveaux. Cependant, la création de nouveaux obstacles d'eau leur compliquera un peu les choses, elle vient maintenant en jeu sur une dizaine de trous. Les équipements de ce club sympathique sont propres et de bonne qualité, sans prétention, on se sent bien accueilli ici.

This course, close to Béziers, immediately gives a pleasing first impression as you drive along a track through the colourful garrigue (Mediterranean shrub) with wild-life all around you. The actual layout, designed by P. Lambert, lives up to this impression. Without any really original ideas or excitement, the 18 holes make for good golfing over flattish terrain, and the local climate and the soil keep the course playable all year. Only the wind can come along and pose a few problems. There are a few very tricky holes (the 7th and 16th, for example), and also some more relaxing numbers to keep the score down and make this a course for everyone. Having said that, the creation of a new water hazard will make life a little more complicated, especially since it is now in play on ten or so holes. The facilities are good and stylish in this very friendly club where visitors very quickly feel one of the family.

Golf de Saint-Thomas — 1992

Route de Pézenas
F - 34500 BEZIERS

Office	Secrétariat	(33) 04 67 39 03 09
Pro shop	Pro-shop	(33) 04 67 39 03 09
Fax	Fax	(33) 04 67 39 10 65
Web	www.golfsaintthomas.com	
Situation	Situation	
Béziers (pop. 71 000), 10 km		
Annual closure	Fermeture annuelle	no
Weekly closure	Fermeture hebdomadaire	no

Fees main season Tarifs haute saison		Full day
	Week days Semaine	**We/Bank holidays** We/Férié
Individual Individuel	44 €	44 €
Couple Couple	88 €	88 €
Under 18 & Students: 27 €		

Caddy	Caddy	no
Electric Trolley	Chariot électrique	no
Buggy	Voiturette	27 € /18 holes
Clubs	Clubs	9 € /full day

Credit cards Cartes de crédit
VISA - CB - Eurocard - MasterCard - AMEX

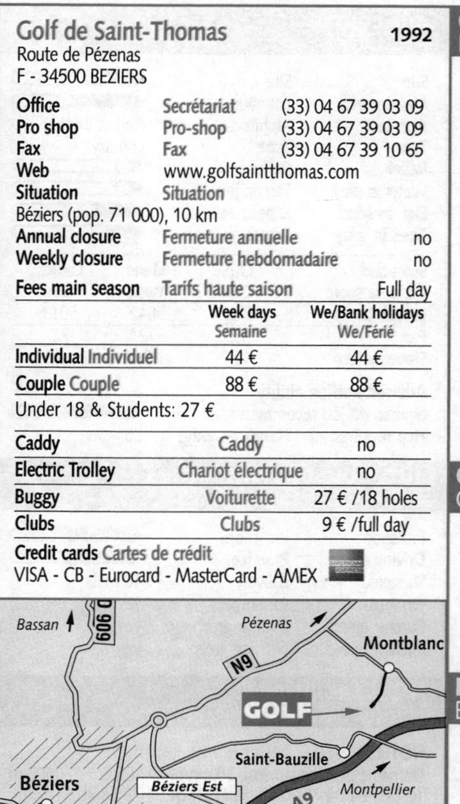

Access Accès : A9, Exit (Sortie) Béziers Est, Expressway (Voie rapide) → Bassan, go through "le Rouge gorge", over bridge, → Golf **Map 13 page 187** Carte 13 Page 187

Golf course PARCOURS — 14/20

Site	Site	
Maintenance	Entretien	
Architect	Architecte	Patrice Lambert
Type	Type	country
Relief	Relief	
Water in play	Eau en jeu	
Exp. to wind	Exposé au vent	
Trees in play	Arbres en jeu	

Scorecard Carte de score	**Chp.** Chp.	**Mens** Mess.	**Ladies** Da.
Length Long.	6131	5729	4737
Par	72	72	72
Slope system	136	124	120

Advised golfing ability 0 12 24 36
Niveau de jeu recommandé
Hcp required Handicap exigé no

Club house & amenities CLUB-HOUSE ET ANNEXES — 7/10

Pro shop	Pro-shop	
Driving range	Practice	
Sheltered	couvert	4 mats
On grass	sur herbe	no, 20 mats open air
Putting-green	putting-green	yes
Pitching-green	pitching green	yes

Hotel facilities ENVIRONNEMENT HOTELIER — 5/10

HOTELS HÔTELS

Impérator , 45 rooms, D 60 € — Béziers
Tel (33) 04 67 49 02 25, Fax (33) 04 67 28 92 30 — 10 km

Champ de Mars, 10 rooms, D 40 € — Béziers
Tel (33) 04 67 28 35 53, Fax (33) 04 67 28 61 42

Château de Lignan, 49 rooms, D 114 € — Lignan-sur-Orb
Tel (33) 04 67 37 91 47, Fax (33) 04 67 37 99 25 — 15 km

RESTAURANTS RESTAURANT

Le Framboisier, Tel (33) 04 67 49 90 00 — Béziers
Le Cep d'Or, Tel (33) 04 67 49 28 09 — Béziers
Château de Lignan — Lignan-sur-Orb
Tel (33) 04 67 37 91 47 — 15 km

SAINTE-BAUME (LA)

14 | 7 | 6

Ce 18 trous aurait pu être une complète réussite si l'on ne trouvait çà et là quelques "idées d'architecte" plus paysagères que golfiques. Alors qu'un parcours commercial doit pouvoir être joué dès la première fois sans cacher ses obstacles, certains trous manquent de franchise, parallèlement à d'autres presque trop faciles. La stratégie n'est alors pas évidente. De fait, on a l'impression d'un ensemble de bonnes idées graphiques, mais pas toujours bien disposées sur le plan du jeu, d'où une impression de manque d'unité. Des améliorations en cours ou en projet devraient y remédier. Les joueurs moyens ou débutants seront sans doute moins sensibles à ces quelques défauts que les joueurs qui attachent une grande importance à la logique des obstacles, au rythme d'un parcours. En dépit de ces appréciations, pour l'utilité de ses installations dans cette région, pour la beauté de l'environnement et la bonne qualité de son entretien, ce parcours mérite largement une visite.

This 18-hole course could have been a total success if it weren't for a few architectural ideas here and there that have more to do with landscaping than with golf. And since a commercial course should be playable first time out without concealing its hazards, there is reason to believe that some holes are a little on the sneaky side, as opposed to others that are almost too easy. The overall impression is that of a whole series of good graphic ideas that are not always well translated into golfing language, hence the feeling of a disjointed layout. Ongoing or planned improvement work should put matters right. Mid-handicappers and beginners will probably be less sensitive to these few flaws than players who attach considerable importance to the logic of hazards and the overall balance of a course. Despite these views, the course is well worth a visit for the utility of facilities in this region, the beauty of the setting and excellent standards of maintenance.

Golf de la Sainte-Baume — 1988

F - 83860 NANS-LES-PINS

Office	Secrétariat	(33) 04 94 78 60 12
Pro shop	Pro-shop	(33) 04 94 78 92 74
Fax	Fax	(33) 04 94 78 63 52
Web	www.opengolfclub.com/gsb/	
Situation	Situation	Marseille, 44 km
Annual closure	Fermeture annuelle	no
Weekly closure	Fermeture hebdomadaire	no

Fees main season Tarifs haute saison	18 holes	
	Week days Semaine	We/Bank holidays We/Férié
Individual Individuel	43 €	43 €
Couple Couple	86 €	86 €

Under 25: 25 € (Weekdays) - 32 € (We)
Seniors: 27 € (thursday/jeudi)

Caddy	Caddy	no
Electric Trolley	Chariot électrique	12 € /18 holes
Buggy	Voiturette	34 € /18 holes
Clubs	Clubs	12 € /full day

Credit cards Cartes de crédit
VISA - CB - Eurocard - MasterCard - DC - JCB - AMEX

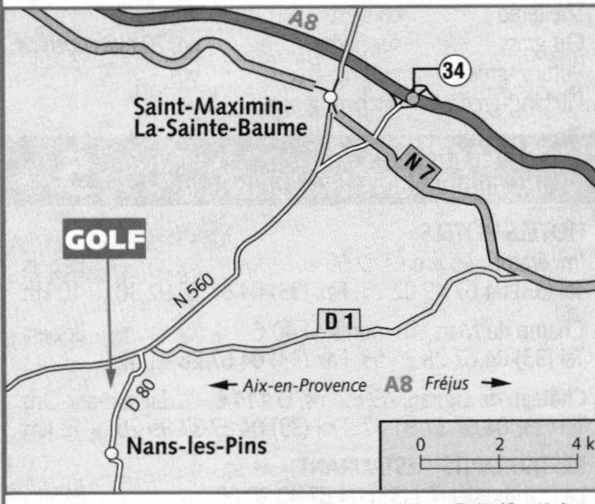

Access Accès : A8 Aix-en-Provence → Nice, Exit (Sortie) Saint-Maximin → La Sainte-Baume, Nans-les-Pins
Map 14 on page 188 Carte 14 Page 188

Golf course PARCOURS — 14/20

Site	Site	
Maintenance	Entretien	
Architect	Architecte	Robert Berthet
Type	Type	country
Relief	Relief	
Water in play	Eau en jeu	
Exp. to wind	Exposé au vent	
Trees in play	Arbres en jeu	

Scorecard Carte de score	Chp. Chp.	Mens Mess.	Ladies Da.
Length Long.	6062	5842	5013
Par	72	72	72
Slope system	124	124	122

Advised golfing ability Niveau de jeu recommandé — 0 12 24 36
Hcp required Handicap exigé — 35

Club house & amenities CLUB-HOUSE ET ANNEXES — 7/10

Pro shop	Pro-shop	
Driving range	Practice	
Sheltered	couvert	10 mats
On grass	sur herbe	yes
Putting-green	putting-green	yes
Pitching-green	pitching green	yes

Hotel facilities ENVIRONNEMENT HOTELIER — 6/10

HOTELS HÔTELS

Domaine de Châteauneuf, 30 rooms, D 165 € — 400 m
Tel (33) 04 94 78 90 06, Fax (33) 04 94 78 63 30

Plaisance, 13 rooms, D 61 € — Saint-Maximin 7 km
Tel (33) 04 94 78 16 74, Fax (33) 04 94 78 18 39

Hôtel de France, 26 rooms, D 59 € — Saint-Maximin
Tel (33) 04 94 78 00 14, Fax (33) 04 94 59 83 80

RESTAURANTS RESTAURANT

Domaine de Châteauneuf ,Tel (33) 04 94 78 90 06 — 400 m

Château de Nans, — Nans-les-Pins
Tel (33) 04 94 78 92 06 — 2 km

SAINTE-MAXIME

13	7	8

Il faut parfois grimper haut (il y a un téléphérique entre le 10 et le 11), et ce parcours est épuisant à pied, mais les vues sur la baie de Saint-Tropez et le massif des Maures récompensent des efforts. Taillé pour une bonne part dans la colline, il n'est pas toujours d'une grande franchise, même si les travaux ont atténué les rebonds indésirables sur des rochers. On comprend que l'architecte Donald Harradine ait adapté son dessin au terrain, mais certains greens aveugles auraient pu être évités. Les fairways sont rarement larges, de nombreux menacent les trajectoires de balle mais la longueur assez réduite du parcours permet de laisser souvent le driver de côté. Il faut soigneusement éviter de jouer en stroke-play, mais on peut beaucoup s'amuser en match-play. Pour les joueurs peu expérimentés, si ce parcours s'avère décourageant, ils pourront profiter pleinement du spectacle splendide.

You sometimes have to scale considerable heights (a cable-car links the 10th and 11th holes) and the course is generally speaking exhausting to walk, but the views over the bay of Saint Tropez and the Maures uplands are more than worth the effort. Mostly cut out of a hill, this can be a deceitful course, even though recent work has reduced the unexpected and unwarranted kicks from rocks. Architect Donald Harradine understandably adapted his layout to the terrain, but certain blind greens could have been avoided. The fairways are seldom wide and numerous pine-trees encroach upon the ball's flight-path, but on this short course you can always leave the driver in the bag. Make a point of not playing stroke-play, you will have much more fun with match-play. A sometimes dispiriting course for inexperienced golfers but they'll love the wonderful view.

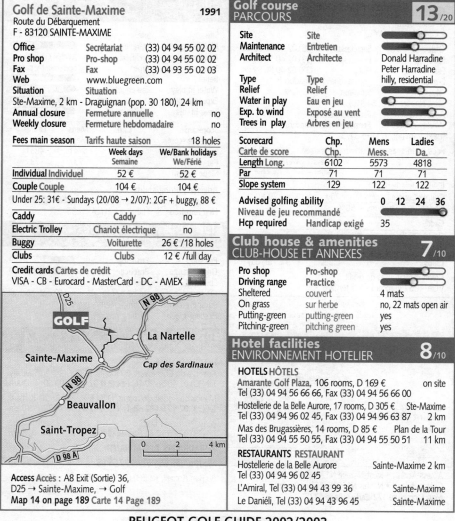

Golf de Sainte-Maxime — 1991

Route du Débarquement
F - 83120 SAINTE-MAXIME

Office	Secrétariat	(33) 04 94 55 02 02
Pro shop	Pro-shop	(33) 04 94 55 02 02
Fax	Fax	(33) 04 93 55 02 03
Web	www.bluegreen.com	
Situation	Situation	

Ste-Maxime, 2 km - Draguignan (pop. 30 180), 24 km

Annual closure	Fermeture annuelle	no
Weekly closure	Fermeture hebdomadaire	no

Fees main season Tarifs haute saison	18 holes	
	Week days Semaine	**We/Bank holidays** We/Férié
Individual Individuel	52 €	52 €
Couple Couple	104 €	104 €

Under 25: 31€ - Sundays (20/08 → 2/07): 2GF + buggy, 88 €

Caddy	Caddy	no
Electric Trolley	Chariot électrique	no
Buggy	Voiturette	26 € /18 holes
Clubs	Clubs	12 € /full day

Credit cards Cartes de crédit
VISA - CB - Eurocard - MasterCard - DC - AMEX

Access Accès : A8 Exit (Sortie) 36,
D25 → Sainte-Maxime, → Golf
Map 14 on page 189 Carte 14 Page 189

Golf course — PARCOURS — 13/20

Site	Site	
Maintenance	Entretien	
Architect	Architecte	Donald Harradine Peter Harradine
Type	Type	hilly, residential
Relief	Relief	
Water in play	Eau en jeu	
Exp. to wind	Exposé au vent	
Trees in play	Arbres en jeu	

Scorecard Carte de score	**Chp.** Chp.	**Mens** Mess.	**Ladies** Da.
Length Long.	6102	5573	4818
Par	71	71	71
Slope system	129	122	122

Advised golfing ability — 0 12 24 36
Niveau de jeu recommandé

Hcp required — Handicap exigé — 35

Club house & amenities — CLUB-HOUSE ET ANNEXES — 7/10

Pro shop	Pro-shop	
Driving range	Practice	
Sheltered	couvert	4 mats
On grass	sur herbe	no, 22 mats open air
Putting-green	putting-green	yes
Pitching-green	pitching green	yes

Hotel facilities — ENVIRONNEMENT HOTELIER — 8/10

HOTELS HÔTELS

Amarante Golf Plaza, 106 rooms, D 169 € — on site
Tel (33) 04 94 56 66 66, Fax (33) 04 94 56 66 00

Hostellerie de la Belle Aurore, 17 rooms, D 305 € — Ste-Maxime
Tel (33) 04 94 96 02 45, Fax (33) 04 94 96 63 87 — 2 km

Mas des Brugassières, 14 rooms, D 85 € — Plan de la Tour
Tel (33) 04 94 55 50 55, Fax (33) 04 94 55 50 51 — 11 km

RESTAURANTS RESTAURANT

Hostellerie de la Belle Aurore — Sainte-Maxime 2 km
Tel (33) 04 94 96 02 45

L'Amiral, Tel (33) 04 94 43 99 36 — Sainte-Maxime

Le Daniéli, Tel (33) 04 94 43 96 45 — Sainte-Maxime

SAVENAY

14 | 5 | 4

Entre Nantes et Saint-Nazaire, et dominant la Loire, Savenay est situé au coeur d'une région aujourd'hui très fournie en golfs de qualité. Un voyage de golf est ainsi agréable pour tous les niveaux, de la Vendée à la côte sud de Bretagne, dans des paysages très caractéristiques de ces régions. Ce parcours plutôt long (complété par un bien utile 9 trous d'entraînement) a été dessiné par Michel Gayon dans un site alternant les trous larges volontiers inspirés des "links" (par leur dessin et l'abondance des bunkers stratégiques), et des trous plus intimes, notamment les 7 et 8, le long d'une pièce d'eau. Les arbres (beaucoup de châtaigniers) sont assez nombreux, mais sans que l'on éprouve une impression d'étouffement. Un petit regret : le grand nombre de trous parallèles. Et un entretien amélioré par les travaux de drainage.

Between Nantes and Saint Nazaire overlooking the Loire river, Savenay stands at the heart of a region which today boasts a number of excellent courses. This makes a golfing holiday to Brittany a pleasant proposition for all, from the Vendée to the southern Breton coastline all in typical settings. This is a rather long course (there is also a 9 hole pitch 'n putt) designed by Michel Gayon, on a site where deliberately wide holes, designed and strategically bunkered in true links style, alternate with more intimate holes, notably the 7th and 8th along a stretch of water. Trees abound (a lot of chestnut trees) but are never too imposing a presence. The one little regret is the number of holes running parallel. Maintenance has been improved by recent drainage work.

Golf de Savenay — 1990

Le Chambeau
F - 44260 SAVENAY

Office	Secrétariat	(33) 02 40 56 88 05
Pro shop	Pro-shop	(33) 02 40 56 88 05
Fax	Fax	(33) 02 40 56 89 04
E-mail	golf.savenay@wanadoo.fr	
Situation	Situation	

Saint-Nazaire (pop. 64 810), 26 km

Annual closure Fermeture annuelle — no
Weekly closure Fermeture hebdomadaire
tuesday (mardi) 1/11 → 31/3

Fees main season Tarifs haute saison — 18 holes

	Week days Semaine	We/Bank holidays We/Férié
Individual Individuel	35 €	35 €
Couple Couple	70 €	70 €

Under 21 & Students: – 50%

Caddy	Caddy	no
Electric Trolley	Chariot électrique	no
Buggy	Voiturette	23 € /18 holes
Clubs	Clubs	9 € /full day

Credit cards Cartes de crédit
VISA - CB - Eurocard - MasterCard

Access Accès : • Saint-Nazaire N171, Exit (Sortie) Châteaubriand • Nantes N165, Exit Blain-Bouvron
Map 6 on page 172 Carte 6 Page 172

Golf course PARCOURS — 14/20

Site	Site	
Maintenance	Entretien	
Architect	Architecte	Michel Gayon
Type	Type	open country, parkland
Relief	Relief	
Water in play	Eau en jeu	
Exp. to wind	Exposé au vent	
Trees in play	Arbres en jeu	

Scorecard Carte de score	Chp. Chp.	Mens Mess.	Ladies Da.
Length Long.	6250	5741	4831
Par	73	73	73
Slope system	141	128	127

Advised golfing ability 0 12 24 36
Niveau de jeu recommandé
Hcp required Handicap exigé 35

Club house & amenities CLUB-HOUSE ET ANNEXES — 5/10

Pro shop	Pro-shop	
Driving range	Practice	
Sheltered	couvert	9 mats
On grass	sur herbe	no, 60 mats open air
Putting-green	putting-green	yes
Pitching-green	pitching green	yes (3)

Hotel facilities ENVIRONNEMENT HOTELIER — 4/10

HOTELS HÔTELS

Auberge du Chêne Vert, 20 rooms, D 38 € — Savenay
Tel (33) 02 40 56 90 16, Fax (33) 02 40 56 99 60 — 1 km

Manoir du Rodoir, 26 rooms, D 84 € — La Roche-Bernard
Tel (33) 02 99 90 82 68, Fax (33) 02 99 90 76 22 — 30 km

Berry, 27 rooms, D 85 € — Saint-Nazaire
Tel (33) 02 40 22 42 61, Fax (33) 02 40 22 45 34 — 23 km

RESTAURANTS RESTAURANT

Moderne, Tel (33) 02 40 22 55 88 — Saint-Nazaire 23 km

Au Bon Accueil, Tel (33) 02 40 22 07 05 — Saint-Nazaire

SEIGNOSSE

17	7	7

Un parcours qui ne laisse personne indifférent et surprend encore à chaque fois. A proximité du parcours très plat d'Hossegor, il se déroule dans un paysage très accidenté, planté de pins et de chênes-liège. Les différences de dénivellation et l'étroitesse des fairways incitent à le conseiller aux joueurs en forme et golfiquement aguerris, qui devront bien étudier leur stratégie. En revanche, il n'est pas très long (notamment les par 3, sauf le 16), et demande un jeu de fers précis, en particulier pour attaquer les drapeaux, car les greens sont très modelés, de dimensions très variées et mettre sa balle loin des trous peut gonfler démesurément le score. Les contours de fairway très travaillés et les abords des greens sont typiquement de von Hagge, de même que l'alternance de bunkers de sable et d'herbe et le dessin des pièces d'eau (sur cinq trous). Souvent spectaculaire et intimidant, il ne se maîtrise pas au premier abord. C'est un parcours follement amusant en match-play. Si on joue bien ici, on peut aller partout.

A course that leaves no-one indifferent and springs a surprise or two every time. Close to the flat course of Hossegor, Seignosse unfolds over very hilly terrain planted with pine-trees and cork oaks. The steep slopes and narrow fairways mean this is a layout for seasoned players on top of their game, who know the meaning of the word strategy. By contrast, the course is short (especially the par 3s except the 16th) and requires precision iron-work, especially when attacking the contoured greens of all sizes. Balls ending up too far from the hole can ruin your card. The rolling fairways and edges of the greens are typical of von Hagge, as are the alternating grass-bunkers and sand-traps and the design of the water hazards (on five holes). Often spectacular and intimidating, most golfers will and do have trouble first time out. A good course and great fun in match-play. If you play well here you will play well anywhere.

Golf de Seignosse — 1989

Avenue du Belvédère
F - 40510 SEIGNOSSE

Office	Secrétariat	(33) 05 58 41 68 30
Pro shop	Pro-shop	(33) 05 58 41 68 30
Fax	Fax	(33) 05 58 41 68 31
Web	www.bluegreen.com	
Situation	Situation	Bayonne, 28 km
Annual closure	Fermeture annuelle	no
Weekly closure	Fermeture hebdomadaire	no

Fees main season Tarifs haute saison	18 holes	
	Week days Semaine	**We/Bank holidays** We/Férié
Individual Individuel	59 €	59 €
Couple Couple	118 €	118 €

Under 21 & Students: – 50%

Caddy	Caddy	no
Electric Trolley	Chariot électrique	no
Buggy	Voiturette	23 € /18 holes
Clubs	Clubs	30 € /18 holes

Credit cards Cartes de crédit
VISA - CB - Eurocard - MasterCard - DC - AMEX

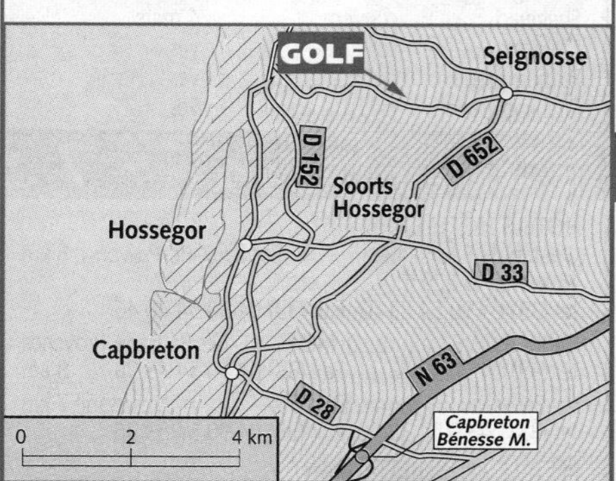

Access Accès : • Bayonne A63 → Bordeaux, Exit (Sortie) Capbreton → Capbreton/Hossegor • Bordeaux A63 → Bayonne, Exit Saint-Geours-de-Marenne → Seignosse

Map 12 on page 184 Carte 12 Page 184

Golf course PARCOURS — 17/20

Site	Site	
Maintenance	Entretien	
Architect	Architecte	Robert von Hagge
Type	Type	forest, hilly
Relief	Relief	
Water in play	Eau en jeu	
Exp. to wind	Exposé au vent	
Trees in play	Arbres en jeu	

Scorecard Carte de score	**Chp.** Chp.	**Mens** Mess.	**Ladies** Da.
Length Long.	6129	5774	5070
Par	72	72	72
Slope system	144	142	137

Advised golfing ability Niveau de jeu recommandé — 0 12 24 36

Hcp required Handicap exigé — no

Club house & amenities CLUB-HOUSE ET ANNEXES — 7/10

Pro shop	Pro-shop	
Driving range	Practice	
Sheltered	couvert	10 mats
On grass	sur herbe	yes
Putting-green	putting-green	yes
Pitching-green	pitching green	yes

Hotel facilities ENVIRONNEMENT HOTELIER — 7/10

HOTELS HÔTELS

Golf Hôtel Blue Green, 45 rooms, D 126 € — on site
Tel (33) 05 58 41 68 40, Fax (33) 05 58 41 68 41

Beauséjour, 45 rooms, D 114 € — Hossegor 5 km
Tel (33) 05 58 43 51 07, Fax (33) 05 58 43 70 13

Les Hortensias du Lac, 19 rooms, D 125 € — Hossegor
Tel (33) 05 58 43 99 00, Fax (33) 05 58 43 42 81

RESTAURANTS RESTAURANT

Les Huîtrières du Lac, Tel (33) 05 58 43 51 48 — Hossegor

Auberge du Cheval Blanc — Bayonne 28 km
Tel (33) 05 59 59 01 33

François Miura, Tel (33) 05 59 59 49 89 — Bayonne

SERVANES

13	7	7

Servanes ne peut renier sa Provence, avec les reliefs blancs et rocailleux des Alpilles, les oliviers, cyprès et platanes, et parfois un méchant coup de mistral, qui devrait empoisonner les golfeurs, mais ils en sont relativement protégés ici. Dans un site de campagne à peu près préservé d'immobilier, Sprecher et Watine ont dessiné un parcours bien paysagé, techniquement honnête, mais sans imagination excessive. Les contours de fairway auraient sans doute pu être mieux travaillés : en Provence, on préfère les sentiers aux boulevards. Autrement, il n'y a pas de grands commentaires à faire, sinon que, tout comme les joueurs de niveau moyen, les joueurs peu expérimentés trouveront ici le calme et de quoi assouvir leur passion naissante dans un cadre magnifique, à proximité du splendide village des Baux de Provence. Quelques départs ont été refaits, et le système d'arrosage très amélioré, ce qui n'est pas inutile dans cette région souvent très ensoleillée. Mais le club house comme l'accueil ne sont pas toujours du meilleur niveau. Cela peut changer.

Servanes is Provence through and through, with the white rocky terrain of the Alpilles, cypress and plane trees, and sometimes a gust of mistral which can play havoc, although golfers are relatively sheltered on this course. On a country site more or less protected from property development, Sprecher and Watine have designed a nicely landscaped course which is technically fair but none too rich in imagination. The fairways could certainly have been better contoured, and in Provence they prefer pathways to boulevards. Otherwise, there is little else to say, except that high-handicappers and beginners alike will find the calm and the course they are looking for to satisfy their nascent enthusiasm for the game. All this in a magnificent setting close to the splendid village of Baux de Provence. A few tee-boxes have been redesigned and the watering system much improved, a useful asset in this sunny part of the world. Unfortunately the club-house and hospitality do not always measure up, but this may change.

Golf Country-Club de Servanes — 1989

Domaine de Servanes
F - 13890 MOURIES

Office	Secrétariat	(33) 04 90 47 59 95
Pro shop	Pro-shop	(33) 04 90 47 65 70
Fax	Fax	(33) 04 90 47 52 58
Web	www.opengolf.com	
Situation	Situation	

Arles (pop. 52 050), 25 km

Annual closure	Fermeture annuelle	no
Weekly closure	Fermeture hebdomadaire	no

Fees main season Tarifs haute saison	Week days Semaine	We/Bank holidays We/Férié
Individual Individuel	41 €	41 €
Couple Couple	82 €	82 €

2 GF + 2 lunches + golf car: 125 € (full day)

Caddy	Caddy	no
Electric Trolley	Chariot électrique	no
Buggy	Voiturette	34 € /18 holes
Clubs	Clubs	15 € /full day

Credit cards Cartes de crédit
VISA - CB - Eurocard - MasterCard - DC - AMEX

Les Baux-de-Provence
Saint-Rémy-de-Provence
D 24
GOLF
D 17
Maussane-les-Alpilles
D 17
Servanes
Mouries
D 5
A54
Arles
D 24
Marseille
Saint-Martin-de-Crau
N 113
A54
0 2 4 km

Access Accès : A54 / N113 Nîmes-Arles, → Marseille, Exit (Sortie) Saint-Martin-de-Crau → Mouriès
Map 14 on page 188 Carte 14 Page 188

Golf course PARCOURS — 13/20

Site	Site	
Maintenance	Entretien	
Architect	Architecte	Thierry Sprecher, Géry Watine
Type	Type	country
Relief	Relief	
Water in play	Eau en jeu	
Exp. to wind	Exposé au vent	
Trees in play	Arbres en jeu	

Scorecard Carte de score	Chp. Chp.	Mens Mess.	Ladies Da.
Length Long.	6121	5690	4811
Par	72	72	72
Slope system	132	123	124

Advised golfing ability Niveau de jeu recommandé — 0 12 24 36
Hcp required Handicap exigé — 35

Club house & amenities CLUB-HOUSE ET ANNEXES — 7/10

Pro shop	Pro-shop	
Driving range	Practice	
Sheltered	couvert	4 mats
On grass	sur herbe	yes
Putting-green	putting-green	yes
Pitching-green	pitching green	yes

Hotel facilities ENVIRONNEMENT HOTELIER — 7/10

HOTELS HÔTELS

Oustau de Baumanière — Les Baux-de-Provence 8 km
15 rooms, D 229 €
Tel (33) 04 90 54 33 07, Fax (33) 04 90 54 40 46

Cabro d'Or, 31 rooms, D 140 € — Les Baux-de-Provence 8 km
Tel (33) 04 90 54 33 21, Fax (33) 04 90 54 45 98

Val Baussenc, 21 rooms, D 105 € — Maussane 7 km
Tel (33) 04 90 54 38 90, Fax (33) 04 90 54 33 36

RESTAURANTS RESTAURANT

Oustau de Baumanière — Les Baux-de-Provence 8 km
Tel (33) 04 90 54 33 07

La Petite France, Tel (33) 04 90 54 41 91 — Maussane 9 km

La Riboto de Taven, Tel (33) 04 90 54 34 23 — Les Baux-de-Provence

SOUFFLENHEIM

16 | 7 | 4

Avec ce parcours, l'Alsace a confirmé son statut de région golfique de qualité, même si les voisins allemands l'ont attaché à Baden-Baden. Bernhard Langer a produit un dessin très technique, où les obstacles sont visuellement et réellement menaçants. La présence de nombreux bunkers de greens et de fairways, comme des obstacles d'eau (sur 14 trous) exige une attention constante et impose un rythme soutenu, mais les joueurs peu expérimentés pourront trouver des solutions et s'y amuser, en jouant des départs avancés. De nombreuses buttes séparent les fairways et entourent la plupart des greens, ajoutant du relief à cet espace naturellement plat, et entouré de forêts. Les greens sont de bonne dimension, souvent bien modelés, ajoutant à l'intérêt du jeu. Quelques plantations et modifications récentes du tracé ont encore amélioré le plaisir d'y jouer. Le parcours n'aime toujours pas les pluies, mais les supporte mieux. Une belle réalisation, pas encore parvenue à complète maturité, mais déjà bien évoluée.

With this course, Alsace has confirmed its status as a great region for golf, even though our German neighbours consider it to be a part of Baden-Baden. Bernhard Langer has created a very technical layout where hazards are visually and truly threatening. The numerous green-side and fairway bunkers and the water hazards (on 14 holes) demand constant care and establish a nice balance, but inexperienced golfers will find the answer and have fun by playing from the front tees. The fairways are separated by numerous sand-hills, which also surround most of the greens, thus adding relief to a naturally flat terrain encircled by a forest. The greens are large and often well contoured, thus adding extra spice to the course. A few plantation programmes and recent changes to the course have improved still further the pleasure of playing here. It still does not like rain, but drainage is better. A fine course which is getting better, although it will take time to fully mature.

Soufflenheim Baden Baden — 1995

Allée du Golf
F - 67620 SOUFFLENHEIM

Office	Secrétariat	(33) 03 88 05 77 00
Pro shop	Pro-shop	(33) 03 88 05 77 00
Fax	Fax	(33) 03 88 05 77 01
Web	www.golfclub-soufflenheim.com	
Situation	Situation	

Strasbourg (pop. 252 260), 40 km - Haguenau, 15 km

Annual closure	Fermeture annuelle	no
Weekly closure	Fermeture hebdomadaire	no

monday (lundi), restaurant closed 01/01 → 01/03

Fees main season Tarifs haute saison		18 holes
	Week days Semaine	**We/Bank holidays** We/Férié
Individual Individuel	48 €	71 €
Couple Couple	96 €	142 €

Under 18: – 50%

Caddy	Caddy	on request
Electric Trolley	Chariot électrique	no
Buggy	Voiturette	26 € /18 holes
Clubs	Clubs	15 € /18 holes

Credit cards Cartes de crédit
VISA - CB - Eurocard - MasterCard - DC

Access Accès : Strasbourg, A4, Exit (Sortie) Karlsruhe-Lauterburg to D300. 15 km, Exit Soufflenheim → Golf
Map 4 on page 169 Carte 4 Page 169

Golf course PARCOURS — 16/20

Site	Site	
Maintenance	Entretien	
Architect	Architecte	Bernhard Langer
Type	Type	forest, open country
Relief	Relief	
Water in play	Eau en jeu	
Exp. to wind	Exposé au vent	
Trees in play	Arbres en jeu	

Scorecard Carte de score	**Chp.** Chp.	**Mens** Mess.	**Ladies** Da.
Length Long.	6357	6053	5217
Par	72	72	72
Slope system	144	140	134

Advised golfing ability Niveau de jeu recommandé — 0 12 24 36

Hcp required Handicap exigé — 36

Club house & amenities CLUB-HOUSE ET ANNEXES — 7/10

Pro shop	Pro-shop	
Driving range	Practice	
Sheltered	couvert	35 mats
On grass	sur herbe	no, 70 mats open air
Putting-green	putting-green	yes (2)
Pitching-green	pitching green	yes

Hotel facilities ENVIRONNEMENT HOTELIER — 4/10

HOTELS HÔTELS

Europe, 75 rooms, D 52 € — Haguenau 14 km
Tel (33) 03 88 93 58 11, Fax (33) 03 88 06 05 43

Kaiserhof, 15 rooms, D 50 € — Haguenau
Tel (33) 03 88 73 43 43, Fax (33) 03 88 73 28 91

RESTAURANTS RESTAURANT

Auberge du Cheval Blanc — Schweighouse-sur-Moder
Tel (33) 03 88 72 76 96 — 18 km

A l'Agneau, Tel (33) 03 88 86 95 55 — Sessenheim 5 km

Au Boeuf, Tel (33) 03 88 86 97 14 — Sessenheim 5 km

Barberousse, Tel (33) 03 88 73 31 09 — Haguenau 14 km

SPÉRONE

17 | 7 | 5

Dans un des deux ou trois sites les plus magnifiques d'Europe, Robert Trent Jones a tracé le parcours en plein maquis, à l'exception de six trous absolument splendides en bord de falaise, d'où l'on découvre la Méditerranée et la Sardaigne en arrière-plan. Pas très long, mais très technique et assez accidenté (voiturette conseillée), ce parcours spectaculaire ne peut laisser indifférent. Si on peut l'estimer difficile pour les joueurs peu expérimentés, on peut en revanche adorer son tracé parfois déconcertant, ses provocations, ses greens très modelés. Avec ses couleurs, ses lumières, les odeurs de la flore, c'est un parcours assez magique, mais parfois injuste quand le vent vient lui donner un air d'Ecosse en plein soleil. Alors, ceux qui maîtrisent mal les balles basses peuvent souffrir ! Une cinquantaine de maisons de belle architecture sont dissimulées dans ce vaste domaine. Sperone a souvent été au centre de l'actualité, il mérite de l'être pour ses grands mérites golfiques. A connaître sans faute.

On one of Europe's two or three most fabulous sites, Robert Trent Jones designed this course amidst gorse and heather, with the exception of six absolutely splendid holes atop the cliffs from where you can see Sardinia in the distance over the shimmering Mediterranean. Not particularly long but very much a course for the technician and hilly to boot (buggy recommended), this spectacular course leaves no-one indifferent. And while it may be considered tough for inexperienced golfers, you have to love the sometimes disconcerting layout, its provocative nature and the switchback greens. With its colours, light and fragrances, this is sheer magic but sometimes a little unjust when the wind blows and brings along a breath of Scottish air in the Corsican sun. In this case, low shots are a must to keep a decent score. Fifty or so villas are hidden on this vast estate, which has often been in the news, mostly for the wrong reasons rather than for being a wonderful golf course. A must.

Golf de Spérone — 1990

Domaine de Spérone
F - 20169 SPERONE

Office	Secrétariat	(33) 04 95 73 17 13
Pro shop	Pro-shop	(33) 04 95 73 17 13
Fax	Fax	(33) 04 95 73 17 85
Web		www.sperone.net
Situation	Situation	Bonifacio (pop. 2 680), 6 km
Annual closure	Fermeture annuelle	6/1→3/2
Weekly closure	Fermeture hebdomadaire	

monday from 01/05 to 30/09 (except holidays)

Fees main season Tarifs haute saison	Week days Semaine	We/Bank holidays We/Férié
	Full day	
Individual Individuel	75 €	75 €
Couple Couple	150 €	150 €

Under 21 & Students: 45 € - 01/09 → 5/06: Green-fee 35€

Caddy	Caddy	no
Electric Trolley	Chariot électrique	no
Buggy	Voiturette	34 € /18 holes
Clubs	Clubs	9 € /full day

Credit cards Cartes de crédit
VISA - CB - Eurocard - MasterCard - DC - AMEX

Figari
Porto-Vecchio
Propriano
Ajaccio
N 198
Golfe de Sta. Manza
Pte de Capicciola
N 196
GOLF
Bonifacio
0 2 4 km

Access Accès : Bonifacio → Phare de Pertusato, → Golf
Map 14 on page 189 Carte 14 Page 189

Golf course PARCOURS — 17/20

Site	Site	
Maintenance	Entretien	
Architect	Architecte	R. Trent Jones Sr
Type	Type	seaside course, hilly
Relief	Relief	
Water in play	Eau en jeu	
Exp. to wind	Exposé au vent	
Trees in play	Arbres en jeu	

Scorecard Carte de score	Chp. Chp.	Mens Mess.	Ladies Da.
Length Long.	6106	5417	4916
Par	72	72	72
Slope system	150	139	137

Advised golfing ability — Niveau de jeu recommandé: 0 12 24 36
Hcp required — Handicap exigé: 28

Club house & amenities CLUB-HOUSE ET ANNEXES — 7/10

Pro shop	Pro-shop	
Driving range	Practice	
Sheltered	couvert	4 mats
On grass	sur herbe	yes
Putting-green	putting-green	yes (2)
Pitching-green	pitching green	yes

Hotel facilities ENVIRONNEMENT HOTELIER — 5/10

HOTELS HÔTELS

A Trama, 25 rooms, D 133 € — Bonifacio
Tel (33) 04 95 73 17 17, Fax (33) 04 95 73 17 79 — 4 km

Genovese, 15 rooms, D 198 € — Bonifacio
Tel (33) 04 95 73 12 34, Fax (33) 04 95 73 09 03 — 6 km

Roy d'Aragon, 31 rooms, D 96 € — Bonifacio
Tel (33) 04 95 73 03 99, Fax (33) 04 95 73 07 94 — 6 km

RESTAURANTS RESTAURANT

Stella d'Oro, Tel (33) 04 95 73 03 63 — Bonifacio 6 km

Marina di Cavu, Tel (33) 04 95 73 14 13 — Calalonga 3 km

STRASBOURG ILLKIRCH Jaune + Rouge

13	7	6

Le golf des Strasbourgeois, avant la création de la Wantzenau et du Kempferhof. L'architecture en est bien plus traditionnelle, avec quelques obstacles d'eau seulement, surtout sur le Rouge, où les arbres ajoutent d'autres difficultés, un paysage moins travaillé. Les trous les plus durs sont groupés au début du Jaune, mais cet ensemble reste rassurant, et ne suscite pas de grandes émotions visuelles ou techniques chez les meilleurs joueurs. En revanche, les nombreux membres y évoluent avec plaisir en famille, d'autant que les fairways sont excellents en toutes saisons. Les greens sont bien défendus, mais il est toujours possible d'y accéder en faisant rouler la balle. Il s'agit là avant tout d'un club pour les locaux, cependant ouvert aux joueurs extérieurs (accès limité en week-end). De passage à Strasbourg, ils y passeront une journée plaisante. Après la rénovation du Club house, des travaux bienvenus sur le parcours en ont rehaussé le niveau.

This was the traditional golf club of Strasbourg before Wantzenau and Kempferhof came along. By comparison, the architecture looks more traditional with only a few water hazards, notably on the Red course, where trees add further difficulties over less elaborate landscape. The hardest holes are grouped at the start of the Yellow course, but the full layout is somewhat reassuring and will hardly cause much visual or technical stirrings amongst the best players. By contrast, the many members enjoy playing here with the family, especially since the fairways are in excellent condition all year round. The greens are well defended but not from the front, thus allowing the easier chipped shot onto the putting surface. This is first and foremost a club for the locals, although the course is open to green-feers (not so easy on week-ends). When passing through Strasbourg, they can spend a pleasant day. After rehabilitation of the Club house, welcome work on the course has improved standards.

Golf de Strasbourg-Ilkirch — 1934

Route du Rhin
F - 67400 ILLKIRCH

Office	Secrétariat	(33) 03 88 66 17 22
Pro shop	Pro-shop	(33) 03 88 67 22 85
Fax	Fax	(33) 03 88 65 05 67
Web	www.golf-strasbourg.com	
Situation	Situation	Strasbourg, 12 km
Annual closure	Fermeture annuelle	22/12→3/1
Weekly closure	Fermeture hebdomadaire	no

wednesday (mercredi): restaurant closed

Fees main season Tarifs haute saison	18 holes	
	Week days Semaine	We/Bank holidays We/Férié
Individual Individuel	38 €	46 € *
Couple Couple	76 €	92 € *

* We, with members only (avec un membre seulement)

Caddy	Caddy	no
Electric Trolley	Chariot électrique	8 € /18 holes
Buggy	Voiturette	30 € /18 holes
Clubs	Clubs	8 € /18 holes

Credit cards Cartes de crédit
VISA - CB - Eurocard - MasterCard

Access Accès : • Strasbourg A35, Exit (Sortie) Baggersee, 1st roundabout → Markolsheim, 2nd roundabout, Expressway, → Golf • Colmar N83, go through Fegersheim → Illkirch
Map 4 on page 169 Carte 4 Page 169

Golf course PARCOURS — 13/20

Site	Site	
Maintenance	Entretien	
Architect	Architecte	Donald Harradine
Type	Type	country
Relief	Relief	
Water in play	Eau en jeu	
Exp. to wind	Exposé au vent	
Trees in play	Arbres en jeu	

Scorecard Carte de score	Chp. Chp.	Mens Mess.	Ladies Da.
Length Long.	6109	5727	4916
Par	73	73	73
Slope system	130	125	128

Advised golfing ability 0 12 24 36
Niveau de jeu recommandé
Hcp required Handicap exigé 35

Club house & amenities CLUB-HOUSE ET ANNEXES — 7/10

Pro shop	Pro-shop	
Driving range	Practice	
Sheltered	couvert	15 mats
On grass	sur herbe	yes (not in winter)
Putting-green	putting-green	yes
Pitching-green	pitching green	yes

Hotel facilities ENVIRONNEMENT HOTELIER — 6/10

HOTELS HÔTELS

Beaucour, 49 rooms, D 145 € — Strasbourg 12 km
Tel (33) 03 88 76 72 00, Fax (33) 03 88 76 72 60

Alsace, 40 rooms, D 52 € — Illkirch 3 km
Tel (33) 03 88 66 41 60, Fax (33) 03 88 67 04 64

Hôtel des Rohan, 36 rooms, D 121 € — Strasbourg
Tel (33) 03 88 32 85 11, Fax (33) 03 88 75 65 37

RESTAURANTS RESTAURANT

La Vieille Enseigne, Tel (33) 03 88 32 58 50 — Strasbourg

Maison des Tanneurs, Tel(33) 03 88 32 79 70 — Strasbourg

Maison Kammerzell et Baumann — Strasbourg 12 km
Tel (33) 03 88 32 42 14

TAULANE

15 | 7 | 4

C'était autrefois un site de golf avant que, des années plus tard, Gary Player remodèle et restructure complètement l'ancien tracé, jamais vraiment ouvert. On reconnaît son souci de faire des parcours accessibles à la majorité des joueurs, et de ne pas trop bouleverser un site, et il a visiblement voulu préserver la beauté du lieu (l'automne y est splendide). Le tracé est très intéressant, sa difficulté globale raisonnable, mais il réclame une bonne technique pour faire un bon score. Il reste à la portée des joueurs de tous niveaux, de préférence en voiturette car les reliefs sont parfois prononcés. Le dessin vous impose le jeu, sans guère d'options différentes, mais le plaisir reste de grande qualité et à dire vrai, on ne joue pas ici tous les jours. Les amoureux de la nature vont adorer Taulane, d'autant que l'hôtel sur place est très agréable. Situé à moyenne altitude, ce parcours n'est ouvert que huit mois par an, dans un site isolé et très naturel donnant une sensation de calme extrême. En été, échapper à la foule et aux chaleurs de la Côte constitue un plaisir supplémentaire.

This was a golf course long before Gary Player, many years later, completely restyled and remodelled the old layout. You can recognise his concern for designing courses that are playable by nearly everyone and for not disrupting natural sites, and here he visibly set out to protect the area's natural beauty (autumn is wonderful). The layout is very interesting and overall difficulty quite reasonable, but a good round here requires a sound technique. Players of all levels will enjoy Taulane, preferably on 4-wheels since some of the slopes are on the steep side. The architecture imposes a certain style of golf with very few options, but the course is fun although maybe not every day. Nature-enthusiasts will love the site, which also boasts a very pleasant hotel. Located at mid-altitude, Taulane is open just eight months a year in an isolated and very natural site which gives a feeling of immense calm. In summer, getting away from the crowds and the heat on the coast makes it even more enjoyable.

Golf de Taulane — 1992

RN 85
F - 83840 LA MARTRE

Office	Secrétariat	(33) 04 93 60 31 30
Pro shop	Pro-shop	(33) 04 93 60 31 30
Fax	Fax	(33) 04 93 60 33 23
Web	www.chateau-taulane.com	
Situation	Situation	
Grasse (pop. 41 380), 50 km		
Annual closure	Fermeture annuelle	1/11→1/4
Weekly closure	Fermeture hebdomadaire	no

Fees main season Tarifs haute saison	Week days Semaine	We/Bank holidays We/Férié
	18 holes	
Individual Individuel	61 €	61 €
Couple Couple	122 €	122 €

Caddy	Caddy	no
Electric Trolley	Chariot électrique	15 € /18 holes
Buggy	Voiturette	34 € /18 holes
Clubs	Clubs	23 € /full day

Credit cards Cartes de crédit
VISA - CB - Eurocard - MasterCard - DC - AMEX

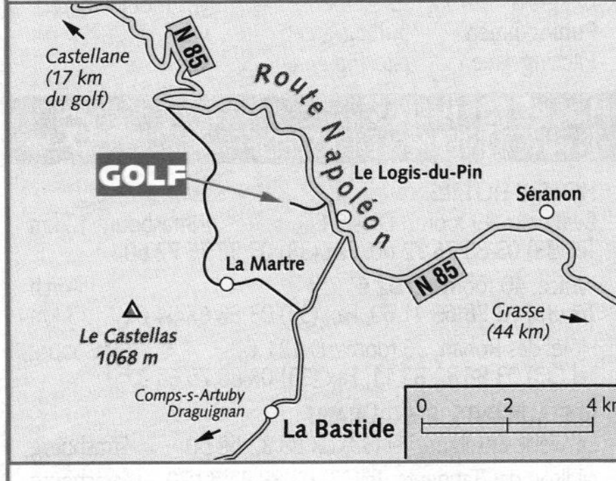

Access Accès : From Nice or Cannes → Grasse/Digne → Le Logis du Pin, "Route Napoléon"
Map 14 on page 189 Carte 14 Page 189

Golf course PARCOURS — 15/20

Site	Site	
Maintenance	Entretien	
Architect	Architecte	Gary Player
Type	Type	forest
Relief	Relief	
Water in play	Eau en jeu	
Exp. to wind	Exposé au vent	
Trees in play	Arbres en jeu	

Scorecard Carte de score	Chp. Chp.	Mens Mess.	Ladies Da.
Length Long.	6269	5822	5341
Par	72	72	72
Slope system	134	131	127

Advised golfing ability / Niveau de jeu recommandé: 0 12 24 36
Hcp required — Handicap exigé: 24 Men, 28 Ladies

Club house & amenities CLUB-HOUSE ET ANNEXES — 7/10

Pro shop	Pro-shop	
Driving range	Practice	
Sheltered	couvert	10 mats
On grass	sur herbe	yes
Putting-green	putting-green	yes
Pitching-green	pitching green	yes

Hotel facilities ENVIRONNEMENT HOTELIER — 4/10

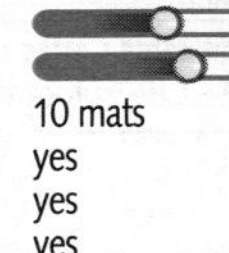

HOTELS HÔTELS
Château de Taulane, 45 rooms, D 204 € — on site
Tel (33) 04 93 40 60 80, Fax (33) 04 93 60 37 48

Château de Trigance, 8 rooms, D 149 € — Trigance 20 km
Tel (33) 04 94 76 91 18, Fax (33) 04 94 85 68 99

Auberge du Teillon, 8 rooms, D 46 € — La Garde 9 km
Tel (33) 04 92 83 60 88, Fax (33) 04 92 83 74 08

RESTAURANTS RESTAURANT
Nouvel Hôtel du Commerce — Castellane 15 km
Tel (33) 04 92 83 61 00

Auberge du Teillon — La Garde 9 km
Tel (33) 04 92 83 60 88

TOULOUSE PALMOLA

15	7	4

Un club vivant et professionnel, où il fait bon s'arrêter. Bien à l'abri du vent, avec de beaux chênes, quelques trouées offrant de jolies vues sur la vallée du Tarn, ce parcours a bien respecté l'environnement. Cette réussite générale rend certainement exigeant. Pour en faire un grand parcours, on souhaiterait par exemple que les bunkers soient un peu plus profonds, ce qui impliquerait une révision des avant-greens. Mais, en l'état, il faut déjà savoir jouer tous les coups, et utiliser tous les clubs du sac : les joueurs de bon handicap apprécieront particulièrement sa technicité. Assez varié pour ne jamais être ennuyeux, le tracé de Michael Fenn a évité les trous parallèles, et offre un rythme de jeu bien équilibré, alternant les trous difficiles et les trous plus reposants. Un golf très familial, avec une bonne politique sportive, qui mérite largement la visite, et garde le sens de la mesure : seul un petit remodelage du trou n° 2 a apporté quelque changement notable.

A very lively, professional club where it is always a pleasure to stop-off. Nicely sheltered from the wind, this is a course that has espoused its environment and is laid out amidst some beautiful oaks. A few holes provide splendid views over the Tarn river. This initial very positive impression makes the visitor a little more demanding when it comes to the rest. For example, a great course would require slightly deeper bunkers and consequently a little re-design work around the greens. But as it is, it demands every shot in the book and probably every club in your bag. Low handicappers in particular will enjoy the course's technical aspect. With enough variety never to be boring, Michael Fenn's layout has avoided parallel holes and provides a nicely balanced course, alternating difficult holes with the not so difficult. A very family-style course and very well organised sports-wise, which is well worth the visit and has retained a sense of measure: only slight restyling of hole N°2 has brought any notable change.

Golf de Toulouse Palmola — 1974

F - 31660 BUZET-SUR-TARN

Office	Secrétariat	(33) 05 61 84 20 50
Pro shop	Pro-shop	(33) 05 61 84 20 50
Fax	Fax	(33) 05 61 84 48 92
Web	golf.palmola	
Situation	Situation	
Toulouse (pop. 358 680), 20 km		
Annual closure	Fermeture annuelle	no
Weekly closure	Fermeture hebdomadaire	
tuesday (mardi)		

Fees main season Tarifs haute saison	Week days Semaine	We/Bank holidays We/Férié
		full day
Individual Individuel	46 €	46 €
Couple Couple	92 €	92 €

Caddy	Caddy	no
Electric Trolley	Chariot électrique	no
Buggy	Voiturette	30 € /18 holes
Clubs	Clubs	23 € /full day

Credit cards Cartes de crédit
VISA - CB - Eurocard - MasterCard - AMEX

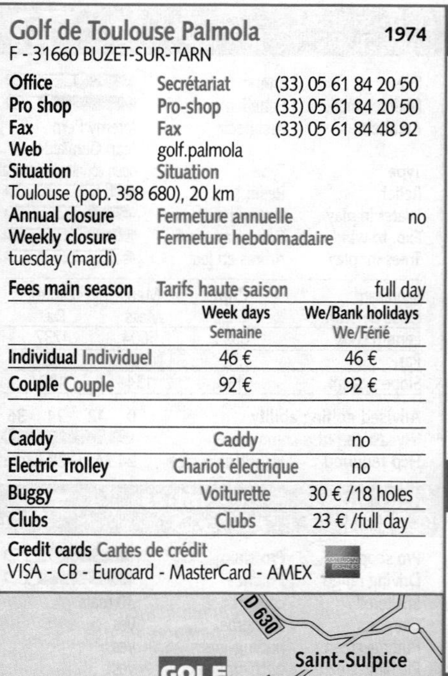

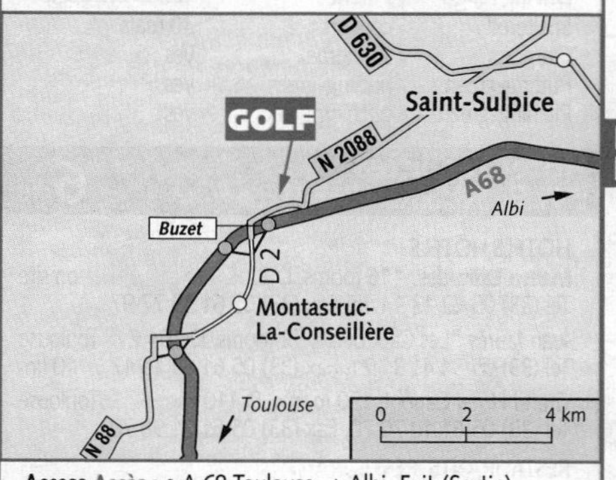

Access Accès : • A 68 Toulouse → Albi, Exit (Sortie) No 4 Gémil-Buzet sur Tarn • Albi → Toulouse, Exit Montastruc la Conseillière, → Albi (N88), → Golf

Map 13 on page 186 Carte 13 Page 186

Golf course PARCOURS — 15/20

Site	Site	
Maintenance	Entretien	
Architect	Architecte	Michael Fenn
Type	Type	forest, residential
Relief	Relief	
Water in play	Eau en jeu	
Exp. to wind	Exposé au vent	
Trees in play	Arbres en jeu	

Scorecard Carte de score	Chp. Chp.	Mens Mess.	Ladies Da.
Length Long.	6156	5949	5290
Par	72	72	72
Slope system	132	131	126

Advised golfing ability / Niveau de jeu recommandé: 0 12 24 36

Hcp required — Handicap exigé — 24-28 (We)

Club house & amenities CLUB-HOUSE ET ANNEXES — 7/10

Pro shop	Pro-shop	
Driving range	Practice	
Sheltered	couvert	4 mats
On grass	sur herbe	yes
Putting-green	putting-green	yes
Pitching-green	pitching green	yes

Hotel facilities ENVIRONNEMENT HOTELIER — 4/10

HOTELS HÔTELS

Grand Hôtel de l'Opéra, 57 rooms, D 213 € — Toulouse
Tel (33) 05 61 21 82 66, Fax (33) 05 61 23 41 04 — 20 km

Beaux Arts, 19 rooms, D 152 € — Toulouse
Tel (33) 05 34 45 42 42, Fax (33) 05 34 45 42 43

Campanile, 70 rooms, D 50 € — L'Union
Tel (33) 05 61 74 00 40, Fax (33) 05 61 09 53 38 — 13 km

RESTAURANTS RESTAURANT

Les Jardins de l'Opéra, Tel (33) 05 61 23 07 76 — Toulouse

Michel Sarran, Tel (33) 05 61 12 32 32 — Toulouse

Auberge de la Pointe — Saint-Sulpice
Tel (33) 05 63 41 80 14 — 10 km

TOULOUSE-SEILH Rouge

15 | 7 | 6

Un Jeremy Pern typique. Partant d'un terrain plat, il a bien modelé ses mouvements de terrain comme ses bunkers, de toutes formes et de toutes dimensions. Les greens sont vastes, avec des reliefs subtils, permettant de multiples positions de drapeaux, certains ont été légèrement modifiés pour les rendre plus accessibles. Les obstacles d'eau jouent aussi un grand rôle dans la stratégie, mais ils sont plus ou moins dangereux selon le vent. Alors, les joueurs prudents ont toujours la solution de jouer à l'écart. Peu boisé à l'origine, il a bénéficié d'un programme de plantations, et fait l'objet de programmes immobiliers, mais pas trop agressifs visuellement. Ce parcours de style américain réclame un jeu très complet, et notamment un petit jeu bien affûté, il joue donc bien son rôle de "formation de golfeurs". Ici, la chance ne peut jouer aucun rôle dans un bon score. Les installations sont fonctionnelles, mais pas toujours très chaleureuses, même s'il y a un progrès en ce sens, ce qui est normal pour un golf commercial...

This is a typical Jeremy Pern layout, starting out with flat terrain and carefully designing-in sloping terrain and bunkers of all shapes and sizes. The greens are huge with subtle breaks, allowing numerous different pin positions, although some have been slightly changed to make them more playable. Water hazards play a major role in game strategy here and can be very dangerous if there is wind around. Otherwise, the cautious player will lay up or play around them. Although there were originally few trees, the plantation programme is beginning to grow as is the number of property developments, which fortunately are not too hard on the eye. Toulouse-Seilh is an American style course requiring an all-round game and some slick short irons, thereby fulfilling its role as a course for "schooling golfers". A good score here owes little or nothing to luck. The facilities are functional but not over-hospitable, even though some progress has been made as it should be with a business venture course like this.

Golf de Toulouse-Seilh Latitudes — 1988

Route de Grenade
F - 31860 SEILH

Office	Secrétariat	(33) 05 62 13 14 14
Pro shop	Pro-shop	(33) 05 62 13 14 14
Fax	Fax	(33) 05 61 42 34 17
Web	www.maeva-latitudes-toulouse.com	
Situation	Situation	

Toulouse (pop. 358 680), 10 km

Annual closure	Fermeture annuelle	no
Weekly closure	Fermeture hebdomadaire	no

Fees main season Tarifs haute saison — full day

	Week days / Semaine	We/Bank holidays / We/Férié
Individual Individuel	26 €	40 €
Couple Couple	52 €	80 €

Special fees in July and August (07/08)

Caddy	Caddy	no
Electric Trolley	Chariot électrique	no
Buggy	Voiturette	18 € /18 holes
Clubs	Clubs	8 € /full day

Credit cards Cartes de crédit
VISA - CB - Eurocard - MasterCard - DC - AMEX

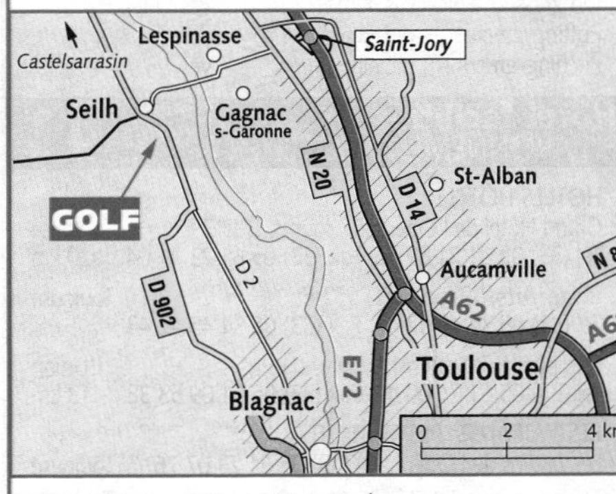

Access Accès : A62 or A61 → Toulouse,
Exit (Sortie) Saint-Jory → Lespinasse → Blagnac, → Golf
Map 12 on page 185 Carte 12 Page 185

Golf course / PARCOURS — 15/20

Site	Site	
Maintenance	Entretien	
Architect	Architecte	Jeremy Pern Jean Garaïalde
Type	Type	open country, residential
Relief	Relief	
Water in play	Eau en jeu	
Exp. to wind	Exposé au vent	
Trees in play	Arbres en jeu	

Scorecard / Carte de score	Chp. / Chp.	Mens / Mess.	Ladies / Da.
Length Long.	6331	5604	4737
Par	72	72	72
Slope system	136	134	128

Advised golfing ability / Niveau de jeu recommandé — 0 12 24 36

Hcp required Handicap exigé — 24 Men, 28 Ladies

Club house & amenities / CLUB-HOUSE ET ANNEXES — 7/10

Pro shop	Pro-shop	
Driving range	Practice	
Sheltered	couvert	30 mats
On grass	sur herbe	yes
Putting-green	putting-green	yes
Pitching-green	pitching green	yes

Hotel facilities / ENVIRONNEMENT HOTELIER — 6/10

HOTELS HÔTELS

Maeva Latitudes, 116 rooms, D 82 € — on site
Tel (33) 05 62 13 14 15, Fax (33) 05 61 59 77 97

Jean Jaurès "Les Capitouls", 52 rooms, D 104 € — Toulouse 10 km
Tel (33) 05 34 41 31 21, Fax (33) 05 61 63 15 17

Grand Hôtel Capoul, 130 rooms, D 110 € — Toulouse
Tel (33) 05 61 10 70 70, Fax (33) 05 61 21 96 70

RESTAURANTS RESTAURANT

Frégate, Tel (33) 05 61 21 62 45 — Toulouse 10 km

Le Pastel, Tel (33) 05 62 87 84 30 — Toulouse-Mirail 18 km

7 Place Saint Sernin, Tel (33) 05 62 30 05 30 — Toulouse

TOUQUET (LE) La Mer

16	6	7

Ce 18 trous était un chef-d'oeuvre. Avec des reliefs modérés, des fairways travaillés, des bunkers redoutables et des greens parfois déconcertants, c'est un links classique, dans une végétation clairsemée, mais bien en jeu. Une bonne partie des trous se déroulent dans des dunes spectaculaires : ici, il faut être humble avec son golf, car erreurs sont immédiatement punies. Et quand le vent s'en mêle, la patience s'impose. Alors, les "manieurs de balles" et les tacticiens prennent le dessus sur les purs frappeurs. Difficile pour les débutants, ce parcours reste généralement passionnant pour les joueurs aguerris, mais on peut avoir des regrets sur la restauration. Le rétablissement d'un tracé proche de celui d'avant-guerre, n'a pas vraiment été fait avec la rigueur ou architecturale nécessaire à toute restauration d'un "monument historique" : on distingue nettement ce qui est original des travaux récents, ce qui est gênant. Plus encore, certains greens (et départs !) ont été modifiés sans nécessité. "La Mer" n'est plus ce qu'elle était. L'autre 18 trous (La Forêt), n'est pas dans la même catégorie, mais reste intéressant.

This 18-hole course was a masterpiece. With moderately undulating and carefully designed fairways, some formidable bunkers and sometimes disconcerting greens, this was your classic links course with only sparse vegetation that was often in play. A tough course for beginners, a great course for the seasoned golfer, but we are none too happy about the way the course has been remodelled. A good number of holes are laid out amongst some spectacular dunes, where mis-hit shots are punished immediately. And when the wind blows, patience is a virtue. Flighters of the ball and the shrewd tactician will find the going easier than the long-hitter. The return to a layout close to the original pre-war design has not really been carried out with the architectural thoroughness required by the restoration of an historical monument. You can clearly distinguish between what is original and is new, which is unfortunate to say the least. More than this, some greens (and tee-boxes) have been needlessly tinkered with. These days, "La Mer" is not what it used to be.The other 18-hole layout (La Forêt) is an enjoyable course to play.

Golf du Touquet — 1904

Avenue du Golf
F - 62520 LE TOUQUET

Office	Secrétariat	(33) 03 21 06 28 00
Pro shop	Pro-shop	(33) 03 21 06 28 00
Fax	Fax	(33) 03 21 06 28 01
Web	www.opengolfclub.com	
Situation	Situation	

Le Touquet (pop. 5 590), 2.5 km - Montreuil (pop. 2 450), 18 km

Annual closure	Fermeture annuelle	no
Weekly closure	Fermeture hebdomadaire	no

Fees main season Tarifs haute saison — 18 holes

	Week days Semaine	We/Bank holidays We/Férié
Individual Individuel	49 €	58 €
Couple Couple	98 €	116 €

Under 25: – 30%

Caddy	Caddy	on request
Electric Trolley	Chariot électrique	no
Buggy	Voiturette	34 € /18 holes
Clubs	Clubs	12 € /full day

Credit cards Cartes de crédit
VISA - CB - Eurocard - MasterCard - AMEX

Access Accès : Le Touquet, → Golf
Map 1 on page 162 Carte 1 Page 162

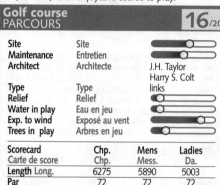

Golf course PARCOURS — 16/20

Site	Site	
Maintenance	Entretien	
Architect	Architecte	J.H. Taylor Harry S. Colt
Type	Type	links
Relief	Relief	
Water in play	Eau en jeu	
Exp. to wind	Exposé au vent	
Trees in play	Arbres en jeu	

Scorecard Carte de score	Chp. Chp.	Mens Mess.	Ladies Da.
Length Long.	6275	5890	5003
Par	72	72	72
Slope system	128	126	123

Advised golfing ability Niveau de jeu recommandé — 0 12 24 36
Hcp required Handicap exigé — 24 Men, 28 Ladies

Club house & amenities CLUB-HOUSE ET ANNEXES — 6/10

Pro shop	Pro-shop	
Driving range	Practice	
Sheltered	couvert	25 mats
On grass	sur herbe	yes
Putting-green	putting-green	yes
Pitching-green	pitching green	yes

Hotel facilities ENVIRONNEMENT HOTELIER — 7/10

HOTELS HÔTELS

Manoir, 41 rooms, D 143 € — on site
Tel (33) 03 21 06 28 28, Fax (33) 03 21 06 28 29

Westminster, 115 rooms, D 183 € — Le Touquet 2,5 km
Tel (33) 03 21 05 48 48, Fax (33) 03 21 05 45 45

Novotel, 149 rooms, D 130 € — Le Touquet 2,5 km
Tel (33) 03 21 09 85 00, Fax (33) 03 21 09 85 10

Château de Montreuil, 14 rooms, D 213 € — Montreuil 10 km
Tel (33) 03 21 81 53 04, Fax (33) 03 21 81 36 43

RESTAURANTS RESTAURANT

Flavio-Club de la Forêt — Le Touquet 2,5 km
Tel (33) 03 21 05 10 22

VAL DE SORNE

14 | 7 | 5

Dans une région pas très riche en golfs, la création de ce golf était bienvenue. Dessiné sur un terrain modérément accidenté par Hugues Lambert dans un style plus américain que britannique, il comporte des obstacles d'eau sur une demi-douzaine de trous. En jouant des départs avancés et même si certains dévers obligent à jouer dans la pente, il est accessible à tous les niveaux, à l'exception du 16, un par 4 difficile dont le green est entouré d'eau. Le déroulement du parcours est assez agréable, sans être d'un tracé vraiment exceptionnel, les arbres sont souvent bien en jeu (comme au 13), mais il vaut mieux le visiter entre mai et octobre, même si des drainages ont été effectués. Les greens sont de dimensions et de difficultés moyenne : leur modelage un peu timide conviendra à tous les handicaps, et leurs défenses ne sont pas trop hermétiques.

This course was most welcome in a region where golf playing facilities are few and far between. Laid out over a moderately hilly terrain by Hugues Lambert in a rather more American style than British, it features water hazards on half a dozen or so holes. From the front-tees, and despite the sloping fairways, the course can be played by golfers of all abilities, with the possible exception of the 16th, a difficult par 4 where the green is surrounded by water. The course unfolds in a pleasant manner without ever being outstanding and trees are often very much in play (on the 13th, for example). And even though drainage work is now complete, the best time to play here is between May and October. The greens are averagely large and difficult but sufficiently flat and bunker-less to appeal to all handicaps.

Golf du Val de Sorne — 1993

Vernantois
F - 39570 LONS-LE-SAUNIER

Office	Secrétariat	(33) 03 84 43 04 80
Pro shop	Pro-shop	(33) 03 84 43 04 80
Fax	Fax	(33) 03 84 47 31 21
Web	www.valdesorne.com	
Situation	Situation	

Lons-le-Saunier (pop. 19 140), 6 km

Annual closure	Fermeture annuelle	no
Weekly closure	Fermeture hebdomadaire	no

Fees main season Tarifs haute saison	18 holes	
	Week days Semaine	**We/Bank holidays** We/Férié
Individual Individuel	37 €	43 €
Couple Couple	74 €	86 €

Under 18: – 50%

Caddy	Caddy	no
Electric Trolley	Chariot électrique	11 € /on request
Buggy	Voiturette	30 €/on request
Clubs	Clubs	12 € /18 holes

Credit cards Cartes de crédit
VISA - CB - Eurocard - MasterCard - DC - AMEX

Access Accès : Lons-le-Saunier → Macornay, then → Vernantois, → Golf
Map 8 on page 176 Carte 8 Page 176

Golf course PARCOURS — 14/20

Site	Site	
Maintenance	Entretien	
Architect	Architecte	Hugues Lambert
Type	Type	parkland
Relief	Relief	
Water in play	Eau en jeu	
Exp. to wind	Exposé au vent	
Trees in play	Arbres en jeu	

Scorecard Carte de score	**Chp.** Chp.	**Mens** Mess.	**Ladies** Da.
Length Long.	6270	6000	5056
Par	72	72	72
Slope system	131	131	128

Advised golfing ability Niveau de jeu recommandé — 0 12 24 36
Hcp required Handicap exigé — no

Club house & amenities CLUB-HOUSE ET ANNEXES — 7/10

Pro shop	Pro-shop	
Driving range	Practice	
Sheltered	couvert	5 mats
On grass	sur herbe	no, 30 mats open air
Putting-green	putting-green	yes
Pitching-green	pitching green	yes

Hotel facilities ENVIRONNEMENT HOTELIER — 5/10

HOTELS HÔTELS

Hôtel du Golf, 36 rooms, D 96 € — Vernantois on site
Tel (33) 03 84 43 04 80, Fax (33) 03 84 47 31 21

Hostellerie des Monts-de-Vaux, 10 rooms, D 158 € — Poligny
Tel (33) 03 84 37 12 50, Fax (33) 03 84 37 09 07

Moulin de Bourgchâteau, 18 rooms, D 69 € — Louhans
Tel (33) 03 85 75 37 12, Fax (33) 03 85 75 45 11 — 26 km

RESTAURANTS RESTAURANT

La Comédie, Tel (33) 03 84 24 20 66 — Lons-le-Saunier 6 km

Auberge de Chavannes, Tel(33) 03 84 47 05 52 — Courlans 8 km

Relais d'Alsace, Tel (33) 03 84 47 24 70 — Lons-le-Saunier 6 km

VAL QUEVEN

15 | 6 | 5

Un site vallonné dans la vallée du Scorff, et en pleine campagne bretonne, ponctuée de beaux arbres, notamment des chênes et châtaigniers, qui protègent bien du vent assez fréquent dans la région. Comme à son habitude, l'architecte Yves Bureau a dessiné un parcours très plaisant et diversifié, bien paysagé et assez large pour être rassurant, assez technique pour renouveler l'intérêt. Les bons scores ne sont pourtant pas si faciles car il faut tenir compte des dénivellations et de la présence de nombreux bunkers bien découpés. Les greens sont de bonne dimension, et bien construits, les obstacles d'eau peu nombreux. Tous les niveaux de jeu peuvent cohabiter ici, les joueurs moyens comme les meilleurs handicaps. Comme souvent en Bretagne, on peut y croiser de nombreux Britanniques. Une curiosité, la présence d'un tumulus antique.

This is a site of rolling landscape in the Scorff valley at the heart of Breton countryside. It is dotted with some fine trees, particularly oak and horse-chestnut, which afford good protection from the frequent wind. As usual, architect Yves Bureau has laid out a very pleasant course, full of variety, well-landscaped and wide enough to reassure most of us, yet technically difficult enough to keep it interesting. Having said that, good scores here are not always easy to come by, courtesy of some steep slopes and numerous neatly outlined bunkers. The greens are of a good size and well designed, and water hazards are rare. All golfers can play together here. And as is often the case in Brittany, the course is a favourite with British golfers. One little curiosity is the presence on the course of a "tumulus" or sepulchral mound.

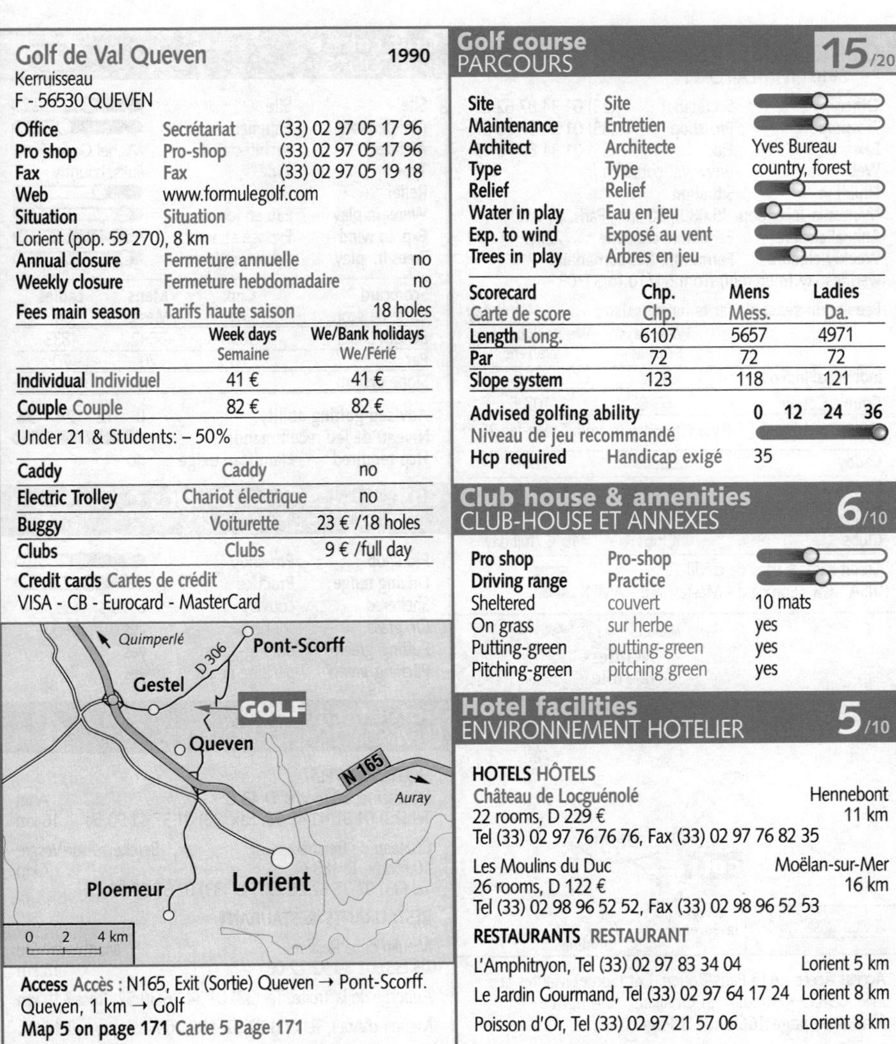

Golf de Val Queven 1990
Kerruisseau
F - 56530 QUEVEN

Office	Secrétariat	(33) 02 97 05 17 96
Pro shop	Pro-shop	(33) 02 97 05 17 96
Fax	Fax	(33) 02 97 05 19 18
Web	www.formulegolf.com	
Situation	Situation	

Lorient (pop. 59 270), 8 km

Annual closure	Fermeture annuelle	no
Weekly closure	Fermeture hebdomadaire	no

Fees main season Tarifs haute saison	**Week days** Semaine	**We/Bank holidays** We/Férié
		18 holes
Individual Individuel	41 €	41 €
Couple Couple	82 €	82 €

Under 21 & Students: – 50%

Caddy	Caddy	no
Electric Trolley	Chariot électrique	no
Buggy	Voiturette	23 € /18 holes
Clubs	Clubs	9 € /full day

Credit cards Cartes de crédit
VISA - CB - Eurocard - MasterCard

Access Accès : N165, Exit (Sortie) Queven → Pont-Scorff. Queven, 1 km → Golf
Map 5 on page 171 Carte 5 Page 171

Golf course PARCOURS — 15/20

Site	Site	
Maintenance	Entretien	
Architect	Architecte	Yves Bureau
Type	Type	country, forest
Relief	Relief	
Water in play	Eau en jeu	
Exp. to wind	Exposé au vent	
Trees in play	Arbres en jeu	

Scorecard Carte de score	**Chp.** Chp.	**Mens** Mess.	**Ladies** Da.
Length Long.	6107	5657	4971
Par	72	72	72
Slope system	123	118	121

Advised golfing ability 0 12 24 36
Niveau de jeu recommandé
Hcp required Handicap exigé 35

Club house & amenities CLUB-HOUSE ET ANNEXES — 6/10

Pro shop	Pro-shop	
Driving range	Practice	
Sheltered	couvert	10 mats
On grass	sur herbe	yes
Putting-green	putting-green	yes
Pitching-green	pitching green	yes

Hotel facilities ENVIRONNEMENT HOTELIER — 5/10

HOTELS HÔTELS

Château de Locguénolé — Hennebont 11 km
22 rooms, D 229 €
Tel (33) 02 97 76 76 76, Fax (33) 02 97 76 82 35

Les Moulins du Duc — Moëlan-sur-Mer 16 km
26 rooms, D 122 €
Tel (33) 02 98 96 52 52, Fax (33) 02 98 96 52 53

RESTAURANTS RESTAURANT

L'Amphitryon, Tel (33) 02 97 83 34 04 — Lorient 5 km
Le Jardin Gourmand, Tel (33) 02 97 64 17 24 — Lorient 8 km
Poisson d'Or, Tel (33) 02 97 21 57 06 — Lorient 8 km

VAUCOULEURS (LA) Les Vallons

15 | 7 | 4

Beaucoup moins boisé que le parcours de "La Rivière", "Les Vallons" est d'un style radicalement différent, où l'architecte Michel Gayon a rendu hommage aux links britanniques. Il s'agit d'une sorte de parcours de bord de mer, sans la mer bien sûr, avec de nombreuses buttes et roughs délimitant bien les fairways, et donnant du relief à un terrain originellement assez plat. Il n'est pas très long, et les longs frappeurs pourront se livrer, mais c'est un parcours plus dangereux et difficile à scorer qu'il n'y paraît, d'autant que le vent y est rarement absent, et que les greens peuvent être parfois complexes à lire. Alors, il faudra exprimer toutes les ressources de son petit jeu pour sauver le score. Bien entretenu, le complexe de La Vaucouleurs est un ensemble à connaître pour sa variété, à jouer plutôt quand les journées sont belles, bien que le présent parcours soit moins sensible que son voisin à l'humidité.

With little or no woodland, "Les Vallons" is radically different from "La Rivière" and is something of a tribute by architect Michel Gayon to British style links golfing. It is certainly a sort of seaside course, without the sea of course, with a number of sand-hills and rough clearly defining the fairways and giving considerable relief to terrain that was originally flat. It is not very long and big-hitters can let fly, but the course is more dangerous and harder to master than it looks, especially since there is nearly always wind around and some of the greens are tricky to read. In this case, only a sharp short game will save your card. Well looked after with good green-keeping, the estate of La Vaucouleurs is a complex worth getting to know for its variety, but better played in dry weather, although this course is less sensitive to the wet than its neighbour.

Golf-Club de la Vaucouleurs — 1989

F - 78910 CIVRY-LA-FORET

Office	Secrétariat	(33) 01 34 87 62 29
Pro shop	Pro-shop	(33) 01 34 87 76 27
Fax	Fax	(33) 01 34 87 70 09
Web	www.vaucouleurs.fr	
Situation	Situation	

Mantes-la-Jolie (pop. 45 080), 20 km - Paris, 61 km

Annual closure Fermeture annuelle 22/12 → 1/1

Weekly closure Fermeture hebdomadaire

wednesday (mercredi) from 01/10 to 31/03

Fees main season Tarifs haute saison — full day

	Week days Semaine	We/Bank holidays We/Férié
Individual Individuel	34 €	57 €
Couple Couple	63 €	107 €

Under 21: 17 € - 34 € (We) / Tuesday (mardi): Green-fee 26 €

Caddy	Caddy	no
Electric Trolley	Chariot électrique	14 € /on request
Buggy	Voiturette	23 € /18 holes
Clubs	Clubs	15 € /full day

Credit cards Cartes de crédit

VISA - CB - Eurocard - MasterCard - AMEX

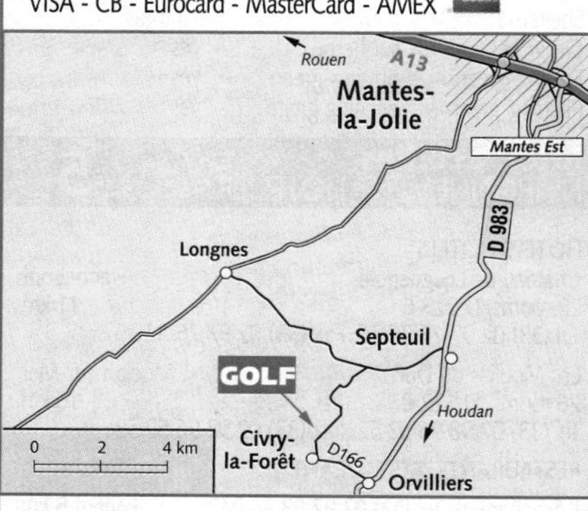

Access Accès : A13 Paris/Rouen, Exit (Sortie) Mantes-la-Jolie, D983 → Houdan. In Orvilliers, turn right → Golf

Map 3 on page 166 Carte 3 Page 166

Golf course — PARCOURS — 15/20

Site	Site	
Maintenance	Entretien	
Architect	Architecte	Michel Gayon
Type	Type	links, country
Relief	Relief	
Water in play	Eau en jeu	
Exp. to wind	Exposé au vent	
Trees in play	Arbres en jeu	

Scorecard Carte de score	Chp. Chp.	Mens Mess.	Ladies Da.
Length Long.	5638	5082	4833
Par	70	70	70
Slope system	115	108	111

Advised golfing ability Niveau de jeu recommandé — 0 12 24 36

Hcp required Handicap exigé — no

Club house & amenities — CLUB-HOUSE ET ANNEXES — 7/10

Pro shop	Pro-shop	
Driving range	Practice	
Sheltered	couvert	6 mats
On grass	sur herbe	yes (summer)
Putting-green	putting-green	yes
Pitching-green	pitching green	yes

Hotel facilities — ENVIRONNEMENT HOTELIER — 4/10

HOTELS HÔTELS

Dousseine, 20 rooms, D 43 € — Anet 16 km
Tel (33) 01 37 41 49 93, Fax (33) 01 37 41 90 54

Château de Berchères — Berchères-sur-Vesgre 7 km
10 rooms, D 183 €
Tel (33) 02 37 82 28 22, Fax (33) 02 37 82 28 23

RESTAURANTS RESTAURANT

Moulin de la Reillère — Mantes-la-Ville 18 km
Tel (33) 01 30 92 22 00

Auberge de la Truite, Tel (33) 01 34 76 30 52 — Rosay 10 km

Manoir d'Anet, Tel (33) 02 37 41 91 05 — Anet 16 km

VILLETTE D'ANTHON Les Sangliers

17 | 7 | 5

Le 18 trous des "Brocards" signé par Michael Fenn est très honnête, et permet à tous les niveaux d'évoluer sans grande presssion. Le plus récent 18 trous (Les Sangliers) a été signé par Hugues Lambert et mérite largement le détour, mais ce sont les joueurs de moins de 24 de handicap qui l'apprécieront davantage. Très long (parfois à l'excès), avec de l'eau en jeu sur la moitié des trous, quelques buttes et pas mal de bunkers, il exige un jeu très complet, et beaucoup de puissance si l'on veut tenir son handicap, même des départs avancés. Ses nombreux obstacles impliquent de le jouer plusieurs fois avant d'en comprendre les aspects stratégiques. Si l'on manque les greens, bien travaillés, on peut parfois y rentrer en roulant, mais il vaut mieux savoir porter la balle. Malgré certains trous un peu faibles, et quelques dessins de bunkers à revoir, c'est incontestablement l'un des tout meilleurs parcours de la région. Très privé, il est difficile d'accès en week-end (sauf l'été).

"Les Brocards" is a fair and unpretentious 18-hole course designed by Michael Fenn and a pleasant round of golf for players of all levels. The more recent 18-hole course ("Les Sangliers"), laid out by Hugues Lambert, is a much more enticing proposition, although a 24 handicap would seem to be the minimum requirement for enjoying the course. Very long (sometimes excessively so) with water on half the holes, a few sand-hills and a lot of bunkers, the course demands an all-round game and power, even from the front tees. The countless hazards imply several exploratory rounds before fully understanding the strategic side to the course. Missed greens can sometimes be reached with chip shots, but controlled lob and pitch shots are important here. Despite a number of rather featureless holes and bunkering that could do with some redesigning in places, this is unquestionably one of the region's very best courses but being private is difficult to play on week-ends (except in summer).

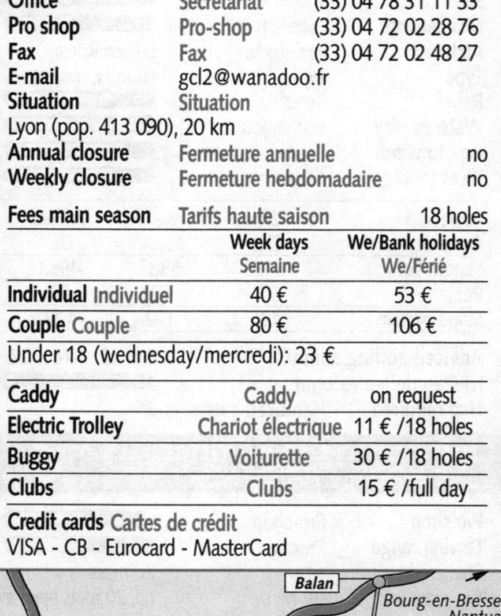

Golf Club de Lyon 1992
F - 38280 VILLETTE-D'ANTHON

Office	Secrétariat	(33) 04 78 31 11 33
Pro shop	Pro-shop	(33) 04 72 02 28 76
Fax	Fax	(33) 04 72 02 48 27
E-mail	gcl2@wanadoo.fr	
Situation	Situation	
Lyon (pop. 413 090), 20 km		
Annual closure	Fermeture annuelle	no
Weekly closure	Fermeture hebdomadaire	no

Fees main season Tarifs haute saison		18 holes
	Week days Semaine	**We/Bank holidays** We/Férié
Individual Individuel	40 €	53 €
Couple Couple	80 €	106 €
Under 18 (wednesday/mercredi): 23 €		
Caddy	Caddy	on request
Electric Trolley	Chariot électrique	11 € /18 holes
Buggy	Voiturette	30 € /18 holes
Clubs	Clubs	15 € /full day

Credit cards Cartes de crédit
VISA - CB - Eurocard - MasterCard

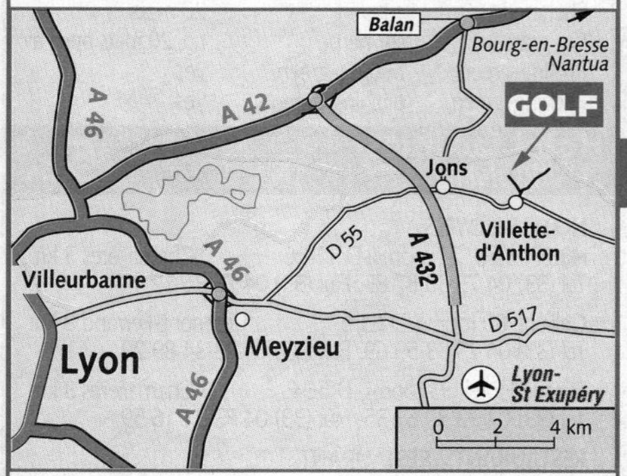

Access Accès : • Lyon, "Rocade Est", Exit (Sortie) Meyzieu le Carreau → Villette d'Anthon • A42 Bourg-en-Bresse Lyon, Exit (Sortie) Balan, → Jons, Villette d'Anthon
Map 11 on page 182 Carte 11 Page 182

Golf course PARCOURS 17/20

Site	Site	
Maintenance	Entretien	
Architect	Architecte	Hugues Lambert
Type	Type	forest, country
Relief	Relief	
Water in play	Eau en jeu	
Exp. to wind	Exposé au vent	
Trees in play	Arbres en jeu	

Scorecard Carte de score	**Chp.** Chp.	**Mens** Mess.	**Ladies** Da.
Length Long.	6727	5883	5033
Par	72	72	72
Slope system	137	125	129

Advised golfing ability Niveau de jeu recommandé — 0 12 24 36
Hcp required Handicap exigé 35

Club house & amenities CLUB-HOUSE ET ANNEXES 7/10

Pro shop	Pro-shop	
Driving range	Practice	
Sheltered	couvert	12 mats
On grass	sur herbe	yes
Putting-green	putting-green	yes
Pitching-green	pitching green	yes (3 greens)

Hotel facilities ENVIRONNEMENT HOTELIER 5/10

HOTELS HÔTELS
Mont-Joyeux, 20 rooms, D 76 € — Meyzieu 12 km
Tel (33) 04 78 04 21 32, Fax (33) 04 72 02 85 72

Auberge de Jons, 25 rooms, D 114 € — Pont-de-Jons 3 km
Tel (33) 04 78 31 29 85, Fax (33) 04 72 02 48 24

Villa Florentine, 19 rooms, D 335 € — Lyon (Vieux-Lyon)
Tel (33) 04 72 56 56 56, Fax (33) 04 72 40 90 56 — 20 km

RESTAURANTS RESTAURANT
Paul Bocuse — Collonges-au-Mont-d'Or
Tel (33) 04 72 42 90 90 — 25 km
Léon de Lyon, Tel (33) 04 72 10 11 12 — Lyon 20 km
Le Jura (Bouchon), Tel (33) 04 78 42 20 57 — Lyon

VOLCANS (LES)

14 | 6 | 5

Situé à près de 900 mètres d'altitude au pied du Puy de Dôme, ce parcours peut parfois être gelé le matin, sauf en été, il faut s'en informer avant de prendre la route. Environné de bouleaux, de pins, de buissons sauvages et de bruyère, il présente une forte montée du 9 au 10, mais pas assez épuisante pour obliger à prendre une voiturette. Le dessin du professionnel local, Lucien Roux, ne prétend certes pas aux plus hautes distinctions, mais il reste plus que correct, avec une bonne utilisation des arbres et des bunkers, quelques greens délicats à double plateau, et un bon rythme de distribution des difficultés. Le parcours peut paraître un peu long du fond, mais les balles portent plus loin en altitude, et les départs avancés (notamment sur les longs par 3) permettent de prendre beaucoup de plaisir dans ce golf sympathique et très familial, situé dans un environnement magnifique et calme, et promis à une belle extension avec neuf trous supplémentaires.

Lying 900 metres above sea level at the foot of the Puy de Dôme, this course is often frost-bound in the morning outside the summer months, so call the secretary before setting out. Surrounded by birch trees, pines, wild bushes and heather, there is steep climb between the 9th and 10th, although not tiring enough to warrant a buggy. Designed by local pro Lucien Roux, the layout cannot and would not claim any of the higher accolades, but it is more than a decent course, with excellent use of trees and bunkers, a few tricky, two-tiered greens and nicely balanced hazards and trouble. The course looks a little long from the back-tees, but the thin air at altitude adds length to the drive. Playing from the front tees (especially the long par 3s) is great fun in this very friendly and family-style club, located in a magnificently calm setting. A further nine holes are planned, which is good news.

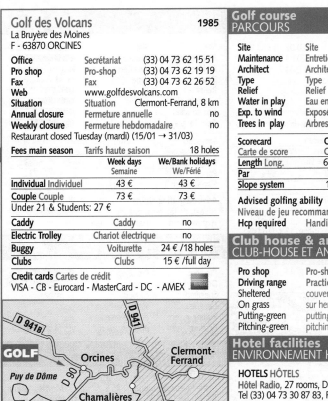

Golf des Volcans — 1985

La Bruyère des Moines
F - 63870 ORCINES

Office	Secrétariat	(33) 04 73 62 15 51
Pro shop	Pro-shop	(33) 04 73 62 19 19
Fax	Fax	(33) 04 73 62 26 52
Web	www.golfdesvolcans.com	
Situation	Situation	Clermont-Ferrand, 8 km
Annual closure	Fermeture annuelle	no
Weekly closure	Fermeture hebdomadaire	no

Restaurant closed Tuesday (mardi) (15/01 → 31/03)

Fees main season Tarifs haute saison	Week days Semaine	We/Bank holidays We/Férié
		18 holes
Individual Individuel	43 €	43 €
Couple Couple	73 €	73 €

Under 21 & Students: 27 €

Caddy	Caddy	no
Electric Trolley	Chariot électrique	no
Buggy	Voiturette	24 € /18 holes
Clubs	Clubs	15 € /full day

Credit cards Cartes de crédit
VISA - CB - Eurocard - MasterCard - DC - AMEX

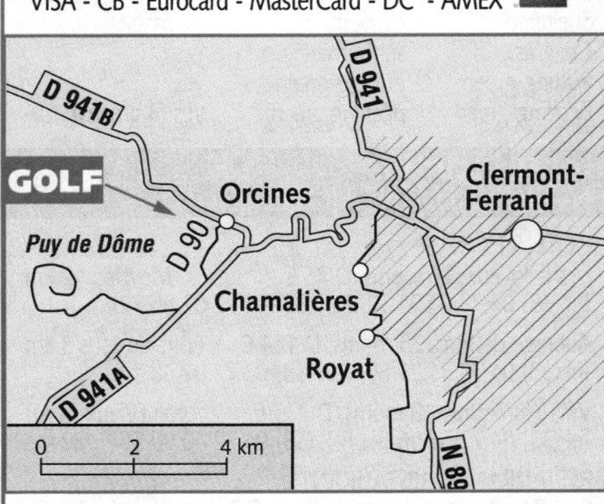

Access Accès : A71, Bourges → Clermont-Ferrand, Exit (Sortie) Clermont-Ferrand Centre → Le Puy-de-Dôme → Orcines
Map 7 on page 175 Carte 7 Page 175

Golf course PARCOURS — 14/20

Site	Site	
Maintenance	Entretien	
Architect	Architecte	Lucien Roux
Type	Type	country, mountain
Relief	Relief	
Water in play	Eau en jeu	
Exp. to wind	Exposé au vent	
Trees in play	Arbres en jeu	

Scorecard Carte de score	Chp. Chp.	Mens Mess.	Ladies Da.
Length Long.	6136	5887	4962
Par	72	72	72
Slope system	125	122	122

Advised golfing ability Niveau de jeu recommandé: 0 12 24 36
Hcp required Handicap exigé: 35

Club house & amenities CLUB-HOUSE ET ANNEXES — 6/10

Pro shop	Pro-shop	
Driving range	Practice	
Sheltered	couvert	20 mats
On grass	sur herbe	no, 20 mats open air
Putting-green	putting-green	yes
Pitching-green	pitching green	yes

Hotel facilities ENVIRONNEMENT HOTELIER — 5/10

HOTELS HÔTELS

Hôtel Radio, 27 rooms, D 114 € — Chamalières 3 km
Tel (33) 04 73 30 87 83, Fax (33) 04 73 36 42 44

Galliéni, 80 rooms, D 63 € — Clermont-Ferrand 8 km
Tel (33) 04 73 93 59 69, Fax (33) 04 73 34 89 29

Europe Hôtel, 33 rooms, D 56 € — Chamalières 3 km
Tel (33) 04 73 37 61 35, Fax (33) 04 73 31 16 59

RESTAURANTS RESTAURANT

Hôtel Radio, Tel (33) 04 73 30 87 33 — Chamalières 3 km

Bernard Andrieux, Tel (33) 04 73 19 25 00 — Durtol 5 km

Emmanuel Hodencq — Clermont-Ferrand 8 km
Tel (33) 04 73 31 23 23

WANTZENAU (LA) | 16 | 6 | 6

C'est la Floride à l'alsacienne, avec un Club House de style résolument local et plutôt réussi. Le paysage est parsemé d'étangs venant en jeu sur neuf des 18 trous, essentiellement au retour, ce qui crée une forte pression sur les joueurs peu expérimentés. On signalera la grande qualité de dessin des par 5, très risqués à attaquer au deuxième coup, et l'habileté de Jeremy Pern à tirer parti d'un espace très plat. Les mouvements de terrain sont subtils, les greens assez vastes, mais leur entrée est généralement ouverte, ce qui permet de jouer la sécurité dans la plupart des cas, quitte à faire confiance à son petit jeu pour sauver le par. Même si l'on est bien loin de tout océan, le vent peut intervenir de manière importante sur ce parcours de très bonne facture, aux obstacles bien visibles, et technique quel que soit le départ choisi. Une belle réalisation

Welcome to Florida in Alsace, where US style golf combines with a rather attractive local-style club-house. The landscape is dotted with lakes in play on 9 of the 18 holes, basically on the back nine, and this puts a lot of pressure on inexperienced players. The par 5s are particularly well-laid out and going for the green in two is a risky business. Architect Jeremy Pern has intelligently made the best of very flat terrain. There has been some clever grading work and the greens are huge and generally undefended up-front, thus allowing players to play safe, even if it means counting on their short game to save par. Although the course is far from any sea, it can get windy and this makes a big difference on what is an excellent course with clearly visible hazards, whatever tees you play from. A fine course.

Golf de la Wantzenau — 1991

CD 302
F - 67610 LA WANTZENAU

Office — Secrétariat — (33) 03 88 96 37 73
Pro shop — Pro-shop — (33) 03 88 96 37 73
Fax — Fax — (33) 03 88 96 34 71
Web — www.golf-wantzenau.com
Situation — Situation
Strasbourg (pop. 252 260), 12 km
Annual closure — Fermeture annuelle — no
Weekly closure — Fermeture hebdomadaire — no
monday (mardi): restaurant closed during winter (hiver)

Fees main season Tarifs haute saison	18 holes	
	Week days Semaine	**We/Bank holidays** We/Férié
Individual Individuel	43 €	61 €
Couple Couple	86 €	122 €

Caddy	Caddy	no
Electric Trolley	Chariot électrique	no
Buggy	Voiturette	30 € /18 holes
Clubs	Clubs	8 € /full day

Credit cards Cartes de crédit
VISA - CB - Eurocard - MasterCard

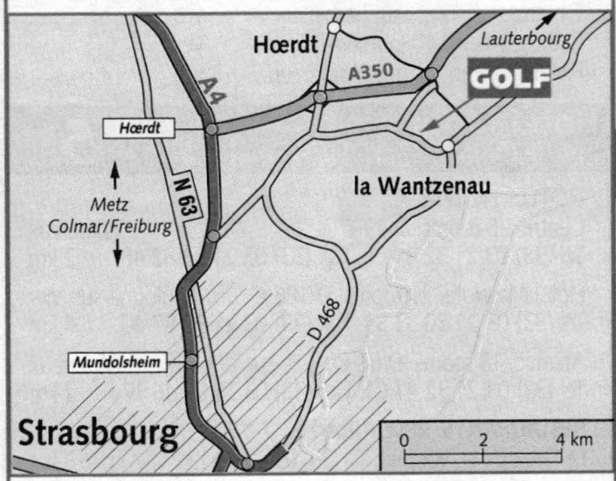

Access Accès : Strasbourg, D468 → La Wantzenau, → Golf
Map 4 on page 169 Carte 4 Page 169

Golf course — PARCOURS — 16/20

Site	Site	
Maintenance	Entretien	
Architect	Architecte	Jeremy Pern Jean Garaïalde
Type	Type	open country, residential
Relief	Relief	
Water in play	Eau en jeu	
Exp. to wind	Exposé au vent	
Trees in play	Arbres en jeu	

Scorecard Carte de score	**Chp.** Chp.	**Mens** Mess.	**Ladies** Da.
Length Long.	6162	5641	4827
Par	72	72	72
Slope system	141	129	128

Advised golfing ability — 0 12 24 36
Niveau de jeu recommandé
Hcp required — Handicap exigé — 35

Club house & amenities — CLUB-HOUSE ET ANNEXES — 6/10

Pro shop	Pro-shop	
Driving range	Practice	
Sheltered	couvert	8 mats
On grass	sur herbe	yes
Putting-green	putting-green	yes
Pitching-green	pitching green	yes

Hotel facilities — ENVIRONNEMENT HOTELIER — 6/10

HOTELS HÔTELS
Relais de la Poste, 18 rooms, D 88 € — La Wantzenau 3 km
Tel (33) 03 88 59 24 80, Fax (33) 03 88 59 24 89
Hôtel Au Moulin, 20 rooms, D 86 € — La Wantzenau
Tel (33) 03 88 59 22 22, Fax (33) 03 88 59 22 00
Holiday Inn, 170 rooms, D 191 € — Strasbourg
Tel (33) 03 88 37 80 00, Fax (33) 03 88 37 07 04 — 10 km

RESTAURANTS RESTAURANT
A la Barrière, Tel (33) 03 88 96 20 23 — La Wantzenau
Au Moulin, Tel (33) 03 88 96 20 01 — La Wantzenau
Pont de l'Ill, Tel (33) 03 88 96 29 44 — La Wantzenau

WIMEREUX

14 | 4 | 5

Si l'on recherche seulement le confort et luxe, il faut passer son chemin, les installations étant spartiates. En revanche, cette simplicité contribue à en faire probablement le parcours français le plus proche des premiers links d'Ecosse, jusqu'aux trous de lapins dans le sol sablonneux. Généralement plat, avec une multitude de profonds bunkers, Wimereux peut présenter un visage aussi souriant et indulgent par beau temps (quand les balles roulent bien) qu'il peut se montrer brutal dès que souffle le vent. Créé en 1907, il a été remanié en 1958 sans trop perdre de son caractère ni de son charme un peu désuet. Ce refus de tout aspect sophistiqué, l'absence d'obstacles d'eau (la mer est à 200 mètres) et d'arbres en jeu peuvent rassurer les amateurs de tous niveaux, qui devront néanmoins éviter les écarts, le grand rough étant redoutable. Des fossés ont été creusés pour évacuer l'eau, ce qui devrait faciliter le jeu après de fortes pluies.

If you are looking for comfort and luxury and nothing else, drive on, as the facilities here are Spartan. By contrast, simplicity probably helps make this the closest French course to the original Scottish links, even as far as the rabbit-holes in the sandy soil. Generally flat with a number of deep bunkers, Wimereux can be as leisurely and forgiving in fine weather (when the ball rolls a long way) as it can be mean and unloving when the wind blows. Created in 1907, it was restyled in 1958 without sacrificing too much of the original character or yesteryear charm. This refusal of anything over-sophisticated, the absence of water hazards (the sea is 200 metres away) and trees in play are enough to reassure golfers of all playing abilities, as long as they keep on the straight and narrow. Be warned, the rough is wicked. Ditches have been dug to drain off surface water and this should make the course more easily playable after heavy rain.

Golf de Wimereux — 1907

Route d'Ambleteuse
F - 62930 WIMEREUX

Office	Secrétariat	(33) 03 21 32 43 20
Pro shop	Pro-shop	(33) 03 21 32 43 20
Fax	Fax	(33) 03 21 33 62 21
E-mail	golf-wimereux@wanadoo.fr	
Situation	Situation	

Boulogne-sur-Mer (pop. 43 670), 6 km

Annual closure	Fermeture annuelle	no
Weekly closure	Fermeture hebdomadaire	no

monday (lundi): restaurant closed from 01/10 to 30/06

Fees main season Tarifs haute saison	18 holes	
	Week days Semaine	**We/Bank holidays** We/Férié
Individual Individuel	35 €	44 €
Couple Couple	63 €	80 €

Students under 25: – 30%

Caddy	Caddy	no
Electric Trolley	Chariot électrique	no
Buggy	Voiturette	30 € /18 holes
Clubs	Clubs	as a loan

Credit cards Cartes de crédit
VISA - CB - Eurocard - MasterCard

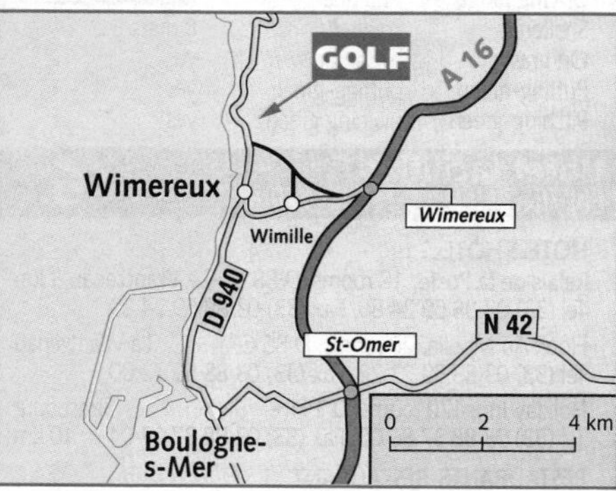

Access Accès : Boulogne s/Mer, D940 → Wimereux
Map 1 on page 162 Carte 1 Page 162

Golf course PARCOURS — 14/20

Site	Site	
Maintenance	Entretien	
Architect	Architecte	Campbell & Hutchinson
Type	Type	links
Relief	Relief	
Water in play	Eau en jeu	
Exp. to wind	Exposé au vent	
Trees in play	Arbres en jeu	

Scorecard Carte de score	**Chp.** Chp.	**Mens** Mess.	**Ladies** Da.
Length Long.	6150	5887	5184
Par	72	72	72
Slope system	132	129	126

Advised golfing ability Niveau de jeu recommandé — 0 12 24 36

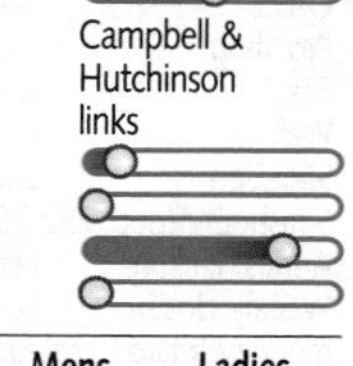

Hcp required Handicap exigé 35

Club house & amenities CLUB-HOUSE ET ANNEXES — 4/10

Pro shop	Pro-shop	
Driving range	Practice	
Sheltered	couvert	10 mats
On grass	sur herbe	yes
Putting-green	putting-green	yes
Pitching-green	pitching green	yes

Hotel facilities ENVIRONNEMENT HOTELIER — 5/10

HOTELS HÔTELS

Centre, 25 rooms, D 49 € — Wimereux
Tel (33) 03 21 32 41 08, Fax (33) 03 21 33 82 48 — 2 km

Hôtel Matelote, 20 rooms, D 186 € — Boulogne-sur-Mer
Tel (33) 03 21 30 33 33, Fax (33) 03 21 30 87 40 — 6 km

Atlantic, 18 rooms, D 88 € — Wimereux
Tel (33) 03 21 32 41 01, Fax (33) 03 21 87 46 17 — 2 km

RESTAURANTS RESTAURANT

Le Relais de la Brocante, Tel (33) 03 21 83 19 31 — Wimille 3 km

Matelote ,Tel (33) 03 21 30 17 97 — Boulogne-sur-Mer 6 km

Liégeoise (Atlantic Hôtel), Tel (33) 03 21 32 41 01 — Wimereux

EUROPE'S TOP 1000 GOLF COURSES

Germany

Seddineer See

Deutschland
Germany

In Deutschland, welches den stärksten Zuwachs ganz Europas aufweist, gibt es heute rund 400 000 Golfer und ca. 600 Plätze. Viele befinden sie sich in der Nähe größerer Städte wie Düsseldorf, Hamburg, Stuttgart, München oder Berlin oder in stark touristisch erschlossenen Regionen wie Bayern, doch auch auf dem Land sind in den letzten Jahren viele Plätze entstand, so dass man in Deutschland fast überall spielen kann. Lediglich die neuen Bundesländer mit Ausnahme von Brandenburg haben noch einen Nachholbedarf. Fast alle sind Privatsclubs, welche jedoch für alle Besucher offen sind, zumindest unter der Woche. An den Wochenenden ist der Zutritt oft beschränkt, was wir denn auch beim jeweiligen Beschreibung vermerkt haben. Für Gruppen sind Reservierungen für das Wochenende daher schwierig, aber einzelne Spieler haben oft die Möglichkeit, mit Clubmitgliedern spielen zu gehen. Rufen Sie vorher an, und mit einem Empfehlungsschreiben Ihres Clubs werden Sie sicherlich eine Chance haben.

Germany today has approx. Registered 400,000 golfers, one of the highest growth rates in Europe, and more than 600 courses. They are mostly situated around the major cities such as Düsseldorf, Hamburg, Stuttgart, München or Berlin, or again in favourite tourist locations like Bavaria, but even on the countryside you find a lot of course. The new states in East Germany have some catching up to except Brandenburg, where you will find a lot of courses around Berlin. The majority of clubs are private, but they all admit visitors, at least during the week, and may sometimes impose restrictions on week-ends. These are mentioned in the Guide. This makes it difficult for groups to book tee-off times at the week-end, but visitors playing alone will often be able to tee-off with members. Phone early and try your luck.

Map No 1
Karte 1
km
0 10 20
Bitche (F)
Soufflenheim (F)
Wantzenau (La) (F)
Strasbourg Illkirch (F)
Kempferhof (Le) (F)
Bâle Hagenthal (F)
Largue (La) (F)
SAARBRÜCKEN
Kaiserslautern
Neustadt-a-d-W
Saarlouis
Völklingen
Neunkirchen
Homburg
Zweibrücken
Pirmasens
Forbach
Sarreguemines
St. Avold
Wissembourg
Haguenau
Saverne
Sarrebourg
Lunéville
Molsheim
Obernai
STRASBOURG
Kehl
Offenburg
Sélestat
St-Dié-des-Vosges
Ribeauvillé
COLMAR
Epinal
Gérardmer
Remiremont
Guebwiller
Thann
MULHOUSE
FREIBURG
Lörrach
Belfort
Montbéliard
BASEL
MICHELIN

St. Leon-Rot
Heilbronn-Hohenlohe
Schloss Nippenburg
Stuttgarter Solitude
Bad Liebenzell
Hechingen-Hohenzollern
Öschberghof
Schloss Langenstein
Oberschwaben Bad Waldsee
Fürstlicher Bad Waldsee
Bodensee-Weissensberg
Lindau-Bad Schachen
Breitenloo (S)
Heilbronn
KARLSRUHE
Pforzheim
STUTTGART
Esslingen
Göppingen
Schwäbisch Gmünd
Schwäbisch Hall
Ludwigsburg
Sindelfingen
Böblingen
Tübingen
Reutlingen
Freudenstadt
Schwenningen
Villingen-
Tuttlingen
Singen
Konstanz
Schaffhausen
Winterthur
Frauenfeld
Ravensburg
Friedrichshafen
Lindau
BADEN-
WÜRTTEMBERG
355
MICHELIN
d'après carte n° 987 - 28ème édition - 2002.
Autorisation n° 0102062.

Map No 2
Karte 2
km
0 10 20
DEUTSCHLAND
BAYERN
Wittelsbacher
Eschenried
Schloss Klingenburg
Augsburg
Münchner-Strasslach
Gut Ludwigsberg
Feldafing
München-Riedhof
Bad Wörishofen
Hohenpähl
Memmingen-Gut Westerhart
Tutzing
Beuerberg
St. Eurach
Iffeldorf
Tegernseer Bad Wiessee
Garmisch-Partenkirchen
Bad Abbach
AUGSBURG
INNSBRUCK
Abenberg
Merkendorf
Hilpoltstein
Parsberg
Gunzenhausen
Pleinfeld
Thalmässing
Berching
Greding
Dietfurt
Hemau
Ellingen
Weißenburg
Beilngries
Wassertrüdingen
Riedenburg
Kelheim
Weltenburg
Treuchtlingen
Pappenheim
Eichstätt
Denkendorf
Oettingen
Neustadt
Abensberg
Wallerstein
Wemding
Lenting
Bopfingen
Nördlingen
Monheim
Ingolstadt
Harburg
Manching
Kaisheim
Neuburg
Karlshuld
Geisenfeld
Neresheim
Donauwörth
Reichertshofen
Langenbruck
Wolnzach
Mainburg
Heidenheim
Rain
Pörnbach
Au
Giengen
Höchstädt
Pöttmes
Pfaffenhofen
Lauingen
Dillingen
Schrobenhausen
Gundelfingen
Meitingen
Wertingen
Allershausen
Freising
Niederstotzingen
Langenau
Aichach
Leipheim
Günzburg
Gersthofen
Dasing
Burgau
Markt Indersdorf
Zusmarshausen
Friedberg
Odelzhausen
Ulm
Göggingen
Sulzemoos
Unterschleissheim
Haunstetten
Dachau
Ismaning
Bobingen
Mering
Karlsfeld
Weißenhorn
Thannhausen
Maisach
Königsbrunn
Krumbach
Fürstenfeldbruck
Germering
Schwabmünchen
Haar
Altenstadt
Gilching
Gräfelfing
Babenhausen
Türkheim
Gauting
Unterhaching
Inning
Buchloe
Landsberg
Utting
Grünwald
Mindelheim
Starnberg
Herrsching
Heimertingen
Steinheim
Bad Wörishofen
Memmingen
Dießen
Wolfratshausen
Ottobeuren
Rott
Weilheim
Wessobrunn
Grönenbach
Schongau
Peißenberg
Penzberg
Obergünzburg
Gmund
Dietmannsried
Hohenpeißenberg
Bad Tölz
Leutkirch
Peiting
Bichl
Bad Wiessee
Marktoberdorf
Benediktbeuern
Kempten
Großweil
Steingaden
Wies
Murnau
Kochel
Roßhaupten
Ohlstadt
Urfeld
Isny
Oberammergau
Vorderriß
Mittelberg
Nesselwang
Linderhof
Walchensee
Wertach
Füssen
Königsschlösser
Oberau
Achenkirch
Pfronten
Ammer-Sattel
Krün
Immenstadt
Oberjoch-P.
Garmisch
Partenkirchen
Pertisau
Sonthofen
Reutte
Mittenwald
Hindelang
Tannheim
Grainau
Zugspitze
2962
Eng
Steibis
Balderschwang
Fischen
Weißenbach
Ehrwald
Scharnitz
Karwendelgebirge
Nebelhorn
2224
Berwang
Lermoos
Seefeld
Hall in Tirol
Oberstdorf
Fernpaß
1209
Telfs
Holzleitner Sattel
Obsteig
Zirl
Riezlern
Hirschegg
Nassereith
Wattens
Volders
Baad
Mittelberg
Elbigenalp
Stams
Silz
Axams
Igls
Europabrücke
Imst
Holzgau
Oetz
Gries im Sellrain
Schönberg
Schröcken
Warth
Steeg
Parseierspitze
Lech
Altmühlsee
Brombachsee
Altmühl
Donau
Lech
Paar
Ammersee
Starnberger See
Isar
Iller
Wörnitz
Romantische Straße
Deutsche Alpenstraße
Alpenstraße
Staffelsee
Forggensee
Plansee
Sylvenstein-Stausee
Achensee
Kleinwalsertal
Inn
MICHELIN

356

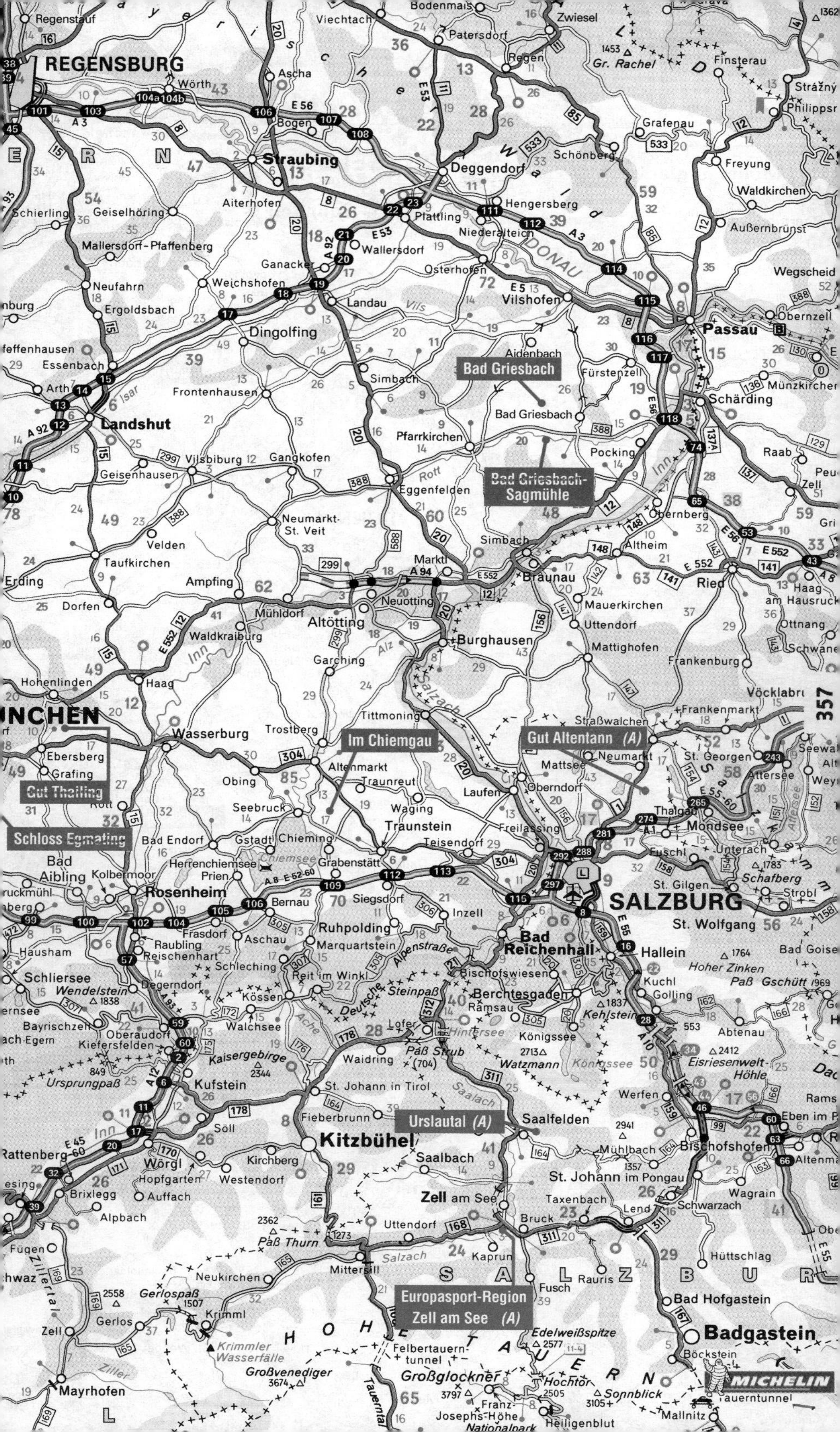
Bad Griesbach
Bad Griesbach-Sagmühle
Im Chiemgau
Gut Altentann (A)
Gut Thailing
Schloss Egmating
Urslautal (A)
Europasport-Region Zell am See (A)
REGENSBURG
Regenstauf
Wörth
Ascha
Viechtach
Bodenmais
Zwiesel
Patersdorf
Regen
Gr. Rachel
Finsterau
Grafenau
Schönberg
Freyung
Waldkirchen
Außernbrünst
Wegscheid
Obernzell
Passau
Straubing
Bogen
Deggendorf
Hengersberg
Plattling
Niederalteich
Wallersdorf
Osterhofen
Vilshofen
Aiterhofen
Geiselhöring
Schierling
Mallersdorf-Pfaffenberg
Neufahrn
Ergoldsbach
Weichshofen
Ganacker
Landau
Dingolfing
Essenbach
Arth
Landshut
Frontenhausen
Simbach
Aidenbach
Fürstenzell
Schärding
Münzkirchen
Pfarrkirchen
Pocking
Raab
Zell
Eggenfelden
Gangkofen
Vilsbiburg
Geisenhausen
Neumarkt-St. Veit
Velden
Taufkirchen
Erding
Dorfen
Ampfing
Mühldorf
Waldkraiburg
Altötting
Neuötting
Marktl
Simbach
Braunau
Altheim
Obernberg
Ried
Haag am Hausruck
Mauerkirchen
Uttendorf
Mattighofen
Burghausen
Garching
Ottnang
Schwanenstadt
Frankenburg
Vöcklabruck
Frankenmarkt
Straßwalchen
Neumarkt
Hohenlinden
Haag
Wasserburg
Trostberg
Tittmoning
Ebersberg
Grafing
Obing
Altenmarkt
Traunreut
Waging
Laufen
Oberndorf
Mattsee
St. Georgen
Attersee
Thalgau
Mondsee
Seebruck
Traunstein
Teisendorf
Freilassing
Bad Endorf
Gstadt
Chieming
Chiemsee
Herrenchiemsee
Prien
Grabenstätt
Bad Aibling
Kolbermoor
Rosenheim
Bernau
Siegsdorf
Inzell
Ruhpolding
Marquartstein
Reit im Winkl
Schleching
Raubling
Reischenhart
Frasdorf
Aschau
Hausham
Schliersee
Wendelstein
Bayrischzell
Degerndorf
Oberaudorf
Kiefersfelden
Kössen
Walchsee
Ursprungpaß
Kaisergebirge
Kufstein
Söll
Wörgl
Hopfgarten
Westendorf
Kirchberg
Kitzbühel
Rattenberg
Brixlegg
Auffach
Alpbach
Fügen
Schwaz
Zillertal
Zell
Gerlos
Gerlospaß
Krimml
Krimmler Wasserfälle
Großvenediger
Mayrhofen
Ziller
Neukirchen
Mittersill
Paß Thurn
Uttendorf
Kaprun
Salzach
Zell am See
Saalbach
Saalfelden
Fieberbrunn
St. Johann in Tirol
Waidring
Lofer
Paß Strub
Saalach
Steinpaß
Deutsche Alpenstraße
Bischofswiesen
Berchtesgaden
Ramsau
Hintersee
Königssee
Watzmann
Kehlstein
Bad Reichenhall
SALZBURG
Hallein
Kuchl
Golling
Fuschl
Unterach
St. Gilgen
Schafberg
Strobl
St. Wolfgang
Bad Goisern
Hoher Zinken
Paß Gschütt
Abtenau
Eisriesenwelt-Höhle
Werfen
Bischofshofen
Mühlbach
St. Johann im Pongau
Schwarzach
Wagrain
Eben im Pongau
Altenmarkt
Lend
Taxenbach
Bruck
Hüttschlag
Rauris
Fusch
Bad Hofgastein
Badgastein
Böckstein
Edelweißspitze
Hochtor
Felbertauern-tunnel
Großglockner
Franz-Josephs-Höhe
Heiligenblut
Sonnblick
Mallnitz
Tauerntunnel
Nationalpark
DONAU
Inn
Isar
Vils
Rott
Alz
Salzach
Ache
HOHE TAUERN
SALZBURG
MICHELIN

Map No 3
Karte 3
km
0 10 20
Essener Oefte
Bergisch Land Wuppertal
Elfrather Mühle
Düsseldorfer
Hubbelrath
Krefelder
Schloss Myllendonk
Gut Lärchenhof
Köln (Refrath)
Spa (Les Fagnes) (B)
Mittelrheinischer
Jakobsberg
Bitburger Land
Grand Ducal de Luxembourg (L)
Kikuoka (L)
Preisch (F)
ESSEN
DUISBURG
Mülheim
Krefeld
WUPPERTAL
Hagen
DÜSSELDORF
Mönchengladbach
Remscheid
Solingen
Leverkusen
KÖLN
BONN
Bad Godesberg
Koblenz
Trier
LUXEMBOURG
RHEINLAND
PFALZ
SAARLAND
MICHELIN

KASSEL
Arnsberg
Meschede
Korbach
Fritzlar
Melsungen
Bad Wildungen
Frankenberg
Marburg
Siegen
Dillenburg
Herborn
Gießen
Wetzlar
Schloss Braunfels
Fürstliches Hofgut Kolnhausen
Lindenhof Bad Vilbel
Hanau-Wilhelmsbad
Hof Trages
Main-Taunus
Frankfurter GC
FRANKFURT
WIESBADEN
MAINZ
Offenbach
Hanau
Aschaffenburg
Darmstadt
Neuhof
Rheinhessen
Domtal-Mommenheim
Nahetal
Biblis Wattenheim
Worms
Ludwigshafen
MANNHEIM
HEIDELBERG
Kaiserslautern
Speyer
Fulda
Alsfeld
Lauterbach
Limburg
Bad Homburg
Bad Nauheim
Friedberg
Worms
Miltenberg
Wertheim
Neustadt-a-d-W
359
MICHELIN

Map No 4
Karte 4
km
0
10
20
THÜRINGEN
Mühlhausen
Bad Tennstedt
Straußfurt
Eckartsberga
Buttstädt
Bad Sulza
Apolda
Weimar
Jena
Bad Langensalza
Gebesee
Buchenwald
ERFURT
Gotha
Eisenach
Herleshausen
Höneback
Berka
Ruhla
Waltershausen
Friedrichroda
Ohrdruf
Arnstadt
Kranichfeld
Bad Berka
Blankenhain
Mellingen
Kahla
Gr. Inselsberg
Bad Liebenstein
Dorndorf
Vacha
Bad Salzungen
Barchfeld
Breitungen
Schmalkalden
Crawinkel
Stadtilm
Rudolstadt
Schwarza
Bad Blankenburg
Oberhof
Ilmenau
Gr. Beerberg
Steinbach-Hallenberg
Zella-Mehlis
Suhl
Gehren
Königsee
Saalfeld
Leutenberg
Rasdorf
Geisa
Hünfeld
Tann
Dermbach
Wasungen
Kaltennordheim
Großbreitenbach
Probstzella
Meiningen
Rohr
Schleusingen
Neuhaus
Ludwigsstadt
Hilders
Melpers
Fladungen
Henneberg
Themar
Rodacherbrunn
Lobenstein
Ehrenberg
Wasser-Kuppe
Hildburghausen
Eisfeld
Steinach
Eußenhausen
Ostheim
Mellrichstadt
Römhild
Sonneberg
Nordhalben
Gersfeld
Rottenbach
Neustadt
Neuhaus-Schierschnitz
Burggrub
Bischofsheim
Linden
Bad Rodach
Kronach
Wallenfels
Bad Königshofen
Trappstadt
Bad Neustadt
Heldburg
Coburg
Obereßfeld
Burgkunstadt
Münnerstadt
Lichtenfels
Vierzehnheiligen
Kulmbach
Bad Kissingen
Hofheim
Staffelstein
Oberfranken
Weismain
Hammelburg
Poppenhausen
Ebern
Schweinfurt
Haßfurt
Bamberg
Breitengüßbach
Bayreuth
Scheßlitz
Hollfeld
Arnstein
Werneck
Eltmann
Hallstadt
Fränkische Schweiz
Waischenfeld
Wiesenttal
Streitberg
Behringersmühle
Gerolzhofen
Volkach
Ebrach
Ebermannstadt
Gössweinstein
Würzburg
Dettelbach
Wiesentheid
Pommersfelden
Schlüsselfeld
Egloffstein
Höchberg
Forchheim
Kitzingen
Biebelried
Iphofen
Höchstadt
Gräfenberg
Reichswald-Nürnberg
Scheinfeld
Erlangen
Forth
Marktbreit
Ochsenfurt
Neustadt-an der Aisch
Herzogenaurach
Heroldsberg
Tauberbischofsheim
Reichsstadt Bad Windsheim
Emskirchen
Lauf
Aub
Uffenheim
Markt Erlbach
Fürth
Rothenbach
Bad Windsheim
Langenzenn
Zirndorf
NÜRNBERG
Fischbach
Bad Mergentheim
Creglingen
Burgbernheim
Großhabersdorf
Stein
Feucht
Weikersheim
Lichtenau-Weickershof
Oberölsbach
Niederstetten
Heilsbronn
Rothenburg ob der Tauber
Lehrberg
Schwabach
Dörzbach
Schrozberg
Ansbach
Allersberg
Leutershausen
Windsbach
Roth
Blaufelden
Abenberg
Künzelsau
Herrieden
Merkendorf
Hilpoltstein
Gerabronn
Bechhofen
Pleinfeld
Brombachsee
Altmühlsee
DEUTSCHLAND
MICHELIN

CHEMNITZ
Karlovy Vary (CZ)
Karlovy Vary
Mariánské Lázně (CZ)
Mariánské Lázně
Schwanhof
REGENSBURG
Zwickau
Gera
Plauen
Hof
Cheb
Chomutov
Weiden
Amberg
Schwandorf
361
MICHELIN

Map No 5
Karte 5
km
0 10 20
Gelpenberg (NL)
Sybrook (NL)
Twente (NL)
Rheine/Mesum
Graafschap (NL)
Wasserburg-Anholt
Elfrather Mühle
Mülheim
Essener Oefte
MICHELIN
Appingedam
Delfzijl
Groningen
Haren
Hoogezand
Veendam
Winschoten
Assen
Emmen
Hoogeveen
Coevorden
Zwolle
Almelo
Hengelo
Enschede
Deventer
Zutphen
Doetinchem
Emmerich
Kleve
Wesel
Moers
Duisburg
Krefeld
Oberhsn
Essen
Mülheim
Bochum
Gelsenkchn
Herne
Dortmund
Hagen
Iserlohn
Recklinghsn
Lünen
Hamm
Münster
Rheine
Nordhorn
Lingen
Meppen
Papenburg
Leer
Cloppenburg
Westerstede
Wiefelstede
Bad Zwischenahn
Ibbenbüren
Greven
Coesfeld
Borken
Bocholt
Dülmen
Dorsten
Marl
Gladbeck
Bottrop
Witten
Unna
Ahlen
Lengerich
Tecklenburg
Steinfurt
Ochtrup
Gronau
Bad Bentheim
Schüttorf
Ahaus
Stadtlohn
Winterswijk
Vreden
Haltern
Lüdinghausen
Drenthe
Overijssel
Nordrhein

Club Zur Vahr (Garlstedt)
BREMEN
Delmenhorst
Osterholz-Scharmbeck
Schwanewede
Vegesack
Achim
Oyten
Rotenburg
Scheeßel
Schneverdingen
Soltau
Wilseder Berg
Egestorf
Munster
Walsrode
Verden
Nienburg
Celle
Isernhagen
Hannover
HANNOVER
Neustadt am Rübenberge
Steinhuder Meer
Wunstorf
Lehrte
Sehnde
Rethmar
Hildesheim
Springe
Hameln
Rinteln
Bückeburg
Minden
Bad Oeynhausen
Herford
Bielefeld
Gütersloh
Rheda-Wiedenbrück
Senne
Detmold
Paderborn
Lippstadt
Brilon
Meschede
Korbach
Warburg
Höxter
Holzminden
Einbeck
Alfeld
Hann.-Münden
KASSEL
Witzenhausen
N I E D E R S A C H S E N
W E S T F A L E N
Weser
Aller
Leine
363
MICHELIN

Map No 6
Karte 6
km
0 10 20
Bad Bevensen
Braunschweig
MICHELIN

BERLIN
POTSDAM
LEIPZIG
BRANDENBURG
Stolper Heide
Schloss Wilkendorf
Semlin am See
Märkischer Potsdam
Berlin-Wannsee
Seddiner See
Motzener See
Scharmützelsee
Herzsprung
Kyritz
Wusterhausen
Neustadt
Bückwitz
Rhinow
Rathenow
Premnitz
Pritzerbe
Plaue
Kirchmöser
Brandenburg
Ziesar
Görzke
Zerbst
Roßlau
Dessau
Alt Ruppin
Neuruppin
Ruppiner See
Fehrbellin
Friesack
Nauen
Wachow
Ketzin
Lindow
Löwenberg
Gransee
Zehdenick
Groß-Schönebeck
Joachimsthal
Werbellinsee
Parsteiner See
Oderberg
Eberswalde
Finowfurt
Finow
Bad Freienwalde
Wriezen
Liebenwalde
Wandlitz
Biesenthal
Lanke
Bernau
Tiefensee
Prötzel
Werneuchen
Strausberg
Blumberg
Altlandsberg
Vogelsdorf
Müncheberg
Rüdersdorf
Kremmen
Oranienburg
Börnicke
Velten
Birkenwerder
Hennigsdorf
Pankow
Tegel
Falkensee
Spandau
Köpenick
Erkner
Tempelhof
Spree
Havel
Babelsberg
Teltow
Werder
Michendorf
Lehnin
Golzow
Wollin
Brück
Belzig
Wiesenburg
Beelitz
Ludwigsfelde
Rangsdorf
Mittenwalde
Königs-Wusterhausen
Friedersdorf
Storkow
Fürstenwalde
Zossen
Trebbin
Wünsdorf
Teupitz
Halbe
Märkisch Buchholz
Neu Lübbenau
Luckenwalde
Baruth
Treuenbrietzen
Niemegk
Jüterbog
Golßen
Dahme
Duben
Lübben
Lübbenau
Luckau
Zahna
Seyda
Wittenberg
Coswig
Wörlitz
Oranienbaum
ELBE
Kemberg
Jessen
Schweinitz
Schwarze Elster
Schönewalde
Schlieben
Sonnewalde
Finsterwalde
Doberlug-Kirchhain
Annaburg
Herzberg
Prettin
Pretzsch
Bad Schmiedeberg
Dommitzsch
Gräfenhainichen
Raguhn
Jeßnitz
Wolfen
Bitterfeld
Zörbig
Brehna
Delitzsch
Landsberg
Bad Düben
Eilenburg
Torgau
Falkenberg
Uebigau
Bad Liebenwerda
Lauchhammer
Schwarzheide
Elsterwerda
Belgern
Schildau
Mühlberg
Gröditz
Strehla
Riesa
Großenhain
Gr. Röder
Dahlen
Oschatz
Wurzen
Taucha
Brandis
Trebsen
Wermsdorf
Mutzschen
Mügeln
Naunhof
Grimma
Leisnig
Colditz
Döbeln
Hartha
Roßwein
Waldheim
Geringswalde
Rochlitz
Geithain
Bad Lausick
Borna
Frohburg
Lommatzsch
Meißen
Coswig
Moritzburg
Radeburg
Radebeul
Nossen
Siebenlehn
Tharandt
Schkeuditz
Leuna
Markranstädt
Markkleeberg
Lützen
Zwenkau
Pegau
Rötha
Böhlen
Groitzsch
Hohenmölsen
Lucka
Teuchern
MICHELIN

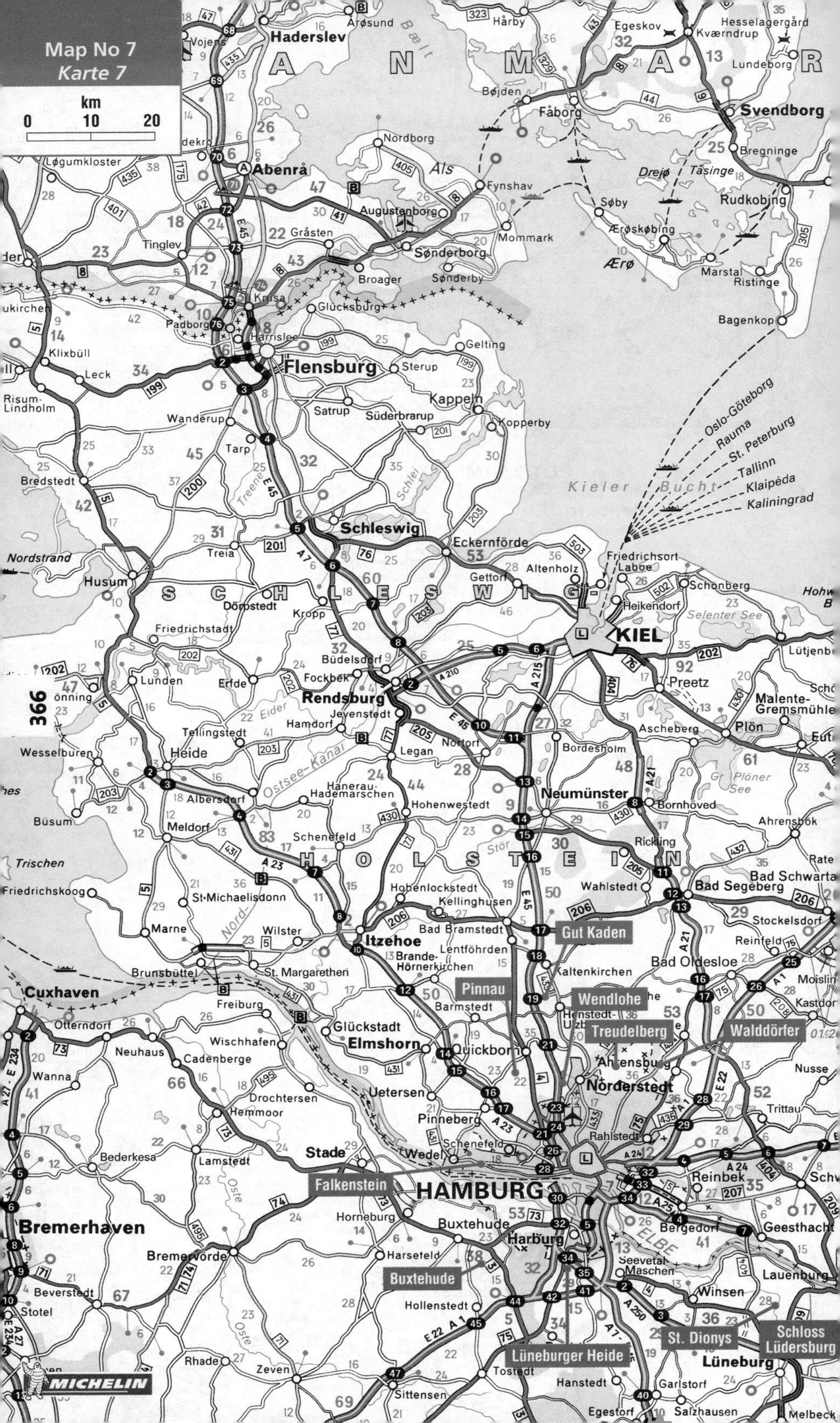
Map No 7
Karte 7
km
0 10 20
Haderslev
Årøsund
Vojens
Hårby
Egeskov
Kværndrup
Hesselagergård
Lundeborg
Bøjden
Fåborg
Svendborg
Bregninge
Nordborg
Als
Fynshav
Drejø
Tåsinge
Rudkøbing
Søby
Ærøskøbing
Ærø
Marstal
Ristinge
Bagenkop
Løgumkloster
Åbenrå
Augustenborg
Gråsten
Tinglev
Sønderborg
Mommark
Broager
Sønderby
Kruså
Padborg
Glücksburg
Harrislee
Flensburg
Klixbüll
Leck
Gelting
Sterup
Risum-Lindholm
Wanderup
Satrup
Süderbrarup
Kappeln
Kopperby
Tarp
Treene
Schlei
Bredstedt
Oslo-Göteborg
Rauma
St. Peterburg
Tallinn
Klaipėda
Kaliningrad
Kieler Bucht
Schleswig
Nordstrand
Treia
Eckernförde
Friedrichsort
Laboe
Husum
Altenholz
Gettorf
Schönberg
S C H L E S W I G -
Dörpstedt
Kropp
Heikendorf
Selenter See
KIEL
Friedrichstadt
Lütjenburg
Büdelsdorf
Fockbek
Rendsburg
Preetz
Lunden
Erfde
Eider
Jevenstedt
Malente-Gremsmühlen
Hamdorf
Plön
Tellingstedt
Nortorf
Ascheberg
Wesselburen
Heide
Legan
Bordesholm
Ostsee-Kanal
Großer Plöner See
Hanerau-Hademarschen
Neumünster
Bornhöved
Büsum
Albersdorf
Hohenwestedt
Meldorf
Schenefeld
Rickling
Ahrensbök
Trischen
H O L S T E I N
Hohenlockstedt
Wahlstedt
Bad Segeberg
Bad Schwartau
Friedrichskoog
St. Michaelisdonn
Kellinghusen
Stockelsdorf
Marne
Nord-Ostsee-Kanal
Wilster
Bad Bramstedt
Gut Kaden
Reinfeld
Itzehoe
Lentföhrden
Bad Oldesloe
Brunsbüttel
St. Margarethen
Brande-Hörnerkirchen
Kaltenkirchen
Pinnau
Wendlohe
Cuxhaven
Freiburg
Barmstedt
Henstedt-Ulzburg
Treudelberg
Walddörfer
Otterndorf
Glückstadt
Elmshorn
Wischhafen
Quickborn
Ahrensburg
Neuhaus
Cadenberge
Wanna
Uetersen
Norderstedt
Nusse
Drochtersen
Hemmoor
Pinneberg
Trittau
Bederkesa
Lamstedt
Stade
Wedel
Schenefeld
Rahlstedt
Falkenstein
HAMBURG
Reinbek
Bremerhaven
Horneburg
Buxtehude
Harburg
Bergedorf
Geesthacht
ELBE
Bremervörde
Harsefeld
Seevetal-Maschen
Lauenburg
Buxtehude
Beverstedt
Winsen
Stotel
Hollenstedt
St. Dionys
Schloss Lüdersburg
Rhade
Lüneburger Heide
Lüneburg
Zeven
Tostedt
Hanstedt
Garlstorf
Sittensen
Egestorf
Salzhausen
Melbeck
MICHELIN

Omø
Smålandsfarvandet
Præstø
Vordingborg
Liselund
Møns Klint
Stege
Aborrebjerg
Møn
Møn (DK)
Bogø
Sønderby
Femø
Østerby
Fejø
Askø
Kragenæs
Stubbekøbing
Nørre-Alslev
FALSTER
Bandholm
Sakskøbing
Nakskov
Søllested
Nykøbing F
Maribo
LOLLAND
Holeby
Rødby
Nysted
Rødby Havn
Gedser
Gedser Odde
OSTSEE
Fehmarnbelt
Puttgarden
Fehmarn
Burg
Fehmarnsund
Großenbrode
Prerow
Darß
Born
Zingst
Der Grabow
Barth
Wustrow
Saaler Bodden
Trelleborg
Löbnitz
Richtenberg
Mecklenburger Bucht
Graal-Müritz
Ribnitz-Damgarten
Oldenburg
Dahme
Warnemünde
Marlow
Tribsees
Malmö
Trelleborg
Helsinki
Tallinn
Kühlungsborn
ROSTOCK
Bad Sülze
Grömitz
Rerik
Bad Doberan
Sanitz
Recknitz
Wustrow
Kröpelin
Tessin
Neustadt
Gnoien
Lübeck-Travemünde
Neubukow
Satow
07-2002
Poel
Boltenhagen
Schwaan
Laage
Travemünde
Klütz
Wismar
MECKLENBURG
Dassow
Neukloster
Neukalen
Grevesmühlen
Bützow
Teterow
Schönberg
Warin
Güstrow
Warnow
Bad Kleinen
Brüel
Malchiner See
Rehna
Mühlen Eichsen
Schweriner See
Sternberg
Schlagbrügge
Gadebusch
Krakow
Roggendorf
Ratzeburg
Lützow
Schwerin
Goldberg
Fleesensee
Mestlin
Waren
Schaalsee
Crivitz
Karow
Malchow
Zarrentin
Elde
Lübz
Plau
Plauer See
Müritz
Wittenburg
Röbel
Spornitz
Parchim
Hagenow
Wöbbelin
Neustadt-Glewe
Vellahn
Pritzier
Marnitz
Meyenburg
Ludwigslust
Freyenstein
Boizenburg
Sude
Zierzow
Ruhner Berge
Lübtheen
Grabow
Putlitz
Neuhaus
Eldena
Elde
Wittstock
Neu Darchau
Pritzwalk
Karstädt
Dömitz
Hitzacker
Perleberg
MICHELIN

CLASSIFICATION OF COURSES
EINTEILUNG DER GOLFPLÄTZE

This classification gives priority consideration to the score awarded to the actual course.

Diese Einteilung berücksichtigt in erster Linie die dem Golfplatz erteilte Note

Course score Note für den Golfplatz				Page Seite
18	6	5	Club zur Vahr (Garlstedt)	393
18	6	7	Falkenstein	399
18	8	7	Scharmützelsee *Nick Faldo*	451
18	9	7	Seddiner See *Südplatz*	461
17	9	9	Bad Griesbach *Brunnwies*	380
17	7	6	Beuerberg	387
17	8	8	Fleesensee	401
17	7	8	Frankfurter GC	402
17	7	8	Fürstlicher GC Bad Waldsee	404
17	9	7	Gut Lärchenhof	409
17	7	7	Gütersloh (Westfälischer GC)	412
17	8	6	Hubbelrath	420
17	6	7	Köln	425
17	7	7	Krefelder	426
17	8	8	Lübeck-Travemünder	430
17	7	7	Mittelrheinischer	435
17	8	6	Motzener See	436
17	6	5	Oberfranken	441
17	8	7	Rethmar	447
17	8	7	Scharmützelsee *Arnold Palmer*	450
17	8	6	Schloss Nippenburg	458
17	7	5	Schloss Wilkendorf	459
17	8	6	Schwanhof	460
17	7	6	St. Dionys	464
17	5	5	Stuttgarter Solitude	469
17	7	6	Wittelsbacher	477
16	7	7	Bergisch Land Wuppertal	385
16	8	9	Berlin-Wannsee	386
16	7	7	Bodensee-Weissensberg	390
16	7	6	Buxtehude	392
16	7	6	Feldafing	400
16	7	6	Gut Grambek	407
16	7	5	Gut Thailing	411
16	8	7	Hamburg-Ahrensburg	413
16	6	6	Hanau-Wilhelmsbad	414
16	7	7	Hannover	415
16	7	6	Iffeldorf	421
16	7	5	Lüneburger Heide	431
16	7	7	München-Riedhof	437
16	7	7	Reichswald-Nürnberg	446
16	8	7	Rheine/Mesum	448
16	7	7	Schloss Braunfels	452
16	8	7	Schloss Langenstein	455
16	7	7	Schloss Myllendonk	457
16	8	7	Semlin am See	462
16	8	7	Senne	463
16	7	6	St. Eurach	465
16	9	7	St. Leon-Rot *"St Leon" Course*	467
16	7	5	Stolper Heide	468
16	7	6	Walddörfer	474
16	7	6	Wendlohe *A-Kurs + B-Kurs*	476
15	7	7	Augsburg	377
15	7	7	Bad Abbach-Deutenhof	378
15	5	7	Bad Bevensen	380
15	9	9	Bad Griesbach-Sagmühle *Sagmühle*	381
15	7	7	Bamberg	384
15	6	7	Biblis Wattenheim *A + B*	388
15	7	8	Bitburger Land	389
15	7	7	Düsseldorfer	395
15	8	7	Essener Oefte	398
15	7	6	Gut Kaden	408
15	6	6	Gut Ludwigsberg	410
15	7	5	Hof Trages	418
15	7	6	Hohenpähl	419
15	7	6	Im Chiemgau	422
15	7	6	Isernhagen	423
15	7	6	Jakobsberg	424
15	7	6	Lichtenau-Weickershof	427
15	7	8	Lindau-Bad Schachen	428
15	6	7	Münchner-Strasslach	438
15	7	7	Neuhof	440
15	6	6	Oberschwaben Bad Waldsee	442

Classification

CLASSIFICATION OF COURSES — EINTEILUNG DER GOLFPLÄTZE

15	7	7	Öschberghof	443
15	7	7	Schloss Egmating	453
15	6	6	Schloss Klingenburg	454
15	7	6	Schloss Lüdersburg *Old/New*	456
15	9	7	St. Leon-Rot *"Rot»"Course*	466
15	6	8	Sylt	470
15	7	6	Tutzing	473
15	7	7	Wasserburg Anholt	475
14	7	6	Abenberg	376
14	7	7	Bad Liebenzell	382
14	6	6	Bad Wörishofen	383
14	6	7	Braunschweig	391
14	7	7	Domtal-Mommenheim	394
14	7	7	Elfrather Mühle	396
14	7	7	Eschenried	397
14	7	6	Fränkische Schweiz	403
14	7	6	Fürstliches Hofgut Kolnhausen	405
14	6	7	Garmisch-Partenkirchen	406
14	6	6	Hechingen-Hohenzollern	416
14	7	8	Heilbronn-Hohenlohe	417
14	8	8	Lindenhof	429
14	7	6	Main-Taunus	432
14	7	6	Märkischer Potsdam	433
14	6	6	Memmingen Gut Westerhart	434
14	8	6	Nahetal	439
14	6	6	Pinnau	444
14	6	7	Reichsstadt Bad Windsheim	445
14	8	7	Rheinhessen	449
14	7	8	Tegernseer Bad Wiessee	471
13	8	7	Treudelberg	472

Classification

HOTELS FACILITIES
EINTEILUNG DES HOTELANGEBOTS DER UMGEBUNG

This classification gives priority consideration to the score awarded to the hotel facilities.

Hotel facility score / Note für das Hotelangebot der Umgebung — Page / Seite

17	9	**9**	Bad Griesbach *Brunnwies*	380
15	9	**9**	Bad Griesbach-Sagmühle *Sagmühle*	381
16	8	**9**	Berlin-Wannsee	386
15	7	**8**	Bitburger Land	389
17	8	**8**	Fleesensee	401
17	7	**8**	Frankfurter GC	402
17	7	**8**	Fürstlicher GC Bad Waldsee	404
14	7	**8**	Heilbronn-Hohenlohe	417
15	7	**8**	Lindau-Bad Schachen	428
14	8	**8**	Lindenhof	429
17	8	**8**	Lübeck-Travemünder	430
15	6	**8**	Sylt	470
14	7	**8**	Tegernseer Bad Wiessee	471
15	7	**7**	Augsburg	377
15	7	**7**	Bad Abbach-Deutenhof	378
15	5	**7**	Bad Bevensen	380
14	7	**7**	Bad Liebenzell	382
15	7	**7**	Bamberg	384
16	7	**7**	Bergisch Land Wuppertal	385
15	6	**7**	Biblis Wattenheim *A + B*	386
16	7	**7**	Bodensee-Weissensberg	390
14	6	**7**	Braunschweig	391
14	7	**7**	Domtal-Mommenheim	394
15	7	**7**	Düsseldorfer	395
14	7	**7**	Elfrather Mühle	386

14	7	**7**	Eschenried	397
15	8	**7**	Essener Oefte	398
18	6	**7**	Falkenstein	399
14	6	**7**	Garmisch-Partenkirchen	406
17	9	**7**	Gut Lärchenhof	409
17	7	**7**	Gütersloh (Westfälischer GC)	412
16	8	**7**	Hamburg-Ahrensburg	413
16	7	**7**	Hannover	415
17	6	**7**	Köln	425
17	7	**7**	Krefelder	426
17	7	**7**	Mittelrheinischer	435
16	7	**7**	München-Riedhof	437
15	6	**7**	Münchner-Strasslach	438
15	7	**7**	Neuhof	440
15	7	**7**	Öschberghof	443
14	6	**7**	Reichsstadt Bad Windsheim	445
16	7	**7**	Reichswald-Nürnberg	446
17	8	**7**	Rethmar	447
16	8	**7**	Rheine/Mesum	448
14	8	**7**	Rheinhessen	449
17	8	**7**	Scharmützelsee *Arnold Palmer*	450
18	8	**7**	Scharmützelsee *Nick Faldo*	451
16	7	**7**	Schloss Braunfels	452
15	7	**7**	Schloss Egmating	453
16	8	**7**	Schloss Langenstein	455
16	7	**7**	Schloss Myllendonk	457
18	9	**7**	Seddiner See *Südplatz*	461
16	8	**7**	Semlin am See	462
16	8	**7**	Senne	463
15	9	**7**	St. Leon-Rot *"Rot" Course*	466
16	9	**7**	St. Leon-Rot *"St Leon" Course*	467
13	8	**7**	Treudelberg	472
15	7	**7**	Wasserburg Anholt	475
14	7	**6**	Abenberg	376
14	6	**6**	Bad Wörishofen	383
17	7	**6**	Beuerberg	387
16	7	**6**	Buxtehude	392
16	7	**6**	Feldafing	400
14	7	**6**	Fränkische Schweiz	403
14	7	**6**	Fürstliches Hofgut Kolnhausen	405
16	7	**6**	Gut Grambek	407
15	7	**6**	Gut Kaden	408
15	6	**6**	Gut Ludwigsberg	411
16	6	**6**	Hanau-Wilhelmsbad	414
14	6	**6**	Hechingen-Hohenzollern	416
15	7	**6**	Hohenpähl	419
17	8	**6**	Hubbelrath	420
16	7	**6**	Iffeldorf	421
15	7	**6**	Im Chiemgau	422
15	7	**6**	Isernhagen	423
15	7	**6**	Jakobsberg	430
15	7	**6**	Lichtenau-Weickershof	427
14	7	**6**	Main-Taunus	432
14	7	**6**	Märkischer Potsdam	433
14	6	**6**	Memmingen Gut Westerhart	434
17	8	**6**	Motzener See	436
14	8	**6**	Nahetal	439
15	6	**6**	Oberschwaben Bad Waldsee	442
14	6	**6**	Pinnau	444
15	6	**6**	Schloss Klingenburg	454
15	7	**6**	Schloss Lüdersburg *Old/New*	456
17	8	**6**	Schloss Nippenburg	458
17	8	**6**	Schwanhof	460
17	7	**6**	St. Dionys	464
16	7	**6**	St. Eurach	465
15	7	**6**	Tutzing	473
16	7	**6**	Walddörfer	474
16	7	**6**	Wendlohe *A-Kurs + B-Kurs*	476
17	7	**6**	Wittelsbacher	477
18	6	**5**	Club zur Vahr (Garlstedt)	393
16	7	**5**	Gut Thailing	411
15	7	**5**	Hof Trages	418
16	7	**5**	Lüneburger Heide	431
17	6	**5**	Oberfranken	441
17	7	**5**	Schloss Wilkendorf	459
16	7	**5**	Stolper Heide	468
17	5	**5**	Stuttgarter Solitude	469

RECOMMENDED GOLFING STAY
FÜR GOLFERIEN EMPFOHLEN

Bad Griesbach *Brunnwies*	17	9	9	380
Bad Griesbach-Sagmühle *Sagmühle*	15	9	9	381
Fleesensee	17	8	8	401
Fürstlicher GC Bad Waldsee	17	7	8	404
Scharmützelsee *Arnold Palmer*	17	8	7	450
Scharmützelsee *Nick Faldo*	18	8	7	451
St. Leon-Rot *"Rot» Cours"*	15	9	7	466
St. Leon-Rot *"St Leon" Course*	16	9	7	467
Lübeck-Travemünder	17	8	8	430

RECOMMENDED GOLFING HOLIDAYS
FÜR EINEN FERIENAUFENTHALT EMPFOHLEN

Bodensee-Weissensberg	16	7	7	390
Garmisch-Partenkirchen	14	6	7	406
Im Chiemgau	15	7	6	422
Lindau-Bad Schachen	15	7	8	428
Lübeck-Travemünder	17	8	8	430
Öschberghof	15	7	7	443
Sylt	15	6	8	472

GÉOGRAPHICAL RELIEF
GELÄNDEBESCHAFFENHEIT DER GOLFPLÄTZE

Bad Wörishofen	14	6	6	383
Biblis Wattenheim *A + B*	15	6	7	390
Eschenried	14	7	7	397
Fürstliches Hofgut Kolnhausen	14	7	6	405
Gütersloh (Westfälischer GC)	17	7	7	412
Hamburg-Ahrensburg	16	8	7	413
Lübeck-Travemünder	17	8	8	430
Rethmar	17	8	7	447
Rheine/Mesum	16	8	7	448
Seddiner See *Südplatz*	18	9	7	461
Senne	16	8	7	4636
St. Leon-Rot *«St Leon» Course*	16	9	7	467
Stolper Heide	16	7	5	468
Wittelsbacher	17	7	6	477

Elfrather Mühle	14	7	7	396
Fürstlicher GC Bad Waldsee	17	7	8	404
Garmisch-Partenkirchen	14	6	7	406
Gut Kaden	15	7	6	408
Gut Lärchenhof	17	9	7	409
Hannover	16	7	7	415
Isernhagen	15	7	6	423

Course				Page
Köln	17	6	7	425
Lindenhof	14	8	8	429
Main-Taunus	14	7	6	432
Öschberghof	15	7	7	443
Pinnau	14	6	6	444
Reichswald-Nürnberg	16	7	7	446
Scharmützelsee *Nick Faldo*	18	8	7	451
Sylt	15	6	8	470
Wasserburg Anholt	15	7	7	475
Wendlohe *A-Kurs + B-Kurs*	16	7	6	476

Course				Page
Abenberg	14	7	6	376
Bad Griesbach-Sagmühle *Sagmühle*	15	9	9	381
Berlin-Wannsee	16	8	9	386
Frankfurter GC	17	7	8	402
Gut Grambek	16	7	6	407
Gut Ludwigsberg	15	6	6	410
Hanau-Wilhelmsbad	16	6	6	414
Hof Trages	15	7	5	418
Krefelder	17	7	7	426
Lichtenau-Weickershof	15	7	6	427
Lindau-Bad Schachen	15	7	8	428
Memmingen Gut Westerhart	14	6	6	434
Neuhof	15	7	7	440
Scharmützelsee *Arnold Palmer*	17	8	7	450
Schloss Braunfels	16	7	7	452
Schloss Lüdersburg *Old/New*	15	7	6	456
Schloss Myllendonk	16	7	7	457
Semlin am See	16	8	7	462
Stuttgarter Solitude	17	5	5	469
Treudelberg	13	8	7	472

Course				Page
Bad Abbach-Deutenhof	15	7	7	378
Beuerberg	17	7	6	387
Bodensee-Weissensberg	16	7	7	390
Club zur Vahr (Garlstedt)	18	6	5	393
Gut Thailing	16	7	5	411
Hohenpähl	15	7	6	419
Im Chiemgau	15	7	6	422
Märkischer Potsdam	14	7	6	433
Mittelrheinischer	17	7	7	435
Motzener See	17	8	6	436
Münchner-Strasslach	15	6	7	438
Reichsstadt Bad Windsheim	14	6	7	445
Schloss Egmating	15	7	7	453
Schloss Klingenburg	15	6	6	454
St. Eurach	16	7	6	465

Course				Page
Bad Bevensen	15	5	7	379
Bad Liebenzell	14	7	7	382
Buxtehude	16	7	6	392
Falkenstein	18	6	7	399
Fränkische Schweiz	14	7	6	403
Hechingen-Hohenzollern	14	6	6	416
Heilbronn-Hohenlohe	14	7	8	417
Hubbelrath	17	8	6	420
Jakobsberg	15	7	6	424
München-Riedhof	16	7	7	437
Nahetal	14	8	6	439
Oberschwaben Bad Waldsee	15	6	6	442
Rheinhessen	14	8	7	449
Schloss Wilkendorf	17	7	5	459
St. Dionys	17	7	6	464
Tegernseer Bad Wiessee	14	7	8	471
Walddörfer	16	7	6	474

Course				Page
Bergisch Land Wuppertal	16	7	7	385
Bitburger Land	15	7	8	389
Braunschweig	14	6	7	391
Domtal-Mommenheim	14	7	7	394
Düsseldorfer	15	7	7	395
Essener Oefte	15	8	7	398
Feldafing	16	7	6	400
Fleesensee	17	8	8	401
Schloss Langenstein	16	8	7	455
Schloss Nippenburg	17	8	6	458
St. Leon-Rot *«Rot» Course*	15	9	7	466

Course				Page
Augsburg	15	7	7	377
Bamberg	15	7	7	384
Lüneburger Heide	16	7	5	431
Oberfranken	17	6	5	441
Schwanhof	17	8	6	460
Tutzing	15	7	6	473

Course				Page
Bad Griesbach *Brunnwies*	17	9	9	380
Iffeldorf	16	7	6	421

TYPE OF COURSE
TYP DES GOLFPLATZES

Country
Bad Bevensen 379, Braunschweig 391, Fränkische Schweiz 403, Hannover 415, Pinnau 444, Schloss Nippenburg 458, Seddiner See *Südplatz* 461, Wendlohe *A-Kurs + B-Kurs* 476.

Forest
Abenberg 376, Augsburg 377, Bad Liebenzell 382, Bergisch Land Wuppertal 385, Berlin-Wannsee 386 Bodensee-Weissensberg 390, Braunschweig 391, Buxtehude 392, Club zur Vahr (Garlstedt) 393, Düsseldorfer 395, Eschenried 397, Essener Oefte 398, Falkenstein 399, Fränkische Schweiz 405, Frankfurter GC 402, Fürstlicher GC Bad Waldsee 404, Hannover 415, Heilbronn-Hohenlohe 417, Hohenpähl 419, Hubbelrath 420, Iffeldorf 421, Isernhagen 423, Köln 425, Krefelder 426, Lüneburger Heide 431, Nahetal 439, Oberfranken 441, Oberschwaben Bad Waldsee 442, Reichswald-Nürnberg 446, Scharmützelsee *Arnold Palmer* 450, Schloss Myllendonk 457, Semlin am See 462, St. Eurach 465, Stuttgarter Solitude 469, Walddörfer 474, Wasserburg Anholt 475, Wittelsbacher 477.

Heathland
Senne 463.

Inland
Rheine/Mesum 448, Schloss Wilkendorf 459.

Links
Scharmützelsee *Nick Faldo* 451, Sylt 470.

Moorland
St. Dionys 464.

Mountain
Feldafing 400, Iffeldorf 421, Tegernseer Bad Wiessee 471, Tutzing 473.

Parkland
Gut Grambek 407, Hanau-Wilhelmsbad 414, Bad Griesbach-Sagmühle *Sagmühle* 381, Bad Wörishofen 383, Beuerberg 387, Fleesensee 401, Garmisch-Partenkirchen 406, Gütersloh (Westfälischer GC) 412, Hamburg-Ahrensburg 413, Hof Trages 418, Lichtenau-Weickershof 427, Lindau-Bad Schachen 428, Märkischer Potsdam 433, Memmingen Gut Westerhart 434, Mittelrheinischer 435, Neuhof 440, Schloss Braunfels 452, Schloss Klingenburg 454, Schloss Lüdersburg *Old/New* 456, Schloss Myllendonk 457, St. Leon-Rot "*Rot*" *Course* 466, Stolper Heide 468.

Seaside course
Lübeck-Travemünder 430.

Hilly
Augsburg 377, Bad Griesbach *Brunnwies* 380, Bamberg 384, Bergisch Land Wuppertal 385, Bitburger Land 389, Hechingen-Hohenzollern 416, Hubbelrath 420, Jakobsberg 424, München-Riedhof 437, Rheinhessen 449, Schloss Langenstein 455, Schwanhof 460, Fleesensee 401, Rethmar 447.

Open Country

Abenberg 376, Bad Abbach-Deutenhof 378, Bad Griesbach *Brunnwies* 380, Bad Liebenzell 382, Bamberg 384, Biblis Wattenheim *A + B* 388, Bitburger Land 389, Buxtehude 392, Domtal-Mommenheim 394, Elfrather Mühle 396, Eschenried 397, Fürstlicher GC Bad Waldsee 404, Fürstliches Hofgut Kolnhausen 405, Gut Kaden 408, Gut Lärchenhof 409, Gut Ludwigsberg 410, Gut Thailing 411, Hechingen-Hohenzollern 416, Heilbronn-Hohenlohe 417, Hof Trages 418, Im Chiemgau 422, Isernhagen 423, Jakobsberg 424, Lindenhof 429, Main-Taunus 432, Memmingen Gut Westerhart 434, Motzener See 436, München-Riedhof 437, Münchner-Strasslach 438, Öschberghof 443, Pinnau 444, Reichsstadt Bad Windsheim 445, Rethmar 447, Rheinhessen 449, Schloss Egmating 453, Schloss Langenstein 455, Schloss Nippenburg 458, Senne 463, St. Leon-Rot *"Rot" Course* 466, Schwanhof 460, Sylt 470, St. Leon-Rot, *"St Leon" Course* 467, Stuttgarter Solitude 469, Treudelberg 472, Wendlohe *A-Kurs + B-Kurs* 476.

Park

Falkenstein 399, Bodensee-Weissensberg 390, Club zur Vahr (Garlstedt) 393, Gut Ludwigsberg 410, Hohenpähl 419, Lübeck-Travemünder 430, Oberfranken 441, Oberschwaben Bad Waldsee 442, Öschberghof 443, Scharmützelsee *Arnold Palmer* 450, Semlin am See 462, Tegernseer Bad Wiessee 471, Walddörfer 474, Wasserburg Anholt 475.

ABENBERG

14 | 7 | 6

Der Golfplatz liegt so nahe bei Nürnberg, dass man sich in dieser deutschen Hochburg des Mittelalters, in der Albrecht Dürer wohnte, gut einquartieren kann. Die Altstadt und das Germanische Nationalmuseum lohnen einen erholsamen Tag zwischen zwei Partien Golf! Die Spielbahn liegt in einem flachen Gelände mit vielen Bäumen. Die riesigen Bäume stellen einen wichtigen Teil der Schwierigkeiten dar, unter anderem verlangen auch die Fairways und die Länge von gewissen Par 4 bei bestimmten Abschlägen eine sehr sorgfältige Auswahl des Schlägers: Wenn man den Ball nicht lange und gerade schlagen kann, muss man einige Bogeys in Kauf nehmen. Die Bunker sind recht zahlreich, aber meist nur um die mittelgrossen, wenig welligen Greens angeordnet. Zwei Greens sind erhöht und zwei auf doppelten Stufen angelegt. Eine ehrliche, offene Anlage, auch wenn die Gestaltung und die Ausprägung der Erhebungen zu wünschen übrig lässt.

The Abenberg course is close enough to Nürnberg for you to establish base-camp in this high spot of Middle-Age Germany, where Albrecht Dürer once lived. The old town and the Germanisches Nationalmuseum are well worth a day's rest between two rounds of golf ! This course is laid out on generally flat terrain in very woody countryside, so big trees are not surprisingly a major factor in the difficulties awaiting you on either side of the fairways. On top of that, the length of some par 4s calls for very careful club selection from a number of tees. If you are not too sure of hitting it long and straight, there'll be a few bogeys in store. Bunkers abound but are basically placed around averagely-sized greens with few contours. Two greens are elevated, two are two-tiered. A very decent course, but perhaps lacking a little contouring work to give the layout greater shape.

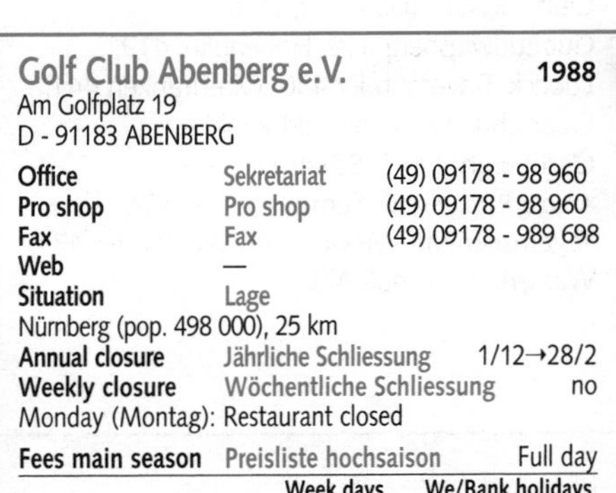

Golf Club Abenberg e.V. — 1988

Am Golfplatz 19
D - 91183 ABENBERG

Office	Sekretariat	(49) 09178 - 98 960
Pro shop	Pro shop	(49) 09178 - 98 960
Fax	Fax	(49) 09178 - 989 698
Web	—	
Situation	Lage	

Nürnberg (pop. 498 000), 25 km

Annual closure	Jährliche Schliessung	1/12→28/2
Weekly closure	Wöchentliche Schliessung	no

Monday (Montag): Restaurant closed

Fees main season Preisliste hochsaison	Week days Woche	We/Bank holidays We/Feiertag
	Full day	
Individual Individuell	36 €	46 €
Couple Ehepaar	72 €	92 €

- 22 years, Students: – 50% on weekdays (Montag-Freitag)

Caddy	Caddy	no
Electric Trolley	Elektrokarren	no
Buggy	Elektrischer Wagen	no
Clubs	Leihschläger	yes

Credit cards Kreditkarten
VISA - Eurocard - MasterCard - AMEX

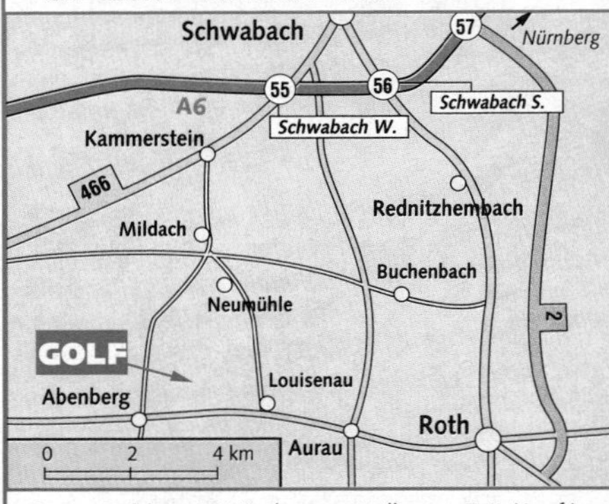

Access Zufahrt : A6 Nürnberg → Heilbronn. Exit (Ausf.) Schwabach West/ Abenberg. B466 → Abenberg
Map 4 on page 360 Karte 4 Seite 360

Golf course PLATZ — 14/20

Site	Lage	
Maintenance	Instandhaltung	
Architect	Architekt	Unknown
Type	Typ	forest, open country
Relief	Begehbarkeit	
Water in play	Platz mit Wasser	
Exp. to wind	Wind ausgesetzt	
Trees in play	Platz mit Bäumen	

Scorecard Scorekarte	Chp. Chp.	Mens Herren	Ladies Damen
Length Länge	6148	5969	5283
Par	72	72	72
Slope system	131	129	130

Advised golfing ability Empfohlene Spielstärke — 0 12 24 36

Hcp required Min. Handicap 36

Club house & amenities KLUBHAUS UND NEBENGEBÄUDE — 7/10

Pro shop	Pro shop	
Driving range	Übungsplatz	
Sheltered	überdacht	6 mats
On grass	auf Rasen	yes
Putting-green	Putting-grün	yes
Pitching-green	Pitching-grün	yes

Hotel facilities HOTEL BESCHREIBUNG — 6/10

HOTELS HOTELS

Burghotel Abenberg, 17 rooms, D 56 € — Abenberg 500 m
Tel (49) 09178 - 982 990, Fax (49) 09178 -982 9910

Hotel-Gasthof Meyerle, 24 rooms, D 61 € — Haag 9 km
Tel (49) 09122 - 51 58, Fax (49) 09122 - 158 58

Zum Heidenberg, 32 rooms, D 71 € — Büchenbach-Kühendorf 4 km
Tel (49) 09171 - 84 40, Fax (49) 09171 - 84 480

RESTAURANTS RESTAURANT

Goldener Stern, Tel (49) 09122 - 2335 — Schwabach 10 km

Zirbelstube, Tel(49) 0911 - 998 820 — Nürnberg-Worzeldorf 25 km

AUGSBURG

15 | 7 | 7

Auf dem Heimatplatz von Bernhard Langer lauert überall Gefahr. Die erste Runde wird man wohl damit beschäftigt sein, die Strategie für die zweite Runde zu analysieren, da die Hindernisse kaum sichtbar sind. Die Bäume dominieren und im Unterholz gehen die Bälle leicht verloren. Auf diesem Platz benötigt man alle Schlagvarianten. Zudem darf die Konzentration nie erlahmen, denn es gibt keine einfachen Löcher. Es ist ein anspruchsvoller, interessanter Platz, die Schwierigkeiten sind gut verteilt und überfordern einen geübteren Spieler nicht. Zögern Sie jedoch nicht, die vorderen Abschläge zu wählen, wenn sie nicht in golferischer oder körperlicher Hochform sind, denn der Platz ist recht anstrengend zu begehen.. Ob man den Golfplatz nun mag oder nicht, zumindest wird man die Ruhe und der Charme dieses Ortes, ganz in der Nähe der schönen Stadt Augsburg, geniessen.

On Bernhard Langer's home course danger lurks everywhere. First time out, you spend your time studying game strategy and how you might apply it for your next visit, as not all the hazards are visible. As the trees are very present and the undergrowth swallows up many a ball, you soon realize that for a good score here, you need flighted shots and constant concentration. Be warned : there is no one easy hole. This is a demanding, competent and exciting course but the difficulties are well spread out and shouldn't be too much for even inexperienced players. Don't think twice about playing from the front tees if your game - and physical fitness - are not in tip-top condition, as Augsburg can be tough on the legs. Whether you like the course or not, you are bound to appreciate the tranquillity and charm of the spot, close to the pretty town of Augsburg.

Golf-Club Augsburg e.V. — 1953

Engelshofer Strasse 2
D - 86399 BOBINGEN-BURGWALDEN

Office	Sekretariat	(49) 08234 - 5621
Pro shop	Pro shop	(49) 08234 - 7311
Fax	Fax	(49) 08234 - 7855
Web	www.golfclubaugsburg.de	
Situation	Lage	Augsburg, 10 km

München (pop. 1 300 000), 78 km

Annual closure	Jährliche Schliessung	no
Weekly closure	Wöchentliche Schliessung	no

Monday (Montag): Restaurant closed

Fees main season Preisliste hochsaison	Week days Woche	We/Bank holidays We/Feiertag
		Full day
Individual Individuell	31 €	46 €
Couple Ehepaar	62 €	92 €

- 21 years/Students: – 50%

Caddy	Caddy	no
Electric Trolley	Elektrokarren	13 €
Buggy	Elektrischer Wagen	no
Clubs	Leihschläger	8 €
Credit cards Kreditkarten		no

Access Zufahrt : A8 München-Augsburg. Exit (Ausf.) Augsburg-West. Exit Gersthofen Süd, B17 → Exit Königsbrunn. Right → Bobingen, Strassberg. Golf → Burgwalden **Map 2 on page 356** Karte 2 Seite 356

Golf course PLATZ — 15/20

Site	Lage	
Maintenance	Instandhaltung	
Architect	Architekt	B. von Limburger, Donald Harradine
Type	Typ	forest, hilly
Relief	Begehbarkeit	
Water in play	Platz mit Wasser	
Exp. to wind	Wind ausgesetzt	
Trees in play	Platz mit Bäumen	

Scorecard Scorekarte	Chp. Chp.	Mens Herren	Ladies Damen
Length Länge	6018	6018	5347
Par	72	72	72
Slope system	133	133	127

Advised golfing ability Empfohlene Spielstärke: 0 12 24 36
Hcp required Min. Handicap: 36

Club house & amenities KLUBHAUS UND NEBENGEBÄUDE — 7/10

Pro shop	Pro shop	
Driving range	Übungsplatz	
Sheltered	überdacht	3 mats
On grass	auf Rasen	yes
Putting-green	Putting-grün	yes
Pitching-green	Pitching-grün	yes

Hotel facilities HOTEL BESCHREIBUNG — 7/10

HOTELS HOTELS

Steigenberger Drei Mohren — Augsburg 10 km
112 rooms, D 179 €
Tel (49) 0821 - 50 360, Fax (49) 0821 - 157 864

Dom Hotel, 52 rooms, D 97 € — Augsburg
Tel (49) 0821 - 343 930, Fax (49) 0821 -3439 3200 — 12 km

Romantik Augsburger Hof, 36 rooms, D 102 € — Augsburg
Tel (49) 0821 - 343 050, Fax (49) 0821 - 343 0555 — 15 km

RESTAURANTS RESTAURANT

Die Ecke ,Tel (49) 0821 - 510 600 — Augsburg 12 km

Fuggerei-Stube, Tel (49) 0821 - 30 870 — Augsburg 12 km

BAD ABBACH-DEUTENHOF

15 | 7 | 7

Dieser Platz liegt südlich der Stadt Regensburg, die in ihrem Stadtbild die Geschichte des Deutschen Kaiserreichs widerspiegelt. Viele Gebäude stammen noch aus dem Mittelalter und der Renaissance. Diese Verbundenheit mit der deutschen Geschichte wird in der Walhalla symbolisiert, einem Denkmal hoch über der Donau, das Ludwig I. von Bayern errrichten liess. Der neue Platz in der Kurstadt Bad Abbach, der auf weit offenem Gelände erbaut wurde, gilt schon heute als einer der besten neuen Plätze in Bayern. Der Platz weist keine Heimtücken auf, hier kann man auf Birdies hoffen, statt ständig Bogeys oder Schlimmeres zu befürchten. Bad Abbach hat sich damit in der Kürze der Zeit einen vorzüglichen Ruf erworben, obwohl es ein wenig abseits der grossen Touristenrouten liegt. Die Schwierigkeiten sind gut über den Platz verteilt. Der Platz ist für Golfer aller Spielstärken gut zubewältigen. Sein einziger Nachteil ist das bergige Gelände, sodass Golfer, die körperlich nicht fit sind, schnell ermüden.

This course is located to the south of the city of Regensburg, one of the high-spots of the history of the German Empire where much of the architecture recalls the Middle Ages and the Renaissance. Such union with German history is equally symbolized by the Walhalla, a sort of memorial overlooking the Danube erected by Louis I of Bavaria. This recent course, laid out in a spa city over rather wide open space, has become established as one of the better new courses in Bavaria. Rather forthright and indulgent to golfers who tend to stumble across birdies rather than actively go looking for them, this Rainer Preismann design tends to bare its teeth more to the reckless golfer. Nicely balanced and with a rather likeable personality, Bad Abbach is making a name for itself on account of its excellent attributes, despite being a little off the busier tourist routes. With difficulties fairly spread around the course and playable by golfers of all levels, its only failing is perhaps the hilly terrain which make this a tiring round of golf for physically unfit players.

378

Golfclub Bad Abbach-Deutenhof — 1996

Gut Deutenhof
D - 93077 BAD ABBACH

Office	Sekretariat	(49) 09405 - 953 20
Pro shop	Pro shop	(49) 09405 - 953 20
Fax	Fax	(49) 09405 - 953 219
Web	www.golf.de/gc-bad-abbach	
Situation	Lage	

Regensburg (pop. 137 000), 10 km

Annual closure	Jährliche Schliessung	no
Weekly closure	Wöchentliche Schliessung	no

Fees main season Preisliste hochsaison	Week days Woche	We/Bank holidays We/Feiertag
		18 holes
Individual Individuell	31 €	41 €
Couple Ehepaar	62 €	82 €

- 21 years/Students: – 50%

Caddy	Caddy	no
Electric Trolley	Elektrokarren	8 €
Buggy	Elektrischer Wagen	23 €
Clubs	Leihschläger	10 €
Credit cards	Kreditkarten	no

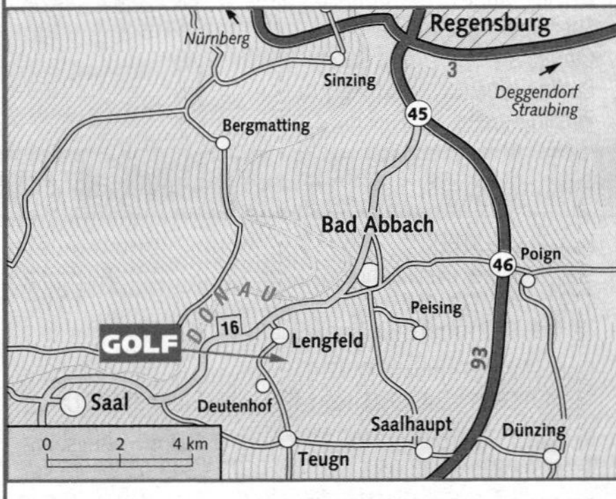

Access Zufahrt : München A93 → Regensburg. Exit (Ausfahrt) Hausen, → Teugn, → Lengfeld. Golf on right side. **Map 2 on page 356** Karte 2 Seite 356

Golf course PLATZ — 15/20

Site	Lage	
Maintenance	Instandhaltung	
Architect	Architekt	Rainer Preismann DeutscheGolfConsult
Type	Typ	open country
Relief	Begehbarkeit	
Water in play	Platz mit Wasser	
Exp. to wind	Wind ausgesetzt	
Trees in play	Platz mit Bäumen	

Scorecard Scorekarte	Chp. Chp.	Mens Herren	Ladies Damen
Length Länge	6150	5817	5179
Par	72	72	72
Slope system	127	121	123

Advised golfing ability Empfohlene Spielstärke — 0 12 24 36

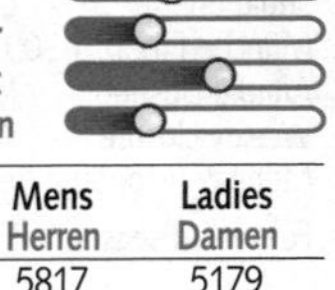

Hcp required Min. Handicap 35

Club house & amenities KLUBHAUS UND NEBENGEBÄUDE — 7/10

Pro shop	Pro shop	
Driving range	Übungsplatz	
Sheltered	überdacht	6 mats
On grass	auf Rasen	yes
Putting-green	Putting-grün	yes
Pitching-green	Pitching-grün	yes

Hotel facilities HOTEL BESCHREIBUNG — 7/10

HOTELS HOTELS

Parkhotel Maximilian, 52 rooms, D 143 € — Regensburg
Tel (49) 0941 - 568 50, Fax (49) 0941 - 529 42 — 10 km

Clubhaus, 12 rooms, D 77 € — Golfclub on site
Tel (49) 09405 - 953 230, Fax (49) 09405 - 953 239

Altstadthotel Arch, 65 rooms, D 107 € — Regensburg
Tel (49) 0941 - 586 60, Fax (49) 0941 -5866 168

RESTAURANTS RESTAURANT

Historisches Eck — Regensburg
Tel (49) 0941 - 58 920

Alte Münz, Tel(49) 0941 - 54 886 — Regensburg

BAD BEVENSEN

15 | 5 | 7

Dieser Platz im ländlichen Norddeutschland wirkt auf den ersten Blick wie ein grosser Bauernhof, eine Atmosphäre wie man sie selten auf modernen Plätzen findet. Hier ist man weit weg von der Hektik der Grossstadt. Die freundliche Umgebung führt leicht dazu, dass man den Platz unterschätzt - ein Fehler. Das Gelände ist ziemlich hügelig, aber gut begehbar. Einige blinde Löchern wollen mit Überlegung attackiert werden. Die Schwierigkeiten sind gut über den Platz verteilt und meist vom Abschlag deutlich zu erkennen. Einziger Schwachpunkt ist das erste Loch, bei dem gute Spieler und Longhitter über eine Pferdekoppel abschlagen müssen. Der Platz ist originell, gut in die Landschaft eingepasst, allerdings werden hohe Handicaps auf diesem Platz Mühe haben, vor allem, wenn sie mit einstelligen Golfern unterwegs. Obwohl der Platz nicht sonderlich lang, ist es keineswegs einfach mit einem guten Ergebnis ins Clubhaus zurückzukehren.

Here were are in the middle of the North German countryside on a course that looks like a huge farm in a rural setting. Bad Bevensen gives new meaning to the expression "getting away from it all". This sort of scenery from another age is something of a rarity on modern golf courses. In such a friendly setting, you might be tempted to underestimate the course, but watch out. The terrain is relatively hilly but definitely walkable, and some virtually blind holes call for extreme caution. Elsewhere, difficulties of all sorts are mostly visible from the tees and cleverly spread around. We did have our reservations about the first hole, where long-hitters have to drive over a horse corral. Original and finely-landscaped, the course as a whole can prove to be awkward when playing amongst players of different abilities, as higher-handicappers will have problems overcoming all the difficulties and keeping up with the others. Despite being on the short side, this is a difficult course to score on.

Golf Club Bad Bevensen e.V. — 1991

Dorfstrasse 22
D - 29575 ALTENMEDINGEN, ORSTEIL SECKLENDORF

Office	Sekretariat	(49) 05821 - 98 250
Pro shop	Pro shop	(49) 05821 - 98 250
Fax	Fax	(49) 05821 - 42 595
Web	www.golf.de/badbevensen	
Situation	Lage	

Lüneburg (pop. 65 000), 24 km

Annual closure	Jährliche Schliessung	no
Weekly closure	Wöchentliche Schliessung	no
Fees main season	Preisliste hochsaison	18 holes

	Week days Woche	We/Bank holidays We/Feiertag
Individual Individuell	31 €	41 €
Couple Ehepaar	62 €	82 €

- 21 Jahre/Studenten: – 50%

Caddy	Caddy	no
Electric Trolley	Elektrokarren	no
Buggy	Elektrischer Wagen	26 €
Clubs	Leihschläger	10 €
Credit cards	Kreditkarten	no

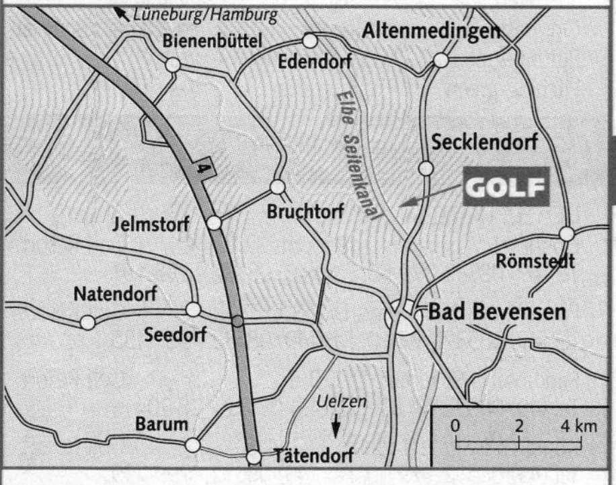

Access Zufahrt : Hamburg, A250 → Lüneburg. B4 → Uelzen. Exit (Ausf.) Bad Bevensen → Secklendorf Altenmedingen. Secklendorf → Golf.

Map 6 on page 364 Karte 6 Seite 364

Golf course PLATZ — 15/20

Site	Lage	
Maintenance	Instandhaltung	
Architect	Architekt	Ulrich Schmidt
Type	Typ	country
Relief	Begehbarkeit	
Water in play	Platz mit Wasser	
Exp. to wind	Wind ausgesetzt	
Trees in play	Platz mit Bäumen	

Scorecard Scorekarte	Chp. Chp.	Mens Herren	Ladies Damen
Length Länge	5808	5808	5163
Par	71	71	71
Slope system	120	120	123

Advised golfing ability Empfohlene Spielstärke — 0 12 24 36

Hcp required Min. Handicap — no

Club house & amenities KLUBHAUS UND NEBENGEBÄUDE — 5/10

Pro shop	Pro shop	
Driving range	Übungsplatz	
Sheltered	überdacht	2 mats
On grass	auf Rasen	yes
Putting-green	Putting-grün	yes
Pitching-green	Pitching-grün	yes

Hotel facilities HOTEL BESCHREIBUNG — 7/10

HOTELS HOTELS

Zur Amtsheide, 101 rooms, D 102 € — Bad Bevensen
Tel (49) 05821 - 8 51, Fax (49) 05821 - 853 38 — 3 km

Grünings Landhaus, 24 rooms, D 128 € — Bad Bevensen
Tel (49) 05821 - 984 00, Fax (49) 05821 - 984 041 — 5 km

Hotel Ascona, 100 rooms, D 102 € — Bad Bevensen
Tel (49) 05821 - 550, Fax (49) 05821 - 427 18 — 3 km

RESTAURANTS RESTAURANT

Zur Linde, Tel (49) 05821 - 7589 — Secklendorf 100 m

Zur Amstheide Tel (49) 05821 - 1249 — Bad Bevensen 3 km

Grünings Restaurant, Tel (49) 05821 - 984 00 — Bad Bevensen

BAD GRIESBACH Brunnwies 17 9 9

Das Golf Resort Bad Griesbach umfasst vier 18-Loch Anlagen. Brunnwies sowie Sagmühle sind die beiden Top-Plätze des Resorts; Uttlau und Lederbach haben ebenfalls ihre Qualitäten, sind aber sehr hügelig (Golfwagen wird empfohlen). Brunnwies ist zwar auch auf unebenem Terrain angelegt, dieser Eindruck wird aber durch die hervorragende Platzgestaltung des Architekten Bernhard Langer weitgehend entschärft. Auffallend ist die sorgfältige Gestaltung des Geländes vom Abschlag zum Grün, wodurch die einzelnen Löchern eine deutliche Form und Definition erhalten. Grosse Beachtung wurde auch der Anlage breiter Fairways, sowie der Fairway- und Grünbunker geschenkt, die noch stärker ins Spiel kommen als die Bäume und das Wasser. Von den hinteren Abschlägen sind einige Löcher sehr lang, aber auch diese Bahnen sind von weiter vorne gespielt durchaus zu bewältigen. Gute Spieler tun sich auf Brunnwies schwerer als Durchschnittsgolfer, genau so soll es sein. Eine faszinierende Anlage mit einem sehr schönen Clubhaus im Stil der lokalen Bauernhöfe.

This enormous resort comprises four 18-hole courses. This and Sagmühle are the two gems, while Uttlau and Lederbach, despite their qualities, are very hilly (buggy recommended). Brunnwies is stepp, too, but the excellence of architect Bernhard Langer tends to keep your mind off geographical considerations. The first thing you notice is the care taken over contouring the terrain, from tee to green, giving clear shape, form and physical definition to holes. There was also concern for wide fairways and fairway and green-side bunkers that are even more in play than the trees or water. From the back tees, some of the holes are long ; moving further forward, though, they are much more reasonable. It's tough for the good player but an easier proposition for the average golfer, so who could ask for more? A spectacular layout with a very pretty club-house in the style of the region's farmhouses.

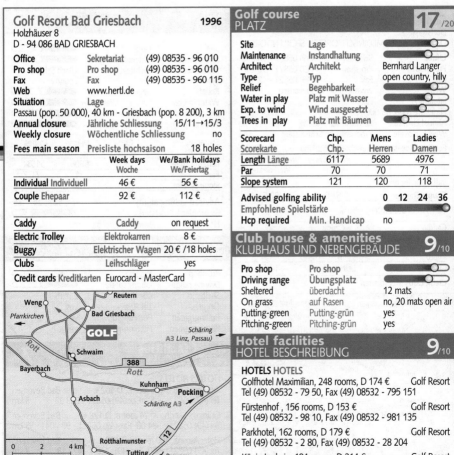

Golf Resort Bad Griesbach — 1996

Holzhäuser 8
D - 94 086 BAD GRIESBACH

Office	Sekretariat	(49) 08535 - 96 010
Pro shop	Pro shop	(49) 08535 - 96 010
Fax	Fax	(49) 08535 - 960 115
Web	www.hertl.de	
Situation	Lage	

Passau (pop. 50 000), 40 km - Griesbach (pop. 8 200), 3 km

Annual closure	Jährliche Schliessung	15/11→15/3
Weekly closure	Wöchentliche Schliessung	no

Fees main season Preisliste hochsaison	Week days Woche	We/Bank holidays We/Feiertag
Individual Individuell	46 €	56 €
Couple Ehepaar	92 €	112 €

18 holes

Caddy	Caddy	on request
Electric Trolley	Elektrokarren	8 €
Buggy	Elektrischer Wagen	20 € /18 holes
Clubs	Leihschläger	yes
Credit cards	Kreditkarten	Eurocard - MasterCard

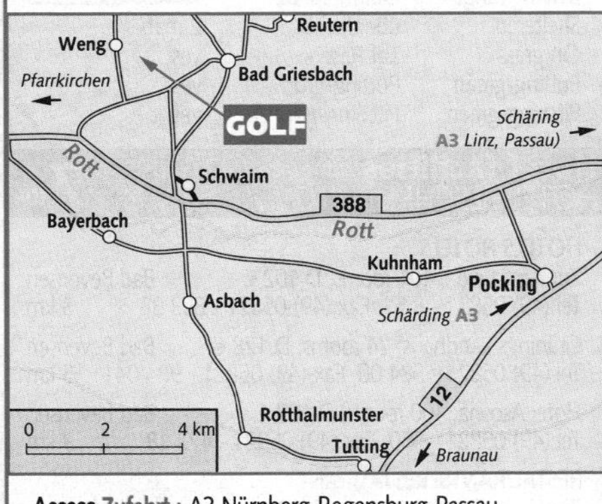

Access Zufahrt : A3 Nürnberg-Regensburg-Passau. Exit (Ausf.) Pocking. B12 and B388 → Bad Griesbach. → Golf
Map 2 on page 357 Karte 2 Seite 357

Golf course PLATZ — 17/20

Site	Lage	
Maintenance	Instandhaltung	
Architect	Architekt	Bernhard Langer
Type	Typ	open country, hilly
Relief	Begehbarkeit	
Water in play	Platz mit Wasser	
Exp. to wind	Wind ausgesetzt	
Trees in play	Platz mit Bäumen	

Scorecard Scorekarte	Chp. Chp.	Mens Herren	Ladies Damen
Length Länge	6117	5689	4976
Par	70	70	71
Slope system	121	120	118

Advised golfing ability Empfohlene Spielstärke — 0 12 24 36

Hcp required Min. Handicap — no

Club house & amenities KLUBHAUS UND NEBENGEBÄUDE — 9/10

Pro shop	Pro shop	
Driving range	Übungsplatz	
Sheltered	überdacht	12 mats
On grass	auf Rasen	no, 20 mats open air
Putting-green	Putting-grün	yes
Pitching-green	Pitching-grün	yes

Hotel facilities HOTEL BESCHREIBUNG — 9/10

HOTELS HOTELS

Golfhotel Maximilian, 248 rooms, D 174 € — Golf Resort
Tel (49) 08532 - 79 50, Fax (49) 08532 - 795 151

Fürstenhof , 156 rooms, D 153 € — Golf Resort
Tel (49) 08532 - 98 10, Fax (49) 08532 - 981 135

Parkhotel, 162 rooms, D 179 € — Golf Resort
Tel (49) 08532 - 2 80, Fax (49) 08532 - 28 204

König Ludwig, 184 rooms, D 214 € — Golf Resort
Tel (49) 08532 - 79 90, Fax (49) 08532 - 799 799

RESTAURANTS RESTAURANT

Fürstenstube, Tel (49) 08532 - 98 10 — Golf Resort

Gutshof Uttlau, Tel (49) 08535 - 1890 — Golf Resort

BAD GRIESBACH-SAGMÜHLE 15 | 9 | 9

Dies ist der älteste der vier Plätze in Deutschlands grösstem Golf-Resort. In etwas Enfernung zu den drei anderen Plätzen gelegen, verläuft Sagmühle auf wesentlich flacherem Gelände im Flusstal der Rott, deren Nebenarm immer wieder die Spielbahnen kreuzt. Wasser, ob als seitliches oder frontales Hindernis, ist die Hauptschwierigkeit auf diesem intelligent konzipierten Golfplatz, der leider häufig recht feucht ist. Um nicht allzuviele Bälle zu verlieren, sollte man daher seine eigenen Schlaglängen gut einschätzen können. Der Platz spielt sich insgesamt nicht allzu lang, sofern man nicht die hinteren Abschläge wählt. Bäume und Bunker sind so in das Platzdesign integriert, dass der Spieler auf der Runde mit allen möglichen Situationen und Hindernissen konfrontiert wird. Die gesamte Anlage, an der Grenze zwischen Bayern und Oberösterreich gelegen, umfasst ausserdem eine riesige Driving Range, eine Golfschule, zwei Kurz-Plätze und bietet zahlreiche weitere Aktivitäten für jeden Geschmack - egal ob Anfänger oder Könner.

This is the "oldest" of the four courses which grace Germany's largest golfing resort. A little out of the way from the three others, it is also much flatter and lies in the valley of the river Rott, a branch of which continually flows in and out of the course. As a frontal or lateral hazard, water is the main difficulty on this intelligently-designed (but often damp) layout, so it helps to know exactly what distance you can cover with each club to avoid losing too many balls. The overall yardage, though, is not excessive providing you steer clear of the back tees. With trees and bunkers, the course appears to be designed to put players in every imaginable situation with every possible hazard. The whole resort, located on the frontier between Bavaria and upper Austria, also features a huge driving range, a golfing school, two small courses and many other activities to keep everyone happy - the good, the not so good and the beginners.

Golf-Club Sagmühle — 1984

Schwaim 52
D - 94 086 BAD GRIESBACH

Office	Sekretariat	(49) 08532 - 2038
Pro shop	Pro shop	(49) 08532 - 7173
Fax	Fax	(49) 08532 - 3165
Web	—	
Situation	Lage	

Passau (pop. 50 000), 40 km - Griesbach (pop. 8 200), 3 km

Annual closure	Jährliche Schliessung	15/11→15/3
Weekly closure	Wöchentliche Schliessung	no

Fees main season Preisliste hochsaison		18 holes
	Week days Woche	**We/Bank holidays** We/Feiertag
Individual Individuell	41 €	46 €
Couple Ehepaar	82 €	92 €

Caddy	Caddy	on request
Electric Trolley	Elektrokarren	8 €
Buggy	Elektrischer Wagen	20 € /18 holes
Clubs	Leihschläger	yes

Credit cards Kreditkarten Eurocard - MasterCard

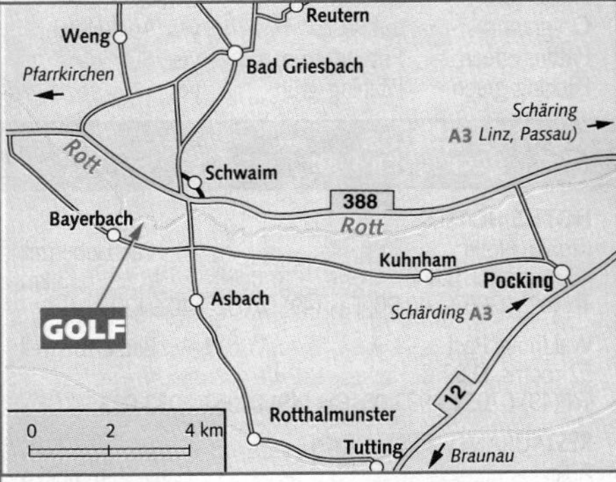

Access Zufahrt : A3 Nürnberg-Regensburg-Passau. Exit (Ausf.) Pocking. B12 and B388 → Bad Griesbach. → Golf
Map 2 on page 357 Karte 2 Seite 357

Golf course PLATZ — 15/20

Site	Lage	
Maintenance	Instandhaltung	
Architect	Architekt	Kurt Rossknecht
Type	Typ	parkland
Relief	Begehbarkeit	
Water in play	Platz mit Wasser	
Exp. to wind	Wind ausgesetzt	
Trees in play	Platz mit Bäumen	

Scorecard Scorekarte	**Chp.** Chp.	**Mens** Herren	**Ladies** Damen
Length Länge	6150	5895	5180
Par	72	72	72
Slope system	125	123	127

Advised golfing ability Empfohlene Spielstärke 0 12 24 36

Hcp required Min. Handicap no

Club house & amenities KLUBHAUS UND NEBENGEBÄUDE — 9/10

Pro shop	Pro shop	
Driving range	Übungsplatz	
Sheltered	überdacht	12 mats
On grass	auf Rasen	no, 20 mats open air
Putting-green	Putting-grün	yes
Pitching-green	Pitching-grün	yes

Hotel facilities HOTEL BESCHREIBUNG — 9/10

HOTELS HOTELS

Golfhotel Maximilian, 248 rooms, D 174 € — Golf Resort
Tel (49) 08532 - 79 50, Fax (49) 08532 - 795 151

Fürstenhof , 156 rooms, D 153 € — Golf Resort
Tel (49) 08532 - 98 10, Fax (49) 08532 - 981 135

Parkhotel, 162 rooms, D 179 € — Golf Resort
Tel (49) 08532 - 2 80, Fax (49) 08532 - 28 204

König Ludwig, 184 rooms, D 214 € — Golf Resort
Tel (49) 08532 - 79 90, Fax (49) 08532 - 799 799

RESTAURANTS RESTAURANT

Fürstenstube, Tel (49) 08532 - 98 10 — Golf Resort

Gutshof Uttlau, Tel (49) 08535 - 1890 — Golf Resort

BAD LIEBENZELL

14	7	7

Der Kurort Bad Liebenzell gilt als eines der nördlichen Tore zum Schwarzwald, der sich zwischen Karlsruhe und Basel erstreckt. Diese Landschaft ist geprägt von Weinbergen, Koniferen, Bauernhöfen, Kirchen und natürlich den berühmten Kuckucksuhren, die einem helfen die Startzeit nicht zu verschlafen. Auf gut 500 m Höhe, inmitten eines wunderschönen Waldgebietes gelegen, macht einem der hügelige Charakter des Platzes sofort klar, dass man sich hier im Mittelgebirge befindet. Der Parcours kann trotzdem gut zu Fuss bewältigt werden. Obwohl erst vor kurzem gebaut, strahlt der Platz bereits eine gewisse Reife aus, wobei spürbar wird, dass von Anfang an auf eine natürliche Einbettung der Anlage in die Umgebung Wert gelegt wurde. Man findet hier alle Arten von Hindernissen vor, von denen sicherlich der Wald und das Rough am gefährlichsten einzuschätzen sind, da es schwierig ist, Bälle von dort wieder herauszuspielen. Besonders wohl fühlen werden sich hier Spieler, die den Ball gerade schlagen, aber auch für alle anderen sollte ein guter Score möglich sein. Ein Platz für alle Spielklassen, der allerdings an die guten Spieler zu geringe Anforderungen stellt.

The spa town of Bad Liebenzell marks one of the northern gateways to the Black Forest (from Karlsruhe to Bâle), in a land of vineyards and conifers, farms and churches, and not forgetting the famous cuckoo clocks to help you make your tee-off time. Located some 500 metres up, this course nestles amid a beautiful part of the forest and is hilly enough to remind players that, although walkable, this is a mid-mountain course. Although recent, the course has already matured, although blending it into the surrounding landscape was obviously a clear priority from the outset. You will find all types of hazard here, the most dangerous unquestionably being the rough and woods, where escape shots are rarely easy. A course for all levels, but perhaps just lacking that little something for the best players.

Golfclub Bad Liebenzell e.V. — 1990

Golfplatz
D - 75378 BAD LIEBENZELL-MONAKAM

Office	Sekretariat	(49) 07052 - 93 250
Pro shop	Pro shop	(49) 07052 - 93 250
Fax	Fax	(49) 07052 - 9325 25
Web	www.gcbl.de	
Situation	Lage	
Pforzheim (pop. 115 000), 15 km		
Annual closure	Jährliche Schliessung	1/11→28/2
Weekly closure	Wöchentliche Schliessung	no

Fees main season Preisliste hochsaison	Full day	
	Week days Woche	**We/Bank holidays** We/Feiertag
Individual Individuell	41 €	51 €
Couple Ehepaar	82 €	102 €

Caddy	Caddy	on request
Electric Trolley	Elektrokarren	4 €
Buggy	Elektrischer Wagen	31 €
Clubs	Leihschläger	5 €
Credit cards Kreditkarten		no

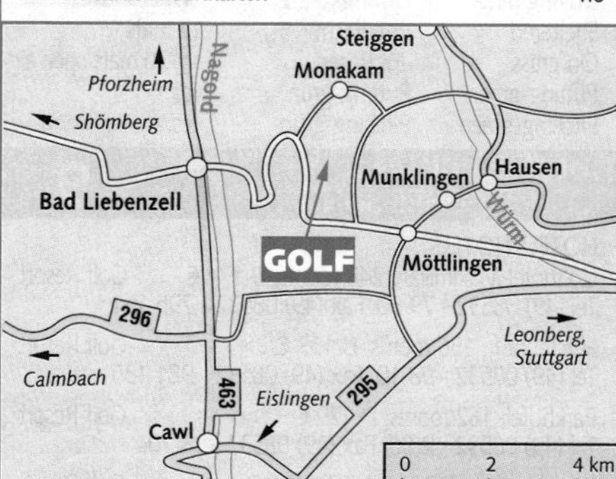

Access Zufahrt : A8 Stuttgart-Karlsruhe.
Exit (Ausf.) Heimsheim. → Bad Liebenzell.
Left → Unterhaugstett. → Golf
Map 1 on page 355 Karte 1 Seite 355

Golf course PLATZ — 14/20

Site	Lage	
Maintenance	Instandhaltung	
Architect	Architekt	unknown
Type	Typ	forest, open country
Relief	Begehbarkeit	
Water in play	Platz mit Wasser	
Exp. to wind	Wind ausgesetzt	
Trees in play	Platz mit Bäumen	

Scorecard Scorekarte	**Chp.** Chp.	**Mens** Herren	**Ladies** Damen
Length Länge	5853	5853	5159
Par	72	72	72
Slope system	132	132	129

Advised golfing ability Empfohlene Spielstärke — 0 12 24 36
Hcp required Min. Handicap — We: 33

Club house & amenities KLUBHAUS UND NEBENGEBÄUDE — 7/10

Pro shop	Pro shop	
Driving range	Übungsplatz	
Sheltered	überdacht	6 mats
On grass	auf Rasen	yes (April-Nov.)
Putting-green	Putting-grün	yes
Pitching-green	Pitching-grün	yes

Hotel facilities HOTEL BESCHREIBUNG — 7/10

HOTELS HOTELS

Kronen Hotel — Bad Liebenzell
43 rooms, D 128 € — 3 km
Tel (49) 07052 - 40 90, Fax (49) 07052 - 40 9420

Waldhotel Post — Bad Liebenzell
52 rooms, D 92 €
Tel (49) 07052 - 932 00, Fax (49) 07052 - 932 099

RESTAURANTS RESTAURANT

Adler — Calw-Stammheim
Tel (49) 07051 - 4287 — 10 km

Häckermühle — Tiefenbronn-Würmtal
Tel (49) 07234 - 6111 — 6 km

BAD WÖRISHOFEN

14	6	6

Dieser Platz hat einserseits weder schlechte Löcher, andererseits fehlt ihm aber auch ein wirklich herausragendes Loch, das einem im Gedächtnis bleibt. Dennoch ermöglichen das flache Terrain sowie andere Vorzüge dieser Anlage, dass man hier ohne zu ermüden 36 Löcher am Tag spielen, und sich dabei ganz auf das eigene Spiel konzentrieren kann. Die Spielstrategie ist offensichtlich. Der Golfplatz ist gut in die Natur integriert und bietet schöne Ausblicke auf den nahen Stausee und die bayerischen Alpen. Zahlreiche Bäume und Büsche grenzen die Löcher gut voneinander ab. Zwar sind einige der Par 4 Löcher recht lang, dafür sind deren Grüns relativ ungeschützt, so dass man trotzdem noch das Par retten kann. Geduldige, methodisch vorgehende Spieler werden hier belohnt. Breite Fairways und nur wenige Wasserhindernisse lassen diesen Golfplatz für alle Spielklassen geeignet erscheinen, jedoch sollte man vorzugsweise unter der Woche spielen, da es am Wochenende ziemlich voll wird.

There is no bad hole here, but there is no signature hole, either, to linger in your memory. Yet the flat terrain and other virtues can mean planning on 36 holes in one day without flagging and with no other worry than the state of your game. Game strategy is pretty obvious. Nicely hidden in its natural surroundings and offering pretty views over Staussee and the Bavarian Alps, this course is enhanced with the lush vegetation of trees and bushes which clearly separate holes. Granted, a number of par 4s are long, but the greens are relatively unguarded to help you save par. Patient and methodical players will feel at home here. Accessible to golfers of all abilities with widish fairways and little water to speak of, this is a course to be recommended during the week. Week-ends are crowded.

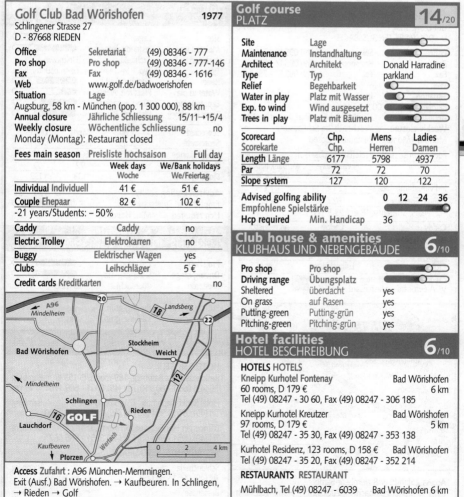

Golf Club Bad Wörishofen 1977

Schlingener Strasse 27
D - 87668 RIEDEN

Office	Sekretariat	(49) 08346 - 777
Pro shop	Pro shop	(49) 08346 - 777-146
Fax	Fax	(49) 08346 - 1616
Web	www.golf.de/badwoerishofen	
Situation	Lage	

Augsburg, 58 km - München (pop. 1 300 000), 88 km

Annual closure	Jährliche Schliessung	15/11→15/4
Weekly closure	Wöchentliche Schliessung	no

Monday (Montag): Restaurant closed

Fees main season Preisliste hochsaison	Full day	
	Week days Woche	**We/Bank holidays** We/Feiertag
Individual Individuell	41 €	51 €
Couple Ehepaar	82 €	102 €

-21 years/Students: – 50%

Caddy	Caddy	no
Electric Trolley	Elektrokarren	no
Buggy	Elektrischer Wagen	yes
Clubs	Leihschläger	5 €
Credit cards Kreditkarten		no

Access Zufahrt : A96 München-Memmingen.
Exit (Ausf.) Bad Wörishofen. → Kaufbeuren. In Schlingen, → Rieden → Golf
Map 2 on page 356 Karte 2 Seite 356

Golf course PLATZ 14/20

Site	Lage	
Maintenance	Instandhaltung	
Architect	Architekt	Donald Harradine
Type	Typ	parkland
Relief	Begehbarkeit	
Water in play	Platz mit Wasser	
Exp. to wind	Wind ausgesetzt	
Trees in play	Platz mit Bäumen	

Scorecard Scorekarte	**Chp.** Chp.	**Mens** Herren	**Ladies** Damen
Length Länge	6177	5798	4937
Par	72	72	70
Slope system	127	120	122

Advised golfing ability Empfohlene Spielstärke 0 12 24 36

Hcp required Min. Handicap 36

Club house & amenities KLUBHAUS UND NEBENGEBÄUDE 6/10

Pro shop	Pro shop	
Driving range	Übungsplatz	
Sheltered	überdacht	yes
On grass	auf Rasen	yes
Putting-green	Putting-grün	yes
Pitching-green	Pitching-grün	yes

Hotel facilities HOTEL BESCHREIBUNG 6/10

HOTELS HOTELS

Kneipp Kurhotel Fontenay Bad Wörishofen
60 rooms, D 179 € 6 km
Tel (49) 08247 - 30 60, Fax (49) 08247 - 306 185

Kneipp Kurhotel Kreutzer Bad Wörishofen
97 rooms, D 179 € 5 km
Tel (49) 08247 - 35 30, Fax (49) 08247 - 353 138

Kurhotel Residenz, 123 rooms, D 158 € Bad Wörishofen
Tel (49) 08247 - 35 20, Fax (49) 08247 - 352 214

RESTAURANTS RESTAURANT

Mühlbach, Tel (49) 08247 - 6039 Bad Wörishofen 6 km
Jagdhof, Tel (49) 08247 - 4879 Schlingen 4 km

BAMBERG

15 | 7 | 7

Schöne Aussicht auf ein Schloss und das Dorf Altenhof, aber die erhöhte Lage hat auch Nachteile. Das Gelände ist extrem hügelig, so dass wir Senioren und konditionsschwachen Spielern diesen Platz nicht empfehlen können, es sei denn sie lassen sich von jemandem die Golftasche tragen. Darüberhinaus müssen vielfach Bälle aus ganz unterschiedlichen Schräglagen gespielt werden, was hohe Anforderungen an die Beherrschung solcher Schläge stellt. Am besten spielt man hier mitten in der Saison, wenn der Schwung gut funktioniert und man konditionell auf der Höhe ist, da einem der Platz wirklich alles abverlangt. Bamberg hat einen hohen technischen Standard, mit vielen Bäumen und einigen gefährlichen Wasserhindernissen. Hier sein Handicap zu spielen ist eine gute Leistung. Lohnt sich kennenzulernen, wenn man gerade in der Gegend ist.

You are greeted here by some pretty vistas over a castle and the village of Altenhof, but the elevated location does have its drawbacks. The terrain is very hilly so we would definitely not advise seniors and players short on physical fitness to come and play here, unless accompanied by someone to carry their bag. Besides, this configuration results in a good number of shots being played from all sorts of slopes, a good test for skill in this department of your game. The best time to play here is in mid-season, when there is less chance of your swing and legs throwing in the towel. You will need all the strength you can muster. With this said, Bamberg is a course of excellent technical standard with lots of trees and a few dangerous water hazards. Playing to your handicap is already a good performance. Well worth getting to know if you are in the region.

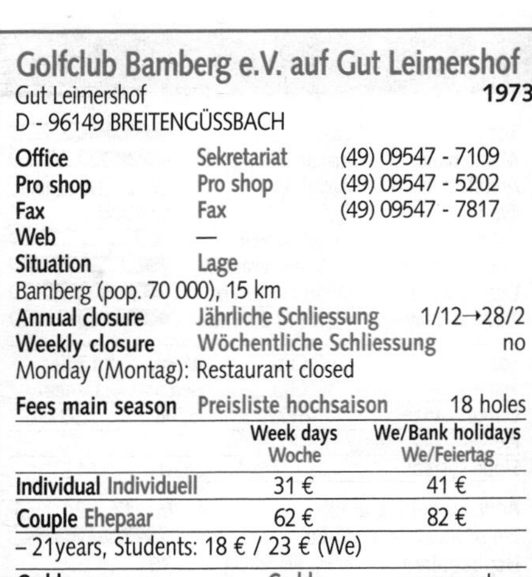

Golfclub Bamberg e.V. auf Gut Leimershof

Gut Leimershof — **1973**
D - 96149 BREITENGÜSSBACH

Office	Sekretariat	(49) 09547 - 7109
Pro shop	Pro shop	(49) 09547 - 5202
Fax	Fax	(49) 09547 - 7817
Web	—	
Situation	Lage	

Bamberg (pop. 70 000), 15 km

Annual closure	Jährliche Schliessung	1/12→28/2
Weekly closure	Wöchentliche Schliessung	no

Monday (Montag): Restaurant closed

Fees main season Preisliste hochsaison — 18 holes	**Week days** Woche	**We/Bank holidays** We/Feiertag
Individual Individuell	31 €	41 €
Couple Ehepaar	62 €	82 €

– 21years, Students: 18 € / 23 € (We)

Caddy	Caddy	on request
Electric Trolley	Elektrokarren	no
Buggy	Elektrischer Wagen	no
Clubs	Leihschläger	yes

Credit cards Kreditkarten
VISA Eurocard - MasterCard - AMEX

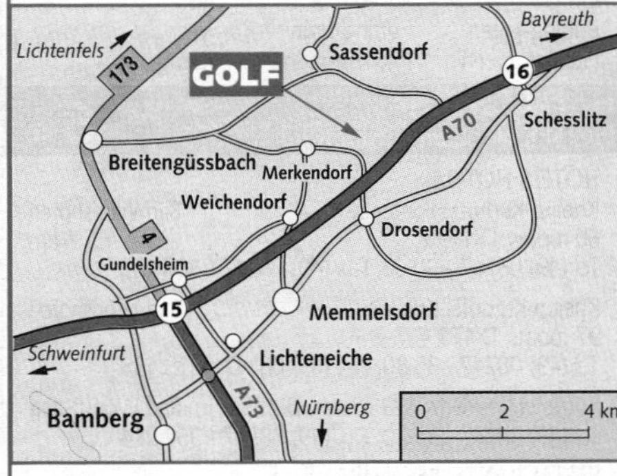

Access Zufahrt : BAB Nürnberg-Bamberg.
B173 → Breitengüssbach. → Zückshut → Hohengüssbach
Map 4 on page 360 Karte 4 Seite 360

Golf course — PLATZ — 15/20

Site	Lage	
Maintenance	Instandhaltung	
Architect	Architekt	Unknown
Type	Typ	open country, hilly
Relief	Begehbarkeit	
Water in play	Platz mit Wasser	
Exp. to wind	Wind ausgesetzt	
Trees in play	Platz mit Bäumen	

Scorecard Scorekarte	**Chp.** Chp.	**Mens** Herren	**Ladies** Damen
Length Länge	6070	6070	5372
Par	72	72	72
Slope system	133	133	132

Advised golfing ability Empfohlene Spielstärke — 0 12 24 36
Hcp required Min. Handicap 35

Club house & amenities — KLUBHAUS UND NEBENGEBÄUDE — 7/10

Pro shop	Pro shop	
Driving range	Übungsplatz	
Sheltered	überdacht	5 mats
On grass	auf Rasen	yes
Putting-green	Putting-grün	yes
Pitching-green	Pitching-grün	yes

Hotel facilities — HOTEL BESCHREIBUNG — 7/10

HOTELS HOTELS

Residenzschloss Bamberg, 189 rooms, D 153 € — Bamberg 15 km
Tel (49) 0951 - 60 910, Fax (49) 0951 - 609 1701

Hotel Sankt Nepomuk, 47 rooms, D 112 € — Bamberg
Tel (49) 0951 - 984 20, Fax (49) 0951 - 984 2100

Bamberger Hof-Bellevue, 50 rooms, D 143 € — Bamberg
Tel (49) 0951 - 985 50, Fax (49) 0951 - 985 562

RESTAURANTS RESTAURANT

Schlencherla — Bamberg
Tel (49) 0951 - 56 060

Bassanese — Bamberg
Tel (49) 0951 - 57 551

BERGISCH LAND WUPPERTAL 16 7 7

Im Grossraum Düsseldorf findet man in Wuppertal einen der besten klassischen Golfplätze des Landes. Der Platz hat sich seit seiner Eröffnung im Jahre 1928 kaum verändert, aber die Länge des Platzes ist auch für den heutigen Standard ausreichend, auch wenn es keine Meisterschaftsabschläge (Tiger Tees) gibt. Der Platz wirkt auf den ersten Blick nicht allzu einschüchternd. Golfer werden nicht mit übergroflen Schwierigkeiten konfrontiert, es werden keine "Carries" über für Durchschnittsgolfer kaum überwindbare Distanzen verlangt. Trotz des hügeligen Geländes sind die meisten Hindernisse, darunter herrliche alte Bäume, immer gut auszumachen. Die Fairways sind relativ breit und werden nur gelegentlich von Wasser gesäumt. Trotzdem erfordert der Platz alle Konzentration, da die Bunker gut platziert und die Grüns nicht einfachz zu lesen sind. Obwohl hier Golfer aller Spielstärken spielen können, ist ein gutes Bruttoergebnis nicht einfach zu erzielen. Dies ist ein klassischer Club-Platz, den man Dutzende Male spielen kann, ohne ihn als langweilig zu empfinden.

In the sprawling greater Düsseldorf area Wuppertal boasts one of the country's great classic golf courses. The course has changed little since it was opened back in 1928, but yardage still meets today's standards and there are no "tiger" tees to talk of. This apparent friendly face is, what's more, an excellent argument, as golfers can come and enjoy playing here without encountering any impossible difficulties or superhuman angles and distances. Despite the hilly terrain, most of the hazards, including some superb trees, are clearly visible at first glance and the fairways are wide with only a few stretches of water to clutter the wide open spaces. But be careful though, as the bunkering is first rate and the greens tricky to read. While golfers of all abilities can play here, carding a good gross score is certainly no foregone conclusion. A real club course that you can play dozens of times and never grow tired of.

Golf Club Bergisch Land Wuppertal 1928

Siebeneickerstrasse 386
D - 42111 WUPPERTAL

Office	Sekretariat	(49) 02053 - 71 77
Pro shop	Pro shop	(49) 02053 - 48 168
Fax	Fax	(49) 02053 - 73 03
Web	—	
Situation	Lage	

Wuppertal (pop. 390 000), 5 km

Annual closure	Jährliche Schliessung	no
Weekly closure	Wöchentliche Schliessung	no

Fees main season Preisliste hochsaison	Week days Woche	We/Bank holidays We/Feiertag (18 holes)
Individual Individuell	41 €	51 € *
Couple Ehepaar	82 €	102 € *

* We: only with members (nur in Mitgliederbegleitung)

Caddy	Caddy	no
Electric Trolley	Elektrokarren	no
Buggy	Elektrischer Wagen	no
Clubs	Leihschläger	no

Credit cards Kreditkarten
VISA - Eurocard - MasterCard - DC - JCB - AMEX

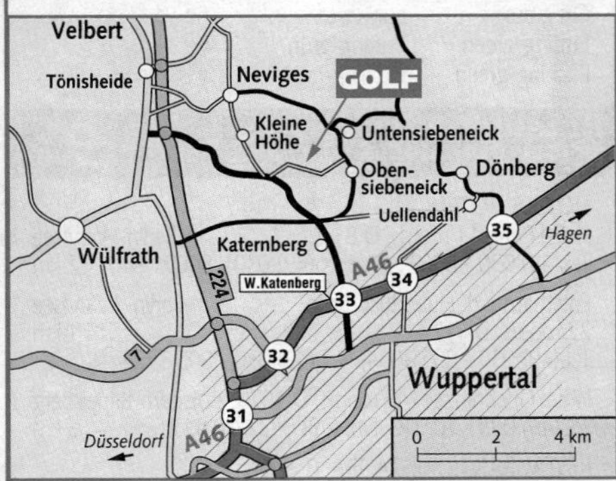

Access Zufahrt : A46. Exit (Ausf.) Wuppertal-Katernberg. → Neviges/Velbert. 2.5 km turn right → Golf.
Map 3 on page 358 Karte 3 Seite 358

Golf course PLATZ 16/20

Site	Lage	
Maintenance	Instandhaltung	
Architect	Architekt	Unknown
Type	Typ	forest, hilly
Relief	Begehbarkeit	
Water in play	Platz mit Wasser	
Exp. to wind	Wind ausgesetzt	
Trees in play	Platz mit Bäumen	

Scorecard Scorekarte	Chp. Chp.	Mens Herren	Ladies Damen
Length Länge	5929	5929	5209
Par	72	72	72
Slope system	134	134	132

Advised golfing ability Empfohlene Spielstärke: 0 12 24 36
Hcp required Min. Handicap 36

Club house & amenities KLUBHAUS UND NEBENGEBÄUDE 7/10

Pro shop	Pro shop	
Driving range	Übungsplatz	
Sheltered	überdacht	
On grass	auf Rasen	yes
Putting-green	Putting-grün	yes
Pitching-green	Pitching-grün	yes

Hotel facilities HOTEL BESCHREIBUNG 7/10

HOTELS HOTELS
Lindner Golfhotel Juliana, Wuppertal-Barmen 7 km
132 rooms, D 128 €
Tel (49) 0202 - 647 50, Fax (49) 0202 - 647 5777

Intercityhotel Kaiserhof Wuppertal-Elberfeld 5 km
160 rooms, D 153 €
Tel (49) 0202 - 43 060, Fax (49) 0202 - 456 959

Villa Christina, 7 rooms, D 102 € Wuppertal-Barmen
Tel (49) 0202 - 621 736, Fax (49) 0202 - 620 499

RESTAURANTS RESTAURANT
Schmitz Jägerhaus Wuppertal-Barmen 12 km
Tel (49) 0202 - 464 602

Jagdhaus Mollenkotten Wuppertal-Barmen 6 km
Tel (49) 0202 - 522 643

BERLIN-WANNSEE 16 8 9

Der Mauerfall und die Wiedervereinigung Deutschlands haben dem Golfsport in der neuen Hauptstadt Auftrieb verliehen, wobei dieser Golfplatz der älteste Berlins ist 1895 angelegt, wurde der Platz in den 20er Jahren von Grund auf umgestaltet und weist für moderne Ansprüche eine ansenhliche Länge auf. Nach der Wiedervereinigung wurden 1994 die neun Löcher des deutschen Clubs und die 18 Löcher des amerikanischen Clubs wieder zusammengelegt, so dass der Club heute über 18 Löcher des Meisterschaftsplatzes und noch einmal 9 Löcher des Schäferbergplatzes verfügt. Die grösste Schwierigkeit ist es, auf den Spielbahnen zu bleiben und die Bäume entlang den Fairways zu vermeiden, allerdings sind die Fairways bis auf wenige Ausnahmen relativ breit. Die Grüns sind teilweise einfach zu lesen und nicht übermässig geschützt. Wasser kommt nur am 17. Loch, einem Par 3, ins Spiel und auch nur für schwächere Spieler. Diese schöne und für alle Spielstärke gut zu spielende Anlage ist eine reizvolle Abwechslung zu den modernen, neuen Anlagen, die um Berlin herum entstanden sind.

It is the oldest course of Berlin, and the ideal base-camp for people looking to combine sport and culture. Designed back in 1895, the course was radically overhauled in the mid-1920s and now features a very decent length to today's standards. In 1994 the 9 holes of the German club and the 18 holes of the American club were reunited, so the club now boasts an 18 hole championship course and the 9-hole Schäferberg Platz (the old back nine of the American club). The basic problem is that of staying on the fairway and avoiding the trees on both sides, but with few exceptions most fairways are of generous width. There is only one water harzard, on hole 17 (Par 3), but it should only come into play for lesser players. The greens are none too difficult to read, well-contoured but not excessively guarded. A very pleasant course to see and play and an excellent companion for the other modern and more demanding courses in the region.

Golf-Club Berlin-Wannsee e.V. 1895

Golfweg 22
D - 14109 BERLIN

Office	Sekretariat	(49) 030 - 806 7060
Pro shop	Pro shop	(49) 030 - 806 70619
Fax	Fax	(49) 030 - 806 70610
Web	www.golf.de/glcbw	
Situation	Lage	

Berlin (pop. 3 500 000), 12 km

Annual closure	Jährliche Schliessung	1/1→31/1
Weekly closure	Wöchentliche Schliessung	no

Monday (Montag): Restaurant closed

Fees main season Preisliste hochsaison	18 holes	
	Week days Woche	**We/Bank holidays** We/Feiertag
Individual Individuell	56 €	*
Couple Ehepaar	112 €	*

* We & holidays: with members (nur in Mitgliederbegleitung)

Caddy	Caddy	no
Electric Trolley	Elektrokarren	13 €
Buggy	Elektrischer Wagen	no
Clubs	Leihschläger	10 €

Credit cards Kreditkarten VISA - Eurocard - Mastercard

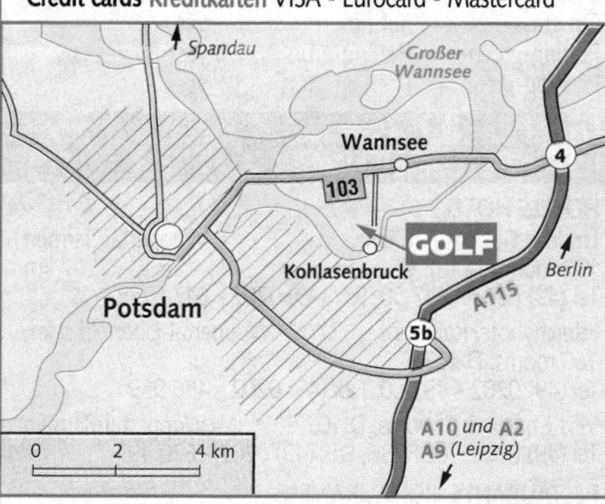

Access Zufahrt : Berlin-Zentrum → Wannsee. Königstrasse, Chausseestrasse, → Kohlhasenbruck (Kohlhasenbrücker Strasse), turn right in Stölpchenweg.
Map 6 on page 365 Karte 6 Seite 365

Golf course PLATZ 16/20

Site	Lage	
Maintenance	Instandhaltung	
Architect	Architekt	FA Harris
Type	Typ	forest
Relief	Begehbarkeit	
Water in play	Platz mit Wasser	
Exp. to wind	Wind ausgesetzt	
Trees in play	Platz mit Bäumen	

Scorecard Scorekarte	**Chp.** Chp.	**Mens** Herren	**Ladies** Damen
Length Länge	5875	5875	4937
Par	72	72	72
Slope system	127	127	125

Advised golfing ability Empfohlene Spielstärke 0 12 24 36
Hcp required Min. Handicap 34

Club house & amenities KLUBHAUS UND NEBENGEBÄUDE 8/10

Pro shop	Pro shop	
Driving range	Übungsplatz	
Sheltered	überdacht	11 mats
On grass	auf Rasen	no
Putting-green	Putting-grün	yes
Pitching-green	Pitching-grün	yes

Hotel facilities HOTEL BESCHREIBUNG 9/10

HOTELS HOTELS

Hotel Petit, 11 rooms, D 81 € — Berlin-Wannsee
Tel (49) 030 - 80691 80, Fax (49) 030 - 80691 840 — 2 km

Forsthaus a.d. Hubertusbrücke — Berlin- Wannsee
22 rooms, D 112 € — 1 km
Tel (49) 030 - 805 3054, Fax (49) 030 - 805 3524

Hotel Griebnitzsee, 40 rooms, D 107 € — Potsdam-Badelsberg
Tel (49) 033 - 70 910, Fax (49) 033 - 70 9111 — 6 km

RESTAURANTS RESTAURANT

Alter Krug, Tel (49) 030 - 832 5089 — Berlin-Dahlem 9 km

Halali, Tel (49) 030 - 805 3125 — Berlin-Wannsee 3 km

BEUERBERG

17 | 7 | 6

Der nationale und internationale Ruf dieses Golfplatzes ist hauptsächlich auf sein aussergewöhnliches Panorama der bayerischen Alpen zurückzuführen. Ihr Anblick tröstet über einen schlechten Score hinweg. Wem es gelingt, seine Aufmerksamkeit nicht nur der Lage und den herrlichen Ausblicken zu widmen, der wird auch vom Platz selbst - einem der besten Entwürfe Donald Harradines - nicht enttäuscht sein. Obwohl recht hoch gelegen, gibt es keine extremen Geländeerhebungen und trotz der vielen Bäume hat man nie den Eindruck, dass diese das Spiel einengen würden. Während die Wasserhindernisse ziemlich bedrohlich wirken, sind die Grüns nur mittelmässig durch Bunker verteidigt. Nach modernen Designkriterien wäre sicherlich eine grössere Anzahl vonw Bunkern angelegt worden, um die besseren Spieler stärker zu fordern. in seinem jetzigen Zustand begünstigt der Platz Spieler mit mittleren und hohen Handicaps. Ein Besuch in Beuerberg lohnt sich in jedem Fall, vor allem auch wegen der hervorragenden Küche. Nach heftigen Regenfällen sollte man den Platz meiden, da er auf Moorboden liegt.

This course's national and international reputation stems widely from the exceptional view here over the Bavarian Alps. The sights can easily make up for a poor score. If you can put the sight and setting to the back of your mind, you won't be disappointed by the course, either, one of the best ever designed by Donald Harradine. Although high up, relief is never excessive, and while trees abound, they never give the impression of narrowness. Rather strangely, there are only three par 3s and five par 5s, but enough short par 4s to hope to bag a few birdies. The water hazards are rather threatening but the greens are only averagely guarded by bunkers: if modern-day criteria were followed, if they had wanted to upset the better players, they might have designed a few more. As it is, the game is made easier for mid- to high-handicappers. Beuerberg is well worth the journey, even more so because the cuisine in the clubhouse is excellent.

Golfclub Beuerberg e.V. — 1983

Gut Sterz
D - 82547 BEUERBERG

Office	Sekretariat	(49) 08179 - 617 728
Pro shop	Pro shop	(49) 08179 - 1229
Fax	Fax	(49) 08179 - 5234
Web	www.golf.de/beuerberg	
Situation	Lage	

München (pop. 1 300 000), 45 km
Wolfratshausen (pop. 16 000), 15 km

Annual closure	Jährliche Schliessung	15/11→15/3
Weekly closure	Wöchentliche Schliessung	no

Fees main season Preisliste hochsaison	18 holes	
	Week days Woche	**We/Bank holidays** We/Feiertag
Individual Individuell	51 €	62 €
Couple Ehepaar	102 €	124 €

Caddy	Caddy	on request
Electric Trolley	Elektrokarren	yes
Buggy	Elektrischer Wagen	no
Clubs	Leihschläger	yes
Credit cards	Kreditkarten	no

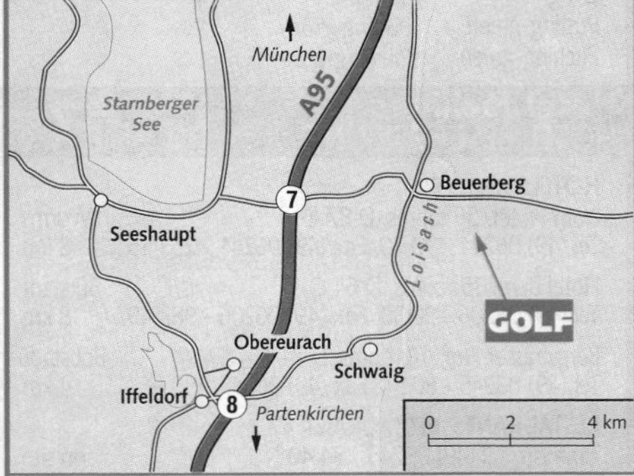

Access Zufahrt : A95 München → Garmisch-Partenkirchen. Exit (Ausf.) Seeshaupt, → Beuerberg
Map 2 on page 356 Karte 2 Seite 356

Golf course — PLATZ — 17/20

Site	Lage	
Maintenance	Instandhaltung	
Architect	Architekt	Donald Harradine
Type	Typ	parkland
Relief	Begehbarkeit	
Water in play	Platz mit Wasser	
Exp. to wind	Wind ausgesetzt	
Trees in play	Platz mit Bäumen	

Scorecard Scorekarte	**Chp.** Chp.	**Mens** Herren	**Ladies** Damen
Length Länge	6250	5820	5204
Par	74	73	73
Slope system	132	132	132

Advised golfing ability Empfohlene Spielstärke — 0 12 24 36
Hcp required Min. Handicap — 36

Club house & amenities — KLUBHAUS UND NEBENGEBÄUDE — 7/10

Pro shop	Pro shop	
Driving range	Übungsplatz	
Sheltered	überdacht	6 mats
On grass	auf Rasen	yes
Putting-green	Putting-grün	yes
Pitching-green	Pitching-grün	yes

Hotel facilities — HOTEL BESCHREIBUNG — 6/10

HOTELS HOTELS

Gut Faistenberg, 10 rooms, D 158 € Eurasburg-Faistenberg
Tel (49) 08179 - 16 16, Fax (49) 08179 - 433 — 7 km

Posthotel Hofherr, 60 rooms, D 89 € — Königsdorf
Tel (49) 08179 - 50 90, Fax (49) 08179 - 659 — 5 km

Jodquellenhof, 71 rooms, D 230 € — Bad Tölz
Tel (49) 08041 - 50 90, Fax (49) 08041 - 509 555 — 15 km

Sprengenöderalm, 8 rooms, D 66 € — Eurasburg
Tel (49) 08179 - 931 00, Fax (49) 08179 - 931 093 — 6 km

RESTAURANTS RESTAURANT

Altes Fährhaus, Tel (49) 08041 - 60 30 — Bad Tölz 15 km

Weinstube Schwaighofer, Tel (49) 08041 - 27 62 — Bad Tölz

BIBLIS WATTENHEIM A + B

15	6	7

Mit seiner freundlichen Atmosphäre und seinem exzellenten Preis-Leistungsverhältnis ist dies einer der kommerziell erfolgreichsten Anlagen, die in den letzten Jahren ihre Abschläge eröffnete. Drei Neun-Loch-Plätze, die man beliebig miteinander kombinieren kann bieten genug Abwechslung um hier einen ganzen Tag zu verbringen. Wir bevorzugen die A+B-Kombination, obwohl gerade der C-Course mit einigen ungewöhnlichen, aber reizvollen Löcher aufwartet. Auf alle Fälle bietet der Platz genug Überraschungen, die die ganze Aufmerksamkeit erfordern und den Blick vom nahegelegenen Atomkraftwerk ablenken. Alle drei Plätze sind flach und leicht begehbar. Die Architektur lehnt sich mit "Target Golf" an amerikanischen Vorbilder an. Wer, besonders bei Wind, auf diesem offenen Platz den Ball mit Fade oder Draw spielen kann, ist im Vorteil. Alles in allem ein reizvoller Platz, der mit zunehmendem Alter nur besser werden kann, ein Platz mit einigen außergewöhnlichen Löchern und ein Platz, der auch höhere Handicaps nicht überfordert.

With a very friendly atmosphere and excellent value for money, this is one of the more successful commercial golf courses opened in recent years. The three nine-hole courses are combinable and can happily take up your whole day, and there is excitement enough to keep your eyes from straying over to a nearby nuclear power plant. We preferred the A & B course combination as the basic 18-hole course, but the C course is well worth a round, especially in match-play because some of the lay-out's unique and amusing holes have a number of surprises in store. All three are flat and never tiring to walk. The style of architecture is distinctly American, with a tendency to prefer target golf, but ability to flight the ball over this wide open space may prove useful, especially in windy conditions. A very handy course to know, one which is imaginative and not too challenging for high-handicappers. It should get even better as it matures.

Golfclub Biblis Wattenheim e.V. — 1998

Golfparkallee 2
D - 68647 BIBLIS-WATTENHEIM

Office	Sekretariat	(49) 06245 - 906 00
Pro shop	Pro shop	(49) 06245 - 906 011
Fax	Fax	(49) 06245 - 906 060
Web	www.golfpark-biblis.de	
Situation	Lage	

Worms (pop. 82 000), 12 km

Annual closure	Jährliche Schliessung	no
Weekly closure	Wöchentliche Schliessung	no

Fees main season Preisliste hochsaison — 18 holes

	Week days Woche	We/Bank holidays We/Feiertag
Individual Individuell	31 €	41 €
Couple Ehepaar	62 €	82 €

Caddy	Caddy	no
Electric Trolley	Elektrokarren	no
Buggy	Elektrischer Wagen	26 € /18 holes
Clubs	Leihschläger	13 € /18 holes

Credit cards Kreditkarten VISA - Eurocard

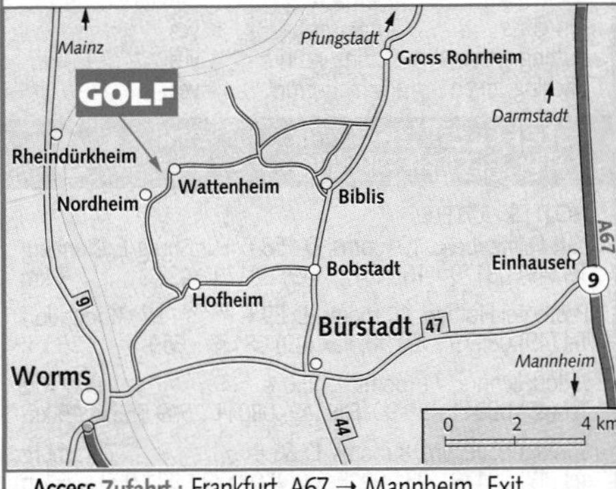

Access Zufahrt : Frankfurt, A67 → Mannheim. Exit (Ausfahrt) Lorsch, then B47 → Worms. In Bürstadt, B44 → Biblis. In Biblis, → Wattenheim.
Map 3 on page 359 Karte 3 Seite 359

Golf course PLATZ — 15/20

Site	Lage	
Maintenance	Instandhaltung	
Architect	Architekt	Hermann Weiland
Type	Typ	open country
Relief	Begehbarkeit	
Water in play	Platz mit Wasser	
Exp. to wind	Wind ausgesetzt	
Trees in play	Platz mit Bäumen	

Scorecard Scorekarte	Chp. Chp.	Mens Herren	Ladies Damen
Length Länge	6318	6096	5349
Par	73	73	73
Slope system	128	127	124

Advised golfing ability Empfohlene Spielstärke — 0 12 24 36

Hcp required Min. Handicap 54

Club house & amenities KLUBHAUS UND NEBENGEBÄUDE — 6/10

Pro shop	Pro shop	
Driving range	Übungsplatz	
Sheltered	überdacht	yes
On grass	auf Rasen	yes
Putting-green	Putting-grün	yes
Pitching-green	Pitching-grün	yes

Hotel facilities HOTEL BESCHREIBUNG — 7/10

HOTELS HOTELS

Dom Hotel, 55 rooms, D 87 € — Worms
Tel (49) 06241 - 90 70, Fax (49) 06241 - 253 15 — 8 km

Hotel Berg, 35 rooms, D 64 € — Bürstadt
Tel (49) 06206 - 98 30, Fax (49) 06206 - 983 49 — 8 km

Bergsträsser Hof, 16 rooms, D 71 € — Bobstadt
Tel (49) 06245 - 80 94, Fax (49) 06245 - 80 96 — 4 km

RESTAURANTS RESTAURANT

Tiramisu, Tel (49) 06245 - 34 40 — on site

Rotisserie Dubs — Rheindürkheim
Tel (49) 06242 - 20 23 — 3 km

Hagenbräu, Tel (49) 06241 - 921 100 — Worms 5 km

BITBURGER LAND

15	7	8

Die Mittelgebirgslandschaft der südlichen Eifel mit den malerischen Tälern ist ein sehr populären Feriengebiet unweit von Luxemburg. Der Platz ist wie zu erwarteen bergig, ein Golfwagen ist zumindest an heiss-schwülen Tagen empfehlenswert, da das Gelände sehr offen ist. Durch die grossen Höhenunterschiede sind drei blinde Löcher entstanden, die die Schlägerwahl sehr schwierig machen, insbesondere am 2. Loch. Abgesehen davon ist die Spielstrategie gut zu erkennen, die Wasserhindernisse sind klar zu erkennen, dennoch wird man sich auf der zweiten Runde leichter tun. ıachen,insbesondere am 2. Loch, einem Par-3-Loch mit wesentlich tiefer liegenden Grün. Weiten Runde leichter tun, da man dann die Grüns sind ziemlich gross und nicht mir allzu viel Konturen, dafür aber gut verteidigt und kaum Sonnenschutz bietet, immer vorgebend klar zu erkennen, dennoch wirweiten Runde leichter tun und dennoch oftmals mit flachen Chips anzuspielen. Karl Grohs entwarf diesen natürlich wirkenden Platz, ohne der Versuchung zu erliegen, denn einen extrem langen Platz zu entwerfen, der schwächere Spiele einschüchter. Golfer aller Spielstärken werden diesen Platz geniessen.

This is a very popular region with tourists and lovers of mountain landscapes and nature, with the typical scenery of the small picturesque valleys in the south of Eifel, not far from Luxembourg. The course is hilly, no surprise there, and a buggy is recommended in hot weather as the terrain is very open and exposed. A few sharp changes in altitude have produced three blind greens, which make club selection a tricky business (particularly on the 2nd hole). Apart from that, game strategy is not what you could call complex (the water hazards are clearly in view) but it will be easier second time around, when the half-obscured bunkers will have lost their element of surprise. The greens are rather large, not too sharply contoured and well guarded, but you can often hit them with low running shots. Karl Grohs designed this course with a good deal of imagination, retaining its natural look and refusing to design in the length that puts so many players off. So golfers of all abilities can have fun, whatever the formula and whatever the stakes.

Golf Resort Bitburger Land — 1994

Zur Weilersheck
D - 54636 WISSMANNSDORF

Office	Sekretariat	(49) 06527 - 927 20
Pro shop	Pro shop	(49) 06527 - 927 216
Fax	Fax	(49) 06527 - 927 230
Web	www.golf.tsx.org	
Situation	Lage	

Trier (pop. 99.000), 30 km

Annual closure	Jährliche Schliessung	no
Weekly closure	Wöchentliche Schliessung	no

Fees main season Preisliste hochsaison	18 holes	
	Week days Woche	**We/Bank holidays** We/Feiertag
Individual Individuell	36 €	46 €
Couple Ehepaar	72 €	92 €

Caddy	Caddy	15 € /on request
Electric Trolley	Elektrokarren	13 €
Buggy	Elektrischer Wagen	26 €
Clubs	Leihschläger	15 €

Credit cards Kreditkarten
VISA - Eurocard - MasterCard - AMEX

Access Zufahrt : • Köln, A1 → Trier. B51 → Bitburg/Prüm. • Koblenz, A48 → Trier → Dreieck Vulkaneifel-Daun, B257 → Bitburg. • Bitburg → Vlanden → "Golf Resort"
Map 3 on page 358 Karte 3 Seite 358

Golf course — PLATZ — 15/20

Site	Lage	
Maintenance	Instandhaltung	
Architect	Architekt	Karl F. Grohs
Type	Typ	open country, hilly
Relief	Begehbarkeit	
Water in play	Platz mit Wasser	
Exp. to wind	Wind ausgesetzt	
Trees in play	Platz mit Bäumen	

Scorecard Scorekarte	**Chp.** Chp.	**Mens** Herren	**Ladies** Damen
Length Länge	6056	6056	5316
Par	72	72	72
Slope system	128	128	128

Advised golfing ability Empfohlene Spielstärke — 0 12 24 36
Hcp required Min. Handicap 36

Club house & amenities — KLUBHAUS UND NEBENGEBÄUDE — 7/10

Pro shop	Pro shop	
Driving range	Übungsplatz	
Sheltered	überdacht	12 mats
On grass	auf Rasen	yes
Putting-green	Putting-grün	yes
Pitching-green	Pitching-grün	yes

Hotel facilities — HOTEL BESCHREIBUNG — 8/10

HOTELS HOTELS

Dorint Hotel & Resort, 100 rooms, D 153 € — Biersdorf
Tel (49) 06569 - 9 90, Fax (49) 06569 - 79 09 — 3.5 km

Waldhaus Seeblick, 21 rooms, D 107 € — Biersdorf
Tel (49) 06569 - 969 90, Fax (49) 06569 - 969 950

Am Wisselbach, 24 rooms, D 92 € — Rittersdorf
Tel (49) 0656 - 195 970, Fax (49) 0656 - 112 293 — 3 km

Blick Instal, 13 rooms, D 51 € — Wissmannsdorf 2 km
Tel (49) 06527 - 3 76, Fax (49) 06527 - 2 47

RESTAURANTS RESTAURANT

Burg Rittersdorf, Tel (49) 06561 - 965 70 — Rittersdorf 3 km

Simonbräu, Tel (49) 06561 - 3333 — Bitburg 6 km

BODENSEE-WEISSENSBERG 16 | 7 | 7

Die Handschrift von Trent Jones ist allein bereits ein Garant für Qualität. Dazu kommt in diesem Fall ein Gelände mit altem Mischwald-Bestand und natürlichen Wasserflächen. Angesichts dieser Vorzüge versteht man die Quelle seiner Inspiriration und das er keinerlei Zugeständnisse an die spielerischen Anforderungen des Platzes machen wollte. Spieler mit hohem Handicap sollten sich daher klaglos darauf einstellen, einige Bälle zu verlieren. Der Platz ist sowohl visuell als auch technisch aussergewöhnlich gut gelungen und hat kaum ein Loch, an dem man sich entspannen könnte. Zu den natürlichen Hindernissen gesellen sich Fairway- und Grünbunker, von denen der Architekt grosszügig Gebrauch gemacht hat. Dennoch ist der Platz fair, da an jedem Loch die Spielstrategie deutlich vorgegeben ist. Spieler, die sich trotzdem an Schlägen versuchen, die ihre Tagesform übersteigen, müssen sich deshalb an der eigenen Nase fassen. Dieser Platz ist ein guter Test und scheint uns aufgrund der umfassenden Anforderungen, die er an die Spieler stellt, besonders geeignet für Wettspiele im Match-Play Format.

The Trent Jones label is already a token of quality. Add to that a site with naturally alternating forest and stretches of water and you will understand his source of inspiration here and his uncompromising refusal of facility. High-handicappers should be ready to lose a lot of balls without complaining. The course is visually and technically just magnificent, with hardly a hole to relax on. Needless to say, the natural hazards have been supplemented by fairway and green-side bunkers generously sprinkled around the course. But this is not a treacherous course, as from each tee game strategy is clear to see and players have only themselves to blame if they attempt to play beyond their current form. This comprehensive course is a tough examination to the most suitable format for amateurs, namely match-play.

Golfclub Bodensee Weissensberg e.V. 1986

Lampertsweiler 51
D - 88138 WEISSENSBERG

Office	Sekretariat	(49) 08389 - 89190
Pro shop	Pro shop	(49) 08389 - 89192
Fax	Fax	(49) 08389 - 89 191
Web	—	
Situation	Lage	

Lindau (pop. 25 000), 7 km - Bregenz (Österreich), 15 km

Annual closure	Jährliche Schliessung	no
Weekly closure	Wöchentliche Schliessung	no

01/11 → 01/04: Restaurant closed

Fees main season Preisliste hochsaison — 18 holes

	Week days / Woche	We/Bank holidays / We/Feiertag
Individual Individuell	41 €	51 €
Couple Ehepaar	82 €	102 €

– 21years, Students: 23 €/60,-

Caddy	Caddy	on request
Electric Trolley	Elektrokarren	no
Buggy	Elektrischer Wagen	no
Clubs	Leihschläger	yes
Credit cards	Kreditkarten	MasterCard

Access Zufahrt : Lindau, → Golf
Map 1 on page 354 Karte 1 Seite 354

Golf course / PLATZ — 16/20

Site	Lage	
Maintenance	Instandhaltung	
Architect	Architekt	R. Trent Jones Sr
Type	Typ	forest, parkland
Relief	Begehbarkeit	
Water in play	Platz mit Wasser	
Exp. to wind	Wind ausgesetzt	
Trees in play	Platz mit Bäumen	

Scorecard / Scorekarte	Chp. / Chp.	Mens / Herren	Ladies / Damen
Length Länge	6079	5848	5185
Par	71	71	71
Slope system	143	141	137

Advised golfing ability 0 12 24 36
Empfohlene Spielstärke
Hcp required Min. Handicap no

Club house & amenities / KLUBHAUS UND NEBENGEBÄUDE — 7/10

Pro shop	Pro shop	
Driving range	Übungsplatz	
Sheltered	überdacht	yes
On grass	auf Rasen	yes
Putting-green	Putting-grün	yes
Pitching-green	Pitching-grün	yes

Hotel facilities / HOTEL BESCHREIBUNG — 7/10

HOTELS HOTELS

Golfhotel Bodensee, 27 rooms, D 153 € — Golf
Tel (49) 08389 - 89 10, Fax (49) 08389 - 89 142

Bayerischer Hof , 100 rooms, D 179 € — Lindau-Insel 7 km
Tel (49) 08382 - 91 50, Fax (49) 08382 - 915 591

Hotel Zum Mohren — Wangen-Neuravensburg 5 km
29 rooms, D 84 €
Tel (49) 07528 - 95 00, Fax (49) 07528 - 95 095

Helvetia, 54 rooms, D 128 € — Lindau-Insel 7 km
Tel (49) 08382 - 91 30, Fax (49) 08382 - 40 04

RESTAURANTS RESTAURANT

Hoyerberg Schlössle, Tel (49) 08382 - 25 295 — Lindau 7 km
Weinstube Frey, Tel (49) 08382 - 52 78 — Lindau-Insel 7 km

BRAUNSCHWEIG

14	6	7

Der Platz ist im typisch britischen Stil konzipiert und vermittelt das Flair eines alten Parks; zudem ist das Gelände für die Gegend recht hügelig. Auffallend sind die geschickt angelegten Fairway- und Grünbunker, welche nicht nur die Löcher optisch voneinander abgrenzen, sondern auch eine sehr wirksame Verteidigung darstellen. Am schwierigsten ist es jedoch seinen Drive gut zu plazieren, was durch eine Reihe sehr enger Fairways erschwert wird. Die dabei geforderte Präzison macht wett, was dem Platz an Länge fehlt. Eine Anzahl blinder Schläge, einige erhöht angelegte Grüns, Höhenunterschiede zwischen Abschlägen und Grüns, sowie relativ kleine Puttflächen erschweren die Schlägerwahl. Braunschweig ist ein spektakulär gestalteter Golfplatz, auf dessen strategisch angelegten Löchern das Spielen grossen Spass macht, wenngleich es Spielern mit mittleren und hohen Handicaps schwer fallen dürfte, hier einen guten Score zu erzielen. Letztere sind gut beraten sich einfach am Spiel zu erfreuen.

A rather hilly course for the region, Braunschweig gives the impression of an old park with a very obvious British style very much to the fore. We noted the clever placing of bunkers (fairway and green) which are as useful for demarcating the layout as they are for protecting it. But the prime difficulty here lies with placing the tee-shot, owing to a number of tight fairways which make up for the course's lack of length. A few blind shots, a number of elevated greens and differences in altitude between tee and green complicate the choice of club, especially since the putting surfaces are generally rather small. A spectacular and prettily landscaped course which is fun to play and very strategic, although mid- and high-handicappers should not bank too much on carding a good score. They are better off just playing for the fun of it.

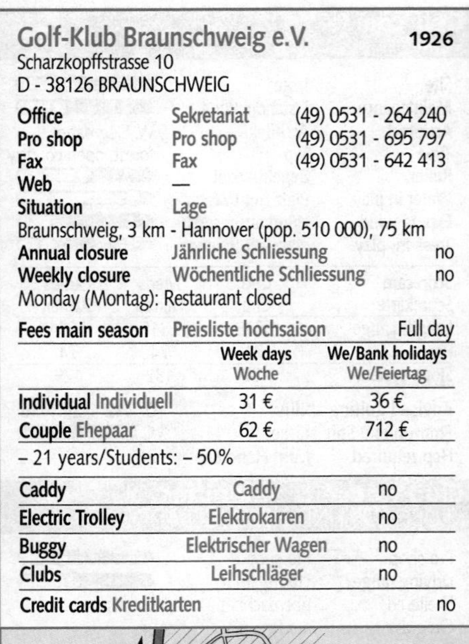

Golf-Klub Braunschweig e.V. — 1926

Scharzkopffstrasse 10
D - 38126 BRAUNSCHWEIG

Office	Sekretariat	(49) 0531 - 264 240
Pro shop	Pro shop	(49) 0531 - 695 797
Fax	Fax	(49) 0531 - 642 413
Web	—	
Situation	Lage	

Braunschweig, 3 km - Hannover (pop. 510 000), 75 km

Annual closure	Jährliche Schliessung	no
Weekly closure	Wöchentliche Schliessung	no

Monday (Montag): Restaurant closed

Fees main season Preisliste hochsaison	Full day	
	Week days Woche	**We/Bank holidays** We/Feiertag
Individual Individuell	31 €	36 €
Couple Ehepaar	62 €	712 €

– 21 years/Students: – 50%

Caddy	Caddy	no
Electric Trolley	Elektrokarren	no
Buggy	Elektrischer Wagen	no
Clubs	Leihschläger	no
Credit cards Kreditkarten		no

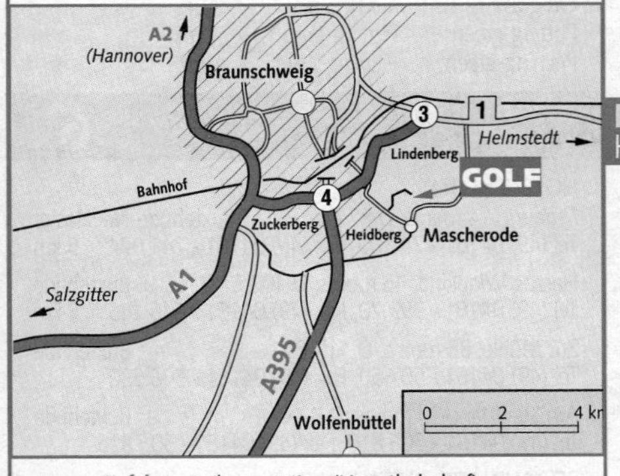

Access Zufahrt : Railway station (Hauptbahnhof), Salzdahlumer Strasse → Krankenhaus
Map 6 on page 364 Karte 6 Seite 364

Golf course PLATZ — 14/20

Site	Lage	
Maintenance	Instandhaltung	
Architect	Architekt	unknown
Type	Typ	country, forest
Relief	Begehbarkeit	
Water in play	Platz mit Wasser	
Exp. to wind	Wind ausgesetzt	
Trees in play	Platz mit Bäumen	

Scorecard Scorekarte	**Chp.** Chp.	**Mens** Herren	**Ladies** Damen
Length Länge	5714	5714	5052
Par	72	72	72
Slope system	124	124	120

Advised golfing ability Empfohlene Spielstärke — 0 12 24 36
Hcp required Min. Handicap — 36

Club house & amenities KLUBHAUS UND NEBENGEBÄUDE — 6/10

Pro shop	Pro shop	
Driving range	Übungsplatz	
Sheltered	überdacht	3 mats
On grass	auf Rasen	yes (summer)
Putting-green	Putting-grün	yes
Pitching-green	Pitching-grün	yes

Hotel facilities HOTEL BESCHREIBUNG — 7/10

HOTELS HOTELS

Stadtpalais, 45 rooms, D 128 € — Braunschweig
Tel (49) 0531 - 241 024, Fax (49) 0531 - 241 025 — 3 km

Play Off, 184 rooms, D 92 € — Braunschweig
Tel (49) 0531 - 26 310, Fax (49) 0531 - 67 119

Fürstenhof, 52 rooms, D 82 € — Braunschweig
Tel (49) 0531 - 791 061, Fax (49) 0531 - 791 064

RESTAURANTS RESTAURANT

Gewandhaus — Braunschweig
Tel (49) 0531 - 242 077

Brabanter Hof — Braunschweig
Tel (49) 0531 - 43 090

BUXTEHUDE

16 | 7 | 6

Ein originelles Beispiel der sehr strengen Architektur Siegmanns, bei dem drei verschiedene Stile vorzufinden sind: Wald, offene Fläche und beinahe alpine Landschaft, wobei letztere körperlich die anstrengendste ist (bei drei Löchern). Der Architekt hat sich dem Gelände gefügt, ohne es stark umzugestalten, daher auch der etwas uneinheitliche Stil. Doch der Platz ist dadurch sehr abwechslungsreich und interessant und die Hindernisse sind von den Abschlägen aus gut sichtbar. Man muss jedoch sein Spiel schnell an die Gegebenheiten anpassen können. Spieler mit weniger guten Reflexen werden etwas Mühe haben. Buxtehude ist sehr lang, daher ergeben seine sechs Par 5 Löcher ein ansprechendes Par 74. Die Greens sind teils erhöht, teils auf Doppelstufen und recht klein, was äusserste Genauigkeit erfordert. Dafür sind ihre Verteidigungen durchaus zu durchbrechen. Geeignet für die ganze Familie, ohne sich allzusehr um den Score zu kümmern.

An original example of Siegmann's very serious style of architecture, where you find three different styles: one in the woods, another in more open countryside and the last virtually up in the hills and physically the most trying (over three holes). The designer has bowed to the landscape more than he has modelled it, hence the impression of a rather unassertive style. In contrast, the course is great fun to play with a lot of variety and clearly visible hazards from the tees. You have to adjust your game quickly, and players with slow reflexes will find it hard work. Buxtehude is very long, but the six par 5s make this a more reasonable par 74. The greens are sometimes elevated and two-tiered, and they are rather small, so extreme accuracy is essential. In contrast, their defences are not unbreachable. Play with all the family and don't worry too much about the score.

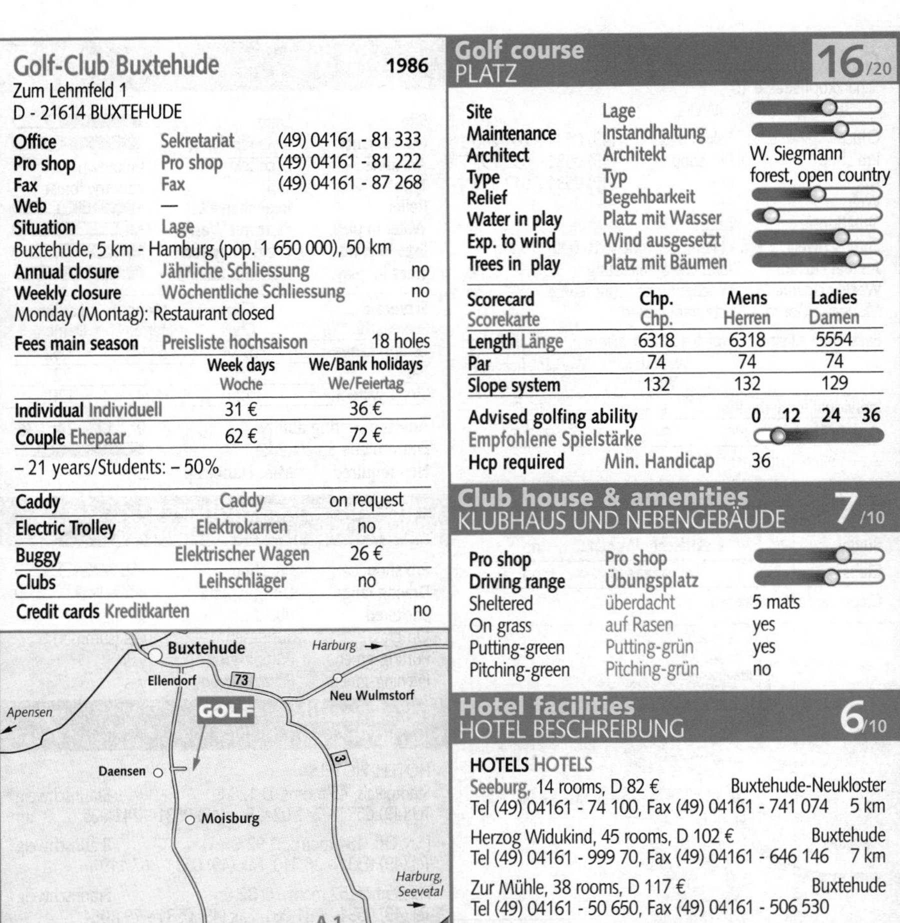

Golf-Club Buxtehude — 1986

Zum Lehmfeld 1
D - 21614 BUXTEHUDE

Office	Sekretariat	(49) 04161 - 81 333
Pro shop	Pro shop	(49) 04161 - 81 222
Fax	Fax	(49) 04161 - 87 268
Web	—	
Situation	Lage	

Buxtehude, 5 km - Hamburg (pop. 1 650 000), 50 km

Annual closure	Jährliche Schliessung	no
Weekly closure	Wöchentliche Schliessung	no

Monday (Montag): Restaurant closed

Fees main season Preisliste hochsaison	**Week days** Woche	**We/Bank holidays** We/Feiertag
	18 holes	
Individual Individuell	31 €	36 €
Couple Ehepaar	62 €	72 €

– 21 years/Students: – 50%

Caddy	Caddy	on request
Electric Trolley	Elektrokarren	no
Buggy	Elektrischer Wagen	26 €
Clubs	Leihschläger	no
Credit cards	Kreditkarten	no

Access Zufahrt : A1 Hamburg-Bremen. Exit (Ausf.) Hollenstedt → Moisburg, Buxtehude. Daensen → Golf
Map 7 on page 366 Karte 7 Seite 366

Golf course — PLATZ — 16/20

Site	Lage	
Maintenance	Instandhaltung	
Architect	Architekt	W. Siegmann
Type	Typ	forest, open country
Relief	Begehbarkeit	
Water in play	Platz mit Wasser	
Exp. to wind	Wind ausgesetzt	
Trees in play	Platz mit Bäumen	

Scorecard Scorekarte	**Chp.** Chp.	**Mens** Herren	**Ladies** Damen
Length Länge	6318	6318	5554
Par	74	74	74
Slope system	132	132	129

Advised golfing ability Empfohlene Spielstärke — 0 12 24 36

Hcp required Min. Handicap — 36

Club house & amenities — KLUBHAUS UND NEBENGEBÄUDE — 7/10

Pro shop	Pro shop	
Driving range	Übungsplatz	
Sheltered	überdacht	5 mats
On grass	auf Rasen	yes
Putting-green	Putting-grün	yes
Pitching-green	Pitching-grün	no

Hotel facilities — HOTEL BESCHREIBUNG — 6/10

HOTELS HOTELS

Seeburg, 14 rooms, D 82 € — Buxtehude-Neukloster
Tel (49) 04161 - 74 100, Fax (49) 04161 - 741 074 — 5 km

Herzog Widukind, 45 rooms, D 102 € — Buxtehude
Tel (49) 04161 - 999 70, Fax (49) 04161 - 646 146 — 7 km

Zur Mühle, 38 rooms, D 117 € — Buxtehude
Tel (49) 04161 - 50 650, Fax (49) 04161 - 506 530

Am Stadtpark, 20 rooms, D 82 € — Buxtehude
Tel (49) 04161 - 506 810, Fax (49) 04161 - 506 815

RESTAURANTS RESTAURANT

Seeburg, Tel (49) 04161 - 82 071 — Buxtehude-Neukloster

Herbstprinz, Tel (49) 04162- 7403 — Jork 8 km

CLUB ZUR VAHR (GARLSTEDT) | 18 | 6 | 5

1905 erbaut, wurde der Platz Anfang der 60er Jahre neu gestaltet. An vier Löchern kommt Wasser ins Spiel; grosse Pinien dominieren den Platzcharakter. Es gibt insgesamt nur zwei Fairway-Bunker, da das Profil der Doglegs die Spielbahnen bereits sehr anspruchvoll macht. Die Grüns sind bemerkenswert gut verteidigt, obschon die sie umgebenden Bunker weder besonders zahlreich noch allzu bedrohlich sind. Angesichts der Tatsache, dass die meisten Schwierigkeiten gut auszumachen sind und das Gelände nur wenige Unebenheiten aufweist, erkennt man, dass die Probleme, die einem dieser Platz bereitet, sehr subtiler Art sein müssen. Dazu gehören Länge, die Beherrschung einer Vielzahl von Schlagvarianten, die Fähigkeit den Ball vom Abschlag aus so zu plazieren, dass man das Grün mit dem zweiten Schlag gut anspielen kann, sowie die Allgegenwärtigkeit von Bäumen und Heidekraut, die alle verunglückten Schläge bestrafen. Nur die sehr guten Spieler werden sich für die hinteren Abschläge entscheiden, wenngleich die sechs Par 5 Löcher gute Gelegenheiten zu einem Birdie bieten. Es ist ein absolutes Vergnügen hier zu spielen.

This is one of Germany's oldest and most celebrated golf courses. Designed in 1905, it was re-modelled in the early 1960s with water on four holes, tall pine-trees virtually everywhere but only two fairway bunkers. They must have thought that the tight dog-legs were already penalizing enough. The greens are remarkably well guarded, even though the protective bunkers are neither too numerous nor too dangerous. If we add to this the fact that most difficulties are clearly visible and relief never more than a gentle roll, you will understand how subtle the problems are here. Length has a lot to do with this, as does the variety of shots to be played, the positioning of each shot to approach the greens from the best angle and the presence of trees and heather, which punish all wayward shots. Only the very good players will choose the back tees, even though the six par 5s are good opportunities for a birdie 4. A real treat to play.

Club zur Vahr e.V., Bremen, Platz Garlstedter Heide — 1905

Am Golfplatz 10 - D - 27711 GARLSTEDT/OHZ

Office	Sekretariat	(49) 0421 - 204 480
Pro shop	Pro shop	(49) 0421 - 231 467
Fax	Fax	(49) 0421 - 244 9248
Web	—	
Situation	Lage	

Bremen (pop. 552 000), 26 km - Bremerhaven, 39 km

Annual closure	Jährliche Schliessung	1/1→1/3
Weekly closure	Wöchentliche Schliessung	no

Monday (Montag): Restaurant closed

Fees main season Preisliste hochsaison	18 holes	
	Week days Woche	**We/Bank holidays** We/Feiertag
Individual Individuell	36 €	36 €
Couple Ehepaar	72 €	72 €

We: with members (nur in Mitgliederbegleitung)

Caddy	Caddy	no
Electric Trolley	Elektrokarren	no
Buggy	Elektrischer Wagen	no
Clubs	Leihschläger	no
Credit cards	Kreditkarten	no

Access Zufahrt : Bremen, A27 → Bremerhaven. Exit (Ausf.) Ihlpol, B6 → Bremerhaven. 10 km until Garlstedt. → Golf on the left.

Map 5 on page 363 Karte 5 Seite 363

Golf course — PLATZ — 18/20

Site	Lage	
Maintenance	Instandhaltung	
Architect	Architekt	B. von Limburger
Type	Typ	forest, parkland
Relief	Begehbarkeit	
Water in play	Platz mit Wasser	
Exp. to wind	Wind ausgesetzt	
Trees in play	Platz mit Bäumen	

Scorecard Scorekarte	**Chp.** Chp.	**Mens** Herren	**Ladies** Damen
Length Länge	6408	6282	5538
Par	74	74	74
Slope system	136	135	132

Advised golfing ability Empfohlene Spielstärke — 0 12 24 36

Hcp required Min. Handicap 36

Club house & amenities — KLUBHAUS UND NEBENGEBÄUDE — 6/10

Pro shop	Pro shop	
Driving range	Übungsplatz	
Sheltered	überdacht	no
On grass	auf Rasen	yes
Putting-green	Putting-grün	yes
Pitching-green	Pitching-grün	yes

Hotel facilities — HOTEL BESCHREIBUNG — 5/10

HOTELS HOTELS

Zum alten Torfkahn, 11 rooms, D 87 € — Osterholz-Scharmbeck
Tel (49) 04791 - 76 08, Fax (49) 04791 - 59 606 — 6 km

Eichenhof, 20 rooms, D 128 € — Worpswede
Tel (49) 04792 - 26 76, Fax (49) 04792 - 44 27 — 18 km

RESTAURANTS RESTAURANT

Tietjen's Hütte — Osterholz-Scharmbeck
Tel (49) 04791 - 24 15 — 9 km

Zum alten Torfkahn — Osterholz-Scharmbeck
Tel (49) 04791 - 76 08 — 6 km

L'Orchidée — Bremen
Tel (49) 0421 - 305 9888 — 25 km

DOMTAL-MOMMENHEIM

14 | 7 | 7

Domtal-Mommenheim ist ein gutes Beispiel für einen Platz, der mit begrenzten Mitteln erbaut wurde. Für das Design zeichnet Siegfried Heinz verantwortlich, der sein Handwerk bei Altmeister Bernhard von Limburger erlernte. Er hatte beim Entwurf vor allem die Mehrzahl der Golfer, also mittlere bis hohe Handicaps, im Auge. Der Platz hat sein Ziel erreicht, Mitglieder und Gastspieler kommen nicht nur aus dem nahegelegenen Mainz. Der Platz wird scheinbar leicht, und dennoch finden auch gute Spieler hier genügend Herausforderung. Dies ist ein Platz, auf dem Longhitter richtig draufhauen können, obwohl es genügend Hindernisse gibt, die aber für gute Spieler selten bedrohlich sind, mit Ausnahme des kurzen 16. Loch (einem Par 3) und dem 18. Loch, bei dem man über Wasser so weit abkürzen kann wie man es sich zutraut. Dennoch muss man den Ball gut treffen, um ein gutes Ergebnis zu erzielen. Alles in allem ist dies ein Platz, auf dem das Spielen in der schönen Umgebung der Weinberge von Rheinhessen richtig Spass macht.

Domtal-Mommenheim is a fine example of a course which was built with a restricted budget, which was designed by owner Siegfried Heinz (who learned his trade as shaper for Bernhard von Limburger) essentially for the vast majority of golfers, i.e. mid-and high-handicappers, and which has successfully reached its target. And by target we don't mean only the inhabitants of Mainz. Yet the apparent facility of this course can be deceiving and good players also have fun playing here. Firstly, long-hitters can open their shoulders because although there is no shortage of hazards they are seldom dangerous, except on the short 16th and on the 18th, where you can cut off as much as you dare over the water hazard. Next, you have to strike the ball well to score well, as shots off-target rarely find any sort of reward. All in all, this is great fun amidst the very pleasant landscape of the Rheinhessen vineyards.

Golf Club Domtal-Mommenheim 1997

Am Golfplatz 1
D - 55278 MOMMENHEIM

Office	Sekretariat	(49) 06138 - 920 20
Pro shop	Pro shop	(49) 06138 - 940 170
Fax	Fax	(49) 06138 - 920 231
Web	www.golf.de/domtal-mommenheim	
Situation	Lage	
Mainz (pop. 186 000), 10 km		
Annual closure	Jährliche Schliessung	no
Weekly closure	Wöchentliche Schliessung	no

Fees main season Preisliste hochsaison		18 holes
	Week days Woche	**We/Bank holidays** We/Feiertag
Individual Individuell	26 €	41 €
Couple Ehepaar	52 €	82 €
– 21 years/Students: – 50%		

Caddy	Caddy	no
Electric Trolley	Elektrokarren	yes
Buggy	Elektrischer Wagen	20 €
Clubs	Leihschläger	13 €
Credit cards Kreditkarten		Eurocard - MasterCard

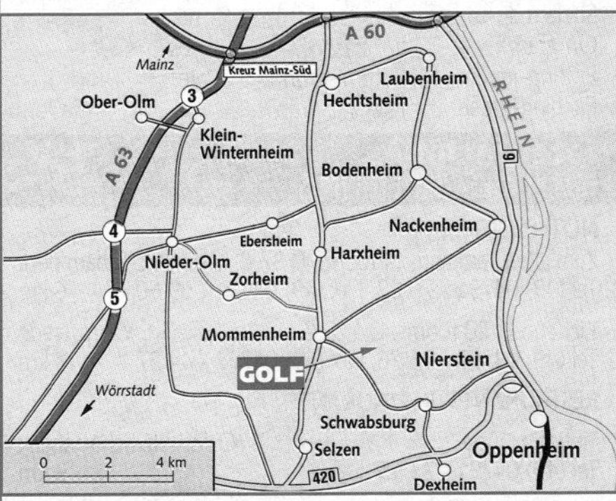

Access Zufahrt : Mainz A63. Exit (Ausf.) Nieder-Olm. → Zornheim, → Mommenheim. 1 km → Schwasburg-Nierstein. → Golf.
Map 3 on page 359 Karte 3 Seite 359

Golf course PLATZ 14/20

Site	Lage	
Maintenance	Instandhaltung	
Architect	Architekt	Siegfried Heinz
Type	Typ	open country
Relief	Begehbarkeit	
Water in play	Platz mit Wasser	
Exp. to wind	Wind ausgesetzt	
Trees in play	Platz mit Bäumen	

Scorecard Scorekarte	**Chp.** Chp.	**Mens** Herren	**Ladies** Damen
Length Länge	6092	5880	5131
Par	72	72	72
Slope system	125	122	118

Advised golfing ability Empfohlene Spielstärke — 0 12 24 36
Hcp required Min. Handicap 54

Club house & amenities KLUBHAUS UND NEBENGEBÄUDE 7/10

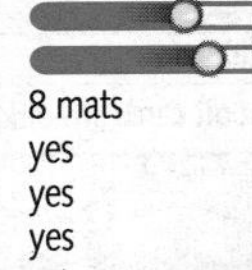

Pro shop	Pro shop	
Driving range	Übungsplatz	
Sheltered	überdacht	8 mats
On grass	auf Rasen	yes
Putting-green	Putting-grün	yes
Pitching-green	Pitching-grün	yes

Hotel facilities HOTEL BESCHREIBUNG 7/10

HOTELS HOTELS

Park Hotel, 55 rooms, D 138 € — Nierstein 5 km
Tel (49) 06133 - 50 80, Fax (49) 06133 - 5083 33

Zum Storchennest, 22 rooms, D 56 € — Mommenheim 1 km
Tel (49) 06138 - 12 33, Fax (49) 06138 - 12 40

Hilton International, 433 rooms, D 204 € — Mainz 15 km
Tel (49) 06131 - 24 50, Fax (49) 06131 - 245 589

RESTAURANTS RESTAURANT

Weingut Nack, — Gau-Bischofsheim 4 km
Tel (49) 06135 - 30 43

Drei Lilien, Tel (49) 06131 - 225 068 — Mainz 10 km

Rats-und Zunftst. Heilig Geist, — Mainz
Tel (49) 06131 - 225 757

DÜSSELDORFER 15 7 7

Der Düsseldorfer Golf Club liegt in Ratingen, wenige Kilometer von der Stadtgrenze der Nordrhein-Westfälischen Landes-hauptstadt. Aber trotz der guten Verkehrsanbindung ist der Platz weit von der Hektik der Grossstadt entfernt. Auf einem dicht bewaldeten, hügeligen Gelände entwarf der englische Architekt Donald Harradine 1961 einen Platz, der nicht nur idyllisch gelegen ist, sondern auch mit seinem abwechslungsreichen Design begeistert. Die Hauptschwierigkeit sind die teilweise engen Spielbahnen, der Wald am Rand der Fairways und die drei Teiche sowie einige seitliche Wasserhindernisse. Alle Schwierigkeiten auf diesem Parkland platz sind vom Abschlag aus zu erkennen, etwas, was vor allem bessere Spieler schätzen. Lediglich beim 15. Loch, einem Par 3 von 148 Länge und 80 Metern Höhenunterschied wird man sich beim erstenmal schwertun. Im Juli 1999 wurden nagelneue Grüns eingeweiht, die wesentlich mehr Ondulationen als die alten aufweisen. Jetzt ist auch das Putten auf diesem Platz interessant und abwechslungsreich. Diesen Platz sollte man sich nicht entgehen lassen.

The Düsseldorfer Golf Club is located in Ratingen, a few kilometers from the city limits of the capital of Northrine-Westfalia. The course is easily reached from Düsseldorf but miles away from the hustle and bustle of the big city. English architect Donald Harradine designed a course in a densely wooded area which is not only idyllic but also a pleasure to play, provided your ball stays out of the forest bordering the sometimes narrow fairways. All difficulties on the parkland style course are visible from the tee boxes, a fact better players appreciate. The 15th, a par 3 of 149 metres and an elevation drop of 80 metres, is perhaps the only hole where first-timers will have a hard time picking the right club. In July 1999, the club opened 18 new greens which have far more contours than the old ones and make putting more of a challenge. This is one course not to be missed.

Düsseldorfer Golf Club e.V. 1961

Rittergut Rommeljansweg - D - 40882 RATINGEN

Office	Sekretariat	(49) 02102 - 81 092
Pro shop	Pro shop	(49) 02102 - 83 683
Fax	Fax	(49) 02102 - 81 782
E-mail	golfclub.mettmann@t-online.de	
Situation	Lage	

Ratingen (pop. 91 000), 1 km - Düsseldorf (pop. 570 000), 10 km

Annual closure	Jährliche Schliessung	20/12→10/2
Weekly closure	Wöchentliche Schliessung	no

Monday (Montag): Restaurant closed

Fees main season Preisliste hochsaison	Full day	
	Week days Woche	**We/Bank holidays** We/Feiertag
Individual Individuell	51 €	36 € *
Couple Ehepaar	102 €	72 € *

* We: with members (nur in Mitgliederbegleitung)
– 21 years/students: – 50 %

Caddy	Caddy	15 € /on request
Electric Trolley	Elektrokarren	10 €
Buggy	Elektrischer Wagen	no
Clubs	Leihschläger	5 €
Credit cards Kreditkarten		no

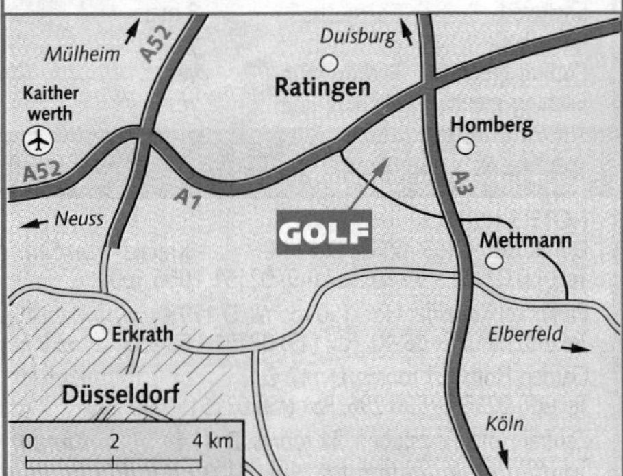

Access Zufahrt : A3, Exit (Ausf.) Ratingen-Wülfrath, → Ratingen. 400 m turn right → Golf
Map 3 on page 358 Karte 3 Seite 358

Golf course PLATZ 15/20

Site	Lage	
Maintenance	Instandhaltung	
Architect	Architekt	Donald Harradine
Type	Typ	forest
Relief	Begehbarkeit	
Water in play	Platz mit Wasser	
Exp. to wind	Wind ausgesetzt	
Trees in play	Platz mit Bäumen	

Scorecard Scorekarte	**Chp.** Chp.	**Mens** Herren	**Ladies** Damen
Length Länge	5781	5781	5105
Par	71	71	71
Slope system	124	124	123

Advised golfing ability Empfohlene Spielstärke 0 12 24 36
Hcp required Min. Handicap 36

Club house & amenities KLUBHAUS UND NEBENGEBÄUDE 7/10

Pro shop	Pro shop	
Driving range	Übungsplatz	
Sheltered	überdacht	4 mats
On grass	auf Rasen	yes
Putting-green	Putting-grün	yes
Pitching-green	Pitching-grün	yes

Hotel facilities HOTEL BESCHREIBUNG 7/10

HOTELS HOTELS

Haus Kronenthal, 30 rooms, D 128 € — Ratingen
Tel (49) 02102 - 85 080, Fax (49) 02102 - 850 850 — 1 km

Allgäuer Hof, 16 rooms, D 97 € — Ratingen
Tel (49) 02102 - 95 410, Fax (49) 02102 - 954 123 — 3 km

Am Düsseldorfer Platz, 49 rooms, D 92 € — Ratingen
Tel (49) 02102 - 20 180, Fax (49) 02102 - 201 850 — 2 km

Breidenbacher Hof, 130 rooms, D 306 € — Düsseldorf
Tel (49) 0211 - 13 030, Fax (49) 0211 - 130 3830 — 15 km

RESTAURANTS RESTAURANT

Haus zum Haus, Tel (49) 02102 - 22 586 — Ratingen 2 km

Auermühle, Tel (49) 02102 - 81 064 — Ratingen 2 km

ELFRATHER MÜHLE

14 | 7 | 7

Eine alte, sorgfältig restaurierte Windmühle beeindruckt den Besucher gleich auf Anhieb. Der Eindruck von dem noch ziemlich jungen Platz ist dagegen weniger überwältigend. Trotzdem rechtfertigt sein allgemeiner Zustand, ihn mal zu spielen. Der Stil ist eher amerikanisch, mit einigen Wasserhindernissen, aber nur wenigen Bäumen, was den Platz sehr windanfällig macht. Es ist hier von Vorteil, den Ball flach schlagen zu können. Gleichzeitig wird es schwierig, die gut verteidigten Grüns anzuspielen, wenn man dem Ball nicht genügend Spin mitgibt. Durch den sandigen Untergrund ist der Platz auch bei nassem Wetter gut bespielbar. Das gesamte Layout wurde mit viel Sorgfalt angelegt, insbesondere die zum Teil in mehreren Stufen aufgebauten Grüns, die sehr interessant zu Lesen sind. Einige recht spektakuläre Löcher heben diesen Platz über das allgemeine Niveau hinaus, allerdings fehlt ihm zu einem wirklich grossartigen Kurs das gewisse Etwas. Dennoch eine gute Anlage, deren hügelige ersten neun Löcher zweifellos anspruchsvoller als die zweiten Neun sind.

An old but very carefully restored windmill gives an excellent first impression. The actual course is not quite as exceptional, but the overall standard makes it worth a round or two, even though the layout is still young. The style is a little on the American side, with a few water hazards in play but very few trees. This adds to the difficulties when the wind gets up. Hitting low balls is an asset here, and it is difficult to reach and stay on certain well-protected greens without enough spin on the ball. The sandy soil also makes this a playable course in wet weather. The whole layout has been carefully designed, especially the greens, which are sometimes multi-tiered and always interesting to read. A number of rather spectacular holes lift the overall standard a little above average, but that little spark of genius, which makes a good course a great course, is missing. A competent course all the same with a hilly and doubtless more demanding front nine.

Golf Club Elfrather Mühle GmbH — 1992

An der Elfrather Mühle 145
D - 47802 KREFELD-TRAAR

Office	Sekretariat	(49) 02151 - 496 910
Pro shop	Pro shop	(49) 02151 - 496 922
Fax	Fax	(49) 02151 - 477 459
Web	—	
Situation	Lage	

Krefeld, 5 km - Düsseldorf (pop. 570 000), 30 km

Annual closure	Jährliche Schliessung	no
Weekly closure	Wöchentliche Schliessung	no

Monday (Montag): Restaurant closed

Fees main season Preisliste hochsaison	18 holes	
	Week days Woche	**We/Bank holidays** We/Feiertag
Individual Individuell	41 €	51 €
Couple Ehepaar	82 €	102 €
Caddy	Caddy	on request
Electric Trolley	Elektrokarren	10 €
Buggy	Elektrischer Wagen	31 €
Clubs	Leihschläger	no

Credit cards Kreditkarten
VISA - Eurocard - MasterCard - DC - AMEX

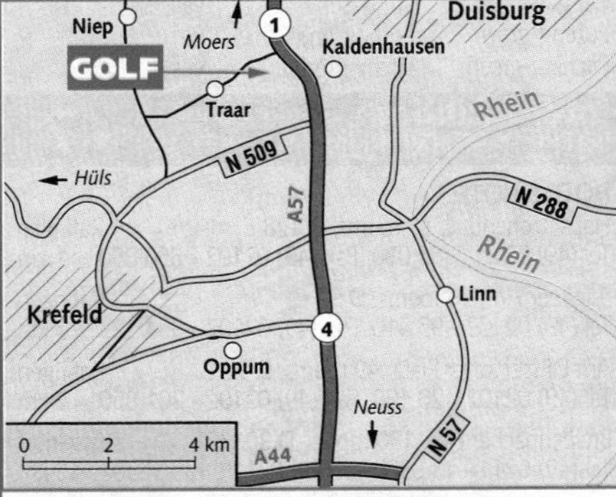

Access Zufahrt : A57 Exit (Ausf.) Krefeld/Gartenstadt. → Krefeld/Gartenstadt. Right in Werner-Voss-Strasse → Traar/Elfrath. Left in An der Elfrather Mühle.
Map 3 on page 358 Karte 3 Seite 358

Golf course — PLATZ — 14/20

Site	Lage	
Maintenance	Instandhaltung	
Architect	Architekt	Ron Kirby Fritz Beindorf
Type	Typ	open country
Relief	Begehbarkeit	
Water in play	Platz mit Wasser	
Exp. to wind	Wind ausgesetzt	
Trees in play	Platz mit Bäumen	

Scorecard Scorekarte	**Chp.** Chp.	**Mens** Herren	**Ladies** Damen
Length Länge	6251	6125	5232
Par	72	72	72
Slope system	121	119	119

Advised golfing ability Empfohlene Spielstärke — 0 12 24 36

Hcp required Min. Handicap — 36/We 28

Club house & amenities — KLUBHAUS UND NEBENGEBÄUDE — 7/10

Pro shop	Pro shop	
Driving range	Übungsplatz	
Sheltered	überdacht	8 mats
On grass	auf Rasen	yes
Putting-green	Putting-grün	yes
Pitching-green	Pitching-grün	yes

Hotel facilities — HOTEL BESCHREIBUNG — 7/10

HOTELS HOTELS

Dorint Hotel, 159 rooms, D 128 € — Krefeld-Traar 5km
Tel (49) 02151 - 95 60, Fax (49) 02151 - 956 100

Parkhotel Krefelder Hof, 150 rooms, D 179 € — Krefeld 5 km
Tel (49) 02151 - 58 40, Fax (49) 02151 - 58 435

Garden Hotel, 51 rooms, D 112 € — Krefeld
Tel (49) 02151 - 590 296, Fax (49) 02151 - 590 299

Zentral Hotel Poststuben, 31 rooms, D 84 € — Krefeld
Tel (49) 02151 - 24 656, Fax (49) 02151 - 802 888

RESTAURANTS RESTAURANT

Koperpot, Tel (49) 02151 - 614 814 — Krefeld
Et Bröckske, Tel(49) 02151 - 29 740 — Krefeld

ESCHENRIED

14 | 7 | 7

Neues und Altes wurde hier vereint. Die "alten" neun baumgesäumten Spielbahnen wurden ergänzt durch weitere neun Löcher in eher offenem Gelände. Letztere bilden die ersten 9 der jetzigen 18-Loch-Anlage. Beim Bau der neuen Löcher wurde weniger Aufmerksamkeit einem einheitlichen Platzcharakter geschenkt, als vielmehr den Grüns, welche aufgrund ihres weitaus aufwendigeren Designs viel interessanter zu spielen sind als die Grüns der alten Bahnen. Die grössten Probleme bereiten den Spielern die Bäume, doch muss man sich ebenso vor den sehr natürlich wirkenden Wasserläufen und Teichen in acht nehmen. Leider ist das Wasser von den kaum erhöhten Abschlägen häufig nicht einsehbar. Insgesamt kommt Wasser aber eher selten ins Spiel und sollte daher auch unerfahrene Spieler nicht allzu sehr abschrecken. Eschenried ist ein gelungener Golfplatz, den zu spielen vor allem unter der Woche empfehlenswert ist, da er an Wochenenden viele Leute aus dem nahen München und Umgebung anzieht.

New and old. The "old" nine-holer through the trees has been supplemented by a second 9-hole course over more open space, which in fact forms the front nine. Nobody really bothered about respecting unity of character, a good job, too, as far as the greens are concerned, which are much better designed, contoured and amusing to play than those on the first nine-hole course. The main problems come from the trees and, just as importantly, the very natural looking streams and ponds. The only regret is that they could have been more visible from the tee, which have no height to speak of. However, water is hardly ever in play and crossing it should not discourage even inexperienced players. A very competent course that is fun to play during the week. Being close to Munich, it is not always easy playing on week-ends.

Golfclub Eschenried — 1983

Kurfürstenweg 10
D - 85232 ESCHENRIED

Office	Sekretariat	(49) 08131 - 87 238
Pro shop	Pro shop	(49) 08131 - 86 786
Fax	Fax	(49) 08131 - 567 418
E-mail	matchpoint@t-online.de	
Situation	Lage	

München (pop. 1 300 000), 15 km

Annual closure	Jährliche Schliessung	1/12→28/2
Weekly closure	Wöchentliche Schliessung	no

Monday (Montag): Restaurant closed

Fees main season Preisliste hochsaison	18 holes	
	Week days Woche	**We/Bank holidays** We/Feiertag
Individual Individuell	41 €	51 €
Couple Ehepaar	82 €	102 €

– 21 years/Students: – 50%

Caddy	Caddy	no
Electric Trolley	Elektrokarren	no
Buggy	Elektrischer Wagen	15 €
Clubs	Leihschläger	15 €
Credit cards Kreditkarten		no

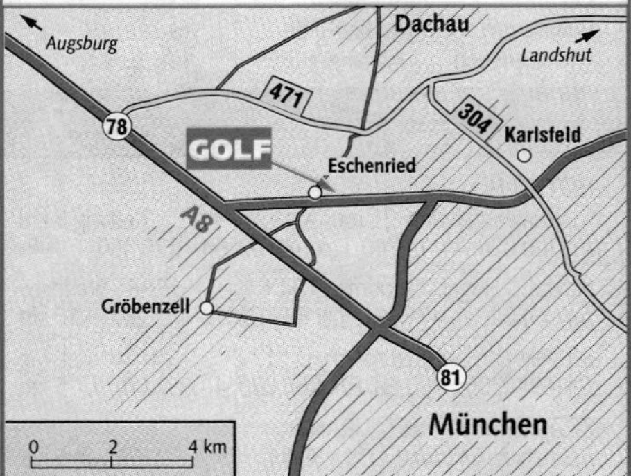

Access Zufahrt : A8 München-Stuttgart. Exit (Ausf.) Langwieder See → Eschenried, → Golf
Map 2 on page 356 Karte 2 Seite 356

Golf course PLATZ — 14/20

Site	Lage	
Maintenance	Instandhaltung	
Architect	Architekt	
Type	Typ	open country, forest
Relief	Begehbarkeit	
Water in play	Platz mit Wasser	
Exp. to wind	Wind ausgesetzt	
Trees in play	Platz mit Bäumen	

Scorecard Scorekarte	**Chp.** Chp.	**Mens** Herren	**Ladies** Damen
Length Länge	5935	5935	5195
Par	72	72	72
Slope system	124	124	127

Advised golfing ability Empfohlene Spielstärke — 0 12 24 36

Hcp required Min. Handicap — no

Club house & amenities KLUBHAUS UND NEBENGEBÄUDE — 7/10

Pro shop	Pro shop	
Driving range	Übungsplatz	
Sheltered	überdacht	yes
On grass	auf Rasen	yes
Putting-green	Putting-grün	yes
Pitching-green	Pitching-grün	yes

Hotel facilities HOTEL BESCHREIBUNG — 7/10

HOTELS HOTELS

Golf Landhaus Eschenried, 16 rooms, D 71 € — Eschenried
Tel (49) 08131 - 850 91, Fax (49) 08131 - 567 418 — on site

Zur Post, 96 rooms, D 128 € — München-Pasing 9 km
Tel (49) 089 - 896 950, Fax (49) 089 - 837 319

Kriemhild, 17 rooms, D 92 € — München-Nymphenburg
Tel (49) 089 - 171 1170, Fax (49) 089 -171 11755 — 10 km

RESTAURANTS RESTAURANT

Schlosswirtschaft zur Schwaige — München-Nymphenburg
Tel (49) 089 - 174 421 — 10 km

Zur Goldenen Gans — München-Pasing
Tel (49) 089 - 837 033 — 8 km

ESSENER OEFTE

15	8	7

Dieser Platz inmitten des Tals der Ruhr, ist ein Hort der Ruhe, ein Golfpark mit einigen tropischen Bäumen und einem Klubhaus in einem alten Schloss, das mehr als tausend Jahre alt ist. Die ersten neun Löcher sind hügelig undziemlich eng mit einigen blinden Löchern, die zweiten Neun sind flachener und offener und geben Longhittern die Möglichkeit, den Frust der ersten Neun loszuwerden, aber sie sollten dabei Vorsicht walten lassen, den auch die Back Nine haben Tücken. Kenner der Kunst des Architekten Bernhard von Limburger erkennen sein unverkennbaren Stil. Die Schwierigkeiten sind gut über den Platz verteilt. Der Platz wirkt etwas altmodisch, aber selbst wenn dies nicht der beste Platz im Land ist, ist er immer noch einer der besten der Gegend.

Right in the Ruhr valley, this course is a heaven of tranquillity, a golf park where you will be surprised by some of the tropical trees, and even more so by the club-house set in a former castle which dates back more than a thousand years. Intelligently, the front nine are steep and not very wide (with several blind greens), the back nine are much flatter and open. Big-hitters can give vent to their frustration that mounts over the front nine, but they should be careful: the difficulties are not only on the first nine holes. Connoisseurs of the skills of Bernhard von Limburger will recognize his golfing insight in the way hazards are spread around the course. Others might find this a little dated, but while this is not the most impressive course in the whole country, it is still one of the very best in this region.

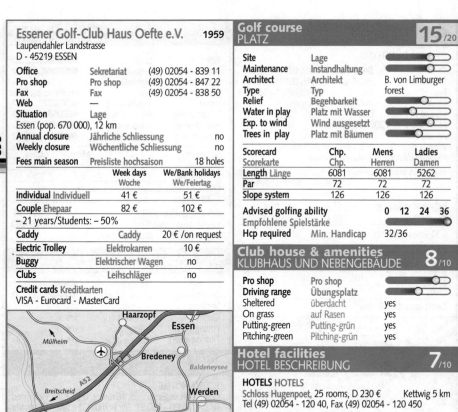

Essener Golf-Club Haus Oefte e.V. 1959

Laupendahler Landstrasse
D - 45219 ESSEN

Office	Sekretariat	(49) 02054 - 839 11
Pro shop	Pro shop	(49) 02054 - 847 22
Fax	Fax	(49) 02054 - 838 50
Web	—	
Situation	Lage	

Essen (pop. 670 000), 12 km

Annual closure	Jährliche Schliessung	no
Weekly closure	Wöchentliche Schliessung	no

Fees main season Preisliste hochsaison 18 holes

	Week days Woche	We/Bank holidays We/Feiertag
Individual Individuell	41 €	51 €
Couple Ehepaar	82 €	102 €

– 21 years/Students: – 50%

Caddy	Caddy	20 € /on request
Electric Trolley	Elektrokarren	10 €
Buggy	Elektrischer Wagen	no
Clubs	Leihschläger	no

Credit cards Kreditkarten
VISA - Eurocard - MasterCard

Access Zufahrt : A52 Essen-Düsseldorf. Exit (Ausf.) Essen-Haarzopf → Werden. Go on E-Werden (Ruhrbrücke), Laupendahler Strasse → E-Kettwig.
Map 3 on page 358 Karte 3 Seite 358

Golf course PLATZ 15/20

Site	Lage	
Maintenance	Instandhaltung	
Architect	Architekt	B. von Limburger
Type	Typ	forest
Relief	Begehbarkeit	
Water in play	Platz mit Wasser	
Exp. to wind	Wind ausgesetzt	
Trees in play	Platz mit Bäumen	

Scorecard Scorekarte	Chp. Chp.	Mens Herren	Ladies Damen
Length Länge	6081	6081	5262
Par	72	72	72
Slope system	126	126	126

Advised golfing ability Empfohlene Spielstärke 0 12 24 36
Hcp required Min. Handicap 32/36

Club house & amenities KLUBHAUS UND NEBENGEBÄUDE 8/10

Pro shop	Pro shop	
Driving range	Übungsplatz	
Sheltered	überdacht	yes
On grass	auf Rasen	yes
Putting-green	Putting-grün	yes
Pitching-green	Pitching-grün	yes

Hotel facilities HOTEL BESCHREIBUNG 7/10

HOTELS HOTELS

Schloss Hugenpoet, 25 rooms, D 230 € Kettwig 5 km
Tel (49) 02054 - 120 40, Fax (49) 02054 - 120 450

Parkhaus Hügel, 13 rooms, D 94 € Essen-Bredeney
Tel (49) 0201 - 471 091, Fax (49) 0201 - 444 207 10 km

Sengelmannshof , 26 rooms, D 117 € Kettwig
Tel (49) 02054 - 60 68, Fax (49) 02054 - 832 00 5 km

RESTAURANTS RESTAURANT

Residence, Tel (49) 02054 - 89 11 Kettwig 5 km

Landhaus Rutherbach, Tel (49) 0201 - 495 246 Kettwig

Parkhaus Hügel Essen-Bredeney
Tel (49) 0201 - 471 091 10 km

FALKENSTEIN

18 | 6 | 7

Ein Klassiker traditioneller, englischer Landschaftsarchitektur, umgeben von Wald (Pinien und weisse Birken) und Heidekraut. Auf den ersten Blick fallen die gestalterischen Feinheiten nicht auf, doch wird der Golfplatz durch sie zunehmend interessanter. Die variantenreichen Löcher und die nüchterne Weite des Platzes auf diesem leicht hügeligen Terrain stellen eine echte Herausforderung dar. Die Hindernisse sind einfach und zugleich raffiniert angelegt. Jeder Schlag muss wohlüberlegt sein und alle spielerischen Aspekte müssen in die ‹berlegungen miteinbezogen werden. Die Greens, teils auf mehreren Stufen, teils erhöht, sind immer gut verteidigt und können die Scores ebenso zunichte machen wie unpräzise Schläge. Gerade Löcher wechseln mit spektakulären Doglegs ab. Falkenstein ist wohl einer der schönsten Golfplätze Europas und wird auch mit viel Liebe gepflegt ein grossartiges Beispiel guter Golfarchitektur. Unglücklicherweise ist der Platz für heutige Profiturnier zu kurz, aber für normale Golfer ist dieser Platz lang genug...

One of the great classics and a traditional British design, set in a forest of pine and silver birch, with heather thrown in for good measure. It is not easy to appreciate the subtlety of the course at first sight, but this serves to make the course more exciting every time. The variety of holes and the forbidding size of the layout on moderately hilly terrain produce a thoroughly good test of golf. Hazards are spread with an equal measure of simplicity and strategic intelligence, and each shot demands a lot of thought in every compartment of the game. Sometimes multi-tiered, often elevated but always well-protected, the greens can ruin your card as easily as fluffed shots. With alternating straight holes and spectacular dog-legs, all in beautiful condition, Falkenstein remains one of Europe's greatest courses and a perfect showpiece for golf design. Unfortunately the course is too short for modern tournament pros, but still long enough for all other golfers.

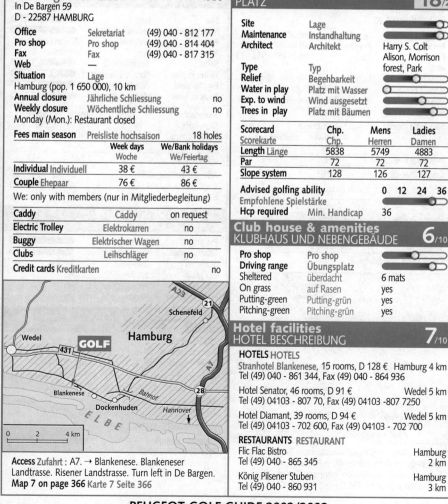

Hamburger Golf Club — 1930

In De Bargen 59
D - 22587 HAMBURG

Office	Sekretariat	(49) 040 - 812 177
Pro shop	Pro shop	(49) 040 - 814 404
Fax	Fax	(49) 040 - 817 315
Web	—	
Situation	Lage	

Hamburg (pop. 1 650 000), 10 km

Annual closure	Jährliche Schliessung	no
Weekly closure	Wöchentliche Schliessung	no

Monday (Mon.): Restaurant closed

Fees main season Preisliste hochsaison	18 holes	
	Week days Woche	**We/Bank holidays** We/Feiertag
Individual Individuell	38 €	43 €
Couple Ehepaar	76 €	86 €

We: only with members (nur in Mitgliederbegleitung)

Caddy	Caddy	on request
Electric Trolley	Elektrokarren	no
Buggy	Elektrischer Wagen	no
Clubs	Leihschläger	no
Credit cards	Kreditkarten	no

Access Zufahrt : A7. → Blankenese. Blankeneser Landtrasse. Risener Landstrasse. Turn left in De Bargen.

Map 7 on page 366 Karte 7 Seite 366

Golf course — PLATZ — 18/20

Site	Lage	
Maintenance	Instandhaltung	
Architect	Architekt	Harry S. Colt Alison, Morrison
Type	Typ	forest, Park
Relief	Begehbarkeit	
Water in play	Platz mit Wasser	
Exp. to wind	Wind ausgesetzt	
Trees in play	Platz mit Bäumen	

Scorecard Scorekarte	**Chp.** Chp.	**Mens** Herren	**Ladies** Damen
Length Länge	5838	5749	4883
Par	72	72	72
Slope system	128	126	127

Advised golfing ability — 0 12 24 36
Empfohlene Spielstärke

Hcp required — Min. Handicap — 36

Club house & amenities — KLUBHAUS UND NEBENGEBÄUDE — 6/10

Pro shop	Pro shop	
Driving range	Übungsplatz	
Sheltered	überdacht	6 mats
On grass	auf Rasen	yes
Putting-green	Putting-grün	yes
Pitching-green	Pitching-grün	yes

Hotel facilities — HOTEL BESCHREIBUNG — 7/10

HOTELS HOTELS

Stranhotel Blankenese, 15 rooms, D 128 € — Hamburg 4 km
Tel (49) 040 - 861 344, Fax (49) 040 - 864 936

Hotel Senator, 46 rooms, D 91 € — Wedel 5 km
Tel (49) 04103 - 807 70, Fax (49) 04103 -807 7250

Hotel Diamant, 39 rooms, D 94 € — Wedel 5 km
Tel (49) 04103 - 702 600, Fax (49) 04103 - 702 700

RESTAURANTS RESTAURANT

Flic Flac Bistro — Hamburg 2 km
Tel (49) 040 - 865 345

König Pilsener Stuben — Hamburg 3 km
Tel (49) 040 - 860 931

FELDAFING

16 | 7 | 6

Feldafing wurde nach Umbau- und Verjüngungsmassnahmen von Heinz Fehring im Jahre 1997 wieder eröffnet, aber es immer noch ein kurzer und enger Platz, allerdings sind die Grüns jetzt stark onduliert. Die Anlage liegt etwas erhöht direkt am Starnberger See, auf einem Gelände, das früher Maximilian II gehörte, dessen Schloss unmittelbar an die Anlage angrenzt. Trotz dieser Lage bletet sich nur selten ein freier Blick auf den See, da der Platz von einer Vielzahl grosser alter Bäume umrahmt wird, die gleichzeitig einen Grossteil der Schwierigkeiten auf diesem Platz darstellen. Bernhard von Limburger hat das ziemlich hügelige Gelände hervorragend zu nutzen verstanden, so dass ein für ihn typisches Design entstanden ist, das sich durch eine nüchtern-eleganten und dabei immer seriösen Stil ausgezeichnet. Feldafing ist ein reizvoller Golfplatz, der sich zudem wunderbar in die ihn umgebende Landschaft einfügt und den man allein schon aus diesem Grund unbedingt kennen lernen sollte.

Feldafing underwent a welcome and successful rejuvenation scheme by Heinz Fehring, but it is still a narrow and short course. Located on an estate formerly belonging to Maximilian II - his castle stands on the edge of the course - Feldafing overlooks the Starnberger See, although the view is not completely clear owing to the very many old trees which form the major share of hazards. Bernhard von Limburger made excellent use of rather hilly terrain (rather tiring when walking) and it is always a pleasure to see his elegant, sober and serious style again. An often spectacular course which blends wonderfully with its natural surroundings. Well worth getting to know.

Golf Club Feldafing e.V. — 1926

Tutzinger Strasse 15
D - 82340 TUTZING

Office	Sekretariat	(49) 08157 - 93 340
Pro shop	Pro shop	(49) 08157 - 93 340
Fax	Fax	(49) 08157 - 933 499
Web	—	
Situation	Lage	München, 40 km
Annual closure	Jährliche Schliessung	no
Weekly closure	Wöchentliche Schliessung	no

Monday (Montag): Restaurant closed

Fees main season Preisliste hochsaison	Week days Woche	We/Bank holidays We/Feiertag
		18 holes
Individual Individuell	56 €	66 €
Couple Ehepaar	112 €	132 €

We: with members (nur in Mitgliederbegleitung)

Caddy	Caddy	on request
Electric Trolley	Elektrokarren	no
Buggy	Elektrischer Wagen	no
Clubs	Leihschläger	yes
Credit cards Kreditkarten		no

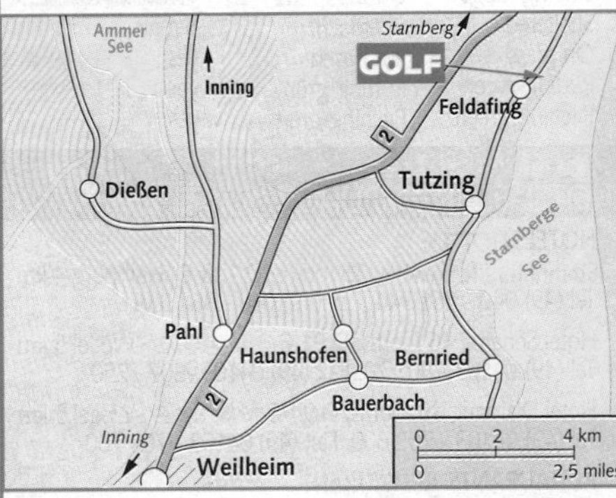

Access Zufahrt : A95 München-Starnberg. Exit (Ausf.) Starnberg. Durch Starnberg. B2 → Pöcking. → Tutzing/Deldafing, right on Tutzinger Strasse. 1 km left, Golf. **Map 2 on page 356** Karte 2 Seite 356

Golf course PLATZ — 16/20

Site	Lage	
Maintenance	Instandhaltung	
Architect	Architekt	B. von Limburger
Type	Typ	mountain
Relief	Begehbarkeit	
Water in play	Platz mit Wasser	
Exp. to wind	Wind ausgesetzt	
Trees in play	Platz mit Bäumen	

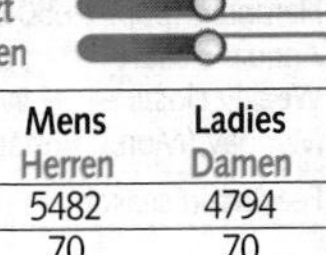

Scorecard Scorekarte	Chp. Chp.	Mens Herren	Ladies Damen
Length Länge	5738	5482	4794
Par	71	70	70
Slope system	128	127	125

Advised golfing ability 0 12 24 36
Empfohlene Spielstärke
Hcp required Min. Handicap 34

Club house & amenities KLUBHAUS UND NEBENGEBÄUDE — 7/10

Pro shop	Pro shop	
Driving range	Übungsplatz	
Sheltered	überdacht	5 mats
On grass	auf Rasen	yes
Putting-green	Putting-grün	yes
Pitching-green	Pitching-grün	yes

Hotel facilities HOTEL BESCHREIBUNG — 6/10

HOTELS HOTELS

Kaiserin Elisabeth, 70 rooms, D 128 € — Feldafing 300 m
Tel (49) 08157 - 930 90, Fax (49) 08157 -930 9133

Forsthaus am See, 21 rooms, 123 € — Pöcking-Possenhofen 2 km
Tel (49) 08157 - 93 010, Fax (49) 08157 - 42 92

Marina, 70 rooms, D 128 € — Bernried 7 km
Tel (49) 08158 - 93 20, Fax (49) 08158 - 71 17

RESTAURANTS RESTAURANT

Forsthaus Ilkahöhe — Tutzing 4 km
Tel (49) 08158 - 8242

FLEESENSEE

17 | 8 | 8

Wie Woburn in England oder PGA de Catalunya in Spanien gehört Fleesensee zu den Plätzen der PGA European Tour. Die Eröffnung des Platzes durch Kanzler Gerhard Schröder in der mecklenburgischen Seenplatte war ein Ereignis, das in ganz Deutschland viel Beachtung fand, besonders da dieses Resort die bisher aufwendigste Tourismus-Projekt in Ostdeutschland darstellt. Zum Resort gehören drei 18-Loch-Plätze, der Par-67-Südplatz, der vorwiegend für jüngere und neue Golfer geeignet ist, der Westplatz im Stil eines Links Courses, der ideal für Durchschnittsgolfer ist und eben der Schlossplatz, der Golfern alles abverlangt. Wasserhindernisse kommen an zehn Löchern ins Spiel, dazu lauern viele Bunker, etliche davon tiefe Topfbunker auf Bälle. Stan Eby hat ein intelligentes Design umgesetzt, das leichte, mittelschwere und extrem schwere Löcher zu einem vorzüglichen Golfplatz kombiniert, ein Platz, der britische und amerikanische Stilelemente kombiniert und trotzdem wie aus einem Guss wirkt. Um allerdings ein gutes Ergebnis zu erzielen, muss man die Grüns genau anspielen. Fleesensee ist eines der besten deutschen Golfresort, eines das mit zunehmendem Alter nur noch besser werden kann.

Fleesensee is a part of the PGA European Tour golf development scheme. The opening of this course in a region of lakes and one of the most picturesque in eastern Germany was quite an event, even more so considering the scope of the project. There are three 18-hole courses: a par 67 much appreciated by younger and new golfers, a par 72 (Westplatz) rather similar in style to a links course and ideal for average golfers to hone their skills, and this one, the most challenging layout where you will need to be on top of your game. Water comes into play on about ten holes and the very many sand-traps, including some deep pot-bunkers, also tend to complicate matters. Stan Eby has done another good job, smoothly combining easy, not so easy and downright difficult holes throughout a very forthright layout which cleverly blends American style golf with a definite British influence. Having said that, you will need some good old "target golf" shots to hit most of the greens. One of Germany's best golfing resorts which can only get better.

Golf & Country Club Fleesensee - Schlossplatz — 2000

Tanneweg 1
D - 17213 GÖHREN-LEBBIN

Office	Sekretariat	(49) 039932 - 80 400
Pro shop	Pro shop	(49) 039932 -204 033
Fax	Fax	(49) 039932 -804 020
Web	www.golfclub-fleesensee.de	
Situation	Lage Malchow (pop. 8 000), 5 km	
Annual closure	Jährliche Schliessung	no
Weekly closure	Wöchentliche Schliessung	no

Fees main season Preisliste hochsaison	18 holes	
	Week days Woche	**We/Bank holidays** We/Feiertag
Individual Individuell	51 €	51 €
Couple Ehepaar	102 €	102 €

Under 16 and Students under 28: – 50%

Caddy	Caddy	no
Electric Trolley	Elektrokarren	13 € /18 holes
Buggy	Elektrischer Wagen	26 € /18 holes
Clubs	Leihschläger	15 € /18 holes

Credit cards Kreditkarten
VISA - Eurocard - AMEX

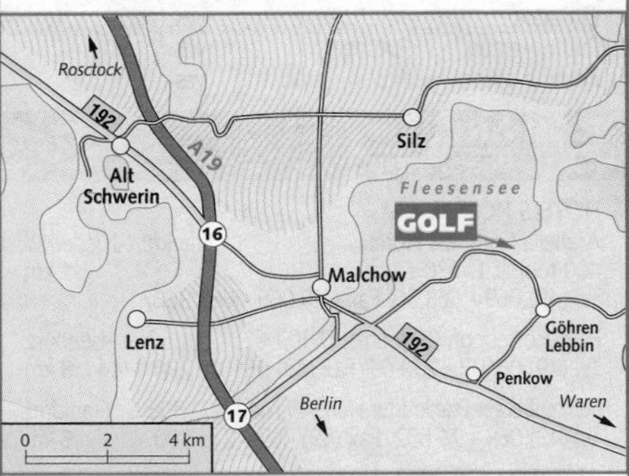

Access Zufahrt : Berlin, A24 → Hamburg. Exit 20, then A19 → Rostock. Exit 17 to Malchow. B192 → Sietow. Golf on left hand side close to Göhren-Lebbin.
Map 7 on page 367 Karte 7 Seite 367

Golf course PLATZ — 17/20

Site	Lage	
Maintenance	Instandhaltung	
Architect	Architekt	Stan Eby PGA European Tour
Type	Typ	parkland, links
Relief	Begehbarkeit	
Water in play	Platz mit Wasser	
Exp. to wind	Wind ausgesetzt	
Trees in play	Platz mit Bäumen	

Scorecard Scorekarte	**Chp.** Chp.	**Mens** Herren	**Ladies** Damen
Length Länge	6335	5919	4877
Par	72	72	72
Slope system	130	126	122

Advised golfing ability Empfohlene Spielstärke — 0 12 24 36
Hcp required Min. Handicap — no

Club house & amenities KLUBHAUS UND NEBENGEBÄUDE — 8/10

Pro shop	Pro shop	
Driving range	Übungsplatz	
Sheltered	überdacht	90 mats, some heated
On grass	auf Rasen	yes
Putting-green	Putting-grün	yes
Pitching-green	Pitching-grün	yes

Hotel facilities HOTEL BESCHREIBUNG — 8/10

HOTELS HOTELS

SAS Radisson Schl. Fleesensee, 184 rooms, D 153 € on site
Tel (49) 039932 - 80 100, Fax (49) 039932-80108010

Robinson Club, 201 rooms, D 237 € — on site
Tel (49) 039932 - 80 200, Fax (49) 039932-8020 100

Dorfhotel, 193 rooms, Apartments 102 € — on site
Tel (49) 039932 - 80 300

RESTAURANTS RESTAURANT

Müritz-Terrasse, Tel (49) 039931 - 8910 — Röbel 15 km
Seestern, Tel (49) 039931 - 58 030 — Röbel 15 km
Reusenhaus, Tel (49) 039931 -666 897 — Waren 15 km

FRANKFURTER GC

17	7	8

Viele Jahre zählte Frankfurt zu den Plätzen, die bis 1989 gut genug waren, die German Open neunmal auszutragen. Doch fehlt dem Platz die Länge, um heute die Longhitter unter den Tourspielern zu testen... Nichtsdestoweniger ist das Spiel auf diesem wunderschön gelegenen Platz ein reines Vergnügen, auch wenn der nahe Flughafen etwas störend wirkt. Das Layout der leicht hügeligen Anlage ist typisch britisch. Kein Wunder, trägt der Platz doch die Handschrift von Colt und Morrison, die Qualität und hohes technisches Können garantiert, was auch in der im Spielverlauf allmählich spürbaren Steigerung der an den Golfer gestellten Anforderungen zum Ausdruck kommt. Durchschnittliche Spieler werden ihren Spass haben, während die besseren Spieler in guter Form sein müssen, um ein für sie gutes Ergebnis zu erzielen. Der Platz erfordert gerade Schläge ebenso wie die Beherrschung unterschiedlicher Ball-Flugkurven, um die vielen Bäumen vermeiden bzw. um diese herumspielen zu können. Die Grüns sind gut geformt, von mittlerer Grösse und gut verteidigt ohne unzugänglich zu sein.

For many a year this was one of the great courses used for the German Open, but nowadays the course is too short to test the long-hitting tour players. Nevertheless, the Frankfurter is a real joy to play for the beauty of its setting, despite the airport being a shade too close for comfort. The layout is sometimes hilly, but never excessively so. It is plainly very British in style, and the Colt and Morrison label is a guarantee of quality and technical skill, with the course gradually getting harder geared to the golfer's ability. Average players will have fun, the better players will need to be on their toes to card a good score. Here, of course, you have to play straight and sometimes flight the ball to avoid, or escape from, the many trees. The greens are well-contoured, medium-sized and reasonably well-protected, although never inaccessible. Since the top soil is sand, the course drains very well and can be played even after heavy rainfall.

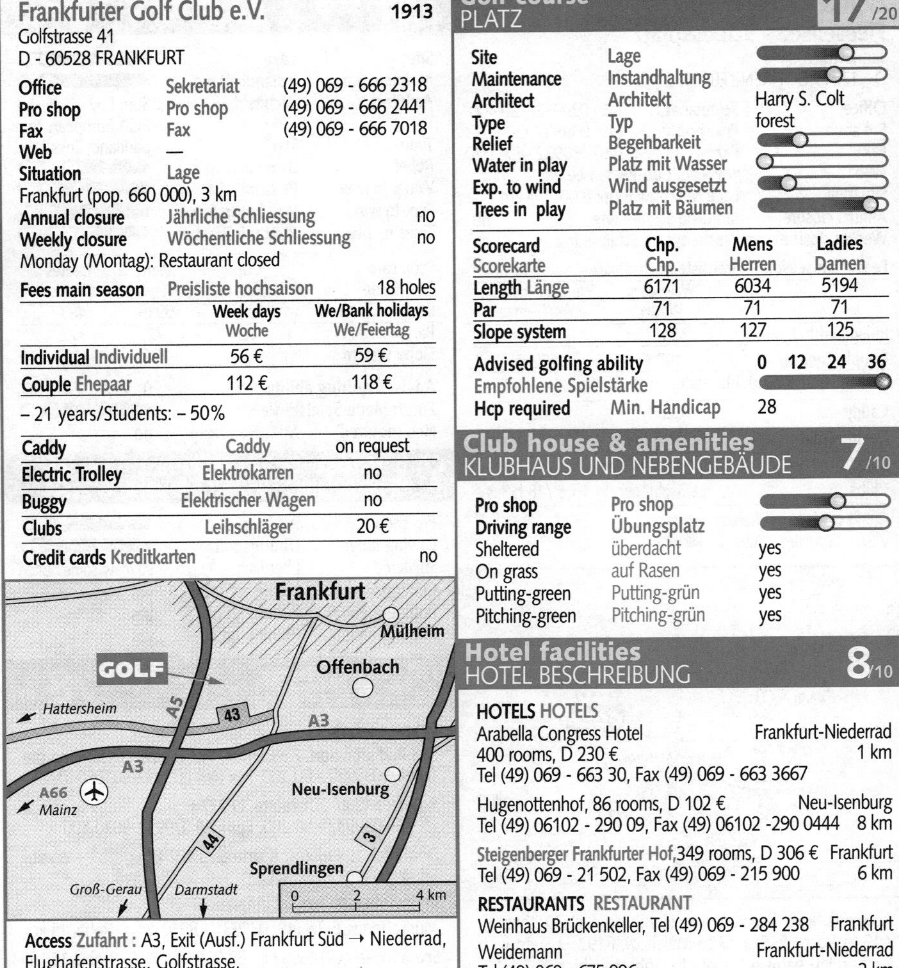

Frankfurter Golf Club e.V. — 1913

Golfstrasse 41
D - 60528 FRANKFURT

Office	Sekretariat	(49) 069 - 666 2318
Pro shop	Pro shop	(49) 069 - 666 2441
Fax	Fax	(49) 069 - 666 7018
Web	—	
Situation	Lage	

Frankfurt (pop. 660 000), 3 km

Annual closure	Jährliche Schliessung	no
Weekly closure	Wöchentliche Schliessung	no

Monday (Montag): Restaurant closed

Fees main season Preisliste hochsaison — 18 holes

	Week days Woche	We/Bank holidays We/Feiertag
Individual Individuell	56 €	59 €
Couple Ehepaar	112 €	118 €

– 21 years/Students: – 50%

Caddy	Caddy	on request
Electric Trolley	Elektrokarren	no
Buggy	Elektrischer Wagen	no
Clubs	Leihschläger	20 €
Credit cards Kreditkarten		no

Access Zufahrt : A3, Exit (Ausf.) Frankfurt Süd → Niederrad, Flughafenstrasse, Golfstrasse.
Map 3 on page 359 Karte 3 Seite 359

Golf course PLATZ — 17/20

Site	Lage	
Maintenance	Instandhaltung	
Architect	Architekt	Harry S. Colt
Type	Typ	forest
Relief	Begehbarkeit	
Water in play	Platz mit Wasser	
Exp. to wind	Wind ausgesetzt	
Trees in play	Platz mit Bäumen	

Scorecard Scorekarte	Chp. Chp.	Mens Herren	Ladies Damen
Length Länge	6171	6034	5194
Par	71	71	71
Slope system	128	127	125

Advised golfing ability Empfohlene Spielstärke — 0 12 24 36

Hcp required Min. Handicap — 28

Club house & amenities KLUBHAUS UND NEBENGEBÄUDE — 7/10

Pro shop	Pro shop	
Driving range	Übungsplatz	
Sheltered	überdacht	yes
On grass	auf Rasen	yes
Putting-green	Putting-grün	yes
Pitching-green	Pitching-grün	yes

Hotel facilities HOTEL BESCHREIBUNG — 8/10

HOTELS HOTELS

Arabella Congress Hotel — Frankfurt-Niederrad
400 rooms, D 230 € — 1 km
Tel (49) 069 - 663 30, Fax (49) 069 - 663 3667

Hugenottenhof, 86 rooms, D 102 € — Neu-Isenburg
Tel (49) 06102 - 290 09, Fax (49) 06102 -290 0444 — 8 km

Steigenberger Frankfurter Hof,349 rooms, D 306 € — Frankfurt
Tel (49) 069 - 21 502, Fax (49) 069 - 215 900 — 6 km

RESTAURANTS RESTAURANT

Weinhaus Brückenkeller, Tel (49) 069 - 284 238 — Frankfurt

Weidemann — Frankfurt-Niederrad
Tel (49) 069 - 675 996 — 2 km

FRÄNKISCHE SCHWEIZ

14	7	6

Die beste Zeit diesen Platz zu spielen ist Ende Frühling, wenn die Apfel- und Kirschbäume in voller Blüte stehen. Seit seiner Erweiterung zur 18-Loch-Anlage ist der GC Fränkische Schweiz, zwischen Nürnberg und Bamberg gelegen, zum beliebten Ziel für Golfer geworden. Die eine Hälfte der Löcher liegt im Wald, die andere in offenerem Gelände, wo auch die längsten Löcher zu finden sind und die Spieler mit langem Drive voll zum Zug kommen. Der Platz ist sehr natürlich angelegt. Wenngleich die Bunker besser modelliert sein könnten, bereiten sie doch auch so den meisten Spielern genug Kopfzerbrechen. Dasselbe gilt auch für die Grüns. Während Gestaltung und Formgebung der Grüns bei älteren Anlagen häufig nicht sehr ausgeprägt ist, hat man sich bei neueren Plätzen in dieser Hinsicht an ein aufwendigeres Design gewöhnt. Zusammenfassend können wir sagen, dass dieser Platz einen recht ausgewogenen Eindruck macht, angenehm zu spielen ist und Golfern aller Spielstärken entgegenkommt. Die Fränkische Schweiz ist zudem eine sehr reizvolle Gegend.

The best season to play here is in late spring, when the apple- and cherry-trees are in blossom. Between Nürnberg and Bamberg, this has been a traditional stop-off for golfers since it was enhanced to 18-hole status in 1989. Half the holes run through the woods, the other half in more open country, where the holes are longer and big-hitters can open their shoulders. The layout is very natural, and while we might have hoped for better contoured bunkers, there is no denying that they do pose a considerable problem for most players. The same observation applies to the greens; while older greens were often a little less elaborate, recent courses have accustomed us to a little more research. With that said, this is a very pleasant and friendly course for players of all levels, and it is well-balanced throughout. Fränkische Schweiz is also a very pretty region...

Golf-Club Fränkische Schweiz e.V. — 1974

Kanndorf 8
D - 91320 EBERMANNSTADT

Office	Sekretariat	(49) 09194 - 4827
Pro shop	Pro shop	(49) 09194 - 4827
Fax	Fax	(49) 09194 - 5410
Web	—	
Situation	Lage	

Nürnberg (pop. 498 000), 45 km - Bamberg, 35 km

Annual closure	Jährliche Schliessung	no
Weekly closure	Wöchentliche Schliessung	no

Fees main season Preisliste hochsaison	Full day	
	Week days Woche	**We/Bank holidays** We/Feiertag
Individual Individuell	31 €	41 €
Couple Ehepaar	62 €	82 €

– 21 years, Students: – 50%

Caddy	Caddy	no
Electric Trolley	Elektrokarren	no
Buggy	Elektrischer Wagen	no
Clubs	Leihschläger	yes
Credit cards	Kreditkarten	no

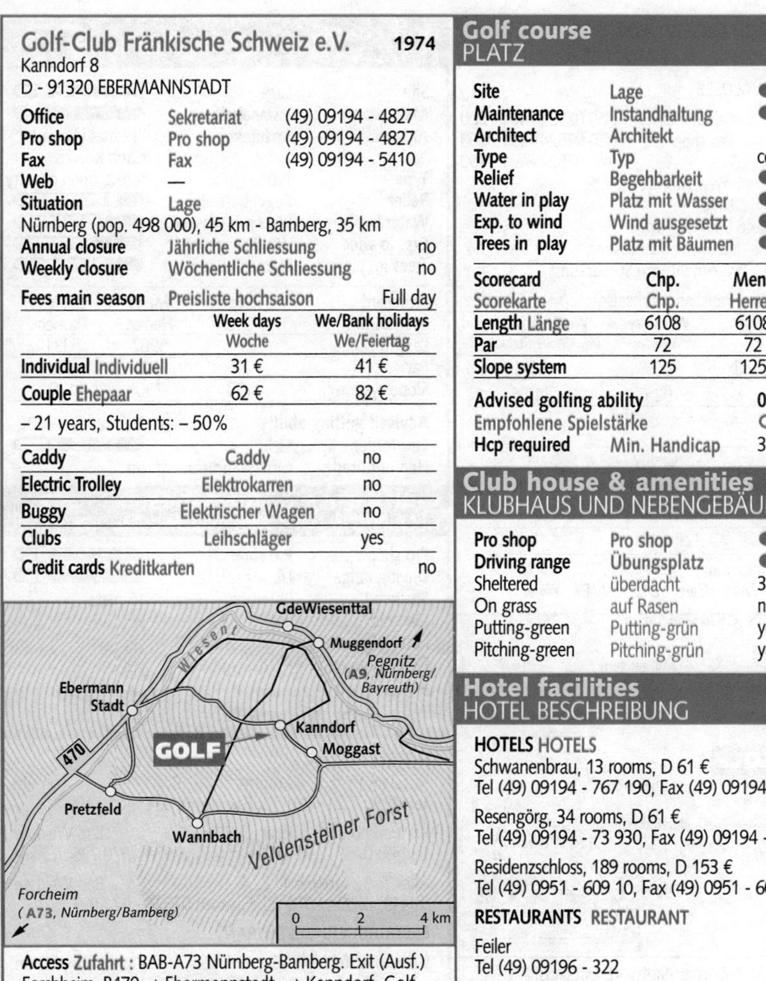

Access Zufahrt : BAB-A73 Nürnberg-Bamberg. Exit (Ausf.) Forchheim. B470 → Ebermannstadt. → Kanndorf, Golf
Map 4 on page 360 Karte 4 Seite 360

Golf course PLATZ — 14/20

Site	Lage	
Maintenance	Instandhaltung	
Architect	Architekt	
Type	Typ	country, forest
Relief	Begehbarkeit	
Water in play	Platz mit Wasser	
Exp. to wind	Wind ausgesetzt	
Trees in play	Platz mit Bäumen	

Scorecard Scorekarte	**Chp.** Chp.	**Mens** Herren	**Ladies** Damen
Length Länge	6108	6108	5375
Par	72	72	72
Slope system	125	125	127

Advised golfing ability Empfohlene Spielstärke — 0 12 24 36
Hcp required Min. Handicap 35

Club house & amenities KLUBHAUS UND NEBENGEBÄUDE — 7/10

Pro shop	Pro shop	
Driving range	Übungsplatz	
Sheltered	überdacht	3 mats
On grass	auf Rasen	no, 10 mats open air
Putting-green	Putting-grün	yes
Pitching-green	Pitching-grün	yes

Hotel facilities HOTEL BESCHREIBUNG — 6/10

HOTELS HOTELS

Schwanenbrau, 13 rooms, D 61 € — Ebermannstadt
Tel (49) 09194 - 767 190, Fax (49) 09194 - 5836 — 2 km

Resengörg, 34 rooms, D 61 € — Ebermannstadt
Tel (49) 09194 - 73 930, Fax (49) 09194 - 739 373

Residenzschloss, 189 rooms, D 153 € — Bamberg
Tel (49) 0951 - 609 10, Fax (49) 0951 - 609 1701 — 35 km

RESTAURANTS RESTAURANT

Feiler — Muggendorf
Tel (49) 09196 - 322 — 4 km

Bierbrunnen — Ebermannstadt
Tel (49) 09194 - 5865 — 5 km

FÜRSTLICHER GC BAD WALDSEE

17	7	8

Dieser 1998 eröffnete Platz liegt nur 50 m vom wesentlich älteren Golf Club Oberschwaben entfernt, den man mit einem Lobwedge über die Bäume leicht erreichen könnte. Doch der neue Platz ist um vieles reizvoller als der alte Nachbarplatz. Der Platz liegt herrlich eingebettet in einer Waldlandschaft. Die dreimalige deutsche Amateurmeister Thomas Himmel und der Pro Carlo Knauss entwarfen den 18-Loch-Platz. Es ist das erste gemeinsame Werk dieser beiden, und es ist ihnen bestens gelungen. Sie haben dem modernen Trend zu immer mehr Länge widerstanden und betonen statt dessen die Werte von intelligentem und strategischem Golf : easy bogey, tough par. Höhepunkt der Runde sind die Löcher 12 bis 16, die sich um einen riesigen ehemaligen Baggersee schlängeln. Da auch noch ein Hotel direkt am Platz liegt, ist Waldsee ideal für einen Kurzurlaub.

You only need a lobwedge over the trees to reach the neighbouring course of the older GC Oberschwaben, located only 50 metres from this course opened in 1998. But in spite of its youth it is better than the old neighbor. The course is beautifully integrated in a wonderful forest. Three-time German Amateur champion Thomas Himmel and Pro Carlo Knauss collaborated on this course for the first time, and they really got it right the first time. Himmel and Knauss resisted the modern trend to extreme length but stress intelligent and strategic golf: easy bogey, tough par. Highlight of the round are the holes 12 through 16 which meander around a flooded gravel pit. With a wonderful hotel on the site Waldsee is an ideal setting for a short break from daily hum-drum.

Fürstlicher Golfclub Bad Waldsee e.V. 1998

Hopfenweiler 14
D - 88339 BAD WALDSEE

Office	Sekretariat	(49) 07524 -401 7200
Pro shop	Pro shop	(49) 07524 -401 7200
Fax	Fax	(49) 07524 -401 7100
Web	www.waldsee-golf.de	
Situation	Lage	

Ravensburg (pop. 46 000), 24 km

Annual closure	Jährliche Schliessung	no
Weekly closure	Wöchentliche Schliessung	no

Fees main season Preisliste hochsaison	18 holes	
	Week days Woche	**We/Bank holidays** We/Feiertag
Individual Individuell	46 €	56 €
Couple Ehepaar	92 €	112 €

Softspikes mandatory

Caddy	Caddy	no
Electric Trolley	Elektrokarren	13 €
Buggy	Elektrischer Wagen	20 €
Clubs	Leihschläger	10 €

Credit cards Kreditkarten
VISA - Eurocard - MasterCard - DC - AMEX

Access Zufahrt : A8 München-Stuttgart. Exit (Ausf.) Ulm-West. B30 → Bodensee. Bad Waldsee → Golf

Map 1 on page 355 Karte 1 Seite 355

Golf course PLATZ — 17/20

Site	Lage	
Maintenance	Instandhaltung	
Architect	Architekt	Thomas Himmel Carlo Knauss
Type	Typ	forest, open country
Relief	Begehbarkeit	
Water in play	Platz mit Wasser	
Exp. to wind	Wind ausgesetzt	
Trees in play	Platz mit Bäumen	

Scorecard Scorekarte	**Chp.** Chp.	**Mens** Herren	**Ladies** Damen
Length Länge	6415	5982	5231
Par	72	72	72
Slope system	130	130	129

Advised golfing ability Empfohlene Spielstärke — 0 12 24 36

Hcp required Min. Handicap — no

Club house & amenities KLUBHAUS UND NEBENGEBÄUDE — 7/10

Pro shop	Pro shop	
Driving range	Übungsplatz	
Sheltered	überdacht	15 mats
On grass	auf Rasen	yes
Putting-green	Putting-grün	yes
Pitching-green	Pitching-grün	yes

Hotel facilities HOTEL BESCHREIBUNG — 8/10

HOTELS HOTELS

Hotel im Hofgut, 40 rooms, D 107 € — on site
Tel (49) 07524 - 401 70, Fax (49) 07524 -401 7100

Kur-Parkhotel, 54 rooms, D 92 € — Bad Waldsee
Tel (49) 07524 - 97 070, Fax (49) 07524 - 970 775 — 2 km

Altes Tor, 27 rooms, D 82 € — Bad Waldsee
Tel (49) 07524 - 971 90, Fax (49) 07524 - 971 997

RESTAURANTS RESTAURANT

Waldhorn, Tel (49) 0751 - 36 120 — Ravensburg 20 km

Krone, Tel (49) 07529 - 1292 — Schlier 25 km

FÜRSTLICHES HOFGUT KOLNHAUSEN 14 7 6

Der Architekt Heinz Fehring wurde stark vom amerikanischen Stil beeinflusst, obwohl die vier nahe beim Clubhaus gelegenen Löcher sich deutlich von den restlichen Spielbahnen unterscheiden. Dies war auch nicht anders zu erwarten, angesichts der Tatsache, dass Bäume kaum ins Spiel kommen und Wasserhindernisse, neben dem Wind natürlich, die Hauptschwierigkeiten dieses Platzes bilden. Daher kam ein "natürlicher" Platz von vornherein gar nicht in Frage. Um mit dem Platz gleich beim ersten Mal zurechtzukommen, empfiehlt es sich, sich eine Birdiekarte (Yardage Book) mitzunehmen, da weder die Spielstrategie deutlich vorgegeben, noch ein Grossteil der Hindernisse vom Abschlag aus erkennbar ist - es gibt sogar fünf blinde Löcher. Das schlimmste und einzig vollkommen misslungene Loch ist das 10. Loch, wo man vor lauter Wasser gar nicht weiss, wo man den Abschlag plazieren soll. Glücklicherweise sind die grösstenteils gut gestalteten Grüns wenigstens voll einsehbar. Allen Durchschnittsgolfern empfehlen wir, von den vorderen Abschlägen zu spielen. Einstellige Golfer sollten jedoch auf die Meisterschaftsabschläge gehen...

Designer Heinz Fehring was visibly influenced by the US style of course, even though the four holes close to the clubhouse are rather different from the rest. It could hardly be otherwise, when trees are hardly ever in play and when water hazards provide the main difficulties (with the wind, of course). There was no question of making this a natural course. First time out, you are best advised to take the yardage book with you to get your bearings. Nothing is obvious, not even the hazards are visible and there are, after all, five blind holes. The worst and only really bad hole is the 10th, where water is everywhere and you have no clue where to place your drive. Fortunately, the greens are in view and by and large they are well designed. We would recommend the front tees for all average players, single figure handicapper can use the championship tees.

Golf- und Land-Club Fürstliches Hofgut Kolnhausen e.V. 1992

D - 35423 LICH

Office	Sekretariat	(49) 06404 - 910 710
Pro shop	Pro shop	(49) 06404 - 910 753
Fax	Fax	(49) 06404 - 910 72
E-mail	licher-golf-club@t-online.de	
Situation	Lage	

Giessen, 15 km - Frankfurt (pop. 660 000), 55 km

Annual closure	Jährliche Schliessung	no
Weekly closure	Wöchentliche Schliessung	no

Monday (Montag): Restaurant closed

Fees main season Preisliste hochsaison	**Week days** Woche	**We/Bank holidays** We/Feiertag
		18 holes
Individual Individuell	41 €	51 €
Couple Ehepaar	82 €	102 €

– 21 years/Students: – 50%

Caddy	Caddy	26 €
Electric Trolley	Elektrokarren	15 €
Buggy	Elektrischer Wagen	no
Clubs	Leihschläger	15 €
Credit cards	Kreditkarten	no

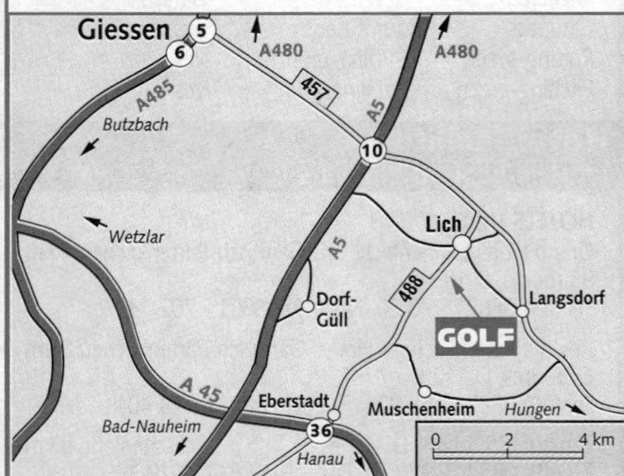

Access Zufahrt : A5 Frankfurt-Kassel. Kambacher Kreuz, A45 → Hanau. Exit (Ausf.) Münzenberg/Lich. → Lich, Golf 5 km.

Map 3 on page 359 Karte 3 Seite 359

Golf course PLATZ 14/20

Site	Lage	
Maintenance	Instandhaltung	
Architect	Architekt	Heinz Fehring
Type	Typ	open country
Relief	Begehbarkeit	
Water in play	Platz mit Wasser	
Exp. to wind	Wind ausgesetzt	
Trees in play	Platz mit Bäumen	

Scorecard Scorekarte	**Chp.** Chp.	**Mens** Herren	**Ladies** Damen
Length Länge	6378	6023	5221
Par	73	72	73
Slope system	124	124	119

Advised golfing ability 0 12 24 36
Empfohlene Spielstärke

Hcp required Min. Handicap 36

Club house & amenities KLUBHAUS UND NEBENGEBÄUDE 7/10

Pro shop	Pro shop	
Driving range	Übungsplatz	
Sheltered	überdacht	6 mats
On grass	auf Rasen	yes
Putting-green	Putting-grün	yes
Pitching-green	Pitching-grün	yes

Hotel facilities HOTEL BESCHREIBUNG 6/10

HOTELS HOTELS

Landhaus Klosterwald, 18 rooms, D 87 € — Lich
Tel (49) 06404 - 91 010, Fax (49) 06404 - 910 134 — 1 km

Alte Klostermühle, 26 rooms, D 97 € — Lich
Tel (49) 06404 - 91 900, Fax (49) 06404 - 919 091

Tandreas, 32 rooms, D 102 € — Giessen
Tel (49) 0641 - 940 70, Fax (49) 0641 - 940 7499 — 20 km

Steinsgarten, 126 rooms, D 128 € — Giessen
Tel (49) 0641 - 38 990, Fax (49) 0641 - 3899 200 — 15 km

RESTAURANTS RESTAURANT

Zum Stern — Butzbach
Tel (49) 06033 - 7977 — 20 km

GARMISCH-PARTENKIRCHEN

14	6	7

In unmittelbarer Nähe zu einem der bekanntesten Winter- und Sommersportorte Europas gelegen, verläuft dieser Platz auf so ebenem Terrain, dass man ihn als Flachland-Platz inmitten einer Alpin-Region bezeichnen kann. Der Platz ist daher auch mühelos zu bewältigen. Trotz der schwierigen Witterungsbedingungen - lange kalte Winter, heisse Sommer - macht der Platz einen sehr gepflegten Eindruck. Um auf diesem Platz gut zu spielen, sollte man nicht allzu sehr streuen, da die Fairways, eingegrenzt durch Bäume, Büsche und Felsen, recht schmal sind. Die Tücken dieses Platzes, der deutlich zu erkennende Hindernisse hat, sind eher psychologischer denn realer Natur. Spieler, die den Ball gerade schlagen, werden die Runde geniessen. Dasselbe gilt für Spieler mit mittlerem Handicap sowie jene, denen es an Länge fehlt. Das 'persönliche Par' ist immer möglich. Einen zusätzlichen Anreiz dieses Ortes bietet das ausgezeichnete Restaurant im Clubhaus mit seiner typisch bayerischen Atmosphäre, in dem man einen schönen Golftag ausklingen lassen sollte.

Very close to one of Europe's most celebrated winter and summer resorts, this course is flat enough to be considered a lowland course transposed to the mountains. You can play it tirelessly. Green-keeping is very decent, given the length of the winters and the hot summers, but this is not a course we would recommend to wild hitters: the fairways are tight and guarded by trees, bushes and rocks. The dangers here are perhaps more psychological than real (hazards are clearly visible) and straight players will enjoy their round. The same might apply to mid-handicappers and players lacking length. On most holes you can play your "personal par" (with handicap strokes). To enjoy your day to the full, pop inside the very country-style club-house and enjoy the excellent restaurant and typically Bavarian atmosphere. It is a great bonus for an excellent site.

Golf-Club Garmisch-Partenkirchen e.V. 1928

Gut Buchwies
D - 82496 OBERAU

Office	Sekretariat	(49) 08824 - 8344
Pro shop	Pro shop	(49) 08824 - 1679
Fax	Fax	(49) 08824 - 325
Web	www.golf.de/garmisch-partenkirchen	
Situation	Lage	München, 81 km
Annual closure	Jährliche Schliessung	1/12→31/3
Weekly closure	Wöchentliche Schliessung	no

Monday (Montag): Restaurant closed

Fees main season Preisliste hochsaison	Week days Woche	We/Bank holidays We/Feiertag
		full day
Individual Individuell	41 €	51 €
Couple Ehepaar	82 €	102 €

– 21 years/Students: – 50%

Caddy	Caddy	on request
Electric Trolley	Elektrokarren	no
Buggy	Elektrischer Wagen	no
Clubs	Leihschläger	10 €

Credit cards Kreditkarten AMEX

Access Zufahrt : A95 and B2 München → Garmisch-Partenkirchen. Exit (Ausf.) Oberau. Left over the Loisach → Gut Buchwies, Golf
Map 2 on page 356 Karte 2 Seite 356

Golf course PLATZ — 14/20

Site	Lage	
Maintenance	Instandhaltung	
Architect	Architekt	unknown
Type	Typ	parkland
Relief	Begehbarkeit	
Water in play	Platz mit Wasser	
Exp. to wind	Wind ausgesetzt	
Trees in play	Platz mit Bäumen	

Scorecard Scorekarte	Chp. Chp.	Mens Herren	Ladies Damen
Length Länge	6093	5893	5140
Par	72	72	72
Slope system	125	122	124

Advised golfing ability Empfohlene Spielstärke — 0 12 24 36
Hcp required Min. Handicap — no

Club house & amenities KLUBHAUS UND NEBENGEBÄUDE — 6/10

Pro shop	Pro shop	
Driving range	Übungsplatz	
Sheltered	überdacht	8 mats
On grass	auf Rasen	yes
Putting-green	Putting-grün	yes
Pitching-green	Pitching-grün	yes

Hotel facilities HOTEL BESCHREIBUNG — 7/10

HOTELS HOTELS

Grand Hotel Sonnenbichl — Garmisch-Partenkirchen 7 km
93 rooms, D 153 €
Tel (49) 08821 - 70 20, Fax (49) 08821 - 702 131

Reindl's Partenkirchner Hof — Garmisch-Partenkirchen 8 km
65 rooms, D 112 €
Tel (49) 08821 - 58 025, Fax (49) 08821 - 73 401

Tonihof, 25 rooms, D 107 € — Eschenlohe 5 km
Tel (49) 08824 - 929 30, Fax (49) 08824 - 929 399

RESTAURANTS RESTAURANT

Husar, Tel (49) 08821 - 1713 — Garmisch-Partenkirchen 8 km

Alpenhof, Tel (49) 08821 - 59 055 — Garmisch-Partenkirchen

GUT GRAMBEK

16 | 7 | 6

Gut Grambek liegt östlich von Hamburg im Naturpark Lauenburgische See inmitten einer für Holstein typischen Landschaft. Das alte Bauernhaus wurde in das heimelige Clubhaus umfunktioniert. Der Parkland-Platz ist relativ flach mit Sandboden, der sich für Golfplätze besser eignet als für Landwirtschaft. Der 1981 eröffnete Platz ist über die Jahre gereift. Durch ständige Verbesserungen gehört er nun zu den besten Plätzen der Region. Der Platz ist kurz, aber dadurch selbst für niedrige Handicaps nicht leicht, da man den Weg durch Wälder, Bunkder, Büschen und Rough finden muss, die jeden Ball, der vom geraden Weg abkommt, verschlucken. Dies gilt selbstverständlich auch für die vielen Wasserhindernisse. Auf diesem Platz ist Präzision gefragt. Wer den Ball mit Draw spielen kann, hat deutliche Vorteile. Ein Platz, den es lohnt, zu spielen.

To the east of Hamburg, Gut Grambek lies in the nature park of Lauenburgische Seen amidst landscapes that are typical of the Holstein countryside. The club-house actually uses the buildings of an old farmhouse. The large park's landscape is rather flat with sandy soil, which makes it better for golfing than for growing crops. Opened in 1981, the course has gradually matured by dint of constant improvement schemes and now deserves to rate amongst the region's best. It could be criticised for its lack of yardage, but this does not make it any easier to play, especially for low-handicappers, who have to pick their way through woods, bunkers, bushes and rough, that are all waiting to snap up the slightly wayward shot, not to mention the rather substantial number of water hazards. Here, accuracy is at a premium, with the ability to draw the ball an added bonus. Well worth playing.

Golf-Club Gut Grambek e.V. — 1981

Schlossstrasse 21
D - 23883 GRAMBEK/MÖLLN

Office	Sekretariat	(49) 04542 - 841 474
Pro shop	Pro shop	(49) 04542 - 841 475
Fax	Fax	(49) 04542 - 841 476
Web	gc.gut.grambek	
Situation	Lage	Mölln (pop. 17 000), 5 km
Annual closure	Jährliche Schliessung	no
Weekly closure	Wöchentliche Schliessung	no

Fees main season Preisliste hochsaison	Week days Woche	We/Bank holidays We/Feiertag
	18 holes	
Individual Individuell	21 €	41 €
Couple Ehepaar	42 €	82 €

Juniors, Students: – 50%

Caddy	Caddy	no
Electric Trolley	Elektrokarren	no
Buggy	Elektrischer Wagen	no
Clubs	Leihschläger	yes

Credit cards Kreditkarten
VISA - Eurocard - MasterCard

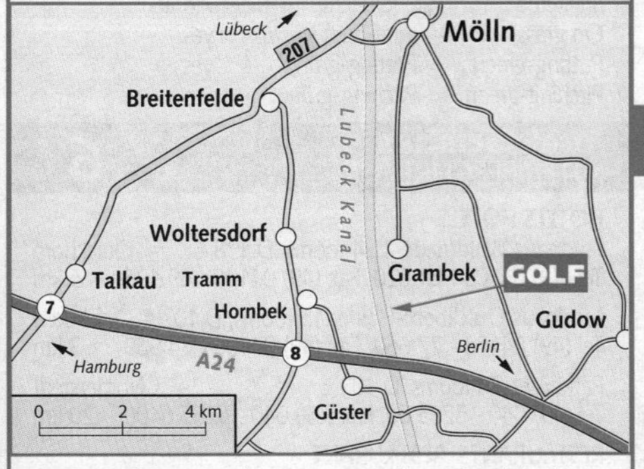

Access Zufahrt : Hamburg, E24 → Berlin. Exit 7 (Ausfahrt 7) Talkau, then B207 → Mölln. Exit Alt Mölln → Mölln. After the bridge over Elbe channel, turn right → Grambek, → Golf. **Map 7 on page 367** Karte 7 Seite 367

Golf course — PLATZ — 16/20

Site	Lage	
Maintenance	Instandhaltung	
Architect	Architekt	Unknown
Type	Typ	pakland
Relief	Begehbarkeit	
Water in play	Platz mit Wasser	
Exp. to wind	Wind ausgesetzt	
Trees in play	Platz mit Bäumen	

Scorecard Scorekarte	Chp. Chp.	Mens Herren	Ladies Damen
Length Länge	5877	5877	5174
Par	71	71	71
Slope system	129	129	126

Advised golfing ability Empfohlene Spielstärke — 0 12 24 36

Hcp required — Min. Handicap — 36

Club house & amenities — KLUBHAUS UND NEBENGEBÄUDE — 7/10

Pro shop	Pro shop	
Driving range	Übungsplatz	
Sheltered	überdacht	3 mats
On grass	auf Rasen	yes
Putting-green	Putting-grün	yes
Pitching-green	Pitching-grün	yes

Hotel facilities — HOTEL BESCHREIBUNG — 6/10

HOTELS HOTELS

Schwanenhof, 31 rooms, D 97 € — Mölln
Tel (49) 04542 - 848 30, Fax (49) 04542 - 848 383 — 7 km

Quellenhof, 18 rooms, D 87 € — Mölln
Tel (49) 04542 - 30 28, Fax (49) 04542 - 72 26

Beim Wasserkrüger, 21 rooms, D 58 € — Mölln
Tel (49) 04542 - 70 91, Fax (49) 04542 - 18 11

RESTAURANTS RESTAURANT

Historischer Ratskeller — Mölln
Tel (49) 04542 - 835 575

GUT KADEN B+C

15	7	6

Der Turnierplatz (B + C) besteht aus 9 der 18 ursprünglichen Bahnen, sowie weiteren 9 Löchern, die 1993 fertiggestellt wurden. Der schöne A-Platz eignet sich für Spieler mit höherem Handicap. Dank der vorhandenen ‹bungseinrichtungen (dazu gehören Indoor Driving Range und Putting Grün) zählt Gut Kaden zu den Anlagen gehobener Klasse. Der Fluss Pinnau durchquert das bei Nässe sehr gut abtrocknende Golfgelände, auf dem es sich zudem sehr angenehm läuft. Der Platz liegt ziemlich offen und ist gespickt mit vielen Wasserhindernissen (6 Löcher mit frontalem Wasser) sowie einer beträchtlichen Anzahl geschickt positionierter Bunker. Diese vielfältigen Gefahren sind jedoch gut erkennbar, so dass ein einziger Besuch genügt, den klug angelegten Spielbahnverlauf schätzen zu lernen, was allerdings nicht als Garantie für einen guten Score misszuverstehen ist. Die richtige Schlägerwahl ist hier ausschlaggebend, besonders beim Anspiel der grossflächigen Grüns, die teilweise auf mehreren Stufen angelegt und sehr gut verteidigt sind. Gutes Putten ist gefragt auf diesem Platz, den man spielen sollte, wenn man in der Nähe ist.

The championship course (B + C) is formed from 9 of the original 18 holes and from a further 9 holer completed in 1993. The pretty A course is more suitable for higher-handicappers. Gut Kaden as a whole is a class set-up, thanks in particular to the practice facilities (which include an indoor driving range and putting-green). Crossed by the river Pinnau, this is an estate that drains well and is pleasant to walk. The course is rather open and brings a large number of water hazards into play (6 holes feature frontal water) plus a considerable number of very well-sited bunkers. But these manifold hazards are clearly visible and a single visit is enough for a player to appreciate the intelligent design, if not to guarantee a good score. Here, the choice of club is of key importance, especially when approaching the large greens that are sometimes multi-tiered and very well-guarded. Make sure your putting is in good shape.

Gut Kaden Golf und Land Club — 1986

Kadener Strasse 9
D - 25486 ALVESLOHE

Office	Sekretariat	(49) 04193 - 99 290
Pro shop	Pro shop	(49) 04193 - 99 290
Fax	Fax	(49) 04193 - 992 919
Web	—	
Situation	Lage	

Quickborn, 5 km - Norderstedt (pop. 70 500), 10 km

Annual closure	Jährliche Schliessung	no
Weekly closure	Wöchentliche Schliessung	no
Fees main season	Preisliste hochsaison	18 holes

	Week days / Woche	We/Bank holidays / We/Feiertag
Individual Individuell	41 €	51 €
Couple Ehepaar	82 €	102 €

Monday (Montag): 20 €/– 21 years: – 50%

Caddy	Caddy	no
Electric Trolley	Elektrokarren	no
Buggy	Elektrischer Wagen	no
Clubs	Leihschläger	no
Credit cards	Kreditkarten	no

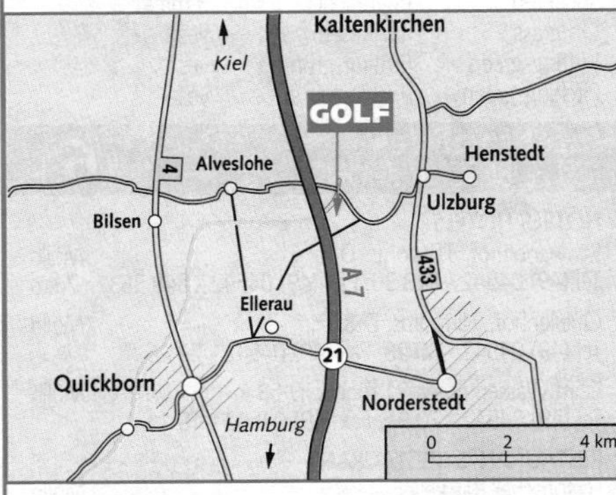

Access Zufahrt : A7 Hamburg-Kiel. Exit (Ausfahrt) Quickborn. Left → Ellerau, Kaltenkirchen. Right → Alveslohe.
Map 7 on page 366 Karte 7 Seite 366

Golf course PLATZ — 15/20

Site	Lage	
Maintenance	Instandhaltung	
Architect	Architekt	Frank Pennink (A+B) Karl F. Grohs (C)
Type	Typ	open country
Relief	Begehbarkeit	
Water in play	Platz mit Wasser	
Exp. to wind	Wind ausgesetzt	
Trees in play	Platz mit Bäumen	

Scorecard Scorekarte	Chp. Chp.	Mens Herren	Ladies Damen
Length Länge	6449	5955	5185
Par	72	72	72
Slope system	123	123	125

Advised golfing ability Empfohlene Spielstärke: 0 12 24 36
Hcp required Min. Handicap: 36

Club house & amenities KLUBHAUS UND NEBENGEBÄUDE — 7/10

Pro shop	Pro shop	
Driving range	Übungsplatz	
Sheltered	überdacht	7 mats
On grass	auf Rasen	yes
Putting-green	Putting-grün	yes
Pitching-green	Pitching-grün	yes

Hotel facilities HOTEL BESCHREIBUNG — 6/10

HOTELS HOTELS

Jagdhaus Waldfrieden, 24 rooms, D 138 € — Quickborn
Tel (49) 04106 - 61 020, Fax (49) 04106 - 69 196 — 5 km

Landhaus Quickborn-Heide, 15 rooms, D 102 € — Quickborn
Tel (49) 04106 - 77 660, Fax (49) 04106 - 74 969 — 3 km

Parkhotel, 78 rooms, D 102 € — Norderstedt
Tel (49) 040 - 5265 60, Fax (49) 040 - 5265 6400 — 20 km

RESTAURANTS RESTAURANT

Jagdhaus Waldfrieden — Quickborn
Tel (49) 04106 - 3771 — 5 km

Restaurant Scheelke — Henstedt-Ulzburg
Tel (49) 04193 - 2207 — 4 km

GUT LÄRCHENHOF

17	9	7

Man muss amriesigen Tor klingeln, damit man eingelassen werden, man muss sich auf eine saftige Rechnung im Restaurant, das einen Stern im Michelin Guide hat, einstellen (Sparsame können im Bistro speisen) und das teuerste Greenfee in Deutschland bezahlen. Aber das Geld ist gut angelegt: Gut Lärchenhof ist einer der eindrucksvollen neuen Plätze in Deutschland. Der Platz ist ein typisches Beispiel für die Arbeit des Architekten Jack Nicklaus. Wie immer bei Nicklaus findert man ein klares Layout mit sorgfältig angelegten Fairways, strategisch gut platzierten Bunkern, aber auch eine Tendenz alles zu auf kreative Art und Weise zu formen, auch wenn der Platz dann nicht mehr allzu natürlich wirkt oder sich harmonisch in die Landschaft fügt. Nicklaus macht Golf zu einem Spektakel, er entwirft Plätze auf den man den Ball mit unterschiedlichen Flugkurven ins Ziel steueren muss, wo man ein vorzügliches kurzes Spiel und ein guten Touch auf den Grüns haben muss, um einen guten Score zu erzielen. Gut Lärchenhof ist ein moderner Platz im wahrsten Sinne des Wortes, der aber trotzdem selbst für durchschnittliche Golfer gut spielbar ist.

You have to ring a bell to get in here, meet a sizeable bill in the restaurant (boasting a 1 star rating in the Michelin Guide) and pay some of the most expensive green-fees in Germany. But the money is well spend in one of the most prestigious new courses in recent years. It is a typical example of the work of its architect, Jack Nicklaus. Obviously you will discover the very strategic use of water and sandtraps, a crisp and clear design, very carefully laid-out fairways and a lot of emphasis on shaping everything on the course in an imaginative and also sometimes artificial style. Nothing is really very natural here or subtly blended into the natural surroundings. Nicklaus likes to turn golf into a spectacle, making each course a setting where you have to bend balls, possess an immaculately honed short game and a perfect putting stroke to card a score. Gut Lärchenhof is a modern course in every sense of the word, but is playable even by only very average golfers.

Golf Club Gut Lärchenhof — 1997

Hahnenstrasse / Gut Lärchenhof
D - 50259 PULHEIM

Office	Sekretariat	(49) 02238 - 923 900
Pro shop	Pro shop	(49) 02238 - 923 170
Fax	Fax	(49)02238 - 923 9010
Web	—	
Situation	Lage	
Köln (pop. 1 005 000), 20 km		
Annual closure	Jährliche Schliessung	no
Weekly closure	Wöchentliche Schliessung	no

Fees main season Preisliste hochsaison	Week days Woche	We/Bank holidays We/Feiertag
		18 holes
Individual Individuell	92 €	92 € *
Couple Ehepaar	184 €	184 € *

* We: with members (nur in Mitgliederbegleitung)

Caddy	Caddy	no
Electric Trolley	Elektrokarren	no
Buggy	Elektrischer Wagen	26 €
Clubs	Leihschläger	yes

Credit cards Kreditkarten VIS - Eurocard - MasterCard

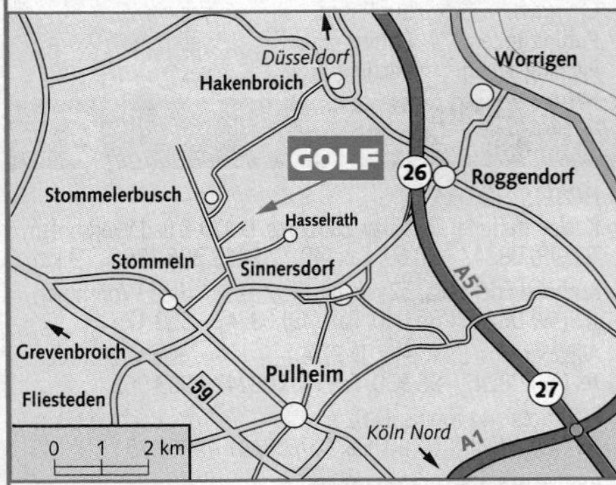

Access Zufahrt : A57, Exit (Ausf.)26 Köln-Worringen, → Simmersdorf, → Stommeln, right → Stommelerbusch. → Gut Lärchenhof
Map 3 on page 358 Karte 3 Seite 358

Golf course PLATZ — 17/20

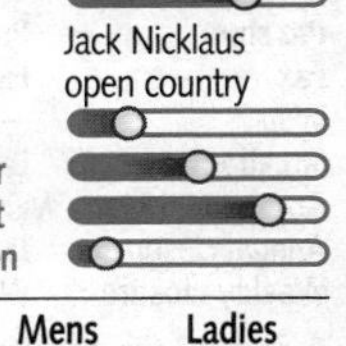

Site	Lage	
Maintenance	Instandhaltung	
Architect	Architekt	Jack Nicklaus
Type	Typ	open country
Relief	Begehbarkeit	
Water in play	Platz mit Wasser	
Exp. to wind	Wind ausgesetzt	
Trees in play	Platz mit Bäumen	

Scorecard Scorekarte	Chp. Chp.	Mens Herren	Ladies Damen
Length Länge	6356	5956	5052
Par	72	72	72
Slope system	132	130	128

Advised golfing ability 0 12 24 36
Empfohlene Spielstärke
Hcp required Min. Handicap 24/28

Club house & amenities KLUBHAUS UND NEBENGEBÄUDE — 9/10

Pro shop	Pro shop	
Driving range	Übungsplatz	
Sheltered	überdacht	7 mats
On grass	auf Rasen	yes
Putting-green	Putting-grün	yes
Pitching-green	Pitching-grün	yes

Hotel facilities HOTEL BESCHREIBUNG — 7/10

HOTELS HOTELS

Ascari, 73 rooms, D 112 € — Pulheim 3 km
Tel (49) 02238 - 80 40, Fax (49) 02238 - 804 140

Königsdorfer Hof, 37 rooms, D 128 € — Frechen 6 km
Tel (49) 02234 - 600 70, Fax (49) 02234 - 600 770

Brauhaus Gäffel, 18 rooms, D 66 € — Stommeln 3 km
Tel (49) 02238 - 2015, Fax (49) 02238 - 3844

RESTAURANTS RESTAURANT

Restaurant Gut Lärchenhof — Golf on site
Tel (49) 02238 - 923 100

Ristorante Ermanno, Tel (49) 02234 - 141 63 — Frechen 6 km

Früh am Dom, Tel (49) 0221 - 50 667 — Köln 20 km

GUT LUDWIGSBERG

15 | 6 | 6

Ein Golfplatz für Sportliche, dessen Clubhaus und Einrichtungen bedauerlicherweise nicht den andernorts üblichen höheren Standards entsprechen. Da die Anlage noch relativ jung ist, bleibt zu hoffen, dass sich dies mit der Zeit ändern wird. Die Lage des Platzes ist eindrucksvoll: An klaren Tagen kann man bis zu 150 km weit sehen, insbesondere Richtung Deutsche Alpenstrasse im Süden, an deren Streckenverlauf von Lindau über Garmisch-Partenkirchen nach Salzburg die verrückten Schlösser Ludwigs II von Bayern einen Besuch lohnen. Architekt Rossknecht hat den weitgehend flachen Parcours mit einer enormen Vielfalt an Hindernissen versehen, wobei alle Arbeiten mit der für ihn üblichen Sorgfalt ausgeführt wurden. Die Grüns sind ausgezeichnet gestaltet, besonders hervorzuheben ist in diesem Zusammenhang das Inselgrün am 18. Loch. Obschon eine harte Nuss von den hinteren Abschlägen, ist der Platz von weiter vorne durchaus für alle Spielstärken geeignet. Zwischen dem 5. und 17. Loch ändert sich der Charakter des Platzes von Parkland hin zu einem eher amerikanischen Stil, wo "target Golf" vom Spieler gefordert wird.

The sporting man's golf course where you might wonder why the clubhouse does not have higher standard facilities. Perhaps they will come in time, as the course is still young. The location is rather remarkable: on a clear day you can see for 150 km, especially toward the Deutsche Alpenstrasse to the south, the road running from Lindau to Garmisch-Partenkirchen and Salzburg, where the crazy castles of Louis II of Bavaria are well worth a visit. The course has been designed on easily walkable terrain, with the usual care associated with a designer such as Rossknecht, who has included every hazard in the book. The greens are particularly well shaped, especially the island green on the 18th. A tough number from the back tees, the course gets a little more human the further forward you go, making it suitable for all levels. From the 5th to the 17th holes, you leave a park style landscape to encounter a more American style of course, where target golf is more the order of the day.

Golfclub zu Gut Ludwigsberg — 1988

Augsburgerstrasse 51
D - 86842 TÜRKHEIM

Office	Sekretariat	(49) 08245 - 3322
Pro shop	Pro shop	(49) 08245 - 3934
Fax	Fax	(49) 08245 - 3789
Web	—	
Situation	Lage	

Augsburg, 35 km - München (pop. 1 300 000), 50 km

Annual closure	Jährliche Schliessung	1/12→31/3
Weekly closure	Wöchentliche Schliessung	no

Fees main season Preisliste hochsaison — 18 holes

	Week days Woche	We/Bank holidays We/Feiertag
Individual Individuell	36 €	46 €
Couple Ehepaar	72 €	92 €

Caddy	Caddy	no
Electric Trolley	Elektrokarren	yes
Buggy	Elektrischer Wagen	yes
Clubs	Leihschläger	yes
Credit cards	Kreditkarten	no

Access Zufahrt : A96/B18 München-Lindau. B18 Exit (Ausf.) Türkheim-Bad Wörishofen. → Ettringen/Schwabmünchen. → Golf

Map 2 on page 356 Karte 2 Seite 356

Golf course PLATZ — 15/20

Site	Lage	
Maintenance	Instandhaltung	
Architect	Architekt	Kurt Rossknecht
Type	Typ	open country, parkland
Relief	Begehbarkeit	
Water in play	Platz mit Wasser	
Exp. to wind	Wind ausgesetzt	
Trees in play	Platz mit Bäumen	

Scorecard Scorekarte	Chp. Chp.	Mens Herren	Ladies Damen
Length Länge	6078	5820	5253
Par	72	72	72
Slope system	123	123	125

Advised golfing ability Empfohlene Spielstärke — 0 12 24 36

Hcp required Min. Handicap — no

Club house & amenities KLUBHAUS UND NEBENGEBÄUDE — 6/10

Pro shop	Pro shop	
Driving range	Übungsplatz	
Sheltered	überdacht	5 mats
On grass	auf Rasen	yes
Putting-green	Putting-grün	yes
Pitching-green	Pitching-grün	yes

Hotel facilities HOTEL BESCHREIBUNG — 6/10

HOTELS HOTELS

Kneipp Kurhotel Fontenay, 60 rooms, D 179 € Bad Wörishofen
Tel (49) 08247 - 30 60, Fax (49) 08247 - 306 185 — 9 km

Kurhotel Edelweiss, 52 rooms, D 97 € — Bad Wörishofen
Tel (49) 08247 - 35 010, Fax (49) 08247 - 350 175

Allgäuer Hof, 32 rooms, D 77 € — Bad Wörishofen
Tel (49) 08247 - 96 990, Fax (49) 08247 - 969 960

Stadthotel, 44 rooms, D 82 € — Buchloe 6 km
Tel (49) 08241 - 50 60, Fax (49) 08241 - 506 135

RESTAURANTS RESTAURANT

Mühlbach, Tel (49) 08247 - 6039 — Bad Wörishofen 9 km

Jagdhof, — Bad Wörishofen-Schlingen
Tel (49) 08247 - 4879 — 13 km

GUT THAILING

16 | 7 | 5

Thailing wirkt aufgrund seiner Nähe, demselben Architekten sowie dem Geländecharakter wie der zweieige Zwilling von Schloss Egmating. Nur das hier, insbesondere auf den zweiten 9 Löchern, weitaus öfter Wasser ins Spiel kommt, was diesem Platz einen ganz eigenständigen Charakter verleiht. Die Fairwaybunker sind aus genehmigungs-rechtlichen Gründen noch nicht mit Sand gefüllt, während die hervorragend geformten Grünbunker die sehr sorgfältig gestalteten Grüns (viele davon sind in mehreren Stufen angelegt) sehr wirkungsvoll verteidigen. Dies ist ein weitgehend offener Golfplatz, dessen umfangreiche Neuanpflanzungen noch einige Jahre brauchen werden, bevor sie eine wirkliche Gefahr darstellen. Man benötigt einige Runden, um mit dem leicht hügeligen Gelände vertraut zu werden. Charakter und Schwierigkeit der Löcher, von denen einige auf Spieler mit hohem Handicap ziemlich einschüchternd wirken können, lassen sich durch mehrere zur Auswahl stehende Abschlag-Boxen verändern. Dies ist eine der vielversprechendsten neuen Anlagen, die zudem bislang noch nicht überlaufen ist.

This is the false twin to Schloss Egmating through closeness, name of designer and character of terrain. Only here, there is much more water in play, emphatically so on one half of the course, thus giving it its own personality. For administrative reasons, the fairway bunkers are still awaiting their sand, but their green-side counterparts are well shaped and jealously guard the very carefully crafted putting surfaces (beware the multi-tiered greens). This is by and large an open space course with a lot of newly-planted saplings, which will need a number of years to grow into a real threat. While you need to play here several times to get to grips with a slightly hilly terrain (but never excessively so), the variety of tee-off areas also changes the character of holes, some of which are pretty intimidating for high-handicappers.

Golfclub Gut Thailing e.V. — 1994

Thailing 4
D - 85643 STEINHÖRIG

Office	Sekretariat	(49) 08094 - 9210
Pro shop	Pro shop	(49) 08094 - 9210
Fax	Fax	(49) 08094 - 9220
Web	www.golf.de/thailing	

Situation Lage
München (pop. 1 300 000), 35 km - Ebersberg, 5 km

Annual closure	Jährliche Schliessung	no
Weekly closure	Wöchentliche Schliessung	no

Fees main season Preisliste hochsaison — 18 holes

	Week days / Woche	We/Bank holidays / We/Feiertag
Individual Individuell	41 €	51 €
Couple Ehepaar	82 €	102 €

Caddy	Caddy	no
Electric Trolley	Elektrokarren	no
Buggy	Elektrischer Wagen	26 €
Clubs	Leihschläger	yes

Credit cards Kreditkarten
Eurocard - Mastercard - AMEX

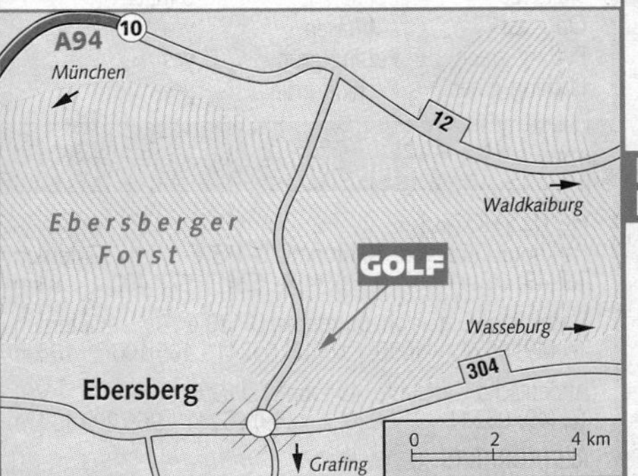

Access Zufahrt : München, A94 → Passau. Forstinning, B12 → Passau. Hohenlinden → Ebersberg. 5,5 km, left → Golf

Map 2 on page 357 Karte 2 Seite 357

Golf course — PLATZ — 16/20

Site	Lage	
Maintenance	Instandhaltung	
Architect	Architekt	Kurt Rossknecht
Type	Typ	open country
Relief	Begehbarkeit	
Water in play	Platz mit Wasser	
Exp. to wind	Wind ausgesetzt	
Trees in play	Platz mit Bäumen	

Scorecard / Scorekarte	Chp. / Chp.	Mens / Herren	Ladies / Damen
Length Länge	6101	5930	5086
Par	72	72	72
Slope system	128	125	124

Advised golfing ability Empfohlene Spielstärke — 0 12 24 36

Hcp required Min. Handicap — 36

Club house & amenities — KLUBHAUS UND NEBENGEBÄUDE — 7/10

Pro shop	Pro shop	
Driving range	Übungsplatz	
Sheltered	überdacht	yes
On grass	auf Rasen	yes
Putting-green	Putting-grün	yes
Pitching-green	Pitching-grün	yes

Hotel facilities — HOTEL BESCHREIBUNG — 5/10

HOTELS HOTELS

Hölzerbräu, 43 rooms, D 87 € — Ebersberg
Tel (49) 08092 - 24 020, Fax (49) 08092 - 24 031 — 5 km

Klostersee, 24 rooms, D 89 € — Ebersberg
Tel (49) 08092 - 82 850, Fax (49) 08092 - 828 550

Huber, 50 rooms, D 77 € — Ebersberg-Oberndorf
Tel (49) 08092 - 21 026, Fax (49) 08092 - 21 442 — 8 km

RESTAURANTS RESTAURANT

Hölzerbrau — Ebersberg
Tel (49) 08092 - 24 020 — 5 km

Klostersee, Tel (49) 08092 - 82 850 — Ebersberg

GÜTERSLOH (WESTFÄLISCHER GC) 17 7 7

Der zwischen Birken und Eichen liegende Platz des Westfälische Golf clubs in Gütersloh geniesst zu recht einen beneidenswerten Ruf. Die Länge des Platzes flösst Respekt ein, ohne die Gesamtlänge eines der modernen Monster aufzuweisen. Doch die von herrlichen alten Bäumen gesäumten Fairways verlangen Präzision, dazu erschweren Wasser-hindernisse (Teiche und Gräben) dem ehrgeizigen Golfer das Leben. Wer seine Schläge den vielen Doglegs anpassen kann, wer sicher einen Draw vom Abschlag spielen kann, ist im Vorteil, während der Fade beim Anspielen der grossen und gut verteidigten Grüns zu bevorzugen ist. Dieser Platz ist einer der besten Arbeiten von Bernhard von Limburger, der in Gütersloh ein abwechslungsreiches Layout entwarf, das alle Bereiche des Spiels testet, ohne übermässig spektakulär zu wirken. Der gesamte Platz strahlt eine nüchterne Eleganz und viel Einfallsreichtum des Architekten aus. Dazu kommt noch die wunderschöne Umgebung, die Ruhe und Stille auf den Spielbahnen, die gut von einander getrennt sind.

Laid out amidst birch and oak trees, this course has gained an enviable reputation. The yardage commands respect without ever making this a modern-day monster course but the ever-present trees form a line of defence which calls for great accuracy, a feat that is not always compatible with big-hitting. What's more, water hazards tend to make life more complicated for the more ambitious golfer. There's no doubt that good benders of the ball will be in their element here; the few dog-legs provide the opportunity to show-off that well-honed draw from the tee before changing to fading the ball to pitch the huge and well-guarded greens. This is one of the great designs from Bernhard von Limburger, an excellent connoisseur of golf but no lover of the more decorative style of course. Everything here is very sober in a sort of austere elegance, yet there is no shortage of imagination in the layout. Add to this the beautiful surroundings, peace and quiet and the isolation of each hole and you will understand why this is a great classic course you can't miss.

Westfälischer Golf Club Gütersloh — 1969

Güterslohertrasse 127
D - 33397 RIETBERG-VARENSELL

Office	Sekretariat	(49) 05244 - 23 40
Pro shop	Pro shop	(49) 05244 - 18 45
Fax	Fax	(49) 05244 - 13 88
Web	—	
Situation	Lage	Gütersloh (pop. 90 000), 8 km
Annual closure	Jährliche Schliessung	no
Weekly closure	Wöchentliche Schliessung	no

Fees main season Preisliste hochsaison	18 holes	
	Week days Woche	**We/Bank holidays** We/Feiertag
Individual Individuell	31 €	41 €
Couple Ehepaar	62 €	82 €

– 21 years/Students: – 50%

Caddy	Caddy	no
Electric Trolley	Elektrokarren	no
Buggy	Elektrischer Wagen	26 €
Clubs	Leihschläger	15 €

Credit cards Kreditkarten
VISA - Eurocard - MasterCard

Access Zufahrt : Hannover A2 → Ruhr. Exit (Ausf.) → Gütersloh. 3rd light, take left on Bruder-Konrad-Strasse, then right → Rietberg. 3.5 km, right → Golf.
Map 5 on page 363 Karte 5 Seite 363

Golf course PLATZ 17/20

Site	Lage	
Maintenance	Instandhaltung	
Architect	Architekt	B. von Limburger
Type	Typ	parkland
Relief	Begehbarkeit	
Water in play	Platz mit Wasser	
Exp. to wind	Wind ausgesetzt	
Trees in play	Platz mit Bäumen	

Scorecard Scorekarte	**Chp.** Chp.	**Mens** Herren	**Ladies** Damen
Length Länge	6135	6044	5303
Par	72	72	72
Slope system	124	124	128

Advised golfing ability Empfohlene Spielstärke — 0 12 24 36
Hcp required Min. Handicap — 35

Club house & amenities KLUBHAUS UND NEBENGEBÄUDE 7/10

Pro shop	Pro shop	
Driving range	Übungsplatz	
Sheltered	überdacht	6 mats
On grass	auf Rasen	yes
Putting-green	Putting-grün	yes
Pitching-green	Pitching-grün	yes

Hotel facilities HOTEL BESCHREIBUNG 7/10

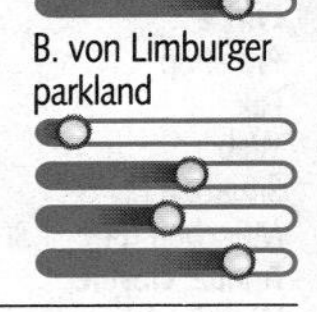

HOTELS HOTELS

Parkhotel Gütersloh, 103 rooms, D 133 € — Gütersloh
Tel (49) 05241 - 8770, Fax (49) 05241 - 877 400 — 8 km

Hotel Stadt Gütersloh, 55 rooms, D 130 € — Gütersloh
Tel (49) 05241 - 1050, Fax (49) 05241 - 105 100 — 10 km

Altdeutsche Gaststätte, 45 rooms, D 89 € — Verl
Tel (49) 05241 - 917 020, Fax (49) 05241 - 966 299 — 15 km

RESTAURANTS RESTAURANT

Büdelsrestaurant-Bürmann's Hof — Verl
Tel (49) 05246 - 7970 — 15 km

Stadthalle — Gütersloh
Tel (49) 05241 - 864 269 — 10 km

HAMBURG-AHRENSBURG

16	8	7

Das Original-Platzdesign von Bernhard von Limburger wurde 1977 von Robert Trent Jones leicht verändert. Diese Änderungen haben den Platz für den Durchschnittsgolfer nicht schwerer gemacht, wenngleich jetzt gelegentlich Wasser zu überwinden ist. Kein Par 4 erreicht 400 Meter, einige sind sogar recht kurz, so dass praktisch alle Eisen zum Einsatz kommen. Trotz des eher flachen Geländes gibt es zwei praktisch blinde Grüns, deren Anspiel "target Golf" erfordert. Diese Anforderung gilt im Grunde generell, da die Grüns durchgehend gut verteidigt sind. Dieser im amerikanischen Stil gestaltete Platz, bei dem alle Schwierigkeiten deutlich sichtbar sind, ist eingebettet in eine parkartige Landschaft, in der sich eine Anzahl exotischer Bäume findet. Auffallend ist auch der Abwechslungsreichtum der Löcher, von denen praktisch jedes auf unterschiedliche Art verteidigt wird, sei es in Form von Büschen, Bäumen, Bunkern und/oder Wasserhindernissen. Man braucht einen kühlen Kopf und gute Ballkontrolle, wenn man hier sein Handicap spielen will.

The original design by Bernhard von Limburger was slightly altered in 1977 by Robert Trent Jones. This has not made it any tougher for average players, even though there is now some water to cross. No one par 4 reaches 400 metres, and some are even short, thus allowing a wide choice of irons. Despite rather flat terrain, two greens are virtually blind and call for some target play, but this is a general feature here owing to the well-guarded greens. In a parkland landscape (with a number of exotic varieties of tree), this is a US-style course with difficulties for all to see. Also noteworthy is the variety of holes, with each having practically its own style of defence: bushes, trees, bunkers and/or water hazards. With a cool head and good ball control, you can hope to play to your handicap.

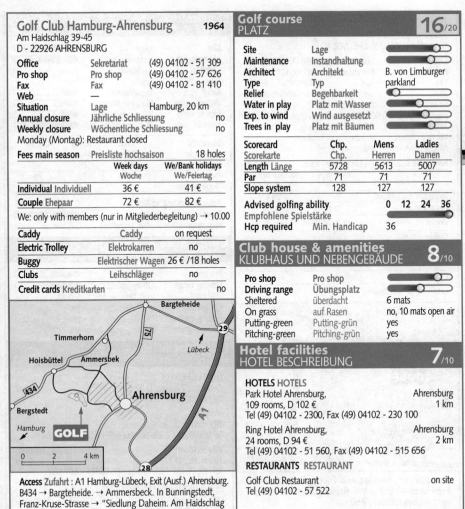

Golf Club Hamburg-Ahrensburg — 1964

Am Haidschlag 39-45
D - 22926 AHRENSBURG

Office	Sekretariat	(49) 04102 - 51 309
Pro shop	Pro shop	(49) 04102 - 57 626
Fax	Fax	(49) 04102 - 81 410
Web	—	
Situation	Lage	Hamburg, 20 km
Annual closure	Jährliche Schliessung	no
Weekly closure	Wöchentliche Schliessung	no

Monday (Montag): Restaurant closed

Fees main season Preisliste hochsaison		18 holes
	Week days Woche	**We/Bank holidays** We/Feiertag
Individual Individuell	36 €	41 €
Couple Ehepaar	72 €	82 €

We: only with members (nur in Mitgliederbegleitung) → 10.00

Caddy	Caddy	on request
Electric Trolley	Elektrokarren	no
Buggy	Elektrischer Wagen	26 € /18 holes
Clubs	Leihschläger	no
Credit cards	Kreditkarten	no

Access Zufahrt **:** A1 Hamburg-Lübeck, Exit (Ausf.) Ahrensburg. B434 → Bargteheide. → Ammersbeck. In Bunningstedt, Franz-Kruse-Strasse → "Siedlung Daheim. Am Haidschlag → Golf **Map 7 on page 366** Karte 7 Seite 366

Golf course PLATZ — 16/20

Site	Lage	
Maintenance	Instandhaltung	
Architect	Architekt	B. von Limburger
Type	Typ	parkland
Relief	Begehbarkeit	
Water in play	Platz mit Wasser	
Exp. to wind	Wind ausgesetzt	
Trees in play	Platz mit Bäumen	

Scorecard Scorekarte	**Chp.** Chp.	**Mens** Herren	**Ladies** Damen
Length Länge	5728	5613	5007
Par	71	71	71
Slope system	128	127	127

Advised golfing ability Empfohlene Spielstärke — 0 12 24 36

Hcp required Min. Handicap — 36

Club house & amenities KLUBHAUS UND NEBENGEBÄUDE — 8/10

Pro shop	Pro shop	
Driving range	Übungsplatz	
Sheltered	überdacht	6 mats
On grass	auf Rasen	no, 10 mats open air
Putting-green	Putting-grün	yes
Pitching-green	Pitching-grün	yes

Hotel facilities HOTEL BESCHREIBUNG — 7/10

HOTELS HOTELS

Park Hotel Ahrensburg, 109 rooms, D 102 € — Ahrensburg 1 km
Tel (49) 04102 - 2300, Fax (49) 04102 - 230 100

Ring Hotel Ahrensburg, 24 rooms, D 94 € — Ahrensburg 2 km
Tel (49) 04102 - 51 560, Fax (49) 04102 - 515 656

RESTAURANTS RESTAURANT

Golf Club Restaurant — on site
Tel (49) 04102 - 57 522

HANAU-WILHELMSBAD

16 | 6 | 6

Der Golfplatz wurde 1939 auf der ehemaligen Fasanenzuchtfarm der Familie Hesse errichtet, ganz in der Nähe von Schloss Wilhelmsbad, einem der zahlreichen Mineral- und Thermalkurorte dieser Gegend. Dieser alte Besitz verfügt über einen grosszügigen alten Baumbestand. Daher rührt auch der Eindruck eines gemütlichen Spaziergangs inmitten eines grossen Parks, den man während der Runde auf dem völlig ebenen Platz gewinnt, dessen 18 Loch ganz mühelos zu Gehen sind. Dank ihres anspruchsvollen Layouts war die Anlage in der Vergangenheit mehrmals Austragungsort der Nationalen offenen Deutschen Golf-Meisterschaften. Die guten Spieler werden versuchen den Amateur-Rekord von 70 Schlägen zu brechen, während die weniger Ehrgeizigen unter uns, von den vorderen Abschlägen aus, einen grossartigen Golftag verbringen können. Da die Runde von Bäumen und einer kleinen Anzahl gefährlicher Wasserhindernisse gewürzt wird, sollten sie nicht zögern, von den vorderen Abschlägen zu spielen. Dies gilt speziell an Loch 7, einem Par 5 von 570 Metern Länge.

This course was designed in 1959 on the former pheasant farm of the Hesse family, close to the castle of Wilhelmsbad, one of the many spas and hydrotherapy centres found in this part of the world. The estate is lavishly lined with old trees, whence the very pleasant impression of a lovely walk in a huge park without any relief to speak of to stop you from walking the 18 holes. The layout is demanding enough for the National German Championships to have been held here several times, and while skilled players will relish the chance to attack the amateur record of 70, the less ambitious amongst us will play from the forward tees and spend a great day's golfing. The trees and a few dangerous water hazards tend to add a little spice to life, so don't shy away from playing the front tees, especially on the 7th hole, a par 5 of some 570 metres (600 yds plus). The course has no unfair difficulties.

Golf-Club Hanau-Wilhelmsbad e.V. 1959

Wilhelmsbader Allee 32
D - 63454 HANAU-WILHELMSBAD

Office	Sekretariat	(49) 06181 - 82 071
Pro shop	Pro shop	(49) 06181 - 81 775
Fax	Fax	(49) 06181 - 86 967
Web	www.golf.de/hanau-wilhelmsbad	
Situation	Lage	

Frankfurt (pop. 660 000), 20 km - Hanau (pop. 90 000), 3 km

Annual closure	Jährliche Schliessung	no
Weekly closure	Wöchentliche Schliessung	no

Monday (Montag): Restaurant closed

Fees main season Preisliste hochsaison — 18 holes

	Week days Woche	We/Bank holidays We/Feiertag
Individual Individuell	46 €	56 €
Couple Ehepaar	92 €	112 €

We: with members only (nur in Mitgliederbegleitung)

Caddy	Caddy	no
Electric Trolley	Elektrokarren	no
Buggy	Elektrischer Wagen	no
Clubs	Leihschläger	15 €
Credit cards Kreditkarten		no

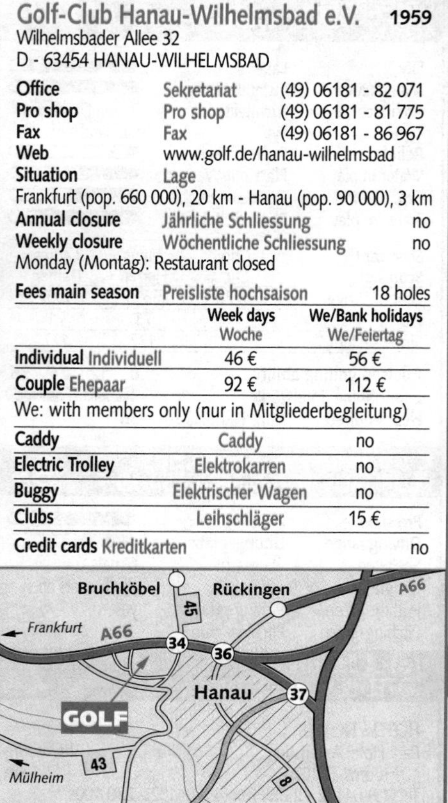

Access Zufahrt : Frankfurt, A66. Exit (Ausf.) Hanau Nord. Right on B8/40 until → Wilhelmsbad. 20 m, right (Wilhelmsbader Allee)
Map 3 on page 359 Karte 3 Seite 359

Golf course PLATZ — 16/20

Site	Lage	
Maintenance	Instandhaltung	
Architect	Architekt	Kothe
Type	Typ	Park
Relief	Begehbarkeit	
Water in play	Platz mit Wasser	
Exp. to wind	Wind ausgesetzt	
Trees in play	Platz mit Bäumen	

Scorecard Scorekarte	Chp. Chp.	Mens Herren	Ladies Damen
Length Länge	6095	5894	5169
Par	73	73	73
Slope system	132	129	130

Advised golfing ability Empfohlene Spielstärke — 0 12 24 36
Hcp required Min. Handicap — 32, We: 28

Club house & amenities KLUBHAUS UND NEBENGEBÄUDE — 6/10

Pro shop	Pro shop	
Driving range	Übungsplatz	
Sheltered	überdacht	5 mats
On grass	auf Rasen	yes
Putting-green	Putting-grün	yes
Pitching-green	Pitching-grün	yes

Hotel facilities HOTEL BESCHREIBUNG — 6/10

HOTELS HOTELS

Golfhotel, 7 rooms, D 92 € — Golf
Tel (49) 06181 - 995 511

Mercure, — Hanau 3 km
137 rooms, D 135 €
Tel (49) 06181 - 305 50, Fax (49) 06181 -305 5444

Villa Stokkum, — Hanau-Steinheim 6 km
135 rooms, D 128 €
Tel (49) 06181 - 66 40, Fax (49) 06181 - 661 580

RESTAURANTS RESTAURANT

Villa Stokkum — Hanau-Steinheim 6 km
Tel (49) 06181 - 66 40

HANNOVER

16 | 7 | 7

Der 1923 gebaute Platz wurde später von Bernhard von Limburger umgestaltet, der seine klassische Handschrift hinterliess. Diese zeigt sich in einem klugen Platzdesign, das sich auszeichnet durch die ebenso angemessene wie geschickte Verwendung von Hindernissen, deren Plazierung gute Schläge nicht betraft. Die Lärmbelästigung durch die nahegelegene Autobahn Köln - Hannover wird von den vielen Bäumen etwas gedämpft, davon abgesehen lohnt sich der Besuch der insgesamt ausgezeichneten Anlage unbedingt. Die bereits erwähnten Bäume verlangen nach geraden Schlägen, um die engen Fairways zu treffen; vielfach ist man sogar gezwungen, einen Fade oder Draw zu spielen, um in die beste Position zu gelangen. Die ziemlich flachen, gut gestalteten Grüns werden von einer Reihe, teilweise sehr tiefer Bunker verteidigt. Die erforderliche Spielstrategie ist offensichtlich, so dass man schon auf der ersten Runde hoffen kann, einen guten Score zu erzielen. Hannover ist einer der besten Plätze der Region und abwechslungsreich genug, um auch bei mehrmaligem Spielen interessant zu bleiben.

Designed in 1923, the course was reshaped by Bernhard von Limburger, who has left his own, very classical stamp with a sensible layout and reasonable use of hazards, always well placed but not too penalising for good shots. The one regret is the closeness of the Cologne-Hannover motorway, but the general excellence of the course makes it well worth visiting, and the very many trees do tend to dampen the noise somewhat. On the downside, these same trees leave the fairways rather narrow, hence the need to play straight or even flight the ball with fade and draw shots to get into the best position. The greens are well designed and relatively flat, but are protected by a host of bunkers, some of which are often very deep. Game strategy is pretty obvious to try and return a goodish card first time out, and the course is varied enough to keep it interesting. This is one of the region's best courses.

Golf-Club Hannover e.V. — 1923

Am Blauen See 120
D - 30823 GARBSEN

Office	Sekretariat	(49) 05137 - 73 068
Pro shop	Pro shop	(49) 05137 - 71 004
Fax	Fax	(49) 05137 - 75 851
Web	—	
Situation	Lage	

Hannover (pop. 510 000), 15 km

Annual closure Jährliche Schliessung 1/1→31/1
Weekly closure Wöchentliche Schliessung
Monday/Montag): Restaurant closed

Fees main season Preisliste hochsaison — Full day

	Week days Woche	We/Bank holidays We/Feiertag
Individual Individuell	31 €	41 €
Couple Ehepaar	62 €	82 €

– 21 years, Students: – 50%

Caddy	Caddy	no
Electric Trolley	Elektrokarren	no
Buggy	Elektrischer Wagen	yes
Clubs	Leihschläger	yes
Credit cards Kreditkarten		no

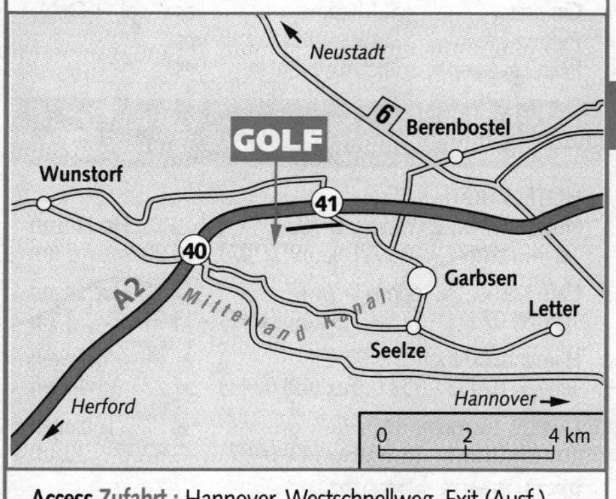

Access Zufahrt : Hannover, Westschnellweg. Exit (Ausf.) Herrenhausen. A2 until Rasthaus "Blauer See". 1,5 km, Golf South of A2 **Map 5 on page 363** Karte 5 Seite 363

Golf course PLATZ — 16/20

Site	Lage	
Maintenance	Instandhaltung	
Architect	Architekt	B. von Limburger
Type	Typ	country, forest
Relief	Begehbarkeit	
Water in play	Platz mit Wasser	
Exp. to wind	Wind ausgesetzt	
Trees in play	Platz mit Bäumen	

Scorecard Scorekarte	**Chp.** Chp.	**Mens** Herren	**Ladies** Damen
Length Länge	5685	5685	5102
Par	71	71	71
Slope system	133	133	131

Advised golfing ability Empfohlene Spielstärke — 0 12 24 36

Hcp required Min. Handicap 34

Club house & amenities KLUBHAUS UND NEBENGEBÄUDE — 7/10

Pro shop	Pro shop	
Driving range	Übungsplatz	
Sheltered	überdacht	3 mats
On grass	auf Rasen	June # Sept.
Putting-green	Putting-grün	yes
Pitching-green	Pitching-grün	yes

Hotel facilities HOTEL BESCHREIBUNG — 7/10

HOTELS HOTELS

Maritim Grand Hotel Hannover — Hannover
300 rooms, D 204 € — 15 km
Tel (49) 0511 - 36 770, Fax (49) 0511 - 325 195

Landhaus am See — Garbsen-Berenbostel
38 rooms, D 102 € — 3 km
Tel (49) 05131 - 468 60, Fax (49) 05131 - 468 666

Hotel Wildhage, 30 rooms, D 69 € — Garbsen-Hevelse
Tel (49) 05137 - 75 033, Fax (49) 05137 - 75 401 — 2 km

RESTAURANTS RESTAURANT

Landhaus Ammann, — Hannover
Tel (49) 0511 - 830 818 — 15 km

Gattopardo, Tel (49) 0511 - 14 375 — Hannover

HECHINGEN-HOHENZOLLERN 14 6 6

Die Nähe zum Schloss der Hohenzollern - dessen Lage weitaus beeindruckender ist als die nicht so alten Gebäude - haben viel zum Ruf und Bekannheitsgrad dieses Golfplatzes beigetragen. Seine idyllische Lage ist für viele, in dieser Hinsicht empfängliche Golfer, ein stichhaltiger Grund, hier zu spielen. Wer seine Aufmerksamkeit von der Umgebung dem Kurs zuwendet, entdeckt einen hübschen Platz mit engen, häufig baumbestandenen Fairways und einer Anzahl gefährlicher Büsche, welche die Hauptschwierigkeit dieser Anlage darstellen. Zwar gibt es auch Fairway- und Grünbunker, jedoch sind diese nicht wirklich gefährlich genug, um gute Spieler ernsthaft daran hindern zu können, die wohlproportionierten, leicht modellierten Grüns anzuspielen. Geeignet für alle Spielklassen, fehlt es diesem Platz ein wenig an Charakter, um den besseren Spielern auch langfristig Vergnügen zu bereiten. Beim Bau der Anlage stand sicherlich im Vordergrund, dass golfende Familien hier Spass haben sollen.

Being so close to the castle of Hohenzollern (even though the site is more impressive than the not-so-old buildings) has done much for the reputation and recognition of this course. Its idyllic setting is also a sound argument for players who are sensitive to this particular aspect of golf. If you can tear your eyes away from the surroundings, you are left facing a pretty course with narrow fairways often protected by trees and, above all, some dangerous bushes, which form the main hazard. The fairway and green-side bunkers are there all right, but are not really dangerous enough to worry good players unduly and prevent them from homing in on nicely-sized and discreetly contoured greens. Accessible to players of all abilities, this course is a little too short of personality to keep the better players happy for too long. Working for the enjoyment of family golf was certainly a major consideration when designing the course.

Golf Club Hechingen-Hohenzollern 1955

Auf dem Hagelwasen, Postfach 1124
D - 72379 HECHINGEN

Office	Sekretariat	(49) 07471 - 2600
Pro shop	Pro shop	(49) 07471 - 62 272
Fax	Fax	(49) 07471 - 14 776
Web	—	
Situation	Lage	

Hechingen, 2 km - Tübingen (pop. 82 000), 25 km

Annual closure	Jährliche Schliessung	1/11→31/3
Weekly closure	Wöchentliche Schliessung	no

Monday (Montag): Restaurant closed

Fees main season Preisliste hochsaison		Full day
	Week days Woche	**We/Bank holidays** We/Feiertag
Individual Individuell	31 €	41 €
Couple Ehepaar	62 €	82 €

– 21 years/Students: – 50%

Caddy	Caddy	no
Electric Trolley	Elektrokarren	yes
Buggy	Elektrischer Wagen	no
Clubs	Leihschläger	5 €
Credit cards	Kreditkarten	no

Access Zufahrt : Stuttgart, B27. Tübingen B27 → Balingen. Hechingen → Burg Hohenzollern, → Hechingen-Weilheim, → Golf
Map 1 on page 355 Karte 1 Seite 355

Golf course PLATZ 14/20

Site	Lage	
Maintenance	Instandhaltung	
Architect	Architekt	Unknown
Type	Typ	open country, hilly
Relief	Begehbarkeit	
Water in play	Platz mit Wasser	
Exp. to wind	Wind ausgesetzt	
Trees in play	Platz mit Bäumen	

Scorecard Scorekarte	**Chp.** Chp.	**Mens** Herren	**Ladies** Damen
Length Länge	6064	6064	5346
Par	72	72	72
Slope system	126	124	122

Advised golfing ability Empfohlene Spielstärke 0 12 24 36

Hcp required Min. Handicap 36

Club house & amenities KLUBHAUS UND NEBENGEBÄUDE 6/10

Pro shop	Pro shop	
Driving range	Übungsplatz	
Sheltered	überdacht	6 mats
On grass	auf Rasen	yes (April → Oct.)
Putting-green	Putting-grün	yes
Pitching-green	Pitching-grün	yes

Hotel facilities HOTEL BESCHREIBUNG 6/10

HOTELS HOTELS

Hotel Brielhof, 25 rooms, D 102 € — Hechingen
Tel (49) 07471 - 40 97, Fax (49) 07471 - 16 908 — 5 km

Café Klaiber, 28 rooms, D 71 € — Hechingen
Tel (49) 07471 - 22 57, Fax (49) 07471 - 13 918 — 3 km

Hamann, 50 rooms, D 92 € — Balingen
Tel (49) 07433 - 95 00, Fax (49) 07433 - 51 23 — 10 km

Domizil, 82 rooms, D 97 € — Tübingen
Tel (49) 07071 - 13 90, Fax (49) 07071 - 13 9250 — 25 km

RESTAURANTS RESTAURANT

Waldhorn, Tel (49) 07071 - 61 270 — Tübingen 30 km

Rosenau, Tel (49) 07071 - 66 466 — Tübingen 25 km

HEILBRONN-HOHENLOHE

14	7	8

Dieser Platz liegt auf dem Land des königlichen Geschlechts der Hohelohes. Die reizvolle Gegend wirkt auch heute noch ländlich. Bei einem Besuch dieser Regikon sollte man einen Abstecher nach Schwäbisch Hall machen und das Hohenloher Freilandmuseum besuchen, ein Freilicht-Museum, dass das ländliche Leben Würtembergs nachstellt. Auf keinen Fall sollte man versäumen, diesen ansprechenden Platz zu spielen. Ein Teil des Platzes, insgesamt sechs Löcher, führt durch den ehemaligen dicht bewaldeten Park des Fürsten. Viele blinde und enge Löcher sowie ein starkes Auf und Ab der Spielbahnen machen die Schwierigkeiten dieses Teils des Platz aus. Der Rest ist offen, mit einigen Wasserhindernisse und herrlichen Ausblicken über das Hohenloher Land. Schade, dass der Platz über keine Fairway-Beregnung verfügt, so dass der Platz nach langen Trockenperioden sehr hart wird. Wenn man in dieser Gegend ist,sollten man den Platz spielen und im Wald & Schlosshotel, der früheren Sommerresidenz des Prinzen von Hohelohe, wohnen und sich von der Küche dieser mit einem Michelin-Stern ausgezeichneten Relais & Châteaux verwöhnen lassen.

This course is situated amidst the possessions of Hohenlohe, one of the German Royal Courts from the Renaissance and age of the Baroque. The area has remained distinctly rural with some very pleasant countryside, and while here you should push on to the pretty town of Schwäbish Hall to the south-east and to the Hohenloher Freilandmuseum, an open-air museum which re-creates the rural life of Wurtemberg. On your way, do not forget to play this pretty course, partly built in a very hilly park full of trees, and partly over flat countryside. A few blind shots make life a little complicated on the way out and you will need to hit it in the right direction to keep your score down. It is a shame about there being no automatic watering system because the ground tends to get very hard after a number of weeks without rain, but there again this is Germany, not the Sahara desert. If you are in the region, it would be a pity not to stop off here for a round and maybe stay at the Wald & Schlosshotel, the former summer residence of a Hohenlohe prince and now a top-rate Relais & Châteaux hotel.

Golf-Club Heilbronn-Hohenlohe — 1964

Hofgasse 4
D - 74639 ZWEIFLINGEN - FRIEDRICHSRUHE

Office	Sekretariat	(49) 07941 - 920 810
Pro shop	Pro shop	(49) 07941 - 920 820
Fax	Fax	(49) 07941 - 920 819
Web	www.friedrichsruhe.de	
Situation	Lage	Heilbronn (pop. 120 000), 35 km
Annual closure	Jährliche Schliessung	no
Weekly closure	Wöchentliche Schliessung	no

Fees main season Preisliste hochsaison		18 holes
	Week days Woche	We/Bank holidays We/Feiertag
Individual Individuell	31 €	46 €
Couple Ehepaar	62 €	92 €

Juniors/Students: – 50%

Caddy	Caddy	no
Electric Trolley	Elektrokarren	no
Buggy	Elektrischer Wagen	26 € /18 holes
Clubs	Leihschläger	yes

Credit cards Kreditkarten
(Pro-shop) VISA - Eurocard - Mastercard - AMEX

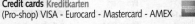

Access Zufahrt **:** A6 Heilbronn/Nürnberg. Exit (Ausfahrt) Öhringen. → Friedrichsruhe/Zweiflingen. Golf on left hand side after Wald & Schlosshotel.
Map 1 on page 355 Karte 1 Seite 355

Golf course — PLATZ — 14/20

Site	Lage	
Maintenance	Instandhaltung	
Architect	Architekt	unknown
Type	Typ	forest, open country
Relief	Begehbarkeit	
Water in play	Platz mit Wasser	
Exp. to wind	Wind ausgesetzt	
Trees in play	Platz mit Bäumen	

Scorecard Scorekarte	Chp. Chp.	Mens Herren	Ladies Damen
Length Länge	6039	5852	5169
Par	72	72	72
Slope system	121	121	124

Advised golfing ability Empfohlene Spielstärke — 0 12 24 36
Hcp required Min. Handicap — 54 (36 We)

Club house & amenities — KLUBHAUS UND NEBENGEBÄUDE — 7/10

Pro shop	Pro shop	
Driving range	Übungsplatz	
Sheltered	überdacht	8 mats
On grass	auf Rasen	no, 80 mats
Putting-green	Putting-grün	yes
Pitching-green	Pitching-grün	yes

Hotel facilities — HOTEL BESCHREIBUNG — 8/10

HOTELS HOTELS

Wald-und Schlosshotel 56 rooms, D 169 € — Friedrichsruhe
Tel (49) 07941 - 608 70, Fax (49) 07941 - 614 68 — on site

Panorama Hotel Waldenburg — Waldenburg 12 km
73 rooms, D 102 €
Tel (49) 07942 - 910 00, Fax (49) 07942- 9100 888

Park Villa, 25 rooms, D 115 € — Heilbronn 28 km
Tel (49) 07131 - 957 00, Fax (49) 07131 - 957 020

RESTAURANTS RESTAURANT

Wald-und Schlosshotel, Tel (49) 07941 - 608 70 — Friedrichsruhe
Münzstube, Tel (49) 07941 - 658 15 — Öhringen 8 km
Ratskeller, Tel (49) 07131 - 846 28 — Heilbronn 28 km

HOF TRAGES

15 | 7 | 5

Kurt Rossknecht hat seinen Ruf als einer der kreativsten Golf-Architekten Europas mit dieser ausgezeichneten Anlage untermauert, die sich als perfekte Ergänzung zu einem der beeindruckendsten Clubhäuser Deutschlands erweist. Der leicht hügelige Platz leugnet nicht die amerikanischen Einflüsse, welche besonders an einer Vielzahl von Wasserhindernissen deutlich werden, die den Spielern, neben einigen durch den Wald verlaufenden Spielbahnen, die grössten Probleme bereiten. Obschon die Schwierigkeiten klar erkennbar sind, muss man doch einige Runden hier spielen, um die vorhandenen strategischen Fallen genau auszumachen. Der Platz ist nicht übermässig lang, so dass Spieler aller Kategorien hier einen schönen Golftag verleben können, sofern sie sich darauf konzentrieren ihr Handicap zu spielen, und keine Schläge unnötig verschenken. Die Grüns sind von guter Qualität, wie auch die gesamte Anlage bereits gut eingewachsen ist. Am 18 Loch, einem schwierigen Par 3, muss man acht geben in Hessen zu bleiben .Wer hier sliced, findet seinen Ball wahrhaft "out of bounds" - nämlich im benachbarten Bayern.

Designer Kurt Rossknecht has asserted his status as one of the most creative course architects in Europe, and this good layout is the perfect complement to one of Germany's most impressive club-houses. Over averagely hilly terrain, the course doesn't try to hide its American influence, and water hazards abound as an obvious danger alongside the stretches through the forest. Even though the difficulties are clearly seen, you need to play the course several times to get a clear picture of the strategic traps. It is not excessively long and players of all levels can spend a good day's golfing if they don't throw strokes away and concentrate on keeping to their handicap. The greens are good and the course has already matured nicely. At the 18th, a tough par 3, be careful to stay in Hesse... if you slice, you will find your ball out of bounds in neighbouring Bavaria!

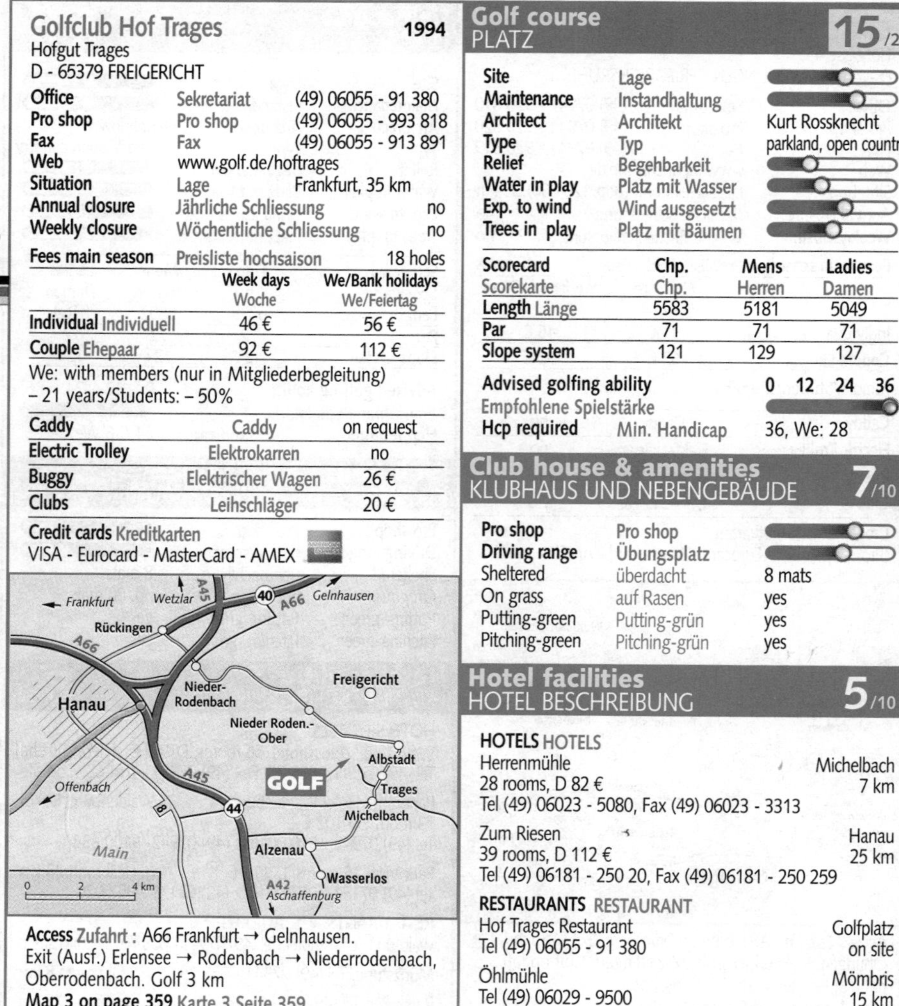

Golfclub Hof Trages — 1994

Hofgut Trages
D - 65379 FREIGERICHT

Office	Sekretariat	(49) 06055 - 91 380
Pro shop	Pro shop	(49) 06055 - 993 818
Fax	Fax	(49) 06055 - 913 891
Web	www.golf.de/hoftrages	
Situation	Lage	Frankfurt, 35 km
Annual closure	Jährliche Schliessung	no
Weekly closure	Wöchentliche Schliessung	no

Fees main season Preisliste hochsaison — 18 holes

	Week days / Woche	We/Bank holidays / We/Feiertag
Individual Individuell	46 €	56 €
Couple Ehepaar	92 €	112 €

We: with members (nur in Mitgliederbegleitung)
– 21 years/Students: – 50%

Caddy	Caddy	on request
Electric Trolley	Elektrokarren	no
Buggy	Elektrischer Wagen	26 €
Clubs	Leihschläger	20 €

Credit cards Kreditkarten
VISA - Eurocard - MasterCard - AMEX

Access Zufahrt : A66 Frankfurt → Gelnhausen. Exit (Ausf.) Erlensee → Rodenbach → Niederrodenbach, Oberrodenbach. Golf 3 km
Map 3 on page 359 Karte 3 Seite 359

Golf course / PLATZ — 15/20

Site	Lage	
Maintenance	Instandhaltung	
Architect	Architekt	Kurt Rossknecht
Type	Typ	parkland, open country
Relief	Begehbarkeit	
Water in play	Platz mit Wasser	
Exp. to wind	Wind ausgesetzt	
Trees in play	Platz mit Bäumen	

Scorecard / Scorekarte	Chp. / Chp.	Mens / Herren	Ladies / Damen
Length Länge	5583	5181	5049
Par	71	71	71
Slope system	121	129	127

Advised golfing ability Empfohlene Spielstärke — 0 12 24 36
Hcp required Min. Handicap — 36, We: 28

Club house & amenities / KLUBHAUS UND NEBENGEBÄUDE — 7/10

Pro shop	Pro shop	
Driving range	Übungsplatz	
Sheltered	überdacht	8 mats
On grass	auf Rasen	yes
Putting-green	Putting-grün	yes
Pitching-green	Pitching-grün	yes

Hotel facilities / HOTEL BESCHREIBUNG — 5/10

HOTELS HOTELS

Herrenmühle — Michelbach 7 km
28 rooms, D 82 €
Tel (49) 06023 - 5080, Fax (49) 06023 - 3313

Zum Riesen — Hanau 25 km
39 rooms, D 112 €
Tel (49) 06181 - 250 20, Fax (49) 06181 - 250 259

RESTAURANTS RESTAURANT

Hof Trages Restaurant — Golfplatz on site
Tel (49) 06055 - 91 380

Öhlmühle — Mömbris 15 km
Tel (49) 06029 - 9500

HOHENPÄHL

15 | 7 | 6

Höhenpähl liegt in einer Parklandschaft zwischen Ammersee und Starnberger See. Trotz der hügeligen Landschaft hat sich Architekt Kurt Rosskneckt bemüht, blinde Löcher möglichst zu vermeiden, was ihm aufgrund der Topographie aber nicht immer gelang. Die gesamte Anlage strahlt viel Ruhe aus, ab und an überquert Wild die Fairways. An Löchern, an denen Bäume und Wasser bereits genug Gefahr darstellen, erschweren nicht noch zusätzlich Bunker das Spiele. Ungeübten Spielern werden im Verlauf der Runde, die eine Vielzahl von Problemen für sie bereithält, deutlich ihre Schwächen aufgezeigt. Dieser meist recht enge Platz verlangt vom Spieler sehr kontrolliertes Golf. Erwähnenswert ist auch die "Ehrlichkeit" des Layouts, abgesehen vom 4. Loch, wo ein vom Abschlag aus nicht sichtbarer Graben das Fairway in Höhe der Drive-Landezone kreuzt. Hohenpähl ist zwar anspruchsvoll, jedoch kein "Monsterplatz". Daher ist Loch 8, die schwerste Bahn des Platzes, an der Bogey ein gutes Ergebnis ist, eher die Ausnahme.

Hohenpähl is located in a park land setting between Ammersee and Starnberger See, two of the most beautiful lakes in Bavaria. In spite of the hilly terrain architect Kurt Rossknecht tried everything to avoid blind holes, but the topography decided otherwise. The site is haven of tranquillity, as the rabbits and deer seem to sense as they bound across the fairways. There are no needless traps here: when the trees and water present an obvious danger, this is never compounded by the addition of bunkers. Inexperienced players will certainly encounter a few problems on the way, but they will also get an insight into their weaknesses. This often narrow course demands good control over your game and its honesty deserves a definite mention, except on the 4th hole where a concealed ditch crosses exactly where the drive should land. Although demanding, Hohenpähl is no monster and only the 8th is really tough going. It's a par 4 but the bogey will do nicely. Well worth knowing.

Golf Club Hohenpähl — 1988

D - 82396 PÄHL

Office	Sekretariat	(49) 08808 - 920 20
Pro shop	Pro shop	(49) 08808 - 1308
Fax	Fax	(49) 08808 - 920 222
Web	www.golf.de/hohenpaehl	
Situation	Lage	

München (pop. 1 300 000), 44 km - Weilheim, 9 km

Annual closure	Jährliche Schliessung	1/11→31/3
Weekly closure	Wöchentliche Schliessung	no

Fees main season Preisliste hochsaison	18 holes	
	Week days Woche	We/Bank holidays We/Feiertag
Individual Individuell	46 €	61 €
Couple Ehepaar	92 €	122 €

We: with members (nur in Mitgliederbegleitung) / - 21 years –50%

Caddy	Caddy	on request
Electric Trolley	Elektrokarren	13 €
Buggy	Elektrischer Wagen	no
Clubs	Leihschläger	13 €
Credit cards	Kreditkarten	no

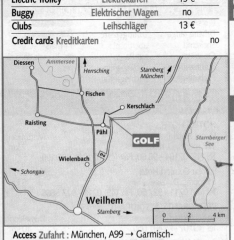

Access Zufahrt : München, A99 → Garmisch-Partenkirchen. Exit (Ausf.) Starnberg. In Starnberg, B2 → Weilheim. Km 41, turn right → Pähl → Golf

Map 2 on page 356 Karte 2 Seite 356

Golf course PLATZ — 15/20

Site	Lage	
Maintenance	Instandhaltung	
Architect	Architekt	Kurt Rossknecht
Type	Typ	forest, parkland
Relief	Begehbarkeit	
Water in play	Platz mit Wasser	
Exp. to wind	Wind ausgesetzt	
Trees in play	Platz mit Bäumen	

Scorecard Scorekarte	Chp. Chp.	Mens Herren	Ladies Damen
Length Länge	5964	5692	5055
Par	71	71	71
Slope system	130	126	125

Advised golfing ability Empfohlene Spielstärke — 0 12 24 36

Hcp required Min. Handicap 36

Club house & amenities KLUBHAUS UND NEBENGEBÄUDE — 7/10

Pro shop	Pro shop	
Driving range	Übungsplatz	
Sheltered	überdacht	yes
On grass	auf Rasen	yes
Putting-green	Putting-grün	yes
Pitching-green	Pitching-grün	yes

Hotel facilities HOTEL BESCHREIBUNG — 6/10

HOTELS HOTELS

Kaiserin Elisabeth, 70 rooms, D 128 € — Feldafing
Tel (49) 08157 - 930 90, Fax (49) 08157 -930 9133 — 15 km

Engelhof, 12 rooms, D 71 € — Tutzing
Tel (49) 08158 - 30 61, Fax (49) 08158 - 67 85 — 4 km

Ammersee Hotel, 40 rooms, D 120 € — Herrsching
Tel (49) 08152 - 968 70, Fax (49) 08152 - 53 74 — 20 km

RESTAURANTS RESTAURANT

Seehaus — Diessen-Riederau
Tel (49) 08807 - 7300 — 12 km

Forsthaus Ilkahöhe — Tutzing
Tel (49) 08158 - 8242 — 12 km

HUBBELRATH

17 | 8 | 6

Hubbelrath gehört zu den Plätzen in Deutschland, die jeder kennen sollte. Er ist gleichzeitig eines der besten Beispiele für das Können Bernhard von Limburgers, dessen Kunst, sich das hier ziemlich hügelige Gelände zunutze zu machen, von wirklich grosser Inspiration zeugt. Aufgrund teilweise nicht immer erkennbarer Schwierigkeiten ist dies ein Platz für erfahrene Spieler. Eine gute Ballkontrolle vorausgesetzt, werden diese mit den Hindernissen besser zurechtkommen als der Rest, auch deswegen, weil sie sich von den vielen blinden Schlägen und Grüns weniger einschüchtern lassen. Die Hindernisse sind ebenso zahlreich wie gefährlich und können den Eindruck eines tückischen Platzes vermitteln. Man braucht schon einige Runden, um den Kurs einigermassen in den Griff zu bekommen, was aber angesichts des Vergnügens hier zu spielen, leicht zu verschmerzen ist. Abgeschirmt von der Hektik des Ruhrgebiets, befindet sich der Platz in erhöhter Lage auf einem bewaldeten Hügel, von wo sich schöne Blicke auf Düsseldorf und Ratingen eröffnen. Hubbelrath offeriert in schöner Umgebung eine sportliche Herausforderung ersten Ranges.

This is one of Germany's courses that everyone should know, and one of the finest testimonies to the skill of Bernhard von Limburger, whose use of a rather hilly terrain can only be described as truly inspired. The sometimes concealed difficulties make this a layout reserved for experienced players; if they know how to control the ball, they will cope with the hazards better than the rest and, importantly, will be somewhat less intimidated by a number of blind shots and greens. The hazards are as numerous as they are truly dangerous and can give you the impression of playing a treacherous course. You certainly need to play several rounds to get to grips with it, but it is always a pleasure to come back here. Sheltered from the rumbling Ruhr region, its elevated location on a wood-covered hill provides some fine views over Düsseldorf and Ratingen. Hubbelrath is a lovely walk and an exciting challenge of the highest order.

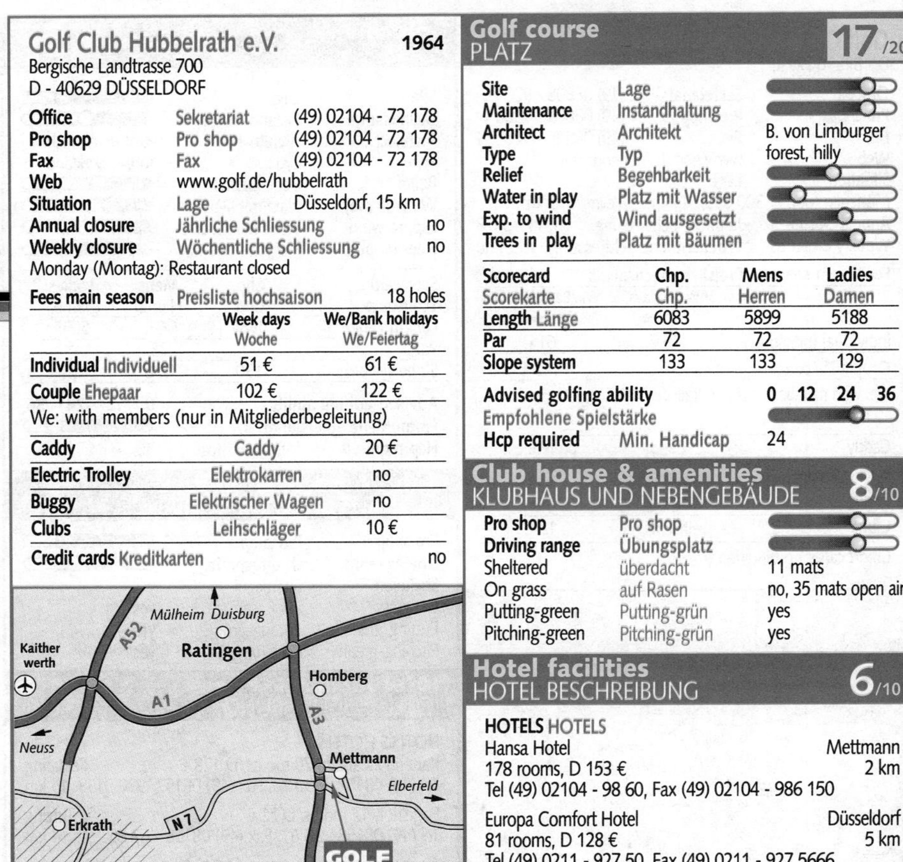

Golf Club Hubbelrath e.V. — 1964

Bergische Landtrasse 700
D - 40629 DÜSSELDORF

Office	Sekretariat	(49) 02104 - 72 178
Pro shop	Pro shop	(49) 02104 - 72 178
Fax	Fax	(49) 02104 - 72 178
Web	www.golf.de/hubbelrath	
Situation	Lage	Düsseldorf, 15 km
Annual closure	Jährliche Schliessung	no
Weekly closure	Wöchentliche Schliessung	no

Monday (Montag): Restaurant closed

Fees main season Preisliste hochsaison		18 holes
	Week days Woche	**We/Bank holidays** We/Feiertag
Individual Individuell	51 €	61 €
Couple Ehepaar	102 €	122 €

We: with members (nur in Mitgliederbegleitung)

Caddy	Caddy	20 €
Electric Trolley	Elektrokarren	no
Buggy	Elektrischer Wagen	no
Clubs	Leihschläger	10 €
Credit cards Kreditkarten		no

Access Zufahrt : Düsseldorf, A3 → Oberhausen. Exit (Ausf.) Düsseldorf-Mettmann. B7 → Mettmann. 800 m, → Golf on the left

Map 3 on page 358 Karte 3 Seite 358

Golf course PLATZ — 17/20

Site	Lage	
Maintenance	Instandhaltung	
Architect	Architekt	B. von Limburger
Type	Typ	forest, hilly
Relief	Begehbarkeit	
Water in play	Platz mit Wasser	
Exp. to wind	Wind ausgesetzt	
Trees in play	Platz mit Bäumen	

Scorecard Scorekarte	**Chp.** Chp.	**Mens** Herren	**Ladies** Damen
Length Länge	6083	5899	5188
Par	72	72	72
Slope system	133	133	129

Advised golfing ability Empfohlene Spielstärke — 0 12 24 36

Hcp required Min. Handicap 24

Club house & amenities KLUBHAUS UND NEBENGEBÄUDE — 8/10

Pro shop	Pro shop	
Driving range	Übungsplatz	
Sheltered	überdacht	11 mats
On grass	auf Rasen	no, 35 mats open air
Putting-green	Putting-grün	yes
Pitching-green	Pitching-grün	yes

Hotel facilities HOTEL BESCHREIBUNG — 6/10

HOTELS HOTELS

Hansa Hotel — Mettmann
178 rooms, D 153 € — 2 km
Tel (49) 02104 - 98 60, Fax (49) 02104 - 986 150

Europa Comfort Hotel — Düsseldorf
81 rooms, D 128 € — 5 km
Tel (49) 0211 - 927 50, Fax (49) 0211 - 927 5666

RESTAURANTS RESTAURANT

Im Schiffchen — Düsseldorf
Tel (49) 0211 - 401 050 — 10 km

Am Weinberg, Tel(49) 0211 - 289 333 — 400 m

Weinhaus Tante Anna — Düsseldorf
Tel (49) 0211 - 131 163 — 15 km

IFFELDORF

16 | 7 | 6

Der zwischen Garmisch-Partenkirchen und München befindliche Teil Bayerns ist gesegnet mit zahlreichen Golfplätzen, von denen viele in die wunderschöne Voralpenlandschaft zwischen offenem Hügelland und Gebirgsszenerie eingebettet sind. Die meisten dieser Kurse sind naturgemäss ziemlich hügelig und damit ein echter Fitness-Test für die meist stadtverwöhnten Golfer. Iffeldorf ist in dieser Hinsicht ganz anders. Die Anlage ist ein ausgezeichnetes Beispiel für einen Golfplatz mit einem guten, wenn auch nicht herausragendem Design, das einerseits der ganzen Familie ungetrübtes Spielvergnügen bereitet, andererseits aber auch den guten Spielern genügend interessante Herausforderungen stellt. Das Layout ist sehr "ehrlich" und man findet die unterschiedlichsten Hindernisse vor, so dass der Kurs auch bei oftmaligem Spielen nicht langweilig wird. Das Sahnestück dieser qualitativ hochwertigen Anlage sind zweifellos die Grüns, die hervorragend gestaltet, von ausreichender Grösse und sorgfältig verteidigt sind.

From Garmisch-Partenkirchen to Munich, Bavaria is full of courses often set in wonderful landscapes between the open countryside and mountain scenery, doubtless a little hilly for town folk a great way to get fit again. The actual course is something else. It is a good example of an excellent golf course, well if not exceptionally designed where all the family can play without any problem and where good players come face to face with interesting challenges. It is a very honest layout where difficulties are evenly spread around the course and varied enough to always enjoy coming back for more. The greens are of the same quality, well designed, reasonably sized and carefully protected.

Golfplatz Iffeldorf e.V. — 1990

Gut Rettenberg 3
D - 82393 IFFELDORF

Office	Sekretariat	(49) 08856 - 9255 55
Pro shop	Pro shop	(49) 08856 - 9255 20
Fax	Fax	(49) 08856 - 9255 59
Web	www.golf.de/iffeldorf	
Situation	Lage	

München (pop. 1 300 000), 50 km - Garmisch-Partenkirchen, 35 km

Annual closure	Jährliche Schliessung	no
Weekly closure	Wöchentliche Schliessung	no

Fees main season Preisliste hochsaison	**Week days** Woche	**We/Bank holidays** We/Feiertag
		18 holes
Individual Individuell	51 €	61 €
Couple Ehepaar	102 €	122 €

Caddy	Caddy	26 €
Electric Trolley	Elektrokarren	13 €
Buggy	Elektrischer Wagen	26 €
Clubs	Leihschläger	10 €

Credit cards Kreditkarten
VISA - Eurocard - JCB

Access Zufahrt : A95 München → Garmisch. Exit (Ausf.) Iffeldorf-Penzberg. → Penzberg, Golf 200 m left towards Gut Rettenberg.
Map 2 on page 356 Karte 2 Seite 356

Golf course PLATZ — 16/20

Site	Lage	
Maintenance	Instandhaltung	
Architect	Architekt	P. Postel
Type	Typ	forest, mountain
Relief	Begehbarkeit	
Water in play	Platz mit Wasser	
Exp. to wind	Wind ausgesetzt	
Trees in play	Platz mit Bäumen	

Scorecard Scorekarte	**Chp.** Chp.	**Mens** Herren	**Ladies** Damen
Length Länge	5904	5904	5234
Par	72	72	72
Slope system	122	122	120

Advised golfing ability Empfohlene Spielstärke — 0 12 24 36
Hcp required Min. Handicap — no

Club house & amenities KLUBHAUS UND NEBENGEBÄUDE — 7/10

Pro shop	Pro shop	
Driving range	Übungsplatz	
Sheltered	überdacht	3 mats
On grass	auf Rasen	yes
Putting-green	Putting-grün	yes
Pitching-green	Pitching-grün	yes

Hotel facilities HOTEL BESCHREIBUNG — 6/10

HOTELS HOTELS

Berggeist, 46 rooms, D 89 € — Penzberg
Tel (49) 08856 - 80 10, Fax (49) 08856 - 81 913 — 4 km

Sterff, 24 rooms, D 71 € — Seeshaupt
Tel (49) 08801 - 906 30, Fax (49) 08856 - 906 340 — 8 km

Gut Faistenberg, 10 rooms, D 158 € — Faistenberg
Tel (49) 08179 - 16 16, Fax (49) 08179 - 433 — 10 km

RESTAURANTS RESTAURANT

La Traviata — Golfplatz
Tel (49) 08856 - 9255 30 — on site

421

IM CHIEMGAU

15 | 7 | 6

Der Golfplatz liegt oberhalb des "bayerischen Meers", wie der Chiemsee als grösster See des bayerischen Voralpenlandes auch häufig genannt wird. Auf einer seiner beiden Inseln findet man das Schloss "Herrenchiemsee", eine der Verrücktheiten König Ludwigs II, der hier eine Kopie von Versailles errichten wollte. Die Gegend ist touristisch stark erschlossen und bietet Nicht-Golfern zahlreiche Freizeitmöglichkeiten, unter denen ein Besuch, im weniger als eine Autostunde entfernten Salzburg, nicht fehlen darf. Der holländische Architekt Dudok van Heel hat hier einen Kurs entworfen, der, ohne grosse technische Schwierigkeiten, ganz auf die Bedürfnisse der Urlauber zugeschnitten ist. Trotzdem ist der Platz anspruchsvoll genug, um nicht uninteressant zu wirken. Nach einigen Runden hat man alle lauernden Gefahren entdeckt, und ist in der Lage, Bunkern und Wasser aus dem Weg zu gehen. Zudem kennt man dann die ideale Spiellinie auf den vielen, von grossen Bäumen gesäumten Fairways. Der Platz hat keine steilen Anstiege und ist somit leicht zu Fuss zu bewältigen. Die Fairways sind von einladender Breite, so dass hier Spieler unterschiedlichen Niveaus problemlos zusammen in einem Flight spielen können. Bessere Spieler sollten sich für die hinteren Abschläge entscheiden.

A course over Chiemsee, or the lake of Bavaria, the region's largest facing the Alps with two pretty islands. One is the site of the "Herrenschiemsee", one of the whimsical notions of King Louis II (and in fact a carbon copy of the Château de Versailles). This is a busy tourist region with a lot to do and see for non-golfers, including a trip to Salzburg (less than an hour's drive). Dutch architect Dudok van Heel has designed a holiday course with no great technical difficulties, but tough enough to keep it interesting. Play it several times and you will discover the awaiting traps, perhaps be able to keep away from the bunkers and water and negotiate a way through the large trees that line many of the holes. With no steep contours, you can walk the course very easily, and as the fairways are deliciously wide, players of all levels can play together, making sure that the best tee off from the back.

Golfclub Im Chiemgau Chieming e.V. 1984

Kötzing 1
D - 83339 CHIEMING

Office	Sekretariat	(49) 08669 - 873 30
Pro shop	Pro shop	(49) 08669 - 873 30
Fax	Fax	(49) 08669 - 873 333
Web	www.golfchieming.de	
Situation	Lage	Chieming, 7 km
Annual closure	Jährliche Schliessung	1/12→31/3
Weekly closure	Wöchentliche Schliessung	no

Monday (Montag): Restaurant closed

Fees main season Preisliste hochsaison	18 holes	
	Week days Woche	**We/Bank holidays** We/Feiertag
Individual Individuell	41 €	56 €
Couple Ehepaar	82 €	112 €

– 21 years/Students: – 50%

Caddy	Caddy	no
Electric Trolley	Elektrokarren	no
Buggy	Elektrischer Wagen	no
Clubs	Leihschläger	18 €
Credit cards	Kreditkarten	no

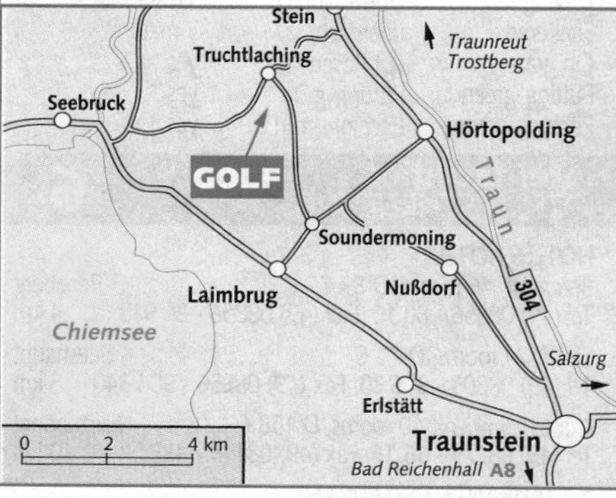

Access Zufahrt : A8 München-Salzburg. Exit (Ausf.) Grabenstätt. In Chieming → Laimgrub, Sondermoning. Left → Hart, Golf → Knesing.
Map 2 on page 357 Karte 2 Seite 357

Golf course PLATZ — 15/20

Site	Lage	
Maintenance	Instandhaltung	
Architect	Architekt	Dudok van Heel
Type	Typ	open country
Relief	Begehbarkeit	
Water in play	Platz mit Wasser	
Exp. to wind	Wind ausgesetzt	
Trees in play	Platz mit Bäumen	

Scorecard Scorekarte	**Chp.** Chp.	**Mens** Herren	**Ladies** Damen
Length Länge	6132	5962	5322
Par	72	72	72
Slope system	133	130	125

Advised golfing ability Empfohlene Spielstärke — 0 12 24 36

Hcp required Min. Handicap 36

Club house & amenities KLUBHAUS UND NEBENGEBÄUDE — 7/10

Pro shop	Pro shop	
Driving range	Übungsplatz	
Sheltered	überdacht	5 mats
On grass	auf Rasen	yes
Putting-green	Putting-grün	yes
Pitching-green	Pitching-grün	yes (2)

Hotel facilities HOTEL BESCHREIBUNG — 6/10

HOTELS HOTELS

Unterwirt, 11 rooms, D 51 € — Chieming
Tel (49) 08664 - 98 460, Fax (49) 08664 - 98 4629 — 6 km

Gut Ising, 105 rooms, D 153 € — Chieming-Ising
Tel (49) 08667 - 7 90, Fax (49) 08667 - 79 432 — 3 km

Park-Hotel Traunsteiner Hof, 59 rooms, D 82 € — Traunstein
Tel (49) 0861 - 988 820, Fax (49) 0861 - 85 12 — 20 km

Eichenhof, 34 rooms, D 161 € — Waging am See
Tel (49) 08681 - 40 30, Fax (49) 08681 - 40 325 — 30 km

RESTAURANTS RESTAURANT

Gut Ising, Tel (49) 08667 - 790 — Chieming-Ising 3 km

Malerwinkel, Tel (49) 08667 - 488 — Seebruck 7 km

ISERNHAGEN

15 | 7 | 6

Ein eher ländlicher Golfplatz, bei dem sich Wald- und Feldflächen abwechseln. Auf den ersten Neun spielt man durch teilweise enge, von alten Bäumen gesäumte Fairways, während die zweiten Neun in offenem Gelände liegen, wo sich hauptsächlich Junganpflanzungen finden. Dadurch gewinnt man den Eindruck, auf zwei unterschiedlichen Kursen zu spielen, auf die man sein Spiel anpassen muss. Während die ersten neun Löcher bei windigen Bedingungen guten Schutz bieten, halten die zweiten Neun für die Spieler einige Überrraschungen bereit. Da die Hindernisse nicht immer deutlich erkennbar sind, bleibt wenig Hoffnung, den Platz auf Anhieb in den Griff zu bekommen. Die Anlage bietet in keiner Hinsicht Aussergewöhnliches, dennoch lohnt ein Besuch, wenn man eh in der Gegend ist. Von den hinteren Abschlägen ist der Platz relativ lang. Wenn man im Familien- oder Freundeskreis unterwegs ist, wo die Spielstärken häufig sehr unterschiedlich sind, empfiehlt es sich deshalb, von etwas weiter vorn zu spielen. Letzteres kommt sicher allen Mitspielern besonders an den wenigen, klug angelegten Wasserhindernissen, entgegen.

This is a country course with alternating woodland and farm landscapes. The course itself chops and changes, from narrow sections through already old trees (the front nine) to wider spaces with smaller saplings (the back nine), giving an impression of two rather different courses to which you need to adapt your game. When the wind blows, you are sheltered up to the 9th hole, but the back nine will have a few surprises in store. And since the hazards are not always clear to see, you can hardly hope to master the course first time around. There is nothing exceptional about the layout, but it is well worth a visit when you are in the region. This is a rather long course from the back tees, so move forward a touch to spend a good day's golfing, especially if you are playing with all the family or among friends of differing abilities. Then you can all cope together with the few very clever water hazards.

Golfclub Isernhagen e.V. — 1983

Gut Lohne
D - 30916 ISERNHAGEN

Office	Sekretariat	(49) 05139 - 89 3185
Pro shop	Pro shop	(49) 05139 - 2998
Fax	Fax	(49) 05139 - 27 033
Web	www.golfclub-isernhagen.de	
Situation	Lage	Hannover, 14 km
Annual closure	Jährliche Schliessung	no
Weekly closure	Wöchentliche Schliessung	no

Monday (Montag): Restaurant closed

Fees main season Preisliste hochsaison	Week days Woche	We/Bank holidays We/Feiertag
		Full day
Individual Individuell	26 €	41 €
Couple Ehepaar	52 €	82 €

Caddy	Caddy	no
Electric Trolley	Elektrokarren	no
Buggy	Elektrischer Wagen	yes
Clubs	Leihschläger	yes
Credit cards	Kreditkarten	no

Access Zufahrt : A7 Exit (Ausf.) Kirchhorst.
In Kirchhorst → Neuwarmbüchen.
Take left → "Golfplatz Gut Lohne"
Map 5 on page 363 Karte 5 Seite 363

Golf course PLATZ — 15/20

Site	Lage	
Maintenance	Instandhaltung	
Architect	Architekt	G. Bruns
Type	Typ	forest, open country
Relief	Begehbarkeit	
Water in play	Platz mit Wasser	
Exp. to wind	Wind ausgesetzt	
Trees in play	Platz mit Bäumen	

Scorecard Scorekarte	Chp. Chp.	Mens Herren	Ladies Damen
Length Länge	6118	6118	5443
Par	72	72	72
Slope system	129	129	126

Advised golfing ability Empfohlene Spielstärke: 0 12 24 36
Hcp required Min. Handicap: 34

Club house & amenities KLUBHAUS UND NEBENGEBÄUDE — 7/10

Pro shop	Pro shop	
Driving range	Übungsplatz	
Sheltered	überdacht	yes
On grass	auf Rasen	yes
Putting-green	Putting-grün	yes
Pitching-green	Pitching-grün	yes

Hotel facilities HOTEL BESCHREIBUNG — 6/10

HOTELS HOTELS

Queens Hotel, 176 rooms, D 112 € — Hannover 14 km
Tel (49) 0511 - 51 030, Fax (49) 0511 - 526 924

Sportpark Hotel, 40 rooms, D 101 € — Hannover
Tel (49) 0511 - 972 840, Fax (49) 0511 - 972 841

Parkhotel Welfenhof — Isernhagen 2 km
110 rooms, D 107 €
Tel (49) 0511 - 65 406, Fax (49) 0511 - 651 050

RESTAURANTS RESTAURANT

Bakkarat im Kasino am Maschsee — Hannover
Tel (49) 0511 - 884 057

Maritim Seeterrassen, Tel (49) 0511 - 884 057 — Hannover

JAKOBSBERG

15 | 7 | 6

Ganz in der Nähe befinden sich auch die Schlösser und der Fels der Lorelei. Der Platz selbst zählt zu den sehr guten Anlagen neueren Datums. Seine grossen Vorzüge liegen in der abwechslungsreichen Gestaltung der Löcher, sowie der klaren Erkennbarkeit der anzuwendenden Spieltaktik. Lediglich der Abschlag an den Löchern 5 und 7 und das Grünanspiel an Loch 17, wo man jeweils sehr auf der Hut sein muss, bilden in dieser Hinsicht eine Ausnahme. Loch 7 ist der einzige Schwachpunkt eines ansonsten sehr ausgewogenen Layouts, bei dem die Hindernisse (Bunker und Wasser) zwar immer im Spiel sind, aber niemals allzu bedrängend wirken. Dies wiederum ermöglicht ein reibungsloses Vorankommen bei Flights, die sich aus Spielern unterschiedlichen Niveaus zusammensetzen, sofern von den, dem Können Aller entsprechenden, Abschlägen gespielt wird. Diesen Golfplatz sollten Sie auf keinen Fall verpassen, zumal die umliegende Region mit ihrer landschaftlichen Schönheit, der Kultur und den Weinbergen ein enormes touristisches Potential bietet.

Located in one of the cradles of German romanticism, overlooking the most boxed-in section of the Rhine valley (the views are superb) and close to the castles and the rock of Loreley, Jakobsberg is one of the very good recent courses. The variety of holes is an asset, as is the clarity of the tactics needed to play here, with the exception of the tee-shot on the 5th and the green on the 17th, which call for particular attention. The 7th is the only weak link on a course that is well-balanced overall, and where difficulties (bunkers and water) are in play but are never too oppressive. This means that players of all levels can get along well together, as long as they are wise enough to choose the right tees. In a region which such fascinating potential for tourists (landscapes, culture and vineyards), this course is a stop-off of considerable merit.

Golf-Club Jakobsberg — 1992

Im Tal der Loreley
D - 56154 BOPPARD-RHENS

Office	Sekretariat	(49) 06742 - 808 491
Pro shop	Pro shop	(49) 06742 - 808 496
Fax	Fax	(49) 06742 - 808 493
Web	www.jakobsberg.de	
Situation	Lage	

Koblenz (pop. 108 000), 10 km

Annual closure	Jährliche Schliessung	no
Weekly closure	Wöchentliche Schliessung	no

Fees main season Preisliste hochsaison	18 holes	
	Week days Woche	**We/Bank holidays** We/Feiertag
Individual Individuell	36 €	46 €
Couple Ehepaar	72 €	92 €

– 21 years/Students: – 50%

Caddy	Caddy	no
Electric Trolley	Elektrokarren	13 €
Buggy	Elektrischer Wagen	26 €
Clubs	Leihschläger	10 €

Credit cards Kreditkarten
VISA - Eurocard - MasterCard - DC - AMEX

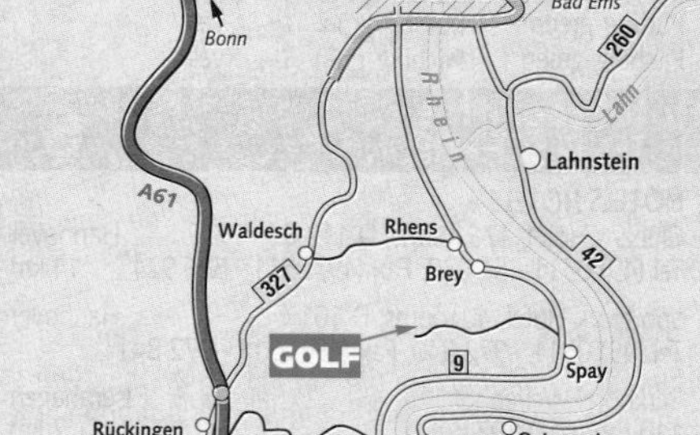

Access Zufahrt : A61 Mainz-Köln/Bonn. Exit (Ausf.) Koblenz-Waldesch, → Rhens, B9 Brey. Turn right → Golf

Map 3 on page 358 Karte 3 Seite 358

Golf course — PLATZ — 15/20

Site	Lage	
Maintenance	Instandhaltung	
Architect	Architekt	Wolfgang Jersombek
Type	Typ	open country, hilly
Relief	Begehbarkeit	
Water in play	Platz mit Wasser	
Exp. to wind	Wind ausgesetzt	
Trees in play	Platz mit Bäumen	

Scorecard Scorekarte	**Chp.** Chp.	**Mens** Herren	**Ladies** Damen
Length Länge	6200	5950	5195
Par	72	72	72
Slope system	126	126	123

Advised golfing ability Empfohlene Spielstärke — 0 12 24 36

Hcp required Min. Handicap — no

Club house & amenities — KLUBHAUS UND NEBENGEBÄUDE — 7/10

Pro shop	Pro shop	
Driving range	Übungsplatz	
Sheltered	überdacht	5 mats
On grass	auf Rasen	yes
Putting-green	Putting-grün	yes
Pitching-green	Pitching-grün	yes

Hotel facilities — HOTEL BESCHREIBUNG — 6/10

HOTELS HOTELS

Golfhotel Jakobsberg — on site
108 rooms, D 138 €
Tel (49) 06742 - 80 80, Fax (49) 06742 - 30 69

Bellevue, 95 rooms, D 123 € — Boppard 12 km
Tel (49) 06742 - 10 20, Fax (49) 06742 - 102 602

Rebstock, 15 rooms, D 102 € — Boppard
Tel (49) 06742 - 4876, Fax (49) 06742 - 4877

RESTAURANTS RESTAURANT

Königstuhl — Rhens 3 km
Tel (49) 02628 - 2244

Stresemann, Tel (49) 0261 - 15 464 — Koblenz 15 km

KÖLN

17 | 6 | 7

Abgeschieden von der Aussenwelt, ist "Refrath" ein typischer Vertreter eines im traditionellen Stil erbauten Golfplatzes, bei dem der Waldcharakter dominiert, ohne das dabei der Eindruck von Weitläufigkeit verloren geht. Longhittern, die sich hier etwas beengt fühlen können, mag er ein wenig kurz erscheinen. Für Normalsterbliche hingegen ist er lang genug, nicht zuletzt weil der Weg zum Grün oft blockiert ist, wenn man die zahlreichen Doglegs nicht von der richtigen Seite anspielt. An Hindernissen gibt es neben einem kleinen Bach, der an einigen Löchern ins Spiel kommt, eine grosse Anzahl geschickt plazierter, teilweise tiefer Bunker, die bei ungenauen Schlägen eine Menge Probleme bereiten können. Spieler, die den Ball gerade schlagen, können zahlreiche Grüns auch mit der Variante "bump and run" anspielen, wenngleich grosses Können erforderlich ist, den Ball auf diese Weise nahe der Fahne zu plazieren. Immer makellos gepflegt, zeichnet sich das klare und ehrliche Layout von Köln besonders durch die abwechslungsreiche Gestaltung seiner Löcher - egal ob Par 5, Par 4 oder Par 3 -aus.

Withdrawn from the outside world, "Refrath" stands for the pure tradition of forest golf courses, without forasmuch being too narrow. It may certainly look a little short for the long-hitters (they might feel a little cramped here), but it is long enough for the common mortal, who will see his or her path to the green irritatingly blocked if they take the dog-legs on the wrong side. Hazard-wise, there is just a little stream that comes into play on a few holes, but the very many bunkers, well located and sometimes very deep, will cause a lot of problems to wayward hitters. The straighter hitters can often bump and run their ball onto the greens, but getting close to the pin needs a lot of skill. Clear, honest and well upkept, Köln stands out for the diversity of its holes, whether playing the par 5s, the par 4s or the three par 3s, all within a remarkable uniformity of style.

Golf- und Land Club Köln — 1906

Golfplatz 2, Bensberg-Refrath
D - 51429 BERGISCH-GLADBACH

Office	Sekretariat	(49) 02204 - 927 60
Pro shop	Pro shop	(49) 02204 - 69 192
Fax	Fax	(49) 02204 - 68 192
E-mail	glckoeln@t-online.de	
Situation	Lage	

Köln (pop. 1 005 000), 20 km - Bergisch-Gladbach, 3 km

Annual closure	Jährliche Schliessung	no
Weekly closure	Wöchentliche Schliessung	no

Monday (Montag): Restaurant closed

Fees main season Preisliste hochsaison		18 holes
	Week days Woche	**We/Bank holidays** We/Feiertag
Individual Individuell	56 €	56 €
Couple Ehepaar	112 €	112 €

We: with members only (nur in Mitgliederbegleitung)

Caddy	Caddy	no
Electric Trolley	Elektrokarren	yes
Buggy	Elektrischer Wagen	no
Clubs	Leihschläger	yes
Credit cards	Kreditkarten	no

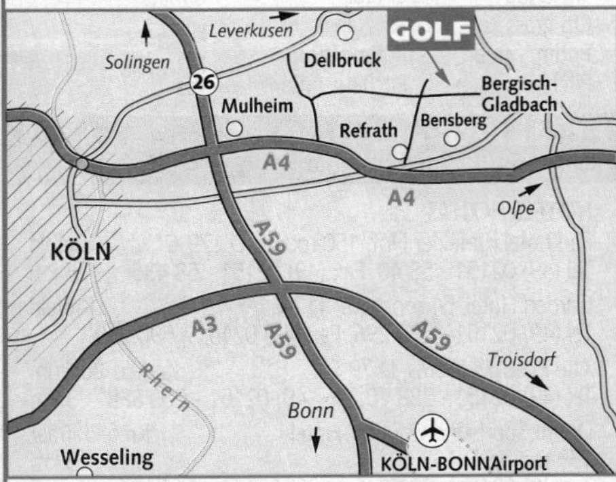

Access Zufahrt : A3 Frankfurt-Köln. Exit (Ausf.) A4 → Olpe. Exit Bergisch-Gladbach-Refrath. B55, 1.5 km. → Bensberg. Dolmanstrasse. Turn right in Altrefratherstr.

Map 3 on page 358 Karte 3 Seite 358

Golf course — PLATZ — 17/20

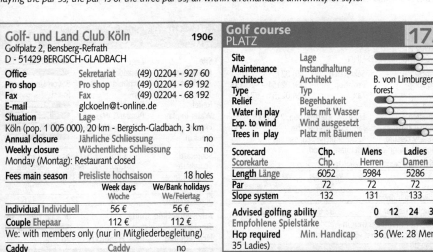

Site	Lage	
Maintenance	Instandhaltung	
Architect	Architekt	B. von Limburger
Type	Typ	forest
Relief	Begehbarkeit	
Water in play	Platz mit Wasser	
Exp. to wind	Wind ausgesetzt	
Trees in play	Platz mit Bäumen	

Scorecard Scorekarte	**Chp.** Chp.	**Mens** Herren	**Ladies** Damen
Length Länge	6052	5984	5286
Par	72	72	72
Slope system	132	131	133

Advised golfing ability Empfohlene Spielstärke — 0 12 24 36

Hcp required Min. Handicap 36 (We: 28 Men, 35 Ladies)

Club house & amenities — KLUBHAUS UND NEBENGEBÄUDE — 6/10

Pro shop	Pro shop	
Driving range	Übungsplatz	
Sheltered	überdacht	6 mats
On grass	auf Rasen	yes
Putting-green	Putting-grün	yes
Pitching-green	Pitching-grün	yes

Hotel facilities — HOTEL BESCHREIBUNG — 7/10

HOTELS HOTELS

Waldhotel Mangold, 21 rooms, D 153 € — Bensberg
Tel (49) 02204 - 95 550, Fax (49) 02204 - 955 560 — 3 km

Gronauer Tannenhof, 34 rooms, D 128 € — Gronau
Tel (49) 02202 - 941 40, Fax (49) 02202 - 941 444 — 3 km

Schlosshotel Lerbach, 54 rooms, D 255 € Bergisch-Gladbach
Tel (49) 02202 - 20 40, Fax (49) 02202 - 204 940 — 3 km

RESTAURANTS RESTAURANT

Restaurant Dieter Müller — Bergisch-Gladbach
Tel (49) 02202 - 2040 — 3 km

Eggemans Bürgerhaus — Bergisch-Gladbach
Tel (49) 02202 - 36 134 — 3 km

KREFELDER

17 | 7 | 7

Der Platz ist somit typisch für eine Zeit, in der den Architekten weder die technischen noch die finanziellen Mittel zur Verfügung standen, das Gelände grundlegend zu verändern. So folgen die Spielbahnen den kleinen, natürlichen Unebenheiten des Geländes und führen durch teilweise sehr enge, baumgesäumte Fairwayschluchten, was den Spielern präzise Schläge abverlangt. Bei den zehn als Dogleg verlaufenden Bahnen erweist sich eine Draw vom Abschlag als sehr hilfreich. Strategische Überlegungen erfordert in erster Linie das Anspiel der Grüns, die mittelgross, leicht gewellt und halbwegs gut verteidigt sind. "Bump and run" Schläge empfehlen sich nur während der Sommermonate, wenn der Boden hart und trocken ist, ansonsten muss man versuchen die Grüns mit hohen Pitch- und Lobschlägen anzugreifen. Putten ist in den seltensten Fällen eine Formsache, doch wird einem dieser Platz in der Hinsicht wenig Ungemach bereiten. Wasser ist kaum im Spiel, so erkennt man schnell, dass dies die Art von Platz ist, an dem Schläge vorwiegend durch unpräzises Spiel eingebüsst werden.

Built more than 60 years ago, this is a "senior" course that is typical of an age when designers did not have the financial resources to change the lie of the land. The course hugs the lightly rolling natural contours and winds its way (sometimes very tightly) through trees, which call for some straight hitting. A draw off the tee will come in handy as well to cope with the ten dog-legs. The basic strategy lies before you reach the greens, since these are mid-sized, moderately contoured and averagely well-guarded but no more. Bump and run shots are recommended only in summer, when the ground is dry enough, otherwise this is a place for pitchers and lobbers. Actual putting is hardly a formality, but there are few nasty surprises in store. As water is only rarely in play, you will soon realize that this is the kind of course where you insidiously drop strokes through lack of accuracy.

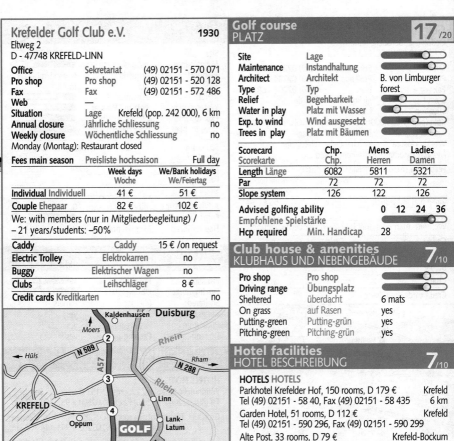

Krefelder Golf Club e.V. — 1930

Eltweg 2
D - 47748 KREFELD-LINN

Office	Sekretariat	(49) 02151 - 570 071
Pro shop	Pro shop	(49) 02151 - 520 128
Fax	Fax	(49) 02151 - 572 486
Web	—	
Situation	Lage	Krefeld (pop. 242 000), 6 km
Annual closure	Jährliche Schliessung	no
Weekly closure	Wöchentliche Schliessung	no

Monday (Montag): Restaurant closed

Fees main season Preisliste hochsaison — Full day

	Week days / Woche	We/Bank holidays / We/Feiertag
Individual Individuell	41 €	51 €
Couple Ehepaar	82 €	102 €

We: with members (nur in Mitgliederbegleitung) / – 21 years/students: –50%

Caddy	Caddy	15 € /on request
Electric Trolley	Elektrokarren	no
Buggy	Elektrischer Wagen	no
Clubs	Leihschläger	8 €
Credit cards	Kreditkarten	no

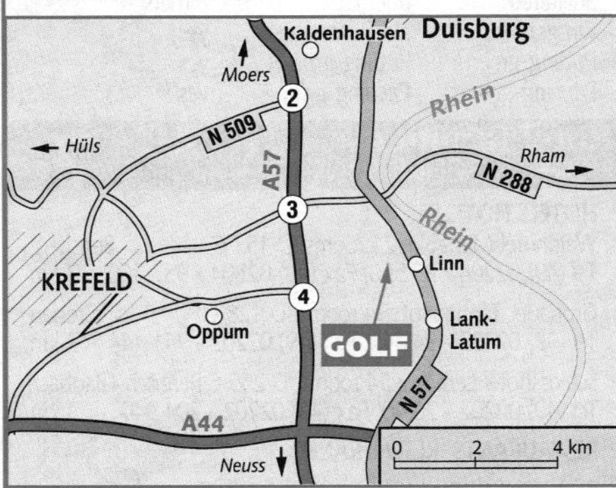

Access Zufahrt : A57 Köln-Moers. Exit (Ausf.) Krefeld-Oppum. First traffic lights turn right, next ones, right again → Autobahnbrücke. → Golf

Map 3 on page 358 Karte 3 Seite 358

Golf course / PLATZ — 17/20

Site	Lage	
Maintenance	Instandhaltung	
Architect	Architekt	B. von Limburger
Type	Typ	forest
Relief	Begehbarkeit	
Water in play	Platz mit Wasser	
Exp. to wind	Wind ausgesetzt	
Trees in play	Platz mit Bäumen	

Scorecard Scorekarte	**Chp.** Chp.	**Mens** Herren	**Ladies** Damen
Length Länge	6082	5811	5321
Par	72	72	72
Slope system	126	122	126

Advised golfing ability Empfohlene Spielstärke — 0 12 24 36

Hcp required Min. Handicap — 28

Club house & amenities / KLUBHAUS UND NEBENGEBÄUDE — 7/10

Pro shop	Pro shop	
Driving range	Übungsplatz	
Sheltered	überdacht	6 mats
On grass	auf Rasen	yes
Putting-green	Putting-grün	yes
Pitching-green	Pitching-grün	yes

Hotel facilities / HOTEL BESCHREIBUNG — 7/10

HOTELS HOTELS

Parkhotel Krefelder Hof, 150 rooms, D 179 € — Krefeld
Tel (49) 02151 - 58 40, Fax (49) 02151 - 58 435 — 6 km

Garden Hotel, 51 rooms, D 112 € — Krefeld
Tel (49) 02151 - 590 296, Fax (49) 02151 - 590 299

Alte Post, 33 rooms, D 79 € — Krefeld-Bockum
Tel (49) 02151 - 588 40, Fax (49) 02151 - 500 888 — 3 km

Dorint Sport-und Country-Hotel — Krefeld-Traar
159 rooms, D 153 € — 15 km
Tel (49) 02151 - 95 60, Fax (49) 02151 - 956 100

RESTAURANTS RESTAURANT

Koperpot, Tel (49) 02151 - 614 814 — Krefeld 8 km
Villa Medici, Tel(49) 02151 - 506 60 — Krefeld

LICHTENAU-WEICKERSHOF 15 | 7 | 6

Der Golfplatz befindet sich in unmittelbarer Nachbarschaft der Kleinstadt Ansbach, deren Ortsbild mit seiner Mischung aus mittelalterlichen und barocken Elementen noch heute an die Familie der Hohenzollern erinnert, denen die Stadt einst Ruhm und höfisches Leben verdankte. Der Platz selbst ist eingebettet in eine typisch fränkische Landschaft. Die ersten neun Löcher führen durch hügeliges Gelände, während die zweiten Neun auf flachem, offenem Terrain liegen. Die Bemühungen um die Erhaltung des natürlichen Ökosystems der zum Golfgelände gehörenden Wälder und Wasserläufe haben dem Platz 1994 einen Sonderpreis für Umweltschutz-Massnahmen eingebracht. Eine respektable Länge sowie zahlreiche Hindernisse lassen den Platz eher für gute Golfer geeignet erscheinen, doch selbst denen wird es nicht leicht fallen wird, hier ihr Handicap zu spielen. Dies liegt zum einen an den recht eigenwilligen, aber gut erkennbaren Hindernissen, wie auch an den enorm grossen, hervorragend gestalteten und gut verteidigten Grüns.

Here, we are next door to Ansbach, a small town mingling memories of the Middle Ages and the baroque era, which owed its fame and court life to a Hohenzollern lineage. The course is located in a typical Franconia landscape, with alternating rolling hills (the front 9) and flat open land (on the way in). It cares enough for its appearance and for the balance of an ecosystem of woods and streams to have won a special award in 1994 for environmental protection. Very respectable yardage and the number of hazards make this a course more for the good golfer, who will be hard pushed to play to his or her handicap owing to the course's peculiar difficulties (well visible first time around) and the greens, which are huge, well-contoured and well-guarded. It doesn't have quite the personality to be rated amongst the best, but it does deserve a serious visit.

Golf- und Landclub Lichtenau-Weickershof e.V. — 1980

Weickershof 1
D - 91586 LICHTENAU

Office	Sekretariat	(49) 09827 - 920 40
Pro shop	Pro shop	(49) 09827 - 7288
Fax	Fax	(49) 09827 - 920 444
Web	www.golf.de/lichtenau-weickershof	
Situation	Lage	

Nürnberg (pop. 498 000), 40 km - Ausbach, 15 km

Annual closure	Jährliche Schliessung	30/11→28/2
Weekly closure	Wöchentliche Schliessung	no

Monday (Montag): Restaurant closed

Fees main season Preisliste hochsaison		Full day
	Week days Woche	**We/Bank holidays** We/Feiertag
Individual Individuell	36 €	46 €
Couple Ehepaar	72 €	92 €
Caddy	Caddy	on request
Electric Trolley	Elektrokarren	yes
Buggy	Elektrischer Wagen	yes
Clubs	Leihschläger	yes

Credit cards Kreditkarten
VISA - Eurocard - MasterCard - AMEX

Access Zufahrt : BAB A6 Nürnberg-Heilbronn.
Exit (Ausf.) Lichtenau. → Golf
Map 4 on page 360 Karte 4 Seite 360

Golf course PLATZ — 15/20

Site	Lage	
Maintenance	Instandhaltung	
Architect	Architekt	unknown
Type	Typ	parkland, country
Relief	Begehbarkeit	
Water in play	Platz mit Wasser	
Exp. to wind	Wind ausgesetzt	
Trees in play	Platz mit Bäumen	

Scorecard Scorekarte	**Chp.** Chp.	**Mens** Herren	**Ladies** Damen
Length Länge	6116	6116	5153
Par	72	72	72
Slope system	126	126	124

Advised golfing ability Empfohlene Spielstärke — 0 12 24 36
Hcp required Min. Handicap — 35

Club house & amenities KLUBHAUS UND NEBENGEBÄUDE — 7/10

Pro shop	Pro shop	
Driving range	Übungsplatz	
Sheltered	überdacht	6 mats
On grass	auf Rasen	yes
Putting-green	Putting-grün	yes
Pitching-green	Pitching-grün	yes

Hotel facilities HOTEL BESCHREIBUNG — 6/10

HOTELS HOTELS

Golfhotel, 7 rooms, D 51 € — on site
Tel (49) 09827 - 920 424, Fax (49) 09827 - 920 424

Am Drechselgarten, 50 rooms, D 112 € — Ansbach 15 km
Tel (49) 0981 - 89 020, Fax (49) 0981 - 8902 605

Gasthof Sonne, 37 rooms, D 77 € — Neuendettelsau 10 km
Tel (49) 09874 - 50 80, Fax (49) 09874 - 508 18

RESTAURANTS RESTAURANT

Weinstube Leidl — Lichtenau 1 km
Tel (49) 09827 - 528

Gasthaus um Hochspessart — Lichtenau 2 km
Tel (49) 09352 - 1228

LINDAU-BAD SCHACHEN 15 7 8

Der Golfplatz wurde rund um das Schloss Schönbühl angelegt, und verfügt über ein modernes, sehr komfortables Clubhaus mit einem hervorragenden Restaurant. Die Lage selbst ist beeindruckend, bietet sie doch schöne Ausblicke über den tiefer gelegenen Bodensee (mit der Insel Mainau) und auf die nahen Alpengipfel. In dieser Region grenzen drei Länder aneinander - Deutschland, Österreich und die Schweiz. Daher rührt die Vielfalt der touristischen Attraktionen, über denen man beinahe den Golfsport vergessen könnte. Dies wäre jedoch schade, denn obwohl der Platz weder in spieltechnischer noch ästhetischer Hinsicht Herausragendes bietet, zählt er doch zum besseren Durchschnitt. Mittelklasse-Spielern, deren Streben einem gemütlichen Golftag gilt, bereitet der Kurs keine grossen Schwierigkeiten. Aus demselben Grund werden ihn bessere Spieler nicht sonderlich aufregend finden. Letzteren sei empfohlen, sich auf der Runde um die schwächeren Golfer in der Familie zu kümmern, ohne Gefahr zu laufen, sich dadurch den eigenen Score zu ruinieren.

This course is laid out around the castle of Schönbühl, with a modern and comfortable club-house which includes a very good restaurant. The site itself is quite remarkable, with some superb views over the Bodensee (with the Mainau Island down below) and the peaks of the Alps. This region lies at the crossroads between three countries - Germany, Austria and Switzerland - so there is much for tourists to see and do, perhaps almost enough to coax you off the golf-course. That would be down below) and the peaks of the Alps. This region lies at the crossroads between three countries - Germany, Austria and Switzerland - so there is much for tourists to see and do, perhaps almost enough to coax you off the golf-course. That would be a shame, because although not an exceptional layout in terms of golfing or style, this course rates well above average. It should hardly pose too many problems for average players whose first desire is to spend a relaxing day, but by the same token it will hardly excite the more proficient golfers. They can make up for it by helping the lesser golfers in the family without too much risk of spoiling their own card.

Golf-Club Lindau-Bad Schachen e.V. 1954

Am Schönbühl 5
D - 88131 LINDAU

Office	Sekretariat	(49) 08382 - 78 090
Pro shop	Pro shop	(49) 08382 - 78 090
Fax	Fax	(49) 08382 - 78 998
Web	—	
Situation	Lage	

Lindau (pop. 25 000), 1.5 km

Annual closure	Jährliche Schliessung	no
Weekly closure	Wöchentliche Schliessung	no

Monday (Montag): Restaurant closed

Fees main season Preisliste hochsaison	Week days Woche	We/Bank holidays We/Feiertag
Individual Individuell	41 €	51 €
Couple Ehepaar	82 €	102 €

18 holes

– 21 years/Students: – 50%

Caddy	Caddy	no
Electric Trolley	Elektrokarren	no
Buggy	Elektrischer Wagen	no
Clubs	Leihschläger	no
Credit cards	Kreditkarten	no

Access Zufahrt : A96 München-Lindau. Exit (Ausf.) Sigmarszell. 3 km → Golf
Map 1 on page 355 Karte 1 Seite 355

Golf course PLATZ 15/20

Site	Lage	
Maintenance	Instandhaltung	
Architect	Architekt	unknown
Type	Typ	parkland
Relief	Begehbarkeit	
Water in play	Platz mit Wasser	
Exp. to wind	Wind ausgesetzt	
Trees in play	Platz mit Bäumen	

Scorecard Scorekarte	Chp. Chp.	Mens Herren	Ladies Damen
Length Länge	5862	5591	4803
Par	71	71	71
Slope system	122	122	123

Advised golfing ability 0 12 24 36
Empfohlene Spielstärke
Hcp required Min. Handicap 36

Club house & amenities KLUBHAUS UND NEBENGEBÄUDE 7/10

Pro shop	Pro shop	
Driving range	Übungsplatz	
Sheltered	überdacht	4 mats
On grass	auf Rasen	no
Putting-green	Putting-grün	yes
Pitching-green	Pitching-grün	yes

Hotel facilities HOTEL BESCHREIBUNG 8/10

HOTELS HOTELS

Bad Schachen, 131 rooms, D 179 € Lindau-Bad Schachen
Tel (49) 08382 - 29 80, Fax (49) 08382 - 25 390 1 km

Parkhotel Eden, 26 rooms, D 92 € Lindau-Bad Schachen
Tel (49) 08382 - 58 16, Fax (49) 08382 - 23 730

Bayerischer Hof, 100 rooms, D 179 € Lindau-Insel
Tel (49) 08382 - 91 50, Fax (49) 08382 - 915 591 2 km

Villino, 16 rooms, D 153 € Lindau-Hoyren
Tel (49) 08382 - 934 50, Fax (49) 08382 - 934 512 1 km

RESTAURANTS RESTAURANT

Hoyerberg Schlössle, Tel (49) 08382 - 25 295 Lindau 1 km
Schachener Hof Tel (49) 08382 - 31 16 Lindau-Bad Schachen

LINDENHOF

14 | 8 | 8

Dieser 1994 eröffnete Platz nahe Frankfurt und des Taunus Mittelgebirges mit herrlichen Wäldern und Mineralwasser-Quellen. Der berühmte Kurort Bad Homburg, die Sommerresidence der preußischen Könige, liegt nur wenige Kilometer entfernt. Bad Vilbel, ebenfalls ein Kurort, ist vor allem durch seine Mineralwasserquellen berühmt. Der Platz liegt im Tal des Nidda und ist flach. Exzellente Drainage macht diesen Platz das ganze Jahr gut bespielbar, zumal das Greenkeeper-Team zahlreicher ist als der deutsche Durchschnitt. Dies ist kein herausragender Platz, aber ein guter, auf dem Golfer aller Spielstärken Spaß haben, obwohl etliche Wasserhindernisse an den Nerven weniger erfahrener Golfer zehren können. Die Schwierigkeiten sind gut über den Platz verteilt. Die ersten Löcher sind relativ leicht, ideal um Selbstvertrauen für den Rest der Runde aufzubauen. Die einzelnen Spielbahnen liegen relativ nah beieinander, trotzdem ist dies ein Platz, den man spielen sollte, wenn man in der Nähe ist.

This course was opened in 1994 close to Frankfurt and the Taunus, a region of low mountains, superb forests and famous spa town of Bad Homburg, the summer residence of the kings of Prussia, and Bad Vilbel, a dainty little spa town with mineral water springs. The site lies prettily in the Nidda valley and is perfectly flat. Excellent drainage makes this a playable course all year round and maintenance is much aided by a larger team of green-keepers than is usual in Germany. At least here they have understood that this is the price to pay for a quality course. This is certainly not a great course, but a good one all the same where all golfers can have fun together, even though some of the water hazards may unnerve the less experienced player. Trouble is well spread around the course, which starts off easily enough to instil early confidence. A little more space to give golfers more elbow room would probably not go amiss, but Lindenhof is still well worth a visit when in the region.

Golfclub Lindenhof, Bad Vilbel — 1995

Lindenhof
D - 61118 BAD VILBEL-DORTELWEIL

Office	Sekretariat	(49) 06101 -5245 200
Pro shop	Pro shop	(49) 06101 -5245 220
Fax	Fax	(49) 06101 -5245 202
E-mail	golfclub.lindenhof@t-online.de	
Situation	Lage	Frankfurt, 12 km
Annual closure	Jährliche Schliessung	no
Weekly closure	Wöchentliche Schliessung	

Monday (montag)

Fees main season Preisliste hochsaison	18 holes	
	Week days Woche	**We/Bank holidays** We/Feiertag
Individual Individuell	41 € *	51 € *
Couple Ehepaar	82 €	102 €

* Hotel guests: 31 € / 41 €

Caddy	Caddy	no
Electric Trolley	Elektrokarren	no
Buggy	Elektrischer Wagen	no
Clubs	Leihschläger	10 € /18 holes

Credit cards Kreditkarten
VISA - Eurocard - MasterCard - AMEX

Access Zufahrt : Frankfurt, A5 → Kassel. Exit (Ausfahrt) Bad Homburg/Bad Vilbel, then A661/B3A → Bad Vilbel . Exit Bad Vilbel, then B3 → Friedberg. In Dortelweil, → Golf. **Map 3 on page 359** Karte 3 Seite 359

Golf course PLATZ — 14/20

Site	Lage	
Maintenance	Instandhaltung	
Architect	Architekt	W. Siegmann
Type	Typ	open country
Relief	Begehbarkeit	
Water in play	Platz mit Wasser	
Exp. to wind	Wind ausgesetzt	
Trees in play	Platz mit Bäumen	

Scorecard Scorekarte	**Chp.** Chp.	**Mens** Herren	**Ladies** Damen
Length Länge	5902	5902	5295
Par	72	72	72
Slope system	119	119	121

Advised golfing ability Empfohlene Spielstärke — 0 12 24 36
Hcp required Min. Handicap — 36 (Week ends)

Club house & amenities KLUBHAUS UND NEBENGEBÄUDE — 8/10

Pro shop	Pro shop	
Driving range	Übungsplatz	
Sheltered	überdacht	8 mats
On grass	auf Rasen	yes
Putting-green	Putting-grün	yes
Pitching-green	Pitching-grün	no

Hotel facilities HOTEL BESCHREIBUNG — 8/10

HOTELS HOTELS

Golfclub Lindenhof Hotel, 19 rooms, D 97 € — on site
Tel (49) 06101 -5245 142, Fax (49) 06101 -5245 141

Golden Tulip City Hotel, 92 rooms, D 128 € — Bad Vilbel 2 km
Tel (49) 06101 - 58 80, Fax (49) 06101 - 588 488

Steigenberger Bad Homburg — Bad Homburg 8 km
169 rooms, D 184 €
Tel (49) 06172 - 18 10, Fax (49) 06172 - 181 630

RESTAURANTS RESTAURANT

Sängers Restaurant ,Tel (49) 06101 - 928 839 — Bad Homburg
Toscana (City Hotel) ,Tel(49) 06101 - 58 80 — Bad Vilbel 2 km
Oberle's, Tel (49) 06172 - 246 62 — Bad Homburg 8 km

LÜBECK-TRAVEMÜNDER

17	8	8

Der Strand von Lübeck liegt in Travemünde, einem Seebad mit einem Kasino... und einem Golfplatz. Da viele Löcher nahe an der Ostsee entlang führen, geniesst man während der Runde herrliche Ausblicke. Trotzdem wirkt der Platz mit den vielen alten, prächtigen Bäumen eher wie ein Park. Das vollständig renovierte Clubhaus steht unter Denkmalsschutz. Seit der Eröffnung der ersten neun Löcher im Jahre 1921 sind die 18 Löcher immer wieder überarbeitet und verändert worden. Am 23. Juni 2001 eröffnete der Club weitere neun Löcher, die von Karl Grohs entworfen wurden. Die 3x9 Löcher (weiss, blau, red) können beliebig kombiniert werden. Die 18 Löcher der weiß-blauen Kombination gelten als eine der schwierigsten Plätze in Deutschland. Der Club nahm außerdem eine neue Driving Range in Betrieb. Beim Bälle schlagen genießt man den Blick auf die Ostsee, eine schönere Aussicht bietet wohl keine andere Übungswiese in Deutschland. Da das Gelände sehr flach ist, ist die Spielstrategie offensichtlich. Dennoch wird man erst nach mehreren Runde die Feinheiten des Platzes kennen.

The beach of Lübeck is Travemünde, a seaside resort with casino... and golf course. With many of the holes close to the Baltic sea, the course offers some great views, but the magnificent trees make this look more like a park, with a club-house listed as an historical monument. The club has opened a third nine hole loop designed by Karl Grohs. The three nines (white, blue and red) can be combined as you please, the white-blue combination is rated one of the most difficult layouts in Germany. On top of the extension the club opened a new driving range where you hit balls towards the Baltic Sea - probably the range with the best view in Germany. Since the terrain is virtually flat, game strategy is pretty clear, although playing several rounds will help you to discover some of the more subtle touches. The imagination and technical thinking that went into this course make it a very pleasant golf and holidays destination for players of all abilities.

Lübeck-Travemünder Golf-Klub e.V. 1928

Kowitzberg 41
D - 23570 LÜBECK-TRAVEMÜNDE

Office	Sekretariat	(49) 04502 - 74 018
Pro shop	Pro shop	(49) 04502 - 73 975
Fax	Fax	(49) 04502 - 72 184
Web	—	
Situation	Lage	Lübeck (pop. 215 000), 19 km
Annual closure	Jährliche Schliessung	no
Weekly closure	Wöchentliche Schliessung	no

Fees main season Preisliste hochsaison	18 holes	
	Week days Woche	**We/Bank holidays** We/Feiertag
Individual Individuell	31 €	41 €
Couple Ehepaar	62 €	82 €

– 21 years/Students: – 50%

Caddy	Caddy	no
Electric Trolley	Elektrokarren	no
Buggy	Elektrischer Wagen	no
Clubs	Leihschläger	15 €

Credit cards Kreditkarten
VISA - Eurocard - MasterCard - DC - AMEX

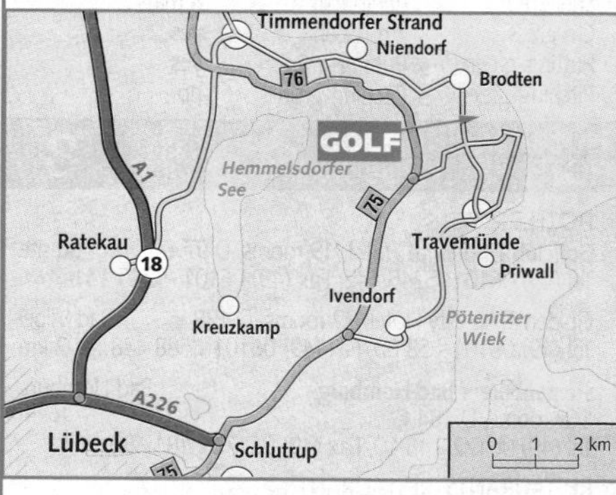

Access Zufahrt : Hamburg A1 → Travemünde. B75 → Travemünde, → Strand/Brodner Ufte, 100 m Kowizberg Str.
Map 7 on page 367 Karte 7 Seite 367

Golf course PLATZ — 17/20

Site	Lage	
Maintenance	Instandhaltung	
Architect	Architekt	Unknown Karl Grohs
Type	Typ	seaside course, parkland
Relief	Begehbarkeit	
Water in play	Platz mit Wasser	
Exp. to wind	Wind ausgesetzt	
Trees in play	Platz mit Bäumen	

Scorecard Scorekarte	**Chp.** Chp.	**Mens** Herren	**Ladies** Damen
Length Länge	6099	6099	5298
Par	73	73	73
Slope system	131	131	134

Advised golfing ability Empfohlene Spielstärke — 0 12 24 36
Hcp required Min. Handicap — 36

Club house & amenities KLUBHAUS UND NEBENGEBÄUDE — 8/10

Pro shop	Pro shop	
Driving range	Übungsplatz	
Sheltered	überdacht	2 bays
On grass	auf Rasen	yes
Putting-green	Putting-grün	yes
Pitching-green	Pitching-grün	yes

Hotel facilities HOTEL BESCHREIBUNG — 8/10

HOTELS HOTELS

Strandperle, 240 rooms, D 157 € — Travemünde
Tel (49) 04502 - 890, Fax (49) 04502 - 744 39 — 1 km

Landhaus Carstens, 27 rooms, D 153 € — Timmendorfer Strand
Tel (49) 04503 - 60 80, Fax (49) 04503 -60 860 — 10 km

Maritim, 240 rooms, D 163 € — Travemünde
Tel (49) 04502 - 8 90, Fax (49) 04502 - 892 020 — 1 km

RESTAURANTS RESTAURANT

Pesel Fischrestaurant — Travemünde
Tel (49) 04502 - 333 0 — 1.5 km

Casabianca, Tel(49) 04502 - 3631 — Travemünde

Hermannshöhe, Tel (49) 04502 - 730 21 — Travemünde

LÜNEBURGER HEIDE 16 7 5

Dieser nicht allzu lange, dafür hügelige und körperlich durchaus anstrengende Golfplatz, sollte von den Spielern in keinem Fall unterschätzt werden. Die geschickte Ausnutzung des Geländes spricht für die hervorragenden Golfkenntnisse der Architekten. Die ersten 11 Löcher sind recht eng von Wald begrenzt, so dass Genauigkeit vom Abschlag hier oberstes Gebot ist. Glücklicherweise reicht anstelle des Drivers häufig schon ein Holz 3 oder ein langes Eisen, um in eine Position zu gelangen, von der aus man die Grüns attackieren kann. Letzteres gilt insbesondere für Spieler, die den Ball gut kontrollieren können. Andererseits sind die Grüns in diesem Teil des Platzes nicht sonderlich gut verteidigt. Bei den restlichen Löchern findet man zwar breitere Fairways vor, dafür sind hier die Grüns teilweise erhöht und auch wesentlich besser geschützt. Ein "ehrlicher" Platz auf dem man, trotz leicht zu lesender Grüns, für einen guten Score hart arbeiten muss.

The very reasonable length of this course (pretty hilly and calling for a degree of physical fitness) should not result in golfers underestimating it before their round. The way the land has been used points to an excellent knowledge of the game by its designers. The first eleven holes are narrowish and laid out in a clearly demarcated forest, so accuracy off the tee is the order of the day. Fortunately, the driver can easily be left in the bag, especially since a 3-wood or a long iron is generally enough to find the right spot to attack the greens, particularly for players who can flight the ball. In contrast, the greens on this part of the course are not too heavily guarded. The fairways then grow wider, but, nothing is ever perfect, the greens are better protected and sometimes elevated, although reading them poses no particular problem. An honest course, but you have to work hard for a good score.

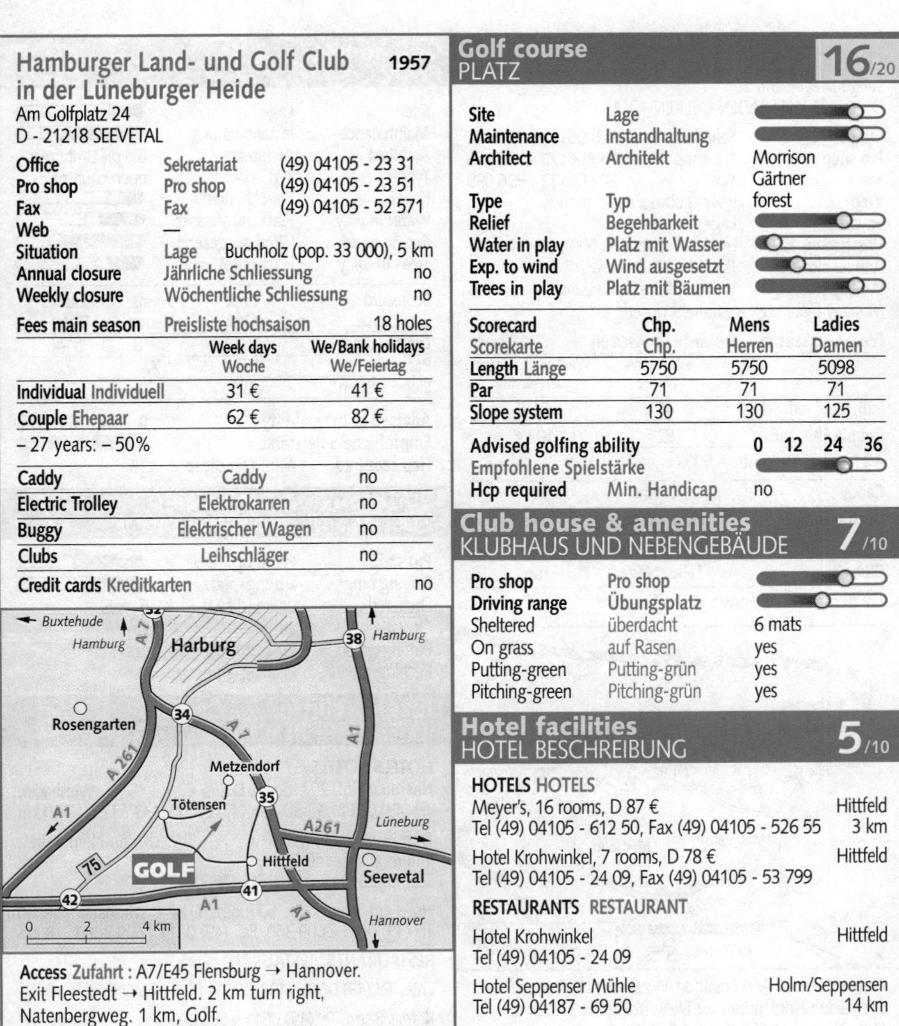

Hamburger Land- und Golf Club in der Lüneburger Heide 1957

Am Golfplatz 24
D - 21218 SEEVETAL

Office	Sekretariat	(49) 04105 - 23 31
Pro shop	Pro shop	(49) 04105 - 23 51
Fax	Fax	(49) 04105 - 52 571
Web	—	
Situation	Lage	Buchholz (pop. 33 000), 5 km
Annual closure	Jährliche Schliessung	no
Weekly closure	Wöchentliche Schliessung	no

Fees main season Preisliste hochsaison	18 holes	
	Week days Woche	**We/Bank holidays** We/Feiertag
Individual Individuell	31 €	41 €
Couple Ehepaar	62 €	82 €

– 27 years: – 50%

Caddy	Caddy	no
Electric Trolley	Elektrokarren	no
Buggy	Elektrischer Wagen	no
Clubs	Leihschläger	no
Credit cards Kreditkarten		no

Access Zufahrt : A7/E45 Flensburg → Hannover. Exit Fleestedt → Hittfeld. 2 km turn right, Natenbergweg. 1 km, Golf.
Map 7 on page 366 Karte 7 Seite 366

Golf course PLATZ 16/20

Site	Lage	
Maintenance	Instandhaltung	
Architect	Architekt	Morrison Gärtner
Type	Typ	forest
Relief	Begehbarkeit	
Water in play	Platz mit Wasser	
Exp. to wind	Wind ausgesetzt	
Trees in play	Platz mit Bäumen	

Scorecard Scorekarte	**Chp.** Chp.	**Mens** Herren	**Ladies** Damen
Length Länge	5750	5750	5098
Par	71	71	71
Slope system	130	130	125

Advised golfing ability Empfohlene Spielstärke: 0 12 24 36

Hcp required Min. Handicap: no

Club house & amenities KLUBHAUS UND NEBENGEBÄUDE 7/10

Pro shop	Pro shop	
Driving range	Übungsplatz	
Sheltered	überdacht	6 mats
On grass	auf Rasen	yes
Putting-green	Putting-grün	yes
Pitching-green	Pitching-grün	yes

Hotel facilities HOTEL BESCHREIBUNG 5/10

HOTELS HOTELS

Meyer's, 16 rooms, D 87 € — Hittfeld 3 km
Tel (49) 04105 - 612 50, Fax (49) 04105 - 526 55

Hotel Krohwinkel, 7 rooms, D 78 € — Hittfeld
Tel (49) 04105 - 24 09, Fax (49) 04105 - 53 799

RESTAURANTS RESTAURANT

Hotel Krohwinkel — Hittfeld
Tel (49) 04105 - 24 09

Hotel Seppenser Mühle — Holm/Seppensen 14 km
Tel (49) 04187 - 69 50

MAIN-TAUNUS

14 | 7 | 6

Die Lage von Main-Taunus zwischen Wiesbaden und Frankfurt ist ein beachtlicher Vorzug, der zum Teil für die nahe Luftwaffenbasis und den häufigen Blick auf eine Zementfabrik entschädigt. Eine weitere Stärke liegt in der Handschrift Bernhard von Limburgers, auch wenn dieser Platz sicherlich nicht zu dessen besten Arbeiten zählt. Die Junganpflanzungen auf diesem offenen Gelände werden in absehbarer Zeit die intime Atmosphäre dieser Anlage noch verstärken. Als Hindernisse sind die Bäume jedoch keineswegs unüberwindlich. Im Gegensatz dazu kann das Wasser durchaus zum Problem werden. Es kommt bei etwa 10 Löchern ins Spiel und ist der Preis, der für einen Golfplatz mitten in einem Vogelschutzgebiet zu zahlen ist. Die nicht übermässig stark bebunkerten Grüns sind von guter Qualität, allerdings mangelt es ihnen nach heutigem Standard etwas an Form und Gestaltung. Dieser klassische Parcours hat ein höchst interessantes und schwieriges Finish, bei dem einem - zumindest auf der ersten Runde - eine Lochbeschreibung sehr gelegen kommt, um die lauernden Hindernisse auszumachen.

The position of Main-Taunus between Wiesbaden and Frankfurt is a considerable advantage, which in part makes up for the closeness of a neighbouring air-base and frequent views of a cement factory. Another strong point is the Bernhard von Limburger label, even though this is not one of his most inspired works. Over this open land, the saplings should eventually add to the intimate atmosphere, but the trees in general are not insurmountable hazards. By contrast, the water can be a problem, coming into play on ten or so holes, a fair price to pay for designing a course in a natural bird reserve. The greens are good but not over-guarded by bunkers, and to modern standards lack a little surface relief. This rather classic design has an intriguing and tough finish, where a map of the course will come in handy to spot the hazards, at least for the first time out.

Golf-Club Main-Taunus e.V. — 1980

Lange Seegewann 2
D - 65205 WIESBADEN-DELKENHEIM

Office	Sekretariat	(49) 06122 - 52 550
Pro shop	Pro shop	(49) 06122 - 935 078
Fax	Fax	(49) 06122 - 936 099
Web	www.golf.de/main-taunus	
Situation	Lage	

Wiesbaden, 12 km - Frankfurt (pop. 660 000), 19 km

Annual closure	Jährliche Schliessung	no
Weekly closure	Wöchentliche Schliessung	no

Monday (Montag): Restaurant closed

Fees main season Preisliste hochsaison — 18 holes

	Week days Woche	We/Bank holidays We/Feiertag
Individual Individuell	41 €	51 €
Couple Ehepaar	82 €	102 €

– 21 years, Students: – 50%

Caddy	Caddy	no
Electric Trolley	Elektrokarren	yes
Buggy	Elektrischer Wagen	yes
Clubs	Leihschläger	no

Credit cards Kreditkarten VISA - Eurocard - MasterCard

Access Zufahrt : A66 Frankfurt-Wiesbaden. Exit (Ausf.) Wiesbaden Nordenstadt. → Delkenheim, Hochheim.
Map 3 on page 359 Karte 3 Seite 359

Golf course PLATZ — 14/20

Site	Lage	
Maintenance	Instandhaltung	
Architect	Architekt	B. von Limburger
Type	Typ	open country
Relief	Begehbarkeit	
Water in play	Platz mit Wasser	
Exp. to wind	Wind ausgesetzt	
Trees in play	Platz mit Bäumen	

Scorecard Scorekarte	Chp. Chp.	Mens Herren	Ladies Damen
Length Länge	6042	5818	5146
Par	72	72	72
Slope system	125	124	121

Advised golfing ability Empfohlene Spielstärke — 0 12 24 36

Hcp required Min. Handicap 36

Club house & amenities KLUBHAUS UND NEBENGEBÄUDE — 7/10

Pro shop	Pro shop	
Driving range	Übungsplatz	
Sheltered	überdacht	6 mats
On grass	auf Rasen	yes
Putting-green	Putting-grün	yes
Pitching-green	Pitching-grün	yes

Hotel facilities HOTEL BESCHREIBUNG — 6/10

HOTELS HOTELS

Nassauer Hof, 207 rooms, D 255 € — Wiesbaden
Tel (49) 0611 - 13 30, Fax (49) 0611 - 133 632 — 10 km

Treff Hotel Rhein-Main — Wiesbaden-Nordenstadt
144 rooms, D 140 € — 5 km
Tel (49) 06122 - 80 10, Fax (49) 06122 - 801 164

Hotel am Schlosspark, 60 rooms, D 82 € — Wiesbaden-Biebrich
Tel (49) 0611 - 609 360, Fax (49) 0611 - 609 3660 — 8 km

RESTAURANTS RESTAURANT

Ente, Tel (49) 0611 - 133 666 — Wiesbaden 10 km

Käfer's Bistro, Tel (49) 0611 - 536 200 — Wiesbaden

MÄRKISCHER POTSDAM

14 | 7 | 6

Der Westen Berlins ist durchzogen von Kanälen und Seen und Potsdam gilt als historisches Zentrum mit dem wunderschönen Schloss Sanssouci und dem beeindruckenden Neuen Palais, die von Friedrich II von Preussen, einem aufgeklärten und kultivierten Herrscher sowie einem Freund Voltaires, erstellt wurden. Eine Besichtigung der Räumlichkeiten und des 300 Hektaren grossen Parks sollte man nicht verpassen. Etwa eine Viertelstunde von Potsdam ist der Golfplatz Märkischer Potsdam, der 1995 von Christian Staedler realisiert wurde. Ein welliges Gelände mit wenig Bäumen, die nie wirklich in die Spielbahn kommen, im Gegensatz zu den Fairway- und Greenbunkern sowie den Wasserhindernissen. Allerdings ist dies kein allzu schwieriger Platz, und die (zahlreichen) Mittelklasse-Spieler werden begeistert sein. Da die Schwierigkeiten gut sichtbar sind, ist es möglich (aber nicht sicher), sein Handicap zu spielen. Ein Platz von durchschnittlich-guter Qualität.

The west of Berlin is a region of canals and lakes, whose historical centre is Potsdam, a city with the extraordinary Schloss Sanssouci and Neues Palais. Both were creations of Frederick II of Prussia, an enlightened and cultured monarch, and friend of Voltaire. Visit both, and the 300 hectares of grounds that go with it. Twenty or so minutes away lies the Märkischer Potsdam course, created in 1995 by Christoph Staedler over relatively hilly terrain. The land is rather woody but trees never really come into play, as opposed to the fairway and green-side bunkers and the water hazards. However, this is not the world's toughest course and golfers of only average ability (and there are quite a few of those !) will love it. And as the difficulties are clearly visible, it is possible (but it is no give-away) to play to your handicap. A generally excellent course.

Märkischer Golfclub Potsdam e.V. — 1995

Schmiedeweg 1
D - 14542 KEMNITZ

Office	Sekretariat	(49) 03327 - 663 70
Pro shop	Pro shop	(49) 03327 - 663 736
Fax	Fax	(49) 03327 - 663 737
Web	www.golf.de/mgc-potsdam	
Situation	Lage	

Potsdam (pop. 140 000), 20 km
Berlin (pop. 3 500 000), 45 km

Annual closure	Jährliche Schliessung	no
Weekly closure	Wöchentliche Schliessung	no

Fees main season Preisliste hochsaison	Week days Woche	We/Bank holidays We/Feiertag
		18 holes
Individual Individuell	41 €	51 €
Couple Ehepaar	82 €	102 €

Caddy	Caddy	no
Electric Trolley	Elektrokarren	no
Buggy	Elektrischer Wagen	26 €
Clubs	Leihschläger	13 €
Credit cards Kreditkarten		no

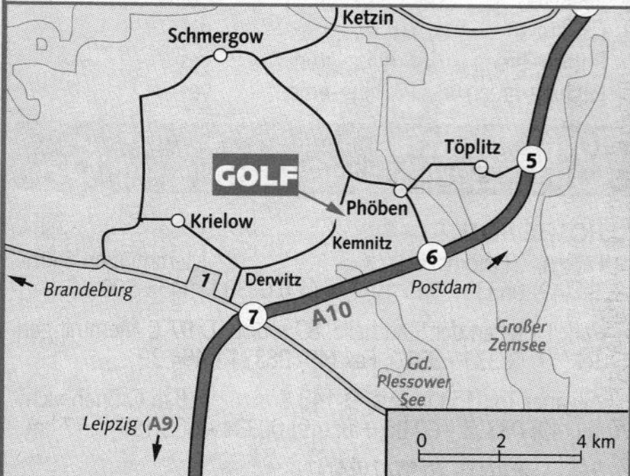

Access Zufahrt : Berlin A115 → Magdeburg. Drewitz A10 → Hamburg (Berliner Ring). Exit (Ausf.) Phöben → Golf.
Map 6 on page 365 Karte 6 Seite 365

Golf course — PLATZ — 14/20

Site	Lage	
Maintenance	Instandhaltung	
Architect	Architekt	Christoph Staedler
Type	Typ	parkland
Relief	Begehbarkeit	
Water in play	Platz mit Wasser	
Exp. to wind	Wind ausgesetzt	
Trees in play	Platz mit Bäumen	

Scorecard Scorekarte	Chp. Chp.	Mens Herren	Ladies Damen
Length Länge	6341	6114	5424
Par	72	72	73
Slope system	123	120	121

Advised golfing ability Empfohlene Spielstärke — 0 12 24 36

Hcp required Min. Handicap — 32

Club house & amenities — KLUBHAUS UND NEBENGEBÄUDE — 7/10

Pro shop	Pro shop	
Driving range	Übungsplatz	
Sheltered	überdacht	6 mats
On grass	auf Rasen	yes
Putting-green	Putting-grün	yes
Pitching-green	Pitching-grün	yes

Hotel facilities — HOTEL BESCHREIBUNG — 6/10

HOTELS HOTELS

Hotel Landgasthof am Golfplatz — Kemnitz 3 km
36 rooms, D 71 €
Tel (49) 03327 - 46 46, Fax (49) 03327 - 464 747

Schlosshotel Cecilienhof, 42 rooms, D 179 € — Potsdam 20 km
Tel (49) 0331 - 37 050, Fax (49) 0331 - 292 498

Seidler Art'otel, 20 km — Potsdam 10 km
Tel (49) 0331 - 981 50, Fax (49) 0331 - 981 5555

RESTAURANTS RESTAURANT

Pegasus, Tel (49) 0331 - 291 506 — Potsdam 20 km

Börse, Tel (49) 0331 - 292 505 — Potsdam

MEMMINGEN GUT WESTERHART 14 6 6

Dieser Platz wurde in einer Region eröffnet, der es an Golfanlagen nicht mangelt. Man findet ihn unweit von München, Augsburg und Ulm gelegen, in der Umgebung der alten Reichsstadt Memmingen, deren Stadtbild noch gut erhaltene Spuren des Mittelalters und der Renaissance trägt. Zum Zeitpunkt unseres Besuches befand sich das Clubhaus noch im Bau. Trotz seines jungen Alters präsentiert sich der Kurs bereits in ausgezeichnetem Zustand, der sich mit der Zeit weiter verbessern sollte. Lediglich der Boden ist noch etwas hart. Die gut gearbeiteten Grüns, die schon dicht mit Gras bewachsen sind, spielen sich etwas weich. Zudem hätte es nicht geschadet, die Grünkörper stärker zu kontourieren, um das Putten, diesen für den Score so ausschlaggebenden Teil des Spiels etwas interssanter zu machen. Während freistehende Bäume nur vereinzelt eine Rolle spielen, kommt dem Wind als Gefahrenelement eine weitaus grössere Bedeutung zu, insbesondere da man auch noch mit dichtem Rough, Büschen, Fairway- und Grünbunkern, sowie einigen Wasserhindernissen fertigwerden muss. Von mittlerem Schwierigkeitsgrad, ohne nenneswerte Erhebungen, eignet sich der Platz für alle Spielstärken.

This course was opened in a region where golfing facilities abound, within the immediate vicinity of Munich, Augsburg and Ulm and close to the former imperial city of Memmingen, which has preserved its vestiges of the past (Middle Ages and Renaissance). When we visited, the club-house was still being built. Despite this being early days, the course is already in excellent condition and should age well (the ground is still a little hard). The well-built greens are already well covered and soft on top, but a little more contouring would not have gone amiss to add a little spice to this department of the game which is so important for scoring. Only a few isolated trees come into play and the wind can be a significant element to be considered, especially with thick rough, bushes, fairway and green-side bunkers and a few water hazards to contend with. Averagely difficult with no significant geographical relief, this is a course for all levels.

Golfclub Memmingen Gut Westerhart e.V. — 1994

Westerhart 1b
D - 87740 BUXHEIM

Office	Sekretariat	(49) 08331 - 71 016
Pro shop	Pro shop	(49) 08331 - 71 016
Fax	Fax	(49) 08331 - 71 018
Web	www.golf.de/memmingen	
Situation	Lage	Ulm (pop. 110 000), 55 km
Annual closure	Jährliche Schliessung	1/11→1/4
Weekly closure	Wöchentliche Schliessung	no

Monday (Montag): Restaurant closed

Fees main season Preisliste hochsaison	18 holes	
	Week days Woche	**We/Bank holidays** We/Feiertag
Individual Individuell	31 €	41 €
Couple Ehepaar	62 €	82 €

Students: – 30%

Caddy	Caddy	no
Electric Trolley	Elektrokarren	3 €
Buggy	Elektrischer Wagen	26 €
Clubs	Leihschläger	5 €
Credit cards Kreditkarten		no

Access Zufahrt : A96 München-Lindau, Exit (Ausf.) Aitrach, B12 → Memmingen, → Westerhart
Map 2 on page 356 Karte 2 Seite 356

Golf course PLATZ 14/20

Site	Lage	
Maintenance	Instandhaltung	
Architect	Architekt	unknown
Type	Typ	parkland, open country
Relief	Begehbarkeit	
Water in play	Platz mit Wasser	
Exp. to wind	Wind ausgesetzt	
Trees in play	Platz mit Bäumen	

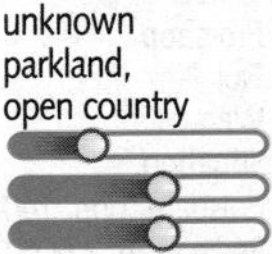

Scorecard Scorekarte	**Chp.** Chp.	**Mens** Herren	**Ladies** Damen
Length Länge	6252	6095	5390
Par	72	72	72
Slope system	124	122	122

Advised golfing ability Empfohlene Spielstärke — 0 12 24 36
Hcp required Min. Handicap 36

Club house & amenities KLUBHAUS UND NEBENGEBÄUDE 6/10

Pro shop	Pro shop	
Driving range	Übungsplatz	
Sheltered	überdacht	10 mats
On grass	auf Rasen	no
Putting-green	Putting-grün	yes
Pitching-green	Pitching-grün	yes

Hotel facilities HOTEL BESCHREIBUNG 6/10

HOTELS HOTELS

Falken, 39 rooms, D 97 € — Memmingen 6 km
Tel (49) 08331 - 945 10, Fax (49) 08331 -9451 500

Park-Hotel an der Stadthalle, 89 rooms, D 97 € Memmingen
Tel (49) 08331 - 9320, Fax (49) 08331 - 484 39

Allgäuer Tor, 153 rooms, D 148 € — Bad Grönenbach 17 km
Tel (49) 08334 - 60 80, Fax (49) 08334 - 608 199

RESTAURANTS RESTAURANT

Weinstube Weber am Bach — Memmingen 6 km
Tel (49) 08331 - 2414

Weinhaus Knöringer, Tel (49) 08331 - 2715 — Memmingen

MITTELRHEINISCHER 17 7 7

Der Mittelrheinische Golfclub liegt gleich neben dem Kurort Bad Ems, wo man sich auf die Behandlung von Hals- und Nasenkrankheiten spezialisiert hat. Der 1928 gebaute Platz ist eingebettet in dichte Vegetation und eröffnet immer wieder schöne Ausblicke auf die Höhenzüge von Eiffel und Taunus. Aufgrund des hügeligen Geländes wird man im Verlauf der Runde mit etwa einem halben Dutzend blinder Schläge konfrontiert. Die Grüns jedoch sind alle gut einsehbar. Leicht gewellt und von mittlerer Grösse bieten sie kaum Anlass für Desaster beim Putten. Golfer, die einen Fade spielen können, haben angesichts der engen Spielbahnen einen kleinen, wenn auch nicht entscheidenden Vorteil. Den Longhittern bieten sich an den fünf Par 5 Löchern gute Birdie-Chancen. Mit ausserdem fünf Par 3 Löchern hat der Platz eine eher ungewöhnliche Konfiguration. Die nicht übermässige Länge des Kurses (nur 9 Löcher verfügen über hintere Abschläge) erleichtert das Miteinander guter und weniger guter Golfer auf einer gemeinsamen Runde. Der Platz lohnt einen Besuch.

The Mittelrheinischer course is located next to the spa of Bad Ems, which specialises in nasal and throat affections. Designed in 1928, the course winds its way through thick vegetation while offering pretty vistas over the Eifel and Taunus uplands. Slightly hilly, the layout entails half a dozen blind shots but all the greens are clearly visible, moderately contoured and of average size (putting disasters are rare). Faders of the ball will enjoy a slight advantage in coping with the narrow fairways, but this is hardly a decisive factor. Long-hitters can look for birdies on the five par 5s; and with five par 3s as well, the course has a rather unusual feel to it. The overall length is very reasonable (there are back tees on 9 holes only) thus making it easier for experienced and inexperienced players to enjoy a round together. Worth knowing.

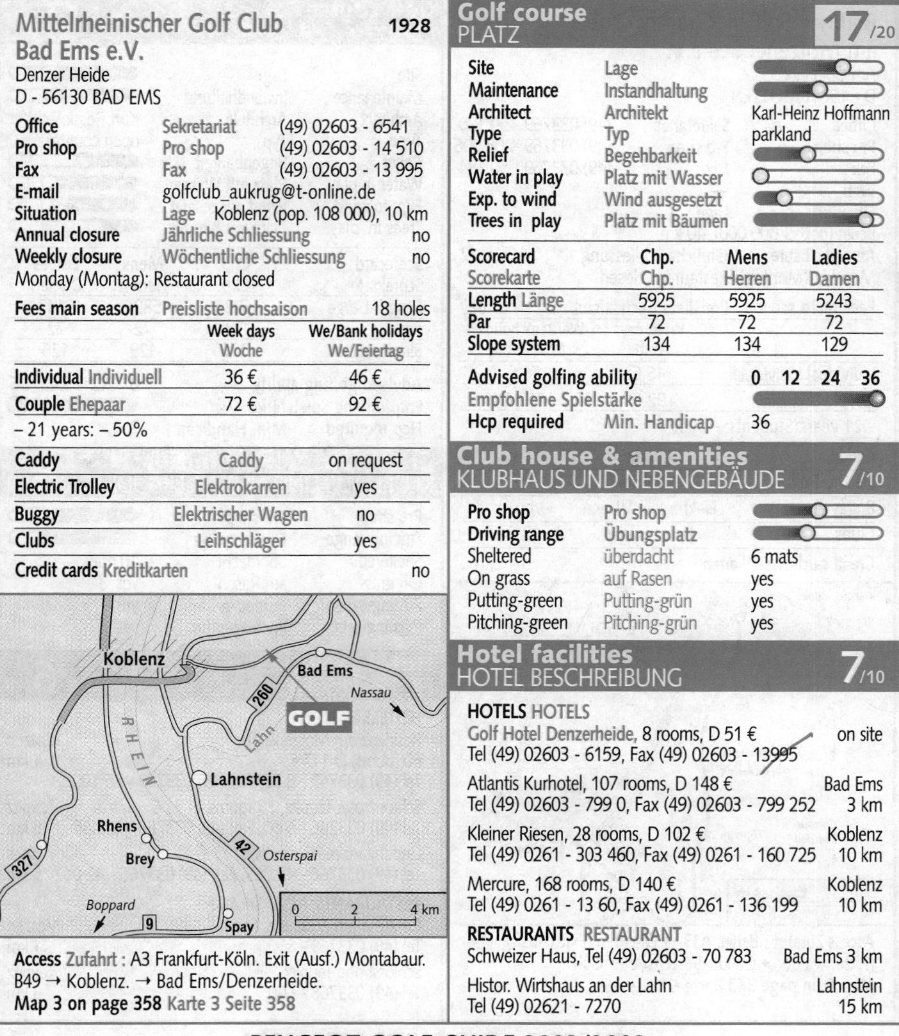

Mittelrheinischer Golf Club Bad Ems e.V. 1928

Denzer Heide
D - 56130 BAD EMS

Office	Sekretariat	(49) 02603 - 6541
Pro shop	Pro shop	(49) 02603 - 14 510
Fax	Fax	(49) 02603 - 13 995
E-mail	golfclub_aukrug@t-online.de	
Situation	Lage	Koblenz (pop. 108 000), 10 km
Annual closure	Jährliche Schliessung	no
Weekly closure	Wöchentliche Schliessung	no

Monday (Montag): Restaurant closed

Fees main season Preisliste hochsaison	18 holes	
	Week days Woche	**We/Bank holidays** We/Feiertag
Individual Individuell	36 €	46 €
Couple Ehepaar	72 €	92 €

– 21 years: – 50%

Caddy	Caddy	on request
Electric Trolley	Elektrokarren	yes
Buggy	Elektrischer Wagen	no
Clubs	Leihschläger	yes
Credit cards Kreditkarten		no

Access Zufahrt : A3 Frankfurt-Köln. Exit (Ausf.) Montabaur. B49 → Koblenz. → Bad Ems/Denzerheide.
Map 3 on page 358 Karte 3 Seite 358

Golf course PLATZ 17/20

Site	Lage	
Maintenance	Instandhaltung	
Architect	Architekt	Karl-Heinz Hoffmann
Type	Typ	parkland
Relief	Begehbarkeit	
Water in play	Platz mit Wasser	
Exp. to wind	Wind ausgesetzt	
Trees in play	Platz mit Bäumen	

Scorecard Scorekarte	**Chp.** Chp.	**Mens** Herren	**Ladies** Damen
Length Länge	5925	5925	5243
Par	72	72	72
Slope system	134	134	129

Advised golfing ability Empfohlene Spielstärke: 0 12 24 36
Hcp required Min. Handicap: 36

Club house & amenities KLUBHAUS UND NEBENGEBÄUDE 7/10

Pro shop	Pro shop	
Driving range	Übungsplatz	
Sheltered	überdacht	6 mats
On grass	auf Rasen	yes
Putting-green	Putting-grün	yes
Pitching-green	Pitching-grün	yes

Hotel facilities HOTEL BESCHREIBUNG 7/10

HOTELS HOTELS

Golf Hotel Denzerheide, 8 rooms, D 51 € — on site
Tel (49) 02603 - 6159, Fax (49) 02603 - 13995

Atlantis Kurhotel, 107 rooms, D 148 € — Bad Ems 3 km
Tel (49) 02603 - 799 0, Fax (49) 02603 - 799 252

Kleiner Riesen, 28 rooms, D 102 € — Koblenz 10 km
Tel (49) 0261 - 303 460, Fax (49) 0261 - 160 725

Mercure, 168 rooms, D 140 € — Koblenz 10 km
Tel (49) 0261 - 13 60, Fax (49) 0261 - 136 199

RESTAURANTS RESTAURANT

Schweizer Haus, Tel (49) 02603 - 70 783 — Bad Ems 3 km

Histor. Wirtshaus an der Lahn — Lahnstein 15 km
Tel (49) 02621 - 7270

MOTZENER SEE

17 | 8 | 6

Dies ist einer der neuen, guten Plätze, die in jüngerer Zeit in Deutschland entstanden sind. Seine hohen technischen Qualitäten werden vor allem den besseren Golfern auffallen. Kurt Rossknecht liess sich beim Bau der Anlage sowohl von amerikanischen wie auch schottischen Stilelementen inspirieren. Entstanden ist dabei ein Platz, der mittels wellenförmiger Fairways und tiefer Bunkerprofile wie die moderne Version eines Linksplatzeses wirkt. Die gut erkennbaren Hindernisse geben die ideale Spiellinie vor. Zudem sind sie so klug positioniert, dass gute Golfschläge nicht bestraft werden. Diese Feststellung gilt im übrigen für das gesamte Layout des Platzes. Allrounder werden diesen Platz ob seines abwechslungsreichen Lochdesigns - an 7 Löchern kommt Wasser ins Spiel - lieben. Je nach Charakter des Loches sind sowohl flache lang ausrollende, als auch hohe Schläge zum Grün gefordert, für deren Ausführung der komplette Schlägersatz herhalten muss. Die grosse Anzahl verschiedener Abschläge erlaubt jedem Golfer eine seiner Spielstärke entsprechende Wahl, aber auch die Möglichkeit je nach Tagesform und Lust zu variieren.

This is one of the best recent courses in Germany, with technical virtues that are more obvious to top level golfers. Kurt Rossknecht was inspired by both American and Scottish styles and has come up with a sort of modernized links (rolling fairways and shaped bunkers). The very clear view of hazards points to the ideal line of play, while their clever positioning and the honest layout never penalizes good golf shots. Good all-round players will love this course, where they can chop and change between low rolled shots and high approaches required by the variety of holes (water is in play on seven holes). Here, you will play every club in the bag. The large number of tees makes this a course that caters to each level of proficiency, and to each player's form and mood... not forgetting that the latter may grow darker with the pin positions on the huge, well-contoured greens.

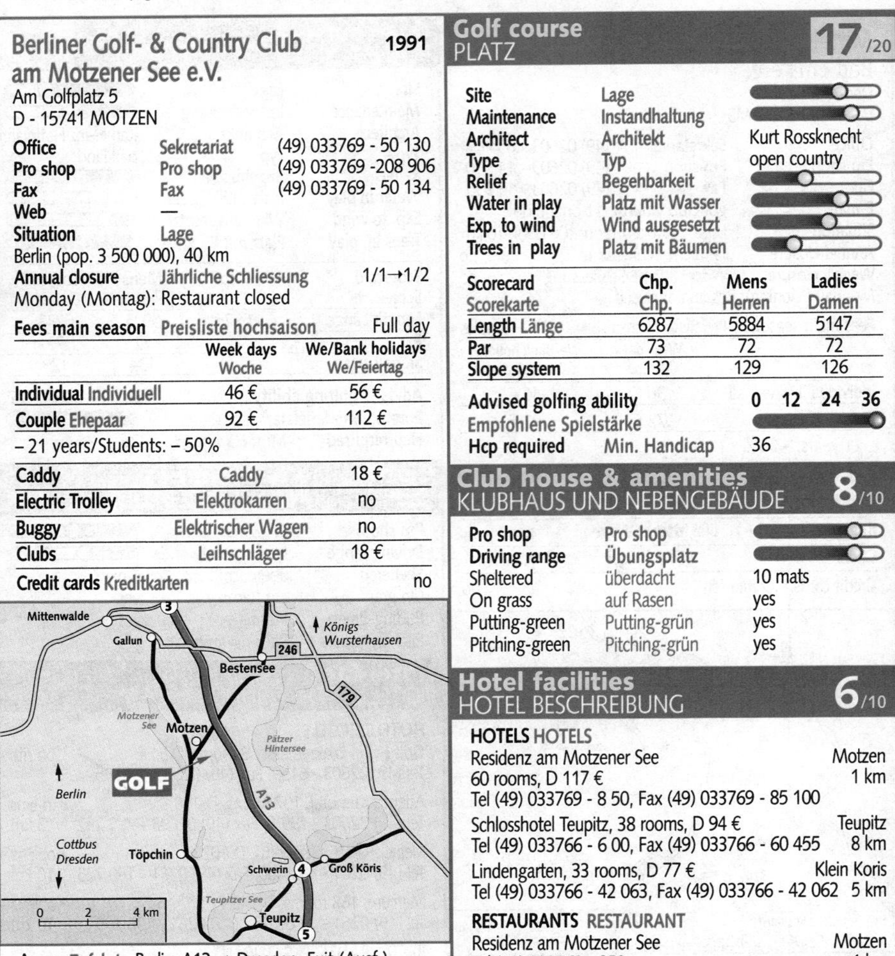

Berliner Golf- & Country Club am Motzener See e.V. — 1991

Am Golfplatz 5
D - 15741 MOTZEN

Office	Sekretariat	(49) 033769 - 50 130
Pro shop	Pro shop	(49) 033769 -208 906
Fax	Fax	(49) 033769 - 50 134
Web	—	
Situation	Lage	

Berlin (pop. 3 500 000), 40 km

Annual closure Jährliche Schliessung — 1/1→1/2

Monday (Montag): Restaurant closed

Fees main season Preisliste hochsaison	Week days Woche	We/Bank holidays We/Feiertag
		Full day
Individual Individuell	46 €	56 €
Couple Ehepaar	92 €	112 €

– 21 years/Students: – 50%

Caddy	Caddy	18 €
Electric Trolley	Elektrokarren	no
Buggy	Elektrischer Wagen	no
Clubs	Leihschläger	18 €
Credit cards Kreditkarten		no

Access Zufahrt : Berlin, A13 → Dresden. Exit (Ausf.) Mittenwalde → Gallun-Bestensee → Golf

Map 6 on page 365 Karte 6 Seite 365

Golf course PLATZ — 17/20

Site	Lage	
Maintenance	Instandhaltung	
Architect	Architekt	Kurt Rossknecht
Type	Typ	open country
Relief	Begehbarkeit	
Water in play	Platz mit Wasser	
Exp. to wind	Wind ausgesetzt	
Trees in play	Platz mit Bäumen	

Scorecard Scorekarte	**Chp.** Chp.	**Mens** Herren	**Ladies** Damen
Length Länge	6287	5884	5147
Par	73	72	72
Slope system	132	129	126

Advised golfing ability Empfohlene Spielstärke — 0 12 24 36

Hcp required Min. Handicap — 36

Club house & amenities KLUBHAUS UND NEBENGEBÄUDE — 8/10

Pro shop	Pro shop	
Driving range	Übungsplatz	
Sheltered	überdacht	10 mats
On grass	auf Rasen	yes
Putting-green	Putting-grün	yes
Pitching-green	Pitching-grün	yes

Hotel facilities HOTEL BESCHREIBUNG — 6/10

HOTELS HOTELS

Residenz am Motzener See — Motzen
60 rooms, D 117 € — 1 km
Tel (49) 033769 - 8 50, Fax (49) 033769 - 85 100

Schlosshotel Teupitz, 38 rooms, D 94 € — Teupitz
Tel (49) 033766 - 6 00, Fax (49) 033766 - 60 455 — 8 km

Lindengarten, 33 rooms, D 77 € — Klein Koris
Tel (49) 033766 - 42 063, Fax (49) 033766 - 42 062 — 5 km

RESTAURANTS RESTAURANT

Residenz am Motzener See — Motzen
Tel (49) 033769 - 850 — 1 km

Schlosshotel Teupitz — Teupitz
Tel (49) 033766 - 600 — 8 km

MÜNCHEN-RIEDHOF

16 | 7 | 7

München-Riedhof liegt in unmittelbarer Nähe zum Starnberger See, einem der grössten bayerischen Seen, auf halbem Weg zwischen München und den bayerischen Alpen. Der von Heinz Fehring entworfene Platz ist vom Layout, dem Pflegezustand und vor allem dem Service her sehr amerikanisch. Greenfeespieler erhalten neben den Pin-Positions auch die Informationen über die "Schnelligkeit" der Grüns (Stimpmeter). Das US-Flair wird durch die vielen Wasserhindernisse (Teiche) verstärkt. Dazu gibt einige Erhebungen im Gelände, die die Schlägerwahl erheblich erschweren. Die Schwierigkeiten sind gut erkennbar. Das gilt auch für die Wasserhindernisse, die für missratene Schläge allerdings weniger Gefahr darstellen, als dies Bäume und Bunker tun. Der grösstenteils spektakuläre, manchmal etwas trügerische Platz bleibt einem gut im Gedächtnis haften, was ein gutes Zeichen ist. Da die Grüns sehr gut verteidigt sind, ist eine gute Ballkontrolle unerlässlich; dennoch werden durchschnittliche Spieler hier ebenso auf ihre Kosten kommmen wie Fortgeschrittene.

The south of Munich is a very privileged region both for sightseeing attractions and the number of courses which offer a wide variety of styles. München-Riedhof is within immediate reach of the Starnberger See, one of Bavaria's largest lakes half-way between Munich and the Bavarian Alps. The course, designed by Heinz Fehring, is not the easiest in the world owing to yardage, water hazards and some steeply contoured terrain, which complicates appreciation of distance. The course is, though, very pleasant to walk around. The difficulties are there to be seen; water is, too, but is not so dangerous for mis-hit shots as the trees and bunkers. Often spectacular and sometimes a wee treacherous, the course sticks in your memory, which is a good sign. As the greens are very well guarded, good ball control is, as always, important, but average players will have as much fun as the experts.

Golfclub München-Riedhof e.V. — 1989

Riedhof 16
D - 85244 EGLING-RIEDHOF

Office	Sekretariat	(49) 08171 - 219 50
Pro shop	Pro shop	(49) 08171 - 219 50
Fax	Fax	(49) 08171 - 219 511
Web	www.golf.de/riedhof	
Situation	Lage	München, 25 km
Annual closure	Jährliche Schliessung	no
Weekly closure	Wöchentliche Schliessung	no

Monday (Montag): Restaurant closed

Fees main season Preisliste hochsaison	18 holes	
	Week days Woche	**We/Bank holidays** We/Feiertag
Individual Individuell	82 €	82 €
Couple Ehepaar	164 €	164 €

We: with members (nur in Mitgliederbegleitung)

Caddy	Caddy	no
Electric Trolley	Elektrokarren	no
Buggy	Elektrischer Wagen	no
Clubs	Leihschläger	no
Credit cards	Kreditkarten	no

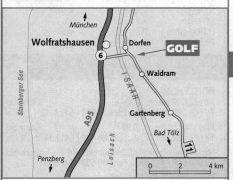

Access Zufahrt : A95 München-Garmisch-Partenkirchen. Exit (Ausf.) Wolfratshausen, → Autobahn Salzburg-Wolfratshausen. → Egling

Map 2 on page 356 Karte 2 Seite 356

Golf course PLATZ — 16/20

Site	Lage	
Maintenance	Instandhaltung	
Architect	Architekt	Heinz Fehring
Type	Typ	open country, hilly
Relief	Begehbarkeit	
Water in play	Platz mit Wasser	
Exp. to wind	Wind ausgesetzt	
Trees in play	Platz mit Bäumen	

Scorecard Scorekarte	**Chp.** Chp.	**Mens** Herren	**Ladies** Damen
Length Länge	6150	6024	5307
Par	72	72	72
Slope system	128	126	126

Advised golfing ability Empfohlene Spielstärke: 0 12 24 36

Hcp required Min. Handicap 34

Club house & amenities KLUBHAUS UND NEBENGEBÄUDE — 7/10

Pro shop	Pro shop	
Driving range	Übungsplatz	
Sheltered	überdacht	10 mats
On grass	auf Rasen	yes
Putting-green	Putting-grün	yes
Pitching-green	Pitching-grün	yes

Hotel facilities HOTEL BESCHREIBUNG — 7/10

HOTELS HOTELS

Thalhammer, 23 rooms, D 87 € — Wolfratshausen 5 km
Tel (49) 08171 - 42 190, Fax (49) 08171 - 76 185

Märchenwald, 14 rooms, D 66 € — Wolfratshausen 5 km
Tel (49) 08171 - 29 096, Fax (49) 08171 - 22 236

Ritterhof, 20 rooms, D 107 € — Grünwald 10 km
Tel (49) 089 - 649 0090, Fax (49) 089 - 649 3012

Schloss Hotel Tannenhof, 21 rooms, D 107 € — Grünwald
Tel (49) 089 - 641 8960, Fax (49) 089 - 641 9303

RESTAURANTS RESTAURANT

Patrizierhof, Tel (49) 08171 - 225 33 — Wolfratshausen 5 km

Vogelbauer, Tel (49) 08171 - 290 63 — Neufahrn 5 km

MÜNCHNER-STRASSLACH 15 6 7

In der Umgebung der Metropole München ist dies wohl einer der meist bespielten Golfplätze. Gastspieler sind am Wochenende nur in Begleitung eines Mitglieds erlaubt... Der Platz wurde 1910 inmitten einer typisch bayerischen Landschaft auf leicht hügeligem Terrain angelegt. Auf dem Platz findet sich eine Anzahl wunderschöner grosser Bäume, die an den Doglegs gefährlich ins Spiel kommen. Einige Seen und Wasserläufe sowie knapp 50 sehr sorgfältig plazierte Bunker komplettieren das Repertoire an Hindernissen. Auf den ersten Blick mag der Platz nicht sonderlich schwierig erscheinen, dieser Eindruck wird sich allerdings im Verlauf der Runde revidieren, nicht zuletzt aufgrund einer Reihe schlecht erkennbarer Hindernisse. Auf der zweiten Runde fühlt man sich schon weitaus wohler, da man dann weiss, wie der Platz taktisch zu spielen ist. Der ausgezeichnete Hauptplatz wird ergänzt durch einen nicht minder guten 9-Loch-Kurzplatz, der allerdings noch einwachsen muss.

Münchner-Strasslach is one of the busiest courses around the magnificent greater metropolitan area of Munich, and playing here on week-ends can be very difficult for green-feers. Created in 1910 over averagely-hilly terrain, the course runs over typically Bavarian landscape, with some beautiful big trees (very dangerous on the dog-legs), a few lakes and streams and a little under 50 carefully-located bunkers. At first sight it doesn't look too difficult, but out on the course it can be quite a handful with a number of hazards hidden from view. Second time out, you feel more comfortable and playing tactics are clearer. A class course supplemented by a very good and shortish 9-holer.

Münchner Golf Club e.V., Strasslach 1910

Tölzerstrasse 95
D - 82064 STRASSLACH

Office	Sekretariat	(49) 08170 - 929 180
Pro shop	Pro shop	(49) 08170 - 7254
Fax	Fax	(49) 08170-929 18120
E-mail	muenchgolfclub@aol.com	
Situation	Lage	

München (pop. 1 300 000), 25 km - Strasslach, 3 km

Annual closure	Jährliche Schliessung	no
Weekly closure	Wöchentliche Schliessung	no

Monday (Montag): Restaurant closed

Fees main season Preisliste hochsaison	18 holes	
	Week days Woche	**We/Bank holidays** We/Feiertag
Individual Individuell	61 €	61 €
Couple Ehepaar	122 €	122 €

We: with members (nur in Mitgliederbegleitung)

Caddy	Caddy	no
Electric Trolley	Elektrokarren	yes
Buggy	Elektrischer Wagen	yes
Clubs	Leihschläger	no
Credit cards Kreditkarten		no

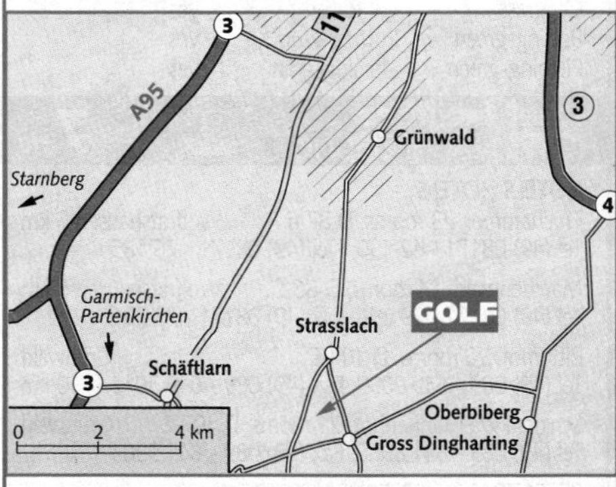

Access Zufahrt : München Süd → Grünwald. In Grünwald → Bad Tölz. Golf on the left.
Map 2 on page 356 Karte 2 Seite 356

Golf course PLATZ 15/20

Site	Lage	
Maintenance	Instandhaltung	
Architect	Architekt	unknown
Type	Typ	open country
Relief	Begehbarkeit	
Water in play	Platz mit Wasser	
Exp. to wind	Wind ausgesetzt	
Trees in play	Platz mit Bäumen	

Scorecard Scorekarte	**Chp.** Chp.	**Mens** Herren	**Ladies** Damen
Length Länge	6169	6169	5457
Par	72	72	72
Slope system	124	124	120

Advised golfing ability 0 12 24 36
Empfohlene Spielstärke
Hcp required Min. Handicap 35

Club house & amenities KLUBHAUS UND NEBENGEBÄUDE 6/10

Pro shop	Pro shop	
Driving range	Übungsplatz	
Sheltered	überdacht	2 mats
On grass	auf Rasen	yes
Putting-green	Putting-grün	yes
Pitching-green	Pitching-grün	yes

Hotel facilities HOTEL BESCHREIBUNG 7/10

HOTELS HOTELS

Ritterhof, 20 rooms, D 107 € — Grünwald
Tel (49) 089 - 649 0090, Fax (49) 089 - 649 3012 — 4 km

Alter Wirt, 50 rooms, D 97 € — Grünwald
Tel (49) 089 - 6419 340, Fax (49) 089 - 6419 3499 — 4 km

Schloss Hotel Tannenhof, 21 rooms, D 107 € — Grünwald
Tel (49) 089 - 641 8960, Fax (49) 089 - 641 9303

RESTAURANTS RESTAURANT

Gasthof zum Wildpark — Strasslach
Tel (49) 08170 - 635 — 1 km

Hubertus — Schäfftlarn
Tel (49) 08178 - 4851 — 5 km

NAHETAL

14 | 8 | 6

Der Golfclub Nahetal wurde 1986 modernisiert, wobei aber die alten Schwierigkeiten erhalten blieben. Erste Notwendigkeit hier ist Präzision, da die Fairways meist nicht sehr breit und zudem von dichtem Wald umgeben sind, was dem Platz den angenehmen Nebeneffekt von Ruhe und Abgeschiedenheit vermittelt. Im vergangenen wurden fast alle Löcher modifiziert und Wasserteiche am 3. Und am 14. Loch gebaut. Der Platz ist sehr ungewöhnlich, da alle zehn Par-4-Löcher und alle vier Par-5-Löcher "blind" sind, d.h. man sieht am Abschlag nur von den Par 3-Löchern die Fahne. Die Spiellinie ist deshalb für bessere Spieler nicht erkennbar. Man benötigt etliche Runden oder die Begleitung eines Platzkenners, um sie herauszufinden. Wer kommt schon auf die Idee am 16. Loch den Ball durch einen Stromleitungsmasten zu schlagen? Das ungewöhnlichste Loch ist wohl das 7. Loch, ein Par 4 von 340 m, wo gute Spieler mit einem Eisen 7 über die hohen Bäume am Knick des Doglegs schlagen und dann ein Eisen 8 zum Grün spielen. Schwächere Spieler müssen gerade schlagen und haben dann noch ein langes Eisen oder ein Fairway-Holz zum Grün. Dafür entschädigt der Ausblick auf den spektakulären Rotenfels für diese architektonische Sünde.

This course has been modernized in 1998, but the difficulties remain the same. The first is the need to play straight, as the fairways are not always wide and are lined with some pretty dense trees with heavy undergrowth, a feature that adds to a pleasant impression of peace and quiet. Last year most holes have been modified and ponds added on holes 3 and 14. The course design is rather unusual since all ten par 4 holes and all four par 5 holes are blind so you can see the flagstick only on the par 3 holes. The line of play is for better players hardly visible, you need several rounds or the advice of a knowledgeable player. Who would think of hitting the drive through an electricity pylon on No. 16 ? The most unusual hole is No. 7, a par 4 of 340 m, where good players hit a 7 iron over the high trees over the turn of the dogleg and a 8 iron into the green. However lesser players have to go the straight route which means hitting a long iron or a fairwood into the green. The spectacular view of the Rotenfels makes up for this sin in golf course design.

Golfclub Nahetal e.V. 1976

Drei Buchen
D - 55583 BAD MÜNSTER AM STEIN-EBERNBURG

Office	Sekretariat	(49) 06708 - 2145
Pro shop	Pro shop	(49) 06708 - 4399
Fax	Fax	(49) 06708 - 1731
Web	www.members.aol.com/nahegolf	
Situation	Lage	Mainz (pop. 186 000), 45 km
Annual closure	Jährliche Schliessung	no
Weekly closure	Wöchentliche Schliessung	no

Monday (Montag): Restaurant closed

Fees main season Preisliste hochsaison	18 holes	
	Week days Woche	We/Bank holidays We/Feiertag
Individual Individuell	36 €	46 €
Couple Ehepaar	72 €	92 €

– 21 years/Students: – 50%

Caddy	Caddy	26 € /on request
Electric Trolley	Elektrokarren	9 €
Buggy	Elektrischer Wagen	26 € (medical)
Clubs	Leihschläger	13 €
Credit cards	Kreditkarten	only Pro Shop

Access Zufahrt : Mainz A60 W, Kreuz Bingen A61 Süd. Exit (Ausf.) Bad Kreuznach. Bad Kreuznach B48 → Bad Münster → Ebernburg. Right in Schlossgartenstr. Right, Wanderweg Dreibuchen. **Map 3 on page 359** Karte 3 Seite 359

Golf course PLATZ 14/20

Site	Lage	
Maintenance	Instandhaltung	
Architect	Architekt	Armin Keller
Type	Typ	forest
Relief	Begehbarkeit	
Water in play	Platz mit Wasser	
Exp. to wind	Wind ausgesetzt	
Trees in play	Platz mit Bäumen	

Scorecard Scorekarte	Chp. Chp.	Mens Herren	Ladies Damen
Length Länge	5888	5888	5159
Par	72	72	72
Slope system	133	133	127

Advised golfing ability Empfohlene Spielstärke: 0 12 24 36

Hcp required Min. Handicap: We: 36

Club house & amenities KLUBHAUS UND NEBENGEBÄUDE 8/10

Pro shop	Pro shop	
Driving range	Übungsplatz	
Sheltered	überdacht	10 mats
On grass	auf Rasen	yes
Putting-green	Putting-grün	yes
Pitching-green	Pitching-grün	yes

Hotel facilities HOTEL BESCHREIBUNG 6/10

HOTELS HOTELS

Parkhotel Kurhaus, 124 rooms, D 112 € — Bad Kreuznach
Tel (49) 0671 - 80 20, Fax (49) 0671 - 354 77 — 12 km

Landhotel Kauzenberg, 47 rooms, D 112 € — Bad Kreuznach
Tel (49) 0671 - 38 000, Fax (49) 0671 - 3800 124 — 4 km

Hotel am Kurpark, 2 km28 rooms, D 92 € — Bad Münster a. Stein
Tel (49) 06708 - 629 000, Fax (49) 06708 -629 0029 — 2 km

RESTAURANTS RESTAURANT

Metzlers Gasthof — Bad Kreuznach-Hackenheim
Tel (49) 0671 - 65 312 — 14 km

Die Kauzenburg, — Bad Kreuznach
Tel (49) 0671 - 380 0801 — 12 km

NEUHOF

15 | 7 | 7

Eines soll gleich zu Beginn gesagt sein, Spieler mit hohem Handicap können von dem, an den ersten Löchern ins Spiel kommenden Wasser, leicht abgeschreckt werden. Alles in allem sind die vorhandenen Schwierigkeiten durchaus dazu angetan, den durchschnittlichen "Hacker" permanent zu beunruhigen. Objektiv betrachtet ist der Platz aber gar nicht so schwierig, doch was heisst das schon in Anbetracht der Tatsache, dass Golf ebenso sehr mit dem Kopf wie mit dem Körper gespielt wird. Einige extrem lange Par 4 Löcher stellen eine anspruchsvolle Aufgabe selbst für bessere Spieler dar, die auch beim Anspiel einiger frontal von Gräben geschützter Grüns, eine harte Nuss zu knacken haben. Die intelligente Plazierung der Hindernisse spricht für den Sachverstand der Architekten. Die sehr amerikanische Platzarchitektur mit dem Merkmal gut erkennbarer Schwierigkeiten verlangt vom Golfer häufig die Entscheidung, entweder auf Angriff oder auf Sicherheit zu spielen. Bevor man daran geht, auf diesem technisch wie auch taktisch anspruchsvollen Layout, ein gutes Zählspiel-Ergebnis zu erreichen, empfiehlt es sich vorher einige Runden Matchplay zu spielen.

Let it be said right away that here, many high-handicappers may well be seriously put off by the water protecting the first holes. By and large there are quite a few difficulties around, enough to prevent the average hacker from ever really feeling confident, although objectively this is not the most difficult course in the world. But no-one needs telling that golf is as much a matter of mind as of body. Some very long par 4s will also be a handful for the better players, who will need to think long and hard before trying to hit several greens guarded by frontal ditches. The designers knew their golf and have laid out hazards intelligently. Rather American in style, Neuhof calls for serious debate over whether to "go for it" or lay up. In this sense the difficulties are clear to see, but before envisioning any idea of a good card from this technical and tactical examination of your golfing skills, you are better off trying a few rounds of matchplay.

Golf Club Neuhof e.V. — 1984

Hofgut Neuhof
D - 63303 DREIEICH

Office	Sekretariat	(49) 06102 - 327 010
Pro shop	Pro shop	(49) 06102 - 33 331
Fax	Fax	(49) 06102 - 327 012
E-mail	golfneuhof@aol.com	
Situation	Lage Frankfurt (pop. 660 000), 15 km	
Annual closure	Jährliche Schliessung	1/1→28/2
Weekly closure	Wöchentliche Schliessung	no

Monday (Montag): Restaurant closed

Fees main season Preisliste hochsaison	18 holes	
	Week days Woche	**We/Bank holidays** We/Feiertag
Individual Individuell	51 €	51 €
Couple Ehepaar	102 €	102 €

We: with members (nur in Mitgliederbegleitung) / – 21 years/Students: – 50%

Caddy	Caddy	on request
Electric Trolley	Elektrokarren	no
Buggy	Elektrischer Wagen	no
Clubs	Leihschläger	5 €
Credit cards	Kreditkarten	no

Access Zufahrt : A3 Frankfurt-Würzburg. Exit (Ausf.) Offenbach-Kreuz. B661 → Langen/Darmstadt. Exit Dreieich-Götzenhaim. 3 km Golf

Map 3 on page 359 Karte 3 Seite 359

Golf course — PLATZ — 15/20

Site	Lage	
Maintenance	Instandhaltung	
Architect	Architekt	Hauser Patrick Merrigan
Type	Typ	parkland
Relief	Begehbarkeit	
Water in play	Platz mit Wasser	
Exp. to wind	Wind ausgesetzt	
Trees in play	Platz mit Bäumen	

Scorecard Scorekarte	**Chp.** Chp.	**Mens** Herren	**Ladies** Damen
Length Länge	6109	5794	5124
Par	72	72	72
Slope system	132	126	126

Advised golfing ability Empfohlene Spielstärke — 0 12 24 36

Hcp required Min. Handicap — 28 Men, 32 Ladies

Club house & amenities — KLUBHAUS UND NEBENGEBÄUDE — 7/10

Pro shop	Pro shop	
Driving range	Übungsplatz	
Sheltered	überdacht	yes
On grass	auf Rasen	yes
Putting-green	Putting-grün	yes
Pitching-green	Pitching-grün	yes

Hotel facilities — HOTEL BESCHREIBUNG — 7/10

HOTELS HOTELS

Kempinski Hotel Gravenbruch — Neu-Isenburg-Gravenbruch
304 rooms, D 230 € — 5 km
Tel (49) 06102 - 50 50, Fax (49) 06102 - 505 900

Holiday Inn, 183 rooms, D 153 € — Neu-Isenbuch
Tel (49) 06102 - 746 0, Fax (49) 06102 - 746 746 — 5 km

Arabella Grand Hotel, 378 rooms, D 317 € — Frankfurt
Tel (49) 069 - 29 810, Fax (49) 069 - 298 1810 — 15 km

RESTAURANTS RESTAURANT

Neuer Haferkasten — Neu-Isenburg
Tel (49) 06102 - 35 329 — 5 km

Grüner Baum, Tel (49) 06102 - 38 318 — Neu-Isenburg

OBERFRANKEN

17 | 6 | 5

Diese ruhige Gegend Frankens wird in erster Linie von Liebhabern barocker Architektur, und mehr noch, von den Besuchern der Bayreuther Festspiele frequentiert. Von wagnerischem Pomp ist beim Golfplatz nichts zu spüren. Oberfranken ist eine klassisch konzipierte Anlage, die sich gut in das unebene Gelände einfügt, und daher vor allem Spielern mit guter Kondition zu empfehlen ist. Schöner, alter Baumbestand schmückt die Landschaft und stellt auf den ersten Blick die Hauptschwierigkeit dar, obschon auch Wasser und Bunker manchmal recht gefährlich werden können. Golfer mittlerer Spielstärke werden sich sicher schwer tun, hier ihr Handicap zu schaffen, obwohl das technische Niveau des Platzes eigentlich von allen Spielern zu meistern ist. Der diskret-elegante Kurs, der sich in der Zeit zwischen spätem Frühling und Frühherbst von seiner schönsten Seite zeigt, zählt zweifellos zu den besten Anlagen der Region.

This peaceful region of Franconia comes alive with visits from lovers of baroque architecture and, more particularly, from "pilgrims" to the Bayreuth Festival. But there's nothing grandiose or Wagnerian about this course, which is very classical in style and naturally hugs a terrain that is hilly enough to recommend it basically for golfers in good physical shape. Beautiful old trees enhance the landscape and at first sight form the main hazards, although water and sand are also sometimes a dangerous proposition. Mid-handicappers will certainly find it hard here to achieve a good score, even though the course is technically speaking within the grasp of most golfers. A discreet and elegant course, Oberfranken is at its best from late spring to early autumn and is one of the region's best golfing stop-offs.

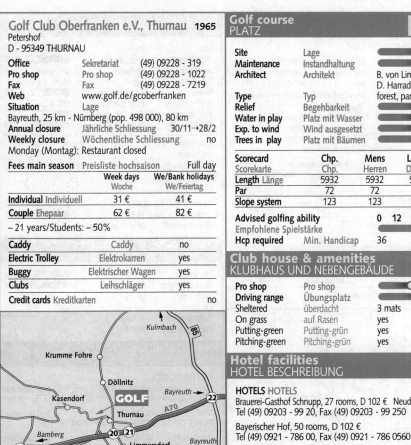

Golf Club Oberfranken e.V., Thurnau 1965

Petershof
D - 95349 THURNAU

Office	Sekretariat	(49) 09228 - 319
Pro shop	Pro shop	(49) 09228 - 1022
Fax	Fax	(49) 09228 - 7219
Web	www.golf.de/gcoberfranken	
Situation	Lage	

Bayreuth, 25 km - Nürnberg (pop. 498 000), 80 km

Annual closure	Jährliche Schliessung	30/11→28/2
Weekly closure	Wöchentliche Schliessung	no

Monday (Montag): Restaurant closed

Fees main season Preisliste hochsaison	Full day	
	Week days Woche	**We/Bank holidays** We/Feiertag
Individual Individuell	31 €	41 €
Couple Ehepaar	62 €	82 €

– 21 years/Students: – 50%

Caddy	Caddy	no
Electric Trolley	Elektrokarren	yes
Buggy	Elektrischer Wagen	yes
Clubs	Leihschläger	yes
Credit cards	Kreditkarten	no

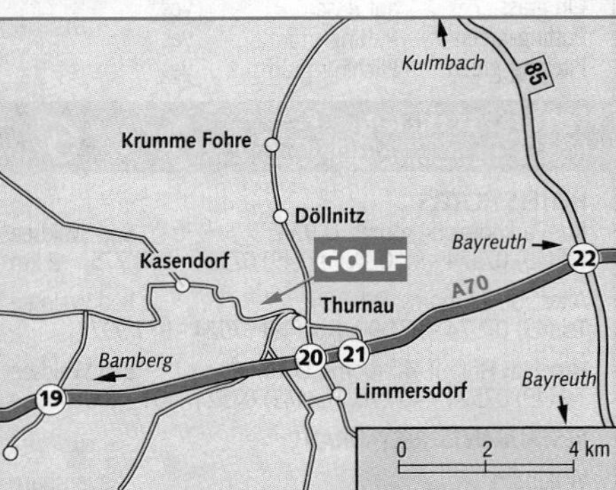

Access Zufahrt : Nürnberg, A9 → Berlin. Exit (Ausf.) Kulmbach-Bayreuth. B505 Exit Thurnau.
Map 4 on page 360 Karte 4 Seite 360

Golf course — PLATZ 17/20

Site	Lage	
Maintenance	Instandhaltung	
Architect	Architekt	B. von Limburger D. Harradine
Type	Typ	forest, parkland
Relief	Begehbarkeit	
Water in play	Platz mit Wasser	
Exp. to wind	Wind ausgesetzt	
Trees in play	Platz mit Bäumen	

Scorecard Scorekarte	**Chp.** Chp.	**Mens** Herren	**Ladies** Damen
Length Länge	5932	5932	5213
Par	72	72	72
Slope system	123	123	121

Advised golfing ability Empfohlene Spielstärke — 0 12 24 36
Hcp required Min. Handicap — 36

Club house & amenities — KLUBHAUS UND NEBENGEBÄUDE 6/10

Pro shop	Pro shop	
Driving range	Übungsplatz	
Sheltered	überdacht	3 mats
On grass	auf Rasen	yes
Putting-green	Putting-grün	yes
Pitching-green	Pitching-grün	yes

Hotel facilities — HOTEL BESCHREIBUNG 5/10

HOTELS HOTELS

Brauerei-Gasthof Schnupp, 27 rooms, D 102 € — Neudrossenfeld
Tel (49) 09203 - 99 20, Fax (49) 09203 - 99 250 — 11 km

Bayerischer Hof, 50 rooms, D 102 € — Bayreuth
Tel (49) 0921 - 786 00, Fax (49) 0921 - 786 0560 — 20 km

Goldener Hirsch, 40 rooms, D 102 € — Bayreuth
Tel (49) 0921 - 23 046, Fax (49) 0921 - 22 483

RESTAURANTS RESTAURANT

Schloss-Restaurant — Neudrossenfeld 10 km
Tel (49) 09203 - 68 368
Schlosshotel Thiergarten, Tel (49) 09209 - 98 40 — Bayreuth

OBERSCHWABEN BAD WALDSEE

15	6	6

Der Platz liegt in einer traditionell bayerischen Umgebung, die einer dicht-bewaldeten Parkanlage ähnelt. Am Kurs werden in Kürze einige Änderungen vorgenommen, von denen wir hoffen, dass sie das Spielvergnügen noch weiter steigern werden. Es gibt hier jeweils fünf Par 3 und Par 5 Löcher, an denen kürzere Spieler genügend gute Chancen aufs Par haben, der Tatsache Rechnung tragend, dass sich der Durchschnitts-Golfer in dieser Hinsicht an Par 4 Löchern häufig am schwersten tut. Aus dem gleichen Grund sollte man die hinteren Abschläge meiden. Der schön gelegene Platz weist eine respektable Länge auf. Senioren empfehlen wir wegen des etwas hügeligen Geländes die Benutzung eines Golfwagens. Die heikelste Passage lauert zwischen Loch 10 und 12. Da der Boden oft feucht ist und ein halbes Dutzend Grüns erhöht liegen, sollte man einen hohen Pitch beherrschen. Insgesamt sind die einen erwartenden Schwierigkeiten keineswegs so bedrohlich, dass Mittelklasse-Spieler sich davon entmutigen lassen. Angenehm zu spielen und abwechslungsreich gestaltet, lohnt die Anlage einen Besuch sowohl der Lage als auch des Layouts wegen.

In a traditional Bavarian setting of densely wooded park-land, we can firstly only hope that the planned alterations will enhance the pleasure of playing here. With five par 5s and five par 3s, the course gives short-hitters the chance to sign for a few pars, knowing full well that the average hacker has the biggest problems with par 4s. In this case, don't opt for the back-tees. Set in a pretty region, the course is a little hilly for senior players (buggy recommended) and respectable in length; the trickiest section awaits you between the 10th and 12th. Since it is often wet and half a dozen greens are elevated, the high pitch shot is a must, but the hardships here are not threatening enough to discourage the average golfer. Pleasant and nicely varied, this course is worth the trip for both the layout and the site.

Golf-Club Oberschwaben Bad Waldsee 1968

Fürstliches Hofgut Hopfenweiler
D - 88339 BAD WALDSEE

Office	Sekretariat	(49) 07524 - 5900
Pro shop	Pro shop	(49) 07524 - 48 778
Fax	Fax	(49) 07524 - 6106
Web	www.golf.de/oberschwaben-badwaldsee	
Situation	Lage	

Ulm (pop. 110 000), 60 km - Ravensburg (pop. 46 000), 20 km

Annual closure	Jährliche Schliessung	1/11→31/3
Weekly closure	Wöchentliche Schliessung	no

Monday (Montag): Restaurant closed

Fees main season Preisliste hochsaison		18 holes
	Week days Woche	**We/Bank holidays** We/Feiertag
Individual Individuell	51 €	51 €
Couple Ehepaar	102 €	102 €

– 21 years/Students: – 50%

Caddy	Caddy	no
Electric Trolley	Elektrokarren	no
Buggy	Elektrischer Wagen	no
Clubs	Leihschläger	yes
Credit cards Kreditkarten		no

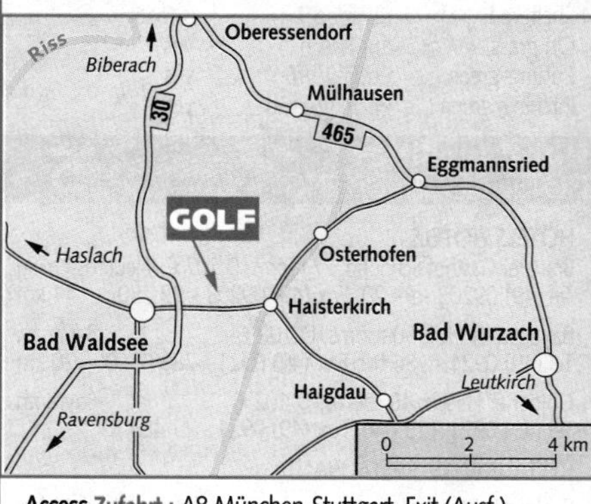

Access Zufahrt : A8 München-Stuttgart. Exit (Ausf.) Ulm-West. B30 → Bodensee. Bad Waldsee → Golf

Map 1 on page 355 Karte 1 Seite 355

Golf course PLATZ — 15/20

Site	Lage	
Maintenance	Instandhaltung	
Architect	Architekt	unknown
Type	Typ	forest, parkland
Relief	Begehbarkeit	
Water in play	Platz mit Wasser	
Exp. to wind	Wind ausgesetzt	
Trees in play	Platz mit Bäumen	

Scorecard Scorekarte	**Chp.** Chp.	**Mens** Herren	**Ladies** Damen
Length Länge	5986	5986	5307
Par	72	72	72
Slope system	133	133	131

Advised golfing ability Empfohlene Spielstärke: 0 12 24 36

Hcp required Min. Handicap 34

Club house & amenities KLUBHAUS UND NEBENGEBÄUDE — 6/10

Pro shop	Pro shop	
Driving range	Übungsplatz	
Sheltered	überdacht	yes
On grass	auf Rasen	yes
Putting-green	Putting-grün	yes
Pitching-green	Pitching-grün	yes

Hotel facilities HOTEL BESCHREIBUNG — 6/10

HOTELS HOTELS

Kur-Parkhotel, 54 rooms, D 92 € — Bad Waldsee
Tel (49) 07524 - 97 070, Fax (49) 07524 - 970 775 — 2 km

Altes Tor, 27 rooms, D 82 € — Bad Waldsee
Tel (49) 07524 - 971 90, Fax (49) 07524 - 971 997

Hotel im Hofgut, 40 rooms, D 107 € — Bad Waldsee
Tel (49) 07524 - 401 70, Fax (49) 07524 -401 7100

RESTAURANTS RESTAURANT

Waldhorn — Ravensburg
Tel (49) 0751 - 36 120 — 20 km

Krone — Schlier
Tel (49) 07529 - 1292 — 25 km

ÖSCHBERGHOF

15 | 7 | 7

Der ideale Ort um ein paar Golftage zu verbringen und die herrlichen Umgebung von Schwarzwald und Donauquelle zu erkunden. Übernachten können Sie im gut ausgestatteten, komfortablen Hotel der Anlage. Der beachtlich lange Platz wird im Verlauf des Jahres um 9 Löcher erweitert. Er verläuft auf relativ ebenem Gelände und kann so leicht zu Fuss bewältigt werden. Obwohl die Hindernisse alle gut erkennbar sind, muss man mehrere Runden spielen um die strategischen Nuancen des Layouts zu begreifen. Ein Wasserlauf kreuzt acht Spielbahnen und bildet eine der Hauptschwierigkeiten, zu denen ebenfalls zahlreiche Bäume und Bunker zählen. Zum Glück sind die Grüns nicht ausgesprochen gut verteidigt, so dass auch der Durchschnitts-Golfer sie einigermassen gut anspielen kann. Der Kurs ist in der Tat so angelegt, dass er nervenschonendes Vergnügen bereitet und schmeichlerische Ergebnisse ermöglicht - ein typischer Urlaubsplatz eben.

An ideal site for a few days golfing, staying in a well-equipped, comfortable hotel (with pool, sauna and jacuzzi) or for exploring this superb region of the Black Forest and sources of the Danube. The course is flat enough for easy walking and during the year will be supplemented by a new 9 holer. It is very reasonable in terms of yardage, but although the hazards are generally visible on each hole, you need several rounds to appreciate the course's strategic "nuances". A stream winds it way across eight holes and forms a major, but not the only, difficulty, as trees and bunkers abound. Fortunately, the greens are not over-protected and approach shots are not too complicated for the average golfer. This is indeed a course designed for enjoyment, where you can card sometimes flattering scores without suffering from nervous exhaustion, so it's just the job the holidays.

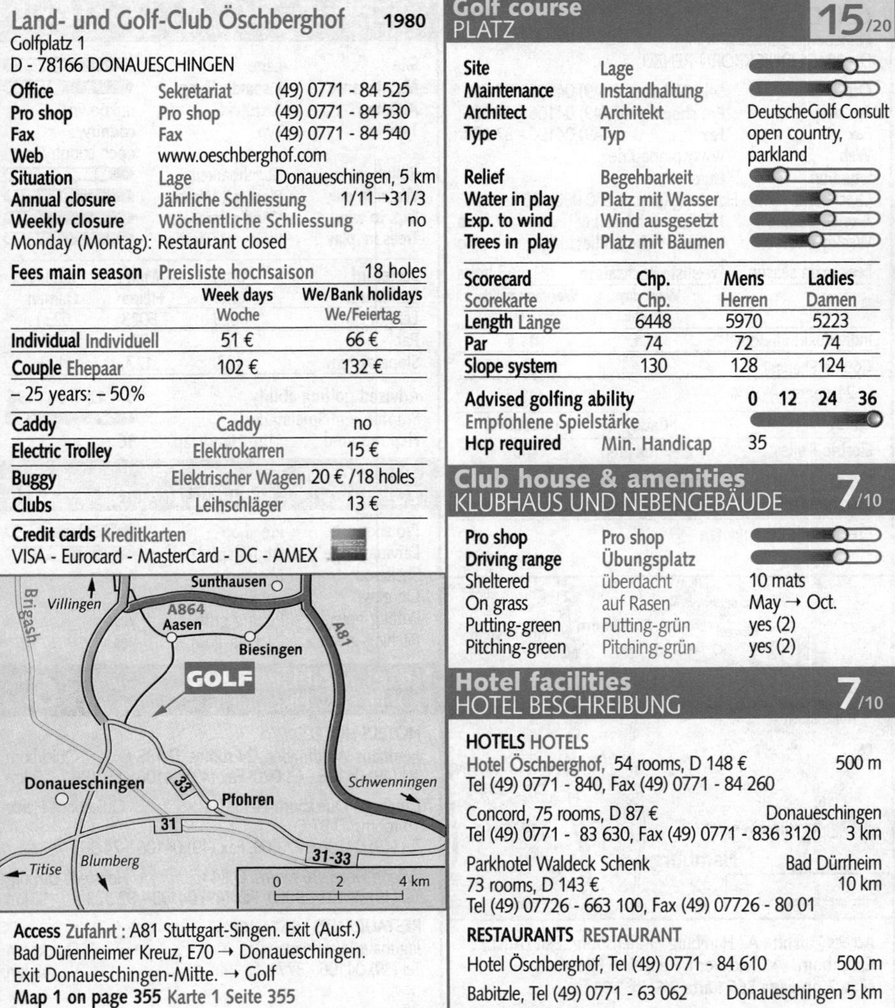

Land- und Golf-Club Öschberghof — 1980

Golfplatz 1
D - 78166 DONAUESCHINGEN

Office	Sekretariat	(49) 0771 - 84 525
Pro shop	Pro shop	(49) 0771 - 84 530
Fax	Fax	(49) 0771 - 84 540
Web	www.oeschberghof.com	
Situation	Lage	Donaueschingen, 5 km
Annual closure	Jährliche Schliessung	1/11→31/3
Weekly closure	Wöchentliche Schliessung	no

Monday (Montag): Restaurant closed

Fees main season Preisliste hochsaison	18 holes	
	Week days Woche	**We/Bank holidays** We/Feiertag
Individual Individuell	51 €	66 €
Couple Ehepaar	102 €	132 €

– 25 years: – 50%

Caddy	Caddy	no
Electric Trolley	Elektrokarren	15 €
Buggy	Elektrischer Wagen	20 € /18 holes
Clubs	Leihschläger	13 €

Credit cards Kreditkarten
VISA - Eurocard - MasterCard - DC - AMEX

Access Zufahrt : A81 Stuttgart-Singen. Exit (Ausf.) Bad Dürenheimer Kreuz, E70 → Donaueschingen. Exit Donaueschingen-Mitte. → Golf

Map 1 on page 355 Karte 1 Seite 355

Golf course PLATZ — 15/20

Site	Lage	
Maintenance	Instandhaltung	
Architect	Architekt	DeutscheGolf Consult
Type	Typ	open country, parkland
Relief	Begehbarkeit	
Water in play	Platz mit Wasser	
Exp. to wind	Wind ausgesetzt	
Trees in play	Platz mit Bäumen	

Scorecard Scorekarte	**Chp.** Chp.	**Mens** Herren	**Ladies** Damen
Length Länge	6448	5970	5223
Par	74	72	74
Slope system	130	128	124

Advised golfing ability Empfohlene Spielstärke — 0 12 24 36
Hcp required Min. Handicap 35

Club house & amenities KLUBHAUS UND NEBENGEBÄUDE — 7/10

Pro shop	Pro shop	
Driving range	Übungsplatz	
Sheltered	überdacht	10 mats
On grass	auf Rasen	May → Oct.
Putting-green	Putting-grün	yes (2)
Pitching-green	Pitching-grün	yes (2)

Hotel facilities HOTEL BESCHREIBUNG — 7/10

HOTELS HOTELS

Hotel Öschberghof, 54 rooms, D 148 € — 500 m
Tel (49) 0771 - 840, Fax (49) 0771 - 84 260

Concord, 75 rooms, D 87 € — Donaueschingen
Tel (49) 0771 - 83 630, Fax (49) 0771 - 836 3120 — 3 km

Parkhotel Waldeck Schenk — Bad Dürrheim
73 rooms, D 143 € — 10 km
Tel (49) 07726 - 663 100, Fax (49) 07726 - 80 01

RESTAURANTS RESTAURANT

Hotel Öschberghof, Tel (49) 0771 - 84 610 — 500 m
Babitzle, Tel (49) 0771 - 63 062 — Donaueschingen 5 km

PINNAU

14 | 6 | 6

Der Platz verdankt seinen Namen dem Fluss Pinnau, der teilweise entlang des Golfgeländes verläuft. Obwohl der Fluss selbst nie ins Spiel kommt, gibt es andere Wasserhindernisse in bedrohlicher Lage vor den Grüns, um unerfahrene Spieler einzuschüchtern, die hier schnell einige Schläge verlieren können. Spielern mit hohen Handicaps machen auch die Grüns zu schaffen, die teilweise stark onduliert sind, aber in gestalterischer Hinsicht zu wünschen übrig lassen. Dieser Platz favorisiert technisch versierte Spieler, die es verstehen, mit den einzeln stehenden Bäumen fertigzuwerden, die vom Architekten geschickt mit ins strategische Kalkül einbezogen wurden. Der flache Platz ist einfach zu Gehen und trocknet gut ab. Golfer aller Spielstärken können sich hier entfalten, wenngleich methodische Spieler gegenüber Longhittern im Vorteil sind. Wenn möglich sollten Sie an der 10 beginnen, da die zweiten Neun etwas weniger interessant sind als der Rest. Wir empfehlen Matchplay, da auf diesem Kurs alles Mögliche passieren kann.

Pinnau takes its name from the river that partly skirts the course. And although this running water never really comes into play, other water hazards in front of the greens are threatening enough to intimidate the more inexperienced players, who can quickly suffer here. High-handicappers will also find the putting surfaces a handful, too, which are sometimes excessively contoured and lacking in inspiration design-wise. With that said, this is a course for the technicians, who will have to cope with strategically located isolated trees, the finest of which have been smartly used by the designer. Flattish and well-drained, the course is a pleasant one to walk, where golfers of all abilities can unfold their game, even though the thoughtful technician will have the upper hand over the long-hitter. If you can, tee off at the 10th, as the back nine are a little less exciting than the rest. And prefer match play, as well, because anything can happen here.

Golf Club An der Pinnau — 1982

Pinneberger Strasse 81a
D - 25451 QUICKBORN-RENZEL

Office	Sekretariat	(49) 04106 - 81 800
Pro shop	Pro shop	(49) 04106 - 60 876
Fax	Fax	(49) 04106 - 82 003
Web	www.pinnau.de	
Situation	Lage	

Quickborn, 1 km - Hamburg (pop. 1 650 000), 25 km

Annual closure	Jährliche Schliessung	no
Weekly closure	Wöchentliche Schliessung	no

Fees main season Preisliste hochsaison	18 holes	
	Week days Woche	**We/Bank holidays** We/Feiertag
Individual Individuell	31 €	41 €
Couple Ehepaar	62 €	82 €

– 21 years: – 50%

Caddy	Caddy	on request
Electric Trolley	Elektrokarren	no
Buggy	Elektrischer Wagen	no
Clubs	Leihschläger	no
Credit cards Kreditkarten		no

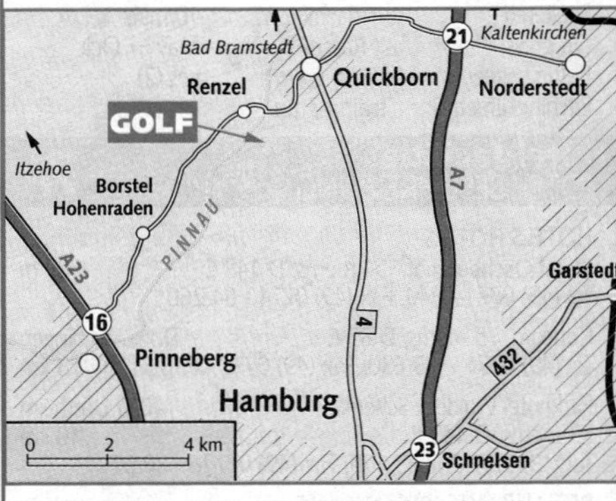

Access Zufahrt : A7 Hamburg → Flensburg. Exit (Ausf.) Quickborn. → Quickborn, Renzel → Pinneberg.
Map 7 on page 366 Karte 7 Seite 366

Golf course PLATZ — 14/20

Site	Lage	
Maintenance	Instandhaltung	
Architect	Architekt	unknown
Type	Typ	country, open country
Relief	Begehbarkeit	
Water in play	Platz mit Wasser	
Exp. to wind	Wind ausgesetzt	
Trees in play	Platz mit Bäumen	

Scorecard Scorekarte	**Chp.** Chp.	**Mens** Herren	**Ladies** Damen
Length Länge	6023	6023	5231
Par	72	72	72
Slope system	127	127	127

Advised golfing ability Empfohlene Spielstärke — 0 12 24 36
Hcp required Min. Handicap 36

Club house & amenities KLUBHAUS UND NEBENGEBÄUDE — 6/10

Pro shop	Pro shop	
Driving range	Übungsplatz	
Sheltered	überdacht	4 mats
On grass	auf Rasen	yes
Putting-green	Putting-grün	yes
Pitching-green	Pitching-grün	yes

Hotel facilities HOTEL BESCHREIBUNG — 6/10

HOTELS HOTELS

Jagdhaus Waldfrieden, 24 rooms, D 138 € — Quickborn
Tel (49) 04106 - 61 020, Fax (49) 04106 - 69 196 — 3 km

Landhaus Quickborn-Heide — Quickborn-Heide
15 rooms, D 97 €
Tel (49) 04106 - 77 660, Fax (49) 04106 - 74 969

Wiking Hotel, 36 rooms, D 84 € — Henstedt-Ulzburg
Tel (49) 04193 - 9080, Fax (49) 04193 - 92 323 — 10 km

RESTAURANTS RESTAURANT

Jagdhaus Waldfrieden — Quickborn
Tel (49) 04106 - 3771 — 3 km

REICHSSTADT BAD WINDSHEIM

14	6	7 Golf

Nahe Würzburg und Nürnberg liegt der Golfplatz an der "Romantischen Strasse", die von Würzburg über Augsburg, durch die Schweiz nach Italien führt, und an deren Weg sich immer wieder Städte und Schlösser aus den Epochen des Mittelalters, der Renaissance und des Barock finden. Gleichermassen erwähnenswert sind die Weinberge (Frankenwein) des Maintals. Falls Sie sich von den kulturellen Attraktionen losreissen können, verpassen Sie auf keinen Fall die Golfplätze dieser Gegend, insbesondere nicht diesen, der ebenso handfest und bodenständig ist wie die regionale Küche. Ebene Flächen wechseln sich ab mit hügeligerem Terrain auf einem Parcours, der insgesamt einen sehr ausgewogenen Eindruck macht. Die Grüns sind enorm gross und sehr gut verteidigt. Es gibt praktisch keine Bäume, was den Platz sehr windanfällig macht. Einige Wasserhindernisse, gefährliche Bunker, Dickicht und Rough tragen dazu bei, dass der Score voraussichtlich ein paar Schläge über dem Handicap liegen wird. Daher sollten unerfahrene Golfer einfach die Runde geniessen ohne allzu sehr auf ihr Ergebnis zu achten.

Very close to Würzburg and Nürnberg, this course is on the route taken by the "Romantic Road", which started out from Würzburg and ran down to Augsburg then on to Switzerland and Italy, crossing towns and castles testifying to the Middle Ages, the Renaissance and the Baroque period. Equally important are the vineyards in the Main valley (Franconia wine). If you can tear yourself away from the cultural fascinations, don't miss the golf courses in this province, especially this one, as serious a layout as the regional cooking. With flat spaces alternating with hillier terrain and well-balanced overall, the course has huge, well-guarded greens, is virtually tree-less and can get very tough when the wind blows. A few water hazards and dangerous bunkers, the thickets and rough are all there to nudge your score a few strokes above your handicap. Inexperienced golfers will enjoy their round even more if they prefer not to count their score.

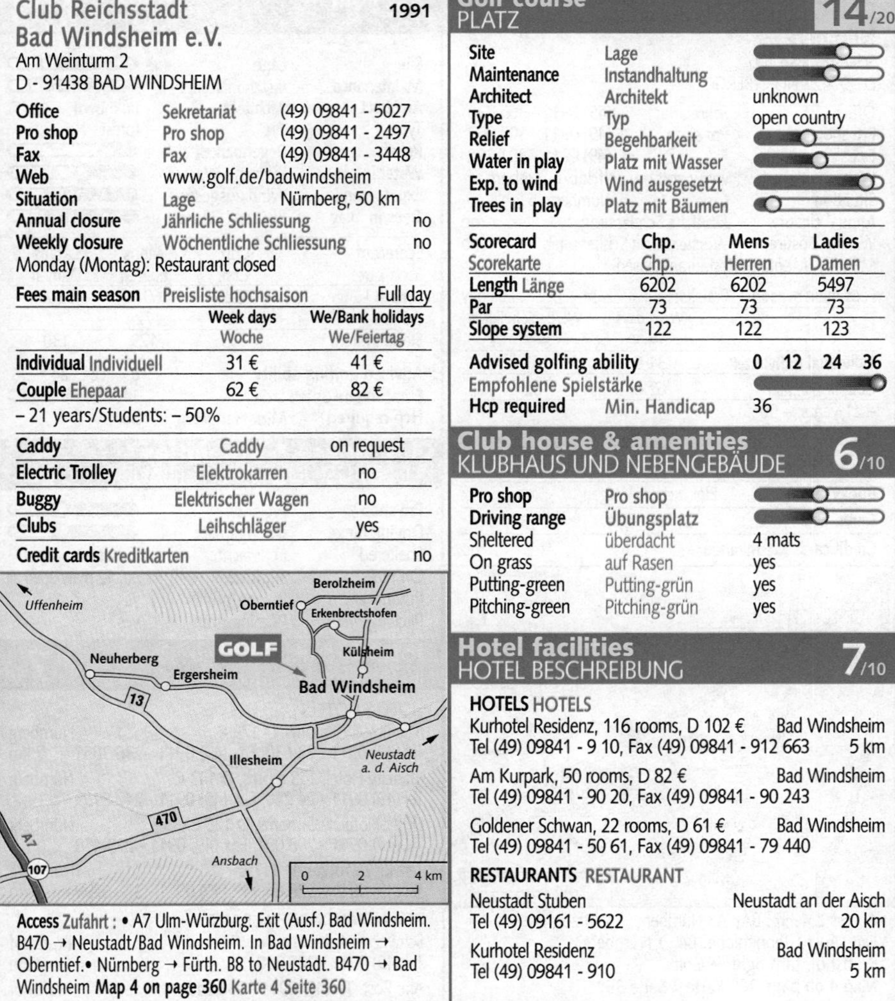

Club Reichsstadt Bad Windsheim e.V. — 1991

Am Weinturm 2
D - 91438 BAD WINDSHEIM

Office	Sekretariat	(49) 09841 - 5027
Pro shop	Pro shop	(49) 09841 - 2497
Fax	Fax	(49) 09841 - 3448
Web	www.golf.de/badwindsheim	
Situation	Lage	Nürnberg, 50 km
Annual closure	Jährliche Schliessung	no
Weekly closure	Wöchentliche Schliessung	no

Monday (Montag): Restaurant closed

Fees main season Preisliste hochsaison	Week days Woche	We/Bank holidays We/Feiertag
	Full day	
Individual Individuell	31 €	41 €
Couple Ehepaar	62 €	82 €

– 21 years/Students: – 50%

Caddy	Caddy	on request
Electric Trolley	Elektrokarren	no
Buggy	Elektrischer Wagen	no
Clubs	Leihschläger	yes
Credit cards	Kreditkarten	no

Access Zufahrt : • A7 Ulm-Würzburg. Exit (Ausf.) Bad Windsheim. B470 → Neustadt/Bad Windsheim. In Bad Windsheim → Oberntief.• Nürnberg → Fürth. B8 to Neustadt. B470 → Bad Windsheim **Map 4 on page 360** Karte 4 Seite 360

Golf course PLATZ — 14/20

Site	Lage	
Maintenance	Instandhaltung	
Architect	Architekt	unknown
Type	Typ	open country
Relief	Begehbarkeit	
Water in play	Platz mit Wasser	
Exp. to wind	Wind ausgesetzt	
Trees in play	Platz mit Bäumen	

Scorecard Scorekarte	Chp. Chp.	Mens Herren	Ladies Damen
Length Länge	6202	6202	5497
Par	73	73	73
Slope system	122	122	123

Advised golfing ability Empfohlene Spielstärke: 0 12 24 36
Hcp required Min. Handicap: 36

Club house & amenities KLUBHAUS UND NEBENGEBÄUDE — 6/10

Pro shop	Pro shop	
Driving range	Übungsplatz	
Sheltered	überdacht	4 mats
On grass	auf Rasen	yes
Putting-green	Putting-grün	yes
Pitching-green	Pitching-grün	yes

Hotel facilities HOTEL BESCHREIBUNG — 7/10

HOTELS HOTELS

Kurhotel Residenz, 116 rooms, D 102 € — Bad Windsheim
Tel (49) 09841 - 9 10, Fax (49) 09841 - 912 663 — 5 km

Am Kurpark, 50 rooms, D 82 € — Bad Windsheim
Tel (49) 09841 - 90 20, Fax (49) 09841 - 90 243

Goldener Schwan, 22 rooms, D 61 € — Bad Windsheim
Tel (49) 09841 - 50 61, Fax (49) 09841 - 79 440

RESTAURANTS RESTAURANT

Neustadt Stuben — Neustadt an der Aisch
Tel (49) 09161 - 5622 — 20 km

Kurhotel Residenz — Bad Windsheim
Tel (49) 09841 - 910 — 5 km

REICHSWALD-NÜRNBERG

16 | 7 | 7

Der Wald spiegelt wohl am besten den Geist der deutschen Romantik wider. Seine Erhaltung und sein Schutz sind zu einem wichtigen gesellschaftlichen Anliegen, insbesondere der Umweltschützer, geworden. Eine ganze Runde in einem solch mächtigen Wald zu spielen, vermittelt einem das Gefühl von Ruhe und Zufriedenheit - es ist, als wäre man ganz alleine auf der Welt. Hier muss man in Topform sein und den Ball kontrolliert schlagen, um den allgegenwärtigen Pinienbäumen aus dem Weg zu gehen und mit dem Drive in eine Position zu gelangen, die einem das Anspiel der gut durch Bunker verteidigten Grüns ermöglicht. Wenn man gut spielt, werden einen die Wasserläufe und Hindernisse, die ein - wenn auch nicht übermässiges - Gefahrenelement darstellen, weniger einschüchtern. Spieler, denen es an Übung und Genauigkeit fehlt, werden vermutlich einen Einbruch erleben, aber schliesslich zwingt sie ja niemand dazu, all ihre Schläge auch zu zählen. Reichswald ist ohne Zweifel einer der besten Plätze der Region, der auch nach oftmaligem Spielen immer wieder Spass macht.

Forests are one of the key constituents of the German romantic soul; their conservation and protection are now one of society's major concerns, especially with the ecologists. Playing a whole course in a forest such as this procures a feeling of incomparable tranquillity and contentment; on the course, you feel as if you are the only soul in the world. Here, you will need to be on top of your game to keep out of the pine-trees and flight your ball to land the drive in the best position to approach the greens (which are well guarded by bunkers). If you're playing well, you won't be too scared of the streams and hazards that add an element of difficulty but never excessively so. Players with little experience and problems of direction will probably suffer, but they don't have to count every stroke, do they ? One of the region's top layouts, this is a spectacular course which is fun to play again and again.

Golf Club Am Reichswald e.V., Nürnberg — 1960

Schiestlstrasse 100
D - 90427 NÜRNBERG

Office	Sekretariat	(49) 0911 - 305 730
Pro shop	Pro shop	(49) 0911 - 305 959
Fax	Fax	(49) 0911 - 301 200
Web	www.golf.de/golfclub-nuernberg	
Situation	Lage	Nürnberg, 5 km
Annual closure	Jährliche Schliessung	no
Weekly closure	Wöchentliche Schliessung	no

Monday (Montag): Restaurant closed

Fees main season Preisliste hochsaison	Week days Woche	We/Bank holidays We/Feiertag
		Full day
Individual Individuell	31 €	41 €
Couple Ehepaar	62 €	82 €

– 21 years: – 50%

Caddy	Caddy	on request
Electric Trolley	Elektrokarren	no
Buggy	Elektrischer Wagen	no
Clubs	Leihschläger	yes
Credit cards	Kreditkarten	no

Access Zufahrt : BAB A3 Nürnberg → Würzburg. Exit (Ausf.) Tennenlohe. B4 → Nürnberg. Kraftshof, turn right → Golf
Map 4 on page 360 Karte 4 Seite 360

Golf course PLATZ — 16/20

Site	Lage	
Maintenance	Instandhaltung	
Architect	Architekt	unknown
Type	Typ	forest
Relief	Begehbarkeit	
Water in play	Platz mit Wasser	
Exp. to wind	Wind ausgesetzt	
Trees in play	Platz mit Bäumen	

Scorecard Scorekarte	Chp. Chp.	Mens Herren	Ladies Damen
Length Länge	6220	6041	5306
Par	72	72	72
Slope system	133	129	130

Advised golfing ability Empfohlene Spielstärke — 0 12 24 36

Hcp required Min. Handicap 36

Club house & amenities KLUBHAUS UND NEBENGEBÄUDE — 7/10

Pro shop	Pro shop	
Driving range	Übungsplatz	
Sheltered	überdacht	3 mats
On grass	auf Rasen	no, 12 mats open air
Putting-green	Putting-grün	yes
Pitching-green	Pitching-grün	yes

Hotel facilities HOTEL BESCHREIBUNG — 7/10

HOTELS HOTELS

Maritim, 319 rooms, D 179 € — Nürnberg
Tel (49) 0911 - 23 630, Fax (49) 0911 - 236 3851 — 7 km

Intercity Hotel, 158 rooms, D 143 € — Nürnberg
Tel (49) 0911 - 24 780, Fax (49) 0911 - 247 8999

Dürer-Hotel, 105 rooms, D 128 € — Nürnberg
Tel (49) 0911 - 208 091, Fax (49) 0911 - 223 458

Tassilo, 79 rooms, D 117 € — Nürnberg
Tel (49) 0911 - 326 66, Fax (49) 0911 - 326 6799 — 5 km

RESTAURANTS RESTAURANT

Schwarzer Adler — Kraftshof
Tel (49) 0911 - 305 858 — 2 km

Alte Post, Tel (49) 0911 - 396 215 — Kraftshof

RETHMAR

17 | 8 | 7

Zweimal neun Löcher (Dunes und Lakes Course) wurden bereits für die Expo 2000 in Hannover fertiggestellt. Die dritten neun Löcher sind derzeit im Bau und werden diesen hervorragenden Golfplatz noch reizvoller gestalten, als er ohnehin schon ist. Der bereits erwähnte Wort Dünen kommt nicht von ungefähr : Der Platz hat die Anmutung eines klassischen Linksplatzes, allerdings erinnern die Dünen mehr an County Louth oder Cruden Bay als an Ballybunion. Der Platz ist mit insgesamt 25 Hektar von Seen und Teichen gespickt, die durch das intelligente Design von Arnold Palmer und Ed Seay ins Spiel gebracht werden. Dieser Platz spiegelt den modernen « Zürück zur Natur-Trend » wider, obwohl man bei vielen Löchern die Wahl hat zwischen der britischen Variante, den Ball rollend zum Grün zu befördern oder die amerikanische Art des hohen Anspiels. Rethmar ist flach und verbirgt kein Hindernis. Der Platz ist geschickt und auffällig gestylt und variiert in seiner Schwierigkeit mit dem Wind. Die Grüns gelten als die besten in Deutschland. Aber nicht nur deshalb gehört Rethmar mittlerweile zu den Plätzen, die selbst die weiteste Anreise rechtfertigen.

Two 9-hole courses (the Dunes and Lakes) have already been built on the 120 hectares of land here for the Hanover World Exposition 2000, while a third 9-hole layout is due to complete what is a superb golfing complex. With dunes on the site, they give the site the links appeal claimed by the designers, although in terms of size the dunes here are more in the style of County Louth or Cruden Bay than Ballybunion. The estate is dotted with 25 hectares of lakes and ponds, deliberately brought into play by Palmer and Seay. This is an example of the ongoing "back to nature" trend in course design, although you often have the choice in the way you approach the greens, rolling the ball in British style or opting for the more American target golf. Rethmar, flat and with nothing to hide, sensibly landscaped and more or less challenging depending on the wind, is fast becoming one of those excellent courses with probably the best greens in Germany sought after by people who are really looking to test their game. Forget the environment.

Rethmar Golf Links e.V. — 1999

Seufzerallee 10
D - 31 319 SEHNDE-RETHMAR

Office	Sekretariat	(49) 05138 - 70 053
Pro shop	Pro shop	(49) 05138 - 70 053
Fax	Fax	(49) 05138 - 613 840
Web	www.rethmar-golf-links.de	
Situation	Lage	
Hannover (pop. 530 000), 20 km		
Annual closure	Jährliche Schliessung	no
Weekly closure	Wöchentliche Schliessung	no
Restaurant closed on Monday (Montag), in Winter		

Fees main season Preisliste hochsaison	Week days Woche	We/Bank holidays We/Feiertag (18 holes)
Individual Individuell	41 €	51 €
Couple Ehepaar	82 €	102 €
Caddy Caddy		13 €
Electric Trolley Elektrokarren		no
Buggy Elektrischer Wagen		20 € /18 holes
Clubs Leihschläger		13 € /18 holes

Credit cards Kreditkarten
VISA - Eurocard - MasterCard - AMEX

Access Zufahrt : Hannover, B65 South (Südschnellweg) → Sehnde. In Sehnde → Peine. In Rethmar, third on the right, Osterkamp, follow → Golf.

Map 5 on page 363 Karte 5 Seite 363

Golf course — PLATZ — 17/20

Site	Lage	
Maintenance	Instandhaltung	
Architect	Architekt	Arnold Palmer, Ed Seay
Type	Typ	open country, links
Relief	Begehbarkeit	
Water in play	Platz mit Wasser	
Exp. to wind	Wind ausgesetzt	
Trees in play	Platz mit Bäumen	

Scorecard Scorekarte	Chp. Chp.	Mens Herren	Ladies Damen
Length Länge	6399	5864	5178
Par	72	72	72
Slope system	133	126	128

Advised golfing ability Empfohlene Spielstärke — 0 12 24 36
Hcp required Min. Handicap 36

Club house & amenities — KLUBHAUS UND NEBENGEBÄUDE — 8/10

Pro shop	Pro shop	
Driving range	Übungsplatz	
Sheltered	überdacht	8 mats
On grass	auf Rasen	yes
Putting-green	Putting-grün	yes
Pitching-green	Pitching-grün	yes

Hotel facilities — HOTEL BESCHREIBUNG — 7/10

HOTELS HOTELS

Rethmar Golf Suites, 16 rooms, D 128 € — on site
Tel (49) 05138 - 700 53, Fax (49) 05138 - 613 840

Gusthof Eucken, 20 rooms, D 77 € — Gross-Lobke 3 km
Tel (49) 05126 - 311 15, Fax (49) 05126 - 311 14

Parkhotel Bilm — Sehnde-Bilm 6 km
50 rooms, D 97 € (w. dinner)
Tel (49) 05138 - 60 90, Fax (49) 05138 - 609 100

RESTAURANTS RESTAURANT

Vitax, Tel (49) 05138 - 16 60 — Sehnde 5 km
Anno, Tel (49) 05128 - 400 225 Hohenhameln-Clauen 8 km

RHEINE/MESUM

16 | 8 | 7

Rheine-Mesum ist einer der Plätze, auf denen man das ganze Jahr auf Grund des sandigen Bodens und der effektiven Drainage vorzüglich spielen kann. Der mittlerweile für seine guten Layouts bekannte Architekt Christoph Städler hat auch hier eine attraktiven Anlage entworfen, bei dem die Schwierigkeiten sehr gut über den gesamten Platz verteilt sind. Städler legte durch geschickte Erdbewegungen und Einbeziehung von Bäumen, Bunkern und Wasserhindernissen einen ausgewogenen, reizvollen Platz in die flache, leicht zu begehende und weitgehend offene Landschaft. Der Wind spielt hier gelegentlich ebenfalls eine Rolle. Alle Schwierigkeiten sind in der Regel vom Abschlag gut zu erkennen, aber eine Birdie-Karte (Yardage Book) ist sehr hilfreich. Das Eröffnungsloch fordert den meisten Spielern schon alles ab, dennoch fühlen sich auch schwächere Spieler auf dem Platz wohl, vorausgesetzt sie wählen die richtigen Abschläge. Ein hübsches Hotel auf dem Platz ergänzt das Angebot dieser überaus gastfreundlichen und service-orientierten Anlage.

This is first and foremost one of the most easily playable courses all year round on account of very sandy subsoil and a particularly efficient drainage system. Course architect Christoph Städtler needs no introduction and is known for his polished style producing attractive courses where difficulties are always very carefully designed into the layout. Here, on open and easily walkable terrain, he has very effectively moved a lot of earth and played with trees, bunkers and water to give the course great balance. The wind also has its say but that's something players have to cope with by themselves. Trouble is generally clearly in view, but the yardage book will be a great help. The first hole is a tough starter, but the average player should not be too worried about the rest, as this is a friendly course as long as you play from the tees that suit your game. A pretty on-site hotel completes the picture and makes this a course well worth the visit.

Golfsportclub Rheine/Mesum — 1998

Wörstrasse 201
D - 48432 RHEINE

Office	Sekretariat	(49) 05975 - 94 90
Pro shop	Pro shop	(49) 05975 - 919 200
Fax	Fax	(49) 05975 - 94 91
Web	www.golfsportclub.de	
Situation	Lage	Rheine (pop. 74 000), 7 km
Annual closure	Jährliche Schliessung	no
Weekly closure	Wöchentliche Schliessung	no

Restaurant closed on Monday (montag), 10 → 03

Fees main season Preisliste hochsaison	18 holes	
	Week days Woche	**We/Bank holidays** We/Feiertag
Individual Individuell	36 €	46 €
Couple Ehepaar	72 €	92 €

Juniors under 18: – 50%

Caddy	Caddy	26 € /on request
Electric Trolley	Elektrokarren	no
Buggy	Elektrischer Wagen	26 € /18 holes
Clubs	Leihschläger	8 € /18 holes

Credit cards Kreditkarten VISA - Eurocard

Access Zufahrt : Münster A1 → Osnabrück. Exit 76 (Ausfahrt 76), then Road 481 to Greven and → Rheine. After Emsdetten, turn → Mesum and Steinfurt. 500 m, turn left → Golf. **Map 5 on page 362** Karte 5 Seite 362

Golf course PLATZ — 16/20

Site	Lage	
Maintenance	Instandhaltung	
Architect	Architekt	Christoph Staedler Euro Golf Projekt
Type	Typ	inland
Relief	Begehbarkeit	
Water in play	Platz mit Wasser	
Exp. to wind	Wind ausgesetzt	
Trees in play	Platz mit Bäumen	

Scorecard Scorekarte	**Chp.** Chp.	**Mens** Herren	**Ladies** Damen
Length Länge	6345	6036	4998
Par	72	72	72
Slope system	120	118	118

Advised golfing ability Empfohlene Spielstärke — 0 12 24 36
Hcp required Min. Handicap 36

Club house & amenities KLUBHAUS UND NEBENGEBÄUDE — 8/10

Pro shop	Pro shop	
Driving range	Übungsplatz	
Sheltered	überdacht	12 mats
On grass	auf Rasen	yes
Putting-green	Putting-grün	yes
Pitching-green	Pitching-grün	yes

Hotel facilities HOTEL BESCHREIBUNG — 7/10

HOTELS HOTELS

Golf Hotel Gut Winterbrock, 8 rooms, D 87 € — on site
Tel (49) 05975 - 919 300, Fax (49) 05975 - 919 301

Altes Gasthaus Borcharding, 14 rooms, D 77 € — Rheine-Mesum 2 km
Tel (49) 05975 - 12 70, Fax (49) 05975 - 35 07

Zum Alten Brunnen, 15 rooms, D 107 € — Rheine 8 km
Tel (49) 05971 - 961 715, Fax (49) 05971 -961 7166

RESTAURANTS RESTAURANT

Altes Gasthaus Borcharding — Rheine-Mesum 2 km
Tel (49) 05975 - 12 70

Mesumer Landhaus, Tel (49) 05975 - 241 — Rheine-Mesum

Zum Alten Brunnen, Tel (49) 05971 - 961 715 — Rheine

RHEINHESSEN

14 | 8 | 7

Mit den Nachbarplätzen von Domtal-Mommenhein und Nahetal in der näheren Umgebung, sind die Weinberg zwischen der Mosel und dem Rhein sind ein lohnenswertes Ausflugsziel. Für Golfer bietet sich ein Aufenthalt im exzellenten Hotel im Klubhaus von Rheinhessen an. Hier, ein wenig abseits der ausgetretenen Pfade, kann man sich entspannen, von der Klubhaus-Terasse das phantastische Panorama der Weinberge geniessen. Der Platz ist keineswegs perfekt, weil zu viele Löcher "blind" sind, ein Fehler, der wie schon in Nahetal leicht hätte vermieden werden können. Ein anderer Negativpunkt ist der Graben und der Teich am 14. Loch, einem Par 5, nach 245 m, genau dort, wo der Drive von guten Spielern landet. Dies zwingt dazu, entweder den Ball kurz abzulegen oder ein unkalkulierbares Risiko einzugehen. Wer hier zum erstenmal spielt, wird die Spielstrategie nicht immer erkennen und viele Überraschungen erleben. Dennoch ist das Layout reizvoll, obwohl die vielen Schräglagen viele Golfer überfordern können.

With Domtal-Mommenheim and Nahetal not far away, plus the vineyards of Nahe between the Moselle and the Rhine this is an attractive region to visit. For golfers, a stay at the excellent hotel in the Rheinhessen clubhouse is most relaxing, a little off the beaten track. The club house overlooks the vineyards and provides a superb panorama for everyone to enjoy, not only wine-lovers. The course itself is by no means perfect, as too many holes are blind, a mistake that could have been avoided both here and at Nahetal. Another rather negative feature is the ditch and pond 245 metres from the 14th tee, just where a good drive should be landing. This forces the golfer to take unreasonable risks or to lay up ridiculously short. People playing here for the first time may well encounter problems of strategy and a number of surprises. Otherwise the layout is pleasant enough, the difficulties are often clearly visible and only the contoured relief might handicap players who are technically not on top of their swing.

Golf Club Rheinhessen Hofgut Wissberg-St. Johann e.V. — 1993

Hofgut Wissberg
D - 55578 ST. JOHANN

Office	Sekretariat	(49) 06701 - 8111
Pro shop	Pro shop	(49) 06701 - 8326
Fax	Fax	(49) 06701 - 8114
Web	—	
Situation	Lage	Mainz (pop. 186 000), 25 km
Annual closure	Jährliche Schliessung	no
Weekly closure	Wöchentliche Schliessung	no

Fees main season Preisliste hochsaison		18 holes
	Week days Woche	**We/Bank holidays** We/Feiertag
Individual Individuell	31 €	46 €
Couple Ehepaar	62 €	92 €

Caddy	Caddy	no
Electric Trolley	Elektrokarren	no
Buggy	Elektrischer Wagen	no
Clubs	Leihschläger	10 €
Credit cards Kreditkarten		no

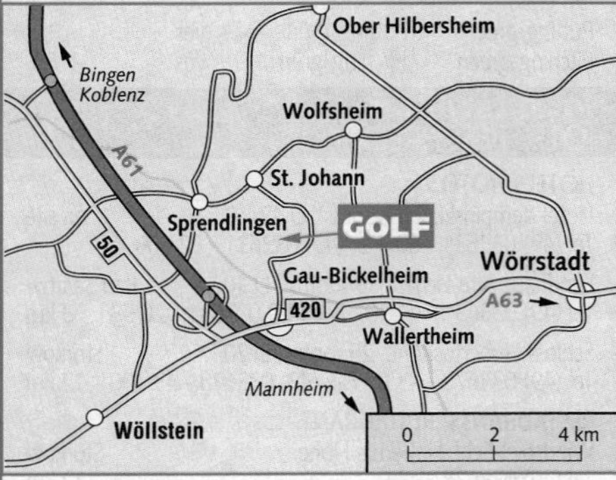

Access Zufahrt : Mainz, A60, A60 until AK Nahetal
Map 3 on page 359 Karte 3 Seite 359

Golf course PLATZ — 14/20

Site	Lage	
Maintenance	Instandhaltung	
Architect	Architekt	Armin Keller
Type	Typ	open country, hilly
Relief	Begehbarkeit	
Water in play	Platz mit Wasser	
Exp. to wind	Wind ausgesetzt	
Trees in play	Platz mit Bäumen	

Scorecard Scorekarte	**Chp.** Chp.	**Mens** Herren	**Ladies** Damen
Length Länge	6225	6046	5320
Par	72	72	72
Slope system	129	138	128

Advised golfing ability Empfohlene Spielstärke — 0 12 24 36
Hcp required Min. Handicap — We: 28/36

Club house & amenities KLUBHAUS UND NEBENGEBÄUDE — 8/10

Pro shop	Pro shop	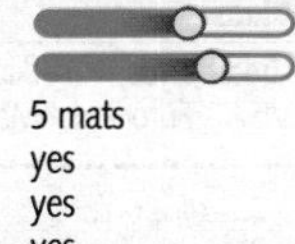
Driving range	Übungsplatz	
Sheltered	überdacht	5 mats
On grass	auf Rasen	yes
Putting-green	Putting-grün	yes
Pitching-green	Pitching-grün	yes

Hotel facilities HOTEL BESCHREIBUNG — 7/10

HOTELS HOTELS

Golf Gasthaus, 23 rooms, D 100 € — on site
Tel (49) 06701 - 916 450, Fax (49) 06701 - 916 455

Landhotel Kauzenberg — Bad Kreuznach
47 rooms, D 112 € — 15 km
Tel (49) 0671 - 38 000, Fax (49) 0671 - 3800 124

Insel-Stuben, 22 rooms, D 92 € — Bad Kreuznach
Tel (49) 0671 - 837 990, Fax (49) 0671 - 837 9955

RESTAURANTS RESTAURANT

Metzlers Gasthof, Tel (49) 0671 - 653 12 — Hackenheim17 km
Krause, Tel (49) 06731 - 61 81 — Alzey 10 km

SCHARMÜTZELSEE Arnold Palmer

17 | 8 | 7

Der erst kürzlich erstellte Golfplatz ist Teil eines 36-Loch Resorts, zu dem auch ein von Nick Faldo entworfener 18-Loch Platz gehört. Die Investoren zögerten nicht, für ihr Projekt die Mitarbeit der Besten in Anspruch zu nehmen und beauftragten Arnold Palmer mit dem Bau seines in Deutschland bislang einzigen Platzes. Der amerikanische Stil des in angelegten Platz ist nur auf den ersten 9 Löchern offensichtlich, die zweiten neun Löcher wirken dagegen wie ein alter klassischer Waldplatz und sind der schönste Teil des Platzes. Das Layout ist gut durchdacht und so machen es die vorhandenen Schwierigkeiten nötig, mehrere Runden hier zu spielen, bis man sich mit der Anlage vertraut fühlt. Natürlich ist der Platz, besonders von den hinteren Abschlägen, auch sehr anspruchsvoll. Mehrere Abschlag-Boxen pro Loch ermöglichen es aber jedem Spieler, eine seinem Niveau entsprechende Wahl zu treffen. Besondere Aufmerksamkeit wurde der Gestaltung der Grüns gewidmet, aber auch der Pflegezustand der gesamten Anlage hebt diesen Platz aus der Masse der deutschen Plätze heraus.

The reunification of Germany has opened up new development in this region between Berlin and Frankfurt an der Oder, particularly close to the huge Scharmützelsee. The present very recent course is part of a 36-hole resort which also includes a Nick Faldo offering. The investors didn't hesitate to call on the best, and this is Germany's only course designed by Arnold Palmer. The American style is only obvious on the front nine, the back nine being more like a traditional German forest course. The design is very intelligent, but the difficulties call for several rounds before getting fully acclimatized. Obviously, it is also very demanding, especially from the back tees, but there are enough tee-boxes for everyone to play the course that suits them best. The greens are especially well-designed and the standard of maintenance of the whole resort makes for two excellent courses.

Sporting Club Berlin Scharmützelsee e.V. 1995

Parkallee 3
D - 15526 BAD SAAROW

Office	Sekretariat	(49) 033631 - 63 300
Pro shop	Pro shop	(49) 033631 - 5628
Fax	Fax	(49) 033631 - 5270
Web	www.sporting-club-berlin.com	
Situation	Lage	Berlin (pop. 3 500 000), 75 km
Annual closure	Jährliche Schliessung	30/11→1/3
Weekly closure	Wöchentliche Schliessung	no

Fees main season Preisliste hochsaison	18 holes	
	Week days Woche	**We/Bank holidays** We/Feiertag
Individual Individuell	36 €	51 €
Couple Ehepaar	72 €	102 €

Caddy	Caddy	15 €
Electric Trolley	Elektrokarren	5 €
Buggy	Elektrischer Wagen	31 €
Clubs	Leihschläger	10 €

Credit cards Kreditkarten
VISA - Eurocard - MasterCard - DC - JCB - AMEX

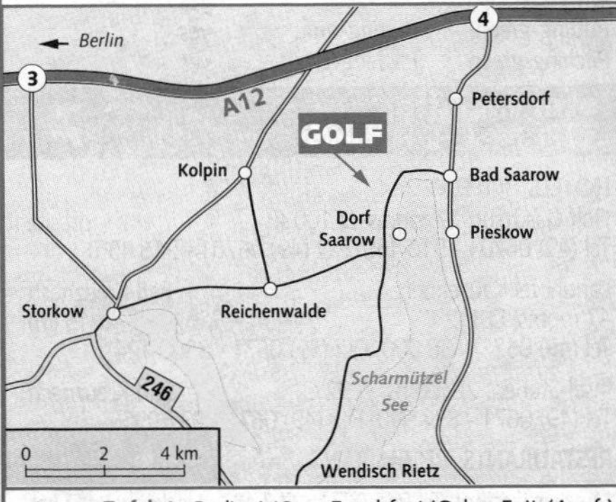

Access Zufahrt : Berlin A12 → Frankfurt/Oder. Exit (Ausf.) Fürstenwalde, → Bad Saarow → Golf.
Map 6 on page 365 Karte 6 Seite 365

Golf course PLATZ — 17/20

Site	Lage	
Maintenance	Instandhaltung	
Architect	Architekt	Arnold Palmer
Type	Typ	forest, parkland
Relief	Begehbarkeit	
Water in play	Platz mit Wasser	
Exp. to wind	Wind ausgesetzt	
Trees in play	Platz mit Bäumen	

Scorecard Scorekarte	**Chp.** Chp.	**Mens** Herren	**Ladies** Damen
Length Länge	6566	6062	5347
Par	72	72	72
Slope system	135	131	128

Advised golfing ability Empfohlene Spielstärke — 0 12 24 36
Hcp required Min. Handicap — no

Club house & amenities KLUBHAUS UND NEBENGEBÄUDE — 8/10

Pro shop	Pro shop	
Driving range	Übungsplatz	
Sheltered	überdacht	14 mats
On grass	auf Rasen	yes
Putting-green	Putting-grün	yes
Pitching-green	Pitching-grün	yes

Hotel facilities HOTEL BESCHREIBUNG — 7/10

HOTELS HOTELS

Hotel Kempinski, 216 rooms , D 174 € — on site
Tel (49) 033631 - 60, Fax (49) 033631 - 62 000

Landhaus Alte Eichen, 39 rooms , D 102 € — Bad Saarow 3 km
Tel (49) 033631 - 41 15, Fax (49) 033631 - 20 58

Schloss Hubertushöhe, 25 rooms, D 204 € — Storkow 12 km
Tel (49) 033678 - 43 0, Fax (49) 033678 - 43 100

RESTAURANTS RESTAURANT

Windspiel-Schl. Hubertus Höhe — Storkow 12 km
Tel (49) 033678 - 43 0

Landhaus Alte Eichen — Bad Saarow 3 km
Tel (49) 033678 - 41 15

SCHARMÜTZELSEE Nick Faldo

18 | 8 | 7

Grosse Champions müssen sich oft den Vorwurf gefallen lassen, Plätze zu gestalten, ohne die dafür erforderliche Zeit und Mühe aufzuwenden. Auf Nick Faldo trifft dies nicht zu, da bei den leider nur wenigen von ihm bislang entworfenen Platzen seine ganz persönliche Handschrift deutlich erkennbar ist. Angesichts des herausragenden Designs dieses auf flachem, offenen Gelände erbauten Golfplatzes wünscht er sich, dass man bald eimal Gelegenheit bekommt, sein Können an einem Streifen "echten" Links-Terrains auszuprobieren. Die natürlichen und künstlichen Unebenheiten des häufig spektakulär und respekteinflössend anmutenden Geländes nutzt er geschickt für sein Spiel mit Links-typischen Elementen. Ungeachtet dessen eignet sich der Platz für Golfer aller Spielstärken (die hinteren Abschläge sind für die Pros reserviert). Obwohl alle Schwierigkeiten gut erkennbar sind, benötigt man sicherlich einige Runden der Gewöhnung, bevor man hoffen darf, diesen Platz mit einem guten Ergebnis zu absolvieren. Viele Pros lobten den Platz nach den German Open 1998 und 1999 als den besten der gesamten europäischen Tour sowohl vom Design als auch vom Pflegezustand.

Great champions are often accused of signing courses without designing them too much. Not so for Nick Faldo, who visibly leaves his mark on the few (too few even) courses he designs. When you see the excellence of this course over a flat, open site, you can hardly wait to see him get to grips with a grand links site. He has toyed with the links idea here, using the natural and artificial undulations of often very spectacular and intimidating terrain. But golfers of all levels can play here easily enough (the back-tees are for the pros). Although the difficulties are clearly there to be seen, you will need to play this course several times (and in match-play) before even thinking about returning a good card at the end of the day. After the German Open of 1998 and 1999, many European Tour players praised the course as the best of the whole PGA European Tour in design and maintenance.

Sporting Club Berlin Scharmützelsee e.V. — 1997

Parkallee 3
D - 15526 BAD SAAROW

Office	Sekretariat	(49) 033631 - 63 300
Pro shop	Pro shop	(49) 033631 - 5628
Fax	Fax	(49) 033631 - 5270
Web	www.sporting-club-berlin.com	
Situation	Lage	Berlin (pop. 3 500 000), 75 km
Annual closure	Jährliche Schliessung	30/11→1/3
Weekly closure	Wöchentliche Schliessung	no

Fees main season Preisliste hochsaison	18 holes	
	Week days Woche	**We/Bank holidays** We/Feiertag
Individual Individuell	36 €	51 €
Couple Ehepaar	72 €	102 €

Caddy	Caddy	15 €
Electric Trolley	Elektrokarren	5 €
Buggy	Elektrischer Wagen	31 €
Clubs	Leihschläger	10 €

Credit cards Kreditkarten
VISA - Eurocard - MasterCard - DC - JCB - AMEX

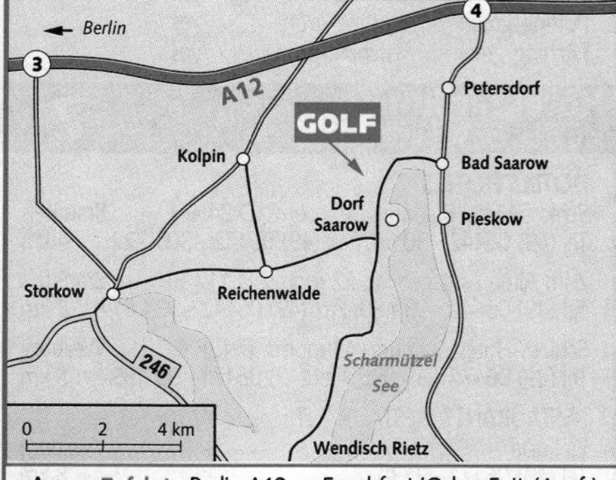

Access Zufahrt : Berlin A12 → Frankfurt/Oder. Exit (Ausf.) Fürstenwalde, → Bad Saarow → Golf.
Map 6 on page 365 Karte 6 Seite 365

Golf course PLATZ — 18/20

Site	Lage	
Maintenance	Instandhaltung	
Architect	Architekt	Nick Faldo
Type	Typ	links
Relief	Begehbarkeit	
Water in play	Platz mit Wasser	
Exp. to wind	Wind ausgesetzt	
Trees in play	Platz mit Bäumen	

Scorecard Scorekarte	**Chp.** Chp.	**Mens** Herren	**Ladies** Damen
Length Länge	6477	6084	5685
Par	72	72	72
Slope system	145	140	137

Advised golfing ability Empfohlene Spielstärke — 0 12 24 36
Hcp required Min. Handicap 28

Club house & amenities KLUBHAUS UND NEBENGEBÄUDE — 8/10

Pro shop	Pro shop	
Driving range	Übungsplatz	
Sheltered	überdacht	14 mats
On grass	auf Rasen	yes
Putting-green	Putting-grün	yes
Pitching-green	Pitching-grün	yes

Hotel facilities HOTEL BESCHREIBUNG — 7/10

HOTELS HOTELS

Hotel Kempinski, 216 rooms , D 174 € — on site
Tel (49) 033631 - 60, Fax (49) 033631 - 62 000

Landhaus Alte Eichen, 39 rooms , D 102 € — Bad Saarow
Tel (49) 033631 - 41 15, Fax (49) 033631 - 20 58 — 3 km

Schloss Hubertushöhe, 25 rooms, D 204 € — Storkow
Tel (49) 033678 - 43 0, Fax (49) 033678 - 43 100 — 12 km

RESTAURANTS RESTAURANT

Windspiel-Schl. Hubertus Höhe — Storkow
Tel (49) 033678 - 43 0 — 12 km

Landhaus Alte Eichen — Bad Saarow
Tel (49) 033678 - 41 15 — 3 km

SCHLOSS BRAUNFELS

16 | 7 | 7

Die alten Bauernhäuser, die einen willkommen heissen, sind gleichermassen beeindruckend wie die Aussicht auf Schloss Braunfels. Der Architekt hat das für einen Golfplatz gut geeignete Gelände absichtlich nur wenig verändert. Die Höhenunterschiede, die einen nicht davon abhalten sollten zu Fuss zu Gehen, spielen eine erheblich Rolle bei der Schlägerwahl, der wiederum eine Schlüsselrolle zukommt beim Anspiel einiger der zahlreichen, erhöht angelegten Grüns. Priorität hat auch die Vermeidung der Bäume und der Wasserhindernisse, letztere kommen an vier Löchern ins Spiel. Schloss Braunfels verlangt von den Spielern sicherlich kein überdurchschnittliches Können, dennoch kann die Fähigkeit den Ball sowohl mit Draw als auch Fade spielen zu können, bei der Endabrechnung von entscheidendem Vorteil sein. Sein Lage, die Umgebung, Vielseitigkeit und dazu ein komfortables Clubhaus - alles Faktoren, die für diesen Platz sprechen. Zudem liegt Wetzlar ganz in der Nähe, die Heimatstadt von Charlotte, der Heldin in Goethes "Werther".

The old farm buildings that welcome you are impressive, as are the views of Braunfels castle. The designer visibly did not want to upset terrain that is easily adaptable to golf. Although easy enough to play on foot, the slopes need to be reckoned with, at least when it comes to choosing the right club, a key factor here for attacking some of the many elevated greens. The first job is to avoid the trees and the water hazards in play on four holes. Schloss Braunfels certainly does not require above-average virtuosity, but being able to flight the ball both ways can be important in the final count. The location, the comfortable club-house, the setting and variety are major assets, as is the closeness to Wetzlar, the town of Charlotte, Goethe's heroine in "Werther".

Golf Club Schloss Braunfels — 1970

Homburger Hof
D - 35619 BRAUNFELS-LAHN

Office	Sekretariat	(49) 06442 - 4530
Pro shop	Pro shop	(49) 06442 - 5752
Fax	Fax	(49) 06442 - 6683
Web	—	
Situation	Lage	

Wetzlar, 15 km - Frankfurt (pop. 660 000), 80 km

Annual closure	Jährliche Schliessung	no
Weekly closure	Wöchentliche Schliessung	no

Monday (Montag): Restaurant closed

Fees main season Preisliste hochsaison	**Week days** Woche	**We/Bank holidays** We/Feiertag
		18 holes
Individual Individuell	36 €	46 €
Couple Ehepaar	72 €	92 €

– 21 years/Students: – 50%

Caddy	Caddy	on request
Electric Trolley	Elektrokarren	no
Buggy	Elektrischer Wagen	no
Clubs	Leihschläger	yes
Credit cards Kreditkarten		no

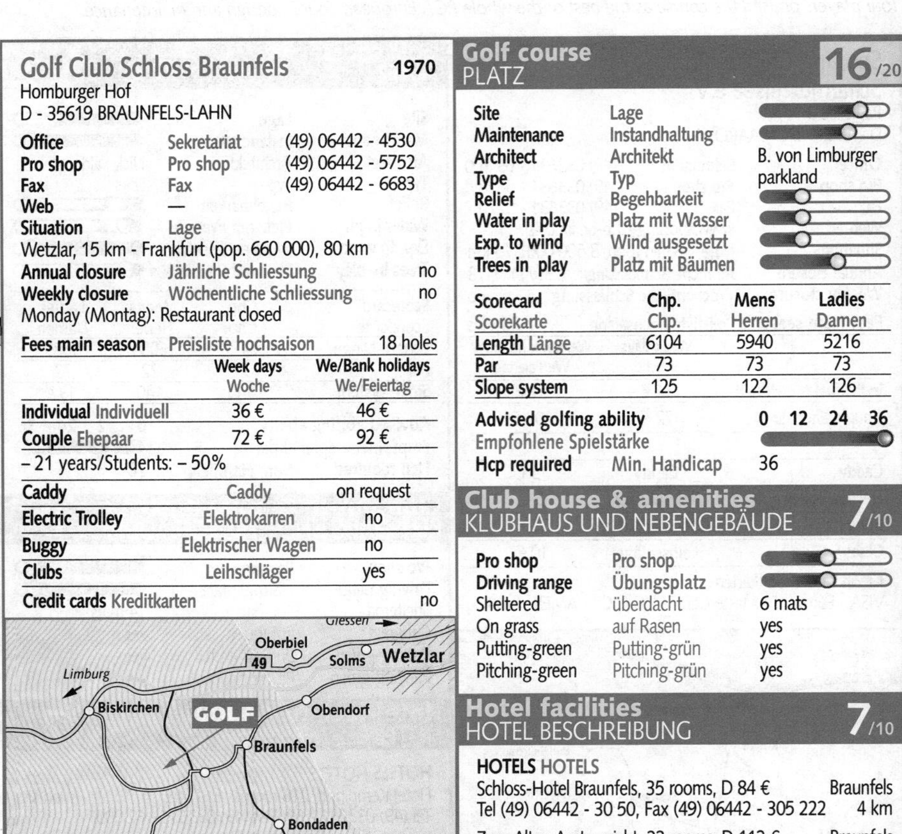

Access Zufahrt : Frankfurt A5 Nord, A45 → Wetzlar. Exit (Ausf.) Wetzlar Ost, B49 → Limburg. Leun, → Braunfels. Restaurant Obermühle, → Golf

Map 3 on page 359 Karte 3 Seite 359

Golf course — PLATZ — 16/20

Site	Lage	
Maintenance	Instandhaltung	
Architect	Architekt	B. von Limburger
Type	Typ	parkland
Relief	Begehbarkeit	
Water in play	Platz mit Wasser	
Exp. to wind	Wind ausgesetzt	
Trees in play	Platz mit Bäumen	

Scorecard Scorekarte	**Chp.** Chp.	**Mens** Herren	**Ladies** Damen
Length Länge	6104	5940	5216
Par	73	73	73
Slope system	125	122	126

Advised golfing ability Empfohlene Spielstärke — 0 12 24 36

Hcp required Min. Handicap 36

Club house & amenities — KLUBHAUS UND NEBENGEBÄUDE — 7/10

Pro shop	Pro shop	
Driving range	Übungsplatz	
Sheltered	überdacht	6 mats
On grass	auf Rasen	yes
Putting-green	Putting-grün	yes
Pitching-green	Pitching-grün	yes

Hotel facilities — HOTEL BESCHREIBUNG — 7/10

HOTELS HOTELS

Schloss-Hotel Braunfels, 35 rooms, D 84 € — Braunfels
Tel (49) 06442 - 30 50, Fax (49) 06442 - 305 222 — 4 km

Zum Alten Amtsgericht, 22 rooms, D 112 € — Braunfels
Tel (49) 06442 - 93 480, Fax (49) 06442 - 934 811 — 3 km

Schloss-Hotel Weilburg, 43 rooms, D 128 € — Weilburg
Tel (49) 06471 - 39 096, Fax (49) 06471 - 39 199 — 8 km

RESTAURANTS RESTAURANT

La Lucia — Weilburg
Tel (49) 06471 - 2130 — 8 km

Zum Alten Amtsgericht — Braunfels
Tel (49) 06442 - 93 480 — 3 km

SCHLOSS EGMATING

15	7	7

Der Architekt Kurt Rossknecht versteht es, den von Ihm entworfenen Anlagen seinen ganz persönlichen Stempel aufzudrücken, was in erster Linie in der sorgfältigen Gestaltung und Positionierung von Bunkern und Grüns zum Ausdruck kommt. Da auf Schloss Egmating wenig Wasser und so gut wie keine Bäume ins Spiel kommen, bilden hier vor allem das hügelige Terrain sowie die Fairway-Bunker den Schwerpunkt der Verteidigung zwischen Abschlag und Grün. Wer glaubt, dass Longhitter hier im Vorteil sind, sollte nicht die Vorzüge eines guten kurzen Spiels sowie die Fähigkeit guter Techniker, den Ball in unterschiedlichen Flugkurven zu spielen, unterschätzen. Letzteres gilt umso mehr, als eine Mischung aus hohen Lob und "bump and run" Schlägen erforderlich ist, um die Grüns anzuspielen. Wenn der Wind weht, ist es recht hilfreich die Flugbahn des Balles richtig einschätzen zu können. Die grosse Anzahl von Abschlägen an jedem Loch macht den Platz für alle Spielstärken zugänglich, solange bei Spielern mit hohem Handicap der Score nicht zu sehr im Vordergund steht. Den Platz sollte man auch in den nächsten Jahren im Auge behalten.

Designer Kurt Rossknecht likes to give courses his own personal stamp, if only through the careful attention he pays to the design of bunkers, to their positioning and to putting surfaces. At Schloss Egmating, water is not a major feature and trees hardly feature at all, so sloping terrain and fairway bunkers form the core of the difficulties en route to the green. You might think that long-hitters would have the upper hand here, but greater rewards often go to the technicians, the flighters of the ball, and even to the short game experts, who have to alternate between high lob and bump and run shots to get home and dry. If the wind blows, a sound knowledge of the science of trajectories will come in handy. The large number of tee-areas makes this a course for all skills, as long as high-handicappers don't worry unduly about a three-figure score. A course well worth watching in the years ahead.

Schloss Egmating — 1990

Schlosstrasse 15
D - 85658 EGMATING

Office	Sekretariat	(49) 08095 - 90 860
Pro shop	Pro shop	(49) 08095 - 908 610
Fax	Fax	(49) 08095 - 9086-66
Web	www.golf.de/egmating	
Situation	Lage	

München (pop. 1 300 000), 25 km - Aying, 3 km

Annual closure	Jährliche Schliessung	1/12→31/3
Weekly closure	Wöchentliche Schliessung	no

Fees main season Preisliste hochsaison	**Week days** Woche	**We/Bank holidays** We/Feiertag
		18 holes
Individual Individuell	51 €	66 €
Couple Ehepaar	102 €	132 €

Caddy	Caddy	on request
Electric Trolley	Elektrokarren	yes
Buggy	Elektrischer Wagen	yes
Clubs	Leihschläger	yes
Credit cards	Kreditkarten	no

Access Zufahrt : München, A99 Ost. Exit (Ausf.) Putzbrunn → Oberpframmen → Golf
Map 2 on page 357 Karte 2 Seite 357

Golf course PLATZ — 15/20

Site	Lage	
Maintenance	Instandhaltung	
Architect	Architekt	Kurt Rossknecht
Type	Typ	open country
Relief	Begehbarkeit	
Water in play	Platz mit Wasser	
Exp. to wind	Wind ausgesetzt	
Trees in play	Platz mit Bäumen	

Scorecard Scorekarte	**Chp.** Chp.	**Mens** Herren	**Ladies** Damen
Length Länge	6368	6116	5324
Par	72	72	72
Slope system	130	132	130

Advised golfing ability Empfohlene Spielstärke: 0 12 24 36
Hcp required Min. Handicap: 36

Club house & amenities KLUBHAUS UND NEBENGEBÄUDE — 7/10

Pro shop	Pro shop	
Driving range	Übungsplatz	
Sheltered	überdacht	yes
On grass	auf Rasen	yes
Putting-green	Putting-grün	yes
Pitching-green	Pitching-grün	yes

Hotel facilities HOTEL BESCHREIBUNG — 7/10

HOTELS HOTELS

Brauereigasthof Aying, 28 rooms, D 153 € — Aying
Tel (49) 08095 - 906 50, Fax (49) 08095 - 906 566 — 3 km

Aigner, 73 rooms, D 128 € — Ottobrunn
Tel (49) 089 - 608 170, Fax (49) 089 -6083 213 — 13 km

Sauerlach Post, 51 rooms, D 107 € — Sauerlach
Tel (49) 08104 - 8 30, Fax (49) 08104 - 83 83 — 10 km

Arabella, 658 rooms, D 306 € — München-Bogenhausen
Tel (49) 089 - 92 640, Fax (49) 089 - 9264 8699 — 25 km

RESTAURANTS RESTAURANT

Tantris, Tel (49) 089 - 362 061 München-Schwabing 25 km

Haflhof, Tel (49) 08093 - 5336 — Egmating 1 km

SCHLOSS KLINGENBURG

15	6	6

In einem alten Schlosspark gelegen ist der Platz mit einer Vielzahl herrlicher Bäume unterschiedlicher Art bestanden. Der Ort strahlt, verstärkt durch den umliegenden Wald, eine Aura von Ruhe und Abgeschiedenheit aus. Obwohl der Kurs angenehm zu spielen ist, bleibt er angesichts der idealen Voraussetzungen, die den Architekten zu einem Meisterwerk hätten beflügeln sollen, etwas hinter den Erwartungen zurück. Dieser schien jedoch mehr darum besorgt einen spielbaren Parcours zu entwerfen als den Platz zu einer echten Herausforderung zu machen. Die wenigen Fairwaybunker haben ein sehr flaches Profil. Bäume, Grünbunker und Wasserhindernisse dagegen stellen eine angemessene Gefahr dar. Abgesehen von den Eröffnungs- und Schlusslöchern verläuft der Platz über relativ ebenes Terrain, auf dem alle Hindernisse gut erkennbar sind. Klingenburgs gut verteidigte Grüns (fünf davon sind blind) verlangen nach "target Golf", so dass Spieler die den Ball faden können einen gewissen Vorteil haben. Theoretisch für Jeden zu bezwingen, bedingt es doch einer guten Form, will man hier einen dem Handicap entsprechenden Score erzielen.

Laid out in old castle grounds, this course has retained some superb varieties of trees, and the impression of peace and tranquillity that exudes from the overall setting is enhanced by the surrounding forest. But while the course is pleasant to play, it doesn't quite come up to expectations. A site as fine as this should have galvanised the architect into creating greater things. He was probably more concerned with designing a pleasant course rather than looking for stiff challenges, so the rare fairway bunkers are virtually flat, and trees, green-side bunkers and water hazards were most likely thought to be too penalising. A somewhat flattish course without any hidden traps, Schloss Klingenburg is more of a target golf course with well-protected greens (some are blind) and will give greater help to people who fade the ball. In theory within the grasp of anyone, you need to be on top of your game to get a good score.

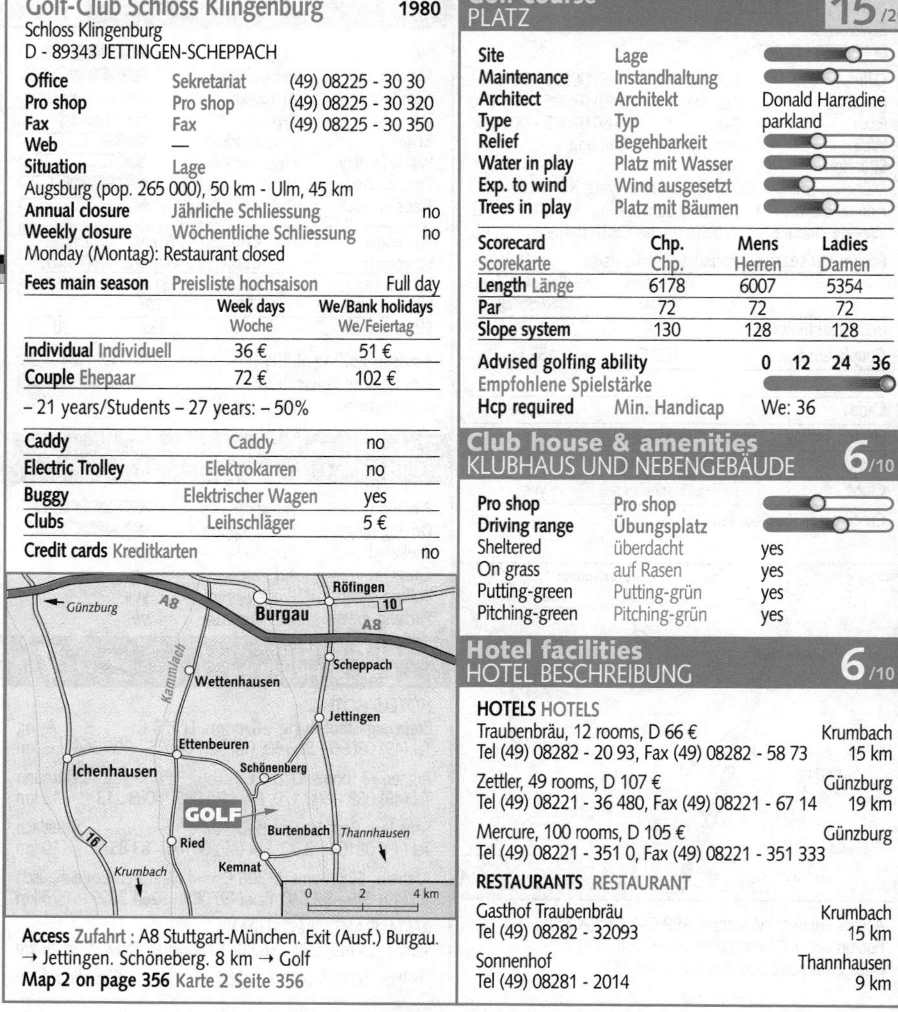

Golf-Club Schloss Klingenburg — 1980

Schloss Klingenburg
D - 89343 JETTINGEN-SCHEPPACH

Office	Sekretariat	(49) 08225 - 30 30
Pro shop	Pro shop	(49) 08225 - 30 320
Fax	Fax	(49) 08225 - 30 350
Web	—	
Situation	Lage	

Augsburg (pop. 265 000), 50 km - Ulm, 45 km

Annual closure	Jährliche Schliessung	no
Weekly closure	Wöchentliche Schliessung	no

Monday (Montag): Restaurant closed

Fees main season Preisliste hochsaison	Week days Woche	We/Bank holidays We/Feiertag
		Full day
Individual Individuell	36 €	51 €
Couple Ehepaar	72 €	102 €

– 21 years/Students – 27 years: – 50%

Caddy	Caddy	no
Electric Trolley	Elektrokarren	no
Buggy	Elektrischer Wagen	yes
Clubs	Leihschläger	5 €
Credit cards	Kreditkarten	no

Access Zufahrt : A8 Stuttgart-München. Exit (Ausf.) Burgau. → Jettingen. Schöneberg. 8 km → Golf
Map 2 on page 356 Karte 2 Seite 356

Golf course PLATZ — 15/20

Site	Lage	
Maintenance	Instandhaltung	
Architect	Architekt	Donald Harradine
Type	Typ	parkland
Relief	Begehbarkeit	
Water in play	Platz mit Wasser	
Exp. to wind	Wind ausgesetzt	
Trees in play	Platz mit Bäumen	

Scorecard Scorekarte	Chp. Chp.	Mens Herren	Ladies Damen
Length Länge	6178	6007	5354
Par	72	72	72
Slope system	130	128	128

Advised golfing ability Empfohlene Spielstärke — 0 12 24 36
Hcp required Min. Handicap — We: 36

Club house & amenities KLUBHAUS UND NEBENGEBÄUDE — 6/10

Pro shop	Pro shop	
Driving range	Übungsplatz	
Sheltered	überdacht	yes
On grass	auf Rasen	yes
Putting-green	Putting-grün	yes
Pitching-green	Pitching-grün	yes

Hotel facilities HOTEL BESCHREIBUNG — 6/10

HOTELS HOTELS

Traubenbräu, 12 rooms, D 66 € — Krumbach
Tel (49) 08282 - 20 93, Fax (49) 08282 - 58 73 — 15 km

Zettler, 49 rooms, D 107 € — Günzburg
Tel (49) 08221 - 36 480, Fax (49) 08221 - 67 14 — 19 km

Mercure, 100 rooms, D 105 € — Günzburg
Tel (49) 08221 - 351 0, Fax (49) 08221 - 351 333

RESTAURANTS RESTAURANT

Gasthof Traubenbräu — Krumbach
Tel (49) 08282 - 32093 — 15 km

Sonnenhof — Thannhausen
Tel (49) 08281 - 2014 — 9 km

SCHLOSS LANGENSTEIN

16	8	7

Die Nähe zur Schweiz und der schönen Stadt Konstanz, sowie prächtige Ausblicke auf den Bodensee verleihen diesem noch recht neuen Golfplatz eine unbestreitbare Anziehungskraft. Der Föhn kann die Ankunft des Frühlings hier etwas beschleunigen, während der Rest von Deutschland noch vor Kälte bibbert. Das ziemlich hügelige Terrain verlangt vom Spieler eine gute Kondition. Trotz der Geländeunebenheiten sind die Hindernisse gut erkennbar und gibt es keine blinden Grüns. Das Schlüsselwort Kontrolle gilt sowohl für den Ball als auch das eigene Spiel, da die "wilderen" Golfer hier häufig ernsthaft in Schwierigkeiten geraten können. Ehrlich gesagt sollten Anfänger und "Hacker" ihre Schläger hier besser im Auto lassen und stattdessen den guten Spielern zuschauen, es sein denn, sie sind bereit die Runde als Teil des Lernprozesses zu betrachten. Gut ausgewogen und kompetent konzipiert ist Schloss Langenstein ein Muss für den der diese schöne Gegend erkundet.

Being very close to Switzerland and to the pretty town of Konstanz, and offering some fabulous views of the Bodensee, this recent course has unquestionable appeal. The foehn wind can bring spring a little early here, while the rest of Germany is still shivering, but you need to be in good shape, even early in the year, because the terrain is rather hilly. Despite the relief, difficulties are rarely hidden from view and no greens are blind. The key word here is control - of your ball and your game - as the wilder players can often end up in serious trouble. To be honest, even though the course makes for a superb walk, beginners and hackers are better off leaving their clubs in the car and watching the good players ply their trade... unless they consider a round here to be part of the learning process. Well-balanced and tastefully designed, Schloss Langenstein is a must if you are exploring this pretty region.

Country Club Schloss Langenstein — 1991

Schloss Langenstein
D - 78359 ORSINGEN-NENZINGEN

Office	Sekretariat	(49) 07774 - 50 651
Pro shop	Pro shop	(49) 07774 - 50 672
Fax	Fax	(49) 07774 - 50 699
Web	www.golf.de/langenstein	
Situation	Lage	Singen (pop. 44 000), 8 km
Annual closure	Jährliche Schliessung	1/12→28/2
Weekly closure	Wöchentliche Schliessung	no

Monday (Montag): Restaurant closed

Fees main season Preisliste hochsaison	18 holes	
	Week days Woche	**We/Bank holidays** We/Feiertag
Individual Individuell	41 €	61 €
Couple Ehepaar	82 €	122 €

– 21 years/Students: – 50%

Caddy	Caddy	no
Electric Trolley	Elektrokarren	13 €
Buggy	Elektrischer Wagen	yes
Clubs	Leihschläger	5 €
Credit cards	Kreditkarten	no

Access Zufahrt : A81 Stuttgart-Singen. Exit (Ausf.) Engen. B31 → Stockach. In Eigeltingen, turn right → Schloss Langenstein.

Map 1 on page 355 Karte 1 Seite 355

Golf course PLATZ — 16/20

Site	Lage	
Maintenance	Instandhaltung	
Architect	Architekt	Unknown
Type	Typ	open country, hilly
Relief	Begehbarkeit	
Water in play	Platz mit Wasser	
Exp. to wind	Wind ausgesetzt	
Trees in play	Platz mit Bäumen	

Scorecard Scorekarte	**Chp.** Chp.	**Mens** Herren	**Ladies** Damen
Length Länge	6341	5961	5268
Par	73	72	72
Slope system	124	124	126

Advised golfing ability Empfohlene Spielstärke — 0 12 24 36

Hcp required Min. Handicap — We: 32/35 (Damen)

Club house & amenities KLUBHAUS UND NEBENGEBÄUDE — 8/10

Pro shop	Pro shop	
Driving range	Übungsplatz	
Sheltered	überdacht	10 mats
On grass	auf Rasen	yes (April → Oct
Putting-green	Putting-grün	yes
Pitching-green	Pitching-grün	yes

Hotel facilities HOTEL BESCHREIBUNG — 7/10

HOTELS HOTELS

Haus Sättele, 15 rooms, D 77 € — Steisslingen
Tel (49) 07738 - 92 200, Fax (49) 07738 - 929 059 — 5 km

Flohr's, 8 rooms, D 123 € — Überlingen
Tel (49) 07731 - 93 230, Fax (49) 07731 - 932 323 — 10 km

Art Villa Am See, 9 rooms, D 128 € — Radolfzell
Tel (49) 07732 - 944 40, Fax (49) 07732 - 944 410 — 3 km

RESTAURANTS RESTAURANT

Flohr's — Überlingen
Tel (49) 07731 - 93 230 — 10 km

Salzburger Stub'n — Rielasingen-Worblingen
Tel (49) 07731 - 27 349 — 12 km

SCHLOSS LÜDERSBURG Old New | 15 | 7 | 6

Die 18 von W. Siegmann entworfenen Löcher wurden vor kurzem um eine von Jack Nicklaus geplante 9-Loch-Anlage erweitert. Sämtliche Löcher können als technisch anspruchsvoll und optisch gelungen bezeichnet werden. Wer jedoch nicht alle 27 Löcher spielen kann, dem empfehlen wir - ohne damit den "Goldenen Bären" beleidigen zu wollen - dem einheitlichen Stil des ursprünglichen Platzes den Vorzug zu geben. Dieser Parcours mit seinen engen, von grossen Bäume gesäumten Spielbahnen wird von einem Wasserlauf durchschnitten, der an 6 Fairways als nur eines von vielen Wasserhindernissen ins Spiel kommt. Von diesen kleinen Boshaftigkeiten sollten sich auch durchschnittliche Spieler nicht abschrecken lassen. Zwar werden diese hier womöglich keinen guten Score erzielen, aber schliesslich hängt der Spass am Golf nicht allein vom Ergebnis ab. Wer die 27 Löcher erfolgreich bewältigen will, darf in seiner Aufmerksamkeit und Konzentration nie nachlassen. Dieser Platz passt gut in eine Region, der es an anspruchsvollen Golfplätzen nicht mangelt. Er wird einem selbst nach häufigem Spielen nie langweilig.

The 18 holes designed by Siegmann have recently been supplemented by a 9 holer laid out by Jack Nicklaus. They are all as technical as they are agreeable to the eye, but if you cannot play all 27, and without wishing to offend the Golden Bear, you are best advised going for the unity of style offered by the original layout. It is rather narrow, lined with large trees and cut by a stream that crosses the fairways six times as one of the many water hazards. However, Schloss Lüdersburg is not spiteful enough to put off the average player. They may not return a fabulous card, but the fun of golf does not depend solely on performance. The 27 holes call for some hard work if they are to be successfully negotiated, enough to keep the player constantly on his toes. In a region where there is no shortage of challenging golf courses, this one is well placed. What's more, you can play it again and again without a minute's boredom.

Golf- und Landclub Schloss Lüdersburg — 1986

Lüdersburger Strasse 21
D - 21379 LÜDERSBURG/LÜNEBURG

Office	Sekretariat	(49) 04139 - 69 700
Pro shop	Pro shop	(49) 04139 - 69 700
Fax	Fax	(49) 04139 - 697 070
Web	www.luedesburg.de	
Situation	Lage	

Lüneburg, 15 km - Hamburg (pop. 1 650 000), 50 km

Annual closure	Jährliche Schliessung	no
Weekly closure	Wöchentliche Schliessung	no
Fees main season	Preisliste hochsaison	18 holes

	Week days / Woche	We/Bank holidays / We/Feiertag
Individual Individuell	26 €	46 €
Couple Ehepaar	52 €	92 €
Caddy	Caddy	no
Electric Trolley	Elektrokarren	no
Buggy	Elektrischer Wagen	yes
Clubs	Leihschläger	yes

Credit cards Kreditkarten
Eurocard - MasterCard

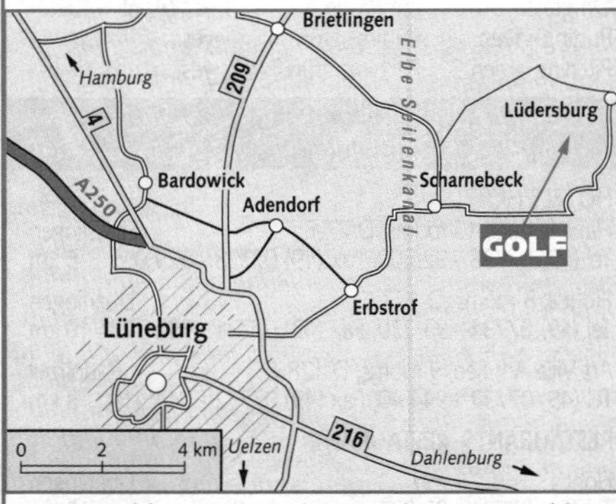

Access Zufahrt : A250 Hamburg-Lüneburg. Exit (Ausfahrt) Lüneburg/Ebersberg. Scranebeck, Lüdersburg.
Map 7 on page 366 Karte 7 Seite 366

Golf course PLATZ — 15/20

Site	Lage	
Maintenance	Instandhaltung	
Architect	Architekt	W. Siegmann Jack Nicklaus
Type	Typ	parkland
Relief	Begehbarkeit	
Water in play	Platz mit Wasser	
Exp. to wind	Wind ausgesetzt	
Trees in play	Platz mit Bäumen	

Scorecard / Scorekarte	Chp. / Chp.	Mens / Herren	Ladies / Damen
Length Länge	6711	5912	5229
Par	73	73	73
Slope system	128	128	126

Advised golfing ability Empfohlene Spielstärke — 0 12 24 36
Hcp required Min. Handicap 36

Club house & amenities KLUBHAUS UND NEBENGEBÄUDE — 7/10

Pro shop	Pro shop	
Driving range	Übungsplatz	
Sheltered	überdacht	yes
On grass	auf Rasen	yes
Putting-green	Putting-grün	yes
Pitching-green	Pitching-grün	yes

Hotel facilities HOTEL BESCHREIBUNG — 6/10

HOTELS HOTELS

Seminaris, 191 rooms, D 115 € — Lüneburg
Tel (49) 04131 - 71 30, Fax (49) 04131 - 71 3727 — 16 km

Hof Reinstorf, 81 rooms, D 120 € — Reinstorf
Tel (49) 04137 - 80 90, Fax (49) 04137 - 80 9100 — 15 km

Heiderose, 21 rooms, D 77 € — Lüneburg
Tel (49) 04131 - 44 410, Fax (49) 04131 - 48 357 — 16 km

Lauenburger Mühle, 34 rooms, D 94 € — Lauenburg
Tel (49) 04153 - 58 90, Fax (49) 04153 - 55 555 — 9 km

RESTAURANTS RESTAURANT

Hof Reinstorf, Tel (49) 04137 - 8090 — Reinstorf 15 km

Zum Heidkrug, Tel (49) 04131 - 31 249 — Lüneburg 16 km

SCHLOSS MYLLENDONK

16 | 7 | 7

Das im Mittelalter erbaute Schloss Myllendonk dient nicht nur als Clubhaus, sondern gibt dem Golfplatz, der im ürigen einen ausgezeichneten Ruf hat, auch seinen Namen. Die schöne Lage täuscht in vielen Fällen über schwerwiegende Schwächen beim Platzdesign hinweg. So enttäuscht uns eine Anzahl sehr nahe beieinander liegender Spielbahnen, trotz der sie begrenzenden schönen Bäume, die das Spiel erschweren. Genaue Drives und kontrolliert geschlagene Bälle sind Voraussetzung, um die Grüns von der besten Position aus angreifen zu können. Aufgrund des sehr ebenen Geländes sind die meisten Hindernisse gut erkennbar. Dies verleiht denen, die hier zum ersten mal spielen, eine gewisse Zuversicht, wenngleich einen das berechtigte Gefühl beschleicht, dass die Wasserläufe und Seen nur darauf lauern, einem das Leben schwer zu machen. Ungeübte Golfer, denen der Platz möglicherweise etwas schwierig erscheint, seien daran erinnert, dass der Score nicht alles ist worum es beim Golf geht.

The castle of Myllendonk, which dates from the Middle Ages, gives this course of excellent repute both its name and its clubhouse. The beauty of the setting can often conceal some glaring errors in design, and while we might regret a number of fairways which are too close to each other, the trees between them are magnificent and really add to the playing difficulty. Accurate driving and flighted shots are vital if you want to have any hope of hitting the greens from the easiest position. As the terrain is very flat, most hazards are clearly visible. This gives the new-comer a certain degree of confidence first time out, even though you can feel that streams and lakes are lying in wait to make life more difficult (a feeling that proves to be true!). Inexperienced golfers might find the layout a little tough, but just tell them that the score is not the only thing in golf...

Golf Club Schloss Myllendonk e.V. 1965
Korschenbroich

Myllendonker Strasse 113
D - 41352 KORSCHENBROICH

Office	Sekretariat	(49) 02161 - 641 049
Pro shop	Pro shop	(49) 02161 - 644 955
Fax	Fax	(49) 02161 - 648 806
Web	www.golf.de/schloss-myllendonk	
Situation	Lage	Düsseldorf, 25 km
Annual closure	Jährliche Schliessung	no
Weekly closure	Wöchentliche Schliessung	no

Monday (Montag): Restaurant closed

Fees main season Preisliste hochsaison	**Week days** Woche	**We/Bank holidays** We/Feiertag
		18 holes
Individual Individuell	46 €	51 €
Couple Ehepaar	92 €	102 €

Caddy	Caddy	no
Electric Trolley	Elektrokarren	no
Buggy	Elektrischer Wagen	no
Clubs	Leihschläger	yes
Credit cards Kreditkarten		no

Access Zufahrt : A44 Exit (Ausf.) Mönchengladbach-Ost → "Gewerbegebiet Üdding". 1 km left in Jakobshöhe Strasse. 600 m, left in Myllendonker Strasse. → Schlosshof-Parkplatz. **Map 3 on page 358** Karte 3 Seite 358

Golf course PLATZ 16/20

Site	Lage	
Maintenance	Instandhaltung	
Architect	Architekt	Donald Harradine
Type	Typ	parkland, forest
Relief	Begehbarkeit	
Water in play	Platz mit Wasser	
Exp. to wind	Wind ausgesetzt	
Trees in play	Platz mit Bäumen	

Scorecard Scorekarte	**Chp.** Chp.	**Mens** Herren	**Ladies** Damen
Length Länge	5971	5539	5255
Par	72	72	72
Slope system	128	131	127

Advised golfing ability Empfohlene Spielstärke — 0 12 24 36

Hcp required Min. Handicap 36

Club house & amenities KLUBHAUS UND NEBENGEBÄUDE 7/10

Pro shop	Pro shop	
Driving range	Übungsplatz	
Sheltered	überdacht	no
On grass	auf Rasen	yes (Summer)
Putting-green	Putting-grün	yes
Pitching-green	Pitching-grün	yes

Hotel facilities HOTEL BESCHREIBUNG 7/10

HOTELS HOTELS

Queens Hotel, 127 rooms, D 143 € Mönchengladbach-Rheydt
Tel (49) 02161 - 93 80, Fax (49) 02161 - 938 807 5 km

Dorint Hotel, 162 rooms, D 153 € Mönchengladbach
Tel (49) 02161 - 89 30, Fax (49) 02161 - 87 231 5 km

Cerano, 67 rooms, D 84 € Mönchengladbach
Tel (49) 02161 - 926 630, Fax (49) 02161 -926 6340

RESTAURANTS RESTAURANT

Michelangelo Mönchengladbach
Tel (49) 02161 - 208 583 5 km

Zur Traube Korschenbroich
Tel (49) 02161 - 670 404 3 km

SCHLOSS NIPPENBURG

17	8	6

Die Bäume am Rande der Spielbahnen sind schon etwas seit der Eröffnung im Jahre 1993 gewachsen, aber es wird noch Jahre dauern ehe sie wirklich zur Gefahr werden. Im Augenblick sind die Bunker, Wasser und das Auf und Ab der Spielbahnen mit vielen Schräglagen die Hauptschwierigkeiten. Es gibt drei erhöhte Grüns und ein halbes Dutzend, die tiefer liegen als die Spielbahn. Wenn der Wind hier bläst, ist der Platz um vieles schwieriger. Bernhard Langer hatte beim Entwurf schottische Küstenplätze im Sinn, aber er hat nicht vergessen, dass Golf kein Spiel nur für Professionals und gute Amateure ist. Wenn der Wind nicht bläst, ist der Platz für die Mehrzahl der Golfer gut spielbar, vorausgesetzt sie kommen mit hängenden Balllagen zurecht. Der einzige Nachtal sind die extrem langen Wege vom Grün zum nächsten Abschlag und der ermüdende, bergauf führende Weg vom Parkplatz zum ultramodernen Clubhaus.

The trees alongside this rather open course have grown since it was first opened in 1993, but it will take a few more years before they really become dangerous. For the moment, the main difficulties are the bunkers, water and contoured landscape which leads to sloping lies, three elevated greens and half a dozen downhill greens. If the wind decides to blow, the course assumes a whole new dimension and requires good ball control if you want to card any sort of score, even though the yardage is reasonable. When designing Schloss Nippenburg, Bernhard Langer obviously had the Scottish links style in mind, but according to the proper tradition he never forgot that golf is not a game reserved only for professionals and good amateur players. If the wind is not blowing the course is not too difficult for the majority of players if they can play sloping lies. The only drawback of the course are the long walks from green to the next tee and the long tiring uphill walk from the parking lot to the ultramodern clubhouse.

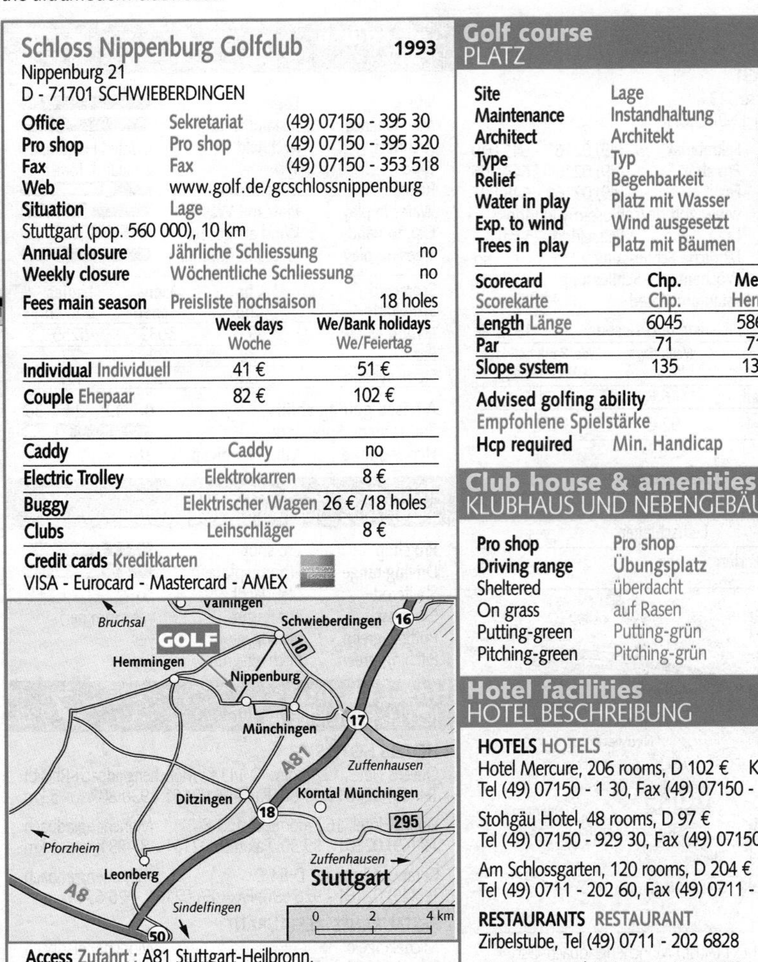

Schloss Nippenburg Golfclub — 1993

Nippenburg 21
D - 71701 SCHWIEBERDINGEN

Office	Sekretariat	(49) 07150 - 395 30
Pro shop	Pro shop	(49) 07150 - 395 320
Fax	Fax	(49) 07150 - 353 518
Web	www.golf.de/gcschlossnippenburg	
Situation	Lage	
Stuttgart (pop. 560 000), 10 km		
Annual closure	Jährliche Schliessung	no
Weekly closure	Wöchentliche Schliessung	no

Fees main season Preisliste hochsaison	**Week days** Woche	**We/Bank holidays** We/Feiertag
	18 holes	
Individual Individuell	41 €	51 €
Couple Ehepaar	82 €	102 €

Caddy	Caddy	no
Electric Trolley	Elektrokarren	8 €
Buggy	Elektrischer Wagen	26 € /18 holes
Clubs	Leihschläger	8 €

Credit cards Kreditkarten
VISA - Eurocard - Mastercard - AMEX

Access Zufahrt : A81 Stuttgart-Heilbronn.
Exit (Ausf.) Stuttgart-Zuffenhausen. B10 → Vaihingen.
Münchingen → Hemmingen. → Golf
Map 1 on page 355 Karte 1 Seite 355

Golf course — PLATZ — 17/20

Site	Lage	
Maintenance	Instandhaltung	
Architect	Architekt	Bernhard Langer
Type	Typ	country, open country
Relief	Begehbarkeit	
Water in play	Platz mit Wasser	
Exp. to wind	Wind ausgesetzt	
Trees in play	Platz mit Bäumen	

Scorecard Scorekarte	**Chp.** Chp.	**Mens** Herren	**Ladies** Damen
Length Länge	6045	5866	5152
Par	71	71	71
Slope system	135	132	130

Advised golfing ability Empfohlene Spielstärke — 0 12 24 36
Hcp required Min. Handicap — no

Club house & amenities — KLUBHAUS UND NEBENGEBÄUDE — 8/10

Pro shop	Pro shop	
Driving range	Übungsplatz	
Sheltered	überdacht	6 mats
On grass	auf Rasen	yes
Putting-green	Putting-grün	yes
Pitching-green	Pitching-grün	yes

Hotel facilities — HOTEL BESCHREIBUNG — 6/10

HOTELS HOTELS

Hotel Mercure, 206 rooms, D 102 € — Korntal-Münchingen
Tel (49) 07150 - 1 30, Fax (49) 07150 - 132 66 — 3 km

Stohgäu Hotel, 48 rooms, D 97 € — Münchingen
Tel (49) 07150 - 929 30, Fax (49) 07150 - 929 399 — 3 km

Am Schlossgarten, 120 rooms, D 204 € — Stuttgart 10 km
Tel (49) 0711 - 202 60, Fax (49) 0711 - 202 6888

RESTAURANTS RESTAURANT

Zirbelstube, Tel (49) 0711 - 202 6828 — Stuttgart 10 km

Di Gennaro, Tel (49) 0711 - 222 9603 — Stuttgart 10 km

Clubhaus Restaurant — Schloss Nippenburg
Tel (49) 07150 - 324 72 — on site

SCHLOSS WILKENDORF

17	7	5

Mit Sandy Lyle, dem sein Landsmann Ross McMurray assistierte, wurde ein weiterer Top-Designer für den Entwurf eines Golfplatzes im Berliner Raum engagiert. Dies ist Lyles erstes Projekt in Kontinental-Europa, und er hat erstklassige Arbeit auf sanft gewellten ehemaligen Ackerland abgeliefert. Der Platz ist perfekt in die Umgebung eingebettet, er wirkt als gäbe es ihn schon seit Ewigkeiten. Alle Spielbahn sind weit von einander getrennt, so daß man sich nie ins Gehege kommt. Neben Bäumen, hohem Rough, wenigen Wasserhindernisse kommen selbstverständlich auch zahlreiche Fairwaybunker ins Spiel, die aber eher unauffällig ins Design integriert sind. Man muß vom Abschlag schon genau hinschauen, um die gut plazierten Sandhindernisse zu erkannen. Die Grüns sind auch relativ flach, dafür aber gut verteidigt. In einer Umfrage unter Berliner Golfern wurde dieser Platz zum besten der Region gewählt, sicherlich auch,weil er nicht ganz so schwierig wie der Faldo- oder der Robert-Trent-Jones-Jr.-Platz am Seddiner See ist. Der Westside Platz ist der einzig öffentliche Platz in Berlin und Brandenburg, man kann also ohne Handicap und Clubmitgliedschaft hier spielen.

This course is laid out across rolling countryside which used to be farm land. The course is new but looks as if it has been around here for years, as it blends beautifully with the environment. Even though the bunkers are threatening they are not as conspicuous as at the nearby courses of Seddiner See South Course or the Faldo course at the Sporting Club Berlin Scharmützelsee. The course boasts wonderful variety, with no two holes alike. One fine example is the short 15th, where the tee shot has to be neatly slotted through a small gap of trees. The only drawback here is the course's relatively remote location to the north east of Berlin. But in spite of the long drive – almost 90 minutes from the centre of Berlin – this is one course not to be missed when in the German capital. The former British Open and US Masters Champion Sandy Lyle has proved that he is as good a golf course designer as he was a player.

Golfclub Schloss Wilkendorf e.V. — 1995

Am Weiher 1
D - 15345 WILKENDORF

Office	Sekretariat	(49) 03341 - 330 960
Pro shop	Pro shop	(49) 03341 -330 6920
Fax	Fax	(49) 03341 - 330 961
E-mail	golfparkschlosswilkendorf@t-online.de	
Situation	Lage	

Berlin (pop. 3 500 000), 70 km - Strausberg, 7 km

Annual closure	Jährliche Schliessung	15/11→15/3
Weekly closure	Wöchentliche Schliessung	no

Monday (Montag): Restaurant closed

Fees main season Preisliste hochsaison	**Week days** Woche	**We/Bank holidays** We/Feiertag
		18 holes
Individual Individuell	33 €	46 €
Couple Ehepaar	66 €	92 €

Caddy	Caddy	no
Electric Trolley	Elektrokarren	13 €
Buggy	Elektrischer Wagen	no
Clubs	Leihschläger	13 €
Credit cards	Kreditkarten	no

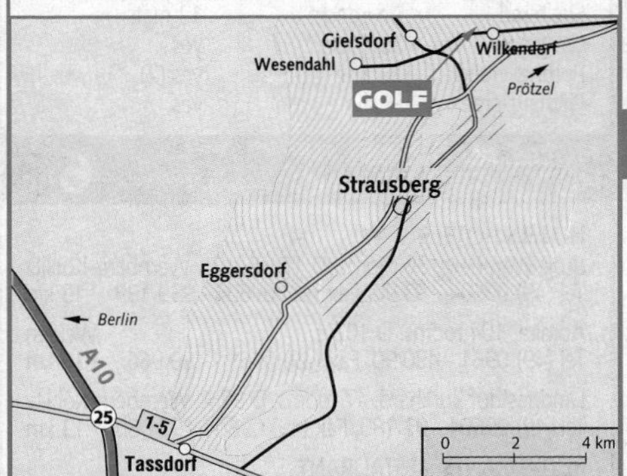

Access Zufahrt : B1-5 Berlin → Frankfurt/Oder to Berliner Ring (A10). 1 km left → Strausberg. → Golf.
Map 6 on page 365 Karte 6 Seite 365

Golf course — PLATZ — 17/20

Site	Lage	
Maintenance	Instandhaltung	
Architect	Architekt	Sandy Lyle
Type	Typ	inland
Relief	Begehbarkeit	
Water in play	Platz mit Wasser	
Exp. to wind	Wind ausgesetzt	
Trees in play	Platz mit Bäumen	

Scorecard Scorekarte	**Chp.** Chp.	**Mens** Herren	**Ladies** Damen
Length Länge	6517	6096	5302
Par	74	72	72
Slope system	131	128	124

Advised golfing ability Empfohlene Spielstärke — 0 12 24 36
Hcp required Min. Handicap — 36

Club house & amenities — KLUBHAUS UND NEBENGEBÄUDE — 7/10

Pro shop	Pro shop	
Driving range	Übungsplatz	
Sheltered	überdacht	16 mats
On grass	auf Rasen	yes
Putting-green	Putting-grün	yes
Pitching-green	Pitching-grün	yes

Hotel facilities — HOTEL BESCHREIBUNG — 5/10

HOTELS HOTELS

Lakeside Hotel, 54 rooms, D 92 € — Strausberg 2 km
Tel (49) 03341 - 346 90, Fax (49) 03341 - 346 915

Schloss Reichenow, 20 rooms, D 102 € — Reichenow 15 km
Tel (49) 033437 - 30 80, Fax (49) 033437 - 30 888

Golfakademie, 5 rooms, D 77 € — Schloss Wilkendorf on site
Tel (49) 03341 - 330 910, Fax (49) 03341 - 330 961

RESTAURANTS RESTAURANT

Stobber Mühle, Tel (49) 033433 - 668 33 — Bucklow 15 km

Goldene Kartoffel — Prötzel 7 km
Tel (49) 0334 - 364 92

SCHWANHOF

17 | 8 | 6

Hier kann man nicht nur vorzüglich Golf spielen, sondern in dem romantischen, mittelalterlichen Hotel Burg Wernberg logieren, das wie der Platz dem deutschen Elektronic-Magnaten Klaus Conrad gehört. Die ruhige ländliches Atmosphäre der bayrischen Oberpfalz nahe Weiden mit seiner Landschaft machen Golf zu einem Vergnügen, besonders, da der Platz für Golfer aller Spielstärken geeignet ist. Auf über 90 Hektar offenen Land haben Jerry Pate und Reinhold Weishaupt einen Topplatz entworfen. Auf den ersten Blick wirken nur das 5. Loch und das 18. Loch mit dem Inselgrün als überaus schwierig, doch testet der Platz mit seinen subtilen Schwierigkeiten selbst Professionals, die ständig hier Turniere der German PGA Tour austragen. Die Fairways sind weit und fehlerverzeihend, ab und an geht es steil bergauf und bergab. Trotz der hügeligen Topografie, die einen Golfwagen bei Hitze empfehlenswert macht, sind alle Hindernisse, meist in der Form gut platzierter Bunker, gut zu erkennen. Der Platz schüchtert nicht ein und wirkt wie die ganze Gegend gastfreundlich. Zusammen mit dem luxuriösen Clubhaus ist dies einer der besten neun deutschen Plätze.

Come here to play golf and enjoy the romantic and chivalrous side of historic Germany with a stay at the nearby Burg Wernberg hotel, owned like the golf course by German electronic magnate Klaus Conrad. The calm, country atmosphere near Weiden along with the landscape add to the pleasure of playing golf, especially as here there is something for everyone. Over 80 hectares of very open land, Jerry Pate and Reinhold Weishaupt have designed a top-class 18-hole course with the emphasis on adapting the layout to golfers of all different abilities. Only the 5th and 18th (island green) holes are perhaps slightly tougher propositions. The fairways are wide and forgiving, sometimes climbing steeply up and down, sufficiently so to warrant a buggy in hot weather. Despite the topography, trouble in store is clearly there to be seen basically in the form of well-located bunkers. Rarely intimidating, hospitable, intelligently designed and well drained, Schwanhof boasts excellent facilities and is one of the finest new courses around.

Golfclub Schwanhof e.V. — 1990

Klaus-Conrad-Allee 1
D - 92706 LUHE-WILDENAU

Office	Sekretariat	(49) 09607 - 92 020
Pro shop	Pro shop	(49) 09607 - 92 020
Fax	Fax	(49) 09607 - 920 248
Web	www.golfclub-schwanhof.de	
Situation	Lage	Weiden (pop. 43 000), 10 km
Annual closure	Jährliche Schliessung	1/1→31/1
Weekly closure	Wöchentliche Schliessung	no

Fees main season Preisliste hochsaison — 18 holes

	Week days Woche	We/Bank holidays We/Feiertag
Individual Individuell	41 €	51 €
Couple Ehepaar	82 €	102 €

Juniors under 18: special prices

Caddy	Caddy	26 €
Electric Trolley	Elektrokarren	10 € /18 holes
Buggy	Elektrischer Wagen	23 € /18 holes
Clubs	Leihschläger	10 € /18 holes

Credit cards Kreditkarten
VISA - Eurocard - MasterCard - DC - AMEX

Access Zufahrt : • München, A93 → Regensburg, then Weiden i.d. Oberpfalz. Exit 26 (Ausfahrt 26) Luhe-Wildenau → Golf Schloss Schwanhof. • Nürnberg, A6 → Amberg. Exit 65 Amberg West. B299/B14 → Hirschau. Left → Luhe-Wildenau. → Golf Schloss Schwanhof. **Map 4 on page 361** Karte 4 Seite 361

Golf course PLATZ — 17/20

Site	Lage	
Maintenance	Instandhaltung	
Architect	Architekt	Jerry Pate, Reinhold Weishaupt
Type	Typ	open country, hilly
Relief	Begehbarkeit	
Water in play	Platz mit Wasser	
Exp. to wind	Wind ausgesetzt	
Trees in play	Platz mit Bäumen	

Scorecard Scorekarte	Chp. Chp.	Mens Herren	Ladies Damen
Length Länge	6034	5696	4916
Par	72	72	72
Slope system	124	122	121

Advised golfing ability Empfohlene Spielstärke — 0 12 24 36

Hcp required Min. Handicap — no

Club house & amenities KLUBHAUS UND NEBENGEBÄUDE — 8/10

Pro shop	Pro shop	
Driving range	Übungsplatz	
Sheltered	überdacht	12 mats
On grass	auf Rasen	yes
Putting-green	Putting-grün	yes (2)
Pitching-green	Pitching-grün	yes

Hotel facilities HOTEL BESCHREIBUNG — 6/10

HOTELS HOTELS

Burg Wernberg, 30 rooms, D 174 € — Wernberg-Köblitz
Tel (49) 09604 - 93 90, Fax (49) 09604 - 939 139 — 13 km

Admira, 104 rooms, D 102 € — Weiden
Tel (49) 0961 - 480 90, Fax (49) 0961 - 480 966 — 10 km

Landgasthof Burkhard, 17 rooms, D 92 € — Wernberg-Köblitz
Tel (49) 09604 - 92 180, Fax (49) 09604 - 921 850 — 13 km

RESTAURANTS RESTAURANT

Kastell Burg Wernberg — Wernberg-Köblitz
Tel (49) 09604 - 9390 — 13 km

Schwanhof, Tel (49) 09607 - 920 20 — on site

SEDDINER SEE Südplatz

18 | 9 | 7

Dies ist der erste, und im Moment auch der einzige Platz in Deutschland, den Robert Trent Jones Jr. entworfen hat. Zusammen mit dem Faldo-Platz am Scharmützelsee ist dies der beste neue Platz in Deutschland. Er besticht vor allem mit seinem Abwechslungsreichtum und vor allem den geschickt platzierten Bunkern, die optisch attraktiv sind und vor allem jedem Loch eine klare Kontur verleihen. Hinzu kommen einige attraktive Wasserhindernisse (vor allem am 9. und 18. Loch). Insgesamt ist dies ein Platz, der jeden Golfer begeistern wird. Durch geschickte Erdbewegungen wirken manchen Hindernisse und Grüns näher oder weiter entfernt als sie tatsächlich sind, deshalb gilt es der Birdie-Karte (Yardage Book) zu vetrauen. Dies ist ein Platz der intelligentes Spiel erfordert, aber für alle Spielstärke schwer ist. Wählen Sie deshalb die richtigen Abschläge, die hinteren "Tiger-Tees" sind ausschließlich für Profis und Longhitter. Unglücklicherweise kann man diesen Südplatz nur in Begleitung eines Mitglieds spielen. Der andere Platz des Clubs, der von Rainer Preismann entworfene Nordplatz ist dagegen ohne Einschränkung für Gastspieler offen. Das luxuriöse Clubhaus und die Übungsreinrichtungen entsprechen dem hohen Standard.

This is the first, and for the moment the only course in Germany designed by Robert Trent Jones Jr. With the "Faldo" course at Scharmützelsee, this is the best of all the recently built layouts for its variety and remarkable bunkering which, although sometimes deceiving to the eye, perfectly outlines the shape of holes over often very open space. If we add the presence of a few attractive water hazards, you get a course of sheer pleasure. Some clever earthwork here and there might give the illusion of hazards and greens being closer or father away than they actually are, so trust the yardage book. This is a very intelligent course that is tough for everyone, so choose your tees wisely: the "tiger" tees are reserved for very long-hitters. Unfortunately, this "South" course can only be played with a member, the other "North" course has no such restrictions but is much more ordinary. Facilities here are on a par with prices: the club house is luxurious and the driving range excellent. A 25 minute drive from Berlin Ku-Damm, this course is a must.

Golf Club Seddiner See — 1997

Zum Weiher 44
D - 1455 WILDENBRUCH

Office	Sekretariat	(49) 033205 - 7320
Pro shop	Pro shop	(49) 033205 - 73 251
Fax	Fax	(49) 033205 - 73 229
Web	—	
Situation	Lage Berlin (pop. 3 500 000), 30 km	
Annual closure	Jährliche Schliessung	no
Weekly closure	Wöchentliche Schliessung	no

Monday (Montag): Restaurant closed

Fees main season Preisliste hochsaison	Week days Woche	We/Bank holidays We/Feiertag
	18 holes	
Individual Individuell	56 € *	66 € *
Couple Ehepaar	112 € *	132 € *

* With members (nur in Mitgliederbegleitung
– 21 years/Students: – 50%

Caddy	Caddy	no
Electric Trolley	Elektrokarren	no
Buggy	Elektrischer Wagen	no
Clubs	Leihschläger	28 €

Credit cards Kreditkarten VISA - Eurocard - AMEX

Access Zufahrt : Berlin, A115 Süd, A10 West.
Exit (Ausf.) 12 → Beelitz
Map 6 on page 365 Karte 6 Seite 365

Golf course PLATZ — 18/20

Site	Lage	
Maintenance	Instandhaltung	
Architect	Architekt	R. Trent Jones Jr
Type	Typ	country
Relief	Begehbarkeit	
Water in play	Platz mit Wasser	
Exp. to wind	Wind ausgesetzt	
Trees in play	Platz mit Bäumen	

Scorecard Scorekarte	Chp. Chp.	Mens Herren	Ladies Damen
Length Länge	6486	6046	5514
Par	72	72	72
Slope system	134	130	131

Advised golfing ability Empfohlene Spielstärke: 0 12 24 36
Hcp required Min. Handicap 34/36

Club house & amenities KLUBHAUS UND NEBENGEBÄUDE — 9/10

Pro shop	Pro shop	
Driving range	Übungsplatz	
Sheltered	überdacht	20 mats
On grass	auf Rasen	yes
Putting-green	Putting-grün	yes
Pitching-green	Pitching-grün	yes

Hotel facilities HOTEL BESCHREIBUNG — 7/10

HOTELS HOTELS

Seidler Art'otel, 123 rooms, D 125 € — Potsdam 15 km
Tel (49) 0331 - 981 50, Fax (49) 0331 - 981 5555

Sol Inn Hotel, 125 rooms, D 98 € — Michendorf 5 km
Tel (49) 033205 - 7 80, Fax (49) 033205 - 78 444

Haus am See, 21 rooms, D 87 € — Ferch 12 km
Tel (49) 033209 - 709 55, Fax (49) 033209 - 704 96

Brandenburger Hof, 82 rooms, D 204 € — Berlin 30 km
Tel (49) 030 - 214 050, Fax (49) 030 - 2140 5100

RESTAURANTS RESTAURANT

Borchardt, Tel (49) 030 - 229 3144 — Berlin 30 km

Opernpalais Königin Luise, Tel (49) 030 - 20 26 83 — Berlin

SEMLIN AM SEE

16 | 8 | 7

Semlin wurde wie auch der Märkische Golfclub Potsdam von Christian Staedler entworfen. Mit ihrem dazugehörigen Hotel entspricht die Anlage einem Resort, und eignet sich somit ausgezeichnet als Wochenend-Ziel für Golfgruppen - auch solche deren Handicaps weit auseinanderklaffen, wenngleich "Hacker" den Platz als etwas zu schwer empfinden mögen. Die Schwierigkeiten sind recht gut erkennbar, so dass man durchaus gleich die erste Runde in Zählspiel absolvieren kann, obschon Matchplay sicherlich genauso viel Spass macht. Das Fehlen gefahrbringender Bäume, die Gestaltung der Grüns und Bunker, sowie das fast völlig ebene Gelände erinnern stark an Florida, damit ist aber nicht eine simple Kopie der dortigen Plätze gemeint. Die Schwierigkeiten sind gut verteilt, so wechseln sich im Verlauf der Runde schwierige und leichtere Löcher miteinander ab. Als sehr hilfreich erweist sich die Fähigkeit den Ball sowohl mit Draw als auch Fade spielen zu können. Die Grüns sind ausgezeichnet und der sandige Boden gewährleistet eine gute Entwässerung.

Like Märkischer Potsdam, Semmlin am See chose Christian Staedler as course architect. This is a sort of resort, with a hotel on site, and can be a very decent week-end destination for a group of golfers, even playing to very different handicaps, although the hackers might find it a little too tough for their liking. The difficulties are visible enough to consider stroke-play first time out, although match-play will be at least just as much fun. The absence of dangerous trees, the design of the greens and bunkers and the very slight physical relief are reminiscent of Florida, but this is no carbon copy. The difficulties are well spread around, with tough holes alternating nicely with easier numbers. Moving the ball (deliberately) both ways will be a great help. The greens are excellent and the sandy soil gives good drainage.

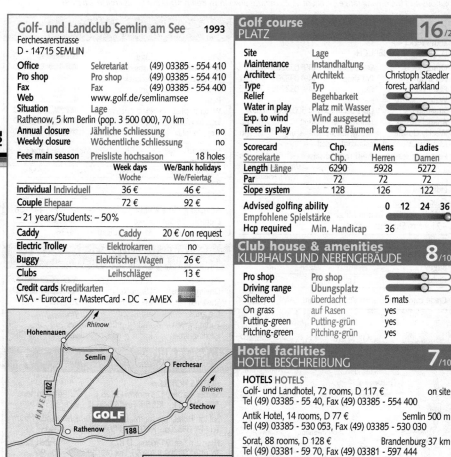

Golf- und Landclub Semlin am See — 1993

Ferchesarerstrasse
D - 14715 SEMLIN

Office	Sekretariat	(49) 03385 - 554 410
Pro shop	Pro shop	(49) 03385 - 554 410
Fax	Fax	(49) 03385 - 554 400
Web	www.golf.de/semlinamsee	
Situation	Lage	

Rathenow, 5 km Berlin (pop. 3 500 000), 70 km

Annual closure	Jährliche Schliessung	no
Weekly closure	Wöchentliche Schliessung	no

Fees main season Preisliste hochsaison — 18 holes

	Week days Woche	We/Bank holidays We/Feiertag
Individual Individuell	36 €	46 €
Couple Ehepaar	72 €	92 €

– 21 years/Students: – 50%

Caddy	Caddy	20 € /on request
Electric Trolley	Elektrokarren	no
Buggy	Elektrischer Wagen	26 €
Clubs	Leihschläger	13 €

Credit cards Kreditkarten
VISA - Eurocard - MasterCard - DC - AMEX

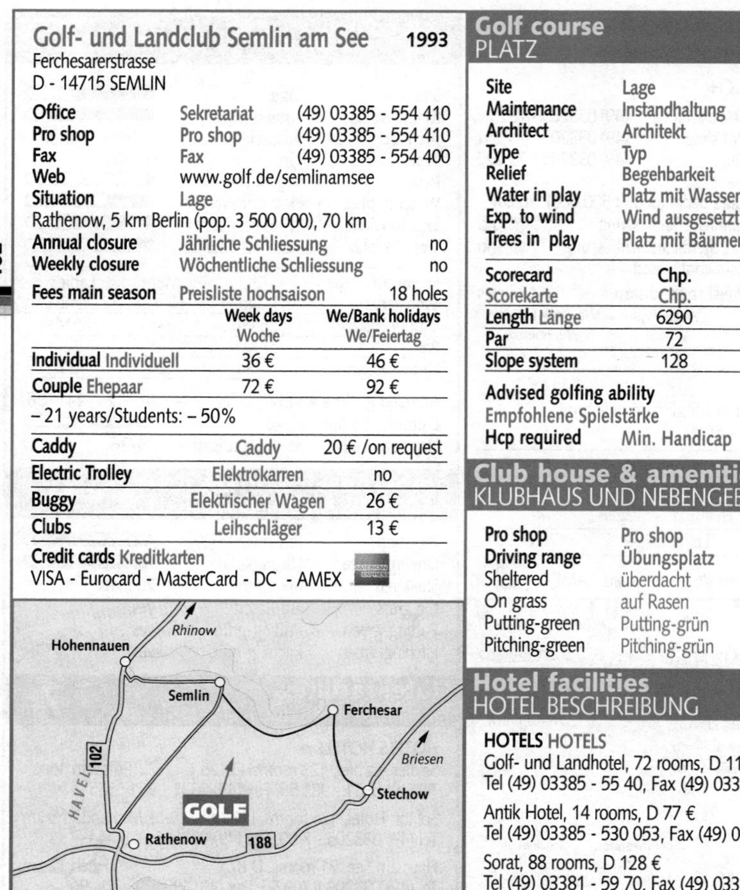

Access Zufahrt : Berlin, B5. Brisen, B188 → Rathenow. Stechow → Ferchesar. → Golf

Map 6 on page 365 Karte 6 Seite 365

Golf course PLATZ — 16/20

Site	Lage	
Maintenance	Instandhaltung	
Architect	Architekt	Christoph Staedler
Type	Typ	forest, parkland
Relief	Begehbarkeit	
Water in play	Platz mit Wasser	
Exp. to wind	Wind ausgesetzt	
Trees in play	Platz mit Bäumen	

Scorecard Scorekarte	Chp. Chp.	Mens Herren	Ladies Damen
Length Länge	6290	5928	5272
Par	72	72	72
Slope system	128	126	122

Advised golfing ability Empfohlene Spielstärke — 0 12 24 36

Hcp required Min. Handicap 36

Club house & amenities KLUBHAUS UND NEBENGEBÄUDE — 8/10

Pro shop	Pro shop	
Driving range	Übungsplatz	
Sheltered	überdacht	5 mats
On grass	auf Rasen	yes
Putting-green	Putting-grün	yes
Pitching-green	Pitching-grün	yes

Hotel facilities HOTEL BESCHREIBUNG — 7/10

HOTELS HOTELS

Golf- und Landhotel, 72 rooms, D 117 € — on site
Tel (49) 03385 - 55 40, Fax (49) 03385 - 554 400

Antik Hotel, 14 rooms, D 77 € — Semlin 500 m
Tel (49) 03385 - 530 053, Fax (49) 03385 - 530 030

Sorat, 88 rooms, D 128 € — Brandenburg 37 km
Tel (49) 03381 - 59 70, Fax (49) 03381 - 597 444

RESTAURANTS RESTAURANT

Golf- und Landhotel — on site
Tel (49) 03385 - 554 412

SENNE

16 | 8 | 7

Dieser Platz liegt in der typischen Senne-Landschaft, die sich mit ihrem Heideboden ideal für Golfplätze eignet. Der Sandboden sorgt dafür, dass der Platz viel Regen aufnehmen kann und ganzjährige auf Sommergrüns bespielbar ist. Der Platz vermittelt den manchmal täuschenden Eindruck von weiten, offenen Fairways, was besonders schwächere Spieler schätzen. Aber auch Longhitter werden sich hier wohlfühlen, doch die vielen Bunker, hohes Rough, einige Bäume und Wasserhindernisse verlangen Präzision. Das gilt besonders für das 13. Loch ein tricky Par 3 oder für das 18. Loch, ein kurzes Par mit einem gut verteidigten Grün. Christoph Städler entwarf ein exzellentes Layout, bei dem sich alle Löcher deutlich voneinander unterscheiden und im Zusammenspiel einen überaus reizvollen Platz ergeben. Das ist allerdings keine Überraschung : Als ehemaliger deutscher Amateur-Nationalspieler versteht Städler viel von Golf. Diese Platz werden Golfer geniessen, selbst wenn der Wind bläst, was in dieser Gegend häufig vorkommt.

This course was laid out in countryside that is typical of the region of Senne on heather-strewn sandy soil, which is so well suited to golf courses, especially when it comes to successfully soaking up the rain. There is a lot of open space, so golfers of all levels can enjoy their round and big hitters really let it rip, even though they could be asking for trouble: watch out for the bunkers, tall rough, a few trees in play and water hazards lining one half of the course. At the 13th for example, a very tricky par 3, or the 18th, a rather short par 4 with a very well guarded green. Christoph Städler has produced an excellent layout where no two holes are alike and where everything seems to neatly fit together. This is hardly surprising, as this former German amateur champion knows a thing or two about golf and golfers. You will enjoy this course, even when the wind starts to blow, a frequent occurrence in these parts.

Senne Golfclub Gut Welschof e.V. — 1992

Augustdorfer Strasse 72
D - 33758 SCHLOSS HOLTE-STUKENBROCK

Office	Sekretariat	(49) 05207 - 920 936
Pro shop	Pro shop	(49) 05207 - 920 936
Fax	Fax	(49) 05207 - 887 88
Web	www.shsonline.de/sennegolfclub	
Situation	Lage	Bielefeld (pop. 325 000), 22 km
Annual closure	Jährliche Schliessung	23/12→6/1
Weekly closure	Wöchentliche Schliessung	no

Restaurant closed on Monday (Montag)

Fees main season Preisliste hochsaison	18 holes	
	Week days Woche	**We/Bank holidays** We/Feiertag
Individual Individuell	31 €	41 €
Couple Ehepaar	62 €	82 €

Caddy	Caddy	no
Electric Trolley	Elektrokarren	no
Buggy	Elektrischer Wagen	26 € /18 holes
Clubs	Leihschläger	15 € /18 holes

Credit cards Kreditkarten
VISA - Eurocard - MasterCard - AMEX

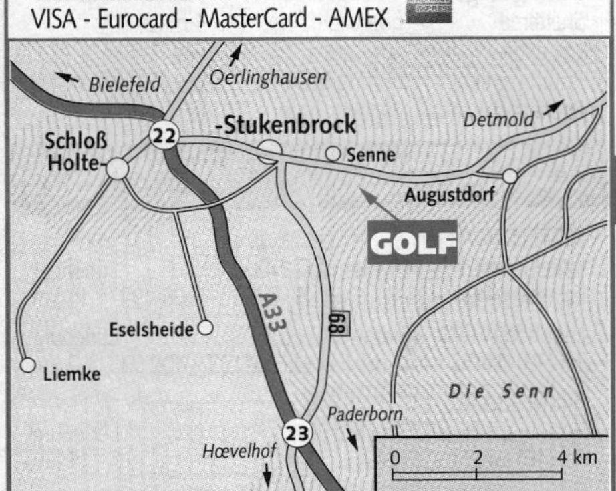

Access Zufahrt : Bielefeld A33 → Paderborn. Exit (Ausfahrt) Schloss Holte-Stukenbrock, then B68. In Stukenbrock → Augustdorf/Detmold. 2.5 km, → Golf.
Map 5 on page 363 Karte 5 Seite 363

Golf course PLATZ — 16/20

Site	Lage	
Maintenance	Instandhaltung	
Architect	Architekt	Christoph Staedler
Type	Typ	heathland, open country
Relief	Begehbarkeit	
Water in play	Platz mit Wasser	
Exp. to wind	Wind ausgesetzt	
Trees in play	Platz mit Bäumen	

Scorecard Scorekarte	**Chp.** Chp.	**Mens** Herren	**Ladies** Damen
Length Länge	6090	5909	5278
Par	72	72	72
Slope system	119	116	119

Advised golfing ability Empfohlene Spielstärke — 0 12 24 36

Hcp required Min. Handicap 36

Club house & amenities KLUBHAUS UND NEBENGEBÄUDE — 8/10

Pro shop	Pro shop	
Driving range	Übungsplatz	
Sheltered	überdacht	6 mats
On grass	auf Rasen	yes
Putting-green	Putting-grün	yes (2)
Pitching-green	Pitching-grün	yes

Hotel facilities HOTEL BESCHREIBUNG — 7/10

HOTELS HOTELS

Senne Hotel, 35 rooms, D 46 € — Schloss Holte-Stukenbroch
Tel (49) 05207 - 81 70, Fax (49) 05207 - 81 70 — 5 km

Westhoff, 32 rooms, D 82 € — Schloss Holte-Stukenbroch
Tel (49) 05207 - 911 00, Fax (49) 05207 - 911 051 — 5 km

Parkhotel Gütersloh, 103 rooms, D 133 € — Gütersloh
Tel (49) 05241 - 8770, Fax (49) 05241 - 877 400 — 23 km

RESTAURANTS RESTAURANT

Altdeutsche Bierstube — Oerlinghausen
Tel (49) 05202 - 35 60 — 5 km

Gasthaus Bockskrug — Gütersloh
Tel (49) 05241 - 543 70 — 23 km

ST. DIONYS

17 | 7 | 6

St. Dionys, in einiger Entfernung zu Hamburg gelegen, bietet einen guten Vorwand zur Erkundung der Lüneburger Heide, einer Moorlandschaft, deren Bild geprägt wird von Pinien, Birken und Heidekraut. Gerade Letzteres taucht diese ansonsten karge Gegend im August und September in üppige Farben. Der Platz selbst weist nur leichte Unebenheiten auf und kann so jedermann empfohlen werden. Die Vegetation ist teilweise sehr dominant, dennoch gibt es auch für Longhitter genügend offene Flächen. Obwohl die gut gestalteten Grüns meist ausgezeichnet verteidigt sind, ist es doch in vielen Fällen möglich, sie flach anzuspielen. Ärgerlich ist die Position einiger Fairwaybunker, durch die gute Schläge bestraft werden können. Es ist nichts Neues, dass für ein gutes Ergebnis lange und gerade Schläge von Bedeutung sind. Diese Feststellung ist hier jedoch - vor allem von den hinteren Abschlägen - ganz besonders zutreffend. Das Vergnügen St. Dionys zu spielen geht weit über den landschaftlichen Reiz der Umgebung hinaus.

St Dionys is some distance from Hamburg, but is a good excuse for discovering the "Lüneburger Heide", moorland dotted with pine-trees and birch, and covered with heather. Both add sumptuous colour to rather austere landscape in August and September. The course itself is only moderately hilly and so can be recommended for everyone. The vegetation is sometimes very much to the fore but there is no lack of open space to attract the big-hitters, and while the greens are generally well-designed and frequently well-guarded, you can often run the ball in. One regret is the layout of some fairway bunkers, which can penalise good shots. Saying you have to play long and straight for a good round is stating the obvious, but here it really is very true, especially from the back tees. The fun of playing St Dionys is more than simply admiring the surroundings.

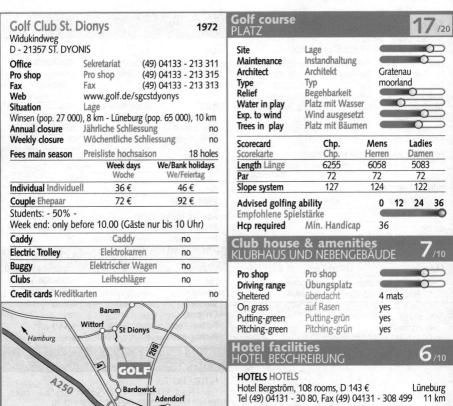

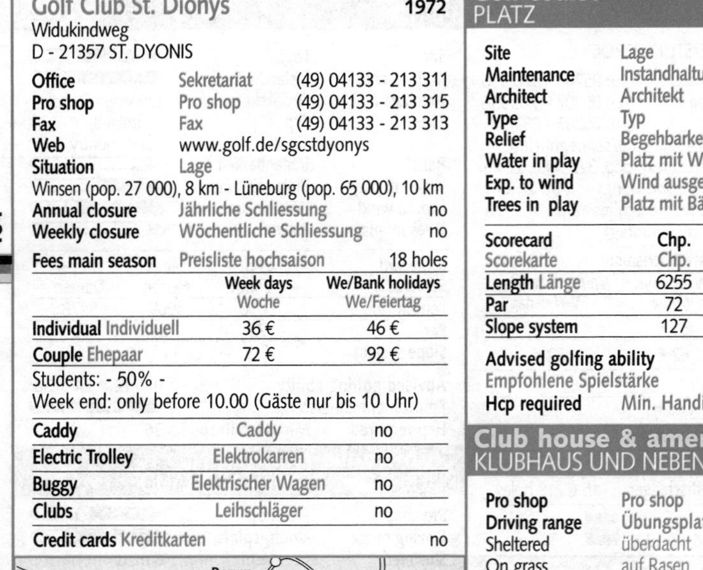

Golf Club St. Dionys — 1972

Widukindweg
D - 21357 ST. DYONIS

Office	Sekretariat	(49) 04133 - 213 311
Pro shop	Pro shop	(49) 04133 - 213 315
Fax	Fax	(49) 04133 - 213 313
Web	www.golf.de/sgcstdyonys	
Situation	Lage	

Winsen (pop. 27 000), 8 km - Lüneburg (pop. 65 000), 10 km

Annual closure	Jährliche Schliessung	no
Weekly closure	Wöchentliche Schliessung	no

Fees main season Preisliste hochsaison	18 holes	
	Week days Woche	**We/Bank holidays** We/Feiertag
Individual Individuell	36 €	46 €
Couple Ehepaar	72 €	92 €

Students: - 50% -
Week end: only before 10.00 (Gäste nur bis 10 Uhr)

Caddy	Caddy	no
Electric Trolley	Elektrokarren	no
Buggy	Elektrischer Wagen	no
Clubs	Leihschläger	no
Credit cards	Kreditkarten	no

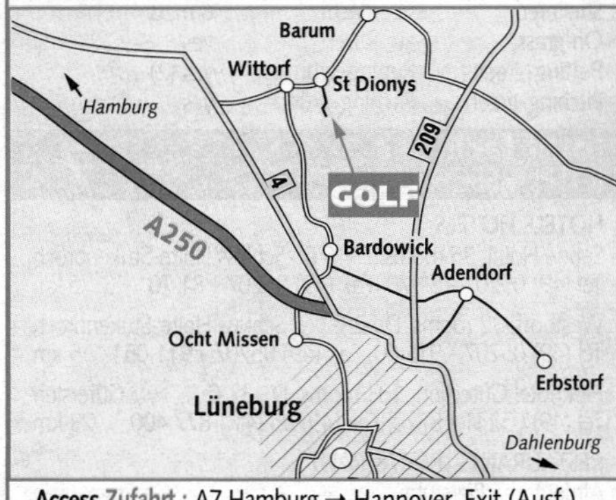

Access Zufahrt : A7 Hamburg → Hannover. Exit (Ausf.) Maschen. A250 → Lüneburg. Exit Winsen Ost. B4 → Lüneburg. Wittorf, left to Barum. → St. Dionys.
Map 7 on page 366 Karte 7 Seite 366

Golf course — PLATZ — 17/20

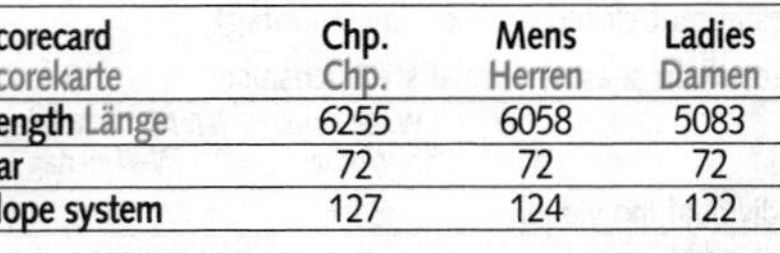

Site	Lage	
Maintenance	Instandhaltung	
Architect	Architekt	Gratenau
Type	Typ	moorland
Relief	Begehbarkeit	
Water in play	Platz mit Wasser	
Exp. to wind	Wind ausgesetzt	
Trees in play	Platz mit Bäumen	

Scorecard Scorekarte	**Chp.** Chp.	**Mens** Herren	**Ladies** Damen
Length Länge	6255	6058	5083
Par	72	72	72
Slope system	127	124	122

Advised golfing ability Empfohlene Spielstärke — 0 12 24 36

Hcp required Min. Handicap — 36

Club house & amenities — KLUBHAUS UND NEBENGEBÄUDE — 7/10

Pro shop	Pro shop	
Driving range	Übungsplatz	
Sheltered	überdacht	4 mats
On grass	auf Rasen	yes
Putting-green	Putting-grün	yes
Pitching-green	Pitching-grün	yes

Hotel facilities — HOTEL BESCHREIBUNG — 6/10

HOTELS HOTELS

Hotel Bergström, 108 rooms, D 143 € — Lüneburg
Tel (49) 04131 - 30 80, Fax (49) 04131 - 308 499 — 11 km

Landhotel Frank, 36 rooms, D 82 € — Lüneburg
Tel (49) 04133 - 400 90, Fax (49) 04133 - 400 933 — 2 km

RESTAURANTS RESTAURANT

Restaurant Hotel Zum Heidkrug — Lüneburg
Tel (49) 04131 - 31 249 — 11 km

Jagdschänke — Lüdersburg
Tel (49) 04153 - 68 422 — 10 km

Kronen-Bauhaus — Lüneburg
Tel (49) 04133 - 713 200 — 11 km

ST. EURACH

16 | 7 | 6

Mit seinem dominierenden Clubhaus, dem Platz, dessen Spielbahnen sich durch Bäume und Wälder winden, und dem Blick auf die Alpen im Hintergrund vermittelt St. Eurach den Eindruck von Exklusivität, der durch das Greenfee bestätigt wird. Der Reiz der umgebenden Natur hinterlässt einen ebenso starken Eindruck wie die sehr traditionelle Platz. Der lange und enge Platz wurde durch die von Bernhard Langer vorgenommenen Veränderungen an den Bunkern zusätzlich erschwert. Dennoch ist der Platz kein Monster und im grossen und ganz fair, d.h. gute Schläge werden belohnt, schlechte bestraft. Die BMW International Open, ein Turnier der europäischen PGA Tour wurde hier von 1994 bis 1996 ausgetragen und der Platz dadurch zu seinem Vorteil verändert.

With the estate dominated by the clubhouse, a course winding its way through trees and the Alps visible in the background on a clear day, St Eurach gives the impression of an exclusive site... an impression confirmed by the green fee (so avoid week-ends). When thinking about it, the natural environment leaves a greater impression than the actual course, and it certainly has the glamour to offset a rather bland personality. When it comes to playing, and we hate to put visitors off, high-handicappers will be hard pushed to enjoy their golf here. The layout is long and narrow, and the alterations made to bunkers by Bernhard Langer have added a little spice, but all this implies complete control of your game if you want to excel. You have to feel easy with all your clubs, including those you need for recovery shots. A demanding course to play when on top of your game. Keep to match-play, there are a lot of surprises in store.

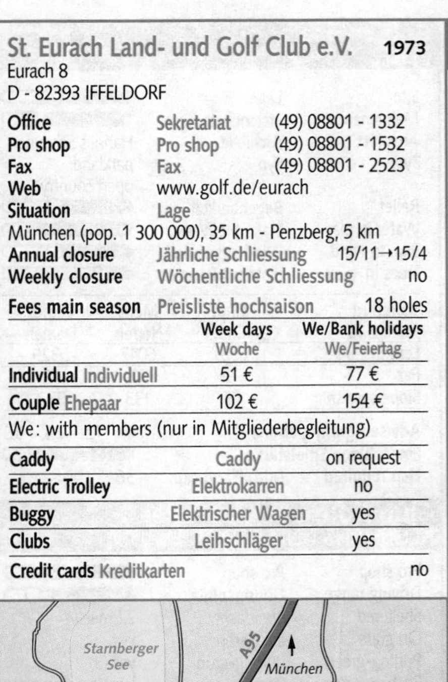

St. Eurach Land- und Golf Club e.V. — 1973

Eurach 8
D - 82393 IFFELDORF

Office	Sekretariat	(49) 08801 - 1332
Pro shop	Pro shop	(49) 08801 - 1532
Fax	Fax	(49) 08801 - 2523
Web	www.golf.de/eurach	
Situation	Lage	

München (pop. 1 300 000), 35 km - Penzberg, 5 km

Annual closure	Jährliche Schliessung	15/11→15/4
Weekly closure	Wöchentliche Schliessung	no

Fees main season Preisliste hochsaison	**Week days** Woche	**We/Bank holidays** We/Feiertag
		18 holes
Individual Individuell	51 €	77 €
Couple Ehepaar	102 €	154 €

We: with members (nur in Mitgliederbegleitung)

Caddy	Caddy	on request
Electric Trolley	Elektrokarren	no
Buggy	Elektrischer Wagen	yes
Clubs	Leihschläger	yes
Credit cards	Kreditkarten	no

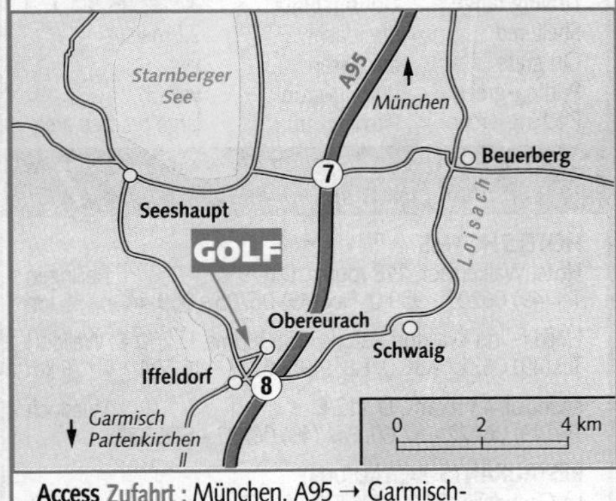

Access Zufahrt : München, A95 → Garmisch-Partenkirchen. Exit (Ausf.) Penzberg → Iffeldorf-Seeshaupt. 1,5 km → Golf on the right.
Map 2 on page 356 Karte 2 Seite 356

Golf course — PLATZ — 16/20

Site	Lage	
Maintenance	Instandhaltung	
Architect	Architekt	Unknown
Type	Typ	forest
Relief	Begehbarkeit	
Water in play	Platz mit Wasser	
Exp. to wind	Wind ausgesetzt	
Trees in play	Platz mit Bäumen	

Scorecard Scorekarte	**Chp.** Chp.	**Mens** Herren	**Ladies** Damen
Length Länge	6430	5907	5267
Par	71	71	74
Slope system	135	131	126

Advised golfing ability Empfohlene Spielstärke — 0 12 24 36

Hcp required Min. Handicap — 28

Club house & amenities — KLUBHAUS UND NEBENGEBÄUDE — 7/10

Pro shop	Pro shop	
Driving range	Übungsplatz	
Sheltered	überdacht	no
On grass	auf Rasen	yes
Putting-green	Putting-grün	yes
Pitching-green	Pitching-grün	yes

Hotel facilities — HOTEL BESCHREIBUNG — 6/10

HOTELS HOTELS

Landgasthof Osterseen, 24 rooms, D 102 € — Iffeldorf
Tel (49) 08856 - 928 60, Fax (49) 08856 - 928 645 — 2 km

Stadthotel Berggeist, 45 rooms, D 89 € — Penzberg
Tel (49) 08856 - 80 10, Fax (49) 08856 - 81 913 — 6 km

Gut Faistenberg — Eurasburg-Faistenberg
10 rooms, D 158 € — 10 km
Tel (49) 08179 - 16 16, Fax (49) 08179 - 433

RESTAURANTS RESTAURANT

Landgasthof Osterseen — Iffeldorf
Tel (49) 08856 - 1011 — 2 km

Stadthotel Berggeist — Penzberg
Tel (49) 08856 - 78 99 — 6 km

ST. LEON-ROT "Rot" Course

15 | 9 | 7

Der Platz gehört Dietmar Hopp, einem der Gründer und ehemaligen Vorstandsvorsitzender von SAP, dem drittgrößten Software-Haus der Welt. Seltsamer weise wurde dieses luxuriöse und ultra-moderne Projekt nicht von einem der bekannten Golfplatz-Architekten, sondern von einem Landschaftsarchitekten entworfen, der nie zuvor in Leben für das Design eines Golfplatzes verantworlich gezeichnet hatte. Deshalb mußte der Platz für die TPC of Europe gründlich überarbeitet werden. Tiger Woods, der die "Deutsche Bank - SAP Open TPC of Europe" auf diesem Platz 1999 und 2001 gewann gefiel der Platz. Nach den vielen Umbauten ist ein Platz entstanden, der zu den besten in Deutschland gehört. Die Hauptschwierigkeit des Platzes sind Wasserhindernisse an neun Löchern (das 7. Loch hat ein Inselgrün) und die viele Biotope, die als seitliches Wasserhinderniss gepflockt sind. Deshalb sind eigentlich nur das erste und das letzte Loch einfach. Diesen Platz wird eben so wenig vergessen, wie das hohe Greenfee.

This is the brain child of Dietmar Hopp, the founder and former chairman of SAP, the third biggest software company of the world. But strangely enough, this luxurious and ultra-modern project was laid out not by a high-tech golf course architect but by a skilled landscape gardener, who had never designed a golf course in his life before. As a result, a good part of the course had to be re-shaped and holes re-routed in order to host the Deutsche Bank-SAP Open in 1999. The result satisfied Tiger Woods, who won the tournament here in 1999 and 2001. After all the alterations, the course has joined the ranks of the best German Courses. An important feature here is not only the presence of water hazards on nine holes (the 7th has an island green), but also the huge areas protected owing to environmental considerations, which are considered as lateral water hazards. If only because, paradoxically, the first and last holes are easy, you will neither forget this course nor the hefty greenfee in a hurry.

Golf Club St. Leon-Rot — 1997

Opelstrasse 30
D - 68789 ST. LEON-ROT

Office	Sekretariat	(49) 06227 - 860 80
Pro shop	Pro shop	(49) 06227 - 860 899
Fax	Fax	(49) 06227 - 860 888
Web	www.golfclub-rot.de	
Situation	Lage	

Heidelberg (pop. 132 000), 15 km

Annual closure	Jährliche Schliessung	no
Weekly closure	Wöchentliche Schliessung	no

Fees main season Preisliste hochsaison — 18 holes

	Week days Woche	We/Bank holidays We/Feiertag
Individual Individuell	61 €	77 €
Couple Ehepaar	122 €	154 €

Students: 31 € / 41 € (Week ends)

Caddy	Caddy	no
Electric Trolley	Elektrokarren	10 € /18 holes
Buggy	Elektrischer Wagen	26 € /18 holes
Clubs	Leihschläger	26 € /18 holes

Credit cards Kreditkarten
VISA - Eurocard

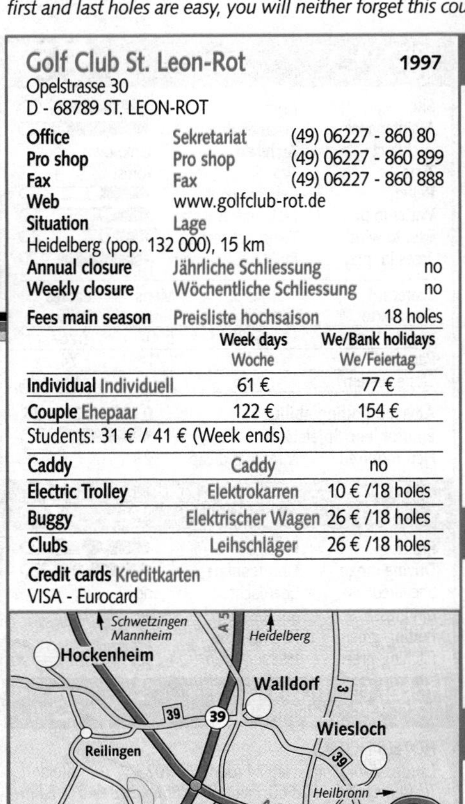

Access Zufahrt : A6 → Heilbronn. Exit (Ausf.) Wiesloch/Rauenberg. → Walldorf. 2nd traffic lights → St. Leon-Rot. 3rd street, turn left in Opelstrasse.
Map 1 on page 355 Karte 1 Seite 355

Golf course PLATZ — 15/20

Site	Lage	
Maintenance	Instandhaltung	
Architect	Architekt	Hannes Schreiner
Type	Typ	parkland, open country
Relief	Begehbarkeit	
Water in play	Platz mit Wasser	
Exp. to wind	Wind ausgesetzt	
Trees in play	Platz mit Bäumen	

Scorecard Scorekarte	Chp. Chp.	Mens Herren	Ladies Damen
Length Länge	6587	6047	5329
Par	72	72	72
Slope system	137	133	133

Advised golfing ability Empfohlene Spielstärke — 0 12 24 36
Hcp required Min. Handicap — 36

Club house & amenities KLUBHAUS UND NEBENGEBÄUDE — 9/10

Pro shop	Pro shop	
Driving range	Übungsplatz	
Sheltered	überdacht	22 mats
On grass	auf Rasen	yes
Putting-green	Putting-grün	yes (3)
Pitching-green	Pitching-grün	large practice area

Hotel facilities HOTEL BESCHREIBUNG — 7/10

HOTELS HOTELS

Hotel Walkershof, 118 rooms, D 179 € — Reilingen
Tel (49) 06205 - 959 0, Fax (49) 06205 - 959 44 — 5 km

Holiday Inn Walldorf Astoria, 158 rooms, D 250 € — Walldorf
Tel (49) 06227 - 36 0, Fax (49) 06227 - 36 504 — 6 km

Mondial, 43 rooms, D 112 € — Wiesloch
Tel (49) 06222 - 57 60, Fax (49) 06222 - 576 333

RESTAURANTS RESTAURANT

La Chandelle, Tel (49) 06222 - 57 60 — Wiesloch
Freihof, Tel (49) 06227 - 25 17 — Wiesloch
Haus Landgraf, Tel (49) 06227 - 40 36 — Walldorf

ST. LEON-ROT "St Leon" 16 | 9 | 7

Dietmar Hopp weder Geld noch Mühe gescheut, um St. Leon zu einem der besten Golfclubs in Deutschland zu machen. Wie bei dem Terre Blanche Projekt in der französischen Provence vertraute er auch beim St. Leon-Platz auf die Design-Arbeit von Dave Thomas. Der englische Architekt ist bekannt dafür, dass er große Erdbewegungen vornimmt, was allerdings dazu führt, dass sich viele seiner Plätze und Löcher ähneln. Dadurch ist es schwierig, sich nach ein paar Tagen an einzelne Löcher zu erinnern. Hier bleiben nur das 2. Loch, das entlang des renaturierten Kraichbachs verläuft und das 4. Loch nachhaltig im Gedächtnis. Der über ein Kilometer lange Kraichbach, die vielen Wasserhindernisse, die zahlreichen Bunker und die großen, stark ondulierten Grüns machen die Hauptschwierigkeit dieses Platzes aus, zumindest so lange wie die angepflanzten Bäume noch relativ klein sind. Auf diesem Platz sollte man den Ball lang und hoch spielen können, Fähigkeiten die eher niedrige Handicaps beherrschen. Alles in allem ein Platz von hoher Qualität und exzellentem Pflegezustand.

No effort was spared by Dietmar Hopp in making this one of Germany's most prestigious golf clubs. As with his Terre Blanche project in the French Provence, he called in course architect Dave Thomas, one of the great earth-shapers of our day and age, despite there sometimes being a little sameness about his work. This can make it difficult to remember individual holes, and here only the 2nd and 4th holes really stick in the mind. Starting with a patch of flat open-land, he has introduced any number of water hazards and brought the little Kraichbach stream back from the dead and into play over more than a kilometre. Add to this very many well designed bunkers and huge greens that are rather well contoured and very well protected, then you get some idea of the difficulties already in play while waiting for the trees to grow. Dave Thomas has clearly chosen sides here, opting for a strategic, penalising and even somewhat athletic style of architecture, because you need to hit it long and hit it high. In other words, skills generally reserved for low-handicappers. All in all, the quality and finish of the whole layout are really excellent.

Golf Club St. Leon-Rot 2000

Opelstrasse 30
D - 68789 ST. LEON-ROT

Office	Sekretariat	(49) 06227 - 860 80
Pro shop	Pro shop	(49) 06227 - 860 899
Fax	Fax	(49) 06227 - 860 888
Web	www.golfclub-rot.de	
Situation	Lage	
Heidelberg (pop. 132 000), 15 km		
Annual closure	Jährliche Schliessung	no
Weekly closure	Wöchentliche Schliessung	no

Fees main season Preisliste hochsaison		18 holes
	Week days Woche	**We/Bank holidays** We/Feiertag
Individual Individuell	82 €	82 €
Couple Ehepaar	164 €	164 €
Students: 31 € / 41 € (Week ends)		
Caddy	Caddy	no
Electric Trolley	Elektrokarren	10 € /18 holes
Buggy	Elektrischer Wagen	26 € /18 holes
Clubs	Leihschläger	26 € /18 holes

Credit cards Kreditkarten
VISA - Eurocard

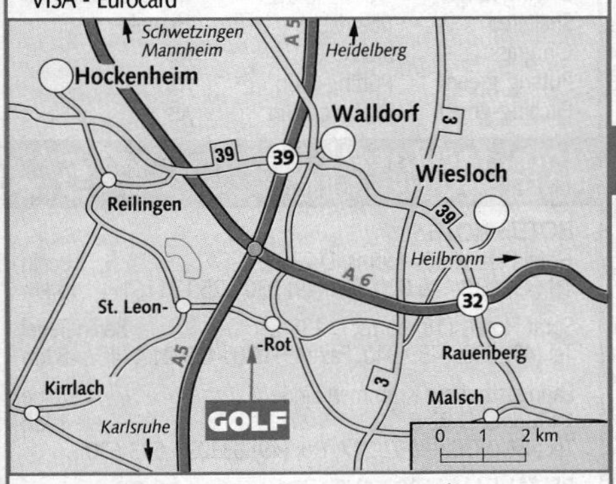

Access Zufahrt : A6 → Heilbronn. Exit (Ausf.) Wiesloch/Rauenberg. → Walldorf. 2nd traffic lights → St. Leon-Rot. 3rd street, turn left in Opelstrasse.
Map 1 on page 355 Karte 1 Seite 355

Golf course PLATZ 16/20

Site	Lage	
Maintenance	Instandhaltung	
Architect	Architekt	Dave Thomas
Type	Typ	open country
Relief	Begehbarkeit	
Water in play	Platz mit Wasser	
Exp. to wind	Wind ausgesetzt	
Trees in play	Platz mit Bäumen	

Scorecard Scorekarte	**Chp.** Chp.	**Mens** Herren	**Ladies** Damen
Length Länge	6518	6142	5020
Par	72	72	72
Slope system	0	0	0

Advised golfing ability Empfohlene Spielstärke — 0 12 24 36
Hcp required Min. Handicap 36

Club house & amenities KLUBHAUS UND NEBENGEBÄUDE 9/10

Pro shop	Pro shop	
Driving range	Übungsplatz	
Sheltered	überdacht	22 mats
On grass	auf Rasen	yes
Putting-green	Putting-grün	yes (3)
Pitching-green	Pitching-grün	large practice area

Hotel facilities HOTEL BESCHREIBUNG 7/10

HOTELS HOTELS

Hotel Walkershof, 118 rooms, D 179 € — Reilingen
Tel (49) 06205 - 959 0, Fax (49) 06205 - 959 44 — 5 km

Holiday Inn Walldorf Astoria — Walldorf
158 rooms, D 250 € — 6 km
Tel (49) 06227 - 36 0, Fax (49) 06227 - 36 504

Mondial, 43 rooms, D 112 € — Wiesloch
Tel (49) 06222 - 57 60, Fax (49) 06222 - 576 333

RESTAURANTS RESTAURANT

La Chandelle, Tel (49) 06222 - 57 60 — Wiesloch
Freihof, Tel (49) 06227 - 25 17 — Wiesloch
Haus Landgraf, Tel (49) 06227 - 40 36 — Walldorf

STOLPER HEIDE

16 | 7 | 5

Stolper Heide ist Bestandteil einer schnell-wachsenden Wohnanlage und ist zweifellos einer der vielversprechendsten Golfplätze in ganz Deutschland. Die Namen Bernhard Langer und Kurt Rossknecht bürgen für ehrlichen Charakter und den Abwechslungsreichtum des Designs, das sich hervorragend an die unterschiedlichen Spielstärken der Golfer anpasst, wenngleich insbesondere die besseren Spieler ihren Spass daran haben werden, die strategischen Herausforderungen des Kurses zu meistern. Auf dem ausgezeichnet und intelligent gestalteten Gelände brauchen die Baüme sicherlich noch Zeit ihr Wachstum zu entfalten, aber bereits jetzt weisen die sorgfältig gearbeiteten Abgrenzungen zwischen Fairway und Rough dem Golfer deutlich die Spiellinie für den nächsten Schlag. Die Schlusslöcher stellen die Spieler vor allem im Match-Play vor eine interessante Aufgabe. Die Pflegezustand des Platzes, besonders im Bereich der sorgfältig gestalteten Grüns, ist bereits ausgezeichnet.

In a fast-growing residential area, Stolper Heide is one of Germany's most promising courses. The names of Bernhard Langer and Rossknecht were sure-fire guarantees for the honesty and variety of this layout and for the way it adapts to different levels of proficiency, although the better players will have the most fun here solving questions of strategy. Well-landscaped and intelligent, the course needs the trees to grow but the careful way in which the fairways and roughs are demarcated means you are never in any doubt as to where the next shot should go. The finishing holes are particularly interesting here if competing in match-play. The green-keeping is already very good, particularly the carefully designed greens.

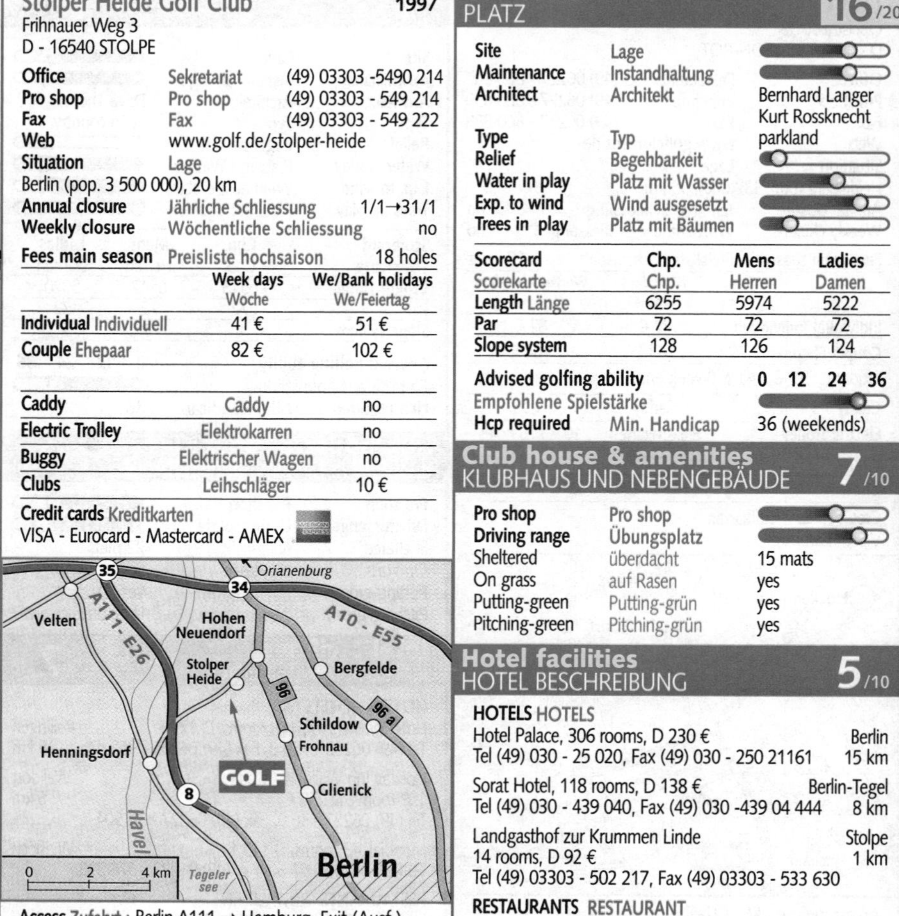

Stolper Heide Golf Club — **1997**
Frihnauer Weg 3
D - 16540 STOLPE

Office	Sekretariat	(49) 03303 -5490 214
Pro shop	Pro shop	(49) 03303 - 549 214
Fax	Fax	(49) 03303 - 549 222
Web	www.golf.de/stolper-heide	
Situation	Lage	

Berlin (pop. 3 500 000), 20 km

Annual closure	Jährliche Schliessung	1/1→31/1
Weekly closure	Wöchentliche Schliessung	no

Fees main season Preisliste hochsaison — 18 holes

	Week days Woche	We/Bank holidays We/Feiertag
Individual Individuell	41 €	51 €
Couple Ehepaar	82 €	102 €

Caddy	Caddy	no
Electric Trolley	Elektrokarren	no
Buggy	Elektrischer Wagen	no
Clubs	Leihschläger	10 €

Credit cards Kreditkarten
VISA - Eurocard - Mastercard - AMEX

Access Zufahrt : Berlin A111 → Hamburg. Exit (Ausf.) Henningsdorf-Stolpe. Left → Stolpe.
Map 6 on page 365 Karte 6 Seite 365

Golf course PLATZ — 16/20

Site	Lage	
Maintenance	Instandhaltung	
Architect	Architekt	Bernhard Langer Kurt Rossknecht
Type	Typ	parkland
Relief	Begehbarkeit	
Water in play	Platz mit Wasser	
Exp. to wind	Wind ausgesetzt	
Trees in play	Platz mit Bäumen	

Scorecard Scorekarte	**Chp.** Chp.	**Mens** Herren	**Ladies** Damen
Length Länge	6255	5974	5222
Par	72	72	72
Slope system	128	126	124

Advised golfing ability Empfohlene Spielstärke — 0 12 24 36
Hcp required Min. Handicap — 36 (weekends)

Club house & amenities KLUBHAUS UND NEBENGEBÄUDE — 7/10

Pro shop	Pro shop	
Driving range	Übungsplatz	
Sheltered	überdacht	15 mats
On grass	auf Rasen	yes
Putting-green	Putting-grün	yes
Pitching-green	Pitching-grün	yes

Hotel facilities HOTEL BESCHREIBUNG — 5/10

HOTELS HOTELS

Hotel Palace, 306 rooms, D 230 € — Berlin 15 km
Tel (49) 030 - 25 020, Fax (49) 030 - 250 21161

Sorat Hotel, 118 rooms, D 138 € — Berlin-Tegel 8 km
Tel (49) 030 - 439 040, Fax (49) 030 -439 04 444

Landgasthof zur Krummen Linde — Stolpe 1 km
14 rooms, D 92 €
Tel (49) 03303 - 502 217, Fax (49) 03303 - 533 630

RESTAURANTS RESTAURANT

Landgasthof zur Krummen Linde — Stolpe 1 km
Tel (49) 03303 - 502 217

STUTTGARTER SOLITUDE

17	5	5

Ein exemplarisches Beispiel für die Arbeit Bernhard von Limburgers, das sehr gut sein Bemühen, den Anforderungen guter Platzarchitektur gerecht zu werden, veranschaulicht. Solitude erweist sich als echter Gütetest für das Können eines Golfers, insbesondere dessen Fähigkeit gerade Drives zu schlagen. Kraftvollen Spielern werden die Fairways - Genauigkeit vorausgesetzt - vergleichsweise breit erscheinen, aber auch das Anspiel der mittelgrossen, erst kürzlich umgebauten Grüns erfordert in vielen Fällen nochmals höchste Präzision. Kürzere Spieler müssen sich vor allem auf gute lange Eisen und ihr kurzes Spiel verlassen können. Dies gilt im besonderen an den langen Par 4 Löchern, die regulär nur schwer zu erreichen sind, sowie den ausgezeichneten Par 3 Löchern. Wasser kommt nur selten ins Spiel, so ist es primär der Wald, der nicht nur den optischen sondern auch den spieltechnischen Charakter dieses Platzes prägt. Dank eines sehr durchdachten Layouts macht der leicht begehbare Kurs einen ausgewogenen Eindruck. Solitude ist eine Anlage, die man kaum ignorieren kann, eignet sich aber eher für die etwas besseren Golfer.

A good example of a von Limburger design and of his concern for the demands of golf. While golf is the examination of a player's abilities, Solitude is a test of value with emphasis on straight driving. If they play straight, powerful hitters will find the fairways comparatively wide, but they will need extreme accuracy to reach a number of mid-sized elevated greens that have been recently reshaped. The shorter-hitters will have to sharpen up their long irons and even their short game on some of the long par 4s, that are tough to hit in regulation, and the very good par 3s. As there is little water to speak of, the course's visual appeal is primarily the forest. The forest is, in fact, the whole point of the course, which is well-balanced, easy on the legs, and a thoroughly well designed affair. It is difficult to overlook Solitude, but it is a course reserved for golfers who can play a bit.

Stuttgarter Golf-Club Solitude — 1968

Am Golfplatz
D - 71297 MÖNSHEIM

Office	Sekretariat	(49) 07044 -911 0410
Pro shop	Pro shop	(49) 07044 -911 0413
Fax	Fax	(49) 07044 -911 0420
Web	www.golf.de/stuttgart-solitude	
Situation	Lage	
Stuttgart (pop. 560 000), 20 km		
Annual closure	Jährliche Schliessung	1/12→31/3
Weekly closure	Wöchentliche Schliessung	no

Fees main season Preisliste hochsaison		Full day
	Week days Woche	**We/Bank holidays** We/Feiertag
Individual Individuell	41 €	51 €
Couple Ehepaar	82 €	102 €

We: only with members (nur in Mitgliederbegleitung)

Caddy	Caddy	on request
Electric Trolley	Elektrokarren	no
Buggy	Elektrischer Wagen	no
Clubs	Leihschläger	no
Credit cards Kreditkarten		no

Access Zufahrt : A8 Stuttgart-Karlsruhe. Exit (Ausf.) Heimsheim-Mönsheim. Golf → Mönsheim
Map 1 on page 355 Karte 1 Seite 355

Golf course — PLATZ — 17/20

Site	Lage	
Maintenance	Instandhaltung	
Architect	Architekt	B. von Limburger
Type	Typ	open country, forest
Relief	Begehbarkeit	
Water in play	Platz mit Wasser	
Exp. to wind	Wind ausgesetzt	
Trees in play	Platz mit Bäumen	

Scorecard Scorekarte	**Chp.** Chp.	**Mens** Herren	**Ladies** Damen
Length Länge	6188	5949	5335
Par	72	72	72
Slope system	131	128	125

Advised golfing ability Empfohlene Spielstärke — 0 12 24 36
Hcp required Min. Handicap 36

Club house & amenities — KLUBHAUS UND NEBENGEBÄUDE — 5/10

Pro shop	Pro shop	
Driving range	Übungsplatz	
Sheltered	überdacht	6 mats
On grass	auf Rasen	yes
Putting-green	Putting-grün	yes
Pitching-green	Pitching-grün	yes

Hotel facilities — HOTEL BESCHREIBUNG — 5/10

HOTELS HOTELS

Parkhotel — Pforzheim 12 km
144 rooms, D 200,-
Tel (49 7231) 1610, Fax (49 7044) 1616 90

Hotel Eiss — Leonberg 15 km
32 rooms, D 87 €
Tel (49) 07152 - 94 40, Fax (49) 07152 - 42 134

RESTAURANTS RESTAURANT

Häckermühle — Tiefenbronn 10 km
Tel (49) 07234 - 6111

Ochsenpost — Tiefenbronn 10 km
Tel (49) 07234 - 920 578

SYLT

15 | 6 | 8

Die nördlichste der friesischen Inseln ist einer der elegantesten Urlaubs,-gebiete in Deutschland. Westerland ist das grösste Seebad Deutschlands, Kampen das exklusivste. Auf dieser seltsam geformten Insel von 40km Länge, die von Klippen, Stränden und Dünen gesäumt ist, erwartet man natürlich einen Links Course. Donald Harradine hat hier eine seiner besten Designs abgeliefert, obwohl der Platz nicht mit den Meisterwerken der Links Courses der Britischen Inseln mithalten kann. Auch auf diesem Küstenplatz ist der Wind einbestimmender Faktor. Der sandige Boden sorgt für hervorragende Drainage, aber diese trockene Bodenbeschaffenheit erschwert die Schläge zum Grün. Um die Bälle auf den Grüns zum Halten zubringen, muss man einkalkulieren wie weit der Ball rollt, wobei bei starkem Wind das Beherrschen von "knock-down-shots" hilfreich ist. Es gibt keine blinden Löcher und Fallen, man sieht immer, wohin man den Ball zu spielen hat. Wer ein hohes Ergebnis mit ins Klubhaus bringt, hat schlecht gespielt ganz so wie es sein sollte. Dieser Platz ist auch ein Naturerlebnis in klarer Seeuft, die prickelnd wie Champagner schmeckt.

This is the northernmost of the North Friesian Islands, next to Denmark, where the largest town, Westerland, is Germany's biggest seaside resort. Over this strangely shaped isle (40 km in length) with alternating cliffs, beaches and dunes, a virtual links course was only to be expected. Donald Harradine has produced here a fine design, even though it doesn't really measure up to the British masterpieces. The wind is a key factor, naturally, as is the joy of breathing air as sharp as chilled champagne. The sand gives ideal turf and perfect draining, but the dryness of the soil and the wind make for difficult approach shots to the green. For the ball to stay on the green, you need to know how to roll it on, taking a chance on the likely trajectory. There are no blind shots here and no traps in what is very varied and well-utilised landscape; you can clearly see what needs to be done and you alone are responsible for any high-scoring.

Golf Club Sylt e.V. — 1982

D - 25996 WENNINGSTEDT

Office	Sekretariat	(49) 04651 -453 11
Pro shop	Pro shop	(49) 04651 -455 22
Fax	Fax	(49) 04651 -456 92
Web	—	
Situation	Lage	
Sylt Island, close to Denmark		
Annual closure	Jährliche Schliessung	no
Weekly closure	Wöchentliche Schliessung	no

470

Fees main season Preisliste hochsaison	18 holes	
	Week days Woche	**We/Bank holidays** We/Feiertag
Individual Individuell	51 €	51 €
Couple Ehepaar	102 €	102 €

Caddy	Caddy	no
Electric Trolley	Elektrokarren	13 €
Buggy	Elektrischer Wagen	no
Clubs	Leihschläger	18 €
Credit cards Kreditkarten		no

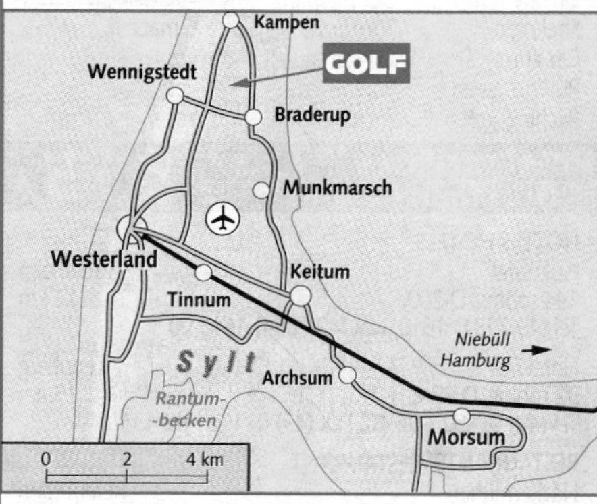

Access Zufahrt : Hamburg E45 to Flensburg, then 199 to Niebüll → Westerland/Sylt, Wennigstedt → List

Map 1 on page 122 Karte 1 Seite 122

Golf course — PLATZ — 15/20

Site	Lage	
Maintenance	Instandhaltung	
Architect	Architekt	Donald Harradine
Type	Typ	links, open country
Relief	Begehbarkeit	
Water in play	Platz mit Wasser	
Exp. to wind	Wind ausgesetzt	
Trees in play	Platz mit Bäumen	

Scorecard Scorekarte	**Chp.** Chp.	**Mens** Herren	**Ladies** Damen
Length Länge	6084	6036	5339
Par	72	72	72
Slope system	128	126	124

Advised golfing ability Empfohlene Spielstärke — 0 12 24 36

Hcp required Min. Handicap — 32

Club house & amenities — KLUBHAUS UND NEBENGEBÄUDE — 6/10

Pro shop	Pro shop	
Driving range	Übungsplatz	
Sheltered	überdacht	20 mats
On grass	auf Rasen	yes
Putting-green	Putting-grün	yes
Pitching-green	Pitching-grün	yes

Hotel facilities — HOTEL BESCHREIBUNG — 8/10

HOTELS HOTELS

Rungholt, 67 rooms, D 194 € — Kampen
Tel (49) 04651 - 4480, Fax (49) 04651 - 44 840 — 3 km

Benen-Diken-Hof, 49 rooms, D 153 € — Keitum
Tel (49) 04651 - 938 30, Fax (49) 04651 -9383 183 — 6 km

Stadt Hamburg, 96 rooms, D 179 € — Westerland
Tel (49) 04651 - 8580, Fax (49) 04651 - 858 220 — 3 km

RESTAURANTS RESTAURANT

Landhaus Nösse — Morsum
Tel (49) 04651 - 819 555 — 10 km

Landhaus Stricker — Tinnum
Tel (49) 04651 - 316 72 — 4 km

Manne Pahl, Tel (49) 04651 - 425 10 — Kempen 3 km

TEGERNSEER BAD WIESSEE 14 | 7 | 8

Der Platz liegt in einer der schönsten Gegenden Deutschland. Der Platz liegt wunderschön oberhalb des Tegernsees. Leider ist der Platz nicht so schön wie die Gegend, der Platz ist eher wegen seiner illustren Mitgliedschaft als wegen seines Designs berühmt. Neun Löcher sind ordentlich, die anderen neun eher schrecklich. Die Platz ist kurz, aber das Anspielen der relativ kleinen Grüns ist extrem schwierig. Das Clubhaus strahlt viel Gemütlichkeit aus. Mit etwas Glück trifft man hier die Reichen und Schönen Deutschlands, von Boris Becker über Gunter Sachs bis hin zu Willy Bogner. Ein Gang durch die Umkleide mit den Namen auf den Spinden erinnert an das deutsche "Who is Who". Der vielbeschäftigte Donald Harradine entwarf den Platz 1960, aber komplett fertiggestellt wurde er erst im Jahr 1984. Der Platz ist recht hügelig, dennoch benötigen nur ältere oder untrainierte Spieler einen Golfwagen.

It is hardly more than an hour's drive to the Austrian border and not much more to visit Innsbrück once you have discovered all the charms of the lake lying at the foot of the course here. While this layout is hardly a world-beater, it does, like its neighbours, have the advantage of an exceptional natural setting. In this sense, Bavaria is a real golfing destination. Designed in 1960 by Donald Harradine, a decidedly prolific architect, it was only really completed in 1984. It shows all the typical features of its designer, who was undoubtedly less concerned with marking his period than many of his colleagues, but it is very British in style as far as understanding the game at all levels is concerned. We sometimes felt he might have contoured the fairways and bunkers a little more, but this sobriety has the advantage of preserving the terrain's natural aspect. The course is rather hilly but only the more elderly or very unfit golfers will need a buggy.

Tegernseer Golf-Club Bad Wiessee e.V. 1960

Robognerhof
D - 83707 BAD WIESSEE

Office	Sekretariat	(49) 08022 - 8769
Pro shop	Pro shop	(49) 08022 - 83 350
Fax	Fax	(49) 08022 - 82 747
Web	—	
Situation	Lage	Bad Tölz, 18 km
Annual closure	Jährliche Schliessung	1/12→31/3
Weekly closure	Wöchentliche Schliessung	no

Monday (Montag): Restaurant closed

Fees main season Preisliste hochsaison	Week days Woche	We/Bank holidays We/Feiertag
		18 holes
Individual Individuell	51 €	66 €
Couple Ehepaar	102 €	132 €

We: ask before coming (begrenzte Spielmöglichkeit)

Caddy	Caddy	26 € /on request
Electric Trolley	Elektrokarren	15 €
Buggy	Elektrischer Wagen	no
Clubs	Leihschläger	18 €
Credit cards Kreditkarten		no

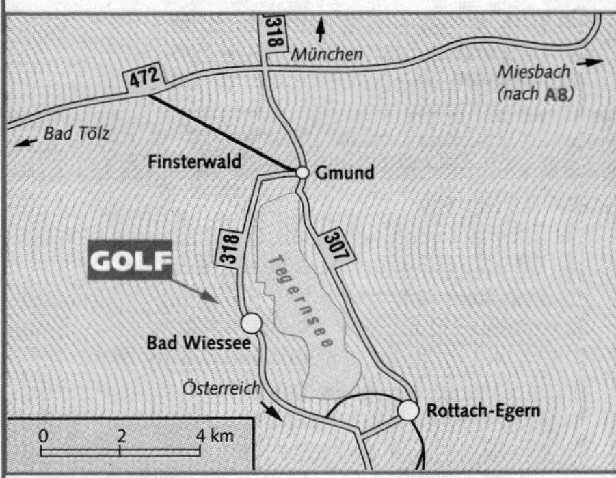

Access Zufahrt : A8 München → Salzburg. Exit (Ausf.) Holzkirchen. 318 → Gmund. In Gmund 318 → Bad Wiessee.
Map 2 on page 356 Karte 2 Seite 356

Golf course PLATZ 14/20

Site	Lage	
Maintenance	Instandhaltung	
Architect	Architekt	Donald Harradine
Type	Typ	mountain, parkland
Relief	Begehbarkeit	
Water in play	Platz mit Wasser	
Exp. to wind	Wind ausgesetzt	
Trees in play	Platz mit Bäumen	

Scorecard Scorekarte	Chp. Chp.	Mens Herren	Ladies Damen
Length Länge	5467	5467	4818
Par	70	70	70
Slope system	126	126	124

Advised golfing ability Empfohlene Spielstärke: 0 12 24 36
Hcp required Min. Handicap 36

Club house & amenities KLUBHAUS UND NEBENGEBÄUDE 7/10

Pro shop	Pro shop	
Driving range	Übungsplatz	
Sheltered	überdacht	no
On grass	auf Rasen	yes
Putting-green	Putting-grün	yes
Pitching-green	Pitching-grün	yes

Hotel facilities HOTEL BESCHREIBUNG 8/10

HOTELS HOTELS
St. Georg Golf Hotel, 28 rooms, D 133 € — Bad Wiessee 500 m
Tel (49) 08022 - 819 700, Fax (49) 08022 - 819 611

Wilhelmy, 22 rooms, D 133 € — Bad Wiessee 1 km
Tel (49) 08022 - 98 680, Fax (49) 08022 - 84 074

Park-Hotel Egerner-Hof — Rottach-Egern 6 km
104 rooms, D 179 €
Tel (49) 08022 - 66 60, Fax (49) 08022 - 666 200

RESTAURANTS RESTAURANT
Freihaus Brenner — Bad Wiessee 1 km
Tel (49) 08022 - 82 004

Altes Fährhaus, Tel (49) 08041 - 60 30 — Bad Tölz 18 km

TREUDELBERG

13 | 8 | 7

Beim Bau dieses Golfplatzes inmitten eines Naturschutzgebietes standen die ökologischen Gesichtspunkte eindeutig im Vordergrund, was zeigt, dass sich Golf und Umwelt durchaus gut vertragen. Treudelberg ist seiner Konzeption nach ein echter Sportclub im Stil amerikanischer Resorts, der aufgrund der angebotenen Palette an Möglichkeiten sicherlich der grösste seiner Art in dieser Region ist. Etwas mehr Charakter würde dem sehr zurückhaltend gestalteten Platz gut zu Gesicht stehen. Da die Anlage sehr stark dem Wind ausgesetzt ist, wären grössere Erdbewegungen wie man sie auch auf flachen Linksplätzen vorfindet, wünschenswert gewesen. Es gibt nur wenig Bäume, dieser Mangel wird aber durch Bunker, zahlreiche Wasserhindernisse sowie, je nach Saison, auch Rough wettgemacht. Ein ganz brauchbarer Platz, auf dem Spieler mit mittleren und hohen Handicaps lernen können, wie man mit Wasserhindernissen zurechtkommt.

This course was laid out in a nature reserve where ecological considerations were top priority. This just goes to show that golf and ecology can get along together. Treudelberg is a real sports club (in the style of US resorts) which is doubtless the largest of its kind in the region, judging by facilities. The course is very discreetly designed, and a little more personality would have been welcome. As exposure to the wind is a dominant factor, we would have liked to see more earth moving and grading, like on links courses, even when flat. Trees are not in great supply, but the bunkers and many water hazards largely make up for that, as does the rough at certain times of year. A useful course where mid- and high-handicappers will learn how to handle water hazards.

Golf & Country Club Treudelberg — 1991

Lehmsaler Landstrasse 45
D - 22397 HAMBURG

Office	Sekretariat	(49) 040 - 60822 500
Pro shop	Pro shop	(49) 040 - 60822 535
Fax	Fax	(49) 040 - 60822 444
Web	www.treudelberg.com	
Situation	Lage	

Hamburg Zentrum (pop. 1 650 000), 15 km
Hamburg-Poppenbüttel, 3 km

Annual closure	Jährliche Schliessung	no
Weekly closure	Wöchentliche Schliessung	no

Fees main season Preisliste hochsaison		18 holes
	Week days Woche	We/Bank holidays We/Feiertag
Individual Individuell	41 €	51 €
Couple Ehepaar	82 €	102 €
Caddy	Caddy	no
Electric Trolley	Elektrokarren	no
Buggy	Elektrischer Wagen	26 €
Clubs	Leihschläger	15 €

Credit cards Kreditkarten
VISA - Eurocard - MasterCard - DC - AMEX

Access Zufahrt : A7 Hamburg-Flesburg. Exit (Ausf.) Schnelsen Nord. Right → Airport (Flughafen). → Poppenbüttel. Left → Lemsahl-Duvenstedt (Ulzburger Strasse), Lemsahler Landstrasse. **Map 7 on page 366** Karte 7 Seite 366

Golf course PLATZ — 13/20

Site	Lage	
Maintenance	Instandhaltung	
Architect	Architekt	Donald Steel
Type	Typ	open country
Relief	Begehbarkeit	
Water in play	Platz mit Wasser	
Exp. to wind	Wind ausgesetzt	
Trees in play	Platz mit Bäumen	

Scorecard Scorekarte	Chp. Chp.	Mens Herren	Ladies Damen
Length Länge	6071	5852	5005
Par	72	72	72
Slope system	131	126	127

Advised golfing ability Empfohlene Spielstärke — 0 12 24 36
Hcp required Min. Handicap — no

Club house & amenities KLUBHAUS UND NEBENGEBÄUDE — 8/10

Pro shop	Pro shop	
Driving range	Übungsplatz	
Sheltered	überdacht	16 mats
On grass	auf Rasen	yes
Putting-green	Putting-grün	yes
Pitching-green	Pitching-grün	yes

Hotel facilities HOTEL BESCHREIBUNG — 7/10

HOTELS HOTELS

Treudelberg Marriott, 135 rooms, D 128 € — on site
Tel (49) 040 - 608 220, Fax (49) 040 - 608 2244

Poppenbütteler Hof — Hamburg-Poppenbüttel
32 rooms, D 112 € — 3 km
Tel (49) 040 - 608 780, Fax (49) 040 - 608 78178

Hafen Hamburg, 234 rooms, D 102 € — Hamburg
Tel (49) 040 - 311 130, Fax (49) 040 - 3111 3755 — 15 km

Baseler Hof, 153 rooms, D 107 € — Hamburg
Tel (49) 040 - 359 060, Fax (49) 040 - 3590 6918

RESTAURANTS RESTAURANT

Ristorante Dante, Tel (49) 040 - 602 0043 — Hamburg-Lemsahl
Treudelberg Marriott, Tel (49) 040 - 608 220 — on site

TUTZING

15 | 7 | 6

Der auf 700 Meter Höhe gelegene Golfplatz ist wie viele andere Kurse dieser Region besonders bei Touristen sehr beliebt. Am schönsten spielt sich Tutzing entweder im Herbst oder aber im Frühling, wenn die Vegetation nach dem Winter wieder voll erblüht ist. Die bayerischen Alpen bilden einen malerischen Hintergrund und verstärken so das Spielvergnügen auf dieser ausgezeichneten Anlage mit zahlreichen Bäumen und einigen hübschen Wasserläufen, welche die Spielbahnen - nicht selten zum Verdruss der Golfer - kreuzen. Der Kurs verfügt über keinerlei aussergewöhnliche aufregende Designelemente, sondern spiegelt vielmehr die Absicht des Architekten wider, in erster Linie einen Platz zu bauen, bei dem das Golfvergnügen im Vordergrund steht. Wenn Sie sich in dieser herrlichen Gegend aufhalten, sollten Sie diesen schön gelegenen Golfplatz und das dazugehörige Clubhaus im Stil eines Chalets keinesfalls links liegen lassen.

At an altitude of 700 metres and like most courses in this region very popular with tourists, Tutzing is particularly pleasant to play from the middle of Spring - when the vegetation is filling out after Winter - to the middle of Autumn. The backdrop of the Bavarian Alps adds to the pleasure of this excellent course with its numerous trees and pretty streams which cross the course, sometimes to the distress of the golfer. Don't look for anything outstandingly exciting design-wise here; this is the work of a serious artist who was thinking first and foremost of golfing pleasure. When you are in this superb region, Tutzing is a course not to be missed and a charming site enhanced by the chalet-style clubhouse.

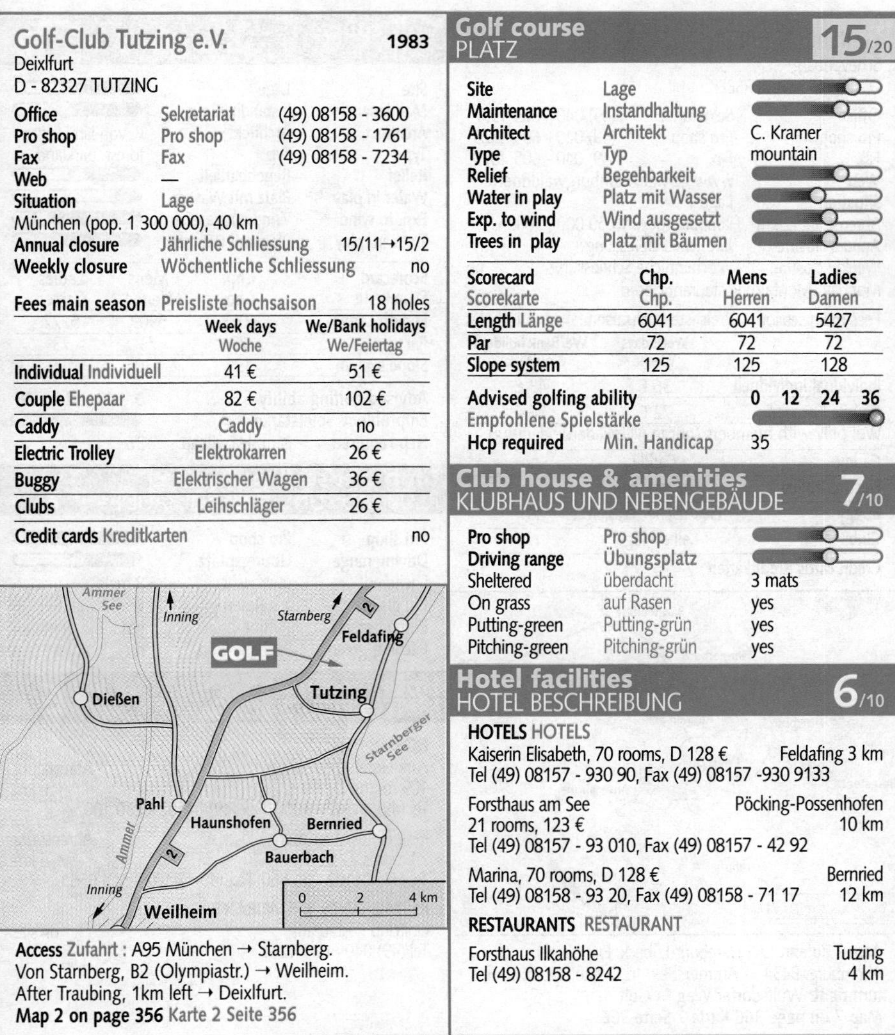

Golf-Club Tutzing e.V. — 1983

Deixlfurt
D - 82327 TUTZING

Office	Sekretariat	(49) 08158 - 3600
Pro shop	Pro shop	(49) 08158 - 1761
Fax	Fax	(49) 08158 - 7234
Web	—	
Situation	Lage	
München (pop. 1 300 000), 40 km		
Annual closure	Jährliche Schliessung	15/11→15/2
Weekly closure	Wöchentliche Schliessung	no

Fees main season Preisliste hochsaison	18 holes	
	Week days Woche	**We/Bank holidays** We/Feiertag
Individual Individuell	41 €	51 €
Couple Ehepaar	82 €	102 €
Caddy Caddy		no
Electric Trolley Elektrokarren		26 €
Buggy Elektrischer Wagen		36 €
Clubs Leihschläger		26 €
Credit cards Kreditkarten		no

Access Zufahrt : A95 München → Starnberg. Von Starnberg, B2 (Olympiastr.) → Weilheim. After Traubing, 1km left → Deixlfurt.
Map 2 on page 356 Karte 2 Seite 356

Golf course PLATZ — 15/20

Site	Lage	
Maintenance	Instandhaltung	
Architect	Architekt	C. Kramer
Type	Typ	mountain
Relief	Begehbarkeit	
Water in play	Platz mit Wasser	
Exp. to wind	Wind ausgesetzt	
Trees in play	Platz mit Bäumen	

Scorecard Scorekarte	**Chp.** Chp.	**Mens** Herren	**Ladies** Damen
Length Länge	6041	6041	5427
Par	72	72	72
Slope system	125	125	128

Advised golfing ability Empfohlene Spielstärke — 0 12 24 36
Hcp required Min. Handicap — 35

Club house & amenities KLUBHAUS UND NEBENGEBÄUDE — 7/10

Pro shop	Pro shop	
Driving range	Übungsplatz	
Sheltered	überdacht	3 mats
On grass	auf Rasen	yes
Putting-green	Putting-grün	yes
Pitching-green	Pitching-grün	yes

Hotel facilities HOTEL BESCHREIBUNG — 6/10

HOTELS HOTELS

Kaiserin Elisabeth, 70 rooms, D 128 € — Feldafing 3 km
Tel (49) 08157 - 930 90, Fax (49) 08157 -930 9133

Forsthaus am See — Pöcking-Possenhofen
21 rooms, 123 € — 10 km
Tel (49) 08157 - 93 010, Fax (49) 08157 - 42 92

Marina, 70 rooms, D 128 € — Bernried
Tel (49) 08158 - 93 20, Fax (49) 08158 - 71 17 — 12 km

RESTAURANTS RESTAURANT

Forsthaus Ilkahöhe — Tutzing
Tel (49) 08158 - 8242 — 4 km

WALLDDÖRFER

16 | 7 | 6

Wie Ahrensburg ist auch Walddörfer am Ufer des Bredenbeker Sees gelegen, inmitten einer Parklandschaft mit für diese Region typischen Hecken und Bäumen. Dutzende unterschiedlicher Baumarten verleihen vielen Spielbahnen ihren ganz eigenen Charakter. Die hügeligen ersten neun Löcher mit ihren durchgehend engen Fairways zwingen speziell beim Abschlag zur Vorsicht. Die Spielbahnen sind zudem noch recht lang; es gibt vier Par 5, drei Par 3 und zwei Par 4 Löcher. Auf den zweiten Neun wird das Gelände flacher und offener. Besonders bei aufkommendem Wind werden sich selbst Longhitter schwer tun ihr Ergebnis zu reparieren, wenn sie auf den ersten Neun zu sehr gestreut haben. Bemerkenswert am Layout von Walddörfer ist, dass es nur sieben Par 4 Löcher gibt. Die gut erkennbaren Schwierigkeiten kommen stark ins Spiel. Das letzte Wort gebührt der ausgezeichneten 18. Bahn, die den würdigen Abschluss einer grossartigen Golfrunde bildet.

Like Ahrensburg, Walddörfer is located on the banks of lake Bredenbeker, in a setting of parkland, hedgerows and trees that are typical of the region. The trees are magnificent, with dozens of varieties giving a distinctive flavour to different holes. The front nine are hilly, with generally narrow fairways calling for care, especially off the tee. The holes are pretty long, too, and there are four par 5s, two par 3s and two par 4s. The landscape then becomes flatter and wider, although big-hitters will still be hard-pushed to repair their card if they were too wayward over the front 9, especially if the unstoppable wind gets up. In all, there are only seven par 4s here, a feature that adds to the originality of Waldörfer. Difficulties are very much in play and generally very visible. One last word should go to the 18th, an excellent hole with which to complete a great round of golf.

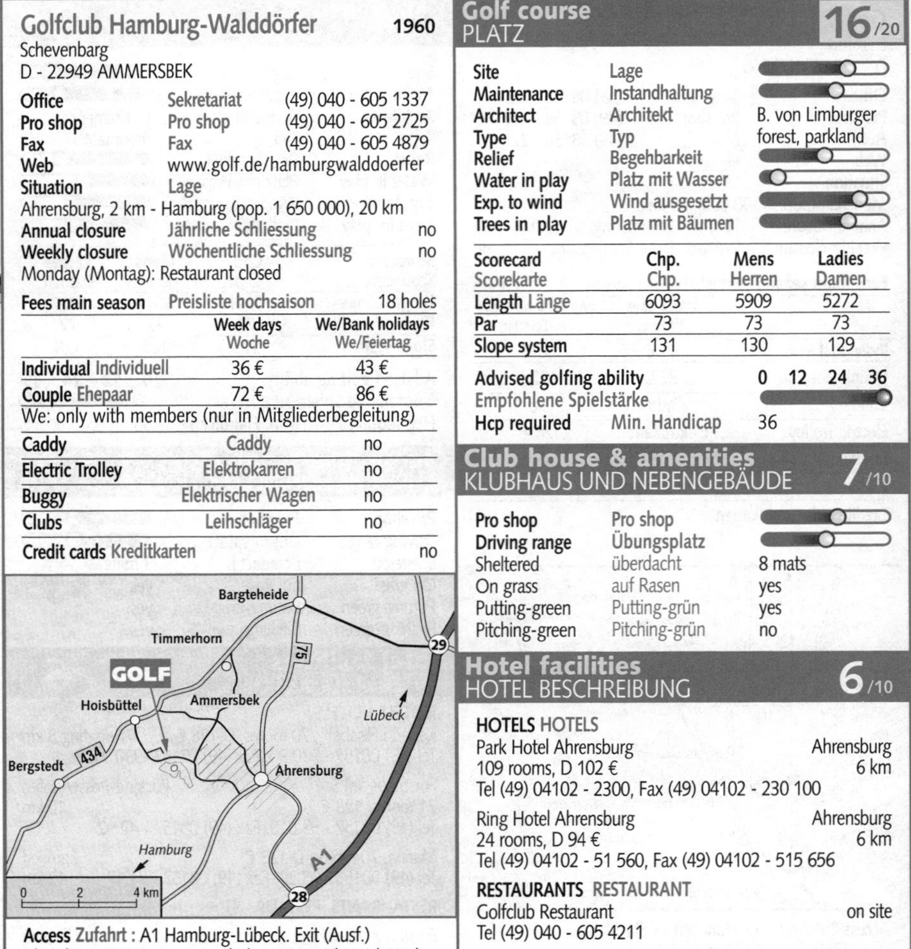

Golfclub Hamburg-Walddörfer — 1960

Schevenbarg
D - 22949 AMMERSBEK

Office	Sekretariat	(49) 040 - 605 1337
Pro shop	Pro shop	(49) 040 - 605 2725
Fax	Fax	(49) 040 - 605 4879
Web	www.golf.de/hamburgwalddoerfer	
Situation	Lage	

Ahrensburg, 2 km - Hamburg (pop. 1 650 000), 20 km

Annual closure	Jährliche Schliessung	no
Weekly closure	Wöchentliche Schliessung	no

Monday (Montag): Restaurant closed

Fees main season / Preisliste hochsaison	Week days / Woche	We/Bank holidays / We/Feiertag
18 holes		
Individual Individuell	36 €	43 €
Couple Ehepaar	72 €	86 €

We: only with members (nur in Mitgliederbegleitung)

Caddy	Caddy	no
Electric Trolley	Elektrokarren	no
Buggy	Elektrischer Wagen	no
Clubs	Leihschläger	no
Credit cards	Kreditkarten	no

Access Zufahrt : A1 Hamburg-Lübeck. Exit (Ausf.) Ahrenburg. B434 → Ammersbek. In Ortsteil Hoisbüttel, turn right: Wulfsdorfer Weg → Golf
Map 7 on page 366 Karte 7 Seite 366

Golf course PLATZ — 16/20

Site	Lage	
Maintenance	Instandhaltung	
Architect	Architekt	B. von Limburger
Type	Typ	forest, parkland
Relief	Begehbarkeit	
Water in play	Platz mit Wasser	
Exp. to wind	Wind ausgesetzt	
Trees in play	Platz mit Bäumen	

Scorecard / Scorekarte	Chp. / Chp.	Mens / Herren	Ladies / Damen
Length Länge	6093	5909	5272
Par	73	73	73
Slope system	131	130	129

Advised golfing ability / Empfohlene Spielstärke: 0 12 24 36

Hcp required — Min. Handicap — 36

Club house & amenities KLUBHAUS UND NEBENGEBÄUDE — 7/10

Pro shop	Pro shop	
Driving range	Übungsplatz	
Sheltered	überdacht	8 mats
On grass	auf Rasen	yes
Putting-green	Putting-grün	yes
Pitching-green	Pitching-grün	no

Hotel facilities HOTEL BESCHREIBUNG — 6/10

HOTELS HOTELS

Park Hotel Ahrensburg — Ahrensburg
109 rooms, D 102 € — 6 km
Tel (49) 04102 - 2300, Fax (49) 04102 - 230 100

Ring Hotel Ahrensburg — Ahrensburg
24 rooms, D 94 € — 6 km
Tel (49) 04102 - 51 560, Fax (49) 04102 - 515 656

RESTAURANTS RESTAURANT

Golfclub Restaurant — on site
Tel (49) 040 - 605 4211

WASSERBURG ANHOLT

15 | 7 | 7

Ein sehr gepflegter, klassischer Parkland Course mit altem Baumbestand in einem Teil des Schlossparks der Anholter Wasserburg. Der Meisterschaftsplatz wurde von Bernhard von Limburger gekonnt in das Landschaftsschutzgebiet Anholter Schweiz mit seinen beiden Flussläufen Issel und Wasserstrang gelegt. Das Platz ist abwechslungsreich und einprägsam, weil jedes der 18 Löcher seinen eigenenen Charakter hat und spezifische Herausforderung bietet. Besonders reizvoll sind die vier Par-3-Löcher, obwohl sie nach modernen Gesichtspunkten nicht sonderlich lang sind (zwischen 119 und 170 m). Dafür sind sie durch Wasser- und Sandhindernisse sehr gut verteidigt. Die anderen Löchern erfordern eine Kombination aus präzisem, langen Spiel und strategischem Geschick.

A very well groomed classical parkland course lined by mature trees located in a part of the old park of the water castle (Wasserschloss) Anholt. This championship course was designed by Bernhard von Limburger who laid out the course masterfully in the environmentally protected area of the Anholter Schweiz with the two streams of Issel and Wolfstrang. The course stays in your mind because each and every hole has its own character and challenge. The four par 3 holes on this course really stand out, even though they are not long by modern standards (between 119 and 170 m), but they are well defended by water hazards and sand traps. All other holes require a combination of long, precise shots and strategic skill.

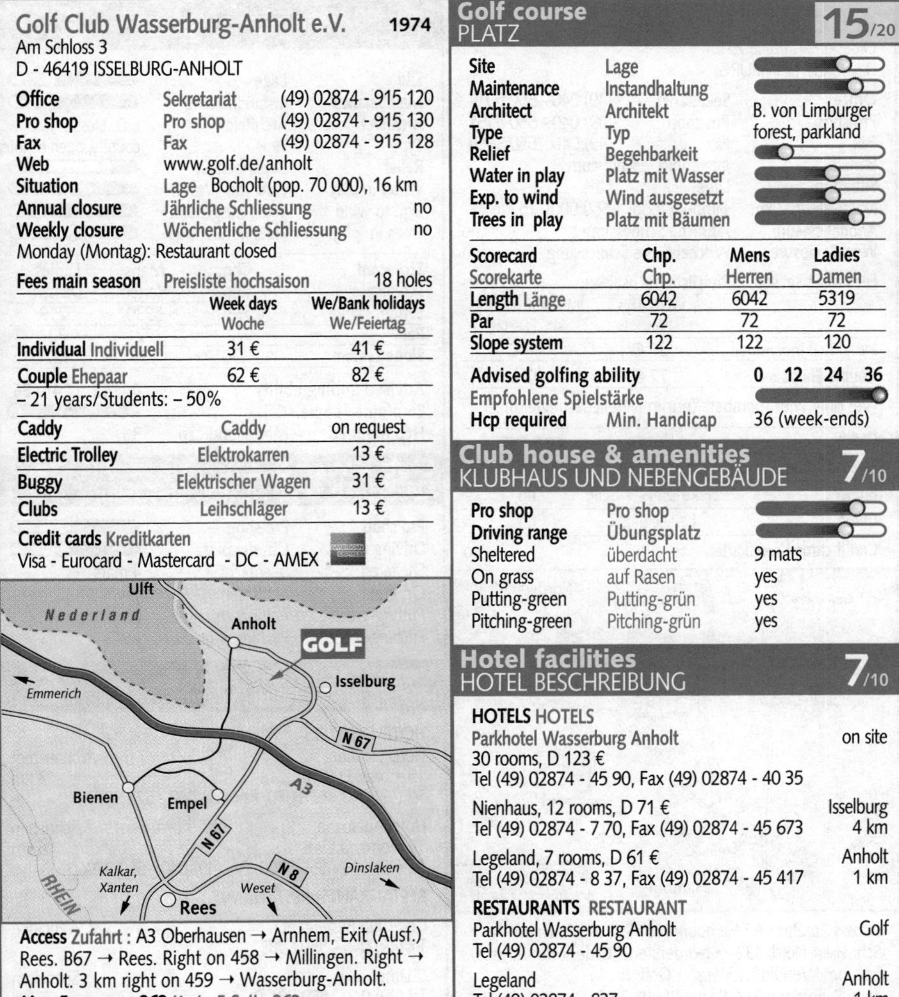

Golf Club Wasserburg-Anholt e.V. **1974**
Am Schloss 3
D - 46419 ISSELBURG-ANHOLT

Office	Sekretariat	(49) 02874 - 915 120
Pro shop	Pro shop	(49) 02874 - 915 130
Fax	Fax	(49) 02874 - 915 128
Web	www.golf.de/anholt	
Situation	Lage	Bocholt (pop. 70 000), 16 km
Annual closure	Jährliche Schliessung	no
Weekly closure	Wöchentliche Schliessung	no

Monday (Montag): Restaurant closed

Fees main season Preisliste hochsaison		18 holes
	Week days Woche	**We/Bank holidays** We/Feiertag
Individual Individuell	31 €	41 €
Couple Ehepaar	62 €	82 €

– 21 years/Students: – 50%

Caddy	Caddy	on request
Electric Trolley	Elektrokarren	13 €
Buggy	Elektrischer Wagen	31 €
Clubs	Leihschläger	13 €

Credit cards Kreditkarten
Visa - Eurocard - Mastercard - DC - AMEX

Access Zufahrt : A3 Oberhausen → Arnhem, Exit (Ausf.) Rees. B67 → Rees. Right on 458 → Millingen. Right → Anholt. 3 km right on 459 → Wasserburg-Anholt.
Map 5 on page 362 Karte 5 Seite 362

Golf course PLATZ — 15/20

Site	Lage	
Maintenance	Instandhaltung	
Architect	Architekt	B. von Limburger
Type	Typ	forest, parkland
Relief	Begehbarkeit	
Water in play	Platz mit Wasser	
Exp. to wind	Wind ausgesetzt	
Trees in play	Platz mit Bäumen	

Scorecard Scorekarte	**Chp.** Chp.	**Mens** Herren	**Ladies** Damen
Length Länge	6042	6042	5319
Par	72	72	72
Slope system	122	122	120

Advised golfing ability Empfohlene Spielstärke — 0 12 24 36
Hcp required Min. Handicap — 36 (week-ends)

Club house & amenities KLUBHAUS UND NEBENGEBÄUDE — 7/10

Pro shop	Pro shop	
Driving range	Übungsplatz	
Sheltered	überdacht	9 mats
On grass	auf Rasen	yes
Putting-green	Putting-grün	yes
Pitching-green	Pitching-grün	yes

Hotel facilities HOTEL BESCHREIBUNG — 7/10

HOTELS HOTELS

Parkhotel Wasserburg Anholt — on site
30 rooms, D 123 €
Tel (49) 02874 - 45 90, Fax (49) 02874 - 40 35

Nienhaus, 12 rooms, D 71 € — Isselburg 4 km
Tel (49) 02874 - 7 70, Fax (49) 02874 - 45 673

Legeland, 7 rooms, D 61 € — Anholt 1 km
Tel (49) 02874 - 8 37, Fax (49) 02874 - 45 417

RESTAURANTS RESTAURANT

Parkhotel Wasserburg Anholt — Golf
Tel (49) 02874 - 45 90

Legeland — Anholt 1 km
Tel (49) 02874 - 837

WENDLOHE A-Kurs + B-Kurs

16	7	6

Die grosszügige Weite Schleswig-Holsteins bildet die ruhige und beschauliche Umgebung für Wendlohe, wo die zahlreichen Bäume kaum beunruhigen, da man seinen Ball auch unter den Bäumen immer in einer guten Lage vorfindet. Wenig Wasser und nur vereinzelte Fairway-Bunker weisen darauf hin, dass die Hauptschwierigkeit im Anspiel der Grüns liegt. Unterschiedlich gross, mit starken Kontouren versehen und teilweise auf mehreren Stufen angelegt, sind diese ohne Frage die interessantesten Grüns weit und breit. Sie sind durchgängig gut verteidigt, sehr schnell aber nie unspielbar. Um sie von der richtigen Position aus anzuspielen, bedarf es sehr präziser Eisenschläge. Deswegen wird es einem auch zumindest auf der ersten Runde schwerfallen, ein seinem Handicap entsprechendes Ergebnis zu spielen. Im Winter ist der Platz etwas feucht. Das Clubhaus erfreut sich einer schönen Terrasse, von der aus man das 18. Loch einsehen kann.

The wide open spaces of Schleswig-Holstein provide a calm and pastoral setting at "Auf der Wendlohe", where trees are hardly a worry. There are enough of them, but you always find your ball well-placed when you meet them. With only a little water and few fairway bunkers, you will guess that the main problem is the approach to the greens. These are unquestionably some of the most interesting putting surfaces to contend with in this part of the world, with different sizes, serious contours and multi-tiering. They are generally fast, well-protected but never unplayable. To approach them from the right position, you need a sharp and accurate iron game. This is why returning a card to reflect your handicap is hardly likely, at least not the first time out. A wee damp in winter, the course boasts a pretty terrace overlooking the 18th hole.

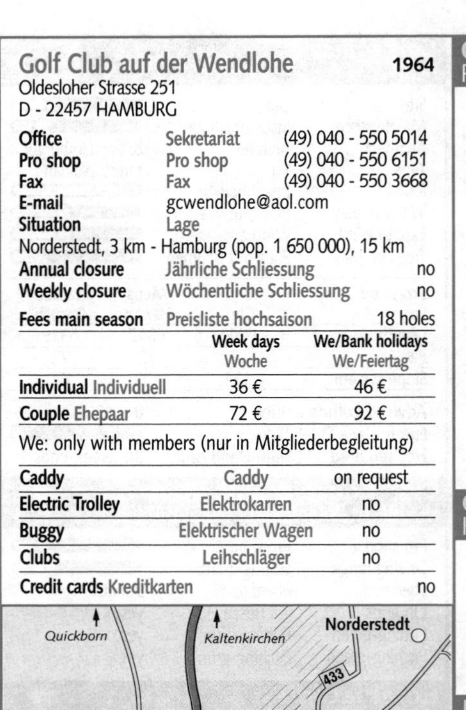

Golf Club auf der Wendlohe — 1964

Oldesloher Strasse 251
D - 22457 HAMBURG

Office	Sekretariat	(49) 040 - 550 5014
Pro shop	Pro shop	(49) 040 - 550 6151
Fax	Fax	(49) 040 - 550 3668
E-mail	gcwendlohe@aol.com	
Situation	Lage	

Norderstedt, 3 km - Hamburg (pop. 1 650 000), 15 km

Annual closure	Jährliche Schliessung	no
Weekly closure	Wöchentliche Schliessung	no

Fees main season Preisliste hochsaison — 18 holes

	Week days Woche	We/Bank holidays We/Feiertag
Individual Individuell	36 €	46 €
Couple Ehepaar	72 €	92 €

We: only with members (nur in Mitgliederbegleitung)

Caddy	Caddy	on request
Electric Trolley	Elektrokarren	no
Buggy	Elektrischer Wagen	no
Clubs	Leihschläger	no
Credit cards	Kreditkarten	no

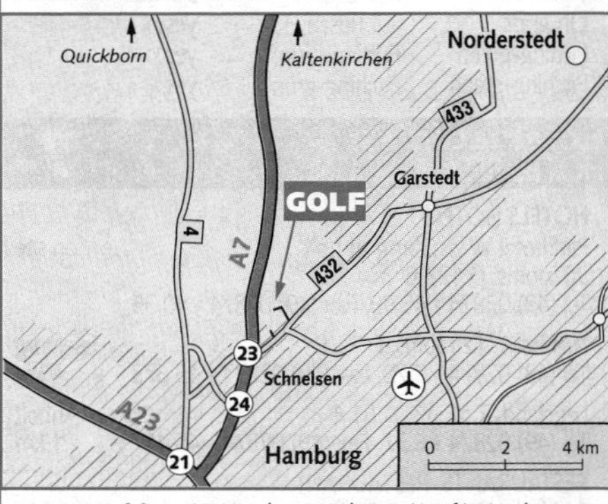

Access Zufahrt : A7 Hamburg-Kiel. Exit (Ausf.) Hamburg-Schnelsen-Nord. 432 → Norderstedt (Oldesloher-Strasse). Left on Wendloher Weg → Golf
Map 7 on page 366 Karte 7 Seite 366

Golf course PLATZ — 16/20

Site	Lage	
Maintenance	Instandhaltung	
Architect	Architekt	E.D. Hess
Type	Typ	country, open country
Relief	Begehbarkeit	
Water in play	Platz mit Wasser	
Exp. to wind	Wind ausgesetzt	
Trees in play	Platz mit Bäumen	

Scorecard Scorekarte	Chp. Chp.	Mens Herren	Ladies Damen
Length Länge	5930	5930	5219
Par	72	72	72
Slope system	130	130	127

Advised golfing ability Empfohlene Spielstärke — 0 12 24 36
Hcp required Min. Handicap 36

Club house & amenities KLUBHAUS UND NEBENGEBÄUDE — 7/10

Pro shop	Pro shop	
Driving range	Übungsplatz	
Sheltered	überdacht	4 mats
On grass	auf Rasen	yes
Putting-green	Putting-grün	yes
Pitching-green	Pitching-grün	yes

Hotel facilities HOTEL BESCHREIBUNG — 6/10

HOTELS HOTELS

Hotel Heuberg — Norderstedt
15 rooms, D 82 € — 3 km
Tel (49) 040 - 528 070, Fax (49) 040 - 523 8067

Hotel Ausspann — Schnelsen
12 rooms, D 89 € — 6 km
Tel (49) 040 - 559 8700, Fax (49) 040 - 559 87060

RESTAURANTS RESTAURANT

Golf Club Restaurant — GC Wendlohe
Tel (49) 040 - 550 8583

Champs — Schnelsen
Tel (49) 040 - 559 791-0 — 6 km

WITTELSBACHER

17 | 7 | 6

Unweit der Donau liegt dieser flache Platz in einer parkähnlichen Landschaft mit wunderschönen alten Bäumen, meist Eichen. Die Hauptschwierigkeit dieses Platzes liegt darin, diesen herrlichen Bäumen und dem extrem dicken Rough aus dem Weg zu gehen. Zudem erschweren drei Wasserhindernisse und 17 strategisch geschickt platzierte Fairway-Bunker das Spiel. Die gut gesicherten Grüns sind von herausragender Qualität Sie sind von teilweise immenser Grösse, so dass man den einen oder anderen 3-Putt einkalkulieren muss. Der Clubpräsident seine Königliche Hoheit Herzog Max in Bayern, der Mitglied des von Pine Valley, des R&A, Muirfield und Royal St. Georges ist, besteht in bester schottischer Tradition darauf, dass die Fairways nicht künstlich bewässert werden und keine Entfernungsmarkierungen aufweisen. Imposant ist das moderne Clubhaus mit Wohnmöglichkeit und einem nahegelegene Dormi-Haus. Ein Platz, den man unbedingt spielen muss, wenn man im Grossraum München-Ingolstadt-Augsburg unterwegs ist.

In countryside along the Danube, this is a flat course surrounded by some really beautiful trees, mainly oak, which give the impression of a large English-style park. The main difficulty here is to stay away from these impressive trees and the heavy, thick rough. Three water hazards and 17 strategically placed fairway bunkers add to the difficulty. The greens are well defended and of excellent quality, but some are simply huge, so getting away without at least one 3-putt is a major feat. The club president and de-facto owner, His Royal Highness Duke Max of Bavaria, who is a member of Pine Valley, the R & A, Muirfield and Royal St. George, insists in the best Scottish traditions that there is no irrigation system for the fairways and no distance markers either. Guests can stay either at the ultra modern clubhouse or in the charming dormy-house located two minutes from the course. This is a course not to be missed, if you are in the greater Munich-Ingolstadt-Augsburg area.

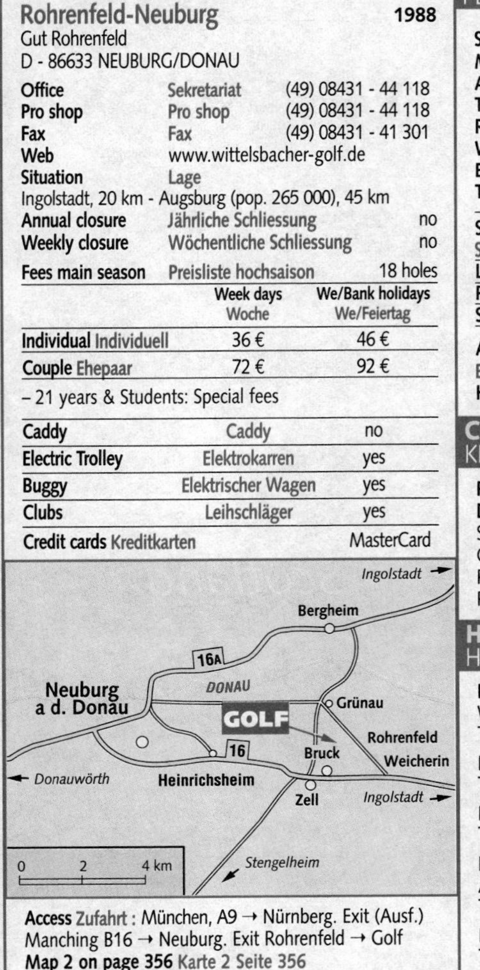

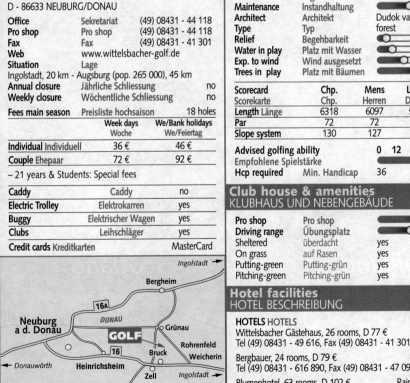

Wittelsbacher Golfclub Rohrenfeld-Neuburg **1988**
Gut Rohrenfeld
D - 86633 NEUBURG/DONAU

Office	Sekretariat	(49) 08431 - 44 118
Pro shop	Pro shop	(49) 08431 - 44 118
Fax	Fax	(49) 08431 - 41 301
Web	www.wittelsbacher-golf.de	
Situation	Lage	

Ingolstadt, 20 km - Augsburg (pop. 265 000), 45 km

Annual closure	Jährliche Schliessung	no
Weekly closure	Wöchentliche Schliessung	no

Fees main season Preisliste hochsaison	18 holes	
	Week days Woche	**We/Bank holidays** We/Feiertag
Individual Individuell	36 €	46 €
Couple Ehepaar	72 €	92 €

– 21 years & Students: Special fees

Caddy	Caddy	no
Electric Trolley	Elektrokarren	yes
Buggy	Elektrischer Wagen	yes
Clubs	Leihschläger	yes
Credit cards Kreditkarten		MasterCard

Access Zufahrt : München, A9 → Nürnberg. Exit (Ausf.) Manching B16 → Neuburg. Exit Rohrenfeld → Golf
Map 2 on page 356 Karte 2 Seite 356

Golf course PLATZ — 17/20

Site	Lage	
Maintenance	Instandhaltung	
Architect	Architekt	Dudok van Heel
Type	Typ	forest
Relief	Begehbarkeit	
Water in play	Platz mit Wasser	
Exp. to wind	Wind ausgesetzt	
Trees in play	Platz mit Bäumen	

Scorecard Scorekarte	**Chp.** Chp.	**Mens** Herren	**Ladies** Damen
Length Länge	6318	6097	5310
Par	72	72	72
Slope system	130	127	125

Advised golfing ability Empfohlene Spielstärke — 0 12 24 36
Hcp required Min. Handicap 36

Club house & amenities KLUBHAUS UND NEBENGEBÄUDE — 7/10

Pro shop	Pro shop	
Driving range	Übungsplatz	
Sheltered	überdacht	yes
On grass	auf Rasen	yes
Putting-green	Putting-grün	yes
Pitching-green	Pitching-grün	yes

Hotel facilities HOTEL BESCHREIBUNG — 6/10

HOTELS HOTELS

Wittelsbacher Gästehaus, 26 rooms, D 77 € — on site
Tel (49) 08431 - 49 616, Fax (49) 08431 - 41 301

Bergbauer, 24 rooms, D 79 € — Neuburg 6 km
Tel (49) 08431 - 616 890, Fax (49) 08431 - 47 090

Blumenhotel, 63 rooms, D 102 € — Rain am Lech 20 km
Tel (49) 09090 - 7 60, Fax (49) 09090 - 76 400

RESTAURANTS RESTAURANT

Arco Schlösschen — Neuburg 6 km
Tel (49) 08431 - 22 85

Im Stadttheater — Ingolstadt 20 km
Tel (49) 0841 - 93 5150

PEUGEOT GOLF GUIDE 2000/2001

EUROPE'S TOP 1000 GOLF COURSES

Great Britain
Ireland

Wales

Ireland

PEUGEOT GOLF GUIDE 2000/2001

Great Britain & Ireland

Travel these days knows no frontiers, or at least very few. From a golfing point of view, the term "Great Britain and Ireland" covers three criteria, namely geography, language and sport. The best players from both islands used to be selected for the Ryder Cup team in years gone by and still are for the Walker Cup and Curtis Cup matches against the United States. A fourth criterion might be unity of style in terms of golf courses, imposed, despite the variety of landscapes, by the pounding seas around each and every coastline. Seas which, miraculously, have left ample space for the great links courses of England, Scotland, Wales, Northern Ireland and the Republic of Ireland.

Some very private courses have now been featured in the Guide. We know full well that the general public will never set foot on them unless especially invited, but there has been widespread demand to see them included in our ranking system. Some readers are also keen to read about them before considering whether or not to become members. This explains why Rye, Loch Lomond and the Carnegie Club at Skibo Castle make a first appearance. But don't waste your time trying to play any of them next week-end, their front gates still remain politely but firmly closed.

When you make choices you necessarily leave yourself open to criticism and amongst the some 3,000 eighteen-hole courses to be found in this home of golf, we will still be accused of having forgotten a number of excellent layouts in Britain and Ireland. Some of them asked not to be included here because they are totally private. But we won't deny the fact that we have also given preference to the more specifically British style course, even though these days they may appear a little outdated in terms of yardage. In the same way, the scores given to clubhouses were awarded in relation to the general standard of club-house found in the British Isles. Some may be considered very low compared to their counterparts in the United States, Japan and even continental Europe. We have considered warmth of atmosphere, respect for tradition and the «golfing» excellence of the site to be of greater importance than marble hallways, thick-pile carpets and gym rooms.

As a general rule, visitors need to be aware of certain local customs. First of all, driving ranges are still few and far between, even though the more recent courses are beginning to think differently. Here people learnt to play out on the course. If you want a few practice swings, bring a bag of balls with you in the boot of your car. Hit them and pick them up yourself on the area provided for practice.

Next, we have done all we can to point out the restrictions on admission to each club, but these may change, as may the minimum handicap required to play the course. We advise you to call in advance every time.

Out on the course, players from Europe will often be surprised at the speed of the game in the UK. Never hesitating to let people play through is one thing, but more importantly they should learn to speed up their own game.

Last but by no means least, always pack a shirt, tie and jacket in your car. Most clubs impose the tie and jacket rule in the bar or restaurant or both, often in the evening but also during the day. So don't get caught out on that one.

One final word: we are sorry to have to report spiralling green-fees at many courses. It is such a pity that these days it is money and not talent or love of golf that opens the front gates to the greatest courses.

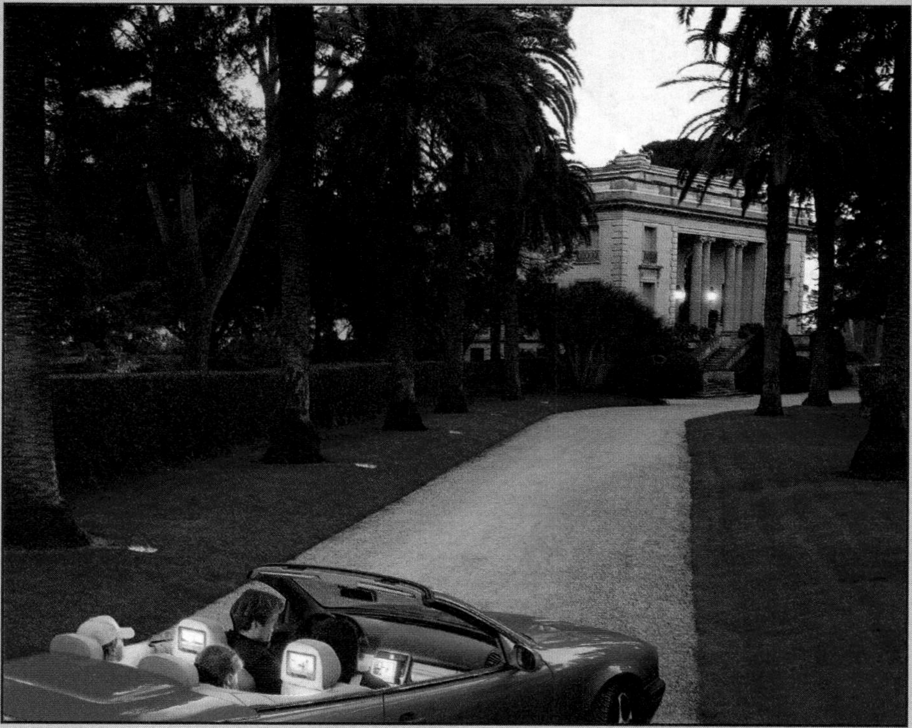

Grande-Bretagne et Irlande

En matière de voyage, il n'y a plus de frontières. L'appellation "Grande-Bretagne et Irlande" a trois justifications. D'abord géographique, ensuite linguistique, et enfin sportive : en golf, on unit les meilleurs joueurs des deux îles, autrefois pour disputer la Ryder Cup, aujourd'hui encore pour jouer la Walker Cup et la Curtis Cup contre les Etats-Unis. On pourrait ajouter en dernier lieu une unité de style de parcours, imposée en dépit des diversités des paysages par les assauts de l'océan, de tous côtés, qui ont par miracle laissé de grands espaces vierges pour y tracer les grands links d'Angleterre, d'Ecosse, du Pays de Galles, d'Irlande et d'Irlande du Nord.

Certains golf très privés sont désormais inclus dans le Guide. Nous savons bien que le public ne peut y avoir accès à moins d'avoir des relations, mais la demande était générale pour les voir inclus dans notre hiérarchie générale, certains lecteurs étant également désireux de la connaître avant d'envisager d'y devenir membres. Ainsi, Rye, Loch Lomond ou le Carnegie Club à Skibo Castle font leur entrée. Inutile de vous y présenter samedi prochain, leur porte restera poliment fermée.

Quand on fait des choix, on est forcément vulnérable aux critiques, et on nous reprochera toujours d'avoir "oublié" certains parcours, en Grande-Bretagne et Irlande, parmi les quelques 3.000 parcours de 18 trous que comptent ces berceaux du golf. Mais nous ne cacherons pas avoir aussi privilégié les parcours les plus spécifiquement britanniques de style, même s'ils peuvent parfois paraître désuets par leur manque de longueur. De la même façon, les notes attribuées aux Club houses ont été attribuées en relation avec leur niveau général dans les îles britanniques : certains d'entre eux seraient jugés très modestes en comparaison avec leurs équivalents les plus luxueux aux Etats-Unis, au Japon, ou même sur le continent. Pour nous, la chaleur de l'ambiance, le respect de la tradition, la qualité «golfique» du lieu a plus d'importance que le marbre, les moquettes et les salles de mise en forme.

En règle générale, les visiteurs doivent être informés de certaines coutumes locales. D'abord, les practices ou driving ranges sont encore rares, même si les récents parcours y pensent. Ici, on apprenait à jouer sur le parcours. Si vous souhaitez vous entraîner, ayez un sac de balles dans votre coffre, que vous ramasserez vous-même sur les zones prévues à cet effet.

Ensuite, nous avons signalé au maximum les restrictions d'accès dans chaque club, mais elles peuvent changer, tout comme les limites de handicap, nous vous conseillons donc de toujours téléphoner à l'avance.

Les joueurs du continent seront souvent surpris par la rapidité de jeu sur les parcours. Qu'ils n'hésitent jamais à laisser passer est une chose, mais qu'ils apprennent surtout à accélérer leur propre rythme.

Enfin, ayez toujours dans votre voiture un petit sac avec une chemise de ville, une cravate et une veste. La plupart des clubs imposent "tie and jacket," au bar, au restaurant, ou les deux, souvent le soir, mais aussi dans la journée. Vous ne serez pas pris au dépourvu.

Enfin, un dernier mort pour regretter l'ascension vertigineuse de beaucoup de green-fees. On regrettera vivement que ce soit l'argent, et pas le talent ou la passion golfique, qui ouvre les portes des plus grands parcours.

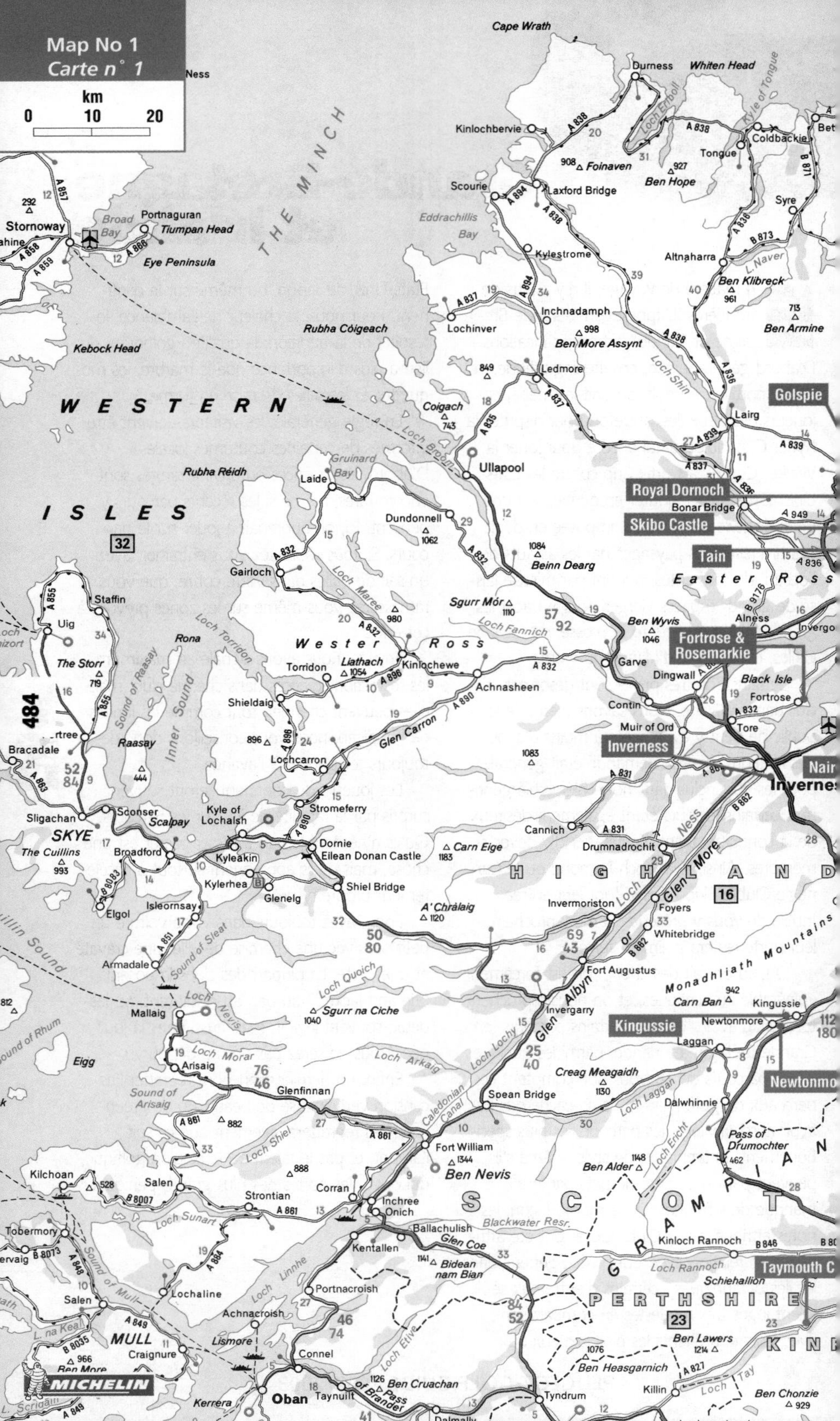
Map No 1
Carte n° 1
km
0 10 20
Cape Wrath
Ness
Durness
Whiten Head
Loch Eriboll
Kyle of Tongue
Kinlochbervie
A 838
Tongue
Coldbackie
Bettyhill
B 871
908 Foinaven
927 Ben Hope
Scourie
A 894
Laxford Bridge
Syre
Eddrachillis Bay
Kylestrome
A 836
B 873
Altnaharra
L. Naver
Ben Klibreck
961
713
Ben Armine
A 837
Lochinver
Inchnadamph
998
Ben More Assynt
Loch Shin
849
Ledmore
Golspie
Coigach
743
A 835
Lairg
A 839
Loch Broom
Gruinard Bay
Ullapool
Royal Dornoch
Laide
Bonar Bridge
A 949
Dundonnell
1062
Skibo Castle
A 832
1084
Beinn Dearg
Tain
A 836
Gairloch
Easter Ross
Loch Maree
B 9176
Sgurr Mór
1110
Loch Fannich
Alness
Invergordon
980
Ben Wyvis
1046
Wester Ross
Fortrose & Rosemarkie
Liathach
1054
Kinlochewe
Torridon
A 896
Garve
Achnasheen
Dingwall
Black Isle
Fortrose
Shieldaig
A 890
Contin
Glen Carron
Tore
Muir of Ord
896
Inverness
Lochcarron
1083
Nairn
Inverness
A 831
B 862
Stromeferry
Kyle of Lochalsh
Cannich
Ness
Drumnadrochit
Dornie
Eilean Donan Castle
Carn Eige
1183
Kyleakin
Glen More
Kylerhea
Glenelg
Shiel Bridge
HIGHLAND
16
Invermoriston
Foyers
A' Chràlaig
1120
Loch
Whitebridge
Monadhliath Mountains
Fort Augustus
Glen Albyn
942
Carn Ban
Kingussie
Invergarry
Kingussie
Newtonmore
Loch Quoich
Sgurr na Ciche
1040
Loch Lochy
Laggan
Newtonmore
Loch Arkaig
Creag Meagaidh
1130
Spean Bridge
Loch Laggan
Dalwhinnie
Caledonian Canal
Pass of Drumochter
462
Fort William
1344
Ben Nevis
1148
Ben Alder
Loch Ericht
GRAMPIAN
SCOTLAND
Inchree
Onich
Blackwater Resr.
Kinloch Rannoch
B 846
Ballachulish
Glen Coe
Kentallen
1141 Bidean nam Bian
Loch Rannoch
Schiehallion
Taymouth Castle
PERTHSHIRE
23
Portnacroish
Loch Linnhe
Loch Etive
1076
Ben Heasgarnich
Ben Lawers
1214
A 827
Killin
Loch Tay
Ben Chonzie
929
Tyndrum
Lochearnhead
Dalmally
Pass of Brander
1126 Ben Cruachan
Taynuilt
Connel
Oban
Kerrera
Lismore
Achnacroish
MULL
Craignure
966
Ben More
Salen
Lochaline
A 849
B 8035
L. na Keal
Sound of Mull
Tobermory
Dervaig
B 8073
A 848
A 884
Loch Sunart
Strontian
A 861
Corran
Salen
B 8007
Kilchoan
528
888
Loch Shiel
Glenfinnan
A 861
882
Sound of Arisaig
Arisaig
Loch Morar
Eigg
Sound of Rhum
812
Mallaig
Loch Nevis
Armadale
Sound of Sleat
A 851
Isleornsay
Elgol
B 8083
Broadford
The Cuillins
993
SKYE
Sligachan
Sconser
Scalpay
Raasay
444
Inner Sound
Sound of Raasay
Rona
Loch Torridon
Bracadale
A 863
Portree
The Storr
719
A 855
Uig
Staffin
Loch Snizort
ISLES
32
WESTERN
Rubha Réidh
Rubha Cóigeach
Kebock Head
THE MINCH
Stornoway
292
A 857
Broad Bay
Portnaguran
Tiumpan Head
A 866
Eye Peninsula
A 858
A 859
MICHELIN

Pentland Firth
Burwick
Dunnet Head
Point
Scrabster
Duncansby Head
Dunnet
A 836
John o' Groats
Thurso
Castletown
Roadside
B 876
A 99
Reiss
Noss Head
A 882
Wick
290
114
183
107
172
Latheron
706
Morven
A 897
Helmsdale
Brora
Brora
Tarbat Ness
Moray Firth
Moray (Old)
Lossiemouth
Nairn Dunbar
Duff House Royal
Elgin
Buckie
Cullen
Kinnairds Head
Banff
Macduff
Fraserburgh
Forres
Fochabers
B 9031
Elgin
Rothes
R. Spey
Keith
Deveron
B 9025
Turriff
Rattray Head
Craigellachie
Dufftown
A 920
Huntly
New Deer
B 9029
Mintlaw
Peterhead
Dava
Grantown on Spey
Huntly
Buchan Ness
Grantown-on-Spey
840
66
109
Cruden Bay
MORAY
Rhynie
Oldmeldrum
Ellon
Dulnain Bridge
19
2
Cruden Bay
Tomintoul
ABERDEEN
Newburgh
Mossat
Inverurie
Stromness
Glenmore Forest Park
Boat of Garten
Don
Kintore
Murcar
Lerwick
Torshavn
Alford
Craigievar Castle
Colnabaichin
871
Aboyne
1
Ben Macdui
Aboyne
Crathes Castle
ABERDEEN
Royal Aberdeen
Braemar
Ballater
Balmoral Castle
Dee
Banchory
Ballater
1155
Banchory
Stonehaven
MOUNTAINS
Devil's Elbow
1068
Glas Maol
N. Esk
89
55
AND ANGUS
3
Edzell
Laurencekirk
Inverbervie
Pitlochry
Marikirk
Montrose
Brechin
Alyth
Kirriemuir
Alyth
Glamis Castle
Forfar
Rattray
Blairgowrie
Dunkeld
Glamis
Meigle
Forfar
Coupar Angus
Sidlaw Hills
Blairgowrie
Letham Grange
Arbroath
Dundee
Monifieth
Carnoustie
485
MICHELIN
d' après cartes n° 401 - 21ème édition, n° 402 - 19ème édition, n° 403 - 23ème édition, n° 404 - 23ème édition - 2001-2002 et n° 986 - 20ème édition - 2002. Autorisation n° 0102062.

Map No 2
Carte n° 2
km
0
10
20
486
Machrie
Machrihanish
Shiskine (Blackwaterfoot)
Turnberry
Buchanan Castle
Loch Lomond
Cardross
Westerwood
Callan
Strathaven
Cairndhu (U)
Portpatrick (Dunskey)
Royal Belfast (U)
Bangor (U)
Clandeboye (U)
Knock (U)
Belvoir Park (U)
Malone (U)
Kirkistown Castle (U)
Ardglass (U)
Royal County Down (U)
MICHELIN
Oban
Taynuilt
Ben Cruachan
Pass of Brander
Tyndrum
Killin
Dalmally
Crianlarich
Lochearnhead
Kerrera
Kilninver
Firth of Lorn
ARGYLL
AND
BUTE
STIRLING
Ben More
Ben Vorlich
Seil
Luing
Arduaine
Toberonochy
Scarba
Inveraray
Tarbet
The Trossachs
Callander
Ben Lomond
Queen Elizabeth Forest Park
Aberfoyle
Furnace
Crinan
Kilmartin
Scalasaig
JURA
Ardlussa
Sound of Jura
Lochgilphead
Ardrishaig
Knapdale
Otter Ferry
Ardentinny
Helensburgh
Drymen
Stirling
Rubha a' Mhail
Beinn an Oir
Port Askaig
Feolin Ferry
Craighouse
Tarbert
Tighnabruaich
Colintraive
Kilcreggan
Dunoon
Gourock
Port Glasgow
Alexandria
Dumbarton
Erskine Bridge
Kirkintilloch
Kilsyth
Bridgend
Beinn Bheigeir
Kennacraig
Portavadie
Rothesay
Innellan
Greenock
Wemyss Bay
Clydebank
Claonaig
Bute
Largs
Johnstone
Paisley
Barrhead
GLASGOW
Gigha I.
Ardbeg
Port Ellen
Lochranza
Millport
Kilbirnie
Beith
Dalry
East Kilbride
Hamilton
Tayinloan
Kintyre
Goat Fell
ARRAN
W. Kilbride
Stewarton
Ardrossan
Saltcoats
Kilwinning
Strathaven
Carradale
Kilbrannan Sound
Brodick
Irvine
Kilmarnock
Lamlash
Troon
Galston
Blackwaterfoot
Prestwick
Mauchline
Machrihanish
Campbeltown
Ayr
Muirkirk
Firth of Clyde
Cumnock
New Cumnock
Southend
Mull of Kintyre
Ailsa Craig
Turnberry
Maybole
Dalmellington
Girvan
AYR
Galloway
DUMFRIES
Cushendun
Red Bay
Glenariff or Waterfoot
Ballantrae
Merrick Forest Park
Antrim Coast
Carnlough
Barrhill
New Galloway
Glenarm
NORTH CHANNEL
Kirkcolm
Cairnryan
Newton Stewart
Larne
Island Magee
Stranraer
Glenluce
Castle Douglas
Gatehouse of Fleet
Ringford
Wigtown
Portpatrick
Kirkcudbright
Carrickfergus
Whitehead
Belfast Lough
Luce Bay
Wigtown Bay
Newtownabbey
Bangor
Port William
Holywood
Donaghadee
Whithorn
Drummore
Isle of Whithorn
Newtownards
Burrow Head
Mull of Galloway
Comber
Greyabbey
Saintfield
Portavogie
Killyleagh
Portaferry
Strangford
DOWN
Downpatrick
Point of Ayre
Ardglass
St John's Point
Dundrum Bay
Newcastle
Ballaugh
Ramsey
Snaefell
Peel
ISLE OF MAN
Douglas

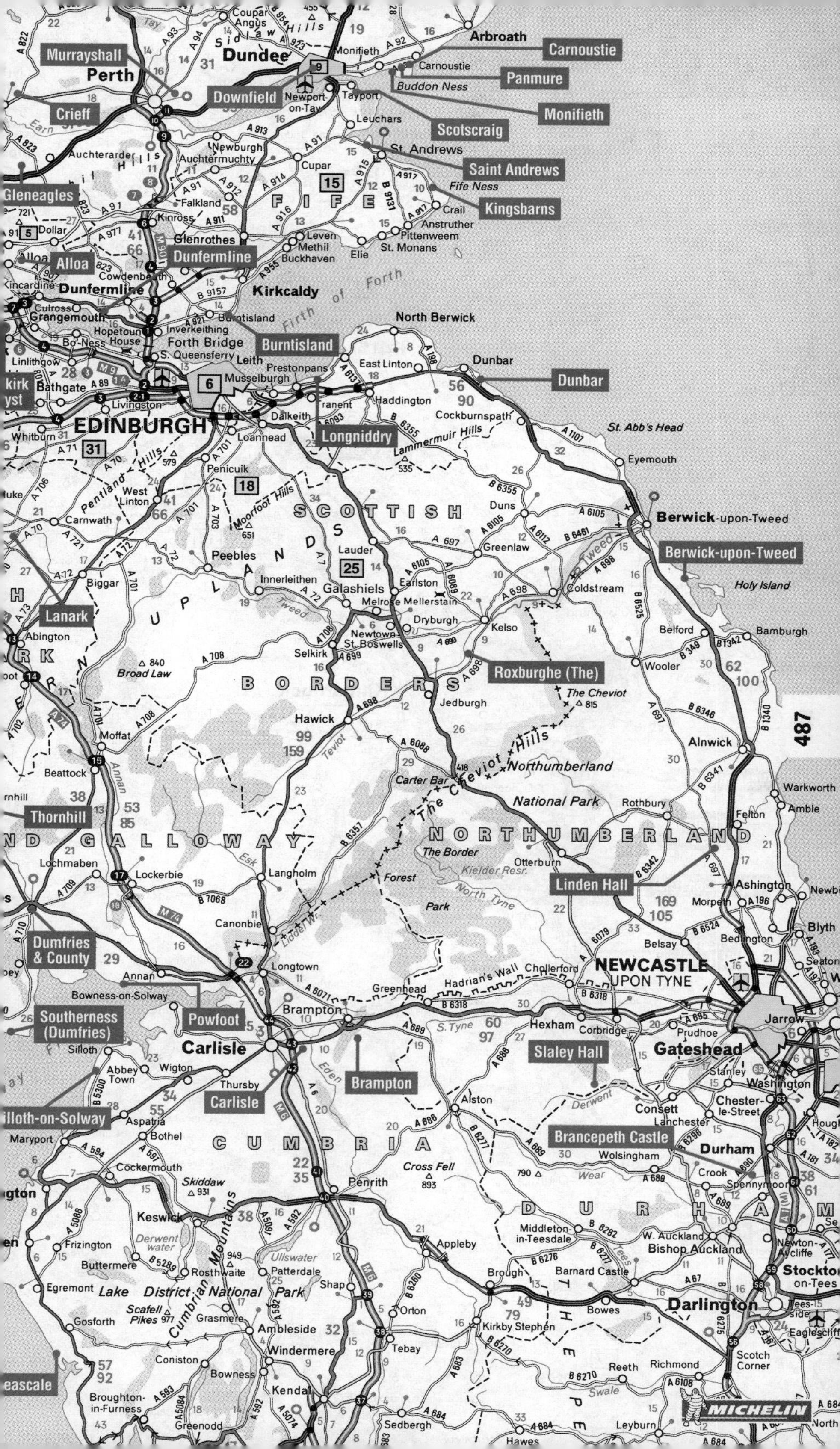

Murrayshall
Carnoustie
Panmure
Monifieth
Downfield
Crieff
Scotscraig
Saint Andrews
Gleneagles
Kingsbarns
Alloa
Dunfermline
Burntisland
Dunbar
Longniddry
Berwick-upon-Tweed
Lanark
Roxburghe (The)
Thornhill
Linden Hall
Dumfries & County
Southerness (Dumfries)
Powfoot
Slaley Hall
Brampton
Carlisle
Silloth-on-Solway
Brancepeth Castle
Seascale
Perth
Dundee
Arbroath
Tayport
Newport-on-Tay
Leuchars
St. Andrews
Cupar
Fife Ness
Crail
Anstruther
Pittenweem
St. Monans
Elie
Leven
Methil
Buckhaven
Glenrothes
Kinross
Falkland
Auchtermuchty
Newburgh
Auchterarder
Dollar
Kirkcaldy
Firth of Forth
North Berwick
East Linton
Haddington
Cockburnspath
St. Abb's Head
Eyemouth
Berwick-upon-Tweed
Holy Island
Bamburgh
Belford
Wooler
Alnwick
Warkworth
Amble
Felton
Rothbury
Morpeth
Ashington
Blyth
Bedlington
Belsay
NEWCASTLE UPON TYNE
Jarrow
Gateshead
Washington
Chester-le-Street
Durham
Spennymoor
Bishop Auckland
W. Auckland
Newton-Aycliffe
Stockton-on-Tees
Darlington
Scotch Corner
Richmond
Leyburn
Hawes
Reeth
Barnard Castle
Bowes
Middleton-in-Teesdale
Wolsingham
Crook
Consett
Lanchester
Stanley
Prudhoe
Corbridge
Hexham
Chollerford
Hadrian's Wall
Greenhead
Otterburn
Kielder Resr.
The Border Forest Park
Northumberland National Park
N O R T H U M B E R L A N D
Cheviot Hills
The Cheviot
Carter Bar
Jedburgh
Kelso
Coldstream
Greenlaw
Duns
Lammermuir Hills
Dalkeith
Musselburgh
Prestonpans
Tranent
Leith
EDINBURGH
Livingston
Bathgate
Linlithgow
Bo'Ness
Grangemouth
Kincardine
Culross
Forth Bridge
S. Queensferry
Inverkeithing
Hopetoun House
Cowdenbeath
Whitburn
Loanhead
Penicuik
Pentland Hills
West Linton
Carnwath
Moorfoot Hills
S C O T T I S H U P L A N D S
Peebles
Innerleithen
Lauder
Earlston
Mellerstain
Galashiels
Melrose
Dryburgh
Newtown St. Boswells
Selkirk
B O R D E R S
Hawick
Broad Law
Biggar
Abington
Moffat
Beattock
Lockerbie
Lochmaben
D G A L L O W A Y
Langholm
Canonbie
Longtown
Annan
Bowness-on-Solway
Brampton
Carlisle
Silloth
Abbey Town
Wigton
Thursby
Aspatria
Maryport
Bothel
Cockermouth
C U M B R I A
Skiddaw
Keswick
Cumbrian Mountains
Derwent water
Buttermere
Rosthwaite
Frizington
Egremont
Lake District National Park
Scafell Pikes
Gosforth
Grasmere
Ambleside
Coniston
Windermere
Bowness
Broughton-in-Furness
Greenodd
Kendal
Sedbergh
Tebay
Orton
Shap
Patterdale
Ullswater
Penrith
Cross Fell
Appleby
Alston
Brough
Kirkby Stephen
D U R H A M
487
MICHELIN

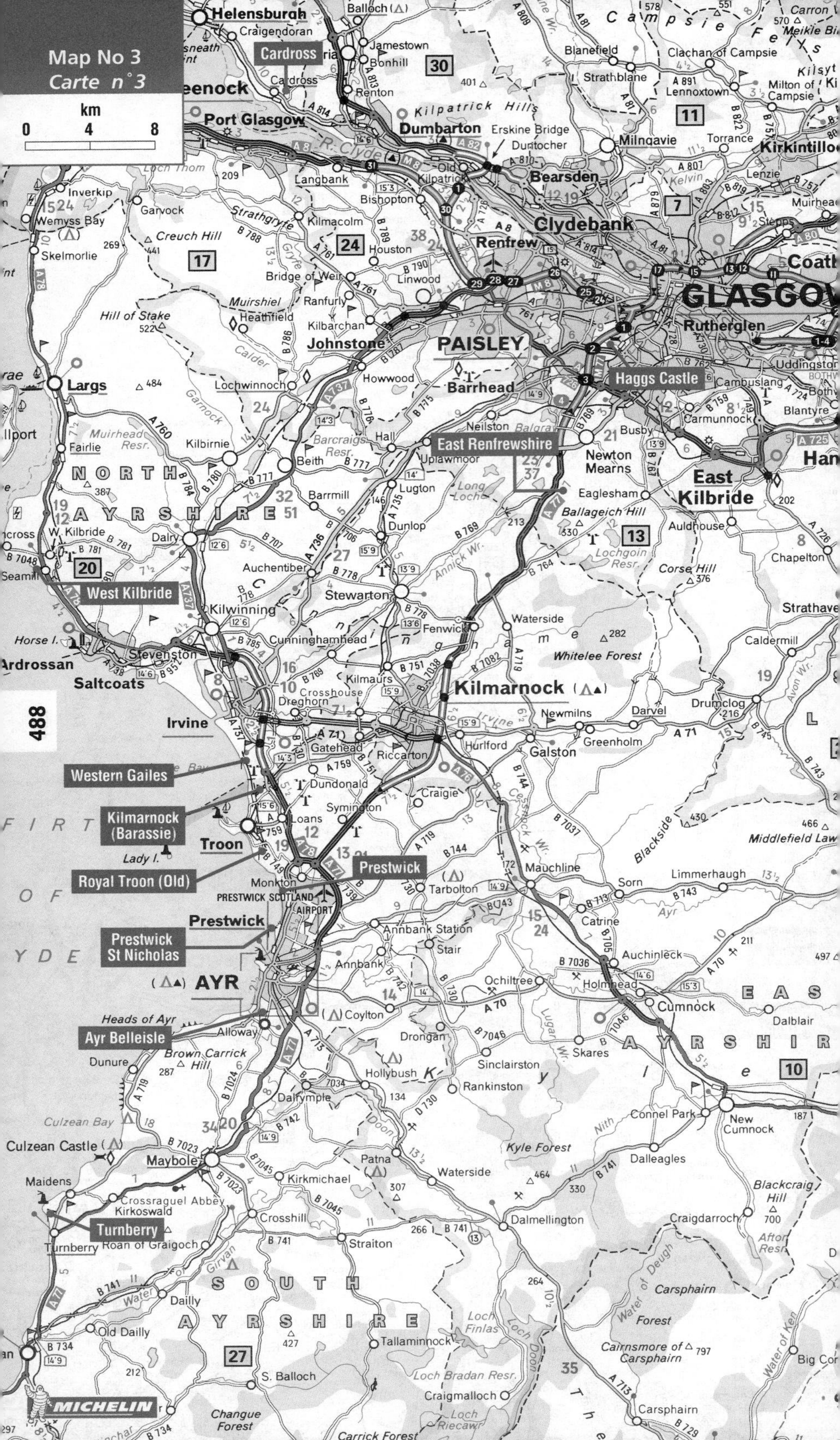

Map No 3
Carte n°3
km
0 4 8
Cardross
Haggs Castle
East Renfrewshire
West Kilbride
Western Gailes
Kilmarnock (Barassie)
Royal Troon (Old)
Prestwick
Prestwick St Nicholas
Ayr Belleisle
Turnberry
Helensburgh
Craigendoran
Balloch
Jamestown
Bonhill
Renton
Dumbarton
Kilpatrick Hills
Port Glasgow
Greenock
Langbank
Bishopton
Erskine Bridge
Duntocher
Old Kilpatrick
Bearsden
Clydebank
Renfrew
Milngavie
Blanefield
Strathblane
Clachan of Campsie
Lennoxtown
Milton of Campsie
Campsie Fells
Torrance
Kirkintilloch
Lenzie
Muirhead
Stepps
GLASGOW
Rutherglen
Cambuslang
Uddingston
Blantyre
Carmunnock
Busby
Newton Mearns
Eaglesham
East Kilbride
Auldhouse
Chapelton
Strathaven
Ballageich Hill
Lochgoin Resr.
Corse Hill
Inverkip
Wemyss Bay
Skelmorlie
Garvock
Creuch Hill
Kilmacolm
Houston
Bridge of Weir
Linwood
Ranfurly
Kilbarchan
Johnstone
PAISLEY
Barrhead
Neilston
Uplawmoor
Howwood
Lochwinnoch
Muirshiel
Heathfield
Hill of Stake
Largs
Fairlie
Muirhead Resr.
Kilbirnie
Beith
Barcraigs Resr.
Hall
Lugton
Long Loch
Dunlop
Barrmill
NORTH AYRSHIRE
Dalry
W. Kilbride
Seamill
Auchentiber
Stewarton
Fenwick
Waterside
Whitelee Forest
Kilwinning
Cunninghamhead
Stevenston
Ardrossan
Saltcoats
Horse I.
Kilmaurs
Crosshouse
Dreghorn
Irvine
Kilmarnock
Newmilns
Darvel
Drumclog
Caldermill
Hurlford
Galston
Greenholm
Gatehead
Riccarton
Dundonald
Craigie
Loans
Symington
Troon
Lady I.
FIRTH OF CLYDE
Monkton
PRESTWICK SCOTLAND AIRPORT
Tarbolton
Mauchline
Sorn
Limmerhaugh
Middlefield Law
Blackside
Catrine
Annbank Station
Stair
Annbank
AYR
Auchinleck
Holmhead
Cumnock
Ochiltree
Heads of Ayr
Alloway
Coylton
Drongan
Dalblair
EAST AYRSHIRE
Brown Carrick Hill
Dunure
Hollybush
Sinclairston
Skares
Rankinston
Dalrymple
New Cumnock
Connel Park
Culzean Bay
Culzean Castle
Maybole
Kirkmichael
Patna
Waterside
Kyle Forest
Dalleagles
Blackcraig Hill
Maidens
Crossraguel Abbey
Kirkoswald
Crosshill
Straiton
Dalmellington
Craigdarroch
Afton Resr.
Turnberry
Roan of Graigoch
SOUTH AYRSHIRE
Dailly
Old Dailly
Tallaminnock
Loch Finlas
Loch Doon
Carsphairn Forest
Cairnsmore of Carsphairn
Loch Bradan Resr.
Craigmalloch
Loch Riecawr
S. Balloch
Changue Forest
Carrick Forest
Carsphairn
Big Cor
MICHELIN

Saint Andrews
St. Andrews
Kingsbarns
Crail
St Andrews Duke's
Ladybank
Lundin
Leven Links
Elie
North Berwick
Muirfield
Gullane
Glen
Luffness New
Whitekirk
Duddingston
Bruntsfield
Longniddry
Royal Burgess
Royal Musselburgh
Baberton
Dalmahoy
Lothianburn
EDINBURGH
FIRTH OF FORTH
Leuchars
Eden Mouth
St. Andrews Bay
Guardbridge
Balmullo
Kilmany
Luthrie
Newburgh
Elcho
Glencarse
Earn
R. Tay
Abernethy
Lindores
Dairsie
Strathkinness
Cath
Boarhills
Kingsbarns
Craighead
Crail
Cupar
Craigtoun
Pitscottie
Hill of Tarvit
Springfield
Ceres
Craigrothie
Scotstarvit Tower
Peat Inn
Dunino
Letham
Pitmedden Forest
Auchtermuchty
Howe of Fife
Ladybank
Kingskettle
Gateside
Strathmiglo
Falkland
Freuchie
Lomond Hills
Backmuir of New Gilston
Largoward
Kellie Castle
Arncroach
Kilconquhar
Pittenweem
Anstruther
Kilrenny
Kirkton of Largo
Lower Largo
Lundin Links
Largo Bay
Elie
Earlsferry
St. Monans
The East Neuk
Milnathort
Kinnesswood
Glenrothes
Markinch
Kennoway
Leven
Windygates
Methil
Buckhaven
E. Wemyss
Scotlandwell
Leslie
Ballingry
Benarty Hill
Kinglassie
Thornton
Lochore
Auchterderran
Crosshill
Cardenden
Kelty
Lochgelly
Cowdenbeath
Kirkcaldy
Auchtertool
Crossgates
Kinghorn
Burntisland
Aberdour
Inchcolm
Oxcars
Inchkeith
Inverkeithing
N. Queensferry
Queensferry
Cramond Island
Dalmeny
Cramond
Kirkliston
Ingliston
Murrayfield
Sighthill
Leith
Restalrig
Portobello
Musselburgh
Prestonpans
Cockenzie and Port Seton
Seton
Tranent
Wallyford
Ormiston
Fidra
Craigleith
Bass Rock
Tantallon Ca
Dirleton
Gullane
Kingston
Aberlady Bay
Aberlady
Drem
Whitekirk
Tyninghame
John Muir
Athelstaneford
Museum of Flight
Longniddry
East
Hailes Cas
Haddington
Traprain Law
Stenton
Garvald
Dunbar Comm
Clints
Gifford
Pencaitland
East Saltoun
Currie
Balerno
Lasswade
Loanhead
Bonnyrigg
Dalkeith
Newtongrange
Roslin
Scottish Mining Museum
Vogrie
Threipmuir Resr.
Rosewell
Gorebridge
Crichton
Pathhead
Humbie
Fala
Lammer Law
Meikle Says Law
Lammermuir
MIDLOTHIAN
Penicuik
Temple
Tynehead
Howgate
Soutra Hill
Leadburn
Carlops
Gilston
Gladhouse Resr.
Moorfoot Hills
Heriot
Oxton
Carfraemill
W. Linton
Lauderdale
The Southern Upland Way
Westruther
Fountainhall
Torquhan
Lauder
Thirlestane
Romannobridge
Eddleston
Stow
Legerwood
Greenknowe Tower
Blyth Bridge
Lyne Wr.
Lyne
Neidpath Castle
Peebles
Glentress
Gala Wr.
Bowland
Langshaw
Earlston
Stobo
Kirkton Manor
Walkerburn
Clovenfords
Galashiels
Smailholm
Cardrona Forest
Innerleithen
Tweed Valley
Elibank and Traquair Forest
Traquair House
Caddonfoot
Abbotsford House
Melrose
Smailholm Tower
Drumelzier
Yair Hill Forest
Dun Rig
Newtown St. Bo
Bowden
Abbey
Newark
SOUTHERN UPLANDS
MICHELIN
489

Map No 4
Carte n° 4
km
0 10 20
Brampton
Carlisle
Slaley Hall
Brancepeth Castle
Seascale
Lytham Green Drive
Fairhaven
Royal Lytham & St Anne's
Pleasington
Clitheroe
Bolton Old Links
Huddersfield (Fixby)
Rudding Park
Sand Moor
Ilkley
Moortown
Alwoodley
Manchester
Royal Liverpool
Caldy
Mere
Wilmslow
Hallamshire
Lindrick
Chesterfield
Coxmoor
Prestbury
Northop Country Park
Carden Park
Hawkstone Park
Notts (Hollinwell)
NEWCASTLE UPON TYNE
Gateshead
Durham
Darlington
CUMBRIA
DURHAM
Penrith
Keswick
Lake District National Park
Cumbrian Mountains
Kendal
Barrow-in-Furness
Morecambe
Lancaster
Yorkshire Dales National Park
NORTH YORKSHIRE
Harrogate
Ripon
LANCASHIRE
BLACKPOOL
Preston
Blackburn
Burnley
BRADFORD
LEEDS
Halifax
Huddersfield
Wakefield
Southport
LIVERPOOL
Birkenhead
Wigan
Bolton
Bury
Rochdale
Oldham
MANCHESTER
Stockport
Warrington
St. Helens
Peak District National Park
SHEFFIELD
Chester
CHESHIRE
Macclesfield
Crewe
Wrexham / Wrecsam
Newcastle-under-Lyme
STOKE-ON-TRENT
DERBY
Derby
Shrewsbury
WREKIN
Stafford
MICHELIN

outh
Shields
DERLAND

Map No 5
Carte n° 5
km
0
10
20
Point of Ayre
Ramsey
Belfast
Douglas
Port Erin
Port St. Mary
Ronaldsway
Castletown
Dublin
St. Bees Head
Egremont
Lake District National Park
Cumbrian
Scafell Pikes 977
Grasmere
Ambleside
Windermere
Gosforth
Seascale
Coniston
Bowness
Kendal
Broughton-in-Furness
Greenodd
Millom
Ulverston
Dalton
Grange-Over-Sands
Carnforth
Barrow-in-Furness
Morecambe
Belfast
Morecambe Bay
Heysham
Fleetwood
Cleveleys
Lytham Green Drive
LANCA
BLACKPOOL
Kirkham
Fairhaven
Lytham St. Anne's
Preston
Royal Lytham & St Anne's
Southport
Leylan
Belfast
Dublin
Ainsdale
Ormskirk
Formby
Skelmersdale
LIVERPOOL
Bootle
St. Helens
Liverpool Bay
Wallasey
Hoylake
Warrington
Birkenhead
Bebington
Widnes
Runcorn
Frodsham
S H S E A
Holyhead
Holyhead / Caergybi
Amlwch
Llanerchymedd
ANGLESEY
Rhosneigr
of Anglesey
Llangefni
Beaumaris
North Wales (Llandudno)
Llandudno (Maesdu)
Great Ormes Head
Llandudno
Royal Liverpool
Colwyn Bay / Bae Colwyn
Rhyl
Prestatyn
Conwy
Penmaenmawr
Bangor
Llanfairfechan
Abergele
Caldy
Holywell
Ellesmere Port
Menai Bridge
Newborough
Bethesda
Conwy
St. Asaph
Flint / Fflint
Queensferry
Carnedd Llewelyn
Denbigh / Dinbych
Mold / Yr Wyddgrug
Caernarfon
Llanberis
Capel Curig
Llanrwst
Chester
Caernarfon Bay
Snowdon
Snowdonia
Betws-y-Coed
Ruthin / Rhuthun
Carden Park
Nefyn & Districk
Pentrefoelas
Northop Country Park
Beddgelert
Blaenau Ffestiniog
Nefyn
Peninsula
Porthmadog
Ffestiniog
Cerrigydrudion
Wrexham / Wrecsam
Ruabon
Criccieth
Penrhyndeudraeth
Corwen
Llangollen
Whitchurch
Pwllheli
Lleyn
Abersoch
Harlech
GWYNEDD
Bala
Ellesmere
berdaron
Royal St David's
and
National
Berwyn
Oswestry
Wem
Hawkstone Park
Llynclys
Barmouth
Dolgellau
Llanfyllin
Cader Idris
Park
Mallwyd
MOUNTAINS
Llanymynech
Shrewsbury
Telford
Tywyn
Aberdovey
Aberdovey
Machynlleth
Welshpool / Y Trallwng
Minsterley
SHROPSHI
Montgomery
Church Stretton
Much Wenlock
Caersws
Cardigan Bay
Aberystwyth
Llanidloes
Newtown / Drenewydd
Bishop's Castle
Severn
Devil's Bridge
Llangurig
Clun
Craven Arms
CAMBRIAN
Llanrhystud
POWYS
Knighton
Ludlow
Aberaeron
CEREDIGION
Rhayader / Rhaeadr
Presteigne
Tregaron
Llandrindod Wells
Kington
Leominster
MICHELIN
Synod Inn
berporth

1 / 400 000
BLACKPOOL
Royal Lytham & St Anne's
Lytham St. Anne's
Fairhaven
Lytham Green Drive
PRESTON
Pleasington
BLACKBURN
SOUTHPORT
Royal Birkdale
Hillside
Southport & Ainsdale
Formby Hall
Formby
Ormskirk
West Lancashire
Chorley
Leyland
WIGAN
Skelmersdale
Kirkby
Crosby
Bootle
ST. HELENS
LIVERPOOL
Wallasey
Royal Liverpool
BIRKENHEAD
Caldy
WARRINGTON
Widnes
Runcorn
Bebington
Ellesmere Port
Delamere Forest
Northop Country Park
CHESTER
Sandiway
Portal
Carden Park
Wrexham / Wrecsam
Flint / Fflint
Mold
Winsford
Nantwich
LIVERPOOL AIRPORT
493
MICHELIN

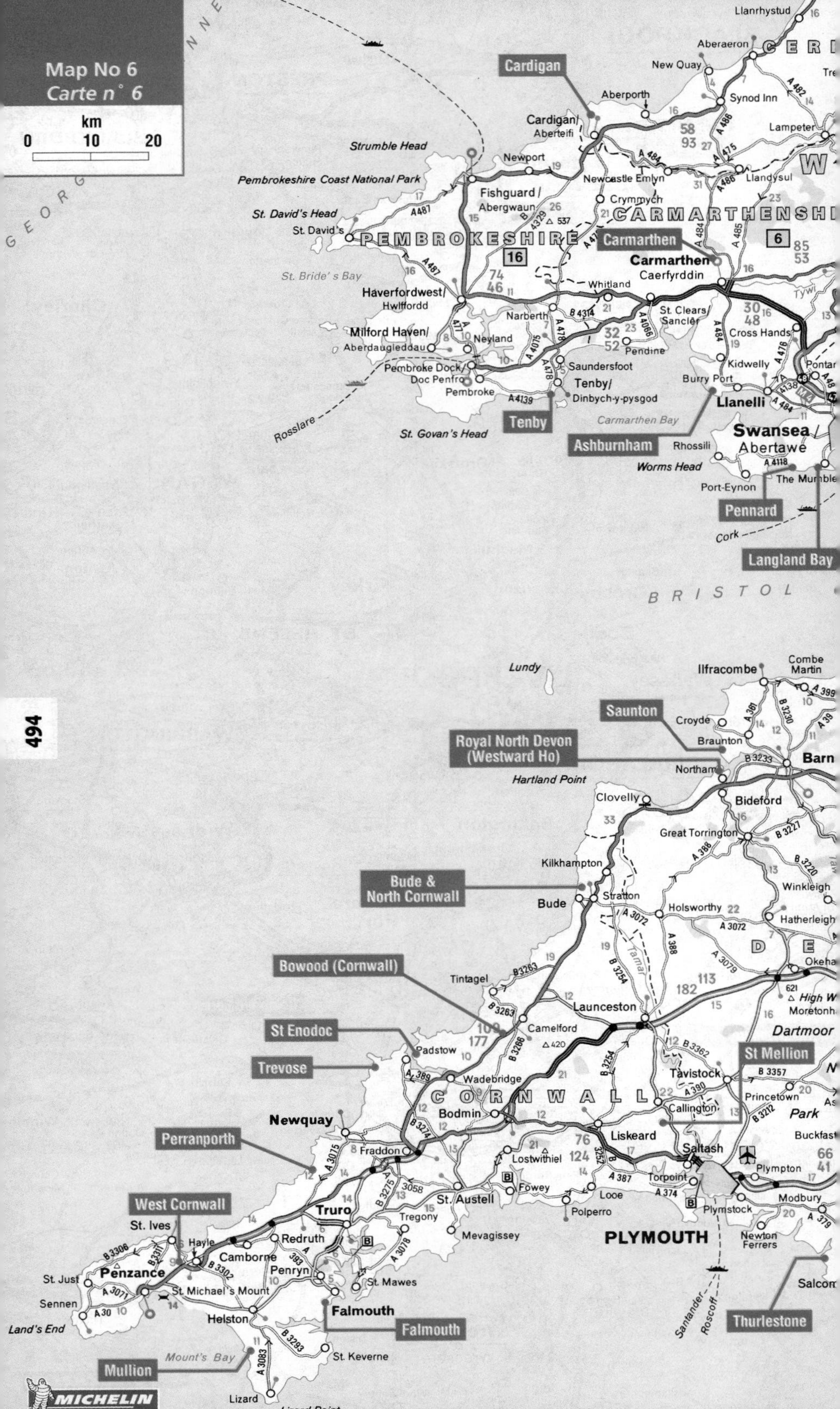

Map No 6
Carte n° 6
km
0
10
20
Cardigan
Carmarthen
Tenby
Ashburnham
Pennard
Langland Bay
Saunton
Royal North Devon (Westward Ho)
Bude & North Cornwall
Bowood (Cornwall)
St Enodoc
Trevose
Perranporth
West Cornwall
Mullion
Falmouth
St Mellion
Thurlestone
PEMBROKESHIRE
CARMARTHENSHI
CORNWALL
Strumble Head
Pembrokeshire Coast National Park
St. David's Head
St. David's
St. Bride's Bay
Haverfordwest/ Hwlffordd
Milford Haven/ Aberdaugleddau
Pembroke Dock/ Doc Penfro
Pembroke
St. Govan's Head
Rosslare
Fishguard / Abergwaun
Newport
Cardigan/ Aberteifi
Aberporth
New Quay
Aberaeron
Llanrhystud
Synod Inn
Lampeter
Newcastle Emlyn
Llandysul
Crymmych
Carmarthen
Caerfyrddin
Whitland
Narberth
Neyland
St. Clears/ Sanclêr
Pendine
Saundersfoot
Tenby/ Dinbych-y-pysgod
Carmarthen Bay
Kidwelly
Cross Hands
Burry Port
Llanelli
Swansea / Abertawe
Rhossili
Worms Head
Port-Eynon
The Mumbles
Cork
BRISTOL
Lundy
Ilfracombe
Combe Martin
Croyde
Braunton
Northam
Hartland Point
Clovelly
Bideford
Great Torrington
Kilkhampton
Stratton
Bude
Holsworthy
Winkleigh
Hatherleigh
Tintagel
Launceston
Camelford
Padstow
Wadebridge
Bodmin
Newquay
Fraddon
Tavistock
Callington
Princetown
Dartmoor
Park
Liskeard
Lostwithiel
Fowey
Looe
Polperro
Torpoint
Saltash
Plympton
Plymstock
PLYMOUTH
Modbury
Newton Ferrers
Salcombe
Santander
Roscoff
St. Austell
Mevagissey
Tregony
Truro
Redruth
Camborne
Penryn
St. Mawes
Falmouth
Hayle
St. Ives
Penzance
St. Just
Sennen
Land's End
St. Michael's Mount
Helston
Mount's Bay
St. Keverne
Lizard
Lizard Point
MICHELIN

494

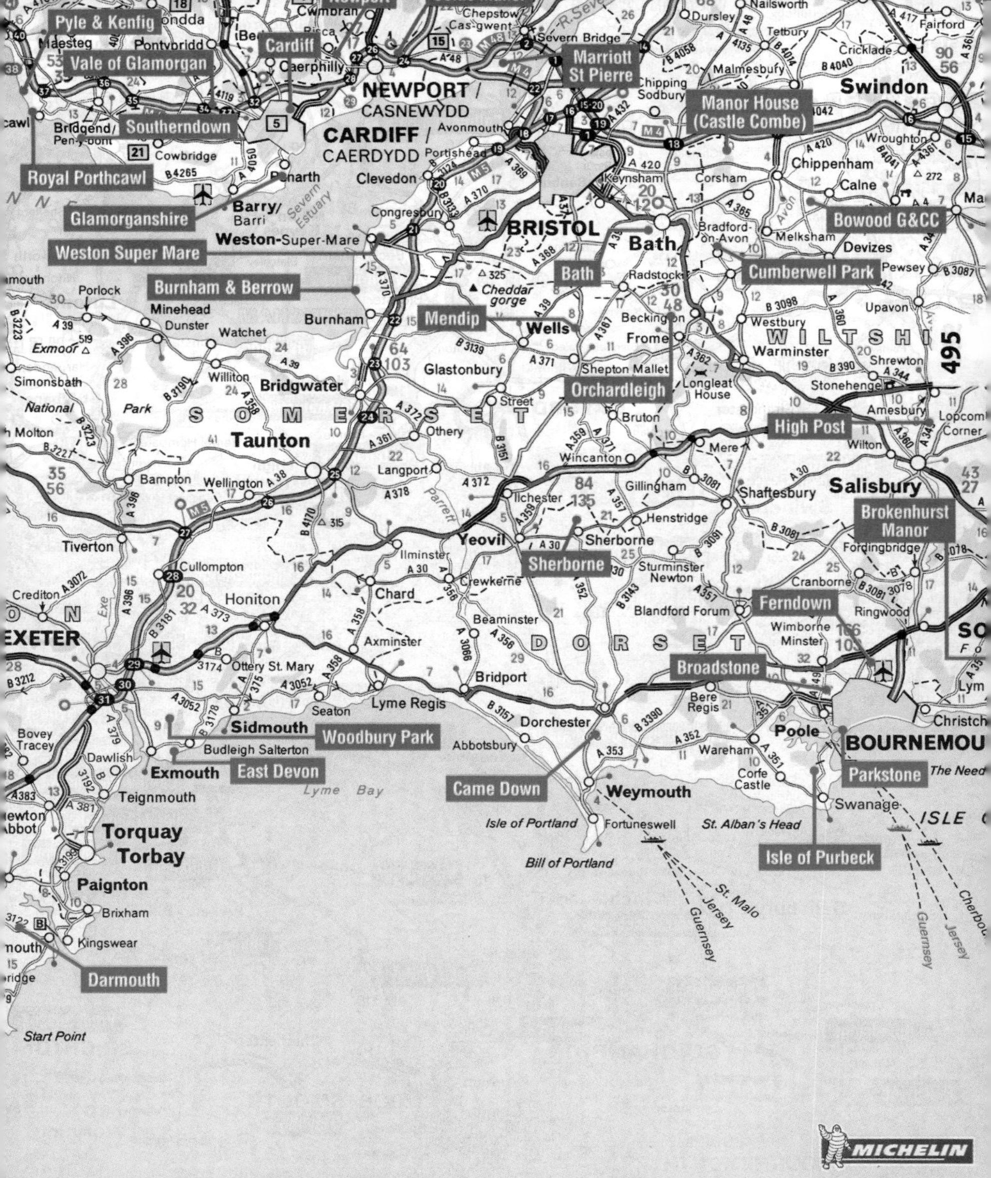
Pyle & Kenfig
Vale of Glamorgan
Cardiff
Marriott St Pierre
Southerndown
Royal Porthcawl
Glamorganshire
Weston Super Mare
Burnham & Berrow
Manor House (Castle Combe)
Bowood G&CC
Bath
Cumberwell Park
Mendip
Orchardleigh
High Post
Brokenhurst Manor
Sherborne
Ferndown
Broadstone
Woodbury Park
East Devon
Came Down
Parkstone
Isle of Purbeck
Darmouth
NEWPORT / CASNEWYDD
CARDIFF / CAERDYDD
BRISTOL
Bath
Swindon
Chippenham
Salisbury
Taunton
Yeovil
EXETER
Torquay Torbay
Paignton
BOURNEMOU
Poole
Weymouth
Dorchester
Sidmouth
Exmouth
Bridgwater
Glastonbury
Wells
Frome
Warminster
Stonehenge
Lyme Bay
Isle of Portland
Bill of Portland
St. Alban's Head
Start Point
S O M E R S E T
D O R S E T
W I L T S H I
495
MICHELIN

Rolls of Monmouth
Ross-on-Wye
Manor House (Castle Combe)
Frilford Heath
Henley
Porters Park
West Berkshire
Badgemore Park
Bowood G&CC
Swinley Forest
Royal Wimbledon
Berkshire (The)
West Byfleet
Cumberwell Park
Newbury and Crookham
North Hants
Camberley Heath
Hankley Common
High Post
West Surrey
Blackmoor
Hindhead
Royal Winchester
Mannings Heath
Liphook
Meon Valley
Brokenhurst Manor
West Sussex
Broadstone
Stoneham
Parkstone
Ferndown
Hayling
Cheltenham
Gloucester
Hereford
Worcester
Swindon
Reading
Newbury
Basingstoke
Salisbury
Winchester
SOUTHAMPTON
PORTSMOUTH
BOURNEMOUTH
BRIGHTON
Worthing
WILTSHIRE
HAMPSHIRE
SURREY
W. SUSSEX
MICHELIN

Boston
Hunstanton
Wells-next-the-Sea
Blakeney
Sheringham
Cromer
Royal Cromer
Royal West Norfolk
(Brancaster)
Hunstanton
Sheringham
The Wash
Holt
Mundesley
Sutterton
Holbeach
Long Sutton
Sandringham
House
Fakenham
Guist
North Walsham
Aylsham
Low Street
Spalding
King's Lynn
NORFOLK
East Dereham
Wisbech
Outwell
Swaffham
Stradsett
Downham Market
Guyhirn
Peterborough
Watton
Wymondham
NORWICH
Acle
Bure
Great
Yarmouth
Gorleston-on-Sea
Yare
March
Whittlesey
Mundford
Attleborough
Thetford
Brandon
Chatteris
Littleport
Lowestoft
Bungay
Beccles
Harleston
Waveney
Ely
Diss
Scole
Earith
St. Ives
Soham
Gt. Ouse
Halesworth
Southwold
Ixworth
Dennington
Yoxford
Bury St. Edmunds
Newmarket
Leiston
Saxmundham
Stowmarket
Cambridge
Gog Magog
Thorpeness
Aldeburgh
Aldeburgh
SUFFOLK
Lavenham
Haverhill
Woodbridge
Woodbridge
IPSWICH
Royston
Saffron
Walden
Clare
Sudbury
Hadleigh
Ipswich
Stour
Finchingfield
Buntingford
Felixstowe Ferry
Halstead
Felixstowe
Stansted
Puckeridge
Great
Dunmow
Braintree
Harwich
Esbjerg
Göteborg
Hoek van H
Hamburg
The Naze
Bishop's
Stortford
Colchester
Walton-on-the-Naze
ESSEX
Ware
Sawbridgeworth
Witham
Frinton-on-Sea
Brightlingsea
Harlow
W. Mersea
Clacton-on-Sea
Hoddesdon
Chelmsford
Epping
Hertfordshire (The)
Maldon
Bradwell-on-Sea
Billericay
Brentwood
Burnham-on-Crouch
Wickford
Foulness Point
Rayleigh
Basildon
Dagenham
Benfleet
Southend-on-Sea
Grays
Thurrock
Thorndon Park
Canvey Island
Dartford
Tilbury
Thames
Grain
Sheerness
Gravesend
Queenborough
Isle of Sheppey
Rochester
Leysdown-on-Sea
North Foreland
Orpington
Swanley
Gillingham
Birchington
Margate
Whitstable
Herne Bay
North Foreland
Chatham
Broadstairs
London Club
Sittingbourne
Faversham
Ramsgate
Canterbury
Prince's
Sandwich
Knole
Sevenoaks
Maidstone
Deal
Royal St George's
Hever
Tonbridge
Downs
Southborough
KENT
Chart Hills
Ashford
Royal Cinque Ports
South Foreland
Royal
Tunbridge Wells
Biddenden
Terminal
Dover
Oostende
Crowborough
Tenterden
Hythe
Folkestone
Tunnel sous la Manche
Channel Tunnel
Royal Ashdown Forest
Hawkhurst
Rye
Haywards Heath
Heathfield
Uckfield
New Romney
Calais
E. SUSSEX
Rye
Lydd
East Sussex
National
Battle
Winchelsea
Dungeness
Cap Blanc Nez
Wissant
Terminal
Guînes
Lewes
Polegate
Bexhill
Hastings
Littlestone
Cap Gris Nez
Ardres
Marquise
Wimereux (F)
Wimereux
Seaford
Eastbourne
Beachy Head
Boulogne
CALAIS

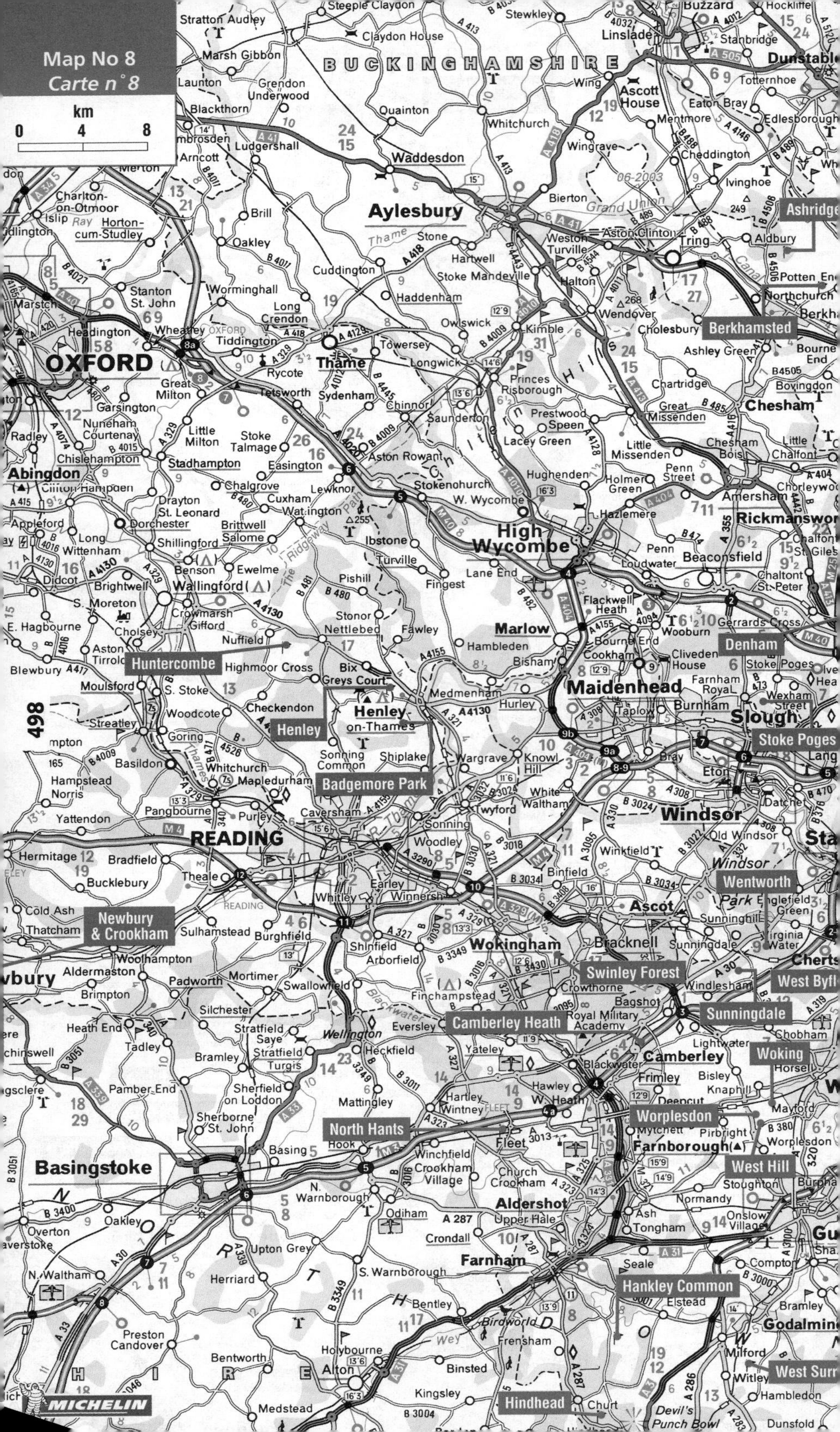

Map No 8
Carte n° 8
km
0 4 8
498
BUCKINGHAMSHIRE
Steeple Claydon
Stratton Audley
Claydon House
Stewkley
Buzzard
Linslade
Hockliffe
Stanbridge
Dunstable
Marsh Gibbon
Launton
Grendon Underwood
Wing
Ascott House
Totternhoe
Eaton Bray
Edlesborough
Blackthorn
Quainton
Whitchurch
Mentmore
Cheddington
Ambrosden
Arncott
Ludgershall
Waddesdon
Wingrave
Ivinghoe
Merton
Charlton-on-Otmoor
Islip
Horton-cum-Studley
Brill
Bierton
Aylesbury
Grand Union
Ashridge
Oakley
Stone
Hartwell
Aston Clinton
Weston Turville
Tring
Aldbury
Stoke Mandeville
Halton
Potten End
Northchurch
Stanton St. John
Worminghall
Cuddington
Haddenham
Long Crendon
Owlswick
Kimble
Wendover
Cholesbury
Berkhamsted
Headington
Wheatley
OXFORD
Tiddington
Thame
Towersey
Longwick
Rycote
Ashley Green
Bourne End
Great Milton
Tetsworth
Sydenham
Princes Risborough
Chartridge
Bovingdon
Garsington
Chinnor
Saunderton
Great Missenden
Chesham
Nuneham Courtenay
Little Milton
Stoke Talmage
Prestwood
Speen
Lacey Green
Little Missenden
Chesham Bois
Chalfont
Radley
Chislehampton
Stadhampton
Easington
Aston Rowant
Abingdon
Clifton Hampden
Chalgrove
Lewknor
Stokenchurch
W. Wycombe
Hughenden
Holmer Green
Penn Street
Chorleywood
Amersham
Drayton St. Leonard
Cuxham
Watlington
Hazlemere
Rickmansworth
Appleford
Dorchester
Brittwell Salome
Ibstone
High Wycombe
Penn
Beaconsfield
Long Wittenham
Shillingford
The Ridgeway Path
Turville
Loudwater
Chalfont St. Giles
Didcot
Benson
Ewelme
Fingest
Lane End
Chalfont St. Peter
Brightwell
Wallingford
Pishill
S. Moreton
Crowmarsh Gifford
Stonor
Fawley
Flackwell Heath
E. Hagbourne
Cholsey
Nettlebed
Marlow
Bourne End
Wooburn
Gerrards Cross
Aston Tirrold
Nuffield
Hambleden
Cookham
Cliveden House
Denham
Blewbury
Huntercombe
Highmoor Cross
Bix
Bisham
Stoke Poges
Moulsford
Greys Court
Maidenhead
Farnham Royal
S. Stoke
Medmenham
Hurley
Wexham Street
Checkendon
Henley-on-Thames
Taplow
Burnham
Slough
Woodcote
Streatley
Henley
Goring
Stoke Poges
Basildon
Whitchurch
Sonning Common
Shiplake
Wargrave
Knowl Hill
Bray
Eton
Hampstead Norris
Mapledurham
Badgemore Park
Datchet
White Waltham
Pangbourne
Purley
Caversham
Twyford
Windsor
Yattendon
READING
Sonning
Woodley
Old Windsor
Hermitage
Bradfield
Winkfield
Binfield
Bucklebury
Theale
Earley
Whitley
Winnersh
Wentworth
Cold Ash
Newbury & Crookham
Ascot
Englefield Green
Thatcham
Sulhamstead
Burghfield
Shinfield
Arborfield
Wokingham
Bracknell
Sunninghill
Sunningdale
Virginia Water
Woolhampton
Swinley Forest
Aldermaston
Padworth
Mortimer
Swallowfield
Finchampstead
Crowthorne
Windlesham
West Byfleet
Brimpton
Blackwater
Bagshot
Sunningdale
Silchester
Eversley
Camberley Heath
Royal Military Academy
Heath End
Stratfield Saye
Wellington
Heckfield
Yateley
Lightwater
Chobham
Woking
Tadley
Bramley
Stratfield Turgis
Blackwater
Camberley
Frimley
Bisley
Horsell
Kingsclere
Pamber End
Sherfield on Loddon
Hartley Wintney
Hawley
W. Heath
Knaphill
Mattingley
Worplesdon
Mytchett
Pirbright
Mayford
Sherborne St. John
North Hants
Hook
Fleet
Farnborough
Basing
Winchfield
Crookham Village
Church Crookham
West Hill
Basingstoke
Stoughton
N. Warnborough
Odiham
Aldershot
Normandy
Oakley
Upper Hale
Ash
Tongham
Onslow Village
Overton
Laverstoke
Crondall
Upton Grey
Farnham
Seale
Compton
N. Waltham
Herriard
S. Warnborough
Hankley Common
Elstead
Bentley
Bramley
Preston Candover
Birdworld
Frensham
Godalming
Holybourne
Bentworth
Binsted
Milford
Alton
Witley
West Surrey
Kingsley
Hindhead
Churt
Hambledon
Medstead
Devil's Punch Bowl
Dunsfold
MICHELIN

Lit. Wymondley
Gt. Offley
Walkern
Westmill
Braughing
Manuden
Stansted Mountfitchet
Elsenham
STANSTED AIRPORT
King's Walden
Stevenage
Puckeridge
LUTON
St. Paul's Walden
Standon
Little Hadham
Bishop's Stortford
BIRCHANGER GREEN
Knebworth
Old Knebworth
Watton at Stone
Kimpton
Datchworth
Much Hadham
Little Hallingbury
Hatfield Forest
Luton Hoo
Codicote
HERTFORDSHIRE
Welwyn
Tewin
Ware
Widford
Hatfield Broad Oak
Hatfield Heath
Harpenden
Hertford
Sawbridgeworth
Wheathampstead
Great Amwell
Sheering
Redbourn
Welwyn Garden City
Stanstead Abbotts
Hertingfordbury
Matching Green
Sandridge
Hoddesdon
St. Albans
Essendon
Roydon
Potter Street
Verulamium
Hatfield
Little Berkhamsted
Broxbourne
Harlow
Moreton
Welham Green
Great Wood
Chiswell Green
London Colney
Brookmans Park
Northaw
South Mimms
Cuffley
Epping
N. Weald Bassett
Abbots Langley
Shenley
Cheshunt
Chipping Ongar
Radlett
SOUTH MIMMS
Potters Bar
Theydon Bois
Aldenham
Hadley Wood
Waltham Abbey
Kelvedon Hatch
Borehamwood
ENFIELD
Epping Forest
Watford
Bushey
Elstree
Loughton
Abridge
Pilgrims Hatch
LONDON GATEWAY
BARNET
Stapleford Abbotts
South Oxhey
Stanmore
Tottenham
Chigwell
Pinner
WALTHAM FOREST
REDBRIDGE
Wealdstone
HARINGEY
HARROW
HAVERING
Wembley
HACKNEY
Hornchurch
Upminster
BRENT
CAMDEN
ISLINGTON
Ilford
BARKING
HILLINGDON
TOWER HAMLETS
AND
NEWHAM
DAGENHAM
EALING
Beckton
LONDON
499
HESTON
HAMMERSMITH
Blackwall Tunnel
THURROCK
Heston
FULHAM
GREENWICH
Dartford Tunnel
HEATHROW AIRPORT
Kew
Erith
Isleworth
LAMBETH
LEWISHAM
BEXLEY
HOUNSLOW
Putney
Dartford
RICHMOND UPON THAMES
WANDSWORTH
Swanscombe
Feltham
Twickenham
Streatham
Sydenham
Sidcup
Ashford
Wimbledon
Wilmington
Darenth
Hampton Court
MERTON
Sunbury
Swanley
Walton on-Thames
KINGSTON UPON THAMES
Mitcham
Farningham
Shepperton
West Wickham
BROMLEY
Cheam
Carshalton
CROYDON
Orpington
Eynsford
Weybridge
Esher
Chessington
SUTTON
Wallington
Claygate
New Addington
West Kingsdown
Ewell
Sanderstead
Cobham
Oxshott
Epsom
Banstead
Warlingham
Biggin Hill
Otford
Kemsing
Wisley
Ashtead
Chipstead
Leatherhead
Tadworth
Woldingham
North Downs
Ightham
Ockham
Kingswood
Caterham
Sevenoaks
Fetcham
Sundridge
East Horsley
Great Bookham
Westerham
Knole
Box Hill
Godstone
Limpsfield
Polesden Lacey
Redhill
Oxted
Chartwell
SURREY
Reigate
South Nutfield
Crockham Hill
Dorking
Gomshall
Westcott
Four Elms
Shere
North Holmwood
Leigh
Salfords
Edenbridge
Chiddingstone
Sutton
Abinger Common
Blindley Heath
Eden
Hever
Penshurst
Leith Hill
Lingfield
Horley
Smallfield
Newdigate
Dormansland
Smart's Hill
Speldhurst
Charlwood
GATWICK AIRPORT
Ockley
Capel
Copthorne
Felbridge
Cranleigh
Crawley
Crawley Down
East Grinstead
Rusper
Turners Hill

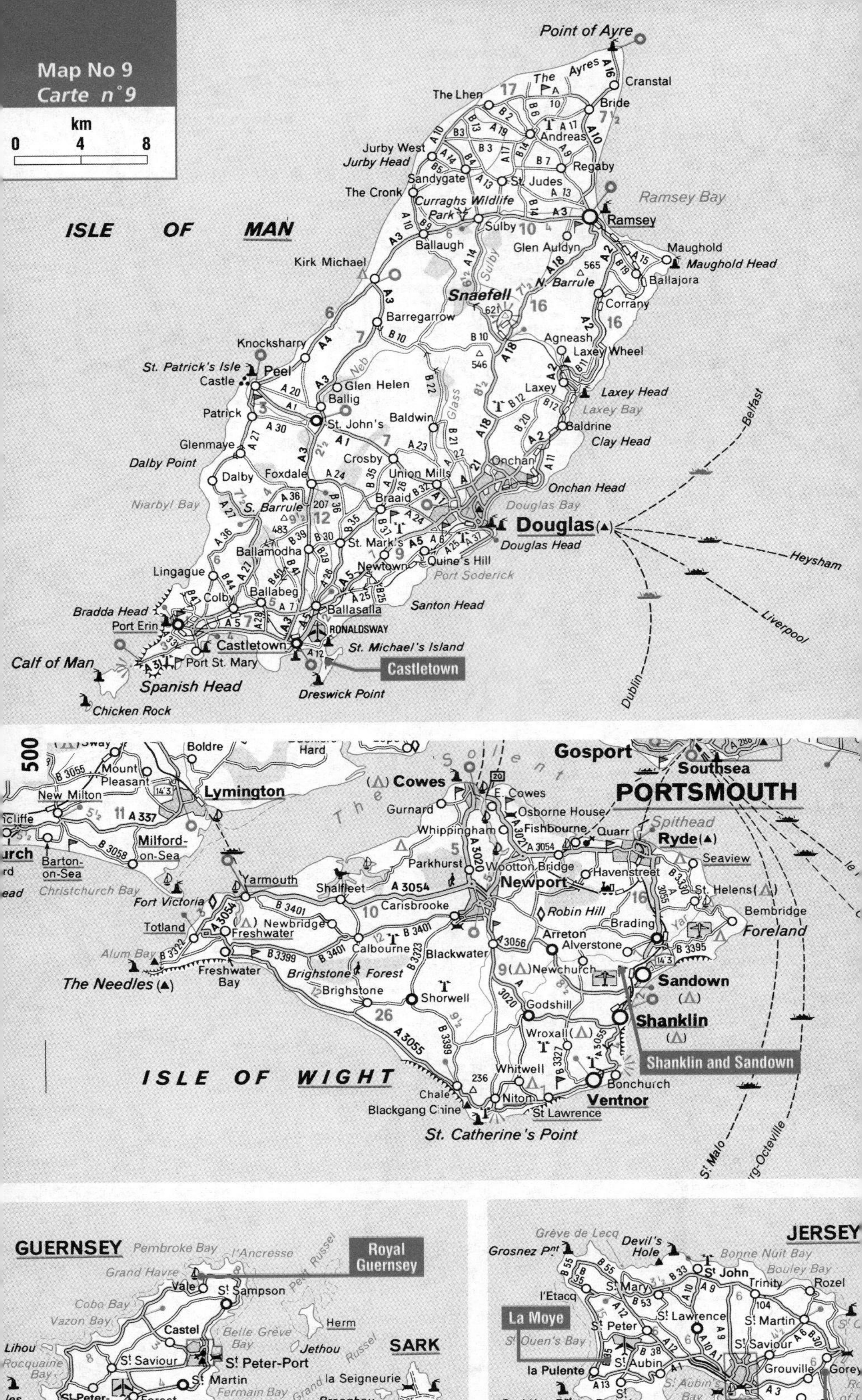
Map No 9
Carte n°9
km
0 4 8
ISLE OF MAN
Point of Ayre
The Ayres
Cranstal
The Lhen
Bride
Andreas
Jurby West
Jurby Head
Regaby
Sandygate
St. Judes
The Cronk
Curraghs Wildlife Park
Ramsey Bay
Ramsey
Sulby
Ballaugh
Glen Auldyn
Maughold
Maughold Head
Kirk Michael
N. Barrule
Ballajora
Snaefell
Corrany
Barregarrow
Agneash
Knocksharry
Laxey Wheel
St. Patrick's Isle
Castle
Peel
Glen Helen
Ballig
Laxey
Laxey Head
Laxey Bay
Patrick
St. John's
Baldwin
Baldrine
Clay Head
Glenmaye
Crosby
Dalby Point
Union Mills
Onchan
Dalby
Foxdale
Onchan Head
Niarbyl Bay
S. Barrule
Braaid
Douglas Bay
Douglas
Douglas Head
St. Mark's
Ballamodha
Quine's Hill
Newtown
Port Soderick
Lingague
Colby
Ballabeg
Bradda Head
Ballasalla
Santon Head
Port Erin
RONALDSWAY
Castletown
St. Michael's Island
Calf of Man
Port St. Mary
Spanish Head
Dreswick Point
Chicken Rock
Belfast
Heysham
Liverpool
Dublin
Boldre
Hard
Gosport
Southsea
Mount Pleasant
New Milton
Lymington
Cowes
E. Cowes
PORTSMOUTH
Gurnard
Osborne House
The Solent
Fishbourne
Quarr
Spithead
Whippingham
Ryde
Barton-on-Sea
Milford-on-Sea
Christchurch Bay
Seaview
Parkhurst
Wootton Bridge
Havenstreet
Yarmouth
Shalfleet
Newport
St. Helens
Fort Victoria
Bembridge
Carisbrooke
Robin Hill
Foreland
Totland
Newbridge
Freshwater
Brading
Arreton
Alverstone
Alum Bay
Calbourne
Blackwater
Newchurch
The Needles
Freshwater Bay
Brighstone Forest
Sandown
Brighstone
Shorwell
Godshill
Shanklin
Wroxall
ISLE OF WIGHT
Whitwell
Bonchurch
Ventnor
Chale
Niton
Blackgang Chine
St Lawrence
St. Catherine's Point
St Malo
GUERNSEY
Pembroke Bay
L'Ancresse
Royal Guernsey
Grand Havre
Vale
St Sampson
Cobo Bay
Vazon Bay
Castel
Belle Grève Bay
Herm
Lihou
St Saviour
Jethou
SARK
Rocquaine Bay
St Peter-Port
St Martin
la Seigneurie
Fermain Bay
les Hanois
St Peter-in-the-Wood
Forest
Brecqhou
Jerbourg Pt
Icart Point
la Coupée
Little Sark
MICHELIN
JERSEY
Grève de Lecq
Devil's Hole
Grosnez Pt
Bonne Nuit Bay
St John
Bouley Bay
Trinity
Rozel
St Mary
L'Etacq
St Lawrence
La Moye
St Martin
St Peter
St Ouen's Bay
St Saviour
St Aubin
la Pulente
Grouville
Gorey
St Aubin's Bay
Corbière Pt
St Brelade
St Helier
St Clément
Noirmont Pt
Green Island
Royal Jers

CLASSIFICATION OF COURSES
CLASSEMENT DES PARCOURS

This classification gives priority consideration to the score awarded to the actual course.

Ce classement donne priorité à la note attribuée au parcours .

Course score / Note du parcours					Page
19	5	6	Carnoustie *Championship*	Sc	708
19	8	5	Ganton	Eng	562
19	8	6	Kingsbarns	Sc	738
19	7	6	Muirfield	Sc	754
19	7	8	Nairn	Sc	757
19	9	7	Royal Birkdale	Eng	618
19	7	7	Royal Dornoch *Championship*	Sc	770
19	7	8	Royal Lytham & St Anne's	Eng	624
19	7	6	Royal Porthcawl	W	812
19	7	5	Royal St George's	Eng	627
19	7	7	Royal Troon *Old Course*	Sc	772
19	9	8	Turnberry *Ailsa Course*	Sc	784
18	7	7	Alwoodley (The)	Eng	513
18	8	6	Blairgowrie *Rosemount*	Sc	698
18	7	6	Burnham & Berrow	Eng	532
18	6	8	Castletown	Eng	538
18	9	7	Celtic Manor *Roman Road*	W	797
18	8	6	Chart Hills	Eng	539
18	7	6	Cruden Bay	Sc	711
18	7	7	Formby	Eng	557
18	9	7	Gleneagles King's	Sc	728
18	7	7	Hillside	Eng	574
18	7	6	Ilkley	Eng	579
18	8	6	Loch Lomond	Sc	744
18	6	4	Machrihanish	Sc	750
18	7	7	Moortown	Eng	599
18	7	8	North Berwick	Sc	760
18	6	6	Notts (Hollinwell)	Eng	604
18	6	6	Pennard	W	809
18	6	7	Prestwick	Sc	765
18	7	8	Royal Aberdeen *Balgownie Links*	Sc	768
18	8	7	Royal Liverpool (Hoylake)	Eng	623
18	6	6	Royal North Devon (Westward Ho!)	Eng	626
18	6	5	Royal St David's	W	813
18	6	6	Rye	Eng	632
18	7	6	Saunton *East Course*	Eng	635
18	5	4	Seascale	Eng	637
18	7	4	Silloth-on-Solway	Eng	643
18	6	5	Southerness	Sc	775
18	8	8	St Andrews *Old Course*	Sc	779
18	7	4	St Enodoc *Church Course*	Eng	646
18	8	8	Sunningdale *New Course*	Eng	651
18	8	8	Sunningdale *Old Course*	Eng	652
18	7	6	Tenby	W	815
18	7	7	Walton Heath *Old Course*	Eng	664
18	8	7	Wentworth *West Course*	Eng	667
18	7	6	West Sussex	Eng	674
18	7	8	Woodhall Spa	Eng	684
17	7	7	Aberdovey	W	792
17	6	5	Ashburnham	W	793
17	8	7	Berkshire (The) *Blue Course*	Eng	519
17	8	7	Berkshire (The) *Red Course*	Eng	520
17	6	5	Blackmoor	Eng	522
17	6	6	Bowood G&CC	Eng	525
17	7	6	Brampton	Eng	526
17	7	7	Broadstone	Eng	528
17	8	7	Buckinghamshire (The)	Eng	530
17	7	7	Caldy	Eng	533
17	8	8	Carden Park *Nicklaus Course*	Eng	536
17	7	7	Carlisle	Eng	537
17	7	7	Clitheroe	Eng	541
17	7	8	Conwy	W	798
17	7	7	Cumberwell Park	Eng	544
17	8	8	Dalmahoy *East Course*	Sc	712
17	6	7	Downfield	Sc	713

CLASSIFICATION OF COURSES

17	8	7	East Sussex National *East Course*	Eng	549
17	7	8	Fairhaven	Eng	550
17	7	7	Ferndown *Old Course*	Eng	553
17	6	7	Forest Pines *Forest + Pines*	Eng	556
17	7	8	Fulford	Eng	560
17	9	7	Gleneagles *PGA Centenary*	Sc	729
17	8	7	Gullane *No 1*	Sc	733
17	7	6	Hunstanton	Eng	577
17	6	8	Kilmarnock (Barassie)	Sc	737
17	7	8	La Moye	Eng	583
17	7	5	Ladybank	Sc	740
17	8	6	Linden Hall	Eng	584
17	6	6	Lindrick	Eng	585
17	7	8	Little Aston	Eng	587
17	7	7	Machrie	Sc	749
17	7	7	Monifieth	Sc	751
17	5	6	Montrose	Sc	752
17	8	7	Moor Park *High Course*	Eng	598
17	5	5	Moray	Sc	753
17	7	6	North Hants	Eng	603
17	6	8	North Wales (Llandudno)	W	807
17	6	5	Panmure	Sc	761
17	8	7	Prestbury	Eng	614
17	7	5	Pyle & Kenfig	W	810
17	6	5	Royal Cinque Ports	Eng	619
17	7	6	Royal West Norfolk (Brancaster)	Eng	628
17	5	7	Sandiway	Eng	634
17	6	4	Seacroft	Eng	636
17	7	5	Seaton Carew	Eng	638
17	7	6	Sherwood Forest	Eng	642
17	5	5	Shiskine (Blackwaterfoot)	Sc	774
17	8	7	Slaley Hall	Eng	644
17	7	7	Southport & Ainsdale	Eng	645
17	8	8	St Andrews *New Course*	Sc	778
17	7	7	St George's Hill	Eng	647
17	9	7	St Mellion *Nicklaus Course*	Eng	648
17	8	8	Stoke Poges	Eng	649
17	6	6	Tain	Sc	781
17	7	7	Trevose *Championship*	Eng	661
17	7	7	Wallasey	Eng	662
17	7	7	West Lancashire	Eng	672
17	5	7	Western Gailes	Sc	787
17	6	7	Whittington Heath	Eng	677
17	7	7	Woburn *Dukes Course*	Eng	679
17	7	7	Woburn *Marquess*	Eng	680
16	7	6	Ashridge	Eng	514
16	5	7	Ayr (Belleisle)	Sc	693
16	6	9	Bath	Eng	516
16	7	7	Beau Desert	Eng	517
16	7	6	Berkhamsted	Eng	518
16	7	6	Bowood (Cornwall)	Eng	524
16	6	6	Camberley Heath	Eng	534
16	9	6	Dartmouth	Eng	545
16	7	8	Duke's Course St Andrews	Sc	716
16	5	6	Dunbar	Sc	718
16	6	7	East Devon	Eng	548
16	6	5	Fortrose & Rosemarkie	Sc	726
16	7	7	Hadley Wood	Eng	564
16	6	6	Hankley Common	Eng	566
16	7	7	Hayling	Eng	569
16	7	6	Hindhead	Eng	575
16	7	5	Holyhead	W	800
16	6	7	Huddersfield (Fixby)	Eng	576
16	7	8	Inverness	Sc	736
16	7	7	Ipswich (Purdis Heath)	Eng	580
16	7	6	Isle of Purbeck	Eng	581
16	7	6	John O'Gaunt	Eng	582
16	6	5	Lanark	Sc	741
16	6	6	Leven	Sc	743
16	7	6	Liphook	Eng	586
16	5	6	Luffness New	Sc	747
16	6	7	Lundin	Sc	748
16	7	7	Manchester	Eng	591
16	8	7	Marriott St Pierre *Old Course*	W	804
16	7	5	Nefyn & District	W	805
16	9	6	Northop Country Park	W	808
16	7	7	Orchardleigh	Eng	605
16	7	8	Parkstone	Eng	608
16	6	6	Perranporth	Eng	610
16	8	6	Pleasington	Eng	611
16	6	4	Powfoot	Sc	764
16	6	7	Prestwick St Nicholas	Sc	766
16	7	9	Royal Burgess	Sc	769
16	7	7	Royal Guernsey	Eng	621
16	7	8	Royal Jersey	Eng	622
16	8	7	Royal Musselburgh	Sc	771

CLASSIFICATION OF COURSES

16	7	8	Royal Wimbledon	Eng	629
16	6	6	Scotscraig	Sc	773
16	7	7	Southerndown	W	814
16	8	8	St Andrews *Jubilee Course*	Sc	777
16	6	8	Swinley Forest	Eng	653
16	9	8	The Belfry *Brabazon*	Eng	655
16	6	4	Thurlestone	Eng	660
16	9	8	Turnberry *Kintyre Course*	Sc	785
16	8	7	Vale of Glamorgan	W	816
16	7	6	Walton Heath *New Course*	Eng	663
16	8	7	Wentworth *East Course*	Eng	666
16	7	6	West Cornwall	Eng	670
16	6	6	West Hill	Eng	671
16	7	5	West Kilbride	Sc	786
16	6	7	Weston-Super-Mare	Eng	675
16	7	6	Wilmslow	Eng	678
16	6	6	Woking	Eng	681
16	7	6	Worplesdon	Eng	685
15	7	6	Alloa	Sc	691
15	6	7	Ballater	Sc	695
15	6	5	Berwick-upon-Tweed	Eng	521
15	8	6	Blairgowrie *Lansdowne*	Sc	697
15	5	7	Bolton Old Links	Eng	523
15	6	6	Brokenhurst Manor	Eng	529
15	7	7	Brora	Sc	700
15	8	9	Bruntsfield	Sc	701
15	6	5	Bude & North Cornwall	Eng	531
15	5	6	Came Down	Eng	535
15	6	5	Cardigan	W	795
15	7	4	Carmarthen	W	796
15	9	7	Carnegie Club (Skibo Castle)	Sc	706
15	6	6	Coxmoor	Eng	543
15	6	6	Crail *Balcomie Links*	Sc	709
15	7	7	Crieff *Ferntower Course*	Sc	710
15	6	7	Delamere Forest	Eng	546
15	7	7	Denham	Eng	547
15	7	9	Duddingston	Sc	714
15	6	6	Duff House Royal	Sc	715
15	7	5	Dumfries & County	Sc	717
15	7	7	Dunfermline	Sc	719
15	6	8	East Renfrewshire	Sc	720
15	7	6	Elgin	Sc	722
15	6	6	Elie	Sc	723
15	6	6	Felixstowe Ferry *Martello Course*	Eng	552
15	8	8	Forest of Arden *Arden Course*	Eng	555
15	9	7	Gleneagles *Queen's*	Sc	730
15	7	8	Gog Magog *Old Course*	Eng	563
15	7	9	Haggs Castle	Sc	734
15	6	8	Hallamshire	Eng	565
15	7	7	Harrogate	Eng	567
15	8	7	Hawkstone Park *Hawkstone*	Eng	568
15	7	7	Hertfordshire (The)	Eng	571
15	6	7	High Post	Eng	573
15	4	5	Kingussie	Sc	739
15	7	7	Langland Bay	W	801
15	7	5	Letham Grange *Old Course*	Sc	742
15	5	8	Llandudno (Maesdu)	W	802
15	9	7	London Golf Club International	Eng	589
15	7	8	Lytham Green Drive	Eng	590
15	8	7	Manor House (Castle Combe)	Eng	593
15	5	7	Mendip	Eng	594
15	8	7	Meon Valley *Meon Course*	Eng	595
15	7	7	Mere	Eng	596
15	6	7	Moor Allerton	Eng	597
15	5	5	Mullion	Eng	600
15	6	6	Murcar	Sc	755
15	7	7	Nairn Dunbar	Sc	758
15	6	7	Newbury & Crookham	Eng	601
15	6	7	Newport	W	806
15	6	7	Pannal	Eng	607
15	8	7	Portal *Championship*	Eng	612
15	7	7	Porters Park	Eng	613
15	6	7	Portpatrick (Dunskey)	Sc	763
15	6	6	Rolls of Monmouth	W	811
15	5	6	Ross-on-Wye	Eng	616
15	7	7	Roxburghe (The)	Sc	767
15	7	6	Royal Cromer	Eng	620
15	6	8	Royal Winchester	Eng	630
15	8	8	Rudding Park	Eng	631
15	7	6	Shanklin & Sandown	Eng	639
15	6	7	Sherborne	Eng	640
15	7	6	Sheringham	Eng	641
15	7	8	Stoneham	Eng	650
15	7	6	Strathaven	Sc	780
15	9	8	The Belfry *PGA National*	Eng	656
15	6	5	Thornhill	Sc	783

15	7	8	Warwickshire (The)	Eng	665
15	7	7	West Berkshire	Eng	668
15	7	7	West Surrey	Eng	673
15	7	7	Whitekirk	Sc	789
15	9	6	Woodbury Park *The Oaks*	Eng	683
14	6	6	Aboyne	Sc	690
14	6	6	Alyth	Sc	692
14	6	8	Baberton	Sc	694
14	7	7	Badgemore Park	Eng	515
14	7	7	Banchory	Sc	696
14	6	7	Boat of Garten	Sc	699
14	6	5	Brancepeth Castle	Eng	527
14	6	6	Buchanan Castle	Sc	702
14	6	6	Burntisland	Sc	703
14	6	8	Cardiff	W	794
14	6	5	Cardross	Sc	705
14	5	6	Carnoustie *Burnside*	Sc	707
14	8	7	Collingtree Park	Eng	542
14	6	3	Edzell	Sc	721
14	6	7	Falmouth	Eng	551
14	6	6	Forfar	Sc	725
14	8	6	Formby Hall	Eng	558
14	7	7	Frilford Heath *Red Course*	Eng	559
14	8	6	Gainsborough-Karsten Lakes	Eng	561
14	7	8	Glamorganshire	W	799
14	7	7	Glen	Sc	727
14	5	4	Golspie	Sc	731
14	6	7	Grantown on Spey	Sc	732
14	6	7	Henley	Eng	570
14	8	8	Hever	Eng	572
14	6	7	Huntercombe	Eng	578
14	6	6	Huntly	Sc	735
14	6	5	Littlestone	Eng	588
14	6	4	Llanymynech	W	803
14	7	6	Longniddry	Sc	745
14	6	8	Lothianburn	Sc	746
14	8	6	Mannings Heath *Waterfall Course*	Eng	592
14	7	8	Murrayshall	Sc	756
14	5	5	Newtonmore	Sc	759
14	6	4	Ormskirk	Eng	606
14	6	7	Pitlochry	Sc	762
14	6	4	Prince's *Himalayas-Shore*	Eng	615
14	7	6	Royal Ashdown Forest	Eng	617
14	3	8	Royal Mid-Surrey *Outer*	Eng	625
14	7	7	Sand Moor	Eng	633
14	8	8	St Andrews *Eden Course*	Sc	776
14	7	6	Tandridge	Eng	654
14	7	5	Thetford	Eng	657
14	7	6	Thorndon Park	Eng	658
14	7	7	Thorpeness	Eng	659
14	6	8	West Byfleet	Eng	669
14	8	6	Westerwood	Sc	788
14	6	6	Wheatley	Eng	676
14	7	7	Woodbridge	Eng	682
13	6	7	Aldeburgh	Eng	512
13	6	7	Callander	Sc	704
13	6	7	Chesterfield	Eng	540
13	6	6	Falkirk Tryst	Sc	724
13	5	5	Filey	Eng	554
13	7	7	North Foreland	Eng	602
13	8	8	Patshull Park Hotel	Eng	609
13	4	6	Taymouth Castle	Sc	782

HOTEL FACILITIES
ENVIRONNEMENT HOTELIER

This classification gives priority consideration to the score awarded to the hotel facilities.

Ce classement donne priorité à la note attribuée à l'environnement hôtelier.

HOTEL FACILITIES SCORE
Note de l'environnement hotelier

Page

16	6	**9**	Bath	Eng	516
15	8	**9**	Bruntsfield	Sc	701
15	7	**9**	Duddingston	Sc	714
15	7	**9**	Haggs Castle	Sc	734
16	7	**9**	Royal Burgess	Sc	769
14	6	**8**	Baberton	Sc	694
17	8	**8**	Carden Park *Nicklaus Course*	Eng	536
14	6	**8**	Cardiff	W	794
18	6	**8**	Castletown	Eng	538
17	7	**8**	Conwy	W	798
17	8	**8**	Dalmahoy *East Course*	Sc	712
16	7	**8**	Duke's Course St Andrews	Sc	716
15	6	**8**	East Renfrewshire	Sc	720
17	7	**8**	Fairhaven	Eng	550
15	8	**8**	Forest of Arden *Arden Course*	Eng	555
17	7	**8**	Fulford	Eng	560
14	7	**8**	Glamorganshire	W	799
15	7	**8**	Gog Magog *Old Course*	Eng	563
15	6	**8**	Hallamshire	Eng	565
14	8	**8**	Hever	Eng	572
16	7	**8**	Inverness	Sc	736
17	6	**8**	Kilmarnock (Barassie)	Sc	737
17	7	**8**	La Moye	Eng	583
17	7	**8**	Little Aston	Eng	587
15	5	**8**	Llandudno (Maesdu)	W	802
14	6	**8**	Lothianburn	Sc	746
15	7	**8**	Lytham Green Drive	Eng	590
14	7	**8**	Murrayshall	Sc	756
19	7	**8**	Nairn	Sc	757
18	7	**8**	North Berwick	Sc	760
17	6	**8**	North Wales (Llandudno)	W	807
16	7	**8**	Parkstone	Eng	608
13	8	**8**	Patshull Park Hotel	Eng	609
18	7	**8**	Royal Aberdeen	Sc	768
16	7	**8**	Royal Jersey	Eng	622
19	7	**8**	Royal Lytham & St Anne's	Eng	624
14	3	**8**	Royal Mid-Surrey *Outer*	Eng	625
16	7	**8**	Royal Wimbledon	Eng	629
15	6	**8**	Royal Winchester	Eng	630
15	8	**8**	Rudding Park	Eng	631
14	8	**8**	St Andrews *Eden Course*	Sc	776
16	8	**8**	St Andrews *Jubilee Course*	Sc	777
17	8	**8**	St Andrews *New Course*	Sc	778
18	8	**8**	St Andrews *Old Course*	Sc	779
17	8	**8**	Stoke Poges	Eng	649
15	7	**8**	Stoneham	Eng	650
18	8	**8**	Sunningdale *New Course*	Eng	651
18	8	**8**	Sunningdale *Old Course*	Eng	652
16	6	**8**	Swinley Forest	Eng	653
16	9	**8**	The Belfry *Brabazon*	Eng	655
15	9	**8**	The Belfry *PGA National*	Eng	656
19	9	**8**	Turnberry *Ailsa Course*	Sc	784
16	9	**8**	Turnberry *Kintyre Course*	Sc	785
15	7	**8**	Warwickshire (The)	Eng	665
14	6	**8**	West Byfleet	Eng	669
18	7	**8**	Woodhall Spa	Eng	684
17	7	**7**	Aberdovey	W	792
13	6	**7**	Aldeburgh	Eng	512
18	7	**7**	Alwoodley (The)	Eng	513
16	5	**7**	Ayr (Belleisle)	Sc	693
14	7	**7**	Badgemore Park	Eng	515
15	6	**7**	Ballater	Sc	695
14	7	**7**	Banchory	Sc	696
16	7	**7**	Beau Desert	Eng	517
17	8	**7**	Berkshire (The) *Blue Course*	Eng	519
17	8	**7**	Berkshire (The) *Red Course*	Eng	520
14	6	**7**	Boat of Garten	Sc	699

CLASSIFICATION OF HOTEL FACILITIES

15	5	**7**	Bolton Old Links	Eng	523
17	7	**7**	Broadstone	Eng	528
15	7	**7**	Brora	Sc	700
17	8	**7**	Buckinghamshire (The)	Eng	530
17	7	**7**	Caldy	Eng	533
13	6	**7**	Callander	Sc	704
17	7	**7**	Carlisle	Eng	537
15	9	**7**	Carnegie Club (Skibo Castle)	Sc	706
18	9	**7**	Celtic Manor *Roman Road*	W	797
13	6	**7**	Chesterfield	Eng	540
17	7	**7**	Clitheroe	Eng	541
14	8	**7**	Collingtree Park	Eng	542
15	7	**7**	Crieff *Ferntower Course*	Sc	710
17	7	**7**	Cumberwell Park	Eng	544
15	6	**7**	Delamere Forest	Eng	546
15	7	**7**	Denham	Eng	547
17	6	**7**	Downfield	Sc	713
15	7	**7**	Dunfermline	Sc	719
16	6	**7**	East Devon	Eng	548
17	8	**7**	East Sussex National *East Course*	Eng	549
14	6	**7**	Falmouth	Eng	551
17	7	**7**	Ferndown *Old Course*	Eng	553
17	6	**7**	Forest Pines *Forest + Pines*	Eng	556
18	7	**7**	Formby	Eng	557
14	7	**7**	Frilford Heath *Red Course*	Eng	559
14	7	**7**	Glen	Sc	727
18	9	**7**	Gleneagles King's	Sc	728
17	9	**7**	Gleneagles *PGA Centenary*	Sc	729
15	9	**7**	Gleneagles *Queen's*	Sc	730
14	6	**7**	Grantown on Spey	Sc	732
17	8	**7**	Gullane *No 1*	Sc	733
16	7	**7**	Hadley Wood	Eng	564
15	7	**7**	Harrogate	Eng	567
15	8	**7**	Hawkstone Park *Hawkstone*	Eng	568
16	7	**7**	Hayling	Eng	569
14	6	**7**	Henley	Eng	570
15	7	**7**	Hertfordshire (The)	Eng	571
15	6	**7**	High Post	Eng	573
18	7	**7**	Hillside	Eng	574
16	6	**7**	Huddersfield (Fixby)	Eng	576
14	6	**7**	Huntercombe	Eng	578
16	7	**7**	Ipswich (Purdis Heath)	Eng	580
15	7	**7**	Langland Bay	W	801
15	9	**7**	London Golf Club *International*	Eng	589
16	6	**7**	Lundin	Sc	748
17	7	**7**	Machrie	Sc	749
16	7	**7**	Manchester	Eng	591
15	8	**7**	Manor House (Castle Combe)	Eng	593
16	8	**7**	Marriott St Pierre *Old Course*	W	804
15	5	**7**	Mendip	Eng	594
15	8	**7**	Meon Valley *Meon Course*	Eng	595
15	7	**7**	Mere	Eng	596
17	7	**7**	Monifieth	Sc	751
15	6	**7**	Moor Allerton	Eng	597
17	8	**7**	Moor Park *High Course*	Eng	598
18	7	**7**	Moortown	Eng	599
15	7	**7**	Nairn Dunbar	Sc	758
15	6	**7**	Newbury & Crookham	Eng	601
15	6	**7**	Newport	W	806
13	7	**7**	North Foreland	Eng	602
16	7	**7**	Orchardleigh	Eng	605
15	6	**7**	Pannal	Eng	607
14	6	**7**	Pitlochry	Sc	762
15	8	**7**	Portal *Championship*	Eng	612
15	7	**7**	Porters Park	Eng	613
15	6	**7**	Portpatrick (Dunskey)	Sc	763
17	8	**7**	Prestbury	Eng	614
18	6	**7**	Prestwick	Sc	765
16	6	**7**	Prestwick St Nicholas	Sc	766
15	7	**7**	Roxburghe (The)	Sc	767
19	9	**7**	Royal Birkdale (The)	Eng	618
19	7	**7**	Royal Dornoch *Championship*	Sc	770
16	7	**7**	Royal Guernsey	Eng	621
18	8	**7**	Royal Liverpool (Hoylake)	Eng	623
16	8	**7**	Royal Musselburgh	Sc	771
19	7	**7**	Royal Troon *Old Course*	Sc	772
14	7	**7**	Sand Moor	Eng	633
17	5	**7**	Sandiway	Eng	634
15	6	**7**	Sherborne	Eng	640
17	8	**7**	Slaley Hall	Eng	644
16	7	**7**	Southerndown	W	814
17	7	**7**	Southport & Ainsdale	Eng	645
17	7	**7**	St George's Hill	Eng	647

506

17	9	**7**	St Mellion *Nicklaus Course*	Eng	648
14	7	**7**	Thorpeness	Eng	659
17	7	**7**	Trevose *Championship*	Eng	661
16	8	**7**	Vale of Glamorgan	W	816
17	7	**7**	Wallasey	Eng	662
18	7	**7**	Walton Heath *Old Course*	Eng	664
16	8	**7**	Wentworth *East Course*	Eng	666
18	8	**7**	Wentworth *West Course*	Eng	667
15	7	**7**	West Berkshire	Eng	668
17	7	**7**	West Lancashire	Eng	672
15	7	**7**	West Surrey	Eng	673
17	5	**7**	Western Gailes	Sc	787
16	6	**7**	Weston-Super-Mare	Eng	675
15	7	**7**	Whitekirk	Sc	789
17	6	**7**	Whittington Heath	Eng	677
17	7	**7**	Woburn *Dukes Course*	Eng	679
17	7	**7**	Woburn *Marquess*	Eng	680
14	7	**7**	Woodbridge	Eng	682
14	6	**6**	Aboyne	Sc	690
15	7	**6**	Alloa	Sc	691
14	6	**6**	Alyth	Sc	692
16	7	**6**	Ashridge	Eng	514
16	7	**6**	Berkhamsted	Eng	518
15	8	**6**	Blairgowrie *Lansdowne*	Sc	697
18	8	**6**	Blairgowrie *Rosemount*	Sc	698
16	7	**6**	Bowood (Cornwall)	Eng	524
17	6	**6**	Bowood G&CC	Eng	525
17	7	**6**	Brampton	Eng	526
15	6	**6**	Brokenhurst Manor	Eng	529
14	6	**6**	Buchanan Castle	Sc	702
18	7	**6**	Burnham & Berrow	Eng	532
14	6	**6**	Burntisland	Sc	703
16	6	**6**	Camberley Heath	Eng	534
15	5	**6**	Came Down	Eng	535
14	5	**6**	Carnoustie *Burnside*	Sc	707
19	5	**6**	Carnoustie *Championship*	Sc	708
18	8	**6**	Chart Hills	Eng	539
15	6	**6**	Coxmoor	Eng	543
15	6	**6**	Crail *Balcomie Links*	Sc	709
18	7	**6**	Cruden Bay	Sc	711
16	9	**6**	Dartmouth	Eng	545
15	6	**6**	Duff House Royal	Sc	715
16	5	**6**	Dunbar	Sc	718
15	7	**6**	Elgin	Sc	722
15	6	**6**	Elie	Sc	723
13	6	**6**	Falkirk Tryst	Sc	724

15	6	**6**	Felixstowe Ferry *Martello Course*	Eng	552
14	6	**6**	Forfar	Sc	725
14	8	**6**	Formby Hall	Eng	558
14	8	**6**	Gainsborough-Karsten Lakes	Eng	561
16	6	**6**	Hankley Common	Eng	566
16	7	**6**	Hindhead	Eng	575
17	7	**6**	Hunstanton	Eng	577
14	6	**6**	Huntly	Sc	735
18	7	**6**	Ilkley	Eng	579
16	7	**6**	Isle of Purbeck	Eng	581
16	7	**6**	John O'Gaunt	Eng	582
19	8	**6**	Kingsbarns	Sc	738
16	6	**6**	Leven	Sc	743
17	8	**6**	Linden Hall	Eng	584
17	6	**6**	Lindrick	Eng	585
16	7	**6**	Liphook	Eng	586
18	8	**6**	Loch Lomond	Sc	744
14	7	**6**	Longniddry	Sc	745
16	5	**6**	Luffness New	Sc	747
14	8	**6**	Mannings Heath *Waterfall Course*	Eng	592
17	5	**6**	Montrose	Sc	752
19	7	**6**	Muirfield	Sc	754
15	6	**6**	Murcar	Sc	755
17	7	**6**	North Hants	Eng	603
16	9	**6**	Northop Country Park	W	808
18	6	**6**	Notts (Hollinwell)	Eng	604
18	6	**6**	Pennard	W	809
16	6	**6**	Perranporth	Eng	610
16	8	**6**	Pleasington	Eng	611
15	6	**6**	Rolls of Monmouth	W	811
15	5	**6**	Ross-on-Wye	Eng	616
14	7	**6**	Royal Ashdown Forest	Eng	617
15	7	**6**	Royal Cromer	Eng	620
18	6	**6**	Royal North Devon (Westward Ho!)	Eng	626
19	7	**6**	Royal Porthcawl	W	812
17	7	**6**	Royal West Norfolk (Brancaster)	Eng	628
18	6	**6**	Rye	Eng	632
18	7	**6**	Saunton *East Course*	Eng	635
16	6	**6**	Scotscraig	Sc	773
15	7	**6**	Shanklin & Sandown	Eng	639
15	7	**6**	Sheringham	Eng	641
17	7	**6**	Sherwood Forest	Eng	642
15	7	**6**	Strathaven	Sc	780

CLASSIFICATION OF HOTEL FACILITIES

17	6	**6**	Tain	Sc	781
14	7	**6**	Tandridge	Eng	654
13	4	**6**	Taymouth Castle	Sc	782
18	7	**6**	Tenby	W	815
14	7	**6**	Thorndon Park	Eng	658
16	7	**6**	Walton Heath *New Course*	Eng	663
16	7	**6**	West Cornwall	Eng	670
16	6	**6**	West Hill	Eng	671
18	7	**6**	West Sussex	Eng	674
14	8	**6**	Westerwood	Sc	788
14	6	**6**	Wheatley	Eng	676
16	7	**6**	Wilmslow	Eng	678
16	6	**6**	Woking	Eng	681
15	9	**6**	Woodbury Park *The Oaks*	Eng	683
16	7	**6**	Worplesdon	Eng	685
17	6	**5**	Ashburnham	W	793
15	6	**5**	Berwick-upon-Tweed	Eng	521
17	6	**5**	Blackmoor	Eng	522
14	6	**5**	Brancepeth Castle	Eng	527
15	6	**5**	Bude & North Cornwall	Eng	531
15	6	**5**	Cardigan	W	795
14	6	**5**	Cardross	Sc	705
15	7	**5**	Dumfries & County	Sc	717
13	5	**5**	Filey	Eng	554
16	6	**5**	Fortrose & Rosemarkie	Sc	726
19	8	**5**	Ganton	Eng	562
16	7	**5**	Holyhead	W	800
15	4	**5**	Kingussie	Sc	739
17	7	**5**	Ladybank	Sc	740
16	6	**5**	Lanark	Sc	741
15	7	**5**	Letham Grange *Old Course*	Sc	742
14	6	**5**	Littlestone	Eng	588
17	5	**5**	Moray	Sc	753
15	5	**5**	Mullion	Eng	600
16	7	**5**	Nefyn & District	W	805
14	5	**5**	Newtonmore	Sc	759
17	6	**5**	Panmure	Sc	761
17	7	**5**	Pyle & Kenfig	W	810
17	6	**5**	Royal Cinque Ports	Eng	619
18	6	**5**	Royal St David's	W	813
19	7	**5**	Royal St George's	Eng	627
17	7	**5**	Seaton Carew	Eng	638
17	5	**5**	Shiskine (Blackwaterfoot)	Sc	774
18	6	**5**	Southerness	Sc	775
14	7	**5**	Thetford	Eng	657
15	6	**5**	Thornhill	Sc	783
16	7	**5**	West Kilbride	Sc	786
15	7	**4**	Carmarthen	W	796
14	5	**4**	Golspie	Sc	731
14	6	**4**	Llanymynech	W	803
18	6	**4**	Machrihanish	Sc	750
14	6	**4**	Ormskirk	Eng	606
16	6	**4**	Powfoot	Sc	764
14	6	**4**	Prince's *Himalayas-Shore*	Eng	615
17	6	**4**	Seacroft	Eng	636
18	5	**4**	Seascale	Eng	637
18	7	**4**	Silloth-on-Solway	Eng	643
18	7	**4**	St Enodoc *Church Course*	Eng	646
16	6	**4**	Thurlestone	Eng	660
14	6	**3**	Edzell	Sc	721

RECOMMENDED GOLFING HOLIDAYS
VACANCES RECOMMANDÉES

Gleneagles King's	18	9	7	728
Gleneagles PGA Centenary	17	9	7	729
Gleneagles Queen's	15	9	7	730
Hayling	16	7	7	569
La Moye	17	7	8	583
Langland Bay	15	7	7	801
Llandudno (Maesdu)	15	5	8	802
North Wales (Llandudno)	17	6	8	807
Pennard	18	6	6	809
Royal Guernsey	16	7	7	621
Royal Jersey	16	7	8	622

RECOMMENDED GOLFING STAY
SEJOUR DE GOLF RECOMMANDÉ

Berkshire (The) *Blue Course*	17	8	7	519
Berkshire (The) *Red Course*	17	8	7	520
Blairgowrie *Lansdowne*	15	8	6	697
Blairgowrie *Rosemount*	18	8	6	698
Burnham & Berrow	18	7	6	532
Carden Park *Nicklaus Course*	17	8	8	536
Carnoustie *Burnside*	14	5	6	707
Carnoustie *Championship*	19	5	6	708
Celtic Manor *Roman Road*	18	9	7	797
Cruden Bay	18	7	6	711
Cumberwell Park	17	7	7	544
Dalmahoy *East Course*	17	8	8	712
East Sussex National *East Course*	17	8	7	549
Ferndown *Old Course*	17	7	7	553
Forest Pines *Forest + Pines*	17	6	7	556
Formby	18	7	7	557
Ganton	19	8	5	562
Gleneagles *King's*	18	9	7	728
Gleneagles *PGA Centenary*	17	9	7	729
Gleneagles *Queen's*	15	9	7	730
Gullane *No 1*	17	8	7	733
Hawkstone Park *Hawkstone*	15	8	7	568
Hillside	18	7	7	574
Isle of Purbeck	16	7	6	581
John O'Gaunt	16	7	6	582
Machrihanish	18	6	4	750
Marriott St Pierre *Old Course*	16	8	7	804
Meon Valley *Meon Course*	15	8	7	595
Moor Park *High Course*	17	8	7	598
Moray	17	5	5	753
Nairn	19	7	8	757
Portal *Championship*	15	8	7	612
Pyle & Kenfig	17	7	5	810
Royal Birkdale	19	9	7	618
Royal Cinque Ports	17	6	5	619
Royal Dornoch *Championship*	19	7	7	770
Royal Liverpool (Hoylake)	18	8	7	623
Royal North Devon (Westward Ho!)	18	6	6	626
Royal Porthcawl	19	7	6	812
Royal St David's	18	6	5	813
Royal St George's	19	7	5	627
Royal Troon *Old Course*	19	7	7	772
Saunton *East Course*	18	7	6	635
Slaley Hall	17	8	7	644
Southport & Ainsdale	17	7	7	645
St Andrews *Eden Course*	14	8	8	776
St Andrews *Jubilee Course*	16	8	8	777
St Andrews *New Course*	17	8	8	778
St Andrews *Old Course*	18	8	8	779
St Enodoc *Church Course*	18	7	4	646
St Mellion *Nicklaus Course*	17	9	7	648
Stoke Poges	17	8	8	649
Sunningdale *New Course*	18	8	8	651
Sunningdale *Old Course*	18	8	8	652
The Belfry *Brabazon*	16	9	8	655
The Belfry *PGA National*	15	9	8	656
Trevose *Championship*	17	7	7	661
Turnberry *Ailsa Course*	19	9	8	784
Turnberry *Kintyre Course*	16	9	8	785
Wallasey	17	7	7	662
Walton Heath *New Course*	16	7	6	663
Walton Heath *Old Course*	18	7	7	664
Warwickshire (The)	15	7	8	665
Wentworth *East Course*	16	8	7	666
Wentworth *West Course*	18	8	7	667
Woburn *Dukes Course*	17	7	7	679
Woburn *Marquess Course*	17	7	7	680
Woodhall Spa	18	7	8	684

EUROPE'S TOP 1000 GOLF COURSES

England

The Royal Birkdale

England
Angleterre

The good news for lovers of golf architecture is the appearance of Rye or Little Aston. Of course you may never play Rye unless invited and accompanied by a member but at least you will know how high it rates in our rankings. Little Aston on the other hand has begun to open up just a little in recent years. Elsewhere, some of the most recent courses have been deliberately overlooked for the time being. Rather than rush in and voice opinions that may well be proved way off the mark by the passing months and years, we have preferred to let them « mature » a little. But you can be sure that they will be reviewed in our next edition. Today more than ever, our choice is neither final nor categorical. Other courses, some of which are relatively ancient, will also feature in the next edition on account of the significant improvements now being made. May our readers rest assured, all the courses included this year are, to coin a wine phrase, great vintages. You will find the greatest links, the top parkland courses, courses which are ranked amongst the best and also those little «gems» which we hope you will be proud to talk about to your friends. And if you happen to come across any others, please let us know…

La bonne nouvelle pour les amateurs d'architecture de golf, c'est l'entrée de Rye ou Little Aston. Certes, vous ne pourrez jamais jouer Rye à moins d'être accompagné par un membre, mais vous saurez au moins à quel niveau il figure dans nos appréciations. De son côté, Little Aston s'est davantage entr'ouvert qu'il y a quelques années. Certains tous récents parcours ne figurent pas non plus ici. Au lieu de nous précipiter et d'émettre des jugements parfois contredits par le temps, nous préférons les voir mûrir un peu. Mais ils seront revus pour la prochaine édition. Aujourd'hui plus que jamais, notre choix n'est ni définitif, ni catégorique. D'autres parcours, même relativement anciens entreront dans ce Guide dans la prochaine édition, parce qu'ils auront fortement progressé. Que les lecteurs soient rassurés, tous les parcours présentés sont, comme on dit en gastronomie, de « bonnes tables. » On y trouve les plus grands links, les meilleurs parkland, les parcours qui figurent dans les grands classements, mais aussi quelques petits joyaux dont nous espérons que vous serez fier de parler ensuite à vos amis. Et si vous en découvrez d'autres, dites-le-nous.

ALDEBURGH

13 | 6 | 7

Music lovers might like to know that the English composer Benjamin Britten lived alongside this course for many years. They can also take advantage of their visit here to attend the music festival (in June) in Aldeburgh's superb Snape Maltings. This course is not a grand tournament layout but it is a pleasant holiday course to be included in any golfing tour around this area. Just avoid coming here after any prolonged dry period because the fairways are not watered and get very hard. With gorse and heather in the wings, the holes don't look all that wide and the wind will probably prompt you to play this as you would a links course. But don't let the benevolence of the site make you lower your concentration, either, as there is no shortage of difficulties waiting to make life really complicated. Luckily, inexperienced players can try the 9-hole "River" course to test their progress without getting lost in the heather.

Les amateurs de musique auront une pensée pour le compositeur Benjamin Britten, qui vécut longtemps à côté du golf. Ils en profiteront pour venir au festival de musique (en juin) dans les superbes Snape Maltings d'Aldeburgh. Le présent parcours n'est pas un très grand tracé de championnat, mais il reste un parcours de vacances agréable à intégrer dans un festival de golf dans la région, en évitant toutefois les longues périodes de sécheresse car les fairways ne sont pas arrosés. Avec la présence de bruyère et d'ajoncs, les trous ne paraissent pas bien larges, et le vent incite à jouer comme sur des links. Et l'amabilité apparente du site ne doit pas inciter à baisser sa garde, car les difficultés ne manquent pas de compliquer la quiétude du golfeur. Heureusement pour les joueurs peu expérimentés, le 9 trous supplémentaire ("River Course") permet de s'aguerrir sans craindre de se perdre dans la bruyère.

Aldeburgh Golf Club — 1884

Saxmundham Road
ENG - ALDEBURGH, Suffolk IP15 5PE

Office	Secrétariat	(44) 01728 - 452 890
Pro shop	Pro-shop	(44) 01728 - 453 309
Fax	Fax	(44) 01728 - 452 937
Web	—	
Situation	Situation	38 km from Ipswich
Annual closure	Fermeture annuelle	no
Weekly closure	Fermeture hebdomadaire	no

512

Fees main season / Tarifs haute saison	18 holes	
	Week days / Semaine	We/Bank holidays / We/Férié
Individual Individuel	£ 45	£ 60
Couple Couple	£ 90	£ 120

£ 35 / £ 40 after 12.00 pm (weekdays / week ends)

Caddy	Caddy	£ 20 /on request
Electric Trolley	Chariot électrique	no
Buggy	Voiturette	£ 10 /18 holes
Clubs	Clubs	£ 7.50 / 18 holes

Credit cards Cartes de crédit
Visa - Mastercard (Pro shop goods only)

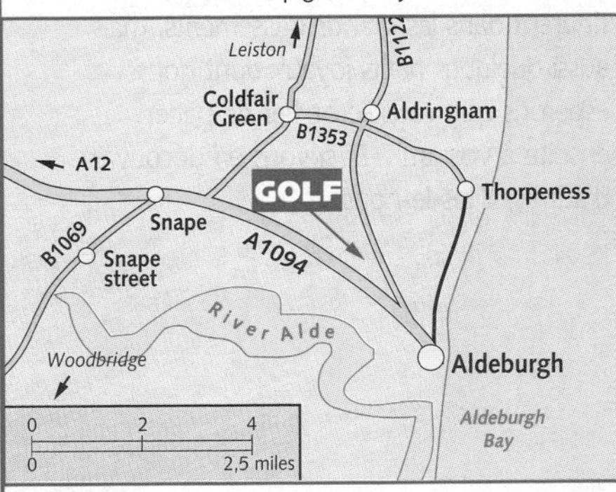

Access Accès : London A12. Ipswich → Felixstowe. Right unto A1094. Course on left of the road before entering Aldeburgh
Map 7 on page 497 Carte 7 Page 497

Golf course / PARCOURS — 13/20

Site	Site	
Maintenance	Entretien	
Architect	Architecte	John Thompson, Willie Fernie
Type	Type	open country, heathland
Relief	Relief	
Water in play	Eau en jeu	
Exp. to wind	Exposé au vent	
Trees in play	Arbres en jeu	

Scorecard / Carte de score	Chp. / Chp.	Mens / Mess.	Ladies / Da.
Length Long.	5698	5238	5238
Par	72	72	74
Slope system	—	—	—

Advised golfing ability / Niveau de jeu recommandé: 0 12 24 36
Hcp required / Handicap exigé: 24

Club house & amenities / CLUB HOUSE ET ANNEXES — 6/10

Pro shop	Pro-shop	
Driving range	Practice	
Sheltered	couvert	no
On grass	sur herbe	yes
Putting-green	putting-green	yes
Pitching-green	pitching green	yes

Hotel facilities / ENVIRONNEMENT HOTELIER — 7/10

HOTELS HÔTELS

Wentworth Hotel, 37 rooms, D £ 120 — Aldeburgh 2 km
Tel (44) 01728 - 452 312, Fax (44) 01728 - 454 343

Uplands Hotel, 20 rooms, D £ 75 — Aldeburgh
Tel (44) 01728 - 452 420, Fax (44) 01728 - 454 872

White Lion, 38 rooms, D £ 70 — Aldeburgh
Tel (44) 01728 - 452 720, Fax (44) 01728 - 452 986

RESTAURANTS RESTAURANT

New Regatta, Tel (44) 01728 - 452 011 — Aldeburgh

Lighthouse, Tel (44) 01728 - 453377 — Aldeburgh

ALWOODLEY (THE)

18	7	7

The recently-built clubhouse has only added to the comfort of this remarkable course, which is a revelation for anyone who has never played here before. You have to admit that the partnership between Harry Colt and Alistair Mackenzie will always appeal to connoisseurs. The greens were relaid along the lines of the original layouts, but to modern American specifications. Likewise, several new tee-boxes have helped to restyle the course without changing any of the strategy involved in coping with hazards. Besides the trees, which come into play only for the really bad shot, heather (always impossible to get out of) and especially the bunkers create most of the trouble. On the fairways, finding sand can cost you half a shot. Around the greens, where access is tight, it can cost even more. A demanding course but the fairest adversary you could hope for. You won't forget it in a long, long while.

Un récent Clubhouse n'a fait qu'ajouter du confort à un parcours remarquable qui sera une révélation pour ceux qui ne le connaissent pas encore. Il faut dire que l'association de Harry Colt et Alister MacKenzie ne peut laisser indifférent les connaisseurs. Les greens ont été refaits suivant les dessins originaux, mais avec les spécifications américaines modernes. De même, quelques nouveaux départs ont permis d'adapter le parcours, sans rien changer à la stratégie par rapport aux obstacles. A côté des bois qui ne sont vraiment en jeu que pour les mauvais coups, la bruyère (il est toujours impossible de s'en extraire) et surtout les bunkers constituent l'essentiel des obstacles. Sur les fairways, ils coûtent un demi-coup. Près des greens, dont les ouvertures sont rendues assez étroites, ils peuvent en coûter plus encore. Ce parcours est exigeant, mais il constitue l'adversaire le plus loyal qui soit. On s'en souviendra longtemps.

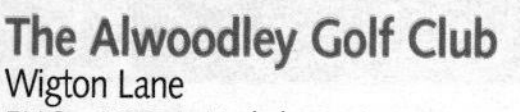

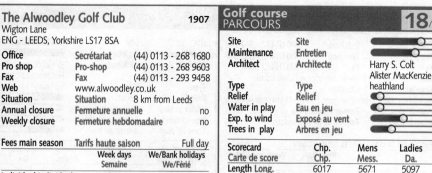

The Alwoodley Golf Club — 1907

Wigton Lane
ENG - LEEDS, Yorkshire LS17 8SA

Office	**Secrétariat**	(44) 0113 - 268 1680
Pro shop	**Pro-shop**	(44) 0113 - 268 9603
Fax	**Fax**	(44) 0113 - 293 9458
Web	www.alwoodley.co.uk	
Situation	**Situation**	8 km from Leeds
Annual closure	**Fermeture annuelle**	no
Weekly closure	**Fermeture hebdomadaire**	no

Fees main season / **Tarifs haute saison**	Full day — Week days / Semaine	We/Bank holidays / We/Férié
Individual Individuel	£ 55	£ 75
Couple Couple	£ 110	£ 150

Caddy	**Caddy**	£ 25 +tip/on request
Electric Trolley	**Chariot électrique**	£ 5 /18 holes
Buggy	**Voiturette**	no
Clubs	**Clubs**	£ 10 /18 holes

Credit cards — **Cartes de crédit**
VISA - Eurocard - MasterCard - DC - AMEX - (not for green fees)

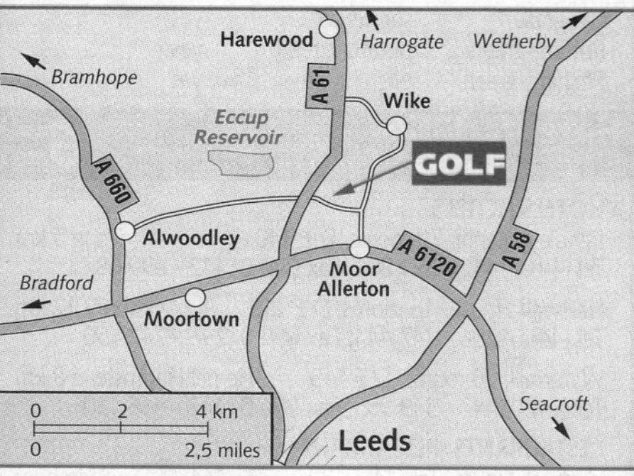

Access Accès : Turn off A61 (→ Harrogate) at traffic lights at Wigton Lane X-roads 8 km N of Leeds.
Map 4 on page 490 Carte 4 Page 490

Golf course — PARCOURS — 18/20

Site	**Site**	
Maintenance	**Entretien**	
Architect	**Architecte**	Harry S. Colt Alister MacKenzie
Type	**Type**	heathland
Relief	**Relief**	
Water in play	**Eau en jeu**	
Exp. to wind	**Exposé au vent**	
Trees in play	**Arbres en jeu**	

Scorecard / **Carte de score**	**Chp.** / **Chp.**	**Mens** / **Mess.**	**Ladies** / **Da.**
Length Long.	6017	5671	5097
Par	72	70	73
Slope system	—	—	—

Advised golfing ability — **Niveau de jeu recommandé** — 0 12 24 36
Hcp required — **Handicap exigé** — no

Club house & amenities — CLUB HOUSE ET ANNEXES — 7/10

Pro shop	**Pro-shop**	
Driving range	**Practice**	
Sheltered	couvert	practice area
On grass	sur herbe	yes
Putting-green	putting-green	yes
Pitching-green	pitching green	yes

Hotel facilities — ENVIRONNEMENT HOTELIER — 7/10

HOTELS HÔTELS

Posthouse, 130 rooms, D £ 90 — Bramhope 6 km
Tel (44) 0870 - 400 9049, Fax (44) 0870 - 284 3451

42 The Calls, 41 rooms, D £ 150 — Leeds 8 km
Tel (44) 0113 - 244 0099, Fax (44) 0113 - 234 4100

Queens, 199 rooms, D £ 125 — Leeds 8 km
Tel (44) 0113 - 243 1323, Fax (44) 0113 - 242 5154

RESTAURANTS RESTAURANT

Pool Court at 42, Tel (44) 0113 - 244 4242 — Leeds 8 km
Leodis, Tel (44) 0113 - 242 1010 — Leeds 8 km
Rascasse, Tel (44) 0113 - 244 6611 — Leeds 8 km

ASHRIDGE

16 | 7 | 6

Not far from the Thames valley, the Chiltern Hills and Whipsnade zoo, the largest wildlife reserve in Europe, Ashridge sits right in the middle of this peaceful, wonderful countryside where the aristocrats of yesteryear built superb castles. The course was opened in 1932 and has undergone only minor changes since, even though Henry Cotton was the club professional for many a year. In a superb parkland setting, the course is pleasantly classical in style with each hole having a distinctly individual character. The designers obviously had the pleasure of week-end golfers in mind, and only the sometimes high rough represents any sort of difficulty. Yardage is very reasonable but some of the par 4s are designed to set a very serious challenge. A very good course for all players, male and female.

Non loin de la vallée de la Tamise, des Chiltern Hills, ou de la réserve d'animaux sauvages de Whipsnade, la plus vaste d'Europe, Ashridge est situé au calme dans cette adorable campagne où les familles aristocrates ont bâti de superbes châteaux. Ce parcours date de 1932, et n'a fait l'objet que de minimes modifications, pas même d'Henry Cotton, qui fut longtemps le professionnel du club. Dans un superbe environnement de parc, le dessin est d'un classicisme satisfaisant, chaque trou ayant pourtant un cacatère individuel bien marqué. Les architectes ont visiblement pensé surtout au plaisir des amateurs en week-end, seul le rough, souvent haut et épais, représentant une difficulté importante. La longueur reste très raisonnable, quelques par 4 pouvant présenter de sérieux challenges par leur dessin. Un très bon parcours adapté à tous les joueurs... et joueuses !

Ashridge Golf Club — 1932

Little Gaddesden -ENG - BERKHAMSTED, Herts HP4 1LY

Office	Secrétariat	(44) 01442 - 842 244
Pro shop	Pro-shop	(44) 01442 - 842 307
Fax	Fax	(44) 01442 - 843 770
Web	www.ashridgegolfclub.ltd.uk	
Situation	Situation	

10 km from Hemel Hemstead (pop. 79 235) 11 km from Aylesbury

Annual closure	Fermeture annuelle	no
Weekly closure	Fermeture hebdomadaire	no

Fees main season Tarifs haute saison	Week days Semaine	We/Bank holidays We/Férié
	18 holes	
Individual Individuel	£ 47	*
Couple Couple	£ 94	*

Full weekdays: £ 65 / * Weekends: members only

Caddy	Caddy	no
Electric Trolley	Chariot électrique	£ 5 /18 holes
Buggy	Voiturette	no
Clubs	Clubs	£ 10 /18 holes

Credit cards Cartes de crédit
Visa - Eurocard - Mastercard - DC - AMEX
(Pro shop goods only)

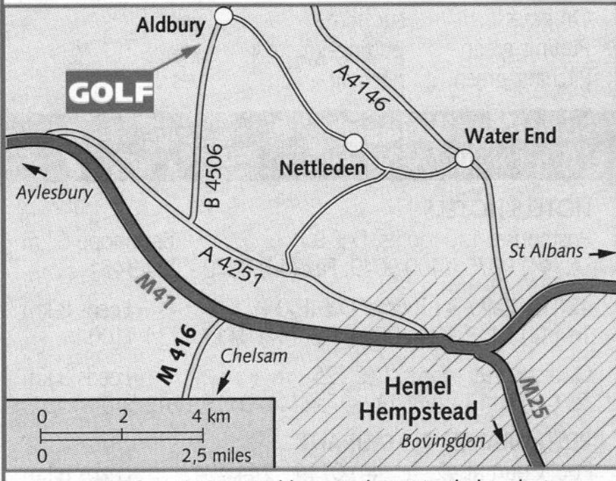

Access Accès : A41 to Berkhamsted. At Northchurch, turn right onto B4506.
Map 8 on page 498 Carte 8 Page 498

Golf course — PARCOURS — 16/20

Site	Site	
Maintenance	Entretien	
Architect	Architecte	Sir Guy Campbell Hutchinson, Hotchkin
Type	Type	parkland
Relief	Relief	
Water in play	Eau en jeu	
Exp. to wind	Exposé au vent	
Trees in play	Arbres en jeu	

Scorecard Carte de score	Chp. Chp.	Mens Mess.	Ladies Da.
Length Long.	5892	5595	5100
Par	72	72	73
Slope system	—	—	—

Advised golfing ability Niveau de jeu recommandé: 0 12 24 36
Hcp required Handicap exigé: certificate

Club house & amenities — CLUB HOUSE ET ANNEXES — 7/10

Pro shop	Pro-shop	
Driving range	Practice	
Sheltered	couvert	no
On grass	sur herbe	yes
Putting-green	putting-green	yes
Pitching-green	pitching green	yes

Hotel facilities — ENVIRONNEMENT HOTELIER — 6/10

HOTELS HÔTELS

Pendley Manor, 70 rooms, D £ 140 — Tring 5 km
Tel (44) 01442 - 891 891, Fax (44) 01442 - 890 687

Hartwell House, 46 rooms, D £ 215 — Aylesbury 12 km
Tel (44) 01296 - 747 444, Fax (44) 01296 - 747 450

Watermill, 75 rooms, D £ 115 — Hemel Hempstead 8 km
Tel (44) 01442 - 349 955, Fax (44) 01442 - 866 130

RESTAURANTS RESTAURANT

Hartwell House, Tel (44) 01296 - 747 444 — Aylesbury

Pendley Manor, Tel (44) 01442 - 891 891 — Tring 5 km

Bottle and Glass, Tel (44) 01296 - 748 488 — Aylesbury

BADGEMORE PARK

14 | 7 | 7

Come here in July and dress up for the royal regattas on the Thames. They are held just after Royal Ascot and just before the international polo tournament at Windsor. All three events could be combined and easily be called the "Hat Festival". Here we are in the magnificent Thames valley that would be fun to discover by boat, but only after a good round of golf here for example, where this recent layout designed by Bob Sandow has quickly forged a fine reputation for itself. The one regret is that there is no driving range, but maybe this reflects a desire not to break with a tradition that has also shaped the style of the course: squat, rather tight and with trees looming skyward. Well-balanced, imaginative and very natural in style, Badgemore Park has been improved, and not only with new tee-boxes.

Il faut venir en juillet pour les régates royales sur la Tamise, où l'on sort les mêmes toilettes qu'au Royal Ascot, quelques jours plus tôt. Pour faire bon poids, on ajoutera l'International Polo à Windsor. L'ensemble pourrait être dénommé "Festival des Chapeaux." Nous sommes ici dans l'adorable vallée de la Tamise, que l'on aimera parcourir en bateau. Après une bonne partie de golf, ici par exemple, où ce récent parcours de Bob Sandow s'est vite fait une bonne réputation. On regrette seulement l'absence de practice, mais c'est peut-être un souci de rester dans la tradition, comme en témoigne le style du parcours, bien ramassé, assez étroit, avec des arbres prenant pas mal de place dans le ciel ! Bien équilibré, imaginatif et très naturel, il est constamment amélioré, après la construction de nouveaux départs.

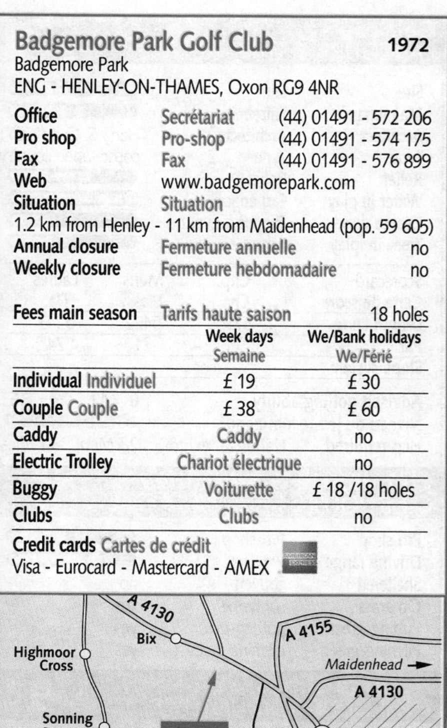

Badgemore Park Golf Club — **1972**

Badgemore Park
ENG - HENLEY-ON-THAMES, Oxon RG9 4NR

Office	Secrétariat	(44) 01491 - 572 206
Pro shop	Pro-shop	(44) 01491 - 574 175
Fax	Fax	(44) 01491 - 576 899
Web	www.badgemorepark.com	
Situation	Situation	

1.2 km from Henley - 11 km from Maidenhead (pop. 59 605)

Annual closure	Fermeture annuelle	no
Weekly closure	Fermeture hebdomadaire	no

Fees main season Tarifs haute saison	18 holes	
	Week days Semaine	**We/Bank holidays** We/Férié
Individual Individuel	£ 19	£ 30
Couple Couple	£ 38	£ 60
Caddy	Caddy	no
Electric Trolley	Chariot électrique	no
Buggy	Voiturette	£ 18 /18 holes
Clubs	Clubs	no

Credit cards Cartes de crédit
Visa - Eurocard - Mastercard - AMEX

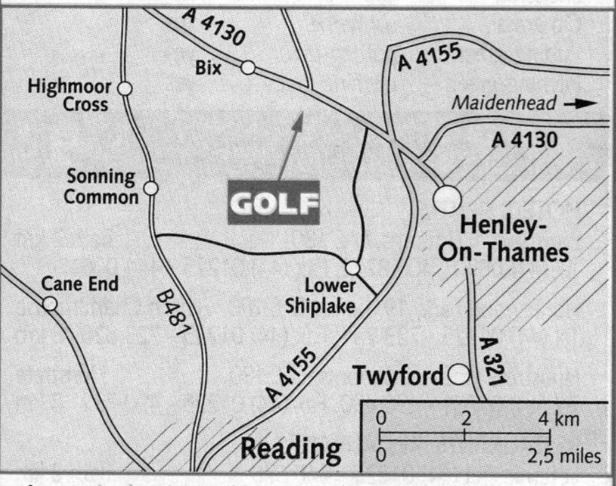

Access Accès : Leave M4 at Jct 8/9, A404, A4130 through Henley-on-Thames. Club house 1.2 km (3/4 m.) after Henley.
Map 8 on page 498 Carte 8 Page 498

Golf course — PARCOURS — 14/20

Site	Site	
Maintenance	Entretien	
Architect	Architecte	Bob Sandow
Type	Type	parkland
Relief	Relief	
Water in play	Eau en jeu	
Exp. to wind	Exposé au vent	
Trees in play	Arbres en jeu	

Scorecard Carte de score	**Chp.** Chp.	**Mens** Mess.	**Ladies** Da.
Length Long.	5500	5082	5036
Par	69	69	72
Slope system	—	—	—

Advised golfing ability 0 12 24 36
Niveau de jeu recommandé
Hcp required Handicap exigé no

Club house & amenities — CLUB HOUSE ET ANNEXES — 7/10

Pro shop	Pro-shop	
Driving range	Practice	
Sheltered	couvert	no
On grass	sur herbe	no
Putting-green	putting-green	yes
Pitching-green	pitching green	yes

Hotel facilities — ENVIRONNEMENT HOTELIER — 7/10

HOTELS HÔTELS

Red Lion, 26 rooms, D £ 135 — Henley 4 km
Tel (44) 01491 - 572 161, Fax (44) 01491 - 410 039

Stonor Arms, 10 rooms, D £ 155 — Stonor 4 km
Tel (44) 01491 - 638 866, Fax (44) 01491 - 638 863

Holiday Inn, 187 rooms, D £ 175 — Maidenhead 11 km
Tel (44) 01628 - 506 000, Fax (44) 01628 - 506 001

RESTAURANTS RESTAURANT

Stonor Arms, Tel (44) 01491 - 638 866 — Stonor 4 km

Villa Marina, Tel (44) 01491 - 575 262 — Henley4 km

Fredrick's, Tel (44) 01628 - 581 000 — Maidenhead

BATH

16 | 6 | 9

A highly reputed spa city for more than two centuries, Bath is essential visiting particularly during the music festival held here in May-June, one of the best times to visit England anyway. Very busy on weekends, Bath has several good courses including this one, located on high ground (and providing some splendid views) and laid out over a former stone quarry. Tips from the locals will help you negotiate a number of blind shots and some sloping fairways, avoid some disconcerting kicks and make allowance for wind that can blow your game away. Their help will only increase your enjoyment on what is a rather forgiving course for hackers and beginners, but where better players will need to keep their wits about them if they want to score as well as they hope to. Hardly a major championship course but one with real personality that is well worth getting to know. After your round, go visit the impressive Roman baths in the city centre.

Ville d'eau de grande réputation depuis deux siècles, Bath est aussi à visiter, au moment du festival de musique en mai-juin, l'une des plus belles périodes pour venir en Angleterre. Très fréquenté en week-end, Bath a plusieurs bons golfs, dont celui-ci, situé sur les hauteurs (avec de très belles vues), et dessiné sur le site d'anciennes carrières de pierre. L'aide des joueurs locaux vous aidera à bien négocier quelques coups aveugles et certains fairways en pente, éviter certains rebonds déconcertants, et tenir compte d'un vent qui peut être assez prononcé. Vous n'en apprécierez que mieux ce tracé assez indulgent pour les joueurs moyens ou peu expérimentés, mais où les bons joueurs devront maintenir leur attention en éveil pour faire des scores à hauteur de leurs espérances. Sans être un parcours de championnat, il présente une personnalité à connaître. Ensuite, allez piquer une tête dans les Bains Romains de la ville.

Bath Golf Club — 1883

Sham Castle, North Road
ENG - BATH, Somerset BA2 6JG

Office	Secrétariat	(44) 01225 - 463 834
Pro shop	Pro-shop	(44) 01225 - 466 953
Fax	Fax	(44) 01225 - 331 027
Web	—	
Situation	Situation	2 km from Bath
20 km from Bristol (pop. 376 146)		
Annual closure	Fermeture annuelle	no
Weekly closure	Fermeture hebdomadaire	Christmas Day

Fees main season Tarifs haute saison	18 holes	
	Week days Semaine	**We/Bank holidays** We/Férié
Individual Individuel	£ 25	£ 30
Couple Couple	£ 50	£ 60
Caddy	Caddy	no
Electric Trolley	Chariot électrique	£ 10 /day
Buggy	Voiturette	no
Clubs	Clubs	£ 12 /day

Credit cards Cartes de crédit
Visa - Eurocard - Mastercard (Pro shop goods only)

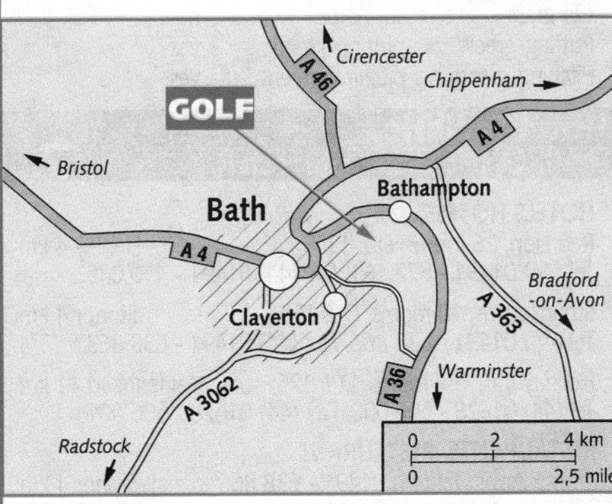

Access Accès : M4 or A36 to Bath. Warminster Road, up North Road, 0,7 km (800 yds) on left up hill. 2 km S of Bath.
Map 6 on page 495 Carte 6 Page 495

Golf course PARCOURS — 16/20

Site	Site	
Maintenance	Entretien	
Architect	Architecte	Harry S. Colt (1937)
Type	Type	copse, open country
Relief	Relief	
Water in play	Eau en jeu	
Exp. to wind	Exposé au vent	
Trees in play	Arbres en jeu	

Scorecard Carte de score	**Chp.** Chp.	**Mens** Mess.	**Ladies** Da.
Length Long.	5795	5422	5243
Par	71	71	74
Slope system	—	—	—

Advised golfing ability Niveau de jeu recommandé — 0 12 24 36
Hcp required Handicap exigé — 28 Men, 36 Ladies

Club house & amenities CLUB HOUSE ET ANNEXES — 6/10

Pro shop	Pro-shop	
Driving range	Practice	
Sheltered	couvert	no
On grass	sur herbe	yes
Putting-green	putting-green	yes
Pitching-green	pitching green	yes

Hotel facilities ENVIRONNEMENT HOTELIER — 9/10

HOTELS HÔTELS
Bath Spa, 103 rooms, D £ 180 — Bath 2 km
Tel (44) 0870 - 400 8222, Fax (44) 01225 - 444 006

Homewood Park, 19 rooms, D £ 180 — Hinton Charterhouse
Tel (44) 01225 - 723 731, Fax (44) 01225 - 723 820 — 8 km

Hunstrete House, 22 rooms, D £ 180 — Hunstrete
Tel (44) 01761 - 490 490, Fax (44) 01225 - 490 732 — 8 km

RESTAURANTS RESTAURANT
Lettonie, Tel (44) 01225 - 446 676 — Bath 2 km
Moody Goose, Tel (44) 01225 - 466 688 — Bath 2 km
Howewood Park — Hinton Charterhouse
Tel (44) 01225 - 723 731 — 8 km

BEAU DESERT

16 | 7 | 7

Opened in 1921, Beau Desert is aptly named, not because of any similarity with the Sahara but because this is an idyllic golfing retreat. For French readers, the word "Beau" could very easily be replaced by "Elégant". This Fowler layout has of course easily embraced a magnificent setting, using the many trees and often digging bunkers (a little in the Harry Colt style) rather than flanking them with sand-hills. This is not a long course but it is narrow, so the choice of club off the tee is important. Most of the time a 3-wood or a long iron will do to get your ball into the right spot for approaching the greens. The rough is generously lined with heather and gorse, as is often the case on a classic style of course such as this which easily soaks up the rain (rainfalls have been known to occur in this part of the world, even in a Desert). An amusing and little known course.

Ouvert en 1921, Beau Desert porte bien son nom. Sauf qu'il ne s'agit pas d'un quelconque Sahara mais plutôt d'un lieu de retraite idyllique. Et si l'on veut traduire "Beau" en français, ce sera aussi le terme d'élégant que l'on utilisera. Le dessin de Fowler s'est bien sûr adapté à un environnement magnifique, utilisant les nombreux arbres, et creusant souvent les bunkers (un peu dans le style de Colt) au lieu de les flanquer de buttes au-dessus du sol. Ce parcours n'est pas bien long, mais il est étroit, ce qui oblige à bien réfléchir sur le club à jouer au départ. La plupart du temps, un bois 3 ou un long fer suffisent pour se placer en bonne position par rapport aux greens. La bruyère et les ajoncs garnissent généreusement les roughs, comme sur ces types de parcours classiques supportant bien la pluie, ce qui semble se produire de temps à autre dans ce pays, même dans un Desert. Un parcours amusant et méconnu.

Beau Desert Golf Club **1921**
Hazel Slade
ENG - CANNOCK, Staffs. WS12 5PJ

Office	Secrétariat	(44) 01543 - 422 626
Pro shop	Pro-shop	(44) 01543 - 422 492
Fax	Fax	(44) 01543 - 451 137
Web	—	
Situation	Situation	5 km from Cannock

25 km from Birmingham (pop. 961 041)

Annual closure	Fermeture annuelle	no
Weekly closure	Fermeture hebdomadaire	no

Fees main season Tarifs haute saison		Full day
	Week days Semaine	**We/Bank holidays** We/Férié
Individual Individuel	£ 38	£ 48
Couple Couple	£ 76	£ 96
Caddy	Caddy	no
Electric Trolley	Chariot électrique	£ 14 /18 holes
Buggy	Voiturette	no
Clubs	Clubs	no

Credit cards Cartes de crédit
(Pro shop only) VISA - Mastercard - AMEX

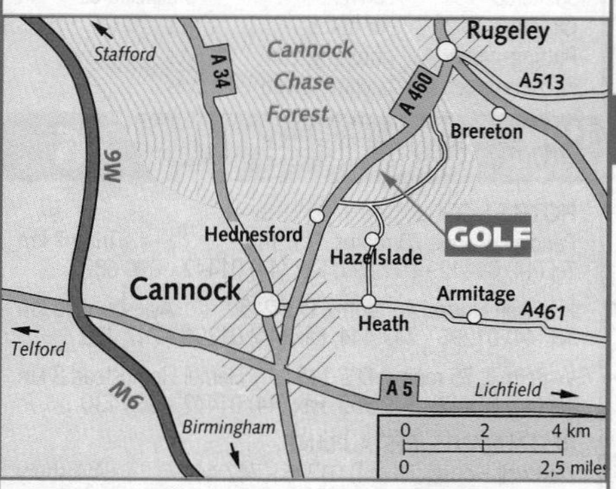

Access Accès : Birmingham, A452 N. A460 Cannock through Hednesford, right at signpost to Hazel Slade, and next left.
Map 7 on page 496 Carte 7 Page 496

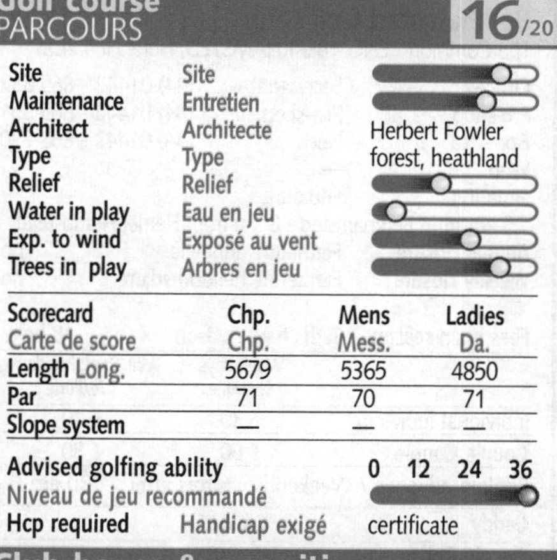

Golf course
PARCOURS **16**/20

Site	Site	
Maintenance	Entretien	
Architect	Architecte	Herbert Fowler
Type	Type	forest, heathland
Relief	Relief	
Water in play	Eau en jeu	
Exp. to wind	Exposé au vent	
Trees in play	Arbres en jeu	

Scorecard Carte de score	**Chp.** Chp.	**Mens** Mess.	**Ladies** Da.
Length Long.	5679	5365	4850
Par	71	70	71
Slope system	—	—	—

Advised golfing ability 0 12 24 36
Niveau de jeu recommandé
Hcp required Handicap exigé certificate

Club house & amenities
CLUB HOUSE ET ANNEXES **7**/10

Pro shop	Pro-shop	
Driving range	Practice	
Sheltered	couvert	10 bays
On grass	sur herbe	no
Putting-green	putting-green	yes
Pitching-green	pitching green	yes

Hotel facilities
ENVIRONNEMENT HOTELIER **7**/10

HOTELS HÔTELS
Roman Way, 56 rooms, D £ 100 — Cannock 5 km
Tel (44) 01543 - 572 121, Fax (44) 01543 - 502 749

Jonathan's, 48 rooms, D £ 150 — Birmingham 25 km
Tel (44) 0121 - 429 3757, Fax (44) 0121 - 434 3107

Asquith House, 10 rooms, D £ 83 — Birmingham 25 km
Tel (44) 0121 - 454 5282, Fax (44) 0121 - 456 4668

Fairlawns, 50 rooms, D £ 105 — Aldridge 8 km
Tel (44) 01922 - 455 122, Fax (44) 01922 - 743 210

RESTAURANTS RESTAURANT
Thrales, Tel (44) 01543 - 255 091 — Lichfield 10 km
Old Farmhouse, Tel (44) 01543 - 490 353 — Armitage 5 km

BERKHAMSTED

16 | 7 | 6

Berkhamsted is one of those courses that is close enough to London to be within easy reach and far enough away so as not to be over-crowded. Even so, you still need to call to book a tee-off time. The new clubhouse is just perfect in terms of comfort but you leave your shoes in the hallway. The landscape here is similar to that at Ashridge, a few miles down the road, and is just as respectable and pleasant. The one big difference is that there are no bunkers. This is logical enough in that bunkers are created by sheep and here there are no sheep, just horses in the woods and lots of people out walking. Fortunately they do not come into play. The absence of sand is largely made good by the bushes and heather and by the dips that you might call grass bunkers. Getting out of them with the desired results is never easy, either. The greens are small and so emphasise the need for accuracy. Worth knowing.

Berkhamsted fait partie de ces clubs assez proches de Londres pour en faciliter l'accès, et assez éloignés pour ne pas être trop surchargés, bien qu'il soit toujours nécessaire de téléphoner à l'avance. Le nouveau Clubhouse est tout à fait confortable, mais on laisse ses clous à la porte. On trouve ici un paysage assez proche de celui d'Ashridge,à quelques kilomètres, et un parcours tout aussi respectable et plaisant. Mais avec une grande différence : ici, aucun bunker ! C'est bien logique, les bunkers ont été créés par des moutons, on ne trouve ici que des chevaux dans les bois, et beaucoup de promeneurs... mais rarement en jeu. Ce manque de sable est largement compensé par les buissons et la bruyère, et par des dépressions que l'on peut appeler "bunkers d'herbe," dont il n'est guère facile de s'extraire avec des résultats garantis. Les greens sont petits, ce qui accentue la nécessité d'être précis. A connaître.

Berkhamsted Golf Club — 1890

The Common - ENG - BERKHAMSTED, Herts HP4 2QB

Office	Secrétariat	(44) 01442 - 865 832
Pro shop	Pro-shop	(44) 01442 - 865 851
Fax	Fax	(44) 01442 - 863 730
Web	—	
Situation	Situation	

1.5 km from Berkhamsted - 8 km from Hemel Hempstead

Annual closure	Fermeture annuelle	no
Weekly closure	Fermeture hebdomadaire	no

Fees main season Tarifs haute saison	Week days Semaine	We/Bank holidays We/Férié
		18 holes
Individual Individuel	£ 30	£ 40
Couple Couple	£ 60	£ 80

Book in advance / Weekends: visitors after 11.30 am

Caddy	Caddy	no
Electric Trolley	Chariot électrique	no
Buggy	Voiturette	no
Clubs	Clubs	£ 10 /18 holes

Credit cards Cartes de crédit
Visa - Mastercard - JCB - AMEX
(Pro shop goods only)

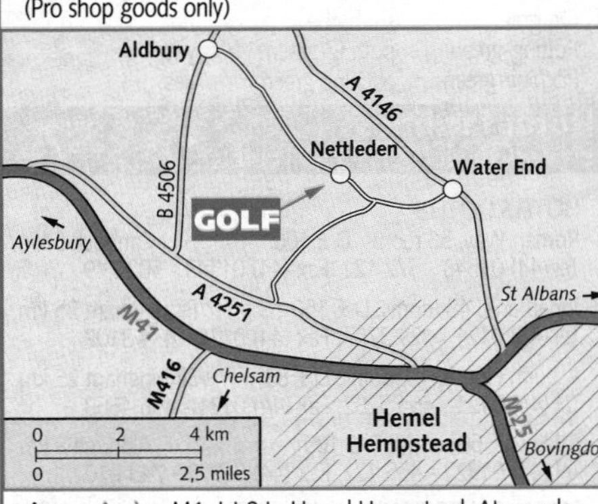

Access Accès : M1, Jct 8 to Hemel Hempstead. At roundabout, take Leighton Buzzard Road. After 4.5 km (3 m.) take Potten End. Turn on left. Golf 4.5 km on left.
Map 8 on page 498 Carte 8 Page 498

Golf course PARCOURS — 16/20

Site	Site	
Maintenance	Entretien	
Architect	Architecte	G.H. Gowring
Type	Type	inland, heathland
Relief	Relief	
Water in play	Eau en jeu	
Exp. to wind	Exposé au vent	
Trees in play	Arbres en jeu	

Scorecard Carte de score	Chp. Chp.	Mens Mess.	Ladies Da.
Length Long.	5945	5580	5161
Par	71	71	73
Slope system	—	—	—

Advised golfing ability Niveau de jeu recommandé — 0 12 24 36
Hcp required Handicap exigé — certificate

Club house & amenities CLUB HOUSE ET ANNEXES — 7/10

Pro shop	Pro-shop	
Driving range	Practice	
Sheltered	couvert	practice area
On grass	sur herbe	yes
Putting-green	putting-green	yes
Pitching-green	pitching green	yes

Hotel facilities ENVIRONNEMENT HOTELIER — 6/10

HOTELS HÔTELS
Pendley Manor, 70 rooms, D £ 140 — Tring 7 km
Tel (44) 01442 - 891 891, Fax (44) 01442 - 890 687

Hartwell House, 46 rooms, D £ 215 — Aylesbury 10 km
Tel (44) 01296 - 747 444, Fax (44) 01296 - 747 450

Watermill, 75 rooms, D £ 115 — Hemel Hempstead 8 km
Tel (44) 01442 - 349 955, Fax (44) 01442 - 866 130

RESTAURANTS RESTAURANT
Hartwell House, Tel (44) 01296 - 747 444 — Aylesbury
Pendley Manor, Tel (44) 01442 - 891 891 — Tring 7 km
Bottle and Glass
Tel (44) 01296 - 748 488 — Aylesbury 12 km

BERKSHIRE (THE) Blue Course

17 | 8 | 7

As it is not always easy to choose between the Red and the Blue courses, play both on either side of lunch. The clubhouse, although renovated, has lost nothing of its charm worthy of characters from P.G. Wodehouse. The trees, not so old but already venerable, are the main setting for this discreet course designed by Herbet Fowler, an equally discreet designer but a real connoisseur of golf (see also Saunton and Walton Heath). The other hazards are fewer in number but just as daunting, for example the bunkers or the stream which crosses several fairways. Here you need every club in your bag, a sign of excellence if ever there was one. Green-keeping is always of the highest standard although without reaching the virtually fanatical levels of preparation that you see all too often these days. Berkshire may not have the "royal" tag but "princely" will do just nicely.

Comme il n'est pas possible de choisir vraiment entre les deux parcours du Berkshire, il faudra jouer les deux, avec une petite visite pour déjeuner à la mi-temps au Clubhouse dont l'intérieur rénové n'a pas perdu son atmosphère digne des héros de P.G. Wodehouse. Les arbres (pas si anciens, mais déjà très vénérables) constituent le décor entourant ce parcours sobrement dessiné par Herbert Fowler, architecte discret, mais toujours aussi connaisseur du jeu de golf (voir aussi Saunton ou Walton Heath). Les autres obstacles ne sont pas très nombreux, mais sont toujours efficaces, comme les bunkers ou le ruisseau traversant plusieurs fairways. Ici, on utilise tous les clubs du sac, c'est un signe de qualité. L'entretien y est de grande qualité, sans les excès de préparation quasi maniaque que l'on voit trop souvent aujourd'hui. Berkshire n'est peut-être pas (ou plus) "Royal," mais il vous offre un plaisir princier.

The Berkshire Golf Club — 1928

Swinley Road
ENG - ASCOT, Berks SL5 8AY

Office	Secrétariat	(44) 01344 - 621 495
Pro shop	Pro-shop	(44) 01344 - 622 351
Fax	Fax	(44) 01344 - 623 328
Web	—	
Situation	Situation	

3 km from Ascot - 5 km from Bracknell (pop. 50 325)

Annual closure	Fermeture annuelle	no
Weekly closure	Fermeture hebdomadaire	no

Fees main season Tarifs haute saison		18 holes
	Week days Semaine	**We/Bank holidays** We/Férié
Individual Individuel	£ 60	*
Couple Couple	£ 120	*

Full weekdays: £ 80 / * No visitors at weekends

Caddy	Caddy	£ 35 /on request
Electric Trolley	Chariot électrique	no
Buggy	Voiturette	£ 25 /18 holes
Clubs	Clubs	£ 20 /18 holes

Credit cards Cartes de crédit
Visa - Mastercard (Pro shop goods only)

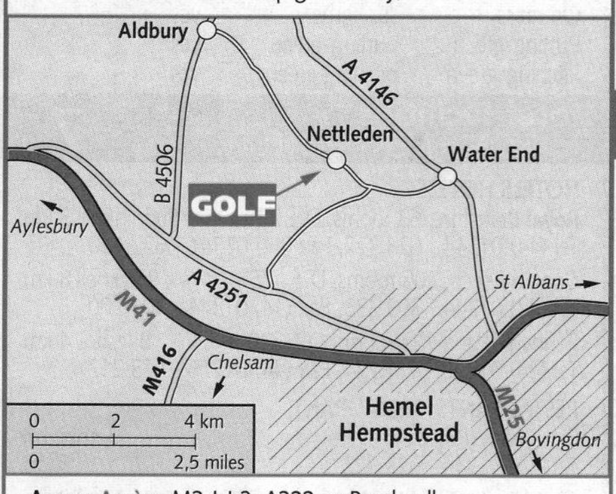

Access Accès : M3 Jct 3. A322 → Bracknell. A332 on right → Ascot. Club house 750 m on left.
Map 8 on page 498 Carte 8 Page 498

Golf course PARCOURS — 17/20

Site	Site	
Maintenance	Entretien	
Architect	Architecte	Herbert Fowler
Type	Type	inland, forest
Relief	Relief	
Water in play	Eau en jeu	
Exp. to wind	Exposé au vent	
Trees in play	Arbres en jeu	

Scorecard Carte de score	**Chp.** Chp.	**Mens** Mess.	**Ladies** Da.
Length Long.	5635	5420	5077
Par	71	71	73
Slope system	—	—	—

Advised golfing ability Niveau de jeu recommandé — 0 12 24 36
Hcp required Handicap exigé Introduction from home club

Club house & amenities CLUB HOUSE ET ANNEXES — 8/10

Pro shop	Pro-shop	
Driving range	Practice	
Sheltered	couvert	no
On grass	sur herbe	yes
Putting-green	putting-green	yes
Pitching-green	pitching green	yes

Hotel facilities ENVIRONNEMENT HOTELIER — 7/10

HOTELS HÔTELS
Royal Berkshire, — Sunninghill 3 km
63 rooms, D £ 220
Tel (44) 01344 - 623 322, Fax (44) 01344 - 627 100

Coppid Beech, 205 rooms, D £ 175 — Bracknell 8 km
Tel (44) 01344 - 303 333, Fax (44) 01344 - 301 200

Hilton, 215 rooms, D £ 235 — Bracknell 5 km
Tel (44) 01344 - 424 801, Fax (44) 01344 - 487 454

RESTAURANTS RESTAURANT
Stateroom (Royal Berkshire) — Sunninghill 3 km
Tel (44) 01344 - 623 322

Jade Fountain, Tel (44) 01344 - 627 070 — Sunninghill

Ciao Ninety, Tel (44) 01344 - 622 285 — Ascot 3 km

BERKSHIRE (THE) Red Course

17 | 8 | 7

If you have only ever played here once, you will probably be hard pushed to remember whether it was the Blue course or the Red. They are not quite twins but the similarities of landscape and in length can be confusing. Here is some valuable help: if you played six par 5s, six par 3s and six par 4s, then you played the Red course. You will need at least all those par 5s (some are trimmed to par 4s for certain top tournaments) to bag some birdies and recover what you will have certainly lost on the par 3s. They are all dangerous and making par can be a real problem should you miss the green. You need a steady game and some straight hitting to do well here, particularly with your longer irons. The pines, chestnut trees and birch trees certainly make for a pretty country setting, but you probably won't find them so appealing when you come to add up your score. And even if you do keep out of the trees, there is still the heather to contend with.

Si vous n'avez joué ici qu'une seule fois, vous avez peu de chances de vous souvenir si c'était le "Blue" ou le "Red." L'un ou l'autre ne sont sans doute pas aussi semblables que des jumeaux, mais même leurs similitudes de longueur peut ajouter à la confusion. Une indication précieuse : si vous avez joué six par 5, six par 3 et six par 4, c'était le "Red." Il faut au moins tous ces par 5 (certains sont ramenés en par 4 dans les grands tournois) pour attraper quelques birdies et récupérer ce que les par 3 vont vous coûter : ils sont tous dangereux et il est très problématique d'y faire le par si vous manquez le green. Il faut ici un jeu solide et bien droit, savoir bien taper les longs fers, car les pins, les châtaigniers et les bouleaux offrent peut-être un cadre bucolique, mais on ne les aime pas toujours autant quand on totalise les scores. Et les éviter ne signifie pas que l'on évitera la bruyère.

The Berkshire Golf Club — 1928

Swinley Road
ENG - ASCOT, Berks SL5 8AY

Office	Secrétariat	(44) 01344 - 621 495
Pro shop	Pro-shop	(44) 01344 - 622 351
Fax	Fax	(44) 01344 - 623 328
Web	—	
Situation	Situation	

3 km from Ascot - 5 km from Bracknell (pop. 50 325)

Annual closure	Fermeture annuelle	no
Weekly closure	Fermeture hebdomadaire	no

Fees main season / Tarifs haute saison	Week days / Semaine	We/Bank holidays / We/Férié
18 holes		
Individual Individuel	£ 60	*
Couple Couple	£ 120	*

Full weekdays: £ 80 / * No visitors at weekends

Caddy	Caddy	£ 35 /on request
Electric Trolley	Chariot électrique	no
Buggy	Voiturette	£ 25 /18 holes
Clubs	Clubs	£ 20 /18 holes

Credit cards Cartes de crédit
Visa - Mastercard (Pro shop goods only)

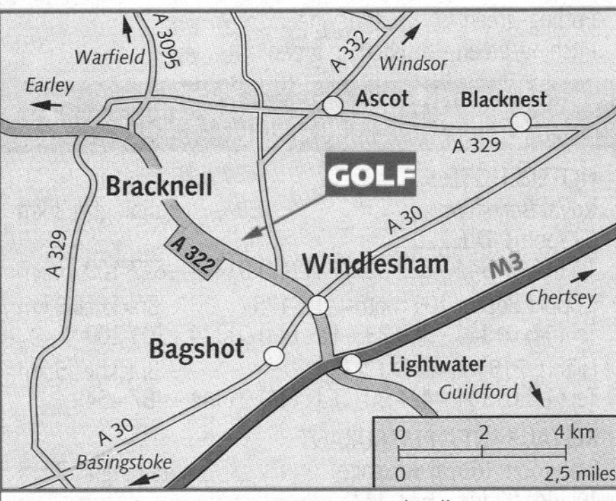

Access Accès : M3 Jct 3. A322 → Bracknell.
A332 on right → Ascot. Club house 750 m on left.
Map 8 on page 498 Carte 8 Page 498

Golf course PARCOURS — 17/20

Site	Site	
Maintenance	Entretien	
Architect	Architecte	Herbert Fowler
Type	Type	inland, forest
Relief	Relief	
Water in play	Eau en jeu	
Exp. to wind	Exposé au vent	
Trees in play	Arbres en jeu	

Scorecard / Carte de score	Chp. / Chp.	Mens / Mess.	Ladies / Da.
Length Long.	5741	5525	5160
Par	72	72	73
Slope system	—	—	—

Advised golfing ability / Niveau de jeu recommandé: 0 12 24 36
Hcp required Handicap exigé Introduction from home club

Club house & amenities CLUB HOUSE ET ANNEXES — 8/10

Pro shop	Pro-shop	
Driving range	Practice	
Sheltered	couvert	no
On grass	sur herbe	yes
Putting-green	putting-green	yes
Pitching-green	pitching green	yes

Hotel facilities ENVIRONNEMENT HOTELIER — 7/10

HOTELS HÔTELS

Royal Berkshire, 63 rooms, D £ 220 — Sunninghill 3 km
Tel (44) 01344 - 623 322, Fax (44) 01344 - 627 100

Coppid Beech, 205 rooms, D £ 175 — Bracknell 8 km
Tel (44) 01344 - 303 333, Fax (44) 01344 - 301 200

Pennyhill Park, 123 rooms, D £ 230 — Bagshot 4 km
Tel (44) 01276 - 471 774, Fax (44) 01276 - 473 217

RESTAURANTS RESTAURANT

Stateroom (Royal Berkshire) — Sunninghill 3 km
Tel (44) 01344 - 623 322

Ciao Ninety, Tel (44) 01344 - 622 285 — Ascot 3 km

Jade Fountain, Tel (44) 01344 - 627 070 — Sunninghill

BERWICK-UPON-TWEED

15 | 6 | 5

A site of endless warring between the English and the Scots, Berwick-upon-Tweed brought peace between both sides and called in designers from both banks of the river Tweed to build a golf course. As you approach, the site looks nothing to write home about, an impression that lasts even as far as the clubhouse, which is simple but functional. The course follows the same style over two wide circles and terrain that is generally on the flat side, with the exception of a few incursions into the sand dunes. This is certainly a less memorable course than others, but its some-what outdated simplicity, a site between the sea and countryside and the peaceful surroundings combine to create an appealing layout. It would be unthinkable not to play here when in the region, but this slumbering "old lady" is still due for some restyling work. In what is an up-and-running project, Dave Thomas has plans to cut out the blind shots and improve the bunkers.

Eternel théâtre des guerres entre Ecossais et Anglais, Berwick-upon-Tweed a fait la paix pour appeler des architectes des deux bords de la Tweed pour s'occuper du parcours. L'arrivée est sans prétention jusqu'au Clubhouse simple, fonctionnel. Le parcours est dans le même style, en deux boucles sur terrain généralement plat, quelques incursions dans les dunes mises à part. Il n'est sans doute pas aussi mémorable que d'autres, mais sa simplicité un peu surannée, une situation entre campagne et mer, la tranquillité de la région lui donnent un charme certain. Il est impensable de ne pas le jouer quand on passe à proximité, mais on attend un réveil de cette "vieille dame." Il semble que ce soit toujours en projet, avec des plans de Dave Thomas pour éliminer les coups aveugles et améliorer les bunkers.

Berwick-upon-Tweed Golf Club — 1890

Goswick, Beal
ENG - BERWICK-UPON-TWEED,

Office	Secrétariat	(44) 01289 - 387 256
Pro shop	Pro-shop	(44) 01289 - 387 380
Fax	Fax	(44) 01289 - 387 256
Web	—	
Situation	Situation	

7 km S of Berwick-upon-Tweed (pop. 26 731)

Annual closure	Fermeture annuelle	no
Weekly closure	Fermeture hebdomadaire	no

Fees main season Tarifs haute saison	18 holes	
	Week days Semaine	**We/Bank holidays** We/Férié
Individual Individuel	£ 25	£ 30
Couple Couple	£ 50	£ 60

Full days: £ 30 / £ 40 (week ends)

Caddy	Caddy	no
Electric Trolley	Chariot électrique	no
Buggy	Voiturette	no
Clubs	Clubs	£ 14 /18 holes

Credit cards Cartes de crédit
Visa - Mastercard (Pro shop goods only)

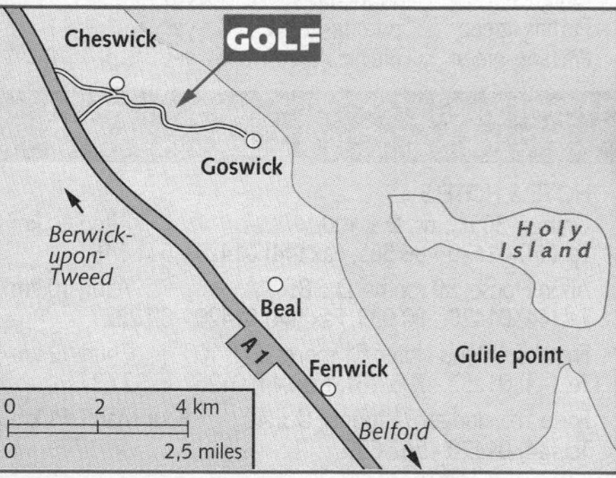

Access Accès : A1 → Berwick-upon-Tweed.
Follow signs after Fenwick village.
Map 2 on page 487 Carte 2 Page 487

Golf course — PARCOURS — 15/20

Site	Site	
Maintenance	Entretien	
Architect	Architecte	James Braid F. Pennink, D. Steel
Type	Type	links
Relief	Relief	
Water in play	Eau en jeu	
Exp. to wind	Exposé au vent	
Trees in play	Arbres en jeu	

Scorecard Carte de score	**Chp.** Chp.	**Mens** Mess.	**Ladies** Da.
Length Long.	5816	5665	5018
Par	72	72	74
Slope system	—	—	—

Advised golfing ability — 0 12 24 36
Niveau de jeu recommandé
Hcp required — Handicap exigé — no

Club house & amenities — CLUB HOUSE ET ANNEXES — 6/10

Pro shop	Pro-shop	
Driving range	Practice	
Sheltered	couvert	no
On grass	sur herbe	yes
Putting-green	putting-green	yes
Pitching-green	pitching green	yes

Hotel facilities — ENVIRONNEMENT HOTELIER — 5/10

HOTELS HÔTELS

Marshall Meadows Country House — Berwick
19 rooms, D £ 100 — 10 km
Tel (44) 01289 - 331 133, Fax (44) 01289 - 331 438

Blue Bell Hotel, — Belford
17 rooms, D £ 90 — 10 km
Tel (44) 01668 - 213 543, Fax (44) 01668 - 213 787

Queenshead, — Berwick
6 rooms, D £ 60 — 10 km
Tel (44) 01289 - 307 852, Fax (44) 01289 - 307 858

Tillmouth Park, 14 rooms, D £ 160 — Cornhill-on-Tweed
Tel (44) 01890 - 882 255, Fax (44) 01890 - 882 540 — 25 km

BLACKMOOR

17 | 6 | 5

Golf is not really about preferring such and such a style of course design, as each has its great side and each its shortcomings. What makes golf such a rich game is the diversity of challenge thrown down to the player. Blackmoor is the perfect example of this, being a very carefully thought out course without the visual gimmickry. Harry Colt placed the hazards, with emphasis as usual on fairness so you see exactly what needs to be done. Given the amount of land available, he preferred a good par 69 to a tricky par 72 and came up with a layout that you will want to play twice in the same day to savour every detail. There are a lot of ditches and especially wonderfully classical bunkers, heather and ubiquitous trees. That sort of description could apply to many other courses, we agree, but Blackmoor has real personality that you meet and feel out on the course.

Il n'est pas question de préférer tel ou tel style d'architecture de golf, chacun a sa grandeur et ses défauts. La richesse du golf vient de cette diversité des défis offerts aux joueurs. Blackmoor est un parfait exemple d'une architecture mûrement pensée, mais sans gadgets visuels. Harry Colt était le maître du placement des obstacles, mais toujours dans un souci de franchise du parcours : on voit ce que l'on doit accomplir. Ici, compte tenu du terrain disponible, il a préféré un bon par 69 à un par 72 "tricky," et l'on aimera le jouer deux fois dans la journée pour mieux en savourer chaque détail. On trouve ici de nombreux fossés, mais surtout, de manière terriblement classique, les bunkers, la bruyère, les arbres omniprésents : c'est une description que l'on pourrait trouver sur bien d'autres parcours... mais Blackmoor a sa véritable personnalité, que vous lrouverez avec votre jeu et votre propre sensibilité.

Blackmoor Golf Club — **1913**

Firgrove Road
ENG - WHITEHILL, Hants GU35 9EH

Office	Secrétariat	(44) 01420 - 472 775
Pro shop	Pro-shop	(44) 01420 - 472 345
Fax	Fax	(44) 01420 - 487 666
Web	www.blackmoorgolf.co.uk	
Situation	Situation	10 km from Alton
Annual closure	Fermeture annuelle	no
Weekly closure	Fermeture hebdomadaire	no

Fees main season Tarifs haute saison	Week days Semaine	We/Bank holidays We/Férié
	18 holes	
Individual Individuel	£ 34	£ 17 *
Couple Couple	£ 68	£ 34 *

* Weekends: only with a member

Caddy	Caddy	no
Electric Trolley	Chariot électrique	£ 5 /18 holes
Buggy	Voiturette	no
Clubs	Clubs	no

Credit cards Cartes de crédit
VISA - MasterCard (not for green fees)

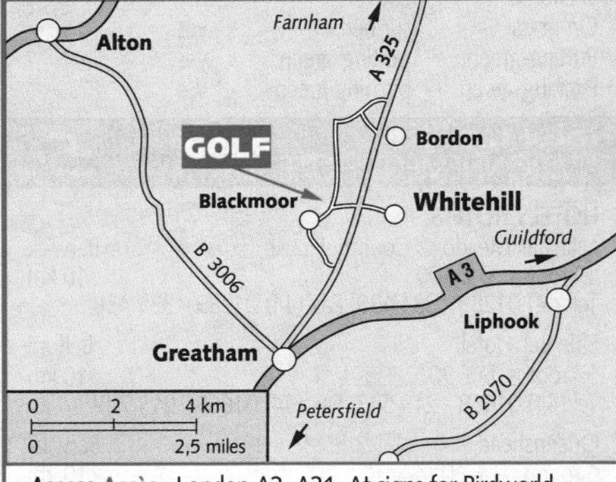

Access Accès : London A3, A31. At signs for Birdworld, A325. Pass Birdworld through Bordon. About 0.75 km out of Bordon, turn right to Blackmoor.
Map 7 on page 496 Carte 7 Page 496

Golf course PARCOURS — 17/20

Site	Site	
Maintenance	Entretien	
Architect	Architecte	Harry S. Colt
Type	Type	inland, heathland
Relief	Relief	
Water in play	Eau en jeu	
Exp. to wind	Exposé au vent	
Trees in play	Arbres en jeu	

Scorecard Carte de score	Chp. Chp.	Mens Mess.	Ladies Da.
Length Long.	5547	5350	5095
Par	69	69	72
Slope system	0	0	0

Advised golfing ability Niveau de jeu recommandé — 0 12 24 36
Hcp required Handicap exigé — 30

Club house & amenities CLUB HOUSE ET ANNEXES — 6/10

Pro shop	Pro-shop	
Driving range	Practice	
Sheltered	couvert	practice area
On grass	sur herbe	yes
Putting-green	putting-green	yes
Pitching-green	pitching green	yes

Hotel facilities ENVIRONNEMENT HOTELIER — 5/10

HOTELS HÔTELS

Grange, 30 rooms, D £ 100 — Alton 10 km
Tel (44) 01420 - 86 565, Fax (44) 01420 - 541 346

Alton House, 39 rooms, D £ 85 — Alton 10 km
Tel (44) 01420 - 80 033, Fax (44) 01420 - 89 222

Frensham Pond Hotel, 51 rooms, D £ 100 — Churt 12 km
Tel (44) 01252 - 795 161, Fax (44) 01252 - 792 631

Forte Travelodge, 31 rooms, D £ 40 — Four Marks 11 km
Tel (44) 01420 - 562 659

RESTAURANTS RESTAURANT

Yew Tree, Tel (44) 01256 - 389 224 — Four Marks 15 km
Grange, Tel (44) 01420 - 86 565 — Alton 10 km

BOLTON OLD LINKS

15 | 5 | 7

Despite the name, this course has neither the sub-soil nor the physical relief of a real links (it is laid out on the side of a hill). Very close to Manchester, it is still a real change of surroundings for local players, except for the few old factory chimneys you can see in the distance. Bolton Old Links actually lies in some pretty English countryside, full of trees, bushes and a few old flint walls, particularly on the 12th hole where there is also a ravine waiting to ruin your card. Note, too, the small and sloping greens on the short par 4s, and the overall difficulty of the putting surfaces in general (the 17th, for instance). Here lie the origins of some of the greens at Augusta, in which Alister Mackenzie had an active hand. This is one of the region's finest tests of golf where, at least for the first time out and especially if it is windy, you shouldn't bother counting your score. Just have a lot of fun.

Ni par le sol, ni par le relief (il est à flanc de colline), ce n'est un vrai "links," mais on donna longtemps aux parcours cette dénomination, par extension. Situé à proximité immédiate de Manchester, il n'en est pas moins dépaysant, n'étaient quelques hautes cheminées d'usine au loin. Bolton Old Links est dans une jolie campagne anglaise, avec plein d'arbres et de buissons, quelques vieux murs de pierre, entre autres au 12, qui comprend également un ravin où votre score peut se perdre. A noter encore, la petite taille et les pentes des greens sur les par 4 courts, mais aussi leur difficulté générale (le 17...). On peut retrouver là l'origine du dessin de quelques greens d'Augusta, auxquels Alister Mackenzie a si efficacement participé. C'est un des meilleurs tests de golf de la région. La première fois, et surtout s'il y a du vent, on ne compte pas son score, et on s'amuse beaucoup.

Bolton Old Links Golf Club — 1891

Chorley Old Road
ENG - BOLTON, Gtr Manchester BL1 5SU

Office	Secrétariat	(44) 01204 - 842 307
Pro shop	Pro-shop	(44) 01204 - 843 089
Fax	Fax	(44) 01204 - 842 307
Web	—	
Situation	Situation	
5 km NW of Bolton (pop. 258 584)		
Annual closure	Fermeture annuelle	no
Weekly closure	Fermeture hebdomadaire	no

Fees main season Tarifs haute saison	Week days Semaine	We/Bank holidays We/Férié
		Full day
Individual Individuel	£ 30	£ 40 *
Couple Couple	£ 60	£ 80 *

* Sunday only, with a reservation

Caddy	Caddy	no
Electric Trolley	Chariot électrique	no
Buggy	Voiturette	no
Clubs	Clubs	no
Credit cards	Cartes de crédit	no

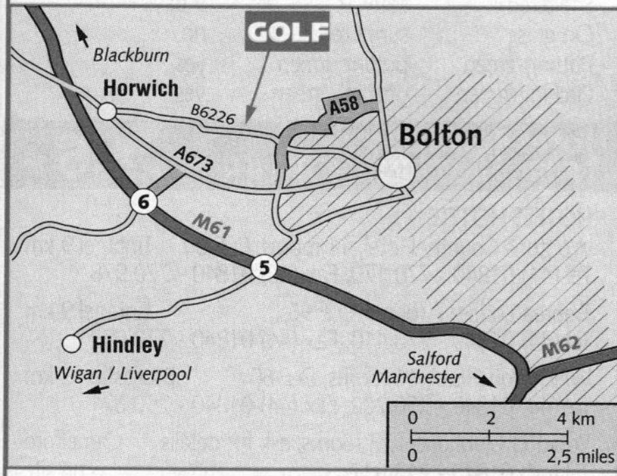

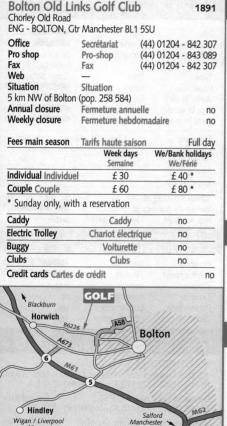

Access Accès : M61 Jct 5, A58 North, then B6226
Map 4 on page 490 Carte 4 Page 490

Golf course — PARCOURS — 15/20

Site	Site	
Maintenance	Entretien	
Architect	Architecte	Alister MacKenzie
Type	Type	inland, open country
Relief	Relief	
Water in play	Eau en jeu	
Exp. to wind	Exposé au vent	
Trees in play	Arbres en jeu	

Scorecard Carte de score	Chp. Chp.	Mens Mess.	Ladies Da.
Length Long.	5830	5490	4995
Par	72	71	73
Slope system	—	—	—

Advised golfing ability Niveau de jeu recommandé: 0 12 24 36
Hcp required Handicap exigé: certificate

Club house & amenities — CLUB HOUSE ET ANNEXES — 5/10

Pro shop	Pro-shop	
Driving range	Practice	
Sheltered	couvert	2 indoor nets
On grass	sur herbe	yes
Putting-green	putting-green	yes
Pitching-green	pitching green	no

Hotel facilities — ENVIRONNEMENT HOTELIER — 7/10

HOTELS HÔTELS

Bolton Moat House, 130 rooms, D £ 115 — Bolton 5 km
Tel (44) 01204 - 879 988, Fax (44) 01204 - 380 777

Last Drop Village, 128 rooms, D £ 120 — Bromley Cross
Tel (44) 01204 - 591 131, Fax (44) 01204 - 304 122

New Pack Horse, 74 rooms, D £ 80 — Bolton 6 km
Tel (44) 01204 - 527 261, Fax (44) 01204 - 364 352

RESTAURANTS RESTAURANT

Bolton Moat House — Bolton 5 km
Tel (44) 01204 - 383 338

Last Drop Village — Bromley Cross 5 km
Tel (44) 01204 - 591 131

BOWOOD (CORNWALL)

16	7	6

Cornwall is traditionally associated with great links courses, but recent additions such as St Mellion have been designed in rather different landscapes. The same goes for Bowood (not to be confused with the Bowood in Wiltshire), a recent course opened in 1992. Laid out in what was once the Black Prince's hunting estate, there are a lot of trees, an unusual feature in Cornwall, many of which the designers have generously brought into play. The style is generally rather British (there is nothing aggressive about this course) although there is a multitude of water hazards in play that most beginners will find rather intimidating. With that said the difficulties are not insurmountable, as long as you can get the ball cleanly up in the air, especially on the 5th hole, a long par 4 with an island green. The clubhouse is huge with pretty views over a country landscape and is to be given 29 rooms to accommodate visitors. Land is also available for housing projects.

On associe la Cornouailles avec les grands links, mais de récentes réalisations comme St Mellion se sont incrites dans des paysages tout différents. C'est le cas de ce Bowood (ne pas confondre avec celui du Wiltshire) ouvert en 1992. Situé dans un ancien domaine de chasse du Prince Noir, on y trouve beaucoup d'arbres (c'est inhabituel dans la région), généreusement mis en jeu par les architectes. Le style est resté assez britannique (le dessin n'est jamais agressif) bien qu'il y ait une multitude d'obstacles d'eau en jeu, que les débutants trouveront intimidants. Cela dit, les difficultés ne sont pas insurmontables... si l'on sait porter la balle, en particulier au 5, un long par 4 avec un green en île. Le Clubhouse est immense, avec de jolies vues sur un paysage rural, et devrait être aménagé avec 29 chambres pour recevoir les visiteurs. Des terrains sont aussi disponibles pour des maisons individuelles.

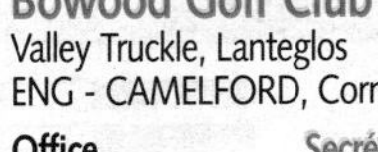

Bowood Golf Club — 1992

Valley Truckle, Lanteglos
ENG - CAMELFORD, Cornwall PL32 9RF

Office	Secrétariat	(44) 01840 - 213 017
Pro shop	Pro-shop	(44) 01840 - 213 017
Fax	Fax	(44) 01840 - 212 622
Web	—	
Situation	Situation	40 km N of Newquay

65 km NW of Plymouth (pop. 245 295)

Annual closure	Fermeture annuelle	no
Weekly closure	Fermeture hebdomadaire	no

Fees main season Tarifs haute saison		18 holes
	Week days Semaine	**We/Bank holidays** We/Férié
Individual Individuel	£ 25	£ 25
Couple Couple	£ 50	£ 50
Caddy	Caddy	no
Electric Trolley	Chariot électrique	no
Buggy	Voiturette	£ 25 /18 holes
Clubs	Clubs	£ 5 /18 holes

Credit cards Cartes de crédit
VISA - Eurocard - MasterCard (Pro-shop & restaurant only)

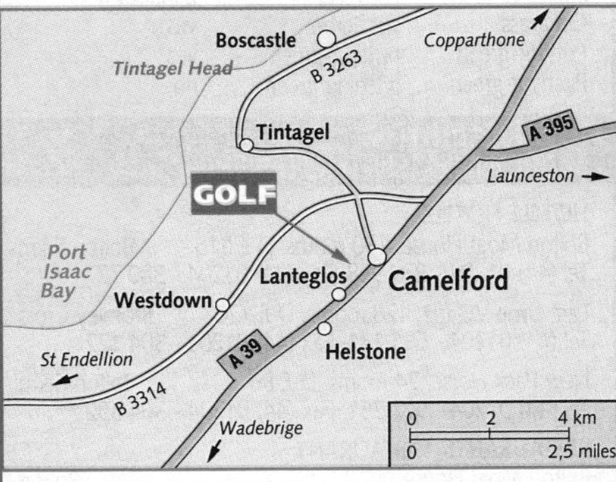

Access Accès : M5, Jct 31 (Exeter), then A30. After Launceston, A395, then A39 South through Camelford. 2 km (1 1/4 m.), turn right on B3266 → Tintagel. First left after garage. **Map 6 on page 494** Carte 6 Page 494

Golf course PARCOURS — 16/20

Site	Site	
Maintenance	Entretien	
Architect	Architecte	Brian Huggett Knott/Bridge
Type	Type	copse, parkland
Relief	Relief	
Water in play	Eau en jeu	
Exp. to wind	Exposé au vent	
Trees in play	Arbres en jeu	

Scorecard Carte de score	**Chp.** Chp.	**Mens** Mess.	**Ladies** Da.
Length Long.	6090	5731	5188
Par	72	72	72
Slope system	—	—	—

Advised golfing ability Niveau de jeu recommandé — 0 12 24 36
Hcp required Handicap exigé — certificate

Club house & amenities CLUB HOUSE ET ANNEXES — 7/10

Pro shop	Pro-shop	
Driving range	Practice	
Sheltered	couvert	9 bays
On grass	sur herbe	no
Putting-green	putting-green	yes
Pitching-green	pitching green	yes

Hotel facilities ENVIRONNEMENT HOTELIER — 6/10

HOTELS HÔTELS

Wootons Country Hotel, 11 rooms, D £ 80 — Tintagel 9 km
Tel (44) 01840 - 770 170, Fax (44) 01840 - 770 978

Trebrea Lodge, 7 rooms, D £ 96 — Tintagel 9 km
Tel (44) 01840 - 770 410, Fax (44) 01840 - 770 092

Wellington Hotel, 16 rooms, D £ 60 — Boscastle 12 km
Tel (44) 01840 - 250 202, Fax (44) 01840 - 250 621

Bowood Clubhouse, 23 rooms, ask for details — Camelford on site
Tel (44) 01840 - 213 017

RESTAURANTS RESTAURANT

Port William, Tel (44) 01840 - 770 230 — Tintagel 8 km

BOWOOD G&CC

17 | 6 | 6

Question: are today's course designers incapable of producing approaches to greens that call for the good old "bump 'n run" shot? Or do they go for the easier option of placing hazards that force players to pitch the greens? We're sorry that Dave Thomas didn't choose to preserve this very British feature here, but his style blends well with the modernity probably required for this sort of course. Bowood is an ambitious resort of a high standard overall where the par 5s are very good, the greens remarkably well defended and where you need to play several rounds before understanding the ins and outs of a very imaginative layout. One word of advice, however: unless you drive straight and long, keep away from the back tees, play further forward and have fun. An impressive resort which is exciting to play, but perhaps not for those continental Europeans who are looking for the traditional English touch of worn tweed and pantaloons.

Les architectes d'aujourd'hui ne sauraient-ils plus dessiner des approches de greens permettant de faire les "bump 'n run" ? C'est plus difficile que de jouer le target -golf, de mettre des obstacles obligeant à faire des coups levés. On regrette que Dave Thomas n'ait pu conserver cet art très britannique, même si son style s'adapte bien à la modernité probablement souhaitée dans ce genre de réalisation. Bowood est un domaine ambitieux, de haute qualité générale, où les par 5 sont très réussis, où les greens sont remarquablement défendus, et où il faut jouer plusieurs fois avant de comprendre les subtilités d'un dessin très imaginatif. Un conseil cependant, ne partez pas des départs reculés, à moins de driver fort et droit. Choisissez de vous amuser, avant tout. Un ensemble impressionnant, passionnant à jouer, mais les continentaux aiment aussi le côté old fashioned et tweed râpé.

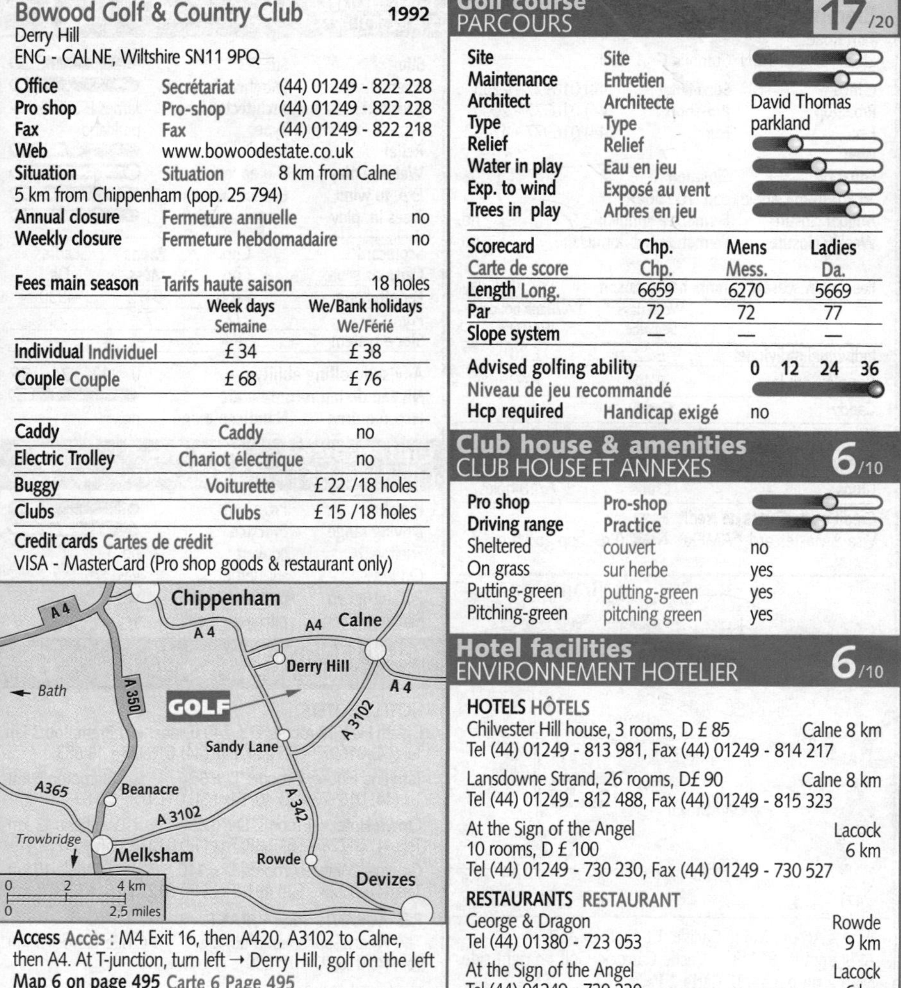

Bowood Golf & Country Club — 1992

Derry Hill
ENG - CALNE, Wiltshire SN11 9PQ

Office	Secrétariat	(44) 01249 - 822 228
Pro shop	Pro-shop	(44) 01249 - 822 228
Fax	Fax	(44) 01249 - 822 218
Web	www.bowoodestate.co.uk	
Situation	Situation	8 km from Calne

5 km from Chippenham (pop. 25 794)

Annual closure	Fermeture annuelle	no
Weekly closure	Fermeture hebdomadaire	no

Fees main season Tarifs haute saison	18 holes	
	Week days Semaine	**We/Bank holidays** We/Férié
Individual Individuel	£ 34	£ 38
Couple Couple	£ 68	£ 76

Caddy	Caddy	no
Electric Trolley	Chariot électrique	no
Buggy	Voiturette	£ 22 /18 holes
Clubs	Clubs	£ 15 /18 holes

Credit cards Cartes de crédit
VISA - MasterCard (Pro shop goods & restaurant only)

Access Accès : M4 Exit 16, then A420, A3102 to Calne, then A4. At T-junction, turn left → Derry Hill, golf on the left
Map 6 on page 495 Carte 6 Page 495

Golf course PARCOURS — 17/20

Site	Site	
Maintenance	Entretien	
Architect	Architecte	David Thomas
Type	Type	parkland
Relief	Relief	
Water in play	Eau en jeu	
Exp. to wind	Exposé au vent	
Trees in play	Arbres en jeu	

Scorecard Carte de score	**Chp.** Chp.	**Mens** Mess.	**Ladies** Da.
Length Long.	6659	6270	5669
Par	72	72	77
Slope system	—	—	—

Advised golfing ability Niveau de jeu recommandé — 0 12 24 36
Hcp required Handicap exigé — no

Club house & amenities CLUB HOUSE ET ANNEXES — 6/10

Pro shop	Pro-shop	
Driving range	Practice	
Sheltered	couvert	no
On grass	sur herbe	yes
Putting-green	putting-green	yes
Pitching-green	pitching green	yes

Hotel facilities ENVIRONNEMENT HOTELIER — 6/10

HOTELS HÔTELS

Chilvester Hill house, 3 rooms, D £ 85 — Calne 8 km
Tel (44) 01249 - 813 981, Fax (44) 01249 - 814 217

Lansdowne Strand, 26 rooms, D£ 90 — Calne 8 km
Tel (44) 01249 - 812 488, Fax (44) 01249 - 815 323

At the Sign of the Angel — Lacock
10 rooms, D £ 100 — 6 km
Tel (44) 01249 - 730 230, Fax (44) 01249 - 730 527

RESTAURANTS RESTAURANT

George & Dragon — Rowde
Tel (44) 01380 - 723 053 — 9 km

At the Sign of the Angel — Lacock
Tel (44) 01249 - 730 230 — 6 km

BRAMPTON

17 | 7 | 6

With Carlisle, this is another little known "gem of a course." The only thing is finding the opportunity to drive as far as this region and the intuition to stop off here. At 1,000 ft. above sea level, it provides some splendid views over the Lake District peaks which soon soothe your sorely tested golfer's nerves. In fact the whole course gives an impression of peace and tranquillity. This is a typical James Braid layout, where the purity of style - there is nothing superfluous on this course - is plain to see: few fairway bunkers, careful thought required for each shot, punishment in keeping with the errors of your ways and rewards for the good shot. You can pitch high balls into the greens but the wisest decision will always be to roll the ball up to the pin (or thereabouts). Fair (despite a few blind shots), direct and clear, the course is rather hilly and at least looks tiring to play. We say "looks" because the senior members walk it several times a week. So maybe you can too.

Non loin de Carlisle, voici encore un petit joyau méconnu. Mais il faut avoir l'occasion de venir dans cette région, et de l'intuition pour s'y arrêter. A 300 mètres d'altitude, il offre des vues superbes sur les montagnes du Lake District, qui vous calmeront vite si vous êtes arrivé sur les nerfs. Tout comme le parcours vous donnera une sensation de paix. C'est un des plus typiques de James Braid. La pureté de son style, où rien n'est inutile, transparaît ici : peu de bunkers de fairway, une exigence de réflexion avant chaque coup, des punitions à la hauteur des fautes, et des récompenses pour les bons coups. Arrivés à proximité des greens, vous aurez la possibilité de faire des balles levées, mais la bonne décison consiste à la faire rouler. Franc (malgré des coups aveugles), direct et clair, ce parcours est assez accidenté et paraît fatigant, mais les membres seniors le jouent à pied plusieurs fois par semaine. Alors...

Brampton Golf Club — 1920

Tarn Road
ENG - BRAMPTON, Cumbria CA8 1HN

Office	Secrétariat	(44) 016977 - 2255
Pro shop	Pro-shop	(44) 016977 - 2000
Fax	Fax	(44) 016977 - 41487
Web		
Situation	Situation	

15 km from Carlisle (pop. 100 562)

Annual closure	Fermeture annuelle	no
Weekly closure	Fermeture hebdomadaire	no

Fees main season / Tarifs haute saison	Week days / Semaine	We/Bank holidays / We/Férié
		Full day
Individual Individuel	£ 22	£ 30
Couple Couple	£ 44	£ 60
Caddy / Caddy		no
Electric Trolley / Chariot électrique		£ 5 /18 holes
Buggy / Voiturette		no
Clubs / Clubs		£ 7 /18 holes

Credit cards Cartes de crédit
Visa - Mastercard - AMEX 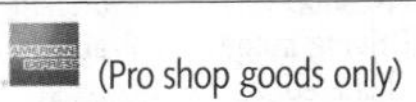 (Pro shop goods only)

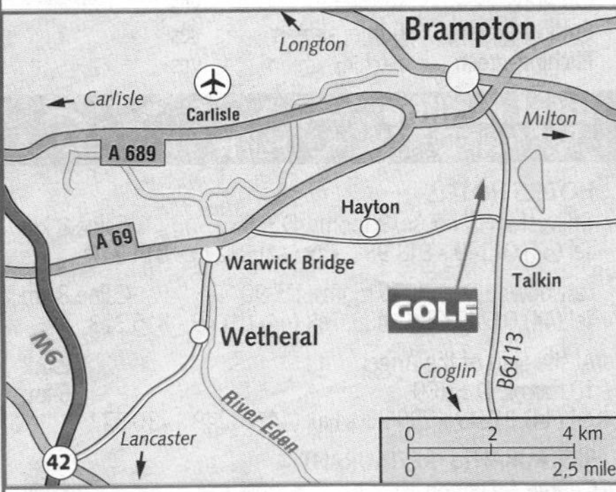

Access Accès : M6 to Carlisle. Jct 43, then A69.
At Brampton, B6413 → Castle Carrock. Golf on right side.
Map 2 on page 487 Carte 2 Page 487

Golf course — PARCOURS — 17/20

Site	Site	
Maintenance	Entretien	
Architect	Architecte	James Braid
Type	Type	parkland
Relief	Relief	
Water in play	Eau en jeu	
Exp. to wind	Exposé au vent	
Trees in play	Arbres en jeu	

Scorecard / Carte de score	Chp. / Chp.	Mens / Mess.	Ladies / Da.
Length Long.	5766	5475	4930
Par	72	72	74
Slope system	—	—	—

Advised golfing ability / Niveau de jeu recommandé — 0 12 24 36
Hcp required / Handicap exigé — no

Club house & amenities — CLUB HOUSE ET ANNEXES — 7/10

Pro shop	Pro-shop	
Driving range	Practice	
Sheltered	couvert	no
On grass	sur herbe	yes
Putting-green	putting-green	yes
Pitching-green	pitching green	yes

Hotel facilities — ENVIRONNEMENT HOTELIER — 6/10

HOTELS HÔTELS

Farlam Hall, 12 rooms, D £ 240 (Dinner inc) Brampton 3 km
Tel (44) 016977 - 46 234, Fax (44) 016977 - 46 683

Tarn End House, 7 rooms, D £ 65 — Brampton 5 km
Tel (44) 016977 - 23 40, Fax (44) 016977 - 20 89

Crown Hotel, 51 rooms, D £ 122 — Wetheral 13 km
Tel (44) 01228 - 561 888, Fax (44) 01228 - 561 637

Crown + Mitre, 97 rooms, D £ 110 — Carlisle 15 km
Tel (44) 01228 - 525 491, Fax (44) 01228 - 514 553

RESTAURANTS RESTAURANT

The Weary Sportsman (Pub) — Castle Carrock 5 km
Tel (44) 016977 - 70 230

No 10, Tel (44) 01228 - 524 183 — Carlisle 15 km

BRANCEPETH CASTLE

14 | 6 | 5

You come here first and foremost to visit Durham, which has retained many vestiges of the Norman conquest, including a castle and an amazing cathedral which in many ways is quite unique. But this course is not to be outshone, as it is laid out around a castle flanked by a church, which both add to the majesty of what is a fine Harry Colt design. A good number of isolated trees are very much in play and seem to detach themselves from the woods like fairway sentinels. A large ravine is another hazard which has to be crossed three times over a wobbling bridge which can only take six players at a time. A very interesting and sometimes surprising course, where the finishing holes should be handled with the utmost care. The whole site is quite superb, so what more could you ask for?

On vient d'abord ici pour visiter Durham, qui conserve de multiples traces de la conquête normande, dont le château et surtout une cathédrale étonnante, dont certains aspects décoratifs sont uniques. Ce parcours n'est pas en reste, car il a trouvé place auprès d'un château flanqué de son église, ce qui apporte plus encore de majesté au beau dessin de Harry Colt. De nombreux arbres isolés sont bien en jeu, et se détachent comme les gardes des bois environnants. Un grand ravin vient également en jeu, et doit être traversé trois fois sur un pont chancelant qui ne peut supporter plus de six personnes à la fois. Un parcours très intéressant, parfois surprenant, et dont les derniers trous doivent être considérés avec attention. L'endroit est superbe, que demander de plus ?

Brancepeth Castle Golf Club — 1924

Brancepeth Village
ENG - DURHAM, Durham DH7 8EA

Office	Secrétariat	(44) 0191 - 378 0075
Pro shop	Pro-shop	(44) 0191 - 378 0183
Fax	Fax	(44) 0191 - 378 3835
Web	—	
Situation	Situation	

6 km W of Durham (pop. 36 937)

Annual closure	Fermeture annuelle	no
Weekly closure	Fermeture hebdomadaire	no

Fees main season / Tarifs haute saison	Week days / Semaine	We/Bank holidays / We/Férié
		Full day
Individual Individuel	£ 30	£ 35
Couple Couple	£ 60	£ 70
Caddy Caddy		no
Electric Trolley Chariot électrique		no
Buggy Voiturette		no
Clubs Clubs		no

Credit cards Cartes de crédit
VISA - Eurocard - MasterCard

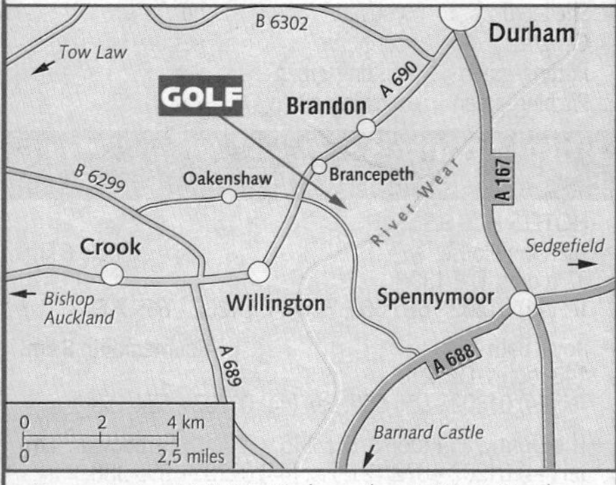

Access Accès : A1 (M) to Durham, then A690 → Crook.
Turn left at crossroads in Brancepeth village.
Take slip road left immediately before Castle gates.
Map 2 on page 487 Carte 2 Page 487

Golf course — PARCOURS — 14/20

Site	Site	
Maintenance	Entretien	
Architect	Architecte	Harry S. Colt
Type	Type	parkland
Relief	Relief	
Water in play	Eau en jeu	
Exp. to wind	Exposé au vent	
Trees in play	Arbres en jeu	

Scorecard / Carte de score	Chp. / Chp.	Mens / Mess.	Ladies / Da.
Length Long.	5720	5720	5312
Par	70	70	75
Slope system	—	—	—

Advised golfing ability / Niveau de jeu recommandé: 0 12 24 36
Hcp required / Handicap exigé: no

Club house & amenities — CLUB HOUSE ET ANNEXES — 6/10

Pro shop	Pro-shop	
Driving range	Practice	
Sheltered	couvert	no
On grass	sur herbe	yes
Putting-green	putting-green	yes
Pitching-green	pitching green	yes

Hotel facilities — ENVIRONNEMENT HOTELIER — 5/10

HOTELS HÔTELS

Royal County — Durham
151 rooms, D £ 150 — 6 km
Tel (44) 0191 - 386 6821, Fax (44) 0191 - 386 0704

Swallow Three Tuns — Durham
50 rooms, D £ 120 — 6 km
Tel (44) 0191 - 386 4326, Fax (44) 0191 - 386 1406

RESTAURANTS RESTAURANT

County (Royal County) — Durham
Tel (44) 0191 - 386 6821 — 6 km

Bistro 21 — Carlisle
Tel (44) 0191 - 384 4354 — 6 km

BROADSTONE

17 | 7 | 7

Some golfers have called Broadstone the Gleneagles of the south. This heather-clad terrain enhanced with pine, birch, oak, chestnut trees and rhododendrons, has kept all the natural appearance of Tom Dunn's original layout, which was later perfected by Harry Colt. Although the holes are often flat, some of the hills are steep and tiring. Never easy to play, the course is a good test for every compartment of your game: length when you need it, accurate ironwork to the rather large but well defended greens, strategy for judging the right distance and flight to avoid the traps, including several dangerous water hazards. If that were not enough, you will also need an excellent short game to make up for mistakes, with lofted or bump 'n roll approach shots, and an acute sense of observation to make the most of the extremely useful experience of local players. Not forgetting your putting and a stop-off at the fountain on the 10th hole, one of the excellent features of a very likeable course.

Certains l'ont appelé le Gleneagles du sud. En terrain de bruyère, orné de pins, bouleaux, chênes, marronniers et rhododendrons, ce terrain a gardé l'aspect naturel du tracé de Tom Dunn, perfectionné et affiné par Harry Colt. Bien que les trous y soient très souvent plats, certaines montées peuvent être assez fatigantes. Peu facile à jouer, c'est un bon test de tous les secteurs de son jeu : la longueur quand il faut porter assez loin la balle, la précision du jeu de fers vers des greens assez grands mais bien protégés, la stratégie quand il faut bien juger des distances et effets pour éviter les obstacles, dont quelques dangereux obstacles d'eau, le petit jeu pour rattraper toutes les fautes, avec des approches levées ou roulées suivant la situation, et l'observation pour tirer profit de l'expérience fort utile des joueurs locaux. Sans oublier le putting ni de s'arrêter à la fontaine du 10, un des attraits d'une très attachante réalisation.

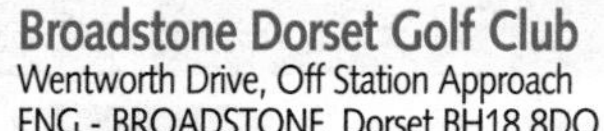

Broadstone Dorset Golf Club — 1898

Wentworth Drive, Off Station Approach
ENG - BROADSTONE, Dorset BH18 8DQ

Office	Secrétariat	(44) 01202 - 692 595
Pro shop	Pro-shop	(44) 01202 - 692 835
Fax	Fax	(44) 01202 - 692 595
Web	—	
Situation	Situation	Bournemouth, 12 km
Annual closure	Fermeture annuelle	no
Weekly closure	Fermeture hebdomadaire	no

528

Fees main season Tarifs haute saison	18 holes	
	Week days Semaine	**We/Bank holidays** We/Férié
Individual Individuel	£ 32	£ 45 *
Couple Couple	£ 64	£ 90 *

Full weekdays: £ 45 / * Only after 3.00 pm

Caddy	Caddy	no
Electric Trolley	Chariot électrique	£ 5 /18 holes
Buggy	Voiturette	no
Clubs	Clubs	yes (ask Pro)

Credit cards Cartes de crédit
(Pro shop goods only) Visa - Mastercard - DC - Amex

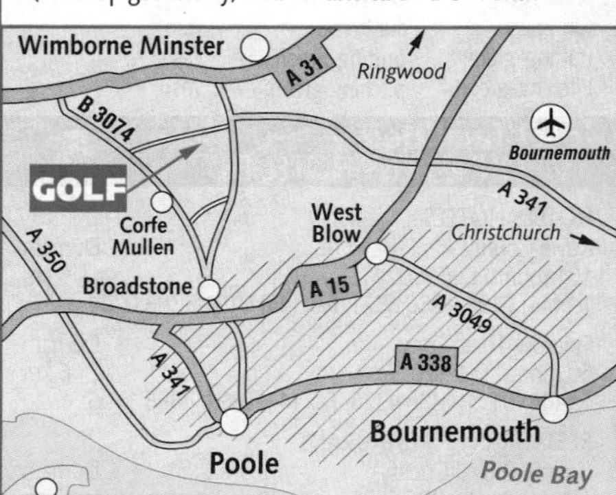

Access Accès : • M3, M27, A31, A349, then Dunyeats Road on the right. • From Poole, B3074, Broadstone Links Road → Blandford, Golf on the right.
Map 6 on page 495 Carte 6 Page 495

Golf course PARCOURS — 17/20

Site	Site	
Maintenance	Entretien	
Architect	Architecte	Tom Dunn Harry S. Colt (1925)
Type	Type	heathland, hilly
Relief	Relief	
Water in play	Eau en jeu	
Exp. to wind	Exposé au vent	
Trees in play	Arbres en jeu	

Scorecard Carte de score	**Chp.** Chp.	**Mens** Mess.	**Ladies** Da.
Length Long.	5746	5547	4975
Par	70	70	72
Slope system	—	—	—

Advised golfing ability 0 12 24 36
Niveau de jeu recommandé

Hcp required Handicap exigé — certificate

Club house & amenities CLUB HOUSE ET ANNEXES — 7/10

Pro shop	Pro-shop	
Driving range	Practice	
Sheltered	couvert	no
On grass	sur herbe	yes
Putting-green	putting-green	yes
Pitching-green	pitching green	yes

Hotel facilities ENVIRONNEMENT HOTELIER — 7/10

HOTELS HÔTELS

Mansion House — Poole 6 km
32 rooms, D £ 130
Tel (44) 01202 - 685 666, Fax (44) 01202 - 665 709

Royal Bath — Bournemouth 8 km
140 rooms, D £ 210
Tel (44) 01202 - 555 555, Fax (44) 01202 - 554 158

The Dormy, 114 rooms, D £ 145 — Ferndown 7 km
Tel (44) 01202 - 872 121, Fax (44) 01202 - 895 388

RESTAURANTS RESTAURANT

La Roche, Tel (44) 01202 - 707 333 — Poole 6 km

Clarks, Tel (44) 01202 - 240 310 — Bournemouth 8 km

BROKENHURST MANOR

15	6	6

Brockenhurst Manor is one of the rare "civilized" spots of the New Forest, one of the finest regions of England over a huge expanse of moorland and oak forest, and a hunting ground for William the Conqueror who helped to create it. The village of Brockenhurst is an excellent starting point for hiking, bicycle rides and horse-trekking, or for playing golf on this Harry Colt course, reached after a very pleasant drive. There is no way you could imagine a course here without trees, and they are a beautiful sight and very much in play, so much so that benders of the ball, in both directions, have a distinct advantage. As is often the case on a Harry Colt layout, the par 3s are wonderful and longer than they look. Another interesting and unusual aspect of this course is that it runs in three loops of 6 holes each, out and back to the club-house. Aside from the trees and bunkers, hazards include a stream which runs along seven holes. Although not really a championship course (it is short), you are guaranteed a great day's golfing.

Brokenhurst Manor est l'un des rares endroits «civilisés» de «New Forest», l'une des plus belles régions d'Angleterre, immense espace de landes et de forêts de chênes, terrain de chasse de Guillaume le Conquérant, qui avait contribué à le créer. Et le village de Brockenhurst est une excellente base de départs pour des randonnées. Ou pour jouer au golf sur ce parcours d'Harry Colt que l'on atteint après une route très plaisante. Ici, on ne pouvait imaginer un parcours sans arbres : ils sont à la fois très beaux visuellement, et très bien mis en jeu. Comme souvent chez Colt, les par 3 sont superbes, et plus longs qu'ils en ont l'air. Autre caractéristique intéressante et inhabituelle, les 18 trous forment trois boucles de six trous revenant au Club house, avec un cours d'eau qui se promène sur sept trous. Bien qu'il ne s'agisse pas vraiment d'un parcours de championnat (il est court), une bonne journée de golf est garantie.

Brokenhurst Manor Golf Club — 1919

Sway Road
ENG - BROCKENHURST, Hants. SO42 7SG

Office	Secrétariat	(44) 01590 - 623 332
Pro shop	Pro-shop	(44) 01590 - 623 092
Fax	Fax	(44) 01590 - 624 140
Web		—
Situation	Situation	Brockenhurst, 2 km

23 km SW of Southampton (pop. 196 864)

Annual closure	Fermeture annuelle	no
Weekly closure	Fermeture hebdomadaire	no
Fees main season	Tarifs haute saison	18 holes

	Week days Semaine	We/Bank holidays We/Férié
Individual Individuel	£ 36	£ 46
Couple Couple	£ 72	£ 92

Full days: £ 46 / £ 62 (week ends)

Caddy	Caddy	no
Electric Trolley	Chariot électrique	no
Buggy	Voiturette	no
Clubs	Clubs	no

Credit cards Cartes de crédit
VISA - MasterCard (not for green fees)

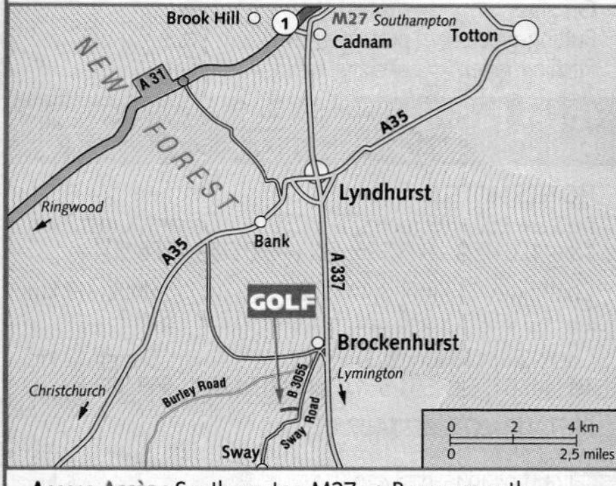

Access Accès : Southampton M27 → Bournemouth.
Exit 1 onto Lyndhurst. → Brockenhurst.
Golf on B0355 (Sway Road)
Map 7 on page 496 Carte 7 Page 496

Golf course PARCOURS — 15/20

Site	Site	
Maintenance	Entretien	
Architect	Architecte	Harry S. Colt
Type	Type	inland
Relief	Relief	
Water in play	Eau en jeu	
Exp. to wind	Exposé au vent	
Trees in play	Arbres en jeu	

Scorecard Carte de score	Chp. Chp.	Mens Mess.	Ladies Da.
Length Long.	5600	5418	5000
Par	70	70	71
Slope system	—	—	—

Advised golfing ability 0 12 24 36
Niveau de jeu recommandé
Hcp required Handicap exigé 24 Men, 36

Club house & amenities CLUB HOUSE ET ANNEXES — 6/10

Pro shop	Pro-shop	
Driving range	Practice	
Sheltered	couvert	2 mats + pract. area
On grass	sur herbe	yes
Putting-green	putting-green	yes
Pitching-green	pitching green	no

Hotel facilities ENVIRONNEMENT HOTELIER — 6/10

HOTELS HÔTELS
Rhinefield House, 34 rooms, D £ 125 — Brockenhurst 7 km
Tel (44) 01590 - 622 922, Fax (44) 01590 - 622 800

Careys Manor, 79 rooms, D £ 130 — Brockenhurst 2 km
Tel (44) 01590 - 623 551, Fax (44) 01590 - 622 799

Thatched Cottage — Brockenhurst 2 km
5 rooms, D £ 130
Tel (44) 01590 - 623 090, Fax (44) 01590 - 623 479

RESTAURANTS RESTAURANT
Simply Poussin — Brockenhurst 2 km
Tel (44) 01590 - 623 063

Thatched Cottage — Brockenhurst 2 km
Tel (44) 01590 - 623 090

BUCKINGHAMSHIRE (THE) 17 | 8 | 7

This is one of those resorts that you find either very pretentious or very cosy. All that's missing is the obligatory fitness centre, but that will come. With this said, you would never judge this John Jacobs course to this sort of criteria. The layout was created with much thought given to today's trends in professional and amateur golfing, forcing the player to take decisions as to the line of fire, the type of shot, whether to attack or whether to play safe. Choosing the right tee-boxes for your game is also an important decision. The woods, isolated trees, lakes and bunkers have been used, created or laid out as if geared to all these technical requirements. Dare we say it, here you get the impression of sitting an examination to ascertain your golf playing skills. As a wily craftsman himself, John Jacobs would not necessarily disagree. We will wait until this course mellows a little and acquires the indulgence of some of the more benign "older" courses.

C'est un de ces complexes que l'on trouvera soit très prétentieux, soit très confortable. Il n'y manque que l'inévitable unité de remise en forme, mais cela ne saurait tarder. Cela dit, le parcours dessiné par John Jacobs ne saurait être jugé sur des critères de goût de ce genre ! Le tracé en a été fait avec beaucoup de réflexion sur les tendances des professionnels et des amateurs, il force à prendre des décisions sur la ligne de jeu, le type de coup, l'attaque ou la sécurité, il force même à choisir les départs adaptés à sa force du jour. Les bois, les arbres isolés, les lacs et les bunkers ont été utilisés ou créés, ou disposés en fonction de ces exigences techniques. Dirons-nous que l'on a un peu l'impression de passer un examen d'aptitude à jouer au golf ? Le fin technicien qu'est Jacobs ne dirait pas forcément non. Nous attendrons que ce parcours vieillisse un peu pour prendre un peu de cette indulgence des bons vieux golfs.

The Buckinghamshire Golf Club — 1992

Denham Court, Denham Court Drive
ENG - DENHAM, Bucks UB9 5BG

Office	Secrétariat	(44) 01895 - 835 777
Pro shop	Pro-shop	(44) 01895 - 835 777
Fax	Fax	(44) 01895 - 835 210
Web	—	
Situation	Situation	London, 25 km
Annual closure	Fermeture annuelle	no
Weekly closure	Fermeture hebdomadaire	no

Fees main season Tarifs haute saison	Week days Semaine	We/Bank holidays We/Férié
		18 holes
Individual Individuel	£ 70	£ 80
Couple Couple	£ 140	£ 160

Booking 48 hrs in advance

Caddy	Caddy	£ 30 /on request
Electric Trolley	Chariot électrique	£ 10 /18 holes
Buggy	Voiturette	no
Clubs	Clubs	£ 25 /18 holes

Credit cards Cartes de crédit
VISA - Eurocard - MasterCard - DC - AMEX

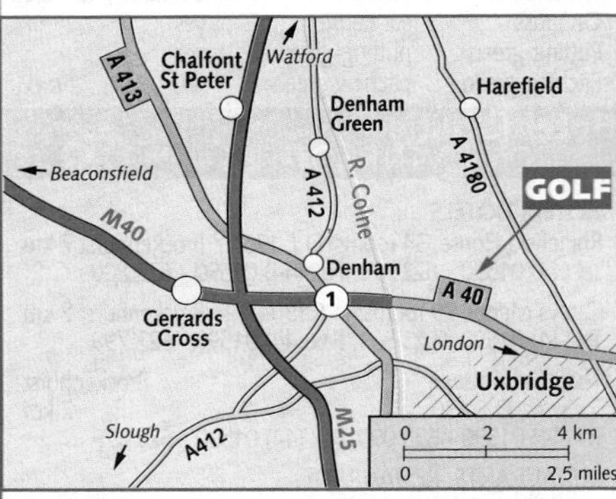

Access Accès : M40 Jct 1. Roundabout on A40, turn into Denham Court Drive, follow signs to the club.
Map 8 on page 498 Carte 8 Page 498

Golf course PARCOURS — 17/20

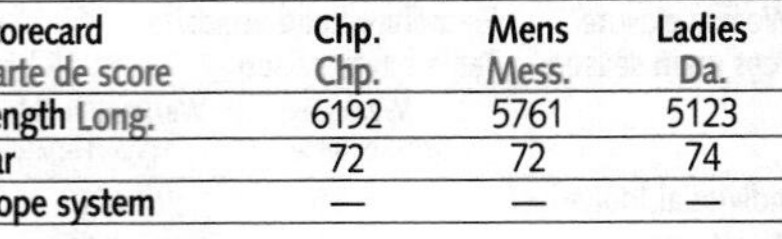

Site	Site	
Maintenance	Entretien	
Architect	Architecte	John Jacobs
Type	Type	parkland
Relief	Relief	
Water in play	Eau en jeu	
Exp. to wind	Exposé au vent	
Trees in play	Arbres en jeu	

Scorecard Carte de score	**Chp.** Chp.	**Mens** Mess.	**Ladies** Da.
Length Long.	6192	5761	5123
Par	72	72	74
Slope system	—	—	—

Advised golfing ability Niveau de jeu recommandé: 0 12 24 36
Hcp required Handicap exigé: no

Club house & amenities CLUB HOUSE ET ANNEXES — 8/10

Pro shop	Pro-shop	
Driving range	Practice	
Sheltered	couvert	
On grass	sur herbe	yes
Putting-green	putting-green	yes
Pitching-green	pitching green	yes

Hotel facilities ENVIRONNEMENT HOTELIER — 7/10

HOTELS HÔTELS

De Vere Bull, 109 rooms, D £ 230 — Gerrards Cross 7 km
Tel (44) 01753 - 885 995, Fax (44) 01753 - 885 504

Copthorne, 219 rooms, D £ 180 — Slough 12 km
Tel (44) 01753 - 516 222, Fax (44) 01753 - 516 237

Courtyard, 149 rooms, D £ 135 — Slough 12 km
Tel (44) 01753 - 551 551, Fax (44) 01753 - 553 333

RESTAURANTS RESTAURANT

Water Hall — Chalfont St Peter 5 km
Tel (44) 01494 - 873 430

Roberto's, Tel (44) 01895 - 632 519 — Ickenham 4 km

Waterfront Brasserie, — Yiewsley 8 km

BUDE & NORTH CORNWALL

15	6	5

Between Tintagel and the pretty harbour of Clovelly, Bude is a popular seaside resort and starting point for walks and treks, especially for bird-watchers who can take the path that runs along the coast. It is also home to a very pretty links course, almost touching the town, where the wind blows as usual and where you find the standard hazards and unpredictable kicks when the ground is dry. A few blind shots and greens add to the pleasure of discovering this course, particularly when you have given up any idea of keeping score. Good technique, good control for knock-down shots and an excellent short game are essential ingredients at Bude, the latter being helpful for short approaches or escapes from some typical links style bunkers. You won't find this course in the League of Champions, but maintenance is good, the greens are excellent and enjoyment is complete. It is also excellent value for money (good for family).

Entre Tintagel et le joli port de Clovelly, Bude est un lieu de vacances balnéaires, mais il faut avoir le sang d'un Britannique pour aller se baigner. C'est aussi un point de départ de promenades, en particulier pour observer les oiseaux en parcourant le sentier qui longe toute la côte. C'est enfin le site d'un très joli links pratiquement en ville, où le vent joue son rôle, mais aussi les hasards de ce genre de parcours, avec des rebonds imprévisibles quand le sol est sec. Quelques coups et greens aveugles ajoutent au plaisir de la découverte, si l'on évite de compter le score. Une bonne technique, une bonne maîtrise des balles basses, un petit jeu excellent s'imposent, ce dernier aussi bien pour les approches roulées que pour s'extraire de quelques bunkers typiques. Bien sûr, Bude & North Cornwall ne joue pas dans la Ligue des Champions, mais l'entretien est très correct, les greens excellents et le plaisir total. Et le rapport qualité/prix reste bon, ce qui est fort appréciable quand on vient en famille.

Bude & North Cornwall Golf Club — 1891

Burn View
ENG - BUDE, Cornwall EX23 8 DA

Office	Secrétariat	(44) 01288 - 352 006
Pro shop	Pro-shop	(44) 01288 - 353 635
Fax	Fax	(44) 01288 - 356 855
Web	www.budegolf.co.uk	
Situation	Situation	70 km from Exeter
Annual closure	Fermeture annuelle	no
Weekly closure	Fermeture hebdomadaire	no

Fees main season Tarifs haute saison	18 holes	
	Week days Semaine	**We/Bank holidays** We/Férié
Individual Individuel	£ 25	£ 30
Couple Couple	£ 50	£ 60

Booking essential (restrictions for visitors)

Caddy	Caddy	no
Electric Trolley	Chariot électrique	no
Buggy	Voiturette	no
Clubs	Clubs	£ 10

Credit cards Cartes de crédit
VISA - Eurocard - MasterCard (Pro shop goods only)

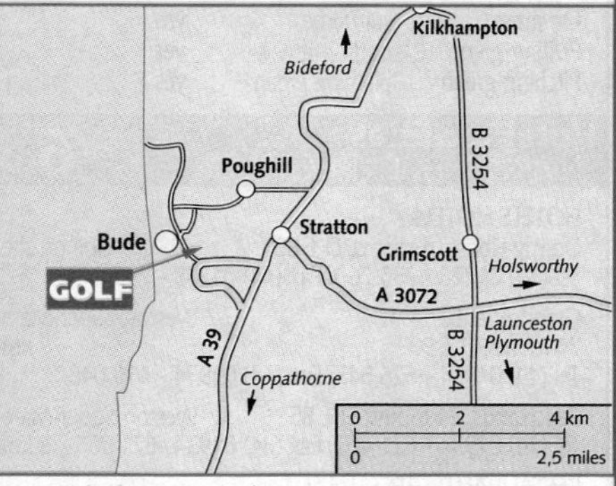

Access Accès : M5 Bristol → Exeter. Exit 27 → Tiverton, Barnstable on A39, then to Bude.
Into town, Golf signposted.
Map 6 on page 494 Carte 6 Page 494

Golf course — PARCOURS — 15/20

Site	Site	
Maintenance	Entretien	
Architect	Architecte	Tom Dunn
Type	Type	seaside course, links
Relief	Relief	
Water in play	Eau en jeu	
Exp. to wind	Exposé au vent	
Trees in play	Arbres en jeu	

Scorecard Carte de score	**Chp.** Chp.	**Mens** Mess.	**Ladies** Da.
Length Long.	5452	5256	4841
Par	71	71	73
Slope system	—	—	—

Advised golfing ability Niveau de jeu recommandé — 0 12 24 36
Hcp required Handicap exigé — certificate

Club house & amenities — CLUB HOUSE ET ANNEXES — 6/10

Pro shop	Pro-shop	
Driving range	Practice	
Sheltered	couvert	practice area
On grass	sur herbe	yes
Putting-green	putting-green	yes
Pitching-green	pitching green	no

Hotel facilities — ENVIRONNEMENT HOTELIER — 5/10

HOTELS HÔTELS

Camelot , 24 rooms, D £ 70 — Bude 1 km
Tel (44) 01288 - 352 361, Fax (44) 01288 - 355 470

Falcon, 26 rooms, D £ 84 — Bude 1 km
Tel (44) 01288 - 352 005, Fax (44) 01288 - 356 359

Hartland, 28 rooms, D £ 84 — Bude 1 km
Tel (44) 01288 - 355 661, Fax (44) 01288 - 355 664

Bude Haven, 11 rooms, D £ 70 — Bude 2 km
Tel (44) 01288 - 352 305, Fax (44) 01288 - 352 305

RESTAURANTS RESTAURANT

Falcon — Bude 1 km
Tel (44) 01288 - 352 005

BURNHAM & BERROW

18 | 7 | 6

Played for many a year by J.H. Taylor, this classic course has been profoundly altered throughout the 20th century, in particular to avoid hitting worshippers as they leave the church set in the middle of the course. The changes also cut out many of the blind shots, thereby reducing a little the glorious uncertainty of golf but giving the layout a more forthright feel as it winds its way between majestic sand-dunes. The plant-life here is superb, especially the orchids, and as on many links courses there are very few water hazards (here on the 6th and behind the 13th holes). Dare we say it, these should only bother the higher handicappers. Generally speaking you have to hit the ball straight, as bushes, rough and bunkers await wayward drives, while hilly slopes and pot-bunkers snap up mis-hit approach shots. As the greens are small and steeply contoured, this is a great course for getting your short game together.

Longtemps arpenté par J.H. Taylor, ce classique a été profondément modifié tout au long de ce siècle, en particulier pour éviter d'envoyer au paradis les fidèles de l'église au milieu du parcours. Les modifications ont aussi permis d'éliminer beaucoup de coups aveugles, retirant un peu de la glorieuse incertitude du golf, mais offrant plus de franchise au tracé, à présent mieux insinué entre des dunes majestueuses. On trouve ici une flore sauvage superbe, notamment des orchidées. Comme sur la plupart des links, il y a peu d'obstacles d'eau (au 6 et derrière le 13), mais ils ne concernent que les handicaps élevés. En général, il faut placer la balle, car les buissons, le rough et les bunkers attendent les drives égarés, les mouvements de terrain et les pot bunkers happent les approches imprécises. Comme les greens sont petits et très mouvementés, on travaille son petit jeu sur ce grand parcours...

Burnham & Berrow Golf Club — 1890

St Christophers Way
ENG - BURNHAM-ON-SEA, Somerset TA8 2PE

Office	Secrétariat	(44) 01278 - 785 760
Pro shop	Pro-shop	(44) 01278 - 785 545
Fax	Fax	(44) 01278 - 795 440
Web	www.BBGC.2-golf.com	
Situation	Situation	50 km SW of Bristol

8 km S of Weston-Super-Mare (pop. 64 935)

Annual closure	Fermeture annuelle	no
Weekly closure	Fermeture hebdomadaire	no

Fees main season Tarifs haute saison	Full day	
	Week days Semaine	**We/Bank holidays** We/Férié
Individual Individuel	£ 40	£ 60
Couple Couple	£ 80	£ 120
Caddy	Caddy	on request
Electric Trolley	Chariot électrique	yes
Buggy	Voiturette	no
Clubs	Clubs	yes

Credit cards Cartes de crédit
Visa - Mastercard (Pro shop goods only)

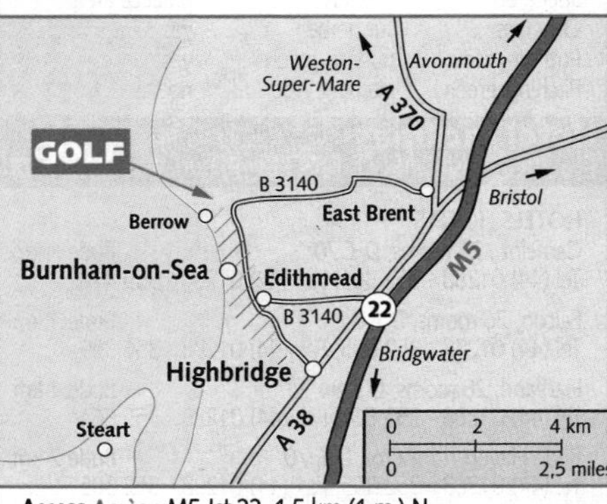

Access Accès : M5 Jct 22, 1,5 km (1 m.) N. of Burnham-on-Sea. Follow signs to Golf.
Map 6 on page 495 Carte 6 Page 495

Golf course — PARCOURS — 18/20

Site	Site	
Maintenance	Entretien	
Architect	Architecte	Unknown
Type	Type	seaside course, links
Relief	Relief	
Water in play	Eau en jeu	
Exp. to wind	Exposé au vent	
Trees in play	Arbres en jeu	

Scorecard Carte de score	**Chp.** Chp.	**Mens** Mess.	**Ladies** Da.
Length Long.	6151	6012	5227
Par	71	71	74
Slope system	—	—	—

Advised golfing ability Niveau de jeu recommandé — 0 12 24 36
Hcp required Handicap exigé — 22 Men, 30 Ladies

Club house & amenities — CLUB HOUSE ET ANNEXES — 7/10

Pro shop	Pro-shop	
Driving range	Practice	
Sheltered	couvert	no
On grass	sur herbe	yes
Putting-green	putting-green	yes
Pitching-green	pitching green	yes

Hotel facilities — ENVIRONNEMENT HOTELIER — 6/10

HOTELS HÔTELS

Dormy House, 4 rooms, D £ 80 — Golf on site
Tel (44) 01278 - 785 760, Fax (44) 01278 - 795 440

Grand Atlantic — Weston-Super-Mare
74 rooms, D £ 90 — 8 km
Tel (44) 01934 - 626 543, Fax (44) 01934 - 415 048

Beachlands, 24 rooms, D £ 85 — Weston-Super-Mare
Tel (44) 01934 - 621 401, Fax (44) 01934 -621 966 — 8 km

RESTAURANTS RESTAURANT

Duets — Weston-Super-Mare
Tel (44) 01934 - 413 428 — 8 km

CALDY

17 | 7 | 7

In a setting formed by the Dee estuary, Flintshire hills and Welsh mountains right in the background, the views from the course provide welcome inspiration, especially towards sun-set. Caldy is a mixture of sloping holes in a parkland setting and links-style seaside holes (3 to 10), and as such offers great variety of style. What's more, being less demanding and less uncompromising than its neighbour, Royal Liverpool, it is not such an intimidating course for the average hacker. Having said that, the number of difficulties (trees, rough, water and sand) makes this a course to be reckoned with, even though the layout is clear and revealing enough for you to know exactly when and where to hit those magic shots. Although slightly hilly in places, no greens are blind but some are elevated, so make allowance for this when choosing your irons. On the downside, lady golfers here seem to be treated as slightly less than 1st class citizens, there are no spectacular dunes to contend with and no long par 4s... but maybe the wind can change all that.

Le décor réunit l'estuaire de la Dee, les collines du Flintshire et les montagnes du Pays de Galles : de quoi inspirer le joueur, surtout au soleil couchant. Avec son mélange de trous en pente, d'esthétique de parc et de links (du 3 au 10), Caldy offre une superbe variété de styles. De plus, n'étant pas aussi exigeant et brutal que son voisin Royal Liverpool, il intimidera moins le joueur moyen. Pourtant le nombre de difficultés (arbres, rough, eau, bunkers) oblige à réfléchir, mais comme on dispose de toutes les cartes en main - le parcours est d'une grande franchise générale - on peut jouer ses atouts au bon moment. En dépit d'un léger relief, on ne trouve pas de greens aveugles, mais certains étant en élévation, il faut bien choisir ses clubs. Si l'on peut regretter quelque chose, c'est le fait que les femmes ne paraissent pas être ici des citoyens de première classe, l'absence de grandes dunes spectaculaires, le manque de longs par 4 - quoiqu'avec le vent...

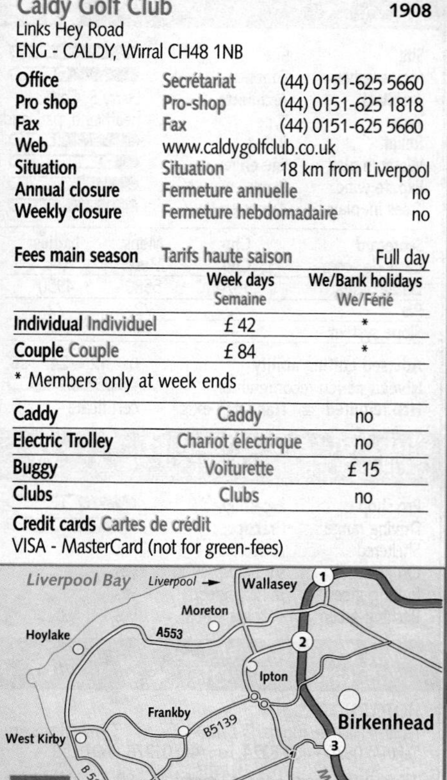

Caldy Golf Club — 1908

Links Hey Road
ENG - CALDY, Wirral CH48 1NB

Office	Secrétariat	(44) 0151-625 5660
Pro shop	Pro-shop	(44) 0151-625 1818
Fax	Fax	(44) 0151-625 5660
Web	www.caldygolfclub.co.uk	
Situation	Situation	18 km from Liverpool
Annual closure	Fermeture annuelle	no
Weekly closure	Fermeture hebdomadaire	no

Fees main season / Tarifs haute saison		Full day
	Week days / Semaine	We/Bank holidays / We/Férié
Individual / Individuel	£ 42	*
Couple / Couple	£ 84	*

* Members only at week ends

Caddy	Caddy	no
Electric Trolley	Chariot électrique	no
Buggy	Voiturette	£ 15
Clubs	Clubs	no

Credit cards Cartes de crédit
VISA - MasterCard (not for green-fees)

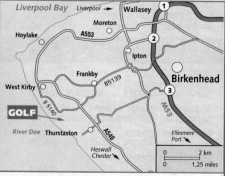

Access Accès : A540 Manchester-Hoylake,
→ left on D 5140 (Caldy Road), 1st left into Croft Drive East, left into Links Hey Road.
Map 5 on page 493 Carte 5 Page 493

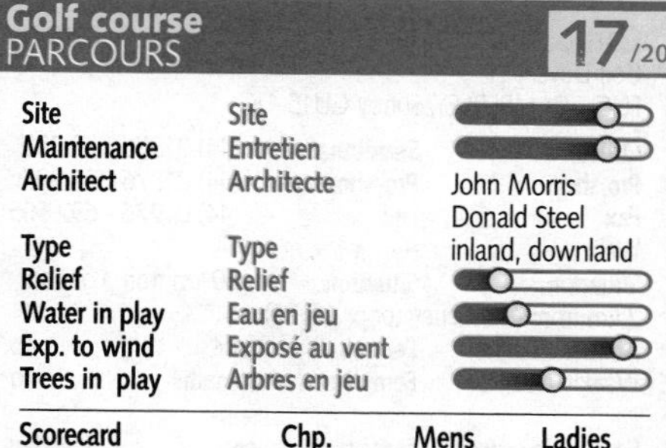

Golf course / PARCOURS — 17/20

Site	Site	
Maintenance	Entretien	
Architect	Architecte	John Morris, Donald Steel
Type	Type	inland, downland
Relief	Relief	
Water in play	Eau en jeu	
Exp. to wind	Exposé au vent	
Trees in play	Arbres en jeu	

Scorecard / Carte de score	Chp. / Chp.	Mens / Mess.	Ladies / Da.
Length Long.	6001	5710	5208
Par	72	72	74
Slope system	—	—	—

Advised golfing ability / Niveau de jeu recommandé — 0 12 24 36
Hcp required / Handicap exigé — certificate

Club house & amenities / CLUB HOUSE ET ANNEXES — 7/10

Pro shop	Pro-shop	
Driving range	Practice	
Sheltered	couvert	
On grass	sur herbe	yes
Putting-green	putting-green	yes
Pitching-green	pitching green	yes

Hotel facilities / ENVIRONNEMENT HOTELIER — 7/10

HOTELS HÔTELS

Grove Hotel, 14 rooms, D £ 90 — Wallasey 10 km
Tel (44) 0151 - 639 3947, Fax (44) 0151 - 639 0028

Leasowe Castle Hotel, 47 rooms, D £ 75 — Moreton 9 km
Tel (44) 0151 - 606 9191, Fax (44) 0151 - 678 5551

Bowler Hat, 32 rooms, D £ 95 — Birkenhead 7 km
Tel (44) 0151 - 652 4931, Fax (44) 0151 - 653 8127

Thornton Hall, 63 rooms, D £ 86 — Thornton Hough 12 km
Tel (44) 0151 - 336 3938, Fax (44) 0151 - 336 7864

RESTAURANTS RESTAURANT

Grove Hotel, Tel (44) 0151 - 630 4558 — Wallasey 10 km
Lee Ho, Tel (44) 0151 - 677 6440 — Moreton 9 km

CAMBERLEY HEATH

16	6	6

This golf-club, lying almost at the intersection between the counties of Surrey, Hampshire and Berkshire, has an impressive club-house from where you get some equally impressive views over a course that winds its way through trees and heather. Virtually free of water (except the 16th hole), this is a fine example of the exceptional skill of architect Harry Colt and his discreet but totally effective bunkering, the use of trees and natural slopes and the often multi-tiered putting surfaces where down-hill putts should be avoided at all costs. The terrain is hilly enough to get the better of tired legs, an important factor on a course where you will need every ounce of strength to cope with the last three holes, which are often decisive for your card. Depending on the tees you choose, the course can change to such an extent that we would recommend (for "friendly" rounds) changing from one day to the next to vary the fun and test your technique. All in all, a very clever layout.

Ce club, au croisement du Surrey, du Hampshire et du Berkshire, offre depuis son imposant Clubhouse un panorama spectaculaire sur le parcours insinué dans les arbres et la bruyère. Pratiquement sans eau (sauf au 16), c'est un grand exemple de l'art exceptionnel de l'architecte Harry Colt, avec son placement sobre et efficace des bunkers, sa mise en jeu des arbres, son utilisation des pentes naturelles du terrain, et les contours fréquemment à plateaux des greens, où il convient absolument d'éviter les putts en descente. Assez accidenté, il éprouvera les jambes des moins résistants, alors que le jeu réclame ici de garder des forces jusqu'au bout : les trois derniers trous peuvent ainsi retourner le résultat d'une compétition. Suivant le choix des départs, le parcours peut changer à tel point que l'on conseillera (en partie amicale) d'en changer d'un jour à l'autre pour varier les plaisirs et tester sa technique sur ce tracé très intelligent.

Camberley Heath Golf Club — 1913

Golf Drive
ENG - CAMBERLEY, Surrey GU15 1JG

Office	Secrétariat	(44) 01276 - 23 258
Pro shop	Pro-shop	(44) 01276 - 27 905
Fax	Fax	(44) 01276 - 692 505
Web	—	
Situation	Situation	60 km from London

2 km from Camberley (pop. 46120)

Annual closure	Fermeture annuelle	no
Weekly closure	Fermeture hebdomadaire	no

Fees main season Tarifs haute saison	Week days Semaine	We/Bank holidays We/Férié
		Full day
Individual Individuel	£ 68	*
Couple Couple	£ 136	*

* Members only at week ends

Caddy	Caddy	£ 20
Electric Trolley	Chariot électrique	no
Buggy	Voiturette	£ 35
Clubs	Clubs	£ 30
Credit cards	Cartes de crédit	no

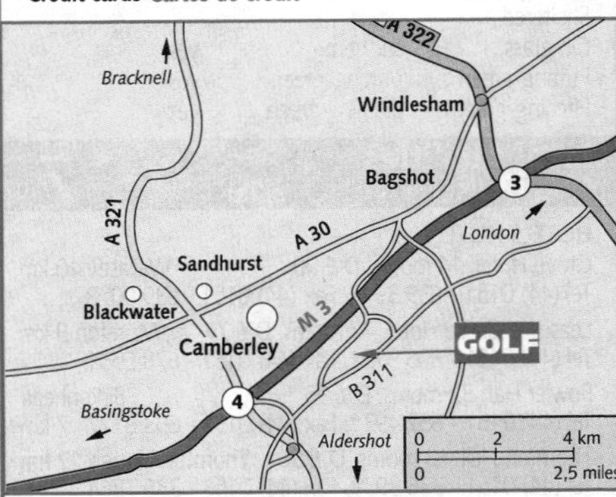

Access Accès : London M3 → Basingstoke. Exit 4 → Frimley. Turn left on Portsmouth Road. Golf on the right at Golf Drive.
Map 8 on page 498 Carte 8 Page 498

Golf course PARCOURS — 16/20

Site	Site	
Maintenance	Entretien	
Architect	Architecte	Harry S. Colt
Type	Type	heathland, parkland
Relief	Relief	
Water in play	Eau en jeu	
Exp. to wind	Exposé au vent	
Trees in play	Arbres en jeu	

Scorecard Carte de score	Chp. Chp.	Mens Mess.	Ladies Da.
Length Long.	5670	5580	4950
Par	72	72	72
Slope system	—	—	—

Advised golfing ability Niveau de jeu recommandé — 0 12 24 36
Hcp required Handicap exigé — certificate

Club house & amenities CLUB HOUSE ET ANNEXES — 6/10

Pro shop	Pro-shop	
Driving range	Practice	
Sheltered	couvert	
On grass	sur herbe	yes
Putting-green	putting-green	yes
Pitching-green	pitching green	yes

Hotel facilities ENVIRONNEMENT HOTELIER — 6/10

HOTELS HÔTELS

Frimley Hall, 86 rooms, D £ 170 — Camberley 3 km
Tel (44) 0870 - 400 8224, Fax (44) 01276 - 691 253

Toby Carvery and Lodge, 43 rooms, D £ 80 — Frimley 3 km
Tel (44) 01276 - 691 939, Fax (44) 01276 - 605 902

Pennyhill Park, 123 rooms, D £ 230 — Bagshot 5 km
Tel (44) 01276 - 471 774, Fax (44) 01276 - 473 217

RESTAURANTS RESTAURANT

Stateroom, Tel (44) 01344 - 623 322 — Ascot 12 km

Ciao Ninety, Tel (44) 01344 - 622 285 — Ascot 12 km

Toby Carvery and Lodge, Tel (44) 01276 - 691 939 — Frimley 3 km

CAME DOWN

15	5	6

From Dorchester, it is just a short drive to the coast and Weymouth, a very old seaside resort where you can still see the vestiges of Maiden castle, a stone-age fortress. Even closer is Came Down golf club, a course designed by Tom Dunn, restyled by J.H. Taylor and fine-tuned by Harry Colt. Three top names in golf course design and three great connoisseurs of golf played at every level, indulgent for the less gifted, demanding for the smarter guys. Laid out on a hill, the course has a few climbs to negotiate but nothing too steep, and naturally reserves a few sloping lies. The advantage of this location is the view over the Dorset countryside and some wide open space where big-hitters can open their shoulders despite the risk of landing in some tall rough. You also have the wind to contend with, so keep the ball low and try to run it in. The greens are excellent but often very slick in summer

De Dorchester, il faut quelques minutes pour rejoindre la côte et Weymouth, une très ancienne station balnéaire, ou voir les vestiges de Maiden Castle, une forteresse de l'Age de pierre. Il en faut encore moins pour jouer le parcours de Came Down, dessiné par Tom Dunn, revu par JH Taylor et peaufiné par Harry Colt. Trois grands noms de l'architecture, trois grands connaisseurs du jeu à tous les niveaux, indulgents pour les élèves peu doués, exigeants pour les premiers de la classe. Situé sur une colline, il réserve quelques moments de montées à pied mais sans rien d'excessif, et quelques positions de balle dans différentes pentes. Avantage de la situation, les points de vue sur la campagne du Dorset, et des espaces très ouverts où les frappeurs pourront se déchaîner, avec quelques risques présentés par les hauts roughs. Il faut aussi savoir jouer avec le vent, c'est-à-dire avec sa balle dans le vent, maîtriser les balles basses, et donc les approches roulées : les greens sont de bonne qualité, et souvent très roulants en été.

Came Down Golf Club — 1904

ENG - CAME, DORCHESTER, Dorset DT2 8 NR

Office	Secrétariat	(44) 01305 - 813 494
Pro shop	Pro-shop	(44) 01305 - 812 670
Fax	Fax	(44) 01305 - 813 494
Web	www.camedowngolfclub.co.uk	
Situation	Situation	

5 km from Dorchester - 10 km from Weymouth (pop. 46 065)

Annual closure	Fermeture annuelle	no
Weekly closure	Fermeture hebdomadaire	no

Fees main season Tarifs haute saison	18 holes	
	Week days Semaine	**We/Bank holidays** We/Férié
Individual Individuel	£ 24	£ 28
Couple Couple	£ 48	£ 56
Caddy	Caddy	no
Electric Trolley	Chariot électrique	no
Buggy	Voiturette	no
Clubs	Clubs	yes

Credit cards Cartes de crédit
VISA - Eurocard - MasterCard (Pro shop goods only)

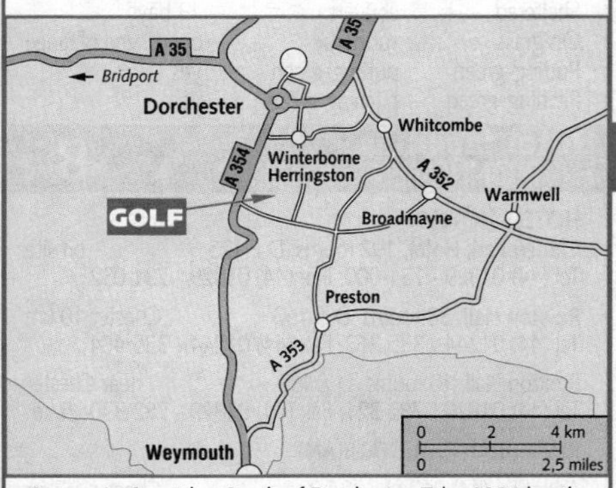

Access Accès : 5 km South of Dorchester. Take A354 head up hill. Keep on same road, Club house on right hand side.
Map 6 on page 495 Carte 6 Page 495

Golf course — PARCOURS — 15/20

Site	Site	
Maintenance	Entretien	
Architect	Architecte	Tom Dunn, J.H. Taylor
Type	Type	open country, hilly
Relief	Relief	
Water in play	Eau en jeu	
Exp. to wind	Exposé au vent	
Trees in play	Arbres en jeu	

Scorecard Carte de score	**Chp.** Chp.	**Mens** Mess.	**Ladies** Da.
Length Long.	5630	5313	5011
Par	70	69	72
Slope system	—	—	—

Advised golfing ability Niveau de jeu recommandé — 0 12 24 36
Hcp required Handicap exigé — certificate

Club house & amenities — CLUB HOUSE ET ANNEXES — 5/10

Pro shop	Pro-shop	
Driving range	Practice	
Sheltered	couvert	practice area
On grass	sur herbe	yes
Putting-green	putting-green	yes
Pitching-green	pitching green	yes

Hotel facilities — ENVIRONNEMENT HOTELIER — 6/10

HOTELS HÔTELS

Wessex Royale, 25 rooms, D £ 70 — Dorchester 5 km
Tel (44) 01305 - 262 660, Fax (44) 01305 - 251 941

Casterbridge, 14 rooms, D £ 85 — Dorchester 5 km
Tel (44) 01305 - 264 043, Fax (44) 01305 - 260 884

Yalbury Cottage, 8 rooms, D £ 82 — Dorchester 5 km
Tel (44) 01305 - 262 382, Fax (44) 01305 - 266 412

Rex, 31 rooms, D £ 98 — Weymouth 10 km
Tel (44) 01305 - 760 400, Fax (44) 01305 - 760 500

RESTAURANTS RESTAURANT

Mock Turtle, Tel (44) 01305 - 264 011 — Dorchester 5 km

Perry's, Tel (44) 01305 - 785 799 — Weymouth 10 km

CARDEN PARK Nicklaus Course 17 | 8 | 8

After Jack Nicklaus Jr., it's his brother Steve who works with dad in his course design business. They have added a second course at the "Cheshire" which, with an on-site hotel, is a great week-end destination. The only problem is the number of golfers here, compounded by the style of this course (the best of the two courses) which is hardly conducive to quick play: water comes into play on more than half the holes. A meandering stream has resulted in double fairways on the 7th and 15th holes, where the risk you are about to take needs even more careful consideration than anywhere else on the course. This is Big Jack's famous "percentage golf". A few large trees complicate things still further, as do the very many bunkers, nearly all large but rather British in style. For once, the architect has not laid out his traditional bunkers with steep walls. Despite this hint of moderation, the course demands target golf, making it a tricky affair for lovers of bump 'n run shot or inveterate toppers of the ball. They will prefer the other course.

Après Jack Nicklaus Jr, c'est son frère Steve qui travaille avec papa. C'est le second parcours du site et, avec l'hôtel sur place, c'est une bonne destination de week-end, assez courue. Le style du présent parcours (le meilleur des deux) ne favorise pas un jeu rapide, avec l'eau en jeu sur une dizaine de trous. Les méandres d'un cours d'eau ont permis de créer des double fairways au 7 et au 15, où l'on devra plus encore qu'ailleurs mesurer les risques avant de jouer : c'est le golf pourcentage cher à Nicklaus. Quelques grands arbres compliquent encore le jeu, ainsi que de nombreux bunkers, souvent grands mais de profils assez britanniques : pour une fois, l'architecte n'a pas trop plaqué ici ses bunkers traditionnels avec des parois abruptes. Malgré cette modération, ce parcours réclame un jeu de cible, ce qui le rend fort délicat pour ceux qui adorent faire rouler la balle, et pour les joueurs sans grande expérience. Ils préfèreront l'autre 18 trous.

Carden Park Hotel, Golf Resort & Spa 1998

ENG - CHESTER, Ches. CH3 9DQ

Office	Secrétariat	(44) 01829 - 731 630
Pro shop	Pro-shop	(44) 01829 - 731 500
Fax	Fax	(44) 01829 - 731 625
Web	www.carden-park.co.uk	
Situation	Situation	25 km S of Chester

15 km W of Nantwich (pop. 11 695)

Annual closure	Fermeture annuelle	no
Weekly closure	Fermeture hebdomadaire	no

536

Fees main season Tarifs haute saison		18 holes
	Week days Semaine	**We/Bank holidays** We/Férié
Individual Individuel	£ 60	£ 60
Couple Couple	£ 120	£ 120

Caddy	Caddy	no
Electric Trolley	Chariot électrique	no
Buggy	Voiturette	£ 15 /18 holes
Clubs	Clubs	£ 10 /18 holes

Credit cards Cartes de crédit
VISA - Eurocard - MasterCard - DC - AMEX

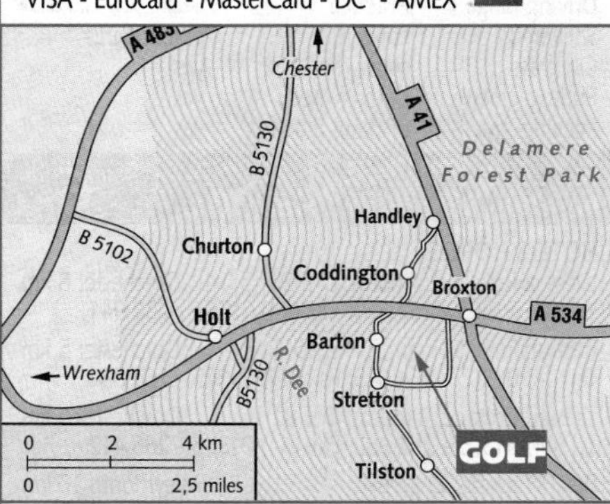

Access Accès : Chester, A41 → Whitchurch.
Broxton roundabout, turn right onto A534 → Wrexham.
Golf approx. 2.5 km (1.5 m) on left side.
Map 4 on page 490 Carte 4 Page 490

Golf course PARCOURS 17/20

Site	Site	
Maintenance	Entretien	
Architect	Architecte	Jack Nicklaus Steve Nicklaus
Type	Type	parkland, inland
Relief	Relief	
Water in play	Eau en jeu	
Exp. to wind	Exposé au vent	
Trees in play	Arbres en jeu	

Scorecard Carte de score	**Chp.** Chp.	**Mens** Mess.	**Ladies** Da.
Length Long.	6341	5672	4690
Par	72	72	72
Slope system	—	—	—

Advised golfing ability 0 12 24 36
Niveau de jeu recommandé
Hcp required Handicap exigé no

Club house & amenities CLUB HOUSE ET ANNEXES 8/10

Pro shop	Pro-shop	
Driving range	Practice	
Sheltered	couvert	13 bays
On grass	sur herbe	oppos. end of range
Putting-green	putting-green	yes
Pitching-green	pitching green	yes

Hotel facilities ENVIRONNEMENT HOTELIER 8/10

HOTELS HÔTELS

Carden Park Hotel, 192 rooms, D £ 125 — on site
Tel (44) 01829 - 731 000, Fax (44) 01829 - 731 032

Rowton Hall, 38 rooms, D £ 150 — Chester 10 km
Tel (44) 01244 - 335 262, Fax (44) 01244 - 335 464

Broxton Hall, 10 rooms, D £ 130 — near Chester
Tel (44) 01829 - 782 321, Fax (44) 01829 - 782 330 — 5 km

RESTAURANTS RESTAURANT

Arkle, Tel (44) 01244 - 324 024 — Chester 15 km

Crabwall Manor, Tel (44) 01244 - 851 666 — Chester 15 km

Blue Bell, Tel (44) 01244 - 317 759 — Chester 15 km

CARLISLE

17 | 7 | 7

As you drive up past the great links courses from Ayrshire to Carlisle and Scotland, forget the M6 motorway and keep to the A6, which crosses the breath-taking scenery of the Lake District and Hadrian's Wall. If it inspires you the way it inspired Keats, Wordsworth or Beatrix Potter, you could be in for a good day's golfing. Carlisle leaves no-one indifferent, and as this a Tom Simpson design, no-one will be too surprised about that. You will find his trade-mark cross-bunkers (Simpson hated topped shots), greens protected by bunkers on the one side, by bumps and hollows on the other, which offer their own particular brand of difficulty. Plus the never-ending need to think with a clear head on the length and direction of the ideal shot before choosing your club. The par 3s here are outstanding and the par 5s no less memorable. The only shortcoming might be the course's overall length, but hopefully would-be designers will think long and hard before making any alterations.

En remontant des grands links de l'Ayrshire vers Carlisle et l'Ecosse, renoncez à la M6 au profit de l'A6, qui traverse les paysages sublimes du Lake District puis le Mur d'Hadrien. Vous y trouverez peut-être l'inspiration, comme Keats, Wordsworth ou Beatrix Potter. Au moins pour le golf, car Carlisle n'est pas un parcours qui laisse indifférent. La signature de Tom Simpson est une garantie. Vous y trouverez ses cross-bunkers car il haïssait les balles toppées, les greens souvent défendus d'un côté par les bunkers, et de l'autre par des creux et des bosses d'où il n'est guère plus facile de jouer, plus la nécessité de réfléchir sur la longueur et la direction du coup idéal avant de choisir un club. Les par 3 sont ici exceptionnels, les par 5 non moins mémorables. Seul défaut, un certain manque de longueur, mais il serait bien dommage de toucher quoi que ce soit sous pétexte de le "moderniser"...

Carlisle Golf Club — 1909

Aglionby
ENG - CARLISLE, Cumbria CA4 8AG

Office	Secrétariat	(44) 01228 - 513 029
Pro shop	Pro-shop	(44) 01228 - 513 241
Fax	Fax	(44) 01228 - 513 303
Web	—	
Situation	Situation	
3 km from Carlisle (pop. 100 562)		
Annual closure	Fermeture annuelle	no
Weekly closure	Fermeture hebdomadaire	no

Fees main season Tarifs haute saison	18 holes	
	Week days Semaine	**We/Bank holidays** We/Férié
Individual Individuel	£ 25	*
Couple Couple	£ 50	*

Full weekdays: £ 40 * No visitors at week ends

Caddy	Caddy	no
Electric Trolley	Chariot électrique	£ 5 /18 holes
Buggy	Voiturette	£ 15 /18 holes
Clubs	Clubs	no
Credit cards Cartes de crédit		no

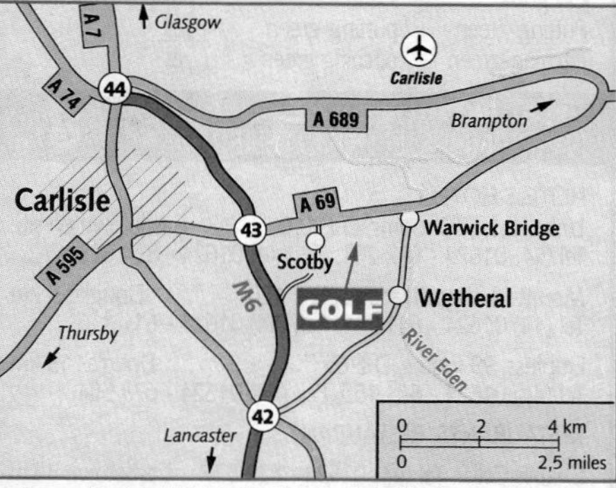

Access Accès : M6 Jct 43, A69 East, Golf 1 km on the right.
Map 2 on page 487 Carte 2 Page 487

Golf course PARCOURS — 17/20

Site	Site	
Maintenance	Entretien	
Architect	Architecte	Tom Simpson, Mackenzie Ross
Type	Type	parkland
Relief	Relief	
Water in play	Eau en jeu	
Exp. to wind	Exposé au vent	
Trees in play	Arbres en jeu	

Scorecard Carte de score	**Chp.** Chp.	**Mens** Mess.	**Ladies** Da.
Length Long.	5601	5408	4945
Par	71	71	73
Slope system	—	—	—

Advised golfing ability Niveau de jeu recommandé: 0 12 24 36
Hcp required Handicap exigé: certificate

Club house & amenities CLUB HOUSE ET ANNEXES — 7/10

Pro shop	Pro-shop	
Driving range	Practice	
Sheltered	couvert	no
On grass	sur herbe	practice area
Putting-green	putting-green	yes
Pitching-green	pitching green	yes

Hotel facilities ENVIRONNEMENT HOTELIER — 7/10

HOTELS HÔTELS

Crown Hotel, 51 rooms, D £ 122 — Wetheral 4 km
Tel (44) 01228 - 561 888, Fax (44) 01228 - 561 637

Cumbrian, 70 rooms, D £ 100 — Carlisle 5 km
Tel (44) 01228 - 531 951, Fax (44) 01228 - 547 799

Cumbria Park, 47 rooms, D £ 120 — Carlisle 5 km
Tel (44) 01228 - 522 887, Fax (44) 01228 - 514 796

Crown + Mitre ,97 rooms, D £ 110 — Carlisle 5 km
Tel (44) 01228 - 525 491, Fax (44) 01228 - 514 553

RESTAURANTS RESTAURANT

No 10, Tel (44) 01228 - 524 183 — Carlisle 5 km

Crown Hotel, Tel (44) 01228 - 561 888 — Wetheral 4 km

CASTLETOWN

18 | 6 | 8

In the middle of the Irish Sea, the Isle of Man is reached by ferry or by air from Blackpool. Castletown is located on a sort of triangular-shaped peninsula surrounded by the sea. They say that on the 17th hole, you are driving in Ireland, Scotland, England or Wales. Whatever, this course is exposed to all winds and only the bunkers give any real shelter. Only a few small dunes and rocks give any relief to this flat, superbly-turfed landscape. After the war, Mackenzie Ross brought Castletown back to life with all the talent he showed at Turnberry and even a touch of genius. This is a golfer's paradise on the edge of a rock, but it can be hell if ever a storm sets in and sends players scampering to seek refuge in the hotel on the course. We would recommend a visit here on a fine summer's day.

En plein milieu de la mer d'Irlande, l'Ile de Man est accessible par ferry ou par avion depuis Blackpool. Castletown est situé sur une sorte de presqu'île en forme de triangle cerné par la mer : on dit que du 17, on peut driver en Irlande, en Ecosse, en Angleterre ou au Pays de Galles. En tout cas, ce parcours est ouvert à tous les vents, et seuls les bunkers forment vraiment des abris. Quelques petites dunes et quelques rochers donnent un semblant de relief à ce paysage plat, mais au gazon superbe. Après la guerre, Mackenzie Ross a rendu Castletown à la vie, avec autant de talent qu'à Turnberry, parfois même une forme de génie. C'est un paradis de golfeur sur un bout de rocher, que seule la tempête peut transformer en enfer, mais il ne reste plus alors qu'à se réfugier à l'hôtel sur le site. On conseillera plutôt de venir par une belle journée d'été.

538

Castletown Golf Club — 1892

Fort Island
ENG - CASTLETOWN, Isle of Man

Office	Secrétariat	(44) 01624 - 822 201
Pro shop	Pro-shop	(44) 01624 - 822 211
Fax	Fax	(44) 01624 - 824 633
Web	—	
Situation	Situation	15 km SW of Douglas
Annual closure	Fermeture annuelle	no
Weekly closure	Fermeture hebdomadaire	no

Fees main season Tarifs haute saison	18 holes	
	Week days Semaine	**We/Bank holidays** We/Férié
Individual Individuel	£ 28.50 *	£ 35
Couple Couple	£ 57 *	£ 70

* Monday → Thursday

Caddy	Caddy	on request
Electric Trolley	Chariot électrique	£ 9 /18 holes
Buggy	Voiturette	£ 20 /18 holes
Clubs	Clubs	£ 8 /18 holes

Credit cards Cartes de crédit
VISA - Eurocard - MasterCard - DC - AMEX

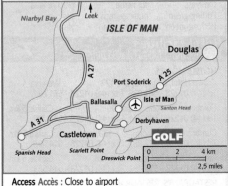

Access Accès : Close to airport
Map 9 on page 500 Carte 9 Page 500

Golf course PARCOURS — 18/20

Site	Site	
Maintenance	Entretien	
Architect	Architecte	Mackenzie Ross
Type	Type	seaside course, links
Relief	Relief	
Water in play	Eau en jeu	
Exp. to wind	Exposé au vent	
Trees in play	Arbres en jeu	

Scorecard Carte de score	**Chp.** Chp.	**Mens** Mess.	**Ladies** Da.
Length Long.	6040	5880	5072
Par	72	72	73
Slope system	—	—	—

Advised golfing ability 0 12 24 36
Niveau de jeu recommandé
Hcp required Handicap exigé no

Club house & amenities CLUB HOUSE ET ANNEXES — 6/10

Pro shop	Pro-shop	
Driving range	Practice	
Sheltered	couvert	no
On grass	sur herbe	practice ground only
Putting-green	putting-green	yes
Pitching-green	pitching green	yes

Hotel facilities ENVIRONNEMENT HOTELIER — 8/10

HOTELS HÔTELS

Links Hotel, 55 rooms, D £ 110 — Castletown on site
Tel (44) 01624 - 822 201, Fax (44) 01624 - 824 633

Mount Murray, 90 rooms, D £ 120 — Douglas 9 km
Tel (44) 01624 - 661 111, Fax (44) 01624 - 611 116

Empress, 99 rooms, D £ 65 — Douglas 15 km
Tel (44) 01624 - 661 155, Fax (44) 01624 - 673 554

RESTAURANTS RESTAURANT

Chablis Cellar, Tel (44) 01624 - 823 527 — Castletown 3 km

The Waterfront, Tel (44) 01624 - 673 222 — Douglas 15 km

Murray's, Tel (44) 01624 - 661 111 — Douglas 9 km

CHART HILLS

18 | 8 | 6

They say you shouldn't always expect champions to be great course designers. Well here, Nick Faldo, backed by the top American specialist Steve Smyers, has produced a masterly layout. We admit that our very high score is intended more for experienced players, and many golfers find this course a little over-elaborate with a touch too much sand and water. Those who are afraid that their game might not be up to such a challenge should head shamelessly straight for the front tees. Only there will they learn how to tame a layout which is psychologically rather than really difficult. It was designed with brilliant, bold and uncompromising intelligence. Upholders of the British tradition for discreet courses will be a little surprised here, that's for sure, but you need visual and technical shocks such as this to keep your game moving. The overall excellence of this resort is outstanding. The green-fee is also a schock...

On ne doit pas toujours espérer des champions qu'ils soient de grands architectes. Epaulé par l'excellent spécialiste américain Steve Smyers, Nick Faldo a réussi un coup de maître. Certes, notre note très favorable est plutôt destinée aux joueurs expérimentés, car beaucoup trouvent ce parcours "trop dessiné," avec un rien trop de sable et un peu trop d'eau. Ceux qui ont peur que leur jeu ne soit pas à la hauteur des défis présentés choisiront sans honte les départs avancés, ils apprendront à apprivoiser ce tracé plus difficile psychologiquement que réellement, conçu avec une brillante intelligence, avec hardiesse, sans concessions. Certes, les tenants de la tradition britannique d'une architecture discrète seront ici surpris, mais il faut des chocs visuels et techniques de ce genre pour progresser. La qualité générale de ce complexe est exceptionnelle, tout comme le montant des greens-fees...

Chart Hills Golf Club — 1993

Weeks Lane
ENG - BIDDENDEN, Kent TN27 8JX

Office	Secrétariat	(44) 01580 - 292 222
Pro shop	Pro-shop	(44) 01580 - 292 148
Fax	Fax	(44) 01580 - 292 233
Web	www.charthills.co.uk	
Situation	Situation	14 km from Ashford

20 km from Maidstone (pop. 136 209)

Annual closure	Fermeture annuelle	no
Weekly closure	Fermeture hebdomadaire	no

Fees main season Tarifs haute saison	Week days Semaine	We/Bank holidays We/Férié
		Full day
Individual Individuel	£ 160	£ 195
Couple Couple	£ 320	£ 390
Caddy Caddy		£ 15 /on request
Electric Trolley Chariot électrique		no
Buggy Voiturette		£ 20 /18 holes
Clubs Clubs		£ 10 /18 holes

Credit cards Cartes de crédit
VISA - MasterCard - AMEX

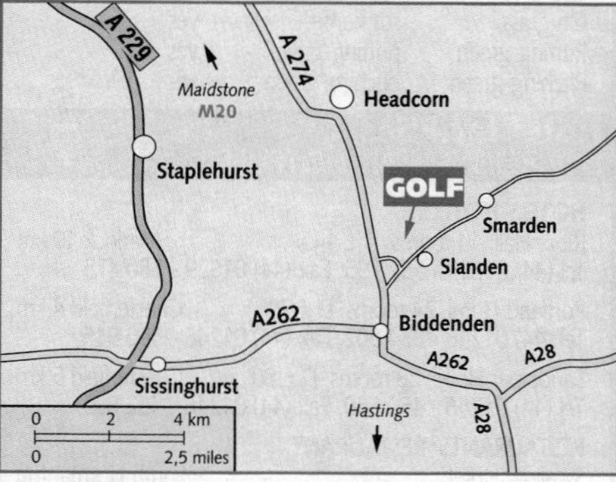

Access Accès : • M20, Jct 6 to Maidstone. A274 → Biddenden. After Headcorn, left at Petrol Station, signpost to Smarden • Ashford, A28 to Tenderden, A262 to Biddenden, A274 → Headcorn. **Map 7 on page 497** Carte 7 Page 497

Golf course — PARCOURS — 18/20

Site	Site	
Maintenance	Entretien	
Architect	Architecte	Nick Faldo Steven Smyers
Type	Type	parkland, open country
Relief	Relief	
Water in play	Eau en jeu	
Exp. to wind	Exposé au vent	
Trees in play	Arbres en jeu	

Scorecard Carte de score	Chp. Chp.	Mens Mess.	Ladies Da.
Length Long.	6375	5780	4980
Par	72	72	72
Slope system	—	—	—

Advised golfing ability Niveau de jeu recommandé — 0 12 24 36
Hcp required Handicap exigé — no

Club house & amenities — CLUB HOUSE ET ANNEXES — 8/10

Pro shop	Pro-shop	
Driving range	Practice	
Sheltered	couvert	no
On grass	sur herbe	yes
Putting-green	putting-green	yes
Pitching-green	pitching green	yes (2)

Hotel facilities — ENVIRONNEMENT HOTELIER — 6/10

HOTELS HÔTELS

Eastwell Manork, 23 rooms, D £ 210 — Ashford 20 km
Tel (44) 01233 - 213 000, Fax (44) 01233 - 213 017

Ashford International, 201 rooms, D £ 100 — Ashford 14 km
Tel (44) 01233 - 219 988, Fax (44) 01233 - 647 743

Pilgrims Rest, 34 rooms, D £ 49 — Ashford 14 km
Tel (44) 01233 - 636 863, Fax (44) 01233 - 610 119

RESTAURANTS RESTAURANT

West House, Tel (44) 01580 - 291 341 — Biddenden 2 km

Alhambra (Ashford Intern.) — Goudhurst 20 km
Tel(44) 01233 - 219 988

Eastwell Manor, Tel (44) 01233 - 219 955 — Ashford 14 km

CHESTERFIELD

13 | 6 | 7

Derbyshire is richly endowed with golf courses in the National Trust region of the Peak District. Admirers of old English mansions won't want to miss Chatsworth castle and the gardens of Capability Brown and Joseph Paxton. Despite the excellence of the site and the parkland style, this course cannot quite match their sophisticated landscaping, as golf architecture is more a matter of strategy than decoration. Although not one of Harry Colt's masterpieces, Chesterfield is a very pleasant course where strategy (see above!) is not always obvious, and where the sometimes hilly terrain calls for careful club selection. Very natural in its layout with some well-guarded greens that can nonetheless be reached in a variety of ways, this versatile course is well worth a round or two. You wouldn't want to play here for ever but it is a good addition to a golfing holiday in the region.

Le Comté de Derbyshire est bien fourni en parcours de golfs, dans cette région du Parc National de Peak District. Les amateurs de vieilles demeures anglaises ne manqueront pas le Château de Chatsworth, et notamment ses jardins de Capability Brown et Joseph Paxton. En dépit de la qualité de son site et de son aspect de grand parc, ce parcours ne saurait lutter avec leurs créations paysagères sophistiquées, l'architecture de golf étant plus affaire de stratégie que de décoration. Sans être un des grands chefs-d'oeuvre de Harry Colt, Chesterfield est un très agréable parcours, où la stratégie (justement) n'est pas toujours évidente, les quelques reliefs du terrain impliquant des ajustements de choix de club. Très naturel dans son aspect, avec des greens bien défendus, mais accessibles de différentes manières, ce parcours très «versatile» mérite que l'on s'y arrête, même si ce n'est pas pour toujours. C'est en tout cas un bon complément à un voyage golfique dans la région.

Chesterfield Golf Club — 1897

ENG - WALTON, CHESTERFIELD, Derbyshire S42 7 LA

Office	Secrétariat	(44) 01246 - 279 256
Pro shop	Pro-shop	(44) 01246 - 276 297
Fax	Fax	(44) 01246 - 276 622
Web	—	
Situation	Situation	20 km from Sheffield
Annual closure	Fermeture annuelle	no
Weekly closure	Fermeture hebdomadaire	no

Fees main season Tarifs haute saison	Week days Semaine	We/Bank holidays We/Férié
18 holes		
Individual Individuel	£ 26	*
Couple Couple	£ 52	*

Full weekdays: £ 35 / * Members only at week ends

Caddy	Caddy	no
Electric Trolley	Chariot électrique	no
Buggy	Voiturette	no
Clubs	Clubs	no

Credit cards Cartes de crédit
(not for green fees)
VISA - Eurocard - MasterCard - AMEX

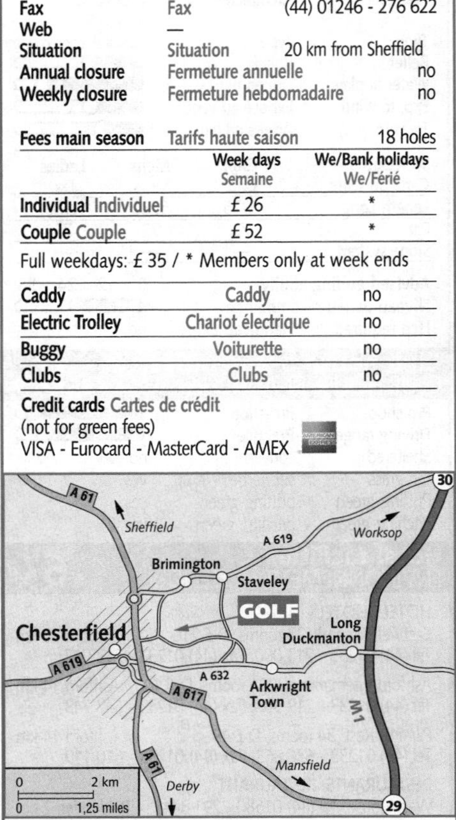

Access Accès : on A 632 (Matlock Road), 3 km from Chesterfield centre town

Map 4 on page 490 Carte 4 Page 490

Golf course PARCOURS — 13/20

Site	Site	
Maintenance	Entretien	
Architect	Architecte	Harry S. Colt
Type	Type	parkland
Relief	Relief	
Water in play	Eau en jeu	
Exp. to wind	Exposé au vent	
Trees in play	Arbres en jeu	

Scorecard Carte de score	Chp. Chp.	Mens Mess.	Ladies Da.
Length Long.	5635	5468	5029
Par	71	71	73
Slope system	—	—	—

Advised golfing ability Niveau de jeu recommandé: 0 12 24 36
Hcp required Handicap exigé: certificate

Club house & amenities CLUB HOUSE ET ANNEXES — 6/10

Pro shop	Pro-shop	
Driving range	Practice	
Sheltered	couvert	
On grass	sur herbe	yes
Putting-green	putting-green	yes
Pitching-green	pitching green	yes

Hotel facilities ENVIRONNEMENT HOTELIER — 7/10

HOTELS HÔTELS

Riber Hall, 14 rooms, D £ 145 — Matlock 10 km
Tel (44) 01629 - 582 795, Fax (44) 01629 - 580 475

Portland Hotel, 24 rooms, D £ 70 — Chesterfield 4 km
Tel (44) 01246 - 234 502, Fax (44) 01246 - 550 915

Sandpiper Hotel, 28 rooms, D £ 80 — Chesterfield 5 km
Tel (44) 01246 - 450 550, Fax (44) 01246 - 452 805

RESTAURANTS RESTAURANT

Swallow Hotel — South Normanton 10 km
Tel (44) 01773 - 812 000

Sitwell Arms — Renishaw 10 km
Tel (44) 01246 - 435 226

CLITHEROE

17 | 7 | 7

The fairways are carpeted with thick turf which prevents balls from ever rolling too far, trees abound but the fairways are wide and the rough not too severe. A few water hazards threaten and readily swallow up any miscued shots, but they are there to be seen and so won't cause any unpleasant surprises. As on many of James Braid's courses, a sharp short game is of the essence, as is skill in rolling the ball. This is another course that deserves rehabilitation, even if its short yardage may not always be to the liking of golfers who hit the ball a long way. But as long-hitters sometimes tend to hook the ball, the out-of-bounds areas down the left on the front 9 will teach them a little respect. The course's location on the edge of the forest of Bowland in the Ribble Valley makes this an ideal site for a few days off the beaten track exploring rivers, old villages, a Roman camp and an abbey or two.

Ce parcours bénéficie d'un gazon dense, ce qui évite aux balles de trop rouler. Les arbres sont très nombreux, mais les fairways sont larges et les roughs peu pénalisants. Quelques obstacles d'eau menacent ou retiennent quelques mauvais coups, mais ils sont bien visibles et ne sauraient causer de mauvaises surprises. De fait, comme sur de nombreux parcours de James Braid, il est essentiel d'avoir un bon petit jeu, en particulier savoir jouer les balles roulées. Encore un parcours à réhabiliter, même si sa longueur le fait regarder avec indifférence par les frappeurs. Comme ce sont souvent des "hookers," les hors-limites à gauche à l'aller leur apprendront le respect. Sa situation en bordure de la forêt de Bowland, au coeur de la Ribble Valley, en fait un site idéal pour quelques jours hors des sentiers battus, à la découverte des rivières et vieux villages, d'un camp romain ou d'une abbaye.

Clitheroe Golf Club — 1932

Whalley Road
ENG - PENDLETON, Lancs BB7 1PP

Office	Secrétariat	(44) 01200 - 422 292
Pro shop	Pro-shop	(44) 01200 - 424 242
Fax	Fax	(44) 01200 - 422 292
Web	—	
Situation	Situation	3 km S of Clitheroe

15 km NE of Blackburn (pop. 136 612)

Annual closure	Fermeture annuelle	no
Weekly closure	Fermeture hebdomadaire	no

Fees main season Tarifs haute saison		Full day
	Week days Semaine	**We/Bank holidays** We/Férié
Individual Individuel	£ 33	£ 39
Couple Couple	£ 66	£ 78
Caddy	Caddy	no
Electric Trolley	Chariot électrique	no
Buggy	Voiturette	no
Clubs	Clubs	no

Credit cards Cartes de crédit (Pro shop goods only)
VISA - Eurocard - MasterCard - DC - JCB - AMEX

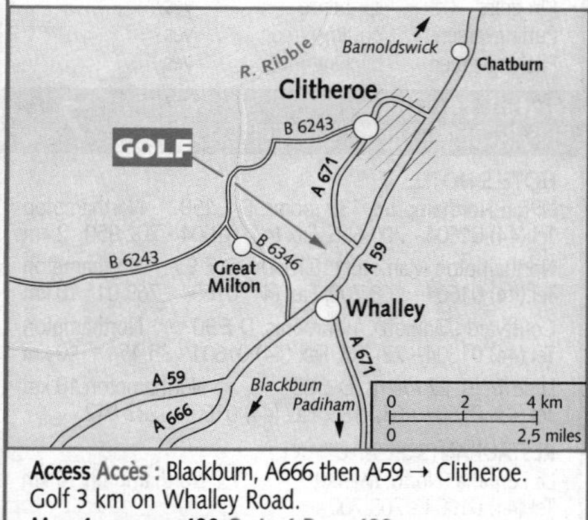

Access Accès : Blackburn, A666 then A59 → Clitheroe. Golf 3 km on Whalley Road.
Map 4 on page 490 Carte 4 Page 490

Golf course PARCOURS — 17/20

Site	Site	
Maintenance	Entretien	
Architect	Architecte	James Braid
Type	Type	parkland
Relief	Relief	
Water in play	Eau en jeu	
Exp. to wind	Exposé au vent	
Trees in play	Arbres en jeu	

Scorecard Carte de score	**Chp.** Chp.	**Mens** Mess.	**Ladies** Da.
Length Long.	5693	5490	4586
Par	71	71	74
Slope system	—	—	—

Advised golfing ability 0 12 24 36
Niveau de jeu recommandé
Hcp required Handicap exigé no

Club house & amenities CLUB HOUSE ET ANNEXES — 7/10

Pro shop	Pro-shop	
Driving range	Practice	
Sheltered	couvert	no
On grass	sur herbe	yes (3 areas)
Putting-green	putting-green	yes
Pitching-green	pitching green	yes

Hotel facilities ENVIRONNEMENT HOTELIER — 7/10

HOTELS HÔTELS

Foxfields, 44 rooms, D £ 100 — Whalley 5 km
Tel (44) 01254 - 822 556, Fax (44) 01254 - 824 613

Northcote Manor, 14 rooms, D £ 110 — Blackburn 8 km
Tel (44) 01254 - 240 555, Fax (44) 01254 - 246 568

Shireburn Arms, 18 rooms, D £ 80 — Clitheroe 3 km
Tel (44) 01254 - 826 518, Fax (44) 01254 - 826 208

RESTAURANTS RESTAURANT

Northcote Manor, Tel (44) 01254 - 240 555 — Blackburn

Paul Heathcote's, Tel(44) 01772 - 784 969 — Longridge18 km

Auctioner, Tel (44) 01200 - 427 153 — Clitheroe 3 km

Foxfields, Tel (44) 01254 - 822 556 — Whalley 5 km

COLLINGTREE PARK

14 | 8 | 7

A corner of the United States in England, a nice change of style for the English but continental Europeans might prefer a little more local colour. With water in play on eight of the 18 holes, numerous well-placed bunkers which lack the "feeling" of what a Simpson, a Colt or a Braid might have produced, and well-balanced difficulties geared to the very many different tee-boxes, Collingtree Park is a good, very pleasant and often very interesting American course but without the often acclaimed visual shocks. It doesn't always blend into the surrounding landscape as well as one might have wished. Johnny Miller was a great player but maybe we expected more of him as a course designer. Problems with the greens probably also weighed in our judgment. At all events, there is no disputing the excellence of practice facilities and services on offer.

Un coin d'Etats-Unis en Angleterre, c'est dépaysant pour les Anglais, mais les continentaux attendent plus de couleur locale. Avec de l'eau en jeu sur huit des 18 trous, des bunkers nombreux, et bien placés, mais aux formes moins "sensuelles" que les créations de Simpson, Braid ou Colt, des difficultés bien balancées suivant les différents (et nombreux) départs, Collingtree Park est un bon parcours à l'américaine, très agréable et souvent très intéressant, mais sans les chocs visuels qui emportent totalement l'adhésion. Son intégration à la nature environnante n'est pas toujours aussi complète qu'on le souhaiterait. Johnny Miller a été un très grand joueur de golf, mais on attendait peut-être davantage de lui comme architecte... Et les problèmes des greens influencent sans doute notre jugement. En tout cas, la qualité remarquable des installations d'entraînement et des services offerts est incontestable.

Collingtree Park Golf Club — 1987

Windingbrook Lane
ENG - NORTHAMPTON NN4 0XN

Office	Secrétariat	(44) 01604 - 700 000
Pro shop	Pro-shop	(44) 01604 - 700 000
Fax	Fax	(44) 01604 - 700 000
Web	www.collingtreeparkgolf.com	
Situation	Situation	Northampton, 10 km
Annual closure	Fermeture annuelle	no
Weekly closure	Fermeture hebdomadaire	no

Fees main season Tarifs haute saison	Full day	
	Week days Semaine	We/Bank holidays We/Férié
Individual Individuel	£ 40	£ 50
Couple Couple	£ 80	£ 100

Booking necessary

Caddy	Caddy	no
Electric Trolley	Chariot électrique	no
Buggy	Voiturette	£ 20 /18 holes
Clubs	Clubs	£ 15 /18 holes

Credit cards Cartes de crédit
VISA - Eurocard - MasterCard - DC - AMEX

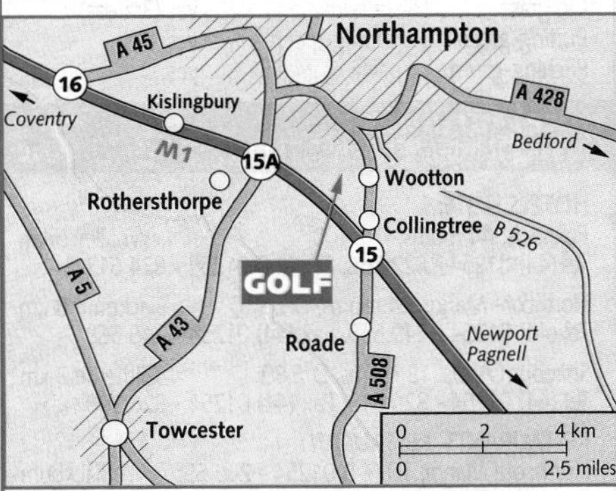

Access Accès : M1 Jct 15, then A508 → Northampton. 10 mins drive, golf on left.
Map 7 on page 496 Carte 7 Page 496

Golf course PARCOURS — 14/20

Site	Site	
Maintenance	Entretien	
Architect	Architecte	Johnny Miller
Type	Type	parkland
Relief	Relief	
Water in play	Eau en jeu	
Exp. to wind	Exposé au vent	
Trees in play	Arbres en jeu	

Scorecard Carte de score	Chp. Chp.	Mens Mess.	Ladies Da.
Length Long.	6217	5598	4860
Par	72	72	73
Slope system	—	—	—

Advised golfing ability Niveau de jeu recommandé: 0 12 24 36
Hcp required Handicap exigé: no

Club house & amenities CLUB HOUSE ET ANNEXES — 8/10

Pro shop	Pro-shop	
Driving range	Practice	
Sheltered	couvert	16 bays (floodlit)
On grass	sur herbe	yes
Putting-green	putting-green	yes
Pitching-green	pitching green	yes

Hotel facilities ENVIRONNEMENT HOTELIER — 7/10

HOTELS HÔTELS

Hilton Northampton, 139 rooms, D £ 150 — Northampton
Tel (44) 01604 - 700 666, Fax (44) 01604 - 702 850 — 2 km

Northampton Marriott, 118 rooms, D £ 95 — Northampton
Tel (44) 01604 - 768 700, Fax (44) 01604 - 769 011 — 10 km

Courtyard (Marriott), 104 rooms, D £ 90 — Northampton
Tel (44) 01604 - 22 777, Fax (44) 01604 - 35 454 — 10 km

Lime Trees, 27 rooms, D £ 85 — Northampton 10 km
Tel (44) 01604 - 632 188, Fax (44) 01604 - 233 012

RESTAURANTS RESTAURANT

La Fontana (North. Marriott) — Northampton 10 km
Tel (44) 01604 - 768 700

French Partridge, Tel (44) 01604 - 870 033 — Horton 7 km

COXMOOR

15 | 6 | 6

With Notts, Sherwood Forest and Coxmoor, this region has three no-nonsense courses, of which the latter lies over moorland and is hilly enough to test your fitness as well as your golfing skills. A good score is there for the taking as long as you avoid the traps on some of the dog-leg holes or carry a number of dangerous hazards, but there could be some nasty surprises in store when you come to add up your score. Strategy here is even more important than the standard of your game and the hazards are generally in clear view from the many elevated tee-boxes. Very pleasant to play with the family or friends, there is an obvious parallel to be drawn with the many similar courses found in Surrey, the one reservation being the sameness of several holes.

Entre Notts, Sherwood Forest et Coxmoor, cette région dispose de trois parcours peu contestables. Celui-ci est dans un espace de landes, et assez accidenté pour tester la forme physique autant que golfique. Un bon score est à votre portée du moment que vous savez déjouer les pièges de certains doglegs ou survoler quelques obstacles dangereux, mais on peut avoir des surprises au moment de l'addition. La stratégie est ici encore plus importante que la qualité du jeu, et les obstacles sont généralement visibles car beaucoup de départs sont en hauteur. Très agréable à jouer avec des amis ou en famille, que ce soit en stroke play ou en match-play, ce parcours est à mettre en parallèle avec de nombreux parcours similaires du Surrey, avec une petite restriction sur la ressemblance de plusieurs trous, qui gêne la précision des souvenirs.

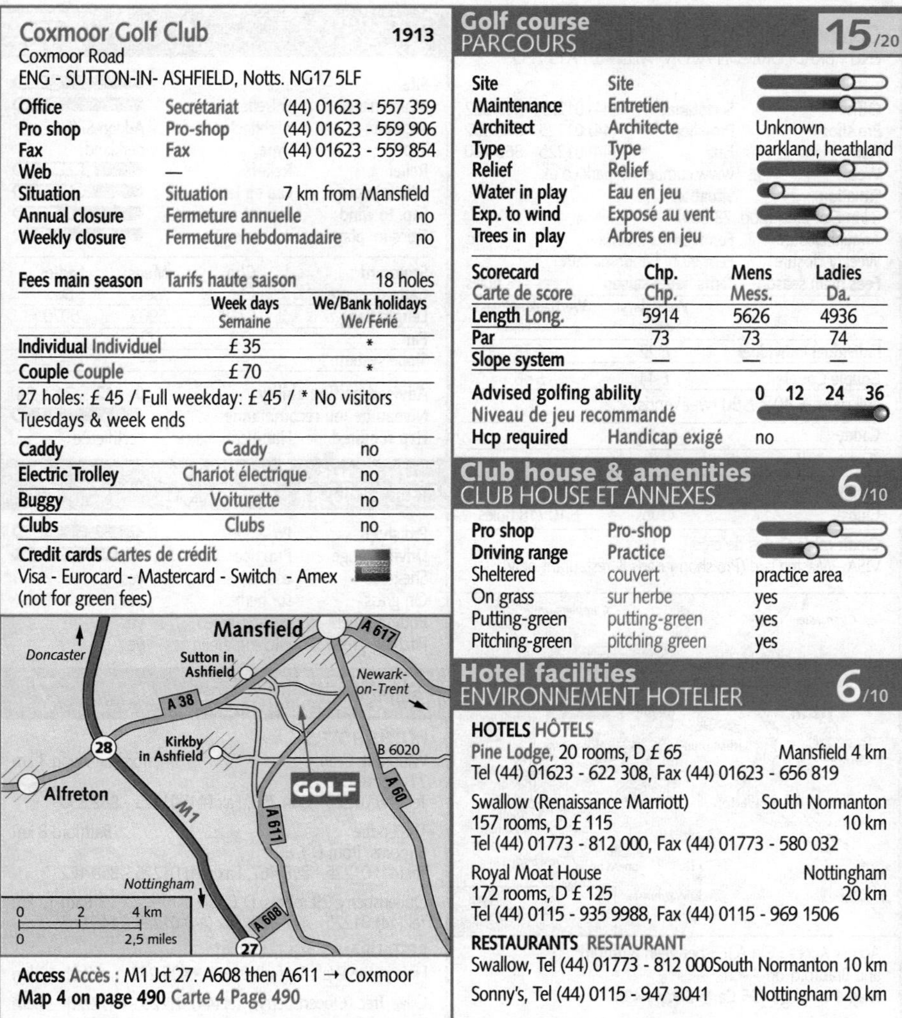

Coxmoor Golf Club — 1913
Coxmoor Road
ENG - SUTTON-IN- ASHFIELD, Notts. NG17 5LF

Office	Secrétariat	(44) 01623 - 557 359
Pro shop	Pro-shop	(44) 01623 - 559 906
Fax	Fax	(44) 01623 - 559 854
Web	—	
Situation	Situation	7 km from Mansfield
Annual closure	Fermeture annuelle	no
Weekly closure	Fermeture hebdomadaire	no

Fees main season Tarifs haute saison	18 holes	
	Week days Semaine	We/Bank holidays We/Férié
Individual Individuel	£ 35	*
Couple Couple	£ 70	*

27 holes: £ 45 / Full weekday: £ 45 / * No visitors Tuesdays & week ends

Caddy	Caddy	no
Electric Trolley	Chariot électrique	no
Buggy	Voiturette	no
Clubs	Clubs	no

Credit cards Cartes de crédit
Visa - Eurocard - Mastercard - Switch - Amex
(not for green fees)

Access Accès : M1 Jct 27. A608 then A611 → Coxmoor
Map 4 on page 490 Carte 4 Page 490

Golf course
PARCOURS — **15**/20

Site	Site	
Maintenance	Entretien	
Architect	Architecte	Unknown
Type	Type	parkland, heathland
Relief	Relief	
Water in play	Eau en jeu	
Exp. to wind	Exposé au vent	
Trees in play	Arbres en jeu	

Scorecard Carte de score	Chp. Chp.	Mens Mess.	Ladies Da.
Length Long.	5914	5626	4936
Par	73	73	74
Slope system	—	—	—

Advised golfing ability Niveau de jeu recommandé — 0 12 24 36
Hcp required Handicap exigé — no

Club house & amenities
CLUB HOUSE ET ANNEXES — **6**/10

Pro shop	Pro-shop	
Driving range	Practice	
Sheltered	couvert	practice area
On grass	sur herbe	yes
Putting-green	putting-green	yes
Pitching-green	pitching green	yes

Hotel facilities
ENVIRONNEMENT HOTELIER — **6**/10

HOTELS HÔTELS
Pine Lodge, 20 rooms, D £ 65 — Mansfield 4 km
Tel (44) 01623 - 622 308, Fax (44) 01623 - 656 819

Swallow (Renaissance Marriott) — South Normanton 10 km
157 rooms, D £ 115
Tel (44) 01773 - 812 000, Fax (44) 01773 - 580 032

Royal Moat House — Nottingham 20 km
172 rooms, D £ 125
Tel (44) 0115 - 935 9988, Fax (44) 0115 - 969 1506

RESTAURANTS RESTAURANT
Swallow, Tel (44) 01773 - 812 000 — South Normanton 10 km
Sonny's, Tel (44) 0115 - 947 3041 — Nottingham 20 km

CUMBERWELL PARK

17 | 7 | 7

From the back tees, this is a tough course with at least two par 5s that are definitely unreachable in two. The designer made up for this, though, by refusing those huge par 3s and preferring shorter but more technical holes. With four short par 4s, you'll find a good number of opportunities to scent some of those evasive birdies. Adrian Stiff has cleverly combined stress and relaxation. In doing so, he has made Cumberwell Park a very pleasant course to play over gently rolling landscape, dotted with elm and oak trees and crossed by a stream that is very much a part of your game. The terrain has been carefully contoured, without overdoing the visual side but with extra concern for enhancing the course within its environment. For the time being, this promising layout is good value for money and its success has prompted the promoters to build a second course of nine good holes. The clubhouse extends a warm welcome and the practice facilities are well above the norm for the UK.

Des départs arrière, c'est un parcours solide, avec au moins deux par 5 pratiquement intouchables en deux, mais l'architecte a compensé en renonçant à ces par 3 interminables, au profit de petits trous plus techniques. Avec quatre par 4 courts, les occasions de birdie ne manqueront pas. Adrian Stiff a bien alterné la tension et la détente, ce qui rend Cumberwell Park très agréable à jouer, dans ce paysage gentiment vallonné et orné de chênes et de pins, où circule un cours d'eau bien mis en jeu. Le modelage du terrain a été fait avec soin, sans excès visuels, mais avec un bon souci de mettre en valeur le parcours dans son environnement. Cette réalisation prometteuse présente pour l'instant un bon rapport qualité/prix, et son succès a incité les promoteurs à construire un second parcours, celui-ci de neuf trous, pour l'instant du moins. Le Clubhouse est accueillant, les installations de practice très au-dessus des normes britanniques.

Cumberwell Park Golf Club — 1994

ENG - BRADFORD-ON-AVON, Wiltshire, BA15 2PQ

Office — Secrétariat — (44) 01225 - 863 322
Pro shop — Pro-shop — (44) 01225 - 862 332
Fax — Fax — (44) 01225 - 868 160
Web — www.cumberwellpark.co.uk
Situation — Situation
8 km E of Bath (pop. 78 689)
Annual closure — Fermeture annuelle — no
Weekly closure — Fermeture hebdomadaire
Fees main season — Tarifs haute saison — 18 holes

	Week days / Semaine	We/Bank holidays / We/Férié
Individual Individuel	£ 22	£ 28
Couple Couple	£ 44	£ 56

Full days: £ 40 / £ 50 (weekends)

Caddy	Caddy	no
Electric Trolley	Chariot électrique	no
Buggy	Voiturette	£ 15 /18 holes
Clubs	Clubs	£ 10 /18 holes

Credit cards Cartes de crédit
VISA - MasterCard (Pro shop goods & restaurant only)

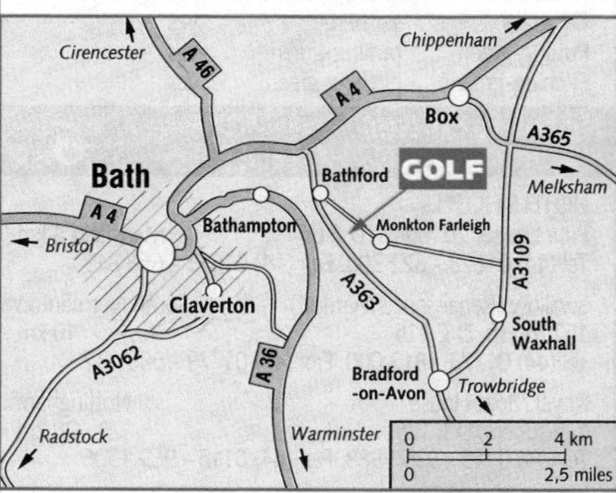

Access Accès : On A363 between Bathford and Bradford-on-Avon
Map 6 on page 495 Carte 6 Page 495

Golf course — PARCOURS — 17/20

Site	Site	
Maintenance	Entretien	
Architect	Architecte	Adrian Stiff
Type	Type	parkland
Relief	Relief	
Water in play	Eau en jeu	
Exp. to wind	Exposé au vent	
Trees in play	Arbres en jeu	

Scorecard Carte de score	**Chp.** Chp.	**Mens** Mess.	**Ladies** Da.
Length Long.	6218	5902	5070
Par	72	72	72
Slope system	—	—	—

Advised golfing ability — 0 12 24 36
Niveau de jeu recommandé
Hcp required — Handicap exigé — certificate

Club house & amenities — CLUB HOUSE ET ANNEXES — 7/10

Pro shop	Pro-shop	
Driving range	Practice	
Sheltered	couvert	yes
On grass	sur herbe	yes
Putting-green	putting-green	yes
Pitching-green	pitching green	yes

Hotel facilities — ENVIRONNEMENT HOTELIER — 7/10

HOTELS HÔTELS

Widbrook Grange — Bradford-on-Avon 3 km
21 rooms, D £ 120
Tel (44) 01225 - 864 750, Fax (44) 01225 - 862 890

The Lodge — Bathford 8 km
6 rooms, from D £ 80
Tel (44) 01225 - 858 467, Fax (44) 01225 - 858 172

Queensberry, 29 rooms, D £ 150 — Bath 12 km
Tel (44) 01225 - 447 928, Fax (44) 01225 - 446 065

RESTAURANTS RESTAURANT

Hole in the Wall, Tel (44) 01225 - 425 242 — Bath 12 km
Olive Tree (Queensberry), Tel (44) 01225 - 447 928 — Bath

DARTMOUTH

16 | 9 | 6

Together with Bowood, this is one of the most promising recent courses in this very romantic region of moorland and heathland. It is also as surprising as the gardens of neighbouring Torquay might appear to foreign visitors... they would do the French Riviera proud. This new course is an inland and rather hilly layout (buggy highly recommended, and the club has 30 for hire). Designer Jeremy Pern has created many very good courses on the continent of Europe (particularly in France) but this is probably one of his very best. He has used land very cleverly indeed, forcing players from the back-tees to carry the ball a long way, particularly to clear the many water hazards. First time out, this is your typical match-play course. The clubhouse (with cottages) is remarkably well equipped with a pool, sauna, jacuzzi and gymnasium.

Avec Bowood, c'est l'une des réalisations prometteuses dans cette région très romantique aux paysages de landes, mais souvent aussi surprenante que les jardins de Torquay, dignes de la Riviéra française, à quelques kilomètres de Dartmouth, d'où partirent les navires des croisades. Ce récent parcours est situé à l'intérieur des terres, et assez accidenté pour ne pas avoir honte d'emprunter une voiturette (il y en a ici plus de 30). L'architecte Jeremy Pern a fait de nombreux très bons parcours sur le continent (en France notamment), et celui-ci est sans doute l'un de ses tout meilleurs, notamment par l'utilisation très intelligente du terrain, obligeant à porter loin la balle des départs arrière, en particulier au-dessus des nombreux obstacles d'eau. La première fois, c'est une découverte, et donc le parcours de match-play typique. Le Clubhouse (avec cottages) est remarquablement équipé, avec piscine, sauna, jaccuzzi et gymnase.

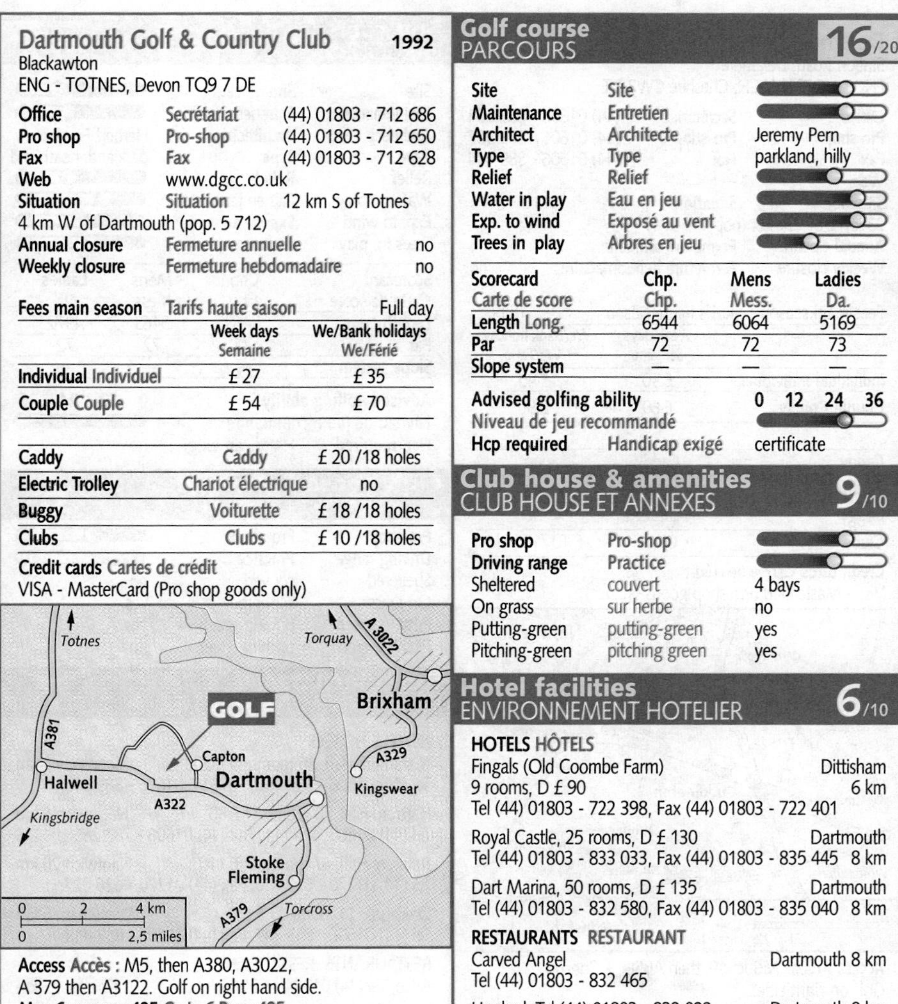

Dartmouth Golf & Country Club **1992**
Blackawton
ENG - TOTNES, Devon TQ9 7 DE

Office	Secrétariat	(44) 01803 - 712 686
Pro shop	Pro-shop	(44) 01803 - 712 650
Fax	Fax	(44) 01803 - 712 628
Web	www.dgcc.co.uk	
Situation	Situation	12 km S of Totnes

4 km W of Dartmouth (pop. 5 712)

Annual closure	Fermeture annuelle	no
Weekly closure	Fermeture hebdomadaire	no

Fees main season Tarifs haute saison		Full day
	Week days Semaine	**We/Bank holidays** We/Férié
Individual Individuel	£ 27	£ 35
Couple Couple	£ 54	£ 70

Caddy	Caddy	£ 20 /18 holes
Electric Trolley	Chariot électrique	no
Buggy	Voiturette	£ 18 /18 holes
Clubs	Clubs	£ 10 /18 holes

Credit cards Cartes de crédit
VISA - MasterCard (Pro shop goods only)

Access Accès : M5, then A380, A3022, A 379 then A3122. Golf on right hand side.
Map 6 on page 495 Carte 6 Page 495

Golf course PARCOURS — 16/20

Site	Site	
Maintenance	Entretien	
Architect	Architecte	Jeremy Pern
Type	Type	parkland, hilly
Relief	Relief	
Water in play	Eau en jeu	
Exp. to wind	Exposé au vent	
Trees in play	Arbres en jeu	

Scorecard Carte de score	**Chp.** Chp.	**Mens** Mess.	**Ladies** Da.
Length Long.	6544	6064	5169
Par	72	72	73
Slope system	—	—	—

Advised golfing ability 0 12 24 36
Niveau de jeu recommandé
Hcp required Handicap exigé certificate

Club house & amenities CLUB HOUSE ET ANNEXES — 9/10

Pro shop	Pro-shop	
Driving range	Practice	
Sheltered	couvert	4 bays
On grass	sur herbe	no
Putting-green	putting-green	yes
Pitching-green	pitching green	yes

Hotel facilities ENVIRONNEMENT HOTELIER — 6/10

HOTELS HÔTELS

Fingals (Old Coombe Farm) — Dittisham
9 rooms, D £ 90 — 6 km
Tel (44) 01803 - 722 398, Fax (44) 01803 - 722 401

Royal Castle, 25 rooms, D £ 130 — Dartmouth
Tel (44) 01803 - 833 033, Fax (44) 01803 - 835 445 — 8 km

Dart Marina, 50 rooms, D £ 135 — Dartmouth
Tel (44) 01803 - 832 580, Fax (44) 01803 - 835 040 — 8 km

RESTAURANTS RESTAURANT

Carved Angel — Dartmouth 8 km
Tel (44) 01803 - 832 465

Hooked, Tel (44) 01803 - 832 022 — Dartmouth 8 km

DELAMERE FOREST

15 | 6 | 7

Here we are at the traditional heart of England and this layout seems to be so symbolic of old English golf that even the card still uses the old term "bogey" instead of "par". It is rather as if the course were gently reminding you that you shouldn't expect miracles on the tougher holes. Let's forget that this should be a par 69 and be proud of playing to our handicap. Designed by Herbert Fowler, this is the perfect heathland course with just the right amount of trees, bunkers (sometimes very deep), heather, a splattering of water and the contours to test your legs and pose a few problems of kicks left and right. There is nothing easy about it, but nothing impossible, either. You can pitch your approach or, preferably, roll it onto the green. Golf here is built into nature and the two lie very comfortably together.

C'est ici le coeur traditionnel de l'Angleterre, et ce parcours est comme le symbole des parcours de golf anglais, au point que la carte de score porte le terme "bogey" au lieu de par, comme pour souligner avec indulgence que l'on n'attend pas de miracles sur les trous difficiles. Oublions donc que ce devrait être un par 69, et soyons fier de jouer notre handicap. Dessiné par Herbert Fowler, c'est le parfait parcours de bruyère, avec les arbres qu'il faut, les bunkers qu'il faut (parfois très profonds), la bruyère bien sûr, quelques soupçons d'eau, des reliefs pour tester les jambes et poser quelques problèmes de rebonds. Rien de facile mais rien d'impossible. On peut y jouer des coups levés, mais plutôt des balles roulées. Le golf est ici logé dans la nature, et il s'y trouve bien à l'aise.

Delamere Forest Golf Club — 1910

Station Road, Delamere
ENG - NORTHWICH, Cheshire CW8 2JE

Office	Secrétariat	(44) 01606 - 883 264
Pro shop	Pro-shop	(44) 01606 - 883 307
Fax	Fax	(44) 01606 - 889 444
Web	—	
Situation	Situation	

23 km E of Chester (pop.115 971)

Annual closure	Fermeture annuelle	no
Weekly closure	Fermeture hebdomadaire	no

Fees main season / Tarifs haute saison	18 holes	
	Week days / Semaine	We/Bank holidays / We/Férié
Individual Individuel	£ 30	£ 45
Couple Couple	£ 60	£ 90

Caddy	Caddy	no
Electric Trolley	Chariot électrique	no
Buggy	Voiturette	no
Clubs	Clubs	£ 10 /18 holes

Credit cards Cartes de crédit
Visa - Mastercard (Pro shop goods only)

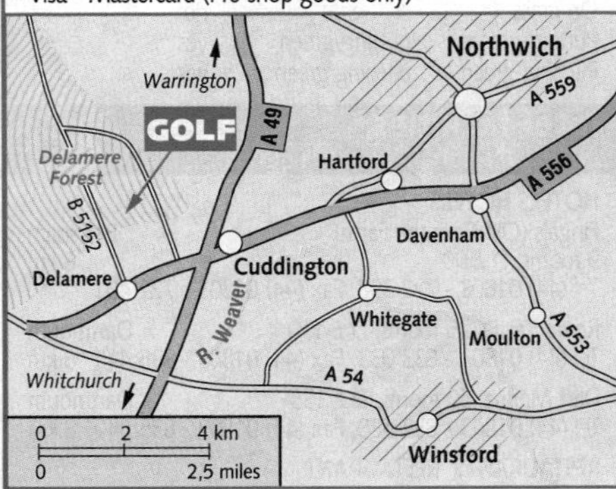

Access Accès : M6 Jct 19, then A556 → Chester.
Golf on right side.
Map 4 on page 490 Carte 4 Page 490

Golf course / PARCOURS — 15/20

Site	Site	
Maintenance	Entretien	
Architect	Architecte	Herbert Fowler
Type	Type	parkland, heathland
Relief	Relief	
Water in play	Eau en jeu	
Exp. to wind	Exposé au vent	
Trees in play	Arbres en jeu	

Scorecard / Carte de score	Chp. / Chp.	Mens / Mess.	Ladies / Da.
Length Long.	5463	5463	4972
Par	72	72	72
Slope system	—	—	—

Advised golfing ability / Niveau de jeu recommandé: 0 12 24 36
Hcp required — Handicap exigé — no

Club house & amenities / CLUB HOUSE ET ANNEXES — 6/10

Pro shop	Pro-shop	
Driving range	Practice	
Sheltered	couvert	no
On grass	sur herbe	yes
Putting-green	putting-green	yes
Pitching-green	pitching green	no

Hotel facilities / ENVIRONNEMENT HOTELIER — 7/10

HOTELS HÔTELS

Nunsmere Hall, 36 rooms, D £ 200 — Sandiway 2 km
Tel (44) 01606 - 889 100, Fax (44) 01606 - 889 055

Hartford Hall, 20 rooms, D £ 80 — Northwich 5 km
Tel (44) 01606 - 75 711, Fax (44) 01606 - 782 285

Rookery Hall, 47 rooms, D £ 110 — Nantwich 20 km
Tel (44) 01270 - 610 016, Fax (44) 01270 - 626 027

Oaklands, 11 rooms, D £ 65 — Weaverham 5 km
Tel (44) 01606 - 853 249, Fax (44) 01606 - 852 419

RESTAURANTS RESTAURANT

Arkle, Tel (44) 01244 - 324 024 — Chester 22 km

Garden House, Tel (44) 01244 - 320 004 — Chester 22 km

DENHAM

15 | 7 | 7

Along with Aberdovey, this is one of the few golf courses to have its own railway station. It also has the type of Clubhouse architecture that reminds you very much of a country residence, and, last but not least, is the type of course that makes you want to take up golf and continue playing for ever. There is nothing particularly spectacular about it, but no Harry Colt course is ever bland. It also has its share of clichés that are typical of other courses he has designed. Here, there are some cleverly placed bunkers but which never bar the entrance to greens (except on the 11th hole), trees but no forest, no hidden terrors, no heather to bury your ball in and no water hazards. It is also a nice length for players who will never hit it as far as Tiger Woods even if they do use high-tech drivers. A course is always an adversary, but this one is fair and most likeable.

C'est un des seuls golfs, avec Aberdovey, qui dispose de sa propre station de chemin de fer. Il a aussi ce genre de Clubhouse dont l'architecture vous donne des idées de maison de campagne. Et c'est enfin le genre de parcours qui donne envie de commencer le golf, et de continuer à l'aimer au point de devenir un jour "oldest member" quelque part. Il n'a rien de très spectaculaire, mais un tracé de Harry Colt n'est jamais banal, même s'il existe des "clichés," typiques d'autres parcours qu'il a dessiné. Ici, il y a des bunkers bien placés mais pas en travers de la route du green (sauf au 11), des arbres mais pas de forêt, rien d'horrible n'est caché, il n'y a pas de bruyère pour happer les balles, pas d'obstacles d'eau, et la longueur est très favorable aux joueurs qui n'auront jamais la puissance de Tiger Woods, même avec un driver high-tech. Si le parcours est l'adversaire du golfeur, Denham est un "jolly good fellow."

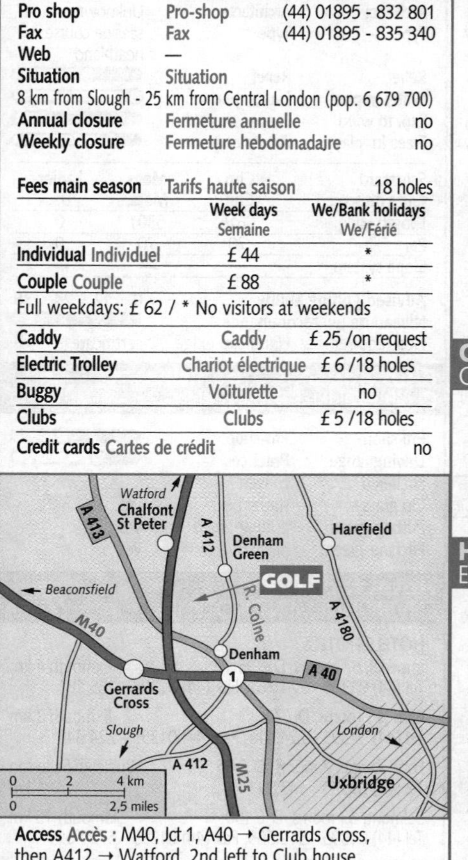

Denham Golf Club **1910**
Tilehouse Lane
ENG - DENHAM, Bucks UB9 5DE

Office	Secrétariat	(44) 01895 - 832 022
Pro shop	Pro-shop	(44) 01895 - 832 801
Fax	Fax	(44) 01895 - 835 340
Web	—	
Situation	Situation	

8 km from Slough - 25 km from Central London (pop. 6 679 700)

Annual closure	Fermeture annuelle	no
Weekly closure	Fermeture hebdomadaire	no

Fees main season Tarifs haute saison	**Week days** Semaine	**We/Bank holidays** We/Férié
		18 holes
Individual Individuel	£ 44	*
Couple Couple	£ 88	*

Full weekdays: £ 62 / * No visitors at weekends

Caddy	Caddy	£ 25 /on request
Electric Trolley	Chariot électrique	£ 6 /18 holes
Buggy	Voiturette	no
Clubs	Clubs	£ 5 /18 holes
Credit cards Cartes de crédit		no

Access Accès : M40, Jct 1, A40 → Gerrards Cross, then A412 → Watford. 2nd left to Club house.
Map 8 on page 498 Carte 8 Page 498

Golf course PARCOURS — 15/20

Site	Site	
Maintenance	Entretien	
Architect	Architecte	Harry S. Colt
Type	Type	parkland
Relief	Relief	
Water in play	Eau en jeu	
Exp. to wind	Exposé au vent	
Trees in play	Arbres en jeu	

Scorecard Carte de score	**Chp.** Chp.	**Mens** Mess.	**Ladies** Da.
Length Long.	5806	5543	5014
Par	70	70	72
Slope system	—	—	—

Advised golfing ability Niveau de jeu recommandé — 0 12 24 36
Hcp required Handicap exigé — 28 Men, 36 Ladies

Club house & amenities CLUB HOUSE ET ANNEXES — 7/10

Pro shop	Pro-shop	
Driving range	Practice	
Sheltered	couvert	practice area
On grass	sur herbe	yes
Putting-green	putting-green	yes
Pitching-green	pitching green	yes

Hotel facilities ENVIRONNEMENT HOTELIER — 7/10

HOTELS HÔTELS

De Vere Bull, 109 rooms, D £ 230 — Gerrards Cross 5 km
Tel (44) 01753 - 885 995, Fax (44) 01753 - 885 504

Copthorne, 219 rooms, D £ 180 — Slough 11 km
Tel (44) 01753 - 516 222, Fax (44) 01753 - 516 237

Courtyard, 149 rooms, D £ 135 — Slough
Tel (44) 01753 - 551 551, Fax (44) 01753 - 553 333

RESTAURANTS RESTAURANT

Water Hall — Chalfont St Peter 3 km
Tel (44) 01494 - 873 430

Roberto's, Tel (44) 01895 - 632 519 — Ickenham 6 km

Waterfront Brasserie — Yiewsley 10 km
Tel (44) 0181 - 899 1733

EAST DEVON

16 | 6 | 7

This is as if a typical Surrey or Berkshire course had been transplanted to the West country. On the cliff tops here, you would think you were playing at Walton Heath or the Berkshire, complete with tall pine-trees, birch trees and gorse. The marine landscape is something of a bonus, rather like the flowers in Spring. Forgetting the unquestionable visual appeal, East Devon is a very good course where, from the back-tees at least, you need a good solid hit, a long carry and some basic skills in flighting the ball through the wind, as the normally harmless hazards (from the front tees) can come dangerously into play. The course is not too hilly but there are still four blind greens and two others that are elevated. Good, accurate players will enjoy themselves (especially between holes 6 and 9) but the higher-handicappers might not enjoy tangling with the gorse and heather on the tougher holes. At least their golfing superiors will have every opportunity to teach them a thing or two about the tactics of golf.

Au sommet de la falaise, on pourrait parfois se croire parfois dans le Surrey ou le Berkshire, quand la bruyère, les grands pins, les bouleaux, les buissons d'ajoncs rappellent Walton Heath ou The Berkshire : les paysages marins sont un cadeau supplémentaire, tout comme les fleurs au printemps. Tout plaisir visuel mis à part, c'est un très bon parcours, où il faut parfois porter solidement la balle depuis les départs arrière du moins, travailler ses balles dans le vent car les obstacles normalement inoffensifs peuvent venir en jeu. Le relief n'est pas trop prononcé, mais il y a quatre greens aveugles et deux autres en élévation. Les joueurs précis prendront pas mal de plaisir ici (entre le 6 et le 9 en particulier), mais les hauts handicaps risquent d'avoir quelques problèmes avec la bruyère et les trous les plus difficiles. Cela dit, leurs aînés en golf se feront un plaisir de les faire profiter de leur expérience tactique du jeu.

The East Devon Golf Club — 1902

North View Road
ENG - BUDLEIGH SALTERTON, Devon EX 9 6DR

Office	Secrétariat	(44) 01395 - 443 370
Pro shop	Pro-shop	(44) 01395 - 445 195
Fax	Fax	(44) 01395 - 445 547
Web	—	
Situation	Situation	2 km from Exmouth

10 km from Exeter (pop. 98 125)

Annual closure	Fermeture annuelle	no
Weekly closure	Fermeture hebdomadaire	Monday

Fees main season Tarifs haute saison	18 holes	
	Week days Semaine	**We/Bank holidays** We/Férié
Individual Individuel	£ 28	£ 36
Couple Couple	£ 56	£ 72

Full days: £ 36 / £42 (week ends)

Caddy	Caddy	no
Electric Trolley	Chariot électrique	£ 8
Buggy	Voiturette	no
Clubs	Clubs	£ 10
Credit cards	Cartes de crédit	no

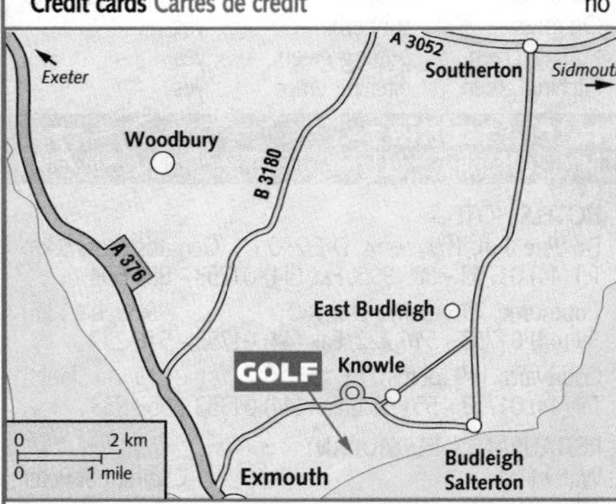

Access Accès : M5 Jct 30, Exmouth A370 onto B3179 Budleigh Satterton, to T Jct. Turn right onto B373C, then B3173. Club on the right hand side before town, on Links Road. **Map 6 on page 495** Carte 6 Page 495

Golf course — PARCOURS — 16/20

Site	Site	
Maintenance	Entretien	
Architect	Architecte	Unknown
Type	Type	seaside course, heathland
Relief	Relief	
Water in play	Eau en jeu	
Exp. to wind	Exposé au vent	
Trees in play	Arbres en jeu	

Scorecard Carte de score	**Chp.** Chp.	**Mens** Mess.	**Ladies** Da.
Length Long.	5616	5301	0
Par	70	70	0
Slope system	—	—	—

Advised golfing ability 0 12 24 36
Niveau de jeu recommandé
Hcp required Handicap exigé certificate

Club house & amenities — CLUB HOUSE ET ANNEXES — 6/10

Pro shop	Pro-shop	
Driving range	Practice	
Sheltered	couvert	
On grass	sur herbe	yes
Putting-green	putting-green	yes
Pitching-green	pitching green	yes

Hotel facilities — ENVIRONNEMENT HOTELIER — 7/10

HOTELS HÔTELS

Imperial, 57 rooms, D £ 95 — Exmouth 4 km
Tel (44) 01395 - 274 761, Fax (44) 01395 - 265 161

Barn ,11 rooms, D £ 68 — Exmouth 3 km
Tel (44) 01395 - 224 411, Fax (44) 01395 - 224 445

Long Range, 7 rooms, D £ 65 — Budleigh Salterton 1 km
Tel (44) 01395 - 443 321

Belmont, 53 rooms, D £ 150 — Sidmouth 10 km
Tel (44) 01395 - 512 555, Fax (44) 01395 - 579 101

RESTAURANTS RESTAURANT

River House, Tel (44) 01395 - 265 147 — Lympstone 8 km

EAST SUSSEX NATIONAL East Course 17 8 7

This is a 36-hole complex, although the more intimate "West" course is reserved more for members. The "East" course is more like a tournament layout with mounds designed for spectators. Designed by the very talented Robert Cupp, the American style is never too loud and you can even sometimes roll your ball onto the green. The many different tee-boxes add to the variety and allow you to approach the course with the caution it deserves first time out, as some of the hazards are hard to spot and game strategy requires some careful thought. Start with a round of match-play, an excellent idea especially since the finishing holes are very impressive. The appeal of the site is supplemented by the hotel on site, a superb driving range and a huge clubhouse.

Cet ensemble comprend 36 trous, mais le parcours "Ouest," plus intime, est à priori réservé aux membres. Celui-ci ressemble davantage à un parcours de tournoi, avec des buttes prévues pour accueillir des spectateurs. Dessiné par le très talentueux Robert Cupp, le style américain n'y est pourtant pas trop agressif, il est parfois même possible d'arriver en roulant sur les greens. La multiplicité des départs permet de renouveler chaque fois les plaisirs, mais aussi, la première fois, de reconnaître prudemment le parcours, car certains obstacles sont peu visibles, et la stratégie du jeu réclame aussi quelque réflexion. Commencer par jouer en match-play sera d'autant plus agréable que le "finish" est excellent. Pour situer la séduction du lieu, ajoutons l'hôtel sur place, un practice superbe et un vaste Clubhouse.

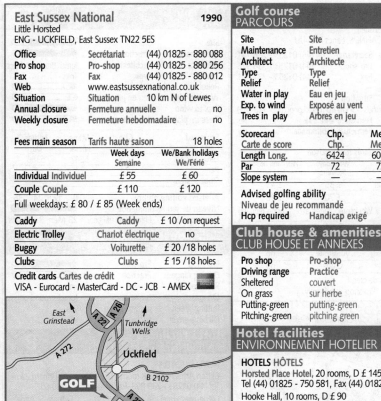

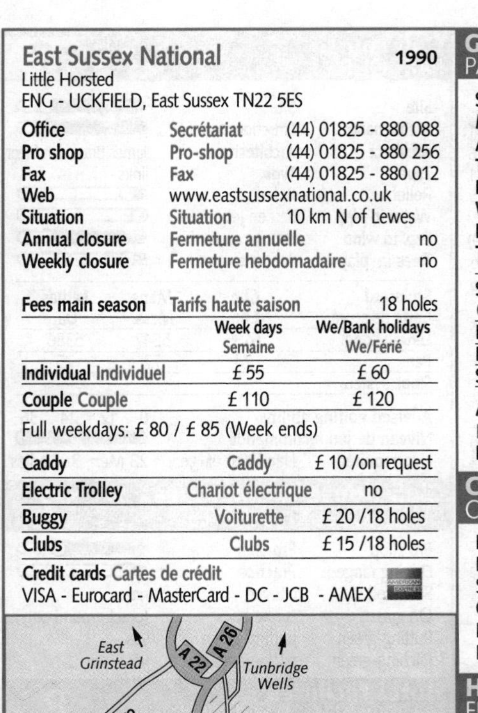

East Sussex National 1990

Little Horsted
ENG - UCKFIELD, East Sussex TN22 5ES

Office	Secrétariat	(44) 01825 - 880 088
Pro shop	Pro-shop	(44) 01825 - 880 256
Fax	Fax	(44) 01825 - 880 012
Web	www.eastsussexnational.co.uk	
Situation	Situation	10 km N of Lewes
Annual closure	Fermeture annuelle	no
Weekly closure	Fermeture hebdomadaire	no

Fees main season Tarifs haute saison	18 holes	
	Week days Semaine	**We/Bank holidays** We/Férié
Individual Individuel	£ 55	£ 60
Couple Couple	£ 110	£ 120
Full weekdays: £ 80 / £ 85 (Week ends)		
Caddy	Caddy	£ 10 /on request
Electric Trolley	Chariot électrique	no
Buggy	Voiturette	£ 20 /18 holes
Clubs	Clubs	£ 15 /18 holes

Credit cards Cartes de crédit
VISA - Eurocard - MasterCard - DC - JCB - AMEX

Access Accès : London, A23 then A22 through East Grinstead, Uckfield. Golf 4.5 km South of Uckfield on A22.
Map 7 on page 497 Carte 7 Page 497

Golf course PARCOURS 17/20

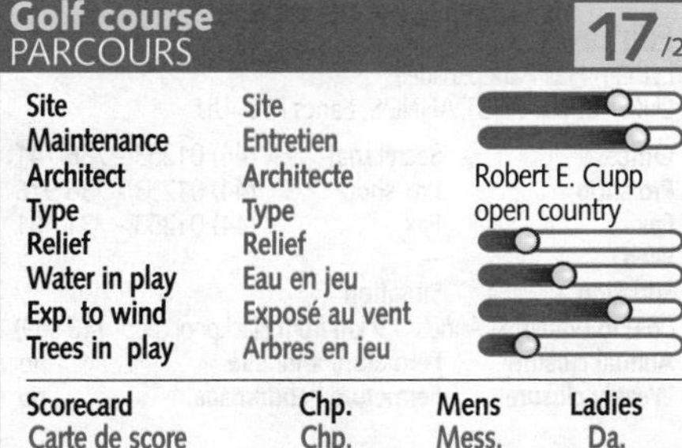

Site	Site	
Maintenance	Entretien	
Architect	Architecte	Robert E. Cupp
Type	Type	open country
Relief	Relief	
Water in play	Eau en jeu	
Exp. to wind	Exposé au vent	
Trees in play	Arbres en jeu	

Scorecard Carte de score	**Chp.** Chp.	**Mens** Mess.	**Ladies** Da.
Length Long.	6424	6084	4764
Par	72	72	72
Slope system	—	—	—

Advised golfing ability Niveau de jeu recommandé 0 12 24 36
Hcp required Handicap exigé certificate

Club house & amenities CLUB HOUSE ET ANNEXES 8/10

Pro shop	Pro-shop	
Driving range	Practice	
Sheltered	couvert	no
On grass	sur herbe	yes
Putting-green	putting-green	yes
Pitching-green	pitching green	yes

Hotel facilities ENVIRONNEMENT HOTELIER 7/10

HOTELS HÔTELS
Horsted Place Hotel, 20 rooms, D £ 145 Uckfield adjacent
Tel (44) 01825 - 750 581, Fax (44) 01825 - 750 459

Hooke Hall, 10 rooms, D £ 90 Uckfield 3 km
Tel (44) 01825 - 761 578, Fax (44) 01825 - 768 025

Shelleys Hotel, 19 rooms, D £ 180 Lewes 10 km
Tel (44) 01273 - 472 361, Fax (44) 01273 - 483 152

RESTAURANTS RESTAURANT
Horsted Place Hotel, Tel (44) 01825 - 750 581 Uckfield adjacent

Shelleys Hotel, Tel (44) 01273 - 472 361 Lewes 10 km

La Scaletta (Hooke Hall), Tel (44) 01825 - 761 578 Uckfield 3 km

FAIRHAVEN

17 | 7 | 8

Golfers who love lush green courses, neatly mown rough, soft greens and trees which shelter from the wind, and who like to get a tan in the process should avoid all the courses on this side of England. On this coast you play golf with all the clubs in your bag, with your head, your technical know-how, all the inspiration you can muster and with locals who will explain where you should hit the ball and where the greens and pins actually are. Fairhaven is simply a great course, not really beautiful from the style point of view, but honest, absorbing, exciting and very well maintained. There are others that have all these attributes but they don't have the pureness of style. To play well here, it's always the same thing: hit it straight, hard and clean. Otherwise don't bother too much counting your strokes, take the gimmies or make full use of the strokes you are given.

Ceux qui aiment les parcours bien verts, les roughs bien tondus, les greens bien mous, les arbres qui abritent du vent, et bronzer en plus, doivent éviter tous les golfs de cette côte d'Angleterre. Ici, on joue au golf avec tous ses clubs et sa tête, avec son bagage technique, avec l'inspiration du moment et avec les joueurs du coin qui vont vous expliquer où sont les points cardinaux, s'il y a des drapeaux au bout des fairways, et où. Fairhaven est simplement un grand parcours pas très très beau (au sens esthétique du terme), mais franc, absorbant, passionnant, très bien entretenu. Il en est d'autres qui ont toutes ces qualités, mais pas la pureté du style. Pour bien le jouer, il faut la même chose, taper droit, fort, nettement. Ou alors ne pas trop s'occuper de compter les coups, ceux que l'on donne et ceux que l'on reçoit.

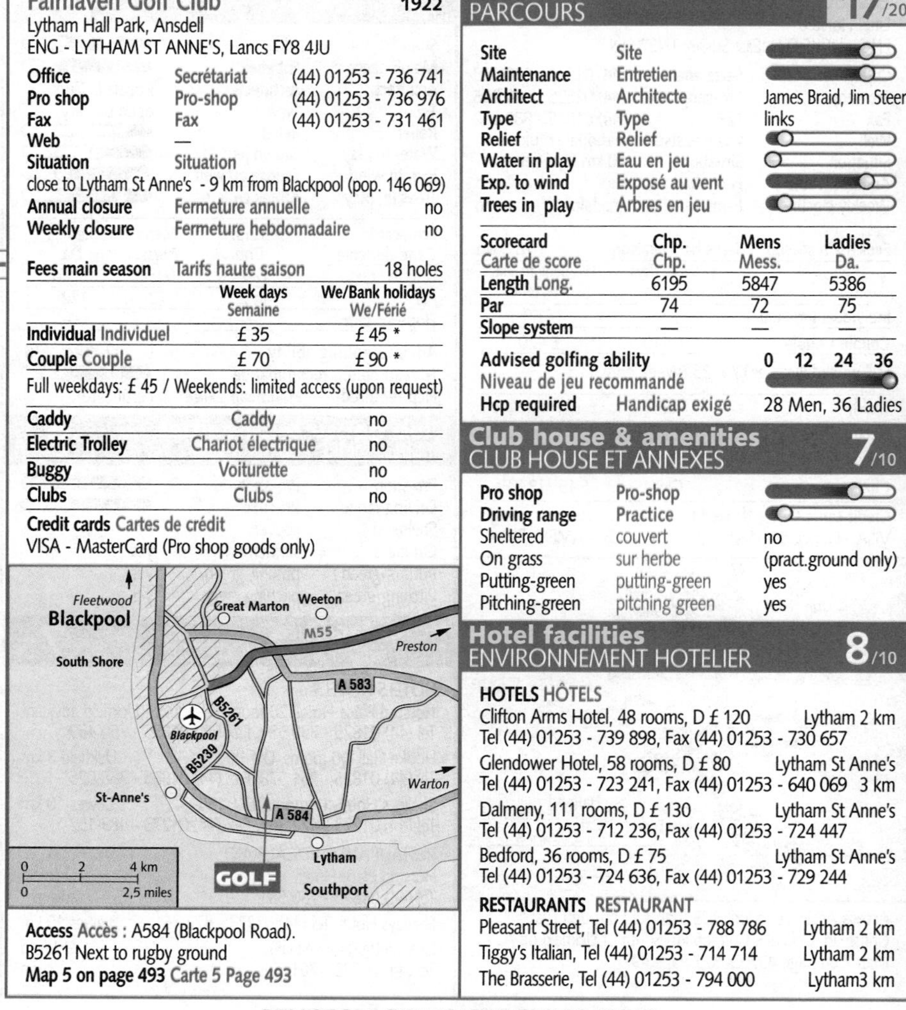

Fairhaven Golf Club — 1922
Lytham Hall Park, Ansdell
ENG - LYTHAM ST ANNE'S, Lancs FY8 4JU

Office	Secrétariat	(44) 01253 - 736 741
Pro shop	Pro-shop	(44) 01253 - 736 976
Fax	Fax	(44) 01253 - 731 461
Web	—	
Situation	Situation	

close to Lytham St Anne's - 9 km from Blackpool (pop. 146 069)

Annual closure	Fermeture annuelle	no
Weekly closure	Fermeture hebdomadaire	no

Fees main season Tarifs haute saison — 18 holes

	Week days Semaine	We/Bank holidays We/Férié
Individual Individuel	£ 35	£ 45 *
Couple Couple	£ 70	£ 90 *

Full weekdays: £ 45 / Weekends: limited access (upon request)

Caddy	Caddy	no
Electric Trolley	Chariot électrique	no
Buggy	Voiturette	no
Clubs	Clubs	no

Credit cards Cartes de crédit
VISA - MasterCard (Pro shop goods only)

Access Accès : A584 (Blackpool Road).
B5261 Next to rugby ground
Map 5 on page 493 Carte 5 Page 493

Golf course PARCOURS — 17/20

Site	Site	
Maintenance	Entretien	
Architect	Architecte	James Braid, Jim Steer
Type	Type	links
Relief	Relief	
Water in play	Eau en jeu	
Exp. to wind	Exposé au vent	
Trees in play	Arbres en jeu	

Scorecard Carte de score	Chp. Chp.	Mens Mess.	Ladies Da.
Length Long.	6195	5847	5386
Par	74	72	75
Slope system	—	—	—

Advised golfing ability Niveau de jeu recommandé — 0 12 24 36
Hcp required Handicap exigé — 28 Men, 36 Ladies

Club house & amenities CLUB HOUSE ET ANNEXES — 7/10

Pro shop	Pro-shop	
Driving range	Practice	
Sheltered	couvert	no
On grass	sur herbe	(pract.ground only)
Putting-green	putting-green	yes
Pitching-green	pitching green	yes

Hotel facilities ENVIRONNEMENT HOTELIER — 8/10

HOTELS HÔTELS

Clifton Arms Hotel, 48 rooms, D £ 120 — Lytham 2 km
Tel (44) 01253 - 739 898, Fax (44) 01253 - 730 657

Glendower Hotel, 58 rooms, D £ 80 — Lytham St Anne's 3 km
Tel (44) 01253 - 723 241, Fax (44) 01253 - 640 069

Dalmeny, 111 rooms, D £ 130 — Lytham St Anne's
Tel (44) 01253 - 712 236, Fax (44) 01253 - 724 447

Bedford, 36 rooms, D £ 75 — Lytham St Anne's
Tel (44) 01253 - 724 636, Fax (44) 01253 - 729 244

RESTAURANTS RESTAURANT

Pleasant Street, Tel (44) 01253 - 788 786 — Lytham 2 km
Tiggy's Italian, Tel (44) 01253 - 714 714 — Lytham 2 km
The Brasserie, Tel (44) 01253 - 794 000 — Lytham3 km

FALMOUTH 14 6 7

The development work here over recent years has significantly raised the standard of this course but fortunately has not made it all that much harder. Meaning that most players can enjoy Falmouth without being put off by excessive difficulties. It would have been a pity to deter holiday-makers and deprive them of some superb views over the sea from atop the cliffs. Even though very good players will enjoy this course, it is to be recommended primarily for 12 handicappers and upwards. In windy weather, it is a different picture altogether, but then it always is on courses as exposed as this. This is when you need to hit those low shots and know how to roll the ball down to the greens. There are a few trees in play all the same, but the main hazards are the bunkers, which also define the fairways and alignment of drives and approach shots. An unpretentious course and golf club (with a good driving range, something of a rarity in Britain) to be included in any decent tour of Cornwall.

Les travaux d'aménagement du parcours au cours des dernières années en ont sensiblement relevé le standard, mais il n'a pas été vraiment durci pour autant. La plupart des joueurs pourront ainsi l'apprécier sans être découragés par d'excessives difficultés. Il aurait été dommage de rebuter les vacanciers, et de les priver de vues superbes sur l'océan, du haut des falaises. Même si les très bons joueurs s'y amuseront, on conseillera surtout Falmouth à partir de 12 de handicap. Quand le vent souffle, c'est une tout autre affaire, mais c'est le cas sur tous les parcours aussi ouverts, il faut alors savoir maîtriser les balles basses et en apprécier le roulement. Quelques arbres sont parfois en jeu, mais les bunkers sont à la fois les principaux obstacles et les repères pour définir les fairways et pour s'aligner. Un parcours et un club sans prétention (avec un bon practice, pour une fois dans le pays), à inscrire dans un grand "tour" de la Cornouailles.

Falmouth Golf Club 1928

Swanpool Road
ENG - FALMOUTH, Cornwall TR11 5 BQ

Office	Secrétariat	(44) 01326 - 311 262
Pro shop	Pro-shop	(44) 01326 - 314 296
Fax	Fax	(44) 01326 - 317 783
Web	www.falmouthgolfclub.co.uk	
Situation	Situation	

1.5 km from Falmouth (pop. 19 217)

Annual closure	Fermeture annuelle	no
Weekly closure	Fermeture hebdomadaire	no

Fees main season Tarifs haute saison	18 holes	
	Week days Semaine	**We/Bank holidays** We/Férié
Individual Individuel	£ 25	£ 25
Couple Couple	£ 50	£ 50
Caddy	Caddy	no
Electric Trolley	Chariot électrique	no
Buggy	Voiturette	£ 15
Clubs	Clubs	£ 8

Credit cards Cartes de crédit
(Pro shop goods only)
VISA - Eurocard - MasterCard - DC - AMEX

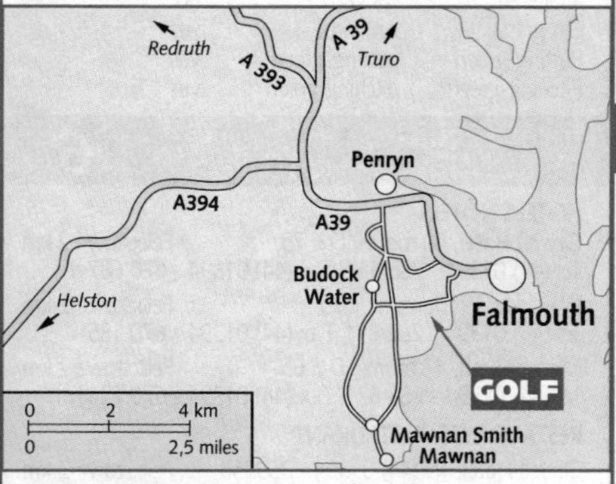

Access Accès : A30 to Truro. → Falmouth.
West of Swanpool Beach. Follow signs.
Map 6 on page 494 Carte 6 Page 494

Golf course PARCOURS 14/20

Site	Site	
Maintenance	Entretien	
Architect	Architecte	Unknown
Type	Type	seaside course, open country
Relief	Relief	
Water in play	Eau en jeu	
Exp. to wind	Exposé au vent	
Trees in play	Arbres en jeu	

Scorecard Carte de score	**Chp.** Chp.	**Mens** Mess.	**Ladies** Da.
Length Long.	5344	5169	4977
Par	71	71	72
Slope system	—	—	—

Advised golfing ability Niveau de jeu recommandé: 0 12 24 36
Hcp required Handicap exigé: certificate

Club house & amenities CLUB HOUSE ET ANNEXES 6/10

Pro shop	Pro-shop	
Driving range	Practice	
Sheltered	couvert	7 bays
On grass	sur herbe	yes
Putting-green	putting-green	yes
Pitching-green	pitching green	yes

Hotel facilities ENVIRONNEMENT HOTELIER 7/10

HOTELS HÔTELS

Royal Duchy, 42 rooms, D £ 130 — Falmouth 1,5 km
Tel (44) 01326 - 313 042, Fax (44) 01326 - 319 420

St Michael's of Falmouth — Falmouth 1,5 km
65 rooms, D £ 80
Tel (44) 01326 - 312 707, Fax (44) 01326 - 211 772

Penmere Manor, 37 rooms, D £ 115 — Falmouth 1,5 km
Tel (44) 01326 - 211 411, Fax (44) 01326 - 317 588

Meudon, 29 rooms, D £ 170 — Mawnan Smith 8 km
Tel (44) 01326 - 250 541, Fax (44) 01326 - 250 543

RESTAURANTS RESTAURANT

Pandora Inn, Tel (44) 01326 - 372 678 — Mylor Bridge 9 km

FELIXSTOWE FERRY Martello Course

15	6	6

This is the fifth oldest club in the history of English golf and a course little known to the majority of golfers on the continent. Yet this is a top notch links course, without the spectacular dunes of the west coast but slightly reminiscent of the courses in Scotland's East Lothian. Re-designed by Henry Cotton after the second world war which left the site in ruins, Tom Dunn's original layout is now a challenge of the highest order despite being rather on the short side. Cut in two by a road, the course's most interesting holes run along the sea-shore. These are the last six holes which make for a highly interesting finish, especially when the wind blows a little (it does happen). A course to bravely go out and pitch into, in the same way as Julie Hall and Jo Hockley, who both learnt their trade here, the hard way.

C'est le cinquième club de l'histoire du golf en Angleterre, et un parcours dont bien peu de continentaux ont entendu parler. C'est pourtant un links de première qualité, sans les dunes spectaculaires de la côte ouest, mais qui n'est pas sans rappeler les parcours de l'East Lothian en Ecosse. Remodelé par Henry Cotton, après la Seconde Guerre Mondiale qui l'avait laissé en ruines, le dessin de Tom Dunn est aujourd'hui redevenu un challenge de premier ordre, même avec sa longueur réduite. Séparé en deux par une route, il offre ses trous les plus intéressants le long de la mer, et ce sont justement les six derniers, ce qui permet un finale des plus intéressants, quand le vent daigne souffler un peu (ce qui arrive). Un parcours à attaquer avec bravoure, comme savent le faire Julie Hall et Jo Hockley, formées ici, à la dure !

Felixstowe Ferry Golf Club — 1880

Ferry Road
ENG - FELIXSTOWE, Suffolk IP11 9RY

Office	Secrétariat	(44) 01394 - 286 834
Pro shop	Pro-shop	(44) 01394 - 283 975
Fax	Fax	(44) 01394 - 273 679
Web	www.felixstoweferry.co.uk	
Situation	Situation	18 km from Ipswich
Annual closure	Fermeture annuelle	no
Weekly closure	Fermeture hebdomadaire	no

Fees main season Tarifs haute saison	18 holes	
	Week days Semaine	**We/Bank holidays** We/Férié
Individual Individuel	£ 30	*
Couple Couple	£ 60	*

* No visitors at weekends.

Caddy	Caddy	no
Electric Trolley	Chariot électrique	£ 5 /18 holes
Buggy	Voiturette	no
Clubs	Clubs	no

Credit cards Cartes de crédit
(Pro shop goods only) Visa - Mastercard - AMEX

Access Accès : Ipswich, A14 → North Felixstowe.
At beach, continue on the left.
Course entrance on the right.
Map 7 on page 497 Carte 7 Page 497

Golf course PARCOURS — 15/20

Site	Site	
Maintenance	Entretien	
Architect	Architecte	Tom Dunn Henry Cotton (1947)
Type	Type	seaside course, links
Relief	Relief	
Water in play	Eau en jeu	
Exp. to wind	Exposé au vent	
Trees in play	Arbres en jeu	

Scorecard Carte de score	**Chp.** Chp.	**Mens** Mess.	**Ladies** Da.
Length Long.	5645	5562	4935
Par	72	72	72
Slope system	—	—	—

Advised golfing ability Niveau de jeu recommandé: 0 12 24 36
Hcp required Handicap exigé: certificate

Club house & amenities CLUB HOUSE ET ANNEXES — 6/10

Pro shop	Pro-shop	
Driving range	Practice	
Sheltered	couvert	no
On grass	sur herbe	yes
Putting-green	putting-green	yes
Pitching-green	pitching green	yes

Hotel facilities ENVIRONNEMENT HOTELIER — 6/10

HOTELS HÔTELS

Orwell Hotel, 58 rooms, D £ 75 — Felixstowe 2 km
Tel (44) 01394 - 285 511, Fax (44) 01394 - 670 687

Waverley, 19 rooms, D £ 75 — Felixstowe 2 km
Tel (44) 01394 - 282 811, Fax (44) 01394 - 670 185

Marlborough, 47 rooms, D £ 65 — Felixstowe 2 km
Tel (44) 01394 - 285 621, Fax (44) 01394 - 670 724

RESTAURANTS RESTAURANT

Orwell Hotel, Tel (44) 01394 - 309955 — Felixstowe 2 km
St Peter's, Tel (44) 01473 - 210810 — Ipswich 18 km
Mortimer's on the Quay, Tel (44) 01473 - 230 225 — Ipswich 18 km

FERNDOWN Old Course

17 | 7 | 7

With sand, heather, pine-trees and conifers, Ferndown is first and foremost a beautiful site with a simple but very functional clubhouse. Once a very dry course during rain-free summers, the course is now watered automatically so that you no longer get those infuriatingly unfair kicks left and right down the fairway, especially on the dog-legs. Be careful with Ferndown, because despite the impression of dealing with a fair and open course, some of the trees are more in play than you think and a number of ditches lie hidden in the rough. Good scores depend a lot on your driving, not only to avoid the dangerous fairway bunkers but also to get the ball in the right spot and have a good shot at the green. Although close to Bournemouth, this is not just a simple holiday course but one that has staged some top tournaments: a little short for the big boys, but ideal for the top ladies.

De sable et de bruyère, orné de pins et de sapins, Ferndown est d'abord un bel endroit, avec un Clubhouse sans prétentions architecturales, mais très fonctionnel. Autrefois très sec lors des étés sans pluie, il bénéficie maintenant d'un arrosage qui a retiré certains rebonds imprévus et souvent injustes, en particulier sur les nombreux doglegs. Il faut se méfier de Ferndown, car on a l'impression d'un parcours très franc, alors que certains arbres sont plus en jeu qu'ils ne paraissent, et des fossés se dissimulent dans les roughs. Les bons scores dépendent beaucoup du driving, pour non seulement éviter les dangereux bunkers de fairway, mais aussi placer la balle en bonne position pour attaquer les greens. Bien que proche de Bournemouth, il vaut bien mieux qu'un simple parcours de vacances. Il fut le théâtre de grandes compétitions : un peu court pour les machos, il était idéal pour les proettes.

Ferndown Golf Club — 1914

119, Golf Links Road -
ENG - FERNDOWN, Dorset BH22 8BU

Office	Secrétariat	(44) 01202 - 874 602
Pro shop	Pro-shop	(44) 01202 - 873 825
Fax	Fax	(44) 01202 - 873 926
Web	www.ferndowngolfclub.co.uk	
Situation	Situation	Bournemouth, 8 km
Annual closure	Fermeture annuelle	no
Weekly closure	Fermeture hebdomadaire	no

Fees main season / Tarifs haute saison	18 holes	
	Week days / Semaine	We/Bank holidays / We/Férié
Individual Individuel	£ 45	£ 50
Couple Couple	£ 90	£ 100

Full days: £ 55 / £ 60 (weekends)

Caddy	Caddy	no
Electric Trolley	Chariot électrique	no
Buggy	Voiturette	£ 20 /18 holes
Clubs	Clubs	£ 15 /18 holes

Credit cards Cartes de crédit
(Pro shop goods only)
Visa - Eurocard - Mastercard - Amex

Access Accès : M3 last exit, then A31 to Trickett's Cross, then A348 to Ferndown, follow signs → Golf.
Map 6 on page 495 Carte 6 Page 495

Golf course PARCOURS — 17/20

Site	Site	
Maintenance	Entretien	
Architect	Architecte	Harold Hilton
Type	Type	inland, heathland
Relief	Relief	
Water in play	Eau en jeu	
Exp. to wind	Exposé au vent	
Trees in play	Arbres en jeu	

Scorecard / Carte de score	Chp. / Chp.	Mens / Mess.	Ladies / Da.
Length Long.	5895	5651	5176
Par	71	71	72
Slope system	—	—	—

Advised golfing ability / Niveau de jeu recommandé: 0 12 24 36
Hcp required / Handicap exigé: 28 Men, 30 Ladies

Club house & amenities CLUB HOUSE ET ANNEXES — 7/10

Pro shop	Pro-shop	
Driving range	Practice	
Sheltered	couvert	no
On grass	sur herbe	yes
Putting-green	putting-green	yes
Pitching-green	pitching green	no

Hotel facilities ENVIRONNEMENT HOTELIER — 7/10

HOTELS HÔTELS

Mansion House, 32 rooms, D £ 130 — Poole 8 km
Tel (44) 01202 - 685 666, Fax (44) 01202 - 665 709

Royal Bath, 140 rooms, D £ 210 — Bournemouth 5 km
Tel (44) 01202 - 555 555, Fax (44) 01202 - 554 158

The Dormy, 114 rooms, D £ 145 — Ferndown 0,5 km
Tel (44) 01202 - 872 121, Fax (44) 01202 - 895 388

RESTAURANTS RESTAURANT

La Roche — Poole 5 km
Tel (44) 01202 - 707 333

Clarks — Bournemouth 5 km
Tel (44) 01202 - 240 310

FILEY

13 | 5 | 5

With the exception of Ganton, there are not all that many very good courses in this region, even though Scarborough was one of the very first English seaside resorts which, like others, has been in slow and steady decline since the end of the war. Not far from Filey (to the south), you will want to visit the white cliffs of Flamborough Head and Bempton, a huge sea-bird reserve. Because nature-lovers are often golf-lovers as well, we would recommend a round here, although don't expect to find the course of the century. It might be beside the sea, but Filey is anything but a links course running through dunes. It plays that way though, firstly because of the wind and secondly because of the sandy soil. The layout is more than a hundred years old and has not been radically altered since, even though any course endures some changes over time. Filey is like hundreds of other courses you find in Britain, offering nothing particularly spectacular or luxurious but a club where golfers cultivate a certain style of life.

Scarborough était l'une des toutes premières stations balnéaires anglaises, mais sa vogue a décliné après la seconde guerre mondiale. Au sud de Filey, on ne manquera pas les falaises calcaires de Flamborough Head et Bempton, énorme colonie d'oiseaux de mer. Les amateurs de nature étant souvent aussi des amoureux de golf, on leur conseillera une visite ici, bien que ce ne soit pas le parcours du siècle. Nous sommes en bord de mer, mais ce parcours n'a rien d'un links au milieu de dunes, bien que le jeu à y développer soit tout à fait comparable, à cause du vent d'abord, bien entendu, mais aussi de la nature sablonneuse du sol. Depuis plus d'un siècle, le dessin n'a pas été vraiment modifié, même si un parcours de golf se transforme. C'est un golf comme on en trouve des centaines dans le pays, sans rien de spectaculaire ou de luxueux, mais où on continue à cultiver une certaine forme de jeu et de convivialité hors des modes.

Filey Golf Club — 1897

West Avenue
ENG - FILEY, North Yorkshire YO14 9BQ

Office	Secrétariat	(44) 01723 - 513 293
Pro shop	Pro-shop	(44) 01723 - 513 134
Fax	Fax	(44) 01723 - 514 952
Web	—	
Situation	Situation	Scarborough, 12 km
Annual closure	Fermeture annuelle	no
Weekly closure	Fermeture hebdomadaire	no

Fees main season Tarifs haute saison	Week days Semaine	We/Bank holidays We/Férié
	18 holes	
Individual Individuel	£ 22	£ 29
Couple Couple	£ 44	£ 58

Full days: £ 28 / £ 31 (week ends)

Caddy	Caddy	no
Electric Trolley	Chariot électrique	£ 5
Buggy	Voiturette	no
Clubs	Clubs	no

Credit cards Cartes de crédit
VISA - Eurocard - MasterCard - AMEX
Switch (not for green fees)

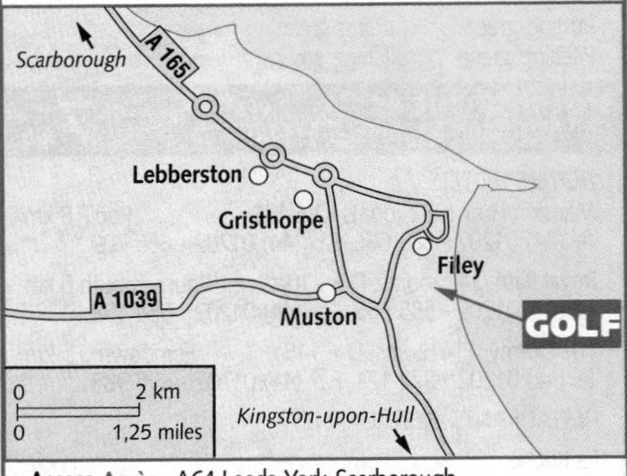

Access Accès : A64 Leeds-York-Scarborough.
After Taxton town, A1039 → Filey. Golf on a private road off end of West Avenue in south end of Filey.
Map 4 on page 490 Carte 4 Page 490

Golf course PARCOURS — 13/20

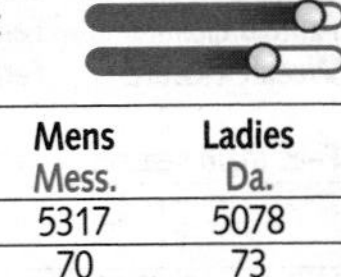

Site	Site	
Maintenance	Entretien	
Architect	Architecte	Unknown
Type	Type	seaside course
Relief	Relief	
Water in play	Eau en jeu	
Exp. to wind	Exposé au vent	
Trees in play	Arbres en jeu	

Scorecard Carte de score	Chp. Chp.	Mens Mess.	Ladies Da.
Length Long.	5501	5317	5078
Par	70	70	73
Slope system	—	—	—

Advised golfing ability 0 12 24 36
Niveau de jeu recommandé
Hcp required Handicap exigé no

Club house & amenities CLUB HOUSE ET ANNEXES — 5/10

Pro shop	Pro-shop	
Driving range	Practice	
Sheltered	couvert	
On grass	sur herbe	yes
Putting-green	putting-green	yes
Pitching-green	pitching green	no

Hotel facilities ENVIRONNEMENT HOTELIER — 5/10

HOTELS HÔTELS

Sea Brink Hotel, 12 rooms, D £ 60 — Filey 2 km
Tel (44) 01723 - 513 257, Fax (44) 01723 - 514 139

White Lodge Hotel, 20 rooms, D £ 94 — Filey 2 km
Tel (44) 01723 - 514 771, Fax (44) 01723 - 516 590

Crown, 83 rooms, D £ 70 — Scarborough 12 km
Tel (44) 01723 - 373 491, Fax (44) 01723 - 362 271

Downcliffe House, 10 rooms, D £ 75 — Filey 2 km
Tel (44) 01723 - 513 310, Fax (44) 01723 - 513 773

RESTAURANTS RESTAURANT

Jade Garden — Scarborough 12 km
Tel (44) 01723 - 369 099

FOREST OF ARDEN Arden

15 | 8 | 8

The very fine hotel today belongs to the Marriott Group, as does the course. The "Aylesford" hotel is very respectable and perfectly complements this "Arden" course, which is technically a very interesting layout, especially for the better player. All in all, it is a very pleasant spot for a few days golfing with a group or with the family, even if you are playing with golfers of very different abilities. We would simply recommend avoiding the wetter months as the soil takes a long time to soak up surface water. "Arden" was designed by Donald Steel and features many different tee-boxes, of which we would advise the yellow tees, at least for your first round, unless you are a good player of long irons. A tricky course overall with quite a few water hazards, trees which neatly outline the fairways and thick rough, Arden gets better and better in what is a very professional golfing resort.

Le très bel hôtel appartient aujourd'hui au groupe Marriott, tout comme les parcours. Le "Aylesford" est fort honorable, et complète agréablement le "Arden," plus intéressant techniquement, en particulier pour les meilleurs joueurs. C'est ainsi un lieu très agréable pour passer quelques jours en groupe ou en famille, même si les niveaux de golf sont très différents. On recommandera simplement d'éviter les mois très humides, car le sol a du mal à évacuer les excès d'eau. Le "Arden" a été dessiné par Donald Steel, qui a fait un tracé avec de multiples départs, dont nous conseillerons les "jaunes," au moins la première fois, à moins d'être un solide joueur de longs fers et de savoir lever la balle. Assez "tricky" en général, avec pas mal d'obstacles d'eau, des arbres sculptant bien les trous, un rough épais, c'est un parcours qui peut encore progresser, dans un complexe très professionnel.

Marriott Forest of Arden Golf Club — 1970

Maxstoke Lane
ENG - MERIDEN, Warwicks. CV7 7HR

Office	Secrétariat	(44) 01676 - 522 335
Pro shop	Pro-shop	(44) 01676 - 522 335
Fax	Fax	(44) 01676 - 523 711
Web	—	
Situation	Situation	Birmingham, 24 km

16 km NW of Coventry (pop. 294 387)

Annual closure	Fermeture annuelle	no
Weekly closure	Fermeture hebdomadaire	no

Fees main season Tarifs haute saison	Week days Semaine	We/Bank holidays We/Férié (18 holes)
Individual Individuel	£ 80	£ 90
Couple Couple	£ 160	£ 180
Caddy Caddy		£ 30 /on request
Electric Trolley Chariot électrique		no
Buggy Voiturette		£ 25 /18 holes
Clubs Clubs		£ 20 /18 holes

Credit cards Cartes de crédit
VISA - Eurocard - MasterCard - DC - AMEX

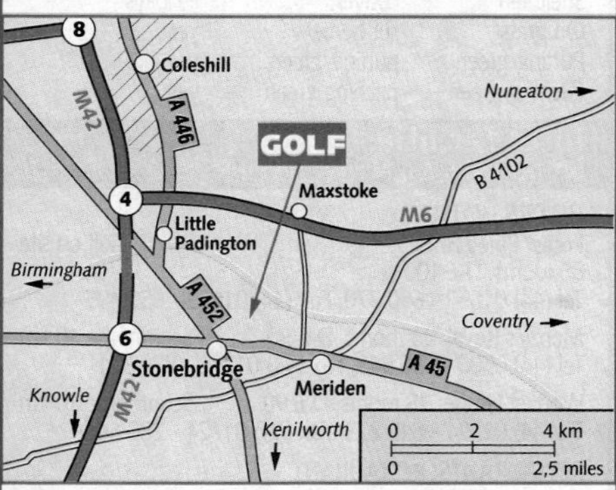

Access Accès : M42 Jct 6, then A45 → Coventry. After 1.5 km (1 m), left into Shepherds Lane, by "Little Chef". Golf 2 km on the left.
Map 7 on page 496 Carte 7 Page 496

Golf course PARCOURS — 15/20

Site	Site	
Maintenance	Entretien	
Architect	Architecte	Donald Steel
Type	Type	parkland
Relief	Relief	
Water in play	Eau en jeu	
Exp. to wind	Exposé au vent	
Trees in play	Arbres en jeu	

Scorecard Carte de score	Chp. Chp.	Mens Mess.	Ladies Da.
Length Long.	6420	5867	5106
Par	72	72	72
Slope system	—	—	—

Advised golfing ability Niveau de jeu recommandé — 0 12 24 36
Hcp required Handicap exigé — no

Club house & amenities CLUB HOUSE ET ANNEXES — 8/10

Pro shop	Pro-shop	
Driving range	Practice	
Sheltered	couvert	6 bays
On grass	sur herbe	no
Putting-green	putting-green	yes
Pitching-green	pitching green	yes

Hotel facilities ENVIRONNEMENT HOTELIER — 8/10

HOTELS HÔTELS
Marriott Forest of Arden Hotel, — Meriden
214 rooms, D £ 160 — on site
Tel (44) 01676 - 522 335, Fax (44) 01676 - 523 711
Manor (De Vere), 112 rooms, D £ 130 — Meriden 3 km
Tel (44) 01676 - 522 735, Fax (44) 01676 - 522 186
Haigs, 23 rooms, D £ 90 — Balsall Common 6 km
Tel (44) 01676 - 533 004, Fax (44) 01676 - 535 132
Hilton Birmingham Metropole Nat. Ex. Centre, Birmingham
793 rooms, D £ 250 — 6 km
Tel (44) 0121 - 780 4242, Fax (44) 0121 - 780 3923

RESTAURANTS RESTAURANT
Sir Edward Elgar's, Tel (44) 0121 - 452 1144 — Birmingham
The Broadwater, Tel (44) 01676 - 522 335 — Merideno

FOREST PINES Forest + Pines

17 | 6 | 7

It is easier than you might think to get a course all wrong when the terrain is not up to standard. Not so here, where the impression is one of a site blessed by Mother Nature and given the able help of John Morgan. He had to know how to trace the right path through a forest, how to define an intelligent layout, adapt the course to players of different levels, individualise the holes while respecting overall harmony, bring hazards into play without penalising the good shots, and keep a few surprises in store so that it's fun to play again and again. There are courses with which you have an affair and courses which you embrace for life. Forest Pines would be in the latter category, but we will wait a while to see whether it stays as good as it is right now as it comes of age. Opened in 1996 and also featuring a good standard 9 hole course ("The Beeches"), this is a resort you cannot afford to miss.

Il est plus facile qu'on ne le croit de rater un parcours alors que le terrain s'y prête. Ici, on peut avoir l'impression que Mère Nature a béni les lieux, mais John Morgan lui a donné un coup de main. Il fallait savoir tracer la route dans la forêt, définir un itinéraire intelligent, adapter son parcours aux différents niveaux de jeu, individualiser les trous tout en conservant une harmonie générale, mettre en jeu les obstacles sans pénaliser les bons coups de golf, et réserver des surprises pour que le plaisir ne soit pas émoussé après la première fois. Il est des parcours avec lesquels on a une liaison et d'autres que l'on épouse. Celui-ci pourrait bien faire partie de la seconde catégorie, même si l'on attend encore un peu pour voir s'il garde sa qualité actuelle en prenant quelques rides. Ouvert en 1996, et proposant également un 9 trous de bonne facture ("Beeches"), c'est un ensemble à connaître sans faute.

Forest Pines — 1996

Ermine Street, Broughton
ENG - BRIGG, Lincs DN20 04Q

Office	Secrétariat	(44) 01652 - 650 756
Pro shop	Pro-shop	(44) 01652 - 650 756
Fax	Fax	(44) 01652 - 650 495
Web	www.forestpines.co.uk	
Situation	Situation	

10 km E of Scunthorpe (pop. 61 550)

Annual closure	Fermeture annuelle	no
Weekly closure	Fermeture hebdomadaire	no

Fees main season Tarifs haute saison	18 holes	
	Week days Semaine	**We/Bank holidays** We/Férié
Individual Individuel	£ 30	£ 30
Couple Couple	£ 60	£ 60

Full days: £ 40

Caddy	Caddy	on request
Electric Trolley	Chariot électrique	no
Buggy	Voiturette	£ 15 /18 holes
Clubs	Clubs	£ 5 /18 holes

Credit cards Cartes de crédit
VISA - Eurocard - MasterCard - Switch - AMEX

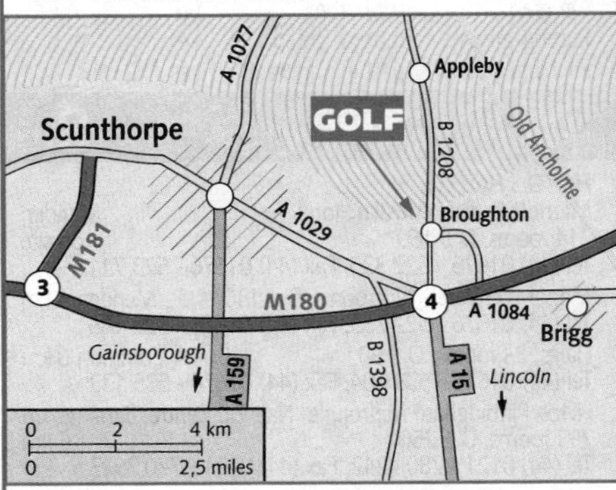

Access Accès : M1, M18 at Jct 32, then M180.
At Jct 4, Golf 2 km North
Map 4 on page 491 Carte 4 Page 491

Golf course PARCOURS — 17/20

Site	Site	
Maintenance	Entretien	
Architect	Architecte	John Morgan
Type	Type	forest
Relief	Relief	
Water in play	Eau en jeu	
Exp. to wind	Exposé au vent	
Trees in play	Arbres en jeu	

Scorecard Carte de score	**Chp.** Chp.	**Mens** Mess.	**Ladies** Da.
Length Long.	6262	5920	5295
Par	73	73	74
Slope system	—	—	—

Advised golfing ability Niveau de jeu recommandé — 0 12 24 36

Hcp required Handicap exigé — certificate

Club house & amenities CLUB HOUSE ET ANNEXES — 6/10

Pro shop	Pro-shop	
Driving range	Practice	
Sheltered	couvert	17 bays
On grass	sur herbe	yes
Putting-green	putting-green	yes
Pitching-green	pitching green	yes

Hotel facilities ENVIRONNEMENT HOTELIER — 7/10

HOTELS HÔTELS

Forest Pines Hotel — Golf on site
86 rooms, D £ 100
Tel (44) 01652 - 650 770, Fax (44) 01652 - 650 495

Menzies Royal, 33 rooms, D £ 90 — Scunthorpe 10 km
Tel (44) 0500 - 636 943, Fax (44) 01773 - 880 321

Wortley House, 38 rooms, D £ 90 — Scunthorpe 10 km
Tel (44) 01724 - 842 223, Fax (44) 01724 - 280 646

RESTAURANTS RESTAURANT

Brigg Hotel + Restaurant — Brigg 7 km
Tel (44) 01652 - 657 633

Forest Pines — Golf on site
Tel (44) 01652 - 650 770

FORMBY

18 | 7 | 7

It is easier to play here as a green-feer (the course is often deserted on weekdays) than to become a member. In this sort of golfing paradise, the latter is perfectly understandable. The layout, soil and dunes bear the hallmark of a links course, but there are trees on a good number of holes, meaning that the wind is not such an important factor as it can be on the region's other links courses. Donald Steel has recently lengthened the course but has taken nothing away from the highly strategic and penalising placing of bunkers, laid out initially by Willie Park then improved upon by Harry Colt. Seen overall, this is a unique and exciting course which offers a permanent challenge. Playing here is a blissful experience, except perhaps for the ladies, who have their own course (a gem) and their own clubhouse. No comment.

Il est plus facile de jouer ici en visiteur (en semaine, c'est souvent désert) que d'y devenir membre. On comprend que ce soit difficile, car Formby est une sorte de paradis. Le dessin, le sol, les dunes sont ceux des links, mais les arbres y sont assez présents sur une bonne partie des trous pour que le vent ne soit pas un facteur aussi terriblement important que sur les autres links de la région. Donald Steel a récemment allongé le parcours, mais sans rien ôter du placement très stratégique et pénalisant des bunkers, établi par Willie Park d'abord, mais surtout par Harry Colt. Au total, le caractère de ce parcours est unique, le jeu passionnant, le challenge permanent. On éprouve ici une impression de bonheur... sauf les Dames, qui ont un parcours à elles (un petit bijou) et leur propre Clubhouse. Sans commentaires.

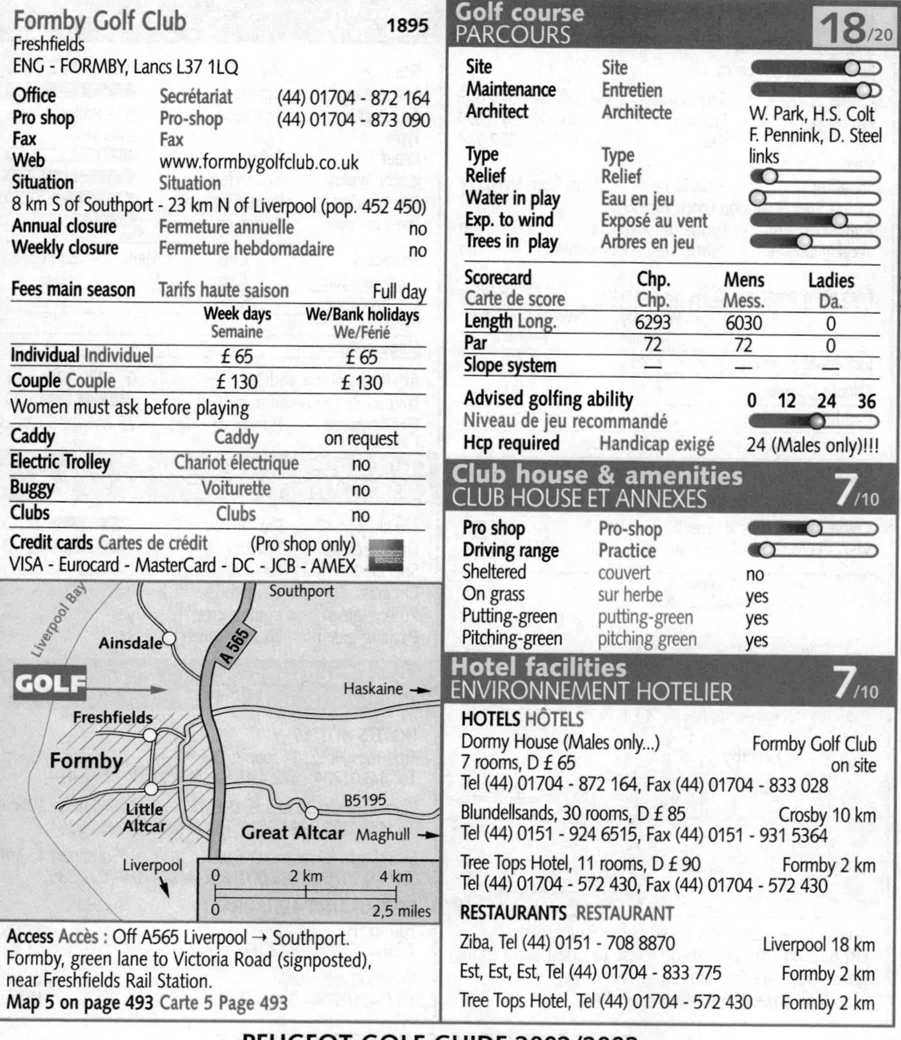

Formby Golf Club **1895**
Freshfields
ENG - FORMBY, Lancs L37 1LQ

Office	Secrétariat	(44) 01704 - 872 164
Pro shop	Pro-shop	(44) 01704 - 873 090
Fax	Fax	
Web	www.formbygolfclub.co.uk	
Situation	Situation	

8 km S of Southport - 23 km N of Liverpool (pop. 452 450)

Annual closure	Fermeture annuelle	no
Weekly closure	Fermeture hebdomadaire	no

Fees main season Tarifs haute saison		Full day
	Week days Semaine	**We/Bank holidays** We/Férié
Individual Individuel	£ 65	£ 65
Couple Couple	£ 130	£ 130

Women must ask before playing

Caddy	Caddy	on request
Electric Trolley	Chariot électrique	no
Buggy	Voiturette	no
Clubs	Clubs	no

Credit cards Cartes de crédit (Pro shop only)
VISA - Eurocard - MasterCard - DC - JCB - AMEX

Access Accès : Off A565 Liverpool → Southport. Formby, green lane to Victoria Road (signposted), near Freshfields Rail Station.
Map 5 on page 493 Carte 5 Page 493

Golf course PARCOURS — 18/20

Site	Site	
Maintenance	Entretien	
Architect	Architecte	W. Park, H.S. Colt F. Pennink, D. Steel
Type	Type	links
Relief	Relief	
Water in play	Eau en jeu	
Exp. to wind	Exposé au vent	
Trees in play	Arbres en jeu	

Scorecard Carte de score	**Chp.** Chp.	**Mens** Mess.	**Ladies** Da.
Length Long.	6293	6030	0
Par	72	72	0
Slope system	—	—	—

Advised golfing ability 0 12 24 36
Niveau de jeu recommandé
Hcp required Handicap exigé 24 (Males only)!!!

Club house & amenities CLUB HOUSE ET ANNEXES — 7/10

Pro shop	Pro-shop	
Driving range	Practice	
Sheltered	couvert	no
On grass	sur herbe	yes
Putting-green	putting-green	yes
Pitching-green	pitching green	yes

Hotel facilities ENVIRONNEMENT HOTELIER — 7/10

HOTELS HÔTELS
Dormy House (Males only...) — Formby Golf Club on site
7 rooms, D £ 65
Tel (44) 01704 - 872 164, Fax (44) 01704 - 833 028

Blundellsands, 30 rooms, D £ 85 — Crosby 10 km
Tel (44) 0151 - 924 6515, Fax (44) 0151 - 931 5364

Tree Tops Hotel, 11 rooms, D £ 90 — Formby 2 km
Tel (44) 01704 - 572 430, Fax (44) 01704 - 572 430

RESTAURANTS RESTAURANT
Ziba, Tel (44) 0151 - 708 8870 — Liverpool 18 km
Est, Est, Est, Tel (44) 01704 - 833 775 — Formby 2 km
Tree Tops Hotel, Tel (44) 01704 - 572 430 — Formby 2 km

FORMBY HALL

14	8	6

Very close to Birkdale, Hillside, Formby and Southport & Ainsdale, this recent country course is anything but a links. So players who don't like the sometimes lunar and often brutal type of landscape found on your typical links course will find a more "human" alternative waiting for them here. There are not too many trees for the moment but a lot have been planted, so the course gets better over the years. There are a whole lot of hazards but the only really surprising traps are the ditches that cross about a dozen fairways. On the flat side and exposed to the wind, Formby Hall seems to call for low shots, but your approach work to the well-defended greens will need some high iron shots as well. Fortunately, the greens are big enough for the balls that run rather than pitch. At all events the members seem to like it here, which augurs well for the future of this still young course.

Si près de Birkdale, Hillside, Formby ou Southport & Ainsdale, ce récent parcours en campagne n'a rien d'un links, mais certains joueurs n'aiment pas trop l'esthétique parfois lunaire, austère, ou même violente de ce type de parcours, ils trouveront ici une alternative plus "humaine." Les arbres n'y sont pas encore nombreux, mais beaucoup ont été plantés, et ce parcours évolue dans le bon sens avec les années. Les obstacles sont nombreux, mais les seuls vraiment surprenants sont les fossés traversant une douzaine de fairways. Assez plat, exposé au vent, Formby Hall semble appeler des balles basses, mais les coups vers les greens bien protégés obligent souvent à les leve., Il faut de toute façon savoir vite les arrêter. Heureusement, ces greens sont assez vastes. En tout cas, les membres semblent apprécier, ce qui rend optimiste quant à la progression de ce parcours encore bien jeune.

Formby Hall Golf Club — 1996

Southport Old Road
ENG - FORMBY, Lancs

Office	Secrétariat	(44) 01704 - 875 699
Pro shop	Pro-shop	(44) 01704 - 875 699
Fax	Fax	(44) 01704 - 832 134
Web	—	
Situation	Situation	21 km from Liverpool

12 km from Southport (pop. 90 959)

Annual closure	Fermeture annuelle	no
Weekly closure	Fermeture hebdomadaire	no

558

Fees main season Tarifs haute saison	Week days Semaine	We/Bank holidays We/Férié
		18 holes
Individual Individuel	£ 35	£ 40
Couple Couple	£ 70	£ 80
Caddy Caddy		on request
Electric Trolley Chariot électrique		no
Buggy Voiturette		£ 20 /18 holes
Clubs Clubs		no

Credit cards Cartes de crédit
VISA - Eurocard - MasterCard - DC - JCB - AMEX

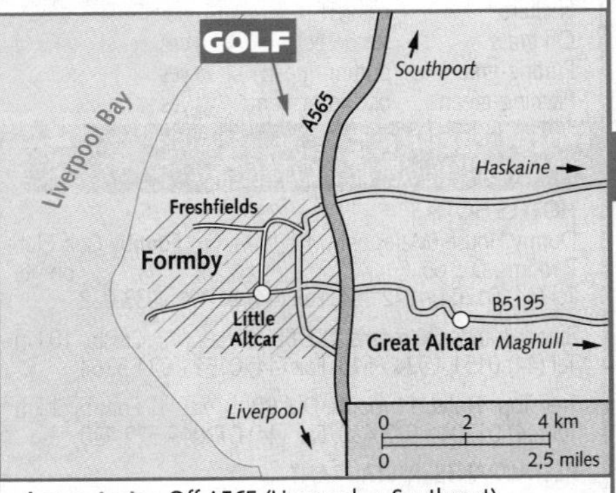

Access Accès : Off A565 (Liverpool → Southport) just beyond Formby turn-off, close to Coast Road traffic lights. Opposite RAF Station at Woodvale.
Map 5 on page 493 Carte 5 Page 493

Golf course — PARCOURS — 14/20

Site	Site	
Maintenance	Entretien	
Architect	Architecte	PGA Projects
Type	Type	parkland
Relief	Relief	
Water in play	Eau en jeu	
Exp. to wind	Exposé au vent	
Trees in play	Arbres en jeu	

Scorecard Carte de score	Chp. Chp.	Mens Mess.	Ladies Da.
Length Long.	6203	5791	5143
Par	72	72	72
Slope system	—	—	—

Advised golfing ability — 0 12 24 36
Niveau de jeu recommandé
Hcp required Handicap exigé — 28 Men, 36 Ladies

Club house & amenities — CLUB HOUSE ET ANNEXES — 8/10

Pro shop	Pro-shop	
Driving range	Practice	
Sheltered	couvert	24 mats
On grass	sur herbe	no
Putting-green	putting-green	yes
Pitching-green	pitching green	yes

Hotel facilities — ENVIRONNEMENT HOTELIER — 6/10

HOTELS HÔTELS

Tree Tops Hotel, 11 rooms, D £ 90 — Formby 5 km
Tel (44) 01704 - 572 430, Fax (44) 01704 - 572 430

Blundellsands, 30 rooms, D £ 85 — Crosby 10 km
Tel (44) 0151 - 924 6515, Fax (44) 0151 - 931 5364

Scarisbrick, 89 rooms, D £ 99 — Southport 15 km
Tel (44) 01704 - 543 000, Fax (44) 01704 - 533 335

RESTAURANTS RESTAURANT

Formby Hall Golf Club — Formby on site
Tel (44) 01704 - 872 164

Warehouse Brasserie — Southport 15 km
Tel (44) 01704 - 544 662

FRILFORD HEATH Red Course

14	7	7

Although the club has three 18-hole courses, the "Red Course" is still the one most people refer to. The first four holes, recent enough to adapt to an impressive number of tee-boxes and greens around the club-house, are a little out of keeping with the rest, especially the bunkering, but the course quickly slips back into the typical style of JH Taylor (albeit restyled by JH Turner). This is a frequently hilly layout and tough going for the physically... and technically unfit golfer. As not all the trouble in store is visible at first sight, the tee-shot here is more important than ever for your final score. Strangely enough for a course as British in style and atmosphere as this one, you are better off hitting high balls (sometimes a risky business when the wind swirls between the trees) either to carry some well-placed fairway bunkers or to hit the well-guarded greens. An often under-estimated course but a class layout in a complex where the number of courses provides peaceful golfing in a busy neighbourhood.

Ce club propose trois 18 trous dont le «Red Course» reste le parcours de référence. Certes, les quatre premiers trous ont été construits afin d'aménager une grande quantité de départs et de greens près du Club house, et détonnent un peu, notamment pour ce qui est du bunkering, mais on retrouve vite le style de JH Taylor, révisé par JH Turner. Le parcours est assez accidenté, difficile pour les joueurs peu entraînés, physiquement... et techniquement. Toutes les difficultés ne sont pas visibles au premier coup d'oeil, alors que la qualité des drives conditionne généralement la qualité du score. Assez curieusement pour un parcours aussi britannique d'ambiance et de style, il vaut mieux faire des trajectoires hautes (aléatoires quand le vent tourbillonne dans les arbres), soit pour porter la balle au dessus de quelques bunkers de fairway bien placés, soit pour rejoindre des greens bien défendus. Un parcours souvent sous-estimé, mais de bonne classe.

Frilford Heath Golf Club 1908
Frilford Heath
ENG - ABINGDON, Oxfordshire OX13 5NW

Office	Secrétariat	(44) 01865 - 390 864
Pro shop	Pro-shop	(44) 01865 - 390 887
Fax	Fax	(44) 01865 - 390 823
Web	www.frilfordheath.co.uk	
Situation	Situation	5 km from Abingdon

12 km from Oxford (pop. 110 103)

Annual closure	Fermeture annuelle	no
Weekly closure	Fermeture hebdomadaire	no

Fees main season Tarifs haute saison		Full day
	Week days Semaine	**We/Bank holidays** We/Férié
Individual Individuel	£ 50	£ 65
Couple Couple	£ 100	£ 130
Caddy	Caddy	on request
Electric Trolley	Chariot électrique	£ 5
Buggy	Voiturette	£ 18
Clubs	Clubs	£ 8.50

Credit cards Cartes de crédit
VISA - MasterCard - DC - AMEX
(Green fees & Pro shop only)

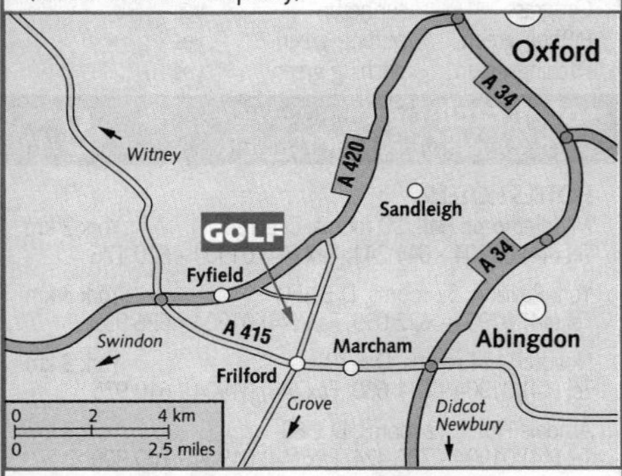

Access Accès : London, M40, A40 → Oxford, A4142 → Abingdon. A415 → Frilford, A338 on right hand side.
Map 7 on page 496 Carte 7 Page 496

Golf course PARCOURS 14/20

Site	Site	
Maintenance	Entretien	
Architect	Architecte	J.H. Taylor
Type	Type	Heathland
Relief	Relief	
Water in play	Eau en jeu	
Exp. to wind	Exposé au vent	
Trees in play	Arbres en jeu	

Scorecard Carte de score	**Chp.** Chp.	**Mens** Mess.	**Ladies** Da.
Length Long.	6159	5931	5234
Par	73	73	73
Slope system	—	—	—

Advised golfing ability Niveau de jeu recommandé: 0 12 24 36
Hcp required Handicap exigé: certificate

Club house & amenities CLUB HOUSE ET ANNEXES 7/10

Pro shop	Pro-shop	
Driving range	Practice	
Sheltered	couvert	practice area only
On grass	sur herbe	yes
Putting-green	putting-green	yes
Pitching-green	pitching green	yes

Hotel facilities ENVIRONNEMENT HOTELIER 7/10

HOTELS HÔTELS
Upper Riches, 31 rooms, D £ 180 — Abingdon 5 km
Tel (44) 0870 - 400 8101, Fax (44) 01235 - 555 182

Bath Place, 13 rooms, D 150 — Oxford 12 km
Tel (44) 01865 - 791 812, Fax (44) 01865 - 791 834

Old Parsonage, 30 rooms, D £ 200 — Oxford 12 km
Tel (44) 01865 - 310 210, Fax (44) 01865 - 311 262

Le Manoir aux Quat'Saisons — Great Milton (A329) 20 km
34 rooms, D £ 450
Tel (44) 01844 - 278 881, Fax (44) 01844 - 278 847

RESTAURANTS RESTAURANT
Gee's, Tel (44) 01865 - 53 540 — Oxford 12 km

FULFORD

17 | 7 | 8

Even before the excellence of the course, Fulford has always been famed for its standard of green-keeping, a reputation enhanced further by the staging here of the English Open and Benson & Hedges International tournaments. Sure, the very low scores carded by the pros have shown that the course might now be a little short for them, but they also holed any number of putts. The greens have always been fast and true, adding to the pleasure of playing here, and the course is definitely long enough for most of us. This is a driver course, not power-wise but in terms of accuracy off the tee, as approach shots must be played from the right spot (bunkers are often on one side of the green only) and will vary according to pin positions. A tactical, technical and fair course for all levels, Fulford has retained its dominant position in York, a superb city to visit with a pedestrians-only centre.

Avant même la qualité de son parcours, Fulford a toujours été renommé pour la qualité de son entretien en général. Et la venue de l'English Open comme celle du Benson & Hedges International ont ensuite accentué cette réputation. Certes, les scores très bas des professionnels ont montré que le parcours était maintenant un peu "court" pour eux, mais ils rentraient aussi beaucoup de putts... Les greens sont toujours rapides et fermes, ce qui n'ajoute qu'un peu plus de plaisir, et le parcours est bien assez "long" pour la majorité d'entre nous. C'est un parcours de driver, pas en termes de puissance, mais de précision, car il faut aborder les greens dans un bon angle (bunkers souvent d'un seul côté), et qui peut varier selon les placements de drapeaux. Tactique et technique, franc et pour tous niveaux, Fulford conserve sa situation dominante à York, qui reste une superbe ville à visiter, avec son centre ville piétonnier.

Fulford Golf Club — 1935

Hessington Lane
ENG - YORK, Yorkshire Y01 5DY

Office	Secrétariat	(44) 01904 - 413 579
Pro shop	Pro-shop	(44) 01904 - 412 882
Fax	Fax	(44) 01904 - 416 918
Web	www.fulfordgolfclub.co.uk	
Situation	Situation	York (pop. 98 745),3 km
Annual closure	Fermeture annuelle	no
Weekly closure	Fermeture hebdomadaire	no

Fees main season Tarifs haute saison	Week days Semaine	We/Bank holidays We/Férié
18 holes		
Individual Individuel	£ 37	*
Couple Couple	£ 74	*

Full weekday: £ 48 / * No visitors at week ends

Caddy	Caddy	no
Electric Trolley	Chariot électrique	£ 5 /18 holes
Buggy	Voiturette	£ 20 /18 holes
Clubs	Clubs	no

Credit cards Cartes de crédit
VISA - MasterCard (not for Green fees)

Access Accès : A19 → Fulford Village.
Heslington Lane on left. Follow signs for University.
Map 4 on page 491 Carte 4 Page 491

Golf course PARCOURS — 17/20

Site	Site	
Maintenance	Entretien	
Architect	Architecte	Charles MacKenzie
Type	Type	parkland
Relief	Relief	
Water in play	Eau en jeu	
Exp. to wind	Exposé au vent	
Trees in play	Arbres en jeu	

Scorecard Carte de score	Chp. Chp.	Mens Mess.	Ladies Da.
Length Long.	6100	5698	4875
Par	72	72	74
Slope system	—	—	—

Advised golfing ability / Niveau de jeu recommandé: 0 12 24 36
Hcp required / Handicap exigé: 28 Men, 36 Ladies

Club house & amenities CLUB HOUSE ET ANNEXES — 7/10

Pro shop	Pro-shop	
Driving range	Practice	
Sheltered	couvert	practice area
On grass	sur herbe	yes
Putting-green	putting-green	yes
Pitching-green	pitching green	yes

Hotel facilities ENVIRONNEMENT HOTELIER — 8/10

HOTELS HÔTELS
Middlethorpe Hall, 30 rooms, D £ 180 — York 2 km
Tel (44) 01904 - 641 241, Fax (44) 01904 - 620 176

York Pavilion, 57 rooms, D £ 150 — York 3 km
Tel (44) 01904 - 622 099, Fax (44) 01904 - 626 939

Novotel, 124 rooms, D £ 79 — York 3 km
Tel (44) 01904 - 611 660, Fax (44) 01904 - 610 925

Arndale Hotel, 12 rooms, D £ 80 — York 3 km
Tel (44) 01904 - 702 424, Fax (44) 01904 - 709 800

RESTAURANTS RESTAURANT
Melton's, Tel (44) 01904 - 634 341 — York 3 km
19 Grape Lane, Tel (44) 01904 - 636 366 — York 3 km

GAINSBOROUGH-KARSTEN LAKES 14 | 8 | 6

This club was purchased in 1985 by Ping, who run a golf equipment factory nearby, so don't be surprised by the manufacturer's dominant presence, particularly in the Pro Shop. The original course, played at a time when the club was called Thonock, has been restyled by Brian Waites and goes very well with this one, a more ambitious affair with a lot of water in play and few trees as yet. A lot have been planted, though, so visually the course gets better. For the moment, the contours of the land and the bunkers do not always give you a clear idea of what you have to do. From the back tees this is a tough proposition which is probably too hard to handle for many average golfers. Further forward, the course is a fair and much more accessible test. A very serious course in a comparatively deserted region golf-wise with an impressive clubhouse (there is an excellent coffee-house for snacks).

Ce club a été acheté en 1985 par Ping, dont l'usine de matériel de golf est située à Gainsborough, on ne sera pas étonné de sentir cette présence, en particulier au Pro-shop ! Le parcours de l'époque où le club s'appelait Thonock avait été remodelé par Brian Waites et complète bien celui-ci, plus ambitieux, avec beaucoup d'eau en jeu, peu d'arbres encore mais les plantations commencent à le faire visuellement évoluer. Pour l'instant, les mouvements de terrain et les bunkers ne précisent pas toujours parfaitement ce qu'il faut faire, le "yardage book" (carnet de parcours) sera utile. Des départs arrière, c'est un solide parcours où beaucoup souffriront, mais les départs avancés proposent un test très franc et accessible à beaucoup. Une réalisation très sérieuse dans une région un peu déserte, avec un Clubhouse impressionnant (excellent Coffee shop pour une petite faim).

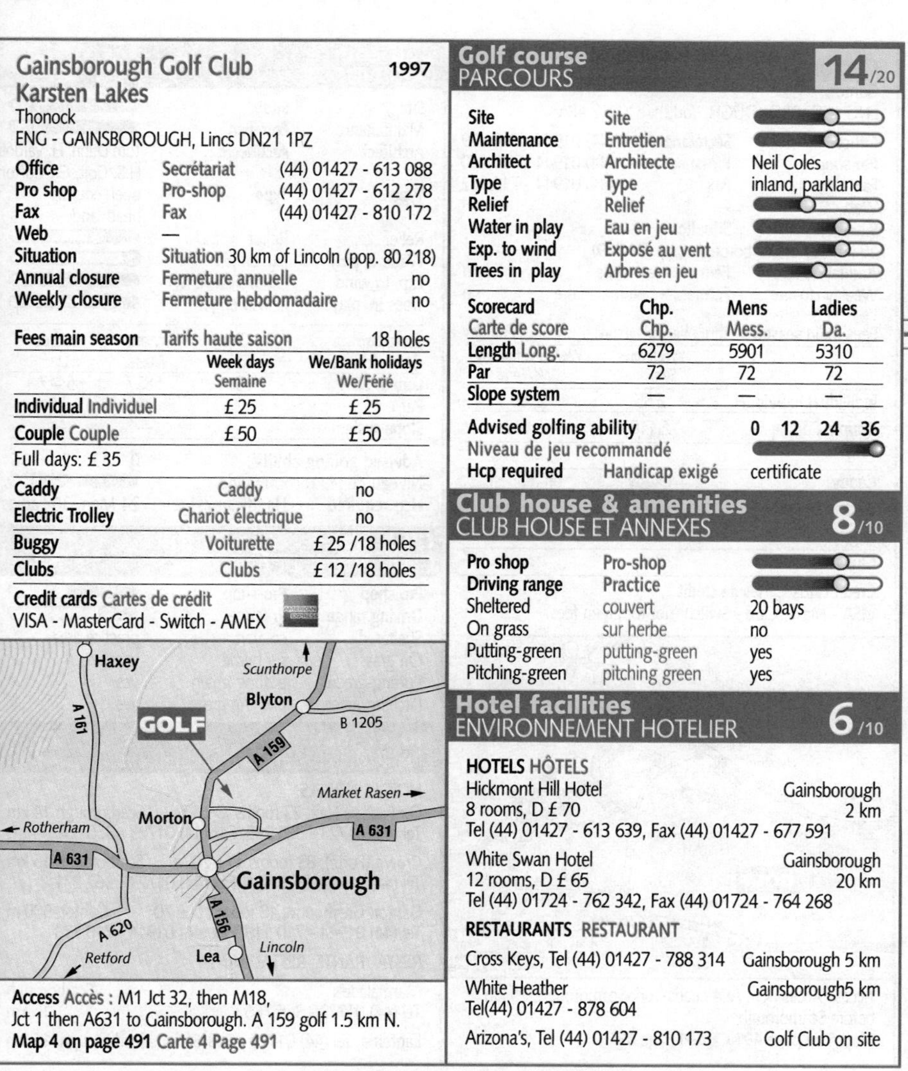

Gainsborough Golf Club Karsten Lakes — 1997

Thonock
ENG - GAINSBOROUGH, Lincs DN21 1PZ

Office	Secrétariat	(44) 01427 - 613 088
Pro shop	Pro-shop	(44) 01427 - 612 278
Fax	Fax	(44) 01427 - 810 172
Web	—	
Situation	Situation 30 km of Lincoln (pop. 80 218)	
Annual closure	Fermeture annuelle	no
Weekly closure	Fermeture hebdomadaire	no

Fees main season / Tarifs haute saison — 18 holes	Week days / Semaine	We/Bank holidays / We/Férié
Individual Individuel	£ 25	£ 25
Couple Couple	£ 50	£ 50

Full days: £ 35

Caddy	Caddy	no
Electric Trolley	Chariot électrique	no
Buggy	Voiturette	£ 25 /18 holes
Clubs	Clubs	£ 12 /18 holes

Credit cards Cartes de crédit
VISA - MasterCard - Switch - AMEX

Access Accès : M1 Jct 32, then M18, Jct 1 then A631 to Gainsborough. A 159 golf 1.5 km N.
Map 4 on page 491 Carte 4 Page 491

Golf course PARCOURS — 14/20

Site	Site	
Maintenance	Entretien	
Architect	Architecte	Neil Coles
Type	Type	inland, parkland
Relief	Relief	
Water in play	Eau en jeu	
Exp. to wind	Exposé au vent	
Trees in play	Arbres en jeu	

Scorecard / Carte de score	Chp. / Chp.	Mens / Mess.	Ladies / Da.
Length Long.	6279	5901	5310
Par	72	72	72
Slope system	—	—	—

Advised golfing ability / Niveau de jeu recommandé: 0 12 24 36
Hcp required / Handicap exigé: certificate

Club house & amenities CLUB HOUSE ET ANNEXES — 8/10

Pro shop	Pro-shop	
Driving range	Practice	
Sheltered	couvert	20 bays
On grass	sur herbe	no
Putting-green	putting-green	yes
Pitching-green	pitching green	yes

Hotel facilities ENVIRONNEMENT HOTELIER — 6/10

HOTELS HÔTELS

Hickmont Hill Hotel — Gainsborough 2 km
8 rooms, D £ 70
Tel (44) 01427 - 613 639, Fax (44) 01427 - 677 591

White Swan Hotel — Gainsborough 20 km
12 rooms, D £ 65
Tel (44) 01724 - 762 342, Fax (44) 01724 - 764 268

RESTAURANTS RESTAURANT

Cross Keys, Tel (44) 01427 - 788 314 — Gainsborough 5 km

White Heather — Gainsborough5 km
Tel(44) 01427 - 878 604

Arizona's, Tel (44) 01427 - 810 173 — Golf Club on site

GANTON

19 | 8 | 5

This is one of the very few inland courses to find favour with links enthusiasts. The sea must have stretched this far in times gone by because you can still find sea-shells in the sand and the soil is of the kind found on every links course. Located between the resort of Scarborough and the superb city of York (a former Viking stronghold), this is a sheer masterpiece of a course where Dunn, Vardon, Harry Colt and C.K. Cotton all had a hand in its design. The links style is all the more obvious in that trees come into play only on a very few holes. Elsewhere, the fairways are bordered by bushes, tall grass and rough, while deep hungry bunkers snap up anything within reach. But all the hazards are there to be seen and the course is not responsible for your shortcomings (or is it?). The slick greens are well-protected but leave the way open for bump 'n roll shots. As we were saying, all that is missing is the sea.

C'est l'un des seuls "inland" à trouver grâce auprès des amoureux des links. Le terrain y est favorable, car la mer devait autrefois venir ici : on a retrouvé des coquillages dans le sable et le sol est celui des links. Entre la station balnéaire de Scarborough et la ville superbe d'York (ancienne place forte viking), il y a ce chef d'oeuvre absolu où Tom Dunn, Harry Vardon, Harry Colt et C.K. Cotton ont apporté successivement leur contribution. Le style de links est d'autant plus flagrant que les arbres ne sont en jeu que sur quelques trous. Ailleurs, les buissons, les hautes herbes du rough délimitent les fairways, de profonds bunkers pleins d'appétit attrapent tout ce qui passe à portée. Mais tous les obstacles sont bien en vue, et le parcours ne peut être considéré comme responsable de vos fautes. Les greens subtils et bien défendus laissent néanmoins la porte ouverte aux approches roulées. Il ne manque que la mer, on vous le disait, mais elle n'est pas loin.

Ganton Golf Club — 1891

Ganton
ENG - SCARBOROUGH, Yorkshire YO12 4PA

Office	Secrétariat	(44) 01944 - 710 329
Pro shop	Pro-shop	(44) 01944 - 710 260
Fax	Fax	(44) 01944 - 710 922
Web	—	
Situation	Situation	

15 km SW of Scarborough (pop. 38 809)

Annual closure	Fermeture annuelle	no
Weekly closure	Fermeture hebdomadaire	no

Fees main season Tarifs haute saison	Week days Semaine	We/Bank holidays We/Férié
	Full day	
Individual Individuel	£ 55	£ 65
Couple Couple	£ 110	£ 130

Caddy	Caddy	on request
Electric Trolley	Chariot électrique	£ 5 /18 holes
Buggy	Voiturette	no
Clubs	Clubs	no

Credit cards Cartes de crédit
VISA - MasterCard - Switch (not for green fees)

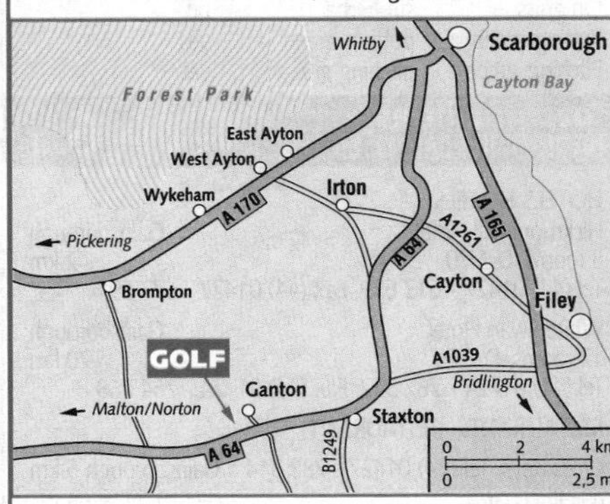

Access Accès : On A64 Leeds-York-Scarborough, 15 km before Scarborough
Map 4 on page 491 Carte 4 Page 491

Golf course — PARCOURS — 19/20

Site	Site	
Maintenance	Entretien	
Architect	Architecte	Tom Dunn, H. Vardon H.S. Colt, CK Cotton
Type	Type	open country, heathland
Relief	Relief	
Water in play	Eau en jeu	
Exp. to wind	Exposé au vent	
Trees in play	Arbres en jeu	

Scorecard Carte de score	Chp. Chp.	Mens Mess.	Ladies Da.
Length Long.	6061	5827	5447
Par	73	73	75
Slope system	—	—	—

Advised golfing ability 0 12 24 36
Niveau de jeu recommandé
Hcp required Handicap exigé 24 Men, 36 Ladies

Club house & amenities — CLUB HOUSE ET ANNEXES — 8/10

Pro shop	Pro-shop	
Driving range	Practice	
Sheltered	couvert	practice area
On grass	sur herbe	yes
Putting-green	putting-green	yes
Pitching-green	pitching green	yes

Hotel facilities — ENVIRONNEMENT HOTELIER — 5/10

HOTELS HÔTELS

Ox Pasture Hall, 23 rooms, D £ 75 — Scarborough 14 km
Tel (44) 01723 - 365 295, Fax (44) 01723 - 355 156

Crown (Forte), 83 rooms, D £ 70 — Scarborough 15 km
Tel (44) 01723 - 373 491, Fax (44) 01723 - 362 271

Ganton Greyhound, 18 rooms, D £ 70 — Ganton 500 m
Tel (44) 01944 - 710 116, Fax (44) 01944 - 710 738

RESTAURANTS RESTAURANT

Marmalade's — Scarborough 15 km
Tel (44) 01723 - 365 766

Lanterna, Tel (44) 01723 - 363 616 — Scarborough, 15 km

GOG MAGOG Old Course

15 | 7 | 8

The landscape in this part of the country is generally so flat that it could hardly have inspired early course designers who probably had little more than ploughs and wheelbarrows to move earth. If you don't play much golf here, you will enjoy visiting Cambridge, Ely, Bury St. Edmonds or the Fens with their windmills. Gog Magog, though, is the exception to the rule and is laid out over some small hills which are easy to walk. The club has a long tradition of hospitality (but is closed to green-feers on weekends) and also a second course, Wandlesbury, which has everything perhaps except the charm of this Old Course. There are not too many trees but they are sometimes placed to block your second shot if the drive is not perfect. A fair and shortish course which rewards good shots, Gog Magog is pleasant to play with friends or with the family, whatever their level.

Le paysage de cette région est en général d'une platitude qui ne pouvait guère inspirer les architectes de golf des origines, qui ne disposaient guère que de charrues et de brouettes pour modeler le terrain. Faute de beaucoup jouer, la visite de Cambridge, d'Ely, de Bury St Edmunds ou les marais des Fens avec leurs moulins à vent sont déjà un dépaysement. Gog Magog est l'exception à la règle, et a trouvé place sur de petites collines assez aimables pour les jambes. Ce club a la longue tradition d'accueil (mais fermé aux visiteurs en week-end) offre un second parcours, Wandlesbury, mais le Old Course garde tout son charme. Les arbres n'y sont pas trop nombreux, mais parfois placés pour bloquer les seconds coups si les drives n'ont pas été parfaits. Honnête, récompensant les bons coups de golf, pas très long, c'est un parcours agréable pour jouer en famille ou avec des amis, quel que soit leur niveau.

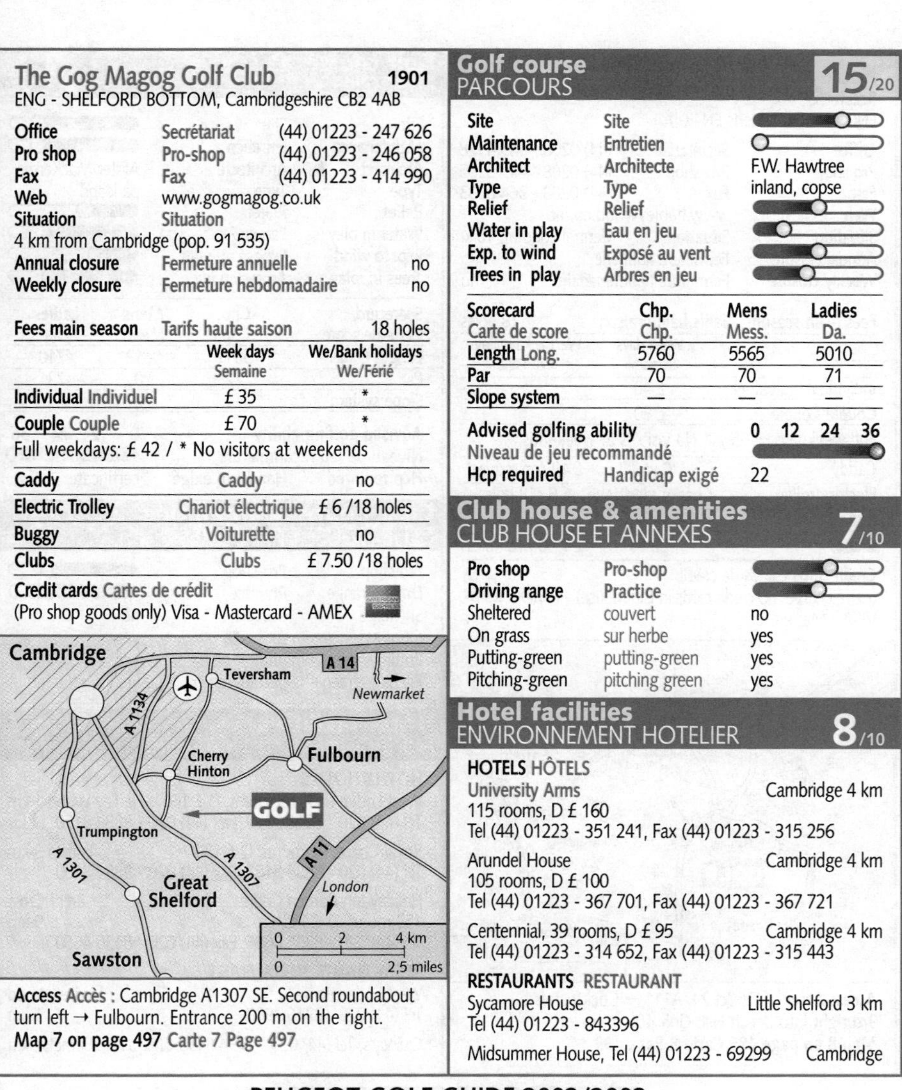

The Gog Magog Golf Club **1901**
ENG - SHELFORD BOTTOM, Cambridgeshire CB2 4AB

Office	Secrétariat	(44) 01223 - 247 626
Pro shop	Pro-shop	(44) 01223 - 246 058
Fax	Fax	(44) 01223 - 414 990
Web	www.gogmagog.co.uk	
Situation	Situation	

4 km from Cambridge (pop. 91 535)

Annual closure	Fermeture annuelle	no
Weekly closure	Fermeture hebdomadaire	no

Fees main season Tarifs haute saison	18 holes	
	Week days Semaine	**We/Bank holidays** We/Férié
Individual Individuel	£ 35	*
Couple Couple	£ 70	*

Full weekdays: £ 42 / * No visitors at weekends

Caddy	Caddy	no
Electric Trolley	Chariot électrique	£ 6 /18 holes
Buggy	Voiturette	no
Clubs	Clubs	£ 7.50 /18 holes

Credit cards Cartes de crédit
(Pro shop goods only) Visa - Mastercard - AMEX

Access Accès : Cambridge A1307 SE. Second roundabout turn left → Fulbourn. Entrance 200 m on the right.
Map 7 on page 497 Carte 7 Page 497

Golf course PARCOURS 15/20

Site	Site	
Maintenance	Entretien	
Architect	Architecte	F.W. Hawtree
Type	Type	inland, copse
Relief	Relief	
Water in play	Eau en jeu	
Exp. to wind	Exposé au vent	
Trees in play	Arbres en jeu	

Scorecard Carte de score	**Chp.** Chp.	**Mens** Mess.	**Ladies** Da.
Length Long.	5760	5565	5010
Par	70	70	71
Slope system	—	—	—

Advised golfing ability Niveau de jeu recommandé 0 12 24 36
Hcp required Handicap exigé 22

Club house & amenities CLUB HOUSE ET ANNEXES 7/10

Pro shop	Pro-shop	
Driving range	Practice	
Sheltered	couvert	no
On grass	sur herbe	yes
Putting-green	putting-green	yes
Pitching-green	pitching green	yes

Hotel facilities ENVIRONNEMENT HOTELIER 8/10

HOTELS HÔTELS
University Arms — Cambridge 4 km
115 rooms, D £ 160
Tel (44) 01223 - 351 241, Fax (44) 01223 - 315 256

Arundel House — Cambridge 4 km
105 rooms, D £ 100
Tel (44) 01223 - 367 701, Fax (44) 01223 - 367 721

Centennial, 39 rooms, D £ 95 — Cambridge 4 km
Tel (44) 01223 - 314 652, Fax (44) 01223 - 315 443

RESTAURANTS RESTAURANT
Sycamore House — Little Shelford 3 km
Tel (44) 01223 - 843396

Midsummer House, Tel (44) 01223 - 69299 — Cambridge

HADLEY WOOD

16 | 7 | 7

Whichever direction you're travelling, London just seems never-ending. The strangest thing is that you start finding golf courses where you would never expect them and, what's more, in calm secluded spots. Less than a mile from Cockfosters tube station, Hadley Wood is one such course, where a very smart clubhouse is surrounded by flowers and bushes whose colours contrast sharply with the grey (or blue) skies. The same elegance and eye for detail are found in what is a very distinguished layout by Alister Mackenzie, landscaped like a garden and whose bunkers, streams and lakes look like items of decoration straight out of a magazine. But deceptive as ever, even the sweetest looking courses can prove deadly and easily end any hope of a good score.

Que l'on aille dans n'importe quelle direction, Londres semble ne jamais finir. Le plus étrange est de parvenir à trouver beaucoup de golfs là où on ne penserait pas en chercher, et à les trouver dans des endroits calmes. Hadley Wood fait partie de ces sites privilégiés, à moins d'un mile du métro Cockfosters. Autour du très beau Clubhouse, fleurs et arbustes témoignent une fois de plus d'un amour des végétaux coloriés qui tranchent avec le ciel gris (et d'ailleurs parfois bleu !). On retrouve cette élégance, ce souci du détail dans le tracé très distingué d'Alister Mackenzie, paysagé comme un jardin, où les bunkers, les petits cours d'eau et les lacs paraissent des éléments d'un décor pour magazine. Mais il faut se méfier des apparences, les dessins les plus évidents peuvent être meurtriers, du moins si l'on tente de faire un bon score.

Hadley Wood Golf Club — 1922

Beech Hill
ENG - BARNET, Herts EN4 0JJ

Office	Secrétariat	(44) 0208 - 449 4328
Pro shop	Pro-shop	(44) 0208 - 449 3285
Fax	Fax	(44) 0208 - 364 8633
Web	www.hadleywood.co.uk	
Situation	Situation	Central London, 16 km
Annual closure	Fermeture annuelle	no
Weekly closure	Fermeture hebdomadaire	no

Fees main season Tarifs haute saison		18 holes
	Week days Semaine	**We/Bank holidays** We/Férié
Individual Individuel	£ 40	*
Couple Couple	£ 80	*

Full weekdays: £ 55 / * No visitors at weekends

Caddy	Caddy	£ 40 /on request
Electric Trolley	Chariot électrique	£ 6 /18 holes
Buggy	Voiturette	no
Clubs	Clubs	£ 7.50 /18 holes

Credit cards Cartes de crédit
(extra charge, no credit cards in Clubhouse) - AMEX
VISA - MasterCard

Access Accès : M25 Jct 24. A111 → Cockfosters.
3rd right into Beech Hill. Golf 400 m on left.
Map 8 on page 499 Carte 8 Page 499

Golf course — PARCOURS — 16/20

Site	Site	
Maintenance	Entretien	
Architect	Architecte	Alister MacKenzie
Type	Type	parkland
Relief	Relief	
Water in play	Eau en jeu	
Exp. to wind	Exposé au vent	
Trees in play	Arbres en jeu	

Scorecard Carte de score	**Chp.** Chp.	**Mens** Mess.	**Ladies** Da.
Length Long.	5811	5612	4710
Par	72	70	73
Slope system	—	—	—

Advised golfing ability Niveau de jeu recommandé — 0 12 24 36
Hcp required Handicap exigé — certificate

Club house & amenities — CLUB HOUSE ET ANNEXES — 7/10

Pro shop	Pro-shop	
Driving range	Practice	
Sheltered	couvert	no
On grass	sur herbe	yes
Putting-green	putting-green	yes
Pitching-green	pitching green	yes

Hotel facilities — ENVIRONNEMENT HOTELIER — 7/10

HOTELS HÔTELS

West Lodge Park, 55 rooms, D £ 160 — Hadley Wood 1 km
Tel (44) 020 - 8216 3900, Fax (44) 020 - 8884 8150

Royal Chace, 92 rooms, D £ 130 — Enfield 3 km
Tel (44) 020 - 8884 8181, Fax (44) 020 - 8884 8150

Holiday Inn Garden Court — Brent Cross 9 km
153 rooms, D £ 145
Tel (44) 020 - 8201 8686, Fax (44) 020 - 8455 4660

RESTAURANTS RESTAURANT

West Lodge Park — Hadley Wood 1 km
Tel (44) 020 - 8216 3900

Quincy's, Tel (44) 020 - 7794 8499 Child's Hill (Barnet) 7 km

HALLAMSHIRE

15 | 6 | 8

As this is probably not the most popular part of Yorkshire with tourists, the courses around Sheffield are played mostly by two types of golfer: the locals and large numbers of travelling businessmen. They will definitely enjoy playing at Hallamshire, which would certainly be better known if located in a more fashionable golfing county like Surrey, for example. This is a course of moorland and woods over rolling but easily walkable terrain, where, surprise, surprise, there is no water. The tall rough is out of play (or should be) and the turf lush and springy, so unless you are here in the middle of a drought you won't have to contend with bad kicks. There are a few blind holes here and there, but if you play with a local golfer from the club, he will guide you around and help you avoid any unpleasant surprises. Hallamshire is a well-balanced course where playing to your handicap is never a foregone conclusion, perhaps owing to a tendency to under-estimate the hazards and ignore the dangers behind a friendly exterior. A very respectable course.

Ce n'est certes pas la partie la plus touristique du Yorkshire, et les parcours aux alentours de Sheffield, mis à part les joueurs locaux, sont surtout fréquentés par les "businessmen" en déplacement. Ils apprécieront Hallamshire, dont la notoriété aurait été plus grande s'il avait par exemple été situé dans le Surrey. Parcours de landes et de bois, dans un paysage animé mais facile à parcourir à pied, il est dénué d'obstacles d'eau, ce qui est rare de nos jours. Le haut rough n'est pas en jeu, le gazon bien souple, les surprises au rebond ne sont à craindre que par sécheresse. On trouve çà et là quelques coups aveugles, mais avec un bon "pilote" habitué du club, pas de mauvaises surprises non plus. Pourtant, il n'est pas si facile de jouer ici son handicap, peut être parce que l'on a tendance à en sous-estimer les difficultés, à ne pas sentir les dents derrière une amabilité de façade. Bien équilibré, c'est un parcours fort respectable.

Hallamshire Golf Club — 1897

The Club House
ENG - SANDYGATE, SHEFFIELD, S. Yorks. S10 44A

Office	Secrétariat	(44) 01142 - 302 153
Pro shop	Pro-shop	(44) 01142 - 305 222
Fax	Fax	(44) 01142 - 305 656
Web	—	
Situation	Situation	

3 km W of Sheffield (pop. 501 202)

Annual closure	Fermeture annuelle	no
Weekly closure	Fermeture hebdomadaire	no

Fees main season Tarifs haute saison	18 holes	
	Week days / Semaine	We/Bank holidays / We/Férié
Individual Individuel	£ 39	£ 43
Couple Couple	£ 78	£ 86
Caddy	Caddy	yes
Electric Trolley	Chariot électrique	no
Buggy	Voiturette	no
Clubs	Clubs	no

Credit cards Cartes de crédit
VISA - MasterCard - Switch (not for green fees)

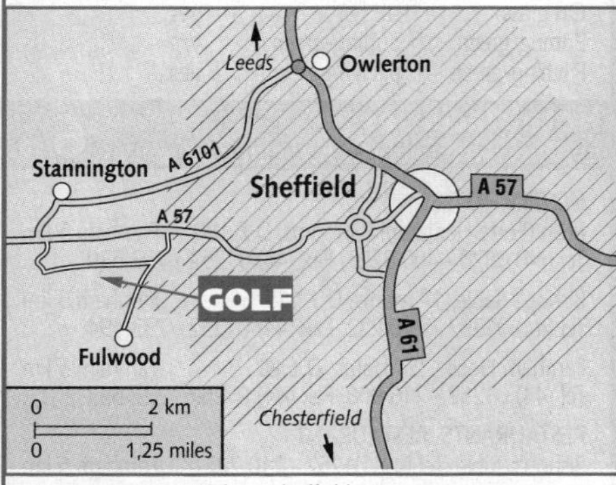

Access Accès : A57 from Sheffield city centre, left fork at Crosspool (pub), 1.5 km to the golf.
Map 4 on page 490 Carte 4 Page 490

Golf course — PARCOURS — 15/20

Site	Site	
Maintenance	Entretien	
Architect	Architecte	Unknown
Type	Type	parkland, hilly
Relief	Relief	
Water in play	Eau en jeu	
Exp. to wind	Exposé au vent	
Trees in play	Arbres en jeu	

Scorecard / Carte de score	Chp. / Chp.	Mens / Mess.	Ladies / Da.
Length Long.	5724	5292	5104
Par	71	71	74
Slope system	—	—	—

Advised golfing ability 0 12 24 36
Niveau de jeu recommandé
Hcp required Handicap exigé — certificate

Club house & amenities — CLUB HOUSE ET ANNEXES — 6/10

Pro shop	Pro-shop	
Driving range	Practice	
Sheltered	couvert	no
On grass	sur herbe	yes
Putting-green	putting-green	yes
Pitching-green	pitching green	yes

Hotel facilities — ENVIRONNEMENT HOTELIER — 8/10

HOTELS HÔTELS
Beauchief Hotel, 50 rooms, D £ 95 — Sheffield 4 km
Tel (44) 0114 - 262 0500, Fax (44) 0114 - 235 0197

Sheffield Moat House, 95 rooms, D £ 120 — Sheffield 8 km
Tel (44) 0114 - 282 9988, Fax (44) 0114 - 237 8140

Swallow Marriott, 116 rooms, D £ 150 — Sheffield 4 km
Tel (44) 0114 - 258 3811, Fax (44) 0114 - 250 0138

RESTAURANTS RESTAURANT
Smith's of Sheffield — Sheffield 4 km
Tel (44) 0114 - 266 6096

Rafters, Tel (44) 0114 - 230 4819 — Sheffield 4 km

Old Vicarage, Tel (44) 0114 - 247 5814 — Ridgeway 13 km

HANKLEY COMMON

16 | 6 | 6

First of all a word of praise for the slick, very fast greens and the flawless green-keeping. Might this be a tribute to Bobby Locke, one of the greatest putters of all time who for years lived right beside this course? Hankley Common used to be very dry in Summer but now has automatic sprinklers which tend to lengthen the course and stress the need for long-hitting. Keep it straight, too, because the fairway bunkers snap up anything remotely off-line, and even if you miss the sand, there's enough heather to keep you busy for longer than you would like, finding ways of getting your ball back into play. The felling of a number of trees has exposed the course to the wind and sometimes gives a part of the course an unexpected links character, with all the technical challenge that that entails. A final word for the beautiful finishing holes, especially the 18th, where our advice is always to take one club more than you think you need to hit the green.

D'abord un mot pour les greens subtils, très rapides et d'un entretien irréprochable, comme en hommage à l'un des meilleurs putters de tous les temps, Bobby Locke, qui habita longtemps à côté d'ici. Longtemps très sec en été, ce parcours bénéficie maintenant de l'arrosage automatique, qui l'a en quelque sorte "allongé," renforçant la nécessité d'être long, et droit car les nombreux bunkers de fairway accueillent avec gourmandise les balles incertaines. Et quand on réussit à les passer, la bruyère est volontaire pour les retenir un certain temps. L'abattage de nombreux arbres a exposé davantage les joueurs au vent, ce qui donne parfois un caractère de links inattendu à certains trous, avec l'exigence technique que cela représente. A signaler enfin, la beauté du final, en particulier du 18ème trou : prenez toujours un club de plus pour jouer le green, vous ne le regretterez pas..

Hankley Common Golf Club — 1895

Tilford Road, Tilford
ENG - FARNHAM, Surrey GU10 2DD

Office	Secrétariat	(44) 01252 - 792 493
Pro shop	Pro-shop	(44) 01252 - 793 761
Fax	Fax	(44) 01252 - 792 493
Web	—	
Situation	Situation	

6 km from Farnham (pop. 30 430)

Annual closure	Fermeture annuelle	no
Weekly closure	Fermeture hebdomadaire	no

Fees main season Tarifs haute saison		18 holes
	Week days Semaine	**We/Bank holidays** We/Férié
Individual Individuel	£ 50	£ 65 *
Couple Couple	£ 100	£ 130 *

Full weekdays: £ 65 / * For 18 holes (ask before)

Caddy	Caddy	no
Electric Trolley	Chariot électrique	no
Buggy	Voiturette	no
Clubs	Clubs	no
Credit cards	Cartes de crédit	no

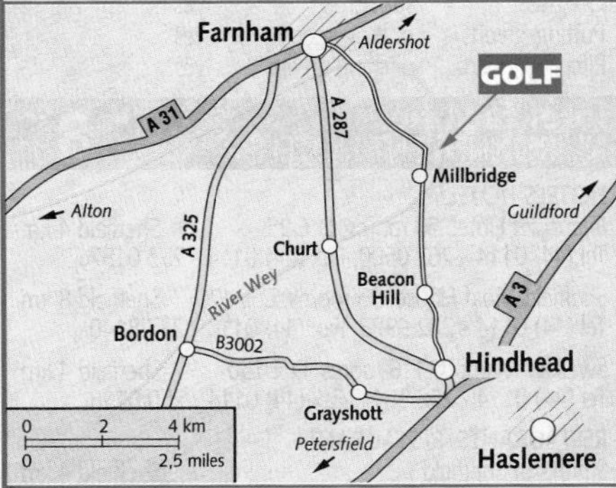

Access Accès : A3 (→ Portsmouth). After Devils Punch Bowl, turn right onto Tilford Road.
Golf Club is approx; 6 km (4 m) on the right.
Map 7 on page 496 Carte 7 Page 496

Golf course PARCOURS — 16/20

Site	Site	
Maintenance	Entretien	
Architect	Architecte	Charles Lawrie
Type	Type	inland, heathland
Relief	Relief	
Water in play	Eau en jeu	
Exp. to wind	Exposé au vent	
Trees in play	Arbres en jeu	

Scorecard Carte de score	**Chp.** Chp.	**Mens** Mess.	**Ladies** Da.
Length Long.	5795	5503	5002
Par	71	71	72
Slope system	—	—	—

Advised golfing ability Niveau de jeu recommandé — 0 12 24 36
Hcp required Handicap exigé — certificate

Club house & amenities CLUB HOUSE ET ANNEXES — 6/10

Pro shop	Pro-shop	
Driving range	Practice	
Sheltered	couvert	no
On grass	sur herbe	yes
Putting-green	putting-green	yes
Pitching-green	pitching green	yes

Hotel facilities ENVIRONNEMENT HOTELIER — 6/10

HOTELS HÔTELS

Bush (Forte Heritage), 83 rooms, D £ 180 — Farnham 5 km
Tel (44) 0870 - 400 8225, Fax (44) 01252 - 733 530

Bishop's Table, 17 rooms, D £ 115 — Farnham 5 km
Tel (44) 01252 - 710 222, Fax (44) 01252 - 733 494

Farnham House, 25 rooms, D £ 80 — Farnham 5 km
Tel (44) 01252 - 716 908, Fax (44) 01252 - 722 583

RESTAURANTS RESTAURANT

Bishop's Table, Tel (44) 01252 - 710 222 — Farnham 5 km

Auberge de France, — Haslemere 10 km
Tel (44) 01428 - 651 251

Banaras (Indian), Tel (44) 01252 - 734 081 — Farnham 5 km

HARROGATE

15 | 7 | 7

This course is close to Knaresborough, one of the oldest towns in the country. The superb surroundings in this region are further enhanced by the spa city of Harrogate, the Yorkshire Dales and the ruins of Fountains Abbey with its gardens and... fountains. There are several superb courses around here, and this is one of them. With neighbouring Pannal, Harrogate is one of Sandy Herd's best layouts on woody terrain (the trees are never too thick) which is hilly enough to conceal one or two difficulties. In other words, strategy is never simple the first time out and errors of positioning or direction can easily require the use of every club you have available. Although not a terribly spectacular course, it is an excellent examination of talent and technique that connoisseurs of the game will appreciate on its merits.

Le présent parcours est tout proche de Knaresborough, une des plus anciennes villes du pays. La ville d'eau d'Harrogate, le Parc National des Yorkshire Dales, ou encore les ruines de l'Abbaye, les temples à l'antique et les jeux d'eau des jardins de Fountains Abbey ajoutent encore à l'agrément de l'environnement superbe de cette région. Elle est pourvue de plusieurs parcours de qualité et celui-ci ne détonne pas auprès d'eux. Avec son voisin Pannal, c'est un des meilleurs tracés de Sandy Herd. Le terrain est boisé mais sans devoir inquiéter les claustrophobes, assez accidenté, ce qui dissimule quelques difficultés. La stratégie n'est alors pas évidente à la première visite, et les erreurs de placement ou de direction peuvent obliger à sortir tous les coups de son sac. Sans être un parcours très spectaculaire, c'est en fait un excellent examen du talent et de la technique, que les bons connaisseurs apprécieront à sa juste valeur.

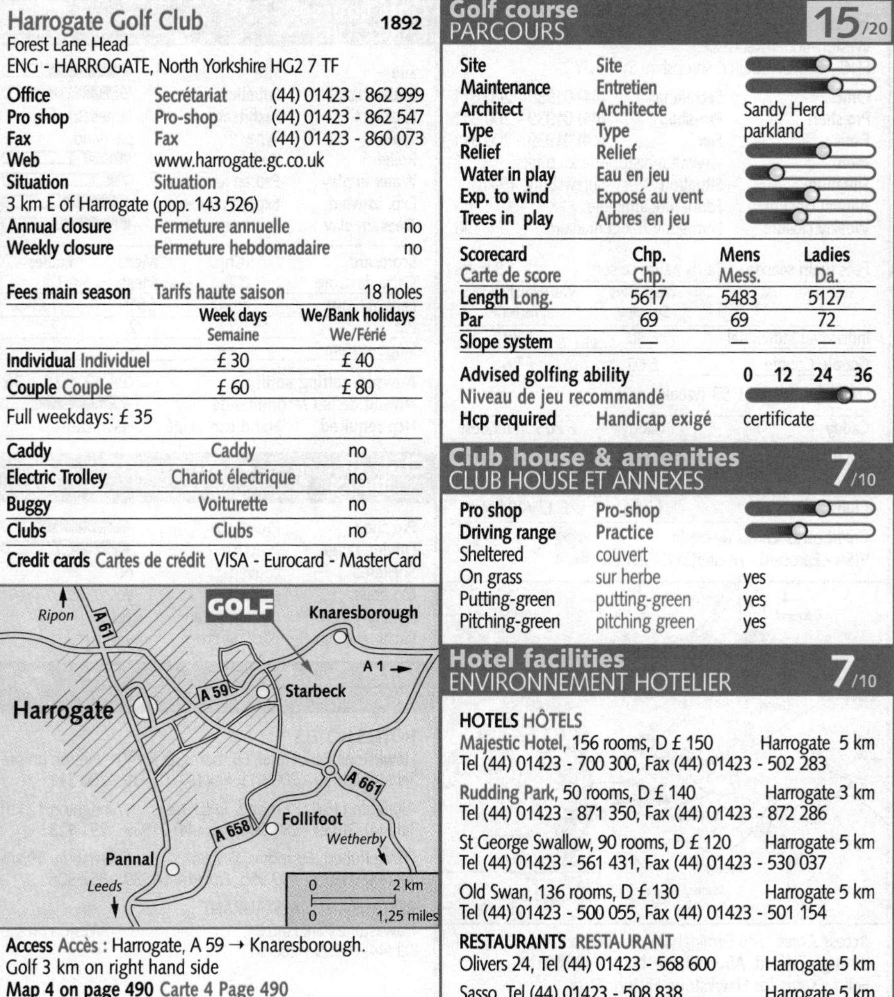

Harrogate Golf Club **1892**
Forest Lane Head
ENG - HARROGATE, North Yorkshire HG2 7 TF

Office	Secrétariat	(44) 01423 - 862 999
Pro shop	Pro-shop	(44) 01423 - 862 547
Fax	Fax	(44) 01423 - 860 073
Web	www.harrogate.gc.co.uk	
Situation	Situation	
3 km E of Harrogate (pop. 143 526)		
Annual closure	Fermeture annuelle	no
Weekly closure	Fermeture hebdomadaire	no

Fees main season Tarifs haute saison		18 holes
	Week days Semaine	**We/Bank holidays** We/Férié
Individual Individuel	£ 30	£ 40
Couple Couple	£ 60	£ 80
Full weekdays: £ 35		

Caddy	Caddy	no
Electric Trolley	Chariot électrique	no
Buggy	Voiturette	no
Clubs	Clubs	no

Credit cards Cartes de crédit VISA - Eurocard - MasterCard

Access Accès : Harrogate, A 59 → Knaresborough.
Golf 3 km on right hand side
Map 4 on page 490 Carte 4 Page 490

Golf course PARCOURS **15**/20

Site	Site	
Maintenance	Entretien	
Architect	Architecte	Sandy Herd
Type	Type	parkland
Relief	Relief	
Water in play	Eau en jeu	
Exp. to wind	Exposé au vent	
Trees in play	Arbres en jeu	

Scorecard Carte de score	**Chp.** Chp.	**Mens** Mess.	**Ladies** Da.
Length Long.	5617	5483	5127
Par	69	69	72
Slope system	—	—	—

Advised golfing ability Niveau de jeu recommandé: 0 12 24 36
Hcp required Handicap exigé: certificate

Club house & amenities CLUB HOUSE ET ANNEXES **7**/10

Pro shop	Pro-shop	
Driving range	Practice	
Sheltered	couvert	
On grass	sur herbe	yes
Putting-green	putting-green	yes
Pitching-green	pitching green	yes

Hotel facilities ENVIRONNEMENT HOTELIER **7**/10

HOTELS HÔTELS

Majestic Hotel, 156 rooms, D £ 150 — Harrogate 5 km
Tel (44) 01423 - 700 300, Fax (44) 01423 - 502 283

Rudding Park, 50 rooms, D £ 140 — Harrogate 3 km
Tel (44) 01423 - 871 350, Fax (44) 01423 - 872 286

St George Swallow, 90 rooms, D £ 120 — Harrogate 5 km
Tel (44) 01423 - 561 431, Fax (44) 01423 - 530 037

Old Swan, 136 rooms, D £ 130 — Harrogate 5 km
Tel (44) 01423 - 500 055, Fax (44) 01423 - 501 154

RESTAURANTS RESTAURANT

Olivers 24, Tel (44) 01423 - 568 600 — Harrogate 5 km

Sasso, Tel (44) 01423 - 508 838 — Harrogate 5 km

HAWKSTONE PARK Hawkstone

15	8	7

A strange place where the "Follies" of Hawkstone Park could be a setting for a video game with caves, secret passages or little monuments, all hidden in lush vegetation. They also say that King Arthur is buried somewhere on this estate. What is certain is that Sandy Lyle learnt how to play here. Today, this is a real resort with a hotel and two courses, including "Hawkestone", which was designed by James Braid, with some of the greens in the style of Alister Mackenzie. The course was restored and adapted to the modern game by Brian Huggett, who also laid out the resort's other 18-hole course. Imaginative, sometimes spectacular, very well landscaped and blending perfectly with its environment, this is a course whose subtleties will probably appeal more to the better golfer. Non-golfers can always visit the pretty town of Shrewsbury in the footsteps of Cadfael, the hero of the medieval murder novels by Ellis Peters.

Etrange endroit où les "Follies" de Hawkstone Park pourraient servir de cadre à un jeu video avec grottes, passages secrets ou petits monuments, tous cachés dans une végétation très riche. On murmure que le Roi Arthur aurait été enterré sur ce domaine, mais la seule chose certaine, c'est que Sandy Lyle a appris le golf ici. C'est aujourd'hui un resort, avec hôtel et deux parcours, dont le "Hawkstone" est un James Braid avec certains greens à la Alister Mackenzie, restauré et adapté au jeu moderne par Brian Huggett, qui a également signé l'autre 18 trous du domaine. Imaginatif, parfois spectaculaire, bien paysagé mais en même temps magnifiquement intégré à son environnement, c'est un parcours dont les joueurs d'un bon niveau apprécieront le plus les subtilités. Les autres pourront chercher dans la jolie ville de Shrewsbury les traces de Frère Cadfael, héros des romans policiers médiévaux d'Ellis Peters.

Hawkstone Park Hotel — 1920

Weston-under-Redcastle
ENG - SHREWSBURY, Shropshire SY4 5UY

Office	Secrétariat	(44) 01939 - 200 611
Pro shop	Pro-shop	(44) 01939 - 200 611
Fax	Fax	(44) 01939 - 200 311
Web	www.hawkstonepark.co.uk	
Situation	Situation	Shrewsbury, 19 km
Annual closure	Fermeture annuelle	no
Weekly closure	Fermeture hebdomadaire	no

Fees main season Tarifs haute saison	18 holes	
	Week days Semaine	**We/Bank holidays** We/Férié
Individual Individuel	£ 30	£ 38
Couple Couple	£ 60	£ 76

Full days: £ 45 / £ 53 (week ends)

Caddy	Caddy	£ 20 /on request
Electric Trolley	Chariot électrique	£ 7.50 /18 holes
Buggy	Voiturette	£ 23 /18 holes
Clubs	Clubs	£ 12 /18 holes

Credit cards Cartes de crédit
VISA - Eurocard - MasterCard - AMEX

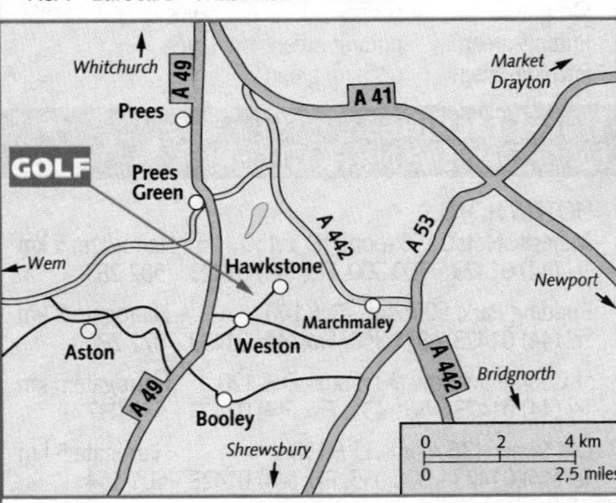

Access Accès : M6 Birmingham → Liverpool. Jct 10A through Telford, A5 → Shrewsbury. A49 North. Follow signs for Hawkstone Historic Park
Map 5 on page 492 Carte 5 Page 492

Golf course PARCOURS — 15/20

Site	Site	
Maintenance	Entretien	
Architect	Architecte	James Braid
Type	Type	parkland
Relief	Relief	
Water in play	Eau en jeu	
Exp. to wind	Exposé au vent	
Trees in play	Arbres en jeu	

Scorecard Carte de score	**Chp.** Chp.	**Mens** Mess.	**Ladies** Da.
Length Long.	5842	5519	5153
Par	72	72	72
Slope system	—	—	—

Advised golfing ability Niveau de jeu recommandé — 0 12 24 36
Hcp required Handicap exigé — certificate

Club house & amenities CLUB HOUSE ET ANNEXES — 8/10

Pro shop	Pro-shop	
Driving range	Practice	
Sheltered	couvert	no
On grass	sur herbe	yes
Putting-green	putting-green	yes
Pitching-green	pitching green	yes

Hotel facilities ENVIRONNEMENT HOTELIER — 7/10

HOTELS HÔTELS

Hawkstone Park Hotel, 65 rooms, D £ 140 — Weston on site
Tel (44) 01939 - 200 611, Fax (44) 01939 - 200 311

Albrighton Hall, 71 rooms, D £ 112 — Albrighton 12 km
Tel (44) 01939 - 291 000, Fax (44) 01939 - 291 123

Prince Rupert, 69 rooms, D £ 85 — Shrewsbury 19 km
Tel (44) 01939 - 499 955, Fax (44) 01939 - 357 306

RESTAURANTS RESTAURANT

Hawkstone Park Hotel — Weston on site
Tel (44) 01939 - 200 611

HAYLING

16 | 7 | 7

The southern coast of England has very few genuine links courses. Rye (totally private) can claim the label, and so can Hayling, whose reputation has never gone beyond England despite being designed by Tom Simpson, a hallmark of quality. As usual, the hazards are remarkably well located with the best route to the green always being the most dangerous (as with Donald Ross). At the same time visibility is 90% perfect so you can get to grips with the course from the first time out. Here you are adapting your game all the time, but that is one of the pleasures of golf. This easy-walking course is ideal for the holidays if you are not too concerned about your card. Close to the beach and a very rich nature reserve, Hayling deserves a good visit.

Cette côte sud de l'Angleterre propose bien peu de sites de vrais links, seul Rye (totalement privé) pouvant prétendre en être vraiment un. Ainsi que Hayling, dont la notoriété n'a pas dépassé les frontières, en dépit de la signature de Tom Simpson, une garantie de qualité. Comme d'habitude avec lui, le placement des obstacles est remarquable, la meilleure route étant toujours la plus dangereuse (comme avec Donald Ross), et la visibilité est à 90 % parfaite, de manière à pouvoir entrer dans le vif du sujet dès la première visite. Les problèmes posés diffèrent d'un trou à l'autre, et d'un vent à l'autre, ce qui oblige à s'adapter sans cesse, mais c'est un des plaisirs du golf. Peu fatigant à marcher, c'est un parcours idéal pour les vacances, si l'on n'est pas trop soucieux de son score. Proche de la plage et d'une très riche réserve naturelle, Hayling mérite une visite attentive.

Hayling Golf Club — 1883

Links Lane
ENG- HAYLING ISLAND, Hampshire PO11 0BX

Office	Secrétariat	(44) 01705 - 464 446
Pro shop	Pro-shop	(44) 01705 - 464 491
Fax	Fax	(44) 01705 - 464 46
Web	www.haylinggolf.co.uk	
Situation	Situation	Portsmouth , 15 km
Annual closure	Fermeture annuelle	no
Weekly closure	Fermeture hebdomadaire	no

Fees main season Tarifs haute saison	18 holes	
	Week days Semaine	We/Bank holidays We/Férié
Individual Individuel	£ 32	£ 42
Couple Couple	£ 64	£ 84

Full day: £ 40 / £ 54 / Weekends: no green-fees before 10.00 am

Caddy	Caddy	no
Electric Trolley	Chariot électrique	£ 7.50 /18 holes
Buggy	Voiturette	no
Clubs	Clubs	no

Credit cards Cartes de crédit
VISA - MasterCard (Pro shop goods only)

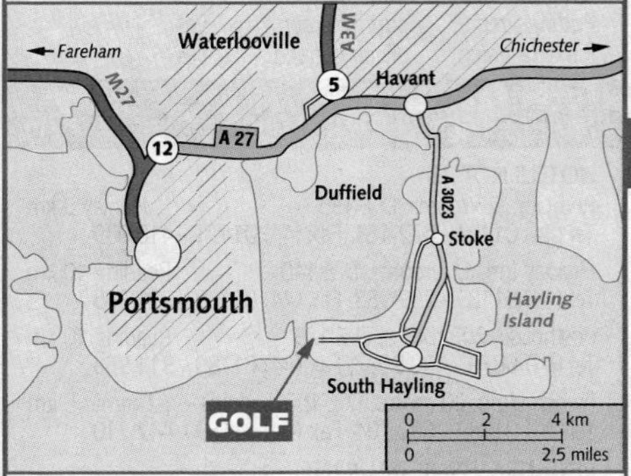

Access Accès : London, A3 → Portsmouth, A27 → Havant. A 3023 to Hayling Island. Seafront, turn right
Map 7 on page 496 Carte 7 Page 496

Golf course PARCOURS — 16/20

Site	Site	
Maintenance	Entretien	
Architect	Architecte	J.H. Taylor Tom Simpson
Type	Type	seaside course, links
Relief	Relief	
Water in play	Eau en jeu	
Exp. to wind	Exposé au vent	
Trees in play	Arbres en jeu	

Scorecard Carte de score	Chp. Chp.	Mens Mess.	Ladies Da.
Length Long.	5870	5675	5220
Par	71	71	74
Slope system	—	—	—

Advised golfing ability Niveau de jeu recommandé — 0 12 24 36
Hcp required Handicap exigé — certificate

Club house & amenities CLUB HOUSE ET ANNEXES — 7/10

Pro shop	Pro-shop	
Driving range	Practice	
Sheltered	couvert	2 mats
On grass	sur herbe	no
Putting-green	putting-green	yes
Pitching-green	pitching green	no

Hotel facilities ENVIRONNEMENT HOTELIER — 7/10

HOTELS HÔTELS

Portsmouth Marriott — Portsmouth 15 km
172 rooms, D £ 90
Tel (44) 023 - 9238 3151, Fax (44) 023 - 9238 8701

Posthouse, 167 rooms, D £ 120 — Portsmouth 15 km
Tel (44) 0870 - 400 9065, Fax (44) 023 - 9275 6715

Seacrest, 26 rooms, D £ 75 — Portsmouth 15 km
Tel (44) 023 - 9273 3192, Fax (44) 023 - 9283 2523

RESTAURANTS RESTAURANT

Bistro Montparnasse — Portsmouth 15 km
Tel (44) 023 - 9281 6754

Lemon Sole, Tel (44) 023 - 9281 1303 — Portsmouth

HENLEY

14 | 6 | 7

We have already talked about this very popular region of Henley (see Badgemore) and the Thames Valley with its pretty villages and timbered houses: the Tudor style is gradually replaced by flint as you move towards the Cotswolds. Another landmark to visit is the Uffington White Horse, carved out of chalk on the hillside. While you are here, play this pretty little Henley course with unpretentious facilities and clubhouse but a well-thought out design by James Braid. There is nothing really distinctive about this course but it makes for a good day's golfing with friends of all different playing levels. You will have a good round relaxing between two more difficult courses in the region, have fun at very little cost and might almost believe you play golf better than you ever thought possible. With that said, proceed with care, as even the most benign course can turn spiteful at times.

Avec Badgemore Park, nous avons évoqué cette région très courue d'Henley et de la vallée de la Tamise, avec les petits villages aux maisons à colombages, qui deviennent peu à peu maisons de pierre à mesure que l'on va vers les Costwolds. Il faudra aussi voir le "Cheval Blanc" d'Uffington, gigantesque figure de craie préhistorique. Et aussi penser à jouer ce joli parcours d'Henley, au Clubhouse et aux installations assez modestes, au dessin bien pensé de James Braid. Certes, il n'offre pas de caractère particulier très notable, mais il permet de passer une bonne journée avec des joueurs de tous niveaux, en guise de détente entre deux parcours plus difficiles, de se faire plaisir à peu de frais, et presque de croire que l'on joue mieux qu'on ne l'imaginait. Il faut cependant faire attention, les parcours les plus souriants ont aussi des dents.

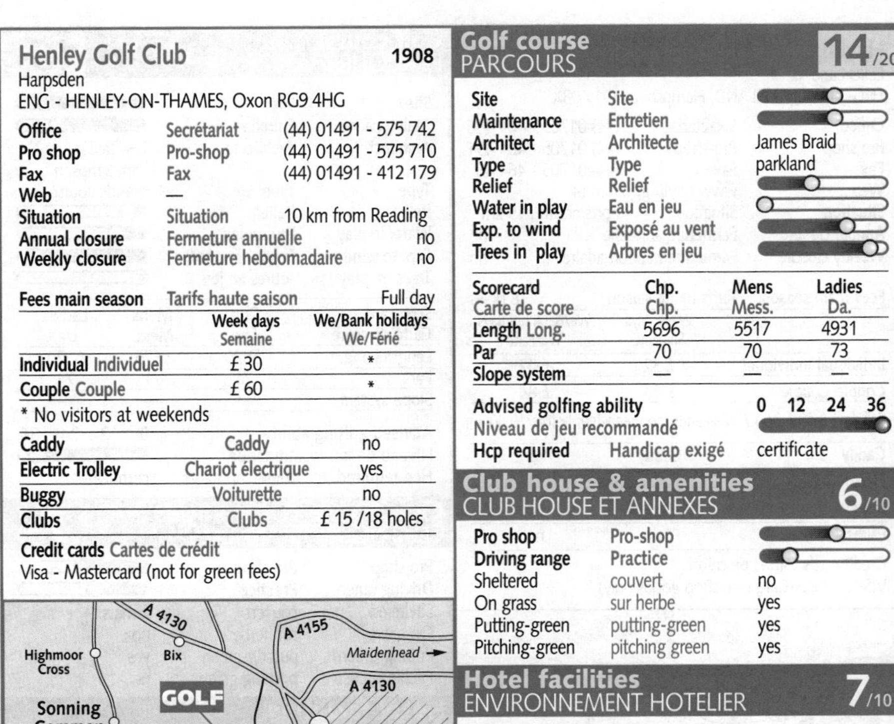

570

Henley Golf Club — 1908

Harpsden
ENG - HENLEY-ON-THAMES, Oxon RG9 4HG

Office	Secrétariat	(44) 01491 - 575 742
Pro shop	Pro-shop	(44) 01491 - 575 710
Fax	Fax	(44) 01491 - 412 179
Web	—	
Situation	Situation	10 km from Reading
Annual closure	Fermeture annuelle	no
Weekly closure	Fermeture hebdomadaire	no

Fees main season Tarifs haute saison		Full day
	Week days Semaine	We/Bank holidays We/Férié
Individual Individuel	£ 30	*
Couple Couple	£ 60	*

* No visitors at weekends

Caddy	Caddy	no
Electric Trolley	Chariot électrique	yes
Buggy	Voiturette	no
Clubs	Clubs	£ 15 /18 holes

Credit cards Cartes de crédit
Visa - Mastercard (not for green fees)

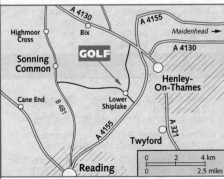

Access Accès : Leave M4 at Jct 8/9, A404, A4130 to Henley-on-Thames, then A4155 → Reading, turn right through Harpsden Village, Golf on the right.
Map 8 on page 498 Carte 8 Page 498

Golf course PARCOURS — 14/20

Site	Site	
Maintenance	Entretien	
Architect	Architecte	James Braid
Type	Type	parkland
Relief	Relief	
Water in play	Eau en jeu	
Exp. to wind	Exposé au vent	
Trees in play	Arbres en jeu	

Scorecard Carte de score	Chp. Chp.	Mens Mess.	Ladies Da.
Length Long.	5696	5517	4931
Par	70	70	73
Slope system	—	—	—

Advised golfing ability Niveau de jeu recommandé — 0 12 24 36
Hcp required Handicap exigé — certificate

Club house & amenities CLUB HOUSE ET ANNEXES — 6/10

Pro shop	Pro-shop	
Driving range	Practice	
Sheltered	couvert	no
On grass	sur herbe	yes
Putting-green	putting-green	yes
Pitching-green	pitching green	yes

Hotel facilities ENVIRONNEMENT HOTELIER — 7/10

HOTELS HÔTELS

Red Lion, 26 rooms, D £ 135 — Henley 3 km
Tel (44) 01491 - 572 161, Fax (44) 01491 - 410 039

Holiday Inn, 112 rooms, D £ 140 — Reading 10 km
Tel (44) 01189 - 259 988, Fax (44) 01189 - 391 665

Posthouse, 202 rooms, D £ 129 — Reading 10 km
Tel (44) 0870 - 400 9067, Fax (44) 01189 - 311 958

French Horn, 20 rooms, D £ 150 — Sonning-on-Thames 5 km
Tel (44) 01189 - 692 204, Fax (44) 01189 - 442 210

RESTAURANTS RESTAURANT

Villa Marina, Tel (44) 01491 - 575 262 — Henley 3 km

French Horn — Sonning-on-Thames 5 km
Tel (44) 01734 - 692 204

HERTFORDSHIRE (THE) | 15 | 7 | 7

The Tudor style architecture of this listed clubhouse gives an excellent first impression when you arrive here. You might expect a traditional course, but in fact you are met with excellent practice facilities and a very modern layout by Nicklaus Design, the company that Jack built. Nicklaus did not actually design this course in person, but over a rather limited area you find the same strategic approach with well designed and often large bunkers, water which comes very much into play but which can be avoided, and huge, well-contoured greens. The front nine are very interesting, the back nine a little less so. The whole layout doubtless still needs to mature. Being so close to London, this very tranquil course deserves more than one visit.

L'architecture Tudor d'un Clubhouse classé donne dès l'arrivée une telle impression de majesté que l'on attend un parcours très traditionnel. En fait, il y a ici de remarquables installations d'entraînement, et un parcours de dessin très moderne, créé par Nicklaus Design, la société du grand joueur et architecte américain, qui n'a pas vraiment signé lui-même le parcours. On y trouve cependant, sur un espace assez réduit, la même approche stratégique, avec des bunkers très dessinés et souvent grands, des obstacles d'eau bien en jeu, mais dont il est possible (et conseillé) de ne pas trop s'approcher, des greens vastes et très travaillés. L'aller est très intéressant, le retour un peu moins. L'ensemble a encore besoin de mûrir, sans aucun doute. Si proche de Londres, ce parcours très tranquille mérite plus qu'une visite.

The Hertfordshire Golf & C.C. — 1995

Broxbournebury Mansion, White Stubbs Lane
ENG - BROXBOURNE, Herts EN10 7 PY

Office	Secrétariat	(44) 01992 - 466 666
Pro shop	Pro-shop	(44) 01992 - 466 666
Fax	Fax	(44) 01992 - 470 326
Web	—	
Situation	Situation	Cheshunt, 5 km
Annual closure	Fermeture annuelle	no
Weekly closure	Fermeture hebdomadaire	no

Fees main season Tarifs haute saison	18 holes	
	Week days Semaine	**We/Bank holidays** We/Férié
Individual Individuel	£ 30	£ 43
Couple Couple	£ 60	£ 86

Full days: £ 38 / £ 43 (week ends)

Caddy	Caddy	no
Electric Trolley	Chariot électrique	no
Buggy	Voiturette	£ 18 (summer)
Clubs	Clubs	£ 10/18 holes

Credit cards Cartes de crédit
VISA - MasterCard (not for green fees)

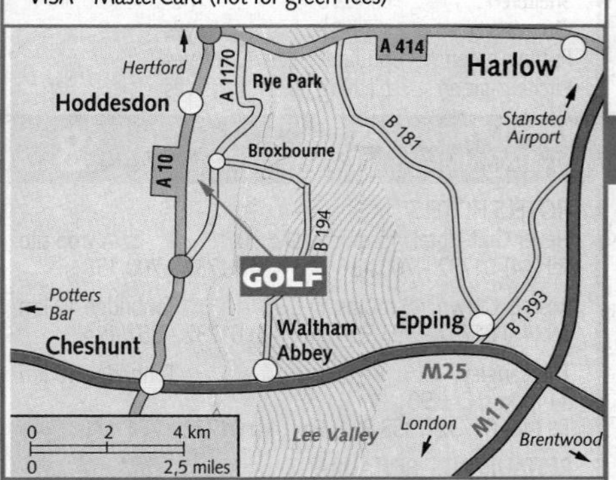

Access Accès : M25. At Jct 25 take A10 → Cambridge. Exit for Turnford, take A1170 to Bell Lane. Turn left, Bell Lane becomes White Stubbs Lane. Course on right.
Map 8 on page 499 Carte 8 Page 499

Golf course PARCOURS — 15/20

Site	Site	
Maintenance	Entretien	
Architect	Architecte	Nicklaus Design
Type	Type	parkland
Relief	Relief	
Water in play	Eau en jeu	
Exp. to wind	Exposé au vent	
Trees in play	Arbres en jeu	

Scorecard Carte de score	**Chp.** Chp.	**Mens** Mess.	**Ladies** Da.
Length Long.	5750	5403	4390
Par	70	70	70
Slope system	—	—	—

Advised golfing ability Niveau de jeu recommandé: 0 12 24 36
Hcp required Handicap exigé: 28 Men, 36 Ladies

Club house & amenities CLUB HOUSE ET ANNEXES — 7/10

Pro shop	Pro-shop	
Driving range	Practice	
Sheltered	couvert	30 bays
On grass	sur herbe	yes (May → Oct)
Putting-green	putting-green	yes
Pitching-green	pitching green	yes

Hotel facilities ENVIRONNEMENT HOTELIER — 7/10

HOTELS HÔTELS

Cheshunt Marriott, 143 rooms, D £ 119 — Cheshunt 4 km
Tel (44) 01992 - 451 245, Fax (44) 01992 - 440 120

Churchgate Manor, 85 rooms, D £ 120 — Old Harlow 12 km
Tel (44) 01279 - 420 246, Fax (44) 01279 - 437 720

Harlow Moat House, 119 rooms, D £ 135 — Harlow 10 km
Tel (44) 01279 - 829 988, Fax (44) 01279 - 635 094

White Horse, 42 rooms, D £ 110 — Hertingfordbury 9 km
Tel (44) 0870 - 400 8114, Fax (44) 01992 - 550 809

RESTAURANTS RESTAURANT

Cheshunt Marriott — Cheshunt
Tel (44) 01992 - 451 245 — 4 km

HEVER

14 | 8 | 8

An impressive site and one of the great new clubs you need to know in the South-West of England which is now so easy to reach courtesy of Eurotunnel for the continentals. The course, clubhouse and hotel have been laid out in the estate of a castle where Ann Boleyn spent her childhood before briefly becoming Henry VIII's second wife. A stream is in play on almost one half of the course before running into the castle lake, but the hazard is psychologically rather than really dangerous. The trees are much more of a problem and those already on the estate have been supplemented by young plantations which will gradually make their presence felt on the fairways and alter the course as the years go by. As a general rule, Nicholson has made good use of existing features, particularly on the dog-legs, and has created enough variety for the course to be constantly enjoyable. Good work and a pretty place to spend a fine day's golfing.

Un site impressionnant, et l'un des grands nouveaux clubs à connaître dans le sud-ouest de l'Angleterre, si facilement accessible maintenant par Eurotunnel pour les continentaux. Le golf, le Clubhouse et l'hôtel ont été créés dans le domaine d'un château où Ann Boleyn passa son enfance, avant d'être la seconde et passagère épouse d'Henry VIII. Le parcours met en jeu sur près de la moitié des trous un cours d'eau se jetant dans le lac du château, mais cet obstacle est plus psychologique que vraiment dangereux. Les arbres le sont bien davantage, et ceux existant dans le parc ont été complétés par de jeunes plantations, qui viendront empiéter sur les fairways et modifier le parcours avec les années. En règle générale, Peter Nicholson a fait bon usage des éléments existant, en particulier sur les doglegs, et donné assez de diversité à son tracé pour que le plaisir soit constamment renouvelé. Du bon travail et un joli endroit pour passer une bonne journée de golf.

Hever Golf Club **1993**
ENG - HEVER, Kent TN8 7NG

Office	Secrétariat	(44) 01732 - 700 771
Pro shop	Pro-shop	(44) 01732 - 700 785
Fax	Fax	(44) 01732 - 700 775
Web	www.hever.com	
Situation	Situation	

3 km from Edenbridge - 10 km from Tonbridge (pop. 101 765)

Annual closure	Fermeture annuelle	no
Weekly closure	Fermeture hebdomadaire	no

Fees main season Tarifs haute saison	18 holes	
	Week days Semaine	**We/Bank holidays** We/Férié
Individual Individuel	£ 35	£ 55
Couple Couple	£ 70	£ 110

Visitors after 11.00 pm on weekends

Caddy	Caddy	no
Electric Trolley	Chariot électrique	no
Buggy	Voiturette	£ 20 /18 holes
Clubs	Clubs	£ 25 /18 holes

Credit cards Cartes de crédit
VISA - MasterCard - AMEX

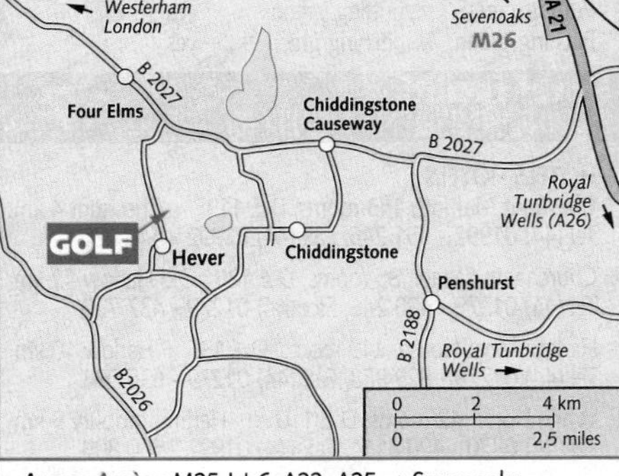

Access Accès : M25 Jct 6, A22, A25 → Sevenoaks. Limpsfield B269 to Crocham Hill, Four Elms, Bough Beech → Hever Castle
Map 7 on page 497 Carte 7 Page 497

Golf course PARCOURS 14/20

Site	Site	
Maintenance	Entretien	
Architect	Architecte	Peter Nicholson
Type	Type	parkland
Relief	Relief	
Water in play	Eau en jeu	
Exp. to wind	Exposé au vent	
Trees in play	Arbres en jeu	

Scorecard Carte de score	**Chp.** Chp.	**Mens** Mess.	**Ladies** Da.
Length Long.	6302	6085	5144
Par	72	72	73
Slope system	—	—	—

Advised golfing ability 0 12 24 36
Niveau de jeu recommandé
Hcp required Handicap exigé certificate

Club house & amenities CLUB HOUSE ET ANNEXES 8/10

Pro shop	Pro-shop	
Driving range	Practice	
Sheltered	couvert	no
On grass	sur herbe	yes
Putting-green	putting-green	yes
Pitching-green	pitching green	yes

Hotel facilities ENVIRONNEMENT HOTELIER 8/10

HOTELS HÔTELS
Hever Golf Hotel, 15 rooms, D £ 90 — on site
Tel (44) 01732 - 700 136, Fax (44) 01732 - 700 138

Rose & Crown, 49 rooms, D £ 95 — Tonbridge 10 km
Tel (44) 01732 - 357 966, Fax (44) 01732 - 357 194

The Langley — Tonbridge 10 km
34 rooms, D £ 90
Tel (44) 01732 - 353 311, Fax (44) 01732 - 771 471

RESTAURANTS RESTAURANT
Honours Mill — Edenbridge 4 km
Tel (44) 01732 - 866757

The Langley — Tonbridge 10 km
Tel (44) 01732 - 353 311

HIGH POST

15 | 6 | 7

Here we are out in the country, with wild peacocks strutting around the clubhouse, jet fighters and trainers flying overhead to disturb your putting stroke, and an obligatory stop at tea-time to taste the delicious cakes. High Post is a hilly course which can be tough on the legs and on your score, but the chalky terrain drains well and doesn't get heavy after rain. The fairways are wide and the rough not too exacting, except when you get too close to the hawthorn bushes. High Post might easily have led a quiet life out of the headlines, except that Peter Alliss drew attention to the course by rating the 9th hole as one of the best 18 holes in England. It is certainly the best without a single grain of sand, and the hollows and grassy sand-hills are often a tougher proposition than bunkers.

Ici, on est à la campagne. Des paons sauvages se promènent autour du Clubhouse, des avions de chasse et d'entraînement vous dérangent quand vous puttez, il faut s'arrêter à l'heure du thé pour déguster quelques fameux cakes. On monte et on descend, ce qui tire sur les jambes comme sur les scores, mais le terrain crayeux est bien draînant, ce qui évite un sol trop lourd par temps de pluie. Les fairways sont larges, les roughs pas trop pénalisants, sauf auprès des nombreux buissons d'aubépine. On pouvait croire que High Post poursuivra sa vie tranquille à l'écart des grandes histoires, quand Peter Alliss attira l'attention sur ce parcours, en classant son 9 parmi les 18 meilleurs trous d'Angleterre. C'est en tout cas le meilleur trou où il n'y ait pas un grain de sable (sinon dans son jeu), et les dépressions ou buttes d'herbe sont souvent moins faciles à négocier que les sorties de bunkers.

High Post Golf Club — 1931

Great Durnford
ENG - SALISBURY, Wiltshire SP4 6AT

Office	Secrétariat	(44) 01722 - 782 356
Pro shop	Pro-shop	(44) 01722 - 782 219
Fax	Fax	(44) 01722 - 782 356
Web	—	
Situation	Situation	6 km N of Salisbury
Annual closure	Fermeture annuelle	no
Weekly closure	Fermeture hebdomadaire	no

Restaurant: limited service on Mondays

Fees main season Tarifs haute saison	18 holes	
	Week days Semaine	**We/Bank holidays** We/Férié
Individual Individuel	£ 28	£ 35
Couple Couple	£ 56	£ 70

Full days: £ 37 / £ 45 (weekeends)

Caddy	Caddy	no
Electric Trolley	Chariot électrique	£ 5 /18 holes
Buggy	Voiturette	no
Clubs	Clubs	no

Credit cards Cartes de crédit
Visa - Mastercard (Pro shop goods only)

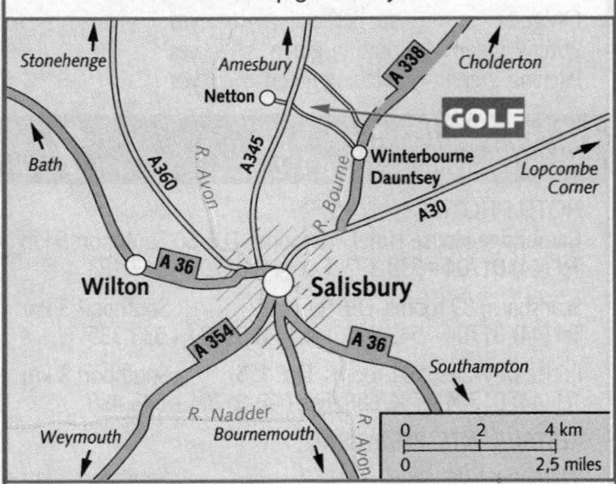

Access Accès : M3 to Southampton, then M27. Jct 2, A36 to Salisbury, then A345 → Amesbury. Golf on right side.
Map 6 on page 495 Carte 6 Page 495

Golf course — PARCOURS — 15/20

Site	Site	
Maintenance	Entretien	
Architect	Architecte	Hawtree & Taylor
Type	Type	copse, open country
Relief	Relief	
Water in play	Eau en jeu	
Exp. to wind	Exposé au vent	
Trees in play	Arbres en jeu	

Scorecard Carte de score	Chp. Chp.	Mens Mess.	Ladies Da.
Length Long.	5738	5490	5172
Par	70	69	73
Slope system	—	—	—

Advised golfing ability Niveau de jeu recommandé — 0 12 24 36
Hcp required Handicap exigé — certificate (W-End)

Club house & amenities — CLUB HOUSE ET ANNEXES — 6/10

Pro shop	Pro-shop	
Driving range	Practice	
Sheltered	couvert	no
On grass	sur herbe	yes
Putting-green	putting-green	yes
Pitching-green	pitching green	yes

Hotel facilities — ENVIRONNEMENT HOTELIER — 7/10

HOTELS HÔTELS

Milford Hall, 35 rooms, D £ 120 — Salisbury 6 km
Tel (44) 01722 - 417 411, Fax (44) 01722 - 419 444

Red Lion Hotel, 53 rooms, D £ 120 — Salisbury 6 km
Tel (44) 01722 - 323 334, Fax (44) 01722 - 325 756

Rose and Crown, 28 rooms, D £ 145 — Harnham 8 km
Tel (44) 01722 - 399 955, Fax (44) 01722 - 339 816

RESTAURANTS RESTAURANT

LXIX — Salisbury 6 km
Tel (44) 01722 - 340 000

Rose and Crown — Harnham 8 km
Tel (44) 01722 - 399 955

573

HILLSIDE

18 | 7 | 7

A quiet course up until 1962, Hillside took on a new dimension with the acquisition of duneland which Fred Hawtree set to work on. A part of the course is lined by pine-trees, forming an unusual setting rather as if the trees had been plucked and placed on a real links. The first holes run along the railway line and set a "down-the-middle" tone from the very beginning. The dunes and tall rough are more concentrated on the back nine (which won the admiration of Jack Nicklaus) and the fairways run between the dune valleys. In such a motley landscape where the wind can have such a diverse influence on the ball, it is not a bad idea to know how it blows in order to stay on track. Highly manicured but still looking very natural, always pleasant to play and walk on with this links-type soil, Hillside is certainly not the best known links course outside England but it is a must to play. A good neighbour for Royal Birkdale.

Parcours tranquille jusqu'en 1962, Hillside a pris une dimension nouvelle avec l'acquisition de terrains travaillés par Fred Hawtree en zone dunaire. De grands pins ornent une partie du parcours, formant un cadre inhabituel, comme un décor posé sur un links authentique. Les premiers trous longent la voie ferrée et annoncent qu'il sera impossible de se relâcher. Les dunes et les haut roughs sont davantage concentrés sur le retour (qui fait l'admiration de Jack Nicklaus... mais aussi la nôtre !), les fairways glissant dans les vallées. Dans un paysage aussi divers où le vent peut influer de manière différente sur la balle, il n'est pas mauvais de connaître les effets pour rester en piste. Très soigné, tout en conservant un aspect naturel, toujours agréable avec ce genre de sol de links si agréable à marcher et à jouer, Hillside n'est sans doute pas le plus connu des links hors des frontières, mais il est inévitable. Un bon voisin pour Royal Birkdale.

Hillside Golf Club — 1923

Hastings Road, Hillside
ENG - SOUTHPORT, Lancs PR8 2 LU

Office	Secrétariat	(44) 01704 - 567169
Pro shop	Pro-shop	(44) 01704 - 568360
Fax	Fax	(44) 01704 - 563192
Web	—	
Situation	Situation	28 km N of Liverpool
Annual closure	Fermeture annuelle	no
Weekly closure	Fermeture hebdomadaire	no

Fees main season Tarifs haute saison	18 holes	
	Week days / Semaine	We/Bank holidays / We/Férié
Individual Individuel	£ 50	£ 65
Couple Couple	£ 100	£ 130

Full days: £ 65 / £ 130 (week ends)

Caddy	Caddy	£ 25 /on request
Electric Trolley	Chariot électrique	no
Buggy	Voiturette	yes
Clubs	Clubs	£ 2 each /18 holes

Credit cards Cartes de crédit
VISA - Eurocard - MasterCard - DC - JCB - AMEX
(not for green-fees)

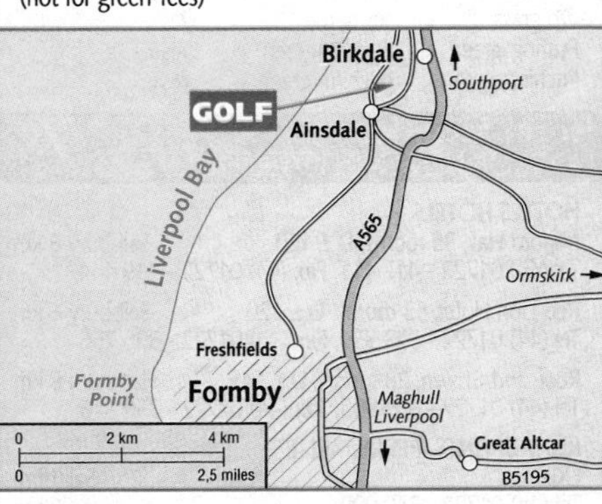

Access Accès : Off A565 Liverpool → Southport, between Hillside railway station and Royal Birkdale gates.
Map 5 on page 493 Carte 5 Page 493

Golf course — PARCOURS — 18/20

Site	Site	
Maintenance	Entretien	
Architect	Architecte	Fred Hawtree (1962)
Type	Type	links
Relief	Relief	
Water in play	Eau en jeu	
Exp. to wind	Exposé au vent	
Trees in play	Arbres en jeu	

Scorecard Carte de score	Chp. Chp.	Mens Mess.	Ladies Da.
Length Long.	6165	5920	5345
Par	72	72	75
Slope system	—	—	—

Advised golfing ability Niveau de jeu recommandé — 0 12 24 36
Hcp required Handicap exigé — certificate

Club house & amenities — CLUB HOUSE ET ANNEXES — 7/10

Pro shop	Pro-shop	
Driving range	Practice	
Sheltered	couvert	no
On grass	sur herbe	yes
Putting-green	putting-green	yes
Pitching-green	pitching green	yes

Hotel facilities — ENVIRONNEMENT HOTELIER — 7/10

HOTELS HÔTELS

Cambridge House Hotel, 16 rooms, D £ 60 — Southport 5 km
Tel (44) 01704 - 538 372, Fax (44) 01704 - 547 183

Scarisbrick, 89 rooms, D £ 99 — Southport 3 km
Tel (44) 01704 - 543 000, Fax (44) 01704 - 533 335

Prince of Wales, 101 rooms, D £ 115 — Southport 3 km
Tel (44) 01704 - 536 688, Fax (44) 01704 - 543 488

RESTAURANTS RESTAURANT

Warehouse Brasserie — Southport 3 km
Tel (44) 01704 - 544 662

Valentino's, Tel (44) 01704 - 538 401 — Southport 3 km

Cloisters (Scarisbrick), Tel (44) 01704 - 535 153 — Southport

HINDHEAD

16 | 7 | 6

For a few days golfing in this region of Surrey, on the border with Hampshire and Sussex, Hindhead is one of a threesome which includes Hankley Common and West Surrey. This is very country landscape and a little tiring if you are pulling your own cart. The two parts of the course are very different, with the first 9 holes played in a valley (rather unusual in Surrey) and the back 9 at the top of a hill. From a visual point of view the front 9 are more memorable, especially the 6th, a 3-par looking down steeply onto a well-protected green. Before your round, go and have a drink at the bar, enjoy the magnificent view over the 18th hole and listen to the locals explaining how to play the course. It all comes down to one pint of best bitter and two ideas: keep it straight and keep out of the heather. They could also tell you to avoid the trees and bushes as well, but one look is enough for that to go without saying.

Pour quelques jours de golf dans cette région du Surrey à la limite du Hampshire et du Sussex, Hindhead apporte sa contribution à Hankley Common et West Surrey, dans un paysage très campagnard, mais un peu fatigant s'il faut aussi tirer son chariot. Les deux parties du parcours sont très différentes, les neuf premiers étant joués dans une vallée (c'est peu habituel dans le Surrey) et les neuf derniers au sommet d'une colline. Visuellement, l'aller est plus mémorable, on se souviendra en particulier du 6, un par 3 au green en contrebas et très défendu. Avant de jouer, allez donc faire un tour au bar où les vues sur le 18 sont magnifiques, et où les locaux vous expliqueront la stratégie du parcours. Elle tient en une pinte et deux idées : restez droit et évitez la bruyère. On ne vous dira pas d'éviter aussi les bois et buissons, cela va sans dire en jetant un seul coup d'oeil.

Hindhead Golf Club — 1904

Churt Road
ENG - HINDHEAD, Surrey GU26 6HX

Office	Secrétariat	(44) 01428 - 604 614
Pro shop	Pro-shop	(44) 01428 - 604 458
Fax	Fax	(44) 01428 - 608 508
Web	—	
Situation	Situation	4 km from Haslemere
Annual closure	Fermeture annuelle	no
Weekly closure	Fermeture hebdomadaire	no

Fees main season Tarifs haute saison	18 holes	
	Week days / Semaine	We/Bank holidays / We/Férié
Individual Individuel	£ 36	£ 47
Couple Couple	£ 72	£ 94

Full days: £ 46 / £ 57 (week ends)

Caddy	Caddy	no
Electric Trolley	Chariot électrique	no
Buggy	Voiturette	no
Clubs	Clubs	no

Credit cards Cartes de crédit
VISA - MasterCard (not for greenfees)

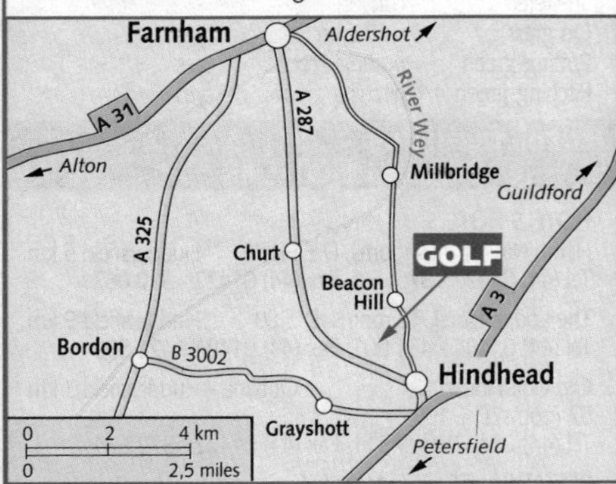

Access Accès : London, A3 (→ Portsmouth). Approx. 9 km (5 m) after Milford, turn right onto A287 → Hindhead, Farnham. After Beacon Hill, golf on right side.
Map 7 on page 496 Carte 7 Page 496

Golf course PARCOURS — 16/20

Site	Site	
Maintenance	Entretien	
Architect	Architecte	J.H. Taylor
Type	Type	inland, heathland
Relief	Relief	
Water in play	Eau en jeu	
Exp. to wind	Exposé au vent	
Trees in play	Arbres en jeu	

Scorecard Carte de score	Chp. Chp.	Mens Mess.	Ladies Da.
Length Long.	5735	5520	4992
Par	70	69	72
Slope system	—	—	—

Advised golfing ability / Niveau de jeu recommandé: 0 12 24 36
Hcp required Handicap exigé: certificate

Club house & amenities CLUB HOUSE ET ANNEXES — 7/10

Pro shop	Pro-shop	
Driving range	Practice	
Sheltered	couvert	2 nets
On grass	sur herbe	yes
Putting-green	putting-green	yes
Pitching-green	pitching green	yes

Hotel facilities ENVIRONNEMENT HOTELIER — 6/10

HOTELS HÔTELS

Pride of the Valley, 16 rooms, D £ 95 — Churt 2 km
Tel (44) 01428 - 605 799, Fax (44) 01428 - 605 875

Lythe Hill, 40 rooms, D £ 120 — Haslemere 6 km
Tel (44) 01428 - 651 251, Fax (44) 01428 - 644 131

Georgian, 24 rooms, D £ 70 — Haslemere 4 km
Tel (44) 01428 - 656 644, Fax (44) 01428 - 645 600

RESTAURANTS RESTAURANT

Undershaw — Hindhead 1 km
Tel (44) 01428 - 604 039

Pride of the Valley, Tel (44) 01428 - 605 799 — Churt 2 km

Auberge de France, Tel (44) 01428 - 651 251 — Haslemere

HUDDERSFIELD (FIXBY) 16 6 7

This was one of the centres of the great industrial revolution in the 19th century. Industries here included coal-mining, today illustrated by the Yorkshire Mining Museum, and textiles, one of the centres of which was Halifax, a few miles down the road. If you are with the family, take the children to visit the Eureka Museum, a sort of living compendium of science. It might take your mind off golf, despite this Huddersfield course, where another youngster, Sandy Herd, learnt how to play well enough to win the British Open in 1902. He must have had pretty sturdy legs too, because this is a very hilly course. Also called Fixby, the layout is lined with trees and strategy is by no means simple because it is so hard to judge the right distances and trajectories you need to place the drive and attack the greens. A classic layout where only good shots get their just desserts. Isn't that how it should be?

C'était une des grandes régions de la révolution industrielle au XIXème siècle. Un bassin minier illustré aujourd'hui par le Musée Minier du Yorkshire, une région d'industrie textile aussi, dont l'une des capitales était Halifax, à quelques kilomètres d'ici. En famille, vous y amènerez aussi vos jeunes enfants au Musée Eureka, une sorte de livre vivant de la science. De quoi vous distraire de votre passion du golf exercée à Huddersfield, où un autre jeune enfant, Sandy Herd, apprit un jeu qui le mena à la victoire au British Open 1902. Il a au moins acquis ici, sur un terrain bien accidenté, les jambes solides nécessaires à de bons appuis du swing. Appelé aussi Fixby, ce parcours est très boisé, la stratégie n'y est pas évidente tant il est difficile d'y juger des distances et des trajectoires nécessaires, pour placer les drives au bon endroit comme pour attaquer les greens. Un parcours au déroulement classique, où seuls les bons coups seront récompensés. C'est l'essentiel.

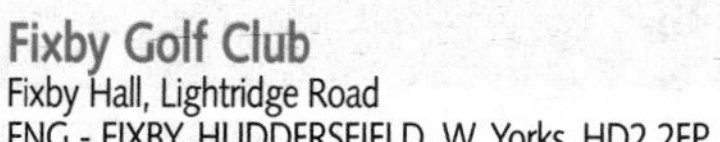

Fixby Golf Club 1891

Fixby Hall, Lightridge Road
ENG - FIXBY, HUDDERSFIELD, W. Yorks. HD2 2EP

Office	Secrétariat	(44) 01484 - 420 110
Pro shop	Pro-shop	(44) 01484 - 426 463
Fax	Fax	(44) 01484 - 424 623
Web	www.huddersfield-golf.co.uk	
Situation	Situation	Huddersfield, 3 km
Annual closure	Fermeture annuelle	no
Weekly closure	Fermeture hebdomadaire	no

Fees main season Tarifs haute saison	18 holes	
	Week days Semaine	We/Bank holidays We/Férié
Individual Individuel	£ 37	£ 47
Couple Couple	£ 74	£ 94

Full days: £ 47 / £ 57 (week ends)

Caddy	Caddy	no
Electric Trolley	Chariot électrique	£ 5
Buggy	Voiturette	no
Clubs	Clubs	no

Credit cards Cartes de crédit
VISA - Eurocard - MasterCard - Switch (Pro shop goods only)

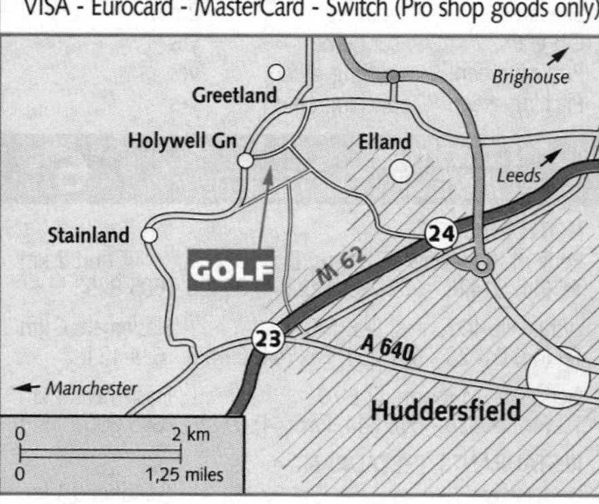

Access Accès : M62 Exit 24 to roundabout. 3rd exit → Brighouse. 1 km to lights, turn right. Turn right again onto Lightridge Road. Golf 500 m on right.
Map 4 on page 490 Carte 4 Page 490

Golf course PARCOURS 16/20

Site	Site	
Maintenance	Entretien	
Architect	Architecte	Unknown
Type	Type	parkland, hilly
Relief	Relief	
Water in play	Eau en jeu	
Exp. to wind	Exposé au vent	
Trees in play	Arbres en jeu	

Scorecard Carte de score	Chp. Chp.	Mens Mess.	Ladies Da.
Length Long.	5825	5470	5020
Par	71	71	71
Slope system	—	—	—

Advised golfing ability 0 12 24 36
Niveau de jeu recommandé

Hcp required Handicap exigé certificate

Club house & amenities CLUB HOUSE ET ANNEXES 6/10

Pro shop	Pro-shop	
Driving range	Practice	
Sheltered	couvert	
On grass	sur herbe	yes
Putting-green	putting-green	yes
Pitching-green	pitching green	yes

Hotel facilities ENVIRONNEMENT HOTELIER 7/10

HOTELS HÔTELS

Hilton Nation, 114 rooms, D £ 90 — Huddersfield 5 km
Tel (44) 01422 - 375 431, Fax (44) 01422 - 310 067

The Lodge Hotel, 12 rooms, D £ 80 — Huddersfield 9 km
Tel (44) 01484 - 431 001, Fax (44) 01484 - 421 590

Old Golf House — Outlane - Huddersfield 3 km
52 rooms, D £ 109
Tel (44) 01422 - 379 311, Fax (44) 01422 - 372 694

RESTAURANTS RESTAURANT

Weaver's Shed, Tel (44) 01484 - 654 284 — Golcar 4 km

Brook's, Tel (44) 01484 - 715 284 — Brighouse 5 km

Maharadjah, Tel (44) 01484 - 535 037 — Huddersfield 4 km

HUNSTANTON

17 | 7 | 6

If you mentioned East Anglia to the majority of continental golfers who are unfamiliar with England, they'd probably think you were talking about a make of car. In fact it is a region and home to some of the country's finest links including Hunstanton, nestling in a superb landscape of dunes, wild grass and scrubby bushes. From the 4th to the 15th holes, after a comparatively placid start, the course winds in every direction and makes that all-important judgment for each shot even more complicated. And just to prove once and for all that golf is an unfair game, this course boasts a famous par 3 hole with a blind green. In contrast, neither the sea nor the beach is out of bounds. Hunstanton plays host to major amateur tournaments, which is only fair dues for this often unorthodox and uplifting course. You might find it more enjoyable if you lose your scoring pencil.

On peut parier que pour les continentaux (qui ne connaissent guère l'Angleterre), East Anglia est le nom d'une voiture du temps passé. Dans cette région, on trouve quelques-uns des plus beaux links du pays, dont Hunstanton, blotti dans un superbe paysage de dunes couronnées d'herbes folles et de buissons touffus. Du 4 au 15, après un départ assez calme, les trous ne cessent de tourner dans toutes les directions, ce qui n'est pas fait pour faciliter le jugement, pourtant plus que nécessaire ici. Pour faire définitivement comprendre que le golf n'est pas un jeu juste, on trouve ici un fameux par 3 avec green aveugle. En revanche, ni la mer ni la plage ne sont hors limites. Hunstanton reçoit de grandes compétitions amateur, c'est justice, avec ce tracé souvent peu orthodoxe, exaltant et d'autant plus amusant si l'on a enfin perdu son crayon pour noter le score.

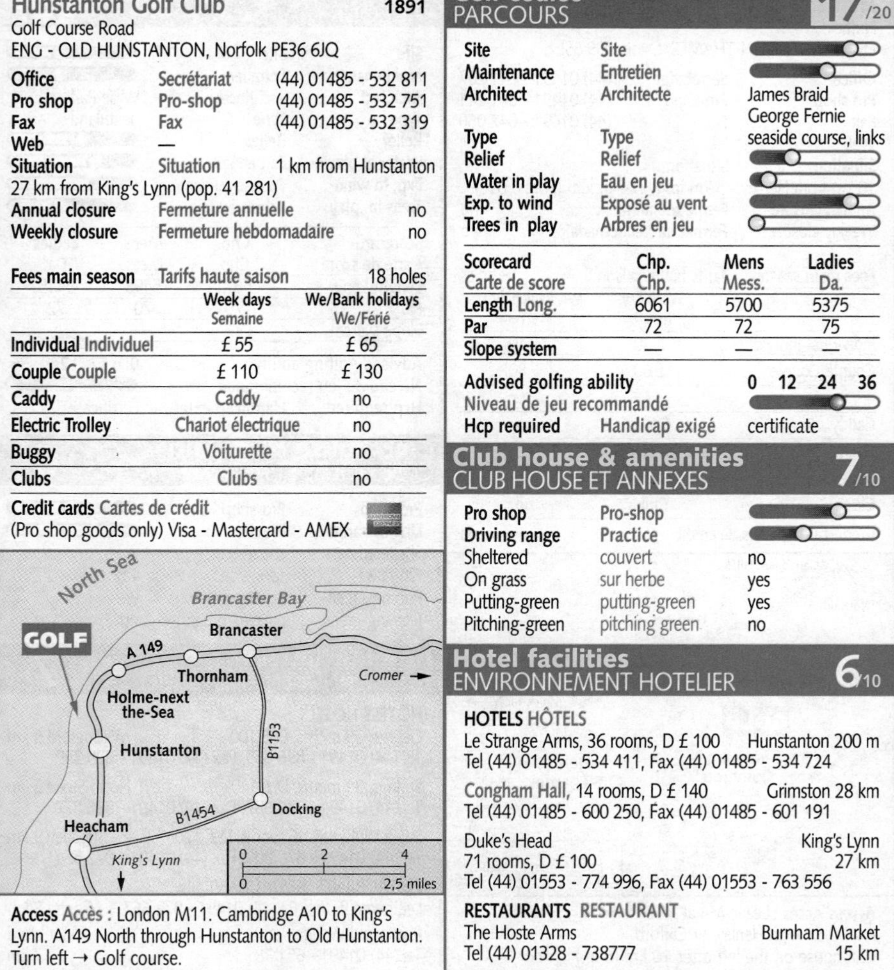

Hunstanton Golf Club — 1891

Golf Course Road
ENG - OLD HUNSTANTON, Norfolk PE36 6JQ

Office	Secrétariat	(44) 01485 - 532 811
Pro shop	Pro-shop	(44) 01485 - 532 751
Fax	Fax	(44) 01485 - 532 319
Web	—	
Situation	Situation	1 km from Hunstanton
27 km from King's Lynn (pop. 41 281)		
Annual closure	Fermeture annuelle	no
Weekly closure	Fermeture hebdomadaire	no

Fees main season Tarifs haute saison	18 holes	
	Week days Semaine	**We/Bank holidays** We/Férié
Individual Individuel	£ 55	£ 65
Couple Couple	£ 110	£ 130
Caddy	Caddy	no
Electric Trolley	Chariot électrique	no
Buggy	Voiturette	no
Clubs	Clubs	no

Credit cards Cartes de crédit
(Pro shop goods only) Visa - Mastercard - AMEX

Access Accès : London M11. Cambridge A10 to King's Lynn. A149 North through Hunstanton to Old Hunstanton. Turn left → Golf course.
Map 4 on page 491 Carte 4 Page 491

Golf course PARCOURS — 17/20

Site	Site	
Maintenance	Entretien	
Architect	Architecte	James Braid, George Fernie
Type	Type	seaside course, links
Relief	Relief	
Water in play	Eau en jeu	
Exp. to wind	Exposé au vent	
Trees in play	Arbres en jeu	

Scorecard Carte de score	**Chp.** Chp.	**Mens** Mess.	**Ladies** Da.
Length Long.	6061	5700	5375
Par	72	72	75
Slope system	—	—	—

Advised golfing ability 0 12 24 36
Niveau de jeu recommandé
Hcp required Handicap exigé certificate

Club house & amenities CLUB HOUSE ET ANNEXES — 7/10

Pro shop	Pro-shop	
Driving range	Practice	
Sheltered	couvert	no
On grass	sur herbe	yes
Putting-green	putting-green	yes
Pitching-green	pitching green	no

Hotel facilities ENVIRONNEMENT HOTELIER — 6/10

HOTELS HÔTELS

Le Strange Arms, 36 rooms, D £ 100 — Hunstanton 200 m
Tel (44) 01485 - 534 411, Fax (44) 01485 - 534 724

Congham Hall, 14 rooms, D £ 140 — Grimston 28 km
Tel (44) 01485 - 600 250, Fax (44) 01485 - 601 191

Duke's Head — King's Lynn
71 rooms, D £ 100 — 27 km
Tel (44) 01553 - 774 996, Fax (44) 01553 - 763 556

RESTAURANTS RESTAURANT

The Hoste Arms — Burnham Market
Tel (44) 01328 - 738777 — 15 km

Rococo, Tel (44) 01553 - 771483 — King's Lynn, 27 km

HUNTERCOMBE

14 | 6 | 7

At the beginning of the century, Daimlers and then a bus would ferry players to and from Henley railway station. Those were the good old days when service and hospitality meant more than they do today. Huntercombe has become a members' course where green-feers are tolerated on week-days only, although from our experience with no great enthusiasm. This is a pity because here is a layout, designed by Willie Park Jr. over heather and gorse, which is an excellent course, demanding an accurate and serious game. On this very classical and so very British course, keep your head down and don't let yourself be distracted by the pretty view over the plain of Oxford. While in the region, spend a good day out in Oxford and visit Blenheim Palace, the castle of the Dukes of Marlborough whose gardens were designed by Capability Brown.

Au début du siècle, des Daimler puis un autobus du club faisaient l'aller-retour jusqu'à la gare d'Henley pour en ramener les joueurs. C'était l'époque héroïque où le service et l'accueil voulaient dire davantage qu'aujourd'hui. Huntercombe est devenu un golf de membres où l'accès en semaine est toléré, mais pas forcément enthousiaste d'après notre expérience. C'est dommage car le tracé de Willie Park Jr en terrain de bruyère est d'excellente qualité, il exige un jeu précis et sérieux, où on ne lèvera la tête que pour admirer de jolis panoramas sur la plaine d'Oxford. Un parcours très classique et terriblement britannique. Dans la région, il ne faudra pas oublier de passer une bonne journée à Oxford et au Blenheim Palace, château des ducs de Marlborough, où les jardins créés par le grand paysagiste Capability Brown vous donneront des idées.

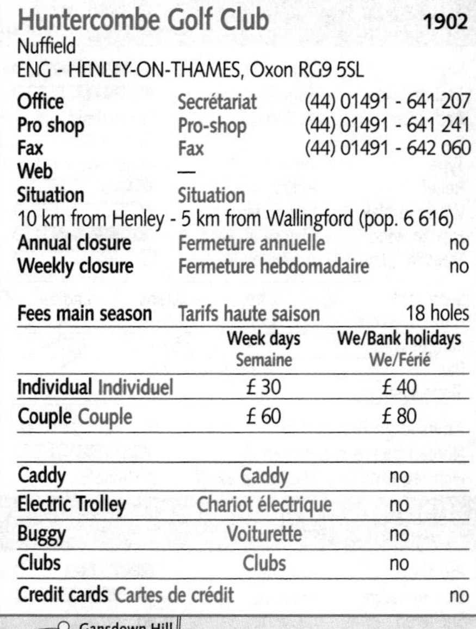

Huntercombe Golf Club — 1902

Nuffield
ENG - HENLEY-ON-THAMES, Oxon RG9 5SL

Office	Secrétariat	(44) 01491 - 641 207
Pro shop	Pro-shop	(44) 01491 - 641 241
Fax	Fax	(44) 01491 - 642 060
Web	—	
Situation	Situation	

10 km from Henley - 5 km from Wallingford (pop. 6 616)

Annual closure	Fermeture annuelle	no
Weekly closure	Fermeture hebdomadaire	no

Fees main season Tarifs haute saison	18 holes	
	Week days Semaine	**We/Bank holidays** We/Férié
Individual Individuel	£ 30	£ 40
Couple Couple	£ 60	£ 80

Caddy	Caddy	no
Electric Trolley	Chariot électrique	no
Buggy	Voiturette	no
Clubs	Clubs	no
Credit cards	Cartes de crédit	no

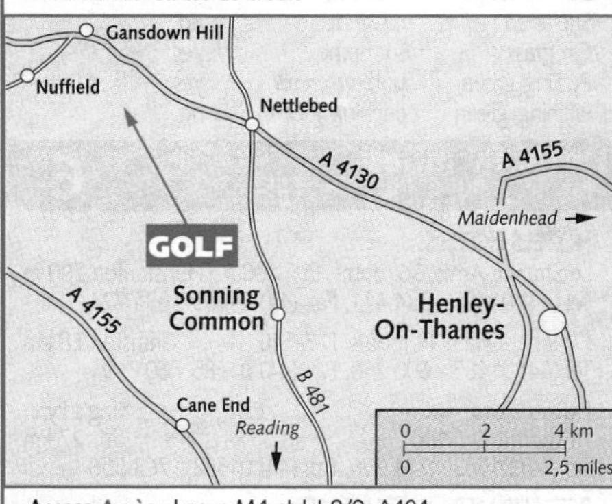

Access Accès : Leave M4 at Jct 8/9, A404, A4130 through Henley, → Oxford. Clubhouse on the left after 10 km (6 m.)
Map 8 on page 498 Carte 8 Page 498

Golf course PARCOURS — 14/20

Site	Site	
Maintenance	Entretien	
Architect	Architecte	Willie Park
Type	Type	heathland
Relief	Relief	
Water in play	Eau en jeu	
Exp. to wind	Exposé au vent	
Trees in play	Arbres en jeu	

Scorecard Carte de score	**Chp.** Chp.	**Mens** Mess.	**Ladies** Da.
Length Long.	5671	5498	5115
Par	70	70	72
Slope system	—	—	—

Advised golfing ability Niveau de jeu recommandé — 0 12 24 36
Hcp required Handicap exigé — certificate

Club house & amenities CLUB HOUSE ET ANNEXES — 6/10

Pro shop	Pro-shop	
Driving range	Practice	
Sheltered	couvert	no
On grass	sur herbe	yes
Putting-green	putting-green	yes
Pitching-green	pitching green	no

Hotel facilities ENVIRONNEMENT HOTELIER — 7/10

HOTELS HÔTELS

George, 39 rooms, D £ 100 — Wallingford 5 km
Tel (44) 01491 - 836 665, Fax (44) 01491 - 825 359

Springs, 31 rooms, D £ 140 — North Stoke 5 km
Tel (44) 01491 - 836 687, Fax (44) 01491 - 836 877

Swan Diplomat, 46 rooms, D £ 120 — Streatley 9 km
Tel (44) 01491 - 878 800, Fax (44) 01491 - 872 554

RESTAURANTS RESTAURANT

Leatherne Bottel, Tel (44) 01491 - 872 667 — Goring 8 km
Beetle and Wedge, Tel (44) 01491 - 651 381 — Moulsford 7 km
Springs, Tel (44) 01491 - 836 687 — North Stoke 5 km

ILKLEY

18 | 7 | 6

Welcome to the beautiful region of the Yorkshire Dales, where you can visit the Wharfe valley and Ilkley, Fountains Abbey and the town of Haworth, home to the Brontë sisters. While you are here, don't forget to play this superb course designed by Colt and Mackenzie, where the river Wharfe threatens your card on seven holes. Flat and laid out in picturesque landscape, Ilkley is a charming course where nothing is easy but where nothing is impossible, either. Just avoid the trees, the fairway bunkers and the traps beside the greens. Nothing could be simpler. The green-side bunkers also tend to obstruct the obvious approach route to what are generally excellent putting surfaces. A good score is by no means a certainty here, as there are only two par 5s for the chance of a birdie, five par 3s and a few long par 4s where you can easily waste precious strokes. Mark James, Gordon Brand and Colin Montgomerie are members here, and this course is good enough to make you feel almost envious.

De cette très belle région, on retiendra le Parc National des Vallées du Yorkshire, dont celle de la Wharfe qui irrigue Ilkley, le très bel et très curieux ensemble religieux et aristocratique de Fountains Abbey, et la ville d'Haworth, foyer des soeurs Brontë. Et l'on n'oubliera pas de jouer ce superbe parcours, dessiné par Colt et Mackenzie, où la Wharfe vient en jeu sur sept trous. Plat et dans un paysage pittoresque, c'est un parcours de charme, où rien n'est facile, mais rien impossible. Il suffit d'éviter les arbres, les bunkers de fairway, les bunkers de greens qui ferment l'entrée de greens généralement en condition parfaite. Un bon score n'est pas donné d'avance car il n'y a que deux par 5 pour espérer des birdies, cinq par 3 et quelques longs par 4 pour gaspiller toute ses réserves. Mark James, Gordon Brand et Colin Montgomerie sont membres ici, on n'est pas loin de les envier.

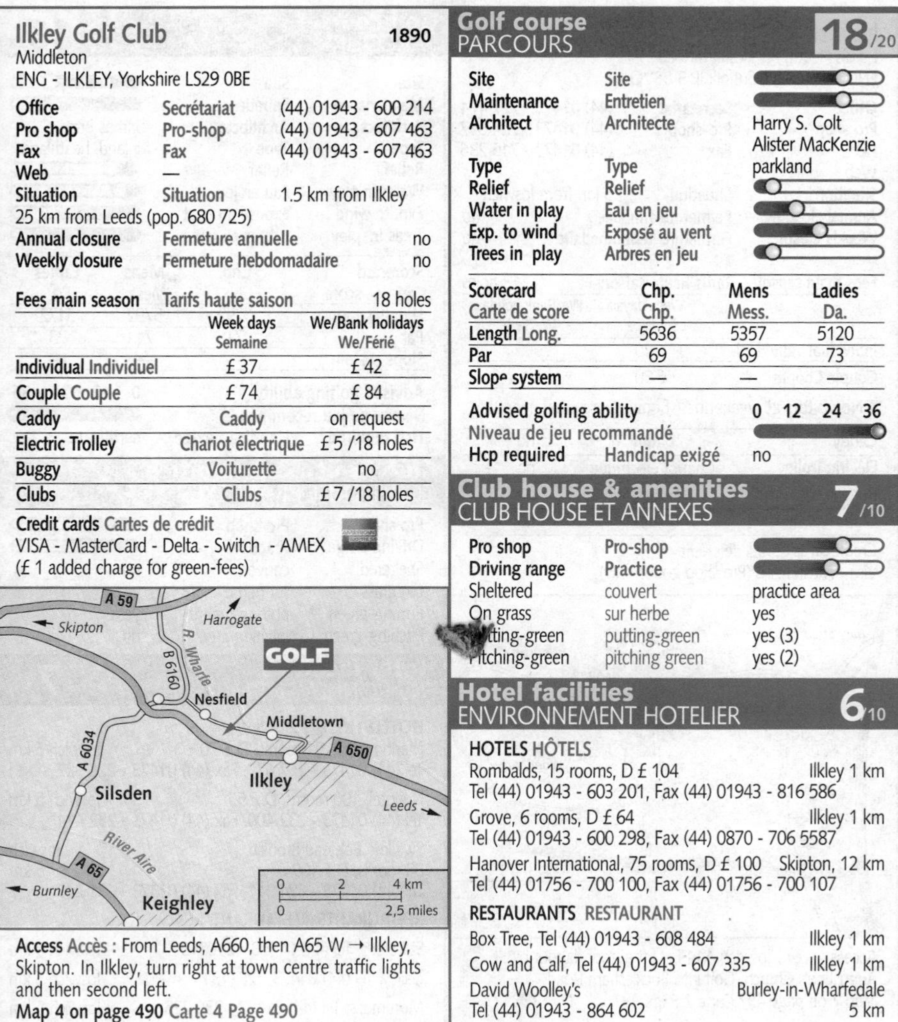

Ilkley Golf Club — 1890

Middleton
ENG - ILKLEY, Yorkshire LS29 0BE

Office	Secrétariat	(44) 01943 - 600 214
Pro shop	Pro-shop	(44) 01943 - 607 463
Fax	Fax	(44) 01943 - 607 463
Web	—	
Situation	Situation	1.5 km from Ilkley

25 km from Leeds (pop. 680 725)

Annual closure	Fermeture annuelle	no
Weekly closure	Fermeture hebdomadaire	no

Fees main season Tarifs haute saison		18 holes
	Week days Semaine	We/Bank holidays We/Férié
Individual Individuel	£ 37	£ 42
Couple Couple	£ 74	£ 84
Caddy	Caddy	on request
Electric Trolley	Chariot électrique	£ 5 /18 holes
Buggy	Voiturette	no
Clubs	Clubs	£ 7 /18 holes

Credit cards Cartes de crédit
VISA - MasterCard - Delta - Switch - AMEX
(£ 1 added charge for green-fees)

Access Accès : From Leeds, A660, then A65 W → Ilkley, Skipton. In Ilkley, turn right at town centre traffic lights and then second left.

Map 4 on page 490 Carte 4 Page 490

Golf course PARCOURS — 18/20

Site	Site	
Maintenance	Entretien	
Architect	Architecte	Harry S. Colt Alister MacKenzie
Type	Type	parkland
Relief	Relief	
Water in play	Eau en jeu	
Exp. to wind	Exposé au vent	
Trees in play	Arbres en jeu	

Scorecard Carte de score	Chp. Chp.	Mens Mess.	Ladies Da.
Length Long.	5636	5357	5120
Par	69	69	73
Slope system	—	—	—

Advised golfing ability Niveau de jeu recommandé: 0 12 24 36

Hcp required Handicap exigé: no

Club house & amenities CLUB HOUSE ET ANNEXES — 7/10

Pro shop	Pro-shop	
Driving range	Practice	
Sheltered	couvert	practice area
On grass	sur herbe	yes
Putting-green	putting-green	yes (3)
Pitching-green	pitching green	yes (2)

Hotel facilities ENVIRONNEMENT HOTELIER — 6/10

HOTELS HÔTELS

Rombalds, 15 rooms, D £ 104 — Ilkley 1 km
Tel (44) 01943 - 603 201, Fax (44) 01943 - 816 586

Grove, 6 rooms, D £ 64 — Ilkley 1 km
Tel (44) 01943 - 600 298, Fax (44) 0870 - 706 5587

Hanover International, 75 rooms, D £ 100 — Skipton, 12 km
Tel (44) 01756 - 700 100, Fax (44) 01756 - 700 107

RESTAURANTS RESTAURANT

Box Tree, Tel (44) 01943 - 608 484 — Ilkley 1 km
Cow and Calf, Tel (44) 01943 - 607 335 — Ilkley 1 km
David Woolley's — Burley-in-Wharfedale
Tel (44) 01943 - 864 602 — 5 km

IPSWICH (PURDIS HEATH) 16 7 7

This is exactly the hide-out you dream of when the wind is too strong to attempt the links course on the coast. It is also the opportunity to discover what is much more than an understudy course, an unthinkable notion for a course designed by James Braid. Even though the great man designed more than a hundred courses, he always succeeded in squeezing the very best out of the land or in creating an extraordinary challenge. Like on the 17th, a par 5 which would be quite harmless if he hadn't placed a few pot bunkers to make you wonder about the length of your second shot. If you decide to lay up, you have a tough third shot on your hands. Then there is the 4th hole where the green is hidden in a vale; if your drive is not just perfect, you have a blind second shot to contend with. Just a few examples to prove that nothing is given away here, and that "old" courses and "old" architects can still teach today's over-confident youngsters a thing or two.

C'est exactement le refuge dont on rêve quand le vent souffle trop pour aller sur les links de la côte. Et c'est l'occasion de découvrir ce qui est bien mieux qu'une doublure. Dire qu'il a été dessiné par James Braid devrait être une signature suffisante. Même s'il a fait des centaines de parcours, il a toujours su tirer du terrain la quintessence, ou alors créer des défis inédits. Comme au 17, un par 5 qui serait anodin s'il n'avait placé quelques pot bunkers pour que l'on s'interroge sur la longueur du second coup : si on décide de rester court, le troisième coup ne sera pas facile ! Prenons le 4, un énorme par 4 où le green est caché dans un vallon : si le drive n'est pas exceptionnel, le second coup est aveugle. De rares exemples pour dire que rien n'est ici donné, que les "vieux" architectes et les "vieux" parcours peuvent encore donner des leçons aux jeunes stars trop sûres d'elles.

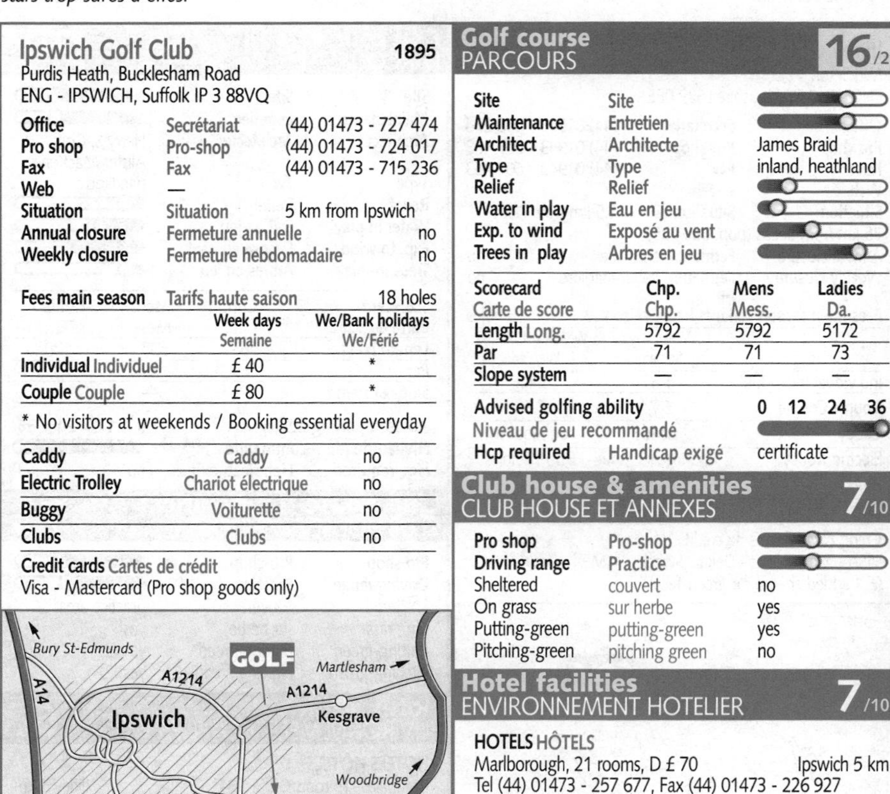

Ipswich Golf Club — 1895

Purdis Heath, Bucklesham Road
ENG - IPSWICH, Suffolk IP 3 88VQ

Office	Secrétariat	(44) 01473 - 727 474
Pro shop	Pro-shop	(44) 01473 - 724 017
Fax	Fax	(44) 01473 - 715 236
Web	—	
Situation	Situation	5 km from Ipswich
Annual closure	Fermeture annuelle	no
Weekly closure	Fermeture hebdomadaire	no

Fees main season Tarifs haute saison	18 holes	
	Week days Semaine	**We/Bank holidays** We/Férié
Individual Individuel	£ 40	*
Couple Couple	£ 80	*

* No visitors at weekends / Booking essential everyday

Caddy	Caddy	no
Electric Trolley	Chariot électrique	no
Buggy	Voiturette	no
Clubs	Clubs	no

Credit cards Cartes de crédit
Visa - Mastercard (Pro shop goods only)

Access Accès : Ipswich A14 E. Left at roundabout by St Augustine's Church. Golf into Bucklesham Road
Map 7 on page 497 Carte 7 Page 497

Golf course PARCOURS 16/20

Site	Site	
Maintenance	Entretien	
Architect	Architecte	James Braid
Type	Type	inland, heathland
Relief	Relief	
Water in play	Eau en jeu	
Exp. to wind	Exposé au vent	
Trees in play	Arbres en jeu	

Scorecard Carte de score	**Chp.** Chp.	**Mens** Mess.	**Ladies** Da.
Length Long.	5792	5792	5172
Par	71	71	73
Slope system	—	—	—

Advised golfing ability Niveau de jeu recommandé — 0 12 24 36
Hcp required Handicap exigé — certificate

Club house & amenities CLUB HOUSE ET ANNEXES 7/10

Pro shop	Pro-shop	
Driving range	Practice	
Sheltered	couvert	no
On grass	sur herbe	yes
Putting-green	putting-green	yes
Pitching-green	pitching green	no

Hotel facilities ENVIRONNEMENT HOTELIER 7/10

HOTELS HÔTELS

Marlborough, 21 rooms, D £ 70 — Ipswich 5 km
Tel (44) 01473 - 257 677, Fax (44) 01473 - 226 927

Novotel, 100 rooms, D £ 55 — Ipswich 5 km
Tel (44) 01473 - 232 400, Fax (44) 01473 - 232 414

Swallow Belstead Brook — Ipswich 5 km
88 rooms, D £ 109
Tel (44) 01473 - 684 241, Fax (44) 01473 - 681 249

RESTAURANTS RESTAURANT

St Peter's, Tel (44) 01473 - 210810 — Ipswich 5 km
Galley, Tel (44) 01473 - 281131 — Ipswich 5 km
Mortimer's, Tel (44) 01473 - 230 225 — Ipswich 5 km

ISLE OF PURBECK

16 | 7 | 6

This is the kind of course where the superb views add a point or two to the artistic score. In the distance are the busy south-coast resorts of Poole and Bournemouth, and the Solent. Here you have all the peace and quiet of superb country landscape on the edge of a natural reserve for plant and bird-lovers. The broom and heather add to the decoration and to the problems awaiting players who are wayward or blown off line by the wind. Design-wise this is not exactly a links course but it does require the same skills of flighting and rolling the ball, of trying to outwit and outfox the course. A pretty site for a long weekend with a very pleasant clubhouse, warm welcome, excellent food and a classy additional 9 hole course where you can leave the less gifted members of the family to discover the joys of golf.

C'est le genre de parcours où la qualité des vues donne un petit point de "note artistique" en plus. Au loin, les stations très fréquentées de Poole, Bournemouth, le Solent. Ici, c'est le calme dans un superbe paysage de campagne, en bordure d'une réserve naturelle pour amoureux de plantes et d'oiseaux. Les genêts et la bruyère apportent un élément de décor, mais pas mal aussi d'empoisonnement aux joueurs peu précis, ou emportés par le vent. Ce parcours n'est pas exactement un links dans son style d'architecture, mais il demande les mêmes qualités, savoir travailler la balle, la faire rouler comme il faut, avoir aussi un peu de ruse, être en quelque sorte plus intelligent que le parcours. Un joli lieu de long week-end, avec un Clubhouse très agréable, un accueil chaleureux, une bonne cuisine et un 9 trous supplémentaire de bonne facture pour que les joueurs les moins compétents de la famille aillent s'amuser, ou pour les aider à s'aguerrir.

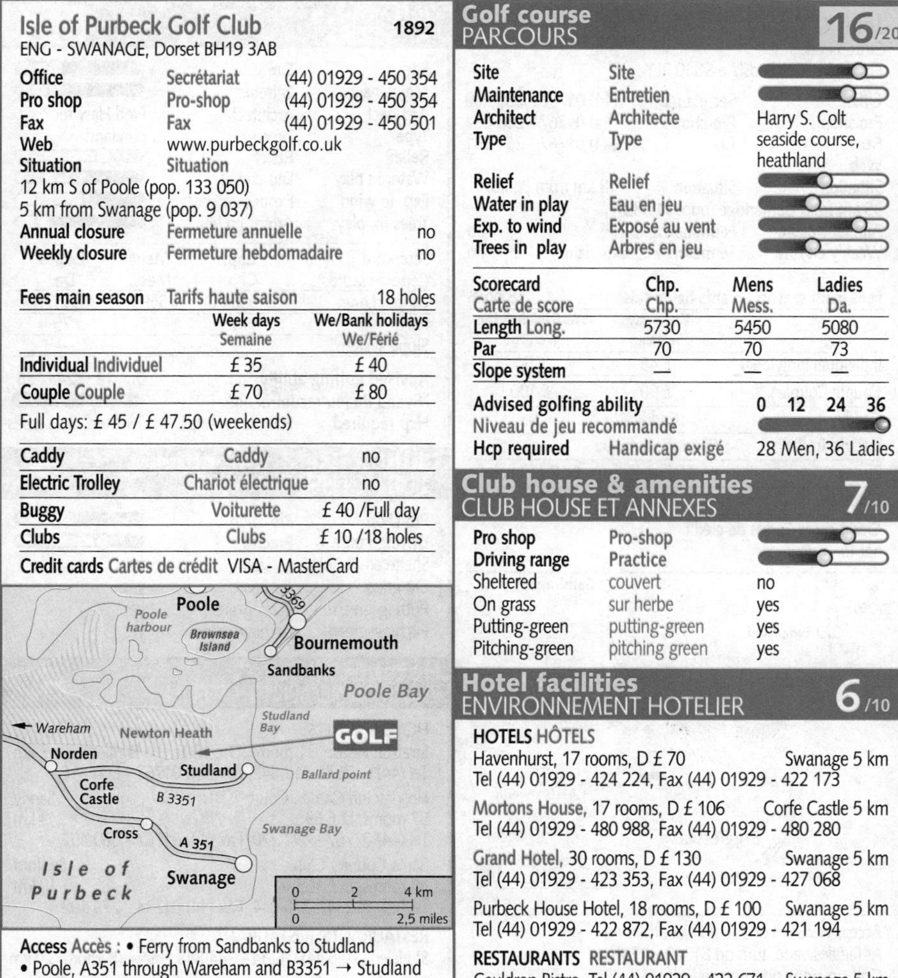

Isle of Purbeck Golf Club **1892**
ENG - SWANAGE, Dorset BH19 3AB

Office	Secrétariat	(44) 01929 - 450 354
Pro shop	Pro-shop	(44) 01929 - 450 354
Fax	Fax	(44) 01929 - 450 501
Web	www.purbeckgolf.co.uk	
Situation	Situation	

12 km S of Poole (pop. 133 050)
5 km from Swanage (pop. 9 037)

Annual closure	Fermeture annuelle	no
Weekly closure	Fermeture hebdomadaire	no

Fees main season Tarifs haute saison	18 holes	
	Week days Semaine	**We/Bank holidays** We/Férié
Individual Individuel	£ 35	£ 40
Couple Couple	£ 70	£ 80

Full days: £ 45 / £ 47.50 (weekends)

Caddy	Caddy	no
Electric Trolley	Chariot électrique	no
Buggy	Voiturette	£ 40 /Full day
Clubs	Clubs	£ 10 /18 holes

Credit cards Cartes de crédit VISA - MasterCard

Access Accès : • Ferry from Sandbanks to Studland
• Poole, A351 through Wareham and B3351 → Studland
Map 6 on page 495 Carte 6 Page 495

Golf course PARCOURS 16/20

Site	Site	
Maintenance	Entretien	
Architect	Architecte	Harry S. Colt
Type	Type	seaside course, heathland
Relief	Relief	
Water in play	Eau en jeu	
Exp. to wind	Exposé au vent	
Trees in play	Arbres en jeu	

Scorecard Carte de score	**Chp.** Chp.	**Mens** Mess.	**Ladies** Da.
Length Long.	5730	5450	5080
Par	70	70	73
Slope system	—	—	—

Advised golfing ability 0 12 24 36
Niveau de jeu recommandé
Hcp required Handicap exigé 28 Men, 36 Ladies

Club house & amenities CLUB HOUSE ET ANNEXES 7/10

Pro shop	Pro-shop	
Driving range	Practice	
Sheltered	couvert	no
On grass	sur herbe	yes
Putting-green	putting-green	yes
Pitching-green	pitching green	yes

Hotel facilities ENVIRONNEMENT HOTELIER 6/10

HOTELS HÔTELS
Havenhurst, 17 rooms, D £ 70 — Swanage 5 km
Tel (44) 01929 - 424 224, Fax (44) 01929 - 422 173

Mortons House, 17 rooms, D £ 106 — Corfe Castle 5 km
Tel (44) 01929 - 480 988, Fax (44) 01929 - 480 280

Grand Hotel, 30 rooms, D £ 130 — Swanage 5 km
Tel (44) 01929 - 423 353, Fax (44) 01929 - 427 068

Purbeck House Hotel, 18 rooms, D £ 100 — Swanage 5 km
Tel (44) 01929 - 422 872, Fax (44) 01929 - 421 194

RESTAURANTS RESTAURANT
Cauldron Bistro, Tel (44) 01929 - 422 671 — Swanage 5 km
The Galley, Tel (44) 01929 - 427 299 — Swanage 5 km

JOHN O'GAUNT

16 | 7 | 6

A great club, as British as you could ever imagine, with two 18-hole courses and a huge and very comfortable clubhouse with wonderful old-style architecture. John O'Gaunt is close enough to London to be within easy reach but far enough not to be too busy, at least during the week. The trees are magnificent and give the course a very park-like appearance, adding style to what is a very discreet layout from Hawtree, at least for the main course. A classic layout which calls for no particular comment but which gives an impression of balance and fulfilment when you play it, especially for lovers of traditional courses that seem to have been around for ever. The other course, Carthagena, opened in 1981, is more of a heatherland course.

Un grand club bien britannique comme on l'imagine, avec deux parcours de 18 trous et un vaste Clubhouse à l'architecture ancienne digne d'une bonne série policière télévisée, et parfaitement confortable. Le club de John O'Gaunt est assez proche de Londres pour être facilement accessible, mais assez loin pour ne pas être trop encombré, en tout cas en semaine. Les arbres y sont magnifiques, donnant une allure de parc, qui convient bien à l'esthétique assez sobre de Fred Hawtree, pour le parcours principal en tout cas. Très classique, c'est le genre de réalisation qui n'appelle pas de commentaires particuliers, mais donne une impression d'équilibre et de plénitude quand on le joue. Pour amoureux des bons parcours traditionnels, qui donnent l'impression d'être là depuis toujours. L'autre parcours, Carthagena, inauguré en 1981, est plus proche d'un style de terre de bruyère.

John O'Gaunt Golf Club — 1948

Sutton Park
ENG - SANDY, Bedshire SG19 2LY

Office	Secrétariat	(44) 01767 - 260 360
Pro shop	Pro-shop	(44) 01767 - 260 094
Fax	Fax	(44) 01767 - 261 381
Web	—	
Situation	Situation	18 km from Bedford

35 km from Cambridge (pop. 91 933)

Annual closure	Fermeture annuelle	no
Weekly closure	Fermeture hebdomadaire	no

Fees main season Tarifs haute saison — 18 holes

	Week days Semaine	We/Bank holidays We/Férié
Individual Individuel	£ 45	£ 50
Couple Couple	£ 90	£ 100
Caddy Caddy		no
Electric Trolley Chariot électrique		no
Buggy Voiturette		£ 18 /18 holes
Clubs Clubs		no

Credit cards Cartes de crédit
not for greenfees

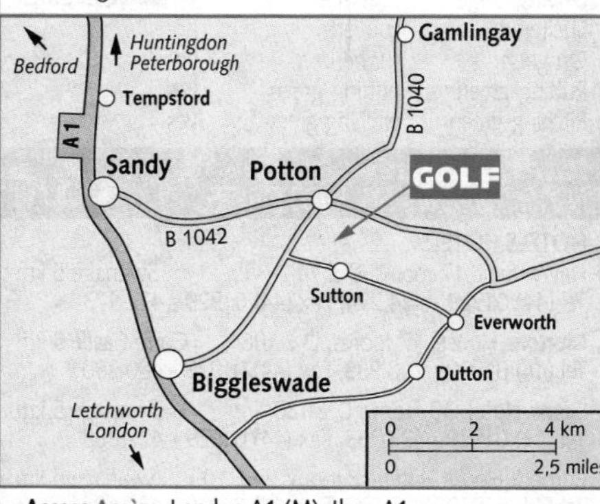

Access Accès : London A1 (M), then A1.
At Biggleswade, turn on B1040 → Potton.
Golf on right side before Potton.
Map 7 on page 496 Carte 7 Page 496

Golf course — PARCOURS — 16/20

Site	Site	
Maintenance	Entretien	
Architect	Architecte	Fred Hawtree
Type	Type	parkland
Relief	Relief	
Water in play	Eau en jeu	
Exp. to wind	Exposé au vent	
Trees in play	Arbres en jeu	

Scorecard Carte de score	Chp. Chp.	Mens Mess.	Ladies Da.
Length Long.	5861	5593	5112
Par	71	71	75
Slope system	—	—	—

Advised golfing ability Niveau de jeu recommandé — 0 12 24 36

Hcp required Handicap exigé — 28 Men, 36 Ladies

Club house & amenities — CLUB HOUSE ET ANNEXES — 7/10

Pro shop	Pro-shop	
Driving range	Practice	
Sheltered	couvert	no
On grass	sur herbe	yes
Putting-green	putting-green	yes
Pitching-green	pitching green	yes

Hotel facilities — ENVIRONNEMENT HOTELIER — 6/10

HOTELS HÔTELS

Stratton House, 31 rooms, D £ 100 — Biggleswade 3 km
Tel (44) 01767 - 312 442, Fax (44) 01767 - 600 416

Holiday Inn Garden Court — Sandy
57 rooms, D £ 69 — 3 km
Tel (44) 01767 - 692 220, Fax (44) 01767 - 680 452

Barns Country Club — Bedford
48 rooms, D £ 155 — 18 km
Tel (44) 01234 - 270 044, Fax (44) 01234 - 273 102

RESTAURANTS RESTAURANT

St Helena, Tel (44) 01234 - 344 848 Elstow (Bedford) 20 km

Barns Country Club, — Bedford
Tel (44) 01767 - 270 044 — 16 km

LA MOYE 17 7 8

Designed by James Braid, La Moye has been considerably lengthened and altered to become the great tournament course of the Channel Islands and long-time home to the Jersey Open. Laid out over the dunes and rolling mounds on the promontory overlooking St Ouen's Bay, it provides an outstanding view and a constantly entertaining challenge. Length and wind together don't make reaching the greens any easier, some of which are blind, all of which are well protected by bunkers or sand-hills. In this setting, only a sharp short game can help save a normal score. If you don't understand how to roll the ball up to the pin ask the pro or some of the local players. During the long evenings of May and early Summer, there are few places on earth where you can get so much pleasure out of playing golf.... no matter how well or badly you are playing.

Dessiné par James Braid, La Moye a été depuis considérablement allongé et modifié, et représente le grand parcours de championnat des iles anglo-normandes, où s'est longtemps disputé le Jersey Open. Tracé sur les dunes et ondulations du promontoire dominant St Ouen's Bay, il offre un panorama exceptionnel et constitue un défi constamment intéressant. Cette longueur combinée au vent ne facilite pas l'accès aux greens, dont certains sont presque aveugles, et tous bien protégés par des bunkers ou les ondulations du terrain. Dans ces conditions, la qualité du petit jeu peut seule garantir un score correct, mais si on n'arrive pas à comprendre comment faire rouler la balle jusqu'au drapeau, il faut demander au pro ou aux joueurs locaux ! Au cours des longues fins de journée du mois de mai jusqu'au début de l'été, il y a peu d'endroits où l'on puisse éprouver autant de plaisir à jouer au golf. Bien ou mal, peu importe.

La Moye Golf Club — 1902

La Moye
ENG - ST BRELADE, Jersey JE3 8GQ

Office	Secrétariat	(44) 01534 - 743 401
Pro shop	Pro-shop	(44) 01534 - 747 166
Fax	Fax	(44) 01534 - 747 289
Web	—	
Situation	Situation	

10 km W of St Helier (pop. 28 123) - 4 km W of St Aubin

Annual closure	Fermeture annuelle	no
Weekly closure	Fermeture hebdomadaire	no

Fees main season / Tarifs haute saison	Week days / Semaine	We/Bank holidays / We/Férié
18 holes		
Individual Individuel	£ 45	£ 50 *
Couple Couple	£ 90	£ 100 *

* only after 2.30 pm during weekends

Caddy	Caddy	no
Electric Trolley	Chariot électrique	£ 5 /18 holes
Buggy	Voiturette	£ 18 /18 holes
Clubs	Clubs	£ 12 /18 holes
Credit cards	Cartes de crédit	VISA - MasterCard

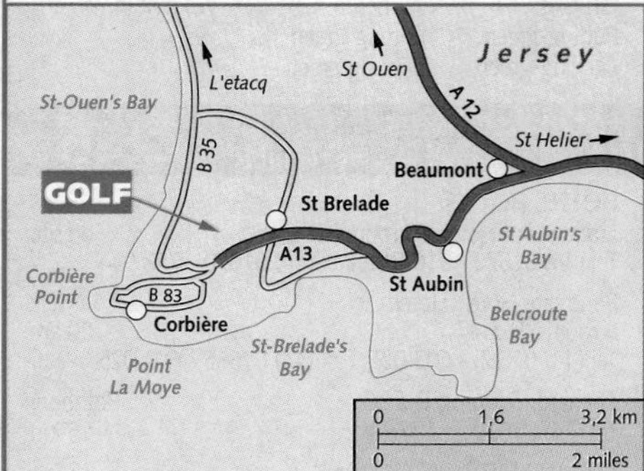

Access Accès : St Helier A1 through St Aubin, then A13 → St Brelade.
Map 9 on page 500 Carte 9 Page 500

Golf course PARCOURS 17/20

Site	Site	
Maintenance	Entretien	
Architect	Architecte	James Braid
Type	Type	seaside course, links
Relief	Relief	
Water in play	Eau en jeu	
Exp. to wind	Exposé au vent	
Trees in play	Arbres en jeu	

Scorecard / Carte de score	Chp. / Chp.	Mens / Mess.	Ladies / Da.
Length Long.	5998	5775	5320
Par	72	72	74
Slope system	—	—	—

Advised golfing ability / Niveau de jeu recommandé: 0 12 24 36

Hcp required — Handicap exigé — 24 Men, 30 Ladies

Club house & amenities CLUB HOUSE ET ANNEXES 7/10

Pro shop	Pro-shop	
Driving range	Practice	
Sheltered	couvert	10 mats
On grass	sur herbe	no
Putting-green	putting-green	yes
Pitching-green	pitching green	yes

Hotel facilities ENVIRONNEMENT HOTELIER 8/10

HOTELS HÔTELS

L'Horizon — St Brelade's Bay 2 km
107 rooms, D £ 200
Tel (44) 01534 - 743 101, Fax (44) 01534 - 746 269

St Brelade's Bay, 80 rooms, D £ 160 — St Brelade's Bay 2 km
Tel (44) 01534 - 746 141, Fax (44) 01534 - 747 278

Sea Crest, 7 rooms, D £130 — Corbière 2 km
Tel (44) 01534 - 746 353, Fax (44) 01534 - 747 316

RESTAURANTS RESTAURANT

The Grill (L'Horizon) — St Brelade's Bay 2 km
Tel (44) 01534 - 743 101

Sea Crest, Tel (44) 01534 - 746 353 — Corbière 2 km

Old Court House Inn, Tel (44) 0134 - 746 433 — St Aubin

LINDEN HALL

17 | 8 | 6

It was the superb hotel of the same name that added this 18-hole course to its estate, which includes a semi-detached pub transformed, quite logically, into a clubhouse. The owners love the end result, and quite rightly so. They wanted a course that was playable by all, an extremely difficult task but one that Jonathan Gaunt managed to achieve. This is a fair course that you can get to grips with right away, as the thick rough and rather frequent hazards (ditches and lakes) only penalise the truly wayward shot. Only two holes really call for high pitching shots, and even then the distances involved are short. Despite the course's tender age, green-keeping is excellent on a site where everything has been done so very professionally. Pleasant to play, challenging from the back tees and set in a very peaceful part of the country where there is a lot to do and see, Linden Hall is one of the excellent surprises to have emerged in recent years.

C'est le superbe hôtel du même nom qui a ajouté ce récent 18 trous à son domaine, en annexant un pub mitoyen transformé (c'était logique) en Clubhouse. Les propriétaires aiment leur réalisation, ils n'ont pas tort. Ils voulaient un parcours jouable par tous, ce qui reste bien le plus difficile, mais Jonathan Gaunt a bien rempli sa tâche. D'abord, c'est un parcours franc, jouable directement, mais le rough épais, comme les assez nombreux obstacles d'eau (fossés et lacs) ne pénalisent que les coups lâchés. Seuls deux trous obligent vraiment à porter la balle, mais ce sont alors de petits coups. L'entretien est excellent en dépit de la jeunesse du parcours, mais les choses ont été faites très professionnellement. Plaisant à jouer, exigeant des départs arrière, situé dans une région très calme avec beaucoup de choses à faire et à voir, c'est une des très bonnes surprises de ces dernières années.

Linden Hall Hotel & Golf Club — 1997

ENG - LONGHORSLEY, Northumberland

Office	Secrétariat	(44) 01670 - 516 611
Pro shop	Pro-shop	(44) 01670 - 788 050
Fax	Fax	(44) 01670 - 788 544
Web	www.lindenhall.co.uk	
Situation	Situation	

10 km from Morpeth - 40 km from Newcastle (pop. 259 541)

Annual closure	Fermeture annuelle	no
Weekly closure	Fermeture hebdomadaire	no

Fees main season Tarifs haute saison	Week days Semaine	We/Bank holidays We/Férié
	18 holes	
Individual Individuel	£ 20	£ 25
Couple Couple	£ 40	£ 50

Full days: £ 33 / £ 40 (week ends)

Caddy	Caddy	no
Electric Trolley	Chariot électrique	no
Buggy	Voiturette	£ 20 /18 holes
Clubs	Clubs	£ 10 /18 holes

Credit cards Cartes de crédit
VISA - Eurocard - MasterCard - DC - JCB

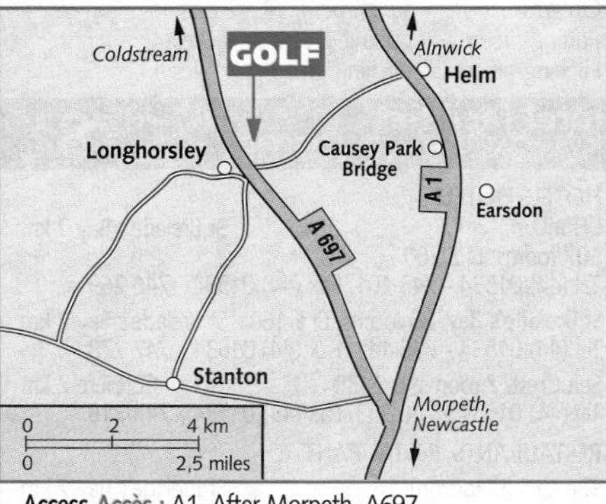

Access Accès : A1. After Morpeth, A697.
Golf at Longhorsley Village.
Map 2 on page 487 Carte 2 Page 487

Golf course — PARCOURS — 17/20

Site	Site	
Maintenance	Entretien	
Architect	Architecte	Jonathan Gaunt
Type	Type	parkland
Relief	Relief	
Water in play	Eau en jeu	
Exp. to wind	Exposé au vent	
Trees in play	Arbres en jeu	

Scorecard Carte de score	**Chp.** Chp.	**Mens** Mess.	**Ladies** Da.
Length Long.	6128	5857	4977
Par	72	72	72
Slope system	—	—	—

Advised golfing ability Niveau de jeu recommandé: 0 12 24 36

Hcp required Handicap exigé: 24 Men, 36 Ladies

Club house & amenities — CLUB HOUSE ET ANNEXES — 8/10

Pro shop	Pro-shop	
Driving range	Practice	
Sheltered	couvert	no
On grass	sur herbe	yes (not in winter)
Putting-green	putting-green	yes
Pitching-green	pitching green	yes

Hotel facilities — ENVIRONNEMENT HOTELIER — 6/10

HOTELS HÔTELS

Linden Hall Hotel, 50 rooms, D £ 150 — on site
Tel (44) 01670 - 516 611, Fax (44) 01670 - 788 544

Bondgate House Hotel — Alnwick
8 rooms, D £ 47 — 20 km
Tel (44) 01665 - 602 025, Fax (44) 01665 - 602 025

Orchard, 6 rooms, D £ 50 — Rothbury
Tel (44) 01669 - 620 684 — 15 km

RESTAURANTS RESTAURANT

Linden Hall Hotel — on site
Tel (44) 01670 - 516 611

LINDRICK

17 | 6 | 6

Lindrick was for a long while the last course where the American Ryder Cup team actually lost. And while it can be considered to be a very short course for the most powerful pros and amateurs, it was once the venue for the British Ladies Open and showed itself to be most suitable for that event. For amateurs, men or women, this is a magnificent test of golf in heather-land shorn of any trees to speak of. It demands a style of play similar to when playing on a links course. Driving is very important, if only to avoid the well-placed bunkers and especially the very tough and highly penalising rough with ball-eating bushes. But the fairways are so wonderfully groomed that you won't want to miss them. Original for its landscape, intelligent for its strategic layout, natural-looking, fun to play and never all that busy, Lindrick is a must.

Lindrick fut longtemps le dernier parcours à avoir vu défaite l'équipe américaine de Ryder Cup. Et s'il peut être considéré comme un parcours très court pour les pros et les amateurs les plus puissants, il fut une fois le théâtre d'un British Open féminin qui le montrait bien adapté aux "proettes". Pour les amateurs, hommes ou femmes, ce magnifique test de golf en pleine terre de bruyère, avec assez peu d'arbres, demande un style de jeu assez analogue à celui des links. Le driving est très important, ne serait-ce que pour éviter les bunkers bien placés, mais surtout un rough très sévère, très pénalisant, avec en supplément des buissons mangeurs de balles. Mais les fairways sont d'une telle qualité que l'on serait assez stupide de les manquer ! Original par son paysage, intelligent par ses aspects stratégiques, naturel dans son aspect, amusant à apprivoiser, et assez peu fréquenté, Lindrick est un "must".

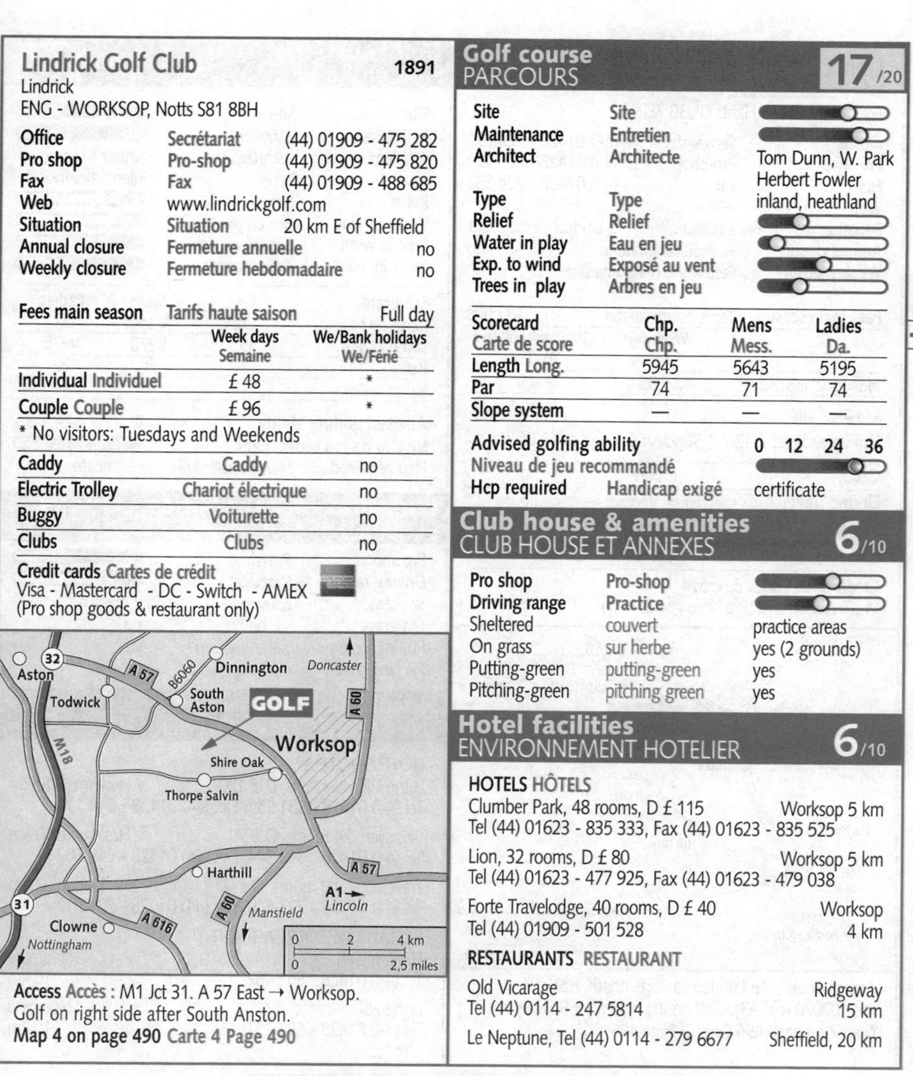

Lindrick Golf Club 1891
Lindrick
ENG - WORKSOP, Notts S81 8BH

Office	Secrétariat	(44) 01909 - 475 282
Pro shop	Pro-shop	(44) 01909 - 475 820
Fax	Fax	(44) 01909 - 488 685
Web	www.lindrickgolf.com	
Situation	Situation	20 km E of Sheffield
Annual closure	Fermeture annuelle	no
Weekly closure	Fermeture hebdomadaire	no

Fees main season Tarifs haute saison	Full day	
	Week days Semaine	We/Bank holidays We/Férié
Individual Individuel	£ 48	*
Couple Couple	£ 96	*

* No visitors: Tuesdays and Weekends

Caddy	Caddy	no
Electric Trolley	Chariot électrique	no
Buggy	Voiturette	no
Clubs	Clubs	no

Credit cards Cartes de crédit
Visa - Mastercard - DC - Switch - AMEX
(Pro shop goods & restaurant only)

Access Accès : M1 Jct 31. A 57 East → Worksop.
Golf on right side after South Anston.
Map 4 on page 490 Carte 4 Page 490

Golf course — PARCOURS — 17/20

Site	Site	
Maintenance	Entretien	
Architect	Architecte	Tom Dunn, W. Park, Herbert Fowler
Type	Type	inland, heathland
Relief	Relief	
Water in play	Eau en jeu	
Exp. to wind	Exposé au vent	
Trees in play	Arbres en jeu	

Scorecard Carte de score	Chp. Chp.	Mens Mess.	Ladies Da.
Length Long.	5945	5643	5195
Par	74	71	74
Slope system	—	—	—

Advised golfing ability 0 12 24 36
Niveau de jeu recommandé
Hcp required Handicap exigé certificate

Club house & amenities — CLUB HOUSE ET ANNEXES — 6/10

Pro shop	Pro-shop	
Driving range	Practice	
Sheltered	couvert	practice areas
On grass	sur herbe	yes (2 grounds)
Putting-green	putting-green	yes
Pitching-green	pitching green	yes

Hotel facilities — ENVIRONNEMENT HOTELIER — 6/10

HOTELS HÔTELS

Clumber Park, 48 rooms, D £ 115 — Worksop 5 km
Tel (44) 01623 - 835 333, Fax (44) 01623 - 835 525

Lion, 32 rooms, D £ 80 — Worksop 5 km
Tel (44) 01623 - 477 925, Fax (44) 01623 - 479 038

Forte Travelodge, 40 rooms, D £ 40 — Worksop 4 km
Tel (44) 01909 - 501 528

RESTAURANTS RESTAURANT

Old Vicarage — Ridgeway 15 km
Tel (44) 0114 - 247 5814

Le Neptune, Tel (44) 0114 - 279 6677 — Sheffield, 20 km

585

LIPHOOK

16 | 7 | 6

Hampshire is one of those counties whose villages, landscape and greenery seem to symbolise the English countryside as seen in films. The drive to Liphook and the hospitality awaiting visitors in the clubhouse are this and more. The designer has bent the course to match the landscape instead of the opposite, maybe because the excavators in service in the 1920s were not up to moving much earth. Liphook is a gem of a course and the hazards penalise absolutely every mis-hit shot. As they are clearly visible, the sanction comes as no surprise. The charming landscape might make you think this to be a kindly course, but nothing could be further from the truth. You need to flight the ball and play with care or else resign yourself to trying to hack your ball out of the heather. Add to this slick subtle greens and you have the full picture: Liphook is an exciting course whose visual discretion cleverly hides the difficulties in store.

Le Hampshire est l'une de ces régions qui symbolisent par leurs villages, leur paysage, leur végétation ce qu'est la campagne anglaise, comme dans les films. L'arrivée au golf de Liphook, comme l'hospitalité du club house vont dans le même sens. L'architecte a plié le parcours au paysage au lieu du contraire, mais il faut bien dire que, dans les années 20, les engins de terrassement ne permettaient pas de bouger beaucoup de terre. Liphook est un petit joyau, et les obstacles pénalisent absolument tous les coups manqués. Comme ils sont bien visibles, on ne saurait en être surpris. Le charme du paysage peut faire penser à un parcours aimable. Ce n'est pas le cas, il faut savoir travailler la balle, jouer avec prudence, ou alors accepter de devoir sortir ses balles de la bruyère. Si l'on ajoute la subtilité des greens, on aura compris : c'est un parcours passionnant, dont la discrétion visuelle cache bien les difficultés.

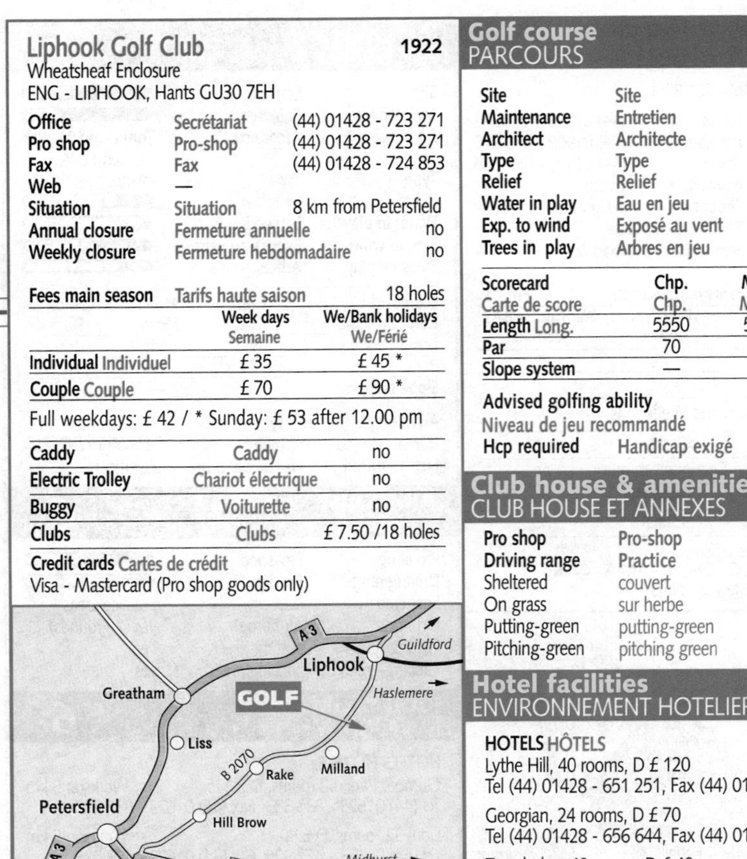

Liphook Golf Club — 1922

Wheatsheaf Enclosure
ENG - LIPHOOK, Hants GU30 7EH

Office	Secrétariat	(44) 01428 - 723 271
Pro shop	Pro-shop	(44) 01428 - 723 271
Fax	Fax	(44) 01428 - 724 853
Web	—	
Situation	Situation	8 km from Petersfield
Annual closure	Fermeture annuelle	no
Weekly closure	Fermeture hebdomadaire	no

Fees main season Tarifs haute saison	18 holes	
	Week days Semaine	**We/Bank holidays** We/Férié
Individual Individuel	£ 35	£ 45 *
Couple Couple	£ 70	£ 90 *

Full weekdays: £ 42 / * Sunday: £ 53 after 12.00 pm

Caddy	Caddy	no
Electric Trolley	Chariot électrique	no
Buggy	Voiturette	no
Clubs	Clubs	£ 7.50 /18 holes

Credit cards Cartes de crédit
Visa - Mastercard (Pro shop goods only)

Access Accès : A3 London to Portsmouth. B2131, then B2070 (old A3). Golf on the right after Railway line
Map 7 on page 496 Carte 7 Page 496

Golf course PARCOURS — 16/20

Site	Site	
Maintenance	Entretien	
Architect	Architecte	Arthur Croome
Type	Type	inland, heathland
Relief	Relief	
Water in play	Eau en jeu	
Exp. to wind	Exposé au vent	
Trees in play	Arbres en jeu	

Scorecard Carte de score	**Chp.** Chp.	**Mens** Mess.	**Ladies** Da.
Length Long.	5550	5270	4975
Par	70	70	72
Slope system	—	—	—

Advised golfing ability Niveau de jeu recommandé — 0 12 24 36
Hcp required Handicap exigé — certificate

Club house & amenities CLUB HOUSE ET ANNEXES — 7/10

Pro shop	Pro-shop	
Driving range	Practice	
Sheltered	couvert	2 mats
On grass	sur herbe	no
Putting-green	putting-green	yes
Pitching-green	pitching green	yes

Hotel facilities ENVIRONNEMENT HOTELIER — 6/10

HOTELS HÔTELS

Lythe Hill, 40 rooms, D £ 120 — Haslemere 10 km
Tel (44) 01428 - 651 251, Fax (44) 01428 - 644 131

Georgian, 24 rooms, D £ 70 — Haslemere 10 km
Tel (44) 01428 - 656 644, Fax (44) 01428 - 645 600

Travelodge, 40 rooms, D £ 40 — Liphook 2 km
Tel (44) 01428 - 727 619, Fax (44) 01428 - 727 619

RESTAURANTS RESTAURANT

Fleur de Sel — Haslemere 10 km
Tel (44) 01428 - 651 462

Lythe Hill — Haslemere 10 km
Tel (44) 01428 - 651 251

LITTLE ASTON

17 | 7 | 8

Always a very traditional club, Little Aston has gradually opened its doors to outside players, who can play the course on weekdays providing they have a decent handicap. Get yours down if need be, because it would be a pity not to play this gem of a course, the quintessence of British parkland golf where just treading the grass is an experience in itself. Now nearly 100 years old, Little Aston is as young as ever, and for the people who may think it a little on the short side, well, perhaps they should let their clubs do the talking. Whatever, nobody can complain about hidden hazards. They are all clearly in view and so traditionally well-placed as to be distinctly unsettling: trees, in play but never excessively so, a hundred or so fairway and greenside bunkers designed to make escapes from sand more than just a mere formality, and two water hazards just to remind you that there is water in this part of the world. Naturally not all the holes are of the same standard, but there is no weak link that could ever undermine the whole layout. Here you live and breathe a sense of measure and sheer quality.

C'était un club très traditionnel, qui s'est peu à peu ouvert aux joueurs extérieurs durant la semaine, du moment qu'ils ont un handicap "correct". Faites des progrès si nécessaire, car il serait dommage de ne pas connaître ce bijou, quintessence du "parkland" britannique, sur un sol où le seul fait de marcher est déjà un plaisir. A près de cent ans, Little Aston est plus jeune que jamais, et si certains le jugeront un peu court, qu'ils le démontrent avec leurs clubs ! En tout cas, que personne ne se plaigne d'un obstacle caché, ils sont tous bien visibles, et si traditionnellement bien placés qu'ils en sont désarmants : les arbres, en jeu mais jamais oppressants, une centaine de bunkers de fairway et de greens, assez bien formés pour qu'en sortir ne soit pas une formalité, deux obstacles d'eau juste pour dire qu'il y a de l'eau dans ce pays. Bien sûr, tous les trous ne sont pas du même niveau, mais aucun n'est faible, ni ne déparre l'ensemble. On respire ici le sens de la mesure et le goût de la qualité.

Little Aston Golf Club — 1908

Streetly
ENG - SUTTON COLDFIELD, West Midlands B74 3AN

Office	Secrétariat	(44) 0121 - 353 2066
Pro shop	Pro-shop	(44) 0121 - 353 0330
Fax	Fax	(44) 0121 - 580 8387
Web	—	
Situation	Situation	Sutton Coldfield, 10 km
Annual closure	Fermeture annuelle	no
Weekly closure	Fermeture hebdomadaire	no

Fees main season Tarifs haute saison	18 holes	
	Week days Semaine	We/Bank holidays We/Férié
Individual Individuel	£ 50	*
Couple Couple	£ 100	*

* No visitors Saturdays & Bank Holidays / Full Weekdays: £ 60

Caddy	Caddy	no
Electric Trolley	Chariot électrique	no
Buggy	Voiturette	no
Clubs	Clubs	no
Credit cards	Cartes de crédit	VISA - MasterCard - DC

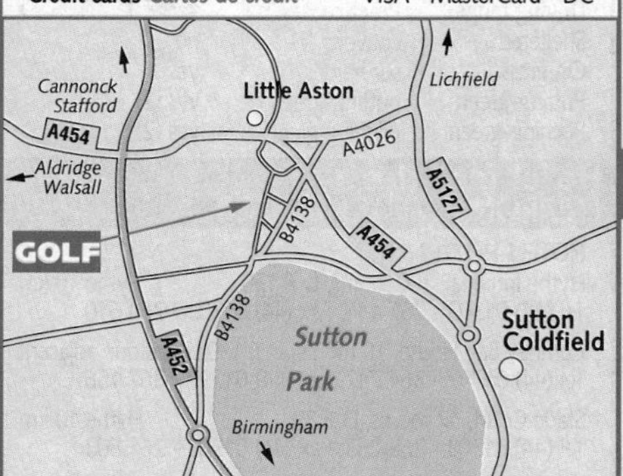

Access Accès : Birmingham A34 (Walsall Road). At Great Barr (Scott Arms pub), turn right at traffic lights → A4041. Go to the fifth roundabout (crossing A452) and take Chester Road (A 452) on the left. 2nd exit through the gates on the righ, Roman Road (private road). Golf on left hand side. **Map 7 on page 496** Carte 7 Page 496

Golf course PARCOURS — 17/20

Site	Site	
Maintenance	Entretien	
Architect	Architecte	Harry Vardon
Type	Type	inland, parkland
Relief	Relief	
Water in play	Eau en jeu	
Exp. to wind	Exposé au vent	
Trees in play	Arbres en jeu	

Scorecard Carte de score	Chp. Chp.	Mens Mess.	Ladies Da.
Length Long.	6003	5758	5179
Par	73	72	74
Slope system	—	—	—

Advised golfing ability Niveau de jeu recommandé: 0 12 24 36

Hcp required Handicap exigé: 24 Men, 36 Ladies

Club house & amenities CLUB HOUSE ET ANNEXES — 7/10

Pro shop	Pro-shop	
Driving range	Practice	
Sheltered	couvert	practice area only
On grass	sur herbe	yes
Putting-green	putting-green	yes
Pitching-green	pitching green	yes

Hotel facilities ENVIRONNEMENT HOTELIER — 8/10

HOTELS HÔTELS

Fairlawns, 50 rooms, D £ 105 — Aldridge c
Tel (44) 01922 - 455 122, Fax (44) 01922 - 743 210

Moor Hall, 74 rooms, D £ 180 — Sutton Coldfield 6 km
Tel (44) 0121 - 308 3751, Fax (44) 0121 - 308 8974

New Hall, 60 rooms, D £ 190 — Sutton Coldfield 7 km
Tel (44) 0121 - 378 2442, Fax (44) 0121 - 378 4637

Jonathan's, 48 rooms, D £ 170 — Brimingham 15 km
Tel (44) 0121 - 429 3757, Fax (44) 0121 - 434 3107

RESTAURANTS RESTAURANT

Sir Edward Elgar's, Tel (44) 0121 - 452 1144 — Birmingham
Gilmore, Tel (44) 0121 - 233 3655 — Hockley, 10 km

LITTLESTONE

14 | 6 | 5

Having failed to get on the very private Rye course, make it along to Littlestone. It is not in the same league, but not to be sniffed at, either. Without ever being boring, the first seven holes are pretty ordinary, at least from a visual viewpoint. It is only after the 8th hole that the landscape really comes to life. And while you won't see any really impressive dunes, you are rarely on the flat with your feet level with your ball. Naturally the wind plays a very important role, especially since it is virtually never blowing in the same direction from the 7th to the 15th holes. The same goes for the last three holes, but here you have other things to worry about. This is a devilishly tough finish to the course, starting with a par 4 and a horrendous second shot, followed by a par 3 where you are likely to need more than one tee shot, and finally a par 5 dotted with bunkers. This is an excellent holiday course in summer. For the rest of the year you will need to shape all kinds of different shots.

Faute de pouvoir aller jouer Rye, aux portes fermement closes, Littlestone est loin d'être négligeable, même s'il n'est pas dans la même catégorie. Les sept premiers trous commencent de manière assez banale, du moins visuellement, même si les architectes ont réussi à ne jamais faire ennuyeux, mais le paysage s'anime à partir du 8. Et si l'on ne verra pas de dunes très impressionnantes, on se retrouve rarement les pieds au même niveau que la balle. Le vent joue un rôle très important, d'autant plus qu'il n'est jamais dans le même sens du 7 au 15. Il sera le même dans les trois derniers trous, mais ce finale est assez diabolique avec un par 4 où le second coup est terrible, puis un par 3 où le coup de départ risque d'être suivi de bien d'autres, et enfin un par 5 constellé de bunkers. En été, c'est un excellent parcours de vacances. Le reste de l'année, il faut savoir fabriquer tous les coups de golf.

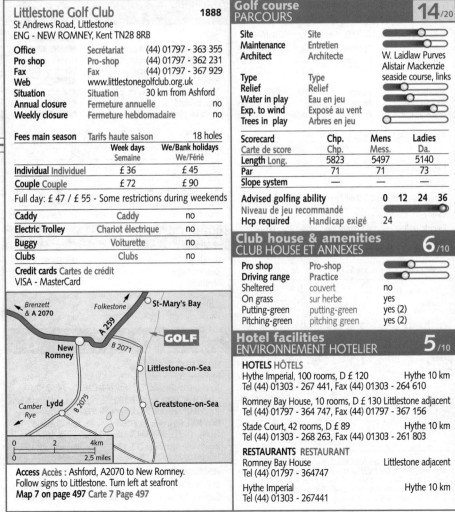

Littlestone Golf Club — 1888

St Andrews Road, Littlestone
ENG - NEW ROMNEY, Kent TN28 8RB

Office	Secrétariat	(44) 01797 - 363 355
Pro shop	Pro-shop	(44) 01797 - 362 231
Fax	Fax	(44) 01797 - 367 929
Web	www.littlestonegolfclub.org.uk	
Situation	Situation	30 km from Ashford
Annual closure	Fermeture annuelle	no
Weekly closure	Fermeture hebdomadaire	no

Fees main season Tarifs haute saison	18 holes	
	Week days Semaine	**We/Bank holidays** We/Férié
Individual Individuel	£ 36	£ 45
Couple Couple	£ 72	£ 90

Full day: £ 47 / £ 55 - Some restrictions during weekends

Caddy	Caddy	no
Electric Trolley	Chariot électrique	no
Buggy	Voiturette	no
Clubs	Clubs	no

Credit cards Cartes de crédit
VISA - MasterCard

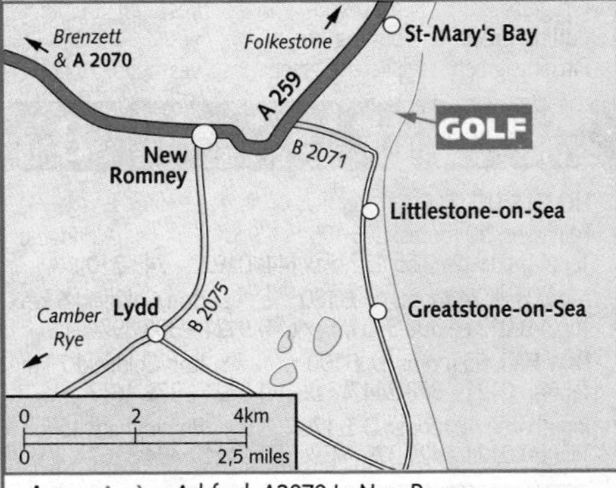

Access Accès : Ashford, A2070 to New Romney. Follow signs to Littlestone. Turn left at seafront
Map 7 on page 497 Carte 7 Page 497

Golf course — PARCOURS — 14/20

Site	Site	
Maintenance	Entretien	
Architect	Architecte	W. Laidlaw Purves Alistair Mackenzie
Type	Type	seaside course, links
Relief	Relief	
Water in play	Eau en jeu	
Exp. to wind	Exposé au vent	
Trees in play	Arbres en jeu	

Scorecard Carte de score	**Chp.** Chp.	**Mens** Mess.	**Ladies** Da.
Length Long.	5823	5497	5140
Par	71	71	73
Slope system	—	—	—

Advised golfing ability — 0 12 24 36
Niveau de jeu recommandé
Hcp required Handicap exigé 24

Club house & amenities — CLUB HOUSE ET ANNEXES — 6/10

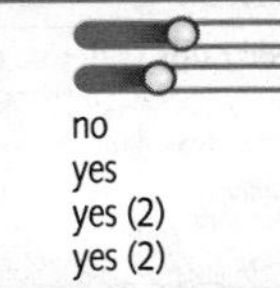

Pro shop	Pro-shop	
Driving range	Practice	
Sheltered	couvert	no
On grass	sur herbe	yes
Putting-green	putting-green	yes (2)
Pitching-green	pitching green	yes (2)

Hotel facilities — ENVIRONNEMENT HOTELIER — 5/10

HOTELS HÔTELS

Hythe Imperial, 100 rooms, D £ 120 — Hythe 10 km
Tel (44) 01303 - 267 441, Fax (44) 01303 - 264 610

Romney Bay House, 10 rooms, D £ 130 — Littlestone adjacent
Tel (44) 01797 - 364 747, Fax (44) 01797 - 367 156

Stade Court, 42 rooms, D £ 89 — Hythe 10 km
Tel (44) 01303 - 268 263, Fax (44) 01303 - 261 803

RESTAURANTS RESTAURANT

Romney Bay House — Littlestone adjacent
Tel (44) 01797 - 364747

Hythe Imperial — Hythe 10 km
Tel (44) 01303 - 267441

LONDON GOLF CLUB International | 15 | 9 | 7

These days, when you want to build a fashionable layout you call in someone like Jack Nicklaus to design it. This is what happened with the "Heritage Course", for members only, but this "International" course, open to all, was left to his Golden Bear company and architect Ron Kirby. The contrary might have been a more preferable option, opening the best of the two courses to players with the ability to play it, but such golfers can seldom afford this kind of membership. At all events, you are best advised to play here when it is dry, as both layouts get very wet in the rain. Having had our gripe, this course is excellent and still wide open, as the trees are young. The wide fairways give welcome breathing space and the huge greens require shots close to the pin to avoid three-putting. The key to a successful round lies with the second shot; the greens are stoutly guarded with sand-traps, and water hazards on four holes. The layout is certainly imaginative and brimming with design know-how, but with a green-fee this high you expect something exceptional.

Quand on veut faire un ensemble à la mode, on demande à Jack Nicklaus de le dessiner. Il l'a fait effectivement pour le "Heritage Course", réservé aux membres et a laissé à son collaborateur Ron Kirby le tracé de celui-ci, "International", ouvert au public. Il aurait été préférable de faire le contraire et d'ouvrir le meilleur des deux parcours aux joueurs susceptibles de le maîtriser, mais ils ont rarement les moyens d'être membres. On conseillera aussi de jouer ici par temps sec, car ces parcours n'aiment pas l'humidité. Cela dit, le présent parcours est d'excellente qualité, très ouvert car les arbres sont petits, avec des fairways larges permettant de se déchaîner, et de vastes greens où il faut viser le drapeau pour ne pas risquer trois putts : la clef du succès réside ici dans les seconds coups. Les défenses de greens sont solides, avec des bunkers ou des obstacles d'eau sur quatre trous. Certes, le dessin est imaginatif, mais pour un tel montant de green-fee, on attend l'exceptionnel.

The London Golf Club — 1993

South Ash Manor Estate
ENG - ASH, Near SEVENOAKS, Kent TN15 7EN

Office	Secrétariat	(44) 01474 - 879 899
Pro shop	Pro-shop	(44) 01474 - 879 899
Fax	Fax	(44) 01474 - 879 912
Web	—	
Situation	Situation	42 km SE of London
Annual closure	Fermeture annuelle	no
Weekly closure	Fermeture hebdomadaire	no

Fees main season Tarifs haute saison	18 holes	
	Week days Semaine	**We/Bank holidays** We/Férié
Individual Individuel	£ 40 *	£ 70 *
Couple Couple	£ 80 *	£ 140 *

* Visitors must play with a member

Caddy	Caddy	£ 30 /on request
Electric Trolley	Chariot électrique	£ 7
Buggy	Voiturette	£ 18
Clubs	Clubs	£ 30

Credit cards Cartes de crédit
VISA- MasterCard - AMEX

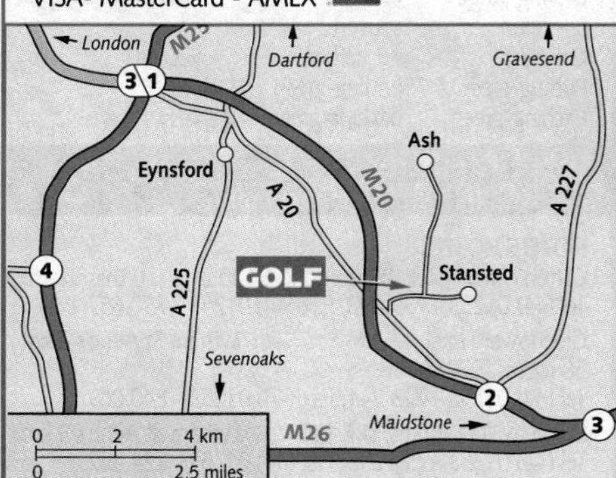

Access Accès : London M20 Exit 2. Turn left → West Kingsdown on A20. 3 km (2 m) on right, sign to Stansted and Golf course. Entrance 100 m on left.
Map 7 on page 497 Carte 7 Page 497

Golf course — PARCOURS — 15/20

Site	Site	
Maintenance	Entretien	
Architect	Architecte	Ron Kirby/Gold. Bear
Type	Type	open country, hilly
Relief	Relief	
Water in play	Eau en jeu	
Exp. to wind	Exposé au vent	
Trees in play	Arbres en jeu	

Scorecard Carte de score	**Chp.** Chp.	**Mens** Mess.	**Ladies** Da.
Length Long.	6305	5917	4945
Par	72	72	72
Slope system	—	—	—

Advised golfing ability 0 12 24 36
Niveau de jeu recommandé
Hcp required Handicap exigé no

Club house & amenities — CLUB HOUSE ET ANNEXES — 9/10

Pro shop	Pro-shop	
Driving range	Practice	
Sheltered	couvert	no
On grass	sur herbe	yes
Putting-green	putting-green	yes
Pitching-green	pitching green	yes

Hotel facilities — ENVIRONNEMENT HOTELIER — 7/10

HOTELS HÔTELS

Brands Hatch Place, 41 rooms, D £ 120 — Fawkham 5 km
Tel (44) 01474 - 872 239, Fax (44) 01474 - 879 652

Brands Hatch Thistle, 121 rooms, D £ 161 — Brands Hatch 5 km
Tel (44) 01474 - 854 900, Fax (44) 01474 - 853 220

Forte Posthouse, 106 rooms, D £ 70 — Wrotham Heath 5 km
Tel (44) 01474 - 883 311, Fax (44) 01474 - 885 850

Anchor & Hope, 6 rooms, D £ 50 (w.breakfast) — Ash 2 km
Tel (44) 01474 - 872 382

RESTAURANTS RESTAURANT

Brands Hatch Place, Tel (44) 01474 - 872 239 — Fawkham
Club's restaurant, Tel (44) 01474 - 879 899 — Club house
Club's restaurant, Tel (44) 01474 - 879 899 — Club house

LYTHAM GREEN DRIVE

15 | 7 | 8

Being close to the popular seaside resort of Blackpool, all the courses in the region are always busy on week-ends and in the Summer. And Summer is the only season when Lytham Green Drive, although not a links course, can be played like one. The rest of the year it plays much longer than the card would suggest as the fairways are heavily grassed. This is, in fact, one of the most immaculately prepared courses we encounter, hence our enthusiasm for the very advanced plans to extend and enlarge a very pretty and very elegant layout. Enjoy the course while it is still playing short, when it looks just great but probably plays a little more easily than you think. Walking the fairways in this sort of manicured park is recreation indeed after the thrills and spills of the coastal links courses.

La proximité de Blackpool, station balnéaire de grand renom et paradis du jeu, assure une importante fréquentation des golfs de la région en week-end et en été. Cette dernière saison est la seule époque où, sans être un links, Lytham Green Drive peut se jouer comme tel. Le reste de l'année, il paraît plus long que la carte ne l'indique, car le gazon est très fourni. Il figure généralement parmi les parcours les plus impeccablement préparés que nous visitions, et l'on ne peut qu'accueillir avec faveur les projets très avancés d'extension et d'agrandissement de ce très joli et très élégant parcours. Profitez des moments où il est encore court, où il est aussi plus séduisant que vraiment difficile : jouer dans un parc aussi manucuré représente une sorte de récréation après avoir connu l'exaltation sur les grands links de la côte.

590

Lytham Green Drive Golf Club — 1922

Ballam Road
ENG - LYTHAM, Lancs FY8 4 LE

Office	Secrétariat	(44) 01253 - 737 390
Pro shop	Pro-shop	(44) 01253 - 737 379
Fax	Fax	(44) 01253 - 731 350
Web	—	
Situation	Situation	10 km from Blackpool
Annual closure	Fermeture annuelle	no
Weekly closure	Fermeture hebdomadaire	no

Fees main season Tarifs haute saison	18 holes	
	Week days / Semaine	We/Bank holidays / We/Férié
Individual Individuel	£ 27	£ 35
Couple Couple	£ 54	£ 70

Full weekdays: £ 35 / Booking essential at weekends (mostly p.m.)

Caddy	Caddy	no
Electric Trolley	Chariot électrique	no
Buggy	Voiturette	no
Clubs	Clubs	£ 10/18 holes
Credit cards	Cartes de crédit	no

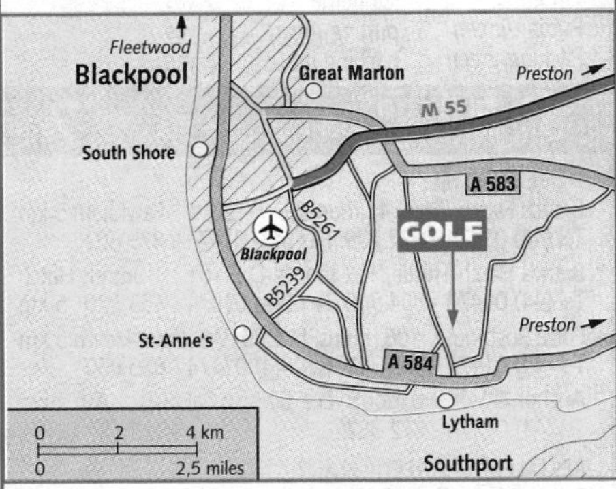

Access Accès : M6, Jct 32, M55 → Blackpool.
Peel Corner lights to Ballam Road. Club on the left.
Map 5 on page 493 Carte 5 Page 493

Golf course — PARCOURS — 15/20

Site	Site	
Maintenance	Entretien	
Architect	Architecte	Sandy Herd, Jim Steer
Type	Type	parkland
Relief	Relief	
Water in play	Eau en jeu	
Exp. to wind	Exposé au vent	
Trees in play	Arbres en jeu	

Scorecard Carte de score	Chp. Chp.	Mens Mess.	Ladies Da.
Length Long.	5543	5390	5057
Par	70	70	73
Slope system	—	—	—

Advised golfing ability / Niveau de jeu recommandé: 0 12 24 36
Hcp required Handicap exigé: 28 Men, 36 Ladies

Club house & amenities — CLUB HOUSE ET ANNEXES — 7/10

Pro shop	Pro-shop	
Driving range	Practice	
Sheltered	couvert	no
On grass	sur herbe	yes
Putting-green	putting-green	yes
Pitching-green	pitching green	yes

Hotel facilities — ENVIRONNEMENT HOTELIER — 8/10

HOTELS HÔTELS

Clifton Arms Hotel, 48 rooms, D £ 120 — Lytham 2 km
Tel (44) 01253 - 739 898, Fax (44) 01253 - 730 657

Glendower Hotel, 58 rooms, D £ 80 — Lytham St Anne's 3 km
Tel (44) 01253 - 723 241, Fax (44) 01253 - 640 069

Dalmeny, 111 rooms, D £ 130 — Lytham St Anne's 3 km
Tel (44) 01253 - 712 236, Fax (44) 01253 - 724 447

RESTAURANTS RESTAURANT

Pleasant Street, Tel (44) 01253 - 788 786 — Lytham 2 km
Tiggy's Italian, Tel (44) 01253 - 714 714 — Lytham 2 km
The Brasserie, Tel (44) 01253 - 794 000 — Lytham 3 km

MANCHESTER

16 | 7 | 7

Very close to the city of Manchester, this fine course is easy to play during the week, particularly for meetings where business and extreme pleasure mix very well indeed. Practice facilities are excellent, which is not always the case in Britain. The layout is not very long but the tee-boxes are well placed to provide each category of player with a good challenge. On an open moorland landscape, the course is very exposed to the wind which can become a major obstacle, particularly on the dog-leg holes, where, as on all Harry Colt courses, you need to think long and hard about where to put your drive to get the right approach to the greens, which are protected by bushes, trees and bunkers. Strategy is to the fore again at the 12th, where hitting the driver will leave you a short approach shot but on a sloping lie, while a 2 iron will leave you on a flat part of the fairway but with a longer approach to the green. A rather hilly course (buggy recommended), Manchester offers some fine views to make up for the difficulty of club selection.

Proche de Manchester, ce beau parcours est très accessible en semaine, notamment pour des réunions d'affaires joignant l'utile au très agréable. Il offre aussi, c'est rare, de bons équipements d'entraînement. Le tracé n'est pas très long, et les départs assez bien placés pour offrir un bon "challenge" à toutes les catégories de joueurs. Dans son paysage de lande, il est très exposé au vent, qui peut devenir l'obstacle essentiel, notamment sur les doglegs où il faut réfléchir sur sa ligne pour avoir les greens ouverts, comme sur beaucoup de dessins d'Harry Colt. Ils sont protégés par des buissons, arbres et bunkers. Stratégie encore au 12, où jouer le drive vous fera jouer un second coup court, mais dans une pente, alors que jouer un fer du départ vous permettra d'avoir les pieds à plat, mais un coup plus long. Assez accidenté, Manchester offre de très belles vues, comme pour compenser la difficulté de sélection de clubs.

Manchester Golf Club — 1882

Hopwood Cottage, Middleton
ENG - MANCHESTER M24 2QP

Office	Secrétariat	(44) 0161 - 643 3202
Pro shop	Pro-shop	(44) 0161 - 643 2638
Fax	Fax	(44) 0161 - 643 9174
Web	—	
Situation	Situation	10km N of Manchester

(pop. 404 861) - 6 km S of Rochdale (pop. 202 164)

Annual closure	Fermeture annuelle	no
Weekly closure	Fermeture hebdomadaire	no

Fees main season Tarifs haute saison	18 holes	
	Week days Semaine	**We/Bank holidays** We/Férié
Individual Individuel	£ 30	*
Couple Couple	£ 60	*

Full weekdays: £ 45

Caddy	Caddy	no
Electric Trolley	Chariot électrique	£ 5/18 holes
Buggy	Voiturette	no
Clubs	Clubs	no
Credit cards	Cartes de crédit	VISA - Eurocard - MasterCard

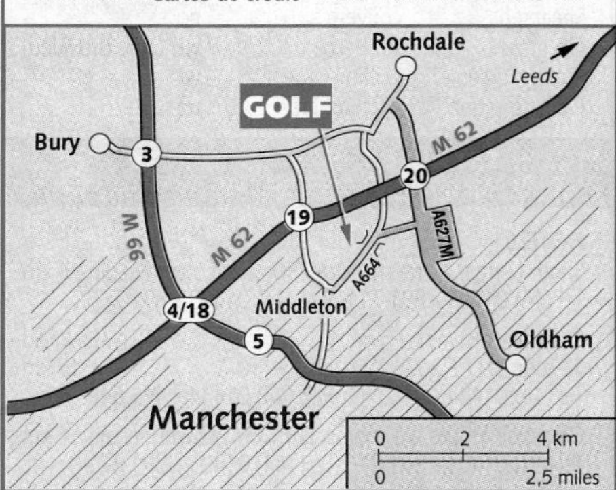

Access Accès : M62 Jct 20, then A627(M) → Oldham.
First exit, follow A664 signs.
Club on the right over humped back bridge.
Map 4 on page 490 Carte 4 Page 490

Golf course — PARCOURS — 16/20

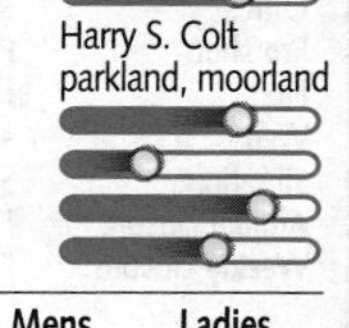

Site	Site	
Maintenance	Entretien	
Architect	Architecte	Harry S. Colt
Type	Type	parkland, moorland
Relief	Relief	
Water in play	Eau en jeu	
Exp. to wind	Exposé au vent	
Trees in play	Arbres en jeu	

Scorecard Carte de score	Chp. Chp.	Mens Mess.	Ladies Da.
Length Long.	5873	5660	5198
Par	72	72	74
Slope system	—	—	—

Advised golfing ability 0 12 24 36
Niveau de jeu recommandé
Hcp required Handicap exigé certificate

Club house & amenities — CLUB HOUSE ET ANNEXES — 7/10

Pro shop	Pro-shop	
Driving range	Practice	
Sheltered	couvert	no
On grass	sur herbe	yes
Putting-green	putting-green	yes
Pitching-green	pitching green	yes

Hotel facilities — ENVIRONNEMENT HOTELIER — 7/10

HOTELS HÔTELS

Royal Toby Lodge, 44 rooms, D £ 93 — Rochdale 7 km
Tel (44) 01706 - 861 861, Fax (44) 01706 - 868 428

Palace, 252 rooms, D £ 160 — Manchester 10 km
Tel (44) 0161 - 288 1111, Fax (44) 0161 - 288 2222

Victoria and Albert — Manchester
158 rooms, D £ 165 — 10 km
Tel (44) 0161 - 832 1188, Fax (44) 0161 - 834 2484

RESTAURANTS RESTAURANT

The French Restaurant — Manchester
Tel (44) 0161 - 236 3333 — 10 km

After Eight — Rochdale
Tel (44) 01706 - 46 432 — 7 km

MANNINGS HEATH Waterfall Course

14	8	6

If we were to give golf course clubhouses a score for artistic content, Mannings Heath would be up there with the front-runners. And a good thing too, because after the 18th hole here you have the one idea of relaxing and putting your feet up. This is a steeply sloping course in a charming corner of Sussex, where golf can be a strenuous exercise (but you knew that already). So buggy and caddie are recommended. Between the woods, the sections of heather and the parkland, find time to admire the landscape and many squirrels, they might give you some valuable inspiration. Although not a long course, you need a good golfing brain to score well. Some drives have to be long enough to be able to see the green for the approach shot (2nd, 4th or 8th holes), while tee-shots on the par 3s need careful thought and execution to avoid the meanders of the Horkins. The 10th hole, with its cascade, is a particularly memorable experience, as is the par 4 11th hole. The second "Kingfisher" course is very pleasant but less testing.

Si l'on devait décerner une note artistique aux club houses, Mannings Heath serait dans le peloton de tête. Tant mieux, car on a l'unique idée de se re-poser dans ce manoir après le 18, tant les ondulations de ce charmant coin de campagne du Sussex font du golf un sport (pour ceux qui en douteraient). Chariot électrique ou caddie conseillé. Entre les bois, les parties de bruyère ou de parc, on doit se donner le temps d'admirer le paysage, et le jeu des écureuils : c'est un bon prétexte pour reprendre ses esprits car, en dépit de sa faible longueur, il ne s'agit pas de jouer sans cervelle. Certains drives doivent être assez longs pour pouvoir ensuite apercevoir le green (2, 4 ou 8), et les coups de départ bien calculés sur les par 3 pour éviter la présence fréquente des méandres du Horkins : on retiendra en particulier le 10 avec sa cascade. Ou encore un par 4, le 11. Le second parcours, Kingfisher, est très plaisant, mais moins décisif.

Mannings Heath Golf Club — 1905

Fullers, Hammerspond Road, Mannings Heath
ENG - HORSHAM, W. Sussex RH13 6PG

Office	Secrétariat	(44) 01403 - 210 228
Pro shop	Pro-shop	(44) 01403 - 210 228
Fax	Fax	(44) 01403 - 270 974
Web	—	
Situation	Situation	12 km SW of Crawley
Annual closure	Fermeture annuelle	no
Weekly closure	Fermeture hebdomadaire	no

Fees main season Tarifs haute saison	18 holes	
	Week days Semaine	We/Bank holidays We/Férié
Individual Individuel	£ 34	£ 56
Couple Couple	£ 68	£ 112

Full days: £ 42 / £ 65 (week ends)

Caddy	Caddy	on request/£ 36
Electric Trolley	Chariot électrique	£ 10 /18 holes
Buggy	Voiturette	£ 26 /18 holes
Clubs	Clubs	£ 20 /18 holes

Credit cards Cartes de crédit
VISA - MasterCard - DC - AMEX

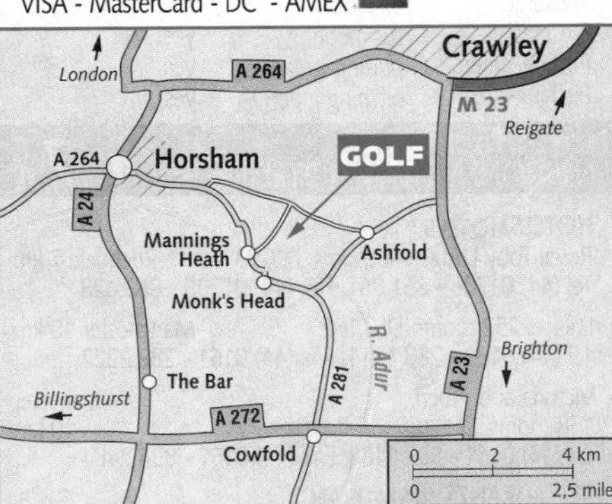

Access Accès : M23 Jct 11, through Pease Pottage to Grouse Lane (left hand side). 5 km (3.5 m.) to T junction, right and first left to Golf.
Map 7 on page 496 Carte 7 Page 496

Golf course PARCOURS — 14/20

Site	Site	
Maintenance	Entretien	
Architect	Architecte	Unknown
Type	Type	inland, heathland
Relief	Relief	
Water in play	Eau en jeu	
Exp. to wind	Exposé au vent	
Trees in play	Arbres en jeu	

Scorecard Carte de score	Chp. Chp.	Mens Mess.	Ladies Da.
Length Long.	5805	5460	4920
Par	73	71	73
Slope system	—	—	—

Advised golfing ability Niveau de jeu recommandé — 0 12 24 36
Hcp required Handicap exigé — certificate

Club house & amenities CLUB HOUSE ET ANNEXES — 8/10

Pro shop	Pro-shop	
Driving range	Practice	
Sheltered	couvert	no
On grass	sur herbe	yes (balls provided)
Putting-green	putting-green	yes
Pitching-green	pitching green	no

Hotel facilities ENVIRONNEMENT HOTELIER — 6/10

HOTELS HÔTELS

South Lodge, 41 rooms, D £ 230 — Lower Beeding 4 km
Tel (44) 01403 - 891 711, Fax (44) 01403 - 891 766

Ockenden Manor — Cuckfield 15 km
22 rooms, D £ 200
Tel (44) 01444 - 416 111, Fax (44) 01444 - 415 549

Cisswood House, 32 rooms, D £ 100 — Lower Beeding 4 km
Tel (44) 01403 - 891 216, Fax (44) 01403 - 891 621

RESTAURANTS RESTAURANT

Ockenden Manor — Cuckfield 15 km
Tel (44) 01444 - 416 111

Cole's, Tel (44) 01403 - 730 456 — Southwater 6 km

MANOR HOUSE (CASTLE COMBE) 15 8 7

It is no coincidence if there are so many buggies here. The superb views from the tee or green come courtesy of some roller-coaster landscape which makes this course something of an ordeal to walk. Designers Alliss and Clark followed the natural lie of the land and evidently had a lot of fun here, alternating pot bunkers or sprawling "sand-traps" and making extensive use of water hazards. All these difficulties are really dangerous because they are so strategic. And the relatively short yardage doesn't mean much when you are constantly shooting uphill or downhill. A spectacular, exciting and, first time out, often a surprising course in a category of its own. You come here for a few days of leisure, staying if you can at Manor House, a pretty piece of architecture with all the most modern amenities. You can also play as a green-feer.

S'il y a autant de voiturettes ici, ce n'est pas par hasard. Les vues superbes du haut des départs ou des greens, c'est au prix de montagnes russes qui rendent le jeu à pied très éprouvant. Les architectes Alliss et Clark ont suivi les contours naturels du terrain et se sont bien amusés dans un tel espace, alternant les "pot" bunkers et de longues étendues de sable, et faisant usage généreux des obstacles d'eau. Toutes ces difficultés sont réellement dangereuses, car très stratégiques, et la longueur relativement faible ne veut pas dire grand chose avec ces changements incessants de niveau. Un parcours spectaculaire, souvent surprenant la première fois, parfois passionnant, et à classer à part. On vient ici passer quelques jours de plaisir, si l'on peut en logeant au Manor House, jolie pièce d'architecture, avec le confort le plus moderne, mais on peut aussi jouer au green-fee.

Manor House (at Castle Combe) 1992

ENG - CASTLE COMBE, Wiltshire SN14 7 PL

Office	Secrétariat	(44) 01249 - 782 982
Pro shop	Pro-shop	(44) 01249 - 783 101
Fax	Fax	(44) 01249 - 782 992
Web	www.exclusivehotels.co.uk	
Situation	Situation	18 km NE of Bath
Annual closure	Fermeture annuelle	no
Weekly closure	Fermeture hebdomadaire	no

Fees main season Tarifs haute saison	18 holes	
	Week days Semaine	**We/Bank holidays** We/Férié
Individual Individuel	£ 40	£ 50
Couple Couple	£ 80	£ 100

Full days: £ 60 / £ 80 (week ends)

Caddy	Caddy	no
Electric Trolley	Chariot électrique	no
Buggy	Voiturette	£ 20 /18 holes
Clubs	Clubs	£ 10 /18 holes

Credit cards Cartes de crédit
VISA - Eurocard - MasterCard
(Pro shop goods & restaurant only)

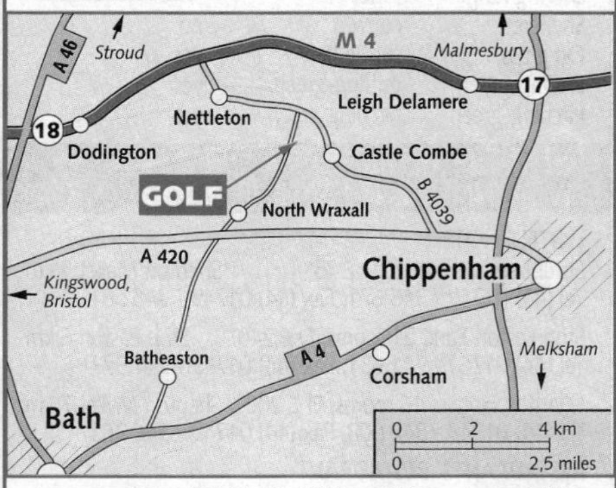

Access Accès : • M4 Jct 17, A350 → Chippenham, A420 on the right, then B4039 N of Castle Combe. • Bath: A46, A420 to Ford, then turn left to Castle Combe.
Map 6 on page 495 Carte 6 Page 495

Golf course PARCOURS 15/20

Site	Site	
Maintenance	Entretien	
Architect	Architecte	Peter Alliss Clive Clark
Type	Type	copse, parkland
Relief	Relief	
Water in play	Eau en jeu	
Exp. to wind	Exposé au vent	
Trees in play	Arbres en jeu	

Scorecard Carte de score	**Chp.** Chp.	**Mens** Mess.	**Ladies** Da.
Length Long.	5496	5298	4659
Par	73	71	72
Slope system	—	—	—

Advised golfing ability Niveau de jeu recommandé: 0 12 24 36
Hcp required Handicap exigé: 28 Men, 36 Ladies

Club house & amenities CLUB HOUSE ET ANNEXES 8/10

Pro shop	Pro-shop	
Driving range	Practice	
Sheltered	couvert	
On grass	sur herbe	yes
Putting-green	putting-green	yes
Pitching-green	pitching green	yes

Hotel facilities ENVIRONNEMENT HOTELIER 7/10

HOTELS HÔTELS
Manor House Hotel, 45 rooms, D £ 220 — on site
Tel (44) 01249 - 782 206, Fax (44) 01249 - 782 159

Castle Inn, 11 rooms, D £ 105 — Castle Combe 1 km
Tel (44) 01249 - 783 030, Fax (44) 01249 - 782 315

White Hart Inn, 11 rooms, D £ 84 — Ford 3 km
Tel (44) 01249 - 782 213, Fax (44) 01249 - 783 075

RESTAURANTS RESTAURANT
Manor House Hotel — on site
Tel (44) 01249 - 782 206

MENDIP

15 | 5 | 7

The highest point of this course is more than 1,000 ft. above sea-level from where you can see as far as Glastonbury and the abbey (you need good eyes), Exmoor (you need binoculars) and Wales. If they add America to the list, then you must be at the bar. Despite the altitude, this is not too hilly a course and the turf is wonderfully springy underfoot. This adds comfort to the pleasure of playing a course where you are rarely on the flat, where you need to think, and where you need some good ironwork and razor-sharp putting: the greens come in all shapes, sizes, slopes and contours and rarely forgive poor reading. Although minor details are always being shuffled around, the original 9 hole course by Vardon, later completed by Frank Pennink, remained unchanged until 1988, when the purchase of new land took the par up to 71. The clubhouse is perhaps not the world's prettiest but the atmosphere inside is very friendly, which is better than the other way around.

Le point le plus haut du parcours est à plus de 300 mètres, d'où l'on voit jusqu'à Glastonbury et son abbaye (il faut de bons yeux), Exmoor (il faut des jumelles) et le Pays de Galles. Mais si l'on vous parle de l'Amérique, c'est que vous êtes au bar. Pourtant, le parcours n'est pas trop accidenté, et le gazon est d'une rare souplesse, ce qui ne fait qu'ajouter le confort au plaisir d'un parcours où l'on n'a pas toujours les pieds à plat, où il faut un peu de tête, un très bon jeu de fers et un putting affûté comme un rasoir, car les greens sont de formes, de tailles, et de reliefs variés, ils ne pardonnent pas une lecture négligente. Tout en remaniant en permanence les détails, le dessin de 9 trous par Vardon, complété par Frank Pennink, est resté inchangé jusqu'en 1988, où l'achat de terrains a permis de porter le par à 71. Le Clubhouse n'est peut-être pas le plus joli du monde mais l'atmosphère y est très amicale. C'est mieux que l'inverse

Mendip Golf Club — 1909

Gurney Slade
ENG - BATH, Somerset BA3 4UT

Office	Secrétariat	(44) 01749 - 840 570
Pro shop	Pro-shop	(44) 01749 - 840 793
Fax	Fax	(44) 01749 - 841 439
Web	www.mendipgolf.co.uk	
Situation	Situation	28 km SW of Bath
Annual closure	Fermeture annuelle	no
Weekly closure	Fermeture hebdomadaire	no

594

Fees main season Tarifs haute saison	18 holes	
	Week days Semaine	**We/Bank holidays** We/Férié
Individual Individuel	£ 21	£ 31
Couple Couple	£ 42	£ 62

Full days: £ 26 / £ 35 (week ends)

Caddy	Caddy	no
Electric Trolley	Chariot électrique	no
Buggy	Voiturette	no
Clubs	Clubs	no

Credit cards Cartes de crédit
Visa - Mastercard (Pro shop goods only)

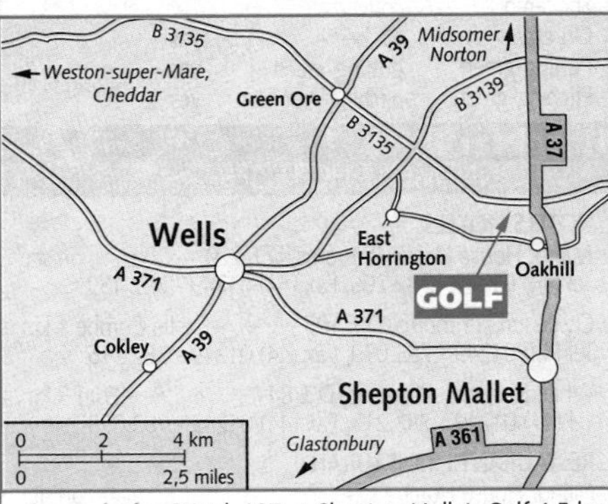

Access Accès : Bristol, A37 → Shepton Mallet, Golf 4.5 km (3 m.) before Shepton Mallet. From Bath, A367.
Map 6 on page 495 Carte 6 Page 495

Golf course PARCOURS — 15/20

Site	Site	
Maintenance	Entretien	
Architect	Architecte	Harry Vardon Frank Pennink (1965)
Type	Type	open country
Relief	Relief	
Water in play	Eau en jeu	
Exp. to wind	Exposé au vent	
Trees in play	Arbres en jeu	

Scorecard Carte de score	**Chp.** Chp.	**Mens** Mess.	**Ladies** Da.
Length Long.	5833	5653	5452
Par	71	71	75
Slope system	—	—	—

Advised golfing ability 0 12 24 36
Niveau de jeu recommandé
Hcp required Handicap exigé no

Club house & amenities CLUB HOUSE ET ANNEXES — 5/10

Pro shop	Pro-shop	
Driving range	Practice	
Sheltered	couvert	no
On grass	sur herbe	yes
Putting-green	putting-green	yes
Pitching-green	pitching green	yes

Hotel facilities ENVIRONNEMENT HOTELIER — 7/10

HOTELS HÔTELS
Shrubbery, 11 rooms, D £ 75 — Shepton Mallet 5 km
Tel (44) 01749 - 346 671, Fax (44) 01749 - 346 581

Ston Easton Park, 21 rooms, D £ 240 — Ston Easton 6 km
Tel (44) 01761 - 241 631, Fax (44) 01749 - 241 377

Charlton House, 16 rooms, D £ 200 — Shepton Mallet 7 km
Tel (44) 01749 - 342 008, Fax (44) 01749 - 346 362

RESTAURANTS RESTAURANT
Mulberry (Charlton House) — Shepton Mallet 7 km
Tel (44) 01749 - 342 008
Shrubbery, Tel (44) 01749 - 346 671 — Shepton Mallet 5 km
Ston Easton Park, Tel (44) 01761 - 241 631 — Ston Easton

MEON VALLEY Meon Course 15 | 8 | 7

This southern area of the Downs is a great site for walks and drives (behind the wheel), stretching out in the direction of Winchester, Chichester, Southampton, Beaulieu, Portsmouth and even the Isle of Wight. What's more, the course hotel is convenient and comfortable with an indoor swimming pool, sauna, fitness centre, etc. And as this "resort" also boasts a second 9-hole course (play it twice from two different sets of tee-box), a few days rest here is time well spent. On the Meon course, only real beginners might find the few small lakes a problem, but everyone should take extra care on the 12th and 18th holes. A ditch runs across a large section of the course but is not always that much in play. Elsewhere, a few isolated trees threaten the tee-shot, trees as a whole are generally in play and bunkers, although sparingly used, are very well located. This is an easily walkable course (except perhaps the climb on hole 13) which does not reveal all the trouble in store at first sight. You have better to use the Yardage book.

Cette partie sud des "Downs" est un site de promenades, à pied, ou même en voiture pour rayonner vers Winchester, Chichester, Southampton, Beaulieu, Portsmouth ou encore l'Ile de Wight. L'hôtel sur le golf est pratique et confortable, avec piscine intérieure, sauna, centre de mise en forme, etc. Et comme ce "resort" comprend un autre 9 trous (jouez-le deux fois de départs très différents !), quelques jours de repos ici seront bien occupés. Sur le "Meon Course", seuls les débutants risquent d'être gênés par quelques petits lacs, mais tous devront s'en méfier au 12 et au 18. Un fossé parcourt une grande partie du terrain, sans être toujours dangereux. A part cela, quelques arbres isolés menacent certains tee-shots, l'ensemble des arbres étant en jeu, et des bunkers bien placés. Assez facile à jouer à pied, ce parcours ne présente pas tous les obstacles au premier abord, il est conseillé de consulter le carnet de parcours.

Marriott Meon Valley Golf & CC — 1976

Sandy Lane
ENG - SHEDFIELD, SOUTHAMPTON SO32 2HQ

Office	Secrétariat	(44) 01329 - 833 455
Pro shop	Pro-shop	(44) 01329 - 836 832
Fax	Fax	(44) 01329 - 834 411
Web	—	
Situation	Situation	Southampton, 18 km
Annual closure	Fermeture annuelle	no
Weekly closure	Fermeture hebdomadaire	no

Fees main season Tarifs haute saison	Week days Semaine	We/Bank holidays We/Férié
	18 holes	
Individual Individuel	£ 36	£ 40
Couple Couple	£ 72	£ 80

Full weekdays: £ 57

Caddy	Caddy	no
Electric Trolley	Chariot électrique	no
Buggy	Voiturette	£ 25
Clubs	Clubs	£ 10

Credit cards Cartes de crédit
VISA - MasterCard - DC - Switch - Connect - AMEX

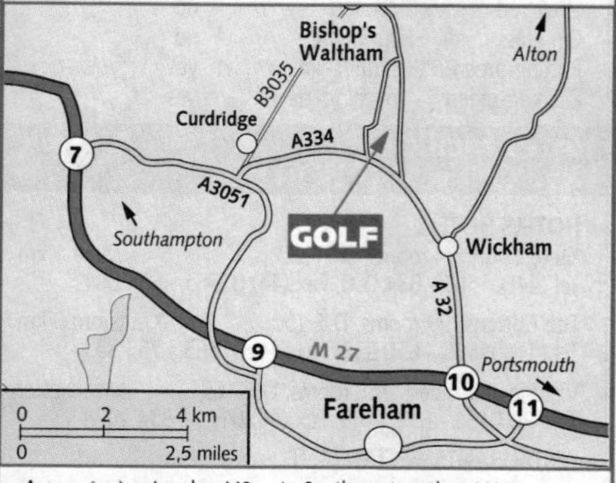

Access Accès : London M3 onto Southampton, then M27 → Portsmouth. Exit Jct 7, first exit for Botley (A334). → Wickham. On passing Wickham Vineyard, Sandy Lane is the next turning on your left. **Map 7 on page 496** Carte 7 Page 496

Golf course PARCOURS 15/20

Site	Site	
Maintenance	Entretien	
Architect	Architecte	Hamilton Stutt
Type	Type	parkland
Relief	Relief	
Water in play	Eau en jeu	
Exp. to wind	Exposé au vent	
Trees in play	Arbres en jeu	

Scorecard Carte de score	Chp. Chp.	Mens Mess.	Ladies Da.
Length Long.	5868	5488	5049
Par	71	71	73
Slope system	—	—	—

Advised golfing ability Niveau de jeu recommandé — 0 12 24 36

Hcp required Handicap exigé — certificate

Club house & amenities CLUB HOUSE ET ANNEXES 8/10

Pro shop	Pro-shop	
Driving range	Practice	
Sheltered	couvert	6 mats
On grass	sur herbe	yes
Putting-green	putting-green	yes
Pitching-green	pitching green	yes

Hotel facilities ENVIRONNEMENT HOTELIER 7/10

HOTELS HÔTELS

Meon Valley Hotel, 112 rooms, D £ 114 — Shedfield on site
Tel (44) 01329 - 833 455, Fax (44) 01329 - 834 411

Old House, 9 rooms, D £ 100 — Wickham 3 km
Tel (44) 01329 - 833 049, Fax (44) 01329 - 833 672

Botley Park, 100 rooms, D £ 150 — Botley 8 km
Tel (44) 01489 - 780 888, Fax (44) 01489 - 789 242

RESTAURANTS RESTAURANT

Treetops (Marriott Hotel) — Shedfield on site
Tel (44) 01329 - 833 455

Old House, Tel (44) 01329 - 833 049 — Wickham 3 km

Kings Head, Tel (44) 01329 - 832 123 — Wickham 3 km

MERE

15 | 7 | 7

Mere was revived 15 years ago when the clubhouse was completely overhauled (adding swimming pools, sauna, tennis courts, etc.), an extensive tree-planting program was begun and the course was given new tee-boxes and a new 18th green. The face-lift has "modernised" the original design by Braid and Duncan - you don't have to love the water hazards on the 7th and 8th holes - and generally enhanced the site with a more challenging finish to the course. Some rolling landscape adds a little variety to the layout where there is a pleasant mix of tight and wider holes. Putting and approach shots can be a tricky business on some of the tiered greens. And your best bet here is to pitch the greens rather than roll the ball. This is one of the most accomplished courses in the region of Manchester, a fair test and always a pleasure to play but only on week-days for visitors.

Mere a été réveillé il y a quinze ans avec une refonte totale du Clubhouse (avec piscines, sauna, tennis, etc), la plantation de nombreux arbres, de nouveaux départs, un nouveau green au 18. Ce rajeunissement a un peu "modernisé" le dessin de Braid et de Duncan - on peut ne pas adorer les obstacles d'eau du 7 et du 8 - mais au profit de l'embellissement général du site, et du renforcement d'un finale très exigeant. Quelques ondulations apportent de la variété au terrain, où le tracé alterne agréablement les trous étroits et les espaces plus larges. Le putting et les approches sont intéressants et délicats à apprécier sur certains greens à plateaux : en général, on devra ici privilégier les coups levés. Dans la région de Manchester, c'est une des réalisations les plus achevées, et ce parcours d'une grande franchise reste un plaisir à jouer. En semaine pour les visiteurs.

Mere Golf & Country Club — 1934

Chester Road, Mere
ENG - KNUTSFORD, Cheshire WA16 6LJ

Office	Secrétariat	(44) 01565 - 830 155
Pro shop	Pro-shop	(44) 01565 - 830 155
Fax	Fax	(44) 01565 - 830 518
Web	www.meregolfclub.com	
Situation	Situation	Manchester, 20 km
Annual closure	Fermeture annuelle	no
Weekly closure	Fermeture hebdomadaire	no

Fees main season / Tarifs haute saison	Week days / Semaine	We/Bank holidays / We/Férié
	Full day	
Individual Individuel	£ 70	£ 75
Couple Couple	£ 140	£ 150

Booking essential

Caddy	Caddy	£ 25 /on request
Electric Trolley	Chariot électrique	no
Buggy	Voiturette	£ 20 /18 holes
Clubs	Clubs	£ 15 /18 holes

Credit cards Cartes de crédit
VISA - Eurocard - MasterCard - DC - AMEX

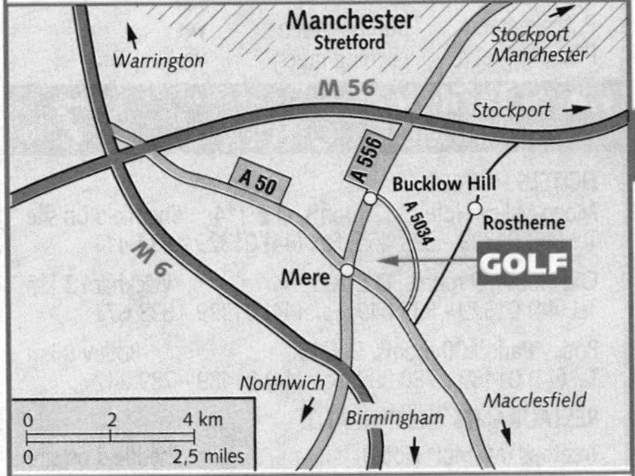

Manchester
Stretford
Warrington
Stockport Manchester
M 56
Stockport
A 556
A 50
Bucklow Hill
A 5034
Rostherne
GOLF
M 6
Mere
Northwich
Birmingham
Macclesfield
0 2 4 km
0 2,5 miles

Access Accès : Manchester, M56 Jct 7. A556 S → Northwich. Golf on left side before A50.
Map 4 on page 490 Carte 4 Page 490

Golf course — PARCOURS — 15/20

Site	Site	
Maintenance	Entretien	
Architect	Architecte	James Braid George Duncan
Type	Type	parkland
Relief	Relief	
Water in play	Eau en jeu	
Exp. to wind	Exposé au vent	
Trees in play	Arbres en jeu	

Scorecard / Carte de score	Chp. / Chp.	Mens / Mess.	Ladies / Da.
Length Long.	6135	5910	5192
Par	71	71	74
Slope system	—	—	—

Advised golfing ability 0 12 24 36
Niveau de jeu recommandé
Hcp required Handicap exigé — certificate

Club house & amenities — CLUB HOUSE ET ANNEXES — 7/10

Pro shop	Pro-shop	
Driving range	Practice	
Sheltered	couvert	no
On grass	sur herbe	no
Putting-green	putting-green	yes
Pitching-green	pitching green	yes

Hotel facilities — ENVIRONNEMENT HOTELIER — 7/10

HOTELS HÔTELS

Mere Court, 34 rooms, D £ 120 — Mere 1 km
Tel (44) 01565 - 831 000, Fax (44) 01565 - 831 001

The Cottons, 99 rooms, D £ 150 — Knutsford 3 km
Tel (44) 01565 - 650 333, Fax (44) 01565 - 755 351

Victoria and Albert, 158 rooms, D £ 165 — Manchester
Tel (44) 0161 - 832 1188, Fax (44) 0161 - 834 2484

RESTAURANTS RESTAURANT

Belle Epoque Brasserie, Tel (44) 01565 - 633 060 — Knutsford
Cafe Maigret, Tel (44) 0161 - 832 1188 — Manchester 20 km
Magnolia (Cottons), Tel (44) 01565 - 650 333 — Knutsford

MOOR ALLERTON

15 | 6 | 7

It is rare indeed to encounter such a concentration of good golf courses in the northern suburbs of Leeds. With Moortown, Sand Moor and Alwoodley, Moor Allerton is the fourth member of a remarkable crop of courses. Here, though, contrary to the typical Yorkshire moor landscape of the three others, the style is much more that of a parkland course. The changes made to the original layout by Robert Trent Jones have accentuated this trait and even given it a slight American flavour. Hazards come in the form of trees and bunkers (well designed and located) completed by very strategically placed stretches of water. To score well you will have to produce a whole range of shots, meaning that the lesser player could have a hard time of things. A few holes stick in the memory, and although there are other, more spectacular courses in the world, this one deserves a round or two. You will enjoy it.

Il est rare de rencontrer une telle concentration de bons parcours de golf que dans la "banlieue nord" de Leeds. Avec Moortown, Sand Moor et Alwoodley, Moor Allerton constitue le quatrième élément d'un quatuor remarquable. Mais, contrairement aux trois premiers, typiques de la lande du Yorkshire, celui-ci revêt une esthétique beaucoup plus nette de parc. Les modifications apportées par Robert Trent Jones au tracé originel ont d'ailleurs accentué ce caractère, l'ont même un peu américanisé. Les obstacles sont constitués par les arbres et les bunkers (très bien dessinés et placés), et complétés par la présence de quelques pièces d'eau tout aussi stratégiquement placés. Il faudra développer ici toute une panoplie de coups de golf pour bien scorer, et les joueurs peu expérimentés s'y sentiront sans doute moins à l'aise que les autres. Quelques trous marquent bien la mémoire, et s'il existe à l'évidence des parcours globalement plus spectaculaires, celui-ci mérite d'être joué et apprécié.

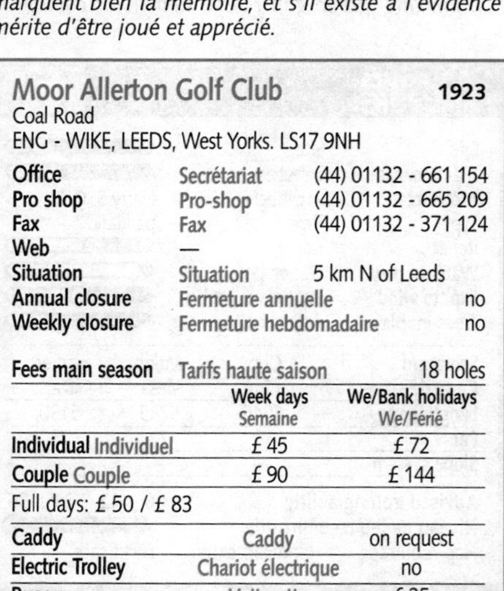

Moor Allerton Golf Club — 1923

Coal Road
ENG - WIKE, LEEDS, West Yorks. LS17 9NH

Office	Secrétariat	(44) 01132 - 661 154
Pro shop	Pro-shop	(44) 01132 - 665 209
Fax	Fax	(44) 01132 - 371 124
Web	—	
Situation	Situation	5 km N of Leeds
Annual closure	Fermeture annuelle	no
Weekly closure	Fermeture hebdomadaire	no

Fees main season Tarifs haute saison	18 holes	
	Week days Semaine	**We/Bank holidays** We/Férié
Individual Individuel	£ 45	£ 72
Couple Couple	£ 90	£ 144

Full days: £ 50 / £ 83

Caddy	Caddy	on request
Electric Trolley	Chariot électrique	no
Buggy	Voiturette	£ 25
Clubs	Clubs	£ 10

Credit cards Cartes de crédit
VISA - Eurocard - MasterCard - AMEX
(Pro shop goods only)

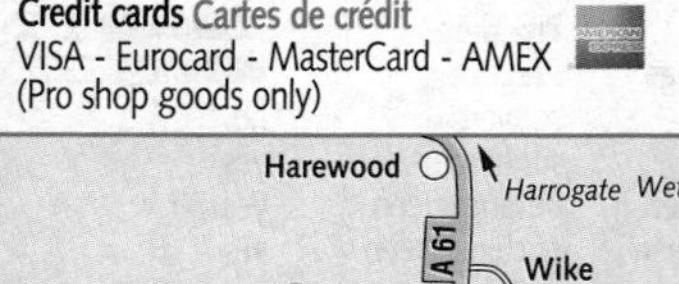

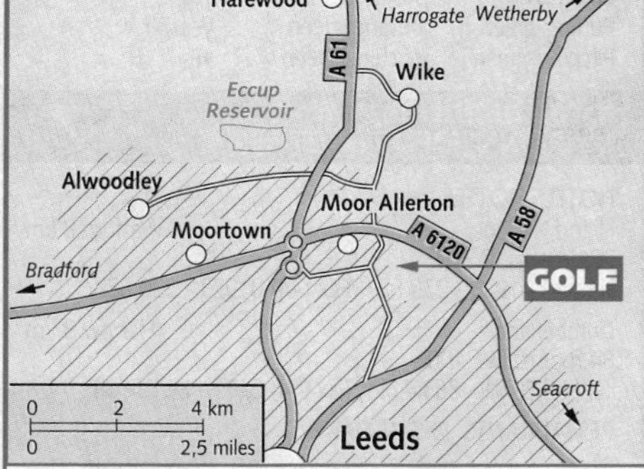

Access Accès : Leeds, A 61 → Harrogate, then A621 → Moor Allerton
Map 4 on page 490 Carte 4 Page 490

Golf course PARCOURS — 15/20

Site	Site	
Maintenance	Entretien	
Architect	Architecte	R. Trent Jones Sr
Type	Type	parkland
Relief	Relief	
Water in play	Eau en jeu	
Exp. to wind	Exposé au vent	
Trees in play	Arbres en jeu	

Scorecard Carte de score	**Chp.** Chp.	**Mens** Mess.	**Ladies** Da.
Length Long.	5823	5526	4878
Par	71	71	73
Slope system	—	—	—

Advised golfing ability 0 12 24 36
Niveau de jeu recommandé
Hcp required Handicap exigé certificate

Club house & amenities CLUB HOUSE ET ANNEXES — 6/10

Pro shop	Pro-shop	
Driving range	Practice	
Sheltered	couvert	12 bays
On grass	sur herbe	yes
Putting-green	putting-green	yes
Pitching-green	pitching green	no

Hotel facilities ENVIRONNEMENT HOTELIER — 7/10

HOTELS HÔTELS

Posthouse Leeds/Bradford — Bramhope 6 km
131 rooms, D £ 89
Tel (44) 0870 - 400 9049, Fax (44) 0113 - 284 3451

Weetwood Hall, 108 rooms, D £ 160 — Leeds 6 km
Tel (44) 0113 - 230 6000, Fax (44) 0113 - 230 6095

42 The Calls, 41 rooms, D £ 150 — Leeds 6 km
Tel (44) 0113 - 244 0099, Fax (44) 0113 - 234 4100

RESTAURANTS RESTAURANT

Leodis Brasserie, Tel (44) 0113 - 242 1010 — Leeds 6 km
Brasserie Forty Four, Tel (44) 0113 - 234 3232 — Leeds 6 km
The Calls Grill, Tel (44) 0113 - 245 3870 — Leeds 6 km

MOOR PARK High Course

17 | 8 | 7

Originally there were three courses here, two of which have survived beneath the impressive and even intimidating shadows of the clubhouse. The shirt and tie rule is so obvious here that you're surprised to see people actually dressed in casual wear on the course. The "West Course" is on the short side but goes very well with the "High" course, where from the 2nd hole onward you realise you'll need some sort of bearings or benchmarks if you are ever going to card a good score. The yardage book will come in handy for knowing where you should put your drive and for identifying the gardens where your ball should not go (especially on the front 9). A Harry Colt course is never a bland affair and this is no exception to the rule. The last nine holes are particularly memorable with three par 3s more than worthy of the designer's reputation. This is most definitely not the place where you could ever imagine golf becoming a sport for all and sundry, but it is one hell of a good course.

Au départ, il y avait trois parcours, dont deux sont restés sous l'ombre impressionnante, et même intimidante d'un Clubhouse où le port d'une cravate paraît tellement aller de soi qu'on la gardera pour jouer (au cas où). Le "West Course" est assez court, mais constitue un bon complément au "High," où dès le 2, on comprend qu'il va falloir trouver ses marques pour espérer ramener un score décent. Le "yardage book" ne sera pas inutile pour savoir où poser le drive, et pour identifier (surtout à l'aller) les jardins où il ne faut pas envoyer sa balle. Un parcours dessiné par Harry Colt n'est jamais indifférent, et celui-ci ne fait pas exception à la règle. on gardera un souvenir particulier des neuf derniers trous, avec trois par 3 à la hauteur de la réputation de l'architecte. Certes, ce n'est pas vraiment le lieu où l'on imagine que le golf puisse s'épanouir comme un sport démocratique, mais c'est un bon parcours !

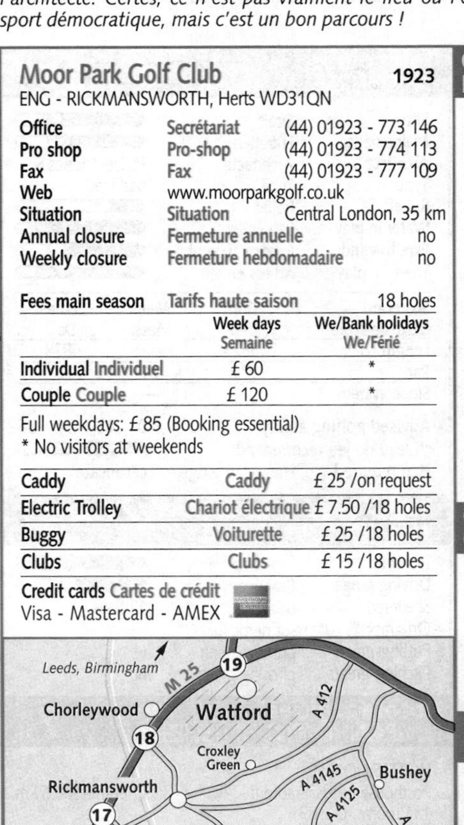

Moor Park Golf Club 1923
ENG - RICKMANSWORTH, Herts WD31QN

Office	Secrétariat	(44) 01923 - 773 146
Pro shop	Pro-shop	(44) 01923 - 774 113
Fax	Fax	(44) 01923 - 777 109
Web	www.moorparkgolf.co.uk	
Situation	Situation	Central London, 35 km
Annual closure	Fermeture annuelle	no
Weekly closure	Fermeture hebdomadaire	no

Fees main season Tarifs haute saison	Week days Semaine	We/Bank holidays We/Férié
		18 holes
Individual Individuel	£ 60	*
Couple Couple	£ 120	*

Full weekdays: £ 85 (Booking essential)
* No visitors at weekends

Caddy	Caddy	£ 25 /on request
Electric Trolley	Chariot électrique	£ 7.50 /18 holes
Buggy	Voiturette	£ 25 /18 holes
Clubs	Clubs	£ 15 /18 holes

Credit cards Cartes de crédit
Visa - Mastercard - AMEX

Access Accès : London, M4 Jct 3, A312, A4180, A404 → Rickmansworth, Golf on the right.
Map 8 on page 498 Carte 8 Page 498

Golf course PARCOURS 17/20

Site	Site	
Maintenance	Entretien	
Architect	Architecte	Harry S. Colt
Type	Type	parkland
Relief	Relief	
Water in play	Eau en jeu	
Exp. to wind	Exposé au vent	
Trees in play	Arbres en jeu	

Scorecard Carte de score	Chp. Chp.	Mens Mess.	Ladies Da.
Length Long.	6045	5735	5130
Par	72	72	73
Slope system	—	—	—

Advised golfing ability / Niveau de jeu recommandé: 0 12 24 36
Hcp required / Handicap exigé: certificate

Club house & amenities CLUB HOUSE ET ANNEXES 8/10

Pro shop	Pro-shop	
Driving range	Practice	
Sheltered	couvert	no
On grass	sur herbe	yes
Putting-green	putting-green	yes
Pitching-green	pitching green	yes

Hotel facilities ENVIRONNEMENT HOTELIER 7/10

HOTELS HÔTELS

Hilton National — Watford 8 km
201 rooms, D £ 99
Tel (44) 01923 - 235 881, Fax (44) 01923 - 220 836

Cumberland — Harrow 8 km
84 rooms, D £ 100
Tel (44) 0181 - 863 4111, Fax (44) 0181 - 861 5668

RESTAURANTS RESTAURANT

Percy's, Tel (44) 0181 - 427 2021 — North Harrow 6 km
Friends, Tel (44) 0181 - 866 0286 — Pinner 5 km
Trattoria Sorrentina, Tel (44) 0181 - 427 9411 — Harrow 8 km

MOORTOWN

18 | 7 | 7

With Alwoodley and Sand Moor, here you have a great threesome of courses close to Leeds, certainly not the prettiest city in England one whose region has a lot to be said for it, especially the city of York. The present course, or at least 16 holes of the present course, were designed by Alister Mackenzie while the last two were added in 1989, giving the whole layout more than respectable yardage and leaving the original style untouched. Classic, well-landscaped and with huge greens in excellent condition, the course gives nothing away. By the same token it doesn't steal strokes, either. Here, you score what you deserved to score. The Ryder Cup was held here for the first time in England, as was a particular English Amateur championship where one player had to hit his third shot on the 18th from inside the bar. A good place to go, but only after you have sunk that final putt.

Avec The Alwoodley et Sand Moor, voici un fameux trio de parcours voisins, à proximité de Leeds, qui n'est sans doute pas la plus belle ville d'Angleterre, mais la région ne manque pas de séductions, en particulier avec York. Le présent parcours a été dessiné par Alister Mackenzie. Du moins 16 de ses trous, car deux nouveaux trous ont été ajoutés en 1989, permettant d'afficher maintenant une longueur fort respectable en regard des canons modernes. Le style original n'en a pas été modifié. Classique, bien paysagé, avec de vastes greens généralement excellents, ce parcours ne fait certes pas de cadeaux, mais il ne vole non plus personne : on y fait exactement le score que l'on mérite. La Ryder Cup 1929 s'y est disputée pour la première fois en Grande-Bretagne, tout comme un English Amateur où un joueur dut taper son troisième coup du 18 depuis l'intérieur du bar. On comprend qu'il y soit allé.

Moortown Golf Club — 1909

Harrogate Road
ENG - LEEDS, W. Yorkshire LS17 7DB

Office	Secrétariat	(44) 0113 - 268 6521
Pro shop	Pro-shop	(44) 0113 - 268 3636
Fax	Fax	(44) 0113 - 268 6521
Web	www.moortowngc.co.uk	
Situation	Situation	8 km N of Leeds
Annual closure	Fermeture annuelle	no
Weekly closure	Fermeture hebdomadaire	no

Fees main season Tarifs haute saison	18 holes	
	Week days Semaine	**We/Bank holidays** We/Férié
Individual Individuel	£ 45	£ 50
Couple Couple	£ 90	£ 100

Full day: £ 50 / £ 60 (weekends)

Caddy	Caddy	no
Electric Trolley	Chariot électrique	£ 7 /18 holes
Buggy	Voiturette	£ 25 /18 holes
Clubs	Clubs	no

Credit cards Cartes de crédit
VISA - Eurocard - MasterCard - DC - Switch
(not for green fees)

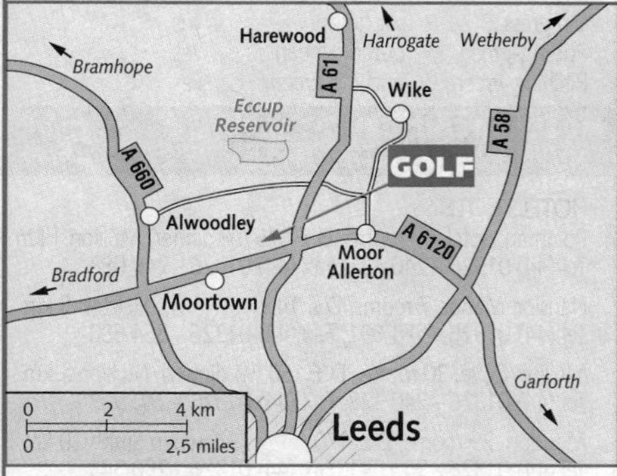

Access Accès : On A61 approx. 8 km (5 m.) N of Leeds
Map 4 on page 490 Carte 4 Page 490

Golf course — PARCOURS — 18/20

Site	Site	
Maintenance	Entretien	
Architect	Architecte	Alister MacKenzie
Type	Type	inland, moorland
Relief	Relief	
Water in play	Eau en jeu	
Exp. to wind	Exposé au vent	
Trees in play	Arbres en jeu	

Scorecard Carte de score	**Chp.** Chp.	**Mens** Mess.	**Ladies** Da.
Length Long.	6390	5883	5398
Par	72	72	75
Slope system	—	—	—

Advised golfing ability Niveau de jeu recommandé — 0 12 24 36
Hcp required Handicap exigé — certificate

Club house & amenities — CLUB HOUSE ET ANNEXES — 7/10

Pro shop	Pro-shop	
Driving range	Practice	
Sheltered	couvert	practice area
On grass	sur herbe	yes
Putting-green	putting-green	yes
Pitching-green	pitching green	yes

Hotel facilities — ENVIRONNEMENT HOTELIER — 7/10

HOTELS HÔTELS

Posthouse, 130 rooms, D £ 90 — Bramhope 5 km
Tel (44) 0870 - 400 9049, Fax (44) 0870 - 284 3451

42 The Calls, 41 rooms, D £ 150 — Leeds 8 km
Tel (44) 0113 - 244 0099, Fax (44) 0113 - 234 4100

Queens, 199 rooms, D £ 125 — Leeds 8 km
Tel (44) 0113 - 243 1323, Fax (44) 0113 - 242 5154

Haleys Hotel, 29 rooms, D £ 130 — Headingley 6 km
Tel (44) 0113 - 278 4446, Fax (44) 0113 - 275 3342

RESTAURANTS RESTAURANT

Pool Court at 42, Tel (44) 0113 - 244 4242 — Leeds 8 km
Leodis, Tel (44) 0113 - 242 1010 — Leeds 8 km
Rascasse, Tel (44) 0113 - 244 6611 — Leeds 8 km

MULLION

15 | 5 | 5

Before teeing it up on this, the southernmost course in England, you will have already enjoyed a very warm welcome and splendid views. The sea is a sight to behold on windy days, when you are better off playing cards than golf, because on this huge, wide open space, the wind can play havoc. Having said that, the weather is often fine down here, and lovers of the open air and inventive golf, even if they are only average golfers, will have a great time. It might take them a while to reach the greens, but they always get there in the end because no shot is impossible. Despite the bushes and huge reed-beds, which make a part of the course a little spongy underfoot, most of the terrain is sandy and the grass excellent. A few dips and hillocks conceal the foot of the pin on occasions but the course in still very honest and open. The good holes include the 6th, the 7th lined with cross-bunkers and the 10th, a par 4 which can be terrifying to play in a head-wind. This is one of those courses where the golfer really feels very close to nature.

Avant d'aborder le parcours le plus septentrional d'Angleterre, on aura remarqué l'accueil très amical, et un panorama splendide sur les falaises et la mer, grandiose les jours de tempête : dans un espace aussi vaste, le vent ne rencontre guère d'obstacles. Mais il y a beaucoup de beaux jours où les amateurs de grand air et d'un golf inventif s'en donneront à coeur joie, même si leur niveau de golf est moyen : s'il faut bien des coups pour arriver au green, aucun d'eux n'est impossible. Une partie du terrain peut être spongieuse avec de vastes roselières, mais la plus grande partie du parcours est sablonneuse, et le gazon excellent. Quelques vallonnements dissimulent certains pieds des drapeaux, mais le parcours est néanmoins d'une grande franchise. On y retiendra parmi bien des bons trous les 6, le 7 avec ses cross-bunkers, la 10 un par 4, qui peut être terrible par vent contraire. Un parcours où le sentiment de communion avec la nature est très fort.

Mullion Golf Club — 1895

ENG - CURY, HELSTON, Cornwall TR12 7BP

Office	Secrétariat	(44) 01326 - 240 685
Pro shop	Pro-shop	(44) 01326 - 241 176
Fax	Fax	(44) 01326 - 240 685
Web	www.mulliongolfclub.co.uk	
Situation	Situation	

25 km from Falmouth (pop. 19 217)

Annual closure	Fermeture annuelle	no
Weekly closure	Fermeture hebdomadaire	no

Fees main season Tarifs haute saison	Week days Semaine	We/Bank holidays We/Férié
		Full day
Individual Individuel	£ 23	£ 28
Couple Couple	£ 46	£ 56

Caddy	Caddy	no
Electric Trolley	Chariot électrique	no
Buggy	Voiturette	£ 15
Clubs	Clubs	no
Credit cards Cartes de crédit		no

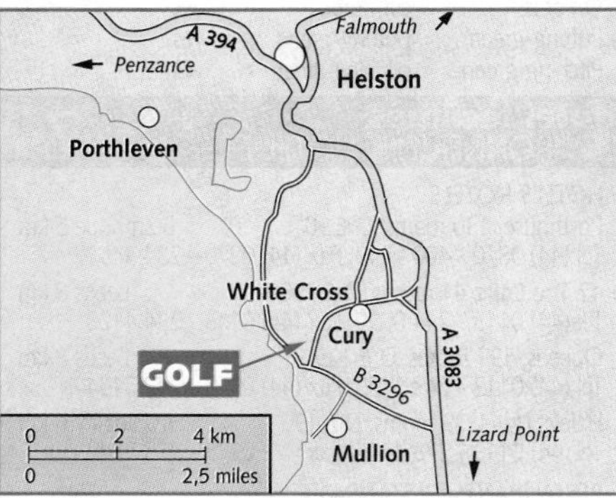

Access Accès : M4, M5 South, A30 → Penzance, → Helston. → Mullion. Follow signs to Golf course.
Map 6 on page 494 Carte 6 Page 494

Golf course — PARCOURS — 15/20

Site	Site	
Maintenance	Entretien	
Architect	Architecte	William Side
Type	Type	seaside course, open country
Relief	Relief	
Water in play	Eau en jeu	
Exp. to wind	Exposé au vent	
Trees in play	Arbres en jeu	

Scorecard Carte de score	Chp. Chp.	Mens Mess.	Ladies Da.
Length Long.	5434	5164	4902
Par	70	70	72
Slope system	—	—	—

Advised golfing ability Niveau de jeu recommandé: 0 12 24 36

Hcp required Handicap exigé: certificate

Club house & amenities — CLUB HOUSE ET ANNEXES — 5/10

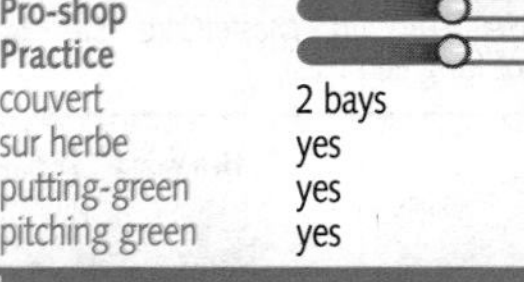

Pro shop	Pro-shop	
Driving range	Practice	
Sheltered	couvert	2 bays
On grass	sur herbe	yes
Putting-green	putting-green	yes
Pitching-green	pitching green	yes

Hotel facilities — ENVIRONNEMENT HOTELIER — 5/10

HOTELS HÔTELS

Polurrian Hotel, 39 rooms, D £ 175 (w. dinner) Mullion 1 km
Tel (44) 01326 - 240 421, Fax (44) 01326 - 240 083

Nansloe Manor, 7 rooms, D £ 140 Helston 8 km
Tel (44) 01326 - 574 691, Fax (44) 01326 - 564 680

Mullion Cove, 30 rooms, D £ 160 (w. dinner) Mullion 1 km
Tel (44) 01326 - 240 328, Fax (44) 01326 - 240 998

Meudon, 29 rooms, D £ 170 Mawnan Smith 20 km
Tel (44) 01326 - 250 541, Fax (44) 01326 - 250 543

RESTAURANTS RESTAURANT

Halzephron Inn, Tel (44) 01326 - 240 406 Gunwalloe 3 km

NEWBURY & CROOKHAM

15	6	7

Horse-racing enthusiasts will already have heard of Newbury, whose racecourse is visible from the 17th hole. But despite being so close, the ground here is far from flat although easy enough to walk. The course was built in 1873, making it one of the oldest in England, and is still popular and busy enough to be closed to non-members on week-ends. Like many of the courses from that period, Newbury & Crookham has a lot of trees and the design has hardly got any younger, but this is not a course to be taken lightly, despite a lack of yardage. It is a very pretty challenge with several holes of the highest order defended by some very well-placed bunkers. There is an obvious need to put your drive in the right place and we would recommend this as a "disciplinary" course for "sprayers". The trees and thick rough will soon get them back on the straight and narrow. The clubhouse is small and not the most cheerful place in the world, but the food is good.

Les amateurs de chevaux connaissent Newbury par son hippodrome, que l'on aperçoit du 17. Malgré ce voisinage, le terrain n'est pas plat, même s'il est facile à jouer à pied. Le parcours a été construit en 1873, ce qui en fait l'un des clubs de golf les plus anciens d'Angleterre, et qui reste assez fréquenté pour qu'il ne soit pas possible d'y jouer en week-end. Comme beaucoup de parcours de cette époque, il est abondamment pourvu d'arbres, et son dessin a seulement été rajeuni, mais son manque de longueur ne doit pas le faire sous-estimer. C'est un très joli challenge, avec plusieurs trous de premier ordre, défendus par des bunkers très bien placés, et la nécessité de placer correctement les drives est évidente : on recommande aux "arroseurs" un petit séjour "disciplinaire" à Newbury & Crookham : les arbres, et aussi un rough épais sauront redresser leurs trajectoires. Le Clubhouse est petit et pas très gai, mais la table est très correcte.

Newbury & Crookham Golf Club — 1873

Burysbank Road, Greenham
ENG - NEWBURY, Berks RG19 8BZ

Office	Secrétariat	(44) 01635 - 40 035
Pro shop	Pro-shop	(44) 01635 - 31 201
Fax	Fax	(44) 01635 - 40 045
Web		—
Situation	Situation	25 km from Reading
Annual closure	Fermeture annuelle	no
Weekly closure	Fermeture hebdomadaire	no

Fees main season Tarifs haute saison	**Week days** Semaine	**We/Bank holidays** We/Férié
		18 holes
Individual Individuel	£ 25	*
Couple Couple	£ 50	*

Full weekdays: £ 30 / * No visitors at weekends

Caddy	Caddy	no
Electric Trolley	Chariot électrique	no
Buggy	Voiturette	no
Clubs	Clubs	on request

Credit cards Cartes de crédit
Visa - Mastercard (Pro shop goods only)

Access Accès : London, M4. Jct 13, A34 South through Newbury. Turn into Newbury Retall Park, 2.5 km SE of Newbury. Golf on left.
Map 7 on page 496 Carte 7 Page 496

Golf course PARCOURS — 15/20

Site	Site	
Maintenance	Entretien	
Architect	Architecte	J.H. Turner
Type	Type	parkland
Relief	Relief	
Water in play	Eau en jeu	
Exp. to wind	Exposé au vent	
Trees in play	Arbres en jeu	

Scorecard Carte de score	**Chp.** Chp.	**Mens** Mess.	**Ladies** Da.
Length Long.	5346	5141	4745
Par	69	69	70
Slope system	—	—	—

Advised golfing ability Niveau de jeu recommandé — 0 12 24 36
Hcp required Handicap exigé — no

Club house & amenities CLUB HOUSE ET ANNEXES — 6/10

Pro shop	Pro-shop	
Driving range	Practice	
Sheltered	couvert	no
On grass	sur herbe	yes
Putting-green	putting-green	yes
Pitching-green	pitching green	yes

Hotel facilities ENVIRONNEMENT HOTELIER — 7/10

HOTELS HÔTELS

Vineyard, 33 rooms, D £ 300 — Newbury 7 km
Tel (44) 01635 - 528 770, Fax (44) 01635 - 528 398

Newbury Manor, 33 rooms, D £ 180 — Newbury 3 km
Tel (44) 01635 - 528 838, Fax (44) 01635 - 523 406

Hilton, 109 rooms, D £ 165 — Newbury 3 km
Tel (44) 01635 - 529 000, Fax (44) 01635 - 529 337

The Chequers, 56 rooms, D £ 140 — Newbury 3 km
Tel (44) 01635 - 38 000, Fax (44) 01635 - 37 170

RESTAURANTS RESTAURANT

Vineyard — Newbury 7 km
Tel (44) 01635 - 528 770

NORTH FORELAND

13	7	7

This virtually tree-less course was designed by Fowler and Simpson at the top of some cliffs, which naturally exposes it to all winds and weathers. Winds in the plural, because there are hardly ever two holes running in the same direction, so keep a cool head and control your shots. Beginners will hardly ever be penalised by the rough because it rarely comes into play for their kind of shots. The same applies to the bunker fairways which will more often punish the mistakes made by longer and better players. So you might call this a logical course. At all events it is an excellent venue for playing with all the family because you will also find a real 18-hole course for children (holes measuring between 70 and 140 yards). And this region is the sunniest and driest in all England. Although many of you may know Margate's reputation as a seaside resort, only the really knowledgeable will know that Charles Dickens used to come on holiday here, in Broadstairs, where he wrote David Copperfield. His house (Bleak House) has been transformed into a museum by the town.

Pratiquement sans arbres, ce parcours a été dessiné par Fowler et Simpson au sommet de la falaise, ce qui l'expose bien sûr au vent. Aux vents, car on ne trouve pratiquement pas deux trous de suite dans le même sens : il faut garder la tête froide et contrôler ses coups. Les joueurs sans expérience seront peu pénalisés car le rough est rarement en jeu pour eux, tout comme les bunkers de fairway, ce qui pénalise surtout les fautes des meilleurs joueurs : voilà un parcours très logique. Et venir en famille est très agréable car l'on trouve également ici un parcours de 18 trous de moins de 130 mètres, à l'échelle des enfants. Et la région est la plus ensoleillée et la moins arrosée d'Angleterre. Si l'on connaît, de réputation, la station balnéaire de Margate, seuls les fanatiques de Charles Dickens savent qu'il prenait ses vacances ici, à Broadstairs, où il écrivit "David Copperfield." La ville a d'ailleurs transformé sa maison (Bleak House) en Musée.

North Foreland Golf Club — 1903

Convent Road
ENG - BROADSTAIRS, Kent CT10 3PU

Office	Secrétariat	(44) 01843 - 862 140
Pro shop	Pro-shop	(44) 01843 - 869 628
Fax	Fax	(44) 01843 - 862 140
Web	—	
Situation	Situation	3 km from Margate
Annual closure	Fermeture annuelle	no
Weekly closure	Fermeture hebdomadaire	no

Fees main season Tarifs haute saison	Week days Semaine	We/Bank holidays We/Férié
18 holes		
Individual Individuel	£ 30	£ 40
Couple Couple	£ 60	£ 80

No visitors Sunday & Monday mornings.
Full weekday: £ 40 / £ 60 (Saturday)

Caddy	Caddy	no
Electric Trolley	Chariot électrique	£ 4 /18 holes
Buggy	Voiturette	£ 15 /18 holes
Clubs	Clubs	£ 2.50 /18 holes

Credit cards Cartes de crédit
Visa - Mastercard - DC (Pro shop goods only)

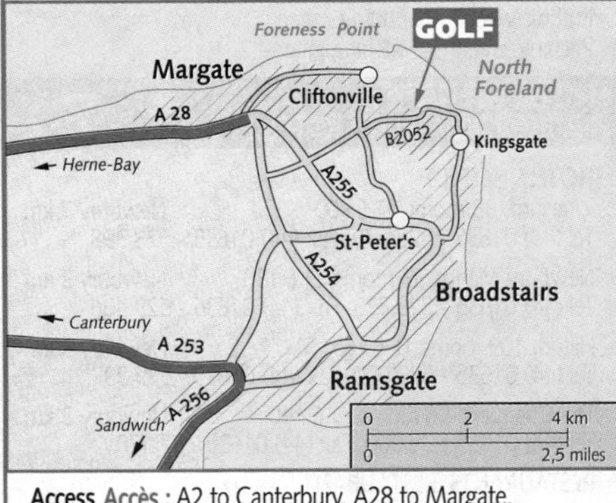

Access Accès : A2 to Canterbury. A28 to Margate, A299 to Kingsgate (past St Peter's Church), B2052
Map 7 on page 497 Carte 7 Page 497

Golf course — PARCOURS — 13/20

Site	Site	
Maintenance	Entretien	
Architect	Architecte	Fowler & Simpson
Type	Type	seaside course
Relief	Relief	
Water in play	Eau en jeu	
Exp. to wind	Exposé au vent	
Trees in play	Arbres en jeu	

Scorecard Carte de score	Chp. Chp.	Mens Mess.	Ladies Da.
Length Long.	5790	5564	5185
Par	71	70	75
Slope system	—	—	—

Advised golfing ability Niveau de jeu recommandé — 0 12 24 36
Hcp required Handicap exigé — certificate or letter

Club house & amenities — CLUB HOUSE ET ANNEXES — 7/10

Pro shop	Pro-shop	
Driving range	Practice	
Sheltered	couvert	no
On grass	sur herbe	yes
Putting-green	putting-green	yes
Pitching-green	pitching green	no

Hotel facilities — ENVIRONNEMENT HOTELIER — 7/10

HOTELS HÔTELS

Castlemere, 36 rooms, D £ 80 — Broadstairs 1 km
Tel (44) 01843 - 861 566, Fax (44) 01843 - 866 379

Bay Tree Hotel, 11 rooms, D £ 55 — Broadstairs 1 km
Tel (44) 01843 - 862 502, Fax (44) 01843 - 860 589

East Horndon, 10 rooms, D £ 60 — Broadstairs 1 km
Tel (44) 01843 - 868 306

Greswolde Hotel, 6 rooms, D £ 50 — Cliftonville 2 km
Tel (44) 01843 - 223 956

RESTAURANTS RESTAURANT

Marchesi, Tel (44) 01843 - 862481 — Broadstairs 1 km

Castlemere, Tel (44) 01843 - 861566 — Broadstairs 1 km

NORTH HANTS

17	7	6

With Blackmoor and Liphook, North Hants completes an excellent clan of courses in a very beautiful part of Hampshire where Harry Colt, Arthur Croome and here James Braid have left their mark. This is a sort of exercise in style with rather similar spaces hewn out of the heather and woods. With Braid, a very great champion in his time, there is always serious emphasis on making each hole different so that the whole course forms a comprehensive examination of a player's ability. If you want to score well, you will need to flight the ball both ways, and while there are few dog-legs here, there is always a right side and a wrong side of the fairway, depending on pin positions. As the greens are very large and protected in proportion to the theoretical length of the approach shot, you will need to be accurate and self-assured. High-handicappers might not feel all that comfortable here but the majority of amateurs will have a lot of fun. North Hants looks great and plays great.

North Hants forme avec Blackmoor et Liphook une excellente famille de parcours dans cette très belle région du Hampshire, où Harry Colt, Arthur Croome et (ici) James Braid ont apposé leur sceau. Entre architectes de haut vol, c'est une sorte d'exercice de style avec des espaces assez similaires, où la bruyère et les bois constituent la matière première. Avec Braid, qui était un très grand champion, on a toujours un grand souci de différencier chaque trou, afin que l'ensemble constitue un examen complet du joueur. Si l'on veut très bien scorer, il faut travailler la balle dans tous les sens. Et s'il y a très peu de doglegs, il y a toujours un "bon" côté du fairway suivant la position du drapeau. Comme les greens sont très grands et protégés en proportion de la longueur théorique du deuxième coup, il faudra être précis et sûr de soi. Les handicaps élevés ne seront pas très à l'aise, mais la majorité des amateurs prendra beaucoup de plaisir. North Hants est beau et bon.

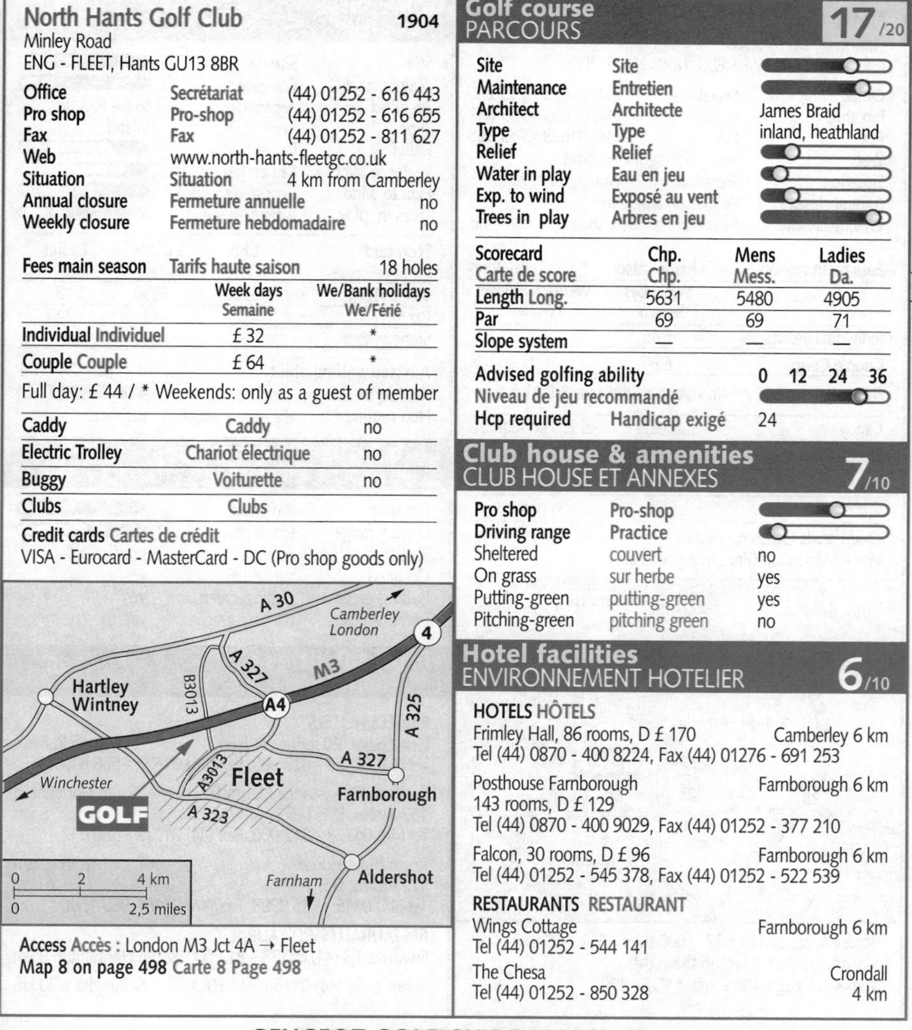

North Hants Golf Club — **1904**

Minley Road
ENG - FLEET, Hants GU13 8BR

Office	Secrétariat	(44) 01252 - 616 443
Pro shop	Pro-shop	(44) 01252 - 616 655
Fax	Fax	(44) 01252 - 811 627
Web	www.north-hants-fleetgc.co.uk	
Situation	Situation	4 km from Camberley
Annual closure	Fermeture annuelle	no
Weekly closure	Fermeture hebdomadaire	no

Fees main season Tarifs haute saison		18 holes
	Week days Semaine	We/Bank holidays We/Férié
Individual Individuel	£ 32	*
Couple Couple	£ 64	*

Full day: £ 44 / * Weekends: only as a guest of member

Caddy	Caddy	no
Electric Trolley	Chariot électrique	no
Buggy	Voiturette	no
Clubs	Clubs	

Credit cards Cartes de crédit
VISA - Eurocard - MasterCard - DC (Pro shop goods only)

Access Accès : London M3 Jct 4A → Fleet
Map 8 on page 498 Carte 8 Page 498

Golf course PARCOURS — 17/20

Site	Site	
Maintenance	Entretien	
Architect	Architecte	James Braid
Type	Type	inland, heathland
Relief	Relief	
Water in play	Eau en jeu	
Exp. to wind	Exposé au vent	
Trees in play	Arbres en jeu	

Scorecard Carte de score	Chp. Chp.	Mens Mess.	Ladies Da.
Length Long.	5631	5480	4905
Par	69	69	71
Slope system	—	—	—

Advised golfing ability Niveau de jeu recommandé — 0 12 24 36

Hcp required Handicap exigé — 24

Club house & amenities CLUB HOUSE ET ANNEXES — 7/10

Pro shop	Pro-shop	
Driving range	Practice	
Sheltered	couvert	no
On grass	sur herbe	yes
Putting-green	putting-green	yes
Pitching-green	pitching green	no

Hotel facilities ENVIRONNEMENT HOTELIER — 6/10

HOTELS HÔTELS

Frimley Hall, 86 rooms, D £ 170 — Camberley 6 km
Tel (44) 0870 - 400 8224, Fax (44) 01276 - 691 253

Posthouse Farnborough — Farnborough 6 km
143 rooms, D £ 129
Tel (44) 0870 - 400 9029, Fax (44) 01252 - 377 210

Falcon, 30 rooms, D £ 96 — Farnborough 6 km
Tel (44) 01252 - 545 378, Fax (44) 01252 - 522 539

RESTAURANTS RESTAURANT

Wings Cottage — Farnborough 6 km
Tel (44) 01252 - 544 141

The Chesa — Crondall 4 km
Tel (44) 01252 - 850 328

NOTTS (HOLLINWELL)

18 | 6 | 6

In a superb setting with a good old clubhouse the way we all like them, this is one inland course to put up there with the very best. Designed by Willie Park Jr. then given bunkers by J.H. Taylor, this is a nicely modelled course typical of a heathland layout which winds it way amidst silver birch and oak trees. There is little water to speak of, but when there is, watch out. Try the 8th hole from the back tees and you will see what we mean. By and large this is a sort of monster where the back-tees are reserved for very good players who know how to flight a ball. It is a little meeker from the front tees, which for the ladies are even too far forward. Notts is also a great course for the rhythm it strikes up, because it has no time for poor shots (except on hole N° 1, the most forgiving). And because you never play the same two shots twice in a row. The members must love it here.

Situé dans un environnement superbe, avec un bon vieux Clubhouse tel qu'on les aime, c'est l'un des parcours "inland" à placer parmi les plus grands. Dessiné à l'origine par Willie Park Jr, son bunkering a ensuite été fait par J.H. Taylor. C'est un parcours bien modelé et typique de terre de bruyère, insinué entre les bouleaux blancs et les chênes. L'eau y est peu abondante, mais de quelle manière au 8, depuis les départs arrière ! En règle générale, c'est une sorte de monstre, et jouer du fond est réservé aux joueurs de très bon niveau, en tout cas ceux qui savent manoeuvrer la balle. Le parcours est plus doux des départs avancés, qui le sont d'ailleurs un peu trop pour les dames, avec leur par 74. Notts est aussi un très grand parcours par le rythme qu'il impose, parce qu'il ne supporte pas les coups médiocres (sauf au 1, le trou le plus indulgent), et parce que l'on ne joue jamais deux fois le même coup deux fois de suite. Les membres doivent s'y régaler...

Notts Golf Club Hollinwell — 1887

Hollinwell, Derby Road
ENG - KIRBY-IN-ASHFIELD, Notts NG17 7QR

Office	Secrétariat	(44) 01623 - 753 225
Pro shop	Pro-shop	(44) 01623 - 753 087
Fax	Fax	(44) 01623 - 753 655
Web	www.nottsgolfclub.com	
Situation	Situation	Nottingham, 20 km
Annual closure	Fermeture annuelle	no
Weekly closure	Fermeture hebdomadaire	no

Fees main season Tarifs haute saison	Week days Semaine	We/Bank holidays We/Férié
	18 holes	
Individual Individuel	£ 45	*
Couple Couple	£ 90	*

Full weekdays: £ 65 / * No visitors at weekends & Bank holidays

Caddy	Caddy	£ 15 /on request
Electric Trolley	Chariot électrique	£ 5 /18 holes
Buggy	Voiturette	no
Clubs	Clubs	on request

Credit cards Cartes de crédit
Visa - Mastercard (Pro Shop goods only)

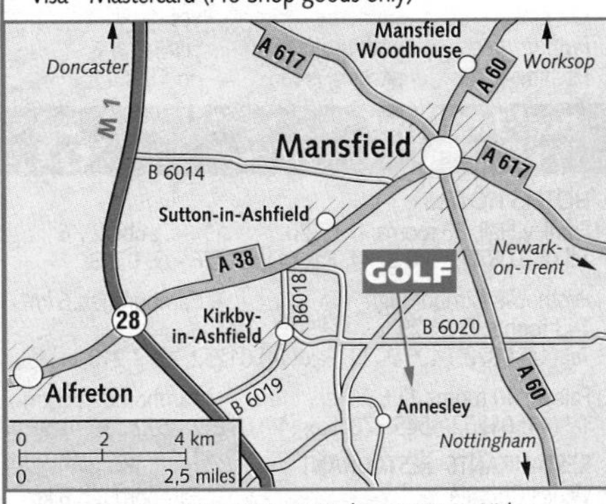

Access Accès : M1 Jct 27. A608 then A611 → Kirby, Mansfield. Golf 3 km on the right.
Map 4 on page 490 Carte 4 Page 490

Golf course PARCOURS — 18/20

Site	Site	
Maintenance	Entretien	
Architect	Architecte	Willie Park Jr
Type	Type	inland
Relief	Relief	
Water in play	Eau en jeu	
Exp. to wind	Exposé au vent	
Trees in play	Arbres en jeu	

Scorecard Carte de score	Chp. Chp.	Mens Mess.	Ladies Da.
Length Long.	6398	6250	5187
Par	72	72	74
Slope system	—	—	—

Advised golfing ability Niveau de jeu recommandé — 0 12 24 36
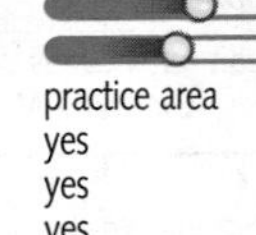

Hcp required Handicap exigé — certificate

Club house & amenities CLUB HOUSE ET ANNEXES — 6/10

Pro shop	Pro-shop	
Driving range	Practice	
Sheltered	couvert	practice area
On grass	sur herbe	yes
Putting-green	putting-green	yes
Pitching-green	pitching green	yes

Hotel facilities ENVIRONNEMENT HOTELIER — 6/10

HOTELS HÔTELS

Pine Lodge, 20 rooms, D £ 65 — Mansfield 8 km
Tel (44) 01623 - 622 308, Fax (44) 01623 - 656 819

Swallow (Renaissance Marriott) — South Normanton 8 km
157 rooms, D £ 115
Tel (44) 01773 - 812 000, Fax (44) 01773 - 580 032

Royal Moat House — Nottingham 20 km
172 rooms, D £ 125
Tel (44) 0115 - 935 9988, Fax (44) 0115 - 969 1506

RESTAURANTS RESTAURANT

Swallow, Tel (44) 01773 - 812 000 — South Normanton 8 km

Sonny's, Tel (44) 0115 - 947 3041 — Nottingham 20 km

ORCHARDLEIGH

16 | 7 | 7

This is an ambitious golf club, but the project of a second course, with an hotel, swimming pool and tennis courts is for now just a project. Close to Bath, and designed by Brian Huggett with the help of Peter McEvoy, this is already a course you will want to get to know. A little on the hilly side with a lot of water in play on six holes, Orchardleigh is an American style course calling for some "target golf" to hit the greens. We are a far cry from the traditional "down to earth" game, but the demands of present-day golfers and the nature of available sites mean that is the way golf seems to be moving. So there are few trees in play but a lot of fairway bunkers, as dangerous as water for high-handicappers (which is a bit of shame). On a peaceful site rich in wildlife and neatly landscaped, this is a sound layout which from a technical angle is very interesting to discover and play.

C'est un club très ambitieux, mais les projets d'un second parcours, avec hôtel, piscine et tennis n'est pour l'instant... qu'un projet. A proximité de Bath, c'est de toute manière un parcours à connaître, dessiné par Brian Huggett avec l'aide de Peter McEvoy. Assez vallonné, mais sans excès, il présente beaucoup d'obstacles d'eau (en jeu sur un tiers des trous), ce qui donne à l'évidence un style américain que la nécessité de jouer du "jeu de cibles" vers les greens accentue encore. Nous sommes loin du "jeu à terre" de la tradition, mais l'exigence des golfeurs d'aujourd'hui, comme la nature des terrains disponibles imposent cette tendance : on trouve ainsi peu d'arbres en jeu, mais de nombreux bunkers de fairway, aussi dangereux que l'eau pour les hauts handicaps (c'est un peu dommage). Dans un site tranquille, riche en vie sauvage et bien paysagé, c'est une solide réalisation, techniquement très intéressante à découvrir et jouer.

Orchardleigh Golf Club — 1996

Near Frome
ENG - BATH, Somerset BA11 2PH

Office	Secrétariat	(44) 01373 - 454 200
Pro shop	Pro-shop	(44) 01373 - 454 200
Fax	Fax	(44) 01373 - 454 202
Web	—	
Situation	Situation	18 km S of Bath
Annual closure	Fermeture annuelle	no
Weekly closure	Fermeture hebdomadaire	no

Fees main season Tarifs haute saison	18 holes	
	Week days Semaine	**We/Bank holidays** We/Férié
Individual Individuel	£ 20	£ 27.50
Couple Couple	£ 40	£ 55

Full weekdays: £ 30

Caddy	Caddy	on request/£ 15
Electric Trolley	Chariot électrique	no
Buggy	Voiturette	£ 20/18 holes
Clubs	Clubs	£ 15/18 holes

Credit cards Cartes de crédit
VISA - MasterCard

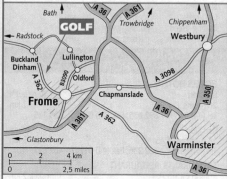

Access Accès : M4 Jct 18, A46 to Bath, then A36 to Frome then A362 → Radstock. 3.5 km NW of Frome, main entrance on right side, before village of Buckland Dinham. **Map 6 on page 495** Carte 6 Page 495

Golf course PARCOURS — 16/20

Site	Site	
Maintenance	Entretien	
Architect	Architecte	Brian Huggett
Type	Type	inland, parkland
Relief	Relief	
Water in play	Eau en jeu	
Exp. to wind	Exposé au vent	
Trees in play	Arbres en jeu	

Scorecard Carte de score	**Chp.** Chp.	**Mens** Mess.	**Ladies** Da.
Length Long.	6198	5691	5026
Par	72	72	73
Slope system	—	—	—

Advised golfing ability Niveau de jeu recommandé — 0 12 24 36
Hcp required Handicap exigé — 28 Men, 36 Ladies

Club house & amenities CLUB HOUSE ET ANNEXES — 7/10

Pro shop	Pro-shop	
Driving range	Practice	
Sheltered	couvert	no
On grass	sur herbe	yes
Putting-green	putting-green	yes
Pitching-green	pitching green	yes

Hotel facilities ENVIRONNEMENT HOTELIER — 7/10

HOTELS HÔTELS

Babington House, 27 rooms, D £ 200 — Frome 1 km
Tel (44) 01373 - 812 266, Fax (44) 01373 - 812 112

Royal Crescent, 45 rooms, D £ 200 — Bath 18 km
Tel (44) 01225 - 823 333, Fax (44) 01225 - 447 427

Bloomfield House, 5 rooms, D £ 95 — Bath 18 km
Tel (44) 01225 - 420 105, Fax (44) 01225 - 481 958

RESTAURANTS RESTAURANT

Mulberry (Charlton House) — Shepton Mallet 12 km
Tel (44) 01749 - 342 008

Babington House, Tel (44) 01373 - 812 266 — Frome 1 km

Bowlish House — Shepton Mallet 12 km
Tel (44) 01749 - 342 022

ORMSKIRK

14 | 6 | 4

Admittedly we are close to the cities of Manchester, Liverpool and Blackburn, but it is still exceptional to see such a concentration of good golf courses in one area. Those on the coast have always attracted the most publicity, but the inland courses have a lot going for them, as well. Take Ormskirk for example, right out in the sticks, far from the hurly-burly of today's modern world. In contrast with links courses, everything here is as green as in those glossy magazines, with birch trees and heather which is a pretty sight indeed... from afar. There is only a single water hazard, on the 3rd hole, but the rough is thick and eats into several fairways. Accurate driving is of the essence, especially on the very many doglegs on which you will have to make a whole range of second shots to reach the greens. The par 3s here are excellent, especially the 14th and 17th holes. Intelligent, natural and very fair, Ormskirk will be a real eye-opener for many golfers.

Certes, nous sommes tout près de Manchester, Liverpool et Blackburn, mais il est exceptionnel de voir une telle concentration de golfs, et de bons golfs. Bien sûr, les parcours de la côte ont bénéficié du maximum de publicité, mais ceux de l'intérieur ne manquent pas d'attraits. Témoin Ormskirk, situé en pleine campagne, très à l'écart des bruits de ce monde. Ici, en contraste avec les links, tout est bien vert comme sur les photos de magazines, avec des bouleaux et la bruyère, si jolie à voir... de loin. Un seul obstacle d'eau, au 3, mais le rough est épais, empiète sur plusieurs fairways, ce qui oblige à la précision des drives, notamment avec les nombreux doglegs qui imposent une très grande variété de seconds coups. On remarquera encore la qualité des par 3, notamment les 14 et 17. Intelligent, naturel et très franc, Ormskirk sera pour beaucoup une découverte.

Ormskirk Golf Club — 1899

Cranes Lane, Lathom
ENG - ORMSKIRK, Lancs L40 5UJ

Office	Secrétariat	(44) 01695 - 572 112
Pro shop	Pro-shop	(44) 01695 - 572 074
Fax	Fax	(44) 01695 - 572 112
Web	—	
Situation	Situation	22 km N of Liverpool
Annual closure	Fermeture annuelle	no
Weekly closure	Fermeture hebdomadaire	no

Fees main season Tarifs haute saison	18 holes	
	Week days Semaine	**We/Bank holidays** We/Férié
Individual Individuel	£ 35	£ 45
Couple Couple	£ 70	£ 90

Full days: £ 40 / £ 50 (week end & wednesday)

Caddy	Caddy	no
Electric Trolley	Chariot électrique	£ 5 /18 holes
Buggy	Voiturette	no
Clubs	Clubs	£ 3 /18 holes

Credit cards Cartes de crédit
VISA - Eurocard - MasterCard - DC - JCB - AMEX
(Pro shop goods only)

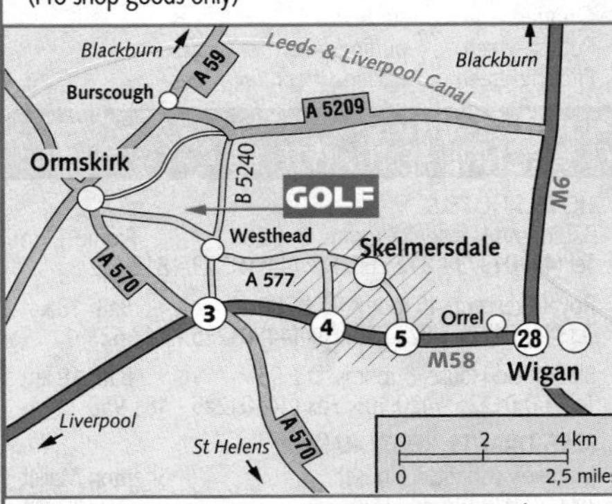

Access Accès : M58 Jct 3. Follow signs to Burscough. First left at T-junction. Right at Hulton Castle Pub. Right at next T-junction. Golf on right.
Map 5 on page 493 Carte 5 Page 493

Golf course — PARCOURS — 14/20

Site	Site	
Maintenance	Entretien	
Architect	Architecte	Harold Hilton
Type	Type	parkland, seaside course
Relief	Relief	
Water in play	Eau en jeu	
Exp. to wind	Exposé au vent	
Trees in play	Arbres en jeu	

Scorecard Carte de score	**Chp.** Chp.	**Mens** Mess.	**Ladies** Da.
Length Long.	5898	5786	5107
Par	70	70	73
Slope system	—	—	—

Advised golfing ability Niveau de jeu recommandé — 0 12 24 36
Hcp required Handicap exigé — certificate

Club house & amenities — CLUB HOUSE ET ANNEXES — 6/10

Pro shop	Pro-shop	
Driving range	Practice	
Sheltered	couvert	no
On grass	sur herbe	yes
Putting-green	putting-green	yes
Pitching-green	pitching green	yes

Hotel facilities — ENVIRONNEMENT HOTELIER — 4/10

HOTELS HÔTELS

Beaufort — Burscough 2 km
20 rooms, D £ 95
Tel (44) 01695 - 892 655, Fax (44) 01695 - 895 135

Red Lion — Newburgh 3 km
13 rooms, D £ 45
Tel (44) 01257 - 462 336, Fax (44) 01257 - 462 827

RESTAURANTS RESTAURANT

Pubs in Ormskirk — Ormskirk 2 km

Beaufort — Burscough 2 km
Tel (44) 01695 - 892 655

PANNAL

15 | 6 | 7

Yorkshire has more specialities than just Yorkshire pudding (which for non-English readers is a sort of batter pastry served with roast-beef, especially on a Sunday). There are also excellent golf courses and the hot springs of Harrogate, which were particularly popular before the first world war. But before trying out the city's superb Turkish baths, spend a day on this very fine course, laid out on a plateau which dominates the surrounding region. This is a typical Yorkshire moorland course, very exposed to the wind but with a lot of trees. The difficulties lie with the thickness of the rough, and your score will depend on how well you drive. Despite the slopes, the course is not tiring to walk, only one green and one drive are blind and only a few elevated greens call for high approach shots. Otherwise you can practice your newly acquired art of rolling the ball onto the green. Green-keeping is very good, the clubhouse elegant and cosy.

Qu'on le sache, le Yorkshire Pudding n'est pas un dessert, mais une pâte à choux servie avec le rôti du dimanche. Le Yorkshire a d'autre spécialités, dont les bons golfs et les sources thermales à Harrogate, très à la mode avant la Grande Guerre. Avant de vous remettre de vos efforts au superbe Sauna Turc de la ville, vous pourrez vous dépenser sur ce très beau parcours, qui vous amène sur un plateau dominant la région. C'est un parcours typique des landes du Comté, très exposé au vent, mais bien arboré. Les difficultés principales tiennent à la densité du rough, et la qualité du drive commande celle du score. En dépit du relief, le parcours n'est pas épuisant, on ne trouve qu'un seul drive et un seul green aveugles, et seules quelques greens surélevés qui appellent des balles levées. Autrement, on peut se livrer à l'amour des balles tendues et des approches roulées. L'entretien est très bon, le Clubhouse élégant et chaleureux.

Pannal Golf Club — 1906

Follifoot Road
ENG - HARROGATE, Yorkshire HG3 1ES

Office	Secrétariat	(44) 01423 - 872 628
Pro shop	Pro-shop	(44) 01423 - 872 620
Fax	Fax	(44) 01423 - 870 043
Web	—	
Situation	Situation	4 km from Harrogate

21 km from Leeds (pop. 680 725)

Annual closure	Fermeture annuelle	no
Weekly closure	Fermeture hebdomadaire	no

Fees main season Tarifs haute saison	18 holes	
	Week days Semaine	**We/Bank holidays** We/Férié
Individual Individuel	£ 40	£ 40
Couple Couple	£ 80	£ 80

Full days: £ 50

Caddy	Caddy	no
Electric Trolley	Chariot électrique	£ 5.50 /18 holes
Buggy	Voiturette	no
Clubs	Clubs	no

Credit cards Cartes de crédit
VISA - Eurocard - MasterCard - Axos (not for green fees)

Access Accès : A61 Leeds → Harrogate.
Map 4 on page 490 Carte 4 Page 490

Golf course PARCOURS — 15/20

Site	Site	
Maintenance	Entretien	
Architect	Architecte	Sandy Herd, Charles MacKenzie
Type	Type	open country, moorland
Relief	Relief	
Water in play	Eau en jeu	
Exp. to wind	Exposé au vent	
Trees in play	Arbres en jeu	

Scorecard Carte de score	**Chp.** Chp.	**Mens** Mess.	**Ladies** Da.
Length Long.	5960	5808	5237
Par	72	72	74
Slope system	—	—	—

Advised golfing ability Niveau de jeu recommandé — 0 12 24 36

Hcp required Handicap exigé — 24 Men, 28 Ladies

Club house & amenities CLUB HOUSE ET ANNEXES — 6/10

Pro shop	Pro-shop	
Driving range	Practice	
Sheltered	couvert	practice area
On grass	sur herbe	yes
Putting-green	putting-green	yes
Pitching-green	pitching green	yes

Hotel facilities ENVIRONNEMENT HOTELIER — 7/10

HOTELS HÔTELS

Rudding Park House Hotel — Rudding Park 3 km
50 rooms, D £ 130
Tel (44) 01423 - 871 350, Fax (44) 01423 - 872 286

Old Swan, 136 rooms, D £ 130 — Harrogate 5 km
Tel (44) 01423 - 500 055, Fax (44) 01423 - 501 154

Crown, 121 rooms, D £ 115 — Harrogate 5 km
Tel (44) 01423 - 567 755, Fax (44) 01423 - 502 284

RESTAURANTS RESTAURANT

Wedgewood Room (Old Swan) — Harrogate 5 km
Tel (44) 01423 - 500 055

Clocktower Brasserie, Tel(44) 01423 - 872 100 Rudding Park

PARKSTONE

16 | 7 | 8

The best time to come here is in Spring, to see how the rhododendrons add colour to the picturesque landscape of heather and pine, or to listen to the ducks quacking as your ball splashes into its watery grave. Parkstone is virtually in town, between Poole and Bournemouth, one of England's most popular seaside resorts. But everything is peace and quiet in a pretty setting where you feel so privileged to be walking the fairways that it is almost unthinkable not to play well. Yet Willie Park, James Braid and Harry Colt used their combined talents to set traps and decorate their work of art with heather from where a decent recovery is nigh on impossible. High-handicappers will certainly not consider this to be a holiday course, but after all there is something to be said for being thrown in at the deep end. They'll learn that this is a good course and if they make it to the 18th (a big par 3) they will do the same as everyone else, take one shot more than they expected.

Ici, il faut venir au printemps quand les rhododendrons ajoutent leurs couleurs de fête du printemps au paysage de bruyères et de pins, et les canards leurs cris de joie quand les balles de golf font des ronds dans l'eau. Parkstone est pratiquement en ville, entre Poole et Bournemouth, une des stations balnéaires les plus fréquentées d'Angleterre. Mais on est ici au calme, dans un joli paysage où il est impossible de mal jouer tant on a le sentiment d'être privilégié. Pourtant, Willie Park, James Braid et Harry Colt se sont ingéniés à tendre des pièges, à décorer leur oeuvre de bruyère dont il est impossible de sortir dignement. Les handicaps un peu élevés ne vont pas trouver qu'il s'agisse d'un parcours de vacances, mais après tout, il faut d'abord apprendre à nager, même au golf. Qu'ils apprennent seulement ce qu'est un bon parcours. Au 18 (un gros par 3), ils feront comme tout le monde, un coup de plus qu'ils n'espérent.

Parkstone Golf Club — 1910

Links Road, Parkstone
ENG - POOLE, Dorset BH14 9QS

Office	Secrétariat	(44) 01202 - 707 138
Pro shop	Pro-shop	(44) 01202 - 708 092
Fax	Fax	(44) 01202 - 706 027
Web	www.parkstonegolfclub.com	
Situation	Situation	2 km E of Poole
Annual closure	Fermeture annuelle	no
Weekly closure	Fermeture hebdomadaire	no

Fees main season Tarifs haute saison — 18 holes

	Week days / Semaine	We/Bank holidays / We/Férié
Individual Individuel	£ 35	£ 45
Couple Couple	£ 70	£ 90

Full days: £ 50 / £ 60 (week ends)

Caddy	Caddy	no
Electric Trolley	Chariot électrique	£ 7 /18 holes
Buggy	Voiturette	no
Clubs	Clubs	£ 8 /day

Credit cards Cartes de crédit
VISA - MasterCard (Pro shop goods only)

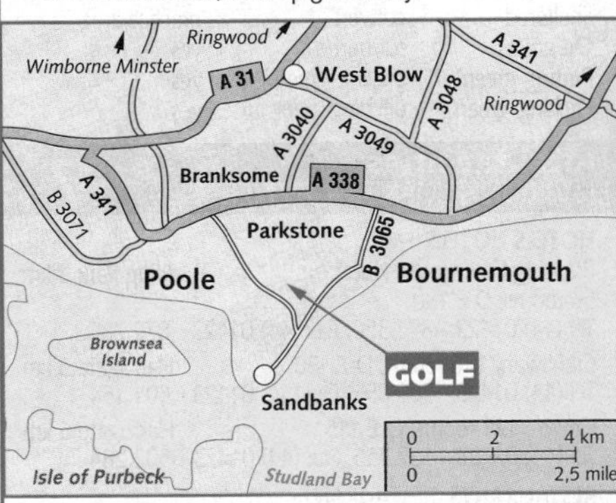

Access Accès : A35 Bournemouth → Poole.
Turn left on St Osmunds Road
Map 6 on page 495 Carte 6 Page 495

Golf course / PARCOURS — 16/20

Site	Site	
Maintenance	Entretien	
Architect	Architecte	Willie Park James Braid
Type	Type	forest, heathland
Relief	Relief	
Water in play	Eau en jeu	
Exp. to wind	Exposé au vent	
Trees in play	Arbres en jeu	

Scorecard / Carte de score	Chp. / Chp.	Mens / Mess.	Ladies / Da.
Length Long.	5690	5405	4952
Par	72	71	71
Slope system	—	—	—

Advised golfing ability / Niveau de jeu recommandé — 0 12 24 36

Hcp required Handicap exigé — 28 Men, 30 Ladies

Club house & amenities / CLUB HOUSE ET ANNEXES — 7/10

Pro shop	Pro-shop	
Driving range	Practice	
Sheltered	couvert	members & green fees
On grass	sur herbe	yes
Putting-green	putting-green	yes
Pitching-green	pitching green	yes

Hotel facilities / ENVIRONNEMENT HOTELIER — 8/10

HOTELS HÔTELS

Haven, 94 rooms, D £ 150 (with dinner) — Sandbanks 2 km
Tel (44) 01202 - 707 333, Fax (44) 01202 - 708 796

Mansion House, 32 rooms, D £ 130 — Poole 2 km
Tel (44) 01202 - 685 666, Fax (44) 01202 - 665 709

East Cliff Court, 70 rooms, D £ 160 — Bournemouth 2 km
Tel (44) 01202 - 554 545, Fax (44) 01202 - 557 456

Miramar, 44 rooms, D £ 140 — Bournemouth 2 km
Tel (44) 01202 - 556 581, Fax (44) 01202 - 291 242

RESTAURANTS RESTAURANT

La Roche, Tel (44) 01202 - 707 333 — Sandbanks 2 km

Benjamin's (Mansion H.), Tel (44) 01202 - 685 666 — Poole

PATSHULL PARK HOTEL

13	8	8

Nature specialists will often talk to you about Capability Brown, no relation to Calamity Jane, but the father-figure of English landscape gardening in the 18th century in reaction to the more austere French-style gardens. Patshull was laid out in an estate planted by the great man and it gives considerable visual appeal to this very discreet and classical course by John Jacobs. The water hazards certainly add a little extra spice. Some of the trees are dangerously in play because they transform a number of straight holes into dog-legs, so you have to play around them. Not too long, Patshull is a pleasant family course to play on foot, although hiring a buggy is not a bad idea, either, at least for carrying your bags. You don't come here to play top tournaments but to spend a day or two's pleasant golfing. The hotel on site is very well appointed with sauna, pool and jacuzzi, and you can also fish here.

Les spécialistes de la nature vous parleront de Capability Brown, qui n'était pas le cousin de Calamity Jane, mais le père du paysage à l'anglaise au XVIIIème siècle, en réaction contre les austères jardins à la française. C'est dans un domaine qu'il a créé que ce parcours a pris place. Il ajoute un attrait visuel indéniable au tracé très sobre et classique de John Jacobs, où les obstacles d'eau apportent un certain piment. Quelques arbres ont été dangereusement mis en jeu, car ils transforment certains trous droits en doglegs. Il faut savoir tourner autour. Pas trop long, Patshull est très agréable à jouer en famille, à pied éventuellement, mais jouer en voiturette n'est pas mal non plus, au moins pour mettre les sacs de golf. Ici, on ne vient pas jouer de grands championnats, mais passer une ou deux bonnes journées. L'hôtel sur place est très bien équipé, avec sauna, piscine, jacuzzi. Il est aussi possible de pêcher. Beau programme.

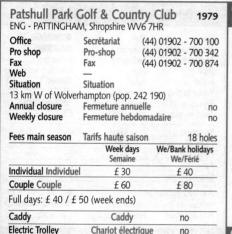

Patshull Park Golf & Country Club — 1979

ENG - PATTINGHAM, Shropshire WV6 7HR

Office	Secrétariat	(44) 01902 - 700 100
Pro shop	Pro-shop	(44) 01902 - 700 342
Fax	Fax	(44) 01902 - 700 874
Web	—	
Situation	Situation	

13 km W of Wolverhampton (pop. 242 190)

Annual closure	Fermeture annuelle	no
Weekly closure	Fermeture hebdomadaire	no

Fees main season Tarifs haute saison	18 holes	
	Week days Semaine	**We/Bank holidays** We/Férié
Individual Individuel	£ 30	£ 40
Couple Couple	£ 60	£ 80

Full days: £ 40 / £ 50 (week ends)

Caddy	Caddy	no
Electric Trolley	Chariot électrique	no
Buggy	Voiturette	£ 19.50 /18 holes
Clubs	Clubs	£ 15 /18 holes

Credit cards Cartes de crédit
VISA - Eurocard - MasterCard - DC - AMEX

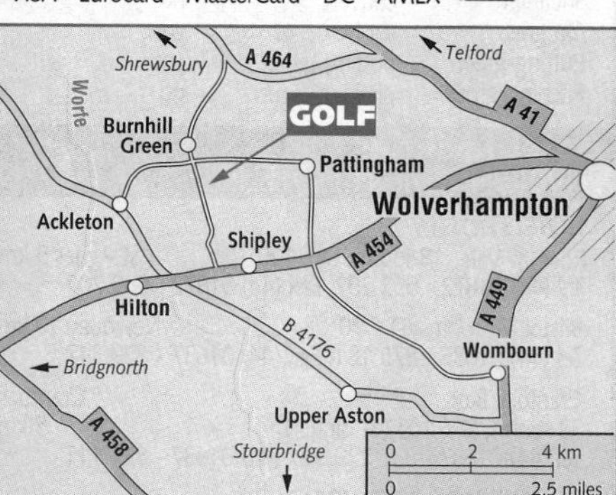

Access Accès : Wolverhampton, A454 → Bridgnorth. Nearly 4 km (2 1/2 m.) until The Mermaid Inn. Turn right after lights (Tinacre Hill) through Pattingham. Turn right at the Church. Golf 2 km on the right. **Map 7 on page 496** Carte 7 Page 496

Golf course — PARCOURS — 13/20

Site	Site	
Maintenance	Entretien	
Architect	Architecte	John Jacobs
Type	Type	parkland
Relief	Relief	
Water in play	Eau en jeu	
Exp. to wind	Exposé au vent	
Trees in play	Arbres en jeu	

Scorecard Carte de score	**Chp.** Chp.	**Mens** Mess.	**Ladies** Da.
Length Long.	5834	5601	5157
Par	72	72	74
Slope system	—	—	—

Advised golfing ability 0 12 24 36
Niveau de jeu recommandé
Hcp required Handicap exigé 27

Club house & amenities — CLUB HOUSE ET ANNEXES — 8/10

Pro shop	Pro-shop	
Driving range	Practice	
Sheltered	couvert	
On grass	sur herbe	yes
Putting-green	putting-green	yes
Pitching-green	pitching green	no

Hotel facilities — ENVIRONNEMENT HOTELIER — 8/10

HOTELS HÔTELS

Patshull Park Hotel, 49 rooms, D £ 90 — on site
Tel (44) 01902 - 700 100, Fax (44) 01902 - 700 874

Hundred House, 10 rooms, D £ 120 — Norton 7 km
Tel (44) 01952 - 730 353, Fax (44) 01952 - 730 355

Park Hall Hotel — Wolverhampton
57 rooms, D £ 75 — 13 km
Tel (44) 01902 - 331 121, Fax (44) 01902 - 344 760

RESTAURANTS RESTAURANT

Old Vicarage — Worfield
Tel (44) 01746 - 716 497 — 6 km

Lakeside Restaurant — on site
Tel (44) 01902 - 700 100

609

PERRANPORTH

16 | 6 | 6

The cliffs and reefs of the west coast of Cornwall sometimes give way to little bays and fine beaches, such as here and the neighbouring holiday resort of Newquay, a surfer's paradise. It's also pretty good for golfers, too, who should make it along here in the same breath as St Enodoc and Trevose. You are in for a relatively easy round if you don't stray from the fairways, but it's a big "if". The "short stuff" is very tight, hilly (with dips, bumps, mounds and hillocks) and difficult to hit. After climbing up the dunes, you can find yourself in long grass, from where good scoring can pose something of a problem. At first glance you might think this an easy course, as there are very few bunkers. Paradoxically it is easier for mid-handicappers than it is for better players, who often prefer to play their approach shots out of sand rather than in thick grass.

Les falaises et les écueils de la côte ouest de Cornouailles laissent parfois place à de petites criques et même des plages, où ont trouvé place des stations de vacances comme Newquay, un paradis des surfeurs. Mais aussi des golfeurs, qui se doivent de venir ici en même temps qu'à St Enodoc et Trevose. Si l'on ne quitte pas les fairways, le jeu y sera relativement aisé. Mais ils sont très étroits, assez mouvementés (des creux et des bosses, des petites buttes et monticules), et on en sort un peu trop facilement. Après avoir grimpé dans les dunes, on peut alors se retrouver dans des herbes bien hautes, d'où un bon score devient problématique. On peut avoir l'illusion qu'il s'agit d'un parcours facile en jetant un premier coup d'oeil, car les bunkers sont peu nombreux : il est paradoxalement plus facile pour les handicaps moyens que pour les bons, qui préfèrent souvent jouer leurs balles dans le sable que dans l'herbe haute...

Perranporth Golf Club — 1929

The Clubhouse, Budnic Hill
ENG - PERRANPOTH, Cornwall TR6 0AB

Office	Secrétariat	(44) 01872 - 573 701
Pro shop	Pro-shop	(44) 01872 - 572 317
Fax	Fax	(44) 01872 - 573 701
Web	—	
Situation	Situation	

10 km S of Newquay (pop. 17 390) - 15 km NW of Truro

Annual closure	Fermeture annuelle	no
Weekly closure	Fermeture hebdomadaire	no

Fees main season Tarifs haute saison		Full day
	Week days Semaine	**We/Bank holidays** We/Férié
Individual Individuel	£ 25	£ 30
Couple Couple	£ 50	£ 60
Caddy	Caddy	no
Electric Trolley	Chariot électrique	no
Buggy	Voiturette	no
Clubs	Clubs	£ 10

Credit cards Cartes de crédit
VISA - Eurocard - MasterCard (Pro shop goods only)

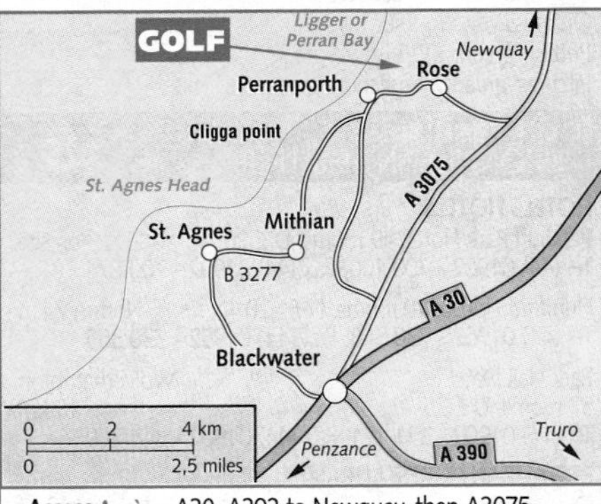

Access Accès : A30, A392 to Newquay, then A3075. At Goonhavern, B3285.
Golf on edge of Perranporth, next to beach
Map 6 on page 494 Carte 6 Page 494

Golf course — PARCOURS — 16/20

Site	Site	
Maintenance	Entretien	
Architect	Architecte	James Braid
Type	Type	seaside course, links
Relief	Relief	
Water in play	Eau en jeu	
Exp. to wind	Exposé au vent	
Trees in play	Arbres en jeu	

Scorecard Carte de score	**Chp.** Chp.	**Mens** Mess.	**Ladies** Da.
Length Long.	5722	5460	4880
Par	72	72	72
Slope system	—	—	—

Advised golfing ability 0 12 24 36
Niveau de jeu recommandé
Hcp required Handicap exigé certificate

Club house & amenities — CLUB HOUSE ET ANNEXES — 6/10

Pro shop	Pro-shop	
Driving range	Practice	
Sheltered	couvert	no
On grass	sur herbe	yes
Putting-green	putting-green	yes
Pitching-green	pitching green	no

Hotel facilities — ENVIRONNEMENT HOTELIER — 6/10

HOTELS HÔTELS

Rose-in-Vale, 18 rooms, D £ 100 — St Agnes 5 km
Tel (44) 01872 - 552 202, Fax (44) 01872 - 552 700

Bristol, 74 rooms, D £ 90 — Newquay 10 km
Tel (44) 01637 - 875 181, Fax (44) 01637 - 879 347

Crantock Bay — Crantock 5 km
33 rooms, D £ 105 (w. dinner)
Tel (44) 01637 - 830 229, Fax (44) 01637 - 831 111

RESTAURANTS RESTAURANT

Pennypots — Truro 15 km
Tel (44) 01209 - 820 347

PLEASINGTON

16 | 8 | 6

611

This is one the region's great parkland courses and has recently treated itself to an impressively sized brand new clubhouse. There are a lot of trees, particularly on the 16th (a par 3) which you have to hit over in order to reach the green, but elsewhere they are rarely in play, except for slicers. The other hazards are the heather and the many large bunkers. Once again, a good score here means you really did play well. You may be lucky once, but rarely twice. Because of the technical challenge here, inexperienced players can expect to sweat a little, so stableford, match-play or a Texas scramble might be a more enjoyable option. This is indeed an excellent course for match-play golf, almost a testimony to the not too distant day and age when match-play was the formula used by all amateur golfers. The general excellence of green-keeping makes a visit here something we would eagerly recommend, despite the proximity of some pretty good links courses.

C'est un des grands parcours "de parc" de cette région, qui s'est offert il y a peu un nouveau Clubhouse de taille impressionnante. On trouve ici beaucoup d'arbres, notamment un au 16 (par 3), qu'il faut survoler pour atteindre le green, mais ils sont rarement très en jeu... sauf pour les sliceurs. Les autres auront plutôt de la bruyère, de grands et nombreux bunkers. Un bon score est forcément la preuve d'un bon jeu. Ici, on peut avoir de la chance une fois, mais rarement deux. En raison de ses exigences techniques, les joueurs peu expérimentés doivent s'attendre à souffrir, on leur conseillera donc le stableford, le match-play ou le scramble ! Car c'est un excellent parcours de match-play, témoin d'un époque pas si lointaine où il s'agissait de la formule de jeu des amateurs. La qualité générale de l'entretien permet de recommander une visite, même si les grands links sont à proximité.

Pleasington Golf Club — 1891

Pleasington
ENG - BLACKBURN, Lancs BB2 5JF

Office	Secrétariat	(44) 01254 - 202 177
Pro shop	Pro-shop	(44) 01254 - 201 630
Fax	Fax	(44) 01254 - 201 028
Web	—	
Situation	Situation	5 km from Blackburn
Annual closure	Fermeture annuelle	no
Weekly closure	Fermeture hebdomadaire	no

Fees main season Tarifs haute saison	Week days Semaine	We/Bank holidays We/Férié
		18 holes
Individual Individuel	£ 36	£ 42
Couple Couple	£ 72	£ 84

Full weekdays: £ 42

Caddy	Caddy	no
Electric Trolley	Chariot électrique	no
Buggy	Voiturette	no
Clubs	Clubs	£ 7.50 /18 holes
Credit cards	Cartes de crédit	no

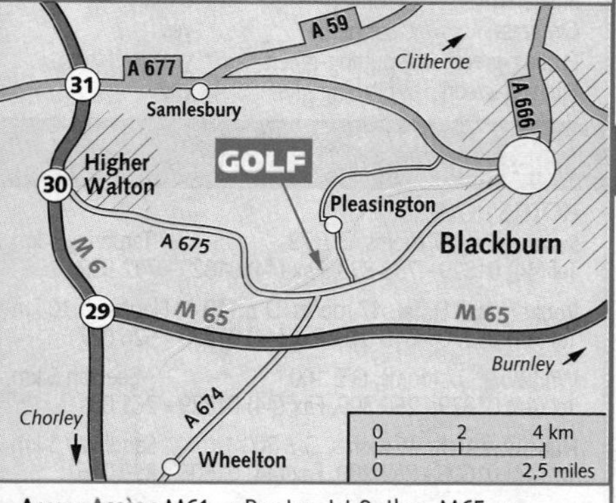

Access Accès : M61 → Preston Jct 9, then M65 → Blackburn. Jct 3, then A674 → Blackburn, to Pleasington Lane. Golf 200 m from Pleasington Station.
Map 5 on page 493 Carte 5 Page 493

Golf course PARCOURS — 16/20

Site	Site	
Maintenance	Entretien	
Architect	Architecte	George Low, Sandy Herd
Type	Type	parkland, heathland
Relief	Relief	
Water in play	Eau en jeu	
Exp. to wind	Exposé au vent	
Trees in play	Arbres en jeu	

Scorecard Carte de score	Chp. Chp.	Mens Mess.	Ladies Da.
Length Long.	5816	5816	5217
Par	71	71	74
Slope system	—	—	—

Advised golfing ability Niveau de jeu recommandé: 0 12 24 36
Hcp required Handicap exigé: no

Club house & amenities CLUB HOUSE ET ANNEXES — 8/10

Pro shop	Pro-shop	
Driving range	Practice	
Sheltered	couvert	no
On grass	sur herbe	practice range only
Putting-green	putting-green	yes
Pitching-green	pitching green	yes

Hotel facilities ENVIRONNEMENT HOTELIER — 6/10

HOTELS HÔTELS

Swallow Trafalgar Hotel — Samlesbury 5 km
78 rooms, D £ 125
Tel (44) 01772 - 877 351, Fax (44) 01772 - 877 424

Forte Posthouse, 121 rooms, D £ 60 — Preston 10 km
Tel (44) 01772 - 259 411, Fax (44) 01772 - 201 923

Millstone, 26 rooms, D £ 108 — Mellor 6 km
Tel (44) 01254 - 813 333, Fax (44) 01254 - 812 628

RESTAURANTS RESTAURANT

Heathcotes Brasserie — Preston 10 km
Tel (44) 01772 - 252 732

Campions, Tel (44) 01772 - 877 641 — Samlesbury 6 km

Golf Club, Tel(44) 01254 - 202 177 — on site

PORTAL Championship

15 | 8 | 7

They needed a big clubhouse here to cater to the number of players on the two 18 hole courses (the second course is the old Oaklands Golf Club). The Championship Course (1989), probably one of Donald Steel's best, is hilly enough for us to recommend a buggy to keep all your strength for playing golf (you will need it). The existing lie of the land was used and enhanced to great effect, completed by some shifting of earth that never clashes with landscape where the impression is more that of a park than open countryside. A little decoration never does any harm, like the little waterfalls on the 15th hole or the plants on the 6th. Owing to the length of this course, you will be hard pushed to play it twice in one day, so you will be pleased to learn that all the hazards are clearly visible, although to avoid them you will have to pitch the ball in high, sometimes flighting it both ways. A fine course.

Il fallait un Clubhouse imposant pour s'accommoder de la fréquentation sur deux 18 trous (le second parcours est l'ancien Oaklands Golf Club). Le Championship Course (1989) est probablement une des meilleures réalisations de Donald Steel, mais on conseillera l'usage d'une voiturette afin de garder assez de forces pour jouer au golf. Le terrain existant a été très bien utilisé et mis en valeur, et complété de mouvements qui ne heurtent jamais un paysage quand même plus proche du parc que de la campagne. Un peu de décoration ne nuit pas, comme les petites cascades du 15 ou les plantations du 6. Comme on jouera difficilement deux fois dans la journée en raison de la longueur du parcours, il faut savoir que tous les obstacles sont bien visibles, mais qu'il vaut mieux savoir bien lever la balle, et parfois la travailler pour réussir. Une belle réalisation.

Portal Golf Club — 1989

Cobblers Cross
ENG - TARPORLEY, Cheshire CW6 0DJ

Office	Secrétariat	(44) 01829 - 733 933
Pro shop	Pro-shop	(44) 01829 - 733 933
Fax	Fax	(44) 01829 - 733 928
Web	www.portalgolf.co.uk	
Situation	Situation	

16 km E of Chester (pop. 115 971)

Annual closure	Fermeture annuelle	no
Weekly closure	Fermeture hebdomadaire	no

Fees main season Tarifs haute saison		18 holes
	Week days Semaine	We/Bank holidays We/Férié
Individual Individuel	£ 50	£ 50
Couple Couple	£ 100	£ 100
Caddy	Caddy	no
Electric Trolley	Chariot électrique	no
Buggy	Voiturette	£ 20 /18 holes
Clubs	Clubs	on request

Credit cards Cartes de crédit
VISA - Eurocard - MasterCard - DC - AMEX

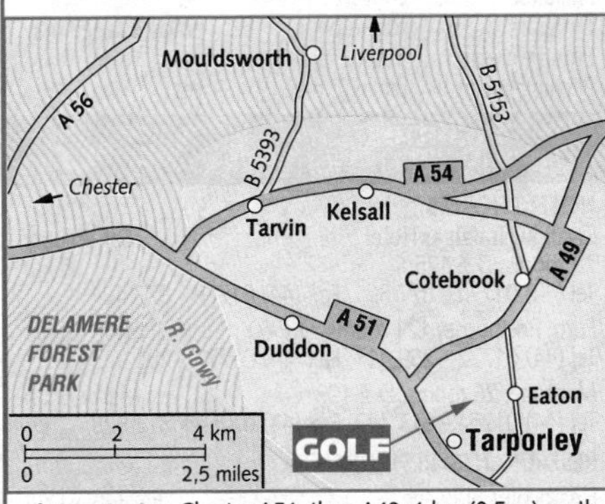

Access Accès : Chester A51, then A49. 1 km (0.5 m) north of Tarporley.
Map 4 on page 490 Carte 4 Page 490

Golf course PARCOURS — 15/20

Site	Site	
Maintenance	Entretien	
Architect	Architecte	Donald Steel
Type	Type	parkland
Relief	Relief	
Water in play	Eau en jeu	
Exp. to wind	Exposé au vent	
Trees in play	Arbres en jeu	

Scorecard Carte de score	Chp. Chp.	Mens Mess.	Ladies Da.
Length Long.	6333	5854	5362
Par	73	73	73
Slope system	—	—	—

Advised golfing ability 0 12 24 36
Niveau de jeu recommandé
Hcp required Handicap exigé no

Club house & amenities CLUB HOUSE ET ANNEXES — 8/10

Pro shop	Pro-shop	
Driving range	Practice	
Sheltered	couvert	6 mats
On grass	sur herbe	yes
Putting-green	putting-green	yes
Pitching-green	pitching green	yes

Hotel facilities ENVIRONNEMENT HOTELIER — 7/10

HOTELS HÔTELS

Swan Hotel, 17 rooms, D £ 73 — Tarporley 5 km
Tel (44) 01829 - 733 838, Fax (44) 01829 - 732 932

Rookery Hall Hotel, 47 rooms, D £ 110 — Nantwich 10 km
Tel (44) 01270 - 610 016, Fax (44) 01270 - 626 027

Wild Boar, 37 rooms, D £ 100 — Beeston 6 km
Tel (44) 01829 - 260 309, Fax (44) 01829 - 261 081

Nunsmere Hall, 36 rooms, D £ 200 — Sandiway 5 km
Tel (44) 01606 - 889 100, Fax (44) 01606 - 889 055

RESTAURANTS RESTAURANT

Swan Hotel, Tel (44) 01829 - 733 838 — Tarporley 5 km

Blue Bell, Tel (44) 01244 - 317 759 — Chester 15 km

PORTERS PARK

15	7	7

This is one of the oldest clubs in Hertfordshire which has recently celebrated its centenary. It was laid out by C.S. Butchart then restyled by J.H. Taylor, especially the bunkering which is remarkable. Bump 'n run shots are frequently a viable option but you often need a good, well-placed drive for the best angle of attack. This is all the more difficult in that high-handicappers seldom have good control over their tee-shots and the contoured fairways here can provide some unpleasant surprises. To make matters worse, a stream comes into play as a frontal hazard on seven holes. Here, either you have the full panoply of shots or you have a sense of improvisation (or both). The second shot also has to be well struck to reach the greens in the best spot. Last but not least, the course finishes with four par 4s of very decent length that can make all the difference whatever formula you are playing. It is great fun playing here (during the week) especially considering the very warm welcome in an impressive and traditional club-house.

Ce club vient de fêter son centenaire. Le parcours dessiné par CS Butchart a été remanié par JH Taylor, en particulier le bunkering, remarquable : les approches roulées sont fréquemment possible, mais l'angle d'attaque doit souvent avoir été préparé par un drive bien placé. C'est d'autant plus difficile que les amateurs contrôlent rarement leurs coups de départ, que les contours des fairways peuvent réserver des surprises, et qu'un cours d'eau vient en jeu sur sept trous de manière frontale. On doit posséder ici un vaste répertoire de coups de golf, savoir improviser. Et pour parvenir aux greens en bonne position, savoir être précis. On ajoutera que ce parcours se termine par quatre par 4 de longueurs respectables, qui feront la différence aussi bien en match-play qu'en stroke-play. C'est un plaisir de jouer ici (en semaine), d'autant que l'accueil est agréable, le Club house imposant et traditionnel, bien qu'il ne soit pas si ancien.

Porters Park Golf Club — 1899

Shenley Hill
ENG - RADLETT, Herts. WD7 7AZ

Office	Secrétariat	(44) 01923 - 854 127
Pro shop	Pro-shop	(44) 01923 - 854 366
Fax	Fax	(44) 01923 - 855 475
Web	—	
Situation	Situation	30 km NW of London
Annual closure	Fermeture annuelle	no
Weekly closure	Fermeture hebdomadaire	no

Fees main season Tarifs haute saison	18 holes	
	Week days Semaine	**We/Bank holidays** We/Férié
Individual Individuel	£ 30	*
Couple Couple	£ 60	*

Full weekdays: £ 45 / * Members only at week ends

Caddy	Caddy	no
Electric Trolley	Chariot électrique	£ 5
Buggy	Voiturette	no
Clubs	Clubs	no

Credit cards Cartes de crédit
VISA - Eurocard - MasterCard - AMEX
(Pro shop goods only)

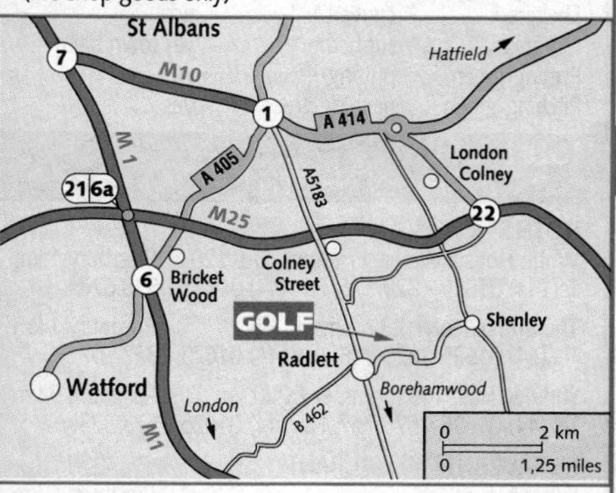

Access Accès : London M1. Exit 5, then first exit along A41. 300m to a big roudabout, → Radlett on B462. At T-junction mini roundabout, turn right, then first left at next roundabout into Shenley Hill. Golf Club 1,5 km. **Map 8 on page 499** Carte 8 Page 499

Golf course — PARCOURS — 15/20

Site	Site	
Maintenance	Entretien	
Architect	Architecte	CS Butchark J.H. Taylor
Type	Type	parkland
Relief	Relief	
Water in play	Eau en jeu	
Exp. to wind	Exposé au vent	
Trees in play	Arbres en jeu	

Scorecard Carte de score	**Chp.** Chp.	**Mens** Mess.	**Ladies** Da.
Length Long.	5741	5440	5032
Par	70	70	73
Slope system	—	—	—

Advised golfing ability Niveau de jeu recommandé: 0 12 24 36
Hcp required Handicap exigé: certificate

Club house & amenities — CLUB HOUSE ET ANNEXES — 7/10

Pro shop	Pro-shop	
Driving range	Practice	
Sheltered	couvert	practice areas
On grass	sur herbe	yes
Putting-green	putting-green	yes
Pitching-green	pitching green	yes

Hotel facilities — ENVIRONNEMENT HOTELIER — 7/10

HOTELS HÔTELS

Hilton National, 201 rooms, D £ 99 — Watford 8 km
Tel (44) 01923 - 235 881, Fax (44) 01923 - 220 836

Edgwarebury, 47 rooms, D £ 180 — Elstree 8 km
Tel (44) 0181 - 953 8227, Fax (44) 0181 - 207 3668

Elstree Moat House — Borehamwood 10 km
131 rooms, D £ 195
Tel (44) 0181 - 214 9988, Fax (44) 0181 - 207 3194

Oaklands Toby, 38 rooms, D £ 85 — Borehamwood 10 km
Tel (44) 0181 - 905 1455, Fax (44) 0181 - 905 1370

RESTAURANTS RESTAURANT

The Cavendish (Edgwarebury) — Elstree 8 km
Tel (44) 0181 - 953 8227

PRESTBURY

17 | 8 | 7

The green-keeper is one of the five "masters" of Britain and his sterling efforts only add to the pleasure of playing one of the very few moorland courses designed by Harry Colt. A huge planting programme has enhanced the course both visually and in terms of giving each hole clearer definition over wide open space. Colt didn't do much to the terrain, he just used it with his usual brilliance, and you might be surprised by some of the sloping fairways. You need an accurate driver here, but the basic work consists in hitting some very-well defended greens which are sometimes tiered, sometimes terraced owing to the lie of the land. You need to play every shot in the book, in every direction. Basically you will want at least one good shot per hole (and some good putts), so you don't have much breathing space. A very sound course that makes an impression on all who play it, although visitors can only tee-off during the week. The ideal time would be a fine Autumn afternoon.

Le greenkeeper est l'un des "Masters" de Grande-Bretagne, et son travail ne fait qu'ajouter au plaisir d'un des seuls dessins de Harry Colt en véritable paysage de lande, auquel un énorme programme de plantations a donné à la fois beauté visuelle et définition des trous dans l'espace. Colt n'a pas beaucoup touché au terrain, il l'a utilisé avec son génie habituel, et certaines inclinaisons des fairways pourront surprendre. Il faut être précis au drive, mais le travail essentiel est dans les approches de greens très protégés, parfois en plateau ou en balcons en raison des mouvements du terrain. Il faut alors savoir jouer tous les coups, et dans tous les sens : il faut au minimum un bon coup de golf par trou (et de bons putts), ce qui ne laisse guère respirer. Un solide parcours qui ne laissera pas indifférent, mais on ne peut le jouer qu'en semaine. A voir par un bel après-midi d'automne.

Prestbury Golf Club — 1921

Macclesfield Road
ENG - PRESTBURY, Cheshire SK10 4BJ

Office	Secrétariat	(44) 01625 - 828 241
Pro shop	Pro-shop	(44) 01625 - 828 242
Fax	Fax	(44) 01625 - 828 241
Web	—	
Situation	Situation	25 km from Manchester
Annual closure	Fermeture annuelle	no
Weekly closure	Fermeture hebdomadaire	no

Fees main season / Tarifs haute saison	Week days / Semaine	We/Bank holidays / We/Férié
Individual Individuel	£ 42	*
Couple Couple	£ 84	*

Full day

* No visitors at weekends

Caddy	Caddy	£ 15 /on request
Electric Trolley	Chariot électrique	£ 5 /18 holes
Buggy	Voiturette	no
Clubs	Clubs	£ 5 /18 holes

Credit cards Cartes de crédit
VISA - Eurocard - MasterCard - DC - AMEX
(Pro shop goods only)

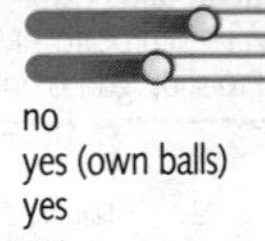

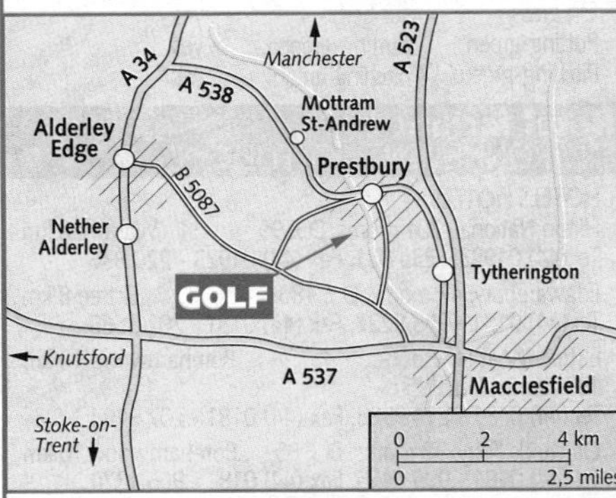

Access Accès : 3 km NW of Macclesfield on A538 off A523.
Map 4 on page 490 Carte 4 Page 490

Golf course / PARCOURS — 17/20

Site	Site	
Maintenance	Entretien	
Architect	Architecte	Harry S. Colt, J. Morrison
Type	Type	inland, open country
Relief	Relief	
Water in play	Eau en jeu	
Exp. to wind	Exposé au vent	
Trees in play	Arbres en jeu	

Scorecard / Carte de score	Chp. / Chp.	Mens / Mess.	Ladies / Da.
Length Long.	5723	5528	4917
Par	71	71	74
Slope system	—	—	—

Advised golfing ability / Niveau de jeu recommandé: 0 12 24 36
Hcp required / Handicap exigé: no

Club house & amenities / CLUB HOUSE ET ANNEXES — 8/10

Pro shop	Pro-shop	
Driving range	Practice	
Sheltered	couvert	no
On grass	sur herbe	yes (own balls)
Putting-green	putting-green	yes
Pitching-green	pitching green	yes

Hotel facilities / ENVIRONNEMENT HOTELIER — 7/10

HOTELS HÔTELS

White House Manor, 11 rooms, D £ 120 — Prestbury 1 km
Tel (44) 01625 - 829 376, Fax (44) 01625 - 828 627

The Bridge Hotel, 23 rooms, D £ 80 — Prestbury 1 km
Tel (44) 01625 - 829 326, Fax (44) 01625 - 827 557

Shrigley Hall, 148 rooms, D £ 200 — Adlington 5 km
Tel (44) 01625 - 575 757, Fax (44) 01625 - 573 323

RESTAURANTS RESTAURANT

White House — Prestbury 1 km
Tel (44) 01625 - 829 376

The Bridge Hotel, Tel (44) 01625 - 829 326 — Prestbury 1 km

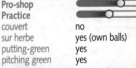

Mauro's, Tel (44) 01625 - 573 898 — Bollington 2 km

PRINCE'S Himalayas-Shore

14 | 6 | 4

Restoration work and alterations since the war, the arranging of the course into 3 nine-hole loops and a commitment to making this a course more for your average golfer have somewhat unseated the original layout by Campbell and Morrison and probably detracted from its overall standard as well. The fairways are wider than they used to be and the bunkers and greens are smaller, thereby reducing the risk of 3-putts. The only really interesting combination is almost certainly "Shore-Himalayas" which, and this is no coincidence, embraces most of the original layout. Of course, alongside Royal St. George and Royal Cinque Ports, a number of less experienced golfers will enjoy their first taste of links golfing with getting too much of a bloody nose. And of course if the wind blows (often a cross-wind here) Prince's can be long and tough. But all the same, the better players will still find the challenge here a little less demanding than it might be. The clubhouse is modern and facilities very respectable.

Les restaurations de l'après-guerre, la disposition en trois boucles de neuf trous, l'adaptation de Prince's aux handicaps moyens ont quelque peu bouleversé le dessin original de Campbell et Morrison. Et l'ont affaibli, il faut bien le dire. Les fairways sont plus larges qu'autrefois, les bunkers souvent plus petits, tout comme les greens : on n'y risque plus trois putts. Et la seule combinaison réellement intéressante est incontestablement "Shore-Himalayas," où l'on trouve, ce n'est pas un hasard, la majorité du tracé d'origine. Certes, à côté de Royal St George's et de Royal Cinque Ports, certains golfeurs peu aguerris aimeront faire leur expérience des links sans trop se casser les dents. Certes, si le vent souffle (souvent en travers), Prince's peut être être long et difficile. Il n'empêche que les meilleurs joueurs trouveront le défi un peu moins agressif qu'il pourrait l'être. Le Clubhouse est moderne, les équipements convenables.

Prince's Golf Club — 1904

ENG - SANDWICH BAY, Kent CT13 9QB

Office	Secrétariat	(44) 01304 - 611 118
Pro shop	Pro-shop	(44) 01304 - 613 797
Fax	Fax	(44) 01304 - 612 000
Web	www.princes/leisure.co.uk	
Situation	Situation	

4 km from Sandwich - 10 km from Deal (pop. 28 504)

Annual closure	Fermeture annuelle	no
Weekly closure	Fermeture hebdomadaire	no

Fees main season Tarifs haute saison	18 holes	
	Week days Semaine	**We/Bank holidays** We/Férié
Individual Individuel	£ 55	£ 60
Couple Couple	£ 110	£ 120

£ 60 / 70 for 36 holes (Weekdays/Week-ends)

Caddy	Caddy	no
Electric Trolley	Chariot électrique	no
Buggy	Voiturette	£ 25 /18 holes
Clubs	Clubs	£ 20

Credit cards Cartes de crédit
VISA - MasterCard - DC

Pegwell Bay
Ramsgate
GOLF
A 257
Canterbury
Sandwich
Sandwich Bay
R. Stour
A 256
Hacklinge
A 258
A2, Dover
Deal
0 2 km
0 1,25 miles

Access Accès : Sandwich, → "The Golf Courses". 3 km Toll gate into Sandwich Bay Estate, left 1 km and left again. Continue 2 km along seafront.
Map 7 on page 497 Carte 7 Page 497

Golf course — PARCOURS — 14/20

Site	Site	
Maintenance	Entretien	
Architect	Architecte	Sir Guy Campbell, John Morrison
Type	Type	seaside course, links
Relief	Relief	
Water in play	Eau en jeu	
Exp. to wind	Exposé au vent	
Trees in play	Arbres en jeu	

Scorecard Carte de score	**Chp.** Chp.	**Mens** Mess.	**Ladies** Da.
Length Long.	5860	5614	5260
Par	71	71	73
Slope system	—	—	—

Advised golfing ability Niveau de jeu recommandé: 0 12 24 36
Hcp required Handicap exigé: no

Club house & amenities — CLUB HOUSE ET ANNEXES — 6/10

Pro shop	Pro-shop	
Driving range	Practice	
Sheltered	couvert	3 mats, members only
On grass	sur herbe	yes
Putting-green	putting-green	yes
Pitching-green	pitching green	yes

Hotel facilities — ENVIRONNEMENT HOTELIER — 4/10

HOTELS HÔTELS

Bell Hotel — Sandwich 4 km
33 rooms, D £ 150
Tel (44) 01304 - 613 388, Fax (44) 01304 - 615 308

Jarvis Marina, 58 rooms, D £ 120 — Ramsgate 12 km
Tel (44) 01843 - 588 276, Fax (44) 01843 - 586 866

San Clu, 44 rooms, D £ 100 — Ramsgate 12 km
Tel (44) 01843 - 592 345, Fax (44) 01843 - 580 157

RESTAURANTS RESTAURANT

Blazing Donkey, Tel (44) 01304 - 617362 — Ham, 7 km
Dunkerleys Restaurant, Tel (44) 01304 - 375016 — Deal 10 km
Hare & Hounds, Tel (44) 01304 - 365 429 — Deal 10 km

ROSS-ON-WYE

15 | 5 | 6

Driving up from London, you will have stopped off at Stratford-upon-Avon (the birthplace of Shakespeare) and then at Gloucester to visit the cathedral and the docks that have now been transformed into a museum. As you pursue your cultural trek on to Hereford, home of the world's first map (in the cathedral), you drive along the very beautiful Wye valley and stop off in the pretty town that has given its name to this golf course. It was laid out in 1964 in a forest with literally thousands of trees, especially birch, which make this pleasant course such a beautiful site with its small, exciting and very well protected greens. There are a few blind shots but overall this is a very fair course with clearly identifiable hazards. Free of traps, well maintained and very pleasant to play, Ross-on-Wye extends a simple but very friendly welcome to green-feers.

Venant de Londres, vous vous serez arrêté à Stratford-upon-Avon (ville natale de Shakespeare), puis à Gloucester pour visiter la cathédrale et les docks transformés en musée. Avant de poursuivre votre quête culturelle à Hereford où l'on trouve la première carte du monde (à la cathédrale), vous devez passer par la très belle vallée de la Wye et vous arrêter dans la jolie ville qui a donné son nom au parcours. Il date de 1964, a été tracé dans une forêt composée de millions d'arbres, en particulier de bouleaux, qui donnent une grande beauté à ce plaisant parcours, avec de petits greens très animés et bien défendus. On trouve quelques coups aveugles, mais l'ensemble est néanmoins très franc, avec des obstacles clairement identifiables. Sans pièges, bien entretenu, très agréable à jouer, Ross-on-Wye bénéficie également d'un accueil simple, mais très amical.

616

Ross-on-Wye Golf Club — 1964

Two Park, Gorsley
ENG - ROSS-ON-WYE, Hereford HR9 7UT

Office	Secrétariat	(44) 01989 - 720 267
Pro shop	Pro-shop	(44) 01989 - 720 439
Fax	Fax	(44) 01989 - 720 212
Web	www.rossonwyegolfclub.co.uk	
Situation	Situation	20 km of Gloucester

(pop. 101 608) - 5 km E of Ross-on-Wye (pop. 9 606)

Annual closure	Fermeture annuelle	no
Weekly closure	Fermeture hebdomadaire	no

Fees main season Tarifs haute saison	18 holes	
	Week days Semaine	**We/Bank holidays** We/Férié
Individual Individuel	£ 34	£ 34
Couple Couple	£ 68	£ 68

Full days: £ 44

Caddy	Caddy	no
Electric Trolley	Chariot électrique	£ 6 /18 holes
Buggy	Voiturette	no
Clubs	Clubs	£ 5 /18 holes

Credit cards Cartes de crédit VISA - MasterCard

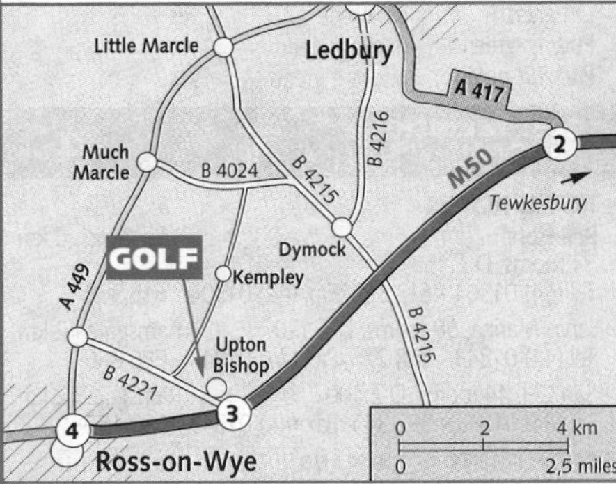

Access Accès : Adjacent Jct 3 of M50.
Map 6 on page 495 Carte 6 Page 495

Golf course PARCOURS — 15/20

Site	Site	
Maintenance	Entretien	
Architect	Architecte	C.K. Cotton
Type	Type	parkland
Relief	Relief	
Water in play	Eau en jeu	
Exp. to wind	Exposé au vent	
Trees in play	Arbres en jeu	

Scorecard Carte de score	**Chp.** Chp.	**Mens** Mess.	**Ladies** Da.
Length Long.	5897	5443	5130
Par	72	72	73
Slope system	—	—	—

Advised golfing ability Niveau de jeu recommandé: 0 12 24 36
Hcp required Handicap exigé: certificate

Club house & amenities CLUB HOUSE ET ANNEXES — 5/10

Pro shop	Pro-shop	
Driving range	Practice	
Sheltered	couvert	no
On grass	sur herbe	yes
Putting-green	putting-green	yes
Pitching-green	pitching green	yes

Hotel facilities ENVIRONNEMENT HOTELIER — 6/10

HOTELS HÔTELS

Chase, 36 rooms, D £ 100 — Ross-on-Wye 6 km
Tel (44) 01989 - 763 161, Fax (44) 01989 - 768 330

Pengethley Manor — Ross-on-Wye 8 km
25 rooms, D £ 120
Tel (44) 01989 - 730 211, Fax (44) 01989 - 730 238

The Royal, 42 rooms, D £ 90 — Ross-on-Wye 4 km
Tel (44) 01989 - 565 105, Fax (44) 01989 - 768 058

RESTAURANTS RESTAURANT

Le Faisan Doré — Ross-on-Wye 6 km
Tel (44) 01989 - 565 751

Le Champignon Sauvage — Cheltenham 30 Km
Tel (44) 01242 - 573 449

ROYAL ASHDOWN FOREST

14	7	6

Players who can't handle sand breathe an almost audible sigh of relief here, where there is not a single bunker in sight. So it could claim to be the most natural course around, as no-one has ever seen a bunker on wholly natural terrain except perhaps on links courses where grazing sheep keep the place in shape. This was the result of an administrative ban but has now become a sort of coquetry. But don't be too relieved, as there is no shortage of difficulties elsewhere: there are pine and birch trees, a stream on several holes, heather, which is even more dangerous than water that often has to be carried with your drive or even your second shot (on the 12th). As a general rule, and with a couple of exceptions, members will tell you to hit the ball high into the greens, which are rather large, very quick in summer and which slope in all directions. A pretty course and a superb clubhouse.

Enfin ! disent les golfeurs qui détestent le sable en arrivant ici. Il n'y a pas un seul bunker, c'est donc le parcours le plus naturel qui soit, car qui a vu des bunkers à l'état naturel, sinon dans les jardins d'enfant et sur les links authentiques où paissent les moutons ? C'était le résultat d'une interdiction administrative, c'est devenu une sorte de coquetterie. Que l'on ne soit pas trop vite soulagé, les difficultés ne manquent pas : les pins et les bouleaux d'abord, un cours d'eau sur plusieurs trous, la bruyère encore, bien plus pénalisante que l'eau, dont il faut souvent franchir des étendues au drive ou même au second coup (au 12). En règle générale, les membres vous souffleront qu'il faut ici lever la balle, sauf pour approcher un ou deux greens. Ceux-ci sont assez grands, avec des pentes dans tous les sens, et très rapides en été. Un joli parcours, avec un superbe Clubhouse.

Royal Ashdown Forest Golf Club **1989**
Chapel Lane, Forest Row
ENG - EAST GRINSTEAD, East Sussex RH18 5LR

Office	Secrétariat	(44) 01342 - 822 018
Pro shop	Pro-shop	(44) 01342 - 822 247
Fax	Fax	(44) 01342 - 825 211
Web	www.royalashdown.co.uk	
Situation	Situation	East Grinstead, 8 km
Annual closure	Fermeture annuelle	no
Weekly closure	Fermeture hebdomadaire	no

Fees main season Tarifs haute saison	18 holes	
	Week days Semaine	**We/Bank holidays** We/Férié
Individual Individuel	£ 45	£ 60
Couple Couple	£ 90	£ 120
Full weekdays: £ 60		

Caddy	Caddy	£ 15
Electric Trolley	Chariot électrique	no
Buggy	Voiturette	no
Clubs	Clubs	£ 10 /18 holes

Credit cards Cartes de crédit
VISA - Eurocard - MasterCard - DC - AMEX
(not for green fees)

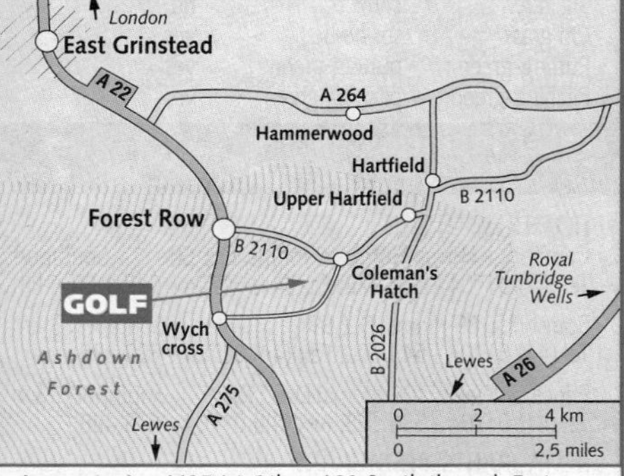

Access Accès : M25 Jct 6 then A22 South through East Grinstead. At Forest Row, turn left into B2110. 0.8 km (1/2 m.) right into Chapel Lane. Top of hill turn left.
Map 7 on page 497 Carte 7 Page 497

Golf course PARCOURS 14/20

Site	Site	
Maintenance	Entretien	
Architect	Architecte	Archdeacon Scott
Type	Type	inland, heathland
Relief	Relief	
Water in play	Eau en jeu	
Exp. to wind	Exposé au vent	
Trees in play	Arbres en jeu	

Scorecard Carte de score	**Chp.** Chp.	**Mens** Mess.	**Ladies** Da.
Length Long.	5712	5675	5032
Par	72	72	73
Slope system	—	—	—

Advised golfing ability 0 12 24 36
Niveau de jeu recommandé
Hcp required Handicap exigé certificate

Club house & amenities CLUB HOUSE ET ANNEXES 7/10

Pro shop	Pro-shop	
Driving range	Practice	
Sheltered	couvert	no
On grass	sur herbe	yes
Putting-green	putting-green	yes
Pitching-green	pitching green	yes

Hotel facilities ENVIRONNEMENT HOTELIER 6/10

HOTELS HÔTELS
Ashdown Park, 107 rooms, D £ 180 Wych Cross 3 km
Tel (44) 01342 - 824 988, Fax (44) 01342 - 826 206

Gravetye Manor, 18 rooms, D £ 250 East Grinstead 8 km
Tel (44) 01342 - 810 567, Fax (44) 01342 - 810 080

Woodbury House, 14 rooms, D £ 95 East Grinstead 5 km
Tel (44) 01342 - 313 657, Fax (44) 01342 - 314 801

RESTAURANTS RESTAURANT
Gravetye Manor East Grinstead 8 km
Tel (44) 01342 - 810 567

Chequers Inn Forest Row 2 km
Tel (44) 01342 - 823 333

ROYAL BIRKDALE (THE) 19 9 7

Royal Birkdale has hosted each and every top tournament: the Open, the Ryder, Walker and Curtis Cups, and the Ladies Open. It has done so more than others probably because this is an open and honest course where you can draw up your strategy according to the wind and not to the imponderables that create the "rough justice" charm of other links. Here, if you stay on the fairway you will avoid any blind shots. If you stray onto the surrounding dunes, you can end up in some very nasty situations indeed. This is a course for the technician and artist, not only the big-hitter. Thomson, Watson, Trevino and Miller have all won here, as did Arnold Palmer, a more refined golfer than some might believe. There is no point in describing what could easily fill a whole book. Suffice it to say that Birkdale is unforgettable and that, like a dinner in a top restaurant, this immense pleasure comes at a price. So make it a full day's golfing on a truly Royal golf course.

Royal Birkdale a reçu toutes les grandes compétitions : le British Open, la Ryder Cup, la Walker Cup, la Curtis Cup, le Ladies British Open... Plus que d'autres sans doute, et on le comprend, parce que sa franchise permet d'établir la stratégie en fonction du vent, et non des impondérables qui font le charme d'autres links, mais pas toujours dans la justice ! Pas de coups aveugles ici, du moins si l'on reste sur le fairway, car les dunes alentour peuvent vous imposer des situations peu confortables. Ce n'est pas un parcours de frappeur, mais de technicien, d'artiste du travail de la balle : Thomson, Watson, Trevino, Miller ont gagné ici, mais aussi Arnold Palmer, plus fin golfeur qu'on ne le croit. Inutile de décrire ce qui prendrait un livre entier, disons seulement que Birkdale est inoubliable, que cet immense plaisir se paie cher, comme un dîner dans un trois étoiles. Alors, prenez la journée, et savourez. Rarement un parcours a autant mérité une accolade "royale."

The Royal Birkdale Golf Club 1897

Waterloo Road
ENG - SOUTHPORT, Lancs PR8 2LX

Office	Secrétariat	(44) 01704 - 567 920
Pro shop	Pro-shop	(44) 01704 - 568 857
Fax	Fax	(44) 01704 - 562 327
Web	www.royalbirkdale.com	
Situation	Situation	30 km N of Liverpool
Annual closure	Fermeture annuelle	no
Weekly closure	Fermeture hebdomadaire	no

Fees main season Tarifs haute saison	Week days Semaine	We/Bank holidays We/Férié
Individual Individuel	£ 108	£ 125 *
Couple Couple	£ 216	£ 250 *

18 holes. * Sunday only / Full weekdays: £ 135

Caddy	Caddy	£ 25 /on request
Electric Trolley	Chariot électrique	£ 8 /18 holes
Buggy	Voiturette	no
Clubs	Clubs	£ 10 /18 holes

Credit cards Cartes de crédit
VISA - Eurocard - MasterCard - DC - JCB - AMEX
(Pro shop goods only)

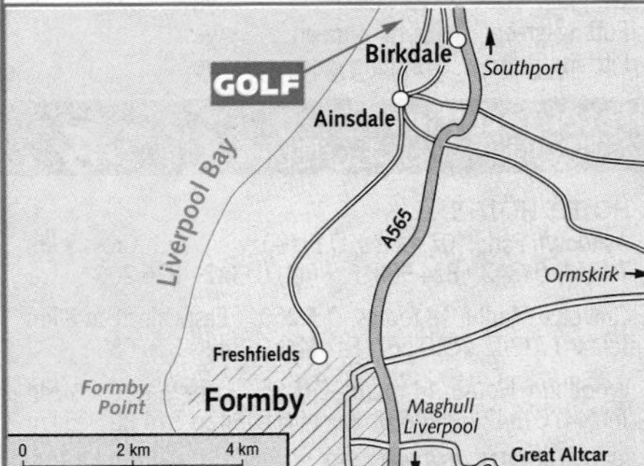

Access Accès : A565 Liverpool → Southport, 1.5 km (1 m.) before Southport.
Map 5 on page 493 Carte 5 Page 493

Golf course PARCOURS 19/20

Site	Site	
Maintenance	Entretien	
Architect	Architecte	F.W. Hawtree, J.H. Taylor
Type	Type	links
Relief	Relief	
Water in play	Eau en jeu	
Exp. to wind	Exposé au vent	
Trees in play	Arbres en jeu	

Scorecard Carte de score	Chp. Chp.	Mens Mess.	Ladies Da.
Length Long.	6290	6021	5195
Par	70	72	75
Slope system	—	—	—

Advised golfing ability Niveau de jeu recommandé 0 12 24 36

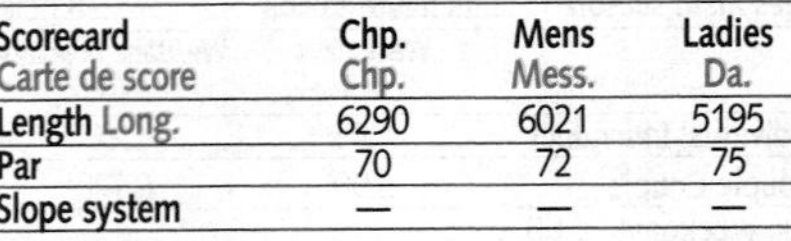

Hcp required Handicap exigé 28 Men, 36 Ladies

Club house & amenities CLUB HOUSE ET ANNEXES 9/10

Pro shop	Pro-shop	
Driving range	Practice	
Sheltered	couvert	no
On grass	sur herbe	yes
Putting-green	putting-green	yes
Pitching-green	pitching green	yes

Hotel facilities ENVIRONNEMENT HOTELIER 7/10

HOTELS HÔTELS
Cambridge House Hotel, 16 rooms, D £ 60 — Southport 6 km
Tel (44) 01704 - 538 372, Fax (44) 01704 - 547 183

Scarisbrick, 89 rooms, D £ 99 — Southport 3 km
Tel (44) 01704 - 543 000, Fax (44) 01704 - 533 335

Prince of Wales, 101 rooms, D £ 115 — Southport 3 km
Tel (44) 01704 - 536 688, Fax (44) 01704 - 543 488

RESTAURANTS RESTAURANT
Warehouse Brasserie ,Tel (44) 01704 - 544 662 — Southport
Valentino's, Tel (44) 01704 - 538 401 — Southport 3 km
Cloisters (Scarisbrick), Tel (44) 01704 - 535 153 — Southport

ROYAL CINQUE PORTS

17 | 6 | 5

Here you are a sliced drive away from the sea but you hardly ever see it. Deal (the course's other name) needs this barrier of dunes to protect the course from the sea-water which is deadly for turf. On a narrow strip of land, dotted with a few dunes and flanked by a little road and houses, you'd think it almost impossible to lay-out such a marvellous course. Less majestic than Royal St. George but more constantly demanding than Prince's, Deal requires the intuition that comes from long years of golfing. For example, knowing that on a particular day a particular shot will need three or even four clubs more. Highly strategic and full of small pot bunkers, this is a lively, clever and smart course which should make you a more intelligent golfer, or else leave you feeling a real fool.

Ici, on est à deux pas de la mer, mais on ne la voit pratiquement jamais. Il faut ce cordon de dunes pour protéger "Deal" (comme on le nomme aussi) des assauts d'eau salée, mortelle pour les gazons. Sur cette étroite langue de terre à peine animée par quelques dunes, longée par une petite route et des maisons, on aurait peine à imaginer pouvoir loger un aussi merveilleux parcours. A deux pas de Royal St George's et de Prince's, moins majestueux que St George's, plus constamment exigeant que Prince's, Royal Cinque Ports réclame l'intuition que donne une longue pratique, pour savoir par exemple qu'il faut aujourd'hui trois ou quatre clubs de plus (ou deux de moins) à cause du vent. Hautement stratégique, plein de petits bunkers où seul un mouton peut tenir, c'est un parcours vivant, astucieux et malin, d'où l'on sort intelligent, ou définitivement stupide.

Royal Cinque Ports Golf Club — 1892

Golf Road
ENG - DEAL, Kent

Office	Secrétariat	(44) 01304 - 374 007
Pro shop	Pro-shop	(44) 01304 - 374 170
Fax	Fax	(44) 01304 - 379 530
Web	—	
Situation	Situation	8 km from Sandwich
Annual closure	Fermeture annuelle	no
Weekly closure	Fermeture hebdomadaire	no

Fees main season Tarifs haute saison	18 holes	
	Week days Semaine	**We/Bank holidays** We/Férié
Individual Individuel	£ 65	£ 65
Couple Couple	£ 130	£ 130

Visitors strictly by arrangement on weekends - Weekdays after 1.00 pm, £ 55

Caddy	Caddy	£ 20 /on request
Electric Trolley	Chariot électrique	£ 5 /18 holes
Buggy	Voiturette	£ 20 /18 holes
Clubs	Clubs	£ 10 /18 holes

Credit cards Cartes de crédit VISA - MasterCard

Access Accès : A2, A258 to Deal. Seafront to the end. Turn left and right into Golf Road
Map 7 on page 497 Carte 7 Page 497

Golf course PARCOURS — 17/20

Site	Site	
Maintenance	Entretien	
Architect	Architecte	Tom Dunn, Guy Campbell
Type	Type	seaside course, links
Relief	Relief	
Water in play	Eau en jeu	
Exp. to wind	Exposé au vent	
Trees in play	Arbres en jeu	

Scorecard Carte de score	**Chp.** Chp.	**Mens** Mess.	**Ladies** Da.
Length Long.	6080	5835	5105
Par	72	70	74
Slope system	—	—	—

Advised golfing ability Niveau de jeu recommandé — 0 12 24 36
Hcp required Handicap exigé — certificate

Club house & amenities CLUB HOUSE ET ANNEXES — 6/10

Pro shop	Pro-shop	
Driving range	Practice	
Sheltered	couvert	no
On grass	sur herbe	yes
Putting-green	putting-green	yes
Pitching-green	pitching green	yes

Hotel facilities ENVIRONNEMENT HOTELIER — 5/10

HOTELS HÔTELS
Royal, 22 rooms, D £ 80 — Deal 1 km
Tel (44) 01304 - 375 555, Fax (44) 01304 - 372 270

Bell Hotel, 33 rooms, D £ 150 — Sandwich 7 km
Tel (44) 01304 - 613 388, Fax (44) 01304 - 615 308

Wallet's Court, 16 rooms, D £ 130 — St Margaret's Bay 8 km
Tel (44) 01304 - 852 424, Fax (44) 01304 - 853 430

RESTAURANTS RESTAURANT
Dunkerleys, Tel (44) 01304 - 375016 — Deal, 1 km
Boathouse Brasserie (Royal Hotel) Tel(44) 01304 - 375 555 — Deal 1 km
Chequers Inn, Tel (44) 01304 - 636296 — Deal on site

ROYAL CROMER

15 | 7 | 6

Royal Cromer is a select location between Yarmouth and Brancaster. Select firstly for its site atop cliffs which alternate with sandy dunes right down the coastline and afford some superb views. Secondly in historical terms, because this is where they thought up the idea of the Curtis Cup between the top British and American ladies. And last but by no means least for the course, which although not a links has the same sort of difficulties including gorse bushes, wind and beautiful bunkering, for which Harry Colt is largely responsible. Although not quite of the same standard as its illustrious neighbours in this region, and without the typical contours of a links course, this layout is well worth a good visit. While you are here, make the most of your time and see the very pretty old town of Norwich.

Entre Yarmouth et Brancaster, Royal Cromer s'est fait une place de choix. Par sa situation d'abord, au sommet des falaises qui alternent sur toute la côte avec les sites dunaires, et qui offrent des vues superbes. Par l'histoire aussi, car c'est là qu'est née l'idée de la future Curtis Cup, entre les meilleures dames amateur de Grande-Bretagne et des USA. Par le parcours enfin, qui n'est pas un links, mais dont les difficultés en sont bien proches, avec les buissons d'ajoncs, le vent, un "bunkering" de toute beauté, dont Harry Colt est sans doute largement responsable. Sans être tout à fait au niveau de ses illustres voisins de la région, sans avoir ces mouvements de terrain typiques des links, ce parcours mérite une visite approfondie. Et tant que vous êtes là, profitez-en pour visiter la très jolie vieille ville de Norwich.

Royal Cromer Golf Club — 1888

Overstrand Road
ENG - CROMER, Norfolk NR27 0JH

Office	Secrétariat	(44) 01263 - 512 884
Pro shop	Pro-shop	(44) 01263 - 512 267
Fax	Fax	(44) 01263 - 512 884
Web	www.royal-cromer.com	
Situation	Situation	

1.5 km from Cromer - 32 km from Norwich (pop. 120 895)

Annual closure	Fermeture annuelle	no
Weekly closure	Fermeture hebdomadaire	no

Fees main season Tarifs haute saison	Week days Semaine	We/Bank holidays We/Férié
		Full day
Individual Individuel	£ 37	£ 42
Couple Couple	£ 74	£ 84
Caddy	Caddy	no
Electric Trolley	Chariot électrique	no
Buggy	Voiturette	no
Clubs	Clubs	no

Credit cards Cartes de crédit
VISA - MasterCard (Pro shop goods only)

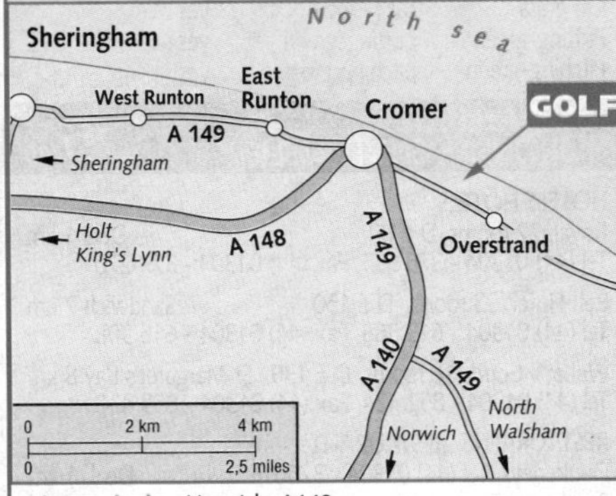

Access Accès : Norwich, A149.
In Cromer, turn right on Coast Road past lighthouse.
Map 7 on page 497 Carte 7 Page 497

Golf course PARCOURS — 15/20

Site	Site	
Maintenance	Entretien	
Architect	Architecte	J.H. Taylor, Harry S. Colt
Type	Type	seaside course, open country
Relief	Relief	
Water in play	Eau en jeu	
Exp. to wind	Exposé au vent	
Trees in play	Arbres en jeu	

Scorecard Carte de score	Chp. Chp.	Mens Mess.	Ladies Da.
Length Long.	5802	5652	5233
Par	72	72	74
Slope system	—	—	—

Advised golfing ability Niveau de jeu recommandé — 0 12 24 36
Hcp required Handicap exigé — certificate

Club house & amenities CLUB HOUSE ET ANNEXES — 7/10

Pro shop	Pro-shop	
Driving range	Practice	
Sheltered	couvert	no
On grass	sur herbe	yes
Putting-green	putting-green	yes
Pitching-green	pitching green	no

Hotel facilities ENVIRONNEMENT HOTELIER — 6/10

HOTELS HÔTELS

Sea Marge, 18 rooms, D £ 80 — Overstrand 1.5 km
Tel (44) 01263 - 579 579, Fax (44) 01263 - 579 524

Links Country Park, 43 rooms, D £ 140 — West Runton 3 km
Tel (44) 01263 - 838 383, Fax (44) 01263 - 838 264

Dormy House, 14 rooms, D £ 90 — West Runton 3 km
Tel (44) 01263 - 835 537, Fax (44) 01263 - 837 537

RESTAURANTS RESTAURANT

Westgate Lodge — Cromer 1.5 km
Tel (44) 01263 - 512840

Links Country Park — West Runton 3 km
Tel (44) 01263 - 838383

ROYAL GUERNSEY

16 | 7 | 7

The Channel Islands are a curious blend of things English and French, with food coming under the latter influence (happily for the French). But golfing here is very British, as seen with this course. Firstly, given the incredible number of players who walks these fairways, Royal Guernsey is very well maintained (but often very dry in Summer). Then it requires good golfing skills and experience of playing in the wind, a capricious element here, often changing directions several times in one round. Under these conditions you don't often damage (pitch) the little greens, at least not as much as one would like. This traditional links course looks as natural as ever despite a number of restyling operations, particularly from Mackenzie Ross and Fred Hawtree. As a bonus, you get splendid views over the sea, the gardens close to the clubhouse... and the cows.

Les îles anglo-normandes (Channel Islands) présentent un curieux mélange d'anglais et de français, cette dernière influence étant aussi sensible (heureusement) sur la cuisine locale. Mais le golf est bien britannique, ce parcours en est l'illustration. D'abord, compte-tenu du nombre incroyable de joueurs qui y passent, il est bien entretenu (mais souvent très sec en été), ensuite, il réclame un jeu très aguerri et une bonne expérience du vent, car celui-ci est capricieux et peut changer plusieurs fois de sens pendant une partie. Dans ces conditions, on n'abîme pas beaucoup les petits greens, du moins aussi rapidement qu'on le voudrait. Parcours de links traditionnel, il continue à paraître naturel, malgré de nombreuses révisions, surtout de Mackenzie Ross et Fred Hawtree. En prime, les vues sont magnifiques, sur la mer, sur les jardins près du Clubhouse... et sur les vaches.

Royal Guernsey Golf Club — 1890

L'Ancresse
ENG - VALE, Guernsey, Channel Islands

Office	Secrétariat	(44) 01481 - 246 523
Pro shop	Pro-shop	(44) 01481 - 245 070
Fax	Fax	(44) 01481 - 243 960
Web	—	
Situation	Situation	St Peter Port, 4.5 km
Annual closure	Fermeture annuelle	no
Weekly closure	Fermeture hebdomadaire	no

Fees main season Tarifs haute saison	Week days Semaine	We/Bank holidays We/Férié
	Full day	
Individual Individuel	£ 38	*
Couple Couple	£ 76	*

* Thursday, Saturday afternoon & Sunday: only with a member

Caddy	Caddy	no
Electric Trolley	Chariot électrique	no
Buggy	Voiturette	no
Clubs	Clubs	£ 7.50 /18 holes

Credit cards Cartes de crédit
VISA - MasterCard (Pro shop goods only)

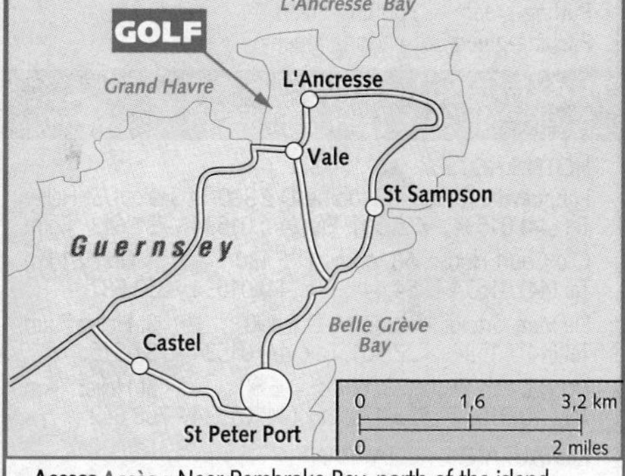

Access Accès : Near Pembroke Bay, north of the island
Map 9 on page 500 Carte 9 Page 500

Golf course PARCOURS — 16/20

Site	Site	
Maintenance	Entretien	
Architect	Architecte	Unknown
Type	Type	seaside course, links
Relief	Relief	
Water in play	Eau en jeu	
Exp. to wind	Exposé au vent	
Trees in play	Arbres en jeu	

Scorecard Carte de score	Chp. Chp.	Mens Mess.	Ladies Da.
Length Long.	5585	5585	5005
Par	70	70	72
Slope system	—	—	—

Advised golfing ability Niveau de jeu recommandé: 0 12 24 36

Hcp required Handicap exigé: no

Club house & amenities CLUB HOUSE ET ANNEXES — 7/10

Pro shop	Pro-shop	
Driving range	Practice	
Sheltered	couvert	no
On grass	sur herbe	no
Putting-green	putting-green	yes
Pitching-green	pitching green	yes

Hotel facilities ENVIRONNEMENT HOTELIER — 7/10

HOTELS HÔTELS

Pembroke Bay, 12 rooms, D £ 98 — L'Ancresse 100 m
Tel (44) 01481 - 247 573, Fax (44) 01481 - 248 838

De Havelet, 34 rooms, D £ 120 — St Peter Port 5 km
Tel (44) 01481 - 722 199, Fax (44) 01481 - 714 057

St Pierre Park, 132 rooms, D £ 170 — St Peter Port 5 km
Tel (44) 01481 - 782 282, Fax (44) 01481 - 712 041

RESTAURANTS RESTAURANT

Victor Hugo, Tel (44) 01481 - 782 282 — St Peter Port 5 km

The Absolute End — St Peter Port 5 km
Tel (44) 01481 - 723 822

Wellington Boot — St Peter Port 5 km
Tel (44) 01481 - 722 199

ROYAL JERSEY

16 | 7 | 8

Harry Vardon was born next door, just before Ted Ray. Add to that the fact that more recently Tommy Horton learnt how to play here and that makes a lot of champions for one club. The views from the impressive club-house are simply magnificent on a course which is a real paradise for golfers, especially players who can produce shots while interpreting every change in land level and get their distances right. In this respect, you are almost better off trusting your eyes than the yardage book. There is no par 4 longer than 400 yards (360 metres), there are five par 3s and only two par 5s at the beginning. Hazards abound and are very well positioned, the deadliest being the sea, at least for slicers. Royal Jersey is very busy in Summer but playable all year because of the warm climate. Spring and Autumn are wonderful times to play here.

Harry Vardon est né à côté, précédant Ted Ray. Si on ajoute que, plus récemment, Tommy Horton a appris le golf ici, cela fait beaucoup de champions pour un seul club. Les vues sont magnifiques depuis l'impressionnant Clubhouse sur ce parcours qui est un véritable paradis pour ceux qui savent fabriquer des coups de golf, en interprétant tous les changements de niveau du terrain, notamment pour les distances. A ce propos, il est presque plus sûr de se fier à ses yeux qu'au carnet de parcours. Aucun par 4 ne dépasse 360 mètres (400 yards), il y a cinq par 3 et seulement deux par 5 placés dès le début, sans doute pour commencer avec le sourire. Les obstacles sont nombreux, très bien placés, le plus redoutable étant la mer, en tout cas pour les sliceurs. Très fréquenté en été, Royal Jersey est jouable toute l'année à cause de la douceur du climat, mais le printemps et l'automne sont particulièrement sublimes.

Royal Jersey Golf Club — 1878

ENG - GROUVILLE, Jersey JE3 9BD

Office	Secrétariat	(44) 01534 - 854 416
Pro shop	Pro-shop	(44) 01534 - 852 234
Fax	Fax	(44) 01534 - 854 684
Web	—	
Situation	Situation	

7 km E of St Helier (pop. 28 123) - 1 km S of Gorey

Annual closure	Fermeture annuelle	no
Weekly closure	Fermeture hebdomadaire	no

Fees main season / Tarifs haute saison	18 holes	
	Week days / Semaine	We/Bank holidays / We/Férié
Individual Individuel	£ 45	£ 45 *
Couple Couple	£ 90	£ 90 *

Full weekdays: £ 75 / * Visitors after 2.30 pm at weekends

Caddy	Caddy	no
Electric Trolley	Chariot électrique	£ 10 /18 holes
Buggy	Voiturette	no
Clubs	Clubs	£ 10 /18 holes

Credit cards Cartes de crédit
VISA - Eurocard - MasterCard - DC (Pro shop goods only)

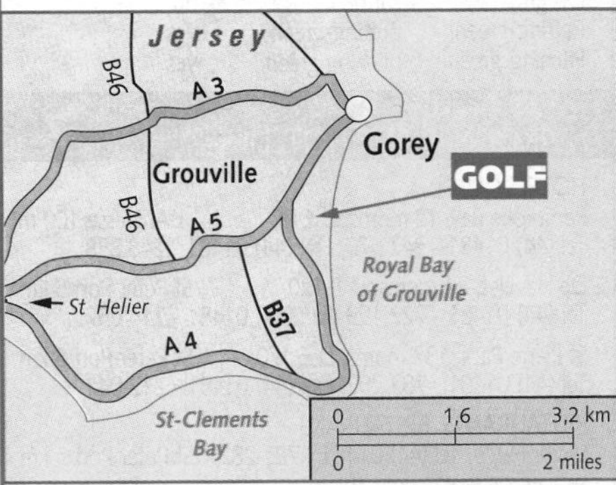

Access Accès : St Helier, A3 → Gorey. Turn right on A4.
Map 9 on page 500 Carte 9 Page 500

Golf course PARCOURS — 16/20

Site	Site	
Maintenance	Entretien	
Architect	Architecte	Unknown
Type	Type	seaside course, links
Relief	Relief	
Water in play	Eau en jeu	
Exp. to wind	Exposé au vent	
Trees in play	Arbres en jeu	

Scorecard / Carte de score	Chp. / Chp.	Mens / Mess.	Ladies / Da.
Length Long.	5480	5480	4890
Par	70	70	71
Slope system	—	—	—

Advised golfing ability / Niveau de jeu recommandé: 0 12 24 36

Hcp required — Handicap exigé — 28 Men, 36 Ladies

Club house & amenities CLUB HOUSE ET ANNEXES — 7/10

Pro shop	Pro-shop	
Driving range	Practice	
Sheltered	couvert	no
On grass	sur herbe	no
Putting-green	putting-green	yes
Pitching-green	pitching green	no

Hotel facilities ENVIRONNEMENT HOTELIER — 8/10

HOTELS HÔTELS

Longueville Manor, 30 rooms, D £ 300 — St Saviour/St Helier 6 km
Tel (44) 01534 - 725 501, Fax (44) 01534 - 731 613

Old Court House, 58 rooms, D £ 130 — Gorey 1 km
Tel (44) 01534 - 854 444, Fax (44) 01534 - 853 587

De Vere Grand, 114 rooms, D £ 190 — St Helier 7 km
Tel (44) 01534 - 722 301, Fax (44) 01534 - 737 815

Hotel De La Plage, 78 rooms, D £ 80 — St Helier 7 km
Tel (44) 01534 - 723 474, Fax (44) 01534 - 768 642

RESTAURANTS RESTAURANT

Longueville Manor, Tel (44) 01534 - 725 501 — St Saviour/St Helier
Jersey Pottery, Tel (44) 01534 - 851119 — Gorey 1 km
La Petite Pomme, Tel (44) 01534 - 766 608 — St Helier 7 km

ROYAL LIVERPOOL (HOYLAKE) | 18 | 8 | 7

Whenever you can, always play a links you don't know with a caddie. With the wind and out-of-bounds (some of which are inside the course), this is particularly true at Hoylake in order to identify certain hazards (the ground is flat) and draw up your game strategy. They say that Hoylake is a match for Carnoustie in terms of difficulty, and they're not wrong, even in fine weather. Here, you need patience, imagination and skill to improvise and invent shots you won't find in golf text-books, particularly on the less spectacular holes where you might be tempted to relax your concentration. There certainly are more spectacular and more baroque-looking courses in the world, but this one is less austere than it looks. Somehow, Hoylake is all a part of English humour; you need wit - a golfing wit - to understand what it's all about. Good news: the British Open has not been held here since 1967, it will be returning in the next future...

Quand c'est possible sur les links que vous ne connaissez pas, prenez un caddie. C'est encore plus vrai ici, avec le vent et les hors-limites (certains sont intérieurs), pour identifier certains obstacles car le terrain est plat, et pour établir une stratégie. On dit que Hoylake tient tête à Carnoustie en matière de difficulté. Ce n'est pas faux, même par beau temps : il faut ici de la patience et de l'imagination, savoir improviser, inventer des coups qui ne sont pas dans les livres. Et surtout sur les trous les moins spectaculaires, où l'on aurait tendance à baisser sa garde. Certes, il est des parcours plus impressionnants, visuellement plus baroques, mais celui-ci est moins sévère qu'il n'y paraît. Quelque part, Hoylake participe de l'humour anglais : il faut un certain esprit pour comprendre. Un esprit de joueur. Les jeunes pros auront l'occasion de le découvrir, car le British Open qui n'était plus venu ici depuis 1967 devrait revenir dans un proche avenir.

Royal Liverpool Golf Club — 1869

Meols Drive, Hoylake
ENG - WIRRAL, Cheshire L47 4AL

Office	Secrétariat	(44) 0151 - 632 6757
Pro shop	Pro-shop	(44) 0151 - 632 5868
Fax	Fax	(44) 0151 - 632 3739
Web	www.royal-liverpool-golf.com	
Situation	Situation	16 km from Liverpool
Annual closure	Fermeture annuelle	no
Weekly closure	Fermeture hebdomadaire	no

Fees main season Tarifs haute saison	18 holes	
	Week days Semaine	**We/Bank holidays** We/Férié
Individual Individuel	£ 70	£ 100
Couple Couple	£ 140	£ 200

Full weekdays: £ 95

Caddy	Caddy	£ 20 + tip
Electric Trolley	Chariot électrique	£ 5 /18 holes
Buggy	Voiturette	no
Clubs	Clubs	£ 15 /18 holes

Credit cards Cartes de crédit
VISA - Eurocard - MasterCard - DC - JCB - AMEX

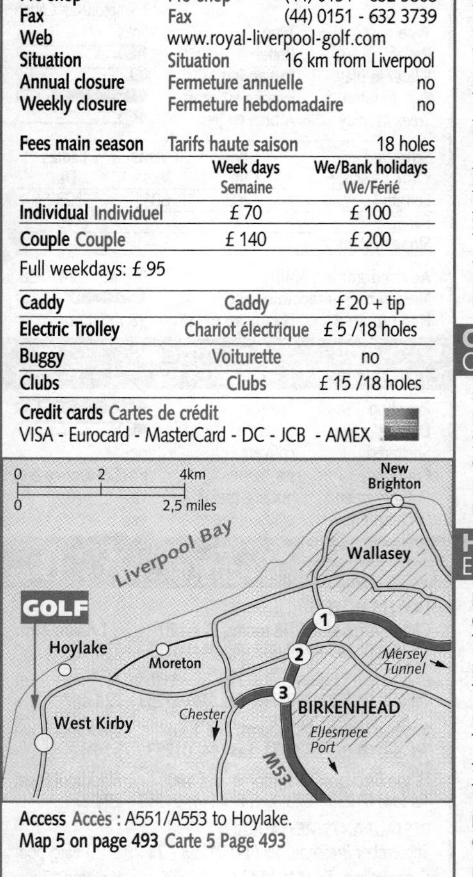

Access Accès : A551/A553 to Hoylake.
Map 5 on page 493 Carte 5 Page 493

Golf course — PARCOURS — 18/20

Site	Site	
Maintenance	Entretien	
Architect	Architecte	Jack Morris
Type	Type	links
Relief	Relief	
Water in play	Eau en jeu	
Exp. to wind	Exposé au vent	
Trees in play	Arbres en jeu	

Scorecard Carte de score	**Chp.** Chp.	**Mens** Mess.	**Ladies** Da.
Length Long.	6345	6139	5180
Par	72	72	74
Slope system	—	—	—

Advised golfing ability Niveau de jeu recommandé — 0 12 24 36

Hcp required Handicap exigé — 24

Club house & amenities — CLUB HOUSE ET ANNEXES — 8/10

Pro shop	Pro-shop	
Driving range	Practice	
Sheltered	couvert	no
On grass	sur herbe	yes (pract. fairway)
Putting-green	putting-green	yes
Pitching-green	pitching green	yes

Hotel facilities — ENVIRONNEMENT HOTELIER — 7/10

HOTELS HÔTELS

Grove Hotel, 14 rooms, D £ 90 — Wallasey 6 km
Tel (44) 0151 - 639 3947, Fax (44) 0151 - 639 0028

Leasowe Castle Hotel, 47 rooms, D £ 75 — Moreton 4 km
Tel (44) 0151 - 606 9191, Fax (44) 0151 - 678 5551

Bowler Hat, 32 rooms, D £ 95 — Birkenhead 8 km
Tel (44) 0151 - 652 4931, Fax (44) 0151 - 653 8127

Thornton Hall, 63 rooms, D £ 86 — Thornton Hough 5 km
Tel (44) 0151 - 336 3938, Fax (44) 0151 - 336 7864

RESTAURANTS RESTAURANT

Grove Hotel, Tel (44) 0151 - 630 4558 — Wallasey 6 km

Lee Ho, Tel (44) 0151 - 677 6440 — Moreton 4 km

ROYAL LYTHAM & ST ANNE'S — 19 | 7 | 8

Like Fairhaven, Royal Lytham doesn't look the most spectacular of courses at first sight, nor the most isolated. It is surrounded by houses and a railway line and has no sea-views. In fact you might think it has done everything to avoid any superfluous cosmetic appearance. But this is a golfer's course, and when the wind blows, it is a monster, almost on a par with Carnoustie, the most brutal of all courses in Britain. Fowler, Colt and Simpson joined forces to make this the ultimate test, the obligatory final examination which was later to be fine-tuned by C.K. Cotton. Pure and tough, it reveals all its hazards but you need to play here fifty times or more to take them all in. Green-keeping is excellent and the greens are slick but prone to push balls towards the deep bunkers. At the end of the day, this style of austerity does have its appeal. For the 2001 Championship, the welcomed removal of poplar trees and the addition of 14 bunkers (bringing the total to 196) have been made under the supervision of Stan Eby, without changing the character of the course. Come here with all the sandwedges you have.

Comme Fairhaven, Royal Lytham ne donne pas au premier abord la plus spectaculaire des impressions, ni celle de l'isolement que proposent souvent les golfs. Entouré par les maisons, la voie ferrée et sans aucune vue sur la mer, c'est un parcours dont on pourrait croire qu'il a évité tout aspect décoratif superflu. C'est un parcours pour golfeurs. Avec le vent, c'est un monstre, l'égal presque de Carnoustie, le plus brutal des parcours de Grande-Bretagne. Fowler, Colt et Simpson se sont alliés pour en faire un test absolu, un examen de passage inévitable, C.K. Cotton l'a enfin peaufiné. Pur, dur, il dévoile tous ses obstacles, mais il faut jouer cinquante fois pour bien assimiler. L'entretien est excellent, les greens subtils, mais ils rejettent volontiers la balle vers de profonds bunkers. Finalement, une telle austérité ne manque pas de charme. Pour le British Open 2001, les peupliers incongrus ont été retirés, et 14 nouveaux bunkers ajoutés par Stan Eby, portant le total à 196. On peut venir ici avec une collection de sandwedges...

Royal Lytham & St Anne's Golf Club 1896

St Patrick's Road South
ENG - LYTHAM, Lancs FY8 3LQ

Office	Secrétariat	(44) 01253 - 724 206
Pro shop	Pro-shop	(44) 01253 - 720 094
Fax	Fax	(44) 01253 - 780 946
Web	—	
Situation	Situation	

Centre of Lytham St Anne's -8 km from Blackpool (pop. 146 069)

Annual closure	Fermeture annuelle	no
Weekly closure	Fermeture hebdomadaire	no

Fees main season Tarifs haute saison	18 holes	
	Week days Semaine	**We/Bank holidays** We/Férié
Individual Individuel	£ 92	*
Couple Couple	£ 184	*

Full weekdays: £ 130 (limited) / * No visitors at weekends

Caddy	Caddy	£ 25 /on request
Electric Trolley	Chariot électrique	no
Buggy	Voiturette	no
Clubs	Clubs	on request

Credit cards Cartes de crédit
VISA - Eurocard - MasterCard - DC - JCB - AMEX

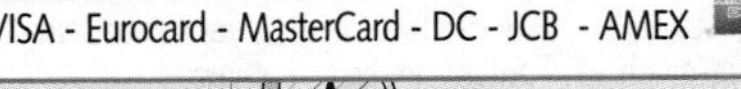

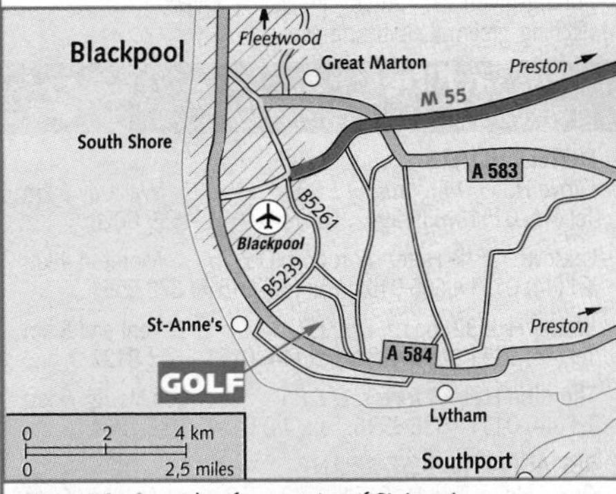

Access Accès : 1 km from centre of St Anne's
Map 5 on page 493 Carte 5 Page 493

Golf course PARCOURS — 19/20

Site	Site	
Maintenance	Entretien	
Architect	Architecte	H. Fowler, H.S. Colt T.Simpson/C.K.Cotton
Type	Type	links
Relief	Relief	
Water in play	Eau en jeu	
Exp. to wind	Exposé au vent	
Trees in play	Arbres en jeu	

Scorecard Carte de score	**Chp.** Chp.	**Mens** Mess.	**Ladies** Da.
Length Long.	6202	6011	5232
Par	71	71	75
Slope system	—	—	—

Advised golfing ability Niveau de jeu recommandé — 0 12 24 36

Hcp required Handicap exigé — 18 maximum

Club house & amenities CLUB HOUSE ET ANNEXES — 7/10

Pro shop	Pro-shop	
Driving range	Practice	
Sheltered	couvert	no
On grass	sur herbe	practice ground only
Putting-green	putting-green	yes
Pitching-green	pitching green	yes

Hotel facilities ENVIRONNEMENT HOTELIER — 8/10

HOTELS HÔTELS

Clifton Arms Hotel, 48 rooms, D £ 120 — Lytham 2 km
Tel (44) 01253 - 739 898, Fax (44) 01253 - 730 657

Dalmeny, 111 rooms, D £ 130 — Lytham St Anne's 2 km
Tel (44) 01253 - 712 236, Fax (44) 01253 - 724 447

Imperial (Forte), 181 rooms, D £ 170 — Blackpool 8 km
Tel (44) 01253 - 23 971, Fax (44) 01253 - 751 784

Hilton Blackpool, 274 rooms, D £ 180 — Blackpool 8 km
Tel (44) 01253 - 623 434, Fax (44) 01253 - 294 371

RESTAURANTS RESTAURANT

September Brasserie, Tel (44) 01253 - 23 282 — Blackpool
Cromwellian, Tel (44) 01772 - 685 680 — Kirkham 13 km

ROYAL MID-SURREY Outer

14	3	8

With two courses (including the "Inner" course which is not quite as good), this is one of the great clubs close to London. Unfortunately it lies beneath a flight route in and out of London airport and so, even though located in a residential area, is less tranquil than it might have been. There is a warm welcome for visitors during the week, a none too frequent occurrence in this part of the country. This generally flat course, designed by J.H. Taylor, has no outstanding difficulty, except perhaps some very tough rough that might test a few weak wrists. Except holes 1 (a long par 3) and 17, this is a very decent course for enjoying your golf even when your swing is not quite in tune. The automatic watering system has considerably improved the standard of green-keeping: this course does not like drought. The clubhouse, so magnificent with enough golfing mementoes for a small museum, has been completely destroyed by fire, and the accomodation is temporary.

Avec deux parcours, dont le "Inner" (intérieur) est moins intéressant, c'est un des grands clubs proches de Londres, mais aussi sur le passage des avions de ligne, ce qui perturbe un endroit autrement très calme, bien qu'il soit situé dans une zone résidentielle. L'accueil est agréable en semaine, ce n'est pas forcément si fréquent dans la région. Généralement plat, le parcours de JH Taylor n'offre pas de difficultés particulières, bien que quelques zones de rough puissent inquiéter les poignets fragiles. Mis à part le 1 (long par 3) et le 17, c'est un très honorable parcours pour se faire plaisir même quand on n'est pas dans son meilleur swing. L'arrosage automatique a permis d'améliorer considérablement son entretien, car il n'aime pas la sécheresse. Le magnifique Club house, avec ses souvenirs de golf, a été totalement détruit au printemps 2001, et les services sont provisoires.

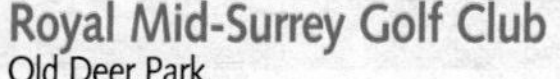

Royal Mid-Surrey Golf Club — 1892

Old Deer Park
ENG - RICHMOND, Surrey TW9 2SB

Office	Secrétariat	(44) 020 - 8940 1894
Pro shop	Pro-shop	(44) 020 - 8940 0459
Fax	Fax	(44) 020 - 8332 2957
Web	www.rmsgc.co.uk	
Situation	Situation	

1 km from Richmond - 15 km from Central London (pop. 6 679 700)

Annual closure	Fermeture annuelle	no
Weekly closure	Fermeture hebdomadaire	no

Fees main season Tarifs haute saison		Full day
	Week days Semaine	**We/Bank holidays** We/Férié
Individual Individuel	£ 68	*
Couple Couple	£ 136	*

* Weekends: with members only

Caddy	Caddy	no
Electric Trolley	Chariot électrique	£ 6 /18 holes
Buggy	Voiturette	no
Clubs	Clubs	£ 7.50 /18 holes
Credit cards Cartes de crédit		not for greenfees

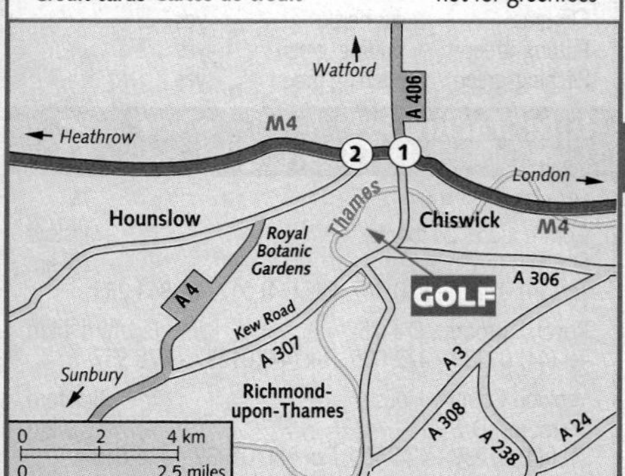

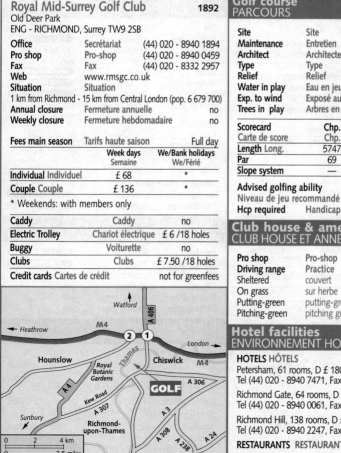

Access Accès : A316, 300 m before Richmond roundabout → London (close to Royal Botanic Gardens).
Map 8 on page 499 Carte 8 Page 499

Golf course PARCOURS — 14/20

Site	Site	
Maintenance	Entretien	
Architect	Architecte	J.H. Taylor
Type	Type	parkland
Relief	Relief	
Water in play	Eau en jeu	
Exp. to wind	Exposé au vent	
Trees in play	Arbres en jeu	

Scorecard Carte de score	**Chp.** Chp.	**Mens** Mess.	**Ladies** Da.
Length Long.	5747	5450	5231
Par	69	69	73
Slope system	—	—	—

Advised golfing ability Niveau de jeu recommandé — 0 12 24 36

Hcp required Handicap exigé — certificate

Club house & amenities CLUB HOUSE ET ANNEXES — 3/10

Pro shop	Pro-shop	
Driving range	Practice	
Sheltered	couvert	4 indoor nets
On grass	sur herbe	yes
Putting-green	putting-green	yes
Pitching-green	pitching green	yes

Hotel facilities ENVIRONNEMENT HOTELIER — 8/10

HOTELS HÔTELS

Petersham, 61 rooms, D £ 180 — Richmond 2 km
Tel (44) 020 - 8940 7471, Fax (44) 020 - 8939 1098

Richmond Gate, 64 rooms, D £ 130 — Richmond 2 km
Tel (44) 020 - 8940 0061, Fax (44) 020 - 8332 0354

Richmond Hill, 138 rooms, D £ 180 — Richmond 2 km
Tel (44) 020 - 8940 2247, Fax (44) 020 - 8940 5424

RESTAURANTS RESTAURANT

Nightingales (Petersham Hotel) — Richmond 2 km
Tel (44) 020 - 8939 1084

McClements — Twickenham 1 km
Tel (44) 020 - 8744 9610

ROYAL NORTH DEVON (WESTWARD HO!) | 18 | 6 | 6

This is the oldest links course in England. If you are disappointed when you set eyes on the flat-looking terrain, you certainly won't be once you are out on the course. It might look gentle, but it doesn't play that way. Take the difficulties for example: tight fairways, invisible ditches, small deep bunkers sometimes lined with railway sleepers, very well protected greens where the approach is sometimes blind and rough with sea-gorse where it is nigh on impossible to get the ball back onto the fairway. Sheep crop the grass and bleat at the top of your back-swing, and then there is the wind. If you can keep the ball low, if you know your strengths and weaknesses, if you stay humble in your ambitions and if someone accompanies you around this huge open space, you can spend a great day and get the impression of having walked around a piece of golfing history.

Le plus vieux links d'Angleterre. L'arrivée à "Westward Ho!" n'est pas des plus exaltante tant le terrain est sans relief, mais votre partie ne va pas en manquer : c'est beaucoup moins tranquille qu'il n'y paraît. D'abord, les difficultés : fairways étroits, fossés invisibles, bunkers petits et profonds, parfois bordés de traverses, greens très défendus et dont l'entrée est parfois aveugle, dans les roughs et buissons de joncs marins d'où il est impossible de sortir. Des moutons broutent le gazon et bêlent quand vous êtes en haut du backswing. Il y a aussi du vent. Si vous savez jouer des balles basses, si vous connaissez bien vos forces et vos faiblesses, si vous envisagez humblement ce parcours, et si quelqu'un vous oriente dans cet immense espace, vous passerez une merveilleuse journée en ayant l'impression d'avoir mis vos pas dans l'histoire.

Royal North Devon Golf Club — 1864

Golf Links Road, Westward Ho!
ENG - BIDEFORD, Devon EX39 7HD

Office	Secrétariat	(44) 01237 - 473 817
Pro shop	Pro-shop	(44) 01237 - 477 598
Fax	Fax	(44) 01237 - 473 456
Web	www.royalnorthdevongolfclub.co.uk	
Situation	Situation	Barnstaple, 12 km
Annual closure	Fermeture annuelle	no
Weekly closure	Fermeture hebdomadaire	no

Fees main season Tarifs haute saison	18 holes	
	Week days Semaine	**We/Bank holidays** We/Férié
Individual Individuel	£ 30	£ 36
Couple Couple	£ 60	£ 72

Full days: £ 36 / £ 40 (weekends)

Caddy	Caddy	no
Electric Trolley	Chariot électrique	no
Buggy	Voiturette	no
Clubs	Clubs	£ 15 /day

Credit cards Cartes de crédit
VISA - Eurocard - MasterCard (everywhere except bar)

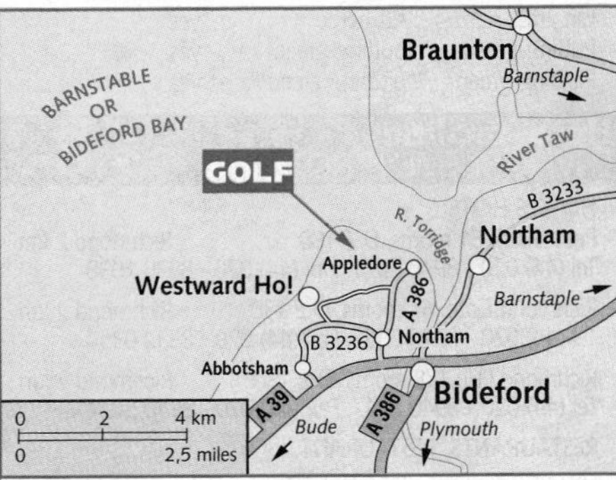

Access Accès : M5 Exit 27, A361 to Barnstaple, then A39 through Northam, take road down Bone Hill past Post Office, keep on left, Clubhouse ahead on hill.
Map 6 on page 494 Carte 6 Page 494

Golf course PARCOURS — 18/20

Site	Site	
Maintenance	Entretien	
Architect	Architecte	Old Tom Morris
Type	Type	links
Relief	Relief	
Water in play	Eau en jeu	
Exp. to wind	Exposé au vent	
Trees in play	Arbres en jeu	

Scorecard Carte de score	**Chp.** Chp.	**Mens** Mess.	**Ladies** Da.
Length Long.	5990	5758	5137
Par	71	72	73
Slope system	—	—	—

Advised golfing ability Niveau de jeu recommandé — 0 12 24 36

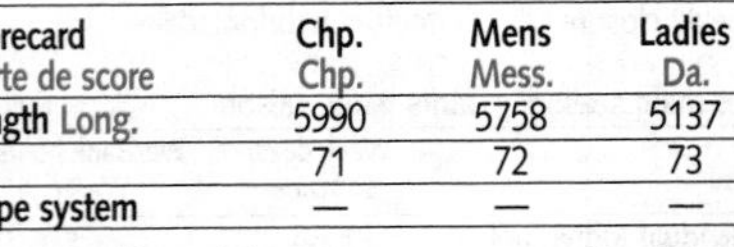

Hcp required Handicap exigé — certificate

Club house & amenities CLUB HOUSE ET ANNEXES — 6/10

Pro shop	Pro-shop	
Driving range	Practice	
Sheltered	couvert	no
On grass	sur herbe	yes
Putting-green	putting-green	yes
Pitching-green	pitching green	yes

Hotel facilities ENVIRONNEMENT HOTELIER — 6/10

HOTELS HÔTELS

Commodore, 20 rooms, D £ 140 (w.dinner) — Instow 7 km
Tel (44) 01271 - 860 347, Fax (44) 01271 - 861 233

Royal, 31 rooms, D £ 75 — Bideford 4 km
Tel (44) 01237 - 472 005, Fax (44) 01237 - 478 957

Yeoldon Country House, 10 rooms, D £ 95 — Bideford 3 km
Tel (44) 01237 - 474 400, Fax (44) 01237 - 476 618

RESTAURANTS RESTAURANT

Yeoldon Country House — Bideford 3 km
Tel (44) 01237 - 474 400

ROYAL ST GEORGE'S

19 | 7 | 5

This is the sort of masterpiece that defies description. If a golf course is to be an adversary offering the toughest resistance to every shot, giving the player the opportunity to shine, sometimes forcing you to take the longer path to get a better shot at your goal, provoking the hardier golfer before breaking him completely but respecting the wise and the knowledgeable, then Royal St. George is one of the very greatest of them all. If we had to find one fault with this regular venue for the British Open, it would be the fact that not all the hazards are clearly visible. Even if you have seen it on TV, you have to play the course a lot to uncover its secrets... but this is a privilege reserved for members only. Although the course is open during the week, we would advise visitors to play with a member, or at least with a caddie. You'll enjoy the experience even more.

Royal St George's est le genre de chef d'oeuvre qui échappe à toute description. Si un parcours de golf doit être un adversaire qui se défende contre tous les coups, offre des chances de briller à son adversaire, oblige parfois à contourner son objectif pour mieux y revenir ensuite, provoque les téméraires pour mieux les détruire, respecte les sages et les savants, Royal St George's est un des très grands parcours de golf. S'il est un seul défaut à ce links où le British Open revient régulièrement, c'est que tous les obstacles ne sont pas clairement visibles : même si on l'a vu à la télévision, il faudrait le jouer tous les jours pour en découvrir les secrets, et seuls les membres ont ce privilège. Bien que le parcours soit ouvert en semaine, on conseillera aux visiteurs de jouer avec eux pour faire plus rapidement connaissance, ou au moins de louer les services d'un caddie. Le plaisir n'en sera que plus grand encore.

Royal St George's Golf Club — 1887

ENG - SANDWICH, Kent CT13 9PB

Office	Secrétariat	(44) 01304 - 613 090
Pro shop	Pro-shop	(44) 01304 - 615 236
Fax	Fax	(44) 01304 - 611 245
Web	—	
Situation	Situation	

2 km from Sandwich - 7 km from Deal (pop. 28 504)

Annual closure	Fermeture annuelle	no
Weekly closure	Fermeture hebdomadaire	no

Fees main season Tarifs haute saison	Week days Semaine	We/Bank holidays We/Férié
		18 holes
Individual Individuel	£ 70	*
Couple Couple	£ 140	*

* No visitors during Weekends
Permission required for Ladies to play

Caddy	Caddy	£ 20 /on request
Electric Trolley	Chariot électrique	no
Buggy	Voiturette	no
Clubs	Clubs	£ 25 /18 holes

Credit cards Cartes de crédit
Visa - Mastercard (Pro shop goods only)

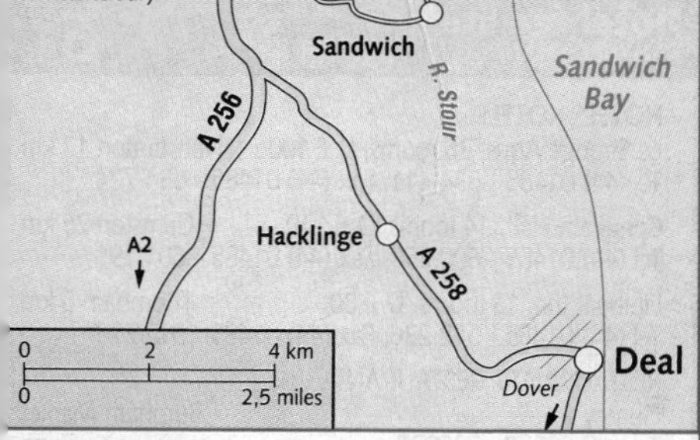

Access Accès : Sandwich → "Golf Courses". 1 km along Sandown Road. Club drive on left after last houses
Map 7 on page 497 Carte 7 Page 497

Golf course — PARCOURS — 19/20

Site	Site	
Maintenance	Entretien	
Architect	Architecte	Dr W. Laidlaw Purves
Type	Type	seaside course, links
Relief	Relief	
Water in play	Eau en jeu	
Exp. to wind	Exposé au vent	
Trees in play	Arbres en jeu	

Scorecard Carte de score	Chp. Chp.	Mens Mess.	Ladies Da.
Length Long.	6174	5904	—
Par	70	70	—
Slope system	—	—	—

Advised golfing ability Niveau de jeu recommandé: 0 12 24 36
Hcp required Handicap exigé: 18 Men, 15 Ladies

Club house & amenities — CLUB HOUSE ET ANNEXES — 7/10

Pro shop	Pro-shop	
Driving range	Practice	
Sheltered	couvert	no
On grass	sur herbe	yes
Putting-green	putting-green	yes
Pitching-green	pitching green	yes

Hotel facilities — ENVIRONNEMENT HOTELIER — 5/10

HOTELS HÔTELS

Bell Hotel, 33 rooms, D £ 150 — Sandwich 2 km
Tel (44) 01304 - 613 388, Fax (44) 01304 - 615 308

Jarvis Marina, 58 rooms, D £ 120 — Ramsgate 12 km
Tel (44) 01843 - 588 276, Fax (44) 01843 - 586 866

Blazing Donkey Country Hotel — Sandwich c
19 rooms, D £ 85
Tel (44) 01304 - 617 362, Fax (44) 01304 - 615 264

RESTAURANTS RESTAURANT

Dunkerleys Restaurant, Tel (44) 01304 - 375016 — Deal 7 km
George and Dragon Inn — Sandwich 2 km
Tel (44) 01304 - 613 106

ROYAL WEST NORFOLK (BRANCASTER)

17	7	6

If you are one of those golfers who go for nature, wildlife and vegetation, this course is for you, set in a landscape of dunes and salt-marshes that flood at every high tide and which are home to a host of wild animals. Brancaster is famous for its railway sleeper bunkers and its devilish greens which are tough to putt on and tough to reach because they are small and often hit with long irons. If it's windy, you can forget it. Get out on the course, by all means, and enjoy what is an uplifting experience for any golfer, but go around in matchplay and play to see who pays for the drink at the bar. You won't want to leave the clubhouse, which has never been anything else but old and smells of wood, woods and balatas. Time has stood still at Brancaster, which is why you feel so privileged to be here. A little on the short side did you say? What the hell.

Si vous êtes de ces golfeurs qui sont aussi amoureux de la nature, de la flore et de la faune, ce parcours est pour vous, dans un paysage de dunes et de marais salés inondés lors des grandes marées, qui abritent une vie sauvage très riche. Brancaster est célèbre pour ses bunkers renforcés par des traverses de chemin de fer, mais aussi pour des greens diaboliques, difficiles à toucher car ils sont petits et souvent attaqués avec de longs fers, et difficiles à putter. Les jours de vent, n'insistez pas : jouez car l'expérience est exaltante, mais en match-play, avec un enjeu à consommer au Clubhouse. Il est vieux depuis toujours, il y règne encore une odeur de bois en bois et de balatas, il fait bon y rester. Ici, le temps s'est arrêté, c'est pourquoi on s'y sent autant privilégié. Le parcours est un peu court ? Et alors...

Royal West Norfolk Golf Club — 1892

ENG - BRANCASTER, Norfolk PE31 8 AY

Office	Secrétariat	(44) 01485 - 210 087
Pro shop	Pro-shop	(44) 01485 - 210 616
Fax	Fax	(44) 01485 - 210 087
Web	—	
Situation	Situation	

12 km from Hunstanton - 30 km from King's Lynn (pop. 41 281)

Annual closure	Fermeture annuelle	no
Weekly closure	Fermeture hebdomadaire	no

Fees main season Tarifs haute saison	Week days Semaine	We/Bank holidays We/Férié
		Full day
Individual Individuel	£ 60	£ 70
Couple Couple	£ 120	£ 140

In August, no visitors unless playing with a member

Caddy	Caddy	on request
Electric Trolley	Chariot électrique	no
Buggy	Voiturette	no
Clubs	Clubs	no

Credit cards Cartes de crédit
Visa - Mastercard (Pro shop goods & green fees)

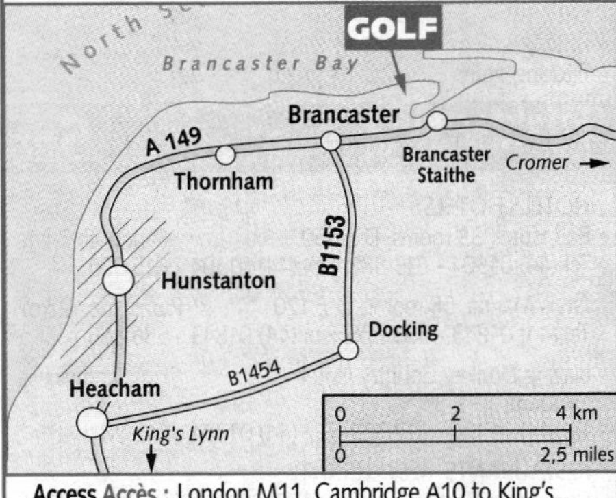

Access Accès : London M11. Cambridge A10 to King's Lynn. A149 North through Hunstanton to Brancaster. Turn left into Beach Road, continue across marsh.
Map 4 on page 491 Carte 4 Page 491

Golf course PARCOURS — 17/20

Site	Site	
Maintenance	Entretien	
Architect	Architecte	Holcombe Ingleby
Type	Type	seaside course, links
Relief	Relief	
Water in play	Eau en jeu	
Exp. to wind	Exposé au vent	
Trees in play	Arbres en jeu	

Scorecard Carte de score	Chp. Chp.	Mens Mess.	Ladies Da.
Length Long.	5785	5785	5334
Par	71	71	75
Slope system	—	—	—

Advised golfing ability Niveau de jeu recommandé — 0 12 24 36
Hcp required Handicap exigé — certificate

Club house & amenities CLUB HOUSE ET ANNEXES — 7/10

Pro shop	Pro-shop	
Driving range	Practice	
Sheltered	couvert	no
On grass	sur herbe	yes
Putting-green	putting-green	yes
Pitching-green	pitching green	no

Hotel facilities ENVIRONNEMENT HOTELIER — 6/10

HOTELS HÔTELS

Le Strange Arms, 36 rooms, D £ 100 — Hunstanton 12 km
Tel (44) 01485 - 534 411, Fax (44) 01485 - 534 724

Congham Hall, 14 rooms, D £ 140 — Grimston 25 km
Tel (44) 01485 - 600 250, Fax (44) 01485 - 601 191

Lifeboat Inn, 13 rooms, D £ 80 — Thornham 5 km
Tel (44) 01485 - 512 236, Fax (44) 01485 - 512 323

RESTAURANTS RESTAURANT

Gurney's — Burnham Market 7 km
Tel (44) 01328 - 738937

The Hoste Arms — Burnham Market 7 km
Tel (44) 01328 - 738777

ROYAL WIMBLEDON

16 | 7 | 8

Being a very private club (but open to green-fees on week-days) and having been upstaged by other courses a little further out of town, Royal Wimbledon probably doesn't have the reputation it deserves. Yet this is the second oldest course in England, a label that naturally still stands despite serious re-styling by Harry Colt, whose layouts always appeal one way or the other. The course is rather hilly but the club does not provide buggies, for some reason. Luckily, the 18 holes are on the short side, so at least you will be hitting short irons into greens defended by some formidable bunkers, always well placed and often deep. The par 3s, holes 5, 13 and 17, fall into this category. To add to the pleasure of this challenge, the putting surfaces are also remarkably well designed and excellent in quality. And you will have all the time in the world to practice your putting stroke on a famous and equally remarkable practice green, rather like the famous one at Saint Andrews.

Parce qu'il s'agit d'un club très privé (accessible en semaine), parce qu'il a été éclipsé par d'autres golfs plus éloignés, plus campagnards aussi, Royal Wimbledon n'a pas la réputation qu'il mérite. Il s'agit pourtant du second golf créé en Angleterre, mais il a été largement remanié par Harry Colt, dont aucun parcours ne laisse indifférent. Il est assez accidenté mais les voiturettes étant sans doute contre la tradition, il n'y en a pas. Heureusement, les 18 trous sont assez courts, car il vaut mieux attaquer les greens avec de petits clubs : les bunkers de défense sont redoutables, bien placés et parfois très profonds. Les par 3 n° 5, 13 et 17 sont notamment très défendus. Pour ajouter encore au plaisir, les greens sont remarquablement dessinés et de très bonne qualité de surface. On a tout le loisir de s'y entraîner sur un célèbre et remarquable putting-green, utilisé pour des compétitions spécifiques, à l'instar de celui de St Andrews.

Royal Wimbledon Golf Club — 1870

Camp Road
ENG - WIMBLEDON SW19

Office	Secrétariat	(44) 020 - 8946 2125
Pro shop	Pro-shop	(44) 020 - 8946 4606
Fax	Fax	(44) 020 - 8944 8652
Web	—	
Situation	Situation	Central London, 14 km
Annual closure	Fermeture annuelle	no
Weekly closure	Fermeture hebdomadaire	no

Fees main season Tarifs haute saison	Week days Semaine	We/Bank holidays We/Férié
18 holes		
Individual Individuel	£ 55	*
Couple Couple	£ 110	*

Full weekdays: £ 75 / * Only with a member at week ends

Caddy	Caddy	£ 25
Electric Trolley	Chariot électrique	£ 12
Buggy	Voiturette	no
Clubs	Clubs	£ 8

Credit cards Cartes de crédit
VISA - Eurocard - MasterCard - DC - AMEX
(Pro shop goods only)

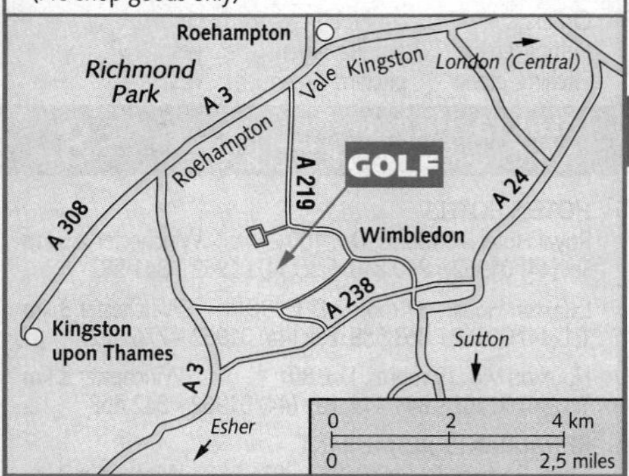

Access Accès : Central London, Fulham Road (A304) → Putney, then Putney Hill, A219 → Caesar's Camp. Golf at Wimbledon Common.
Map 8 on page 499 Carte 8 Page 499

Golf course — PARCOURS — 16/20

Site	Site	
Maintenance	Entretien	
Architect	Architecte	Harry S. Colt
Type	Type	inland, parkland
Relief	Relief	
Water in play	Eau en jeu	
Exp. to wind	Exposé au vent	
Trees in play	Arbres en jeu	

Scorecard Carte de score	Chp. Chp.	Mens Mess.	Ladies Da.
Length Long.	5712	5712	5015
Par	70	70	72
Slope system	—	—	—

Advised golfing ability Niveau de jeu recommandé — 0 12 24 36
Hcp required Handicap exigé — certificate

Club house & amenities — CLUB HOUSE ET ANNEXES — 7/10

Pro shop	Pro-shop	
Driving range	Practice	
Sheltered	couvert	
On grass	sur herbe	yes
Putting-green	putting-green	yes
Pitching-green	pitching green	yes

Hotel facilities — ENVIRONNEMENT HOTELIER — 8/10

HOTELS HÔTELS

Cannizaro House, 45 rooms, D £ 250 — Wimbledon
Tel (44) 020 - 8879 1464, Fax (44) 020 - 8879 7338

Forte Travelodge, 32 rooms, D £ 60 — Morden
Tel (44) 020 - 8640 8227, Fax (44) 020 - 8640 8227 — 5 km

Kingston Lodge — Kingston-upon-Thames
64 rooms, D £ 180 — 2 km
Tel (44) 020 - 8541 4481, Fax (44) 020 - 8547 1013

RESTAURANTS RESTAURANT

Gravier's — Kingston-upon-Thames
Tel (44) 020 - 8549 5557 — 4 km

Sonny's, Tel (44) 020 - 8748 0393 — Barnes 5 km

Nightingales, Tel (44) 020 - 8939 1084 — Richmond 6 km

ROYAL WINCHESTER 15 | 6 | 8

The famous Winchester cathedral has the longest nave in Europe and bears vestiges of Norman architecture. It is one of the treasures to be found in this city, others including the legendary Round Table, which was actually built several centuries late! This J.H. Taylor course is also a piece of history, dating from the last century, where you might get the impression you can play a bit until it comes to counting your score. On each tee you will need to think long and hard about the direction of your shot and the club you should play in order to avoid the bunkers. Here the finer technicians of the game are probably better rewarded than thoughtless big-hitters. At least the trees are not too much in play, but there is wind to contend with. A pleasant course to walk (except the 10th), this excellent layout has hardly aged at all, except in yardage, but none of us will lose much sleep about that. Well worth getting to know.

La célèbre cathédrale de Winchester aurait la plus longue nef d'Europe. Elle porte de nombreuses traces de l'architecture normande, mais elle n'est qu'un des trésors d'une très belle ville, dont la Table Ronde de la légende, mais qui fut fabriquée des siècles après ! Le parcours de JH Taylor est aussi une pièce d'histoire plus que centenaire, où l'on aura l'illusion de pouvoir bien jouer jusqu'au moment de compter le score. Sur chaque départ, il faut bien réfléchir à la fois à la trajectoire et au club à utiliser pour ne pas risquer les bunkers. Ici, ce sont les fins techniciens qui seront récompensés, et pas les frappeurs sans cervelle ! Au moins, les arbres ne sont guère en jeu, ce qui laisse d'ailleurs le champ libre aux caprices du vent. Agréable à marcher (sauf le 10), cette excellente réalisation n'a guère pris de l'âge que pour sa longueur, mais cela ne gênera pas grand-monde. A connaître.

Royal Winchester Golf Club 1888

Sarum Road
ENG - WINCHESTER, Hants SO22 5QE

Office	Secrétariat	(44) 01962 - 852 462
Pro shop	Pro-shop	(44) 01962 - 852 473
Fax	Fax	(44) 01962 - 865 048
Web	—	
Situation	Situation	Winchester, 2.5 km
Annual closure	Fermeture annuelle	no
Weekly closure	Fermeture hebdomadaire	no

Fees main season Tarifs haute saison	18 holes	
	Week days Semaine	**We/Bank holidays** We/Férié
Individual Individuel	£ 33	*
Couple Couple	£ 66	*

Full weekdays: £ 42 / * Weekends: only as a guest of member

Caddy	Caddy	no
Electric Trolley	Chariot électrique	no
Buggy	Voiturette	no
Clubs	Clubs	£ 5 /18 holes

Credit cards Cartes de crédit
VISA - MasterCard

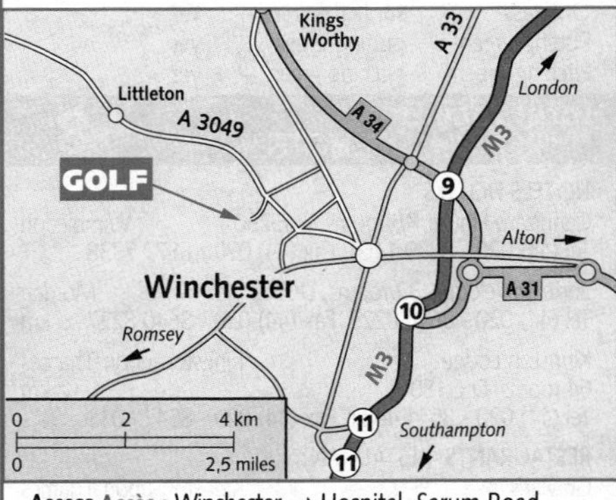

Access Accès : Winchester, → Hospital, Sarum Road, Golf on the right
Map 7 on page 496 Carte 7 Page 496

Golf course PARCOURS 15/20

Site	Site	
Maintenance	Entretien	
Architect	Architecte	J.H. Taylor
Type	Type	inland
Relief	Relief	
Water in play	Eau en jeu	
Exp. to wind	Exposé au vent	
Trees in play	Arbres en jeu	

Scorecard Carte de score	**Chp.** Chp.	**Mens** Mess.	**Ladies** Da.
Length Long.	5585	5416	4950
Par	71	71	72
Slope system	—	—	—

Advised golfing ability Niveau de jeu recommandé — 0 12 24 36
Hcp required Handicap exigé — certificate

Club house & amenities CLUB HOUSE ET ANNEXES 6/10

Pro shop	Pro-shop	
Driving range	Practice	
Sheltered	couvert	no
On grass	sur herbe	yes
Putting-green	putting-green	yes
Pitching-green	pitching green	yes

Hotel facilities ENVIRONNEMENT HOTELIER 8/10

HOTELS HÔTELS

Royal Hotel, 75 rooms, D £ 100 — Winchester 2.5 km
Tel (44) 01962 - 840 840, Fax (44) 01962 - 841 582

Lainston House, 37 rooms, D £ 130 — Winchester 3 km
Tel (44) 01962 - 863 588, Fax (44) 01962 - 776 672

Hotel du Vin, 19 rooms, D £ 80 — Winchester 3 km
Tel (44) 01962 - 841 414, Fax (44) 01962 - 842 458

RESTAURANTS RESTAURANT

Chesil Rectory, Tel (44) 01962 - 851 555 — Winchester 3 km

Bistro (Hotel du Vin) — Winchester
Tel(44) 01962 - 841 414

Nine the Square, Tel (44) 01962 - 864 004 — Winchester

RUDDING PARK

15 | 8 | 8

Faced with administrative restrictions, there was the choice between giving up the ghost or simple ingenuity. Designer Martin Hawtree chose the second option and here has produced one of his best courses. As no bunkers were allowed except in woody areas, there are only 6 greenside bunkers but the edges of the putting surfaces are well contoured with slopes and hollows and the trees are brought into play to be more strategic than decorative. As far as your game is concerned, approach shots are tricky and putting calls for some inspired play. Water has also been cleverly brought into the frame, although on several holes the ladies may have problems carrying it. 9,000 trees have recently been planted to enhance the quality of the design. It will be interesting to see how this interesting project matures, particularly with such a pleasant hotel on site A last word: Rudding Park won a national Amazone Environmental Competition.

Devant les restrictions administratives, on a le choix entre l'abandon et l'ingéniosité. L'architecte Martin Hawtree a choisi la deuxième solution et produit là un de ses meilleurs ouvrages. Comme il était interdit de mettre des bunkers sauf dans les zones boisées, on ne trouve ici que six bunkers de greens, mais les alentours des surfaces de putting sont modelés en reliefs et en creux, et les arbres mis en jeu de manière encore plus stratégique que décorative. Sur le plan du jeu, les approches sont beaucoup plus délicates, et les greens très modelés demandent de l'inspiration. Les obstacles d'eau ont aussi été mis en jeu avec intelligence, mais certaines dames auront peut-être du mal à les franchir sur certains trous en portant la balle. 9.000 arbres ayant été récemment plantés pour rehausser le tracé, on suivra de près la maturation de ce projet intéressant, d'autant que l'hôtel sur place est très bien équipé et tout à fait agréable. Un dernier mot pour souligner que Rudding Park a remporté une importante distinction nationale pour son souci de l'environnement.

Rudding Park Golf Club — 1995

Rudding Park, Follifoot
ENG - HARROGATE, Yorkshire HG3 1DJ

Office	Secrétariat	(44) 01423 - 872 100
Pro shop	Pro-shop	(44) 01254 - 872 100
Fax	Fax	(44) 01254 - 873 011
Web	www.ruddingpark.com	
Situation	Situation	22 km from Leeds
Annual closure	Fermeture annuelle	no
Weekly closure	Fermeture hebdomadaire	no

Fees main season Tarifs haute saison	Week days / Semaine	We/Bank holidays / We/Férié
18 holes		
Individual Individuel	£ 19.50	£ 23
Couple Couple	£ 39	£ 46

Full days: £ 30 / £ 40 (week ends)

Caddy	Caddy	no
Electric Trolley	Chariot électrique	no
Buggy	Voiturette	no
Clubs	Clubs	£ 7.50/18 holes

Credit cards Cartes de crédit
VISA - Eurocard - MasterCard - JCB - AMEX

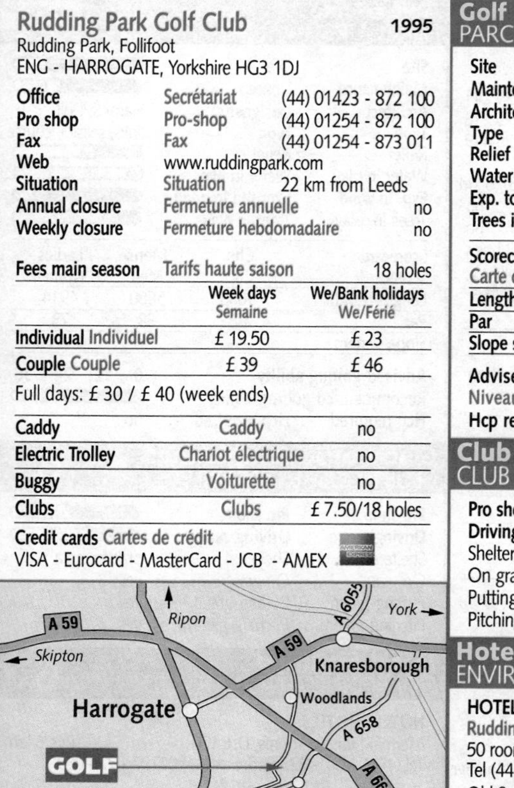

Access Accès : Leeds → Harrogate on A61, then A658 (Harrogate by-pass), follow brown tourist signs for Rudding Park. **Map 4 on page 490** Carte 4 Page 490

Golf course PARCOURS — 15/20

Site	Site	
Maintenance	Entretien	
Architect	Architecte	Martin Hawtree
Type	Type	parkland
Relief	Relief	
Water in play	Eau en jeu	
Exp. to wind	Exposé au vent	
Trees in play	Arbres en jeu	

Scorecard Carte de score	Chp. Chp.	Mens Mess.	Ladies Da.
Length Long.	6184	5873	5167
Par	72	72	72
Slope system	—	—	—

Advised golfing ability Niveau de jeu recommandé: 0 12 24 36
Hcp required Handicap exigé: 28 Men, 36 Ladies

Club house & amenities CLUB HOUSE ET ANNEXES — 8/10

Pro shop	Pro-shop	
Driving range	Practice	
Sheltered	couvert	18 bays
On grass	sur herbe	yes
Putting-green	putting-green	yes
Pitching-green	pitching green	yes

Hotel facilities ENVIRONNEMENT HOTELIER — 8/10

HOTELS HÔTELS

Rudding Park House Hotel, 50 rooms, D £ 130 — Rudding Park adjacent
Tel (44) 01423 - 871 350, Fax (44) 01423 - 872 286

Old Swan, 136 rooms, D £ 130 — Harrogate 5 km
Tel (44) 01423 - 500 055, Fax (44) 01423 - 501 154

Crown, 121 rooms, D £ 115 — Harrogate 5 km
Tel (44) 01423 - 567 755, Fax (44) 01423 - 502 284

RESTAURANTS RESTAURANT

Wedgewood Room (Old Swan) — Harrogate 5 km
Tel (44) 01423 - 500 055

Clocktower Brasserie, — Rudding Park
Tel (44) 01423 - 872 100

The Bistro, Tel (44) 01423 - 530 708 — Harrogate 5 km

RYE

18 | 6 | 6

This course is a masterpiece of links golf architecture on a par with the (almost) neighbouring courses at Deal and Sandwich. It is also a formidable test of golf with a par 68, which seems harmless enough until you actually read the scorecard. There is only one par 5 and that is hole No 1, looking as if to get the birdie holes out of the way from the word go. This is followed by five par 3s with tiered greens stretching from 140 to almost 200 metres, and twelve par 4s, half of which are around the 420-yard mark. Add a touch of wind then save your best for the closing holes, which finish with a magnificent 18th hole. You don't have much chance to relax here, with the first headache being the choice of club, compounded by the obligation not only to carry fourteen clubs but also to be able to play each one in ten different ways. Rye is a must, but the club is so private that it is virtually impossible to get on, but you never know. Maybe in the pretty medieval town of the same name (also well worth a visit) you will run into a club member. If you do, treat him nice, he could do you a huge favour.

Ce parcours est l'un des chefs-d'œuvre de l'architecture de links, au même titre que ses (presque) voisins de la région de Deal et Sandwich. C'est aussi un redoutable test de golf, avec un par 68 qui paraît anodin tant que l'on ne regarde pas la carte de score. Un seul par 5 ici, le premier trou, comme pour se débarrasser tout de suite des trous à birdie, mais cinq par 3 étagés de 140 à presque 200 mètres, et douze par 4, dont la moitié flirte avec les 400 mètres. Ajoutez le vent, et gardez des forces pour le finale, culminant dans un 18 de toute beauté. On ne trouvera guère ici d'occasions de se reposer, la migraine commençant dès le choix du club, accentuée par l'obligation d'en avoir non seulement quatorze, mais aussi dix manières de jouer chacun d'entre eux. Il faut jouer Rye, et c'est presque impossible tant le club est privé. Mais sait-on jamais, peut-être rencontrerez-vous dans la jolie petite ville médiévale du même nom (qui vaut aussi le déplacement) un membre du club. Si cela vous arrive, traitez-le bien, c'est quelqu'un d'intéressant !

Rye Golf Club — 1894

Camber
ENG - RYE, East Sussex TN31 7QS

Office	Front desk	(44) 01797 - 225 241
Pro shop	Pro shop	(44) 01797 - 225 218
Fax	Fax	(44) 01797 - 228 419
Web	—	
Situation	Location	Rye (pop. 3708), 6 km
Annual closure	Annual closing	no
Weekly closure	Weekly closing	no
Fees main season	Fees main season	18 holes

	Week days / Week days	We/Bank holidays / We/Legal holidays
Individual Single player	*	*
Couple Couple	*	*

* Strictly for members and their guests / or introduction of a member

Caddy	Caddy	no
Electric Trolley	Electric trolley	no
Buggy	Buggy	no
Clubs	Clubs	no

Credit cards Credit cards
Pro shop only

Access Access : A259 Hastings → Folkestone.
After Rye, turn right → Camber.
After 5 km, golf on right hand side.
Map 7 on page 497 Map 7 Page 497

Golf course — PARCOURS — 18/20

Site	Site	
Maintenance	Upkeep	
Architect	Designer(s)	Harry S. Colt
Type	Type	links, seaside course
Relief	Relief	
Water in play	Water in play	
Exp. to wind	Exposed to wind	
Trees in play	Trees in play	

Scorecard Scorecard	Chp. / Chp.	Mens / Men	Ladies / Women
Length Length	5680	5680	4914
Par	68	68	73
Slope system	—	—	—

Advised golfing ability Recommended golfing ability — 0 12 24 36
Hcp required Hcp required — no

Club house & amenities — CLUB HOUSE ET ANNEXES — 6/10

Pro shop	Pro shop	
Driving range	Driving range	
Sheltered	Sheltered	practice area
On grass	On grass	yes
Putting-green	Putting-green	yes
Pitching-green	Pitching-green	yes

Hotel facilities — ENVIRONNEMENT HOTELIER — 6/10

HOTELS HOTELS

Mermaid Inn, 31 rooms, D £ 120 — Rye 6 km
Tel (44) 01797 - 223 065, Fax (44) 01797 - 225 069

George, 21 rooms, D 120 — Rye 6 km
Tel (44) 01797 - 222 114, Fax (44) 01797 - 224 065

Broomhill Lodge, 12 rooms, D £ 90 — Rye 6 km
Tel (44) 01797 - 280 421, Fax (44) 01797 - 280 402

RESTAURANTS RESTAURANTS

Mermaid Inn, Tel (44) 01797 - 223 065 — Rye 6 km
Flushing Inn, Tel (44) 01797 - 223 292 — Rye 6 km
Landgate Bistro Tel (44) 01797 - 222 829 — Rye 6 km

SAND MOOR

14 | 7 | 7

Modern clubhouses unquestionably lack the charm of their older counterparts but they are more comfortable. Following this same modern trend, many clubs have also laid out driving ranges (instead of the small practice arezas), if only to cater to the ever greater number of players. In 1961, Sand Moor was given a face-lift and at the same time re-styled, adhering most respectfully to the layout of Alister MacKenzie on one side of Alwoodley Lane. The land is rather hilly, but as the use of buggies requires a medical certificate we will simply recommend an electric trolley. Laid out over moorland, the feeling of space here is very pleasant and the rough not too hard on your game, but some of the bunches of trees and carefully placed fairway bunkers do their job very well. We noted the excellence of the par 3s on what is a very good test of golf, albeit a little on the short side for the better players.

Les Clubhouses modernes manquent sans doute un peu du charme des anciens, mais ils sont souvent beaucoup plus confortables et fonctionnels. De même, à la place des rudimentaires "practice areas", bien des clubs ont aménagé des espaces d'entraînement, ne serait-ce que pour répondre à l'élargissement du public. En 1961, Sand Moor s'est ainsi rajeuni et en a profité pour remodeler - avec beaucoup de respect d'ailleurs - le tracé d'Alister Mackenzie, d'un seul côté d'Alwoodley Lane. Le terrain est assez accidenté, mais seul un certificat médical permettant de jouer en voiturette, on conseillera le chariot électrique. En terre de lande, la sensation d'espace est ici très agréable, le rough n'est pas trop pénalisant, mais certains bouquets d'arbres et des bunkers de fairway judicieusement placés ne manquent pas de jouer leur rôle. A remarquer enfin, la qualité des pars 3. Un très bon test de golf, un peu court pour les meilleurs joueurs.

Sand Moor Golf Club — 1926

Alwoodley Lane
ENG - LEEDS, W. Yorkshire LS17 7DJ

Office	Secrétariat	(44) 0113 - 268 5180
Pro shop	Pro-shop	(44) 0113 - 268 3925
Fax	Fax	(44) 0113 - 268 5180
Web	—	
Situation	Situation	

8 km N of Leeds (pop. 680 722)

Annual closure	Fermeture annuelle	no
Weekly closure	Fermeture hebdomadaire	no

Fees main season Tarifs haute saison	18 holes	
	Week days Semaine	**We/Bank holidays** We/Férié
Individual Individuel	£ 38	*
Couple Couple	£ 76	*

Full weekdays: £ 48 / * No visitors at week ends

Caddy	Caddy	no
Electric Trolley	Chariot électrique	£ 5 /18 holes
Buggy	Voiturette	no
Clubs	Clubs	on request

Credit cards Cartes de crédit VISA - Eurocard - MasterCard
(+ 4% for green fees, not in Club house)

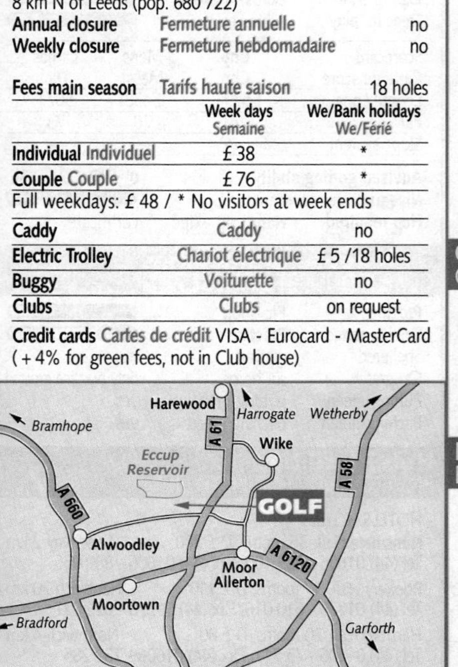

Access Accès : Leeds, A61 North, left into Alwoodley Lane, Golf 0.8 km (1/2 m.) on right hand side.
Map 4 on page 490 Carte 4 Page 490

Golf course — PARCOURS — 14/20

Site	Site	
Maintenance	Entretien	
Architect	Architecte	Alister MacKenzie
Type	Type	parkland
Relief	Relief	
Water in play	Eau en jeu	
Exp. to wind	Exposé au vent	
Trees in play	Arbres en jeu	

Scorecard Carte de score	**Chp.** Chp.	**Mens** Mess.	**Ladies** Da.
Length Long.	5851	5464	5092
Par	71	71	73
Slope system	—	—	—

Advised golfing ability Niveau de jeu recommandé — 0 12 24 36
Hcp required Handicap exigé — certificate

Club house & amenities — CLUB HOUSE ET ANNEXES — 7/10

Pro shop	Pro-shop	
Driving range	Practice	
Sheltered	couvert	practice area
On grass	sur herbe	yes
Putting-green	putting-green	yes
Pitching-green	pitching green	yes

Hotel facilities — ENVIRONNEMENT HOTELIER — 7/10

HOTELS HÔTELS

Posthouse, 130 rooms, D £ 90 — Bramhope 6 km
Tel (44) 0870 - 400 9049, Fax (44) 0870 - 284 3451

42 The Calls, 41 rooms, D £ 150 — Leeds 8 km
Tel (44) 0113 - 244 0099, Fax (44) 0113 - 234 4100

Queens, 199 rooms, D £ 125 — Leeds 8 km
Tel (44) 0113 - 243 1323, Fax (44) 0113 - 242 5154

Haleys Hotel, 29 rooms, D £ 130 — Headingley 7 km
Tel (44) 0113 - 278 4446, Fax (44) 0113 - 275 3342

RESTAURANTS RESTAURANT

Pool Court at 42, Tel (44) 0113 - 244 4242 — Leeds 8 km
Leodis, Tel (44) 0113 - 242 1010 — Leeds 8 km
Rascasse, Tel (44) 0113 - 244 6611 — Leeds 8 km

SANDIWAY

17 | 5 | 7

Sandiway stands in a little compact group of courses to the east of Chester, the others being Mere and the similarly styled Delamere Forest. If Sandiway was in the western suburbs of London it would surely be better known than it is, but there again for a golfer there is something gratifying about being able to talk about little gems that no-one else has ever set eyes upon. With lots of trees lining sloping fairways, keeping your ball in play is anything but easy, so think twice before taking the driver out of the bag. This very varied course demands good tactics and skill in flighting the ball... at least when it comes to getting out of trouble. A very pretty course and a very intelligent one, too, which demands the same quality from the people who play it.

Sandiway tient bien sa place dans un petit groupe compact à l'est de Chester, qui comprend également Mere et Delamere Forest, le second nommé lui étant le plus comparable par son paysage et son style. Sans nul doute, s'il était dans la banlieue ouest de Londres, ce parcours serait bien plus connu, mais, pour un golfeur, c'est très gratifiant de pouvoir parler des trésors que les autres n'ont jamais vu ! Avec beaucoup d'arbres délimitant les trous, et des fairways souvent en pente, il n'est pas évident d'y garder sa balle en sécurité, il faudra donc réfléchir avant d'empoigner son driver. Très varié, ce parcours exige une tactique solide et souvent de savoir travailler la balle... au moins pour s'extraire des problèmes. Ce très joli parcours est d'une grande intelligence, il en demande aussi aux joueurs.

Sandiway Golf Club — 1921

Chester Road, Sandiway
ENG - NORTHWICH, Cheshire CW8 20 J

Office	Secrétariat	(44) 01606 - 883 247
Pro shop	Pro-shop	(44) 01606 - 883 180
Fax	Fax	(44) 01606 - 883 548
Web	—	
Situation	Situation	25 km E of Chester
Annual closure	Fermeture annuelle	no
Weekly closure	Fermeture hebdomadaire	no

634

Fees main season Tarifs haute saison	18 holes	
	Week days Semaine	**We/Bank holidays** We/Férié
Individual Individuel	£ 40	£ 45
Couple Couple	£ 80	£ 90

Full days: £ 45 / £ 50 (week ends)

Caddy	Caddy	no
Electric Trolley	Chariot électrique	£ 5 /18 holes
Buggy	Voiturette	no
Clubs	Clubs	no

Credit cards Cartes de crédit
VISA - Eurocard - MasterCard - AMEX
(Pro shop goods only)

Access Accès : Manchester M56. Jct 7, A556 → Northwich, Chester. Golf on left side after Northwich.
Map 4 on page 490 Carte 4 Page 490

Golf course PARCOURS — 17/20

Site	Site	
Maintenance	Entretien	
Architect	Architecte	Ted Ray
Type	Type	parkland
Relief	Relief	
Water in play	Eau en jeu	
Exp. to wind	Exposé au vent	
Trees in play	Arbres en jeu	

Scorecard Carte de score	**Chp.** Chp.	**Mens** Mess.	**Ladies** Da.
Length Long.	5791	5438	5071
Par	70	70	73
Slope system	—	—	—

Advised golfing ability 0 12 24 36
Niveau de jeu recommandé
Hcp required Handicap exigé certificate

Club house & amenities CLUB HOUSE ET ANNEXES — 5/10

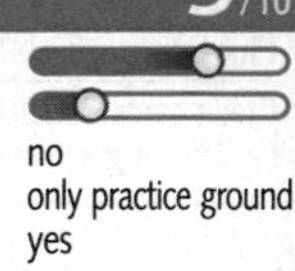

Pro shop	Pro-shop	
Driving range	Practice	
Sheltered	couvert	no
On grass	sur herbe	only practice ground
Putting-green	putting-green	yes
Pitching-green	pitching green	yes

Hotel facilities ENVIRONNEMENT HOTELIER — 7/10

HOTELS HÔTELS

Nunsmere Hall, 36 rooms, D £ 200 — Sandiway 2 km
Tel (44) 01606 - 889 100, Fax (44) 01606 - 889 055

Rookery Hall, 47 rooms, D £ 110 — Nantwich 20 km
Tel (44) 01270 - 610 016, Fax (44) 01270 - 626 027

Hartford Hall, 20 rooms, D £ 80 — Northwich 4 km
Tel (44) 01606 - 75 711, Fax (44) 01606 - 782 285

Tall Trees Lodge, 20 rooms, D £ 43 — Weaverham 3 km
Tel (44) 01606 - 790 824, Fax (44) 01606 - 791 330

RESTAURANTS RESTAURANT

Nunsmere Hall, Tel (44) 01606 - 889 100 — Sandiway 2 km

Rookery Hall, Tel (44) 01270 - 610 016 — Nantwich 20 km

SAUNTON East Course

18	7	6

Saunton does not carry the Royal Seal but if it did it would be well deserved. Harry Vardon dreamed of retiring here, but he was just a professional wasn't he? As such he must have appreciated the amazing balance of the East course, the more fluent of the two. If you play from the back tees, the first four holes will most likely cause irreparable damage to your card. Likewise, if you don't watch out, the last five will finish it off completely. The other holes are not quite so devastating, but the worst danger here is being caught off-guard. Winding between magnificent dunes with sheltered greens, all 18 holes at Saunton make for fantastic golf if you play from the tees that suit your level. The humbler you are, the more fun you will have. Especially since the greens are real beauties.

Si Saunton n'a pas eu droit à l'annoblissement royal, il ne le mérite pas moins : Harry Vardon rêvait de s'y retirer, mais peut-être n'était-il qu'un professionnel ? Comme tel, il dut apprécier le rythme étonnant de ce parcours Est, le plus éloquent des deux. Quand vous jouez des départs arrière, les quatre premiers trous vont dévorer votre carte, comme les cinq derniers la détruiront définitivement si vous n'y restez pas attentif. Les autres trous sont moins brutaux, mais le pire danger est de baisser la garde. Insinués entre des dunes magnifiques, les greens bien à l'abri, les trous de Saunton apportent un plaisir fou, si l'on joue des départs correspondant à son niveau : plus vous serez humble, plus vous prendrez du plaisir. Et d'autant plus que les greens sont un véritable régal.

Saunton Golf Club — 1897

Saunton
ENG - BRAUNTON EX33 1LG

Office	Secrétariat	(44) 01271 - 812 436
Pro shop	Pro-shop	(44) 01271 - 812 013
Fax	Fax	(44) 01271 - 814 241
Web	www.sauntongolf.co.uk	
Situation	Situation	

3 km W of Braunton -8 km W of Barnstaple (pop. 20 740)

Annual closure	Fermeture annuelle	no
Weekly closure	Fermeture hebdomadaire	no

Fees main season Tarifs haute saison	18 holes	
	Week days Semaine	**We/Bank holidays** We/Férié
Individual Individuel	£ 45	£ 45
Couple Couple	£ 90	£ 90

Full weekdays: £ 65 / Fees include lunch

Caddy	Caddy	on request
Electric Trolley	Chariot électrique	£ 5 /18 holes
Buggy	Voiturette	£ 10 /18 holes
Clubs	Clubs	£ 15 /18 holes

Credit cards Cartes de crédit
VISA - MasterCard (Pro shop goods only)

Access Accès : M5 Jct 27, then A361 to Barnstaple, then A361 to Braunton. Follow signs to Saunton, golf on the left.
Map 6 on page 494 Carte 6 Page 494

Golf course — PARCOURS — 18/20

Site	Site	
Maintenance	Entretien	
Architect	Architecte	Herbert Fowler
Type	Type	seaside course, links
Relief	Relief	
Water in play	Eau en jeu	
Exp. to wind	Exposé au vent	
Trees in play	Arbres en jeu	

Scorecard Carte de score	**Chp.** Chp.	**Mens** Mess.	**Ladies** Da.
Length Long.	6123	5800	4555
Par	73	71	74
Slope system	—	—	—

Advised golfing ability 0 12 24 36
Niveau de jeu recommandé

Hcp required Handicap exigé certificate

Club house & amenities — CLUB HOUSE ET ANNEXES — 7/10

Pro shop	Pro-shop	
Driving range	Practice	
Sheltered	couvert	no
On grass	sur herbe	yes (own balls)
Putting-green	putting-green	yes
Pitching-green	pitching green	yes

Hotel facilities — ENVIRONNEMENT HOTELIER — 6/10

HOTELS HÔTELS

Preston House, 12 rooms, D £ 100 — Saunton, on site
Tel (44) 01271 - 890 472, Fax (44) 01271 - 890 555

Kittiwell House, 12 rooms, D £ 75 — Croyde, 3 km
Tel (44) 01271 - 890 247, Fax (44) 01271 - 890 469

RESTAURANTS RESTAURANT

Lynwood House — Barnstaple, 8 km
Tel (44) 01271 - 43 695

Whiteleaf at Croyde — Croyde, 3 km
Tel (44) 01271 - 890 266

SEACROFT

17 | 6 | 4

Moving up the coast, this is the only real links course after Hunstanton. The one further on is Seaton Carew which unfortunately lies in such surroundings that only local golfers really enjoy playing there. The landscape at Seacroft will hardly have you gasping with admiration but it is agreeable enough to give this course a pleasant setting. All the holes are neatly laid out in single file, out and in, except the disorderly 6th hole. This makes club selection a little easier when the wind is howling and forces you to hit low shots. In fine weather, you can hit any shot, which makes life easier for those of you who like to hit the ball high. Whatever, the very strategic bunkering here requires a clear-cut tactical approach to every round, but the hazards are visible enough for you to do so. Varied, very authentic and traditional, this is a course you should try.

En remontant la côte, c'est le seul vrai links après Hunstanton, et le suivant sera Seaton Carew, hélas situé dans un tel environnement que seuls les golfeurs locaux y trouveront du plaisir. Les paysages de Seacroft ne vous arracheront pas des cris d'admiration, mais ils sont assez plaisants pour offrir un décor agréable au parcours. Tous les trous sont sagement rangés en file indienne, en aller et retour, mis à part un indiscipliné, le 6. Cet ordre facilite le choix de clubs quand il y a du vent, qui seul vous obligera aux balles basses. Par beau temps, tous les coups sont permis, ce qui peut faciliter le travail de ceux qui savent surtout lever la balle. En tous les cas, le placement très stratégique des bunkers implique de bien définir la tactique de jeu, mais les obstacles sont assez visibles pour ce faire. Varié, très authentique et traditionnel, c'est un parcours à découvrir.

Seacroft Golf Club **1895**

Drummond Road
ENG - SKEGNESS, Lincolnshire PE25 3AU

Office	Secrétariat	(44) 01754 - 763 020
Pro shop	Pro-shop	(44) 01754 - 769 624
Fax	Fax	(44) 01754 - 769 624
Web	www.seacroft/golfclub.co.uk	
Situation	Situation	30 km NE of Boston
Annual closure	Fermeture annuelle	no
Weekly closure	Fermeture hebdomadaire	no

Fees main season Tarifs haute saison	18 holes	
	Week days Semaine	**We/Bank holidays** We/Férié
Individual Individuel	£ 26	£ 31
Couple Couple	£ 52	£ 62

Full days: £ 36 / £ 41 (week ends)

Caddy	Caddy	no
Electric Trolley	Chariot électrique	no
Buggy	Voiturette	no
Clubs	Clubs	no

Credit cards Cartes de crédit
VISA - Eurocard - MasterCard - DC - AMEX
(Pro shop goods only)

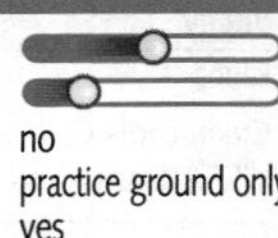

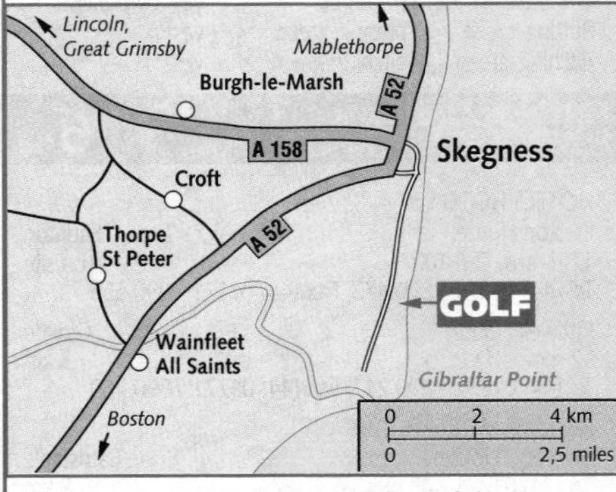

Access Accès : A52 to Skegness. 1.5 km S of Skegness alongside Gibraltar Road Bird Sanctuary.
Map 4 on page 491 Carte 4 Page 491

Golf course PARCOURS — 17/20

Site	Site	
Maintenance	Entretien	
Architect	Architecte	Tom Dunn
Type	Type	seaside course, links
Relief	Relief	
Water in play	Eau en jeu	
Exp. to wind	Exposé au vent	
Trees in play	Arbres en jeu	

Scorecard Carte de score	**Chp.** Chp.	**Mens** Mess.	**Ladies** Da.
Length Long.	5831	5421	5275
Par	71	71	73
Slope system	—	—	—

Advised golfing ability Niveau de jeu recommandé: 0 12 24 36
Hcp required Handicap exigé: certificate

Club house & amenities CLUB HOUSE ET ANNEXES — 6/10

Pro shop	Pro-shop	
Driving range	Practice	
Sheltered	couvert	no
On grass	sur herbe	practice ground only
Putting-green	putting-green	yes
Pitching-green	pitching green	yes

Hotel facilities ENVIRONNEMENT HOTELIER — 4/10

HOTELS HÔTELS

Crown Hotel, — Skegness 400 m
27 rooms, D £ 80
Tel (44) 01754 - 610 760, Fax (44) 01754 - 610 847

Vine Hotel — Skegness 1 km
21 rooms, D £ 80
Tel (44) 01754 - 610 611, Fax (44) 01754 - 769 845

North Shore — Skegness 1 km
36 rooms, D £ 90
Tel (44) 01754 - 763 298, Fax (44) 01754 - 761 902

RESTAURANTS RESTAURANT

Crown Hotel — Skegness 400 m
Tel (44) 01754 - 610 760

SEASCALE

18 | 5 | 4

A strange place where the Sellafield power station ought to give golfers at least the energy to turn their backs on the cooling towers. When you think of how much flak golf courses get from some environmentalists, it makes you wonder why they don't protect courses from this sort of eyesore. Seascale is a hidden gem, away from the world and off the beaten track. You can talk about this course in glowing terms, no-one will ever argue. An imposing but subtle layout, and odd in that the railway line runs between the course and the sea, Seascale is anything but a fashionable course, just one to severely test any player's capacity for invention and adaptability. As on every links course, you either act positively or suffer the consequences, depending on the state of your game. If you do not know Seascale, then enter it now into your list of best little-known courses.

Etrange endroit où la centrale électrique de Sellafield devrait surtout donner l'énergie aux golfeurs de lui tourner le dos. Quand on sait à quel point on peut ennuyer les golfs avec les problèmes d'environnement, pourquoi ne pas préserver aussi les golfs des pollutions visuelles ? Seascale est un joyau caché, à l'écart du monde et des sentiers battus et, quand vous en parlerez avec émotion, personne ne viendra vous contredire. Puissant et subtil, assez curieux dans la mesure où le chemin de fer passe entre le golf et la mer, Seascale est tout sauf un parcours "fashionable." Il met en oeuvre la capacité d'invention et d'adaptation des joueurs. Comme sur les links, on agit ou on subit, suivant sa forme du moment. Si vous ne le connaissez pas, c'est un parcours à inscrire à votre tableau de chasse des meilleurs parcours méconnus.

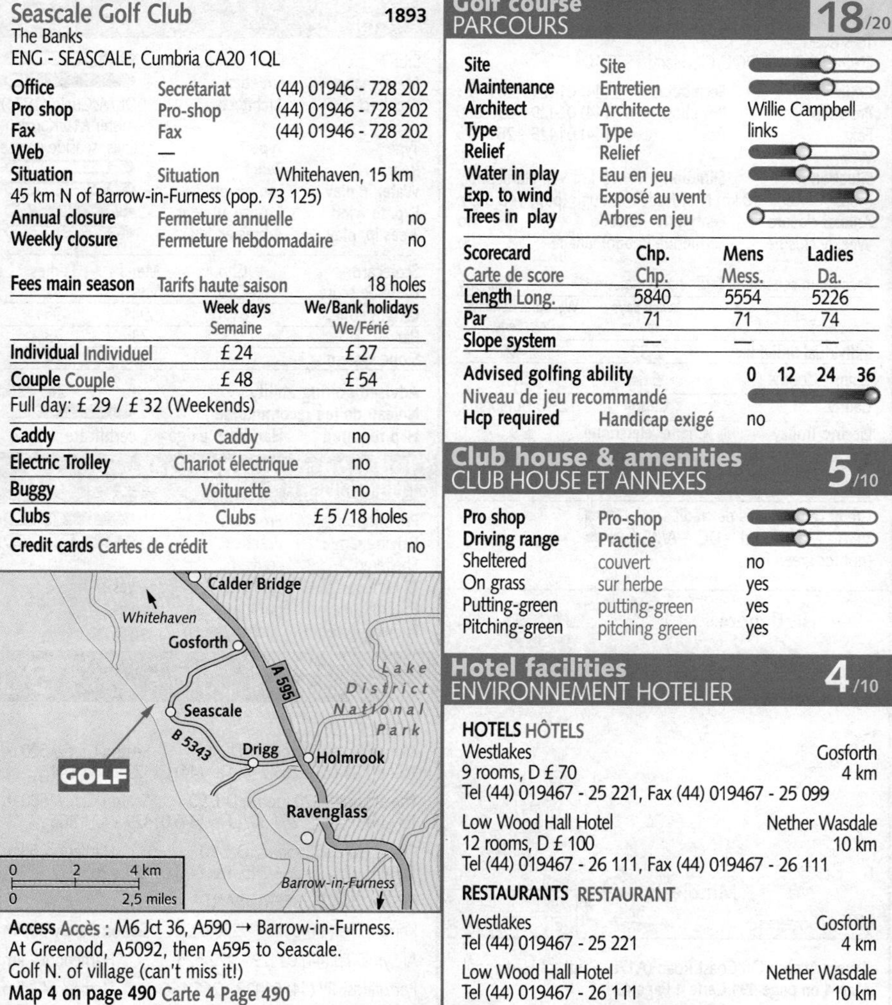

Seascale Golf Club **1893**
The Banks
ENG - SEASCALE, Cumbria CA20 1QL

Office	Secrétariat	(44) 01946 - 728 202
Pro shop	Pro-shop	(44) 01946 - 728 202
Fax	Fax	(44) 01946 - 728 202
Web	—	
Situation	Situation	Whitehaven, 15 km

45 km N of Barrow-in-Furness (pop. 73 125)

Annual closure	Fermeture annuelle	no
Weekly closure	Fermeture hebdomadaire	no

Fees main season Tarifs haute saison	18 holes	
	Week days Semaine	**We/Bank holidays** We/Férié
Individual Individuel	£ 24	£ 27
Couple Couple	£ 48	£ 54

Full day: £ 29 / £ 32 (Weekends)

Caddy	Caddy	no
Electric Trolley	Chariot électrique	no
Buggy	Voiturette	no
Clubs	Clubs	£ 5 /18 holes
Credit cards	Cartes de crédit	no

Access Accès : M6 Jct 36, A590 → Barrow-in-Furness. At Greenodd, A5092, then A595 to Seascale. Golf N. of village (can't miss it!)
Map 4 on page 490 Carte 4 Page 490

Golf course PARCOURS — 18/20

Site	Site	
Maintenance	Entretien	
Architect	Architecte	Willie Campbell
Type	Type	links
Relief	Relief	
Water in play	Eau en jeu	
Exp. to wind	Exposé au vent	
Trees in play	Arbres en jeu	

Scorecard Carte de score	**Chp.** Chp.	**Mens** Mess.	**Ladies** Da.
Length Long.	5840	5554	5226
Par	71	71	74
Slope system	—	—	—

Advised golfing ability 0 12 24 36
Niveau de jeu recommandé

Hcp required Handicap exigé no

Club house & amenities CLUB HOUSE ET ANNEXES — 5/10

Pro shop	Pro-shop	
Driving range	Practice	
Sheltered	couvert	no
On grass	sur herbe	yes
Putting-green	putting-green	yes
Pitching-green	pitching green	yes

Hotel facilities ENVIRONNEMENT HOTELIER — 4/10

HOTELS HÔTELS

Westlakes — Gosforth 4 km
9 rooms, D £ 70
Tel (44) 019467 - 25 221, Fax (44) 019467 - 25 099

Low Wood Hall Hotel — Nether Wasdale 10 km
12 rooms, D £ 100
Tel (44) 019467 - 26 111, Fax (44) 019467 - 26 111

RESTAURANTS RESTAURANT

Westlakes — Gosforth 4 km
Tel (44) 019467 - 25 221

Low Wood Hall Hotel — Nether Wasdale 10 km
Tel (44) 019467 - 26 111

SEATON CAREW

17 | 7 | 5

The industrial surroundings are certainly not the most pleasant setting for a golf course, but no keen golfer can afford to miss playing this course and getting to grips with the wile and cunning of Alister MacKenzie, the layout's devilishly clever architect. The four holes added by Frank Pennink for spice and variety were laid out in the same spirit. Although rather flat, the course comprises several strings of sand-dunes, just to bother the inaccurate hitter, plus the thickets, bushes and buckthorns that go with them. For all the qualities of this championship course, it is not what you would call intimidating, especially the outward nine. Lesser players might prefer to watch how their betters negotiate the back nine, where certain shots calls for good ball-striking and long carries. This is particularly true on the 17th, probably the trickiest hole of all (and the most deceitful) with a terribly difficult approach shot to an elevated green. And just in case you needed reminding, the wind might also have its say in the final reckoning.

Certes, l'environnement industriel n'est pas des plus réjouissants, mais aucun golfeur acharné ne saurait passer à côté de ce parcours sans affronter les astuces et les ruses d'Alister Mackenzie, son diabolique architecte. Et les quatre trous ajoutés par Frank Pennink, pour varier les plaisirs, ont été créés dans le même esprit. Assez plat, il comprend néanmoins, pour mieux ennuyer le golfeur imprécis, quelques cordons dunaires, avec les arbustes touffus, les buissons et les nerpruns qui vont avec. En dépit de ses qualités de parcours de championnat, il n'est pourtant pas intimidant, en particulier l'aller. Les joueurs peu expérimentés regarderont plutôt leurs «maîtres» négocier le retour, où certains coups demandent des balles solides coups, bien portées. Notamment le 17, sans doute le trou le plus délicat (et le moins franc) de Seaton Carew, par son approche des plus difficiles d'un green surélévé. Et le vent...

Seaton Carew Golf Club — 1925

Tees Road
ENG - HARTLEPOOL, Cleveland TS25 1DE

Office	Secrétariat	(44) 01429 - 261 473
Pro shop	Pro-shop	(44) 01429 - 890 660
Fax	Fax	(44) 01429 - 261 473
Web	—	
Situation	Situation	5 km S of Hartlepool,

(pop. 90 409) - 10 km N of Middlesbrough (pop. 140 849)

Annual closure	Fermeture annuelle	no
Weekly closure	Fermeture hebdomadaire	no

Fees main season Tarifs haute saison — Full day

	Week days Semaine	We/Bank holidays We/Férié
Individual Individuel	£ 32	£ 42
Couple Couple	£ 64	£ 84
Caddy Caddy		£ 10 (Juniors)
Electric Trolley Chariot électrique		£ 3
Buggy Voiturette		£ 16
Clubs Clubs		£ 10

Credit cards Cartes de crédit
VISA - MasterCard - DC - AMEX
(not for green fees)

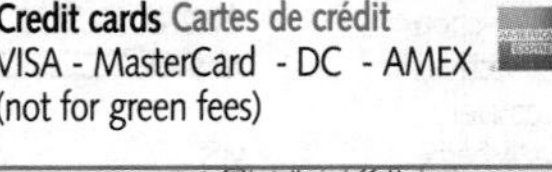

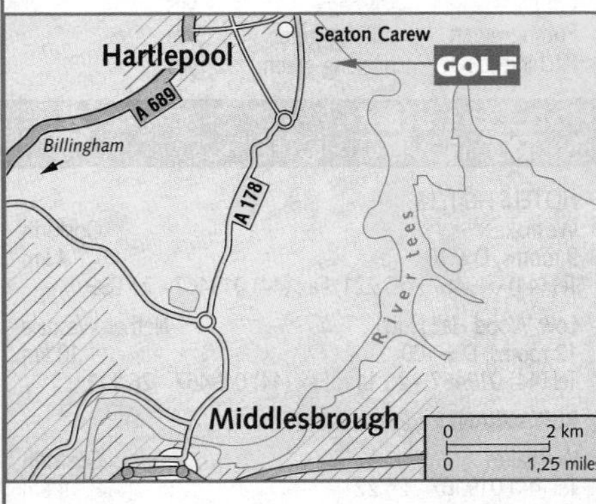

Access Accès : On Coast Road (A178) South of Hartlepool
Map 4 on page 491 Carte 4 Page 491

Golf course — PARCOURS — 17/20

Site	Site	
Maintenance	Entretien	
Architect	Architecte	Dr McCuaig (1874) Alister MacKenzie
Type	Type	links, seaside course
Relief	Relief	
Water in play	Eau en jeu	
Exp. to wind	Exposé au vent	
Trees in play	Arbres en jeu	

Scorecard Carte de score	Chp. Chp.	Mens Mess.	Ladies Da.
Length Long.	6170	5941	4951
Par	73	73	73
Slope system	—	—	—

Advised golfing ability 0 12 24 36
Niveau de jeu recommandé
Hcp required Handicap exigé — certificate

Club house & amenities — CLUB HOUSE ET ANNEXES — 7/10

Pro shop	Pro-shop	
Driving range	Practice	
Sheltered	couvert	
On grass	sur herbe	yes
Putting-green	putting-green	yes
Pitching-green	pitching green	yes

Hotel facilities — ENVIRONNEMENT HOTELIER — 5/10

HOTELS HÔTELS

Marine Hotel, 25 rooms, D £ 85 — Seaton Carew 500 m
Tel (44) 01429 - 266 244, Fax (44) 01429 - 864 144

The Staincliffe, 20 rooms, D £ 90 — Seaton Carew 500 m
Tel (44) 01429 - 264 301, Fax (44) 01429 - 421 366

Grand Hotel, 50 rooms, D £ 90 — Hartlepool 5 km
Tel (44) 01429 - 266 345, Fax (44) 01429 - 265 217

RESTAURANTS RESTAURANT

Krimo's, Tel (44) 01429 - 290 022 — Seaton Carew 500 m

Al Syros, Tel (44) 01429 - 272 525 — Hartlepool 2 km

Portofinos, Tel (44) 01429 - 266 166 — Hartlepool 3 km

SHANKLIN & SANDOWN

15	7	6

Shanklin & Sandown is the best of the seven courses on the Isle of Wight. It is short, naturally, as designers at the turn of the century were wiser than they are today. They weren't unaware of the fact that big-hitters make up only a minority of golfers and that wind can really bother simply anyone, whether blowing with or against the ball. A part of this layout is similar to links golfing, another part is more inland in style with some impressive heather and broom. Despite a distinctly hilly character, there are only three blind drives, otherwise playing strategy is clear. The sole element of chance is the stance and lie, sometimes difficult to negotiate for players who are used to flat courses. With tight fairways and well placed bunkers, we would recommend this course to players who have some control over their ball. Beginners here could easily spend all day looking for theirs.

Shanklin & Sandown se détache parmi les sept parcours de l'Ile de Wight. Il est bien sûr assez court, mais les architectes du début du siècle étaient des sages. Ils n'ignoraient pas que les bons frappeurs ne sont pas les plus nombreux, et que le vent a tendance à gêner tout le monde, qu'il souffle contre ou avec vous. Ce parcours comporte une partie apparentée aux links et une partie "inland" avec une très belle végétation de bruyère et de genêts. On ne trouve ici, en dépit d'un certain relief, que trois drives aveugles. Autrement, la stratégie à mettre en oeuvre est assez claire, la part de hasard étant préservée par des stances parfois difficiles pour ceux qui jouent habituellement les pieds à plat. Avec ses fairways étroits et ses bunkers très bien placés, on le recommandera à ceux qui savent déjà contrôler la balle car les débutants peuvent passer la journée à chercher la leur !

Shanklin & Sandown Golf Club — 1900

The Fairway Lake
ENG - SANDOWN, Isle of Wight PO36 9 PR

Office	Secrétariat	(44) 01983 - 403 217
Pro shop	Pro-shop	(44) 01983 - 404 424
Fax	Fax	(44) 01983 - 403 217
Web	—	
Situation	Situation	Isle of Wight (pop. 124 580)
Annual closure	Fermeture annuelle	no
Weekly closure	Fermeture hebdomadaire	no

Fees main season Tarifs haute saison	18 holes	
	Week days Semaine	We/Bank holidays We/Férié
Individual Individuel	£ 25	£ 30
Couple Couple	£ 50	£ 60

Saturday: only after 1.00 pm / Sunday: after 9.00 am

Caddy	Caddy	no
Electric Trolley	Chariot électrique	no
Buggy	Voiturette	no
Clubs	Clubs	no

Credit cards Cartes de crédit
VISA - MasterCard (Pro shop goods only)

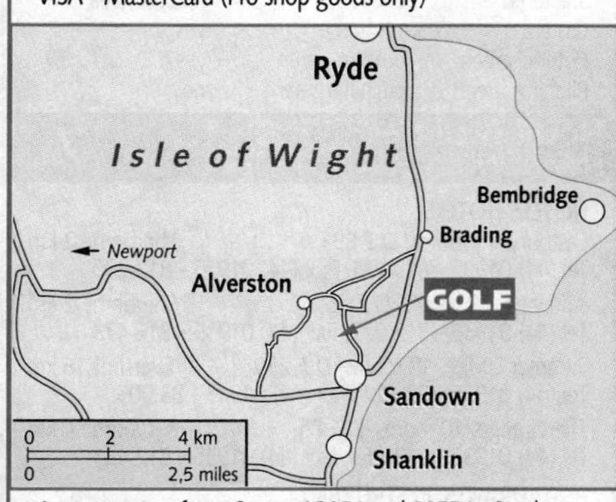

Access Accès : from Cowes A3054 and 3055 to Sandown. Avenue Road on left, then Broadway, Lake Hill on the right, The Fairway on the right.
Map 9 on page 500 Carte 9 Page 500

Golf course PARCOURS — 15/20

Site	Site	
Maintenance	Entretien	
Architect	Architecte	James Braid, M. Cowper
Type	Type	links, parkland
Relief	Relief	
Water in play	Eau en jeu	
Exp. to wind	Exposé au vent	
Trees in play	Arbres en jeu	

Scorecard Carte de score	Chp. Chp.	Mens Mess.	Ladies Da.
Length Long.	5456	5223	4960
Par	70	70	72
Slope system	—	—	—

Advised golfing ability / Niveau de jeu recommandé: 0 12 24 36
Hcp required / Handicap exigé: certificate

Club house & amenities CLUB HOUSE ET ANNEXES — 7/10

Pro shop	Pro-shop	
Driving range	Practice	
Sheltered	couvert	no
On grass	sur herbe	yes
Putting-green	putting-green	yes
Pitching-green	pitching green	yes

Hotel facilities ENVIRONNEMENT HOTELIER — 6/10

HOTELS HÔTELS

Brunswick, 35 rooms, D £ 88 — Shanklin 2 km
Tel (44) 01983 - 863 245, Fax (44) 01983 - 863 398

Royal Hotel, 55 rooms, D £ 150 — Ventnor 6 km
Tel (44) 01983 - 852 186, Fax (44) 01983 - 855 395

Bourne Hall Country, 30 rooms, D £ 83 — Shanklin 2 km
Tel (44) 01983 - 862 820, Fax (44) 01983 - 865 138

Rylstone Manor, 8 rooms, D £ 78 — Shanklin 2 km
Tel (44) 01983 - 862 806

RESTAURANTS RESTAURANT

Bourne Hall Country, Tel (44) 01983 - 862820 — Shanklin

Royal Hotel, Tel (44) 01983 - 852 186 — Ventnor 6 km

SHERBORNE

15 | 6 | 7

For a little culture, drive into town. In the 16th century, the transformation of Sherborne Abbey into a school led to the building being saved at a time when Henry VIII's break with Rome was resulting in the dissolution of monasteries and often the destruction of some of Britain's finest landmarks. For the golf, drive into this course, about a mile from the city of Sherborne, is testimony to the design skills of James Braid over a country landscape. It was completed in 1936 on a layout dating from 1894. The course is not too hilly but the slopes do pose a few questions, particularly on the sloping fairways of holes 6 and 13. The five par 3s are all excellent holes. The greens are average in size, never blind but do have some stiff slopes at the front on half a dozen holes. This is a fair test and a good family course.

Pour la culture, on ira en ville : au XVIè siècle la transformation de l'abbaye de Sherborne en école a permis de la préserver, après que la rupture d'Henry VIII avec Rome ait eu pour conséquence la dissolution des monastères, leur abandon et souvent la destruction de monuments magnifiques dans toute la Grande-Bretagne. Pour le golf, ce parcours à deux kilomètres de Sherborne reste un bon témoignage de l'architecture de James Braid en paysage de campagne, réalisé en 1936 à partir d'un tracé de 1894. Les reliefs ne sont pas assez importants mais ils permettent d'apporter quelques éléments d'interrogation, en particulier avec les fairways en pente au 6 et au 13. A remarquer aussi, la qualité des cinq par 3. Les greens sont de taille moyenne, jamais aveugles mais avec des pentes sévères en début de surface, sur une demi-douzaine de trous. Aucun green n'est aveugle, ce qui confirme la franchise de ce bon parcours familial.

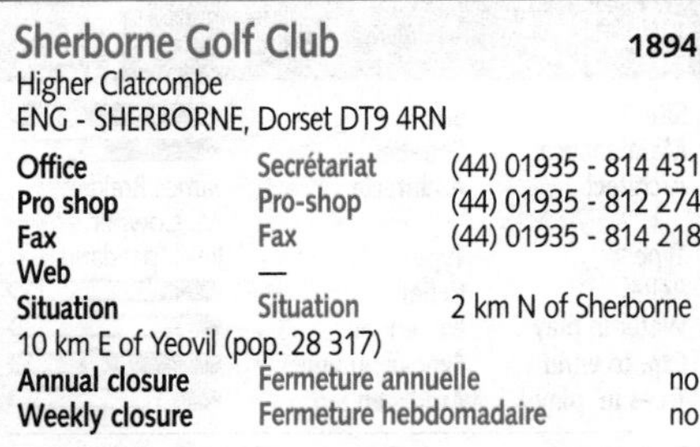

Sherborne Golf Club — 1894

Higher Clatcombe
ENG - SHERBORNE, Dorset DT9 4RN

Office	Secrétariat	(44) 01935 - 814 431
Pro shop	Pro-shop	(44) 01935 - 812 274
Fax	Fax	(44) 01935 - 814 218
Web	—	
Situation	Situation	2 km N of Sherborne

10 km E of Yeovil (pop. 28 317)

Annual closure	Fermeture annuelle	no
Weekly closure	Fermeture hebdomadaire	no

Fees main season Tarifs haute saison	Week days Semaine	We/Bank holidays We/Férié
		Full day
Individual Individuel	£ 28	£ 36
Couple Couple	£ 56	£ 72

Caddy	Caddy	no
Electric Trolley	Chariot électrique	no
Buggy	Voiturette	no
Clubs	Clubs	ask Pro

Credit cards Cartes de crédit
VISA - MasterCard (Pro shop goods only)

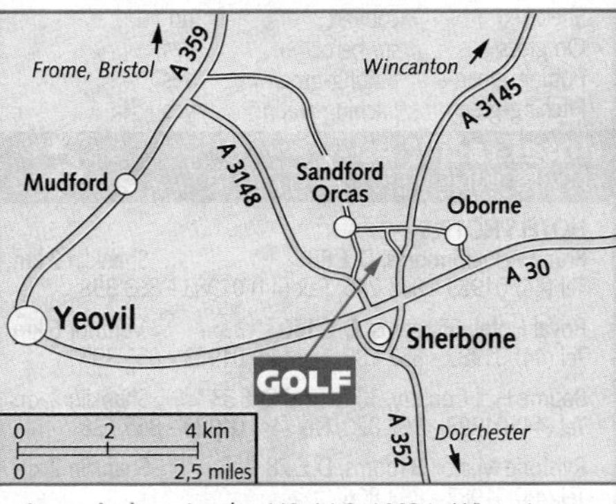

Access Accès : • London M3, Jct 8, A303 to Wincanter, A357 then B3145 → Sherborne. • Bristol A37 to Yeovil, A30 to Sherborne, then B3145 → Wincanton.
Map 6 on page 495 Carte 6 Page 495

Golf course / PARCOURS — 15/20

Site	Site	
Maintenance	Entretien	
Architect	Architecte	James Braid (1936)
Type	Type	parkland
Relief	Relief	
Water in play	Eau en jeu	
Exp. to wind	Exposé au vent	
Trees in play	Arbres en jeu	

Scorecard Carte de score	Chp. Chp.	Mens Mess.	Ladies Da.
Length Long.	5377	5220	5018
Par	70	70	73
Slope system	—	—	—

Advised golfing ability Niveau de jeu recommandé: 0 12 24 36

Hcp required Handicap exigé: certificate

Club house & amenities / CLUB HOUSE ET ANNEXES — 6/10

Pro shop	Pro-shop	
Driving range	Practice	
Sheltered	couvert	practice area
On grass	sur herbe	yes
Putting-green	putting-green	yes
Pitching-green	pitching green	no

Hotel facilities / ENVIRONNEMENT HOTELIER — 7/10

HOTELS HÔTELS

Eastbury, 14 rooms, D £ 89 — Sherborne 2 km
Tel (44) 01935 - 813 131, Fax (44) 01935 - 817 296

Antelope, 19 rooms, D £ 75 — Sherborne 2 km
Tel (44) 01935 - 812 077, Fax (44) 01935 - 816 473

Summer Lodge, 18 rooms, D £ 230 — Evershot 16 km
Tel (44) 01935 - 83 424, Fax (44) 01935 - 83 005

The Grange, 10 rooms, D £ 85 — Oborne 4 km
Tel (44) 01935 - 813 463, Fax (44) 01935 - 817 464

RESTAURANTS RESTAURANT

Pheasants, Tel (44) 01935 - 815 252 — Sherborne 2 km
Eastbury, Tel (44) 01935 - 813 131 — Sherborne 2 km
The Grange Tel (44) 01935 - 813 463 — Oborne 4 km

SHERINGHAM

15 | 7 | 6

Less well known than Royal West Norfolk and Hunstanton, Sheringham (together with Royal Cromer) is one of the excellent courses along this magnificent northern coast of East Anglia. Once you have actually found the entrance to the course, some of the views from atop chalk cliffs are quite magnificent. This is not a links course but the wind plays an even more important role in that there are no dunes to offer any shelter. The professionals find Sheringham a little on the short side but the course is looked upon with the greatest respect by the best amateur golfers, for whom the need to improvise and shape shots is an even more essential factor than length. Bunkers play a key role in the definition of each hole and in strategy, but so do the heather and gorse. At least there are no hidden traps on this Tom Dunn layout (created in 1891), and it is perhaps this fairness which deserves our greatest respect.

Moins connu que Royal West Norfolk et Hunstanton, Sheringham est avec Royal Cromer l'un des excellents parcours de cette magnifique côte nord de l'East Anglia, et offre des vues exceptionnelles, du haut de ses falaises de craie... une fois que l'on a trouvé l'entrée du golf. Bien sûr, ce n'est pas un véritable links, mais le vent y joue un rôle encore plus important : il n'y a pas de dunes pour s'en abriter ! Les professionnels le trouvent un peu court, mais c'est un tracé hautement respecté par les meilleurs amateurs, pour qui la nécessité de savoir créer des coups de golf est un facteur plus essentiel que la distance. Les bunkers jouent un rôle important dans la définition des trous et la stratégie, mais peut-être plus encore les buissons d'ajoncs et de fougère. Au moins n'y a t-il aucun piège caché sur ce dessin de Tom Dunn (en 1891), et cette honnêteté mérite le plus grand respect.

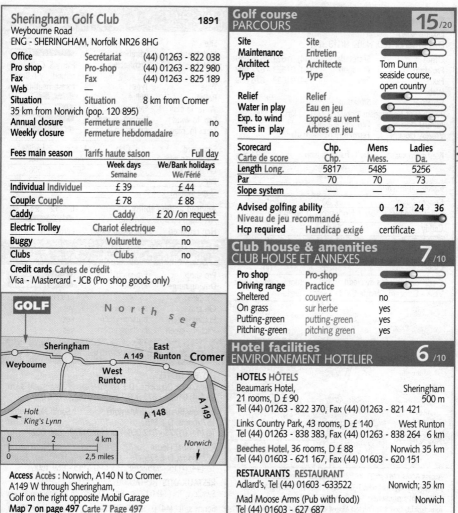

Sheringham Golf Club — 1891

Weybourne Road
ENG - SHERINGHAM, Norfolk NR26 8HG

Office	Secrétariat	(44) 01263 - 822 038
Pro shop	Pro-shop	(44) 01263 - 822 980
Fax	Fax	(44) 01263 - 825 189
Web	—	
Situation	Situation	8 km from Cromer

35 km from Norwich (pop. 120 895)

Annual closure	Fermeture annuelle	no
Weekly closure	Fermeture hebdomadaire	no

Fees main season Tarifs haute saison	Week days Semaine	We/Bank holidays We/Férié
		Full day
Individual Individuel	£ 39	£ 44
Couple Couple	£ 78	£ 88
Caddy Caddy		£ 20 /on request
Electric Trolley Chariot électrique		no
Buggy Voiturette		no
Clubs Clubs		no

Credit cards Cartes de crédit
Visa - Mastercard - JCB (Pro shop goods only)

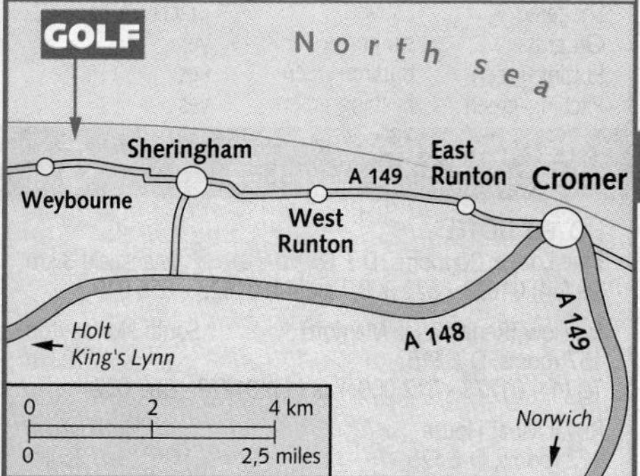

Access Accès : Norwich, A140 N to Cromer.
A149 W through Sheringham,
Golf on the right opposite Mobil Garage
Map 7 on page 497 Carte 7 Page 497

Golf course — PARCOURS — 15/20

Site	Site	
Maintenance	Entretien	
Architect	Architecte	Tom Dunn
Type	Type	seaside course, open country
Relief	Relief	
Water in play	Eau en jeu	
Exp. to wind	Exposé au vent	
Trees in play	Arbres en jeu	

Scorecard Carte de score	Chp. Chp.	Mens Mess.	Ladies Da.
Length Long.	5817	5485	5256
Par	70	70	73
Slope system	—	—	—

Advised golfing ability Niveau de jeu recommandé: 0 12 24 36
Hcp required Handicap exigé: certificate

Club house & amenities — CLUB HOUSE ET ANNEXES — 7/10

Pro shop	Pro-shop	
Driving range	Practice	
Sheltered	couvert	no
On grass	sur herbe	yes
Putting-green	putting-green	yes
Pitching-green	pitching green	yes

Hotel facilities — ENVIRONNEMENT HOTELIER — 6/10

HOTELS HÔTELS

Beaumaris Hotel, 21 rooms, D £ 90 — Sheringham 500 m
Tel (44) 01263 - 822 370, Fax (44) 01263 - 821 421

Links Country Park, 43 rooms, D £ 140 — West Runton 6 km
Tel (44) 01263 - 838 383, Fax (44) 01263 - 838 264

Beeches Hotel, 36 rooms, D £ 88 — Norwich 35 km
Tel (44) 01603 - 621 167, Fax (44) 01603 - 620 151

RESTAURANTS RESTAURANT

Adlard's, Tel (44) 01603 -633522 — Norwich; 35 km

Mad Moose Arms (Pub with food)) — Norwich
Tel (44) 01603 - 627 687

SHERWOOD FOREST

17	7	6

Here we are in Robin Hood country where you can visit the cities of Nottingham and Lincoln and what is left of Sherwood Forest. As you might expect, trees are the main feature on this course and they play a major role throughout. It will be surprising if you don't have to play at least one swirling recovery to get back onto the fairway (the undergrowth is cut back short). Otherwise Harry Colt and James Braid have laid out bunkers as effectively as usual, including around the greens which can be approached in different ways, according to their line of defence. A rather traditional course but with a back 9 that can upset your score. Having spent many years in the shadow of Notts Hollinwell, this hilly course deserves a little limelight of its own.

Nous voici dans le monde de Robin des Bois. Entre une visite à Nottingham et une excursion vers Lincoln, la forêt de Sherwood n'est plus inquiétante que pour les imaginations d'enfants. Comme on pouvait s'y attendre, les arbres constituent l'essentiel du décor de ce parcours, mais un décor qui joue les rôles principaux. Il serait étonnant que vous n'ayiez jamais à jouer de balles à effet pour vous en extraire (les sous-bois sont bien dégagés). Autrement, Harry Colt et James Braid ont développé leur jeu de bunkers toujours aussi efficace, y compris autour des greens. Ceux-ci peuvent cependant être attaqués de différentes manières, selon les lignes de défense. Un parcours assez traditionnel, mais la difficulté du retour peut perturber le score. Longtemps à l'ombre de Notts (Hollinwell), ce parcours très vallonné mérite d'être placé en pleine lumière.

Sherwood Forest Golf Club — 1895

Eakring Road
ENG - MANSFIELD, Notts. NG18 3EW

Office	Secrétariat	(44) 01623 - 626 689
Pro shop	Pro-shop	(44) 01623 - 627 403
Fax	Fax	(44) 01623 - 626 689
Web	—	
Situation	Situation	

25 km N of Nottingham (pop. 270 222) - 3 km E of Mansfield

Annual closure	Fermeture annuelle	no
Weekly closure	Fermeture hebdomadaire	no

Fees main season Tarifs haute saison	18 holes	
	Week days Semaine	**We/Bank holidays** We/Férié
Individual Individuel	£ 40	*
Couple Couple	£ 80	*

Full weekdays: £ 55 / * No visitors at w/ends

Caddy	Caddy	no
Electric Trolley	Chariot électrique	£ 5 /18 holes
Buggy	Voiturette	no
Clubs	Clubs	no

Credit cards Cartes de crédit (not for green fees)
VISA - Eurocard - MasterCard - Switch - Delta

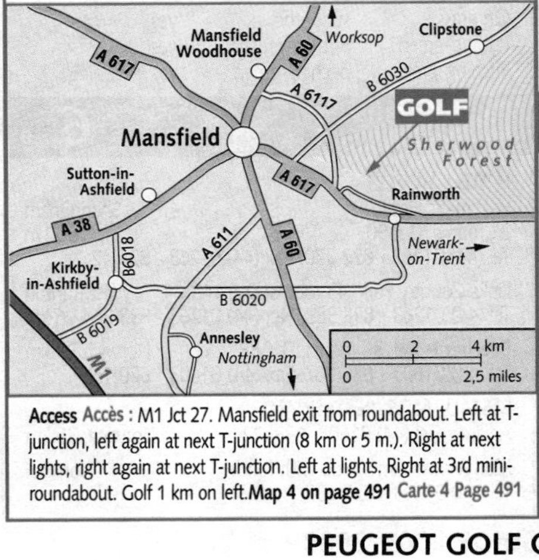

Access Accès : M1 Jct 27. Mansfield exit from roundabout. Left at T-junction, left again at next T-junction (8 km or 5 m.). Right at next lights, right again at next T-junction. Left at lights. Right at 3rd mini-roundabout. Golf 1 km on left. **Map 4 on page 491** Carte 4 Page 491

Golf course PARCOURS — 17/20

Site	Site	
Maintenance	Entretien	
Architect	Architecte	Harry S. Colt remod. by J. Braid
Type	Type	forest, heathland
Relief	Relief	
Water in play	Eau en jeu	
Exp. to wind	Exposé au vent	
Trees in play	Arbres en jeu	

Scorecard Carte de score	**Chp.** Chp.	**Mens** Mess.	**Ladies** Da.
Length Long.	6028	5654	5082
Par	71	71	73
Slope system	—	—	—

Advised golfing ability Niveau de jeu recommandé: 0 12 24 36
Hcp required Handicap exigé: certificate

Club house & amenities CLUB HOUSE ET ANNEXES — 7/10

Pro shop	Pro-shop	
Driving range	Practice	
Sheltered	couvert	practice area
On grass	sur herbe	yes
Putting-green	putting-green	yes
Pitching-green	pitching green	yes

Hotel facilities ENVIRONNEMENT HOTELIER — 6/10

HOTELS HÔTELS

Pine Lodge, 20 rooms, D £ 65 — Mansfield 3 km
Tel (44) 01623 - 622 308, Fax (44) 01623 - 656 819

Swallow (Renaissance Marriott) — South Normanton 18 km
157 rooms, D £ 115
Tel (44) 01773 - 812 000, Fax (44) 01773 - 580 032

Royal Moat House — Nottingham 25 km
172 rooms, D £ 125
Tel (44) 0115 - 935 9988, Fax (44) 0115 - 969 1506

RESTAURANTS RESTAURANT

Swallow, Tel (44) 01773 - 812 000 — South Normanton 18 km
Sonny's, Tel (44) 0115 - 947 3041 — Nottingham 25 km

SILLOTH-ON-SOLWAY

18 | 7 | 4

A course to take in on your way from Liverpool to Scotland, or from Glasgow to England, together with Southerness just opposite on the other side of Solway Firth. Keep looking in this direction, too, because the industrial complex nearby is something of an eyesore. The course's location in the middle of nowhere has kept Silloth from staging any top tournaments, but this does have it advantages: being a quiet course and frequented mostly only by the inhabitants of Carlisle, its overall condition is simply marvellous. It has its enthusiasts, who rate this amongst their top-five links courses, and understandably so. The well-contoured fairways rarely have you standing on flat ground, fairway bunkers have been replaced by heather and gorse, the approaches to greens are tight and putting surfaces are tricky. Bring your best game here and a suitcase because you won't want to leave. Play Silloth before it becomes too fashionable.

Un parcours à inclure dans un voyage de Liverpool vers l'Ecosse, ou de Glasgow vers l'Angleterre, avec celui de Southerness, juste en face, de l'autre côté du Solway Firth. Regardez plutôt de ce côté, car le complexe industriel à proximité n'est pas beau du tout. Sa situation à l'écart de tout a empêché Silloth d'avoir beaucoup de grands championnats, mais il y a un avantage : peu fréquenté, sinon par les habitants de Carlisle, il est dans un état généralement merveilleux. Il a ses amoureux, qui le classent dans leur "Top 5" des links, et on les comprend. Les fairways bien modelés vous mettent rarement à plat, les bunkers de fairway sont remplacés par la bruyère et les ajoncs, les entrées de greens sont étroites, leurs surfaces subtiles. A Silloth-on-Solway, il faut amener son meilleur jeu, et sa valise, car on aura envie de rester... A jouer avant qu'il ne devienne à la mode.

Silloth-on-Solway Golf Club — 1892

ENG - SILLOTH-ON-SOLWAY, Cumbria CA5 4AT

Office	Secrétariat	(44) 016973 - 31 304
Pro shop	Pro-shop	(44) 016973 - 32 404
Fax	Fax	(44) 016973 - 31 782
Web	—	
Situation	Situation	

40 km from Carlisle (pop. 100 562)

Annual closure	Fermeture annuelle	no
Weekly closure	Fermeture hebdomadaire	no

Fees main season Tarifs haute saison	Week days Semaine	We/Bank holidays We/Férié
		Full day
Individual Individuel	£ 26	£ 35 *
Couple Couple	£ 52	£ 70 *

* 18 holes only

Caddy	Caddy	no
Electric Trolley	Chariot électrique	no
Buggy	Voiturette	no
Clubs	Clubs	£ 10 /18 holes

Credit cards Cartes de crédit
VISA - Eurocard - MasterCard - DC - AMEX

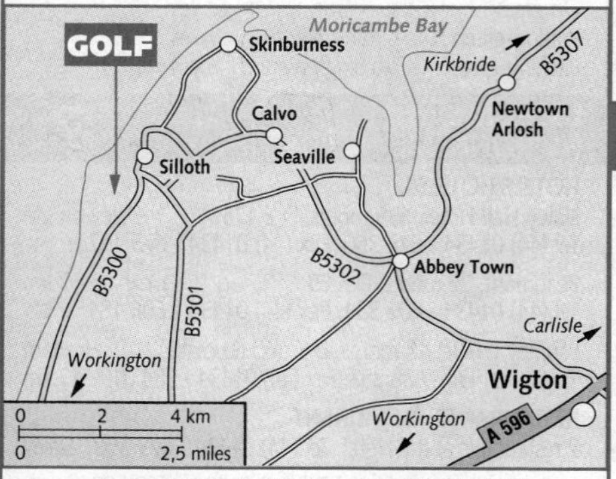

Access Accès : M6 to Carlisle, then A595 & A596. At Wigton, B5302 to Silloth Promenade. Go right 200 m.
Map 2 on page 487 Carte 2 Page 487

Golf course — PARCOURS — 18/20

Site	Site	
Maintenance	Entretien	
Architect	Architecte	Willie Park
Type	Type	links
Relief	Relief	
Water in play	Eau en jeu	
Exp. to wind	Exposé au vent	
Trees in play	Arbres en jeu	

Scorecard Carte de score	Chp. Chp.	Mens Mess.	Ladies Da.
Length Long.	5952	5721	5203
Par	72	72	75
Slope system	—	—	—

Advised golfing ability — 0 12 24 36
Niveau de jeu recommandé
Hcp required Handicap exigé — certificate

Club house & amenities — CLUB HOUSE ET ANNEXES — 7/10

Pro shop	Pro-shop	
Driving range	Practice	
Sheltered	couvert	no
On grass	sur herbe	yes
Putting-green	putting-green	yes
Pitching-green	pitching green	yes

Hotel facilities — ENVIRONNEMENT HOTELIER — 4/10

HOTELS HÔTELS

Silloth Golf Hotel, 22 rooms, D £ 65 — Silloth 200 m
Tel (44) 016973 - 31 438, Fax (44) 016973 - 32 582

The Skinburness, 33 rooms, D £ 90 — Silloth on site
Tel (44) 016973 - 32 332, Fax (44) 016973 - 32 549

Crown + Mitre, 97 rooms, D £ 110 — Carlisle 40 km
Tel (44) 01228 - 525 491, Fax (44) 01228 - 514 553

RESTAURANTS RESTAURANT

The Skinburness — Silloth on site
Tel (44) 016973 - 32 332

643

SLALEY HALL

17 | 8 | 7

The Woburn of the north or the Gleneagles of the south, it doesn't matter either way. Slaley Hall is one of those courses that has brought life to a region where good courses were comparatively few and far between. The vegetation is typical of the north, with a good number of pine-trees lining the fairways or adding dark colour to contrast with the lighter greens of the fairways and putting surfaces, the sand in the bunkers and the lakes. Familiar colours to golfers, certainly, but here they just look smarter than anywhere else. The many different playing options add variety to the fun of playing here; you can change the complexion of the course by switching tee-boxes but still keep the same panoply of hazards, including fairway bunkers whose shape (Dave Thomas style) gives this magnificent English style park a little American touch. If you are feeling tired after the very challenging finishing holes, the clubhouse and hotel offer all the facilities of a major golfing resort, enhanced still further with a second course.

Woburn du nord ou Gleneagles du sud, peu importe, Slaley Hall fait partie, des golfs qui ont un peu réveillé une région assez pauvre en grands parcours. La végétation est néanmoins plus typique du nord, avec les nombreux sapins bordant les fairways ou fournissant des couleurs sombres harmonisées à celles des greens et des fairways, au sable des bunkers et aux lacs. Ce sont des couleurs familières aux golfeurs, mais ici plus soignées que partout ailleurs. De multiples options de jeu permettent de varier les plaisirs : d'un jour à l'autre, changez de difficultés en changeant de tees, tout en conservant une panoplie d'obstacles, les formes des bunkers de fairway (à la Dave Thomas !) apportant une touche américaine à ce beau parc à l'anglaise. Si vous êtes un peu fatigué après un finale exigeant, le Clubhouse et l'hôtel offrent tous les services d'un grand "resort", encore amélioré avec un second parcours.

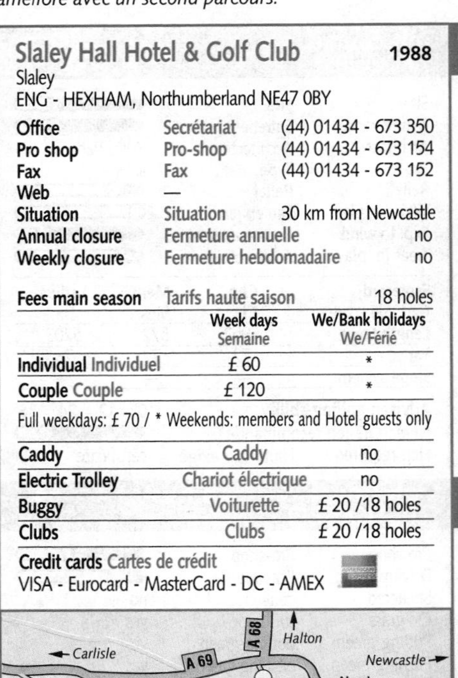

Slaley Hall Hotel & Golf Club 1988

Slaley
ENG - HEXHAM, Northumberland NE47 0BY

Office	Secrétariat	(44) 01434 - 673 350
Pro shop	Pro-shop	(44) 01434 - 673 154
Fax	Fax	(44) 01434 - 673 152
Web	—	
Situation	Situation	30 km from Newcastle
Annual closure	Fermeture annuelle	no
Weekly closure	Fermeture hebdomadaire	no

Fees main season	Tarifs haute saison	18 holes
	Week days Semaine	**We/Bank holidays** We/Férié
Individual Individuel	£ 60	*
Couple Couple	£ 120	*

Full weekdays: £ 70 / * Weekends: members and Hotel guests only

Caddy	Caddy	no
Electric Trolley	Chariot électrique	no
Buggy	Voiturette	£ 20 /18 holes
Clubs	Clubs	£ 20 /18 holes

Credit cards Cartes de crédit
VISA - Eurocard - MasterCard - DC - AMEX

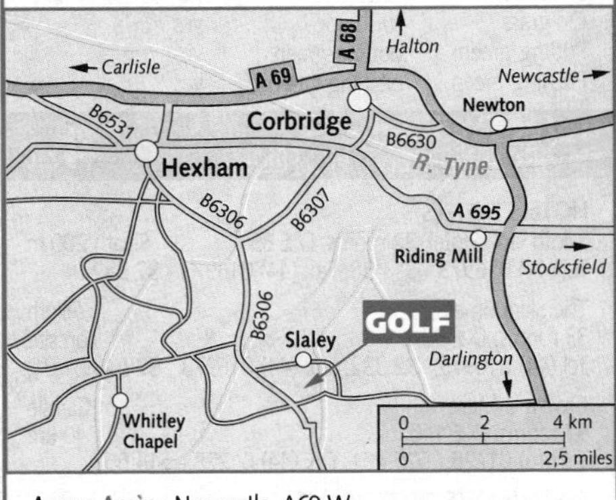

Access Accès : Newcastle, A69 W, turn to Hexham, then B6306 to Slaley.
Map 2 on page 487 Carte 2 Page 487

Golf course PARCOURS 17/20

Site	Site	
Maintenance	Entretien	
Architect	Architecte	David Thomas
Type	Type	parkland
Relief	Relief	
Water in play	Eau en jeu	
Exp. to wind	Exposé au vent	
Trees in play	Arbres en jeu	

Scorecard Carte de score	**Chp.** Chp.	**Mens** Mess.	**Ladies** Da.
Length Long.	6320	6085	5255
Par	72	72	75
Slope system	—	—	—

Advised golfing ability 0 12 24 36
Niveau de jeu recommandé
Hcp required Handicap exigé 24 Men, 36 Ladies

Club house & amenities CLUB HOUSE ET ANNEXES 8/10

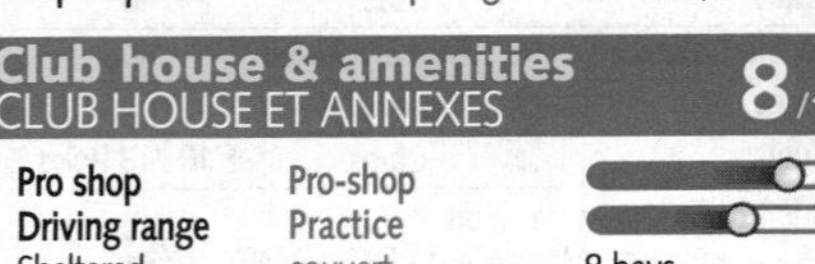

Pro shop	Pro-shop	
Driving range	Practice	
Sheltered	couvert	8 bays
On grass	sur herbe	yes
Putting-green	putting-green	yes
Pitching-green	pitching green	yes

Hotel facilities ENVIRONNEMENT HOTELIER 7/10

HOTELS HÔTELS

Slaley Hall Hotel, 139 rooms, D £ 175 — Slaley on site
Tel (44) 01434 - 673 350, Fax (44) 01434 - 673 152

Beaumont, 25 rooms, D £ 85 — Hexham 12 km
Tel (44) 01434 - 602 331, Fax (44) 01434 - 606 184

Langley Castle, 18 rooms, D £ 165 (in castle) — Hexham 12 km
Tel (44) 01434 - 688 888, Fax (44) 01434 - 684 019

RESTAURANTS RESTAURANT

2 restaurants at the Hotel, Tel (44) 01434 - 673 350 — Slaley

Josephine (Langley Castle) Tel (44) 01434 - 688 888

Ramblers Country House, Tel(44) 01434 - 632 424 — Corbridge 15 km

SOUTHPORT & AINSDALE 17 | 7 | 7

Although it has staged the Ryder Cup and the British Ladies Open, this course has suffered from being overshadowed by its towering neighbours Birkdale and Hillside, although actually there is little to choose between them. It may look short, but only to the better players. For the rest of us it has yardage enough, especially since driving these tight fairways is never easy. The paths to the greens are never very wide, either, and call for bump 'n run shots which can make the job even tougher. In contrast, game strategy will vary with the wind and always be clear: you see exactly what needs to be done. Whether you play here twice or a hundred times, it is always as exciting as that very first day in an elegant, traditional and warm atmosphere.

Bien qu'il ait reçu la Ryder Cup et le British Ladies Open, ce parcours a souffert de l'ombre de ses puissants voisins, Birkdale et Hillside, mais sans vraiment devoir leur envier grand'chose. Il peut paraître court, mais seulement aux meilleurs joueurs : il est bien assez long pour la plupart d'entre nous, en particulier par ce que driver sur ces fairways étroits n'est guère facile. Les entrées de greens ne sont pas toujours très larges, mais on doit les approcher en roulant, ce qui ne facilite pas non plus la tâche. En revanche, la stratégie peut varier en fonction du vent, mais elle apparaît toujours clairement : on voit exactement ce que l'on doit faire. Que l'on joue deux fois ou cent fois, le plaisir est comme au premier jour dans ce club à l'ambiance élégante, traditionnelle et chaleureuse.

Southport & Ainsdale Golf Club 1922

Bradshaws Lane, Ainsdale
ENG - SOUTHPORT, Lancs PR8 3LG

Office	Secrétariat	(44) 01704 - 578 092
Pro shop	Pro-shop	(44) 01704 - 577 316
Fax	Fax	(44) 01704 - 570 896
Web	www.sagolfclub.co.uk	
Situation	Situation	26 km N of Liverpool
Annual closure	Fermeture annuelle	no
Weekly closure	Fermeture hebdomadaire	no

Fees main season Tarifs haute saison		18 holes
	Week days Semaine	We/Bank holidays We/Férié
Individual Individuel	£ 45	£ 60 *
Couple Couple	£ 90	£ 120 *

* Limited access at weekends / Full weekdays: £ 60

Caddy	Caddy	£ 20 /on request
Electric Trolley	Chariot électrique	no
Buggy	Voiturette	no
Clubs	Clubs	£ 7.50 /day

Credit cards Cartes de crédit
VISA - Eurocard - MasterCard - DC - JCB - AMEX

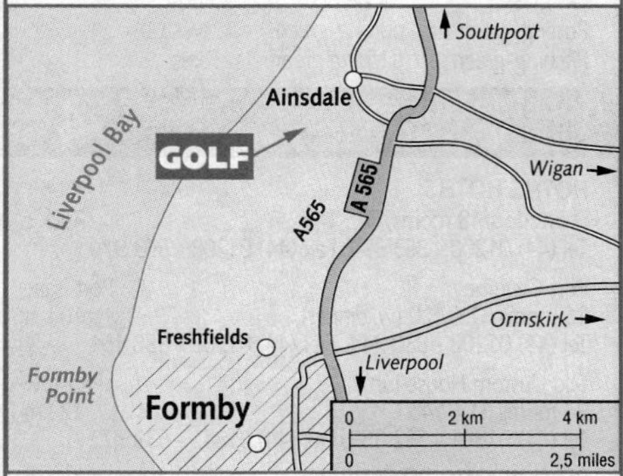

Southport
Ainsdale
GOLF
Liverpool Bay
A565
A 565
Wigan →
Ormskirk →
Freshfields
Liverpool
Formby Point
Formby
0 2 km 4 km
0 2,5 miles

Access Accès : A565 Liverpool → Southport. Ainsdale Village centre, turn left on Bradswhaws Lane
Map 5 on page 493 Carte 5 Page 493

Golf course PARCOURS 17/20

Site	Site	
Maintenance	Entretien	
Architect	Architecte	James Braid
Type	Type	links
Relief	Relief	
Water in play	Eau en jeu	
Exp. to wind	Exposé au vent	
Trees in play	Arbres en jeu	

Scorecard Carte de score	Chp. Chp.	Mens Mess.	Ladies Da.
Length Long.	5950	5924	5052
Par	72	72	74
Slope system	—	—	—

Advised golfing ability 0 12 24 36
Niveau de jeu recommandé
Hcp required Handicap exigé 28 Men, 36 Ladies

Club house & amenities CLUB HOUSE ET ANNEXES 7/10

Pro shop	Pro-shop	
Driving range	Practice	
Sheltered	couvert	no
On grass	sur herbe	yes
Putting-green	putting-green	yes
Pitching-green	pitching green	yes

Hotel facilities ENVIRONNEMENT HOTELIER 7/10

HOTELS HÔTELS

Cambridge House Hotel — Southport 6 km
16 rooms, D £ 60
Tel (44) 01704 - 538 372, Fax (44) 01704 - 547 183

Scarisbrick, 89 rooms, D £ 99 — Southport 5 km
Tel (44) 01704 - 543 000, Fax (44) 01704 - 533 335

Prince of Wales, 101 rooms, D £ 115 — Southport 5 km
Tel (44) 01704 - 536 688, Fax (44) 01704 - 543 488

RESTAURANTS RESTAURANT

Warehouse Brasserie — Southport 5 km
Tel (44) 01704 - 544 662

Valentino's, Tel (44) 01704 - 538 401 — Southport

Cloisters (Scarisbrick), Tel (44) 01704 - 535 153 — Southport

ST ENODOC Church Course

18 | 7 | 4

You will remember three things about this course: the wonderful views over the Cornish coast and the Camel estuary, the little church on the 10th hole, dug out of the sand 60 years ago, and Himalaya, a giant hill-shaped bunker standing some 80 feet high where you watch golfers walk up and down in a vain attempt to get their ball back in the fairway. But this is not the only hill over steeply undulating terrain, which can be tiring for the fainter-hearted. Some greens are difficult to reach other than with lofted shots, meaning that good scores go to good players. Beginners will spend their time in the dunes and the very thick rough. St. Enodoc is a superb golfing arena, with special mention going to the final holes where you play for the match and an excellent meal in the clubhouse.

Vous vous souviendrez au moins de trois choses : les vues magnifiques sur la côte de Cornouailles et le Camel Estuary, la petite église au 10, tirée du sable il y a 60 ans, et l'Himalaya, gigantesque bunker en forme de colline de 25 mètres de haut, d'où il est distrayant de regarder les joueurs monter et descendre sans parvenir à sortir leur balle. Mais ce n'est pas la seule colline d'un terrain très mouvementé, parfois assez fatigant pour les plus faibles. Certains greens sont difficiles à atteindre autrement qu'avec des balles levées, ce qui réserve les bons scores aux bons joueurs. Les débutants passeront leur vie dans les dunes et dans les roughs très épais. St Enodoc est une superbe arène pour jouer, avec une mention particulière pour les derniers trous quand on y joue le match et un très bon repas au Clubhouse.

St Enodoc Golf Club — 1890

Rock
ENG - WADEBRIDGE, Cornwall PL2T 6LD

Office	Secrétariat	(44) 01208 - 863 216
Pro shop	Pro-shop	(44) 01208 - 862 402
Fax	Fax	(44) 01208 - 862 976
Web	—	
Situation	Situation	32 km from Bodmin
Annual closure	Fermeture annuelle	no
Weekly closure	Fermeture hebdomadaire	no

Fees main season Tarifs haute saison	Full day	
	Week days Semaine	**We/Bank holidays** We/Férié
Individual Individuel	£ 50 *	£ 55
Couple Couple	£ 100 *	£ 110

* 18 holes: £ 35

Caddy	Caddy	no
Electric Trolley	Chariot électrique	£ 9 /day
Buggy	Voiturette	no
Clubs	Clubs	£ 10 /18 holes

Credit cards Cartes de crédit
Visa - Mastercard (Pro shop goods only)

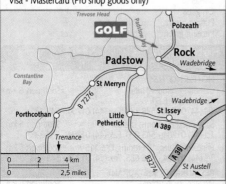

Access Accès : A30 Exeter to Bodmin, then A389 to Wadebridge, follow signs to Rock, drive through Rock, past Boat Club and Matiner's pub, sharp right uphill to Clubhouse (signposted) **Map 6 on page 494** Carte 6 Page 494

Golf course PARCOURS — 18/20

Site	Site	
Maintenance	Entretien	
Architect	Architecte	James Braid
Type	Type	seaside course, links
Relief	Relief	
Water in play	Eau en jeu	
Exp. to wind	Exposé au vent	
Trees in play	Arbres en jeu	

Scorecard Carte de score	**Chp.** Chp.	**Mens** Mess.	**Ladies** Da.
Length Long.	5619	5450	5115
Par	69	69	73
Slope system	—	—	—

Advised golfing ability Niveau de jeu recommandé — 0 12 24 36
Hcp required Handicap exigé — certificate

Club house & amenities CLUB HOUSE ET ANNEXES — 7/10

Pro shop	Pro-shop	
Driving range	Practice	
Sheltered	couvert	no
On grass	sur herbe	no
Putting-green	putting-green	yes (2)
Pitching-green	pitching green	yes

Hotel facilities ENVIRONNEMENT HOTELIER — 4/10

HOTELS HÔTELS

St Enodoc, 18 rooms, D £ 145 — Rock c
Tel (44) 01208 - 863 394, Fax (44) 01208 - 863 970

Port Gaverne — Port Isaac
16 rooms, D £ 120 (w. dinner) — 10 km
Tel (44) 01208 - 880 244, Fax (44) 01208 - 880 151

Old Custom House Inn — Padstow
24 rooms, D £ 145 — 12 km
Tel (44) 01841 - 532 359, Fax (44) 01841 - 533 372

RESTAURANTS RESTAURANT

Porthilly Grill (St Enodoc) — St Kew
Tel (44) 01208 - 863 394 — c

The Seafood, Tel (44) 01841 - 532 700 — Padstow 12 km

ST GEORGE'S HILL

17 | 7 | 7

Come and play here in May. If you're game lets you down, you'll probably find some consolation in the rhododendrons in full bloom, whose colours contrast with the purple heather, silver birch and pines to produce a wonderful setting for a superb course designed by Harry Colt. For those of you who are not as fit as you were, this is a very hilly course. If you run out of puff, make it back to the clubhouse and admire the superb views. Actually on the course, the changes of gradient and the slopes call for a little reconnoitring before hoping to card a good score, especially since the greens are very quick, full of breaks and sometimes multi-tiered. A few blind drives or tee-shots to steeply sloping fairways also require extreme accuracy. St George's Hill is not only picturesque, it is also one of the country's very good inland golf courses.

Venez donc au mois de mai. Si votre jeu vous a déçu, vous vous consolerez à la vue des rhododendrons en pleine floraison, dont les couleurs s'ajoutent aux bruyères pourpres, aux bouleaux blancs, aux pins et aux sapins pour offrir un cadre somptueux au superbe dessin de Harry Colt. Hélas pour ceux qui n'ont pas une excellente forme, ce parcours est très physique. Ils pourront toujours rester au Clubhouse, qui offre des vues superbes. Quant au parcours, ses changements de niveaux et ses pentes exigent une petite reconnaissance préalable avant d'espérer un bon score, d'autant plus que les greens sont rapides, très mouvementés, parfois à plusieurs plateaux. Quelques drives aveugles ou vers des fairways en dévers demandent aussi beaucoup de précision. St George's Hill n'est pas seulement pittoresque, c'est aussi un des très bons parcours "inland" du pays.

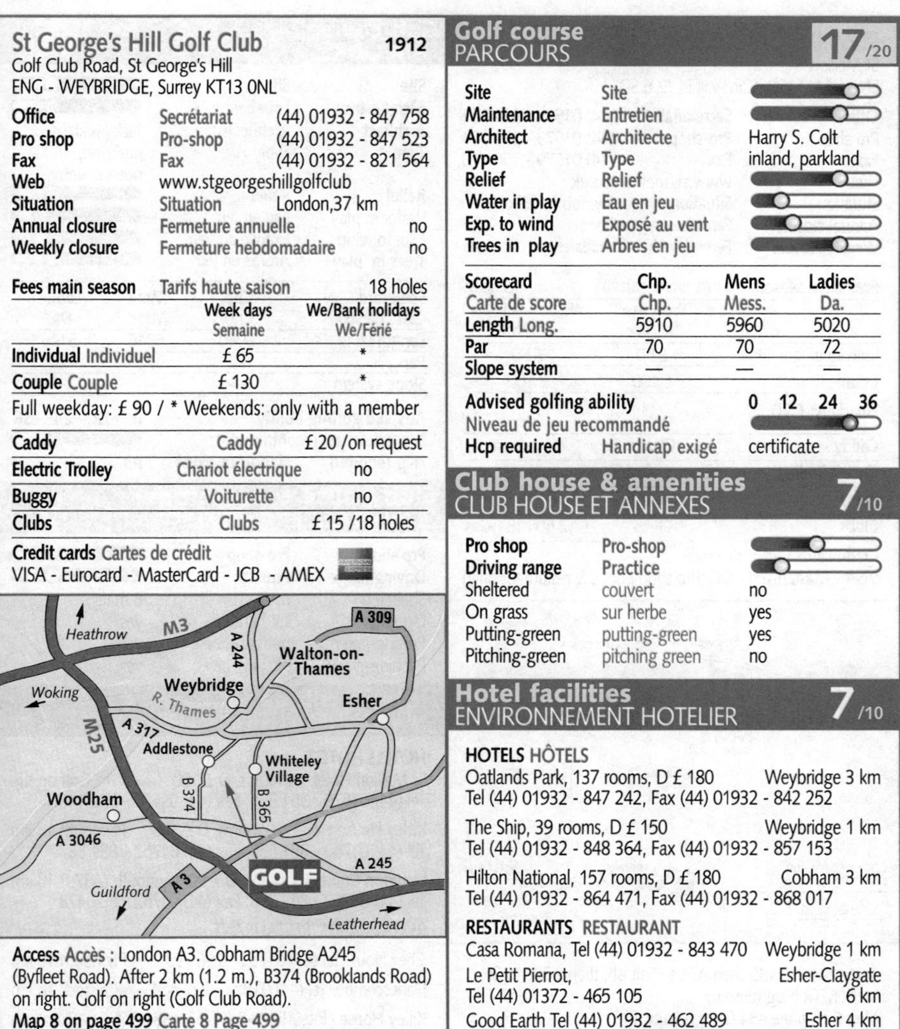

St George's Hill Golf Club — 1912

Golf Club Road, St George's Hill
ENG - WEYBRIDGE, Surrey KT13 0NL

Office	Secrétariat	(44) 01932 - 847 758
Pro shop	Pro-shop	(44) 01932 - 847 523
Fax	Fax	(44) 01932 - 821 564
Web	www.stgeorgeshillgolfclub	
Situation	Situation	London,37 km
Annual closure	Fermeture annuelle	no
Weekly closure	Fermeture hebdomadaire	no

Fees main season Tarifs haute saison	18 holes	
	Week days Semaine	**We/Bank holidays** We/Férié
Individual Individuel	£ 65	*
Couple Couple	£ 130	*

Full weekday: £ 90 / * Weekends: only with a member

Caddy	Caddy	£ 20 /on request
Electric Trolley	Chariot électrique	no
Buggy	Voiturette	no
Clubs	Clubs	£ 15 /18 holes

Credit cards Cartes de crédit
VISA - Eurocard - MasterCard - JCB - AMEX

Access Accès : London A3. Cobham Bridge A245 (Byfleet Road). After 2 km (1.2 m.), B374 (Brooklands Road) on right. Golf on right (Golf Club Road).
Map 8 on page 499 Carte 8 Page 499

Golf course — PARCOURS — 17/20

Site	Site	
Maintenance	Entretien	
Architect	Architecte	Harry S. Colt
Type	Type	inland, parkland
Relief	Relief	
Water in play	Eau en jeu	
Exp. to wind	Exposé au vent	
Trees in play	Arbres en jeu	

Scorecard Carte de score	**Chp.** Chp.	**Mens** Mess.	**Ladies** Da.
Length Long.	5910	5960	5020
Par	70	70	72
Slope system	—	—	—

Advised golfing ability Niveau de jeu recommandé — 0 12 24 36
Hcp required Handicap exigé — certificate

Club house & amenities — CLUB HOUSE ET ANNEXES — 7/10

Pro shop	Pro-shop	
Driving range	Practice	
Sheltered	couvert	no
On grass	sur herbe	yes
Putting-green	putting-green	yes
Pitching-green	pitching green	no

Hotel facilities — ENVIRONNEMENT HOTELIER — 7/10

HOTELS HÔTELS

Oatlands Park, 137 rooms, D £ 180 — Weybridge 3 km
Tel (44) 01932 - 847 242, Fax (44) 01932 - 842 252

The Ship, 39 rooms, D £ 150 — Weybridge 1 km
Tel (44) 01932 - 848 364, Fax (44) 01932 - 857 153

Hilton National, 157 rooms, D £ 180 — Cobham 3 km
Tel (44) 01932 - 864 471, Fax (44) 01932 - 868 017

RESTAURANTS RESTAURANT

Casa Romana, Tel (44) 01932 - 843 470 — Weybridge 1 km
Le Petit Pierrot, Tel (44) 01372 - 465 105 — Esher-Claygate 6 km
Good Earth Tel (44) 01932 - 462 489 — Esher 4 km

ST MELLION Nicklaus Course

17 | 9 | 7

This is a Jack Nicklaus course and golfers who know his style in the United States will recognise the way in which he has bent and twisted the Cornish countryside to fit his requirements. Turning around a hill which is the setting for another 18 hole course, St. Mellion is exposed to all winds and weathers which will make the course even more difficult than usual. Let's be honest here: even from the front tees this course will be beyond most average players. The bunkers, water and lakes are impressive enough to put off any visitor. Equally true though is the fact that it mellows a little more each time you play it. Maybe because you pay less attention to features such as the many tiny, multi-tiered greens. This is a course you cannot pass by, especially given the club's outstanding facilities, but it is not exactly what you would call a holiday course and there is little local colour to talk of. A must to play to form your own opinion. And test the state of your game.

D'accord, St Mellion est signé Jack Nicklaus. Ceux qui connaissent ses parcours aux USA reconnaîtront qu'il a voulu plier le paysage de Cornouailles à ses volontés. Tournant autour d'une colline où est logé un autre 18 trous, celui-ci est exposé à tous les vents, ce qui renforce encore sa difficulté. Disons-le franchement, même des départs avancés, ce parcours n'est pas à la portée des joueurs moyens. Les bunkers, les cours d'eau, les lacs impressionnent assez pour refroidir le visiteur. Il est vrai que ce parcours s'adoucit à mesure qu'on le joue, on remarque moins que certains greens sont minuscules, beaucoup à plateaux. Il est impossible d'ignorer ce golf, d'autant que les équipements sont remarquables, mais ce n'est pas exactement un parcours de vacances, et l'on cherchera vainement une couleur vraiment locale. A connaître absolument, pour se faire une opinion. Et tester son jeu.

St Mellion International — 1987

St Mellion
ENG - SALTASH, Cornwall PL12 6 SD

Office	Secrétariat	(44) 01579 - 351 351
Pro shop	Pro-shop	(44) 01579 - 350 724
Fax	Fax	(44) 01579 - 350 116
Web	www.st/mellion.co.uk	
Situation	Situation	Plymouth, 16 km
Annual closure	Fermeture annuelle	no
Weekly closure	Fermeture hebdomadaire	no

Fees main season Tarifs haute saison	18 holes	
	Week days Semaine	**We/Bank holidays** We/Férié
Individual Individuel	£ 50	£ 50
Couple Couple	£ 100	£ 100

Full days: £ 70

Caddy	Caddy	on request
Electric Trolley	Chariot électrique	no
Buggy	Voiturette	£ 18 /18 holes
Clubs	Clubs	£ 12.50 /18 holes

Credit cards Cartes de crédit
VISA - MasterCard - DC (Pro shop goods & restaurant only)

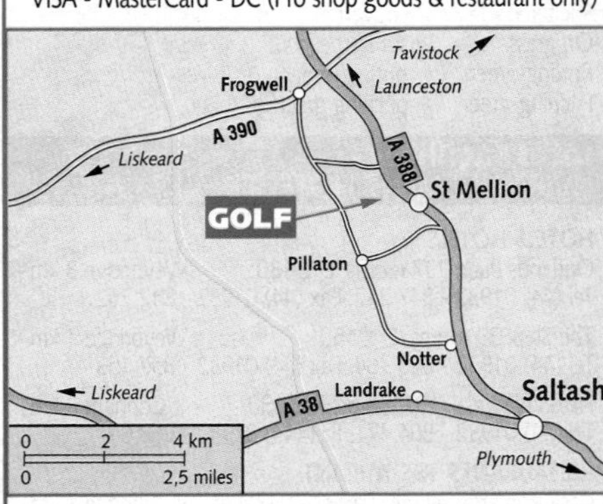

Access Accès : M5 then A38 to Saltash, then A388 to St Mellion. Golf signposted.
Map 6 on page 494 Carte 6 Page 494

Golf course PARCOURS — 17/20

Site	Site	
Maintenance	Entretien	
Architect	Architecte	Jack Nicklaus
Type	Type	parkland, open country
Relief	Relief	
Water in play	Eau en jeu	
Exp. to wind	Exposé au vent	
Trees in play	Arbres en jeu	

Scorecard Carte de score	**Chp.** Chp.	**Mens** Mess.	**Ladies** Da.
Length Long.	6080	5846	5146
Par	72	72	73
Slope system	—	—	—

Advised golfing ability Niveau de jeu recommandé — 0 12 24 36
Hcp required Handicap exigé — no

Club house & amenities CLUB HOUSE ET ANNEXES — 9/10

Pro shop	Pro-shop	
Driving range	Practice	
Sheltered	couvert	6 mats
On grass	sur herbe	yes
Putting-green	putting-green	yes
Pitching-green	pitching green	yes

Hotel facilities ENVIRONNEMENT HOTELIER — 7/10

HOTELS HÔTELS

St Mellion Hotel, 24 rooms, D £ 100 — Golf on site
Tel (44) 01579 - 351 351, Fax (44) 01579 - 350 116

Kitley House Hotel, 20 rooms, D £ 140 — Plymouth 18 km
Tel (44) 01752 - 881 555, Fax (44) 01752 - 881 667

Langdon Court, 18 rooms, D £ 90 — Plymouth (A379) 18 km
Tel (44) 01752 - 862 358, Fax (44) 01752 - 863 428

RESTAURANTS RESTAURANT

Chez Nous, Tel (44) 01752 - 266 793 — Plymouth 16 km
Danescombe, Tel (44) 01822 - 832 414 — Calstock 16 km
Kitley House Hotel, Tel (44) 01752 - 881 555 — Plymouth

STOKE POGES

17 | 8 | 8

Agreed, at this price the week-end green-fee is a little high, but we suppose they have to find some sort of deterrent. The most surprising thing here is not the price nor the Clubhouse, re-designed to cater to the addition of a new 9-hole course, hotel rooms and a swimming pool. No, what really surprises the visitor is the absence of heather, found on every other course in the region virtually without exception. We are in the purest "park-land" style, where fairways lined with splendid trees cover space that only Harry Colt could have turned into such a clever course. Everyone talks about the 7th hole, an exemplary par 3, but the rest are no less exciting. With Colt you always have to weigh up the pros and cons of each shot, look twice and watch out for illusions such as hazards that are too visible. If you want to talk about the course, there are some excellent restaurants in the clubhouse.

D'accord, à ce prix en week-end, c'est cher, mais le tarif doit être surtout dissuasif ! Ce qui est le plus surprenant ici, ce n'est pas cela, ni le Clubhouse, bien refait, avec un nouveau 9 trous, des chambres d'hôtel et une piscine. Ce qui est le plus étonnant, c'est qu'il n'y a pas ici de bruyère, comme dans tous les autres parcours de la région, pratiquement sans exception. Nous sommes dans le style "parkland" le plus pur, avec des fairways décorés d'arbres splendides, dans un espace dont seul un Harry Colt pouvait tirer un parcours d'une telle intelligence. On parle toujours du 7, un par 3 exemplaire, mais les autres ne sont pas moins passionnants à envisager. Avec Colt, il faut toujours regarder à deux fois, se méfier des illusions comme des obstacles trop visibles, il faut toujours peser le pour et le contre de chaque coup. Pour en parler, il y a les excellents restaurants du Clubhouse...

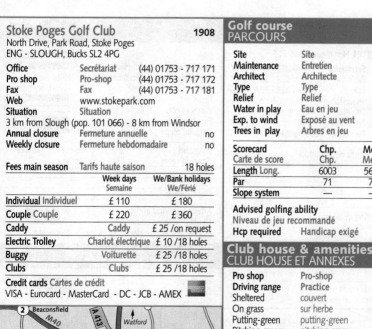

Stoke Poges Golf Club — 1908
North Drive, Park Road, Stoke Poges
ENG - SLOUGH, Bucks SL2 4PG

Office	Secrétariat	(44) 01753 - 717 171
Pro shop	Pro-shop	(44) 01753 - 717 172
Fax	Fax	(44) 01753 - 717 181
Web	www.stokepark.com	
Situation	Situation	

3 km from Slough (pop. 101 066) - 8 km from Windsor

Annual closure	Fermeture annuelle	no
Weekly closure	Fermeture hebdomadaire	no

Fees main season Tarifs haute saison — 18 holes

	Week days Semaine	We/Bank holidays We/Férié
Individual Individuel	£ 110	£ 180
Couple Couple	£ 220	£ 360
Caddy Caddy		£ 25 /on request
Electric Trolley Chariot électrique		£ 10 /18 holes
Buggy Voiturette		£ 25 /18 holes
Clubs Clubs		£ 25 /18 holes

Credit cards Cartes de crédit
VISA - Eurocard - MasterCard - DC - JCB - AMEX

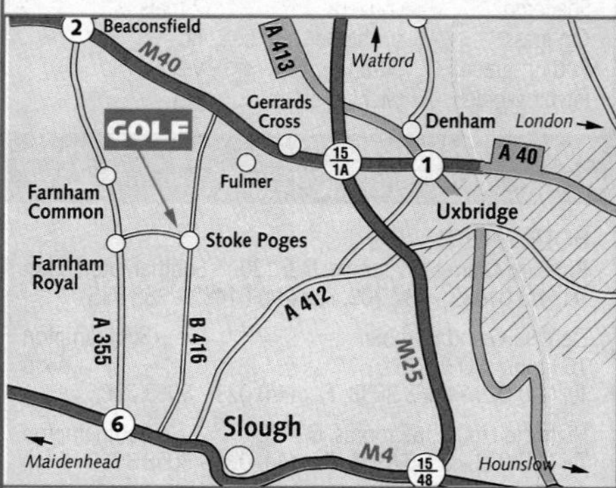

Access Accès : M4 Jct 6 at Slough, A355 → Beaconsfield. At double mini roundabout in Farnham Royal turn right into Park Road.
Map 8 on page 498 Carte 8 Page 498

Golf course PARCOURS — 17/20

Site	Site	
Maintenance	Entretien	
Architect	Architecte	Harry S. Colt
Type	Type	parkland
Relief	Relief	
Water in play	Eau en jeu	
Exp. to wind	Exposé au vent	
Trees in play	Arbres en jeu	

Scorecard Carte de score	Chp. Chp.	Mens Mess.	Ladies Da.
Length Long.	6003	5682	5280
Par	71	71	74
Slope system	—	—	—

Advised golfing ability Niveau de jeu recommandé — 0 12 24 36

Hcp required Handicap exigé — 28 Men, 36 Ladies

Club house & amenities CLUB HOUSE ET ANNEXES — 8/10

Pro shop	Pro-shop	
Driving range	Practice	
Sheltered	couvert	no
On grass	sur herbe	yes
Putting-green	putting-green	yes
Pitching-green	pitching green	yes

Hotel facilities ENVIRONNEMENT HOTELIER — 8/10

HOTELS HÔTELS

Stoke Park, 20 rooms, D from £ 245 — Stoke Poges on site
Tel (44) 01753 - 717171, Fax (44) 01753 - 717181

Copthorne, 219 rooms, D £ 180 — Slough 5 km
Tel (44) 01753 - 516 222, Fax (44) 01753 - 516 237

Courtyard, 149 rooms, D £ 135 — Slough 5 km
Tel (44) 01753 - 551 551, Fax (44) 01753 - 553 333

Burnham Beeches, 82 rooms, D £ 150 — Burnham 4 km
Tel (44) 01628 - 429 955, Fax (44) 01628 - 603 994

RESTAURANTS RESTAURANT

Waldo's, Tel (44) 01628 - 668 561 — Taplow 6 km

Club house (3 restaurants) — Stoke Poges on site
Tel (44) 01753 - 717171

STONEHAM

15 | 7 | 8

A lack of yardage did not prevent Stoneham from staging the first British Masters in 1946 or the Brabazon Trophy in 1993. We'll simply say that this is a good par 70 for golfers who know the course well and pay more attention to their overall score, rather than concentrating on playing to par on each individual hole. At all events, the fairway bunkers should not bother too many players and should ideally be moved to restore their original purpose. The main hazards are now the heather and gorse-bushes, together with the slopes and hills on a site that can be tiring to walk on a number of holes (the 3rd and 18th). This course poses enough problems for us to recommend it first and foremost to experienced players, who will appreciate the uncompromising severity of the challenge. Last but not least, although so close to the port of Southampton, the course is a haven of peace and quiet.

Son manque de longueur n'a pas empêché Stoneham de recevoir le premier British Masters en 1946, ainsi que le Brabazon Trophy en 1993. Nous dirons simplement que c'est un bon par 70 pour ceux qui le connaissent bien et font plus attention au par total qu'au par de chaque trou. En tout cas, les bunkers de fairway ne gêneront pas grand-monde, il faudrait les déplacer pour leur restituer leur fonction originelle. Ce sont la bruyère et les buissons d'ajoncs qui sont maintenant les obstacles principaux, avec les changements de niveau ou même les ondulations d'un terrain assez fatigant sur quelques trous (3 et 18). Ce parcours pose assez de problèmes pour qu'on le conseille d'abord aux joueurs expérimentés, qui apprécieront la rigueur sans concession du défi présenté. Enfin, si près du port de Southampton, on est ici parfaitement au calme.

Stoneham Golf Club — 1908

Monks Wood Close
ENG - SOUTHAMPTON, Hampshire SO16 3TT

Office	Secrétariat	(44) 023 - 8076 9272
Pro shop	Pro-shop	(44) 023 - 8076 8397
Fax	Fax	(44) 023 - 8076 6320
Web	www.stonehamgolfclub.org.co.uk	
Situation	Situation	Southampton
Annual closure	Fermeture annuelle	no
Weekly closure	Fermeture hebdomadaire	no

Fees main season Tarifs haute saison	18 holes	
	Week days Semaine	**We/Bank holidays** We/Férié
Individual Individuel	£ 32	£ 44
Couple Couple	£ 64	£ 88

Full days: £ 36 / £ 55 (week ends)

Caddy	Caddy	no
Electric Trolley	Chariot électrique	£ 10/18 holes
Buggy	Voiturette	no
Clubs	Clubs	no

Credit cards Cartes de crédit
Visa - Mastercard (Pro shop goods only)

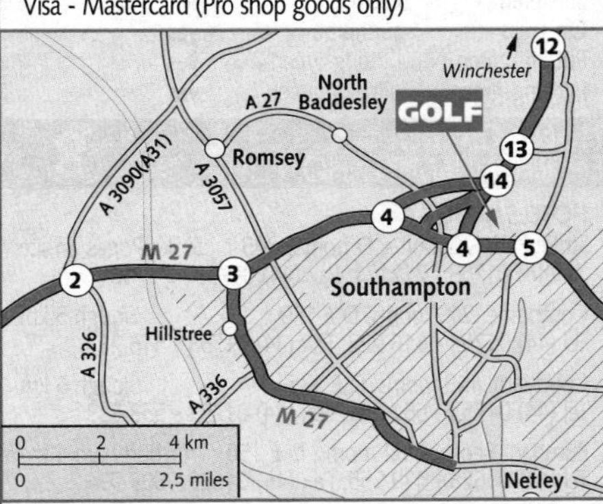

Access Accès : M27 Jct 5. Drive towards Southampton. Turn right at first traffic lights on A27 (Bassett Green Road). 1.2 km, turn right into Golf Club.
Map 7 on page 496 Carte 7 Page 496

Golf course — PARCOURS — 15/20

Site	Site	
Maintenance	Entretien	
Architect	Architecte	Willie Park
Type	Type	inland, heathland
Relief	Relief	
Water in play	Eau en jeu	
Exp. to wind	Exposé au vent	
Trees in play	Arbres en jeu	

Scorecard Carte de score	**Chp.** Chp.	**Mens** Mess.	**Ladies** Da.
Length Long.	5680	5360	4809
Par	72	72	71
Slope system	—	—	—

Advised golfing ability Niveau de jeu recommandé — 0 12 24 36
Hcp required Handicap exigé — certificate

Club house & amenities — CLUB HOUSE ET ANNEXES — 7/10

Pro shop	Pro-shop	
Driving range	Practice	
Sheltered	couvert	2 mats
On grass	sur herbe	no
Putting-green	putting-green	yes
Pitching-green	pitching green	yes

Hotel facilities — ENVIRONNEMENT HOTELIER — 8/10

HOTELS HÔTELS

Botleigh Grange, 59 rooms, D £ 120 — Southampton 5 km
Tel (44) 01489 - 787 700, Fax (44) 01489 - 788 535

De Vere Grand Harbour — Southampton 4 km
169 rooms, D £ 130
Tel (44) 023 - 8063 3033, Fax (44) 023 - 8063 3066

Highfield House, 66 rooms, D £ 100 — Southampton 4 km
Tel (44) 023 - 8035 9955, Fax (44) 023 - 8058 3910

RESTAURANTS RESTAURANT

Botley Grange — Southampton 5 km
Tel (44) 01489 - 787 700

Old Manor House, Tel (44) 01794 - 517 353 — Romsey 12 km

SUNNINGDALE New Course

18	8	8

When you find two great courses at the same Club, you always have a slight preference. But don't be disappointed if you cannot play the "Old" course, its "New" counterpart is just as good and some excellent players even prefer it. If you forget the less enchanting and more "manly" landscape, the "New" course has a lot to be said for it. It allows more aggressive driving, although placing the ball is still crucially important. You need to avoid the fairway bunkers (the edges of which are very high), a very dangerous pond on the 15th, and a few wicked ditches. Your ironwork will have to be up to scratch, too, to hit the right spot on greens which readily cast off any mis-hit approach shots. Technical and tactical, lovely to walk but not so easy to score on, this is one of Harry Colt's vintage courses. Make it a whole day here at this very chic Club so you can play both courses.

Quand on trouve deux grands parcours dans le même golf, on a toujours une légère préférence. Que ceux qui ne pourraient jouer le "Old" ne soient pas déçus, le "New" est d'une qualité très comparable, certains excellents joueurs le préférant même. Si l'on fait abstraction d'un paysage moins charmeur, plus "viril," le New ne manque pas d'arguments. Il autorise des drives plus agressifs, mais le placement de la balle reste crucial : il faut éviter les bunkers de fairway (leurs rebords sont très hauts), une mare très dangereuse au 15, quelques fossés pernicieux, et avoir un excellent jeu de fers pour placer la balle en bonne position sur les greens, qui rejettent sans hésiter les balles un peu approximatives. Technique, tactique, très agréable à marcher, pas facile à scorer, c'est un des bons crus de son architecte Harry Colt. Prenez donc la journée pour jouer les deux parcours de ce club très chic.

Sunningdale Golf Club — 1922

Ridgemount Road
ENG - SUNNINGDALE, Berks SL5 9RW

Office	Secrétariat	(44) 013 - 4461 2681
Pro shop	Pro-shop	(44) 013 - 4462 0128
Fax	Fax	(44) 013 - 4462 4154
Web	—	
Situation	Situation	5 km from Ascot
Annual closure	Fermeture annuelle	no
Weekly closure	Fermeture hebdomadaire	no

Fees main season Tarifs haute saison	18 holes	
	Week days Semaine	**We/Bank holidays** We/Férié
Individual Individuel	£ 85	*
Couple Couple	£ 170	*

Full weekdays: £ 145 / * Visitors from Monday to Thursday (Booking essential)

Caddy	Caddy	£ 30 /on request
Electric Trolley	Chariot électrique	no
Buggy	Voiturette	£ 25 /18 holes
Clubs	Clubs	no

Credit cards Cartes de crédit
VISA - MasterCard (Pro shop & green fees only)

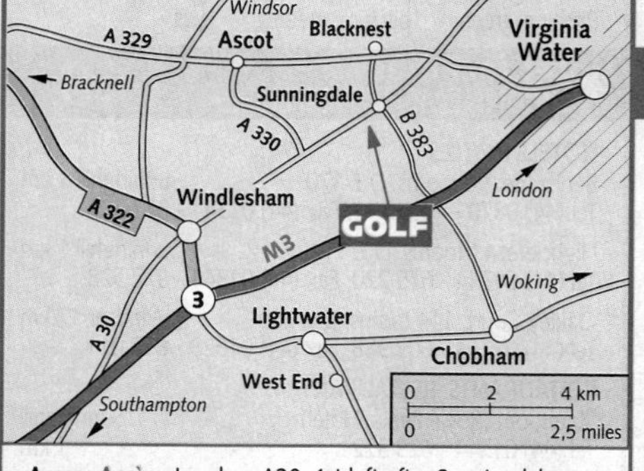

Access Accès : London, A30. 1st left after Sunningdale level crossing. Club 300 m on left.
Map 8 on page 498 Carte 8 Page 498

Golf course PARCOURS — 18/20

Site	Site	
Maintenance	Entretien	
Architect	Architecte	Harry S. Colt
Type	Type	forest, heathland
Relief	Relief	
Water in play	Eau en jeu	
Exp. to wind	Exposé au vent	
Trees in play	Arbres en jeu	

Scorecard Carte de score	**Chp.** Chp.	**Mens** Mess.	**Ladies** Da.
Length Long.	6022	5798	5256
Par	71	71	74
Slope system	—	—	—

Advised golfing ability Niveau de jeu recommandé — 0 12 24 36
Hcp required Handicap exigé — 18 Men, 24 Ladies

Club house & amenities CLUB HOUSE ET ANNEXES — 8/10

Pro shop	Pro-shop	
Driving range	Practice	
Sheltered	couvert	no
On grass	sur herbe	yes
Putting-green	putting-green	yes
Pitching-green	pitching green	yes

Hotel facilities ENVIRONNEMENT HOTELIER — 8/10

HOTELS HÔTELS

Berystede, 90 rooms, D £ 170 — Sunninghill 1 km
Tel (44) 0870 - 400 8111, Fax (44) 01344 - 872 301

Highclere, 11 rooms, D £ 110 — Sunninghill 1 km
Tel (44) 01344 - 625 220, Fax (44) 01344 - 872 528

Oakley Court, 114 rooms, D £ 200 — Windsor 12 km
Tel (44) 01753 - 609 988, Fax (44) 01628 - 637 011

RESTAURANTS RESTAURANT

Stateroom (Royal Berks. Hotel) — Sunninghill 1 km
Tel (44) 01344 - 623 322

Ciao Ninety, Tel (44) 01344 - 622 285 — Ascot 3 km

Jade Fountain, Tel (44) 01344 - 627 070 — Sunninghill 1 km

SUNNINGDALE Old Course

18 | 8 | 8

This is one of those courses where the impression of space unfolding before you is as inviting as it is deceptive. In a magnificent setting, the trees are a sight to behold and are enhanced by heather which has invaded all the rough. When in flower it all looks wonderful, although you might wish you'd never set eyes on it when trying to hack your ball back onto the fairway. Laid out on ideal sandy soil, Sunningdale may lack yardage but is still a model of course design. This is one of Willie Park's masterpieces, such is the need for accuracy and inspiration, for a constant choice of tactics and for control over the full panoply of shots, particularly near the greens. But on a fine day when the ball rolls and rolls and when the greens are at their sublime best, scores can be flattering. This "Old Lady" has boundless charm and appeal.

C'est l'un des parcours où l'impression d'espace devant soi invite au jeu, mais elle peut être aussi trompeuse que la séduction du lieu. Les arbres sont un spectacle, mis en valeur par la bruyère qui envahit tous les roughs, magnifique quand elle prend ses couleurs, impossible quand il faut en déloger sa balle. Construit sur cette terre sablonneuse qui fait de si bons golfs, Sunningdale manque peut-être de longueur, mais reste un modèle d'architecture, et l'un des chefs-d'oeuvre de Willie Park, tant il réclame de précision et d'inspiration, tant il offre constamment des choix tactiques, tant il oblige à disposer de la gamme complète des coups de golf, notamment au petit jeu. Mais en un beau jour d'été où les balles n'en finissent pas de rouler, et où les greens sont à leur sommet, les scores peuvent être flatteurs. Cette "Old Lady" sait toujours se laisser séduire.

Sunningdale Golf Club — 1901

Ridgemount Road
ENG - SUNNINGDALE, Berks SL5 9RW

Office	Secrétariat	(44) 013 - 4461 2681
Pro shop	Pro-shop	(44) 013 - 4462 0128
Fax	Fax	(44) 013 - 4462 4154
Web	—	
Situation	Situation	5 km from Ascot
Annual closure	Fermeture annuelle	no
Weekly closure	Fermeture hebdomadaire	no

Fees main season Tarifs haute saison	Week days Semaine	We/Bank holidays We/Férié
	18 holes	
Individual Individuel	£ 120	*
Couple Couple	£ 240	*

Full weekdays: £ 145 / Visitors: Monday-Thursday only (Booking essential)

Caddy	Caddy	£ 30 /on request
Electric Trolley	Chariot électrique	no
Buggy	Voiturette	£ 25 /18 holes
Clubs	Clubs	no

Credit cards Cartes de crédit
VISA - MasterCard (Pro shop & green fees only)

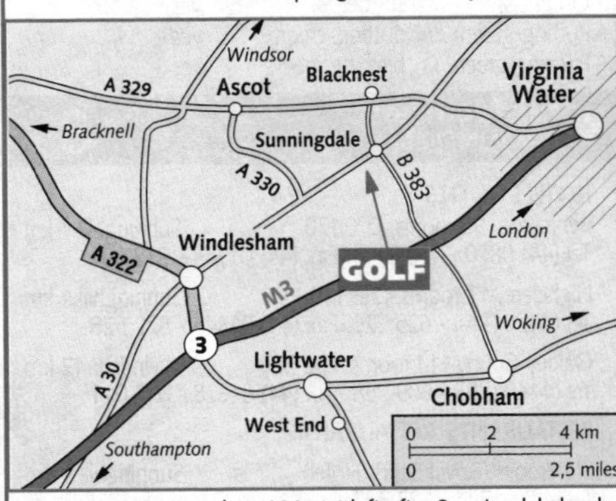

Access Accès : London, A30. 1st left after Sunningdale level crossing. Club 300 m on left.
Map 8 on page 498 Carte 8 Page 498

Golf course PARCOURS — 18/20

Site	Site	
Maintenance	Entretien	
Architect	Architecte	Willie Park
Type	Type	forest, heathland
Relief	Relief	
Water in play	Eau en jeu	
Exp. to wind	Exposé au vent	
Trees in play	Arbres en jeu	

Scorecard Carte de score	Chp. Chp.	Mens Mess.	Ladies Da.
Length Long.	5948	5707	5242
Par	72	70	74
Slope system	—	—	—

Advised golfing ability Niveau de jeu recommandé — 0 12 24 36
Hcp required Handicap exigé — 18 Men, 24 Ladies

Club house & amenities CLUB HOUSE ET ANNEXES — 8/10

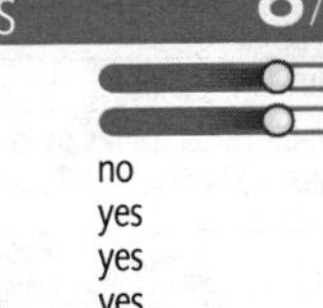

Pro shop	Pro-shop	
Driving range	Practice	
Sheltered	couvert	no
On grass	sur herbe	yes
Putting-green	putting-green	yes
Pitching-green	pitching green	yes

Hotel facilities ENVIRONNEMENT HOTELIER — 8/10

HOTELS HÔTELS

Berystede, 90 rooms, D £ 170 — Sunninghill 1 km
Tel (44) 0870 - 400 8111, Fax (44) 01344 - 872 301

Highclere, 11 rooms, D £ 110 — Sunninghill 1 km
Tel (44) 01344 - 625 220, Fax (44) 01344 - 872 528

Oakley Court, 114 rooms, D £ 200 — Windsor 12 km
Tel (44) 01753 - 609 988, Fax (44) 01628 - 637 011

RESTAURANTS RESTAURANT

Stateroom (Royal Berks. Hotel) — Sunninghill 1 km
Tel (44) 01344 - 623 322

Ciao Ninety, Tel (44) 01344 - 622 285 — Ascot 3 km

Jade Fountain, Tel (44) 01344 - 627 070 — Sunninghill 1 km

SWINLEY FOREST

16	6	8

A striking feature is the impression of wide open space despite the impressive mass of trees: the fairways are actually wide and only hugely mis-hit drives can cause real problems for the second shot. Having said that, you will need to be more accurate if you want to hit the greens from the best position and stay on the putting surface, as uncannily they tend to pick out the well-hit shots and reject the rest. As usual with Harry Colt, the tee-boxes, bunkers and greens are at once carefully designed and well-positioned. Here more than ever, try not to count those golfing birdies before they are hatched; granted, the course is not long but it is a par 69 with five par 3s and some long par 4s, the kind of holes which add to your score rather than lower it. Last but not least, we should emphasize that this is a gentleman's club (no Ryder cup here!) where ladies and dogs are nonetheless welcome and where the rules of admission may be relaxed with a prior telephone call to the Secretary.

L'impression d'espace ouvert est frappante, en dépit de la masse imposante des arbres : les fairways sont effectivement larges, et seuls les drives très égarés peuvent vous préoccuper pour le second coup. Cela dit, il convient d'être plus précis si l'on veut attaquer les greens en bonne position, et y rester, car ils ont assez tendance à trier les bonnes balles et rejeter les moins bonnes. Comme d'habitude avec Harry Colt, les départs comme les bunkers de fairway et de green sont soignés dans leur dessin comme dans leur placement. Il convient aussi de ne pas préjuger de son score avant de l'avoir fait : le parcours n'est pas long, mais c'est un par 69, avec 5 par 3 et quelques longs par 4, le genre de trous qui font les additions plus que les soustractions. Soulignons que c'est un club très "gentlemen" où femmes et chiens sont néanmoins bienvenus, et que les règles d'entrée peuvent s'assouplir avec un coup de téléphone poli au Secretary.

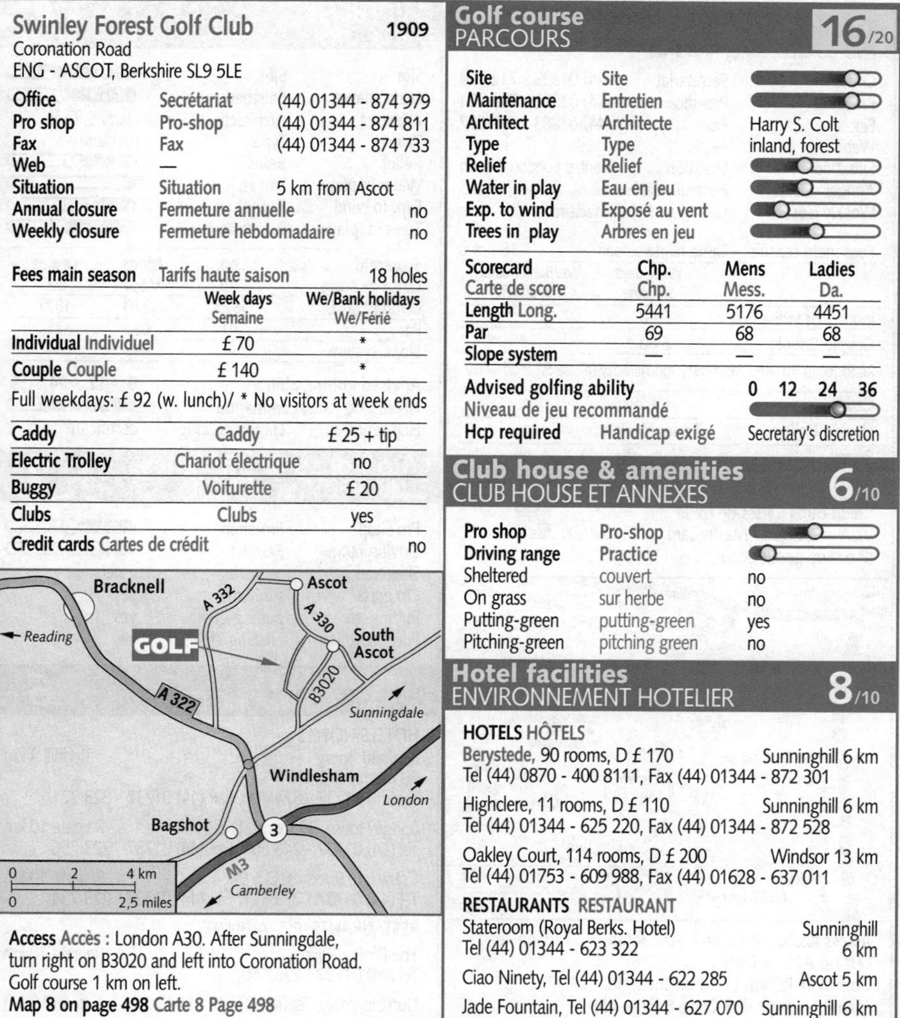

Swinley Forest Golf Club — 1909

Coronation Road
ENG - ASCOT, Berkshire SL9 5LE

Office	Secrétariat	(44) 01344 - 874 979
Pro shop	Pro-shop	(44) 01344 - 874 811
Fax	Fax	(44) 01344 - 874 733
Web	—	
Situation	Situation	5 km from Ascot
Annual closure	Fermeture annuelle	no
Weekly closure	Fermeture hebdomadaire	no

Fees main season Tarifs haute saison	Week days Semaine	We/Bank holidays We/Férié
18 holes		
Individual Individuel	£ 70	*
Couple Couple	£ 140	*

Full weekdays: £ 92 (w. lunch)/ * No visitors at week ends

Caddy	Caddy	£ 25 + tip
Electric Trolley	Chariot électrique	no
Buggy	Voiturette	£ 20
Clubs	Clubs	yes
Credit cards	Cartes de crédit	no

Access Accès : London A30. After Sunningdale, turn right on B3020 and left into Coronation Road. Golf course 1 km on left.

Map 8 on page 498 Carte 8 Page 498

Golf course PARCOURS — 16/20

Site	Site	
Maintenance	Entretien	
Architect	Architecte	Harry S. Colt
Type	Type	inland, forest
Relief	Relief	
Water in play	Eau en jeu	
Exp. to wind	Exposé au vent	
Trees in play	Arbres en jeu	

Scorecard Carte de score	Chp. Chp.	Mens Mess.	Ladies Da.
Length Long.	5441	5176	4451
Par	69	68	68
Slope system	—	—	—

Advised golfing ability / Niveau de jeu recommandé: 0 12 24 36

Hcp required / Handicap exigé: Secretary's discretion

Club house & amenities CLUB HOUSE ET ANNEXES — 6/10

Pro shop	Pro-shop	
Driving range	Practice	
Sheltered	couvert	no
On grass	sur herbe	no
Putting-green	putting-green	yes
Pitching-green	pitching green	no

Hotel facilities ENVIRONNEMENT HOTELIER — 8/10

HOTELS HÔTELS

Berystede, 90 rooms, D £ 170 — Sunninghill 6 km
Tel (44) 0870 - 400 8111, Fax (44) 01344 - 872 301

Highclere, 11 rooms, D £ 110 — Sunninghill 6 km
Tel (44) 01344 - 625 220, Fax (44) 01344 - 872 528

Oakley Court, 114 rooms, D £ 200 — Windsor 13 km
Tel (44) 01753 - 609 988, Fax (44) 01628 - 637 011

RESTAURANTS RESTAURANT

Stateroom (Royal Berks. Hotel) — Sunninghill 6 km
Tel (44) 01344 - 623 322

Ciao Ninety, Tel (44) 01344 - 622 285 — Ascot 5 km

Jade Fountain, Tel (44) 01344 - 627 070 — Sunninghill 6 km

TANDRIDGE

14 | 7 | 6

A little road leads you one of England's prettiest clubhouses in pure Tudor style. The actual course offers not only some wonderful views over Surrey, Sussex and Kent, but also an exhilarating sensation of open space where most of the tee-boxes are elevated and give a very clear idea of the strategy required. The downside to this hilly landscape is that the course is tiring to walk over the last 9 holes. Tandridge is a rather short course and the wide fairways are an invitation to use your driver, but a few bushes, trees and sometimes very thick rough severely penalise wayward hitting. When approaching the greens, watch out for the bunkers, which are placed well forward. The result is an optical illusion which makes club selection more difficult than usual. The members' favourite hole here is the 14th, where you drive into a valley before hitting your approach shot up the hill towards a very well protected green. Tandridge is a model of simplicity and intelligence, Harry Colt style.

Une petite route vous mène à l'un des plus jolis Clubhouses d'Angleterre, en style Tudor. Le parcours offre non seulement des vues imprenables sur le Surrey, le Sussex et le Kent, mais aussi un sentiment d'espace tout à fait exaltant, car la plupart des départs sont ici en hauteur, donnant une idée très claire de la stratégie. Mais ce relief a l'inconvénient d'être un peu fatigant sur les neuf derniers trous. Tandridge est assez court, et la largeur des fairways permet de sortir souvent le driver, mais quelques buissons, les arbres et un rough parfois dense peuvent punir sévèrement les coups lâchés. A l'approche des greens, il faut remarquer les bunkers placés très en avant, rendant la sélection des clubs difficile en raison des illusions d'optique. Le trou favori des membres est ici le 14, où l'on drive dans une vallée pour remonter ensuite vers un green très défendu : c'est un modèle de simplicité et d'intelligence "à la Colt."

Tandridge Golf Club — 1925

ENG - OXTED, Surrey RH8 9NQ

Office	Secrétariat	(44) 01883 - 712 274
Pro shop	Pro-shop	(44) 01883 - 713 701
Fax	Fax	(44) 01883 - 730 537
Web	—	
Situation	Situation	Central London, 30 km
Annual closure	Fermeture annuelle	no
Weekly closure	Fermeture hebdomadaire	no

Fees main season Tarifs haute saison	18 holes	
	Week days Semaine	**We/Bank holidays** We/Férié
Individual Individuel	£ 40 *	*
Couple Couple	£ 80 *	*

Restricted to Monday, Wednesday and Thursday (please call in advance)

Caddy	Caddy	no
Electric Trolley	Chariot électrique	no
Buggy	Voiturette	no
Clubs	Clubs	£ 5 /18 holes

Credit cards Cartes de crédit
VISA - Eurocard - MasterCard - DC - AMEX
(Pro shop goods only)

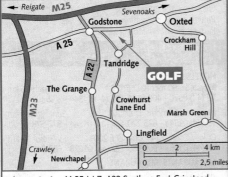

Access Accès : M 25 Jct 7. A22 South → East Grinstead.
Left on A25 → Oxted.
Golf Club 1.5 km (1 m) on the right.
Map 8 on page 499 Carte 8 Page 499

Golf course PARCOURS — 14/20

Site	Site	
Maintenance	Entretien	
Architect	Architecte	Harry S. Colt
Type	Type	parkland
Relief	Relief	
Water in play	Eau en jeu	
Exp. to wind	Exposé au vent	
Trees in play	Arbres en jeu	

Scorecard Carte de score	**Chp.** Chp.	**Mens** Mess.	**Ladies** Da.
Length Long.	5625	5270	4877
Par	70	68	71
Slope system	—	—	—

Advised golfing ability Niveau de jeu recommandé — 0 12 24 36
Hcp required Handicap exigé — certificate

Club house & amenities CLUB HOUSE ET ANNEXES — 7/10

Pro shop	Pro-shop	
Driving range	Practice	
Sheltered	couvert	2 nets
On grass	sur herbe	yes
Putting-green	putting-green	yes
Pitching-green	pitching green	yes

Hotel facilities ENVIRONNEMENT HOTELIER — 6/10

HOTELS HÔTELS

Nutfield Priory — Redhill 9 km
60 rooms, D £ 150
Tel (44) 01737 - 824 400, Fax (44) 01737 - 823 321

Bridge House, 39 rooms, D £ 110 — Reigate 10 km
Tel (44) 01737 - 246 801, Fax (44) 01737 - 223 756

Cranleigh, 9 rooms, D £ 99 — Reigate 10 km
Tel (44) 01737 - 223 417, Fax (44) 01737 - 223 734

RESTAURANTS RESTAURANT

The Dining Room — Reigate 10 km
Tel (44) 01737 - 226 650

Nutfield Priory, Tel (44) 01737 - 824 400 — Redhill 9 km

THE BELFRY Brabazon

16	9	8

If you don't know how important politics is in the choice of Ryder Cup sites, then you won't understand why this course (as others) has hosted the event so many times. This is a resort that is generally quite remarkable with a huge hotel, a whole number of activities on site and three 18-hole golf courses. The Brabazon is a good average parkland course, and as the rough is kept cropped most of the time to speed up play, these flat 18 holes lose something of their character. Actually, two holes here have built the course's reputation; the 10th, a driveable par 4 from the front tees (remember the Ryder Cup) but which most amateurs try to reach from the back. And the 18th, a remarkable high-risk par 4 where the bogey is generally enough to win your match. Having said that, this is a very pleasant and well-balanced course . However, when paying this sort of money to play, the golfer is entitled to expect a higher standard of technical challenge and a little more excitement. The remodeling have been successful.

Si l'on ne sait pas à quel point la politique est essentielle dans le choix des sites de la Ryder Cup, on ne comprend pas pourquoi ce parcours (comme d'autres) a reçu tant de fois cette épreuve mythique. Car s'il s'agit d'un "resort" de remarquable qualité générale, avec un immense hôtel et trois 18 trous, le "Brabazon Course" est dans la bonne moyenne des parcours "parkland" du genre. De plus, le rough étant bien coupé la plupart du temps pour accélérer le jeu, ces 18 trous perdent une partie de leur définition. En fait, deux trous ici ont fait la réputation du parcours, le 10, drivable des départs rouges (comme en Ryder Cup), mais que tous les amateurs essaient de driver des départs arrière, et le 18, remarquable par 4 à hauts risques, où un bogey est souvent suffisant pour gagner un match. Cela dit, c'est quand même un parcours très agréable et bien équilibré, mais on est en droit d'attendre un niveau technique et émotionnel aussi élevé que le green-fee... Le remodelage a cependant bien relevé le niveau du parcours.

The Belfry — 1977

ENG - WISHAW, North Warwickshire B76 9PR

Office	Secrétariat	(44) 01675 - 470 033
Pro shop	Pro-shop	(44) 01675 - 470 301
Fax	Fax	(44) 01675 - 470 178
Web	www.devereonline.co.uk	
Situation	Situation	
10 km from Birmingham (pop. 961 041)		
Annual closure	Fermeture annuelle	no
Weekly closure	Fermeture hebdomadaire	no

Fees main season Tarifs haute saison	18 holes	
	Week days Semaine	**We/Bank holidays** We/Férié
Individual Individuel	£ 120	£ 120
Couple Couple	£ 240	£ 240

Caddy	Caddy	£ 25
Electric Trolley	Chariot électrique	no
Buggy	Voiturette	£ 30
Clubs	Clubs	£ 15

Credit cards Cartes de crédit
VISA - Eurocard - MasterCard - DC - AMEX

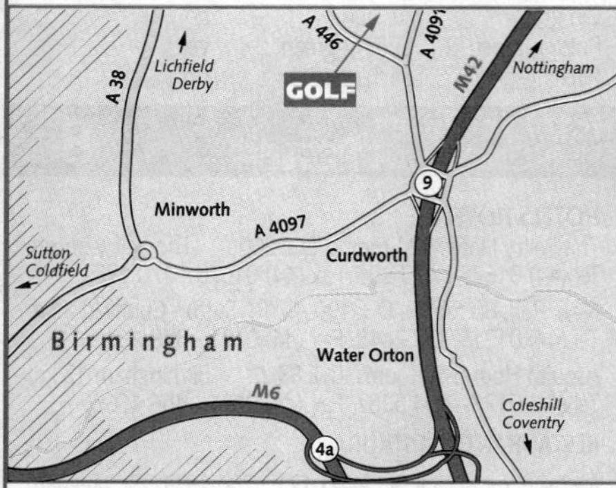

Access Accès : From London: M42 Exit 9.
Follow signs to Belfry From Birmingham: A38 to M6, then M42 North at Jct 4A. Exit 9 on M42. Follow signs to Belfry.
Map 7 on page 496 Carte 7 Page 496

Golf course PARCOURS — 16/20

Site	Site	
Maintenance	Entretien	
Architect	Architecte	Peter Alliss, Dave Thomas (remod.)
Type	Type	open country, parkland
Relief	Relief	
Water in play	Eau en jeu	
Exp. to wind	Exposé au vent	
Trees in play	Arbres en jeu	

Scorecard Carte de score	**Chp.** Chp.	**Mens** Mess.	**Ladies** Da.
Length Long.	6407	6052	5205
Par	72	72	73
Slope system	—	—	—

Advised golfing ability Niveau de jeu recommandé — 0 12 24 36

Hcp required Handicap exigé — 24 Men, 32 Women

Club house & amenities CLUB HOUSE ET ANNEXES — 9/10

Pro shop	Pro-shop	
Driving range	Practice	
Sheltered	couvert	17 bays
On grass	sur herbe	no
Putting-green	putting-green	yes
Pitching-green	pitching green	no

Hotel facilities ENVIRONNEMENT HOTELIER — 8/10

HOTELS HÔTELS

The Belfry Hotel, 324 rooms, D £ 200 — on site
Tel (44) 01675 - 470 301, Fax (44) 01675 - 470 178

New Hall, 60 rooms, D £ 190 — Sutton Coldfield
Tel (44) 0121 - 378 2442, Fax (44) 0121 - 378 4637 — 7 km

Jonathan's, 48 rooms, D £ 150 — Birmingham
Tel (44) 0121 - 429 3757, Fax (44) 0121 - 434 3107 — 12 km

RESTAURANTS RESTAURANT

Metro Bar and Grill — Birmingham 10 km
Tel (44) 0121 - 200 1911

Gilmore, Tel (44) 0121 - 233 3655 — Birmingham

French Restaurant, Tel (44) 01675 - 470 301 — on site

THE BELFRY PGA National

15 | 9 | 8

It is already clear that with the short and tall rough left to grow freely the course would acquire greater definition on terrain that has little natural appeal and where the saplings still have a lot of growing to do. The slight movements of terrain carried out when creating the course would be given more shape and the whole course be more visually attractive. But, as with the Brabazon, the authorities that be have their sights set on a middle-class clientele with money to spend. They also want to enjoy their golf, so scaring them off with tall rough is out of the question. We would recommend that they and others play from the front tees, as a number of water hazards turn very dangerous from the tips (particularly the 4th and 8th). The bunkers have been carefully designed (Dave Thomas style) and decisively brought into play, although some greens can still be reached with bump 'n roll shots. The green-fee is less expensive (well, a little) than at the Brabazon and the layout is almost more likeable than its elder, so much so that perhaps a composite 18 hole setting from the two courses might provide a battlefield with some excitement for the next Ryder Cup.

On devine ici qu'en laissant pousser les roughs et haut roughs, on donnerait un peu plus de mouvement à un terrain sans intérêt naturel, tant que les arbres plantés n'ont pas vraiment grandi. Les légers mouvements de terrain qui ont été créés prendraient qplus d'acuité, et l'oeil serait aussi plus intéressé. Mais, comme pour le "Brabazon", on vise ici une clientèle de niveau moyen, assez argentée, et peut être désireuse de se faire plaisir. On leur conseillera d'ailleurs les départs avancés, car certains obstacles d'eau sont très dangereux depuis le fond (4 et 8 notamment). Les bunkers sont dessinés avec soin (à la Dave Thomas), mis en jeu avec détermination, bien qu'il soit parfois possible de rejoindre les greens en roulant. Le green-fee est (un peu) moins élevé qu'au "Brabazon", et on a presque plus de sympathie pour ce tracé, au point qu'un 18 trous composite des deux ne serait pas si mal pour une Ryder Cup.

The Belfry — 1997

ENG - WISHAW, North Warwickshire B76 9PR

Office	Secrétariat	(44) 01675 - 470 033
Pro shop	Pro-shop	(44) 01675 - 470 301
Fax	Fax	(44) 01675 - 470 178
Web	www.devereonline.co.uk	
Situation	Situation	

10 km from Birmingham (pop. 961 041)
7 km from Sutton Coldfield (pop. 106 001)

Annual closure	Fermeture annuelle	no
Weekly closure	Fermeture hebdomadaire	no

Fees main season Tarifs haute saison — 18 holes

	Week days / Semaine	We/Bank holidays / We/Férié
Individual Individuel	£ 60	£ 60
Couple Couple	£ 120	£ 120
Caddy Caddy		£ 25
Electric Trolley Chariot électrique		no
Buggy Voiturette		£ 30
Clubs Clubs		£ 15

Credit cards Cartes de crédit
VISA - Eurocard - MasterCard - DC - AMEX

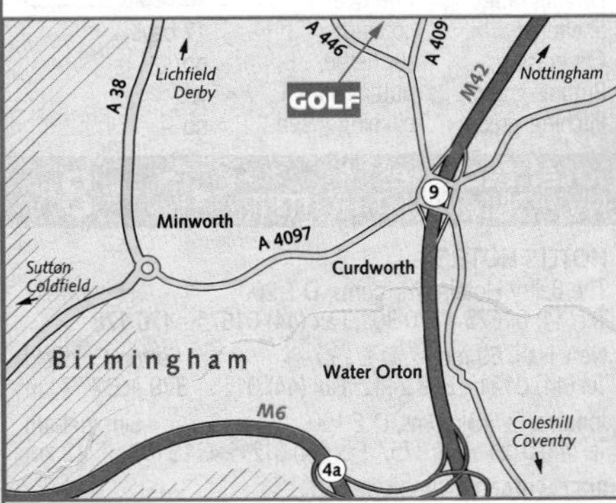

Access Accès : From London: M42 Exit 9.
Follow signs to Belfry From Birmingham: A38 to M6, then M42 North at Jct 4A. Exit 9 on M42. Follow signs to Belfry.
Map 7 on page 496 Carte 7 Page 496

Golf course — PARCOURS — 15/20

Site	Site	
Maintenance	Entretien	
Architect	Architecte	Dave Thomas
Type	Type	open country, parkland
Relief	Relief	
Water in play	Eau en jeu	
Exp. to wind	Exposé au vent	
Trees in play	Arbres en jeu	

Scorecard / Carte de score	Chp. / Chp.	Mens / Mess.	Ladies / Da.
Length Long.	6365	6064	5175
Par	72	72	73
Slope system	—	—	—

Advised golfing ability Niveau de jeu recommandé: 0 12 24 36
Hcp required Handicap exigé: 24 Men, 32 Ladies

Club house & amenities — CLUB HOUSE ET ANNEXES — 9/10

Pro shop	Pro-shop	
Driving range	Practice	
Sheltered	couvert	17 bays
On grass	sur herbe	no
Putting-green	putting-green	yes
Pitching-green	pitching green	no

Hotel facilities — ENVIRONNEMENT HOTELIER — 8/10

HOTELS HÔTELS

The Belfry Hotel, 324 rooms, D £ 200 — The Belfry on site
Tel (44) 01675 - 470 301, Fax (44) 01675 - 470 178

New Hall, 60 rooms, D £ 190 — Sutton Coldfield 7 km
Tel (44) 0121 - 378 2442, Fax (44) 0121 - 378 4637

Asquith House, 10 rooms, D £ 83 — Birmingham 12 km
Tel (44) 0121 - 454 5282, Fax (44) 0121 - 456 4668

RESTAURANTS RESTAURANT

Metro Bar and Grill, Tel (44) 0121 - 200 1911 — Birmingham

Gilmore, Tel (44) 0121 - 233 3655 — Birmingham10 km

French Restaurant, Tel (44) 01675 - 470 301 — The Belfry on site

THETFORD

14 | 7 | 5

Between the pretty Georgian town of Swaffham, the national stud-farm of Newmarket, the Neolithic site of Grimes Graves and the beautiful medieval town of Norwich, you might find the time to play this 1912 course which was restyled and lengthened by Donald Steel in 1985. A pity perhaps that the fairways are so wide, but they do prompt the bigger-hitters to open their shoulders and dispatch their ball into the waiting fairway bunkers. There are trees, of course, but not all that close to the fairways. When they do come close, it is to complicate your second shot. Very pretty, calm, well-balanced and with pleasant springy turf over sandy sub-soil, Thetford is not the course of the century but it does enable golfers of all levels to play together very easily. For the less experienced player, however, we would shamelessly recommend the front tees.

Entre les visites de la jolie ville georgienne de Swaffham, du haras national de Newmarket, du site néolithique de Grimes Graves et de la belle ville médiévale de Norwich, il vous restera probablement quelques heures pour jouer ce parcours de 1912, mais remodelé et allongé par Donald Steel en 1985. On regrette que les fairways soient très larges, mais ils incitent les frappeurs à se déchaîner... et à expédier leurs balles dans les bunkers de fairway ! Certes, on trouve aussi des arbres, mais ils ne sont pas très proches des fairways, et quand ils le sont, c'est plutôt pour gêner les seconds coups. Très joli, très calme, bien équilibré, avec un gazon très agréable sur un sol de sable et de tourbe, Thetford n'est pas le parcours du siècle, mais il permet au moins à tous les niveaux d'évoluer en bonne harmonie. On conseillera cependant aux joueurs peu expérimentés de choisir sans honte les départs avancés

Thetford Golf Club — 1912

Brandon Road
ENG - THETFORD, Norfolk IP24 3NE

Office	Secrétariat	(44) 01842 - 752 258
Pro shop	Pro-shop	(44) 01842 - 752 662
Fax	Fax	(44) 01842 - 766 212
Web	—	
Situation	Situation	Cambridge, 50 km
Annual closure	Fermeture annuelle	no
Weekly closure	Fermeture hebdomadaire	no

Fees main season Tarifs haute saison	18 holes	
	Week days Semaine	**We/Bank holidays** We/Férié
Individual Individuel	£ 34	*
Couple Couple	£ 68	*

* No visitors at weekends & public holidays - Booking essential

Caddy	Caddy	no
Electric Trolley	Chariot électrique	no
Buggy	Voiturette	no
Clubs	Clubs	no

Credit cards Cartes de crédit
(Pro shop goods only) Visa - Mastercard - AMEX

Access Accès : London M11. Jct 9, A11 → Norwich. Thetford Bypass B1107 → Brandon, Golf 500 m on the left.
Map 7 on page 497 Carte 7 Page 497

Golf course — PARCOURS — 14/20

Site	Site	
Maintenance	Entretien	
Architect	Architecte	C.H. Mayo Donald Steel (1985)
Type	Type	inland, forest
Relief	Relief	
Water in play	Eau en jeu	
Exp. to wind	Exposé au vent	
Trees in play	Arbres en jeu	

Scorecard Carte de score	**Chp.** Chp.	**Mens** Mess.	**Ladies** Da.
Length Long.	6190	5970	5405
Par	72	72	74
Slope system	—	—	—

Advised golfing ability — 0 12 24 36
Niveau de jeu recommandé

Hcp required Handicap exigé — no

Club house & amenities — CLUB HOUSE ET ANNEXES — 7/10

Pro shop	Pro-shop	
Driving range	Practice	
Sheltered	couvert	no
On grass	sur herbe	yes
Putting-green	putting-green	yes
Pitching-green	pitching green	yes

Hotel facilities — ENVIRONNEMENT HOTELIER — 5/10

HOTELS HÔTELS

The Thomas Paine Hotel, 13 rooms, D £ 70 — Thetford 2 km
Tel (44) 01842 - 755 631, Fax (44) 01842 - 766 505

Strattons, 6 rooms, D £ 120 — Swaffham 25 km
Tel (44) 01760 - 723 845, Fax (44) 01760 - 720 458

Angel, 43 rooms, D £ 95 — Bury St Edmunds 20 km
Tel (44) 01284 - 714 000, Fax (44) 01284 - 714 001

RESTAURANTS RESTAURANT

Angel, Tel (44) 01284 - 714 000 — Bury St Edmunds 20 km
Strattons, Tel (44) 01760 - 723 845 — Swaffham 25 km
Theobalds, Tel (44) 01359 - 231 707 — Ixworth 17 km

THORNDON PARK

14	7	6

Essex is not really a golfing county like Surrey, for example, on the other side of London. But some of the courses here do stand out, like this one, laid out in 1920 over a former hunting estate which sports a gigantic neo-classical mansion where everyone seems to speak in whispered tones. The clubhouse is more modern and less imposing, but jacket and tie are required. This is one course of the hundreds designed by Harry Colt, as intelligent in its layout, as imaginative in its use of the land and as fair and open as the others. When you realise how few technical resources they had at the time (1920), it makes you think how much many modern designers could learn from this style of layout. Of course, like many British courses from another age, this one lacks length but the vast majority of players won't complain. A course for everyone, even the best.

L'Essex n'est pas vraiment une région à golf comme peut l'être le Surrey par exemple, de l'autre côté de Londres. Mais quelques parcours se distinguent comme celui-ci, créé en 1920 dans un ancien domaine de chasse orné d'une gigantesque bâtisse néo-classique que l'on dénomme "mansion," et dans laquelle on doit parler à voix basse. Le Clubhouse est plus moderne, moins imposant, mais on y porte veste et cravate. C'est un parcours parmi les centaines créés par Harry Colt, aussi intelligent dans son déroulement, imaginatif dans son utilisation du terrain, aussi franc et honnête que les autres. Quand on imagine le manque de moyens techniques à l'époque (1920), bien des architectes modernes devraient y prendre des leçons. Bien sûr, comme la plupart des parcours britanniques d'autrefois, il manque de longueur, mais l'immense majorité des joueurs ne s'en plaindra pas. Pour tous, même les meilleurs.

Thordon Park Golf Club — 1920

Ingrave
ENG - BRENTWOOD, Essex CM13 3RH

Office	Secrétariat	(44) 01277 - 811 666
Pro shop	Pro-shop	(44) 01277 - 810 736
Fax	Fax	(44) 01277 - 810 645
Web	—	
Situation	Situation	London, 35 km
Annual closure	Fermeture annuelle	no
Weekly closure	Fermeture hebdomadaire	no

Fees main season Tarifs haute saison	18 holes	
	Week days Semaine	**We/Bank holidays** We/Férié
Individual Individuel	£ 35	*
Couple Couple	£ 70	*

Full weekdays: £ 50 (Booking essential)
* No visitors at weekends

Caddy	Caddy	no
Electric Trolley	Chariot électrique	no
Buggy	Voiturette	no
Clubs	Clubs	£ 5 /18 holes

Credit cards Cartes de crédit
Visa - Mastercard (Pro shop goods only)

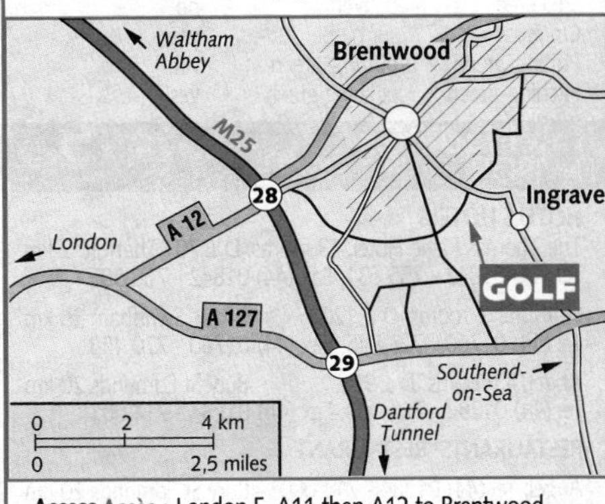

Access Accès : London E, A11 then A12 to Brentwood. A 128 SE → East Horndon. Golf on the right.
Map 7 on page 497 Carte 7 Page 497

Golf course — PARCOURS — 14/20

Site	Site	
Maintenance	Entretien	
Architect	Architecte	Harry S. Colt
Type	Type	parkland, inland
Relief	Relief	
Water in play	Eau en jeu	
Exp. to wind	Exposé au vent	
Trees in play	Arbres en jeu	

Scorecard Carte de score	**Chp.** Chp.	**Mens** Mess.	**Ladies** Da.
Length Long.	5845	5620	4580
Par	71	71	72
Slope system	—	—	—

Advised golfing ability 0 12 24 36
Niveau de jeu recommandé
Hcp required Handicap exigé — certificate

Club house & amenities — CLUB HOUSE ET ANNEXES — 7/10

Pro shop	Pro-shop	
Driving range	Practice	
Sheltered	couvert	no
On grass	sur herbe	yes
Putting-green	putting-green	yes
Pitching-green	pitching green	no

Hotel facilities — ENVIRONNEMENT HOTELIER — 6/10

HOTELS HÔTELS

Marygreen Manor, 43 rooms, D £ 134 — Brentwood 6 km
Tel (44) 01277 - 225 252, Fax (44) 01277 - 262 809

Posthouse Brentwood, 145 rooms, D £ 130 — Brentwood
Tel (44) 0870 - 400 9012, Fax (44) 01277 - 264 264

Travelodge, 22 rooms, D £ 50 — East Horndon
Tel (44) 01277 - 810 819, Fax (44) 01277 - 810 819 — 4 km

The Heybridge, 22 rooms, D £ 125 — Ingatestone
Tel (44) 01277 - 355 355, Fax (44) 01277 - 353 288 — 12 km

RESTAURANTS RESTAURANT

Marygreen Manor, Tel (44) 01277 - 225 252 — Brentwood

Posthouse Brentwood, Tel (44) 0870 - 400 9012 — Brentwood

THORPENESS

14 | 7 | 7

Thorpeness is just outside Aldeburgh, not far from Minsmere nature reserve in Dunwich, where you can watch an incredible variety of birds. The hotel-clubhouse is excellent and makes this a fine destination, especially since there is an abundance of good courses round and about (Ipswich, Aldeburgh, Woodbridge, Felixstowe Ferry, etc.). This one was initially designed in 1923 by James Braid and slightly re-shaped in 1965. Here, you keep out of the heather and avoid the lupins, very pretty when in flower but not the ideal place to put your ball. An uncomplicated layout, prepared to make life easier for the average golfer, but one which requires good placing of the ball, so don't think twice about playing an iron off the tee (except perhaps for the half a dozen long par 4s). Other landmarks to cap a very pleasant day's golfing are a windmill, a curious "house in the clouds" and an unsightly nuclear power station in the distance.

Thorpeness est juste à l'extérieur d'Aldeburgh, non loin de la réserve naturelle de Minsmere à Dunwich, d'où l'on peut observer une incroyable variété d'oiseaux. L'Hôtel-Clubhouse est de grande qualité, ce qui en fait une destination tout à fait agréable, d'autant que les bons parcours alentour ne manquent pas (Ipswich, Aldeburgh, Woodbridge, Felixstowe Ferry...). Celui-ci a été dessiné par James Braid en 1923, et légèrement retouché vers 1965. On veillera à éviter les bruyères et les buissons de lupin, très jolis en fleur, mais dont il vaut mieux ne pas s'approcher avec une balle de golf. Ce tracé sans histoires, préparé pour faciliter les choses, nécessite avant tout un bon placement : il ne faut pas hésiter à jouer des fers au départ, sauf sur la demi-douzaine de longs par 4. Pour décorer une très agréable journée, un moulin à vent, un curieuse "maison dans les nuages," et une centrale nucléaire au loin, pas bien belle.

Thorpeness Golf Club — 1923

ENG - THORPENESS, Suffolk IP16 4NH

Office	Secrétariat	(44) 01728 - 452 176
Pro shop	Pro-shop	(44) 01728 - 454 926
Fax	Fax	(44) 01728 - 453 869
Web	www.thorpeness.co.uk	
Situation	Situation	

3 km from Aldeburgh - 39 km from Ipswich (pop. 130 157)

Annual closure	Fermeture annuelle	no
Weekly closure	Fermeture hebdomadaire	no

Fees main season Tarifs haute saison	18 holes	
	Week days Semaine	**We/Bank holidays** We/Férié
Individual Individuel	£ 32.50	£ 37.50
Couple Couple	£ 65	£ 75

Caddy	Caddy	no
Electric Trolley	Chariot électrique	£ 5 /18 holes
Buggy	Voiturette	£ 30 /18 holes
Clubs	Clubs	no

Credit cards Cartes de crédit
VISA - MasterCard

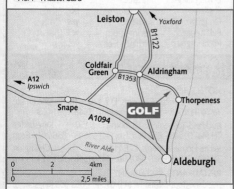

Access Accès : Ipswich A12 → Saxmundham. Turn right on B119 → Leiston. At Leiston, turn right on B1353
Map 7 on page 497 Carte 7 Page 497

Golf course PARCOURS — 14/20

Site	Site	
Maintenance	Entretien	
Architect	Architecte	James Braid
Type	Type	seaside course, open country
Relief	Relief	
Water in play	Eau en jeu	
Exp. to wind	Exposé au vent	
Trees in play	Arbres en jeu	

Scorecard Carte de score	**Chp.** Chp.	**Mens** Mess.	**Ladies** Da.
Length Long.	5645	5674	4922
Par	69	69	74
Slope system	—	—	—

Advised golfing ability Niveau de jeu recommandé: 0 12 24 36
Hcp required Handicap exigé: certificate

Club house & amenities CLUB HOUSE ET ANNEXES — 7/10

Pro shop	Pro-shop	
Driving range	Practice	
Sheltered	couvert	no
On grass	sur herbe	yes
Putting-green	putting-green	yes
Pitching-green	pitching green	yes

Hotel facilities ENVIRONNEMENT HOTELIER — 7/10

HOTELS HÔTELS

Thorpeness GC Hotel, 30 rooms, D £ 95 — Thorpeness on site
Tel (44) 01728 - 452 176, Fax (44) 01728 - 453 868

Wentworth Hotel, 37 rooms, D £ 120 — Aldeburgh 4 km
Tel (44) 01728 - 452 312, Fax (44) 01728 - 454 343

Brudenell, 47 rooms, D £ 110 — Aldeburgh 4 km
Tel (44) 01728 - 452 071, Fax (44) 01728 - 454 082

RESTAURANTS RESTAURANT

Thorpeness GC Hotel — Thorpeness on site
Tel (44) 01728 - 452 176

New Regatta, Tel (44) 01728 - 452 011 — Aldeburgh 4 km

THURLESTONE

16 | 6 | 4

This is a magnificent spot where you savour every moment along a rugged coastline with rocky cliffs and pounding waves. This course is beside the sea, but most of the holes are pretty high up. Only the dunes are missing to make this a text-book links course, although the sandy soil is just right and the layout well worthy of the label. After much hesitation, the original short 9 hole course was happily extended and altered by Harry Colt; the back 9 are 1,000 yards longer than the front 9 and have added a good deal of zip to the course. The first seven holes are short, rather treacherous and very technical in style, while the remainder are longer and more open but still to be played with care and caution when the wind blows. In windy weather, punchers of the ball will have fun while the others can always divide their score by two or else admire the landscape and visit the region.

C'est un magnifique endroit à savourer chaque instant le long d'une côte tourmentée, avec d'impressionnantes falaises où la mer livre ses assauts. Ce parcours est situé en bordure de mer, mais la plupart des trous sont bien en hauteur. Il ne manque que les dunes pour en faire un links comme dans les livres, mais le sol sablonneux a la qualité requise, et le dessin est à la hauteur. Après bien des hésitations, le petit 9 trous initial fut heureusement modifié et agrandi par Harry Colt : le retour est près de 1000 mètres plus long que l'aller et a donné de la vigueur au tracé. Les sept premiers trous sont courts, assez traîtres et très techniques, les suivants plus longs et ouverts, à négocier avec attention et prudence quand le vent souffle. Les "puncheurs" de balles pourront alors s'y régaler, les autres diviseront leur score par deux, à moins de se contenter d'admirer le paysage ou de visiter la région.

660

Thurlestone Golf Club — 1897

Thurlestone
ENG - KINGSBRIDGE, S. Devon TQ7 3NZ

Office	Secrétariat	(44) 01548 - 560 405
Pro shop	Pro-shop	(44) 01548 - 560 715
Fax	Fax	(44) 01548 - 560 405
Web	—	
Situation	Situation	

6 km W of Kingsbridge (pop. 5 081) - 8 km W of Salcombe

Annual closure	Fermeture annuelle	no
Weekly closure	Fermeture hebdomadaire	no

Fees main season Tarifs haute saison		18 holes
	Week days Semaine	**We/Bank holidays** We/Férié
Individual Individuel	£ 30	£ 30
Couple Couple	£ 60	£ 60
Caddy	Caddy	no
Electric Trolley	Chariot électrique	£ 10 /day
Buggy	Voiturette	no
Clubs	Clubs	£ 10 /day

Credit cards Cartes de crédit
Visa - Mastercard (Pro shop goods only)

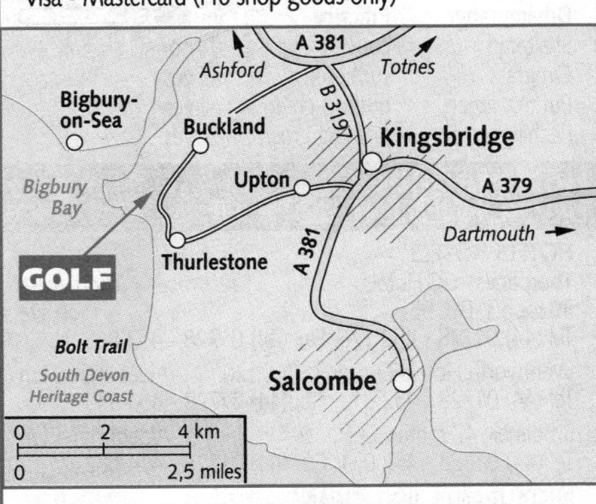

Access Accès : M5, then A38, A382 to Newton Abbott, then A381 through Totnes and Kingsbridge. In Sutton, → South Milton and Thurlestone. Follow signs.
Map 6 on page 494 Carte 6 Page 494

Golf course PARCOURS — 16/20

Site	Site	
Maintenance	Entretien	
Architect	Architecte	Harry S. Colt
Type	Type	seaside course, open country
Relief	Relief	
Water in play	Eau en jeu	
Exp. to wind	Exposé au vent	
Trees in play	Arbres en jeu	

Scorecard Carte de score	**Chp.** Chp.	**Mens** Mess.	**Ladies** Da.
Length Long.	5770	5626	5086
Par	71	71	73
Slope system	—	—	—

Advised golfing ability Niveau de jeu recommandé — 0 12 24 36
Hcp required Handicap exigé — 28 Men, 36 Ladies

Club house & amenities CLUB HOUSE ET ANNEXES — 6/10

Pro shop	Pro-shop	
Driving range	Practice	
Sheltered	couvert	no
On grass	sur herbe	yes
Putting-green	putting-green	yes
Pitching-green	pitching green	yes

Hotel facilities ENVIRONNEMENT HOTELIER — 4/10

HOTELS HÔTELS

Thurlestone Hotel, 67 rooms, D £ 170 — Thurlestone on site
Tel (44) 01548 - 560 382, Fax (44) 01548 - 561 069

Buckland-Tout-Saints, 10 rooms, D £ 150 — Kingsbridge
Tel (44) 01548 - 853 055, Fax (44) 01548 - 856 261 — 6 km

White House, 7 rooms, D £ 110 — Chillington
Tel (44) 01548 - 580 580, Fax (44) 01548 - 581 124 — 15 km

RESTAURANTS RESTAURANT

Buckland-Tout-Saints, Tel (44) 01548 - 853 055 — Kingsbridge

Sloop Inn (Pub w. food) — Bantham2 km
Tel (44) 01548 - 560 489

Margaret Amelia, Tel (44) 01548 - 560 382 — on site

TREVOSE Championship

17 | 7 | 7

With tighter fairways and rough as wild as the tops of the dunes, Trevose would be much more difficult. But this is first and foremost a holiday location, where regular golfers return each year with their children. The kids eventually get to play the "big" 18-hole course after cutting their teeth on the two 9-holers. Spectacular, charming and technical, Trevose is a course for golfers of all levels where the best players will never grow tired. This Harry Colt layout is highly strategic and very honest, even though not all the hazards are visible, but there are seldom any really unpleasant surprises. They say that a friendly atmosphere adds to the pleasure of playing golf, and that is certainly true here, even with the wind. And that King Arthur met Merlin the Wizard nearby. It might even have been over a meal in the clubhouse, because the food is excellent.

Avec des fairways plus étroits, un rough aussi sauvage que les sommets des dunes, Trevose serait bien plus difficile encore. Mais c'est d'abord un lieu de vacances, où les habitués reviennent chaque année, avec les enfants qui finissent un jour par passer au "grand" 18 trous après avoir débuté et pris de l'expérience sur les deux 9 trous, parfaits pour la famille. Spectaculaire, plein de charme, technique, Trevose est un parcours pour tous les niveaux, où les meilleurs ne s'ennuient jamais. Le dessin de Harry Colt est très stratégique et très franc, même si les obstacles ne sont pas tous bien visibles, mais on a rarement de mauvaises surprises. On dit qu'une atmosphère amicale contribue au plaisir du jeu, c'est bien le cas ici, même avec le vent. Le Roi Arthur aurait rencontré l'Enchanteur Merlin dans les environs, c'était peut-être ici au Clubhouse, car les repas sont excellents.

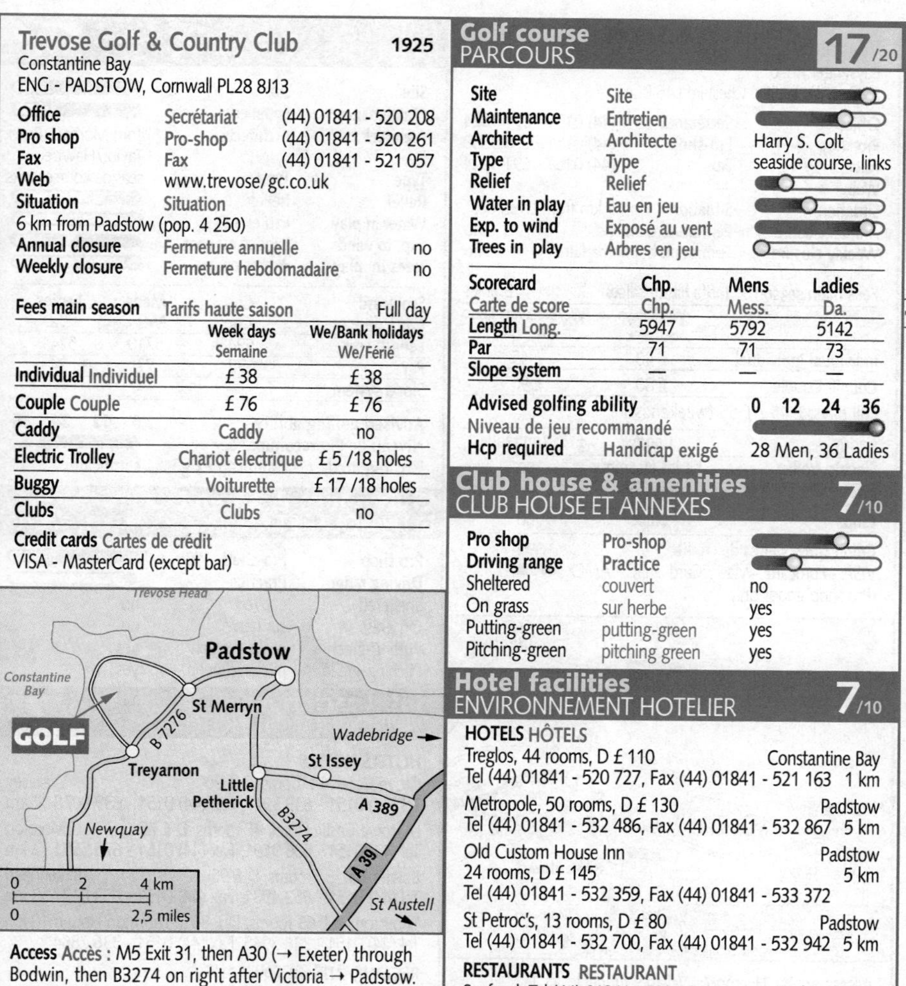

Trevose Golf & Country Club — 1925

Constantine Bay
ENG - PADSTOW, Cornwall PL28 8J13

Office	Secrétariat	(44) 01841 - 520 208
Pro shop	Pro-shop	(44) 01841 - 520 261
Fax	Fax	(44) 01841 - 521 057
Web	www.trevose/gc.co.uk	
Situation	Situation	

6 km from Padstow (pop. 4 250)

Annual closure	Fermeture annuelle	no
Weekly closure	Fermeture hebdomadaire	no

Fees main season Tarifs haute saison		Full day
	Week days Semaine	**We/Bank holidays** We/Férié
Individual Individuel	£ 38	£ 38
Couple Couple	£ 76	£ 76

Caddy	Caddy	no
Electric Trolley	Chariot électrique	£ 5 /18 holes
Buggy	Voiturette	£ 17 /18 holes
Clubs	Clubs	no

Credit cards Cartes de crédit
VISA - MasterCard (except bar)

Access Accès : M5 Exit 31, then A30 (→ Exeter) through Bodwin, then B3274 on right after Victoria → Padstow. → St Merryn. Follow signs to golf.
Map 6 on page 494 Carte 6 Page 494

Golf course — PARCOURS — 17/20

Site	Site	
Maintenance	Entretien	
Architect	Architecte	Harry S. Colt
Type	Type	seaside course, links
Relief	Relief	
Water in play	Eau en jeu	
Exp. to wind	Exposé au vent	
Trees in play	Arbres en jeu	

Scorecard Carte de score	**Chp.** Chp.	**Mens** Mess.	**Ladies** Da.
Length Long.	5947	5792	5142
Par	71	71	73
Slope system	—	—	—

Advised golfing ability / Niveau de jeu recommandé: 0 12 24 36
Hcp required Handicap exigé: 28 Men, 36 Ladies

Club house & amenities — CLUB HOUSE ET ANNEXES — 7/10

Pro shop	Pro-shop	
Driving range	Practice	
Sheltered	couvert	no
On grass	sur herbe	yes
Putting-green	putting-green	yes
Pitching-green	pitching green	yes

Hotel facilities — ENVIRONNEMENT HOTELIER — 7/10

HOTELS HÔTELS

Treglos, 44 rooms, D £ 110 — Constantine Bay
Tel (44) 01841 - 520 727, Fax (44) 01841 - 521 163 — 1 km

Metropole, 50 rooms, D £ 130 — Padstow
Tel (44) 01841 - 532 486, Fax (44) 01841 - 532 867 — 5 km

Old Custom House Inn — Padstow
24 rooms, D £ 145 — 5 km
Tel (44) 01841 - 532 359, Fax (44) 01841 - 533 372

St Petroc's, 13 rooms, D £ 80 — Padstow
Tel (44) 01841 - 532 700, Fax (44) 01841 - 532 942 — 5 km

RESTAURANTS RESTAURANT

Seafood, Tel (44) 01841 - 532 485 — Padstow 5 km
St Petroc's Bistro, Tel (44) 01841 - 532 700 — Padstow 5 km

WALLASEY

17 | 7 | 7

What with coastal erosion having washed away three of the original holes and the problems of ownership which caused some bad blood and the need to borrow less favourable terrain, the course has evolved considerably since its creation. Today, everything seems to have settled down. Laid out on more hilly landscape than its (near) neighbour Hoylake, Wallasey requires a lot of serious thought as to where to place your drive in order to attack the greens from the best position and keep well away from the dunes, bushes and fairway bunkers (few in number but the penalty is always high). With that said, the pleasure you get from hitting good recovery shots on this sort of course is such that you might almost stray off the straight and narrow deliberately in order to add to your fond memories. So try match-play, or even the stableford points system, whose homonymous inventor came from Wallasey and certainly knew a thing or two about the problems of counting a score once you reach a certain number.

L'érosion de la côte ayant supprimé trois des trous originaux, des problèmes de propriété ayant empoisonné le club, le parcours a évolué depuis sa création, devant emprunter des terrains moins favorables, mais tout cela semble résolu. Dans un paysage plus mouvementé que celui de son (presque) voisin Royal Liverpool, Wallasey demande quelque réflexion sur le placement des drives afin d'attaquer les greens en bonne position, et ne pas se retrouver dans les dunes, les buissons, les bunkers de fairway - peu nombreux mais pénalisants. Cela dit, le plaisir de réussir les recoveries sur ce genre de parcours est tel que l'on pourrait presque faire exprès de s'égarer pour se fabriquer des souvenirs ! Alors, jouez en match-play, ou en stableford, l'inventeur de la formule qui porte son nom venait d'ici, il savait donc à quoi s'en tenir sur la difficulté de compter à partir d'un certain chiffre.

Wallasey Golf Club — 1891

Bayswater Road
ENG - WALLASEY, Cheshire L45 8LA

Office	Secrétariat	(44) 0151 - 691 1024
Pro shop	Pro-shop	(44) 0151 - 638 3888
Fax	Fax	(44) 0151 - 691 1024
Web	—	
Situation	Situation	5 km from Liverpool
Annual closure	Fermeture annuelle	no
Weekly closure	Fermeture hebdomadaire	no

662

Fees main season Tarifs haute saison	18 holes	
	Week days Semaine	**We/Bank holidays** We/Férié
Individual Individuel	£ 40	£ 45
Couple Couple	£ 80	£ 90

Full days: £ 45 / £ 55 (weekends)

Caddy	Caddy	£ 25 /on request
Electric Trolley	Chariot électrique	no
Buggy	Voiturette	no
Clubs	Clubs	no

Credit cards Cartes de crédit
VISA - Eurocard - MasterCard - DC - AMEX
(Pro shop goods only)

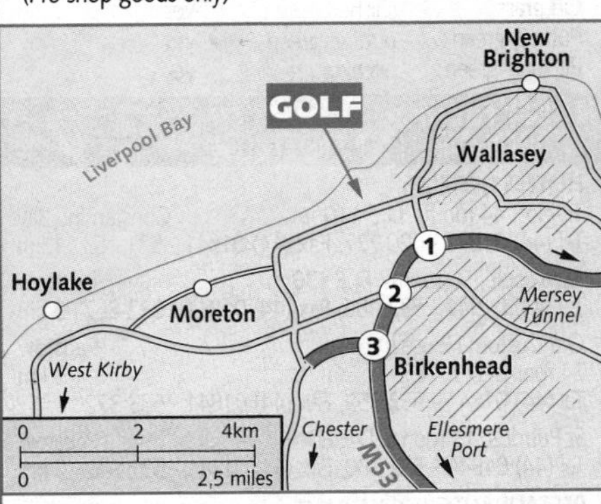

Access Accès : Liverpool, Wallasey tunnel to Jct 1.
Follow signs to New Brighton. Golf on A 551.
Map 5 on page 493 Carte 5 Page 493

Golf course PARCOURS — 17/20

Site	Site	
Maintenance	Entretien	
Architect	Architecte	Tom Morris/J. Braid Taylor/Hawtree...
Type	Type	seaside course, links
Relief	Relief	
Water in play	Eau en jeu	
Exp. to wind	Exposé au vent	
Trees in play	Arbres en jeu	

Scorecard Carte de score	**Chp.** Chp.	**Mens** Mess.	**Ladies** Da.
Length Long.	5946	5710	5241
Par	72	72	74
Slope system	—	—	—

Advised golfing ability Niveau de jeu recommandé — 0 12 24 36
Hcp required Handicap exigé — certificate

Club house & amenities CLUB HOUSE ET ANNEXES — 7/10

Pro shop	Pro-shop	
Driving range	Practice	
Sheltered	couvert	no
On grass	sur herbe	no
Putting-green	putting-green	yes
Pitching-green	pitching green	yes

Hotel facilities ENVIRONNEMENT HOTELIER — 7/10

HOTELS HÔTELS

Grove Hotel, 14 rooms, D £ 90 — Wallasey
Tel (44) 0151 - 639 3947, Fax (44) 0151 - 639 0028 — 2 km

Leasowe Castle Hotel, 47 rooms, D £ 75 — Moreton
Tel (44) 0151 - 606 9191, Fax (44) 0151 - 678 5551 — 2 km

Bowler Hat, 32 rooms, D £ 95 — Birkenhead
Tel (44) 0151 - 652 4931, Fax (44) 0151 - 653 8127 — 3 km

Thornton Hall, 63 rooms, D £ 86 — Thornton Hough 10 km
Tel (44) 0151 - 336 3938, Fax (44) 0151 - 336 7864

RESTAURANTS RESTAURANT

Grove Hotel, Tel (44) 0151 - 630 4558 — Wallasey 2 km
Lee Ho, Tel (44) 0151 - 677 6440 — Moreton 2 km

WALTON HEATH New Course 16 | 7 | 6

The history of Walton Heath is closely tied to politics, with many members being Ministers (including Winston Churchill in his younger days) or Peers. The Prince of Wales was club captain in 1935, but apparently that was not enough for the club to receive the royal seal. Soil and space are both ideal here, despite being so close to London, but sand and heather land were of no use to farmers in those days. The wind can be an important factor here, as the course is high up. There are trees, but they don't detract from a great feeling of open space, or relieve the anxiety as you eye the ubiquitous heather and wonder how on earth anyone could ever get out of there. It is especially dangerous on the 12th hole, where you need a long drive to have any hope of reaching a very well-protected green. Although this "New" course is not easy, the members will tell you that it is two shots easier than its "Old" neighbour. We suggest you check that out for yourself.

L'histoire de Walton Heath est étroitement liée à la politique, avec quantité de membres ministres, dont Winston Churchill, ou appartenant à la Chambre des Lords. Le Prince de Galles en a été capitaine en 1935, sans que le club en soit annobli pour autant. Les parcours ont eu un sol idéal, et de l'espace, même à proximité de Londres car les terres de sable et de bruyère étaient inutilisées pour l'agriculture. Le vent y est un facteur important, car nous sommes ici en hauteur. Malgré la présence des arbres, on éprouve une grande sensation d'espace, avec un soupçon d'inquiétude devant l'omniprésence de la bruyère, dont aucun traité ne vous enseigne comment en sortir. Elle est spécialement dangereuse au 12, où il faut un long drive pour espérer toucher le green très défendu. Bien que ce "New" ne soit pas facile, les membres vous diront qu'il est de deux coups plus facile que le "Old." A vérifier par vous-même !

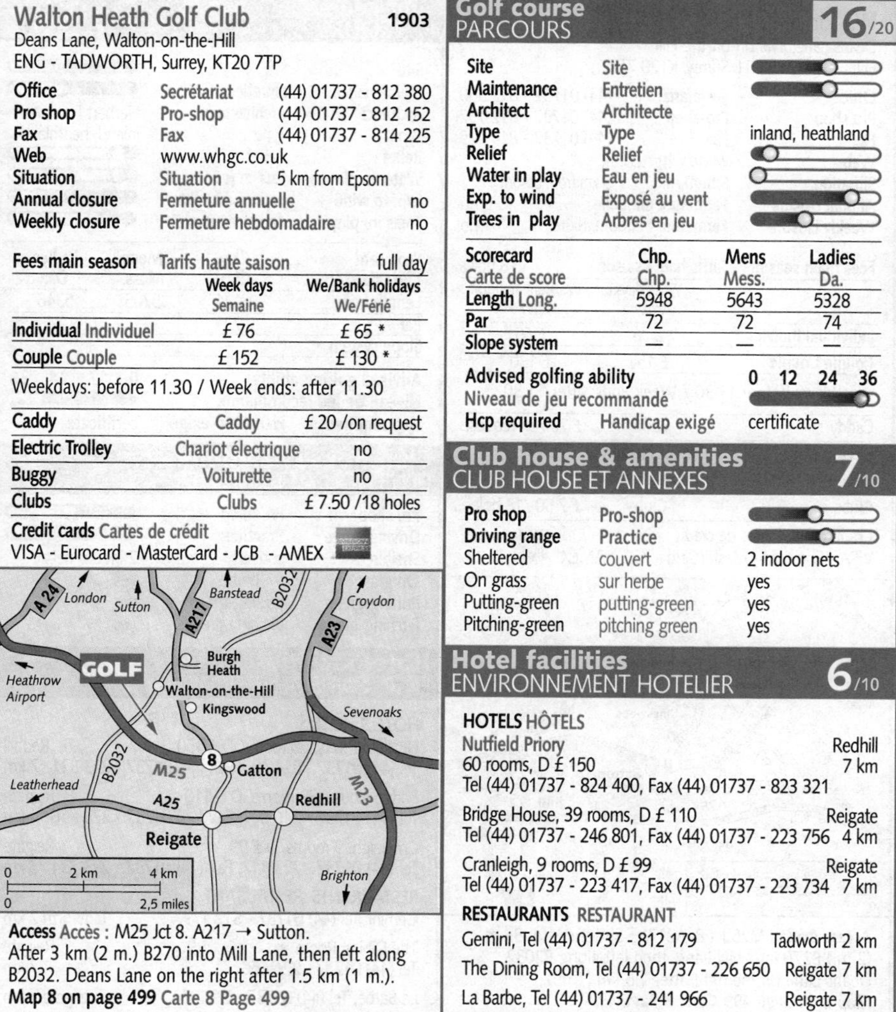

Walton Heath Golf Club — 1903
Deans Lane, Walton-on-the-Hill
ENG - TADWORTH, Surrey, KT20 7TP

Office	Secrétariat	(44) 01737 - 812 380
Pro shop	Pro-shop	(44) 01737 - 812 152
Fax	Fax	(44) 01737 - 814 225
Web	www.whgc.co.uk	
Situation	Situation	5 km from Epsom
Annual closure	Fermeture annuelle	no
Weekly closure	Fermeture hebdomadaire	no

Fees main season Tarifs haute saison	full day	
	Week days Semaine	We/Bank holidays We/Férié
Individual Individuel	£ 76	£ 65 *
Couple Couple	£ 152	£ 130 *

Weekdays: before 11.30 / Week ends: after 11.30

Caddy	Caddy	£ 20 /on request
Electric Trolley	Chariot électrique	no
Buggy	Voiturette	no
Clubs	Clubs	£ 7.50 /18 holes

Credit cards Cartes de crédit
VISA - Eurocard - MasterCard - JCB - AMEX

Access Accès : M25 Jct 8. A217 → Sutton.
After 3 km (2 m.) B270 into Mill Lane, then left along B2032. Deans Lane on the right after 1.5 km (1 m.).
Map 8 on page 499 Carte 8 Page 499

Golf course PARCOURS — 16/20

Site	Site	
Maintenance	Entretien	
Architect	Architecte	
Type	Type	inland, heathland
Relief	Relief	
Water in play	Eau en jeu	
Exp. to wind	Exposé au vent	
Trees in play	Arbres en jeu	

Scorecard Carte de score	Chp. Chp.	Mens Mess.	Ladies Da.
Length Long.	5948	5643	5328
Par	72	72	74
Slope system	—	—	—

Advised golfing ability Niveau de jeu recommandé — 0 12 24 36
Hcp required Handicap exigé — certificate

Club house & amenities CLUB HOUSE ET ANNEXES — 7/10

Pro shop	Pro-shop	
Driving range	Practice	
Sheltered	couvert	2 indoor nets
On grass	sur herbe	yes
Putting-green	putting-green	yes
Pitching-green	pitching green	yes

Hotel facilities ENVIRONNEMENT HOTELIER — 6/10

HOTELS HÔTELS
Nutfield Priory — Redhill 7 km
60 rooms, D £ 150
Tel (44) 01737 - 824 400, Fax (44) 01737 - 823 321

Bridge House, 39 rooms, D £ 110 — Reigate 4 km
Tel (44) 01737 - 246 801, Fax (44) 01737 - 223 756

Cranleigh, 9 rooms, D £ 99 — Reigate 7 km
Tel (44) 01737 - 223 417, Fax (44) 01737 - 223 734

RESTAURANTS RESTAURANT
Gemini, Tel (44) 01737 - 812 179 — Tadworth 2 km
The Dining Room, Tel (44) 01737 - 226 650 — Reigate 7 km
La Barbe, Tel (44) 01737 - 241 966 — Reigate 7 km

WALTON HEATH Old Course

18 | 7 | 7

Herbert Fowler designed the courses for this club where James Braid was the first professional. He was here for 50 years and although his name does not figure anywhere, it would be hard to imagine him never having retouched the original layout here and there, or never having given others the benefit of his invaluable advice. With the soft turf, the layout and even the sensation of space, you might think yourself on a links course, if it weren't for the pine, birch and oak trees, and the heather. And when the wind blows (this is the highest spot in Surrey), the illusion is complete. The wide, deep bunkers are a feature you'll remember for many a month, as they outline the holes to perfection and attract any ball sailing slightly off course. The greens are well grassed, fast, fair and particularly well defended. A difficult course with its very own character, but every golfer will improve his game here as long as he remembers the one basic rule of golf... humility.

Herbert Fowler a dessiné les parcours de ce club dont James Braid a été le premier professionnel. Il y est resté pendant plus de 50 ans, et si son nom n'apparaît pas, on imagine mal qu'il n'ait jamais eu à retoucher çà et là le dessin originel, ou à donner quelques précieux conseils. Par la qualité du gazon comme par le dessin ou même la sensation d'espace, on pourait se croire sur un links, n'était la présence de pins, de bouleaux, de chênes et de bruyère. Et quand le vent souffle (c'est le plus haut point du Surrey), l'illusion est complète. Les bunkers larges et profonds sont un élément dont on se souvient, tant ils dessinent les trous à la perfection, tout en attirant les balles un peu trop écartées. Les greens sont bien fournis, rapides et francs, et surtout très défendus. C'est un parcours difficile, au caractère bien marqué, mais tous les joueurs y feront des progrès s'ils l'abordent avec modestie.

Walton Heath Golf Club 1903

Deans Lane, Walton-on-the-Hill
ENG - TADWORTH, Surrey, KT20 7TP

Office	Secrétariat	(44) 01737 - 812 380
Pro shop	Pro-shop	(44) 01737 - 812 152
Fax	Fax	(44) 01737 - 814 225
Web	www.whgc.co.uk	
Situation	Situation	5 km from Epsom
Annual closure	Fermeture annuelle	no
Weekly closure	Fermeture hebdomadaire	no

Fees main season Tarifs haute saison	18 holes	
	Week days Semaine	**We/Bank holidays** We/Férié
Individual Individuel	£ 76	£ 65 *
Couple Couple	£ 152	£ 130 *

Weekdays: before 11.30 / Week ends: after 11.30

Caddy	Caddy	£ 20 /on request
Electric Trolley	Chariot électrique	no
Buggy	Voiturette	no
Clubs	Clubs	£ 7.50 /18 holes

Credit cards Cartes de crédit
VISA - Eurocard - MasterCard - JCB - AMEX

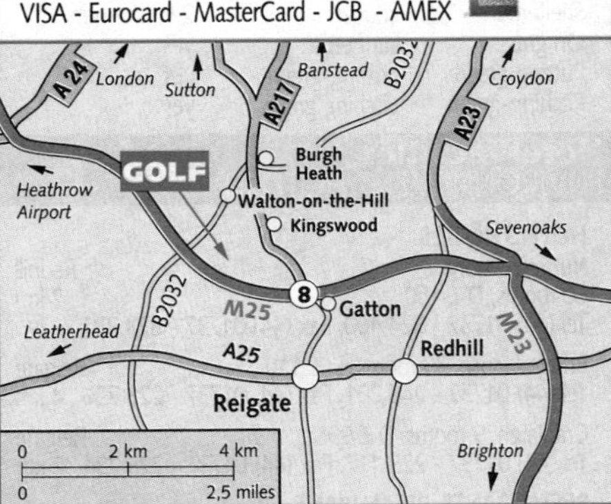

Access Accès : M25 Jct 8. A217 → Sutton. After 3 km (2 m.) B270 into Mill Lane, then left along B2032. Deans Lane on the right after 1.5 km (1 m.).
Map 8 on page 499 Carte 8 Page 499

Golf course PARCOURS 18/20

Site	Site	
Maintenance	Entretien	
Architect	Architecte	Herbert Fowler
Type	Type	inland, heathland
Relief	Relief	
Water in play	Eau en jeu	
Exp. to wind	Exposé au vent	
Trees in play	Arbres en jeu	

Scorecard Carte de score	**Chp.** Chp.	**Mens** Mess.	**Ladies** Da.
Length Long.	6121	5705	5346
Par	72	71	74
Slope system	—	—	—

Advised golfing ability Niveau de jeu recommandé: 0 12 24 36
Hcp required Handicap exigé: certificate

Club house & amenities CLUB HOUSE ET ANNEXES 7/10

Pro shop	Pro-shop	
Driving range	Practice	
Sheltered	couvert	2 indoor nets
On grass	sur herbe	yes
Putting-green	putting-green	yes
Pitching-green	pitching green	yes

Hotel facilities ENVIRONNEMENT HOTELIER 7/10

HOTELS HÔTELS

Nutfield Priory, 60 rooms, D £ 150 — Redhill
Tel (44) 01737 - 824 400, Fax (44) 01737 - 823 321 — 7 km

Bridge House, 39 rooms, D £ 110 — Reigate
Tel (44) 01737 - 246 801, Fax (44) 01737 - 223 756 — 4 km

Cranleigh, 9 rooms, D £ 99 — Reigate
Tel (44) 01737 - 223 417, Fax (44) 01737 - 223 734 — 7 km

RESTAURANTS RESTAURANT

Gemini, Tel (44) 01737 - 812 179 — Tadworth 2 km

The Dining Room — Reigate
Tel (44) 01737 - 226 650 — 7 km

La Barbe, Tel (44) 01737 - 241 966 — Reigate 7 km

WARWICKSHIRE (THE) 15 7 8

This is a complex of four inter-combinable nine-hole courses. The East and North courses are rather hilly, the South and West courses are simply sloping. Karl Litten's design is unashamedly American with a lot of dangerous water hazards (except on the North where there are more trees). Carefully placing your shots is important, and if you are an attacking player you should follow your instinct, as any hesitation can cost you dearly. The greens must be attacked with high shots, but when we visited they were very firm and so will surely cause problems for average-players. The length of each hole is such that we would suggest the forward tees for all except the very good player, and would recommend beginners to head for the pitch 'n putt course. With a very flexible combination of courses, spectacular golf and very modern facilities, this is a very well designed resort but not quite as hospitable as it could be. Our advice: rent a buggy and shoot 36 holes.

C'est un ensemble de quatre fois neuf trous combinables, l'Est et le Nord étant assez accidentés, le Sud et l'Ouest simplement ondulés. L'architecture de Karl Litten est américaine sans honte, avec beaucoup d'obstacles d'eau dangereux (sauf sur le Nord, plus arboré). Il est partout nécessaire de bien placer la balle, mais aussi d'attaquer sans réserves si on a ce caractère, car les hésitations ne pardonnent pas. Les greens doivent être attaqués comme des cibles, mais ils étaient très fermes lors de notre visite, ce qui ne facilitait pas la tâche des joueurs moyens. La longueur de chacun des neuf trous incite à ne recommander les départs arrière qu'aux très bons amateurs, et à conseiller aux presque débutants d'aller sur le parcours de par 3. Flexible dans ses combinaisons, spectaculaire, avec des équipements très modernes, c'est un ensemble très bien conçu, mais pas vraiment chaleureux. Notre conseil : 36 trous en voiturette.

The Warwickshire — 1993

Leek Wootton
ENG - WARWICK, Warwickshire CV35 7QT

Office	Secrétariat	(44) 01926 - 409 409
Pro shop	Pro-shop	(44) 01926 - 409 409
Fax	Fax	(44) 01926 - 408 409
Web	www.clubhouse.com	
Situation	Situation	

5 km N of Warwick - 13 km S of Coventry (pop. 294 387)

Annual closure	Fermeture annuelle	no
Weekly closure	Fermeture hebdomadaire	no

Fees main season Tarifs haute saison	18 holes	
	Week days Semaine	**We/Bank holidays** We/Férié
Individual Individuel	£ 35	£ 45
Couple Couple	£ 70	£ 90

Caddy	Caddy	£ 30 /on request
Electric Trolley	Chariot électrique	no
Buggy	Voiturette	£ 20 /18 holes
Clubs	Clubs	£ 12.50 /18 holes

Credit cards Cartes de crédit
VISA - Eurocard - MasterCard - AMEX

Access Accès : M40 Jct 15, then A46 → Coventry. Follow signs to Leek Wootton (B4115).
Map 7 on page 196 Carte 7 Page 196

Golf course — PARCOURS — 15/20

Site	Site	
Maintenance	Entretien	
Architect	Architecte	Karl Litten
Type	Type	parkland
Relief	Relief	
Water in play	Eau en jeu	
Exp. to wind	Exposé au vent	
Trees in play	Arbres en jeu	

Scorecard Carte de score	**Chp.** Chp.	**Mens** Mess.	**Ladies** Da.
Length Long.	6500	6000	5000
Par	72	72	72
Slope system	—	—	—

Advised golfing ability Niveau de jeu recommandé — 0 12 24 36
Hcp required Handicap exigé — certificate

Club house & amenities — CLUB HOUSE ET ANNEXES — 7/10

Pro shop	Pro-shop	
Driving range	Practice	
Sheltered	couvert	10 bays
On grass	sur herbe	no
Putting-green	putting-green	yes
Pitching-green	pitching green	yes

Hotel facilities — ENVIRONNEMENT HOTELIER — 8/10

HOTELS HÔTELS

Chesford Grange, 154 rooms, D £ 130 — Kenilworth
Tel (44) 01926 - 859 331, Fax (44) 01926 - 859 075 — 3 km

Clarendon House, 30 rooms, D £ 90 — Kenilworth
Tel (44) 01926 - 857 668, Fax (44) 01926 - 850 669 — 3 km

Mallory Court — Royal Leamington Spa
18 rooms, D £ 220 — 4 km
Tel (44) 01926 - 330 214, Fax (44) 01926 - 451 714

RESTAURANTS RESTAURANT

Simpson's, Tel (44) 01926 - 864 567 — Kenilworth 4 km

Bosquet, Tel (44) 01926 - 852 463 — Kenilworth 4 km

Amor's — Royal Leamington Spa 4 km
Tel (44) 01926 - 778 744

WENTWORTH East Course

16 | 8 | 7

If you don't get lost in the very comfortable and totally gigantic clubhouse at Wentworth (a little over the top, maybe?), try to forget the West course and go for the East. This was the first course laid out at Wentworth by Harry Colt and many prefer it to its illustrious neighbour. It simply has not had the benefit of the same rejuvenation programmes nor maybe the same standard of green-keeping, but the soil is more pleasant (sand) and drier, and the heather adds a touch of colour. It is difficult to explain other than that we felt this a more «cheerful» layout, without the same severity that you find on the West course. Very fair and with some very amusing greens, this course has been under-estimated for too long. The full Wentworth complex has been supplemented with a third course, «Edinburgh», which despite everything it has to offer is not necessarily worth a green-fee of some £ 100!

Si vous ne vous êtes pas perdu dans le Clubhouse très confortable et totalement gigantesque (un peu "too much ?") de Wentworth, tournez un jour le dos au "West" et dirigez-vous vers "l'East." Ce fut le premier des parcours dessinés par Harry Colt à Wentworth, et beaucoup le préfèrent à son illustre voisin. Il n'a simplement pas bénéficié des mêmes programmes de rajeunissement, ni peut-être du même entretien, mais le sol y est plus agréable (c'est du sable), plus sec, et la bruyère ajoute une touche de couleur. Il est difficile d'expliquer autrement qu'en disant qu'il est plus «souriant,»dénué de cette sévérité que l'on peut trouver au parcours West. Franc, avec des greens souvent amusants, ce parcours a été trop longtemps sous-estimé. Cet ensemble de Wentworth a été complété par un troisième parcours, "Edinburgh" qui, en dépit de ses qualités, ne vaut absolument pas un green-fee d'une centaine de Livres..

Wentworth Golf Club — 1924

Wentworth Drive
ENG - VIRGINIA WATER, Surrey GU25 4 LS

Office	Secrétariat	(44) 01344 - 842 201
Pro shop	Pro-shop	(44) 01344 - 843 353
Fax	Fax	(44) 01344 - 842 804
Web	www.wentworthclub.com	
Situation	Situation	7 km from Ascot
Annual closure	Fermeture annuelle	no
Weekly closure	Fermeture hebdomadaire	no

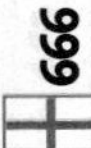

666

Fees main season Tarifs haute saison	Week days Semaine	We/Bank holidays We/Férié
18 holes		
Individual Individuel	£ 105	£ 105
Couple Couple	£ 210	£ 210

Caddy	Caddy	£ 25 /on request
Electric Trolley	Chariot électrique	no
Buggy	Voiturette	£ 35 /18 holes
Clubs	Clubs	£ 25 /18 holes

Credit cards Cartes de crédit
VISA - Eurocard - MasterCard - DC - AMEX

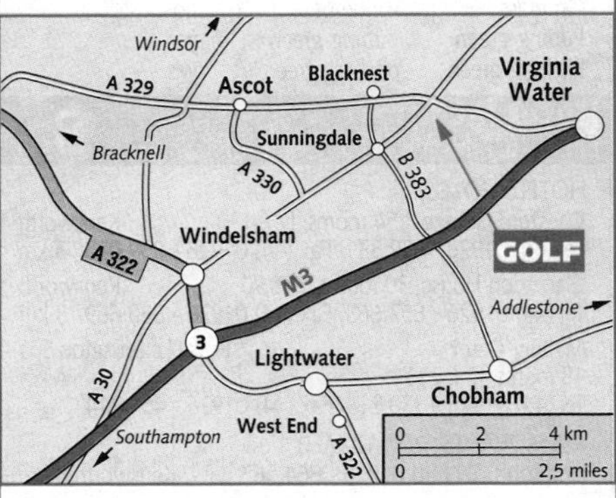

Access Accès : London, A30.
Left road opposite A329 turning to Ascot.
Map 8 on page 498 Carte 8 Page 498

Golf course PARCOURS — 16/20

Site	Site	
Maintenance	Entretien	
Architect	Architecte	Harry S. Colt
Type	Type	inland, forest
Relief	Relief	
Water in play	Eau en jeu	
Exp. to wind	Exposé au vent	
Trees in play	Arbres en jeu	

Scorecard Carte de score	Chp. Chp.	Mens Mess.	Ladies Da.
Length Long.	5558	5354	4855
Par	68	68	72
Slope system	—	—	—

Advised golfing ability Niveau de jeu recommandé — 0 12 24 36

Hcp required Handicap exigé — 28 Men, 36 Ladies

Club house & amenities CLUB HOUSE ET ANNEXES — 8/10

Pro shop	Pro-shop	
Driving range	Practice	
Sheltered	couvert	10 mats
On grass	sur herbe	yes
Putting-green	putting-green	yes
Pitching-green	pitching green	yes

Hotel facilities ENVIRONNEMENT HOTELIER — 7/10

HOTELS HÔTELS

Royal Berkshire, 63 rooms, D £ 220 — Sunninghill
Tel (44) 01344 - 623 322, Fax (44) 01344 - 627 100 — 3 km

Berystede, 90 rooms, D £ 170 — Sunninghill
Tel (44) 0870 - 400 8111, Fax (44) 01344 - 872 301 — 5 km

Great Fosters, 39 rooms, D £ 175 — Egham
Tel (44) 01784 - 433 822, Fax (44) 01784 - 472 455 — 5 km

Thames Lodge, 78 rooms, D £ 150 — Staines
Tel (44) 0870 - 400 8121, Fax (44) 01784 - 454 858 — 10 km

RESTAURANTS RESTAURANT

Stateroom (Royal Berkshire) — Sunninghill
Tel (44) 01344 - 623 322 — 3 km

WENTWORTH West Course 18 8 7

This is one of those courses that has become familiar to many through the staging here every year of the PGA and the World Match-Play Championships. The price of the green-fee is such that you'd better get here in good shape if you really want to enjoy your day. Another solution is to take advantage of the special rates and play between October and March, although the landscape is not always very pretty at that time of year. You just get a clearer view of some of the superb houses on this very exclusive site. The "West" course is a great test of golf, where the yardage book will prove most handy to get a clearer idea of the position of difficulties, particularly some not very visible ditches. The positioning of hazards here is subtlety itself and nothing is left to chance. Your game must be absolutely tip-top, with a lot of inspiration to boot in the tricky run from the 13th to the 15th holes. Our judgment is a little more reserved for the two par 5s at the end of a course which is unquestionably one of the best inland layouts in England.

Ce parcours est de ceux que la télévision a rendus familiers, grâce au PGA Championship et au World Match-Play qui s'y disputent tous les ans. Et le prix du green-fee est tel qu'il faut y arriver en forme pour vraiment savourer sa journée, ou alors profiter de tarifs spéciaux d'octobre à mars. Mais le paysage n'est pas très gai à cette période, sauf que les vues sont plus dégagées sur les superbes maisons de ce domaine très exclusif. Le parcours "Ouest" est un grand test de golf, où le carnet de parcours sera fort utile pour identifier les difficultés, notamment des fossés pas très visibles. Le placement des obstacles est d'une subtilité exceptionnelle, et rien de bon ici n'est dû au hasard. Il faut un jeu absolument complet, et beaucoup d'inspiration dans le très délicat passage du 13 au 15. On sera plus réservé sur les deux par 5 clôturant ce parcours, qui reste incontestablement l'un des meilleurs "inland" du pays.

Wentworth Golf Club — 1926

Wentworth Drive
ENG - VIRGINIA WATER, Surrey GU25 4 LS

Office	Secrétariat	(44) 01344 - 842 201
Pro shop	Pro-shop	(44) 01344 - 843 353
Fax	Fax	(44) 01344 - 842 804
Web	www.wentworthclub.com	
Situation	Situation	7 km from Ascot
Annual closure	Fermeture annuelle	no
Weekly closure	Fermeture hebdomadaire	no

Fees main season Tarifs haute saison	18 holes	
	Week days Semaine	**We/Bank holidays** We/Férié
Individual Individuel	£ 200	£ 200
Couple Couple	£ 400	£ 400

Caddy	Caddy	£ 25 /on request
Electric Trolley	Chariot électrique	no
Buggy	Voiturette	£ 35 /18 holes
Clubs	Clubs	£ 25 /18 holes

Credit cards Cartes de crédit
VISA - Eurocard - MasterCard - DC - AMEX

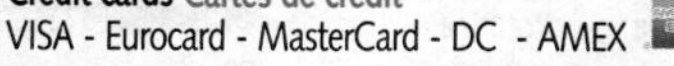

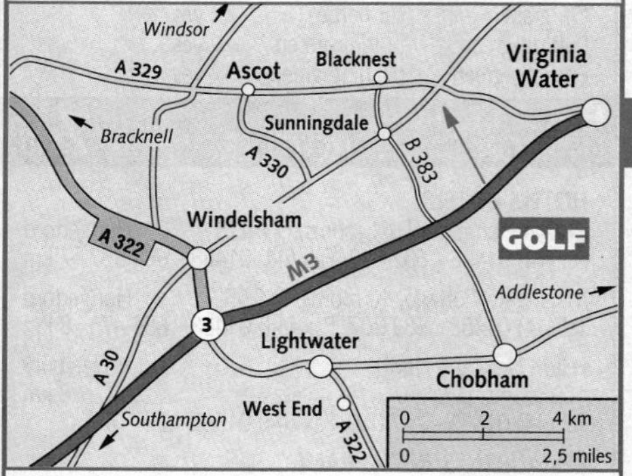

Access Accès : London, A30.
Left road opposite A329 turning to Ascot.
Map 8 on page 498 Carte 8 Page 498

Golf course PARCOURS 18/20

Site	Site	
Maintenance	Entretien	
Architect	Architecte	Harry S. Colt
Type	Type	inland, forest
Relief	Relief	
Water in play	Eau en jeu	
Exp. to wind	Exposé au vent	
Trees in play	Arbres en jeu	

Scorecard Carte de score	**Chp.** Chp.	**Mens** Mess.	**Ladies** Da.
Length Long.	6261	6008	5440
Par	73	73	75
Slope system	—	—	—

Advised golfing ability Niveau de jeu recommandé — 0 12 24 36
Hcp required Handicap exigé — 24 Men, 32 Ladies

Club house & amenities CLUB HOUSE ET ANNEXES 8/10

Pro shop	Pro-shop	
Driving range	Practice	
Sheltered	couvert	10 mats
On grass	sur herbe	yes
Putting-green	putting-green	yes
Pitching-green	pitching green	yes

Hotel facilities ENVIRONNEMENT HOTELIER 7/10

HOTELS HÔTELS

Royal Berkshire, 63 rooms, D £ 220 — Sunninghill
Tel (44) 01344 - 623 322, Fax (44) 01344 - 627 100 — 3 km

Berystede , 90 rooms, D £ 170 — Sunninghill
Tel (44) 0870 - 400 8111, Fax (44) 01344 - 872 301 — 5 km

Great Fosters, 39 rooms, D £ 175 — Egham
Tel (44) 01784 - 433 822, Fax (44) 01784 - 472 455 — 5 km

Thames Lodge, 78 rooms, D £ 150 — Staines
Tel (44) 0870 - 400 8121, Fax (44) 01784 - 454 858 — 10 km

RESTAURANTS RESTAURANT

Left Bank (Runnymede Hotel) — Egham
Tel (44) 01784 - 437 400 — 5 km

WEST BERKSHIRE

15 | 7 | 7

Without wishing to appear "reactionary", there are a number of trends in modern course design which don't always go down very well. Take the length of the par 5s here, for example, and particularly hole N°5, which is a full 635 yards. Admittedly professional golfers hit the ball further than they used to, but this can be a windy course, the ground can often be wet and while the normal tee-boxes bring everything down to more human proportions, there must be a happy medium somewhere for good golfers who don't have to be huge-hitters. It is a pity that such an ambitious facility, with some magnificent views, seems to have forgotten somewhat that playing golf is about enjoyment, that the aim of the game is not for a golfer to end up on his knees with his swing in tatters. Even though the course is flat, you will appreciate this very interesting and often captivating layout much more in a buggy, competing with friends more than with the course.

Sans être un vieux réactionnaire, on peut ne pas apprécier certaines tendances des architectes modernes. Ici, tous les par 5 le sont vraiment, le trou n°5 atteignant 570 mètres (635 yards). Il est vrai que les pros tapent plus fort qu'avant, mais le vent est moins rare ici que les grands champions, le sol peut être humide (non ?), et si les départs "normaux" ramènent les trous à des proportions normales, il y a sans doute un juste milieu pour les golfeurs d'un bon niveau sans carrure d'athlètes. Il est dommage qu'un équipement aussi ambitieux, offrant des vues magnifiques, ait un peu oublié la dimension de plaisir du joueur, ou, en tout cas, qu'il ne doit pas finir à genoux et le swing en compote. Même si le terrain est très plat, on appréciera beaucoup plus en voiturette ce tracé intéressant et souvent captivant, en dehors de tout esprit de compétition, sauf bien sûr avec les amis.

West Berkshire Golf Club — 1978

Chaddleworth
ENG - NEWBURY, Berks RG16 0HS

Office	Secrétariat	(44) 01488 - 638 574
Pro shop	Pro-shop	(44) 01488 - 638 851
Fax	Fax	(44) 01488 - 638 781
Web	—	
Situation	Situation	

8 km NW from Newbury (pop. 136 700) - 7 km NE of Hungerford

Annual closure	Fermeture annuelle	no
Weekly closure	Fermeture hebdomadaire	no

Fees main season Tarifs haute saison — 18 holes

	Week days Semaine	We/Bank holidays We/Férié
Individual Individuel	£ 25	£ 35
Couple Couple	£ 50	£ 70

Full weekdays: £ 35 / * Visitors after 12.00 pm at weekends

Caddy	Caddy	no
Electric Trolley	Chariot électrique	no
Buggy	Voiturette	£ 10 /18 holes
Clubs	Clubs	£ 10 /18 holes

Credit cards Cartes de crédit VISA - MasterCard

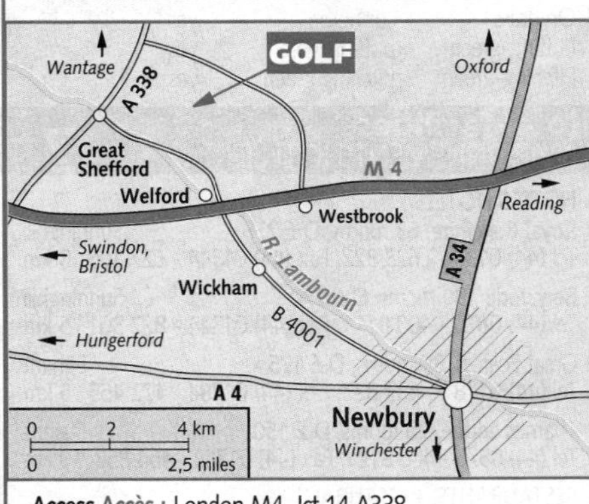

Access Accès : London M4. Jct 14 A338, → RAF Welford, Club house on right.
Map 7 on page 496 Carte 7 Page 496

Golf course — PARCOURS — 15/20

Site	Site	
Maintenance	Entretien	
Architect	Architecte	John Stagg
Type	Type	open country
Relief	Relief	
Water in play	Eau en jeu	
Exp. to wind	Exposé au vent	
Trees in play	Arbres en jeu	

Scorecard Carte de score	**Chp.** Chp.	**Mens** Mess.	**Ladies** Da.
Length Long.	6353	5618	5200
Par	73	73	74
Slope system	—	—	—

Advised golfing ability — 0 12 24 36
Niveau de jeu recommandé
Hcp required Handicap exigé — no

Club house & amenities — CLUB HOUSE ET ANNEXES — 7/10

Pro shop	Pro-shop	
Driving range	Practice	
Sheltered	couvert	no
On grass	sur herbe	yes
Putting-green	putting-green	yes
Pitching-green	pitching green	yes

Hotel facilities — ENVIRONNEMENT HOTELIER — 7/10

HOTELS HÔTELS

Bear at Hungerford, 41 rooms, D £ 125 — Hungerford
Tel (44) 01488 - 682 512, Fax (44) 01488 - 684 357 — 7 km

Marshgate Cottage, 10 rooms, D £ 55 — Hungerford
Tel (44) 01488 - 682 307, Fax (44) 01488 - 685 475 — 8 km

Hilton Newbury North — Newbury
109 rooms, D £ 150 — 8 km
Tel (44) 01635 - 247 010, Fax (44) 01635 - 247 077

RESTAURANTS RESTAURANT

Just William's — Hungerford
Tel (44) 01488 - 681 199 — 7 km

Blue Boar Inn, Tel (44) 01635 - 248 236 — Newbury 4 km

WEST BYFLEET

14 | 6 | 8

Although the club-house is situated close to the road, you still get the impression of being in the heart of Surrey's tree-covered countryside and find it hard to imagine that in such green surroundings a drought virtually killed the fairways here some years back. This is a rather flat course where the difficulties are clearly visible, but no-one ever said that seeing was avoiding. It is made even narrower than the trees suggest by the position of fairway bunkers, especially on the 16th, where the fairway slopes towards the sand hazards. This long hole is part of an excellent finishing stretch with the 15th, ending in a very undulating green, the 17th, a very well-guarded par 3, and the 18th, where you can risk it and go for the green in two. These last four holes are in fact what make West Byfleet a good course rather than just a pretty one, although it is still not quite in the very top class. The course being open on week-ends is in pleasant contrast with the other top courses in the region, but book a tee-time all the same.

Bien que le club house soit situé près de la route, on garde l'impression d'être effectivement dans les belles parties boisées de la campagne du Surrey. C'est un parcours assez plat où les difficultés sont bien visibles mais il ne suffit pas de les voir pour les éviter : il est rendu plus étroit encore que les arbres ne l'indiquent par le placement des bunkers de fairway, en particulier au 16 où les pentes du fairway inclinent vers ces obstacles. Ce long trou fait partie d'un finale de très bonne qualité, avec le 15 et son green très modelé du 15, le 17 (par 3) avec ses solides défenses, le 18, où l'on peut être tenté d'attaquer le green en deux, mais avec des risques. ce sont en fait ces quatre trous qui font passer West Byfleet du statut de joli parcours à celui de bon parcours. Et le fait qu'il soit ouvert en week-end tranche singulièrement avec les autres grands parcours de la région, mais il est prudent de réserver un départ.

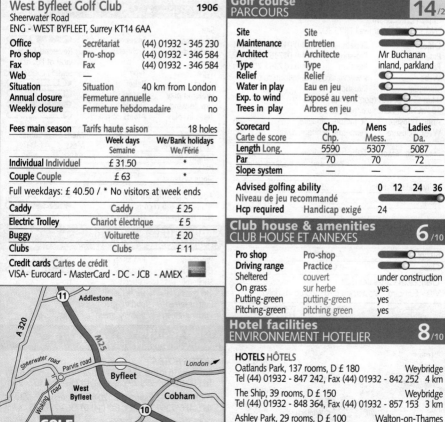

West Byfleet Golf Club — 1906

Sheerwater Road
ENG - WEST BYFLEET, Surrey KT14 6AA

Office	Secrétariat	(44) 01932 - 345 230
Pro shop	Pro-shop	(44) 01932 - 346 584
Fax	Fax	(44) 01932 - 346 584
Web	—	
Situation	Situation	40 km from London
Annual closure	Fermeture annuelle	no
Weekly closure	Fermeture hebdomadaire	no

Fees main season Tarifs haute saison	18 holes	
	Week days Semaine	**We/Bank holidays** We/Férié
Individual Individuel	£ 31.50	*
Couple Couple	£ 63	*

Full weekdays: £ 40.50 / * No visitors at week ends

Caddy	Caddy	£ 25
Electric Trolley	Chariot électrique	£ 5
Buggy	Voiturette	£ 20
Clubs	Clubs	£ 11

Credit cards Cartes de crédit
VISA- Eurocard - MasterCard - DC - JCB - AMEX

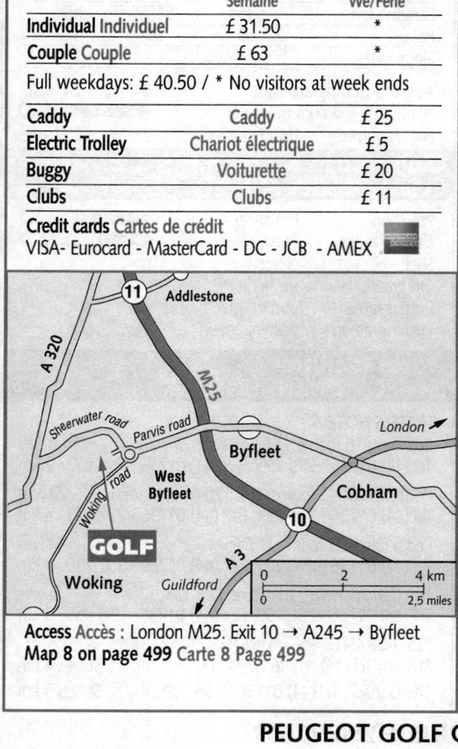

Access Accès : London M25. Exit 10 → A245 → Byfleet
Map 8 on page 499 Carte 8 Page 499

Golf course — PARCOURS — 14/20

Site	Site	
Maintenance	Entretien	
Architect	Architecte	Mr Buchanan
Type	Type	inland, parkland
Relief	Relief	
Water in play	Eau en jeu	
Exp. to wind	Exposé au vent	
Trees in play	Arbres en jeu	

Scorecard Carte de score	**Chp.** Chp.	**Mens** Mess.	**Ladies** Da.
Length Long.	5590	5307	5087
Par	70	70	72
Slope system	—	—	—

Advised golfing ability Niveau de jeu recommandé — 0 12 24 36
Hcp required Handicap exigé 24

Club house & amenities — CLUB HOUSE ET ANNEXES — 6/10

Pro shop	Pro-shop	
Driving range	Practice	
Sheltered	couvert	under construction
On grass	sur herbe	yes
Putting-green	putting-green	yes
Pitching-green	pitching green	yes

Hotel facilities — ENVIRONNEMENT HOTELIER — 8/10

HOTELS HÔTELS

Oatlands Park, 137 rooms, D £ 180 — Weybridge
Tel (44) 01932 - 847 242, Fax (44) 01932 - 842 252 — 4 km

The Ship, 39 rooms, D £ 150 — Weybridge
Tel (44) 01932 - 848 364, Fax (44) 01932 - 857 153 — 3 km

Ashley Park, 29 rooms, D £ 100 — Walton-on-Thames
Tel (44) 01932 - 220 196, Fax (44) 01932 - 248 721 — 7 km

RESTAURANTS RESTAURANT

Casa Romana — Weybridge
Tel (44) 01932 - 843 470 — 3 km

Edwinns — Sheperton
Tel (44) 01932 - 223 543 — 8 km

WEST CORNWALL

16 | 7 | 6

On the first hole at West Cornwall, you understand the religious and sporting nature of the game of golf, as you line up your drive on the steeple of the village church, the birthplace of Jim Barnes, one of the few British golfers to have won both the British and the US Opens. The course has not changed much since his time. It is rather short and a little devious in that the sloping terrain can easily draw your ball off the fairway. At the same time the railway line exerts a strange attraction on slicers over four holes. Once you are out of "Calamity Corner", where two par 3s and a short par 4 (holes 5 to 7) have ruined many a card, you will need a cool head for the remaining 11 holes in the dunes, up until the 18th, where you are in for a gentle landing downhill. A very natural and imaginative course, West Cornwall is excellent golfing before visiting the pretty fishing village and the artists of Saint Ives.

Le premier trou de West Cornwall permet de comprendre la nature religieuse et sportive du golf, il faut s'aligner sur le clocher de l'église du village où est né Jim Barnes, l'un des rares Britanniques à avoir remporté le British et l'US Open. Et le parcours n'a pas dû changer beaucoup. Assez court, il n'est pas d'une parfaite franchise, car les pentes peuvent sortir la balle du fairway, et la voie ferrée attire étrangement les sliceurs sur quatre trous. Une fois sorti indemne de "Calamity Corner," où deux par 3 et un minuscule par 4 (du 5 au 7) ont détruit bien des cartes, il faut garder son sang-froid pour les onze trous restant, toujours dans les dunes, et jusqu'au 18, un atterrissage en douceur et en descente. Très naturel et imaginatif, West Cornwall est à connaître, avant de visiter St Ives, joli village de pêcheurs et d'artistes.

West Cornwall Golf Club — 1889

Church Lane, Lelant
ENG - ST IVES, Cornwall TR26 3D2

Office	Secrétariat	(44) 01736 - 753 401
Pro shop	Pro-shop	(44) 01736 - 753 177
Fax	Fax	(44) 01736 - 753 401
Web	www.westcornwallgolfclub.co.uk	
Situation	Situation	

3 km SE of St Ives (pop. 7 254)
16 km NE of Penzance (pop. 20 284)

Annual closure	Fermeture annuelle	no
Weekly closure	Fermeture hebdomadaire	no

Fees main season Tarifs haute saison	Week days Semaine	We/Bank holidays We/Férié
Full day		
Individual Individuel	£ 25	£ 35
Couple Couple	£ 50	£ 70

Caddy	Caddy	no
Electric Trolley	Chariot électrique	no
Buggy	Voiturette	no
Clubs	Clubs	£ 10 /day

Credit cards Cartes de crédit
Visa - Eurocard - Mastercard (Pro shop goods only)

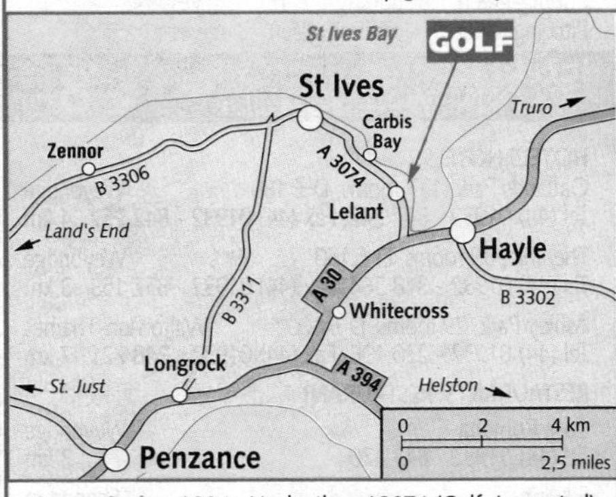

Access Accès : A30 to Hayle, then A3074 (Golf signposted)
Map 6 on page 494 Carte 6 Page 494

Golf course — PARCOURS — 16/20

Site	Site	
Maintenance	Entretien	
Architect	Architecte	Reverend Tyack, vicar of Lelant...
Type	Type	seaside course, links
Relief	Relief	
Water in play	Eau en jeu	
Exp. to wind	Exposé au vent	
Trees in play	Arbres en jeu	

Scorecard Carte de score	Chp. Chp.	Mens Mess.	Ladies Da.
Length Long.	5354	5180	4890
Par	69	69	73
Slope system	—	—	—

Advised golfing ability Niveau de jeu recommandé — 0 12 24 36
Hcp required Handicap exigé — 28 Men, 36 Ladies

Club house & amenities — CLUB HOUSE ET ANNEXES — 7/10

Pro shop	Pro-shop	
Driving range	Practice	
Sheltered	couvert	no
On grass	sur herbe	yes
Putting-green	putting-green	yes
Pitching-green	pitching green	yes

Hotel facilities — ENVIRONNEMENT HOTELIER — 6/10

HOTELS HÔTELS

Boskerris, 16 rooms, D £ 145 (with dinner) — Carbis Bay
Tel (44) 01736 - 795 295, Fax (44) 01736 - 798 632 — 2 km

Porthminster, 43 rooms, D £ 120 (with dinner) — St Ives
Tel (44) 01736 - 795 221, Fax (44) 01736 - 797 043 — 4 km

Ped'n Olva, 33 rooms, D £ 65 — St Ives
Tel (44) 01736 - 796 222, Fax (44) 01736 - 797 710 — 4 km

The Garrack Hotel, 16 rooms, D £ 135 — St Ives
Tel (44) 01736 - 796 199, Fax (44) 01736 - 798 955 — 3 km

RESTAURANTS RESTAURANT

Russets, Tel (44) 01736 - 794 700 — St Ives 4 km
The Garrack, Tel (44) 01736 - 796 199 — St Ives 3 km

WEST HILL

16 | 6 | 6

This is the third of a compact threesome of courses, the other two being virtual neighbours Woking and Worplesdon. In fact these are three courses belonging to the same club, and each has its own personality. We suppose you are bound to prefer one of the three, but each to his own, as they say. West Hill is very short and only moderately contoured over land strewn with pines, birch and conifers. The heather narrows the fairways and even cuts them in two on the 5th and 17th holes, two par 5s where that age-old decision arises once again: do I carry the hazard or lay up short? In fact the whole course calls for constant thought on the best way of driving, hitting the second shot and approaching the greens. This is why it is always such fun to play. A natural and well-landscaped course whose sandy soil drains easily, West Hill has inimitable charm, matched only perhaps by the other two "Ws"...

C'est le troisième d'un trio compact, avec Woking et Worplesdon, pratiquement voisins. Comme s'il s'agissait de trois parcours d'un même club, alors que chacun a préservé sa personnalité. Que l'on préfère l'un à l'autre est inévitable, mais "chacun a son goût." West Hill est très court, avec un relief très modéré, et un espace arboré de pins, de bouleaux et de sapins. La bruyère rétrécit les fairways, et vient parfois même les interrompre comme au 5 et au 17, deux par 5 où il faut prendre la décision de risquer de passer ou de rester court. L'ensemble du parcours demande une réflexion constante sur la meilleure façon de driver, de jouer le second coup, d'approcher, c'est pourquoi il reste aussi amusant. Naturel et bien paysagé, bien draînant avec son sol sablonneux, West Hill a un charme inimitable, sauf par les deux autres "W," peut-être...

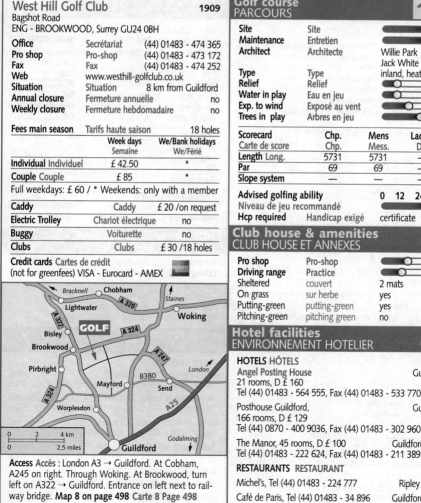

West Hill Golf Club — 1909

Bagshot Road
ENG - BROOKWOOD, Surrey GU24 0BH

Office	Secrétariat	(44) 01483 - 474 365
Pro shop	Pro-shop	(44) 01483 - 473 172
Fax	Fax	(44) 01483 - 474 252
Web	www.westhill-golfclub.co.uk	
Situation	Situation	8 km from Guildford
Annual closure	Fermeture annuelle	no
Weekly closure	Fermeture hebdomadaire	no

Fees main season Tarifs haute saison	Week days Semaine	We/Bank holidays We/Férié
		18 holes
Individual Individuel	£ 42.50	*
Couple Couple	£ 85	*

Full weekdays: £ 60 / * Weekends: only with a member

Caddy	Caddy	£ 20 /on request
Electric Trolley	Chariot électrique	no
Buggy	Voiturette	no
Clubs	Clubs	£ 30 /18 holes

Credit cards Cartes de crédit
(not for greenfees) VISA - Eurocard - AMEX

Access Accès : London A3 → Guildford. At Cobham, A245 on right. Through Woking. At Brookwood, turn left on A322 → Guildford. Entrance on left next to railway bridge. **Map 8 on page 498** Carte 8 Page 498

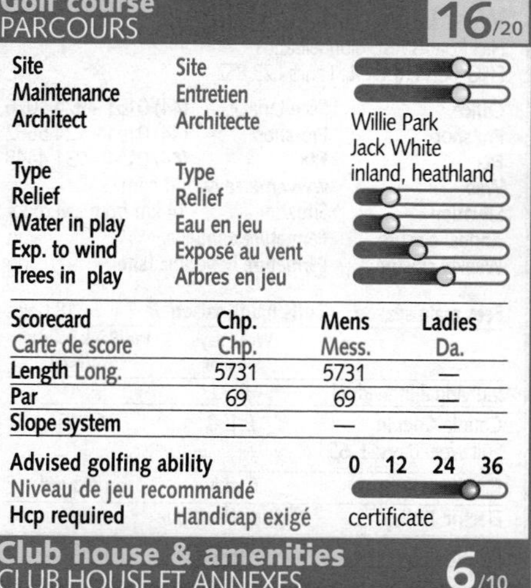

Golf course — PARCOURS — 16/20

Site	Site	
Maintenance	Entretien	
Architect	Architecte	Willie Park Jack White
Type	Type	inland, heathland
Relief	Relief	
Water in play	Eau en jeu	
Exp. to wind	Exposé au vent	
Trees in play	Arbres en jeu	

Scorecard Carte de score	Chp. Chp.	Mens Mess.	Ladies Da.
Length Long.	5731	5731	—
Par	69	69	—
Slope system	—	—	—

Advised golfing ability Niveau de jeu recommandé — 0 12 24 36

Hcp required Handicap exigé — certificate

Club house & amenities — CLUB HOUSE ET ANNEXES — 6/10

Pro shop	Pro-shop	
Driving range	Practice	
Sheltered	couvert	2 mats
On grass	sur herbe	yes
Putting-green	putting-green	yes
Pitching-green	pitching green	no

Hotel facilities — ENVIRONNEMENT HOTELIER — 6/10

HOTELS HÔTELS

Angel Posting House — Guildford 8 km
21 rooms, D £ 160
Tel (44) 01483 - 564 555, Fax (44) 01483 - 533 770

Posthouse Guildford, — Guildford 8 km
166 rooms, D £ 129
Tel (44) 0870 - 400 9036, Fax (44) 01483 - 302 960

The Manor, 45 rooms, D £ 100 — Guildford 8 km
Tel (44) 01483 - 222 624, Fax (44) 01483 - 211 389

RESTAURANTS RESTAURANT

Michel's, Tel (44) 01483 - 224 777 — Ripley 10 km
Café de Paris, Tel (44) 01483 - 34 896 — Guildford 8 km

WEST LANCASHIRE

17 | 7 | 7

The string of great courses running from Liverpool to Southport is unmatched anywhere in the world. And although West Lancashire is undoubtedly one of them, it has seldom staged top tournaments. The views over the Mersey estuary and the Welsh mountains are superb from the clubhouse, yet are less visible from the actual course, which lies sheltered behind a line of dunes. This is not a very hilly course, a fact that tends to give it an air of austerity but also its very own personality. What's more, this impression of infinity makes it very difficult to judge distances. It is already a tough task choosing the right club for the wind, avoiding bunkers, many of which just swallow up your ball, and getting to grips with firm, subtle and very slick greens. But despite everything, game strategy is pretty obvious, even though a few hazards are hard to spot from the tee-boxes.

Nulle part au monde on ne trouve une telle succession de grands parcours que de Liverpool à Southport. West Lancashire y figure sans conteste, alors qu'il a rarement reçu de grandes épreuves. Du Clubhouse, les vues sont superbes sur l'estuaire de la Mersey et les montagnes du Pays de Galles, mais on les voit peu du parcours, à l'abri derrière un cordon de dunes. Le relief n'est pas ici très prononcé, ce qui lui donne un caractère d'austérité, mais aussi sa personnalité. De plus, cette impression d'infinité rend très difficile le jugement des distances : il est déjà délicat de choisir les bons clubs en fonction du vent, d'éviter les bunkers, dont beaucoup sont d'une grande voracité, de négocier des greens fermes, subtils et très rapides. La stratégie est malgré tout assez évidente, alors que certains obstacles sont peu visibles des départs.

West Lancashire Golf Club 1873

Hall Road West, Blundellsands
ENG - LIVERPOOL, Lancs L23 8SZ

Office	Secrétariat	(44) 0151 - 924 1076
Pro shop	Pro-shop	(44) 0151 - 924 5662
Fax	Fax	(44) 0151 - 931 4448
Web	www.merseyworld.com	
Situation	Situation	14 km from Liverpool
Annual closure	Fermeture annuelle	no
Weekly closure	Fermeture hebdomadaire	no

Fees main season / Tarifs haute saison	18 holes	
	Week days / Semaine	We/Bank holidays / We/Férié
Individual Individuel	£ 50	£ 70
Couple Couple	£ 100	£ 140

Full weekdays: £ 65

Caddy	Caddy	on request
Electric Trolley	Chariot électrique	no
Buggy	Voiturette	no
Clubs	Clubs	£ 5 /18 holes

Credit cards Cartes de crédit
VISA - Eurocard - MasterCard - DC - JCB - AMEX
(Pro shop goods only)

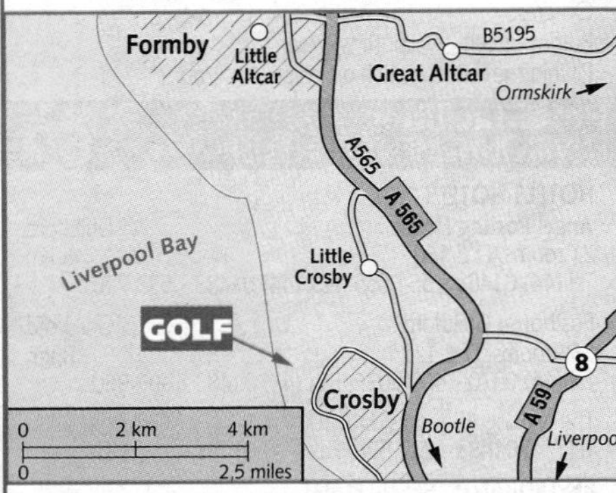

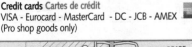

Access Accès : Liverpool, A565 to Crosby.
+Follow signs to club by Hall Road Rail Station
Map 5 on page 493 Carte 5 Page 493

Golf course PARCOURS 17/20

Site	Site	
Maintenance	Entretien	
Architect	Architecte	Unknown until 1960 C.K. Cotton (1960)
Type	Type	links
Relief	Relief	
Water in play	Eau en jeu	
Exp. to wind	Exposé au vent	
Trees in play	Arbres en jeu	

Scorecard / Carte de score	Chp. / Chp.	Mens / Mess.	Ladies / Da.
Length Long.	6086	5594	5135
Par	72	70	73
Slope system	—	—	—

Advised golfing ability Niveau de jeu recommandé: 0 12 24 36

Hcp required Handicap exigé: 28 Men, 36 Ladies

Club house & amenities CLUB HOUSE ET ANNEXES 7/10

Pro shop	Pro-shop	
Driving range	Practice	
Sheltered	couvert	no
On grass	sur herbe	yes
Putting-green	putting-green	yes
Pitching-green	pitching green	yes

Hotel facilities ENVIRONNEMENT HOTELIER 7/10

HOTELS HÔTELS

Blundellsands, 30 rooms, D £ 85 — Crosby
Tel (44) 0151 - 924 6515, Fax (44) 0151 - 931 5364 — 3 km

Atlantic Tower Thistle, 226 rooms, D £ 134 — Liverpool
Tel (44) 0151 - 227 4444, Fax (44) 0151 - 236 3973 — 15 km

Liverpool Moat House, 263 rooms, D £ 135 — Liverpool
Tel (44) 0151 - 471 9988, Fax (44) 0151 - 709 2706

Tree Tops Hotel, 11 rooms, D £ 90 — Formby
Tel (44) 01704 - 572 430, Fax (44) 01704 - 572 430 — 10 km

RESTAURANTS RESTAURANT

60 Hope Street, Tel (44) 0151 - 707 6060 — Liverpool 15 km

Blundellsands, Tel (44) 0151 - 924 6515 — Crosby 3 km

WEST SURREY

15 | 7 | 7

West Surrey is one of those courses where you soon start feeling excited about your game as all the hazards and the tactics you need to overcome them are crystal clear. This is important, because placing the drive is of prime importance if you want a relatively simple approach shot. So players who are playing to form should card their handicap and perhaps even better if they excel on the greens. In Summer the course gets a little harder because the fairways are not watered and the ball will roll on easily into the long thick rough from where only a wedge can be of any use. With this said, there are not many other hazards to contend with. With a longer outward 9 and tight back 9, there is something for every kind of player, and the long-hitters who keep out of the trees will enjoy a number of birdie opportunities on the par 5s.

West Surrey est de ces parcours où l'on éprouve vite de bonnes sensations, parce que l'on voit aussi clairement les obstacles que la tactique à mettre en oeuvre. C'est important car le placement du drive est essentiel pour garantir un second coup assez facile. Ainsi, les joueurs qui sont à leur bon niveau joueront normalement leur handicap, et mieux même s'ils sont inspirés sur les greens. En été, le parcours est plus difficile car les fairways ne sont pas arrosés, et l'on roule assez facilement dans des roughs longs et épais, d'où on ne peut souvent sortir qu'avec un wedge. Cela dit, il n'y a pas beaucoup d'autres obstacles. Avec un aller plus long, mais un retour plus étroit, tous les types de joueurs sont bien servis, et les longs frappeurs sachant éviter les arbres trouveront de belles occasions de birdies sur les par 5.

West Surrey Golf Club — 1910

Enton Green - ENG - GODALMING, Surrey GU8 5AF

Office	Secrétariat	(44) 01483 - 421 275
Pro shop	Pro-shop	(44) 01483 - 417 278
Fax	Fax	(44) 01483 - 415 419
Web	www.wsgc.co.uk	
Situation	Situation	6 km from Guildford
Annual closure	Fermeture annuelle	no
Weekly closure	Fermeture hebdomadaire	Tuesday 08 → 12

Fees main season Tarifs haute saison	18 holes	
	Week days Semaine	**We/Bank holidays** We/Férié
Individual Individuel	£ 27	£ 36
Couple Couple	£ 54	£ 72

Full days: £ 36 / £ 48 (week ends) / Restrictions at weekends (please call)

Caddy	Caddy	no
Electric Trolley	Chariot électrique	£ 6 /18 holes
Buggy	Voiturette	no
Clubs	Clubs	£ 10 /18 holes

Credit cards Cartes de crédit
VISA - Eurocard - MasterCard - DC - JCB - AMEX
(not for green fees)

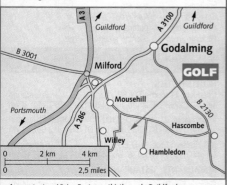

Access Accès : A3 (→ Portsmouth) through Guildford. Turn left to Milford. At traffic lights turn left onto A 3100 (→Portsmouth). Right onto Station Lane. Golf 3 km down (2 m.) on right side. **Map 8 on page 498** Carte 8 Page 498

Golf course PARCOURS — 15/20

Site	Site	
Maintenance	Entretien	
Architect	Architecte	Herbert Fowler
Type	Type	parkland
Relief	Relief	
Water in play	Eau en jeu	
Exp. to wind	Exposé au vent	
Trees in play	Arbres en jeu	

Scorecard Carte de score	**Chp.** Chp.	**Mens** Mess.	**Ladies** Da.
Length Long.	5633	5842	4970
Par	71	71	72
Slope system	—	—	—

Advised golfing ability Niveau de jeu recommandé — 0 12 24 36
Hcp required Handicap exigé — certificate

Club house & amenities CLUB HOUSE ET ANNEXES — 7/10

Pro shop	Pro-shop	
Driving range	Practice	
Sheltered	couvert	no
On grass	sur herbe	yes (summer)
Putting-green	putting-green	yes
Pitching-green	pitching green	yes

Hotel facilities ENVIRONNEMENT HOTELIER — 7/10

HOTELS HÔTELS

Devil's Punchbowl, 36 rooms, D £ 100 — Hindhead 8 km
Tel (44) 01428 - 606 565, Fax (44) 01428 - 605 713

The Manor, 45 rooms, D £ 100 — Guildford 7 km
Tel (44) 01483 - 222 624, Fax (44) 01483 - 211 389

Angel Posting House and Livery — Guildford 7 km
21 rooms, D £ 160
Tel (44) 01483 - 564 555, Fax (44) 01483 - 533 770

Bramley Grange, 45 rooms, D £ 120 — Bramley 3 km
Tel (44) 01483 - 893 434, Fax (44) 01483 - 893 835

RESTAURANTS RESTAURANT

White Horse ,Tel (44) 01483 - 208 258 — Hascombe 3 km
Café de Paris, Tel(44) 01483 - 34 896 — Guildford 7 km

WEST SUSSEX

18 | 7 | 6

The good news for most amateurs is that West Sussex is not a long course. The bad news is that there is only one par 5, hole N°1, where your swing might not quite be in the right groove to hit the green in two. There are also a number of holes where you will hope to get by unscathed, for example the 6th and 15th, two tough par 3s where you need to carry water, and the 16th, a beautiful par 4 whose green looks depressingly tiny beyond a wide ravine. Here, you have every opportunity to shoot a good round as long as your game is in tip-top condition, and although the greens are very well protected, there is often an easy way in. You need to play every shot there is, one at a time, firstly in your mind, then with your club. This absolute gem of a course does not have the recognition it deserves, but the people here seem to have opted for the sweet life, preferring to leave the limelight for others.

La bonne nouvelle pour la plupart des amateurs, c'est que West Sussex n'est pas bien long ! La mauvaise, c'est qu'il y a un seul par 5, et c'est le 1, où l'on n'est généralement pas assez assoupli pour vraiment attaquer le green en deux. Il y a aussi quelques trous dont il faut sortir indemne, comme le 6 et le 15, deux solides par 3 où il faut passer l'eau, ou le 16, très beau par 4 dont le green paraît minuscule au delà d'un large ravin. Autrement, il est ici beaucoup d'occasions de réussir si l'on a amené son meilleur jeu, d'autant que les greens sont bien protégés, mais qu'ils laissent très souvent une ouverture. Il faut ici savoir jouer tous les coups, et un seul à la fois, d'abord avec sa tête puis avec son club. Ce merveilleux petit bijou n'a pas la notoriété qu'il mérite, mais, ici, on a choisi de vivre heureux, sans souci des projecteurs trop violents.

West Sussex Golf Club — 1931

ENG - PULBOROUGH, West Sussex RH20 2EN

Office	Secrétariat	(44) 01798 - 875 563
Pro shop	Pro-shop	(44) 01798 - 872 426
Fax	Fax	(44) 01798 - 875 563
Web	—	
Situation	Situation	25 km from Brighton
Annual closure	Fermeture annuelle	no
Weekly closure	Fermeture hebdomadaire	no

Fees main season Tarifs haute saison	18 holes	
	Week days Semaine	We/Bank holidays We/Férié
Individual Individuel	£ 47.50	*
Couple Couple	£ 95	*

Full weekdays: £ 57.50 / * No visitors on Friday & week ends

Caddy	Caddy	no
Electric Trolley	Chariot électrique	£ 5/18 holes
Buggy	Voiturette	no
Clubs	Clubs	£ 7.50/18 holes

Credit cards Cartes de crédit
VISA - MasterCard (Pro shop goods only)

Pulborough
A 29
Billingshurst
Horsham
London
GOLF
A 24
A 29
West Chiltington
Chichester
Storrington
A 283
Washington
0 2 4 km
0 2,5 miles
Worthing

Access Accès : M25 Jct 9, A24 → Worthing.
At Washington, A283 on the right through Storrington → Pulborough. Golf course on the right.
Map 7 on page 496 Carte 7 Page 496

Golf course PARCOURS — 18/20

Site	Site	
Maintenance	Entretien	
Architect	Architecte	Sir Guy Campbell C.K. Hutchinson
Type	Type	inland, heathland
Relief	Relief	
Water in play	Eau en jeu	
Exp. to wind	Exposé au vent	
Trees in play	Arbres en jeu	

Scorecard Carte de score	Chp. Chp.	Mens Mess.	Ladies Da.
Length Long.	5600	5320	5020
Par	68	68	73
Slope system	—	—	—

Advised golfing ability 0 12 24 36
Niveau de jeu recommandé
Hcp required Handicap exigé — certificate

Club house & amenities CLUB HOUSE ET ANNEXES — 7/10

Pro shop	Pro-shop	
Driving range	Practice	
Sheltered	couvert	1 mat
On grass	sur herbe	yes
Putting-green	putting-green	yes
Pitching-green	pitching green	yes

Hotel facilities ENVIRONNEMENT HOTELIER — 6/10

HOTELS HÔTELS

Chequers, 11 rooms, D £ 90 — Pulborough
Tel (44) 01798 - 872 486, Fax (44) 01798 - 872 715 — 3 km

Roundabout, 23 rooms, D £ 100 — West Chiltington
Tel (44) 01798 - 813 838, Fax (44) 01798 - 812 962 — 2 km

Mill House, 11 rooms, D £ 90 — Ashington
Tel (44) 01903 - 892 426, Fax (44) 01903 - 892 855 — 10 km

RESTAURANTS RESTAURANT

Fleur de Sel, Tel (44) 01903 - 742 331 — Storrington 4 km
Old Forge, Tel (44) 01903 - 743 402 — Storrington 4 km
Roundabout Hotel — West Chiltington
Tel (44) 01798 - 813 838 — 2 km

WESTON-SUPER-MARE

16	6	7

The beginning of the course is not so simple, between the sand-dunes and out-of-bounds. If the wind is blowing, don't go for the pin, you will be asking for trouble. The 15th is also surpri-ng, because you have to cut the ball over an out-of-bounds area. Try and get a round with some local layers so they can tell you about the traps that are not always clearly in view. For example, the rough is ne-er the same from one season to the next and even disappears altogether in the Winter (hardly the best time come here anyway). Facing the Welsh coast, Weston-Super-Mare provides some spectacular views over ie Bristol Channel and the general flatness of the course means you can easily play 36 holes in a day when n holiday. Similar to Saunton in style but without offering quite the same challenge, this is a course in the rand links tradition.

e début du parcours n'est pas si simple, entre les dunes et le hors-limites. S'il y a du vent, ne jouez pas di-ctement les drapeaux, vous risquez des problèmes. Le 15 est aussi surprenant, où il faut couper au-dessus u hors-limites. Essayez donc de faire une partie avec des joueurs locaux, ils vous en apprendront les pièges as toujours bien visibles, notamment que le rough n'est jamais le même suivant la saison, et qu'il est ab-ent en hiver. Mais il est vari que l'on vient rarement ici en cette période de l'année. En face du Pays de alles, Weston-super-Mare offre des vues spectaculaires sur le Bristol Channel. Son absence de relief en it un parcours idéal pour jouer 36 trous en vacances. Assez proche par son style de Saunton, sans pré-ndre à son exigence, c'est un parcours de grande tradition de links.

Weston-Super-Mare Golf Club 1892

Uphill Road North
ENG - WESTON-SUPER-MARE, Bristol BS23 4NQ

Office	Secrétariat	(44) 01934 - 626 968
Pro shop	Pro-shop	(44) 01934 - 633 360
Fax	Fax	(44) 01934 - 626 968
Web	www.wsmgolfclub.com	
Situation	Situation	23 km SW of Bristol
Annual closure	Fermeture annuelle	no
Weekly closure	Fermeture hebdomadaire	no

Fees main season / Tarifs haute saison	Week days / Semaine	We/Bank holidays / We/Férié
	Full day	
Individual Individuel	£ 24	£ 35
Couple Couple	£ 48	£ 70

Full days: £ 35 / £ 45 (week ends)

Caddy	Caddy	no
Electric Trolley	Chariot électrique	no (but batteries)
Buggy	Voiturette	no
Clubs	Clubs	yes (ask pro)

Credit cards Cartes de crédit
Visa - Mastercard (Pro shop goods only)

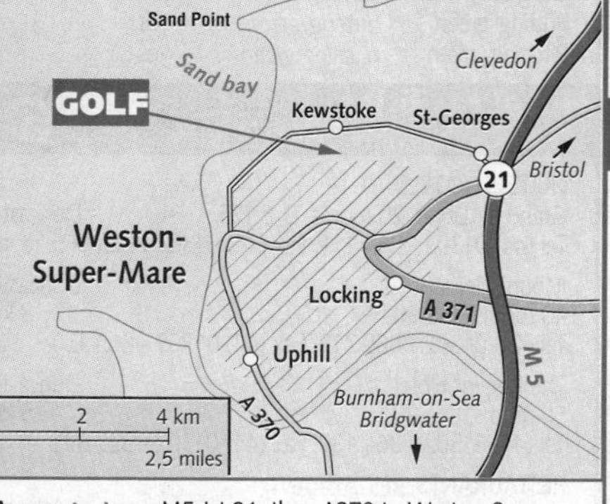

Access Accès : • M5 Jct 21, then A370 to Weston-Super-Mare. Follow signs. • From Bristol centre, A370.
Map 6 on page 495 Carte 6 Page 495

Golf course PARCOURS 16/20

Site	Site	
Maintenance	Entretien	
Architect	Architecte	Tom Dunn
Type	Type	seaside course, links
Relief	Relief	
Water in play	Eau en jeu	
Exp. to wind	Exposé au vent	
Trees in play	Arbres en jeu	

Scorecard / Carte de score	Chp. / Chp.	Mens / Mess.	Ladies / Da.
Length Long.	5651	5540	5006
Par	70	70	72
Slope system	—	—	—

Adv' ed golfing ability / Niveau de jeu recommandé: 0 12 24 36
Hcp required / Handicap exigé: certificate

Club house & amenities CLUB HOUSE ET ANNEXES 6/10

Pro shop	Pro-shop	
Driving range	Practice	
Sheltered	couvert	no
On grass	sur herbe	yes
Putting-green	putting-green	yes
Pitching-green	pitching green	yes

Hotel facilities ENVIRONNEMENT HOTELIER 7/10

HOTELS HÔTELS

Beachlands, 24 rooms, D £ 85 — Weston-Super-Mare
Tel (44) 01934 - 621 401, Fax (44) 01934 -621 966 — adjacent

Grand Atlantic — Weston-Super-Mare
74 rooms, D £ 90 — 2 km
Tel (44) 01934 - 626 543, Fax (44) 01934 - 415 048

Commodore, 19 rooms, D £ 95 — Weston-Super-Mare
Tel (44) 01934 - 415 778, Fax (44) 01934 - 636 483 — 2 km

RESTAURANTS RESTAURANT

Duets — Weston-Super-Mare
Tel (44) 01934 - 413 428 — 3 km

Claremont Vaults — Weston-Super-Mare 2 km

WHEATLEY

14 | 6 | 6

This course is on the edge of the city of Doncaster, one of England's more famous horse-racing v nues. And although there are many houses all around, you forget all about them once out on t course. The club-house, recently refurbished, is simple with no superfluous frills or outstanding architecture, y the restaurant serves good food, something you don't always find in British club-houses. The peat and sandy s provide good drainage and top quality grass, especially since the fairways are protected in winter: players hit th shots off a little mat. This tree-lined course is easily walkable despite a few slopes on the back nine, where you fi most of the difficulties; trouble is evenly spread over alternating tricky and easier holes to ensure a pleasa rhythm to your round. This is a good course to play with all the family, although the best players looking for a te ting challenge might end up a little frustrated.

Ce parcours est à la limite de la ville de Doncaster, assez connue par les amateurs de chevaux de course. Bi qu'il y ait de nombreuses maisons alentour, on les oublie totalement une fois sur le parcours. Le Club house a é récemment rénové, mais reste simple, sans luxe excessif ni architecture très remarquable. Cependant, le resta rant est de bonne qualité, ce qui n'est pas toujours le cas dans les golfs britanniques, il faut bien le dire. Le sol sable et de tourbe assure un bon drainage, et un gazon de bonne qualité, d'autant que les fairways sont protég en hiver : les joueurs tapent leurs coups à partir de petits tapis ! Le parcours bien boisé est facile à jouer à pie malgré quelques petits reliefs au retour. C'est là que l'on trouve d'ailleurs les trous les plus problématiques, alo que les difficultés sont bien réparties, l'alternance de trous faciles et de trous délicats assurant un rythme de j agréable. C'est un bon parcours à jouer pour la détente, les meilleurs joueurs seront un peu frustrés dans leurs a tentes de grands défis.

Wheatley Golf Club — 1923

Armthorpe Road
ENG - DONCASTER, S. Yorkshire DN2 5QB

Office	Secrétariat	(44) 01302 - 831 655
Pro shop	Pro-shop	(44) 01302 - 834 085
Fax	Fax	(44) 01302 - 812 736
Web	—	
Situation	Situation	

2 km from Doncaster (pop. 288 854)

Annual closure	Fermeture annuelle	no
Weekly closure	Fermeture hebdomadaire	no

Fees main season Tarifs haute saison — 18 holes

	Week days Semaine	We/Bank holidays We/Férié
Individual Individuel	£ 27	£ 38
Couple Couple	£ 54	£ 76

Full weekdays: £ 33

Caddy	Caddy	no
Electric Trolley	Chariot électrique	no
Buggy	Voiturette	no
Clubs	Clubs	no

Credit cards Cartes de crédit
VISA - Eurocard - MasterCard - JCB - Switch - AMEX

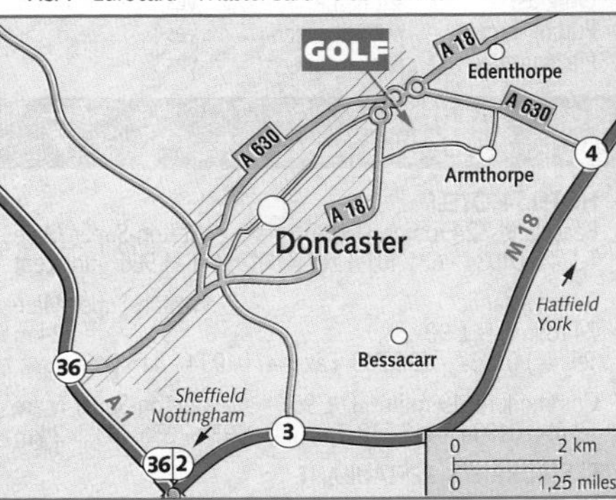

Access Accès : Doncaster → Hatfield, then Armthorpe Road on right hand side.
Map 4 on page 491 Carte 4 Page 491

676

Golf course PARCOURS — 14/2

Site	Site	
Maintenance	Entretien	
Architect	Architecte	Unknown
Type	Type	parkland
Relief	Relief	
Water in play	Eau en jeu	
Exp. to wind	Exposé au vent	
Trees in play	Arbres en jeu	

Scorecard Carte de score	Chp. Chp.	Mens Mess.	Ladies Da.
Length Long.	5765	5598	5237
Par	71	71	73
Slope system	—	—	—

Advised golfing ability 0 12 24 36
Niveau de jeu recommandé
Hcp required Handicap exigé — certificate

Club house & amenities CLUB HOUSE ET ANNEXES — 6/10

Pro shop	Pro-shop	
Driving range	Practice	
Sheltered	couvert	
On grass	sur herbe	yes
Putting-green	putting-green	yes
Pitching-green	pitching green	yes

Hotel facilities ENVIRONNEMENT HOTELIER — 6/10

HOTELS HÔTELS

Grand St. Leger, 20 rooms, D £ 125 — Doncaste
Tel (44) 01302 - 364 111, Fax (44) 01302 - 329 865 — 3 km

Mount Pleasant — Doncaste
40 rooms, D £ 90 — 8 km
Tel (44) 01302 - 868 219, Fax (44) 01302 - 865 130

The Regent Hotel — Doncaste
50 rooms, D £ 90 — 5 km
Tel (44) 01302 - 364 180, Fax (44) 01302 - 322 331

RESTAURANTS RESTAURANT

Mount Pleasant, Tel (44) 01302 - 868 696 — Doncaster 8 km
The Bistro — Doncaster 3 km
Hamilton's, Tel(44) 01302 - 760 770 — Doncaster 3 km

WHITTINGTON HEATH

17	6	7

This is the kind of course you would like to keep to yourself. Very much underrated and often completely unknown, it is a sort of delectable gem that long-hitters will look down upon until they reach the 14th tee. In a none too impressive site of heathland and on the springy turf that comes with peat, the layout was designed by Harry Colt, who knew a thing or two about teasing dog-legs. Missing the open side of the fairway calls for some acrobatics through or over the trees, or some sheepish save-shots back into play. If you score well it's because you thought it out well. The greens are well defended, distinctly well contoured, pretty huge and a pleasure to putt on. What lingers here is an impression of happiness, of having discovered something personal, but which you have to share with others...

C'est le genre de parcours que l'on aimerait garder pour soi. Très sous-estimé, souvent complètement ignoré, c'est une sorte de délicieux petit bijou que les longs frappeurs regarderont de haut jusqu'au moment où ils parviendront au départ du 14. Dans un site de terre de bruyère pas spécialement impressionnant, sur ce gazon élastique que donne un sol de tourbe, le tracé est signé Harry Colt, qui savait notamment faire des doglegs provoquants, où manquer l'ouverture oblige à des coups d'acrobate, ou encore à des retours penauds en sécurité sur le fairway. Et si l'on a bien scoré, c'est que l'on a bien pensé. Bien défendus, très travaillés, et plutôt vastes, les greens sont un plaisir à négocier. C'est cette impression de bonheur qui reste ici, d'avoir découvert quelque chose, même si on est loin d'être le seul...

Whittington Heath Golf Club — 1886

Tamworth Road
ENG - LICHFIELD, Staffs WS14 9PW

Office	Secrétariat	(44) 01543 - 432 317
Pro shop	Pro-shop	(44) 01543 - 432 261
Fax	Fax	(44) 01543 - 432 317
Web	—	
Situation	Situation	

6 km from Lichfield - 20 km from Birmingham (pop. 961 041)

Annual closure	Fermeture annuelle	no
Weekly closure	Fermeture hebdomadaire	no

Fees main season Tarifs haute saison	18 holes	
	Week days Semaine	**We/Bank holidays** We/Férié
Individual Individuel	£ 30	*
Couple Couple	£ 60	*

Full weekdays: £ 40 / * No visitors at w/ends

Caddy	Caddy	no
Electric Trolley	Chariot électrique	no
Buggy	Voiturette	no
Clubs	Clubs	no

Credit cards Cartes de crédit
Visa - Mastercard (Pro shop & green fees)

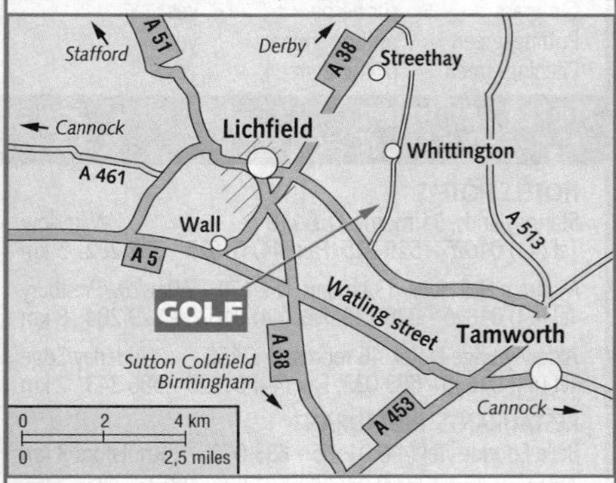

Access Accès : On A51, 4 km from Lichfield Station
Map 7 on page 496 Carte 7 Page 496

Golf course PARCOURS — 17/20

Site	Site	
Maintenance	Entretien	
Architect	Architecte	Harry S. Colt
Type	Type	inland, heathland
Relief	Relief	
Water in play	Eau en jeu	
Exp. to wind	Exposé au vent	
Trees in play	Arbres en jeu	

Scorecard Carte de score	**Chp.** Chp.	**Mens** Mess.	**Ladies** Da.
Length Long.	5841	5542	5117
Par	70	70	72
Slope system	—	—	—

Advised golfing ability Niveau de jeu recommandé — 0 12 24 36
Hcp required Handicap exigé — 65, C.J. Poxon

Club house & amenities CLUB HOUSE ET ANNEXES — 6/10

Pro shop	Pro-shop	
Driving range	Practice	
Sheltered	couvert	no
On grass	sur herbe	no
Putting-green	putting-green	yes
Pitching-green	pitching green	yes

Hotel facilities ENVIRONNEMENT HOTELIER — 7/10

HOTELS HÔTELS

Little Barrow, 24 rooms, D £ 80 — Lichfield
Tel (44) 01543 - 414 500, Fax (44) 01543 - 415 734 — 6 km

Travel Inn, 40 rooms, D £ 41 — Tamworth
Tel (44) 01827 - 54 414, Fax (44) 01827 - 310 420 — 5 km

New Hall, 60 rooms, D £ 190 — Sutton Coldfield
Tel (44) 0121 - 378 2442, Fax (44) 0121 - 378 4637 — 15 km

The Olde Corner House, 23 rooms, D £ 85 — Lichfield
Tel (44) 01543 - 372 182, Fax (44) 01543 - 372 211 — 6 km

RESTAURANTS RESTAURANT

Thrales, Tel (44) 01543 - 255 091 — Lichfield 6 km
New Hall ,Tel (44) 0121 - 378 2442 Sutton Coldfield 15 km

WILMSLOW

16 | 7 | 6

In a typical landscape of rural Cheshire, golf at Wilmslow is a civilized affair with distinct disdain for the ostentatious. Although there is a pleasantly old-fashioned feel to the course, maintenance is definitely modern and probably the best in the region. It is generally prepared in such a way as to not intimidate the less experienced players while providing a respectable challenge for low-handicappers. They can start by attempting to drive the green on hole N°1, cutting the corner of this par 4 by hitting it over the trees. The most surprising thing here is the unity of style, even though a dozen or so architects have altered the layout in their own way, from James Braid to Tom Simpson to Fred Hawtree to Dave Thomas. At least no-one thought of removing the many cross-bunkers that modern-day architects hardly know how to use any more. A course with all the components of a good test of golf, a stiff challenge for the better player, a "human" course that neither flatters the hacker nor demands too much of single-figure handicappers.

Dans un paysage typique du Cheshire rural, le golf à Wilmslow est chose civilisée, dédaignant toute ostentation. Bien que l'on ait ici une sensation agréablement "old fashion", rien de tel dans l'entretien du parcours, l'un des meilleurs de la région sur ce plan. Il est généralement préparé de manière à ne pas intimider le joueur peu aguerri, tout en offrant des défis respectables aux meilleurs. Le plus surprenant ici est l'unité de style, bien qu'une bonne dizaine d'architectes se soient penchés sur ce dessin, de James Braid à Tom Simpson, de Fred Hawtree à Dave Thomas. Au moins personne n'aura songé à en effacer les nombreux "cross-bunkers" que les architectes modernes ne savent plus guère mettre en oeuvre. Un parcours avec tous les éléments d'un bon test, résistant bien aux meilleurs, un parcours à l'échelle humaine, ni pour faire briller les mauvais joueurs à bon compte, ni pour demander l'impossible aux bons.

Wilmslow Golf Club — 1903

Great Warford, Mobberley
ENG - KNUTSFORD, Cheshire WA16 7AY

Office	Secrétariat	(44) 01565 - 872 148
Pro shop	Pro-shop	(44) 01565 - 873 620
Fax	Fax	(44) 01565 - 872 172
Web	—	
Situation	Situation	20 km S of Manchester
Annual closure	Fermeture annuelle	no
Weekly closure	Fermeture hebdomadaire	no

Fees main season Tarifs haute saison	Week days Semaine	We/Bank holidays We/Férié
18 holes		
Individual Individuel	£ 40	£ 50
Couple Couple	£ 80	£ 100

Full weekdays: £ 50

Caddy	Caddy	no
Electric Trolley	Chariot électrique	£ 7
Buggy	Voiturette	no
Clubs	Clubs	£ 10

Credit cards Cartes de crédit
VISA - MasterCard (Pro shop goods only)

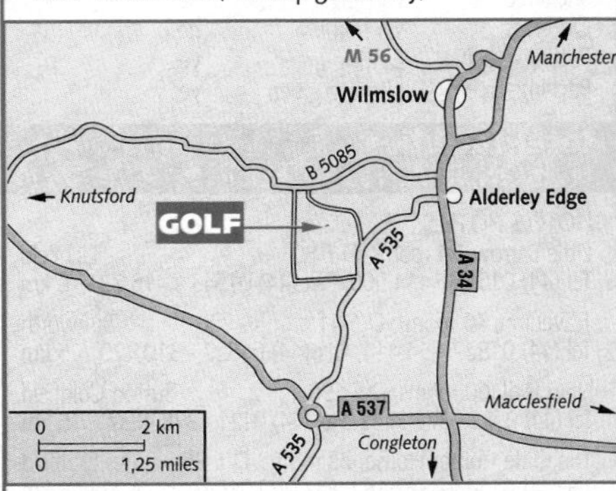

Access Accès : Manchester A34 onto Wilmslow, then B5085 → Mobberley, Knutsford, turn left → David Lewis Centre for Epilepsy, Golf course on left hand side.
Map 4 on page 490 Carte 4 Page 490

Golf course PARCOURS — 16/20

Site	Site	
Maintenance	Entretien	
Architect	Architecte	S. Herd, J. Braid T. Simpson, G.Duncan
Type	Type	inland, open country
Relief	Relief	
Water in play	Eau en jeu	
Exp. to wind	Exposé au vent	
Trees in play	Arbres en jeu	

Scorecard Carte de score	Chp. Chp.	Mens Mess.	Ladies Da.
Length Long.	6044	6044	5293
Par	72	72	74
Slope system	—	—	—

Advised golfing ability Niveau de jeu recommandé: 0 12 24 36
Hcp required Handicap exigé: certificate

Club house & amenities CLUB HOUSE ET ANNEXES — 7/10

Pro shop	Pro-shop	
Driving range	Practice	
Sheltered	couvert	practice area
On grass	sur herbe	yes
Putting-green	putting-green	yes
Pitching-green	pitching green	yes

Hotel facilities ENVIRONNEMENT HOTELIER — 6/10

HOTELS HÔTELS

Stanneylands, 31 rooms, D £ 118 — Wilmslow
Tel (44) 01625 - 525 225, Fax (44) 01625 - 537 282 — 5 km

Mottram Hall Hotel, 132 rooms, D £ 170 — Wilmslow/Prestbury
Tel (44) 01625 - 828 135, Fax (44) 01625 - 829 284 — 8 km

Alderley Edge Hotel, 46 rooms, D £ 150 — Alderley Edge
Tel (44) 01625 - 583 033, Fax (44) 01625 - 586 343 — 2 km

RESTAURANTS RESTAURANT

Belle Epoque ,Tel (44) 01565 - 633 060 — Knutsford 3 km
Alderley Edge, Tel (44) 01625 - 583 033 — Alderley Edge 2 km
Bank Square (booking ess.) — Wilmslow
Tel (44) 01625 - 539 754 — 5 km

WOBURN Duke's Course

17 | 7 | 7

In a very elegant setting with an equally comfortable clubhouse, the three courses at Woburn are pleasantly sited well away from the noise of the outside world. The Duchess course is above average but not in the same league as the Duke's, made famous by the British Masters and the Women's British Open, and the new "Marquess". Except for the first few holes, this one is a rather flat layout which winds its way through a beautiful old forest of pine and chestnut trees, sufficiently in play for the rough not to be too difficult. The sandy soil makes for pleasant golfing all the year round, enhanced by the excellence of the greens, which are never easy to read. The holes all have a distinct individual character but without detracting from a pleasant unity of style. The back-tees are for very good players only, especially from the 13th onward, where some of the par-4s are quite formidable. In such a serious layout, the only regret might be a slight lack of fantasy (maybe a touch of British humour might help).

D'une grande élégance générale, l'ensemble des trois parcours de Woburn bénéficie d'une situation bien à l'écart du monde. Le parcours "Duchess" est honorable, mais ne saurait lutter avec le "Duke's," rendu célèbre par le British Masters et le Women's British Open, et le nouveau "Marquess". Assez plat, sauf dans ses premiers trous, le Duke's est insinué dans une belle et ancienne forêt, où dominent les pins et les châtaigniers, assez présents dans le jeu pour que les roughs ne soient pas trop difficiles. Le sol sablonneux le rend très agréable à jouer toute l'année, et la qualité des greens, pas faciles à lire, augmente encore ce plaisir. Les trous sont bien individualisés, tout en offrant une bonne unité de style. On ne conseillera les départs arrière qu'aux très bons joueurs, surtout à partir du 13, où quelques par 4 sont redoutables. Sur un tracé aussi sérieux, on regrettera peut-être un léger manque de fantaisie (d'humour anglais?)

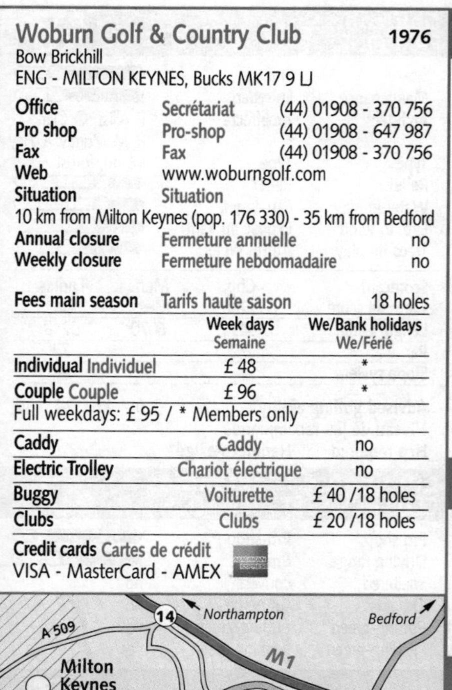

Woburn Golf & Country Club — 1976

Bow Brickhill
ENG - MILTON KEYNES, Bucks MK17 9 LJ

Office	Secrétariat	(44) 01908 - 370 756
Pro shop	Pro-shop	(44) 01908 - 647 987
Fax	Fax	(44) 01908 - 370 756
Web	www.woburngolf.com	
Situation	Situation	

10 km from Milton Keynes (pop. 176 330) - 35 km from Bedford

Annual closure	Fermeture annuelle	no
Weekly closure	Fermeture hebdomadaire	no

Fees main season Tarifs haute saison	18 holes	
	Week days / Semaine	We/Bank holidays / We/Férié
Individual Individuel	£ 48	*
Couple Couple	£ 96	*

Full weekdays: £ 95 / * Members only

Caddy	Caddy	no
Electric Trolley	Chariot électrique	no
Buggy	Voiturette	£ 40 /18 holes
Clubs	Clubs	£ 20 /18 holes

Credit cards Cartes de crédit
VISA - MasterCard - AMEX

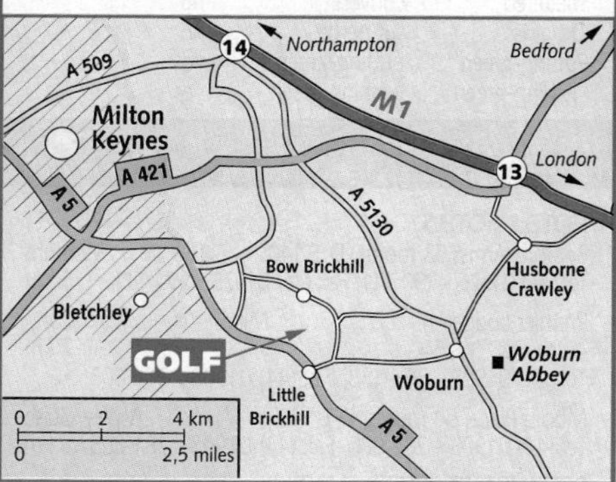

Access Accès : London M1 North. Jct 13 into Woburn Sands. Left to Woburn. After 0.75 km (1/2 m), right at sign.
Map 7 on page 496 Carte 7 Page 496

Golf course — PARCOURS — 17/20

Site	Site	
Maintenance	Entretien	
Architect	Architecte	Charles Lawrie
Type	Type	inland, forest
Relief	Relief	
Water in play	Eau en jeu	
Exp. to wind	Exposé au vent	
Trees in play	Arbres en jeu	

Scorecard Carte de score	Chp. Chp.	Mens Mess.	Ladies Da.
Length Long.	6264	5898	5454
Par	72	72	75
Slope system	—	—	—

Advised golfing ability Niveau de jeu recommandé — 0 12 24 36
Hcp required Handicap exigé — 28 Men, 36 Ladies

Club house & amenities — CLUB HOUSE ET ANNEXES — 7/10

Pro shop	Pro-shop	
Driving range	Practice	
Sheltered	couvert	no
On grass	sur herbe	no
Putting-green	putting-green	yes
Pitching-green	pitching green	yes

Hotel facilities — ENVIRONNEMENT HOTELIER — 7/10

HOTELS HÔTELS

Bedford Arms, 53 rooms, D £ 140 — Woburn
Tel (44) 01525 - 290 441, Fax (44) 01525 - 290 432 — 5 km

Premier Lodge — Milton Keynes/Caldecotte
40 rooms, D £ 50 — 7 km
Tel (44) 01908 - 366 188, Fax (44) 01908 - 366 603

Moore Place, 54 rooms, D £ 120 — Aspley Guise
Tel (44) 01908 - 282 000, Fax (44) 01908 - 281 888 — 6 km

RESTAURANTS RESTAURANT

Paris House, Tel (44) 01525 - 290 692 — Woburn 5 km
The Birch (Pub w. food), Tel(44) 01525 - 290 295 — Woburn
Bell Inn, Tel (44) 01525 - 290 280 — Woburn

WOBURN Marquess

17 | 7 | 7

Compared with the well-known Duke's Course, this new "Marquess" layout puts more emphasis on driving, one of the key's to playing golf at the highest level today. It is also much wider and provides a striking contrast with the other two courses which grace this huge estate. Its character stems primarily from the surroundings, lined with pine-trees like its neighbours, but also oak, chestnut, beech or spruce trees. Some of them stand out from the backdrop of forest to infringe on your game without actually blocking your view. This just means that you have to flight the ball or take a few calculated risks. The greens are pretty huge and well-contoured and have been shaped to provide a number of highly interesting pin-positions. Their contours and areas around the greens have been carefully designed and call for reflection before hitting an approach shot. One might have wished for a little more sophistication in bunker design, but the architects deliberately adhered to a certain British tradition in this respect. Interestingly, the only water hazards are to be found on hole No 12.

Par rapport au Duke's Course bien connu, ce nouveau "Marquess" met l'accent sur le driving, l'une des clefs du jeu de haut niveau moderne. Mais il est aussi beaucoup plus large et offre un vrai contraste avec les deux autres parcours de ce vaste domaine. Son caractère, c'est d'abord l'environnement, avec des pins comme chez ses voisins, mais plus encore des chênes, châtaigniers, hêtres ou épicéas. Certains d'entre eux se détachent de l'arrière-plan forestier pour venir interférer sur le jeu sans obstruer la vue, obligeant à travailler la balle ou à mesurer les risques. Les greens sont assez vastes et ondulés, avec pas mal de positions intéressantes de drapeaux. Leurs contours et leurs alentours ont été bien travaillés, ce qui oblige à une certaine réflexion avant de jouer les approches. On aurait peut-être pu souhaiter un dessin un peu plus sophistiqué des bunkers, mais les architectes sont volontairement restés dans une certaine tradition britannique de dessin. A noter que les seuls obstacles d'eau se trouvent au 12.

Woburn Golf & Country Club — 1999

Bow Brickhill
ENG - MILTON KEYNES, Bucks MK17 9 LJ

Office	Secrétariat	(44) 01908 - 370 756
Pro shop	Pro-shop	(44) 01908 - 647 987
Fax	Fax	(44) 01908 - 370 756
Web	www.woburngolf.com	
Situation	Situation	

10 km from Milton Keynes (pop. 176 330) - 35 km from Bedford

Annual closure	Fermeture annuelle	no
Weekly closure	Fermeture hebdomadaire	no

Fees main season Tarifs haute saison	**Week days** Semaine	**We/Bank holidays** We/Férié
Individual Individuel		*
Couple Couple		*

18 holes

Softspikes only / * Members only

Caddy	Caddy	no
Electric Trolley	Chariot électrique	no
Buggy	Voiturette	£ 40 /18 holes
Clubs	Clubs	£ 20 /18 holes

Credit cards Cartes de crédit
VISA - MasterCard - AMEX

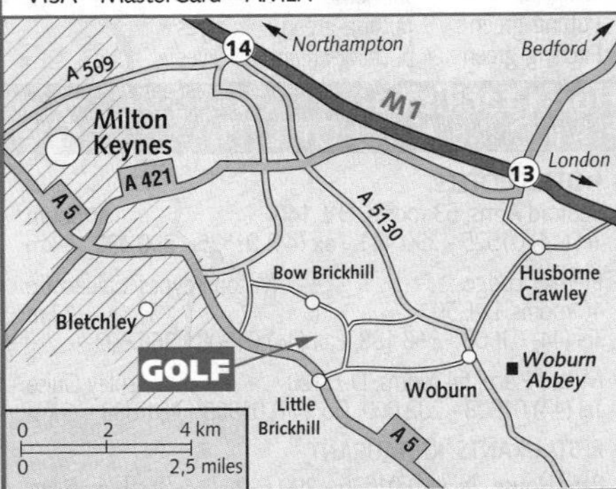

Access Accès : London M1 North. Jct 13 into Woburn Sands. Left to Woburn. After 0.75 km (1/2 m), right at sign.
Map 7 on page 496 Carte 7 Page 496

Golf course PARCOURS — 17/20

Site	Site	
Maintenance	Entretien	
Architect	Architecte	P. Alliss, C. Clark R. McMurray, A. Hay
Type	Type	inland, forest
Relief	Relief	
Water in play	Eau en jeu	
Exp. to wind	Exposé au vent	
Trees in play	Arbres en jeu	

Scorecard Carte de score	**Chp.** Chp.	**Mens** Mess.	**Ladies** Da.
Length Long.	6493	6070	5248
Par	72	72	72
Slope system	—	—	—

Advised golfing ability — 0 12 24 36
Niveau de jeu recommandé
Hcp required Handicap exigé

Club house & amenities CLUB HOUSE ET ANNEXES — 7/10

Pro shop	Pro-shop	
Driving range	Practice	
Sheltered	couvert	no
On grass	sur herbe	no
Putting-green	putting-green	yes
Pitching-green	pitching green	yes

Hotel facilities ENVIRONNEMENT HOTELIER — 7/10

HOTELS HÔTELS

Bedford Arms, 53 rooms, D £ 140 — Woburn 5 km
Tel (44) 01525 - 290 441, Fax (44) 01525 - 290 432

Premier Lodge — Milton Keynes/Caldecotte
40 rooms, D £ 50 — 7 km
Tel (44) 01908 - 366 188, Fax (44) 01908 - 366 603

Moore Place, 54 rooms, D £ 120 — Aspley Guise 6 km
Tel (44) 01908 - 282 000, Fax (44) 01908 - 281 888

RESTAURANTS RESTAURANT

Paris House, Tel (44) 01525 - 290 692 — Woburn 5 km
The Birch (Pub w. food), Tel (44) 01525 - 290 295 — Woburn
Bell Inn, Tel (44) 01525 - 290 280 — Woburn

WOKING

16 | 6 | 6

The second of the threesome of "Ws", we could almost write the same report for each one, although each does have its own personality. Here it all starts with the clubhouse, as British as a cric-et pavilion where you drink tea after your round. Otherwise the landscape is the same as on the other two ourses, with heather just about everywhere you look. Isn't it about time someone invented a special "hea-her wedge" to help get balls back onto the fairway? And heather it is that puts the most pressure on your ee-shot here, where apprehension will always be your worst enemy. Add to this first class bunkering and ery subtle, medium-sized greens that need time and patience to figure out and you realise that although a ery fair proposition, Woking is a difficult course for carding a good score. A charming site, but watch out or its bite...

vec West Hill et Worplesdon, ce sont de faux triplés. On pourrait d'ailleurs imaginer le même texte, avec ois copies. Chacun a son caractère. Celui-ci commence par son Clubhouse, à ce point British que l'on magine un pavillon de cricket, où l'on boit le thé à la fin de la partie. Sinon, le paysage est analogue, avec ne omniprésente bruyère dont il faudra bien que quelqu'un dessine un jour un "heather wedge" pour en ortir. C'est d'ailleurs cette possibilité qui met tant de pression sur les coups de départ : en golf aussi, la eur est mauvaise conseillère. Et si l'on ajoute un bunkering de premier ordre, ainsi que des greens de taille oyenne, mais d'une telle subtilité qu'il faut du temps et de la patience pour les comprendre, on se doute ue, en dépit de sa franchise, Woking n'est pas un parcours évident à scorer. Derrière le charme du lieu, il y de solides mâchoires.

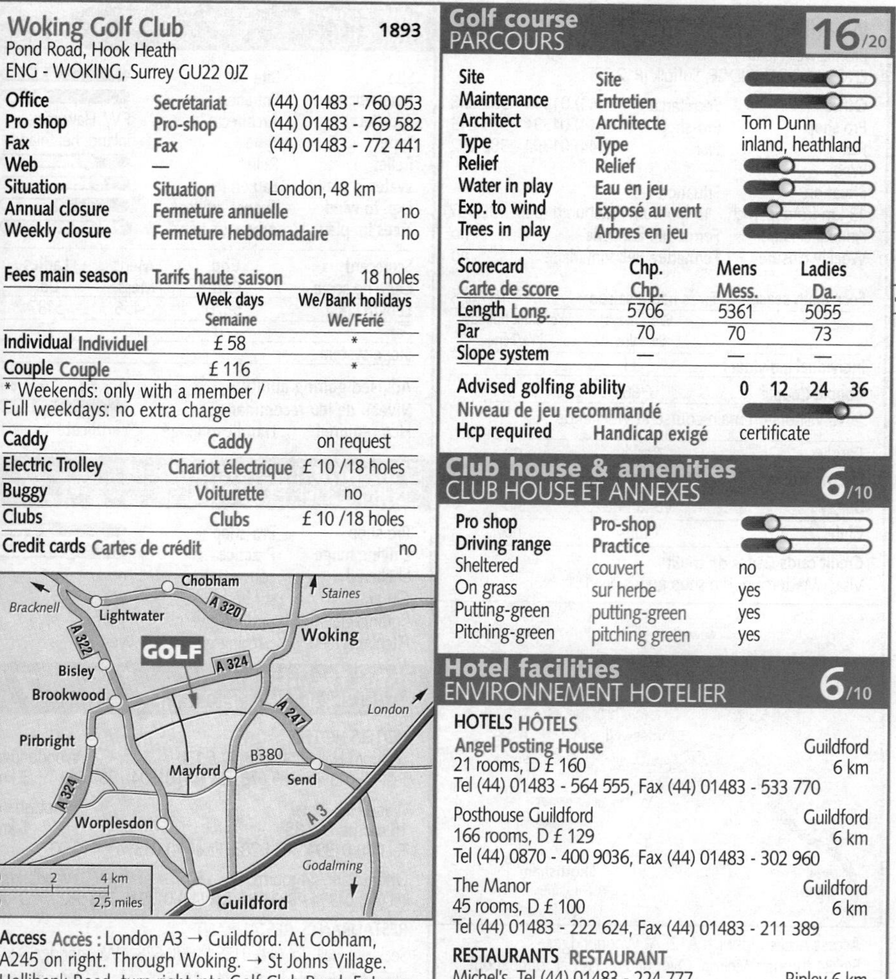

Woking Golf Club — 1893

Pond Road, Hook Heath
ENG - WOKING, Surrey GU22 0JZ

Office	Secrétariat	(44) 01483 - 760 053
Pro shop	Pro-shop	(44) 01483 - 769 582
Fax	Fax	(44) 01483 - 772 441
Web	—	
Situation	Situation	London, 48 km
Annual closure	Fermeture annuelle	no
Weekly closure	Fermeture hebdomadaire	no

Fees main season Tarifs haute saison	18 holes	
	Week days / Semaine	We/Bank holidays / We/Férié
Individual Individuel	£ 58	*
Couple Couple	£ 116	*

* Weekends: only with a member / Full weekdays: no extra charge

Caddy	Caddy	on request
Electric Trolley	Chariot électrique	£ 10 /18 holes
Buggy	Voiturette	no
Clubs	Clubs	£ 10 /18 holes
Credit cards	Cartes de crédit	no

Access Accès : London A3 → Guildford. At Cobham, A245 on right. Through Woking. → St Johns Village. Hollibank Road, turn right into Golf Club Road. Entrance on right at end. **Map 8 on page 498** Carte 8 Page 498

Golf course — PARCOURS — 16/20

Site	Site	
Maintenance	Entretien	
Architect	Architecte	Tom Dunn
Type	Type	inland, heathland
Relief	Relief	
Water in play	Eau en jeu	
Exp. to wind	Exposé au vent	
Trees in play	Arbres en jeu	

Scorecard Carte de score	Chp. Chp.	Mens Mess.	Ladies Da.
Length Long.	5706	5361	5055
Par	70	70	73
Slope system	—	—	—

Advised golfing ability 0 12 24 36
Niveau de jeu recommandé
Hcp required Handicap exigé — certificate

Club house & amenities — CLUB HOUSE ET ANNEXES — 6/10

Pro shop	Pro-shop	
Driving range	Practice	
Sheltered	couvert	no
On grass	sur herbe	yes
Putting-green	putting-green	yes
Pitching-green	pitching green	yes

Hotel facilities — ENVIRONNEMENT HOTELIER — 6/10

HOTELS HÔTELS

Angel Posting House — Guildford 6 km
21 rooms, D £ 160
Tel (44) 01483 - 564 555, Fax (44) 01483 - 533 770

Posthouse Guildford — Guildford 6 km
166 rooms, D £ 129
Tel (44) 0870 - 400 9036, Fax (44) 01483 - 302 960

The Manor — Guildford 6 km
45 rooms, D £ 100
Tel (44) 01483 - 222 624, Fax (44) 01483 - 211 389

RESTAURANTS RESTAURANT

Michel's, Tel (44) 01483 - 224 777 — Ripley 6 km

Café de Paris, Tel (44) 01483 - 34 896 — Guildford 6 km

WOODBRIDGE

14 | 7 | 7

Since 1893, Woodbridge has moved with the times and got equipped with a modern clubhous in the early 1970s. Once much wider, the course has become much tighter as the trees hav grown, a factor rarely given full consideration but one which can and will significantly change the designer original intentions. A lot of courses should be studying the question right now. As it happens, the trees Woodbridge hardly make it the ideal course for wayward hitters or beginners, unless they can master a 1 iro off the tee, which for the latter at least is hardly likely. This is a pity because here you have a very good test golf where many holes widen out after the driving area and things get a little easier if you stay out of the hea ther. Those of you who can flight the ball either way will enjoy Woodbridge, a fine course and an excelle test, but never an ordeal. Very pleasant to play with the family, for fun.

Depuis 1893, Woodbridge a évolué avec le temps, et s'est doté d'un Clubhouse moderne vers 1970. Autrefo large, le parcours est devenu beaucoup plus étroit avec la croissance des arbres : c'est un élément rareme pris en compte, alors qu'il peut beaucoup modifier les intentions originales des architectes. Cette questic doit en tout cas se poser pour beaucoup de parcours. En l'occurrence, ce détail empêche de conseill Woodbridge aux frappeurs pas trop précis et aux débutants, à moins qu'ils ne soient des maîtres du fer 1, qui serait étonnant, du moins chez les débutants. C'est dommage car c'est un très bon test de golf, beaucou de trous s'élargissent après la zone de drive, et les choses vont mieux si l'on a évité la bruyère. Les tr vailleurs de balle s'amuseront beaucoup sur ce beau parcours, un bon test sans être une bataille, et tr agréable à jouer en famille, pour le plaisir.

682

Woodbridge Golf Club — 1893

Bromeswell Heath
ENG - WOODBRIDGE, Suffolk IP12 2PF

Office	Secrétariat	(44) 01394 - 382 038
Pro shop	Pro-shop	(44) 01394 - 383 213
Fax	Fax	(44) 01394 - 382 392
Web	—	
Situation	Situation	

13 km from Ipswich - 15 km from Aldeburgh (pop. 130 157)

Annual closure	Fermeture annuelle	no
Weekly closure	Fermeture hebdomadaire	no

Fees main season Tarifs haute saison	18 holes	
	Week days Semaine	**We/Bank holidays** We/Férié
Individual Individuel	£ 33	*
Couple Couple	£ 66	*

* No visitors on main course at weekends

Caddy	Caddy	no
Electric Trolley	Chariot électrique	no
Buggy	Voiturette	no
Clubs	Clubs	no

Credit cards Cartes de crédit
Visa - Mastercard (Pro shop goods only)

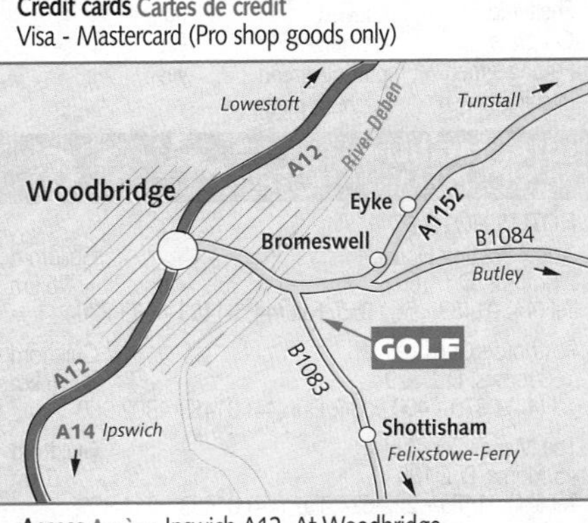

Access Accès : Ipswich A12. At Woodbridge, B1084 through Melton. Over bridge. Left at roundabout. Golf course 200 m on the right.
Map 7 on page 497 Carte 7 Page 497

Golf course — PARCOURS — 14/20

Site	Site	
Maintenance	Entretien	
Architect	Architecte	F.W. Hawtree
Type	Type	inland, heathland
Relief	Relief	
Water in play	Eau en jeu	
Exp. to wind	Exposé au vent	
Trees in play	Arbres en jeu	

Scorecard Carte de score	**Chp.** Chp.	**Mens** Mess.	**Ladies** Da.
Length Long.	5670	5456	5137
Par	70	70	73
Slope system	—	—	—

Advised golfing ability Niveau de jeu recommandé — 0 12 24 36
Hcp required Handicap exigé — certificate

Club house & amenities — CLUB HOUSE ET ANNEXES — 7/10

Pro shop	Pro-shop	
Driving range	Practice	
Sheltered	couvert	no
On grass	sur herbe	yes
Putting-green	putting-green	yes
Pitching-green	pitching green	yes

Hotel facilities — ENVIRONNEMENT HOTELIER — 7/10

HOTELS HÔTELS

Seckford Hall, 32 rooms, D £ 130 — Woodbridge 3 km
Tel (44) 01394 - 385 678, Fax (44) 01394 - 380 610

Wood Hall Hotel — Shottisham 6 km
15 rooms, D £ 85
Tel (44) 01394 - 411 283, Fax (44) 01394 - 410 007

Ufford Park, 44 rooms, D £ 130 — Woodbridge 3 km
Tel (44) 01394 - 383 555, Fax (44) 01394 - 383 582

RESTAURANTS RESTAURANT

Seckford Hall, Tel (44) 01394 - 385678 — Woodbridge 3 km
Ufford Park, Tel (44) 01394 - 383555 — Woodbridge
The Captain's Table, Tel (44) 01394 - 383 145 — Woodbridge

WOODBURY PARK The Oaks

15 | 9 | 6

As this course belongs to Nigel Mansell, it is only logical to drive around it rather than walk. It is actually pretty hilly but it won't wear you out, at least not physically. Mentally, chronic hookers might find their ball in deep trouble on at least one half of the holes. Opened in 1992, this 18-hole course is still maturing, although the well-wooded countryside has retained its typical Devonshire landscape. Holes through the woods alternate with holes over open space where water hazards beckon (on 7 holes). Add to this some pretty huge and deep bunkers with high lips and you can feel a very distinct American influence where target golf is the order of the day. There is no way you can roll your ball onto the greens. This is a very interesting test where you should play from the tee-boxes designed for your level of ability. Beginners will certainly feel more comfortable on the neighbouring 9-holer, unless they prefer a little fishing, the swimming pool, tennis courts or aerobics available in this very well equipped resort.

Comme ce golf appartient à Nigel Mansell, il est assez logique de le jouer en voiture ! Il est effectivement assez accidenté mais pas épuisant, sauf mentalement pour les spécialistes du hook, qui risquent la sortie de route sur une bonne moitié des trous. Ouvert en 1992, le 18 trous n'a pas encore atteint sa maturité, même si le paysage bien boisé a gardé son style de campagne typique du Devon. Il alterne les trous très boisés et les espaces plus ouverts, où les obstacles d'eau sont dangereux (sur sept trous). Si l'on ajoute les bunkers plutôt vastes, profonds avec des faces très relevées, on a ici une sensation très nette d'influence américaine, et il n'est pas question de faire rouler la balle. C'est un test très intéressant, si l'on joue les départs à son niveau. Les débutants seront plus à l'aise sur le 9 trous voisin, à moins de se livrer aux plaisirs de la pêche, de la piscine, du tennis ou de l'aréobic que propose ce club très bien équipé.

Woodbury Park Golf & Country Club 1992

Woodbury Castle, Woodbury
ENG - EXETER EX5 1JJ

Office	Secrétariat	(44) 01395 - 233 382
Pro shop	Pro-shop	(44) 01395 - 233 382
Fax	Fax	(44) 01395 - 233 384
Web	www.woodburypark.co.uk	
Situation	Situation	

9 km SE of Exeter (pop. 98 125)

Annual closure	Fermeture annuelle	no
Weekly closure	Fermeture hebdomadaire	no

Fees main season Tarifs haute saison		18 holes
	Week days Semaine	**We/Bank holidays** We/Férié
Individual Individuel	£ 30	£ 40
Couple Couple	£ 60	£ 80

Full days: £ 60 / £ 80 (week ends)

Caddy	Caddy	no
Electric Trolley	Chariot électrique	no
Buggy	Voiturette	£ 20 /18 holes
Clubs	Clubs	£ 12.50 /18 holes

Credit cards Cartes de crédit
VISA - MasterCard

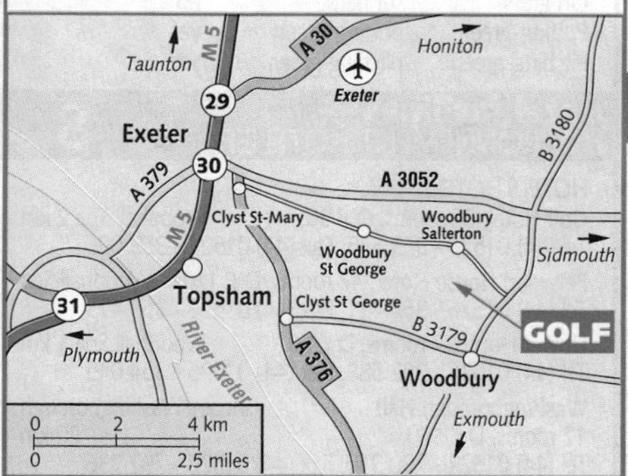

Access Accès : M5 Jct 30. A376 to Sidmouth/Exmouth. Take A3052 to Sidmouth. Turn right at Half Way House Inn.
Map 6 on page 495 Carte 6 Page 495

Golf course PARCOURS 15/20

Site	Site	
Maintenance	Entretien	
Architect	Architecte	J. Hamilton Stutt
Type	Type	inland, parkland
Relief	Relief	
Water in play	Eau en jeu	
Exp. to wind	Exposé au vent	
Trees in play	Arbres en jeu	

Scorecard Carte de score	**Chp.** Chp.	**Mens** Mess.	**Ladies** Da.
Length Long.	6252	6030	5201
Par	72	72	73
Slope system	—	—	—

Advised golfing ability Niveau de jeu recommandé: 0 12 24 36
Hcp required Handicap exigé: certificate

Club house & amenities CLUB HOUSE ET ANNEXES 9/10

Pro shop	Pro-shop	
Driving range	Practice	
Sheltered	couvert	18 bays
On grass	sur herbe	yes
Putting-green	putting-green	yes (3)
Pitching-green	pitching green	yes

Hotel facilities ENVIRONNEMENT HOTELIER 6/10

HOTELS HÔTELS

Rougemont Thistle, 88 rooms, D £ 75 — Exeter 9 km
Tel (44) 01392 - 54 982, Fax (44) 01392 - 420 928

Royal Clarence Hotel, 57 rooms, D £ 135 — Exeter 9 km
Tel (44) 01392 - 319 955, Fax (44) 01392 - 439 423

Barton Cross Hotel — Stoke Canon 15 km
8 rooms, D £ 90
Tel (44) 01392 - 841 245, Fax (44) 01392 - 841 942

RESTAURANTS RESTAURANT

Michael Caines (R. Clarence) — Exeter 9 km
Tel (44) 01392 - 310 031

Barton Cross Hotel, Tel (44) 01392 - 841 245 — Exeter 15 km

Brazz, Tel (44) 01392 - 252 525 — Exeter 9 km

WOODHALL SPA Hotchkin

18 | 7 | 8

Woodhall Spa is still a very important leisure and holiday centre, like a sort of wood-strewn oasis in the middle of the Lincolnshire countryside with a large training centre and two courses (the other one, "Bracken", is a Donald Steel design) acquired by the English Golf Union in 1995. The Hotchkin course is regularly ranked amongst the best in Britain. Originally laid out by Vardon and Colt amidst pines, birch-trees and heather on ideal sandy soil, it was re-designed by the owner, Hotchkin. The number one requirement is to keep your drive in play and the ball alive in order to square up to some of the toughest second (and third) shots you could imagine. You then avoid the bunkers: you can spend quite some time there, especially on the par 3s. Might we add that to avoid putting beginners off the game altogether, here they will be better off watching or carrying someone's bag. Hiring a caddie is also money well spent.

Ancienne ville d'eau, Woodhall Spa est resté un centre de loisirs et de vacances important, comme une sorte d'oasis boisée au milieu de la campagne du Lincolnshire, à l'instar de Pinehurst aux USA. Avec deux parcours (le second est de Donald Steel) et un centre d'entraînement cet ensemble récemment acquis par la Fédération Anglaise de Golf est de toute beauté. Le Hotchkin est régulièrement classé parmi les meilleurs de Grande-Bretagne et le mérite largement. Tracé par Vardon et Colt dans les pins, les bouleaux et la bruyère, sur un sol sablonneux idéal, il a été redessiné par le propriétaire, Hotchkin. Il exige d'abord de garder la balle en jeu du départ, afin d'être encore vivant pour affronter quelques-uns des deuxièmes coups les plus difficiles qui soient (comme les troisièmes !), où il importe d'éviter des bunkers où l'on peut rester longtemps, notamment sur les par 3. On ajoutera seulement que les débutants doivent porter le sac des autres joueurs s'ils ne veulent pas se décourager, et que prendre un caddie est un bon investissement.

Woodhall Spa Golf Club — 1905

The Broadway
ENG - WOODHALL SPA, Lincolnshire LN10 6PU

Office	Secrétariat	(44) 01526 - 352 511
Pro shop	Pro-shop	(44) 01526 - 352 511
Fax	Fax	(44) 01526 - 352 778
Web	www.englishgolfunion.org	
Situation	Situation	21 km E of Lincoln
Annual closure	Fermeture annuelle	no
Weekly closure	Fermeture hebdomadaire	no

Fees main season Tarifs haute saison	18 holes	
	Week days / Semaine	We/Bank holidays / We/Férié
Individual Individuel	£ 40	£ 40
Couple Couple	£ 80	£ 80

Full day £ 60

Caddy	Caddy	£ 20 /on request
Electric Trolley	Chariot électrique	no
Buggy	Voiturette	no
Clubs	Clubs	no

Credit cards Cartes de crédit
VISA - MasterCard - Switch - AMEX

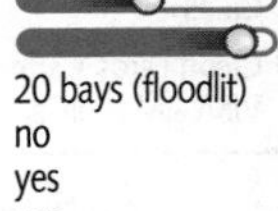

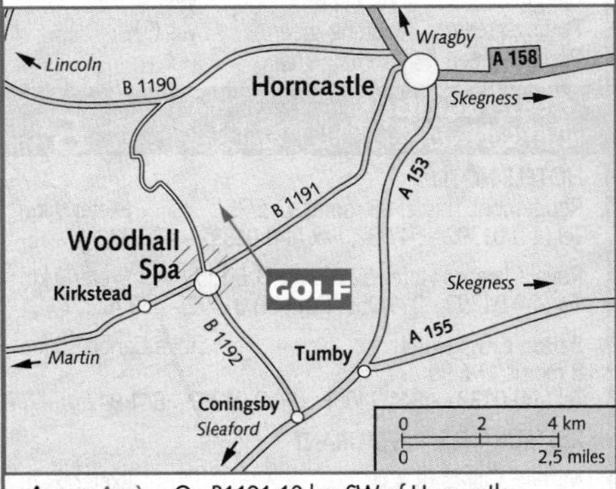

Access Accès : On B1191 10 km SW of Horncastle
Map 4 on page 491 Carte 4 Page 491

Golf course — PARCOURS — 18/20

Site	Site	
Maintenance	Entretien	
Architect	Architecte	Col. S.V. Hotchkin
Type	Type	inland, heathland
Relief	Relief	
Water in play	Eau en jeu	
Exp. to wind	Exposé au vent	
Trees in play	Arbres en jeu	

Scorecard Carte de score	Chp. Chp.	Mens Mess.	Ladies Da.
Length Long.	6250	5897	5203
Par	73	71	73
Slope system	—	—	—

Advised golfing ability 0 12 24 36
Niveau de jeu recommandé
Hcp required Handicap exigé 20 Men, 30 Women

Club house & amenities — CLUB HOUSE ET ANNEXES — 7/10

Pro shop	Pro-shop	
Driving range	Practice	
Sheltered	couvert	20 bays (floodlit)
On grass	sur herbe	no
Putting-green	putting-green	yes
Pitching-green	pitching green	yes

Hotel facilities — ENVIRONNEMENT HOTELIER — 8/10

HOTELS HÔTELS

Golf Hotel, 50 rooms, D £ 90 — Woodhall Spa 2 km
Tel (44) 01526 - 353 535, Fax (44) 01526 - 353 096

Petwood House Hotel, 47 rooms, D £ 110 — Woodhall Spa
Tel (44) 01526 - 352 411, Fax (44) 01526 - 353 473

Dower House, 7 rooms, D £ 60 — Woodhall Spa 1 km
Tel (44) 01526 - 352 588, Fax (44) 01526 - 354 045

Washingborough Hall — Lincoln/Washingborough
12 rooms, D £ 100 — 20 km
Tel (44) 01522 - 790 340, Fax (44) 01522 - 792 936

RESTAURANTS RESTAURANT

The Magpies, — Horncastle
Tel (44) 01507 - 527 004 — 10 km

WORPLESDON

16 | 7 | 6

This is the third of the three "Ws" around Woking, designed by John Abercromby, who worked with, amongst others, the inimitable Tom Simpson. On arriving you notice the winding first hole and the beautiful houses around the course. You never grow tired of that sensation of privilege you get from playing golf over wide open spaces. A watering system has further enhanced green-keeping, and the greens are very quick, so you'd better stay on the right side of the slopes and the right tier of the multi-tiered greens. If you are looking for a brilliant score, the pin placements here will dictate game strategy. While West Hill and Woking are, in a way, courses where the tee-shot is all-important, Worplesdon calls for excellence on your second shot. Choosing between the three would be like having to refuse the starter, main course or dessert in a good restaurant.

C'est le troisième de la trinité de Woking, cette fois dessiné par John Abercromby, qui a travaillé notamment avec l'inimitable Tom Simpson. En arrivant, on remarque d'une part les méandres du premier trou, et la beauté des maisons environnantes. On ne saurait être insensible à cette sensation de privilège que donne le golf dans de beaux espaces. Et l'arrosage a fait encore progresser l'entretien. Les greens sont souvent très rapides, ce qui implique d'être du bon côté des pentes, et sur le bon plateau quand il y en a plusieurs. Le placement des drapeaux va en fait dicter toute la stratégie si l'on veut faire un score brillant. Si West Hill et Woking sont, un peu, des parcours de mise en jeu, Worplesdon est un parcours de seconds coups. On ne choisira pas plus qu'on ne refuse l'entrée, le plat ou le dessert dans un bon restaurant...

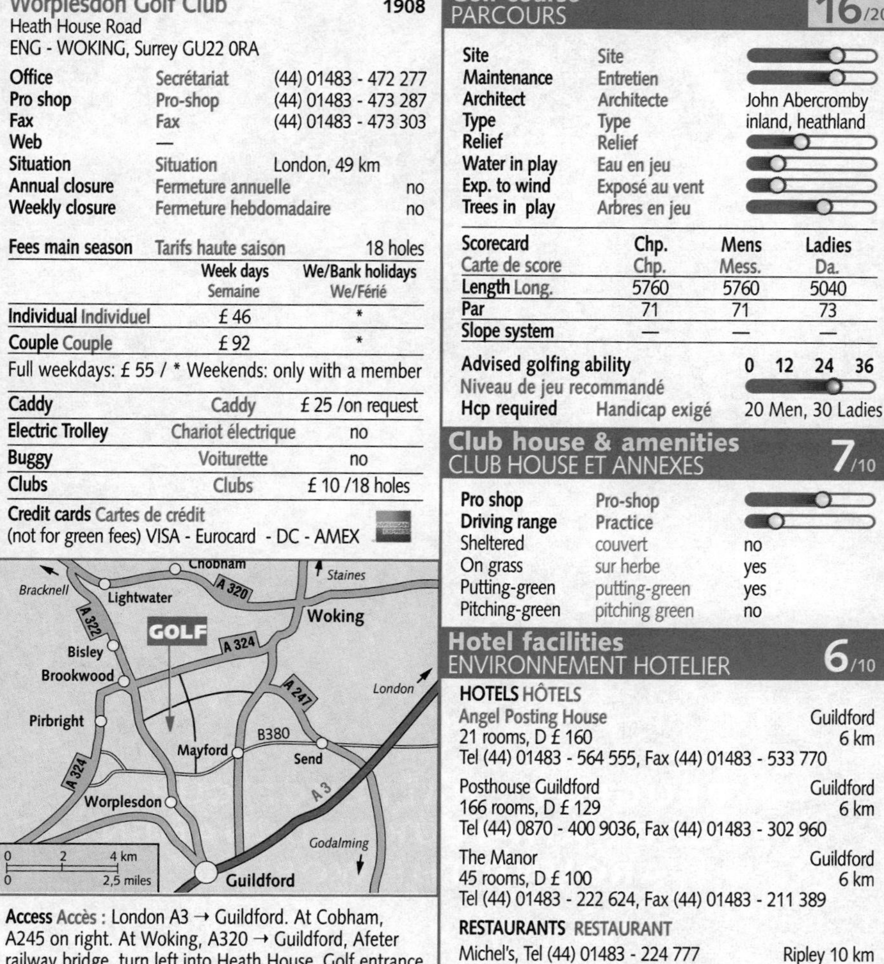

Worplesdon Golf Club — 1908

Heath House Road
ENG - WOKING, Surrey GU22 0RA

Office	Secrétariat	(44) 01483 - 472 277
Pro shop	Pro-shop	(44) 01483 - 473 287
Fax	Fax	(44) 01483 - 473 303
Web	—	
Situation	Situation	London, 49 km
Annual closure	Fermeture annuelle	no
Weekly closure	Fermeture hebdomadaire	no

Fees main season Tarifs haute saison	18 holes	
	Week days Semaine	**We/Bank holidays** We/Férié
Individual Individuel	£ 46	*
Couple Couple	£ 92	*

Full weekdays: £ 55 / * Weekends: only with a member

Caddy	Caddy	£ 25 /on request
Electric Trolley	Chariot électrique	no
Buggy	Voiturette	no
Clubs	Clubs	£ 10 /18 holes

Credit cards Cartes de crédit
(not for green fees) VISA - Eurocard - DC - AMEX

Access Accès : London A3 → Guildford. At Cobham, A245 on right. At Woking, A320 → Guildford, Afeter railway bridge, turn left into Heath House. Golf entrance on right. **Map 8 on page 498** Carte 8 Page 498

Golf course — PARCOURS — 16/20

Site	Site	
Maintenance	Entretien	
Architect	Architecte	John Abercromby
Type	Type	inland, heathland
Relief	Relief	
Water in play	Eau en jeu	
Exp. to wind	Exposé au vent	
Trees in play	Arbres en jeu	

Scorecard Carte de score	**Chp.** Chp.	**Mens** Mess.	**Ladies** Da.
Length Long.	5760	5760	5040
Par	71	71	73
Slope system	—	—	—

Advised golfing ability Niveau de jeu recommandé — 0 12 24 36
Hcp required Handicap exigé — 20 Men, 30 Ladies

Club house & amenities — CLUB HOUSE ET ANNEXES — 7/10

Pro shop	Pro-shop	
Driving range	Practice	
Sheltered	couvert	no
On grass	sur herbe	yes
Putting-green	putting-green	yes
Pitching-green	pitching green	no

Hotel facilities — ENVIRONNEMENT HOTELIER — 6/10

HOTELS HÔTELS

Angel Posting House — Guildford 6 km
21 rooms, D £ 160
Tel (44) 01483 - 564 555, Fax (44) 01483 - 533 770

Posthouse Guildford — Guildford 6 km
166 rooms, D £ 129
Tel (44) 0870 - 400 9036, Fax (44) 01483 - 302 960

The Manor — Guildford 6 km
45 rooms, D £ 100
Tel (44) 01483 - 222 624, Fax (44) 01483 - 211 389

RESTAURANTS RESTAURANT

Michel's, Tel (44) 01483 - 224 777 — Ripley 10 km

Café de Paris, Tel (44) 01483 - 34 896 — Guildford 6 km

Scotland

Muirfield

Scotland
Ecosse

As a country, Scotland is a small in terms of land surface but quite exceptional when it comes to golf, with courses sometimes laid out one after the other in an uninterrupted sequence on either side of the country. There are huge clusters of links course on both the east and the west coasts of Ayrshire.

Here we have included the great links courses but also some lesser known gems around Glasgow and Edinburgh, or between Aberdeen and Inverness. But besides the links courses – Scotland's pride and joy – we have also elected to present a number of inland clubs, some of which have been laid out over areas of immense beauty, for example in the Highlands. Naturally, some people might consider their yardage to be bordering on the "ridiculous" by today's standards, but they are certainly more than a match for your average long-hitter.

As here we are at the very heart of golf, we could quite easily have included "North Inch" in Perth, a course that was played by King James VI in 1603, or again Askernish on the isle of South Uist, but rather than opt for history or unusual surroundings, we preferred Shiskine in Blackwaterfoot which, although only having twelve holes, remains an amazing reference in course design and for the game of golf. This is particularly relevant at a time when the temptation from America or influence from south of the border has pushed green-fees upward, and when golf in Scotland has always been and most of the time always will be a game for everyone.

Courses like Loch Lomond or Carnegie Club at Skibo Castle have built up a huge reputation and we wanted to include them here simply to meet the demand from very many of our readers. It is always difficult, if not impossible, to play them, but you never know the kind of policy they may be adopting in the years ahead. A lot of money has been spent, but the lure of sunnier climes and changes of season are the same as ever. In Scotland, golf courses have always been created by Mother Nature helped by the genius of a few brilliant architects, and golf is a shining light for all. Some courses are snow-bound in Winter, it sometimes rains and the wind can play havoc. But while the best time to play is from April to September, you can tee-off virtually all year... just don't forget to pack a few thick sweaters.

You don't come to Scotland the way you would fly to the Caribbean. You come here to play, breathe and live golf. This is perhaps best symbolised by Kingsbarns, which combines as ever the spirit behind links golf and today's modern techniques. The course makes a spectacular first appearance in this year's edition.

Scotland
Ecosse

L'Ecosse est un petit pays en superficie mais un exceptionnel pays de golf, où les parcours peuvent se succéder de manière pratiquement ininterrompue sur les grandes concentrations de links des côtes Est comme de la côte de l'Ayrshire à l'Ouest.

Nous avons inclus ici les plus grands links, mais aussi de petites merveilles moins connues, rassemblés autour de Glasgow et d'Edimbourg, mais aussi d'Aberdeen à Inverness. En dehors des links qui ont fait la gloire de l'Ecosse, nous avons aussi choisi de vous présenter des parcours " inland", dont la plupart ont été comme posés sur des espaces d'une intense beauté, comme dans les Highlands. Bien sûr, on pourra estimer leur longueur parfois "ridicule", mais en ramener un bon score n'est pas à la portée du premier cogneur venu.

Sans aucun doute, comme nous sommes au cœur du golf, nous aurions presque pu inclure le "North Inch" de Perth, sur un terrain où a joué le roi James VI en 1603, ou encore Askernish dans l'île de South Uist, mais, quitte à être historique ou dépaysant, nous avons préféré Shiskine à Blackwaterfoot, qui compte peut-être douze trous, mais constitue une étonnante référence d'architecture et de jeu. Il n'est pas inutile de rappeler les fondamentaux du dessin de parcours, ou tout au moins les grands témoignages du passé, à l'heure où la tentation américaine ou l'exemple des grands clubs modernes anglais ont poussé les green-fees vers le haut, alors même que le golf en Ecosse a toujours été un jeu pour tous, et le reste, fort heureusement, la plupart du temps.

Des parcours comme Loch Lomond ou Carnegie Club à Skibo Castle étaient de fameuse réputation, nous avons voulu les faire figurer ici, parce que de nombreux lecteurs nous le demandaient. Il est toujours difficile voire impossible de les jouer, mais sait-on jamais quelle politique ils adopteront dans les prochaines années... Beaucoup d'argent y a été investi, mais la course du soleil et le rythme des saisons n'ont guère changé. En Ecosse, les golfs ont toujours été faits par la nature et quelques architectes de génie, le soleil du golf brille pour tous, certains parcours sont enneigés en hiver, la pluie tombe parfois, le vent souffle aussi, et si la meilleure saison va d'avril à septembre, on peut jouer pratiquement toute l'année... avec de gros pulls dans la valise.

On ne vient pas en Ecosse comme dans les Caraïbes. On vient ici pour jouer au golf, pour respirer le golf, vivre le golf. Le symbole en est peut-être Kingsbarns, associant comme jamais l'esprit des links et les techniques modernes, il fait son entrée ici, de manière spectaculaire.

ABOYNE

14 | 6 | 6

There is no shortage of golf courses in the region of Deeside, each one having its own character often shaped by the setting. Aboyne is a real park and is by and large flat, except on the edge of the course where the holes run around a small hill and the slopes from the 11th to the 14th holes take us into more rocky countryside. Reassuringly, particularly for your game strategy, the course is free of hidden hazards as no-one likes to fall into that sort of trap the first time they play a new course. There are though just a few elevated or tiered greens that might cause you trouble. Generally speaking, Aboyne is a little similar to Ballater, only with a little more variety in hole layout.

Cette région du Deeside ne manque pas de parcours de golf, chacun avec son propre caractére, souvent fonction de l'environnement. Aboyne est un véritable parc, généralement plat. Sauf à l'extrémité du parcours où les trous tournent autour d'une petite colline et ces quelques reliefs du 11 au 14 qui nous amènent dans un paysage de lande rocailleuse. Quand on joue un parcours pour la première fois, il n'est pas toujours agréable d'être piégé par des obstacles cachés, mais ici, ce n'est pas le cas, ce qui peut rassurer sur la stratégie à mettre en oeuvre. Seuls quelques greens surélevés, ou à plateau peuvent causer quelques surprises. En règle général, Aboyne est un peu similaire de caractère avec Ballater, mais avec un peu plus de variété de dessin des trous.

Aboyne Golf Club **1883**
Formaston Park
SCO - ABOYNE, Aberdeenshire AB34 5 HE

Office	Secrétariat	(44) 013398 -870 78
Pro shop	Pro-shop	(44) 013398 -863 28
Fax	Fax	(44) 013398 -875 92
Web	—	
Situation	Situation	

48 km W of Aberdeen (pop. 204 885)
19 km W of Banchory (pop. 6 230)

Annual closure	Fermeture annuelle	no
Weekly closure	Fermeture hebdomadaire	no

Fees main season Tarifs haute saison 18 holes

	Week days Semaine	We/Bank holidays We/Férié
Individual Individuel	£ 19	£ 25
Couple Couple	£ 38	£ 50

Full days: £ 22 - £ 28 (Weekends)

Caddy	Caddy	on request
Electric Trolley	Chariot électrique	no
Buggy	Voiturette	no
Clubs	Clubs	yes

Credit cards Cartes de crédit Eurocard - MasterCard

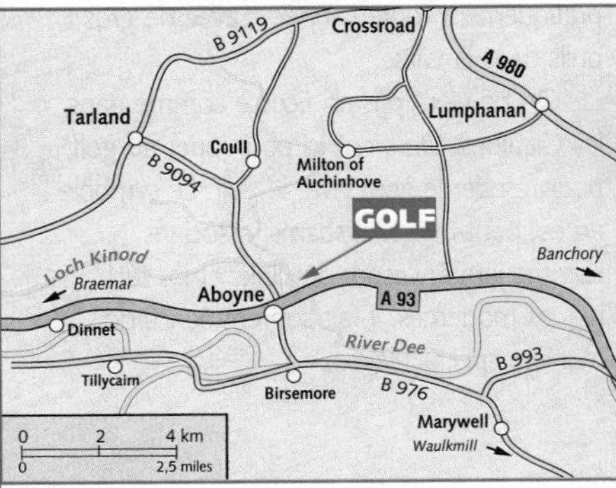

Access Accès : Aberdeen, A93. In Aboyne, turn off to right at club entrance.
Map 1 on page 487 Carte 1 Page 487

Golf course PARCOURS 14/20

Site	Site	
Maintenance	Entretien	
Architect	Architecte	Archie Simpson
Type	Type	parkland
Relief	Relief	
Water in play	Eau en jeu	
Exp. to wind	Exposé au vent	
Trees in play	Arbres en jeu	

Scorecard Carte de score	Chp. Chp.	Mens Mess.	Ladies Da.
Length Long.	5447	5112	4906
Par	68	67	72
Slope system	0	0	0

Advised golfing ability 0 12 24 36
Niveau de jeu recommandé
Hcp required Handicap exigé no

Club house & amenities CLUB HOUSE ET ANNEXES 6/10

Pro shop	Pro-shop	
Driving range	Practice	
Sheltered	couvert	no
On grass	sur herbe	no
Putting-green	putting-green	yes
Pitching-green	pitching green	yes

Hotel facilities ENVIRONNEMENT HOTELIER 6/10

HOTELS HÔTELS
Struan Hall, 4 rooms, D £ 57 — Aboyne c
Tel (44) 01339 - 887 241, Fax (44) 01339 - 887 241

Hilton Craigendarroch, 45 rooms, D £ 150 — Ballater
Tel (44) 013397 - 55 858, Fax (44) 013397 - 55 447 14 km

Glen Lui, 19 rooms, D £ 80 — Ballater 14 km
Tel (44) 013397 - 55 402, Fax (44) 013397 - 55 545

RESTAURANTS RESTAURANT
The Boat Inn (Pub) — Aboyne c
Tel (44) 01339 - 886 137

Conservatory (Darroch Learg) — Ballater 14 km
Tel (44) 01339 - 755 443

ALLOA

15 | 7 | 6

Alloa is one of a bunch of very good inland courses in Scotland, in a region little known by golfing tourists. You shouldn't pass through here without stopping off and playing this fine course, once again restyled by James Braid. Where hasn't the man left his mark in Scotland? If you are a "collector" of James Braid courses, you will recognise his strategic placing of bunkers denoting an astute knowledge of both the game at the highest level and of average players' abilities, a rare feature from a former champion such as he. While there are courses for driving and courses for approach shots, this one demands both to reach greens which are sometimes elevated and even blind and call for special care. This is a hilly course so physical fitness will help.

Alloa fait partie du petit peloton des très bons parcours "inland" d'Ecosse, dans une région assez peu connue des touristes golfiques. Il ne faudrait pas passer par là sans connaître cette belle réalisation, une fois de plus remaniée par James Braid, mais où n'est-il pas intervenu ? Si vous "collectionnez" tous ses parcours, vous retrouverez ici un placement stratégique des obstacles, dénotant une connaissance aiguë du jeu au plus haut niveau mais aussi des joueurs moyens, ce qui est plus rare de la part d'un ancien champion comme lui. S'il est des parcours de drives et des parcours de "seconds coups," celui-ci exige autant des départs aux greens, avec une attention particulière pour attaquer ces derniers, parfois surélevés, voire aveugles. Le relief est ici bien marqué, attention à venir en bonne forme physique.

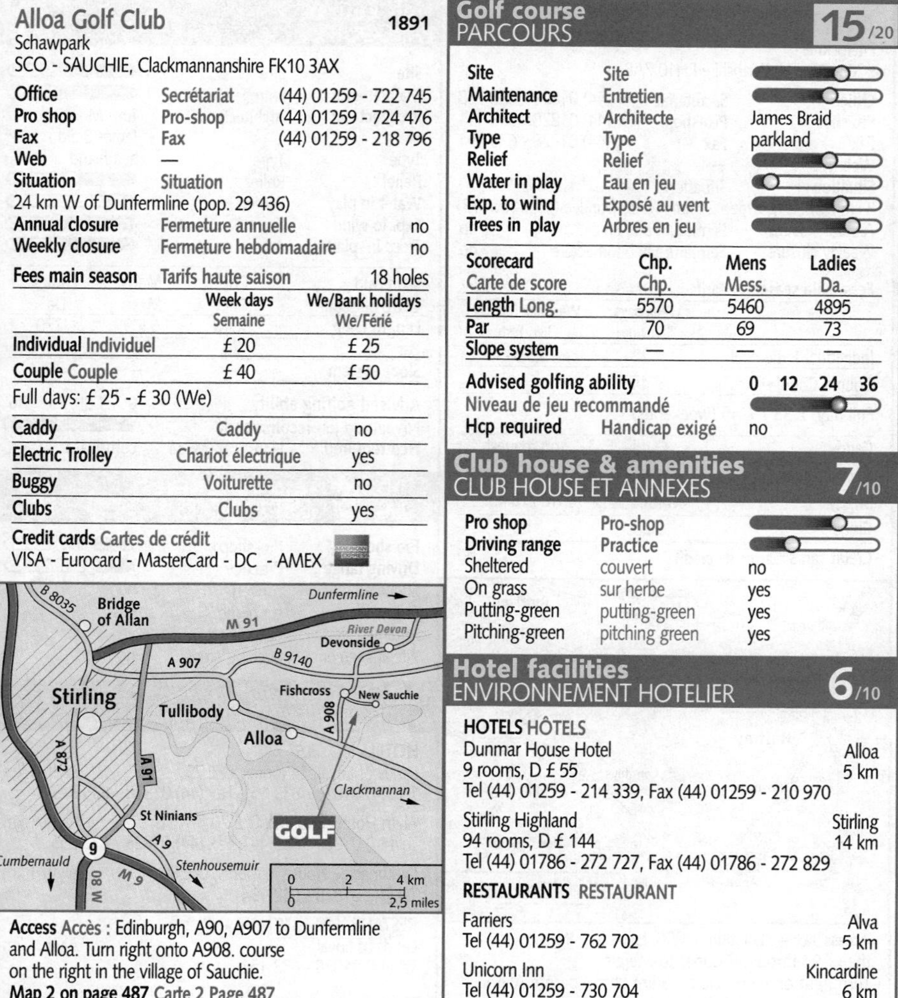

Alloa Golf Club **1891**
Schawpark
SCO - SAUCHIE, Clackmannanshire FK10 3AX

Office	Secrétariat	(44) 01259 - 722 745
Pro shop	Pro-shop	(44) 01259 - 724 476
Fax	Fax	(44) 01259 - 218 796
Web	—	
Situation	Situation	

24 km W of Dunfermline (pop. 29 436)

Annual closure	Fermeture annuelle	no
Weekly closure	Fermeture hebdomadaire	no

Fees main season Tarifs haute saison		18 holes
	Week days Semaine	**We/Bank holidays** We/Férié
Individual Individuel	£ 20	£ 25
Couple Couple	£ 40	£ 50

Full days: £ 25 - £ 30 (We)

Caddy	Caddy	no
Electric Trolley	Chariot électrique	yes
Buggy	Voiturette	no
Clubs	Clubs	yes

Credit cards Cartes de crédit
VISA - Eurocard - MasterCard - DC - AMEX

Access Accès : Edinburgh, A90, A907 to Dunfermline and Alloa. Turn right onto A908. course on the right in the village of Sauchie.
Map 2 on page 487 Carte 2 Page 487

Golf course PARCOURS — 15/20

Site	Site	
Maintenance	Entretien	
Architect	Architecte	James Braid
Type	Type	parkland
Relief	Relief	
Water in play	Eau en jeu	
Exp. to wind	Exposé au vent	
Trees in play	Arbres en jeu	

Scorecard Carte de score	**Chp.** Chp.	**Mens** Mess.	**Ladies** Da.
Length Long.	5570	5460	4895
Par	70	69	73
Slope system	—	—	—

Advised golfing ability Niveau de jeu recommandé — 0 12 24 36
Hcp required Handicap exigé — no

Club house & amenities CLUB HOUSE ET ANNEXES — 7/10

Pro shop	Pro-shop	
Driving range	Practice	
Sheltered	couvert	no
On grass	sur herbe	yes
Putting-green	putting-green	yes
Pitching-green	pitching green	yes

Hotel facilities ENVIRONNEMENT HOTELIER — 6/10

HOTELS HÔTELS

Dunmar House Hotel — Alloa 5 km
9 rooms, D £ 55
Tel (44) 01259 - 214 339, Fax (44) 01259 - 210 970

Stirling Highland — Stirling 14 km
94 rooms, D £ 144
Tel (44) 01786 - 272 727, Fax (44) 01786 - 272 829

RESTAURANTS RESTAURANT

Farriers — Alva 5 km
Tel (44) 01259 - 762 702

Unicorn Inn — Kincardine 6 km
Tel (44) 01259 - 730 704

ALYTH

14 | 6 | 6

Within the immediate vicinity of Blairgowrie, Dundee and Perth, the Alyth course does not have the fame it deserves, partly because fame today comes through hosting top tournaments. This course now is too short for that but is way above average in terms of appeal. With good, well protected greens, endless trees and heather edging the fairways and dangerous bunkers, Alyth requires great accuracy and is ideal for getting your ironwork into good shape. A few very good holes and some superb views over the Perthshire countryside add extra appeal to a guaranteed good day's golfing. The region of Angus also offers a variety facilities for leisure and excursions.

A proximité immédiate de Blairgowrie, Dundee et Perth, le parcours d'Alyth n'a pas connu la notoriété qu'il mérite, en partie parce qu'elle se fait aujourd'hui en recevant de grands tournois et que celui-ci est resté dans l'ombre. Ce parcours est aujourd'hui trop court pour les grandes épreuves, mais son intérêt est nettement au-dessus de la moyenne. Avec de bons greens correctement défendus contre les assauts, des arbres nombreux et la bruyère bordant les fairways, des bunkers dangereux, il demande une grande précision, et c'est idéal pour travailler son jeu de fers. Quelques très bons trous et des vues superbes sur la campagne du Perthshire ajoutent un intérêt supplémentaire à une bonne journée de golf garanti sans souffrances. Et cette région de l'Angus offre de multiples opportunités de loisirs et d'excursions.

692

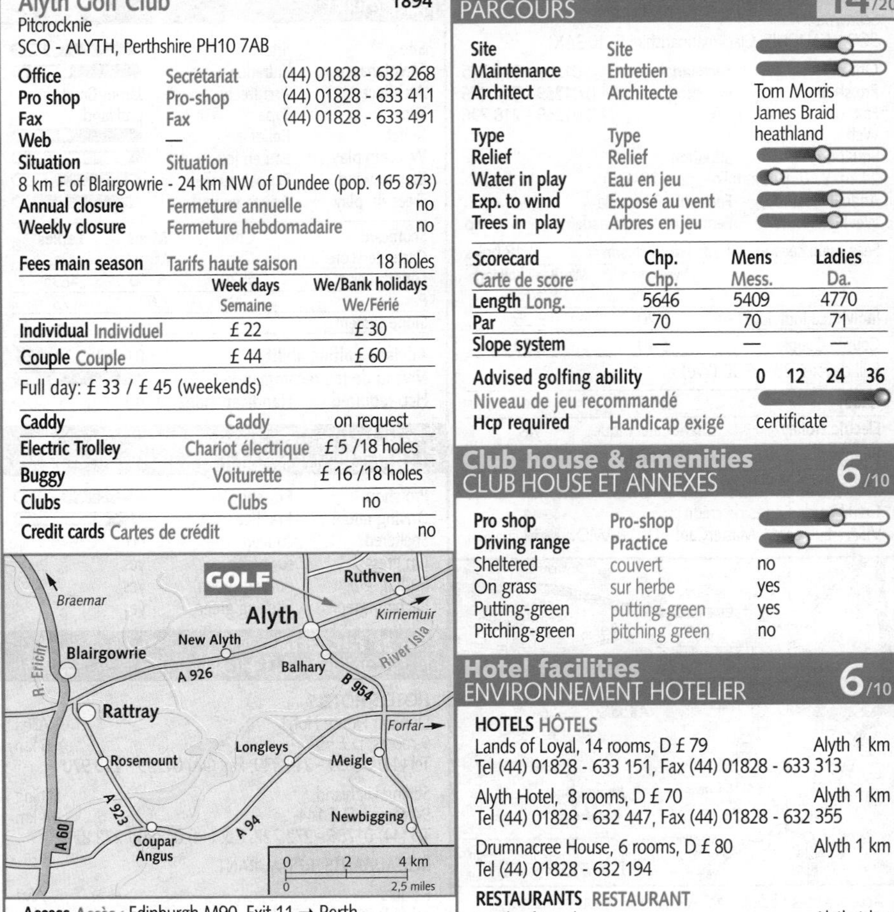

Alyth Golf Club 1894
Pitcrocknie
SCO - ALYTH, Perthshire PH10 7AB

Office	Secrétariat	(44) 01828 - 632 268
Pro shop	Pro-shop	(44) 01828 - 633 411
Fax	Fax	(44) 01828 - 633 491
Web	—	
Situation	Situation	

8 km E of Blairgowrie - 24 km NW of Dundee (pop. 165 873)

Annual closure	Fermeture annuelle	no
Weekly closure	Fermeture hebdomadaire	no

Fees main season Tarifs haute saison	Week days Semaine	We/Bank holidays We/Férié
	18 holes	
Individual Individuel	£ 22	£ 30
Couple Couple	£ 44	£ 60

Full day: £ 33 / £ 45 (weekends)

Caddy	Caddy	on request
Electric Trolley	Chariot électrique	£ 5 /18 holes
Buggy	Voiturette	£ 16 /18 holes
Clubs	Clubs	no
Credit cards	Cartes de crédit	no

Access Accès : Edinburgh M90, Exit 11 → Perth, then A94 through Coupar to Meigle. Turn right on B954. Golf 1.5 km (1 m.) before Alyth.
Map 1 on page 485 Carte 1 Page 485

Golf course PARCOURS — 14/20

Site	Site	
Maintenance	Entretien	
Architect	Architecte	Tom Morris James Braid
Type	Type	heathland
Relief	Relief	
Water in play	Eau en jeu	
Exp. to wind	Exposé au vent	
Trees in play	Arbres en jeu	

Scorecard Carte de score	**Chp.** Chp.	**Mens** Mess.	**Ladies** Da.
Length Long.	5646	5409	4770
Par	70	70	71
Slope system	—	—	—

Advised golfing ability Niveau de jeu recommandé — 0 12 24 36
Hcp required Handicap exigé — certificate

Club house & amenities CLUB HOUSE ET ANNEXES — 6/10

Pro shop	Pro-shop	
Driving range	Practice	
Sheltered	couvert	no
On grass	sur herbe	yes
Putting-green	putting-green	yes
Pitching-green	pitching green	no

Hotel facilities ENVIRONNEMENT HOTELIER — 6/10

HOTELS HÔTELS

Lands of Loyal, 14 rooms, D £ 79 — Alyth 1 km
Tel (44) 01828 - 633 151, Fax (44) 01828 - 633 313

Alyth Hotel, 8 rooms, D £ 70 — Alyth 1 km
Tel (44) 01828 - 632 447, Fax (44) 01828 - 632 355

Drumnacree House, 6 rooms, D £ 80 — Alyth 1 km
Tel (44) 01828 - 632 194

RESTAURANTS RESTAURANT

Lands of Loyal — Alyth 1 km
Tel (44) 01828 - 633 151

AYR (BELLEISLE)

16 | 5 | 7

Most of the visitors to this region head for Prestwick, Royal Troon and Turnberry and might easily neglect a number of little gems of which this is a typical example. Designed by James Braid (who else?) in 1927 to meet the huge demand for new courses, Belleisle was laid out in a public park close to the sea but without the features of a links. This is nonetheless a challenging course with a lot of character where there is something almost odd about the views over the sea in the setting of trees. With no hidden dangers, golfing can be enjoyed without fear as long as you choose the right clubs and the right way of playing them. The weather will decide whether you aim high or low. An ideal course for week-end golfing when the "big" courses are crowded.

La plupart des visiteurs de la région se concentrent sur Prestwick, Royal Troon et Turnberry, et risquent de négliger quelques petits joyaux de moindre réputation. En voici un exemple typique. Dessiné par James Braid en 1927 pour satisfaire une demande galopante de nouveaux parcours, Belleisle a été créé dans un parc public proche de la mer, mais sans les caractéristiques des links. Il n'empêche qu'il s'agit d'un parcours exigeant, avec beaucoup de caractère, où certains points de vue sur l'eau ont quelque chose d'étrange dans cet environnement d'arbres. Sans dissimuler aucun de ses dangesr, ce parcours peut être immédiatement dégusté sans crainte, du moment que l'on y choisità la fois les bons clubs et la bonne manière de s'en servir. Suivant le temps, on pourra y jouer balles roulées ou balles levées. Idéal pour jouer en week-end quand les "grands" sont très difficiles d'accès.

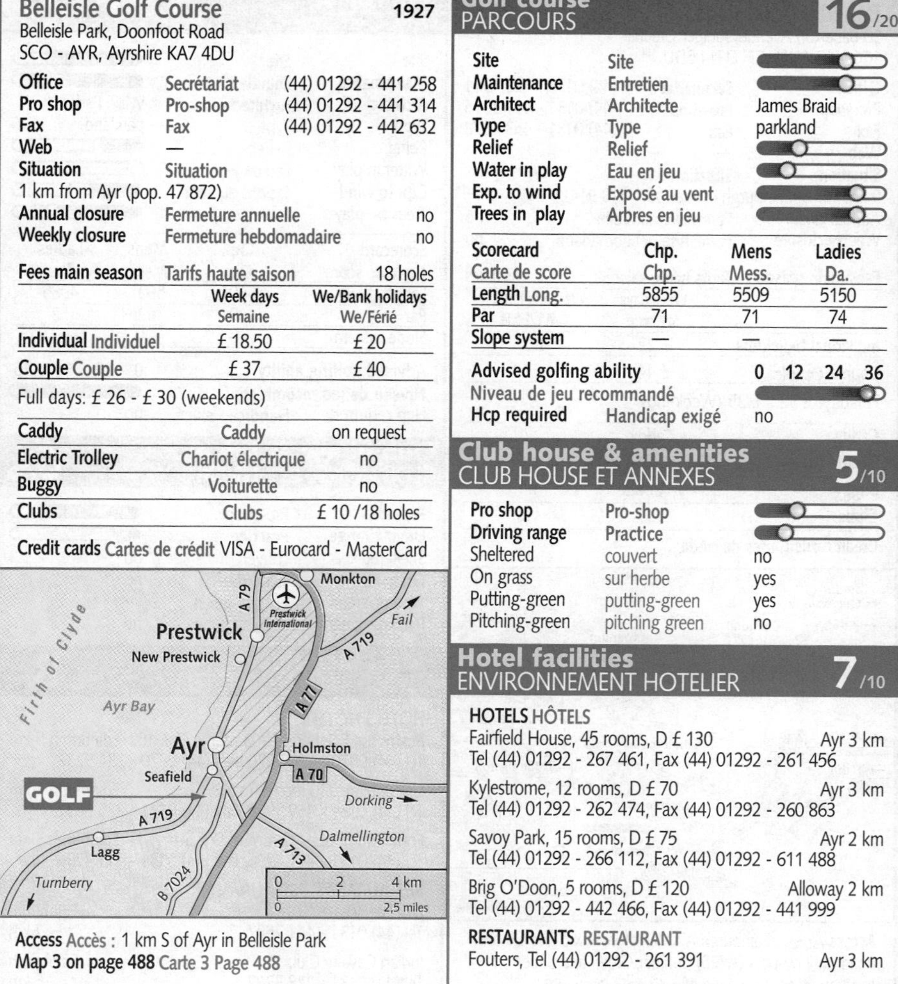

Belleisle Golf Course — 1927

Belleisle Park, Doonfoot Road
SCO - AYR, Ayrshire KA7 4DU

Office	Secrétariat	(44) 01292 - 441 258
Pro shop	Pro-shop	(44) 01292 - 441 314
Fax	Fax	(44) 01292 - 442 632
Web	—	
Situation	Situation	

1 km from Ayr (pop. 47 872)

Annual closure	Fermeture annuelle	no
Weekly closure	Fermeture hebdomadaire	no

Fees main season Tarifs haute saison	18 holes	
	Week days Semaine	**We/Bank holidays** We/Férié
Individual Individuel	£ 18.50	£ 20
Couple Couple	£ 37	£ 40

Full days: £ 26 - £ 30 (weekends)

Caddy	Caddy	on request
Electric Trolley	Chariot électrique	no
Buggy	Voiturette	no
Clubs	Clubs	£ 10 /18 holes

Credit cards Cartes de crédit VISA - Eurocard - MasterCard

Access Accès : 1 km S of Ayr in Belleisle Park
Map 3 on page 488 Carte 3 Page 488
(Map 3 on page 488)

Golf course PARCOURS — 16/20

Site	Site	
Maintenance	Entretien	
Architect	Architecte	James Braid
Type	Type	parkland
Relief	Relief	
Water in play	Eau en jeu	
Exp. to wind	Exposé au vent	
Trees in play	Arbres en jeu	

Scorecard Carte de score	**Chp.** Chp.	**Mens** Mess.	**Ladies** Da.
Length Long.	5855	5509	5150
Par	71	71	74
Slope system	—	—	—

Advised golfing ability 0 12 24 36
Niveau de jeu recommandé
Hcp required Handicap exigé no

Club house & amenities CLUB HOUSE ET ANNEXES — 5/10

Pro shop	Pro-shop	
Driving range	Practice	
Sheltered	couvert	no
On grass	sur herbe	yes
Putting-green	putting-green	yes
Pitching-green	pitching green	no

Hotel facilities ENVIRONNEMENT HOTELIER — 7/10

HOTELS HÔTELS

Fairfield House, 45 rooms, D £ 130 — Ayr 3 km
Tel (44) 01292 - 267 461, Fax (44) 01292 - 261 456

Kylestrome, 12 rooms, D £ 70 — Ayr 3 km
Tel (44) 01292 - 262 474, Fax (44) 01292 - 260 863

Savoy Park, 15 rooms, D £ 75 — Ayr 2 km
Tel (44) 01292 - 266 112, Fax (44) 01292 - 611 488

Brig O'Doon, 5 rooms, D £ 120 — Alloway 2 km
Tel (44) 01292 - 442 466, Fax (44) 01292 - 441 999

RESTAURANTS RESTAURANT

Fouters, Tel (44) 01292 - 261 391 — Ayr 3 km

BABERTON

14 | 6 | 8

While the family is visiting Edinburgh or doing some shopping, you'll have the time to play 18 holes at Baberton to the south-west of the city. Created in 1893 and designed by the great Wille Park Jnr, this is no longer a tournament course but some of the par 4s and par 3s are anything but easy. Without being really dangerous, the trees, bunkers and ditches are in play just enough to bother average players, who make up the major share of green-feers here during the week. The trees are particularly beautiful especially in their Autumn colours, when we visited. Don't be surprised if you're late getting back, as the Clubhouse reserves a warm welcome to all. The best idea would be for the family to come and meet you there.

Pendant que la famille visite Edinburgh ou fait du shopping, vous avez le temps de faire 18 trous à Baberton, au sud-ouest de la ville. Fondé en 1893 et dessiné par le grand Willie Park Jr, ce n'est plus aujourd'hui un parcours de championnat, bien que certains de ses par 4 et ses cinq par 3 ne soient pas des plus faciles. Sans être vaiment dangereux, les arbres, les bunkers et les fossés sont assez en jeu pour inquiéter le joueur moyen, qui fournit l'essentiel de la clientèle extérieure en semaine. Les arbres sont ici particulièrement beaux, spécialement dans leurs teintes d'automne. Et si vous êtes en retard pour rejoindre les vôtres, vous avez une excuse, le Clubhouse est accueillant. La bonne idée, c'est de vous donner rendez-vous ici.

Baberton Golf Club **1893**

50 Baberton Avenue, Juniper Green
SCO - EDINBURGH EH14 5DU

Office	Secrétariat	(44) 0131 - 453 4911
Pro shop	Pro-shop	(44) 0131 - 453 3555
Fax	Fax	(44) 0131 - 453 4678
Web	—	
Situation	Situation	

9 km SW of Edinburgh centre (pop. 418 914)

Annual closure	Fermeture annuelle	no
Weekly closure	Fermeture hebdomadaire	no

Fees main season Tarifs haute saison		18 holes
	Week days Semaine	We/Bank holidays We/Férié
Individual Individuel	£ 22	£ 25
Couple Couple	£ 44	£ 50

Full day: £ 32 / £ 35 (Weekends)

Caddy	Caddy	no
Electric Trolley	Chariot électrique	no
Buggy	Voiturette	no
Clubs	Clubs	yes
Credit cards	Cartes de crédit	no

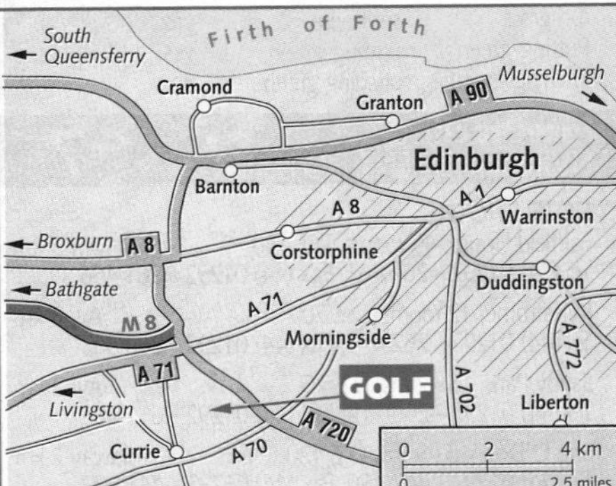

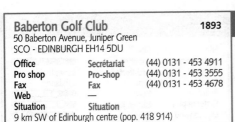

Access Accès : Edinburgh A70 Slateford Road and Lanark Road until by-pass (A720), Juniper Green and Baberton Junction. **Map 3 on page 489** Carte 3 Page 489

Golf course PARCOURS — 14/20

Site	Site	
Maintenance	Entretien	
Architect	Architecte	Willie Park
Type	Type	parkland
Relief	Relief	
Water in play	Eau en jeu	
Exp. to wind	Exposé au vent	
Trees in play	Arbres en jeu	

Scorecard Carte de score	Chp. Chp.	Mens Mess.	Ladies Da.
Length Long.	5601	5601	4985
Par	69	69	72
Slope system	—	—	—

Advised golfing ability Niveau de jeu recommandé: 0 12 24 36

Hcp required Handicap exigé: no

Club house & amenities CLUB HOUSE ET ANNEXES — 6/10

Pro shop	Pro-shop	
Driving range	Practice	
Sheltered	couvert	no
On grass	sur herbe	no
Putting-green	putting-green	yes
Pitching-green	pitching green	no

Hotel facilities ENVIRONNEMENT HOTELIER — 8/10

HOTELS HÔTELS

Posthouse Edinburgh, 303 rooms, D £ 109 Edinburgh 5 km
Tel (44) 0870 - 400 9026, Fax (44) 0870 - 334 9237

Caledonian, 236 rooms, D £ 295 Edinburgh 7 km
Tel (44) 0131 - 459 9988, Fax (44) 0131 - 225 6632

Forte Travelodge, 72 rooms, D £ 50 Edinburgh 3 km
Tel (44) 0131 - 441 4296, Fax (44) 0131 - 441 4296

RESTAURANTS RESTAURANT

Mackenzies Edinburgh 2 km
Tel (44) 0131 - 441 2587

Indian Cavalry Club Edinburgh 5 km
Tel (44) 0131 - 228 3282

BALLATER

15 | 6 | 7

Here we are just a few miles from Balmoral Castle, the Royal Family's summer residence, in a beautiful region of the Highlands along the banks of the river Dee, which borders the course. The area is more popular for tourism than golf, or even for fishing or hunting from Spring to late Autumn only (at 2,000 ft. above sea level, the winter weather always has the final say). The course, rather hilly although never too exhausting to walk on a soft carpet of grass, winds its way through heather, broom and trees. James Braid and Harry Vardon added their personal touch to a very pleasant layout, where the land has been used very intelligently. This may not be the world's most difficult course but playing here certainly is time well spent.

Nous ne sommes qu'à quelques kilomètres du château de Balmoral, la résidence d'été de la famille royale, dans une des très belles régions des Highlands, en bordure de la rivière Dee qui sert de limite au parcours. On vient généralement ici davantage pour le tourisme que pour le golf, ou encore pour la pêche et la chasse, à partir du printemps et jusqu'à la fin de l'automne, car nous sommes après tout à 600 mètres d'altitude. Les reliefs du parcours sont assez prononcés, bien que l'ensemble ne soit pas épuisant, grâce à un gazon très fourni, insinué dans la bruyère, les genêts et les arbres. James Braid et Harry Vardon ont apporté leur touche personnelle à un dessin très agréable, où le terrain a été utilisé avec beaucoup d'à-propos. Ce n'est peut-être pas le parcours le plus difficile du monde, mais on n'y perdra jamais son temps.

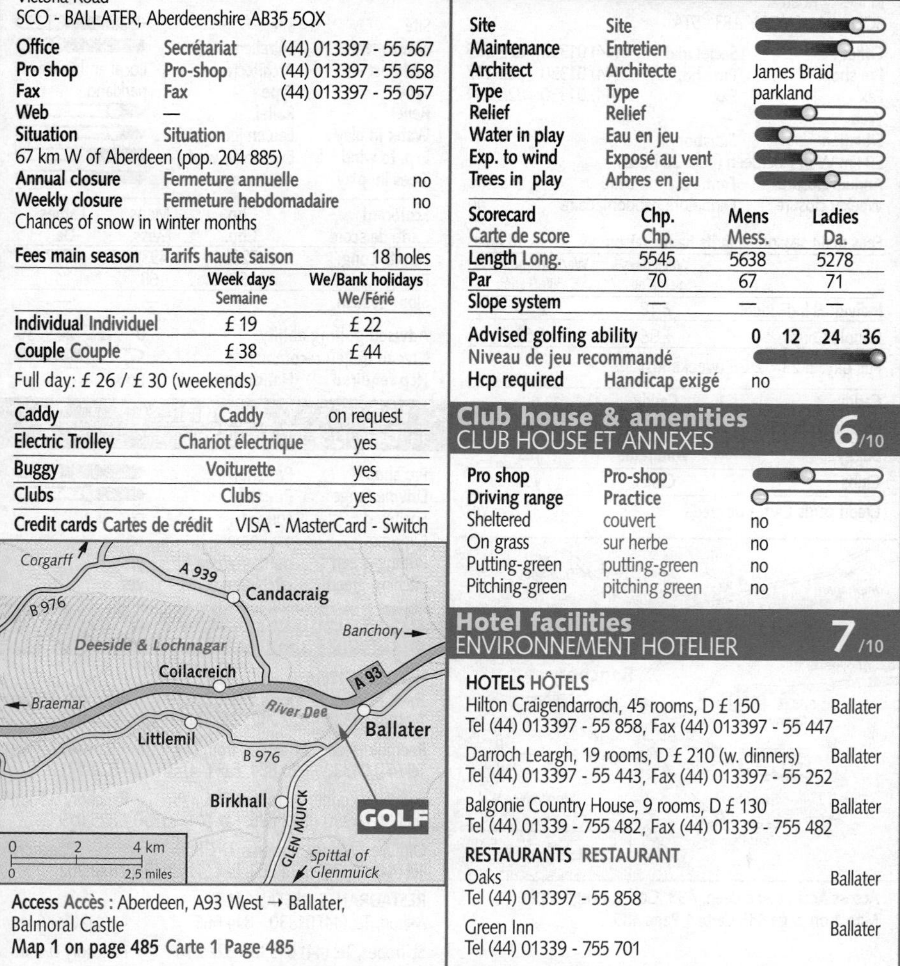

Ballater Golf Club — 1892

Victoria Road
SCO - BALLATER, Aberdeenshire AB35 5QX

Office	Secrétariat	(44) 013397 - 55 567
Pro shop	Pro-shop	(44) 013397 - 55 658
Fax	Fax	(44) 013397 - 55 057
Web	—	
Situation	Situation	

67 km W of Aberdeen (pop. 204 885)

Annual closure	Fermeture annuelle	no
Weekly closure	Fermeture hebdomadaire	no

Chances of snow in winter months

Fees main season Tarifs haute saison	18 holes	
	Week days Semaine	**We/Bank holidays** We/Férié
Individual Individuel	£ 19	£ 22
Couple Couple	£ 38	£ 44

Full day: £ 26 / £ 30 (weekends)

Caddy	Caddy	on request
Electric Trolley	Chariot électrique	yes
Buggy	Voiturette	yes
Clubs	Clubs	yes
Credit cards	Cartes de crédit	VISA - MasterCard - Switch

Access Accès : Aberdeen, A93 West → Ballater, Balmoral Castle
Map 1 on page 485 Carte 1 Page 485

Golf course — PARCOURS — 15/20

Site	Site	
Maintenance	Entretien	
Architect	Architecte	James Braid
Type	Type	parkland
Relief	Relief	
Water in play	Eau en jeu	
Exp. to wind	Exposé au vent	
Trees in play	Arbres en jeu	

Scorecard Carte de score	**Chp.** Chp.	**Mens** Mess.	**Ladies** Da.
Length Long.	5545	5638	5278
Par	70	67	71
Slope system	—	—	—

Advised golfing ability — Niveau de jeu recommandé: 0 12 24 36

Hcp required — Handicap exigé: no

Club house & amenities — CLUB HOUSE ET ANNEXES — 6/10

Pro shop	Pro-shop	
Driving range	Practice	
Sheltered	couvert	no
On grass	sur herbe	no
Putting-green	putting-green	no
Pitching-green	pitching green	no

Hotel facilities — ENVIRONNEMENT HOTELIER — 7/10

HOTELS HÔTELS

Hilton Craigendarroch, 45 rooms, D £ 150 — Ballater
Tel (44) 013397 - 55 858, Fax (44) 013397 - 55 447

Darroch Leargh, 19 rooms, D £ 210 (w. dinners) — Ballater
Tel (44) 013397 - 55 443, Fax (44) 013397 - 55 252

Balgonie Country House, 9 rooms, D £ 130 — Ballater
Tel (44) 01339 - 755 482, Fax (44) 01339 - 755 482

RESTAURANTS RESTAURANT

Oaks — Ballater
Tel (44) 013397 - 55 858

Green Inn — Ballater
Tel (44) 01339 - 755 701

BANCHORY

14 | 7 | 7

Starting out from Aberdeen, the A93 runs up the Grampian mountains alongside the river Dee. You won't be alone in making this climb, the salmon have been doing it for centuries, as you will probably see from the Brigg O'Feugh, an 18th century bridge in the middle of the village of Banchory. The splendours of Royal Deeside include this golf course, which lies right alongside the river. Recently restyled by some keen local golfers, this is a combination of wide open space and tree-lined fairways. Big-hitting is not always an essential virtue on this ideal holiday course, but the par 3s are long (except the 16th) and tricky. The best is certainly hole N°11 (180 yards/162 metres) with OB to the left and a burn in front of the green. There are also half a dozen or so short par 4s that are fun to play. Non-golfers have lots to do in this region and can even take an indiscreet look at Balmoral Castle, the Queen's summer residence.

En partant d'Aberdeen, la A93 s'enfonce dans les Grampians, en longeant la rivière Dee. Vous ne serez pas seul à remonter, les saumons le font aussi depuis des siècles, comme on peut les apercevoir du Brigg o'Feugh, un pont du XVIIIè siècle au milieu du village de Banchory. Parmi les splendeurs du Royal Deeside, ce parcours qui longe la rivière, récemment remanié par des enthousiastes golfeurs locaux associe les espaces ouverts avec des fairways bordés d'arbres. La force de frappe n'est pas une qualité obligatoire sur ce parcours idéal pour des vacances, mais les par 3 sont longs (sauf le 16) et délicats. Le meilleur d'entre eux est sans doute le 11, de 162 mètres (180 yards), avec hors-limites à gauche et un "burn" devant le green. On remarquera aussi une demi-douzaine de courts par 4 très amusants. Quant aux non golfeurs, ils ne manqueront pas de sources d'intérêt dans cette région, et jetteront un coup d'oeil indiscret sur le Château de Balmoral, résidence d'été de la Reine.

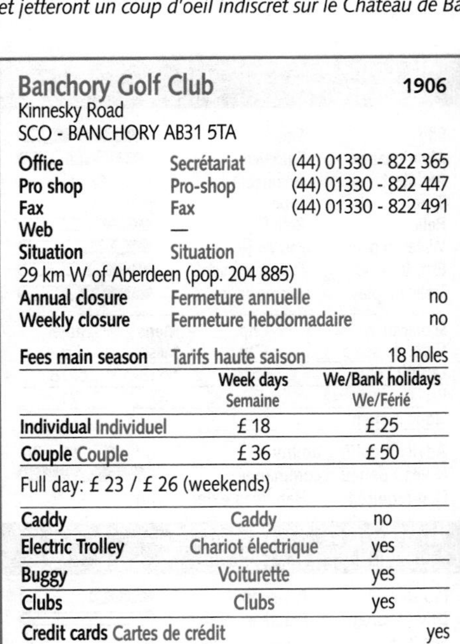

Banchory Golf Club — 1906

Kinnesky Road
SCO - BANCHORY AB31 5TA

Office	Secrétariat	(44) 01330 - 822 365
Pro shop	Pro-shop	(44) 01330 - 822 447
Fax	Fax	(44) 01330 - 822 491
Web	—	
Situation	Situation	

29 km W of Aberdeen (pop. 204 885)

Annual closure	Fermeture annuelle	no
Weekly closure	Fermeture hebdomadaire	no

Fees main season Tarifs haute saison		18 holes
	Week days Semaine	**We/Bank holidays** We/Férié
Individual Individuel	£ 18	£ 25
Couple Couple	£ 36	£ 50

Full day: £ 23 / £ 26 (weekends)

Caddy	Caddy	no
Electric Trolley	Chariot électrique	yes
Buggy	Voiturette	yes
Clubs	Clubs	yes
Credit cards	Cartes de crédit	yes

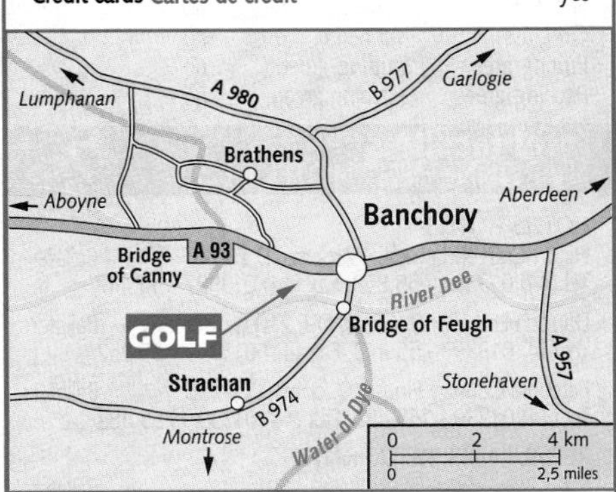

Access Accès : Aberdeen, A93, Golf in village centre.
Map 1 on page 485 Carte 1 Page 485

Golf course — PARCOURS — 14/20

Site	Site	
Maintenance	Entretien	
Architect	Architecte	Local enthusiasts
Type	Type	parkland
Relief	Relief	
Water in play	Eau en jeu	
Exp. to wind	Exposé au vent	
Trees in play	Arbres en jeu	

Scorecard Carte de score	**Chp.** Chp.	**Mens** Mess.	**Ladies** Da.
Length Long.	5203	4939	4707
Par	69	68	71
Slope system	—	—	—

Advised golfing ability — 0 12 24 36
Niveau de jeu recommandé

Hcp required Handicap exigé — no

Club house & amenities — CLUB HOUSE ET ANNEXES — 7/10

Pro shop	Pro-shop	
Driving range	Practice	
Sheltered	couvert	no
On grass	sur herbe	no
Putting-green	putting-green	yes
Pitching-green	pitching green	yes

Hotel facilities — ENVIRONNEMENT HOTELIER — 7/10

HOTELS HÔTELS

Tor-Na-Coille, 22 rooms, from D £ 130 — Banchory 0.5 km
Tel (44) 01330 - 822 242, Fax (44) 01330 - 824 012

Raemoir House, 21 rooms, from D £ 110 — Banchory 5 km
Tel (44) 01330 - 824 884, Fax (44) 01330 - 822 171

Banchory Lodge, 22 rooms, D £ 175 — Banchory 0.5 km
Tel (44) 01330 - 822 625, Fax (44) 01330 - 825 019

Old West Manse, 3 rooms, D £ 55 — Banchory
Tel (44) 01330 - 822 202, Fax (44) 01330 - 822 202

RESTAURANTS RESTAURANT

Milton, Tel (44) 01330 - 844 566 — Crathes 6 km

St Tropez, Tel (44) 01330 - 822 216 — Banchory 0.5 km

BLAIRGOWRIE Lansdowne 15 | 8 | 6

In a magnificent resort located in some of Scotland's finest countryside, this course designed by Thomas and Alliss in 1974 brought a welcome alternative to the famous Rosemount course. There is of course a definite American influence in this layout over a thickly treed landscape (pine-trees especially). The fairways are narrow and then the heather makes things a little more complicated, but the designers have often left a few open corridors to the greens to make things easier for Scottish golfers who are not always experts at lofting the ball. We would have liked a little more breathing space for the tee-shot, as players who are neither too long nor too straight will have a tough time if they choose to play from the back tees. The course has aged well even though some might find this still just a touch artificial.

Dans ce magnifique ensemble situé dans un des très beaux paysages d'Ecosse, ce parcours de Dave Thomas et Peter Alliss a apporté en 1974 une alternative bienvenue au fameux Rosemount Course. Bien sûr, on trouve une certaine influence américaine dans leur dessin tracé dans un paysage très boisé (surtout des pins). Les fairways sont étroits, la bruyère complique ensuite les choses, mais les architectes ont souvent laissé quelques passages en ouverture des greens pour faciliter le travail des joueurs écossais pas toujours habitués aux balles levées. On aimerait parfois une plus grande sensation d'espace au moment de driver, car les joueurs ni très longs, ni très droits souffriront s'ils choisissent les départs reculés. Le parcours a bien vieilli, mais on peut toujours le trouver un rien artificiel.

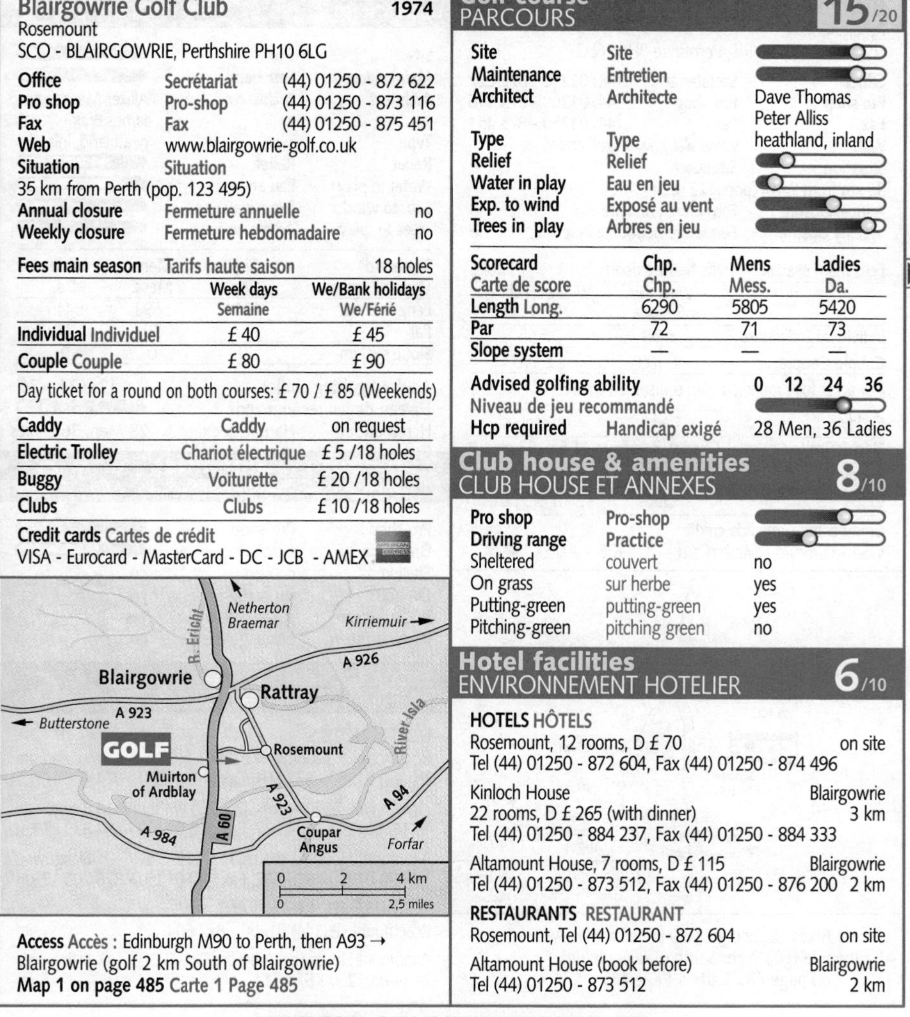

Blairgowrie Golf Club — 1974

Rosemount
SCO - BLAIRGOWRIE, Perthshire PH10 6LG

Office	Secrétariat	(44) 01250 - 872 622
Pro shop	Pro-shop	(44) 01250 - 873 116
Fax	Fax	(44) 01250 - 875 451
Web	www.blairgowrie-golf.co.uk	
Situation	Situation	

35 km from Perth (pop. 123 495)

Annual closure	Fermeture annuelle	no
Weekly closure	Fermeture hebdomadaire	no

Fees main season Tarifs haute saison	Week days Semaine	We/Bank holidays We/Férié
		18 holes
Individual Individuel	£ 40	£ 45
Couple Couple	£ 80	£ 90

Day ticket for a round on both courses: £ 70 / £ 85 (Weekends)

Caddy	Caddy	on request
Electric Trolley	Chariot électrique	£ 5 /18 holes
Buggy	Voiturette	£ 20 /18 holes
Clubs	Clubs	£ 10 /18 holes

Credit cards Cartes de crédit
VISA - Eurocard - MasterCard - DC - JCB - AMEX

Access Accès : Edinburgh M90 to Perth, then A93 → Blairgowrie (golf 2 km South of Blairgowrie)
Map 1 on page 485 Carte 1 Page 485

Golf course PARCOURS 15/20

Site	Site	
Maintenance	Entretien	
Architect	Architecte	Dave Thomas, Peter Alliss
Type	Type	heathland, inland
Relief	Relief	
Water in play	Eau en jeu	
Exp. to wind	Exposé au vent	
Trees in play	Arbres en jeu	

Scorecard Carte de score	Chp. Chp.	Mens Mess.	Ladies Da.
Length Long.	6290	5805	5420
Par	72	71	73
Slope system	—	—	—

Advised golfing ability 0 12 24 36
Niveau de jeu recommandé
Hcp required Handicap exigé 28 Men, 36 Ladies

Club house & amenities CLUB HOUSE ET ANNEXES 8/10

Pro shop	Pro-shop	
Driving range	Practice	
Sheltered	couvert	no
On grass	sur herbe	yes
Putting-green	putting-green	yes
Pitching-green	pitching green	no

Hotel facilities ENVIRONNEMENT HOTELIER 6/10

HOTELS HÔTELS
Rosemount, 12 rooms, D £ 70 — on site
Tel (44) 01250 - 872 604, Fax (44) 01250 - 874 496

Kinloch House — Blairgowrie
22 rooms, D £ 265 (with dinner) — 3 km
Tel (44) 01250 - 884 237, Fax (44) 01250 - 884 333

Altamount House, 7 rooms, D £ 115 — Blairgowrie
Tel (44) 01250 - 873 512, Fax (44) 01250 - 876 200 — 2 km

RESTAURANTS RESTAURANT
Rosemount, Tel (44) 01250 - 872 604 — on site

Altamount House (book before) — Blairgowrie
Tel (44) 01250 - 873 512 — 2 km

BLAIRGOWRIE Rosemount 18 8 6

For many golfers this is one of the best British inland courses. It's a pity they had to sacrifice two or three holes to cater to the building of the Lansdowne course but James Braid had already altered the original layout by Alister MacKenzie. Despite this, Rosemount has lost nothing of its charm and of the marvellous feeling of tranquillity you get when playing here, as each hole is clearly separated from the others by a thick row of trees. The wildlife and flora add to the beauty of the spot, particularly in Autumn, and to this excellent course where you need to play in every direction. Beneath its kindly exterior, Rosemount cleverly conceals perhaps not the hazards but at least its difficulties. And as it is never tiring to play, it is worth more than the one visit.

C'est pour beaucoup de joueurs l'un des meilleurs parcours "inland" de Grande-Bretagne. On regrette un peu que deux ou trois trous aient été sacrifiés au moment de la construction du Lansdowne Course, mais James Braid avait déjà retouché auparavant le travail original d'Alister MacKenzie. Rosemount n'a rien perdu pour autant de son charme, et de la merveilleuse sensation de paix qu'on y éprouve, chaque trou étant nettement séparé des autres par d'épais rideaux d'arbres. La vie sauvage et la flore ajoutent encore à la beauté du lieu, notamment en automne. Qui plus est, c'est un excellent parcours où il faut savoir jouer dans tous les sens, et qui cache bien sous des dehors souriants, sinon ses obstacles, du moins ses difficultés. Comme il n'est pas non plus fatigant à jouer, il mérite bien mieux qu'une simple visite.

Blairgowrie Golf Club — 1889

Rosemount
SCO - BLAIRGOWRIE, Perthshire PH10 6LG

Office	Secrétariat	(44) 01250 - 872 622
Pro shop	Pro-shop	(44) 01250 - 873 116
Fax	Fax	(44) 01250 - 875 451
Web	www.blairgowrie-golf.co.uk	
Situation	Situation	

35 km from Perth (pop. 123 495)

Annual closure	Fermeture annuelle	no
Weekly closure	Fermeture hebdomadaire	no

Fees main season Tarifs haute saison	18 holes	
	Week days Semaine	**We/Bank holidays** We/Férié
Individual Individuel	£ 50	£ 55
Couple Couple	£ 100	£ 110

Day ticket for a round on both courses: £ 70 / £ 85 (Weekends)

Caddy	Caddy	on request
Electric Trolley	Chariot électrique	£ 5 /18 holes
Buggy	Voiturette	£ 20 /18 holes
Clubs	Clubs	£ 10 /18 holes

Credit cards Cartes de crédit
VISA - Eurocard - MasterCard - DC - JCB - AMEX

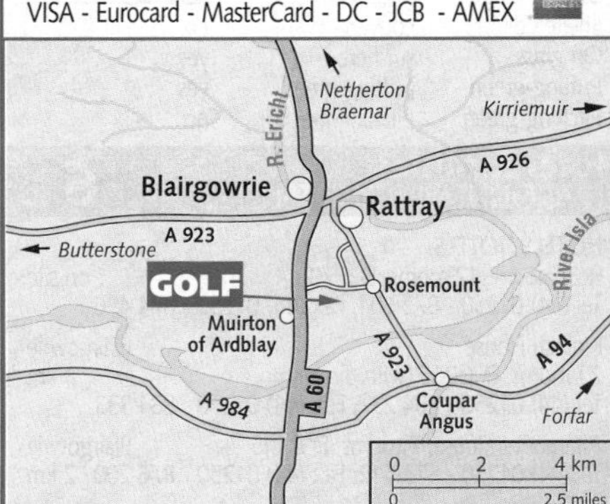

Access Accès : Edinburgh M90 to Perth, then A93 → Blairgowrie (golf 2 km South of Blairgowrie)
Map 1 on page 485 Carte 1 Page 485

Golf course PARCOURS — 18/20

Site	Site	
Maintenance	Entretien	
Architect	Architecte	Alister MacKenzie James Braid
Type	Type	heathland, inland
Relief	Relief	
Water in play	Eau en jeu	
Exp. to wind	Exposé au vent	
Trees in play	Arbres en jeu	

Scorecard Carte de score	**Chp.** Chp.	**Mens** Mess.	**Ladies** Da.
Length Long.	6014	5693	5445
Par	72	70	74
Slope system	0	0	0

Advised golfing ability Niveau de jeu recommandé — 0 12 24 36

Hcp required Handicap exigé — 28 Men, 36 Ladies

Club house & amenities CLUB HOUSE ET ANNEXES — 8/10

Pro shop	Pro-shop	
Driving range	Practice	
Sheltered	couvert	no
On grass	sur herbe	yes
Putting-green	putting-green	yes
Pitching-green	pitching green	no

Hotel facilities ENVIRONNEMENT HOTELIER — 6/10

HOTELS HÔTELS

Rosemount, 12 rooms, D £ 70 — on site
Tel (44) 01250 - 872 604, Fax (44) 01250 - 874 496

Kinloch House, 22 rooms, D £ 265 (with dinner) — Blairgowrie
Tel (44) 01250 - 884 237, Fax (44) 01250 - 884 333 — 3 km

Altamount House, 7 rooms, D £ 115 — Blairgowrie
Tel (44) 01250 - 873 512, Fax (44) 01250 - 876 200 — 2 km

RESTAURANTS RESTAURANT

Rosemount, Tel (44) 01250 - 872 604 — on site

Altamount House (book before) — Blairgowrie
Tel (44) 01250 - 873 512 — 2 km

BOAT OF GARTEN

14	6	7

Boat of Garten is the gateway to the Cairngorms, with some of the highest peaks in the UK. It lies close to a wildlife reserve and only a few miles from the ski resort of Aviemore where the steam train is a popular attraction. Deer and osprey are often seen on the course, and are worth the visit on their own. The local distilleries are also popular with visitors. The golf course is a little hilly over the first two or three holes, but thereafter is easy to walk and enjoys some spectacular scenery. The rolling fairways often present hanging lies in the manner of seaside golf courses. James Braid's layout is first class and the 6th hole is one of the most memorable in all of Scottish golf. It's the perfect holiday course.

A proximité immédiate d'une réserve naturelle créée pour protéger les orfraies, et à quelques kilomètres de la station de ski d'Aviemore, reliée par un charmant train à vapeur, Boat of Garten est une sorte de porte d'entrée dans les Cairngorns, qui figurent parmi les plus hautes montagnes de Grande-Bretagne. La flore et la faune de cette région valent largement le déplacement, mais les distilleries locales sont tout aussi appréciées par les visiteurs. Le parcours de Boat of Garten est un peu accidenté dans les premiers trous, mais il s'assagit ensuite et sa qualité générale en fait plus qu'une distraction annexe ou un prétexte à admirer de spectaculaires panoramas. Les fairways présentent souvent des ondulations dignes des golfs de bord de mer, et le dessin de James Braid est globalement de première qualité, notamment au 6, l'un des meilleurs trous de toute l'Ecosse. Un parcours de vacances, mais de bonnes vacances.

Boat of Garten Golf Club — 1932

SCO - BOAT OF GARTEN, Inverness-shire PH24 3BQ

Office	**Secrétariat**	(44) 01479 - 831 282
Pro shop	**Pro-shop**	(44) 01479 - 831 282
Fax	**Fax**	(44) 01479 - 831 523
E-mail	boatgolf@enterprise.net	
Situation	**Situation**	

8 km from Aviemore - 48 km SE of Inverness (pop. 62 186)

Annual closure	**Fermeture annuelle**	1/11→1/4
Weekly closure	**Fermeture hebdomadaire**	no

Fees main season **Tarifs haute saison** 18 holes	**Week days** Semaine	**We/Bank holidays** We/Férié
Individual Individuel	£ 25	£ 30
Couple Couple	£ 50	£ 60

Full day: £ 30 / £ 35 (weekends)

Caddy	**Caddy**	£ 20 /on request
Electric Trolley	**Chariot électrique**	£ 5 /18 holes
Buggy	**Voiturette**	no
Clubs	**Clubs**	£ 5 /18 holes

Credit cards Cartes de crédit
VISA - MasterCard - Delta - JCB

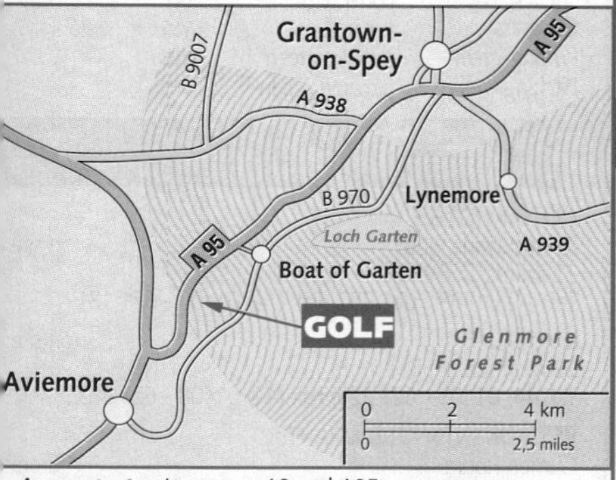

Access Accès : Inverness, A9 and A95.
2 km North of Aviemore. Follow signs to village.
Map 1 on page 485 Carte 1 Page 485

Golf course PARCOURS — 14/20

Site	**Site**	
Maintenance	**Entretien**	
Architect	**Architecte**	James Braid
Type	**Type**	heathland
Relief	**Relief**	
Water in play	**Eau en jeu**	
Exp. to wind	**Exposé au vent**	
Trees in play	**Arbres en jeu**	

Scorecard Carte de score	**Chp.** Chp.	**Mens** Mess.	**Ladies** Da.
Length Long.	5340	5340	4640
Par	69	69	71
Slope system	—	—	—

Advised golfing ability 0 12 24 36
Niveau de jeu recommandé
Hcp required **Handicap exigé** certificate

Club house & amenities CLUB HOUSE ET ANNEXES — 6/10

Pro shop	**Pro-shop**	
Driving range	**Practice**	
Sheltered	couvert	no
On grass	sur herbe	no
Putting-green	putting-green	yes
Pitching-green	pitching green	yes

Hotel facilities ENVIRONNEMENT HOTELIER — 7/10

HOTELS HÔTELS

The Boat Hotel — Boat of Garten 1 km
35 rooms, D £ 130 (with dinner)
Tel (44) 01479 - 831 258, Fax (44) 01479 - 831 414

Muckrach Lodge, 13 rooms, from D £ 125 — Dulnain Bridge 3 km
Tel (44) 01479 - 851 257, Fax (44) 01479 - 851 325

Auchendean Lodge, 7 rooms, D £ 94 — Dulnain Bridge 3 km
Tel (44) 01479 - 851 347, Fax (44) 01479 - 851 347

RESTAURANTS RESTAURANT

The Boat Hotel — Boat of Garten 1 km
Tel (44) 01479 - 831 258

Muckrach Lodge — Dulnain Bridge 3 km
Tel (44) 01479 - 851 257

BROLA

15	7	7

This course is found no further than the end of the world, a little after Dornoch and Golspie, where th length of the days in summer could almost let you play all three in the same day. Brora is one of th great traditional links, fine-tuned in 1924 after a design by James Braid. Electric fences protect all the green from the sheep employed to keep the grass cropped. The tee-boxes and greens are often elevated, built betwee dunes of between 5 and 12 metres high, and the texture of the turf is particularly pleasant, especially for putting Although rather short, Brora is not an easy course, even though sometimes you might prefer slightly more penalisin rough (especially for the guys you're playing with). This is a club of perfect hospitality, where the 19th hole is both re ward and consolation. More should be said about this side of Brora to people who are not curious enough to com and discover the course.

Ce n'est pas plus loin que le bout du monde, un peu après Dornoch et Golspie, là où la longueur des journées d début d'été vous permettraient presque de jouer les trois le même jour. Brora est un des grands links traditionnel peaufiné en 1924 d'après un dessin de James Braid. Des clôtures électriques préservent chaque green des mouton chargés de tondre. Les départs et greens sont souvent surélevés, construits entre des dunes de 5 à 12 mètres de hau la texture du gazon particulièrement agréable, notamment au putting. Bien qu'assez court, Brora n'est pas un pa cours facile, même si l'on souhaiterait parfois (pour ses adversaires !) un rough plus pénalisant. Un club à la parfait hospitalité, où le 19ème trou est à la fois récompense et consolation, dont on aimera parler à ceux qui ne sont pa assez curieux pour le connaître.

Brora Golf Club — 1891

Golf Road
SCO - BRORA, Highland KW9 6QS

Office	Secrétariat	(44) 01408 - 621 417
Pro shop	Pro-shop	(44) 01408 - 621 473
Fax	Fax	(44) 01408 - 622 157
Web	www.highlandgolf.com	
Situation	Situation	

85 km N of Inverness (pop. 62 186)

Annual closure	Fermeture annuelle	no
Weekly closure	Fermeture hebdomadaire	no

Fees main season Tarifs haute saison — 18 holes

	Week days Semaine	We/Bank holidays We/Férié
Individual Individuel	£ 25	£ 30
Couple Couple	£ 50	£ 60

Second round on the same day: £ 10

Caddy	Caddy	£ 25 /on request
Electric Trolley	Chariot électrique	yes
Buggy	Voiturette	£ 15 /18 holes
Clubs	Clubs	£ 10 /18 holes

Credit cards Cartes de crédit
VISA - Access - Delta

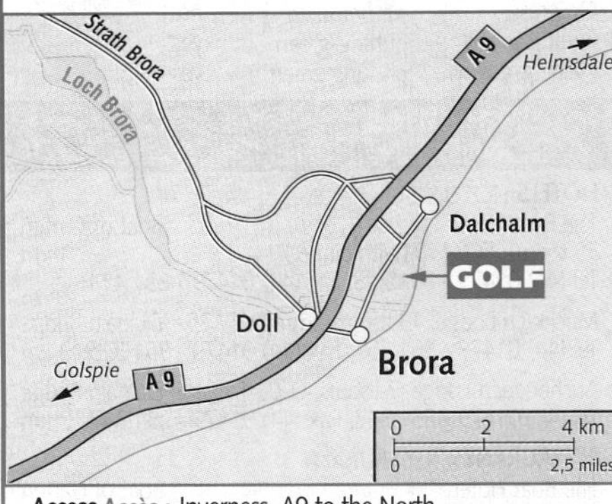

Access Accès : Inverness, A9 to the North
Map 1 on page 485 Carte 1 Page 485

Golf course PARCOURS — 15/20

Site	Site	
Maintenance	Entretien	
Architect	Architecte	James Braid
Type	Type	links
Relief	Relief	
Water in play	Eau en jeu	
Exp. to wind	Exposé au vent	
Trees in play	Arbres en jeu	

Scorecard Carte de score	Chp. Chp.	Mens Mess.	Ladies Da.
Length Long.	5499	5285	4746
Par	69	69	70
Slope system	—	—	—

Advised golfing ability Niveau de jeu recommandé — 0 12 24 36
Hcp required Handicap exigé — no

Club house & amenities CLUB HOUSE ET ANNEXES — 7/10

Pro shop	Pro-shop	
Driving range	Practice	
Sheltered	couvert	no
On grass	sur herbe	yes
Putting-green	putting-green	yes
Pitching-green	pitching green	yes

Hotel facilities ENVIRONNEMENT HOTELIER — 7/10

HOTELS HÔTELS

Royal Marine Hotel — on site
22 rooms, D £ 138
Tel (44) 01408 - 621 252, Fax (44) 01408 - 621 181

Links Hotel — on site
22 rooms, D £ 98
Tel (44) 01408 - 621 225, Fax (44) 01408 - 621 383

RESTAURANTS RESTAURANT

Garden Room — Brora 1 km
Tel (44) 01408 - 621 252

Brora Golf Club — on site
Tel (44) 01408 - 621 417

BRUNTSFIELD

15 | 8 | 9

For many continental Europeans, playing golf virtually in town is a unique experience. This club used to be right in the middle of Edinburg but has since moved to the outskirts where space is a little less cramped. Willie Park and the great Alistair Mackenzie are responsible for a very pleasant layout at the edge of some hills but where steep slopes have been avoided. This park-style course is generally in excellent condition with immaculate fairways and not over-sized greens. In addition to traditional bunkers, trees are often a dangerous hazard if you play without thinking. This course is a good test for everyone before they square up to more formidable tests on either side of the Forth. Enjoy the excellent restaurant.

Pour bien des continentaux, jouer au golf quasiment en ville est une expérience unique. Ce club était autrefois en plein milieu d'Edinburgh, mais il a émigré à la périphérie, moins à l'étroit. Willie Park et le grand Alister Mackenzie sont responsables d'un tracé très plaisant, en bordure de collines, mais où les fortes pentes ont été évitées. Ce véritable parc est généralement en excellente condition, avec des fairways impeccables et des greens pas très vastes. En plus des bunkers traditionnels, les arbres constituent souvent des obstacles dangereux, si l'on ne réfléchit pas assez. C'est un bon test pour tous, avant d'affronter des adversaires plus redoutables, d'un côté ou de l'autre du Forth. A signaler enfin, l'excellent restaurant.

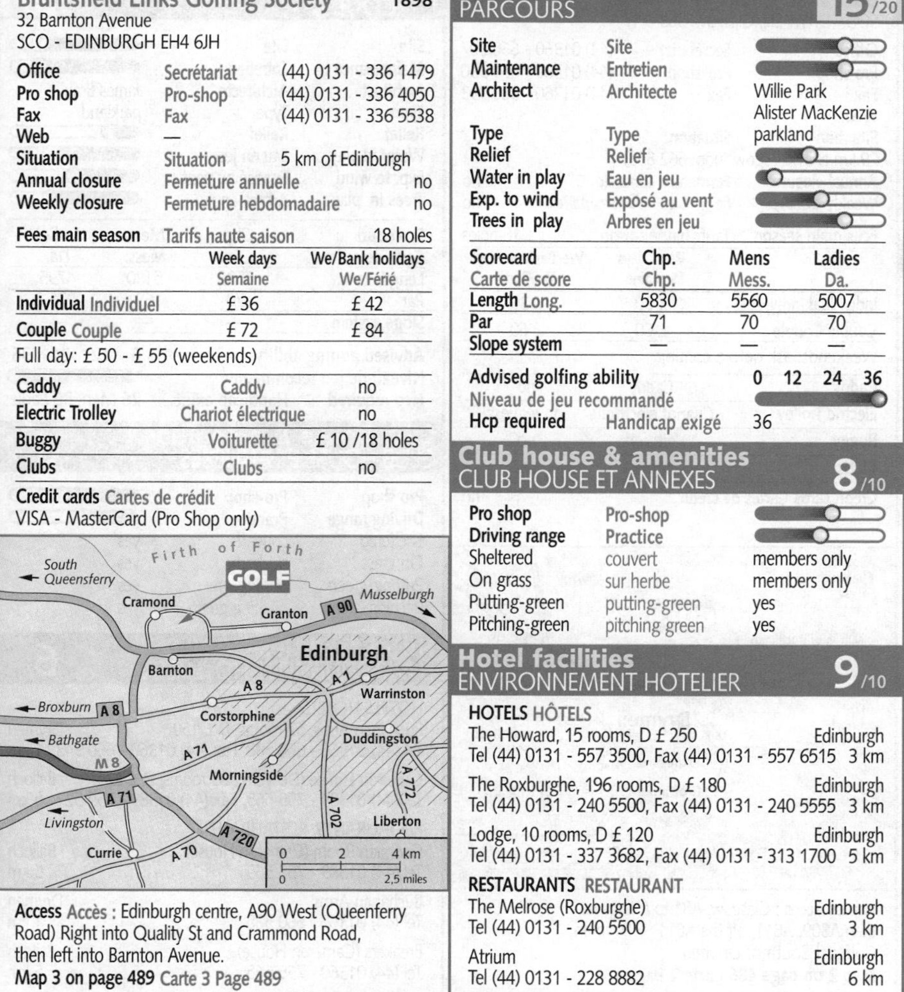

Bruntsfield Links Golfing Society **1898**
32 Barnton Avenue
SCO - EDINBURGH EH4 6JH

Office	Secrétariat	(44) 0131 - 336 1479
Pro shop	Pro-shop	(44) 0131 - 336 4050
Fax	Fax	(44) 0131 - 336 5538
Web	—	
Situation	Situation	5 km of Edinburgh
Annual closure	Fermeture annuelle	no
Weekly closure	Fermeture hebdomadaire	no

Fees main season Tarifs haute saison		18 holes
	Week days Semaine	**We/Bank holidays** We/Férié
Individual Individuel	£ 36	£ 42
Couple Couple	£ 72	£ 84

Full day: £ 50 - £ 55 (weekends)

Caddy	Caddy	no
Electric Trolley	Chariot électrique	no
Buggy	Voiturette	£ 10 /18 holes
Clubs	Clubs	no

Credit cards Cartes de crédit
VISA - MasterCard (Pro Shop only)

Access Accès : Edinburgh centre, A90 West (Queenferry Road) Right into Quality St and Crammond Road, then left into Barnton Avenue.
Map 3 on page 489 Carte 3 Page 489

Golf course PARCOURS **15**/20

Site	Site	
Maintenance	Entretien	
Architect	Architecte	Willie Park Alister MacKenzie
Type	Type	parkland
Relief	Relief	
Water in play	Eau en jeu	
Exp. to wind	Exposé au vent	
Trees in play	Arbres en jeu	

Scorecard Carte de score	**Chp.** Chp.	**Mens** Mess.	**Ladies** Da.
Length Long.	5830	5560	5007
Par	71	70	70
Slope system	—	—	—

Advised golfing ability Niveau de jeu recommandé: 0 12 24 36
Hcp required Handicap exigé: 36

Club house & amenities CLUB HOUSE ET ANNEXES **8**/10

Pro shop	Pro-shop	
Driving range	Practice	
Sheltered	couvert	members only
On grass	sur herbe	members only
Putting-green	putting-green	yes
Pitching-green	pitching green	yes

Hotel facilities ENVIRONNEMENT HOTELIER **9**/10

HOTELS HÔTELS
The Howard, 15 rooms, D £ 250 — Edinburgh
Tel (44) 0131 - 557 3500, Fax (44) 0131 - 557 6515 — 3 km

The Roxburghe, 196 rooms, D £ 180 — Edinburgh
Tel (44) 0131 - 240 5500, Fax (44) 0131 - 240 5555 — 3 km

Lodge, 10 rooms, D £ 120 — Edinburgh
Tel (44) 0131 - 337 3682, Fax (44) 0131 - 313 1700 — 5 km

RESTAURANTS RESTAURANT
The Melrose (Roxburghe) — Edinburgh
Tel (44) 0131 - 240 5500 — 3 km

Atrium — Edinburgh
Tel (44) 0131 - 228 8882 — 6 km

BUCHANAN CASTLE

14 | 6 | 6

While Donald Ross or Tom Simpson might define their designer art as the straight hole, James Braid prefers the dog-leg. Here on the former training grounds for the horses of the Dukes of Montrose, Braid designed a good dozen holes, which were shortened somewhat to cater to members who found the layout a little too difficult. The site is almost flat and so easy on the legs, but keep away from the thick rough which can be really sticky in wet weather. The river Endrick, although theoretically out of reach for normal shots, seems to attract balls like a magnet and it is true that your average hacker is pretty good at going where he never wanted to. Since this course is close to Loch Lomond, Scotland's most private course, come and dream here. You will be made most welcome.

Si l'aboutissement de l'art de Donald Ross ou de Tom Simpson en tant qu'architectes, c'est le trou rectiligne, celui de James Braid, c'est le dog-leg. Ici, sur les anciennes pistes d'entraînement des chevaux des Ducs de Montrose, il en a dessiné une bonne dizaine. Un peu raccourcis depuis, car on estimait que son tracé était trop difficile pour les membres. Le terrain est pratiquement plat, ce qui le rend facile à marcher, mais il vaut mieux échapper aux roughs, très épais quand le temps est à la pluie. Mais rien n'oblige à y aller ! La rivière Endrick est théoriquement hors de portée des coups normaux, mais elle semble avoir un effet magnétique, tant il est vrai que les golfeurs moyens réussissent surtout à aller là où ils ne veulent pas aller. Comme ce parcours est proche de Loch Lomond, le club le plus fermé d'Ecosse, venez rêver ici, vous serez les bienvenus.

Buchanan Castle Golf Club — 1936

SCO - DRYMEN, Glasgow G63 0HY

Office	Secrétariat	(44) 01360 - 660 307
Pro shop	Pro-shop	(44) 01360 - 660 330
Fax	Fax	(44) 01360 - 660 993
Web	—	
Situation	Situation	
29 km N of Glasgow (pop. 662 853)		
Annual closure	Fermeture annuelle	no
Weekly closure	Fermeture hebdomadaire	no

Fees main season Tarifs haute saison	18 holes	
	Week days Semaine	**We/Bank holidays** We/Férié
Individual Individuel	£ 30	£ 30
Couple Couple	£ 60	£ 60

Weekends: ask before coming

Caddy	Caddy	no
Electric Trolley	Chariot électrique	on request
Buggy	Voiturette	no
Clubs	Clubs	yes
Credit cards Cartes de crédit		no

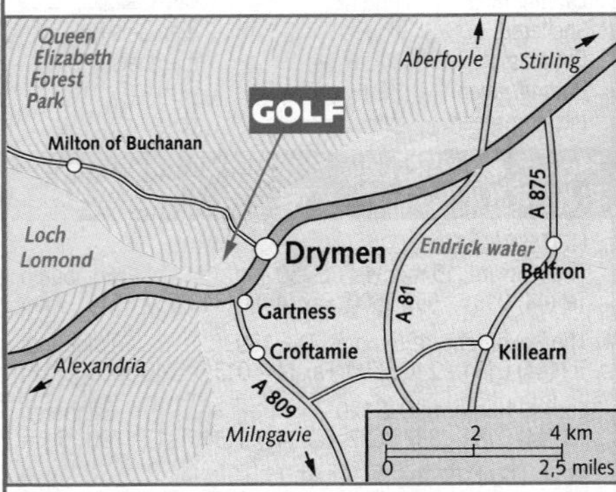

Access Accès : Glasgow, A81 to Milngavie, then A809, A811, off the A811 → Drymen, Golf just South of Drymen.
Map 2 on page 486 Carte 2 Page 486

Golf course — PARCOURS — 14/20

Site	Site	
Maintenance	Entretien	
Architect	Architecte	James Braid
Type	Type	parkland
Relief	Relief	
Water in play	Eau en jeu	
Exp. to wind	Exposé au vent	
Trees in play	Arbres en jeu	

Scorecard Carte de score	**Chp.** Chp.	**Mens** Mess.	**Ladies** Da.
Length Long.	5538	5180	4795
Par	70	68	71
Slope system	—	—	—

Advised golfing ability Niveau de jeu recommandé — 0 12 24 36

Hcp required Handicap exigé — 26 Men, 36 Ladies

Club house & amenities — CLUB HOUSE ET ANNEXES — 6/10

Pro shop	Pro-shop	
Driving range	Practice	
Sheltered	couvert	yes
On grass	sur herbe	yes
Putting-green	putting-green	yes
Pitching-green	pitching green	yes

Hotel facilities — ENVIRONNEMENT HOTELIER — 6/10

HOTELS HÔTELS

Buchanan Arms, 52 rooms, D £ 150 — Drymen
Tel (44) 01360 - 660 588, Fax (44) 01360 - 660 943 — 1 km

Cameron House (De Vere), 89 rooms, D £ 225 — Balloch
Tel (44) 01389 - 755 565, Fax (44) 01389 - 759 522 — 5 km

RESTAURANTS RESTAURANT

Georgian Room (Cameron House) — Balloch
Tel (44) 01389 - 755 565 — 5 km

Buchanan Arms — Drymen
Tel (44) 01360 - 660 588 — 1 km

Breakers (Cameron House) — Balloch
Tel (44) 01360 - 755 565 — 5 km

BURNTISLAND

14	6	6

The club was founded in 1797 but the course dates back to the end of the 19th century. Laid out by Willie Park Jr., it was restyled by the inevitable James Braid. At the time, this was one of the few courses to open on a Sunday. Built on a little hill overlooking the Firth of Forth, it is still very walkable but a number of elevated greens call for very careful club selection. Likewise, the natural topology has been used with great skill, as you might expect from the afore-mentioned architects. Alongside the many links courses along the coast leading up to Saint Andrews, Burntisland provides the alternative of a parkland style which is highly satisfactory to look at and to play. A candidly open course when the wind stays away, it can turn nasty when the weather gets rough, as all the holes seem to be laid out in different directions. So on a windy day this is a good test for technique and for your nerves. The club-house is modern, functional and unpretentious with a warm welcome.

Le Club a été fondé en 1797 mais le parcours date de la fin du XIXème siècle. Tracé par Willie Park Jr, il a été remanié par l'inévitable James Braid. A l'époque, c'était l'un des seul parcours du pays ouvert le dimanche. Il est construit sur une petite colline dominant le Firth of Forth, mais reste tout à fait jouable à pied. Cependant, quelques greens en élévation exigent un choix de club très exact. De même, les contours du terrain ont été utilisés avec beaucoup de savoir-faire, comme on peut l'attendre de tels architectes. A côté des nombreux links de la côte menant jusqu'à St Andrews, Burntisland offre l'alternative d'une esthétique "parkland" très satisfaisante visuellement et golfiquement. Assez franc quand il n'y pas de vent, ce parcours peut devenir plus méchant s'il souffle, car les trous changent sans cesse d'orientation. C'est alors un bon test pour la technique et les nerfs. Le Clubhouse est moderne, fonctionnel et sans prétention, l'accueil chaleureux.

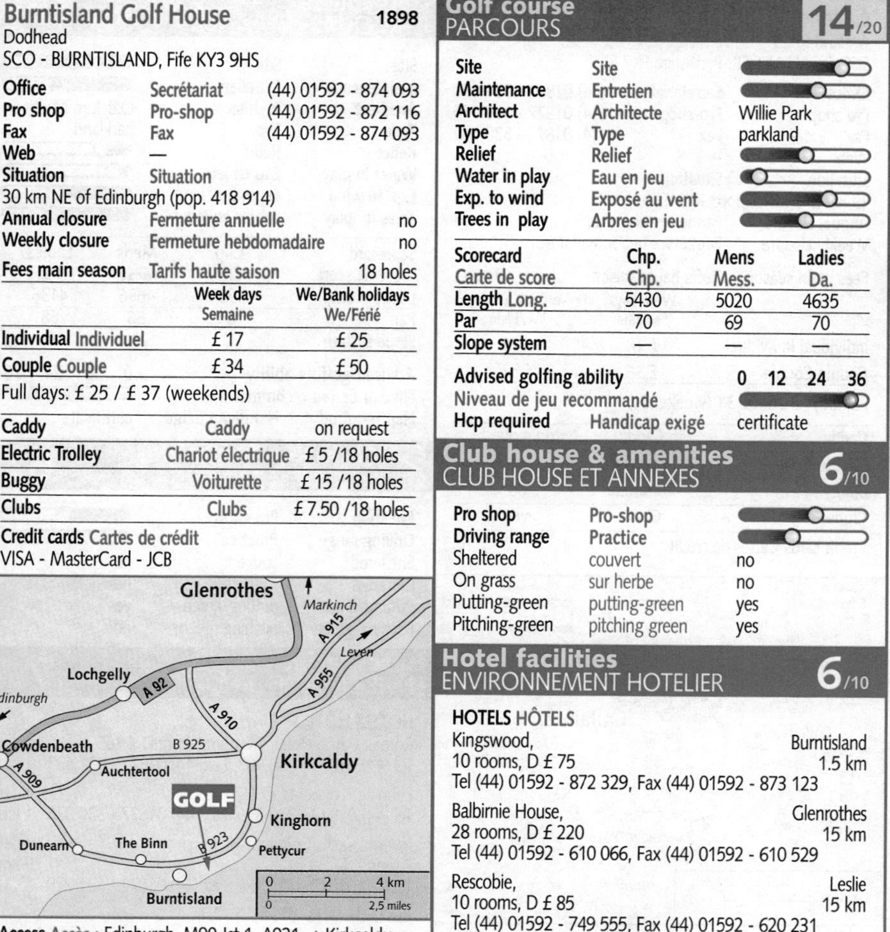

Burntisland Golf House **1898**
Dodhead
SCO - BURNTISLAND, Fife KY3 9HS

Office	Secrétariat	(44) 01592 - 874 093
Pro shop	Pro-shop	(44) 01592 - 872 116
Fax	Fax	(44) 01592 - 874 093
Web	—	
Situation	Situation	

30 km NE of Edinburgh (pop. 418 914)

Annual closure	Fermeture annuelle	no
Weekly closure	Fermeture hebdomadaire	no

Fees main season Tarifs haute saison	18 holes	
	Week days Semaine	**We/Bank holidays** We/Férié
Individual Individuel	£ 17	£ 25
Couple Couple	£ 34	£ 50

Full days: £ 25 / £ 37 (weekends)

Caddy	Caddy	on request
Electric Trolley	Chariot électrique	£ 5 /18 holes
Buggy	Voiturette	£ 15 /18 holes
Clubs	Clubs	£ 7.50 /18 holes

Credit cards Cartes de crédit
VISA - MasterCard - JCB

Access Accès : Edinburgh, M90 Jct 1, A921 → Kirkcaldy, Golf on B923, 1.5 km (1 m.) East of Burntisland.
Map 3 on page 489 Carte 3 Page 489

Golf course PARCOURS 14/20

Site	Site	
Maintenance	Entretien	
Architect	Architecte	Willie Park
Type	Type	parkland
Relief	Relief	
Water in play	Eau en jeu	
Exp. to wind	Exposé au vent	
Trees in play	Arbres en jeu	

Scorecard Carte de score	**Chp.** Chp.	**Mens** Mess.	**Ladies** Da.
Length Long.	5430	5020	4635
Par	70	69	70
Slope system	—	—	—

Advised golfing ability Niveau de jeu recommandé 0 12 24 36
Hcp required Handicap exigé certificate

Club house & amenities CLUB HOUSE ET ANNEXES 6/10

Pro shop	Pro-shop	
Driving range	Practice	
Sheltered	couvert	no
On grass	sur herbe	no
Putting-green	putting-green	yes
Pitching-green	pitching green	yes

Hotel facilities ENVIRONNEMENT HOTELIER 6/10

HOTELS HÔTELS

Kingswood, Burntisland
10 rooms, D £ 75 1.5 km
Tel (44) 01592 - 872 329, Fax (44) 01592 - 873 123

Balbirnie House, Glenrothes
28 rooms, D £ 220 15 km
Tel (44) 01592 - 610 066, Fax (44) 01592 - 610 529

Rescobie, Leslie
10 rooms, D £ 85 15 km
Tel (44) 01592 - 749 555, Fax (44) 01592 - 620 231

King Malcolm Thistle, Dunfermline
48 rooms, D £ 120 15 km
Tel (44) 01383 - 722 611, Fax (44) 01383 - 730 865

CALLANDER

13 | 6 | 7

This is the region of Trossachs, dotted with hills and lochs and a lot of wild-life, including deer which come down from the Perthshire hills in spring to graze on the fairways. It is also the region which inspired Walter Scott and Daniel Defoe and helped create the character of Rob Roy. In fact, the museum celebrating this popular hero is situated in Callander. The golf-course of the same name is laid out over an idyllic site which is ideal for spending a few days holiday without feeling too bad about your game. Old Tom Morris help build this course, and as on most courses that stretch back almost to the origins of golf, length is not a vital factor. Having said that, the par 3s take some reaching and there are seven of them to contend with here. There is also only one par 5, so the tempo is a little different from usual. The dangers include several ditches and other hazards, which call for some careful shot-making. Open and uncomplicated, this is hardly your unforgettable course but we would defy anyone not to have fun playing it.

C'est la région des Trossachs, parsemée de collines et de lochs, avec une faune importante : au printemps, les cerfs descendent des collines du Perthshire pour brouter sur le parcours. C'est aussi une région qui a inspiré Walter Scott, et Daniel Defoe avec le personnage de Rob Roy. Le Musée célébrant ce héros poulaire se trouve d'ailleurs à Callander. Le parcours du même nom se trouve dans un site idyllique, idéal pour passer quelques jours de vacances sans trop faire honte à ses clubs. Old Tom Morris a participé à sa construction. Comme sur les parcours encore proches des origines, la longueur n'est pas l'élément essentiel, bien que les par 3 soient souvent très respectables de ce point de vue. Il y en a sept ici, et un seul par 5, ce qui créée un rythme de jeu assez inhabituel. Plusieurs fossés et autres obstacles d'eau demandent un travail de balle très réfléchi et attentif. Franc et sans complication, ce n'est certes pas un parcours inoubliable, mais on défie quiconque de ne pas y prendre plaisir.

Callander Golf Club — 1890

Aveland Road
SCO - CALLANDER, Perthshire FK7 8EN

Office	Secrétariat	(44) 01877 - 330 090
Pro shop	Pro-shop	(44) 01877 - 330 975
Fax	Fax	(44) 01877 - 330 062
Web	—	
Situation	Situation	

19 km of Stirling (pop. 30 515)

Annual closure	Fermeture annuelle	no
Weekly closure	Fermeture hebdomadaire	no

Fees main season Tarifs haute saison	Week days Semaine	We/Bank holidays We/Férié
18 holes		
Individual Individuel	£ 18	£ 26
Couple Couple	£ 36	£ 52

Full day: £ 26 - £ 31 (weekends)

Caddy	Caddy	on request
Electric Trolley	Chariot électrique	yes
Buggy	Voiturette	no
Clubs	Clubs	yes
Credit cards	Cartes de crédit	no

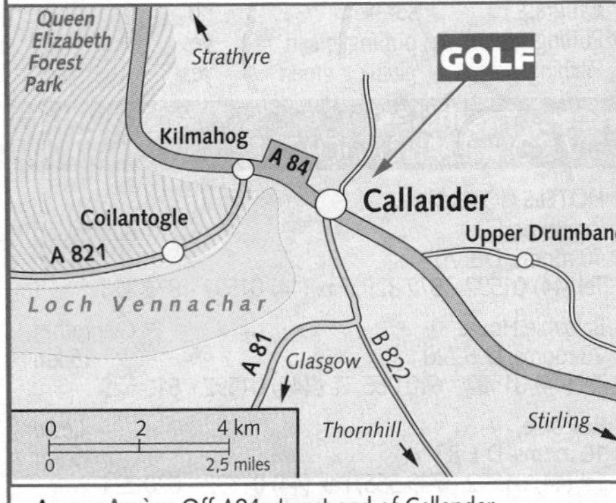

Access Accès : Off A84 at east end of Callander
Map 2 on page 486 Carte 2 Page 486

Golf course — PARCOURS — 13/20

Site	Site	
Maintenance	Entretien	
Architect	Architecte	Old Tom Morris
Type	Type	parkland
Relief	Relief	
Water in play	Eau en jeu	
Exp. to wind	Exposé au vent	
Trees in play	Arbres en jeu	

Scorecard Carte de score	Chp. Chp.	Mens Mess.	Ladies Da.
Length Long.	4903	4636	4136
Par	63	66	68
Slope system	0	0	0

Advised golfing ability Niveau de jeu recommandé — 0 12 24 36
Hcp required Handicap exigé — certificate

Club house & amenities — CLUB HOUSE ET ANNEXES — 6/10

Pro shop	Pro-shop	
Driving range	Practice	
Sheltered	couvert	no
On grass	sur herbe	no
Putting-green	putting-green	yes
Pitching-green	pitching green	no

Hotel facilities — ENVIRONNEMENT HOTELIER — 7/10

HOTELS HÔTELS

Roman Camp Hotel, 14 rooms, from D £ 165 — Callander
Tel (44) 01877 - 330 003, Fax (44) 01877 - 331 533 — 1 km

Lubnaig, 10 rooms, D £ 76 — Callander
Tel (44) 01877 - 330 376, Fax (44) 01877 - 330 376 — 1 km

Invertrossachs Country House — Callander
3 rooms, D £ 130 — 9 km
Tel (44) 01877 - 311 126, Fax (44) 01877 - 331 229

RESTAURANTS RESTAURANT

The Restaurant (Roman Camp) — Callander
Tel (44) 01877 - 330 003 — 1 km

Braeval Old Mill, Tel (44) 01877 - 382 711 Aberfoyle 12 km

CARDROSS

14	6	5

To the south of Loch Lomond, this course provides some pretty views over the Firth of Clyde and the countryside around Dumbarton. Laid out in moderately hilly parkland landscape, it is a good test of golf for players of all abilities, even though the course is hardly the latest thing in modern golf design. The main ifficulty lies with the classic and very numerous bunkers. The heavy clay soil can get sticky in winter and the very thick urf stops the ball from rolling very far in spring and summer. Under these conditions, every yard of fairway really ounts. The course was laid out in 1904 by Willie Fernie from Troon, and the changes made since then have not changed the spirit of this old and respectable golf club. Other clubs in the region certainly enjoy a better reputation and probably have more spectacular courses than this (and higher green-fees, too), but the frankness of this layout, the pleasure of playing here and the way the course is adapted to players of all abilities, make this a pretty useful round of golf when you are in the region (except on week-ends).

u sud du Loch Lomond, ce parcours offre de jolis panoramas sur le Firth of Clyde et la campagne de Dumbarton. racé dans un paysage de parc modérément accidenté, c'est un bon test de golf pour tous niveaux, même s'il n'est pas u tout dernier modernisme. Ce sont d'ailleurs de classiques et nombreux bunkers qui sont la principale difficulté. Le errain argileux est assez lourd en hiver, et son gazon très fourni empêche les balles de rouler beaucoup à la belle saison : dans ces conditions, chaque mètre du parcours compte. Le dessin en a été fait en 1904 par Willie Fernie, de roon, et les changements apportés depuis n'ont pas modifié l'esprit de ce vieux et respectable Club de golf. Certes, 'autres Clubs de la région ont des réputations mieux établies, et sans doute des parcours plus spectaculaires (et aussi ux green-fees plus élevés), mais la franchise de celui-ci, l'agrément du lieu, l'adaptation à tous les types de joueurs n font un golf utile (sauf en week-end) quand on se trouve dans cette région.

Cardross Golf Club — 1904

Main Road
SCO - CARDROSS, Dumbarton G82 5LB

Office	Secrétariat	(44) 01389 - 841 754
Pro shop	Pro-shop	(44) 01389 - 841 350
Fax	Fax	(44) 01389 - 841 754
Web	—	
Situation	Situation	

8 km W of Dumbarton - 30 km NW of Glasgow (pop. 662 853)

Annual closure	Fermeture annuelle	no
Weekly closure	Fermeture hebdomadaire	no

Fees main season / Tarifs haute saison	18 holes	
	Week days / Semaine	We/Bank holidays / We/Férié
Individual Individuel	£ 28	*
Couple Couple	£ 56	*

* No visitors at weekends / Full weekday: £ 40

Caddy	Caddy	on request
Electric Trolley	Chariot électrique	no
Buggy	Voiturette	no
Clubs	Clubs	£ 12 /18 holes

Credit cards Cartes de crédit
VISA (Pro Shop only)

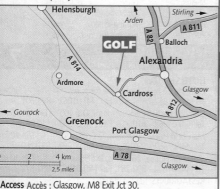

Access Accès : Glasgow, M8 Exit Jct 30, then A814 to Cardross
Map 3 on page 488 Carte 3 Page 488

Golf course / PARCOURS — 14/20

Site	Site	
Maintenance	Entretien	
Architect	Architecte	Willie Fernie, James Braid
Type	Type	parkland
Relief	Relief	
Water in play	Eau en jeu	
Exp. to wind	Exposé au vent	
Trees in play	Arbres en jeu	

Scorecard / Carte de score	Chp. / Chp.	Mens / Mess.	Ladies / Da.
Length Long.	5887	5607	5238
Par	71	71	76
Slope system	0	0	0

Advised golfing ability / Niveau de jeu recommandé: 0 12 24 36
Hcp required / Handicap exigé: no

Club house & amenities / CLUB HOUSE ET ANNEXES — 6/10

Pro shop	Pro-shop	
Driving range	Practice	
Sheltered	couvert	no
On grass	sur herbe	yes
Putting-green	putting-green	yes
Pitching-green	pitching green	yes

Hotel facilities / ENVIRONNEMENT HOTELIER — 5/10

HOTELS HÔTELS

Cameron House, 96 rooms, D £ 220 — Balloch 8 km
Tel (44) 01389 - 755 565, Fax (44) 01389 - 759 522

Travelodge, 32 rooms, D £ 60 — Dunbarton 8 km
Tel (44) 01389 - 765 202

RESTAURANTS RESTAURANT

Georgian Room (Cameron House) — Balloch 8 km
Tel (44) 01389 - 755 565

CARNEGIE CLUB (SKIBO CASTLE) 15 9 7

This Donald Steel designed links course is set on the grounds of the famous Skibo Castle, once t home of Andrew Carnegie and now a private international member's club. There are very few tee tim available, they can only be booked by prior arrangement . The original course was built in 1898. Dona Steel has retained very little from the original blueprint and has laid out this links course over limited space and magr ficent countryside, surrounded on three sides by the sea. At the same time, he has preserved a number of very nat ral areas where you can see some very rare species of lichen growing on stony surfaces. There are also salt marsh widgeons, greylag geese and otters, making this a paradise for bird and animal lovers. The actual course perha lacks a little audacity, but nobody is going to knock Steel forkeeping to sobriety and tradition. He has respected t soul of the site and left the panache to the rest of the property. Strictly reserved for members only, this very luxurio estate sometimes opens up to the outside world, for golf or for weddings... Just ask Madonna.

Ce parcours de links a été tracé en 1898 sur le domaine du Skibo Castle, appartenant à Andrew Carnegie. C'e maintenant un club international très privé, avec peu de départs possibles pour les visiteurs. Donald Steel a conse vé peu de choses de l'original, traçant son links dans un espace limité et un paysage magnifique, entouré sur tr côtés par la mer. En même temps, il a préservé des zones très naturelles, où poussent de très rares espèces lichens sur la surface des pierres. On trouve aussi des marais salants, des canards siffleurs,des oies cendrées, d loutres, et c'est un paradis pour les amoureux des oiseaux. Le parcours lui-même manque sans doute un peu d'a dace, mais peut-on vraiment reprocher à Steel d'avoir joué la sobriété et la tradition, bref, l'esprit du lieu, laissa le panache à la propriété elle-même. Très réservé à ses membres, ce domaine très luxueux peut s'ouvrir parfois l'extérieur, pour le golf ou pour s'y marier, comme Madonna...

The Carnegie Club 1995

Skibo Castle
SCO - DORNOCH, Sutherland IV25 3RQ

Office	Secrétariat	(44) 01862 - 894 600
Pro shop	Pro-shop	(44) 01862 - 894 600
Fax	Fax	(44) 01862 - 894 601
Web	www.carnegieclubs.com	
Situation	Situation	

7 km W. of Dornoch (pop. 2042) - 56 km from Inverness

Annual closure	Fermeture annuelle	no
Weekly closure	Fermeture hebdomadaire	no

Fees main season Tarifs haute saison		18 holes
	Week days Semaine	**We/Bank holidays** We/Férié
Individual Individuel	£ 130	*
Couple Couple	£ 260	*

A few times available per year. * For members.

Caddy	Caddy	on request
Electric Trolley	Chariot électrique	no
Buggy	Voiturette	on request
Clubs	Clubs	yes

Credit cards Cartes de crédit
VISA - Eurocard - MasterCard - DC - AMEX

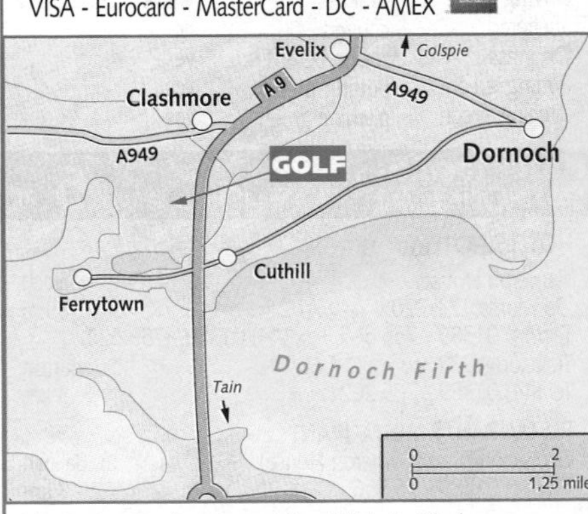

Access Accès : Inverness, A9 → Wick, In Clashmore, turn left on A949.
Map 1 on page 484 Carte 1 Page 484

Golf course PARCOURS 15/2

Site	Site	
Maintenance	Entretien	
Architect	Architecte	Donald Steel Tom Mackenzie
Type	Type	seaside course, link
Relief	Relief	
Water in play	Eau en jeu	
Exp. to wind	Exposé au vent	
Trees in play	Arbres en jeu	

Scorecard Carte de score	**Chp.** Chp.	**Mens** Mess.	**Ladies** Da.
Length Long.	6004	5566	4893
Par	71	71	71
Slope system	—	—	—

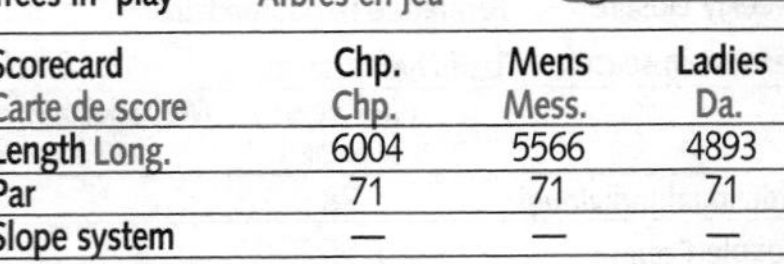

Advised golfing ability 0 12 24 36
Niveau de jeu recommandé
Hcp required Handicap exigé no

Club house & amenities CLUB HOUSE ET ANNEXES 9/10

Pro shop	Pro-shop	
Driving range	Practice	
Sheltered	couvert	no
On grass	sur herbe	yes
Putting-green	putting-green	yes
Pitching-green	pitching green	yes

Hotel facilities ENVIRONNEMENT HOTELIER 7/1(

HOTELS HÔTELS
Carnegie Club, 32 rooms, ask for prices — on site
Tel (44) 01862 - 894 600, Fax (44) 01862 - 894 601
Dornoch Castle Hotel, 17 rooms, D £ 100 — Dornoch 5 km
Tel (44) 01862 - 810 216, Fax (44) 01862 - 810 981
Mansfield House, 19 rooms, D £ 170 — Tain 10 km
Tel (44) 01862 - 892 052, Fax (44) 01862 - 892 260
Morangie House, 26 rooms, D £ 95 — Tain 10 km
Tel (44) 01862 - 892 281, Fax (44) 01862 - 892 872

RESTAURANTS RESTAURANT
Carnegie Club, Tel (44) 01862 - 894 600 — on site
Mansfield House, Tel (44) 01862 - 892 052 — Tain
Morangie House, Tel (44) 01862 - 892 281 — Tain 10 km

CARNOUSTIE Burnside

14	5	6

Of course you don't come here only to play this "Burnside Course", but if you consider this simply as a warm-up round before playing the Championship course, then watch out: this is not a layout for beginners. It is certainly much shorter than its prestigious older companion but does have enough difficulties for it to hold its head high. It is laid out in a similar setting, the only blemish being that it runs alongside the railway track. Bunkers form the main line of defence, but there is also a number of trees which accentuate the countryside appearance found here and there on the Championship course. On a site that could contain in all almost a dozen courses, this layout more than does itself justice. And the appeal of the environment benefits from the hotel opened for the British Open in 1999.

Certes, on ne vient pas ici uniquement pour jouer ce "Burnside Course", mais s'il s'agit simplement de s'échauffer avant de jouer le "Championship", méfiance car ce n'est pas un parcours pour débutants. Il est certes beaucoup plus court que son prestigieux aîné, mais présente assez de difficultés pour garder la tête haute. Il est d'ailleurs situé dans un environnement similaire, son seul défaut étant de longer davantage la voie ferrée. Les bunkers constituent la défense essentielle, avec aussi pas mal d'arbres, ce qui accentue un aspect campagne que l'on retrouve çà et là sur le "Championship." Dans un site qui pourrait au total contenir une bonne dizaine de parcours, celui-ci est plus qu'honorable. Et la séduction autrefois incertaine de l'environnement a bénéficié de l'inauguration d'un hôtel pour le mémorable British Open 1999.

Carnoustie Golf Links — 1914

Links Parade
SCO- CARNOUSTIE, Angus, DD7 7JE

Office	Secrétariat	(44) 01241 - 853 789
Pro shop	Pro-shop	
Fax	Fax	(44) 01241 - 852 720
Web	www.carnoustie.co.uk	
Situation	Situation	

17 km NE of Dundee (pop. 165 873) - 9 km SW of Abroath

Annual closure	Fermeture annuelle	no
Weekly closure	Fermeture hebdomadaire	no

Fees main season Tarifs haute saison		18 holes
	Week days Semaine	**We/Bank holidays** We/Férié
Individual Individuel	£ 25	£ 25
Couple Couple	£ 50	£ 50

Caddy	Caddy	£ 30
Electric Trolley	Chariot électrique	no
Buggy	Voiturette	no
Clubs	Clubs	nearby Pro shop

Credit cards Cartes de crédit
VISA - Eurocard - MasterCard - AMEX

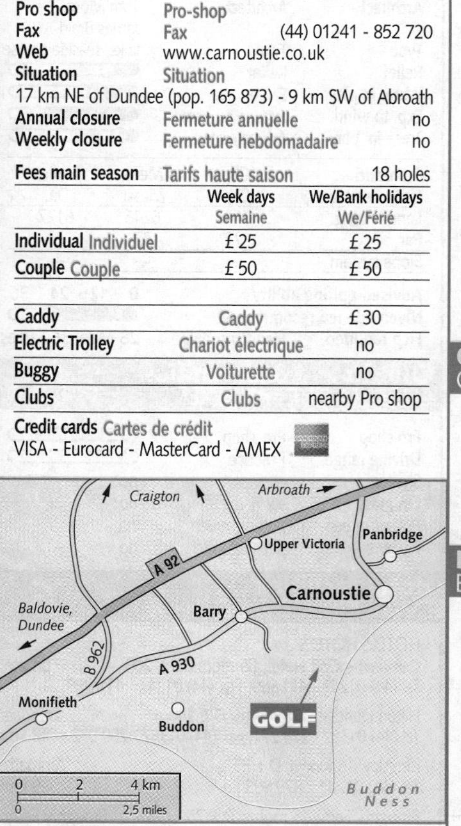

Access Accès : Dundee, A92 and A930
Map 2 on page 487 Carte 2 Page 487

Golf course PARCOURS — 14/20

Site	Site	
Maintenance	Entretien	
Architect	Architecte	Unknown
Type	Type	links
Relief	Relief	
Water in play	Eau en jeu	
Exp. to wind	Exposé au vent	
Trees in play	Arbres en jeu	

Scorecard Carte de score	**Chp.** Chp.	**Mens** Mess.	**Ladies** Da.
Length Long.	5478	5478	5478
Par	68	68	72
Slope system	—	—	—

Advised golfing ability Niveau de jeu recommandé — 0 12 24 36
Hcp required Handicap exigé — no

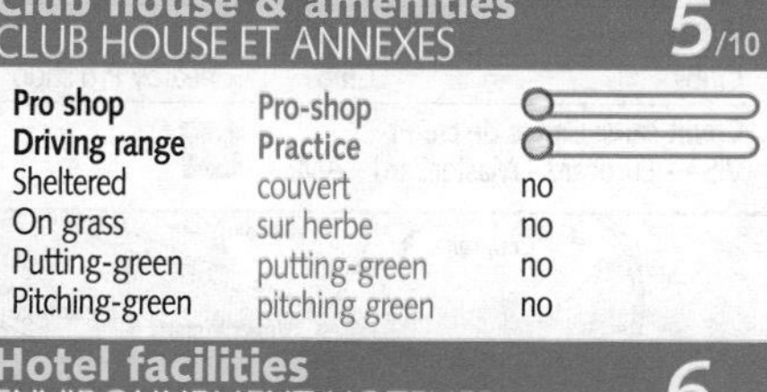

Club house & amenities CLUB HOUSE ET ANNEXES — 5/10

Pro shop	Pro-shop	
Driving range	Practice	
Sheltered	couvert	no
On grass	sur herbe	no
Putting-green	putting-green	no
Pitching-green	pitching green	no

Hotel facilities ENVIRONNEMENT HOTELIER — 6/10

HOTELS HÔTELS

Carnoustie Golf Hotel, 85 rooms, D £ 200 — Carnoustie on site
Tel (44) 01241 - 411 999, Fax (44) 01241 - 411 998

Hilton Dundee, 128 rooms, D £ 140 — Dundee 18 km
Tel (44) 01382 - 229 271, Fax (44) 01382 - 200 072

Kingsley, 16 rooms, D £ 35 — Arbroath 9 km
Tel (44) 01241 - 879 933

Broughty Ferry, 15 rooms, D £ 75 — Broughty Ferry 12 km
Tel (44) 01382 - 480 027, Fax (44) 01382 - 477 660

RESTAURANTS RESTAURANT

11 Park Avenue — Carnoustie 3 km
Tel (44) 01241 - 853 336

CARNOUSTIE Championship 19 | 5 | 6

The return of the British Open to Carnoustie saw the historic 18th hole disaster of Jean van de Velde and a surprise win for Paul Lawrie, a little unusual in a history marked by wins from such greats as Armour, Cotton, Ben Hogan, Gary Player and Tom Watson. Contrary to many links courses, this one is very difficult without the wind. When the wind does blow, it can be a real brute. There are no large dunes, just a sort of space where the sea has apparently withdrawn to leave room for a few streams, bushes, a little scrub and long grass. Designers have successively added a few very nasty bunkers, very tricky greens and optical illusions that make club choice very difficult. If you survive the first 15 holes, the last three can easily finish you off. For this inhuman greatness, some prefer Carnoustie to the Old Course at St Andrews. There is little to choose...

Le retour du British Open à Carnoustie en 1999 a vu le désastre historique de Jean van de Velde et la victoire surprise de Paul Lawrie, assez insolites après les succès ici de légendes telles que Armour, Cotton, Ben Hogan, Gary Player et Tom Watson. Au contraire de beaucoup de links qui ne prennent leur vraie dimension que dans un vent violent, celui-ci est très difficile même quand il n'y en a pas. Et s'il souffle, c'est carrément une brute. Pas de grandes dunes ici, mais une sorte d'espace d'où la mer se serait retirée doucement pour laisser place à quelques ruisseaux, aux buissons, à de rares arbustes, aux longues herbes. Les architectes y ont successivement ajouté quelques bunkers très méchants, des greens d'une grande subtilité, et des illusions d'optique qui rendent très difficile le choix de clubs. Et si l'on a survécu à quinze trous, les trois derniers peuvent vous achever. Pour cette grandeur inhumaine, certains préfèrent Carnoustie au "Old Course" de St Andrews... Il n'est certes pas inférieur.

Carnoustie Golf Links — 1842

Links Parade
SCO- CARNOUSTIE, Angus, DD7 7JE

Office Secrétariat (44) 01241 - 853 789
Pro shop Pro-shop
Fax Fax (44) 01241 - 852 720
Web www.carnoustie.co.uk
Situation Situation
17 km NE of Dundee (pop. 165 873) - 9 km SW of Abroath
Annual closure Fermeture annuelle — no
Weekly closure Fermeture hebdomadaire — no

Fees main season / Tarifs haute saison	Week days / Semaine	We/Bank holidays / We/Férié
18 holes		
Individual Individuel	£ 60	£ 85
Couple Couple	£ 120	£ 170

Caddy	Caddy	£ 30
Electric Trolley	Chariot électrique	no
Buggy	Voiturette	no
Clubs	Clubs	nearby Pro shop

Credit cards Cartes de crédit
VISA - Eurocard - MasterCard - AMEX

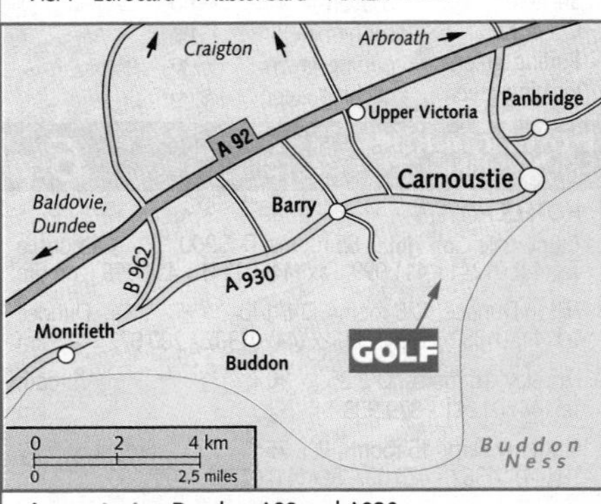

Access Accès : Dundee, A92 and A930
Map 2 on page 487 Carte 2 Page 487

Golf course PARCOURS — 19/20

Site	Site	
Maintenance	Entretien	
Architect	Architecte	Tom Morris, James Braid
Type	Type	links, seaside course
Relief	Relief	
Water in play	Eau en jeu	
Exp. to wind	Exposé au vent	
Trees in play	Arbres en jeu	

Scorecard / Carte de score	Chp. / Chp.	Mens / Mess.	Ladies / Da.
Length Long.	6643	6246	6127
Par	72	72	73
Slope system	—	—	—

Advised golfing ability 0 12 24 36
Niveau de jeu recommandé
Hcp required Handicap exigé 28 Men, 36 Ladies

Club house & amenities CLUB HOUSE ET ANNEXES — 5/10

Pro shop	Pro-shop	
Driving range	Practice	
Sheltered	couvert	no
On grass	sur herbe	no
Putting-green	putting-green	no
Pitching-green	pitching green	no

Hotel facilities ENVIRONNEMENT HOTELIER — 6/10

HOTELS HÔTELS
Carnoustie Golf Hotel, 85 rooms, D £ 200 — on site
Tel (44) 01241 - 411 999, Fax (44) 01241 - 411 998

Hilton Dundee, 128 rooms, D £ 140 — Dundee
Tel (44) 01382 - 229 271, Fax (44) 01382 - 200 072 — 18 km

Kingsley, 16 rooms, D £ 35 — Arbroath
Tel (44) 01241 - 879 933 — 9 km

Broughty Ferry, 15 rooms, D £ 75 — Broughty Ferry
Tel (44) 01382 - 480 027, Fax (44) 01382 - 477 660 — 12 km

RESTAURANTS RESTAURANT
11 Park Avenue, Tel (44) 01241 - 853 336 Carnoustie 3 km

CRAIL Balcomie Links

15 | 6 | 6

The Balcomie Links in the ancient burgh of Crail not far from St Andrews itself, is one of Scotland's finest golfing treasures. This is not one of the country's longest courses but it is one of its most popular and draws visitors from every corner of the world, year after year, to enjoy a very special challenge to add to wonderful views across St Andrews Bay. Several fairways wind their way along golden sandy beaches and rocky outcrops along the Forth foreshore. The club itself is the seventh oldest in the world, having been founded in 1786. It may be an old club, but its is very modern in its thinking and outlook. The club brought in American architect Gil Hanse to build a second course in Crail - the Craighead Links. This is a different animal altogether from the Balcomie course, and already has earned a reputation for its severity of challenge and for depth of its rough.

Balcomie Links est à ranger parmi les richesses du golf écossais. Construit dans le "burgh" de Crail, non loin de St Andrews, ce n'est pas l'un des plus longs parcours du pays, mais sa popularité lui attire des visiteurs du monde entier, venus relever ses nombreux défis, tout en admirant le merveilleux spectacle de St Andrews Bay. Le relief de la côte Est de l'Ecosse est moins mouvementé que celui de la côte Ouest, soumise à toutes les tempêtes, mais on trouvera plusieurs trous le long de plages dorées ponctuées d'affleurements rocheux le long du rivage du Forth. Le reste du parcours, plus "inland," n'est pas moins exposé au vent, il est assez intéressant pour que l'on reste concentré jusqu'à la fin. Crail est le septième plus ancien club de l'histoire du golf (il a été fondé en 1786), mais son ancienneté ne l'empêche pas d'être parmi les plus accueillants de tout le pays, et il ne refuse pas la modernité. Ainsi, Crail a demandé à l'architecte américain Gil Hanse de construire un second 18 trous, Craighead Links. Dans un autre style que Balcomie Links, il a conquis sa réputation par son exigence, et aussi la densité de ses roughs.

Crail Golfing Society — 1895

Balcomie Clubhouse, Fifeness
SCO - CRAIL, Fife KY10 3XN

Office	Secrétariat	(44) 01333 - 450 686
Pro shop	Pro-shop	(44) 01333 - 450 960
Fax	Fax	(44) 01333 - 450 416
Web	—	
Situation	Situation	

14 km S of St Andrews (pop. 11 136)

Annual closure	Fermeture annuelle	no
Weekly closure	Fermeture hebdomadaire	no

Fees main season Tarifs haute saison — 18 holes

	Week days / Semaine	We/Bank holidays / We/Férié
Individual Individuel	£ 30	£ 35
Couple Couple	£ 60	£ 70

Caddy	Caddy	on request
Electric Trolley	Chariot électrique	yes
Buggy	Voiturette	medical reasons only
Clubs	Clubs	£ 15 /18 holes

Credit cards Cartes de crédit
VISA - Eurocard - MasterCard - JCB

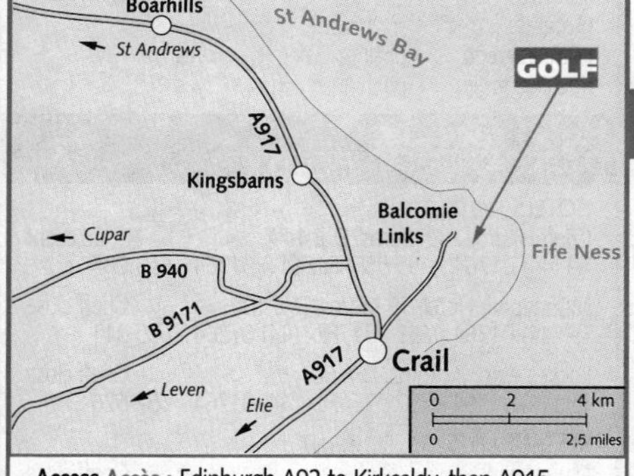

Access Accès : Edinburgh A92 to Kirkcaldy, then A915 through Leven, B942 and A 917 through Crail until Golf Hotel, turn right → Golf.
Map 3 on page 489 Carte 3 Page 489

Golf course PARCOURS — 15/20

Site	Site	
Maintenance	Entretien	
Architect	Architecte	Tom Morris
Type	Type	links
Relief	Relief	
Water in play	Eau en jeu	
Exp. to wind	Exposé au vent	
Trees in play	Arbres en jeu	

Scorecard / Carte de score	Chp. / Chp.	Mens / Mess.	Ladies / Da.
Length Long.	5330	4908	4707
Par	69	67	70
Slope system	—	—	—

Advised golfing ability — 0 12 24 36
Niveau de jeu recommandé
Hcp required Handicap exigé — no

Club house & amenities CLUB HOUSE ET ANNEXES — 6/10

Pro shop	Pro-shop	
Driving range	Practice	
Sheltered	couvert	no
On grass	sur herbe	no
Putting-green	putting-green	yes
Pitching-green	pitching green	no

Hotel facilities ENVIRONNEMENT HOTELIER — 6/10

HOTELS HÔTELS

Balcomie Links — Crail
15 rooms, D £ 70 — 1 km
Tel (44) 01333 - 450 237, Fax (44) 01333 - 450 540

Croma, 8 rooms, D £ 60 — Crail
Tel (44) 01333 - 450 239 — 1 km

Smugglers Inn — Anstruther
9 rooms, D £ 65 — 6 km
Tel (44) 01333 - 310 506, Fax (44) 01333 - 312 706

RESTAURANTS RESTAURANT

The Cellar — Anstruther
Tel (44) 01333 - 310 378 — 6 km

CRIEFF Ferntower Course

15	7	7

The Crieff Golf Club is built largely on the side of a hill and therefore the challenge is at times as much a physical as a golfing one. Most golfers will need shaping their shots or choosing the right strategy with due consideration given to the slopes. Old Tom Morris laid out the original nine-hole course which was extended to 18 by Robert Simpson at the beginning of the First World War. James Braid made alterations to the layout in the 1920's but very little now remains of the changes he recommended following extensive alterations to the Ferntower course and the creation of the nine-hole Dornock course. The Ferntower Course in its present layout only dates back to 1980. Familiarity with the layout is a big advantage here. Visitors are assured of a warm and hospitable welcome. The people at Crieff really do make you feel at home.

Déjà, on ne saurait conseiller Crieff à ceux dont les jambes sont faibles, car il a été construit largement à flanc de colline, et le défi est parfois tout aussi physique que golfique. Les pentes doivent d'ailleurs souvent être prises en considération pour établir une stratégie efficace, comme pour choisir les meilleures trajectoires. Old Tom Morris lui-même a tracé le 9-trous original, porté à 18 trous par Robert Simpson au début de la Première Guerre Mondiale. James Braid a aussi effectué un certain nombre de modifications dans les années 1920, mais il reste peu de choses de ces éléments d'origine, suite à la modification du tracé du Ferntower Course et de la construction d'un 9-trous supplémentaire, le Dornock Course. Les travaux définitifs ont été achevés en 1980, mais ils ont été assez bien menés pour que l'on n'ait pas trop de disparités de style. Il est utile de jouer plusieurs fois pour bien comprendre ce tracé, mais on le fera avec plaisir quand on constate la qualité de la réception et de l'accueil : on se sent ici en famille.

Crieff Golf Club — 1891

Perth Road
SCO - CRIEFF, Perthshire PH7 3LR

Office	Secrétariat	(44) 01764 - 652 397
Pro shop	Pro-shop	(44) 01764 - 652 909
Fax	Fax	(44) 01764 - 655 096
Web	—	
Situation	Situation	

27 km W of Perth (pop. 123 495)

Annual closure	Fermeture annuelle	no
Weekly closure	Fermeture hebdomadaire	no

Fees main season Tarifs haute saison	Week days Semaine	We/Bank holidays We/Férié
		18 holes
Individual Individuel	£ 20	£ 25
Couple Couple	£ 40	£ 50

Full Weekdays: £ 33

Caddy	Caddy	no
Electric Trolley	Chariot électrique	no
Buggy	Voiturette	£ 15 /18 holes
Clubs	Clubs	£ 7.50 /18 holes

Credit cards Cartes de crédit
VISA - Mastercard - Access (only in Pro shop)

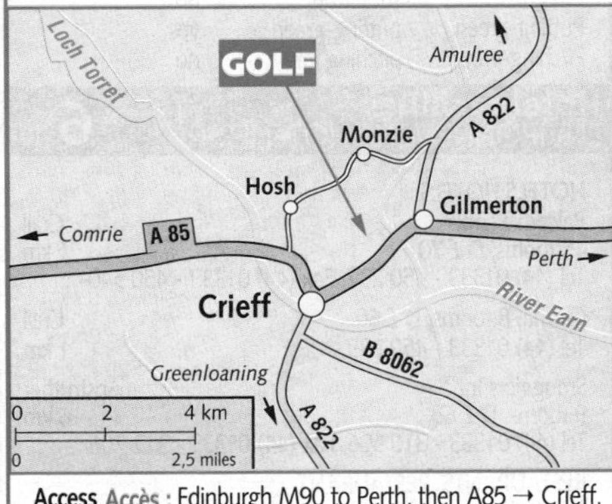

Access Accès : Edinburgh M90 to Perth, then A85 → Crieff. Golf on right at the edge of town.
Map 2 on page 487 Carte 2 Page 487

Golf course PARCOURS — 15/20

Site	Site	
Maintenance	Entretien	
Architect	Architecte	Bob Simpson James Braid
Type	Type	parkland
Relief	Relief	
Water in play	Eau en jeu	
Exp. to wind	Exposé au vent	
Trees in play	Arbres en jeu	

Scorecard Carte de score	Chp. Chp.	Mens Mess.	Ladies Da.
Length Long.	5830	5830	5830
Par	71	71	76
Slope system	—	—	—

Advised golfing ability Niveau de jeu recommandé — 0 12 24 36
Hcp required Handicap exigé — certificate

Club house & amenities CLUB HOUSE ET ANNEXES — 7/10

Pro shop	Pro-shop	
Driving range	Practice	
Sheltered	couvert	no
On grass	sur herbe	yes
Putting-green	putting-green	yes
Pitching-green	pitching green	yes

Hotel facilities ENVIRONNEMENT HOTELIER — 7/10

HOTELS HÔTELS

Crieff Hydro, 209 rooms, D £ 140 — adjacent
Tel (44) 01764 - 655 555, Fax (44) 01764 - 653 087

Murraypark Hotel, 19 rooms, D £ 100 — Crieff close
Tel (44) 01764 - 653 731, Fax (44) 01764 - 655 311

Lockes Acre, 7 rooms, D £ 60 — Crieff close
Tel (44) 01764 - 652 526, Fax (44) 01764 - 652 526

RESTAURANTS RESTAURANT

Murraypark — Crieff close
Tel (44) 01764 - 653 731

Crieff Hydro — adjacent
Tel (44) 01764 - 655 555

CRUDEN BAY

18 | 7 | 6

This is one of the very few Tom Simpson courses in Scotland, a masterpiece on a par with County Louth, another hidden gem but this time in Ireland. They say that Slain Castle in the background inspired Bram Stoker for his Dracula. Well you'll find drama enough here and maybe blood on your card too when the wind starts to blow and the designer, as if in a game of chess, takes your pieces one by one as the course unwinds. You will find every challenge to test your game: subtle, well-protected greens, strategic fairway bunkers, deep green-side bunkers, burns, blind shots, majestic long holes or teasing shorter ones. There was once a grand hotel on the site but it was demolished, a fact that might explain the relative anonymity from which Cruden Bay deserves to emerge... but don't tell anybody.

C'est un des seuls parcours de Tom Simpson en Ecosse, un véritable chef-d'oeuvre à mettre à côté de County Louth, lui aussi un des joyaux cachés du golf, mais d'Irlande cette fois. On dit que Slain Castle, en arrière plan du lieu, a inspiré Bram Stoker pour son "Dracula." Nul doute qu'il y aura aussi des drames et du sang sur les cartes de score quand le vent souffle un peu, et que la patiente partie d'échec de l'architecte avec les joueurs tourne à la déconfiture de ceux-ci. Greens subtils et bien défendus, bunkers de fairway stratégiques, profonds bunkers de green, petits "burns" piégeux, coups aveugles, longs trous majestueux ou petits trous provocants : on a ici tous les défis pour mettre son jeu à l'épreuve. Il y avait autrefois un grand hôtel sur place, il a été détruit, ce qui explique le relatif anonymat dont Cruden Bay mérite de sortir. Mais n'en parlez à personne...

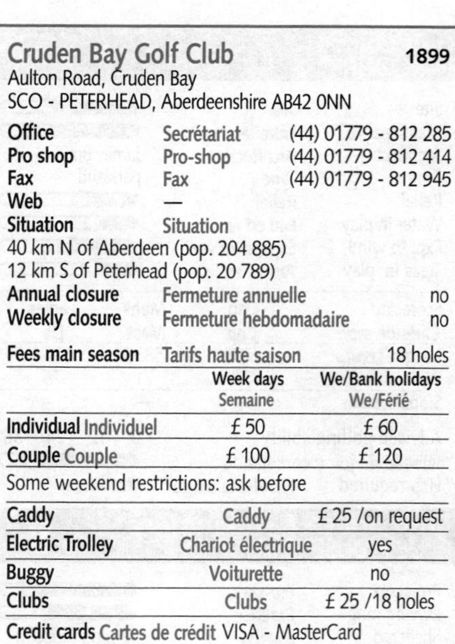

Cruden Bay Golf Club **1899**
Aulton Road, Cruden Bay
SCO - PETERHEAD, Aberdeenshire AB42 0NN

Office	Secrétariat	(44) 01779 - 812 285
Pro shop	Pro-shop	(44) 01779 - 812 414
Fax	Fax	(44) 01779 - 812 945
Web	—	
Situation	Situation	

40 km N of Aberdeen (pop. 204 885)
12 km S of Peterhead (pop. 20 789)

Annual closure	Fermeture annuelle	no
Weekly closure	Fermeture hebdomadaire	no

Fees main season Tarifs haute saison	18 holes	
	Week days Semaine	We/Bank holidays We/Férié
Individual Individuel	£ 50	£ 60
Couple Couple	£ 100	£ 120

Some weekend restrictions: ask before

Caddy	Caddy	£ 25 /on request
Electric Trolley	Chariot électrique	yes
Buggy	Voiturette	no
Clubs	Clubs	£ 25 /18 holes
Credit cards	Cartes de crédit	VISA - MasterCard

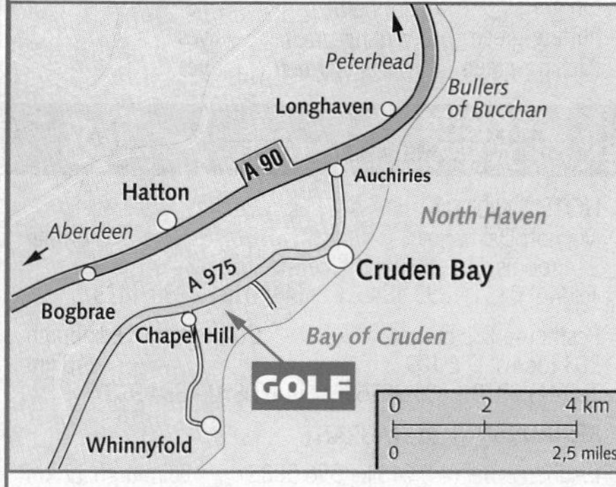

Access Accès : A92 through Aberdeen, then A975 → Peterhead to Cruden Bay.
Map 1 on page 485 Carte 1 Page 485

Golf course PARCOURS 18/20

Site	Site	
Maintenance	Entretien	
Architect	Architecte	Tom Simpson
Type	Type	links
Relief	Relief	
Water in play	Eau en jeu	
Exp. to wind	Exposé au vent	
Trees in play	Arbres en jeu	

Scorecard Carte de score	Chp. Chp.	Mens Mess.	Ladies Da.
Length Long.	5820	5480	5243
Par	70	70	74
Slope system	—	—	—

Advised golfing ability Niveau de jeu recommandé: 0 12 24 36
Hcp required Handicap exigé: certificate

Club house & amenities CLUB HOUSE ET ANNEXES 7/10

Pro shop	Pro-shop	
Driving range	Practice	
Sheltered	couvert	10 mats
On grass	sur herbe	yes
Putting-green	putting-green	yes
Pitching-green	pitching green	yes

Hotel facilities ENVIRONNEMENT HOTELIER 6/10

HOTELS HÔTELS

Waterside Inn, 69 rooms, D £ 90 — Peterhead 13 km
Tel (44) 01779 - 471 121, Fax (44) 01779 - 470 670

Udny Arms, 26 rooms, D £ 82 — Newburgh 10 km
Tel (44) 01358 - 789 444, Fax (44) 01779 - 789 012

Ardoe House, 112 rooms, D £ 110 — Aberdeeen 35 km
Tel (44) 01224 - 860 600, Fax (44) 01224 - 861 283

RESTAURANTS RESTAURANT

Udny Arms — Newburgh 10 km
Tel (44) 01358 - 789 444

Waterside Inn — Peterhead 13 km
Tel (44) 01779 - 471 121

DALMAHOY East Course

17 | 8 | 8

With two 18-hole courses, one of which is in the international league, this golfing complex controlled by Marriott is a very high class resort with a full-facility hotel, particularly for non-golfers (tennis, swimming pool, fitness, etc.). The East Course, designed by James Braid, has played host to some major tournaments, including the Solheim Cup in 1992. Although some aspects of the course are reminiscent of a links, here we are in a beautiful park where trees are important not so much as dangerous hazards but for outlining the holes. Water comes into play but only on two holes. So really if you drive straight you're half-way there, but only half-way. You need some accurate ironwork to hit the well-protected greens, so a few rudiments of target golf will more than come in handy. A good test of golf.

Avec deux parcours de 18 trous, dont un de classe internationale, cet ensemble contrôlé par Marriott est devenu un complexe de tout premier ordre avec un hôtel très bien équipé, notamment pour les non-golfeurs, qui auront de quoi s'occcuper en vous attendant: tennis, piscine, mise en forme, etc... Dessiné par James Braid, l'East Course a accueilli de grandes épreuves, dont la Solheim Cup en 1992. Bien que certains aspects puissent rappeler les links, nous sommes ici dans un parc de toute beauté, où les arbres jouent un certain rôle, mais ils définissent plus les trous qu'ils ne constituent des obstacles dangereux. L'eau n'est en jeu que sur deux trous. De fait, si l'on drive bien, on aura fait une bonne partie du chemin vers un bon score, mais c'est loin d'être suffisant : il faut être d'autant plus précis que les greens sont bien défendus, ce qui exige parfois de connaître les secrets du "target golf". Un bon test de golf.

Marriott Dalmahoy Golf & Country Club 1927

Kirknewton
SCO - EDINBURGH EH27 8EB

Office	Secrétariat	(44) 0131 - 333 1845
Pro shop	Pro-shop	(44) 0131 - 333 1845
Fax	Fax	(44) 0131 - 333 1433
Web	—	
Situation	Situation	

12 km SW of Edinburgh (pop. 418 914)

Annual closure	Fermeture annuelle	no
Weekly closure	Fermeture hebdomadaire	no

Fees main season Tarifs haute saison	Week days Semaine	We/Bank holidays We/Férié
		18 holes
Individual Individuel	£ 65*	£ 80*
Couple Couple	£ 130	£ 160

* For non residents

Caddy	Caddy	on request/£ 25
Electric Trolley	Chariot électrique	no
Buggy	Voiturette	£ 25 /18 holes
Clubs	Clubs	£ 25 /18 holes

Credit cards Cartes de crédit
VISA - Eurocard - MasterCard - DC - AMEX

Access Accès : From Edinburgh, on A 71 → Livingston
Map 3 on page 489 Carte 3 Page 489

Golf course PARCOURS 17/20

Site	Site	
Maintenance	Entretien	
Architect	Architecte	James Braid
Type	Type	parkland
Relief	Relief	
Water in play	Eau en jeu	
Exp. to wind	Exposé au vent	
Trees in play	Arbres en jeu	

Scorecard Carte de score	Chp. Chp.	Mens Mess.	Ladies Da.
Length Long.	6030	5836	5356
Par	72	71	75
Slope system	—	—	—

Advised golfing ability 0 12 24 36
Niveau de jeu recommandé
Hcp required Handicap exigé certificate

Club house & amenities CLUB HOUSE ET ANNEXES 8/10

Pro shop	Pro-shop	
Driving range	Practice	
Sheltered	couvert	12 bays (floodlit)
On grass	sur herbe	no
Putting-green	putting-green	yes
Pitching-green	pitching green	yes

Hotel facilities ENVIRONNEMENT HOTELIER 8/10

HOTELS HÔTELS

Marriott Dalmahoy — on site
214 rooms, D £ 261 with green-fee/dinner
Tel (44) 0131 - 333 1845, Fax (44) 0131 - 333 1433

Posthouse Edinburgh — Costorphine / Edinburgh 10 km
303 rooms, D £ 109
Tel (44) 0870 - 400 9026, Fax (44) 0870 - 334 9237

RESTAURANTS RESTAURANT

L'Auberge, Tel (44) 0131 - 556 5888 — Edinburgh 12 km
Yumi (Japanese), Tel (44) 0131 - 337 2173 — Edinburgh 9 km
Channings, Tel (44) 0131 - 315 2225 — Edinburgh 10 km

DOWNFIELD

17 | 6 | 7

Located in the north-west confines of Dundee, Downfield is without a doubt one of the very great British inland courses, even though it is still little known outside of Scotland and even less so to players from continental Europe. If you are in the region it would be a great pity to miss it. C.K. Cotton has designed an uncompromising challenge in an already very heavily wooded area. The course's park style means that the ball doesn't roll much so each yard of the course really counts on your card. Only good drivers can hope to get a good score, as long they keep on the straight and narrow. But short-game experts will feel very welcome here, as well. At an equal distance from St Andrews and Carnoustie, this is an excellent stop-over and a serious test of golf, more sheltered from the wind.

Situé aux limites nord-ouest de Dundee, Downfield est sans conteste un des très bons parcours "inland" de Grande-Bretagne, bien qu'il reste peu connu en dehors des limites de l'Ecosse, et ne parlons même pas des joueurs du continent. Mais il serait fort dommage de le négliger si l'on passe dans les environs. C.K. Cotton a créé un défi sans compromis dans un espace déjà très boisé. La nature de parc implique que la balle roule peu sur les fairways, et chaque mètre de ce parcours compte sur la carte. Seuls les bons drivers peuvent espérer un score honorable, du moment qu'ils parviennnet à ne pas trop s'égarer. Mais les maîtres du petit jeu sont aussi les bienvenus ici. A égale distance de Carnoustie et de St Andrews, voici une halte de qualité, et un sérieux test de golf... plus à l'abri du vent que ses deux presque voisins.

Downfield Golf Club — 1932

Turnberry Avenue
SCO - DUNDEE DD2 3QP

Office	Secrétariat	(44) 01382 - 825 595
Pro shop	Pro-shop	(44) 01382 - 889 246
Fax	Fax	(44) 01382 - 813 111
Web	—	
Situation	Situation	
3 km from Dundee (pop. 165 873)		
Annual closure	Fermeture annuelle	no
Weekly closure	Fermeture hebdomadaire	no

Fees main season Tarifs haute saison		18 holes
	Week days Semaine	**We/Bank holidays** We/Férié
Individual Individuel	£ 33	£ 34
Couple Couple	£ 66	£ 68
Caddy	Caddy	£ 20
Electric Trolley	Chariot électrique	£ 8 /18 holes
Buggy	Voiturette	£ 18 /18 holes
Clubs	Clubs	£ 12 /18 holes
Credit cards Cartes de crédit		yes

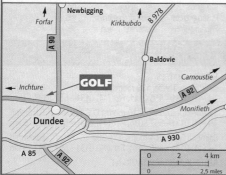

Access Accès : In Dundee, A90 Kingsway (Ring Road. A923 Coupar Angus Road. 50 m, right Faraday St, 1st left on Harrison Rd. 200 m, T junction, left onto Dalamhoy Dr. 400 m, left. **Map 1 on page 485** Carte 1 Page 485

Golf course — PARCOURS — 17/20

Site	Site	
Maintenance	Entretien	
Architect	Architecte	C.K. Cotton
Type	Type	parkland
Relief	Relief	
Water in play	Eau en jeu	
Exp. to wind	Exposé au vent	
Trees in play	Arbres en jeu	

Scorecard Carte de score	**Chp.** Chp.	**Mens** Mess.	**Ladies** Da.
Length Long.	6208	5702	5330
Par	73	70	74
Slope system	—	—	—

Advised golfing ability Niveau de jeu recommandé — 0 12 24 36

Hcp required Handicap exigé — no

Club house & amenities — CLUB HOUSE ET ANNEXES — 6/10

Pro shop	Pro-shop	
Driving range	Practice	
Sheltered	couvert	no
On grass	sur herbe	yes
Putting-green	putting-green	yes
Pitching-green	pitching green	yes

Hotel facilities — ENVIRONNEMENT HOTELIER — 7/10

HOTELS HÔTELS

Swallow Hotel, 105 rooms, D £ 115 — Dundee 3 km
Tel (44) 01382 - 641 122, Fax (44) 01382 - 568 340

Hilton Dundee, 128 rooms, D £ 140 — Dundee 5 km
Tel (44) 01382 - 229 271, Fax (44) 01382 - 200 072

Travel Inn, 40 rooms, D £ 41 — Dundee 5 km
Tel (44) 01382 - 203 240, Fax (44) 01382 - 203 237

RESTAURANTS RESTAURANT

Birkhill Inn — Dundee 2 km
Tel (44) 01382 - 581 297

Beefeater, Tel (44) 01382 - 561 115 — Dundee5 km

Raffles, Tel (44) 01382 - 226 344 — Dundee 4 km

DUDDINGSTON

15 | 7 | 9

One of the good Edinburgh courses, of which there are several dozen. The club has a good sporting reputation with an encouraging policy for young golfers that is none too common in the often crowded big city clubs. Located immediately behind Arthur's Seat to the east of the castle, this is a park course with the meanders of Braid's burn to make life a misery for golfers who like a round without hazards. The trees are also dangerously in play when there are no fairway bunkers. This moderately hilly course is well worth playing, especially since the designers always kept the cohorts of average players very much in mind. In the olden days it was often thus. A very pleasant course and a hospitable club, but only on weekdays.

L'un des bons parcours d'Edinburgh, qui en compte plusieurs dizaines pratiquement en ville. Celui-ci s'est fait une bonne réputation sportive, avec une politique en direction des jeunes, pas toujours si courante dans les grands clubs citadins, souvent très fréquentés. Situé immédiatement derrière Arthur's Seat, à l'est du château, c'est un golf de parc, avec les méandres du Braid's burn pour empoisonner la vie de ceux qui aiment la vie sans obstacles. Et les arbres viennent aussi dangereusement en jeu quand les bunkers de fairway manquent à l'appel. D'un relief modéré, c'est un parcours à connaître, d'autant que les architectes n'ont jamais perdu de vue les armées de joueurs moyens. Mais il est vrai que l'on y pensait davantage autrefois. Un parcours très plaisant, et un club accueillant, mais seulement en semaine.

Duddingston Golf Club — 1895

Duddingston Road West
SCO - EDINBURGH EH15 3QD

Office	Secrétariat	(44) 0131 - 661 7688
Pro shop	Pro-shop	(44) 0131 - 661 4301
Fax	Fax	(44) 0131 - 652 6057
Web	—	
Situation	Situation	

3 km E of Edinburgh centre (pop. 418 914)

Annual closure	Fermeture annuelle	no
Weekly closure	Fermeture hebdomadaire	no

Fees main season Tarifs haute saison	18 holes	
	Week days Semaine	**We/Bank holidays** We/Férié
Individual Individuel	£ 35	*
Couple Couple	£ 70	*

* Members only

Caddy	Caddy	no
Electric Trolley	Chariot électrique	no
Buggy	Voiturette	yes
Clubs	Clubs	yes
Credit cards	Cartes de crédit	yes

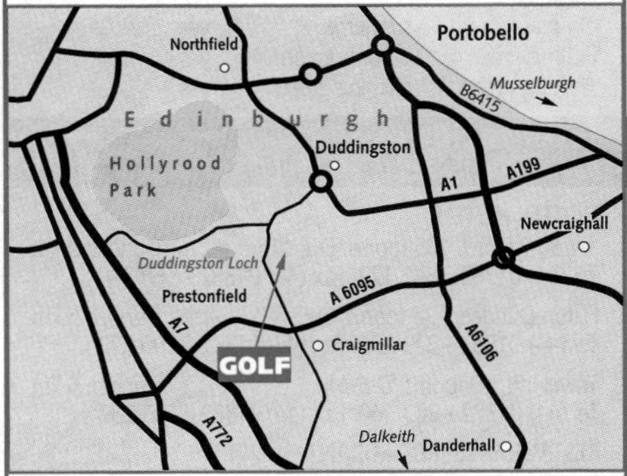

Access Accès : Edinburgh Princes Street, Regent Road, London Road, turn off right to Willowbrae Road, right to Duddingston Road West (near Duddingston Loch).
Map 3 on page 489 Carte 3 Page 489

Golf course — PARCOURS — 15/20

Site	Site	
Maintenance	Entretien	
Architect	Architecte	Willie Park
Type	Type	parkland
Relief	Relief	
Water in play	Eau en jeu	
Exp. to wind	Exposé au vent	
Trees in play	Arbres en jeu	

Scorecard Carte de score	**Chp.** Chp.	**Mens** Mess.	**Ladies** Da.
Length Long.	5826	5580	4996
Par	71	71	69
Slope system	—	—	—

Advised golfing ability — Niveau de jeu recommandé: 0 12 24 36
Hcp required — Handicap exigé: no

Club house & amenities — CLUB HOUSE ET ANNEXES — 7/10

Pro shop	Pro-shop	
Driving range	Practice	
Sheltered	couvert	no
On grass	sur herbe	no
Putting-green	putting-green	yes
Pitching-green	pitching green	yes

Hotel facilities — ENVIRONNEMENT HOTELIER — 9/10

HOTELS HÔTELS

King James Thistle, 139 rooms, D £ 155 — Edinburgh
Tel (44) 0131 - 556 0111, Fax (44) 0131 - 557 5333 — 3 km

17 Abercromby Place , 10 rooms, D £ 120 — Edinburgh
Tel (44) 0131 - 557 8036, Fax (44) 0131 - 558 3453 — 5 km

Balmoral Forte, 164 rooms, D £ 300 — Edinburgh
Tel (44) 0131 - 556 2414, Fax (44) 0131 - 557 3747 — 5 km

RESTAURANTS RESTAURANT

Number One — Edinburgh
Tel (44) 0131 - 622 8831 — 4 km

Kelly's — Edinburgh
Tel (44) 0131 - 668 3847 — 5 km

DUFF HOUSE ROYAL

15	6	6

There are courses you play in tournaments and courses you prefer for a bright stroll. This is one of the latter, where enjoyment comes first. Although designer Alister MacKenzie also laid out great championship courses like Augusta and Cypress Point, here he was looking above all else to satisfy golfers of all levels. The difficulties are there, certainly (clever bunkering, trees or the estuary of the river Deveron) but they are never insurmountable or unavoidable. So you can hope to reach the green without too much to-do, keeping to your handicap on rather flat terrain, but be careful not to waste those precious handicap strokes: the greens are often two-tiered with tricky slopes and are well protected.

Il y a des parcours pour s'affronter en compétition et d'autres plus propices à d'intelligentes balades. Celui-ci fait évidemment partie de la seconde catégorie, celle du golf-plaisir avant tout. Certes, l'architecte Alister MacKenzie a aussi créé Augusta et Cypress Point, immenses parcours de championnats, mais il a surtout cherché ici à satisfaire tous les niveaux. Les difficultés sont présentes (bunkering intelligent, arbres, ou l'embouchure de la rivière Deveron) mais jamais insurmontables ou impossibles à éviter. On peut ainsi espérer arriver paisiblement jusqu'au green en utilisant sagement ses points de handicap sur un terrain assez plat, mais il faut rester attentif à ne pas les gâcher : les greens sont souvent ici à double plateau, avec des pentes subtiles. Ils sont aussi bien protégés.

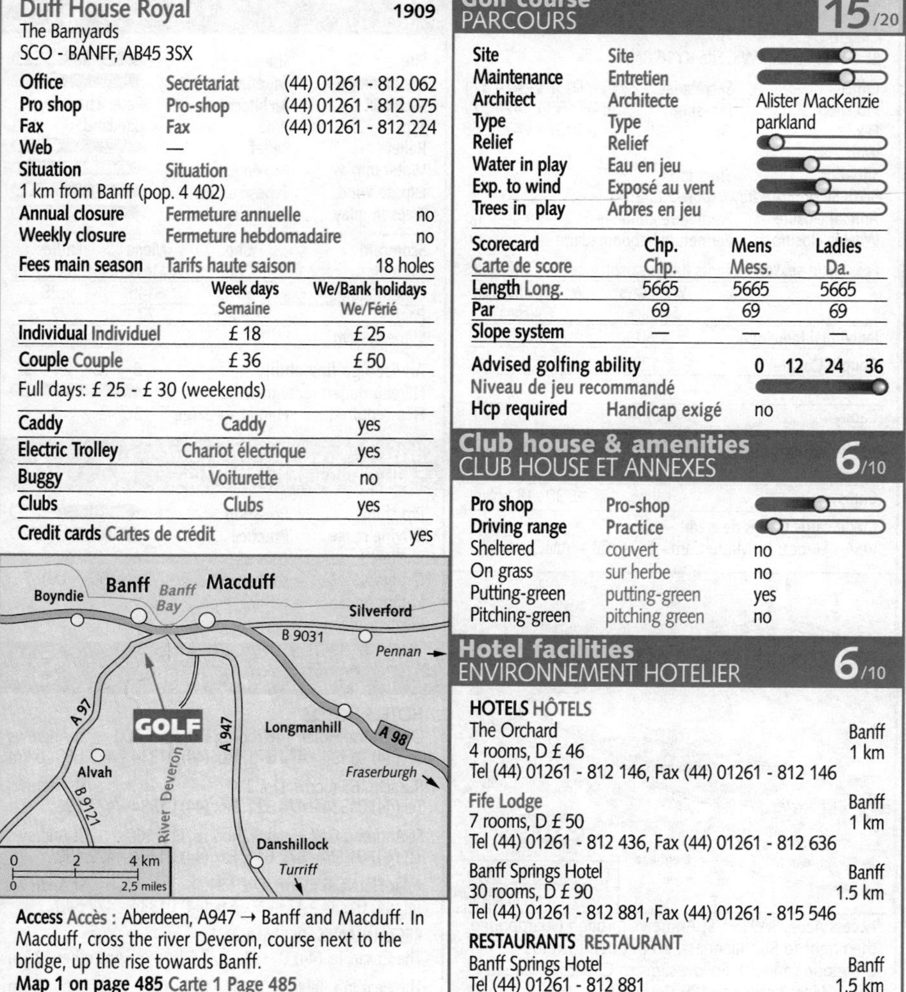

Duff House Royal **1909**
The Barnyards
SCO - BANFF, AB45 3SX

Office	Secrétariat	(44) 01261 - 812 062
Pro shop	Pro-shop	(44) 01261 - 812 075
Fax	Fax	(44) 01261 - 812 224
Web	—	
Situation	Situation	
1 km from Banff (pop. 4 402)		
Annual closure	Fermeture annuelle	no
Weekly closure	Fermeture hebdomadaire	no

Fees main season Tarifs haute saison		18 holes
	Week days Semaine	**We/Bank holidays** We/Férié
Individual Individuel	£ 18	£ 25
Couple Couple	£ 36	£ 50

Full days: £ 25 - £ 30 (weekends)

Caddy	Caddy	yes
Electric Trolley	Chariot électrique	yes
Buggy	Voiturette	no
Clubs	Clubs	yes
Credit cards Cartes de crédit		yes

Access Accès : Aberdeen, A947 → Banff and Macduff. In Macduff, cross the river Deveron, course next to the bridge, up the rise towards Banff.
Map 1 on page 485 Carte 1 Page 485

Golf course PARCOURS 15/20

Site	Site	
Maintenance	Entretien	
Architect	Architecte	Alister MacKenzie
Type	Type	parkland
Relief	Relief	
Water in play	Eau en jeu	
Exp. to wind	Exposé au vent	
Trees in play	Arbres en jeu	

Scorecard Carte de score	**Chp.** Chp.	**Mens** Mess.	**Ladies** Da.
Length Long.	5665	5665	5665
Par	69	69	69
Slope system	—	—	—

Advised golfing ability 0 12 24 36
Niveau de jeu recommandé
Hcp required Handicap exigé no

Club house & amenities CLUB HOUSE ET ANNEXES 6/10

Pro shop	Pro-shop	
Driving range	Practice	
Sheltered	couvert	no
On grass	sur herbe	no
Putting-green	putting-green	yes
Pitching-green	pitching green	no

Hotel facilities ENVIRONNEMENT HOTELIER 6/10

HOTELS HÔTELS

The Orchard — Banff
4 rooms, D £ 46 — 1 km
Tel (44) 01261 - 812 146, Fax (44) 01261 - 812 146

Fife Lodge — Banff
7 rooms, D £ 50 — 1 km
Tel (44) 01261 - 812 436, Fax (44) 01261 - 812 636

Banff Springs Hotel — Banff
30 rooms, D £ 90 — 1.5 km
Tel (44) 01261 - 812 881, Fax (44) 01261 - 815 546

RESTAURANTS RESTAURANT

Banff Springs Hotel — Banff
Tel (44) 01261 - 812 881 — 1.5 km

DUKE'S COURSE ST ANDREWS 16 | 7 | 8

Five times British Open winner Peter Thompson designed this course at the request of the Old Course Hotel. It was intended for hotel patrons owing to the problem of getting firm guaranteed tee-off times on the adjacent Old Course. Contrary to its illustrious neighbour, the Duke's Course is 3 miles inland and very different in character. It is situated on high land offering magnificent views over the old town of St Andrews and the mountains to the north beyond the bay of St Andrews. Owing to the steep slopes and distances between green and next tee, we would advise a buggy, something that would certainly be seen as sacrilege on the "real" St Andrews. Difficult, intelligent and well landscaped, the Duke's is a solid test of golf, best played from the front tees.

Cinq fois vainqueur du British Open, Peter Thomson a dessiné ce parcours à la demande du Old Course Hotel et à l'intention de ses clients, en raison de la difficulté d'obtenir des départs garantis sur le "Old Course" jouxtant cet hôtel. Contrairement à son illustre voisin, le "Duke's" est un parcours intérieur situé à 5 km de la mer, et d'un caractère très différent. Il a été tracé sur un terrain élevé, propose des vues magnifiques sur la vieille ville de St Andrews, et sur les montagnes au nord au delà de la baie de St Andrews. A cause du relief et des distances entre greens et départs, on conseillera l'usage de la voiturette, qui serait une hérésie sur le "vrai" St Andrews. Difficile, intelligent, bien paysagé, le "Duke's" propose un solide test de golf, où l'on conseillera les départs avancés.

The Duke's Golf Club — 1995

Craigton
SCO - ST ANDREWS, Fife KY16 8NS

Office	Secrétariat	(44) 01334 - 474 371
Pro shop	Pro-shop	(44) 01334 - 474 371
Fax	Fax	(44) 01334 - 477 668
Web	—	
Situation	Situation	

5 km SE of St Andrews (pop. 11 136)

Annual closure	Fermeture annuelle	no
Weekly closure	Fermeture hebdomadaire	no

Fees main season Tarifs haute saison	Week days Semaine	We/Bank holidays We/Férié (18 holes)
Individual Individuel	£ 60	£ 75
Couple Couple	£ 120	£ 150

Caddy	Caddy	no
Electric Trolley	Chariot électrique	no
Buggy	Voiturette	£ 35 /18 holes
Clubs	Clubs	£ 30 /18 holes

Credit cards Cartes de crédit
VISA - Eurocard - MasterCard - DC - JCB - AMEX

Access Accès : A91 → St Andrews through Guardbridge, then right to Strathkinness, go through towards Craigtoun (on left). Follow signs to Craigtoun Country Park). **Map 3 on page 489** Carte 3 Page 489

Golf course — PARCOURS 16/20

Site	Site	
Maintenance	Entretien	
Architect	Architecte	Peter Thomson
Type	Type	parkland
Relief	Relief	
Water in play	Eau en jeu	
Exp. to wind	Exposé au vent	
Trees in play	Arbres en jeu	

Scorecard Carte de score	Chp. Chp.	Mens Mess.	Ladies Da.
Length Long.	6616	6145	5528
Par	72	72	72
Slope system	—	—	—

Advised golfing ability Niveau de jeu recommandé — 0 12 24 36

Hcp required Handicap exigé 36

Club house & amenities — CLUB HOUSE ET ANNEXES 7/10

Pro shop	Pro-shop	
Driving range	Practice	
Sheltered	couvert	no
On grass	sur herbe	yes (05 → 09)
Putting-green	putting-green	yes
Pitching-green	pitching green	yes

Hotel facilities — ENVIRONNEMENT HOTELIER 8/10

HOTELS HÔTELS

Old Course Hotel, 146 rooms, D from £ 300 — St Andrews
Tel (44) 01334 - 474 371, Fax (44) 01334 - 477 668 — 5 km

Rusacks, 68 rooms, D £ 210 — St Andrews
Tel (44) 01334 - 474 321, Fax (44) 01334 - 477 896

St Andrews Golf Hotel, 22 rooms, D £ 160 — St Andrews
Tel (44) 01334 - 472 611, Fax (44) 01334 - 472 188

Aslar House, 5 rooms, D £ 62 — St Andrews
Tel (44) 01334 - 473 460, Fax (44) 01334 - 477 540

RESTAURANTS RESTAURANT

The Cellar, Tel (44) 01333 - 477 540 — Ansruther 12 km

The Peat Inn, Tel (44) 01334 - 840 206 — Peat Inn 8 km

DUMFRIES & COUNTY

15 | 7 | 5

This is one of the best courses in south-west Scotland, a region too often neglected by foreign tourists. Off the beaten track, Dumfries & County is generally in excellent condition and very pleasant on the eye with the river Nith alongside the course. This adds a pastoral note to a very tree-bound landscape. Designed by Willie Fernie, this is one of those collection of courses which will probably never mark the history of golf design but which you are glad to have played. An unpretentious layout, it is happy to be just a rather difficult course to test the average player, kind enough not to put off the rather less experienced golfer and clever enough to tease the experts. The one hole no-one will forget is the tiny 14th, a par-3.

C'est un des meilleurs parcours du sud-ouest de l'Ecosse, une région trop souvent négligée par les touristes étrangers. Hors des sentiers battus, Dumfries & County est généralement en excellente condition, et très plaisant visuellement, où la rivière Nith, le long du terrain, ajoute une note pastorale à un paysage très arboré. Dessiné par Willie Fernie, il fait partie de cet ensemble de golfs qui ne marqueront sans doute pas l'histoire de l'architecture de golf, mais que l'on est heureux de connaître et surtout d'avoir joué. Sans prétention aucune, il se contente d'être un parcours assez difficile pour tester les joueurs moyens, assez aimable pour ne pas rebuter les joueurs peu expérimentés, assez astucieux pour provoquer les experts. Ils garderont au minimum le souvenir du minuscule 14, un par 3.

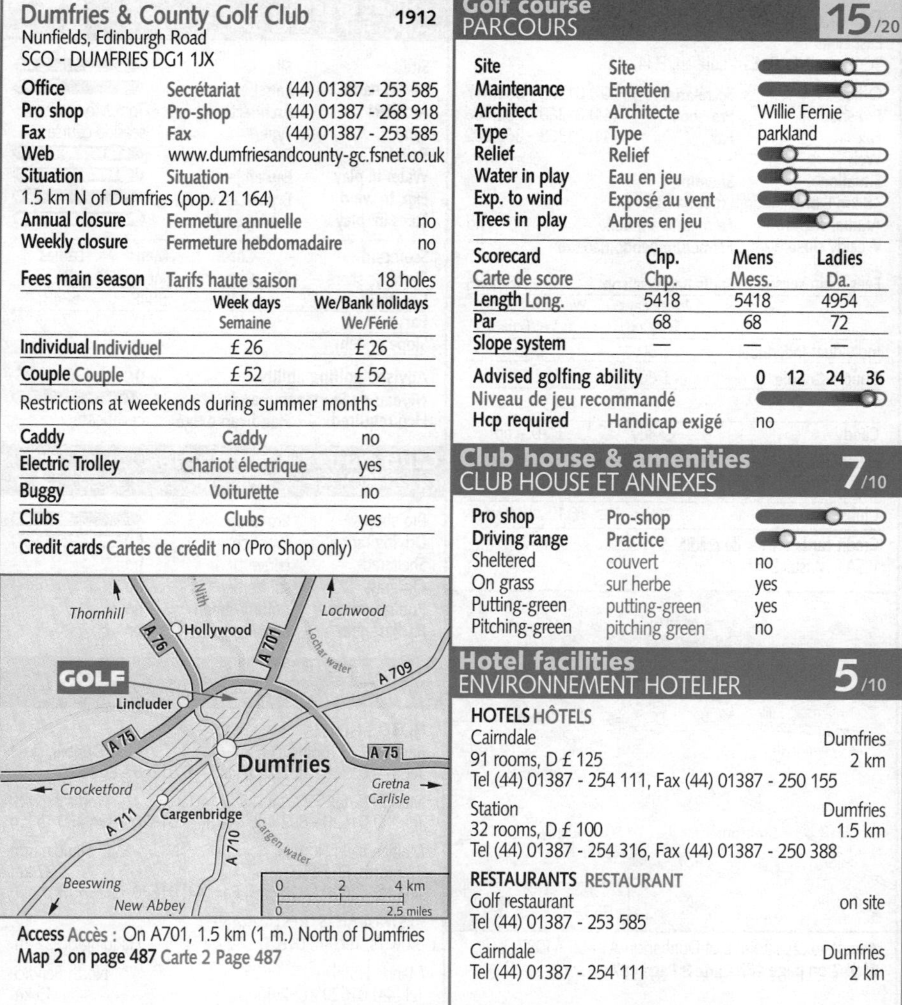

Dumfries & County Golf Club **1912**
Nunfields, Edinburgh Road
SCO - DUMFRIES DG1 1JX

Office	Secrétariat	(44) 01387 - 253 585
Pro shop	Pro-shop	(44) 01387 - 268 918
Fax	Fax	(44) 01387 - 253 585
Web	www.dumfriesandcounty-gc.fsnet.co.uk	
Situation	Situation	
1.5 km N of Dumfries (pop. 21 164)		
Annual closure	Fermeture annuelle	no
Weekly closure	Fermeture hebdomadaire	no

Fees main season Tarifs haute saison	18 holes	
	Week days Semaine	**We/Bank holidays** We/Férié
Individual Individuel	£ 26	£ 26
Couple Couple	£ 52	£ 52

Restrictions at weekends during summer months

Caddy	Caddy	no
Electric Trolley	Chariot électrique	yes
Buggy	Voiturette	no
Clubs	Clubs	yes
Credit cards	Cartes de crédit	no (Pro Shop only)

Access Accès : On A701, 1.5 km (1 m.) North of Dumfries
Map 2 on page 487 Carte 2 Page 487

Golf course PARCOURS **15/20**

Site	Site	
Maintenance	Entretien	
Architect	Architecte	Willie Fernie
Type	Type	parkland
Relief	Relief	
Water in play	Eau en jeu	
Exp. to wind	Exposé au vent	
Trees in play	Arbres en jeu	

Scorecard Carte de score	**Chp.** Chp.	**Mens** Mess.	**Ladies** Da.
Length Long.	5418	5418	4954
Par	68	68	72
Slope system	—	—	—

Advised golfing ability 0 12 24 36
Niveau de jeu recommandé
Hcp required Handicap exigé no

Club house & amenities CLUB HOUSE ET ANNEXES **7/10**

Pro shop	Pro-shop	
Driving range	Practice	
Sheltered	couvert	no
On grass	sur herbe	yes
Putting-green	putting-green	yes
Pitching-green	pitching green	no

Hotel facilities ENVIRONNEMENT HOTELIER **5/10**

HOTELS HÔTELS
Cairndale — Dumfries
91 rooms, D £ 125 — 2 km
Tel (44) 01387 - 254 111, Fax (44) 01387 - 250 155
Station — Dumfries
32 rooms, D £ 100 — 1.5 km
Tel (44) 01387 - 254 316, Fax (44) 01387 - 250 388

RESTAURANTS RESTAURANT
Golf restaurant — on site
Tel (44) 01387 - 253 585
Cairndale — Dumfries
Tel (44) 01387 - 254 111 — 2 km

DUNBAR

16 | 5 | 6

One of the classic courses of East Lothian, nestling on a narrow strip of land along a rocky seashore hardly big enough for two fairways. This means that you have not only the sea but also a wall and out-of-bounds to contend with, so when the wind blows you just might feel you haven't a friend on earth. In this case do what all amateurs used to do and go around in match-play, a very exciting format on this type of course. The most memorable part of the course is from the 7th to the 16th holes, as the holes close to the clubhouse are rather squeezed together. This is where the Firth of Forth becomes the North Sea and the view of this mass of water adds to the pleasure of playing golf in the bracing sea-air.

C'est un des parcours classiques de l'East Lothian, blotti sur une étroite bande le long d'un rivage rocheux, avec à peine assez de place pour placer deux fairways côte-à-côte. Ce qui implique non seulement que la mer est en jeu, mais aussi qu'il y ait un mur et des hors-limites. Autrement dit, les jours de vent, les joueurs peuvent avoir l'impression de n'avoir que des adversaires. On leur conseillera alors de se réfugier dans la formule de tous les amateurs d'autrefois, le match-play, toujours très excitant sur des parcours de ce style. Ici, on retiendra particulièrement le passage du 7 au 16, les trous à proximité immédiate du Clubhouse étant plus resserrés. C'est ici que le Firth of Forth devient vraiment la Mer du Nord, et la vue de cette immensité ajoute encore au plaisir du jeu de golf dans un air vivifiant.

Dunbar Golf Club — 1856

East Links
SCO - DUNBAR, East Lothian, EH42 1LL

Office	Secrétariat	(44) 01368 - 862 317
Pro shop	Pro-shop	(44) 01368 - 862 086
Fax	Fax	(44) 01368 - 865 202
Web	—	
Situation	Situation	

48 km E of Edinburgh (pop. 418 914)

Annual closure	Fermeture annuelle	no
Weekly closure	Fermeture hebdomadaire	no

Fees main season Tarifs haute saison	Week days Semaine	We/Bank holidays We/Férié
18 holes		
Individual Individuel	£ 30	£ 35
Couple Couple	£ 60	£ 70

Caddy	Caddy	£ 20 + tip
Electric Trolley	Chariot électrique	£ 6 /18 holes
Buggy	Voiturette	no
Clubs	Clubs	£ 10 /18 holes

Credit cards Cartes de crédit
VISA - MasterCard

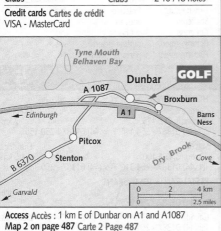

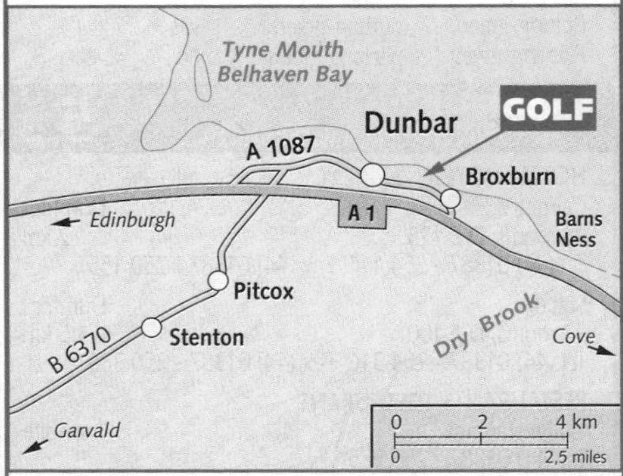

Access Accès : 1 km E of Dunbar on A1 and A1087
Map 2 on page 487 Carte 2 Page 487

Golf course PARCOURS — 16/20

Site	Site	
Maintenance	Entretien	
Architect	Architecte	Tom Morris
Type	Type	seaside course
Relief	Relief	
Water in play	Eau en jeu	
Exp. to wind	Exposé au vent	
Trees in play	Arbres en jeu	

Scorecard Carte de score	Chp. Chp.	Mens Mess.	Ladies Da.
Length Long.	5848	5848	5848
Par	71	71	74
Slope system	—	—	—

Advised golfing ability Niveau de jeu recommandé: 0 12 24 36
Hcp required Handicap exigé: certificate

Club house & amenities CLUB HOUSE ET ANNEXES — 5/10

Pro shop	Pro-shop	
Driving range	Practice	
Sheltered	couvert	no
On grass	sur herbe	no
Putting-green	putting-green	no
Pitching-green	pitching green	no

Hotel facilities ENVIRONNEMENT HOTELIER — 6/10

HOTELS HÔTELS

Bayswell, 13 rooms, D £ 79 — Dunbar, close
Tel (44) 01368 - 862 225, Fax (44) 01368 - 862 225

Marine Hotel, 79 rooms, D £ 140 — North Berwick
Tel (44) 01620 - 892 406, Fax (44) 01620 - 894 480 15 km

Maitlandfield House — Haddington
22 rooms, D £ 150 — 22 km
Tel (44) 01620 - 826 513, Fax (44) 01620 - 826 713

RESTAURANTS RESTAURANT

Brown's, Tel (44) 01620 - 822 254 — Haddington 22 km

Marine Hotel — North Berwick
Tel (44) 01620 - 892 406 — 15 km

DUNFERMLINE

15	7	7

This city was the capital of Scotland up until 1603 and still carries the vestiges of its prestigious past. Now while the kingdom of Fife is famous for its links, shaped by nature over several hundred years, this particular course is an inland layout which has much to be said for it but without quite the same nobility. Tradition here goes back more than 110 years, and although the course was constructed at the beginning of the 1950s, no great change was made to the 600 year-old clubhouse. Trees and bunkers form the traditional hazards of a well-balanced course which is moderately hilly and fun for all. In short, this is your standard middle-of-the-road course that will sometimes have you raring to go. The watchword here is always fun.

La ville fut la capitale de l'Ecosse jusqu'en 1603, et conserve les vestiges d'un aussi prestigieux passé. Mais si le royaume de Fife est célèbre par ses links patinés depuis des siècles par la nature, le présent parcours "inland" ne manque pas de qualités non plus, sans prétendre pour autant à tant de noblesse. Sa tradition remonte à plus de 110 ans, et bien que le parcours lui-même ait été créé au début des années 1950, l'on a peu touché au Clubhouse, qui date, lui, de plus de six siècles. Les arbres et les bunkers forment les obstacles traditionnels d'un parcours bien équilibré dans ses difficultés, modérément mouvementé, amusant pour tous les niveaux. Bref, un modèle de golf "middle-of-the-road," que l'on pourrait parfois avoir envie de violenter un peu, mais le maître mot est ici le plaisir...

Dunfermline Golf Club — 1887

Pitfirrane, Crossford
SCO - DUNFERMLINE, Fife KY12 8QW

Office	Secrétariat	(44) 01383 - 723 534
Pro shop	Pro-shop	(44) 01383 - 729 061
Fax	Fax	(44) 01383 - 723 534
Web	—	
Situation	Situation	

3 km W of Dunfermline (pop.29 436)
27 km NW of Edinburgh (pop. 418 914)

Annual closure	Fermeture annuelle	no
Weekly closure	Fermeture hebdomadaire	no

Fees main season Tarifs haute saison	18 holes	
	Week days Semaine	We/Bank holidays We/Férié
Individual Individuel	£ 21	£ 25*
Couple Couple	£ 42	£ 50

Caddy	Caddy	no
Electric Trolley	Chariot électrique	no
Buggy	Voiturette	no
Clubs	Clubs	no
Credit cards	Cartes de crédit	no

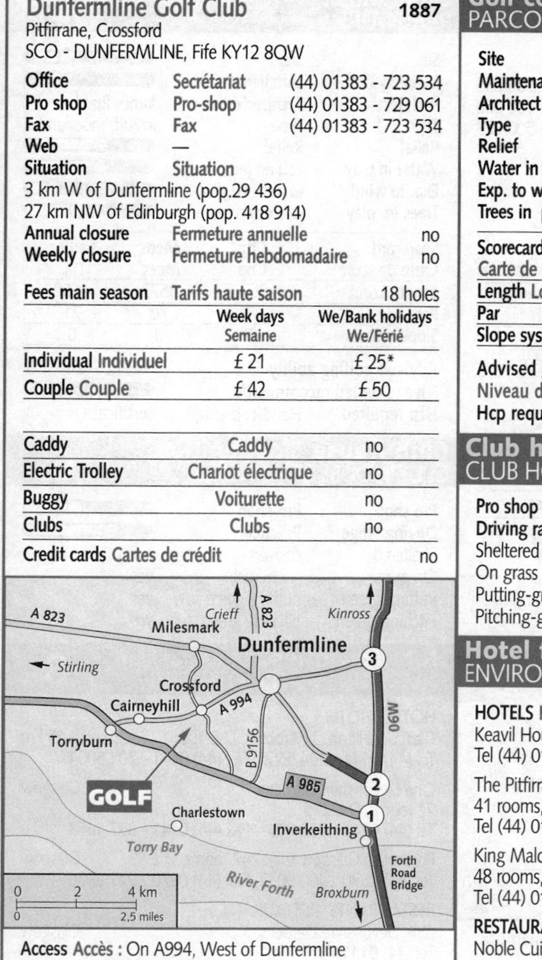

Access Accès : On A994, West of Dunfermline
Map 2 on page 487 Carte 2 Page 487

Golf course PARCOURS — 15/20

Site	Site	
Maintenance	Entretien	
Architect	Architecte	Stutt & Co
Type	Type	parkland
Relief	Relief	
Water in play	Eau en jeu	
Exp. to wind	Exposé au vent	
Trees in play	Arbres en jeu	

Scorecard Carte de score	Chp. Chp.	Mens Mess.	Ladies Da.
Length Long.	5575	5263	4917
Par	72	70	72
Slope system	—	—	—

Advised golfing ability / Niveau de jeu recommandé: 0 12 24 36
Hcp required / Handicap exigé: certificate

Club house & amenities CLUB HOUSE ET ANNEXES — 7/10

Pro shop	Pro-shop	
Driving range	Practice	
Sheltered	couvert	no
On grass	sur herbe	yes
Putting-green	putting-green	yes
Pitching-green	pitching green	yes

Hotel facilities ENVIRONNEMENT HOTELIER — 7/10

HOTELS HÔTELS

Keavil House Hotel, 47 rooms, D £ 125 — Crossford 0,5 km
Tel (44) 01383 - 736 258, Fax (44) 01383 - 621 600

The Pitfirrane Arms Hotel — Crossford
41 rooms, D from £ 52
Tel (44) 01383 - 736 132, Fax (44) 01383 - 621 760

King Malcolm Thistle Hotel — Dunfermline 4 km
48 rooms, D £ 120
Tel (44) 01383 - 722 611, Fax (44) 01383 - 730 865

RESTAURANTS RESTAURANT

Noble Cuisine, Tel (44) 01383 - 620 555 — Dunfermline
King Malcolm, Tel (44) 01383 - 722 611 — Dunfermline

EAST RENFREWSHIRE

15	6	8

Although close to Glasgow, this course is located away from any residential area. We are out in the country on Scottish moorland with its typical covering of whin (gorse) and heather, very many trees and a stream that crosses the course, running down the side of the fairways and sometimes cutting across them at strategic distances. This was only to be expected from James Braid. It is very easy to see your ball end up there if you don't give enough thought to flight and roll. Mid-handicappers, though, can always choose a line of flight without too many risks, although the experts will be keen to flex their muscles. In a word, a good score here is not as easy as all that. The clubhouse is spacious but the course crowded enough for us to advise you to book your tee-off time in advance.

Bien qu'il soit proche de Glasgow, ce parcours est situé en dehors de toute zone résidentielle. Nous sommes à la campagne, dans la lande écossaise, avec une végétation typique d'ajoncs et de bruyère, de nombreux arbres, mais aussi un ruisseau qui parcourt l'espace, longeant les fairways ou venant les interrompre, de manière stratégique, ccomme on pouvait l'attendre de James Braid. Il est très facile d'y voir les balles y terminer leur course si l'on n'a pas réfléchi un peu sur leur portée et leur roulement. Cependant, les handicaps moyens peuvent toujours choisir des lignes de jeu sans grands risques, alors que les experts voudront montrer leurs muscles. Bref, il n'est pas si facile de scorer ici. Le Clubhouse est spacieux, mais le parcours assez fréquenté pour que l'on conseille de réserver les départs à l'avance.

East Renfrewshire Golf Course — 1923

Pilmuir, Newton Mearns
SCO - GLASGOW G77 6RT

Office	Secrétariat	(44) 01355 - 500 256
Pro shop	Pro-shop	(44) 01355 - 500 206
Fax	Fax	(44) 01355 - 500 323
Web	—	
Situation	Situation	

15 km S of centre of Glasgow (pop. 622 853)

Annual closure	Fermeture annuelle	no
Weekly closure	Fermeture hebdomadaire	no

Fees main season Tarifs haute saison — 18 holes

	Week days / Semaine	We/Bank holidays / We/Férié
Individual Individuel	£ 30	£ 30
Couple Couple	£ 60	£ 60

Full day: £ 40

Caddy	Caddy	no
Electric Trolley	Chariot électrique	no
Buggy	Voiturette	no
Clubs	Clubs	yes

Credit cards Cartes de crédit
VISA - Eurocard - MasterCard - DC - AMEX

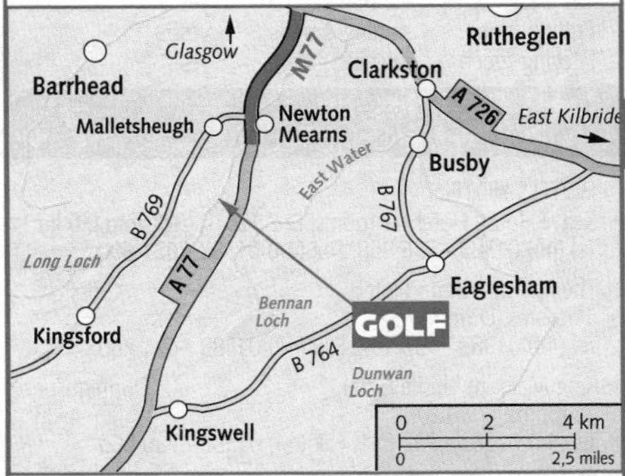

Access Accès : Glasgow M8 and M77/A77 → Kilmarnock. Club on the right shortly after Newton Mearns.
Map 3 on page 488 Carte 3 Page 488

Golf course / PARCOURS — 15/20

Site	Site	
Maintenance	Entretien	
Architect	Architecte	James Braid
Type	Type	inland, moorland
Relief	Relief	
Water in play	Eau en jeu	
Exp. to wind	Exposé au vent	
Trees in play	Arbres en jeu	

Scorecard / Carte de score	Chp. / Chp.	Mens / Mess.	Ladies / Da.
Length Long.	5577	5577	4668
Par	70	70	71
Slope system	0	0	0

Advised golfing ability Niveau de jeu recommandé — 0 12 24 36
Hcp required Handicap exigé — certificate

Club house & amenities / CLUB HOUSE ET ANNEXES — 6/10

Pro shop	Pro-shop	
Driving range	Practice	
Sheltered	couvert	no
On grass	sur herbe	yes
Putting-green	putting-green	yes
Pitching-green	pitching green	yes

Hotel facilities / ENVIRONNEMENT HOTELIER — 8/10

HOTELS HÔTELS

Glasgow Hilton, 319 rooms, D £ 190 — Glasgow 15 km
Tel (44) 0141 - 204 5555, Fax (44) 0141 - 204 5004

One Devonshire Gardens — Glasgow
27 rooms, D £ 275
Tel (44) 0141 - 339 2001, Fax (44) 0141 - 337 1663

Posthouse Glasgow City, 247 rooms, D £ 99 — Glasgow
Tel (44) 0870 - 400 9032, Fax (44) 0870 - 221 8986

RESTAURANTS RESTAURANT

One Devonshire Gardens — Glasgow
Tel (44) 0141 - 339 2001

Buttery, Tel (44) 0141 - 221 8188 — Glasgow

EDZELL

14 | 6 | 3

This course is located virtually in town, or should we say village, as Edzell has often been voted "the best preserved village in Scotland". It was certainly one of the most stylishly frequented for many a year, as princes and maharajahs would come here for the fishing and hunting at the edge of the Highlands, and certainly to play this course designed in 1895 by Bob Simpson of Carnoustie. Laid out over gorse-land, this is a gem of a course, with a wide variety of holes, small, well-kept greens, soft fairways and hazards of all shapes and sizes, including bunkers, a steep-banked river and trees. This is one of the places in Scotland where you can still feel "out of time", as you are so far away from the main roads. Don't expect a Japanese-style clubhouse on this kind of course; what really matters here is hospitality, and here you will find that a plenty.

Ce parcours est pratiquement en ville. Ou en village plutôt, car Edzell a été souvent élu comme "le village le mieux préservé d'Ecosse." Il fut longtemps aussi le "mieux" fréquenté, car princes et maharadjahs venaient ici pêcher, chasser en bordure des Highlands, et sans doute aussi jouer sur ce parcours créé en 1895 par Bob Simpson de Carnoustie. Tracé en terre de bruyère, c'est un petit bijou, avec des trous très variés, de petits greens bien entretenus, des fairways souples et des obstacles en tous genres, depuis les bunkers jusqu'à la rivière et ses rives abruptes en passant par les bois. C'est un des endroits d'Ecosse où l'on peut le plus se croire hors du temps, parce qu'on se retrouve aussi à l'écart des grandes routes. Dans ce genre de golf, que l'on n'attende pas un Clubhouse à la japonaise : l'essentiel est dans la chaleur de l'accueil.

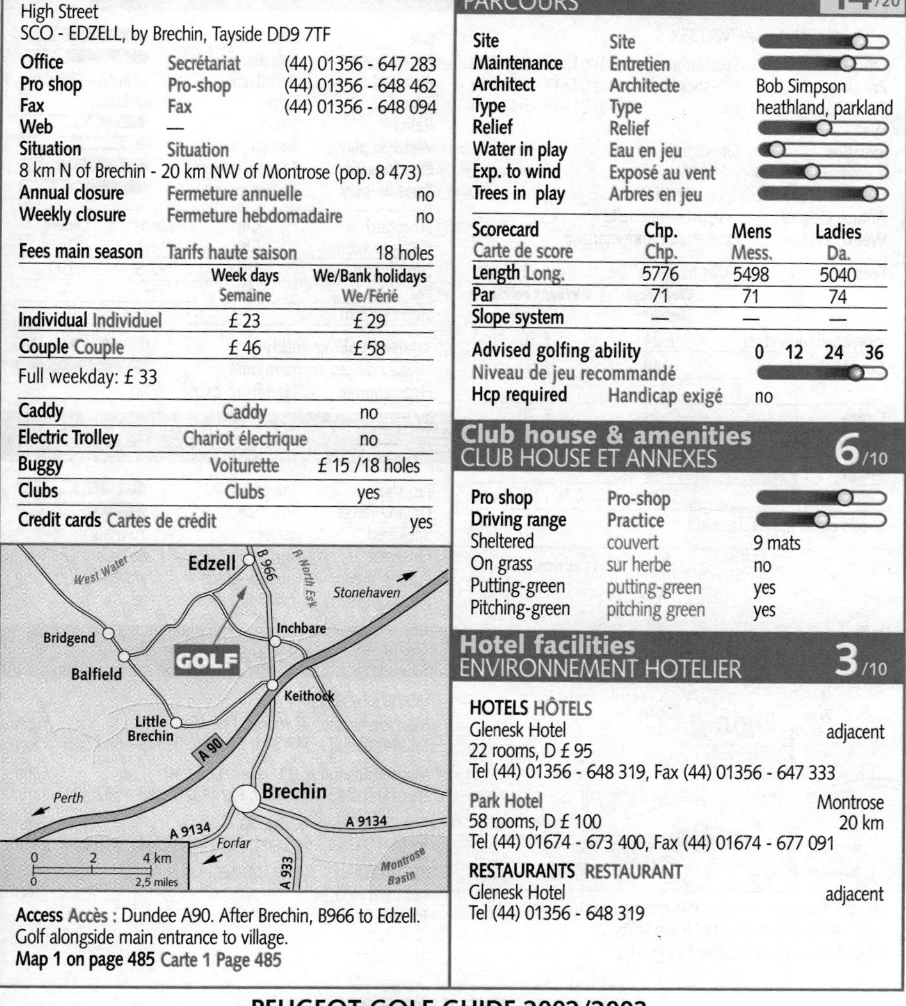

The Edzell Golf Club — 1895

High Street
SCO - EDZELL, by Brechin, Tayside DD9 7TF

Office	Secrétariat	(44) 01356 - 647 283
Pro shop	Pro-shop	(44) 01356 - 648 462
Fax	Fax	(44) 01356 - 648 094
Web	—	
Situation	Situation	

8 km N of Brechin - 20 km NW of Montrose (pop. 8 473)

Annual closure	Fermeture annuelle	no
Weekly closure	Fermeture hebdomadaire	no

Fees main season Tarifs haute saison		18 holes
	Week days Semaine	We/Bank holidays We/Férié
Individual Individuel	£ 23	£ 29
Couple Couple	£ 46	£ 58

Full weekday: £ 33

Caddy	Caddy	no
Electric Trolley	Chariot électrique	no
Buggy	Voiturette	£ 15 /18 holes
Clubs	Clubs	yes
Credit cards	Cartes de crédit	yes

Access Accès : Dundee A90. After Brechin, B966 to Edzell. Golf alongside main entrance to village.
Map 1 on page 485 Carte 1 Page 485

Golf course — PARCOURS — 14/20

Site	Site	
Maintenance	Entretien	
Architect	Architecte	Bob Simpson
Type	Type	heathland, parkland
Relief	Relief	
Water in play	Eau en jeu	
Exp. to wind	Exposé au vent	
Trees in play	Arbres en jeu	

Scorecard Carte de score	Chp. Chp.	Mens Mess.	Ladies Da.
Length Long.	5776	5498	5040
Par	71	71	74
Slope system	—	—	—

Advised golfing ability — Niveau de jeu recommandé: 0 12 24 36
Hcp required — Handicap exigé: no

Club house & amenities — CLUB HOUSE ET ANNEXES — 6/10

Pro shop	Pro-shop	
Driving range	Practice	
Sheltered	couvert	9 mats
On grass	sur herbe	no
Putting-green	putting-green	yes
Pitching-green	pitching green	yes

Hotel facilities — ENVIRONNEMENT HOTELIER — 3/10

HOTELS HÔTELS
Glenesk Hotel — adjacent
22 rooms, D £ 95
Tel (44) 01356 - 648 319, Fax (44) 01356 - 647 333

Park Hotel — Montrose 20 km
58 rooms, D £ 100
Tel (44) 01674 - 673 400, Fax (44) 01674 - 677 091

RESTAURANTS RESTAURANT
Glenesk Hotel — adjacent
Tel (44) 01356 - 648 319

ELGIN

15 | 7 | 6

This course has the enviable reputation of being one of the best inland courses in northern Scotland. At all events it is a very good test of golf, and although its length may seem a little outdated, there is only the one par 5 and this can often dash any hope of carding a good score. Precision is at a premium here, but hazards are in good view and so can help you recover an efficient game strategy. Eight of the par-4s are longer than 390 yards, so you can understand Elgin's reputation for being a serious examination of every green-feer's talent. For want of beating any records, you can always enjoy the view over the old city of Elgin to the north (well worth a visit) and to the south the superb Cairngorm Mountains (well worth exploring).

Ce parcours a la réputation enviable d'être l'un des meilleurs parcours "inlands" du nord de l'Ecosse. C'est en tout cas un très bon test de golf, et si sa longueur peut le faire paraître désuet, ce n'est après tout qu'un par 69, qui ne comporte qu'un seul par 5, ce qui complique bien souvent l'espérance d'un bon score. Il faut être ici très précis, mais les obstacles sont assez en vue pour établir rapidement une stratégie efficace. Huit des par 4 mesurant plus de 360 mètres, on comprend que la réputation de Elgin soit aussi d'être un sérieux examen du talent des visiteurs. A défaut de battre tous les records, ceux-ci pourront se livrer à la contemplation du panorama sur la vieille cité d'Elgin au nord (à visiter) et, au sud, sur les superbes Cairngorm Mountains (à explorer).

Elgin Golf Club — **1926**
Birnie Road
SCO - ELGIN, Moray IV30 3SX

Office	Secrétariat	(44) 01343 - 542 338
Pro shop	Pro-shop	(44) 01343 - 542 884
Fax	Fax	(44) 01343 - 542 341
Web	—	
Situation	Situation	

1 km from Elgin (pop. 11 855)
62 km E of Inverness (pop. 62 186)

Annual closure	Fermeture annuelle	no
Weekly closure	Fermeture hebdomadaire	no

Fees main season Tarifs haute saison	18 holes	
	Week days Semaine	**We/Bank holidays** We/Férié
Individual Individuel	£ 24	£ 30
Couple Couple	£ 48	£ 60

Caddy	Caddy	£ 20
Electric Trolley	Chariot électrique	no
Buggy	Voiturette	no
Clubs	Clubs	£ 10 /18 holes
Credit cards	Cartes de crédit	yes

Access Accès : Aberdeen or Inverness A96 to Elgin. Golf on A941 just South of town limits
Map 1 on page 485 Carte 1 Page 485

Golf course PARCOURS — 15/20

Site	Site	
Maintenance	Entretien	
Architect	Architecte	John MacPherson
Type	Type	parkland
Relief	Relief	
Water in play	Eau en jeu	
Exp. to wind	Exposé au vent	
Trees in play	Arbres en jeu	

Scorecard Carte de score	**Chp.** Chp.	**Mens** Mess.	**Ladies** Da.
Length Long.	5834	5608	5290
Par	69	69	74
Slope system	—	—	—

Advised golfing ability Niveau de jeu recommandé — 0 12 24 36
Hcp required Handicap exigé — no

Club house & amenities CLUB HOUSE ET ANNEXES — 7/10

Pro shop	Pro-shop	
Driving range	Practice	
Sheltered	couvert	16 mats
On grass	sur herbe	no
Putting-green	putting-green	yes
Pitching-green	pitching green	no

Hotel facilities ENVIRONNEMENT HOTELIER — 6/10

HOTELS HÔTELS

Mansion House, 23 rooms, D £ 150 — Elgin 1 km
Tel (44) 01343 - 548 811, Fax (44) 01343 - 547 916

Mansefield House, 21 rooms, D £ 110 — Elgin
Tel (44) 01343 - 540 883, Fax (44) 01343 - 552 491

The Croft, 3 rooms, D £ 50 — Elgin 2 km
Tel (44) 01343 - 546 004, Fax (44) 01343 - 546 004

RESTAURANTS RESTAURANT

Mansion House — Elgin
Tel (44) 01343 - 548 811

ELIE

15 | 6 | 6

This is where James Braid learnt his golf, and you can understand why he became such a great champion and such a good course designer. Elie is a delightful course, as picturesque as they come with a number of rural features that will stay for ever, notably its location virtually in the middle of the village. But if you get the impression you are in for a pleasure cruise, watch out. The traps here are as frequent as the number of shots that, although not completely blind, do raise a few questions and eyebrows. Exposure to the wind is so fierce that there is no point in worrying about the theoretical par for each hole. It changes from one day to the next. Likewise you'll learn how to bump and run the ball by asking the locals who are always willing to give advice. One of the region's most amusing courses.

C'est ici que James Braid a appris le golf, l'on comprend qu'il soit devenu un si grand champion, et un si bon architecte. Elie est un délicieux parcours, aussi pittoresque que possible, avec certains aspects rustiques à préserver, notamment sa situation quasiment au milieu du village. Mais si l'on a l'impression de s'y livrer à une partie de plaisir, il faut méfiance garder. Les pièges sont ici aussi nombreux que les coups sinon aveugles, du moins bien soulignés de points d'interrogation. L'exposition au vent est tellement importante qu'il ne faut pas se soucier du par théorique de chaque trou, il change d'un jour à l'autre. De même on y apprendra à faire rouler la balle, en demandant aux joueurs locaux, qui n'hésitent jamais à livrer leurs bons conseils... avec l'accent. L'un des plus amusants parcours de la région.

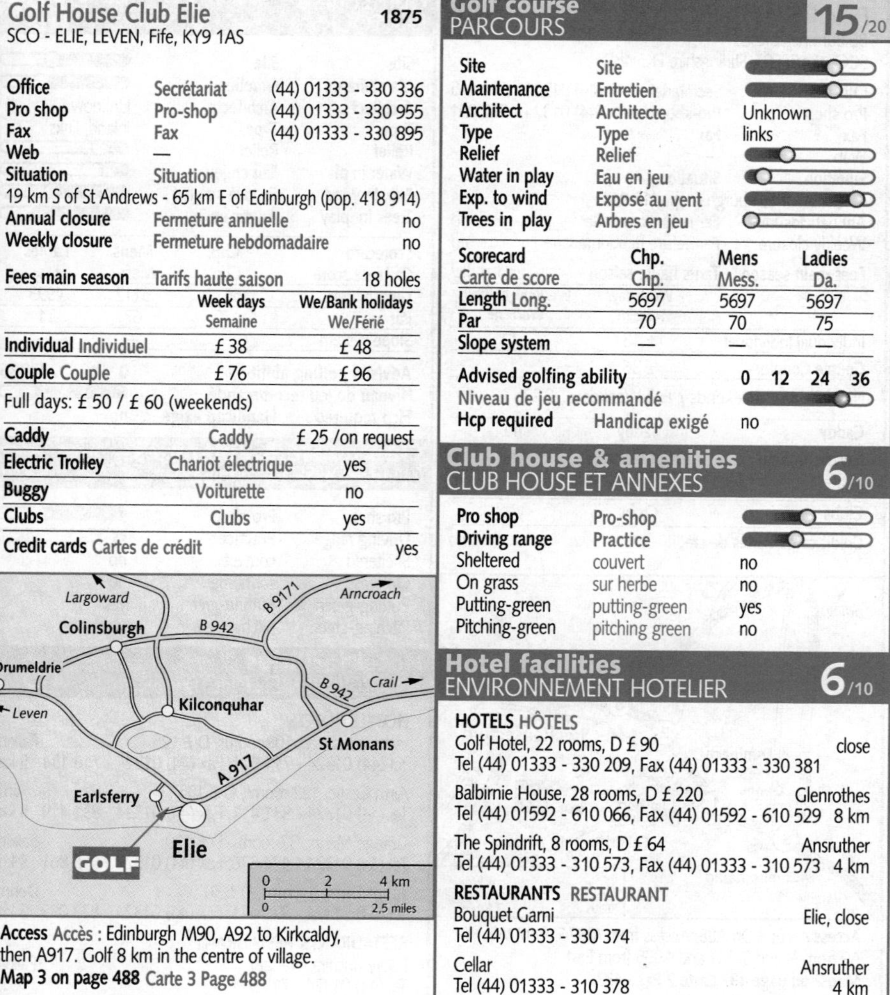

Golf House Club Elie — 1875

SCO - ELIE, LEVEN, Fife, KY9 1AS

Office	Secrétariat	(44) 01333 - 330 336
Pro shop	Pro-shop	(44) 01333 - 330 955
Fax	Fax	(44) 01333 - 330 895
Web	—	
Situation	Situation	

19 km S of St Andrews - 65 km E of Edinburgh (pop. 418 914)

Annual closure	Fermeture annuelle	no
Weekly closure	Fermeture hebdomadaire	no

Fees main season Tarifs haute saison — 18 holes

	Week days / Semaine	We/Bank holidays / We/Férié
Individual Individuel	£ 38	£ 48
Couple Couple	£ 76	£ 96

Full days: £ 50 / £ 60 (weekends)

Caddy	Caddy	£ 25 /on request
Electric Trolley	Chariot électrique	yes
Buggy	Voiturette	no
Clubs	Clubs	yes
Credit cards	Cartes de crédit	yes

Access Accès : Edinburgh M90, A92 to Kirkcaldy, then A917. Golf 8 km in the centre of village.

Map 3 on page 488 Carte 3 Page 488

Golf course — PARCOURS — 15/20

Site	Site	
Maintenance	Entretien	
Architect	Architecte	Unknown
Type	Type	links
Relief	Relief	
Water in play	Eau en jeu	
Exp. to wind	Exposé au vent	
Trees in play	Arbres en jeu	

Scorecard / Carte de score	Chp. / Chp.	Mens / Mess.	Ladies / Da.
Length Long.	5697	5697	5697
Par	70	70	75
Slope system	—	—	—

Advised golfing ability / Niveau de jeu recommandé — 0 12 24 36

Hcp required — Handicap exigé — no

Club house & amenities — CLUB HOUSE ET ANNEXES — 6/10

Pro shop	Pro-shop	
Driving range	Practice	
Sheltered	couvert	no
On grass	sur herbe	no
Putting-green	putting-green	yes
Pitching-green	pitching green	no

Hotel facilities — ENVIRONNEMENT HOTELIER — 6/10

HOTELS HÔTELS

Golf Hotel, 22 rooms, D £ 90 — close
Tel (44) 01333 - 330 209, Fax (44) 01333 - 330 381

Balbirnie House, 28 rooms, D £ 220 — Glenrothes
Tel (44) 01592 - 610 066, Fax (44) 01592 - 610 529 — 8 km

The Spindrift, 8 rooms, D £ 64 — Ansruther
Tel (44) 01333 - 310 573, Fax (44) 01333 - 310 573 — 4 km

RESTAURANTS RESTAURANT

Bouquet Garni — Elie, close
Tel (44) 01333 - 330 374

Cellar — Ansruther
Tel (44) 01333 - 310 378 — 4 km

FALKIRK TRYST

13 | 6 | 6

This is not the most engaging site for golf. With a cricket pitch right in the middle, here you have th two most mysterious games ever invented by man sitting side by side. The course was built over seve ral stages on flat terrain in the village of Larbert. The first three holes form a sort of loop. From N° 4 to N 10 (plus the 18th), you have another set of holes, then a third running from hole number 11 to 17. On this course where the rhythm of the layout is strange to say the least, the par 3s are called "short holes", even though two o them are in the region of 200 yards and the three others never shorter than 165 yards. By contrast, two of the thre par 5s provide a reasonable opportunity for a birdie. When it comes to counting your score, you will see tha playing to your handicap is anything but easy, an annoying state of affairs when considering how flat and short th course is overall. Lovers of spectacular courses probably would not play here every day, but a round from time t time is always time well spent.

Ce n'est pas le site le plus engageant. Avec un terrain de cricket au milieu de ce golf, voici côte-à-côte les deu jeux les plus mystérieux que l'homme ait inventé. Le parcours a été créé en plusieurs temps sur cet espace pla dans le village de Larbert. Les trois premiers trous forment une boucle. Du 4 au 10 (avec le 18), nous avons encor un autre ensemble, le troisième allant du 11 au 17. Dans cette réalisation au rythme un peu étrange, les par 3 sor appelés "short holes" en anglais, ils n'ont rien de court, deux d'entre eux dépassent les 180 mètres, les trois autre ne sont jamais inférieurs à 150 mètres. Deux des trois par 5 fournissent néanmoins de raisonnables occasions d birdie. A l'heure des comptes, il n'est guère facile de jouer son handicap, ce qui est d'autant plus vexant que le te rain est plat et l'ensemble plutôt court. Certes, les amateurs de parcours spectaculaires ne joueront pas ici tous le jours, mais une visite de temps en temps n'est jamais du temps perdu.

Falkirk Tryst Golf Club — 1885

86 Burn,head Road
SCO - LARBERT, Stirlingshire FK5 4BD

Office	Secrétariat	(44) 01324 - 562 415
Pro shop	Pro-shop	(44) 01324 - 562 091
Fax	Fax	
Web	—	
Situation	Situation	

40 km W of Edinburgh (pop. 418 914)

Annual closure	Fermeture annuelle	no
Weekly closure	Fermeture hebdomadaire	no

Fees main season Tarifs haute saison		full day
	Week days Semaine	We/Bank holidays We/Férié
Individual Individuel	£ 18	*
Couple Couple	£ 36	*

No visitors at weekends / Full Weekdays: £ 27

Caddy	Caddy	no
Electric Trolley	Chariot électrique	yes
Buggy	Voiturette	no
Clubs	Clubs	yes
Credit cards	Cartes de crédit	no

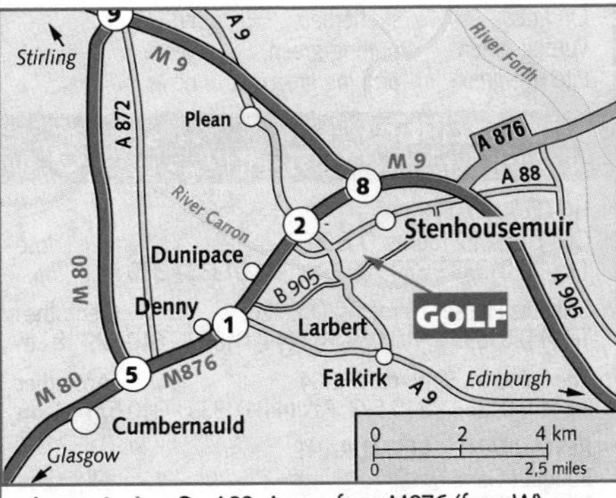

Access Accès : On A88. Access from M876 (from W), A9 from N and S, M9 and A905 from East.
Map 2 on page 487 Carte 2 Page 487

Golf course — PARCOURS — 13/20

Site	Site	
Maintenance	Entretien	
Architect	Architecte	Unknown
Type	Type	inland, links
Relief	Relief	
Water in play	Eau en jeu	
Exp. to wind	Exposé au vent	
Trees in play	Arbres en jeu	

Scorecard Carte de score	Chp. Chp.	Mens Mess.	Ladies Da.
Length Long.	5532	5112	4993
Par	70	67	71
Slope system	—	—	—

Advised golfing ability — Niveau de jeu recommandé: 0 12 24 36
Hcp required — Handicap exigé: no

Club house & amenities — CLUB HOUSE ET ANNEXES — 6/10

Pro shop	Pro-shop	
Driving range	Practice	
Sheltered	couvert	no
On grass	sur herbe	no
Putting-green	putting-green	yes
Pitching-green	pitching green	yes

Hotel facilities — ENVIRONNEMENT HOTELIER — 6/10

HOTELS HÔTELS

Inchyra Grange, 108 rooms, D £ 125 — Falkirk 5 km
Tel (44) 01324 - 711 911, Fax (44) 01324 - 716 134

Airth Castle, 122 rooms, D £ 195 — Airth 5 km
Tel (44) 01324 - 831 411, Fax (44) 01324 - 831 419

Grange Manor, 37 rooms, D £ 120 — Falkirk 3 km
Tel (44) 01324 - 474 836, Fax (44) 01324 - 665 861

Topps Farm, 8 rooms, D £ 50 — Denny 5 km
Tel (44) 01324 - 822 471, Fax (44) 01324 - 823 099

RESTAURANTS RESTAURANT

Priory (Inchira Grange) — Falkirk 5 km
Tel (44) 01324 - 711 911

FORFAR

14 | 6 | 6

Old Tom Morris came from Forfar to lay out the first nine holes of this course in beautiful landscape dotted with heather. In 1925, the Club asked James Braid to come and complete the course, which he did for the princely sum of £10. At that rate you can understand why the man travelled Scotland far and wide, designing hundreds of courses and managing to earn his living as a golf-course designer. Today, the course has been enhanced by some tall pine-trees, but you can still feel Tom Morris' beloved springy turf underfoot. Not a long course - although it is only a par 69 with just the one par 5 - it is still exciting to play, especially the par 3s and a number of blind shots for a few extra thrills. If you are in the region, Forfar is well worth a visit.

Old Tom Morris vint de Saint Andrews pour tracer les neuf premiers trous de ce parcours dans un beau paysage parsemé de bruyère. En 1925, le Club demanda à James Braid de le compléter, ce qu'il fit pour la modique somme de dix Livres. A ce tarif, on comprend qu'il ait sillonné l'Ecosse pour dessiner une multitude de parcours et parvenir à gagner sa vie d'architecte de golf ! Aujourd'hui, de grands pins viennent agrémenter le tracé, mais on y trouve toujours ce sol élastique que Tom Morris aimait tant. De longueur assez modeste - mais c'est un par 69 avec un seul par 5 - il n'en est pas moins passionnant à jouer, en particulier avec ses très beaux par 3, et quelques coups aveugles pour donner un peu d'émotions. Si vous êtes dans la région, Forfar mérite bien une halte.

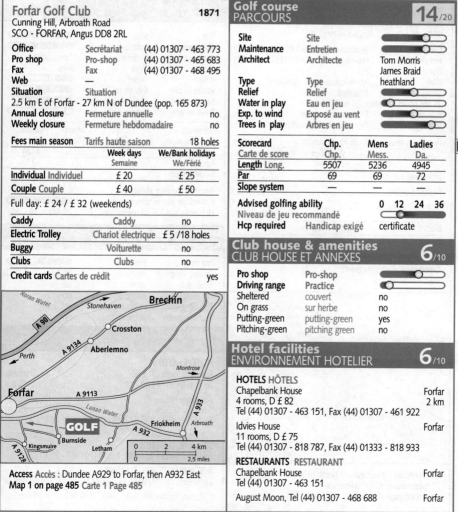

Forfar Golf Club **1871**
Cunning Hill, Arbroath Road
SCO - FORFAR, Angus DD8 2RL

Office	Secrétariat	(44) 01307 - 463 773
Pro shop	Pro-shop	(44) 01307 - 465 683
Fax	Fax	(44) 01307 - 468 495
Web	—	
Situation	Situation	

2.5 km E of Forfar - 27 km N of Dundee (pop. 165 873)

Annual closure	Fermeture annuelle	no
Weekly closure	Fermeture hebdomadaire	no

Fees main season Tarifs haute saison		18 holes
	Week days Semaine	**We/Bank holidays** We/Férié
Individual Individuel	£ 20	£ 25
Couple Couple	£ 40	£ 50

Full day: £ 24 / £ 32 (weekends)

Caddy	Caddy	no
Electric Trolley	Chariot électrique	£ 5 /18 holes
Buggy	Voiturette	no
Clubs	Clubs	no
Credit cards Cartes de crédit		yes

Access Accès : Dundee A929 to Forfar, then A932 East
Map 1 on page 485 Carte 1 Page 485

Golf course PARCOURS 14/20

Site	Site	
Maintenance	Entretien	
Architect	Architecte	Tom Morris James Braid
Type	Type	heathland
Relief	Relief	
Water in play	Eau en jeu	
Exp. to wind	Exposé au vent	
Trees in play	Arbres en jeu	

Scorecard Carte de score	**Chp.** Chp.	**Mens** Mess.	**Ladies** Da.
Length Long.	5507	5236	4945
Par	69	69	72
Slope system	—	—	—

Advised golfing ability — Niveau de jeu recommandé: 0 12 24 36
Hcp required — Handicap exigé: certificate

Club house & amenities CLUB HOUSE ET ANNEXES 6/10

Pro shop	Pro-shop	
Driving range	Practice	
Sheltered	couvert	no
On grass	sur herbe	no
Putting-green	putting-green	yes
Pitching-green	pitching green	no

Hotel facilities ENVIRONNEMENT HOTELIER 6/10

HOTELS HÔTELS
Chapelbank House — Forfar
4 rooms, D £ 82 — 2 km
Tel (44) 01307 - 463 151, Fax (44) 01307 - 461 922

Idvies House — Forfar
11 rooms, D £ 75
Tel (44) 01307 - 818 787, Fax (44) 01333 - 818 933

RESTAURANTS RESTAURANT
Chapelbank House — Forfar
Tel (44) 01307 - 463 151

August Moon, Tel (44) 01307 - 468 688 — Forfar

FORTROSE & ROSEMARKIE

16 | 6 | 5

This delightful course is sited on a promontory on Black Isle and gives a magnificent view over Cromarty Firth. It's shortish length might make you feel that only accuracy is of any importance here, and that's true if the wind keeps low, which is rare. Twice restyled by James Braid, it uses the land in remarkable fashion and is extremely dangerous in the way the sea comes into play. You will need a broad pair of shoulders to keep your score down on an off-day, but you don't have to keep score. Doubtless a little kinder than its neighbours Royal Dornoch and Nairn, this gently rolling course is magic for everyone, and remarkable value for money. On the 17th, watch out for the stone marking the tomb of the "last" Scottish witch. Was she really the last?

Ce délicieux parcours est situé sur un promontoire sur la Black Isle et offre un spectacle magnifique sur le Cromarty Firth. Sa longueur très modérée pourrait faire croire que seule va compter la précision. C'est vrai si le vent ne souffle pas, ce qui est bien rare. Révisé à deux reprises par James Braid, il utilise le terrain de manière remarquable, et met en jeu la mer de manière fort dangereuse. Il faut certes avoir les épaules larges pour serrer le score quand le jeu n'est pas au rendez-vous... mais après tout, on n'est pas toujours obligé de compter les coups. Moins brutal sans doute que ses voisins Royal Dornoch et Nairn, ce parcours gentiment ondulé est un régal pour tous, avec un rapport qualité/prix remarquable. A remarquer au 17, la pierre marquant la tombe de la "dernière" sorcière d'Ecosse. La dernière, vraiment ?

Fortrose & Rosemarkie — 1888

Ness Road East, Fortrose
SCO - BLACK ISLE, Ross-shire IV10 8SE

Office	Secrétariat	(44) 01381 - 620 529
Pro shop	Pro-shop	(44) 01381 - 620 733
Fax	Fax	—
Web	www.fortrosegolfclub.co.uk	
Situation	Situation	

21 km NE of Inverness (pop. 62 186)

Annual closure	Fermeture annuelle	no
Weekly closure	Fermeture hebdomadaire	no

Fees main season Tarifs haute saison — 18 holes

	Week days Semaine	We/Bank holidays We/Férié
Individual Individuel	£ 21	£ 32
Couple Couple	£ 42	£ 64

Caddy	Caddy	no
Electric Trolley	Chariot électrique	no
Buggy	Voiturette	on request
Clubs	Clubs	on request

Credit cards Cartes de crédit
VISA - MasterCard

Access Accès : Inverness, A9 North to Tore. At roundabout, A382 to Fortrose

Map 1 on page 484 Carte 1 Page 484

Golf course PARCOURS — 16/20

Site	Site	
Maintenance	Entretien	
Architect	Architecte	James Braid
Type	Type	links
Relief	Relief	
Water in play	Eau en jeu	
Exp. to wind	Exposé au vent	
Trees in play	Arbres en jeu	

Scorecard Carte de score	Chp. Chp.	Mens Mess.	Ladies Da.
Length Long.	5295	5000	4824
Par	71	71	71
Slope system	—	—	—

Advised golfing ability Niveau de jeu recommandé — 0 12 24 36

Hcp required Handicap exigé — 28 Men, 36 Ladies

Club house & amenities CLUB HOUSE ET ANNEXES — 6/10

Pro shop	Pro-shop	
Driving range	Practice	
Sheltered	couvert	no
On grass	sur herbe	no
Putting-green	putting-green	yes
Pitching-green	pitching green	no

Hotel facilities ENVIRONNEMENT HOTELIER — 5/10

HOTELS HÔTELS

Royal, 10 rooms, D £ 55 — Cromarty 15 km
Tel (44) 01381 - 600 217

Ballyfeary House — Inverness 25 km
5 rooms, D £ 76
Tel (44) 01463 - 235 572, Fax (44) 01463 - 717 583

Craigmonie Hotel — Inverness
35 rooms, D £ 118
Tel (44) 01463 - 231 649, Fax (44) 01463 - 233 720

RESTAURANTS RESTAURANT

La Riviera, Tel (44) 01463 - 223 777 — Inverness

Culloden House, Tel (44) 01463 - 790 461 — Inverness

GLEN

14 | 7 | 7

This is the "East Links" of North Berwick, less well known than its neighbour doubtless because it is less of a complete links and has several inland holes. It is laid out over two levels but is still easy on the legs. Designed at the turn of the century and tastefully restyled by MacKenzie Ross with a considerate thought for all players, it offers some splendid views over the Firth of Forth and over the famous bird reserve of Bass Rock in the open sea. It is not over-long (compared as always with today's standards) but is still a stiff test of golf, especially with the wind which although not too blustery is never far away. Green-feers will at least remember the drive from the 18th tee, from a severely elevated tee, and the excitement of a number of blind shots.

C'est le "East Links" de North Berwick, moins connu que son voisin, sans doute parce qu'il a un caractère moins totalement "links", avec plusieurs trous nettement "inland." Construit sur deux niveaux, il n'est pas fatigant à jouer. Créé au début du siècle, remanié par Mackenzie Ross avec beaucoup de goût et de souci d'adaptation à tous les joueurs, il propose de superbes vues sur le Firth of Forth et sur la fameuse réserve d'oiseaux du Bass Rock, au large. Bien qu'il ne soit pas très long (toujours en regard des célèbres critères modernes), c'est néanmoins un solide test de jeu, spécialement avec le vent, pas toujours violent, mais toujours présent. Les visiteurs garderont d'ici au moins le souvenir du drive du 18, depuis un départ très en hauteur, et celui de quelques émotions sur certains coups aveugles.

Glen Golf Club — 1906

Tantallon Terrace
SCO - NORTH BERWICK, East Lothian EH39 4LE

Office	Secrétariat	(44) 01620 - 892 726
Pro shop	Pro-shop	(44) 01620 - 892 726
Fax	Fax	(44) 01620 - 895 447
Web	—	
Situation	Situation	

25 km E of Edinburgh (pop. 418 914)

Annual closure	Fermeture annuelle	no
Weekly closure	Fermeture hebdomadaire	no

Fees main season / Tarifs haute saison	18 holes	
	Week days / Semaine	We/Bank holidays / We/Férié
Individual Individuel	£ 20	£ 27
Couple Couple	£ 40	£ 54

Caddy	Caddy	on request
Electric Trolley	Chariot électrique	£ 5 /18 holes
Buggy	Voiturette	no
Clubs	Clubs	£ 10 /18 holes

Credit cards Cartes de crédit
VISA - Mastercard

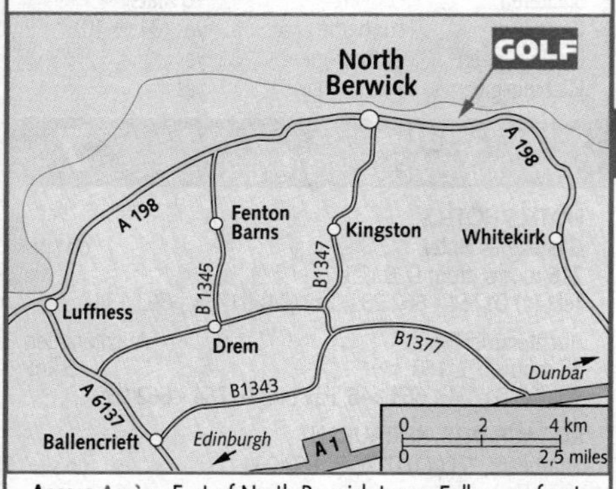

Access Accès : East of North Berwick town. Follow seafront road from harbour. Course signposted.
Map 3 on page 489 Carte 3 Page 489

Golf course / PARCOURS — 14/20

Site	Site	
Maintenance	Entretien	
Architect	Architecte	Mackenzie Ross
Type	Type	seaside course
Relief	Relief	
Water in play	Eau en jeu	
Exp. to wind	Exposé au vent	
Trees in play	Arbres en jeu	

Scorecard / Carte de score	Chp. / Chp.	Mens / Mess.	Ladies / Da.
Length Long.	5485	5251	5039
Par	69	69	72
Slope system	—	—	—

Advised golfing ability / Niveau de jeu recommandé: 0 12 24 36
Hcp required / Handicap exigé: no

Club house & amenities / CLUB HOUSE ET ANNEXES — 7/10

Pro shop	Pro-shop	
Driving range	Practice	
Sheltered	couvert	no
On grass	sur herbe	yes
Putting-green	putting-green	yes
Pitching-green	pitching green	yes

Hotel facilities / ENVIRONNEMENT HOTELIER — 7/10

HOTELS HÔTELS

Marine Hotel — North Berwick, 3 km
79 rooms, D £ 140
Tel (44) 01620 - 892 406, Fax (44) 01620 - 894 480

Nether Abbey — North Berwick
16 rooms, D £ 55
Tel (44) 01620 - 892 802

RESTAURANTS RESTAURANT

Tantallon Inn — North Berwick, 0.5 km
Tel (44) 01620 - 892 238

The Grange — North Berwick, 1 km
Tel (44) 01620 - 895 894

GLENEAGLES King's

18 | 9 | 7

You come here as a true golfing fanatic, and to hell with the cost. The Gleneagles hotel, an absolute must, is a genuine palace hotel in an idyllic region of the Highlands. At the end of the first world war, James Braid designed the first two 18-hole courses - the King's and Queen's - while the third, the PGA Centenary, was laid out by Jack Nicklaus. The King's Course is without a doubt the finest of the three, magnificently crafted from the surrounding landscape, winding its way through trees, bushes and hills and teeming with wildlife. The course has one essential quality, namely the variety of holes and a sort of indefinable logic in its balance. The artistry in the shapes of greens and bunkers only adds to the visual and technical pleasure of playing this challenging, very technical and remarkably well-groomed course. Exposure to the wind may vary considerably, depending on how protected the fairways are.

On vient ici en passionné du golf, en décidant de ne pas compter ses sous. Le Gleneagles Hotel, point de passage obligatoire, est un véritable palace, dans une région idyllique des Highlands. A la fin de la première Guerre Mondiale, James Braid dessina les deux premiers 18 trous, le King's et le Queen's, le troisième, le PGA Centenary, ayant été créé par Jack Nicklaus. Le premier nommé reste sans doute le plus savoureux des trois. Magnifiquement sculpté dans la campagne environnante, insinué au milieu des arbres, des buissons, des collines, parcourus d'une vie animale intense, il a une qualité essentielle, la variété des trous et une sorte de logique indéfinissable de rythme. Et la sensualité des formes des greens ou des bunkers ne fait qu'ajouter au plaisir visuel et technique de ce parcours exigeant, très technique, remarquablement entretenu. L'exposition au vent peut varier considérablement, suivant que les fairways sont ou non protégés.

Gleneagles Hotel & Golf Courses 1919

Gleneagles Hotel
SCO - AUCHTERARDER, Perthshire PH3 1NF

Office	Secrétariat	(44) 01764 - 694 469
Pro shop	Pro-shop	(44) 01764 - 694 362
Fax	Fax	(44) 01764 - 694 383
Web	www.gleneagles.com	
Situation	Situation	

30 km SW of Perth - 85 km NW of Edinburgh (pop. 418 914)

Annual closure	Fermeture annuelle	no
Weekly closure	Fermeture hebdomadaire	no

Fees main season Tarifs haute saison — 18 holes

	Week days / Semaine	We/Bank holidays / We/Férié
Individual Individuel	£ 100 *	£ 100 *
Couple Couple	£ 200	£ 200

Residents greenfees: £ 85

Caddy	Caddy	£ 30
Electric Trolley	Chariot électrique	no
Buggy	Voiturette	no
Clubs	Clubs	£ 30 /18 holes

Credit cards Cartes de crédit
VISA - Eurocard - MasterCard - DC - JCB - AMEX

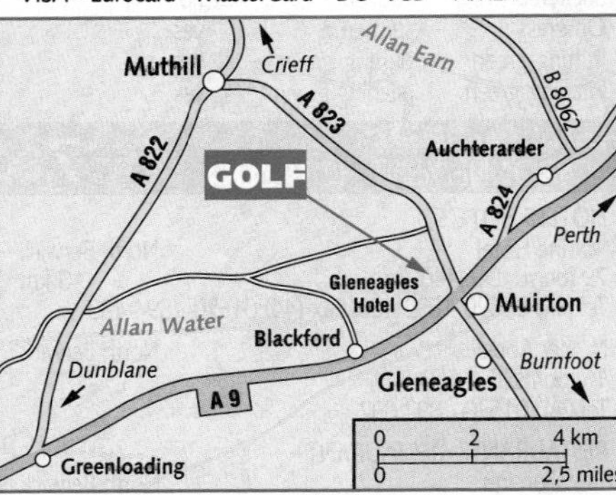

Access Accès : • Glasgow A80, M9, A9. Turn left at junction with A823 signed Crieff & Gleneagles • Edinburgh M90. Jct 2, then A823 through Dunfermline, → Crieff.
Map 2 on page 488 Carte 2 Page 488

Golf course PARCOURS 18/20

Site	Site	
Maintenance	Entretien	
Architect	Architecte	James Braid
Type	Type	moorland
Relief	Relief	
Water in play	Eau en jeu	
Exp. to wind	Exposé au vent	
Trees in play	Arbres en jeu	

Scorecard Carte de score	Chp. Chp.	Mens Mess.	Ladies Da.
Length Long.	6111	5824	5286
Par	70	70	75
Slope system	—	—	—

Advised golfing ability Niveau de jeu recommandé — 0 12 24 36

Hcp required Handicap exigé — no

Club house & amenities CLUB HOUSE ET ANNEXES 9/10

Pro shop	Pro-shop	
Driving range	Practice	
Sheltered	couvert	10 mats
On grass	sur herbe	yes (04 → 10)
Putting-green	putting-green	yes
Pitching-green	pitching green	yes

Hotel facilities ENVIRONNEMENT HOTELIER 7/10

HOTELS HÔTELS

Gleneagles Hotel — on site
216 rooms, from D £ 125
Tel (44) 01764 - 662 231, Fax (44) 01764 - 662 134

Auchterarder House — Auchterarder 5 km
15 rooms, F £ 160
Tel (44) 01764 - 663 646, Fax (44) 01764 - 662 939

RESTAURANTS RESTAURANT

Strathearn, Tel (44) 01764 - 662 231 — on site

Dormy Clubhouse Restaurant — on site
Tel (44) 01764 - 662 231

Restaurant Andrew Fairlie, Tel (44) 01764 - 694 267 on site

GLENEAGLES PGA Centenary 17 | 9 | 7

This course was built to complement the King's and Queen's courses. It was designed by Jack Nicklaus and clearly aimed at appealing to the American visitors who visit the internationally famous hotel. After having been called "Monarch", the name has been changed in 2001 to the PGA Centenary Course. Created as a venue for championship golf, it has natural amphitheatres round every hole which not only create a sense of grandeur but also excellent viewing areas for spectators. The course is memorable for its dramatic and open views of the nearby Ochil Hills and Glendevon. Five tees on each hole make it both the longest and the shortest playing course at the resort, to accommodate all levels of ability. The course is of an excellent strategic standard, even though Nicklaus was visibly thinking more of the proficient golfer than the less experienced hacker. The superb setting will silence even those people who feel that the difference in style with the other two courses is over the top.

Ce parcours a été construit ici pour accompagner le King's et le Queen's. Dessiné par Jack Nicklaus, il est visiblement destinée à retenir les visiteurs américains qui adorent cet hôtel mondialement célèbre. L'appellation de "Monarch" a été modifiée au profit de "PGA Centenary". Conçu pour recevoir des championnats, il est entouré d'amphithéâtres naturels, qui ne créent pas seulement un sentiment de grandeur, mais offrent aussi une excellente visibilité aux spectateurs. Les aperçus des Ochil Hills et du Glendevon ajoutent encore du prestige au lieu. Cinq tees de départ permettent d'en faire le parcours le plus long comme le plus court du domaine, pour accommoder tous les niveaux de jeu. Nettement américain de dessin, parfois un peu artificiel dans ce paysage, il est d'une excellente qualité stratégique, même si Nicklaus a visiblement plus pensé aux bons joueurs qu'aux moins expérimentés. L'environnement superbe fera taire même ceux qui estiment la différence esthétique excessive par rapport aux deux autres parcours.

Gleneagles Hotel & Golf Courses — 1993

Gleneagles Hotel
SCO - AUCHTERARDER, Perthshire PH3 1NF

Office	Secrétariat	(44) 01764 - 694 469
Pro shop	Pro-shop	(44) 01764 - 694 362
Fax	Fax	(44) 01764 - 694 383
Web	www.gleneagles.com	
Situation	Situation	

30 km SW of Perth - 85 km NW of Edinburgh (pop. 418 914)

Annual closure	Fermeture annuelle	no
Weekly closure	Fermeture hebdomadaire	no

Fees main season Tarifs haute saison		full day
	Week days Semaine	**We/Bank holidays** We/Férié
Individual Individuel	£ 100 *	£ 100 *
Couple Couple	£ 200	£ 200

Residents greenfees: £ 85

Caddy	Caddy	£ 30
Electric Trolley	Chariot électrique	no
Buggy	Voiturette	£ 30/PGA C'ry. only
Clubs	Clubs	£ 30 /18 holes

Credit cards Cartes de crédit
VISA - Eurocard - MasterCard - DC - JCB - AMEX

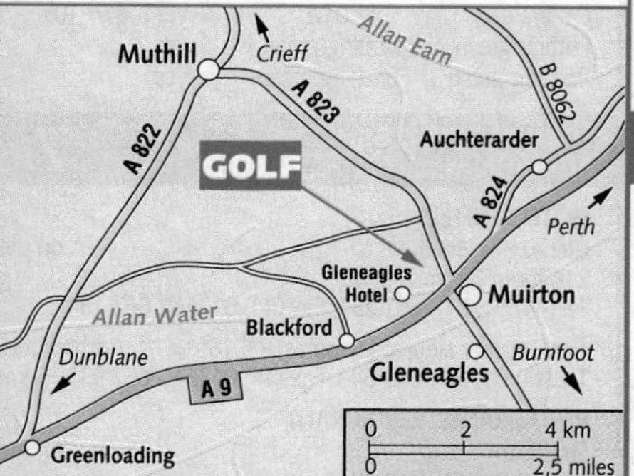

Access Accès : • Glasgow A80, M9, A9. Turn left at junction with A823 signed Crieff & Gleneagles • Edinburgh M90. Jct 2, then A823 through Dunfermline, → Crieff.
Map 2 on page 488 Carte 2 Page 488

Golf course PARCOURS — 17/20

Site	Site	
Maintenance	Entretien	
Architect	Architecte	Jack Nicklaus
Type	Type	moorland
Relief	Relief	
Water in play	Eau en jeu	
Exp. to wind	Exposé au vent	
Trees in play	Arbres en jeu	

Scorecard Carte de score	**Chp.** Chp.	**Mens** Mess.	**Ladies** Da.
Length Long.	6380	5521	5128
Par	72	72	72
Slope system	—	—	—

Advised golfing ability 0 12 24 36
Niveau de jeu recommandé

Hcp required Handicap exigé no

Club house & amenities CLUB HOUSE ET ANNEXES — 9/10

Pro shop	Pro-shop	
Driving range	Practice	
Sheltered	couvert	10 mats
On grass	sur herbe	yes (04 → 10)
Putting-green	putting-green	yes
Pitching-green	pitching green	yes

Hotel facilities ENVIRONNEMENT HOTELIER — 7/10

HOTELS HÔTELS

Gleneagles Hotel, 216 rooms, from D £ 125 — on site
Tel (44) 01764 - 662 231, Fax (44) 01764 - 662 134

Auchterarder House, 15 rooms, F £ 160 — Auchterarder
Tel (44) 01764 - 663 646, Fax (44) 01764 - 662 939 — 5 km

RESTAURANTS RESTAURANT

Strathearn — on site
Tel (44) 01764 - 662 231

Dormy Clubhouse Restaurant — on site
Tel (44) 01764 - 662 231

Restaurant Andrew Fairlie — on site
Tel (44) 01764 - 694 267

GLENEAGLES Queen's

15 | 9 | 7

The Queens Course has rather lived in the shadow of its more famous sister, the King's Course ove the years, but this beautifully designed James Braid layout is a wonderful golf course in its own right Were it standing on its own in another location, it would undoubtedly have received far more acclain than it already has. It is not as long or ultimately taxing as its sister courses, but it still represents a wonderful chal lenge and shares the magical surroundings of this very special place. There are many fine and demanding holes her enhanced with attractive stretches of water. And while it is more reassuring because it offers less resistance to goo golfers, it is still essential playing it when you are here. From Spring to late Autumn, when the sun is shining in thi corner of Perthshire, there are few more idyllic spots to be found in the whole of world golf.

Dans un grand ensemble de parcours, il y a souvent un parcours que l'on réserve aux moins bons joueurs, ou qu figure comme un repos pour le guerrier. Le "Queen's" a vécu longtemps dans l'ombre de son voisin le "King's" mais le splendide tracé de James Braid mérite à lui seul le déplacement. N'importe où ailleurs, ce très bon parcour aurait été bien plus acclamé qu'il ne l'a été jusqu'ici. Il n'est pas aussi long, aussi difficile, aussi exposé que se deux compagnons, mais ce n'en est pas moins bien mieux qu'un faire-valoir. Dans le même environnement su blime, on trouve ici de nombreux trous très exigeants, rehaussés visuellement par des points d'eau. Et s'il rassur par une moindre résistance aux efforts, il n'en est pas moins incontournable quand on se trouve ici. Du printemp à la fin de l'automne, il y a peu de plus beaux endroits au monde que cette région du Perthshire pour séjourner e jouer au golf, même si l'on trouve ailleurs de plus grands chefs-d'oeuvre au plan technique.

Gleneagles Hotel & Golf Courses — 1917

Gleneagles Hotel
SCO - AUCHTERARDER, Perthshire PH3 1NF

Office	Secrétariat	(44) 01764 - 694 469
Pro shop	Pro-shop	(44) 01764 - 694 362
Fax	Fax	(44) 01764 - 694 383
Web	www.gleneagles.com	
Situation	Situation	

30 km SW of Perth - 85 km NW of Edinburgh (pop. 418 914)

Annual closure	Fermeture annuelle	no
Weekly closure	Fermeture hebdomadaire	no

Fees main season Tarifs haute saison		full day
	Week days Semaine	**We/Bank holidays** We/Férié
Individual Individuel	£ 100 *	£ 100 *
Couple Couple	£ 200	£ 200

Residents greenfees: £ 85

Caddy	Caddy	£ 30
Electric Trolley	Chariot électrique	no
Buggy	Voiturette	£ 30 /PGA C'ry. only
Clubs	Clubs	£ 30 /18 holes

Credit cards Cartes de crédit
VISA - Eurocard - MasterCard - DC - JCB - AMEX

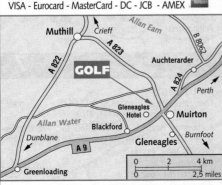

Access Accès : • Glasgow A80, M9, A9. Turn left at junction with A823 signed Crieff & Gleneagles • Edinburgh M90. Jct 2, then A823 through Dunfermline, → Crieff.
Map 2 on page 488 Carte 2 Page 488

Golf course — PARCOURS — 15/20

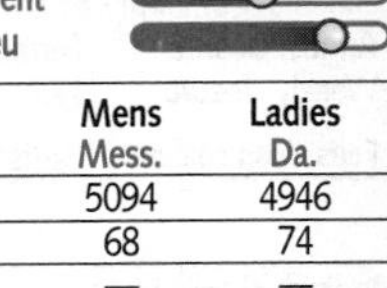

Site	Site	
Maintenance	Entretien	
Architect	Architecte	James Braid
Type	Type	moorland
Relief	Relief	
Water in play	Eau en jeu	
Exp. to wind	Exposé au vent	
Trees in play	Arbres en jeu	

Scorecard Carte de score	**Chp.** Chp.	**Mens** Mess.	**Ladies** Da.
Length Long.	5369	5094	4946
Par	68	68	74
Slope system	—	—	—

Advised golfing ability Niveau de jeu recommandé: 0 12 24 36

Hcp required Handicap exigé: no

Club house & amenities — CLUB HOUSE ET ANNEXES — 9/10

Pro shop	Pro-shop	
Driving range	Practice	
Sheltered	couvert	10 mats
On grass	sur herbe	yes (04 → 10)
Putting-green	putting-green	yes
Pitching-green	pitching green	yes

Hotel facilities — ENVIRONNEMENT HOTELIER — 7/10

HOTELS HÔTELS

Gleneagles Hotel — on site
216 rooms, from D £ 125
Tel (44) 01764 - 662 231, Fax (44) 01764 - 662 134

Auchterarder House, 15 rooms, F £ 160 — Auchterarder 5 km
Tel (44) 01764 - 663 646, Fax (44) 01764 - 662 939

RESTAURANTS RESTAURANT

Strathearn — on site
Tel (44) 01764 - 662 231

Dormy Clubhouse Restaurant — on site
Tel(44) 01764 - 662 231

Restaurant Andrew Fairlie, Tel (44) 01764 - 694 267 — on site

GOLSPIE

14 | 5 | 4

Golspie is particularly interesting for the shape and layout of the course. Over limited space, you start off virtually in a park before moving on to pure links holes (not necessarily the best), then into woods and heather before returning to park landscape. There is no shortage of interesting holes of all shapes and sizes, with some very long and very short par 4s, five par 3s and just the one par 5. A very pleasant course to play on holiday, far from the crowds who flock to more fashionable and less remote venues, Golspie also offers some beautiful views over the coast, north and south. A word should go the excellent green-keeping despite only very few staff working on the course. Play here in Summer, when the wind keeps away, before playing Brora and Dornoch.

Golspie est particulièrement intéressant en raison de sa conformation. Sur un espace restreint, on part quasiment d'un parc pour passer ensuite par des trous de pur links (ce ne sont pas forcément les meilleurs comme on pourrait l'imaginer), puis dans les bois, la bruyère et enfin revenir au parc. Les trous intéressants ne manquent pas ici, dans tous les genres car on trouve des longs par 4 mais aussi de très courts, cinq par 3 et un seul par 5. Très agréable à jouer en vacances, loin de la foule qui choisit des endroits plus à la mode, ou moins lointains, Golspie offre en outre des vues très belles sur la côte, au nord comme au sud. On signalera enfin l'excellente qualité de l'entretien, malgré un personnel très restreint. A jouer en été, quand le vent est amical, et avant de jouer Brora et Dornoch.

Golspie Golf Club — 1889

Ferry Road
SCO - GOLSPIE, Sutherland KW10 6ST

Office	Secrétariat	(44) 01408 - 633 266
Pro shop	Pro-shop	(44) 01408 - 633 266
Fax	Fax	(44) 01408 - 633 393
Web	—	
Situation	Situation	

18 km N of Dornoch - 80 km N of Inverness (pop. 62 186)

Annual closure	Fermeture annuelle	no
Weekly closure	Fermeture hebdomadaire	no

Fees main season Tarifs haute saison	18 holes	
	Week days Semaine	**We/Bank holidays** We/Férié
Individual Individuel	£ 25	£ 25
Couple Couple	£ 30	£ 30

Caddy	Caddy	on request
Electric Trolley	Chariot électrique	no
Buggy	Voiturette	no
Clubs	Clubs	yes

Credit cards Cartes de crédit
VISA - MasterCard - Switch - Delta

Access Accès : Off the main A9. Turn right after railway crossing. Golf on the sea side.
Map 1 on page 485 Carte 1 Page 485

Golf course — PARCOURS — 14/20

Site	Site	
Maintenance	Entretien	
Architect	Architecte	James Braid (1926)
Type	Type	links, parkland
Relief	Relief	
Water in play	Eau en jeu	
Exp. to wind	Exposé au vent	
Trees in play	Arbres en jeu	

Scorecard Carte de score	**Chp.** Chp.	**Mens** Mess.	**Ladies** Da.
Length Long.	5360	5167	4766
Par	68	68	71
Slope system	—	—	—

Advised golfing ability Niveau de jeu recommandé — 0 12 24 36
Hcp required Handicap exigé — no

Club house & amenities — CLUB HOUSE ET ANNEXES — 5/10

Pro shop	Pro-shop	
Driving range	Practice	
Sheltered	couvert	n,o
On grass	sur herbe	yes
Putting-green	putting-green	yes
Pitching-green	pitching green	no

Hotel facilities — ENVIRONNEMENT HOTELIER — 4/10

HOTELS HÔTELS

Ben Bhraggie — Golspie close
7 rooms, D £ 36
Tel (44) 01408 - 633 242, Fax (44) 01408 - 634 277

Sutherland Arms — Golspie close
14 rooms, D £ 56
Tel (44) 01408 - 633 234, Fax (44) 01408 - 633 234

Golf Links — Golspie close
9 rooms, D £ 55
Tel (44) 01408 - 633 408

RESTAURANTS RESTAURANT

Taste Buds, Tel (44) 01408 - 633 022 — Golspie, close

GRANTOWN ON SPEY

14	6	7

This is the kind of course you want to show those golfers who know only the links courses in Scotland. But why go and play mountain courses, you may ask? Firstly because they are located in superb, untamed regions and then because they are flat enough not to tire the legs of people who spend the rest of the year behind a desk. And perhaps you'll find more things to do outside golf (for non-golfers) in the Highlands than beside the sea. Close to Boat of Garten and Aviemore, this course was designed by Willie Park and James Braid. It has no needless complications, is very short (even for a par 68), is quick to play and is playable by golfers of all levels. The best players might find it a little on the easy side, but there is nothing to stop them from trying to beat the course record (60), or play more than once.

Le genre de parcours à mettre sous les yeux de ceux qui ne connaissent de l'Ecosse que les paysages de links. Pourquoi aller jouer ses parcours de montagne ? D'abord parce qu'ils se trouvent dans des régions superbes et sauvages, ensuite parce qu'ils sont souvent, paradoxalement, assez plats pour ne pas effrayer ceux qui passent leur vie dans un bureau. Parce que l'on trouve peut-être plus d'activités annexes (pour ceux qui ne jouent pas) dans les Highlands qu'en bord de mer. A proximité de Boat of Garten et d'Aviemore, des réserves des Cairngorns, ce parcours de Willie Park et Braid est sans complications inutiles, très court (même pour un par 68), rapide à jouer et bien adapté à tous les niveaux. Les meilleurs le trouveront un peu limité pour eux, mais rien ne les empêche de battre le record (60), et de le jouer plusieurs fois !

Grantown on Spey Golf Club — 1890

Golf Course Road
SCO - GRANTOWN ON SPEY, Morayshire PH26 3HY

Office	Secrétariat	(44) 01479 - 872 079
Pro shop	Pro-shop	(44) 01479 - 872 079
Fax	Fax	(44) 01479 - 873 725
Web	www.grantownonspeygolfclub.co.uk	
Situation	Situation	

56 km SE of Inverness (pop. 62 186)

Annual closure	Fermeture annuelle	no
Weekly closure	Fermeture hebdomadaire	no

Clubhouse closed 11 → 03 inclusive

Fees main season Tarifs haute saison	Week days Semaine	We/Bank holidays We/Férié
		Full day
Individual Individuel	£ 20	£ 25
Couple Couple	£ 40	£ 50

Caddy	Caddy	no
Electric Trolley	Chariot électrique	no
Buggy	Voiturette	£ 10 /18 holes
Clubs	Clubs	£ 18 /18 holes

Credit cards Cartes de crédit VISA - Eurocard - MasterCard

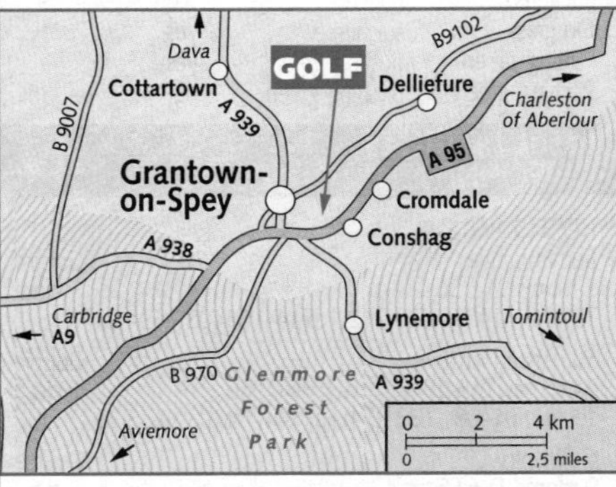

Access Accès : Inverness, A9, A938 & A95 to Grantown. Course lies off the road to Nairn and Forres, on NE side of Grantown
Map 1 on page 485 Carte 1 Page 485

Golf course — PARCOURS — 14/20

Site	Site	
Maintenance	Entretien	
Architect	Architecte	A.C. Brown/W. Park, James Braid
Type	Type	parkland
Relief	Relief	
Water in play	Eau en jeu	
Exp. to wind	Exposé au vent	
Trees in play	Arbres en jeu	

Scorecard Carte de score	Chp. Chp.	Mens Mess.	Ladies Da.
Length Long.	5198	4930	4801
Par	70	69	72
Slope system	—	—	—

Advised golfing ability Niveau de jeu recommandé: 0 12 24 36

Hcp required Handicap exigé: no

Club house & amenities — CLUB HOUSE ET ANNEXES — 6/10

Pro shop	Pro-shop	
Driving range	Practice	
Sheltered	couvert	no
On grass	sur herbe	no
Putting-green	putting-green	yes
Pitching-green	pitching green	no

Hotel facilities — ENVIRONNEMENT HOTELIER — 7/10

HOTELS HÔTELS

Muckrach Lodge, 13 rooms, from D £ 125 — Dulnain Bridge
Tel (44) 01479 - 851 257, Fax (44) 01479 - 851 325 — 5 km

Culdearn House — Grantown
9 rooms, D £ 150 (w. dinner) — 0.5 km
Tel (44) 01479 - 872 106, Fax (44) 01479 - 873 641

Ravenscourt House, 8 rooms, D £ 80 — Grantown
Tel (44) 01479 - 872 286, Fax (44) 01479 - 873 260

RESTAURANTS RESTAURANT

Craggan Mill, Tel (44) 01479 - 872 288 — Grantown 0.5 km

La Taverna ,Tel (44) 01479 - 810 636 — Aviemore 22 km

GULLANE No 1

17 | 8 | 7

Of the three courses at Gullane, the N° 1 is unquestionably the most spectacular and the most challenging in golfing terms, although its two neighbours are a pleasant alternative on holiday or for less experienced golfers in the family. The slow climb along an impressive hill takes you gradually up above the Firth of Forth until you can make out the famous Muirfield links not far away. But Gullane is much more than an observatory. Wide open spaces, where only the tall rough can break the feeling of immensity, accommodate a high class course where the work of anonymous designers consisted primarily in laying out the greens, digging the bunkers (often deep) and leaving time do the rest. If you want to enjoy rather than endure this often austere course, give it everything you've got.

Des trois parcours de Gullane, le 1 est sans conteste le plus spectaculaire et le plus exigeant au plan golfique, bien que ses deux voisins constituent une alternative heureuse en vacances, ou séduisent les membres moins expérimentés de la famille ou du groupe. La lente montée le long d'une imposante colline permet de s'élever peu à peu au-dessus du Firth of Forth, jusqu'à distinguer non loin les fameux links de Muirfield. Mais Gullane est bien plus qu'un observatoire. Les vastes espaces, où seul le haut rough peut rompre le sentiment d'immensité, accueillent un parcours de haute volée, où le travail anonyme des architectes a surtout consisté à aménager les greens, creuser les bunkers (souvent profonds) et laisser faire le temps. Ici, sur ce tracé souvent austère, on exprime tout son golf, ou on le subit...

Gullane Golf Club — 1844

West Links Road
SCO - GULLANE, East Lothian EH31 2BB

Office	Secrétariat	(44) 01620 - 842 255
Pro shop	Pro-shop	(44) 01620 - 842 255
Fax	Fax	(44) 01620 - 842 327
E-mail	gullane@compuserve.com	
Situation	Situation	

29 km E of Edinburgh (pop. 418 914)

Annual closure	Fermeture annuelle	no
Weekly closure	Fermeture hebdomadaire	no

Fees main season Tarifs haute saison	18 holes	
	Week days Semaine	**We/Bank holidays** We/Férié
Individual Individuel	£ 65	£ 80
Couple Couple	£ 130	£ 160

Full Weekdays: £ 90

Caddy	Caddy	£ 25 /on request
Electric Trolley	Chariot électrique	no
Buggy	Voiturette	£ 20 /18 holes
Clubs	Clubs	£ 20 /18 holes

Credit cards Cartes de crédit
VISA - Eurocard - MasterCard - AMEX

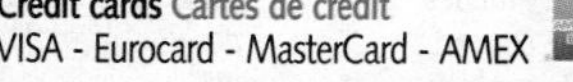

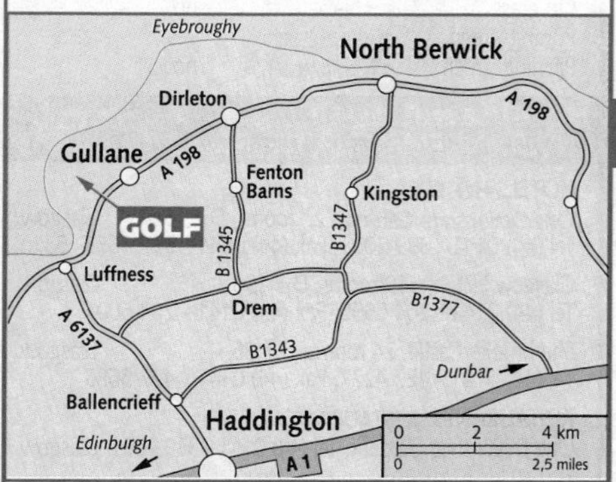

Access Accès : Edinburgh A198 to Gullane
Map 3 on page 489 Carte 3 Page 489

Golf course PARCOURS — 17/20

Site	Site	
Maintenance	Entretien	
Architect	Architecte	Unknown
Type	Type	seaside course, links
Relief	Relief	
Water in play	Eau en jeu	
Exp. to wind	Exposé au vent	
Trees in play	Arbres en jeu	

Scorecard Carte de score	**Chp.** Chp.	**Mens** Mess.	**Ladies** Da.
Length Long.	5884	5530	5530
Par	71	71	75
Slope system	—	—	—

Advised golfing ability Niveau de jeu recommandé: 0 12 24 36
Hcp required Handicap exigé: 24 Men, 30 Ladies

Club house & amenities CLUB HOUSE ET ANNEXES — 8/10

Pro shop	Pro-shop	
Driving range	Practice	
Sheltered	couvert	no
On grass	sur herbe	yes
Putting-green	putting-green	yes
Pitching-green	pitching green	yes

Hotel facilities ENVIRONNEMENT HOTELIER — 7/10

HOTELS HÔTELS

Mallard Hotel, 18 rooms, D £ 76 — Gullane
Tel (44) 01620 - 843 288, Fax (44) 01620 - 843 200 — 2 km

Brown's Hotel — Haddington
5 rooms, D £ 120 — 3 km
Tel (44) 01620 - 822 254, Fax (44) 01620 - 822 254

Maitlandfield House — Haddington
22 rooms, D £ 150 — 3 km
Tel (44) 01620 - 826 513, Fax (44) 01620 - 826 713

RESTAURANTS RESTAURANT

Brown's — Haddington
Tel (44) 01620 - 822 254 — 3 km

HAGGS CASTLE

15 | 7 | 9

The fine layout of this well-known Glaswegian club unwinds between rows of fully grown trees a few miles to the south-west of the city centre. It is one of the easiest-to-reach courses around Glasgow, useful to know in that although a private club, it willingly welcomes visitors during the week. Of course it doesn't offer the array of technical challenges found on the great championship courses but it has often been used for some very high level tournaments which testify to its status. The Scottish Open was one such before it moved on to Gleneagles and then Carnoustie. Good drivers will feel easy here, the others will need all their expertise to reach the well-protected greens which pitch well. There are very few bump 'n run shots to be played here, rather more in the American target golf style, despite the very British nature of the course overall.

Le beau tracé de ce club bien connu de Glasgow s'étire entre des rangées d'arbres bien adultes, à quelques kilomètres au sud-ouest du centre ville. C'est un des golfs de Glasgow les plus faciles d'accès. Et d'autant plus que, bien qu'il soit privé, il accueille volontiers les visteurs en semaine. Certes, le parcours ne présente pas la variété des défis techniques des plus grands parcours de championnat, mais il a souvent été utilisé pour de très bonnes épreuves, ce qui témoigne de son rang : nous ne citerons que le Scottish Open, qui émigra ensuite à Gleneagles puis Carnoustie. Les bons drivers y seront ici à l'aise. Les autres devront témoigner de virtuosité pour rejoindre des greens bien protégés, mais qui tiennent bien la balle. Ici, peu de "bump'n run," mais plutôt un jeu de cible à l'américaine, malgré le caractère général très britannique de l'ensemble.

Haggs Castle Golf Club — 1910

70 Dumbreck Road
SCO - GLASGOW G41 4SN

Office	Secrétariat	(44) 0141 - 427 0480
Pro shop	Pro-shop	(44) 0141 - 427 3355
Fax	Fax	(44) 0141 - 427 1157
Web	—	
Situation	Situation	

5 km SW of Glasgow centre (pop. 662 853)

Annual closure	Fermeture annuelle	no
Weekly closure	Fermeture hebdomadaire	no

Fees main season Tarifs haute saison	Week days Semaine	We/Bank holidays We/Férié
Individual Individuel	£ 35	*
Couple Couple	£ 70	*

18 holes. No visitors at weekends

Caddy	Caddy	on request
Electric Trolley	Chariot électrique	no
Buggy	Voiturette	on request
Clubs	Clubs	on request
Credit cards	Cartes de crédit	no

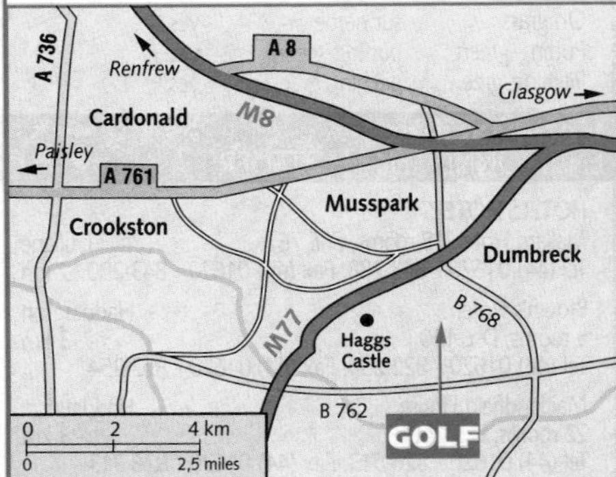

Access Accès : A7 end of Jct 1 off M77. SW of Glasgow city centre.
Map 3 on page 488 Carte 3 Page 488

Golf course — PARCOURS — 15/20

Site	Site	
Maintenance	Entretien	
Architect	Architecte	Unknown
Type	Type	parkland
Relief	Relief	
Water in play	Eau en jeu	
Exp. to wind	Exposé au vent	
Trees in play	Arbres en jeu	

Scorecard Carte de score	Chp. Chp.	Mens Mess.	Ladies Da.
Length Long.	884	5389	4962
Par	72	69	73
Slope system	—	—	—

Advised golfing ability Niveau de jeu recommandé: 0 12 24 36
Hcp required Handicap exigé: certificate

Club house & amenities — CLUB HOUSE ET ANNEXES — 7/10

Pro shop	Pro-shop	
Driving range	Practice	
Sheltered	couvert	no
On grass	sur herbe	no
Putting-green	putting-green	yes
Pitching-green	pitching green	no

Hotel facilities — ENVIRONNEMENT HOTELIER — 9/10

HOTELS HÔTELS

One Devonshire Gardens, 27 rooms, D £ 275 — Glasgow
Tel (44) 0141 - 339 2001, Fax (44) 0141 - 337 1663 — 5 km

Glasgow Hilton, 319 rooms, D £ 190 — Glasgow
Tel (44) 0141 - 204 5555, Fax (44) 0141 - 204 5004

Sherbrooke Castle, 24 rooms, D £ 85 — Glasgow
Tel (44) 0141 - 427 4227, Fax (44) 0141 - 427 5685

RESTAURANTS RESTAURANT

One Devonshire Gardens, Tel (44) 0141 - 339 2001 — Glasgow

The Restaurant at Corinthian — Glasgow
Tel (44) 0141 - 552 1101

Rogano, Tel (44) 0141 - 248 4055 — Glasgow

HUNTLY

14 | 6 | 6

This may not be the masterpiece of the century when it comes to course design, and as a course off the beaten track, you wouldn't expect it to be. But if you want to know what everyday golf is like in Scotland, come along to Huntly. You'll easily find a playing partner and learn things about the country that you will never find in any book. Flattish and running alongside the river Deveron (in play on a few holes), this is an excellent course for playing with the family or on holiday, and one where you can card a flattering score without deceiving yourself. But be careful, the trees and often very thick rough can humble anyone who takes this course too lightly. You might not want to travel 500 km just to play a round of golf here, but if you did you would spend a great day, somewhere between Aberdeen and Nairn.

D'accord, ce n'est pas le chef-d'oeuvre du siècle en matière d'architecture de golf, mais on ne saurait en rechercher autant à l'écart des chemins très fréquentés du golf. Cependant, pour celui qui veut connaître le golf des Ecossais au quotidien, Huntly est un des parcours à choisir, où il trouvera facilement des partenaires de jeu, et apprendra à connaître le pays en dehors des livres. Peu accidenté, le long de la rivière Deveron qui joue son rôle sur quelques-uns des trous, c'est un excellent parcours pour jouer en famille et en vacances, où il est possible de faire un score flatteur sans se faire d'illusions sur sa propre valeur. Mais il faut faire attention, les arbres et un rough souvent épais peuvent étrangler celui qui prendrait ce parcours à la légère. Certes, on ne fait pas 500 kilomètres pour venir ici, mais il n'empêche que vous passerez une bonne journée ici, disons entre Aberdeen et Nairn.

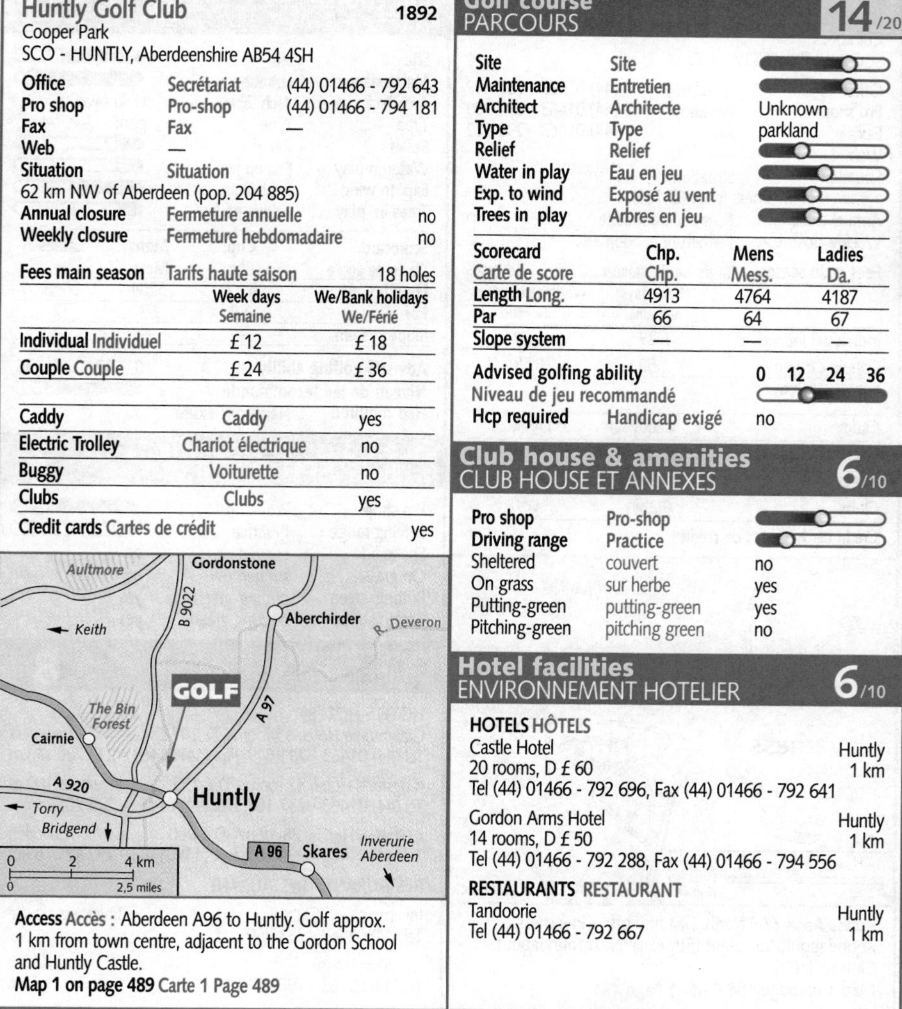

Huntly Golf Club — **1892**
Cooper Park
SCO - HUNTLY, Aberdeenshire AB54 4SH

Office	Secrétariat	(44) 01466 - 792 643
Pro shop	Pro-shop	(44) 01466 - 794 181
Fax	Fax	—
Web	—	
Situation	Situation	

62 km NW of Aberdeen (pop. 204 885)

Annual closure	Fermeture annuelle	no
Weekly closure	Fermeture hebdomadaire	no

Fees main season Tarifs haute saison	18 holes	
	Week days Semaine	**We/Bank holidays** We/Férié
Individual Individuel	£ 12	£ 18
Couple Couple	£ 24	£ 36

Caddy	Caddy	yes
Electric Trolley	Chariot électrique	no
Buggy	Voiturette	no
Clubs	Clubs	yes
Credit cards	Cartes de crédit	yes

Access Accès : Aberdeen A96 to Huntly. Golf approx. 1 km from town centre, adjacent to the Gordon School and Huntly Castle.
Map 1 on page 489 Carte 1 Page 489

Golf course — PARCOURS — 14/20

Site	Site	
Maintenance	Entretien	
Architect	Architecte	Unknown
Type	Type	parkland
Relief	Relief	
Water in play	Eau en jeu	
Exp. to wind	Exposé au vent	
Trees in play	Arbres en jeu	

Scorecard Carte de score	**Chp.** Chp.	**Mens** Mess.	**Ladies** Da.
Length Long.	4913	4764	4187
Par	66	64	67
Slope system	—	—	—

Advised golfing ability Niveau de jeu recommandé — 0 12 24 36
Hcp required Handicap exigé — no

Club house & amenities — CLUB HOUSE ET ANNEXES — 6/10

Pro shop	Pro-shop	
Driving range	Practice	
Sheltered	couvert	no
On grass	sur herbe	yes
Putting-green	putting-green	yes
Pitching-green	pitching green	no

Hotel facilities — ENVIRONNEMENT HOTELIER — 6/10

HOTELS HÔTELS

Castle Hotel — Huntly 1 km
20 rooms, D £ 60
Tel (44) 01466 - 792 696, Fax (44) 01466 - 792 641

Gordon Arms Hotel — Huntly 1 km
14 rooms, D £ 50
Tel (44) 01466 - 792 288, Fax (44) 01466 - 794 556

RESTAURANTS RESTAURANT

Tandoorie — Huntly 1 km
Tel (44) 01466 - 792 667

INVERNESS

16 | 7 | 8

The completion of a new, first-rate club-house has provided an additional argument for this often underrated course in the capital of the Scottish highlands. The site is excellent with views over the hills on either side of Loch Ness, and the occasional glimpse over Moray Firth. The course is lined by any number of trees (not always as tall as you might imagine), the fairways are generously wide and it takes a pretty wild mis-hit to reach the tall rough. On this moderately hilly terrain, there is only one really blind shot, from the 16th tee. Otherwise the layout is very frank and hides nothing. Pleasant to play in normal weather, it can turn nasty under championship conditions, when a tough round can turn distinctly nightmarish on the 14th, one of the toughest par 4s in the north of Scotland. Inverness certainly does not have the layout or setting to claim parity with Nairn or Dornoch, but in its own style it can and does hold its head high.

L'achèvement d'un nouveau Clubhouse de premier ordre a apporté un argument de plus à ce parcours souvent sous-estimé, celui de la capitale des Highlands. Le site est de grande qualité, avec les vues sur les collines de part et d'autre du Loch Ness, et des aperçus sur le Firth de temps à autre. De nombreux arbres longent le parcours, pas toujours immenses d'ailleurs, les fairawys sont de largeur généreuse, et il faut faire des efforts pour s'égarer dans le haut rough. Sur ce terrain modérément accidenté, on ne trouve qu'un seul coup vraiment aveugle, au drive du 16. Sinon, le dessin est d'une grande franchise. Agréable en temps normal, il peut montrer les dents en conditions de championnat, culminant au 14, l'un des par 4 les plus difficiles du nord de l'Ecosse. Certes, Inverness ne prétend ni par son dessin, ni par son cadre à être l'égal de Nairn ou de Dornoch, mais dans son propre style, il peut tenir la tête haute.

Inverness Golf Club — 1908

Culcabock
SCO - INVERNESS IV2 3XQ

Office	Secrétariat	(44) 01463 - 239 882
Pro shop	Pro-shop	(44) 01463 - 231 989
Fax	Fax	(44) 01463 - 239 882
Web	—	
Situation	Situation	

1,5 km S of Inverness (pop. 62 186)

Annual closure	Fermeture annuelle	no
Weekly closure	Fermeture hebdomadaire	no
Fees main season	Tarifs haute saison	18 holes

	Week days Semaine	We/Bank holidays We/Férié
Individual Individuel	£ 29	£ 29
Couple Couple	£ 58	£ 58

Full day: £ 39

Caddy	Caddy	on request
Electric Trolley	Chariot électrique	no
Buggy	Voiturette	yes
Clubs	Clubs	yes
Credit cards	Cartes de crédit	no

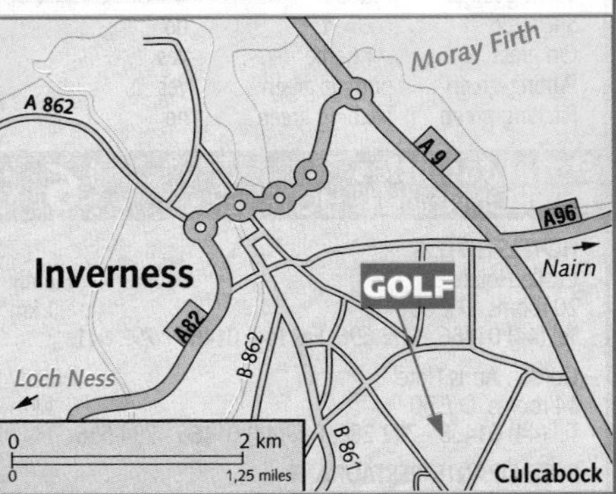

Access Accès : A9 North. First turn off → Inverness. Roundabout, turn right (5th exit). Next roundabout, Club on left.
Map 1 on page 484 Carte 1 Page 484

Golf course PARCOURS — 16/20

Site	Site	
Maintenance	Entretien	
Architect	Architecte	Unknown
Type	Type	park
Relief	Relief	
Water in play	Eau en jeu	
Exp. to wind	Exposé au vent	
Trees in play	Arbres en jeu	

Scorecard Carte de score	Chp. Chp.	Mens Mess.	Ladies Da.
Length Long.	5700	5204	5068
Par	69	67	72
Slope system	—	—	—

Advised golfing ability Niveau de jeu recommandé — 0 12 24 36

Hcp required Handicap exigé — 35

Club house & amenities CLUB HOUSE ET ANNEXES — 7/10

Pro shop	Pro-shop	
Driving range	Practice	
Sheltered	couvert	no
On grass	sur herbe	no
Putting-green	putting-green	yes
Pitching-green	pitching green	yes

Hotel facilities ENVIRONNEMENT HOTELIER — 8/10

HOTELS HÔTELS

Craigmonie Hotel, 35 rooms, D £ 118 — Inverness
Tel (44) 01463 - 231 649, Fax (44) 01463 - 233 720 — 1 km

Kingsmills Hotel, 82 rooms, D £ 155 — Inverness 100 m
Tel (44) 01463 - 237 166, Fax (44) 01463 - 225 208

Culloden House, 28 rooms, D £ 200 — Culloden
Tel (44) 01463 - 790 461, Fax (44) 01463 - 792 181 — 6 km

RESTAURANTS RESTAURANT

Inverness Golf Club — Inverness on site
Tel (44) 01463 - 233 259

Culloden House — Culloden
Tel (44) 01463 - 790 461 — 6 km

KILMARNOCK (BARASSIE) | 17 | 6 | 8

Much closer to the holiday resort of Troon than to Kilmarnock, Barassie is also much more than a friendly leisure course. Although near the sea it often feels like an inland course, but don't let that fool you. This is an impressive challenge even for the best players and each visit is the opportunity to discover new surprises and enjoy it again and again. A few blind shots add a little spice to the fun and the difficulties are evenly spread around the course. You'll need the full range of shots here to see you home, but then again you do on virtually every course of this type. Testimony to the excellence of this layout is the fact that this is one of the courses for the final qualification rounds when the British Open is played at Troon. It has also hosted some of the greatest amateur tournaments. Essential visiting when in this region that is spoilt for great courses.

Bien plus près de la station de vacances de Troon que de Kilmarnock, Barassie est beaucoup plus qu'un aimable parcours de loisirs. Bien qu'il soit proche de la mer, il offre parfois la sensation d'être un vrai parcours "inland," mais il ne faut pas se laisser piéger : il présente un imposant défi, même aux meilleurs, et chaque visite est l'occasion de surprises, et d'un plaisir renouvelé. Quelques coups aveugles ajoutent un peu de piment, les difficultés sont très bien équilibrées, et il faudra toute la panoplie de coups du sac pour en sortir, mais c'est pratiquement le cas sur tous les parcours de ce type. Témoin de sa qualité, c'est l'un des parcours des ultimes qualifications quand le British Open se joue à Royal Troon, il a aussi été le site de grandes compétitions amateur. A ne pas manquer dans cette région richissime en grands golfs.

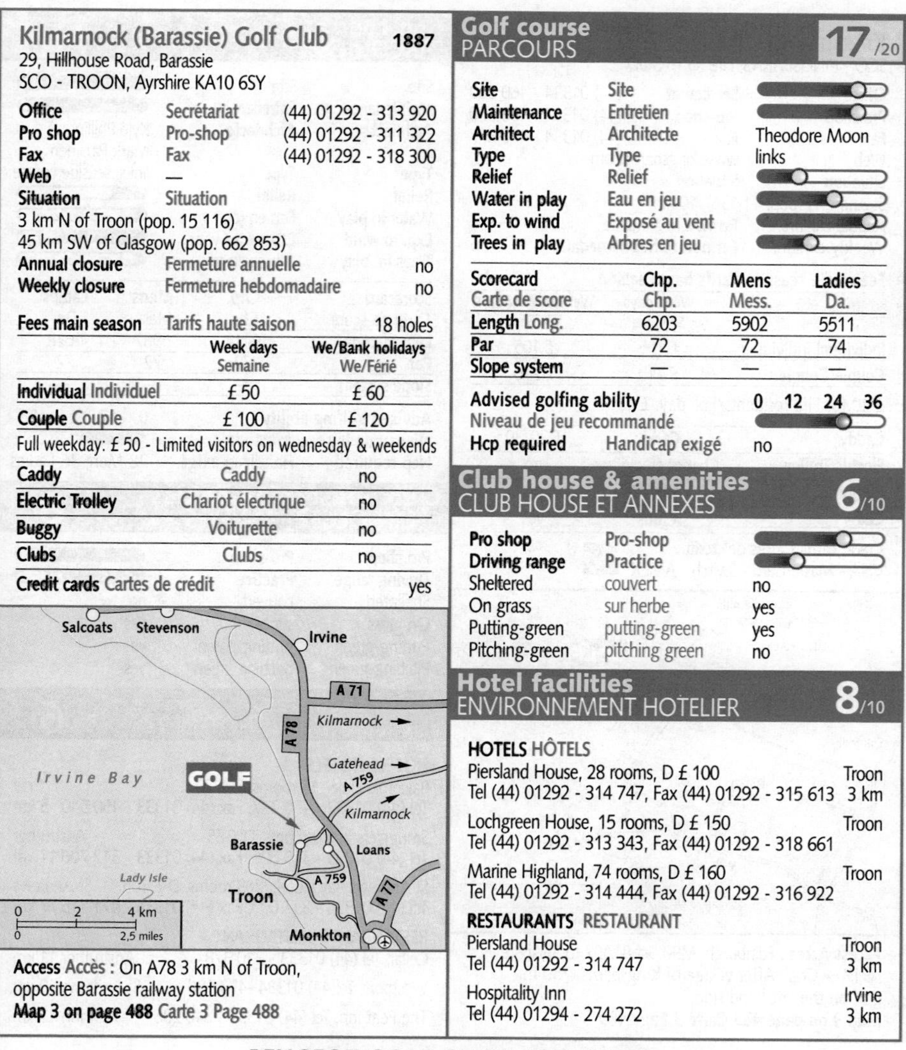

Kilmarnock (Barassie) Golf Club — 1887

29, Hillhouse Road, Barassie
SCO - TROON, Ayrshire KA10 6SY

Office	Secrétariat	(44) 01292 - 313 920
Pro shop	Pro-shop	(44) 01292 - 311 322
Fax	Fax	(44) 01292 - 318 300
Web	—	
Situation	Situation	

3 km N of Troon (pop. 15 116)
45 km SW of Glasgow (pop. 662 853)

Annual closure	Fermeture annuelle	no
Weekly closure	Fermeture hebdomadaire	no

Fees main season Tarifs haute saison	18 holes	
	Week days Semaine	**We/Bank holidays** We/Férié
Individual Individuel	£ 50	£ 60
Couple Couple	£ 100	£ 120

Full weekday: £ 50 - Limited visitors on wednesday & weekends

Caddy	Caddy	no
Electric Trolley	Chariot électrique	no
Buggy	Voiturette	no
Clubs	Clubs	no
Credit cards	Cartes de crédit	yes

Access Accès : On A78 3 km N of Troon, opposite Barassie railway station
Map 3 on page 488 Carte 3 Page 488

Golf course PARCOURS — 17/20

Site	Site	
Maintenance	Entretien	
Architect	Architecte	Theodore Moon
Type	Type	links
Relief	Relief	
Water in play	Eau en jeu	
Exp. to wind	Exposé au vent	
Trees in play	Arbres en jeu	

Scorecard Carte de score	**Chp.** Chp.	**Mens** Mess.	**Ladies** Da.
Length Long.	6203	5902	5511
Par	72	72	74
Slope system	—	—	—

Advised golfing ability Niveau de jeu recommandé — 0 12 24 36
Hcp required Handicap exigé — no

Club house & amenities CLUB HOUSE ET ANNEXES — 6/10

Pro shop	Pro-shop	
Driving range	Practice	
Sheltered	couvert	no
On grass	sur herbe	yes
Putting-green	putting-green	yes
Pitching-green	pitching green	no

Hotel facilities ENVIRONNEMENT HOTELIER — 8/10

HOTELS HÔTELS

Piersland House, 28 rooms, D £ 100 — Troon
Tel (44) 01292 - 314 747, Fax (44) 01292 - 315 613 — 3 km

Lochgreen House, 15 rooms, D £ 150 — Troon
Tel (44) 01292 - 313 343, Fax (44) 01292 - 318 661

Marine Highland, 74 rooms, D £ 160 — Troon
Tel (44) 01292 - 314 444, Fax (44) 01292 - 316 922

RESTAURANTS RESTAURANT

Piersland House — Troon
Tel (44) 01292 - 314 747 — 3 km

Hospitality Inn — Irvine
Tel (44) 01294 - 274 272 — 3 km

KINGSBARNS

19 | 8 | 6

Promoter Mark Parsinen and Art Dunkley called in Kyle Phillips to design this genuine masterpiece. They have proven that it is possible to blend the classic early days of golf course architecture with the technology of modern days. Kingsbarns has everything of a real links course withoutever going over the top: just formidable bunkers, bushes and sometimes fearfulrough, a few ditches running down to the sea and crossing your path, and greenswhich hug the natural terrain. The out and in design is reminiscent of SaintAndrews but with a sense of space found more at courses like Muirfield orCarnoustie, all made better by the fact that almost every hole overlooks thesea. Then there is the sheer variety of holes which blend to form a coherentwhole, the golfing challenge and excellence of realisation (this is pure linksturf). As the site is one of the last capable of hosting a real links course,they could neither damage nor undermine it. Kingsbarns is an authentic "coupde maître" that has already gained an international reputation and a devoted following.

Les promoteurs Mark Parsinen et Art Dunkley ont fait appel à Kyle Phillips pour créer cet authentique chef-d'œuvre. Ils prouvent qu'il était parfaitement possible d'associer la grande tradition classique avec les technologies modernes. On trouve ainsi tous les composants des vrais links, sans pour autant que ce soit un catalogue : bunkers redoutables, buissons et rough très dangereux, quelques fossés qui vont vers la mer et croisent votre route, des greens qui épousent le terrain. La forme en aller-retour est réminiscente de St Andrews, mais avec un sens de l'espace que l'on trouve davantage à Muirfield ou Carnoustie, et accentué par le fait qu'on domine la mer pratiquement sur chaque trou. Ajoutons la diversité des trous, harmonieusement fondus dans un ensemble cohérent, l'exigence du jeu à fournir, la qualité de la réalisation (un vrai gazon de links). Le site étant l'un des derniers à pouvoir accueillir un links, il ne fallait ni l'endommager, ni l'affaiblir. Kingsbarns est un vrai coup de maître qui a déjà ses admirateurs et fanatiques.

Kingsbarns Golf Links — 2001

SCO - KINGSBARNS, Fife KY16 8QD

Office	Secrétariat	(44) 01334 - 460 860
Pro shop	Pro-shop	(44) 01334 - 460 860
Fax	Fax	(44) 01334 - 460 877
Web	www.kingsbarns.com	
Situation	Situation	

St Andrews (pop. 11 136), 10 km

Annual closure	Fermeture annuelle	30/11→1/4
Weekly closure	Fermeture hebdomadaire	no

Fees main season Tarifs haute saison		18 holes
	Week days Semaine	**We/Bank holidays** We/Férié
Individual Individuel	£ 105	£ 105
Couple Couple	£ 210	£ 210

£ 40 for Fife residents/Full day: £ 155

Caddy	Caddy	£ 20/30
Electric Trolley	Chariot électrique	no
Buggy	Voiturette	no
Clubs	Clubs	yes

Credit cards Cartes de crédit
VISA - MasterCard - Switch - AMEX

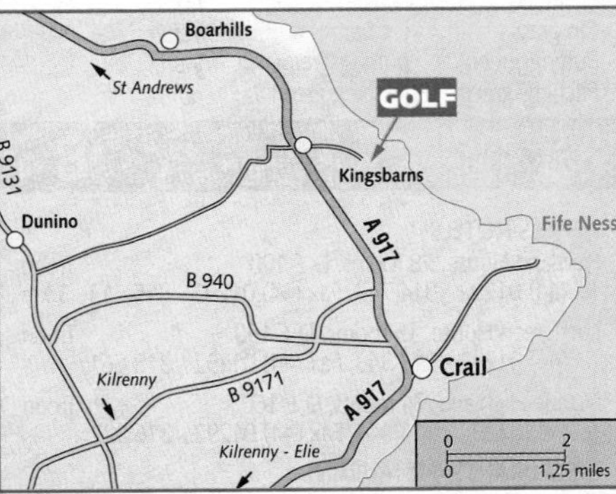

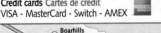

Access Accès : Edinburgh, M90, Jct 8, A92 to St Andrews, A917 → Crail. After village of Kingsbarns, 750 m, golf on the left hand side
Map 3 on page 489 Carte 3 Page 489

Golf course — PARCOURS — 19/20

Site	Site	
Maintenance	Entretien	
Architect	Architecte	Kyle Phillips, Mark Parsinen
Type	Type	links, seaside course
Relief	Relief	
Water in play	Eau en jeu	
Exp. to wind	Exposé au vent	
Trees in play	Arbres en jeu	

Scorecard Carte de score	**Chp.** Chp.	**Mens** Mess.	**Ladies** Da.
Length Long.	6414	5987	4628
Par	72	72	72
Slope system	—	—	—

Advised golfing ability Niveau de jeu recommandé: 0 12 24 36
Hcp required Handicap exigé: 28 Men, 36 Ladies

Club house & amenities — CLUB HOUSE ET ANNEXES — 8/10

Pro shop	Pro-shop	
Driving range	Practice	
Sheltered	couvert	no
On grass	sur herbe	yes
Putting-green	putting-green	yes
Pitching-green	pitching green	yes

Hotel facilities — ENVIRONNEMENT HOTELIER — 6/10

HOTELS HÔTELS

Balcomie Links, 15 rooms, D £ 70 — Crail
Tel (44) 01333 - 450 237, Fax (44) 01333 - 450 540 — 5 km

Smugglers Inn, 9 rooms, D £ 65 — Anstruther
Tel (44) 01333 - 310 506, Fax (44) 01333 - 312 706 — 11 km

St Andrews Bay Hotel, 209 rooms, D £ 105 — St Andrews
Tel (44) 01334 - 837 000, Fax (44) 01334 - 471 115 — 7 km

RESTAURANTS RESTAURANT

Cellar, Tel (44) 01333 - 310 378 — Anstruther 11 km
Westport, Tel(44) 01334 -473 186 — St Andrews 10 km
The Peat Inn, Tel (44) 01334 - 840 206 — Peat Inn 12 km

KINGUSSIE

15 | 4 | 5

This Highlands course, located at 1,000 ft. above sea level, provides some breath-taking views over Speyside and the Cairngorms. The river Gynack crosses the course and comes into play on several occasions. Kingussie was originally designed on farmland, and Harry Vardon has made so much out of it that you'd willingly believe he had shifted tons of earth. He was unable to avoid a few blind shots over rather hilly terrain, but they are few and far between. The course is not really too tiring, either; the designer was a great champion and knew what can be asked of an amateur golfer. On this terrain of peat and moor-land, the ball never rolls much so the course plays every yard of its length. With a charming setting and warm welcome, Kingussie is a good holiday course.

Situé à environ 300 mètres d'altitude, ce parcours des Highlands offre de vastes panoramas sur le Speyside et les montagnes des Cairngorns. La rivière Gynack parcourt le site, venant en jeu sur quelques trous. A l'origine, ce parcours a été dessiné sur un terrain réservé à l'élevage, et Harry Vardon en a tiré un tel parti que l'on pourrait croire qu'il a déplacé des tonnes de terre. Dans un espace assez accidenté, il n'a pu éviter quelques coups aveugles, mais ils sont bien rares. De plus, on ne peut pas dire que ce parcours soit épuisant : l'architecte était un grand champion, il savait ce qu'on peut demander à un amateur. Sur ce terrain de tourbe et de lande, la balle ne roule jamais beaucoup, ce qui rend à peine plus long ce parcours. Le charme de l'environnement, comme l'accueil font de Kingussie un bon golf de vacances.

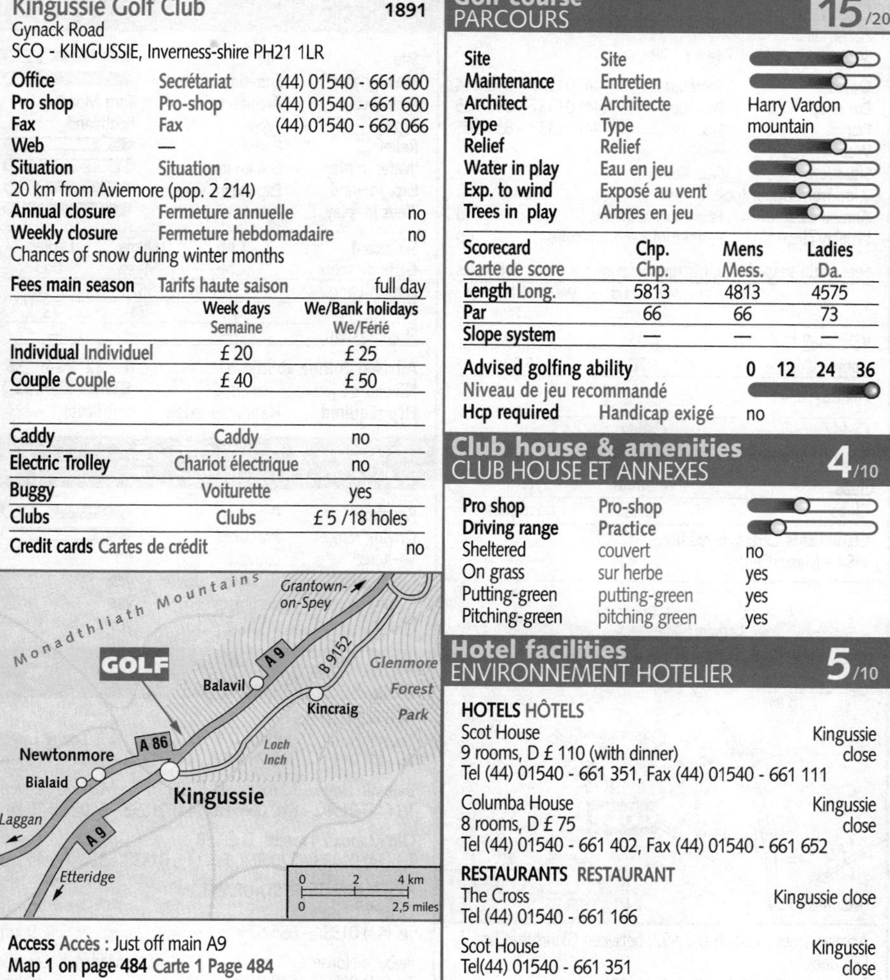

Kingussie Golf Club — 1891

Gynack Road
SCO - KINGUSSIE, Inverness-shire PH21 1LR

Office	Secrétariat	(44) 01540 - 661 600
Pro shop	Pro-shop	(44) 01540 - 661 600
Fax	Fax	(44) 01540 - 662 066
Web	—	
Situation	Situation	

20 km from Aviemore (pop. 2 214)

Annual closure	Fermeture annuelle	no
Weekly closure	Fermeture hebdomadaire	no

Chances of snow during winter months

Fees main season Tarifs haute saison — full day

	Week days Semaine	We/Bank holidays We/Férié
Individual Individuel	£ 20	£ 25
Couple Couple	£ 40	£ 50

Caddy	Caddy	no
Electric Trolley	Chariot électrique	no
Buggy	Voiturette	yes
Clubs	Clubs	£ 5 /18 holes
Credit cards	Cartes de crédit	no

Access Accès : Just off main A9
Map 1 on page 484 Carte 1 Page 484

Golf course PARCOURS — 15/20

Site	Site	
Maintenance	Entretien	
Architect	Architecte	Harry Vardon
Type	Type	mountain
Relief	Relief	
Water in play	Eau en jeu	
Exp. to wind	Exposé au vent	
Trees in play	Arbres en jeu	

Scorecard Carte de score	**Chp.** Chp.	**Mens** Mess.	**Ladies** Da.
Length Long.	5813	4813	4575
Par	66	66	73
Slope system	—	—	—

Advised golfing ability Niveau de jeu recommandé — 0 12 24 36
Hcp required Handicap exigé — no

Club house & amenities CLUB HOUSE ET ANNEXES — 4/10

Pro shop	Pro-shop	
Driving range	Practice	
Sheltered	couvert	no
On grass	sur herbe	yes
Putting-green	putting-green	yes
Pitching-green	pitching green	yes

Hotel facilities ENVIRONNEMENT HOTELIER — 5/10

HOTELS HÔTELS

Scot House — Kingussie close
9 rooms, D £ 110 (with dinner)
Tel (44) 01540 - 661 351, Fax (44) 01540 - 661 111

Columba House — Kingussie close
8 rooms, D £ 75
Tel (44) 01540 - 661 402, Fax (44) 01540 - 661 652

RESTAURANTS RESTAURANT

The Cross — Kingussie close
Tel (44) 01540 - 661 166

Scot House — Kingussie close
Tel(44) 01540 - 661 351

739

LADYBANK

17	7	5

Although not a links, Ladybank is used as a qualifying course for the British Open when held at St Andrews. In other words it is held in high esteem by the game's governing bodies, and deserves to be. Amidst pine-trees, heather and gorse, this is a technical challenge of the highest order where accuracy is at a premium. You are best advised to keep well away from the formidable rough here where you can lose balls, clubs and perhaps even players too! But while good players may suffer, the humbler hacker can get by with a minimum of careful thought. With superb use of the land, pleasantly contoured fairways and well-defended greens where there is always one safe way in, Ladybank really is worth the trip.

Bien qu'il ne s'agisse pas d'un links, Ladybank est utilisé comme parcours de qualification pour le British Open quand il a lieu à St Andrews. C'est dire qu'il est tenu en haute estime par les pouvoirs sportifs. Il le mérite amplement. Au milieu des pins, de la bruyère et des ajoncs, c'est un défi technique de première grandeur, où la précision est d'abord essentielle, car il vaut mieux ne pas s'égarer dans les roughs redoutables où l'on perd les balles, les clubs et sans doute aussi les joueurs ! Mais si les bons joueurs peuvent souffrir, les joueurs plus humbles et modestes tireront leur épingle du jeu avec un minimum de réflexion. Par sa superbe utilisation du terrain, son relief agréable, ses greens bien défendus mais qui laissent toujours une porte ouverte, Ladybank mérite vraiment le détour.

Ladybank Golf Club — 1879

Annsmuir
SCO - LADYBANK, Fife KY7 7RA

Office	Secrétariat	(44) 01337 - 830 814
Pro shop	Pro-shop	(44) 01337 - 830 725
Fax	Fax	(44) 01337 - 831 505
Web	—	
Situation	Situation	

9 km from Cupar (pop. 8 174)

Annual closure	Fermeture annuelle	no
Weekly closure	Fermeture hebdomadaire	no

Fees main season Tarifs haute saison	**Week days** Semaine	**We/Bank holidays** We/Férié
18 holes		
Individual Individuel	£ 35	£ 40
Couple Couple	£ 70	£ 80

Full day: £ 45

Caddy	Caddy	no
Electric Trolley	Chariot électrique	no
Buggy	Voiturette	yes (2)
Clubs	Clubs	on request

Credit cards Cartes de crédit
VISA - MasterCard

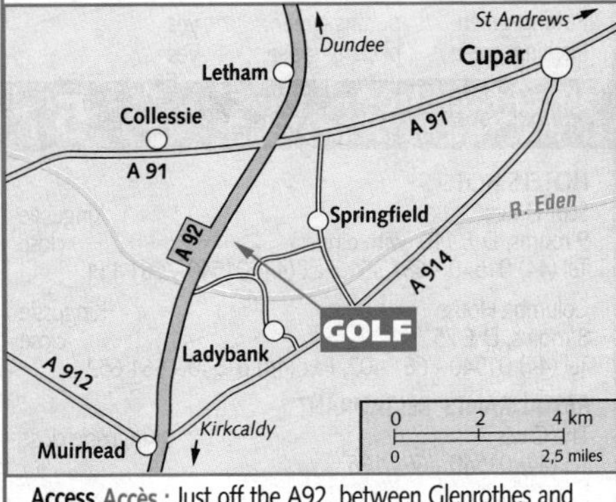

Access Accès : Just off the A92, between Glenrothes and Dundee
Map 3 on page 489 Carte 3 Page 489

Golf course PARCOURS — 17/20

Site	Site	
Maintenance	Entretien	
Architect	Architecte	Tom Morris
Type	Type	heathland
Relief	Relief	
Water in play	Eau en jeu	
Exp. to wind	Exposé au vent	
Trees in play	Arbres en jeu	

Scorecard Carte de score	**Chp.** Chp.	**Mens** Mess.	**Ladies** Da.
Length Long.	6079	5670	5330
Par	71	71	73
Slope system	—	—	—

Advised golfing ability Niveau de jeu recommandé: 0 12 24 36
Hcp required Handicap exigé: certificate

Club house & amenities CLUB HOUSE ET ANNEXES — 7/10

Pro shop	Pro-shop	
Driving range	Practice	
Sheltered	couvert	no
On grass	sur herbe	yes
Putting-green	putting-green	yes
Pitching-green	pitching green	yes

Hotel facilities ENVIRONNEMENT HOTELIER — 5/10

HOTELS HÔTELS

Crusoe Hotel, 16 rooms, D £ 90 — Lower Largo
Tel (44) 01333 - 320 759, Fax (44) 01333 - 320 865 15 km

Balbinie House, 30 rooms, D £ 200 — Markinch, Leven
Tel (44) 01592 - 610 066, Fax (44) 01592 - 610 529 10 km

Old Manor, 24 rooms, D £ 188 — Leven
Tel (44) 01333 - 320 368, Fax (44) 01333 - 320 911 15 km

RESTAURANTS RESTAURANT

Ostler's Close — Cupar
Tel (44) 01334 - 655 574 — 9 km

Balbinie House — Markinch, Levenx
Tel (44) 01592 - 610 066 — 10 km

LANARK 16 6 5

They say that the total length of courses designed by James Braid exceeds the combined length and width of Great Britain. That's probably true inasmuch as he basically retouched a lot of existing courses. This layout was designed by Old Tom Morris, another prolific designer, but at the time "designing" was primarily a question of laying out the route of the course and the position of bunkers and greens. The course was then completed by the work of nature. Lanark is one of those courses where golf seems always to have been a part of the scene on land of heather and moorland which make such excellent playing surfaces. Not overly long, moderately hilly and with only one or two blind shots, this is a no-nonsense course and a serious test for all levels. A genuinely hidden treasure of Scottish golf.

On dit que la longueur totale des parcours dessinés par James Braid totalise plus de la longueur et de la largeur de la Grande-Bretagne. C'est probablement vrai, dans la mesure où il en a dessiné beaucoup, mais il a essentiellement retouché beaucoup de parcours existants. Celui-ci avait été tracé par Old Tom Morris, lui aussi architecte très prolifique : mais, à son époque, l'architecture de golf consistait avant tout à définir l'itinéraire du parcours, l'emplacement des greens et bunkers. Un parcours devait s'arranger avec la nature. Lanark est l'un de ces sites où le golf paraît avoir toujours été présent, en terre de bruyère et de lande qui fait de bons tapis de jeu. Pas trop long, avec un relief modéré, et seulement un ou deux coups aveugles, c'est un parcours sans autres histoires que celles que l'on y fait, un test sérieux pour tous niveaux. Un petit bijou bien caché du golf écossais.

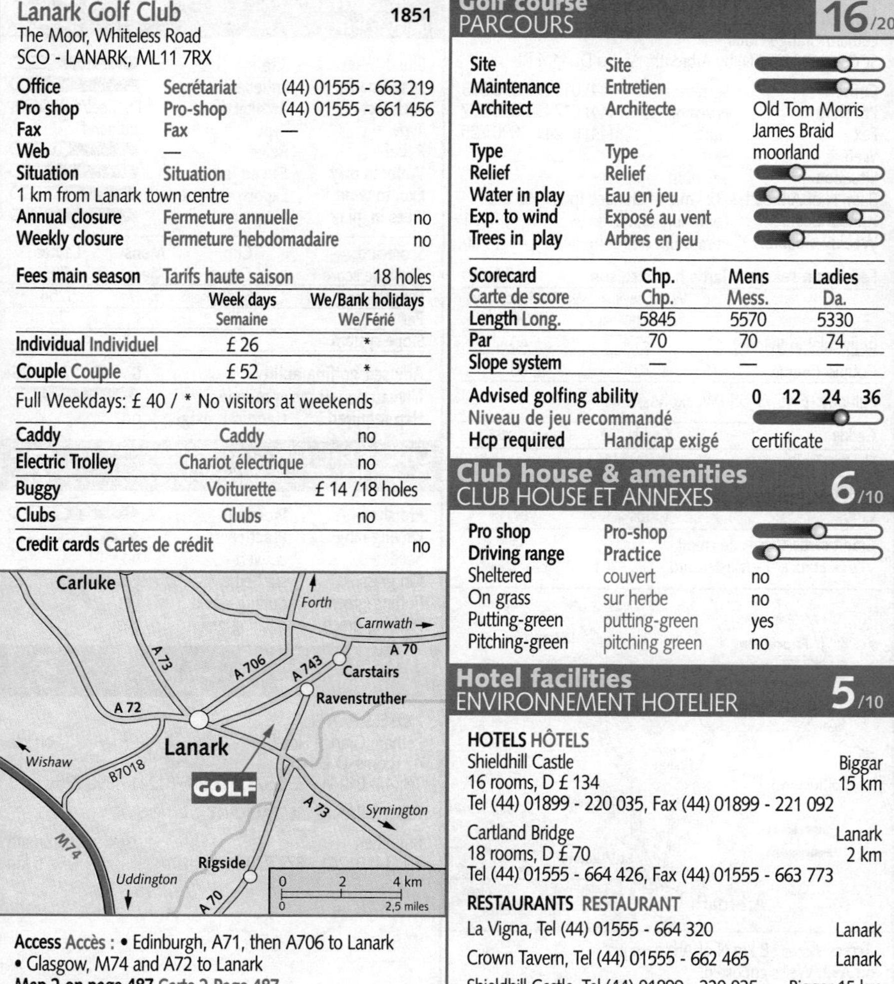

Lanark Golf Club — 1851

The Moor, Whiteless Road
SCO - LANARK, ML11 7RX

Office	Secrétariat	(44) 01555 - 663 219
Pro shop	Pro-shop	(44) 01555 - 661 456
Fax	Fax	—
Web	—	
Situation	Situation	

1 km from Lanark town centre

Annual closure	Fermeture annuelle	no
Weekly closure	Fermeture hebdomadaire	no

Fees main season Tarifs haute saison	18 holes	
	Week days Semaine	**We/Bank holidays** We/Férié
Individual Individuel	£ 26	*
Couple Couple	£ 52	*

Full Weekdays: £ 40 / * No visitors at weekends

Caddy	Caddy	no
Electric Trolley	Chariot électrique	no
Buggy	Voiturette	£ 14 /18 holes
Clubs	Clubs	no
Credit cards	Cartes de crédit	no

Access Accès : • Edinburgh, A71, then A706 to Lanark • Glasgow, M74 and A72 to Lanark
Map 2 on page 487 Carte 2 Page 487

Golf course — PARCOURS 16/20

Site	Site	
Maintenance	Entretien	
Architect	Architecte	Old Tom Morris James Braid
Type	Type	moorland
Relief	Relief	
Water in play	Eau en jeu	
Exp. to wind	Exposé au vent	
Trees in play	Arbres en jeu	

Scorecard Carte de score	**Chp.** Chp.	**Mens** Mess.	**Ladies** Da.
Length Long.	5845	5570	5330
Par	70	70	74
Slope system	—	—	—

Advised golfing ability Niveau de jeu recommandé — 0 12 24 36
Hcp required Handicap exigé — certificate

Club house & amenities — CLUB HOUSE ET ANNEXES 6/10

Pro shop	Pro-shop	
Driving range	Practice	
Sheltered	couvert	no
On grass	sur herbe	no
Putting-green	putting-green	yes
Pitching-green	pitching green	no

Hotel facilities — ENVIRONNEMENT HOTELIER 5/10

HOTELS HÔTELS

Shieldhill Castle — Biggar 15 km
16 rooms, D £ 134
Tel (44) 01899 - 220 035, Fax (44) 01899 - 221 092

Cartland Bridge — Lanark 2 km
18 rooms, D £ 70
Tel (44) 01555 - 664 426, Fax (44) 01555 - 663 773

RESTAURANTS RESTAURANT

La Vigna, Tel (44) 01555 - 664 320 — Lanark
Crown Tavern, Tel (44) 01555 - 662 465 — Lanark
Shieldhill Castle, Tel (44) 01899 - 220 035 — Biggar 15 km

LETHAM GRANGE Old Course

15 | 7 | 5

This course was opened in 1987 at the foot of the splendid Letham Grange Hotel and was designed by gentleman farmer Ken Smith who drew his inspiration from the Augusta National course, hoping that one day this might become known as the Scottish Augusta. In actual fact there are very few similarities but this is nonetheless a pretty and rather challenging layout with tree-lined fairways and a few rather dangerous water hazards. The course is rather hilly in places, which means a few blind shots. Target golf is virtually an obligation here, and this is why you don't always get the impression of playing in Scotland. But despite everything, it is fun playing here with friends of all levels, of whom the least experienced will probably enjoy more the second, shorter course.

Ce parcours a été créé en 1987 au pied du splendide Letham Grange Hotel, et dessiné par Ken Smith, un gentleman farmer qui s'inspira d'Augusta National en espérant que ce parcours pourrait un jour être appelé le "Augusta d'Ecosse". sans vouloir le chagriner, on trouve peu de ressemblances avec le parcours du Masters, mais c'est malgré tout un joli tracé, assez exigeant, aux fairways bordés d'arbres, avec quelques obstacles d'eau assez dangereux. Le relief est parfois assez prononcé, ce qui implique quelques coups aveugles. Ici, le target golf est quasiment une obligation, c'est pourquoi on n'a pas forcément l'impression de se trouver en Ecosse. Malgré tout, on aura plaisir à évoluer ici avec des amis de tous niveaux, dont les moins expérimentés aimeront jouer le second parcours, plus court.

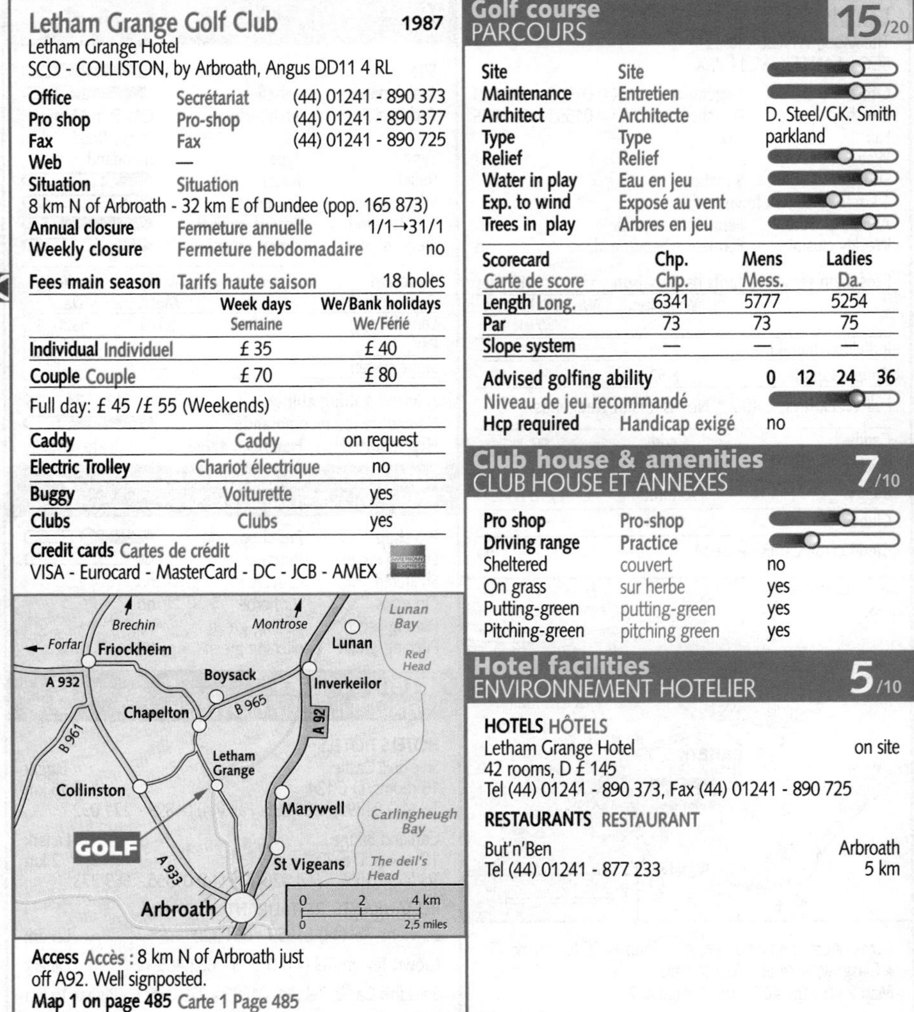

Letham Grange Golf Club — 1987

Letham Grange Hotel
SCO - COLLISTON, by Arbroath, Angus DD11 4 RL

Office	Secrétariat	(44) 01241 - 890 373
Pro shop	Pro-shop	(44) 01241 - 890 377
Fax	Fax	(44) 01241 - 890 725
Web	—	
Situation	Situation	

8 km N of Arbroath - 32 km E of Dundee (pop. 165 873)

Annual closure	Fermeture annuelle	1/1→31/1
Weekly closure	Fermeture hebdomadaire	no

Fees main season Tarifs haute saison	18 holes	
	Week days Semaine	**We/Bank holidays** We/Férié
Individual Individuel	£ 35	£ 40
Couple Couple	£ 70	£ 80

Full day: £ 45 /£ 55 (Weekends)

Caddy	Caddy	on request
Electric Trolley	Chariot électrique	no
Buggy	Voiturette	yes
Clubs	Clubs	yes

Credit cards Cartes de crédit
VISA - Eurocard - MasterCard - DC - JCB - AMEX

Access Accès : 8 km N of Arbroath just off A92. Well signposted.
Map 1 on page 485 Carte 1 Page 485

Golf course — PARCOURS — 15/20

Site	Site	
Maintenance	Entretien	
Architect	Architecte	D. Steel/GK. Smith
Type	Type	parkland
Relief	Relief	
Water in play	Eau en jeu	
Exp. to wind	Exposé au vent	
Trees in play	Arbres en jeu	

Scorecard Carte de score	**Chp.** Chp.	**Mens** Mess.	**Ladies** Da.
Length Long.	6341	5777	5254
Par	73	73	75
Slope system	—	—	—

Advised golfing ability Niveau de jeu recommandé — 0 12 24 36
Hcp required Handicap exigé — no

Club house & amenities — CLUB HOUSE ET ANNEXES — 7/10

Pro shop	Pro-shop	
Driving range	Practice	
Sheltered	couvert	no
On grass	sur herbe	yes
Putting-green	putting-green	yes
Pitching-green	pitching green	yes

Hotel facilities — ENVIRONNEMENT HOTELIER — 5/10

HOTELS HÔTELS
Letham Grange Hotel — on site
42 rooms, D £ 145
Tel (44) 01241 - 890 373, Fax (44) 01241 - 890 725

RESTAURANTS RESTAURANT
But'n'Ben — Arbroath 5 km
Tel (44) 01241 - 877 233

LEVEN

16 | 6 | 6

The original course was shared with the Lundin Golf Club. But when the railways arrived in the region, the course was split nine holes on one side and nine on the other, with each club creating an extra nine holes. So instead of one good course, here we have two, as adjacent now as they were in the past. Most of the holes at Leven are pure links style, but two or three are close to the heather-bound inland courses that are so common in both Scotland and England. Here again the wind has a say in things, because Leven is distinctly vulnerable when played by long-hitters and skilled technicians in fine weather. In this case even the least experienced players will have fun, although the last few holes can easily upset their card. The least they should do is avoid the deep fairway bunkers and the traps around the green.

Le parcours original a été partagé avec le Lundin Golf Club, à l'arrivée du chemin de fer dans la région. Chacun étant reparti de son côté avec neuf trous a créé neuf autres trous. Au lieu d'un seul bon parcours, en voilà deux, toujours mitoyens. La plupart de trous de Leven ont un caractère de pur links, mais deux ou trois sont assez proches des parcours inland de bruyère, que l'on trouve souvent en Ecosse comme en Angleterre. Là encore, le vent fait la différence, car Leven s'avère assez fragile face aux solides frappeurs et aux bons techniciens quand le temps est beau. Alors, même les moins expérimentés y trouveront leur plaisir, mais les derniers trous peuvent leur créer des problèmes. Qu'ils évitent en tous cas les profonds bunkers de fairway comme ceux qui défendent les greens.

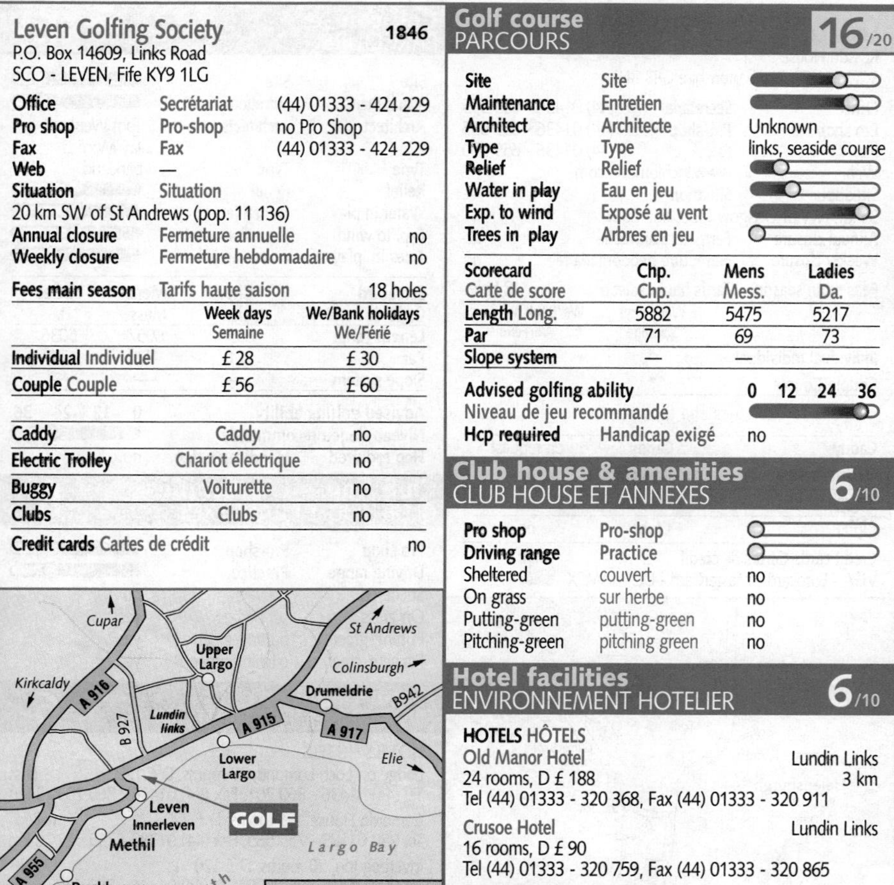

Leven Golfing Society — 1846

P.O. Box 14609, Links Road
SCO - LEVEN, Fife KY9 1LG

Office	Secrétariat	(44) 01333 - 424 229
Pro shop	Pro-shop	no Pro Shop
Fax	Fax	(44) 01333 - 424 229
Web	—	
Situation	Situation	

20 km SW of St Andrews (pop. 11 136)

Annual closure	Fermeture annuelle	no
Weekly closure	Fermeture hebdomadaire	no

Fees main season Tarifs haute saison		18 holes
	Week days Semaine	**We/Bank holidays** We/Férié
Individual Individuel	£ 28	£ 30
Couple Couple	£ 56	£ 60

Caddy	Caddy	no
Electric Trolley	Chariot électrique	no
Buggy	Voiturette	no
Clubs	Clubs	no
Credit cards	Cartes de crédit	no

Access Accès : Edinburgh, M90 then A92 (Jct3), A955. Golf East of Leven, on Promenade.
Map 3 on page 489 Carte 3 Page 489

Golf course PARCOURS — 16/20

Site	Site	
Maintenance	Entretien	
Architect	Architecte	Unknown
Type	Type	links, seaside course
Relief	Relief	
Water in play	Eau en jeu	
Exp. to wind	Exposé au vent	
Trees in play	Arbres en jeu	

Scorecard Carte de score	**Chp.** Chp.	**Mens** Mess.	**Ladies** Da.
Length Long.	5882	5475	5217
Par	71	69	73
Slope system	—	—	—

Advised golfing ability Niveau de jeu recommandé — 0 12 24 36

Hcp required Handicap exigé — no

Club house & amenities CLUB HOUSE ET ANNEXES — 6/10

Pro shop	Pro-shop	
Driving range	Practice	
Sheltered	couvert	no
On grass	sur herbe	no
Putting-green	putting-green	no
Pitching-green	pitching green	no

Hotel facilities ENVIRONNEMENT HOTELIER — 6/10

HOTELS HÔTELS

Old Manor Hotel — Lundin Links, 3 km
24 rooms, D £ 188
Tel (44) 01333 - 320 368, Fax (44) 01333 - 320 911

Crusoe Hotel — Lundin Links
16 rooms, D £ 90
Tel (44) 01333 - 320 759, Fax (44) 01333 - 320 865

RESTAURANTS RESTAURANT

Old Manor Hotel — Lundin Links
Tel (44) 01333 - 320 368

Scotland's Larder — Lower Largo, 5 km
Tel (44) 01333 - 360 414

LOCH LOMOND

18 | 8 | 6

Loch Lomond is the preserve of a mainly international membership who play there only occasionally. Alone or with their guests, they enjoy the privilege of strolling down the quiet fairways of one of the world's most beautiful courses. This has definitely raised a few eyebrows in Scotland, a country where golf has always been considered the right of all and not the (happy) few. In between time, the Solheim Cup 2000 and the Scottish Open have made the course more familiar to TV viewers. This is a course of the highest standard, at once open and challenging, spectacular and blending beautifully into the landscape, long and technically hard work in a setting that has successfully preserved the site's natural flora and fauna. There are though one or two minor flaws, like the way the course suffers in rainy weather and a style that is a little too American for this part of the world. We have respect enough for the course architects, but have they shown enough respect for the bonnie heart of Scotland ? Tom Weiskopf believes that this course is his lasting memorial to golf. No-one could argue with him...

Loch Lomond est la chasse gardée de membres venat du monde entier, qui ne jouent ici que de temps à autre. Seuls, avec leurs invités, ils ont le droit de fouler les fairways tranquilles de l'un des plus beaux parcours du monde. Ainsi, le club a encouru quelques critiques en Ecosse, pays où le droit de jouer au golf est considéré comme le droit de tous, et non de "happy few", mais la Solheim Cup 2000 et le Scottish Open l'on fait largement connaître aux téléspectateurs. A la fois franc et exigeant, spectaculaire et bien insinué dans le paysage, long et technique, c'est un parcours du plus haut niveau, qui a su aussi préserver la faune et la flore du lieu. On y trouvera quelques bémols, une certaine fragilité par temps de pluie, et un style peut-être un peu trop américain pour le lieu. Nous respectons les architectes, ont-t-il assez respecté l'âme du pays ? De son côté, Tom Weiskopf estime que c'est sa meilleure contribution au golf. Pourquoi en discuter ?

Loch Lomond Golf Club — 1993

Rossdu House
SCO - LUSS, Dunbartonshire G83 8NT

Office	Secrétariat	(44) 01436 - 655 555
Pro shop	Pro-shop	(44) 01436 - 655 555
Fax	Fax	(44) 01436 - 655 500
Web	www.lochlomond.com	
Situation	Situation	

35 km NW of Glasgow (pop. 662 853)

Annual closure	Fermeture annuelle	no
Weekly closure	Fermeture hebdomadaire	no

Fees main season Tarifs haute saison — 18 holes

	Week days / Semaine	We/Bank holidays / We/Férié
Individual Individuel	*	*
Couple Couple	*	*

* Strictly for members and their guests

Caddy	Caddy	on request
Electric Trolley	Chariot électrique	no
Buggy	Voiturette	no
Clubs	Clubs	no

Credit cards Cartes de crédit
VISA - Eurocard - MasterCard - DC - AMEX

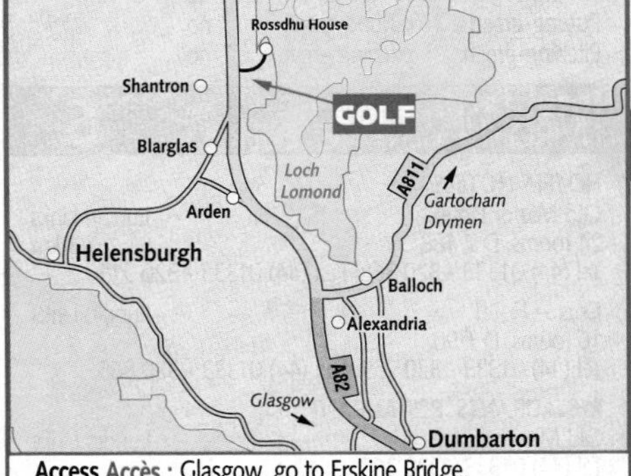

Rossdhu House
Shantron
GOLF
Blarglas
Loch Lomond
A811
Gartocharn
Drymen
Arden
Helensburgh
Balloch
Alexandria
A82
Glasgow
Dumbarton

Access Accès : Glasgow, go to Erskine Bridge, A82 → Alexandria, Luss. After Alexandria, golf on right hand side.

Map 2 on page 486 Carte 2 Page 486

Golf course PARCOURS — 18/20

Site	Site	
Maintenance	Entretien	
Architect	Architecte	Tom Weiskopf Jay Morrish
Type	Type	parkland
Relief	Relief	
Water in play	Eau en jeu	
Exp. to wind	Exposé au vent	
Trees in play	Arbres en jeu	

Scorecard Carte de score	Chp. Chp.	Mens Mess.	Ladies Da.
Length Long.	6354	6057	5036
Par	71	72	74
Slope system	—	—	—

Advised golfing ability Niveau de jeu recommandé — 0 12 24 36
Hcp required Handicap exigé — no

Club house & amenities CLUB HOUSE ET ANNEXES — 8/10

Pro shop	Pro-shop	
Driving range	Practice	
Sheltered	couvert	no
On grass	sur herbe	yes
Putting-green	putting-green	yes
Pitching-green	pitching green	yes

Hotel facilities ENVIRONNEMENT HOTELIER — 6/10

HOTELS HÔTELS

Lodge on Loch Lomond, 29 rooms, D £ 129 — Luss
Tel (44) 01436 - 860 201, Fax (44) 01436 - 860 203 — 3 km

Cameron House, 96 rooms, D £ 220 — Balloch
Tel (44) 01389 - 755 565, Fax (44) 01389 - 759 522 — 6 km

Inverbeg Inn, 20 rooms, D £ 120 — Luss
Tel (44) 01436 - 860 678, Fax (44) 01436 - 860 686

RESTAURANTS RESTAURANT

Georgian Room (Cameron House) — Balloch
Tel (44) 01389 - 755 565 — 6 km

Lodge on Loch Lomond, Tel (44) 01436 - 860 201 — Luss

Inverbegg Inn, Tel (44) 01436 - 860 678 — Luss

LONGNIDDRY

14 | 7 | 6

According to legend, Mary Queen of Scots played golf "over the fields of Seton" in 1567 in the vicinity of the present Longniddry course, shortly after the dead of her husband Lord Darnley, incurring the wrath of the Church as a result. The original course here was designed by Harry S. Colt some 350 years later, and formally opened for play in 1922. James Braid and MacKenzie Ross made alterations to the course which in more recent times has undergone another makeover, this time at the hands of architect Donald Steel. Many of the cross-bunkers from the original design have now been relocated further from the teeing areas to take account of advances in technology. The course is now less penal for the bogey golfer and more challenging for the scratch golfer. It give always an impression of tranquillity, beauty and elegance, and a breath-taking view over the Firth of Forth. Longniddry is as much parkland as links, and is unusual in not having any par 5 holes, even if some of the long par 4s could be considered as such. The greens are good and receptive to well-hit approach shots, whether pitched or rolled.

La légende veut que Mary Reine d'Ecosse ait joué au golf dans les environs en 1567, au lendemain de la mort de son mari Lord Darnley. 350 ans plus tard, Harry Colt dessina le parcours original, ouvert en 1922 et retouché ensuite par James Braid et Mackenzie Ross. Récemment, l'architecte Donald Steel a été chargé de réviser le tracé, notamment en reportant un certain nombre de "cross-bunkers" plus loin des départs, pour mieux répondre aux défis des progrès du matériel de golf. Le parcours pénalise maintenant moins les joueurs moyens, et davantage les meilleurs. Il n'a rien perdu de son atmosphère de calme, de beauté et d'élégance. Avec sa vue imprenable sur le Firth of Forth, Longniddry est aussi bien un parc qu'un links, il a aussi la particularité de ne pas avoir de par 5 à proprement parler, même si certains longs par 4 pourraient prétendre à ce titre. Les greens, de bonne qualité, sont réceptifs à des approches bien jouées, éventuellement roulées, on peut seulement regretter que certains greens à double plateau aient disparu.

Longniddry Golf Club — 1922

SCO - LONGNIDDRY, East Lothian EH32 0NL

Office	Secrétariat	(44) 01875 - 852 241
Pro shop	Pro-shop	(44) 01875 - 852 228
Fax	Fax	(44) 01875 - 853 371
Web	www.longniddrygolfclub.co.uk	
Situation	Situation	

19 km E of Edinburgh (pop. 418 914)

Annual closure	Fermeture annuelle	no
Weekly closure	Fermeture hebdomadaire	no

Fees main season / Tarifs haute saison	18 holes	
	Week days / Semaine	We/Bank holidays / We/Férié
Individual Individuel	£ 35	£ 45
Couple Couple	£ 70	£ 90

Full weekdays: £ 48

Caddy	Caddy	£ 15 /on request
Electric Trolley	Chariot électrique	no
Buggy	Voiturette	yes
Clubs	Clubs	on request

Credit cards Cartes de crédit
VISA - MasterCard - AMEX

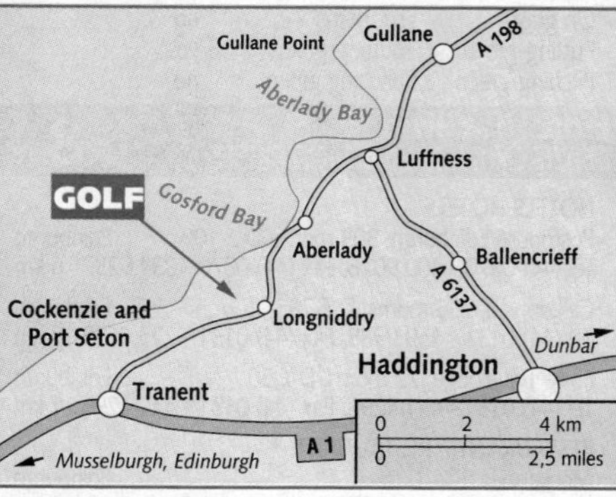

Access Accès : Edinburgh, A1, A198.
Course reached via Links Road at North of the village.
Map 3 on page 489 Carte 3 Page 489

Golf course — PARCOURS — 14/20

Site	Site	
Maintenance	Entretien	
Architect	Architecte	Harry S. Colt, Ross / Braid
Type	Type	parkland
Relief	Relief	
Water in play	Eau en jeu	
Exp. to wind	Exposé au vent	
Trees in play	Arbres en jeu	

Scorecard / Carte de score	Chp. / Chp.	Mens / Mess.	Ladies / Da.
Length Long.	5634	5425	5207
Par	68	68	73
Slope system	—	—	—

Advised golfing ability / Niveau de jeu recommandé: 0 12 24 36

Hcp required — Handicap exigé: 28 Men, 36 Ladies

Club house & amenities — CLUB HOUSE ET ANNEXES — 7/10

Pro shop	Pro-shop	
Driving range	Practice	
Sheltered	couvert	no
On grass	sur herbe	yes
Putting-green	putting-green	yes
Pitching-green	pitching green	yes

Hotel facilities — ENVIRONNEMENT HOTELIER — 6/10

HOTELS HÔTELS

Mallard Hotel, 18 rooms, D £ 76 — Gullane
Tel (44) 01620 - 843 288, Fax (44) 01620 - 843 200 10 km

Brown's Hotel, 5 rooms, D £ 120 — Haddington
Tel (44) 01620 - 822 254, Fax (44) 01620 - 822 254 12 km

Maitlandfield House, 22 rooms, D £ 150 — Haddington
Tel (44) 01620 - 826 513, Fax (44) 01620 - 826 713

RESTAURANTS RESTAURANT

Greywalls Hotel — Gullane
Tel (44) 01620 - 842 144 — 10 km

LOTHIANBURN

14 | 6 | 8

Lying to the south of Edinburgh at the boundary with the Pentland Hills, this course has undergone many a change since its inception in 1893. Four such major alterations were made by James Braid and the last change in 1993 seems to have given the course its final complexion (but who knows?). The terrain is full of slopes, some of which are really steep (especially out in the middle section), so we would recommend this to fit players only. The reward is the beauty of vistas over the Firth of Forth from atop the hill. The course has a number of excellent holes, whose contours seem to follow those of the natural terrain. The downside is that you need to play here several times to establish any sort of game strategy. As on any unknown course, give matchplay a shot first time around.

Au sud d'Edinburgh et à la limite des Pentland Hills, ce parcours créé en 1893 a connu bien des modifications, dont au moins quatre majeures sous la direction de James Braid, et une dernière en 1993 qui semble lui avoir donné son caractère définitif (mais sait-on jamais ?). Le terrain est très vallonné, parfois de façon assez brutale (surtout dans la partie centrale) et l'on ne conseillera qu'aux joueurs en forme de s'y mesurer. La récompense, c'est la beauté des points de vue sur le Firth of Forth, au sommet de la colline. On trouve ici bon nombre d'excellents trous de golf, dont le tracé a suivi les contours des reliefs. Mais le revers de la médaille, c'est qu'il faut avoir joué plusieurs fois pour bien établir une stratégie. Comme sur tous les parcours inconnus, jouez au début en match-play...

Lothianburn Golf Club — 1893

106A Biggar Road
SCO - EDINBURGH EH10 7DU

Office	Secrétariat	(44) 0131 - 445 5067
Pro shop	Pro-shop	(44) 0131 - 445 2288
Fax	Fax	—
Web	—	
Situation	Situation	

limits of Edinburgh city (pop. 418 914)

Annual closure	Fermeture annuelle	no
Weekly closure	Fermeture hebdomadaire	no

Fees main season Tarifs haute saison	18 holes	
	Week days / Semaine	We/Bank holidays / We/Férié
Individual Individuel	£ 16.50	£ 22.50
Couple Couple	£ 33	£ 45

Full days: £ 22.50 / £ 27.50 (Weekends)

Caddy	Caddy	no
Electric Trolley	Chariot électrique	yes
Buggy	Voiturette	no
Clubs	Clubs	yes

Credit cards Cartes de crédit
(Pro Shop only)

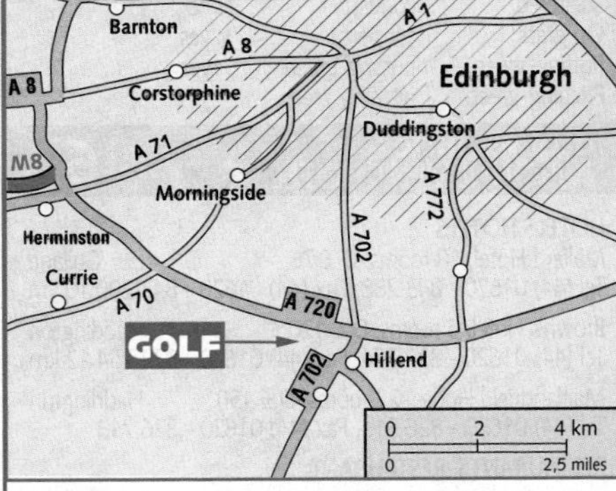

Access Accès : City by-pass. Lothianburn exit.
Map 3 on page 489 Carte 3 Page 489

Golf course / PARCOURS — 14/20

Site	Site	
Maintenance	Entretien	
Architect	Architecte	James Braid
Type	Type	hilly
Relief	Relief	
Water in play	Eau en jeu	
Exp. to wind	Exposé au vent	
Trees in play	Arbres en jeu	

Scorecard Carte de score	Chp. / Chp.	Mens / Mess.	Ladies / Da.
Length Long.	5096	5096	4463
Par	71	71	70
Slope system	—	—	—

Advised golfing ability 0 12 24 36
Niveau de jeu recommandé
Hcp required Handicap exigé 28 Men/Ladies

Club house & amenities / CLUB HOUSE ET ANNEXES — 6/10

Pro shop	Pro-shop	
Driving range	Practice	
Sheltered	couvert	no
On grass	sur herbe	no
Putting-green	putting-green	yes
Pitching-green	pitching green	no

Hotel facilities / ENVIRONNEMENT HOTELIER — 8/10

HOTELS HÔTELS

Posthouse Edinburgh, 303 rooms, D £ 109 — Edinburgh
Tel (44) 0870 - 400 9026, Fax (44) 0870 - 334 9237 — 6 km

Caledonian, 236 rooms, D £ 295 — Edinburgh
Tel (44) 0131 - 459 9988, Fax (44) 0131 - 225 6632 — 8 km

Forte Travelodge, 72 rooms, D £ 50 — Edinburgh
Tel (44) 0131 - 441 4296, Fax (44) 0131 - 441 4296 — 1 km

RESTAURANTS RESTAURANT

Mackenzies — Edinburgh
Tel (44) 0131 - 441 2587 — 2 km

Indian Cavalry Club — Edinburgh
Tel (44) 0131 - 228 3282 — 5 km

LUFFNESS NEW

16	5	6

Arriving here, you seem to be carrying on from Gullane in a whole cluster of courses the equivalent of which is to be found only at St Andrews or Pinehurst. Although Luffness New is not as well known as its neighbours or even nearby Muirfield, it is a course of great character which is always in perfect condition (the greens are famous for this). It rewards the good shots and punishes the bad ones, the way it should be not always is. The wind is an important factor but the direction changes at almost every hole. With a network of bunkers and formidable, omnipresent rough, carding a good score here is the sign of a talented player. Even if you are short of talent, you'll still have fun.

En arrivant ici, on se retrouve dans la continuité des parcours de Gullane, et dans une véritable galaxie dont on ne retrouve l'équivalent qu'à St Andrews ou, plus encore, Pinehurst. Bien que Luffness New n'ait pas la notoriété de ses voisins ou, plus encore, de Muirfield tout proche, c'est un parcours de caractère fort, toujours en bon état (ses greens sont célèbres), qui récompense les bons coups et punit les mauvais, ce qui devrait toujours être le cas, mais n'est pas si fréquent. Le vent y est un facteur important, mais l'orientation change pratiquement à chaque trou. Avec le réseau de bunkers et un rough aussi redoutable qu'omniprésent, signer un bon score ici est une preuve de talent. Si l'on en manque, on s'y amusera aussi beaucoup.

Luffness New Golf Club — 1894

SCO - ABERLADY EH32 0QA

Office	Secrétariat	(44) 01620 - 843 336
Pro shop	Pro-shop	(44) 01620 - 843 114
Fax	Fax	(44) 01620 - 842 933
Web	—	
Situation	Situation	

27 km E of Edinburgh (pop. 418 914)

Annual closure	Fermeture annuelle	no
Weekly closure	Fermeture hebdomadaire	no

Fees main season Tarifs haute saison	18 holes	
	Week days Semaine	**We/Bank holidays** We/Férié
Individual Individuel	£ 37.50	*
Couple Couple	£ 75	*

Full weekday: £ 55
* No visitors at weekends / Restrictions for Ladies (ask)

Caddy	Caddy	no
Electric Trolley	Chariot électrique	no
Buggy	Voiturette	no
Clubs	Clubs	no
Credit cards	Cartes de crédit	no

Access Accès : Edinburgh A1. Near Tranent, A198 through Longniddry and Aberlady.
Turn off right to Luffness Clubhouse.
Map 3 on page 489 Carte 3 Page 489

Golf course — PARCOURS — 16/20

Site	Site	
Maintenance	Entretien	
Architect	Architecte	Tom Morris
Type	Type	links
Relief	Relief	
Water in play	Eau en jeu	
Exp. to wind	Exposé au vent	
Trees in play	Arbres en jeu	

Scorecard Carte de score	**Chp.** Chp.	**Mens** Mess.	**Ladies** Da.
Length Long.	5510	5510	5510
Par	69	69	73
Slope system	0	0	0

Advised golfing ability 0 12 24 36
Niveau de jeu recommandé
Hcp required Handicap exigé certificate

Club house & amenities — CLUB HOUSE ET ANNEXES — 5/10

Pro shop	Pro-shop	
Driving range	Practice	
Sheltered	couvert	no
On grass	sur herbe	no
Putting-green	putting-green	yes
Pitching-green	pitching green	no

Hotel facilities — ENVIRONNEMENT HOTELIER — 6/10

HOTELS HÔTELS

Mallard Hotel, 18 rooms, D £ 76 — Gullane
Tel (44) 01620 - 843 288, Fax (44) 01620 - 843 200 — 4 km

Brown's Hotel, 5 rooms, D £ 120 — Haddington
Tel (44) 01620 - 822 254, Fax (44) 01620 - 822 254 — 5 km

Maitlandfield House — Haddington
22 rooms, D £ 150
Tel (44) 01620 - 826 513, Fax (44) 01620 - 826 713

RESTAURANTS RESTAURANT

Brown's — Haddington
Tel (44) 01620 - 822 254

747

LUNDIN

16 | 6 | 7

The twin brother to Leven Links, Lundin was born from a split in 1868, where each course took 9 holes and went their own way up to 18. Don't wait for the annual tournament that bring both courses together, just try and play this course which originated beside the sea. Restyled like so many other courses by James Braid, this is a good old links - there is even an old railway track running through the middle - used for the qualifying rounds when the British Open is held at Saint Andrews. You'll find some holes in heathland, particularly the 12th and 13th holes, where the view over the Forth is impressive, from the confines of Edinburgh to Muirfield, just opposite. On the course the major hazard is the wind, and let's hope that the watering system is not over-used. Soft terrain kills a little of the subtlety of playing a links course and requires less creativity from the golfer.

Frère jumeau de Leven Links, Lundin est né d'une scission en 1868, chacun gardant neuf trous et complétant son parcours. N'attendez pas la compétition annuelle qui les réunit, essayez aussi de jouer ce parcours des origines le long de la mer. Remodelé comme bien d'autres par James Braid, c'est un vrai bon links (avec même une ancienne voie ferrée au milieu) utilisé pour les qualifications du British Open quand il est à Saint Andrews. Mais on y trouve aussi des trous en terrain de bruyère, en particulier au 12 et au 13, d'où la vue est impressionnante sur le Forth, des confins d'Edimbourg à Muirfield, en face. Sur le parcours, le vent est le principal obstacle, mais on peut souhaiter que l'arrosage ne soit pas trop utilisé, car un terrain mou retire un peu de leur subtilité aux links, et exige moins de créativité.

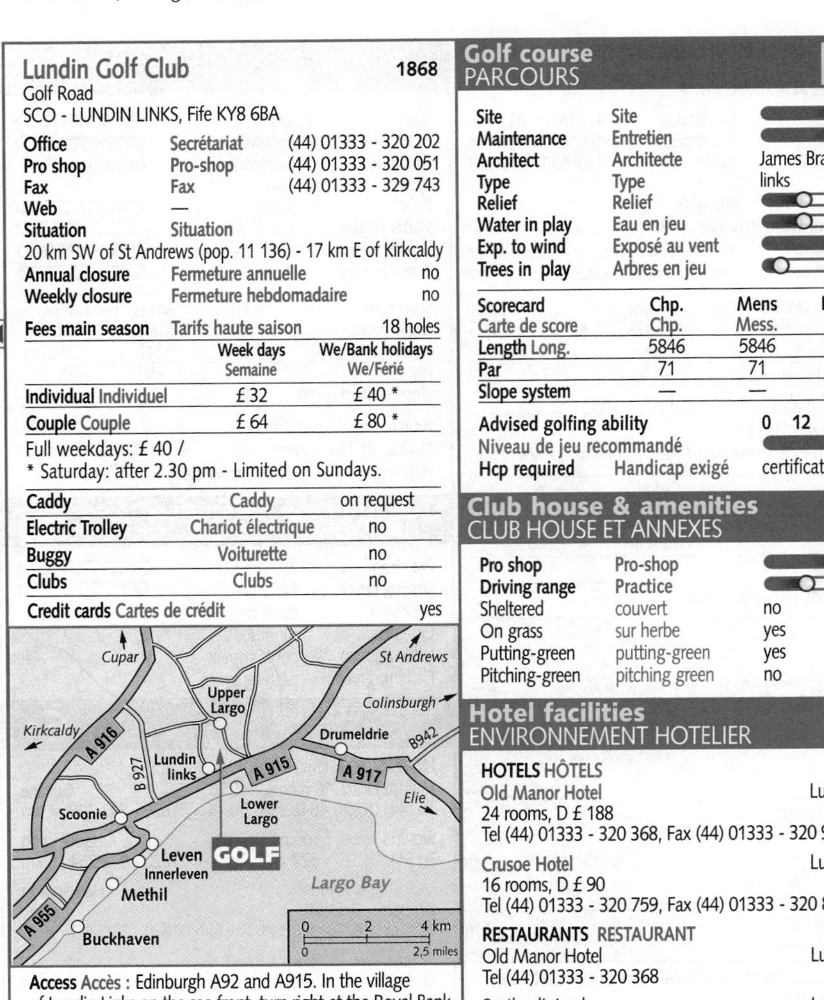

Lundin Golf Club — 1868

Golf Road
SCO - LUNDIN LINKS, Fife KY8 6BA

Office	Secrétariat	(44) 01333 - 320 202
Pro shop	Pro-shop	(44) 01333 - 320 051
Fax	Fax	(44) 01333 - 329 743
Web	—	
Situation	Situation	

20 km SW of St Andrews (pop. 11 136) - 17 km E of Kirkcaldy

Annual closure	Fermeture annuelle	no
Weekly closure	Fermeture hebdomadaire	no

Fees main season Tarifs haute saison	Week days Semaine	We/Bank holidays We/Férié
		18 holes
Individual Individuel	£ 32	£ 40 *
Couple Couple	£ 64	£ 80 *

Full weekdays: £ 40 /
* Saturday: after 2.30 pm - Limited on Sundays.

Caddy	Caddy	on request
Electric Trolley	Chariot électrique	no
Buggy	Voiturette	no
Clubs	Clubs	no
Credit cards	Cartes de crédit	yes

Access Accès : Edinburgh A92 and A915. In the village of Lundin Links on the sea front, turn right at the Royal Bank of Scotland, thereafter first right and second left.
Map 3 on page 489 Carte 3 Page 489

Golf course PARCOURS — 16/20

Site	Site	
Maintenance	Entretien	
Architect	Architecte	James Braid
Type	Type	links
Relief	Relief	
Water in play	Eau en jeu	
Exp. to wind	Exposé au vent	
Trees in play	Arbres en jeu	

Scorecard Carte de score	Chp. Chp.	Mens Mess.	Ladies Da.
Length Long.	5846	5846	5846
Par	71	71	75
Slope system	—	—	—

Advised golfing ability Niveau de jeu recommandé — 0 12 24 36
Hcp required Handicap exigé — certificate

Club house & amenities CLUB HOUSE ET ANNEXES — 6/10

Pro shop	Pro-shop	
Driving range	Practice	
Sheltered	couvert	no
On grass	sur herbe	yes
Putting-green	putting-green	yes
Pitching-green	pitching green	no

Hotel facilities ENVIRONNEMENT HOTELIER — 7/10

HOTELS HÔTELS

Old Manor Hotel — Lundin Links 0.4 km
24 rooms, D £ 188
Tel (44) 01333 - 320 368, Fax (44) 01333 - 320 911

Crusoe Hotel — Lundin Links 0,3 km
16 rooms, D £ 90
Tel (44) 01333 - 320 759, Fax (44) 01333 - 320 865

RESTAURANTS RESTAURANT

Old Manor Hotel — Lundin Links 0.4 km
Tel (44) 01333 - 320 368

Scotland's Larder — Lower Largo 0.3 km
Tel (44) 01333 - 360 414

MACHRIE

17 | 7 | 7

So far away from the "civilised" world, this course, where designer Willie Campbell worked wonders, could but adapt to existing terrain. With a 100-year-old hotel or small cottages, there is no shortage of accommodation or pleasure facilities, aided by some exceptional pure malt whiskies smoked over a peat fire, even tastier when drunk after some wholesome sporting activities. The beaches are superb and the views equally magnificent and romantic. The fairways lie like a carpet and form nothing less than a good, pure and authentic golf course. There are few places in the world that feel so different to what you know already as Machrie. You can get here by boat, but it's a long haul, or by plane in a quick hop from Glasgow.

Autant à l'écart du monde "civilisé", ce parcours ne pouvait que s'adapter au terrain existant, et l'architecte Willie Campbell en a tiré des merveilles. Avec un hôtel plus que centenaire ou de petits cottages, le lieu ne manque pas de possibilités d'accueil, ni de plaisirs : on y distille alentour d'exceptionnels whiskies pur malt fumé à la tourbe, on s'y livre à de saines activités sportives avant de les déguster. Les plages sont superbes, les vues magnifiques, romantiques. Le parcours est posé comme un tapis sur le sol, c'est un pur, vrai et bon parcours de golf. Il est peu d'endroits au monde qui soient si "différents" de tout ce que l'on connaît. On peut y aller en bateau, mais c'est long, ou en avion : c'est un saut de puce depuis Glasgow.

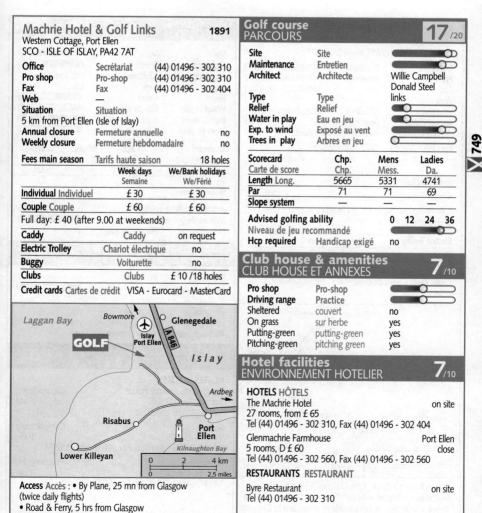

Machrie Hotel & Golf Links 1891

Western Cottage, Port Ellen
SCO - ISLE OF ISLAY, PA42 7AT

Office	Secrétariat	(44) 01496 - 302 310
Pro shop	Pro-shop	(44) 01496 - 302 310
Fax	Fax	(44) 01496 - 302 404
Web	—	
Situation	Situation	

5 km from Port Ellen (Isle of Islay)

Annual closure	Fermeture annuelle	no
Weekly closure	Fermeture hebdomadaire	no

Fees main season Tarifs haute saison	Week days Semaine	We/Bank holidays We/Férié
		18 holes
Individual Individuel	£ 30	£ 30
Couple Couple	£ 60	£ 60

Full day: £ 40 (after 9.00 at weekends)

Caddy	Caddy	on request
Electric Trolley	Chariot électrique	no
Buggy	Voiturette	no
Clubs	Clubs	£ 10 /18 holes
Credit cards	Cartes de crédit	VISA - Eurocard - MasterCard

Laggan Bay
Bowmore
Glenegedale
Islay Port Ellen
A 846
GOLF
Islay
Ardbeg
Risabus
Port Ellen
Lower Killeyan
Kilnaughton Bay
0 2 4 km
0 2,5 miles

Access Accès : • By Plane, 25 mn from Glasgow (twice daily flights)
• Road & Ferry, 5 hrs from Glasgow
Map 2 on page 486 Carte 2 Page 486

Golf course PARCOURS 17/20

Site	Site	
Maintenance	Entretien	
Architect	Architecte	Willie Campbell Donald Steel
Type	Type	links
Relief	Relief	
Water in play	Eau en jeu	
Exp. to wind	Exposé au vent	
Trees in play	Arbres en jeu	

Scorecard Carte de score	Chp. Chp.	Mens Mess.	Ladies Da.
Length Long.	5665	5331	4741
Par	71	71	69
Slope system	—	—	—

Advised golfing ability Niveau de jeu recommandé 0 12 24 36
Hcp required Handicap exigé no

Club house & amenities CLUB HOUSE ET ANNEXES 7/10

Pro shop	Pro-shop	
Driving range	Practice	
Sheltered	couvert	no
On grass	sur herbe	yes
Putting-green	putting-green	yes
Pitching-green	pitching green	yes

Hotel facilities ENVIRONNEMENT HOTELIER 7/10

HOTELS HÔTELS

The Machrie Hotel — on site
27 rooms, from £ 65
Tel (44) 01496 - 302 310, Fax (44) 01496 - 302 404

Glenmachrie Farmhouse — Port Ellen close
5 rooms, D £ 60
Tel (44) 01496 - 302 560, Fax (44) 01496 - 302 560

RESTAURANTS RESTAURANT

Byre Restaurant — on site
Tel (44) 01496 - 302 310

MACHRIHANISH

18 | 6 | 4

The road you take to reach here is as long as it is picturesque, the only problem being that you can't stay for ever. The course is superb, as are the distilleries and the hospitality of the inhabitants of Kintyre here at the ends of the world. So step into this wide open space "created by the Almighty to play golf", as Old Tom Morris would say, who knew a good sales pitch when he saw one and could design a course or two. He obviously lent our Good Lord a hand here to make this marvellous test of golf between the dunes and the foot of the hills. With a simply beautiful first hole, a par 4 over the sea, where the men will envy the ladies. For the fairer sex this is a par 5, for many male players too. You won't regret a single second of your visit here.

La route pour arriver ici est aussi longue que splendide. Le seul problème est qu'il faut ensuite repartir. S'arracher à Machrihanish est d'autant plus dur que si le parcours est superbe, les distilleries ne le sont pas moins, et l'accueil des habitants du Kintyre d'autant plus agréable que l'on est au bout de l'ancien monde, et du monde tout court. Alors, immergez-vous dans un espace "créé par le Tout-Puissant pour jouer au golf" comme disait Old Tom Morris qui avait le sens du commerce, et du dessin de golf aussi. Car il est évidemment venu en aide au Seigneur pour en faire un merveilleux test de golf entre les dunes et le pied des collines. Avec un premier trou de toute beauté, un par 4 à jouer au-dessus de la mer où les hommes jalouseront les dames : c'est pour elles un par 5... pour beaucoup d'hommes aussi ! Vous ne regretterez rien du voyage.

Machrihanish Golf Club — 1876

Machrihanish
SCO - CAMPBELTOWN, Argyll PA28 6PT

Office	Secrétariat	(44) 01586 - 810 213
Pro shop	Pro-shop	(44) 01586 - 810 277
Fax	Fax	(44) 01586 - 810 221
Web	—	
Situation	Situation	Campbeltown, 8 km
Annual closure	Fermeture annuelle	no
Weekly closure	Fermeture hebdomadaire	no

Fees main season Tarifs haute saison	full day	
	Week days Semaine	**We/Bank holidays** We/Férié
Individual Individuel	£ 40*	£ 60*
Couple Couple	£ 80*	£ 120*

* Weekdays: Sunday to Friday /18 holes, weekdays only: £ 30

Caddy	Caddy	on request
Electric Trolley	Chariot électrique	no
Buggy	Voiturette	no
Clubs	Clubs	yes

Credit cards Cartes de crédit
VISA - MasterCard

Access Accès : • By air: from Glasgow, 15 mn flight to Machrihanish Airport. • By car: 3 hrs drive by A82, A83, via Tarbet, Inverraray... or Ferry to Isle of Arran, and to Claonaig.
Map 2 on page 486 Carte 2 Page 486

Golf course / PARCOURS — 18/20

Site	Site	
Maintenance	Entretien	
Architect	Architecte	Old Tom Morris
Type	Type	links
Relief	Relief	
Water in play	Eau en jeu	
Exp. to wind	Exposé au vent	
Trees in play	Arbres en jeu	

Scorecard Carte de score	**Chp.** Chp.	**Mens** Mess.	**Ladies** Da.
Length Long.	5670	5425	5025
Par	70	70	72
Slope system	—	—	—

Advised golfing ability Niveau de jeu recommandé — 0 12 24 36
Hcp required Handicap exigé — no

Club house & amenities / CLUB HOUSE ET ANNEXES — 6/10

Pro shop	Pro-shop	
Driving range	Practice	
Sheltered	couvert	no
On grass	sur herbe	yes
Putting-green	putting-green	yes
Pitching-green	pitching green	yes

Hotel facilities / ENVIRONNEMENT HOTELIER — 4/10

HOTELS HÔTELS

Balegreggan Country House — Campbeltown 8 km
4 rooms, from D £ 70
Tel (44) 01586 - 552 062

Seafield — Campbeltown 8 km
9 rooms, D £ 75
Tel (44) 01586 - 554 385, Fax (44) 01586 - 552 741

Ardell House — Machrihanish close
9 rooms, D £ 62
Tel (44) 01586 - 810 235, Fax (44) 01586 - 810 235

MONIFIETH

17 | 7 | 7

We know that golf was played here in the first half of the 17th century but the first signs of a real course really date from 1850. Like nearby Carnoustie, the course is shared by five different clubs, as is the Ashludie Course, a little more modest and restful but nonetheless interesting. The wide open spaces of the "great" course naturally leaves it exposed to the wind, but anything else would come as a great surprise. Classic and discreet in design with no hidden traps, Monifieth is respectable in length and deserves to be better known outside Scotland. This is one of the best surprises that any visitor could hope to find on the east coast. A course for connoisseurs but pleasant for players of all levels.

On sait que le golf a été pratiqué ici dès la première moitié du XVIIème siècle, mais les premiers signes d'un véritable parcours ne remontent pas plus loin que 1850. Comme les tout proches parcours de Carnoustie, celui-ci est partagé par cinq clubs différents, de même que le "Ashludie Course", plus modeste et reposant, mais néanmoins intéressant. Les vastes espaces où s'épanouit le "grand" parcours l'exposent bien sûr au vent, mais c'est le contraire qui serait étonnant. D'une architecture classique et sobre, sans pièges dissimulés, et d'une longueur très respectable, Monifieth mériterait de connaître une meilleure notoriété hors des frontières, et c'est l'une des meilleures surprises que les visiteurs pourront trouver de ce côté de l'Ecosse. Un parcours pour connaisseurs, mais agréable à tous niveaux de jeu.

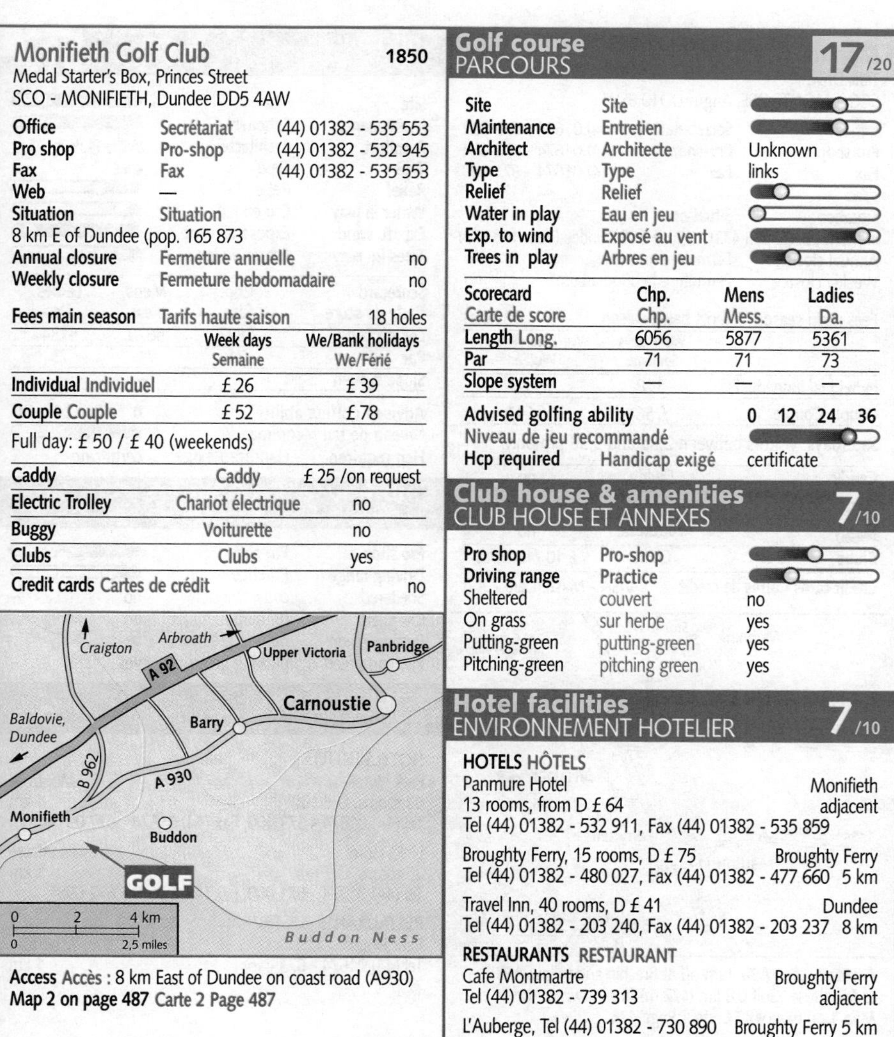

Monifieth Golf Club — 1850

Medal Starter's Box, Princes Street
SCO - MONIFIETH, Dundee DD5 4AW

Office	Secrétariat	(44) 01382 - 535 553
Pro shop	Pro-shop	(44) 01382 - 532 945
Fax	Fax	(44) 01382 - 535 553
Web	—	
Situation	Situation	

8 km E of Dundee (pop. 165 873

Annual closure	Fermeture annuelle	no
Weekly closure	Fermeture hebdomadaire	no

Fees main season Tarifs haute saison	Week days Semaine	We/Bank holidays We/Férié
		18 holes
Individual Individuel	£ 26	£ 39
Couple Couple	£ 52	£ 78

Full day: £ 50 / £ 40 (weekends)

Caddy	Caddy	£ 25 /on request
Electric Trolley	Chariot électrique	no
Buggy	Voiturette	no
Clubs	Clubs	yes
Credit cards	Cartes de crédit	no

Access Accès : 8 km East of Dundee on coast road (A930)
Map 2 on page 487 Carte 2 Page 487

Golf course PARCOURS — 17/20

Site	Site	
Maintenance	Entretien	
Architect	Architecte	Unknown
Type	Type	links
Relief	Relief	
Water in play	Eau en jeu	
Exp. to wind	Exposé au vent	
Trees in play	Arbres en jeu	

Scorecard Carte de score	Chp. Chp.	Mens Mess.	Ladies Da.
Length Long.	6056	5877	5361
Par	71	71	73
Slope system	—	—	—

Advised golfing ability Niveau de jeu recommandé — 0 12 24 36
Hcp required Handicap exigé — certificate

Club house & amenities CLUB HOUSE ET ANNEXES — 7/10

Pro shop	Pro-shop	
Driving range	Practice	
Sheltered	couvert	no
On grass	sur herbe	yes
Putting-green	putting-green	yes
Pitching-green	pitching green	yes

Hotel facilities ENVIRONNEMENT HOTELIER — 7/10

HOTELS HÔTELS

Panmure Hotel — Monifieth
13 rooms, from D £ 64 — adjacent
Tel (44) 01382 - 532 911, Fax (44) 01382 - 535 859

Broughty Ferry, 15 rooms, D £ 75 — Broughty Ferry
Tel (44) 01382 - 480 027, Fax (44) 01382 - 477 660 — 5 km

Travel Inn, 40 rooms, D £ 41 — Dundee
Tel (44) 01382 - 203 240, Fax (44) 01382 - 203 237 — 8 km

RESTAURANTS RESTAURANT

Cafe Montmartre — Broughty Ferry
Tel (44) 01382 - 739 313 — adjacent

L'Auberge, Tel (44) 01382 - 730 890 — Broughty Ferry 5 km

MONTROSE

17 | 5 | 6

A great classic shared by three golf clubs, as is Carnoustie a few miles down the coast. If the history books are right, then this is the 5th oldest club in the world and golf has been played on the grounds of the Earl of Montrose since the 16th century. It is true that there is tradition in the air here, with a tinge of austerity as well. Here you'll find all the finest components that go to make up a great links course: deep bunkers, wonderfully soft soil, bushes and towering dunes covered by wild grass that shape the winding fairways and greens. Very reasonable in length, although this can change in a matter of minutes when the wind blows, this excellent course (complemented by the little Broomfield Course) has been a little neglected for the benefit of more powerful neighbours, but the course is so steeped in history that it should be a part of your own experience.

Un grand classique partagé par trois clubs de golf, comme Carnoustie, quelques kilomètres plus bas sur la côte. L'histoire voudrait que ce soit le cinquième club du monde, et que l'on ait joué sur ces terres du Marquis de Montrose depuis le XVIè siècle. Il est vrai que l'on respire ici la tradition, non sans une certaine austérité. On trouve ici à l'état pur ce qui fait la grandeur des links, de profonds bunkers, un sol merveilleusement souple, des buissons, de hautes dunes envahies d'herbes folles entre lesquelles s'insinuent les fairways et les greens. De longueur très raisonnable, mais que le vent peut bien sûr métamorphoser d'un instant à l'autre, cet excellent parcours (complété par le petit Broomfield Course) a été un peu négligé au profit de puissants voisins, mais il témoigne de toute une histoire, et doit faire partie de la vôtre.

Montrose Links Trust — 1562

Traill Drive
SCO - MONTROSE, Angus DD10 8SW

Office	Secrétariat	(44) 01674 - 672 932
Pro shop	Pro-shop	(44) 01674 - 672 634
Fax	Fax	(44) 01674 - 671 800
Web	—	
Situation	Situation	

in Montrose (pop. 8 473) - 35 km E of Dundee (pop. 165 873)

Annual closure	Fermeture annuelle	no
Weekly closure	Fermeture hebdomadaire	no

Fees main season Tarifs haute saison	18 holes	
	Week days Semaine	**We/Bank holidays** We/Férié
Individual Individuel	£ 28	£ 32*
Couple Couple	£ 56	£ 64*

Saturdays: visitors between 2.35 and 3.38 pm only.

Caddy	Caddy	no
Electric Trolley	Chariot électrique	£ 5 /18 holes
Buggy	Voiturette	no
Clubs	Clubs	£ 10 /18 holes
Credit cards	Cartes de crédit	VISA - MasterCard - JCB

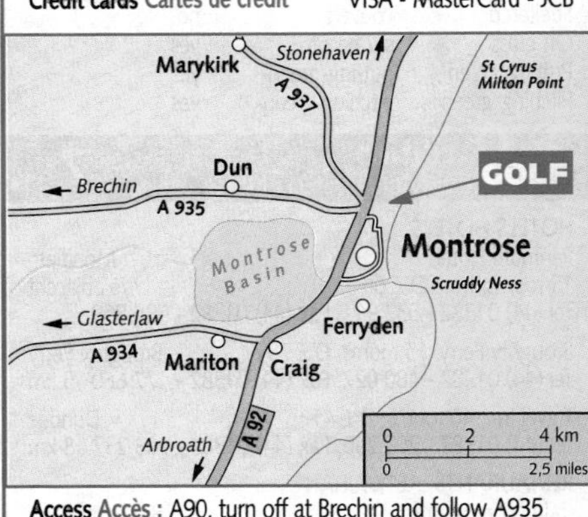

Access Accès : A90, turn off at Brechin and follow A935 to Montrose. Golf 0.8 km (1/2 m) from town centre.
Map 1 on page 485 Carte 1 Page 485

Golf course — PARCOURS — 17/20

Site	Site	
Maintenance	Entretien	
Architect	Architecte	Willie Park Jr
Type	Type	links
Relief	Relief	
Water in play	Eau en jeu	
Exp. to wind	Exposé au vent	
Trees in play	Arbres en jeu	

Scorecard Carte de score	**Chp.** Chp.	**Mens** Mess.	**Ladies** Da.
Length Long.	5887	5670	5134
Par	71	71	73
Slope system	—	—	—

Advised golfing ability Niveau de jeu recommandé — 0 12 24 36
Hcp required Handicap exigé — certificate

Club house & amenities — CLUB HOUSE ET ANNEXES — 5/10

Pro shop	Pro-shop	
Driving range	Practice	
Sheltered	couvert	no
On grass	sur herbe	no
Putting-green	putting-green	yes
Pitching-green	pitching green	yes

Hotel facilities — ENVIRONNEMENT HOTELIER — 6/10

HOTELS HÔTELS

Park Hotel — Montrose 1 km
58 rooms, D £ 100
Tel (44) 01674 - 673 400, Fax (44) 01674 - 677 091

Links Hotel — Montrose 1 km
25 rooms, D £ 80
Tel (44) 01674 - 671 000, Fax (44) 01674 - 672 698

RESTAURANTS RESTAURANT

Park Hotel — Montrose 1 km
Tel (44) 01674 - 673 415

MORAY

17 | 5 | 5

This is not the best known links in Scotland but it is a good one. Firstly for its antiquated charm, because like the Old Course at St Andrews, it starts and ends in town, in Lossiemouth, the name by which the course is also sometimes known. A large part of this "old" course was designed by Old Tom Morris, although patient changes have given the layout its present-day look, custom-made for the requirements of modern golf. Players of all levels will enjoy this course, and the less experienced golfers can get acquainted with the subtle side of links golf without too much to worry about. Moray is also home to the "New Course" designed by Henry Cotton, a very pleasant layout but without the cachet of its "old" stablemate. We would also emphasise the mildness of the climate here and the superb views over the Moray Firth. Highly recommended.

Ce n'est pas le plus connu des links d'Ecosse, mais ce n'est pas le moindre. Par son charme désuet d'abord : comme le Old Course de St Andrews, il commence et s'achève en ville, à Lossiemouth, qui lui a donné parfois son nom. Ce "Old" a en grande partie été conçu par Old Tom Morris, mais de patientes modifications lui ont donné son visage actuel, parfaitement adapté aux exigences du golf moderne. Cependant, les joueurs de tous niveaux y prendront plaisir, et les moins expérimentés pourront s'y familiariser avec les subtilités du golf de links sans être trop intimidés. De plus, on trouve également à Moray le "New Course" dessiné par Henry Cotton, très agréable mais moins empreint de grandeur que le "Old." On soulignera enfin la douceur du climat local, et les vues superbes sur le Moray Firth. Visite conseillée !

Moray Golf Club — 1889

Stotfield Road
SCO - LOSSIEMOUTH, Moray JV31 6QS

Office	Secrétariat	(44) 01343 - 812 018
Pro shop	Pro-shop	(44) 01343 - 813 330
Fax	Fax	(44) 01343 - 815 102
Web	—	
Situation	Situation	
9 km N of Elgin (pop. 11 855)		
Annual closure	Fermeture annuelle	no
Weekly closure	Fermeture hebdomadaire	no

Fees main season / Tarifs haute saison	Week days / Semaine	We/Bank holidays / We/Férié
		18 holes
Individual Individuel	£ 30	£ 40
Couple Couple	£ 60	£ 80

Full days: £ 40 - £ 50 (weekends)

Caddy	Caddy	on request
Electric Trolley	Chariot électrique	no
Buggy	Voiturette	no
Clubs	Clubs	yes
Credit cards	Cartes de crédit	only Pro-shop

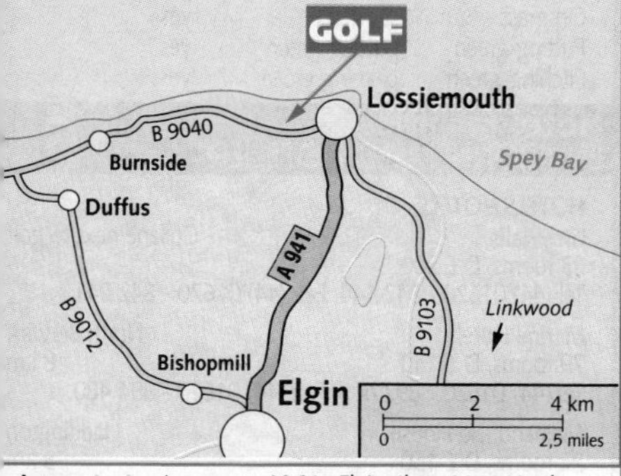

Access Accès : Inverness, A96 to Elgin, then A941 North.
Map 1 on page 485 Carte 1 Page 485

Golf course PARCOURS — 17/20

Site	Site	
Maintenance	Entretien	
Architect	Architecte	Old Tom Morris
Type	Type	links
Relief	Relief	
Water in play	Eau en jeu	
Exp. to wind	Exposé au vent	
Trees in play	Arbres en jeu	

Scorecard / Carte de score	Chp. / Chp.	Mens / Mess.	Ladies / Da.
Length Long.	6066	5735	5580
Par	71	70	75
Slope system	—	—	—

Advised golfing ability / Niveau de jeu recommandé: 0 12 24 36
Hcp required / Handicap exigé: 24

Club house & amenities CLUB HOUSE ET ANNEXES — 5/10

Pro shop	Pro-shop	
Driving range	Practice	
Sheltered	couvert	no
On grass	sur herbe	no
Putting-green	putting-green	yes
Pitching-green	pitching green	yes

Hotel facilities ENVIRONNEMENT HOTELIER — 5/10

HOTELS HÔTELS

Stotfield, 45 rooms, D £ 80 — Lossiemouth adajcent
Tel (44) 01343 - 812 011, Fax (44) 01343 - 814 820

Mansion House — Elgin 9 km
23 rooms, D £ 150
Tel (44) 01343 - 548 811, Fax (44) 01343 - 547 916

Laichmoray, 35 rooms, D £ 80 — Elgin 9 km
Tel (44) 01343 - 540 045, Fax (44) 01343 - 540 055

RESTAURANTS RESTAURANT

1629 Restaurant, — Lossiemouth 1 km
Tel (44) 01343 - 813 743

Mansion House, Tel (44) 01343 - 548 811 — Elgin 9 km

MUIRFIELD

19 | 7 | 6

The course of the Honourable Company of Edinburg Golfers, who drew up the first collection ‹ the rules of golf, is first and foremost one of the great courses used for the British Open. Winne here include Nicklaus, Trevino and Faldo, three players of very different talent, suggesting that grea courses adapt to all styles of play. While there are no spectacular dunes and no sea in the immediate vicinity fc this to be labelled a reference links course, the thick and very tall rough, deep bunkering that reflects a shrew golfing mind, narrow (but welcoming) fairways and tricky greens where you need magic fingers, make it a re ference course, full stop. The course asks a lot of players when it comes to shaping the right shot. A good shc is rewarded but any flaw is a shortcut to disaster. This is a great test of golf. The clubhouse is superb, historical very instructive and a great place to eat.

Le parcours de l'Honourable Company of Edinburgh Golfers, qui a établi le premier recueil de règles de golf e surtout l'un des grands parcours du British Open, où ont triomphé notamment Nicklaus, Trevino et Faldo, tro hommes aux talents dissemblables, comme quoi les grands golfs s'adaptent à tous les types de jeu. S'il manqu de dunes spectaculaires et de proximité immédiate de la mer pour être un links de référence, les roughs épais e très hauts, de profonds bunkers placés avec une très grande connaissance du jeu, des fairways étroits (mais ac cueillants), des greens subtils où il faut avoir des doigts de fée en font une référence. Ici, on exige beaucoup d joueur afin qu'il fasse le coup qui convient. Un bon coup est récompensé, mais toute défaillance amène un de sastre. Un grand test de golf. Le Club house est superbe, historiquement très instructif, et la table excellente.

Honourable Company of Edinburgh Golfers **1891**

Muirfield
SCO - GULLANE, E. Lothian, EH31 2EG

Office	Secrétariat	(44) 01620 - 842 123
Pro shop	Pro-shop	no Pro shop
Fax	Fax	(44) 01620 - 842 977
E-mail	hceg@btinternet.com	
Situation	Situation	

30 km E of Edinburgh (pop. 418 914)

Annual closure	Fermeture annuelle	no
Weekly closure	Fermeture hebdomadaire	no

Fees main season Tarifs haute saison		full day
	Week days Semaine	**We/Bank holidays** We/Férié
Individual Individuel	£ 85	*
Couple Couple	£ 170	*

Always ask for availability / * No visitors at weekends

Caddy	Caddy	on request
Electric Trolley	Chariot électrique	no
Buggy	Voiturette	limited use
Clubs	Clubs	no
Credit cards Cartes de crédit		no

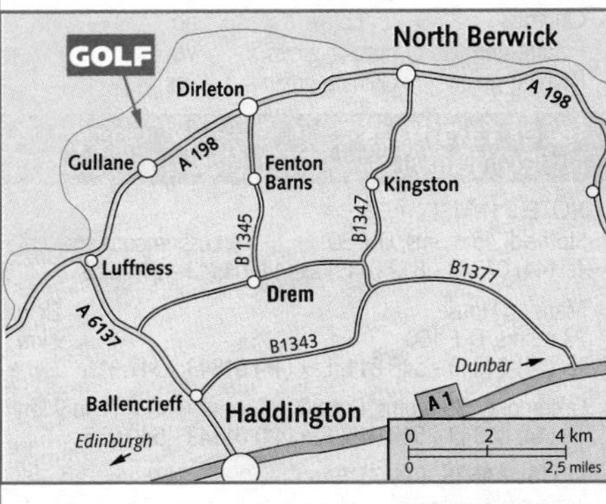

Access Accès : Edinburgh A198 along Firth of Forth. Turn left at the end of Gullane, follow signs to Greywalls Hotel.
Map 3 on page 489 Carte 3 Page 489

Golf course PARCOURS — 19/20

Site	Site	
Maintenance	Entretien	
Architect	Architecte	Tom Morris Harry S. Colt
Type	Type	links
Relief	Relief	
Water in play	Eau en jeu	
Exp. to wind	Exposé au vent	
Trees in play	Arbres en jeu	

Scorecard Carte de score	**Chp.** Chp.	**Mens** Mess.	**Ladies** Da.
Length Long.	6336	6007	—
Par	73	73	—
Slope system	—	—	—

Advised golfing ability Niveau de jeu recommandé — 0 12 24 36

Hcp required Handicap exigé — certificate

Club house & amenities CLUB HOUSE ET ANNEXES — 7/10

Pro shop	Pro-shop	
Driving range	Practice	
Sheltered	couvert	practice area only
On grass	sur herbe	yes
Putting-green	putting-green	yes
Pitching-green	pitching green	yes

Hotel facilities ENVIRONNEMENT HOTELIER — 6/10

HOTELS HÔTELS

Greywalls — Gullane next to golf
23 rooms, D £ 200
Tel (44) 01620 - 842 144, Fax (44) 01620 - 842 241

Marine Hotel — North Berwick 8 km
79 rooms, D £ 140
Tel (44) 01620 - 892 406, Fax (44) 01620 - 894 480

Maitlandfield House — Haddington 3 km
22 rooms, D £ 150
Tel (44) 01620 - 826 513, Fax (44) 01620 - 826 713

RESTAURANTS RESTAURANT

Greywalls, Tel (44) 01620 - 842 144 — Gullane next to golf

MURCAR

15 | 6 | 6

Murcar lies next door to Royal Aberdeen but although it may never have the Royal seal, there are many who rate it just as highly as its more famous neighbour. But if they say that mongrels are a tougher species than pedigrees, then Murcar is definitely a course not to be missed. It is a first class challenge even when the wind does not blow and must never be taken lightly. Not quite as long as Royal Aberdeen, the terrain is similar in many ways. There are three par 3s, two par 5s and 13 par 4s. The latter include a group of short par 4s that are devilishly tricky and often produce as many bogeys as pars for the unwary. Naturally you won't find the tremendous challenges that await you on the monster courses in Scotland, but Murcar deserves much more than just a quick look. It should be on everyone's itinerary in this part of Scotland which has an abundance of great courses. Recent work on the course has now brought it back to excellent condition.

Murcar jouxte le parcours de Royal Aberdeen et n'a pas eu droit à l'annoblissement. Mais si on dit que les bâtards sont les plus vigoureux, Murcar est effectivement un parcours à ne pas manquer. C'est un défi de premier ordre à relever, à ne jamais prendre à la légère, même quand le vent ne souffle pas. A peine plus court que son voisin, il s'en rapproche par de nombreux aspects. La distribution des trous est assez inhabituelle, avec trois par 3, deux par 5 et treize par 4, dont ces démoniaques petits trous techniques que l'on croit pouvoir driver et qui vous mettent à genoux. Certes, l'on n'attendra pas ici d'aussi formidables défis que dans le groupe des grands monstres d'Ecosse, mais Murcar mérite beaucoup mieux qu'un simple regard. Il devrait figurer sur l'itinéraire de tout golfeur voyageant dans cette partie d'Ecosse, qui ne manque pas de grands parcours, d'autant que des améliorations récentes lui ont rendu sa qualité d'entretien.

Murcar Golf Club — 1909

Bridge of Don
SCO - ABERDEEN, Aberdeenshire AB23 8BD

Office	Secrétariat	(44) 01224 - 704 354
Pro shop	Pro-shop	(44) 01224 - 704 370
Fax	Fax	(44) 01224 - 704 354
Web	www.murcar.co.uk	
Situation	Situation	
8 km N of Aberdeen (pop. 204 885)		
Annual closure	Fermeture annuelle	no
Weekly closure	Fermeture hebdomadaire	no

Fees main season Tarifs haute saison	18 holes	
	Week days Semaine	**We/Bank holidays** We/Férié
Individual Individuel	£ 40	£ 50
Couple Couple	£ 80	£ 100

Caddy	Caddy	on request
Electric Trolley	Chariot électrique	no
Buggy	Voiturette	no
Clubs	Clubs	yes
Credit cards	Cartes de crédit	yes

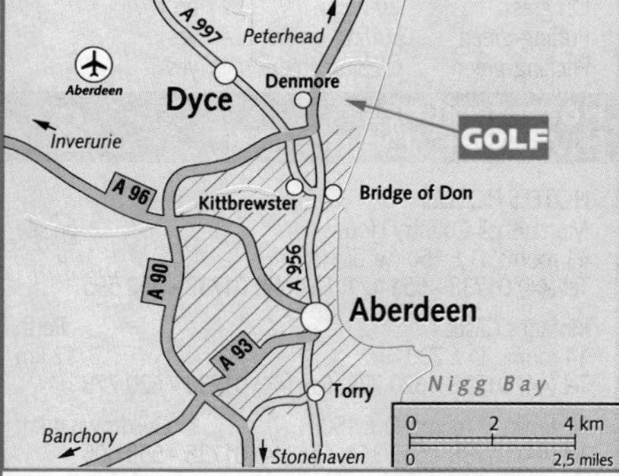

Access Accès : Aberdeen, A92 → Peterhead.
Signposted to right.
Map 1 on page 485 Carte 1 Page 485

Golf course — PARCOURS — 15/20

Site	Site	
Maintenance	Entretien	
Architect	Architecte	Archie Simpson, James Braid
Type	Type	links
Relief	Relief	
Water in play	Eau en jeu	
Exp. to wind	Exposé au vent	
Trees in play	Arbres en jeu	

Scorecard Carte de score	**Chp.** Chp.	**Mens** Mess.	**Ladies** Da.
Length Long.	5659	5229	4981
Par	71	68	72
Slope system	—	—	—

Advised golfing ability 0 12 24 36
Niveau de jeu recommandé
Hcp required Handicap exigé: certificate

Club house & amenities — CLUB HOUSE ET ANNEXES — 6/10

Pro shop	Pro-shop	
Driving range	Practice	
Sheltered	couvert	no
On grass	sur herbe	yes
Putting-green	putting-green	yes
Pitching-green	pitching green	yes

Hotel facilities — ENVIRONNEMENT HOTELIER — 6/10

HOTELS HÔTELS

Marcliffe at Piffodels, 42 rooms, D £ 275 — Aberdeen
Tel (44) 01224 - 861 000, Fax (44) 01224 - 868 860 — 9 km

Travel Inn, 40 rooms, D £ 41 — Murcar close
Tel (44) 01224 - 821 217, Fax (44) 01224 - 706 869

Simpson's, 35 rooms, D £ 140 — Aberdeen
Tel (44) 01224 - 327 777, Fax (44) 01224 - 327 700 — 9 km

Ardoe House — Aberdeen
Tel (44) 01224 - 860 600, Fax (44) 01224 - 861 283 — 16 km

RESTAURANTS RESTAURANT

Courtyard on the Lane, Tel (44) 01224 - 213 795 — Aberdeen
Silver Darling, Tel (44) 01224 - 576 229 — Aberdeen

MURRAYSHALL

14 | 7 | 8

Located in a well-forested setting not far from Perth, this country course was opened in 1981 and has quickly built up an excellent reputation among local players for its pleasant site, the hazards and the challenge of playing here. This is by no means an easy course but is one of those layouts which quickly help you forget a bad score. If your card is bad, there's no blaming the course. Game strategy is obvious from the first time out, difficulties are evenly spread around the course with just the right balance of stress and relaxation, and the greens are well designed and protected. This is one of the best-equipped golf clubs you can find, with a real driving range and a very comfortable hotel.

Situé dans un environnement bien boisé non loin de Perth, ce parcours campagnard né en 1981 s'est vite bâti une excellente réputation parmi les joueurs de la région, en raison de l'agrément du site, mais aussi des difficultés présentées et du "challenge" offert. Ce n'est certes pas un parcours facile, mais il fait partie de ceux qui vous font vite oublier un mauvais score. En tout cas, on ne pourra pas en accuser le parcours. La stratégie de jeu y est assez évidente dès la première visite, les difficultés sont bien réparties, avec ce qu'il faut de tension et de détente, les greens bien dessinés et bien défendus. Le Club est l'un des mieux équipés que l'on puisse trouver, notamment avec un vrai pratice et un hôtel très confortable.

Murrayshall Golf Club — 1981

Murrayshall Country House Hotel
SCO - SCONE, Perthshire PH2 7PH

Office	Secrétariat	(44) 01738 - 551 171
Pro shop	Pro-shop	(44) 01738 - 554 804
Fax	Fax	(44) 01738 - 552 595
Web	—	
Situation	Situation	

8 km NE of Perth (pop. 123 495)

Annual closure	Fermeture annuelle	no
Weekly closure	Fermeture hebdomadaire	no

Fees main season Tarifs haute saison — 18 holes

	Week days / Semaine	We/Bank holidays / We/Férié
Individual Individuel	£ 27	£ 30
Couple Couple	£ 54	£ 60

Full days: £ 30 - £ 45 (weekends)

Caddy	Caddy	£ 15 /on request
Electric Trolley	Chariot électrique	£ 7.50 /18 holes
Buggy	Voiturette	£ 20 /18 holes
Clubs	Clubs	£ 15 /18 holes

Credit cards Cartes de crédit
VISA - Eurocard - MasterCard - AMEX

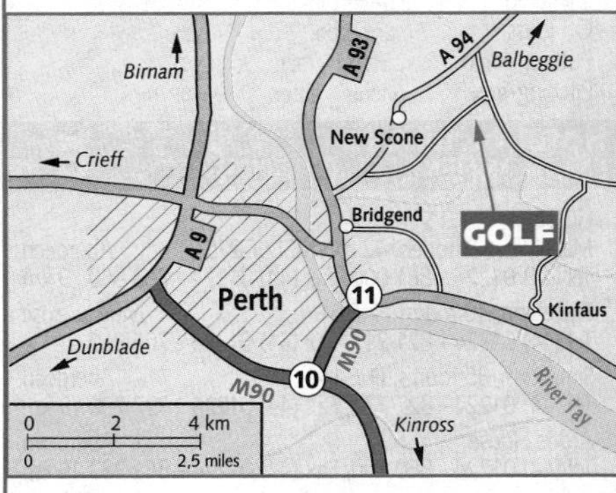

Access Accès : Edinburgh M90 to Perth, then A94 → Coupar Angus, Golf at Scone.
Map 2 on page 487 Carte 2 Page 487

Golf course — PARCOURS — 14/20

Site	Site	
Maintenance	Entretien	
Architect	Architecte	Hamilton Stutt
Type	Type	parkland
Relief	Relief	
Water in play	Eau en jeu	
Exp. to wind	Exposé au vent	
Trees in play	Arbres en jeu	

Scorecard / Carte de score	Chp. / Chp.	Mens / Mess.	Ladies / Da.
Length Long.	5797	5540	4786
Par	73	73	73
Slope system	—	—	—

Advised golfing ability / Niveau de jeu recommandé: 0 12 24 36

Hcp required Handicap exigé: no

Club house & amenities — CLUB HOUSE ET ANNEXES — 7/10

Pro shop	Pro-shop	
Driving range	Practice	
Sheltered	couvert	11 mats
On grass	sur herbe	no
Putting-green	putting-green	yes
Pitching-green	pitching green	yes

Hotel facilities — ENVIRONNEMENT HOTELIER — 8/10

HOTELS HÔTELS

Murrayshall Country House — on site
41 rooms, D £ 150 (w. dinner)
Tel (44) 01738 - 551 171, Fax (44) 01738 - 552 595

Kinfauns Castle — Perth 12 km
14 rooms, D £ 200
Tel (44) 01738 - 620 777, Fax (44) 01738 - 620 778

Newmiln, 7 rooms, D £ 150 — Guildtown 4 km
Tel (44) 01738 - 552 364, Fax (44) 01738 - 553 505

RESTAURANTS RESTAURANT

Old Masters, Tel (44) 01738 - 551 171 — on site

Let's Eat, Tel (44) 01738 - 643 377 — Perth 8 km

NAIRN

19 | 7 | 8

This is one of the great Scottish links and for many a year was one of the country's best guarded secrets. The heather, broom and gorse complete a fine collection of hazards preying on your ball once you have avoided the traps along the Moray Firth. But on the whole Nairn is a remarkable challenge, notably with greens that are often firm and very quick. If you add James Braid's high class bunkering, you'll understand that you don't drive past without stopping off a day or three to test your game on the long golfing road that leads the visitor from Aberdeen to Inverness then to Dornoch and beyond. The landscape is maybe plainer than on other courses in the region, but it is also a little more sheltered, if that is the right word.

C'est l'un des grands links d'Ecosse et ce fut longtemps l'un de ses secrets les mieux gardés. La bruyère, les genêts et les ajoncs complètent une belle collection d'entraves à la liberté des balles, une fois que l'on a déjoué les pièges le long du Moray Firth. Mais Nairn est dans l'ensemble un défi remarquable, avec notamment des greens souvent fermes et très rapides. Si l'on ajoute la contribution majeure de James Braid, un "bunkering" de haute volée, on aura compris que l'on ne saurait passer devant la porte sans s'arrêter un bon moment pour tester sa forme, sur la longue route golfique menant d'Aberdeen à Inverness puis Dornoch et au-delà. Le paysage est moins mouvementé que sur d'autres parcours de la région, mais il est aussi un peu plus abrité... si l'on peut dire.

Nairn Golf Club — 1887

Seabank Road
SCO - NAIRN, IV12 4HB

Office	Secrétariat	(44) 01667 - 453 208
Pro shop	Pro-shop	(44) 01667 - 452 787
Fax	Fax	(44) 01667 - 456 328
Web	—	
Situation	Situation	24 km E of Inverness
Annual closure	Fermeture annuelle	no
Weekly closure	Fermeture hebdomadaire	no

Fees main season Tarifs haute saison	Week days Semaine	We/Bank holidays We/Férié
		18 holes
Individual Individuel	£ 70	£ 70
Couple Couple	£ 140	£ 140

Caddy	Caddy	£ 25 /on request
Electric Trolley	Chariot électrique	no
Buggy	Voiturette	no
Clubs	Clubs	£ 15 /18 holes

Credit cards Cartes de crédit
VISA - MasterCard - AMEX

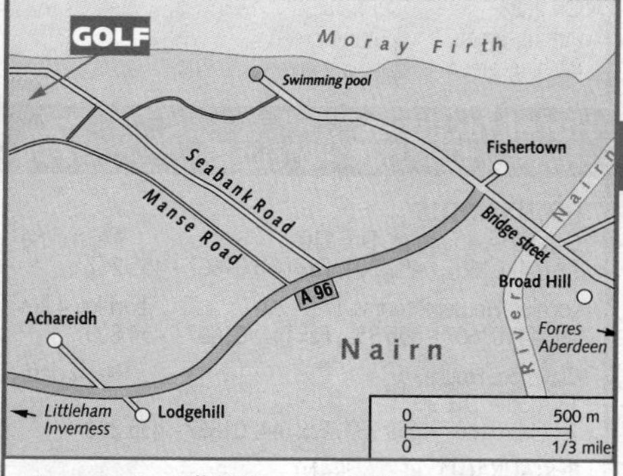

Access Accès : Off A96 Inverness to Nairn road. Golf to the West of town centre.
Map 1 on page 485 Carte 1 Page 485

Golf course — PARCOURS — 19/20

Site	Site	
Maintenance	Entretien	
Architect	Architecte	Old Tom Morris James Braid
Type	Type	links
Relief	Relief	
Water in play	Eau en jeu	
Exp. to wind	Exposé au vent	
Trees in play	Arbres en jeu	

Scorecard Carte de score	Chp. Chp.	Mens Mess.	Ladies Da.
Length Long.	6035	5787	5162
Par	72	71	75
Slope system	—	—	—

Advised golfing ability Niveau de jeu recommandé — 0 12 24 36
Hcp required Handicap exigé — certificate

Club house & amenities — CLUB HOUSE ET ANNEXES — 7/10

Pro shop	Pro-shop	
Driving range	Practice	
Sheltered	couvert	no
On grass	sur herbe	yes
Putting-green	putting-green	yes
Pitching-green	pitching green	no

Hotel facilities — ENVIRONNEMENT HOTELIER — 8/10

HOTELS HÔTELS
Golf View, 45 rooms, D £ 110 — Nairn close
Tel (44) 01667 - 452 301, Fax (44) 01667 - 455 267

Clifton House, 12 rooms, D £ 107 — Nairn close
Tel (44) 01667 - 453 119, Fax (44) 01667 - 452 836

Boath House — Nairn 3 km
7 rooms, D from £ 175
Tel (44) 01667 - 454 896, Fax (44) 01667 - 454 896

RESTAURANTS RESTAURANT
Longhouse, Tel (44) 01667 - 455 532 — Nairn close
Golf View Hotel, Tel (44) 01667 - 452 301 — Nairn close

NAIRN DUNBAR

15 | 7 | 7

The Nairn Dunbar Golf Club perhaps lives slightly in the shadow of its more widely known sister on the other side of town, but this beautiful links course should not be left off the visitor's itinerary. It is long enough to test the best players and yet is perfectly enjoyable for all standard of players. Accuracy is the key here because of the high stands of gorse that line many of the fairways. It is a course that demands the use of every club in the bag and the gorse has the added advantage of creating a wonderful feeling of solitude on most of the holes. It is a very friendly club and there are fine views across the links from the magnificent new clubhouse. Among many fine holes, the formidable par four 10th remains firmly in the memory for most visitors to this delightful stretch of Morayshire coastline.

Le parcours du Nairn Dunbar Golf Club vit peut-être dans l'ombre de son célèbre cousin situé de l'autre côté de la ville, mais il serait très dommage pour le voyageur, même pressé, de ne pas l'inclure dans son itinéraire de golfeur. Près de la mer et de l'embouchure de la rivière, il a été intelligemment adapté au site, avec beaucoup d'esprit d'invention. Il est assez long pour exiger beaucoup des meilleurs joueurs, mais reste parfaitement agréable pour tous les autres. Ce parcours demande la maîtrise de tous les clubs du sac et la précision y est essentielle, en raison de la végétation qui longe la plupart des trous, ce qui a par ailleurs l'avantage de donner aux joueurs une merveilleuse sensation de solitude. Le club est très accueillant, ce qui permet de profiter avec plus de plaisir encore de vues magnifiques depuis le nouveau et superbe clubhouse. Parmi bien d'autres trous, le 10, un formidable par 4, restera sans aucun doute dans la mémoire des visiteurs de cette merveilleuse région de la côte du Morayshire.

Nairn Dunbar Golf Club — 1899

Lochloy Road
SCO - NAIRN, IV12 5AE

Office	Secrétariat	(44) 01667 - 452 741
Pro shop	Pro-shop	(44) 01667 - 453 964
Fax	Fax	(44) 01667 - 456 897
Web	www.nairndunbar.com	
Situation	Situation	

25 km E of Inverness (pop. 62 186)

Annual closure	Fermeture annuelle	no
Weekly closure	Fermeture hebdomadaire	no

Fees main season Tarifs haute saison	18 holes	
	Week days Semaine	**We/Bank holidays** We/Férié
Individual Individuel	£ 33	£ 40
Couple Couple	£ 66	£ 80

Full days: £ 42 /£ 53 (weekends)

Caddy	Caddy	on request
Electric Trolley	Chariot électrique	no
Buggy	Voiturette	£ 18 /18 holes
Clubs	Clubs	£ 12 /18 holes
Credit cards	Cartes de crédit	VISA - Access

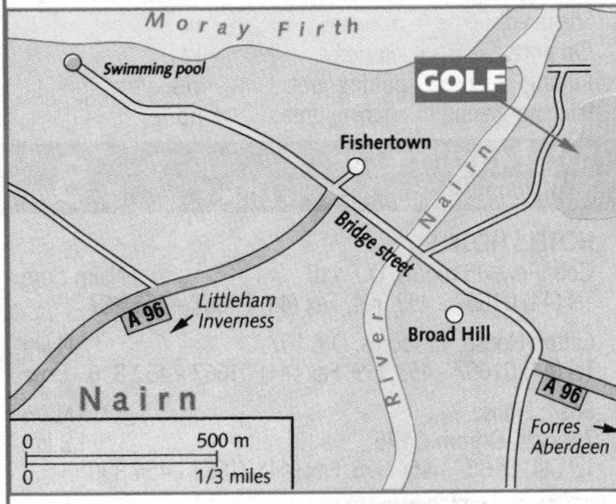

Access Accès : Inverness A96 through Nairn.
Golf at the end of town.
Map 1 on page 485 Carte 1 Page 485

Golf course PARCOURS — 15/20

Site	Site	
Maintenance	Entretien	
Architect	Architecte	Unknown
Type	Type	links
Relief	Relief	
Water in play	Eau en jeu	
Exp. to wind	Exposé au vent	
Trees in play	Arbres en jeu	

Scorecard Carte de score	**Chp.** Chp.	**Mens** Mess.	**Ladies** Da.
Length Long.	6048	5663	5164
Par	72	72	75
Slope system	—	—	—

Advised golfing ability 0 12 24 36
Niveau de jeu recommandé

Hcp required Handicap exigé no

Club house & amenities CLUB HOUSE ET ANNEXES — 7/10

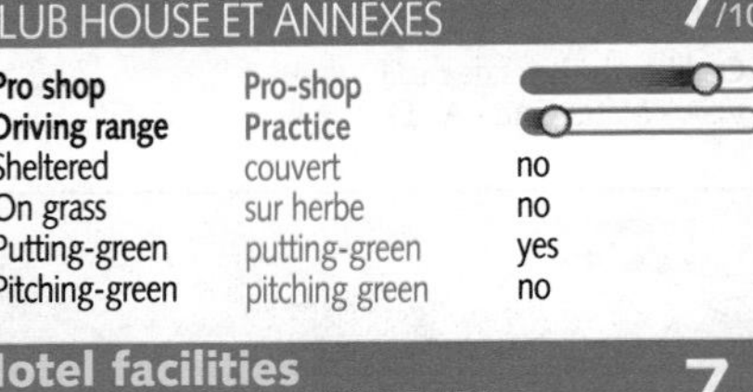

Pro shop	Pro-shop	
Driving range	Practice	
Sheltered	couvert	no
On grass	sur herbe	no
Putting-green	putting-green	yes
Pitching-green	pitching green	no

Hotel facilities ENVIRONNEMENT HOTELIER — 7/10

HOTELS HÔTELS

Golf View, 45 rooms, D £ 110 — Nairn close
Tel (44) 01667 - 452 301, Fax (44) 01667 - 455 267

Lochloy House, 8 rooms, D £ 120 — Lochloy 4 km
Tel (44) 01667 - 455 355, Fax (44) 01667 - 454 809

Claymore House — Nairn close
13 rooms, D £ 90
Tel (44) 01667 - 453 731, Fax (44) 01667 - 455 290

RESTAURANTS RESTAURANT

Longhouse, Tel (44) 01667 - 455 532 — Nairn close

Golf View, Tel (44) 01667 - 452 301 — Nairn close

NEWTONMORE

14	5	5

The neighbour to Kingussie and a good complementary course to play when spending a few days in the beautiful region of the Cairngorms. A large part of the course is laid out in the plain of the river Spey, which runs alongside several holes. The first and last two holes are on higher land with heather that is fortunately cut back, while the others run through heavier and flatter terrain generously lined with copses of conifers. Over the years, James Braid's original layout has been lengthened but this is by no means a monster. The different holes are well designed with a certain emphasis on variety, but there is nothing to get too excited about. The bottom-line is that this is a very pleasant course for holidays and the family in a magnificent setting. The club-house is not over-large but Scottish hospitality means everything here.

C'est le voisin de Kingussie, et un bon complément quand on passe quelques jours dans cette belle région des Cairngorms. Le parcours est situé en grande partie dans la plaine de la rivière Spey, qui longe plusieurs trous. Les deux premiers et deux derniers trous se trouvent plus en hauteur, en terre de bruyère assez dégagée, alors que les autres trous, en terrain plus lourd et plus plat, sont généreusement boisés de bosquets de conifères. Au fil des ans, le parcours originale de James Braid a été allongé, sans être pour autant un monstre, loin de là. Les différents trous sont bien dessinés, avec un certain souci de variété, mais les émotions restent assez limitées. En fait, il s'agit d'un très agréable parcours à faire en vacances et en famille, dans un cadre magnifique. Le Clubhouse n'est pas grand, mais l'hospitalité écossaise n'y est pas un vain mot.

Newtonmore Golf Club **1893**
Golf Course Road
SCO - NEWTONMORE, Highland PH20 1AT

Office	Secrétariat	(44) 01540 - 673 328
Pro shop	Pro-shop	(44) 01540 - 673 878
Fax	Fax	(44) 01540 - 673 878
Web	—	
Situation	Situation	

68 km S of Inverness (pop. 62 186) - 4 km S of Kingussie

Annual closure	Fermeture annuelle	no
Weekly closure	Fermeture hebdomadaire	no
Fees main season	Tarifs haute saison	18 holes

	Week days Semaine	We/Bank holidays We/Férié
Individual Individuel	£ 16	£ 18
Couple Couple	£ 32	£ 36

Caddy	Caddy	on request
Electric Trolley	Chariot électrique	no
Buggy	Voiturette	£ 14 /18 holes
Clubs	Clubs	yes
Credit cards Cartes de crédit		no

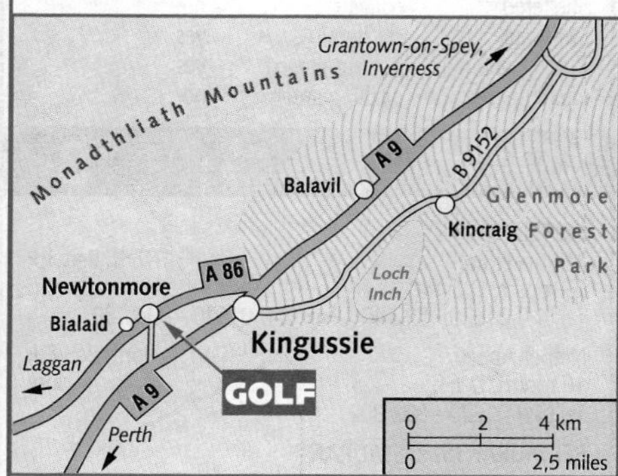

Access Accès : Inverness, A9 through Kingussie.
Golf 100 m from centre of Newtonmore
Map 1 on page 484 Carte 1 Page 484

Golf course
PARCOURS **14**/20

Site	Site	
Maintenance	Entretien	
Architect	Architecte	James Braid
Type	Type	inland
Relief	Relief	
Water in play	Eau en jeu	
Exp. to wind	Exposé au vent	
Trees in play	Arbres en jeu	

Scorecard Carte de score	Chp. Chp.	Mens Mess.	Ladies Da.
Length Long.	5487	4950	4813
Par	70	67	73
Slope system	—	—	—

Advised golfing ability 0 12 24 36
Niveau de jeu recommandé
Hcp required Handicap exigé no

Club house & amenities
CLUB HOUSE ET ANNEXES **5**/10

Pro shop	Pro-shop	
Driving range	Practice	
Sheltered	couvert	no
On grass	sur herbe	no
Putting-green	putting-green	yes
Pitching-green	pitching green	no

Hotel facilities
ENVIRONNEMENT HOTELIER **5**/10

HOTELS HÔTELS
Scot House — Kingussie
9 rooms, D £ 110 (w. dinner) — 4 km
Tel (44) 01540 - 661 351, Fax (44) 01540 - 661 111

Avondale, 6 rooms, D £ 42 — Kingussie
Tel (44) 01540 - 661 731

The Cross, 9 rooms, D £ 150 — Kingussie
Tel (44) 01540 - 661 166, Fax (44) 01540 - 661 080

Columba House, 8 rooms, D £ 75 — Kingussie
Tel (44) 01540 - 661 402, Fax (44) 01540 - 661 652

RESTAURANTS RESTAURANT
The Cross, Tel (44) 01540 - 661 166 — Kingussie

NORTH BERWICK

18 | 7 | 8

This is probably one of the courses that is closest to the origins of the game, where you start off along the beach trying to avoid passers-by who watch without a smile. It's then onto a wide strip of land with a few, reasonably high dunes, and a wall you'll have to get over one day to reach the green. Although this is flattish terrain, there are a few blind holes. North Berwick was modelled by mother nature and the sands of time, although they did need an architect (unknown) to build "Perfection (a par 4) and the famous "Redan", a diabolical and often imitated par 3. At once archaic and very modern, seemingly friendly but ferocious when the wind blows (any high ball can be disastrous), North Berwick slowly unveils its secrets which you can only discover with a good measure of patience and humility.

C'est probablement l'un des parcours les plus proches des origines, où l'on commence le long de la plage en essayant d'éviter les promeneurs qui vous regardent sans rire, on se promène ensuite dans une large bande de terrain avec quelques dunes pas trop hautes. Il y a un mur au-dessus duquel il faudra passer un jour pour atteindre le green. Il y a quelques coups aveugles bien que le terrain soit assez plat. C'est la nature et les siècles qui ont modelé North Berwick, mais il a bien fallu un architecte (inconnu) pour faire le "Perfection" (par 4) et le célèbre "Redan", par 3 diabolique souvent copié. A la fois archaïque et très moderne, apparemment aimable et sauvage quand le vent le balaie (toute balle haute provoque un désastre), North Berwick révèle lentement ses secrets. Il faut savoir les découvrir avec patience et humilité.

North Berwick Golf Club — 1832

New Club House, Beach Road
SCO - NORTH BERWICK, East Lothian, EH39 4BB

Office	Secrétariat	(44) 01620 - 892 135
Pro shop	Pro-shop	(44) 01620 - 893 233
Fax	Fax	(44) 01620 - 893 274
E-mail		nbgc_sec@compuserve.com
Situation	Situation	

37 km E of Edinburgh (pop. 418 914)

Annual closure	Fermeture annuelle	no
Weekly closure	Fermeture hebdomadaire	no
Fees main season	Tarifs haute saison	18 holes

	Week days / Semaine	We/Bank holidays / We/Férié
Individual Individuel	£ 40	£ 60
Couple Couple	£ 80	£ 120

Full days: £ 60 / £ 80 (weekends)

Caddy	Caddy	£ 25 /on request
Electric Trolley	Chariot électrique	no
Buggy	Voiturette	no
Clubs	Clubs	£ 10 /18 holes

Credit cards Cartes de crédit
VISA - MasterCard

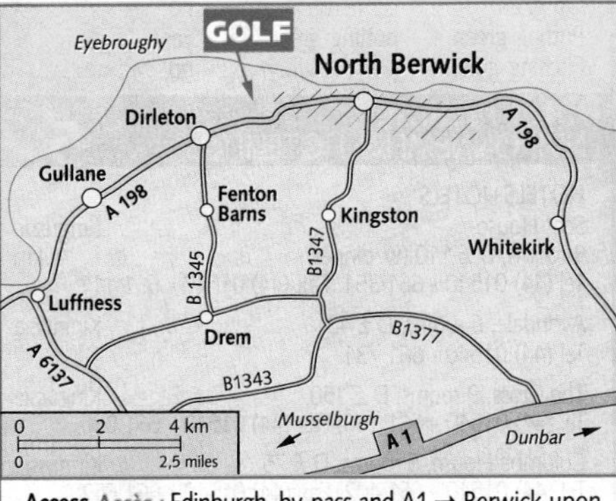

Access Accès : Edinburgh, by-pass and A1 → Berwick upon Tweed. Exit for A198, follow to North Berwick.
Map 3 on page 489 Carte 3 Page 489

Golf course / PARCOURS — 18/20

Site	Site	
Maintenance	Entretien	
Architect	Architecte	Unknown
Type	Type	links
Relief	Relief	
Water in play	Eau en jeu	
Exp. to wind	Exposé au vent	
Trees in play	Arbres en jeu	

Scorecard / Carte de score	Chp. / Chp.	Mens / Mess.	Ladies / Da.
Length Long.	5842	5490	5233
Par	71	70	74
Slope system	—	—	—

Advised golfing ability / Niveau de jeu recommandé — 0 12 24 36
Hcp required Handicap exigé — 25 Men, 35 Ladies

Club house & amenities / CLUB HOUSE ET ANNEXES — 7/10

Pro shop	Pro-shop	
Driving range	Practice	
Sheltered	couvert	no
On grass	sur herbe	yes
Putting-green	putting-green	yes
Pitching-green	pitching green	no

Hotel facilities / ENVIRONNEMENT HOTELIER — 8/10

HOTELS HÔTELS

Marine Hotel — North Berwick
79 rooms, D £ 140 — adjacent
Tel (44) 01620 - 892 406, Fax (44) 01620 - 894 480

Nether Abbey — North Berwick
16 rooms, D £ 55 — close
Tel (44) 01620 - 892 802

RESTAURANTS RESTAURANT

Marine Hotel — North Berwick
Tel (44) 01620 - 892 406 — adjacent

The Grange — North Berwick
Tel (44) 01620 - 895 894 — close

PANMURE

17	6	5

Although this course has paled somewhat in the shadow of neighbouring Carnoustie, Panmure (like the other neighbour Monifieth) does not fall far short from featuring in the same class. Anywhere else it would be very highly rated, so take advantage of your stay in the region to play it. In a rather hilly landscape, sometimes even dotted with oddly-shaped dunes, you'll have to be pretty hot with your bump and run shots, regardless of wind direction, in order to control the flight of your shots even though from first reading the card you might think that the course has nothing over-difficult to offer. The greens are extremely well protected and the putting surface is always tricky but never impossible. A classic and very forthright links to which access is restricted on weekends but where a warm welcome awaits the visitor on weekdays.

Bien qu'il ait un peu pâli du puissant voisinage de Carnoustie, il manque peu de chose à Panmure (tout comme à Monifieth, son autre voisin) pour figurer dans la même classe. Partout ailleurs, il serait hautement considéré : profitez d'être dans la région pour le découvrir. Dans un paysage assez mouvementé, parfois même orné de petites dunes de formes curieuses, il vous faudra savoir jouer les balles roulées, que le vent soit dans n'importe quel sens, pour bien contrôler vos trajectoires de balles, même si la lecture de la carte peut faire penser que les difficultés ne sont pas immenses. Les greens sont très bien défendus, leurs surfaces subtiles mais sans exagérations. Un links classique d'une grande franchise, où l'accès est limité en week-end, mais l'accueil chaleureux en semaine.

Panmure Golf Club — 1845

Barry
SCO- CARNOUSTIE, Angus DD7 7RT

Office	Secrétariat	(44) 01241 - 855 120
Pro shop	Pro-shop	(44) 01241 - 852 460
Fax	Fax	(44) 01241 - 859 737
Web	—	
Situation	Situation	

16 km E of Dundee (pop. 165 873)

Annual closure	Fermeture annuelle	no
Weekly closure	Fermeture hebdomadaire	no

Fees main season Tarifs haute saison		18 holes
	Week days Semaine	**We/Bank holidays** We/Férié
Individual Individuel	£ 35	£ 35 *
Couple Couple	£ 70	£ 70 *

* Not Saturdays - Full Weekday: £ 50

Caddy	Caddy	on request
Electric Trolley	Chariot électrique	no
Buggy	Voiturette	£ 20 /18 holes
Clubs	Clubs	yes

Credit cards Cartes de crédit
VISA - Eurocard - MasterCard - JCB

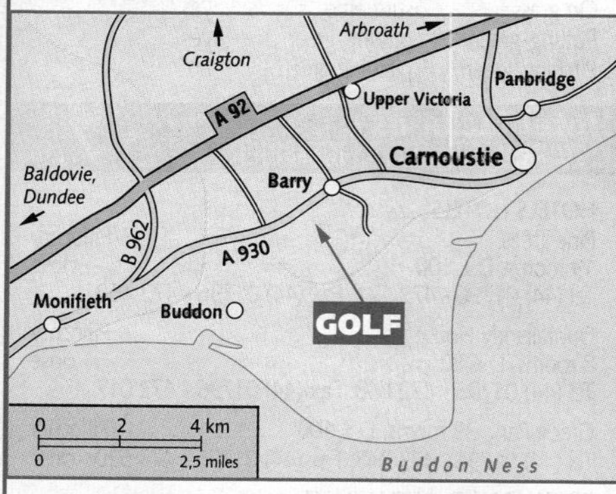

Access Accès : Dundee A930 to Barry Village. Golf 1 km
Map 2 on page 487 Carte 2 Page 487

Golf course PARCOURS — 17/20

Site	Site	
Maintenance	Entretien	
Architect	Architecte	Unknown
Type	Type	links
Relief	Relief	
Water in play	Eau en jeu	
Exp. to wind	Exposé au vent	
Trees in play	Arbres en jeu	

Scorecard Carte de score	**Chp.** Chp.	**Mens** Mess.	**Ladies** Da.
Length Long.	5925	5538	5215
Par	70	70	73
Slope system	—	—	—

Advised golfing ability 0 12 24 36
Niveau de jeu recommandé

Hcp required Handicap exigé no

Club house & amenities CLUB HOUSE ET ANNEXES — 6/10

Pro shop	Pro-shop	
Driving range	Practice	
Sheltered	couvert	1 mat
On grass	sur herbe	yes (own balls)
Putting-green	putting-green	yes
Pitching-green	pitching green	yes

Hotel facilities ENVIRONNEMENT HOTELIER — 5/10

HOTELS HÔTELS

Carnoustie Golf Hotel — Carnoustie
85 rooms, D £ 200 — 16 km
Tel (44) 01241 - 411 999, Fax (44) 01241 - 411 998

Hilton Dundee, 128 rooms, D £ 140 — Dundee
Tel (44) 01382 - 229 271, Fax (44) 01382 - 200 072 — 6 km

Kingsley, 16 rooms, D £ 35 — Arbroath
Tel (44) 01241 - 879 933 — 10 km

Broughty Ferry, 15 rooms, D £ 75 — Broughty Ferry
Tel (44) 01382 - 480 027, Fax (44) 01382 - 477 660

RESTAURANTS RESTAURANT
11 Park Avenue, Tel (44) 01241 - 853 336 Carnoustie 3 km

PITLOCHRY

14 | 6 | 7

A visit here in Winter would probably come as something as a surprise, as even at a moderate altitude, snow is not rare. This little town, one of Queen Victoria's favourite destinations, is surrounded by hills edged with pine-trees and looks it best in Summer, when nature and the course are in full bloom and the salmon are on their way up to Loch Faskally. Accommodation here is both extensive and good standard and there is even a theatre. The actual course lies on a hill above Pitlochry, and although the first few holes are something of a climb, the layout soon levels out and the view from the top of the course really is worth the effort. Slopes have been used so intelligently that you don't always notice them, and while tee-boxes and greens are frequently at the same level, you'll find a few surprises in store as you progress from one to the other. Interestingly, the bunkers here contain quartz sand.

Venir par ici en hiver pourrait bien vous surprendre. Même à une altitude modérée, il n'est pas rare d'y voir de la neige. Les collines bordées de pins entourent la petite ville, que la reine Victoria adorait. Il faut venir ici en été, quand la végétation est à sa plénitude, et que les saumons remontent le Loch Faskally. L'hébergement est ici aussi abondant que de qualité, on trouve même un théâtre. Le parcours est situé sur une colline au-dessus de Pitlochry, le début est physiquement assez difficile, mais les choses s'arrangent rapidement, et la vue du haut du parcours valait cet effort. On ne remarque pas toujours les pentes, car elles sont intelligemment utilisées, les départs et les greens sont fréquemment au même niveau, mais on peut trouver quelques surprises entre les deux. A remarquer, le sable de quartz dans les bunkers.

Pitlochry Golf Club — 1909

Golf Course Road
SCO - PITLOCHRY, TH16 5QY

Office	Secrétariat	(44) 01796 - 472 314
Pro shop	Pro-shop	(44) 01796 - 472 792
Fax	Fax	(44) 01796 - 473 599
Web	—	
Situation	Situation	

45 km N of Perth (pop. 123 495) close to Pitlochry (Pop. 3 126)

Annual closure	Fermeture annuelle	no
Weekly closure	Fermeture hebdomadaire	no

Chances of snow during winter months

Fees main season Tarifs haute saison — 18 holes

	Week days / Semaine	We/Bank holidays / We/Férié
Individual Individuel	£ 18	£ 21
Couple Couple	£ 36	£ 42

Full day: £ 26 /£ 32 (Weekends)

Caddy	Caddy	no
Electric Trolley	Chariot électrique	yes
Buggy	Voiturette	no
Clubs	Clubs	yes
Credit cards	Cartes de crédit	yes

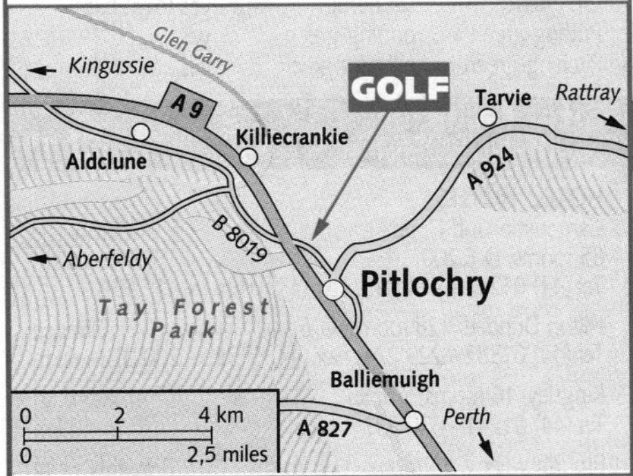

Access Accès : Edinburgh M90 then A9 to Pitlochry. Turn uphill at sign in middle of town.
Map 1 on page 485 Carte 1 Page 485

Golf course / PARCOURS — 14/20

Site	Site	
Maintenance	Entretien	
Architect	Architecte	W. Fernie
Type	Type	mountain
Relief	Relief	
Water in play	Eau en jeu	
Exp. to wind	Exposé au vent	
Trees in play	Arbres en jeu	

Scorecard / Carte de score	Chp. / Chp.	Mens / Mess.	Ladies / Da.
Length Long.	5290	5290	5290
Par	69	69	72
Slope system	—	—	—

Advised golfing ability — 0 12 24 36
Niveau de jeu recommandé
Hcp required Handicap exigé — certificate

Club house & amenities / CLUB HOUSE ET ANNEXES — 6/10

Pro shop	Pro-shop	
Driving range	Practice	
Sheltered	couvert	no
On grass	sur herbe	yes
Putting-green	putting-green	yes
Pitching-green	pitching green	no

Hotel facilities / ENVIRONNEMENT HOTELIER — 7/10

HOTELS HÔTELS

Pine Trees — Pitlochry close
19 rooms, D £ 100
Tel (44) 01796 - 472 121, Fax (44) 01796 - 472 460

Dunfallandy House — Pitlochry close
8 rooms, D £ 80
Tel (44) 01796 - 472 648, Fax (44) 01796 - 472 017

Green Park, 39 rooms, D £ 100 — Pitlochry close
Tel (44) 01796 - 473 248, Fax (44) 01796 - 473 520

RESTAURANTS RESTAURANT

East Haugh House, — Pitlochry 4 km
Tel (44) 01796 - 473 121

PORTPATRICK (DUNSKEY)

15	6	7

This course dominates the little village of Portpatrick from atop the cliffs overlooking the Irish sea, with views stretching to the distant Isle of Man, the Irish coast and the Mull of Kintyre. Although close to the ocean, this is not a dunes links, although the scrub and bushes are just as dangerous. Because of its location it is very exposed to the prevailing south-westerlies, and of course overcoming, or at least accepting, this element is essential, particularly when it comes to club selection. Make full allowance for side-winds or head-winds or any possible combination of the two. This is a pretty spot to spend a holiday, especially as the little 9-holer is ideal for beginners to cut their teeth or even for non-golfers in the family to hit a ball or two. It is also the opportunity to discover a little known region of Scotland.

Ce parcours domine le petit village de Portpatrick du haut des falaises dominant la mer d'Irlande, avec des vues dans le lointain sur l'Ile de Man, la côte irlandaise et le Mull of Kintyre. Il est proche de l'océan, mais ce n'est pas un links dans les dunes, bien que les bosquets et arbustes y jouent un rôle identique. A cause de sa situation, il est très exposé aux vents dominants de sud-ouest. Bien sûr, savoir maîtriser - ou au moins accepter - cet élément est ici une nécessité, notamment au moment du choix des clubs : prévoir large par vent contre ou latéral, ou toutes combinaisons imaginables des deux. C'est un joli endroit où passer pendant les vacances, d'autant que le petit 9-trous est idéal pour aguerrir les débutants, voire initier les non-golfeurs de la famille. C'est aussi l'occasion de découvrir une région peu connue d'Ecosse...

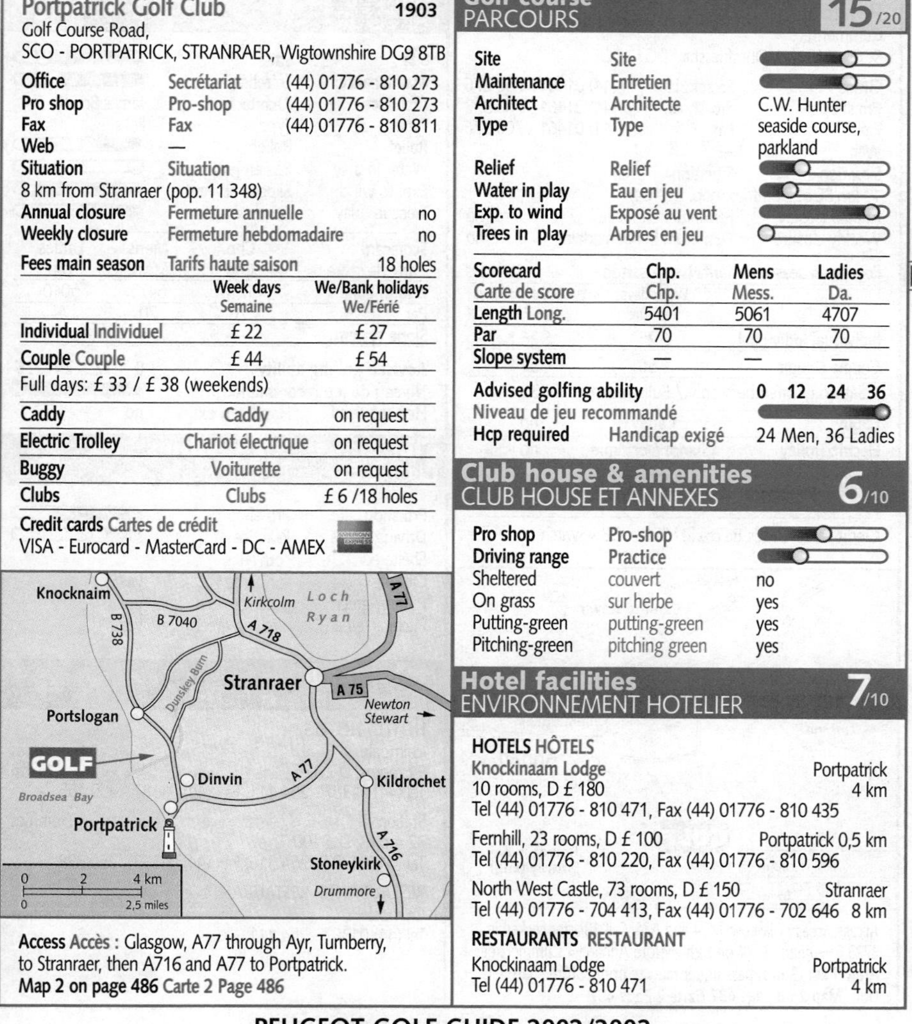

Portpatrick Golf Club **1903**
Golf Course Road,
SCO - PORTPATRICK, STRANRAER, Wigtownshire DG9 8TB

Office	Secrétariat	(44) 01776 - 810 273
Pro shop	Pro-shop	(44) 01776 - 810 273
Fax	Fax	(44) 01776 - 810 811
Web	—	
Situation	Situation	

8 km from Stranraer (pop. 11 348)

Annual closure	Fermeture annuelle	no
Weekly closure	Fermeture hebdomadaire	no

Fees main season Tarifs haute saison	18 holes	
	Week days Semaine	**We/Bank holidays** We/Férié
Individual Individuel	£ 22	£ 27
Couple Couple	£ 44	£ 54

Full days: £ 33 / £ 38 (weekends)

Caddy	Caddy	on request
Electric Trolley	Chariot électrique	on request
Buggy	Voiturette	on request
Clubs	Clubs	£ 6 /18 holes

Credit cards Cartes de crédit
VISA - Eurocard - MasterCard - DC - AMEX

Access Accès : Glasgow, A77 through Ayr, Turnberry, to Stranraer, then A716 and A77 to Portpatrick.
Map 2 on page 486 Carte 2 Page 486

Golf course PARCOURS — 15/20

Site	Site	
Maintenance	Entretien	
Architect	Architecte	C.W. Hunter
Type	Type	seaside course, parkland
Relief	Relief	
Water in play	Eau en jeu	
Exp. to wind	Exposé au vent	
Trees in play	Arbres en jeu	

Scorecard Carte de score	**Chp.** Chp.	**Mens** Mess.	**Ladies** Da.
Length Long.	5401	5061	4707
Par	70	70	70
Slope system	—	—	—

Advised golfing ability 0 12 24 36
Niveau de jeu recommandé
Hcp required Handicap exigé 24 Men, 36 Ladies

Club house & amenities CLUB HOUSE ET ANNEXES — 6/10

Pro shop	Pro-shop	
Driving range	Practice	
Sheltered	couvert	no
On grass	sur herbe	yes
Putting-green	putting-green	yes
Pitching-green	pitching green	yes

Hotel facilities ENVIRONNEMENT HOTELIER — 7/10

HOTELS HÔTELS
Knockinaam Lodge — Portpatrick 4 km
10 rooms, D £ 180
Tel (44) 01776 - 810 471, Fax (44) 01776 - 810 435

Fernhill, 23 rooms, D £ 100 — Portpatrick 0,5 km
Tel (44) 01776 - 810 220, Fax (44) 01776 - 810 596

North West Castle, 73 rooms, D £ 150 — Stranraer 8 km
Tel (44) 01776 - 704 413, Fax (44) 01776 - 702 646

RESTAURANTS RESTAURANT
Knockinaam Lodge — Portpatrick 4 km
Tel (44) 01776 - 810 471

POWFOOT

16 | 6 | 4

It has often been said that the finest turf in the world is to be found close to Solway Firth. Whatever, the grass at Powfoot does nothing to undermine that claim. And although the course is not specifically a links, the type of soil here means you play it as if it were. There is a lot of gorse to worry wayward hitters, although the fairways are wide enough for players to open their shoulders, as long as the wind behaves itself. Mid- and high-handicappers can rest assured: this is a friendly layout and they shouldn't be over-awed by the one or two blind shots. The surprises in store from off-target shots are more often pleasant than unpleasant. The better players will need to think harder to keep the ball straight and avoid the very many bunkers, which were laid out by James Braid. Need we say more? Excellent golfing.

On a souvent dit que l'on trouvait les meilleurs gazons du monde près du Solway Firth. Celui de Powfoot prouve en tout cas que ce n'est pas faux. Et bien que le parcours ne soit pas spécifiquement un links, la nature du sol fait qu'on le joue comme tel. Les ajoncs sont ici abondants pour inquiéter les joueurs imprécis, mais les fairways sont assez larges pour qu'ils oublient leurs craintes, tant que le vent ne souffle pas trop... Que les joueurs de handicap moyen ou élevé se rassurent, c'est un tracé des plus amicaux, et les quelques coups aveugles ne devraient pas trop les préoccuper : ils auront plus de bonnes surprises que de mauvaises avec leurs écarts imprévus ! Les meilleurs joueurs devront réfléchir davantage à garder la balle assez droite, à éviter les nombreux bunkers : James Braid les a disposés, il n'est pas nécessaire d'en dire plus. Une halte de qualité.

Powfoot Golf Club — 1903

Cummertrees
SCO - ANNAN, Dumfriesshire DG12 5QE

Office	Secrétariat	(44) 01461 - 700 276
Pro shop	Pro-shop	(44) 01461 - 700 327
Fax	Fax	(44) 01461 - 700 276
Web	—	
Situation	Situation	

19 km SE of Dumfries (pop. 21 164)

Annual closure	Fermeture annuelle	no
Weekly closure	Fermeture hebdomadaire	no

Fees main season Tarifs haute saison	18 holes	
	Week days Semaine	**We/Bank holidays** We/Férié
Individual Individuel	£ 25	£ 26 *
Couple Couple	£ 50	£ 52 *

* Saturday: members only / Full weekday: £ 32

Caddy	Caddy	no
Electric Trolley	Chariot électrique	no
Buggy	Voiturette	no
Clubs	Clubs	no

Credit cards Cartes de crédit VISA - JCB - Switch

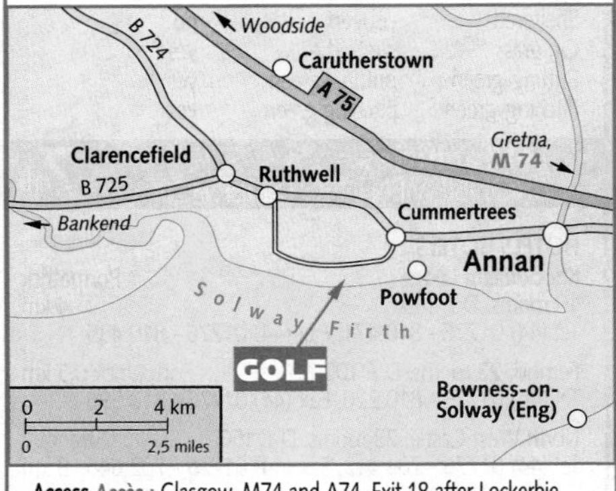

Access Accès : Glasgow, M74 and A74. Exit 18 after Lockerbie, B723 → Annan. B724 on right before Annan → Cummertrees. After 5 km (3 m.), pass under railway bridge, turn sharp left → Golf. **Map 2 on page 487** Carte 2 Page 487

Golf course PARCOURS — 16/20

Site	Site	
Maintenance	Entretien	
Architect	Architecte	James Braid
Type	Type	links
Relief	Relief	
Water in play	Eau en jeu	
Exp. to wind	Exposé au vent	
Trees in play	Arbres en jeu	

Scorecard Carte de score	**Chp.** Chp.	**Mens** Mess.	**Ladies** Da.
Length Long.	5710	5475	5010
Par	70	70	74
Slope system	—	—	—

Advised golfing ability Niveau de jeu recommandé: 0 12 24 36

Hcp required Handicap exigé: no

Club house & amenities CLUB HOUSE ET ANNEXES — 6/10

Pro shop	Pro-shop	
Driving range	Practice	
Sheltered	couvert	
On grass	sur herbe	yes
Putting-green	putting-green	yes
Pitching-green	pitching green	yes

Hotel facilities ENVIRONNEMENT HOTELIER — 4/10

HOTELS HÔTELS

Cairndale — Dumfries 15 km
91 rooms, D £ 125
Tel (44) 01387 - 254 111, Fax (44) 01387 - 250 155

Station — Dumfries
32 rooms, D £ 100
Tel (44) 01387 - 254 316, Fax (44) 01387 - 250 388

RESTAURANTS RESTAURANT

Cairndale — Dumfries
Tel (44) 01387 - 254 111

PRESTWICK

18 | 6 | 7

This was the first course used for the British Open but was withdrawn from the course rotation in 1925 for being too short and perhaps, too, for a number of eccentric features such as the blind par-3 fifth hole or the second shot on the 17th, where the green is nowhere to be seen. But no lover of authentic golf will miss playing this delightful and one-of-a-kind links course which is kept in excellent condition. Like many courses in Scotland, it unwinds between a railway track and the sea. It has been lengthened since the days when there were only twelve holes but this has added to the course's variety if not its unity. The bunkers here are particularly tough, especially the famous Cardinal, which cuts hole N°3 in two. Prestwick thrives on hospitality (on week-days) and memories of the past that you can't and won't miss in the clubhouse.

Ce fut le premier parcours du British Open, mais il fut retiré de la rotation des parcours en 1925, pour sa longueur insuffisante, mais peut-être aussi quelques aspects excentriques comme le 5, un par 3 aveugle, ou le second coup du 17, où le green n'est pas plus visible. Mais aucun amoureux de golfeur uthentique ne manquera de jouer ce links savoureux et unique en son genre, où l'entretien est d'excellente qualité. Comme beaucoup de parcours en Ecosse, il se déroule entre la voie ferrée et la mer. Il a été allongé depuis l'époque où il ne comptait que 12 trous, mais cela a contribué à ajouter à sa variété, sinon à son unité. Les bunkers ici sont particulièrement féroces, notamment le fameux Cardinal, qui coupe le 3 en deux parties. Prestwick cultive l'hospitalité (en semaine) et les souvenirs des temps passés, que vous ne manquerez pas au Club house.

Prestwick Golf Club — 1851

2 Links Road
SCO - PRESTWICK, Ayrshire KA9 1QG

Office	Secrétariat	(44) 01292 - 477 404
Pro shop	Pro-shop	(44) 01292 - 479 483
Fax	Fax	(44) 01292 - 477 255
Web	—	
Situation	Situation	

4 km N of Ayr - 50 km SW of Glasgow (pop. 662 853)

Annual closure	Fermeture annuelle	no
Weekly closure	Fermeture hebdomadaire	no

Fees main season Tarifs haute saison	18 holes	
	Week days Semaine	**We/Bank holidays** We/Férié
Individual Individuel	£ 80	*
Couple Couple	£ 160	*

* No visitors at week ends / Full Weekdays: £ 120

Caddy	Caddy	on request
Electric Trolley	Chariot électrique	yes
Buggy	Voiturette	no
Clubs	Clubs	yes

Credit cards Cartes de crédit
(Pro shop) VISA - MasterCard - AMEX

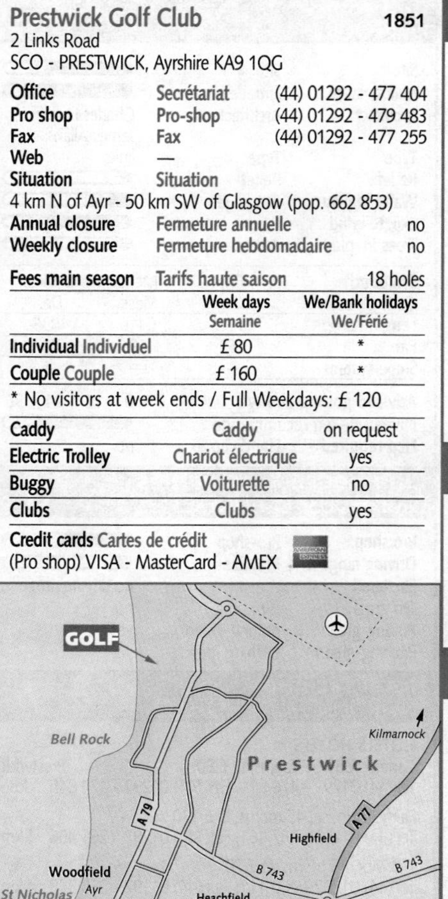

Access Accès : A77, take road to Prestwick, Golf adjacent to railway station
Map 3 on page 488 Carte 3 Page 488

Golf course — PARCOURS — 18/20

Site	Site	
Maintenance	Entretien	
Architect	Architecte	Unknown
Type	Type	links
Relief	Relief	
Water in play	Eau en jeu	
Exp. to wind	Exposé au vent	
Trees in play	Arbres en jeu	

Scorecard Carte de score	**Chp.** Chp.	**Mens** Mess.	**Ladies** Da.
Length Long.	6068	6068	—
Par	72	72	—
Slope system	—	—	—

Advised golfing ability 0 12 24 36
Niveau de jeu recommandé
Hcp required Handicap exigé certificate

Club house & amenities — CLUB HOUSE ET ANNEXES — 6/10

Pro shop	Pro-shop	
Driving range	Practice	
Sheltered	couvert	no
On grass	sur herbe	yes
Putting-green	putting-green	yes
Pitching-green	pitching green	yes

Hotel facilities — ENVIRONNEMENT HOTELIER — 7/10

HOTELS HÔTELS

Parkstone, 22 rooms, D £ 75 — Prestwick
Tel (44) 01292 - 477 286, Fax (44) 01292 - 477 671 — close

Fairfield House, 45 rooms, D £ 130 — Ayr
Tel (44) 01292 - 267 461, Fax (44) 01292 - 261 456 — 4 km

Kylestrome, 12 rooms, D £ 70 — Ayr
Tel (44) 01292 - 262 474, Fax (44) 01292 - 260 863 — 3 km

RESTAURANTS RESTAURANT

Fouters, Tel (44) 01292 - 261 391 — Ayr 4 km

The Ivy House, Tel (44) 01655 - 442 336 — Alloway 8 km

PRESTWICK ST NICHOLAS 16 | 6 | 7

The reputation of the other Prestwick course has doubtless helped keep this course out of the limelight. That might be so with non-Scots, but the local players know that this is not just another course but one that should be included when making an intelligent and exhaustive survey of good courses in Ayrshire. This is a genuine typical Scottish links laid out between the sea and a railway line, both of which come into play depending on where the wind is blowing from. While some of the natural bunkers can keep you out of the wind, you'll have to get out of them sooner or later to affront the tricky slopes of the huge greens, which are often firm and slick. With difficulties spread evenly over the 18 holes, don't put too much faith in the lengths written on the card. You can certainly play to your handicap here, but it's no walk-over either.

La réputation de l'autre Prestwick a sans doute maintenu celui-ci dans une certaine obscurité, au moins auprès des étrangers car les joueurs de la région savent qu'il ne s'agit pas là d'un parcours indifférent, à inclure dans une exploration intelligente et exhaustive des bons parcours de l'Ayrshire. Il s'agit là d'un vrai et typique "Scottish links," situé entre la mer et le chemin de fer, qui viennent tous deux en jeu selon que le vent souffle d'un côté ou de l'autre. Et si certains bunkers naturels vous fourniront un abri, il faudra pourtant bien en sortir un jour pour affronter les subtils reliefs de greens vastes, souvent fermes et bien roulants. Avec des difficultés bien réparties tout au long des 18 trous, il ne faut pas se fier aux longueurs inscrites sur la carte. Certes, on peut jouer ici son handicap, mais ce n'est pas donné d'avance.

Prestwick St Nicholas Golf Club 1892

Grangemuir Road
SCO - PRESTWICK, Ayrshire KA9 1SN

Office	Secrétariat	(44) 01292 - 477 608
Pro shop	Pro-shop	(44) 01292 - 473 904
Fax	Fax	(44) 01292 - 473 900
Web	—	
Situation	Situation	

3 km N of Ayr - 51 km SW of Glasgow (pop. 662 853)

Annual closure	Fermeture annuelle	no
Weekly closure	Fermeture hebdomadaire	no

Fees main season Tarifs haute saison	18 holes	
	Week days Semaine	**We/Bank holidays** We/Férié
Individual Individuel	£ 30.50	£ 35.50 *
Couple Couple	£ 61	£ 71 *

Full weekdays: £ 50.50 / * Visitors at weekends: Sunday pm only

Caddy	Caddy	on request
Electric Trolley	Chariot électrique	no
Buggy	Voiturette	no
Clubs	Clubs	yes
Credit cards	Cartes de crédit	yes

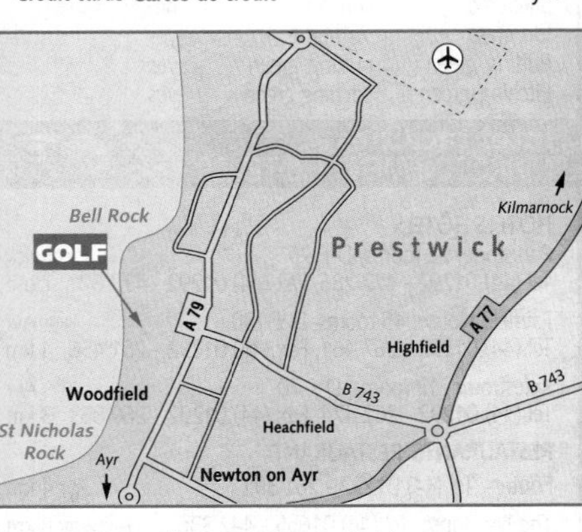

Access Accès : Glasgow, A77 to Prestwick
Map 3 on page 488 Carte 3 Page 488

Golf course PARCOURS 16/20

Site	Site	
Maintenance	Entretien	
Architect	Architecte	Charles Hunter James Allan
Type	Type	links
Relief	Relief	
Water in play	Eau en jeu	
Exp. to wind	Exposé au vent	
Trees in play	Arbres en jeu	

Scorecard Carte de score	**Chp.** Chp.	**Mens** Mess.	**Ladies** Da.
Length Long.	5416	5416	4836
Par	69	69	70
Slope system	—	—	—

Advised golfing ability Niveau de jeu recommandé: 0 12 24 36
Hcp required Handicap exigé: no

Club house & amenities CLUB HOUSE ET ANNEXES 6/10

Pro shop	Pro-shop	
Driving range	Practice	
Sheltered	couvert	no driving range
On grass	sur herbe	no
Putting-green	putting-green	yes
Pitching-green	pitching green	yes

Hotel facilities ENVIRONNEMENT HOTELIER 7/10

HOTELS HÔTELS

Carlton Toby, 37 rooms, D £ 80 — Prestwick
Tel (44) 01292 - 476 811, Fax (44) 01292 - 474 845 — close

Fairfield House, 45 rooms, D £ 130 — Ayr
Tel (44) 01292 - 267 461, Fax (44) 01292 - 261 456 — 4 km

Pickwick, 15 rooms, D £ 70 — Ayr
Tel (44) 01292 - 260 111, Fax (44) 01292 - 285 348 — 4 km

RESTAURANTS RESTAURANT

Fouters — Ayr
Tel (44) 01292 - 261 391 — 4 km

ROXBURGHE (THE)

15 | 7 | 7

The Duke and Duchess of Roxburghe were personally involved in the decoration and style of the Roxburghe Hotel and everyone should visit their "home sweet home", i.e. the hundreds of rooms in the Floors Castle. Fishing, clay pigeon-shooting, riding and tennis are some of the activities on offer on this estate located very close to the English border, plus an 18-hole course designed by Dave Thomas alongside a river, following the natural relief of the estate and alternating stretches in the forest and the attractive park (the course is not always easy to walk). Modern in style with many different hazards, it demands target golf more than your usual bump and run shots. A high-class location for a sporting holiday in very pretty countryside. Excellent practice for your game.

Le Duc et la Duchesse de Roxburghe ont mis eux-même la main à la décoration et au style de l'hôtel Roxburghe, et l'on ne manquera pas de visiter leur "sweet home", c'est-à-dire les centaines de pièces du Floors Castle. Pêche, tir au pigeon d'argile, équitation et tennis sont quelques-unes des activités proposées dans ce domaine tout proche de la frontière avec l'Angleterre, auxquelles s'ajoute un 18 trous dessiné par Dave Thomas en bordure de rivière. Il suit les reliefs naturels du domaine et alterne passages en forêt et esthétique de parc (le parcours n'est pas toujours facile à marcher). De style moderne, avec de multiples obstacles, exigeant un jeu de cible plus que des coups roulés, c'est un lieu de vacances sportives de très bonne facture, dans un très joli paysage. Très beau practice, ce qui n'est pas si fréquent en Ecosse !

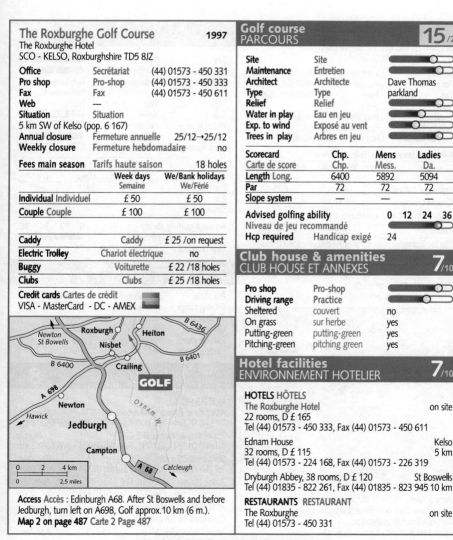

The Roxburghe Golf Course — 1997

The Roxburghe Hotel
SCO - KELSO, Roxburghshire TD5 8JZ

Office	Secrétariat	(44) 01573 - 450 331
Pro shop	Pro-shop	(44) 01573 - 450 333
Fax	Fax	(44) 01573 - 450 611
Web	—	
Situation	Situation	

5 km SW of Kelso (pop. 6 167)

Annual closure	Fermeture annuelle	25/12→25/12
Weekly closure	Fermeture hebdomadaire	no

Fees main season Tarifs haute saison	18 holes	
	Week days Semaine	**We/Bank holidays** We/Férié
Individual Individuel	£ 50	£ 50
Couple Couple	£ 100	£ 100

Caddy	Caddy	£ 25 /on request
Electric Trolley	Chariot électrique	no
Buggy	Voiturette	£ 22 /18 holes
Clubs	Clubs	£ 25 /18 holes

Credit cards Cartes de crédit
VISA - MasterCard - DC - AMEX

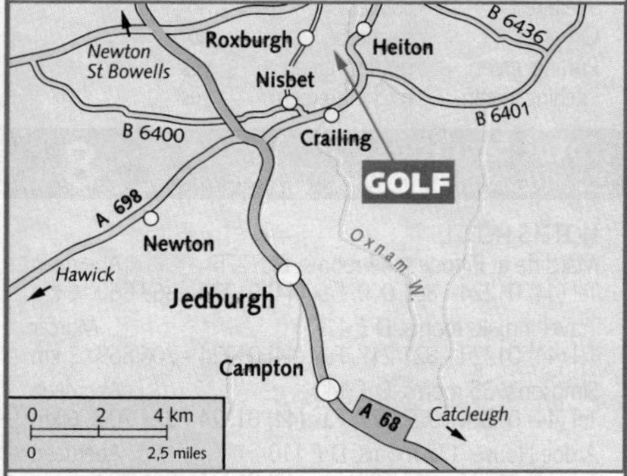

Newton St Bowells
Roxburgh
Heiton
Nisbet
B 6436
B 6401
B 6400
Crailing
GOLF
A 698
Newton
Hawick
Jedburgh
Oxnam W.
Campton
A 68
Catcleugh
0 2 4 km
0 2,5 miles

Access Accès : Edinburgh A68. After St Boswells and before Jedburgh, turn left on A698, Golf approx.10 km (6 m.).
Map 2 on page 487 Carte 2 Page 487

Golf course PARCOURS — 15/20

Site	Site	
Maintenance	Entretien	
Architect	Architecte	Dave Thomas
Type	Type	parkland
Relief	Relief	
Water in play	Eau en jeu	
Exp. to wind	Exposé au vent	
Trees in play	Arbres en jeu	

Scorecard Carte de score	**Chp.** Chp.	**Mens** Mess.	**Ladies** Da.
Length Long.	6400	5892	5094
Par	72	72	72
Slope system	—	—	—

Advised golfing ability 0 12 24 36
Niveau de jeu recommandé
Hcp required Handicap exigé 24

Club house & amenities CLUB HOUSE ET ANNEXES — 7/10

Pro shop	Pro-shop	
Driving range	Practice	
Sheltered	couvert	no
On grass	sur herbe	yes
Putting-green	putting-green	yes
Pitching-green	pitching green	yes

Hotel facilities ENVIRONNEMENT HOTELIER — 7/10

HOTELS HÔTELS
The Roxburghe Hotel — on site
22 rooms, D £ 165
Tel (44) 01573 - 450 333, Fax (44) 01573 - 450 611

Ednam House — Kelso 5 km
32 rooms, D £ 115
Tel (44) 01573 - 224 168, Fax (44) 01573 - 226 319

Dryburgh Abbey, 38 rooms, D £ 120 — St Boswells 10 km
Tel (44) 01835 - 822 261, Fax (44) 01835 - 823 945

RESTAURANTS RESTAURANT
The Roxburghe — on site
Tel (44) 01573 - 450 331

ROYAL ABERDEEN Balgownie Links

18 | 7 | 8

A page of golf was written here, less than 2 miles from the "city of granite". Royal Aberdeen originated in 1780, was the world's sixth golf club and the first to adopt the 5-minute rule when looking for your ball. You probably won't lose yours as long as you play "Balgownie" (its more familiar name) carefully, avoid the bushes and tall grass and, in a word, stay in the fairway. You'll probably have a tougher time distinguishing the fairways amongst the dunes, keeping a solid swing when the wind blows a little too hard, or remembering to turn around at the 9th, as the holes that continue belong to Murcar. A little off the beaten golf-trotter track, this is one of the great classics for every links-collector, fun to play every time.

A seulement 3 km de la "ville de granit" s'est tournée une page du golf : le Royal Aberdeen trouve ses origines en 1780, c'est le sixième club du monde et le premier à avoir adopté la règle de cinq minutes pour chercher une balle. Mais on ne risque pas trop d'en perdre si l'on joue sagement "Balgownie" (comme on le connaît mieux), en évitant les buissons et les hautes herbes. Bref si l'on ne quitte pas le fairway. On perdra davantage la tête à repérer certains fairways parmi les dunes, à garder un swing solide quand le vent souffle un peu trop fort, ou si l'on oublie de revenir en arrière au 9 : les trous qui suivent appartiennent à Murcar. Un peu en dehors des sentiers touristiques du golf, c'est un des grands classiques quand on fait collection de links. Et c'est toujours un plaisir d'y revenir.

Royal Aberdeen Golf Club — 1888

Balgownie, Links Road, Bridge of Don
SCO- ABERDEEN AB23 8AT

Office	Secrétariat	(44) 01224 - 702 571
Pro shop	Pro-shop	(44) 01224 - 702 221
Fax	Fax	(44) 01224 - 826 591
Web	—	
Situation	Situation	3 km from Aberdeen
Annual closure	Fermeture annuelle	no
Weekly closure	Fermeture hebdomadaire	no

Fees main season Tarifs haute saison	Week days Semaine	We/Bank holidays We/Férié
		18 holes
Individual Individuel	£ 65	£ 75 *
Couple Couple	£ 130	£ 150 *

* after 15.30 / Full weekdays: £ 90

Caddy	Caddy	on request
Electric Trolley	Chariot électrique	£ 6 /18 holes
Buggy	Voiturette	no
Clubs	Clubs	£ 10 /18 holes

Credit cards Cartes de crédit
VISA - Eurocard - MasterCard - JCB

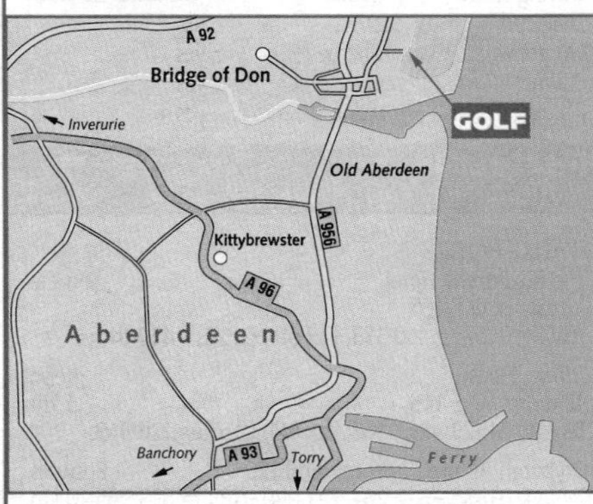

Access Accès : 3 km N of Aberdeen on A92. Cross River Don, on right at first traffic lights, on Links Road to golf course.
Map 1 on page 485 Carte 1 Page 485

Golf course PARCOURS — 18/20

Site	Site	
Maintenance	Entretien	
Architect	Architecte	Bob Simpson James Braid
Type	Type	links
Relief	Relief	
Water in play	Eau en jeu	
Exp. to wind	Exposé au vent	
Trees in play	Arbres en jeu	

Scorecard Carte de score	Chp. Chp.	Mens Mess.	Ladies Da.
Length Long.	5915	5915	—
Par	70	70	—
Slope system	—	—	—

Advised golfing ability Niveau de jeu recommandé: 0 12 24 36
Hcp required Handicap exigé: 24

Club house & amenities CLUB HOUSE ET ANNEXES — 7/10

Pro shop	Pro-shop	
Driving range	Practice	
Sheltered	couvert	no
On grass	sur herbe	no
Putting-green	putting-green	yes
Pitching-green	pitching green	yes

Hotel facilities ENVIRONNEMENT HOTELIER — 8/10

HOTELS HÔTELS

Marcliffe at Piffodels, 42 rooms, D £ 275 — Aberdeen
Tel (44) 01224 - 861 000, Fax (44) 01224 - 868 860 — 6 km

Travel Inn, 40 rooms, D £ 41 — Murcar
Tel (44) 01224 - 821 217, Fax (44) 01224 - 706 869 — 3 km

Simpson's, 35 rooms, D £ 140 — Aberdeen
Tel (44) 01224 - 327 777, Fax (44) 01224 - 327 700 — 6 km

Ardoe House, 112 rooms, D £ 110 — Aberdeen
Tel (44) 01224 - 860 600, Fax (44) 01224 - 861 283 — 5 km

RESTAURANTS RESTAURANT

Courtyard on the Lane, Tel (44) 01224 - 213 795 — Aberdeen
Silver Darling, Tel (44) 01224 - 576 229 — Aberdeen

ROYAL BURGESS

16 | 7 | 9

This club was formed in 1735 and played the Brunstfield Links behind Edinburgh Castle. Today it lies adjoined to the Brunstfield Club (whose history runs parallel to this club) in the north-west of the city in magnificently laid out park landscape. The work of Old Tom Morris and then James Braid, this course has its own very personal character with alternating old trees and young saplings standing alone or in clumps. Accuracy is recommended, needless to say, as for many golfers this is a "second-shot" course where you have to be so efficient to hit the greens or save your score when you miss them. The putting surfaces are such a pleasure to play that sometimes you would like to putt a little more often. Well worth knowing, but not easy to reach.

Ce club a été formé en 1735, et aurait eu comme parcours les Bruntsfield Links derrière le Château d'Edinburgh. Toujours est-il qu'il est aujourd'hui mitoyen au Club de Bruntsfield (dont l'histoire est parallèle), au nord-ouest de la ville, et dans un paysage de parc magnifiquement sculpté. Dû aux crayons bien connus de Old Tom Morris, puis de James Braid, ce parcours possède un caractère très personnel, avec son alternance d'arbres anciens et de jeunes pousses, solitaires ou en bosquets. Inutile de dire que la précision est recommandée, car c'est pour beaucoup un parcours "de seconds coups," tant il faut être efficace pour rejoindre les greens, et pour sauver le score quand on les a manqués. Les surfaces de putting sont d'ailleurs un tel régal que l'on aimerait devoir faire plein de putts ! A connaître, mais l'accès n'y est pas facile.

Royal Burgess Golfing Society of Edinburgh — 1894

181 Whitehouse Road, Barnton
SCO - EDINBURGH EH4 6BY

Office	Secrétariat	(44) 0131 - 339 2075
Pro shop	Pro-shop	(44) 0131 - 339 6474
Fax	Fax	(44) 0131 - 339 3712
Web	—	
Situation	Situation	Edinburgh, 5 km
Annual closure	Fermeture annuelle	no
Weekly closure	Fermeture hebdomadaire	no

Fees main season Tarifs haute saison	18 holes	
	Week days Semaine	**We/Bank holidays** We/Férié
Individual Individuel	£ 42	*
Couple Couple	£ 84	*

* Weekends: members only
Restrictions for Ladies (ask before)

Caddy	Caddy	on request
Electric Trolley	Chariot électrique	yes
Buggy	Voiturette	no
Clubs	Clubs	yes
Credit cards	Cartes de crédit	yes

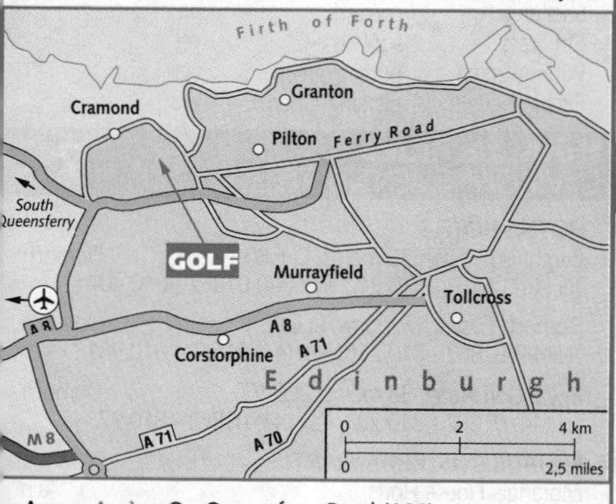

Access Accès : On Queensferry Road (A90).
Turn right at Barnton roundabout on Whitehouse Road.
Map 3 on page 489 Carte 3 Page 489

Golf course — PARCOURS — 16/20

Site	Site	
Maintenance	Entretien	
Architect	Architecte	Tom Morris James Braid
Type	Type	parkland
Relief	Relief	
Water in play	Eau en jeu	
Exp. to wind	Exposé au vent	
Trees in play	Arbres en jeu	

Scorecard Carte de score	**Chp.** Chp.	**Mens** Mess.	**Ladies** Da.
Length Long.	5838	5500	—
Par	71	71	—
Slope system	—	—	—

Advised golfing ability Niveau de jeu recommandé: 0 12 24 36
Hcp required Handicap exigé: 24

Club house & amenities — CLUB HOUSE ET ANNEXES — 7/10

Pro shop	Pro-shop	
Driving range	Practice	
Sheltered	couvert	no
On grass	sur herbe	yes
Putting-green	putting-green	yes
Pitching-green	pitching green	no

Hotel facilities — ENVIRONNEMENT HOTELIER — 9/10

HOTELS HÔTELS

The Howard, 15 rooms, D £ 250 — Edinburgh 5 km
Tel (44) 0131 - 557 3500, Fax (44) 0131 - 557 6515

The Roxburghe, 196 rooms, D £ 180 — Edinburgh
Tel (44) 0131 - 240 5500, Fax (44) 0131 - 240 5555

Lodge, 10 rooms, D £ 120 — Edinburgh
Tel (44) 0131 - 337 3682, Fax (44) 0131 - 313 1700

RESTAURANTS RESTAURANT

The Melrose (Roxburghe) — Edinburgh
Tel (44) 0131 - 240 5500

Atrium, Tel (44) 0131 - 228 8882 — Edinburgh

ROYAL DORNOCH Championship 19 7 7

Golf has been played here since about 1616, but it was Old Tom Morris and particularly the admirable Donald Ross who had the honour of really designing the course before John Sutherland added the final gloss. For untamed natural beauty and the challenge it offers any player, Royal Dornoch is one of the world's greatest courses. Located away from any large towns, this is a haven of peace and tranquillity in a unique atmosphere where you can chew long and hard over your technical flaws and the philosophy of golf. In fact it is only this isolation that has kept this gem of a course from being on the British Open rotation. In July you might often see some of the top champions who come here to re-acclimatise themselves to links golfing, the beginning and the end for every true golfer. Two of the greatest fans of Dornoch and none other than Tom Watson and Ben Crenshaw.

Le golf a été pratiqué sur le site depuis 1616 environ, mais ce fut à Old Tom Morris et surtout à l'admirable Donald Ross que revinrent l'honneur de dessiner vraiment le parcours, plus tard peaufiné par John Sutherland. Pour sa beauté sauvage et naturelle, pour les défis qu'il présente aux joueurs, Royal Dornoch est un des plus grands parcours au monde. Situé à l'écart des grandes villes, c'est un havre de paix à l'atmosphère unique où l'on peut méditer sur ses faiblesses techniques et la philosophie du jeu, et seul cet isolement a pu empêcher cette merveille d'être l'un des parcours du British Open. En juillet, il n'est pas rare d'y croiser de grands champions, venus se réacclimater au jeu sur les links, l'alpha et l'oméga du vrai golfeur. Tom Watson et Ben Crenshaw notamment n'ont pas été les moins élogieux sur "Dornoch."

Royal Dornoch Golf Club — 1877

Golf Road
SCO - DORNOCH, Sutherland IV25 3LW

Office	Secrétariat	(44) 01862 - 810 219
Pro shop	Pro-shop	(44) 01862 - 810 902
Fax	Fax	(44) 01862 - 810 792
Web	www.royaldornoch.com	
Situation	Situation	

72 km N of Inverness (pop. 62 186)

Annual closure	Fermeture annuelle	no
Weekly closure	Fermeture hebdomadaire	no

Fees main season Tarifs haute saison — 18 holes

	Week days / Semaine	We/Bank holidays / We/Férié
Individual Individuel	£ 55	£ 65
Couple Couple	£ 110	£ 130

GF £ 60 for Championship + Struie courses

Caddy	Caddy	£ 30 /on request
Electric Trolley	Chariot électrique	£ 5 /18 holes
Buggy	Voiturette	£ 20 /18 holes
Clubs	Clubs	£ 15 /18 holes

Credit cards Cartes de crédit VISA - MasterCard

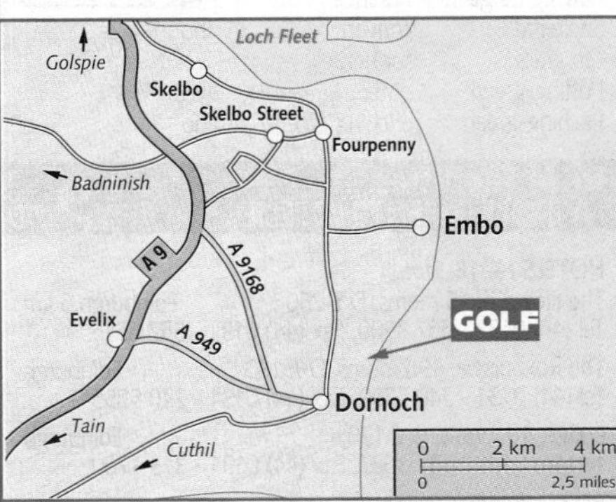

Access Accès : Inverness A9 North → Wick.
Golf on A949 to the east of the town.
Map 1 on page 484 Carte 1 Page 484

Golf course PARCOURS — 19/20

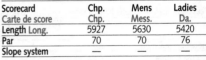

Site	Site	
Maintenance	Entretien	
Architect	Architecte	Old Tom Morris Donald Ross
Type	Type	links
Relief	Relief	
Water in play	Eau en jeu	
Exp. to wind	Exposé au vent	
Trees in play	Arbres en jeu	

Scorecard / Carte de score	Chp. / Chp.	Mens / Mess.	Ladies / Da.
Length Long.	5927	5630	5420
Par	70	70	76
Slope system	—	—	—

Advised golfing ability Niveau de jeu recommandé — 0 12 24 36
Hcp required Handicap exigé — 24 Men, 39 Ladies

Club house & amenities CLUB HOUSE ET ANNEXES — 7/10

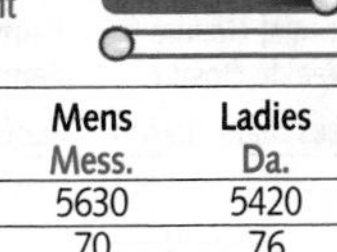

Pro shop	Pro-shop	
Driving range	Practice	
Sheltered	couvert	no
On grass	sur herbe	yes
Putting-green	putting-green	yes
Pitching-green	pitching green	yes

Hotel facilities ENVIRONNEMENT HOTELIER — 7/10

HOTELS HÔTELS

Burghfield House, 30 rooms, D £ 80 — Dornoch
Tel (44) 01862 - 810 212, Fax (44) 01862 - 810 404

Dornoch Castle, 17 rooms, D £ 80 — Dornoch
Tel (44) 01862 - 810 216, Fax (44) 01862 - 810 981

Royal Golf Hotel, 33 rooms, D £ 150 — Dornoch
Tel (44) 01862 - 810 283, Fax (44) 01862 - 810 923

RESTAURANTS RESTAURANT

Morangie House Hotel, — Tain
Tel (44) 01862 - 892 281 — 10 km

2 Quail, Tel (44) 01862 - 811 811 — Dornoch

ROYAL MUSSELBURGH

16 | 8 | 7

The club was founded in 1774 but we imagine that golf was played at the Old Musselburgh long before that. That course still exists but its original tenants left on one side to form the Muirfield club and on the other to open this course in 1925. This is not a links but a park course laid out around a majestic barony used as the clubhouse. James Braid designed the first layout, but in 1939 the Club asked Mungo park to give it a thorough overhaul. The very many trees form impressive lines of defence completed by some very effective bunkering to swallow any wayward shot. This is not a long course but there is only one par 5, something that generally speaking bothers the long-hitters on the look-out for "easy" birdies. This well-balanced course is a pleasant alternative when you have had enough of wind howling over the dunes.

Le Club a été fondé en 1774, mais on présume que le "Old Musselburgh" avait vu jouer au golf bien avant. Il existe toujours mais ses premiers locataires sont partis d'un côté créer Muirfield, et de l'autre celui-ci, en 1925. Il ne s'agit pas d'un links, mais d'un golf de parc, autour d'une majestueuse baronnie utilisée comme Club-house. James Braid créa le premier tracé, mais le Club demanda en 1939 à Mungo Park de le réviser sérieusement. Les nombreux arbres forment des défenses imposantes, complétées par un bunkering très efficace pour recueillir les coups un peu égarés. Ce n'est pas un parcours bien long, mais il n'a qu'un seul par 5, ce qui gêne en général beaucoup les frappeurs en quête de birdies faciles. Bien équilibré, c'est une bonne alternative quand on est un peu saoûlé par le vent dans les dunes.

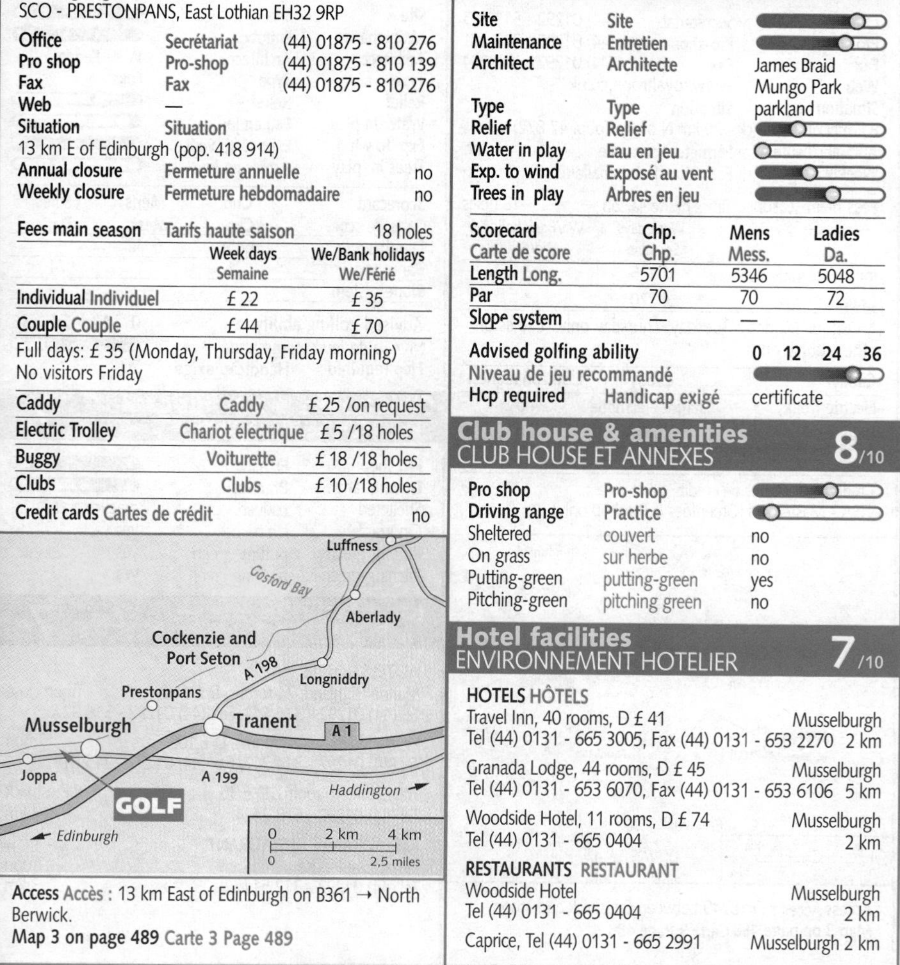

Royal Musselburgh Golf Club — 1926

Prestongrange House
SCO - PRESTONPANS, East Lothian EH32 9RP

Office	Secrétariat	(44) 01875 - 810 276
Pro shop	Pro-shop	(44) 01875 - 810 139
Fax	Fax	(44) 01875 - 810 276
Web	—	
Situation	Situation	

13 km E of Edinburgh (pop. 418 914)

Annual closure	Fermeture annuelle	no
Weekly closure	Fermeture hebdomadaire	no

Fees main season Tarifs haute saison	18 holes	
	Week days Semaine	We/Bank holidays We/Férié
Individual Individuel	£ 22	£ 35
Couple Couple	£ 44	£ 70

Full days: £ 35 (Monday, Thursday, Friday morning)
No visitors Friday

Caddy	Caddy	£ 25 /on request
Electric Trolley	Chariot électrique	£ 5 /18 holes
Buggy	Voiturette	£ 18 /18 holes
Clubs	Clubs	£ 10 /18 holes
Credit cards Cartes de crédit		no

Access Accès : 13 km East of Edinburgh on B361 → North Berwick.
Map 3 on page 489 Carte 3 Page 489

Golf course PARCOURS — 16/20

Site	Site	
Maintenance	Entretien	
Architect	Architecte	James Braid, Mungo Park
Type	Type	parkland
Relief	Relief	
Water in play	Eau en jeu	
Exp. to wind	Exposé au vent	
Trees in play	Arbres en jeu	

Scorecard Carte de score	Chp. Chp.	Mens Mess.	Ladies Da.
Length Long.	5701	5346	5048
Par	70	70	72
Slope system	—	—	—

Advised golfing ability 0 12 24 36
Niveau de jeu recommandé
Hcp required Handicap exigé — certificate

Club house & amenities CLUB HOUSE ET ANNEXES — 8/10

Pro shop	Pro-shop	
Driving range	Practice	
Sheltered	couvert	no
On grass	sur herbe	no
Putting-green	putting-green	yes
Pitching-green	pitching green	no

Hotel facilities ENVIRONNEMENT HOTELIER — 7/10

HOTELS HÔTELS
Travel Inn, 40 rooms, D £ 41 — Musselburgh
Tel (44) 0131 - 665 3005, Fax (44) 0131 - 653 2270 — 2 km

Granada Lodge, 44 rooms, D £ 45 — Musselburgh
Tel (44) 0131 - 653 6070, Fax (44) 0131 - 653 6106 — 5 km

Woodside Hotel, 11 rooms, D £ 74 — Musselburgh
Tel (44) 0131 - 665 0404 — 2 km

RESTAURANTS RESTAURANT
Woodside Hotel — Musselburgh
Tel (44) 0131 - 665 0404 — 2 km

Caprice, Tel (44) 0131 - 665 2991 — Musselburgh 2 km

ROYAL TROON Old Course

19 | 7 | 7

This course is the most remarkable of the five courses around Troon and has staged many a British Open. It also offers magnificent views of the Firth of Clyde towards the Isle of Arran and the Mull of Kintyre, lulling you into a false sense of tranquillity. On this tremendous links course, the outward 9 may seem comparatively easy, but the back 9 is one of the most horrendous in the world of golf. It is the wind that makes all the difference, especially as here it is often a side wind adding even more spice to the course. At the famous "postage-stamp" hole, the green can seem more like a pin-head when the wind is playing tricks. All those golfers who love Castles in Spain, huge trees bathed in sunlight and flattering scores can be on their way. Sure there's the Gulf Stream nearby, and sure you'll see more impressive dunes elsewhere, but this is no place for the mild or meek-hearted.

Ce parcours est le plus remarquable des cinq parcours autour de Troon, et a été le théâtre de nombreux British Open. Il offre des vues magnifiques au-delà du Firth of Clyde vers l'Ile d'Arran et le Mull of Kintyre, dans une trompeuse tranquillité. Sur ce formidable links, l'aller peut paraître assez facile et le retour un des plus féroces au monde. Mais le vent fera la différence, d'autant qu'il est souvent en travers, et ajoute encore à l'intérêt du parcours : au fameux "Postage Stamp", le green est encore plus petit qu'un timbre-poste quand il souffle. Que ceux qui aiment les châteaux en Espagne, les grands arbres baignés de soleil et les scores flatteurs passent leur chemin. Certes, le Gulf Stream passe par ici, certes, les dunes peuvent être encore plus impressionnantes ailleurs, mais on n'est pas ici au royaume de la douceur.

Royal Troon Golf Club — 1878

SCO - TROON, Ayrshire KA10 6EP

Office	Secrétariat	(44) 01292 - 311 555
Pro shop	Pro-shop	(44) 01292 - 313 281
Fax	Fax	(44) 01292 - 318 204
Web	www.royaltroon.co.uk	
Situation	Situation	

8 km N of Prestwick - 20 km N of Ayr (pop. 47 872)

Annual closure	Fermeture annuelle	no
Weekly closure	Fermeture hebdomadaire	no

Fees main season / Tarifs haute saison	18 holes	
	Week days / Semaine	We/Bank holidays / We/Férié
Individual Individuel	£ 135	*
Couple Couple	£ 270	*

* Visitors: Monday, Tuesday, Thursday only. Ladies on other course only.

Caddy	Caddy	L 30 /on request
Electric Trolley	Chariot électrique	no
Buggy	Voiturette	no
Clubs	Clubs	£ 25 /18 holes

Credit cards Cartes de crédit
VISA - Mastercard (Greenfees & Proshop only)

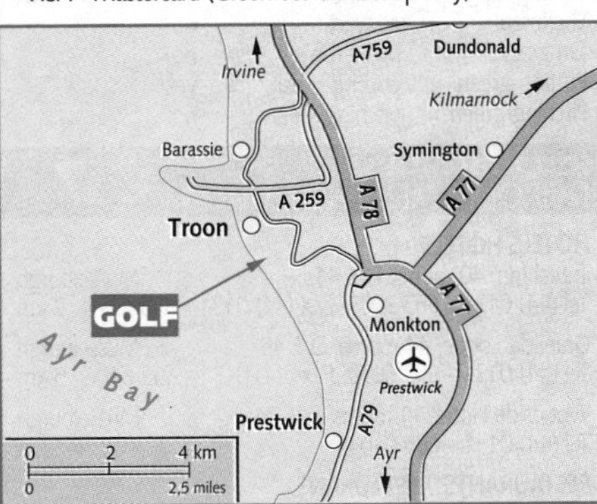

Access Accès : On B749 between Pretswick and Troon
Map 3 on page 488 Carte 3 Page 488

Golf course — PARCOURS — 19/20

Site	Site	
Maintenance	Entretien	
Architect	Architecte	Willie Fernie
Type	Type	links
Relief	Relief	
Water in play	Eau en jeu	
Exp. to wind	Exposé au vent	
Trees in play	Arbres en jeu	

Scorecard / Carte de score	Chp. / Chp.	Mens / Mess.	Ladies / Da.
Length Long.	6458	6042	—
Par	71	71	74
Slope system	—	—	—

Advised golfing ability / Niveau de jeu recommandé: 0 12 24 36
Hcp required / Handicap exigé: 20

Club house & amenities — CLUB HOUSE ET ANNEXES — 7/10

Pro shop	Pro-shop	
Driving range	Practice	
Sheltered	couvert	practice area
On grass	sur herbe	yes
Putting-green	putting-green	yes
Pitching-green	pitching green	yes

Hotel facilities — ENVIRONNEMENT HOTELIER — 7/10

HOTELS HÔTELS

Marine Highland, 74 rooms, D £ 160 — Troon close
Tel (44) 01292 - 314 444, Fax (44) 01292 - 316 922

Piersland House, 28 rooms, D £ 100 — Troon
Tel (44) 01292 - 314 747, Fax (44) 01292 - 315 613

Travel Inn, 40 rooms, D £ 35 — Prestwick 4 km
Tel (44) 01292 - 678 262

RESTAURANTS RESTAURANT

Highgrove House — Troon 3 km
Tel (44) 01292 - 312 511

SCOTSCRAIG

16 | 6 | 6

This is one of Scotland's oldest courses, whose reputation has not really benefited from the closeness of St Andrews, at least not with outsiders. The road that gets you here is nothing special, but when you reach the course, all that changes. A little links and a little inland with heather, this is a course that is none too tiring to play but one which requires a lot of concentration to play well. The wind plays a vital role, it must be said, but so do the deep bunkers and the well-contoured greens which, like the course as a whole, are in good condition. Scotscraig has been used as a qualifying course for the British Open, which speaks volumes for its quality as a test of golf, but this doesn't stop less experienced players from having a go themselves.

C'est un des plus anciens golfs d'Ecosse, dont la réputation n'a pas vraiment bénéficié de la proximité de St Andrews, en tout cas auprès des étrangers à la région. La route d'arrivée n'est pas merveilleuse, mais tout change dès que l'on arrive. Un peu links, un peu inland avec de la bruyère, c'est un parcours peu fatigant à jouer mais qui demande beaucoup d'attention pour être maîtrisé. Le vent y joue un rôle essentiel, faut-il le dire, mais aussi les profonds bunkers, les greens bien modelés et généralement en bon état, comme le parcours. Scotscraig a été utilisé comme parcours qualificatif pour le British Open, c'est le signe de sa qualité de test, mais que cela n'empêche pas les joueurs moins expérimentés de l'affronter.

Scotscraig Golf Club — 1817

Golf Road
SCO - TAYPORT, Fife DD6 9DZ

Office	Secrétariat	(44) 01382 - 552 515
Pro shop	Pro-shop	(44) 01382 - 552 855
Fax	Fax	(44) 01382 - 553 130
Web	—	
Situation	Situation	St Andrews, 16 km
Annual closure	Fermeture annuelle	no
Weekly closure	Fermeture hebdomadaire	no

Fees main season Tarifs haute saison	18 holes	
	Week days Semaine	We/Bank holidays We/Férié
Individual Individuel	£ 35	£ 40
Couple Couple	£ 70	£ 80

Full weekday: £ 35

Caddy	Caddy	on request
Electric Trolley	Chariot électrique	£ 6 /18 holes
Buggy	Voiturette	£ 18 /18 holes
Clubs	Clubs	£ 15 /18 holes

Credit cards Cartes de crédit
VISA - Mastercard - AMEX

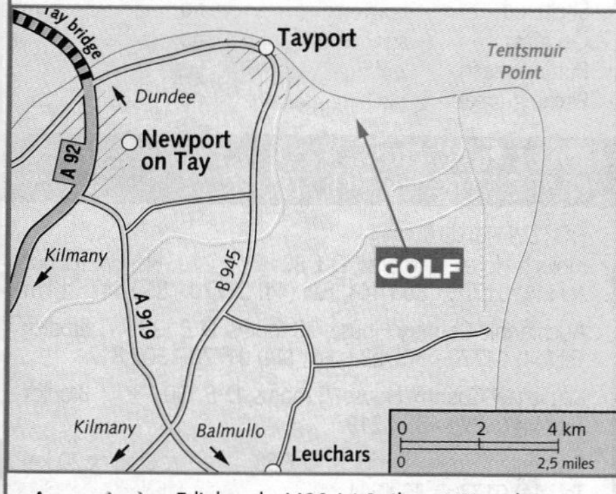

Access Accès : Edinburgh, M90 Jct 3, then A92 and A914 → Dundee. Before Tay Bridge, turn right to Tayport on B945. Golf signposted to left in Tayport.
Map 2 on page 487 Carte 2 Page 487

Golf course PARCOURS — 16/20

Site	Site	
Maintenance	Entretien	
Architect	Architecte	James Braid (1920)
Type	Type	links, heathland
Relief	Relief	
Water in play	Eau en jeu	
Exp. to wind	Exposé au vent	
Trees in play	Arbres en jeu	

Scorecard Carte de score	Chp. Chp.	Mens Mess.	Ladies Da.
Length Long.	5960	5960	5960
Par	69	69	74
Slope system	—	—	—

Advised golfing ability 0 12 24 36
Niveau de jeu recommandé
Hcp required Handicap exigé certificate

Club house & amenities CLUB HOUSE ET ANNEXES — 6/10

Pro shop	Pro-shop	
Driving range	Practice	
Sheltered	couvert	no
On grass	sur herbe	yes
Putting-green	putting-green	yes
Pitching-green	pitching green	no

Hotel facilities ENVIRONNEMENT HOTELIER — 6/10

HOTELS HÔTELS

Hilton Dundee, 128 rooms, D £ 140 — Dundee
Tel (44) 01382 - 229 271, Fax (44) 01382 - 200 072 — 7 km

Shaftesbury, 12 rooms, D £ 80 — Dundee
Tel (44) 01382 - 669 216, Fax (44) 01382 - 641 598

Travel Inn, 40 rooms, D £ 41 — Dundee
Tel (44) 01382 - 203 240, Fax (44) 01382 - 203 237

RESTAURANTS RESTAURANT

Hilton Dundee — Dundee
Tel (44) 01382 - 229 271

SHISKINE (BLACKWATERFOOT)

17	5	5

This is the one exception to our rule of featuring only 18-hole courses. Shiskine has only twelve but it is one of the most frequently visited courses by the world's golf designers. There is one blind shot on virtually each hole and signals in every direction telling players when it is safe to play. This is golf in its original pure style and enjoyment (but also with its own idiosyncrasies). The sheep are there to crop the sprinkler-free fairways, which haven't changed at all since the course first opened. That was when Willie Fernie brought the very best out of a space of land without even the most primitive excavator to call on. The greens are amazingly good, when you finally reach them. You need to play here a hundred times in order to fully understand the ins and outs of the course, but who's objecting.

La seule exception à notre règle de ne signaler que des parcours de 18 trous. Le Shiskine n'a que douze trous, mais c'est un des parcours les plus visités par les architectes du monde entier. On trouve un coup aveugle sur pratiquement chaque trou, et des signaux dans tous les sens pour préciser aux joueurs quand ils peuvent jouer en toute sécurité. C'est ici le golf dans sa pureté et son plaisir originels (mais aussi ses excès baroques), avec des moutons pour tondre des fairways sans arrosage, qui n'ont pas bougé depuis la création. Alors, Willie Fernie avait tiré la quintessence d'un espace où il ne disposait pas du moindre engin de terrassement. Les greens y sont d'une surprenante qualité... quand on y parvient enfin. Il faut jouer ici cent fois pour comprendre toutes les astuces, mais on ne demande que çà.

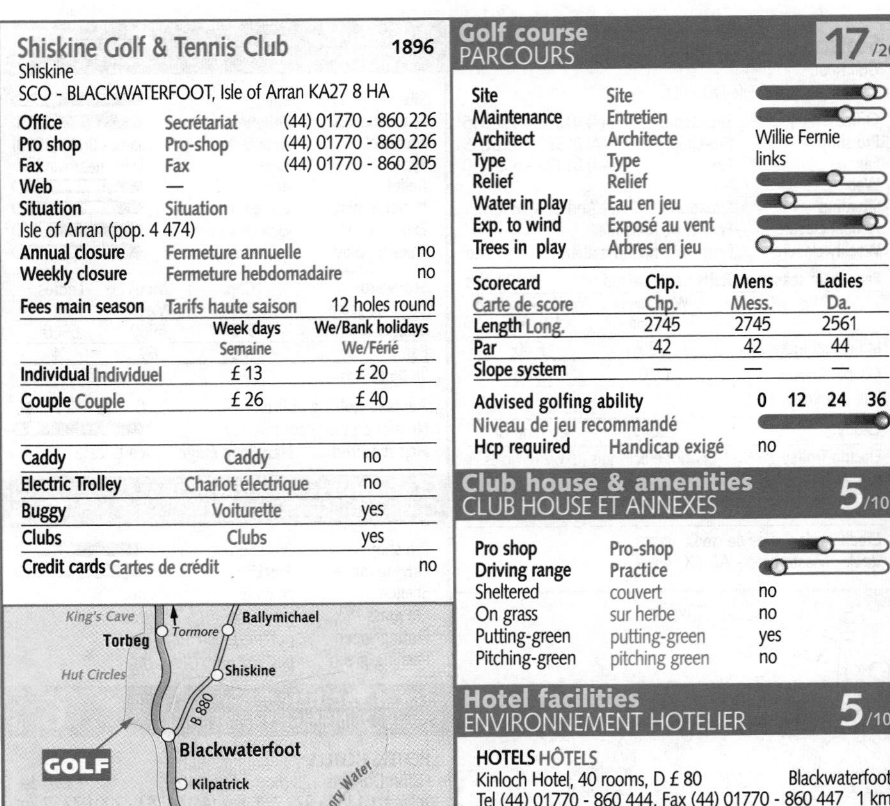

Shiskine Golf & Tennis Club — 1896

Shiskine
SCO - BLACKWATERFOOT, Isle of Arran KA27 8 HA

Office	Secrétariat	(44) 01770 - 860 226
Pro shop	Pro-shop	(44) 01770 - 860 226
Fax	Fax	(44) 01770 - 860 205
Web	—	
Situation	Situation	
Isle of Arran (pop. 4 474)		
Annual closure	Fermeture annuelle	no
Weekly closure	Fermeture hebdomadaire	no

Fees main season Tarifs haute saison	Week days Semaine	We/Bank holidays We/Férié
	12 holes round	
Individual Individuel	£ 13	£ 20
Couple Couple	£ 26	£ 40

Caddy	Caddy	no
Electric Trolley	Chariot électrique	no
Buggy	Voiturette	yes
Clubs	Clubs	yes
Credit cards	Cartes de crédit	no

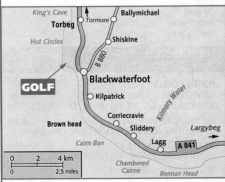

Access Accès : Ferry from Ardrossan to Brodick. Cross island via String Road (20 km) to village of Blackwaterfoot.
Map 2 on page 486 Carte 2 Page 486

Golf course PARCOURS — 17/20

Site	Site	
Maintenance	Entretien	
Architect	Architecte	Willie Fernie
Type	Type	links
Relief	Relief	
Water in play	Eau en jeu	
Exp. to wind	Exposé au vent	
Trees in play	Arbres en jeu	

Scorecard Carte de score	Chp. Chp.	Mens Mess.	Ladies Da.
Length Long.	2745	2745	2561
Par	42	42	44
Slope system	—	—	—

Advised golfing ability / Niveau de jeu recommandé: 0 12 24 36
Hcp required / Handicap exigé: no

Club house & amenities CLUB HOUSE ET ANNEXES — 5/10

Pro shop	Pro-shop	
Driving range	Practice	
Sheltered	couvert	no
On grass	sur herbe	no
Putting-green	putting-green	yes
Pitching-green	pitching green	no

Hotel facilities ENVIRONNEMENT HOTELIER — 5/10

HOTELS HÔTELS

Kinloch Hotel, 40 rooms, D £ 80 — Blackwaterfoot
Tel (44) 01770 - 860 444, Fax (44) 01770 - 860 447 — 1 km

Auchrannie Country House, 28 rooms, D £ 122 — Brodick
Tel (44) 01770 - 302 234, Fax (44) 01770 - 302 812

Kilmichael Country House, 5 rooms, D £ 130 — Brodick
Tel (44) 01770 - 302 219

Dunvegan House, 9 rooms, D £ 58 — Brodick 20 km
Tel (44) 01770 - 302 811

RESTAURANTS RESTAURANT

Carraigh Mhor — Lamlash
Tel (44) 01770 - 600 453 — 22 km

SOUTHERNESS

18	6	5

A course for connoisseurs off the traditional golfing trail but your journey will be more than rewarded by a superb day out. This is one of the most recent links to date in Scotland, designed by Mackenzie Ross while he was working on Turnberry. The excellence of the design, very elaborate despite the course's natural look, quickly caught the attention of the better players, who appreciate the distinctive layout and the variety of challenge, with a special mention for the 12th, one of the finest par 4s in Scotland. Golfing here can be very enjoyable when the weather is fine, but that doesn't happen all that often. What's more, the holes are always running in different directions, thus calling for constant improvisation. Generally flat with only a few welcome slopes and difficulties that are always visible, this course is well worth the trip.

Un golf de connaisseurs, à l'écart des sentiers traditionnels, mais le déplacement sera récompensé par une superbe journée. C'est l'un des derniers en date des links d'Ecosse, dessiné par Mackenzie Ross alors qu'il ressuscitait Turnberry au même moment. La qualité du dessin, très travaillé malgré son apparence naturelle, a vite attiré l'attention des bons joueurs. Ils apprécient la distinction du tracé, la diversité des défis proposés, avec une mention particulière pour le 12, un des plus beaux par 4 d'Ecosse. Le golf peut ici être très plaisant quand le temps est calme, mais ce n'est pas si fréquent. De plus, les trous vont dans des directions toujours différentes, ce qui oblige à un sens constant de l'improvisation. Généralement plat, avec quelques ondulations bienvenues, mais des difficultés toujours visibles, ce parcours vaut le voyage.

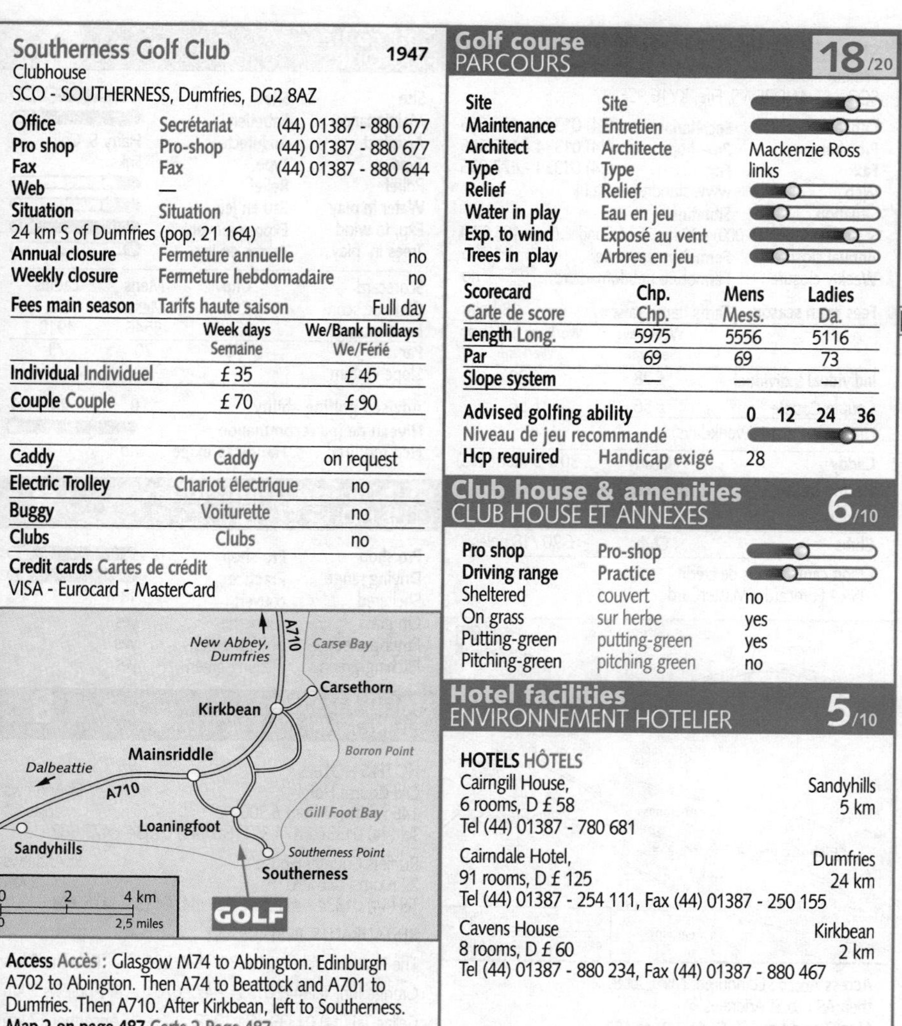

Southerness Golf Club — 1947
Clubhouse
SCO - SOUTHERNESS, Dumfries, DG2 8AZ

Office	Secrétariat	(44) 01387 - 880 677
Pro shop	Pro-shop	(44) 01387 - 880 677
Fax	Fax	(44) 01387 - 880 644
Web	—	
Situation	Situation	
24 km S of Dumfries (pop. 21 164)		
Annual closure	Fermeture annuelle	no
Weekly closure	Fermeture hebdomadaire	no

Fees main season Tarifs haute saison	Week days Semaine	We/Bank holidays We/Férié
		Full day
Individual Individuel	£ 35	£ 45
Couple Couple	£ 70	£ 90

Caddy	Caddy	on request
Electric Trolley	Chariot électrique	no
Buggy	Voiturette	no
Clubs	Clubs	no

Credit cards Cartes de crédit
VISA - Eurocard - MasterCard

Access Accès : Glasgow M74 to Abbington. Edinburgh A702 to Abington. Then A74 to Beattock and A701 to Dumfries. Then A710. After Kirkbean, left to Southerness.
Map 2 on page 487 Carte 2 Page 487

Golf course PARCOURS — 18/20

Site	Site	
Maintenance	Entretien	
Architect	Architecte	Mackenzie Ross
Type	Type	links
Relief	Relief	
Water in play	Eau en jeu	
Exp. to wind	Exposé au vent	
Trees in play	Arbres en jeu	

Scorecard Carte de score	Chp. Chp.	Mens Mess.	Ladies Da.
Length Long.	5975	5556	5116
Par	69	69	73
Slope system	—	—	—

Advised golfing ability Niveau de jeu recommandé — 0 12 24 36
Hcp required Handicap exigé 28

Club house & amenities CLUB HOUSE ET ANNEXES — 6/10

Pro shop	Pro-shop	
Driving range	Practice	
Sheltered	couvert	no
On grass	sur herbe	yes
Putting-green	putting-green	yes
Pitching-green	pitching green	no

Hotel facilities ENVIRONNEMENT HOTELIER — 5/10

HOTELS HÔTELS

Cairngill House, 6 rooms, D £ 58 — Sandyhills 5 km
Tel (44) 01387 - 780 681

Cairndale Hotel, 91 rooms, D £ 125 — Dumfries 24 km
Tel (44) 01387 - 254 111, Fax (44) 01387 - 250 155

Cavens House, 8 rooms, D £ 60 — Kirkbean 2 km
Tel (44) 01387 - 880 234, Fax (44) 01387 - 880 467

ST ANDREWS Eden Course

14 | 8 | 8

Notably shorter than its three most prestigious neighbours, the Eden Course is a very respectful course and probably, if not the most forthright then at least the least difficult of the three to figure out first time around, even though the wind will always be there to make things a little harder. This is a more conventional course, laid out in two loops of 9 holes, but the hazards are intelligently placed with a good number of bunkers from which average players will find escaping a little easier than on the other courses around here. Don't underestimate the Eden course, it can be fun playing here when everyone is swarming over the other courses of the golf factory that St Andrews has now become.

Notablement plus court que ses trois voisins les plus prestigieux, l'Eden Course est cependant un parcours plus qu'honorable, et probablement sinon le plus franc des trois, du moins le moins difficile à déchiffrer au premier abord, même si le vent vient tout autant y compliquer les choses. De fait, c'est un parcours plus conventionnel, au point même d'avoir deux boucles de 9 trous, mais les obstacles sont intelligemment placés, les bunkers sont assez nombreux, mais les joueurs moyens pourront en sortir un jour (ce n'est pas toujours facile sur les autres parcours du site !). Il ne faut pas le sous-estimer, et le plaisir de jouer ici n'est pas négligeable quand tout le monde s'agite dans les autres ateliers de cette véritable usine à golf que St Andrews est devenu.

St Andrews Links **1914**

Pilmour House
SCO - ST ANDREWS, Fife, KY16 9SF

Office	Secrétariat	(44) 01334 - 466 666
Pro shop	Pro-shop	(44) 01334 - 466 666
Fax	Fax	(44) 01334 - 477 036
Web	www.standrews.org.uk	
Situation	Situation	

St Andrews (pop.15 000) - 30 km SE of Dundee (pop. 165 873)

Annual closure	Fermeture annuelle	no
Weekly closure	Fermeture hebdomadaire	no

Fees main season Tarifs haute saison		18 holes
	Week days Semaine	We/Bank holidays We/Férié
Individual Individuel	£ 28	£ 28
Couple Couple	£ 56	£ 56

Under 16/ £ 14 (weekdays)

Caddy	Caddy	£ 30 + 5 (adm. fee)
Electric Trolley	Chariot électrique	no
Buggy	Voiturette	no
Clubs	Clubs	£ 20 /18 holes

Credit cards Cartes de crédit
VISA - Eurocard - MasterCard

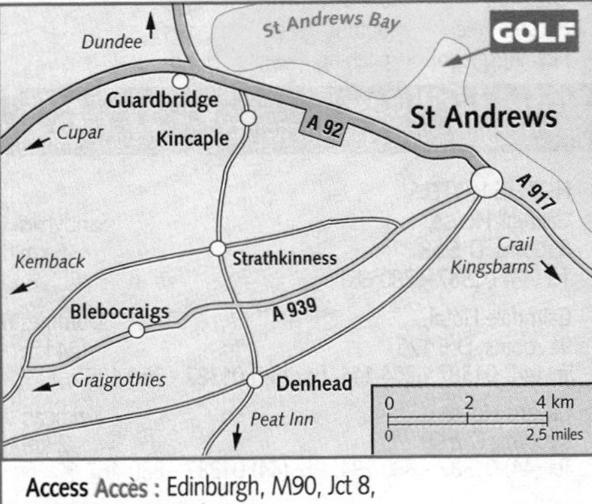

Access Accès : Edinburgh, M90, Jct 8, then A91 to St Andrews.
Map 3 on page 489 Carte 3 Page 489

Golf course PARCOURS — 14/20

Site	Site	
Maintenance	Entretien	
Architect	Architecte	Harry S. Colt
Type	Type	links
Relief	Relief	
Water in play	Eau en jeu	
Exp. to wind	Exposé au vent	
Trees in play	Arbres en jeu	

Scorecard Carte de score	Chp. Chp.	Mens Mess.	Ladies Da.
Length Long.	5546	5546	4910
Par	70	70	73
Slope system	—	—	—

Advised golfing ability 0 12 24 36
Niveau de jeu recommandé
Hcp required Handicap exigé no

Club house & amenities CLUB HOUSE ET ANNEXES — 8/10

Pro shop	Pro-shop	
Driving range	Practice	
Sheltered	couvert	14 mats
On grass	sur herbe	yes
Putting-green	putting-green	yes
Pitching-green	pitching green	yes

Hotel facilities ENVIRONNEMENT HOTELIER — 8/10

HOTELS HÔTELS

Old Course Hotel — St Andrews adjacent
146 rooms, D from £ 300
Tel (44) 01334 - 474 371, Fax (44) 01334 - 477 668

Rufflets Country House — St Andrews 2 km
22 rooms, D £ 190
Tel (44) 01334 - 472 594, Fax (44) 01334 - 478 703

RESTAURANTS RESTAURANT

The Peat Inn, Tel (44) 01334 - 840 206 — Peat Inn 8 km
Grange Inn, Tel (44) 01334 - 472 670 — St Andrews 2 km
Cellar, Tel (44) 01333 - 310 378 — Ansruther 17 km

ST ANDREWS Jubilee Course 16 | 8 | 8

Having celebrated its centenary in 1997, the Jubilee Course has been given a recent face-lift and is now the longest course at St Andrews. Although laid out in a single stretch with no return to the Club House at the 9th, there are no double fairways. The course is a little more hilly and gives some pretty viewpoints in a region which is rather flat. There is little in the way of vegetation on the holes close to the sea if you except tall grass, but this layout requires accurate driving and a lot of concentration. Like the others, the course is run by St Andrews Links Management and the Links Trust which built a very well equipped clubhouse open to all. Needless to say any trip should be organised in advance, especially between April and September.

Centenaire en 1997, le "Jubilee" a bénéficié d'une récente cure de rajeunissement qui en a fait le plus long des parcours de St Andrews. On ne trouve pas ici les fameux double fairways, bien que le parcours se déroule aussi d'un seul trait, sans retour au Club-house au 9. On trouve aussi davantage de relief, et donc quelques jolis points de vue dans une région somme toute peu accidentée. Les trous proches de la mer ont une végétation assez limitée, les hautes herbes mises à part, mais l'ensemble demande des drives précis, et généralement beaucoup d'attention. Comme les autres, ce parcours est géré par le St Andrews Links Management, et le Links Trust, qui a construit un Club-house de très bien équipé, et ouvert à tous. Inutile de dire qu'il est nécessaire d'organiser son voyage à l'avance, surtout d'avril à septembre.

St Andrews Links **1897**
Pilmour House
SCO - ST ANDREWS, Fife, KY16 9SF

Office	Secrétariat	(44) 01334 - 466 666
Pro shop	Pro-shop	(44) 01334 - 466 666
Fax	Fax	(44) 01334 - 477 036
Web	www.standrews.org.uk	
Situation	Situation	

St Andrews (pop. 15 000) - 30 km SE of Dundee (pop. 165 873

Annual closure	Fermeture annuelle	no
Weekly closure	Fermeture hebdomadaire	no

Fees main season Tarifs haute saison	18 holes	
	Week days Semaine	We/Bank holidays We/Férié
Individual Individuel	£ 37	£ 37
Couple Couple	£ 74	£ 74

Under 16: £ 18 (Weekdays)

Caddy	Caddy	£ 30 + 5 (adm. fee)
Electric Trolley	Chariot électrique	no
Buggy	Voiturette	no
Clubs	Clubs	£ 20 /18 holes

Credit cards Cartes de crédit
VISA - Eurocard - MasterCard

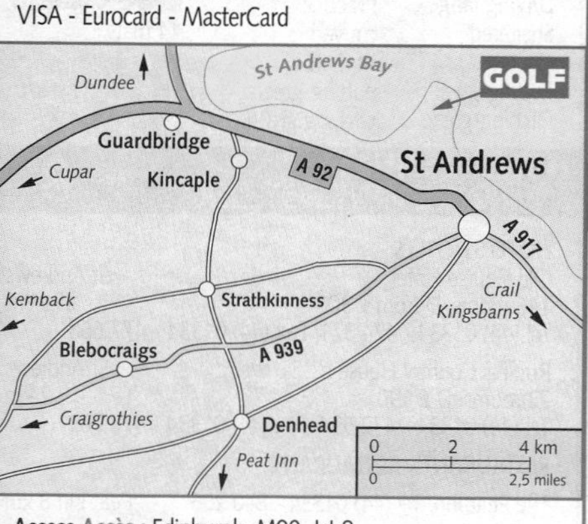

Access Accès : Edinburgh, M90, Jct 8, then A91 to St Andrews.
Map 3 on page 489 Carte 3 Page 489

Golf course PARCOURS 16/20

Site	Site	
Maintenance	Entretien	
Architect	Architecte	Old Tom Morris Auchterlonie/Steel
Type	Type	links
Relief	Relief	
Water in play	Eau en jeu	
Exp. to wind	Exposé au vent	
Trees in play	Arbres en jeu	

Scorecard Carte de score	Chp. Chp.	Mens Mess.	Ladies Da.
Length Long.	6125	6125	5440
Par	72	72	75
Slope system	—	—	—

Advised golfing ability 0 12 24 36
Niveau de jeu recommandé
Hcp required Handicap exigé no

Club house & amenities CLUB HOUSE ET ANNEXES 8/10

Pro shop	Pro-shop	
Driving range	Practice	
Sheltered	couvert	14 mats
On grass	sur herbe	yes
Putting-green	putting-green	yes
Pitching-green	pitching green	yes

Hotel facilities ENVIRONNEMENT HOTELIER 8/10

HOTELS HÔTELS

Old Course Hotel — St Andrews adjacent
146 rooms, D from £ 300
Tel (44) 01334 - 474 371, Fax (44) 01334 - 477 668

Rufflets Country House — St Andrews 2 km
22 rooms, D £ 190
Tel (44) 01334 - 472 594, Fax (44) 01334 - 478 703

RESTAURANTS RESTAURANT

The Peat Inn, Tel (44) 01334 - 840 206 — Peat Inn 8 km
Grange Inn, Tel (44) 01334 - 472 670 — St Andrews 2 km
Cellar, Tel (44) 01333 - 310 378 — Ansruther 17 km

ST ANDREWS New Course

17 | 8 | 8

Fortunately, there are several other excellent golf courses at St Andrews when it is impossible to play the Old Course. The New Course is one of them and does not settle for playing second fiddle to its illustrious neighbour. Some local players even consider this their favourite course. At all events it is a very demanding layout, rather similar to the Old Course in its general physiognomy and the way it demands technical skill and powers of invention. Here you don't play the club you need for such and such a distance, rather the club that will roll the ball up to the pin. Hazard-wise there are no trees, naturally, only threatening thick gorse and bunkers like those on the Old Course which collect any ball coming their way. The greens are huge and undulating and the turf a pleasure to walk and play on.

Heureusement, quand il est impossible de jouer le "Old Course", il reste plusieurs excellents autres parcours à St Andrews. Le "New" est de ceux-là, et bien plus que le second violon de son voisin géographique immédiat. On trouve même des joueurs locaux pour en faire leur favori ! C'est en tout cas un parcours très exigeant, assez proche de son aîné pour sa physionomie générale et pour ce qu'il réclame de qualités techniques et de capacités d'invention. Ici, on ne joue pas le club qu'il faut pour telle distance, mais celui qui fera arriver la balle en roulant jusqu'au drapeau. Côté obstacles, pas d'arbres bien sûr, mais des ajoncs menaçants et denses, et aussi des bunkers comme ceux du "Old", qui recueillent toutes les balles qui passent aux alentours. Les greens sont très vastes et ondulés, et le gazon un plaisir à fouler et à jouer.

St Andrews Links — 1895

Pilmour House
SCO - ST ANDREWS, Fife, KY16 9SF

Office	Secrétariat	(44) 01334 - 466 666
Pro shop	Pro-shop	(44) 01334 - 466 666
Fax	Fax	(44) 01334 - 477 036
Web	www.standrews.org.uk	
Situation	Situation	

St Andrews (pop. 15 000) - 30 km SE of Dundee (pop. 165 873)

Annual closure	Fermeture annuelle	no
Weekly closure	Fermeture hebdomadaire	

Fees main season Tarifs haute saison	18 holes	
	Week days Semaine	We/Bank holidays We/Férié
Individual Individuel	£ 42	£ 42
Couple Couple	£ 84	£ 84

Under 16: £ 21 (Weekdays)

Caddy	Caddy	£ 30 + 5 (adm. fee)
Electric Trolley	Chariot électrique	no
Buggy	Voiturette	no
Clubs	Clubs	£ 20 /18 holes

Credit cards Cartes de crédit
VISA - Eurocard - MasterCard

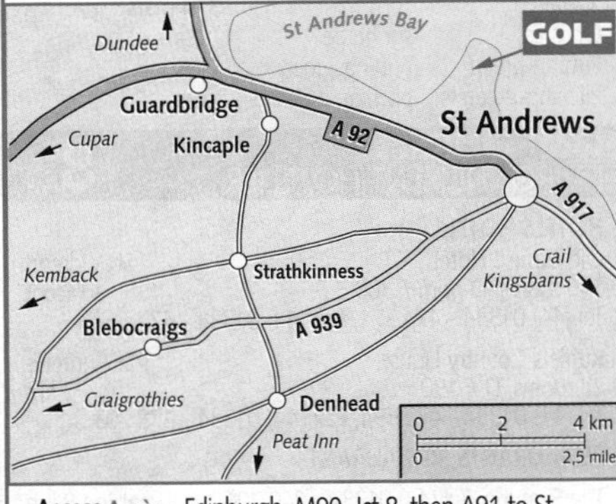

Access Accès : Edinburgh, M90, Jct 8, then A91 to St Andrews.
Map 3 on page 489 Carte 3 Page 489

Golf course PARCOURS — 17/20

Site	Site	
Maintenance	Entretien	
Architect	Architecte	W. Hall Blyth Old Tom Morris
Type	Type	links
Relief	Relief	
Water in play	Eau en jeu	
Exp. to wind	Exposé au vent	
Trees in play	Arbres en jeu	

Scorecard Carte de score	Chp. Chp.	Mens Mess.	Ladies Da.
Length Long.	5945	5945	5393
Par	71	71	76
Slope system	—	—	—

Advised golfing ability Niveau de jeu recommandé — 0 12 24 36
Hcp required Handicap exigé — no

Club house & amenities CLUB HOUSE ET ANNEXES — 8/10

Pro shop	Pro-shop	
Driving range	Practice	
Sheltered	couvert	14 mats
On grass	sur herbe	yes
Putting-green	putting-green	yes
Pitching-green	pitching green	yes

Hotel facilities ENVIRONNEMENT HOTELIER — 8/10

HOTELS HÔTELS

Old Course Hotel — St Andrews
146 rooms, D from £ 300 — adjacent
Tel (44) 01334 - 474 371, Fax (44) 01334 - 477 668

Rufflets Country House — St Andrews
22 rooms, D £ 190 — 2 km
Tel (44) 01334 - 472 594, Fax (44) 01334 - 478 703

RESTAURANTS RESTAURANT

The Peat Inn, Tel (44) 01334 - 840 206 — Peat Inn 8 km
Grange Inn, Tel(44) 01334 - 472 670 — St Andrews 2 km
Cellar, Tel (44) 01333 - 310 378 — Ansruther 17 km

ST ANDREWS Old Course

18 | 8 | 8

Is there anything left to write about the Old Course? The world's most famous venue is a public course even though you do need to be patient if you want to play here. It is well thought of to say that this is the greatest course in the British Isles, so often in the public eye that when you come here for the first time you get the impression you have already played it. Be wise and take a caddy, as the devilish subtleties, traps, double fairways and double greens make every decision a tough one. The work of no real designer, the Old Course has been shaped by the passing centuries, the wind, champions and green-keepers. The atmosphere alone is enough to intimidate or even terrorise amateurs stepping onto the first tee. But if you disregard the "religiousness" of this hallowed site there are, dare we say it, many more challenging links courses when the weather is calm (may the gods of golf forgive us). You cannot not play the Old Course.

Est-il encore possible d'écrire sur l'Old Course ? Le plus célèbre parcours du monde, est un golf public, même s'il faut de la patience pour pouvoir le jouer. Il est bien vu de dire que c'est le plus grand parcours des Iles Britanniques, tellement montré qu'on a l'impression de déjà l'avoir joué quand on vient pour la première fois. Mais il reste prudent de prendre un caddie car ses diaboliques subtilités, ses pièges, ses double fairways et double greens rendent difficiles toutes les décisions. Sans véritable architecte, le "Old" a été admirablement façonné par les siècles, le vent, les champions, les green-keepers, et rien que son atmosphère rend les amateurs sinon terrorisés, du moins intimidés au départ du 1. Si l'on fait abstraction de la "religiosité du lieu", il est des links bien plus exigeants, quand le temps est calme. Mais a t-on le droit de le dire sans aller en enfer? L'Old Course est inévitable.

St Andrews Links
Pilmour House
SCO - ST ANDREWS, Fife, KY16 9SF

Office	Secrétariat	(44) 01334 - 466 666
Pro shop	Pro-shop	(44) 01334 - 466 666
Fax	Fax	(44) 01334 - 477 036
Web	www.standrews.org.uk	
Situation	Situation	

St Andrews (pop. 15 000) - 30 km SE of Dundee (pop. 165 873)

Annual closure	Fermeture annuelle	no
Weekly closure	Fermeture hebdomadaire	Sunday

Fees main season Tarifs haute saison		18 holes
	Week days Semaine	We/Bank holidays We/Férié
Individual Individuel	£ 85	£ 85
Couple Couple	£ 170	£ 170

Caddy	Caddy	£ 30 + 5 (adm. fee)
Electric Trolley	Chariot électrique	no
Buggy	Voiturette	no
Clubs	Clubs	£ 20 /18 holes

Credit cards Cartes de crédit
VISA - Eurocard - MasterCard

Access Accès : Edinburgh, M90, Jct 8, then A91 to St Andrews.
Map 3 on page 489 Carte 3 Page 489

Golf course PARCOURS **18/20**

Site	Site	
Maintenance	Entretien	
Architect	Architecte	Unknown
Type	Type	links
Relief	Relief	
Water in play	Eau en jeu	
Exp. to wind	Exposé au vent	
Trees in play	Arbres en jeu	

Scorecard Carte de score	**Chp.** Chp.	**Mens** Mess.	**Ladies** Da.
Length Long.	6403	5990	5430
Par	72	72	76
Slope system	—	—	—

Advised golfing ability Niveau de jeu recommandé: 0 12 24 36
Hcp required Handicap exigé: 24 Men, 36 Ladies

Club house & amenities CLUB HOUSE ET ANNEXES **8/10**

Pro shop	Pro-shop	
Driving range	Practice	
Sheltered	couvert	14 mats
On grass	sur herbe	yes
Putting-green	putting-green	yes
Pitching-green	pitching green	yes

Hotel facilities ENVIRONNEMENT HOTELIER **8/10**

HOTELS HÔTELS
Old Course Hotel — St Andrews adjacent
146 rooms, D from £ 300
Tel (44) 01334 - 474 371, Fax (44) 01334 - 477 668

Rufflets Country House — St Andrews 2 km
22 rooms, D £ 190
Tel (44) 01334 - 472 594, Fax (44) 01334 - 478 703

RESTAURANTS RESTAURANT
The Peat Inn, Tel (44) 01334 - 840 206 — Peat Inn 8 km
Grange Inn, Tel (44) 01334 - 472 670 — St Andrews 2 km
Cellar, Tel (44) 01333 - 310 378 — Ansruther 17 km

STRATHAVEN

15 | 7 | 6

Located some 22 miles from Glasgow, this is one of those gems tucked away in the west of Scotland. It is an inland course with more than a touch of heathland in a layout which winds its way between fir trees and long established woodland. The layout was extended to 18 holes in 1965 in a style that is very much in keeping with the original course. Bunkers are strategically located and the rough very penalising, both of which call for careful game strategy. For many, this is a course for accurate drivers, sometimes a little treacherous, which needs to be played several times over before getting to grips with the traps and appreciating its many qualities. Even when you reach the very tricky greens, you are still not through because you need a magic putter here to pick up strokes. Many high-level tournaments have been played here, a token of the course's overall excellence.

A quelques 45 km de Glasgow, c'est un des petits bijoux cachés à l'ouest de l'Ecosse, et un parcours "inland" dont le dessin s'insinue entre les sapins et un paysage boisé. Le tracé a été porté à 18 trous en 1965, dans un style qui reste très cohérent avec l'original. Les bunkers sont stratégiquement placés et le rough très pénalisant, ce qui oblige à bien réfléchir sur la tactique à mettre en oeuvre. C'est pour beaucoup un parcours de drives précis, parfois un peu traître, et il faut jouer plusieurs fois pour en comprendre à la fois les pièges et en savourer toutes les qualités. Et une fois arrivé sur des greens très subtils, le travail n'est pas fini, il faut un toucher d'orfèvre pour y gagner des points. De nombreux bons tournois ont été disputés ici, c'est une véritable marque de qualité.

Strathaven Golf Club — 1908

Overton Avenue, Glasgow Road
SCO - STRATHAVEN, Strathclyde, ML10 6NL

Office	Secrétariat	(44) 01357 - 520 421
Pro shop	Pro-shop	(44) 01357 - 521 812
Fax	Fax	(44) 01357 - 520 539
Web	—	
Situation	Situation	

12 km SE of East Kilbride (pop. 73 378)

Annual closure	Fermeture annuelle	no
Weekly closure	Fermeture hebdomadaire	no

Fees main season Tarifs haute saison		full day
	Week days Semaine	**We/Bank holidays** We/Férié
Individual Individuel	£ 35	*
Couple Couple	£ 70	*

* Weekends: members only

Caddy	Caddy	no
Electric Trolley	Chariot électrique	no
Buggy	Voiturette	yes
Clubs	Clubs	no
Credit cards	Cartes de crédit	no

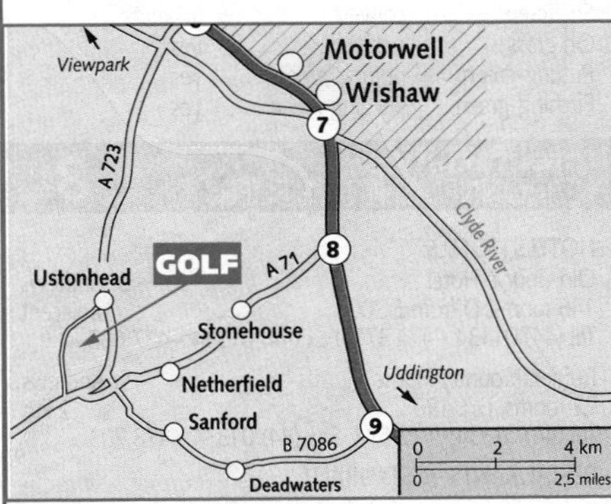

Access Accès : Glasgow, A726.
Golf in the outskirts of Strathaven city.
Map 3 on page 488 Carte 3 Page 488

Golf course PARCOURS — 15/20

Site	Site	
Maintenance	Entretien	
Architect	Architecte	Willie Fernie, J.R. Stutt
Type	Type	parkland
Relief	Relief	
Water in play	Eau en jeu	
Exp. to wind	Exposé au vent	
Trees in play	Arbres en jeu	

Scorecard Carte de score	**Chp.** Chp.	**Mens** Mess.	**Ladies** Da.
Length Long.	5665	5665	5066
Par	71	71	73
Slope system	—	—	—

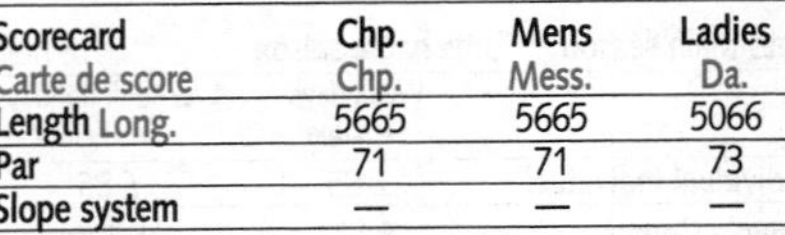

Advised golfing ability 0 12 24 36
Niveau de jeu recommandé
Hcp required Handicap exigé 28 Men, 36 Ladies

Club house & amenities CLUB HOUSE ET ANNEXES — 7/10

Pro shop	Pro-shop	
Driving range	Practice	
Sheltered	couvert	no
On grass	sur herbe	no
Putting-green	putting-green	yes
Pitching-green	pitching green	no

Hotel facilities ENVIRONNEMENT HOTELIER — 6/10

HOTELS HÔTELS

Strathaven Hotel, 22 rooms, D £ 85 — Strathaven
Tel (44) 01357 - 521 778, Fax (44) 01357 - 520 789 — 2 km

Crutherland Country House — East Kilbride
74 rooms, D £ 105 — 5 km
Tel (44) 01355 - 237 633, Fax (44) 01355 - 220 855

Bruce; 65 rooms, D £ 95 — East Kilbride
Tel (44) 01355 - 229 771, Fax (44) 01355 - 242 216 — 2 km

RESTAURANTS RESTAURANT

Hilton East Kilbride — East Kilbride
Tel (44) 01355 - 236 300 — 5 km

Waterside Inn — Strathaven

TAIN

17 | 6 | 6

Although it doesn't have the aura of Dornoch, Tain is worth much more than just a casual visit. All the more so in that green-keeping here is on a par with that found at "posher" courses. The site is superb and very quiet and the alternating heather and seaside holes produce a variety of landscapes, but playing here always requires a shrewd brain. Nothing is given away and players constantly have to adapt to new problems. The greens are never very large and the tricky breaks can be disastrous if you're not really careful. The new clubhouse should enhance still further the enjoyment of playing here, especially considering the value for money and warm welcome.

Sans avoir l'aura de Dornoch, Tain mérite néanmoins bien plus qu'un regard distrait. Et d'autant plus que l'entretien rivalise généralement avec celui de parcours plus huppés. Le site en est superbe et très tranquille, l'alternance de trous de links et de trous dans la bruyère apporte une variété de paysages, mais le jeu doit constamment être réfléchi. Rien n'est donné, et le joueur doit sans cesse s'adapter à de nouveaux problèmes. Les greens ne sont jamais très grands, et leurs subtiles ondulations peuvent provoquer des désastres si l'on n'y prête pas attention. Le nouveau Club house devrait augmenter encore le plaisir que l'on éprouve ici, d'autant que le rapport qualité-prix-accueil est très favorable !

Tain Golf Club — 1890

Chapel Road
SCO - TAIN, Ross-shire, IV19 1JE

Office	Secrétariat	(44) 01862 - 892 314
Pro shop	Pro-shop	(44) 01862 - 893 313
Fax	Fax	(44) 01862 - 892 099
Web	—	
Situation	Situation	

56 km N of Inverness (pop. 62 186) - 1 km of Tain (pop. 4 540)

Annual closure	Fermeture annuelle	no
Weekly closure	Fermeture hebdomadaire	no
Fees main season	Tarifs haute saison	18 holes

	Week days / Semaine	We/Bank holidays / We/Férié
Individual Individuel	£ 30	£ 36
Couple Couple	£ 60	£ 72

Full day: £ 36 (Weekday)/£ 46 pp (We)

Caddy	Caddy	on request
Electric Trolley	Chariot électrique	yes
Buggy	Voiturette	£ 20/18 holes
Clubs	Clubs	yes
Credit cards	Cartes de crédit	VISA - MasterCard

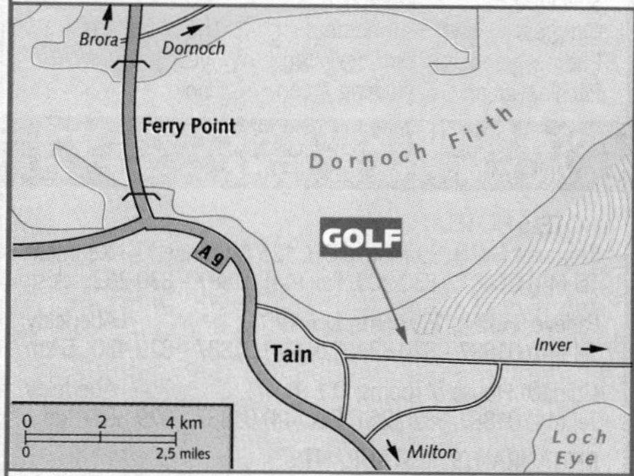

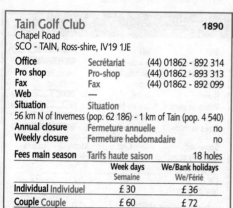

Access Accès : Inverness, A9 → Dornoch to Tain. From Tain town centre, down Castle Brae over railway, past cemetery

Map 1 on page 484 Carte 1 Page 484

Golf course / PARCOURS — 17/20

Site	Site	
Maintenance	Entretien	
Architect	Architecte	Tom Morris
Type	Type	links, heathland
Relief	Relief	
Water in play	Eau en jeu	
Exp. to wind	Exposé au vent	
Trees in play	Arbres en jeu	

Scorecard / Carte de score	Chp. / Chp.	Mens / Mess.	Ladies / Da.
Length Long.	5764	5500	5090
Par	71	70	73
Slope system	—	—	—

Advised golfing ability / Niveau de jeu recommandé: 0 12 24 36

Hcp required Handicap exigé: no

Club house & amenities / CLUB HOUSE ET ANNEXES — 6/10

Pro shop	Pro-shop	
Driving range	Practice	
Sheltered	couvert	no
On grass	sur herbe	no
Putting-green	putting-green	yes
Pitching-green	pitching green	yes

Hotel facilities / ENVIRONNEMENT HOTELIER — 6/10

HOTELS HÔTELS

Morangie House, 26 rooms, D £ 95 — Tain 0.5 km
Tel (44) 01862 - 892 281, Fax (44) 01862 - 892 872

Mansfield House, 19 rooms, D £ 170 — Tain
Tel (44) 01862 - 892 052, Fax (44) 01862 - 892 260

Golf View House, 5 rooms, D £ 50 — Tain
Tel (44) 01862 - 892 856, Fax (44) 01862 - 892 172

Glenmorangie House, 9 rooms, D £ 260 — Cadboll 14 km
Tel (44) 01862 - 871 671, Fax (44) 01862 - 871 625

RESTAURANTS RESTAURANT

Morangie Hotel, Tel (44) 01862 - 892 281 — Tain

Mansfield House, Tel (44) 01862 - 892 052 — Tain

TAYMOUTH CASTLE

13 | 4 | 6

This course is located in the alluvial plain on the banks of the river Tay, right next to the Loch of the same name. James Braid made the best possible use of limited space and restricted potential for contouring generally flat terrain. But even he was hard put to avoid a number of up and down holes and a hint of monotony. Whenever the course moves on to higher ground, the standard of the holes follows suit. In such an attractive region as this, the landscape is an added value of prime importance with the surrounding woods and hills. As the winter months are pretty wet here, even by Scottish standards, the best time to play is in summer or early autumn, for the colours. Most of the very many trees line and define the fairways, but some interfere to the point where they may be considered as hazards. Hit the ball in the right direction off the tee to keep out of trouble. This is not a great course, but there are few others in the immediate neighbourhood and, when all is said and done, this is a good layout despite the overall sobriety.

Ce parcours est situé dans la plaine alluviale au bord de la rivière Tay, et tout près du Loch. James Braid a tiré le meilleur parti possible d'un espace assez limité et de possibilités restreintes de modelage d'un terrain généralement plat. Mais il lui était difficile d'éviter un certain nombre d'allers et retour et une légère monotonie. Dès que le parcours s'élève un peu, la qualité des trous fait de même. Dans une région aussi attrayante, le paysage est une valeur ajoutée de premier ordre, avec les bois et les collines environnants. Les mois d'hiver étant assez humides - même pour un Ecossais - on viendra ici en été ou en début d'automne, pour les couleurs. La plupart des nombreux arbres longent et définissent les fairways, mais certains empiètent assez pour prendre le statut d'obstacles : il est laors sage de bien étudier la trajectoire des coups de départ. En définitive, ce n'est pas un "grand" parcours, mais il y en a peu dans les environs immédiats, et celui-ci est de qualité, dans sa sobriété.

Taymouth Castle Golf Course — 1923

Kenmore
SCO - ABERFELDY, Perthshire PH15 2NT

Office	Secrétariat	(44) 01887 - 830 228
Pro shop	Pro-shop	(44) 01887 - 830 228
Fax	Fax	(44) 01887 - 830 765
Web	—	
Situation	Situation	

60 km NW of Perth (pop. 123 495) - 9 km W of Aberfeldy

Annual closure	Fermeture annuelle	no
Weekly closure	Fermeture hebdomadaire	no

Clubhouse closed 11 → 03

Fees main season / Tarifs haute saison	18 holes	
	Week days / Semaine	We/Bank holidays / We/Férié
Individual Individuel	£ 17	£ 21
Couple Couple	£ 34	£ 42
Caddy Caddy	no	
Electric Trolley Chariot électrique	no	
Buggy Voiturette	£ 15 /18 holes	
Clubs Clubs	£ 10 /18 holes	
Credit cards Cartes de crédit	no	

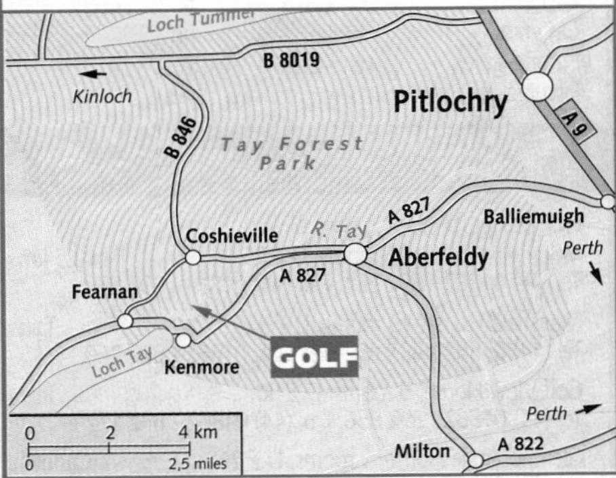

Access Accès : Perth, A9 North to Ballinluig, then A827 through Aberfeldy. Kenmore is approx. 9 km farther on the same road.
Map 1 on page 485 Carte 1 Page 485

Golf course / PARCOURS — 13/20

Site	Site	
Maintenance	Entretien	
Architect	Architecte	James Braid
Type	Type	parkland
Relief	Relief	
Water in play	Eau en jeu	
Exp. to wind	Exposé au vent	
Trees in play	Arbres en jeu	

Scorecard / Carte de score	Chp. / Chp.	Mens / Mess.	Ladies / Da.
Length Long.	5520	5220	4598
Par	69	69	72
Slope system	—	—	—

Advised golfing ability / Niveau de jeu recommandé: 0 12 24 36
Hcp required / Handicap exigé: no

Club house & amenities / CLUB HOUSE ET ANNEXES — 4/10

Pro shop	Pro-shop	
Driving range	Practice	
Sheltered	couvert	no
On grass	sur herbe	no
Putting-green	putting-green	yes
Pitching-green	pitching green	no

Hotel facilities / ENVIRONNEMENT HOTELIER — 6/10

HOTELS HÔTELS

Kenmore Hotel, 39 rooms, D £ 125 (w. dinner) — Kenmore
Tel (44) 01887 - 830 205, Fax (44) 01887 - 830 262 — close

Farleyer House, 19 rooms, D £ 120 — Aberfeldy
Tel (44) 01887 - 820 332, Fax (44) 01887 - 829 430 — 5 km

Guinach House, 7 rooms, D £ 91 — Aberfeldy
Tel (44) 01887 - 820 251, Fax (44) 01887 - 829 6077 km

RESTAURANTS RESTAURANT

Farleyer House — Aberfeldy
Tel (44) 01887 - 820 332 — 5 km

Kenmore Hotel — Kenmore
Tel (44) 01887 - 830 205

THORNHILL

15 | 6 | 5

After the city, seaside and sometimes upland courses, here we are out in the country with some pretty views over the surrounding hills. Created by Willie Fernie and then restyled in 1979, this is a very short but rather technical layout designed more for families or friendly rounds but also completed with remarkable concern for quality. You need to be accurate because the greens are small and often treacherous and multi-tiered. This is an easy walk, but it is still very much a rural park and its difficulties shouldn't be taken lightly. Judging by the success of the club's prodigal son Andrew Coltart, this is a good course to learn on. The clubhouse of this "village course" is unpretentious but warm. Close by, art enthusiasts will visit Drumlanrig Castle which houses a fine collection of paintings and mementoes of Bonnie Prince Charlie.

Après les golfs des villes, du bord de mer, des montagnes parfois aussi, nous voici à la campagne, avec de jolies vues sur les collines alentour. Créé par Willie Fernie, remanié en 1979, c'est un tracé très court, assez technique, très orienté vers le jeu en famille ou entre amis, mais avec un souci de qualité à remarquer. Il faut être précis, car les greens sont petits, souvent assez traîtres, parfois à plateaux. Peu accidenté, il conserve néanmoins un caractère de parc rural, et il ne faut pas prendre à la légère ses difficultés. Si l'on en juge par la réussite de l'enfant du club, Andrew Coltart, c'est un parcours formateur. Le Clubhouse de ce "golf de village" est modeste, mais chaleureux. A proximité, les amateurs d'art visiteront le Drumlanrig Castle, avec une riche collection de peinture et des souvenirs du Bonnie Prince Charlie.

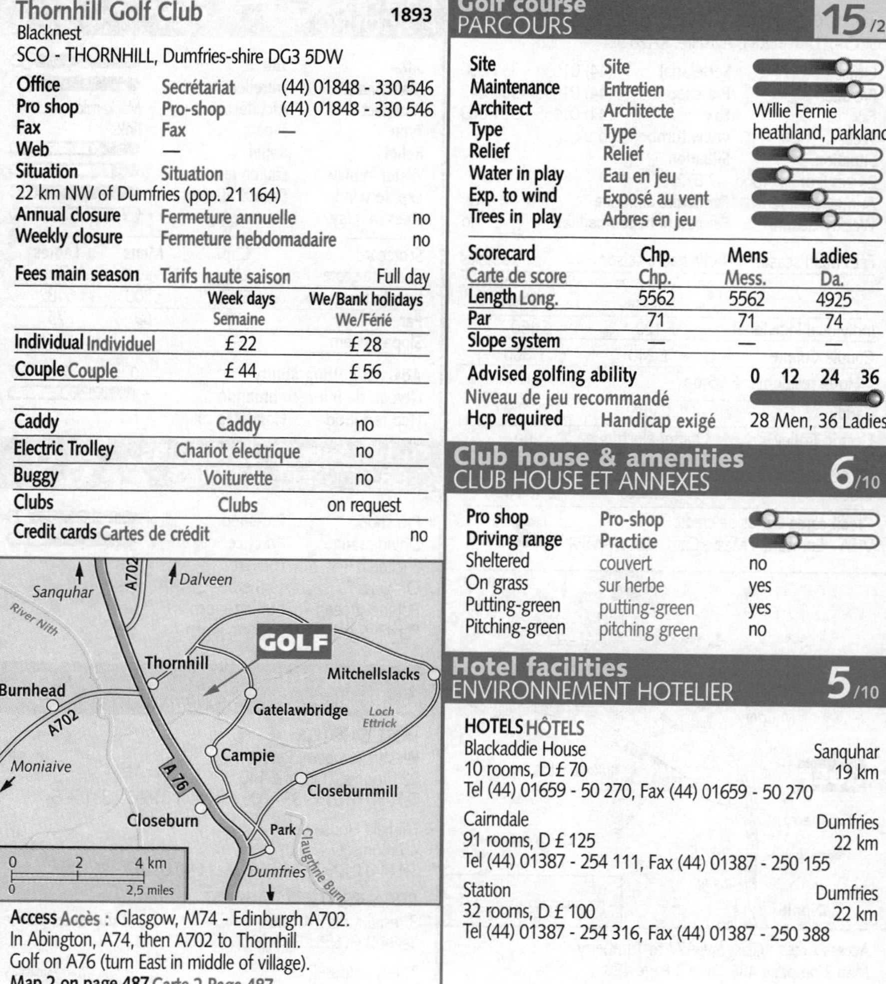

Thornhill Golf Club — **1893**
Blacknest
SCO - THORNHILL, Dumfries-shire DG3 5DW

Office	Secrétariat	(44) 01848 - 330 546
Pro shop	Pro-shop	(44) 01848 - 330 546
Fax	Fax	—
Web	—	
Situation	Situation	

22 km NW of Dumfries (pop. 21 164)

Annual closure	Fermeture annuelle	no
Weekly closure	Fermeture hebdomadaire	no

Fees main season Tarifs haute saison — Full day

	Week days / Semaine	We/Bank holidays / We/Férié
Individual Individuel	£ 22	£ 28
Couple Couple	£ 44	£ 56

Caddy	Caddy	no
Electric Trolley	Chariot électrique	no
Buggy	Voiturette	no
Clubs	Clubs	on request
Credit cards	Cartes de crédit	no

Access Accès : Glasgow, M74 - Edinburgh A702.
In Abington, A74, then A702 to Thornhill.
Golf on A76 (turn East in middle of village).
Map 2 on page 487 Carte 2 Page 487

Golf course PARCOURS — 15/20

Site	Site	
Maintenance	Entretien	
Architect	Architecte	Willie Fernie
Type	Type	heathland, parkland
Relief	Relief	
Water in play	Eau en jeu	
Exp. to wind	Exposé au vent	
Trees in play	Arbres en jeu	

Scorecard Carte de score	**Chp.** Chp.	**Mens** Mess.	**Ladies** Da.
Length Long.	5562	5562	4925
Par	71	71	74
Slope system	—	—	—

Advised golfing ability Niveau de jeu recommandé — 0 12 24 36
Hcp required Handicap exigé — 28 Men, 36 Ladies

Club house & amenities CLUB HOUSE ET ANNEXES — 6/10

Pro shop	Pro-shop	
Driving range	Practice	
Sheltered	couvert	no
On grass	sur herbe	yes
Putting-green	putting-green	yes
Pitching-green	pitching green	no

Hotel facilities ENVIRONNEMENT HOTELIER — 5/10

HOTELS HÔTELS

Blackaddie House — Sanquhar 19 km
10 rooms, D £ 70
Tel (44) 01659 - 50 270, Fax (44) 01659 - 50 270

Cairndale — Dumfries 22 km
91 rooms, D £ 125
Tel (44) 01387 - 254 111, Fax (44) 01387 - 250 155

Station — Dumfries 22 km
32 rooms, D £ 100
Tel (44) 01387 - 254 316, Fax (44) 01387 - 250 388

TURNBERRY Ailsa Course

19 | 9 | 8

Regularly playing host to the British Open has forged this course's reputation as one of the world's greatest championship venues. The course is located at the southernmost end of a majestic series of links in Ayrshire and offers a splendid view over the Isle of Arran, the dark and mysterious Mull of Kintyre and the rock of Ailsa. Try and play here in fine weather (it happens more often than you might imagine) as the wind can make this a hellish course to handle. After an almost innocent first few holes, you soon find the sea down the left for the 8 most spectacular holes with the famous lighthouse, but the finish is no less gripping. Brought back to life after the war thanks to the work of MacKenzie Ross, the Ailsa course is challenging, untamed and beguiling. It simply has to be experienced at least once in a lifetime, at any price (and here it is not just any price). A course to savour from end to end, without worrying too much about your card.

La venue régulière du British Open a fait sa réputation parmi les plus grands parcours de championnat au monde. Situé dans la partie la plus au sud d'une série majestueuse de links de l'Ayrshire, il offre un spectacle splendide sur l'île d'Arran, le sombre et mystérieux Mull of Kintyre et le rocher d'Ailsa. A savourer par beau temps (plus fréquent qu'on ne le croit !), car le vent peut transformer le parcours en enfer du jeu. Après un départ presque innocent, on trouve vite la mer à main gauche, pour les huit trous les plus spectaculaires, avec le célèbre phare, mais la conclusion n'est pas moins prenante. Ressuscité après la guerre grâce au travail de Mackenzie Ross, l'Ailsa est exigeant, sauvage, enchanteur, il constitue une expérience à connaître au moins une fois dans sa vie, à n'importe quel prix (c'est effectivement le cas...). Un parcours à savourer de bout en bout, sans trop penser au score.

Turnberry Hotel Golf Courses — 1906

SCO - TURNBERRY, Ayrshire, KA26 9LT

Office	Secrétariat	(44) 01655 - 331 000
Pro shop	Pro-shop	(44) 01655 - 334 043
Fax	Fax	(44) 01655 - 331 069
Web	www.turnberry.co.uk	
Situation	Situation	

24 km S of Ayr (pop. 47 872)

Annual closure	Fermeture annuelle	no
Weekly closure	Fermeture hebdomadaire	no

784

Fees main season Tarifs haute saison	Week days Semaine	We/Bank holidays We/Férié
		18 holes
Individual Individuel	£ 120 *	£ 150 *
Couple Couple	£ 240	£ 300

* Hotel residents: £ 95 pp

Caddy	Caddy	£ 25
Electric Trolley	Chariot électrique	no
Buggy	Voiturette	no
Clubs	Clubs	£ 40 /day

Credit cards Cartes de crédit
VISA - Eurocard - MasterCard - DC - AMEX

Access Accès : Glasgow, A77 to Turnberry
Map 3 on page 488 Carte 3 Page 488

Golf course — PARCOURS — 19/20

Site	Site	
Maintenance	Entretien	
Architect	Architecte	Mackenzie Ross, 1945
Type	Type	links
Relief	Relief	
Water in play	Eau en jeu	
Exp. to wind	Exposé au vent	
Trees in play	Arbres en jeu	

Scorecard Carte de score	Chp. Chp.	Mens Mess.	Ladies Da.
Length Long.	6279	5800	5182
Par	70	69	75
Slope system	—	—	—

Advised golfing ability Niveau de jeu recommandé — 0 12 24 36
Hcp required Handicap exigé — no

Club house & amenities — CLUB HOUSE ET ANNEXES — 9/10

Pro shop	Pro-shop	
Driving range	Practice	
Sheltered	couvert	yes
On grass	sur herbe	yes
Putting-green	putting-green	yes
Pitching-green	pitching green	yes

Hotel facilities — ENVIRONNEMENT HOTELIER — 8/10

HOTELS HÔTELS

Westin Turnberry Resort — on site
221 rooms, D from £ 140
Tel (44) 01655 - 331 000, Fax (44) 01655 - 331 706

Fairfield House — Ayr 24 km
45 rooms, D £ 130
Tel (44) 01292 - 267 461, Fax (44) 01292 - 261 456

RESTAURANTS RESTAURANT

3 restaurants / 4 bars — at the Hotel on site
Tel (44) 01655 - 331 000

The Ivy House, — Alloway 20 km
Tel (44) 01655 - 442 336

TURNBERRY Kintyre Course

16 | 9 | 8

The Kintyre Course was opened to great acclaim in the summer of 2001 and provides a perfect complement to its more illustrious sister. Building on the challenge laid down by the famous old Arran Course - a course of very considerable merit - the Kintyre is links golf at its exhilarating best. Created in 1909, the Arran was rebuilt on two previous occasions before architect Donald Steel was brought in to undertake a complete redesign in 1999. The alterations were so comprehensive that a change of name was warranted, with Kintyre maintaining a geographic link to the famous Mull of Kintyre across the water in Turnberry. The unveiling of the new course has introduced a new dimension complete with spectacular views and a magical setting. Kintyre will no more de considered as a second fiddle, or only as a warm-up round before playing the Ailsa course. Okay, you have to dig into your savings to play and stay in the impressive grand hotel, but if there are places in this world where pecuniary considerations come last, this has to be one of them.

Le Kyntire Course a été inauguré en été 2001, et s'est placé comme le parfait complément de son illustre voisin, le Ailsa Course. Bâti à la place du fameux vieux "Arran Course", parcours de grand mérite, soit dit en passant, le Kintyre représente un grand exemple d'architecture de links, plus encore que son prédécesseur. Créé en 1909, l'Arran a été remodelé en deux occasions, avant que l'architecte Donald Steel entreprenne un travil fondamental en 1999. Les changements ont été si importants qu'un changement de nom était nécessaire, celui de Kintyre assurant le lien évident avec le Mull of Kintyre, au large de Turnberry. C'est une nouvelle dimension que l'on trouve ici, avec des vues spectaculaires, une mise en scène remarquable et un challenge renouvelé. Kintyre ne saurait être considéré comme un parcours de second ordre, où l'on vient s'échauffer avant de jouer le "Ailsa Course". Plus que jamais, il faut casser sa tirelire pour séjourner dans le magnifique hôtel et jouer ici, mais Turnberry fait peut-être partie des endroits sans prix.

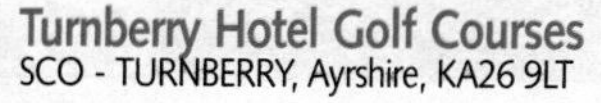

Turnberry Hotel Golf Courses

SCO - TURNBERRY, Ayrshire, KA26 9LT

Office	Secrétariat	(44) 01655 - 331 000
Pro shop	Pro-shop	(44) 01655 - 334 043
Fax	Fax	(44) 01655 - 331 069
Web	www.turnberry.co.uk	
Situation	Situation	

24 km S of Ayr (pop. 47 872)

Annual closure	Fermeture annuelle	no
Weekly closure	Fermeture hebdomadaire	no

Fees main season Tarifs haute saison		18 holes
	Week days Semaine	**We/Bank holidays** We/Férié
Individual Individuel	£ 95 *	£ 95 *
Couple Couple	£ 190	£ 190

* Hotel residents: £ 80 pp

Caddy	Caddy	£ 25
Electric Trolley	Chariot électrique	no
Buggy	Voiturette	no
Clubs	Clubs	£ 40 /day

Credit cards Cartes de crédit
VISA - Eurocard - MasterCard - DC - AMEX

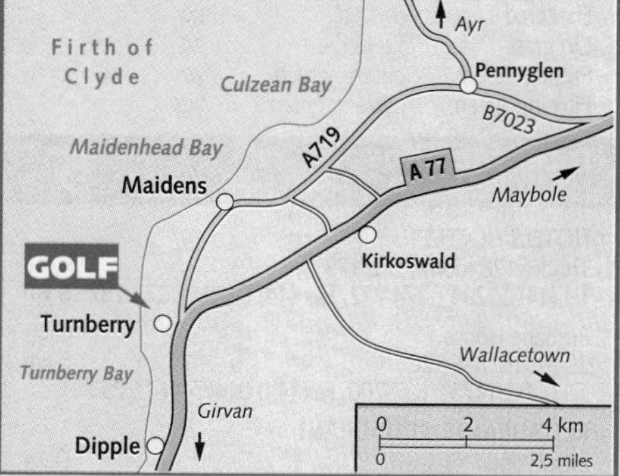

Access Accès : Glasgow, A77 to Turnberry
Map 3 on page 488 Carte 3 Page 488

Golf course PARCOURS — 16/20

Site	Site	
Maintenance	Entretien	
Architect	Architecte	Mackenzie Ross, 1945 Donald Steel, 1999
Type	Type	links
Relief	Relief	
Water in play	Eau en jeu	
Exp. to wind	Exposé au vent	
Trees in play	Arbres en jeu	

Scorecard Carte de score	**Chp.** Chp.	**Mens** Mess.	**Ladies** Da.
Length Long.	6268	5854	5004
Par	72	72	73
Slope system	—	—	—

Advised golfing ability Niveau de jeu recommandé: 0 12 24 36
Hcp required Handicap exigé: no

Club house & amenities CLUB HOUSE ET ANNEXES — 9/10

Pro shop	Pro-shop	
Driving range	Practice	
Sheltered	couvert	yes
On grass	sur herbe	yes
Putting-green	putting-green	yes
Pitching-green	pitching green	yes

Hotel facilities ENVIRONNEMENT HOTELIER — 8/10

HOTELS HÔTELS

Westin Turnberry Resort — on site
221 rooms, D from £ 140
Tel (44) 01655 - 331 000, Fax (44) 01655 - 331 706

Fairfield House — Ayr 24 km
45 rooms, D £ 130
Tel (44) 01292 - 267 461, Fax (44) 01292 - 261 456

RESTAURANTS RESTAURANT

3 restaurants / 4 bars — at the Hotel on site
Tel (44) 01655 - 331 000

The Ivy House — Alloway 20 km
Tel (44) 01655 - 442 336

WEST KILBRIDE

16 | 7 | 5

A very pretty course on the Ayrshire coast, without the claim to fame of its prestigious neighbours but always very welcoming on weekdays. The site is as magnificent as it is peaceful, with superb views over the Isle of Arran, Ailsa Craig and the north-west hills. But this 18-hole course is worth much more than its scenery. A very reasonable length makes this interesting prey for good golfers and the best players will find more than one opportunity to shine. The spread of difficulties makes for a well-balanced round of golf with only a single burn to interrupt the links landscape: bunkers that look to have been here since time began, thick bushes and the few trees that the wind has left standing. And of course the sea, whose incursions often tend to complicate the job of club officials.

Un très joli parcours de la côte de l'Ayrshire, sans prétendre aux grands titres de gloire de ses prestigieux voisins, mais toujours accueillant en semaine. Le site est aussi magnifique et très tranquille, avec des vues superbes sur l'Ile d'Arran, Ailsa Craig et les collines du nord-ouest. Mais ce 18 trous vaut mieux que son panorama. Sa longueur très raisonnable en fait une proie intéressante pour les golfeurs de niveau honorable, et les meilleurs y trouveront plus d'une occasion de s'y casser les dents. Le répartition des difficultés offre un bon rythme de jeu, un "burn" venant seul rompre leur nature propre aux links : des bunkers qui paraissent là depuis l'éternité, des buissons bien épais, quelques arbres ayant résisté au vent. Et à la mer, dont l'action vient parfois compliquer la tâche des responsables du Club.

The West Kilbride Golf Club — 1893

33-35 Fullerton Drive, Seamill
SCO - WEST KILBRIDE, Ayrshire KA23 9HT

Office	Secrétariat	(44) 01294 - 823 911
Pro shop	Pro-shop	(44) 01294 - 823 042
Fax	Fax	(44) 01294 - 823 573
Web	—	
Situation	Situation	Glasgow, 56 km
Annual closure	Fermeture annuelle	no
Weekly closure	Fermeture hebdomadaire	no

786

Fees main season Tarifs haute saison	18 holes	
	Week days Semaine	We/Bank holidays We/Férié
Individual Individuel	£ 25	*
Couple Couple	£ 50	*

Full weekday: £ 38 / No visitors at weekends

Caddy	Caddy	no
Electric Trolley	Chariot électrique	yes
Buggy	Voiturette	no
Clubs	Clubs	£ 5 /18 holes

Credit cards Cartes de crédit
VISA - Eurocard - MasterCard - DC - JCB - AMEX

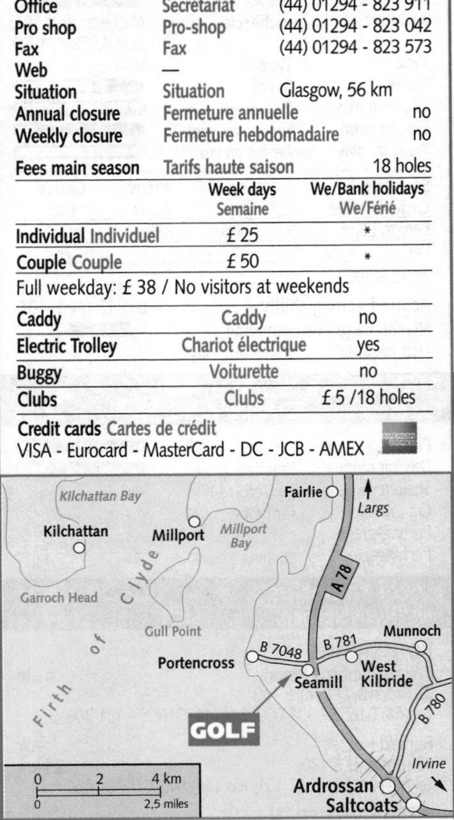

Kilchattan Bay
Kilchattan
Millport
Millport Bay
Fairlie
Largs
Garroch Head
Firth of Clyde
A 78
Gull Point
Portencross
B 7048
B 781
Munnoch
Seamill
West Kilbride
GOLF
B 780
Irvine
Ardrossan
Saltcoats
0 2 4 km
0 2,5 miles

Access Accès : Glasgow, A80 → Airport. At Jct 29, A737 through Paisley, Beith. After Dalry turn right on B781. In West Kilbride, turn right towards the sea.

Map 3 on page 488 Carte 3 Page 488

Golf course — PARCOURS — 16/20

Site	Site	
Maintenance	Entretien	
Architect	Architecte	Tom Morris James Braid
Type	Type	links
Relief	Relief	
Water in play	Eau en jeu	
Exp. to wind	Exposé au vent	
Trees in play	Arbres en jeu	

Scorecard Carte de score	Chp. Chp.	Mens Mess.	Ladies Da.
Length Long.	5898	5898	5292
Par	71	71	72
Slope system	—	—	—

Advised golfing ability — 0 12 24 36
Niveau de jeu recommandé
Hcp required Handicap exigé — certificate

Club house & amenities — CLUB HOUSE ET ANNEXES — 7/10

Pro shop	Pro-shop	
Driving range	Practice	
Sheltered	couvert	no
On grass	sur herbe	no
Putting-green	putting-green	yes
Pitching-green	pitching green	yes

Hotel facilities — ENVIRONNEMENT HOTELIER — 5/10

HOTELS HÔTELS

Thistle, 128 rooms, D £ 178 — Irvine
Tel (44) 01294 - 274 272, Fax (44) 01294 - 277 287 — 6 km

Brisbane House — Largs
23 rooms, D £ 120 — 5 km
Tel (44) 01475 - 687 200, Fax (44) 01475 - 676 295

RESTAURANTS RESTAURANT

Braidwoods — Dalry
Tel (44) 01294 - 833 544 — 6 km

Lagoon (Thistle) — Irvine
Tel (44) 01294 - 274 272 — 6 km

WESTERN GAILES

17 | 5 | 7

Between the seaside dunes and the railway lines, Western Gailes is one of the best links down the whole coast of Scotland. Totally exposed to the prevailing south-west wind, it subtly changes its nature even if the wind varies just a few degrees. There are only three par 3s, every one more difficult than it looks. Rather strangely for a course that is hardly much wider than two fairways, the clubhouse is almost in the middle. This means you play one half of the front 9 and one half of the back 9 with the wind behind you, and holes 5 to 13 with the wind in your face. This calls for some careful thinking over the line of play and attack. This private club welcomes visitors, even of the female variety, although there are no ladies tees. We'll just say that for them, this is an excellent par 74.

Entre les dunes de bord de mer et la voie ferrée, Western Gailes est un des meilleurs links de toute cette côte de l'Ecosse. Totalement exposé aux vents dominants de sud-ouest, il change subtilement de caractère selon que l'orientation se modifie de quelques degrés seulement. Il n'y a que trois par 3 ici, mais tous plus difficiles qu'ils ne paraissent. Assez curieusement pour un parcours guère plus large que deux fairways, le Club-house est presqu'au milieu : on joue ainsi la moitié de l'aller et la moitié du retour vent avec, et toute la partie du 5 au 13 vent contre, ce qui exige pas mal de réflexion sur la ligne de jeu... et la façon de négocier. Ce club privé est accueillant aux visiteurs, même féminins, bien qu'elles n'aient pas ici de départs spécifiques : disons que c'est pour elles un excellent par 74.

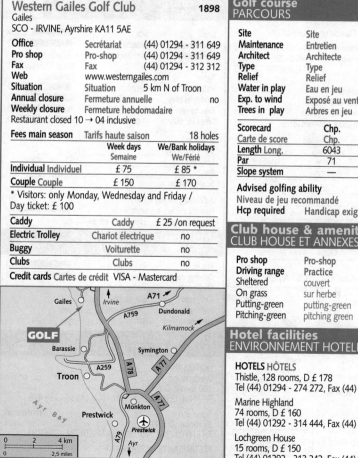

Western Gailes Golf Club — 1898

Gailes
SCO - IRVINE, Ayrshire KA11 5AE

Office	Secrétariat	(44) 01294 - 311 649
Pro shop	Pro-shop	(44) 01294 - 311 649
Fax	Fax	(44) 01294 - 312 312
Web	www.westerngailes.com	
Situation	Situation	5 km N of Troon
Annual closure	Fermeture annuelle	no
Weekly closure	Fermeture hebdomadaire	

Restaurant closed 10 → 04 inclusive

Fees main season Tarifs haute saison	18 holes	
	Week days Semaine	We/Bank holidays We/Férié
Individual Individuel	£ 75	£ 85 *
Couple Couple	£ 150	£ 170

* Visitors: only Monday, Wednesday and Friday / Day ticket: £ 100

Caddy	Caddy	£ 25 /on request
Electric Trolley	Chariot électrique	no
Buggy	Voiturette	no
Clubs	Clubs	no
Credit cards	Cartes de crédit	VISA - Mastercard

Access Accès : On A78, 3 km S of junction with A 71.
Map 3 on page 488 Carte 3 Page 488

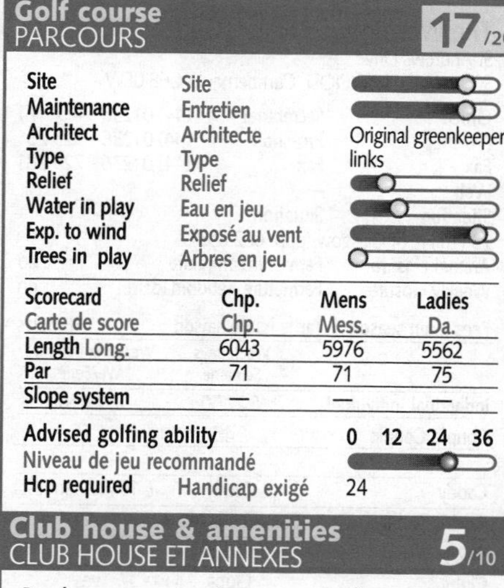

Golf course PARCOURS — 17/20

Site	Site	
Maintenance	Entretien	
Architect	Architecte	Original greenkeeper
Type	Type	links
Relief	Relief	
Water in play	Eau en jeu	
Exp. to wind	Exposé au vent	
Trees in play	Arbres en jeu	

Scorecard Carte de score	Chp. Chp.	Mens Mess.	Ladies Da.
Length Long.	6043	5976	5562
Par	71	71	75
Slope system	—	—	—

Advised golfing ability Niveau de jeu recommandé — 0 12 24 36
Hcp required Handicap exigé 24

Club house & amenities CLUB HOUSE ET ANNEXES — 5/10

Pro shop	Pro-shop	
Driving range	Practice	
Sheltered	couvert	small practice area
On grass	sur herbe	no
Putting-green	putting-green	yes
Pitching-green	pitching green	yes

Hotel facilities ENVIRONNEMENT HOTELIER — 7/10

HOTELS HÔTELS

Thistle, 128 rooms, D £ 178 — Irvine 2 km
Tel (44) 01294 - 274 272, Fax (44) 01294 - 277 287

Marine Highland — Troon 5 km
74 rooms, D £ 160
Tel (44) 01292 - 314 444, Fax (44) 01292 - 316 922

Lochgreen House — Troon 5 km
15 rooms, D £ 150
Tel (44) 01292 - 313 343, Fax (44) 01292 - 318 661

RESTAURANTS RESTAURANT

Highgrove House — Troon 3 km
Tel (44) 01292 - 312 511

WESTERWOOD

14 | 8 | 6

This is one of the very ambitious projects of recent years, designed by Dave Thomas and Seve Ballesteros in search of commercial success. The site is beautiful with an excellent hotel atop a hill, guaranteeing a scenic view and exposure to the wind. The course unwinds around the hotel but is never very hilly. The only real regret is that the course gets very wet when it rains and stays very dry for the rest of the time, which doesn't make playing very easy either way. You have to play long and straight, the greens are very well protected and the wind can make life complicated even in the middle of the trees. An often interesting and sometimes even spectacular course which is well worth playing in fine weather. Still in its infancy, Westerwood can only get better.

C'est l'un des projets très ambitieux de ces dernières années, avec les signatures de Dave Thomas et Seve Ballesteros pour rechercher le succès commercial. Le site est très beau, avec un excellent hôtel au sommet d'une colline, ce qui garantit le panorama, mais aussi l'exposition au vent. Le parcours se déroule à son pied, mais les reliefs ne sont pas très importants. Le seul vrai regret que l'on puisse avoir est qu'il soit très humide quand il a plu, et très sec par ailleurs, ce qui ne facilite pas le jeu dans un cas comme dans l'autre. Car il faut être long, précis, les greens sont très bien défendus et le vent peut compliquer les choses, même au milieu des arbres. Un parcours souvent intéressant, parfois même spectaculaire et qui vaut la peine d'être découvert par beau temps. Mais il est encore jeune et ne peut que progresser.

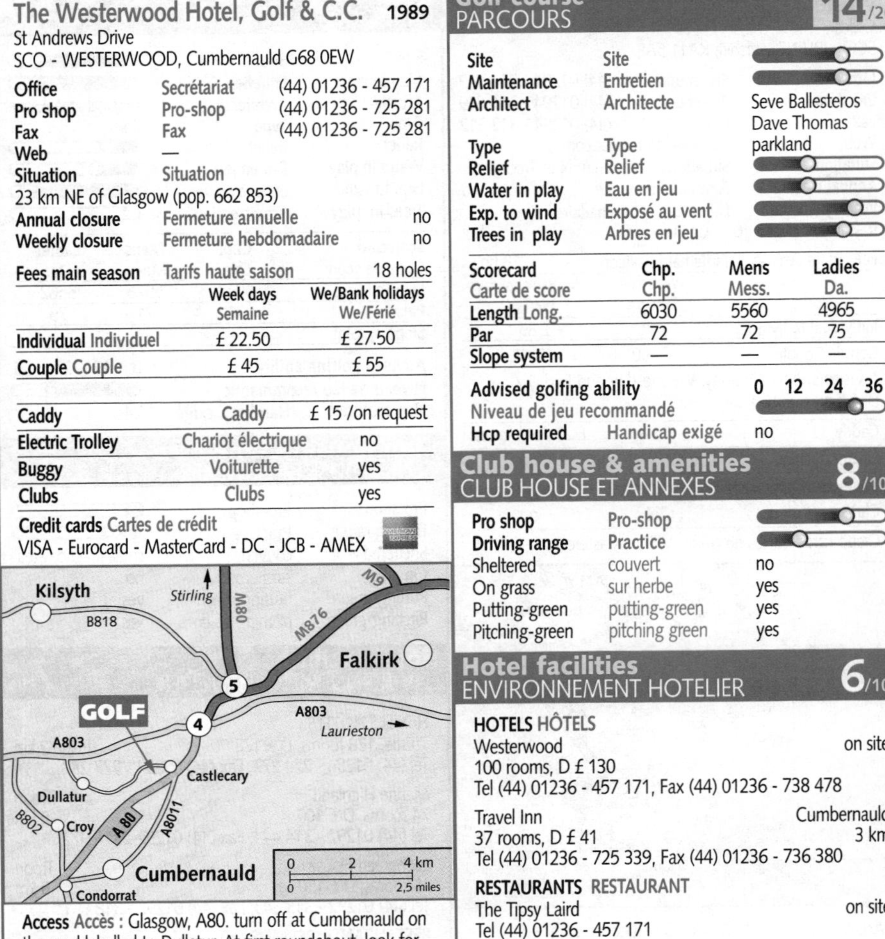

The Westerwood Hotel, Golf & C.C. 1989

St Andrews Drive
SCO - WESTERWOOD, Cumbernauld G68 0EW

Office	Secrétariat	(44) 01236 - 457 171
Pro shop	Pro-shop	(44) 01236 - 725 281
Fax	Fax	(44) 01236 - 725 281
Web	—	
Situation	Situation	

23 km NE of Glasgow (pop. 662 853)

Annual closure	Fermeture annuelle	no
Weekly closure	Fermeture hebdomadaire	no

Fees main season Tarifs haute saison		18 holes
	Week days Semaine	We/Bank holidays We/Férié
Individual Individuel	£ 22.50	£ 27.50
Couple Couple	£ 45	£ 55

Caddy	Caddy	£ 15 /on request
Electric Trolley	Chariot électrique	no
Buggy	Voiturette	yes
Clubs	Clubs	yes

Credit cards Cartes de crédit
VISA - Eurocard - MasterCard - DC - JCB - AMEX

Access Accès : Glasgow, A80. turn off at Cumbernauld on the road labelled to Dullatur. At first roundabout, look for Westerwood sign (not obvious!).
Map 2 on page 486 Carte 2 Page 486

Golf course PARCOURS 14/20

Site	Site	
Maintenance	Entretien	
Architect	Architecte	Seve Ballesteros Dave Thomas
Type	Type	parkland
Relief	Relief	
Water in play	Eau en jeu	
Exp. to wind	Exposé au vent	
Trees in play	Arbres en jeu	

Scorecard Carte de score	Chp. Chp.	Mens Mess.	Ladies Da.
Length Long.	6030	5560	4965
Par	72	72	75
Slope system	—	—	—

Advised golfing ability / Niveau de jeu recommandé: 0 12 24 36
Hcp required / Handicap exigé: no

Club house & amenities CLUB HOUSE ET ANNEXES 8/10

Pro shop	Pro-shop	
Driving range	Practice	
Sheltered	couvert	no
On grass	sur herbe	yes
Putting-green	putting-green	yes
Pitching-green	pitching green	yes

Hotel facilities ENVIRONNEMENT HOTELIER 6/10

HOTELS HÔTELS
Westerwood — on site
100 rooms, D £ 130
Tel (44) 01236 - 457 171, Fax (44) 01236 - 738 478

Travel Inn — Cumbernauld 3 km
37 rooms, D £ 41
Tel (44) 01236 - 725 339, Fax (44) 01236 - 736 380

RESTAURANTS RESTAURANT
The Tipsy Laird — on site
Tel (44) 01236 - 457 171

WHITEKIRK

15 | 7 | 7

In a region where there are many high quality courses, the Whitekirk promoters scored a significant victory over those who thought there wouldn't be enough space for another one. This course is a fine example of what can still be done with a restricted budget but with the determination to offer visitors excellent value for money. Practice facilities are of a standard seldom found in the UK, the greens are excellent, the layout very varied and the views (free of charge) over the Firth of Forth are magnificent. Naturally this layout cannot really match the genuine links courses found in the vicinity here, but it is a very serious design and strategy is immediately obvious without any hidden traps. This is essential for a "pay-as-you-play" course.

Dans une région présentant des parcours d'une telle qualité, les promoteurs de Whitekirk ont remporté une belle victoire sur ceux qui estimaient qu'il n'y avait plus de place disponible. Ce parcours est un bon exemple de ce que l'on peut encore faire avec un budget limité, mais avec la détermination d'offrir un bon rapport qualité-prix aux visiteurs de passage. Ils y trouveront des installations d'entraînement d'une rare qualité en Grande-Bretagne, des greens excellents, un tracé très varié et (gratuitement) de très belles vues sur le Firth of Forth. Certes, ce parcours ne peut tout à fait lutter avec les véritables links que l'on peut trouver alentour, mais son dessin a été sérieusement réalisé, la stratégie est immédiatement évidente, sans pièges dissimulés, ce qui est essentiel pour un parcours "pay-as-you-play."

Whitekirk Golf Course — 1995

Whitekirk
SCO - Nr NORTH BERWICK, E. Lothian EH39 5PR

Office	Secrétariat	(44) 01620 - 870 300
Pro shop	Pro-shop	(44) 01620 - 870 300
Fax	Fax	(44) 01620 - 870 330
Web	www.whitekirk.com	
Situation	Situation	North Berwick, 5 km
Annual closure	Fermeture annuelle	no
Weekly closure	Fermeture hebdomadaire	no

Fees main season / Tarifs haute saison	18 holes	
	Week days / Semaine	We/Bank holidays / We/Férié
Individual / Individuel	£ 20	£ 25
Couple / Couple	£ 40	£ 50

Full days: £ 30 / £ 40 (weekends)

Caddy	Caddy	on request
Electric Trolley	Chariot électrique	yes
Buggy	Voiturette	£ 15 /18 holes
Clubs	Clubs	£ 10 /18 holes

Credit cards Cartes de crédit
VISA - Eurocard - MasterCard

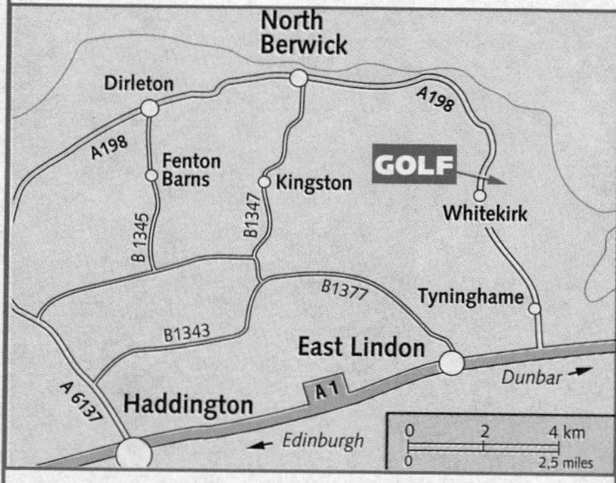

Access Accès : Edinburgh A1 → Berwick-upon-Tweed. After East Linton, A198 on the left. Golf on left side after Whitekirk village.
Map 3 on page 489 Carte 3 Page 489

Golf course / PARCOURS — 15/20

Site	Site	
Maintenance	Entretien	
Architect	Architecte	Cameron Sinclair
Type	Type	open country
Relief	Relief	
Water in play	Eau en jeu	
Exp. to wind	Exposé au vent	
Trees in play	Arbres en jeu	

Scorecard / Carte de score	Chp. / Chp.	Mens / Mess.	Ladies / Da.
Length Long.	5842	5645	4835
Par	72	72	72
Slope system	—	—	—

Advised golfing ability / Niveau de jeu recommandé: 0 12 24 36
Hcp required / Handicap exigé: no

Club house & amenities / CLUB HOUSE ET ANNEXES — 7/10

Pro shop	Pro-shop	
Driving range	Practice	
Sheltered	couvert	no
On grass	sur herbe	yes
Putting-green	putting-green	yes
Pitching-green	pitching green	yes

Hotel facilities / ENVIRONNEMENT HOTELIER — 7/10

HOTELS HÔTELS

Marine Hotel — North Berwick 5 km
79 rooms, D £ 140
Tel (44) 01620 - 892 406, Fax (44) 01620 - 894 480

Bayswell — Dunbar 12 km
13 rooms, D £ 79
Tel (44) 01368 - 862 225, Fax (44) 01368 - 862 225

RESTAURANTS RESTAURANT

Marine — North Berwick 5 km
Tel (44) 01620 - 892 406

Whitekirk Restaurant — Golf on site
Tel (44) 01620 - 870 300

EUROPE'S TOP 1000 GOLF COURSES

Wales

Royal Porthcawl

Wales
Pays de Galles

In the British Isles, Wales is not the best known country for golf, at least to players on the continent, who are often only familiar with those courses seen on the television during the British Open or other top tournaments. Yet Wales has one of the highest concentrations of great courses seen anywhere in the world. The problem is that they are sometimes so far away from any major city that it is virtually impossible for them to organise any of the world's top tournaments.

You won't find the sunny climes of Spain here, but the Gulf Stream does bring a lot of mild weather and a few spots of rain are always good for the skin. This means that there are very few tourists, which can only be good news for golf-trotters, who often have hundreds of acres of forest, miles of rugged coastline or sandy beaches and splendid landscapes all to themselves. And these are courses where you will have more than one opportunity to find playing partners and to get to know the Welsh people, who are the very picture of their country: sometimes a little rough on the edges, discreet, always proud and profoundly hospitable. All they need do is tell the rest of the world that their golf courses are first-rate, but they are only now starting to get involved in big publicity and promotion campaigns. If a great life means a hidden existence out-of-the-way, then real happiness is right here.

Dans les Iles Britanniques, le Pays de Galles n'est pas le pays le plus connu pour le golf, en tout cas par les continentaux, qui ne connaissent souvent que les parcours vus à la télévision au moment de championnats comme le British Open. Pourtant, le Pays de Galles réunit l'une des plus fortes concentrations de grands parcours par rapport au nombre total, mais ils sont parfois tellement à l'écart des grandes métropoles qu'il est presque impossible d'y organiser les plus grandes compétitions.

Ici, on ne trouve pas la chaleur de l'Espagne, mais le Gulf Stream adoucit le climat, et les quelques gouttes de pluie attendrissent la peau. S'il y a peu de touristes, tant mieux : on a souvent pour soi tout seul des centaines d'hectares de forêt, des kilomètres de côtes sauvages ou de plages, des paysages splendides, et des parcours de golf où l'on aura l'occasion de trouver des compagnons de jeu, de découvrir des Gallois à l'image de leur pays, rudes parfois, discrets, chaleureux et fiers. Il leur reste à faire savoir que leurs parcours sont de première grandeur, mais ils commencent seulement à se lancer dans de grandes campagnes de promotion.
S'il faut être bien caché pour vivre heureux, le bonheur est ici.

ABERDOVEY

17	7	7

You can get here by train, bringing your clubs with you, a throw-back to the times when courses were always close to railway tracks. The line here does indeed run alongside the course but not enough to make a nuisance of itself. And that's probably good news, because this layout, which has benefited from the flair of designers Fowler, Colt and Braid, is one of the best in Wales. Located in the Dovey estuary at the foot of some hills, this is a flat course lying alongside the pretty resort of Aberdovey, hence the rather crowded fairways in Summer. As the Old Course at St. Andrews, the holes are in a straight line out and in, thus making play a little easier in the wind. Yet the shifting landscape and dunes bring variety and sometimes even surprises like at the 3rd, a par 3 where the green is totally out of view. Aberdovey is Ian Woosnam's retreat between tournaments. So if it suits him, it'll probably suit you, too.

On peut venir en train avec ses clubs, ce qui rappelle le temps où les golfs étaient près du chemin de fer. Certes, il longe tout le parcours, mais pas assez souvent pour être une nuisance. Heureusement, car ce tracé, où des gloires comme Herbert Fowler, Harry Colt et James Braid ont laissé leur "patte" est un des meilleurs du pays. Dans l'embouchure de la Dovey, au pied des collines, c'est un parcours plat, à côté de la jolie station balnéaire d'Aberdovey, d'où une forte fréquentation en été. A l'instar du Old Course de St Andrews, les trous sont pratiquement alignés en aller et retour, ce qui facilite le jeu quand il y a du vent, mais les mouvements du terrain et les dunes apportent de la variété, parfois même de la surprise comme au 3, un par 3 où le green est totalement dissimulé. Pour Ian Woosnam, Aberdovey est une retraite entre les tournois. Si c'est bien pour lui, ce ne sera pas mal pour vous.

Aberdovey Golf Club — 1892

WAL - ABERDOVEY, Gwynedd LL35 0RT

Office	Secrétariat	(44) 01654 - 767 493
Pro shop	Pro-shop	(44) 01654 - 767 602
Fax	Fax	(44) 01654 - 767 027
Web	—	
Situation	Situation	

5 km NW of Aberdovey - 140 km from Cardiff (pop. 279 055)

Annual closure	Fermeture annuelle	no
Weekly closure	Fermeture hebdomadaire	no

Fees main season Tarifs haute saison	18 holes	
	Week days Semaine	**We/Bank holidays** We/Férié
Individual Individuel	£ 30*	£ 35*
Couple Couple	£ 60	£ 70

* Full day: £ 42/£ 48

Caddy	Caddy	no
Electric Trolley	Chariot électrique	yes
Buggy	Voiturette	yes
Clubs	Clubs	no

Credit cards Cartes de crédit
VISA - MasterCard (Green fees & goods, only at Pro shop)

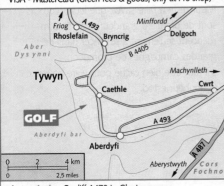

Access Accès : Cardiff A470 to Glantwymyn, then A489 to Machynlleth, A493 through Aberdyfi. Golf course NW near Railway Station.
Map 5 on page 492 Carte 5 Page 492

Golf course — PARCOURS — 17/20

Site	Site	
Maintenance	Entretien	
Architect	Architecte	Braid, Fowler, Colt
Type	Type	seaside course, links
Relief	Relief	
Water in play	Eau en jeu	
Exp. to wind	Exposé au vent	
Trees in play	Arbres en jeu	

Scorecard Carte de score	**Chp.** Chp.	**Mens** Mess.	**Ladies** Da.
Length Long.	5865	5551	5314
Par	71	71	74
Slope system	—	—	—

Advised golfing ability / Niveau de jeu recommandé: 0 12 24 36
Hcp required Handicap exigé: certificate

Club house & amenities — CLUB HOUSE ET ANNEXES — 7/10

Pro shop	Pro-shop	
Driving range	Practice	
Sheltered	couvert	no
On grass	sur herbe	yes
Putting-green	putting-green	yes
Pitching-green	pitching green	yes

Hotel facilities — ENVIRONNEMENT HOTELIER — 7/10

HOTELS HÔTELS

Plas Penhelig Country House — Aberdovey
11 rooms, D £ 132 (w. dinner) — 6 km
Tel (44) 01654 - 767 676, Fax (44) 01654 - 767 783

Trefeddian, 48 rooms, D £ 134 (w. dinner) — Aberdovey
Tel (44) 01654 - 767 213, Fax (44) 01654 - 767 777 — 3 km

Penhelig Arms, 10 rooms, D £ 79 — Aberdovey
Tel (44) 01654 - 767 215, Fax (44) 01654 - 767 690 — 5 km

Ynishir Hall, 8 rooms, D £ 190 — Machynlleth 15 km
Tel (44) 01654 - 781 209, Fax (44) 01654 - 781 366

RESTAURANTS RESTAURANT

Plas Penhelig Country House — Aberdovey
Tel (44) 01654 - 767 676 — 6 km

ASHBURNHAM

17 | 6 | 5

Located to the west of Llanelli and not so far from Swansea, this is one of the oldest courses in Wales, overlooking Camarthen Bay. The fairways are very busy in Summer, so be warned. The first and last two holes have a rather marked inland character, but for the rest of the course you have the prevailing south-westerlies to contend with. Holes 3 to 8 run parallel to the sea with a head-wind, holes 9 to 15 are played with the wind behind you. With tight fairways, dangerous rough and other unwelcome but easily identifiable hazards, you play here with your clubs and your brains. The greens are on the large side and equally difficult to read, which would explain why the course record here is only 70. Even though players of all levels can measure up to this test, the least experienced should not hold out too much hope when the wind roars (except perhaps for learning how to play with it).

Situé à l'ouest de Llanelli, et pas si loin de Swansea, ce parcours très fréquenté en été, et l'un des plus anciens du Pays de Galles, domine la baie de Carmarthen. Les deux premiers et deux derniers trous ont un caractère inland assez marqué. Ensuite, il faut jouer avec le vent dominant, car les trous du 3 ou 8 sont joués parallèlement à la mer et vent contre, les trous 9 à 15 se jouent vent avec... Avec les fairways étroits, un rough et des obstacles bien dangereux, mais aussi bien identifiables, il faut jouer avec ses clubs, mais aussi sa tête. Les greens sont assez grands, mais aussi très difficiles à lire, ce qui explique que le record ne soit ici que de 70. Et même si les joueurs de tous niveaux trouveront le test à leur mesure, les moins expérimentés ne doivent pas trop espérer quand le vent souffle (sinon apprendre à jouer...)

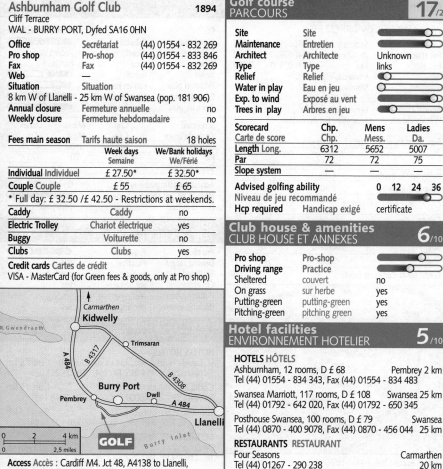

Ashburnham Golf Club — 1894

Cliff Terrace
WAL - BURRY PORT, Dyfed SA16 0HN

Office	Secrétariat	(44) 01554 - 832 269
Pro shop	Pro-shop	(44) 01554 - 833 846
Fax	Fax	(44) 01554 - 832 269
Web	—	
Situation	Situation	

8 km W of Llanelli - 25 km W of Swansea (pop. 181 906)

Annual closure	Fermeture annuelle	no
Weekly closure	Fermeture hebdomadaire	no

Fees main season Tarifs haute saison	18 holes	
	Week days Semaine	**We/Bank holidays** We/Férié
Individual Individuel	£ 27.50*	£ 32.50*
Couple Couple	£ 55	£ 65

* Full day: £ 32.50 /£ 42.50 - Restrictions at weekends.

Caddy	Caddy	no
Electric Trolley	Chariot électrique	yes
Buggy	Voiturette	no
Clubs	Clubs	yes

Credit cards Cartes de crédit
VISA - MasterCard (for Green fees & goods, only at Pro shop)

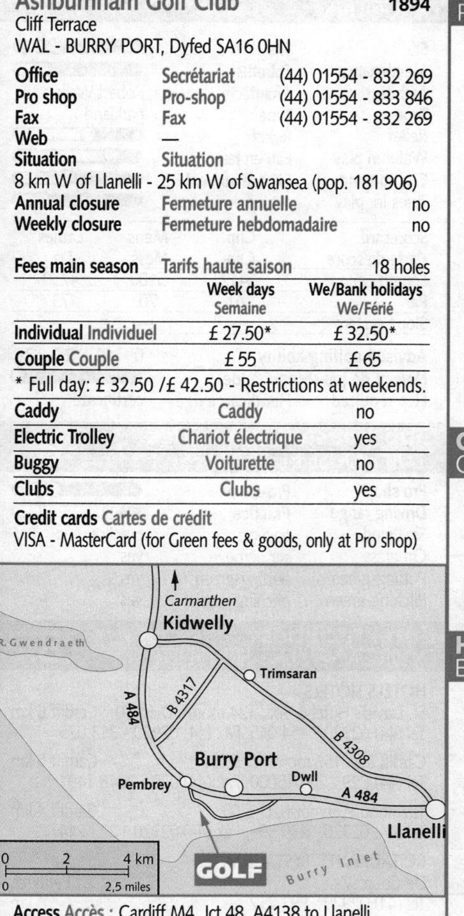

Access Accès : Cardiff M4. Jct 48, A4138 to Llanelli, then A484 to Burry Port.
Map 6 on page 494 Carte 6 Page 494

Golf course PARCOURS — 17/20

Site	Site	
Maintenance	Entretien	
Architect	Architecte	Unknown
Type	Type	links
Relief	Relief	
Water in play	Eau en jeu	
Exp. to wind	Exposé au vent	
Trees in play	Arbres en jeu	

Scorecard Carte de score	**Chp.** Chp.	**Mens** Mess.	**Ladies** Da.
Length Long.	6312	5652	5007
Par	72	72	75
Slope system	—	—	—

Advised golfing ability Niveau de jeu recommandé: 0 12 24 36
Hcp required Handicap exigé: certificate

Club house & amenities CLUB HOUSE ET ANNEXES — 6/10

Pro shop	Pro-shop	
Driving range	Practice	
Sheltered	couvert	no
On grass	sur herbe	yes
Putting-green	putting-green	yes
Pitching-green	pitching green	yes

Hotel facilities ENVIRONNEMENT HOTELIER — 5/10

HOTELS HÔTELS

Ashburnham, 12 rooms, D £ 68 — Pembrey 2 km
Tel (44) 01554 - 834 343, Fax (44) 01554 - 834 483

Swansea Marriott, 117 rooms, D £ 108 — Swansea 25 km
Tel (44) 01792 - 642 020, Fax (44) 01792 - 650 345

Posthouse Swansea, 100 rooms, D £ 79 — Swansea 25 km
Tel (44) 0870 - 400 9078, Fax (44) 0870 - 456 044

RESTAURANTS RESTAURANT

Four Seasons — Carmarthen 20 km
Tel (44) 01267 - 290 238

Hanson's — Swansea 25 km
Tel (44) 01792 - 466 200

CARDIFF

14 | 6 | 8

This course is virtually in the middle of town, one but not the only reason why it is impossible to play here without being accompanied by a member. Quite simply, this is an excellent course, even considered by some to be one of the three best inland courses in Wales, despite the relatively short yardage. This very well maintained course is a classic example of parkland golfing, where the growing trees have gradually become a crucial factor. A few water hazards and particularly the very cleverly arranged green-side bunkers make the golfer's job a whole lot more difficult. What's more, the greens are medium-sized only, thus calling for even greater accuracy. In this respect it is interesting to note that modern courses seldom require any more virtuosity than their elders, just a little more power. From the back tees here, there are some short and some long par 4s, but virtually nothing in between. A great and appealing challenge.

Ce parcours est pratiquement situé en pleine ville. Mais ce n'est pas seulement pour cela qu'il est impossible d'y jouer en week-end autrement qu'avec un membre, c'est parce qu'il s'agit aussi d'un excellent parcours. Certains le considèrent même comme l'un des trois meilleurs parcours "inland" du Pays de Galles, bien qu'il soit plutôt côté "court" que côté "long". Très bien entretenu, c'est un exemple classique de "parkland", dans lequel la croissance des arbres en a fait progressivement un facteur de jeu crucial. Quelques obstacles d'eau et surtout des bunkers de green disposés de manière très intelligente rendent la tâche plus complexe. De plus, ces greens sont de taille plutôt moyenne, ce qui oblige plus encore à être précis. Il est d'ailleurs intéressant de constater que les parcours modernes ne réclament guère plus de virtuosité que les anciens, juste un peu plus de puissance. On remarquera d'ailleurs que, des départs arrière, il y a ici des par 4 courts et longs mais pratiquement pas de longueur moyenne. Un bon et beau "challenge".

Cardiff Golf Club — 1921

Sherborne Avenue
WAL - CYNCOED, CARDIFF CF2 6SJ

Office	Secrétariat	(44) 02920 - 753 067
Pro shop	Pro-shop	(44) 02920 - 754 772
Fax	Fax	(44) 02920 - 752 134
Web	www.cardiffgolf.com	
Situation	Situation	

3 km N. of Cardiff (pop. 279 055)

Annual closure	Fermeture annuelle	no
Weekly closure	Fermeture hebdomadaire	no

Fees main season Tarifs haute saison	Week days Semaine	We/Bank holidays We/Férié
		Full day
Individual Individuel	£ 35	£ 40*
Couple Couple	£ 70	£ 80*

* We: only with a member

Caddy	Caddy	no
Electric Trolley	Chariot électrique	no
Buggy	Voiturette	no
Clubs	Clubs	yes
Credit cards	Cartes de crédit	no

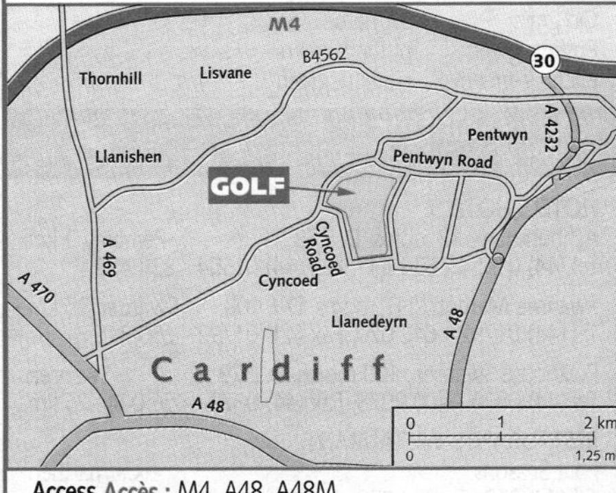

Access Accès : M4, A48, A48M
Map 6 on page 495 Carte 6 Page 495

Golf course PARCOURS — 14/20

Site	Site	
Maintenance	Entretien	
Architect	Architecte	Robert Walker
Type	Type	parkland
Relief	Relief	
Water in play	Eau en jeu	
Exp. to wind	Exposé au vent	
Trees in play	Arbres en jeu	

Scorecard Carte de score	Chp. Chp.	Mens Mess.	Ladies Da.
Length Long.	5412	5180	4750
Par	70	70	73
Slope system	—	—	—

Advised golfing ability 0 12 24 36
Niveau de jeu recommandé
Hcp required Handicap exigé certificate

Club house & amenities CLUB HOUSE ET ANNEXES — 6/10

Pro shop	Pro-shop	
Driving range	Practice	
Sheltered	couvert	practice area
On grass	sur herbe	yes
Putting-green	putting-green	yes
Pitching-green	pitching green	yes

Hotel facilities ENVIRONNEMENT HOTELIER — 8/10

HOTELS HÔTELS

St. David's Hotel & Spa, 124 rooms, D £ 170 — Cardiff 6 km
Tel (44) 02920 - 454 045, Fax (44) 02920 - 313 075

Cardiff Bay, 156 rooms, D £ 150 — Cardiff 5 km
Tel (44) 029 - 2047 5000, Fax (44) 029 - 2048 1491

Townhouse, 9 rooms, D £ 60 — Cardiff 4 km
Tel (44) 02920 - 239 399, Fax (44) 02920 - 223 214

RESTAURANTS RESTAURANT

De Courcey's — Pentyrch
Tel (44) 02920 - 892 232 — 4 km

Woods Brasserie, Tel (44) 02920 - 492 400 — Cardiff 6 km

Le Cassoulet, Tel (44) 02920 - 221 905 — Cardiff 5 km

CARDIGAN

15 | 6 | 5

This is not the best known Welsh course, but it does bear comparison with Tenby or Glamorganshire. The club-house buildings, although not the smartest in the world, are at least functional, while the view over the sea, particularly from the 16th, costs nothing even for the "never-break-a-hundred" hacker. The club dates back to 1895, but the course has been restyled several times, the last effort being conducted by Hawtree and Sons without altering the feel of the original. Yardage is in line with modern-day requirements, while the gorse and fern form the most obvious hazards for mis-hits; your ball somehow always seem to end up there whenever the wind blows it off course. In fact, this is a subtle blend of a links course, cliffs and pasture-land on a rather hilly setting, but the greens can generally be reached with low shots, at least if you work your way between the bunkers. A high standard course, with a special mention going to the visual and technical excellence of the last three holes.

Ce n'est pas le plus connu des parcours gallois, mais il peut soutenir la comparaison avec des parcours tels que Tenby ou Glamorganshire. Certes, les bâtiments du Clubhouse ne sont pas les plus stylés du monde, mais il sont au moins fonctionnels. Quant à la vue sur l'Océan, en particulier au départ du 16, elle est offerte, même aux mauvais joueurs. Le club date de 1895, mais le parcours a été plusieurs fois remanié, la dernière fois par le cabinet Hawtree & Sons sans en modifier l'esprit. Sa longueur répond à présent aux critères modernes. Les ajoncs et les fougères constituent l'une des menaces les plus flagrantes pour les balles, et si le vent les détourne, c'est toujours vers les obstacles. En fait, c'est un mélange assez subtil de links, de parcours de falaise, de pâturages, le tout assez accidenté, mais les greens acceptent en général les approches roulées, du moins si les bunkers les laissent passer. Dans ce parcours de bon niveau, on soulignera enfin la qualité visuelle et technique des trois derniers trous.

Cardigan Golf Club — 1928

Gwbert on Sea
WAL - CARDIGAN SA43 1PR

Office	Secrétariat	(44) 01239 - 621 775
Pro shop	Pro-shop	(44) 01239 - 615 359
Fax	Fax	(44) 01239 - 621 775
Web	—	
Situation	Situation	

3 km from Cardigan (pop. 4 409)

Annual closure	Fermeture annuelle	no
Weekly closure	Fermeture hebdomadaire	no

Fees main season Tarifs haute saison	Week days Semaine	We/Bank holidays We/Férié
		Full day
Individual Individuel	£ 20	£ 25
Couple Couple	£ 40	£ 50
Caddy Caddy		no
Electric Trolley Chariot électrique		no
Buggy Voiturette		£ 15
Clubs Clubs		yes

Credit cards Cartes de crédit
VISA - Eurocard - MasterCard

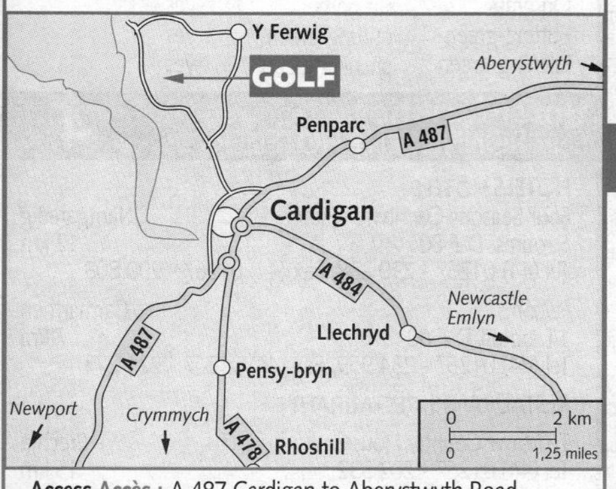

Access Accès : A 487 Cardigan to Aberystwyth Road. Fork left at War Memorial, 2 km.
Map 6 on page 494 Carte 6 Page 494

Golf course — PARCOURS — 15/20

Site	Site	
Maintenance	Entretien	
Architect	Architecte	I.E. Grant Hawtree & Son
Type	Type	links, meadowland
Relief	Relief	
Water in play	Eau en jeu	
Exp. to wind	Exposé au vent	
Trees in play	Arbres en jeu	

Scorecard Carte de score	Chp. Chp.	Mens Mess.	Ladies Da.
Length Long.	6019	5784	5022
Par	72	72	74
Slope system	—	—	—

Advised golfing ability — 0 12 24 36
Niveau de jeu recommandé
Hcp required Handicap exigé — certificate

Club house & amenities — CLUB HOUSE ET ANNEXES — 6/10

Pro shop	Pro-shop	
Driving range	Practice	
Sheltered	couvert	practice area
On grass	sur herbe	yes
Putting-green	putting-green	yes
Pitching-green	pitching green	no

Hotel facilities — ENVIRONNEMENT HOTELIER — 5/10

HOTELS HÔTELS

Gwbert Hotel, 16 rooms, D £ 127 — Gwbert-on-Sea 1 km
Tel (44) 01239 - 612 638, Fax (44) 01239 - 621 474

Penrallt, 16 rooms, D £ 100 — Aberporth 10 km
Tel (44) 01239 - 810 227, Fax (44) 01239 - 811 375

Penbontbren Farm, 10 rooms, D £ 91 — Cardigan 3 km
Tel (44) 01239 - 810 248, Fax (44) 01239 - 811 129

RESTAURANTS RESTAURANT

Penbontbren Farm — Cardigan 3 km
Tel (44) 01239 - 810 248

Gwbert Hotel, — Gwbert-on-Sea 1 km
Tel (44) 01239 - 612 638

CARMARTHEN

15 | 7 | 4

If you have the time, have a drink or (even better) take lunch after your round facing one of the most splendid sights to be seen on the Welsh coast. This should offer some consolation for shooting over your handicap on a course that J.H. Taylor obviously had great fun building. Don't be fooled by the yardage, relatively short except for the first hole, an intimidating long and tough par 4. And watch out for the 17th, where the two-tiered green is treacherous enough to ruin any card. With this said, if you can move the ball both ways, have a certain instinct for the game and a fair degree of humility, approach this course with serious but modest pretentions. There are no gimmicks here, no needless trimmings and no huge back-fills of earth: it is quite simply a great test of golf, pleasant to walk despite the rolling terrain and a peaceful site out in the countryside. It gets pretty wet here in winter so try to make it in spring or summer.

Si vous en avez le temps, prenez un verre ou (encore mieux) déjeunez après votre parcours devant l'un des plus beaux panoramas que l'on puisse trouver sur la campagne galloise. Cela vous consolera de ne pas avoir cassé le par sur un parcours que J.H. Taylor a dû prendre beaucoup de plaisir à dessiner. Sa longueur modérée ne doit pas faire illusion. D'ailleurs, le parcours commence par un long et difficile par 4 pour vous intimider, et le 17 se termine par un green à double plateau, assez traître pour vous casser la carte. Mais si vous avez quelque talent du maniement de balle, l'instinct du jeu, et une certaine humilité, prenez ce parcours avec sérieux et modestie. pas de "gimmicks" ici, pas de décoration inutile, pas de grands mouvements de terrain, c'est tout simplement un très bon test de golf, agréable à marcher en dépit de ses ondulations, un lieu de calme aussi en pleine campagne. Il peut être humide en hiver, venez plutôt aux beaux jours.

Carmarthen Golf Club — 1928

Rhydymarchog, Blaen-y-Coed Road
WAL - CARMARTHEN SA33 6EH

Office	Secrétariat	(44) 01267 - 281 588
Pro shop	Pro-shop	(44) 01267 - 281 493
Fax	Fax	(44) 01267 - 281 214
Web	—	
Situation	Situation	

6 km NW of Carmarthen

Annual closure	Fermeture annuelle	no
Weekly closure	Fermeture hebdomadaire	no

Fees main season Tarifs haute saison	18 holes	
	Week days Semaine	We/Bank holidays We/Férié
Individual Individuel	£ 20	£ 25
Couple Couple	£ 40	£ 50

Half price when playing with a member

Caddy	Caddy	no
Electric Trolley	Chariot électrique	
Buggy	Voiturette	
Clubs	Clubs	yes
Credit cards	Cartes de crédit	VISA - MasterCard

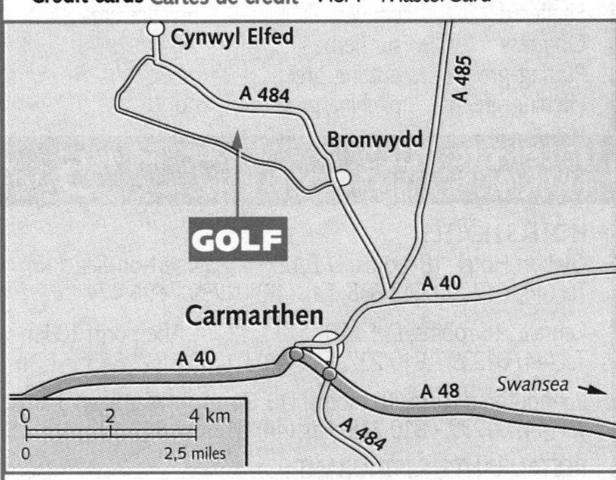

Access Accès : M4, A48 to Carmarthen, A40 → Abergwilli, then A484 North, left on Blaen-y-Coed road.
Map 6 on page 494 Carte 6 Page 494

Golf course — PARCOURS — 15/20

Site	Site	
Maintenance	Entretien	
Architect	Architecte	J.H. Taylor
Type	Type	parkland
Relief	Relief	
Water in play	Eau en jeu	
Exp. to wind	Exposé au vent	
Trees in play	Arbres en jeu	

Scorecard Carte de score	Chp. Chp.	Mens Mess.	Ladies Da.
Length Long.	5621	5433	4815
Par	71	71	72
Slope system	—	—	—

Advised golfing ability Niveau de jeu recommandé — 0 12 24 36
Hcp required Handicap exigé — certificate

Club house & amenities — CLUB HOUSE ET ANNEXES — 7/10

Pro shop	Pro-shop	
Driving range	Practice	
Sheltered	couvert	large practice area
On grass	sur herbe	yes
Putting-green	putting-green	yes
Pitching-green	pitching green	yes

Hotel facilities — ENVIRONNEMENT HOTELIER — 4/10

HOTELS HÔTELS

Four Seasons Cwmtwrch Hotel — Nantgaredig
6 rooms, D £ 80 — 12 km
Tel (44) 01267 - 290 238, Fax (44) 01267 - 290 808

Falcon — Carmarthen
14 rooms, D £ 60 — 7 km
Tel (44) 01267 - 234 959, Fax (44) 01267 - 221 277

RESTAURANTS RESTAURANT

Ty Mawr Country House — Brechfa
Tel (44) 01267 - 202 332 — 15 km

Four Seasons (Cwmtwrch Hotel) — Carmarthen
Tel (44) 01267 - 290 238 — 7 km

CELTIC MANOR Roman Road

18	9	7

The total budget of £ 100 million of this ambitious complexhas provided great facilities and a great course, too. After the first two layouts designed by Robert Trent Jones Jr. (of Welsh stock), a third, "Wentwood Hills", has recently been opened using the same architect. At some 6,700 metres in length, the course is patently reserved more for experienced golfers. We will leave it time to mature a little, although we can only be favourably disposed to a layout where nothing has been spared to make Celtic Manor a hugely successful venture. Average players can continue to enjoy "Roman Road", where as the name suggests you find the remains of a Roman road and even an ancient school for gladiators, although the battles fought here nowadays are of a more peaceful nature with a little white ball. Over a rolling landscape (buggy advisable for some), the architect has laid out a very American style course, forcing the golfer to fight his or her way over, through or across lakes, ravines, trees,streams and huge bunkers to finally get the ball onto some vast and finely contoured greens.

Le budget total de 100 millions de Livres de cet ambitieux complexe n'a pas oublié le golf. Après les deux premiers parcours dessinés par le Gallois d'origine Robert Trent Jones Jr, le troisième ("Wentwood Hills") vient d'être ouvert, toujours avec le même architecte. Avec 6700 mètres, sa longueur le réserve aux golfeurs expérimentés. Nous le laisserons prendre un peu de maturité, avec un préjugé favorable, rien n'ayant été épargné pour faire de Celtic Manor une réussite. Les joueurs moyens continueront à apprécier "Roman Road", où l'on trouve les restes d'une voie romaine, et même d'une école de gladiateurs, mais on va batailler ici de manière plus pacifique. Dans ce paysage vallonné (voiturette conseillée pour les moins en forme), l'architecte a placé un parcours très américain de style, obligeant à négocier son itinéraire avec des lacs, des ravins, des bois, des cours d'eau, des immenses bunkers, pour enfin poser sa balle sur de vastes greens très travaillés.

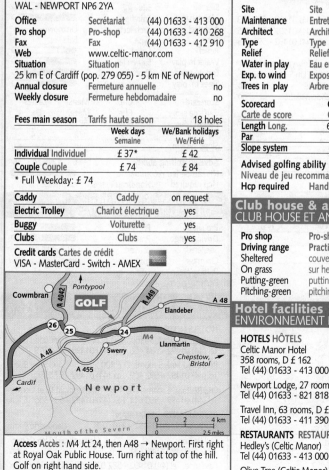

Celtic Manor — 1995

Coldra Woods
WAL - NEWPORT NP6 2YA

Office	Secrétariat	(44) 01633 - 413 000
Pro shop	Pro-shop	(44) 01633 - 410 268
Fax	Fax	(44) 01633 - 412 910
Web	www.celtic-manor.com	
Situation	Situation	

25 km E of Cardiff (pop. 279 055) - 5 km NE of Newport

Annual closure	Fermeture annuelle	no
Weekly closure	Fermeture hebdomadaire	no

Fees main season Tarifs haute saison	18 holes	
	Week days Semaine	**We/Bank holidays** We/Férié
Individual Individuel	£ 37*	£ 42
Couple Couple	£ 74	£ 84

* Full Weekday: £ 74

Caddy	Caddy	on request
Electric Trolley	Chariot électrique	yes
Buggy	Voiturette	yes
Clubs	Clubs	yes

Credit cards Cartes de crédit
VISA - MasterCard - Switch - AMEX

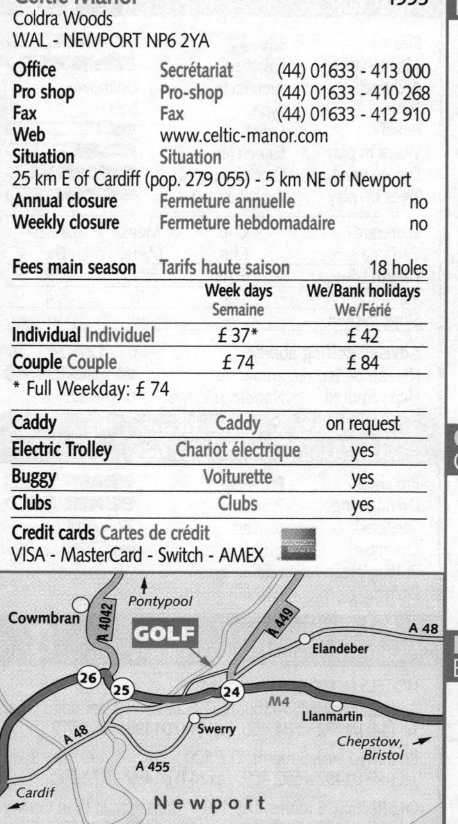

Access Accès : M4 Jct 24, then A48 → Newport. First right at Royal Oak Public House. Turn right at top of the hill. Golf on right hand side.
Map 6 on page 495 Carte 6 Page 495

Golf course — PARCOURS — 18/20

Site	Site	
Maintenance	Entretien	
Architect	Architecte	R. Trent Jones Jr
Type	Type	parkland
Relief	Relief	
Water in play	Eau en jeu	
Exp. to wind	Exposé au vent	
Trees in play	Arbres en jeu	

Scorecard Carte de score	**Chp.** Chp.	**Mens** Mess.	**Ladies** Da.
Length Long.	6371	5998	4430
Par	70	70	70
Slope system	—	—	—

Advised golfing ability — 0 12 24 36
Niveau de jeu recommandé
Hcp required Handicap exigé — certificate

Club house & amenities — CLUB HOUSE ET ANNEXES — 9/10

Pro shop	Pro-shop	
Driving range	Practice	
Sheltered	couvert	28 floodlit bays
On grass	sur herbe	yes
Putting-green	putting-green	yes
Pitching-green	pitching green	yes

Hotel facilities — ENVIRONNEMENT HOTELIER — 7/10

HOTELS HÔTELS

Celtic Manor Hotel — Golf o
358 rooms, D £ 162
Tel (44) 01633 - 413 000, Fax (44) 01633 - 412 910

Newport Lodge, 27 rooms, D £ 85 — Newport 5 km
Tel (44) 01633 - 821 818, Fax (44) 01633 - 856 360

Travel Inn, 63 rooms, D £ 41 — Newport 5 km
Tel (44) 01633 - 411 390, Fax (44) 01633 - 411 376

RESTAURANTS RESTAURANT

Hedley's (Celtic Manor) — on site
Tel (44) 01633 - 413 000

Olive Tree (Celtic Manor), Tel (44) 01633 - 413 000 on site

CONWY

17	7	8

Sections of the artificial port for the 1944 Normandy landings were built behind the green on the 2nd hole. This is only one page of history amongst many others, as the city has even held onto its medieval ramparts. The course is much flatter than its counterparts on the western and southern coasts, but there is never any question of tedium thanks to subtle shifts in landscape and the ubiquitous gorse. Naturally, you can add to this the course's own specific headaches, including length from the back tees. Playing further forward can put it within easier reach. In every case this is a perfectly honest layout, where the penalty to pay matches the gravity of your mis-hit. Very natural and with obvious personality, Conwy deserves a prolonged and respectful visit.

Derrière le green du 2 ont été construites en 1943 des portions du port artificiel du débarquement de 1944. Ce n'est qu'une page d'histoire parmi d'autres, car la ville a conservé jusqu'à ses remparts médiévaux. Le parcours est beaucoup plus plat que ceux des côtes ouest et sud, mais il échappe à la monotonie grâce à de subtils mouvements de terrain, et aussi à l'omniprésence de buissons d'ajoncs. Il faut encore y ajouter les difficultés propres du parcours, très long des départs les plus reculés, mais plus accessible des départs avancés. En tous les cas, il est d'une parfaite franchise, les punitions étant à la hauteur de la gravité des fautes commises. Très naturel, avec son évidente personnalité, Conwy mérite une visite aussi prolongée que respectueuse.

Conwy (Caernarvonshire) Golf Club — 1890

Morfa
WAL - CONWY, Gwynedd LL32 8 ER

Office	Secrétariat	(44) 01492 - 592 423
Pro shop	Pro-shop	(44) 01492 - 593 225
Fax	Fax	(44) 01492 - 593 363
Web	—	
Situation	Situation	Colwyn Bay, 8 km 4 km S of Llandudno
Annual closure	Fermeture annuelle	no
Weekly closure	Fermeture hebdomadaire	no

Fees main season Tarifs haute saison		18 holes
	Week days Semaine	**We/Bank holidays** We/Férié
Individual Individuel	£ 25*	£ 32*
Couple Couple	£ 50	£ 64

* Full day: £ 30 /£ 37

Caddy	Caddy	no
Electric Trolley	Chariot électrique	yes
Buggy	Voiturette	yes
Clubs	Clubs	yes
Credit cards Cartes de crédit		no

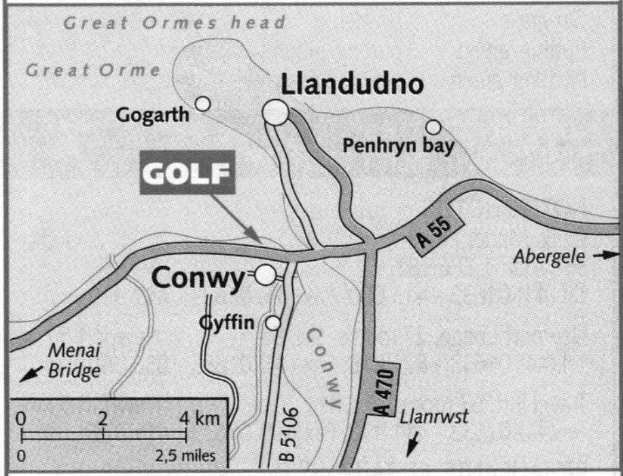

Great Ormes head
Great Orme
Llandudno
Gogarth
Penhryn bay
GOLF
A 55
Abergele
Conwy
Gyffin
Conwy
Menai Bridge
A 470
B 5106
Llanrwst
0 2 4 km
0 2,5 miles

Access Accès : A55 to Conwy and follow signs to Conwy Marina.
Map 5 on page 492 Carte 5 Page 492

Golf course — PARCOURS — 17/20

Site	Site	
Maintenance	Entretien	
Architect	Architecte	Unknown
Type	Type	links
Relief	Relief	
Water in play	Eau en jeu	
Exp. to wind	Exposé au vent	
Trees in play	Arbres en jeu	

Scorecard Carte de score	**Chp.** Chp.	**Mens** Mess.	**Ladies** Da.
Length Long.	6049	5819	5299
Par	72	72	74
Slope system	—	—	—

Advised golfing ability Niveau de jeu recommandé: 0 12 24 36
Hcp required Handicap exigé: certificate

Club house & amenities — CLUB HOUSE ET ANNEXES — 7/10

Pro shop	Pro-shop	
Driving range	Practice	
Sheltered	couvert	28 floodlit bays
On grass	sur herbe	yes
Putting-green	putting-green	yes
Pitching-green	pitching green	yes

Hotel facilities — ENVIRONNEMENT HOTELIER — 8/10

HOTELS HÔTELS
Bodysgallen Hall, 36 rooms, D £ 240 — Llandudno 6 km
Tel (44) 01492 - 584 466, Fax (44) 01492 - 582 519

Berthlwyd Hall, 5 rooms, D £ 100 — Conwy 3 km
Tel (44) 01492 - 592 409, Fax (44) 01492 - 572 290

Old Rectory, 6 rooms, D £ 130 — Llansanffraid Glan Conwy
Tel (44) 01492 - 580 611, Fax (44) 01492 - 584 555 — 6 km

RESTAURANTS RESTAURANT
Martin's, Tel (44) 01492 - 870 070 — Llandudno 6 km

Old Rectory — Llansanffraid Glan Conwy
Tel (44) 01492 - 580 611 — 6 km

Paysanne, Tel (44) 01492 - 582 079 — Deganwy 5 km

GLAMORGANSHIRE

14 | 7 | 8

This is the fourth oldest club in Wales and the first inland course. Perched above the Bristol Channel, it provides some splendid views over Glamorgan and Monmouthshire, and over the English counties on the other side as well. The architect is unknown, but he sure knew his job. Aside from links courses, this is how our ancestors enjoyed their golfing; forget the acres of white sand, the shining blue lakes and manicured grass. Tee it up, hit the approach from whatever position you happen to be in and try and stop your ball on firm, slick greens. With this said, the general condition of the course is excellent but here they prefer the course to be good and play well rather than just look beautiful. This is a totally forthright course where you can't lie about your game or hide any chinks in the armour: it is tradition in its finest and most vivid form, with some golfing history to boot. This is where Dr. Frank Stableford invented the scoring system that bears his name. For the moment, however, we still don't know where Mssrs Foursome and Medal used to play...

C'est le quatrième plus ancien Club du Pays de Galles et le tout premier "inland". Du haut de son perchoir au dessus du Bristol Channel, il offre des vues sur le Glamorgan et le Monmouthshire, mais aussi sur trois Comtés anglais. On ne connaît pas son architecte mais il connaissait son métier. Mis à part les links, c'est ainsi que nos ancêtres vivaient le golf : oubliez les hectares de sable blanc, les lacs aux hauts bleues, les brins de gazon au garde-à-vous. Tapez la balle sur le tee, puis jouez votre approche comme sa position vous l'impose, et tâchez d'arrêter votre balle sur un green ferme et roulant. Cela dit, l'état général du parcours est excellent, mais rien n'est fait pour faire "beau" au détriment de "bien". La franchise du parcours est absolue, et vous ne pourrez pas mentir avec lui, maquiller vos défauts, c'est la tradition dans ce qu'elle a de mieux, et de plus vivant. En plus, vous avez l'histoire : c'est ici que le Dr Frank Stableford inventa la formule de jeu qui porte son nom. En revanche, on ne sait toujours pas où jouaient MM. Foursome et Stroke Play.

The Glamorganshire Golf Club — 1890

Lavernock Road
ENG - PENARTH CF64 5UP

Office	Secrétariat	(44) 02920 - 701 185
Pro shop	Pro-shop	(44) 02920 - 707 401
Fax	Fax	(44) 02920 - 701 185
Web	www.theglamorganshiregolfclub.com	
Situation	Situation	

16 km from Cardiff (pop. 279 055)

Annual closure	Fermeture annuelle	no
Weekly closure	Fermeture hebdomadaire	no

Fees main season Tarifs haute saison	Full day	
	Week days Semaine	**We/Bank holidays** We/Férié
Individual Individuel	£ 30	£ 35
Couple Couple	£ 60	£ 70
Caddy	Caddy	no
Electric Trolley	Chariot électrique	no
Buggy	Voiturette	£ 20
Clubs	Clubs	yes

Credit cards Cartes de crédit
VISA - MasterCard

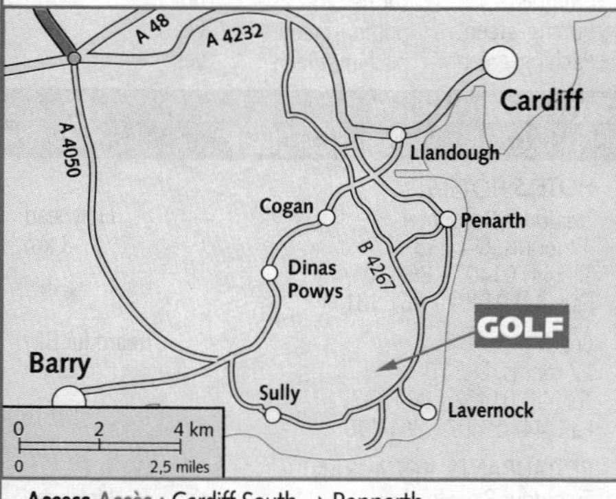

Access Accès : Cardiff South → Pennarth.
B 4267 → Golf
Map 6 on page 495 Carte 6 Page 495

Golf course PARCOURS — 14/20

Site	Site	●●●●○
Maintenance	Entretien	●●●●○
Architect	Architecte	Unknown
Type	Type	parkland
Relief	Relief	●○○○○
Water in play	Eau en jeu	●○○○○
Exp. to wind	Exposé au vent	●●●●○
Trees in play	Arbres en jeu	●●●●○

Scorecard Carte de score	**Chp.** Chp.	**Mens** Mess.	**Ladies** Da.
Length Long.	5451	5281	4916
Par	70	70	72
Slope system	—	—	—

Advised golfing ability Niveau de jeu recommandé — 0 12 24 36
Hcp required Handicap exigé — certificate

Club house & amenities CLUB HOUSE ET ANNEXES — 7/10

Pro shop	Pro-shop	●●●●○
Driving range	Practice	●○○○○
Sheltered	couvert	practice area
On grass	sur herbe	yes
Putting-green	putting-green	yes
Pitching-green	pitching green	yes

Hotel facilities ENVIRONNEMENT HOTELIER — 8/10

HOTELS HÔTELS

Mount Sorrel, 41 rooms, D £ 95 — Barry 7 km
Tel (44) 01446 - 740 069, Fax (44) 01446 - 746 600

Egerton Grey Country House, 10 rooms, D £ 130 — Barry 14 km
Tel (44) 01446 - 711 666, Fax (44) 01446 - 711 690

Ferrier's Hotel, 26 rooms, D £ 50 — Cardiff 16 km
Tel (44) 01222 - 383 413, Fax (44) 01222 - 383 413

Clare Court Hotel, 8 rooms, D £ 40 — Cardiff
Tel (44) 01222 - 344 839, Fax (44) 01222 - 665 856

RESTAURANTS RESTAURANT

Quayle's, Tel (44) 029 - 2034 1264 — Cardiff
Armless Dragon, Tel (44) 029 - 2038 2357 — Cardiff

HOLYHEAD

16 | 7 | 5

A bridge has made Anglesey a peninsula and Trearddur Bay (as Holyhead is properly known) a better known course. Local players will tell you some horrible stories about lost golfers and terrifying scores, but Wales is also known as a land of tall stories. This course is difficult in the wind, but that is true for all links courses. It is short enough not to have staged very many prestigious tournaments, and rather hilly with tight, neatly contoured fairways. The natural rough is often dotted with thick heather, broom, gorse and even ferns, so it is an honest test for players of all levels (it was designed by James Braid, which says it all) with some of the best greens in the country. Exciting to play, intelligent and imaginative, Holyhead is well worth going out of your way for, and in Summer is quite superb.

Le pont a fait d'Anglesey une presqu'île, et de "Trearddur Bay" (comme on appelle Holyhead) une oeuvre mieux connue. Les joueurs locaux vous raconteront quelques horribles histoires sur des golfeurs perdus et des scores terrifiants, mais le Pays de Galles est aussi celui des contes de fées. Ce parcours est difficile par grand vent, mais c'est le cas de tous les links. Assez court, ce qui explique qu'il n'ait pas reçu beaucoup de championnats très prestigieux, pas trop accidenté, il a des fairways étroits, bien modelés, des roughs naturels souvent parsemés d'une dense végétation de bruyère, de genêts, d'ajoncs et même de fougères. C'est un test d'une grande franchise pour tous les niveaux (il est signé James Braid, une référence), avec des greens parmi les meilleurs du pays. Superbe au printemps et en été, excitant à jouer, intelligent et imaginatif, Holyhead mérite le détour.

Holyhead (Caergybi) Golf Club — 1912

Lon Carreg Fawr, Trearddur Bay
WAL - HOLYHEAD, Gwynedd LL65 2YG

Office	Secrétariat	(44) 01407 - 763 279
Pro shop	Pro-shop	(44) 01407 - 762 022
Fax	Fax	(44) 01407 - 763 279
Web	www. holyheadgolfclub.com	
Situation	Situation	3 km S of Holyhead
Annual closure	Fermeture annuelle	no
Weekly closure	Fermeture hebdomadaire	no

Fees main season Tarifs haute saison	Week days Semaine	We/Bank holidays We/Férié
	18 holes	
Individual Individuel	£ 19*	£ 25*
Couple Couple	£ 38	£ 50

Full day: £ 25/£29

Caddy	Caddy	no
Electric Trolley	Chariot électrique	no
Buggy	Voiturette	no
Clubs	Clubs	yes

Credit cards Cartes de crédit
VISA - Mastercard (Pro shop only)

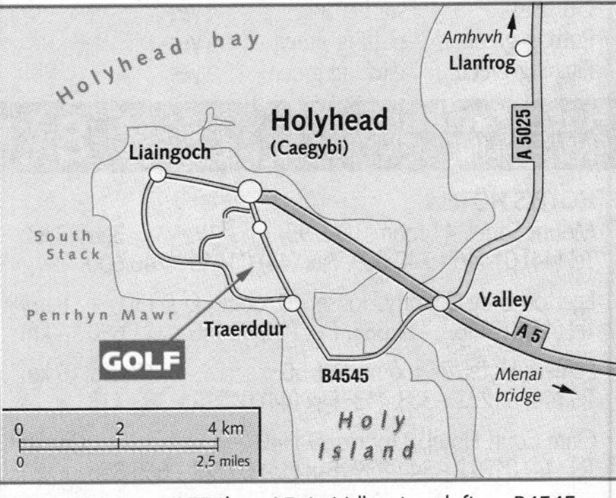

Access Accès : A55 then A5. In Valley, turn left on B4545.
Map 5 on page 494 Carte 5 Page 494

Golf course PARCOURS — 16/20

Site	Site	
Maintenance	Entretien	
Architect	Architecte	James Braid
Type	Type	heathland
Relief	Relief	
Water in play	Eau en jeu	
Exp. to wind	Exposé au vent	
Trees in play	Arbres en jeu	

Scorecard Carte de score	Chp. Chp.	Mens Mess.	Ladies Da.
Length Long.	5922	5180	4825
Par	71	68	72
Slope system	—	—	—

Advised golfing ability 0 12 24 36
Niveau de jeu recommandé
Hcp required Handicap exigé — certificate

Club house & amenities CLUB HOUSE ET ANNEXES — 7/10

Pro shop	Pro-shop	
Driving range	Practice	
Sheltered	couvert	no
On grass	sur herbe	no
Putting-green	putting-green	yes
Pitching-green	pitching green	yes

Hotel facilities ENVIRONNEMENT HOTELIER — 5/10

HOTELS HÔTELS

Trearddur Bay Hotel — Holyhead 3 km
42 rooms, D £ 113
Tel (44) 01407 - 860 301,
Fax (44) 01407 - 861 181

Beach — Trearddur Bay 3 km
27 rooms, D £ 70
Tel (44) 01407 - 860 332,
Fax (44) 01407 - 861 140

RESTAURANTS RESTAURANT

Trearddur Bay Hotel — Holyhead 3 km
Tel (44) 01407 - 860 301

LANGLAND BAY

15 | 7 | 7

This course is located in the Mumbles, a water sports centre at the entrance to the Gower peninsula, a listed site. Although rather hilly in places, Langland Bay is perfectly walkable, offering a splendid enough view to fire any imagination. However the small greens, a bunch of bunkers and threatening rough quickly bring you back to golfing reality. The hazards were clearly forged with the course and are dangerous without being downright treacherous. Everything is on an open table in front of you, so it is up to you to cross swords with the hazards in the great tradition of openness and challenge that remains the James Braid hallmark. Imaginative but totally natural, the course has unique charm, and although yardage is short to today's standards, par (gross or net) is never a walk-over. A number of international players are members here, so they too must find this course to their liking and to their standard.

Ce parcours est situé dans les Mumbles, centre de sports nautiques, et à l'entrée de la péninsule de Gower, qui est un site classé. Le site est assez accidenté à certains endroits mais il est assez facile de jouer à pied. La vue splendide va vite vous occuper, mais de petits greens, une quantité de bunkers et un rough menaçant vous ramènent vite aux réalités du parcours. Les obstacles ont été bien fondus dans le parcours, ils sont dangereux sans être traîtres. Tout est exposé devant vous, à vous de combattre les périls, dans la grande tradition de franchise et d'exigence mesurée de James Braid. Imaginatif tout en restant naturel, c'est un parcours au charme unique, et bien qu'il manque de longueur selon nos critères du jour, il n'est guère facile d'attaquer le par (en brut ou en net) avec toutes les chances de succès. Le club compte nombre de joueurs internationaux parmi ses membres, ils doivent sans doute trouver ce parcours à leur goût et à leur niveau.

Langland Bay Golf Club — 1901

The Mumbles
WAL - SWANSEA SA3 4QR

Office	Secrétariat	(44) 01792 - 361 721
Pro shop	Pro-shop	(44) 01792 - 366 186
Fax	Fax	(44) 01792 - 361 082
Web	—	
Situation	Situation	

10 km S. of Swansea (pop. 181 906)

Annual closure	Fermeture annuelle	no
Weekly closure	Fermeture hebdomadaire	no

Fees main season / Tarifs haute saison	Week days / Semaine	We/Bank holidays / We/Férié
	Full day	
Individual Individuel	£ 28	£ 30
Couple Couple	£ 56	£ 60

Caddy	Caddy	no
Electric Trolley	Chariot électrique	no
Buggy	Voiturette	no
Clubs	Clubs	no
Credit cards	Cartes de crédi	no

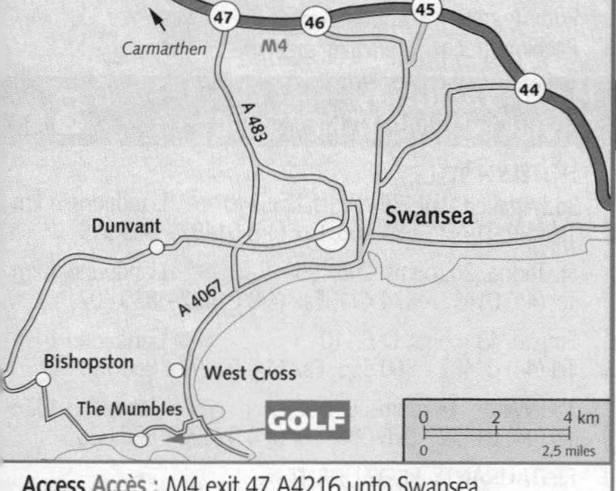

Access Accès : M4 exit 47 A4216 unto Swansea, then A4216 and to the end of A4067. Then → The Mumbles.
Map 6 on page 494 Carte 6 Page 494

Golf course / PARCOURS — 15/20

Site	Site	
Maintenance	Entretien	
Architect	Architecte	James Braid
Type	Type	seaside course, parkland
Relief	Relief	
Water in play	Eau en jeu	
Exp. to wind	Exposé au vent	
Trees in play	Arbres en jeu	

Scorecard / Carte de score	Chp. / Chp.	Mens / Mess.	Ladies / Da.
Length Long.	5272	5146	4804
Par	70	70	73
Slope system	—	—	—

Advised golfing ability / Niveau de jeu recommandé: 0 12 24 36
Hcp required / Handicap exigé: certificate

Club house & amenities / CLUB HOUSE ET ANNEXES — 7/10

Pro shop	Pro-shop	
Driving range	Practice	
Sheltered	couvert	practice area
On grass	sur herbe	yes
Putting-green	putting-green	yes
Pitching-green	pitching green	yes

Hotel facilities / ENVIRONNEMENT HOTELIER — 7/10

HOTELS HÔTELS

St. Annes, 33 rooms, D £ 70 — The Mumbles 1 km
Tel (44) 01792 - 369 147, Fax (44) 01792 - 360 537

Norton House, 15 rooms, D £ 90 — The Mumbles 1 km
Tel (44) 01792 - 404 891, Fax (44) 01792 - 403 210

Swansea Marriott, 117 rooms, D £ 108 — Swansea 10 km
Tel (44) 01792 - 642 020, Fax (44) 01792 - 650 345

Fairy Hill, 8 rooms, D £ 225 — Llanrhidian 12 km
Tel (44) 01792 - 390 139, Fax (44) 01792 - 391 358

RESTAURANTS RESTAURANT

Dermott's, Tel (44) 01792 - 459 050 — Swansea 10 km
L'Amuse, Tel (44) 01792 - 366 006 — The Mumbles 1 km

LLANDUDNO (MAESDU) 15 5 8

This seaside resort owes it existence and reputation to the railways. It has preserved a very Victorian feel and physiognomy, still resisting the flash modern age of cars, motorcycles and planes. Yet there is nothing stuffy about this corner of the world, the air along the huge pier and sheltered promenades is far too keen for that. The course was created in the early part of the 20th century, designed by a one Tom Jones (whatever happened to him?) in a superb setting and beautiful parkland style with a few links features to add a little extra spice. This is yet another example of traditional architecture given few resources to shift earth but a great deal of imagination in using existing terrain. Trees, bunkers and a few well-placed ponds provide the main ingredients of a pleasant challenge, where holiday-makers can have fun and good amateur golfers let rip. A particularly high mark should go to the excellence of maintenance, especially the greens.

Cette station balnéaire a dû à la fois sa construction et sa notoriété au chemin de fer. Elle en gardé un esprit et une physionomie très victoriens, résistant au modernisme et au clinquant, à l'heure de l'automobile, de la moto et de l'avion. Rien pourtant ici ne sent la poussière, l'air est trop vif le long de l'immense jetée et des promenades abritées. Ce parcours est né au début du XXème siècle, sous le crayon d'un Tom Jones qui n'a guère laissé de traces indélébiles. Celui-ci bénéficie d'un environnement superbe, d'une esthétique de golf "parkland" avec quelques traits de links pour épicer le plat. C'est encore un bon exemple de l'architecture traditionnelle, disposant de peu de moyens pour remuer la terre, mais de pas mal d'imagination pour utiliser le terrain existant. Des arbres, des bunkers, et quelques mares bien placées fournissent les éléments d'un challenge agréable, où les vacanciers pourront s'amuser, et les bons amateurs se déchaîner. La qualité de l'entretien et en particulier des greens est à noter.

Llandudno (Maesdu) Golf Club — 1915

Hospital Road
WAL - LLANDUDNO LL30 1HU

Office	Secrétariat	(44) 01492 - 876 450
Pro shop	Pro-shop	5 195450
Fax	Fax	(44) 01492 - 871 570
Web		—
Situation	Situation	

1,5 km S of Llandudno (pop. 18 647)

Annual closure	Fermeture annuelle	no
Weekly closure	Fermeture hebdomadaire	no

Fees main season / Tarifs haute saison	Full day Week days / Semaine	We/Bank holidays / We/Férié
Individual Individuel	£ 25	£ 30
Couple Couple	£ 50	£ 60

Caddy	Caddy	no
Electric Trolley	Chariot électrique	no
Buggy	Voiturette	£ 16
Clubs	Clubs	yes
Credit cards	Cartes de crédit	no

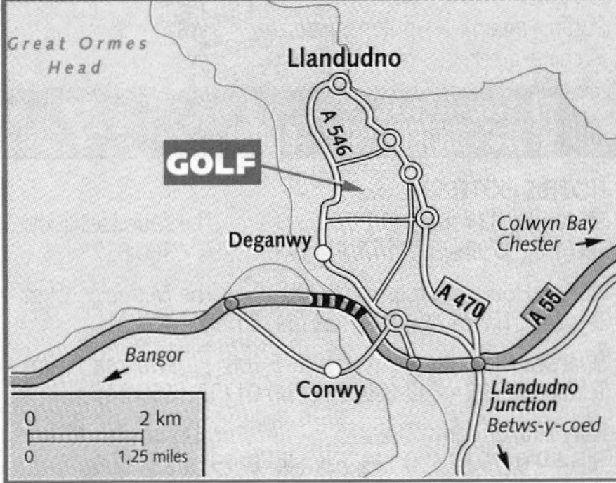

Access Accès : Manchester & Liverpool, A55, then A470 to Llandudno. Golf near the Hospital.
Map 5 on page 494 Carte 5 Page 494

Golf course / PARCOURS — 15/20

Site	Site	
Maintenance	Entretien	
Architect	Architecte	Tom Jones
Type	Type	parkland
Relief	Relief	
Water in play	Eau en jeu	
Exp. to wind	Exposé au vent	
Trees in play	Arbres en jeu	

Scorecard / Carte de score	Chp. / Chp.	Mens / Mess.	Ladies / Da.
Length Long.	5891	5630	5095
Par	72	72	75
Slope system	—	—	—

Advised golfing ability / Niveau de jeu recommandé: 0 12 24 36
Hcp required / Handicap exigé: certificate

Club house & amenities / CLUB HOUSE ET ANNEXES — 5/10

Pro shop	Pro-shop	
Driving range	Practice	
Sheltered	couvert	practice area
On grass	sur herbe	yes
Putting-green	putting-green	yes
Pitching-green	pitching green	yes

Hotel facilities / ENVIRONNEMENT HOTELIER — 8/10

HOTELS HÔTELS

Bodysgallen Hall, 36 rooms, D £ 240 — Llandudno 4 km
Tel (44) 01492 - 584 466, Fax (44) 01492 - 582 519

St. Tudno, 20 rooms, D £ 195 — Llandudno 1 km
Tel (44) 01492 - 874 411, Fax (44) 01492 - 860 407

Empire, 43 rooms, D £ 110 — Llandudno 1 km
Tel (44) 01492 - 860 555, Fax (44) 01492 - 860 791

The Wilton, 14 rooms, D £ 52 — Llandudno 1 km
Tel (44) 01492 - 876 086, Fax (44) 01492 - 876 086

RESTAURANTS RESTAURANT

Martin's, Tel (44) 01492 - 870 070 — Llandudno 1 km

Richard's Bistro, Tel (44) 01492 - 877 924 — Llandudno 1 km

LLANYMYNECH

14	6	4

This course is important for several reasons. Firstly, its name is nigh on impossible to pronounce, secondly this is the site where the former Great Britain was defeated by the Romans after some heroic resistance, thirdly a small part of the course is in England and a larger part in Wales, and lastly this is where the young Woosnam learned the game. On top of that it also happens to be a good golf course, where the natural topology has been utilized with excellent insight into the game of golf and a marked degree of wisdom. As a result, a number of greens are elevated and a few ditches look safely far away but are in fact much closer and are just waiting for your ball to come their way. The perspectives here can be deceiving, therefore, even though the hilly terrain is easily walkable. Varied and pleasing to the eye, there is no let-up here if you want to card a good score, but you can also have fun with friends or the family. In short, a real good course becoming increasingly popular and busy.

Ce golf est important pour plusieurs raisons. D'abord, son nom est impossible. Puis, c'est ici que le roi de l'ancienne Grande Bretagne fut défait par les Romains après une héroïque résistance. Ensuite, le parcours est minoritairement en Angleterre, majoritairement au Pays de Galles. Enfin, c'est ici que le jeune Ian Woosnam a exercé ses premiers talents. Tout cela dit, c'est aussi un bon parcours de golf, où les accidents variés du terrain ont été utilisés avec un bon sens du jeu, mais aussi une certaine sagesse. Quelques greens sont ainsi surélevés, quelques fossés vous paraissent bien lointains, mais ils sont très proches pour les balles. Les perspectives offertes par les dénivellées sont parfois trompeuses, même si les reliefs ne sont pas un obstacle au jeu à pied. Varié, plaisant visuellement, il ne permet guère de répit si l'on veut bien scorer. mais on peut aussi s'y amuser entre amis ou en famille. Bref, un vrai bon golf, de plus en plus connu, et donc fréquenté.

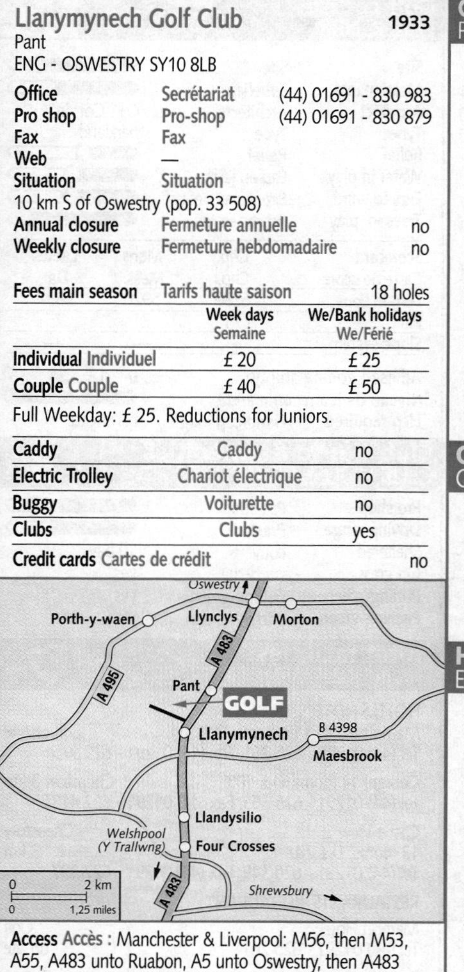

Llanymynech Golf Club — 1933

Pant
ENG - OSWESTRY SY10 8LB

Office	Secrétariat	(44) 01691 - 830 983
Pro shop	Pro-shop	(44) 01691 - 830 879
Fax	Fax	
Web	—	
Situation	Situation	

10 km S of Oswestry (pop. 33 508)

Annual closure	Fermeture annuelle	no
Weekly closure	Fermeture hebdomadaire	no

Fees main season Tarifs haute saison	18 holes	
	Week days Semaine	**We/Bank holidays** We/Férié
Individual Individuel	£ 20	£ 25
Couple Couple	£ 40	£ 50

Full Weekday: £ 25. Reductions for Juniors.

Caddy	Caddy	no
Electric Trolley	Chariot électrique	no
Buggy	Voiturette	no
Clubs	Clubs	yes
Credit cards	Cartes de crédit	no

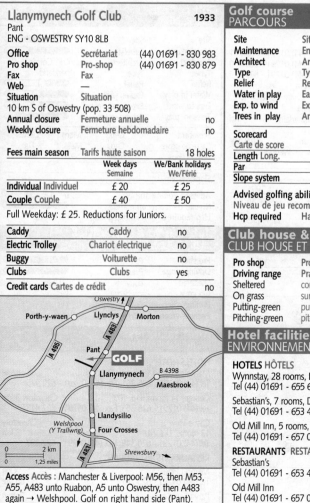

Access Accès : Manchester & Liverpool: M56, then M53, A55, A483 unto Ruabon, A5 unto Oswestry, then A483 again → Welshpool. Golf on right hand side (Pant).
Map 5 on page 494 Carte 5 Page 494

Golf course PARCOURS — 14/20

Site	Site	
Maintenance	Entretien	
Architect	Architecte	Unknown
Type	Type	open country, upland
Relief	Relief	
Water in play	Eau en jeu	
Exp. to wind	Exposé au vent	
Trees in play	Arbres en jeu	

Scorecard Carte de score	**Chp.** Chp.	**Mens** Mess.	**Ladies** Da.
Length Long.	5503	5310	4695
Par	70	70	71
Slope system	—	—	—

Advised golfing ability Niveau de jeu recommandé — 0 12 24 36

Hcp required Handicap exigé — no

Club house & amenities CLUB HOUSE ET ANNEXES — 6/10

Pro shop	Pro-shop	
Driving range	Practice	
Sheltered	couvert	practice area
On grass	sur herbe	yes
Putting-green	putting-green	yes
Pitching-green	pitching green	yes

Hotel facilities ENVIRONNEMENT HOTELIER — 4/10

HOTELS HÔTELS

Wynnstay, 28 rooms, D £ 95 — Oswestry 10 km
Tel (44) 01691 - 655 621, Fax (44) 01691 - 670 606

Sebastian's, 7 rooms, D £ 60 — Oswestry 10 km
Tel (44) 01691 - 653 452, Fax (44) 01691 - 653 452

Old Mill Inn, 5 rooms, D £ 40 — Llanforda 8 km
Tel (44) 01691 - 657 058

RESTAURANTS RESTAURANT

Sebastian's — Oswestry 10 km
Tel (44) 01691 - 653 452

Old Mill Inn — Llanforda 8 km
Tel (44) 01691 - 657 058

MARRIOTT ST PIERRE Old Course 16 8 7

Purchasing this course allowed the Marriott group to rejuvenate and put the whole site centre-stage, with notably the arrival of the Solheim Cup in 1996. With a hotel now set up in the little 14th century manor here, the venue has become a leading resort which comprises two courses, the best known and most demanding of which is the "Old Course", named thus because it dates from only 1961. Designed by Ken Cotton, this has all the style of a typical park-land course where the finishing holes bring a lot of water into play. It is certainly not the world's most subtle course, but this honesty has the advantage of letting the golfer feel immediately at home and of carding the score he or she really deserves. We would advise green-feers not to go for the back-tees, especially on the 18th, a huge par 3.

L'achat de ce golf par le groupe Marriott a permis un rajeunissement notable, mais lui a aussi donné un coup de projecteur accentué par la venue de la Solheim Cup 1996. Avec son hôtel installé dans un petit manoir du XIVème siècle, c'est devenu un "resort" important, qui comprend deux parcours dont le plus connu et le plus exigeant est le le "Old Course," dénommé ainsi bien qu'il ne date que de 1961. Dessiné par Ken Cotton, c'est un parcours typique de l'esthétique des parcs, avec un finale où l'eau est très en jeu. Ce n'est sans doute pas le parcours le plus subtil du monde, mais cette franchise a l'avantage de permettre immédiatement de s'y sentir à l'aise, et de faire le score que l'on mérite vraiment. On conseillera aux visiteurs de ne pas choisir les départs arrière, surtout au 18, énorme par 3.

Marriott St Pierre Hotel & Country Club 1961

St Pierre Park
WAL - CHEPSTOW, Gwent NP6 6YA

Office	Secrétariat	(44) 01291 - 625 261
Pro shop	Pro-shop	(44) 01291 - 621 400
Fax	Fax	(44) 01291 - 629 975
Web	www.marriott.com	
Situation	Situation	20 km E of Newport
Annual closure	Fermeture annuelle	no
Weekly closure	Fermeture hebdomadaire	no

Fees main season Tarifs haute saison		full day
	Week days Semaine	**We/Bank holidays** We/Férié
Individual Individuel	£ 50*	£ 50*
Couple Couple	£ 100	£ 100

* Weekends: ask before coming / * Residents: £ 40

Caddy	Caddy	on request
Electric Trolley	Chariot électrique	yes
Buggy	Voiturette	yes
Clubs	Clubs	yes

Credit cards Cartes de crédit
VISA - Eurocard - DC - AMEX

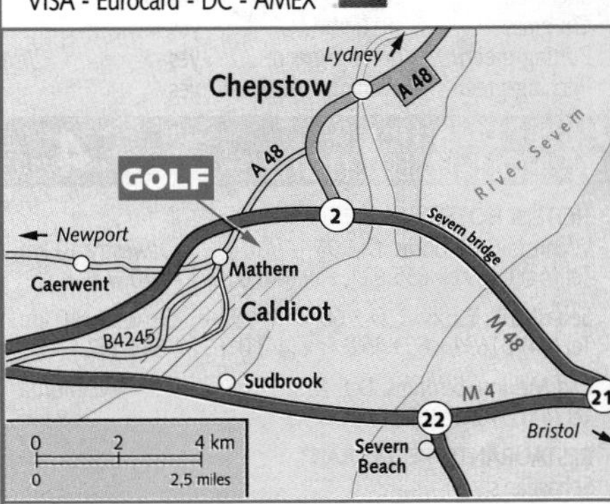

Access Accès : Newport A48 → Chepstow.
Golf 3 km (2 m. before Chepstow).
Map 6 on page 495 Carte 6 Page 495

Golf course PARCOURS 16/20

Site	Site	
Maintenance	Entretien	
Architect	Architecte	C.K. Cotton
Type	Type	parkland
Relief	Relief	
Water in play	Eau en jeu	
Exp. to wind	Exposé au vent	
Trees in play	Arbres en jeu	

Scorecard Carte de score	**Chp.** Chp.	**Mens** Mess.	**Ladies** Da.
Length Long.	6280	5920	5337
Par	71	71	75
Slope system	—	—	—

Advised golfing ability 0 12 24 36
Niveau de jeu recommandé
Hcp required Handicap exigé certificate

Club house & amenities CLUB HOUSE ET ANNEXES 8/10

Pro shop	Pro-shop	
Driving range	Practice	
Sheltered	couvert	10 bays
On grass	sur herbe	yes
Putting-green	putting-green	yes
Pitching-green	pitching green	yes

Hotel facilities ENVIRONNEMENT HOTELIER 7/10

HOTELS HÔTELS

Marriott Hotel, 148 rooms, D £ 104 — Golf on site
Tel (44) 01291 - 625 261, Fax (44) 01291 - 629 975

George, 14 rooms, D £ 100 — Chepstow 3 km
Tel (44) 01291 - 625 363, Fax (44) 01291 - 627 418

Castle View — Chepstow 3 km
13 rooms, D £ 70
Tel (44) 01291 - 620 349, Fax (44) 01291 - 627 397

RESTAURANTS RESTAURANT

Marriott Hotel — Golf on site
Tel (44) 01291 - 625 261

Parva Farmhouse — Tintern 8 km
Tel (44) 01291 - 689 411

NEFYN & DISTRICT

16 | 7 | 5

This course is hardly close to the major tourist routes, but the site at least deserves a visit. Perched atop cliffs, it is very similar to a links course although some holes prefer heather to dunes. The course was founded in 1907, re-styled by J.H. Taylor and James Braid and completed in 1993. The site also houses a 9-holer between two sea inlets. The 18 hole course is no walk-over but never too tough or unfair. You also have to play every shot in the book, compounded by the fact that you often have a choice between playing safe or "going for it". The latter option can turn out to be foolhardy indeed on certain blind-shots. Never mind, you can stop off at the pub close to the 12th hole to boost your sagging spirits before squaring up to a wonderful finish, of which for us the 15th is the crowning moment. Maintenance is excellent and the club-house extends a warm welcome.

Ce parcours de Nefyn & District n'est pas exactement sur les autoroutes de touristes, mais le site au moins mérite une visite. Perché sur les falaises, il est apparenté à un links, bien que certains trous soient assez proches des terrains de bruyère. Ce golf a été fondé en 1907, remanié par J.H. Taylor et James Braid, et achevé en 1993. On y trouve aussi un petit 9 trous entre deux bras de mer. Le 18 trous n'est pas facile, mais n'est jamais trop sévère ni injuste. On doit d'autant plus y jouer toute la gamme des coups de golf que l'on a souvent le choix entre la sécurité et l'héroïsme, qui peut s'avérer folie sur certains coups aveugles. Mais on peut faire une halte pour reprendre ses esprits au pub non loin du green du 12, afin d'affronter un très beau finish, dont le 15 est pour nous le sommet. L'entretien est de très bonne qualité, et le Clubhouse très chaleureux.

Nefyn & District Golf Club — 1907

Morfa Nefyn
WAL - PWLLHELI, Gwynedd LL53 6DA

Office	Secrétariat	(44) 01758 - 720 966
Pro shop	Pro-shop	(44) 01758 - 720 102
Fax	Fax	(44) 01758 - 720 476
Web	www.nefyn/golf/club.com	
Situation	Situation	Caernarfon, 32 km
Annual closure	Fermeture annuelle	no
Weekly closure	Fermeture hebdomadaire	no

Fees main season Tarifs haute saison	18 holes	
	Week days Semaine	**We/Bank holidays** We/Férié
Individual Individuel	£ 28*	£ 33*
Couple Couple	£ 56	£ 66

* Full day: £ 33 - £ 38

Caddy	Caddy	on request
Electric Trolley	Chariot électrique	yes
Buggy	Voiturette	£ 15 /18 holes
Clubs	Clubs	yes

Credit cards Cartes de crédit
VISA - MasterCard (Pro shop only)

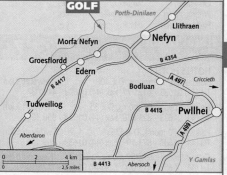

Access Accès : North coast Lleyn Peninsula, on B4417
Map 5 on page 494 Carte 5 Page 494

Golf course PARCOURS — 16/20

Site	Site	
Maintenance	Entretien	
Architect	Architecte	James Braid J.H. Taylor
Type	Type	seaside course, links
Relief	Relief	
Water in play	Eau en jeu	
Exp. to wind	Exposé au vent	
Trees in play	Arbres en jeu	

Scorecard Carte de score	**Chp.** Chp.	**Mens** Mess.	**Ladies** Da.
Length Long.	5958	5750	5420
Par	71	71	75
Slope system	—	—	—

Advised golfing ability 0 12 24 36
Niveau de jeu recommandé
Hcp required Handicap exigé certificate

Club house & amenities CLUB HOUSE ET ANNEXES — 7/10

Pro shop	Pro-shop	
Driving range	Practice	
Sheltered	couvert	no
On grass	sur herbe	yes
Putting-green	putting-green	yes
Pitching-green	pitching green	yes

Hotel facilities ENVIRONNEMENT HOTELIER — 5/10

HOTELS HÔTELS

Caeau Capel Hotel — Nefyn 2 km
18 rooms, D £ 75
Tel (44) 01758 - 720 240, Fax (44) 01758 - 720 750

Plas Bodegroes — Pwllheli 12 km
11 rooms, D £ 110 (w/dinner)
Tel (44) 01758 - 612 363, Fax (44) 01758 - 701 247

White House, 13 rooms, D £ 110 — Abersoch 25 km
Tel (44) 01758 - 713 427, Fax (44) 01758 - 713 512

RESTAURANTS RESTAURANT

Plas Bodegroes, Tel (44) 01758 - 612 363 — Pwllheli 12 km
Caeau Capel, Tel (44) 01758 - 720 240 — Nefyn 2 km

NEWPORT

15 | 6 | 7

A week's golfing in the Cardiff and Swansea region can be a week of playing a different course every day and of getting to know some superb and visually very contrasting layouts. Between St. Pierre and Porthcawl, close to Celtic Manor, the Newport course is one of the best examples of a park-land golf course you could ever hope to find. What's more, green-keeping is excellent and the welcome from both the clubhouse and members is warm and friendly. They are rightly extremely proud of a varied layout with very reasonable yardage, spread over rolling landscape which is very pleasant to walk. You won't find any breath-taking designer ploys or excesses, just a sort of sobriety in a pretty country landscape. A quality course, quite simply.

Une semaine de golf dans la région de Cardiff et Swansea peut permettre de ne jamais jouer deux fois le même parcours, et d'en jouer de superbes, d'esthétiques très différentes, voire opposées. Entre St Pierre et Porthcawl, près de Celtic Manor, le parcours de Newport est l'un des meilleurs exemples de golfs de parcs que l'on puisse trouver. Ce qui ne gâte rien, l'entretien y est toujours très soigné, et l'accueil, du club comme des membres, très amical et chaleureux. Ils sont fiers à juste raison d'un tracé très varié, et de longueur très raisonnable sur un terrain vallonné, mais où il est agréable de jouer à pied. On ne trouvera pas ici de trouvailles architecturales à couper le souffle, ni d'excès, mais une sorte de sobriété dans un joli paysage de campagne. La qualité, tout simplement.

Newport Golf Club — 1903

Great Oak, Rogerstone
WAL - NEWPORT, Gwent NP1 9FX

Office	Secrétariat	(44) 01633 - 892 643
Pro shop	Pro-shop	(44) 01633 - 893 271
Fax	Fax	(44) 01633 - 896 676
Web	—	
Situation	Situation	

6 km W of Newport (pop.133 318)

Annual closure	Fermeture annuelle	no
Weekly closure	Fermeture hebdomadaire	no

Fees main season Tarifs haute saison	Week days Semaine	We/Bank holidays We/Férié
		18 holes
Individual Individuel	£ 30	£ 40*
Couple Couple	£ 60	£ 80*

* Weekends: ask before coming

Caddy	Caddy	no
Electric Trolley	Chariot électrique	yes
Buggy	Voiturette	no
Clubs	Clubs	yes
Credit cards	Cartes de crédit	no

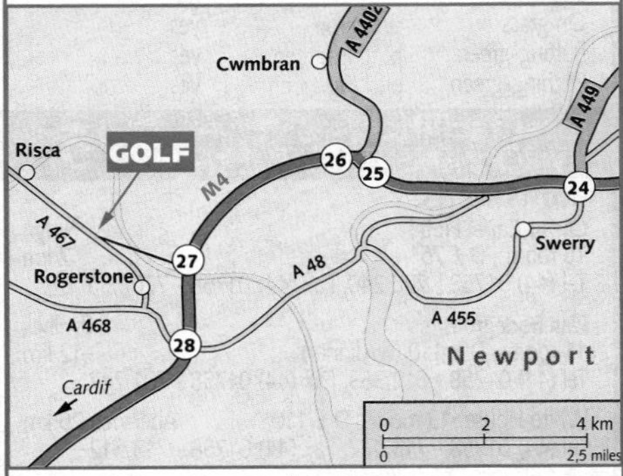

Cwmbran
A 4402
A 449
Risca
GOLF
M4
26
25
24
A 467
27
Swerry
A 48
Rogerstone
A 468
A 455
28
Newport
Cardif
0 2 4 km
0 2,5 miles

Access Accès : M4 Jct 27, then B4591.
Golf 1 km (1/2 m) W of exit.
Map 6 on page 495 Carte 6 Page 495

Golf course PARCOURS — 15/20

Site	Site	
Maintenance	Entretien	
Architect	Architecte	Unknown
Type	Type	parkland
Relief	Relief	
Water in play	Eau en jeu	
Exp. to wind	Exposé au vent	
Trees in play	Arbres en jeu	

Scorecard Carte de score	Chp. Chp.	Mens Mess.	Ladies Da.
Length Long.	5852	5632	5195
Par	72	72	74
Slope system	—	—	—

Advised golfing ability Niveau de jeu recommandé: 0 12 24 36
Hcp required Handicap exigé: certificate

Club house & amenities CLUB HOUSE ET ANNEXES — 6/10

Pro shop	Pro-shop	
Driving range	Practice	
Sheltered	couvert	no
On grass	sur herbe	yes
Putting-green	putting-green	yes
Pitching-green	pitching green	yes

Hotel facilities ENVIRONNEMENT HOTELIER — 7/10

HOTELS HÔTELS

Holiday Inn, 119 rooms, D £ 108 — Newport 3 km
Tel (44) 01633 - 412 777, Fax (44) 01633 - 413 087

Newport Lodge, 27 rooms, D £ 85 — Newport 3 km
Tel (44) 01633 - 821 818, Fax (44) 01633 - 856 360

Parkway, 70 rooms, D £ 125 — Cwmbran 6 km
Tel (44) 01633 - 871 199, Fax (44) 01633 - 869 160

Celtic Manor Hotel, 358 rooms, D £ 162 — Newport 5 km
Tel (44) 01633 - 413 000, Fax (44) 01633 - 412 910

RESTAURANTS RESTAURANT

Owens (Celtic Manor) — Newport 5 km
Tel (44) 01633 - 413 000

NORTH WALES (LLANDUDNO) 17 | 6 | 8

Llandudno is the seaside resort where a one Charles Dodgson, alias Lewis Carroll, treated his friends' children to readings of the stories that were to become Alice in Wonderland. It is also a resort where you can also ride on one of the few cable-car tramways in the world - there is another in San Francisco - to get to Great Orme's Head and see the Bronze Age copper mines. You will also find this rather little known links course, described by none other than Henry Cotton as a "gem". After a hesitant start, you are plunged into a landscape of dunes through which the course somehow winds it way. The front nine stretch alongside a railway line, the back nine return along the coastline, but the holes never run one behind the other; the direction they head in can cause a few surprises on your card. From one day to the next, a capricious wind can make life extremely complicated. There are good and bad things you will remember about this course, things like blind shots or weird ball positions and stances. Not forgetting the gorse, heather and a few deep bunkers.

Llandudno, c'est la station balnéaire où Charles Dodgson, alias Lewis Carroll, racontait aux enfants de ses amis les histoires qui allaient former Alice au Pays des Merveilles. C'est aussi là que l'on peut prendre l'un des seuls tramways à câble du monde, avec celui de San Francisco, pour monter au Great Orme's Head, avec ses mines de cuivre de l'Age du Bronze. C'est enfin le site de ce links assez méconnu, décrit par Henry Cotton comme un "joyau". Après un départ hésitant, on plonge dans un paysage de dunes où se coule le parcours. Les neuf premiers trous longent une voie ferrée, les neuf derniers reviennent le long de la mer, mais les trous ne sont pas les uns derrière les autres, et leur orientation peut causer des surprises sur la carte. D'un jour à l'autre, les caprices du vent peuvent encore compliquer les choses. On se souviendra ici du bon et du mauvais caractère du parcours, qui peuvent vous réserver aussi bien des coups aveugles que des positions de balle (et de stance) bizarres. Ajoutons quelques buissons de bruyère et d'ajoncs, et quelques profonds bunkers.

North Wales Golf Club — 1894

72 Brynian Road
WAL - WEST SHORE, LLANDUDNO LL30 2 DZ

Office	Secrétariat	(44) 01492 - 875 325
Pro shop	Pro-shop	(44) 01492 - 876 878
Fax	Fax	(44) 01492 - 875 325
Web	www.northwales.uk.com	
Situation	Situation	
1 km from Llandudno (pop. 18 647)		
Annual closure	Fermeture annuelle	no
Weekly closure	Fermeture hebdomadaire	no

Fees main season Tarifs haute saison	Full day	
	Week days Semaine	**We/Bank holidays** We/Férié
Individual Individuel	£ 25	£ 35
Couple Couple	£ 50	£ 70

Caddy	Caddy	no
Electric Trolley	Chariot électrique	no
Buggy	Voiturette	£ 25
Clubs	Clubs	yes
Credit cards	Cartes de crédit	no

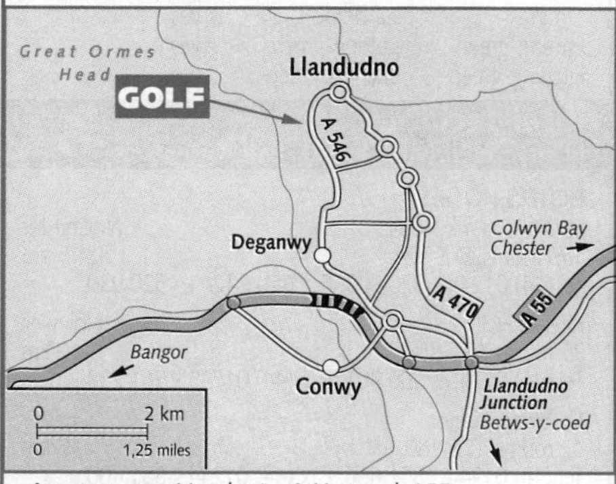

Access Accès : Manchester & Liverpool, A55, then A470 to Llandudno.
Golf 1 km West of Llandudno on West Shore
Map 5 on page 494 Carte 5 Page 494

Golf course PARCOURS 17/20

Site	Site	
Maintenance	Entretien	
Architect	Architecte	Unknown
Type	Type	links
Relief	Relief	
Water in play	Eau en jeu	
Exp. to wind	Exposé au vent	
Trees in play	Arbres en jeu	

Scorecard Carte de score	**Chp.** Chp.	**Mens** Mess.	**Ladies** Da.
Length Long.	5623	5331	5072
Par	71	71	73
Slope system	—	—	—

Advised golfing ability Niveau de jeu recommandé — 0 12 24 36
Hcp required Handicap exigé — certificate

Club house & amenities CLUB HOUSE ET ANNEXES 6/10

Pro shop	Pro-shop	
Driving range	Practice	
Sheltered	couvert	practice area
On grass	sur herbe	yes
Putting-green	putting-green	yes
Pitching-green	pitching green	yes

Hotel facilities ENVIRONNEMENT HOTELIER 8/10

HOTELS HÔTELS

Imperial, 100 rooms, D £ 115 — Llandudno 1 km
Tel (44) 01492 - 877 466, Fax (44) 01492 - 878 043

Tan Lan, 17 rooms, D £ 54 — Llandudno 1 km
Tel (44) 01492 - 860 221, Fax (44) 01492 - 870 219

Bryn Derwen, 10 rooms, D £ 84 — Llandudno 1 km
Tel (44) 01492 - 876 804, Fax (44) 01492 - 876 804

Lighthouse, 3 rooms, D £ 110 — Llandudno 4 km
Tel (44) 01492 - 876 819, Fax (44) 01492 - 876 668

RESTAURANTS RESTAURANT

Number 1's Bistro, Tel (44) 01492 - 875 424 — Llandudno 1 km
Garden Room, Tel (44) 01492 - 874 411 — Llandudno 1 km

NORTHOP COUNTRY PARK

16	9	6

The club-house is opulent and spacious, the adjacent hotel is luxurious, the park is a beauty and maintenance virtually faultless. The course is recent but has already hosted many high-level tournaments like the British Girls. It was designed by John Jacobs, one of the legendary names in modern golf instruction but not always as inspired as you might imagine when it comes to laying out a course. Here, though, he was at his best, even though a little more extravagance in the graphics of the layout might sometimes have been welcome over what is a spectacular complex. Nevertheless, the whole course has been carefully designed in a rather classic British style and it is becoming better and better as each passing year adds to its maturity. One decisive advantage here is that nothing is concealed from view and both reward and sanction are equal to the risk taken or mistake made. You can almost feel the teacher behind the architect. Amongst other excellent holes, the 8th is most memorable, a downhill par 5, together with the 16th, a slight dog-leg with trees and water on the right and in front of the green.

Le Clubhouse est riche et grand, l'hôtel adjacent est luxueux, le parc est beau, l'entretien presque sans fautes. Le parcours est récent, mais il a déjà reçu de nombreuses bonnes épreuves, comme le British Girls. Son auteur est John Jacobs, l'une des légendes de l'enseignement moderne de golf, mais pas toujours aussi inspiré qu'on pourrait l'imaginer dans ses dessins de parcours. Ici, il est à son meilleur, même si on pourrait souhaiter parfois un peu plus de "folie" graphique dans un ensemble par ailleurs spectaculaire. Il reste que l'ensemble est très soigné, assez classiquement britannique, et que chaque année ajoutant de la maturité, il se bonifie en vieillissant. Avantage décisif : rien n'est caché ici, et la récompense comme la punition sont à la hauteur du risque pris ou de la faute commise. On sent bien là l'enseignant derrière l'architecte ! Entre autres trous de qualité, on se souviendra du 8, un par 5 en descente, comme du 16, un léger dog-leg avec des arbres, de l'eau à droite comme devant le green.

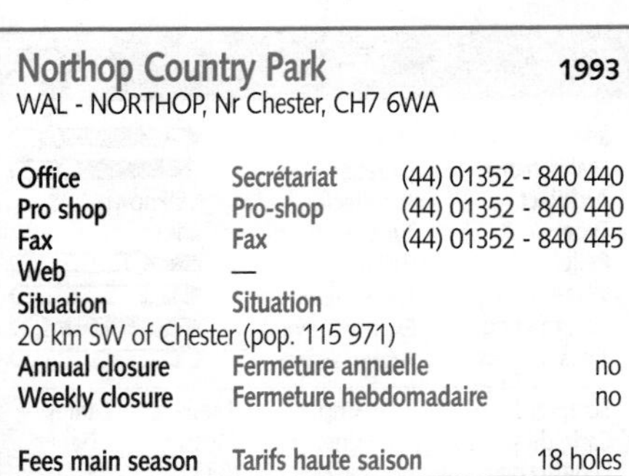

Northop Country Park — **1993**

WAL - NORTHOP, Nr Chester, CH7 6WA

Office	Secrétariat	(44) 01352 - 840 440
Pro shop	Pro-shop	(44) 01352 - 840 440
Fax	Fax	(44) 01352 - 840 445
Web	—	
Situation	Situation	

20 km SW of Chester (pop. 115 971)

Annual closure	Fermeture annuelle	no
Weekly closure	Fermeture hebdomadaire	no

Fees main season Tarifs haute saison	18 holes	
	Week days Semaine	We/Bank holidays We/Férié
Individual Individuel	£ 30*	£ 35*
Couple Couple	£ 60	£ 70

* Full day: £ 40 - £ 50

Caddy	Caddy	no
Electric Trolley	Chariot électrique	no
Buggy	Voiturette	£ 15
Clubs	Clubs	£ 10
Credit cards Cartes de crédit		VISA - MasterCard

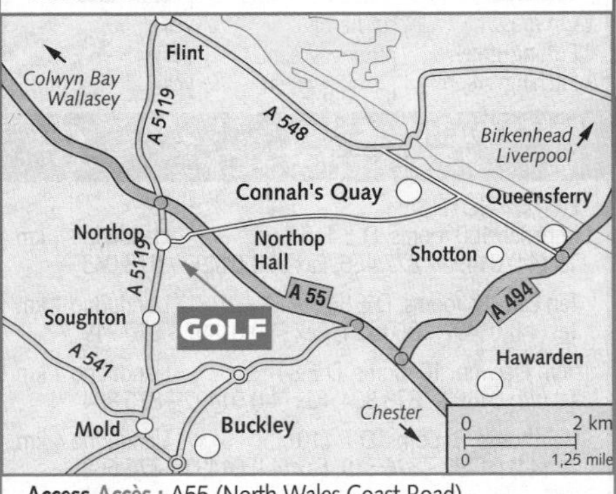

Access Accès : A55 (North Wales Coast Road).
Exit at Northop Connah's Quay.
Northop Country Park is on left side of exit road.
Map 5 on page 494 Carte 5 Page 494

Golf course PARCOURS — 16/20

Site	Site	
Maintenance	Entretien	
Architect	Architecte	John Jacobs
Type	Type	parkland
Relief	Relief	
Water in play	Eau en jeu	
Exp. to wind	Exposé au vent	
Trees in play	Arbres en jeu	

Scorecard Carte de score	Chp. Chp.	Mens Mess.	Ladies Da.
Length Long.	6128	5765	4945
Par	72	72	72
Slope system	—	—	—

Advised golfing ability Niveau de jeu recommandé — 0 12 24 36

Hcp required Handicap exigé — yes

Club house & amenities CLUB HOUSE ET ANNEXES — 9/10

Pro shop	Pro-shop	
Driving range	Practice	
Sheltered	couvert	6 bays
On grass	sur herbe	yes
Putting-green	putting-green	yes
Pitching-green	pitching green	yes

Hotel facilities ENVIRONNEMENT HOTELIER — 6/10

HOTELS HÔTELS

St David's Park Hotel — Nr Chester 15 km
145 rooms, D £ 124
Tel (44) 01244 - 520 800, Fax (44) 01244 - 520 930

Kinsale Hall — Holywell 10 km
35 rooms, D £ 85
Tel (44) 01745 - 560 001, Fax (44) 01745 - 561 298

Crabwall Manor — Chester 15 km
42 rooms, D £ 150
Tel (44) 01244 - 851 666, Fax (44) 01244 - 851 400

RESTAURANTS RESTAURANT

Crabwall Manor, Tel (44) 01244 - 851 666 — Chester 15 km

Arkle, Tel (44) 01244 - 324 024 — Chester 15 km

PENNARD

18 | 6 | 6

Firstly there are the superb views over a rugged coastline, the sea, smugglers' beaches and dunes, then the countryside with remains of castles. In a highly romantic setting, don't ever let this course catch you napping. At first sight it can be intimidating with steep hills that make club selection a delicate business (there are a few blind shots to contend with) but the difficulties are not insurmountable even for a mid-handicapper, unless the wind begins to blow a little too hard. In calm weather, Pennard certainly could not claim to be a major championship course, but it is incredibly enjoyable both visually and technically. And when you do finally get to grips with it, you feel that you could be a good player. Green-keeping is of a very high standard, and the greens are slick and firm all year round (Winters are very mild here). Discovery recommended.

D'abord il y a des vues superbes sur les côtes découpées, la mer, des plages de contrebandiers, les dunes, la campagne, des châteaux en ruines. Dans un site hautement romantique, il ne faut pas rêver pour jouer ce parcours. Il peut intimider au premier abord avec ses reliefs qui compliquent notamment la sélection des clubs (quelques coups aveugles), mais ses difficultés ne sont pas insurmontables, même pour un joueur moyen, sauf si le vent se met à souffler un peu fort. Certes, par temps calme, Pennard ne saurait prétendre être un parcours de grands championnats, mais il procure un plaisir fou, visuellement et techniquement. Et quand vous parvenez à l'apprivoiser, vous avez l'impression d'être un grand joueur. L'entretien est ici très soigné, les greens rapides et fermes toute l'année (les hivers sont assez doux). A découvrir !

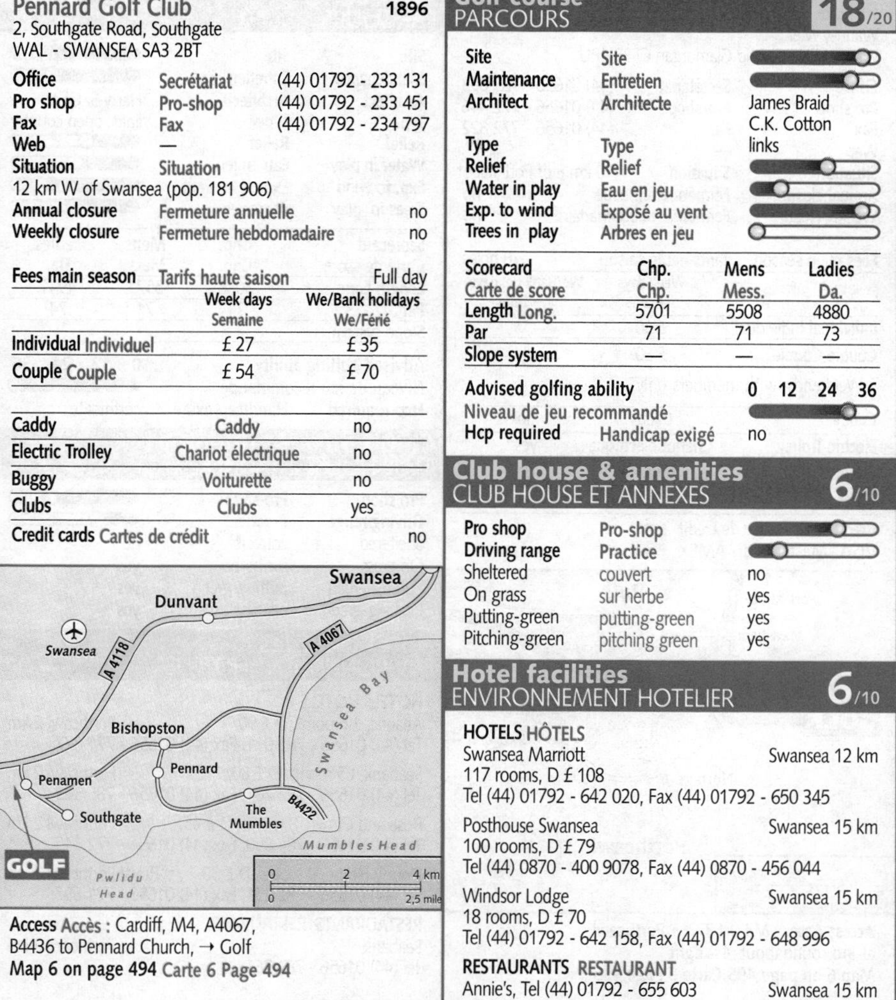

Pennard Golf Club — 1896

2, Southgate Road, Southgate
WAL - SWANSEA SA3 2BT

Office	Secrétariat	(44) 01792 - 233 131
Pro shop	Pro-shop	(44) 01792 - 233 451
Fax	Fax	(44) 01792 - 234 797
Web	—	
Situation	Situation	

12 km W of Swansea (pop. 181 906)

Annual closure	Fermeture annuelle	no
Weekly closure	Fermeture hebdomadaire	no

Fees main season Tarifs haute saison	Week days Semaine	We/Bank holidays We/Férié
		Full day
Individual Individuel	£ 27	£ 35
Couple Couple	£ 54	£ 70

Caddy	Caddy	no
Electric Trolley	Chariot électrique	no
Buggy	Voiturette	no
Clubs	Clubs	yes
Credit cards	Cartes de crédit	no

Access Accès : Cardiff, M4, A4067, B4436 to Pennard Church, → Golf
Map 6 on page 494 Carte 6 Page 494

Golf course PARCOURS — 18/20

Site	Site	
Maintenance	Entretien	
Architect	Architecte	James Braid C.K. Cotton
Type	Type	links
Relief	Relief	
Water in play	Eau en jeu	
Exp. to wind	Exposé au vent	
Trees in play	Arbres en jeu	

Scorecard Carte de score	Chp. Chp.	Mens Mess.	Ladies Da.
Length Long.	5701	5508	4880
Par	71	71	73
Slope system	—	—	—

Advised golfing ability Niveau de jeu recommandé — 0 12 24 36
Hcp required Handicap exigé — no

Club house & amenities CLUB HOUSE ET ANNEXES — 6/10

Pro shop	Pro-shop	
Driving range	Practice	
Sheltered	couvert	no
On grass	sur herbe	yes
Putting-green	putting-green	yes
Pitching-green	pitching green	yes

Hotel facilities ENVIRONNEMENT HOTELIER — 6/10

HOTELS HÔTELS

Swansea Marriott — Swansea 12 km
117 rooms, D £ 108
Tel (44) 01792 - 642 020, Fax (44) 01792 - 650 345

Posthouse Swansea — Swansea 15 km
100 rooms, D £ 79
Tel (44) 0870 - 400 9078, Fax (44) 0870 - 456 044

Windsor Lodge — Swansea 15 km
18 rooms, D £ 70
Tel (44) 01792 - 642 158, Fax (44) 01792 - 648 996

RESTAURANTS RESTAURANT

Annie's, Tel (44) 01792 - 655 603 — Swansea 15 km

PYLE & KENFIG

17 | 7 | 5

There is not much missing at Pyle & Kenfig for this to rank amongst the very great courses. For once, a course of this type returns to the clubhouse at the 9th and in doing so emphasises the difference between the front and back nines, separated by a road. Although the outward half is not to be sniffed at, it doesn't have the dune landscape of the epic back nine, which has a single par 5 but some beefy par 3s and huge par 4s (from hole 16 to 18 with a head-wind to boot). The greatest difficulties are the rough, the positions you can get yourself into when straying off the fairway and the cleverly placed pot bunkers. The greens are on the flat side and generally reachable with bump and run shots, luckily for the players, because they are of course often very exposed to the wind. Not an easy course, but very forthright.

Il ne manque pas grand-chose à Pyle & Kenfig pour être dans la cour des très grands parcours. Pour une fois, un parcours de type links revient au Clubhouse au 9, cela ne fait que souligner la différence entre l'aller et le retour, séparés par une route. Bien que l'aller ne soit pas négligeable, il lui manque le caractère dunaire d'un retour héroïque, où l'on trouve un seul par 5, mais des par 3 très musclés et d'énormes par 4 (du 16 au 18, contre les vents dominants). Les plus grandes difficultés sont les roughs, les positions où l'on se trouve par rapport à la balle (quand on s'égare hors des fairways), et de profonds bunkers (trop) bien placés. Les greens sont assez plats, leur accès généralement possible en roulant, ce qui est fort heureux car l'exposition au vent est bien sûr importante. Un parcours pas facile, mais franc.

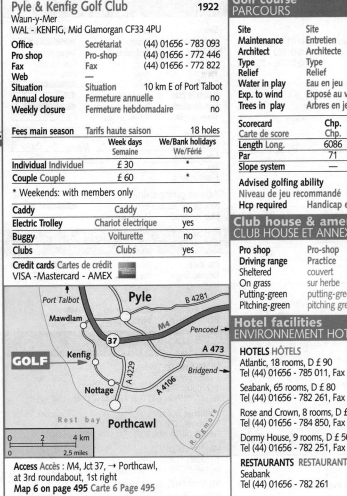

Pyle & Kenfig Golf Club — 1922

Waun-y-Mer
WAL - KENFIG, Mid Glamorgan CF33 4PU

Office	Secrétariat	(44) 01656 - 783 093
Pro shop	Pro-shop	(44) 01656 - 772 446
Fax	Fax	(44) 01656 - 772 822
Web	—	
Situation	Situation	10 km E of Port Talbot
Annual closure	Fermeture annuelle	no
Weekly closure	Fermeture hebdomadaire	no

Fees main season Tarifs haute saison	18 holes	
	Week days Semaine	We/Bank holidays We/Férié
Individual Individuel	£ 30	*
Couple Couple	£ 60	*

* Weekends: with members only

Caddy	Caddy	no
Electric Trolley	Chariot électrique	yes
Buggy	Voiturette	no
Clubs	Clubs	yes

Credit cards Cartes de crédit
VISA -Mastercard - AMEX

Access Accès : M4, Jct 37, → Porthcawl, at 3rd roundabout, 1st right
Map 6 on page 495 Carte 6 Page 495

Golf course PARCOURS — 17/20

Site	Site	
Maintenance	Entretien	
Architect	Architecte	Harry S. Colt
Type	Type	links, open country
Relief	Relief	
Water in play	Eau en jeu	
Exp. to wind	Exposé au vent	
Trees in play	Arbres en jeu	

Scorecard Carte de score	Chp. Chp.	Mens Mess.	Ladies Da.
Length Long.	6086	5571	4941
Par	71	71	74
Slope system	—	—	—

Advised golfing ability Niveau de jeu recommandé — 0 12 24 36
Hcp required Handicap exigé — certificate

Club house & amenities CLUB HOUSE ET ANNEXES — 7/10

Pro shop	Pro-shop	
Driving range	Practice	
Sheltered	couvert	no
On grass	sur herbe	yes
Putting-green	putting-green	yes
Pitching-green	pitching green	yes

Hotel facilities ENVIRONNEMENT HOTELIER — 5/10

HOTELS HÔTELS

Atlantic, 18 rooms, D £ 90 — Porthcawl 2 km
Tel (44) 01656 - 785 011, Fax (44) 01656 - 771 877

Seabank, 65 rooms, D £ 80 — Porthcawl 2 km
Tel (44) 01656 - 782 261, Fax (44) 01656 - 785 363

Rose and Crown, 8 rooms, D £ 45 — Porthcawl 2 km
Tel (44) 01656 - 784 850, Fax (44) 01656 - 772 345

Dormy House, 9 rooms, D £ 50 — Royal Porthcawl 2 km
Tel (44) 01656 - 782 251, Fax (44) 01656 - 771 687

RESTAURANTS RESTAURANT

Seabank — Porthcawl 2 km
Tel (44) 01656 - 782 261

ROLLS OF MONMOUTH (THE) 15 | 6 | 6

You sometimes wonder why some good courses never reach the sort of stardom they might deserve. Here, despite the excellent road from Birmingham to Cardiff running close by, the reason might be the absence of any top tournament. From another angle, this tranquillity is a blessing for players who love to feel alone in the world. Although laid out over "rolling" landscape, the course's name comes from the Rolls family (as in Royce), whose estate overlooks the course. It is sited around a forest-covered hill in a parkland landscape lined with some superb trees. Walking can be a little hard on the legs but there are buggies to give you the time to admire the landscape and wild-life or to drive on and reconnoitre some of the blind shots that await you. As far as the course's very own personality is concerned, you'll remember best of all the magnificent par 3s.

On se demande pourquoi de bons parcours restent à l'écart de la célébrité. Dans le cas présent, l'excellente route de Birmingham à Cardiff passant pourtant à côté, il manque peut-être un grand tournoi. D'un autre côté, cette tranquillité est une bénédiction pour les joueurs, qui adorent être seuls au monde, c'est bien connu. Certes le terrain est "rolling," mais le nom vient de la famille Rolls (comme Royce) dont la propriété domine le parcours, dessiné autour d'une grande colline boisée, dans un paysage de parc et de bois superbes. Marcher peut-être ici fatigant, mais il y a des voiturettes pour se donner le temps d'admirer le paysage et la vie sauvage, ou d'aller repérer les lieux sur les quelques coups aveugles. Pour ce qui est de la personnalité du parcours, on se souviendra notamment des très beaux par 3.

The Rolls of Monmouth — 1982

The Hendre
WAL - MONMOUTH, Gwent NP5 4HG

Office	Secrétariat	(44) 01600 - 715 353
Pro shop	Pro-shop	(44) 01600 - 715 353
Fax	Fax	(44) 01600 - 713 115
Web	—	
Situation	Situation	58 km NE of Cardiff
Annual closure	Fermeture annuelle	no
Weekly closure	Fermeture hebdomadaire	no

Fees main season Tarifs haute saison	18 holes	
	Week days Semaine	**We/Bank holidays** We/Férié
Individual Individuel	£ 34	£ 38
Couple Couple	£ 68	£ 76

Monday offer: £ 26

Caddy	Caddy	no
Electric Trolley	Chariot électrique	yes
Buggy	Voiturette	£ 25 /18 holes
Clubs	Clubs	no

Credit cards Cartes de crédit VISA - DC - AMEX

Access Accès : Cardiff, M4 East, Jct 24, then A449 to Monmouth. Golf on B4233 (Abergavenny Road), 5 km W of Monmouth.
Map 6 on page 495 Carte 6 Page 495

Golf course PARCOURS 15/20

Site	Site	
Maintenance	Entretien	
Architect	Architecte	Urbis Planning
Type	Type	parkland, hilly
Relief	Relief	
Water in play	Eau en jeu	
Exp. to wind	Exposé au vent	
Trees in play	Arbres en jeu	

Scorecard Carte de score	Chp. Chp.	Mens Mess.	Ladies Da.
Length Long.	6127	5718	5215
Par	72	72	75
Slope system	—	—	—

Advised golfing ability 0 12 24 36
Niveau de jeu recommandé
Hcp required Handicap exigé no

Club house & amenities CLUB HOUSE ET ANNEXES 6/10

Pro shop	Pro-shop	
Driving range	Practice	
Sheltered	couvert	no
On grass	sur herbe	yes
Putting-green	putting-green	yes
Pitching-green	pitching green	yes

Hotel facilities ENVIRONNEMENT HOTELIER 6/10

HOTELS HÔTELS

Riverside — Monmouth 6 km
17 rooms, D £ 70
Tel (44) 01600 - 715 577, Fax (44) 01600 - 712 668

Penyclawdd Court — Llanfihangel Crucorney 10 km
3 rooms, D £ 100
Tel (44) 01873 - 890 719, Fax (44) 01873 - 890 848

Llansantffraed Court — Abergavenny 10 km
21 rooms, D £ 98
Tel (44) 01873 - 840 678, Fax (44) 01873 - 840 674

RESTAURANTS RESTAURANT

Clytha Arms, Tel (44) 01873 - 840 206 — Raglan 8 km

ROYAL PORTHCAWL

19 | 7 | 6

The is the most famous course in Wales and does full honour to its reputation. Royal Porthcawl is an absolute must for great course "trophy-hunters". It is, of course, a links, although half a dozen very distinctive holes are more heather-land in style and are played on a sort of high plateau overlooking the Bristol Channel. Contrary to many links, where holes are often laid out in line, the holes here shoot out in all directions and make club selection a real headache, depending on the wind. This is a part of what goes to make up the greatness and test value of this layout, where the slightest technical shortcoming will cost you dearly, and where the uninterrupted view over the sea might make you wish you had gone to the beach instead. A true masterpiece, beautifully maintained, which has staged some memorable Curtis Cup and Walker Cup matches and several British Amateur Championships.

C'est le plus fameux parcours du Pays de Galles, il honore dignement sa réputation, et doit figurer dans le "tableau" des chasseurs de grands golfs. C'est évidemment un links, bien qu'une demi-douzaine de trous de caractère un peu plus "terre de bruyère" trouvent place sur une sorte de haut plateau dominant le Canal de Bristol. Au contraire de nombreux links, dont les trous sont souvent alignés, ceux-ci tournent dans toutes les directions, à vous donner le vertige quant au choix de clubs suivant le vent. C'est une part de ce qui fait la grandeur et la valeur de test de ce parcours, où la moindre faiblesse technique se paie cher, où la vue constante de la mer peut vous faire regretter de ne pas avoir choisi d'aller à la plage. Un vrai chef-d'oeuvre merveilleusement entretenu, où se sont déroulées de mémorables Curtis Cup et Walker Cup, ainsi que plusieurs British Amateur.

Royal Porthcawl Golf Club — 1891

WAL - PORTHCAWL, Mid Glamorgan CF36 3VW

Office	Secrétariat	(44) 01656 - 782 251
Pro shop	Pro-shop	(44) 01656 - 773 702
Fax	Fax	(44) 01656 - 771 687
Web	www.golf-in-wales.com	
Situation	Situation	

40 km W of Cardiff (pop. 279 055) - 10 km E of Port Talbot

Annual closure	Fermeture annuelle	no
Weekly closure	Fermeture hebdomadaire	no

Fees main season Tarifs haute saison	18 holes	
	Week days Semaine	We/Bank holidays We/Férié
Individual Individuel	£ 45*	£ 60*
Couple Couple	£ 90	£ 120

* Full day: £ 55 /£ 70
Weekends & Wednesdays: with members only

Caddy	Caddy	on request
Electric Trolley	Chariot électrique	yes
Buggy	Voiturette	no
Clubs	Clubs	yes

Credit cards Cartes de crédit VISA - MasterCard

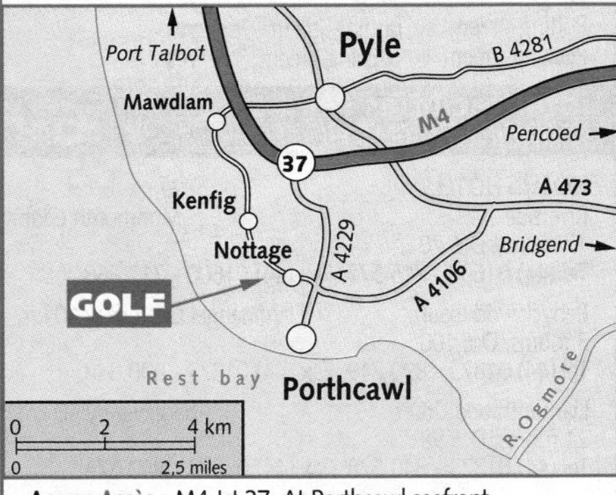

Access Accès : M4 Jct 37. At Porthcawl seafront, right → Locks Common, then left.
Map 6 on page 495 Carte 6 Page 495

Golf course PARCOURS — 19/20

Site	Site	
Maintenance	Entretien	
Architect	Architecte	Charles Gibson
Type	Type	links
Relief	Relief	
Water in play	Eau en jeu	
Exp. to wind	Exposé au vent	
Trees in play	Arbres en jeu	

Scorecard Carte de score	Chp. Chp.	Mens Mess.	Ladies Da.
Length Long.	6083	5608	5231
Par	72	72	75
Slope system	—	—	—

Advised golfing ability Niveau de jeu recommandé: 0 12 24 36
Hcp required Handicap exigé: certificate

Club house & amenities CLUB HOUSE ET ANNEXES — 7/10

Pro shop	Pro-shop	
Driving range	Practice	
Sheltered	couvert	2 bays
On grass	sur herbe	yes
Putting-green	putting-green	yes
Pitching-green	pitching green	yes

Hotel facilities ENVIRONNEMENT HOTELIER — 6/10

HOTELS HÔTELS

Atlantic, 18 rooms, D £ 90 — Porthcawl 1 km
Tel (44) 01656 - 785 011, Fax (44) 01656 - 771 877

Seabank, 65 rooms, D £ 80 — Porthcawl 3 km
Tel (44) 01656 - 782 261, Fax (44) 01656 - 785 363

Rose and Crown — Porthcawl 2 km
8 rooms, D £ 45
Tel (44) 01656 - 784 850, Fax (44) 01656 - 772 345

Dormy House, 9 rooms, D £ 50 — Royal Porthcawl o
Tel (44) 01656 - 782 251, Fax (44) 01656 - 771 687

RESTAURANTS RESTAURANT

Seabank — Porthcawl 2 km
Tel (44) 01656 - 782 261

ROYAL ST DAVID'S

18 | 6 | 5

Overlooked by the extraordinary medieval Harlech castle with a fortified stairway running down to the sea, this course (named after the patron saint of Wales) is more majestic than ever. The pros say this is the toughest par 69 in the world, but one thing is sure: for the ordinary mortal, playing 3 strokes over your handicap is already a right "royal" exploit. The constant changes in hole direction are a further disruptive factor for golfers who already have to contend with the optical illusions created by the dune environment and the sensation of space. The shot you need to master here is of course the low ball and you need a good measure of flair to place your bump 'n run shots close to the pin. High shots will more often than not end up in spots where your recovery can be "most amusing". A great course.

Dominé par l'extraordinaire château médiéval d'Harlech, avec son escalier fortifié allant jusqu'à la mer, ce parcours (portant le nom du patron du Pays de Galles) acquiert une majesté supplémentaire. Les professionnels disent qu'il s'agit du par 69 le plus difficile du monde. Une chose est sûre, pour le commun des mortels, jouer trois au-dessus de son handicap est déjà "royal". Les changements constants d'orientation des trous perturbent les joueurs, déjà aux prises avec les illusions de distance que donne l'environnement de dunes, mais aussi la sensation d'espace. Le coup à maîtriser est bien sûr la balle basse, et il faut beaucoup de flair pour placer les obligatoires "bump'n run" à proximité du trou. Quant aux balles hautes, elles terminent leur course dans des endroits d'où il est amusant de s'extraire. Un grand parcours.

Royal St David's Golf Club — 1894

WAL - HARLECH, Gwynedd LL46 2UB

Office	Secrétariat	(44) 01766 - 780 361
Pro shop	Pro-shop	(44) 01766 - 780 851
Fax	Fax	(44) 01766 - 781 110
Web	www.royalstdavids.co.uk	
Situation	Situation	3 km from Harlech
Annual closure	Fermeture annuelle	no
Weekly closure	Fermeture hebdomadaire	no

Fees main season / Tarifs haute saison	18 holes	
	Week days / Semaine	We/Bank holidays / We/Férié
Individual / Individuel	£ 30*	£ 35*
Couple / Couple	£ 60	£ 70

* Full day: £ 40 - £ 45 / Booking essential at weekends

Caddy	Caddy	no
Electric Trolley	Chariot électrique	yes
Buggy	Voiturette	yes
Clubs	Clubs	yes

Credit cards Cartes de crédit
VISA - Mastercard

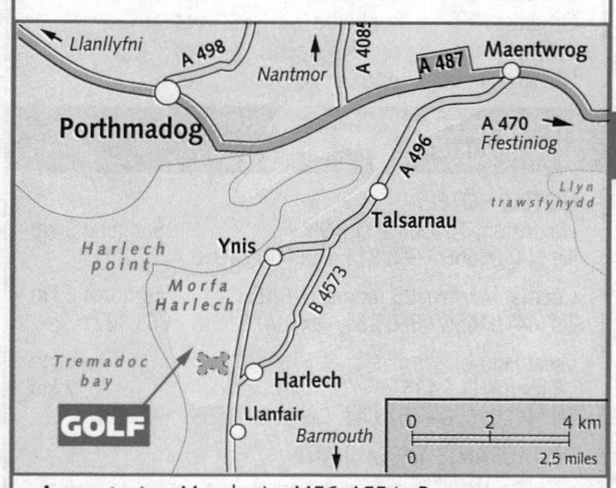

Access Accès : Manchester M56, A55 to Bangor, then A487 South to Porthmadog, A470 and A496 → Harlech. Golf on right side before Harlech.
Map 5 on page 494 Carte 5 Page 494

Golf course — PARCOURS — 18/20

Site	Site	
Maintenance	Entretien	
Architect	Architecte	Unknown
Type	Type	links
Relief	Relief	
Water in play	Eau en jeu	
Exp. to wind	Exposé au vent	
Trees in play	Arbres en jeu	

Scorecard / Carte de score	Chp. / Chp.	Mens / Mess.	Ladies / Da.
Length Long.	5848	5713	5266
Par	69	69	74
Slope system	—	—	—

Advised golfing ability / Niveau de jeu recommandé: 0 12 24 36
Hcp required / Handicap exigé: certificate

Club house & amenities — CLUB HOUSE ET ANNEXES — 6/10

Pro shop	Pro-shop	
Driving range	Practice	
Sheltered	couvert	no
On grass	sur herbe	yes
Putting-green	putting-green	yes
Pitching-green	pitching green	yes

Hotel facilities — ENVIRONNEMENT HOTELIER — 5/10

HOTELS HÔTELS

Maes y Neuadd, 16 rooms, D £ 180 — Harlech 1 km
Tel (44) 01766 - 780 200, Fax (44) 01766 - 780 211

Castle Cottage — Harlech
6 rooms, D £ 52 — 3 km
Tel (44) 01766 - 780 479Estuary Motel — Harlech
10 rooms, D £ 52 — 2 km
Tel (44) 01766 - 771 155, Fax (44) 01766 - 771 697

RESTAURANTS RESTAURANT

Maes y Neuadd — Harlech
Tel (44) 01766 - 780 200 — 1 km

Castle Cottage — Harlech
Tel (44) 01766 - 780 479 — 1 km

SOUTHERNDOWN

16 | 7 | 7

A good number of specialists lent a hand in laying out this course, including Fernie, Vardon, Braid, Fowler, Willie Park, H.S. Colt and, more recently Donald Steel. Perched high up overlooking Porthcawl, Southerndown has resisted any attempts at serious human interference and stayed very natural in style. And it is true that the land was ideal for the building of a golf course. The fairways are cropped by sheep, who never go on strike and work most methodically. Very British in its sloping and hilly design but never over-tiring on the legs, this is not a links because the terrain is clay (well drained) but there are more bushes than trees in play. Still, you are playing links-style golf here, hitting searing low shots. A tough test from the back tees, a little easier from the front and all in all, well worth getting to know.

Bien des spécialistes se sont penchés sur ce parcours : Fernie, Vardon, Braid, Fowler, Willie Park, H.S. Colt et dernièrement Donald Steel. Perché haut et dominant Porthcawl, Southerndown a pourtant réussi à se préserver des atteintes et rester très naturel: il est vrai que le terrain se prêtait idéalement à la construction d'un golf. Les fairways sont d'ailleurs tondus par les moutons, qui ne font jamais grève et travaillent avec méthode ! Très britannique dans son dessin typique des terrains en pente, mais sans fatigue excessive, ce n'est pas un links, parce que le terrain est argileux (bien drainé) et bien que l'on y trouve plus de buissons que d'arbres en jeu, mais il faut utiliser le même type de jeu, avec des balles pénétrantes et basses. Difficile des départs arrière, il s'adoucit quand on avance un peu. A connaître.

Southerndown Golf Club — 1905

Ewenny
WAL - BRIDGEND, Mid. Glam. CF32 0QP

Office	Secrétariat	(44) 01656 - 880 476
Pro shop	Pro-shop	(44) 01656 - 880 326
Fax	Fax	(44) 01656 - 880 371
Web	www.southerndowngolf.com	
Situation	Situation	

5 km SW of Bridgend (pop. 14 311)

Annual closure	Fermeture annuelle	no
Weekly closure	Fermeture hebdomadaire	no

Fees main season Tarifs haute saison	18 holes	
	Week days Semaine	**We/Bank holidays** We/Férié
Individual Individuel	£ 25*	£ 35*
Couple Couple	£ 50	£ 70

* Full day: £ 30 - £ 40 / Weekends: ask before coming

Caddy	Caddy	no
Electric Trolley	Chariot électrique	no
Buggy	Voiturette	no
Clubs	Clubs	yes
Credit cards	Cartes de crédit	no

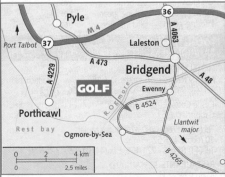

Access Accès : On the coast road Bridgend to Ogmore-by-Sea. Turn off at Pelican Inn (opp. Ogmore Castle)
Map 6 on page 495 Carte 6 Page 495

Golf course PARCOURS — 16/20

Site	Site	
Maintenance	Entretien	
Architect	Architecte	Willie Fernie
Type	Type	downland
Relief	Relief	
Water in play	Eau en jeu	
Exp. to wind	Exposé au vent	
Trees in play	Arbres en jeu	

Scorecard Carte de score	**Chp.** Chp.	**Mens** Mess.	**Ladies** Da.
Length Long.	5840	5395	5049
Par	70	69	74
Slope system	—	—	—

Advised golfing ability Niveau de jeu recommandé: 0 12 24 36
Hcp required Handicap exigé: certificate

Club house & amenities CLUB HOUSE ET ANNEXES — 7/10

Pro shop	Pro-shop	
Driving range	Practice	
Sheltered	couvert	no
On grass	sur herbe	yes
Putting-green	putting-green	yes
Pitching-green	pitching green	yes

Hotel facilities ENVIRONNEMENT HOTELIER — 7/10

HOTELS HÔTELS

Heronston, 75 rooms, D £ 95 — Bridgend 3 km
Tel (44) 01656 - 668 811, Fax (44) 01656 - 767 391

Coed-y-Mwstwr, 23 rooms, D £ 155 — Coychurch 6 km
Tel (44) 01656 - 860 261, Fax (44) 01656 - 863 122

Great House — Laleston
16 rooms, D £ 135 — 7 km
Tel (44) 01656 - 657 644, Fax (44) 01656 - 668 892

RESTAURANTS RESTAURANT

Frolics, Tel (44) 01656 - 880 127 — Southerndown 3 km

Leicester's (Great House) — Laleston
Tel (44) 01656 - 657 644 — 7 km

TENBY

18 | 7 | 6

Firstly there is a landscape of pot-holed dunes, looking as if they have been stirred by the wind for years on end. And then comes the course, fashioned by men and nature for centuries with the sporadic help of James Braid, as witnessed by the contours of some of the greens and the location of the many bunkers. There are very few continental golfers who have heard much about Welsh courses. This one is a must as you travel around the magnificent coastline of this very likeable country. Depending on the weather, the course can turn into a major championship test or a superb walk in the bracing sea-air. This is the time to test your creativity and invent special shots, because you will often end up in situations that are completely new to you. Tenby is a surprising, honest and charming course to play.

D'abord, il y a un paysage de dunes agitées comme par des années de bombardements, un parcours façonné par les hommes et la nature pendant plus d'un siècle, avec l'aide sporadique de James Braid, visible par les contours de certains greens, et le placement de nombreux bunkers. Rares sont les golfeurs du continent qui ont entendu parler des parcours du Pays de Galles. Celui-ci est incontournable dans un circuit des côtes magnifiques de ce pays attachant. Suivant le temps, il prendra des allures de grand test de championnat, ou de superbe promenade dans un air vivifiant. C'est alors le moment de tester votre créativité, d'inventer des coups de golf, parce que vous serez souvent dans des situations inconnues. Surprenant et franc, Tenby est aussi un parcours de charme.

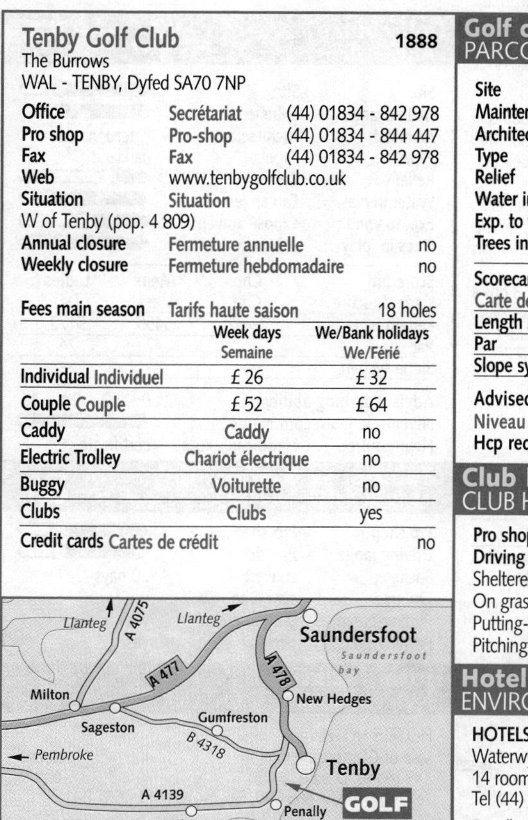

Tenby Golf Club — 1888

The Burrows
WAL - TENBY, Dyfed SA70 7NP

Office	Secrétariat	(44) 01834 - 842 978
Pro shop	Pro-shop	(44) 01834 - 844 447
Fax	Fax	(44) 01834 - 842 978
Web	www.tenbygolfclub.co.uk	
Situation	Situation	
W of Tenby (pop. 4 809)		
Annual closure	Fermeture annuelle	no
Weekly closure	Fermeture hebdomadaire	no

Fees main season Tarifs haute saison	Week days Semaine	We/Bank holidays We/Férié
		18 holes
Individual Individuel	£ 26	£ 32
Couple Couple	£ 52	£ 64
Caddy Caddy		no
Electric Trolley Chariot électrique		no
Buggy Voiturette		no
Clubs Clubs		yes
Credit cards Cartes de crédit		no

Access Accès : Cardiff, M4 West, A48, A477, A478 to Tenby. Golf near railway station.
Map 6 on page 494 Carte 6 Page 494

Golf course / PARCOURS — 18/20

Site	Site	
Maintenance	Entretien	
Architect	Architecte	James Braid
Type	Type	links
Relief	Relief	
Water in play	Eau en jeu	
Exp. to wind	Exposé au vent	
Trees in play	Arbres en jeu	

Scorecard / Carte de score	Chp. / Chp.	Mens / Mess.	Ladies / Da.
Length Long.	5767	5120	4943
Par	69	68	73
Slope system	—	—	—

Advised golfing ability / Niveau de jeu recommandé: 0 12 24 36
Hcp required / Handicap exigé: certificate

Club house & amenities / CLUB HOUSE ET ANNEXES — 7/10

Pro shop	Pro-shop	
Driving range	Practice	
Sheltered	couvert	no
On grass	sur herbe	yes
Putting-green	putting-green	yes
Pitching-green	pitching green	yes

Hotel facilities / ENVIRONNEMENT HOTELIER — 6/10

HOTELS HÔTELS

Waterwynch House, — Tenby 3 km
14 rooms, D £ 100
Tel (44) 01834 - 842 464, Fax (44) 01834 - 845 076

Penally Abbey, — Penally 2 km
12 rooms, D £ 136
Tel (44) 01834 - 843 033, Fax (44) 01834 - 844 714

Atlantic, — Tenby 2 km
42 rooms, D £ 130
Tel (44) 01834 - 842 881, Fax (44) 01834 - 842 881

Broadmead, — Tenby 3 km
20 rooms, D £ 62
Tel (44) 01834 - 842 641, Fax (44) 01834 - 845 757

VALE OF GLAMORGAN

16 | 8 | 7

This resort, with hotel, fitness and beauty centre, indoor squash and tennis courts, gymnasiums and swimming pools, was built to compete with the resorts of Marriott St Pierre and Celtic Manor. Add to this a high-tech training facility and suddenly you are light-years away from a traditional golf-club where you bring your own balls to hit across a field before making for the first tee. Will this evolution produce better players? That's not the point; here the aim is to host big events, even though the course is a little of the short side. Ten holes feature water in play, thus giving a slight American flavour to what is otherwise a very British country setting, and calling for target golf on virtually every hole. Luckily, the architect also remembered that a course needs players all year, which is why even though the yardage is reasonable overall, the front tees provide an intriguing challenge which remains within the bounds of human possibility. The character of the location and excellence of the Lake Course mean this is recommended golfing every time. Another 9-hole layout (the Hensol Course) is perfect for beginners to build up their confidence.

Ce complexe avec hôtel, centre de mise en forme et de beauté, squash et tennis indoor, gymnases et autres piscines est destiné à lutter avec les complexes de Marriott St Pierre et de Celtic Manor. Si l'on ajoute un centre d'entraînement high tech, nous voilà très loin du club traditionnel où l'on amène ses propres balles pour taper dans un champ avant d'aller sur le parcours. Cela fera t-il de plus grands joueurs ? La question n'est pas là. Ici, on vise à accueillir de grandes épreuves, bien que l'ensemble soit un peu court. Dix trous ont de l'eau en jeu, ce qui donne un caractère un peu américain à un paysage autrement très britannique, et impose un jeu de cible pratiquement sur tous les trous. Heureusement, l'architecte a aussi pensé qu'il faut des joueurs toute l'année, c'est pourquoi, même si la longueur générale est raisonnable, les départs avancés procurent un challenge intéressant, mais sans rien d'inhumain. Le caractère du lieu et la qualité de ce "Lake Course" incitent à le recommander. Un autre 9 trous (Hensol Course) permet aux joueurs golfiquement timides de prendre de l'assurance.

Vale of Glamorgan Golf & Country Club 1994

Hensol Park
WAL - HENSOL, near BRIDGEND CF7 8JY

Office	Secrétariat	(44) 01443 - 665 899
Pro shop	Pro-shop	(44) 01443 - 665 899
Fax	Fax	(44) 01443 - 667 801
Web	www.vale/hotel.com	
Situation	Situation	32 km from Cardiff
Annual closure	Fermeture annuelle	no
Weekly closure	Fermeture hebdomadaire	no

Fees main season Tarifs haute saison	18 holes	
	Week days Semaine	**We/Bank holidays** We/Férié
Individual Individuel	£ 30	£ 30*
Couple Couple	£ 60	£ 60

* We: with members / Soft spikes mandatory

Caddy	Caddy	no
Electric Trolley	Chariot électrique	no
Buggy	Voiturette	yes
Clubs	Clubs	yes

Credit cards Cartes de crédit
VISA - Eurocard - MasterCard - DC - AMEX

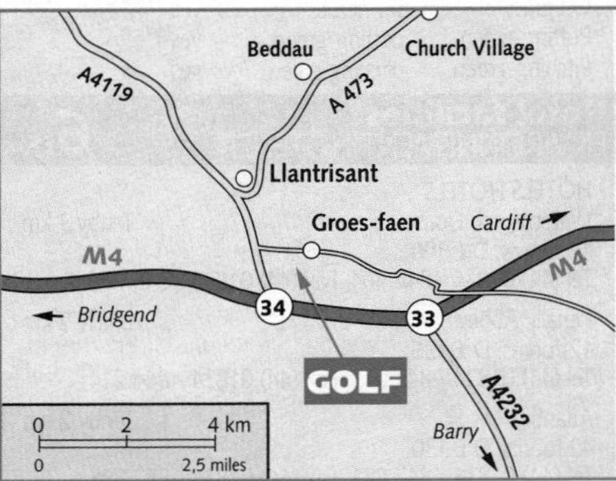

Access Accès : Just off Junction 34 of M4
Map 6 on page 495 Carte 6 Page 495

Golf course PARCOURS 16/20

Site	Site	
Maintenance	Entretien	
Architect	Architecte	Peter Johnson
Type	Type	parkland
Relief	Relief	
Water in play	Eau en jeu	
Exp. to wind	Exposé au vent	
Trees in play	Arbres en jeu	

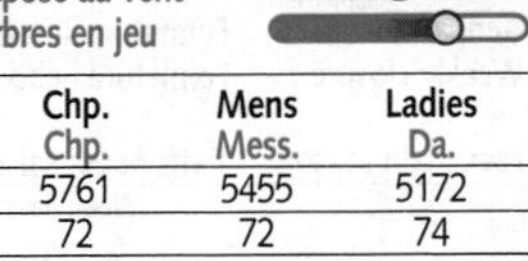

Scorecard Carte de score	**Chp.** Chp.	**Mens** Mess.	**Ladies** Da.
Length Long.	5761	5455	5172
Par	72	72	74
Slope system	—	—	—

Advised golfing ability Niveau de jeu recommandé — 0 12 24 36
Hcp required Handicap exigé — certificate

Club house & amenities CLUB HOUSE ET ANNEXES 8/10

Pro shop	Pro-shop	
Driving range	Practice	
Sheltered	couvert	20 bays
On grass	sur herbe	no
Putting-green	putting-green	yes
Pitching-green	pitching green	yes

Hotel facilities ENVIRONNEMENT HOTELIER 7/10

HOTELS HÔTELS

Vale of Glamorgan Hotel — Hensol, on site
143 rooms, D £ 80
Tel (44) 01443 - 665 899, Fax (44) 01443 - 667 801

Greyhound Inn — Llantrisant, 6 km
10 rooms, D £ 68
Tel (44) 01291 - 672 505, Fax (44) 01291 - 673 255

Coed-y-Mwstwr — Coychurch, 12 km
23 rooms, D £ 155
Tel (44) 01656 - 860 261, Fax (44) 01656 - 863 122

Forte Travelodge — Pencoed, 8 km
40 rooms, D £ 40
Tel (44) 01656 - 864 404, Fax (44) 01656 - 864 404

EUROPE'S TOP 1000 GOLF COURSES

Ireland
Northern Ireland

Ballybunion

Ireland & Northern Ireland

Irlande & Irlande du Nord

Here, we have included in succession courses from the Republic of Ireland and Northern Ireland. There is no rush in this part of the world, and even to meet high demand from tourists you can count the number of recently opened courses on the fingers of one hand.

Of these, we have included Ring of Kerry, Esker Hills and the Headfort New Course. When trimming the list down to 100, we deliberately focused on the most representative layouts, especially the links courses, which continental golfers seldom have the chance to play locally.

With nearly 280 eighteen-hole and 100 nine-hole courses or 220,000 registered players, there is no shortage of space for visitors, and Ireland is a golfing destination renowned the world over. You will always be made most welcome, but don't expect to find any magnificent driving ranges (you often find just rough practice areas where you can hit your own balls), or sumptuous club-houses. Here, modern facilities and luxury come second to the excellence of the course and warm hospitality. A letter of introduction from your own club is never a bad idea, and also remember to book your tee-off times.

Vous trouverez ici, successivement, les parcours de la République d'Irlande et d'Irlande du Nord. Ici, rien de sert de se presser, et même pour répondre à une demande touristique forte, seuls quelques parcours ont été construits récemment.

Parmi eux, nous avons inclus Ring of Kerry, Esker Hills et le New Course d'Headfort. Pour choisir les 100 meilleurs des golfs irlandais, nous avons volontairement mis l'accent sur les plus représentatifs, en particulier les links, que les golfeurs continentaux ont rarement l'habitude de trouver chez eux.

Avec près de 280 parcours de 18 trous et 100 de 9 trous pour 220.000 joueurs licenciés, la place ne manque pas pour les visiteurs, et le territoire de l'Irlande est une destination touristique connue du monde entier. Vous y serez toujours le bienvenu, mais ne vous attendez pas à trouver des practices magnifiques (on trouve souvent de simples zones où l'on tape ses propres balles), ni toujours des Club-house somptueux). Ici, le modernisme et le luxe passent après la qualité du parcours et la chaleur de l'accueil. Une lettre d'introduction de votre club n'est jamais inutile. Pensez aussi à réserver vos départs à l'avance.

Map No 1
Carte n°1

km
0 10 20

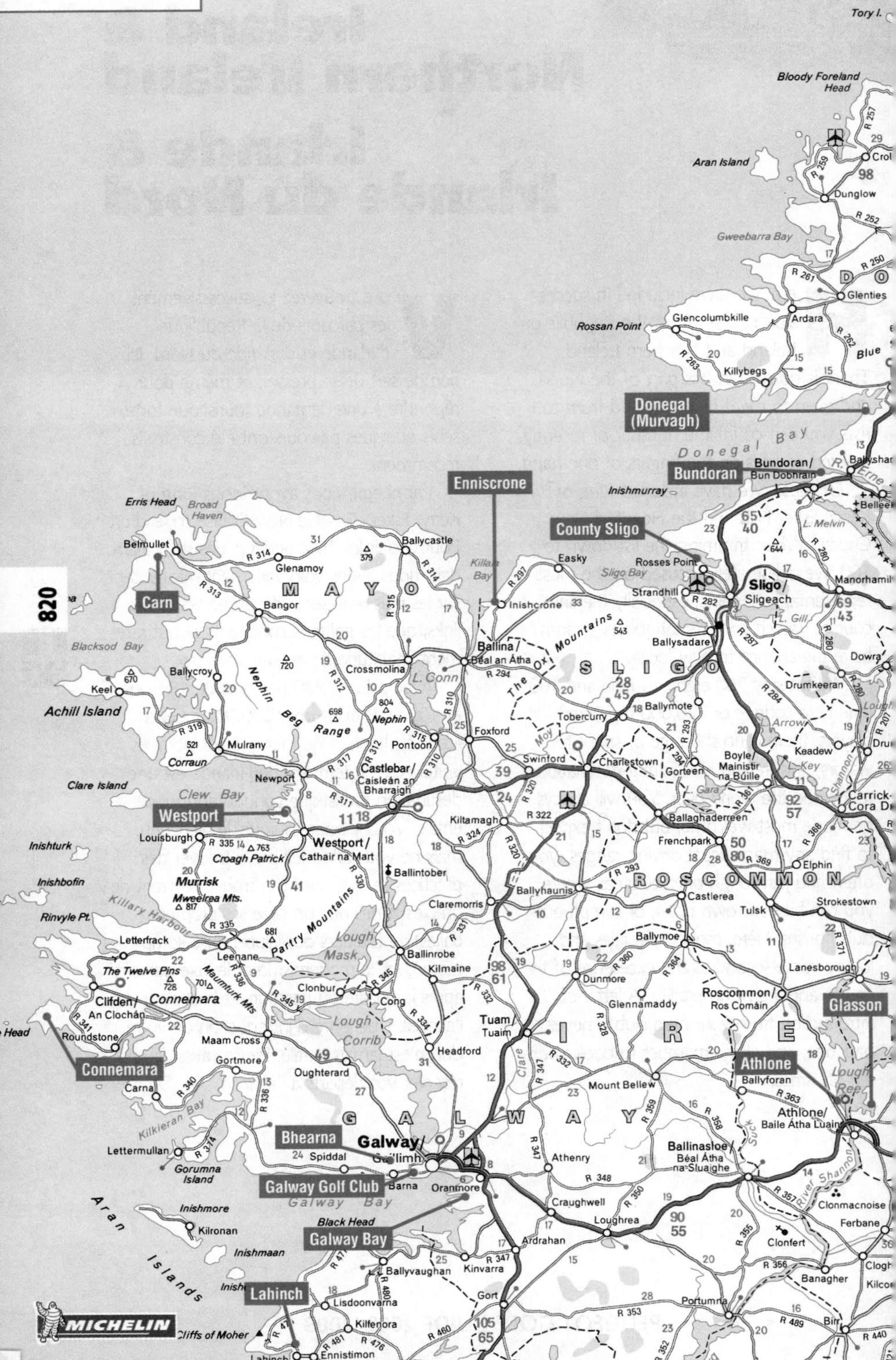

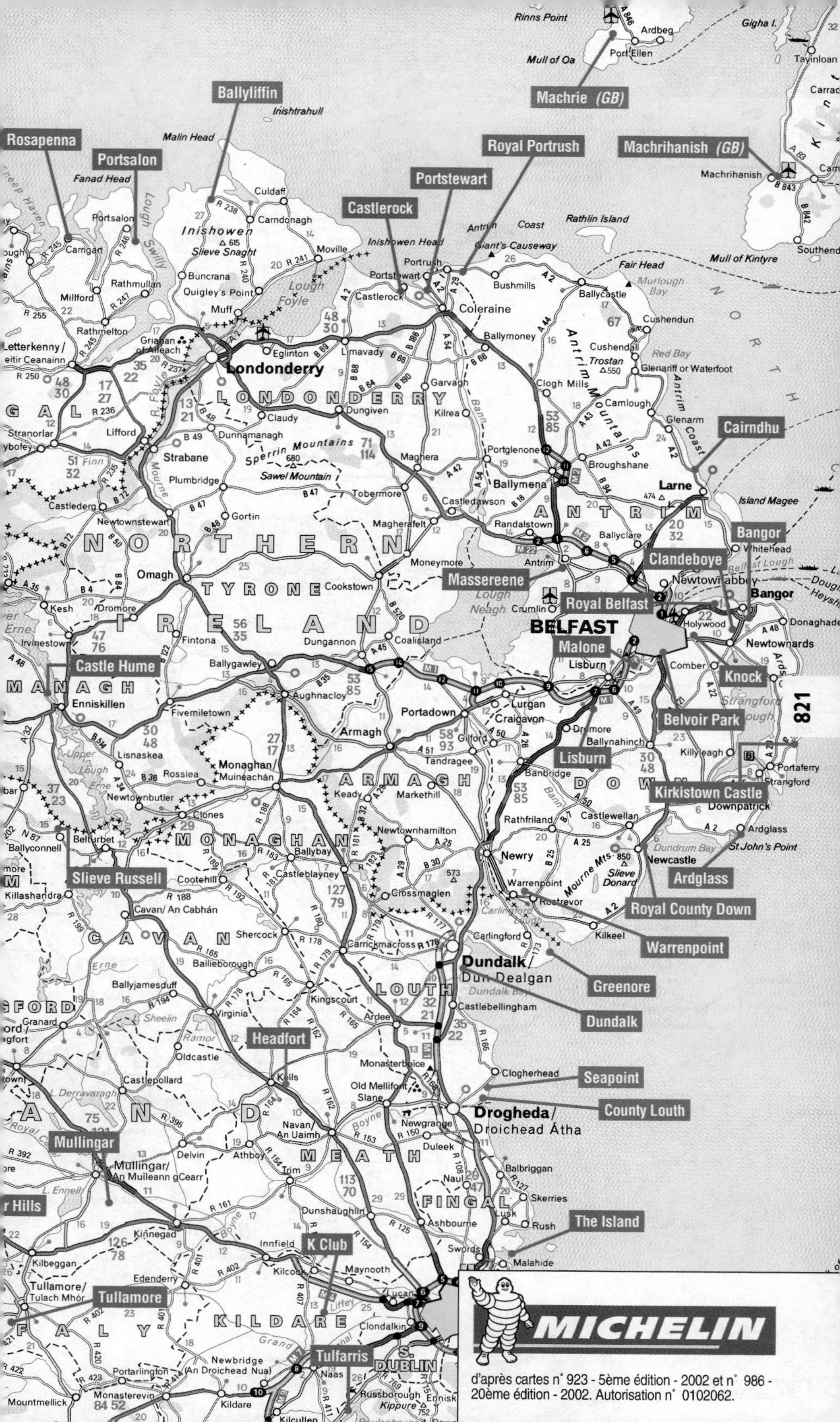
Machrie (GB)
Ballyliffin
Rosapenna
Portsalon
Royal Portrush
Machrihanish (GB)
Portstewart
Castlerock
Cairndhu
Bangor
Clandeboye
Massereene
Royal Belfast
Malone
Castle Hume
Knock
Belvoir Park
Lisburn
Kirkistown Castle
Slieve Russell
Ardglass
Royal County Down
Warrenpoint
Greenore
Dundalk
Headfort
Seapoint
County Louth
Mullingar
The Island
K Club
Tullamore
Tulfarris
NORTHERN IRELAND
LONDONDERRY
TYRONE
ANTRIM
ARMAGH
DOWN
MONAGHAN
CAVAN
LOUTH
MEATH
FINGAL
KILDARE
Londonderry
BELFAST
Dundalk/ Dún Dealgan
Drogheda/ Droichead Átha
MICHELIN
d'après cartes n° 923 - 5ème édition - 2002 et n° 986 - 20ème édition - 2002. Autorisation n° 0102062.

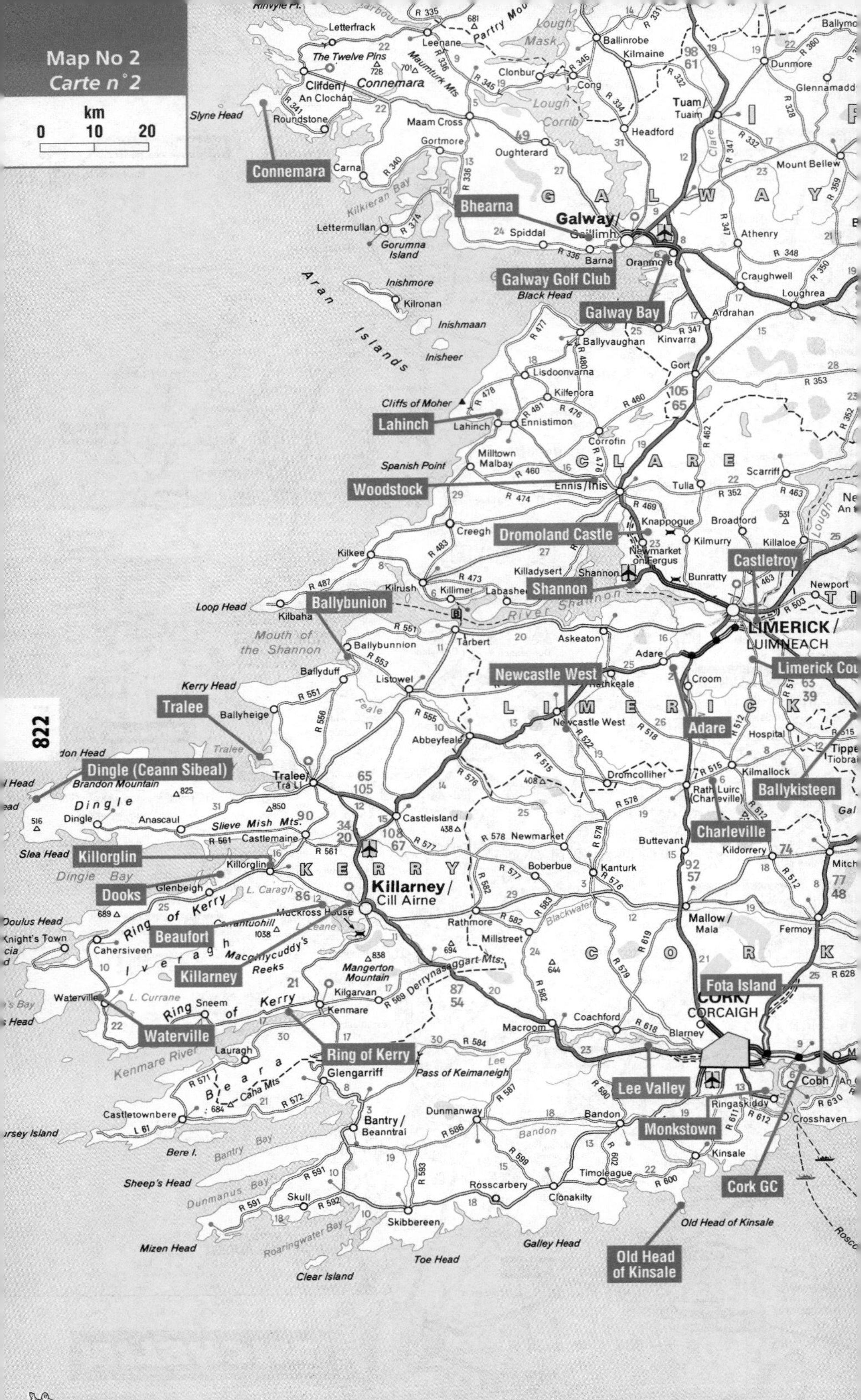

Map No 2
Carte n°2

km
0 10 20

Connemara
Bhearna
Galway Golf Club
Galway Bay
Lahinch
Woodstock
Dromoland Castle
Castletroy
Shannon
Ballybunion
Newcastle West
Limerick Cou
Tralee
Adare
Dingle (Ceann Sibeal)
Ballykisteen
Charleville
Killorglin
Dooks
Beaufort
Killarney
Fota Island
Waterville
Ring of Kerry
Lee Valley
Monkstown
Cork GC
Old Head of Kinsale

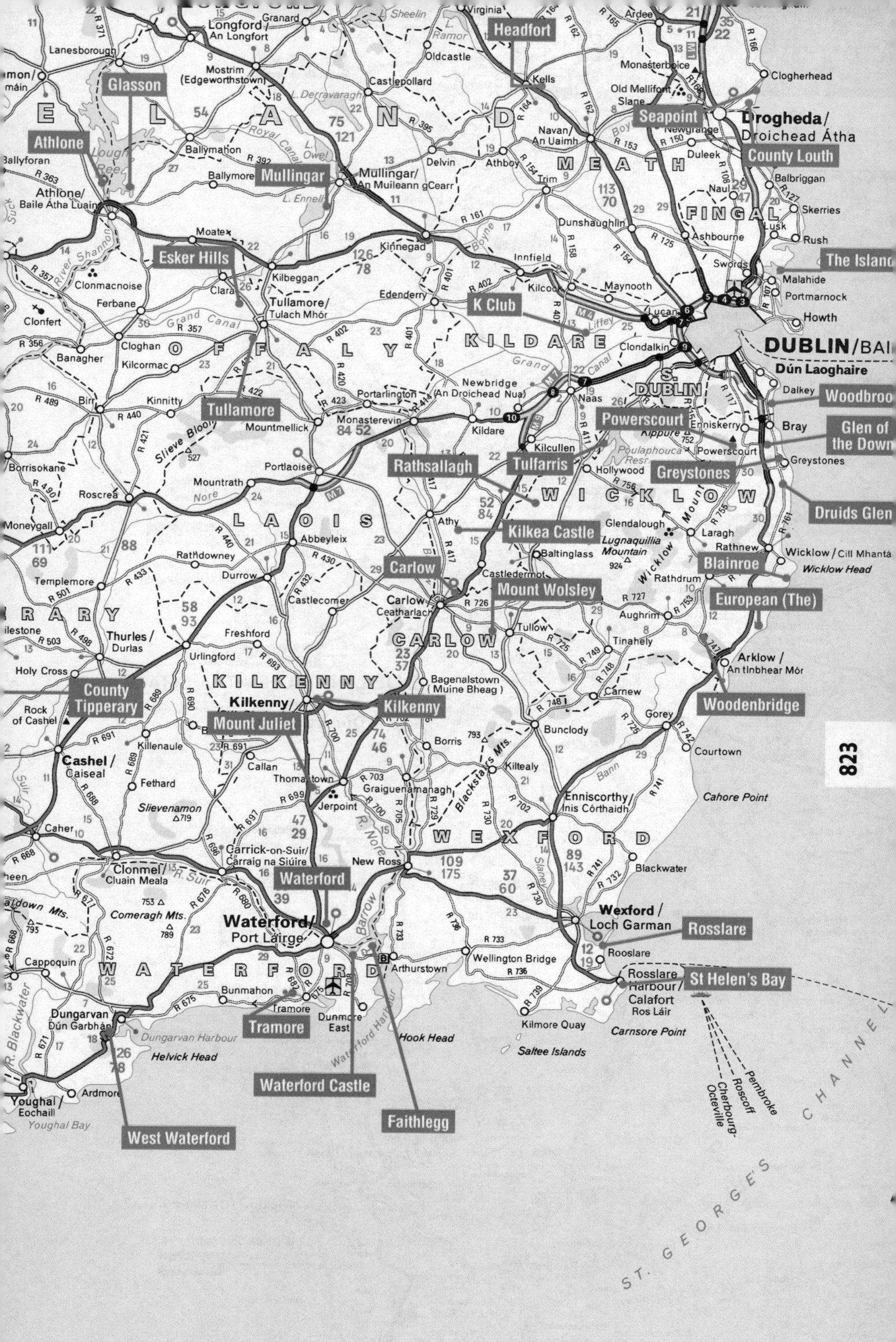
Headfort
Glasson
Athlone
Mullingar
Seapoint
County Louth
Esker Hills
The Island
K Club
Tullamore
Powerscourt
Woodbrook
Glen of the Downs
Rathsallagh
Tulfarris
Greystones
Druids Glen
Kilkea Castle
Carlow
Blainroe
Mount Wolsley
European (The)
County Tipperary
Kilkenny
Mount Juliet
Woodenbridge
Waterford
Rosslare
St Helen's Bay
Tramore
Waterford Castle
Faithlegg
West Waterford
MEATH
FINGAL
KILDARE
OFFALY
S. DUBLIN
WICKLOW
LAOIS
CARLOW
KILKENNY
WEXFORD
WATERFORD
DUBLIN
Drogheda / Droichead Átha
ST. GEORGE'S CHANNEL

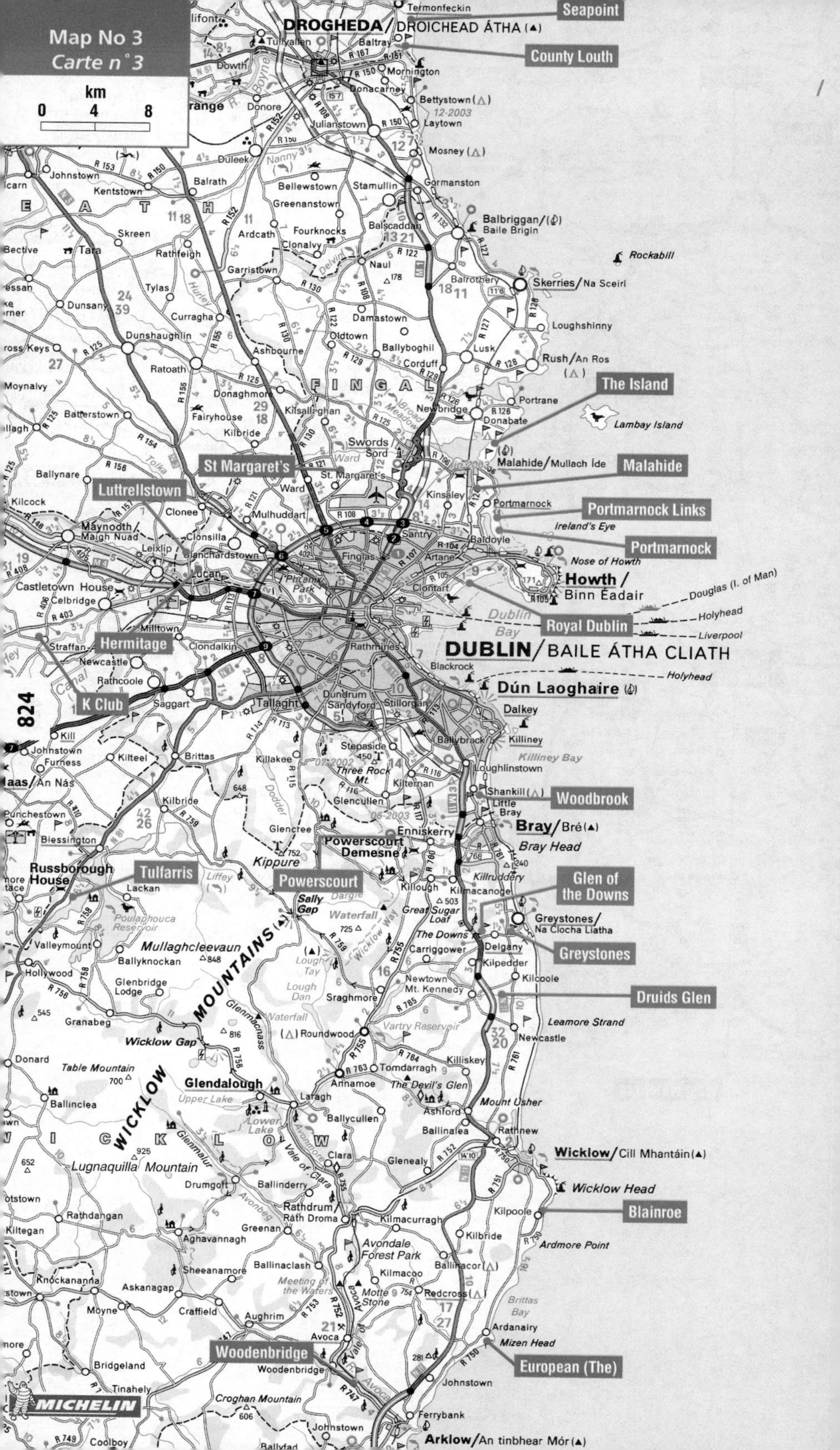

Map No 3
Carte n° 3
km
0 4 8
Seapoint
County Louth
DROGHEDA/DROICHEAD ÁTHA
Termonfeckin
Tullyallen
Baltray
Mornington
Donacarney
Bettystown
12-2003
Laytown
Julianstown
Donore
Duleek
Mosney
Gormanston
Johnstown
Kentstown
Balrath
Bellewstown
Stamullin
Greenanstown
Balbriggan/Baile Brigin
Balscaddan
Fourknocks
Ardcath
Clonalvy
Naul
Skreen
Tara
Bective
Rathfeigh
Garristown
Rockabill
Balrothery
Skerries/Na Sceirí
Tylas
Dunsany
Curragha
Damastown
Oldtown
Loughshinny
Dunshaughlin
Ashbourne
Ballyboghil
Corduff
Lusk
Rush/An Ros
Ratoath
FINGAL
The Island
Moynalvy
Donaghmore
Portrane
Batterstown
Fairyhouse
Kilsallaghan
Newbridge
Donabate
Lambay Island
Kilbride
Swords
Sord
Ballynare
St Margaret's
St. Margaret's
Malahide/Mullach Íde
Malahide
Luttrellstown
Ward
Kinsaley
Kilcock
Clonee
Mulhuddart
Portmarnock
Portmarnock Links
Maynooth/Maigh Nuad
Ireland's Eye
Clonsilla
Santry
Baldoyle
Portmarnock
Leixlip
Blanchardstown
Finglas
Artane
Nose of Howth
Lucan
Phoenix Park
Howth/Binn Éadair
Castletown House
Celbridge
Clontarf
Douglas (I. of Man)
Dublin Bay
Royal Dublin
Holyhead
Milltown
Liverpool
Straffan
Hermitage
Clondalkin
Rathmines
DUBLIN/BAILE ÁTHA CLIATH
Newcastle
Blackrock
Holyhead
Rathcoole
Dundrum
Dún Laoghaire
K Club
Saggart
Tallaght
Sandyford
Stillorgan
Dalkey
824
Kill
Ballybrack
Killiney
Johnstown
Furness
Kilteel
Brittas
Killakee
Stepaside
Killiney Bay
Naas/An Nás
Three Rock Mt.
Kilternan
Loughlinstown
Glencullen
Shankill
Woodbrook
Punchestown
Kilbride
Little Bray
Bray/Bré
Blessington
Glencree
Enniskerry
Powerscourt Demesne
Bray Head
Russborough House
Tulfarris
Kippure
Powerscourt
Killruddery
Lackan
Sally Gap
Killough
Kilmacanogue
Glen of the Downs
Poulaphouca Reservoir
Waterfall
Great Sugar Loaf
Greystones/Na Clocha Liatha
Valleymount
Mullaghcleevaun
MOUNTAINS
Wicklow Way
The Downs
Delgany
Greystones
Ballyknockan
Lough Tay
Carriggower
Kilpedder
Hollywood
Kilcoole
Glenbridge Lodge
Lough Dan
Newtown Mt. Kennedy
Druids Glen
Sraghmore
Granabeg
Glenmacnass
Waterfall
Vartry Reservoir
Leamore Strand
Wicklow Gap
Roundwood
Newcastle
Donard
Table Mountain
Tomdarragh
Killiskey
Annamoe
The Devil's Glen
Glendalough
Upper Lake
Laragh
Mount Usher
Ballinclea
Ashford
Lower Lake
Ballycullen
Rathnew
WICKLOW
Ballinalea
Glenmalur
Clara
Wicklow/Cill Mhantáin
Lugnaquilla Mountain
Vale of Clara
Glenealy
Drumgoff
Ballinderry
Wicklow Head
Avonbeg
Rathdrum/Ráth Droma
Blainroe
Rathdangan
Kilmacurragh
Kilpoole
Kiltegan
Greenan
Aghavannagh
Kilbride
Avondale Forest Park
Ardmore Point
Sheeanamore
Ballinaclash
Ballinacor
Knockananna
Kilmacoo
Askanagap
Meeting of the Waters
Motte Stone
Redcross
Brittas Bay
Moyne
Craffield
Aughrim
Ardanairy
Avoca
Mizen Head
Woodenbridge
Bridgeland
European (The)
Johnstown
Tinahely
Croghan Mountain
MICHELIN
Ferrybank
Coolboy
Johnstown
Ballyfad
Arklow/An tInbhear Mór

GOLF COURSES IN IRELAND & NORTHERN IRELAND
PARCOURS EN IRLANDE & IRLANDE DU NORD

This classification gives priority consideration to the score awarded to the actual course.

Ce classement donne priorité à la note attribuée au parcours.

Course score Note du parcours					Page
19	7	6	Ballybunion *Old Course*	I	831
19	7	8	Portmarnock	I	887
19	6	7	Royal County Down	NI	925
19	7	7	Royal Portrush *Dunluce Links*	NI	926
18	5	6	County Louth	I	847
18	5	6	European (The)	I	860
18	9	8	Mount Juliet	I	883
18	7	6	Tralee	I	902
17	6	5	Ballyliffin *Glashedy Links*	I	833
17	4	4	County Sligo	I	848
17	8	6	Enniscrone	I	858
17	8	8	K Club	I	871
17	6	6	Lahinch	I	877
17	7	8	Portmarnock Links	I	888
17	6	7	Waterville	I	908
16	7	6	Ballybunion *Cashen (New Course)*	I	830
16	6	7	Carlow	I	840
16	6	6	Castlerock	NI	916
16	6	6	Donegal (Murvagh)	I	852
16	9	7	Druids Glen	I	855
16	7	6	Fota Island	I	862
16	7	7	Glasson	I	865
16	5	8	Grange	I	867
16	7	8	Killarney *Killeen Course*	I	874
16	7	7	Old Head	I	886
16	5	5	Portsalon	I	889
16	7	7	Portstewart *Strand Course*	NI	923
16	7	6	Rosapenna	I	893
16	8	7	Royal Dublin	I	895
16	7	7	St Margaret's	I	900
16	7	6	Woodenbridge	I	911
15	6	7	Adare	I	828
15	6	5	Ballyliffin *Old Course*	I	834
15	5	3	Belmullet	I	837
15	5	6	Belvoir Park	NI	914
15	6	6	Clandeboye *Dufferin Course*	NI	917
15	6	6	Connemara	I	845
15	3	5	Cork GC	I	846
15	7	5	County Tipperary	I	849
15	5	4	Dingle Links (Ceann Sibeal)	I	851
15	5	5	Dooks	I	853
15	6	6	Dundalk	I	856
15	6	6	Headfort *New Course*	I	869
15	6	8	Hermitage	I	870
15	6	6	Kilkea Castle	I	872
15	7	8	Killarney *Mahony's Point*	I	875
15	6	5	Kirkistown Castle	NI	918
15	7	6	Knock	NI	919
15	7	6	Limerick County	I	879
15	7	6	Lisburn	NI	920
15	7	7	Luttrellstown	I	880
15	6	7	Monkstown	I	882
15	5	5	Mullingar	I	885
15	7	7	Powerscourt	I	890
15	7	7	Ring of Kerry	I	892
15	7	7	Royal Belfast	NI	924
15	6	6	Seapoint	I	896
15	8	6	Slieve Russell	I	898
15	7	7	The Island	I	901
15	7	6	Tulfarris	I	904
15	6	5	Tullamore	I	905
15	7	7	Westport	I	909
15	7	6	Woodbrook	I	910
14	6	4	Ardglass	NI	912
14	7	6	Ballykisteen	I	832
14	6	6	Bangor	NI	913
14	7	7	Bearna	I	835
14	5	5	Courtown	I	850
14	7	8	Dromoland Castle	I	854
14	6	6	Esker Hills	I	859
14	7	6	Galway Bay	I	863

Classification

GOLF COURSES IN IRELAND AND NORTHERN IRELAND

14	6	5	Greenore	I	868
14	6	5	Killorglin	I	876
14	5	6	Massereene	NI	922
14	7	6	Rathsallagh	I	891
14	6	6	St Helen's Bay	I	899
14	6	6	Waterford	I	906
14	5	6	Waterford Castle	I	907
13	6	6	Athlone	I	829
13	6	7	Beaufort	I	836
13	6	6	Blainroe	I	838
13	6	7	Bundoran	I	839
13	6	5	Cairndhu	NI	915
13	6	8	Castle	I	841
13	6	6	Castletroy	I	842
13	4	6	Charleville	I	843
13	6	8	Citywest	I	844
13	7	8	Elm Park	I	857
13	7	7	Faithlegg	I	861
13	6	6	Galway GC	I	864
13	6	7	Glen of the Downs	I	866
13	7	6	Kilkenny	I	873
13	7	6	Lee *Valley*	I	878
13	7	8	Malahide *Red + Blue + Yellow*	I	881
13	6	6	Malone	NI	921
13	6	5	Mount Wolseley	I	884
13	5	6	Rosslare	I	894
13	7	7	Royal Portrush *Valley*	NI	927
13	6	6	Shannon	I	897
13	7	6	Tramore	I	903
13	6	5	Warrenpoint	NI	928

RECOMMENDED GOLFING STAY
SEJOUR DE GOLF RECOMMANDÉ

Ballybunion *Old Course/Cashen*	19	7	6	831
Ballyliffin *Glashedy Links*	17	6	5	833
Ballyliffin *Old Course*	15	6	5	834
County Louth	18	5	6	847
County Sligo	17	4	4	848
Druids Glen	16	9	7	855
European (The)	18	5	6	860
Headfort *New Course*	15	6	6	869
K Club	17	8	8	871
Killarney *Killeen Course*	16	7	8	874
Killarney *Mahony's Point*	15	7	8	875
Lahinch	17	6	6	877
Mount Juliet	18	9	8	883
Portmarnock	19	7	8	887
Portmarnock Links	17	7	8	888
Portstewart *Strand Course*	16	7	7	923
Royal County Down	19	6	7	925
Royal Dublin	16	8	7	895
Royal Portrush *Dunluce Links*	19	7	7	926
Royal Portrush *Valley*	13	7	7	927
Tralee	18	7	6	902
Waterville	17	6	7	908

RECOMMENDED GOLFING HOLIDAYS
VACANCES RECOMMANDÉES

Connemara & Galway 835/845/863/864 - Cork 846 - Killarney & Kerry 831/874/892/908

TYPE OF COURSE
TYPE DE PARCOURS

Copse
Clandeboye *Dufferin Course* 917.

Forest
Woodenbridge 911.

Hilly
Lee *Valley* 878, Warrenpoint 928.

Inland
Adare 828, Bangor 913, Charleville 843, Clandeboye *Dufferin Course* 917, Dundalk 856, Esker Hills 859, Glen of the Downs 866, Headfort *New Course* 869, K Club 871, Lee *Valley* 878, Malone 921, Massereene 922, Powerscourt 890, Rathsallagh 891, St Marga-ret's 900, Woodbrook 910

Links
Ballybunion *Cashen (New Course)* 830, Ballybunion *Old Course* 831, Ballyliffin *Glashedy Links* 833, Ballyliffin *Old Course* 834, Belmullet 837, Bundoran 839, Castlerock 916, Connemara 845, County Louth 847, County Sligo 848, Dingle Links (Ceann Sibeal) 851 Donegal (Murvagh) 852, Dooks 853, Enniscrone 858, European (The) 860, Kirkistown Castle 918, Lahinch 877, Portmarnock 887, Portmarnock Links 888, Portsalon 889, Portstewart *Strand Course* 923, Rosapenna 893, Rosslare 894, Royal County Down 925, Royal Dublin 895, Royal Portrush *Dunluce Links* 926, Royal Portrush *Valley* 927, Seapoint 896, St Helen's Bay 899, The Island 901, Tralee 902, Waterville 908.

Open country
Bearna 835.

Parkland
Adare 828, Athlone 829, Ballykisteen 832, Beaufort 836, Belvoir Park 914, Blainroe 838, Cairndhu 915, Carlow 840, Castle 841, Castletroy 842, Charleville 843, Citywest 844, Cork GC 846, County Tipperary 849, Courtown 850, Dromoland Castle 854, Druids Glen 855, Dundalk 856, Elm Park 857, Esker Hills 859, Faithlegg 861, Fota Island 862, Galway GC 864, Glasson 865, Grange 867, Headfort *New Course* 869, Hermitage 870, K-Club 871, Kilkea Castle 872, Kilkenny 873, Killarney *Killeen Course* 874, Killarney *Mahony's Point* 875, Killorglin 876, Kirkistown Castle 918, Knock 919, Limerick County 879, Lisburn 920, Luttrellstown 880, Malahide *Red + Blue + Yellow* 881, Malone 921, Massereene 922, Monkstown 882, Mount Juliet 883, Mount Wolseley 884, Mullingar 885, Powerscourt 890, Rathsallagh 891, Ring of Kerry 892, Royal Belfast 924, Shannon 897, Slieve Russell 898, St Helen's Bay 899, St Margaret's 900, Tramore 903, Tulfarris 904, Tullamore 905, Warrenpoint 928, Waterford 906, Waterford Castle 907, Westport 909, Woodenbridge, 911.

Seaside course
Ardglass 912, Ballyliffin *Glashedy Links* 833, Blainroe 838, Cairndhu 915, Castlerock 916, Dooks 853, Dingle Links (Ceann Sibeal) 851, Enniscrone 858, Galway Bay 863, Galway GC 864, Greenore 868, Old Head 886, Ring of Kerry 892, Rosslare 894, Tramore 903, Westport 909.

ADARE

15 | 6 | 7

From time to time, being iconoclastic can make a pleasant change. There could be no doubting that Adare was designed by Robert Trent Jones, because this could just as easily be a course on the Costa del Sol. In other words, there is no real "feeling" with the Irish landscape, probably on account of the over-extensive earthworks and grading used to shape the course, the give-away bunker designs and the huge water hazard on the front 9, which cost a fortune to build. But this is still a great course once you forget its artificial side, which anyway is less apparent on the way in. Here, golfers have to cope with the river Maigue and indigenous trees such as oak, beech, pine and cedar. There is no hidden trap, which only emphasises the psychological fear factor. Long and challenging, the course is almost certainly too tough for high-handicappers on account of the very many hazards. Even the better players will find it hard going.

De temps à autre, il n'est pas désagréable d'être iconoclaste: Adare a certes été dessiné par Robert Trent Jones, mais pourrait tout aussi bien se trouver sur la Costa del Sol. Autrement dit, on ne trouvera pas ici de véritable "sympathie" avec le paysage irlandais, en raison sans doute de mouvements de terrain trop importants, de dessin de bunkers trop révélateurs de leur auteur, de l'immense obstacle d'eau de l'aller, dont l'aménagement a coûté une fortune. Mais il reste un grand parcours de golf, dont on oubliera le côté parfois artificiel, d'ailleurs moins sensible au retour: il met essentiellement en jeu la rivière Maigue, et les arbres natifs du lieu : chênes, hêtres, pins ou cèdres. Aucun piège n'est caché, ce qui accentue le facteur psychologique de crainte. Long et exigeant, ce parcours reste sans doute très difficile pour les handicaps élevés, en raison de la multiplicité des obstacles, les autres n'y connaîtront guère de repos...

Adare Golf Club — 1995

Adare Manor
IRL - ADARE, Co Limerick

Office	Secrétariat	(353) 061 - 395 044
Pro shop	Pro-shop	(353) 061 - 395 044
Fax	Fax	(353) 061 - 396 987
Web	www.adaremanor.ie	
Situation	Situation	Limerick, 10 km
Annual closure	Fermeture annuelle	no
Weekly closure	Fermeture hebdomadaire	no

Fees main season Tarifs haute saison	18 holes	
	Week days Semaine	**We/Bank holidays** We/Férié
Individual Individuel	76 €	76 €
Couple Couple	152 €	152 €

Special fees for early tee-times

Caddy	Caddy	20 € /18 holes
Electric Trolley	Chariot électrique	no
Buggy	Voiturette	38 € /18 holes
Clubs	Clubs	15 € /18 holes

Credit cards Cartes de crédit
VISA - Eurocard - MasterCard - AMEX

N 69 · Limerick Luimneach · N 20 · Foynes Faing · GOLF · Adare Átha Dara · Reaver Maigue · N 21 · R519 · Newcastle West An Caisleán Nua · Ballingarry Baile an Gharraí · N 20 · Mallow Mala · Bruff An Brú · 0 2 4 km · 0 2,5 miles

Access Accès : Limerick, N7 → Adare. Patrick's Well, straight through the fork in road, first left in village at gates, right to proshop
Map 2 on page 822 Carte 2 Page 822

Golf course — PARCOURS — 15/20

Site	Site	
Maintenance	Entretien	
Architect	Architecte	R. Trent Jones Sr
Type	Type	inland, parkland
Relief	Relief	
Water in play	Eau en jeu	
Exp. to wind	Exposé au vent	
Trees in play	Arbres en jeu	

Scorecard Carte de score	**Chp.** Chp.	**Mens** Mess.	**Ladies** Da.
Length Long.	6489	5993	4925
Par	72	72	72
Slope system	—	—	—

Advised golfing ability 0 12 24 36
Niveau de jeu recommandé
Hcp required Handicap exigé 28 Men, 36 Ladies

Club house & amenities — CLUB HOUSE ET ANNEXES — 6/10

Pro shop	Pro-shop	
Driving range	Practice	
Sheltered	couvert	no
On grass	sur herbe	yes
Putting-green	putting-green	yes
Pitching-green	pitching green	yes

Hotel facilities — ENVIRONNEMENT HOTELIER — 7/10

HOTELS HÔTELS

Adare Manor Hotel — on site
64 rooms, D 356 €
Tel (353) 061 - 396 566, Fax (353) 061 - 396 124

Woodlands Hotel — Adare 2 km
57 rooms, D 114 €
Tel (353) 061 - 396 118, Fax (353) 061 - 396 073

Dunraven Arms Hotel, 66 rooms, D 190 € — Adare 0.5 km
Tel (353) 061 - 396 633, Fax (353) 061 - 396 541

RESTAURANTS RESTAURANT

Wild Geese — Adare 1 km
Tel (353) 061 - 396 451

Dunraven Arms, Tel (353) 061 - 396 633 — Adare 0.5 km

ATHLONE

13 | 6 | 6

The gently rolling course of Athlone is magnificently sited on a peninsula overlooking Lough Ree. An old course that was remodelled in the late 1930s, the lack of yardage might lead to the better players under-estimating its difficulty and will invite them to play from the back-tees. It demands a wide variety of shots, especially when the wind blows from the lake, and skills in flighting the ball will help. The woods are on the outskirts of the course, as are most of the water hazards, although some isolated trees can come into play. Otherwise, you just avoid the bunkers, whose only criticism is the bland uniformity in design and shape. The greens are generally in good condition and moderately contoured, but they do tend to be soft in winter... It's not the best season in Ireland anyway. Long-hitters will have fun on the three rather short par 5s, but accuracy is always important. Watch out for some tight fairways.

Doucement vallonné, le parcours d'Athlone dispose d'une situation magnifique sur une péninsule dominant le Lough Ree. Déjà ancien, bien que révisé à la fin des années 30, son manque de longueur ne doit pas le faire sous estimer par les joueurs de bon niveau, à qui on conseillera bien sûr les départs arrière. Il demande une grande variété de coups, surtout quand le vent vient du lac, il faut alors savoir travailler la balle. Les bois sont à la périphérie du parcours, de même que la plupart des obstacles d'eau, mais certains arbres isolés peuvent parfois venir en jeu. Autrement, pour bien scorer, il suffit d'éviter les bunkers, auxquels on peut simplement reprocher une certaine uniformité de dessin et de forme. Les greens sont généralement en bonne condition et de relief modéré, mais ils peuvent être assez mous en hiver, qui n'est pas il est vrai la meilleure saison. Les longs frappeurs s'amuseront sur trois par 5 assez courts, mais ne devront pas oublier la précision, les fairways peuvent être étroits.

Athlone Golf Club — 1892

Hodson Bay
IRL - ATHLONE, Co. Westmeath

Office	Secrétariat	(353) 0902 - 92 073
Pro shop	Pro-shop	(353) 0902 - 94 285
Fax	Fax	(353) 0902 - 94 080
Web		—
Situation	Situation	
5 km from Athlone (pop. 7 691)		
Annual closure	Fermeture annuelle	no
Weekly closure	Fermeture hebdomadaire	no

Fees main season / Tarifs haute saison	Week days / Semaine	We/Bank holidays / We/Férié
18 holes		
Individual Individuel	32 €	32 €
Couple Couple	64 €	64 €
Caddy Caddy	13 € /on request	
Electric Trolley Chariot électrique	no	
Buggy Voiturette	19 €	
Clubs Clubs	13 €	

Credit cards Cartes de crédit
VISA - MasterCard

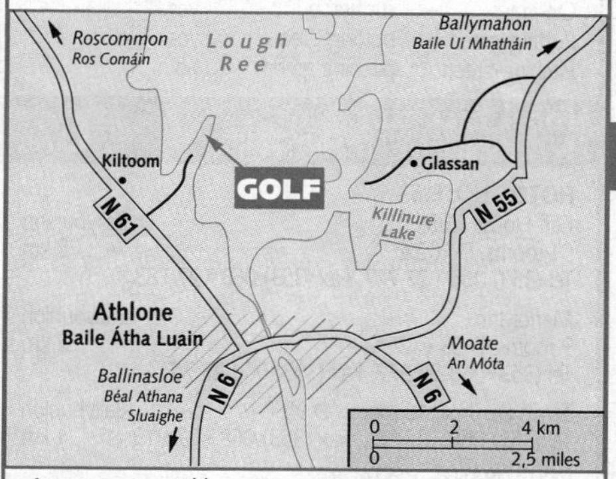

Access Accès : Athlone, N61 → Roscommon.
Golf beside Hodson Bay Hotel
Map 2 on page 823 Carte 2 Page 823

Golf course — PARCOURS — 13/20

Site	Site	
Maintenance	Entretien	
Architect	Architecte	J. McAllister Fred Hawtree
Type	Type	parkland
Relief	Relief	
Water in play	Eau en jeu	
Exp. to wind	Exposé au vent	
Trees in play	Arbres en jeu	

Scorecard / Carte de score	Chp. / Chp.	Mens / Mess.	Ladies / Da.
Length Long.	5922	5773	5104
Par	71	71	75
Slope system	—	—	—

Advised golfing ability / Niveau de jeu recommandé: 0 12 24 36
Hcp required / Handicap exigé: no

Club house & amenities — CLUB HOUSE ET ANNEXES — 6/10

Pro shop	Pro-shop	
Driving range	Practice	
Sheltered	couvert	no
On grass	sur herbe	yes
Putting-green	putting-green	yes
Pitching-green	pitching green	yes

Hotel facilities — ENVIRONNEMENT HOTELIER — 6/10

HOTELS HÔTELS

Hodson Bay Hotel — Athlone, beside golf
100 rooms, D 140 €
Tel (353) 0902 - 80 500, Fax (353) 0902 - 80 520

Prince of Wales Hotel — Athlone 6 km
73 rooms, D 102 €
Tel (353) 0902 - 72 626, Fax (353) 0902 - 75 658

Shamrock Lodge, 25 rooms, D 102 € — Athlone 5 km
Tel (353) 0902 - 92 601

RESTAURANTS RESTAURANT

Cornloft, Tel (353) 0902 - 94 753 — on road 362 6 km
Le Chateau, Tel (353) 0902 - 94 517 — Athlone 5 km

BALLYBUNION Cashen (New Course) | 16 | 7 | 6

Designing a new course in a mythical site such as this can be fatal to any course architect. But Robert Trent Jones has already designed enough great courses of his own to shrug off any mention of comparison, and his personality told him not to ape the old course, even though the dune-peppered landscape is similar (and sometimes even more impressive). The result here is a course that is slightly harder to decipher, where there is less room for intuition and more for knowledge of distance when choosing your clubs. A little American touch, even though approach shots can still be played "British" style. However, he has made maximum use of the terrain's natural contours and limited earthworks, while giving each hole its own individual character. The course's forceful personality (it is not everyone's cup of tea) would make this a must anywhere else, but here it lives in the shadow of the "Old Course".

Pour un architecte, signer un nouveau parcours dans un site aussi mythique peut être meurtrier. Robert Trent Jones avait déjà créé assez de grands parcours pour ne pas craindre la comparaison, et sa personnalité ne l'incitait pas à essayer de singer le "Old", bien que le paysage dunaire soit similaire (parfois plus impressionnant encore). De fait, il a créé un parcours plus complexe à déchiffrer, où la place de l'intuition est moins importante que la connaissance des distances pour choisir les clubs. Une petite touche américaine... même si les petites approches peuvent être souvent jouées "à la britannique". Cependant, il a su utiliser au maximum les contours naturels du terrain et limiter les terrassements, tout en donnant la touche de caractère individuel à chaque trou. La forte personnalité de ce parcours (qui ne fait pas toujours l'unanimité) en ferait n'importe où ailleurs un "must", mais le "Old" lui fait forcément ombrage.

Ballybunion Golf Club 1971

Sandhill Road
IRL - BALLYBUNION, Co Kerry

Office	Secrétariat	(353) 068 - 27 146
Pro shop	Pro-shop	(353) 068 - 27 146
Fax	Fax	(353) 068 - 27 387
Web	www.ballybuniongolfclub.ie	
Situation	Situation	

1 km from Ballybunion (pop. 1 346)

Annual closure	Fermeture annuelle	no
Weekly closure	Fermeture hebdomadaire	no

Fees main season Tarifs haute saison	18 holes	
	Week days Semaine	**We/Bank holidays** We/Férié
Individual Individuel	51 €	51 €
Couple Couple	102 €	102 €

91 € for both courses (same day)

Caddy	Caddy	32 € /18 holes
Electric Trolley	Chariot électrique	no
Buggy	Voiturette	no
Clubs	Clubs	32 € /18 holes

Credit cards Cartes de crédit VISA - MasterCard

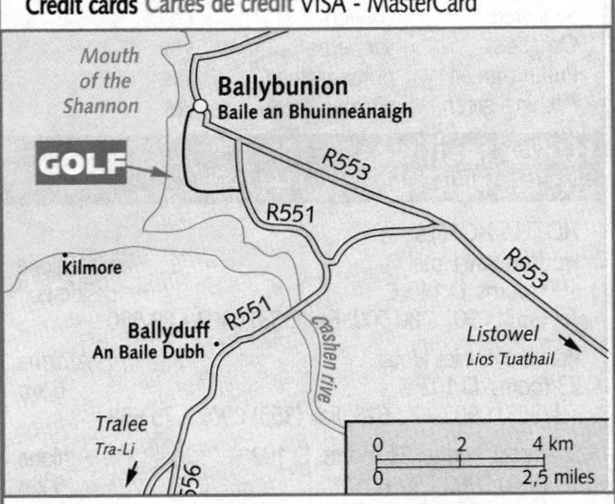

Access Accès : Limerick, N21 → Newcastle West, → Listowel, → Ballybunion
Map 2 on page 822 Carte 2 Page 822

Golf course PARCOURS 16/20

Site	Site	
Maintenance	Entretien	
Architect	Architecte	Robert Trent Jones
Type	Type	links
Relief	Relief	
Water in play	Eau en jeu	
Exp. to wind	Exposé au vent	
Trees in play	Arbres en jeu	

Scorecard Carte de score	**Chp.** Chp.	**Mens** Mess.	**Ladies** Da.
Length Long.	5830	5350	5160
Par	72	72	72
Slope system	—	—	—

Advised golfing ability Niveau de jeu recommandé 0 12 24 36
Hcp required Handicap exigé 24 Men, 36 Ladies

Club house & amenities CLUB HOUSE ET ANNEXES 7/10

Pro shop	Pro-shop	
Driving range	Practice	
Sheltered	couvert	
On grass	sur herbe	yes
Putting-green	putting-green	yes
Pitching-green	pitching green	no

Hotel facilities ENVIRONNEMENT HOTELIER 6/10

HOTELS HÔTELS

Cliff House Hotel — Ballybunion 2 km
51 rooms, D 102 €
Tel (353) 068 - 27 777, Fax (353) 068 - 27 783

Manor Inn — Ballybunion 2 km
9 rooms, D 63 €
Tel (353) 068-27 577, Fax (353) 068-27 757

Teach De Broc, 10 rooms, D 95 € — Ballybunion 1 km
Tel (353) 068 - 27 581, Fax (353) 068 - 27 919

RESTAURANTS RESTAURANT

Three Mermaids — Listowel 15 km
Tel (353) 068 - 21 184

Harty-Costello Tel (353) 068 - 27 129 — Ballybunion 1 km

BALLYBUNION Old Course

19 | 7 | 6

There are some courses you could write a book about, where anything less you know will fail to do them justice. The old course at Ballybunion is one such course. On a windless day (a rare occurrence), it's not easy playing here. In a strong wind, it can be hell. But losing out to a living masterpiece such as this is sheer bliss. The numbers on your card lose all their significance: there are no such things as par 3s, par 4s or par 5s, all that matters is survival. After a few almost ordinary holes (relatively speaking), the pulse starts to quicken on the 6th. The rest is one long epic adventure where you need ball control in every direction, skills with every club in the bag and technique for high and low shots alike. At the same time you'll admire the layout. Lost between huge sand dunes, the fairway looks so narrow, the greens tiny and the bunkers absolutely ruthless. Tom Watson considers this ultimate test of technique and inspiration to be the greatest course in the world. Suffice it to say, every golfer will have to check it out for himself or herself, one day or another.

Faute de pouvoir écrire un livre sur certains parcours, il faudrait ne rien en dire. Le "Old Course" de Ballybunion est de ceux-là. Sans vent (c'est rare), il n'est pas facile. Il devient infernal par vent fort, mais quel bonheur d'être battu par un chef-d'oeuvre aussi vivant. Alors, les chiffres inscrits sur la carte ne signifient plus rien: plus de par 3, 4 ou 5, il s'agit de survivre. Après quelques trous presque anodins (c'est relatif !), le pouls s'accélère à partir du 6, la suite n'est plus qu'une longue épopée, où il faut travailler la balle dans tous les sens, jouer tous les clubs et tous les coups, maîtriser les balles hautes comme les balles au ras du sol. Et admirer le génie du dessin. Perdus dans d'immenses dunes, le fairway paraît bien étroit, les greens minuscules, les bunkers sans pitié. Tom Watson considère cet examen suprême de la technique et de l'inspiration comme le plus grand parcours du monde. Il reste au sommet du monde, et tout golfeur doit le vérifier un jour.

Ballybunion Golf Club — 1893

Sandhill Road
IRL - BALLYBUNION, Co Kerry

Office	Secrétariat	(353) 068 - 27 146
Pro shop	Pro-shop	(353) 068 - 27 146
Fax	Fax	(353) 068 - 27 387
Web	www.ballybuniongolfclub.ie	
Situation	Situation	

1 km from Ballybunion (pop. 1 346)

Annual closure	Fermeture annuelle	no
Weekly closure	Fermeture hebdomadaire	no

Fees main season Tarifs haute saison	18 holes	
	Week days Semaine	**We/Bank holidays** We/Férié
Individual Individuel	95 €	95 €
Couple Couple	190 €	190 €

91 € for both courses (same day)

Caddy	Caddy	32 € /18 holes
Electric Trolley	Chariot électrique	no
Buggy	Voiturette	no
Clubs	Clubs	32 € /18 holes

Credit cards Cartes de crédit VISA - MasterCard

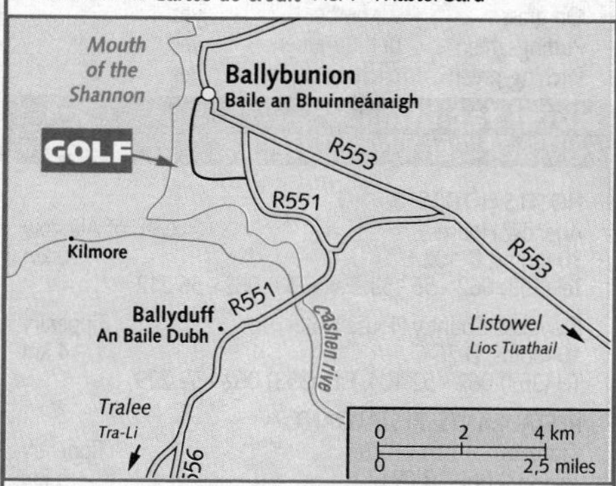

Access Accès : Limerick, N21 → Newcastle West, → Listowel, → Ballybunion
Map 2 on page 822 Carte 2 Page 822

Golf course — PARCOURS — 19/20

Site	Site	
Maintenance	Entretien	
Architect	Architecte	L. Hewson, T. Simpson
Type	Type	links
Relief	Relief	
Water in play	Eau en jeu	
Exp. to wind	Exposé au vent	
Trees in play	Arbres en jeu	

Scorecard Carte de score	**Chp.** Chp.	**Mens** Mess.	**Ladies** Da.
Length Long.	6241	6201	5004
Par	71	71	74
Slope system	0	0	0

Advised golfing ability 0 12 24 36
Niveau de jeu recommandé

Hcp required Handicap exigé 28 Men, 36 Ladies

Club house & amenities — CLUB HOUSE ET ANNEXES — 7/10

Pro shop	Pro-shop	
Driving range	Practice	
Sheltered	couvert	
On grass	sur herbe	yes
Putting-green	putting-green	yes
Pitching-green	pitching green	no

Hotel facilities — ENVIRONNEMENT HOTELIER — 6/10

HOTELS HÔTELS

Cliff House Hotel — Ballybunion 2 km
51 rooms, D 102 €
Tel (353) 068 - 27 777, Fax (353) 068 - 27 783

Manor Inn, 9 rooms, D 63 € — Ballybunion 2 km
Tel (353) 068-27 577, Fax (353) 068-27 757

Teach De Broc, 10 rooms, D 95 € — Ballybunion 1 km
Tel (353) 068 - 27 581, Fax (353) 068 - 27 919

RESTAURANTS RESTAURANT

Three Mermaids, Tel (353) 068 - 21 184 — Listowel 15 km

Harty-Costello, Tel (353) 068 - 27 129 — Ballybunion 1 km

BALLYKISTEEN

14	7	6

Laid out over a former horse farm and riding stables, Ballykisteen looks like a large park where trees and water form the main hazards. But the designers (Des Smyth and Declan Branigan) spared a thought for everyone. The further back you tee off, the narrower the fairways become, and the great number of tees means you can adapt each round to your ability. The course calls for every shot in the book: here a fade, there a draw. The greens are guarded to allow either the good old bump and run shots, or the new-style target shot approaches. Water is in play on ten holes, but with varying degrees of difficulty. It is at its worst on the 15th (with out-of-bounds to the left), one of Ireland's most demanding par 3s - the bogey should be gratefully accepted. Forthright and well-balanced, Ballykisteen still lacks in yardage, but who's really complaining?

Réalisé dans un ancien élevage de chevaux, Ballykisteen présente un caractère de grand parc, où les arbres et l'eau constituent les dangers. Mais les architectes (le champion irlandais Des Smyth et Declan Branigan) ont pensé à tout le monde. Plus on recule de départ, plus le parcours est étroit, et la multiplicité des départs permet de se faire un parcours "à sa main. Le dessin exige tous les coups de golf : certains trous demandent une balle en fade, un nombre égal réclame le draw. Et les défenses de green autorisent soit des balles roulées (bump and run), soit des balles levées (target golf). L'eau vient en jeu sur dix trous, mais avec différents niveaux de difficulté. Elle est au maximum sur le 15 (avec hors-limites à gauche), un des plus exigeants par 3 d'Irlande : le bogey y est très acceptable ! Honnête et bien équilibré, Ballykisteen manque toujours un peu de longueur, mais qui s'en plaindra ?

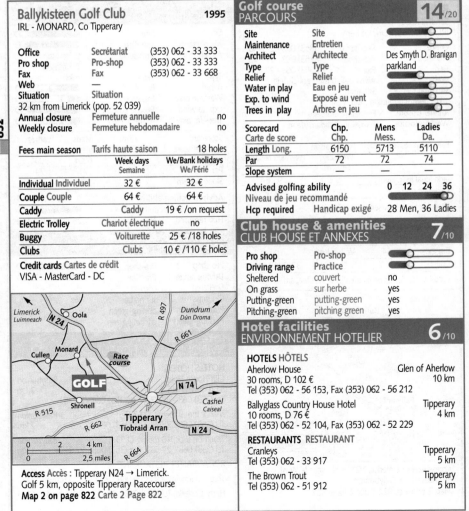

Ballykisteen Golf Club — 1995

IRL - MONARD, Co Tipperary

Office	Secrétariat	(353) 062 - 33 333
Pro shop	Pro-shop	(353) 062 - 33 333
Fax	Fax	(353) 062 - 33 668
Web	—	
Situation	Situation	

32 km from Limerick (pop. 52 039)

Annual closure	Fermeture annuelle	no
Weekly closure	Fermeture hebdomadaire	no

Fees main season Tarifs haute saison	Week days Semaine	We/Bank holidays We/Férié
		18 holes
Individual Individuel	32 €	32 €
Couple Couple	64 €	64 €
Caddy Caddy		19 € /on request
Electric Trolley Chariot électrique		no
Buggy Voiturette		25 € /18 holes
Clubs Clubs		10 € /110 € holes

Credit cards Cartes de crédit
VISA - MasterCard - DC

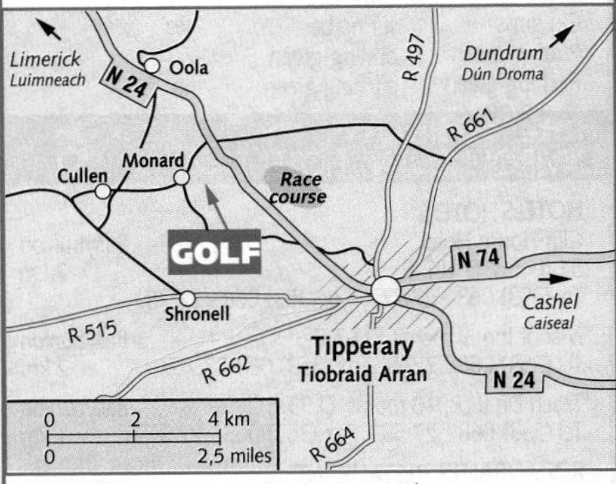

Access Accès : Tipperary N24 → Limerick.
Golf 5 km, opposite Tipperary Racecourse
Map 2 on page 822 Carte 2 Page 822

Golf course — PARCOURS — 14/20

Site	Site	
Maintenance	Entretien	
Architect	Architecte	Des Smyth D. Branigan
Type	Type	parkland
Relief	Relief	
Water in play	Eau en jeu	
Exp. to wind	Exposé au vent	
Trees in play	Arbres en jeu	

Scorecard Carte de score	Chp. Chp.	Mens Mess.	Ladies Da.
Length Long.	6150	5713	5110
Par	72	72	74
Slope system	—	—	—

Advised golfing ability Niveau de jeu recommandé — 0 12 24 36
Hcp required Handicap exigé — 28 Men, 36 Ladies

Club house & amenities — CLUB HOUSE ET ANNEXES — 7/10

Pro shop	Pro-shop	
Driving range	Practice	
Sheltered	couvert	no
On grass	sur herbe	yes
Putting-green	putting-green	yes
Pitching-green	pitching green	yes

Hotel facilities — ENVIRONNEMENT HOTELIER — 6/10

HOTELS HÔTELS

Aherlow House — Glen of Aherlow 10 km
30 rooms, D 102 €
Tel (353) 062 - 56 153, Fax (353) 062 - 56 212

Ballyglass Country House Hotel — Tipperary 4 km
10 rooms, D 76 €
Tel (353) 062 - 52 104, Fax (353) 062 - 52 229

RESTAURANTS RESTAURANT

Cranleys — Tipperary 5 km
Tel (353) 062 - 33 917

The Brown Trout — Tipperary 5 km
Tel (353) 062 - 51 912

BALLYLIFFIN Glashedy Links

17	6	5

This recent course outstrips its neighbour in terms of technical play. The landscape is even more moon-like, with massive dunes, but a little grading work has resulted in levelling out a number of drive landing areas and in creating a collection of fairway and green-side bunkers that you are sure to encounter every now and then. This course grabs you by the throat from the word go and doesn't let you go. You need to hit low shots into the wind and with the wind, otherwise your ball will float upwards like a feather. You need to know how to fade and draw the ball to get around the dog-legs, you need brains and nerves to approach the greens, to stay on the putting surface and make the putt. You need a cool head to go fetch your ball instead of admiring the landscape (especially Glashedy Rock, off the coast). You need to play here and spend some time on the course to measure what you are capable of. One of the best courses in Ireland.

Ce parcours relativement récent dépasse son voisin en matière de technicité. Le paysage est encore plus lunaire, avec des dunes massives, où quelques terrassements ont permis d'adoucir certaines zones d'arrivée de drive, mais aussi de creuser une collection de bunkers de fairway et de green que l'on ne manquera pas d'expérimenter. Ce parcours vous prend à la gorge dès les premiers trous, et ne vous lâchera plus. Il faudra faire des balles basses, contre le vent, mais aussi avec, pour ne pas les voir voler comme des plumes. Il faudra maîtriser les effets de fade et de draw pour négocier les dog-legs, il faudra de la science et des nerfs pour attaquer les greens, pour y rester, et pour putter. Il faudra du sang-froid pour revenir à sa balle au lieu d'admirer le paysage (notamment sur le Glashedy Rock, au large). Il faudra jouer ici, y faire une retraite de golf pour mesurer vos capacités. Décidément, ce parcours fait partie des meilleurs du pays.

Ballyliffin Golf Club — 1995

IRL - BALLYLIFFIN, Co Donegal

Office	Secrétariat	(353) 077 - 76 119
Pro shop	Pro-shop	(353) 077 - 76 119
Fax	Fax	(353) 077 - 76 672
Web	www.ballyliffingolfclub.com	
Situation	Situation	

40 km from Derry (72 334), 160 km from Belfast (279 237)

Annual closure	Fermeture annuelle	no
Weekly closure	Fermeture hebdomadaire	no

Fees main season / Tarifs haute saison	18 holes	
	Week days / Semaine	We/Bank holidays / We/Férié
Individual / Individuel	51 €	51 €
Couple / Couple	102 €	102 €

Caddy	Caddy	13 € /on request
Electric Trolley	Chariot électrique	no
Buggy	Voiturette	25 € /18 holes
Clubs	Clubs	13 €

Credit cards Cartes de crédit
VISA - Eurocard - MasterCard - Access

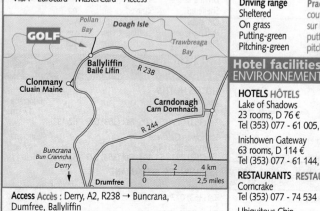

Access Accès : Derry, A2, R238 → Buncrana, Dumfree, Ballyliffin
Map 1 on page 821 Carte 1 Page 821

Golf course / PARCOURS — 17/20

Site	Site	
Maintenance	Entretien	
Architect	Architecte	Pat Ruddy Tom Craddock
Type	Type	links, seaside course
Relief	Relief	
Water in play	Eau en jeu	
Exp. to wind	Exposé au vent	
Trees in play	Arbres en jeu	

Scorecard / Carte de score	Chp. / Chp.	Mens / Mess.	Ladies / Da.
Length Long.	6422	6196	5275
Par	72	73	72
Slope system	—	—	—

Advised golfing ability Niveau de jeu recommandé: 0 12 24 36
Hcp required Handicap exigé: 28 Men, 36 Ladies

Club house & amenities / CLUB HOUSE ET ANNEXES — 6/10

Pro shop	Pro-shop	
Driving range	Practice	
Sheltered	couvert	no
On grass	sur herbe	yes
Putting-green	putting-green	yes
Pitching-green	pitching green	yes

Hotel facilities / ENVIRONNEMENT HOTELIER — 5/10

HOTELS HÔTELS

Lake of Shadows — Buncrana 17 km
23 rooms, D 76 €
Tel (353) 077 - 61 005, Fax (353) 077 - 62 131

Inishowen Gateway — Buncrana 17 km
63 rooms, D 114 €
Tel (353) 077 - 61 144, Fax (353) 077 - 62 278

RESTAURANTS RESTAURANT

Corncrake — Carndonagh 12 km
Tel (353) 077 - 74 534

Ubiquitous Chip — Buncrana 16 km
Tel (353) 077 - 62 530

BALLYLIFFIN Old Course

15 | 6 | 5

The trip to the northern tip of Ireland is not the easiest in the world, but this one of the country's finest golfing destinations, with two excellent courses. Summer days are very long here, enough to give anyone more than their fill of golf, no matter how tempting a proposition these courses may be. Nick Faldo called the Old Links here "the most natural course ever" when making a surprise visit that did much for the site's recognition. Here, you play the ball where it lies, on rolling fairways between the rough, sometimes with no visible limits, and rarely on the flat. The landscape has an amazing austere beauty to it, between the ocean, hills and endless stretches of dunes, tall grass and bushes, dotted with the odd white house in the distance. In this huge sanctuary of tranquillity, every player cuts his own path, as if he were the first to play here. A bit short, did you say? That's just the way it is, and no more.

Le voyage à l'extrême nord de l'Irlande n'est pas des plus faciles, mais le fait qu'il y ait ici deux 18 trous en fait une des plus belles destinations du pays. Les journées d'été y sont très longues, assez pour se donner une... indigestion de golf, alors que ces parcours sont bien digestes ! Le "Old Links" a été qualifié par Nick Faldo de "Golf le plus naturel qui soit" lors d'une visite surprise qui a beaucoup fait pour la notoriété du lieu. Ici, on joue la balle où elle est, sur des fairways ondulant entre les roughs, parfois sans limite visible, où l'on joue rarement la balle à plat. Le paysage est stupéfiant d'austère beauté, entre les flots de l'océan, les collines et des étendues infinies de dunes, de buissons, d'herbes hautes, ponctuées par de rares maisons blanches dans le lointain. Dans cet espace immense de paix, chacun trace son chemin, comme s'il était le premier à jouer ici. Le parcours est un peu court ? Il est ce qu'il est, c'est tout.

Ballyliffin Golf Club — 1947

IRL - BALLYLIFFIN, Co Donegal

Office Secrétariat (353) 077 - 76 119
Pro shop Pro-shop (353) 077 - 76 119
Fax Fax (353) 077 - 76 672
Web www.ballyliffingolfclub.com
Situation Situation
40 km from Derry (72 334), 160 km from Belfast (279 237)
Annual closure Fermeture annuelle — no
Weekly closure Fermeture hebdomadaire — no

Fees main season Tarifs haute saison	18 holes	
	Week days Semaine	**We/Bank holidays** We/Férié
Individual Individuel	30 €	34 €
Couple Couple	60 €	68 €

Caddy	Caddy	13 € /on request
Electric Trolley	Chariot électrique	no
Buggy	Voiturette	25 € /18 holes
Clubs	Clubs	13 €

Credit cards Cartes de crédit
VISA - Eurocard - MasterCard - Access

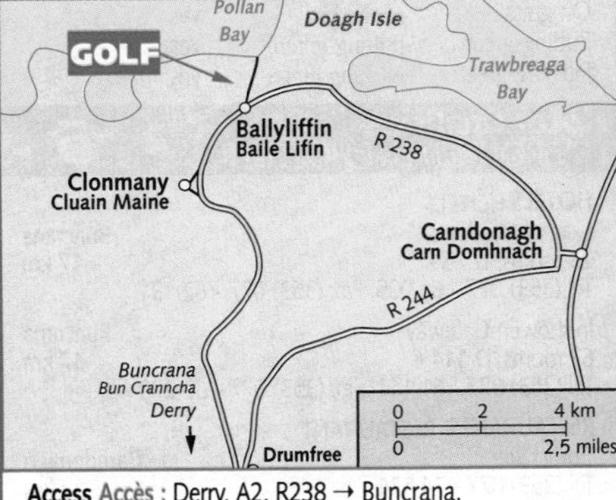

Access Accès : Derry, A2, R238 → Buncrana, Dumfree, Ballyliffin
Map 1 on page 821 Carte 1 Page 821

Golf course PARCOURS — 15/20

Site	Site	
Maintenance	Entretien	
Architect	Architecte	unknown
Type	Type	links
Relief	Relief	
Water in play	Eau en jeu	
Exp. to wind	Exposé au vent	
Trees in play	Arbres en jeu	

Scorecard Carte de score	**Chp.** Chp.	**Mens** Mess.	**Ladies** Da.
Length Long.	5951	5661	4859
Par	71	71	71
Slope system	—	—	—

Advised golfing ability Niveau de jeu recommandé — 0 12 24 36
Hcp required Handicap exigé — Men 28, Ladies 36

Club house & amenities CLUB HOUSE ET ANNEXES — 6/10

Pro shop	Pro-shop	
Driving range	Practice	
Sheltered	couvert	no
On grass	sur herbe	yes
Putting-green	putting-green	yes
Pitching-green	pitching green	yes

Hotel facilities ENVIRONNEMENT HOTELIER — 5/10

HOTELS HÔTELS

Lake of Shadows — Buncrana 17 km
23 rooms, D 76 €
Tel (353) 077 - 61 005, Fax (353) 077 - 62 131

Inishowen Gateway — Buncrana 17 km
63 rooms, D 114 €
Tel (353) 077 - 61 144, Fax (353) 077 - 62 278

RESTAURANTS RESTAURANT

Corncrake — Carndonagh 12 km
Tel (353) 077 - 74 534

Ubiquitous Chip — Buncrana 16 km
Tel (353) 077 - 62 530

BEARNA

14 | 7 | 7

This course was laid out over a marsh with granite subsoil (which protrudes here and there), but intensive draining was carried out before the course was built, which is one reason why it is in excellent condition. The relatively hilly site is magnificent, between the Bay of Galway and the hills of County Clare in the distance, countryside which was one of the major areas affected by the great famine of the 19th century. Although in the middle of the countryside with many water hazards to contend with, the style of this R.J. Browne layout has a strong links flavour, meaning that golfers who prefer seaside courses will feel the most comfortable over these 18 holes, where the difficulties gradually pile up as you progress. This is perhaps not the best course in the world but the peaceful setting, the keen air, the wild beauty of the nature all around and the sheer pleasure of playing here make it a rather unique layout, a good round of golf next to the Galway courses before moving on up to Connemara.

Ce parcours a été construit sur un marécage avec un sous-sol de granit (qui affleure çà et là), mais un drainage intensif a précédé la construction du parcours, d'où sa très bonne condition. Le site relativement vallonné est magnifique, entre la baie de Galway et les collines du County Clare au loin, et la campagne, un des sites historiques de la grande famine au XIXème siècle. Bien qu'en pleine campagne, avec de nombreux obstacles d'eau, le style du parcours dessiné par RJ Browne dégage un fort parfum de links. De fait, ce sont les amoureux des parcours en bord de mer qui se sentiront le plus à l'aise dans la montée en puissance de ces 18 trous, où les difficultés augmentent à mesure que l'on progresse. Ce n'est peut être pas le meilleur parcours du monde, mais la tranquillité du lieu, l'air vif, la sauvage beauté de la nature environnante, le plaisir de jouer ici rendent ce parcours assez unique, à jouer à côté de ceux de Galway, et avant de continuer sa route jusqu'au Connemara.

Bearna Golf Club — 1996

Corboley
IRL - BARNA, Co. Galway

Office	Secrétariat	(353) 091 - 592 677
Pro shop	Pro-shop	(353) 091 - 592 677
Fax	Fax	(353) 091 - 592 674
E-mail	bearnagc@eircom.ie	
Situation	Situation	
Galway (pop. 57 241), 11 km		
Annual closure	Fermeture annuelle	no
Weekly closure	Fermeture hebdomadaire	no

Fees main season Tarifs haute saison	18 holes	
	Week days Semaine	**We/Bank holidays** We/Férié
Individual Individuel	38 €	47 €
Couple Couple	76 €	94 €
Caddy Caddy	25 € /on request	
Electric Trolley Chariot électrique	no	
Buggy Voiturette	25 € /18 holes	
Clubs Clubs	13 € /18 holes	

Credit cards Cartes de crédit
VISA - Eurocard - MasterCard - DC - AMEX

Clifden
An Clochàn
N 59
GOLF
R 338
Galway
Gaillimh
Lough Inch
R 337
R 336
Barna
Bearna
Salthill
Bóthar na Trá
Galway bay
Spiddle
An Spidéal
0 2 km
0 1,25 miles

Access Accès : Galway, R338/337/336 → Spiddle.
At the end of Barna (Bearna), turn right → Golf
Map 1 on page 820 Carte 1 Page 820

Golf course — PARCOURS — 14/20

Site	Site	
Maintenance	Entretien	
Architect	Architecte	R.J. Browne
Type	Type	open country
Relief	Relief	
Water in play	Eau en jeu	
Exp. to wind	Exposé au vent	
Trees in play	Arbres en jeu	

Scorecard Carte de score	**Chp.** Chp.	**Mens** Mess.	**Ladies** Da.
Length Long.	6174	5746	4684
Par	72	72	70
Slope system	—	—	—

Advised golfing ability Niveau de jeu recommandé: 0 12 24 36
Hcp required Handicap exigé: no

Club house & amenities — CLUB HOUSE ET ANNEXES — 7/10

Pro shop	Pro-shop	
Driving range	Practice	
Sheltered	couvert	12 bays
On grass	sur herbe	yes
Putting-green	putting-green	yes
Pitching-green	pitching green	yes

Hotel facilities — ENVIRONNEMENT HOTELIER — 7/10

HOTELS HÔTELS

Connemara Coast Hotel — Galway 10 km
112 rooms, D 178 €
Tel (353) 091 - 592 108, Fax (353) 091 - 592 065

Twelve Pins Lodge Hotel — Bearna 2,5 km
18 rooms, D 127 €
Tel (353) 091 - 592 368, Fax (353) 091 - 592 185

Ardilaun Hotel, 89 rooms, D 152 € — Galway 10 km
Tel (353) 091 - 521 433, Fax (353) 091 - 521 546

RESTAURANTS RESTAURANT

Donnellys, Tel — Barna 3 km

Corboley, Tel (353) 091 - 592 866 — Barnao

BEAUFORT

13 | 6 | 7

It was not so easy to create a new course within the immediate vicinity of Killarney, but with such a superb setting (the Mcgillicuddy Reeks form an impressive backdrop) and even the ruins of castle Gore to add a touch of history to the back nine, the appeal of the site could only enhance the actual course. Designed by Arthur Springs over pleasantly rolling and woody terrain, this recent course has mellowed, and is really in good condition. Of special note are the excellence of the par 3s (especially the 8th), the care taken over the placement of hazards, especially the bunkers, the use of trees and the variety of greens, sometimes elevated or multi-tiered and requiring some accurate ironwork. You can seldom roll the ball here. A few blind shots call for a careful choice of line, but things are generally rather obvious. A pleasant course for all.

Il n'était pas si facile de créer un nouveau golf à proximité immédiate de celui de Killarney, mais la séduction du lieu ne pouvait que profiter au parcours lui-même avec une situation aussi favorable (les Mcgillicuddy Reeks sont en toile de fond), et même les ruines du Castle Core, pour donner une touche d'histoire aux neuf derniers trous. Dessiné par Arthur Springs sur un terrain agréablement vallonné et boisé, ce récent parcours a gagné en maturité, mais sa condition est très correcte. On y remarquera en particulier la qualité des pars 3 (notamment le 8), le soin apporté au placement des obstacles, des bunkers en particulier, la mise en jeu des arbres et la diversité des greens, parfois surélevés ou à plateaux, obligeant à un jeu de fers précis : il est rarement possible de faire rouler la balle. Certains coups aveugles obligent à bien choisir la ligne de jeu, mais elle reste assez évidente. Un parcours agréable pour tous.

Beaufort Golf Club — 1994

IRL - BEAUFORT, Co. Kerry

Office	Secrétariat	(353) 064 - 44 440
Pro shop	Pro-shop	(353) 064 - 44 440
Fax	Fax	(353) 064 - 44 752
Web	www.globalgolf.com	
Situation	Situation	

11 km W of Killarney (pop. 8 809),
10 km E of Killorglin (pop. 1 278)

Annual closure	Fermeture annuelle	no
Weekly closure	Fermeture hebdomadaire	no

Fees main season Tarifs haute saison	**Week days** Semaine	**We/Bank holidays** We/Férié
18 holes		
Individual Individuel	44 €	57 €
Couple Couple	88 €	114 €
Caddy Caddy		25 € /on request
Electric Trolley Chariot électrique		no
Buggy Voiturette		38 €
Clubs Clubs		13 €

Credit cards Cartes de crédit
VISA - MasterCard - AMEX

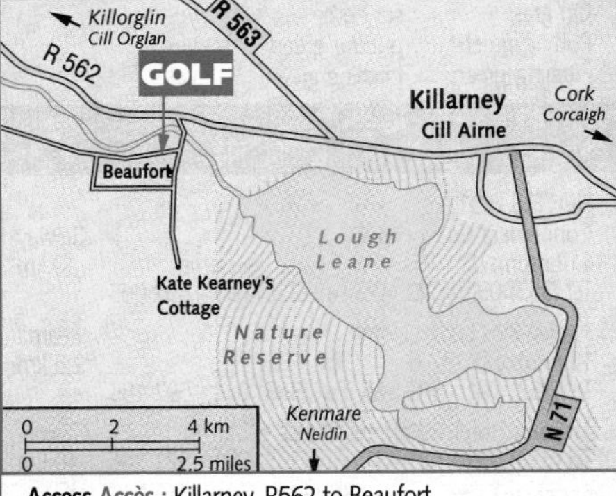

Access Accès : Killarney, R562 to Beaufort.
Golf signposted
Map 2 on page 822 Carte 2 Page 822

Golf course PARCOURS — 13/20

Site	Site	
Maintenance	Entretien	
Architect	Architecte	Arthur Spring
Type	Type	parkland
Relief	Relief	
Water in play	Eau en jeu	
Exp. to wind	Exposé au vent	
Trees in play	Arbres en jeu	

Scorecard Carte de score	**Chp.** Chp.	**Mens** Mess.	**Ladies** Da.
Length Long.	6005	5535	4803
Par	71	71	71
Slope system	—	—	—

Advised golfing ability Niveau de jeu recommandé — 0 12 24 36
Hcp required Handicap exigé — no

Club house & amenities CLUB HOUSE ET ANNEXES — 6/10

Pro shop	Pro-shop	
Driving range	Practice	
Sheltered	couvert	no
On grass	sur herbe	no
Putting-green	putting-green	yes
Pitching-green	pitching green	no

Hotel facilities ENVIRONNEMENT HOTELIER — 7/10

HOTELS HÔTELS

Dunloe Castle — Beaufort 2 km
120 rooms, D 165 €
Tel (353) 064 - 44 111, Fax (353) 064 - 44 583

Hotel Europe — Killarney 6 km
205 rooms, D 165 €
Tel (353) 064 - 31 900, Fax (353) 064 - 32 118

Aghadoe Heights, 60 rooms, D 229 € — Killarney 7 km
Tel (353) 064 - 31 766, Fax (353) 064 - 31 345

RESTAURANTS RESTAURANT

Fredrick's at the Heights — Killarney 7 km
Tel (353) 064 - 31 766

Gaby's, Tel (353) 064 - 32 519 — Killarney 11 km

BELMULLET

15 | 5 | 3

Also known by the name of Carn, this is yet another world's end course, with impressive views over the rocky coast to the north of Mayo and Blacksod Bay. It is also one of the most recent designs by Eddie Hackett (over 80 years old). The course is very hilly, so we would advise a buggy for all seniors if they want to keep a cool head. Everyone else would be well advised to study the course closely (without counting their score first time out), because a lot of shots and greens turn blind if you are too far off the fairway, and the eight dog-legs are difficult to cope with if you don't get the right distance and angle for the green. Belmullet is an exciting prospect in match-play, because miracles are as frequent as disasters. However, this course is not to everyone's liking, especially to players who like parks with a pretty castle in the middle, but it is an essential experience in a site very exposed to the wind. But then, which links is not?

Egalement connu sous le nom de Cran, avec d'impressionnants panoramas sur la côte sauvage au nord du Mayo et Blacksod Bay, c'est encore un parcours au bout du monde, et l'un des plus récents de Eddie Hackett (à plus de 80 ans). Comme il est très accidenté, on conseillera aux seniors de prendre une voiturette, s'ils veulent garder la tête froide. Et à tout le monde de bien l'étudier (sans compter leur score la première fois) car beaucoup de coups et de greens seront aveugles s'ils s'écartent trop du fairway, et les huit doglegs seront difficiles à négocier si l'on évalue mal les distances pour avoir l'ouverture. En match-play, Belmullet est passionnant, car les miracles sont aussi fréquents que les désastres. Ce parcours toujours aussi excitant ne plaira pas à tout le monde, notamment à ceux qui aiment les parcs avec joli château, mais c'est une expérience à vivre, dans un site très exposé au vent, mais que serait un links sans vent ?

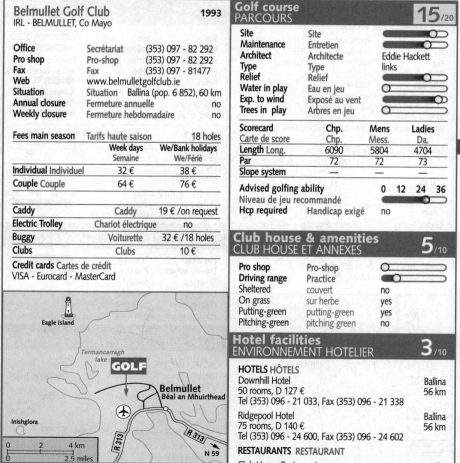

Belmullet Golf Club — 1993

IRL - BELMULLET, Co Mayo

Office	Secrétariat	(353) 097 - 82 292
Pro shop	Pro-shop	(353) 097 - 82 292
Fax	Fax	(353) 097 - 81477
Web	www.belmulletgolfclub.ie	
Situation	Situation	Ballina (pop. 6 852), 60 km
Annual closure	Fermeture annuelle	no
Weekly closure	Fermeture hebdomadaire	no

Fees main season Tarifs haute saison	**Week days** Semaine	**We/Bank holidays** We/Férié
		18 holes
Individual Individuel	32 €	38 €
Couple Couple	64 €	76 €

Caddy	Caddy	19 € /on request
Electric Trolley	Chariot électrique	no
Buggy	Voiturette	32 € /18 holes
Clubs	Clubs	10 €

Credit cards Cartes de crédit
VISA - Eurocard - MasterCard

Access Accès : Ballina, N59 to Bangor.
R313 to Belmullet. → Airport. Golf on the right
Map 1 on page 822 Carte 1 Page 822

Golf course — PARCOURS — 15/20

Site	Site	
Maintenance	Entretien	
Architect	Architecte	Eddie Hackett
Type	Type	links
Relief	Relief	
Water in play	Eau en jeu	
Exp. to wind	Exposé au vent	
Trees in play	Arbres en jeu	

Scorecard Carte de score	**Chp.** Chp.	**Mens** Mess.	**Ladies** Da.
Length Long.	6090	5804	4704
Par	72	72	73
Slope system	—	—	—

Advised golfing ability — Niveau de jeu recommandé: 0 12 24 36
Hcp required — Handicap exigé: no

Club house & amenities — CLUB HOUSE ET ANNEXES — 5/10

Pro shop	Pro-shop	
Driving range	Practice	
Sheltered	couvert	no
On grass	sur herbe	yes
Putting-green	putting-green	yes
Pitching-green	pitching green	no

Hotel facilities — ENVIRONNEMENT HOTELIER — 3/10

HOTELS HÔTELS

Downhill Hotel — Ballina 56 km
50 rooms, D 127 €
Tel (353) 096 - 21 033, Fax (353) 096 - 21 338

Ridgepool Hotel — Ballina 56 km
75 rooms, D 140 €
Tel (353) 096 - 24 600, Fax (353) 096 - 24 602

RESTAURANTS RESTAURANT

Club House Restaurant — on site
Tel (353) 097 - 82 292

The River Boat Inn — Ballina 60 km
Tel (353) 096 - 22 183

BLAINROE

13 | 6 | 6

A seaside course but not a true links, with pronounced hilly relief between the 2nd and 8th holes before becoming a little easier. The architects have made good use of difficult terrain for golf but were unable to prevent the 6th, 7th and 14th from being rather tricky little numbers. The 4 closing holes more than make up for this minor shortcoming. In a region where there is no shortage of very good courses, Blainroe compares well. Water is in play on two holes only, news that will delight those players who have been playing with the same ball all season, and the basic difficulties, excluding the wind, are the 58 bunkers, all more strategic than really penalising. When the ground is dry, the greens are open enough to allow rolled shots. Players of all abilities can enjoy their golf here, but single-figure handicappers might prefer to wait for the wind to make this a tougher challenge.

Un parcours de bord de mer, mais sans être vraiment un links, avec des reliefs prononcés entre le 2 et le 8, mais ensuite nettement assagis. Les architectes ont fait bon usage d'un terrain difficile à adapter au golf, et n'ont pu éviter de rendre le 6, le 7 et le 14 assez "tricky", mais les quatre derniers trous rachètent ces faiblesses ponctuelles. Dans une région où les très bons parcours ne manquent pas, Blainroe s'est taillé une place très honorable. L'eau n'y vient en jeu que sur deux trous, ce qui ne manquera pas de plaire à ceux qui jouent avec la même balle depuis des années, et les difficultés essentielles (en dehors du vent) sont les 58 bunkers, tous plus stratégiques que vraiment pénalisants. Quand le terrain est sec, les greens sont assez ouverts pour permettre de faire rouler la balle. Tous les niveaux de jeu peuvent s'exprimer ici, mais les meilleurs attendront que le vent souffle pour affronter un challenge plus à leur mesure.

Blainroe Golf Club — 1978

IRL - BLAINROE, Co. Wicklow

Office	Secrétariat	(353) 0404 - 68 168
Pro shop	Pro-shop	(353) 0404 - 68 168
Fax	Fax	(353) 0404 - 69 369
Web	—	
Situation	Situation	

6 km S of Wicklow (pop. 6 416)
51 km from Dublin (pop. 481 854)

Annual closure	Fermeture annuelle	no
Weekly closure	Fermeture hebdomadaire	no

Fees main season Tarifs haute saison	18 holes	
	Week days Semaine	**We/Bank holidays** We/Férié
Individual Individuel	44 €	57 €
Couple Couple	76 €	94 €
Caddy	Caddy	25 € /on request
Electric Trolley	Chariot électrique	no
Buggy	Voiturette	no
Clubs	Clubs	15 €

Credit cards Cartes de crédit
VISA - MasterCard - AMEX

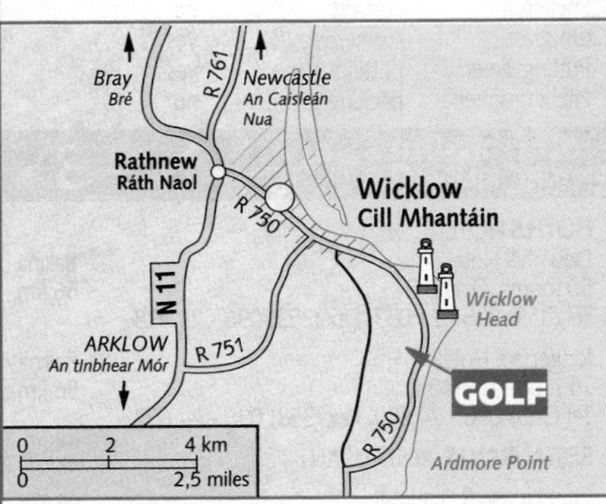

Access Accès : Dublin, N11 to Wicklow.
R750 (Coast Road) to Golf.
Map 3 on page 824 Carte 3 Page 824

Golf course — PARCOURS — 13/20

Site	Site	
Maintenance	Entretien	
Architect	Architecte	Hawtree & Sons
Type	Type	seaside course, parkland
Relief	Relief	
Water in play	Eau en jeu	
Exp. to wind	Exposé au vent	
Trees in play	Arbres en jeu	

Scorecard Carte de score	**Chp.** Chp.	**Mens** Mess.	**Ladies** Da.
Length Long.	6175	6070	5365
Par	72	72	74
Slope system	—	—	—

Advised golfing ability 0 12 24 36
Niveau de jeu recommandé
Hcp required Handicap exigé no

Club house & amenities — CLUB HOUSE ET ANNEXES — 6/10

Pro shop	Pro-shop	
Driving range	Practice	
Sheltered	couvert	no
On grass	sur herbe	yes
Putting-green	putting-green	yes
Pitching-green	pitching green	yes

Hotel facilities — ENVIRONNEMENT HOTELIER — 6/10

HOTELS HÔTELS

Tinakilly House Hotel — Rathnew 10 km
29 rooms, D 190 €
Tel (353) 0404 - 69 274, Fax (353) 0404 - 67 806

Blainroe Golf Hotel — adjacent
10 rooms, D 114 €
Tel (353) 0404 - 67 500, Fax (353) 0404 - 69 737

Grand Hotel, 32 rooms, D 102 € — Wicklow 6 km
Tel (353) 0404 - 67 337, Fax (353) 0404 - 69 607

RESTAURANTS RESTAURANT

The Old Rectory, Tel (353) 0404 - 67 048 — Wicklow 6 km
The Bakery, Tel (353) 0404 - 66 770 — Wicklow 6 km

BUNDORAN

13 | 6 | 7

The shortest courses are not always the easiest, often lacking par 5s to make those coveted birdies. Bundoran is one such number, and is also a part of history, being over 100 years old. Between the wars, the course was reshaped and toughened up by the grand champion Harry Vardon (the designer of Little Aston and the first designer of Woodhall Spa in England). Alternating parkland country with links holes, this is a good quality test that is ideal for a few rounds with friends or the family. Of course, with the wind, which can blow very hard indeed, things may get tough. Visitors enjoy a picturesque setting with several holes running alongside the ocean (you can even see people surfing) and some superb beaches. When exploring for golf in the north-west of Ireland - which is making itself a nice little international reputation - Bundoran is a highly recommendable stop-off.

Les parcours les plus courts ne sont pas toujours les plus faciles, car ils ont généralement peu de pars 5 pour faire des birdies ! Bundoran en fait partie. Tout comme il appartient à l'histoire, car il a plus d'un siècle d'existence. Entre les deux guerres, il a été remodelé et durci par le grand champion Harry Vardon (l'auteur de Little Aston et le premier architecte de Woodhall Spa, en Angleterre). Alternant les paysages de parc et les vrais trous de links, c'est un test de bonne qualité, idéal pour quelques bonnes parties de golf entre amis ou en famille, mais qui (bien sûr) prend de la puissance avec le vent, parfois très fort ici. Il fait profiter ses visiteurs d'une situation pittoresque, avec plusieurs trous le long de l'océan (on y voit souvent des surfeurs) et de superbes plages. Dans une exploration golfique du Nord-Ouest de l'Irlande, qui commence à acquérir une réputation internationale, Bundoran est une halte très recommandable.

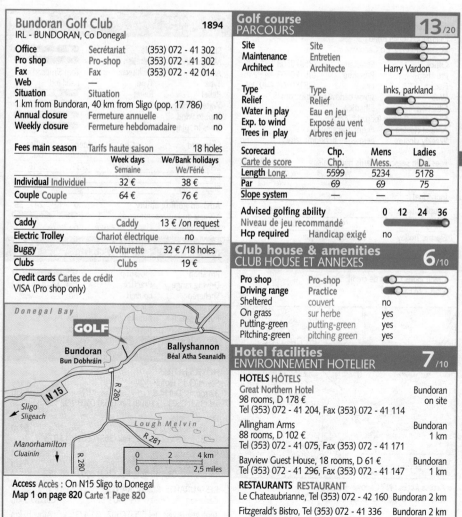

Bundoran Golf Club — 1894

IRL - BUNDORAN, Co Donegal

Office	Secrétariat	(353) 072 - 41 302
Pro shop	Pro-shop	(353) 072 - 41 302
Fax	Fax	(353) 072 - 42 014
Web	—	
Situation	Situation	

1 km from Bundoran, 40 km from Sligo (pop. 17 786)

Annual closure	Fermeture annuelle	no
Weekly closure	Fermeture hebdomadaire	no

Fees main season Tarifs haute saison	Week days Semaine	We/Bank holidays We/Férié
	18 holes	
Individual Individuel	32 €	38 €
Couple Couple	64 €	76 €

Caddy	Caddy	13 € /on request
Electric Trolley	Chariot électrique	no
Buggy	Voiturette	32 € /18 holes
Clubs	Clubs	19 €

Credit cards Cartes de crédit
VISA (Pro shop only)

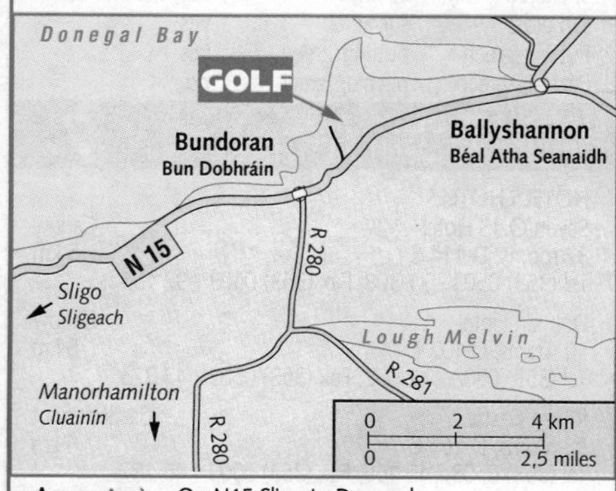

Access Accès : On N15 Sligo to Donegal
Map 1 on page 820 Carte 1 Page 820

Golf course — PARCOURS — 13/20

Site	Site	
Maintenance	Entretien	
Architect	Architecte	Harry Vardon
Type	Type	links, parkland
Relief	Relief	
Water in play	Eau en jeu	
Exp. to wind	Exposé au vent	
Trees in play	Arbres en jeu	

Scorecard Carte de score	Chp. Chp.	Mens Mess.	Ladies Da.
Length Long.	5599	5234	5178
Par	69	69	75
Slope system	—	—	—

Advised golfing ability Niveau de jeu recommandé — 0 12 24 36

Hcp required Handicap exigé — no

Club house & amenities — CLUB HOUSE ET ANNEXES — 6/10

Pro shop	Pro-shop	
Driving range	Practice	
Sheltered	couvert	no
On grass	sur herbe	yes
Putting-green	putting-green	yes
Pitching-green	pitching green	yes

Hotel facilities — ENVIRONNEMENT HOTELIER — 7/10

HOTELS HÔTELS

Great Northern Hotel — Bundoran on site
98 rooms, D 178 €
Tel (353) 072 - 41 204, Fax (353) 072 - 41 114

Allingham Arms — Bundoran 1 km
88 rooms, D 102 €
Tel (353) 072 - 41 075, Fax (353) 072 - 41 171

Bayview Guest House, 18 rooms, D 61 € — Bundoran 1 km
Tel (353) 072 - 41 296, Fax (353) 072 - 41 147

RESTAURANTS RESTAURANT

Le Chateaubrianne, Tel (353) 072 - 42 160 — Bundoran 2 km
Fitzgerald's Bistro, Tel (353) 072 - 41 336 — Bundoran 2 km

CARLOW

16 | 6 | 7

There are some designers that always arouse our curiosity. Alongside Braid, Colt or Mackenzie, one such is Tom Simpson, whose philosophy has been taken up by numerous modern course architects, but not always so successfully. For Simpson, a course must be demanding for champions, less and less difficult the further forward the tee, and the most dangerous hazards should be designed to worry the very best players. This spirit abounds at Carlow, where virtually nothing has changed since the earliest days. It could be lengthened, that's for sure, but this par 70 stands up very well to every assault. All the difficulties are visible, but the strategic and aesthetic subtleties appear only gradually: the bunkering, the shaping of the fairways and the use of a little elevated land and rare water hazards reveal an in-depth knowledge of the game of golf. A engaging course, off the beaten track.

Il est des signatures qui éveillent la curiosité. A côté de Braid, Colt ou Mackenzie, Tom Simpson est de celles-là. Sa philosophie a été reprise par de nombreux architectes modernes, pas toujours avec un tel succès : un parcours doit être exigeant pour les champions, de moins en moins difficile à mesure que l'on avance de départ, et les obstacles les plus dangereux doivent inquiéter avant tout les premiers nommés, les meilleurs. On retrouve cet esprit à Carlow, où pratiquement rien n'a changé depuis les origines. Certes, on pourrait allonger un peu ce parcours, mais ce par 70 résiste de toute façon aux assauts. Toutes les difficultés sont visibles, mais les subtilités stratégiques et esthétiques n'apparaissent que progressivement : le placement des bunkers, le travail de modelage des fairways, l'utilisation des quelques élévations de terrain et des rares obstacles d'eau révèlent une connaissance profonde du jeu. Un parcours attachant, hors des sentiers battus.

Carlow Golf Club — 1937

Deerpark, Dublin Road
IRL - CARLOW, Co Carlow

Office	Secrétariat	(353) 0503 - 31 695
Pro shop	Pro-shop	(353) 0503 - 41 745
Fax	Fax	(353) 0503 - 40 065
Web	www.carlowgolfclub.com	
Situation	Situation	

5 km from Carlow (pop. 11 721)

Annual closure	Fermeture annuelle	no
Weekly closure	Fermeture hebdomadaire	no

Fees main season Tarifs haute saison	18 holes	
	Week days Semaine	**We/Bank holidays** We/Férié
Individual Individuel	44 €	57 €
Couple Couple	88 €	114 €
Caddy	Caddy	25 € /on request
Electric Trolley	Chariot électrique	no
Buggy	Voiturette	25 € /18 holes
Clubs	Clubs	13 €

Credit cards Cartes de crédit
VISA - MasterCard

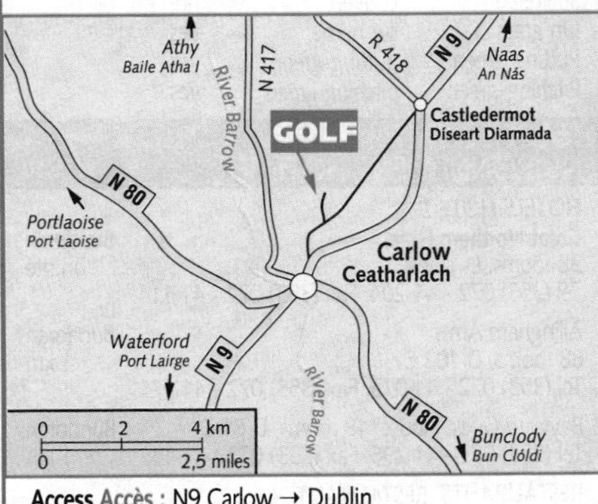

Access Accès : N9 Carlow → Dublin
Map 2 on page 823 Carte 2 Page 823

Golf course / PARCOURS — 16/20

Site	Site	
Maintenance	Entretien	
Architect	Architecte	Tom Simpson
Type	Type	parkland
Relief	Relief	
Water in play	Eau en jeu	
Exp. to wind	Exposé au vent	
Trees in play	Arbres en jeu	

Scorecard Carte de score	**Chp.** Chp.	**Mens** Mess.	**Ladies** Da.
Length Long.	5844	5731	5218
Par	70	70	75
Slope system	—	—	—

Advised golfing ability Niveau de jeu recommandé — 0 12 24 36
Hcp required Handicap exigé — no

Club house & amenities / CLUB HOUSE ET ANNEXES — 6/10

Pro shop	Pro-shop	
Driving range	Practice	
Sheltered	couvert	no
On grass	sur herbe	yes
Putting-green	putting-green	yes
Pitching-green	pitching green	no

Hotel facilities / ENVIRONNEMENT HOTELIER — 7/10

HOTELS HÔTELS

Seven Oaks Hotel — Carlow
32 rooms, D 114 € — 5 km
Tel (353) 0503 - 31 308, Fax (353) 0503 - 32 155

Dolmen Hotel — Carlow
40 rooms, D 102 € — 5 km
Tel (353) 0503 - 42 002, Fax (353) 0503 - 42 375

Kilkea Castle — Castledermot
38 rooms, D 165 € — 8 km
Tel (353) 0503 - 45 156, Fax (353) 0503 - 45 187

RESTAURANTS RESTAURANT

Carlovian, Tel (353) 0503 - 30 911 — Carlow 3 km
Tonlegee House, Tel (353) 0507 - 31 473 — Athy 15 km

CASTLE

13	6	8

Here we are virtually in town, enough to turn green with envy many a continental city-dweller who has to drive miles and miles to find a course. Here, though, you still feel a distinct change of surroundings after a very pleasant drive up to a pretty club-house. The course, designed by Harry Colt, is already old and weathered by the years; the trees and grass have a sort of polished sheen look to them, rather like on old furniture. The rather flat layout is like a pleasant walk in a large park, with trees placed (or used) strategically so that they don't actually form a wood. Visually, they look even more dangerous. Equally well "placed" are the fairway and green-side bunkers, but it is fair to say that here you seldom have a truly long shot to play, which makes it even more annoying to miss the smallish greens when you have a short iron in hand. A good old top class course, well-maintained and very pleasant for a round with the family... or to show off your skills with lesser players than yourself.

On est pratiquement en pleine ville, ce qui rendra jaloux bien des golfeurs du continent qui doivent faire des dizaines de kilomètres pour trouver un parcours à jouer. Pourtant, on a ici une certaine impression de dépaysement, après une arrivée très agréable sur le site et la vision d'un joli Club house. Dû au crayon expert de Harry Colt, ce parcours déjà ancien est poli par les années, les arbres et le gazon ont cette sorte de "patine" que l'on associe aux meubles anciens. Assez plat, le tracé constitue une sorte de promenade dans un grand parc, les arbres étant davantage placés (ou utilisés) stratégiquement qu'ils ne constituent des bois à proprement parler. Ils n'en paraissent que plus dangereux visuellement. Tout aussi "bien" placés, les bunkers de fairway et bunkers de greens, mais il faut dire que l'on a rarement de longs coups à jouer ici : il n'en est que plus vexant de manquer les greens (ils ne sont pas très grands) quand on n'a que de petits fers en main. Un bon vieux parcours de bonne classe, bien entretenu, très agréable à jouer en famille... ou pour briller devant des amis moins expérimentés.

Castle Golf Club — 1913

Woodside Drive
IRL - RATHFARNHAM - DUBLIN 14

Office	Secrétariat	(353) 01 - 490 4207
Pro shop	Pro-shop	(353) 01 - 490 4207
Fax	Fax	(353) 01 - 490 0264
E-mail	leslie@castlegolfclub-dublin.com	
Situation	Situation	

Dublin (pop. 481 854), 6 km from city centre

Annual closure	Fermeture annuelle	no
Weekly closure	Fermeture hebdomadaire	no

Fees main season Tarifs haute saison	18 holes	
	Week days Semaine	**We/Bank holidays** We/Férié
Individual Individuel	56 €	56 €
Couple Couple	112 €	112 €
Caddy	Caddy	25 €
Electric Trolley	Chariot électrique	6 € /18 holes
Buggy	Voiturette	no
Clubs	Clubs	no

Credit cards Cartes de crédit
VISA - Eurocard - MasterCard - DC - AMEX

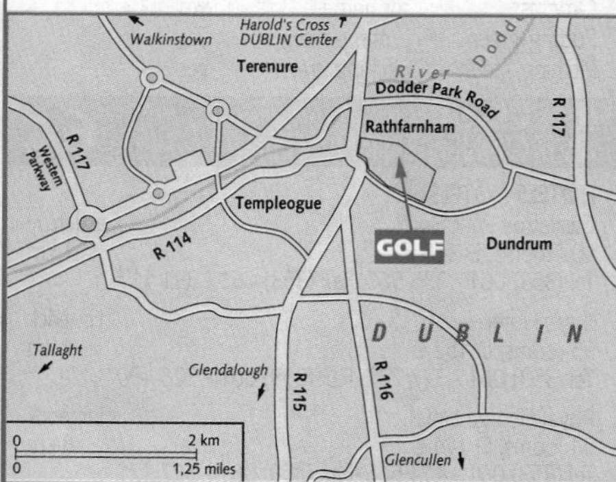

Access Accès : In Dublin, → Castle, Harold's Cross Road, Lower Dodder Park Road, Woodside Drive (Golf at Rathfarnham). **Map 3 on page 824** Carte 3 Page 824

Golf course — PARCOURS — 13/20

Site	Site	
Maintenance	Entretien	
Architect	Architecte	Harry S. Colt
Type	Type	parkland
Relief	Relief	
Water in play	Eau en jeu	
Exp. to wind	Exposé au vent	
Trees in play	Arbres en jeu	

Scorecard Carte de score	**Chp.** Chp.	**Mens** Mess.	**Ladies** Da.
Length Long.	5733	5508	5104
Par	70	70	72
Slope system	—	—	—

Advised golfing ability Niveau de jeu recommandé: 0 12 24 36

Hcp required Handicap exigé: no

Club house & amenities — CLUB HOUSE ET ANNEXES — 6/10

Pro shop	Pro-shop	
Driving range	Practice	
Sheltered	couvert	no
On grass	sur herbe	yes (practice area)
Putting-green	putting-green	yes
Pitching-green	pitching green	no

Hotel facilities — ENVIRONNEMENT HOTELIER — 8/10

HOTELS HÔTELS

Rathmines Capital Hotel, 54 rooms, D 114 € — Rathmines
Tel (353) 01 - 496 6966, Fax (353) 01 - 491 0603 — 6 km

Orwell Lodge Hotel, 10 rooms, D 127 € — Rathgae
Tel (353) 01 - 497 7258, Fax (353) 01 - 497 9913 — 3 km

Red Cow Morans Hotel, 1233 rooms, D 190 € — Clondalkin
Tel (353) 01 - 459 3650, Fax (353) 01 - 459 1588 — 14 km

RESTAURANTS RESTAURANT

Johnnie Foxes, Tel (353) 01 - 295 5647 — Glencullen 17 km

Yellow House, Tel(353) 01 - 493 2994 — Rathfarnham 5 km

Killakee Restaurant, Tel (353) 01 - 493 2645 — Rathfarnham

CASTLETROY

13 | 6 | 6

Here is a good example of a course where maintenance can change everything. After a few years of comparative neglect, Castletroy can once again boast the manicured label with clearly cut fairways, making it a whole different course. The new greens have been re-laid on sand, leading to a slight difference from the rest in terms of roll and pitch, but nothing to shout about. It is always pleasant to feel this impression of a huge park with trees that are always dangerous. In fact they outline the holes more than form a real wood, but they still swallow up any mis-hit drive with great relish. Accuracy is the watchword here, with OB on holes 1 & 2 calling for tidy shot-making from the outset, whatever the club. This is particularly true on hole N°12, an excellent dog-leg with an elevated and highly contoured green, or the 13th, a pretty par 3 with a small green way down below. And as the more you play here the more you enjoy the course, Castletroy should on the itinerary of demanding golfers.

Un bon exemple de parcours où l'entretien peut tout changer. Après quelques années difficiles, Castletroy est redevenu bien "manucuré", ses fairways nettement dessinés, et tout change. les nouveaux greens ont été refaits sur du sable, ce qui provoque un peu de différence de roulement et de tenue avec les autres, mais cela ne choque pas. On retrouvera avec plaisir cette impression de grand parc, avec des arbres toujours dangereux. Il s'agit pourtant plus de définition des trous que de véritables bois, mais ils accueillent avec un plaisir évident les drives un peu écartés! La précision est d'ailleurs le maître mot, avec les hors-limites aux 1 et 2 qui vous imposent d'entrée la rigueur, avec le nombre de coups différents qu'il convient de savoir jouer. En particulier pour négocier des trous délicats comme le 12, excellent dog-leg avec green en hauteur et très travaillé, ou le 13, joli par 3 avec un petit green en contrebas. Et comme plus on joue ici, plus on apprécie le parcours, Castletroy a vraiment fait son retour sur les itinéraires des golfeurs exigeants.

Castletroy Golf Club — 1937

IRL - CASTLETROY, Co. Limerick

Office	Secrétariat	(353) 061 - 335 261
Pro shop	Pro-shop	(353) 061 - 330 450
Fax	Fax	(353) 061 - 335 373
E-mail	cgc@iol.ie	
Situation	Situation	

3.5 km from Limerick (pop. 52 039)

Annual closure	Fermeture annuelle	no
Weekly closure	Fermeture hebdomadaire	no

Fees main season Tarifs haute saison	Week days Semaine	We/Bank holidays We/Férié
18 holes		
Individual Individuel	32 €	38 €
Couple Couple	64 €	76 €

Caddy	Caddy	25 €
Electric Trolley	Chariot électrique	8 € /18 holes
Buggy	Voiturette	25 € /18 holes
Clubs	Clubs	13 €

Credit cards Cartes de crédit
VISA - MasterCard - DC AMEX

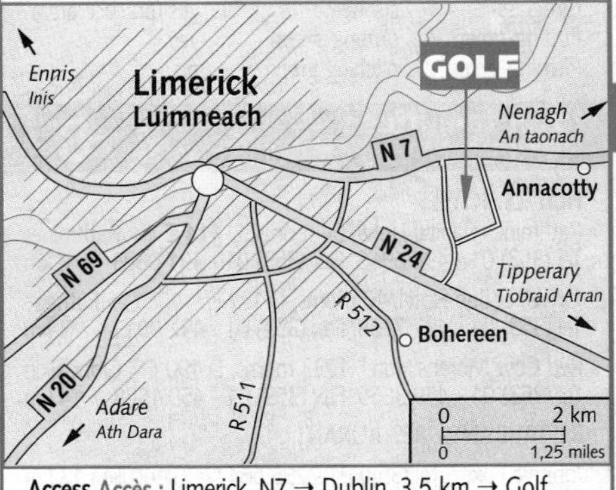

Access Accès : Limerick, N7 → Dublin. 3.5 km → Golf
Map 2 on page 822 Carte 2 Page 822

Golf course PARCOURS — 13/20

Site	Site	
Maintenance	Entretien	
Architect	Architecte	Eddie Hackett
Type	Type	parkland
Relief	Relief	
Water in play	Eau en jeu	
Exp. to wind	Exposé au vent	
Trees in play	Arbres en jeu	

Scorecard Carte de score	Chp. Chp.	Mens Mess.	Ladies Da.
Length Long.	5793	5617	5256
Par	71	71	75
Slope system	—	—	—

Advised golfing ability Niveau de jeu recommandé: 0 12 24 36

Hcp required Handicap exigé: no

Club house & amenities CLUB HOUSE ET ANNEXES — 6/10

Pro shop	Pro-shop	
Driving range	Practice	
Sheltered	couvert	3 mats
On grass	sur herbe	yes
Putting-green	putting-green	yes
Pitching-green	pitching green	yes

Hotel facilities ENVIRONNEMENT HOTELIER — 6/10

HOTELS HÔTELS

Castletroy Park Hotel — Castletroy 1 km
107 rooms, D 165 €
Tel (353) 061 - 335 566, Fax (353) 061 - 331 117

Jury's Hotel — Limerick 4 km
95 rooms, D 152 €
Tel (353) 061 - 327 777, Fax (353) 061 - 326 400

Royal George Hotel — Limerick 8 km
54 rooms, D 114 €
Tel (353) 061 - 414 566, Fax (353) 061 - 317 171

RESTAURANTS RESTAURANT

Moll Darby's, Tel (353) 061 - 411 511 — Limerick 4 km

Freddy's Bistro, Tel (353) 061 - 418 749 — Limerick 4 km

CHARLEVILLE

13 | 4 | 6

One of the good courses to the north of Cork. The extra 9 holes make it even more pleasant to play. At the heart of the Golden Vale at the foot of the Ballyhoura Mountains, this is one of Ireland's best known farming regions and a good opportunity to note that the Irish are not just a people of sailors and fishermen. On this subject, the nearby Blackwater river is one of the finest sites in Ireland for tickling trout. This very busy course is in excellent condition (greens and fairways) but the bunkers are average only and rainy days are not ideal for playing here. The very many trees are often dangerous and clearly suggest a 3-wood rather than the driver. As the course is relatively short, this is not too much of a problem. It was designed more for club members than for over-demanding green-feers, but if you are in the region, you won't be disappointed.

L'un des bons parcours de 18 trous au nord de Cork, avec un 9 trous supplémentair, qui en augmente encore l'agrément. Au coeur de la "Golden Vale", au pied des Ballyhoura Mountains, c'est l'une des régions agricoles les plus connues d'Irlande, une bonne occasion de vérifier que les Irlandais ne sont pas seulement un peuple de marins et de pêcheurs. A ce propos, la proche rivière Blackwater est l'un des meilleurs sites d'Irlande pour taquiner le poisson. Ce parcours très fréquenté est en excellente condition (greens et fairways), mais les bunkers sont simplement moyens, et les périodes pluvieuses ne sont pas idéales. Les arbres abondants sont souvent dangereux, ils incitent à laisser le driver dans le sac : comme le parcours n'est pas long, ce n'est pas un problème. Il a été conçu davantage pour les membres d'un club que pour des visiteurs trop exigeants. Si vous passez dans la région, vous ne serez pas déçu.

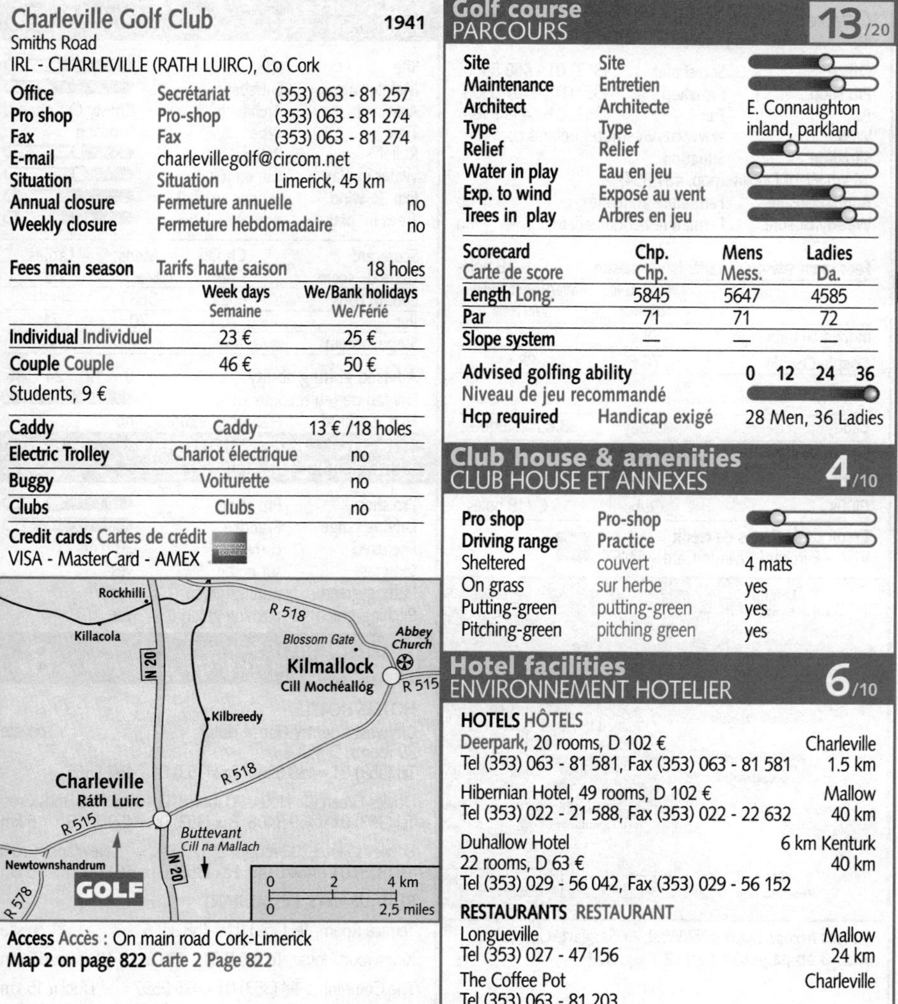

Charleville Golf Club — 1941

Smiths Road
IRL - CHARLEVILLE (RATH LUIRC), Co Cork

Office	Secrétariat	(353) 063 - 81 257
Pro shop	Pro-shop	(353) 063 - 81 274
Fax	Fax	(353) 063 - 81 274
E-mail	charlevillegolf@circom.net	
Situation	Situation	Limerick, 45 km
Annual closure	Fermeture annuelle	no
Weekly closure	Fermeture hebdomadaire	no

Fees main season / Tarifs haute saison	Week days / Semaine	We/Bank holidays / We/Férié
18 holes		
Individual Individuel	23 €	25 €
Couple Couple	46 €	50 €
Students, 9 €		

Caddy	Caddy	13 € /18 holes
Electric Trolley	Chariot électrique	no
Buggy	Voiturette	no
Clubs	Clubs	no

Credit cards Cartes de crédit
VISA - MasterCard - AMEX

Access Accès : On main road Cork-Limerick
Map 2 on page 822 Carte 2 Page 822

Map 2 on page 822 Carte 2 Page 822

Golf course — PARCOURS — 13/20

Site	Site	
Maintenance	Entretien	
Architect	Architecte	E. Connaughton
Type	Type	inland, parkland
Relief	Relief	
Water in play	Eau en jeu	
Exp. to wind	Exposé au vent	
Trees in play	Arbres en jeu	

Scorecard / Carte de score	Chp. / Chp.	Mens / Mess.	Ladies / Da.
Length Long.	5845	5647	4585
Par	71	71	72
Slope system	—	—	—

Advised golfing ability / Niveau de jeu recommandé: 0 12 24 36
Hcp required / Handicap exigé: 28 Men, 36 Ladies

Club house & amenities — CLUB HOUSE ET ANNEXES — 4/10

Pro shop	Pro-shop	
Driving range	Practice	
Sheltered	couvert	4 mats
On grass	sur herbe	yes
Putting-green	putting-green	yes
Pitching-green	pitching green	yes

Hotel facilities — ENVIRONNEMENT HOTELIER — 6/10

HOTELS HÔTELS

Deerpark, 20 rooms, D 102 € — Charleville 1.5 km
Tel (353) 063 - 81 581, Fax (353) 063 - 81 581

Hibernian Hotel, 49 rooms, D 102 € — Mallow 40 km
Tel (353) 022 - 21 588, Fax (353) 022 - 22 632

Duhallow Hotel — 6 km Kenturk 40 km
22 rooms, D 63 €
Tel (353) 029 - 56 042, Fax (353) 029 - 56 152

RESTAURANTS RESTAURANT

Longueville — Mallow 24 km
Tel (353) 027 - 47 156

The Coffee Pot — Charleville
Tel (353) 063 - 81 203

CITYWEST

13 | 6 | 8

This is a green-fee course easily playable on week-ends and boasting good practice facilities (20 mats on the driving range are lit-up). It is a whole different picture from the recent, very fashionable private clubs in the region of Dublin. Christy O'Connor Jr. has cleverly made the most of limited space, where imposing trees provided a good working base and pleasant setting. Intelligent but not unduly stressful deployment of water, the use of some natural topography to lay a number of greens and careful bunkering have resulted in a varied, interesting and instructive course: here you have to play every shot in the book, but everyone can try their luck once in a while. Visually, some holes like the 8th and 9th definitely look a little artificial in this landscape, but time changes all that. A very useful addition at a time when fashion seems to be swinging a little too much in favour of upmarket courses.

C'est un parcours au green-fee, facilement accessible en week-end et pourvu de bonnes installations d'entraînement (20 postes du driving range sont éclairés). Rien à voir avec les récents grands clubs privés très "fashionable" de la région de Dublin. Mais Christy O'Connor Jr a astucieusement tiré parti d'un espace limité, où l'implantation d'arbres déjà imposants a fourni à la fois une base de travail et un environnement plaisant. Une mise en place intelligente mais pas trop stressante d'obstacles d'eau, l'utilisation de quelques reliefs naturels pour implanter certains greens, un bunkering soigné ont contribué à en faire un parcours varié, intéressant et formateur : ici, on doit jouer tous les coups de golf, mais tous les golfeurs pourront tenter leur chance. Visuellement, certains trous comme le 8 et le 9 paraissent certes un peu artificiels dans le paysage, mais le temps commence à effacer cela. Une réalisation fort utile, en un temps où l'on a un peu trop tendance à privilégier le "haut de gamme".

Citywest Golf Club — 1994

IRL - SAGGART, Co Dublin

Office	Secrétariat	(353) 01 - 458 8566
Pro shop	Pro-shop	(353) 01 - 401 0900
Fax	Fax	(353) 01 - 458 8565
Web	www.citywesthotel-ireland.com	
Situation	Situation	
16 km W. of Dublin	(pop. 481 854)	
Annual closure	Fermeture annuelle	no
Weekly closure	Fermeture hebdomadaire	no

Fees main season Tarifs haute saison	18 holes	
	Week days Semaine	**We/Bank holidays** We/Férié
Individual Individuel	38 €	44 €
Couple Couple	76 €	88 €

Hotel guests: 25 €

Caddy	Caddy	38 € /on request
Electric Trolley	Chariot électrique	no
Buggy	Voiturette	25 € /18 holes
Clubs	Clubs	15 € /18 holes

Credit cards Cartes de crédit
VISA - Eurocard - MasterCard - AMEX

Access Accès : Dublin, N7 West. → Saggart. Golf 2 km
Map 3 on page 824 Carte 3 Page 824

Golf course PARCOURS — 13/20

Site	Site	
Maintenance	Entretien	
Architect	Architecte	Christy O'Connor Jr
Type	Type	parkland
Relief	Relief	
Water in play	Eau en jeu	
Exp. to wind	Exposé au vent	
Trees in play	Arbres en jeu	

Scorecard Carte de score	**Chp.** Chp.	**Mens** Mess.	**Ladies** Da.
Length Long.	6022	5683	4910
Par	70	70	71
Slope system	—	—	—

Advised golfing ability 0 12 24 36
Niveau de jeu recommandé
Hcp required Handicap exigé no

Club house & amenities CLUB HOUSE ET ANNEXES — 6/10

Pro shop	Pro-shop	
Driving range	Practice	
Sheltered	couvert	20 mats
On grass	sur herbe	yes
Putting-green	putting-green	yes
Pitching-green	pitching green	yes

Hotel facilities ENVIRONNEMENT HOTELIER — 8/10

HOTELS HÔTELS

Citywest Country House Hotel — on site
39 rooms, D 152 €
Tel (353) 01 - 458 8566, Fax (353) 01 - 458 8565

Doyles Green Isle Hotel, 90 rooms, D 102 € — Newlands Cross
Tel (353) 01 - 459 3406, Fax (353) 01 - 459 2178 — 5 km

Bowley's Hotel,200 rooms, D 127 € — Newlands Cross
Tel (353) 01 - 464 0140, Fax (353) 01 - 464 0900 — 5 km

RESTAURANTS RESTAURANT

Terrace Room, Tel (353) 01 - 458 8566 — on site

Kingswood House, Tel (353) 01 - 459 2428 — Naas Road 2 km

The Common's, Tel (353) 01 - 475 2597 — Dublin 15 km

CONNEMARA

15 | 6 | 6

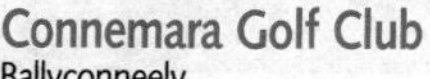

An exceptional, terribly romantic and mind-soothing site set between the ocean and national park mountains. Here, you are transported hundreds of years back in history, and the actual course looks as if it has always been a part of the picture. For a long while we rued the total absence of any relief over the first few holes and the serious business only really starts at the 8th. Then come a number of gems (the 8th, 9th and 13th) and all the closing holes from the 15th onward. Nine additional and pretty spectacular holes can now replace the original front 9, although the best idea is to play all 27. Whichever holes you play, this layout effectively reminds you of the real state of your game and experience will come in handy if you want to card a good score. The fairway bunkers are more or less dangerous, depending on the wind, and the same goes for the rough and some formidable thickets (often around the greens) which are more or less in play.

Le site est exceptionnel, romantique et apaisant, entre l'Océan et les montagnes du Parc National. On est transporté des milliers d'années en arrière, et le golf lui-même donne l'impression d'avoir toujours été là. On a longtemps pu regretter le manque total de relief et de spectacle dans les premiers trous où les choses sérieuses ne commençaient vraiment qu'à partir du 8. On trouvait ensuite quelques joyaux (8, 9, 13) et toute le finale à partir du 15. Neuf trous supplémentaires et assez spectaculaires peuvent maintenant remplacer l'aller, le mieux étant évidemment de jouer l'ensemble, malgré un léger manque d'unité. Quel que soit le tracé, le parcours vous rappelle à la réalité de votre golf, et il faut de l'expérience pour scorer. Selon le vent, la situation change du tout au tout, les bunkers de fairway, le rough et de redoutables buissons (souvent autour des greens) venant plus ou moins en jeu.

Connemara Golf Club

Ballyconneely
IRL - CLIFDEN, Co Galway

Office	Secrétariat	(353) 095 - 23 602
Pro shop	Pro-shop	(353) 095 - 23 502
Fax	Fax	(353) 095 - 23 662
Web	www.golfclubireland.com/connemara	
Situation	Situation	
16 km from Clifden (pop. 920)		
Annual closure	Fermeture annuelle	no
Weekly closure	Fermeture hebdomadaire	no

Fees main season Tarifs haute saison		18 holes
	Week days Semaine	**We/Bank holidays** We/Férié
Individual Individuel	44 €	51 €
Couple Couple	88 €	102 €
Caddy	Caddy	25 € /on request
Electric Trolley	Chariot électrique	13 € /18 holes
Buggy	Voiturette	32 € /18 holes
Clubs	Clubs	23 € /23 € holes

Credit cards Cartes de crédit
VISA - Eurocard - MasterCard

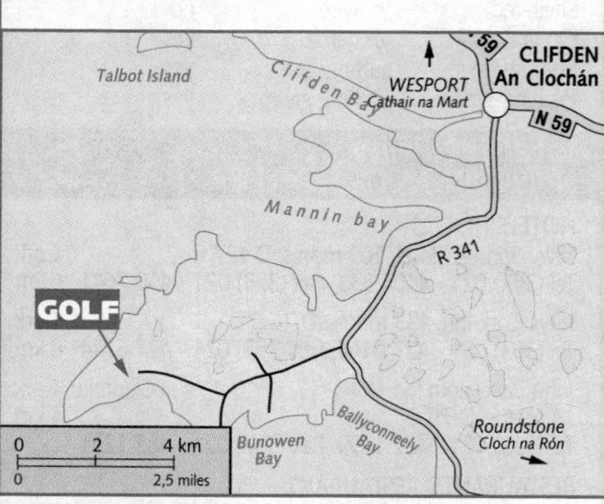

Access Accès : Galway N59 → Clifden.
16 km S of Clifden, golf in seaside village of Ballyconneely **Map 1 on page 820** Carte 1 Page 820

Golf course PARCOURS 15/20

Site	Site	
Maintenance	Entretien	
Architect	Architecte	Eddie Hackett
Type	Type	links
Relief	Relief	
Water in play	Eau en jeu	
Exp. to wind	Exposé au vent	
Trees in play	Arbres en jeu	

Scorecard Carte de score	**Chp.** Chp.	**Mens** Mess.	**Ladies** Da.
Length Long.	6611	6263	5055
Par	72	72	72
Slope system	—	—	—

Advised golfing ability Niveau de jeu recommandé: 0 12 24 36
Hcp required Handicap exigé: 28 Men, 36 Ladies

Club house & amenities CLUB HOUSE ET ANNEXES 6/10

Pro shop	Pro-shop	
Driving range	Practice	
Sheltered	couvert	no
On grass	sur herbe	yes
Putting-green	putting-green	yes
Pitching-green	pitching green	no

Hotel facilities ENVIRONNEMENT HOTELIER 6/10

HOTELS HÔTELS

Abbeyglen Castle Hotel — Clifden 16 km
32 rooms, D 152 €
Tel (353) 095 - 21 201, Fax (353) 095 - 21 797

Rock Glen, 29 rooms, D 152 € — Clifden 16 km
Tel (353) 095 - 21 035, Fax (353) 095 - 21 737

Erriseask Hotel, 13 rooms, D 114 € — Ballyconneely 5 km
Tel (353) 095 - 23 553, Fax (353) 095 - 23 639

RESTAURANTS RESTAURANT

O'Grady's Seafood — Clifden 16 km
Tel (353) 095 - 21 450

High Moors, Tel(353) 095 - 21 342 — Clifden 16 km

CORK GC

15 | 3 | 5

This course, which is more than 100 years old, was remodelled by Alistair Mackenzie, one of the great names from the classical era (he was the joint designer of Augusta, no less). Although well off the beaten golfer's track, Cork G.C. is well worth the visit. Located in a park on an island opposite the port of Cork, this is a marvellously technical course and you are constantly amazed at how easy it can be to drop so many strokes on such an honest and apparently benign course. But here, placing the drive is crucial, hazards are magnificently well placed and the putting surfaces are not easy to read. Water comes into play on only a few holes (ditches), but the rough can be as formidable as a huge lake. This very prettily landscaped and very well kept course has victoriously weathered the passing of time. Discover or return to Cork G.C. before setting out to explore the very many sights to see in this pretty region.

Ce parcours plus que centenaire a été remodelé par Alistair Mackenzie, l'un des grands architectes de l'ère classique (c'est le co-auteur d'Augusta). Bien qu'il figure à l'écart des grands circuits golfiques, il mérite largement la visite. Dans un paysage de parc et situé dans une petite île face au port de Cork, c'est une petite merveille de technicité, et l'on s'étonne constamment de perdre autant de points sur un tracé aussi franc et apparemment aimable. Mais le placement des drives y est crucial, les obstacles sont magnifiquement placés, les surfaces de green sont peu faciles à lire. L'eau ne vient en jeu que sur quelques trous (fossés), mais le rough peut être tout aussi redoutable que l'immense lac. Ce parcours très joliment paysagé et très bien entretenu a victorieusement subi les atteintes du temps. A découvrir, ou redécouvrir, avant d'explorer les richesses touristiques de cette jolie région.

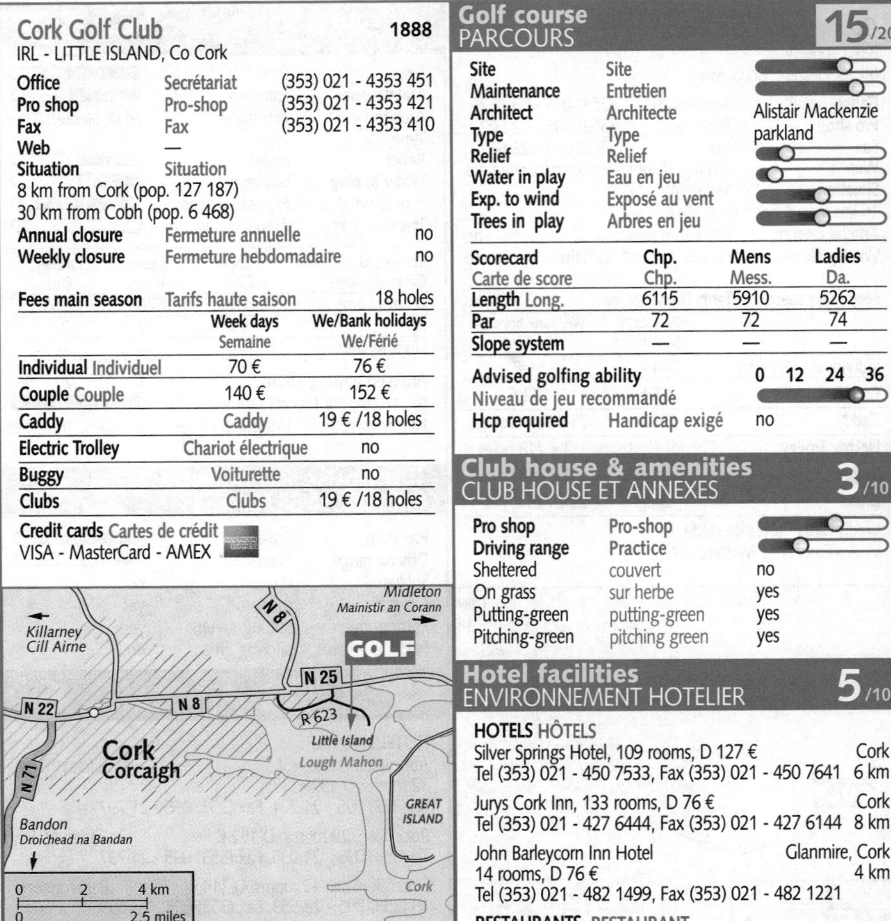

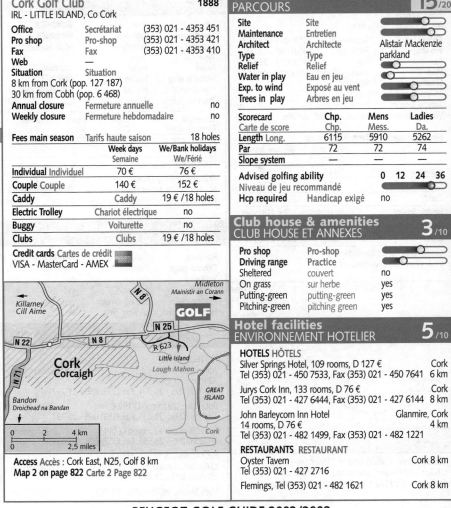

Cork Golf Club — 1888
IRL - LITTLE ISLAND, Co Cork

Office	Secrétariat	(353) 021 - 4353 451
Pro shop	Pro-shop	(353) 021 - 4353 421
Fax	Fax	(353) 021 - 4353 410
Web	—	
Situation	Situation	

8 km from Cork (pop. 127 187)
30 km from Cobh (pop. 6 468)

Annual closure	Fermeture annuelle	no
Weekly closure	Fermeture hebdomadaire	no

Fees main season Tarifs haute saison — 18 holes

	Week days / Semaine	We/Bank holidays / We/Férié
Individual Individuel	70 €	76 €
Couple Couple	140 €	152 €
Caddy Caddy		19 € /18 holes
Electric Trolley Chariot électrique		no
Buggy Voiturette		no
Clubs Clubs		19 € /18 holes

Credit cards Cartes de crédit
VISA - MasterCard - AMEX

Access Accès : Cork East, N25, Golf 8 km
Map 2 on page 822 Carte 2 Page 822

Golf course / PARCOURS — 15/20

Site	Site	
Maintenance	Entretien	
Architect	Architecte	Alistair Mackenzie
Type	Type	parkland
Relief	Relief	
Water in play	Eau en jeu	
Exp. to wind	Exposé au vent	
Trees in play	Arbres en jeu	

Scorecard Carte de score	Chp. / Chp.	Mens / Mess.	Ladies / Da.
Length Long.	6115	5910	5262
Par	72	72	74
Slope system	—	—	—

Advised golfing ability / Niveau de jeu recommandé — 0 12 24 36
Hcp required Handicap exigé — no

Club house & amenities / CLUB HOUSE ET ANNEXES — 3/10

Pro shop	Pro-shop	
Driving range	Practice	
Sheltered	couvert	no
On grass	sur herbe	yes
Putting-green	putting-green	yes
Pitching-green	pitching green	yes

Hotel facilities / ENVIRONNEMENT HOTELIER — 5/10

HOTELS HÔTELS

Silver Springs Hotel, 109 rooms, D 127 € — Cork
Tel (353) 021 - 450 7533, Fax (353) 021 - 450 7641 — 6 km

Jurys Cork Inn, 133 rooms, D 76 € — Cork
Tel (353) 021 - 427 6444, Fax (353) 021 - 427 6144 — 8 km

John Barleycorn Inn Hotel — Glanmire, Cork
14 rooms, D 76 € — 4 km
Tel (353) 021 - 482 1499, Fax (353) 021 - 482 1221

RESTAURANTS RESTAURANT

Oyster Tavern — Cork 8 km
Tel (353) 021 - 427 2716

Flemings, Tel (353) 021 - 482 1621 — Cork 8 km

COUNTY LOUTH

18	5	6

How do you explain the fame of a golf course? County Louth (or Baltray) has never hosted major international tournaments, is not one of the star courses in the south-west of Ireland and is an hour's drive from Dublin, where there is no shortage of top courses. But recognition comes from being known by the connoisseurs. While some courses may be controversial, this one is acclaimed by all. The dunes may not be as Dantesque as elsewhere and all the difficulties are there to be seen, but this course needs a humble and clear-headed approach and close observation of each detail to appreciate the aristocratic grandeur of the whole layout. Designer Tom Simpson was perhaps the greatest strategist of all for the placing and design of bunkers, and here you recognise his cachet from hole 1 to 18. Whichever direction the wind blows, it is always in play. The fairways are comparatively wide but the rough and thickets are deadly. This sheer gem always deserves both respect and glory.

A quoi tient la célébrité d'un parcours ? County Louth (ou Baltray) n'a pas reçu de grandes compétitions internationales, ne fait pas partie des vedettes du Sud-Ouest, est à une heure de Dublin, où les grands parcours ne manquent pas. Mais on reconnaît un connaisseur s'il le connaît. S'il est des parcours controversés, celui-ci fait l'unanimité. Certes, les dunes n'y sont pas aussi dantesques qu'ailleurs, on distingue toutes les difficultés, mais il faut l'aborder avec humilité et lucidité, en observer chaque détail pour apprécier la grandeur aristocratique de l'ensemble. L'architecte Tom Simpson était peut-être le plus grand stratège du placement et du dessin même des bunkers : on reconnaît sa signature du premier au dernier trou. Quelle que soit la direction du vent, il s'en trouve toujours en jeu. Les fairways sont relativement larges, mais les roughs et les buissons sont redoutables. Ce pur joyau mérite toujours le respect, et la gloire.

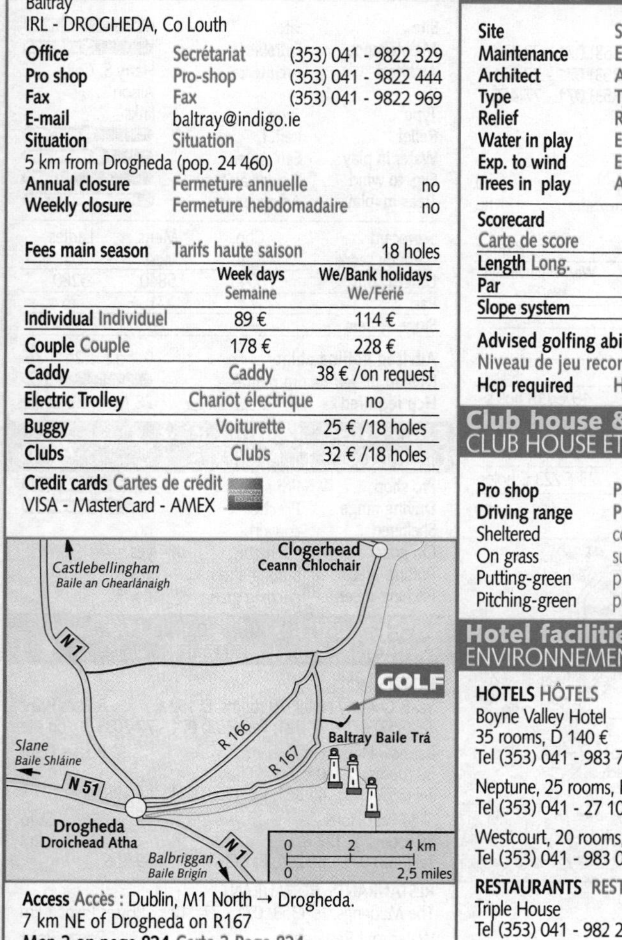

County Louth Golf Club — **1892**
Baltray
IRL - DROGHEDA, Co Louth

Office	Secrétariat	(353) 041 - 9822 329
Pro shop	Pro-shop	(353) 041 - 9822 444
Fax	Fax	(353) 041 - 9822 969
E-mail	baltray@indigo.ie	
Situation	Situation	
5 km from Drogheda (pop. 24 460)		
Annual closure	Fermeture annuelle	no
Weekly closure	Fermeture hebdomadaire	no

Fees main season Tarifs haute saison	18 holes	
	Week days Semaine	**We/Bank holidays** We/Férié
Individual Individuel	89 €	114 €
Couple Couple	178 €	228 €
Caddy Caddy		38 € /on request
Electric Trolley Chariot électrique		no
Buggy Voiturette		25 € /18 holes
Clubs Clubs		32 € /18 holes

Credit cards Cartes de crédit
VISA - MasterCard - AMEX

Access Accès : Dublin, M1 North → Drogheda.
7 km NE of Drogheda on R167
Map 3 on page 824 Carte 3 Page 824

Golf course PARCOURS — 18/20

Site	Site	
Maintenance	Entretien	
Architect	Architecte	Tom Simpson (1937)
Type	Type	links
Relief	Relief	
Water in play	Eau en jeu	
Exp. to wind	Exposé au vent	
Trees in play	Arbres en jeu	

Scorecard Carte de score	**Chp.** Chp.	**Mens** Mess.	**Ladies** Da.
Length Long.	6113	5952	5740
Par	73	73	75
Slope system	—	—	—

Advised golfing ability Niveau de jeu recommandé — 0 12 24 36
Hcp required Handicap exigé — no

Club house & amenities CLUB HOUSE ET ANNEXES — 5/10

Pro shop	Pro-shop	
Driving range	Practice	
Sheltered	couvert	no
On grass	sur herbe	yes
Putting-green	putting-green	yes
Pitching-green	pitching green	yes

Hotel facilities ENVIRONNEMENT HOTELIER — 6/10

HOTELS HÔTELS

Boyne Valley Hotel — Drogheda
35 rooms, D 140 € — 5 km
Tel (353) 041 - 983 7737, Fax (353) 041 - 983 9188

Neptune, 25 rooms, D 57 € — Bettystown
Tel (353) 041 - 27 107, Fax (353) 041 - 27 243 — 10 km

Westcourt, 20 rooms, D 102 € — Drogheda
Tel (353) 041 - 983 0965, Fax (353) 041 - 983 0970 — 5 km

RESTAURANTS RESTAURANT

Triple House — Termonfeckin 3 km
Tel (353) 041 - 982 2616

Little Strand, Tel — Clogherhead 5 km

COUNTY SLIGO

17 | 4 | 4

From the fairways, magnificent views over the Atlantic, the bay of Drumcliff and Ben Bulben warrant a trip to Rosses Point. But this is also home to one of Ireland's greatest golf courses. As windless days are few and far between, the elements are an overriding factor: the fairways are wide enough, but balls too far left or right are snapped up by the bunkers and rough, both equally penalising. With this said, and if we exclude two or three blind shots, all the hazards are clearly visible and the player knows perfectly well what needs to be done to avoid them. It is simply a question of doing it! Golfers with little experience or even less nerve can choose their own tees, they are all well placed to vary the shape of the course. With 9 holes overlooking the site and the other half in a valley, you can look forward to a few climbs (nothing too exhausting) and elevated greens, but none are blind. A great links to savour, yard by yard.

Depuis le parcours, les vues magnifiques sur l'Atlantique, la baie de Drumcliff et le mont Ben Bulben justifieraient le voyage à Rosses Point. Mais c'est aussi l'un des plus grands parcours d'Irlande. Comme les jours sans vent sont rares, c'est un facteur dominant : les fairways sont assez larges, mais un petit écart amène vite la balle dans les roughs et les bunkers, tout aussi pénalisants. Cela dit, à l'exception de deux ou trois coups aveugles, tous les obstacles sont visibles, et l'on sait parfaitement ce qu'il faut éviter, à défaut de le faire ! Les golfeurs peu expérimentés ou pas trop courageux pourront choisir leurs tees de départ, ils sont tous très bien placés pour varier le parcours. Avec une moitié des trous dominant le site et l'autre moitié dans une vallée, on peut s'attendre à quelques montées (elles ne sont pas épuisantes), et à quelques greens surélevés, mais aucun n'est aveugle. Un grand links à savourer mètre par mètre.

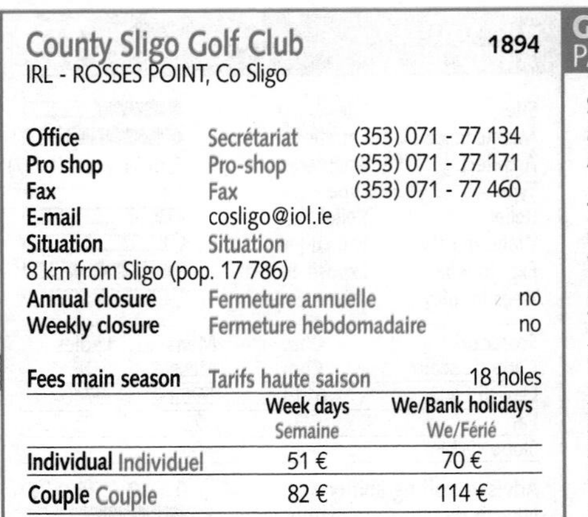

County Sligo Golf Club — 1894

IRL - ROSSES POINT, Co Sligo

Office	Secrétariat	(353) 071 - 77 134
Pro shop	Pro-shop	(353) 071 - 77 171
Fax	Fax	(353) 071 - 77 460
E-mail	cosligo@iol.ie	
Situation	Situation	

8 km from Sligo (pop. 17 786)

Annual closure	Fermeture annuelle	no
Weekly closure	Fermeture hebdomadaire	no

Fees main season Tarifs haute saison		18 holes
	Week days Semaine	**We/Bank holidays** We/Férié
Individual Individuel	51 €	70 €
Couple Couple	82 €	114 €

Caddy	Caddy	19 € /18 holes
Electric Trolley	Chariot électrique	13 € /18 holes
Buggy	Voiturette	32 € /18 holes
Clubs	Clubs	23 € /23 € holes
Credit cards Cartes de crédit		no

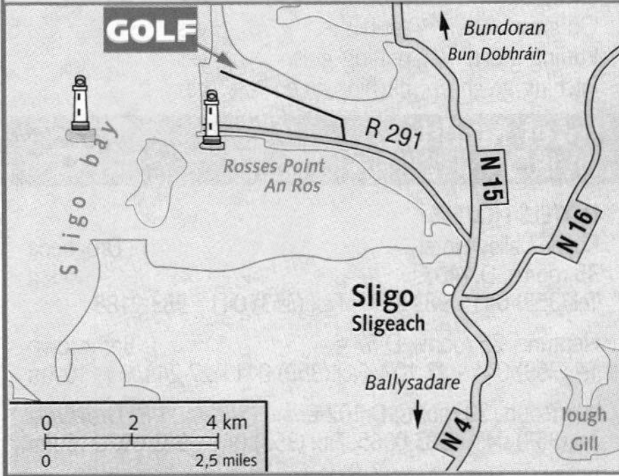

Access Accès : N15, 8 km NW of Sligo
Map 1 on page 820 Carte 1 Page 820

Golf course PARCOURS — 17/20

Site	Site	
Maintenance	Entretien	
Architect	Architecte	Harry S. Colt Alison
Type	Type	links
Relief	Relief	
Water in play	Eau en jeu	
Exp. to wind	Exposé au vent	
Trees in play	Arbres en jeu	

Scorecard Carte de score	**Chp.** Chp.	**Mens** Mess.	**Ladies** Da.
Length Long.	6043	5840	5280
Par	71	71	75
Slope system	—	—	—

Advised golfing ability Niveau de jeu recommandé: 0 12 24 36

Hcp required Handicap exigé: 28 Men, 36 Ladies

Club house & amenities CLUB HOUSE ET ANNEXES — 4/10

Pro shop	Pro-shop	
Driving range	Practice	
Sheltered	couvert	no
On grass	sur herbe	yes
Putting-green	putting-green	yes
Pitching-green	pitching green	no

Hotel facilities ENVIRONNEMENT HOTELIER — 4/10

HOTELS HÔTELS

Yeats Country Hotel, 79 rooms, D 152 € — Rosses Point
Tel (353) 071 - 77 221, Fax (353) 071 - 77 203 — on site

Ballincar House Hotel — Rosses Point
30 rooms, D 140 € — 4 km
Tel (353) 071 - 45 361, Fax (353) 071 - 44 198

Sligo Park Hotel — Sligo
89 rooms, D 127 € — 8 km
Tel (353) 071 - 60 291, Fax (353) 071 - 69 556

RESTAURANTS RESTAURANT

The Moorings, Tel (353) 071 - 77 112 — Rosses Point 1 km

Waterfront Restaurant — Rosses Point
Tel (353) 071 - 77 122

COUNTY TIPPERARY

15 | 7 | 5

A long way to Tipperary? Not from Shannon, Cork or Dublin at any rate, although this course is rather off the traditional golfing track and it's a pity, because professional golfer Philip Walton has also shown himself to be a good course architect. He has used the natural contours well, along with the lakes and the river that cross the course rather dangerously on the 4th, and there are visible signs of the so-called American influence, particularly around the greens. These have been carefully designed and call more for lofted approaches rather than the traditional British style run shots. Designed for all levels of play, this rather, but never excessively, long course (even from the back) was designed on rolling terrain (easily walkable) around an 18th century manor, now converted into a hotel.. As a result, this is a very agreeable week-end destination in the peaceful Irish countryside.

De Shannon, de Cork ou de Dublin, ce n'est pas une longue route pour aller à Tipperary... Pourtant, ce parcours reste en dehors des circuits golfiques traditionnels, et c'est dommage, car l'excellent professionnel Philip Walton s'y révèle également bon architecte. Il a ainsi très bien utilisé les contours naturels, les lacs et la rivière qui traverse de manière dangereuse le 4, avec une influence de l'architecture dite américaine que l'on retrouve dans le dessin des greens, très travaillés, et qui appellent davantage un jeu de balles levées que des "bump 'n run" à la britannique. Conçu pour tous les niveaux de jeu, ce parcours assez long, mais sans excès (même du fond) a été construit sur un terrain assez ondulé (facile à marcher) autour d'un manoir du XVIIIème siècle transformé en hôtel, ce qui en fait une destination de week-end tout à fait acceptable, dans le calme de la campagne irlandaise.

County Tipperary Golf & C.C. — 1993

Dundrum House Hotel
IRL - DUNDRUM, Co Tipperary

Office	Secrétariat	(353) 062 - 71 116
Pro shop	Pro-shop	(353) 062 - 71 116
Fax	Fax	(353) 062 - 71 366
Web	www.dundrumhousehotel.com	
Situation	Situation	

8 km N of Tipperary, 9 km W of Cashel

Annual closure	Fermeture annuelle	no
Weekly closure	Fermeture hebdomadaire	no

Fees main season Tarifs haute saison		18 holes
	Week days Semaine	**We/Bank holidays** We/Férié
Individual Individuel	44 €	51 €
Couple Couple	88 €	102 €
Caddy Caddy		no
Electric Trolley Chariot électrique		6 €
Buggy Voiturette		38 € /18 holes
Clubs Clubs		19 € /18 holes

Credit cards Cartes de crédit
VISA - MasterCard - AMEX

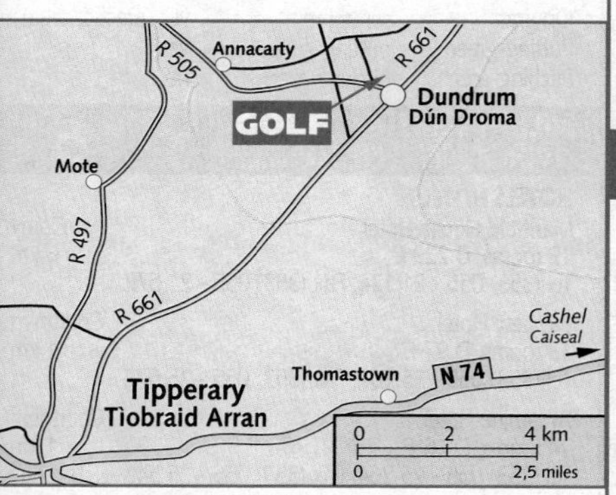

Access Accès : • Dublin N7 to Portlaoise. N8 to Cashel. R505 to Dundrum
• Cork N8 to Cashel. R505 to Dundrum
Map 2 on page 823 Carte 2 Page 823

Golf course — PARCOURS — 15/20

Site	Site	
Maintenance	Entretien	
Architect	Architecte	Philip Walton
Type	Type	parkland
Relief	Relief	
Water in play	Eau en jeu	
Exp. to wind	Exposé au vent	
Trees in play	Arbres en jeu	

Scorecard Carte de score	**Chp.** Chp.	**Mens** Mess.	**Ladies** Da.
Length Long.	6150	5800	4800
Par	72	72	72
Slope system	—	—	—

Advised golfing ability 0 12 24 36
Niveau de jeu recommandé
Hcp required Handicap exigé no

Club house & amenities — CLUB HOUSE ET ANNEXES — 7/10

Pro shop	Pro-shop	
Driving range	Practice	
Sheltered	couvert	no
On grass	sur herbe	no
Putting-green	putting-green	yes
Pitching-green	pitching green	no

Hotel facilities — ENVIRONNEMENT HOTELIER — 5/10

HOTELS HÔTELS

Dundrum House Hotel — Dundrum on site
60 rooms, D 127 €
Tel (353) 062 - 71 116, Fax (353) 062 - 71 366

Cashel Palace, 23 rooms, D 140 € — Cashel 8 km
Tel (353) 062 - 62 707, Fax (353) 062 - 62 521

Rectory House Hotel, 10 rooms, D 70 € — Dundrum 2 km
Tel (353) 062 - 71 266, Fax (353) 062 - 71 115

RESTAURANTS RESTAURANT

Rosemore, — Dundrum House Hotel on site
Tel (353) 062 - 71 116

Venue Restaurant, Tel(353) 062 - 71 717 Dundrum on site

COURTOWN

14 | 5 | 5

Alongside the monster-length courses in this region like The European and Druid's Glen, albeit in different styles, the parkland landscape and unpretentiousness of the Courtown course is like a breath of fresh air. Although the course lies close to the sea, trees form a natural shelter from the frequent wind, even though in return off-target big-hitters might find them a little too big for comfort. Add to this country scene the rolling contours of small hills and you get a course that is pleasant and varied: no two holes are the same. With medium-sized greens that are thickly grassed and true, plus a nice balance between holes presumed to be easy and others that are more demanding, Courtown is one of those good but somewhat old-fashioned courses - compared to today's modern designs - that everyone enjoys playing, even if you would never drive 200 miles out of your way to do so. After a cheerful welcome in the club-house, no-one at least will feel too intimidated on the first tee.

A côté des monstres de longueur que peuvent être, dans cette région et dans des styles différents, The European et Druids Glen, la longueur réduite, le paysage de parc et l'absence de prétention d'un Courtown constituent une sorte de respiration. Bien que le parcours soit très près de la mer, les arbres constituent un abri naturel contre un vent souvent présent, même si, en contrepartie, les frappeurs auront affaire à ces adversaires de (grande) taille. Et quand on ajoute à ce tableau champêtre les ondulations mesurées de petites collines, on obtient un ensemble agréable et varié : il n'y a pas deux trous identiques. Avec des greens de taille moyenne mais bien garnis et francs, un bon équilibre entre les trous présumés faciles et d'autres plus exigeants, Courtown fait partie de ces bons parcours un peu surranés par rapport à une certaine modernité de la conception que chacun a plaisir à jouer même si l'on ne fait pas 500 km de route rien que pour le visiter. Après une entrée souriante dans le club, personne au moins n'y sera trop intimidé au départ du 1.

Courtown Golf Club — 1936

IRL - COURTOWN, GOREY, Co. Wexford

Office Secrétariat (353) 055 - 25 166
Pro shop Pro-shop (353) 055 - 25 166
Fax Fax (353) 055 - 25 553
Web www.courtowngolfclub.com
Situation Situation
6 km from Gorey (pop. 2 150)
95 km from Dublin (pop. 481 854)
Annual closure Fermeture annuelle — no
Weekly closure Fermeture hebdomadaire — no

Fees main season Tarifs haute saison	18 holes	
	Week days Semaine	**We/Bank holidays** We/Férié
Individual Individuel	38 €	44 €
Couple Couple	76 €	88 €
Caddy Caddy	no	
Electric Trolley Chariot électrique	no	
Buggy Voiturette	32 € /18 holes	
Clubs Clubs	25 € /18 holes	

Credit cards Cartes de crédit
Visa - MasterCard (not in the bar)

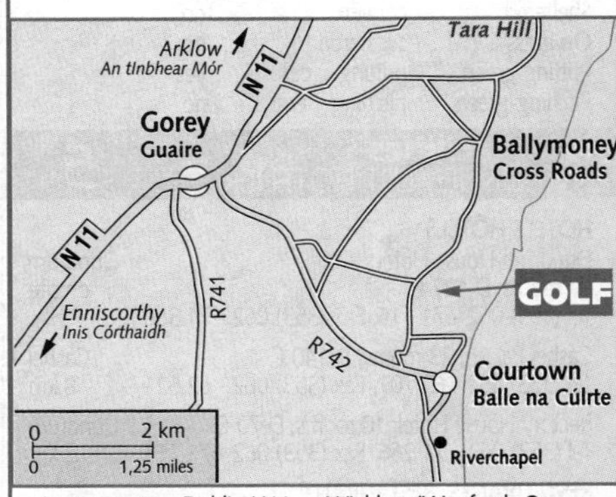

Access Accès : Dublin N11 → Wicklow/Wexford. Gorey, R742 → Courtown, Golf on the left.
Map 2 on page 823 Carte 2 Page 823

Golf course PARCOURS — 14/20

Site Site
Maintenance Entretien
Architect Architecte — Harris & Associates
Type Type — parkland
Relief Relief
Water in play Eau en jeu
Exp. to wind Exposé au vent
Trees in play Arbres en jeu

Scorecard Carte de score	**Chp.** Chp.	**Mens** Mess.	**Ladies** Da.
Length Long.	5898	5725	4981
Par	71	71	73
Slope system	—	—	—

Advised golfing ability Niveau de jeu recommandé — 0 12 24 36
Hcp required Handicap exigé — no

Club house & amenities CLUB HOUSE ET ANNEXES — 5/10

Pro shop Pro-shop
Driving range Practice
Sheltered couvert — no
On grass sur herbe — yes (practice area)
Putting-green putting-green — yes
Pitching-green pitching green — no

Hotel facilities ENVIRONNEMENT HOTELIER — 5/10

HOTELS HÔTELS

Marlfield House Hotel — Gorey 6 km
19 rooms, D 229 €
Tel (353) 055 - 21 124, Fax (353) 055 - 21 572

Bayview Hotel — Courtown 1 km
13 rooms, D 97 €
Tel (353) 055 - 25 307, Fax (353) 055 - 25 576

Ardamine Hotel — Courtown 1 km
24 rooms, D 46 €
Tel (353) 055 - 25 264, Fax (353) 055 - 25 548

RESTAURANTS RESTAURANT

Marlfield House, Tel (353) 055 - 21 124 — Gorey 6 km
The Old Rectory, Tel (353) 0404 - 67 048 — Wicklow 40 km

DINGLE LINKS (CEANN SIBEAL) 15 | 5 | 4

The first thing here is the magic of an outstanding site, overlooking Dingle Bay, the Blasket Islands and Mount Brandon, on a peninsula where you can find the vestiges of the stone age or the beginnings of Christianity. The many panels in Gaelic only add to the impression of a journey back in time. Designed by Eddie Hackett and Christy O'Connor Jnr., this course looks as if it has always been here, and is a real pleasure to play on long summer days, even if the wind blows or if it rains a little (this may sometimes occur in Ireland). Without pretending to be in the same league as Ballybunion or Waterville, this is an interesting course for everyone, where emphasis should be laid on trying to play low shots. The main difficulty is making clean contact with the ball on sandy soil, escaping from bunkers and avoiding a meandering stream which comes into play on about ten holes. A delightful experience.

D'abord, il y a la magie d'une situation exceptionnelle sur la baie de Dingle, les Blasket Islands et le Mount Brandon, dans une péninsule où l'on trouve des vestiges de l'Age de pierre ou des débuts du christianisme. La présence de nombreux panneaux en gaëlique accentue encore cette impression de voyage en remontant le temps. Créé par Eddie Hackett et Christy O'Connor Jr, ce parcours paraît avoir toujours été là, et c'est un plaisir d'y jouer pendant les longues journées d'été, même si le vent souffle, ou s'il pleut un peu (ce qui arrive parfois en Irlande). Sans prétendre appartenir à la même division que Ballybunion ou Waterville, c'est un parcours intéressant pour tous, où l'on jouera de préférence des balles basses, où la principale difficulté consiste à bien contacter la balle sur le sol sablonneux, à s'échapper des bunkers, et à éviter les méandres d'un cours d'eau, en jeu sur une dizaine de trous. Une expérience de charme.

Golf Chumann Cean Sibeal — 1972

Ballyoughteragh
IRL - BALLYFERRITER, Co Kerry

Office	Secrétariat	(353) 066 - 915 6255
Pro shop	Pro-shop	(353) 066 - 915 6255
Fax	Fax	(353) 066 - 915 6409
Web	www.dingle-golf.com	
Situation	Situation	

2 km from Ballyferriter, 16 km from Dingle

Annual closure	Fermeture annuelle	no
Weekly closure	Fermeture hebdomadaire	no

Fees main season / Tarifs haute saison	18 holes	
	Week days / Semaine	We/Bank holidays / We/Férié
Individual Individuel	57 €	57 €
Couple Couple	114 €	114 €
Caddy Caddy	13 € /on request	
Electric Trolley Chariot électrique	no	
Buggy Voiturette	32 € /18 holes	
Clubs Clubs	15 €	

Credit cards Cartes de crédit
VISA - MasterCard

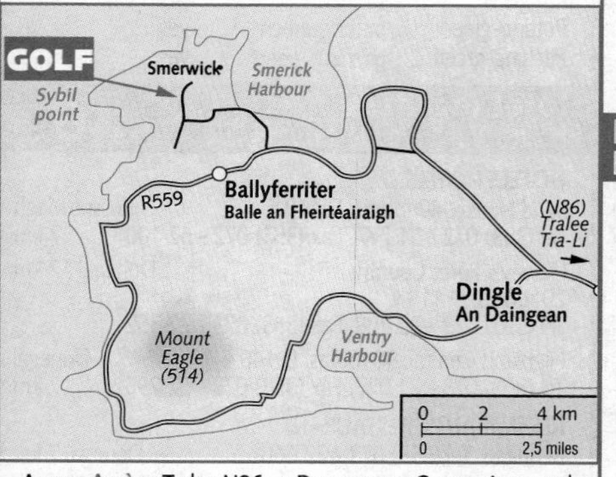

Access Accès : Tralee N86 → Derrymore, Camp, Anascaul, Dingle. R559 → Ballynana, Ballyferriter (Dingle Peninsula) **Map 2 on page 822** Carte 2 Page 822

Golf course PARCOURS — 15/20

Site	Site	
Maintenance	Entretien	
Architect	Architecte	Eddie Hackett, Christy O'Connor Jr
Type	Type	seaside course, links
Relief	Relief	
Water in play	Eau en jeu	
Exp. to wind	Exposé au vent	
Trees in play	Arbres en jeu	

Scorecard / Carte de score	Chp. / Chp.	Mens / Mess.	Ladies / Da.
Length Long.	6030	5870	4700
Par	72	72	73
Slope system	—	—	—

Advised golfing ability Niveau de jeu recommandé: 0 12 24 36
Hcp required Handicap exigé: no

Club house & amenities CLUB HOUSE ET ANNEXES — 5/10

Pro shop	Pro-shop	
Driving range	Practice	
Sheltered	couvert	no
On grass	sur herbe	yes
Putting-green	putting-green	yes
Pitching-green	pitching green	no

Hotel facilities ENVIRONNEMENT HOTELIER — 4/10

HOTELS HÔTELS

Dingle Skellig Hotel — Dingle 16 km
100 rooms, D 127 €
Tel (353) 066 - 915 0200, Fax (353) 066 - 915 1501

Benners Hotel, 24 rooms, D 102 € — Dingle 16 km
Tel (353) 066 - 915 1638, Fax (353) 066 - 915 1412

Dun an Oir Golf Hotel, 20 rooms, D 63 € — on site
Tel (353) 066 - 915 6133, Fax (353) 066 - 915 6153

RESTAURANTS RESTAURANT

Doyle's Seafood Bar — Dingle 16 km
Tel (353) 066 - 915 1174

Beginish, Tel (353) 066 - 915 1588 — Dingle 16 km

DONEGAL (MURVAGH)

16 | 6 | 6

Be warned, this is not a course for the faint-hearted. A word of advice: if your driving is not in tip-top condition, and unless you couldn't give the proverbial two hoots about playing 10 strokes over your handicap, avoid the back tees. The tiger tees are definitely no-go, except if you have the wind behind you all the way (and St Patrick to watch over you). You guessed it, this is the longest course in all of Ireland. Some of the par 4s are real monsters, not to mention the 16th, a par 3, that is inaccessible to the common run of people. From the front tees, however, it is a little easier, and the effort of walking over hilly terrain will be rewarded by a great day's golfing. The greens are often open to bump and runs, and the short game experts can have a whale of a time. The surrounding dunes and general layout make this a very good, spectacular and exciting links course, but emphasis is more on the roughness of the course than on the finesse you find with the really great courses of this type. The Clubhouse has been rebuilt, better than ever, with nice views from the bar.

Ce n'est pas un parcours de gamins. Un bon conseil : à moins d'avoir réglé votre driving à la perfection, de vous moquer éperdument de jouer dix coups au-dessus de votre handicap, évitez les départs arrière. A moins d'avoir vent avec sur tous les trous (il faut St Patrick pour veiller sur vous), évitez les départs de championnat, c'est le plus long parcours d'Irlande. Quelques par 4 sont de véritables monstres, sans même parler du 16, un par 3 inaccessible au commun des mortels. Cela dit, il s'adoucit un peu des départs avancés, et les efforts de la marche sur ce terrain accidenté seront récompensés par une belle journée de golf. Les greens sont souvent accessibles en roulant, et les virtuoses du petit jeu pourront s'y régaler. L'environnement de dunes, et le tracé général en font un très bon links, spectaculaire et excitant, mais l'accent a été mis davantage sur la rudesse que sur la finesse des plus grands parcours du genre. Le Clubhouse a été bien reconstruit, avec de jolies vues depuis le bar.

Donegal Golf Club — 1960

IRL - LAGHY, Co Donegal

Office	Secrétariat	(353) 073 - 34 054
Pro shop	Pro-shop	(353) 073 - 34 054
Fax	Fax	(353) 073 - 34 377
Web	www.donegalgolfclub.ie	
Situation	Situation	
7 km from Donegal (pop. 2 296)		
Annual closure	Fermeture annuelle	no
Weekly closure	Fermeture hebdomadaire	no

Fees main season Tarifs haute saison	18 holes	
	Week days Semaine	**We/Bank holidays** We/Férié
Individual Individuel	38 €	51 €
Couple Couple	76 €	102 €

Caddy	Caddy	15 € /on request
Electric Trolley	Chariot électrique	13 €
Buggy	Voiturette	25 € /18 holes
Clubs	Clubs	no
Credit cards	Cartes de crédit	no

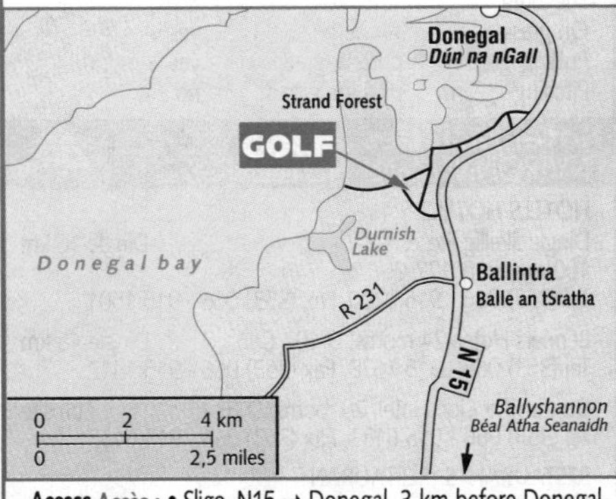

Access Accès : • Sligo, N15 → Donegal. 3 km before Donegal, turn left to Mullinasole/Murvagh peninsula • Donegal N15 South →Ballyshannon. Laghy, turn right to Mullinasole/ Murvagh peninsula **Map 1 on page 820** Carte 1 Page 820

Golf course — PARCOURS — 16/20

Site	Site	
Maintenance	Entretien	
Architect	Architecte	Eddie Hackett
Type	Type	links
Relief	Relief	
Water in play	Eau en jeu	
Exp. to wind	Exposé au vent	
Trees in play	Arbres en jeu	

Scorecard Carte de score	**Chp.** Chp.	**Mens** Mess.	**Ladies** Da.
Length Long.	6574	6249	5253
Par	73	73	75
Slope system	—	—	—

Advised golfing ability — 0 12 24 36
Niveau de jeu recommandé

Hcp required Handicap exigé — 28 Men, 36 Ladies

Club house & amenities — CLUB HOUSE ET ANNEXES — 6/10

Pro shop	Pro-shop	
Driving range	Practice	
Sheltered	couvert	no
On grass	sur herbe	yes
Putting-green	putting-green	yes
Pitching-green	pitching green	yes

Hotel facilities — ENVIRONNEMENT HOTELIER — 6/10

HOTELS HÔTELS

Sand House, 40 rooms, D 140 € — Rossnowlagh 7 km
Tel (353) 072 - 51 777, Fax (353) 072 - 52 100

Harvey's Point Country — Donegal 12 km
20 rooms, D 114 €
Tel (353) 073 - 22 208, Fax (353) 073 - 22 352

Highland Central, 90 rooms, D 140 € — Donegal 7 km
Tel (353) 073 - 21 027, Fax (353) 073 - 22 295

RESTAURANTS RESTAURANT

Belshade, Tel (353) 073 - 22 660 — Donegal 7 km

The Castle Bar, Tel (353) 073 - 21 062 — Donegal 7 km

Harvey's Point Country, — Donegal 12 km
Tel (353) 073 - 22 208

DOOKS

15 | 5 | 5

A very good links course, whose international fame has been eclipsed somewhat by its prestigious neighbours. While this course alone may not warrant a long journey, it would be a shame not to include Dooks in any golfing itinerary to south-west Ireland. It is an excellent practice outing before getting to grips with some even more difficult courses nearby. Opened in the 19th century, it was completed in 1973 by Eddie Hackett, with praiseworthy concern for preserving unity of style. There are no gigantic dunes here, just endless mounds and dales which add to the course's character and complicate the round just enough to keep everyone happy. Not very long but often narrow, Dooks gets tougher with the wind. The greens are not huge but are well-guarded, so accuracy and a sharp short game are the order of the day, with excellent scope for bump and run approach shots. The one or two blind shots merely add to the excitement.

Un très bon parcours de links, dont la notoriété internationale a été éclipsée par de prestigieux voisins. S'il ne justifie pas à lui seul un long voyage, il serait fort dommage de ne pas l'intégrer à un séjour golfique dans le Sud-Ouest de l'Irlande. C'est même un très bon galop d'entraînement avant d'affronter des adversaires encore plus difficiles. Créé au siècle dernier, il a été complété en 1973 par Eddie Hackett, avec un louable souci de lui conserver son unité. On ne trouve pas ici de dunes gigantesques, mais les nombreuses buttes et dépressions ajoutent à son caractère, et compliquent assez le jeu pour plaire à tous. Pas très long, mais souvent étroit, il prend de la force avec le vent. Les greens ne sont pas immenses, et bien protégés, il convient alors d'être très exact, ou de sortir son meilleur petit jeu, en favorisant ces approches roulées qui sont un des plaisirs des links, avec quelques coups aveugles pour se donner des émotions.

Dooks Golf Club — 1889

IRL - GLENBEIGH, Co Kerry

Office	Secrétariat	(353) 066 - 976 8205
Pro shop	Pro-shop	(353) 066 - 976 8205
Fax	Fax	(353) 066 - 976 8476
Web	www.dooks.com	
Situation	Situation	

24 km from Killarney (pop. 8 809)
8 km from Killorglin (pop. 1 278)

Annual closure	Fermeture annuelle	no
Weekly closure	Fermeture hebdomadaire	no

Fees main season Tarifs haute saison	18 holes	
	Week days Semaine	**We/Bank holidays** We/Férié
Individual Individuel	38 €	38 €
Couple Couple	76 €	76 €
Caddy	Caddy	19 € /on request
Electric Trolley	Chariot électrique	10 € /110 € holes
Buggy	Voiturette	32 € /18 holes
Clubs	Clubs	no

Credit cards Cartes de crédit
VISA - Eurocard - MasterCard - AMEX

Access Accès : Killarney N72 → Killorglin. N70 → Glenbeigh (Ring of Kerry). Golf 3 km from Glenbeigh

Map 2 on page 822 Carte 2 Page 822

Golf course — PARCOURS — 15/20

Site	Site	
Maintenance	Entretien	
Architect	Architecte	Eddie Hackett
Type	Type	links, seaside course
Relief	Relief	
Water in play	Eau en jeu	
Exp. to wind	Exposé au vent	
Trees in play	Arbres en jeu	

Scorecard Carte de score	**Chp.** Chp.	**Mens** Mess.	**Ladies** Da.
Length Long.	6010	5702	4848
Par	70	70	70
Slope system	—	—	—

Advised golfing ability Niveau de jeu recommandé — 0 12 24 36

Hcp required Handicap exigé — 24 Men, 36 Ladies

Club house & amenities — CLUB HOUSE ET ANNEXES — 5/10

Pro shop	Pro-shop	
Driving range	Practice	
Sheltered	couvert	no
On grass	sur herbe	no
Putting-green	putting-green	yes
Pitching-green	pitching green	no

Hotel facilities — ENVIRONNEMENT HOTELIER — 5/10

HOTELS HÔTELS

Ard Na Sidhe — Caragh Lake, Killorglin 5 km
20 rooms, D 216 €
Tel (353) 066 - 976 9105, Fax (353) 066 - 976 9282

Towers Hotel — Glenbeigh 3 km
28 rooms, D 102 €
Tel (353) 066 - 976 8212, Fax (353) 066 - 976 8260

Foxtrot, 4 rooms, D 51 € — Glenbeigh 3 km
Tel (353) 066 - 976 8417, Fax (353) 066 - 976 8552

RESTAURANTS RESTAURANT

Bianconi Inn, Tel (353) 066 - 976 1146 — Killorglin 11 km

Nicks, Tel (353) 066 - 976 1219 — Killorglin11 km

DROMOLAND CASTLE

14 | 7 | 8

Give Robert Trent Jones Snr. a big lake (in play on many of the holes) and a reasonably sized parkland estate, and he will produce a course that is well above average. He probably lacked a bit of space here to create the length he usually gives his courses, so he laid more emphasis on the technical side. Being able to flight the ball is a decisive advantage here. Although only very slightly hilly, certain rolling fairways have resulted in blind tee shots, but the greens and traps along the way are clearly visible for the second shot (or at least they should be). River Rine also comes into play on several holes. People who are used to Trent Jones courses will recognise his strategic style for locating bunkers and the work made on and around the greens, which are always fascinating to putt on. Dromoland Castle has earned itself a very handy reputation, particularly thanks to the work made on the course in recent years.

Donnez un grand lac (en jeu sur de nombreux trous) et un parc de taille raisonnable à Robert Trent Jones Sr, il saura vous faire un parcours nettement au dessus de la moyenne. Il a sans doute manqué un peu d'espace pour lui donner la longueur habituelle de ses parcours, il a donc mis davantage l'accent sur la technicité. Ainsi, savoir travailler la balle est un avantage décisif. Bien que le relief soit limité, certaines ondulations du terrain ont imposé des départs aveugles, mais les greens et leurs défenses sont bien visibles au second coup. A signaler aussi la mise en jeu de la rivière Rine sur plusieurs trous. Les habitués des parcours de Trent Jones reconnaîtront son style stratégique de placement de bunkers, ainsi que le travail efffectué sur les greens, toujours intéressants à putter. Dromoland Castle confirme sa très bonne réputation, en particulier grâce au travail effectué sur le parcours depuis quelques années.

Dromoland Castle Golf Club — 1985

IRL - NEWMARKET-ON-FERGUS, Co Clare

Office	Secrétariat	(353) 061 - 368 444
Pro shop	Pro-shop	(353) 061 - 368 444
Fax	Fax	(353) 061 - 363 355
Web	www.dromoland.ie	
Situation	Situation	

28 km from Limerick (pop. 52 039)
11 km from Ennis (pop. 15 333)

Annual closure	Fermeture annuelle	no
Weekly closure	Fermeture hebdomadaire	no

Fees main season Tarifs haute saison	18 holes	
	Week days Semaine	**We/Bank holidays** We/Férié
Individual Individuel	51 €	57 €
Couple Couple	102 €	114 €
Caddy	Caddy	19 € /18 holes
Electric Trolley	Chariot électrique	no
Buggy	Voiturette	38 € /18 holes
Clubs	Clubs	13 €

Credit cards Cartes de crédit
VISA - Eurocard - MasterCard - DC - AMEX

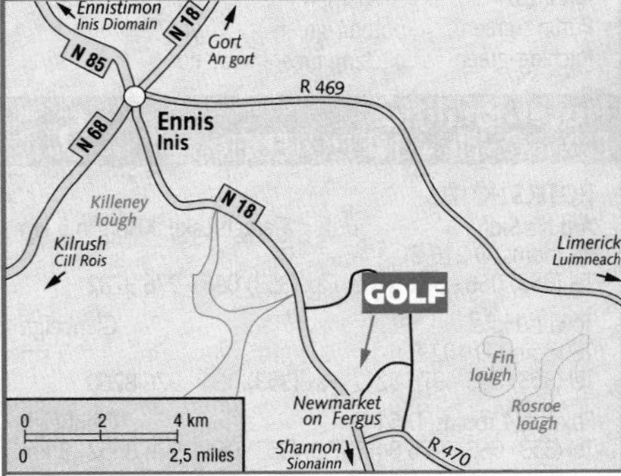

Access Accès : Limerick, N18 → Ennis. Outside Newmarket-on-Fergus, right → Dromoland Castle

Map 2 on page 822 Carte 2 Page 822

Golf course — PARCOURS — 14/20

Site	Site	
Maintenance	Entretien	
Architect	Architecte	R. Trent Jones Sr
Type	Type	parkland
Relief	Relief	
Water in play	Eau en jeu	
Exp. to wind	Exposé au vent	
Trees in play	Arbres en jeu	

Scorecard Carte de score	**Chp.** Chp.	**Mens** Mess.	**Ladies** Da.
Length Long.	5719	5646	5542
Par	71	71	71
Slope system	—	—	—

Advised golfing ability Niveau de jeu recommandé — 0 12 24 36
Hcp required Handicap exigé — no

Club house & amenities — CLUB HOUSE ET ANNEXES — 7/10

Pro shop	Pro-shop	
Driving range	Practice	
Sheltered	couvert	no
On grass	sur herbe	yes
Putting-green	putting-green	yes
Pitching-green	pitching green	yes

Hotel facilities — ENVIRONNEMENT HOTELIER — 8/10

HOTELS HÔTELS

Dromoland Castle Hotel, 73 rooms, D 256 € — on site
Tel (353) 061 - 368 144, Fax (353) 061 - 363 355

Clare Inn — Newmarket-on-Fergus 1,5 km
121 rooms, D 102 €
Tel (353) 061 - 368 161, Fax (353) 061 - 368 622

Bunratty Shamrock Hotel — Bunratty 12 km
115 rooms, D 163 €
Tel (353) 061 - 361 177, Fax (353) 061 - 471 252

RESTAURANTS RESTAURANT

Earl of Thomond, Tel (353) 061 - 368 144 — on site

Weavers Inn — Newmarket-on-Fergus 1,5 km
Tel(353) 061 - 368 482

DRUIDS GLEN

16 | 9 | 7

You might easily imagine the club-house here in a chic suburb of London. It is certainly impressive for comfort, but it lacks Irish warmth. Likewise, you might find this course just about anywhere in the United States, and the very American style is compounded by the necessity to be practised in the art of target golf. These remarks come to mind only because of the course's stated cultural identity, as the problem for any foreign visitor is to decipher the signposts showing the way here - they are all written in Gaelic. With this said, we are talking about an excellent and often intimidating course, notably the 12th, 13th and 14th (another Amen corner), the only holes that are really hilly and often less challenging than they look, at least if you avoid playing the "tiger-tees" and stick more or less to the fairway. Very spectacular and always extremely well kept, this luxury course is well worth a close inspection.

On imaginerait bien le Club-house dans la banlieue chic de Londres. Il est certes impressionnant de confort, mais il manque la chaleur irlandaise. De même, on pourrait trouver le parcours n'importe où aux USA, son style très américain étant accentué par la nécessité de jouer un "target golf". Ces remarques ne viennent à l'esprit qu'en raison de l'identité culturelle affichée : le problème pour un étranger est de déchiffrer les panneaux pour y parvenir, ceux-ci étant exclusivement rédigés en gaëlique. Cela dit, il reste un excellent parcours, souvent très intimidant, notamment aux 12, 13 et 14 (l'Amen Corner), seuls trous au relief vraiment accidenté, mais souvent moins exigeant qu'il n'y paraît, si l'on évite du moins les départs de championnat, et si l'on ne s'écarte pas trop de la piste. Très spectaculaire, et toujours aussi remarquablement entretenu, ce parcours de grand luxe mérite une visite attentive.

Druids Glen Golf Club — 1995

IRL - NEWTOWN MOUNT KENNEDY, Co Wicklow

Office	Secrétariat	(353) 01 - 287 3600
Pro shop	Pro-shop	(353) 01 - 287 3600
Fax	Fax	(353) 01 - 287 3699
Web	www.druidsglen.ie	
Situation	Situation	

2 km from Kilcoole - 35 km from Dublin (pop. 481 854)

Annual closure	Fermeture annuelle	no
Weekly closure	Fermeture hebdomadaire	no

Fees main season Tarifs haute saison	18 holes	
	Week days Semaine	**We/Bank holidays** We/Férié
Individual Individuel	114 €	114 €
Couple Couple	228 €	228 €

Softspikes only - Before 9.30 am, 83 €

Caddy	Caddy	32 € /on request
Electric Trolley	Chariot électrique	no
Buggy	Voiturette	38 € /18 holes
Clubs	Clubs	19 € /18 holes

Credit cards Cartes de crédit
VISA - Eurocard - DC - AMEX

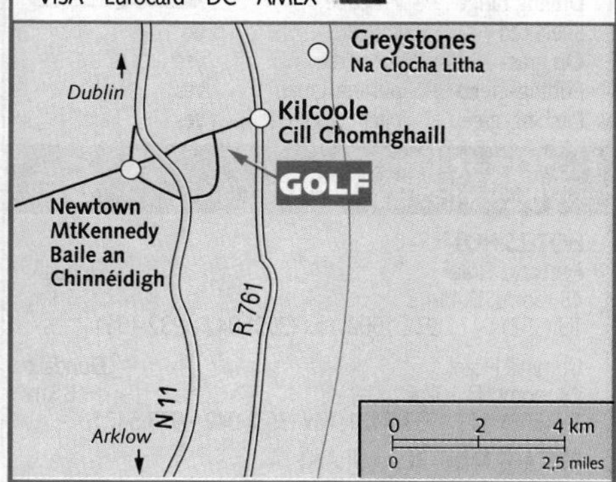

Access Accès : Dublin, N11 South.
Turn left at Newtown Mt Kennedy (signpost). Golf 2 km
Map 3 on page 824 Carte 3 Page 824

Golf course — PARCOURS — 16/20

Site	Site	
Maintenance	Entretien	
Architect	Architecte	Pat Ruddy M. Craddock
Type	Type	parkland
Relief	Relief	
Water in play	Eau en jeu	
Exp. to wind	Exposé au vent	
Trees in play	Arbres en jeu	

Scorecard Carte de score	**Chp.** Chp.	**Mens** Mess.	**Ladies** Da.
Length Long.	6416	5997	4773
Par	72	72	72
Slope system	—	—	—

Advised golfing ability 0 12 24 36
Niveau de jeu recommandé

Hcp required Handicap exigé no

Club house & amenities — CLUB HOUSE ET ANNEXES — 9/10

Pro shop	Pro-shop	
Driving range	Practice	
Sheltered	couvert	no
On grass	sur herbe	yes
Putting-green	putting-green	yes
Pitching-green	pitching green	yes

Hotel facilities — ENVIRONNEMENT HOTELIER — 7/10

HOTELS HÔTELS

Glenview Hotel, 73 rooms, D 178 € — Glen of the Downs
Tel (353) 01 - 287 3399, Fax (353) 01 - 287 7511 — 8 km

Tinakilly House Hotel — Rathnew
29 rooms, D 190 € — 15 km
Tel (353) 0404 - 69 274, Fax (353) 0404 - 67 806

Hunter's Hotel, 16 rooms, D 140 € — Rathnew
Tel (353) 0404 - 40 106, Fax (353) 0404 - 40 338 — 15 km

RESTAURANTS RESTAURANT

Hungry Monk — Greystones
Tel (353) 01 - 287 5759 — 6 km

Cooper's, Tel (353) 01 - 287 3914 — Greystones 6 km

DUNDALK

15 | 6 | 6

On a road linking some of the very greatest Irish courses, Dundalk is located between County Louth and Royal County Down. You certainly won't be wasting your time stopping off here, in the shadow of the Cooley Mountains and with the Mountains of Mourne in the background. Rejuvenated by Alliss and Thomas, this is still one of the country's most under-rated inland courses. Firstly, it is a course to test your driver, with a few long and very tough par 4s and strategically located fairway bunkers. The architects have also tightened the entrances to many of the greens, thus attaching greater importance to spot-on second shots, which are, nonetheless, made easier by the elimination of blind approaches. A generally very open course, you need to get into your stride right away, as many of the difficulties are concentrated over the first seven holes. With little difference between the white and yellow tees, there's every chance that inexperienced golfers will find this tough going score-wise.

Sur une route des très grands parcours d'Irlande, Dundalk se situe entre County Louth et Royal County Down, mais l'on ne perdra pas son temps en marquant une halte ici, à l'ombre des Cooley Mountains, avec au loin les Mountains of Mourne. Rajeuni par Peter Alliss et Dave Thomas, c'est toujours l'un des "inland " les plus sous-estimés du pays. C'est d'abord un parcours pour tester les drivers, avec quelques longs par 4 très difficiles, et des bunkers de fairway très stratégiques. Les architectes ont aussi rétréci les entrées de beaucoup de greens, ce qui accentue la nécessité de seconds coups précis, mais facilités par l'élimination des coups aveugles. Généralement très ouvert, il oblige à prendre vite le rythme, avec une forte concentration des difficultés sur les sept premiers trous. Il y a peu de différences entre les départs arrière et les départs hommes normaux : les golfeurs peu expérimentés auront du mal à y scorer...

Dundalk Golf Club — 1904

Blackrock
IRL - DUNDALK, Co Louth

Office	Secrétariat	(353) 042 - 932 731
Pro shop	Pro-shop	(353) 042 - 932 731
Fax	Fax	(353) 042 - 932 2022
Web	www.eiresoft.com/dundalkgc	
Situation	Situation	
5 km S. of Dundalk	(pop. 25 762)	
Annual closure	Fermeture annuelle	no
Weekly closure	Fermeture hebdomadaire	no

Fees main season Tarifs haute saison		full day
	Week days Semaine	**We/Bank holidays** We/Férié
Individual Individuel	38 €	44 €
Couple Couple	76 €	88 €
Caddy	Caddy	13 € /18 holes
Electric Trolley	Chariot électrique	13 € /18 holes
Buggy	Voiturette	32 € /18 holes
Clubs	Clubs	19 € /18 holes

Credit cards Cartes de crédit
VISA - Eurocard - MasterCard

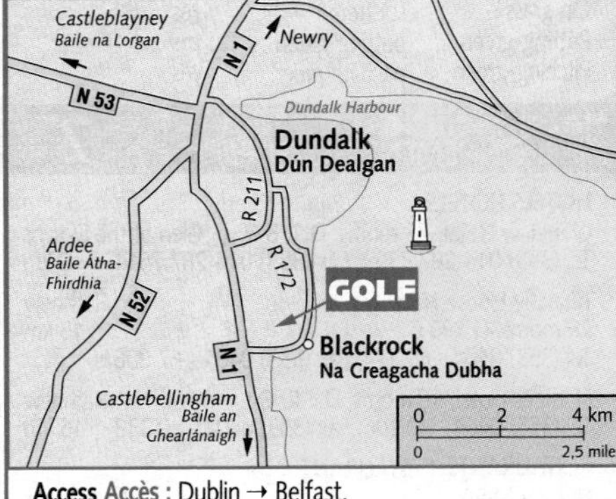

Access Accès : Dublin → Belfast,
1 km N. of Blackrock Village
Map 1 on page 821 Carte 1 Page 821

Golf course PARCOURS — 15/20

Site	Site	
Maintenance	Entretien	
Architect	Architecte	T. Shannon Alliss & Thomas
Type	Type	inland, parkland
Relief	Relief	
Water in play	Eau en jeu	
Exp. to wind	Exposé au vent	
Trees in play	Arbres en jeu	

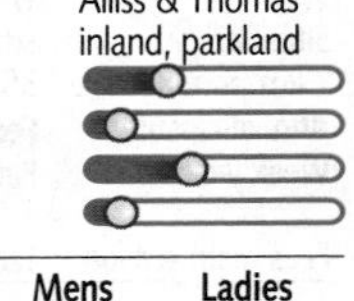

Scorecard Carte de score	**Chp.** Chp.	**Mens** Mess.	**Ladies** Da.
Length Long.	6160	6028	5134
Par	72	72	73
Slope system	—	—	—

Advised golfing ability Niveau de jeu recommandé — 0 12 24 36
Hcp required Handicap exigé — 28 Men, 36 Ladies

Club house & amenities CLUB HOUSE ET ANNEXES — 6/10

Pro shop	Pro-shop	
Driving range	Practice	
Sheltered	couvert	no
On grass	sur herbe	yes
Putting-green	putting-green	yes
Pitching-green	pitching green	yes

Hotel facilities ENVIRONNEMENT HOTELIER — 6/10

HOTELS HÔTELS

Fairways Hotel — Dundalk
48 rooms, D 114 € — 1 km
Tel (353) 042 - 932 1500, Fax (353) 042 - 932 1511

Derryhill Hotel — Dundalk
23 rooms, D 102 € — 8 km
Tel (353) 042 - 933 5471, Fax (353) 042 - 933 5471

RESTAURANTS RESTAURANT

Mashie + Spoon — on site
Tel (353) 042 - 932 2255

Jade Garden — Dundalk
Tel (353) 042 - 933 0378 — 5 km

ELM PARK

13	7	8

After an impressive drive up to the club-house past twenty or so tennis courts, you feel very much in a club here, where silence is almost guaranteed by the vicinity of St. Vincent's Hospital and the keen air of Dublin Bay. Strangely enough, the course begins with a par 3 that is not to be under-estimated, as two trees threaten the tee shot. In fact they give you some idea of the landscape ahead, compounded by a meandering stream which is in play on almost half the holes and devours any mis-hit shot. The city park atmosphere is confirmed by the virtual absence of rough, so it's fair to say that a good score is a distinct possibility. Yet the impression of this being an easy course is soon dented by some well-located bunkers and greens in any number of shapes and contours that call for cool-thinking when planning your approach shot. Variety is also to the fore in the layout of each hole, with things coming to a head over the finishing holes where a whole string of difficulties can easily ruin your card or swing the match.

Après une arrivée impressionnante et la vue d'une vingtaine de courts de tennis, on se sent bien dans un club où le silence est presque garanti par la proximité de St. Vincent's Hospital, et l'air vif par Dublin Bay. Assez curieusement, le parcours débute par un par 3 à ne pas sous-estimer, deux arbres menaçant le tee-shot. Ils donnent d'ailleurs une idée de l'environnement à venir, auquel s'ajoutent vite les méandres d'un petit cours d'eau, en jeu sur près de la moitié des trous, et fort gourmand en balles. L'atmosphère de grand parc citadin est confirmée par l'absence quasi totale de rough dans le jeu, favorisant la qualité des scores, il faut bien le dire. Cependant, l'impression de facilité est vite contrée par des bunkers bien placés, et par la variété de formes et d'ondulations des greens, obligeant à réfléchir sur le choix du type d'approche. De fait, la variété est aussi au niveau du tracé de chaque trou, en plaçant un accent aigu sur le finale, où l'enchaînement des difficultés dans les derniers trous peut facilement faire basculer un score ou un match.

Elm Park Golf Club — 1925

Nutley House, Nutley Lane
IRL - DONNYBROOK, DUBLIN 4

Office	Secrétariat	(353) 01 - 269 3438
Pro shop	Pro-shop	(353) 01 - 269 2650
Fax	Fax	(353) 01 - 269 4505
E-mail	office@elmparkgolfclub.ie	
Situation	Situation	
Dublin (pop. 481 854), 7 km		
Annual closure	Fermeture annuelle	no
Weekly closure	Fermeture hebdomadaire	no

Fees main season Tarifs haute saison	18 holes	
	Week days Semaine	**We/Bank holidays** We/Férié
Individual Individuel	57 €	70 €
Couple Couple	114 €	140 €
Caddy Caddy	25 €	
Electric Trolley Chariot électrique	no	
Buggy Voiturette	on request	
Clubs Clubs	15 €	

Credit cards Cartes de crédit
VISA - Eurocard - MasterCard

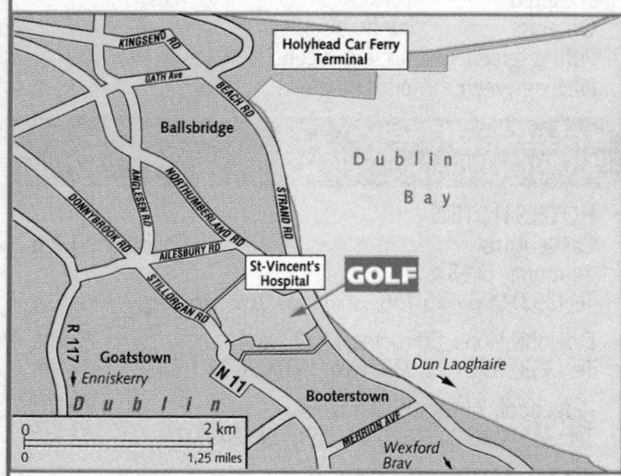

Access Accès : Dublin → Dun Laoghaire. Stillorgan Road (dual carriage way), turn off onto Nutley Lane. Golf course besides St. Vincent's Hospital.
Map 3 on page 824 Carte 3 Page 824

Golf course — PARCOURS — 13/20

Site	Site	
Maintenance	Entretien	
Architect	Architecte	Unknown
Type	Type	parkland
Relief	Relief	
Water in play	Eau en jeu	
Exp. to wind	Exposé au vent	
Trees in play	Arbres en jeu	

Scorecard Carte de score	**Chp.** Chp.	**Mens** Mess.	**Ladies** Da.
Length Long.	5355	5150	4974
Par	69	69	72
Slope system	—	—	—

Advised golfing ability Niveau de jeu recommandé: 0 12 24 36
Hcp required Handicap exigé: no

Club house & amenities — CLUB HOUSE ET ANNEXES — 7/10

Pro shop	Pro-shop	
Driving range	Practice	
Sheltered	couvert	6 mats
On grass	sur herbe	yes
Putting-green	putting-green	yes
Pitching-green	pitching green	yes

Hotel facilities — ENVIRONNEMENT HOTELIER — 8/10

HOTELS HÔTELS

Doyne Montrose Hotel, 179 rooms, D 102 € — Dublin
Tel (353) 01 - 269 3311, Fax (353) 01 - 269 1164 — 2 km

Jurys Hotel, 394 rooms, D 241 € — Dublin
Tel (353) 01 - 660 5000, Fax (353) 01 - 660 5540 — 5 km

Burlington Hotel, 451 rooms, D 229 € — Dublin
Tel (353) 01 - 660 5222, Fax (353) 01 - 660 3172 — 6 km

RESTAURANTS RESTAURANT

Da Vincenzo, Tel (353) 01 - 660 9906 — Dublin 3 km
Beaufield News, Tel (353) 01 - 288 0375 — Skillorgan 3 km
Roly's Bistro, Tel (353) 01 - 668 2611 — Dublin 5 km

ENNISCRONE

17 | 8 | 6

For many a year, Enniscrone was one of the least known links in Ireland. The rediscovery of this region has pulled it out of the shadows, as has the opening of nine new holes, a welcome addition in that the course sometimes lacked the subtle features associated with the greatest links courses. It is well worth the trip even though it can be a little tiring to walk. Some holes here have been redesigned and added to, while a whole series of holes have been laid out in the sand-dunes by Donald Steel, who has succeeded in preserving the feel of the original design by Eddie Hackett dating from 1974. Excursions into a lunar and quite spectacular landscape are much more adventurous, and your driving and ironwork here will need to be both daring and accurate. The wind off the sea can easily make Enniscrone doubly challenging and spoil the ambitions of many a hardy soul; in this case only experienced players can hope to make any impression. The others can say that they played a great course while the whole party sit down to admire the setting sun.

Enniscrone a longtemps été l'un des links les plus méconnus d'Irlande. La redécouverte de cette région l'a placé au premier plan, ainsi que la création de neuf nouveaux trous , très bienvenue car le parcours manquait parfois des subtilités des plus grands links. Il mérite plus encore le détour, même s'il reste parfois un peu fatigant à pied. Certains trous existants ont été revus et complétés, et toute une série de trous construits dans les dunes par Donald Steel, qui a su préserver l'esprit du dessin d'Eddie Hackett effectué en 1974. Les voyages dans un paysage à la fois lunaire et spectaculaire sont bien plus aventureux, où le driving comme le jeu de fers devront être aussi audacieux que précis. Le vent venu de l'océan tout proche peut facilement doubler l'exigence d'Enniscrone et contrecarrer les ambitions des téméraires : seuls les joueurs expérimentés pourront alors espérer s'imposer. Les autres pourront se dire qu'ils ont joué un beau parcours, tout en contemplant avec leurs vainqueurs le coucher du soleil.

Enniscrone Golf Club — 1925

IRL - ENNISCRONE, Co Sligo

Office	Secrétariat	(353) 096 - 36 297
Pro shop	Pro-shop	(353) 096 - 36 297
Fax	Fax	(353) 096 - 36 657
Web		www.homepage.eircom.net/~enniscronegolf
Situation	Situation	

13 km N of Ballina (pop. 6 852)

Annual closure	Fermeture annuelle	no
Weekly closure	Fermeture hebdomadaire	no

Fees main season Tarifs haute saison	18 holes	
	Week days Semaine	We/Bank holidays We/Férié
Individual Individuel	38 €	51 €
Couple Couple	76 €	102 €

Caddy	Caddy	13 € /18 holes
Electric Trolley	Chariot électrique	no
Buggy	Voiturette	25 € /18 holes
Clubs	Clubs	15 €

Credit cards Cartes de crédit
VISA - Eurocard - Mastercard

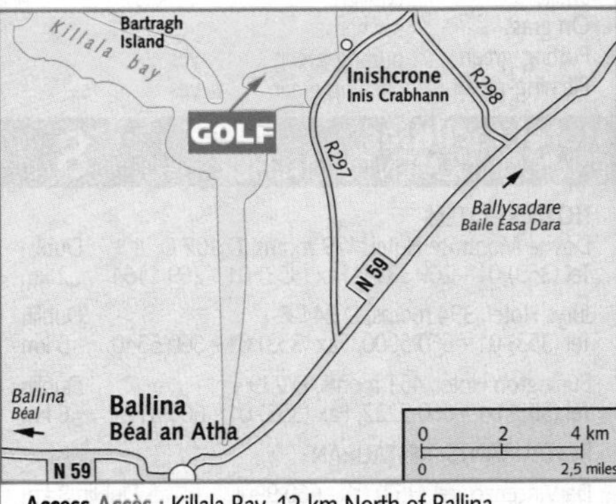

Access Accès : Killala Bay, 12 km North of Ballina
Map 1 on page 820 Carte 1 Page 820

Golf course PARCOURS — 17/20

Site	Site	
Maintenance	Entretien	
Architect	Architecte	Eddie Hackett
Type	Type	seaside course, links
Relief	Relief	
Water in play	Eau en jeu	
Exp. to wind	Exposé au vent	
Trees in play	Arbres en jeu	

Scorecard Carte de score	Chp. Chp.	Mens Mess.	Ladies Da.
Length Long.	6190	5900	5050
Par	72	72	73
Slope system	—	—	—

Advised golfing ability Niveau de jeu recommandé — 0 12 24 36

Hcp required Handicap exigé — 28 Men, 36 Ladies

Club house & amenities CLUB HOUSE ET ANNEXES — 8/10

Pro shop	Pro-shop	
Driving range	Practice	
Sheltered	couvert	6 mats
On grass	sur herbe	yes
Putting-green	putting-green	yes
Pitching-green	pitching green	no

Hotel facilities ENVIRONNEMENT HOTELIER — 6/10

HOTELS HÔTELS

Castle Arms — Enniscrone 1 km
24 rooms, D 63 €
Tel (353) 096 - 36 156, Fax (353) 096 - 36 156

Downhill Hotel, 50 rooms, D 127 € — Ballina 13 km
Tel (353) 096 - 21 033, Fax (353) 096 - 21 338

Ridgepool, 71 rooms, D 152 € — Ballina 13 km
Tel (353) 096 24 600, Fax (353) 096 24 602

RESTAURANTS RESTAURANT

Clark's, Tel (353) 096 - 36 405 — Enniscrone adjacent

Alpine Hotel — Enniscrone adjacent
Tel (353) 096 - 36 252

ESKER HILLS

14	6	6

The terrain here was perfect for building a golf course, full of sand and gravel deposited by an ancient glacier. The drainage system is obviously excellent, running ground-water off to the natural lakes used abundantly by Christy O'Connor Jr., who has also made excellent use of the many pre-existing trees. Winding their way through alternating hillocks and valleys, the course's very distinctive 18 holes have retained their pleasantly natural appearance. As usual with O'Connor, the fairways are wide open, bunkers are carefully shaped and placed, and the greens are on the large size without any excessive contouring so as to allow every kind of approach shot. As all hazards are generally in full view, you will enjoy playing here first time out and certainly leave you wanting to come back here to this central part of Ireland, the cradle of Irish civilisation. When you do, you will want to stop off at nearby Kilbeggan, home to a famous whiskey museum, a beverage which, so we were told, is as inseparable from life as golf itself.

Le terrain était très favorable à la construction d'un parcours, avec une large proportion de sable et de gravier déposés par un ancien glacier. Evidemment, le drainage y est excellent, vers des lacs naturels utilisés par Christy O'Connor Jr avec gourmandise, tout comme pas mal d'arbres déjà sur place. De petites collines et vallées alternent, où s'insinuent 18 trous bien caractérisés, qui ont conservé un caractère plaisament naturel. Comme d'habitude avec l'architecte, les fairways sont généreux, les bunkers bien travaillés et positionnés, les greens assez grands et sans ondulations excessives appellent tous les types d'approches. Et comme les obstacles sont généralement bien visibles, dès la première fois, on prendra plaisir à jouer, pour se donner le goût de revenir dans cette région du centre, berceau de la civilisation irlandaise. En s'arrêtant à Kilbeggan, tout proche, où se trouve un fameux musée du whiskey, aussi inséparable de la vie que le golf, nous dit-on.

Esker Hills Golf Club — 1996

IRL - TULLAMORE, Co. Offaly

Office	Secrétariat	(353) 0506 - 55 999
Pro shop	Pro-shop	(353) 0506 - 55 999
Fax	Fax	(353) 0506 - 55 021
Web	www.eskerhillsgolf.com	
Situation	Situation	

5 km N. of Tullamore (pop. 9 220)

Annual closure	Fermeture annuelle	no
Weekly closure	Fermeture hebdomadaire	no

Fees main season Tarifs haute saison	18 holes Week days Semaine	We/Bank holidays We/Férié
Individual Individuel	25 €	34 €
Couple Couple	50 €	68 €

Caddy	Caddy	25 € /on request
Electric Trolley	Chariot électrique	9 €
Buggy	Voiturette	25 €
Clubs	Clubs IR£ 10	

Credit cards Cartes de crédit
VISA - MasterCard

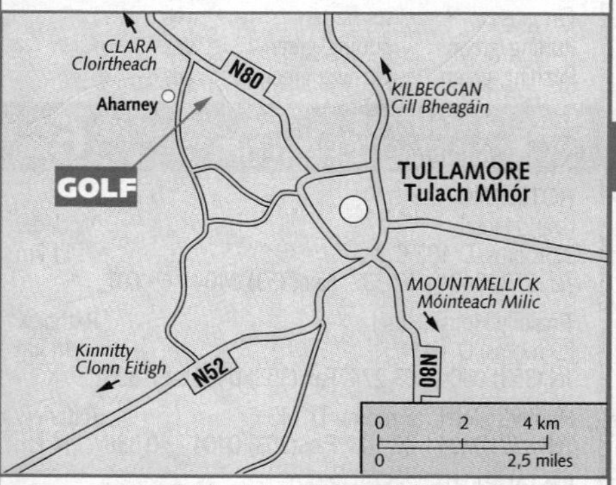

Access Accès : Dublin, N4 → Kinnegad. N6 → Kilbeggan. N52 → Tullamore then N80 North → Clara.
Map 2 on page 823 Carte 2 Page 823

Golf course PARCOURS — 14/20

Site	Site	
Maintenance	Entretien	
Architect	Architecte	Christy O'Connor Jr
Type	Type	parkland, inland
Relief	Relief	
Water in play	Eau en jeu	
Exp. to wind	Exposé au vent	
Trees in play	Arbres en jeu	

Scorecard Carte de score	Chp. Chp.	Mens Mess.	Ladies Da.
Length Long.	6003	5563	4540
Par	71	71	72
Slope system	—	—	—

Advised golfing ability Niveau de jeu recommandé — 0 12 24 36
Hcp required Handicap exigé — no

Club house & amenities CLUB HOUSE ET ANNEXES — 6/10

Pro shop	Pro-shop	
Driving range	Practice	
Sheltered	couvert	no
On grass	sur herbe	no
Putting-green	putting-green	yes
Pitching-green	pitching green	yes

Hotel facilities ENVIRONNEMENT HOTELIER — 6/10

HOTELS HÔTELS

Bridge House Hotel — Tullamore 5 km
72 rooms, D 140 €
Tel (353) 0506-22 000, Fax (353) 0506-25 690

Tullamore Court Hotel — Tullamore 10 km
72 rooms, D 190 €
Tel (353) 0506-46 666, Fax (353) 0506-46 677

Moorhill House Hotel, 12 rooms, D 76 € — Tullamore 8 km
Tel (353) 0506 - 21 395, Fax (353) 0506 - 52 424

RESTAURANTS RESTAURANT

Moorhill House, Tel (353) 0506 - 21 395 — Tullamore 8 km
Tullamore Court, Tel (353) 0506-46 666 — Tullamore 10 km

EUROPEAN (THE)

18 | 5 | 6

How a site like this remained unknown until the late 1980s will always be a mystery. The creation of "The European" was the work of Pat Ruddy, a professional, enthusiast, journalist and course designer. This is his masterpiece, and looks almost hand-made. Between the dunes, the beach, the fairways, the greens and the bunkers bolstered by railway line sleepers (the sand-wedge is the only way out), there was just enough room for a little marsh and a water hazard that is as worrying as it is unexpected. This course is a great trip to the land of golf where each round is so varied, so demanding and so exciting that no-one would care to mention the layout's one or two weaknesses. It takes time to appreciate the course's finer points, but the only thing on your mind when leaving is knowing when you can come back. The atmosphere of freshness and golfing purism that reigns here is the icing on the cake, as opposed to clubs where personal wealth seems to be the only criterion for playing. But the green-fee is now very high, as it is everywhere else...

Comment un site aussi magnifique est resté ignoré jusqu'à la fin des années 1980 restera un éternel mystère. La création de "The European" est dûe à Pat Ruddy, enthousiaste professionnel, journaliste et architecte. C'est son chef-d'oeuvre, donnant l'impression d'avoir été fait à la main. Entre les dunes, la plage, les fairways, les greens et des bunkers renforcés de traverses de chemin de fer (sandwedge obligatoire), il restait à peine place pour un petit marais, et pour un obstacle d'eau aussi préoccupant qu'inattendu. Ce parcours est un grand voyage au pays du golf, où l'on n'a pas le courage de relever quelques faiblesses de dessin tant le jeu y est varié, exigeant, excitant. Il faut du temps pour en apprécier toutes les nuances, mais on a une seule idée en le quittant, c'est d'y revenir. L'atmosphère de fraîcheur et de purisme golfique qui règne ici est la cerise sur un gâteau, à l'opposé de clubs où la fortune paraît le seul critère pour jouer. Il est vrai aussi que le green-fee n'est plus donné...

The European Club — 1989

IRL - BRITTAS BAY, Co Wicklow

Office Secrétariat (353) 0404 - 47 415
Pro shop Pro-shop (353) 0404 - 47 415
Fax Fax (353) 0404 - 47 449
E-mail info@theeuropeanclunb.com
Situation Situation
12 km from Wicklow (pop. 6 416), 10 km from Arklow
Annual closure Fermeture annuelle — no
Weekly closure Fermeture hebdomadaire — no

860

Fees main season Tarifs haute saison	18 holes	
	Week days Semaine	We/Bank holidays We/Férié
Individual Individuel	102 €	102 €
Couple Couple	204 €	204 €

Caddy Caddy	19 € /18 holes
Electric Trolley Chariot électrique	no
Buggy Voiturette	32 € /18 holes
Clubs Clubs	25 € /18 holes

Credit cards Cartes de crédit
VISA - Eurocard - MasterCard

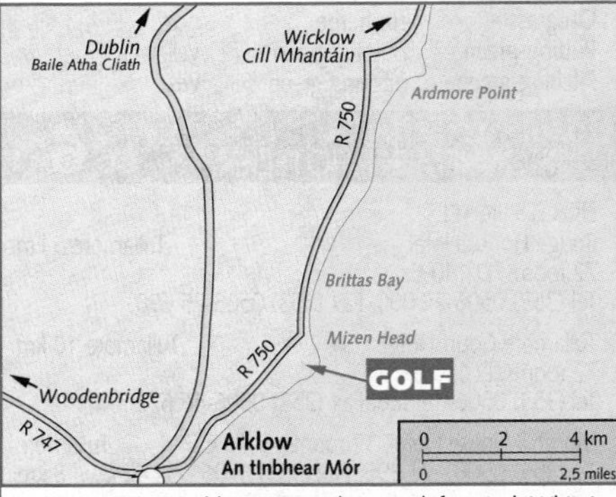

Access Accès : Dublin, N11. 56 km turn left at Jack White's Inn. Turn right at T Junction → Brittas Bay. 2 km
Map 3 on page 824 Carte 3 Page 824

Golf course PARCOURS — 18/20

Site	Site	
Maintenance	Entretien	
Architect	Architecte	Pat Ruddy
Type	Type	links
Relief	Relief	
Water in play	Eau en jeu	
Exp. to wind	Exposé au vent	
Trees in play	Arbres en jeu	

Scorecard Carte de score	Chp. Chp.	Mens Mess.	Ladies Da.
Length Long.	6187	5922	5153
Par	71	71	71
Slope system	—	—	—

Advised golfing ability Niveau de jeu recommandé — 0 12 24 36
Hcp required Handicap exigé — no

Club house & amenities CLUB HOUSE ET ANNEXES — 5/10

Pro shop	Pro-shop	
Driving range	Practice	
Sheltered	couvert	under construction
On grass	sur herbe	yes
Putting-green	putting-green	yes
Pitching-green	pitching green	yes

Hotel facilities ENVIRONNEMENT HOTELIER — 6/10

HOTELS HÔTELS

Grand Hotel — Wicklow 11 km
32 rooms, D 102 €
Tel (353) 0404 - 67 337, Fax (353) 0404 - 69 607

Tinakilly House Hotel — Rathnew 14 km
29 rooms, D 190 €
Tel (353) 0404 - 69 274, Fax (353) 0404 - 67 806

Hunter's Hotel, 16 rooms, D 140 € — Rathnew 14 km
Tel (353) 0404 - 40 106, Fax (353) 0404 - 40 338

RESTAURANTS RESTAURANT

Old Rectory, Tel (353) 0404 - 67 048 — Wicklow 12 km
Tinakilly House, Tel (353) 0404 - 69 274 — Rathnew 14 km

FAITHLEGG

13 | 7 | 7

The south-eastern coast is not the most popular with golftrotters, and that's a good reason for discovering the region once you have visited the rest. Faithlegg was laid out over a former estate, as you can see with the old trees, which outline the fairways, the enclosure wall and the gardens. They add extra style and difficulties to the course as a whole. The architect has designed a very varied layout with no excessively steep hills, although some hazards are hardly visible and so complicate matters slightly in terms of strategy. With this said, they only await the really wayward shot. This is an averagely difficult and very competent course, the one criticism being the very ordinary bunkers with sand a little on the coarse side. However, you can get round the course quickly, as the rough is lenient and the undergrowth kept neatly trimmed. Faithlegg has been the site of the Irish Ladies Open.

La côte Sud-Est n'est pas la plus fréquentée par les touristes golfiques, c'est une bonne raison de l'explorer quand vous aurez parcouru les régions plus classiques. Faithlegg a été construit dans une ancienne propriété, comme on le remarque avec les arbres très adultes qui définissent les trous, le mur d'enceinte et les jardins : ils apportent une beauté supplémentaire et quelques difficultés au parcours. L'architecte a conçu un tracé très varié, sans reliefs excessifs, certains obstacles d'eau par exemple ne sont guère visibles, ce qui complique légèrement la stratégie, mais ils ne recueillent que les balles très écartées du bon chemin. De difficulté moyenne, c'est une réalisation sérieuse. On peut cependant estimer que la forme des bunkers ne sort pas de l'ordinaire, et que le sable pourrait être plus fin. En revanche, la vitesse de jeu est garantie par la clémence des roughs et le bon entretien des sous-bois. Ce parcours a reçu l'Irish Ladies Open.

Faithlegg Golf Club — 1992

IRL - FAITHLEGG, Co. Waterford

Office	Secrétariat	(353) 051 - 382 241
Pro shop	Pro-shop	(353) 051 - 382 241
Fax	Fax	(353) 051 - 382 664
Web	—	
Situation	Situation	
7 km from Waterford (pop. 42 540)		
Annual closure	Fermeture annuelle	no
Weekly closure	Fermeture hebdomadaire	no

Fees main season Tarifs haute saison	18 holes	
	Week days Semaine	**We/Bank holidays** We/Férié
Individual Individuel	32 €	44 €
Couple Couple	64 €	88 €

Caddy	Caddy	13 € /on request
Electric Trolley	Chariot électrique	no
Buggy	Voiturette	25 € /18 holes
Clubs	Clubs	13 €

Credit cards Cartes de crédit
VISA - MasterCard

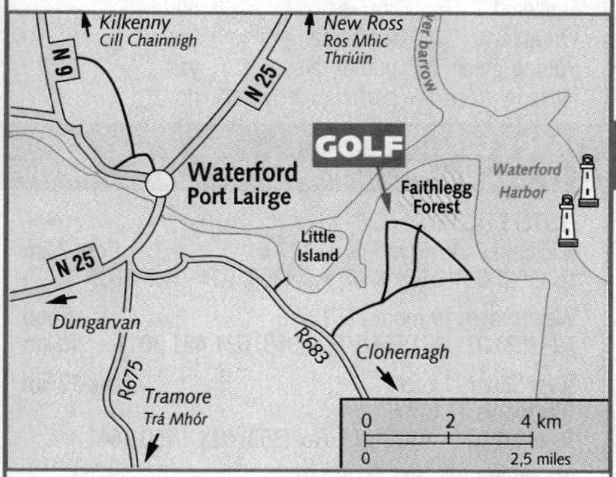

Access Accès : Waterford, R683
Map 2 on page 823 Carte 2 Page 823

Golf course — PARCOURS — 13/20

Site	Site	
Maintenance	Entretien	
Architect	Architecte	Patrick Merrigan
Type	Type	parkland
Relief	Relief	
Water in play	Eau en jeu	
Exp. to wind	Exposé au vent	
Trees in play	Arbres en jeu	

Scorecard Carte de score	**Chp.** Chp.	**Mens** Mess.	**Ladies** Da.
Length Long.	6057	5712	5160
Par	72	72	73
Slope system	—	—	—

Advised golfing ability Niveau de jeu recommandé: 0 12 24 36
Hcp required Handicap exigé: no

Club house & amenities — CLUB HOUSE ET ANNEXES — 7/10

Pro shop	Pro-shop	
Driving range	Practice	
Sheltered	couvert	no
On grass	sur herbe	yes
Putting-green	putting-green	yes
Pitching-green	pitching green	no

Hotel facilities — ENVIRONNEMENT HOTELIER — 7/10

HOTELS HÔTELS

Faithlegg Hotel, 82 rooms, D 178 € — Waterford
Tel (353) 051 382 000, Fax (353) 051 382 010 — on site

Tower Hotel, 141 rooms, D 114 € — Waterford
Tel (353) 051 - 875 801, Fax (353) 051 - 870 129 — 7 km

Granville Hotel, 74 rooms, D 102 € — Waterford
Tel (353) 051 - 305 555, Fax (353) 051 - 305 566 — 7 km

RESTAURANTS RESTAURANT

Dwyer's — Waterford
Tel (353) 051 - 77 478 — 7 km

Prendiville's — Waterford
Tel (353) 051 - 78 851 — 7 km

FOTA ISLAND

16	7	6

This is the brainchild of Kevin Mulcahy, the son of the founder of Waterville, and now the property of Mt Juliet owners. It is not a links, but it makes no difference, and the designers McEvoy and O'Connor Jnr. have made a point of including some seaside features like pot bunkers and a double green, amongst the many other difficulties. For the new owners and the venue of the Irish Open, Jeff Howes has remodeled all the greens, and redesigned more or less 8 holes. You often see water (as far as the port of Cork) but it still only comes into play on half a dozen holes. The other hazards are primarily trees, green-side bunkers and a few stone walls here and there. This course is now more suitable for better players, who can make their choice between lofted and ground shots. Here, you hone your short game and play with your brains. You will also see a few ostriches, monkeys or llamas roaming in the adjacent natural park.

C'est l'enfant de Kevin Mulcahy, fils du fondateur de Waterville, et racheté depuis par les propriétaires de Mt Juliet. Que ce ne soit pas un links n'enlève rien à ses qualités, et les architectes McEvoy et O'Connor Jr n'ont pas manqué d'en citer quelques traits, comme quelques pot-bunkers et un double-green, parmi bien d'autres difficultés. Pour les nouveaux occupants des lieux et l'organisation ici de l'Irish Open, Jeff Howes a remodelé tous les greens et plus ou moins huit trous. On voit souvent l'eau (jusqu'au port de Cork), elle ne vient réellement en jeu que sur une demi-douzaine de trous, et de manière dangereuse au 12, au 14 et au 18. Les autres obstacles sont principalement de grands arbres, les bunkers de green et un petit mur çà et là. Ce parcours conviendra mieux encore maintenant aux joueurs de bon niveau, qui sauront faire le choix entre les balles portées (target golf) et les approches roulées. Ici, on travaille son petit jeu, on joue avec sa tête et on peut apercevoir quelques autruches, singes ou lamas en balade hors du parc naturel adjacent.

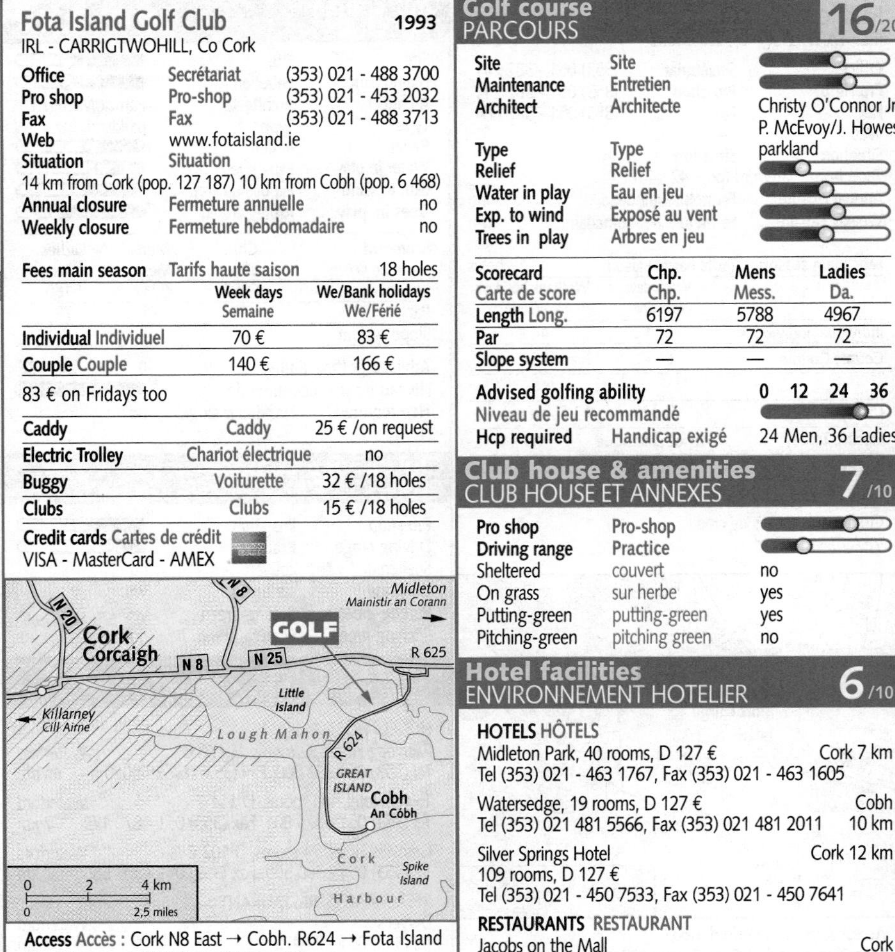

Fota Island Golf Club — 1993

IRL - CARRIGTWOHILL, Co Cork

Office	Secrétariat	(353) 021 - 488 3700
Pro shop	Pro-shop	(353) 021 - 453 2032
Fax	Fax	(353) 021 - 488 3713
Web	www.fotaisland.ie	
Situation	Situation	

14 km from Cork (pop. 127 187) 10 km from Cobh (pop. 6 468)

Annual closure	Fermeture annuelle	no
Weekly closure	Fermeture hebdomadaire	no

Fees main season Tarifs haute saison	18 holes	
	Week days Semaine	**We/Bank holidays** We/Férié
Individual Individuel	70 €	83 €
Couple Couple	140 €	166 €

83 € on Fridays too

Caddy	Caddy	25 € /on request
Electric Trolley	Chariot électrique	no
Buggy	Voiturette	32 € /18 holes
Clubs	Clubs	15 € /18 holes

Credit cards Cartes de crédit
VISA - MasterCard - AMEX

Access Accès : Cork N8 East → Cobh. R624 → Fota Island
Map 2 on page 822 Carte 2 Page 822

Golf course PARCOURS — 16/20

Site	Site	
Maintenance	Entretien	
Architect	Architecte	Christy O'Connor Jr P. McEvoy/J. Howes
Type	Type	parkland
Relief	Relief	
Water in play	Eau en jeu	
Exp. to wind	Exposé au vent	
Trees in play	Arbres en jeu	

Scorecard Carte de score	**Chp.** Chp.	**Mens** Mess.	**Ladies** Da.
Length Long.	6197	5788	4967
Par	72	72	72
Slope system	—	—	—

Advised golfing ability Niveau de jeu recommandé — 0 12 24 36
Hcp required Handicap exigé — 24 Men, 36 Ladies

Club house & amenities CLUB HOUSE ET ANNEXES — 7/10

Pro shop	Pro-shop	
Driving range	Practice	
Sheltered	couvert	no
On grass	sur herbe	yes
Putting-green	putting-green	yes
Pitching-green	pitching green	no

Hotel facilities ENVIRONNEMENT HOTELIER — 6/10

HOTELS HÔTELS

Midleton Park, 40 rooms, D 127 € — Cork 7 km
Tel (353) 021 - 463 1767, Fax (353) 021 - 463 1605

Watersedge, 19 rooms, D 127 € — Cobh 10 km
Tel (353) 021 481 5566, Fax (353) 021 481 2011

Silver Springs Hotel — Cork 12 km
109 rooms, D 127 €
Tel (353) 021 - 450 7533, Fax (353) 021 - 450 7641

RESTAURANTS RESTAURANT

Jacobs on the Mall — Cork 14 km
Tel (353) 021 - 452 1530

Trade Winds, Tel (353) 021 481 3754 — Cobh, 10 km

GALWAY BAY

14 | 7 | 6

Overlooking the Atlantic and the town of Galway, this recent course provides some outstanding viewpoints, but don't let them blur your judgment. The terrain given to Christy O'Connor Jnr. was naturally nothing more than ordinary, but he has made a great job of it and designed in a lot of appeal at the expense of some highly appropriate earthworks. As usual, the bunkers are very well placed and ready to collect any ball that doesn't quite manage to short-cut the dog-legs. There are also three lakes, but there are in play on three holes only. The many tee-off areas spread the range of difficulties, but only the back tees make this a severe test. The general difficulties are clearly visible and game strategy is obvious; this is important because the wind can turn nasty and make it even more essential to know how to play with it and against it. Welcome to a course designed with considerable talent, lacking only that intangible touch of greatness that separates the excellent from the exceptional.

Dominant l'océan et la ville de Galway, ce récent parcours offre des points de vue exceptionnels. Mais ils ne doivent pas influencer le jugement ! Le terrain mis à la disposition de Christy O'Connor Jr était naturellement assez ordinaire, il en a tiré un très bon parti, et l'a même rendu séduisant, au prix de travaux de terrassement très adéquats. Ses bunkers sont comme d'habitude très bien placés, et prêts à accueillir ceux qui ne parviennent pas à couper les dog-legs. De même, trois lacs sont mis en jeu, mais sur trois trous seulement. Les nombreux départs proposent un éventail de difficultés, seuls les départs arrière rendent ce parcours sévère. Les difficultés générales sont bien visibles, et la stratégie de jeu évidente : c'est important car le vent peut devenir méchant, et renforcer encore la nécessité de savoir jouer avec et contre lui. Un parcours réalisé avec talent, auquel ne manque que l'indéfinissable grandeur qui fait les exceptions.

Galway Bay Golf & Country Club — 1993

Renville
IRL - ORANMORE, Co Galway

Office	Secrétariat	(353) 091 - 790 500
Pro shop	Pro-shop	(353) 091 - 790 503
Fax	Fax	(353) 091 - 790 510
Web	www.gbaygolf.com	
Situation	Situation	

5 km from Oranmore - 13 km from Galway (pop. 57 241)

Annual closure	Fermeture annuelle	no
Weekly closure	Fermeture hebdomadaire	no

Fees main season Tarifs haute saison	18 holes	
	Week days Semaine	**We/Bank holidays** We/Férié
Individual Individuel	51 €	57 €
Couple Couple	102 €	114 €

57 € on Fridays too

Caddy	Caddy	25 € /on request
Electric Trolley	Chariot électrique	no
Buggy	Voiturette	25 € /18 holes
Clubs	Clubs	13 €

Credit cards Cartes de crédit
VISA - Eurocard - MasterCard

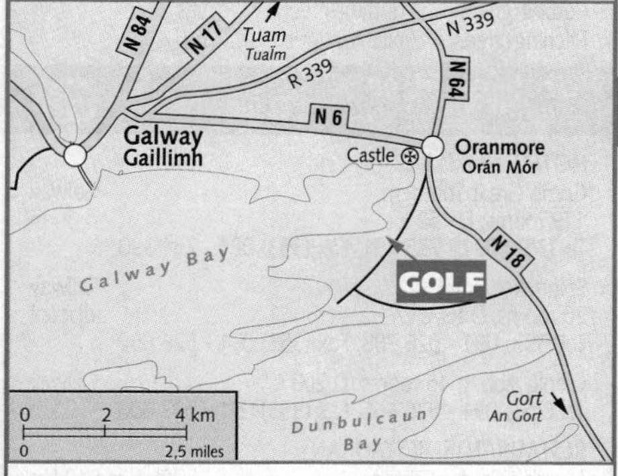

Access Accès : Galway N6 → Oranmore, → Renville
Map 1 on page 820 Carte 1 Page 820

Golf course PARCOURS — 14/20

Site	Site	
Maintenance	Entretien	
Architect	Architecte	Christy O'Connor Jr
Type	Type	seaside course
Relief	Relief	
Water in play	Eau en jeu	
Exp. to wind	Exposé au vent	
Trees in play	Arbres en jeu	

Scorecard Carte de score	**Chp.** Chp.	**Mens** Mess.	**Ladies** Da.
Length Long.	6533	6091	5205
Par	72	72	74
Slope system	—	—	—

Advised golfing ability Niveau de jeu recommandé — 0 12 24 36

Hcp required Handicap exigé — 28 Men, 36 Ladies

Club house & amenities CLUB HOUSE ET ANNEXES — 7/10

Pro shop	Pro-shop	
Driving range	Practice	
Sheltered	couvert	no
On grass	sur herbe	yes
Putting-green	putting-green	yes
Pitching-green	pitching green	yes

Hotel facilities ENVIRONNEMENT HOTELIER — 6/10

HOTELS HÔTELS

Galway Bay Golf & CC, — on site
92 rooms, D 229 €
Tel (353) 065 - 682 3000, Fax (353) 065 - 682 3759

Galway Ryan, 96 rooms, D 165 € — Galway
Tel (353) 091 - 753 181, Fax (353) 091 - 753 187 — 9 km

Oranmore Lodge Hotel — Oranmore
40 rooms, D 114 € — 5 km
Tel (353) 091 - 794 400, Fax (353) 091 - 790 227

RESTAURANTS RESTAURANT

Paddy Burkes, Tel (353) 091 - 796 226 — Clarinbridge 7 k

Galway Bay Golf Club, Tel (353) 091 - 790 500 — on site

GALWAY GC

13 | 6 | 6

We always expect a lot from a great designer such as Alistair Mackenzie, but there's no denying the fact that Galway GC is now in need of a little careful remodelling from a modern designer who can enhance the course's style and spirit. The trees have obviously grown considerably since 1923, compounding the course's general tightness, the only real difficulty for the modern player. Precision play and flighting the ball take precedence over length, to the extent that long-hitters can leave the driver firmly in the bag and card a better score in return. On the other hand, average players will doubtless find the course long enough as it is. The space available was used to good effect and there are a lot of bunkers which are never excessively penalising. If we add to all this the superb views over Galway Bay, Burren and the Aran islands, plus the very busy city of Galway, then there is a welcome for you here.

On attend beaucoup de la signature d'un très grand architecte tel que Alister Mackenzie, mais il faut bien reconnaître que ce parcours mériterait un "lifting" attentif de la part d'un architecte moderne soucieux de lui conserver son esthétique et son esprit. Les arbres ont dû beaucoup pousser depuis 1923, accentuant l'étroitesse du parcours, seule véritable difficulté pour un joueur d'aujourd'hui. La précision et le travail de balle prennent nettement le pas sur la longueur, au point que les longs joueurs pourront laisser le driver dans le sac, avec une incidence favorable sur leur score. En revanche, les joueurs moyens trouveront sans doute la longueur du parcours suffisante ! L'espace disponible a été bien utilisé, le bunkering est important, mais rarement de manière trop pénalisante. Si l'on ajoute les points de vue superbes sur la baie de Galway, le Burren et les Iles d'Arran, et la proximité de la ville très animée de Galway... bienvenue ici.

Galway Golf Club — 1893

Blackrock
IRL - SALTHILL, GALWAY, Co Galway

Office	Secrétariat	(353) 091 - 522 033
Pro shop	Pro-shop	(353) 091 - 523 038
Fax	Fax	(353) 091 - 522 033
Web	—	
Situation	Situation	

2 km from Galway (pop. 57 241)

Annual closure	Fermeture annuelle	no
Weekly closure	Fermeture hebdomadaire	no

Fees main season Tarifs haute saison	Week days Semaine	We/Bank holidays We/Férié (18 holes)
Individual Individuel	32 €	38 €
Couple Couple	64 €	76 €
Caddy Caddy		19 € /on request
Electric Trolley Chariot électrique		6 € /18 holes
Buggy Voiturette		32 € /18 holes
Clubs Clubs		10 € /110 € holes

Credit cards Cartes de crédit
VISA - MasterCard

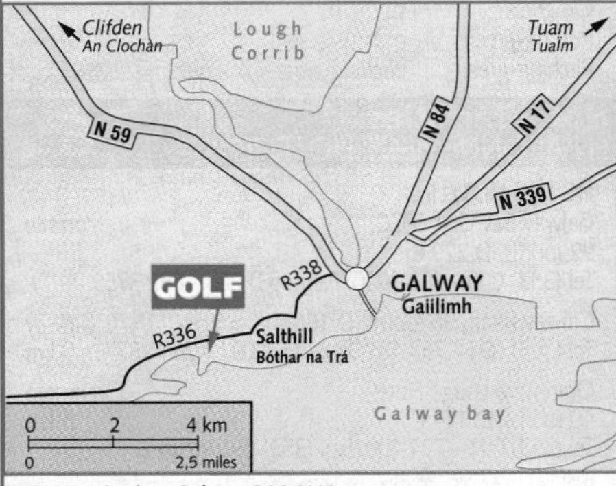

Access Accès : Galway R336 West.
Golf at the end of the Promenade at Salthill.
Map 1 on page 820 Carte 1 Page 820

Golf course PARCOURS — 13/20

Site	Site	
Maintenance	Entretien	
Architect	Architecte	Alistair Mackenzie
Type	Type	seaside course, parkland
Relief	Relief	
Water in play	Eau en jeu	
Exp. to wind	Exposé au vent	
Trees in play	Arbres en jeu	

Scorecard Carte de score	Chp. Chp.	Mens Mess.	Ladies Da.
Length Long.	5832	5598	4752
Par	70	71	73
Slope system	—	—	—

Advised golfing ability Niveau de jeu recommandé: 0 12 24 36
Hcp required Handicap exigé: 28 Men, 36 Ladies

Club house & amenities CLUB HOUSE ET ANNEXES — 6/10

Pro shop	Pro-shop	
Driving range	Practice	
Sheltered	couvert	no
On grass	sur herbe	yes
Putting-green	putting-green	yes
Pitching-green	pitching green	no

Hotel facilities ENVIRONNEMENT HOTELIER — 6/10

HOTELS HÔTELS

Corrib Great Southern — Galway 1 km
179 rooms, D 152 €
Tel (353) 091 - 755 281, Fax (353) 091 - 751 390

Spinnaker Hotel — Galway adjacent
20 rooms, D 89 €
Tel (353) 091 - 526 788, Fax (353) 091 - 526 650

Glenlo Abbey, 45 rooms, D 203 € — Galway 2 km
Tel (353) 091 - 526 666, Fax (353) 091 - 527 800

RESTAURANTS RESTAURANT

Moran's Oyster Cottage — Kilcolgan 10 km
Tel (353) 091 - 796 113

Cavey's Westwood, Tel (353) 091 - 21 442 — Galway 3 km

GLASSON

16 | 7 | 7

Very positively adapting a course to players of all abilities is something you would expect from a fine connoisseur of amateur and professional golf such as Christy O'Connor Jnr. Given a remarkable site, long a favourite haunt of hikers and cyclists, he visibly rose to the occasion, and the views over Lough Ree are as magnificent as his deployment of the course on several holes. Other lakes add to both the course's scenic beauty and difficulty. And if we add to this a lot of very careful design on and around the greens, intelligently placed bunkers and the general balance of the layout, you will understand that this is one of the finest recent additions to the collection of Irish courses and one that will leave nobody indifferent. A little hilly but not excessively so, Glasson calls for a very precise game strategy and a cool head at all times. One further detail: you can reach the 18th tee by boat from Athlone.

On pouvait attendre d'un fin connaisseur du golf amateur et professionnel comme Christy O'Connor Jr qu'il adapte un parcours de manière très sûre à tous les niveaux de jeu. Disposant d'un site remarquable, depuis longtemps connu des amateurs de randonnées cyclistes et pédestres, il en a visiblement été exalté, et les vues sur le Lough Ree sont aussi magnifiques que sa mise en jeu sur quelques trous. D'autres lacs contribuent aussi bien à la beauté scénique du parcours qu'à sa difficulté. Et si l'on ajoute le travail très soigné des greens, le placement intelligent des bunkers et l'équilibre général du tracé, on aura compris qu'il s'agit d'une des meilleures additions récentes à la collection des golfs irlandais, et qui ne peut laisser indifférent. Un peu accidenté, mais sans excès, Glasson demande une stratégie de jeu très précise et de garder la tête froide. Pour l'anecdote, on peut parvenir en bateau au départ du 18, depuis Athlone.

Glasson Golf Club — 1993

Glasson
IRL - ATHLONE, Co West Meath

Office	Secrétariat	(353) 0902 - 85 120
Pro shop	Pro-shop	(353) 0902 - 85 120
Fax	Fax	(353) 0902 - 85 444
Web	www.glassongolf.ie	
Situation	Situation	

9 km from Athlone (pop. 7 691)

Annual closure	Fermeture annuelle	no
Weekly closure	Fermeture hebdomadaire	no

Fees main season Tarifs haute saison	18 holes	
	Week days Semaine	**We/Bank holidays** We/Férié
Individual Individuel	32 €	38 €
Couple Couple	64 €	76 €
Caddy Caddy	25 € /on request	
Electric Trolley Chariot électrique	9 €	
Buggy Voiturette	38 € /18 holes	
Clubs Clubs	19 € /18 holes	

Credit cards Cartes de crédit
VISA - MasterCard

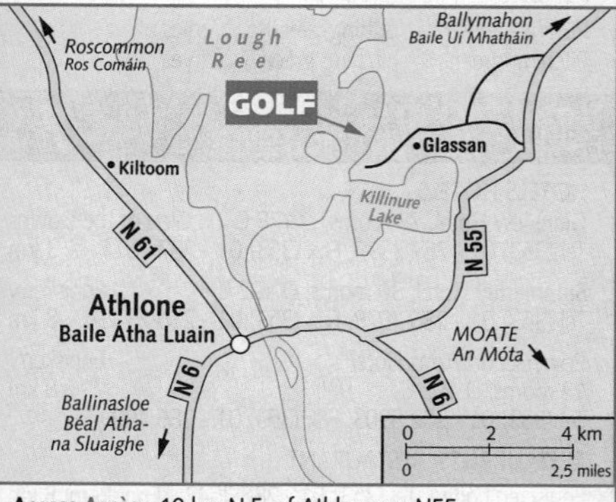

Access Accès : 10 km N.E. of Athlone on N55.
Cavan road
Map 2 on page 823 Carte 2 Page 823

Golf course — PARCOURS — 16/20

Site	Site	
Maintenance	Entretien	
Architect	Architecte	Christy O'Connor Jr
Type	Type	parkland
Relief	Relief	
Water in play	Eau en jeu	
Exp. to wind	Exposé au vent	
Trees in play	Arbres en jeu	

Scorecard Carte de score	**Chp.** Chp.	**Mens** Mess.	**Ladies** Da.
Length Long.	6510	6083	5100
Par	72	72	73
Slope system	—	—	—

Advised golfing ability Niveau de jeu recommandé — 0 12 24 36
Hcp required Handicap exigé — 24 Men, 36 Ladies

Club house & amenities — CLUB HOUSE ET ANNEXES — 7/10

Pro shop	Pro-shop	
Driving range	Practice	
Sheltered	couvert	no
On grass	sur herbe	yes
Putting-green	putting-green	yes
Pitching-green	pitching green	yes

Hotel facilities — ENVIRONNEMENT HOTELIER — 7/10

HOTELS HÔTELS

Glasson Golf Hotel, 30 rooms, D 178 € — Athlone on site
Tel (353) 0902 - 85 120, Fax (353) 0902 - 85 444

Hodson Bay Hotel — Athlone 12 km
100 rooms, D 140 €
Tel (353) 0902 - 80 500, Fax (353) 0902 - 80 520

Prince of Wales, 75 rooms, D 127 € — Athlone 9 km
Tel (353) 0902 - 72 626, Fax (353) 0902 - 75 658

RESTAURANTS RESTAURANT

Wineport, Tel (353) 0902 - 85 466 — Glassan 3 km

Glasson Village — Glassan/Athlone 2 km
Tel (353) 0902 - 85 001

GLEN OF THE DOWNS

13 | 6 | 7

This is a recent addition to a very large number of courses in County Wicklow, but its condition already makes it look much older. Laid out about 200 ft above sea level, it provides some splendid views over the Irish Sea and surrounding hills. The slopes are a feature of the course, which nonetheless is still definitely walkable. Architect Peter McEvoy, a remarkable golfer himself, has very carefully used the natural topology and the trees and ponds to produce a pretty layout. Likewise, the greens are sometimes elevated; if not, they are well guarded by bunkers. Straightforwardness is a valuable asset here on a course where golfing psychology is important: the hazards are often less dangerous than they seem. Although we could not rank Glen of the Downs in the top pack of courses in Ireland, it is still very pleasant and even more so with a new club-house.

Dans le Co. Wicklow, c'est une récente addition à un ensemble de parcours déjà fort important, mais son état est déjà celui d'un parcours bien plus ancien. Situé à une soixantaine de mètres au-dessus du niveau de la mer, il offre des vues splendides à la fois sur la Mer d'Irlande et sur les collines de la région. Ces reliefs sont d'ailleurs une marque du parcours, bien qu'il soit très jouable à pied. L'architecte (et très grand joueur) Peter McEvoy a très habilement utilisé ces accidents naturels, ainsi que les arbres et les petites mares pour poser joliment son tracé. De même, les greens sont parfois surélevés et bien défendus par des bunkers quand ils ne le sont pas. La franchise est de mise dans ce parcours, avec un aspect psychologique important : les obstacles sont souvent moins dangereux qu'on ne le croit. Bien qu'on ne puisse classer Glen of the Downs dans le peloton de tête des parcours d'Irlande, il n'en reste pas moins très agréable, avec un vaste club house.

Glen of the Downs Golf Club — 1997

IRL - DELGANY, Co Wicklow

Office	Secrétariat	(353) 01 - 287 0065
Pro shop	Pro-shop	(353) 01 - 287 6240
Fax	Fax	(353) 01 - 287 0063
Web	—	
Situation	Situation	
Dublin (pop. 481 854), 30 km		
Annual closure	Fermeture annuelle	no
Weekly closure	Fermeture hebdomadaire	no

Fees main season Tarifs haute saison	18 holes	
	Week days Semaine	**We/Bank holidays** We/Férié
Individual Individuel	51 €	63 €
Couple Couple	102 €	126 €

Caddy	Caddy	no
Electric Trolley	Chariot électrique	13 € /18 holes
Buggy	Voiturette	32 € /18 holes
Clubs	Clubs	19 €

Credit cards Cartes de crédit
VISA - MasterCard - DC - AMEX 

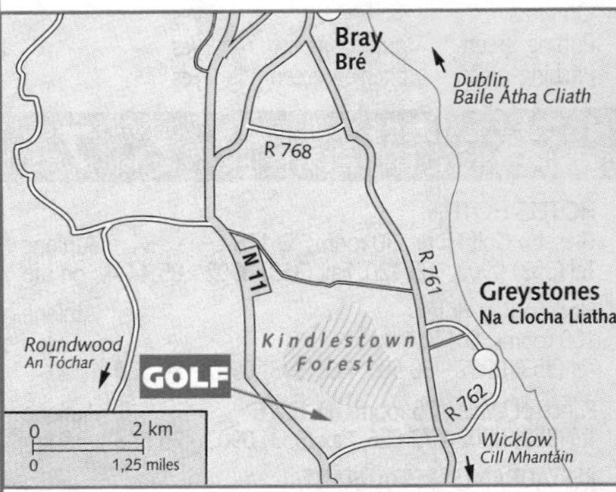

Access Accès : Dublin, N11 → Wicklow/Wexford. Kilmacanogue → Greystones. → Glen of the Downs.
Map 3 on page 824 Carte 3 Page 824

Golf course PARCOURS — 13/20

Site	Site	
Maintenance	Entretien	
Architect	Architecte	Peter McEvoy
Type	Type	inland
Relief	Relief	
Water in play	Eau en jeu	
Exp. to wind	Exposé au vent	
Trees in play	Arbres en jeu	

Scorecard Carte de score	**Chp.** Chp.	**Mens** Mess.	**Ladies** Da.
Length Long.	5830	5410	4780
Par	71	71	71
Slope system	—	—	—

Advised golfing ability Niveau de jeu recommandé — 0 12 24 36

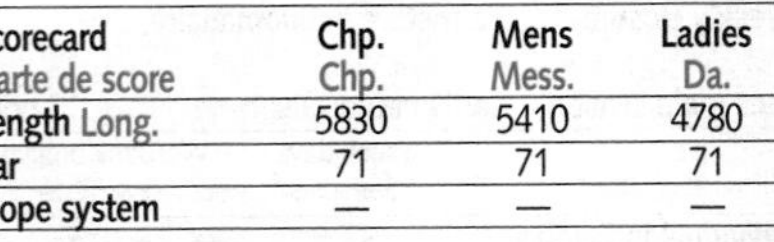

Hcp required Handicap exigé — no

Club house & amenities CLUB HOUSE ET ANNEXES — 6/10

Pro shop	Pro-shop	
Driving range	Practice	
Sheltered	couvert	no
On grass	sur herbe	no
Putting-green	putting-green	yes
Pitching-green	pitching green	yes

Hotel facilities ENVIRONNEMENT HOTELIER — 7/10

HOTELS HÔTELS

Glenview Hotel, 73 rooms, D 178 € — Glen of the Downs
Tel (353) 01 - 287 3399, Fax (353) 01 - 287 7511 — 3 km

Summerhill Hotel, 30 rooms, D 102 € — Enniskerry
Tel (353) 01 - 286 7928, Fax (353) 01 - 286 79 29 — 8 km

Powerscourt Arms Hotel — Enniskerry
12 rooms, D 102 € — 8 km
Tel (353) 01 - 282 8903, Fax (353) 01 - 286 4909

RESTAURANTS RESTAURANT

Enniscree Lodge, Tel (353) 01 - 286 3542 — Enniskerry 8 km

Tinakilly House, Tel (353) 0404 - 69 274 — Rathnew 15 km

Cooper's, Tel (353) 01 - 287 3914 — Greystones 5 km

GRANGE

16 | 5 | 8

The great James Braid created fewer courses in Ireland than in Scotland, but alongside Tullamore or Mullingar, Grange is one of his more excellent designs. No wonder then that the club has a large number of members to make week-end green-fees a difficult proposition. Here in the city they preserve tradition, at least for having retained the wooden club-house built in the 1940s and kept the design of the course as close as possible to the original. You will appreciate the very subtle bunkering and the strategic use of water on the 18th. By and large, the course looks to be tight and tough all the way, in fact only the first 6 holes really fit this category. But the impression of narrowness never leaves you: James Braid knew a thing a two about the psychology of your average golfer. But there again, the trees have doubtless grown a lot over the past one hundred years or so. Some of the greens are elevated (depending on terrain topology), all are well guarded and only a handful can really be reached by rolling the ball in. All in all, a classic course you will never grow weary of.

Le grand James Braid n'a pas créé autant de parcours en Irlande qu'en Ecosse mais, à côté de Tullamore ou Mullingar, Grange figure parmi ses excellentes créations, et le nombre de membres est assez important pour qu'il soit très difficile de le jouer en week-end. On y cultive la tradition, au moins pour avoir conservé le Club house en bois construit dans les années 40, et le dessin du parcours aussi original qu'il était possible. On appréciera en particulier le bunkering très subtil, l'utilisation stratégique d'un cours d'eau au 18. En règle générale, le parcours paraît étroit et difficile, bien que seuls les six premiers trous le soient vraiment, mais l'impression d'étroitesse demeure : James Braid connaissait très bien la psychologie de l'amateur. D'un autre côté, les arbres ont sans doute aussi beaucoup poussé depuis près de cent ans... Côté greens, quelques uns sont en élévation (suivant le terrain), la plupart sont bien défendus, seule une poignée étant vraiment accessibles en roulant. En résumé, un classique dont il est difficile de se lasser.

Grange Golf Club — 1910

IRL - RATHFARNHAM, DUBLIN 16

Office	Secrétariat	(353) 01 - 493 2889
Pro shop	Pro-shop	(353) 01 - 493 2299
Fax	Fax	(353) 01 - 493 2832
Web	—	
Situation	Situation	

Dublin (pop. 481 854), 10 km

Annual closure	Fermeture annuelle	no
Weekly closure	Fermeture hebdomadaire	no

Fees main season Tarifs haute saison	Week days Semaine	We/Bank holidays We/Férié
	18 holes	
Individual Individuel	51 €	57 €
Couple Couple	102 €	114 €

No green-fees on Saturdays

Caddy	Caddy	19 €
Electric Trolley	Chariot électrique	no
Buggy	Voiturette	no
Clubs	Clubs	13 €

Credit cards Cartes de crédit
VISA - MasterCard - DC - AMEX

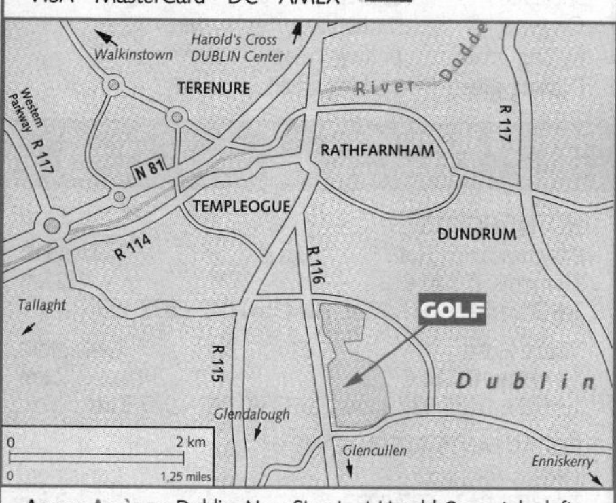

Access Accès : • Dublin, New Street, at Harold Cross, take left on Harold Cross Road. Left on Grange Road. • Or Western Parkway to the end, straight on Knocklyon, Scholars, Taylor Lane, Grange Road. **Map 3 on page 824** Carte 3 Page 824

Golf course PARCOURS — 16/20

Site	Site	
Maintenance	Entretien	
Architect	Architecte	James Braid
Type	Type	parkland
Relief	Relief	
Water in play	Eau en jeu	
Exp. to wind	Exposé au vent	
Trees in play	Arbres en jeu	

Scorecard Carte de score	Chp. Chp.	Mens Mess.	Ladies Da.
Length Long.	5517	5420	5154
Par	68	68	73
Slope system	—	—	—

Advised golfing ability / Niveau de jeu recommandé: 0 12 24 36
Hcp required / Handicap exigé

Club house & amenities CLUB HOUSE ET ANNEXES — 5/10

Pro shop	Pro-shop	
Driving range	Practice	
Sheltered	couvert	no
On grass	sur herbe	yes (practice area)
Putting-green	putting-green	yes
Pitching-green	pitching green	yes

Hotel facilities ENVIRONNEMENT HOTELIER — 8/10

HOTELS HÔTELS

Rathmines Capital Hotel, 54 rooms, D 114 € — Rathmines
Tel (353) 01 - 496 6966, Fax (353) 01 - 491 0603 — 5 km

Orwell Lodge Hotel, 10 rooms, D 127 € — Rathgae
Tel (353) 01 - 497 7258, Fax (353) 01 - 497 9913 — 12 km

Red Cow Morans Hotel, 1233 rooms, D 190 € — Clondalkin
Tel (353) 01 - 459 3650, Fax (353) 01 - 459 1588 — 7 km

RESTAURANTS RESTAURANT

Johnnie Foxes, Tel (353) 01 - 295 5647 — Glencullen 15 km

Yellow House, Tel (353) 01 - 493 2994 — Rathfarnham 3 km

Killakee Restaurant, Tel (353) 01 - 493 2645 — Rathfarnham 8 km

GREENORE

14 | 6 | 5

This age-old course, completed and overhauled by Eddie Hackett, is a mixture of wooded inland course and links, resulting in a lot of variety and an original appearance. There are even surprises in store, with the presence of the old disused railway line, whose infrastructure offers protection from the Irish sea and serves as a platform (no pun intended) for four elevated tees. If you like surprises, this course harbours a number of traps and is no walk-over first time out. Six greens are blind, there is a double green (2 and 10), a few hazards are invisible on several holes, a ditch makes its presence felt on four holes and there are ponds for a watery grave on three others. Fortunately, if you miss the fairway, the rough is perfectly playable. Laid out along Carlingford Lough, close to the pretty fishing village of Carlingford (an oyster centre), this is a very amusing, far from easy and rather uncommon course.

Ce parcours centenaire complété et (joliment) révisé par Eddie Hackett est un mélange de parcours inland boisé et de links, ce qui lui donne à la fois beaucoup de variété et un visage assez original. Il est même surprenant à cause de la présence d'une ancienne ligne de chemin de fer, aujourd'hui désaffectée, dont l'infrastructure protège de la mer d'Irlande, et sert de base pour quatre départs surélevés. Si vous aimez les surprises, ce parcours recèle pas mal de pièges, et n'est pas évident à jouer à première vue : six greens sont aveugles, on trouve un double green (2 et 10), quelques obstacles sont invisibles sur plusieurs trous, un fossé vient en jeu sur quatre trous, et des mares sur trois trous. Heureusement, si l'on manque les fairways, le rough reste tout à fait jouable. Le long du Carlingford Lough, près du joli village de pêcheurs de Carlingford (la capitale des huîtres), c'est un parcours très amusant, pas facile et dépaysant.

Greenore Golf Club — 1896

IRL - GREENORE, Co Louth

Office	Secrétariat	(353) 042 - 937 3678
Pro shop	Pro-shop	(353) 042 - 937 3678
Fax	Fax	(353) 042 - 937 3678
Web	—	
Situation	Situation	

12 km from Dundalk (pop. 25 762)
16 km from Newry (pop. 21 633)

Annual closure	Fermeture annuelle	no
Weekly closure	Fermeture hebdomadaire	no

Fees main season Tarifs haute saison	Week days Semaine	We/Bank holidays We/Férié
		18 holes
Individual Individuel	25 €	36 €
Couple Couple	50 €	72 €

Caddy	Caddy	no
Electric Trolley	Chariot électrique	no
Buggy	Voiturette	32 € /18 holes
Clubs	Clubs	no
Credit cards	Cartes de crédit	no

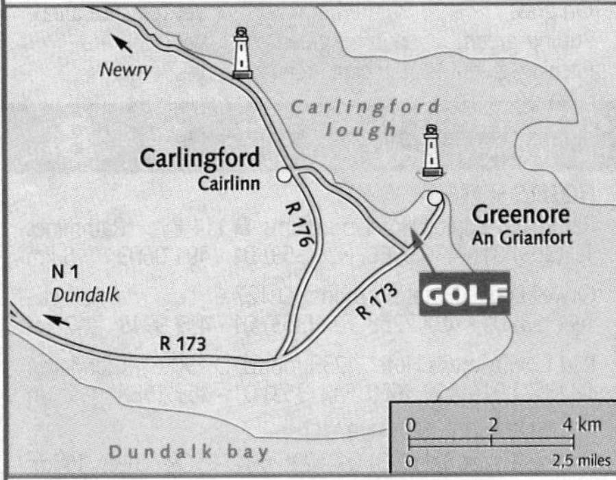

Access Accès : Dublin, N1 to Dundalk. Out of Dundalk, turn right on R173 to Greenore. Golf 12 km
Map 1 on page 821 Carte 1 Page 821

Golf course PARCOURS — 14/20

Site	Site	
Maintenance	Entretien	
Architect	Architecte	Eddie Hackett
Type	Type	seaside course
Relief	Relief	
Water in play	Eau en jeu	
Exp. to wind	Exposé au vent	
Trees in play	Arbres en jeu	

Scorecard Carte de score	Chp. Chp.	Mens Mess.	Ladies Da.
Length Long.	5954	5700	5198
Par	71	71	74
Slope system	—	—	—

Advised golfing ability Niveau de jeu recommandé — 0 12 24 36

Hcp required Handicap exigé — 24 Men, 36 Ladies

Club house & amenities CLUB HOUSE ET ANNEXES — 6/10

Pro shop	Pro-shop	
Driving range	Practice	
Sheltered	couvert	no
On grass	sur herbe	yes
Putting-green	putting-green	yes
Pitching-green	pitching green	no

Hotel facilities ENVIRONNEMENT HOTELIER — 5/10

HOTELS HÔTELS

Ballymascanlon Hotel — Dundalk
36 rooms, D 140 € — 12 km
Tel (353) 042 - 937 1124, Fax (353) 042 - 937 1598

Village Hotel — Carlingford
13 rooms, D 114 € — 2 km
Tel (353) 042 - 937 3116, Fax (353) 042 - 937 3144

RESTAURANTS RESTAURANT

Jordans Townhouse — Carlingford
Tel (353) 042 - 937 3223 — 3 km

McKevitts Village — Carlingford
Tel (353) 042 - 937 3116 — 3 km

HEADFORT New Course

15 | 6 | 6

The nearby Kells monastery was where the enlightened "Book of Kells" manuscript was written, a famous document now exhibited in Dublin. Although slightly less colourful, the two Headfort courses also give substantial food for thought and make for some excellent golfing. The "Old Course" was already well known, but its traditional inland style never really made this a course to top your list of priorities. The course's intrinsic qualities have been put into perspective by the opening of a second, more original layout, designed by Christy O'Connor Jr.. He has created a daring combination of British tradition and more American audacity with water hazards on twelve holes and the bringing into play of the Blackwater river. But being a man well schooled in golf at all levels, O'Connor has laid out neatly profiled bunkers designed not so much to over-penalise the average hacker, more to challenge the better golfer. The course is very long and full of trees, thus adding extra appeal to the site. Somewhat off the beaten track, this is a pretty destination with two very contrasting 18-hole courses.

C'est au monastère tout proche de Kells que fut élaboré le célèbre manuscrit enluminé "Book of Kells" exposé à Dublin. Moins colorés, les parcours d'Headfort n'en élèvent pas moins l'esprit par leur style. Le "Old Course," était déjà bien connu, mais son côté inland traditionnel ne rendait pas vraiment urgent un long détour. Il voit ses qualités propres mises en valeur par un second 18 trous, d'architecture plus originale. On retrouvera le style de Christy O'Connor Jr mélangeant avec goût la tradition britannique avec une audace plus américaine, avec la présence de l'eau sur une douzaine de trous, en particulier par la mise en valeur de la rivière Blackwater. Mais avec sa grande connaissance du jeu à tous niveaux, O'Connor a disposé des bunkers bien profilés avec le souci de ne pas trop pénaliser les joueurs moyens, tout en opposant des défis aux meilleurs. Très long, ce parcours est aussi bien arboré, ce qui ajoute à l'intérêt du lieu. En dehors des sentiers golfiques, une jolie destination et 36 trous très contrastés.

Headfort Golf Club — 2001

IRL - KELLS, Co Meath

Office	Secrétariat	(353) 046 - 40857
Pro shop	Pro-shop	(353) 046 - 40639
Fax	Fax	(353) 046 - 49282
Web	—	
Situation	Situation	

16 km N. of Navan (pop. 3 447)

Annual closure	Fermeture annuelle	no
Weekly closure	Fermeture hebdomadaire	no

Fees main season Tarifs haute saison		18 holes
	Week days Semaine	**We/Bank holidays** We/Férié
Individual Individuel	44 €	44 €
Couple Couple	88 €	88 €

Caddy	Caddy	on request
Electric Trolley	Chariot électrique	9 €
Buggy	Voiturette	38 €
Clubs	Clubs	19 €

Credit cards Cartes de crédit
VISA - MasterCard

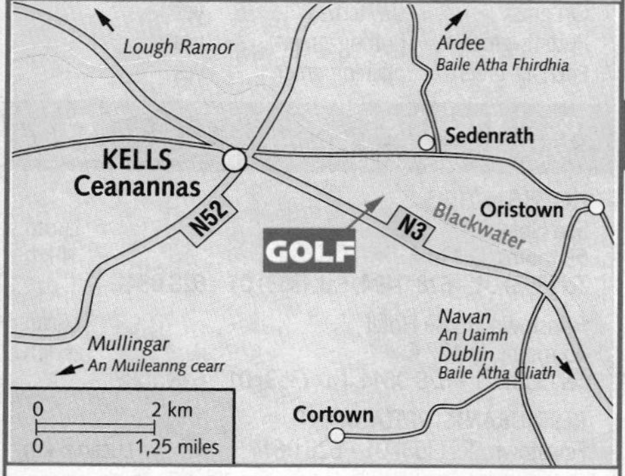

Access Accès : Dublin, N3 → Navan → Kells (Ceannánas)
Map 2 on page 823 Carte 2 Page 823

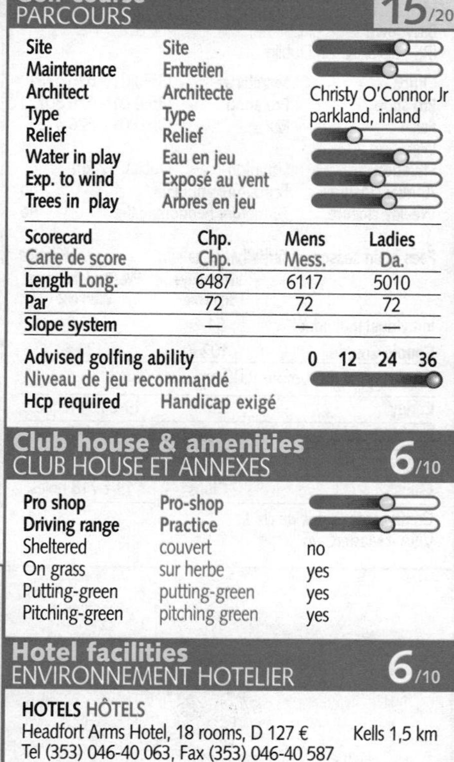

Golf course — PARCOURS — 15/20

Site	Site	
Maintenance	Entretien	
Architect	Architecte	Christy O'Connor Jr
Type	Type	parkland, inland
Relief	Relief	
Water in play	Eau en jeu	
Exp. to wind	Exposé au vent	
Trees in play	Arbres en jeu	

Scorecard Carte de score	**Chp.** Chp.	**Mens** Mess.	**Ladies** Da.
Length Long.	6487	6117	5010
Par	72	72	72
Slope system	—	—	—

Advised golfing ability — 0 12 24 36
Niveau de jeu recommandé
Hcp required — Handicap exigé

Club house & amenities — CLUB HOUSE ET ANNEXES — 6/10

Pro shop	Pro-shop	
Driving range	Practice	
Sheltered	couvert	no
On grass	sur herbe	yes
Putting-green	putting-green	yes
Pitching-green	pitching green	yes

Hotel facilities — ENVIRONNEMENT HOTELIER — 6/10

HOTELS HÔTELS

Headfort Arms Hotel, 18 rooms, D 127 € — Kells 1,5 km
Tel (353) 046-40 063, Fax (353) 046-40 587

Ardboyne Hotel, 29 rooms, D 127 € — Navan 18 km
Tel (353) 046-23 119, Fax (353) 046-22 355

Newgrange Hotel, 36 rooms, D 127 € — Navan 18 km
Tel (353) 046-74 100, Fax (353) 046-73 977

Ma Dwyers Guest House, 9 rooms, D 63 € — Navan 18 km
Tel (353) 046-77 992, Fax (353) 046-77 995

RESTAURANTS RESTAURANT

Southbank Bistro, Tel (353) 046-72 406 — Navan 15 km

Headfort Arms Hotel, Tel (353) 046-74 100 — Kells 1,5 km

HERMITAGE

15 | 6 | 8

This course has led a quiet existence since the turn of the century and continues to figure regularly amongst the better Irish golf courses. There is nothing of the links about it, sure, but its park-landscape configuration (the trees are superb) on the banks of the Liffey, the moderately hilly relief (two or three steep climbs) and the closeness to Dublin make this a very interesting stop-off. It is not very long (especially from the normal tees) but it does require a lot of precision play and probably every club in your bag. A few blind shots and greens add a little uncertainty to it all, and the 10th (a par 3 along the Liffey river) is an exciting prospect with the green way down below you. You shouldn't under-estimate Hermitage, it is capable of baring its teeth to anyone who is not permanently on his or her toes. This is a very fine example of an inland course and has hosted a number of top tournaments. It may not always stand up to the best player, but it has lost none of its charm.

Ce golf vit paisiblement depuis le début du siècle, et continuer à figurer régulièrement parmi les bons parcours d'Irlande. Certes, il n'a rien d'un links, mais sa configuration de grand parc (les arbres sont superbes) en bordure de la Liffey, son relief modéré (deux ou trois fortes montées) et sa proximité de Dublin en font une étape fort intéressante. Il n'est pas très long (surtout des départs normaux), mais il demande pas mal de précision, et l'utilisation probable de tous les clubs du sac. Quelques coups et un green aveugles ajoutent un peu d'incertitude, et le 10 (un par 3 le long de la Liffey) amène quelque émotion, avec son green très en contrebas du départ. On ne doit pas sous-estimer Hermitage, il est capable de montrer les dents à ceux qui négligeraient de conserver en permanence leur concentration. Ce très bel exemple de parcours "inland" a reçu de grandes compétitions, il conserve son charme, sinon sa résistance aux meilleurs joueurs.

Hermitage Golf Club — 1902

Ballydowd
IRL - LUCAN, Co Dublin

Office	Secrétariat	(353) 01 - 626 4781
Pro shop	Pro-shop	(353) 01 - 626 8072
Fax	Fax	(353) 01 - 626 4781
Web	—	
Situation	Situation	Dublin, 12 km
Annual closure	Fermeture annuelle	no
Weekly closure	Fermeture hebdomadaire	no

Fees main season Tarifs haute saison	18 holes	
	Week days Semaine	**We/Bank holidays** We/Férié
Individual Individuel	51 €	66 €
Couple Couple	102 €	132 €

Weekdays: 27 € before 9.00 am

Caddy	Caddy	19 € /on request
Electric Trolley	Chariot électrique	6 €
Buggy	Voiturette	no
Clubs	Clubs	13 € /18 holes

Credit cards Cartes de crédit
VISA - MasterCard

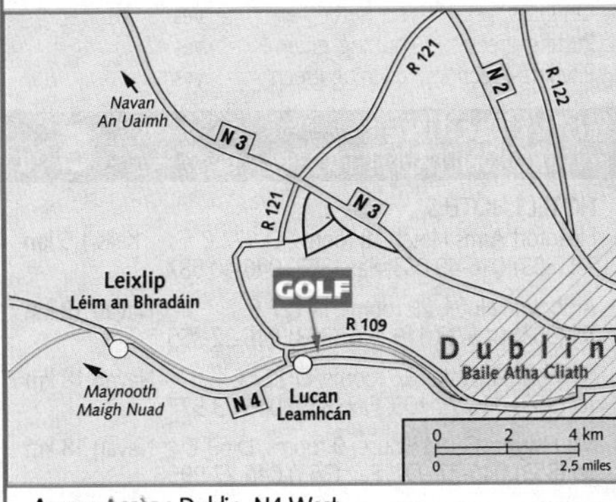

Access Accès : Dublin, N4 West
Map 3 on page 824 Carte 3 Page 824

Golf course PARCOURS — 15/20

Site	Site	
Maintenance	Entretien	
Architect	Architecte	M. McKenna
Type	Type	parkland
Relief	Relief	
Water in play	Eau en jeu	
Exp. to wind	Exposé au vent	
Trees in play	Arbres en jeu	

Scorecard Carte de score	**Chp.** Chp.	**Mens** Mess.	**Ladies** Da.
Length Long.	6051	5833	5215
Par	71	71	75
Slope system	—	—	—

Advised golfing ability Niveau de jeu recommandé — 0 12 24 36

Hcp required Handicap exigé — 24 Men, 36 Ladies

Club house & amenities CLUB HOUSE ET ANNEXES — 6/10

Pro shop	Pro-shop	
Driving range	Practice	
Sheltered	couvert	no
On grass	sur herbe	yes
Putting-green	putting-green	yes
Pitching-green	pitching green	yes

Hotel facilities ENVIRONNEMENT HOTELIER — 8/10

HOTELS HÔTELS

Spa Hotel — Lucan 4 km
53 rooms, D 114 €
Tel (353) 01 - 628 0494, Fax (353) 01 - 628 0841

Finnstown House Hotel — Lucan 6 km
45 rooms, D 127 €
Tel (353) 01 - 628 0644, Fax (353) 01 - 628 1088

RESTAURANTS RESTAURANT

Finnstown, Tel (353) 01 - 628 0644 — Lucan 6 km
Ryans, Tel (353) 01 - 820 8210 — Dublin 6 km
Patrick Guilbaud, Tel (353) 01 - 676 4192 — Dublin 12 km

K CLUB

17 | 8 | 8

This is one of the most ambitious projects ever carried out in Ireland. Straffan House has been converted into a top luxury hotel and a course built without counting the cost, the whole piece co-ordinated by the Jefferson Smurfit group, one of the country's most dynamic entrepreneurs. Arnold Palmer pitched and won the official tender to design the course and has come up with one of his most exacting layouts. In length and tactical difficulty, it is reminiscent of Bay Hill in Florida. Only the most accomplished golfers can hope to cope without feeling too disillusioned about their game. Even from the front tees, this is an uncompromising challenge, so don't waste time counting your strokes, or even your balls if you start flirting too boldly with the water, especially over the closing holes. What with the closeness of the river Liffey, we would suggest you play here in summer, despite the excellent drainage. After your game, be happy: a beer is cheaper than a green-fee.

C'est l'une des plus ambitieuses réalisations jamais effectuées en Irlande, avec la transformation de la Straffan House en hôtel de grand luxe, et la construction d'un parcours où l'argent n'a pas été compté, sous la houlette du Jefferson Smurfit Group, l'une des entreprises les plus dynamiques du pays. Arnold Palmer est sorti vainqueur du concours d'architectes, il a livré l'un des ses parcours les plus exigeants : par sa longueur et ses difficultés tactiques, il n'est pas sans rappeler Bay Hill en Floride. Et seul les golfeurs accomplis pourront prétendre le négocier sans trop perdre d'illusions sur leur golf. Même des départs avancés, il reste un challenge sans concessions, on évitera donc de compter ses coups, et parfois même ses balles, si l'on flirte trop audacieusement avec l'eau, notamment dans les derniers trous. En dépit d'importants drainages, la proximité de la rivière Liffey incite à le recommander surtout en été. Après avoir joué, prenez une bière au bar, elle est moins chère que le green-fee.

The K Club — 1991

IRL - STRAFFAN, Co Kildare

Office	Secrétariat	(353) 01 - 601 7300
Pro shop	Pro-shop	(353) 01 - 601 7321
Fax	Fax	(353) 01 - 601 7399
Web	www.kclub.ie	
Situation	Situation	
34 km W of Dublin	(pop. 481 854)	
Annual closure	Fermeture annuelle	no
Weekly closure	Fermeture hebdomadaire	no

Fees main season Tarifs haute saison	18 holes	
	Week days Semaine	**We/Bank holidays** We/Férié
Individual Individuel	222 €	222 €
Couple Couple	444 €	444 €

Caddy	Caddy	32 € /on request
Electric Trolley	Chariot électrique	13 €
Buggy	Voiturette	38 € /18 holes
Clubs	Clubs	38 € /18 holes

Credit cards Cartes de crédit
VISA - Eurocard - MasterCard - DC - AMEX

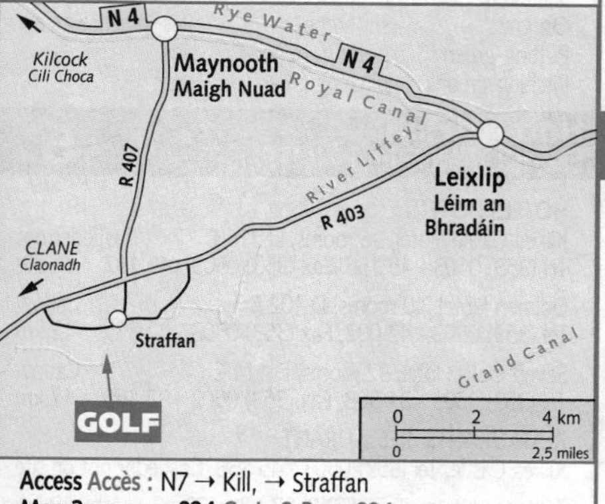

Access Accès : N7 → Kill, → Straffan
Map 3 on page 824 Carte 3 Page 824

Golf course — PARCOURS — 17/20

Site	Site	
Maintenance	Entretien	
Architect	Architecte	Arnold Palmer
Type	Type	inland, parkland
Relief	Relief	
Water in play	Eau en jeu	
Exp. to wind	Exposé au vent	
Trees in play	Arbres en jeu	

Scorecard Carte de score	**Chp.** Chp.	**Mens** Mess.	**Ladies** Da.
Length Long.	6519	6063	4990
Par	72	72	73
Slope system	—	—	—

Advised golfing ability Niveau de jeu recommandé — 0 12 24 36
Hcp required Handicap exigé — 28 Men, 36 Ladies

Club house & amenities — CLUB HOUSE ET ANNEXES — 8/10

Pro shop	Pro-shop	
Driving range	Practice	
Sheltered	couvert	no
On grass	sur herbe	yes
Putting-green	putting-green	yes
Pitching-green	pitching green	yes

Hotel facilities — ENVIRONNEMENT HOTELIER — 8/10

HOTELS HÔTELS

Kildare Hotel and Country Club — on site
45 rooms, D 406 €
Tel (353) 01 - 627 3333, Fax (353) 01 - 627 3312

Leixlip House Hotel — Leixlip 10 km
16 rooms, D 152 €
Tel (353) 01 - 624 2268, Fax (353) 01 - 624 4177

Moyglare Manor, 16 rooms, D 190 € — Maynooth 10 km
Tel (353) 01 - 628 63 51, Fax (353) 01 - 628 5405

RESTAURANTS RESTAURANT

The Legends, Tel (353) 01 - 627 3111 — K Club on site
The Burly Turk, Tel (353) 01 - 627 3111 — K Club on site

KILKEA CASTLE

15 | 6 | 6

At first sight, this is an impressive complex. Kilkea Castle is the oldest inhabited castle in Ireland and provides a splendid setting for this golf and hotel resort, where you can also try your hand at archery, clay-pigeon shooting and horse-riding, one of Ireland's national sports. Seen in comparison with the hotel's facilities, the green-fee is by no means prohibitive and in any case is in line with the very respectful quality of the course. The architects have used the natural terrain, streams and ponds for purposes of effect and also for game strategy. Existing trees are reasonably in play and new plantations should enhance the scenery and nature of hazards still further. They also tried to please everyone, so less experienced players always have the chance to stay away from trouble while others will face up to the challenge without too much trepidation. And while some US-style holes call for target shots, others welcome the good old bump 'n run as long as the clayey soil is dry enough.

Au premier regard, l'ensemble est impressionnant. Kilkea Castle est le plus ancien château habité d'Irlande, il constitue un cadre splendide à cet ensemble golf et hôtel, où l'on peut également pratiquer le tir à l'arc, le tir au pigeon d'argile et l'équitation, un des sports nationaux de l'Irlande. En comparaison des équipements de l'hôtel, le green-fee n'est pas ici prohibitif, en tout cas par rapport à la très honorable qualité du parcours. Les architectes ont utilisé le terrain naturel, les cours d'eau et les mares avec beaucoup de sens de l'effet, mais aussi de la stratégie du jeu. Les arbres existants du domaine sont raisonnablement en jeu, et de nouvelles plantations devraient encore faire évoluer le décor et la nature des obstacles. On a aussi cherché ici à contenter tout le monde, tous les niveaux de jeu. Ainsi, les joueurs les moins aguerris ont toujours des possibilités de rester à l'écart des problèmes, les autres affronteront sans trop de peur les défis du lieu. De même, s'il faut parfois maîtriser les balles levées sur les trous "à l'américaine", d'autres trous permettent un jeu "bump' n' run", si le terrain argileux est du moins assez sec.

Kilkea Castle Golf Club — 1994

IRL - CASTLEDERMOT, Co. Kildare

Office	Secrétariat	(353) 0503 - 45 555
Pro shop	Pro-shop	(353) 0503 - 45 555
Fax	Fax	(353) 0503 - 45 505
Web	www.kilkeacastlehotelgolf.net	
Situation	Situation	
Dublin (pop. 481 854), 65 km		
Annual closure	Fermeture annuelle	no
Weekly closure	Fermeture hebdomadaire	no

Fees main season Tarifs haute saison	18 holes	
	Week days Semaine	**We/Bank holidays** We/Férié
Individual Individuel	38 €	44 €
Couple Couple	76 €	88 €
Caddy	Caddy	32 € /on request
Electric Trolley	Chariot électrique	no
Buggy	Voiturette	no
Clubs	Clubs	19 €

Credit cards Cartes de crédit
VISA - Eurocard - MasterCard - AMEX

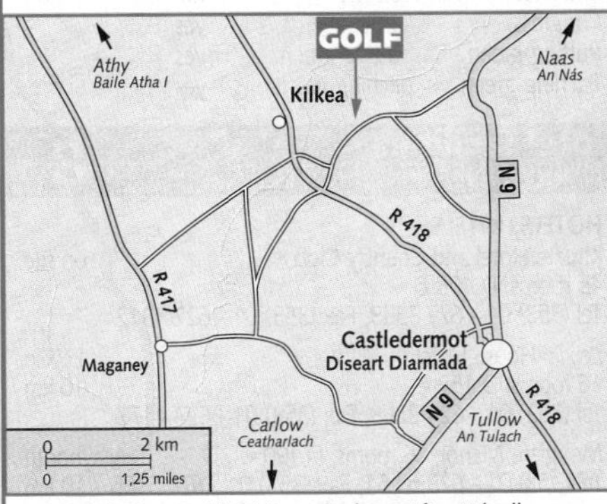

Access Accès : Dublin, N9 → Carlow. After Kilcullen, Ballymount, turn off at High Cross → Kilkea Castle.
Map 2 on page 822 Carte 2 Page 822

Golf course — PARCOURS — 15/20

Site	Site	
Maintenance	Entretien	
Architect	Architecte	Andrew Gilbert, Jim Cassidy
Type	Type	parkland
Relief	Relief	
Water in play	Eau en jeu	
Exp. to wind	Exposé au vent	
Trees in play	Arbres en jeu	

Scorecard Carte de score	**Chp.** Chp.	**Mens** Mess.	**Ladies** Da.
Length Long.	6097	5891	5076
Par	70	70	72
Slope system	—	—	—

Advised golfing ability Niveau de jeu recommandé: 0 12 24 36
Hcp required Handicap exigé: no

Club house & amenities — CLUB HOUSE ET ANNEXES — 6/10

Pro shop	Pro-shop	
Driving range	Practice	
Sheltered	couvert	no
On grass	sur herbe	yes (practice area
Putting-green	putting-green	yes
Pitching-green	pitching green	yes

Hotel facilities — ENVIRONNEMENT HOTELIER — 6/10

HOTELS HÔTELS

Kilkea Castle Hotel, 36 rooms, D 216 € — Castledermot
Tel (353) 0503 - 45 156, Fax (353) 0503 - 45 187 — on site

Dolmen Hotel, 40 rooms, D 102 € — Carlow
Tel (353) 0503 - 42 002, Fax (353) 0503 - 42 375 — 12 km

Seven Oaks Hotel, 32 rooms, D 114 € — Carlow
Tel (353) 0503 - 31 308, Fax (353) 0503 - 32 155 — 12 km

RESTAURANTS RESTAURANT

Kilkea Castle, Tel (353) 0503 - 45 156 — Castledermot on site

Tonlegee House, Tel (353) 0507 - 31 473 — Athy 19 km

Rathsallagh House, Tel (353) 045 - 403 112 — Dunlavin, 36 km

KILKENNY

13 | 7 | 6

The thousands of trees planted in the 1960s and 1970s have grown and compounded the difficulty of this course. But being on the short side, it is within the grasp of most golfers, although the best will see this more as a good practice course rather than a top-level test of skill. Here, then, is the opportunity to look after the rest of the family or the lesser players in the group. They will, though, need to be careful on the par 3s, on the 11th, a long par 4, and on the closing holes, which can spoil a good card. The main hazards are generally speaking the trees, which neatly outline the holes, the fairway bunkers (they can be punishing at times) and the sand around the greens. The greens themselves are forthright, medium-sized and not bumpy enough to be really difficult to read. This is a pleasant day's golfing over terrain where holes alternate over flat and rolling landscape.

La croissance des milliers d'arbres plantés dans les années 60 et 70 a accru la difficulté de ce parcours. Cependant, sa faible longueur le place à la portée de tous les niveaux de jeu, mais les meilleurs doivent le considérer comme un bon parcours d'entraînement, et non comme un test de première grandeur : ce sera l'occasion pour eux de s'occuper des autres joueurs de la famille ou du groupe ! Mais ils devront être vigilants sur les pars 3, sur le 11 (un long par 4) et sur les derniers trous, qui peuvent endommager un bon score. Les principaux obstacles sont en général les arbres, qui définissent bien les trous, les bunkers de fairway (ils pourraient être plus punitifs), et les bunkers défendant les greens. Ces derniers sont francs, de taille moyenne, ne sont pas assez accidentés pour être vraiment difficiles à lire. Et comme le relief du terrain alterne les trous plats et les trous plus vallonnés, c'est une agréable promenade.

Kilkenny Golf Club — 1896

IRL - GLENDINE, Co Kilkenny

Office	Secrétariat	(353) 056 - 65 400
Pro shop	Pro-shop	(353) 056 - 61 730
Fax	Fax	(353) 056 - 23 593
Web	—	
Situation	Situation	

Kilkenny (pop. 8 507), 1.5 km

Annual closure	Fermeture annuelle	no
Weekly closure	Fermeture hebdomadaire	no

Fees main season / Tarifs haute saison	Week days / Semaine	We/Bank holidays / We/Férié
18 holes		
Individual Individuel	34 €	41 €
Couple Couple	68 €	82 €

Caddy	Caddy	15 €
Electric Trolley	Chariot électrique	13 € /18 holes
Buggy	Voiturette	25 € /18 holes
Clubs	Clubs	13 €

Credit cards Cartes de crédit
VISA - MasterCard

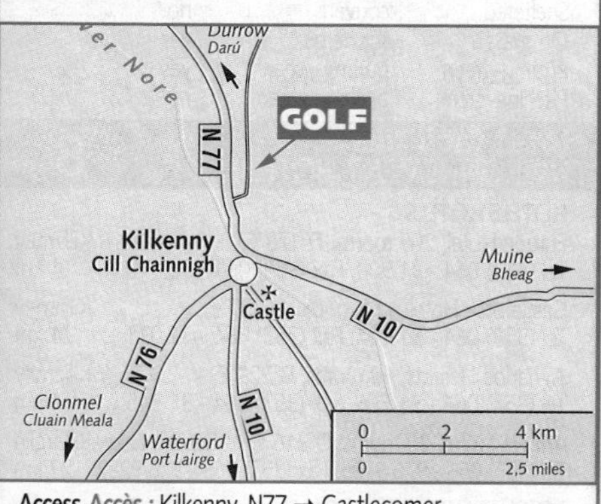

Access Accès : Kilkenny, N77 → Castlecomer.
Golf 1.5 km
Map 2 on page 823 Carte 2 Page 823

Golf course PARCOURS — 13/20

Site	Site	
Maintenance	Entretien	
Architect	Architecte	unknown
Type	Type	parkland
Relief	Relief	
Water in play	Eau en jeu	
Exp. to wind	Exposé au vent	
Trees in play	Arbres en jeu	

Scorecard Carte de score	Chp. Chp.	Mens Mess.	Ladies Da.
Length Long.	5857	5600	5112
Par	71	71	73
Slope system	—	—	—

Advised golfing ability / Niveau de jeu recommandé: 0 12 24 36
Hcp required / Handicap exigé: no

Club house & amenities CLUB HOUSE ET ANNEXES — 7/10

Pro shop	Pro-shop	
Driving range	Practice	
Sheltered	couvert	no
On grass	sur herbe	yes
Putting-green	putting-green	yes
Pitching-green	pitching green	no

Hotel facilities ENVIRONNEMENT HOTELIER — 6/10

HOTELS HÔTELS

Mount Juliet House — Thomastown 16 km
32 rooms, D 229 €
Tel (353) 056 - 73 000, Fax (353) 056 - 73 019

Hotel Kilkenny — Kilkenny 3 km
60 rooms, D 152 €
Tel (353) 056 - 62 000, Fax (353) 056 - 65 984

Newpark Hotel, 84 rooms, D 140 € — Kilkenny 3 km
Tel (353) 056 - 22 122, Fax (353) 056 - 61 111

RESTAURANTS RESTAURANT

Zuni Restaurant, Tel (353) 056 - 23 999 — Kilkenny 2 km
Lacken House, Tel (353) 056 - 61 085 — Kilkenny 3 km

KILLARNEY Killeen Course

16 | 7 | 8

Although the closing holes here are not quite as spectacular as those on its illustrious neighbour, Killeen is generally considered to be the most challenging course of this remarkable complex. It staged the Irish Open in 1991 and 1992, when Nick Faldo triumphed. Some of the original holes designed by Sir Guy Campbell are included here, but the basic layout is the work of Eddie Hackett and Billy O'Sullivan. The landscape is that of a huge park with every imaginable hazard. Let's start with the trees: from the back tees, the fairways look and are narrow, and demand very accurate driving. As you move forward, they obligingly become a little wider. The path to the green is dotted with strategically placed bunkers, and water hazards also play a significant role. While it is difficult to prefer one or the other of the Killarney courses (everyone to his own), the purists say that Killeen just has the edge.

Bien qu'il ne produise pas un finish aussi spectaculaire que son voisin, le Killeen Course est généralement considéré comme le plus exigeant de ce remarquable complexe. C'est d'ailleurs celui qui a reçu l'Irish Open, notamment en 1991 et 1992 quand Nick Faldo s'y imposa. Quelques-uns des trous du tracé original de Sir Guy Campbell ont été repris ici, mais l'essentiel en est dû à Eddie Hackett et Billy O'Sullivan. Le paysage est celui d'un vaste parc, avec tous les obstacles imaginables. A commencer par les arbres : des départs arrière, les fairways paraissent étroits et imposent un driving très précis, mais ils s'élargissent amicalement pour les départs plus avancés. Le chemin des greens est alors très fourni en bunkers stratégiques, et les obstacles d'eau jouent également un rôle important. S'il est difficile de préférer l'un ou l'autre parcours de Killarney (chacun son goût), celui-ci est un soupçon supérieur selon les puristes.

Killarney Golf Club — 1971

O'Mahoney's Point
IRL - KILLARNEY, Co Kerry

Office	Secrétariat	(353) 064 - 31 034
Pro shop	Pro-shop	(353) 064 - 31 165
Fax	Fax	(353) 064 - 33 065
Web	www.killarney-golf.com	
Situation	Situation	

3 km from Killarney (pop. 8 809)

Annual closure	Fermeture annuelle	no
Weekly closure	Fermeture hebdomadaire	no

Fees main season Tarifs haute saison	Week days Semaine	We/Bank holidays We/Férié
	18 holes	
Individual Individuel	63 €	63 €
Couple Couple	126 €	126 €

Caddy	Caddy	25 € /18 holes
Electric Trolley	Chariot électrique	3 € /18 holes
Buggy	Voiturette	no
Clubs	Clubs	20 € /18 holes

Credit cards Cartes de crédit
VISA - Eurocard - MasterCard - DC - AMEX

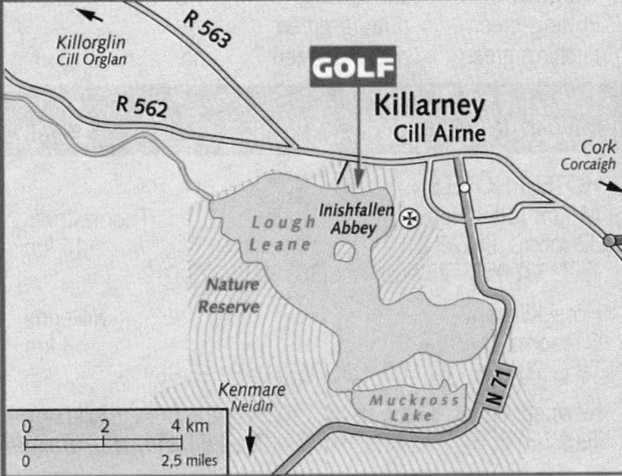

Access Accès : Killarney W, 3 km on R562 → Killorglin
Map 2 on page 822 Carte 2 Page 822

Golf course PARCOURS — 16/20

Site	Site	
Maintenance	Entretien	
Architect	Architecte	Eddie Hackett, Billy O'Sullivan
Type	Type	parkland
Relief	Relief	
Water in play	Eau en jeu	
Exp. to wind	Exposé au vent	
Trees in play	Arbres en jeu	

Scorecard Carte de score	Chp. Chp.	Mens Mess.	Ladies Da.
Length Long.	6474	5993	4928
Par	72	72	74
Slope system	—	—	—

Advised golfing ability — 0 12 24 36
Niveau de jeu recommandé
Hcp required Handicap exigé — 28 Men, 36 Ladies

Club house & amenities CLUB HOUSE ET ANNEXES — 7/10

Pro shop	Pro-shop	
Driving range	Practice	
Sheltered	couvert	no
On grass	sur herbe	yes
Putting-green	putting-green	yes
Pitching-green	pitching green	no

Hotel facilities ENVIRONNEMENT HOTELIER — 8/10

HOTELS HÔTELS

Europe Hotel, 205 rooms, D 178 € — Killarney
Tel (353) 064 - 31 900, Fax (353) 064 - 32 118 — 1 km

Castlerosse Hotel, 114 rooms, D 127 € — Killarney
Tel (353) 064 - 31 144, Fax (353) 064 - 31 031 — 1 km

Aghadoe Heights, 60 rooms, D 229 € — Killarney
Tel (353) 064 - 31 766, Fax (353) 064 - 31 345 — 1 km

Ard Na Sidhe, 20 rooms, D 216 € — Caragh Lake, Killorglin
Tel (353) 066 - 976 9105, Fax (353) 066 - 976 9282 — 22 km

RESTAURANTS RESTAURANT

Dingle's, Tel (353) 064 - 31 079 — Killarney 4 km

Failte Restaurant, Tel (353) 064 - 33 404 — Killarney 4 km

KILLARNEY Mahony's Point

15 | 7 | 8

A lively place to be at night, this charming little town is a major tourist centre and an ideal holiday stop-off to explore the lakes in the National Park, the Kerry mountains... and the prestigious golf courses of south-west Ireland. The three 18-hole courses at Killarney are a part of these, and golfers often tend to show a slight sentimental preference for this one, especially the 3 closing holes, which include the 18th, a tough par 3 magnificently set alongside Lough Leane. Try and arrange to play here in the early evening to watch the sun set, when the surrounding forests blossom in the colours of autumn (play Killeen in the morning). A rather short course, it is less of a handful than it looks at first sight, but it does require a careful short game around very well-guarded greens. The beauty of the environment, the trees and the layout add to the pleasure of your day spent here, and the best players in your group will enjoy a good round without having to dig too deeply into their reserves.

Très animée le soir, cette charmante petite ville est un grand centre touristique, un lieu de séjour idéal pour explorer les lacs du National Park, les monts du Kerry... et pour aller jouer les prestigieux parcours du Sud-Ouest. Les trois 18 trous de Killarney en font partie, et les joueurs ont souvent une petite préférence sentimentale pour celui-ci, notamment pour les trois derniers trous, dont le magnifique 18, un par 3 difficile et magnifiquement situé le long du Lough Leane : il faut s'arranger pour le jouer au coucher du soleil, quand les forêts environnantes prennent leurs couleurs d'automne (jouer Killeen le matin). Assez court, ce parcours est moins difficile à négocier qu'il n'y paraît à première vue, mais il réclame un petit jeu attentif, car les greens sont bien défendus. La beauté de l'environnement, des arbres et du dessin ajoute au plaisir de la journée, et les meilleurs joueurs du groupe auront plaisir à briller sans trop puiser dans leurs réserves.

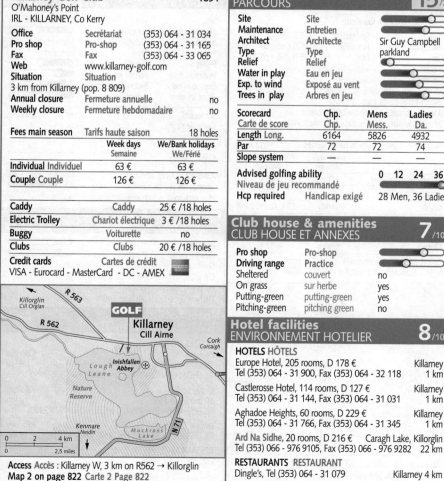

Killarney Golf Club — 1891

O'Mahoney's Point
IRL - KILLARNEY, Co Kerry

Office	Secrétariat	(353) 064 - 31 034
Pro shop	Pro-shop	(353) 064 - 31 165
Fax	Fax	(353) 064 - 33 065
Web	www.killarney-golf.com	
Situation	Situation	
3 km from Killarney (pop. 8 809)		
Annual closure	Fermeture annuelle	no
Weekly closure	Fermeture hebdomadaire	no

Fees main season Tarifs haute saison	**Week days** Semaine	**We/Bank holidays** We/Férié
		18 holes
Individual Individuel	63 €	63 €
Couple Couple	126 €	126 €

Caddy	Caddy	25 € /18 holes
Electric Trolley	Chariot électrique	3 € /18 holes
Buggy	Voiturette	no
Clubs	Clubs	20 € /18 holes

Credit cards Cartes de crédit
VISA - Eurocard - MasterCard - DC - AMEX

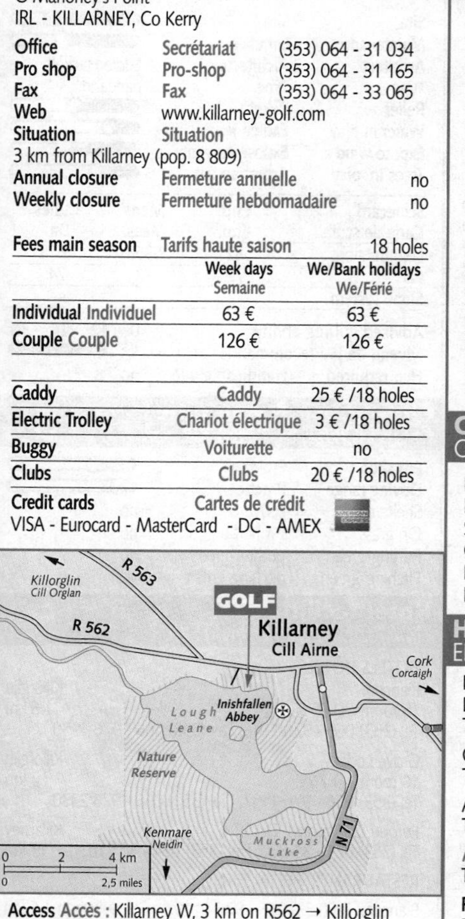

Access Accès : Killarney W, 3 km on R562 → Killorglin
Map 2 on page 822 Carte 2 Page 822

Golf course PARCOURS — 15/20

Site	Site	
Maintenance	Entretien	
Architect	Architecte	Sir Guy Campbell
Type	Type	parkland
Relief	Relief	
Water in play	Eau en jeu	
Exp. to wind	Exposé au vent	
Trees in play	Arbres en jeu	

Scorecard Carte de score	**Chp.** Chp.	**Mens** Mess.	**Ladies** Da.
Length Long.	6164	5826	4932
Par	72	72	74
Slope system	—	—	—

Advised golfing ability Niveau de jeu recommandé — 0 12 24 36
Hcp required Handicap exigé — 28 Men, 36 Ladies

Club house & amenities CLUB HOUSE ET ANNEXES — 7/10

Pro shop	Pro-shop	
Driving range	Practice	
Sheltered	couvert	no
On grass	sur herbe	yes
Putting-green	putting-green	yes
Pitching-green	pitching green	no

Hotel facilities ENVIRONNEMENT HOTELIER — 8/10

HOTELS HÔTELS

Europe Hotel, 205 rooms, D 178 € — Killarney
Tel (353) 064 - 31 900, Fax (353) 064 - 32 118 — 1 km

Castlerosse Hotel, 114 rooms, D 127 € — Killarney
Tel (353) 064 - 31 144, Fax (353) 064 - 31 031 — 1 km

Aghadoe Heights, 60 rooms, D 229 € — Killarney
Tel (353) 064 - 31 766, Fax (353) 064 - 31 345 — 1 km

Ard Na Sidhe, 20 rooms, D 216 € — Caragh Lake, Killorglin
Tel (353) 066 - 976 9105, Fax (353) 066 - 976 9282 — 22 km

RESTAURANTS RESTAURANT

Dingle's, Tel (353) 064 - 31 079 — Killarney 4 km

Failte Restaurant, Tel (353) 064 - 33 404 — Killarney 4 km

KILLORGLIN

14 | 6 | 5

As the courses in this region are very busy, catering to not only tourists but also the locals, this course was more than welcome. It was designed by the busiest of all Irish designers, Eddie Hackett. Running on the side of hill, the terrain overlooks Dingle Bay (the weaker souls will find the course tiring to walk) and gives golfers some pretty viewpoints over the estuary, the Slieve Mish Mountains opposite and Macgillicuddy's Reeks to the west. Although not outstanding, Killorglin is well worth a visit, especially for a round with friends or the family, without undue suffering (except, of course, when the wind gets up). The difficulties are easily seen but are more psychological than real. You can even play to your handicap first time round, providing you don't misjudge your approach shots - some greens are elevated, others multi-tiered.

Les parcours de la région étant très fréquentés, non seulement par les touristes, mais aussi par la clientèle locale, ce parcours a été plus que bienvenu. C'est le plus occupé des architectes irlandais, Eddie Hackett, qui en est l'auteur. A flanc de colline, le terrain domine la baie de Dingle (les plus fatigués souffriront à pied), ce qui offre aux joueurs quelques jolis points de vue sur cet estuaire, comme sur les Slieve Mish Mountains en face et, à l'ouest, sur les Macgilliguddy Reeks. Sans être exceptionnel, le parcours de Killorglin mérite la visite, notamment pour y faire une partie amicale ou en famille, sans trop souffrir, sauf quand le vent souffle fort, bien sûr. Les difficultés sont aisément identifiables, mais sont plus psychologiques que réelles. Dès la première fois, on peut y jouer son handicap, à condition de bien juger ses approches : certains greens sont surélevés et quelques-uns à plateaux.

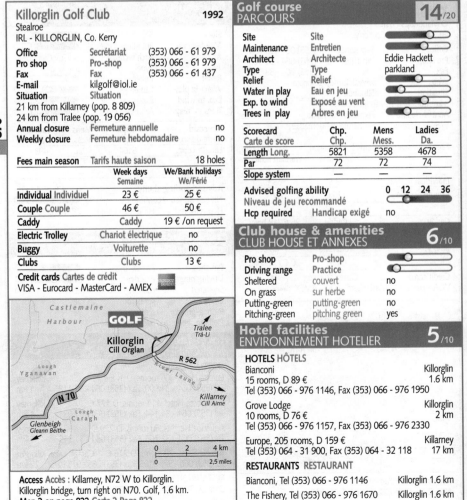

Killorglin Golf Club — 1992

Stealroe
IRL - KILLORGLIN, Co. Kerry

Office	Secrétariat	(353) 066 - 61 979
Pro shop	Pro-shop	(353) 066 - 61 979
Fax	Fax	(353) 066 - 61 437
E-mail	kilgolf@iol.ie	
Situation	Situation	

21 km from Killarney (pop. 8 809)
24 km from Tralee (pop. 19 056)

Annual closure	Fermeture annuelle	no
Weekly closure	Fermeture hebdomadaire	no

Fees main season Tarifs haute saison	18 holes	
	Week days Semaine	**We/Bank holidays** We/Férié
Individual Individuel	23 €	25 €
Couple Couple	46 €	50 €
Caddy Caddy	19 € /on request	
Electric Trolley Chariot électrique	no	
Buggy Voiturette	no	
Clubs Clubs	13 €	

Credit cards Cartes de crédit
VISA - Eurocard - MasterCard - AMEX

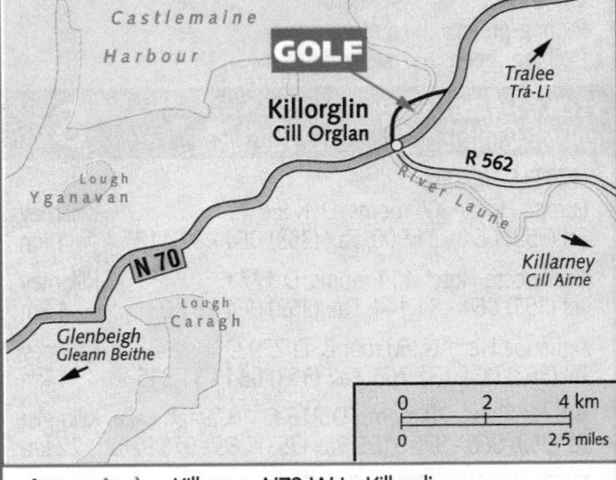

Access Accès : Killarney, N72 W to Killorglin. Killorglin bridge, turn right on N70. Golf, 1.6 km.
Map 2 on page 822 Carte 2 Page 822

Golf course — PARCOURS — 14/20

Site	Site	
Maintenance	Entretien	
Architect	Architecte	Eddie Hackett
Type	Type	parkland
Relief	Relief	
Water in play	Eau en jeu	
Exp. to wind	Exposé au vent	
Trees in play	Arbres en jeu	

Scorecard Carte de score	**Chp.** Chp.	**Mens** Mess.	**Ladies** Da.
Length Long.	5821	5358	4678
Par	72	72	74
Slope system	—	—	—

Advised golfing ability Niveau de jeu recommandé — 0 12 24 36
Hcp required Handicap exigé — no

Club house & amenities — CLUB HOUSE ET ANNEXES — 6/10

Pro shop	Pro-shop	
Driving range	Practice	
Sheltered	couvert	no
On grass	sur herbe	no
Putting-green	putting-green	no
Pitching-green	pitching green	yes

Hotel facilities — ENVIRONNEMENT HOTELIER — 5/10

HOTELS HÔTELS

Bianconi — Killorglin
15 rooms, D 89 € — 1.6 km
Tel (353) 066 - 976 1146, Fax (353) 066 - 976 1950

Grove Lodge — Killorglin
10 rooms, D 76 € — 2 km
Tel (353) 066 - 976 1157, Fax (353) 066 - 976 2330

Europe, 205 rooms, D 159 € — Killarney
Tel (353) 064 - 31 900, Fax (353) 064 - 32 118 — 17 km

RESTAURANTS RESTAURANT

Bianconi, Tel (353) 066 - 976 1146 — Killorglin 1.6 km
The Fishery, Tel (353) 066 - 976 1670 — Killorglin 1.6 km

LAHINCH

17 | 6 | 6

Lahinch has long held pride of place in the collection of great courses in south-west Ireland. The surrounding dunes invite visual comparison with Ballybunion, although it is not quite as challenging. For example, if you can keep on the straight and narrow here, approach shots to the greens are altogether an easier matter, with bump and run shots a distinct possibility. But you need to know the course to cope, to appreciate the effects of the wind, to identify where hazards are placed and to come to terms with the sand-dunes, where balls can end up in some unusual positions. Care is rewarded on this spectacular layout, where high variety is the watchword and where flighters of the ball will have fun (beginners probably much less so). Look out for the extraordinary 5th and 6th holes, the first a par 5, where the second shot has to fly over a huge dune, the latter a par 3 with a blind green.

Dans la collection des grands parcours du sud-ouest de l'Irlande, Lahinch tient depuis longtemps une belle place. Son environnement de grandes dunes le rapproche visuellement de Ballybunion, bien qu'il ne soit pas aussi exigeant. Par exemple, si l'on parvient à rester droit, les approches des greens y sont moins complexes, ceux-ci étant généralement accessibles avec des coups roulés. Mais il faut bien connaître ce parcours pour le négocier, apprécier les effets du vent, identifier la place des obstacles, composer avec les dunes, où la balle peut se trouver dans des situations "intéressantes". La prudence sera récompensée sur ce tracé spectaculaire et d'une très grande variété, où les virtuoses des effets de balle s'amuseront beaucoup (les débutants beaucoup moins). A signaler, les extraordinaires trous 5 et 6, un par 5 où le second coup doit survoler une énorme dune, et un par 3 avec un green aveugle. A connaître.

Lahinch Golf Club — 1892

IRL - LAHINCH, Co Clare

Office	Secrétariat	(353) 065 - 708 1003
Pro shop	Pro-shop	(353) 065 - 708 1003
Fax	Fax	(353) 065 - 708 1592
Web	www.lahinchgolf.com	
Situation	Situation	

0.5 km from Lahinch (pop. 580) 32 km from Ennis (pop. 15 333)

Annual closure	Fermeture annuelle	no
Weekly closure	Fermeture hebdomadaire	no

Fees main season Tarifs haute saison	18 holes	
	Week days Semaine	**We/Bank holidays** We/Férié
Individual Individuel	76 €	76 €
Couple Couple	152 €	152 €

Green-fees on Castle Course: 38 €

Caddy	Caddy	25 € /18 holes
Electric Trolley	Chariot électrique	10 €
Buggy	Voiturette	no
Clubs	Clubs	19 € /18 holes

Credit cards Cartes de crédit
VISA - Eurocard - MasterCard

Access Accès : N18 Limerick → Ennis,
N85 Ennis → Ennistymon, → Lahinch, 3 km
Map 2 on page 822 Carte 2 Page 822

Golf course — PARCOURS — 17/20

Site	Site	
Maintenance	Entretien	
Architect	Architecte	Old Tom Morris Alistair MacKenzie
Type	Type	links
Relief	Relief	
Water in play	Eau en jeu	
Exp. to wind	Exposé au vent	
Trees in play	Arbres en jeu	

Scorecard Carte de score	**Chp.** Chp.	**Mens** Mess.	**Ladies** Da.
Length Long.	6123	5890	4997
Par	72	72	74
Slope system	—	—	—

Advised golfing ability Niveau de jeu recommandé: 0 12 24 36

Hcp required Handicap exigé: 28 Men, 36 Ladies

Club house & amenities — CLUB HOUSE ET ANNEXES — 6/10

Pro shop	Pro-shop	
Driving range	Practice	
Sheltered	couvert	no
On grass	sur herbe	yes
Putting-green	putting-green	yes
Pitching-green	pitching green	no

Hotel facilities — ENVIRONNEMENT HOTELIER — 6/10

HOTELS HÔTELS

Aberdeen Arms, 55 rooms, D 63 € — Lahinch
Tel (353) 065 - 708 1100, Fax (353) 065 - 708 1228

Atlantic Hotel, 14 rooms, D 89 € — Lahinch
Tel (353) 065 - 708 1049, Fax (353) 065 - 708 1029

Falls Hotel, 100 rooms, D 89 € — Ennistymon
Tel (353) 065 - 707 1004, Fax (353) 065 - 707 1367 — 3 km

RESTAURANTS RESTAURANT

Mr Eamons — Lahinch
Tel (353) 065 - 708 1050

Aberdeen Arms, Tel (353) 065 - 708 1100 — Lahinch

LEE VALLEY

13 | 7 | 6

A rather hilly site for players out of condition or those who have taken a little too kindly to delicious Irish food and drink. Over this pleasantly landscaped and country style terrain, Christy O'Connor Jnr has produced a perfectly honest layout, where good shots are rewarded. It still needs getting to know to cope with some tricky holes, like the 10th or the tough 18th, to keep away from the numerous water hazards (on the 8th and 15th especially), and to read the greens, which are sometimes a real handful. There are many different tee-off areas, so the course adjusts easily to players of all abilities and to how you might be feeling on any one particular day. Lee Valley will present its final face once the trees have grown, but it is already one of the busiest courses in the region, which goes to prove that players like to come back here.

Un site parfois bien accidenté pour les joueurs en forme physique moyenne... ou qui auront un peu trop goûté les spécialités irlandaises. Sur ce terrain au paysage très agréable et campagnard, mais pas idéal pour un golf, Christy O'Connor Jr a produit un dessin d'une parfaite honnêteté, où les bons coups de golf sont récompensés, même si une bonne connaissance du terrain permet de mieux négocier quelques trous, comme le 10 ou le difficile 18, d'échapper aux nombreux obstacles d'eau, au 8 et au 15 notamment, et enfin de bien interpréter les greens, parfois d'une grande subtilité. La multiplicité des départs permet d'adapter facilement le parcours à tous les niveaux de jeu, ou à l'inspiration du jour. Lee Valley prendra son véritable visage quand tous les arbres auront poussé, mais c'est déjà l'un des parcours les plus fréquentés de la région, ce qui prouve que les joueurs aiment y revenir.

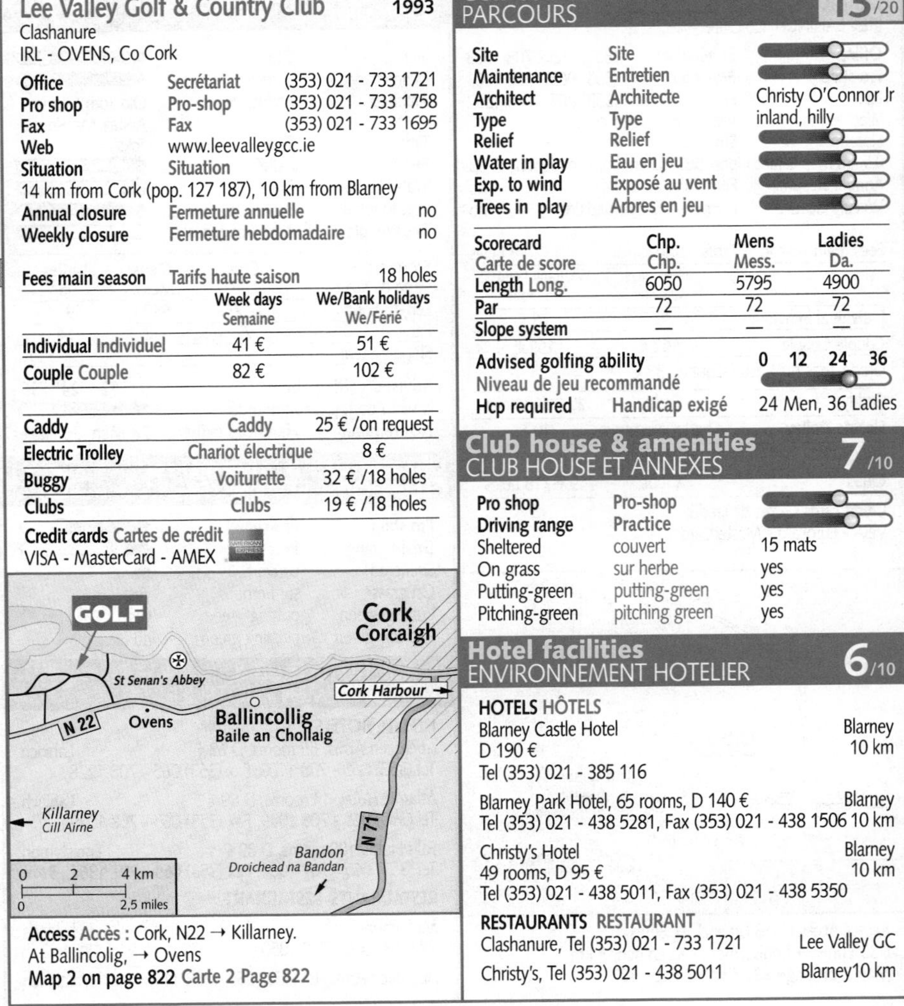

Lee Valley Golf & Country Club — 1993

Clashanure
IRL - OVENS, Co Cork

Office	Secrétariat	(353) 021 - 733 1721
Pro shop	Pro-shop	(353) 021 - 733 1758
Fax	Fax	(353) 021 - 733 1695
Web	www.leevalleygcc.ie	
Situation	Situation	

14 km from Cork (pop. 127 187), 10 km from Blarney

Annual closure	Fermeture annuelle	no
Weekly closure	Fermeture hebdomadaire	no

878

Fees main season Tarifs haute saison	Week days Semaine	We/Bank holidays We/Férié
	18 holes	
Individual Individuel	41 €	51 €
Couple Couple	82 €	102 €

Caddy	Caddy	25 € /on request
Electric Trolley	Chariot électrique	8 €
Buggy	Voiturette	32 € /18 holes
Clubs	Clubs	19 € /18 holes

Credit cards Cartes de crédit
VISA - MasterCard - AMEX

Access Accès : Cork, N22 → Killarney.
At Ballincolig, → Ovens
Map 2 on page 822 Carte 2 Page 822

Golf course — PARCOURS — 13/20

Site	Site	
Maintenance	Entretien	
Architect	Architecte	Christy O'Connor Jr
Type	Type	inland, hilly
Relief	Relief	
Water in play	Eau en jeu	
Exp. to wind	Exposé au vent	
Trees in play	Arbres en jeu	

Scorecard Carte de score	Chp. Chp.	Mens Mess.	Ladies Da.
Length Long.	6050	5795	4900
Par	72	72	72
Slope system	—	—	—

Advised golfing ability 0 12 24 36
Niveau de jeu recommandé
Hcp required Handicap exigé — 24 Men, 36 Ladies

Club house & amenities — CLUB HOUSE ET ANNEXES — 7/10

Pro shop	Pro-shop	
Driving range	Practice	
Sheltered	couvert	15 mats
On grass	sur herbe	yes
Putting-green	putting-green	yes
Pitching-green	pitching green	yes

Hotel facilities — ENVIRONNEMENT HOTELIER — 6/10

HOTELS HÔTELS

Blarney Castle Hotel — Blarney 10 km
D 190 €
Tel (353) 021 - 385 116

Blarney Park Hotel, 65 rooms, D 140 € — Blarney 10 km
Tel (353) 021 - 438 5281, Fax (353) 021 - 438 1506

Christy's Hotel — Blarney 10 km
49 rooms, D 95 €
Tel (353) 021 - 438 5011, Fax (353) 021 - 438 5350

RESTAURANTS RESTAURANT

Clashanure, Tel (353) 021 - 733 1721 — Lee Valley GC
Christy's, Tel (353) 021 - 438 5011 — Blarney10 km

LIMERICK COUNTY

15 | 7 | 6

The cottages on site are an excellent base camp for exploring the courses in this region, especially this one. Des Smyth has used the terrain to good effect, but we will have to wait until the trees grow to see how it will look in the end. For the moment, the saplings are obviously not a problem, but the same cannot be said for the collection of bunkers and obligatory water hazards found on modern courses. Very difficult from the back tees, it is a little kinder further forward, from where we recommend you play unless you are a long driver. A few tees and greens are played blind, which requires good knowledge of the course to fix any definite strategy, especially on the back 9, which happens to be much flatter than the first half of the course. The greens are hospitable but certain pin positions can make them a tricky proposition. This very competent layout is already rated amongst the country's top twenty or thirty inland courses.

Les cottages sur place en font une bonne base pour explorer les golfs de la région, et notamment celui-ci. Des Smyth a bien utilisé le terrain, mais il faudra attendre qu'il prenne son visage définitif, le temps que grandissent les nombreux arbres plantés. Pour l'instant, ils ne sont pas un facteur de difficulté, au contraire de la collection de bunkers et d'obstacles d'eau incontournables dans les parcours modernes. Très difficile des départs arrière, il est plus amical des autres, on les conseillera, à moins d'avoir affaire à de bons frappeurs. Quelques départs et greens sont aveugles, imposant une bonne connaissance du parcours pour avoir une stratégie précise, notamment au retour, qui est en revanche plus plat que l'aller. Les greens sont accueillants, mais certaines positions de drapeau peuvent les rendre très délicats. Cette très solide réalisation figure déjà parmi les vingt ou trente meilleurs parcours inland du pays.

Limerick County Golf & Country Club 1994

IRL - BALLYNEETY, Co Limerick

Office	Secrétariat	(353) 061 - 351 881
Pro shop	Pro-shop	(353) 061 - 351 881
Fax	Fax	(353) 061 - 351 384
Web	www.limerickcounty.com	
Situation	Situation	

11 km from Limerick (pop. 52 039)

Annual closure	Fermeture annuelle	no
Weekly closure	Fermeture hebdomadaire	no

Fees main season Tarifs haute saison	Week days Semaine	We/Bank holidays We/Férié
	18 holes	
Individual Individuel	38 €	44 €
Couple Couple	76 €	88 €

Weekdays: 12.50 € before 9.30 am

Caddy	Caddy	19 € /on request
Electric Trolley	Chariot électrique	13 € /18 holes
Buggy	Voiturette	32 € /18 holes
Clubs	Clubs	19 € /18 holes

Credit cards Cartes de crédit
VISA - MasterCard

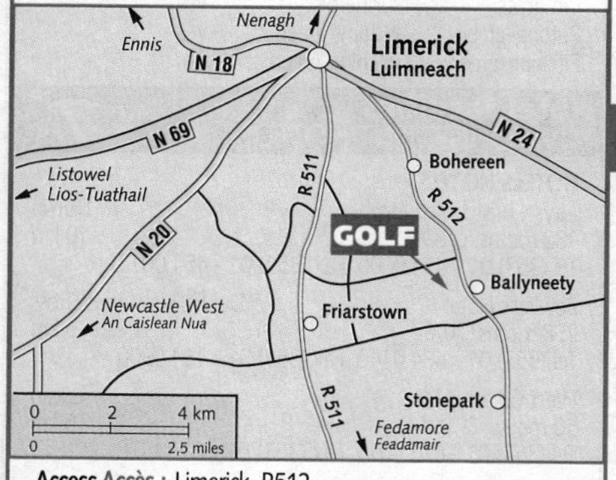

Access Accès : Limerick, R512
Map 2 on page 822 Carte 2 Page 822

Golf course — PARCOURS — 15/20

Site	Site	
Maintenance	Entretien	
Architect	Architecte	Des Smyth
Type	Type	parkland
Relief	Relief	
Water in play	Eau en jeu	
Exp. to wind	Exposé au vent	
Trees in play	Arbres en jeu	

Scorecard Carte de score	Chp. Chp.	Mens Mess.	Ladies Da.
Length Long.	6194	5784	5050
Par	72	72	73
Slope system	—	—	—

Advised golfing ability — 0 12 24 36
Niveau de jeu recommandé

Hcp required Handicap exigé — 28 Men, 36 Ladies

Club house & amenities — CLUB HOUSE ET ANNEXES — 7/10

Pro shop	Pro-shop	
Driving range	Practice	
Sheltered	couvert	20 mats
On grass	sur herbe	yes
Putting-green	putting-green	yes
Pitching-green	pitching green	yes

Hotel facilities — ENVIRONNEMENT HOTELIER — 6/10

HOTELS HÔTELS

Castletroy Park Hotel — Limerick 8 km
107 rooms, D 165 €
Tel (353) 061 - 335 566, Fax (353) 061 - 331 117

Jury's Hotel — Limerick 11 km
95 rooms, D 152 €
Tel (353) 061 - 327 777, Fax (353) 061 - 326 400

Limerick Ryan Hotel, 180 rooms, D 80 € — Limerick 11 km
Tel (353) 061 - 453 922, Fax (353) 061 - 326 333

RESTAURANTS Restaurant

Moll Darby's, Tel (353) 061 - 411 511 — Limerick 11 km

Freddy's Bistro, Tel (353) 061 - 418 749 — Limerick 11 km

LUTTRELLSTOWN

15	7	7

In the grounds of a famous castle hotel, whose illustrious guests have included Queen Victoria, Fred Astaire, Ronald Reagan and Rainiers of Monaco, this recent course was designed by Nicholas Bielenberg. It is laid out in a huge park, where age-old trees add beauty and majesty to a matchless atmosphere of tranquility. The few straight up and down holes are rather a pity, although the fairways are clearly separated by trees and water. These two elements are the main hazards here, especially the many lakes and ponds, which call for long, lofted shots (on about half a dozen holes). This might not be too much to the liking of high-handicappers, but target golf buffs will have fun. The geographical relief is only very slight and enough to give each hole clear definition. Very long from the tiger-tees, this is a stiff challenge for any golfer, although much more approachable from the front tees.

Dans le domaine d'un célèbre Château-hôtel, qui a reçu des gloires telles que la Reine Victoria, Fred Astaire, Ronald Reagan ou Rainier de Monaco, ce récent parcours a été dessiné par Nicholas Bielenberg, dans un immense parc avec des arbres centenaires, qui ajoutent leur beauté et leur majesté à une atmosphère incomparable de tranquillité. On peut regretter certains allers et retours du tracé, malgré que les fairways soient bien séparés par les bois et l'eau. Ces deux éléments constituent des difficultés évidentes, notamment les nombreux lacs et mares, qui obligent souvent à porter la balle (sur une demi-douzaine de trous environ). Si cela ne plaira guère aux handicaps élevés, les habitués du "target golf" auront de quoi s'amuser. Le relief est très modéré, et suffisant pour assurer une bonne définition des trous. Très long des départs de championnat, ce parcours reste un "challenge", mais plus abordable, des départs avancés.

Luttrellstown Golf & Country Club — 1993

IRL - CLONSILLA, Co Dublin

Office	Secrétariat	(353) 01 - 808 9988
Pro shop	Pro-shop	(353) 01 - 808 9988
Fax	Fax	(353) 01 - 820 5218
Web	www.luttrellstown.ie	
Situation	Situation	

10 km from Dublin (pop. 481 854)

Annual closure	Fermeture annuelle	no
Weekly closure	Fermeture hebdomadaire	no

Fees main season — Tarifs haute saison	Week days / Semaine	We/Bank holidays / We/Férié
18 holes		
Individual Individuel	76 €	83 €
Couple Couple	152 €	166 €

Caddy	Caddy	25 € /on request
Electric Trolley	Chariot électrique	no
Buggy	Voiturette	32 € /18 holes
Clubs	Clubs	19 € /18 holes

Credit cards Cartes de crédit
VISA - MasterCard - AMEX - DC 

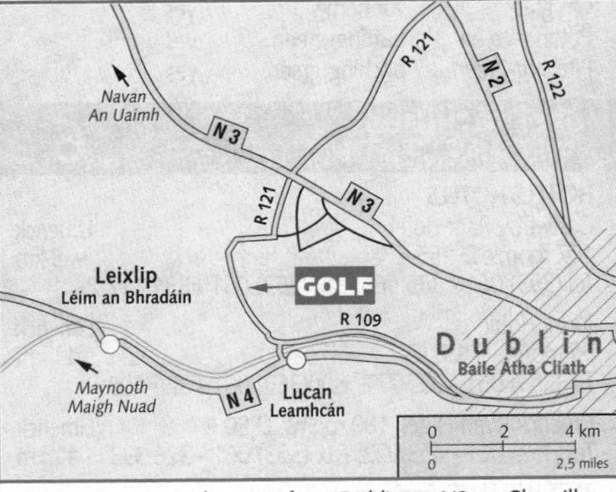

Access Accès : 10 km NW from Dublin on N3 → Clonsilla
Map 3 on page 824 Carte 3 Page 824

Golf course — PARCOURS — 15/20

Site	Site	
Maintenance	Entretien	
Architect	Architecte	Nicholas Bielenberg
Type	Type	parkland
Relief	Relief	
Water in play	Eau en jeu	
Exp. to wind	Exposé au vent	
Trees in play	Arbres en jeu	

Scorecard / Carte de score	Chp. / Chp.	Mens / Mess.	Ladies / Da.
Length Long.	6384	6032	5246
Par	72	72	72
Slope system	—	—	—

Advised golfing ability — Niveau de jeu recommandé: 0 12 24 36
Hcp required — Handicap exigé: 24 Men, 36 Ladies

Club house & amenities — CLUB HOUSE ET ANNEXES — 7/10

Pro shop	Pro-shop	
Driving range	Practice	
Sheltered	couvert	no
On grass	sur herbe	yes
Putting-green	putting-green	yes
Pitching-green	pitching green	no

Hotel facilities — ENVIRONNEMENT HOTELIER — 7/10

HOTELS HÔTELS

Jurys Christchurch Inn — Dublin 10 km
182 rooms, D 89 €
Tel (353) 01 - 454 0000, Fax (353) 01 - 454 0012

Bewley's Hotel — Dublin/Newlands Cross 5 km
258 rooms, 70 €
Tel (353) 01 - 464 0140, Fax (353) 01 - 464 0900

West County Hotel — Lucan 5 km
50 rooms, D 114 €
Tel (353) 01 - 626 4011, Fax (353) 01 - 623 1378

RESTAURANTS RESTAURANT

Annadale, Tel (353) 01 - 628 0622 — Lucan 4 km

Scott's, Tel (353) 01 - 821 3482 — Castleknock 3 km

MALAHIDE Red + Blue + Yellow

13 | 7 | 8

If you want to play every Eddie Hackett course in Ireland, you sure have a lot of golfing to do. With the experience of age, he was very kind here with the average week-enders, who return the compliment and come to play here in droves on 27 holes combinable in every different way. In addition to the actual layout, the wind and wetness of the terrain can seriously dent any hopes of a good card. First time around, a number of blinds shots should require some reconnaissance work, but the course is by no means hilly. Bunkering is high quality, as is the use of water hazards, especially on the par 3s. Another side to the course's resistance is the elevation of certain greens, calling for some accurate ironwork. Once on the green, the surfaces are easy to read (perhaps too easy ?). A recent course, Malahide has matured and is always good fun in amongst the region's great links courses.

Si vous voulez jouer tous les parcours d'Eddie Hackett en Irlande, vous n'avez pas fini... Avec l'expérience de l'âge, il a été ici très amical avec les golfeurs moyens : ils le lui rendent bien et viennent nombreux sur les 27 trous, combinables à volonté. En dehors du tracé lui-même, le vent et l'humidité du terrain peuvent perturber les prétentions à bien scorer. La première fois, certains coups aveugles nécessitent une certaine reconnaissance, mais le parcours est facilement jouable à pied. Le "bunkering" est de grande qualité, de même que l'utilisation des obstacles d'eau, notamment sur les pars 3. Autre facteur de résistance du parcours, l'élévation de certains greens, qui oblige à des coups de fer très exacts, mais les surfaces de putting ne sont guère complexes à lire (pas assez ?). De construction récente, Malahide a pris de la maturité, c'est toujours une bonne récréation entre les grands links de la région.

Malahide Golf Club — 1991

Beechwood, The Grange
IRL - MALAHIDE, Co Dublin

Office	Secrétariat	(353) 01 - 846 1611
Pro shop	Pro-shop	(353) 01 - 846 0002
Fax	Fax	(353) 01 - 846 1270
E-mail	malgc@club.ie	
Situation	Situation	

18 km from Dublin (pop 481 854)

Annual closure	Fermeture annuelle	no
Weekly closure	Fermeture hebdomadaire	no

Fees main season Tarifs haute saison		18 holes
	Week days Semaine	We/Bank holidays We/Férié
Individual Individuel	57 €	83 €
Couple Couple	114 €	166 €

Caddy	Caddy	32 € /on request
Electric Trolley	Chariot électrique	no
Buggy	Voiturette	25 € /18 holes
Clubs	Clubs	25 € /18 holes

Credit cards Cartes de crédit
VISA - Eurocard - MasterCard - AMEX

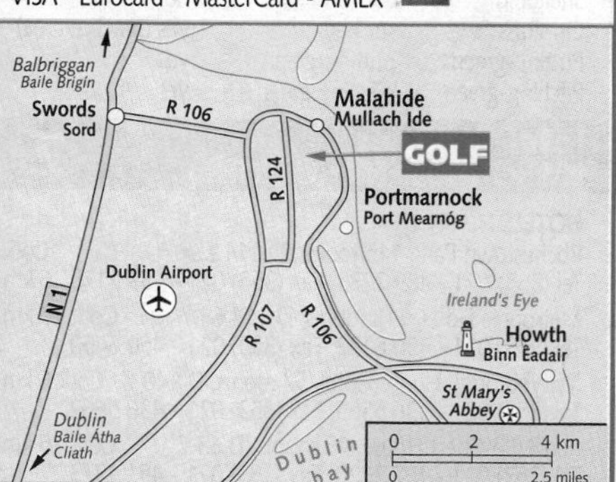

Access Accès : Dublin to Portmarnock Village. Left turn at traffic lights beside Church. Golf 3 km from there.
Map 3 on page 824 Carte 3 Page 824

Golf course PARCOURS — 13/20

Site	Site	
Maintenance	Entretien	
Architect	Architecte	Eddie Hackett
Type	Type	parkland
Relief	Relief	
Water in play	Eau en jeu	
Exp. to wind	Exposé au vent	
Trees in play	Arbres en jeu	

Scorecard Carte de score	Chp. Chp.	Mens Mess.	Ladies Da.
Length Long.	6066	5742	5146
Par	71	70	74
Slope system	—	—	—

Advised golfing ability Niveau de jeu recommandé — 0 12 24 36
Hcp required Handicap exigé — Men 28, Ladies 36

Club house & amenities CLUB HOUSE ET ANNEXES — 7/10

Pro shop	Pro-shop	
Driving range	Practice	
Sheltered	couvert	no
On grass	sur herbe	yes
Putting-green	putting-green	yes
Pitching-green	pitching green	no

Hotel facilities ENVIRONNEMENT HOTELIER — 8/10

HOTELS HÔTELS

Grand Hotel, 100 rooms, D 229 € — Malahide 1 km
Tel (353) 01 - 845 0000, Fax (353) 01 - 845 0987

Portmarnock Links Hotel — Portmarnock 4 km
110 rooms, D 254 €
Tel (353) 01 - 846 0611, Fax (353) 01 - 846 2442

White Sands Hotel — Portmarnock 2 km
10 rooms, D 127 €
Tel (353) 01 - 846 0003, Fax (353) 01 - 846 0420

RESTAURANTS RESTAURANT

Bon Appetit, Tel (353) 01 - 845 0314 — Malahide 1 km
Colonnade, Tel (353) 01 - 845 0000 — Malahide 1 km

MONKSTOWN

15	6	7

This course was built in the early 20th century then restyled in 1971, but it remains on the short side, probably much to the pleasure of the majority of golfers, no matter how modern their equipment. The two parts of the course are distinctly different, with the outward 9 overlooking Cork harbour. Indeed, variety is one of the course's strong points, giving numerous opportunities to try different shots. The majority of hazards are clearly visible from the tee, but the architects could not or would not avoid a number of blind shots, imposed by the sloping terrain. The overall topology and the position of trees call for some long, hard thinking, as do the 80 bunkers, all of which are very much in play. Add to this the setting provided by an old 17th century castle and the excellence of the greens - long considered to be the best in the country - and you will understand why Monkstown deserves to find out just how good a golfer you are.

Créé au début du XXème siècle, ce parcours a été remanié en 1971, mais est resté assez court, ce qui n'est pas pour déplaire à la majorité des joueurs, quel que soit leur armement golfique moderne. Les deux parties de ce parcours sont sensiblement différentes, avec les 9 premiers trous dominant le port de Cork. La variété est d'ailleurs l'un des points forts de ce tracé, ce qui offre parallèlement une très grande variété d'occasions de coups différents. La plus grande partie des obstacles sont bien visibles du départ, mais les architectes n'ont pas pu ou voulu éviter certains coups aveugles, que la configuration du terrain pouvait imposer. Les contours du terrain comme la position des arbres imposent une certaine réflexion, de même que la présence de 80 bunkers dont aucun n'est en dehors du jeu. Si l'on ajoute le décor formé par un vieux château du XVIIè siècle et la qualité des greens, longtemps considérés comme les meilleurs du pays, on aura compris que Monkstown mérite de connaître la qualité de votre golf.

Monkstown Golf Club — 1908

Parkgarry
IRL - MONKSTOWN, Co. Cork

Office	Secrétariat	(353) 021 - 484 1376
Pro shop	Pro-shop	(353) 021 - 484 1686
Fax	Fax	(353) 021 - 484 1722
Web	—	
Situation	Situation	

Cork (pop. 127 187), 12 km

Annual closure	Fermeture annuelle	no
Weekly closure	Fermeture hebdomadaire	no

Fees main season Tarifs haute saison	18 holes	
	Week days Semaine	**We/Bank holidays** We/Férié
Individual Individuel	38 €	44 €
Couple Couple	76 €	88 €

Caddy	Caddy	25 €
Electric Trolley	Chariot électrique	13 € /18 holes
Buggy	Voiturette	25 €
Clubs	Clubs	15 €

Credit cards Cartes de crédit
VISA - MasterCard - AMEX

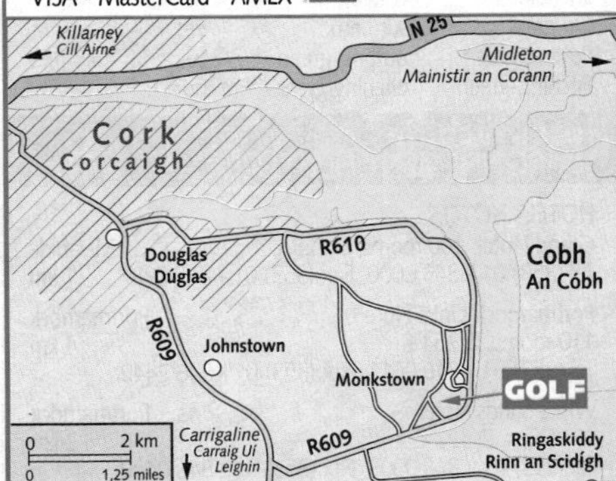

Access Accès : Cork, South East along R610 → Glenbrook/Monkstown
Map 2 on page 822 Carte 2 Page 822

Golf course — PARCOURS — 15/20

Site	Site	
Maintenance	Entretien	
Architect	Architecte	Peter O'Hare T. Carey, B. Murphy
Type	Type	parkland
Relief	Relief	
Water in play	Eau en jeu	
Exp. to wind	Exposé au vent	
Trees in play	Arbres en jeu	

Scorecard Carte de score	**Chp.** Chp.	**Mens** Mess.	**Ladies** Da.
Length Long.	5669	5441	4862
Par	70	70	73
Slope system	—	—	—

Advised golfing ability — Niveau de jeu recommandé: 0 12 24 36
Hcp required — Handicap exigé: no

Club house & amenities — CLUB HOUSE ET ANNEXES — 6/10

Pro shop	Pro-shop	
Driving range	Practice	
Sheltered	couvert	no
On grass	sur herbe	yes (practice area)
Putting-green	putting-green	yes
Pitching-green	pitching green	yes

Hotel facilities — ENVIRONNEMENT HOTELIER — 7/10

HOTELS HÔTELS

Rochestown Park, 115 rooms, D 114 € — Cork 6 km
Tel (353) 021 - 489 2233, Fax (353) 021 - 489 2178

Metropole Hotel, 113 rooms, D 114 € — Cork 10 km
Tel (353) 021 - 450 8122, Fax (353) 021 - 450 6450

Maryborough House Hotel, 57 rooms, D 140 € — Cork 6 km
Tel (353) 021 - 436 5555, Fax (353) 021 - 436 5662

Redclyffe Guest House, 13 rooms, D 63 € — Cork 15 km
Tel (353) 021 - 427 3220, Fax (353) 021 - 481 1373

RESTAURANTS RESTAURANT

The Bosun, Tel (353) 021 - 842 172 — Monkstown 3 km
Gregory's — Carrigaline 12 km

MOUNT JULIET

18 | 9 | 8

There is hardly a country in the world where Jack Nicklaus has not left his mark as a course designer, with, it should be said, mixed success. If he claims to be the greatest course designer, our reply is that there are probably many better than he around the world. It all depends on what a designer can squeeze out of a given space. At Mount Juliet, Nicklaus was presented with a magnificent estate, profusely covered with oak, lime and beech trees. A lot of use has been found for water (there is even a waterfall) and very US-style bunkers, or sand-traps, as they say. The greens, vast and well-designed, only add to the difficulties of a course which demands a complete game from start to finish and, in particular an aptitude for target golf. The many different tee-off areas cater to players of differing abilities, but given the overall length the back-tees should most definitely be reserved for single-figure handicappers. Spectacular and remarkable intelligent, this is an excellent Nicklaus vintage.

Il n'est guère de pays au monde où Jack Nicklaus n'ait laissé sa trace en tant qu'architecte, avec - il faut bien le dire - des bonheurs divers. Et s'il annonce vouloir être le plus grand architecte, on répondra qu'il y a beaucoup de meilleurs architectes du monde ! Tout dépend du parti qu'ils tirent d'un espace. A Mount Juliet, il a trouvé une magnifique propriété, généreusement occupée par les chênes, les tilleuls, les hêtres. Un généreux usage a été fait de l'eau (il y a même une cascade), et de bunkers au profil très américain. Et les greens eux-mêmes, vastes et bien travaillés, ajoutent aux difficultés : ce parcours exige un jeu complet, du départ au dernier trou, et singulièrement un jeu de "target golf". La diversité des départs permet de l'adapter aux possibilités des joueurs, mais sa longueur réserve les départs arrière aux handicaps à un chiffre. Spectaculaire et remarquablement intelligent, c'est un excellent Nicklaus...

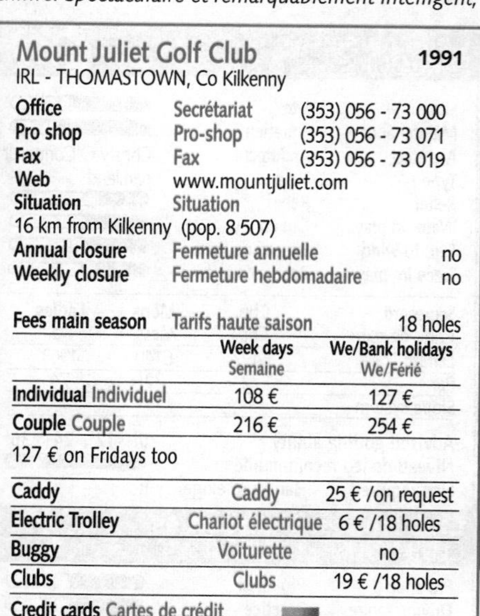

Mount Juliet Golf Club — 1991

IRL - THOMASTOWN, Co Kilkenny

Office	Secrétariat	(353) 056 - 73 000
Pro shop	Pro-shop	(353) 056 - 73 071
Fax	Fax	(353) 056 - 73 019
Web	www.mountjuliet.com	
Situation	Situation	
16 km from Kilkenny (pop. 8 507)		
Annual closure	Fermeture annuelle	no
Weekly closure	Fermeture hebdomadaire	no

Fees main season Tarifs haute saison	18 holes	
	Week days Semaine	**We/Bank holidays** We/Férié
Individual Individuel	108 €	127 €
Couple Couple	216 €	254 €

127 € on Fridays too

Caddy	Caddy	25 € /on request
Electric Trolley	Chariot électrique	6 € /18 holes
Buggy	Voiturette	no
Clubs	Clubs	19 € /18 holes

Credit cards Cartes de crédit
VISA - MasterCard - DC - AMEX

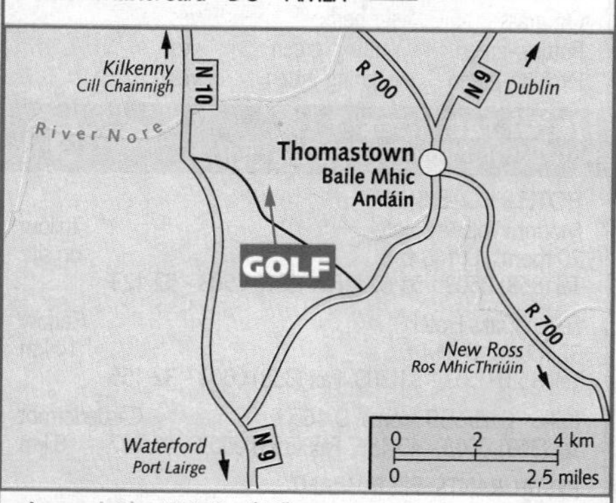

Access Accès : N10 S. of Kilkenny
N9 S. of Carlow
Map 2 on page 823 Carte 2 Page 823

Golf course — PARCOURS — 18/20

Site	Site	
Maintenance	Entretien	
Architect	Architecte	Jack Nicklaus
Type	Type	parkland
Relief	Relief	
Water in play	Eau en jeu	
Exp. to wind	Exposé au vent	
Trees in play	Arbres en jeu	

Scorecard Carte de score	**Chp.** Chp.	**Mens** Mess.	**Ladies** Da.
Length Long.	7111	6705	5554
Par	72	72	73
Slope system	—	—	—

Advised golfing ability Niveau de jeu recommandé — 0 12 24 36

Hcp required Handicap exigé — 28 Men, 36 Ladies

Club house & amenities — CLUB HOUSE ET ANNEXES — 9/10

Pro shop	Pro-shop	
Driving range	Practice	
Sheltered	couvert	5 bays
On grass	sur herbe	yes
Putting-green	putting-green	yes
Pitching-green	pitching green	yes

Hotel facilities — ENVIRONNEMENT HOTELIER — 8/10

HOTELS HÔTELS

Mount Juliet House — Thomastown on site
32 rooms, D 229 €
Tel (353) 056 - 73 000, Fax (353) 056 - 73 019

Kilkenny Ormonde Hotel — Kilkenny 17 km
112 rooms, D 140 €
Tel (353) 056 - 23 900, Fax (353) 056 - 23 977

Newpark Hotel, 84 rooms, D 140 € — Kilkenny 17 km
Tel (353) 056 - 22 122, Fax (353) 056 - 61 111

RESTAURANTS RESTAURANT

Parliament House, Tel (353) 056 - 63 666 — Kilkenny 16 km
Langtons, Tel (353) 056 - 65 133 — Kilkenny 16 km

MOUNT WOLSELEY

13 | 6 | 5

This recent course is quite typical of the style of Christy O'Connor Jr., with water hazards – water coming into play on eleven holes, especially on the outward nine – and fairway bunkers which some might feel often unfairly penalise good shots. High-level lady players will also feel frustrated as their tee-boxes are often too far forward (a frequent feature these days). Some men will find the backtees too far backward (it is also a frequent feature these days!). However this very likeable course is most welcome in a lovely region and the overall honesty of the layout is conducive to attacking golf without the fear of too many unpleasant surprises. We noted the variety of design and protection for the greens, thus allowing all sorts of approach shots. The course is in very respectable condition.

Ce récent parcours est tout à fait typique du style architectural de Christy O'Connor Jr, avec ses obstacles d'eau (en jeu sur onze trous, surtout à l'aller) et ses bunkers de fairway, mais on peut trouver que ces derniers pénalisent souvent les bons coups. Les femmes de bon niveau seront aussi frustrées, car leurs départs sont souvent trop avancés (c'est aujourd'hui fréquent). Quant aux hommes, ils pourront trouver en revanche leurs backtees trop éloignés (c'est aujourd'hui tout aussi fréquent!). Cela dit, cette sympathique réalisation est bienvenue dans une région très agréable, et la franchise générale du tracé permet de l'attaquer sans trop de crainte des mauvaises surprises. Il faut enfin remarquer la variété de dessin et de défense des greens, ce qui permet toutes sortes d'approches. L'état du parcours est très honorable.

Mount Wolseley Golf Club — 1996

IRL - TULLOW, Co. Carlow

Office	Secrétariat	(353) 0503 - 51 674
Pro shop	Pro-shop	(353) 0503 - 51 674
Fax	Fax	(353) 0503 - 52 123
Web		www.golfclubireland.com/mountwolseley.htm
Situation	Situation	
Annual closure	Fermeture annuelle	no
Weekly closure	Fermeture hebdomadaire	no

80 km S of Dublin (pop. 481 854)
14 km E of Carlow (pop. 11 721)

Fees main season Tarifs haute saison — 18 holes

	Week days Semaine	We/Bank holidays We/Férié
Individual Individuel	44 €	51 €
Couple Couple	88 €	102 €
Caddy Caddy		25 € /on request
Electric Trolley Chariot électrique		6 € /18 holes
Buggy Voiturette		32 € /18 holes
Clubs Clubs		19 € /18 holes

Credit cards Cartes de crédit
VISA - MasterCard - DC - AMEX

Access Accès : Dublin, N9 → Carlow.
In Castledermot, R418 to Tullow
Map 2 on page 823 Carte 2 Page 823

Golf course PARCOURS — 13/20

Site	Site	
Maintenance	Entretien	
Architect	Architecte	Christy O'Connor Jr
Type	Type	parkland
Relief	Relief	
Water in play	Eau en jeu	
Exp. to wind	Exposé au vent	
Trees in play	Arbres en jeu	

Scorecard Carte de score	Chp. Chp.	Mens Mess.	Ladies Da.
Length Long.	6497	6140	4963
Par	72	72	74
Slope system	—	—	—

Advised golfing ability Niveau de jeu recommandé — 0 12 24 36
Hcp required Handicap exigé — no

Club house & amenities CLUB HOUSE ET ANNEXES — 6/10

Pro shop	Pro-shop	
Driving range	Practice	
Sheltered	couvert	
On grass	sur herbe	yes
Putting-green	putting-green	yes
Pitching-green	pitching green	yes

Hotel facilities ENVIRONNEMENT HOTELIER — 5/10

HOTELS HÔTELS

Mount Wolseley Hotel — Tullow on site
20 rooms, D 140 €
Tel (353) 0503 - 51 674, Fax (353) 0503 - 52 123

Seven Oaks Hotel — Carlow 14 km
32 rooms, D 114 €
Tel (353) 0503 - 31 308, Fax (353) 0503 - 32 155

Kilkea Castle 38 rooms, D 165 € — Castledermot 8 km
Tel (353) 0503 - 45 156, Fax (353) 0503 - 45 187

RESTAURANTS RESTAURANT

Mount Wolseley Hotel, — Tullow on site
Tel (353) 0503 - 51674

Kilkea Castle, Tel (353) 0503 - 45 156 — Castledermot 8 km

MULLINGAR

15 | 5 | 5

James Braid, who reshaped this course in 1937, considered Mullingar to be one of his best designs. A little on the short side today (there was little space available at the time), this is still a very popular course with Irish players, although it has still to gain an international reputation. It shouldn't leave foreigners feeling too lost, as you can find similar courses in the UK and on the continent, which only show how typical an inland design this is. The one slight difference would be the need to go for target golf, as the greens are very well guarded up front. The hazards are dangerous and call for precision play (the par 3s are excellent). Skills in working the ball both ways, although not decisive, do give an advantage here. A pleasant course for all levels (the ladies tees are nicely well forward) and one you won't be sorry to discover. It has been recently lengthened and re-bunkered.

James Braid, qui remodela ce parcours en 1937, le considérait comme un de ses meilleurs dessins. Aujourd'hui un peu court (l'espace disponible était réduit), c'est malgré tout un golf très populaire auprès des joueurs irlandais, mais sa réputation internationale reste à établir. Il ne devrait pas trop dépayser les étrangers, car on pourrait trouver aussi bien en Grande-Bretagne que sur le continent des parcours similaires, tant il est typique de l'esthétique et de l'architecture des "inland". Une seule à dans cette appréciation : il vaut mieux jouer des balles de "target golf", car les greens sont bien défendus frontalement. Les obstacles sont dangereux, obligeant à un jeu précis (les pars 3 sont excellents), et si l'on sait travailler la balle, l'avantage sera sinon décisif, du moins important. Un parcours plaisant, pour tous niveaux (les départs dames sont gentiment avancés) et que l'on ne sera pas déçu de découvrir. Il a été récemment allongé, et son bunkering revu.

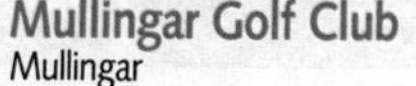

Mullingar Golf Club — 1894

Mullingar
IRL - BELVEDERE, Co West Meath

Office	Secrétariat	(353) 044 - 48 366
Pro shop	Pro-shop	(353) 044 - 40 088
Fax	Fax	(353) 044 - 41 499
Web	—	
Situation	Situation	

5 km from Mullingar (pop. 8 040)

Annual closure	Fermeture annuelle	no
Weekly closure	Fermeture hebdomadaire	no

Fees main season / Tarifs haute saison	18 holes	
	Week days / Semaine	We/Bank holidays / We/Férié
Individual Individuel	32 €	38 €
Couple Couple	64 €	76 €

Caddy	Caddy	no
Electric Trolley	Chariot électrique	6 € /18 holes
Buggy	Voiturette	32 € /18 holes
Clubs	Clubs	13 € /18 holes
Credit cards	Cartes de crédit	no

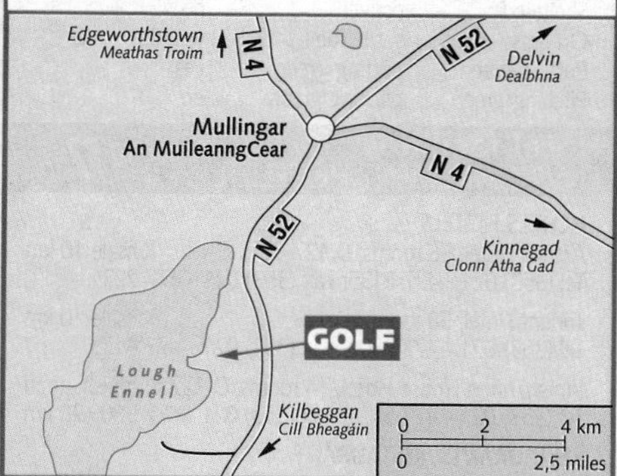

Access Accès : Dublin, M4 / N4 → Mullingar.
In Mullingar, R52 to Belvedere
Map 2 on page 823 Carte 2 Page 823

Golf course / PARCOURS — 15/20

Site	Site	
Maintenance	Entretien	
Architect	Architecte	James Braid
Type	Type	parkland
Relief	Relief	
Water in play	Eau en jeu	
Exp. to wind	Exposé au vent	
Trees in play	Arbres en jeu	

Scorecard / Carte de score	Chp. / Chp.	Mens / Mess.	Ladies / Da.
Length Long.	5913	5450	4991
Par	72	72	74
Slope system	—	—	—

Advised golfing ability / Niveau de jeu recommandé: 0 12 24 36
Hcp required / Handicap exigé: 28 Men, 36 Ladies

Club house & amenities / CLUB HOUSE ET ANNEXES — 5/10

Pro shop	Pro-shop	
Driving range	Practice	
Sheltered	couvert	no
On grass	sur herbe	yes
Putting-green	putting-green	yes
Pitching-green	pitching green	no

Hotel facilities / ENVIRONNEMENT HOTELIER — 5/10

HOTELS HÔTELS

Bloomfield House — Mullingar
33 rooms, D 89 €
Tel (353) 044 - 40 894, Fax (353) 044 - 43 767

Greville Arms — Mullingar 5 km
40 rooms, D 102 €
Tel (353) 044 - 48 563, Fax (353) 044 - 48 052

RESTAURANTS RESTAURANT

Hacketts — Mullingar 5 km
Tel (353) 044 - 49 755

Oscars — Mullingar 5 km
Tel (353) 044 - 44 909

OLD HEAD

16 | 7 | 7

Like a boat leaving its harbour, this new course is exposed to all winds. So there was really little point in adding an array of difficulties to those already inherent in an excellent and virtually sea-bound setting and the architects don't overtask the players'strength. Perched atop cliffs but not really a links course in the strict sense of the term, this is still one of the most exciting courses to play at the present time. The number of tee-boxes helps adapt the course to its strengths and the forces of nature, but you are best advised to opt for match-play rather than aim to score to your handicap. The pretty town of Kinsale deserved a class course, and here it is, laid out by a host of designers (Kirby, Carr, Merrigan, Hackett and Higgins). Not surprisingly, the purist may point of a little lack of unity in style.

Comme un navire sortant du port, ce nouveau parcours est exposé à tous les vents. On admirera la sagesse des architectes, car il n'était pas utile d'ajouter une profusion de difficultés à celles imposées par un site exceptionnel, pratiquement encerclé par la mer. Situé au sommet des falaises, sans être un links à proprement parler, il n'en est pas moins l'un des plus excitants à jouer actuellement. Le nombre de tees permet d'adapter le parcours à ses forces et celles de la nature, mais il vaudra mieux y jouer en match-play que de faire la course derrière son handicap. La jolie ville de Kinsale méritait un parcours de grande classe. Dessiné par une armée d'architectes (Kirby, Carr, Merrigan, Hackett et Higgins), il manquera cependant un peu d'unité de style aux yeux des puristes...

Old Head Golf Links — 1997

IRL - KINSALE, Co. Cork

Office	Secrétariat	(353) 021 - 477 8444
Pro shop	Pro-shop	(353) 021 - 477 8444
Fax	Fax	(353) 021 - 477 8567
E-mail	info@oldheadgolf.ie	
Situation	Situation	

10 km S of Kinsale (pop. 2 007)
48 km from Cork (pop. 127 187)

Annual closure	Fermeture annuelle	no
Weekly closure	Fermeture hebdomadaire	no

Fees main season Tarifs haute saison		18 holes
	Week days Semaine	We/Bank holidays We/Férié
Individual Individuel	241 €	241 €
Couple Couple	482 €	482 €
Caddy	Caddy	32 € /on request
Electric Trolley	Chariot électrique	no
Buggy	Voiturette	51 € /18 holes
Clubs	Clubs	38 € /18 holes

Credit cards Cartes de crédit
VISA - MasterCard - DC - AMEX

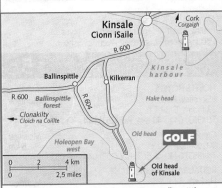

Access Accès : Cork → Kinsale, R 600 → Ballinspittle
Map 2 on page 822 Carte 2 Page 822

Golf course PARCOURS — 16/20

Site	Site	
Maintenance	Entretien	
Architect	Architecte	Ron Kirby, Joe Carr P. Merrigan...
Type	Type	seaside course
Relief	Relief	
Water in play	Eau en jeu	
Exp. to wind	Exposé au vent	
Trees in play	Arbres en jeu	

Scorecard Carte de score	Chp. Chp.	Mens Mess.	Ladies Da.
Length Long.	6080	5657	4827
Par	72	72	72
Slope system	—	—	—

Advised golfing ability / Niveau de jeu recommandé: 0 12 24 36

Hcp required / Handicap exigé: no

Club house & amenities CLUB HOUSE ET ANNEXES — 7/10

Pro shop	Pro-shop	
Driving range	Practice	
Sheltered	couvert	no
On grass	sur herbe	yes (03 → 10)
Putting-green	putting-green	yes
Pitching-green	pitching green	no

Hotel facilities ENVIRONNEMENT HOTELIER — 7/10

HOTELS HÔTELS

Actons Hotel, 56 rooms, D 127 € — Kinsale 10 km
Tel (353) 021 - 477 2135, Fax (353) 021 - 477 2231

Trident Hotel, 58 rooms, D 127 € — Kinsale 10 km
Tel (353) 021 - 477 2301, Fax (353) 021 - 477 4173

Innishannon House Hotel, 14 rooms, D 127 € — Innishannon 20 km
Tel (353) 021 - 477 5121, Fax (353) 021 - 477 5609

RESTAURANTS RESTAURANT

The Vintage, Tel (353) 021 - 477 2502 — Kinsale 10 km
Blue Haven Hotel, Tel (353) 021 - 477 4075 — Kinsale
The White House — Kinsale
Tel (353) 021 - 477 2125

PORTMARNOCK 19 | 7 | 8

A masterpiece. Straight to the point, honest, blunt and diabolical when the wind blows. While Ballybunion can sometimes appear a little baroque, Portmarnock posts an almost austere classicism. There is not one hazard too many, and not one too few to collect wayward shots, not to mention the rough, which is knee-high in places. The greens are huge, subtly contoured and formidably well-guarded. Every shot has to be perfect, from tee to final putt, otherwise stick your tail between your legs and accept that what you get is no more than what you give, with no chance of blaming a single hidden difficulty. If there is one course in this world to be admired for its power, visual amazement, intelligence and variety within unity of style, then it has to be Portmarnock. It is also a great lesson in sobriety for all the world's golf-course designers. You haven't lived if you haven't played Portmarmock at least once. There again, you could also spend your whole life playing here. Almost good value for (so much) money.

Un chef-d'oeuvre. Direct, franc, brutal, et diabolique quand le vent souffle. Si Ballybunion peut paraître parfois baroque, Portmarnock est d'un classicisme presque austère. Il n'y a pas un obstacle superflu, mais il n'en manque pas un pour recevoir les coups égarés, sans même parler d'un rough qui peut monter jusqu'aux genoux. Les greens sont vastes, leurs contours subtils, leurs défenses redoutables. Tous les coups doivent être parfaits, du départ au dernier putt, sinon, il faut faire preuve d'humilité, accepter de ne recevoir que ce que vous donnez, sans pouvoir accuser une seule difficulté cachée. S'il est un parcours admirable par sa puissance, sa grandeur visuelle, son intelligence, sa diversité à l'intérieur même d'une unité de style, c'est Portmarnock. C'est aussi une grande leçon de sobriété pour tous les architectes du monde. On ne saurait vivre sans avoir joué ici une fois, on pourrait aussi y passer sa vie. Disons que le rapport qualité/green fee est presque bon.

Portmarnock Golf Club — 1894

IRL - PORTMARNOCK, Co. Dublin

Office	Secrétariat	(353) 01 - 846 2968
Pro shop	Pro-shop	(353) 01 - 846 2634
Fax	Fax	(353) 01 - 846 2601
Web	www.portmarnockgolfclub.ie	
Situation	Situation 16 km NE of Dublin (pop. 481 854)	
Annual closure	Fermeture annuelle	no
Weekly closure	Fermeture hebdomadaire	no

Fees main season Tarifs haute saison — 18 holes

	Week days Semaine	We/Bank holidays We/Férié
Individual Individuel	127 €	159 €
Couple Couple	254 €	318 €

No women at weekend or public holidays !!!

Caddy	Caddy	32 € /on request
Electric Trolley	Chariot électrique	6 € /18 holes
Buggy	Voiturette	no
Clubs	Clubs	20 € /full day

Credit cards Cartes de crédit
VISA - Eurocard - MasterCard - DC - AMEX

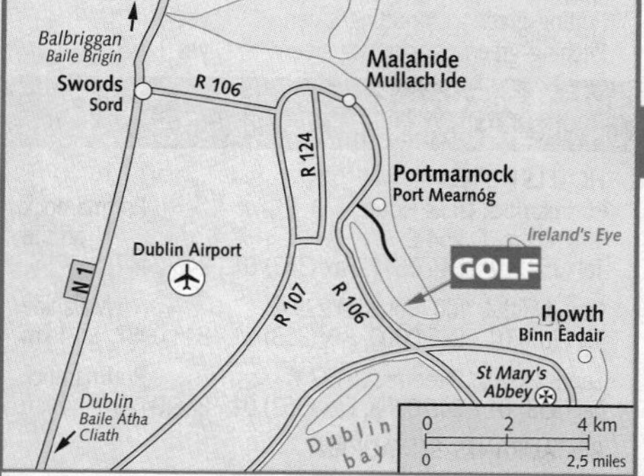

Access Accès : Baldoyle, Portmarnock Village. Golf Links bar, turn right. Golf 1,5 km
Map 3 on page 824 Carte 3 Page 824

Golf course PARCOURS — 19/20

Site	Site	
Maintenance	Entretien	
Architect	Architecte	WG Pikeman George Ross
Type	Type	links
Relief	Relief	
Water in play	Eau en jeu	
Exp. to wind	Exposé au vent	
Trees in play	Arbres en jeu	

Scorecard Carte de score	Chp. Chp.	Mens Mess.	Ladies Da.
Length Long.	6656	6251	5304
Par	72	72	72
Slope system	—	—	—

Advised golfing ability Niveau de jeu recommandé — 0 12 24 36

Hcp required Handicap exigé — 28 Men, 36 Ladies

Club house & amenities CLUB HOUSE ET ANNEXES — 7/10

Pro shop	Pro-shop	
Driving range	Practice	
Sheltered	couvert	no
On grass	sur herbe	yes
Putting-green	putting-green	yes
Pitching-green	pitching green	yes

Hotel facilities ENVIRONNEMENT HOTELIER — 8/10

HOTELS HÔTELS

Grand Hotel Malahide, 100 rooms, D 229 € — Malahide
Tel (353) 01 - 845 0000, Fax (353) 01 - 845 0987 — 5 km

Marine Hotel, 26 rooms, D 152 € — Sutton
Tel (353) 01 - 832 2613, Fax (353) 01 - 839 04 42 — 5 km

Portmarnock Hotel & Golf Links — Portmarnock
110 rooms, D 146 € — 1 km
Tel (353) 01 - 846 0611, Fax (353) 01 - 846 2442

RESTAURANTS RESTAURANT

Colonnade — Grand Hotel, Malahide 5 km
Tel (353) 01 - 845 0000

Meridian Restaurant — Marine Hotel, Sutton
Tel (353) 01 - 839 0000 — 5 km

PORTMARNOCK LINKS

17 | 7 | 8

Assuming such a prestigious name was a stiff task, but Bernhard Langer and Stan Eby accepted the challenge and came up with a great course. Only history will tell how great, but their initial achievement was to approach the site with a degree of modesty, and to learn from others - including its illustrious neighbour and other gems such as Carnoustie and Muirfield - without copying a single thing. There is nothing visually excessive and no signature hole, just a natural layout in unforgiving, changing landscape. While the first holes are visually unimpressive, their technical challenge is something else. From the 8th hole onward, the terrain becomes a little more lively and the choice of club a little tougher in a spectacular landscape of dunes. There is no water (to speak of) and no trees, either, nothing but bushes, dangerous rough, magnificently designed and located bunkers and greens that are really exciting to play. The result is more than anyone could ever have hoped for.

Il était difficile de porter un nom de golf aussi prestigieux. Bernhard Langer et Stan Eby ont relevé le défi, et réussi un grand parcours. L'histoire dira sa place exacte, mais la réussite première est d'avoir abordé modestement ce site, de n'avoir rien copié tout en retenant les leçons de l'illustre voisin, mais aussi de merveilles telles que Carnoustie ou Muirfield. Rien ici d'excessif visuellement, pas de trou-signature, rien que le déroulement naturel dans un paysage rude et changeant. Si les premiers trous ne sont pas visuellement impressionnants, quels challenges techniques ils présentent ! A partir du 8, le terrain devient plus animé, le choix de club plus difficile dans un paysage spectaculaire de dunes. Ici, pas d'eau (ou presque), pas d'arbres, rien que des buissons, un rough dangereux, des bunkers magnifiquement dessinés et placés, des greens passionnants à jouer. Le résultat dépasse les espérances, et en plus vieillit bien.

Portmarnock Hotel & Golf Links — 1995

IRL - PORTMARNOCK, Co Dublin

Office	Secrétariat	(353) 01 - 846 1800
Pro shop	Pro-shop	(353) 01 - 846 1800
Fax	Fax	(353) 01 - 846 1077
E-mail	golf@portmarnock.com	
Situation	Situation	

8 km from Dublin (pop. 481 854)

Annual closure	Fermeture annuelle	no
Weekly closure	Fermeture hebdomadaire	no

Fees main season Tarifs haute saison	Week days Semaine	We/Bank holidays We/Férié
18 holes		
Individual Individuel	95 €	102 €
Couple Couple	190 €	204 €

Hotel guests: 38 €

Caddy	Caddy	32 € /on request
Electric Trolley	Chariot électrique	no
Buggy	Voiturette	no
Clubs	Clubs	25 € /18 holes

Credit cards Cartes de crédit
VISA - MasterCard - AMEX

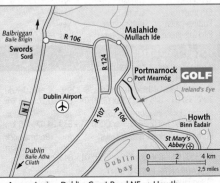

Balbriggan / Baile Brigin
Swords / Sord
R 106
Malahide / Mullach Ide
R 124
Portmarnock / Port Mearnóg
GOLF
Ireland's Eye
Dublin Airport
N1
R 107
R 106
Howth / Binn Éadair
St Mary's Abbey
Dublin / Baile Átha Cliath
Dublin bay
0 2 4 km
0 2,5 miles

Access Accès : Dublin, Coast Road NE → Howth.
Map 3 on page 824 Carte 3 Page 824

Golf course PARCOURS — 17/20

Site	Site	
Maintenance	Entretien	
Architect	Architecte	Bernhard Langer
Type	Type	links
Relief	Relief	
Water in play	Eau en jeu	
Exp. to wind	Exposé au vent	
Trees in play	Arbres en jeu	

Scorecard Carte de score	Chp. Chp.	Mens Mess.	Ladies Da.
Length Long.	6195	5909	4987
Par	71	71	71
Slope system	—	—	—

Advised golfing ability Niveau de jeu recommandé — 0 12 24 36

Hcp required Handicap exigé — 24 Men, 36 Ladies

Club house & amenities CLUB HOUSE ET ANNEXES — 7/10

Pro shop	Pro-shop	
Driving range	Practice	
Sheltered	couvert	yes
On grass	sur herbe	yes
Putting-green	putting-green	yes
Pitching-green	pitching green	yes

Hotel facilities ENVIRONNEMENT HOTELIER — 8/10

HOTELS HÔTELS

Portmarnock Links Hotel — Portmarnock
110 rooms, D 254 € — on site
Tel (353) 01 - 846 0611, Fax (353) 01 - 846 2442

Grand Hotel, 100 rooms, D 229 € — Malahide
Tel (353) 01 - 845 0000, Fax (353) 01 - 845 0987 — 4 km

Sands Hotel, 10 rooms, D 127 € — Portmarnock
Tel (353) 01 - 846 0003, Fax (353) 01 - 846 0420 — 1 km

RESTAURANTS RESTAURANT

Bon Appetit, Tel (353) 01 - 845 0314 — Malahide 4 km

Old Street Wine Bar, Tel (353) 01 - 845 1882 — Malahide

Ostborne (at Hotel), Tel (353) 01 846 0611 — on site

PORTSALON

16 | 5 | 5

Portsalon is an outstanding site, between the beach of Ballymostocker bay, one of the world's finest, and the Knockalla mountains. This age-old course is today run by local Irishmen, which means a friendly welcome guaranteed every time. The course is a shortish links with no real geographical relief, and so is ideal for a romantic stroll, even for the non-golfers in the family. The terrain has stayed very natural, with unpredictable kicks that are all part of the fun of golf, when they bounce and rebound in the right direction. The rough is not too severe and the bunkers are nicely, but not excessively, in play. Golfers who are new to the game will enjoy the opportunity here to learn about the architecture of a links course, without undue suffering, especially continental Europeans, who have little contact with this style of golf. The water on the 3rd and 15th shouldn't bother them too much, either. The wind is, of course, an element to be reckoned with, but it puts colour into your cheeks and gives you a hearty appetite for after the round.

Portsalon bénéficie d'une situation exceptionnelle, entre la plage de Ballymostocker Bay, l'une des plus belles du monde, et les Knockalla Mountains. Ce golf centenaire est aujourd'hui géré par des Irlandais locaux, c'est une garantie d'accueil amical. Le parcours est un links de longueur réduite, sans relief trop prononcé, ce qui permet une promenade romantique, même pour les non-golfeurs de la famille. Le terrain est resté très naturel, avec les rebonds imprévisibles qui font le plaisir du jeu... quand ils sont favorables. Le rough n'est pas trop sévère, les bunkers bien en jeu, mais sans excès. Les golfeurs peu expérimentés auront ici une belle occasion d'apprendre à aimer sans douleur l'architecture de links, notamment les Européens du continent, peu familiarisés avec elle. Et la présence de l'eau, au 3 et au 15, ne devrait pas trop les gêner. Bien sûr, le vent est un élément important, mais il donne bonne mine et ouvre l'appétit.

Portsalon Golf Club — 1881

Portsalon
IRL - FANAD, Co Donegal

Office	Secrétariat	(353) 074 - 59 459
Pro shop	Pro-shop	(353) 074 - 59 459
Fax	Fax	(353) 074 - 59 459
Web	—	
Situation	Situation	

50 km from Derry (pop. 72 334)
32 km from Letterkenny (pop. 7 606)

Annual closure	Fermeture annuelle	no
Weekly closure	Fermeture hebdomadaire	no

Fees main season Tarifs haute saison	18 holes	
	Week days Semaine	**We/Bank holidays** We/Férié
Individual Individuel	25 €	32 €
Couple Couple	50 €	64 €
Caddy Caddy	13 € /18 holes	
Electric Trolley Chariot électrique	6 € /18 holes	
Buggy Voiturette	no	
Clubs Clubs	no	
Credit cards Cartes de crédit	no	

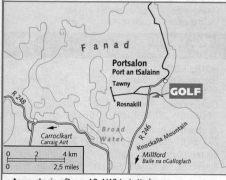

Fanad
Portsalon
Port an tSalainn
Tawny
Rosnakill
GOLF
R 248
R 246
Broad Water
Knockalla Mountain
Carroclkart
Carraig Airt
Millford
Baile na nGalloglach
0 2 4 km
0 2,5 miles

Access Accès : Derry, A2, N13 to Letterkenny.
R245 to Rathmelton, Milford.
R246 to Portsalon (Fanad Peninsula)
Map 1 on page 821 Carte 1 Page 821

Golf course — PARCOURS — 16/20

Site	Site	
Maintenance	Entretien	
Architect	Architecte	Mr Thompson
Type	Type	links
Relief	Relief	
Water in play	Eau en jeu	
Exp. to wind	Exposé au vent	
Trees in play	Arbres en jeu	

Scorecard Carte de score	**Chp.** Chp.	**Mens** Mess.	**Ladies** Da.
Length Long.	5354	5354	4499
Par	69	69	70
Slope system	—	—	—

Advised golfing ability Niveau de jeu recommandé: 0 12 24 36
Hcp required Handicap exigé: no

Club house & amenities — CLUB HOUSE ET ANNEXES — 5/10

Pro shop	Pro-shop	
Driving range	Practice	
Sheltered	couvert	no
On grass	sur herbe	no
Putting-green	putting-green	yes
Pitching-green	pitching green	no

Hotel facilities — ENVIRONNEMENT HOTELIER — 5/10

HOTELS HÔTELS

Rathmullan House, 21 rooms, D 140 € — Rathmullan
Tel (353) 074 - 59 115, Fax (353) 074 - 58 200 — 10 km

Fort Royal Hotel, 15 rooms, D 63 € — Rathmullan
Tel (353) 074 - 58 100, Fax (353) 074 - 58 103 — 10 km

Castle Grove Hotel, 8 rooms, D 127 € — Letterkenny
Tel (353) 074 - 51 118, Fax (353) 074 - 51 384 — 30 km

RESTAURANTS RESTAURANT

Portsalon Store — Portsalon
Tel (353) 074 - 59 107 — 1 km

Rosapenna Hotel — Downings
Tel (353) 074 - 55 301

POWERSCOURT

15 | 7 | 7

This is a magnificent site alongside the little town of Enniskerry, the gateway to the "Military Road" that crosses the wild landscape of the Wicklow Mountains in the immediate vicinity of Powerscourt Castle (hence the name of the course). The course winds it way around a majestic estate over some sharp slopes that might make a buggy advisable for senior players. Amateur champion Peter McEvoy has produced a championship course that is as honest as it is technically demanding, where water comes into play on only two holes (including the superb 16th hole, a par 3 and obvious tribute to the 12th at Augusta). The main hazards are the large trees and very strategically placed bunkers. Powerscourt is still a very young course but the sand-based greens are already in excellent condition ; for the moment, the fairways still need to gain a little firmness and the back-tees are best left alone...

C'est un site magnifique, à côté de la petite ville d'Enniskerry, porte d'entrée de la "Military Road" traversant les paysages sauvages des Wicklow Mountains, à proximité immédiate du Château de Powerscourt, dont le golf a emprunté le nom. Le parcours a été insinué dans cet espace majestueux, au prix de quelques reliefs incitant à conseiller une voiturette aux seniors. Le grand champion amateur Peter McEvoy en a fait un parcours de championnat aussi franc qu'exigeant techniquement, où l'eau n'est en jeu que sur deux trous (dont le superbe 16, un par 3 en référence évidente au 12 d'Augusta). Les grands arbres constituent les principaux obstacles, avec des bunkers très stratégiques. Powerscourt est très jeune encore, mais les greens en sable sont déjà en excellente condition, alors que les fairways ont besoin d'acquérir un peu de fermeté : il vaut mieux ne pas jouer des départs arrière pour l'instant...

Powerscourt Golf Club — 1996

Powerscourt Estate
IRL - ENNISKERRY, Co Wicklow

Office	Secrétariat	(353) 01 - 204 6033
Pro shop	Pro-shop	(353) 01 - 204 6033
Fax	Fax	(353) 01 - 286 3561
Web	www.powerscourt.ie	
Situation	Situation	

19 km S of Dublin (pop. 481 854)
1 km from Enniskerry (pop. 1 275)

Annual closure	Fermeture annuelle	no
Weekly closure	Fermeture hebdomadaire	no

Fees main season Tarifs haute saison — 18 holes

	Week days Semaine	We/Bank holidays We/Férié
Individual Individuel	95 €	95 €
Couple Couple	190 €	190 €

Caddy	Caddy	32 € /on request
Electric Trolley	Chariot électrique	no
Buggy	Voiturette	44 € /18 holes
Clubs	Clubs	32 € /18 holes

Credit cards Cartes de crédit
VISA - MasterCard - Laser - AMEX

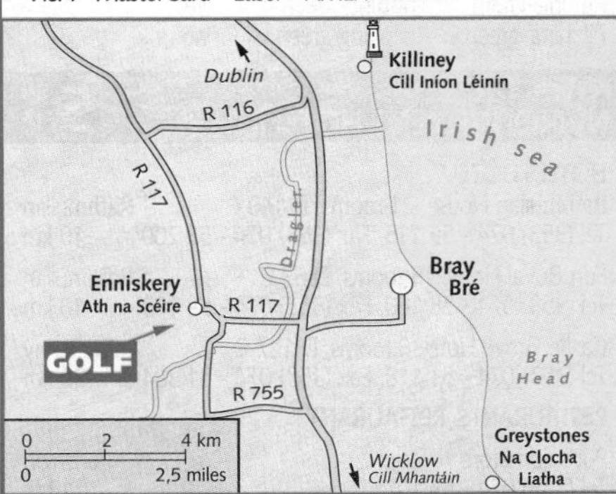

Access Accès : N11, South of Bray
Map 3 on page 824 Carte 3 Page 824

Golf course PARCOURS — 15/20

Site	Site	
Maintenance	Entretien	
Architect	Architecte	Peter McEvoy
Type	Type	inland, parkland
Relief	Relief	
Water in play	Eau en jeu	
Exp. to wind	Exposé au vent	
Trees in play	Arbres en jeu	

Scorecard Carte de score	Chp. Chp.	Mens Mess.	Ladies Da.
Length Long.	6410	5858	5322
Par	72	72	75
Slope system	—	—	—

Advised golfing ability Niveau de jeu recommandé — 0 12 24 36
Hcp required Handicap exigé — no

Club house & amenities CLUB HOUSE ET ANNEXES — 7/10

Pro shop	Pro-shop	
Driving range	Practice	
Sheltered	couvert	no
On grass	sur herbe	yes
Putting-green	putting-green	yes
Pitching-green	pitching green	yes

Hotel facilities ENVIRONNEMENT HOTELIER — 7/10

HOTELS HÔTELS

Summerhill Hotel, 30 rooms, D 102 € — Enniskerry
Tel (353) 01 - 286 7928, Fax (353) 01 - 286 79 29 — close

Glenview Hotel, 73 rooms, D 178 € — Delgany
Tel (353) 01 - 287 3399, Fax (353) 01 - 287 7511 — 13 km

Apartments at Powerscourt, D 102 € — Enniskerry
Tel (353) 01 - 204 6033, Fax (353) 01 - 276 1303 — on site

RESTAURANTS RESTAURANT

Roly's Bistro, Tel (353) 01 - 668 2611 — Dublin 15 km
Cooper's, Tel (353) 01 - 287 3914 — Greystones 13 km
Hungry Monk, Tel (353) 01 - 287 5759 — Greystones 13 km

RATHSALLAGH

14 | 7 | 6

Welcome to a huge park, where the age-old trees provide a sumptuous splash of colour come Autumn. Away from the madding crowd, the trees here are in fact a real factor to complicate the course and your game. The slopes are sometimes steep and might hinder some senior players, but they also add to the problem of club selection. This is compounded by well-guarded and cleverly designed greens, where you can rarely get home without lofting the ball. A noticeable feature is the variety of the holes, with more than a few slight dog-legs that ideally call for some flighted shots (when the ground is damp the course plays very long). There is water on seven holes, and it is often dangerous. Although generally honest and open, the course nonetheless harbours a few traps, including the 6th, a par 5 peppered with bunkers, ponds and ditches and a tricky hole to master. Other features are the difficulty of the closing holes and the very family atmosphere that reigns throughout the club.

Un immense parc avec des arbres centenaires, dont les couleurs automnales sont somptueuses. A l'écart des bruits du monde, leur présence est un facteur de difficulté effective dans le jeu. Les dénivellées sont parfois importantes, et peuvent poser des problèmes aux seniors, mais aussi pour bien choisir son club, et d'autant plus que les greens sont très défendus, très travaillés : on peut rarement y entrer en faisant rouler la balle. On remarquera aussi la variété des trous, avec pas mal de légers dog-legs obligeant à travailler ses effets (le parcours est très long quand le sol est humide). L'eau est présente sur sept trous, souvent de manière dangereuse. Généralement assez franc, ce parcours recèle néanmoins quelques pièges, dont le 6, un par 5 truffé de bunkers, de mares et de fossés, et bien délicat à décrypter. A signaler aussi, la difficulté des derniers trous, et l'atmosphère très familiale qui règne ici.

Rathsallagh Golf Club — 1995

IRL - DUNLAVIN, Co Wicklow

Office	Secrétariat	(353) 045 - 403 316
Pro shop	Pro-shop	(353) 045 - 403 316
Fax	Fax	(353) 045 - 403 295
Web	www.rathsallagh.com	
Situation	Situation	
4 km from Dunlavin	(pop. 693)	
Annual closure	Fermeture annuelle	no
Weekly closure	Fermeture hebdomadaire	no

Fees main season Tarifs haute saison	Week days Semaine	We/Bank holidays We/Férié (18 holes)
Individual Individuel	70 €	83 €
Couple Couple	140 €	166 €

Weekdays: 25 € before 9.30 am

Caddy	Caddy	on request
Electric Trolley	Chariot électrique	13 € /18 holes
Buggy	Voiturette	38 € /18 holes
Clubs	Clubs	32 € /18 holes

Credit cards Cartes de crédit
VISA - MasterCard

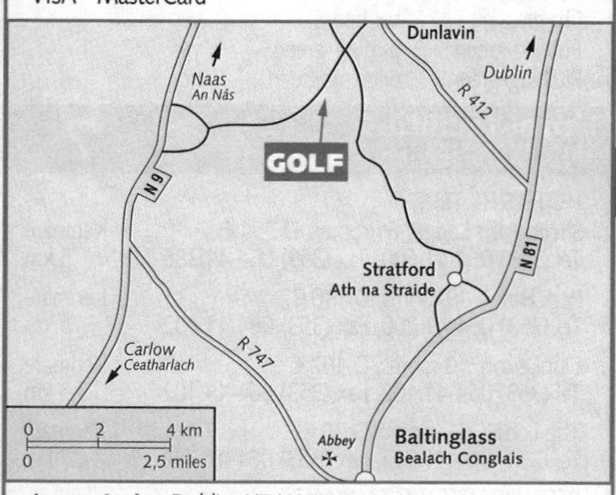

Access Accès : Dublin, N7 West.
N9 → Waterford. → Dunlavin
Map 2 on page 823 Carte 2 Page 823

Golf course — PARCOURS — 14/20

Site	Site	
Maintenance	Entretien	
Architect	Architecte	Peter McEvoy, Ch. O'Connor Jr
Type	Type	inland, parkland
Relief	Relief	
Water in play	Eau en jeu	
Exp. to wind	Exposé au vent	
Trees in play	Arbres en jeu	

Scorecard Carte de score	Chp. Chp.	Mens Mess.	Ladies Da.
Length Long.	6321	5940	5033
Par	72	72	73
Slope system	—	—	—

Advised golfing ability 0 12 24 36
Niveau de jeu recommandé
Hcp required Handicap exigé 28 Men, 36 Ladies

Club house & amenities — CLUB HOUSE ET ANNEXES — 7/10

Pro shop	Pro-shop	
Driving range	Practice	
Sheltered	couvert	2 mats
On grass	sur herbe	yes
Putting-green	putting-green	yes
Pitching-green	pitching green	no

Hotel facilities — ENVIRONNEMENT HOTELIER — 6/10

HOTELS HÔTELS

Rathsallagh House — on site
17 rooms, D 260 €
Tel (353) 045 - 403 112, Fax (353) 045 - 403 343

Kilkea Castle — Castledermot 20 km
38 rooms, D 165 €
Tel (353) 0503 - 45 156, Fax (353) 0503 - 45 187

RESTAURANTS RESTAURANT

Rathsallagh House, Tel (353) 045 - 403 112 — on site

Priory Inn — Carlow-Kilkenny Road 4 km
Tel (353) 045 - 403 355

RING OF KERRY

15 | 7 | 7

A drive around Kerry is a must. One of the world's most picturesque roads from Killarney to Killarney has been further enhanced from the golfer's point of view with a new course overlooking the bay and jagged cliffs of Kenmare and backed by the MacGillicuddy Reeks and the Caha Mountains. In this quite spectacular setting, Eddie Hackett has designed a very beautiful course with emphasis both on testing the better golfer and, at the same time, on showing respect for all golf-lovers, even the less skilled and the less ambitious. Here, the many different tee-boxes provide the flexibility needed to adapt a course to playing ability and strengths. Water has been intelligently brought into play without ever overdoing things, and the same goes for the vegetation. Players should, though, be wary of being lured into a false sense impression of security and pleasure by the wonderful scenery. You need to be on top of your game at all times to make any impression on a course which is easier once you get to know some of the more subtle aspects of the layout. Definitely a course to play.

Le tour du Kerry est un incontournable. L'une des plus belles routes du monde, de Killarney à Killarney, s'est enrichie pour les golfeurs d'une nouvelle halte, dominant la baie de Kenmare et ses dentellières, et adossée aux MacGillicuddy Reeks et aux Caha Mountains. Dans ce site spectaculaire, Eddie Hackett a dessiné un très beau parcours, soucieux à la fois de tester les meilleurs, mais avec, parallèlement, un grand respect de tous les amoureux du golf, même s'ils sont moins expérimentés ou ambitieux. Bien des architectes tentent cette gageure, bien peu la réussissent vraiment. L'eau a été mise en jeu avec intelligence, mais sans excès non plus, de même que la végétation. Que l'on se méfie quand même de l'impression de sécurité et de plaisir du paysage, il est nécessaire de rester vigilant pour réussir, et une connaissance un peu approfondie des subtilités du dessin ne sera pas inutile. A connaître.

892

Ring of Kerry Golf Club — 1998

IRL - TEMPLENOE, Kenmare, Co. Kerry

Office	Secrétariat	(353) 064 - 42 000
Pro shop	Pro-shop	(353) 064 - 42 000
Fax	Fax	(353) 064 - 42 533
Web	www.ringofkerrygolf.com	
Situation	Situation	

6 km W of Kenmare (pop. 1 420)

Annual closure	Fermeture annuelle	no
Weekly closure	Fermeture hebdomadaire	no

Fees main season / Tarifs haute saison	Week days / Semaine	We/Bank holidays / We/Férié
18 holes		
Individual Individuel	63 €	63 €
Couple Couple	126 €	126 €

Caddy	Caddy	on request
Electric Trolley	Chariot électrique	no
Buggy	Voiturette	38 €
Clubs	Clubs IR£ 20	

Credit cards Cartes de crédit
VISA - MasterCard - DC - AMEX

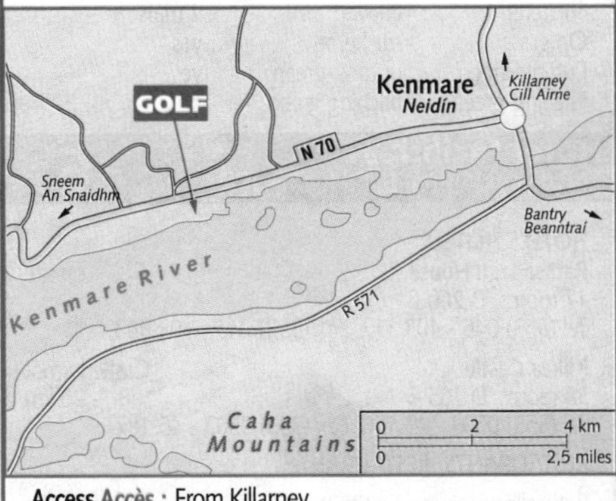

Access Accès : From Killarney, Ring of Kerry through Kenmare, then → Templenoe
Map 2 on page 822 Carte 2 Page 822

Golf course — PARCOURS — 15/20

Site	Site	
Maintenance	Entretien	
Architect	Architecte	Eddie Hackett
Type	Type	seaside, parkland
Relief	Relief	
Water in play	Eau en jeu	
Exp. to wind	Exposé au vent	
Trees in play	Arbres en jeu	

Scorecard / Carte de score	Chp. / Chp.	Mens / Mess.	Ladies / Da.
Length Long.	6127	5742	4997
Par	71	71	71
Slope system	—	—	—

Advised golfing ability / Niveau de jeu recommandé: 0 12 24 36

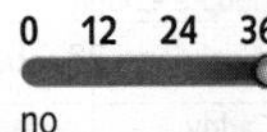

Hcp required Handicap exigé: no

Club house & amenities — CLUB HOUSE ET ANNEXES — 7/10

Pro shop	Pro-shop	
Driving range	Practice	
Sheltered	couvert	no
On grass	sur herbe	yes
Putting-green	putting-green	yes
Pitching-green	pitching green	no

Hotel facilities — ENVIRONNEMENT HOTELIER — 7/10

HOTELS HÔTELS

Sheen Falls Lodge, 61 rooms, D 254 € — Kenmare 5 km
Tel (353) 064-41 600, Fax (353) 064-41 386

Park Hotel, 49 rooms, D 330 € — Kenmare 5 km
Tel (353) 064-41 200, Fax (353) 064-41 402

Dunkerron, 10 rooms, D 102 € — Kenmare 3,5 km
Tel (353) 064-41 102, Fax (353) 064-41 102

The Lodge, 11 rooms, D 76 € — Kenmare 7 km
Tel (353) 064-41 512, Fax (353) 064-42 724

RESTAURANTS RESTAURANT

D'Arcy's, Tel (353) 064-41 589 — Kenmare 5 km

The Lime Tree — Kenmare 5 km
Tel (353) 064-41 225

ROSAPENNA

16 | 7 | 6

Originally designed by Old Tom Morris in 1893, Rosapenna was reshaped by James Braid and Harry Vardon in 1906 before Eddie Hackett added the final touches in 1993. With names like these, the course should, on the face of it, be quite something, and it is. This is one of the obligatory stop-offs in the long trek of exploring golfing treasures in the north-west of Ireland, often unknown to foreign tourists but not so to the Irish themselves. Playing on a links is like going back to the origins of the game, when intuition and inspiration held the upper hand over pure technique, when the size of your score was merely relative because match-play was the formula that reigned supreme with amateur golfers. Exposure to the wind makes Rosapenna a tricky number to play, and even if the traps are seldom hidden, playing here several times makes it easier to choose tactics. Lack of experience could be a serious setback for high-handicappers. Great value for money.

D'abord dessiné par Old Tom Morris en 1893, Rosapenna a bénéficié des aménagements de James Braid et Harry Vardon en 1906, avant que Eddie Hackett lui donne la dernière touche en 1993. Avec de tels signataires, ce parcours ne peut laisser indifférent, à priori ! Il constitue effectivement l'un des étapes obligées dans une longue exploration des trésors golfiques du Nord-Ouest, souvent ignorés par les touristes étrangers, alors que les Irlandais en ont pris souvent le chemin. Jouer sur un links, c'est retrouver les origines du jeu, où l'intuition et l'inspiration prenaient le pas sur la technique pure, où l'importance du score était toute relative quand le match-play était la formule reine des amateurs. L'exposition au vent rend forcément Rosapenna délicat à jouer, et même si les pièges sont rarement dissimulés, jouer plusieurs fois améliore les choix tactiques. Le manque d'expérience pourra gêner les golfeurs très moyens. Le rapport qualité/prix est imbattable.

Rosapenna Hotel & Golf Links — 1893

IRL - DOWNINGS, Co Donegal

Office	Secrétariat	(353) 074 - 55 301
Pro shop	Pro-shop	(353) 074 - 55 301
Fax	Fax	(353) 074 - 55 128
Web	—	
Situation	Situation	

40 km from Letterkenny (pop. 7 606)

Annual closure	Fermeture annuelle	no
Weekly closure	Fermeture hebdomadaire	no

Fees main season Tarifs haute saison	18 holes	
	Week days Semaine	**We/Bank holidays** We/Férié
Individual Individuel	32 €	38 €
Couple Couple	64 €	76 €

Caddy	Caddy	on request
Electric Trolley	Chariot électrique	no
Buggy	Voiturette	32 € /18 holes
Clubs	Clubs	13 €

Credit cards Cartes de crédit
VISA - Eurocard - MasterCard - DC

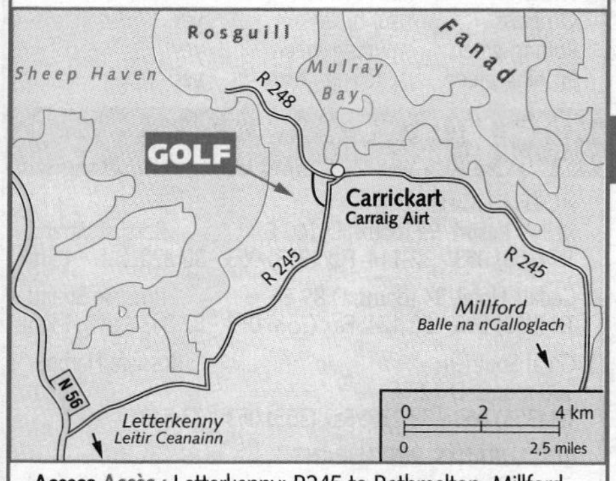

Access Accès : Letterkenny: R245 to Rathmelton, Millford, Cranford, Carrigart. Golf 2 km → Rosapenna
Map 1 on page 821 Carte 1 Page 821

Golf course — PARCOURS — 16/20

Site	Site	
Maintenance	Entretien	
Architect	Architecte	Old Tom Morris Braid, Vardon
Type	Type	links
Relief	Relief	
Water in play	Eau en jeu	
Exp. to wind	Exposé au vent	
Trees in play	Arbres en jeu	

Scorecard Carte de score	**Chp.** Chp.	**Mens** Mess.	**Ladies** Da.
Length Long.	5950	5644	4555
Par	71	70	74
Slope system	—	—	—

Advised golfing ability 0 12 24 36
Niveau de jeu recommandé
Hcp required Handicap exigé — Men 24, Ladies 36

Club house & amenities — CLUB HOUSE ET ANNEXES — 7/10

Pro shop	Pro-shop	
Driving range	Practice	
Sheltered	couvert	6 mats
On grass	sur herbe	yes
Putting-green	putting-green	yes
Pitching-green	pitching green	yes

Hotel facilities — ENVIRONNEMENT HOTELIER — 6/10

HOTELS HÔTELS

Rosapenna Hotel, 46 rooms, D 140 € — on site
Tel (353) 074 - 55 301, Fax (353) 074 - 55 128

Arnold's Hotel, 34 rooms, D 114 € — Dunfanaghy 25 km
Tel (353) 074 - 36 208, Fax (353) 074 - 36 352

Shandon Hotel, 55 rooms, D 140 € — Marble Hill 13 km
Tel (353) 074 - 36 137, Fax (353) 074 - 36 430

RESTAURANTS RESTAURANT

Rosapenna Hotel — on site
Tel (353) 074 - 55 301

The Cove — Dunfanaghy 25 km
Tel (353) 074 - 36 300

ROSSLARE

13 | 5 | 6

This course is located on a peninsula, and what with there being no trees to protect it, is clearly exposed to the wind. This element makes any links course an exciting proposition and adds to the pleasure when you can keep control. It can, though, easily upset the more inexperienced player. This is the main difficulty at Rosslare, which otherwise can appear a little dated to top level players. The bunkers are more strategic than really penalising and the well-watered greens will still hold slightly miscued shots, but before reaching them you need an accurate tee-shot to avoid the unforgiving rough. One particular feature here is the excellence of the par 3s and the closing holes along the sea, which are superb fun in matchplay. Today better suited to holiday golf than tournaments, Rosslare is a good course on which to become acclimatised with links golf.

La situation de ce parcours sur une péninsule et l'absence d'arbres protecteurs impliquent une forte exposition au vent. Cet élément rend très excitants les parcours de links, et renforce le plaisir quand on réussit à en maîtriser les effets. Mais il tourne la tête des joueurs peu expérimentés ! C'est la principale difficulté de Rosslare, autrement un peu désuet au regard des joueurs du meilleur niveau. Les bunkers sont plus stratégiques que vraiment pénalisants, l'arrosage des greens a facilité la réception des coups imparfaits, mais il faut encore de la précision au drive pour pouvoir les attaquer, car le rough peut être méchant. On distinguera particulièrement ici la qualité des pars 3, et celle des derniers trous le long de la mer, qui offrent un espace superbe en match-play. Aujourd'hui mieux adapté à un golf de vacances que de championnat, Rosslare est un bon parcours pour se familiariser avec l'architecture de links.

Rosslare Golf Club — 1905

IRL - ROSSLARE STRAND, Co Wicklow

Office	Secrétariat	(353) 053 - 32 113
Pro shop	Pro-shop	(353) 053 - 32 238
Fax	Fax	(353) 053 - 32 203
Web	www.iol.ie/~rgolfclub	
Situation	Situation	

18 km from Wexford (pop. 9 533)

Annual closure	Fermeture annuelle	no
Weekly closure	Fermeture hebdomadaire	no

Fees main season / Tarifs haute saison	18 holes	
	Week days / Semaine	We/Bank holidays / We/Férié
Individual Individuel	38 €	51 €
Couple Couple	76 €	102 €

Caddy	Caddy	no
Electric Trolley	Chariot électrique	6 € /18 holes
Buggy	Voiturette	32 € /18 holes
Clubs	Clubs	8 €

Credit cards Cartes de crédit
VISA

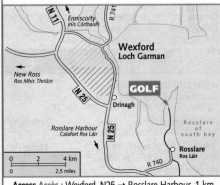

Access Accès : Wexford, N25 → Rosslare Harbour. 1 km after Killinick, left on R740 to Rosslare.
Golf → Rosslare Point/Burrow
Map 2 on page 823 Carte 2 Page 823

Golf course / PARCOURS — 13/20

Site	Site	
Maintenance	Entretien	
Architect	Architecte	unknown
Type	Type	seaside course, links
Relief	Relief	
Water in play	Eau en jeu	
Exp. to wind	Exposé au vent	
Trees in play	Arbres en jeu	

Scorecard / Carte de score	Chp. / Chp.	Mens / Mess.	Ladies / Da.
Length Long.	5920	5650	5075
Par	72	72	73
Slope system	—	—	—

Advised golfing ability 0 12 24 36
Niveau de jeu recommandé
Hcp required Handicap exigé — no

Club house & amenities / CLUB HOUSE ET ANNEXES — 5/10

Pro shop	Pro-shop	
Driving range	Practice	
Sheltered	couvert	no
On grass	sur herbe	yes
Putting-green	putting-green	yes
Pitching-green	pitching green	yes

Hotel facilities / ENVIRONNEMENT HOTELIER — 6/10

HOTELS HÔTELS

Kelly's Resort, 99 rooms, D 140 € — Rosslare Strand
Tel (353) 053 - 32 114, Fax (353) 053 - 32 222 — 1 km

Cedars Hotel, 34 rooms, D 89 € — Rosslare Strand
Tel (353) 053 - 32 124, Fax (353) 053 - 32 243 — 1 km

Great Southern — Rosslare Harbour
100 rooms, D 127 € — 4 km
Tel (353) 053 - 33 233, Fax (353) 053 - 33 543

RESTAURANTS RESTAURANT

Ocean Bed Seafood Restaurant — Wexford
Tel (353) 053 - 23 935 — 20 km

Kelly's Resort — Rosslare Strand
Tel (353) 053 - 32 114 — 1 km

ROYAL DUBLIN

16 | 8 | 7

Although not inside the very closed club of exceptional golf courses, Royal Dublin is an excellent example of a classic links, peppered with deep fairway and green-side bunkers (sometimes very penalising indeed) and a number of bushes, but these are often more decorative or useful for gauging distance than really dangerous. Although the terrain is none too hilly, there are a couple of blind drives but nothing blind when approaching the greens. You could almost call this a kind course if the prevailing wind wasn't blowing in your face on the way in. This makes the back 9 an even trickier proposition, which demands certain skills in drawing the ball, a feat that many will find harder than others. A very natural looking course and very busy, being so close to Dublin, this layout has started to show its age and still needs a little restyling (especially in terms of yardage) if it is to recover its great championship course status.

Bien qu'il n'appartienne pas au club très fermé des parcours exceptionnels, Royal Dublin est un excellent exemple de links classique, avec ses profonds bunkers de fairway et de greens (parfois très pénalisants), des buissons, mais souvent plus décoratifs ou utiles comme points de repère que vraiment dangereux. Bien que le terrain soit peu accidenté, on trouve ici quelques drives aveugles, mais aucun green de la sorte. On pourrait presque le qualifier d'aimable si le vent dominant n'était contraire au retour, ce qui rend cette partie du parcours encore plus délicate, exigeant notamment une bonne maîtrise des effets de draw, ce qui n'est pas donné à tout le monde ! Très naturel d'aspect, très fréquenté aussi en raison de sa proximité de Dublin, ce parcours porte un peu son âge, mais a toujours besoin d'un lifting (notamment au niveau de la longueur), s'il souhaite retrouver un statut de parcours de grand championnat.

Royal Dublin Golf Club — 1885

Bull Island
IRL - DUBLIN 3

Office	Secrétariat	(353) 01 - 833 6346
Pro shop	Pro-shop	(353) 01 - 833 6477
Fax	Fax	(353) 01 - 833 6504
E-mail	jlambe@theroyaldublingolfclub.com	
Situation	Situation	Dublin (pop. 481 854)
Annual closure	Fermeture annuelle	no
Weekly closure	Fermeture hebdomadaire	no

Fees main season Tarifs haute saison	18 holes	
	Week days Semaine	**We/Bank holidays** We/Férié
Individual Individuel	102 €	114 €
Couple Couple	204 €	228 €

No Ladies on Week-ends and Public Holidays!!!

Caddy	Caddy	25 € /on request
Electric Trolley	Chariot électrique	13 € /18 holes
Buggy	Voiturette	32 € /18 holes
Clubs	Clubs	29 € /18 holes

Credit cards Cartes de crédit
VISA - MasterCard - DC - AMEX

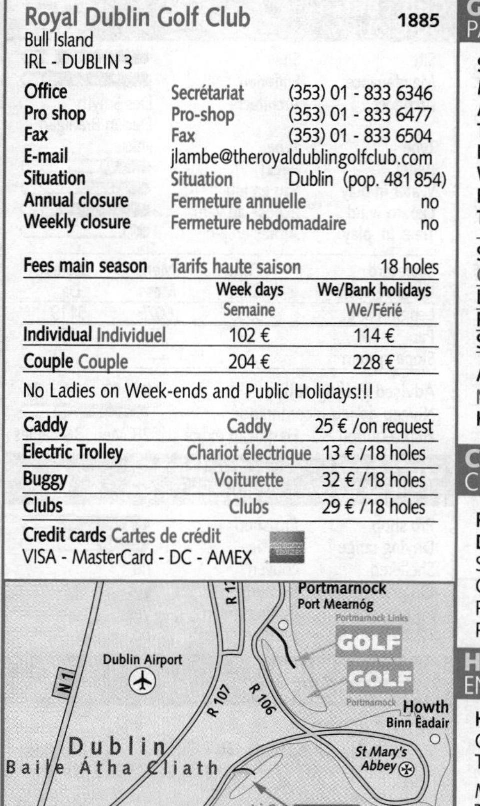

Access Accès : Dublin City, Coast road → Howth.
Bull Island Bridge, turn right
Map 3 on page 824 Carte 3 Page 824

Golf course — PARCOURS — 16/20

Site	Site	●●●●○
Maintenance	Entretien	●●●●○
Architect	Architecte	H.S. Colt
Type	Type	links
Relief	Relief	●●○○○
Water in play	Eau en jeu	●○○○○
Exp. to wind	Exposé au vent	●●●●○
Trees in play	Arbres en jeu	●○○○○

Scorecard Carte de score	**Chp.** Chp.	**Mens** Mess.	**Ladies** Da.
Length Long.	6281	6030	5439
Par	72	72	74
Slope system	—	—	—

Advised golfing ability Niveau de jeu recommandé: 0 12 24 36 (36)
Hcp required Handicap exigé: 28 Men, 36 Ladies

Club house & amenities — CLUB HOUSE ET ANNEXES — 8/10

Pro shop	Pro-shop	●●●●○
Driving range	Practice	●●○○○
Sheltered	couvert	no
On grass	sur herbe	yes
Putting-green	putting-green	yes
Pitching-green	pitching green	yes

Hotel facilities — ENVIRONNEMENT HOTELIER — 7/10

HOTELS HÔTELS

Clontarf Castle Hotel, 111 rooms, D 127 € — Dublin/Clontarf
Tel (353) 01 - 833 2321, Fax (353) 01 - 833 0418 — 2 km

Marine Hotel, 26 rooms, D 152 € — Sutton
Tel (353) 01 - 832 2613, Fax (353) 01 - 839 04 42 — 7 km

Grand Hotel Malahide, 100 rooms, D 229 € — Malahide
Tel (353) 01 - 845 0000, Fax (353) 01 - 845 0987 — 10 km

RESTAURANTS RESTAURANT

Picasso, Tel (353) 01 - 853 1120 — Dublin/Clontarf 2 km

Dollymount House — Dublin/Clontarf 8 km
Tel(353) 01 - 833 2492

Roly's Bistro, Tel (353) 01 - 668 2611 — Dublin 13 km

SEAPOINT

15 | 6 | 6

From the 14th at County Louth, you can see practically all the neighbouring course of Seapoint. Here, it is a return to similar moonscape scenery, but with a large section of the course winding through heather and a more rural landscape. This is rather an attractive contrast, and gives the impression of a course gradually building up speed through to the closing holes, all very spectacular and exciting when using the match-play format. The wind often has a word or two to say, and good ball control is required, especially with the tee shot, in order to avoid the fairway bunkers and get a good view of the greens to keep out of the often dangerous green-side traps. These greens are large and distinguished more by general slopes than by individual contouring. By and large, the difficulties are clearly visible (water comes into play on the 4th and 9th holes), so at least you can start out here with a degree of confidence. Well worth knowing.

Depuis le 14 de County Louth, on aperçoit pratiquement tout le parcours voisin de Seapoint. On y retrouve au retour un paysage dunaire analogue, alors qu'une grande partie se déroule dans la bruyère et un paysage plus rural. Ce contraste est d'ailleurs assez séduisant, et donne une impression de montée en puissance progressive, jusqu'aux derniers trous, très spectaculaires et excitants en match-play. Le vent joue souvent un rôle et il faut un bon contrôle de balle, en particulier depuis les départs, pour éviter les bunkers de fairway et avoir une ouverture suffisante sur les greens pour échapper à leurs bunkers, souvent dangereux. Ces greens sont largement dimensionnés, et caractérisés davantage par des pentes générales que par des ondulations ponctuelles. En règle générale, les difficultés sont bien visibles (eau en jeu au 4 et au 9), ce qui permet d'aborder Seapoint avec un minimum de confiance. A connaître.

Seapoint Golf Club — 1993

IRL - TERMONFECKIN, Co Louth

Office	Secrétariat	(353) 041 - 982 2333
Pro shop	Pro-shop	(353) 041 - 988 1066
Fax	Fax	(353) 041 - 982 2331
Web	www.seapoint.com	
Situation	Situation	
8 km from Drogheda (pop. 24 460)		
Annual closure	Fermeture annuelle	no
Weekly closure	Fermeture hebdomadaire	no

Fees main season Tarifs haute saison	Week days Semaine	We/Bank holidays We/Férié
	18 holes	
Individual Individuel	38 €	51 €
Couple Couple	76 €	102 €

Caddy	Caddy	25 € /on request
Electric Trolley	Chariot électrique	no
Buggy	Voiturette	25 € /18 holes
Clubs	Clubs	13 € /18 holes

Credit cards Cartes de crédit
VISA - MasterCard

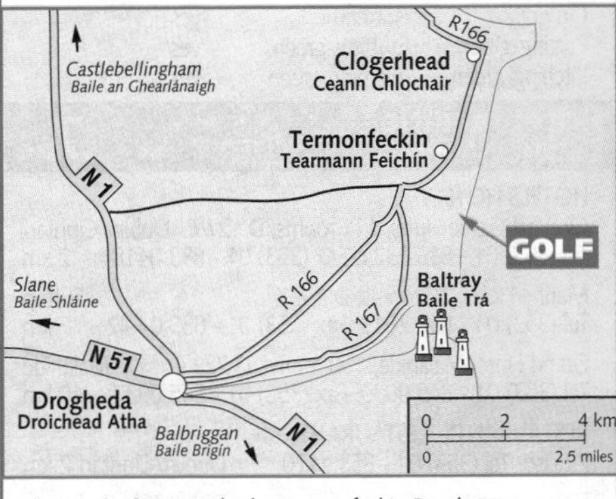

Access Accès : Drogheda, Termonfeckin Road
Map 3 on page 824 Carte 3 Page 824

Golf course PARCOURS — 15/20

Site	Site	
Maintenance	Entretien	
Architect	Architecte	Des Smyth, Declan Branigan
Type	Type	links
Relief	Relief	
Water in play	Eau en jeu	
Exp. to wind	Exposé au vent	
Trees in play	Arbres en jeu	

Scorecard Carte de score	Chp. Chp.	Mens Mess.	Ladies Da.
Length Long.	6339	6075	5119
Par	72	72	73
Slope system	—	—	—

Advised golfing ability Niveau de jeu recommandé — 0 12 24 36
Hcp required Handicap exigé — 28 Men, 36 Ladies

Club house & amenities CLUB HOUSE ET ANNEXES — 6/10

Pro shop	Pro-shop	
Driving range	Practice	
Sheltered	couvert	no
On grass	sur herbe	yes
Putting-green	putting-green	yes
Pitching-green	pitching green	no

Hotel facilities ENVIRONNEMENT HOTELIER — 6/10

HOTELS HÔTELS

Boyne Valley, 37 rooms, D 140 € — Drogheda
Tel (353) 041 - 983 7737, Fax (353) 041 - 983 9188 — 8 km

West Court House, 27 rooms, D 102 € — Drogheda 15 km
Tel (353) 041 - 983 0965, Fax (353) 041 - 983 0970

Neptune Hotel, 38 rooms, D 127 € — Bettystown
Tel (353) 041 - 982 7107, Fax (353) 041 - 982 7412 — 10 km

RESTAURANTS RESTAURANT

Triple House — Termonfeckin 1 km
Tel (353) 041 - 982 2616

Donegans, Tel (353) 041 - 983 7383 — Monasterboice 5 km

SHANNON

13 | 6 | 6

Located close to Shannon airport, this is a good starting point for a golfing holiday in the region, with enough difficulties to get you into your stride. High handicappers, though, might not feel so confident about it. In a park landscape, the trees are always in play, but there are not enough of them to trouble even the most claustrophobic player, despite the tightness of some fairways. The essential difficulties are the bunkers and many water hazards, which call for some straight driving and good club selection for the second shot. Most holes give you the choice of lofted approaches or rolled shots. But just following the layout is not enough here, you need to take the initiative. With well-spread hazards and a pleasant variety of holes, this complete course requires some powerful hitting when playing from the back-tees. A very competent course in its style.

Situé près de l'aéroport de Shannon, c'est un bon point de départ pour un séjour golfique dans la région, avec assez de difficultés pour prendre le bon rythme, mais les handicaps élevés auront du mal à se mettre en confiance. Dans un paysage de parc, les arbres entrent en jeu, et si certains trous sont étroits, ils ne sont pas assez nombreux pour gêner les claustrophobes. Les difficultés essentielles sont les bunkers et les nombreux obstacles d'eau, qui imposent pas mal de précision au drive, et un choix de club précis aux seconds coups. Sur la plupart des trous, on peut avoir les options de porter la balle ou de jouer des balles roulées. Il ne suffit pas ici de se laisser porter par le tracé, encore faut-il prendre des initiatives. Avec ses obstacles bien répartis et une bonne variété des trous, ce parcours complet demande aussi quelque puissance si l'on choisit les départs arrière. Une solide réalisation dans son genre.

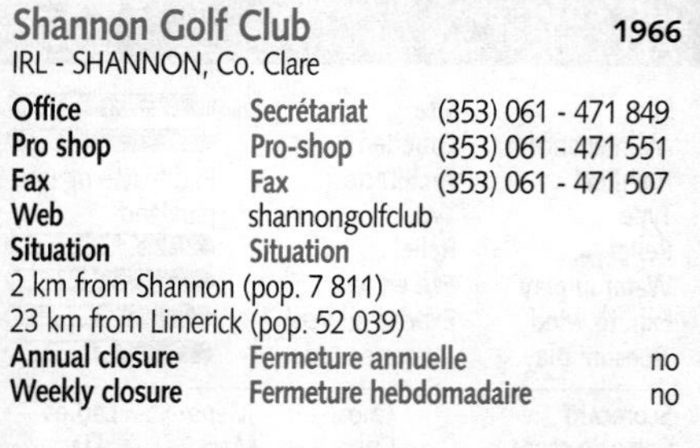

Shannon Golf Club — 1966

IRL - SHANNON, Co. Clare

Office	Secrétariat	(353) 061 - 471 849
Pro shop	Pro-shop	(353) 061 - 471 551
Fax	Fax	(353) 061 - 471 507
Web	shannongolfclub	
Situation	Situation	

2 km from Shannon (pop. 7 811)
23 km from Limerick (pop. 52 039)

Annual closure	Fermeture annuelle	no
Weekly closure	Fermeture hebdomadaire	no

Fees main season Tarifs haute saison	Week days Semaine	We/Bank holidays We/Férié
	18 holes	
Individual Individuel	38 €	44 €
Couple Couple	76 €	88 €

Caddy	Caddy	32 € /on request
Electric Trolley	Chariot électrique	13 € /18 holes
Buggy	Voiturette	32 € /18 holes
Clubs	Clubs	19 €

Credit cards Cartes de crédit
VISA - MasterCard

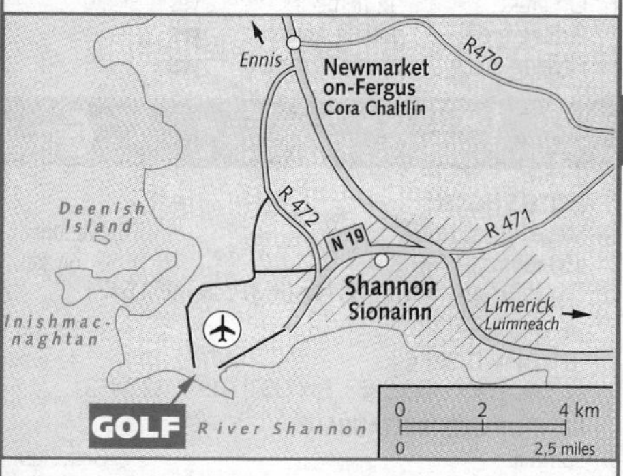

Access Accès : Limerick, N18 → Ennis.
N19 to Shannon. Golf 800 m from Shannon Airport.
Map 2 on page 822 Carte 2 Page 822

Golf course — PARCOURS — 13/20

Site	Site	
Maintenance	Entretien	
Architect	Architecte	John D. Harris
Type	Type	parkland
Relief	Relief	
Water in play	Eau en jeu	
Exp. to wind	Exposé au vent	
Trees in play	Arbres en jeu	

Scorecard / Carte de score	Chp. / Chp.	Mens / Mess.	Ladies / Da.
Length Long.	6186	5863	5209
Par	72	72	74
Slope system	—	—	—

Advised golfing ability 0 12 24 36
Niveau de jeu recommandé
Hcp required Handicap exigé — Men 24, Ladies 36

Club house & amenities — CLUB HOUSE ET ANNEXES — 6/10

Pro shop	Pro-shop	
Driving range	Practice	
Sheltered	couvert	no
On grass	sur herbe	yes
Putting-green	putting-green	yes
Pitching-green	pitching green	yes

Hotel facilities — ENVIRONNEMENT HOTELIER — 6/10

HOTELS HÔTELS

Great Southern Hotel — Shannon Airport 1 km
115 rooms, D 127 €
Tel (353) 061 - 471 122, Fax (353) 061 - 471 982

Fitzpatrick Shamrock Hotel — Bunratty 9 km
115 rooms, D 159 €
Tel (353) 061 - 361 177, Fax (353) 061 - 471 252

West County Inn, 110 rooms, D 102 € — Ennis 20 km
Tel (353) 065 - 28 421, Fax (353) 065 - 28 801

RESTAURANTS RESTAURANT

MacCloskey's, Tel (353) 061 - 364 082 — Bunratty 9 km
Mr Pickwick's, Tel (353) 061 - 364 290 — Shannon 2 km

SLIEVE RUSSELL

15 | 8 | 6

The early 1990s saw the advent of a fine group of excellent new courses in Ireland, often tied in with hotels. Slieve Russell is one such project in a region that hitherto had earned a reputation as being a paradise for anglers, and whose isolation should appeal to golfers who want to get away from the world for a few days spent in the heart of nature. The landscape is park-land in style, but certain geographical features are reminiscent of a links course. Two large lakes come into play, joined by a stretch of water which lurks just as threateningly, and complete a full barrage of difficulties: sometimes very thick rough, thickets, fairway and green-side bunkers and greens with sometimes very pronounced contours. Of the more memorable holes, we noted the excellence of the par 3s (especially the 16th), the 2nd, where the water is already upon you, and the 13th, a magnificent par 5 alongside Lough Rud. This course has very quickly forged itself a pretty fine reputation, and understandably so.

Le début des années 90 a vu naître en Irlande un bon groupe d'excellents nouveaux parcours, souvent associés à des hôtels. Slieve Russell est de ceux-ci, dans une région jusqu'ici réputée comme un paradis des pêcheurs, et dont l'isolement devrait séduire les golfeurs qui veulent se retirer du monde, du moins en pleine nature et au moins quelques jours. Il se trouve dans un paysage de parc, mais certains reliefs font parfois penser aux links. Deux grands lacs viennent en jeu, réunis par un cours d'eau tout aussi menaçant, et complètent un arsenal de difficultés : rough parfois épais, buissons, bunkers de fairway et de greens, ceux-ci protégeant des greens au relief parfois prononcé. Parmi quelques trous mémorables, on soulignera la qualité des par 3 (notamment le 16), du 2, où l'eau est déjà présente, et du 13, un magnifique par 5 le long du Lough Rud. Ce parcours s'est vite fait une jolie réputation, on comprend pourquoi.

Slieve Russell Golf Club — 1992

IRL - BALLYCONNELL, Co Cavan

Office	Secrétariat	(353) 049 - 952 6458
Pro shop	Pro-shop	(353) 049 - 952 6444
Fax	Fax	(353) 049 - 952 6640
Web	www.quinn-group.com	
Situation	Situation	

Belturbet, 11 km. 25 km from Cavan (pop. 3 509)

Annual closure	Fermeture annuelle	no
Weekly closure	Fermeture hebdomadaire	no

Fees main season Tarifs haute saison	Week days Semaine	We/Bank holidays We/Férié
	18 holes	
Individual Individuel	57 €	70 €
Couple Couple	114 €	140 €

Hotel residents : 24 € (W/D) and 33 € (W/E)

Caddy	Caddy	25 € /on request
Electric Trolley	Chariot électrique	no
Buggy	Voiturette	32 € /18 holes
Clubs	Clubs	19 € /18 holes

Credit cards Cartes de crédit
VISA - Eurocard - MasterCard - DC

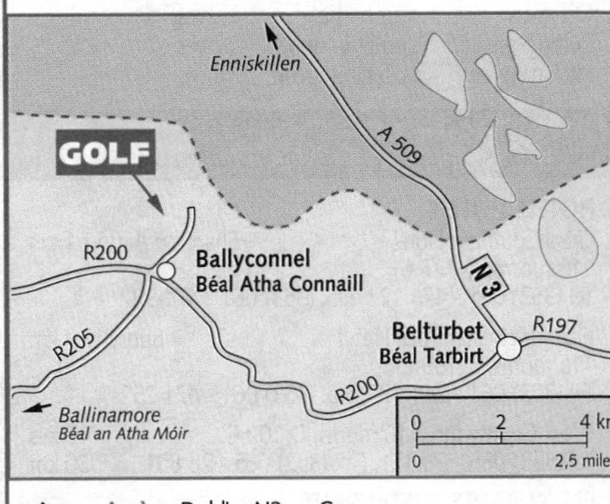

Access Accès : Dublin, N3 → Cavan. Belturbet, R200 → Ballyconnell
Map 1 on page 821 Carte 1 Page 821

Golf course — PARCOURS — 15/20

Site	Site	
Maintenance	Entretien	
Architect	Architecte	Paddy Merrigan
Type	Type	parkland
Relief	Relief	
Water in play	Eau en jeu	
Exp. to wind	Exposé au vent	
Trees in play	Arbres en jeu	

Scorecard Carte de score	Chp. Chp.	Mens Mess.	Ladies Da.
Length Long.	6449	6018	4849
Par	72	72	72
Slope system	—	—	—

Advised golfing ability Niveau de jeu recommandé: 0 12 24 36
Hcp required Handicap exigé: no

Club house & amenities — CLUB HOUSE ET ANNEXES — 8/10

Pro shop	Pro-shop	
Driving range	Practice	
Sheltered	couvert	no
On grass	sur herbe	yes
Putting-green	putting-green	yes
Pitching-green	pitching green	yes

Hotel facilities — ENVIRONNEMENT HOTELIER — 6/10

HOTELS HÔTELS

Slieve Russell Hotel, 150 rooms, D 190 € — Ballyconnell, on site
Tel (353) 049 - 952 6442, Fax (353) 049 - 952 6474

Hotel Kilmore, 39 rooms, D 102 € — Cavan, 12 km
Tel (353) 049 - 433 2288, Fax (353) 049 - 433 2458

RESTAURANTS RESTAURANT

Summit, Tel (353) 049 - 26 444 — Golf Club, on site

Erin Bistro — Belturbet 11 km

ST HELEN'S BAY

14 | 6 | 6

Some 6,000 trees have been planted at St Helen's Bay, and they will of course underline the park landscape of a part of this course. Philip Walton, who made his golf-designer debut here, visibly had the amateur golfer in mind. Sure, there is water on six holes, but it is more psychologically scaring than terribly dangerous, the fairway bunkers are on the lenient side and the greens (moderately sized) are well defended but leave a way open for rolled approach shots, if preferred to lofted pitches. From the 14th hole onward, you are in links country, and the going gets tougher as you progress. The coup de grâce awaits you at the 17th and 18th holes, where your card can end in tatters... or maybe not, since you have had 16 holes to hone your swing. One of the major assets of this course is its versatility, and it gives a lot of pleasure to players of all levels. We should mention, in closing, that the "wall of famine", dating from 1846, comes into play on three holes.

6.000 arbres ont été plantés à St Helen's Bay, qui vont accentuer le paysage de parc d'une partie du parcours. Philip Walton, dont c'est le premier dessin, a visiblement pensé aux amateurs. Certes, l'eau vient en jeu sur six trous, mais de manière plus psychologique que terriblement dangereuse, les bunkers de fairway ne sont pas trop pénalisants, les greens (de dimension confortable) sont bien défendus, mais on peut en aborder la plupart en faisant rouler la balle, ou en la portant, au choix. A partir du 14, nous voici dans un paysage de links, dont la difficulté va croissant, pour culminer au 17 et au 18, deux trous pour détruire sa carte, ou pour la soigner : vous avez 16 trous pour vous y préparer ! La versatilité du parcours est l'un de ses arguments majeurs, il donne beaucoup de plaisir aux joueurs de tous niveaux. Pour l'anecdote, soulignons la mise en jeu sur trois trous du "mur de la famine", qui remonte à 1846.

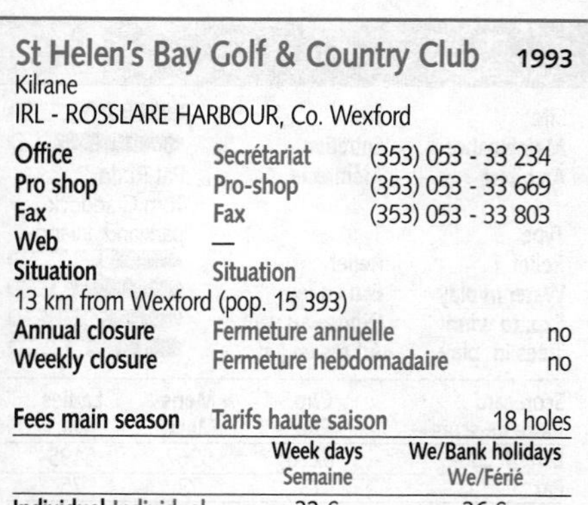

St Helen's Bay Golf & Country Club 1993
Kilrane
IRL - ROSSLARE HARBOUR, Co. Wexford

Office	Secrétariat	(353) 053 - 33 234
Pro shop	Pro-shop	(353) 053 - 33 669
Fax	Fax	(353) 053 - 33 803
Web	—	
Situation	Situation	

13 km from Wexford (pop. 15 393)

Annual closure	Fermeture annuelle	no
Weekly closure	Fermeture hebdomadaire	no

Fees main season Tarifs haute saison		18 holes
	Week days Semaine	**We/Bank holidays** We/Férié
Individual Individuel	32 €	36 €
Couple Couple	64 €	72 €

Caddy	Caddy	13 € /18 holes
Electric Trolley	Chariot électrique	8 €
Buggy	Voiturette	25 € /18 holes
Clubs	Clubs	10 €

Credit cards Cartes de crédit
VISA - Eurocard - MasterCard - AMEX

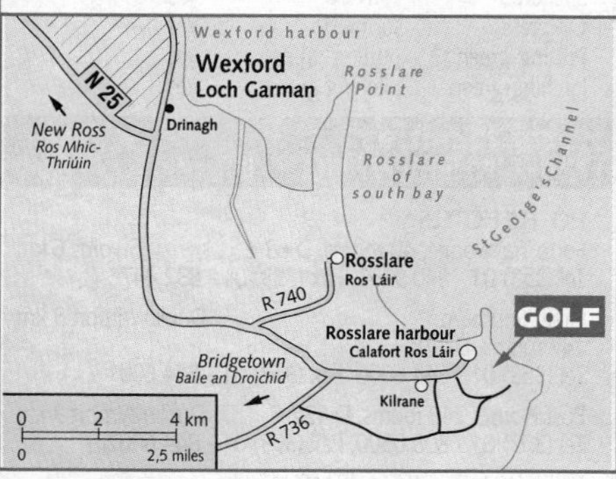

Access Accès : Dublin, N11 to Wexford.
N25 to Rosslare Harbour
Map 2 on page 823 Carte 2 Page 823

Golf course PARCOURS 14/20

Site	Site	
Maintenance	Entretien	
Architect	Architecte	Philip Walton
Type	Type	links, parkland
Relief	Relief	
Water in play	Eau en jeu	
Exp. to wind	Exposé au vent	
Trees in play	Arbres en jeu	

Scorecard Carte de score	**Chp.** Chp.	**Mens** Mess.	**Ladies** Da.
Length Long.	6091	5813	4967
Par	72	72	72
Slope system	—	—	—

Advised golfing ability Niveau de jeu recommandé: 0 12 24 36
Hcp required Handicap exigé: no

Club house & amenities CLUB HOUSE ET ANNEXES 6/10

Pro shop	Pro-shop	
Driving range	Practice	
Sheltered	couvert	no
On grass	sur herbe	yes
Putting-green	putting-green	yes
Pitching-green	pitching green	no

Hotel facilities ENVIRONNEMENT HOTELIER 6/10

HOTELS HÔTELS

Kelly's Resort, 99 rooms, D 140 € — Rosslare Strand
Tel (353) 053 - 32 114, Fax (353) 053 - 32 222 — 5 km

Great Southern, 100 rooms, D 127 € — Rosslare Harbour
Tel (353) 053 - 33 233, Fax (353) 053 - 33 543 — 4 km

Cedars Hotel, 34 rooms, D 89 € — Rosslare Strand
Tel (353) 053 - 32 124, Fax (353) 053 - 32 243 — 5 km

RESTAURANTS RESTAURANT

Coopers — Killinick
Tel (353) 053 - 58 942 — 6 km

Lobster Pot — Carne
Tel (353) 053 - 31 110 — 3 km

ST MARGARET'S

16 | 7 | 7

Before designing Druid's Glen, Pat Ruddy and Tom Craddock gave Dublin one of its best inland courses, at the expense of significant earthwork, as the former farming land was singularly lacking in geographical relief. They evidently had champion golfers in mind, but didn't forget the average amateur player either. Yet despite the many different tee-off areas, they haven't really managed to make it easy. Many of the greens are very well-guarded, and the style of golf is more American than British, meaning a lot of lofted iron shots, long and short. There are a few memorable holes, like the 8th or 12th, two real par 5s reachable only in three, and the 7th and 18th, two grand par 4s. These are all holes where water lurks dangerously. Elsewhere, the bunkers are comparatively flat and so don't set too many problems, even for players who have an aversion to sand. A course well worth getting to know.

Avant de produire Druids Glen, Pat Ruddy et Tom Craddock ont donné à Dublin l'un de ses meilleurs parcours intérieurs, au prix de terrassements importants, car ces anciens terrains agricoles manquaient singulièrement de relief. S'ils ont pensé aux champions, ils n'ont pas oublié les amateurs moyens, mais ils n'ont pas vraiment réussi, malgré le nombre de départs, à le rendre facile. Il faut dire que de nombreux greens sont très défendus, et que l'on joue plus un golf à l'américaine qu'à la "britannique", avec l'obligation de porter haut les coups de fer, y compris les petites approches. Quelques trous sont mémorables, comme le 8 et le 12, deux véritables par 5 à trois coups, le 7 et surtout le 18, deux par 4 de grand style. Ce sont tous des trous où l'eau est dangereuse. Ailleurs, les bunkers sont relativement plats, ce qui ne pose pas trop de problèmes, même à ceux qui n'adorent pas le sable. Un parcours à connaître.

St Margaret's Golf & Country Club — 1992

IRL - ST MARGARET'S, Co Dublin

Office	Secrétariat	(353) 01 - 864 0400
Pro shop	Pro-shop	(353) 01 - 864 0400
Fax	Fax	(353) 01 - 864 0289
Web	www.st-margarets.net	
Situation	Situation	

20 km from Dublin (pop. 481 854)
10 km from Malahide (pop. 13 539)

Annual closure	Fermeture annuelle	no
Weekly closure	Fermeture hebdomadaire	no

Fees main season Tarifs haute saison	18 holes	
	Week days Semaine	**We/Bank holidays** We/Férié
Individual Individuel	57 €	63 €
Couple Couple	114 €	126 €

Caddy	Caddy	32 € /18 holes
Electric Trolley	Chariot électrique	no
Buggy	Voiturette	32 € /18 holes
Clubs	Clubs	19 € /18 holes

Credit cards Cartes de crédit
VISA - MasterCard - AMEX

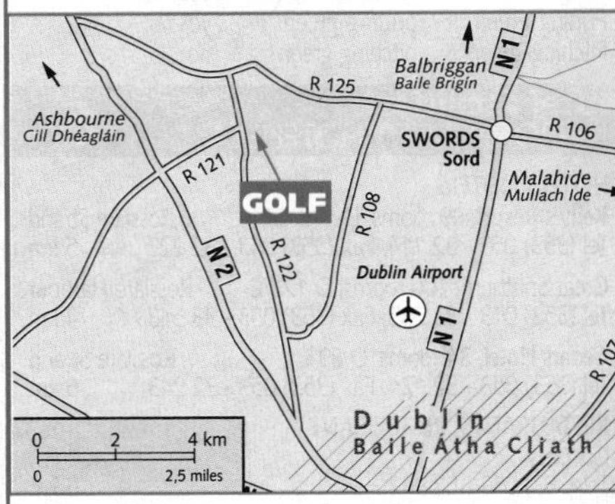

Access Accès : 6 km W. of Dublin Airport
Map 3 on page 824 Carte 3 Page 824

Golf course PARCOURS — 16/20

Site	Site	
Maintenance	Entretien	
Architect	Architecte	Pat Ruddy, Tom Craddock
Type	Type	parkland, inland
Relief	Relief	
Water in play	Eau en jeu	
Exp. to wind	Exposé au vent	
Trees in play	Arbres en jeu	

Scorecard Carte de score	**Chp.** Chp.	**Mens** Mess.	**Ladies** Da.
Length Long.	6226	5967	5195
Par	73	73	75
Slope system	—	—	—

Advised golfing ability Niveau de jeu recommandé — 0 12 24 36
Hcp required Handicap exigé — 24 Men, 36 Ladies

Club house & amenities CLUB HOUSE ET ANNEXES — 7/10

Pro shop	Pro-shop	
Driving range	Practice	
Sheltered	couvert	yes
On grass	sur herbe	yes
Putting-green	putting-green	yes
Pitching-green	pitching green	yes

Hotel facilities ENVIRONNEMENT HOTELIER — 7/10

HOTELS HÔTELS

Forte Travelodge, 40 rooms, D 63 € — Swords 6 km
Tel (353) 01 - 840 9233, Fax (353) 01 - 832 4476

Great Southern — Dublin Airport 3 km
147 rooms, D 178 €
Tel (353) 01 - 844 6000, Fax (353) 01 - 844 6001

Post House, 249 rooms, D 127 € — Dublin Airport 3 km
Tel (353) 01 - 808 0500, Fax (353) 01 - 844 6002

RESTAURANTS RESTAURANT

Red Bank, Tel (353) 01 - 849 1005k — Skerries 15 km
Old School House, Tel (353) 01 - 840 2846 — Swords 8 km

THE ISLAND

15 | 7 | 7

A hundred years after it was first created, the original design here was drastically remodelled by Fred Hawtree and Eddie Hackett. In the past, you could only reach the course by boat. Now, they have made it meaner but removed some of its beauty in the process. In contrast, there are no more blind greens, even though the terrain is hilly (but not too punishing). A kind course when there is little or no wind, The Island can turn nasty when the wind blows, especially on the holes close to the sea. This is when you need the deliberate low shot and, if that were not enough, the ability to stop the ball on the greens at the same time. Here you learn how to fashion every shot in the book, so much so that this club has schooled an impressive list of top men and lady players, which goes to show that power play on its own is not enough. The ideal venue for the region's golfing technicians.

Cent ans après sa naissance, Fred Hawtree et Eddie Hackett ont révisé de manière drastique le dessin original d'un parcours auquel on ne pouvait autrefois accéder qu'en barque. Ils lui ont donné de la rudesse, mais retiré un peu de beauté. En revanche, il n'y a plus de greens aveugles, même si le terrain est un peu accidenté (pas de manière punitive). Assez aimable par vent faible ou nul, The Island peut devenir très méchant par vent fort, en particulier sur les trous proches de la mer, il faut alors maîtriser les balles basses, mais ce n'est pas suffisant, il faut en même temps arrêter la balle sur les greens. Ici, on apprend à fabriquer tous les coups de golf. Tellement bien que ce club a formé une liste impressionnante de joueurs et surtout de bonnes joueuses, comme quoi la puissance ne suffit pas. The Island semble bien être l'un des grands rendez-vous des techniciens de la région.

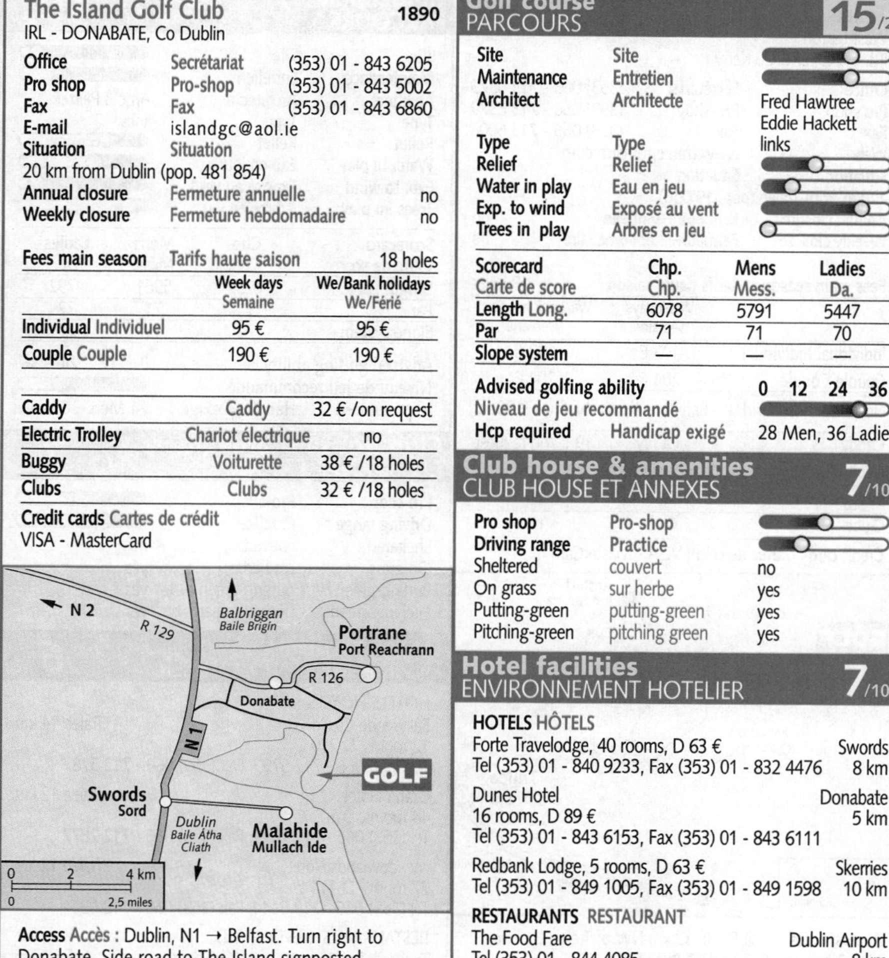

The Island Golf Club — 1890

IRL - DONABATE, Co Dublin

Office Secrétariat (353) 01 - 843 6205
Pro shop Pro-shop (353) 01 - 843 5002
Fax Fax (353) 01 - 843 6860
E-mail islandgc@aol.ie
Situation Situation
20 km from Dublin (pop. 481 854)
Annual closure Fermeture annuelle: no
Weekly closure Fermeture hebdomadaire: no

Fees main season Tarifs haute saison	Week days Semaine	We/Bank holidays We/Férié
		18 holes
Individual Individuel	95 €	95 €
Couple Couple	190 €	190 €

Caddy	Caddy	32 € /on request
Electric Trolley	Chariot électrique	no
Buggy	Voiturette	38 € /18 holes
Clubs	Clubs	32 € /18 holes

Credit cards Cartes de crédit
VISA - MasterCard

Access Accès : Dublin, N1 → Belfast. Turn right to Donabate. Side road to The Island signposted.
Map 3 on page 824 Carte 3 Page 824

Golf course PARCOURS — 15/20

Site	Site	
Maintenance	Entretien	
Architect	Architecte	Fred Hawtree Eddie Hackett
Type	Type	links
Relief	Relief	
Water in play	Eau en jeu	
Exp. to wind	Exposé au vent	
Trees in play	Arbres en jeu	

Scorecard Carte de score	Chp. Chp.	Mens Mess.	Ladies Da.
Length Long.	6078	5791	5447
Par	71	71	70
Slope system	—	—	—

Advised golfing ability Niveau de jeu recommandé: 0 12 24 36
Hcp required Handicap exigé: 28 Men, 36 Ladies

Club house & amenities CLUB HOUSE ET ANNEXES — 7/10

Pro shop	Pro-shop	
Driving range	Practice	
Sheltered	couvert	no
On grass	sur herbe	yes
Putting-green	putting-green	yes
Pitching-green	pitching green	yes

Hotel facilities ENVIRONNEMENT HOTELIER — 7/10

HOTELS HÔTELS

Forte Travelodge, 40 rooms, D 63 € — Swords 8 km
Tel (353) 01 - 840 9233, Fax (353) 01 - 832 4476

Dunes Hotel — Donabate 5 km
16 rooms, D 89 €
Tel (353) 01 - 843 6153, Fax (353) 01 - 843 6111

Redbank Lodge, 5 rooms, D 63 € — Skerries 10 km
Tel (353) 01 - 849 1005, Fax (353) 01 - 849 1598

RESTAURANTS RESTAURANT

The Food Fare — Dublin Airport 8 km
Tel (353) 01 - 844 4085

Giovanni's, Tel (353) 01 - 845 1733 — Malahide 8 km

TRALEE

18 | 7 | 6

Give a golfer terrain like this and he will give you a course to match his designer skills, imagination and audacity. Arnold Palmer had no shortage of the latter and he learnt the former; Tralee (with the complicity of mother nature) is one of his greatest courses. The front 9 unwind partly atop a cliff overhanging the ocean, which comes dangerously into play if direction and accuracy are wayward. The back 9 are even more impressive, amidst huge dunes in their natural state. Here, you often need to carry the ball a long way and you will be best advised to play from the front tees if your drive and long ironwork are not quite up to scratch. A heroic course, not always as refined in diabolical details as say Ballybunion, Portrush or County Down, but essential visiting for every true golfing enthusiast.

Donnez un terrain comme celui-ci à un golfeur, il vous fera un parcours à la hauteur de ses connaissances d'architecte, de son imagination et de son audace. Le champion Arnold Palmer ne manquait pas de ces dernières qualités, il a appris les premières et Tralee (avec la complicité de la nature) est l'une de ses plus grandes réussites. L'aller se déroule partiellement au sommet d'une falaise longeant l'océan, qui vient dangereusement en jeu si l'on manque de direction et de précision. Le retour est plus impressionnant encore, au milieu d'énormes dunes à l'état sauvage. Là, il faut souvent porter loin la balle, et l'on aura intérêt à choisir les départs avancés si la qualité du drive et des longs fers n'est pas à la hauteur des défis. Un parcours héroïque, pas toujours aussi raffiné dans les détails diaboliques que Ballybunion, Portrush ou County Down, mais incontournable pour tout véritable amoureux du golf.

902

Tralee Golf Club — 1895

West Barron
IRL - ARDFERT, Co Kerry

Office	Secrétariat	(353) 066 - 713 6379
Pro shop	Pro-shop	(353) 066 - 713 6379
Fax	Fax	(353) 066 - 713 6008
Web	www.traleegolfclub.com	
Situation	Situation	

12 km from Tralee (pop. 19 056)

Annual closure	Fermeture annuelle	no
Weekly closure	Fermeture hebdomadaire	no

Fees main season Tarifs haute saison	Week days Semaine	We/Bank holidays We/Férié
Individual Individuel	102 €	102 €
Couple Couple	204 €	204 €

18 holes

No visitors on Sunday - Early tee times: 44 € (→9.30am)

Caddy	Caddy	19 € /on request
Electric Trolley	Chariot électrique	no
Buggy	Voiturette	no
Clubs	Clubs	no

Credit cards Cartes de crédit VISA - MasterCard

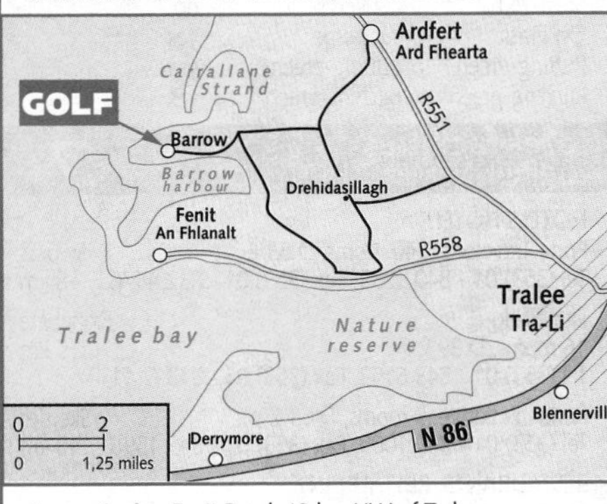

Access Accès : Fenit Road, 12 km NW of Tralee
Map 2 on page 822 Carte 2 Page 822

Map 2 on page 822 Carte 2 Page 822

Golf course PARCOURS — 18/20

Site	Site	
Maintenance	Entretien	
Architect	Architecte	Arnold Palmer
Type	Type	links
Relief	Relief	
Water in play	Eau en jeu	
Exp. to wind	Exposé au vent	
Trees in play	Arbres en jeu	

Scorecard Carte de score	Chp. Chp.	Mens Mess.	Ladies Da.
Length Long.	6252	5961	4792
Par	71	71	72
Slope system	—	—	—

Advised golfing ability Niveau de jeu recommandé — 0 12 24 36

Hcp required Handicap exigé — 24 Men, 36 Ladies

Club house & amenities CLUB HOUSE ET ANNEXES — 7/10

Pro shop	Pro-shop	
Driving range	Practice	
Sheltered	couvert	no
On grass	sur herbe	yes
Putting-green	putting-green	yes
Pitching-green	pitching green	yes

Hotel facilities ENVIRONNEMENT HOTELIER — 6/10

HOTELS HÔTELS

Ballyseede Castle — Tralee 14 km
12 rooms, D 210 €
Tel (353) 066 - 712 5799, Fax (353) 066 - 712 5287

Grand Hotel — Tralee 12 km
44 rooms, D 102 €
Tel (353) 066 - 712 1499, Fax (353) 066 - 712 2877

Meadowlands Hotel — Tralee 12 km
27 rooms, D 114 €
Tel (353) 066 - 718 0444, Fax (353) 066 - 718 0964

RESTAURANTS RESTAURANT

Tankard, Tel (353) 066 - 713 6349 — Tralee 2 km

Oyster Tavern, Tel (353) 066 - 713 6102 — Tralee 3 km

TRAMORE

13 | 7 | 6

Tramore is first and foremost an impressive site by the sea, which in the past caused more than a few problems in stormy weather. The present course has no links holes and is much better protected. The clay soil and heathery terrain drain the course well owing to its elevated position, and the sloping terrain makes an easy walk. This is a driver's course, where long-hitters have an obvious advantage. However, while they can open their shoulders on the first few holes, they will need to keep on the straight and narrow coming home, where the course gets much narrower. Generally speaking, the hazards (especially trees) are placed to catch wayward shots, and players lacking power should avoid the back-tees. Tramore is suitable for players of all levels, but there is just a touch of extra difficulty on the last four holes, especially on the 16th, where a little stream comes into play rather dangerously.

Tramore, c'est d'abord une situation impressionnante en bord de mer, qui a posé autrefois bien des problèmes lors de grandes tempêtes. Le parcours actuel n'a pas de trous de links, il est beaucoup mieux protégé. Le sol d'argile et de terre de bruyère est bien drainant en raison de sa situation surélevée, et les pentes du terrain sont assez favorables à la marche. C'est un parcours pour driver où les joueurs longs seront évidemment avantagés, mais s'ils pourront se déchaîner dans les premiers trous, ils devront aussi être droits vers la fin, bien plus étroite. En règle générale, les obstacles (surtout les arbres) sont placés pour recevoir les coups écartés, les joueurs pas trop puissants auront intérêt à ne pas jouer des départs arrière. Tramore convient à tous les niveaux de jeu, avec une nuance de difficulté supplémentaire sur les quatre derniers trous, particulièrement au 16, où un ruisseau vient en jeu de manière dangereuse.

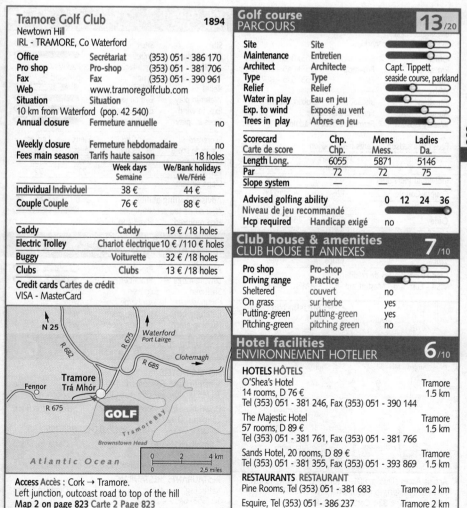

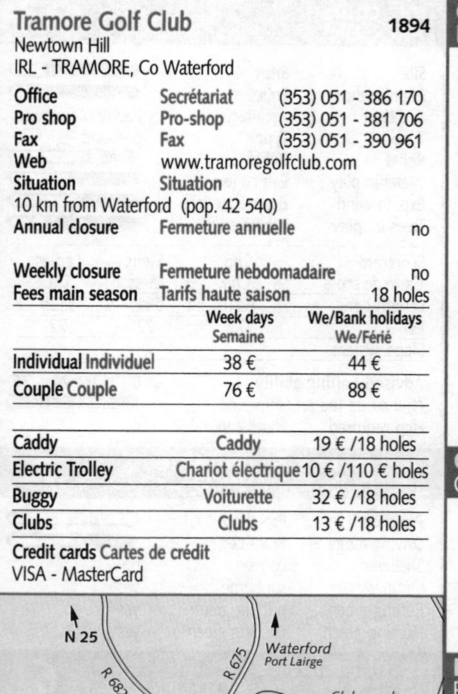

Tramore Golf Club — 1894

Newtown Hill
IRL - TRAMORE, Co Waterford

Office	Secrétariat	(353) 051 - 386 170
Pro shop	Pro-shop	(353) 051 - 381 706
Fax	Fax	(353) 051 - 390 961
Web	www.tramoregolfclub.com	
Situation	Situation	

10 km from Waterford (pop. 42 540)

Annual closure	Fermeture annuelle	no
Weekly closure	Fermeture hebdomadaire	no
Fees main season	Tarifs haute saison	18 holes

	Week days / Semaine	We/Bank holidays / We/Férié
Individual Individuel	38 €	44 €
Couple Couple	76 €	88 €

Caddy	Caddy	19 € /18 holes
Electric Trolley	Chariot électrique	10 € /110 € holes
Buggy	Voiturette	32 € /18 holes
Clubs	Clubs	13 € /18 holes

Credit cards Cartes de crédit
VISA - MasterCard

Access Accès : Cork → Tramore.
Left junction, outcoast road to top of the hill
Map 2 on page 823 Carte 2 Page 823

Golf course PARCOURS — 13/20

Site	Site	
Maintenance	Entretien	
Architect	Architecte	Capt. Tippett
Type	Type	seaside course, parkland
Relief	Relief	
Water in play	Eau en jeu	
Exp. to wind	Exposé au vent	
Trees in play	Arbres en jeu	

Scorecard / Carte de score	Chp. / Chp.	Mens / Mess.	Ladies / Da.
Length Long.	6055	5871	5146
Par	72	72	75
Slope system	—	—	—

Advised golfing ability / Niveau de jeu recommandé: 0 12 24 36
Hcp required Handicap exigé: no

Club house & amenities CLUB HOUSE ET ANNEXES — 7/10

Pro shop	Pro-shop	
Driving range	Practice	
Sheltered	couvert	no
On grass	sur herbe	yes
Putting-green	putting-green	yes
Pitching-green	pitching green	no

Hotel facilities ENVIRONNEMENT HOTELIER — 6/10

HOTELS HÔTELS

O'Shea's Hotel — Tramore 1.5 km
14 rooms, D 76 €
Tel (353) 051 - 381 246, Fax (353) 051 - 390 144

The Majestic Hotel — Tramore 1.5 km
57 rooms, D 89 €
Tel (353) 051 - 381 761, Fax (353) 051 - 381 766

Sands Hotel, 20 rooms, D 89 € — Tramore 1.5 km
Tel (353) 051 - 381 355, Fax (353) 051 - 393 869

RESTAURANTS RESTAURANT

Pine Rooms, Tel (353) 051 - 381 683 — Tramore 2 km
Esquire, Tel (353) 051 - 386 237 — Tramore 2 km

TULFARRIS

15	7	6

With an hotel on site, this course is very attractively located on the shores of lake Blessington and the layout, restyled and completed by P.J. Merrigan, is well suited to all levels of golfing ability. The fairways are wide, with bold routes to beckon the long-hitters and safer ways forward for the lesser players, and the use of trees, sand and water as hazards is cleverly balanced. In this respect, the fairway and green-side bunkers are particularly well located. The design successfully manages to retain a certain local colour despite the "foreign" architectural influences, because the natural landscape has been left unspoilt. High-handicappers will certainly find it something of a stiff challenge, but they will be glad to have had a go. This still very young course has a brilliant future ahead of it, and we would not be at all surprised if it were to become one of Ireland's very best inland courses.

Avec un hôtel sur place, ce golf est des plus séduisants. Sa situation en bordure du lac de Blessington est très plaisante, le tracé remodelé et complété par P.J. Merrigan est bien adapté à tous les niveaux de jeu, avec des fairways larges, des chemins audacieux pour les frappeurs, et d'autres plus sûrs pour les joueurs plus modestes, une utilisation très équilibrée des arbres, de l'eau et du sable comme obstacles : les bunkers de fairways et de greens sont particulièrement bien placés. Le dessin réussit à conserver une certaine couleur "locale" en dépit d'influences architecturales "étrangères", parce que le paysage naturel n'a pas été bouleversé. Certes, les joueurs peu expérimentés trouveront le challenge un peu au-desus de leur niveau, mais ils seront heureux de l'avoir affronté. Encore très jeune, ce parcours d'avenir doit devenir l'un des meilleurs "inland" du pays.

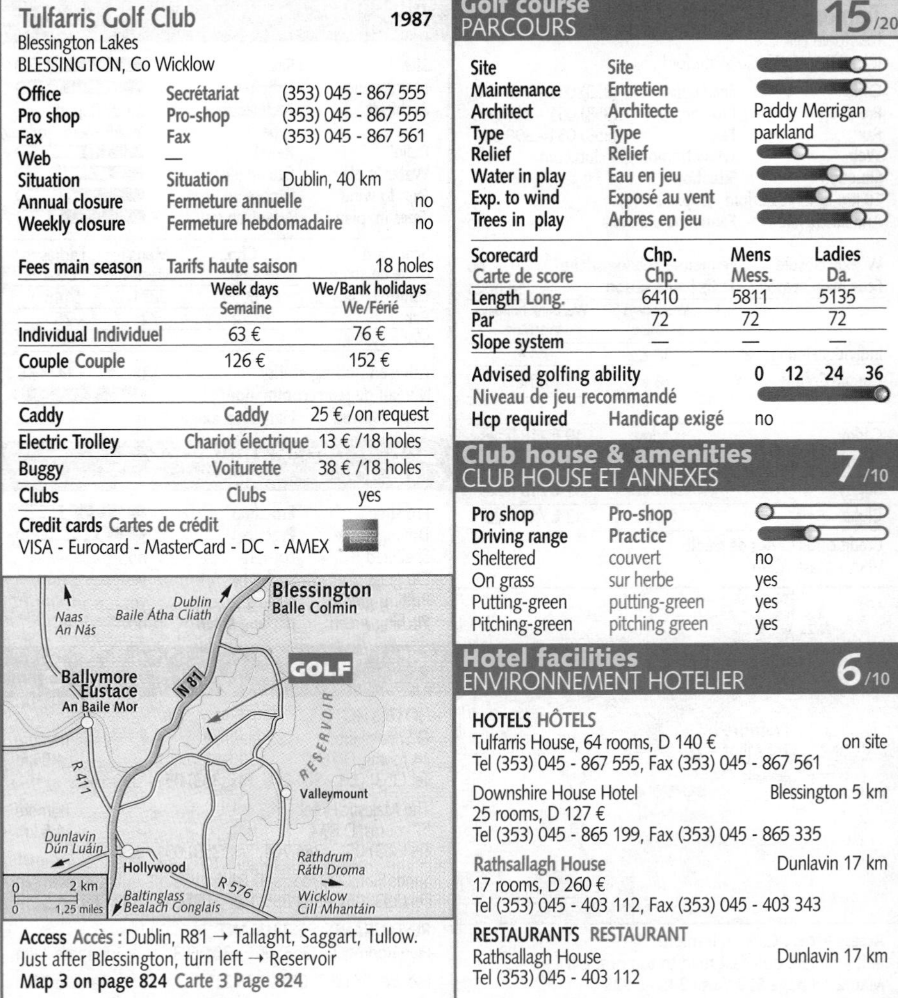

Tulfarris Golf Club 1987
Blessington Lakes
BLESSINGTON, Co Wicklow

Office	Secrétariat	(353) 045 - 867 555
Pro shop	Pro-shop	(353) 045 - 867 555
Fax	Fax	(353) 045 - 867 561
Web	—	
Situation	Situation	Dublin, 40 km
Annual closure	Fermeture annuelle	no
Weekly closure	Fermeture hebdomadaire	no

Fees main season Tarifs haute saison	Week days Semaine	We/Bank holidays We/Férié
	18 holes	
Individual Individuel	63 €	76 €
Couple Couple	126 €	152 €

Caddy	Caddy	25 € /on request
Electric Trolley	Chariot électrique	13 € /18 holes
Buggy	Voiturette	38 € /18 holes
Clubs	Clubs	yes

Credit cards Cartes de crédit
VISA - Eurocard - MasterCard - DC - AMEX

Access Accès : Dublin, R81 → Tallaght, Saggart, Tullow. Just after Blessington, turn left → Reservoir
Map 3 on page 824 Carte 3 Page 824

Golf course PARCOURS 15/20

Site	Site	
Maintenance	Entretien	
Architect	Architecte	Paddy Merrigan
Type	Type	parkland
Relief	Relief	
Water in play	Eau en jeu	
Exp. to wind	Exposé au vent	
Trees in play	Arbres en jeu	

Scorecard Carte de score	Chp. Chp.	Mens Mess.	Ladies Da.
Length Long.	6410	5811	5135
Par	72	72	72
Slope system	—	—	—

Advised golfing ability Niveau de jeu recommandé: 0 12 24 36
Hcp required Handicap exigé: no

Club house & amenities CLUB HOUSE ET ANNEXES 7/10

Pro shop	Pro-shop	
Driving range	Practice	
Sheltered	couvert	no
On grass	sur herbe	yes
Putting-green	putting-green	yes
Pitching-green	pitching green	yes

Hotel facilities ENVIRONNEMENT HOTELIER 6/10

HOTELS HÔTELS

Tulfarris House, 64 rooms, D 140 € — on site
Tel (353) 045 - 867 555, Fax (353) 045 - 867 561

Downshire House Hotel — Blessington 5 km
25 rooms, D 127 €
Tel (353) 045 - 865 199, Fax (353) 045 - 865 335

Rathsallagh House — Dunlavin 17 km
17 rooms, D 260 €
Tel (353) 045 - 403 112, Fax (353) 045 - 403 343

RESTAURANTS RESTAURANT

Rathsallagh House — Dunlavin 17 km
Tel (353) 045 - 403 112

TULLAMORE

15	6	5

This has long been one of Ireland's very good inland courses (it is over 100 years old). Reviewed by James Braid in 1926, it has been rejuvenated by Paddy Merrigan and given a planting programme involving 5,000 trees to add to the surrounding forest (oak and beech trees). So trees should become an even more significant factor here, alongside the classic bunkers and a meandering stream. The shape of the fairways brings the rough into play in a very honest way, only really penalising the truly wayward shot. The clearly visible hazards clearly show the best way forward, a friendly gesture which is repeated right around this very open and forthright course. And even though yardage is low, this is still a course where scoring can be difficult; you need to be very accurate to get to a good position on averagely sized greens, which pitch and bite nicely. This is a flat course, and an interesting day's golf.

C'est depuis longtemps (il est centenaire) l'un des très bons parcours inland. Revu par James Braid en 1926, il a fait l'objet d'un rajeunissement par Paddy Merrigan, et d'un programme de plantations de 5.000 arbres, alors que la forêt l'entoure (chênes et hêtres). Les arbres devraient donc devenir un facteur encore plus important, à côté des bunkers classiques et des méandres d'un ruisseau. Le dessin des fairways met en jeu le rough, mais de façon très honnête, ne pénalisant vraiment que les coups très écartés. Les obstacles bien visibles indiquent clairement la ligne de jeu, cet aspect amical se confirme sur ce parcours d'une grande franchise. Il reste cependant difficile d'y réaliser un très bon score, même si la longueur est réduite : il faut beaucoup de précision pour être en bonne position sur des greens de taille moyenne, mais assez réceptifs. Si l'on ajoute que ce parcours est plat, le détour est intéressant.

Tullamore Golf Club — 1896

Brookfield
IRL - TULLAMORE, Co Offaly

Office	Secrétariat	(353) 0506 - 21 439
Pro shop	Pro-shop	(353) 0506 - 51 757
Fax	Fax	(353) 0506 - 51 757
Web	—	
Situation	Situation	Dublin, 90 km

2 km from Tullamore (pop. 9 221)

Annual closure	Fermeture annuelle	no
Weekly closure	Fermeture hebdomadaire	no

Fees main season Tarifs haute saison	18 holes	
	Week days Semaine	**We/Bank holidays** We/Férié
Individual Individuel	38 €	38 €
Couple Couple	76 €	76 €

Caddy	Caddy	19 € /on request
Electric Trolley	Chariot électrique	no
Buggy	Voiturette	no
Clubs	Clubs	13 € /18 holes
Credit cards	Cartes de crédit	no

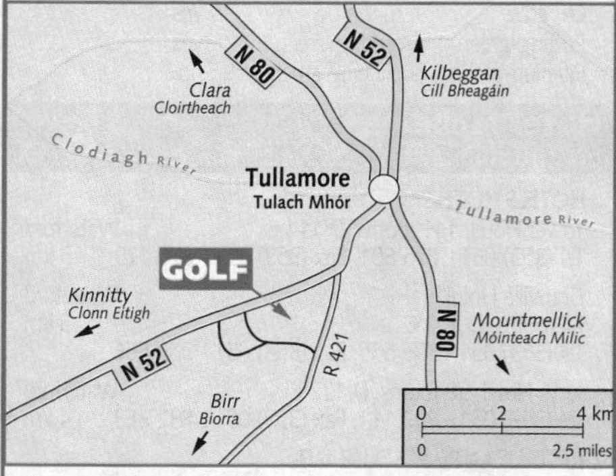

Access Accès : Dublin N4 → Kinnegad. N6 → Kilbeggan. N52 → Tullamore. R421 → Kinnitty, 2 km from Tullamore. **Map 2 on page 823** Carte 2 Page 823

Golf course — PARCOURS — 15/20

Site	Site	
Maintenance	Entretien	
Architect	Architecte	James Braid, Paddy Merrigan
Type	Type	parkland
Relief	Relief	
Water in play	Eau en jeu	
Exp. to wind	Exposé au vent	
Trees in play	Arbres en jeu	

Scorecard Carte de score	**Chp.** Chp.	**Mens** Mess.	**Ladies** Da.
Length Long.	5779	5555	5070
Par	71	71	74
Slope system	—	—	—

Advised golfing ability 0 12 24 36
Niveau de jeu recommandé

Hcp required Handicap exigé no

Club house & amenities — CLUB HOUSE ET ANNEXES — 6/10

Pro shop	Pro-shop	
Driving range	Practice	
Sheltered	couvert	no
On grass	sur herbe	yes
Putting-green	putting-green	yes
Pitching-green	pitching green	yes

Hotel facilities — ENVIRONNEMENT HOTELIER — 5/10

HOTELS HÔTELS

Moorhill House Hotel, 12 rooms, D 76 € — Tullamore
Tel (353) 0506 - 21 395, Fax (353) 0506 - 52 424 — 3 km

Bridge House Hotel, 72 rooms, D 140 € — Tullamore
Tel (353) 0506-22 000, Fax (353) 0506-25 690 — 5 km

Tullamore Court Hotel — Tullamore
72 rooms, D 190 € — 5 km
Tel (353) 0506-46 666, Fax (353) 0506-46 677

RESTAURANTS RESTAURANT

Moorhill House, Tel (353) 0506 - 21 395 — Tullamore 2 km

Sli Dala — Kinnitty 20 km
Tel (353) 0509 - 37 318

WATERFORD

14 | 6 | 6

The first nine holes, designed by the great Willie Park Jnr., were completed by the no less great James Braid. From these two we would have expected a course to resist the skilled player and show a kinder face to the less experienced golfer. This is indeed the case, but today its yardage might seem a little on the short side. Likewise, although the fairway bunkers are strategically well placed, their design has faded over the years. This is perfect on a day when you want golf to be fun. In contrast, the green-side bunkers are well-placed to gather the wayward shot, and you will need to play some sharp short and medium irons. The greens are medium-sized, slightly contoured and are virtually all elevated above ground level, thus emphasising the need for accuracy. This pleasant course leaves a pleasant memory thanks to the 18th hole, a downhill par 4 with a splendid scenic view from the tee.

Les neuf premiers trous conçus par le grand Willie Park Jr ont été complétés par le non moins grand James Braid. On pouvait attendre d'eux un parcours résistant aux efforts des joueurs de haut niveau, et plus amical pour les moins expérimentés. C'est effectivement le cas, mais on peut trouver aujourd'hui sa longueur insuffisante, de même que, si le placement des bunkers de fairway est très stratégique, leur dessin s'est affadi au cours des années. Le jour où l'on a envie que le golf soit amusant, c'est parfait ! En revanche, les bunkers de green sont bien placés pour accueillir les coups insuffisants de précision, et l'on devra bien toucher ses petits et moyens fers. Les greens sont de surface moyenne, faiblement ondulés, mais ils sont pratiquement tous au-dessus du niveau du sol, ce qui accentue la nécessité d'être précis. De ce plaisant parcours, on retiendra le 18, un par 4 en descente avec une vue panoramique splendide depuis le départ.

Waterford Golf Club — 1934

IRL - NEWRATH, Co Waterford

Office	Secrétariat	(353) 051 - 876 748
Pro shop	Pro-shop	(353) 051 - 854 256
Fax	Fax	(353) 051 - 853 405
Web	—	
Situation	Situation	

3 km from Waterford (pop. 42 540)

Annual closure	Fermeture annuelle	no
Weekly closure	Fermeture hebdomadaire	no

Fees main season Tarifs haute saison	Week days Semaine	We/Bank holidays We/Férié
18 holes		
Individual Individuel	32 €	38 €
Couple Couple	64 €	76 €

Caddy	Caddy	no
Electric Trolley	Chariot électrique	no
Buggy	Voiturette	25 € /18 holes
Clubs	Clubs	19 € /18 holes
Credit cards	Cartes de crédit	no

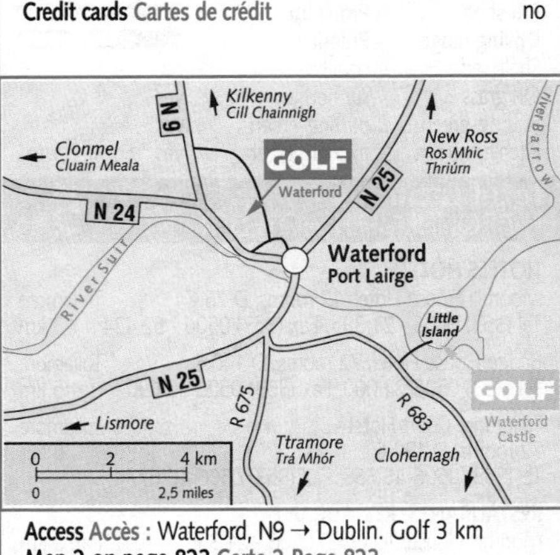

Access Accès : Waterford, N9 → Dublin. Golf 3 km

Map 2 on page 823 Carte 2 Page 823

Golf course PARCOURS — 14/20

Site	Site	
Maintenance	Entretien	
Architect	Architecte	Willie Park Jr James Braid
Type	Type	parkland
Relief	Relief	
Water in play	Eau en jeu	
Exp. to wind	Exposé au vent	
Trees in play	Arbres en jeu	

Scorecard Carte de score	Chp. Chp.	Mens Mess.	Ladies Da.
Length Long.	5722	5491	5168
Par	71	71	74
Slope system	—	—	—

Advised golfing ability / Niveau de jeu recommandé: 0 12 24 36

Hcp required / Handicap exigé: no

Club house & amenities CLUB HOUSE ET ANNEXES — 6/10

Pro shop	Pro-shop	
Driving range	Practice	
Sheltered	couvert	no
On grass	sur herbe	yes
Putting-green	putting-green	yes
Pitching-green	pitching green	no

Hotel facilities ENVIRONNEMENT HOTELIER — 6/10

HOTELS HÔTELS

Tower Hotel, 141 rooms, D 114 € — Waterford
Tel (353) 051 - 875 801, Fax (353) 051 - 870 129 — 5 km

Granville Hotel — Waterford
74 rooms, D 102 € — 5 km
Tel (353) 051 - 305 555, Fax (353) 051 - 305 566

Jurys Hotel, 98 rooms, D 127 € — Waterford
Tel (353) 051 - 832 111, Fax (353) 051 - 832 863 — 4 km

RESTAURANTS RESTAURANT

Granville Hotel — Waterford
Tel (353) 051 - 855 111 — 5 km

Prendiville's, Tel (353) 051 - 78 851 — Waterford 7 km

WATERFORD CASTLE

14 | 5 | 6

A few minutes on a ferry to cross the Suir river, and there you are in a sanctuary of peace and quiet where, if you break into your piggy bank, you can enjoy a dream stay at the on-site hotel and admire some of the walls, which date back to the middle ages. This is perhaps not the course where you would spend the rest of your golfing days, but despite its young age it is in excellent condition and shouldn't be overlooked when in the region. The architects have worked wonders with the physical relief (none too hilly) and the trees which neatly demarcate the holes. This is not really a championship course, but the hazards have been placed to worry the very good players more than the average week-end golfer, who will, or should, have fun here. The large greens make it essential to choose the right club to get close to the pin. A number of water hazards add to the course's appeal.

Quelques minutes de ferry pour traverser la rivière Suir, et vous voilà dans une enclave de tranquillité où vous pourrez faire un séjour de rêve à l'hôtel sur place (certains des murs remontent au Moyen-Age) si vous cassez un peu la tirelire... Le parcours n'est peut-être pas celui que l'on choisirait pour passer le reste de sa vie, mais il est en très bon état malgré sa jeunesse, et ne saurait être ignoré quand on visite la région. Les architectes ont tiré un excellent parti des reliefs (peu importants) du terrain, et des nombreux arbres pour définir les trous dans l'espace. Il ne s'agit pas vraiment d'un parcours de championnat, mais les obstacles ont été placés pour perturber plutôt les très bons joueurs que les joueurs moyens, qui s'y amuseront beaucoup. Les greens, de grande dimension, obligent à faire les bons choix de clubs pour se trouver près des drapeaux. Les obstacles d'eau ajoutent à l'intérêt de ce parcours.

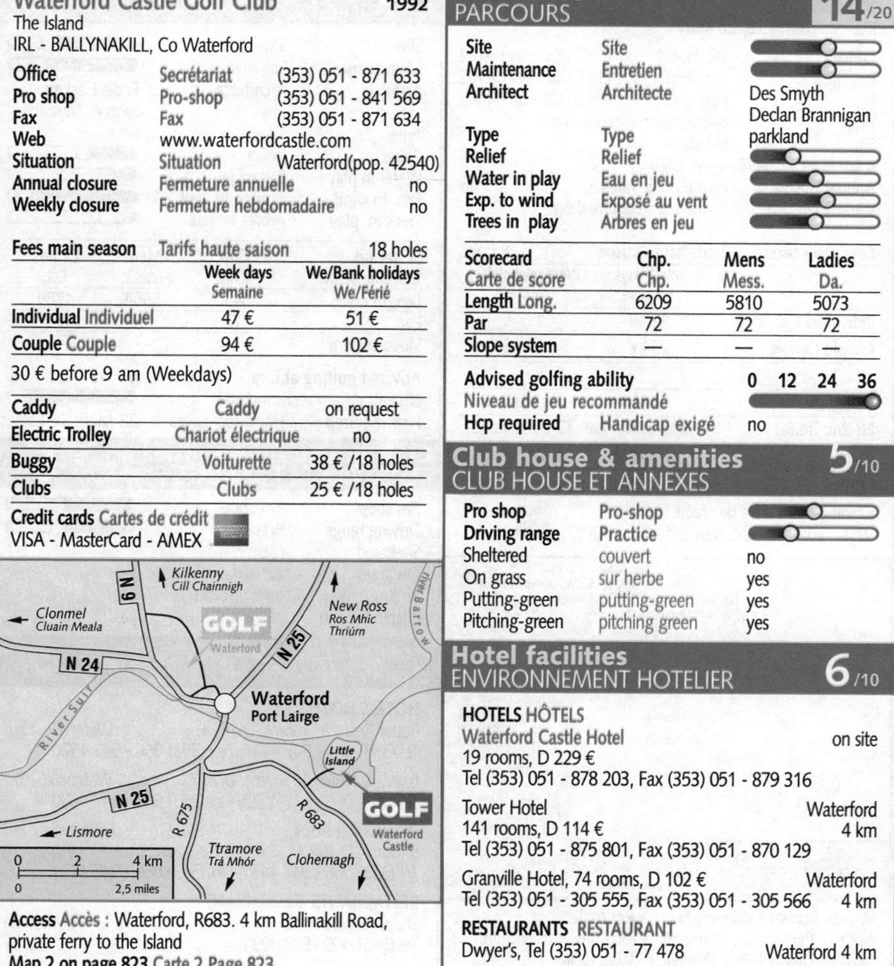

Waterford Castle Golf Club — 1992

The Island
IRL - BALLYNAKILL, Co Waterford

Office	Secrétariat	(353) 051 - 871 633
Pro shop	Pro-shop	(353) 051 - 841 569
Fax	Fax	(353) 051 - 871 634
Web	www.waterfordcastle.com	
Situation	Situation	Waterford(pop. 42540)
Annual closure	Fermeture annuelle	no
Weekly closure	Fermeture hebdomadaire	no

Fees main season / Tarifs haute saison	18 holes	
	Week days / Semaine	We/Bank holidays / We/Férié
Individual Individuel	47 €	51 €
Couple Couple	94 €	102 €

30 € before 9 am (Weekdays)

Caddy	Caddy	on request
Electric Trolley	Chariot électrique	no
Buggy	Voiturette	38 € /18 holes
Clubs	Clubs	25 € /18 holes

Credit cards Cartes de crédit
VISA - MasterCard - AMEX

Access Accès : Waterford, R683. 4 km Ballinakill Road, private ferry to the Island
Map 2 on page 823 Carte 2 Page 823

Golf course PARCOURS — 14/20

Site	Site	
Maintenance	Entretien	
Architect	Architecte	Des Smyth Declan Brannigan
Type	Type	parkland
Relief	Relief	
Water in play	Eau en jeu	
Exp. to wind	Exposé au vent	
Trees in play	Arbres en jeu	

Scorecard / Carte de score	Chp. / Chp.	Mens / Mess.	Ladies / Da.
Length Long.	6209	5810	5073
Par	72	72	72
Slope system	—	—	—

Advised golfing ability 0 12 24 36
Niveau de jeu recommandé
Hcp required Handicap exigé no

Club house & amenities CLUB HOUSE ET ANNEXES — 5/10

Pro shop	Pro-shop	
Driving range	Practice	
Sheltered	couvert	no
On grass	sur herbe	yes
Putting-green	putting-green	yes
Pitching-green	pitching green	yes

Hotel facilities ENVIRONNEMENT HOTELIER — 6/10

HOTELS HÔTELS

Waterford Castle Hotel — on site
19 rooms, D 229 €
Tel (353) 051 - 878 203, Fax (353) 051 - 879 316

Tower Hotel — Waterford 4 km
141 rooms, D 114 €
Tel (353) 051 - 875 801, Fax (353) 051 - 870 129

Granville Hotel, 74 rooms, D 102 € — Waterford 4 km
Tel (353) 051 - 305 555, Fax (353) 051 - 305 566

RESTAURANTS RESTAURANT

Dwyer's, Tel (353) 051 - 77 478 — Waterford 4 km
Waterford Castle, Tel (353) 051 - 878 203 — on site

WATERVILLE

17 | 6 | 7

The pleasure of playing Waterville starts on the road, the "Ring of Kerry", which you first take from the south, from Killarney. The first nine holes unwind over very flat countryside, but the remainder, snaking their way through sand dunes, are impressive to say the least. The design work, no matter how natural it might look today, was considerable: there are no blind holes, virtually flat fairways and almost no dog-legs (except the 16th). But with sometimes blustery side-winds, you need to know how to flight the ball to keep it in play. If we add to this the fact that the putting surfaces are a little less enigmatic than those at Ballybunion, for example, the overall problem here stems from its length (a "man's course", as they say), plus the technical side to the second shot once the drive has avoided the rough and a number of fairway bunkers. A great course, to be played off the front tees.

Le plaisir de jouer Waterville commence sur la route, le "Ring of Kerry" qu'il faut prendre d'abord par le sud, depuis Killarney. Les neuf premiers trous se déroulent dans un paysage de campagne très plat, mais la suite, insinuée dans les dunes, est impressionnante. Le travail architectural, pour naturel qu'il paraisse aujourd'hui, a été important : pas de trous aveugles, des fairways quasiment plats, quasiment aucun dog-leg (sauf le 16). Mais il faudra savoir travailler la balle pour la garder en jeu, avec des vents latéraux souvent violents. Si l'on ajoute que les surfaces de greens ne sont pas aussi énigmatiques qu'elles peuvent l'être à Ballybunion par exemple, la difficulté générale de Waterville tient certes beaucoup à sa longueur, comme on l'a dit ("un parcours d'hommes" !), on peut aussi parler de la technicité des seconds coups, une fois que le drive a évité les roughs et certains bunkers de fairway. Un grand parcours, à jouer des départs avancés.

Waterville — 1889

IRL - WATERVILLE, Co Kerry

Office	Secrétariat	(353) 066 - 947 4102
Pro shop	Pro-shop	(353) 066 - 947 4102
Fax	Fax	(353) 066 - 947 4482
Web	www.watervillegolf.com	
Situation	Situation	
4 km from Waterville (pop. 466)		
Annual closure	Fermeture annuelle	no
Weekly closure	Fermeture hebdomadaire	no

Fees main season Tarifs haute saison	Week days Semaine	We/Bank holidays We/Férié
	18 holes	
Individual Individuel	127 €	127 €
Couple Couple	254 €	254 €

Caddy	Caddy	on request
Electric Trolley	Chariot électrique	13 € /18 holes
Buggy	Voiturette	44 € /18 holes
Clubs	Clubs	13 € /18 holes

Credit cards Cartes de crédit
VISA - Eurocard - MasterCard - DC - AMEX

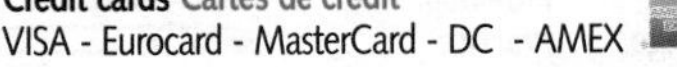

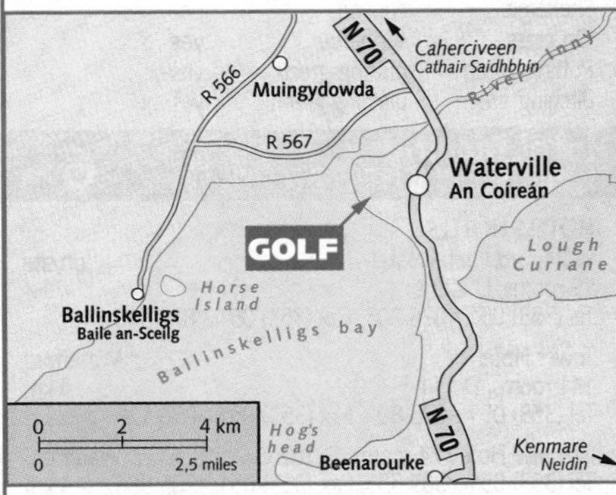

Access Accès : • Killarney N71 → Kenmate.
N70 → Parknasilla, Waterville • Killarney → Killorglin.
N70 → Glenbeigh, Cahirciveen, Waterville
Map 2 on page 822 Carte 2 Page 822

Golf course — PARCOURS — 17/20

Site	Site	
Maintenance	Entretien	
Architect	Architecte	Eddie Hackett John A. Mulcahy
Type	Type	links
Relief	Relief	
Water in play	Eau en jeu	
Exp. to wind	Exposé au vent	
Trees in play	Arbres en jeu	

Scorecard Carte de score	Chp. Chp.	Mens Mess.	Ladies Da.
Length Long.	6430	5954	4789
Par	72	73	73
Slope system	—	—	—

Advised golfing ability Niveau de jeu recommandé — 0 12 24 36
Hcp required Handicap exigé — 28 Men, 36 Ladies

Club house & amenities — CLUB HOUSE ET ANNEXES — 6/10

Pro shop	Pro-shop	
Driving range	Practice	
Sheltered	couvert	
On grass	sur herbe	yes
Putting-green	putting-green	yes
Pitching-green	pitching green	yes

Hotel facilities — ENVIRONNEMENT HOTELIER — 7/10

HOTELS HÔTELS

Butler Arms, 35 rooms, D 152 € — Waterville 2 km
Tel (353) 066 - 947 4144, Fax (353) 066 - 947 4520

Bayview Hotel, 10 rooms, D 76 € — Waterville 2 km
Tel (353) 066 - 947 4122, Fax (353) 066 - 947 4680

Brookhaven House — Waterville 2 km
5 rooms, D 102 €
Tel (353) 066 - 947 4431, Fax (353) 066 - 947 4724

RESTAURANTS RESTAURANT

Sheilin Seafood — Waterville nearby
Tel (353) 066 - 947 4231

Smugglers Inn, Tel (353) 066 - 947 4330 — Waterville,nearby

WESTPORT

15 | 7 | 7

Although located on the edge of Clew Bay, this is essentially a parkland course. For many players, it will be the opportunity to catch their breath between Connemara and Carn or Enniscrone, and to find a little shelter when the wind is playing havoc elsewhere. The views here are just magnificent, between the bay and the blessed mountain of Croagh Patrick, where Ireland's patron saint spent 40 days of fasting and prayer. We wouldn't ask golfers to do the same, as they'll need all their strength to cope with this top-class course. The only slight shortcoming is the relative blandness of the first few holes, but the challenge grows stronger on the way in, with a special mention going to the very pretty 14th, a par 3, and especially the 15th, a splendid and very long par 5 along the bay. The hazards are visibly in play and clear enough to make strategy pretty obvious on your first visit.

Bien qu'il soit situé en bordure de la Clew Bay, ce parcours présente un caractère de parc. Ce sera pour beaucoup de joueurs l'occasion de reprendre leur souffle entre Connemara et Carn ou Enniscrone, et de trouver quelque abri, quand le vent joue un rôle important. Les vues sont ici magnifiques, entre la baie et la "montagne sacrée", le Croagh Patrick, où le saint patron de l'Irlande aurait passé 40 jours de jeûne et de prières. On n'en demandera pas autant aux golfeurs, qui ont besoin de toutes leurs forces sur ce parcours de qualité. La seule nuance dans ce jugement, c'est la relative faiblesse des premiers trous, mais le challenge devient plus exigeant au retour, avec une mention particulière pour le 14, très joli par 3, et surtout le 15, un splendide par 5 très long en bordure de la baie. Les obstacles sont honnêtement en jeu, et assez visibles pour que la stratégie soit évidente dès la première visite.

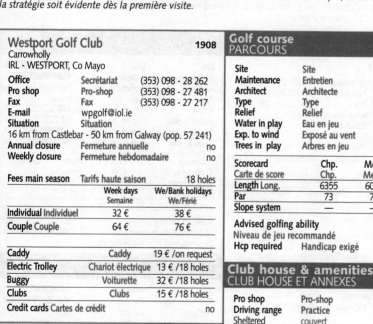

Westport Golf Club — 1908

Carrowholly
IRL - WESTPORT, Co Mayo

Office	Secrétariat	(353) 098 - 28 262
Pro shop	Pro-shop	(353) 098 - 27 481
Fax	Fax	(353) 098 - 27 217
E-mail		wpgolf@iol.ie
Situation	Situation	

16 km from Castlebar - 50 km from Galway (pop. 57 241)

Annual closure	Fermeture annuelle	no
Weekly closure	Fermeture hebdomadaire	no

Fees main season Tarifs haute saison	Week days Semaine	We/Bank holidays We/Férié
		18 holes
Individual Individuel	32 €	38 €
Couple Couple	64 €	76 €

Caddy	Caddy	19 € /on request
Electric Trolley	Chariot électrique	13 € /18 holes
Buggy	Voiturette	32 € /18 holes
Clubs	Clubs	15 € /18 holes
Credit cards	Cartes de crédit	no

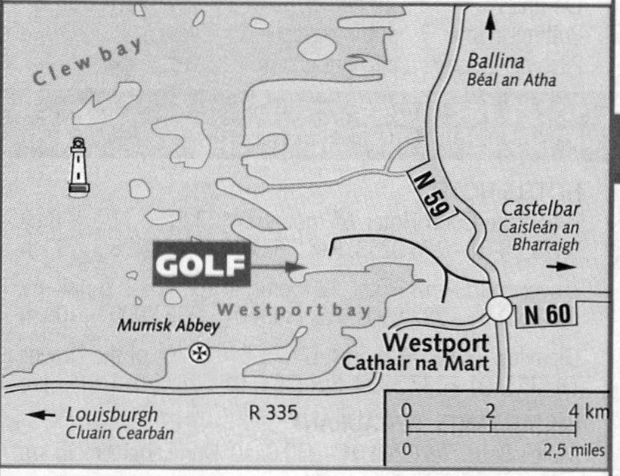

Access Accès : 4 km from Westport on Newport Road
Map 1 on page 820 Carte 1 Page 820

Golf course PARCOURS — 15/20

Site	Site	
Maintenance	Entretien	
Architect	Architecte	Fred Hawtree
Type	Type	seaside course, parkland
Relief	Relief	
Water in play	Eau en jeu	
Exp. to wind	Exposé au vent	
Trees in play	Arbres en jeu	

Scorecard Carte de score	Chp. Chp.	Mens Mess.	Ladies Da.
Length Long.	6355	6095	5233
Par	73	73	74
Slope system	—	—	—

Advised golfing ability / Niveau de jeu recommandé: 0 12 24 36
Hcp required / Handicap exigé: no

Club house & amenities CLUB HOUSE ET ANNEXES — 7/10

Pro shop	Pro-shop	
Driving range	Practice	
Sheltered	couvert	no
On grass	sur herbe	yes
Putting-green	putting-green	yes
Pitching-green	pitching green	no

Hotel facilities ENVIRONNEMENT HOTELIER — 7/10

HOTELS HÔTELS

Hotel Westport, 49 rooms, D 114 € — Westport 4 km
Tel (353) 098 - 25 122, Fax (353) 098 - 26 739

Olde Railway Hotel, 27 rooms, D 89 € — Westport 4 km
Tel (353) 098 - 25 166, Fax (353) 098 - 25 090

Castlecourt Hotel — Westport 4 km
140 rooms, D 102 €
Tel (353) 098 - 25 444, Fax (353) 098 - 25 444

RESTAURANTS RESTAURANT

Ardmore House, Tel (353) 098 - 25 994 — Westport 4 km
The Moorings, Tel (353) 098 - 25 874 — Westport 4 km

606

WOODBROOK

15 | 7 | 6

This course was for many a year a star attraction to the south of Dublin, often hosting the Carroll's Irish Open in the 1960s and the Irish Senior Open in 1998. Complete re-laying of the tees and greens some years ago, under the supervision of Peter McEvoy, has helped to restore the course's prestige and raise the challenge that awaits you. Clearly, the alternating inland and seaside holes provide a close examination of the talent of skilled players and the lesser player too, because the layout is reasonably playable by golfers of all abilities. This rather flat course overlooks the Irish sea from atop cliffs, even though only holes 10 to 12 actually run along the coast. Although there are no huge difficulties, the wind can make life tricky, especially since the trees do little to break it. The only flaw is the Dublin to Wexford railway line, but this type of interference was commonplace in the past and together with the old-style club-house helps to create a site full of the charm of yesteryear.

Ce golf a longtemps été une vedette au sud de Dublin, recevant souvent le Carroll's Irish Open dans les années 60, et l'Irish Senior Open en 1998. Une réfection complète des départs et des greens il y a quelques années, sous l'autorité de Peter McEvoy, a contribué à lui rendre son prestige et à augmenter la qualité du défi. Il faut dire que l'alternance des trous inland et des trous de bord de mer permet un examen complet du talent des bons joueurs. Comme des moins bons d'ailleurs, car ce parcours est raisonnablement jouable à tous les niveaux. Assez plat, il domine du haut des falaises la mer d'Irlande, bien que seuls les trous du 10 au 12 longent effectivement la côte. Les difficultés ne sont pas immenses, mais le vent peut notamment compliquer les choses, d'autant que les arbres présents ne constituent pas vraiment des remparts. Seul défaut, le passage de la voie de chemin de fer Dublin-Wexford, mais ce genre d'interférence était autrefois fréquent, et contribue comme le "old style" du Clubhouse à donner au lieu un certain charme d'antan.

Woodbrook Golf Club — 1926

Dublin Road
IRL - BRAY, Co. Wicklow

Office	Secrétariat	(353) 01 - 282 4799
Pro shop	Pro-shop	(353) 01 - 282 4799
Fax	Fax	(353) 01 - 282 4799
Web	www.woodbrook.ie	
Situation	Situation	
Dublin (pop. 481 854), 20 km		
Annual closure	Fermeture annuelle	no
Weekly closure	Fermeture hebdomadaire	no

910

Fees main season Tarifs haute saison	Week days Semaine	We/Bank holidays We/Férié
		18 holes
Individual Individuel	70 €	83 €
Couple Couple	140 €	166 €
Caddy	Caddy	25 €
Electric Trolley	Chariot électrique	no
Buggy	Voiturette	no
Clubs	Clubs	19 €

Credit cards Cartes de crédit
VISA - MasterCard - DC - AMEX

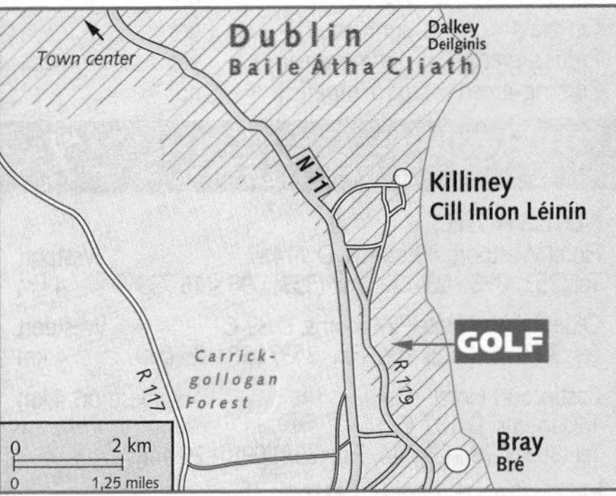

Access Accès : Dublin, N11. R761 → Bray.
1.5 km before Bray → Woodbrook Golf Club
Map 3 on page 824 Carte 3 Page 824

Golf course PARCOURS — 15/20

Site	Site	
Maintenance	Entretien	
Architect	Architecte	Peter McEvoy (remod)
Type	Type	inland
Relief	Relief	
Water in play	Eau en jeu	
Exp. to wind	Exposé au vent	
Trees in play	Arbres en jeu	

Scorecard Carte de score	Chp. Chp.	Mens Mess.	Ladies Da.
Length Long.	6362	6276	5609
Par	72	72	74
Slope system	—	—	—

Advised golfing ability Niveau de jeu recommandé: 0 12 24 36
Hcp required Handicap exigé: no

Club house & amenities CLUB HOUSE ET ANNEXES — 7/10

Pro shop	Pro-shop	
Driving range	Practice	
Sheltered	couvert	no
On grass	sur herbe	yes (practice area)
Putting-green	putting-green	yes
Pitching-green	pitching green	yes

Hotel facilities ENVIRONNEMENT HOTELIER — 6/10

HOTELS HÔTELS

Woodland Court Hotel, 65 rooms, D 127 € — Bray
Tel (353) 01 - 276 0258, Fax (353) 01 - 276 0298 — 3 km

Powerscourt Arms Hotel, 12 rooms, D 102 € — Enniskerry
Tel (353) 01 - 282 8903, Fax (353) 01 - 286 4909 — 10 km

Glenview Hotel, 73 rooms, D 178 € — Glen of the Downs
Tel (353) 01 - 287 3399, Fax (353) 01 - 287 7511 — 12 km

RESTAURANTS RESTAURANT

Morels Bistro, Tel (353) 01 - 230 0210 — Dun Laoghaire 15 km

Enniscree Lodge, Tel (353) 01 - 286 3542 — Enniskerry 15 km

Tinakilly Country House, — Rathnew
Tel (353) 0404 - 69 274 — 30 km

WOODENBRIDGE

16 | 7 | 6

Woodenbrige is located in the very pretty Vale of Avoca, famous for its tweeds, and essential visiting in the spring when the cherry trees are in full blossom. You will be following in the footsteps of the poet Thomas Moore. Created 100 years ago, this fine course became very popular when Paddy Merrigan upgraded it to 18 holes in 1993. The only vegetation are the few trees, here and there (woods outline the course's boundaries), which come very much into play from time to time, but the main hazards are the bunkers (none too penalising) and water, notably the river Avoca, which naturally abounds in this region. There are no unpleasant surprises for visitors, as the difficulties are clearly visible from each tee and add to the course's overall honesty. There is no great need to flight your shots, and only the variety of approach shots (lofted or run) call for real talent.

Woodenbridge est situé dans la très jolie Vallée d'Avoca, célèbre pour ses tweeds, et qu'il faut voir au printemps, quand les cerisiers sont en fleurs : vous y suivrez les traces du poète Thomas Moore. Créé il y a cent ans, ce bon parcours est devenu très populaire quand Paddy Merrigan l'a porté à 18 trous en 1993. La seule végétation est ici constituée par des arbres çà et là (les bois marquant les limites du golf), ils sont parfois très en jeu, mais les obstacles principaux sont les bunkers (pas trop pénalisants quand on s'y retrouve) et des obstacles d'eau - notamment la rivière Avoca - naturellement abondants dans cette région. Les visiteurs ne risquent pas de mauvaises surprises, les difficultés sont bien visibles de chaque départ, ajoutant à la franchise générale du tracé. Il n'est pas utile de beaucoup travailler la balle, seule la variété des approches (balles levées ou balles roulées) exigeant un certain talent.

Woodenbridge Golf Club — 1897

Woodenbridge
IRL - ARKLOW, Co Wicklow

Office	Secrétariat	(353) 0402 - 35 202
Pro shop	Pro-shop	(353) 0402 - 35 202
Fax	Fax	(353) 0402 - 31 402
Web	—	
Situation	Situation	

74 km from Dublin (pop. 481 854) - 7 km from Arklow

Annual closure	Fermeture annuelle	no
Weekly closure	Fermeture hebdomadaire	no

Fees main season Tarifs haute saison	**Week days** Semaine	**We/Bank holidays** We/Férié
18 holes		
Individual Individuel	51 €	63 €
Couple Couple	83 €	95 €

Caddy	Caddy	25 € /on request
Electric Trolley	Chariot électrique	no
Buggy	Voiturette	25 € /18 holes
Clubs	Clubs	no
Credit cards	Cartes de crédit	no

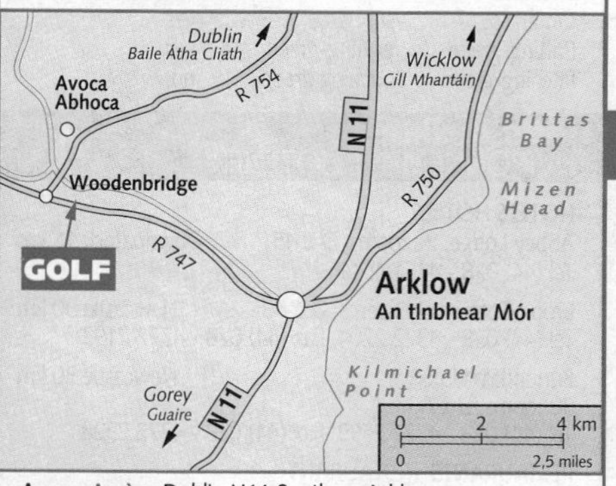

Access Accès : Dublin N11 South → Arklow.
7 km NW of Arklow on R747
Map 3 on page 824 Carte 3 Page 824

Golf course PARCOURS — 16/20

Site	Site	
Maintenance	Entretien	
Architect	Architecte	Paddy Merrigan, 1993
Type	Type	forest, parkland
Relief	Relief	
Water in play	Eau en jeu	
Exp. to wind	Exposé au vent	
Trees in play	Arbres en jeu	

Scorecard Carte de score	**Chp.** Chp.	**Mens** Mess.	**Ladies** Da.
Length Long.	6350	6074	5490
Par	71	71	72
Slope system	—	—	—

Advised golfing ability Niveau de jeu recommandé — 0 12 24 36
Hcp required Handicap exigé — 24 Men, 36 Ladies

Club house & amenities CLUB HOUSE ET ANNEXES — 7/10

Pro shop	Pro-shop	
Driving range	Practice	
Sheltered	couvert	no
On grass	sur herbe	yes
Putting-green	putting-green	yes
Pitching-green	pitching green	no

Hotel facilities ENVIRONNEMENT HOTELIER — 6/10

HOTELS HÔTELS

Woodenbridge Hotel, 12 rooms, D 102 € — Arklow 1 km
Tel (353) 0402 - 35 146, Fax (353) 0402 - 35 573

Valley Hotel, 10 rooms, D 89 € — Woodenbridge 1 km
Tel (353) 0402 - 35 200, Fax (353) 0402 - 35 542

Arklow Bay Hotel — Arklow 7 km
38 rooms, D 102 €
Tel (353) 0402 - 32 309, Fax (353) 0402 - 32 300

RESTAURANTS RESTAURANT

Sheepwalk House, Tel (353) 0402 - 35 189 — Avoca 8 km

Mitchell's — Laragh, Glendalough 28 km
Tel (353) 0404 - 45 302

ARDGLASS

14 | 6 | 4

In this region, occupied by the Vikings, pirates and smugglers, you will also find the vestiges of a castle built by the Normans alongside the club-house. Other good news for non-golfers is the nearby Strangford Lough, a real sanctuary for birds. But back to golf. As the course runs impressively atop coastal cliffs, this is one of the country's finest sites, with a view as far as the Isle of Man (on a clear day). Worth seeing, and worth playing, too. An age-old course from an unknown architect, this is a good layout and links course with no steep relief and none of those enormous dunes that can have such an effect on easily influenced players. You need to play several rounds to grasp the subtleties of the course, because there are quite a few blind drives and so a high risk of ending up in the rough or bushes, that do your card no good at all. And that's no to mention the exposure to the wind, which hardly helps matters. The bunkers are rather small, as are the greens. First time out, have fun with a match-play round.

Dans ce pays occupé par les Vikings, les pirates et les contrebandiers, on trouve aussi, à côté du Club-house, les vestiges d'un château bâti par les Normands. A proximité, le Strangford Lough est un véritable sanctuaire d'oiseaux. Et comme la situation du parcours sur de hautes falaises est impressionnante, c'est un des grands sites du pays, avec une vue jusqu'à l'Ile de Man (quand il fait beau). A voir mais aussi à jouer. Centenaire, et d'architecte inconnu, c'est un bon tracé, un links au relief très modéré, mais sans les dunes énormes qui peuvent ailleurs effrayer les joueurs influençables. Il faut plusieurs visites pour en comprendre les subtilités, on trouve pas mal de départs aveugles, avec le risque de se retrouver dans un rough ou des buissons dangereux pour le score. Et l'exposition au vent n'arrange rien en ce domaine. Les bunkers sont assez petits, mais les greens aussi... La première fois, amusez-vous en match-play.

Ardglass Golf Club — 1896

Castle Place
NIR - ARDGLASS, Co Down BT30 7 TP

Office	Secrétariat	(44) 028 - 4484 1219
Pro shop	Pro-shop	(44) 028 - 4484 1022
Fax	Fax	(44) 028 - 4484 1841
Web	www.ardglass.force9.co.uk	
Situation	Situation	

11 km from Downpatrick- 48 km from Belfast (pop. 279 237)

Annual closure	Fermeture annuelle	no
Weekly closure	Fermeture hebdomadaire	no

Fees main season Tarifs haute saison	18 holes	
	Week days Semaine	**We/Bank holidays** We/Férié
Individual Individuel	£ 22	£ 25
Couple Couple	£ 44	£ 50

Caddy	Caddy	£ 15 /on request
Electric Trolley	Chariot électrique	no
Buggy	Voiturette	no
Clubs	Clubs	£ 6

Credit cards Cartes de crédit
VISA - MasterCard (Pro shop only)

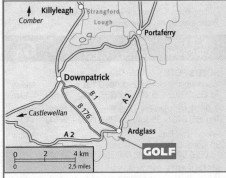

Access Accès : Belfast, A24, A7 to Downpatrick. B1 to Ardglass. → Golf
Map 1 on page 821 Carte 1 Page 821

Golf course PARCOURS — 14/20

Site	Site	
Maintenance	Entretien	
Architect	Architecte	
Type	Type	seaside course
Relief	Relief	
Water in play	Eau en jeu	
Exp. to wind	Exposé au vent	
Trees in play	Arbres en jeu	

Scorecard Carte de score	**Chp.** Chp.	**Mens** Mess.	**Ladies** Da.
Length Long.	5500	5500	4765
Par	70	70	70
Slope system	0	0	0

Advised golfing ability Niveau de jeu recommandé — 0 12 24 36

Hcp required Handicap exigé — Men 24, Ladies 36

Club house & amenities CLUB HOUSE ET ANNEXES — 6/10

Pro shop	Pro-shop	
Driving range	Practice	
Sheltered	couvert	no
On grass	sur herbe	yes
Putting-green	putting-green	yes
Pitching-green	pitching green	no

Hotel facilities ENVIRONNEMENT HOTELIER — 4/10

HOTELS HÔTELS

Abbey Lodge, 22 rooms, D £ 45 — Downpatrick 11 km
Tel (44) 028 - 4461 4511

Brook Cottage, 12 rooms, D £ 46 — Newcastle 30 km
Tel (44) 028 - 4372 2204, Fax (44) 028 - 4372 2193

Burrendale Hotel — Newcastle 30 km
50 rooms, D £ 80
Tel (44) 028 - 4372 2599, Fax (44) 028 - 4372 2328

RESTAURANTS RESTAURANT

Aldo's, Tel (44) 028 - 4384 1315 — Ardglass 1 km

Seaford Inn, Tel (44) 028 - 4381 2232 — Seaford 22 km

BANGOR

14 | 6 | 6

The course is located virtually in the city of Bangor, David Feherty's home town, where, so they say, you'll see the finest landscapes in the whole of Northern Ireland. Bird-watching enthusiasts are just a few minutes away from the boat that takes them to the Copeland Islands, inhabited only by birds, and you are not far from the pretty town of Newtownards. Inveterate golfers, on the other hand, will enjoy playing on this course, rather off the beaten track, a little dated in terms of yardage but great fun to play all the same. James Braid laid out a few elevated greens, others being multi-tiered, plus a few fairway bunkers that are both strategic and punishing. Some of the dog-legs (the 5th, 13th, 14th and 15th holes) call for very accurate driving. In all, a course where you would probably not spend the rest of your life playing, but a good addition to the region's other courses.

Le golf est situé pratiquement dans la ville de Bangor, ville natale du champion David Feherty, où l'on trouve paraît-il les plus beaux paysages d'Irlande du Nord. Les amateurs d'ornithologie n'auront que quelques minutes à faire pour embarquer à destination des Copeland Islands, où ne vivent plus que des oiseaux, ou pour découvrir la jolie ville de Newtownards. Quant aux golfeurs invétérés, ils pourront s'exprimer sur ce parcours hors des sentiers battus, un peu daté en ce qui concerne la longueur, mais très amusant au demeurant. James Braid y a disposé quelques greens surélevés, d'autres à double plateau, et quelques bunkers de fairway à la fois stratégiques et punitifs. Certains dog-legs (5, 13, 14 et 15) demandent un driving très précis pour être maîtrisés. Au total, un parcours sur lequel on ne jouerait peut-être pas toute sa vie, mais un bon complément aux autres parcours de la région.

Bangor Golf Club — 1903

Broadway
NIR - BANGOR, Co. Down BT20 4RH

Office	Secrétariat	(44) 028 - 9127 0922
Pro shop	Pro-shop	(44) 028 - 9146 2164
Fax	Fax	(44) 028 - 9145 3394
Web	www.clubnetusga.co.uk	
Situation	Situation	

10 km from Newtownards - 20 km from Belfast (pop. 279 237)

Annual closure	Fermeture annuelle	no
Weekly closure	Fermeture hebdomadaire	no

Fees main season Tarifs haute saison — 18 holes

	Week days Semaine	We/Bank holidays We/Férié
Individual Individuel	£ 25	£ 28
Couple Couple	£ 30	£ 56

Saturday: members only

Caddy	Caddy	no
Electric Trolley	Chariot électrique	no
Buggy	Voiturette	no
Clubs	Clubs	£ 10 /18 holes

Credit cards Cartes de crédit
VISA - Access - MasterCard

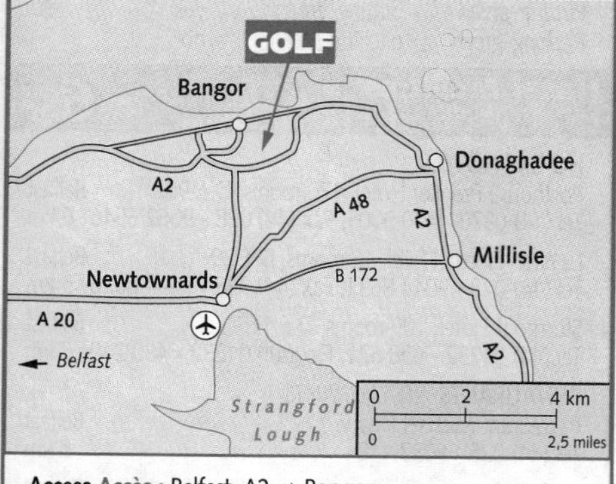

Access Accès : Belfast, A2 → Bangor
Map 1 on page 821 Carte 1 Page 821

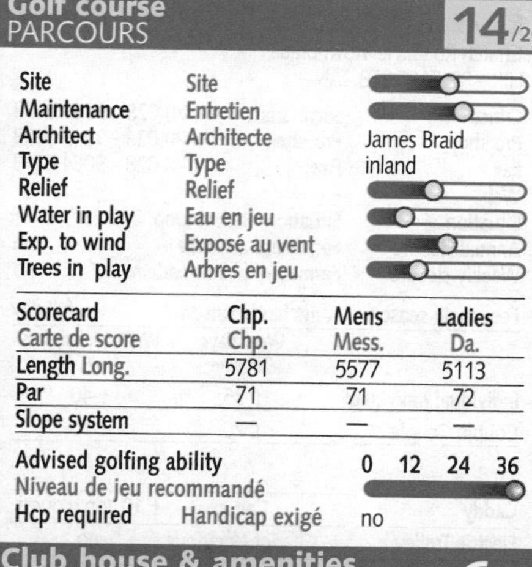

Golf course / PARCOURS — 14/20

Site	Site	
Maintenance	Entretien	
Architect	Architecte	James Braid
Type	Type	inland
Relief	Relief	
Water in play	Eau en jeu	
Exp. to wind	Exposé au vent	
Trees in play	Arbres en jeu	

Scorecard Carte de score	**Chp.** Chp.	**Mens** Mess.	**Ladies** Da.
Length Long.	5781	5577	5113
Par	71	71	72
Slope system	—	—	—

Advised golfing ability / Niveau de jeu recommandé — 0 12 24 36
Hcp required Handicap exigé — no

Club house & amenities / CLUB HOUSE ET ANNEXES — 6/10

Pro shop	Pro-shop	
Driving range	Practice	
Sheltered	couvert	no
On grass	sur herbe	yes
Putting-green	putting-green	yes
Pitching-green	pitching green	yes

Hotel facilities / ENVIRONNEMENT HOTELIER — 6/10

HOTELS HÔTELS

Royal Hotel, 50 rooms, D £ 80 — Bangor 1.5 km
Tel (44) 028 - 9127 1866, Fax (44) 028 - 9146 7810

Crawfordsburn Inn — Crawfordsburn 5 km
33 rooms, D £ 90
Tel (44) 028 - 9185 3255, Fax (44) 028 - 9185 2775

Cairn Bay Lodge, 5 rooms, £ 55 — Bangor 1.5 km
Tel (44) 028 - 9146 7636, Fax (44) 028 - 9145 7728

RESTAURANTS RESTAURANTS

Shanks, Tel (44) 028 - 9185 3313 — Bangor 8 km
Jenny Watts, Tel (44) 028 - 9127 0401 — Bangor 2.5 km

BELVOIR PARK

15 | 5 | 6

The energetic rejuvenation of this course has turned it into one of the region's hidden gems in the region of Belfast, without ever affecting the intelligence of Harry Colt's original layout. Very reasonable in length, it is a real pleasure to play in this lush green park, well protected from the city noise by woods and thick curtains of trees, which also separate the fairways and call for unfailing accuracy. Despite everything, the fairways are of a fair width, and while there are fairway bunkers, their design rarely makes them dangerous. Ditches on the 10th and 12th are the only water hazards, but they play a key role. The course is generally not too hilly, except on the 3rd and 17th, the latter being a part of a very difficult finish, where many a card can fall apart. Fun to play and very prettily landscaped, Belvoir Park is rated amongst the country's finest inland courses.

Le rajeunissement énergique de ce parcours en a fait l'un des petits bijoux cachés de la région de Belfast, sans pour autant altérer l'intelligence du tracé original de Harry Colt, d'une longueur très raisonnable. C'est un plaisir d'évoluer dans ce grand parc en pleine verdure, bien protégé des bruits de la ville par de petits bois et d'épais rideaux d'arbres, séparant bien les fairways, tout en impliquant une certaine précision. Malgré tout, les fairways restent d'une largeur très acceptable, et si les bunkers y sont présents, leur dessin les rend rarement très dangereux. Les fossés au 10 et au 12 sont les seuls obstacles d'eau, mais ils y jouent un rôle fondamental. Le parcours est généralement de relief très modéré, sauf au 3 et au 17, ce dernier trou faisant partie d'un "finish" très difficile, où bien des cartes vont s'alourdir. Amusant à jouer, très joliment paysagé, Belvoir Park figure parmi les très bons parcours "inland" du pays.

Belvoir Park Golf Club — 1927

Church Road, Newtownbreda
NIR - BELFAST BT8 4AN

Office	Secrétariat	(44) 028 - 9049 1693
Pro shop	Pro-shop	(44) 028 - 9049 1693
Fax	Fax	(44) 028 - 9064 6113
Web	—	
Situation	Situation	Belfast (pop. 279 237), 5 km
Annual closure	Fermeture annuelle	no
Weekly closure	Fermeture hebdomadaire	no

Fees main season Tarifs haute saison	full day	
	Week days Semaine	We/Bank holidays We/Férié
Individual Individuel	£ 35	£ 40
Couple Couple	£ 70	£ 80

Caddy	Caddy	£ 10 /on request
Electric Trolley	Chariot électrique	no
Buggy	Voiturette	£ 20 /18 holes
Clubs	Clubs	£ 10 /18 holes
Credit cards	Cartes de crédit	no

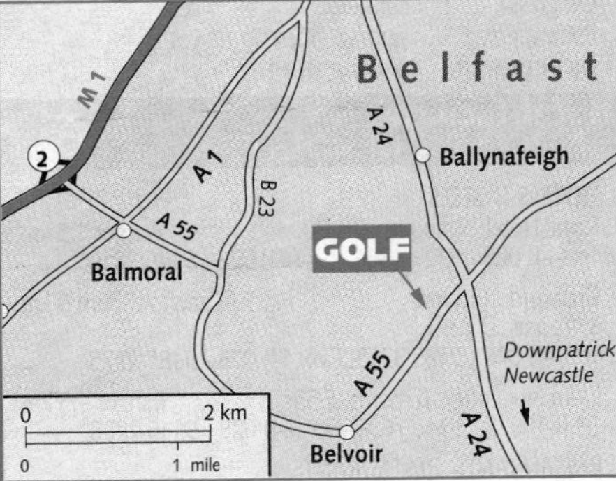

Access Accès : Belfast A24 → Saintfield. Turn off Ormeau Road (Newtownbreda)
Map 1 on page 821 Carte 1 Page 821

Golf course PARCOURS — 15/20

Site	Site	
Maintenance	Entretien	
Architect	Architecte	Harry S. Colt
Type	Type	parkland
Relief	Relief	
Water in play	Eau en jeu	
Exp. to wind	Exposé au vent	
Trees in play	Arbres en jeu	

Scorecard Carte de score	Chp. Chp.	Mens Mess.	Ladies Da.
Length Long.	5958	5739	5152
Par	71	70	73
Slope system	—	—	—

Advised golfing ability / Niveau de jeu recommandé: 0 12 24 36
Hcp required / Handicap exigé: 24 Men, 36 Ladies

Club house & amenities CLUB HOUSE ET ANNEXES — 5/10

Pro shop	Pro-shop	
Driving range	Practice	
Sheltered	couvert	no
On grass	sur herbe	yes
Putting-green	putting-green	yes
Pitching-green	pitching green	no

Hotel facilities ENVIRONNEMENT HOTELIER — 6/10

HOTELS HÔTELS

Posthouse Premier Hotel, 170 rooms, D £ 90 — Belfast
Tel (44) 0870 - 400 9005, Fax (44) 028 - 9062 6546 — 6 km

La Mon House Hotel, 46 rooms, D £ 70 — Belfast
Tel (44) 028 - 9044 8631, Fax (44) 028 - 9044 8026 — 5 km

Stormont Hotel, 109 rooms, D £ 115 — Belfast
Tel (44) 01232 - 658 621, Fax (44) 01232 - 480 240 — 5 km

RESTAURANTS RESTAURANTS

Restaurant Michael Deane — Belfast
Tel (44) 028 - 9033 1134 — 5 km

La Belle Epoque — Belfast
Tel (44) 028 - 9032 3244 — 5 km

CAIRNDHU

13 | 6 | 5

There are trees here, but if you hit your ball into the woods, you are almost certainly out of bounds. Cairndhu is a seaside course (not really a links) along the Antrim coast road. This is the beginner's road leading from Belfast to the great links courses in the north, and the views are often quite spectacular. Excellence of setting and environment are, though, virtually a constant factor throughout Ireland. Don't be too put out when setting eyes on the contours and relief of the first few holes, things calm down a little after the 4th hole and the terrain gently rolls, nothing more. The course demands some straight driving and accurate approach shots, especially when homing in on a number of small greens, although "average" hitters will basically be playing mid to short irons. Don't place too much faith in your own instinct for gauging distances, because here they can be misleading. The architect has made the most of the terrain and it would be a pity not to get to known a course like this.

Il y a des arbres, mais si vous envoyez votre balle dans les bois, elle est sans doute hors limites. Cairndhu est un parcours de bord de mer (pas vraiment un links), le long de l'Antrim Coast Road. C'est le chemin des écoliers pour aller de Belfast aux grands links du nord, et les vues y sont parfois spectaculaires, mais cette qualité d'environnement est quasiment une constante dans toute l'Irlande. A moins d'être cardiaque, ne vous affolez pas trop à la vue du relief des premiers trous, il s'adoucit après le 4 pour laisser place à de sobres ondulations. Ce parcours réclame de la précision au drive et aux approches, particulièrement pour attaquer certains greens de petite taille, mais les frappeurs "normaux" auront alors essentiellement à jouer des moyens et petits fers. Ne vous fiez pas trop à votre instinct pour les distances, il peut vous tromper. L'architecte a tiré un bon parti du terrain, il serait dommage de ne pas le connaître.

Cairndhu Golf Club — 1928

192 Coast Road, Ballygally
NIR - LARNE, Co Antrim

Office	Secrétariat	(44) 028- 2858 3324
Pro shop	Pro-shop	(44) 028- 2858 3324
Fax	Fax	(44) 028- 2858 3324
Web	cairndhu	
Situation	Situation	

6 km from Larne (pop. 17 575)

Annual closure	Fermeture annuelle	no
Weekly closure	Fermeture hebdomadaire	no

Fees main season Tarifs haute saison	Week days Semaine	We/Bank holidays We/Férié
		18 holes
Individual Individuel	£ 20	£ 25
Couple Couple	£ 30	£ 40

Caddy	Caddy	on request
Electric Trolley	Chariot électrique	no
Buggy	Voiturette	no
Clubs	Clubs	£ 15 /18 holes

Credit cards Cartes de crédit
VISA - Eurocard - MasterCard (Golf club only)

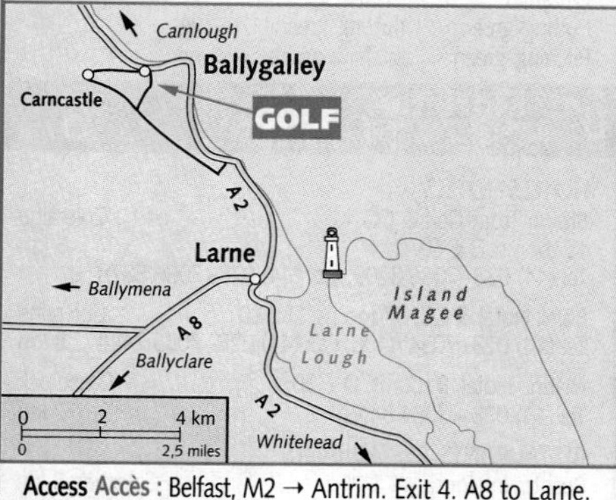

Access Accès : Belfast, M2 → Antrim. Exit 4. A8 to Larne. A2 to Ballygally

Map 1 on page 821 Carte 1 Page 821

Golf course PARCOURS — 13/20

Site	Site	
Maintenance	Entretien	
Architect	Architecte	T. Morrison
Type	Type	seaside course, parkland
Relief	Relief	
Water in play	Eau en jeu	
Exp. to wind	Exposé au vent	
Trees in play	Arbres en jeu	

Scorecard Carte de score	Chp. Chp.	Mens Mess.	Ladies Da.
Length Long.	5500	5436	4861
Par	70	70	73
Slope system	—	—	—

Advised golfing ability Niveau de jeu recommandé — 0 12 24 36

Hcp required Handicap exigé — no

Club house & amenities CLUB HOUSE ET ANNEXES — 6/10

Pro shop	Pro-shop	
Driving range	Practice	
Sheltered	couvert	no
On grass	sur herbe	yes
Putting-green	putting-green	yes
Pitching-green	pitching green	no

Hotel facilities ENVIRONNEMENT HOTELIER — 5/10

HOTELS HÔTELS

Ballygally Castle Hotel, 30 rooms, D £ 80 — Balligally
Tel (44) 028 - 2858 3212, Fax (44) 028 - 2858 3681 — 3 km

Magheramorne House, 22 rooms, D £ 90 — Larne
Tel (44) 028 - 2827 9444, Fax (44) 028 - 2826 0138 — 6 km

Londonderry Arms Hotel, 21 rooms, D £ 80 — Carnlough
Tel (44) 028 - 2888 5255, Fax (44) 028 - 2888 5263 — 18 km

RESTAURANTS RESTAURANTS

Lynden Heights — Ballygally
Tel (44) 028 - 2858 3560 — 3 km

Halfway House — Ballygally
Tel (44) 028- 2858 3265 — 2 km

CASTLEROCK

16 | 6 | 6

Already at a venerable age, Castlerock is certainly not one of the best known links courses, but it would be shame to overlook it. It certainly won't disappoint the better players, and it is also more within the reach of mid- to high-handicappers than its prestigious neighbours. This is a great introduction for people who have never played links golf ; it has a very natural look to it, is in a beautifully wild setting and has the traditional difficulties found on this type of course. The bunkers, though, are appreciably less severe than elsewhere. To maintain the suspense, you will find a few blind drives, but the hazards everywhere are visible enough for you to forget, temporarily at least, that golf is a sport where there's no justice. Smallish greens call for great precision, and if you miss them you will have the opportunity to put your newly-honed short game to the test. Another important factor here is the warm welcome in the clubhouse.

Ayant déjà atteint un âge vénérable, Castlerock ne figure sans doute pas parmi les links les plus connus, mais il serait bien regrettable de le négliger. Il ne décevra en rien les meilleurs joueurs, mais il est aussi davantage à la portée du golfeur de handicap moyen ou élevé que ses voisins prestigieux. Pour ceux qui n'ont jamais joué un links, c'est une bonne initiation, par son aspect très naturel, la beauté sauvage de son environnement de dunes, et les difficultés traditionnelles de ce type de parcours : les bunkers sont notamment moins sévères qu'ailleurs. Pour maintenir le suspense, on trouve quelques drives aveugles, mais les obstacles sont partout assez visibles pour ne pas trop s'apercevoir que le golf est un sport sans justice. Des greens de surface assez réduite obligent à une certaine précision. Si on les manque, ce sera l'occasion de mettre en valeur sa virtuosité au petit jeu. La qualité de l'accueil est aussi à souligner.

Castlerock Golf Club — 1901

Circular Road
NIR - CASTLEROCK, Co Derry

Office	Secrétariat	(44) 028 - 7084 8314
Pro shop	Pro-shop	(44) 028 - 7084 8314
Fax	Fax	(44) 028 - 7084 9440
E-mail		castlerock18@hotmail.com
Situation	Situation	

90 km from Belfast (pop. 279 237) - 9 km from Coleraine

Annual closure	Fermeture annuelle	no
Weekly closure	Fermeture hebdomadaire	no

Fees main season Tarifs haute saison	18 holes	
	Week days Semaine	**We/Bank holidays** We/Férié
Individual Individuel	£ 40	£ 60
Couple Couple	£ 60	£ 110

Caddy	Caddy	£ 20 /on request
Electric Trolley	Chariot électrique	no
Buggy	Voiturette	no
Clubs	Clubs	£ 15 /on request

Credit cards Cartes de crédit
(Pro shop only) VISA - MasterCard - AMEX

Portrush
Portstewart
A 2
Bushmills
Downhill
Castlerock
Limavady
The Ulster Way
A 2
GOLF
Coleraine
0 2 4 km
0 2,5 miles

Access Accès : Belfast M2 North → Antrim. Turn right to A26 → Ballymena/Coleraine. Coleraine A2 → Castlerock

Map 1 on page 821 Carte 1 Page 821

Golf course PARCOURS — 16/20

Site	Site	
Maintenance	Entretien	
Architect	Architecte	Ben Sayers
Type	Type	links, seaside course
Relief	Relief	
Water in play	Eau en jeu	
Exp. to wind	Exposé au vent	
Trees in play	Arbres en jeu	

Scorecard Carte de score	**Chp.** Chp.	**Mens** Mess.	**Ladies** Da.
Length Long.	6115	5850	5299
Par	73	73	75
Slope system	—	—	—

Advised golfing ability Niveau de jeu recommandé — 0 12 24 36

Hcp required Handicap exigé — 28 Men, 36 Ladies

Club house & amenities CLUB HOUSE ET ANNEXES — 6/10

Pro shop	Pro-shop	
Driving range	Practice	
Sheltered	couvert	no
On grass	sur herbe	yes
Putting-green	putting-green	yes
Pitching-green	pitching green	no

Hotel facilities ENVIRONNEMENT HOTELIER — 6/10

HOTELS HÔTELS

Brown Trout Golf & CC — Coleraine 6 km
15 rooms, D £ 60
Tel (44) 028- 7086 8209, Fax (44) 028- 7086 8878

Bohill Hotel & CC, 37 rooms, D £ 80 — Coleraine 8 km
Tel (44) 028- 7034 4406, Fax (44) 028- 7035 2424

Marine Hotel, 9 rooms, D £ 50 — Castlerock 2 km
Tel (44) 028 - 7084 8456

RESTAURANTS RESTAURANTS

Bushtown House — Coleraine 8 km
Tel (44) 028 - 7035 8367

The Lodge, Tel (44) 028 - 7034 4848 — Coleraine

CLANDEBOYE Dufferin Course

15	6	6

Standing alongside the short and amusing "Ava Course", Clandeboye is a layout of greater calibre in its variety and technical demands on players. Yardage is definitely no difficulty, especially for the long-hitters (they will enjoy the wide fairways), but players who are too short might have problems in carrying the ball. What's more, the uneven soil can also create some interesting lies. Game strategy is pretty obvious, as the difficulties are easily identifiable from the tee, albeit in a sometimes intimidating way. There is just the one blind green here, and the few elevated greens call for accurately and cleanly hit approach shots, especially since the putting surfaces are rather firm. Add to this the water, stream and ditches and you will realise that playing to your handicap here requires careful thought and attention.

A côté du "Ava Course", court et assez amusant, Clandeboye propose ici un parcours de plus grand calibre, par sa diversité et ses exigences techniques. Sa longueur n'est certes pas un facteur de difficulté particulière, en particulier pour les longs frappeurs (ils pourront se déchaîner sur des fairways larges), mais certains joueurs courts risquent d'avoir des problèmes quand il faut porter la balle. Par ailleurs, le sol irrégulier provoque quelques positions de balle intéressantes. La stratégie est assez évidente, les difficultés étant facilement identifiables de chaque départ, mais elles peuvent intimider. On trouve ici un seul green aveugle, quelques greens surélevés, les approches devront y être d'autant plus précises et les coups bien touchés que les surfaces de putting sont souvent assez fermes. Ajoutons la présence de cours d'eau et de fossés, et vous aurez compris que jouer son handicap demande de la réflexion et de l'attention.

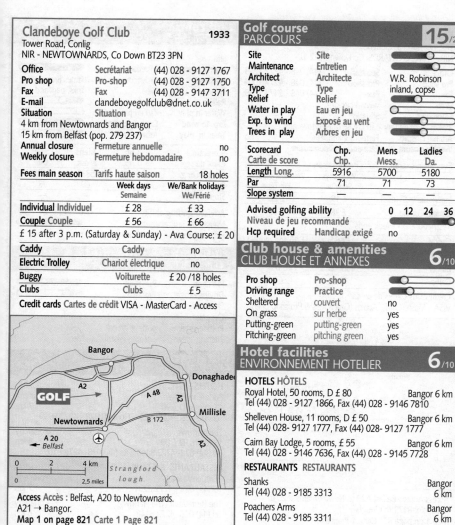

Clandeboye Golf Club — 1933

Tower Road, Conlig
NIR - NEWTOWNARDS, Co Down BT23 3PN

Office	Secrétariat	(44) 028 - 9127 1767
Pro shop	Pro-shop	(44) 028 - 9127 1750
Fax	Fax	(44) 028 - 9147 3711
E-mail	clandeboyegolfclub@dnet.co.uk	
Situation	Situation	

4 km from Newtownards and Bangor
15 km from Belfast (pop. 279 237)

Annual closure	Fermeture annuelle	no
Weekly closure	Fermeture hebdomadaire	no

Fees main season Tarifs haute saison		18 holes
	Week days Semaine	**We/Bank holidays** We/Férié
Individual Individuel	£ 28	£ 33
Couple Couple	£ 56	£ 66

£ 15 after 3 p.m. (Saturday & Sunday) - Ava Course: £ 20

Caddy	Caddy	no
Electric Trolley	Chariot électrique	no
Buggy	Voiturette	£ 20 /18 holes
Clubs	Clubs	£ 5

Credit cards Cartes de crédit VISA - MasterCard - Access

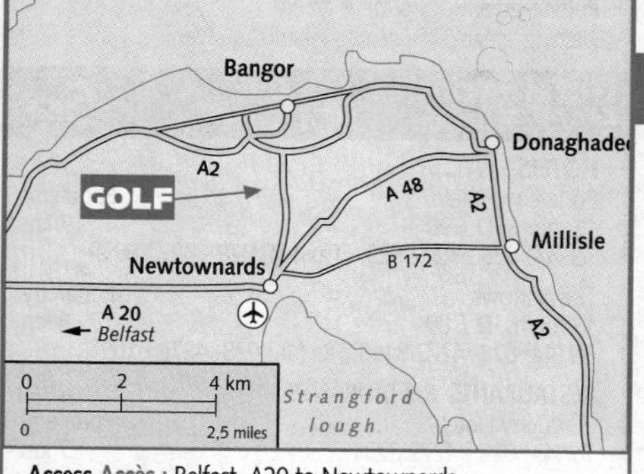

Access Accès : Belfast, A20 to Newtownards.
A21 → Bangor.
Map 1 on page 821 Carte 1 Page 821

Golf course PARCOURS — 15/20

Site	Site	
Maintenance	Entretien	
Architect	Architecte	W.R. Robinson
Type	Type	inland, copse
Relief	Relief	
Water in play	Eau en jeu	
Exp. to wind	Exposé au vent	
Trees in play	Arbres en jeu	

Scorecard Carte de score	**Chp.** Chp.	**Mens** Mess.	**Ladies** Da.
Length Long.	5916	5700	5180
Par	71	71	73
Slope system	—	—	—

Advised golfing ability Niveau de jeu recommandé — 0 12 24 36
Hcp required Handicap exigé — no

Club house & amenities CLUB HOUSE ET ANNEXES — 6/10

Pro shop	Pro-shop	
Driving range	Practice	
Sheltered	couvert	no
On grass	sur herbe	yes
Putting-green	putting-green	yes
Pitching-green	pitching green	yes

Hotel facilities ENVIRONNEMENT HOTELIER — 6/10

HOTELS HÔTELS

Royal Hotel, 50 rooms, D £ 80 — Bangor 6 km
Tel (44) 028 - 9127 1866, Fax (44) 028 - 9146 7810

Shelleven House, 11 rooms, D £ 50 — Bangor 6 km
Tel (44) 028- 9127 1777, Fax (44) 028- 9127 1777

Cairn Bay Lodge, 5 rooms, £ 55 — Bangor 6 km
Tel (44) 028 - 9146 7636, Fax (44) 028 - 9145 7728

RESTAURANTS RESTAURANTS

Shanks — Bangor 6 km
Tel (44) 028 - 9185 3313

Poachers Arms — Bangor 6 km
Tel (44) 028 - 9185 3311

KIRKISTOWN CASTLE

15 | 6 | 5

With breath-taking views over the Irish Sea, gently contoured landscape and a sandy soil, you can understand why James Braid exclaimed "if only this spot were within 50 miles of London !" Not far from the sea but closer to a lush park-land style than anything else, it does nonetheless have something of the links about it, not to mention the wind, which blows wherever it wants to and magnifies every error and difficulty. The course's bunkering is particularly remarkable, but the green-side bunkers generally leave a way open for bump and run shots, which are just the job for firm greens like these. This pretty course is a high-class design, which is only to be expected from its architect, and offers a refreshing and quaintly old-fashioned alternative to modern layouts splattered with water hazards. Even with a par 69 and low yardage, this friendly course is well worth a visit.

Avec ses vues admirables et imprenables sur la mer d'Irlande, son relief très modéré et un sol sablonneux, on comprend que James Braid en ait dit : "Si seulement ce terrain se trouvait à moins de 50 miles de Londres !" Non loin de la mer, mais plus proche d'un parc que d'un véritable links, il en présente malgré tout certains aspects, sans parler du vent, qui souffle où il veut, mais qui amplifie toutes les erreurs et les difficultés. Le bunkering de ce parcours est particulièrement remarquable, mais les bunkers de greens laissent généralement une ouverture, ce qui permet de jouer les "bump and run" bien adaptés à des greens fermes. Ce joli parcours bénéficie d'un dessin de haut niveau, que l'on pouvait attendre de son architecte, et offre une alternative rafraîchissante et un peu surranée aux tracés modernes envahis d'obstacles d'eau. Même avec un par 69 et sa longueur réduite, ce parcours tout à fait amical mérite une visite.

918

Kirkistown Castle — 1902

142, Main Road, Cloughey
NIR - NEWTOWNARDS, Co Down BT22 1JA

Office	Secrétariat	(44) 048 - 4277 1233
Pro shop	Pro-shop	(44) 048 - 4277 1004
Fax	Fax	(44) 048 - 2477 1699
Web	www.kcgc.org	
Situation	Situation	

38 km SE of Bangor - 30 km SE of Newtownards

Annual closure	Fermeture annuelle	no
Weekly closure	Fermeture hebdomadaire	no

Fees main season / Tarifs haute saison	Week days / Semaine	We/Bank holidays / We/Férié
18 holes		
Individual Individuel	£ 19	£ 26
Couple Couple	£ 38	£ 52

Restrictions on Week ends

Caddy	Caddy	£ 15 /on request
Electric Trolley	Chariot électrique	no
Buggy	Voiturette	no
Clubs	Clubs	£ 10

Credit cards Cartes de crédit
VISA - MasterCard - Access (Green fees & Pro shop only)

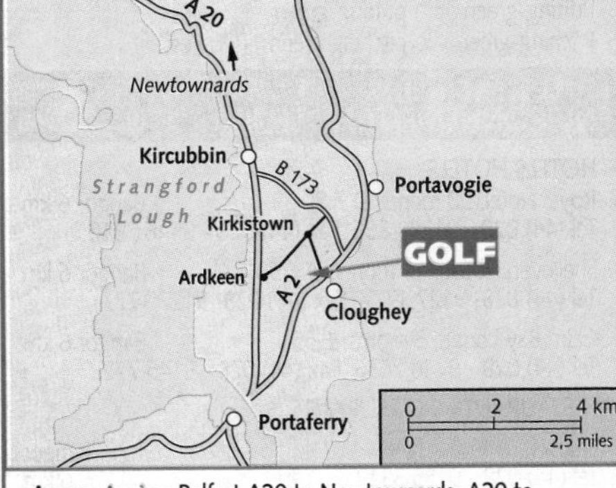

Access Accès : Belfast A20 to Newtownards. A20 to Kircubbin. B173 to Cloughey
Map 1 on page 821 Carte 1 Page 821

Golf course / PARCOURS — 15/20

Site	Site	
Maintenance	Entretien	
Architect	Architecte	James Braid
Type	Type	links, parkland
Relief	Relief	
Water in play	Eau en jeu	
Exp. to wind	Exposé au vent	
Trees in play	Arbres en jeu	

Scorecard / Carte de score	Chp. / Chp.	Mens / Mess.	Ladies / Da.
Length Long.	5550	5335	5120
Par	70	69	73
Slope system	—	—	—

Advised golfing ability / Niveau de jeu recommandé: 0 12 24 36
Hcp required / Handicap exigé: no

Club house & amenities / CLUB HOUSE ET ANNEXES — 6/10

Pro shop	Pro-shop	
Driving range	Practice	
Sheltered	couvert	no
On grass	sur herbe	yes
Putting-green	putting-green	yes
Pitching-green	pitching green	yes

Hotel facilities / ENVIRONNEMENT HOTELIER — 5/10

HOTELS HÔTELS

Portaferry Hotel — Portaferry 7 km
11 rooms, D £ 90
Tel (44) 028 - 4272 8231, Fax (44) 028 - 4272 8999

The Narrows — Portaferry 6 km
13 rooms, D £ 80
Tel (44) 028- 4272 8148, Fax (44) 028- 4272 8105

RESTAURANTS RESTAURANTS

Portaferry Hotel — Portaferry 7 km
Tel (44) 028 - 4272 8231

The Restaurant (The Narrows) — Portaferry 6 km
Tel (44) 028- 4272 8148

KNOCK

15 | 7 | 6

This is a generally flat course with a hill in the middle, which you climb twice, although climb is hardly the word. As with all courses close to Belfast, Knock is very busy on week-ends and the week-days are quieter for green-feers. They will have a lot of fun here, unless their swing is off-colour or they start spraying their drives. If you do go into the woods, a little recovery shot back to the fairway is all you can hope for. Most of the holes are lined with trees, which make for a peaceful setting, but wayward hitters will suffer the consequences. The hazards are clearly visible and you feel confident from the very first visit ; all you need do is avoid the meanders of two streams which come and go over the course. Although not one of the country's most spectacular and original courses, Knock is at the very least extremely pleasant to play, perhaps more so for mid-handicappers than for the more proficient golfers.

C'est un parcours généralement plat, avec une colline en son centre, que l'on grimpe deux fois, mais il ne s'agit certes pas d'une escalade ! Comme tous les golfs à proximité de Belfast, il est très fréquenté en week-end, mais la semaine est plus calme pour les visiteurs. Il s'y amuseront beaucoup, sauf si leur swing est malade ce jour là et qu'ils "arrosent" au drive : il leur faudra bien souvent se contenter de se recentrer s'ils se sont un peu enfoncés dans les bois. La plupart des trous sont bordés d'arbres, ce qui garantit une tranquillité certaine, mais il faut en subir les conséquences. Les obstacles sont ici bien visibles, on se sent en confiance dès la première visite, il suffira d'éviter les méandres de deux cours d'eau qui vont et viennent sur le parcours. S'il ne figure pas parmi les golfs les plus spectaculaires et originaux du pays, Knock est du moins très agréable à jouer, peut-être davantage pour les joueurs moyens que pour les meilleurs.

Knock Golf Club — 1895

Summerfield, Dundonald
NIR - BELFAST BT16 OQX

Office	Secrétariat	(44) 028 - 9048 3251
Pro shop	Pro-shop	(44) 028 - 9048 3825
Fax	Fax	(44) 028 - 9048 3251
Web	—	
Situation	Situation	

7 km from Belfast (pop. 279 237) - 9 km from Newtownards

Annual closure	Fermeture annuelle	no
Weekly closure	Fermeture hebdomadaire	no

Fees main season Tarifs haute saison	18 holes	
	Week days Semaine	**We/Bank holidays** We/Férié
Individual Individuel	£ 23	£ 27
Couple Couple	£ 46	£ 54

Caddy	Caddy	no
Electric Trolley	Chariot électrique	no
Buggy	Voiturette	no
Clubs	Clubs	£ 10 /18 holes
Credit cards	Cartes de crédit	no

Access Accès : Belfast, A20 → Newtownards
Map 1 on page 821 Carte 1 Page 821

Golf course PARCOURS — 15/20

Site	Site	
Maintenance	Entretien	
Architect	Architecte	Harry Colt, McKenzie, Allison
Type	Type	parkland
Relief	Relief	
Water in play	Eau en jeu	
Exp. to wind	Exposé au vent	
Trees in play	Arbres en jeu	

Scorecard Carte de score	**Chp.** Chp.	**Mens** Mess.	**Ladies** Da.
Length Long.	5800	5615	5205
Par	70	70	73
Slope system	—	—	—

Advised golfing ability 0 12 24 36
Niveau de jeu recommandé
Hcp required Handicap exigé no

Club house & amenities CLUB HOUSE ET ANNEXES — 7/10

Pro shop	Pro-shop	
Driving range	Practice	
Sheltered	couvert	no
On grass	sur herbe	yes
Putting-green	putting-green	yes
Pitching-green	pitching green	yes

Hotel facilities ENVIRONNEMENT HOTELIER — 6/10

HOTELS HÔTELS

Stormont, 110 rooms, D £ 150 — Belfast
Tel (44) 028 - 9065 8621, Fax (44) 028 - 9048 0240 — 4 km

Strangford Arms, 40 rooms, D £ 80 — Newtownards
Tel (44) 028 - 9081 4141, Fax (44) 028 - 9081 8846 — 10 km

Park Avenue, 70 rooms, D £ 90 — Belfast
Tel (44) 028 - 9065 6520, Fax (44) 028 - 9047 1417 — 8 km

RESTAURANTS RESTAURANTS

Duke of York — Belfast
Tel (44) 028 - 9024 1062 — 9 km

Strand — Belfast
Tel (44) 028 - 9068 2266 — 9 km

LISBURN

15 | 7 | 6

A beautiful tree-lined drive leads to the Lisburn Golf Club, and sets the mood. Here, you are in the wide open space of park-land and meadows, with the feeling of tranquillity that prevails throughout the Irish countryside. But don't let such bucolic thoughts go to your head, as this course is far-from-easy, especially from the back tees. With that said, the men's yellow and ladies tees are well forward, so most golfers can breathe easily. Created in 1905, Lisburn was overhauled by Fred Hawtree, whose strategic positioning of fairway and green-side bunkers is clear to see, although the latter seldom block the front of the greens. The terrain is rather flat and only one hole could really be called blind, the 17th, a tricky hole before finishing on a spectacular downhill par 3, itself something of a rarity. This very pretty layout is well worth visiting if you are up Belfast way.

Une belle allée bordée d'arbres conduit au Golf de Lisburn, et donne l'ambiance. Nous allons nous trouver dans un espace de grand parc et de prairies, avec le sentiment de tranquillité associé à la campagne irlandaise. Mais il ne faudra pas se laisser endormir par des pensées bucoliques, ce parcours n'est pas des plus faciles, notamment du fond, mais les départs hommes et dames sont assez avancés pour que la majorité des golfeurs s'y trouve à l'aise. Créé en 1905, il a été révisé par Fred Hawtree, dont on peut remarquer le positionnement stratégique des bunkers de fairway et de greens, mais ces derniers masquent rarement l'entrée des greens. Le terrain est assez plat, et un seul green peut être considéré comme aveugle, au 17, un trou délicat, avant de finir par un par 3 spectaculaire en descente : une disposition très rare sur un parcours. Cette très jolie réalisation mérite le détour si vous passez à Belfast.

Lisburn Golf Club — **1905**
68 Eglantine Road
NIR - LISBURN, Co Antrim

Office	Secrétariat	(44) 028 - 9267 7216
Pro shop	Pro-shop	(44) 028 - 9267 7216
Fax	Fax	(44) 028 - 9260 3608
E-mail	lisburngolfclub@aol.com	
Situation	Situation	

14 km from Belfast (pop. 279 237) - 4 km from Lisburn

Annual closure	Fermeture annuelle	no
Weekly closure	Fermeture hebdomadaire	no

Fees main season Tarifs haute saison		18 holes
	Week days Semaine	**We/Bank holidays** We/Férié
Individual Individuel	£ 30	£ 35
Couple Couple	£ 60	£ 70

Caddy	Caddy	no
Electric Trolley	Chariot électrique	no
Buggy	Voiturette	no
Clubs	Clubs	£ 15 /18 holes

Credit cards Cartes de crédit
VISA - MasterCard (Pro shop goods only)

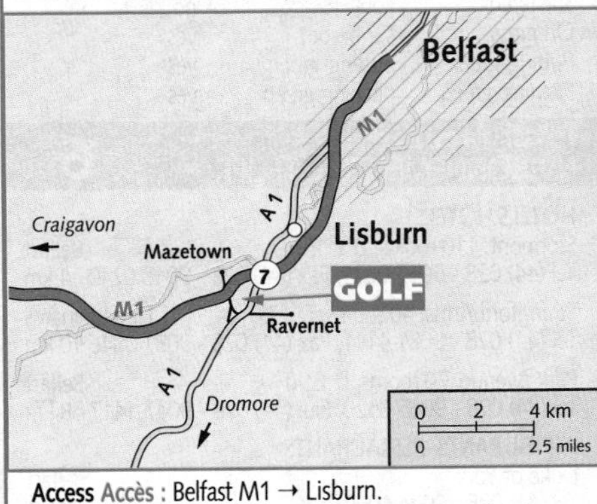

Access Accès : Belfast M1 → Lisburn.
Turn left to A1 → Hillsborough. Golf 4 km S of Lisburn
Map 1 on page 821 Carte 1 Page 821

Golf course PARCOURS — 15/20

Site	Site	
Maintenance	Entretien	
Architect	Architecte	Fred Hawtree
Type	Type	parkland
Relief	Relief	
Water in play	Eau en jeu	
Exp. to wind	Exposé au vent	
Trees in play	Arbres en jeu	

Scorecard Carte de score	**Chp.** Chp.	**Mens** Mess.	**Ladies** Da.
Length Long.	6075	5754	5049
Par	72	72	72
Slope system	—	—	—

Advised golfing ability Niveau de jeu recommandé — 0 12 24 36
Hcp required Handicap exigé — 24 Men, 36 Ladies

Club house & amenities CLUB HOUSE ET ANNEXES — 7/10

Pro shop	Pro-shop	
Driving range	Practice	
Sheltered	couvert	no
On grass	sur herbe	yes
Putting-green	putting-green	yes
Pitching-green	pitching green	yes

Hotel facilities ENVIRONNEMENT HOTELIER — 6/10

HOTELS HÔTELS

Aldergrove International — Belfast 12 km
108 rooms, D £ 90
Tel (44) 028 - 9442 2033, Fax (44) 028 - 9442 3500

Posthouse Premier — Belfast 4 km
170 rooms, D £ 90
Tel (44) 0870 - 400 9005, Fax (44) 028 - 9062 6546

RESTAURANTS RESTAURANTS

Tidy Doffer — Hillsborough 2 km
Tel (44) 028 - 9268 9188

Cayenne — Belfast 12 km
Tel (44) 028 - 9033 1532

MALONE

13 | 6 | 6

A course with forty bunkers, both necessary and sufficient, as water hazards also play a significant role on certain holes : the 7th, 15th and 16th, a pretty and short par 3 where the tee-box and green bite into a large lake, and again on the 18th, a superb par 4 where slicers might spend a few nervous moments. Created in 1895, the Malone Golf Club moved to this pleasantly rolling terrain in the early 1960s. It is a typical Fred Hawtree design with well-guarded greens of all different sizes, but with the front door left open for crisply hit rolled shots. The existing natural setting was hardly touched, the course being a frank and finely landscaped layout designed around the trees. Of course, visitors used to the British inland style will hardly notice any particular local character, but if you are in the region, you will find this a challenge of high standard.

On trouve une quarantaine de bunkers ici, à la fois nécessaires et suffisants, car les obstacles d'eau jouent un grand rôle, au 7, au 15, au 16, joli par 3 court où le départ et le green empiètent sur un lac de neuf hectares, et encore au 18, superbe par 4 où les slicers risquent d'éprouver des émotions fortes. Créé en 1895, le club de Malone a émigré sur ce terrain agréablement vallonné au début des années 60, avec un dessin assez typique de Fred Hawtree, avec des greens de dimensions variées, bien défendus, mais laissant souvent la porte ouverte aux approches roulées bien touchées. Il n'a guère modifié la nature existante, mais y a inscrit un tracé bien paysagé en fonction des arbres, et d'une parfaite franchise. Certes, les visiteurs habitués au style britannique "inland" ne trouveront pas ici de caractère local très fort, mais si vous vous trouvez dans la région, vous trouverez ici un challenge de très bonne qualité.

Malone Golf Club — 1895

240, Upper Malone Road
NIR - DUNMURRY, Co Belfast BT17 9LB

Office	Secrétariat	(44) 028 - 9061 2758
Pro shop	Pro-shop	(44) 028 - 9061 4917
Fax	Fax	(44) 028 - 9043 1394
Web	www.malonegolfclub.com	
Situation	Situation 8 km S of Belfast (pop. 279 237)	
Annual closure	Fermeture annuelle	no
Weekly closure	Fermeture hebdomadaire	no

Fees main season Tarifs haute saison	18 holes	
	Week days Semaine	**We/Bank holidays** We/Férié
Individual Individuel	£ 33	£ 40
Couple Couple	£ 66	£ 80

Caddy	Caddy	£ 15 /on request
Electric Trolley	Chariot électrique	£ 5 /18 holes
Buggy	Voiturette	£ 20 /18 holes
Clubs	Clubs	£ 10

Credit cards Cartes de crédit
VISA - Eurocard - MasterCard - AMEX
(Green-fees & Pro shop only)

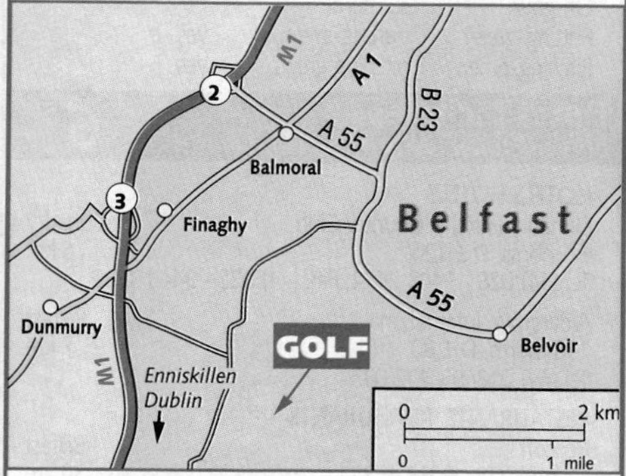

Access Accès : Belfast. B23 (Upper Malone Road)
Map 1 on page 821 Carte 1 Page 821

Golf course — PARCOURS — 13/20

Site	Site	
Maintenance	Entretien	
Architect	Architecte	Fred Hawtree
Type	Type	inland, parkland
Relief	Relief	
Water in play	Eau en jeu	
Exp. to wind	Exposé au vent	
Trees in play	Arbres en jeu	

Scorecard Carte de score	**Chp.** Chp.	**Mens** Mess.	**Ladies** Da.
Length Long.	6084	5680	5213
Par	71	71	72
Slope system	—	—	—

Advised golfing ability 0 12 24 36
Niveau de jeu recommandé
Hcp required Handicap exigé no

Club house & amenities — CLUB HOUSE ET ANNEXES — 6/10

Pro shop	Pro-shop	
Driving range	Practice	
Sheltered	couvert	no
On grass	sur herbe	yes
Putting-green	putting-green	yes
Pitching-green	pitching green	yes

Hotel facilities — ENVIRONNEMENT HOTELIER — 6/10

HOTELS HÔTELS

Posthouse Premier, 170 rooms, D £ 90 — Belfast
Tel (44) 0870 - 400 9005, Fax (44) 028 - 9062 6546 — 7 km

Wellington Park, 50 rooms, D £ 100 — Belfast
Tel (44) 028 - 9038 1111, Fax (44) 028 - 9066 5410 — 7 km

Beechlawn House, 42 rooms, D £ 80 — Dunmurry
Tel (44) 028 - 9060 2010, Fax (44) 028 - 9060 2080 — 2 km

RESTAURANTS RESTAURANT

Roscoff — Belfast
Tel (44) 028 - 9033 1532 — 6 km

Nicks Warehouse — Belfast
Tel (44) 028 - 9043 9690 — 7 km

MASSEREENE

14 | 5 | 6

The course's location on the banks of Lough Neagh, the largest lake in the British Isles, is a convincing argument in its favour. There are others. Created in 1895, the course was tampered with on several occasions before Fred Hawtree came along in 1961 and brought some order and consistency to the layout. There are any number of trees here, many of which have been planted and are already of an age to come clearly into play (especially on the 17th). The front 9, on clay, can be heavy going in winter, but the back 9 are laid out over sandy soil which drains easily when it rains. There are a lot of hazards, basically bunkers (and water on the 16th), not always very deep but always well-placed and clearly visible. The variety in the size and shape of greens adds to the diversity of holes, and while beginners will unquestionably suffer, good players can test their driving accuracy. A course worth discovering.

Sa situation en bordure du Lough Neagh, le plus grand lac des Iles Britanniques, est un argument de taille (si l'on peut dire). Ce n'est pas le seul. Fondé en 1895, il a été modifié à de multiples reprises, avant que Fred Hawtree vienne mettre un peu d'ordre et de cohérence dans le tracé, en 1961. On trouve de nombreux arbres, dont beaucoup ont été plantés, mais ils ont assez atteint leur maturité pour venir nettement en jeu (spécialement au 17). L'aller, sur un sol argileux, peut être assez mou en hiver, mais le retour bénéficie d'un sol sablonneux, et bien drainant en cas de pluie. Les obstacles sont nombreux, essentiellement les bunkers (de l'eau au 16), mais pas très profonds, toujours bien placés et bien visibles. La variété de dimension et de forme des greens contribue à la diversité des trous, et si les débutants souffriront sans doute, les bons joueurs pourront y tester la précision de leurs drives. Un parcours à découvrir.

Massereene Golf Club — 1895

51 Lough Road
NIR - ANTRIM BT41 4OQ

Office	Secrétariat	(44) 028 - 9442 8096
Pro shop	Pro-shop	(44) 028 - 9446 4074
Fax	Fax	(44) 028 - 9448 7661
Web	—	
Situation	Situation	

1.5 km from Antrim - 35 km from Belfast (pop. 279 237)

Annual closure	Fermeture annuelle	no
Weekly closure	Fermeture hebdomadaire	no

Fees main season Tarifs haute saison — 18 holes

	Week days Semaine	We/Bank holidays We/Férié
Individual Individuel	£ 25	£ 30
Couple Couple	£ 50	£ 60

Caddy	Caddy	on request
Electric Trolley	Chariot électrique	no
Buggy	Voiturette	no
Clubs	Clubs	£ 15 /18 holes

Credit cards Cartes de crédit
VISA - MasterCard (Green-fees & Pro shop only)

Access Accès : A26 S of Antrim. 1 km, right turn at leisure center. Golf 1.5 km along this road
Map 1 on page 821 Carte 1 Page 821

Golf course PARCOURS — 14/20

Site	Site	
Maintenance	Entretien	
Architect	Architecte	Fred Hawtree
Type	Type	inland, parkland
Relief	Relief	
Water in play	Eau en jeu	
Exp. to wind	Exposé au vent	
Trees in play	Arbres en jeu	

Scorecard Carte de score	Chp. Chp.	Mens Mess.	Ladies Da.
Length Long.	5980	5760	5048
Par	72	72	72
Slope system	—	—	—

Advised golfing ability 0 12 24 36
Niveau de jeu recommandé
Hcp required Handicap exigé no

Club house & amenities CLUB HOUSE ET ANNEXES — 5/10

Pro shop	Pro-shop	
Driving range	Practice	
Sheltered	couvert	no
On grass	sur herbe	no
Putting-green	putting-green	yes
Pitching-green	pitching green	yes

Hotel facilities ENVIRONNEMENT HOTELIER — 6/10

HOTELS HÔTELS

Dunadry Hotel & Country Club — Dunadry 6 km
67 rooms, D £ 120
Tel (44) 028 - 9443 2474, Fax (44) 028 - 9443 3389

Aldergrove International — Belfast 7 km
108 rooms, D £ 80
Tel (44) 01849 - 422 033

RESTAURANTS RESTAURANTS

Roscoff — Belfast 30 km
Tel (44) 028 - 9033 1532

Dunadry Hotel — Dunadry 6 km
Tel (44) 028 - 9443 2474

PORTSTEWART Strand Course

16 | 7 | 7

The seaside resorts of Portrush and Portstewart are very busy, but foreign tourists come here for the golf. Kept in the shadows of its illustrious neighbour for many a year, the Portstewart (Championship) course has been recently restyled and toughened up, and is now a very respectable test of golf which unquestionably deserves a good visit. Seven new holes have been built over an area of what were virgin dunes, and the old holes were used as a base for a 9 holer, which has completed a second 18 hole course (the "Old" course). From the back tees Portstewart is a very competent course with a dangerous collection of bunkers, but you can still play to your handicap... when the wind is just a breeze and the fairways roll well. The most intimidating hole is the first, a par 4, where you probably will have to make do with the bogey. The next holes are spectacular but not quite as fearsome as they look. Make a point of playing here.

Les stations balnéaires de Portrush et Portstewart sont très fréquentées, mais les touristes étrangers viennent pour jouer au golf ! Longtemps à l'ombre de son illustre voisin, le parcours de Portstewart (Championship) a été récemment rajeuni et durci, c'est maintenant devenu un test fort respectable, qui mérite sans discussion le détour. Sept nouveaux trous ont été construits dans un espace de dunes autrefois vierge, et les anciens trous ont servi de base pour un 9 trous, complétant un autre 18 trous (le "Old"). Des départs arrière, c'est devenu un très solide parcours, avec notamment une collection dangereuse de bunkers, mais il reste possible d'y jouer son handicap... quand le vent s'appelle brise, et quand les fairways roulent bien. Le trou le plus intimidant est le 1, un par 4 où il faut savoir se contenter d'un bogey. Les trous sont ensuite très spectaculaires, mais un peu moins terribles qu'ils ne paraissent. A connaître sans faute.

Portstewart Golf Club — 1894

117, Strand Road
NIR - PORTSTEWART BT55 7PG

Office	Secrétariat	(44) 028 - 7083 2015
Pro shop	Pro-shop	(44) 028 - 7083 2601
Fax	Fax	(44) 028 - 7083 4097
Web	www.portstewartgc.co.uk	
Situation	Situation	

Belfast (pop. 279 237), 75 km - Coleraine (pop. 20 721), 8 km

Annual closure	Fermeture annuelle	no
Weekly closure	Fermeture hebdomadaire	no

Fees main season Tarifs haute saison	18 holes	
	Week days Semaine	**We/Bank holidays** We/Férié
Individual Individuel	£ 55	£ 75
Couple Couple	£ 110	£ 150

Caddy	Caddy	£ 25 /on request
Electric Trolley	Chariot électrique	£ 8 /18 holes
Buggy	Voiturette	no
Clubs	Clubs	£ 10 /18 holes

Credit cards Cartes de crédit VISA - MasterCard

Portrush · Portstewart · A 2 · Bushmills · GOLF · A 2 · A 37 · Coleraine · Limavady · 0 2 4 km · 0 2,5 miles

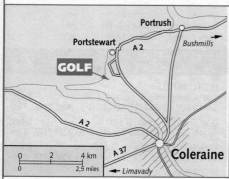

Access Accès : Belfast M2 North to Antrim.
Turn right on A26 to Ballymena and Coleraine.
Coleraine A2 → Portstewart
Map 1 on page 821 Carte 1 Page 821

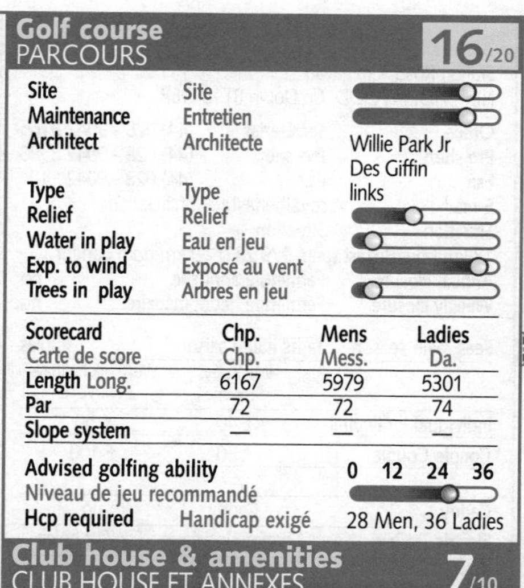

Golf course PARCOURS — 16/20

Site	Site	
Maintenance	Entretien	
Architect	Architecte	Willie Park Jr Des Giffin
Type	Type	links
Relief	Relief	
Water in play	Eau en jeu	
Exp. to wind	Exposé au vent	
Trees in play	Arbres en jeu	

Scorecard Carte de score	**Chp.** Chp.	**Mens** Mess.	**Ladies** Da.
Length Long.	6167	5979	5301
Par	72	72	74
Slope system	—	—	—

Advised golfing ability 0 12 24 36
Niveau de jeu recommandé

Hcp required Handicap exigé 28 Men, 36 Ladies

Club house & amenities CLUB HOUSE ET ANNEXES — 7/10

Pro shop	Pro-shop	
Driving range	Practice	
Sheltered	couvert	no
On grass	sur herbe	yes
Putting-green	putting-green	yes
Pitching-green	pitching green	no

Hotel facilities ENVIRONNEMENT HOTELIER — 7/10

HOTELS HÔTELS

Edgewater, 31 rooms, D £ 90 — adjacent
Tel (44) 028 - 7083 3314, Fax (44) 028 - 7083 2224

Causeway Coast Hotel, 21 rooms, D £ 100 — Portrush
Tel (44) 028 - 7082 2435, Fax (44) 028 - 7082 4495 — 5 km

Comfort Hotel, 50 rooms, D £ 100 — Portrush
Tel (44) 028 - 7052 6100, Fax (44) 028 - 7052 6160 — 8 km

RESTAURANTS RESTAURANTS

Cromore Halt — Portstewart
Tel (44) 028 - 7083 6888 — 2 km

Ramore Wine Bar — Portrush
Tel (44) 028 - 7082 4313 — 4 km

ROYAL BELFAST

15 | 7 | 7

As you might expect from a course with a regal title in a capital city, Royal Belfast is a rather exclusive club, but it is certainly not impossible to play here (especially during the week) if you book a tee-off time. Although you shouldn't expect the warm atmosphere of a vacation club in Florida, it would be a shame not to play the oldest established club in Ireland, not only for historical reasons but also because of the good course, modified slightly in the 1920s by Harry Colt. Although clearly visible, the hazards are genuinely dangerous (there is a total of 61 bunkers) and need extreme precision if they are to be avoided. So this is hardly what you would call a course for beginners. In addition, the greens are well-guarded and should be approached from exactly the right angle to keep your score down. Course upkeep is excellent.

Comme on peut l'attendre d'un golf avec un titre de noblesse et situé dans une capitale, Royal Belfast est un club assez exclusif, mais il n'est certes pas impossible d'y jouer (surtout en semaine) en réservant à l'avance. Bien sûr, il ne faut pas y attendre l'ambiance chaleureuse d'un club de vacances en Floride ! Il serait malgré tout dommage de ne pas visiter le plus ancien club établi en Irlande, non seulement pour raisons historiques, mais aussi parce qu'il dispose d'un bon parcours, auquel Harry Colt a apporté quelques modifications dans les années 20. Bien que les obstacles soient visibles, ils sont effectivement dangereux (il y a 61 bunkers au total), et demandent une grande précision pour être évités. De fait, ce n'est pas exactement un parcours pour débutants ! De plus, les greens sont bien protégés, et il faut les aborder avec un angle d'attaque correct pour préserver un bon score. L'entretien est excellent.

Royal Belfast Golf Club — 1891

Station Road, Craigavad
NIR - HOLYWOOD, Co Down BT18 OBP

Office	Secrétariat	(44) 028 - 9042 8165
Pro shop	Pro-shop	(44) 028 - 9042 8586
Fax	Fax	(44) 028 - 9042 1404
E-mail		royalbelfastgc@btclick.com
Situation	Situation	

13 km from Belfast (pop. 279 237) - 9 km from Bangor

Annual closure	Fermeture annuelle	no
Weekly closure	Fermeture hebdomadaire	no

Fees main season Tarifs haute saison	18 holes	
	Week days Semaine	**We/Bank holidays** We/Férié
Individual Individuel	£ 40	£ 50
Couple Couple	£ 80	£ 100

Caddy	Caddy	no
Electric Trolley	Chariot électrique	£ 7 /18 holes
Buggy	Voiturette	no
Clubs	Clubs	yes

Credit cards Cartes de crédit
VISA - MasterCard (Green-fees & Pro shop only)

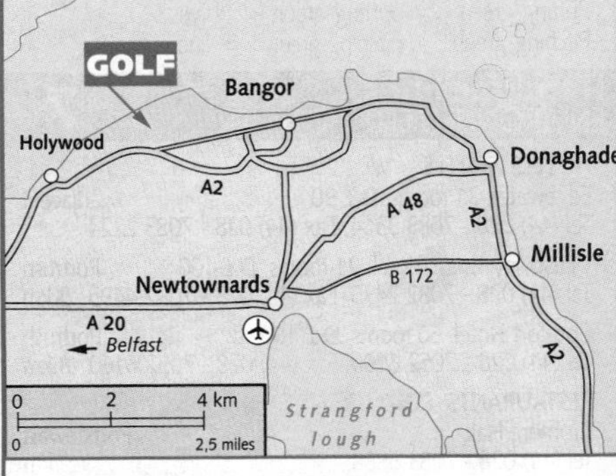

Access Accès : Belfast, A2 → Bangor.
Map 1 on page 821 Carte 1 Page 821

Golf course — PARCOURS — 15/20

Site	Site	
Maintenance	Entretien	
Architect	Architecte	Harry S. Colt
Type	Type	parkland
Relief	Relief	
Water in play	Eau en jeu	
Exp. to wind	Exposé au vent	
Trees in play	Arbres en jeu	

Scorecard Carte de score	**Chp.** Chp.	**Mens** Mess.	**Ladies** Da.
Length Long.	5676	5575	5000
Par	71	70	72
Slope system	—	—	—

Advised golfing ability Niveau de jeu recommandé — 0 12 24 36

Hcp required Handicap exigé — 24 Men, 36 Ladies

Club house & amenities — CLUB HOUSE ET ANNEXES — 7/10

Pro shop	Pro-shop	
Driving range	Practice	
Sheltered	couvert	
On grass	sur herbe	yes
Putting-green	putting-green	yes
Pitching-green	pitching green	no

Hotel facilities — ENVIRONNEMENT HOTELIER — 7/10

HOTELS HÔTELS

Corr's Corner Hotel, 30 rooms, D £ 90 — Belfast
Tel (44) 028 - 9084 9221, Fax (44) 028 - 9083 2118 — 7 km

Duke's Hotel, 21 rooms, D £ 80 — Belfast
Tel (44) 028 - 9023 6666, Fax (44) 028 - 9023 7177 — 8 km

Wellington Hotel, 75 rooms, D £ 80 — Belfast
Tel (44) 028 - 9038 1111, Fax (44) 028 - 9066 5410 — 8 km

RESTAURANTS RESTAURANTS

Sullivans — Holywood
Tel (44) 028 - 9042 1000 — 6 km

Shanks — Bangor
Tel (44) 028 - 9185 3313 — 9 km

ROYAL COUNTY DOWN 19 6 7

Choosing between Ballybunnion, Royal Portrush, Portmarnock and Royal County Down is like trying to give an order of preference to four children. This is a masterly links, with enough blind shots and tricky greens to make a caddie well worthwhile on your first visit. Designed by Old Tom Morris, the course has been modernised with no loss of character or majesty, and without the hazards losing their strategic role : the rough, bushes, bunkers and huge dunes collect poor or over-ambitious shots. For a decent score, your game has to be up to the standard demanded by the course, and a degree of humility will also help you to come to terms with the hazards, without which the game of golf would be boring. If you can, tee off from the 10th ; despite their excellence, the last 9 holes are a little less impressive than the front 9, which wind their way through sand dunes. This is, perhaps, the only hint of a blemish on an otherwise perfect masterpiece.

Choisir entre Ballybunion, Royal Portrush, Portmarnock et Royal County Down, c'est comme classer ses quatre enfants par ordre de préférence. Celui-ci est un links magistral, avec assez de coups aveugles et des greens assez délicats à lire pour inciter à prendre un caddie la première fois. Conçu par Old Tom Morris, ce parcours a été modernisé sans perdre son caractère et sa grandeur, sans que les obstacles perdent leur rôle stratégique : les roughs, les buissons, les bunkers, les immenses dunes reccueillent tous les coups médiocres ou trop audacieux. Il faut un jeu à la hauteur du parcours pour y scorer décemment, mais aussi beaucoup d'humilité pour accepter les hasards sans lesquels le golf serait bien ennuyeux. Si l'on peut, on commencera par le retour : en dépit de leur qualité golfique, ses derniers trous ne sont pas aussi impressionnnants que les autres, insinués dans les dunes. C'est la seule petite ombre à un tableau de maître.

Royal County Down — 1889

NIR - NEWCASTLE, Co Down

Office	Secrétariat	(44) 028 - 4372 3314
Pro shop	Pro-shop	(44) 028 - 4372 2419
Fax	Fax	(44) 028 - 4372 9281
Web	www.royalcountydown.org	
Situation	Situation	

48 km S of Belfast (pop. 279 237) - 1 km from Newcastle

Annual closure	Fermeture annuelle	no
Weekly closure	Fermeture hebdomadaire	no

Fees main season Tarifs haute saison	18 holes	
	Week days Semaine	**We/Bank holidays** We/Férié
Individual Individuel	£ 95	£ 105
Couple Couple	£ 190	£ 210

No visitors on Sundays

Caddy	Caddy	£ 25 /18 holes
Electric Trolley	Chariot électrique	£ 7.50 /18 holes
Buggy	Voiturette	no
Clubs	Clubs	£ 15 /18 holes

Credit cards Cartes de crédit
VISA - MasterCard - AMEX

Downpatrick
A 24
Ballynahinch
Belfast
A 25
Clough
Castlewellan
A 2
GOLF
Dundrum Bay
A 25
Newcastle
Annalong
A 2
0 2 4 km
0 2,5 miles

Access Accès : Belfast A24, 50 km through Newcastle on A2
Map 1 on page 821 Carte 1 Page 821

Golf course — PARCOURS — 19/20

Site	Site	
Maintenance	Entretien	
Architect	Architecte	Old Tom Morris
Type	Type	links
Relief	Relief	
Water in play	Eau en jeu	
Exp. to wind	Exposé au vent	
Trees in play	Arbres en jeu	

Scorecard Carte de score	**Chp.** Chp.	**Mens** Mess.	**Ladies** Da.
Length Long.	6335	6084	5672
Par	71	71	76
Slope system	—	—	—

Advised golfing ability Niveau de jeu recommandé — 0 12 24 36

Hcp required Handicap exigé — 28 Men, 36 Ladies

Club house & amenities — CLUB HOUSE ET ANNEXES — 6/10

Pro shop	Pro-shop	
Driving range	Practice	
Sheltered	couvert	
On grass	sur herbe	yes
Putting-green	putting-green	yes
Pitching-green	pitching green	no

Hotel facilities — ENVIRONNEMENT HOTELIER — 7/10

HOTELS HÔTELS

Slieve Donard Hotel, 130 rooms, D £ 120 Newcastle 500 m
Tel (44) 028 - 4372 3681, Fax (44) 028 - 4372 4830

Glasdrumman Hotel — Glasdrumman 11 km
10 rooms, D £ 120
Tel (44) 028 - 4376 8585, Fax (44) 028 - 4376 7041

The Burrendale Hotel — Newcastle 1 km
68 rooms, D £ 100
Tel (44) 028 - 4372 2599, Fax (44) 028 - 4372 2328

RESTAURANTS RESTAURANTS

The Pavillion, Tel (44) 028 - 4372 6239 — adjacent
Mario's, Tel (44) 028 - 4372 3912 — Newcastle 1 km

ROYAL PORTRUSH Dunluce Links

19 | 7 | 7

Being so close to the Giant's Causeway effectively brings to mind how a course can dwarf your golf. The Dunluce course is rated as one of Ireland's greatest courses, a fact you can easily check for yourself. Over an area covered with enormous dunes, the course comes and goes in a perfectly nothing-to-hide manner. In fact, it never leaves you alone and not a single hole fails to impress, so woe betide the golfer who drops his guard. You need not only extreme skill with club and ball, but also nerves of steel so as not to shrink from the difficulties you are sure to encounter sooner or later. Even the greens, with some tantalising slopes, demand unfailing concentration. You need a certain level of golfing ability to appreciate the subtler sides to this devilish course, which really snarls when the wind gets up. Harry Colt considered this to be his masterpiece. It is, quite simply, a masterpiece.

La proximité de la "Chaussée des Géants" fait penser que l'on est un nain, golfiquement parlant du moins. Le "Dunluce" de Royal Portrush passe pour être l'un des plus grands parcours d'Irlande, vous le vérifierez aisément. Dans un espace occupé par d'énormes dunes, le parcours va et vient avec une franchise parfaite. Il n'est pas un trou pour vous laisser tranquille ou indifférent, pour vous permettre de baisser la garde. Il faut non seulement une grande maîtrise de ses clubs et du maniement de la balle, mais aussi des nerfs d'acier pour ne pas fléchir devant les difficultés, à un moment ou à un autre. Même les greens exigent une concentration sans faille, avec leurs pentes déconcertantes. Il faut un certain niveau de jeu pour apprécier les subtilités de ce parcours démoniaque, dont les dents sont encore plus acérées avec le vent. Harry Colt le considérait comme "son" chef-d'oeuvre. C'est un chef d'oeuvre, tout simplement.

Royal Portrush Golf Club — 1888

Bushmills Road
NIR - PORTRUSH, Co Antrim

Office	Secrétariat	(44) 028 - 7082 2311
Pro shop	Pro-shop	(44) 028 - 7082 3335
Fax	Fax	(44) 028 - 7082 3139
Web	www.royalportrushgolfclub.com	
Situation	Situation	

90 km from Belfast (pop. 279 237)
8 km N of Coleraine (pop. 20 721)

Annual closure	Fermeture annuelle	no
Weekly closure	Fermeture hebdomadaire	no

926

Fees main season Tarifs haute saison	Week days Semaine	We/Bank holidays We/Férié
		18 holes
Individual Individuel	£ 80	£ 90
Couple Couple	£ 160	£ 180

Additional round: £ 25 (any day)

Caddy	Caddy	£ 25 /on request
Electric Trolley	Chariot électrique	£ 8 /18 holes
Buggy	Voiturette	£ 25 /18 holes
Clubs	Clubs	£ 15 /18 holes

Credit cards Cartes de crédit VISA - MasterCard

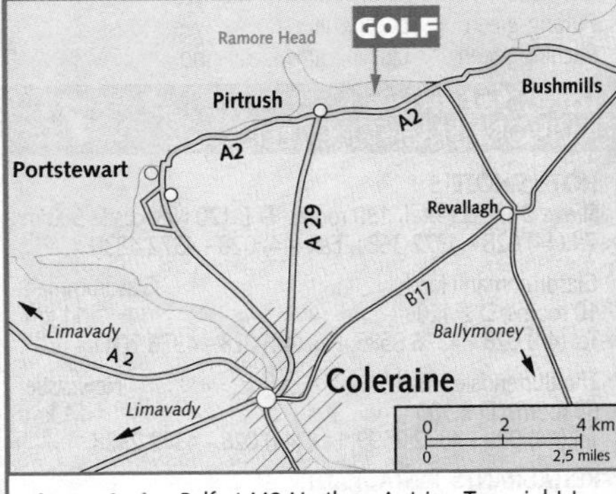

Access Accès : Belfast M2 North → Antrim. Turn right to A26 → Ballymena/Coleraine. Coleraine → Portrush
Map 1 on page 821 Carte 1 Page 821

Golf course PARCOURS — 19/20

Site	Site	
Maintenance	Entretien	
Architect	Architecte	Harry S. Colt
Type	Type	links
Relief	Relief	
Water in play	Eau en jeu	
Exp. to wind	Exposé au vent	
Trees in play	Arbres en jeu	

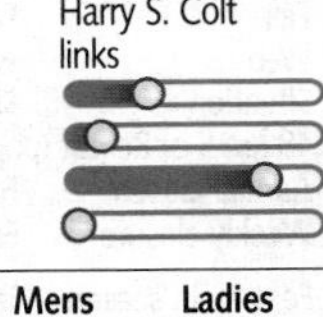

Scorecard Carte de score	Chp. Chp.	Mens Mess.	Ladies Da.
Length Long.	6137	6000	5601
Par	72	72	75
Slope system	—	—	—

Advised golfing ability Niveau de jeu recommandé — 0 12 24 36

Hcp required Handicap exigé — 24 Men, 36 Ladies

Club house & amenities CLUB HOUSE ET ANNEXES — 7/10

Pro shop	Pro-shop	
Driving range	Practice	
Sheltered	couvert	no
On grass	sur herbe	yes
Putting-green	putting-green	yes
Pitching-green	pitching green	yes

Hotel facilities ENVIRONNEMENT HOTELIER — 7/10

HOTELS HÔTELS

O'Neills Causeway Coast Hotel — Portrush 1 km
101 rooms, D £ 100
Tel (44) 028 - 7082 2435, Fax (44) 028 - 7082 4495

Comfort Hotel, 50 rooms, D £ 100 — Portrush 2 km
Tel (44) 028 - 7052 6100, Fax (44) 028 - 7052 6160

Magherabuoy House Hotel — Portrush 2 km
38 rooms, D £ 100
Tel (44) 028 - 7082 3507, Fax (44) 028 - 7082 4687

RESTAURANTS RESTAURANTS

Ramore, Tel (44) 028 - 7082 4313 — Portrush 2 km

Some Place Else — Portrush 2 km
Tel (44) 028 - 7082 4945

ROYAL PORTRUSH Valley

13 | 7 | 7

How can we assess the "second course" at Portrush ? Would we rate it a very good course if it went by any other name ? The answer is seemingly yes, even though it is some way from the greatness and majesty of Dunluce Links. Located, as its name suggests, in a valley between dunes, there are, strangely enough, no more than twenty bunkers, and the par 3s are particularly devoid of sand. Otherwise, the rolling terrain, rough, bushes and wind are trouble enough to upset most players, especially when the end-targets are as small as they generally are here. The nature of the terrain will also pose a few problems for players who are used to the immaculately prepared fairways of inland courses. As with all links courses, this is a test of ball-play and feeling, and the natural setting only adds to the appeal. Golfers who end up discovering this course by chance are generally surprised at the overall excellence of the layout. A very good practice course.

Comment juger le "second parcours" de Royal Portrush ? S'il portait un autre nom, serait-il considéréé comme un très bon parcours ? A l'évidence oui, même s'il est loin de la grandeur et de la majesté du "Dunluce Links". Situé comme son nom l'indique dans une vallée entre les dunes, il ne compte curieusement qu'une vingtaine de bunkers, particulièrement sur les par 3. Autrement, les ondulations du terrain, les roughs, les buissons et le vent suffisent amplement à troubler les joueurs, surtout quand les cibles finales sont petites, ce qui est généralement le cas. Et la nature du terrain posera forcément des problèmes aux joueurs habitués aux fairways impeccablement garnis des parcours intérieurs. Comme tous les links, celui-ci est un test de toucher de balle, et son aspect naturel ajoute à la séduction. Ceux qui sont amenés à le découvrir par hasard sont généralement surpris de sa qualité générale. Un bon parcours d'entraînement.

Royal Portrush Golf Club — 1889

Bushmills Road
NIR - PORTRUSH, Co Antrim

Office	Secrétariat	(44) 028 - 7082 2311
Pro shop	Pro-shop	(44) 028 - 7082 3335
Fax	Fax	(44) 028 - 7082 3139
Web	www.royalportrushgolfclub.com	
Situation	Situation	

90 km from Belfast (pop. 279 237)
8 km N of Coleraine (pop. 20 721)

Annual closure	Fermeture annuelle	no
Weekly closure	Fermeture hebdomadaire	no

Fees main season Tarifs haute saison	18 holes	
	Week days Semaine	**We/Bank holidays** We/Férié
Individual Individuel	£ 30	£ 35
Couple Couple	£ 60	£ 70

Additional round: £ 10

Caddy	Caddy	£ 25 /on request
Electric Trolley	Chariot électrique	£ 8 /18 holes
Buggy	Voiturette	£ 25 /18 holes
Clubs	Clubs	£ 15 /18 holes

Credit cards Cartes de crédit VISA - MasterCard

Ramore Head
GOLF
Pirtrush
Bushmills
A2
Portstewart
A 29
Revallagh
B17
Limavady
A 2
Ballymoney
Coleraine
Limavady
0 2 4 km
2.5 miles

Access Accès : Belfast M2 North → Antrim. Turn right to A26 → Ballymena/Coleraine. Coleraine → Portrush
Map 1 on page 821 Carte 1 Page 821

Golf course PARCOURS — 13/20

Site	Site	
Maintenance	Entretien	
Architect	Architecte	
Type	Type	links
Relief	Relief	
Water in play	Eau en jeu	
Exp. to wind	Exposé au vent	
Trees in play	Arbres en jeu	

Scorecard Carte de score	**Chp.** Chp.	**Mens** Mess.	**Ladies** Da.
Length Long.	5700	5450	4995
Par	70	68	72
Slope system	—	—	—

Advised golfing ability Niveau de jeu recommandé: 0 12 24 36
Hcp required Handicap exigé: no

Club house & amenities CLUB HOUSE ET ANNEXES — 7/10

Pro shop	Pro-shop	
Driving range	Practice	
Sheltered	couvert	no
On grass	sur herbe	yes
Putting-green	putting-green	yes
Pitching-green	pitching green	yes

Hotel facilities ENVIRONNEMENT HOTELIER — 7/10

HOTELS HÔTELS

O'Neills Causeway Coast Hotel — Portrush 1 km
101 rooms, D £ 100
Tel (44) 028 - 7082 2435, Fax (44) 028 - 7082 4495

Comfort Hotel — Portrush 2 km
50 rooms, D £ 100
Tel (44) 028 - 7052 6100, Fax (44) 028 - 7052 6160

Magherabuoy House Hotel — Portrush 2 km
38 rooms, D £ 100
Tel (44) 028 - 7082 3507, Fax (44) 028 - 7082 4687

RESTAURANTS RESTAURANTS

Ramore, Tel (44) 028 - 7082 4313 — Portrush 2 km
Some Place Else, Tel (44) 028 - 7082 4945 — Portrush 2 km

WARRENPOINT

13 | 6 | 5

The setting for the Warrenpoint course, between mountains and Carringford bay, provides some breathtaking scenery and gives a marvellous sensation of space. To appreciate it fully, though, you will need to disregard the noise of the adjacent road, which is a shame. This is otherwise a very pleasant course, maybe more for mid- to high-handicappers than for the more skilled exponents, who might feel a little frustrated if expecting an adversary measuring up to their ability. But we need courses for every taste and anyway, there is no shortage of tough courses in Ireland. This layout requires no great length off the tee (which is a reserved privilege, anyway) but it does call for a sharp and subtle short game, as some approaches and bunkers around the greens are tricky. But these difficulties are generally on either side of the greens, so you can lay up short and stay out of trouble. A pleasant stop-off on "hard-working" holidays.

La situation du golf de Warrenpoint, entre les montagnes et la baie de Carringford permet des points de vue majestueux, donnant une sensation merveilleuse d'espace, mais il faut, pour en profiter, faire abstraction du bruit de la route adjacente... C'est dommage, car ce parcours est autrement très agréable, peut-être davantage encore pour les handicaps moyens et élevés, alors que les meilleurs joueurs seront un peu frustrés s'ils attendent un adversaire à la mesure de leur talent. Mais il faut des golfs pour tous les goûts, et le pays ne manque pas de parcours difficiles. Celui-ci ne requiert pas une grande longueur (elle n'est pas donnée à tout le monde), mais plutôt de la finesse de petit jeu, car certains abords de greens sont délicats, de même que les bunkers. Mais ces difficultés sont plutôt de part et d'autre des greens, ce qui autorise à jouer court pour ne pas en souffrir. Une halte sympathique pour des vacances studieuses.

Warrenpoint Golf Club — 1893

Lower Dromore Road
NIR - WARRENPOINT, Co Down BT34 3LN

Office	Secrétariat	(44) 028 - 4175 3695
Pro shop	Pro-shop	(44) 028 - 4175 2371
Fax	Fax	(44) 028 - 4175 2918
E-mail	warrenpointgolfclub@talk21.com	
Situation	Situation	

50 km from Belfast (pop. 279 237) - 8 km from Newry

Annual closure	Fermeture annuelle	no
Weekly closure	Fermeture hebdomadaire	no

Fees main season Tarifs haute saison — 18 holes

	Week days Semaine	We/Bank holidays We/Férié
Individual Individuel	£ 18	£ 24
Couple Couple	£ 36	£ 48

Caddy	Caddy	no
Electric Trolley	Chariot électrique	£ 10 /18 holes
Buggy	Voiturette	no
Clubs	Clubs	£ 10

Credit cards Cartes de crédit VISA (Pro shop only)

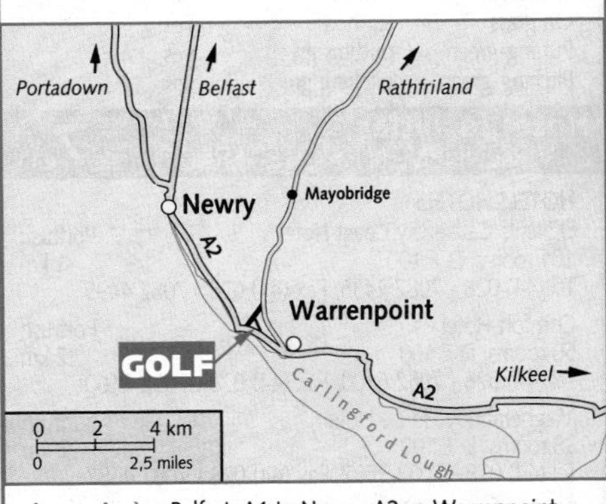

Access Accès : Belfast, A1 to Newry. A2 → Warrenpoint.
Map 1 on page 821 Carte 1 Page 821

Golf course — PARCOURS — 13/20

Site	Site	
Maintenance	Entretien	
Architect	Architecte	
Type	Type	parkland, hilly
Relief	Relief	
Water in play	Eau en jeu	
Exp. to wind	Exposé au vent	
Trees in play	Arbres en jeu	

Scorecard Carte de score	Chp. Chp.	Mens Mess.	Ladies Da.
Length Long.	6161	5778	5377
Par	71	71	72
Slope system	—	—	—

Advised golfing ability Niveau de jeu recommandé — 0 12 24 36

Hcp required Handicap exigé — no

Club house & amenities — CLUB HOUSE ET ANNEXES — 6/10

Pro shop	Pro-shop	
Driving range	Practice	
Sheltered	couvert	no
On grass	sur herbe	yes
Putting-green	putting-green	yes
Pitching-green	pitching green	no

Hotel facilities — ENVIRONNEMENT HOTELIER — 5/10

HOTELS HÔTELS

Canal Court Hotel — Newry 12 km
50 rooms, D £ 100
Tel (44) 028 - 3025 1234, Fax (44) 028 - 3025 1177

Mourne Country — Newry 12 km
41 rooms, D £ 70
Tel (44) 028 - 3026 7922, Fax (44) 028 - 3026 0896

RESTAURANTS RESTAURANTS

The Brass Monkey — Newry 8 km
Tel (44) 028 - 3026 3176

Aylesfort House — Warrenpoint 100 m
Tel (44) 028 - 4177 2255

EUROPE'S TOP 1000 GOLF COURSES

Italy

Biella

Italia
Italy

E'difficile immaginare un paese più piacevole e con il clima migliore dell'Italia, nel quale la storie si trova ovunque intorno a te ma si integra perfettamente con la vita moderna superattiva. Anche se l'inverno può essere abbastanza freddo al nord, a parte nella regione dei laghi, il golf è uno sport che si pratica tutto l'anno. Per il momento ci sono solo poco più di 100 campi e neanche 70.000 giocatori. Mentre la Spagna e il Portogallo hanno riempito le loro coste di campi e turisti-golfisti, l'Italia ha trascurato questo aspetto ed ha costruito percorsi principalmente per la popolazione locale, in particolar modo intorno alle città più importanti e sopratutto nel nord del paese.
E' veramente un piacere giocare a golf qui, oltretutto, di solito si trovano club-houses molto eleganti e ben attrezzate che sono il punto d'incontro della buona società e dove si mangia molto bene. Si dice che il golf sia un'arte di vivere: in Italia lo è certamente.

It is hard to imagine a more agreeable country and favourable climate than Italy, where history is all around you and closely integrated with very active modern-day life. Even though the winters can be rather cold in the north, excepting the lakes region, golf is an all-year sport. Yet, there are only about a hundred courses and not even 70,000 players. While Spain and Portugal have covered their coastlines with courses and touring golfers, Italy has neglected this side of the equation and has built courses mainly for local populations and particularly around major cities, mainly in the North of the country. It is such a pleasure playing golf here, though, with generally very elegant and well-equipped club-houses which make a point of cultivating social life and great food. They say that golf is an art of living; in Italy it certainly is.

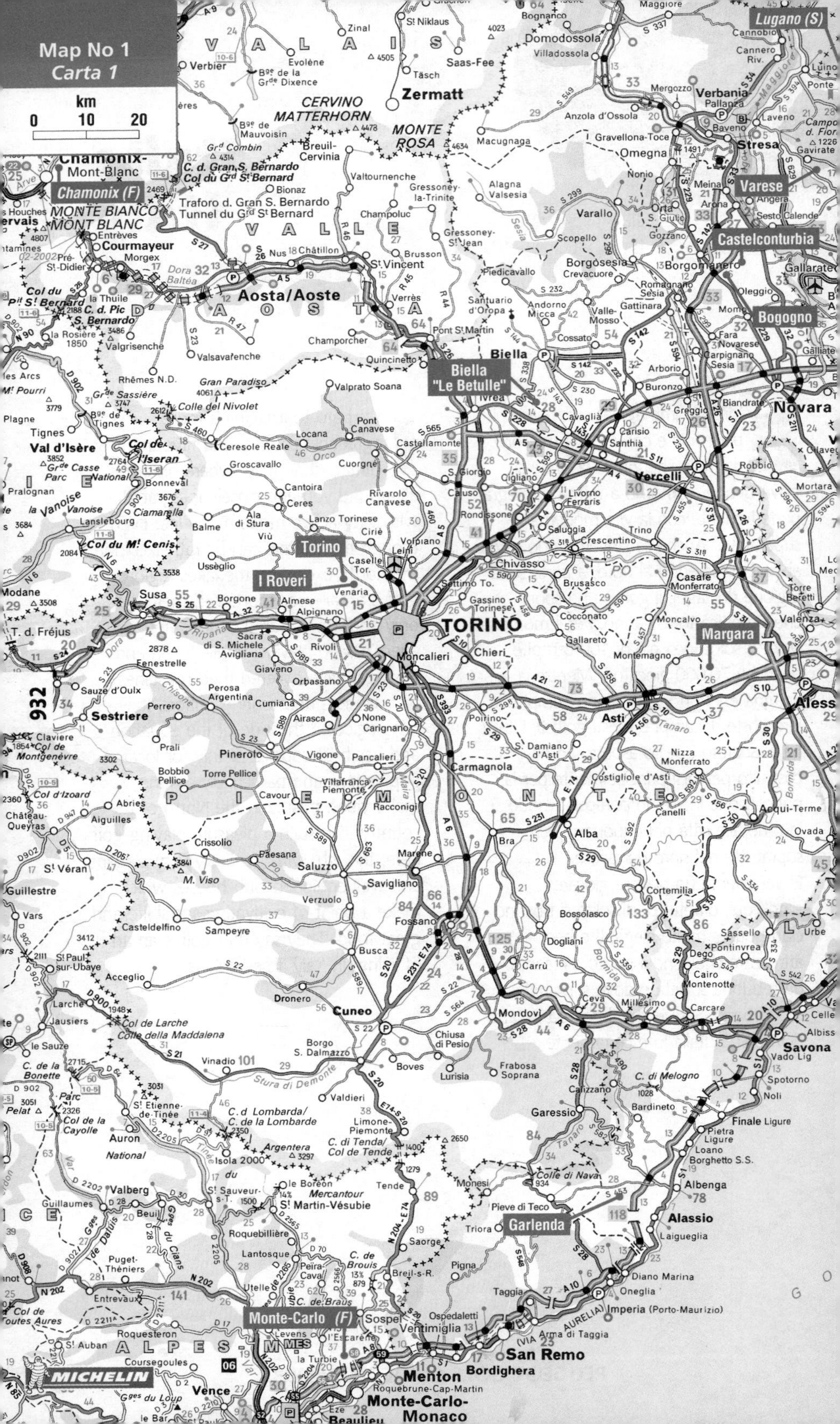

Map No 1
Carta 1
km
0 10 20
Lugano (S)
Chamonix (F)
Varese
Castelconturbia
Bogogno
Biella "Le Betulle"
Torino
I Roveri
Margara
Garlenda
Monte-Carlo (F)
V A L A I S
V A L L E
D A O S T A
P I E M O N T E
Chamonix-Mont-Blanc
MONTE BIANCO
MONT BLANC
Courmayeur
Aosta/Aoste
Zermatt
CERVINO MATTERHORN
MONTE ROSA
Domodossola
Verbania-Pallanza
Stresa
Omegna
Biella
Ivrea
Novara
Vercelli
Chivasso
TORINO
Moncalieri
Chieri
Asti
Alba
Bra
Carmagnola
Pinerolo
Sestriere
Susa
Saluzzo
Savigliano
Fossano
Cuneo
Mondovì
Casale Monferrato
Valenza
Acqui-Terme
Savona
Albenga
Alassio
Imperia (Porto-Maurizio)
San Remo
Bordighera
Ventimiglia
Menton
Monte-Carlo-Monaco
Vence
Val d'Isère
Col du Mt Cenis
Gran Paradiso
Col de Tende
Isola 2000
St Martin-Vésubie
A L P E S - M A R I T I M E S
MICHELIN
932

933
LUGANO
Como
Lecco
Bergamo
Brescia
MILANO
Pavia
Piacenza
Cremona
Mantova
PARMA
Reggio nell' Emilia
Verona
GENOVA
La Spezia
Rapallo
Lucca
Massa
Carrara
Viareggio
"L'Albenza" Bergamo
Villa d'Este
Monticello
Barlassina
Milano
La Pinetina
Le Robinie
Molinetto
Ambrosiano
Castello di Tolcinasco
Palazzo Arzaga
Franciacorta
Gardagolf
Verona
Rapallo
Barcelona.Palma
Tunis
Cagliari
Porto-Torres
Olbia-Arbatax
Palermo
Bastia
Ile-Rousse
DI GENOVA
MICHELIN
d'après carte n° 988 - 25ème édition - 2002.
Autorisation n° 0102062.

Map No 2
Carta 2
km
0 10 20
934
Asolo
Verona
Padova
Montecchia
Venezia
Albarella
Modena
Bologna
Cervia
Cortina d'Ampezzo
Bolzano/Bozen
Trento
Rovereto
Belluno
Treviso
Vicenza
VERONA
PADOVA
VENEZIA
Mestre
Chioggia
Rovigo
FERRARA
MODENA
BOLOGNA
RAVENNA
Pordenone
Mantova
Imola
Faenza
MICHELIN

Hermagor
Arnoldstein
Faak
St. Jakob im Rosental
Ferlach
Eisenkappel
Topla
Črna na K.
Croce Carnico
Gail
Naßfeld-Paß
P^so di Pramollo
Rodkoren
Planina
Loibltunnel
Seebergsattel / Jezerski vrh
Solčava
Logarska Dolina
Radegunda
Paularo
Pontebba
Tarvisio
Rateče
Gozd.M.
Jesenice
Ljubelj
Ljubno
Mozirje
Paluzza
Kranjska Gora
Mojstrana
Zg. Jezersko
Grintavec
Luče
Letuš
Arta Terme
Predel
P^so di Predil
Sella Nevea
Triglav
Bled
Lesce
Tržič
Gornji Grad
Log
Trenta
Preddvor
Golnik
Krvavec
Črnivec
Vransko
Tolmezzo
Chiusaforte
P^so di Nevea
Radovljica
Stahovica
Šmartno
M. Canin
Bovec
Socka
Pokljuka
Sava
Kamnik
Trojane
Carnia
P^so di Tanamea
Žaga
Bohinj
Bled (SLO)
Sp. Brnik
Lukovica p K.
Trbovlje
Krn
Ribčev Laz
Bohinjska Bistrica
Železniki
Kranj
Izlake
Trnovo
Vogel
Menges
Zagorje ob Savi
Gemona d. Friuli
Robič
Kobarid
Kandrše
Moravče
Osoppo
Soča
Tolmin
Škofja Loka
Domžale
Tarcento
Gorenja Vas
Medvode
Litija
Most na Soči
Grahovo
Cerkno
Črni Vrh
Tricesimo
S. Daniele d. Fr.
Polhov Gradec
LJUBLJANA
Martignacco
Cividale d. Friuli
Kanal
Idrijca
Žiri
Ivančna gorica
Škofljica
Udine
Lokve
M. Goljaki
Idrija
Vrhnika
Podpeč
Ig
Grosuplje
Višnja gora
Campoformido
Godovič
Cormons
Nova Gorica
Logatec
Rakitna
Turjak
Krška vas
Kalce
Borovnica
Žužemberk
Pozzuolo
Gorizia
Ajdovščina
Col
Videm
Codroipo
Palmanova
Gradisca d'Is.
Vipava
Planina
Postojnska jama
Vel. Lašče
Struge
Castions di S.
Nova vas
Cerknica
Ribnica
S. Giorgio di N.
Štanjel
Postojna
Bloška polica
Sodražica
Dolenja vas
Monfalcone
Ronchi
Muzzana d. Turgnano
Cervignano d. Fr.
Aquileia
Duino
Sistiana
Sežana
Razdrto
Senožeče
Lož
Pudob
Debeli vrh
Marano
Ausso Corno
Divača
Pivka
Cerkniško jez.
Prezid
Latisana
Opicina
Lipica
TRIESTE
Basovizza
Knežak
Sneżnik
Štalcerji
Lignano Sabbiadoro
Grado
Kozina
Ribnica
Ilirska Bistrica
Čabar
Lignano
Golfo di Trieste
Muggia
Reka
Gerovo
Bibione
Ankaran
Slavnik
Obrov
Brod na Kupi
Izola / Isola
Podgrad
Rupa
Risnjak
Delnice
Caorle
Piran / Pirano
Koper / Capodistria
Hrastovlje
Vodice
Klana
Crni Lug
Savudrija
Portorož / Portorose
Ćićarija
G.Jelenje
Lokve
Buzet
Matulji
Umag
Buje
Plavnik
Istarske Toplice
Opatija
Bakar
Mrkopalj
Fužine
Livade
Motovun
Vranja
Učka
RIJEKA
Bakarac
Lovran
Medveja
Kraljevica
Višnjada
Tar
Mirna
Novigrad
Pazin
Moščenička Draga
Voz
Omišajl
Moščenice
Njivice
Selce
Šilo
Poreč
Baderna
Pićan
Dobrinj
Brestovac
Porozina
Klenovica
Plomin
Malinska
Gorice
Žminij
Labin
Milohnići
Vrbnik
Vrsar
Kanfanar
Dragozetići
Valbiska
Krk
Punat
Valalta
Rovinj
Barban
Raša
Rabac
Predoščica
Obzova
Koromačno
Merag
Bale
Cres
Plavnik
Rakalj
Vodnjan
Valun
Grgur
Fažana
Marčana
Venezia
Brijun
Supetarska Draga
Martinšćica
Vrana
Pula
Šišan
Štivan
Belej
Rab
Premantura
Medulin
CRES
Rt Kamenjak
Kvarner
Osor
Punta Križa
Nerezine
Unije
Čunski
Lošinj
Mali Lošinj
Veli Lošinj
Susak
Susak
Ilovik
Silba
Ancona
Premuda
Premuda

Map No 3
Carta 3
km
0 10 20
Le Pavoniere
Poggio dei Medici
Firenze Ugolino
Cosmopolitan
Punta Ala
FIRENZE
LIVORNO
Pisa
Lucca
Pistoia
Prato
Siena
Arezzo
Grosseto
Civitavecchia
Imola
Faenza
Forlì
Massa
Pietrasanta
Camaiore
Viareggio
Montecatini-Terme
Empoli
S. Miniato
Pontedera
Cascina
Volterra
S. Gimignano
Poggibonsi
Colle di Val d'Elsa
Monteriggioni
Castellina in Chianti
Greve
Montevarchi
Montepulciano
Chianciano Terme
Pienza
Montalcino
Buonconvento
Cecina
Rosignano Marittimo
Castiglioncello
Piombino
Follonica
Portoferraio
Isola d'Elba
I. Pianosa
I. di Montecristo
I. d. Giglio
Giglio Porto
I. di Giannutri
Orbetello
Porto S. Stefano
Port'Ercole
Promontorio dell'Argentario
Castiglione della Pescaia
Marina di Grosseto
Scansano
Manciano
Pitigliano
Albinia
Capalbio
Ansedonia
Montalto di Castro
Tarquinia
Massa Marittima
Larderello
Roccastrada
Paganico
Arcidosso
M. Amiata
Abbadia S. Salvatore
S. Quirico d'Orcia
Sinalunga
Asciano
Borgo S. Lorenzo
Barberino di Mugello
Fiesole
Sesto fior.
Bagno a Ripoli
Impruneta
Vallombrosa
Bibbiena
Poppi
Stia
Camaldoli
Colline Metallifere
Toscana
Olbia
Arbatax
Golfo Aranci
Cagliari
Bastia
Palermo
MICHELIN

Cervia
Cesenatico
Bellaria
Viserba
Rimini
Miramare
Savignano sul Rubicone
Santarcangelo di Rom.
Riccione
Cattolica
Gabicce Mare
Verucchio
Sogliano al Rubicone
S. Marino
Pesaro
Gradara
Morciano di Rom.
Montecchio
Fano
San Leo
Mercatino Conca
Marotta
Macerata Feltria
Mercatale
Carpegna
Belforte all'Isauro
Urbino
Fossombrone
Mondolfo
Senigallia
Mondavio
Falconara Maritt.
Ancona
Mali Losinj
Zadar
Šibenik
Split
Hvar
Kérkira (Corfu)
Igoumenitsa
Pátra (Patrasso)
Sestino
Urbania
Corinaldo
Chiaravalle
Ostra
Sirolo
Numana
S. Angelo in Vado
Acqualagna
Piobbico
S. Marcello
Montecarotto
Pergola
Jesi
Moie
Cagli
Apecchio
Bocca Trabaria
Arcevia
Osimo
Castelfidardo
Loreto
Porto Recanati
Recanati
S. Giustino
M. Catria
Cupramontana
Filottrano
Sassoferrato
Città di Castello
Pietralunga
Scheggia
Cingoli
Villa Potenza
Potenza Picena
Fabriano
Borgo Tufico
Macerata
Civitanova Marche
Treia
Porto S. Elpidio
Gubbio
S. Severino Marche
Sforzacosta
Corridonia
S. Elpidio a Mare
Osteria di Gatto
Tolentino
Montegranaro
Porto S. Giorgio
Umbertide
Mengara
Matelica
Fermo
Campodonico
Castelraimondo
Antognolla
Gualdo Tadino
Montegiorgio
Mercatale
Tuoro sul T.
Valfabbrica
Caldarola
Monterubbiano
Pedaso
Camerino
S. Ginesio
Magione
Perugia
Bosco
Muccia
Montefiore d. Aso
Servigliano
Lago Trasimeno
Nocera Umbra
Assisi
Parco
Sarnano
Ripatransone
Grottammare
S. Bened
Fiastra
Colfiorito
Montalto d. Marche
Sta Maria d. Angeli
Spello
Amandola
Nazionale
Comunanza
Offida
Deruta
Foligno
Visso
dei Monti
Ascoli Piceno
Tavernelle
Bevagna
M. Vettore
Montegallo
Nereto
Marsciano
Trevi
Civitella d. T.
Castelluccio
Arquata d. T.
Montefalco
Triponzo
Norcia
Sibillini
Acquasanta Terme
Campli
Valle Castellana
Massa Martana
Teramo
Spoleto
Cascia
Prato
Todi
Monteluco
Ceppo
Montorio al Vomano
Villa Vomano
Orvieto
Monteleone di Spoleto
Amatrice
Acquasparta
Cittareale
L. di Campotosto
Baschi
Castiglione in T.
San Gemini
Leonessa
Isola d. Gr. Sasso d'It.
Bisenti
Prati di Tivo
Bagnoregio
Lugnano in T.
Terni
Posta
Gran Sasso d'Italia
Montereale
Penne
Amelia
Attigliano
Piediluco
M. Terminillo
Terminillo
Borbona
Valico b. Capannelle
Campo Imperatore
Farindola
Montefiascone
Narni
Greccio
Pizzoli
Assergi
Catigna
Orte
Rieti
Cittaducale
Antrodoco
Castel d. Monte
Viterbo
Soriano nel Cimino
Contigliano
L'Aquila
Barisciano
Vignanello
Velino
Navelli
Capestrano
Borghetto
Magliano Sabina
Fiamignano
L. di Vico
Montenero S.
Rocca Sinibalda
Rocca di Mezzo
Vetralla
Ronciglione
Pescorocchiano
Ovindoli
Civita Castellana
Poggio Mirteto
Borgorose
M. Velino
Castelvecchio Subequo
Magliano de Marsi
Celano
Le Querce
Sutri
Rignano Fl.
Orvinio
Forca Caruso
Fiano R.
Carsoli
Tagliacozzo
Pescina
Trevignano R.
L. di Bracciano
Castelnuovo di Porto
Mandela
Avezzano
Manziana
Bracciano
Palombara S.
Monterotondo
Capistrello
Sasso
Guidonia
Marco Simone
Trasacco
Cerveteri
Mentana
Tivoli
Castel Madama
Subiaco
Civitella Roveto
Olgiata
Settebagni
Villa Adriana
Balsorano
Palidoro
ROMA
Ladispoli
Roma Acquasanta
Palestrina
Parco de' Medici
Fiuggi
Fregene
Frascati
Castelgandolfo
Valmontone
Paliano
Anagni
Alatri
Sora
Fiumicino
Ostia Antica
Marino
Rocca di Papa
Castel Gondolfo
M. Cavo
Artena
Colleferro
Ferentino
Segni
Isola del Liri
Abbazia di Casamari
MICHELIN

Map No 4
Carta 4
km
0 10 20
938
Dubrovnik
Bar
BARI
Trani
Bisceglie
Molfetta
Giovinazzo
Canosa di Puglia
Andria
Corato
Terlizzi
Ruvo di P.
Bitonto
Palo d. Colle
Modugno
Mola di Bari
Capurso
Polignano a Mare
Rutigliano
Monopoli
Castel d. Monte
Minervino Murge
Bitetto
Sannicandro di Bari
Adelfia
Conversano
Casamassima
Castellana Grotte
Turi
Fasano
Torre Canne
Acquaviva d. Fonti
Sammichele
Putignano
Alberobello
Cassano d. Murge
Spinazzola
Cisternino
Ostuni
Carovigno
Noci
Locorotondo
Gioia d. Colle
Altamura
Santeramo in Colle
Gravina in Puglia
Martina Franca
S. Vito d. Normanni
Genzano di Lucania
Ceglie Messapica
P U G L I A
Irsina
Matera
Mottola
Massafra
Francavilla Fontana
Grottaglie
Castellaneta
Laterza
Ginosa
Palagiano
Tolve
Grassano
Tricarico
Miglionico
Montescaglioso
TARANTO
S. Giorgio Ionico
Sava
Oria
Manduria
Albano di Luc.
Pso Croce d. Scrivano
Accettura
S. Mauro Forte
Ferrandina
Bernalda
Lido di Metaponto
Lido Silvana
Riva dei Tessali
B A S I L I C A T A
Laurenzana
Stigliano
Pisticci
Craco
Corleto Perticara
Nuovo
M. Volturino
Viggiano
Scanzano
Tursi
Policoro
Colobraro
Rotondella
Nova Siri
Moliterno
Senise
Agri
Sinni
Basento
Bradano
G O L F O
D I T A R A N
M. Sirino
Lagonegro
Latronico
Oriolo
Francavilla in Sinni
Terranova di Pollino
Lauria
Parco Nazionale
Rotonda
M. Pollino
Cerchiara di Cal.
Trebisacce
Frascineto
Mormanno
Morano Cal.
Castrovillari
Cassano allo Ionio
Sibari
Papasidero
del Pollino
Scalea
Lungro
Firmo
Spezzano Albanese
Verbicaro
Diamante
Belvedere Marittimo
Roggiano Gravina
Tarsia
Corigliano Calabro
Rossano
S. Demetrio Corone
Sta Sofia d'Epiro
Cariati
S. Marco Argentano
Bisignano
Longobucco
Campana
Cetraro
Torano Cast.
Acri
Cirò
Cirò Marina
Terme Luigiane
Luzzi
C A L A B R I A
Fuscaldo
Montalto Uffugo
Rose
L. di Cecita
Camigliatello S.
Savelli
Strongoli
Paola
Spezzano d. Sila
M. Botte Donato
S. Giovanni in Fiore
Rende
Cosenza
Lorica
S. Lucido
Neto
Crotone
C. d'Ascione
L A S I L A
Lago
Rogliano
M. Gariglione
Petilia Policastro
Colosimi
Villaggio Mancuso
Mesoraca
Cutro
Grimaldi
Amantea
Sersale
Taverna
Isola di Capo Rizzuto
Soveria Mannelli
Campora S. Giovanni
Nocera Terinese
Falerna
Sambiase
Tiriolo
Catanzaro
MICHELIN

Arcipelago della Maddalena
Bocche di Bonifacio
I. Maddalena
La Maddalena
I. Caprera
Formia
Napoli
Sta Teresa Gallura
Palau
Baia Sardinia
Porto Cervo
Pevero
Livorno
Civitavecchia
La Spezia
Genova
Costa Smeralda
Arzachena
Porto Rotondo
Golfo Aranci
Isola Asinara
Ajaccio
Marseille
Propriano
Golfo dell' Asinara
Luogosanto
Trinità d'Agultu e V.
S. Antonio
Olbia
I. Tavolara
Falcone
Stintino
Castelsardo
Aggius
Calangianus
Tempio Pausania
Pta Balistreri
Telti
Loiri
Monti
Porto Torres
Platamona Lido
Sedini
Sorso
Sennori
Nulvi
Martis
Osilo
Lago del Coghinas
Padru
M. Nieddu
Sassari
Ploaghe
Oschiri
Palmadula
Alà d. Sardi
Posada
La Caletta
Olmedo
Uri
Ozieri
Pattada
Buddusò
Lodè
Siniscola
Fertilia
Alghero
Grotta di Nettuno
Ittiri
Thiesi
Mores
Pta Catirina
Bitti
Villanova Monteleone
Romana
Foresta di Burgos
Bultei
Bono
Orune
Cedrino
Bonorva
Pozzomaggiore
Montresta
Tirso
Nuoro
Orosei
Bolotana
Cala Gonone
Dorgali
Oliena
Golfo di Orosei
Bosa
Suni
Macomer
Ottana
Orani
Sarule
Parco Nazionale del Golfo Orosei e del Gennargentu
Orgosolo
Cuglieri
Sedilo
Gavoi
Genna Cruxi
M. Ferru
Abbasanta
Santu Lussurgiu
Ghilarza
Lago Omodeo
Fonni
Pso di Caravai
939
Sta Caterina Pittinuri
Is Arenas
Narbolia
Milis
Sorgono
Tonara
Desulo
Monti del Gennargentu
Riola Sardo
Tramatza
Fordongianus
Aritzo
Arbatax
Tortolì
Cabras
Samugheo
Simaxis
Marina di Torre Grande
Oristano
Lanusei
S. Giovanni di Sinis
Sta Giusta
Laconi
Seulo
Seui
Jerzu
Golfo di Oristano
Nurallao
Arborea
Ales
Terralba
Barumini
Isili
Uras
Mandas
Sardara
L. di Mulargia
Sanluri
Furtei
Ballao
Flumendosa
Guspini
S. Gavino Monreale
Senorbì
S. Nicolò Gerrei
Arbus
S. Andrea Frius
Villasalto
S. Vito
Gonnosfanadiga
Muravera
M. Linas
Villacidro
Serramanna
Fluminimaggiore
Monastir
Dolianova
Villasor
P. Serpeddì
S. Sperate
Sestu
Mannu
Domusnovas
Iglesias
Siliqua
Assemini
Selargius
Castiadas
Elmas
Quarto S. Elena
Gonnesa
Villamassargia
CAGLIARI
Portoscuso
Carbonia
Narcao
I. di S. Pietro
M. is Caravius
Golfo di Cagliari
Villasimius
Capo Carbonara
Carloforte
S. Giovanni Suergiu
Calasetta
Is Mola
Sarroch
S. Antioco
Giba
Pula
I. di S. Antioco
Sta Margherita
Teulada
Porto Pino
Civitavecchia
Napoli
Trapani-Palermo
Tunis
Genova
MICHELIN

Per chi ha sete
di emozioni.
PREMIUM BEER
EXPORT LAGER
PREMIUM
BIRRA
BEER
Nastro
Azzurro
Export Lager
EXPORT
1846
QUALITY
PERONI
Il gusto vincente.

CLASSIFICATION OF COURSES
CLASSIFICA DEI PERCORSI

This classification gives priority consideration to the score awarded to the actual course.

Questa classifica è ordinata secondo il punteggio assegnato al percorso.

Course score / Giudizio sul percorso — Page / Pagina

Score			Course	Page
18	7	8	Biella - Le Betulle	950
18	8	8	Castelconturbia *Giallo + Azzurro*	954
17	8	7	Bogogno *Bonora*	951
17	8	7	Bogogno *Del Conte*	952
17	7	7	I Roveri	963
17	2	6	Is Arenas	964
17	7	8	Is Molas	965
17	8	7	Le Querce	968
17	8	8	Pevero	981
16	7	7	Bergamo - L'Albenza *Blu + Giallo*	949
16	9	8	Milano	973
16	8	6	Olgiata	978
16	8	9	Roma - Acquasanta	987
16	8	7	Torino - La Mandria *Percorso Blu*	988
16	7	9	Venezia	990
16	9	8	Villa D'Este	992
15	8	7	Antognolla	945
15	9	8	Arzaga	946
15	7	7	Castelgandolfo	955
15	8	8	Gardagolf	961
15	8	8	Le Robinie	969
15	8	8	Marco Simone	971
15	7	7	Poggio dei Medici	982
14	8	8	Albarella	943
14	8	7	Barlassina	948
14	8	7	Castello di Tolcinasco	956
14	6	7	Cosmopolitan	958
14	7	8	Franciacorta	960
14	7	8	Garlenda	962
14	8	8	Le Pavoniere	967
14	7	7	Lignano	970
14	8	7	Monticello	977
14	8	8	Padova	979
14	6	8	Punta Ala	983
14	8	7	Varese	989
13	7	7	Ambrosiano	944
13	7	7	Asolo	947
13	7	7	Bologna	953
13	6	9	Cervia	957
13	8	9	Firenze - Ugolino	959
13	7	8	La Pinetina	966
13	7	7	Margara	972
13	7	7	Modena	974
13	8	8	Molinetto	975
13	8	8	Montecchia	976
13	6	9	Parco de' Medici	980
13	8	8	Rapallo	984
13	6	8	Rimini	985
13	7	7	Riva dei Tessali	986
13	7	8	Verona	991

Classification

RECOMMENDED GOLFING STAY
SOGGIORNO GOLFISTICO CONSIGLIATI

Course	Score			Page
Bogogno *Bonora*	17	8	7	951
Bogogno *Del Conte*	17	8	7	952
Castelconturbia *Giallo + Azzurro*	18	8	8	954
I Roveri	17	7	7	963
Torino - La Mandria *Percorso Blu*	16	8	7	988

HOTELS FACILITIES
SERVIZI ALBERGHIERI

This classification gives priority consideration to the score awarded to the hotel facilities.

Questa classifica è ordinata secondo il punteggio assegnato ai servizi alberghieri.

hotel facility score
Giudizio sul offerta alberghiera

Page
Pagina

13	6	**9**	Cervia	957
13	8	**9**	Firenze - Ugolino	959
13	6	**9**	Parco de' Medici	980
16	8	**9**	Roma - Acquasanta	987
16	7	**9**	Venezia	990
14	8	**8**	Albarella	943
15	9	**8**	Arzaga	946
18	7	**8**	Biella - Le Betulle	950
18	8	**8**	Castelconturbia	
			Giallo + Azzurro	954
14	7	**8**	Franciacorta	960
15	8	**8**	Gardagolf	961
14	7	**8**	Garlenda	962
17	7	**8**	Is Molas	965
13	7	**8**	La Pinetina	966
14	8	**8**	Le Pavoniere	967
15	8	**8**	Le Robinie	969
15	8	**8**	Marco Simone	971
16	9	**8**	Milano	973
13	8	**8**	Molinetto	975
13	8	**8**	Montecchia	976
14	8	**8**	Padova	979
17	8	**8**	Pevero	981
14	6	**8**	Punta Ala	983
13	8	**8**	Rapallo	984
13	6	**8**	Rimini	985
13	7	**8**	Verona	991
16	9	**8**	Villa D'Este	992
13	7	**7**	Ambrosiano	944
15	8	**7**	Antognolla	945
13	7	**7**	Asolo	947
14	8	**7**	Barlassina	948
16	7	**7**	Bergamo - L'Albenza	
			Blu + Giallo	949
17	8	**7**	Bogogno *Bonora*	951
17	8	**7**	Bogogno *Del Conte*	952
13	7	**7**	Bologna	953
15	7	**7**	Castelgandolfo	955
14	8	**7**	Castello di Tolcinasco	956
14	6	**7**	Cosmopolitan	958
17	7	**7**	I Roveri	963
17	8	**7**	Le Querce	968
14	7	**7**	Lignano	970
13	7	**7**	Margara	972
13	7	**7**	Modena	974
14	8	**7**	Monticello	977
15	7	**7**	Poggio dei Medici	982
13	7	**7**	Riva dei Tessali	986
16	8	**7**	Torino - La Mandria	
			Percorso Blu	988
14	8	**7**	Varese	989
17	2	**6**	Is Arenas	964
16	8	**6**	Olgiata	978

ALBARELLA

14 | 8 | 8

Situato in una piccola isola nel delta del Po, vicino a Venezia e a Padova è un golf ben conosciuto in Italia, in particolare perchè ha ospitato numerosi tornei internazionali. E' stato costruito su un terreno molto aperto dove la vegetazione è poco significativa, molto vicino al mare ed alla spiaggia. Circondato da piccole dune di sabbia, il percorso può far pensare ad un links. Il gioco può cambiare radicalmente quando soffia forte il vento e capita abbastanza spesso, ma questa caratteristica tipicamente britannica qui ha i suoi limiti: l'Adriatico non è il Mare del Nord o l'Atlantico! Infatti questo è un piacevolissimo percorso di vacanza, ben tenuto e dove può facilmente giocare tutta la famiglia. Le difficoltà sono solitamente ben visibili e i rilievi praticamente inesistenti. I più critici possono dire che manca un pò di movimento, ma evidentemente Harris e Croze hanno pensato prima ai dilettanti quando hanno disegnato il percorso. Il record del campo è 63, ma anche i migliori giocatori dovranno essere al massimo della forma per riuscire a far meglio.

Albarella, located on a small peninsula in the estuary of the river Po near Venice and Padova, is one of Italy's best known courses, primarily because it has hosted a considerable number of international tournaments. It is laid out on open terrain with little in the way of vegetation, close to the sea and beaches. Surrounded by small sand-dunes, certain aspects of this course are reminiscent of a typical links course. The way it plays can certainly change drastically when the wind blows, a frequent occurrence here, but this British side to the course has its limits, as this is, after all, the Adriatic not the North Sea or the Atlantic. In actual fact this is a very good holiday course, which is well kept and easy to play with all the family. Hazards are clearly visible and there is no relief to speak of. The more critically-minded might feel that the course could have been given more shape, but John Harris and Marco Croze obviously had amateur golfers in mind when designing the layout. Even though the course record is 63, the better players will have to be on top of their game if they want to card low scores.

Circolo Golf Albarella — 1972

Isola di Albarella
I - 45010 ROSOLINA (RO)

Office	Segreteria	(39) 0426 330 124
Pro shop	Pro shop	(39) 0426 330 896
Fax	Fax	(39) 0426 330 830
Web	www.isoladialbarella.it	
Situation	Localita'	

Chioggia (pop. 52 039) 24 km, Venezia (pop. 277305), 45 km

Annual closure	Chiusura annuale	no
Weekly closure	Chiusura settimanale	tuesday

Fees main season Tariffe alta stagione		18 holes
	Week days Settimana	**We/Bank holidays** Feriale/Festivo
Individual Individuale	41 €	52 €
Couple Coppia	82 €	104 €
Caddy	Caddy	no
Electric Trolley	Carello elettrico	no
Buggy	Car	31 €
Clubs	Bastoni	26 €

Credit cards Carte di credito
VISA - Eurocard - MasterCard

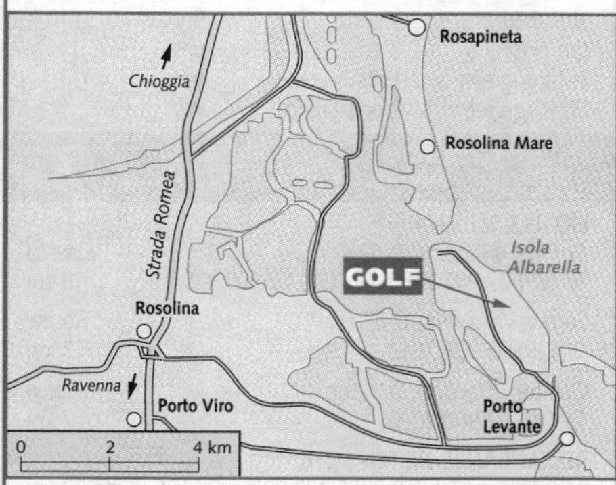

Access Itinerario : A4 Milano-Venezia. Exit (Uscita) Padova Est. S516 → Chioggia. In Chioggia, Strada Romea → Ravenna. After Rosolina, turn left to Isola Albarella, then → Golf **Map 2 on page 934** Carta 2 Pagina 934

Golf course — PERCORSO — 14/20

Site	Paesaggio	
Maintenance	Manutenzione	
Architect	Architetto	John Harris Marco Croze
Type	Tipologia	links, residential
Relief	Relievo terreno	
Water in play	Acqua in gioco	
Exp. to wind	Esposto al vento	
Trees in play	Alberi in gioco	

Scorecard Carta-score	**Chp.** Camp.	**Mens** Uomini	**Ladies** Donne
Length Lunghezza	6100	6100	5370
Par	72	72	72
Slope system	—	—	—

Advised golfing ability Livello di gioco consigliato: 0 12 24 36
Hcp required Handicap richiesto 34

Club house & amenities — CLUB HOUSE E SERVIZI — 8/10

Pro shop	Pro shop	
Driving range	Campo pratica	
Sheltered	coperto	4 mats
On grass	in erba	yes
Putting-green	Putting-green	yes
Pitching-green	Green-pratica	yes

Hotel facilities — ALBERGHI — 8/10

HOTELS ALBERGHI

Hotel Capo Nord, 41 rooms, D 83 € — Albarella
Tel (39) 0426 330 139 — 3 km

Club house, 22 rooms, D 103 € — on site
Tel (39) 0426 367 811, Fax (39) 0426 330 628

RESTAURANTS RISTORANTE

Sottovento — Norge Polesine
Tel (39) 0426 340 138 — 12,5 km

Due Leoni — Ariano nel Polesine
Tel (39) 0426 372 129 — 25 km

Al Monte — Rosolina
Tel (39) 0426 337 132 — 10 km

AMBROSIANO

13 | 7 | 7

Questo percorso di recente costruzione è molto vicino a Milano ma anche poco distante da Pavia, nella quale università hanno studiato nientemeno che il Petrarca e Leonardo da Vinci. La città è stata una roccaforte dei Visconti che stabilirono il loro mausoleo a nord della città, alla Certosa di Pavia, una straordinaria chiesa lombarda tra il gotico e il rinascimentale. A qualche chilometro di distanza c'è l'Ambrosiano e coloro che non amano più di tanto la storia e l'antichità potranno fare questo percorso anche due volte al giorno. Siccome è particolarmente piatto e con pochi alberi, non è facile capire subito la strategia di gioco e visualizzare i suoi tranelli. La disposizione intelligente dei numerosi ostacoli ne fa un percorso divertente e di qualità anche se il paesaggio non è eccezionale. E' decisamente più delicato dalle partenze di campionato.

Sure, this recent course is close to Milan, but it is also not far from Pavia, at whose university Petrarch and Leonardo da Vinci studied in days gone by. This was also one of the strongholds of the Visconti, who built their mausoleum to the north of the city at Certosa di Pavia (Charterhouse of Pavia), an extraordinary Lombardy-style church somewhere between the Gothic and Renaissance styles. It is also just a few miles from Ambrosiano. Golfers who have no time for history or old buildings can play this course twice in a day. Being virtually shorn of trees, it is hard to immediately appreciate game strategy and visualize the traps. The clever layout of the very many hazards makes this a very amusing and high quality course, even though the landscape is nothing to write home about. It is, however, a much trickier proposition when played from the tiger tees.

Golf Club Ambrosiano — 1994

Cascina Bertacca
I - 20080 BUBBIANO (MI)

Office	Segreteria	(39) 02 9084 0820
Pro shop	Pro shop	(39) 02 9084 0820
Fax	Fax	(39) 02 9084 9365
E-mail	gcambros@tin.it	
Situation	Localita'	

Milano (pop. 1 032 808), 29 km, Pavia (pop. 74 065), 30 km

Annual closure	Chiusura annuale	no
Weekly closure	Chiusura settimanale	tuesday

Fees main season Tariffe alta stagione		full day
	Week days Settimana	**We/Bank holidays** Feriale/Festivo
Individual Individuale	36 €	57 €
Couple Coppia	72 €	114 €
Caddy	Caddy	no
Electric Trolley	Carello elettrico	no
Buggy	Car	31 €
Clubs	Bastoni	15 €

Credit cards Carte di credito
VISA - Eurocard - MasterCard - CartaSi

Access Itinerario : A7 Milano-Genova, Exit (Uscita) Binasco, right → Motta Visconti. 7 km, → Bubbiano. → Golf.
Map 1 on page 933 Carta 1 Pagina 933

Golf course — PERCORSO — 13/20

Site	Paesaggio	
Maintenance	Manutenzione	
Architect	Architetto	Cornish & Silva
Type	Tipologia	country
Relief	Relievo terreno	
Water in play	Acqua in gioco	
Exp. to wind	Esposto al vento	
Trees in play	Alberi in gioco	

Scorecard Carta-score	**Chp.** Camp.	**Mens** Uomini	**Ladies** Donne
Length Lunghezza	6281	6047	5316
Par	72	72	72
Slope system	—	—	—

Advised golfing ability 0 12 24 36
Livello di gioco consigliato
Hcp required Handicap richiesto no

Club house & amenities — CLUB HOUSE E SERVIZI — 7/10

Pro shop	Pro shop	
Driving range	Campo pratica	
Sheltered	coperto	5 mats
On grass	in erba	yes
Putting-green	Putting-green	yes
Pitching-green	Green-pratica	yes

Hotel facilities — ALBERGHI — 7/10

HOTELS ALBERGHI

Corona, 48 rooms, D 62 € — Binasco
Tel (39) 02 905 2280, Fax (39) 02 905 4353 — 8 km

Europa, 40 rooms, D 62 € — Rosate
Tel (39) 02 908 7612 — 3 km

Comtur, 49 rooms, D 129 € — Binasco
Tel (39) 02 900 2020 — 7 km

RESTAURANTS RISTORANTE

Al Cassinino, Tel (39) 0382 422 097 — Pavia (Str. 35) 22 km
I Castagni Tel (39) 0381 42 860 — Vigevano 16 km
Re Artù, Tel (39) 02 908 5123 — Gaggiano15 km

ANTOGNOLLA 15 | 8 | 7

Il posto è veramente molto bello, con il castello che domina questo tranquillo e ondulato paesaggio dell'Umbria. Le antiche fattorie di pietra sono sparse qua e là nella pianura e sulle colline coperte soprattutto di olivi, elemento fondamentale delle cucina italiana. Siamo vicino a Perugia ma anche a Cortona, al lago Trasimeno e, ovviamente, ad Assisi. Qui, in un luogo veramente bello, Robert Trent Jones Jr ha disegnato il percorso muovendosi a piccoli passi per conservare l'armonia del paesaggio. Il terreno, molto aperto è anche molto mosso tanto che le sue pendenze faranno girare la testa ai giocatori sia sui fairway che in green! I bunkers sono molto ben disegnati e gli ostacoli d'acqua sono numerosi ma non onnipresenti per non andare contro la natura del posto. Qui non si richiedono colpi particolari e ci si può lasciar andare al proprio gioco. Abbastanza onesto e non troppo duro dalle partenze avanzate, Antognolla sembra avere un ottimo avvenire.

An impressive site with a castle overlooking the quiet rolling countryside of Umbria. The plain and wood-covered hills are dotted with the old stones of former farmhouses plus any number of olive trees. Here you are not far from Perugia, Cortona, Lago Trasimeno and, of course, Assisi. Robert Trent Jones Jr has crafted this course across a superb piece of land, seemingly working section by section to give the layout a sense of rhythm. On terrain that is rather open but still hilly, eye-catching features include often severely sloping fairways and greens, well-designed bunkers and the obligatory water hazards, which although dangerous are never omnipresent, simply because the soul of the site never called for it. One reassuring thing is that you do not necessarily have to "steer" the ball that much, as there is room enough to open the shoulders and perhaps stray just a little from the straight and narrow. Antognolla is a an honest-to-goodness course, never too "mean" when played from the front tees, and one which promises much for the future.

Antognolla Golf & Country Club 1998

Strada San Giovanni del Pantano, Loc. Antognolla
I - 06070 PERUGIA

Office	Segreteria	(39) 075 605 9563
Pro shop	Pro shop	(39) 075 605 9563
Fax	Fax	(39) 075 605 9562
Web	www.antognolla.com	
Situation	Localita' Perugia (pop. 156 673), 15 km	
Annual closure	Chiusura annuale	no
Weekly closure	Chiusura settimanale	no

Fees main season Tariffe alta stagione		Full day
	Week days Settimana	We/Bank holidays Feriale/Festivo
Individual Individuale	44 €	62 €
Couple Coppia	88 €	124 €

Caddy	Caddy	no
Electric Trolley	Carello elettrico	no
Buggy	Car	yes
Clubs	Bastoni	15 €

Credit cards Carte di credito
VISA - Eurocard - MasterCard - JCB - AMEX

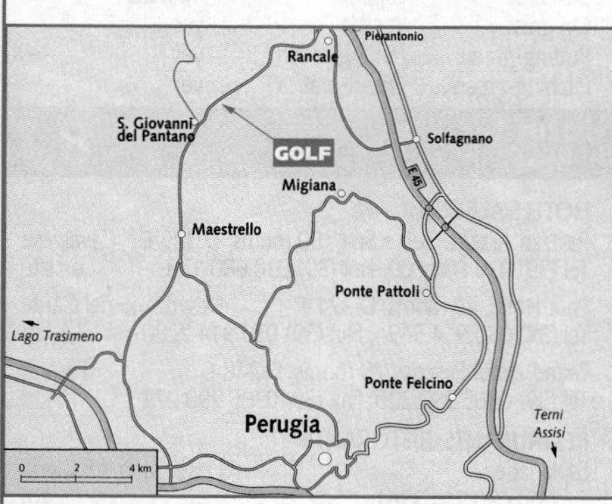

Access Itinerario : A1 Firenze-Roma. Exit (Uscita) Valdichiana. → Perugia, Exit (Uscita) Magione. ss 75bis. 3 km turn left → Umbertide. Follow signs to golf
Map 3 on page 937 Carta 3 Pagina 937

Golf course PERCORSO 15/20

Site	Paesaggio	
Maintenance	Manutenzione	
Architect	Architetto	R. Trent Jones Jr
Type	Tipologia	hilly, open country
Relief	Relievo terreno	
Water in play	Acqua in gioco	
Exp. to wind	Esposto al vento	
Trees in play	Alberi in gioco	

Scorecard Carta-score	Chp. Camp.	Mens Uomini	Ladies Donne
Length Lunghezza	6228	5873	5164
Par	71	71	71
Slope system	—	—	—

Advised golfing ability 0 12 24 36
Livello di gioco consigliato
Hcp required Handicap richiesto 34

Club house & amenities CLUB HOUSE E SERVIZI 8/10

Pro shop	Pro shop	
Driving range	Campo pratica	
Sheltered	coperto	no
On grass	in erba	yes
Putting-green	Putting-green	yes
Pitching-green	Green-pratica	yes

Hotel facilities ALBERGHI 7/10

HOTELS ALBERGHI

Castello dell'Oscano — Cenerente 11 km
26 rooms, D 165 €
Tel (39) 075 584 371, Fax (39) 075 690 666

Colle della Trinità, 50 rooms, D 103 € — Perugia 15 km
Tel (39) 075 517 2048, Fax (39) 075 517 1197

Brufani, 75 rooms, D 258 € — Perugia 15 km
Tel (39) 075 573 2541, Fax (39) 075 572 0210

RESTAURANTS RISTORANTE

Osteria del Bartolo, Tel (39) 075 573 1561 — Perugia 15 km
Da Settimio, Tel (39) 075 847 6000 — Magione 18 km
L'Abbatia di Montecorone — Umbertide 10 km

ARZAGA

15 | 9 | 8

Dopo i numerosi percorsi di assoluta qualità sorti nella regione dei laghi in Lombardia, abbiamo assistito alla nascita di una vera destinazione golfistica circondata da un magnifico paesaggio e a due passi da grandi città turistiche, commerciali e artistiche come Milano o ancora Brescia e Verona. Il nuovo golf di Palazzo Arzaga si trova tra queste due ultime città, appena sopra al lago di Garda. Il primo percorso è stato aperto nel 1998, con l'intenzione di creare un complesso ambizioso, con un hotel extra lusso nell' antica villa della tenuta, campi da tennis, un centro estetico delle famose Terme di Saturnia. Il primo percorso, c'è n'è un altro firmato da Gary Player che ha per il momento solo 9 buche, èstato disegnato dal figlio di Jack Nicklaus in stile assolutamente americano, con pochi alberi in gioco, ma con molti ostacoli d'acqua e bunkers piazzati strategicamente sia in fairway che intorno ai greens.Questi ultimi con le loro pendenze contribuiscono a rendere difficile la riuscita di un buono score. Questo percorso, grazie ai numerosi tees di partenza, è divertente per i giocatori di ogni livello e si può giocare in ogni stagione dell'anno in condizioni ottime del terreno.

With so many top class courses in the region of the Lombardy lakes, we could be witnessing the birth of a real golfing destination, set in dream landscapes within the immediate vicinity of major tourist, business and cultural cities such as Milan or even Brescia and Verona. The new Palazzo Arzaga course lies between these two cities just above lake Garda. This is an ambitious resort opened in 1998 with a sumptuous hotel in a patrician villa, tennis courts, a spa as at Saturnia and swimming pool (reserved for members). In this very fine site, which will eventually comprise 36 holes of golf (Gary Player is designing a second course), Jack Nicklaus Junior has designed a bltantly American-styled layout with few trees coming into play but a lot of water and sand. The greens are huge, sometimes tiered and elevated and contoured enough to compound the task of carding a good score here. Still, the course is playable by everyone but needs a little maturing before moving up from the rating of "good" course to "great" course.

Arzaga Golf Club — 1998

Loc. Carzago
I - 25080 CAVALGESE DELLA RIVIERA

Office	Segreteria	(39) 030 680 600
Pro shop	Pro shop	(39) 030 680 6171
Fax	Fax	(39) 030 680 178
Web	www.palazzoarzaga.com	
Situation	Localita'	

Brescia (pop. 191 317), 28 km, Verona (pop. 255 268), 45 km

Annual closure	Chiusura annuale	no
Weekly closure	Chiusura settimanale	no

Fees main season Tariffe alta stagione — 18 holes

	Week days Settimana	We/Bank holidays Feriale/Festivo
Individual Individuale	52 €	72 €
Couple Coppia	104 €	144 €
Caddy Caddy	no	
Electric Trolley Carello elettrico	8 €	
Buggy Car	31 €	
Clubs Bastoni	21 €	

Credit cards Carte di credito
VISA - Eurocard - MasterCard - DC - CartaSì - AMEX

Access Itinerario : A4 Milano-Venezia. Exit (Uscita) Desenzano. Turn left, then left again → Brescia. → Sedena. 2 km turn right. 300 m to the left.

Map 1 on page 933 Carta 1 Pagina 933

Golf course — PERCORSO — 15/20

Site	Paesaggio	
Maintenance	Manutenzione	
Architect	Architetto	Jack Nicklaus Jr
Type	Tipologia	country
Relief	Relievo terreno	
Water in play	Acqua in gioco	
Exp. to wind	Esposto al vento	
Trees in play	Alberi in gioco	

Scorecard Carta-score	Chp. Camp.	Mens Uomini	Ladies Donne
Length Lunghezza	6062	5885	5220
Par	72	72	72
Slope system	—	—	—

Advised golfing ability 0 12 24 36
Livello di gioco consigliato
Hcp required Handicap richiesto 34

Club house & amenities — CLUB HOUSE E SERVIZI — 9/10

Pro shop	Pro shop	
Driving range	Campo pratica	
Sheltered	coperto	10 mats
On grass	in erba	yes
Putting-green	Putting-green	yes
Pitching-green	Green-pratica	yes

Hotel facilities — ALBERGHI — 8/10

HOTELS ALBERGHI

Palazzo Arzaga Golf e Spa, 80 rooms, D 325 € — Cavalgese
Tel (39) 030 680 600, Fax (39) 030 680 178 — on site

Park Hotel, 49 rooms, D 121 € — Desenzano del Garda
Tel (39) 030 914 3494, Fax (39) 030 914 2280 — 7,5 km

Grand Hotel Fasano, 75 rooms, D 248 € — Fasano
Tel (39) 0365 290 220, Fax (39) 0365 290 221 — 15 km

RESTAURANTS RISTORANTE

Esplanade, — Desenzano del Garda
Tel (39) 030 914 3361 — 7,5 km

Cavallino, Tel (39) 030 912 0217 — Desenzano del Garda

Locanda Santa Giulia — Padenghe sul Garda
Tel (39) 030 99 950 — 5 km

ASOLO

13 | 7 | 7

Con la sua ubicazione vicino a Vicenza, Treviso, Padova, Venezia ed anche all'Austria, Asolo è uno dei percorsi da conoscere quando si visita questa superba regione del Veneto. A questa lista di famose cittadine ci sono da aggiungere Asolo con i suoi castelli e i suoi palazzi e Bassano del Grappa, conosciuta per le sue piccole case dipinte, le sue ceramiche e... la grappa! Questo percorso è immerso in un posto molto bello ed ampio e comprende tre percorsi di 9 buche combinabili tra loro in diversi percorsi di 18 buche. Stan Eby, della European Golf Design, ha concepito questo tracciato dove le difficoltà sono ben distribuite ed è quindi accessibile ai giocatori di ogni livello. Tutto qui è stato fatto con grande serietà e con una buona conoscenza sulle capacità diverse dei giocatori, ma gli amanti dei percorsi di carattere avrebbero preferito un po' più di audacia nel disegno. Asolo resta comunque un campo da visitare quando si è nella regione.

Being close to Vicenza, Treviso, Padova, Venice and even Switzerland, Asolo is a course to play when exploring this superb region of Veneto. We can add Asolo to this list of famous cities, with fortress and palaces, and Bassano del Grappa, famous for its little painted houses, porcelain and... Grappa liqueur! The golf course is spread over a very beautiful and uncluttered site and will shortly comprise three combinable 9 hole courses to form several different 18-hole layouts. Stan Eby from European Golf Design designed this course, which is well-balanced in the difficulties it presents, playable by golfers of all abilities but not always necessarily very exciting. Everything has been done very thoroughly here, with good insight into different levels of golfing skill, although golfers who like more personalized courses might have preferred a little more daring here and there. Nonetheless, Asolo is still a course that deserves a visit when in the region.

Asolo Golf Club — 1997

Via Ronche
I - 31034 CAVASO DEL TOMBA (TV)

Office	Segreteria	(39) 0423 942 000
Pro shop	Pro shop	(39) 0423 942 217
Fax	Fax	(39) 0423 543 226
Web	www.asologolf.com	
Situation	Localita'	

Treviso (pop. 81.328), 35 km, Bassano del Grappa, 15 km

Annual closure	Chiusura annuale	no
Weekly closure	Chiusura settimanale	tuesday

Fees main season Tariffe alta stagione		full day
	Week days Settimana	**We/Bank holidays** Feriale/Festivo
Individual Individuale	41 €	62 €
Couple Coppia	82 €	124 €
Caddy	Caddy	21 €
Electric Trolley	Carello elettrico	no
Buggy	Car	31 €
Clubs	Bastoni	15 €

Credit cards Carte di credito
VISA - Eurocard - MasterCard - DC - Cartasi - AMEX

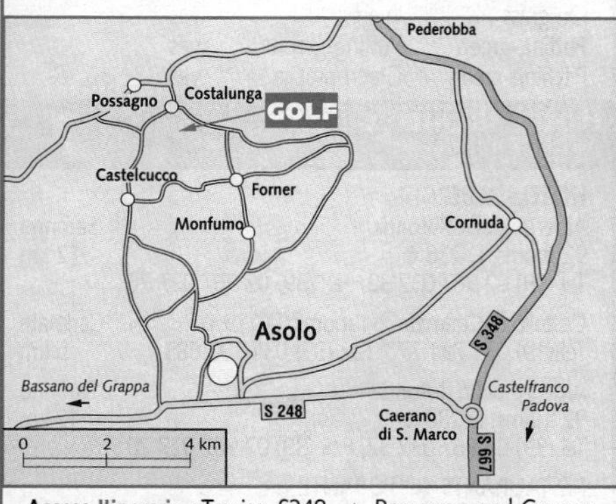

Access Itinerario : Treviso, S348, → Possagno and Cavaso del Tomba. Golf 2 km after Cavaso.
Map 2 on page 934 Carta 2 Pagina 934

Golf course — PERCORSO — 13/20

Site	Paesaggio	
Maintenance	Manutenzione	
Architect	Architetto	European Golf Design
Type	Tipologia	country
Relief	Relievo terreno	
Water in play	Acqua in gioco	
Exp. to wind	Esposto al vento	
Trees in play	Alberi in gioco	

Scorecard Carta-score	**Chp.** Camp.	**Mens** Uomini	**Ladies** Donne
Length Lunghezza	6242	5873	5161
Par	72	72	72
Slope system	—	—	—

Advised golfing ability 0 12 24 36
Livello di gioco consigliato
Hcp required Handicap richiesto 34

Club house & amenities — CLUB HOUSE E SERVIZI — 7/10

Pro shop	Pro shop	
Driving range	Campo pratica	
Sheltered	coperto	10 mats
On grass	in erba	yes
Putting-green	Putting-green	yes
Pitching-green	Green-pratica	yes

Hotel facilities — ALBERGHI — 7/10

HOTELS ALBERGHI

Villa Cipriani 31 rooms, D 411 € — Asolo 8 km
Tel (39) 0423 523 411, Fax (39) 0423 952 095

Golf Club, 11 rooms, D 72 € — on site
Tel (39) 0423 942 000, Fax (39) 0423 543 226

Hotel Duse, 14 rooms, D 129 € — Asolo 7 km
Tel (39) 0423 55 241, Fax (39) 0423 950 404

RESTAURANTS RISTORANTE

Belvedere — Bassano del Grappa 15 km
Tel (39) 0424 524 988

Ai Due Archi, Tel (39) 0423 952 201 — Asolo 8 km

Tavernetta, Tel (39) 0423 952 273 — Asolo 8 km

BARLASSINA

14 | 8 | 7

Aperto nel 1956, il disegno dell'architetto inglese John Morrison è stato modificato nel 1988, per quel che riguarda il tracciato di alcune buche e di molti greens. E' situato in una regione abbastanza ondulata ad un ventina di chilometri a nord di Milano, poco distante dalle strade che portano verso il lago di Como. La natura è particolarmente piacevole e le buche sono ritagliate in mezzo agli alberi anche se i fairways sono sempre abbastanza larghi. Gli alberi qui sono in gioco senza essere veramente pericolosi, sono soprattutto un elemento di decoro e uníaggiunta al fascino visivo del campo. In questo grande parco, scegliere di andare a piedi è sempre la cosa più piacevole e non è necessario essere un gran campione per divertirsi perchè non sono richiesti colpi particolarmente tecnici. Detto questo, se partirete dai tees di campionato dovrete sbagliare molto poco se vorrete fare un buono score. Tra i numerosi percorsi intorno a Milano, Barlassina merita una visita ma non durante il week-end dove il gioco è riservato ai soci.

Opened in 1956, this layout from British architect John Morrison was altered in 1988 with changes made to a number of holes and to the configuration of several greens. It is located over rolling countryside some twenty or so kilometres to the north of Milan, just off the road leading to Lake Como. The surroundings are pleasant indeed and the course full of trees, but still with rather wide fairways. Although in play, the trees are not all that dangerous and serve more as decoration and an addition to the course's visual appeal. In this large park, the walk is all the more enjoyable in that you don't have to be a top champion to tame the course, or know how to hit the so-called technical shots. With that said, if you play from the tips, you have little room for error if you want to score well. Of the many courses around Milan, Barlassina is well worth a visit, except on week-ends when the course is reserved for members only.

Barlassina Country Club — 1956

Via Privata Golf 42
I - 20030 BIRAGO DI CAMNAGO (MI)

Office	Segreteria	(39) 0362 560 621
Pro shop	Pro shop	(39) 0362 560 621
Fax	Fax	(39) 0362 560 934
E-mail	bccgolf@ntt.it	
Situation	Localita'	

Milano (pop. 1 300 977), 26 km - Como, 25 km

Annual closure	Chiusura annuale	no
Weekly closure	Chiusura settimanale	monday

Fees main season Tariffe alta stagione	18 holes	
	Week days Settimana	**We/Bank holidays** Feriale/Festivo
Individual Individuale	57 €	80 €
Couple Coppia	114 €	160 €

Green-fees on week days only (settimana)

Caddy	Caddy	18 €
Electric Trolley	Carello elettrico	no
Buggy	Car	no
Clubs	Bastoni	10 €
Credit cards Carte di credito		no

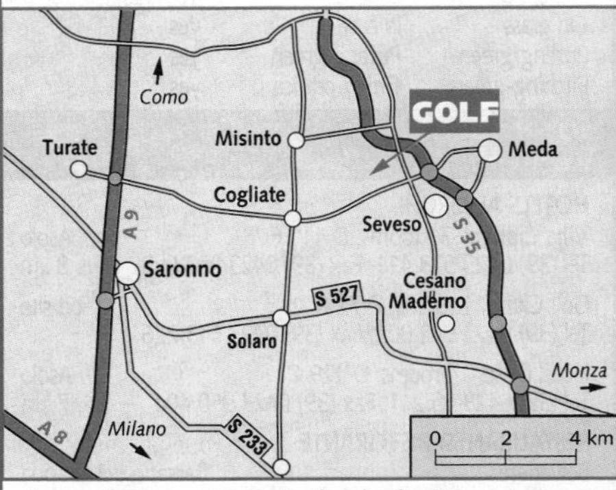

Access Itinerario : Milano North, take the S35 → Como. Exit (Uscita Seveso/Barlassina.
Map 1 on page 933 Carta 1 Pagina 933

Golf course / PERCORSO — 14/20

Site	Paesaggio	
Maintenance	Manutenzione	
Architect	Architetto	J. Morrison
Type	Tipologia	parkland
Relief	Relievo terreno	
Water in play	Acqua in gioco	
Exp. to wind	Esposto al vento	
Trees in play	Alberi in gioco	

Scorecard Carta-score	**Chp.** Camp.	**Mens** Uomini	**Ladies** Donne
Length Lunghezza	6197	6197	5418
Par	72	72	72
Slope system	—	—	—

Advised golfing ability 0 12 24 36
Livello di gioco consigliato
Hcp required Handicap richiesto 34

Club house & amenities / CLUB HOUSE E SERVIZI — 8/10

Pro shop	Pro shop	
Driving range	Campo pratica	
Sheltered	coperto	8 mats
On grass	in erba	yes
Putting-green	Putting-green	yes
Pitching-green	Green-pratica	yes

Hotel facilities / ALBERGHI — 7/10

HOTELS ALBERGHI

Albergo della Rotonda — Saronno 12 km
92 rooms, D 238 €
Tel (39) 02 967 032 32, Fax (39) 02 967 027 70

Castello di Carimate, 54 rooms, D 119 € — Carimate 5 km
Tel (39) 031 791 770, Fax (39) 031 790 683

Albergo della Rotonda — Saronno 12 km
92 rooms, D 238 €
Tel (39) 02 967 032 32, Fax (39) 02 967 027 70

RESTAURANTS RISTORANTE

Osteria del Pomiroeu Tel (39) 0362 237 973 — Seregno 7 km
Le Querce Tel (39) 031 731 336 — Cantù 15 km
La Rimessa Tel (39) 031 749 668 — Mariano Comense 6 km

BERGAMO - L'ALBENZA Blu + Giallo

16	7	7

Se le 9 buche "blu" e le 9 buche "gialle" sono considerate il percorso di campionato, le 9 buche "rosse" costituiscono un'alternativa di qualità all'uno o all'altro e aggiungono un tocco in più ad un disegno che è già molto interessante con i suoi par 4 e suoi par 5 duri da raggiungere in due colpi. E' sicuramente la varietà una delle chiavi del successo dell'Albenza che alterna passaggi tra i boschi a spazi aperti, buche lunghe a buche corte, colpi di assoluta precisione e approcci a correre in perfetto stile "British". Bisogna saper "lavorare" la palla in entrambe le direzioni per avere dei colpi al green più facili e riflettere bene sulla scelta dei bastoni. Un percorso molto "educativo" se si giudica la carriera e il gioco molto completo di Costantino Rocca, che ha cominciato qui come caddie prima di diventare uno dei migliori giocatori del mondo.

If we consider the "blue" and "yellow" 9-hole courses to be the 18 hole championship course, the "red" course is an excellent alternative to both and adds a little more spice to a layout that is pretty hot as it is, in particular on account of the par 4s and the par 5s that are tough to reach in two. Talking of spice, variety is certainly one of the key assets of "L'Albenza", which winds its way now through the woods, now over open space, alternating short and long holes, or target golf and the more British bump and run approach. You often have to work the ball one way or the other for an easier shot at the greens, and club choice requires careful thinking. This is a very "educational" course, judging by the career and very complete game of Costantino Rocca, who started off here as a caddie before becoming one of the world's best golfers. A colourful figure, Rocca could easily have figured in the "Commedia dell'Arte" which, as it happens, was founded in Bergamo.

Golf Club Bergamo - L'Albenza 1961

Via Longoni 12
I - 24030 ALMENNO SAN BARTOLOMEO (BG)

Office	Segreteria	(39) 035 640 028
Pro shop	Pro shop	(39) 035 643 288
Fax	Fax	(39) 035 643 066
E-mail	albenzagolf@tiscalinet.it	
Situation	Localita'	

Bergamo (pop. 117.619) 15 km Brescia (pop. 191 317), 50 km

Annual closure	Chiusura annuale	no
Weekly closure	Chiusura settimanale	monday

Fees main season Tariffe alta stagione		18 holes
	Week days Settimana	**We/Bank holidays** Feriale/Festivo
Individual Individuale	46 €	67 €
Couple Coppia	92 €	134 €

Caddy	Caddy	21 €
Electric Trolley	Carello elettrico	8 €
Buggy	Car	36 €
Clubs	Bastoni	5 €

Credit cards Carte di credito VISA - DC - CartaSi

Access Itinerario : A4 Milano-Venezia, Exit (Uscita) Capriate. Turn right → Ponte San Pietro. At old house, turn left → Lecco. 2 km right → Almenno San Bartolomeo. Golf on left hand side. **Map 1 on page 933** Carta 1 Pagina 933

Golf course PERCORSO 16/20

Site	Paesaggio	
Maintenance	Manutenzione	
Architect	Architetto	Cotton & Sutton
Type	Tipologia	forest
Relief	Relievo terreno	
Water in play	Acqua in gioco	
Exp. to wind	Esposto al vento	
Trees in play	Alberi in gioco	

Scorecard Carta-score	**Chp.** Camp.	**Mens** Uomini	**Ladies** Donne
Length Lunghezza	6220	6100	5368
Par	72	72	72
Slope system	—	—	—

Advised golfing ability 0 12 24 36
Livello di gioco consigliato

Hcp required Handicap richiesto 34

Club house & amenities CLUB HOUSE E SERVIZI 7/10

Pro shop	Pro shop	
Driving range	Campo pratica	
Sheltered	coperto	12 mats
On grass	in erba	yes
Putting-green	Putting-green	yes
Pitching-green	Green-pratica	yes

Hotel facilities ALBERGHI 7/10

HOTELS ALBERGHI

Castello di Clanezzo, 12 rooms, D 103 € — Clanezzo 3 km
Tel (39) 035 641 567, Fax (39) 035 641 567

Starhotel Cristallo Palace — Bergamo 15 km
90 rooms, D 201 €
Tel (39) 035 311 211, Fax (39) 035 312 031

Radisson SAS Hotel, 80 rooms, D 201 € — Bergamo 15 km
Tel (39) 035 308 111, Fax (39) 035 308 308

RESTAURANTS RISTORANTE

Ponte di Briolo, Tel (39) 035 611 197 — Valbrembo 5 km

Trattoria del Tone, Tel (39) 035 613 166 — Curno 8 km

Caprese, Tel (39) 035 611 148 — Mozzo 6 km

BIELLA - LE BETULLE

18 | 7 | 8

Biella è il più grande centro italiano della lana e dei tessuti che hanno fatto la gloria della moda italiana ed è anche la sede di uno dei più discreti ma grandiosi golf della penisola. Qui il disegno del campo passa in secondo piano rispetto alla bellezza del paesaggio e di un terreno che sembrano essere fatti apposta per il golf, ma con la maestria di un architetto come John Morrison è stata raggiunta la perfezione. Il percorso è stato allungato nel corso degli anni per rispondere alle esigenze del gioco moderno, ma vi consigliamo di giocare dai tees normali a meno di non avere una tecnica da grande campione. In questo percorso si respira un'atmosfera assolutamente britannica , dove sono in gioco bunkers piazzati strategicamente, fossi diabolici e un'infinità di querce, castagni e betulle. A tutto questo si aggiunge una varietà notevole: qui infatti sobrietà, non vuol mai dire monotonia. E' sicuramente un eccellente banco di prova in un ambiente superbo, può essere un pò difficile per i giocatori inesperti. Da conoscere, ancor meglio alloggiando nella "Dormy House" nel circolo.

Biella is one of Italy's wool and fabric production centres that have made such a name for Italian design. It is also the site of one of the more discreet but also one of the greatest golf courses in the whole of Italy, a course where architectural design plays second fiddle to the beauty of the landscape and terrain that were just made for golf. Yet it still took the designer skills of John Morrison to perfect the chemistry. The course has since been lengthened to meet the demands of the modern game, but unless you have the technique of a budding champion, we would recommend the normal tees to avoid needless suffering. There is a very British feel to this course, which brings strategically located bunkers into play, along with diabolic ditches and no end of oak, chestnut and birch trees. Add to all this a remarkable touch of variety and you'll realize that here, sobriety does not necessarily mean monotony. All in all, a great test of golf in superb surroundings, but maybe a little too tough for inexperienced players. For an even more enjoyable experience, try and stay in the course's "Dormy House" hotel.

Golf Club Biella - Le Betulle — 1958

Località Valcarrozza
I - 13887 MAGNANO (BI)

Office	Segreteria	(39) 015 679 151
Pro shop	Pro shop	(39) 015 679 151
Fax	Fax	(39) 015 679 276
Web	—	
Situation	Localita'	

Biella (pop. 47 353), 18 km - Torino (pop. 903 705), 75 km

Annual closure	Chiusura annuale	no
Weekly closure	Chiusura settimanale	monday

Fees main season Tariffe alta stagione	18 holes	
	Week days Settimana	**We/Bank holidays** Feriale/Festivo
Individual Individuale	46 €	67 €
Couple Coppia	92 €	134 €
Caddy Caddy		yes
Electric Trolley Carello elettrico		no
Buggy Car		36 €
Clubs Bastoni		15 €

Credit cards Carte di credito VISA - AMEX

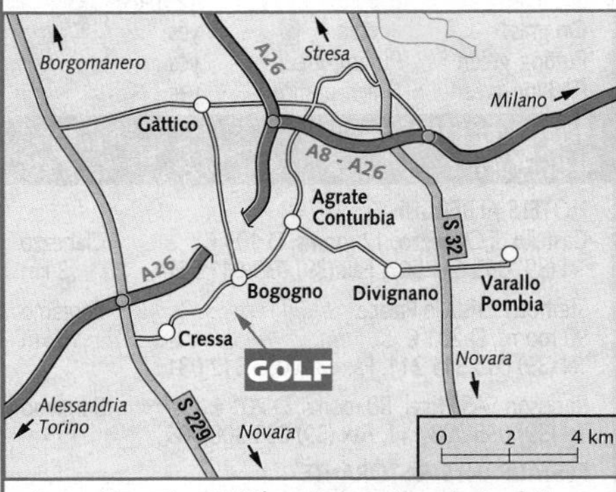

Access Itinerario : A4 Milano-Torino, A5 → Aosta. Exit (Uscita) Albiano, → Biella. Cross the S228 and take S338 → Biella. Golf 2 km

Map 1 on page 932 Carta 1 Pagina 932

Golf course PERCORSO — 18/20

Site	Paesaggio	
Maintenance	Manutenzione	
Architect	Architetto	John Morrison
Type	Tipologia	forest
Relief	Relievo terreno	
Water in play	Acqua in gioco	
Exp. to wind	Esposto al vento	
Trees in play	Alberi in gioco	

Scorecard Carta-score	**Chp.** Camp.	**Mens** Uomini	**Ladies** Donne
Length Lunghezza	6497	6125	5390
Par	73	73	73
Slope system	—	—	—

Advised golfing ability 0 12 24 36
Livello di gioco consigliato

Hcp required Handicap richiesto 34

Club house & amenities CLUB HOUSE E SERVIZI — 7/10

Pro shop	Pro shop	
Driving range	Campo pratica	
Sheltered	coperto	10 mats
On grass	in erba	yes
Putting-green	Putting-green	yes
Pitching-green	Green-pratica	yes

Hotel facilities ALBERGHI — 8/10

HOTELS ALBERGHI

Dormy House, 20 rooms, D 77 € — Magnano
Tel (39) 015 679 151, Fax (39) 015 679 276 — on site

Cascina Era, 29 rooms, D 108 € — Sandigliano 15 km
Tel (39) 015 249 3085, Fax (39) 015 249 3266

Astoria, 50 rooms, D 98 € — Biella 18 km
Tel (39) 015 402 750, Fax (39) 015 849 1691

Augustus, 38 rooms, D 83 € Tel (39) 015 27 554 — Biella

RESTAURANTS RISTORANTE

La Bessa, Tel (39) 015 679 186 — Magnano 4 km

Prinz Grill da Beppe e Teresio — Biella 18 km
Tel (39) 015 23 876

San Paolo, Tel (39) 015 8493 236 — Biella 18 km

BOGOGNO Bonora

17 | 8 | 7

Il grande successo delle prime 18 buche meritava un seguito che ha permesso di realizzare uno dei migliori complessi di 36 buche di tutta Europa e sicuramente di questa regione che pur non manca di grandi percorsi. Bonora è formato da nove buche del primo percorso aperto e nove nuove buche, che sono anche le più difficili, disegnate in uno spazio molto aperto con molti ostacoli d'acqua. Più lungo e delicato del suo vicino "del Conte" obbliga ad una grande, lunga e bella avventura perché non si torna in club-house fino alla 18a e ultima buca. Ma come sempre con il suo architetto Robert von Hagge, questo percorso sa essere divertente, non nasconde ostacoli ingiusti e sa ricompensare i buoni colpi anche se è molto impegnativo per i giocatori normali, quelli che non ambiscono ad una carriera da pro! Comunque... quando si ama non si fanno i conti, e qui è molto divertente sperimentare le proprie capacità senza mettersi lo score in tasca. Spettacolare e molto ben realizzato, Bonora migliorerà ancor più con gli anni a venire.

The very successful outcome of the first 18-hole course called for a repeat performance, and the result has been to form one of the best 36-hole golf resorts to be found anywhere in Europe and more particularly in this region, where there is no shortage of excellent layouts. "Bonora" combines nine holes from the original course with nine new and more difficult holes laid out over wide open space with a whole lot of water hazards. Longer and harder to play than its neighbour, it takes the golfer on a long and beautiful trek through golfing country because you only return to the club-house as you walk up the 18th hole. But as always with architect Robert von Hagge, this is a consistently pleasant course to play, one that does not conceal unfair traps and but which does reward good shots, even though it is a tough proposition for the normal good player, i.e. golfers who are not looking to turn professional by the year's end. Inexperienced golfers can gauge the progress they still need to make. In other words, because feelings always matter more than figures, you should firstly take time out to widen your range of shots before thinking about carding a good score. Spectacular and well-designed, Bonora should get better and better as it grows older.

Circolo Golf Bogogno — 2000

Via S. Isidoro 1
I - 28010 BOGOGNO (NO)

Office	Segreteria	(39) 0322 863 794
Pro shop	Pro shop	(39) 0322 863 339
Fax	Fax	(39) 0322 863 798
Web	www.golfbogogno.it	
Situation	Localita'	

Novara (pop. 102 037), 30 km
Milano (pop. 1 300 977), 66 km

Annual closure	Chiusura annuale	no
Weekly closure	Chiusura settimanale	no

Fees main season Tariffe alta stagione	Week days Settimana	We/Bank holidays Feriale/Festivo
	18 holes	
Individual Individuale	62 €	80 €
Couple Coppia	124 €	160 €
Caddy Caddy		21 €
Electric Trolley Carello elettrico		10 €
Buggy Car		36 €
Clubs Bastoni		18 €

Credit cards Carte di credito VISA - DC - CartaSì

Access Itinerario : A4 Milano-Torino, Exit (Uscita) Novara. Then S229 → Borgomanero. About 29 km, turn right → Cressa. 800 m turn left to Bogogno.
Map 1 on page 932 Carta 1 Pagina 932

Golf course PERCORSO — 10/20

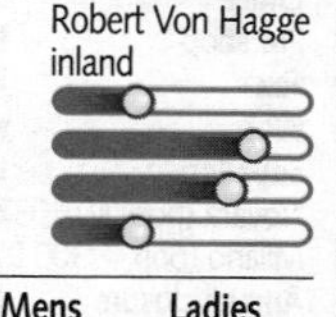

Site	Paesaggio	
Maintenance	Manutenzione	
Architect	Architetto	Robert Von Hagge
Type	Tipologia	inland
Relief	Relievo terreno	
Water in play	Acqua in gioco	
Exp. to wind	Esposto al vento	
Trees in play	Alberi in gioco	

Scorecard Carta-score	Chp. Camp.	Mens Uomini	Ladies Donne
Length Lunghezza	6284	5880	4907
Par	72	72	72
Slope system	—	—	—

Advised golfing ability Livello di gioco consigliato: 0 12 24 36
Hcp required Handicap richiesto 34

Club house & amenities CLUB HOUSE E SERVIZI — 8/10

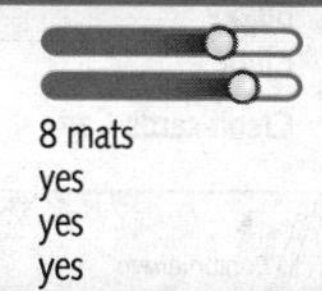

Pro shop	Pro shop	
Driving range	Campo pratica	
Sheltered	coperto	8 mats
On grass	in erba	yes
Putting-green	Putting-green	yes
Pitching-green	Green-pratica	yes

Hotel facilities ALBERGHI — 7/10

HOTELS ALBERGHI

San Rocco, 74 rooms, D 238 € — Orta San Giulio
Tel (39) 0322 911 977, Fax (39) 0322 911 964 — 20 km

Residence Isotta, 16 rooms, D 62 € — Veruno
Tel (39) 0322 830 502, Fax (39) 0322 830 708 — 3 km

Golf Hotel Castelconturbia — Agrate Conturbia
19 rooms, D 93 € — 3 km
Tel (39) 0322 832 337, Fax (39) 0322 832 428

RESTAURANTS RISTORANTE

Pinocchio, — Borgomanero
Tel (39) 0322 82 273 — 6 km

Il Bersagliere — Borgomanero
Tel (39) 0322 82 277 — 6 km

BOGOGNO Del Conte

17 | 8 | 7

Nato nel 1996, Bogogno si è subito imposto come uno dei campi più spettacolari d' Italia e d'altronde c'era da aspettarselo da un architetto come Robert von Hagge che non è certamente un "minimalista". Bisogna comunque dire che i suoi movimenti del terreno non sono mai inutili, sono fatti per variare le prospettive, rendere le buche più difficili e nello stesso tempo isolarle una dall'altra quando il terreno è particolarmente piatto. L'impatto visuale è un altro degli elementi molto importanti per von Hagge e qui a Bogogno rivela un aspetto quasi scozzese... Ma siamo in Italia, culla del teatro: lo sfondo delle Alpi e del Monte Rosa è stato valorizzato al massimo nel disegno del percorso. I giocatori avranno ampi spazi per muoversi ma dovranno stare attenti perchè non è sempre facile interpretarne le difficoltà. Bisogna avere i nervi saldi e un buon mestiere per tenere sulla distanza e preservare un buono score. Il "del Conte" unisce come l'altro percorso "Bonora" nove buche della prima realizzazione e nove buche più recenti.

Opened in 1996, Bogogno immediately became established as one of the most spectacular courses in Italy. This was only to be expected from course architect Robert von Hagge, who is hardly known for dabbling with "minimalism". It should be said, though, that the way he shapes a course is never gratuitous and that any shifting of earth is done to add variety, throw in a difficulty or two or isolate holes when the land is flat. The visual aspect is also very important and the topography this creates gives the course an almost Scottish flavour. But here we are in Italy, the land of theatre: the backdrop of the Alps and Monte Rosa is highlighted by the course's graphic beauty. The actors here will find wide open spaces which are fun to play in but not always easy to perform well with. You will need a strong nerve and good experience to last the course and keep your score down. Like its neighbour "Bonora", this "Conte" course combines nine holes from the original course with nine new holes.

Circolo Golf Bogogno — 1996

Via S. Isidoro 1
I - 28010 BOGOGNO (NO)

Office	Segreteria	(39) 0322 863 794
Pro shop	Pro shop	(39) 0322 863 339
Fax	Fax	(39) 0322 863 798
Web	www.golfbogogno.it	
Situation	Localita'	

Novara (pop. 102 037), 30 km
Milano (pop. 1 300 977), 66 km

Annual closure	Chiusura annuale	no
Weekly closure	Chiusura settimanale	monday

Fees main season Tariffe alta stagione	Week days Settimana	We/Bank holidays Feriale/Festivo
18 holes		
Individual Individuale	62 €	80 €
Couple Coppia	124 €	160 €
Caddy Caddy		21 €
Electric Trolley Carello elettrico		10 €
Buggy Car		36 €
Clubs Bastoni		18 €

Credit cards Carte di credito VISA - DC - CartaSì

Access Itinerario : A4 Milano-Torino, Exit (Uscita) Novara. Then S229 → Borgomanero. About 29 km, turn right → Cressa. 800 m turn left to Bogogno.
Map 1 on page 932 Carta 1 Pagina 932

Golf course PERCORSO — 17/20

Site	Paesaggio	
Maintenance	Manutenzione	
Architect	Architetto	Robert von Hagge
Type	Tipologia	country, forest
Relief	Relievo terreno	
Water in play	Acqua in gioco	
Exp. to wind	Esposto al vento	
Trees in play	Alberi in gioco	

Scorecard Carta-score	Chp. Camp.	Mens Uomini	Ladies Donne
Length Lunghezza	6485	5755	4947
Par	72	72	72
Slope system	—	—	—

Advised golfing ability Livello di gioco consigliato — 0 12 24 36
Hcp required Handicap richiesto 34

Club house & amenities CLUB HOUSE E SERVIZI — 8/10

Pro shop	Pro shop	
Driving range	Campo pratica	
Sheltered	coperto	8 mats
On grass	in erba	yes
Putting-green	Putting-green	yes
Pitching-green	Green-pratica	yes

Hotel facilities ALBERGHI — 7/10

HOTELS ALBERGHI

San Rocco, 74 rooms, D 238 € — Orta San Giulio
Tel (39) 0322 911 977, Fax (39) 0322 911 964 — 20 km

Residence Isotta, 16 rooms, D 62 € — Veruno
Tel (39) 0322 830 502, Fax (39) 0322 830 708 — 3 km

Golf Hotel Castelconturbia — Agrate Conturbia
19 rooms, D 93 € — 3 km
Tel (39) 0322 832 337, Fax (39) 0322 832 428

RESTAURANTS RISTORANTE

Pinocchio, — Borgomanero
Tel (39) 0322 82 273 — 6 km

Il Bersagliere — Borgomanero
Tel (39) 0322 82 277 — 6 km

BOLOGNA

13 | 7 | 7

Bologna, da secoli punto di ritrovo per gli studenti di tutto il mondo, non è una delle città italiane di maggior attrazione turistica anche se non scarseggia di monumenti e musei importanti. E' anche uno dei centri più significativi per l'enogastronomia del paese e se si aggiunge la sua attività industriale e quella della vicina Modena c'è da chiedersi come mai questa regione non sia più ricca di percorsi di golf. Aperto da più di 40 anni, questo percorso è stato disegnato da Henry Cotton e John Harris su di un terreno ondulato ai piedi degli Appennini. Il suo aspetto generale ricorda i percorsi britannici dell'interno con i greens ben difesi dai bunkers, ma senza un disegno particolarmente originale. Non si verrà qui per vedere paesaggi mozzafiato ma, il giusto grado di difficoltà rende il percorso piacevole per la grande maggioranza dei giocatori. Soltanto ai migliori mancherà il sapore della sfida più dura.

For centuries, Bologna has been one of the top cities for students, and although not one of Italy's leading tourist destinations, there is no shortage of significant landmarks and museums. It is also one the country's top areas for food and drink. If we add to this the region's industrial activity and that of the neighbouring city of Modena, then the scarcity of golf courses might come as something of a surprise. Opened some forty years ago, this course was laid out by Henry Cotton and John Harris over rolling terrain at the foot of the Apennines. Its overall shape is reminiscent of British inland courses, with greens well protected by bunkers and nothing particularly original about the layout as a whole. You certainly wouldn't come here just for thrills or striking visual beauty, but the moderation in the layout of hazards makes this a pleasant course for almost every player. Only the very best might rue the absence of a tougher challenge.

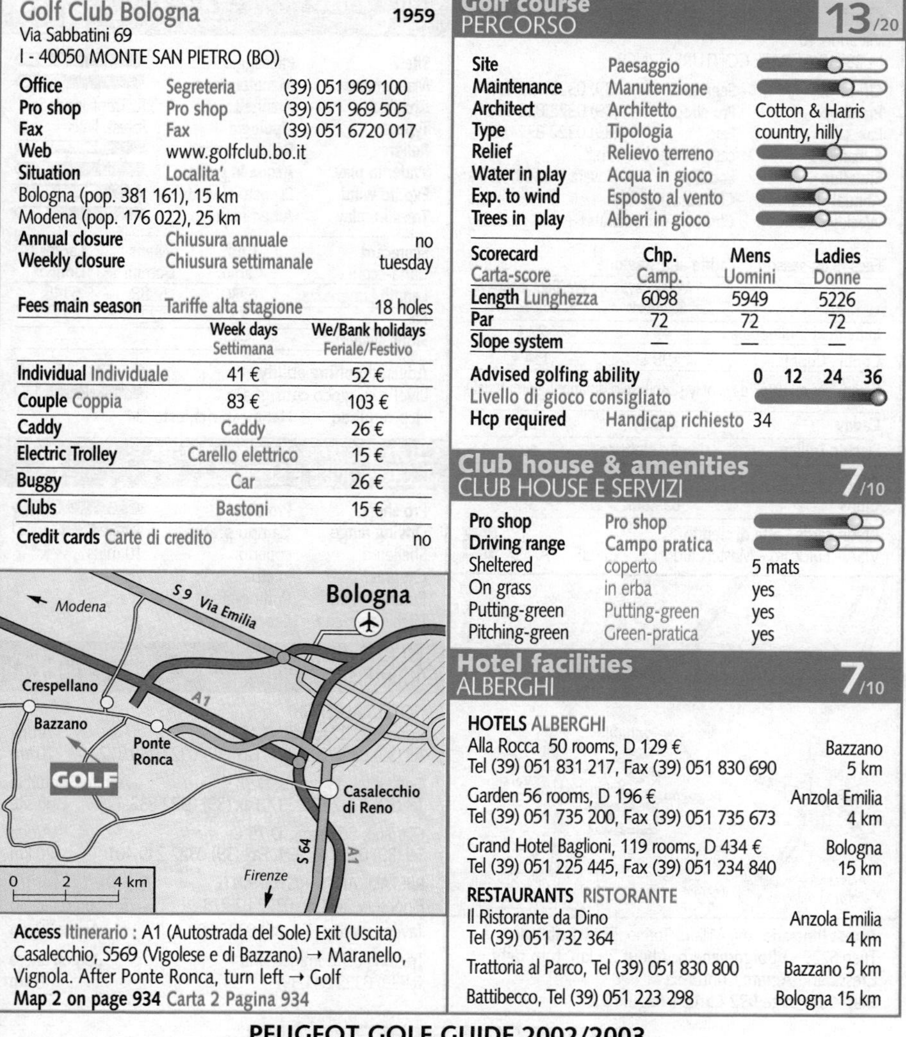

Golf Club Bologna — 1959

Via Sabbatini 69
I - 40050 MONTE SAN PIETRO (BO)

Office	Segreteria	(39) 051 969 100
Pro shop	Pro shop	(39) 051 969 505
Fax	Fax	(39) 051 6720 017
Web	www.golfclub.bo.it	
Situation	Localita'	

Bologna (pop. 381 161), 15 km
Modena (pop. 176 022), 25 km

Annual closure	Chiusura annuale	no
Weekly closure	Chiusura settimanale	tuesday

Fees main season Tariffe alta stagione		18 holes
	Week days Settimana	**We/Bank holidays** Feriale/Festivo
Individual Individuale	41 €	52 €
Couple Coppia	83 €	103 €
Caddy	Caddy	26 €
Electric Trolley	Carello elettrico	15 €
Buggy	Car	26 €
Clubs	Bastoni	15 €
Credit cards Carte di credito		no

Access Itinerario : A1 (Autostrada del Sole) Exit (Uscita) Casalecchio, S569 (Vigolese e di Bazzano) → Maranello, Vignola. After Ponte Ronca, turn left → Golf
Map 2 on page 934 Carta 2 Pagina 934

Golf course — PERCORSO — 13/20

Site	Paesaggio	
Maintenance	Manutenzione	
Architect	Architetto	Cotton & Harris
Type	Tipologia	country, hilly
Relief	Relievo terreno	
Water in play	Acqua in gioco	
Exp. to wind	Esposto al vento	
Trees in play	Alberi in gioco	

Scorecard Carta-score	**Chp.** Camp.	**Mens** Uomini	**Ladies** Donne
Length Lunghezza	6098	5949	5226
Par	72	72	72
Slope system	—	—	—

Advised golfing ability Livello di gioco consigliato — 0 12 24 36
Hcp required Handicap richiesto 34

Club house & amenities — CLUB HOUSE E SERVIZI — 7/10

Pro shop	Pro shop	
Driving range	Campo pratica	
Sheltered	coperto	5 mats
On grass	in erba	yes
Putting-green	Putting-green	yes
Pitching-green	Green-pratica	yes

Hotel facilities — ALBERGHI — 7/10

HOTELS ALBERGHI

Alla Rocca 50 rooms, D 129 € — Bazzano 5 km
Tel (39) 051 831 217, Fax (39) 051 830 690

Garden 56 rooms, D 196 € — Anzola Emilia 4 km
Tel (39) 051 735 200, Fax (39) 051 735 673

Grand Hotel Baglioni, 119 rooms, D 434 € — Bologna 15 km
Tel (39) 051 225 445, Fax (39) 051 234 840

RESTAURANTS RISTORANTE

Il Ristorante da Dino — Anzola Emilia 4 km
Tel (39) 051 732 364

Trattoria al Parco, Tel (39) 051 830 800 — Bazzano 5 km

Battibecco, Tel (39) 051 223 298 — Bologna 15 km

CASTELCONTURBIA Giallo+Azzurro

18 | 8 | 8

Anche se i tre percorsi di 9 buche sono intercambiabili tra loro per fare percorsi differenti, è il tracciato "blu e giallo" quello che è stato scelto per l'Open d'Italia dispuato qui nel 1991 e nel 1998. La firma di Robert Trent Jones si riconosce ovunque e non solo per i bunkers frastagliati. L'aspetto strategico qui è particolarmente importante e bisogna stare attenti alla larghezza ingannevole dei fairways, anche se, c'è sempre una parte ideale da dove attaccare meglio i greens che per la verità sono grandi ma con dislivelli e pendenze spesso diaboliche. Il gioco qui consiste sia nel cercare di evitare gli errori giocando in difesa che nell' attaccare con decisione. Castelconturbia richiede prima molta riflessione e dopo la capacità di metterla in atto: i giocatori inesperti hanno la vita difficile! Il percorso si snoda su un pendio senza rilievi particolari ma alcuni greens sopraelevati richiedono un'attenzione speciale. E' un complesso superbo impossibile da ignorare.

Although the three 9 hole courses can be combined to produce different layouts, the blue and yellow courses were the two chosen for the Italian Open in 1991 and 1998. The hallmark of Robert Trent Jones is omnipresent, and not only in the jagged sand traps. The strategic aspect is particularly important, and watch out for the deceiving width of fairways. Remember, too, that there is always the right side from which to attack greens in the best position, especially since the greens in question are pretty huge with diabolical slopes and breaks. Golf here consists in cutting out mistakes and in stopping short of all-out attack. Castelconturbia requires a lot of thought and the ability to turn thought into deed, so inexperienced players will find it hard going. The course is on the flat side, although some of the raised greens require special care. A superb resort, not to be missed.

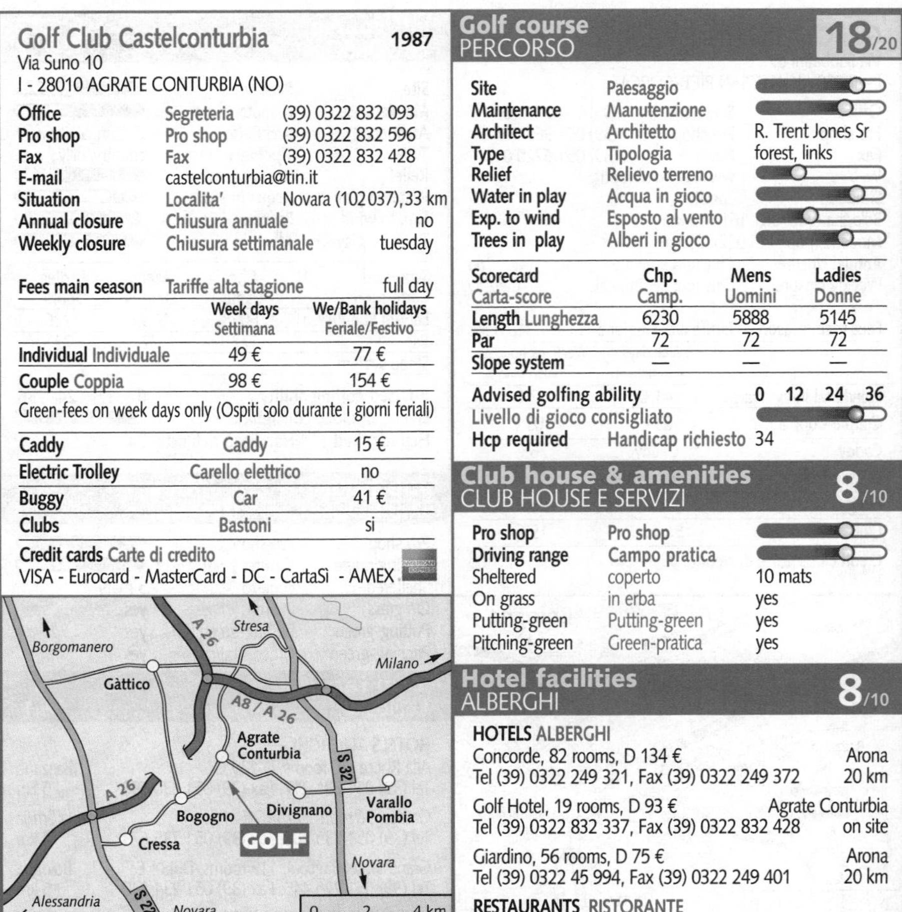

Golf Club Castelconturbia 1987

Via Suno 10
I - 28010 AGRATE CONTURBIA (NO)

Office	Segreteria	(39) 0322 832 093
Pro shop	Pro shop	(39) 0322 832 596
Fax	Fax	(39) 0322 832 428
E-mail	castelconturbia@tin.it	
Situation	Localita'	Novara (102 037), 33 km
Annual closure	Chiusura annuale	no
Weekly closure	Chiusura settimanale	tuesday

Fees main season Tariffe alta stagione		full day
	Week days Settimana	**We/Bank holidays** Feriale/Festivo
Individual Individuale	49 €	77 €
Couple Coppia	98 €	154 €

Green-fees on week days only (Ospiti solo durante i giorni feriali)

Caddy	Caddy	15 €
Electric Trolley	Carello elettrico	no
Buggy	Car	41 €
Clubs	Bastoni	si

Credit cards Carte di credito
VISA - Eurocard - MasterCard - DC - CartaSì - AMEX

Access Itinerario : A4 Milano-Torino, Exit (Uscita) Novara. Then S229 → Borgomanero. About 29 km, turn right → Cressa and Agrate Conturbia.
Map 1 on page 932 Carta 1 Pagina 932

Golf course PERCORSO 18/20

Site	Paesaggio	
Maintenance	Manutenzione	
Architect	Architetto	R. Trent Jones Sr
Type	Tipologia	forest, links
Relief	Relievo terreno	
Water in play	Acqua in gioco	
Exp. to wind	Esposto al vento	
Trees in play	Alberi in gioco	

Scorecard Carta-score	**Chp.** Camp.	**Mens** Uomini	**Ladies** Donne
Length Lunghezza	6230	5888	5145
Par	72	72	72
Slope system	—	—	—

Advised golfing ability Livello di gioco consigliato — 0 12 24 36
Hcp required Handicap richiesto 34

Club house & amenities CLUB HOUSE E SERVIZI 8/10

Pro shop	Pro shop	
Driving range	Campo pratica	
Sheltered	coperto	10 mats
On grass	in erba	yes
Putting-green	Putting-green	yes
Pitching-green	Green-pratica	yes

Hotel facilities ALBERGHI 8/10

HOTELS ALBERGHI

Concorde, 82 rooms, D 134 € — Arona
Tel (39) 0322 249 321, Fax (39) 0322 249 372 — 20 km

Golf Hotel, 19 rooms, D 93 € — Agrate Conturbia
Tel (39) 0322 832 337, Fax (39) 0322 832 428 — on site

Giardino, 56 rooms, D 75 € — Arona
Tel (39) 0322 45 994, Fax (39) 0322 249 401 — 20 km

RESTAURANTS RISTORANTE

Pinocchio, Tel (39) 0322 82 273 — Borgomanero

Taverna Pittore, Tel (39) 0322 293 366 — Arona 20 km

Trattoria dei Commercianti — Borgomanero
Tel(39) 0322 841 392 — 6 km

CASTELGANDOLFO

15 | 7 | 7

Questo piccolo paese è famoso per essere la residenza estiva del Papa, in un'antica regione vulcanica, dove il clima è particolarmente mite. E' stata in passato una zona molto importante, conosciuta con il nome di Alba Longa, che la leggenda narra sia stata fondata da Enea e che si sia poi opposta a Roma nella guerra tra Orazi e Curiazi. Questo percorso è l'ideale per un match-play, perchè qui Robert Trent Jones non ha risparmiato le sue insidie, soprattutto quelle di un grande lago che entra in gioco pericolosamente in diverse buche. In più in questo paesaggio di pini marittimi e olivi che addolciscono il rigore del paesaggio e quello del sole, ritroverete i soliti difficili bunkers e i greens a volte indecifrabili dell'architetto americano. Per rilassarsi la club-house è veramente molto piacevole in un'antica villa del XVII secolo, ben restaurata, que domina su tutto il percorso.

This little town is known for being the Pope's summer residence in a formerly volcanic region with a warm, balmy climate. It is importantly the site of Alba Longa which, according to legend was founded by Aeneas and then opposed Rome in the fighting with the Horatii and the Curiatii. So this layout is ideal for head-to-head match-play, as there is no shortage of traps spread around the course by Robert Trent Jones, especially a lake which comes into play most dangerously on several holes. Otherwise, you find the usual bunkers and often hard-to-read greens favoured by the American architect in a landscape of maritime pines and olive trees, which temper the course and the sunshine too. For relaxation after your round, the club-house is a real treat, a well-restored former 17th century patrician villa which overlooks the whole course.

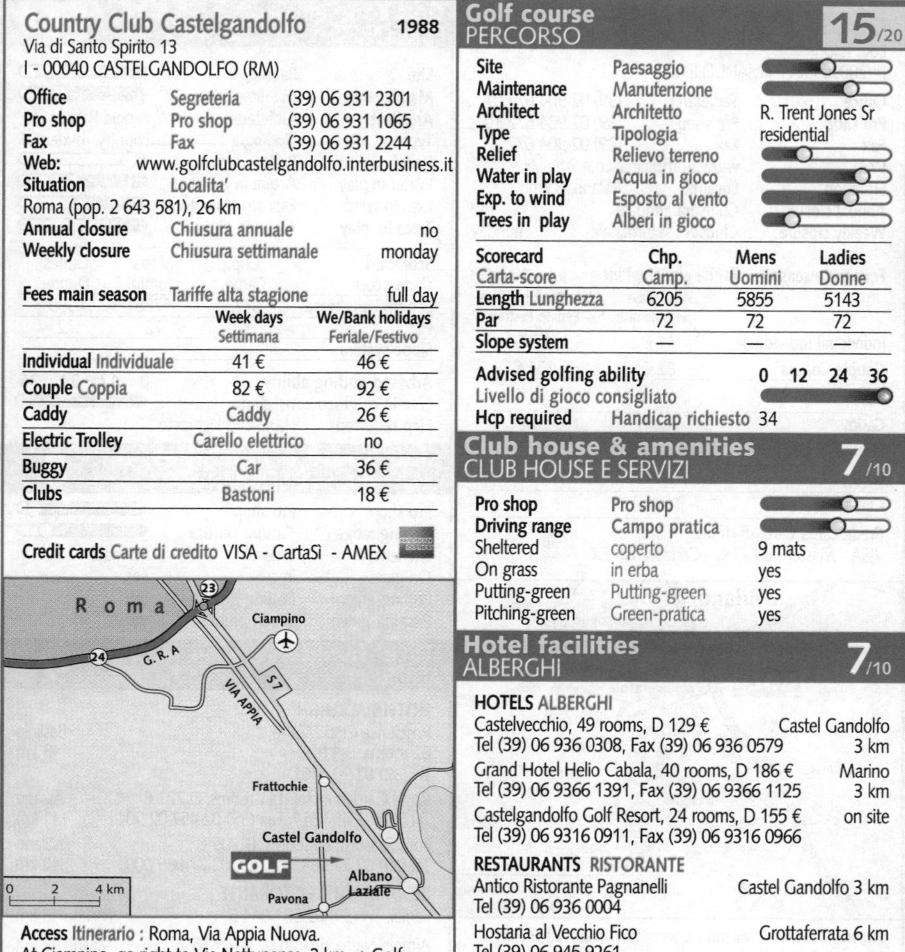

Country Club Castelgandolfo **1988**
Via di Santo Spirito 13
I - 00040 CASTELGANDOLFO (RM)

Office	Segreteria	(39) 06 931 2301
Pro shop	Pro shop	(39) 06 931 1065
Fax	Fax	(39) 06 931 2244
Web:		www.golfclubcastelgandolfo.interbusiness.it
Situation	Localita'	
Roma (pop. 2 643 581), 26 km		
Annual closure	Chiusura annuale	no
Weekly closure	Chiusura settimanale	monday

Fees main season Tariffe alta stagione	**Week days** Settimana	full day **We/Bank holidays** Feriale/Festivo
Individual Individuale	41 €	46 €
Couple Coppia	82 €	92 €
Caddy Caddy		26 €
Electric Trolley Carello elettrico		no
Buggy Car		36 €
Clubs Bastoni		18 €

Credit cards Carte di credito VISA - CartaSì - AMEX

Access Itinerario : Roma, Via Appia Nuova.
At Ciampino, go right to Via Nettunense. 2 km → Golf.
Map 3 on page 937 Carta 3 Pagina 937

Golf course PERCORSO — 15/20

Site	Paesaggio	
Maintenance	Manutenzione	
Architect	Architetto	R. Trent Jones Sr
Type	Tipologia	residential
Relief	Relievo terreno	
Water in play	Acqua in gioco	
Exp. to wind	Esposto al vento	
Trees in play	Alberi in gioco	

Scorecard Carta-score	**Chp.** Camp.	**Mens** Uomini	**Ladies** Donne
Length Lunghezza	6205	5855	5143
Par	72	72	72
Slope system	—	—	—

Advised golfing ability 0 12 24 36
Livello di gioco consigliato
Hcp required Handicap richiesto 34

Club house & amenities CLUB HOUSE E SERVIZI — 7/10

Pro shop	Pro shop	
Driving range	Campo pratica	
Sheltered	coperto	9 mats
On grass	in erba	yes
Putting-green	Putting-green	yes
Pitching-green	Green-pratica	yes

Hotel facilities ALBERGHI — 7/10

HOTELS ALBERGHI

Castelvecchio, 49 rooms, D 129 € — Castel Gandolfo
Tel (39) 06 936 0308, Fax (39) 06 936 0579 — 3 km

Grand Hotel Helio Cabala, 40 rooms, D 186 € — Marino
Tel (39) 06 9366 1391, Fax (39) 06 9366 1125 — 3 km

Castelgandolfo Golf Resort, 24 rooms, D 155 € — on site
Tel (39) 06 9316 0911, Fax (39) 06 9316 0966

RESTAURANTS RISTORANTE

Antico Ristorante Pagnanelli — Castel Gandolfo 3 km
Tel (39) 06 936 0004

Hostaria al Vecchio Fico — Grottaferrata 6 km
Tel (39) 06 945 9261

Da Mario - La Cavola d'Oro — Grottaferrata 8 km
Tel (39) 06 9431 5755

CASTELLO DI TOLCINASCO

14 | 8 | 7

Per i grandi giocatori che si sono messi a disegnare campi da golf, la chiave del successo è sempre stata la qualità dei loro ingegneri ed architetti. Gary Player ha imparato dalla cattiva esperienza e così Jack Nicklaus che non sempre ha firmato opere ben riuscite. Anche Arnold Palmer ha avuto dei periodi incerti ma il Castello di Tolcinasco fa parte delle sue opere di buona qualità pur non essendo eccezionale. Questo terreno molto aperto a sud di Milano si prestava per un tracciato all'americana che comprende 3 percorsi di 9 buche intercambiabili tra loro, dove grossi bunkers e ostacoli d'acqua costituiscono la maggior parte delle difficoltà, obbligando a giocare un golf molto preciso. Impegnativo dai tees più arretrati, questo percorso (un po' artificiale) diventa nettamente più facile dalle partenze avanzate, dimostrando che si può tener conto di tutti i livelli di gioco anche se si vuole disegnare un percorso da campionato. I dilettanti medi si divertiranno molto qui, anche con lo score in tasca.

For the game's top players who have moved into course design, the key to success has always been the excellence of their engineers and architects. Gary Player learnt from experience, and so has Jack Nicklaus, whose courses have not always been top rate. Arnold Palmer has had a few patchy periods as well, but Castello di Tolcinasco is a layout of high, not to say outstanding quality. This rather open terrain to the south of Milan was just perfect for an American-style layout. It features now three 9-hole courses, where the majority of hazards are huge sand traps and water, which call for accurate target golf. Tough from the back tees, this course (a little artificial, it might be said) becomes a little more human the further forward you move, which just goes to show that you can take account of all levels of playing ability yet still design a good tournament course. Whatever, average mid-handicappers will have a lot of fun here, even if they count their score.

Castello di Tolcinasco G & CC — 1993

Loc. Tolcinasco
I - 20090 PIEVE EMANUELE (MI)

Office	Segreteria	(39) 02 904 672 01
Pro shop	Pro shop	(39) 02 904 672 10
Fax	Fax	(39) 02 904 672 26
Web	www.golftolcinasco.it	
Situation	Localita'	Milano, 8 km
Annual closure	Chiusura annuale	no
Weekly closure	Chiusura settimanale	monday

956

Fees main season Tariffe alta stagione	Week days Settimana	We/Bank holidays Feriale/Festivo
	18 holes	
Individual Individuale	41 €	62 €
Couple Coppia	82 €	124 €

Softspikes only

Caddy	Caddy	26 €
Electric Trolley	Carello elettrico	no
Buggy	Car	31 €
Clubs	Bastoni	no

Credit cards Carte di credito
VISA - MasterCard - DC - CartaSì - AMEX

Access Itinerario : Milano Duomo, Via Torino, C° di Porto Ticinese, C° San Gottardo, straight in Via dei Missaglia. At traffic lights go left. 3 km, Castello di Tolcinasco.
Map 1 on page 933 Carta 1 Pagina 933

Golf course PERCORSO — 14/20

Site	Paesaggio	
Maintenance	Manutenzione	
Architect	Architetto	Arnold Palmer
Type	Tipologia	country, residential
Relief	Relievo terreno	
Water in play	Acqua in gioco	
Exp. to wind	Esposto al vento	
Trees in play	Alberi in gioco	

Scorecard Carta-score	Chp. Camp.	Mens Uomini	Ladies Donne
Length Lunghezza	6322	5788	4999
Par	72	72	72
Slope system	—	—	—

Advised golfing ability Livello di gioco consigliato — 0 12 24 36
Hcp required Handicap richiesto

Club house & amenities CLUB HOUSE E SERVIZI — 8/10

Pro shop	Pro shop	
Driving range	Campo pratica	
Sheltered	coperto	15 mats
On grass	in erba	yes
Putting-green	Putting-green	yes
Pitching-green	Green-pratica	yes

Hotel facilities ALBERGHI — 7/10

HOTELS ALBERGHI

Residence Club Milano 62 rooms, D 114 € Tel (39) 02 907 461	Basiglio 3 km
Royal Garden Hotel, 111 rooms, D 222 € Tel (39) 02 457 811, Fax (39) 02 457 02 901	Assago 11 km
Four Seasons, 89 rooms, D 705 € Tel (39) 02 77 088, Fax (39) 02 77 085 000	Milano 12 km

RESTAURANTS RISTORANTE

Sadler, Tel (39) 02 581 044 51	Milano 13 km
Aimo e Nadia, Tel(39) 02 416 886	Milano 12 km
Alfredo - Gran San Bernardo Tel (39) 02 331 9000	Milano 10 km

CERVIA

13 | 6 | 9

Questa parte della Costa Adriatica è una delle più affollate e più divertenti in assoluto. La fama di Cesenatico, Riccione e Milano Marittima ha varcato le frontiere e questo percorso è nato come ulteriore attrazione per coloro che amano le vacanze sportive. Non bisogna poi dimenticare la vicinanza con Ravenna, i suoi monumenti e i suoi famosi mosaici che figurano tra i tesori mondiali. Tracciato su un terreno piatto, tra i pini e sulle dune sabbiose, il percorso disegnato da Marco Croze riprende i tratti tipici dei links ma con un vago sapore americano che ne elimina l'aspetto selvaggio dei percorsi scozzesi. L'architetto ha apparentemente voluto aggiungere un tocco di "italianità", una sorta di eleganza nel disegno, a volte persino un po' eccessiva. Solo il vento può inasprire la sfida offerta ai giocatori. Detto questo, Cervia resta un percorso molto piacevole sul quale giocare, perchè gli ostacoli pur essendo sempre in gioco non sono mai scoraggianti nè insormontabili.

This section of the Adriatic coast is one of the most popular and entertaining (great fun to be had) along the whole Mediterranean basin. The reputation of Cesenatico, Riccione and especially Milano Marittima has spread abroad and this course should logically be an extra attraction for people who prefer the more sporting style of holiday. Let's not forget either nearby Ravenna, whose monuments and mosaics feature amongst the world's treasures. Spread over flat terrain amidst both pine trees and sandy dunes, this Marco Croze layout has some of the features of a real links course but also a slight American flavour, but you won't find the raw brutality of a Scottish links. The architect has apparently looked to add a little "Italian touch", a sort of elegance of design which sometimes goes a little over the top. In this case, only the wind can stiffen the challenge. With this said, Cervia is a very pleasant course to play, especially since all the hazards are in play and are never dissuasive or insurmountable. The architect was asked to design a course that is fun for all to play and that is exactly what he did.

Adriatic Golf Club Cervia — 1985

Via Jelenia Gora 6
I - 48016 MILANO MARITTIMA (RA)

Office	Segreteria	(39) 0544 992 786
Pro shop	Pro shop	(39) 0544 993 788
Fax	Fax	(39) 0544 993 410
Web	www.golfcervia.com	
Situation	Localita'	

Ravenna (pop. 137 721), 22 km, Forlì (pop. 107 461), 28 km

Annual closure	Chiusura annuale	no
Weekly closure	Chiusura settimanale	monday

Fees main season Tariffe alta stagione		18 holes
	Week days Settimana	**We/Bank holidays** Feriale/Festivo
Individual Individuale	44 €	52 €
Couple Coppia	88 €	104 €
Caddy Caddy		on request, 21 €
Electric Trolley Carello elettrico		no
Buggy Car		28 €
Clubs Bastoni		13 €

Credit cards Carte di credito
VISA - Eurocard - MasterCard - DC - CartaSì - AMEX

Access Itinerario : A14 Bologna-Rimini. Exit (Uscita) Cesena. → Cervia, → Pineta and Milano Marittima. → Golf

Map 2 on page 934 Carta 2 Pagina 934

Golf course PERCORSO — 13/20

Site	Paesaggio	
Maintenance	Manutenzione	
Architect	Architetto	Marco Croze
Type	Tipologia	seaside course, parkland
Relief	Relievo terreno	
Water in play	Acqua in gioco	
Exp. to wind	Esposto al vento	
Trees in play	Alberi in gioco	

Scorecard Carta-score	**Chp.** Camp.	**Mens** Uomini	**Ladies** Donne
Length Lunghezza	6296	6029	5185
Par	72	72	72
Slope system	—	—	—

Advised golfing ability Livello di gioco consigliato — 0 12 24 36

Hcp required Handicap richiesto 34

Club house & amenities CLUB HOUSE E SERVIZI — 6/10

Pro shop	Pro shop	
Driving range	Campo pratica	
Sheltered	coperto	5 mats
On grass	in erba	yes
Putting-green	Putting-green	yes
Pitching-green	Green-pratica	yes

Hotel facilities ALBERGHI — 9/10

HOTELS ALBERGHI

Mare e Pineta, 170 rooms, D 181 € — Milano Marittima
Tel (39) 0544 992 262, Fax (39) 0544 992 739 — 500 m

Deanna Golf Hotel, 68 rooms, D 93 € — Milano Marittima
Tel (39) 0544 991 365, Fax (39) 0544 994 251 — 300 m

Grand Hotel Cervia, 56 rooms, D 253 € — Cervia
Tel (39) 0544 970 500, Fax (39) 0544 972 086 — 1 km

RESTAURANTS RISTORANTE

Al Caminetto, — Milano Marittima
Tel (39) 0544 994 479 — 500 m

Dal Marinio, Tel (39) 0544 975 479 — Milano Marittima 500 m

Al Teatro, Tel (39) 0544 716 39 — Cervia 1 km

COSMOPOLITAN

14 | 6 | 7

Un viaggio intelligente alla scoperta dell'Italia deve passare obbligatoriamente da Pisa per visitare la famosa Torre di marmo bianco ma anche i magnifici altri edifici della piazza del Duomo, con il Battistero, il Camposanto e ovviamente il Duomo, in stile puramente romanico. Scendendo verso Livorno, città portuale molto viva, si può fare una sosta al Cosmopolitan, un percorso aperto abbastanza di recente. E' stato disegnato da David Mezzacane su un terreno piatto e senza alberi e lo stile links era quindi sicuramente il migliore per dare carattere a questo percorso dove soltanto il posizionamento degli ostacoli d'acqua ha un leggero sapore americano. Nell'insieme il posto conserva un aspetto selvaggio del tutto inaspettato. E' abbastanza difficile giocarsi il proprio handicap soprattutto quando tira vento e ancor più se si gioca dalle partenze arretrate anche se la larghezza dei fairways e la buona dimensione dei greens perdonano gli errori dei giocatori inesperti.

A smart trip to discover the joys of Italy has to include a visit to Pisa to see the famous white marble bell-tower and the other fantastic buildings on the Piazza del Duomo, with the Battistero, Camposanto (closed cemetery), and of course the Duomo, all built primarily in pure Roman style. Driving down towards Livorno, a very lively harbour town, you can stop off at the recently opened Cosmopolitan course designed by David Mezzacane over flat and tree-less terrain. A links style was essential here to create some sort of lively addition to the open space, and only the introduction of a few water hazards gives this a slight American flavour. Despite everything, the whole course has retained an unexpected very natural appearance. Playing to your handicap here is a tall order, especially when the wind blows and even more so when playing from the back-tees. Yet the wide fairways and nicely-sized greens help forgive the shortcomings of inexperienced players.

Cosmopolitan Golf & Country Club 1993

Via Pisorno 60
56018 TIRRENIA (PI)

Office	Segreteria	(39) 050 33 633
Pro shop	Pro shop	(39) 050 384 002
Fax	Fax	(39) 050 384 707
Web	www.cosmopolitangolf.it	
Situation	Localita'	

Pisa (pop. 92 379), 18 km, Livorno (pop. 161 673), 11 km

Annual closure	Chiusura annuale	no
Weekly closure	Chiusura settimanale	monday

Fees main season Tariffe alta stagione		full day
	Week days Settimana	**We/Bank holidays** Feriale/Festivo
Individual Individuale	41 €	46 €
Couple Coppia	82 €	92 €
Caddy	Caddy	no
Electric Trolley	Carello elettrico	no
Buggy	Car	31 €
Clubs	Bastoni	13 €

Credit cards Carte di credito
VISA - Eurocard - MasterCard - DC - CartaSì - AMEX

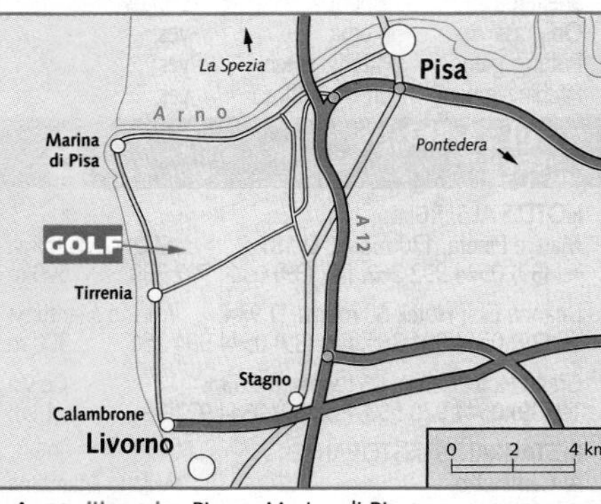

Access Itinerario : Pisa → Marina di Pisa.
→ Tirrenia and Livorno
Map 3 on page 936 Carta 3 Pagina 936

Golf course PERCORSO 14/20

Site	Paesaggio	
Maintenance	Manutenzione	
Architect	Architetto	David Mezzacane
Type	Tipologia	links
Relief	Relievo terreno	
Water in play	Acqua in gioco	
Exp. to wind	Esposto al vento	
Trees in play	Alberi in gioco	

Scorecard Carta-score	**Chp.** Camp.	**Mens** Uomini	**Ladies** Donne
Length Lunghezza	6291	5830	5125
Par	72	72	72
Slope system	—	—	—

Advised golfing ability Livello di gioco consigliato 0 12 24 36
Hcp required Handicap richiesto 34

Club house & amenities CLUB HOUSE E SERVIZI 6/10

Pro shop	Pro shop	
Driving range	Campo pratica	
Sheltered	coperto	no
On grass	in erba	yes
Putting-green	Putting-green	yes
Pitching-green	Green-pratica	yes

Hotel facilities ALBERGHI 7/10

HOTELS ALBERGHI

Grand Hotel Golf 77 rooms, D 163 € — Tirrenia
Tel (39) 050 37 545, Fax (39) 050 32 111

San Francesco, 25 rooms, D 145 € — Tirrenia
Tel (39) 050 33 572, Fax (39) 050 33 630 — 1 km

Europa Park Hotel, 13 rooms, D 77 € — Pisa
Tel (39) 050 500 732, Fax (39) 050 554 930 — 18 km

RESTAURANTS RISTORANTE

Dante e Ivana, Tel (39) 050 32 549 — Tirrenia 1 km

Al Ristoro dei Vecchi Macelli — Pisa
Tel (39) 050 20 424 — 18 km

A Casa Mia, Tel (39) 050 879 265 — Pisa 12 km

FIRENZE - UGOLINO

13	8	9

Il Circolo Golf Firenze aperto all'inizio del secolo si è insediato in questo luogo soltanto nel 1933. Disegnato dallo studio Blandford & Gannon è stato modificato in seguito da Piero Mancinelli. Il posto è particolarmente piacevole e dunque è garantita una bella giornata di golf. Si consiglia l'uso del golf cart ai giocatori non in perfetta forma fisica, perchè il terreno è molto mosso. Per i professionisti di oggi, l'Ugolino manca un poco di lunghezza ma resta un buon percorso di gara per i dilettanti tra i quali la precisione conta ben più che la forza bruta. Ci sono dei par 3 abbastanza lunghi ma anche una lunga serie di corti par 4 dove si è lecito pensare al birdie, senza peraltro riuscire a farne molti perchè i greens sono generalmente piccoli, ben disegnati e ben difesi. L'Ugolino non è certamente un esempio di modernità, ma merita una visita anche se un viaggio a Firenze, una delle città più belle al mondo, lascia poco tempo per lo sport. Vale la pena di provarlo ... insieme ad un bicchiere di Chianti.

The Circolo Golf Firenze (Florence Golf Club) is the oldest in Italy but the present course opened here only in 1933. Designed by Blandford & Gannon, it was subsequently altered by Piero Mancinelli. This is a very pleasant site with a great day's golfing assured. We would simply advise a buggy for players whose physical condition is not what it was, as the course is rather hilly. For today's professionals, Ugolino is doubtless a little short, but this is still an excellent course for amateur tournaments, where accuracy counts for much more than brute strength. The par 3s are rather long, but there is also an impressive group of short par 4s, where you might be tempted to think about birdies. Whether or not you make them remains in some doubt, as the greens are generally small, well contoured and well protected. Ugolino is by no means an example of modernity but it certainly deserves a visit, even if a trip to Florence, one of the world's finest cities, leaves little time for sport. Certainly worth a try... together, of course, with a glass of local Chianti wine.

Circolo Golf Ugolino — 1933

Via Chiantigiana 3
I - 50015 GRASSINA (FI)

Office	Segreteria	(39) 055 2301 009
Pro shop	Pro shop	(39) 055 2301 278
Fax	Fax	(39) 055 2301 141
E-mail	golf.ugolino@ntt.it	
Situation	Localita'	
Firenze (pop. 376 662), 12 km		
Annual closure	Chiusura annuale	no
Weekly closure	Chiusura settimanale	monday

Fees main season Tariffe alta stagione	Full day	
	Week days Settimana	**We/Bank holidays** Feriale/Festivo
Individual Individuale	57 €	72 €
Couple Coppia	114 €	144 €
Caddy	Caddy	no
Electric Trolley	Carello elettrico	no
Buggy	Car	36 €
Clubs	Bastoni	15 €

Credit cards Carte di credito VISA - Cartasì - AMEX

Access Itinerario : A1 Exit (Uscita) Firenze South (Sud). Turn right to Grassina then S222 (Chiantigiana). Golf 4 km on the left. **Map 3 on page 936** Carta 3 Pagina 936

Golf course PERCORSO — 13/20

Site	Paesaggio	
Maintenance	Manutenzione	
Architect	Architetto	Blandford & Gannon
Type	Tipologia	hilly
Relief	Relievo terreno	
Water in play	Acqua in gioco	
Exp. to wind	Esposto al vento	
Trees in play	Alberi in gioco	

Scorecard Carta-score	**Chp.** Camp.	**Mens** Uomini	**Ladies** Donne
Length Lunghezza	5800	5676	4994
Par	72	72	72
Slope system	—	—	—

Advised golfing ability 0 12 24 36
Livello di gioco consigliato
Hcp required Handicap richiesto 34

Club house & amenities CLUB HOUSE E SERVIZI — 8/10

Pro shop	Pro shop	
Driving range	Campo pratica	
Sheltered	coperto	12 mats
On grass	in erba	yes
Putting-green	Putting-green	yes
Pitching-green	Green-pratica	yes

Hotel facilities ALBERGHI — 9/10

HOTELS ALBERGHI

Poggio del Golf, 33 rooms, D 98 € — Grassina
Tel (39) 055 230 551, Fax (39) 055 230 1081 — 300 m

Brunelleschi, 89 rooms, D 289 € — Firenze
Tel (39) 055 27 370, Fax (39) 055 219 653 — 12 km

G. Hotel Villa Cora, 33 rooms, D 491 € — Firenze
Tel (39) 055 229 8451, Fax (39) 055 229 086 — 5 km

RESTAURANTS RISTORANTE

Enoteca Pinchiorri, Tel (39) 055 242 777 — Firenze 12 km
Il Padellino, Tel (39) 055 858 388 — Greve in Chianti 5 km
Cibreo, Tel(39) 055 234 1100 — Firenze 12 km

FRANCIACORTA

14 | 7 | 8

Il golf di Franciacorta si trova vicino al lago d'Iseo che anche se non è il più celebre dei grandi laghi italiani, merita di essere conosciuto per il suo aspetto selvaggio, così come merita una visita il Monte Isola che si trova in mezzo al lago e dal quale si gode un panorama superbo delle Alpi. Con il "Domaine Imperial" in Svizzera e Il Parco di Roma, questo percorso è uno dei rari esempi in Europa dello stile, spesso controverso (ma sempre fedele allo spirito del golf) di Pete Dye, che qui ha collaborato con Marco Croze, uno dei più prolifici architetti italiani. E' stato tracciato su un terreno mosso ma non troppo faticoso. Lo stile è decisamente americano con ostacoli d'acqua su circa la metà delle buche e con due greens in un'isola: ci si può scordare di arrivare a rotolo! Malgrado ciò i giocatori medi si potranno divertire molto perchè le difficoltà sono ben visibili e la strategia di gioco evidente.

The Golf de Franciacorta is situated close to Lake Iseo. This is not the most famous of the Italian "Great Lakes", but the wild scenery here is well worth seeing, as is the Monte Isola, located in the middle of the lake and offering superb views over the Alps. Along with the Domaine Impérial in Switzerland and Parco di Roma, this course is one of the rare examples in Europe of the often controversial style (but always true to the spirit of golf) of American designer Pete Dye, who here worked together with Marco Croze, one of the more prolific Italian course architects. The course is laid out on slightly hilly but never tiring terrain. The style is blatantly American, with water on almost half the holes and two island greens, so you can forget the bump and run shots. Despite this, average players can have a lot of fun, as all the difficulties are clear to see and game strategy is obvious.

Golf di Franciacorta — 1986

Loc. Castagnola
I - 25040 CORTE FRANCA (BS)

Office	Segreteria	(39) 030 984 167
Pro shop	Pro shop	(39) 030 9828 330
Fax	Fax	(39) 030 984 343
E-mail	franciacortagolfclub@libero.it	
Situation	Localita'	

Brescia (pop. 191 317), 28 km, Bergamo, 32 km

Annual closure	Chiusura annuale	no
Weekly closure	Chiusura settimanale	tuesday

Fees main season Tariffe alta stagione		18 holes
	Week days Settimana	**We/Bank holidays** Feriale/Festivo
Individual Individuale	36 €	52 €
Couple Coppia	72 €	104 €

Caddy	Caddy	no
Electric Trolley	Carello elettrico	no
Buggy	Car	31 €
Clubs	Bastoni	21 €

Credit cards Carte di credito VISA - Mastercard

Access Itinerario : A4 Milano-Venezia. Exit (Uscita) Rovato, turn left then right → Iseo. 6 km → golf on left hand side
Map 1 on page 933 Carta 1 Pagina 933

Golf course — PERCORSO — 14/20

Site	Paesaggio	
Maintenance	Manutenzione	
Architect	Architetto	Pete Dye Marco Croze
Type	Tipologia	country
Relief	Relievo terreno	
Water in play	Acqua in gioco	
Exp. to wind	Esposto al vento	
Trees in play	Alberi in gioco	

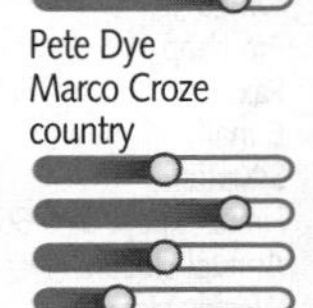

Scorecard Carta-score	**Chp.** Camp.	**Mens** Uomini	**Ladies** Donne
Length Lunghezza	5924	5762	5095
Par	72	72	72
Slope system	—	—	—

Advised golfing ability 0 12 24 36
Livello di gioco consigliato
Hcp required Handicap richiesto 34

Club house & amenities — CLUB HOUSE E SERVIZI — 7/10

Pro shop	Pro shop	
Driving range	Campo pratica	
Sheltered	coperto	4 mats
On grass	in erba	yes
Putting-green	Putting-green	yes
Pitching-green	Green-pratica	yes

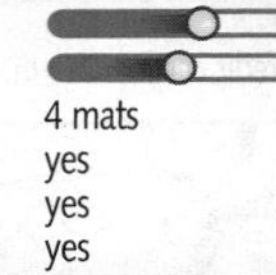

Hotel facilities — ALBERGHI — 8/10

HOTELS ALBERGHI

L'Albereta, 38 rooms, from D 238 € — Erbusco 9 km
Tel (39) 030 776 0550, Fax (39) 030 776 0573

Relais Franciacorta, 44 rooms, D 165 € — Corte Franca 3 km
Tel (39) 030 988 4234, Fax (39) 030 988 4224

Franciacorta Golf Hotel 43 rooms, D 114 € — Paratico 8 km
Tel (39) 035 913 333, Fax (39) 035 913 600

RESTAURANTS RISTORANTE

Gualtiero Marchesi (Albereta) — Erbusco 9 km
Tel (39) 030 7760 562

Santa Giulia, Tel (39) 030 9828 348 — Timoline 2 km

La Mongolfiera dei Sodi, Tel (39) 030 7268 303 — Erbusco

GARDAGOLF

15 | 8 | 8

Grazie alla protezione delle Dolomiti che mitigano il vento, il lago di Garda vanta un clima formidabile, particolarmente dolce d'inverno. Per la sua ubicazione appena sopra al lago, la sua vista spettacolare e la sua vicinanza a Brescia, Bergamo e Milano, Gardagolf ha fatto in fretta ad ottenere un grande successo, tanto che può essere ora difficile riuscire a giocare nel week-end. Ma questa regione ha tante altre attrattive per trascorrerci più giorni se non addirittura settimane. Disegnato dallo Studio Cotton, Penninck & Steel, con 9 buche piatte e 9 buche in collina è considerato difficile dai tees di campionato (uomini e donne), ma nessuno vi obbligherà a partire da lì. L'acqua entra in gioco su circa un terzo delle buche e i bunkers sia del fairway che dei greens sono stati piazzati intelligentemente. Qui non bisogna fare colpi particolari e i giocatori lunghi ne trarranno beneficio, tanto più che i greens non richiedono studi particolari essendo generalmente piatti. Un buon percorso in una bellissima regione.

Protected by the Dolomites, which cut out the wind, Lake Garda enjoys a wonderful climate which is surprisingly mild in winter. Located above the lake, spectacular in more ways than one and located close to Brescia, Bergamo and Milan, Gardagolf has rapidely become a popular venue and week-end green-fees can be hard to come by. Nonetheless, this region has appeal enough to spend several days or even weeks looking around. Designed by architects Cotton, Penninck & Steel, with nine flat holes and nine hilly numbers, the course is considered to be hard from the back tees (men and ladies) but there is no obligation to play from the tips. Water is in play on half a dozen holes and the green-side and fairway bunkers are cleverly located. There is no great need to work the ball in any direction, and straight-hitters should do well, especially as the greens have no hidden perils and are generally rather flat. A good course in a superb region.

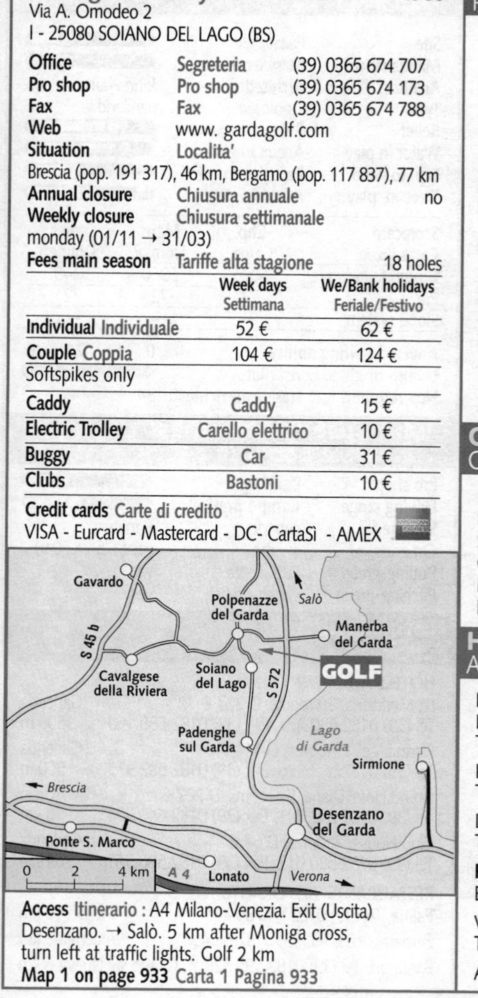

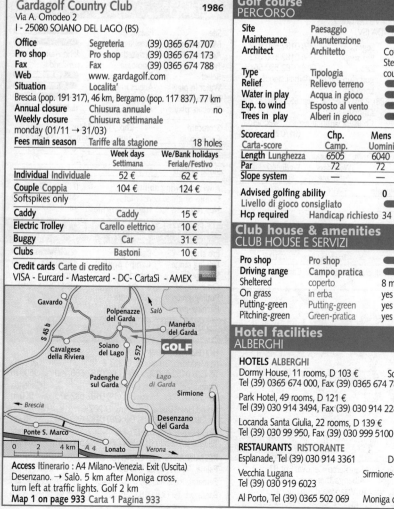

Gardagolf Country Club — 1986

Via A. Omodeo 2
I - 25080 SOIANO DEL LAGO (BS)

Office	Segreteria	(39) 0365 674 707
Pro shop	Pro shop	(39) 0365 674 173
Fax	Fax	(39) 0365 674 788
Web	www. gardagolf.com	
Situation	Localita'	

Brescia (pop. 191 317), 46 km, Bergamo (pop. 117 837), 77 km

Annual closure Chiusura annuale — no

Weekly closure Chiusura settimanale
monday (01/11 → 31/03)

Fees main season Tariffe alta stagione — 18 holes

	Week days Settimana	We/Bank holidays Feriale/Festivo
Individual Individuale	52 €	62 €
Couple Coppia	104 €	124 €

Softspikes only

Caddy	Caddy	15 €
Electric Trolley	Carello elettrico	10 €
Buggy	Car	31 €
Clubs	Bastoni	10 €

Credit cards Carte di credito
VISA - Eurcard - Mastercard - DC- CartaSì - AMEX

Access Itinerario : A4 Milano-Venezia. Exit (Uscita) Desenzano. → Salò. 5 km after Moniga cross, turn left at traffic lights. Golf 2 km

Map 1 on page 933 Carta 1 Pagina 933

Golf course PERCORSO — 15/20

Site	Paesaggio	
Maintenance	Manutenzione	
Architect	Architetto	Cotton, Pennink Steel & Partners
Type	Tipologia	country
Relief	Relievo terreno	
Water in play	Acqua in gioco	
Exp. to wind	Esposto al vento	
Trees in play	Alberi in gioco	

Scorecard Carta-score	Chp. Camp.	Mens Uomini	Ladies Donne
Length Lunghezza	6505	6040	5353
Par	72	72	72
Slope system	—	—	—

Advised golfing ability Livello di gioco consigliato — 0 12 24 36

Hcp required Handicap richiesto 34

Club house & amenities CLUB HOUSE E SERVIZI — 8/10

Pro shop	Pro shop	
Driving range	Campo pratica	
Sheltered	coperto	8 mats
On grass	in erba	yes
Putting-green	Putting-green	yes
Pitching-green	Green-pratica	yes

Hotel facilities ALBERGHI — 8/10

HOTELS ALBERGHI

Dormy House, 11 rooms, D 103 € — Soiano del Garda
Tel (39) 0365 674 000, Fax (39) 0365 674 788 — on site

Park Hotel, 49 rooms, D 121 € — Desenzano
Tel (39) 030 914 3494, Fax (39) 030 914 2280 — 5 km

Locanda Santa Giulia, 22 rooms, D 139 € — Padenghe
Tel (39) 030 99 950, Fax (39) 030 999 5100 — 3 km

RESTAURANTS RISTORANTE

Esplanade, Tel (39) 030 914 3361 — Desenzano 5 km

Vecchia Lugana — Sirmione-Lugana 16 km
Tel (39) 030 919 6023

Al Porto, Tel (39) 0365 502 069 — Moniga del Garda 5 km

GARLENDA

14 | 7 | 8

Questo percorso è nato dal desiderio di fare della Riviera italiana una sorta di Costa del Sol o piuttosto della Riviera francese così piena di campi da golf ma purtroppo questo progetto molto intelligente non è andato avanti. Garlenda è stato costruito sulle colline che dominano le stazioni balneari di Alassio e Albenga ed è un percorso abbastanza corto che non spaventa i giocatori mediocri. John Harris lo ha disegnato con gusto rispettando il paesaggio, da una parte all'altra del fiume Lerrone che attraversa la 13 un lungo par 3. Gli alberi sono di ostacolo in numerose buche e invitano i giocatori a compiere colpi ad effetto in numerose buche per avvicinarsi il più possibile ai greens, spesso di piccole dimensioni ma disegnati senza troppe difficoltà. Divertente per giocare con la famiglia e con gli amici anche di livello molto diverso, Garlenda non pretende di essere un grande percorso da campionato, ma offre una buona occasione per giocare in questa regione e trascorrere un piacevole soggiorno a "La Meridiana" (Relais-Châteaux) o nelle camere sopra il club house.

This course was born from the desire to make the Italian Riviera a match for the Spanish Costa Del Sol or even the French Riviera, where golf courses abound. Unfortunately, this clever project never quite made it and the development of tourism in Italy has never focused on golf. This course was built in the hills overlooking the resorts of Albenga and Alassio, and is short enough to avoid scaring off the average golfer. John Harris designed the lay-out with taste and good landscaping sense on either side of the river Lerrone, which crosses the 13th hole, a long par 3. Trees are a threat on many holes and sometimes invite the player to work the ball both ways in order to get as close as possible to the greens, which are often small but designed without too many difficulties. Fun to play with the family and friends, even of very different abilities, Garlenda does not claim to be a great championship course but offers a fine opportunity to play and even stay in this part of Italy, courtesy of the "La Meridiana" (Relais-Châteaux hotel) and rooms belonging to the club.

Golf Club Garlenda — 1965

Piazzetta Galleani - Via del Golf 7
I - 17033 GARLENDA (SV)

Office	Segreteria	(39) 0182 580 012
Pro shop	Pro shop	(39) 0182 580 012
Fax	Fax	(39) 0182 580 561
E-mail	golf.club.garlenda@mail.sirio.it	
Situation	Localita'	

Albenga (pop. 22 688), 8 km - Genova (pop. 659 754), 75 km

Annual closure	Chiusura annuale	no
Weekly closure	Chiusura settimanale	wednesday (01/09 → 30/06)

Fees main season Tariffe alta stagione — 18 holes

	Week days Settimana	We/Bank holidays Feriale/Festivo
Individual Individuale	41 €	67 €
Couple Coppia	82 €	134 €
Caddy	Caddy	18 €
Electric Trolley	Carello elettrico	5 €
Buggy	Car	31 €
Clubs	Bastoni	10 €

Credit cards Carte di credito VISA - DC - CartaSì

Access Itinerario : A10 San-Remo-Genova. Exit (Uscita) Albenga. Turn right → Albenga then right at turnabout under the motorway to Villanova d'Albenga and Garlenda. **Map 1 on page 932** Carta 1 Pagina 932

Golf course PERCORSO — 14/20

Site	Paesaggio	
Maintenance	Manutenzione	
Architect	Architetto	John Harris
Type	Tipologia	parkland
Relief	Relievo terreno	
Water in play	Acqua in gioco	
Exp. to wind	Esposto al vento	
Trees in play	Alberi in gioco	

Scorecard Carta-score	Chp. Camp.	Mens Uomini	Ladies Donne
Length Lunghezza	6095	5960	5240
Par	72	72	72
Slope system	—	—	—

Advised golfing ability Livello di gioco consigliato — 0 12 24 36

Hcp required Handicap richiesto 34

Club house & amenities CLUB HOUSE E SERVIZI — 7/10

Pro shop	Pro shop	
Driving range	Campo pratica	
Sheltered	coperto	8 mats
On grass	in erba	yes (1/5 → 30.9)
Putting-green	Putting-green	yes
Pitching-green	Green-pratica	yes

Hotel facilities ALBERGHI — 8/10

HOTELS ALBERGHI

La Meridiana, 30 rooms, D 227 € — Garlenda 500 m
Tel (39) 0182 580 271, Fax (39) 0182 580 150

Hermitage, 11 rooms, D 114 € — Garlenda 500 m
Tel (39) 0182 582 976, Fax (39) 0182 582 975

Grand Hotel Diana, 52 rooms, D 207 € — Alassio 10 km
Tel (39) 0182 642 701, Fax (39) 0182 640 304

Club House, 7 rooms, D 57 € — Garlenda on site
Tel (39) 0182 580 012, Fax (39) 0182 580 561

RESTAURANTS RISTORANTE

Palma, Tel (39) 0182 640 314 — Alassio 10 km
Pernambucco, Tel (39) 0182 53 458 — Albenga 8 km
Bar Sport, Tel (39) 0182 595 323 — Cisano sul Nueva 6 km

I ROVERI

17 | 7 | 7

Questa antica riserva di caccia era il luogo ideale per la costruzione di un ambizioso complesso golfistico alle porte di Torino dove gli alberi secolari avrebbero sia isolato le buche una dall'altra, che creato una barriera naturale alle ambizioni dei giocatori poco precisi. Qui ci sono 27 buche ma il terzo percorso è decisamente sottotono rispetto alle 18 buche da campionato disegnate da Trent Jones e quindi sono utili soprattutto ai principianti. Nel percorso ufficiale, a parte la lunghezza , si noterà il piazzamento molto strategico degli ostacoli d'acqua, nonchè la posizione e il disegno molto elaborato dei bunkers. Qui bisogna saper giocare tutti i colpi ma soprattutto fare traiettorie alte, "all'americana", perchè è molto raro poter attaccare i greens, molto ben difesi, facendo rotolare la palla. Una volta arrivati, le numerosissime pendenze possono dare notevoli problemi di putting. I Roveri è senza dubbio uno dei più bei percorsi d'Italia.

This former hunting estate was the ideal setting for building an ambitious golfing resort close to Turin. The age-old trees both demarcate and isolate the holes and form a natural barrier to the ambitions of wayward hitters. There are 27 holes here, although the par-3 course is a notch below the other two 9-hole layouts, probably to help the club's members who are just starting out. On the "championship" 18 hole course (designed by Trent Jones), yardage aside, you will notice the very strategic deployment of water and the very carefully plotted position and design of bunkers. You have to know how to hit it every way here, especially those US-style target golf shots, since you don't get much chance to roll the ball onto very well defended greens. Once there, the putting surfaces are nicely contoured and can pose a number of problems. I Roveri is definitely one of the very best courses in Italy.

I Roveri Golf Club — 1971

Rotta Cerbiatta 24
I - 10070 FIANO TORINESE (TO)

Office	Segreteria	(39) 011 923 5719
Pro shop	Pro shop	(39) 011 923 5223
Fax	Fax	(39) 011 923 5669
E-mail	roveri2000@tiscalinet.it	
Situation	Localita'	

Torino (pop. 903 705), 16 km

Annual closure	Chiusura annuale	no
Weekly closure	Chiusura settimanale	monday

Fees main season / Tariffe alta stagione	18 holes	
	Week days / Settimana	We/Bank holidays / Feriale/Festivo
Individual Individuale	52 €	72 €
Couple Coppia	104 €	144 €

Caddy	Caddy	yes
Electric Trolley	Carello elettrico	no
Buggy	Car	41 €
Clubs	Bastoni	no
Credit cards	Carte di credito	no

Access Itinerario : Milano to Torino, A4 - A45 Exit (Uscita) Venaria. → Lanzo. Golf to the left.
Map 1 on page 932 Carta 1 Pagina 932

Golf course — PERCORSO — 17/20

Site	Paesaggio	
Maintenance	Manutenzione	
Architect	Architetto	R. Trent Jones Sr
Type	Tipologia	forest, residential
Relief	Relievo terreno	
Water in play	Acqua in gioco	
Exp. to wind	Esposto al vento	
Trees in play	Alberi in gioco	

Scorecard / Carta-score	Chp. / Camp.	Mens / Uomini	Ladies / Donne
Length Lunghezza	6566	6218	5471
Par	72	72	72
Slope system	—	—	—

Advised golfing ability / Livello di gioco consigliato: 0 12 24 36
Hcp required Handicap richiesto 34

Club house & amenities — CLUB HOUSE E SERVIZI — 7/10

Pro shop	Pro shop	
Driving range	Campo pratica	
Sheltered	coperto	6 mats
On grass	in erba	yes
Putting-green	Putting-green	yes
Pitching-green	Green-pratica	yes

Hotel facilities — ALBERGHI — 7/10

HOTELS ALBERGHI

Jet Hotel, 79 rooms, D 145 € — Caselle Torinese
Tel (39) 011 991 3733, Fax (39) 011 996 1544 — 8 km

Hotel Atlantic, 110 rooms, D 165 € — Borgaro Torinese
Tel (39) 011 450 0055, Fax (39) 011 470 1783 — 13 km

Gotha Hotel, 44 rooms, D 108 € — Cirié
Tel (39) 011 921 2059, Fax (39) 011 920 3661 — 4 km

RESTAURANTS RISTORANTE

Dolce Stil Novo, Tel (39) 011 921 1110 — Cirié 7 km
Mario, Tel (39) 011 920 3490 — Cirié 7 km
Antica Zecca, Tel (39) 011 996 1403 — Caselle Torinese 8 km
Balbo, Tel (39) 011 839 5775 — Torino 16 km

IS ARENAS

17 | 2 | 6

Il club-house e le strutture erano ancora provvisori al momento della nostra visita che ha ampiamente meritato la deviazione, come anche tutto questo tratto di costa occidentale che conserva tracce dell'epoca preistorica. A parte Oristano, dalla quale il golf è molto vicino, si può dire che non sia veramente distante da nessuna delle altre grandi città, ma da queste parti, come in Corsica, le distanze si misurano con il tempo piuttosto che con la distanza! I promotori di Is Arenas hanno scelto un terreno non particolarmente mosso dove la costa si alterna tra dune sabbiose, pineta e macchia mediterranea. Gli ostacoli d'acqua sono parecchi e pericolosi ed oltre ad essere un elemento fondamentale del gioco offrono una gradevole sensazione di freschezza; l'intenso profumo e il miscuglio di colori della vegetazione sono una piacevolezza in più da aggiungere a quella del gioco. Questo percorso maestoso che porta la firma di von Hagge, Baril e Smelek esige intelligenza nella strategia di gioco, esperienza nel vento (e qui ce n'è sovente) e qualche finezza; in poche parole è richiesto di giocare veramente a golf!

The club-house and facilities were still only temporary affairs when we visited, but the course is well worth a visit, as is the whole of this west coast, which still bears the signs of successive invasions dating from prehistoric times. From nearby Oristano, you are never far from anywhere, but as in Corsica, a journey here is measured in hours, not in miles. The promoters of Is Arenas have chosen a flattish location, whose seaside features are illustrated by a few sand-dunes alternating with forest and scrub-land. The very many and often dangerous water hazards are naturally a part of the course but also provide a refreshing touch, at least from a visual angle. Added to the scents and colours of the flowers and plant-life, they make your round of golf all the more enjoyable. This is a majestic and challenging layout designed by von Hagge, Baril and Smelek. It requires clever thinking, some experience of playing in the wind (it is often very breezy), some down-to-earth course management with regards to the state of your own game and a touch of finesse. This is a course that simply asks you to "play golf".

Is Arenas Golf & Country Club 2000

Loc. Pineta Is Arenas
I - 09070 NARBOLIA (OR)

Office	Segreteria	(39) 0783 52 108
Pro shop	Pro shop	(39) 0783 52 108
Fax	Fax	(39) 0783 52 235
Web	www.isarenas.it	
Situation	Localita'	

Oristano (pop. 33 007), 18 km

Annual closure	Chiusura annuale	no
Weekly closure	Chiusura settimanale	no

Fees main season Tariffe alta stagione	18 holes	
	Week days Settimana	**We/Bank holidays** Feriale/Festivo
Individual Individuale	52 €	67 €
Couple Coppia	104 €	134 €
Caddy	Caddy	no
Electric Trolley	Carello elettrico	no
Buggy	Car	36 €
Clubs	Bastoni	15 €

Credit cards Carte di credito
VISA - Eurocard - MasterCard - DC - JCB

Access Itinerario : Cagliari ss 131 → Sassari. 104 km → Tramatza. San Vero Milis ss 292 → Cuglieri. Km 113,400 turn left on a small road → "Centro Operativo Is Arenas". Follow signs to golf. **Map 4 on page 939** Carta 4 Pagina 939

Golf course PERCORSO 17/20

Site	Paesaggio	
Maintenance	Manutenzione	
Architect	Architetto	Robert Von Hagge Smelek, Barril
Type	Tipologia	seaside course
Relief	Relievo terreno	
Water in play	Acqua in gioco	
Exp. to wind	Esposto al vento	
Trees in play	Alberi in gioco	

Scorecard Carta-score	**Chp.** Camp.	**Mens** Uomini	**Ladies** Donne
Length Lunghezza	6327	5947	4889
Par	72	72	72
Slope system	—	—	—

Advised golfing ability 0 12 24 36
Livello di gioco consigliato
Hcp required Handicap richiesto 34

Club house & amenities CLUB HOUSE E SERVIZI 2/10

Pro shop	Pro shop	
Driving range	Campo pratica	
Sheltered	coperto	6 mats
On grass	in erba	yes
Putting-green	Putting-green	yes
Pitching-green	Green-pratica	yes

Hotel facilities ALBERGHI 6/10

HOTELS ALBERGHI

Mistral 2, 132 rooms, D 83 € — Oristano
Tel (39) 0783 210 389, Fax (39) 0783 211 000 — 18 km

Sa Mola, 20 rooms, D 67 € — Bonárcado
Tel (39) 0783 56 580 — 18 km

RESTAURANTS RISTORANTE

Il Faro, Tel (39) 0783 70 002	Oristano 18 km
Leopardi, Tel (39) 0783 290 303	Cabras 15 km
Da Giovanni, Tel (39) 0783 22 051	Torre Grande 10 km
Cocco e Dessì, Tel(39) 0783 300 720	Oristano 18 km
Sa Funtà, Tel(39) 0783 290 685	Cabras 10 km

IS MOLAS

17 | 7 | 8

E' uno dei tre (eccellenti) percorsi di 18 buche in Sardegna, vicino al capoluogo dell'isola, Cagliari. Anche se non si trova esattamente in riva al mare, ne subisce nettamente l'influenza: ancor più delle difficoltà del tracciato, il vento è il fattore decisivo del gioco. Il percorso è decisamente lungo, ma di solito è abbastanza duro e quindi la palla rotola molto ma rende più pericolosi gli ostacoli d'acqua. Disegnato dai britannici Cotton e Pennink, il percorso è stato costruito con la supervisione di Piero Mancinelli uno dei più grandi architetti italiani. Ben equilibrato nel tracciato, Is Molas si è ben integrato con l'aspetto originale del terreno ed ha conservato un aspetto naturale, tra il mare e le colline boschive. Spettacolare e originale, è un campo sia bello da vedere che appassionante per giocarci e per chi non gioca a golf c'è un mare incomparabile a due passi. A questo si aggiunge un nuovo percorso di 18 buche già agibile che renderà questa destinazione sempre più attraente.

This is one of the three excellent 18-hole courses in Sardinia, close to Cagliari, the island's "capital". Although not exactly beside the sea, the course clearly comes under its influence, and the wind is a key factor when playing here, just as much as the difficulties of the layout and the hazards. The course's very respectable length also has to be considered, even though the fairways often roll a lot and make the water hazards more dangerous in the process. Designed by British designers Cotton and Pennink, the course was actually built under the supervision of Piero Mancinelli, one of the great Italian course architects of our day and age. A well-balanced layout, Is Molas has successfully hugged the contours of the terrain and retained its very natural appearance between the sea and tree-covered hills. Spectacular and original, the course is at once pleasant to look at and exciting to play. For non-golfers, there is all the fun of the seaside just next door. There is a project of another 18-hole course here, which should add to the seduction of this place.

Circolo Golf Is Molas — 1975

Loc. Is Molas
I - SANTA MARGHERITA DI PULA (CA)

Office	Segreteria	(39) 070 924 1013
Pro shop	Pro shop	(39) 070 924 1070
Fax	Fax	(39) 070 924 1015
Web	www.ismolas.it	
Situation	Localita'	

Cagliari (pop. 165 926), 35 km

Annual closure	Chiusura annuale	no
Weekly closure	Chiusura settimanale	no

Fees main season Tariffe alta stagione		Full day
	Week days Settimana	**We/Bank holidays** Feriale/Festivo
Individual Individuale	52 €	62 €
Couple Coppia	104 €	124 €
Caddy	Caddy	15 €
Electric Trolley	Carello elettrico	no
Buggy	Car	31 €
Clubs	Bastoni	15 €

Credit cards Carte di credito
VISA - Eurocard - MasterCard - DC - CartSì - AMEX

Access Itinerario : Cagliari, S195 south to Pula.
3 km after Pula, turn right → Golf
Map 4 on page 939 Carta 4 Pagina 939

Golf course — PERCORSO — 17/20

Site	Paesaggio	
Maintenance	Manutenzione	
Architect	Architetto	Cotton, Pennink Piero Mancinelli
Type	Tipologia	country
Relief	Relievo terreno	
Water in play	Acqua in gioco	
Exp. to wind	Esposto al vento	
Trees in play	Alberi in gioco	

Scorecard Carta-score	**Chp.** Camp.	**Mens** Uomini	**Ladies** Donne
Length Lunghezza	6383	6197	5395
Par	72	72	72
Slope system	—	—	—

Advised golfing ability 0 12 24 36
Livello di gioco consigliato
Hcp required Handicap richiesto 34

Club house & amenities — CLUB HOUSE E SERVIZI — 7/10

Pro shop	Pro shop	
Driving range	Campo pratica	
Sheltered	coperto	5 mats
On grass	in erba	yes
Putting-green	Putting-green	yes
Pitching-green	Green-pratica	yes

Hotel facilities — ALBERGHI — 8/10

HOTELS ALBERGHI

Is Molas Golf Hotel, 83 rooms, D 222 € — Is Molas
Tel (39) 070 924 1006, Fax (39) 070 924 1002 — on site

Costa dei Fiori, 62 rooms, D 336 € — Santa Margherita
Tel (39) 070 924 5333, Fax (39) 070 924 5335 — 5 km

Nora Club Hotel, 25 rooms, D 129 € — Pula
Tel (39) 070 924 421, Fax (39) 070 924 42257 — 4 km

Sant'Efis, 42 rooms, D 207 € — Pula
Tel (39) 070 924 5370, Fax (39) 070 924 5373 — 3 km

RESTAURANTS RISTORANTE

Su Gunventeddu, Tel (39) 070 920 9092 — Nora-Pula 3 km

Urru, Tel (39) 070 921 491 — S. Margherita di Pula 5 km

LA PINETINA

13	7	8

Se avete scelto di alloggiare nelle camere del golf, Como è lontano solo una quindicina di chilometri. Gli amanti di storia e di architettura apprezzeranno la ricchezza del Duomo costruito nel XIV secolo e anche la sobrietà romanica della Basilica di Sant'Abbondio e di San Fedele. Dopo potrete ritrovare la quiete alla Pinetina, un percorso disegnato da John Harris e Gianni Albertini e costruito in due tempi su un terreno molto scosceso che lo rende abbastanza stancante a piedi (è consigliato il golf cart). Grazie alla sua ubicazione offre degli scorci magnifici sulle montagne. Come dice il suo nome, i fairways sono bordati da numerosissimi pini che obbligano i colpi maldestri a ritornare sui propri passi; qualche ostacolo d'acqua complica ancor più la situazione. Quando ci si ha giocato un po' di volte, si riesce ad interpretare meglio questo tracciato abbastanza "tricky" e si può pensare di fare un buono score, trascorrendo una piacevole giornata di golf.

Although we decided to stay in the course's own guestrooms, lake Como is a mere fifteen kilometres down the road. Lovers of history and architecture will appreciate the wealth of Duomo, built during 14th century, and the Romanesque sobriety of the Basilica di Sant'Abbondio and San Fedele. Then it is on to the peace and quiet of La Pinetina, a course designed by John Harris and Gianni Albertini over two stages and hilly terrain which results in this being a tiring course to walk (buggy recommended). The good thing, naturally, is the magnificent view over the mountains. As its name would suggest, the fairways here are lined with pine-trees and wayward balls will need bending back to the short stuff. Then a few water hazards make life a little difficult, as well. After several rounds here, you have a clearer insight into this rather tricky layout and you can even think about carding a good score and having a great day's golfing in the process.

La Pinetina Golf Club — 1971

Via al Golf 4
I - 22070 APPIANO GENTILE (CO)

Office	Segreteria	(39) 031 933 202
Pro shop	Pro shop	(39) 031 890 857
Fax	Fax	(39) 031 890 342
E-mail	pinetina@ntt.it	
Situation	Localita'	

Como (pop. 82 989), 15 km Milano (pop. 1 300 977), 35 km

Annual closure	Chiusura annuale	no
Weekly closure	Chiusura settimanale	tuesday

Fees main season Tariffe alta stagione		18 holes
	Week days Settimana	**We/Bank holidays** Feriale/Festivo
Individual Individuale	36 €	57 €
Couple Coppia	72 €	114 €
Caddy	Caddy	21 €
Electric Trolley	Carello elettrico	no
Buggy	Car	37 €
Clubs	Bastoni	15 €

Credit cards Carte di credito VISA - CartSì - AMEX

Access Itinerario : Milano A8, A9 → Como, Exit (Uscita) Lomazzo, turn right → Guanzate and Appiano Gentile.
Map 1 on page 933 Carta 1 Pagina 933

Golf course PERCORSO — 13/20

Site	Paesaggio	
Maintenance	Manutenzione	
Architect	Architetto	John Harris G. Albertini
Type	Tipologia	forest, hilly
Relief	Relievo terreno	
Water in play	Acqua in gioco	
Exp. to wind	Esposto al vento	
Trees in play	Alberi in gioco	

Scorecard Carta-score	**Chp.** Camp.	**Mens** Uomini	**Ladies** Donne
Length Lunghezza	5922	5684	5233
Par	71	71	71
Slope system	—	—	—

Advised golfing ability 0 12 24 36
Livello di gioco consigliato
Hcp required Handicap richiesto 34

Club house & amenities CLUB HOUSE E SERVIZI — 7/10

Pro shop	Pro shop	
Driving range	Campo pratica	
Sheltered	coperto	6 mats
On grass	in erba	yes
Putting-green	Putting-green	yes
Pitching-green	Green-pratica	yes

Hotel facilities ALBERGHI — 8/10

HOTELS ALBERGHI

Golf Club, 11 rooms, D 57 € Tel (39) 031 930 931, Fax (39) 031 890 342	Appiano Gentile on ite
Canturio, 30 rooms, D 103 € Tel (39) 031 716 035, Fax (39) 031 720 211	Cantù 5 km
Hotel Sigma, 52 rooms, D 85 € Tel (39) 031 700 589, Fax (39) 031 720 440	Cantù 5 km

RESTAURANTS RISTORANTE

In, Tel (39) 031 935 702	Fenegrò 8 km
Antico Ostello Lombardo, Tel (39) 0331 842 832	Tradate 4 km
Tradate, Tel (39) 0331 841 401	Tradate 4 km

LE PAVONIERE

14	8	8

Dopo aver visitato bene Firenze è ora di girare verso ovest. Scoprire Montecatini Terme, una piacevole stazione termale ideale per rimettersi in forma dopo le abbuffate di bistecca alla fiorentina o di troppo Chianti e sopratutto Prato che ha sempre vissuto all'ombra di Firenze, ma alla quale non mancano certo le qualità. In particolare meritano una visita il Duomo, il Palazzo Pretorio o la stupefacente fortezza del Castello dell' Imperatore. E perchè no, ad una decina di chilometri, Le Pavoniere, aperto nel 1996 e disegnato da Arnold Palmer come il Castello di Tolcinasco in Lombardia. Si ritrova qui l'ispirazione sempre molto strategica del campione americano, dove gli ostacoli sono messi in gioco con grande intelligenza e con una buona conoscenza delle possibilità dei giocatori di ogni livello, anche se i più inesperti rischiano di soffrire un po'. Anche se piatto, questo percorso nasconde qualche sottigliezza che consente di non annoiarsi mai e i greens sono abbastanza grandi da offrire tante posizioni di bandiere diverse.

After a good look at Florence, it is time to head west of the city and discover Montecatini Terme, a pretty spa resort for treating people suffering from too much Bistecca alla Fiorentina or Chianti, and particularly Prato, for many a year overshadowed by Florence but nonetheless a town of many attractions. Visit Duomo, the Palazzo Pretorio, or the amazing fortress of Castello dell'Imperatore. Or again, a few miles further on, play Le Pavoniere, opened in 1986 and designed by Arnold Palmer, as was Castello di Tolcinasco in Lombardy. You can feel Arnie's highly strategic inspiration, where hazards are very cleverly brought into play, and his excellent knowledge of players of differing abilities. All the same, the less experienced players might suffer a little here anyway. Although rather flat, the course is subtle enough to be played and enjoyed often, and the greens big enough to offer very many different pin positions.

Golf Club Le Pavoniere — 1986

Via della Fattoria 6/29, Loc. Tavola
I - 50040 PRATO

Office	Segreteria	(39) 0574 620 855
Pro shop	Pro shop	(39) 0574 620 855
Fax	Fax	(39) 0574 624 558
E-mail	golfclublepavoniere@conmet.it	
Situation	Localita' Firenze (pop. 376 662), 20 km	
Annual closure	Chiusura annuale	no
Weekly closure	Chiusura settimanale	monday (01/10 → 31/03)

Fees main season Tariffe alta stagione		18 holes
	Week days Settimana	**We/Bank holidays** Feriale/Festivo
Individual Individuale	52 €	62 €
Couple Coppia	104 €	124 €
Softspikes only		
Caddy	Caddy	26 €
Electric Trolley	Carello elettrico	no
Buggy	Car	31 €
Clubs	Bastoni	15 €

Credit cards Carte di credito
VISA - Eurocard - MasterCard - DC - CartaSi - AMEX

Access Itinerario : A11 Exit (Uscita) Prato Ovest. Take right → Poggio a Caiano. Right → Tavola. After four traffic lights, don't turn left, take the dead end way (senza uscita) **Map 3 on page 936** Carta 3 Pagina 936

Golf course — PERCORSO — 14/20

Site	Paesaggio	
Maintenance	Manutenzione	
Architect	Architetto	Arnold Palmer
Type	Tipologia	parkland, open country
Relief	Relievo terreno	
Water in play	Acqua in gioco	
Exp. to wind	Esposto al vento	
Trees in play	Alberi in gioco	

Scorecard Carta-score	**Chp.** Camp.	**Mens** Uomini	**Ladies** Donne
Length Lunghezza	6465	6137	5323
Par	72	72	72
Slope system	—	—	—

Advised golfing ability Livello di gioco consigliato — 0 12 24 36
Hcp required Handicap richiesto 34

Club house & amenities — CLUB HOUSE E SERVIZI — 8/10

Pro shop	Pro shop	
Driving range	Campo pratica	
Sheltered	coperto	12 mats
On grass	in erba	yes
Putting-green	Putting-green	yes
Pitching-green	Green-pratica	yes

Hotel facilities — ALBERGHI — 8/10

HOTELS ALBERGHI

Hermitage, 58 rooms, D 93 € — Poggio a Caiano
Tel (39) 055 877 040, Fax (39) 055 879 7057 — 5 km

Paggeria Medicea, 37 rooms, D 129 € — Prato
Tel (39) 055 875 141, Fax (39) 055 875 1470 — 10 km

San Marco, 40 rooms, D 85 € — Prato
Tel (39) 0574 21 321, Fax (39) 0574 22 378 — 10 km

RESTAURANTS RISTORANTE

Il Piraña, Tel (39) 0574 25 746 — Prato 10 km

Da Delfina, Tel (39) 055 871 8119 — Artimino 15 km

Biagio Pignatta, Tel (39) 055 875 1406 — Artimino 10 km

LE QUERCE

17 | 8 | 7

Dopo aver visitato bene Firenze è ora di girare verso ovest. Scoprire Montecatini Terme, una piacevole stazione termale ideale per rimettersi in forma dopo le abbuffate di bistecca alla fiorentina o di troppo Chianti e sopratutto Prato che ha sempre vissuto all'ombra di Firenze, ma alla quale non mancano certo le qualità. In particolare meritano una visita il Duomo, il Palazzo Pretorio o la stupefacente fortezza del Castello dell' Imperatore. E perchè no, ad una decina di chilometri, Le Pavoniere, aperto nel 1996 e disegnato da Arnold Palmer come il Castello di Tolcinasco in Lombardia. Si ritrova qui l'ispirazione sempre molto strategica del campione americano, dove gli ostacoli sono messi in gioco con grande intelligenza e con una buona conoscenza delle possibilità dei giocatori di ogni livello, anche se i più inesperti rischiano di soffrire un po'. Anche se piatto, questo percorso nasconde qualche sottigliezza che consente di non annoiarsi mai e i greens sono abbastanza grandi da offrire tante posizioni di bandiere diverse.

Le Querce is a course lined with oak-trees, which was opened in 1990 as a national golf centre for the Italian Golf Federation but also as a private club. The hosting of the World Cup here in 1991 highlighted the course's many qualities, but the not-so-good players can handle this okay as long they keep well away from the back tees. Playing from the tips is a very demanding experience for both power and precision. This is a very open course, though, and game strategy with respect to the dangers and hazards is clear enough. The sloping terrain calls for thoughtful club selection, because while the greens are on the large side, they are well guarded and steeply contoured; putting here is never easy if you are too far from the hole. To finish, make a note of two stretches which can make or break your card: 4 through 6 and 13 through 15... two "Amen Corners" and a natural state of affairs being so close to the Holy City.

Golf Club Le Querce — 1990

Via Cassia Km 44,500
I - 01015 SUTRI (VT)

Office	Segreteria	(39) 0761 600 789
Pro shop	Pro shop	(39) 0761 600 789
Fax	Fax	(39) 0761 600 142
Web	www.golfclublequerce.it	
Situation	Localita'	

Viterbo (pop. 60 212), 31 km - Roma (pop. 2 643 581), 51 km

Annual closure	Chiusura annuale	no
Weekly closure	Chiusura settimanale	no

Fees main season Tariffe alta stagione	full day	
	Week days Settimana	**We/Bank holidays** Feriale/Festivo
Individual Individuale	41 €	52 €
Couple Coppia	82 €	104 €
Caddy	Caddy	no
Electric Trolley	Carello elettrico	8 €
Buggy	Car	26 €
Clubs	Bastoni	5 €

Credit cards Carte di credito VISA - CartaSi - AMEX

Access Itinerario : Roma, Via Cassia. Before Monterosi, at the end of a long and straight road, take left → Golf.
Map 3 on page 937 Carta 3 Pagina 937

Golf course PERCORSO — 17/20

Site	Paesaggio	
Maintenance	Manutenzione	
Architect	Architetto	Jim Fazio
Type	Tipologia	open country, hilly
Relief	Relievo terreno	
Water in play	Acqua in gioco	
Exp. to wind	Esposto al vento	
Trees in play	Alberi in gioco	

Scorecard Carta-score	**Chp.** Camp.	**Mens** Uomini	**Ladies** Donne
Length Lunghezza	6462	6052	5305
Par	72	72	72
Slope system	—	—	—

Advised golfing ability Livello di gioco consigliato — 0 12 24 36

Hcp required Handicap richiesto 34

Club house & amenities CLUB HOUSE E SERVIZI — 8/10

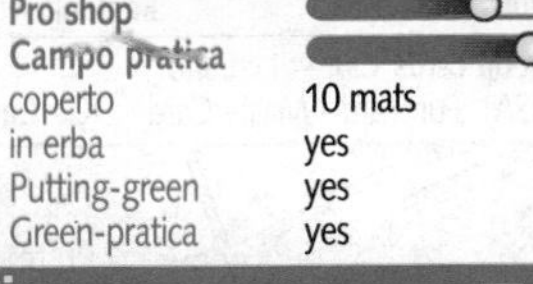

Pro shop	Pro shop	
Driving range	Campo pratica	
Sheltered	coperto	10 mats
On grass	in erba	yes
Putting-green	Putting-green	yes
Pitching-green	Green-pratica	yes

Hotel facilities ALBERGHI — 7/10

HOTELS ALBERGHI

Golf Club, 24 rooms, D 62 € — loc. San Martino
Tel (39) 0761 608 979, Fax (39) 0761 600 142 — on site

Il Borgo di Sutri, 21 rooms, D 124 € — Sutri
Tel (39) 0761 608 690, Fax (39) 0761 608 308 — 2 km

Hotel Salus e delle Terme — Viterbo
100 rooms, D 124 € — 31 km
Tel (39) 0761 3581, Fax (39) 0761 354 262

RESTAURANTS RISTORANTE

La Taverna, Tel (39) 0761 600 131 — Sutri 4 km

Il Vescovado, Tel (39) 0761 608 811 — Sutri5 km

Casa Tuscia, Tel (39) 0761 555 070 — Nepi 5 km

LE ROBINIE

15 | 8 | 8

A metà strada tra Milano, Varese e il lago Maggiore, Le Robinie è uno dei più recenti golf italiani ed anche uno dei più prestigiosi grazie alla firma di Jack Nicklaus. Esistono architetti di meno fascino e forse ancora più creativi ma l'Orso d'Oro continua ad essere un marchio di grande qualità anche se si può obiettare che tutti i suoi percorsi seguano un po' lo stesso modello secondo l'ingegnere che ha effettivamente seguito i lavori. Su un terreno così piatto, l'esperienza americana è stata di grande utilità e i lavori di movimentazione sono stati veramente di prim'ordine con numerosi ostacoli d'acqua creati per recuperare terra e riportarla in modo da ottenere tanti anfiteatri che dominano le buche. Molto lavoro è stato dedicato al disegno di bunkers e greens e il risultato grafico è di assoluto rilievo. Dalle partenze di campionato questo percorso è consigliato solo ai giocatori esperti, per gli altri, i tees normali sono l'ideale per trascorrere una bella giornata di golf.

Mid-way between Milan, Varese and the unavoidable Lake Maggiore, Le Robinie is one of Italy's more recent courses and one of the most prestigious too, courtesy of its designer Jack Nicklaus. There are other, less fashionable and perhaps more creative architects, but the Golden Bear label is a quality guarantee even if all his courses do tend to follow more or less the same model, depending on the engineer. On terrain as flat as this, American experience is useful indeed and the excavation work made to contour the course was quite remarkable, including many water hazards in order to recover the earth which has been arranged to form amphitheatres around the holes. A lot of thought also went into the shapes of bunkers and greens, giving a very graphic look to the whole layout. From the back tees, this very open and forthright course is for experienced players only. Further forward and you are in for a great day's golfing.

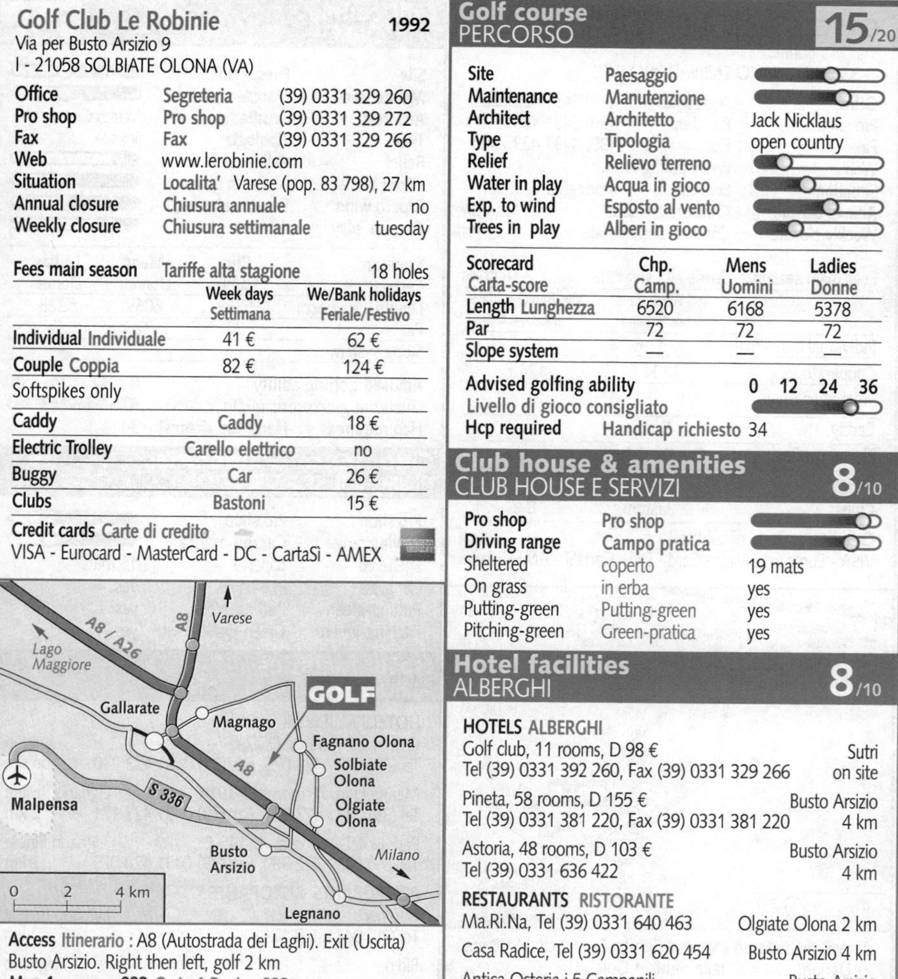

Golf Club Le Robinie — 1992

Via per Busto Arsizio 9
I - 21058 SOLBIATE OLONA (VA)

Office	Segreteria	(39) 0331 329 260
Pro shop	Pro shop	(39) 0331 329 272
Fax	Fax	(39) 0331 329 266
Web	www.lerobinie.com	
Situation	Localita' Varese (pop. 83 798), 27 km	
Annual closure	Chiusura annuale	no
Weekly closure	Chiusura settimanale	tuesday

Fees main season Tariffe alta stagione	Week days Settimana	We/Bank holidays Feriale/Festivo
	18 holes	
Individual Individuale	41 €	62 €
Couple Coppia	82 €	124 €
Softspikes only		

Caddy	Caddy	18 €
Electric Trolley	Carello elettrico	no
Buggy	Car	26 €
Clubs	Bastoni	15 €

Credit cards Carte di credito
VISA - Eurocard - MasterCard - DC - CartaSì - AMEX

Access Itinerario : A8 (Autostrada dei Laghi). Exit (Uscita) Busto Arsizio. Right then left, golf 2 km
Map 1 on page 933 Carta 1 Pagina 933

Golf course — PERCORSO — 15/20

Site	Paesaggio	
Maintenance	Manutenzione	
Architect	Architetto	Jack Nicklaus
Type	Tipologia	open country
Relief	Relievo terreno	
Water in play	Acqua in gioco	
Exp. to wind	Esposto al vento	
Trees in play	Alberi in gioco	

Scorecard Carta-score	Chp. Camp.	Mens Uomini	Ladies Donne
Length Lunghezza	6520	6168	5378
Par	72	72	72
Slope system	—	—	—

Advised golfing ability Livello di gioco consigliato — 0 12 24 36
Hcp required Handicap richiesto 34

Club house & amenities — CLUB HOUSE E SERVIZI — 8/10

Pro shop	Pro shop	
Driving range	Campo pratica	
Sheltered	coperto	19 mats
On grass	in erba	yes
Putting-green	Putting-green	yes
Pitching-green	Green-pratica	yes

Hotel facilities — ALBERGHI — 8/10

HOTELS ALBERGHI

Golf club, 11 rooms, D 98 € — Sutri
Tel (39) 0331 392 260, Fax (39) 0331 329 266 — on site

Pineta, 58 rooms, D 155 € — Busto Arsizio
Tel (39) 0331 381 220, Fax (39) 0331 381 220 — 4 km

Astoria, 48 rooms, D 103 € — Busto Arsizio
Tel (39) 0331 636 422 — 4 km

RESTAURANTS RISTORANTE

Ma.Ri.Na, Tel (39) 0331 640 463 — Olgiate Olona 2 km

Casa Radice, Tel (39) 0331 620 454 — Busto Arsizio 4 km

Antica Osteria i 5 Campanili — Busto Arsizio
Tel (39) 0331 630 493 — 4 km

LIGNANO

14 | 7 | 7

Lignano è una stazione balneare di primaria importanza in Friuli, sulle rive dell'Adriatico ed è più o meno a metà strada tra Venezia e Trieste. La spiaggia lunga otto chilometri, è l'ideale per trascorrere piacevoli soggiorni con la famiglia nei paesi di Lignano Sabbiadoro o di Lignano Pineta. Il golfista potrà quindi dedicarsi al suo gioco preferito senza rimorsi quando i bambini sono al mare. Il percorso, disegnato da Marco Croze è particolarmente piatto, con pochi alberi ed è una combinazione tra lo stile "links" con un disegno ben studiato di fairways e bunkers e lo stile "Florida" con gli ostacoli d'acqua che entrano in gioco. Abbastanza difficile dalle partenze arretrate quando soffia vento, è più facile giocarsi l'handicap se si mette da parte il proprio orgoglio e ci si accontenta di partire davanti. Bisogna giocare due o tre volte per apprezzare le sottigliezze del percorso, ma non ci si annoierà restando qualche giorno.

Lignano is one of the topmost seaside resorts in Friuli on the shores of the Adriatic, about half-way between Venice and Trieste. The 5-mile long beach is perfect for very pleasant family holidays in the small towns of Lignano Sabbiadoro or Lignano Pineta. You guessed it, golfers can go about their favourite pastime with a clear conscience when the children are on the beach. This course, designed by Marco Croze, is virtually flat with few trees. It combines a sort of links style, where terrain has been cleverly contoured and given some large bunkers, with some very Floridian features when the water hazards come into play. A rather tough proposition from the back tees when the wind blows, it is easier to play to your handicap when swallowing your pride and not being too ambitious (i.e. opt for the front tees). You need two or three rounds to appreciate the finer points of this layout, but you won't get bored playing here if you are around for several days.

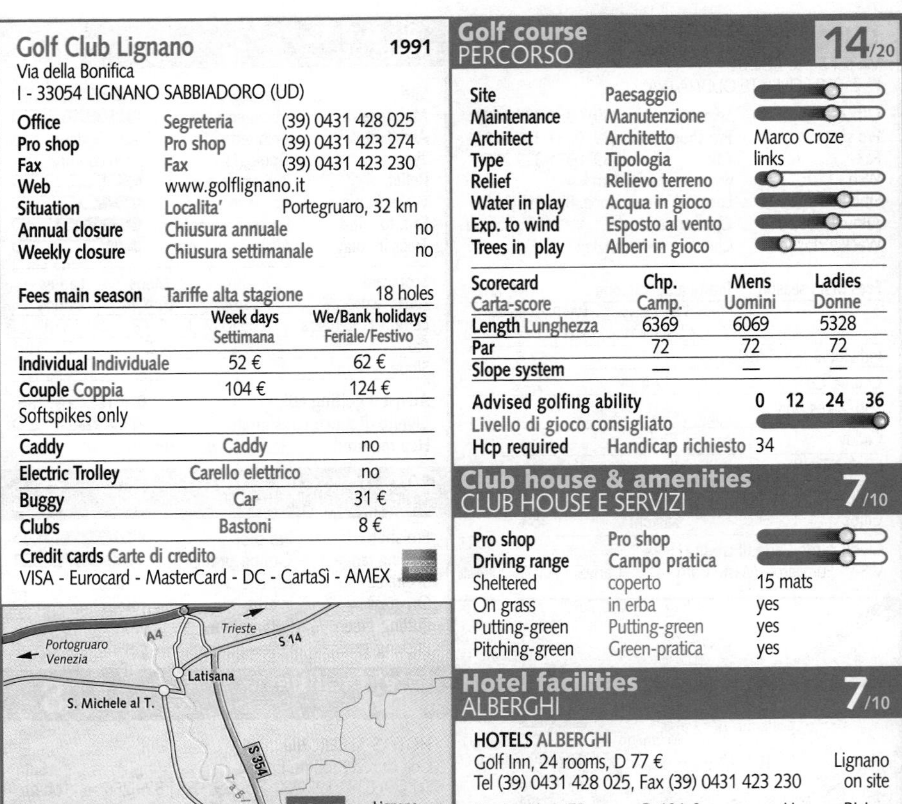

Golf Club Lignano — 1991

Via della Bonifica
I - 33054 LIGNANO SABBIADORO (UD)

Office	Segreteria	(39) 0431 428 025
Pro shop	Pro shop	(39) 0431 423 274
Fax	Fax	(39) 0431 423 230
Web	www.golflignano.it	
Situation	Localita'	Portegruaro, 32 km
Annual closure	Chiusura annuale	no
Weekly closure	Chiusura settimanale	no

Fees main season Tariffe alta stagione	18 holes	
	Week days Settimana	We/Bank holidays Feriale/Festivo
Individual Individuale	52 €	62 €
Couple Coppia	104 €	124 €

Softspikes only

Caddy	Caddy	no
Electric Trolley	Carello elettrico	no
Buggy	Car	31 €
Clubs	Bastoni	8 €

Credit cards Carte di credito
VISA - Eurocard - MasterCard - DC - CartaSì - AMEX

Access Itinerario : A4 Venezia-Trieste, Exit (Uscita) Latisana, → Lignano. 24 km, take right → Golf.
Map 2 on page 936 Carta 2 Pagina 936

Golf course PERCORSO — 14/20

Site	Paesaggio	
Maintenance	Manutenzione	
Architect	Architetto	Marco Croze
Type	Tipologia	links
Relief	Relievo terreno	
Water in play	Acqua in gioco	
Exp. to wind	Esposto al vento	
Trees in play	Alberi in gioco	

Scorecard Carta-score	Chp. Camp.	Mens Uomini	Ladies Donne
Length Lunghezza	6369	6069	5328
Par	72	72	72
Slope system	—	—	—

Advised golfing ability 0 12 24 36
Livello di gioco consigliato
Hcp required Handicap richiesto 34

Club house & amenities CLUB HOUSE E SERVIZI — 7/10

Pro shop	Pro shop	
Driving range	Campo pratica	
Sheltered	coperto	15 mats
On grass	in erba	yes
Putting-green	Putting-green	yes
Pitching-green	Green-pratica	yes

Hotel facilities ALBERGHI — 7/10

HOTELS ALBERGHI

Golf Inn, 24 rooms, D 77 € — Lignano on site
Tel (39) 0431 428 025, Fax (39) 0431 423 230

Marina Uno, 78 rooms, D 191 € — Lignano Riviera 2 km
Tel (39) 0431 427 171, Fax (39) 0431 427 171

Park Hotel, 44 rooms, D 145 € — Lignano Pineta 2 km
Tel (39) 0431 422 380, Fax (39) 0431 428 079

RESTAURANTS RISTORANTE

Newport — Lignano Riviera 2 km
Tel (39) 0431 427 171

Bidin — Lignano 2 km
Tel (39) 0431 71 988

MARCO SIMONE

15 | 8 | 8

Si può scommettere che ben pochi turisti stranieri che vengono a visitare Roma hanno mai sentito parlare di Tivoli. Invece è uno dei posti più magici che si possano immaginare, soprattutto per i giardini e le fontane di Villa d'Este e per la ricchezza archeologica di Villa Adriana, antica dimora dell'imperatore Adriano. Le 27 buche del golf Marco Simone si trovano a meno di 10 chilometri in una campagna molto ondulata (è consigliato il golf cart). A ridosso di un antico castello di proprietà della stilista Laura Biagiotti, la club-house è immensa e i servizi lussuosi con tennis, piscina e centro bellezza che sono però riservati ai soci. Il percorso disegnato con molta fantasia da Jim Fazio ha il merito di essere difficile dalle partenze di campionato ma è studiato intelligentemente per diventare più facile man mano che si accorciano le partenze.Gli ostacoli d'acqua così come le forme dei greens e dei bunkers gli confluiscono uno stile americano, mitigato dal paesaggio della campagna romana. Un gran bel percorso ormai maturo.

You can bet that very few foreign tourists coming to visit Rome have heard of Tivoli. Yet it is one of the most magic spots imaginable, particularly with the gardens and fountains of la Villa d'Este or the archaeological wealth of the Villa Adriana, the former mansion of Emperor Hadrian. The 27 holes that grace the Marco Simone golf course are less than 10 kilometres away, laid out over steeply rolling countryside (buggy recommended). Leaning against a former castle belonging to designer Laura Biagiotti, the club-house is huge and facilities luxurious, including tennis courts, swimming pool and health centre, but reserved for members only. The course, designed with much imagination by architect Jim Fazio, has the merit of being tough from the back tees but easier the further forward you go, which is only logical. Water hazards and the shaping of greens and bunkers create a very American feel, tempered only by the landscape of the Roman countryside. A very good course, already mature.

Golf Marco Simone — **1991**
Via di Marco Simone 84/88
I - 00012 GUIDONIA MONTECELLO (RM)

Office	Segreteria	(39) 0774 366 469
Pro shop	Pro shop	(39) 0774 367 060
Fax	Fax	(39) 0774 366 476
E-mail	golfclubmarcosimone@ntt.it	
Situation	Localita'	

Tivoli (pop. 52 809), 9 km - Roma (pop. 2 643 581), 37 km

Annual closure	Chiusura annuale	no
Weekly closure	Chiusura settimanale	tuesday

Fees main season Tariffe alta stagione		18 holes
	Week days Settimana	**We/Bank holidays** Feriale/Festivo
Individual Individuale	41 €	62 €
Couple Coppia	82 €	124 €
Caddy	Caddy	yes
Electric Trolley	Carello elettrico	no
Buggy	Car	36 €
Clubs	Bastoni	15 €

Credit cards Carte di credito
VISA - Eurocard - MasterCard - DC - CartaSi - AMEX

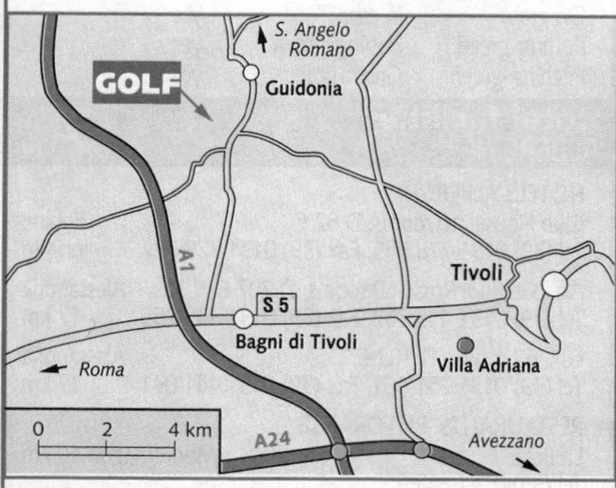

Access Itinerario : Roma, "Grande Raccordo Anulare" (Ring road), Exit (Uscita) 11, → Mentana. → Guidonia.
Map 3 on page 937 Carta 3 Pagina 937

Golf course
PERCORSO — **15/20**

Site	Paesaggio	
Maintenance	Manutenzione	
Architect	Architetto	Jim Fazio
Type	Tipologia	country, hilly
Relief	Relievo terreno	
Water in play	Acqua in gioco	
Exp. to wind	Esposto al vento	
Trees in play	Alberi in gioco	

Scorecard Carta-score	**Chp.** Camp.	**Mens** Uomini	**Ladies** Donne
Length Lunghezza	6343	6037	5320
Par	72	72	72
Slope system	—	—	—

Advised golfing ability Livello di gioco consigliato — 0 12 24 36
Hcp required Handicap richiesto 34

Club house & amenities
CLUB HOUSE E SERVIZI — **8/10**

Pro shop	Pro shop	
Driving range	Campo pratica	
Sheltered	coperto	10 mats
On grass	in erba	yes
Putting-green	Putting-green	yes
Pitching-green	Green-pratica	yes

Hotel facilities
ALBERGHI — **8/10**

HOTELS ALBERGHI

Grand Hotel Duca d'Este 176 rooms, D 155 € Tel (39) 0774 3883, Fax (39) 0774 388 101	Bagni di Tivoli 5 km
Torre Sant'Angelo, 31 rooms, D 129 € Tel (39) 0774 332 533, Fax (39) 0774 332 533	Tivoli 9 km
Sirene, 40 rooms, D 134 € Tel (39) 0774 330 605, Fax (39) 0774 330 608	Villa Adriana 7 km
Golf Club Marco Simone, 27 rooms, apartments Tel (39) 0774 366 469, Fax (39) 0774 366 476	Guidonia on site

RESTAURANTS RISTORANTE

Adriano, Tel (39) 0774 382 235	Villa Adriana 7 km
Antiqua Host. dei Carrettieri, Tel (39) 0774 330 159	Tivoli 9 km

MARGARA

13 | 7 | 7

Questo golf è situato in una regione industriale fuori dalle rotte turistiche, fatta eccezione per il periodo del Palio o della festa del vino ad Asti (in settembre). Partendo da Torino ci si può arrivare attraversando il Monferrato che merita una sosta nei suoi castelli per degustare i famosi vini piemontesi come il Barolo ed il Barbera. In questa occasione o durante un viaggio d'affari, una visita a Margara non è certo tempo perso. Si può anche soggiornare nell'immensa costruzione che ospita il club-house e dalla quale si gode la vista di tutto il percorso. Tre percorsi di 9 buche sono combinabili tra loro e sono stati disegnati dal professionista Agostino Reale e da Glauco Lolli Ghetti, proprietario della tenuta. Il percorso è abbastanza mosso e questo obbliga a scegliere attentamente i bastoni. Gli ostacoli sono quelli classici con molti bunkers e senza grandi movimenti e una curiosità alla buca 11, dove il green è interamente circondato da un fosso.

This course is located in an industrial part of the country, off the tourist trail, except during the period of Palio or the Wine Festival in Asti (September). Starting out from Turin, you can also take the Monferrato road with its castles and taste all the wines of Piedmont, including the famous Barolo and Barbera. On such an occasion, or during a business trip, a visit to Margara is time well spent. You can even stay here in the impressive club-house buildings, which overlook almost all the course. There are three combinable 9-hole courses, designed by the professional player Agostino Reale and Glauco Lolli Ghetti, son of the proprietor of this former farming estate. The course is a little hilly and so calls for careful club selection. Hazards are standard affairs with some slightly unimaginative bunkering and one curiosity at the 11th hole, where the green is completely surrounded by a ditch.

972

Golf Club Margara — 1975

Via Tenuta Margara 25
I - 15043 FUBINE (AL)

Office	Segreteria	(39) 0131 778 555
Pro shop	Pro shop	(39) 0131 778 555
Fax	Fax	(39) 0131 778 772
Web	—	
Situation	Localita'	

Alessandria (pop. 90 289), 17 km
Asti (pop. 73 159), 29 km

Annual closure	Chiusura annuale	no
Weekly closure	Chiusura settimanale	monday

Fees main season Tariffe alta stagione — 18 holes

	Week days Settimana	We/Bank holidays Feriale/Festivo
Individual Individuale	36 €	57 €
Couple Coppia	72 €	114 €
Caddy Caddy		no
Electric Trolley Carello elettrico		yes
Buggy Car		26 €
Clubs Bastoni		si

Credit cards Carte di credito VISA - CartaSi

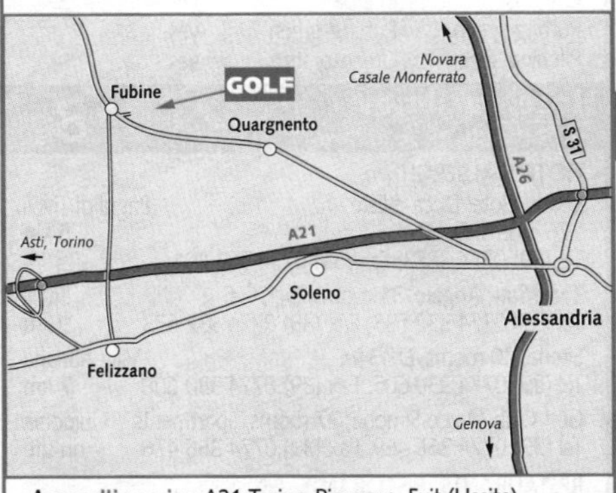

Access Itinerario : A21 Torino-Piacenza. Exit (Uscita) Felizzano. Turn left on S10. In Felizzano take left → Fubine. 3 km → golf **Map 1 on page 932** Carta 1 Pagina 932

Golf course PERCORSO — 13/20

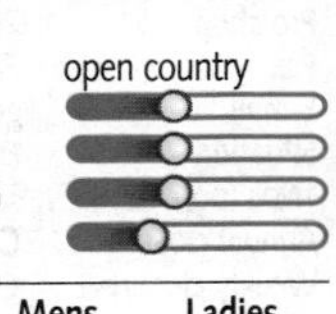

Site	Paesaggio	
Maintenance	Manutenzione	
Architect	Architetto	
Type	Tipologia	open country
Relief	Relievo terreno	
Water in play	Acqua in gioco	
Exp. to wind	Esposto al vento	
Trees in play	Alberi in gioco	

Scorecard Carta-score	Chp. Camp.	Mens Uomini	Ladies Donne
Length Lunghezza	6198	6045	5319
Par	72	72	72
Slope system	—	—	—

Advised golfing ability Livello di gioco consigliato — 0 12 24 36
Hcp required Handicap richiesto 34

Club house & amenities CLUB HOUSE E SERVIZI — 7/10

Pro shop	Pro shop	
Driving range	Campo pratica	
Sheltered	coperto	10 mats
On grass	in erba	yes
Putting-green	Putting-green	yes
Pitching-green	Green-pratica	yes

Hotel facilities ALBERGHI — 7/10

HOTELS ALBERGHI

Club House, 10 rooms, D 52 € — Fubine on site
Tel (39) 0131 778 555, Fax (39) 0131 778 772

Alli Due Buoi Rossi, 50 rooms, D 207 € — Alessandria 17 km
Tel (39) 0131 445 252, Fax (39) 0131 445 255

Lux, 52 rooms, D 103 € — Alessandria 17 km
Tel (39) 0131 251 661, Fax (39) 0131 441 091

RESTAURANTS RISTORANTE

La Braja — Montemagno 10 km
Tel (39) 0141 653 925

La Fermata, Tel (39) 0131 251 350 — Alessandria17 km

Castello di Lajone — Piepasso (Quattordio) 10 km
Tel (39) 0131 773 692

MILANO

16 | 9 | 8

Situato in prossimità del capoluogo lombardo dentro al Parco di Monza, è sicuramente uno dei circoli italiani più prestigiosi che ama coltivare le tradizioni come conferma l'incontro annuale dei suoi soci con quelli del Royal & Ancient Golf Club of St. Andrews. Glannon e Blanford lo hanno disegnato su di un terreno piatto, dove gli alberi maestosi sono sia il mezzo per isolarsi completamente in una sorta di piacevole esclusività che un'impenetrabile barriera per evitare i principianti maldestri. I numerosi bunkers difendono molto bene i greens che sono di medie dimensioni, leggermente ondulati e solitamente ben tenuti. Giocando qui si ha la sensazione di muoversi in un parco immenso dove il silenzio viene meno soltanto nei giorni in cui si disputano le corse sul circuito di Monza. Con i suoi bei percorsi, per un totale di 27 buche, che si adattano a tutti i livelli di gioco e con la sua grande club-house funzionale e lussuosa che ha sostituito il vecchio casino di caccia, il Golf Club Milano ha ancora davanti a sè un florido avvenire.

Located close to the capital of Lombardy in the Parco di Monza, this is obviously one of the most prestigious Italian clubs cultivating real golfing tradition, as testified by the annual encounter with the members of the Royal & Ancient at St Andrews. Gannon and Blanford laid the course out over flat terrain, where majestic trees create both a feeling of isolation and pleasant exclusivity, and a formidable line of defence for hitters who slug rather than think. The very many bunkers ably defend the average-sized greens that are slightly contoured and very well maintained. Here you get the feeling of playing in a huge park, where the silence is disturbed only on those days when the Monza race-track is in action. With good courses (27 holes in all) well suited to all standards of play, plus a huge, functional and luxurious club-house, which has replaced the former hunting lodge, the Golf Club Milano has a great future in store.

Golf Club Milano — 1928

Viale Mulini San Giorgio 7
I - 20052 PARCO DI MONZA (MI)

Office	Segreteria	(39) 039 303 081
Pro shop	Pro shop	(39) 039 304 561
Fax	Fax	(39) 039 304 427
Web	www.golfmilano.it	
Situation	Localita'	

Milano (pop. 1 300 977), 25 km, Bergamo, 29 km

Annual closure	Chiusura annuale	no
Weekly closure	Chiusura settimanale	monday

Fees main season Tariffe alta stagione		18 holes
	Week days Settimana	**We/Bank holidays** Feriale/Festivo
Individual Individuale	52 €	77 €
Couple Coppia	104 €	154 €

Caddy	Caddy	15 €
Electric Trolley	Carello elettrico	no
Buggy	Car	31 €
Clubs	Bastoni	15 €

Credit cards Carte di credito VISA - DC

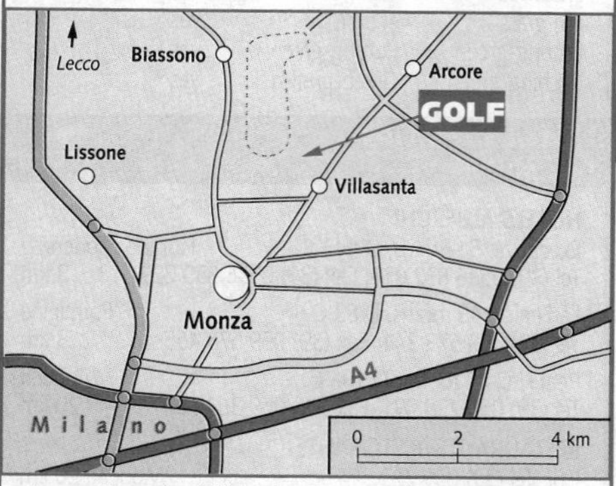

Access Itinerario : Milano A4, Tangenziale Est. Exit (Uscita) Vimercate. Take left → Villasanta. Cross road to Lecco, → Villasanta. First traffic lights, turn right → San Giorgio. → Parco di Monza, Golf **Map 1 on page 933** Carta 1 Pagina 933

Golf course — PERCORSO — 16/20

Site	Paesaggio	
Maintenance	Manutenzione	
Architect	Architetto	Blandford & Gannon
Type	Tipologia	parkland
Relief	Relievo terreno	
Water in play	Acqua in gioco	
Exp. to wind	Esposto al vento	
Trees in play	Alberi in gioco	

Scorecard Carta-score	**Chp.** Camp.	**Mens** Uomini	**Ladies** Donne
Length Lunghezza	6403	6239	5509
Par	72	72	72
Slope system	—	—	—

Advised golfing ability 0 12 24 36
Livello di gioco consigliato
Hcp required Handicap richiesto 34

Club house & amenities — CLUB HOUSE E SERVIZI — 9/10

Pro shop	Pro shop	
Driving range	Campo pratica	
Sheltered	coperto	8 mats
On grass	in erba	yes
Putting-green	Putting-green	yes
Pitching-green	Green-pratica	yes

Hotel facilities — ALBERGHI — 8/10

HOTELS ALBERGHI

De La Ville, 61 rooms, D 212 € — Monza 2 km
Tel (39) 039 382 581, Fax (39) 039 367 647

Della Regione, 90 rooms, D 155 € — Monza 2 km
Tel (39) 039 387 205, Fax (39) 039 380 254

Sant' Eustorgio, 35 rooms, D 119 € — Arcore 4 km
Tel (39) 039 601 3718, Fax (39) 039 617 531

RESTAURANTS RISTORANTE

Osteria del Pomiroeu — Seregno 6 km
Tel (39) 0362 237 973

Pierino Penati — Viganò 17 km
Tel (39) 039 956 020

Derby Grill, Tel (39) 039 382 581 — Monza 5 km

MODENA

13 | 7 | 7

Le scarpe, i treni e soprattutto le automobili (con la Ferrari a Maranello) hanno fatto la fama di Modena... così come il suo Duomo e la bella raccolta di quadri della Galleria Estense. Aperto nel 1987, il percorso del Modena Golf & Country Club è stato disegnato da Bernhard Langer, senza dubbio all'epoca della sua collaborazione con Buckley. Più tardi il campione tedesco si è molto evoluto perfezionandosi nel suo mestiere di architetto. Il suo disegno segue fedelmente gli aspetti del terreno poco movimentato dove gli alberi non sono un pericolo. La strategia di gioco è evidente da subito. Gli ostacoli sono costituiti maggiormente dai bunkers e dall'acqua molto presente e in particolare su due par 3 e alla 18 dove l'audacia può essere ricompensata o può distruggere un buono score. E' un percorso ideale per un circolo che ha soci di diverso livello, anche se i giocatori migliori resteranno un pò delusi e i cultori dei campi naturali lo troveranno un po' troppo artificiale. E' sicuramente destinato a migliorare nel tempo.

Footwear, rolling stock and particularly cars (Ferrari in Maranello) have forged the reputation of Modena... together with the Duomo and the fine collection of paintings at the Galleria Estense. Created in 1987, the Modena Golf & Country Club course was designed by Bernhard Langer, certainly during the period when he was working with Buckley. Since then, the German champion has covered a lot of ground and acquired maturity in his work as a course architect. Here, the design faithfully hugs the contours of rather flat terrain, where trees are not a danger. Playing strategy is obvious as soon as you are on the course. Hazards are basically the bunkers and very present water hazards, especially on two of the par 3s and at the end, on the 18th, where daring may be rewarded or simply ruin your card. This is a real members' course where playing levels are necessarily very different, and where the more skilled player might feel a little frustrated. Lovers of natural courses will find this layout a little artificial, but one which matures well with age.

Modena Golf & Country Club — 1987

Via Castelnuovo Rangone 4
I - 41050 COLOMBARO DI FORMIGINE (MO)

Office	Segreteria	(39) 0359 553 482
Pro shop	Pro shop	(39) 0359 553 696
Fax	Fax	(39) 0359 553 696
E-mail	modenagolf@tiscalinet.it	
Situation	Localita'	

Modena (pop 176 022), 20 km, Bologna (pop 381 161), 40 km

Annual closure	Chiusura annuale	no
Weekly closure	Chiusura settimanale	tuesday

Fees main season Tariffe alta stagione — 18 holes

	Week days Settimana	We/Bank holidays Feriale/Festivo
Individual Individuale	31 €	46 €
Couple Coppia	62 €	92 €

Caddy	Caddy	no
Electric Trolley	Carello elettrico	no
Buggy	Car	31 €
Clubs	Bastoni	10 €

Credit cards Carte di credito
VISA - Eurocard - MasterCard - DC - CartaSì - AMEX

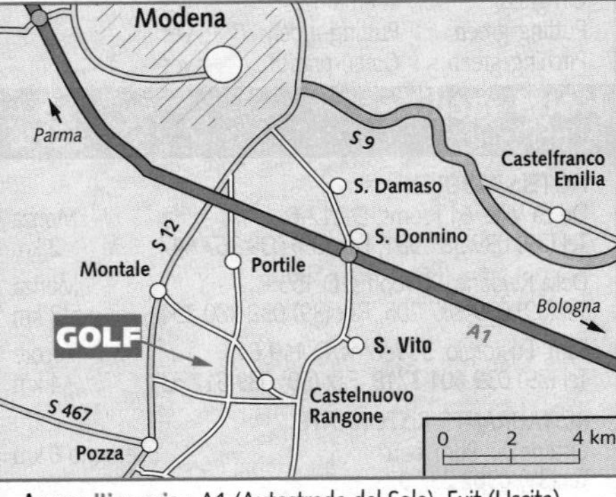

Access Itinerario : A1 (Autostrada del Sole), Exit (Uscita) Modena Sud. Go right → Modena for 5 km. A12 to the left. 12 km, Golf on the left hand side.
Map 2 on page 934 Carta 2 Pagina 934

Golf course — PERCORSO — 13/20

Site	Paesaggio	
Maintenance	Manutenzione	
Architect	Architetto	Bernhard Langer
Type	Tipologia	open country
Relief	Relievo terreno	
Water in play	Acqua in gioco	
Exp. to wind	Esposto al vento	
Trees in play	Alberi in gioco	

Scorecard Carta-score	Chp. Camp.	Mens Uomini	Ladies Donne
Length Lunghezza	6423	6097	5350
Par	72	72	72
Slope system	—	—	—

Advised golfing ability Livello di gioco consigliato — 0 12 24 36
Hcp required Handicap richiesto 34

Club house & amenities — CLUB HOUSE E SERVIZI — 7/10

Pro shop	Pro shop	
Driving range	Campo pratica	
Sheltered	coperto	10 mats
On grass	in erba	yes
Putting-green	Putting-green	yes
Pitching-green	Green-pratica	yes

Hotel facilities — ALBERGHI — 7/10

HOTELS ALBERGHI

Executive, 51 rooms, D 142 € — Fiorano Modenese
Tel (39) 0536 832 010, Fax (39) 0536 830 229 — 3 km

La Fenice, 48 rooms, D 83 € — Formigine
Tel (39) 059 573 344, Fax (39) 059 573 455 — 3 km

Real Fini, 87 rooms, D 186 € — Modena
Tel (39) 059 238 091, Fax (39) 059 364 804 — 20 km

RESTAURANTS RISTORANTE

Fini, Tel (39) 059 223 314 — Modena 20 km

Arnaldo-Clinica Gastronomica — Rubiera
Tel (39) 059 626 124 — 10 km

Borso d'Este, Tel (39) 059 214 114 — Modena 20 km

MOLINETTO

13 | 8 | 8

E' uno dei numerosi e più recenti golf intorno a Milano, sulla strada di Gongonzola... Aperto nel 1983, il percorso ha acquisito un'ottima reputazione ospitando soltando due anni dopo l'inaugurazione un'edizione dell'Open d'Italia. Da allora ha continuato ad apportare migliorie al percorso soprattutto per quanto riguarda i movimenti del terreno. E' stato tracciato su un terreno assolutamente piatto con numerosi piccoli laghi che entrano in gioco molto spesso. I fairways sono abbastanza stretti in seguito alla scarsa lunghezza del percorso e i greens di medie dimensioni sono abbastanza ben disegnati e ben difesi. Al Molinetto i promotori hanno cercato di raggiungere un bacino d'utenza molto vasto e non necessariamente composto da golfisti provetti per formare un grande circolo plurisportivo. Lo confermano la presenza di un campo pratica di grandi dimensioni, di una piscina e anche di numerosissimi campi da tennis.

This is one of the many and most recent golf courses of Milan on the road to Gorgonzola... Since is was opened in 1983, Molinetto has acquired an excellent reputation and even hosted the Italian Open after just two years. Since then, it has undergone a number of significant improvements, especially in terms of contouring. It is laid out over a plain with a whole number of little lakes that are frequently in play. The fairways are rather narrow, which may seem logical given the course's short yardage; likewise, the greens are not enormous but rather well designed and protected. Here again, the promoters set their sights on a wide customer base, without necessarily much experience of golf, in order to create a multi-sports club; whence the huge driving range, swimming pool and any number of tennis courts.

Molinetto Country Club — 1982

SS. Padana Superiore 11
I - 20063 CERNUSCO SUL NAVIGLIO (MI)

Office	Segreteria	(39) 02 92 105 128
Pro shop	Pro shop	(39) 02 92 149 954
Fax	Fax	(39) 02 92 106 635
E-mail	molinetto.c.c@ntt.it	
Situation	Localita'	
Milano (pop. 1300 977), 6 km		
Annual closure	Chiusura annuale	no
Weekly closure	Chiusura settimanale	monday

Fees main season Tariffe alta stagione		18 holes
	Week days Settimana	**We/Bank holidays** Feriale/Festivo
Individual Individuale	41 €	52 €
Couple Coppia	82 €	104 €
Caddy	Caddy	no
Electric Trolley	Carello elettrico	5 €
Buggy	Car	no
Clubs	Bastoni	yes

Credit cards Carte di credito
VISA - DC - CartaSì - AMEX

Access Itinerario : Milano, Via Palmanova → Vimodrome. S11 → Cernusco and Gorgonzola. Golf on the left hand side **Map 1 on page 933** Carta 1 Pagina 933

Golf course PERCORSO — 13/20

Site	Paesaggio	
Maintenance	Manutenzione	
Architect	Architetto	S. Carrera L. Rota Caremoli
Type	Tipologia	country, residential
Relief	Relievo terreno	
Water in play	Acqua in gioco	
Exp. to wind	Esposto al vento	
Trees in play	Alberi in gioco	

Scorecard Carta-score	**Chp.** Camp.	**Mens** Uomini	**Ladies** Donne
Length Lunghezza	5901	5901	5193
Par	71	71	71
Slope system	—	—	—

Advised golfing ability 0 12 24 36
Livello di gioco consigliato
Hcp required Handicap richiesto 34

Club house & amenities CLUB HOUSE E SERVIZI — 8/10

Pro shop	Pro shop	
Driving range	Campo pratica	
Sheltered	coperto	4 mats
On grass	in erba	yes
Putting-green	Putting-green	yes
Pitching-green	Green-pratica	yes

Hotel facilities ALBERGHI — 8/10

HOTELS ALBERGHI

Concorde, 37 rooms, D 77 € — Cernusco sul Naviglio 1 km
Tel (39) 02 921 005 49

Jolly Hotel Milano 149 rooms, D 155 € — Segrate (Milano) 10 km
Tel (39) 02 2175, Fax (39) 02 264 101 15

Country Hotel Borromeo — Peschiera Borromeo 10 km
75 rooms, D 207 €
Tel (39) 02 547 5121, Fax (39) 02 553 007 08

RESTAURANTS RISTORANTE

Vecchia Filanda, Tel (39) 02 924 9200 Cernusco sul Naviglio
San Martino, Tel (39) 0363 490 75 — Treviglio 18 km
Osteria dei Fauni, Tel (39) 02 269 214 11 — Segrate 7 km

MONTECCHIA

13 | 8 | 8

Questo percorso è stato aperto nel 1992 vicino alle stazioni termali di Abano Terme e Montegrotto e soprattutto a due passi dalla bella città di Padova, che per tanto tempo ha vissuto all'ombra della vicina Venezia. Gli affreschi di Mantegna e Giotto sono una visita da non mancare e se qui è abitudine pregare S. Antonio per salvare i naufraghi i più religiosi potranno provare a farlo anche a Montecchia per cercare di evitare gli ostacoli d'acqua disseminati in questo tracciato di Tom Macauley! Non ha avuto un compito facile su un terreno così piatto dove ha creato movimenti scavando e aggiungendo terra altrove. Le qualità tecniche rendono il percorso accessibile a giocatori di ogni livello, anche rimane un lieve difetto di uniformità. Non è un percorso che rimane impresso nella mente, a meno che non ci si abbia giocato varie volte. Un altro percorso di 9 buche aggiunge maggior interesse a questo circolo molto piacevole.

This course was opened in 1992 close to the spa resorts of Abano Terme and Montegrotto Terme, and particularly within the vicinity of the fine city of Padua, which spent many a year in the shadows of neighbouring Venice. The frescoes of Mantegna and Giotto are exciting visiting. While in earlier times they used to pray to Saint Antonio de Padua for shipwrecked mariners, prayers can still be heard in Montecchia to avoid the water hazards that are very much in play on this Tom Macauley layout. Designing the course was no easy job on such flat land, but he succeeded in contouring the fairways by digging here to add over there. However, the technical qualities of the course, playable by golfers of all abilities, cannot conceal a slight problem of uniformity. This is not a layout that sticks in the mind, unless of course you play it several times. A 9-hole layout has added to the appeal of what is a very pleasant course.

Golf della Montecchia — 1992

Via Montecchia 16
I - 35030 SELVAZZANO DENTRO (PD)

Office	Segreteria	(39) 049 805 5550
Pro shop	Pro shop	(39) 049 805 5965
Fax	Fax	(39) 049 805 5737
E-mail	golfmontecchia@tin.it	
Situation	Localita'	

Padova (pop. 211 391), 7 km, Venezia (pop. 277 305), 42 km

Annual closure	Chiusura annuale	no
Weekly closure	Chiusura settimanale	monday

Fees main season Tariffe alta stagione	Week days Settimana	We/Bank holidays Feriale/Festivo (18 holes)
Individual Individuale	52 €	62 €
Couple Coppia	104 €	124 €
Caddy	Caddy	no
Electric Trolley	Carello elettrico	no
Buggy	Car	34 €
Clubs	Bastoni	15 €

Credit cards Carte di credito
VISA - Eurocard - MasterCard - DC - CartaSì - AMEX

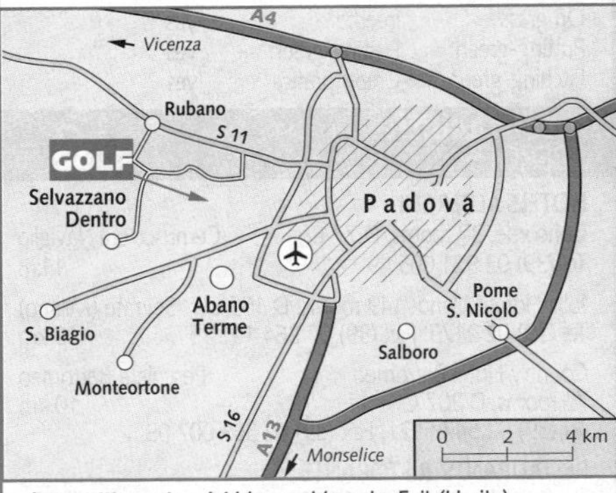

Access Itinerario : A4 Verona-Venezia. Exit (Uscita) Padova-Ovest. Take the Corso Australia, right to Tencarola, right again → Selvazzano Dentro. → Golf
Map 2 on page 934 Carta 2 Pagina 934

Golf course PERCORSO — 13/20

Site	Paesaggio	
Maintenance	Manutenzione	
Architect	Architetto	Tom Macauley
Type	Tipologia	open country
Relief	Relievo terreno	
Water in play	Acqua in gioco	
Exp. to wind	Esposto al vento	
Trees in play	Alberi in gioco	

Scorecard Carta-score	Chp. Camp.	Mens Uomini	Ladies Donne
Length Lunghezza	6318	6078	5326
Par	72	72	72
Slope system	—	—	—

Advised golfing ability Livello di gioco consigliato — 0 12 24 36
Hcp required Handicap richiesto 34

Club house & amenities CLUB HOUSE E SERVIZI — 8/10

Pro shop	Pro shop	
Driving range	Campo pratica	
Sheltered	coperto	12 mats
On grass	in erba	yes
Putting-green	Putting-green	yes
Pitching-green	Green-pratica	yes

Hotel facilities ALBERGHI — 8/10

HOTELS ALBERGHI

La Piroga, 62 rooms, D 114 € — Selvazzano Dentro
Tel (39) 049 637 966, Fax (39) 049 637 460 — 3 km

Bristol Buja, 128 rooms, D 124 € — Abano Terme
Tel (39) 049 866 9390, Fax (39) 049 667 910 — 6 km

La Residence, 112 rooms, D 127 € — Abano Terme
Tel (39) 049 824 7777, Fax (39) 049 866 8396 — 6 km

RESTAURANTS RISTORANTE

Da Mario, Tel (39) 049 794 090 — Montegrotto Terme 6 km
Relais, Tel (39) 049 805 5323 — Selvazzano Dentro 2 km
Casa Vecia, Tel (39) 049 860 0138 — Monterosso 8 km

MONTICELLO

14 | 8 | 7

E' uno dei grandi classici italiani, reso celebre sia dai numerosi Open d'Italia che qui sono stati organizzati, che per la manutenzione molto accurata dei suoi due percorsi di 18 buche. A pochi chilometri, il bellissimo lago di Como rende questo posto perfetto per trascorrere un fine settimana o una piacevole vacanza. Il percorso «rosso» è stato inaugurato nel 1975 in una pianura ornata da varie specie di alberi con le Alpi in sottofondo e malgrado le difficoltà siano ben visibili e distribuite con saggezza per non infastidire troppo i giocatori medi e testare l'intelligenza e la tattica dei migliori, Monticello aveva il punto debole nel disegno poco tecnico dei greens. Per questo all'inizio del 2001 sono iniziati i lavori di modifica progettati da Graham Cooke che prevedono nei prossimi due anni un restyling di entrambi i percorsi. Le novità più salienti riguarderanno il green della 7, par 3 impegnativo e di grande effetto e i greens della 9 e della 18 che saranno collegati da un lago.

This is one of the great classic courses in Italy, made famous by the Italian Open championships held here and by the very meticulous maintenance and green-keeping on both 18-hole courses. The wonderful lake Como, a few miles down the road, makes this a great spot for a week-end or longer holiday. The "Rosso" course is laid out in a plain lined with little copses and with the Alps as a backdrop. The difficulties are clearly in view and judiciously spread in order to avoid overwhelming the average player. Instead, they test the intelligence and tactical sense of the better golfers. What's more, only the better player will feel easy playing from the back-tees, particularly on the two very long par 3s, one green of which is surrounded by water (hole N° 7). Elsewhere, the fairways are rather wide, the rough can be dangerous and the most frequently encountered hazards are bunkers and trees. A good course but one which might have deserved a little more imagination from a graphical viewpoint.

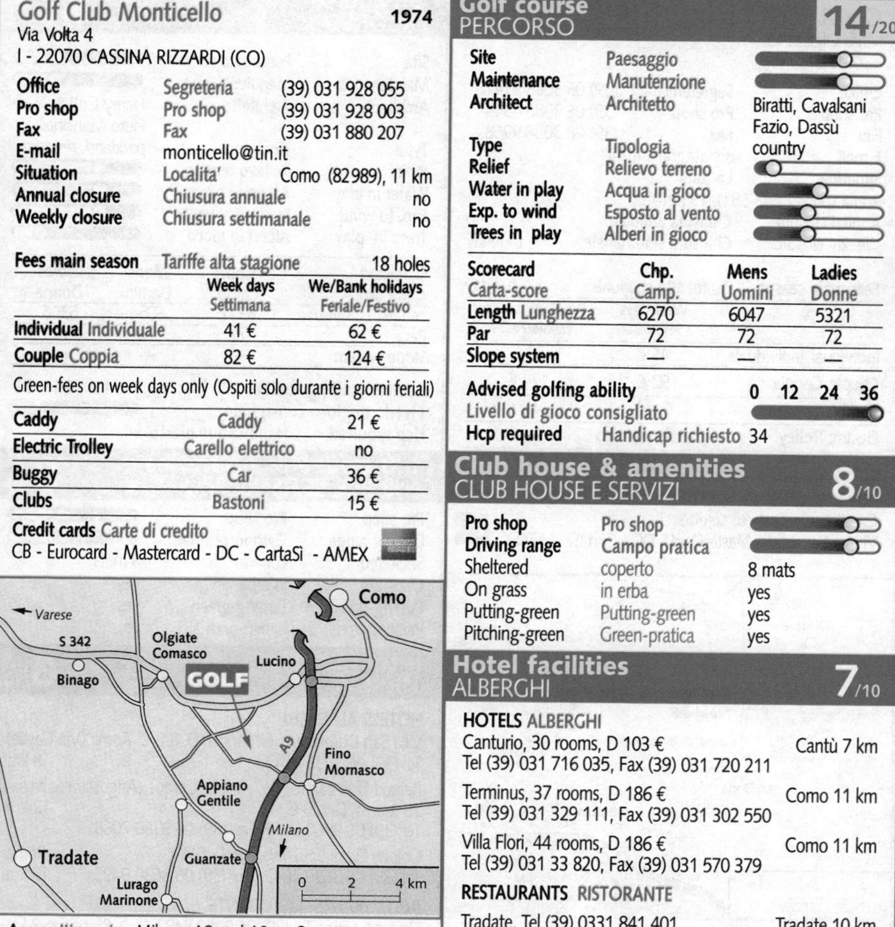

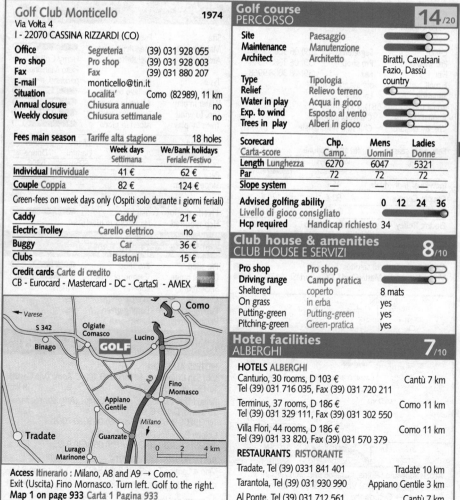

Golf Club Monticello — 1974

Via Volta 4
I - 22070 CASSINA RIZZARDI (CO)

Office	Segreteria	(39) 031 928 055
Pro shop	Pro shop	(39) 031 928 003
Fax	Fax	(39) 031 880 207
E-mail	monticello@tin.it	
Situation	Localita'	Como (82989), 11 km
Annual closure	Chiusura annuale	no
Weekly closure	Chiusura settimanale	no

Fees main season Tariffe alta stagione	**Week days** Settimana	**We/Bank holidays** Feriale/Festivo
		18 holes
Individual Individuale	41 €	62 €
Couple Coppia	82 €	124 €

Green-fees on week days only (Ospiti solo durante i giorni feriali)

Caddy	Caddy	21 €
Electric Trolley	Carello elettrico	no
Buggy	Car	36 €
Clubs	Bastoni	15 €

Credit cards Carte di credito
CB - Eurocard - Mastercard - DC - CartaSì - AMEX

Access Itinerario : Milano, A8 and A9 → Como.
Exit (Uscita) Fino Mornasco. Turn left. Golf to the right.
Map 1 on page 933 Carta 1 Pagina 933

Golf course — PERCORSO — 14/20

Site	Paesaggio	
Maintenance	Manutenzione	
Architect	Architetto	Biratti, Cavalsani Fazio, Dassù
Type	Tipologia	country
Relief	Relievo terreno	
Water in play	Acqua in gioco	
Exp. to wind	Esposto al vento	
Trees in play	Alberi in gioco	

Scorecard Carta-score	**Chp.** Camp.	**Mens** Uomini	**Ladies** Donne
Length Lunghezza	6270	6047	5321
Par	72	72	72
Slope system	—	—	—

Advised golfing ability Livello di gioco consigliato — 0 12 24 36
Hcp required Handicap richiesto 34

Club house & amenities — CLUB HOUSE E SERVIZI — 8/10

Pro shop	Pro shop	
Driving range	Campo pratica	
Sheltered	coperto	8 mats
On grass	in erba	yes
Putting-green	Putting-green	yes
Pitching-green	Green-pratica	yes

Hotel facilities — ALBERGHI — 7/10

HOTELS ALBERGHI

Canturio, 30 rooms, D 103 € — Cantù 7 km
Tel (39) 031 716 035, Fax (39) 031 720 211

Terminus, 37 rooms, D 186 € — Como 11 km
Tel (39) 031 329 111, Fax (39) 031 302 550

Villa Flori, 44 rooms, D 186 € — Como 11 km
Tel (39) 031 33 820, Fax (39) 031 570 379

RESTAURANTS RISTORANTE

Tradate, Tel (39) 0331 841 401 — Tradate 10 km
Tarantola, Tel (39) 031 930 990 — Appiano Gentile 3 km
Al Ponte, Tel (39) 031 712 561 — Cantù 7 km

OLGIATA

16 | 8 | 6

Costruito nella proprietà della scuderia che ha dato cavalli come Nearco e Ribot, questo grande circolo romano comprende 27 buche disegnate da Charles Kenneth Cotton e realizzate da Piero Mancinelli. Il percorso principale di 18 buche ha ricevuto tutti gli elogi in occasione delle due edizioni della World Cup nel 1968 e nel 1984. E' un percorso classico, dove l'acqua interviene soltanto su due buche perchè i maggiori ostacoli sono i numerosi alberi e i bunkers. Nei fairways questi ultimi sono penalizzanti sopratutto per i giocatori migliori e questa è una buona notizia per i visitatori. Abbastanza piatto ha tuttavia qualche buca con il drive cieco, ma senza eccessi: generalmente questo percorso non nasconde le sue difficoltà. Ogni buca ha il suo carattere e questo vi aiuterà a ricordarle. Inoltre c'è sempre una piacevole sensazione di spazio e di isolamento tra un fairway e l'altro. Uno dei grandi percorsi italiani.

Built over a former horse-rearing estate which produced such horses as Nearco and Ribot, this great Roman club boasts 27 holes designed by Charles Kenneth Cotton and laid out by Piero Mancinelli. The main 18-hole course was much acclaimed during the 1968 and 1984 World Cups held here. This is a classic course, where water comes into play only on two holes and where the main hazards are the very many trees and bunkers. In the fairways, bunkers are most penalizing for the better players, which might reassure visitors. Rather flat, there are nonetheless a few holes where you are driving blind, but within reason: generally speaking, this course reveals what it has in store. Interestingly, each hole has its own character, so you remember them well. Each hole, too, gives a great sensation of space and isolation from one fairway to another. One of the great Italian courses.

Olgiata Golf Club — 1961

Largo Olgiata 15
I - 00123 ROMA

Office	Segreteria	(39) 06 3088 9141
Pro shop	Pro shop	(39) 06 3088 4344
Fax	Fax	(39) 06 3088 9968
E-mail		olgiatagolf@ntt.it
Situation	Localita'	

Roma (pop. 2 643 581), 19 km

Annual closure	Chiusura annuale	no
Weekly closure	Chiusura settimanale	monday

Fees main season / Tariffe alta stagione	Week days / Settimana	We/Bank holidays / Feriale/Festivo
		full day
Individual Individuale	46 €	62 €
Couple Coppia	92 €	124 €
Caddy / Caddy		no
Electric Trolley / Carello elettrico		no
Buggy / Car		31 €
Clubs / Bastoni		10 €

Credit cards Carte di credito
VISA - Eurocard - MasterCard - DC - CartaSì - AMEX

Access Itinerario : Roma, "Grande Raccordo Anulare" (Ring road), Exit (Uscita) Via Cassia. S493 to the left → Bracciano, → Golf on the right.

Map 3 on page 937 Carta 3 Pagina 937

Golf course PERCORSO — 16/20

Site	Paesaggio	
Maintenance	Manutenzione	
Architect	Architetto	Henry Cotton, Piero Mancinelli
Type	Tipologia	parkland, residential
Relief	Relievo terreno	
Water in play	Acqua in gioco	
Exp. to wind	Esposto al vento	
Trees in play	Alberi in gioco	

Scorecard / Carta-score	Chp. / Camp.	Mens / Uomini	Ladies / Donne
Length Lunghezza	6347	6054	5306
Par	72	72	72
Slope system	—	—	—

Advised golfing ability / Livello di gioco consigliato: 0 12 24 36
Hcp required / Handicap richiesto 34

Club house & amenities CLUB HOUSE E SERVIZI — 8/10

Pro shop	Pro shop	
Driving range	Campo pratica	
Sheltered	coperto	8 mats
On grass	in erba	yes
Putting-green	Putting-green	yes
Pitching-green	Green-pratica	yes

Hotel facilities ALBERGHI — 6/10

HOTELS ALBERGHI

Villa San Dominique, 62 rooms, D 108 € — Roma (Via Cassia) 8 km
Tel (39) 06 3036 0147

Relais I Due Laghi — Le Cerque (Anguillara Sabazia) 12 km
25 rooms, D 129 €
Tel (39) 06 9960 7059, Fax (39) 06 9960 7068

Colony Flaminio, 74 rooms, D 134 € — Roma 12 km
Tel (39) 06 3630 1843, Fax (39) 06 3630 9495

RESTAURANTS RISTORANTE

Vino e Camino,Tel (39) 06 9980 3433 — Bracciano 8 km
Chalet del Lago, Tel (39) 06 9960 7053 — Anguillara Sabazia
Il Grottino da Norina, Tel(39) 06 996 8181 — Anguillara Sabazia

PADOVA

14 | 8 | 8

E' il campo più vicino a Montecchia, realizzato su un terreno praticamente piatto ai piedi dei Colli Euganei, colline di origine vulcanica colme di frutteti e vigneti da dove sgorgano calde sorgenti, conosciute fin dall'epoca dei Romani che hanno dato origine ad un gran numero di stazioni termali tra le quali Abano Terme ed altre nelle vicinanze. Il percorso disegnato da John Harris è di buona qualità e si adatta alla maggioranza dei giocatori. Qualche ostacolo d'acqua è stato scavato in modo da poter recuperare terra per effettuare movimenti in superficie e sono particolarmente pericolosi nelle buche tra la 5 e la 8. Agli alberi esistenti, sono stati aggiunti molti altri arbusti e cespugli che crescono lentamente ma sono una garanzia per il futuro. Il tracciato non esige virtuosismi particolari e i migliori giocatori qui potranno fare buoni risultati con una certa facilità. Un percorso abbastanza corto, di solito molto frequentato nei week-end (la club-house è molto grande ed ha 15 camere a disposizione) e piacevole per giocarci con tutta la famiglia.

This is the neighbouring course to Montecchia, on flat terrain at the foot of the Colli Euganei, volcanic hills dotted with orchards and vineyards and the source of hot springs already appreciated by the ancient Romans. They spawned a number of spa resorts, including Abano Terme and others in the same region. This course, designed by John Harris, is quality golfing and ideal for most players. A few water hazards have been dug out to collect some welcome earth with which to contour the course elsewhere, and are particularly dangerous from hole 5 to hole 8. The existing vegetation has been supplemented by many others trees and bushes, which are growing slowly but surely. The layout does not require any special skills and the best players might card a good score without being unduly tested. A rather short course, often busy on week-ends (the club-house is huge with 15 guestrooms) and pleasant to play with all the family.

Golf Club Padova — 1964

Via Noiera 57
I - 35030 VALSANZIBIO DI GALZIGNANO TERME (PA)

Office	Segreteria	(39) 049 913 0078
Pro shop	Pro shop	(39) 049 913 1140
Fax	Fax	(39) 049 913 1193
Web	www.golfpadova.it	
Situation	Localita'	

Padova (pop. 211 391), 17 km, Venezia (pop. 277 305), 40 km

Annual closure	Chiusura annuale	no
Weekly closure	Chiusura settimanale	monday

Fees main season Tariffe alta stagione		18 holes
	Week days Settimana	**We/Bank holidays** Feriale/Festivo
Individual Individuale	52 €	62 €
Couple Coppia	104 €	124 €

Green-fees on week days only (Ospiti solo durante i giorni feriali)

Caddy	Caddy	no
Electric Trolley	Carello elettrico	yes
Buggy	Car	26 €
Clubs	Bastoni	no

Credit cards Carte di credito VISA - CartaSi

Access Itinerario : A13 Padova-Bologna. Exit (Uscita) Terme Euganee. In Battaglia Terme, turn right. 6 km, Galzignano. Turn left → Valsanzibio. Golf on the left
Map 2 on page 934 Carta 2 Pagina 934

Golf course — PERCORSO — 14/20

Site	Paesaggio	
Maintenance	Manutenzione	
Architect	Architetto	John Harris
Type	Tipologia	country
Relief	Relievo terreno	
Water in play	Acqua in gioco	
Exp. to wind	Esposto al vento	
Trees in play	Alberi in gioco	

Scorecard Carta-score	**Chp.** Camp.	**Mens** Uomini	**Ladies** Donne
Length Lunghezza	6053	5920	5328
Par	72	72	72
Slope system	—	—	—

Advised golfing ability Livello di gioco consigliato: 0 12 24 36
Hcp required Handicap richiesto 34

Club house & amenities — CLUB HOUSE E SERVIZI — 8/10

Pro shop	Pro shop	
Driving range	Campo pratica	
Sheltered	coperto	10 mats
On grass	in erba	yes
Putting-green	Putting-green	yes
Pitching-green	Green-pratica	yes

Hotel facilities — ALBERGHI — 8/10

HOTELS ALBERGHI

Majestic Hotel Terme, 116 rooms, D 160 € — Galzignano Terme 1 km
Tel (39) 049 919 4000, Fax (39) 049 919 4250

Sporting Hotel Terme — Galzignano Terme 1 km
110 rooms, D 212 €
Tel (39) 049 919 5000, Fax (39) 049 919 5250

Green Park Hotel Terme — Galzignano Terme 1 km
93 rooms, D 129 €
Tel (39) 049 919 7000, Fax (39) 049 919 7250

RESTAURANTS RISTORANTE

Club House, Tel (39) 049 913 0215 — on site
Antico Brolo, Tel (39) 049 664 555 — Padova 17 km
La Montanella, Tel (39) 0429 718 200 — Arquà Petrarca 3 km

979

PARCO DE' MEDICI

13 | 6 | 9

Il percorso di 18 buche è stato completato da altre 9 buche (par 34) ed è stato parzialmente costruito su di una tenuta di caccia usata da Papa Leone X nel XV secolo. E'facilmente raggiungibile essendo molto vicino sia dal centro di Roma e dall'aeroporto. Il terreno è molto piatto e la sua monotonia è rotta da qualche movimento del terreno e da tanti laghi, rifugio di numerosi uccelli... Ma anche di un gran numero di palline dei giocatori imprecisi! Abbastanza lungo dalle partenze arretrate è molto più facile quando si ha la modestia di partire dalle partenze avanti anche se non vi lascerà un ricordo indelebile. Disegnato da David Mezzacane e Peter Fazio, Parco de' Medici rappresenta bene l'architettura moderna molto strategica dove, con grandi greens ben protetti, bisogna giocare preferibilmente un "target golf". Una grande club-house, un albergo a 5 stelle, una piscina e due tennis in erba completano questa struttura di buon livello.

The 18-hole course has been supplemented by a 9-holer (par 34) and was partly laid out over a former hunting estate belonging to Pope Leon X in the 15th century. For easy access, the course is within the immediate vicinity of downtown Rome and the airport. The terrain is very flat but the monotony is broken by contouring and the very many stretches of water that are home to a good many birds and a resting place for even more balls if you don't hit it straight. Rather long from the back-tees and very exposed to the wind, the layout is much easier when you are humble enough to move further forward, but somehow it doesn't leave a lasting impression. Designed by David Mezzacane and Peter Fazio, Parco de' Medici clearly portrays the highly strategic modern style of course architecture with large, well-guarded greens and a preference for target golf. A huge club-house, grand hotel, a pool and two grass tennis courts complete the very high standard facilities here.

Golf Club Parco de' Medici 1990
Viale Parco de' Medici 165/167
I - 00148 ROMA

Office	Segreteria	(39) 06 655 3477
Pro shop	Pro shop	(39) 06 655 3477
Fax	Fax	(39) 06 655 3344
Web	www.sheraton.com	
Situation	Localita'	

close to Roma (pop. 2 643 581)

Annual closure	Chiusura annuale	no
Weekly closure	Chiusura settimanale	tuesday

Fees main season Tariffe alta stagione	18 holes	
	Week days Settimana	**We/Bank holidays** Feriale/Festivo
Individual Individuale	46 €	52 €
Couple Coppia	92 €	104 €
Caddy	Caddy	26 €
Electric Trolley	Carello elettrico	no
Buggy	Car	26 €
Clubs	Bastoni	13 €

Credit cards Carte di credito
VISA - Eurocard - MasterCard - DC - CartaSì - AMEX

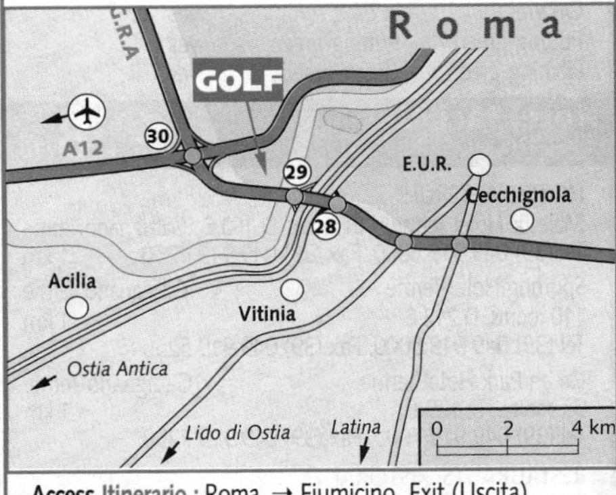

Access Itinerario : Roma, → Fiumicino, Exit (Uscita) Magliana Vecchia. → Golf
Map 3 on page 937 Carta 3 Pagina 937

Golf course PERCORSO — 13/20

Site	Paesaggio	
Maintenance	Manutenzione	
Architect	Architetto	David Mezzacane
Type	Tipologia	residential
Relief	Relievo terreno	
Water in play	Acqua in gioco	
Exp. to wind	Esposto al vento	
Trees in play	Alberi in gioco	

Scorecard Carta-score	**Chp.** Camp.	**Mens** Uomini	**Ladies** Donne
Length Lunghezza	6303	5908	5200
Par	71	71	71
Slope system	—	—	—

Advised golfing ability 0 12 24 36
Livello di gioco consigliato
Hcp required Handicap richiesto 34

Club house & amenities CLUB HOUSE E SERVIZI — 6/10

Pro shop	Pro shop	
Driving range	Campo pratica	
Sheltered	coperto	9 mats
On grass	in erba	yes
Putting-green	Putting-green	yes
Pitching-green	Green-pratica	yes

Hotel facilities ALBERGHI — 9/10

HOTELS ALBERGHI

Sheraton Golf Parco de' Medici — Roma 300 m
285 rooms, D 173 €
Tel (39) 06 658 588, Fax (39) 06 658 587 42

Holiday Inn Parco de' Medici — Roma 500 m
317 rooms, D 284 €
Tel (39) 06 65 581, Fax (39) 06 657 7005

Dei Congressi, 105 rooms, D 165 € — Roma 10 km
Tel (39) 06 592 6021, Fax (39) 06 591 1903

RESTAURANTS RISTORANTE

Checchino del 1887, Tel (39) 06 574 6318 — Roma 12 km
Il Convivio, Tel (39) 06 686 9432 — Roma 12 km
Quinzi Gabrieli, Tel (39) 06 687 9389 — Roma 12 km

PEVERO

17 | 8 | 8

Questa regione chiamata Costa Smeralda è stata lanciata turisticamente nel 1961, sotto la spinta di un gruppo di investitori guidati da Karim Aga Khan. E' diventata una delle regioni favorite dal "jet-set" con alberghi da sogno, porti turistici, tennis-club e con il Golf del Pevero, fiore all'occhiello del luogo, all'esatto opposto del non meno famoso (e più recente) Golf di Sperone in Corsica. I due campi sono stati disegnati da Robert Trent Jones. Il Pevero è sontuoso, scavato in mezzo alle rocce coperte di vegetazione boscosa, interrotte da baie stupende e da un mare dai mille colori. Il disegno è assolutamente strategico dove la lunghezza è relativa, ma ci vuole tecnica di prim'ordine per fare un buono score. E' un percorso fantastico per un match-play soprattutto quando il vento soffia forte e... capita molto spesso. In questo caso contare i propri colpi (sicuramente molti più di quanti vi aspettiate) diventa inopportuno. E' comunque un luogo di vacanza da sogno.

This region, known as the Costa Smeralda, began to be exploited as tourist material in 1961, spurred on by Karim Aga Khan and a consortium of investors. It has become one of the jet-set's favourite playgrounds with its palace hotels, marinas, tennis clubs and the site's crowning glory, the Pevero golf course, lying almost directly opposite the no less famous (and more recent) Golf de Sperone in Corsica. Both were designed by Robert Trent Jones. The Pevero site is simply sumptuous, between tree-covered hills, a rocky coastline broken only by some splendid coves and a sea of ever changing colour. This layout is highly strategic, yardage is a matter of relative importance and a good score calls for the virtuosity of a fine technician. This is a marvellous course for match-play golf, especially when the wind blows, as it does on occasions. In this case counting your strokes (certainly more than you bargained for) is meaningless. A dream holiday location.

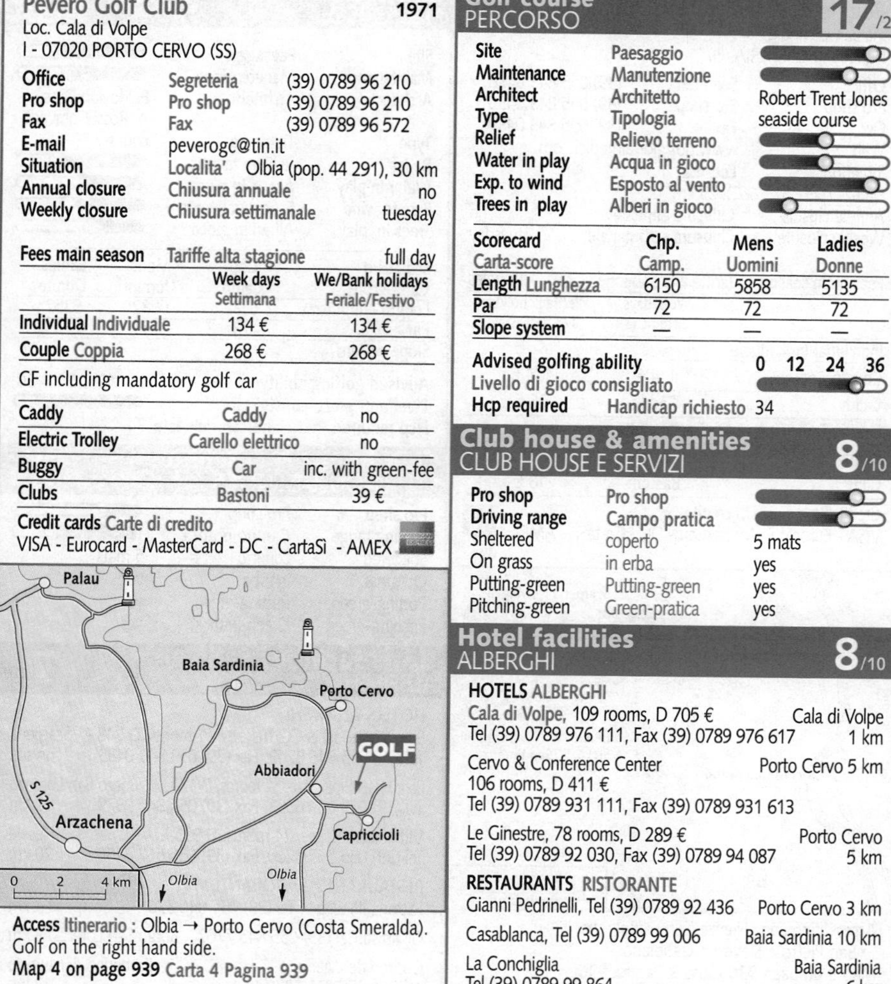

Pevero Golf Club **1971**
Loc. Cala di Volpe
I - 07020 PORTO CERVO (SS)

Office	Segreteria	(39) 0789 96 210
Pro shop	Pro shop	(39) 0789 96 210
Fax	Fax	(39) 0789 96 572
E-mail	peverogc@tin.it	
Situation	Localita'	Olbia (pop. 44 291), 30 km
Annual closure	Chiusura annuale	no
Weekly closure	Chiusura settimanale	tuesday

Fees main season Tariffe alta stagione		full day
	Week days Settimana	We/Bank holidays Feriale/Festivo
Individual Individuale	134 €	134 €
Couple Coppia	268 €	268 €

GF including mandatory golf car

Caddy	Caddy	no
Electric Trolley	Carello elettrico	no
Buggy	Car	inc. with green-fee
Clubs	Bastoni	39 €

Credit cards Carte di credito
VISA - Eurocard - MasterCard - DC - CartaSì - AMEX

Access Itinerario : Olbia → Porto Cervo (Costa Smeralda). Golf on the right hand side.
Map 4 on page 939 Carta 4 Pagina 939

Golf course PERCORSO — 17/20

Site	Paesaggio	
Maintenance	Manutenzione	
Architect	Architetto	Robert Trent Jones
Type	Tipologia	seaside course
Relief	Relievo terreno	
Water in play	Acqua in gioco	
Exp. to wind	Esposto al vento	
Trees in play	Alberi in gioco	

Scorecard Carta-score	**Chp.** Camp.	**Mens** Uomini	**Ladies** Donne
Length Lunghezza	6150	5858	5135
Par	72	72	72
Slope system	—	—	—

Advised golfing ability 0 12 24 36
Livello di gioco consigliato
Hcp required Handicap richiesto 34

Club house & amenities CLUB HOUSE E SERVIZI — 8/10

Pro shop	Pro shop	
Driving range	Campo pratica	
Sheltered	coperto	5 mats
On grass	in erba	yes
Putting-green	Putting-green	yes
Pitching-green	Green-pratica	yes

Hotel facilities ALBERGHI — 8/10

HOTELS ALBERGHI

Cala di Volpe, 109 rooms, D 705 € — Cala di Volpe 1 km
Tel (39) 0789 976 111, Fax (39) 0789 976 617

Cervo & Conference Center — Porto Cervo 5 km
106 rooms, D 411 €
Tel (39) 0789 931 111, Fax (39) 0789 931 613

Le Ginestre, 78 rooms, D 289 € — Porto Cervo 5 km
Tel (39) 0789 92 030, Fax (39) 0789 94 087

RESTAURANTS RISTORANTE

Gianni Pedrinelli, Tel (39) 0789 92 436 — Porto Cervo 3 km

Casablanca, Tel (39) 0789 99 006 — Baia Sardinia 10 km

La Conchiglia — Baia Sardinia 6 km
Tel (39) 0789 99 864

POGGIO DEI MEDICI

15 | 7 | 7

Firenze possiede qualcosa in più oltre alla sua città: ha anche una campagna meravigliosa, dolce e affascinante dove ogni cosa è dotata di naturale armonia. Immersi in queste colline coperte di vigneti, olivi, pini e cipressi, in una regione dove si mangia molto bene e si producono vini stupendi, vi potrà capitare di pensare che il tempo si sia fermato. Il nome di questo golf (la collina dei Medici) riassume la storia e il paesaggio di Firenze. Bisognerà aspettare che gli alberi crescano ancora per vedere l'aspetto definitivo di questo percorso. E' stato inaugurato nel 1992 in una distesa molto vasta ed è stato disegnato dal campione italiano Baldovino Dassù e dall' architetto Alvise Rossi Fioravanti. Hanno dimostrato grande fantasia per come è stato utilizzato il terreno, come sono stati disegnati fairways e greens e per come sono stati fatti entrare in gioco gli ostacoli: rough, sabbia e acqua. Molto ondulato, esige una buona forma fisica e, a meno che non abbiate un handicap con una sola cifra, sarà meglio giocare dalle partenze normali.

Florence is a little more than just the city of Florence; there is also some wonderfully sweet and charming countryside where everything is visual and natural harmony. In the middle of hills covered with vines, olive, pine and cypress trees, and in a land of sophisticated food and admirable wines, you could be forgiven for thinking that time has stood still. The name of this course ("The Hill of the Medici") sums up both the history and landscape of Florence. However, the trees here will need to grow a little before the course fully matures. It was opened in 1992 over very wide open space and designed by the Italian champion Baldovino Dassù and course architect Alvise Rossi Fioravanti. They have showed a great deal of imagination in the way they used the terrain, contoured the fairways and greens and brought hazards into play, namely rough, sand and water. A very hilly course which is better played by the fitter golfer, and a difficult one, too, where the front tees are to be advised unless you can boast a single-figure handicap. If you only have time for the one round, match-play is the best solution for enjoyable golf.

Poggio dei Medici Golf Club — 1992

Via San Gavino 27
I - 50038 SCARPERIA (FI)

Office	Segreteria	(39) 055 843 0436
Pro shop	Pro shop	(39) 055 843 0436
Fax	Fax	(39) 055 843 0439
Web	www.poggiodeimedici.com	
Situation	Localita'	

Firenze (pop. 376 662), 25 km

Annual closure	Chiusura annuale	no
Weekly closure	Chiusura settimanale	tuesday

Fees main season Tariffe alta stagione		18 holes
	Week days Settimana	We/Bank holidays Feriale/Festivo
Individual Individuale	57 €	67 €
Couple Coppia	114 €	134 €
Caddy Caddy		26 €
Electric Trolley Carello elettrico		no
Buggy Car		31 €
Clubs Bastoni		18 €

Credit cards Carte di credito
VISA - Eurocard - MasterCard- DC - CartaSì - AMEX

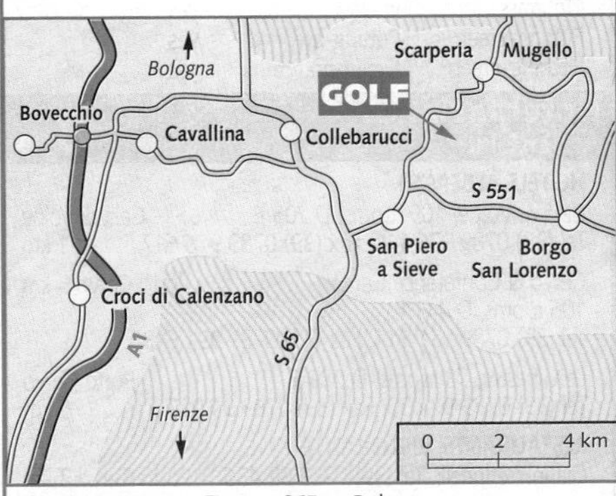

Access Itinerario : Firenze, S65 → Bologna, → San Pietro a Sieve, → Gabbiano.
Map 3 on page 936 Carta 3 Pagina 936

Golf course — PERCORSO — 15/20

Site	Paesaggio	
Maintenance	Manutenzione	
Architect	Architetto	Baldovino Dassù A. Rossi Fioravanti
Type	Tipologia	country
Relief	Relievo terreno	
Water in play	Acqua in gioco	
Exp. to wind	Esposto al vento	
Trees in play	Alberi in gioco	

Scorecard Carta-score	Chp. Camp.	Mens Uomini	Ladies Donne
Length Lunghezza	6338	6082	5352
Par	73	73	73
Slope system	—	—	—

Advised golfing ability Livello di gioco consigliato — 0 12 24 36
Hcp required Handicap richiesto 34

Club house & amenities — CLUB HOUSE E SERVIZI — 7/10

Pro shop	Pro shop	
Driving range	Campo pratica	
Sheltered	coperto	5 mats
On grass	in erba	yes
Putting-green	Putting-green	yes
Pitching-green	Green-pratica	yes

Hotel facilities — ALBERGHI — 7/10

HOTELS ALBERGHI

Sonesta Resort & CC Tuscany 31 rooms, D 248 € — Scarperia
Tel (39) 055 846 8249, Fax (39) 055 843 0439 — on site

Park Hotel Ripaverde, 51 rooms, D 170 € — Borgo San Lorenzo
Tel (39) 055 849 6003, Fax (39) 055 845 9379 — 8 km

Villa San Michele, 24 rooms, D 935 € — Fiesole
Tel (39) 055 567 8200, Fax (39) 055 567 8250 — 20 km

RESTAURANTS RISTORANTE

Fattoria Il Palagio, Tel (39) 055 846 376 — Scarperia 2 km

Gli artisti, Tel (39) 055 845 7707 — Borgo San Lorenzo 8 km

Cosimo de' Medici — Barberino di Mugello
Tel (39) 055 842 0370 — 3 km

PUNTA ALA

14 | 6 | 8

Non lontano dalla città storica di Siena (che merita una visita di qualche giorno), in faccia alla Corsica, vicino ad altre importanti stazioni balneari, Punta Ala è un luogo di vacanze di prim' ordine per tutta la famiglia. L'ottima qualità del suo golf permette quindi oltre al divertimento la possibilità di un'impegnativa giornata di golf. Disegnato da Giulio Cavalsani all'inizio degli anni '60 si snoda su di un terreno molto ondulato (il golf-cart è consigliato) che obbliga ad una costante concentrazione. La presenza interminabile di alberi, complica ancora di più la situazione per coloro che cercano di fare un buono score: diventa allora indispensabile saper "lavorare" bene la palla in tutte le direzioni per uscire dalla pineta quando si è finiti dentro. Abbastanza lungo dalle partenze arretrate, Punta Ala è decisamente più piacevole dalle partenze normali. Un campo divertente, in un posto molto tranquillo.

Not far from the historical city of Sienna (worth a visit of several days), opposite Corsica and next to some top seaside resorts, Punta Ala is a first-rate holiday destination for all the family. The excellence of the golf course also means that golfers can both have fun and get down to some serious golfing. Designed by Giulio Cavalsani in the early 1960s, it is laid out over some very hilly terrain (buggy recommended) which calls for unwavering concentration. In addition, the unending presence of trees complicates matters still further if you are looking, say, to break 90. You simply have to be able to work the ball in all directions to get that mis-hit ball safely out of the pine trees. Rather a long course from the back tees, Punta Ala is much kinder when you tee off further forward. A pretty course in a very calm setting.

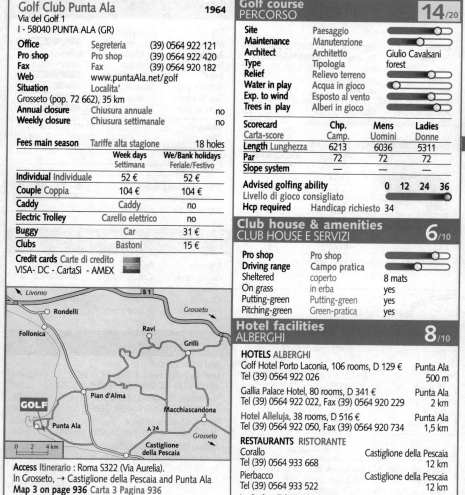

Golf Club Punta Ala **1964**
Via del Golf 1
I - 58040 PUNTA ALA (GR)

Office	Segreteria	(39) 0564 922 121
Pro shop	Pro shop	(39) 0564 922 420
Fax	Fax	(39) 0564 920 182
Web	www.puntaAla.net/golf	
Situation	Localita'	

Grosseto (pop. 72 662), 35 km

Annual closure	Chiusura annuale	no
Weekly closure	Chiusura settimanale	no

Fees main season Tariffe alta stagione	**Week days** Settimana	**We/Bank holidays** Feriale/Festivo 18 holes
Individual Individuale	52 €	52 €
Couple Coppia	104 €	104 €
Caddy Caddy		no
Electric Trolley Carello elettrico		no
Buggy Car		31 €
Clubs Bastoni		15 €

Credit cards Carte di credito
VISA- DC - CartaSi - AMEX

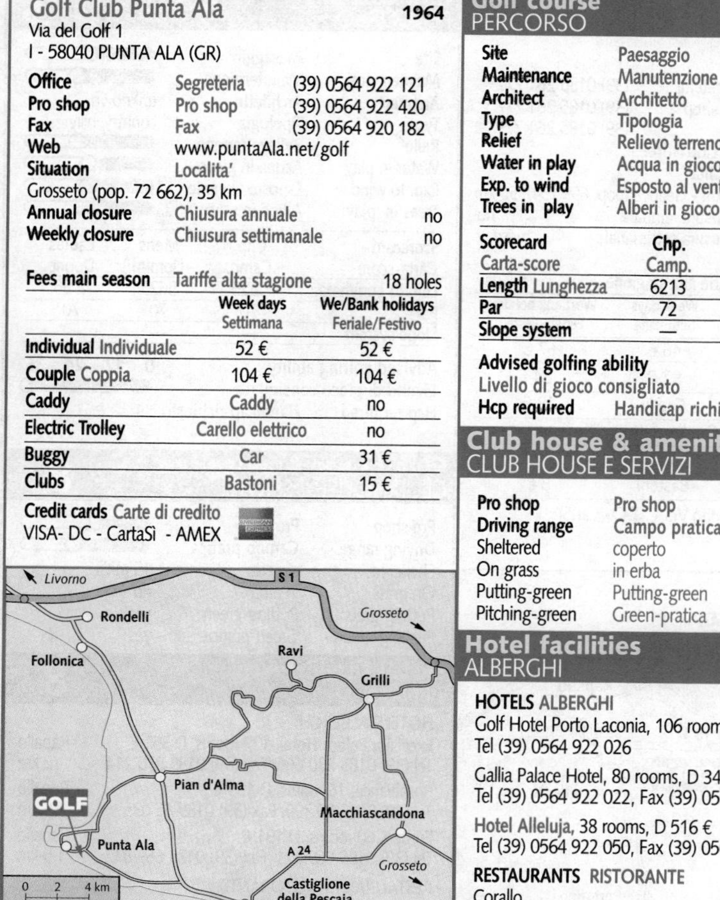

Access Itinerario : Roma S322 (Via Aurelia).
In Grosseto, → Castiglione della Pescaia and Punta Ala
Map 3 on page 936 Carta 3 Pagina 936

Golf course PERCORSO — 14/20

Site	Paesaggio	
Maintenance	Manutenzione	
Architect	Architetto	Giulio Cavalsani
Type	Tipologia	forest
Relief	Relievo terreno	
Water in play	Acqua in gioco	
Exp. to wind	Esposto al vento	
Trees in play	Alberi in gioco	

Scorecard Carta-score	**Chp.** Camp.	**Mens** Uomini	**Ladies** Donne
Length Lunghezza	6213	6036	5311
Par	72	72	72
Slope system	—	—	—

Advised golfing ability 0 12 24 36
Livello di gioco consigliato
Hcp required Handicap richiesto 34

Club house & amenities CLUB HOUSE E SERVIZI — 6/10

Pro shop	Pro shop	
Driving range	Campo pratica	
Sheltered	coperto	8 mats
On grass	in erba	yes
Putting-green	Putting-green	yes
Pitching-green	Green-pratica	yes

Hotel facilities ALBERGHI — 8/10

HOTELS ALBERGHI

Golf Hotel Porto Laconia, 106 rooms, D 129 € — Punta Ala 500 m
Tel (39) 0564 922 026

Gallia Palace Hotel, 80 rooms, D 341 € — Punta Ala 2 km
Tel (39) 0564 922 022, Fax (39) 0564 920 229

Hotel Alleluja, 38 rooms, D 516 € — Punta Ala 1,5 km
Tel (39) 0564 922 050, Fax (39) 0564 920 734

RESTAURANTS RISTORANTE

Corallo — Castiglione della Pescaia 12 km
Tel (39) 0564 933 668

Pierbacco — Castiglione della Pescaia 12 km
Tel (39) 0564 933 522

Lo Scalino Tel (39) 0564 922 168 — Punta Ala 1 km

RAPALLO

13 | 8 | 8

Come molti golf europei, anche Rapallo è nato vicino ad un luogo di villeggiatura ed è situato nella parte orientale della Riviera, più mossa e selvaggia della parte occidentale, da Genova a Ventimiglia. Rapallo è una delle più eleganti stazioni balneari italiane e il percorso si snoda sulle colline che la circondano. Di lunghezza ridotta, ma rispettabile al momento della costruzione negli anni '30, il percorso non ha che due par 5 (la 2 e la 7) quattro par 3 e dodici par 4 tra i 255 e i 385 metri. L'architetto ha seguito armoniosamente i movimenti del terreno per disegnare il campo facendo entrare in gioco alberi e corsi d'acqua come ostacoli naturali. I greens di taglia piccola obbligano ad una precisione assoluta dato che sono anche molto ben difesi. Un golf piacevole per fare una partita tra amici e relativamente facile dalle partenze normali. Una buona occasione per fare bella figura!

Like many continental golf courses, Rapallo was designed near a holiday centre on the eastern side of the Riviera, a steeper and wilder section of coastline than further west, running from Genoa to Ventimiglia. Rapallo is one of Italy's most elegant seaside resorts and the golf course is laid out over the hills that overlook the town below. Today considered a short course (although this sort of yardage was quite respectable in the 1930s when it was first laid out), Rapallo has only two par 5s (the 2nd and 7th holes), four par 3s and twelve par 4s of between 255 and 385 metres. The architect used the terrain's natural contours to build a smoothly flowing layout, playing with trees and water as natural hazards. The small greens calls for accurate approach shots, especially since they are well guarded. A pleasant course for a round with friends and relatively easy from the front tees. A good opportunity to shine without too much effort.

Cicolo Golf e Tennis Rapallo — 1930

Via Mameli 377
I - 16035 RAPALLO (GE)

Office	Segreteria	(39) 0185 261 777
Pro shop	Pro shop	(39) 0185 261 777
Fax	Fax	(39) 0185 261 779
E-mail	golfclub@ifree.it	
Situation	Localita'	

Rapallo (pop. 28 176), 2 km - Genova (pop. 659 754), 50 km

Annual closure	Chiusura annuale	no
Weekly closure	Chiusura settimanale	tuesday

Fees main season Tariffe alta stagione — full day

	Week days / Settimana	We/Bank holidays / Feriale/Festivo
Individual Individuale	46 €	67 €
Couple Coppia	92 €	134 €
Caddy	Caddy	18 €
Electric Trolley	Carello elettrico	no
Buggy	Car	34 €
Clubs	Bastoni	8 €

Credit cards Carte di credito VISA - DC - CartSì

Access Itinerario : A12 Genova-Livorno. Exit (Uscita) Rapallo → Centro Cittadino. Golf 200 m on the right.
Map 1 on page 933 Carta 1 Pagina 933

Golf course — PERCORSO — 13/20

Site	Paesaggio	
Maintenance	Manutenzione	
Architect	Architetto	unknown
Type	Tipologia	country, hilly
Relief	Relievo terreno	
Water in play	Acqua in gioco	
Exp. to wind	Esposto al vento	
Trees in play	Alberi in gioco	

Scorecard Carta-score	Chp. Camp.	Mens Uomini	Ladies Donne
Length Lunghezza	5625	5625	4955
Par	70	70	70
Slope system	—	—	—

Advised golfing ability Livello di gioco consigliato — 0 12 24 36
Hcp required Handicap richiesto 34

Club house & amenities — CLUB HOUSE E SERVIZI — 8/10

Pro shop	Pro shop	
Driving range	Campo pratica	
Sheltered	coperto	15 mats
On grass	in erba	no
Putting-green	Putting-green	yes
Pitching-green	Green-pratica	yes

Hotel facilities — ALBERGHI — 8/10

HOTELS ALBERGHI

Excelsior Palace Hotel, 127 rooms, D 351 € — Rapallo 2 km
Tel (39) 0185 230 666, Fax (39) 0185 230 214

Rosabianca, 16 rooms, D 155 € — Rapallo 1,5 km
Tel (39) 0185 50 390, Fax (39) 0185 65 035

Europa, 60 rooms, D 191 € — Rapallo 1,5 km
Tel (39) 0185 669 521, Fax (39) 0185 669 847

RESTAURANTS RISTORANTE

Hostaria Vecchia Rapallo, — Rapallo 2 km
Tel (39) 0185 50 053

Luca, Tel (39) 0185 60 323 — Rapallo 2,5 km

U Giancu, Tel (39) 0185 260 505 — Rapallo 1.5 km

RIMINI

13 | 6 | 8

Rimini non ha la pretesa di essere uno dei grandi percorsi del nostro tempo ma, in un luogo di villeggiatura, è stato concepito soprattutto con lo scopo di far divertire i giocatori senza appesantire troppo i loro scores! Il posto è il punto di partenza ideale sia per una puntata verso le famose spiagge dell'Adriatico che per andare alla scoperta delle ricchezze culturali di Ravenna e Ferrara. Rimini ha dei tesori propri ereditati in particolar modo dalla famiglia Malatesta che è stata esempio di rara raffinatezza ma anche di estrema crudeltà. Questo percorso si trova nell'entroterra, in una regione magnifica proprio ai piedi della Repubblica di San Marino nella valle della Marecchia. Il disegno di Brian Silva è abbastanza classico, facile da interpretare: sin dalla prima volta non sarà difficile decifrare i suoi segreti. Abbastanza piatto consente di andare a piedi senza stancarsi ma non deve essere sottovalutato; gli alberi e soprattutto gli ostacoli d'acqua sono sempre in gioco diventando a volte pericolosi. Ben disegnato, il golf di Rimini non ha una personalità spiccata ma la sua onestà e la bellezza del paesaggio piaceranno sicuramente.

Rimini would never claim to be one of the greatest courses in the world, but in this holiday region the idea was to provide a layout that does not leave you dead and buried and which actually gives you the chance to card a good score. This site is also a good starting point for exploring not only the beaches of the Adriatic but also the cultural heritage of Ravenna and Ferrara. Rimini also has treasures of its own, inherited most notably from the Malatesta family, which unashamedly embraced both cruelty and refinement. The course is located just inland in a magnificent region along the edge of the Marecchia valley overlooked by the Republic of San Marino. Brian Silva's layout is in the classic style with no real surprises. It is rather flat and easy on the feet, but definitely not a course to be sniffed at. Woods, and mainly water hazards come into play and sometimes loom dangerously. A well-designed layout that hardly stands head and shoulders above the rest, but as a plain honest golf course you will enjoy it. Not to mention the site's outstanding beauty.

Rimini Golf Club — 1993

Via Tenuta 109
I - 47827 VILLA VERUCCHIO

Office	Segreteria	(39) 0541 678 122
Pro shop	Pro shop	(39) 0541 678 122
Fax	Fax	(39) 0541 670 572
Web	www.riminigolf.com	
Situation	Localita'	
Rimini (pop. 131 062), 14 km		
Annual closure	Chiusura annuale	no
Weekly closure	Chiusura settimanale	no

Fees main season Tariffe alta stagione	18 holes	
	Week days Settimana	**We/Bank holidays** Feriale/Festivo
Individual Individuale	46 €	57 €
Couple Coppia	92 €	114 €
Caddy Caddy	no	
Electric Trolley Carello elettrico	no	
Buggy Car	31 €	
Clubs Bastoni	13 €	

Credit cards Carte di credito
VISA - Eurocard - MasterCard- DC - JCB - AMEX

Access Itinerario : A14 Bologna-Ancona. Exit (Uscita) Rimini Nord → Verucchio. At Santarcangelo, → Villa Verucchio. 10 km turn right.

Map 3 on page 937 Carta 3 Pagina 937

Golf course PERCORSO — 13/20

Site	Paesaggio	
Maintenance	Manutenzione	
Architect	Architetto	Brian Silva
Type	Tipologia	open country
Relief	Relievo terreno	
Water in play	Acqua in gioco	
Exp. to wind	Esposto al vento	
Trees in play	Alberi in gioco	

Scorecard Carta-score	**Chp.** Camp.	**Mens** Uomini	**Ladies** Donne
Length Lunghezza	6145	6145	5407
Par	72	72	72
Slope system	—	—	—

Advised golfing ability 0 12 24 36
Livello di gioco consigliato
Hcp required Handicap richiesto 34

Club house & amenities CLUB HOUSE E SERVIZI — 6/10

Pro shop	Pro shop	
Driving range	Campo pratica	
Sheltered	coperto	27 mats
On grass	in erba	yes
Putting-green	Putting-green	yes
Pitching-green	Green-pratica	yes

Hotel facilities ALBERGHI — 8/10

HOTELS ALBERGHI

Case Rosse, 6 rooms, D 72 € — on site
Tel (39) 0541 678 123, Fax (39) 0541 678 876

Hotel National, 86 rooms, D 160 € — Rimini 15 km
Tel (39) 0541 390 944, Fax (39) 0541 390 954

Villa Adriatica, 85 rooms, D 72 € — Rimini 14 km
Tel (39) 0541 545 99

RESTAURANTS RISTORANTE

Pesce Azzurro — Villa Verucchio 500 m
Tel (39) 0541 678 237

Acero Rosso — Rimini 15 km
Tel (39) 0541 535 77

Ro' e Buni Tel (39) 0541 678 484 — Villa Verucchio

RIVA DEI TESSALI

13 | 7 | 7

Questa parte della Puglia non è la più conosciuta dai turisti stranieri, anche se assistere alla processione della settimana Santa a Taranto (indispensabile per entrare nella dimensione religiosa del profondo sud) o andare a visitare più a nord la stupefacente città di Matera sarebbero da non perdere. A Taranto c'è anche il Museo Archeologico Nazionale che fa rivivere in modo particolare la presenza greca in questa parte d'Europa. Infine la costa, disseminata di spiagge immense, come il lido di Metaponto, fa di questa zona un luogo di vacanza di tutto rispetto. Il percorso di Riva dei Tessali è uno dei rari nel sud Italia dove i numerosissimi alberi assicurano l'ombra, molto spesso gradita e nello stesso tempo sono una delle principali difficoltà del percorso insieme agli ostacoli d'acqua. Disegnato da Marco Croze, non è molto lungo ma i greens di medie dimensioni sono ben difesi. Non è il percorso più spettacolare del mondo, ma ha il privilegio di essere alla portata di tutti.

The region of Apulia is hardly the part of Italy best known to foreign tourists, yet the Holy Week processions in Taranto (they give great insight into the depth of religious feeling in southern Italy) and a trip to the amazing town of Metera with its troglodyte dwellings further north are essential visiting. Taranto also boasts a Museo Archeologico Nazionale, which recalls the presence of the ancient Greeks in this part of Europe. Last but not least, the beach-lined seaboard, for example the Lido di Metaponto, makes this a remarkable holiday destination. Riva dei Tessali is one of the rare golf courses to be found in the south of Italy, where the very many trees offer welcome shade and provide one of the course's main difficulties, together with water. Designed by Marco Croze, the course is on the short side and has average-sized greens that are well defended. Not the most spectacular layout in the world but at least playable by everyone.

Golf Club Riva dei Tessali — 1968

I - 74011 CASTELLANETA (TA)

Office	Segreteria	(39) 099 843 9251
Pro shop	Pro shop	(39) 099 843 9251
Fax	Fax	(39) 099 843 1844
Web	www.rivadeitessali.it	
Situation	Localita'	
Taranto (pop. 208 214), 34 km		
Annual closure	Chiusura annuale	no
Weekly closure	Chiusura settimanale	tuesday

Fees main season Tariffe alta stagione		18 holes
	Week days Settimana	**We/Bank holidays** Feriale/Festivo
Individual Individuale	41 €	41 €
Couple Coppia	82 €	82 €
Caddy	Caddy	yes
Electric Trolley	Carello elettrico	no
Buggy	Car	21 €
Clubs	Bastoni	13 €

Credit cards Carte di credito VISA - CartaSì - AMEX

Access Itinerario : Bari A14 → Taranto. At the end of motorway, go to Palagiano. S106dir, turn right on S106. 18 km, → Riva dei Tessali
Map 4 on page 938 Carta 4 Pagina 938

Golf course — PERCORSO — 13/20

Site	Paesaggio	
Maintenance	Manutenzione	
Architect	Architetto	Marco Croze
Type	Tipologia	copse
Relief	Relievo terreno	
Water in play	Acqua in gioco	
Exp. to wind	Esposto al vento	
Trees in play	Alberi in gioco	

Scorecard Carta-score	**Chp.** Camp.	**Mens** Uomini	**Ladies** Donne
Length Lunghezza	5947	5709	5095
Par	72	72	72
Slope system	—	—	—

Advised golfing ability Livello di gioco consigliato 0 12 24 36
Hcp required Handicap richiesto 34

Club house & amenities — CLUB HOUSE E SERVIZI — 7/10

Pro shop	Pro shop	
Driving range	Campo pratica	
Sheltered	coperto	no
On grass	in erba	yes
Putting-green	Putting-green	yes
Pitching-green	Green-pratica	yes

Hotel facilities — ALBERGHI — 7/10

HOTELS ALBERGHI

Riva dei Tessali Golf Hotel — Castellaneta Marina 2,5 km
70 rooms, D 129 €
Tel (39) 099 843 9251, Fax (39) 099 843 1844

Grand Hotel Delfino, 198 rooms, D 103 € — Taranto 34 km
Tel (39) 099 732 3232, Fax (39) 099 730 4654

Residence Club Hotel, 20 rooms, D 176 € — Castellaneta on site
Tel (39) 099 843 9811, Fax (39) 099 843 9001

RESTAURANTS RISTORANTE

Da Fifina, Tel (39) 0835 543 134 — Bernalda 10 km

Al Vecchio Frantoio — Bernalda 10 km
Tel(39) 0835 543 546

ROMA - ACQUASANTA

16 | 8 | 9

In una campagna così calma e serafica, non si potrebbe mai immaginare di essere a un passo dal centro di Roma e a poche centinaia di metri da Cinecittà. Invece siamo sulla via Appia "nuova" a fianco di quella "antica" e la vista dell'Acquedotto che portava l'acqua alla capitale dell'Impero ci riporta alla mente la storia che circonda questa parte d'Italia. Il percorso dell'Acquasanta ne fa parte, perchè è il più vecchio golf d'Italia, dove sono passate tutte le teste coronate e gli attori del cinema. E' un grande percorso vecchio stile inserito in una vegetazione superba ma non soffocante. Dolcemente ondulato è attraversato da piccoli corsi d'acqua piazzati quasi sempre davanti ai greens. E' molto vario nel disegno e proprio per questo giocando qui non ci si annoia mai. Spettacolare e nello stesso tempo naturale il percorso si integra delicatamente nel paesaggio tipico della campagna romana. Quando il golf è Dolce Vita...

In countryside as lazy and as peaceful as this, it is hard to believe you are so close to the centre of Rome and a few hundred metres from Cinecitta. Maybe we are on the "new" Via Appia, alongside the old one. The view from the aqueduct that carried spring water to the capital of the Roman empire is a constant reminder of the history that surrounds this part of Italy. The Acquasanta course is all part of it, being the oldest club in Italy and one that has entertained kings, princes and movie stars. Above all, it is a great old-style course in a superb setting of plants and trees, although the latter are never too present. This is a pleasantly sloping course crossed by streams, often just in front of the greens. And thanks to the variety of the layout, you never tire of playing here. Both spectacular and natural, the course blends delicately into the landscape of typical Roman countryside. Golf very much "dolce vita" style.

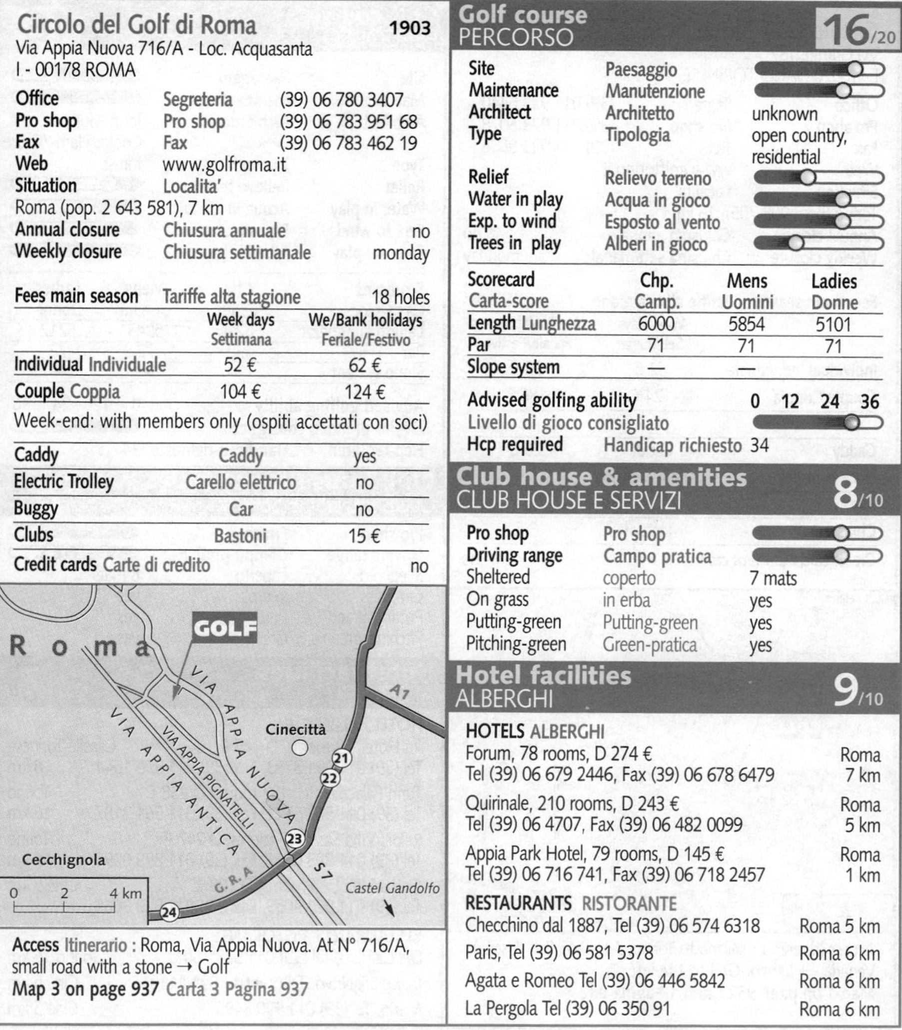

Circolo del Golf di Roma — 1903

Via Appia Nuova 716/A - Loc. Acquasanta
I - 00178 ROMA

Office	Segreteria	(39) 06 780 3407
Pro shop	Pro shop	(39) 06 783 951 68
Fax	Fax	(39) 06 783 462 19
Web	www.golfroma.it	
Situation	Localita'	
Roma (pop. 2 643 581), 7 km		
Annual closure	Chiusura annuale	no
Weekly closure	Chiusura settimanale	monday

Fees main season Tariffe alta stagione	18 holes	
	Week days Settimana	**We/Bank holidays** Feriale/Festivo
Individual Individuale	52 €	62 €
Couple Coppia	104 €	124 €

Week-end: with members only (ospiti accettati con soci)

Caddy	Caddy	yes
Electric Trolley	Carello elettrico	no
Buggy	Car	no
Clubs	Bastoni	15 €
Credit cards Carte di credito		no

Access Itinerario : Roma, Via Appia Nuova. At N° 716/A, small road with a stone → Golf
Map 3 on page 937 Carta 3 Pagina 937

Golf course PERCORSO — 16/20

Site	Paesaggio	
Maintenance	Manutenzione	
Architect	Architetto	unknown
Type	Tipologia	open country, residential
Relief	Relievo terreno	
Water in play	Acqua in gioco	
Exp. to wind	Esposto al vento	
Trees in play	Alberi in gioco	

Scorecard Carta-score	**Chp.** Camp.	**Mens** Uomini	**Ladies** Donne
Length Lunghezza	6000	5854	5101
Par	71	71	71
Slope system	—	—	—

Advised golfing ability Livello di gioco consigliato — 0 12 24 36
Hcp required Handicap richiesto 34

Club house & amenities CLUB HOUSE E SERVIZI — 8/10

Pro shop	Pro shop	
Driving range	Campo pratica	
Sheltered	coperto	7 mats
On grass	in erba	yes
Putting-green	Putting-green	yes
Pitching-green	Green-pratica	yes

Hotel facilities ALBERGHI — 9/10

HOTELS ALBERGHI

Forum, 78 rooms, D 274 € Tel (39) 06 679 2446, Fax (39) 06 678 6479	Roma 7 km
Quirinale, 210 rooms, D 243 € Tel (39) 06 4707, Fax (39) 06 482 0099	Roma 5 km
Appia Park Hotel, 79 rooms, D 145 € Tel (39) 06 716 741, Fax (39) 06 718 2457	Roma 1 km

RESTAURANTS RISTORANTE

Checchino dal 1887, Tel (39) 06 574 6318	Roma 5 km
Paris, Tel (39) 06 581 5378	Roma 6 km
Agata e Romeo Tel (39) 06 446 5842	Roma 6 km
La Pergola Tel (39) 06 350 91	Roma 6 km

TORINO - LA MANDRIA Percorso Blu

16 | 8 | 7

E' il fratello maggiore e il vicino di casa de I Roveri, un complesso di 36 buche dove il percorso migliore è quello "Blu". Di lunghezza assolutamente rispettabile è stato disegnato da John Morrison prima di subire recentemente qualche modifica sotto la supervisione di Graham Cooke. Gli alberi secolari sono un pò ovunque, ma la larghezza dei fairways è sufficiente per non sentirsi soffocati. I bunkers difendono bene i greens di questo percorso dal deciso carattere britannico. Alcuni ostacoli d'acqua naturali sono stati fatti entrare in gioco con intelligenza, ma è comunque è sempre facile rimediare i propri errori. E' un percorso dove si cammina senza stancarsi, immerso in una natura molto estremamente piacevole e inoltre è sufficientemente impegnativo per i giocatori bassi di handicap senza essere troppo difficile per i giocatori mediocri. Il percorso "giallo" è immerso nella stessa natura ericorda un pò lo stesso disegno ma ha più acqua in gioco.

This is the elderly neighbour to "I Roveri", a 36 hole resort the most challenging section of which is the "Percorso Blu". With very respectable yardage, it was designed by John Morrison and underwent a number of more recent changes under the supervision of Graham Cooke. Age-old trees are almost everywhere but the fairways are wide enough to avoid any risk of claustrophobia. The greens are well defended by bunkers on a course that has classic British character. A few stretches of water have been cleverly brought into play, but here again it is always possible to make up for your mistakes. In all, this gives an easily walkable, very pleasant and well-landscaped course that is demanding enough for low-handicap golfers and not too tough for high-handicappers. The other course, the "Percorso giallo" is more or less the same sort of layout only with more water in play.

Circolo Golf Torino — 1924

Via Grange 137
I - 10070 FIANO TORINESE

Office	Segreteria	(39) 011 923 5440
Pro shop	Pro shop	(39) 011 923 6028
Fax	Fax	(39) 011 923 5886
Web	www.golftorino.it	
Situation	Localita'	

Torino (pop. 903 705), 16 km

Annual closure	Chiusura annuale	no
Weekly closure	Chiusura settimanale	monday

Fees main season Tariffe alta stagione	18 holes	
	Week days Settimana	We/Bank holidays Feriale/Festivo
Individual Individuale	62 €	93 €
Couple Coppia	124 €	186 €

Caddy	Caddy	26 €
Electric Trolley	Carello elettrico	5 €
Buggy	Car	26 €
Clubs	Bastoni	8 €
Credit cards Carte di credito		no

Access Itinerario : Milano to Torino, A4 - A45 Exit (Uscita) Venaria. → Lanzo. Golf to the left.

Map 1 on page 932 Carta 1 Pagina 932

Golf course PERCORSO — 16/20

Site	Paesaggio	
Maintenance	Manutenzione	
Architect	Architetto	John Morrison Cooke/Harris/Croze
Type	Tipologia	forest
Relief	Relievo terreno	
Water in play	Acqua in gioco	
Exp. to wind	Esposto al vento	
Trees in play	Alberi in gioco	

Scorecard Carta-score	Chp. Camp.	Mens Uomini	Ladies Donne
Length Lunghezza	6216	5943	5212
Par	72	72	72
Slope system	—	—	—

Advised golfing ability 0 12 24 36
Livello di gioco consigliato
Hcp required Handicap richiesto 34

Club house & amenities CLUB HOUSE E SERVIZI — 8/10

Pro shop	Pro shop	
Driving range	Campo pratica	
Sheltered	coperto	8 mats
On grass	in erba	yes
Putting-green	Putting-green	yes
Pitching-green	Green-pratica	yes

Hotel facilities ALBERGHI — 7/10

HOTELS ALBERGHI

Jet Hotel, 79 rooms, D 145 € — Caselle Torinese
Tel (39) 011 991 3733, Fax (39) 011 996 1544 — 8 km

Turin Palace Hotel, 123 rooms, D 238 € — Torino
Tel (39) 011 562 5511, Fax (39) 011 561 2187 — 16 km

Relais Villa Sassi, 17 rooms, D 217 € — Torino
Tel (39) 011 898 0556, Fax (39) 011 898 0095 — 16 km

Gotha Hotel, 44 rooms, D 108 € — Cirié 5 km
Tel (39) 011 921 2059, Fax (39) 011 920 3661

RESTAURANTS RISTORANTE

Del Cambio, Tel (39) 011 543 760 — Torino 16 km
Dolce Stil Novo, Tel (39) 011 921 1110 — Cirié 5 km
Mario, Tel (39) 011 920 3490 — Cirié 5 km

VARESE

14 | 8 | 7

Varese è una città dallo sviluppo abbastanza recente, situata tra il lago di Lugano e Milano. Il campo da golf è stato costruito appena sopra al lago di Varese, che è uno dei più piccoli laghi lombardi dove il clima è particolarmente mite e soleggiato. I golfisti più religiosi non potranno fare a meno di una visita al Sacro Monte, luogo di pellegrinaggio alla Vergine Maria da dove si può godere un fantastico panorama sui laghi e le montagne. Questa regione non è solamente turistica e questo percorso merita una visita per la sua particolarità. Non è molto lungo, ma il terreno molto mosso richiede una buona forma fisica e una buona padronanza dei colpi in situazioni delicate e nei pendii. La scelta del bastone non è mai facile perchè parecchi greens sono sopraelevati e siccome molti hanno anche due livelli, la precisione diventa un obbligo. Se il vostro giro non è andato molto bene, vi consolerete facilmente rilassandovi nella superba club-house (un antico monastero) e ammirando la bellezza del paesaggio.

Varese is a city that has developed only recently, located between Lake Lugano and Milan. This course was built above Lake Varese, one of the smallest lakes in Lombardy, where the climate is particularly mild and sunny. The more religious-minded golfer won't want to miss visiting the Sacro Monte, the site of a great pilgrimage to the Virgin Mary plus the added bonus of wonderful views over lakes and mountains. This region is not only a tourist destination, it also worth visiting for the originality of this course. It might not be very long but the hilly terrain requires a certain level of fitness and control when hitting the ball from tricky situations and sloping lies. Club selection is seldom straightforward, especially since a number of greens are elevated and many are two-tiered, making accuracy a must. If your round didn't go so well, the superb club-house (a former monastery) offers solace and consolation from where you can admire the beautiful landscape.

Golf Club Varese — 1934

Via Vitorio Veneto 32
I - 21020 LUVINATE (VA)

Office	Segreteria	(39) 0332 229 302
Pro shop	Pro shop	(39) 0332 821 043
Fax	Fax	(39) 0332 222 107
E-mail	golf.varese@ntt.it	
Situation	Localita'	

Varese (pop. 83 798), 5 km - Milano (pop. 1 300 977), 55 km

Annual closure	Chiusura annuale	no
Weekly closure	Chiusura settimanale	monday

Fees main season Tariffe alta stagione	**Week days** Settimana	**We/Bank holidays** Feriale/Festivo
		18 holes
Individual Individuale	41 €	62 €
Couple Coppia	82 €	124 €

Caddy	Caddy	21 €
Electric Trolley	Carello elettrico	no
Buggy	Car	31 €
Clubs	Bastoni	10 €

Credit cards Carte di credito VISA - CartaSì

Access Itinerario : Varese, Via Manzoni, Via Sacco, Via S. Sanvito → Gavirate/Laveno. 5 km → Golf
Map 1 on page 932 Carta 1 Pagina 932

Golf course — PERCORSO — 14/20

Site	Paesaggio	
Maintenance	Manutenzione	
Architect	Architetto	Cecil R. Blandford Peter Gannon
Type	Tipologia	parkland, hilly
Relief	Relievo terreno	
Water in play	Acqua in gioco	
Exp. to wind	Esposto al vento	
Trees in play	Alberi in gioco	

Scorecard Carta-score	**Chp.** Camp.	**Mens** Uomini	**Ladies** Donne
Length Lunghezza	6105	5942	5238
Par	72	72	72
Slope system	—	—	—

Advised golfing ability Livello di gioco consigliato — 0 12 24 36

Hcp required Handicap richiesto 34

Club house & amenities — CLUB HOUSE E SERVIZI — 8/10

Pro shop	Pro shop	
Driving range	Campo pratica	
Sheltered	coperto	15 mats
On grass	in erba	no
Putting-green	Putting-green	yes
Pitching-green	Green-pratica	no

Hotel facilities — ALBERGHI — 7/10

HOTELS ALBERGHI

Palace Hotel, 112 rooms, D 258 € — Varese
Tel (39) 0332 312 600, Fax (39) 0332 312 870 — 4 km

City Hotel, 47 rooms, D 129 € — Varese
Tel (39) 0332 281 304, Fax (39) 0332 232 882 — 4 km

Bel Sit, 30 rooms, D 62 € — Comerio
Tel (39) 0332 737 705 — 7 km

RESTAURANTS RISTORANTE

Lago Maggiore, Tel (39) 0332 231 183 — Varese 5 km

Da Annetta, Tel (39) 0332 490 230 — Capolago 5 km

Al Vecchio Convento — Varese
Tel (39) 0332 261 005 — 5 km

989

VENEZIA

16 | 7 | 9

Si dice che Venezia sia magica all'alba e a notte fonda, quindi rimane tutta la giornata per giocare a golf su questo percorso nell'estremità ovest del Lido, di fronte alla città dei Dogi, in una stazione balneare molto elegante dove c'è anche uno dei pochissimi casinò italiani. Ma questo percorso è molto più di qualcosa dove cercare la vostra fortuna al gioco del golf. Disegnato da Cruikshank e rivisto da C.K. Cotton e Marco Croze, si snoda su terreno di dune sabbiose in mezzo a pioppi, pini ed olivi. La sua architettura tipicamente britannica si è perfettamente armonizzata negli anni e non costringe a porsi troppi problemi tattici quando non si è in forma. Bisogna comunque fare attenzione: in un ambiente così piacevole, gli errori si fanno facilmente e possono costare cari sullo score o in un match-play. Qualche ostacolo d'acqua e spesso il vento aggiungono un po' di sale in più a questo eccellente "piatto" golfistico.

As Venice is sheer magic at dawn and nightfall, you have the whole day in between to play this course at the far western tip of the Lido, opposite the city of Doges, a very chic seaside resort which is also home to one of the rare casinos to be found in Italy. This course, however, is much more than just space in which you can try your luck at golf. Designed by Cruikshank and restyled by C.K. Cotton and Marco Croze, it stretches over dune land amidst poplar, pine and olive trees. The obvious British architecture here has aged well and you find yourself rather happy not to have to ask too many tactical questions when your game is off-colour. Caution is required nonetheless, as mistakes can occur so easily in such a pleasant setting and prove costly for your card or match-play score. A few water hazards and frequent wind add a little spice to this excellent feast of golf.

Circolo Golf Venezia — 1928

Via del Forte
I - 30011 ALBERONI (VE)

Office	Segreteria	(39) 041 731 333
Pro shop	Pro shop	(39) 041 276 0361
Fax	Fax	(39) 041 731 339
Web	www.digilander.iol.it/circologolfvenezia	
Situation	Localita'	Venezia, 11 km
Annual closure	Chiusura annuale	no
Weekly closure	Chiusura settimanale	monday

Fees main season Tariffe alta stagione — full day

	Week days / Settimana	We/Bank holidays / Feriale/Festivo
Individual Individuale	46 €	52 €
Couple Coppia	92 €	104 €

Week-end : 2 days 72 € (indiv.)/ 124 € (couple)

Caddy	Caddy	31 €
Electric Trolley	Carello elettrico	no
Buggy	Car	no
Clubs	Bastoni	13 €

Credit cards Carte di credito
VISA- DC - CartaSi - AMEX

Access Itinerario : Venezia to Lido with vaporetto
Map 2 on page 934 Carta 2 Pagina 934

Golf course — PERCORSO — 16/20

Site	Paesaggio	
Maintenance	Manutenzione	
Architect	Architetto	CK Cotton/Cruikshank Marco Croze
Type	Tipologia	seaside course
Relief	Relievo terreno	
Water in play	Acqua in gioco	
Exp. to wind	Esposto al vento	
Trees in play	Alberi in gioco	

Scorecard Carta-score	Chp. Camp.	Mens Uomini	Ladies Donne
Length Lunghezza	6199	6039	5353
Par	72	72	72
Slope system	—	—	—

Advised golfing ability Livello di gioco consigliato — 0 12 24 36
Hcp required Handicap richiesto 34

Club house & amenities — CLUB HOUSE E SERVIZI — 7/10

Pro shop	Pro shop	
Driving range	Campo pratica	
Sheltered	coperto	5 mats
On grass	in erba	yes
Putting-green	Putting-green	yes
Pitching-green	Green-pratica	yes

Hotel facilities — ALBERGHI — 9/10

HOTELS ALBERGHI

Danieli, 233 rooms, D 653 € — Venezia
Tel (39) 041 522 6480, Fax (39) 041 520 0208 — 11 km

Excelsior, 193 rooms, D 566 € — Venezia Lido
Tel (39) 041 526 0201, Fax (39) 041 526 7276 — 3 km

Cà del Borgo 8 rooms, D 243 € — Venezia Lido (Malamocco)
Tel (39) 041 770 749, Fax (39) 041 770 744 — 3 km

RESTAURANTS RISTORANTE

Trattoria Favorita, Tel (39) 041 526 1626 — Venezia Lido 3 km
Andri, Tel (39) 041 526 5482 — Venezia Lido 12 km
Osteria da Fiore, Tel (39) 041 721 308 — Venezia 11 km
Al Vecio Cantier, Tel (39) 041 526 8130 — Venezia Lido 3 km

VERONA

13 | 7 | 8

Se amate le storie d'amore struggenti, non c' è posto più adatto di Verona, teatro del tragico amore di Romeo e Giulietta. Autentiche o create per gli animi sensibili, la casa in via Cappello e la tomba di Giulietta meritano un giro dopo un'opera all'Arena o un caffè in Piazza delle Erbe. Da ogni parte la guardiate, Verona è una città bellissima resa ancor più attraente dalla sua vicinanza con il lago di Garda. Il golf club Verona è stato fondato nel 1963 e il percorso è stato realizzato in due tempi da John Harris in uno stile assolutamente britannico secondo quello dell'architetto. Molto mosso, obbliga i giocatori meno in forma ad usare il golf cart e a stare molto attenti ad attaccare i greens sopraelevati (ed anche un green cieco). Le prime nove buche sono abbastanza strette e "tricky" con qualche pericoloso fuori limite mentre le buche di ritorno sono più larghe e con qualche ostacolo d'acqua ma consentono di non compromettere un buono score ottenuto sulle prime.

When you love tear-jerking tales of love and grief, you can hardly wish for a better setting than Verona, home to the tragic story of Romeo and Juliette. The house (Via Cappello) and tomb of Juliette are worth going out your way for, after an opera at the Arenas or a coffee on the Piazza delle Erbe. Whichever way you look at it, Verona is a superb city made even more attractive by the closeness of Lake Garda. The Verona Golf Club was founded in 1963 and the course laid out in two stages by John Harris, in a British parkland style consistent with the architect's own style. Very hilly, this course warrants a buggy for the more unfit golfer and a lot of concentration to hit some elevated greens (and one blind green as well). The first holes are rather narrow and tricky to negotiate - some dangerous out-of-bounds await the mis-hit shot - while the back 9 are wider with a few water hazards and shouldn't do too much damage to your card if you have scored well over the front nine.

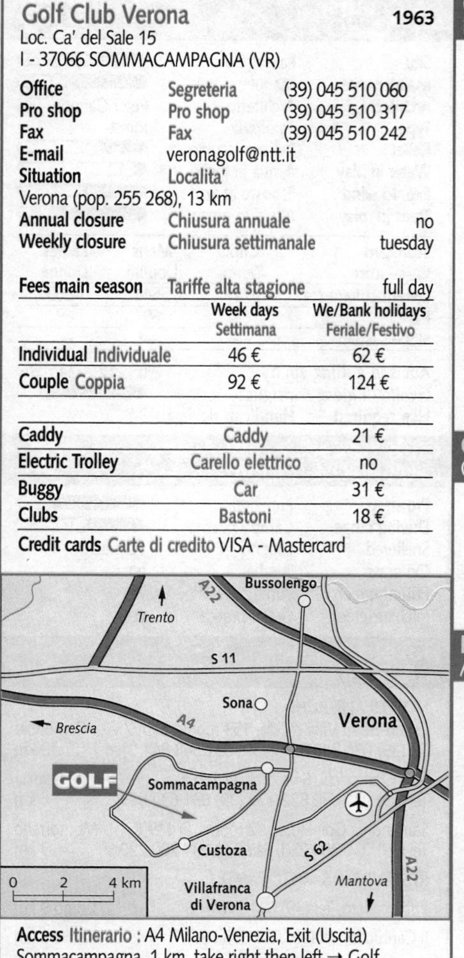

Golf Club Verona — 1963

Loc. Ca' del Sale 15
I - 37066 SOMMACAMPAGNA (VR)

Office	Segreteria	(39) 045 510 060
Pro shop	Pro shop	(39) 045 510 317
Fax	Fax	(39) 045 510 242
E-mail	veronagolf@ntt.it	
Situation	Localita'	
Verona (pop. 255 268), 13 km		
Annual closure	Chiusura annuale	no
Weekly closure	Chiusura settimanale	tuesday

Fees main season Tariffe alta stagione	full day	
	Week days Settimana	**We/Bank holidays** Feriale/Festivo
Individual Individuale	46 €	62 €
Couple Coppia	92 €	124 €

Caddy	Caddy	21 €
Electric Trolley	Carello elettrico	no
Buggy	Car	31 €
Clubs	Bastoni	18 €

Credit cards Carte di credito VISA - Mastercard

Access Itinerario : A4 Milano-Venezia, Exit (Uscita) Sommacampagna. 1 km, take right then left → Golf.
Map 2 on page 934 Carta 2 Pagina 934

Golf course PERCORSO — 13/20

Site	Paesaggio	
Maintenance	Manutenzione	
Architect	Architetto	John Harris
Type	Tipologia	country
Relief	Relievo terreno	
Water in play	Acqua in gioco	
Exp. to wind	Esposto al vento	
Trees in play	Alberi in gioco	

Scorecard Carta-score	**Chp.** Camp.	**Mens** Uomini	**Ladies** Donne
Length Lunghezza	6037	6037	5241
Par	72	72	72
Slope system	—	—	—

Advised golfing ability 0 12 24 36
Livello di gioco consigliato
Hcp required Handicap richiesto 34

Club house & amenities CLUB HOUSE E SERVIZI — 7/10

Pro shop	Pro shop	
Driving range	Campo pratica	
Sheltered	coperto	12 mats
On grass	in erba	yes
Putting-green	Putting-green	yes
Pitching-green	Green-pratica	yes

Hotel facilities ALBERGHI — 8/10

HOTELS ALBERGHI

Saccardi Quadrante Europe — Caselle di Sommacampagna
120 rooms, D 165 € — 5 km
Tel (39) 045 858 1400, Fax (39) 045 858 1402

Gabbia d'Oro — Verona
27 rooms, D 351 € — 13 km
Tel (39) 045 800 3060, Fax (39) 045 590 293

Locanda Merica, 11 rooms, D 77 € — Sommacampagna
Tel (39) 045 515 160, Fax (39) 045 515 344 — 5 km

RESTAURANTS RISTORANTE

Il Desco, Tel (39) 045 595 358 — Verona 13 km
Merica, Tel (39) 045 515 160 — Sommacampagna 2 km
Maffei, Tel (39) 045 801 0015 — Verona 13 km

VILLA D'ESTE

16 | 9 | 8

Disegnato nel 1926 da Peter Gannon, Villa d'Este è diventato rapidamente uno dei gioielli golfistici italiani. Merito è anche della sua posizione vicino al magnifico lago di Como, che si snoda in lunghezza e dove i piccoli porticcioli si succedono ai giardini esotici delle sue ville da sogno. La più bella è stata trasformata a Cernobbio in uno dei più affascinanti hotel, luogo di soggiorno ideale... Se non si hanno problemi di portafoglio. Villa d'Este è un percorso abbastanza mosso che si snoda ai bordi del piccolo lago di Montorfano in mezzo a pini, castani e querce ma dove si può facilmente giocare anche a piedi. Non è lungo, ma per fare un buono score bisogna mettere a punto una tecnica eccellente e saper fare colpi elaborati soprattutto nei par 3. Ci sono solo due par 5 ma entrambi offrono buone possibilità per un birdie. Una club-house di gran classe aggiunge il tocco finale a questo posto tranquillo ed elegante.

Designed in 1926 by Peter Gannon, Villa d'Este has rapidly become one of the gems of Italian golf courses, much of which is due to a location close to the long Lake Como, where small harbours give way to exotic gardens around superb villas. The finest of these villas in Cernobbio has been transformed into one of the most charming hotels you could wish to find, the ideal site for a holiday... if not on too tight a budget. Villa d'Este, alongside the small lake of Montorfano, is a rather hilly course set amidst pine, chestnut and birch trees but is easily walkable all the same. Yardage is not too demanding but you need to develop good technique to play well here, bending the ball both ways especially on the six par 3s. There are only two par 5s but both offer a real chance of a birdie. A superb club-house adds the final touch to this tranquil and elegant site.

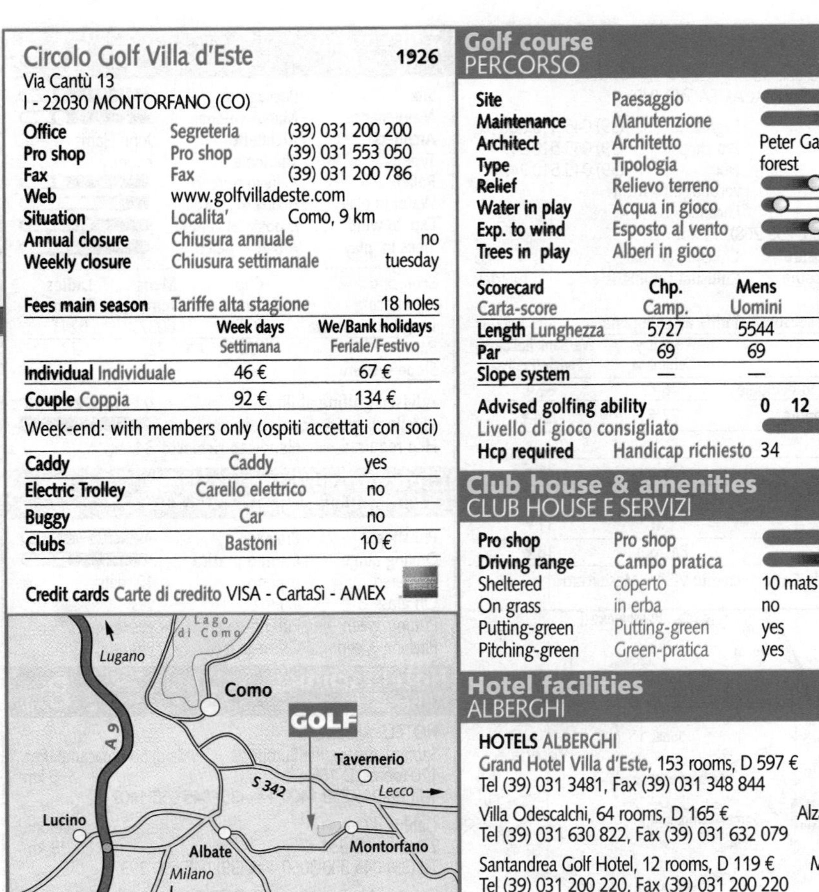

Circolo Golf Villa d'Este — 1926

Via Cantù 13
I - 22030 MONTORFANO (CO)

Office	Segreteria	(39) 031 200 200
Pro shop	Pro shop	(39) 031 553 050
Fax	Fax	(39) 031 200 786
Web	www.golfvilladeste.com	
Situation	Localita'	Como, 9 km
Annual closure	Chiusura annuale	no
Weekly closure	Chiusura settimanale	tuesday

Fees main season Tariffe alta stagione — 18 holes

	Week days Settimana	We/Bank holidays Feriale/Festivo
Individual Individuale	46 €	67 €
Couple Coppia	92 €	134 €

Week-end: with members only (ospiti accettati con soci)

Caddy	Caddy	yes
Electric Trolley	Carello elettrico	no
Buggy	Car	no
Clubs	Bastoni	10 €

Credit cards Carte di credito VISA - CartaSì - AMEX

Access Itinerario : A9 → Como. Exit (Uscita) Como-Sud. Turn right → Cantù. 5 km → Montorfano. Golf on left hand side. **Map 1 on page 933** Carta 1 Pagina 933

Golf course — PERCORSO — 16/20

Site	Paesaggio	
Maintenance	Manutenzione	
Architect	Architetto	Peter Gannon
Type	Tipologia	forest
Relief	Relievo terreno	
Water in play	Acqua in gioco	
Exp. to wind	Esposto al vento	
Trees in play	Alberi in gioco	

Scorecard Carta-score	Chp. Camp.	Mens Uomini	Ladies Donne
Length Lunghezza	5727	5544	4869
Par	69	69	69
Slope system	—	—	—

Advised golfing ability Livello di gioco consigliato — 0 12 24 36

Hcp required Handicap richiesto 34

Club house & amenities — CLUB HOUSE E SERVIZI — 9/10

Pro shop	Pro shop	
Driving range	Campo pratica	
Sheltered	coperto	10 mats
On grass	in erba	no
Putting-green	Putting-green	yes
Pitching-green	Green-pratica	yes

Hotel facilities — ALBERGHI — 8/10

HOTELS ALBERGHI

Grand Hotel Villa d'Este, 153 rooms, D 597 € — Cernobbio
Tel (39) 031 3481, Fax (39) 031 348 844 — 13 km

Villa Odescalchi, 64 rooms, D 165 € — Alzate Brianza
Tel (39) 031 630 822, Fax (39) 031 632 079 — 6 km

Santandrea Golf Hotel, 12 rooms, D 119 € — Montorfano
Tel (39) 031 200 220, Fax (39) 031 200 220 — 3 km

RESTAURANTS RISTORANTE

Imbarcadero, Tel (39) 031 270 166 — Como 9 km
Il Cantuccio, Tel (39) 031 628 736 — Albavilla 8 km
Crotto del Lupo Tel (39) 031 570 881 — Como 9 km
Al Ponte Tel (39) 031 712 561 — Cantù 3 km

The Netherlands

EUROPE'S TOP 1000 GOLF COURSES

Haagsche

Nederland
The Netherlands

Met meer dan 175.000 spelers behoort Nederland tot de landen van Europa met een sterke groei. Er zijn meer dan 70 18-holes-banen, die logischerwijze vooral rond de grote steden liggen. Wat betekent dat het er vooral in de weekends druk kan zijn. Maar de afstanden van de ene naar de andere kant van dit land zijn nooit erg groot en het wegennet is vrij dicht, waardoor je een groot gebied rond de verblijfplaats kunt bereiken. Naast de 'grote' banen aan de kust heeft het land golftechnisch nog meer in zijn mars, met banen die vaak goed in het landschap zijn opgenomen. Het is een weinig bekende bestemming, die vooral in de zomer ontdekt moet worden.

The Netherlands, with 175,000 golfers, is one of the countries in Europe where golf is developing fast. There are about 70 eighteen-hole courses, naturally spread around large cities, thus implying busy week-ends. But here, distances from one end of the country to the other are never too great, and the very dense road system makes for easy travelling round and about your holiday location. Alongside the great seaside courses, the country has a number of solid arguments to attract golf-trotters, with courses that, more often than not, blend in very tastefully with the natural landscape. This is still a little known destination, and one well worth discovering during the warmer months.

Map No 1
Carte n° 1
km
0 10 20
Amsterdam
Houtrak
Kennemer
Noordwijk
Haagsche
Broekpolder
Cromstrijen
Grevelingenhout
Goes
Wouwse Plantage
Royal Zoute (B)
Royal Latem (B)
Royal Antwerp (B)
Hilversum
Lage Vuursche
De Pan
Hoge
Anderstein
Batouwe
Efteling
Oosterhout
Toxandria
Gendersteyn
Eindhoven
Limburg (B)
Den Helder
Texel
Vlieland
Harlingen
Stavoren
IJsselmeer
Markermeer
Alkmaar
Haarlem
Zandvoort
IJmuiden
AMSTERDAM
Hilversum
UTRECHT
Amersfoort
Leiden
Scheveningen
DEN HAAG
('S-GRAVENHAGE)
Delft
Gouda
ROTTERDAM
Schiedam
Vlaardingen
Europoort
Hoek van Holland
Dordrecht
Breda
Tilburg
Roosendaal
Middelburg
Vlissingen
Goes
Bergen op Zoom
Knokke-Heist
Terneuzen
(ANVERS)
ANTWERPEN
BRUGGE
GENT
(GAND)
St-Niklaas
Mechelen
Lier
Turnhout
Leuven (Louvain)
BRUXELLES
Aalst
Oudenaarde
Hasselt
Genk
NOORD-HOLLAND
ZUID-HOLLAND
UTRECHT
ZEELAND
NOORD-BRABANT
ANTWERPEN
OOST-VLAANDEREN
VLAAMS-BRABANT
LIMBURG
FLEVOLAND
Newcastle
Kingston upon Hull
Harwich
MICHELIN

GRONINGEN
Assen
Emmen
Zwolle
Deventer
Enschede
Hengelo
Almelo
Apeldoorn
ARNHEM
Nordhorn
Lingen
Meppen
Rheine
Münster
Cloppenburg
Bocholt
Recklinghsn
Gelsenkchn
DORTMUND
ESSEN
Bochum
DUISBURG
Krefeld
Mönchengladbach
DÜSSELDORF
WUPPERTAL
Hagen
Solingen
KÖLN
AACHEN
Maastricht
Heerlen
Venlo
D R E N T H E
O V E R I J S S E L
N O R D R H E I N
L I M B U R G
Lauswolt
Sint Nicolaasga
Gelpenberg
Sybrook
Twente
Nunspeet
Rheine/
Mesum
Graafschap
Rosendael
Wasserburg-Anholt (D)
Rijk van
Nijmegen
Essener Oefte (D)
Bergisch Land
Wuppertal (D)
Mülheim (D)
Elfrather Mühle (D)
Hubbelrath (D)
Krefelder (D)
Düsseldorfer (D)
Schloss Myllendonk (D)
Herkenbosch
Gut Lärchenhof (D)
Spiegelven (B)
Zuid Limburgse
997
MICHELIN
d'après carte n° 987 - 28ème édition - 2002.
Autorisation n° 0102062.

CLASSIFICATION OF COURSES
RANKSCHIKKING VAN DE BANEN

This classification gives priority consideration to the score awarded to the actual course.

Deze rangschikking houdt eerst en vooral rekening met hetcijfer, dat aan het baan werd toegekend.

Courses score / Cijfer van de banen			Course	Page / Blz
18	8	6	Eindhoven	1006
18	7	8	Haagsche	1012
18	8	8	Kennemer	1017
18	7	8	Noordwijk	1020
17	7	7	Lage Vuursche	1018
16	8	5	Cromstrijen	1003
16	8	7	De Pan	1004
16	8	5	Efteling	1005
16	7	6	Herkenbosch	1013
16	7	7	Hilversum	1014
16	8	8	Houtrak	1016
15	7	7	Amsterdam	999
15	7	3	Batouwe	1001
15	7	6	Broekpolder	1002
15	7	7	Gendersteyn	1008
15	7	6	Goes	1009
15	7	6	Graafschap	1010
15	6	7	Hoge Kleij	1015
15	5	6	Nunspeet *North/East*	1021
15	7	7	Oosterhout	1022
15	7	7	Rosendael	1024
15	7	5	Sint Nicolaasga	1025
15	6	6	Sybrook	1026
15	7	6	Twente	1028
15	7	6	Wouwse Plantage	1029
14	7	6	Anderstein	1000
14	4	5	Gelpenberg	1007
14	7	4	Grevelingenhout	1011
14	6	7	Lauswolt	1019
14	6	5	Rijk van Nijmegen *Nijmeegse Baan*	1023
14	7	6	Toxandria	1027
14	7	8	Zuid Limburgse	1030

RECOMMENDED GOLFING STAY
AAN TE RADEN VAKANTIEVERBLIJF

Course				Page
Haagsche	18	7	8	1012
Kennemer	18	8	8	1017
Noordwijk	18	7	8	1020
Rijk van Nijmegen	14	6	5	1023
Efteling	16	8	5	1005

AMSTERDAM

15 | 7 | 7

Toen de oude Amsterdamse de helft van zijn holes aan de Spoorwegen verloor, vertrok de club naar een nieuw, open terrein aan de westkant van de stad (soms een beetje rumoerig door de overvliegende vliegtuigen). Aanvankelijk waren er problemen waardoor alle greens moesten worden gerenoveerd. Die ingreep en het verder groeien van de jonge aanplant, zullen de baan sterk verbeteren. De eerste zeven holes zijn niet om over naar huis te schrijven, met alleen de fairway bunkers en de wind als moeilijkheidsfactor. Dan wordt het spannender met twee par-4 holes en water. Water speelt ook een belangrijke rol op de tweede negen, vooral op de 14e (een par-5 dogleg met twee vijvers) en de 18e waar de green wordt afgeschermd door water. Een prachtige slothole. De baan is niet te druk.

When the old Amsterdam Golf Club lost half of its holes to the railways, the club moved out into a very open area to the west of the city (sometimes a little noisy because of the airport). Owing to a number of serious problems, the greens have all been re-laid and their maturity should do much to improve the terrain still further; the same goes for the newly planted trees and bushes. The seven first holes are not much to write home about, the only difficulties being the bunker fairways and wind. Then, it gets a little more exciting with two par 4s and water hazards. Water, in fact, is very much to the fore on the way in, especially on the 14th (a par 5 dog-leg with two ponds and two ditches) and the 18th, where the green is again guarded by water to make an excellent final hole. The course is not too crowded.

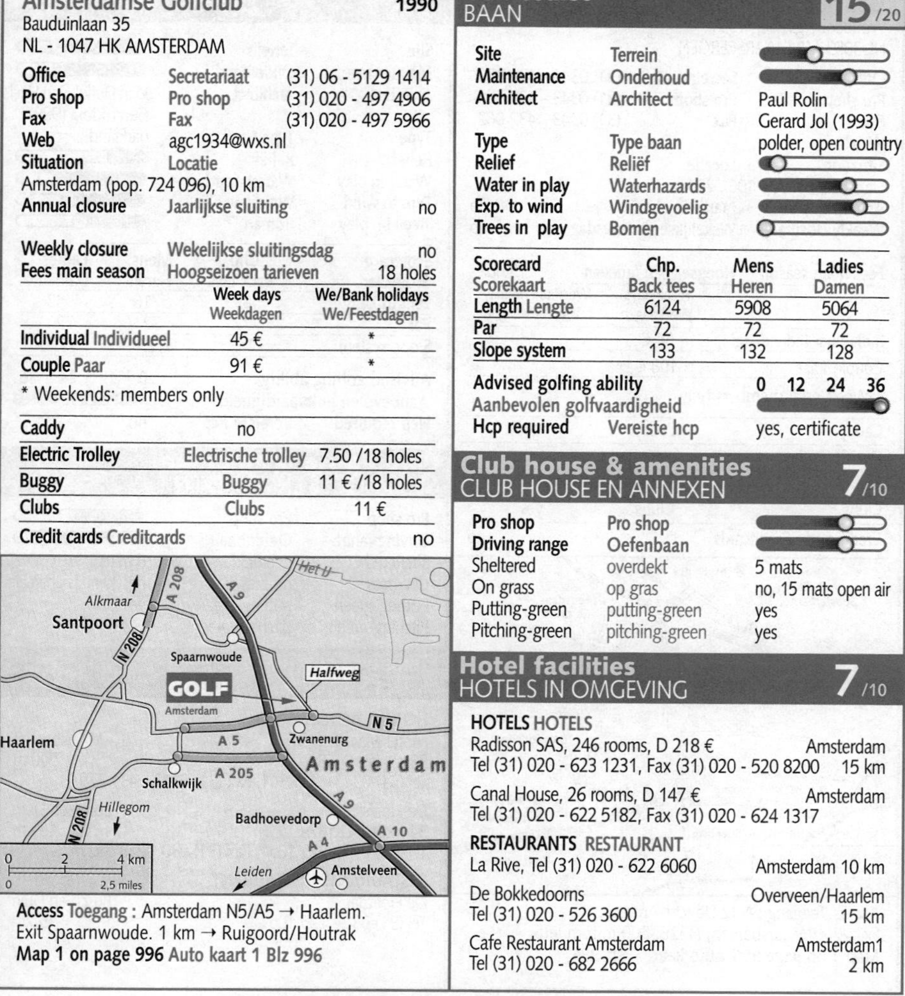

Amsterdamse Golfclub — 1990

Bauduinlaan 35
NL - 1047 HK AMSTERDAM

Office	Secretariaat	(31) 06 - 5129 1414
Pro shop	Pro shop	(31) 020 - 497 4906
Fax	Fax	(31) 020 - 497 5966
Web	agc1934@wxs.nl	
Situation	Locatie	
Amsterdam (pop. 724 096), 10 km		
Annual closure	Jaarlijkse sluiting	no
Weekly closure	Wekelijkse sluitingsdag	no
Fees main season	Hoogseizoen tarieven	18 holes

	Week days Weekdagen	We/Bank holidays We/Feestdagen
Individual Individueel	45 €	*
Couple Paar	91 €	*

* Weekends: members only

Caddy		no
Electric Trolley	Electrische trolley	7.50 /18 holes
Buggy	Buggy	11 € /18 holes
Clubs	Clubs	11 €
Credit cards Creditcards		no

Access Toegang : Amsterdam N5/A5 → Haarlem. Exit Spaarnwoude. 1 km → Ruigoord/Houtrak
Map 1 on page 996 Auto kaart 1 Blz 996

Golf course — BAAN — 15/20

Site	Terrein	
Maintenance	Onderhoud	
Architect	Architect	Paul Rolin, Gerard Jol (1993)
Type	Type baan	polder, open country
Relief	Reliëf	
Water in play	Waterhazards	
Exp. to wind	Windgevoelig	
Trees in play	Bomen	

Scorecard Scorekaart	**Chp.** Back tees	**Mens** Heren	**Ladies** Damen
Length Lengte	6124	5908	5064
Par	72	72	72
Slope system	133	132	128

Advised golfing ability Aanbevolen golfvaardigheid — 0 12 24 36
Hcp required Vereiste hcp — yes, certificate

Club house & amenities — CLUB HOUSE EN ANNEXEN — 7/10

Pro shop	Pro shop	
Driving range	Oefenbaan	
Sheltered	overdekt	5 mats
On grass	op gras	no, 15 mats open air
Putting-green	putting-green	yes
Pitching-green	pitching-green	yes

Hotel facilities — HOTELS IN OMGEVING — 7/10

HOTELS HOTELS

Radisson SAS, 246 rooms, D 218 € — Amsterdam
Tel (31) 020 - 623 1231, Fax (31) 020 - 520 8200 — 15 km

Canal House, 26 rooms, D 147 € — Amsterdam
Tel (31) 020 - 622 5182, Fax (31) 020 - 624 1317

RESTAURANTS RESTAURANT

La Rive, Tel (31) 020 - 622 6060 — Amsterdam 10 km

De Bokkedoorns — Overveen/Haarlem
Tel (31) 020 - 526 3600 — 15 km

Cafe Restaurant Amsterdam — Amsterdam1
Tel (31) 020 - 682 2666 — 2 km

999

ANDERSTEIN

14 | 7 | 6

De spoorweg en de A12 op de achtergrond van een aantal holes zouden niet teveel de aandacht van de vele kwaliteiten van deze baan moeten afleiden. Het vroegere familiedomein is omgetoverd in een 18-holes baan, met het clubhuis in de gerestaureerde en onlangs nog eens gerenoveerde boerenstal. Bij de uitbreiding zijn acht van de oorspronkelijke holes intact gebleven. Die zijn vrij smal omdat er in eerste aanleg niet veel ruimte was. Van de tien nieuwe holes liggen er vijf in open land. Het zijn doglegs met brede fairways, twee grote vijvers en strategisch geplaatste fairway bunkers. De overige vijf liggen meer tussen de bomen, zoals de oorspronkelijke holes. Alles bij elkaar is het een aantrekkelijke baan geworden, met allerlei moeilijkheden. Allereerst al de noodzaak om aan de grote variteit in holes te wennen. Je moet er eigenlijk meerdere keren spelen om de baan te gaan begrijpen. Doe dit vooral door de week, want in de weekenden zijn er veel leden op de been/baan.

The railway line and road that form a backdrop to some holes here should not conceal the many virtues of this course. The erstwhile family property was extended and built into a private 18 hole course, and the old farmhouse, now the clubhouse, has recently been restored. Eight of the first nine holes have been preserved and are very narrow - they were built over a restricted amount of space. Of the ten new holes, five run through wide open land in the form of dog-legs with broad fairways, two major water hazards and strategically located fairway bunkers. The other five are in woodland, like the original holes. In all, this has become a very attractive course, offering all sorts of difficulty, the first of which is to get accustomed to the very different nature of each hole. You definitely need to play here several times to understand the course. If you do, make it a week-day, as there are a lot of members at week-ends.

Golfclub Anderstein — 1987

Woudenbergseweg 13 A
NL 3953 ME MAARSBERGEN

Office	Secretariaat	(31) 0343 - 431 330
Pro shop	Pro shop	(31) 0343 - 431 560
Fax	Fax	(31) 0343 - 432 062
Web	—	
Situation	Locatie	

Utrecht (pop. 234 106), 20 km

Annual closure	Jaarlijkse sluiting	no
Weekly closure	Wekelijkse sluitingsdag	no

Fees main season Hoogseizoen tarieven	18 holes	
	Week days Weekdagen	We/Bank holidays We/Feestdagen
Individual Individueel	54 €	*
Couple Paar	108 €	*

* Week-end: members only

Caddy	Caddy	no
Electric Trolley	Electrische trolley	no
Buggy	Buggy	no
Clubs	Clubs	yes
Credit cards	Creditcards	no

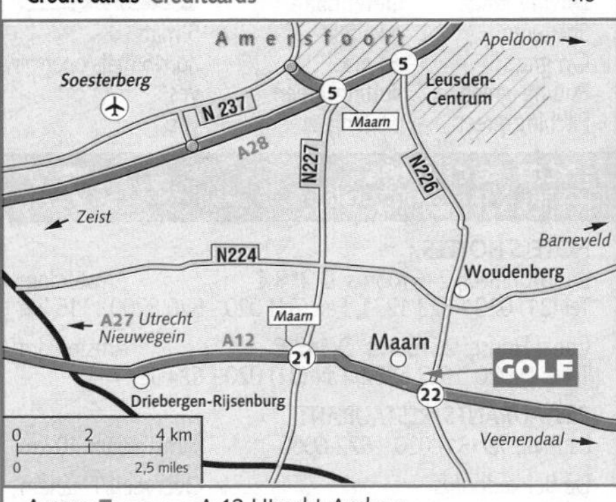

Access Toegang : A 12 Utrecht-Arnhem.
Exit 22 → Maarsbergen, N226. 500 m turn left
Map 1 on page 996 Auto kaart 1 Blz 996

Golf course BAAN — 14/20

Site	Terrein	
Maintenance	Onderhoud	
Architect	Architect	Joan Dudok van Heel Gerard Jol (1989)
Type	Type baan	parkland
Relief	Reliëf	
Water in play	Waterhazards	
Exp. to wind	Windgevoelig	
Trees in play	Bomen	

Scorecard Scorekaart	Chp. Back tees	Mens Heren	Ladies Damen
Length Lengte	5899	5716	4943
Par	72	72	72
Slope system	133	129	123

Advised golfing ability Aanbevolen golfvaardigheid: 0 12 24 36
Hcp required Vereiste hcp: no

Club house & amenities CLUB HOUSE EN ANNEXEN — 7/10

Pro shop	Pro shop	
Driving range	Oefenbaan	
Sheltered	overdekt	6 mats
On grass	op gras	no, 20 mats open air
Putting-green	putting-green	yes
Pitching-green	pitching-green	yes

Hotel facilities HOTELS IN OMGEVING — 6/10

HOTELS HOTELS

Motel Maarsbergen — Maarsbergen
38 rooms, D 68 € — 500 m
Tel (31) 0343 - 431 341, Fax (31) 0343 - 431 379

De Hoefslag — Bosch en Duin
34 rooms, D 147 € — 15 km
Tel (31) 030 - 225 1051, Fax (31) 030 - 228 5821

RESTAURANTS RESTAURANT

De Hoefslag — Bosch en Duin
Tel (31) 030 - 225 1051 — 15 km

BATOUWE

15 | 7 | 3

Deze nieuwe baan ligt in open terrein, midden tussen de grote rivieren. Bij de aanleg stonden er al een handjevol bomen en die zijn goed in het ontwerp ingepast. Ze staan langs de fairways of beschermen enkele greens, waardoor spelers twee keer moeten denken voordat ze een driver uit de tas halen. Er komen heel wat waterhazards in het spel, zoals op de 15e, een par-3 met een eilandgreen, of de 18e waar water de green beschermd tegen mislukte approaches. De negen andere holes hebben gewoon veel bunkers vooral op de fairways, zeker op twee holes. Honderden jonge bomen zijn aangeplant, maar die zijn nog niet groot genoeg om veel bescherming tegen de wind te bieden. Hoewel de baan vrij kort is, zijn het vooral de elementen, zoals wind en water, die dwingen tot een nauwkeurige clubkeuze. De beste tijd om Batouwe te spelen is in het voorjaar, als de fruitbomen in de Betuwe in bloei staan.

This recent course has been laid out over wide open space between the main rivers in the centre of Holland. There were a handful of trees, and these have been intelligently used by the designer. They line certain fairways and protect a number of greens, forcing players to think twice before taking the driver out of the bag. A lot of water hazards come into play, like on the par 3 15th, with an island green, or the 18th, where water protects the green from mis-hit approach shots. Most of the other holes just have lots of bunkers, especially of the fairway variety, numerous on two holes in particular. Hundreds of other trees have been planted but are no size as yet, so there is precious little protection from the wind - even though the course itself is on the short side, the elements are a key factor here for choosing the right club. The best time to play Batouwe is in the Spring, when the region's fruit trees are in full blossom.

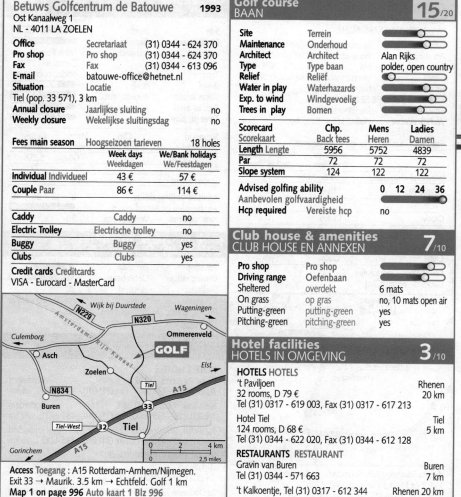

Betuws Golfcentrum de Batouwe — 1993

Ost Kanaalweg 1
NL - 4011 LA ZOELEN

Office	Secretariaat	(31) 0344 - 624 370
Pro shop	Pro shop	(31) 0344 - 624 370
Fax	Fax	(31) 0344 - 613 096
E-mail	batouwe-office@hetnet.nl	
Situation	Locatie	
Tiel (pop. 33 571), 3 km		
Annual closure	Jaarlijkse sluiting	no
Weekly closure	Wekelijkse sluitingsdag	no

Fees main season Hoogseizoen tarieven	**Week days** Weekdagen	**We/Bank holidays** We/Feestdagen
	18 holes	
Individual Individueel	43 €	57 €
Couple Paar	86 €	114 €

Caddy	Caddy	no
Electric Trolley	Electrische trolley	no
Buggy	Buggy	yes
Clubs	Clubs	yes

Credit cards Creditcards
VISA - Eurocard - MasterCard

Access Toegang : A15 Rotterdam-Arnhem/Nijmegen.
Exit 33 → Maurik. 3.5 km → Echtfeld. Golf 1 km
Map 1 on page 996 Auto kaart 1 Blz 996

Golf course — BAAN — 15/20

Site	Terrein	
Maintenance	Onderhoud	
Architect	Architect	Alan Rijks
Type	Type baan	polder, open country
Relief	Reliëf	
Water in play	Waterhazards	
Exp. to wind	Windgevoelig	
Trees in play	Bomen	

Scorecard Scorekaart	**Chp.** Back tees	**Mens** Heren	**Ladies** Damen
Length Lengte	5956	5752	4839
Par	72	72	72
Slope system	124	122	122

Advised golfing ability Aanbevolen golfvaardigheid — 0 12 24 36
Hcp required Vereiste hcp — no

Club house & amenities — CLUB HOUSE EN ANNEXEN — 7/10

Pro shop	Pro shop	
Driving range	Oefenbaan	
Sheltered	overdekt	6 mats
On grass	op gras	no, 10 mats open air
Putting-green	putting-green	yes
Pitching-green	pitching-green	yes

Hotel facilities — HOTELS IN OMGEVING — 3/10

HOTELS HOTELS

't Paviljoen — Rhenen 20 km
32 rooms, D 79 €
Tel (31) 0317 - 619 003, Fax (31) 0317 - 617 213

Hotel Tiel — Tiel 5 km
124 rooms, D 68 €
Tel (31) 0344 - 622 020, Fax (31) 0344 - 612 128

RESTAURANTS RESTAURANT

Gravin van Buren — Buren 7 km
Tel (31) 0344 - 571 663

't Kalkoentje, Tel (31) 0317 - 612 344 — Rhenen 20 km

BROEKPOLDER

15 | 7 | 6

Hier vindt u een voorbeeld van een nog vrij nieuwe baan, waar de oorspronkelijk nogal kale ruimte geleidelijk aan voller en rijker wordt. Na de aanleg in 1983 zijn bomen en struiken nu bijna volgroeid hetgeen zowel bescherming tegen de wind biedt als een visuele verbetering is. De ontwikkeling van de baan wordt versterkt door recente ingrepen die wat oorspronkelijke zwaktes hebben opgeheven. Waterhazards komen op vijf holes in het spel en vormen met de sloten de belangrijkste hindernissen. Ook bunkers spelen een rol in de verdediging van de grote greens. Sommige holes zijn behoorlijk aan de lange kant, maar toch is de baan geschikt voor spelers van alle niveaus. Broekpolder ligt maar een paar meter boven het zeeniveau, maar dat is voldoende om een paar mooie vergezichten over de omliggende polders op te leveren, met de haveninstallatie van Rotterdam op de achtergrond.

Here is an example of a recently built course, where the original barren space is gradually becoming richer, visibly developing and maturing year in year out. Since 1983, the trees and bushes are already almost full grown, bringing greater protection from the wind and visual improvement. The course's evolution has also been marked by recent changes, which have put right some of the flaws exposed by the course's immaturity. The water hazards come into play on four holes, and, with a number of ditches, form the main difficulties. The bunkers, too, provide a firm line of defence for the large greens. We might add that some of the holes are on the long side, but overall the course can be played by golfers of all levels. Broekpolder is only a few metres above sea level, but that's enough to provide some pretty views over the surrounding lakes and fields, with the port of Rotterdam in the background.

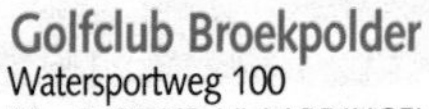

Golfclub Broekpolder — 1983

Watersportweg 100
NL - 3138 HD VLAARDINGEN

Office	Secretariaat	(31) 010 - 249 5566
Pro shop	Pro shop	(31) 010 - 474 7610
Fax	Fax	(31) 010 - 474 4094
E-mail	secretariaat@golfclubbroekpolder.nl	
Situation	Locatie	

Rotterdam (pop. 598 521), 12 km

1002

Annual closure	Jaarlijkse sluiting	no
Weekly closure	Wekelijkse sluitingsdag	no

Fees main season Hoogseizoen tarieven	Week days Weekdagen	We/Bank holidays We/Feestdagen
18 holes		
Individual Individueel	59 €	73 €
Couple Paar	118 €	146 €

Caddy	Caddy	no
Electric Trolley	Electrische trolley	no
Buggy	Buggy	no
Clubs	Clubs	yes

Credit cards Creditcards
Eurocard - MasterCard

Access Toegang : A20 Rotterdam → Vlaardingen.
Exit 8 → Broekpolderweg, Golf 3 km
Map 1 on page 996 Auto kaart 1 Blz 996

Golf course BAAN — 15/20

Site	Terrein	
Maintenance	Onderhoud	
Architect	Architect	Frank Pennink Gerard Jol (1991)
Type	Type baan	polder, open country
Relief	Reliëf	
Water in play	Waterhazards	
Exp. to wind	Windgevoelig	
Trees in play	Bomen	

Scorecard Scorekaart	Chp. Back tees	Mens Heren	Ladies Damen
Length Lengte	6429	6004	5252
Par	72	72	72
Slope system	129	124	125

Advised golfing ability Aanbevolen golfvaardigheid: 0 12 24 36
Hcp required Vereiste hcp: 30

Club house & amenities CLUB HOUSE EN ANNEXEN — 7/10

Pro shop	Pro shop	
Driving range	Oefenbaan	
Sheltered	overdekt	20 mats
On grass	op gras	no, 20 mats open air
Putting-green	putting-green	yes
Pitching-green	pitching-green	yes

Hotel facilities HOTELS IN OMGEVING — 6/10

HOTELS HOTELS

Delta, 78 rooms, D 102 € — Vlaardingen
Tel (31) 010 - 434 5477, Fax (31) 010 - 434 9525 — 5 km

New York, 73 rooms, D 93 € — Rotterdam
Tel (31) 010 - 439 0500, Fax (31) 010 - 484 2701 — 20 km

Parkhotel, 187 rooms, D 127 € — Rotterdam
Tel (31) 010 - 436 3611, Fax (31) 010 - 436 4212 — 15 km

RESTAURANTS RESTAURANT

Parkheuvel — Rotterdam 15 km
Tel (31) 010 - 475 0011

La Duchesse Tel (31) 010 - 426 4626 — Schiedam 10 km

CROMSTRIJEN

16 | 8 | 5

Deze nog vrij nieuwe baan, niet ver van Rotterdam, ligt in een wijd open gebied. Weliswaar dichtbij een autoweg, maar ook met fraaie vergezichten over de omliggende weidegebieden. De plaatselijke autoriteiten keurden de aanleg van een golfbaan goed op voorwaarde dat die open zou staan voor iedereen. Het resultaat daarvan is een openbare 9-holes baan naast een besloten 18-holes baan. Het meest opvallende natuurlijke element wordt gevormd door vier rijen met hoge bomen. De stukken water daartussen zijn uitgebouwd tot een klein meertje, dat meerdere keren in het spel komt. Een andere moeilijkheidsfactor bestaat uit de 75 strategisch geplaatste bunkers en, natuurlijk, uit de wind. Er is veel jonge aanplant, bedoeld om deze vlakke baan een beetje vorm te geven. De greens zijn groot, goed gevormd, goed ontworpen en sterk bewaakt. De baan is door Tom McAuley ontworpen voor alle type golfers en wordt zeer goed onderhouden baan. Naarmate de baan rijpt, zal het een van de meeste interessante banen van het land worden. Het clubhuis straalt al de allure uit die bij die status past.

This recent course, situated not far from Rotterdam, is laid out in wide open space, close to a motorway but with scenic views over farmland. The local authorities agreed to building the course as long as it was open to everyone. The result is a public 9-holer next to a private 18-hole course. The most striking natural elements are the four rows of trees. The patches of water have been extended to form a real lake, which comes into play several times. The other hazards are the 75 strategically placed bunkers and, of course, the wind. A great many shrubs have been planted as well, to give this flat course a little relief. The greens are huge, well-contoured, well-designed and very safely- guarded. As it matures, this Tom McAuley course, designed for all golfers and very well upkept, should become one of the most interesting in Holland. The clubhouse already has the majestic allure worthy of such a status.

Golfclub Cromstrijen — 1991

Veerweg 26
NL - 3281 LX NUMANSDORP

Office	Secretariaat	(31) 0186 - 654 336
Pro shop	Pro shop	(31) 0186 - 654 336
Fax	Fax	(31) 0186 - 654 681
E-mail	g.c.cromstrijen@hetnet.nl	
Situation	Locatie	Rotterdam, 20 km

Dordrecht (pop. 113 394), 15 km

Annual closure	Jaarlijkse sluiting	no
Weekly closure	Wekelijkse sluitingsdag	no

Fees main season Hoogseizoen tarieven	full day	
	Week days Weekdagen	We/Bank holidays We/Feestdagen
Individual Individueel	48 €	*
Couple Paar	96 €	*

* Weekends: members only

Caddy	Caddy	no
Electric Trolley	Electrische trolley	no
Buggy	Buggy	no
Clubs	Clubs	11 €
Credit cards	Creditcards	no

Access Toegang : Rotterdam A29.
Exit 22 → Havens Numansdorp, → Veenhaven
Map 1 on page 996 Auto kaart 1 Blz 996

Golf course — BAAN — 16/20

Site	Terrein	
Maintenance	Onderhoud	
Architect	Architect	Tom MacAuley
Type	Type baan	open country
Relief	Reliëf	
Water in play	Waterhazards	
Exp. to wind	Windgevoelig	
Trees in play	Bomen	

Scorecard Scorekaart	Chp. Back tees	Mens Heren	Ladies Damen
Length Lengte	6128	5894	5023
Par	72	72	72
Slope system	120	122	122

Advised golfing ability Aanbevolen golfvaardigheid — 0 12 24 36
Hcp required Vereiste hcp — no

Club house & amenities — CLUB HOUSE EN ANNEXEN — 8/10

Pro shop	Pro shop	
Driving range	Oefenbaan	
Sheltered	overdekt	12 mats
On grass	op gras	no, 6 mats open air
Putting-green	putting-green	yes
Pitching-green	pitching-green	yes

Hotel facilities — HOTELS IN OMGEVING — 5/10

HOTELS HOTELS

Het Wapen van Willemstad — Willemstad 8 km
6 rooms, D 60 €
Tel (31) 0168 - 473 450, Fax (31) 0168 - 473 705

Zuiderparkhotel — Rotterdam 20 km
117 rooms, D 91 €
Tel (31) 010 - 485 0055, Fax (31) 010 - 485 6304

RESTAURANTS RESTAURANT

Wapen van Willemstad — Willemstad 8 km
Tel (31) 0168 - 473 450

Kasteel van Rhoon — Rhoon 15 km
Tel (31) 010 - 501 8896

DE PAN

16	8	7

Harry Colt heeft zijn stempel op meerdere banen in Nederland gezet en zijn ontwerpen zijn altijd een plezierige ervaring. Een korte bootreis was voor hem voldoende om hier naartoe te komen vanuit zijn geboorteland Engeland, waar hij ook een aantal meesterwerken afleverde (Sunningdale, Wentworth en Ganton, bijvoorbeeld). Hij was onder andere een van de eerste grote ontwerpers van banen in het binnenland. De Pan is een van die uitstekende voorbeelden van zijn vermogen net het juiste aantal hazards op te nemen om wat pikants aan het spel toe te voegen. Op heel natuurlijke wijze werkend met de omgeving en altijd een paar strategische verrassingen toevoegend, zoals een aantal fascinerende doglegs en veeleisende par-3 holes. De baan heeft meer glooiing dan je zou verwachten zo midden in Holland. De belangrijkste obstakels om te ontwijken zijn de bomen en een paar goed geplaatste bunkers. De fraai vorm gegeven greens worden goed bewaakt, maar sommigen zijn van elke verdediging ontbloot. Weggestopt in de bossen, ver van alle lawaai, is deze aantrekkelijke baan er een die u echt aan uw collectie moet toevoegen.

You often find the mark of Harry Colt in the Netherlands, and it's always a pleasure. Coming here was a short boat trip from his native England, where he also produced a number of masterpieces (Sunningdale, Wentworth and Ganton, for example). Among other things, he was one of the first great designers of inland courses. This is one excellent example of his skill in placing just the right number of hazards needed to add a little spice to the game, working very naturally with the surroundings and always adding a few strategic surprises, such as a number of compelling dog-legs and tough par 3s. The course undulates a little more than you might expect in this part of Holland, and the major hazards to be avoided are the trees and a few well-located bunkers. The nicely contoured greens are well-guarded, but some have no defence at all. Tucked away in the woods far from any noise, this fine course is most definitely one to add to your collection.

Utrechtse Golf Club De Pan — 1929

Amersfoortseweg 1
NL - 3735 LJ BOSCH EN DUIN

Office	Secretariaat	(31) 030 - 695 6427
Pro shop	Pro shop	(31) 030 - 695 6427
Fax	Fax	(31) 030 - 696 3769
E-mail	golfclubdepan@wxs.nl	
Situation	Locatie	

Utrecht (pop. 234 106), 10 km

Annual closure	Jaarlijkse sluiting	no
Weekly closure	Wekelijkse sluitingsdag	no

Fees main season Hoogseizoen tarieven	18 holes	
	Week days Weekdagen	**We/Bank holidays** We/Feestdagen
Individual Individueel	45 €	*
Couple Paar	90 €	*

* Weekends: members only

Caddy	Caddy	no
Electric Trolley	Electrische trolley	no
Buggy	Buggy	no
Clubs	Clubs	no
Credit cards	Creditcards	no

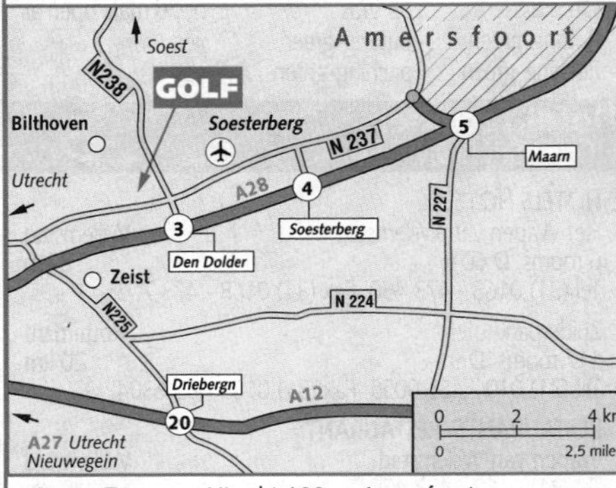

Access Toegang : Utrecht A28 → Amersfoort, Exit 3 → Den Dolder. 500 m left. 1.7 km parallel road
Map 1 on page 996 Auto kaart 1 Blz 996

Golf course BAAN — 16/20

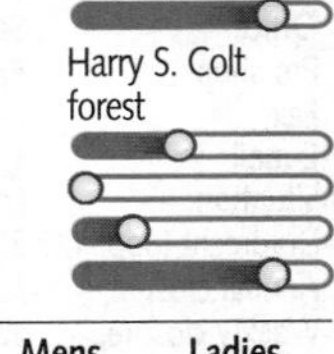

Site	Terrein	
Maintenance	Onderhoud	
Architect	Architect	Harry S. Colt
Type	Type baan	forest
Relief	Reliëf	
Water in play	Waterhazards	
Exp. to wind	Windgevoelig	
Trees in play	Bomen	

Scorecard Scorekaart	**Chp.** Back tees	**Mens** Heren	**Ladies** Damen
Length Lengte	6070	5707	4951
Par	72	72	72
Slope system	127	123	122

Advised golfing ability Aanbevolen golfvaardigheid — 0 12 24 36
Hcp required Vereiste hcp — 28

Club house & amenities CLUB HOUSE EN ANNEXEN — 8/10

Pro shop	Pro shop	
Driving range	Oefenbaan	
Sheltered	overdekt	6 mats
On grass	op gras	no, 4 mats open air
Putting-green	putting-green	yes
Pitching-green	pitching-green	yes

Hotel facilities HOTELS IN OMGEVING — 7/10

HOTELS HOTELS

De Hoefslag — Bosch en Duin
34 rooms, D 147 € — 1 km
Tel (31) 030 - 225 1051, Fax (31) 030 - 228 5821

Kerkebosch — Zeist
30 rooms, D 107 € — 5 km
Tel (31) 030 - 691 4734, Fax (31) 030 - 691 3114

RESTAURANTS RESTAURANT

De Hoefslag — Bosch en Duin
Tel (31) 030 - 225 1051 — 1 km

Wilhelmina Park — Utrecht
Tel (31) 030 - 251 0693 — 10 km

EFTELING

16 | 8 | 5

Deze nieuwe baan is onderdeel van het bekende, gelijknamige attractiepark (ideaal voor de niet-golfers in de familie), waarvan sommige onderdelen vanaf de fairways te zien zijn. De baan ligt in een landelijke omgeving met aan weerszijden een natuurgebied. Veel open ruimtes waardoor de richting en kracht van de wind een grote rol spelen, omdat maar vier holes beschermd liggen. Bij gebrek aan bomen is water de belangrijkste hindernis, in de vorm van grote vijvers langs de baan of voor de green. Op de derde hole kronkelt een kreekje door de fairway, waardoor spelers voor de keuze worden gesteld rechts of links te houden. De greens zijn groot, goed gevormd en beschermd door handig geplaatste bunkers omgeven door heuveltjes en andere vormen van aarden wallen. Met smaak ontworpen door Donald Steel. Een prettige en boeiende baan geschikt voor spelers van alle nivo's. Goed aangelegd en goed onderhouden.

This very recent course is part of the celebrated "De Efteling" theme park (ideal for non-golfers in the family), which you can actually see from the fairways. The whole piece is located in a rural spot surrounded by two nature reserves. There is a lot of very open space here, which gives great importance to the direction and strength of the wind, as only four holes are protected. For want of trees, water is the main hazard to cope with, in the shape of large ponds lining the fairways or in front of the greens. At the 3rd, a stretch of water winds its way down the fairway, forcing players to choose from which side of the fairway they want to play the hole. The greens are huge, well-contoured and protected by cleverly placed bunkers surrounded by mounds and other forms of earthwork. Tastefully designed by Donald Steel, this is a very pleasant and entertaining course for golfers of all abilities. Well built and well upkept.

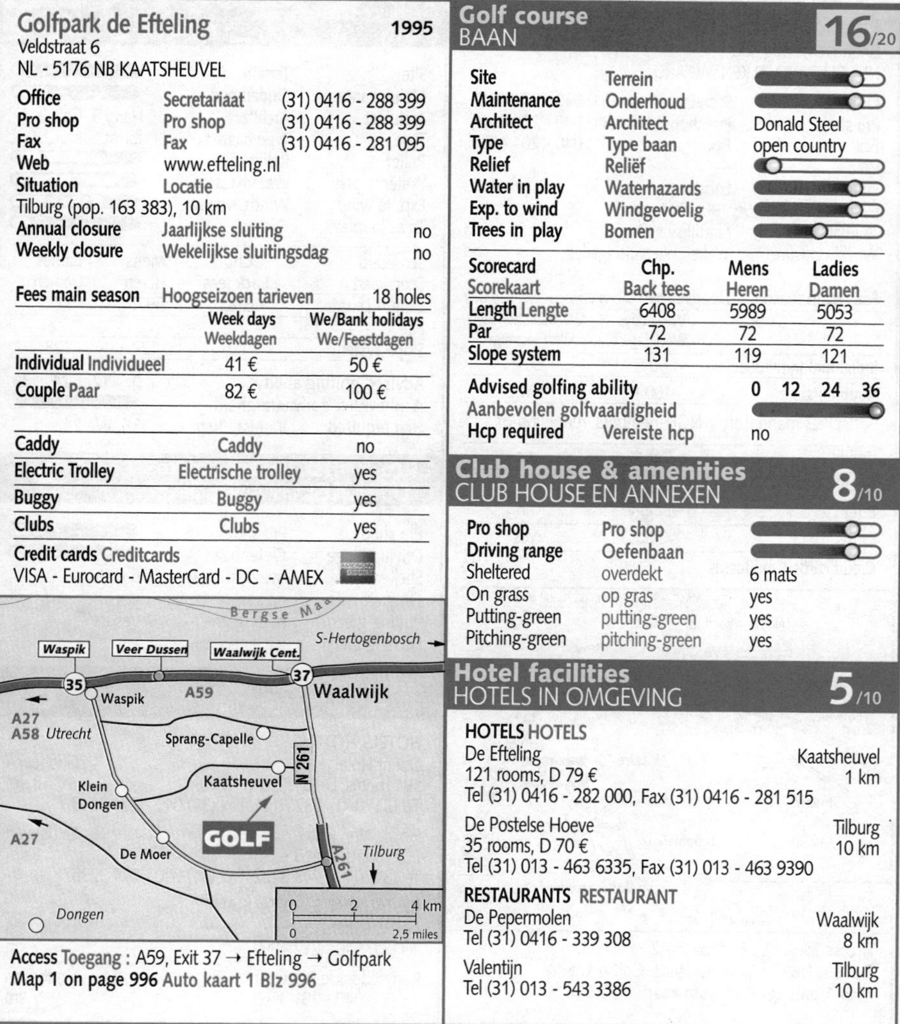

Golfpark de Efteling — 1995

Veldstraat 6
NL - 5176 NB KAATSHEUVEL

Office	Secretariaat	(31) 0416 - 288 399
Pro shop	Pro shop	(31) 0416 - 288 399
Fax	Fax	(31) 0416 - 281 095
Web	www.efteling.nl	
Situation	Locatie	
Tilburg (pop. 163 383), 10 km		
Annual closure	Jaarlijkse sluiting	no
Weekly closure	Wekelijkse sluitingsdag	no

Fees main season / Hoogseizoen tarieven		18 holes
	Week days / Weekdagen	We/Bank holidays / We/Feestdagen
Individual Individueel	41 €	50 €
Couple Paar	82 €	100 €

Caddy	Caddy	no
Electric Trolley	Electrische trolley	yes
Buggy	Buggy	yes
Clubs	Clubs	yes

Credit cards Creditcards
VISA - Eurocard - MasterCard - DC - AMEX

Access Toegang : A59, Exit 37 → Efteling → Golfpark
Map 1 on page 996 Auto kaart 1 Blz 996

Golf course / BAAN — 16/20

Site	Terrein	
Maintenance	Onderhoud	
Architect	Architect	Donald Steel
Type	Type baan	open country
Relief	Reliëf	
Water in play	Waterhazards	
Exp. to wind	Windgevoelig	
Trees in play	Bomen	

Scorecard / Scorekaart	Chp. / Back tees	Mens / Heren	Ladies / Damen
Length Lengte	6408	5989	5053
Par	72	72	72
Slope system	131	119	121

Advised golfing ability / Aanbevolen golfvaardigheid: 0 12 24 36
Hcp required / Vereiste hcp: no

Club house & amenities / CLUB HOUSE EN ANNEXEN — 8/10

Pro shop	Pro shop	
Driving range	Oefenbaan	
Sheltered	overdekt	6 mats
On grass	op gras	yes
Putting-green	putting-green	yes
Pitching-green	pitching-green	yes

Hotel facilities / HOTELS IN OMGEVING — 5/10

HOTELS HOTELS

De Efteling — Kaatsheuvel 1 km
121 rooms, D 79 €
Tel (31) 0416 - 282 000, Fax (31) 0416 - 281 515

De Postelse Hoeve — Tilburg 10 km
35 rooms, D 70 €
Tel (31) 013 - 463 6335, Fax (31) 013 - 463 9390

RESTAURANTS RESTAURANT

De Pepermolen — Waalwijk 8 km
Tel (31) 0416 - 339 308

Valentijn — Tilburg 10 km
Tel (31) 013 - 543 3386

EINDHOVEN

18 | 8 | 6

Een van de beste banen in het binnenland met een nivo van onderhoud dat overeenkomt met de hoge kwaliteit van de geboden faciliteiten. De baan ligt midden in een prachtig bos met beekjes en vennetjes. Twee lussen van negen holes omcirkelen grote stukken bos, waardoor spelers een gevoel van afzonde-ring en rust krijgen dat zeer bevorderlijk voor de concentratie is. Hoewel de fairways breed zijn - goed nieuws voor krachtpatsers - is het oppassen geblazen voor de doglegs, die vragen om met effect gesla-gen ballen, zowel naar links als naar rechts. Dit is een baan voor technisch ervaren spelers, met goed ontwor-pen greens, bewaakt door grote bunkers. Kenmerkend voor Harry Colt, duidelijk een van de grootste golf-ar-chitecten uit de eerste helft van deze eeuw. Zijn ontwerpen zijn veeleisend voor de goede, maar toch ook mild voor de stomme slagen van de gemiddelde speler. Een aardig element is het grote ven voor het clubhuis dat in de zomer als openlucht zwembad fungeert.

One of Holland's best inland courses with a standard upkeep to match the general quality of facilities. The course is laid out in a magnificent forest with streams and ponds. The trees are right in the middle of the two parts of the course, out and in, and this gives players an impression of isolation and tranquillity that can be very useful for concentration. Although the fairways are wide - good news for big-hitters - still watch out for the dog-legs winding left and right and calling for a number of flighted shots in both directions. This is a course for skilled technicians, with well designed putting surfaces and greens well-guarded by large bunkers, another dis-tinctive feature of Harry Colt, definitely one of the greatest course designers from the first half of the century. His layouts demand a great deal from good players but are somehow more lenient on duff shots from the ave-rage hacker. Another attractive feature is the large open-air swimming pool in front of the clubhouse.

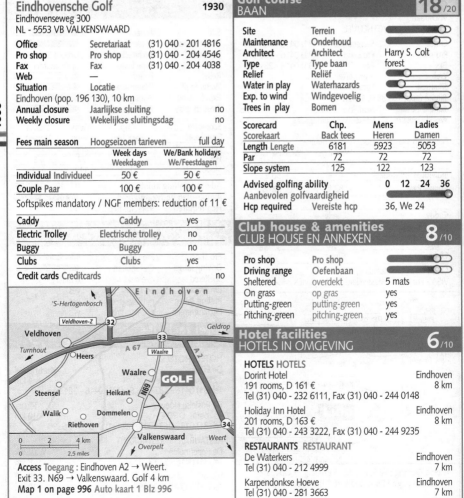

Eindhovensche Golf — 1930

Eindhovenseweg 300
NL - 5553 VB VALKENSWAARD

Office	Secretariaat	(31) 040 - 201 4816
Pro shop	Pro shop	(31) 040 - 204 4546
Fax	Fax	(31) 040 - 204 4038
Web	—	
Situation	Locatie	

Eindhoven (pop. 196 130), 10 km

Annual closure	Jaarlijkse sluiting	no
Weekly closure	Wekelijkse sluitingsdag	no

Fees main season Hoogseizoen tarieven	Week days Weekdagen	We/Bank holidays We/Feestdagen
		full day
Individual Individueel	50 €	50 €
Couple Paar	100 €	100 €

Softspikes mandatory / NGF members: reduction of 11 €

Caddy	Caddy	yes
Electric Trolley	Electrische trolley	no
Buggy	Buggy	no
Clubs	Clubs	yes
Credit cards Creditcards		no

Access Toegang : Eindhoven A2 → Weert. Exit 33. N69 → Valkenswaard. Golf 4 km
Map 1 on page 996 Auto kaart 1 Blz 996

Golf course BAAN — 18/20

Site	Terrein	
Maintenance	Onderhoud	
Architect	Architect	Harry S. Colt
Type	Type baan	forest
Relief	Reliëf	
Water in play	Waterhazards	
Exp. to wind	Windgevoelig	
Trees in play	Bomen	

Scorecard Scorekaart	Chp. Back tees	Mens Heren	Ladies Damen
Length Lengte	6181	5923	5053
Par	72	72	72
Slope system	125	122	123

Advised golfing ability Aanbevolen golfvaardigheid: 0 12 24 36
Hcp required Vereiste hcp: 36, We 24

Club house & amenities CLUB HOUSE EN ANNEXEN — 8/10

Pro shop	Pro shop	
Driving range	Oefenbaan	
Sheltered	overdekt	5 mats
On grass	op gras	yes
Putting-green	putting-green	yes
Pitching-green	pitching-green	yes

Hotel facilities HOTELS IN OMGEVING — 6/10

HOTELS HOTELS

Dorint Hotel — Eindhoven
191 rooms, D 161 € — 8 km
Tel (31) 040 - 232 6111, Fax (31) 040 - 244 0148

Holiday Inn Hotel — Eindhoven
201 rooms, D 163 € — 8 km
Tel (31) 040 - 243 3222, Fax (31) 040 - 244 9235

RESTAURANTS RESTAURANT

De Waterkers — Eindhoven
Tel (31) 040 - 212 4999 — 7 km

Karpendonkse Hoeve — Eindhoven
Tel (31) 040 - 281 3663 — 7 km

GELPENBERG

14 | 4 | 5

Zoals veel banen in Nederland is de Gelpenberg in twee fasen tot stand gekomen. En zoals vaker liggen negen holes in een bosgebied en de andere in vroeger agrarisch, meer open terrein. Hier zijn de eerste negen holes betrekkelijk smal, met bomen als voornaamste hindernis. Middenin het bos liggen flinke stukken hei, die op vier holes in het spel komen en voldoende problemen geven om het praktisch ontbreken van fairway-bunkers te verklaren. Omdat er zes doglegs bij zijn, is een goede strategie en effectvolle slagen (in de goede richting) een 'must'. De tweede negen zijn veel breder, maar ook meer beïnvloed door de wind. Een klein meertje komt op drie holes in het spel, net als een paar grote fairway bunkers, zoals op de 18e. De bunker die op de slothole de fairway doorkruist moet een van de grootste van Europa zijn. Een baan die het waard is gespeeld te worden, door spelers van elk nivo.

Like several courses in the Netherlands, Gelpenberg was designed in two stages. Like the others, you find nine holes amidst an old forest and the others on former farming land, which is much more open. Here, the front 9 are tight, with trees as the main hazards, so take care to avoid them. In the middle of the forest, there is a huge area of heather, which comes into play on four holes and causes enough difficulty to explain the virtual absence of fairway bunkers. And as there are 6 dog-legs to cope with, choosing the right strategy and flighting the ball (in the right direction) are important. The back 9 are much wider, but also much exposed to the wind. A small lake comes into play on three holes, as do some large fairway bunkers, notably on the 18th. The bunker splitting the fairway on this final hole must be one of the largest in Europe. A course well worth getting to know, for players of all levels.

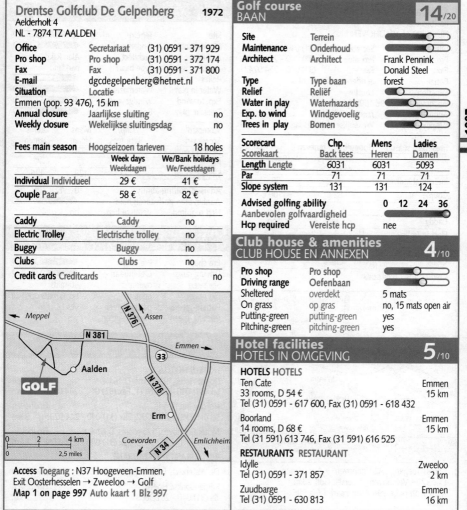

Drentse Golfclub De Gelpenberg — 1972

Aelderholt 4
NL - 7874 TZ AALDEN

Office	Secretariaat	(31) 0591 - 371 929
Pro shop	Pro shop	(31) 0591 - 372 174
Fax	Fax	(31) 0591 - 371 800
E-mail	dgcdegelpenberg@hetnet.nl	
Situation	Locatie	
Emmen (pop. 93 476), 15 km		
Annual closure	Jaarlijkse sluiting	no
Weekly closure	Wekelijkse sluitingsdag	no

Fees main season Hoogseizoen tarieven	18 holes	
	Week days Weekdagen	**We/Bank holidays** We/Feestdagen
Individual Individueel	29 €	41 €
Couple Paar	58 €	82 €

Caddy	Caddy	no
Electric Trolley	Electrische trolley	no
Buggy	Buggy	no
Clubs	Clubs	no
Credit cards Creditcards		no

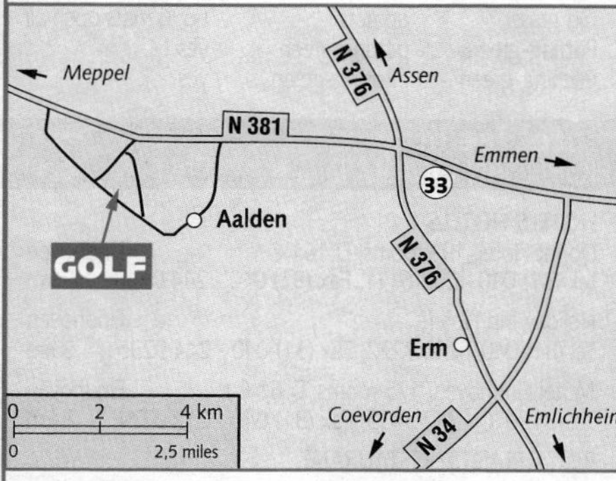

Access Toegang : N37 Hoogeveen-Emmen, Exit Oosterhesselen → Zweeloo → Golf
Map 1 on page 997 Auto kaart 1 Blz 997

Golf course — BAAN — 14/20

Site	Terrein	
Maintenance	Onderhoud	
Architect	Architect	Frank Pennink, Donald Steel
Type	Type baan	forest
Relief	Reliëf	
Water in play	Waterhazards	
Exp. to wind	Windgevoelig	
Trees in play	Bomen	

Scorecard Scorekaart	**Chp.** Back tees	**Mens** Heren	**Ladies** Damen
Length Lengte	6031	6031	5093
Par	71	71	71
Slope system	131	131	124

Advised golfing ability Aanbevolen golfvaardigheid — 0 12 24 36
Hcp required Vereiste hcp — nee

Club house & amenities — CLUB HOUSE EN ANNEXEN — 4/10

Pro shop	Pro shop	
Driving range	Oefenbaan	
Sheltered	overdekt	5 mats
On grass	op gras	no, 15 mats open air
Putting-green	putting-green	yes
Pitching-green	pitching-green	yes

Hotel facilities — HOTELS IN OMGEVING — 5/10

HOTELS HOTELS

Ten Cate — Emmen 15 km
33 rooms, D 54 €
Tel (31) 0591 - 617 600, Fax (31) 0591 - 618 432

Boorland — Emmen 15 km
14 rooms, D 68 €
Tel (31 591) 613 746, Fax (31 591) 616 525

RESTAURANTS RESTAURANT

Idylle — Zweeloo 2 km
Tel (31) 0591 - 371 857

Zuudbarge — Emmen 16 km
Tel (31) 0591 - 630 813

GENDERSTEYN

15 | 7 | 7

Deze baan is aangelegd in een landelijk gebied, tussen een autoweg en wat industrie. Alhoewel ook een aantal holes verborgen ligt in de bossen, waardoor een vredige atmosfeer is geschapen. Hoewel de baan nog jong is, ogen de bomen zeer volwassen. De fairways mogen wat korter gemaaid (er is nauwelijks een semi-rough). Twee vijvers en een paar kleine vennetjes komen op verschillende manieren in het spel, zoals op de 6e, een par-3 waarvan de tee (niet de green) op een eiland ligt. De tweede negen strekken zich uit over een tot 20 meter verhoogd stuk land, zodat spelers worden geconfronteerd met blinde slagen en sterk hellende fairways. Het hoogste punt levert een fraai uitzicht over de omgeving op. Het vormt een welkome onderbreking van het vlakke deel van de baan. De greens kunnen lastig zijn, afhankelijk van de pin-positie en een aantal afslagen zijn veeleisend, maar er is altijd ruimte om een veilige weg te vinden. Geschikt voor alle type golfers.

This course is laid out in a rural zone between a motorway and industrial estate, although several holes are tucked away in a woodland area and help give the site something of a peaceful atmosphere. Although still very young, the trees create an air of maturity, even though the grass is not yet mown short enough (there is no semi-rough). Two lakes and several little ponds come into play in different ways, like on the 6th, a par 3 where the tee is an island (but not the green). The back 9 are built over a plot of fallow land some 20 metres high, where players are confronted with a few blind shots and many sloping lies. This altitude offers some pretty views over the region and breaks up the rather flat nature of the course. The greens can be difficult, depending on the pin positions, and a number of drives can be tricky, but there is always room to play safe. For golfers of all levels.

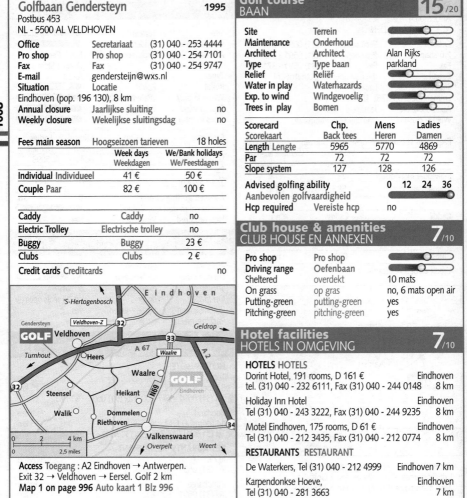

Golfbaan Gendersteyn — 1995

Postbus 453
NL - 5500 AL VELDHOVEN

Office	Secretariaat	(31) 040 - 253 4444
Pro shop	Pro shop	(31) 040 - 254 7101
Fax	Fax	(31) 040 - 254 9747
E-mail	gendersteijn@wxs.nl	
Situation	Locatie	

Eindhoven (pop. 196 130), 8 km

Annual closure	Jaarlijkse sluiting	no
Weekly closure	Wekelijkse sluitingsdag	no

Fees main season Hoogseizoen tarieven	18 holes	
	Week days Weekdagen	**We/Bank holidays** We/Feestdagen
Individual Individueel	41 €	50 €
Couple Paar	82 €	100 €

Caddy	Caddy	no
Electric Trolley	Electrische trolley	no
Buggy	Buggy	23 €
Clubs	Clubs	2 €
Credit cards Creditcards		no

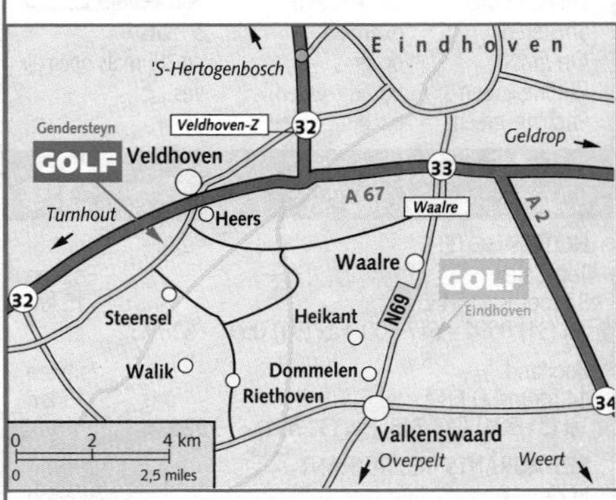

Access Toegang : A2 Eindhoven → Antwerpen.
Exit 32 → Veldhoven → Eersel. Golf 2 km
Map 1 on page 996 Auto kaart 1 Blz 996

Golf course BAAN — 15/20

Site	Terrein	
Maintenance	Onderhoud	
Architect	Architect	Alan Rijks
Type	Type baan	parkland
Relief	Reliëf	
Water in play	Waterhazards	
Exp. to wind	Windgevoelig	
Trees in play	Bomen	

Scorecard Scorekaart	**Chp.** Back tees	**Mens** Heren	**Ladies** Damen
Length Lengte	5965	5770	4869
Par	72	72	72
Slope system	127	128	126

Advised golfing ability 0 12 24 36
Aanbevolen golfvaardigheid
Hcp required Vereiste hcp — no

Club house & amenities CLUB HOUSE EN ANNEXEN — 7/10

Pro shop	Pro shop	
Driving range	Oefenbaan	
Sheltered	overdekt	10 mats
On grass	op gras	no, 6 mats open air
Putting-green	putting-green	yes
Pitching-green	pitching-green	yes

Hotel facilities HOTELS IN OMGEVING — 7/10

HOTELS HOTELS

Dorint Hotel, 191 rooms, D 161 € — Eindhoven
tel. (31) 040 - 232 6111, Fax (31) 040 - 244 0148 — 8 km

Holiday Inn Hotel — Eindhoven
Tel (31) 040 - 243 3222, Fax (31) 040 - 244 9235 — 8 km

Motel Eindhoven, 175 rooms, D 61 € — Eindhoven
Tel (31) 040 - 212 3435, Fax (31) 040 - 212 0774 — 8 km

RESTAURANTS RESTAURANT

De Waterkers, Tel (31) 040 - 212 4999 — Eindhoven 7 km

Karpendonkse Hoeve, — Eindhoven
Tel (31) 040 - 281 3663 — 7 km

GOES

15 | 7 | 6

Van een afstand lijkt deze baan misschien op een van de vele nieuwe 'polderbanen'. Maar als je op de fairways loopt vallen direct de glooiingen en heuveltjes op, die elke slag een beetje moeilijker dan normaal kunnen maken. Deze heuveltjes zijn gemaakt met de grond die vrijkwam bij het graven van de waterpartijen die op dertien holes in het spel komen. Soms alleen langs de kant van de fairway, maar in veel gevallen vlak voor de green. Water is niet de enige hindernis om rekening mee te houden. Er ligt een flink aantal bunkers op strategische plaatsen. De greens zijn alle wat glooiend, maar zonder de overdreven contouren die je op veel nieuwe banen tegenkomt. Als afsluiting van het hele project is een ruim nieuw clubhuis gebouwd, dat een fraai uitzicht over de baan biedt.

From a distance, Goes may look like one of the many new courses in the flat Dutch "polderland". But once walking its fairways you will notice the subtle undulations and hills that frequently make your next shot a little more awkward. These slopes result from the clever use of soil dug out to create the many water hazards that come into play, sometimes edging the fairway but on several occasions in front of the greens. And water is not the only hazard to cope with, as a fair number of bunkers are strategically located on the fairways. The greens are rather distinctly contoured but don't have the excessive bumps often seen on today's new courses. Now that the new clubhouse has opened its doors, the facilities are complete and up-to-standard.

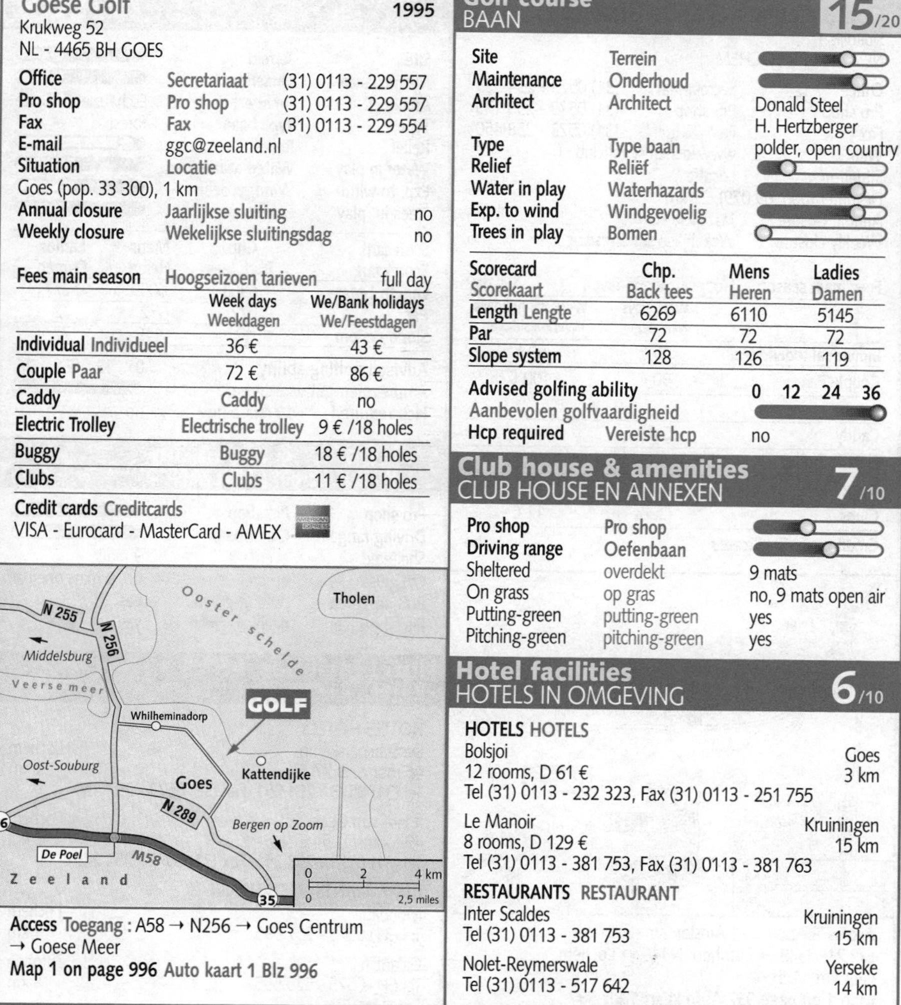

Goese Golf — 1995
Krukweg 52
NL - 4465 BH GOES

Office	Secretariaat	(31) 0113 - 229 557
Pro shop	Pro shop	(31) 0113 - 229 557
Fax	Fax	(31) 0113 - 229 554
E-mail	ggc@zeeland.nl	
Situation	Locatie	
Goes (pop. 33 300), 1 km		
Annual closure	Jaarlijkse sluiting	no
Weekly closure	Wekelijkse sluitingsdag	no

Fees main season Hoogseizoen tarieven	full day	
	Week days Weekdagen	**We/Bank holidays** We/Feestdagen
Individual Individueel	36 €	43 €
Couple Paar	72 €	86 €
Caddy Caddy		no
Electric Trolley Electrische trolley		9 € /18 holes
Buggy Buggy		18 € /18 holes
Clubs Clubs		11 € /18 holes

Credit cards Creditcards
VISA - Eurocard - MasterCard - AMEX

Access Toegang : A58 → N256 → Goes Centrum → Goese Meer
Map 1 on page 996 Auto kaart 1 Blz 996

Golf course — BAAN — 15/20

Site	Terrein	
Maintenance	Onderhoud	
Architect	Architect	Donald Steel H. Hertzberger
Type	Type baan	polder, open country
Relief	Reliëf	
Water in play	Waterhazards	
Exp. to wind	Windgevoelig	
Trees in play	Bomen	

Scorecard Scorekaart	**Chp.** Back tees	**Mens** Heren	**Ladies** Damen
Length Lengte	6269	6110	5145
Par	72	72	72
Slope system	128	126	119

Advised golfing ability Aanbevolen golfvaardigheid — 0 12 24 36
Hcp required Vereiste hcp — no

Club house & amenities — CLUB HOUSE EN ANNEXEN — 7/10

Pro shop	Pro shop	
Driving range	Oefenbaan	
Sheltered	overdekt	9 mats
On grass	op gras	no, 9 mats open air
Putting-green	putting-green	yes
Pitching-green	pitching-green	yes

Hotel facilities — HOTELS IN OMGEVING — 6/10

HOTELS HOTELS

Bolsjoi — Goes 3 km
12 rooms, D 61 €
Tel (31) 0113 - 232 323, Fax (31) 0113 - 251 755

Le Manoir — Kruiningen 15 km
8 rooms, D 129 €
Tel (31) 0113 - 381 753, Fax (31) 0113 - 381 763

RESTAURANTS RESTAURANT

Inter Scaldes — Kruiningen 15 km
Tel (31) 0113 - 381 753

Nolet-Reymerswale — Yerseke 14 km
Tel (31) 0113 - 517 642

GRAAFSCHAP 15 7 6

Het specifieke karakter van deze goed ontworpen baan is de afwisseling tussen open en bebost terrein, een typische eigenschap van het hele gebied. Het uit zich hier in het feit dat bijna de helft van de holes begint in een open stuk en eindigt temidden van bomen. Of andersom. In tegenstelling tot veel nieuwe banen is hier weinig grond verzet, zelfs niet voor de waterhazards die klein en heel natuurlijk zijn. De meeste fairways zijn breed en mild voor afgedwaalde ballen, maar enkele losse bomen kunnen voor flinke problemen zorgen. In combinatie met de wind (in de open gedeelten) kunnen zij elke hoop op een goede score de nek omdraaien. Ondanks het ontbreken van reliëf valt er van prachtige vergezichten te genieten, vooral in de herfst. De greens zijn middelgroot, niet moeilijk te lezen en over het algemeen niet spectaculair. Wel afdoende bewaakt door bunkers.

The full character of this competently designed course lies with its alternating forest and open landscape, a frequent feature throughout the region. It is plain to see on almost half the holes, which start under the open sky and end up in the trees, or inversely. As opposed to many recent courses, there has been little artificial moving of earth, even for the water hazards that are small and very natural. Most of the fairways are wide and forgiving for wayward shots, but several isolated trees can spell serious trouble. Combined with the wind (in the more exposed sections), they can dash any hope of playing to your handicap, a feat that otherwise is more than possible. Despite the lack of relief, there are some beautiful views to be had here, especially in the Autumn. The greens are mid-sized, pretty easy to read and generally, but none too imaginatively, well-guarded by a brace of bunkers.

Golf & Country Club De Graafschap 0

Sluitdijk 4
NL - 7241 RR LOCHEM

Office	Secretariaat	(31) 0573 - 254 323
Pro shop	Pro shop	(31) 0573 - 258 179
Fax	Fax	(31) 0573 - 258 450
Web	www.lochemsegolfclub.nl	
Situation	Locatie	

Deventer (pop. 69 079), 22 km

Annual closure	Jaarlijkse sluiting	no
Weekly closure	Wekelijkse sluitingsdag	no

Fees main season / Hoogseizoen tarieven	Week days / Weekdagen	We/Bank holidays / We/Feestdagen
		full day
Individual Individueel	45 €	50 €
Couple Paar	90 €	100 €

Caddy	Caddy	no
Electric Trolley	Electrische trolley	no
Buggy	Buggy	no
Clubs	Clubs	11 €
Credit cards	Creditcards	no

Access Toegang : A1 Amsterdam -Enschede. Exit 23. N348 → Zutphen. N346 → Lochem. Golf km 11.5
Map 1 on page 997 Auto kaart 1 Blz 997

Golf course / BAAN 15/20

Site	Terrein	
Maintenance	Onderhoud	
Architect	Architect	Eschauzier & Thate
Type	Type baan	forest
Relief	Reliëf	
Water in play	Waterhazards	
Exp. to wind	Windgevoelig	
Trees in play	Bomen	

Scorecard / Scorekaart	Chp. / Back tees	Mens / Heren	Ladies / Damen
Length Lengte	6303	6059	5277
Par	72	72	72
Slope system	122	119	72

Advised golfing ability / Aanbevolen golfvaardigheid: 0 12 24 36
Hcp required / Vereiste hcp: no

Club house & amenities / CLUB HOUSE EN ANNEXEN 7/10

Pro shop	Pro shop	
Driving range	Oefenbaan	
Sheltered	overdekt	9 mats
On grass	op gras	no, 9 mats open air
Putting-green	putting-green	yes
Pitching-green	pitching-green	yes

Hotel facilities / HOTELS IN OMGEVING 6/10

HOTELS HOTELS

De Scheperskamp — Lochem 3 km
46 rooms, D 77 €
Tel (31) 0573 - 254 051, Fax (31) 0573 - 257 150

't Hof van Gelre — Lochem 3 km
49 rooms, D 54 €
Tel (31) 0573 - 253 351, Fax (31) 0573 - 254 245

RESTAURANTS RESTAURANT

Mondani — Lochem 3 km
Tel (31) 0573 - 257 595

Galantijn — Zutphen 8 km
Tel (31) 0575 - 525 555

GREVELINGENHOUT

14	7	4

Wat kunt u anders verwachten in de provincie Zeeland dan een straffe wind? Grevelingenhout is ontworpen in een mooi gebied langs de rivierendelta, waar zeilen de traditionele sport is. Het is de eerste golfbaan in Nederland waar ook gewoond kan worden, al zijn de huizen op de vrij kleine stukken grond niet altijd wonderen van architectuur. Zij zijn gescheiden van de baan door vijvertjes en sloten, die op bijna alle holes in het spel komen. We hopen maar dat de aangeplante bomen en struiken de bewoners, en de spelers, geleidelijk wat meer privacy zullen bieden. Dit is een goede golfbaan om spelers aan water te laten wennen. Dat komt op fraaie wijze in het spel op de 12e (een par-3) over een vijver en de 9e en de 18e, die een dubbelgreen delen, bewaakt door water. Het zal niet verbazen dat al die nattigheid het grootste obstakel vormt, samen met de wind. Het zou spelers ertoe kunnen aanzetten juist hier matchplay te spelen.

What else would you expect in the province of Zeeland than persistent wind? Grevelingenhout was designed in a pretty region along the delta, where sailing is the traditional sport. This is Holland's first residential course, although the houses built on small plots of land are hardly wonders of architecture. They are separated from the fairways by ponds and other stretches of water, which come into play on most holes. We can only hope that the newly planted trees and bushes will offer the inhabitants, and players, a little more privacy. This is a good course for accustoming all golfers to the problems posed by water, which is excellently brought into play on the 12th (a par 3 over water) and the 9th and 18th holes, which share a very well-guarded double green. Water is, not surprisingly, the key difficulty here, together with the wind we talked about, and this should incite most golfers to opt for the match-play format.

Golfclub Grevelingenhout — 1989

Oudendijk 3
NL - 4311 NA BRUINISSE

Office	Secretariaat	(31) 0111 - 482 650
Pro shop	Pro shop	(31) 0111 - 482 650
Fax	Fax	(31) 0111 - 481 566
E-mail	golfclub@grevelingenhout.nl	
Situation	Locatie	

Goes (pop. 33 281), 30 km - Rotterdam (pop. 598 521), 50 km

Annual closure	Jaarlijkse sluiting	no
Weekly closure	Wekelijkse sluitingsdag	no

Fees main season Hoogseizoen tarieven		full day
	Week days Weekdagen	**We/Bank holidays** We/Feestdagen
Individual Individueel	41 €	50 €
Couple Paar	82 €	100 €

Caddy	Caddy	no
Electric Trolley	Electrische trolley	yes
Buggy	Buggy	yes
Clubs	Clubs	yes
Credit cards Creditcards		no

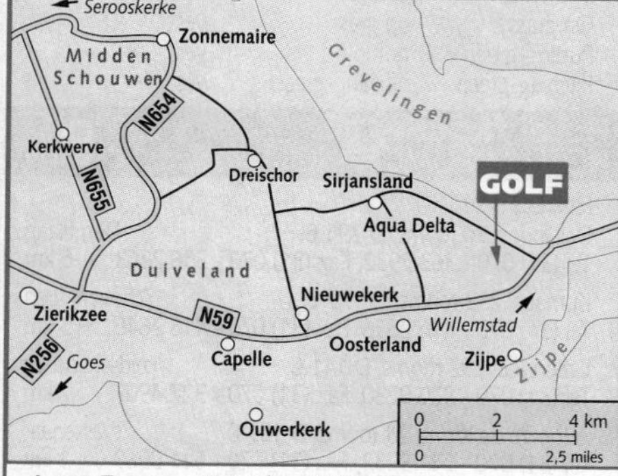

Access Toegang : Rotterdam A29,
Exit Middelharnis, N59 → Zierikzee. Exit Aquadelta
Map 1 on page 996 Auto kaart 1 Blz 996

Golf course — BAAN — 14/20

Site	Terrein	
Maintenance	Onderhoud	
Architect	Architect	Donald Harradine
Type	Type baan	parkland
Relief	Reliëf	
Water in play	Waterhazards	
Exp. to wind	Windgevoelig	
Trees in play	Bomen	

Scorecard Scorekaart	**Chp.** Back tees	**Mens** Heren	**Ladies** Damen
Length Lengte	6193	5951	5144
Par	72	72	72
Slope system	128	128	124

Advised golfing ability Aanbevolen golfvaardigheid — 0 12 24 36
Hcp required Vereiste hcp — no

Club house & amenities — CLUB HOUSE EN ANNEXEN — 7/10

Pro shop	Pro shop	
Driving range	Oefenbaan	
Sheltered	overdekt	6 mats
On grass	op gras	no, 6 mats open air
Putting-green	putting-green	yes
Pitching-green	pitching-green	yes

Hotel facilities — HOTELS IN OMGEVING — 4/10

HOTELS HOTELS

Mondragon — Zierikzee 10 km
8 rooms, D 91 €
Tel (31) 0111 - 413 051, Fax (31) 0111 - 415 997

Schuddebeurs — Schuddebeurs 15 km
21 rooms, D 79 €
Tel (31) 0111 - 415 651, Fax (31) 0111 - 413 103

RESTAURANTS RESTAURANT

De drie Morianen — Zierikzee 10 km
Tel (31) 0111 - 412 931

Mondragon — Zierikzee 10 km
Tel (31) 0111 - 412 670

1011

HAAGSCHE

18 | 7 | 8

De Hollandse kust leent zich uitstekend voor de aanleg van prachtige banen en deze is daar een goed voorbeeld van. Naar het ontwerp van de architecten Colt en Alison die borg stonden voor een uitdagend ontwerp. Het is maar goed dat de lengte niet overdreven is, want het komt vaak voor dat je slagen verliest in dichte struiken of in diepe bunkers. Maar als u door de wind met rust gelaten wordt en alle aandacht aan uw swing kunt besteden, dan hebt u een goede kans een mooi resultaat te sco-ren. Zoals je in de duinen kan verwachten zijn er maar weinig echt vlakke stukken op de fairways. Veel uphill of downhill slagen dus, plus interessante situaties rond de greens. De Haagsche heeft talloze internationale wedstrijden (waaronder het Dutch Open) mogen ontvangen. Het is de moeite waard hier een dag voor uit te trekken. Zowaar een linksbaan zonder het Kanaal te hoeven oversteken.

The Dutch coast is a marvellous site for building great courses, and this is one of the finest. The cachet of designers Colt and Alison speaks volumes for the challenging style of this layout. Although not excessively long, there are more than enough opportunities to drop shots, in the thickets lining the fairways or in the pot bunkers. If the wind leaves you alone, with just your problems of swing to cope with, you will have every chance of returning a good score. As you might expect among sand dunes, there are few really flat lies on the fairways, a lot of shots uphill and down, and some tantalising situations around the greens. Haagsche has hosted a number of international events (including the Dutch Open) and, with its counter-parts along the coast, deserves a special golfing holiday. Here is a great links to play without having to ferry across the Channel.

Koninklijke Haagsche Golf & Countryclub

1938
Groot Haesenbroekseweg 22
NL - 2243 EC WASSENAAR

Office	Secretariaat	(31) 070 - 517 9607
Pro shop	Pro shop	(31) 070 - 517 9822
Fax	Fax	(31) 070 - 514 0171
Web	—	
Situation	Locatie	

Den Haag (pop. 445 279), 4 km

Annual closure	Jaarlijkse sluiting	no
Weekly closure	Wekelijkse sluitingsdag	no

Fees main season Hoogseizoen tarieven	Week days Weekdagen	We/Bank holidays We/Feestdagen
		full day
Individual Individueel	82 €	*
Couple Paar	164 €	*

* Weekends: members only

Caddy	Caddy	no
Electric Trolley	Electrische trolley	no
Buggy	Buggy	no
Clubs	Clubs	no
Credit cards Creditcards		no

Access Toegang : A44 → Wassenaar
Map 1 on page 996 Auto kaart 1 Blz 996

Golf course BAAN — 18/20

Site	Terrein	
Maintenance	Onderhoud	
Architect	Architect	Harry S. Colt, Allison
Type	Type baan	links
Relief	Reliëf	
Water in play	Waterhazards	
Exp. to wind	Windgevoelig	
Trees in play	Bomen	

Scorecard Scorekaart	Chp. Back tees	Mens Heren	Ladies Damen
Length Lengte	6142	5674	5006
Par	72	72	72
Slope system	131	129	126

Advised golfing ability Aanbevolen golfvaardigheid — 0 12 24 36
Hcp required Vereiste hcp — 26

Club house & amenities CLUB HOUSE EN ANNEXEN — 7/10

Pro shop	Pro shop	
Driving range	Oefenbaan	
Sheltered	overdekt	12 mats
On grass	op gras	yes
Putting-green	putting-green	yes
Pitching-green	pitching-green	yes

Hotel facilities HOTELS IN OMGEVING — 8/10

HOTELS HOTELS

Des Indes, 70 rooms, D 295 € — Den Haag
Tel (31) 070 - 363 2932, Fax (31) 070 - 356 2863 — 5 km

Kurhaus, 233 rooms, D 179 € — Scheveningen
Tel (31) 070 - 416 2636, Fax (31) 070 - 416 2646 — 5 km

Green Park, 92 rooms, D 141 € — Leidschendam
Tel (31) 070 - 320 9280, Fax (31) 070 - 327 4907 — 7 km

Auberge de Kievit, 23 rooms, D 159 € — Wassenaar
Tel (31) 070 - 511 9232, Fax (31) 070 - 511 0969 — 1 km

RESTAURANTS RESTAURANT

Auberge de Kievit, Tel (31) 070 - 511 9232 — Wassenaar
't Ganzenest, Tel (31) 070 - 389 6709 — Den Haag 5 km

HERKENBOSCH

16 | 7 | 6

Dit is waarschijnlijk een van de laatste keren dat de aanleg van een baan in zulke bebost terrein werd toegestaan. In dit geval was het verkrijgen van een kapvergunning iets makkelijker, omdat het om mijnhout ging. Er is nog steeds veel daarvan blijven staan, en die bomen zijn de belangrijkste hindernis, vooral op de smallere holes en de vele doglegs. De begroeiing onder de bomen kan heel dicht zijn, hetgeen een extra afstraffing van onnauwkeurige slagen oplevert (neem wat extra ballen mee als u niet zo zuiver slaat). Dit is het enige zwakke punt in wat verder een knappe baan is, waarvan een deel over een heuvel is gedrapeerd, hetgeen resulteert in moeilijke uphill en downhill slagen. Er ligt daarentegen niet zoveel water. Al komt wat er ligt wel duidelijk in het spel, zoals op de fraaie 11e hole. De greens zijn tamelijk groot, goed ontworpen en goed bewaakt.

This is probably one of the last courses that the authorities will allow to be built in such a wooded area. Permission to fell trees was granted because they were lean pines planted for the mining industry. There are a lot of them left and they form the main hazard, especially on a number of tight holes and numerous dog-legs. The undergrowth is thick to say the least and adds an extra and perhaps unwarranted difficulty, given that mis-hit shots are already punished enough (bring a stock of balls if you are wayward off the tee). This is the only real flaw in what is an intelligent course, a part of which hugs a steepish hill, thus giving some tricky holes uphill and down. In contrast, there is little water to bother you, although what there is well in play, as on the very fine 11th hole. The greens are rather large, well-contoured and well-guarded.

Burggolf Herkenbosch — 1992

Stationsweg 100
NL - 6075 CD HERKENBOSCH

Office	Secretariaat	(31) 0475 - 529 529
Pro shop	Pro shop	(31) 0475 - 535 804
Fax	Fax	(31) 0475 - 533 580
E-mail	nlhoef01@ey.nl	
Situation	Locatie	

Roermond (pop. 43 110), 5 km

Annual closure	Jaarlijkse sluiting	no
Weekly closure	Wekelijkse sluitingsdag	no

Fees main season Hoogseizoen tarieven	18 holes	
	Week days Weekdagen	**We/Bank holidays** We/Feestdagen
Individual Individueel	45 €	54 €
Couple Paar	90 €	108 €

Caddy	Caddy	no
Electric Trolley	Electrische trolley	yes
Buggy	Buggy	yes
Clubs	Clubs	yes

Credit cards Creditcards
VISA - Eurocard - MasterCard

Access Toegang : A2 Maastricht-Weert-Eindhoven.
Exit 40. N68, A68 → Roermond.
N68, N281 → Herkenbosch → Golf
Map 1 on page 997 Auto kaart 1 Blz 997

Golf course — BAAN — 16/20

Site	Terrein	
Maintenance	Onderhoud	
Architect	Architect	Joan Dudok van Heel B. Steensels
Type	Type baan	forest
Relief	Reliëf	
Water in play	Waterhazards	
Exp. to wind	Windgevoelig	
Trees in play	Bomen	

Scorecard Scorekaart	**Chp.** Back tees	**Mens** Heren	**Ladies** Damen
Length Lengte	6141	5758	4981
Par	72	72	72
Slope system	137	136	129

Advised golfing ability Aanbevolen golfvaardigheid — 0 12 24 36

Hcp required Vereiste hcp — We: 36

Club house & amenities — CLUB HOUSE EN ANNEXEN — 7/10

Pro shop	Pro shop	
Driving range	Oefenbaan	
Sheltered	overdekt	6 mats
On grass	op gras	no, 10 mats open air
Putting-green	putting-green	yes
Pitching-green	pitching-green	yes

Hotel facilities — HOTELS IN OMGEVING — 6/10

HOTELS HOTELS

Kasteeltje Hattem, 11 rooms, D 132 € — Roermond 5 km
Tel (31) 0475 - 319 222, Fax (31) 0475 - 319 292

Landhotel Cox, 54 rooms, D 84 € — Roermond 5 km
Tel (31) 0475 - 329 966, Fax (31) 0475 - 325 142

Boshotel, 60 rooms, D 68 € — Vlodrop 3 km
Tel (31) 0475 - 534 959, Fax (31) 0475 - 534 580

RESTAURANTS RESTAURANT

Kasteel Daelenbroek — Herkenbosch 2 km
Tel (31) 0475 - 532 465

La Cascade, Tel (31) 0475 - 319 274 — Roermond 5 km

HILVERSUM

16 | 7 | 7

Sinds deze baan aan het begin van de eeuw is aangelegd, heeft hij een aantal ingrijpende wijzigingen ondergaan. Hoewel sommige van die aanpassingen twijfelachtig zijn, blijft Hilversum wat het altijd is geweest: een verbluffend voorbeeld van een goed ontwerp voor een baan in het binnenland. Door de vele oude bomen zijn de meeste fairways behoorlijk smal, waardoor ze precisie en effectvolle slagen vereisen. De zanderige heuvels, die vaak tot slagen van glooiende hellingen dwingen, verhogen het technisch aspect van het spel. De spaarzame fairway-bunkers zijn goed geplaatst en moeilijk, de middelgrote greens worden goed bewaakt en de heidevelden voegen extra moeilijkheden aan de baan toe. De baan is heel rustig (de enige verstoring kan komen van fietsers of ruiters) en heeft het onderhoudsnivo de laatste tijd sterk verbeterd. Dat zou te maken kunnen hebben met het Dutch Open dat hier vanaf 1994 wordt gespeeld.

Since it was created at the turn of the century, this course has undergone a number of significant changes. Although some of these are questionable, the course is still the strikingly good example of excellent inland design it always has been. Owing to the very many old trees, some fairways are very tight and require precision and flighted shots. The sandy slopes, which often call for shots played from sloping lies, augment the technical aspect of golf here. The few fairway bunkers you come across are still well-placed and tough, the mid-sized greens are well-guarded and the heather adds an extra difficulty to the course. Very quiet (the only disturbance here might come from cyclists or horse-riders), Hilversum has significantly improved its standard of course upkeep: to prove it, the Dutch Open has been played here since 1994.

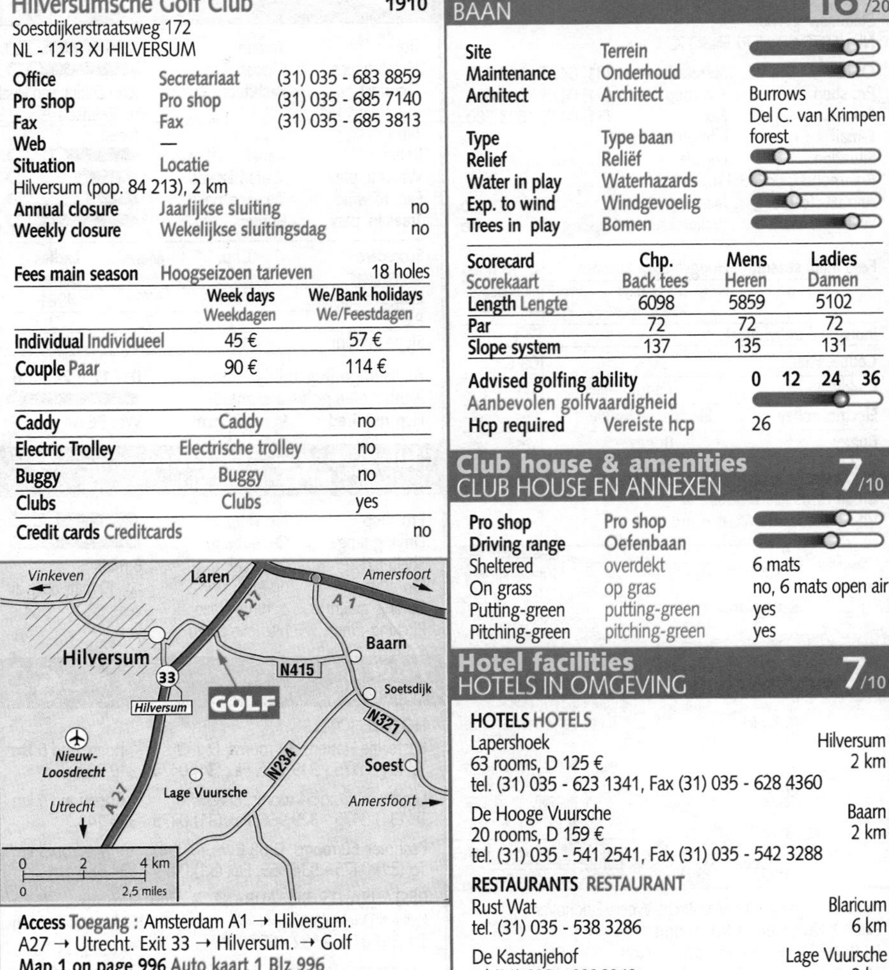

Hilversumsche Golf Club 1910

Soestdijkerstraatsweg 172
NL - 1213 XJ HILVERSUM

Office	Secretariaat	(31) 035 - 683 8859
Pro shop	Pro shop	(31) 035 - 685 7140
Fax	Fax	(31) 035 - 685 3813
Web	—	
Situation	Locatie	

Hilversum (pop. 84 213), 2 km

Annual closure	Jaarlijkse sluiting	no
Weekly closure	Wekelijkse sluitingsdag	no

Fees main season Hoogseizoen tarieven — 18 holes

	Week days / Weekdagen	We/Bank holidays / We/Feestdagen
Individual Individueel	45 €	57 €
Couple Paar	90 €	114 €

Caddy	Caddy	no
Electric Trolley	Electrische trolley	no
Buggy	Buggy	no
Clubs	Clubs	yes
Credit cards	Creditcards	no

Access Toegang : Amsterdam A1 → Hilversum. A27 → Utrecht. Exit 33 → Hilversum. → Golf
Map 1 on page 996 Auto kaart 1 Blz 996

Golf course / BAAN — 16/20

Site	Terrein	
Maintenance	Onderhoud	
Architect	Architect	Burrows Del C. van Krimpen
Type	Type baan	forest
Relief	Reliëf	
Water in play	Waterhazards	
Exp. to wind	Windgevoelig	
Trees in play	Bomen	

Scorecard Scorekaart	**Chp.** Back tees	**Mens** Heren	**Ladies** Damen
Length Lengte	6098	5859	5102
Par	72	72	72
Slope system	137	135	131

Advised golfing ability Aanbevolen golfvaardigheid — 0 12 24 36

Hcp required Vereiste hcp — 26

Club house & amenities / CLUB HOUSE EN ANNEXEN — 7/10

Pro shop	Pro shop	
Driving range	Oefenbaan	
Sheltered	overdekt	6 mats
On grass	op gras	no, 6 mats open air
Putting-green	putting-green	yes
Pitching-green	pitching-green	yes

Hotel facilities / HOTELS IN OMGEVING — 7/10

HOTELS HOTELS

Lapershoek — Hilversum 2 km
63 rooms, D 125 €
tel. (31) 035 - 623 1341, Fax (31) 035 - 628 4360

De Hooge Vuursche — Baarn 2 km
20 rooms, D 159 €
tel. (31) 035 - 541 2541, Fax (31) 035 - 542 3288

RESTAURANTS RESTAURANT

Rust Wat — Blaricum 6 km
tel. (31) 035 - 538 3286

De Kastanjehof — Lage Vuursche 3 km
tel.(31) 035 - 666 8248

HOGE KLEIJ

15 | 6 | 7

Deze opvallende baan, in het midden van het land, was een van de eerste van een serie nieuwe privé banen die begin jaren '80 werden aangelegd. Een groot deel van de baan ligt temidden van bestaande bossen, de rest in meer open terrein. Door dat laatste biedt de Hoge Klej een groter gevoel van ruimte dan de 'oudere' buren Hilversum en De Pan. Op enkele holes is goed gebruik gemaakt van de hoogteverschillen, terwijl de overige holes vrij vlak zijn. Dat maakt de baan toegankelijk voor elk nivo speler. Het mag dan geen spectaculaire baan zijn, er zitten een paar mooie holes tussen, met een grote variteit in vormen, maten en moeilijkheden. Maar dat kun je verwachten van ontwerpers en kenners als Steel en Pennink, die zich nooit druk maken om al te subtiele details. De oefenfaciliteiten houden gelijke tred met de kwaliteit van de baan en hetzelfde kan worden gezegd van het clubhuis (met een goed restaurant).

This remarkable course, in the centre of Holland, was one of the first of a series of new private courses built in the first half of the 1980s. A large section was laid out in trees, the rest in wide open spaces, and this gives "Hoge Kleij" a much more definite impression of space than its elder neighbours at Hilversum and De Pan. The differences in level on several holes have been cleverly used, while the rest of the course is flat, making it easier for players of all levels and ages. This is hardly a spectacular course, but there are some competent holes here and a wide variety of shapes, sizes and difficulties. Again, this is only to be expected from designers and fine connoisseurs of golf such as Steel and Pennink, who never care unduly about excessively sophisticated details. Practice facilities are consistent with the standard of the course design, and the same can be said for the clubhouse (with a good restaurant).

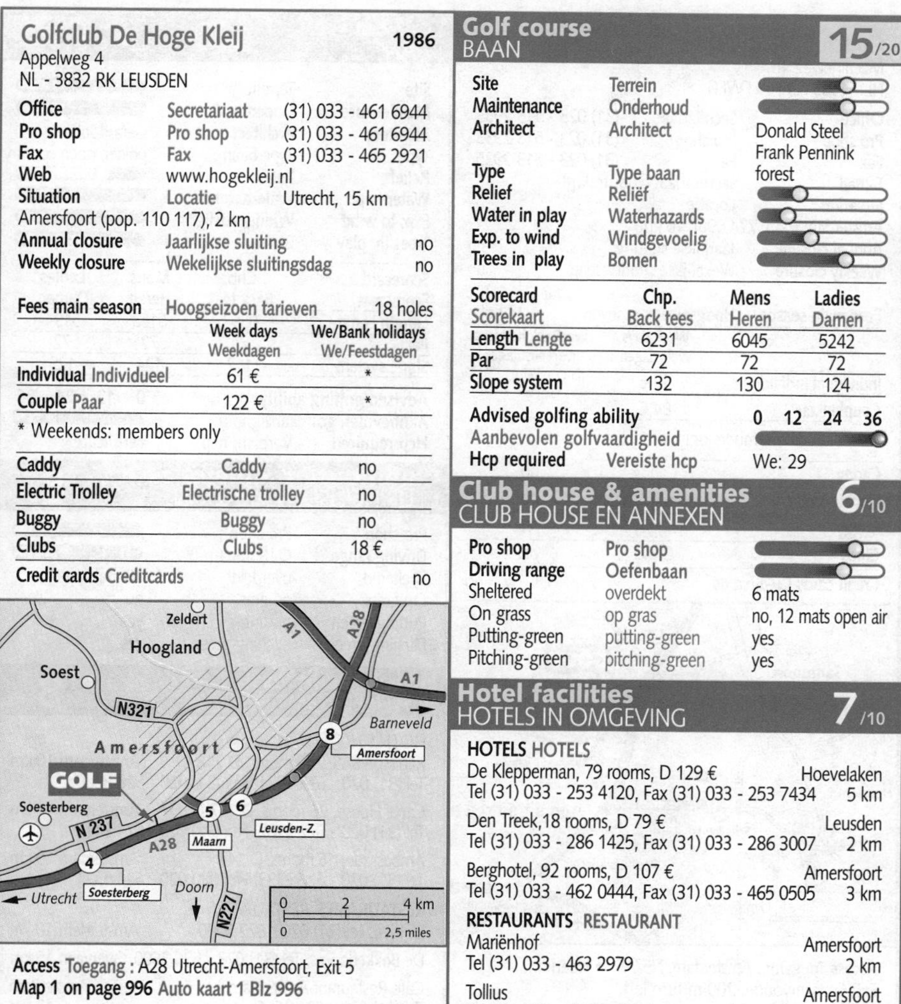

Golfclub De Hoge Kleij — 1986

Appelweg 4
NL - 3832 RK LEUSDEN

Office	Secretariaat	(31) 033 - 461 6944
Pro shop	Pro shop	(31) 033 - 461 6944
Fax	Fax	(31) 033 - 465 2921
Web	www.hogekleij.nl	
Situation	Locatie	Utrecht, 15 km

Amersfoort (pop. 110 117), 2 km

Annual closure	Jaarlijkse sluiting	no
Weekly closure	Wekelijkse sluitingsdag	no

Fees main season Hoogseizoen tarieven	18 holes	
	Week days Weekdagen	**We/Bank holidays** We/Feestdagen
Individual Individueel	61 €	*
Couple Paar	122 €	*

* Weekends: members only

Caddy	Caddy	no
Electric Trolley	Electrische trolley	no
Buggy	Buggy	no
Clubs	Clubs	18 €
Credit cards Creditcards		no

Access Toegang : A28 Utrecht-Amersfoort, Exit 5
Map 1 on page 996 Auto kaart 1 Blz 996

Golf course — BAAN — 15/20

Site	Terrein	
Maintenance	Onderhoud	
Architect	Architect	Donald Steel Frank Pennink
Type	Type baan	forest
Relief	Reliëf	
Water in play	Waterhazards	
Exp. to wind	Windgevoelig	
Trees in play	Bomen	

Scorecard Scorekaart	**Chp.** Back tees	**Mens** Heren	**Ladies** Damen
Length Lengte	6231	6045	5242
Par	72	72	72
Slope system	132	130	124

Advised golfing ability Aanbevolen golfvaardigheid — 0 12 24 36
Hcp required Vereiste hcp — We: 29

Club house & amenities — CLUB HOUSE EN ANNEXEN — 6/10

Pro shop	Pro shop	
Driving range	Oefenbaan	
Sheltered	overdekt	6 mats
On grass	op gras	no, 12 mats open air
Putting-green	putting-green	yes
Pitching-green	pitching-green	yes

Hotel facilities — HOTELS IN OMGEVING — 7/10

HOTELS HOTELS

De Klepperman, 79 rooms, D 129 € — Hoevelaken
Tel (31) 033 - 253 4120, Fax (31) 033 - 253 7434 — 5 km

Den Treek,18 rooms, D 79 € — Leusden
Tel (31) 033 - 286 1425, Fax (31) 033 - 286 3007 — 2 km

Berghotel, 92 rooms, D 107 € — Amersfoort
Tel (31) 033 - 462 0444, Fax (31) 033 - 465 0505 — 3 km

RESTAURANTS RESTAURANT

Mariënhof — Amersfoort
Tel (31) 033 - 463 2979 — 2 km

Tollius — Amersfoort
Tel (31) 033 - 465 1793 — 2 km

HOUTRAK

16 | 8 | 8

Deze aantrekkelijke baan is aangelegd in de eerste drooglegging van het IJ (net als de naastgelegen baan van de Amsterdamse Golfclub) en zal, zolang de aangebrachte beplanting nog bescheiden is, het karakter van een polderbaan hebben. Maar geleidelijk zal dat veel gevarieerder worden. Ook al omdat bij de aanleg optimaal gebruik is gemaakt van de oude bomen die nog net op een puntje van het terrein staan, waar nu een volledige par-3 in verscholen ligt. En er zijn twaalfhonderd vrachtwagens met verse grond aangevoerd, waarmee licht glooiende contouren zijn geschapen. Verder zijn er heel wat waterpartijen, die vooral aan de buitenkant van het terrein zorgen voor een natuurlijke overgang naar de weilanden. Vanuit het iets hoger gelegen clubhuis is er een prachtig zicht op zes holes die van of naar dit centrale punt lopen.

This attractive course was built in the first land-recovery of the IJ-estuary (just like the adjacent course of the Amsterdamse Golfclub). So as long as the newly planted trees and bushes are still small, it will be ranked as a "polderbaan". But the nature of the course will gradually change, if only because of the clever use that has been made of some remaining trees in a corner of the terrain, now hiding a full par-3 hole. In addition, more than 1200 truckloads of new soil were brought in and used to create slight undulations, and there are various ponds serving as water hazards. On the outskirts of the course, they provide a natural transition to the surrounding meadowlands. From the somewhat elevated clubhouse you enjoy a magnificent view over six holes running in or out.

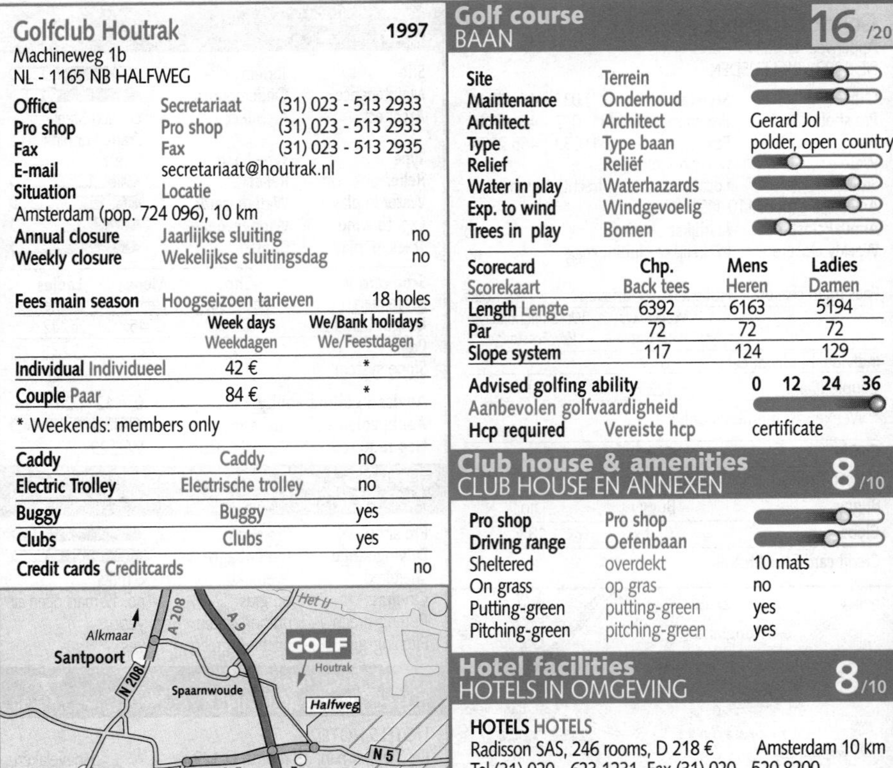

Golfclub Houtrak — 1997

Machineweg 1b
NL - 1165 NB HALFWEG

Office	Secretariaat	(31) 023 - 513 2933
Pro shop	Pro shop	(31) 023 - 513 2933
Fax	Fax	(31) 023 - 513 2935
E-mail	secretariaat@houtrak.nl	
Situation	Locatie	

Amsterdam (pop. 724 096), 10 km

Annual closure	Jaarlijkse sluiting	no
Weekly closure	Wekelijkse sluitingsdag	no

Fees main season Hoogseizoen tarieven	18 holes	
	Week days Weekdagen	**We/Bank holidays** We/Feestdagen
Individual Individueel	42 €	*
Couple Paar	84 €	*

* Weekends: members only

Caddy	Caddy	no
Electric Trolley	Electrische trolley	no
Buggy	Buggy	yes
Clubs	Clubs	yes
Credit cards	Creditcards	no

Access Toegang : Amsterdam, N5/A5 → Haarlem. Exit Spaarnwoude. 200 m turn left.
Map 1 on page 996 Auto kaart 1 Blz 996

Golf course BAAN — 16/20

Site	Terrein	
Maintenance	Onderhoud	
Architect	Architect	Gerard Jol
Type	Type baan	polder, open country
Relief	Reliëf	
Water in play	Waterhazards	
Exp. to wind	Windgevoelig	
Trees in play	Bomen	

Scorecard Scorekaart	**Chp.** Back tees	**Mens** Heren	**Ladies** Damen
Length Lengte	6392	6163	5194
Par	72	72	72
Slope system	117	124	129

Advised golfing ability Aanbevolen golfvaardigheid — 0 12 24 36
Hcp required Vereiste hcp — certificate

Club house & amenities CLUB HOUSE EN ANNEXEN — 8/10

Pro shop	Pro shop	
Driving range	Oefenbaan	
Sheltered	overdekt	10 mats
On grass	op gras	no
Putting-green	putting-green	yes
Pitching-green	pitching-green	yes

Hotel facilities HOTELS IN OMGEVING — 8/10

HOTELS HOTELS

Radisson SAS, 246 rooms, D 218 € — Amsterdam 10 km
Tel (31) 020 - 623 1231, Fax (31) 020 - 520 8200

Canal House, 26 rooms, D 147 € — Amsterdam 10 km
Tel (31) 020 - 622 5182, Fax (31) 020 - 624 1317

Ambassade, 46 rooms, D 147 € — Amsterdam 10 km
Tel (31) 020 - 626 2333, Fax (31) 020 - 624 5321

RESTAURANTS RESTAURANT

La Rive, Tel (31) 020 - 622 6060 — Amsterdam 10 km
De Bokkedoorns, Tel (31) 023 - 526 3600 — Overveen 15 km
Cafe Restaurant Amsterdam — Amsterdam
Tel (31) 020 - 682 2666 — 12 km

KENNEMER

18 | 8 | 8

Als Holland een vlak land is, dan liggen hier haar bergen. Duintoppen, wind en sobere vegetatie zijn de kenmerken van een echte linksbaan. De Kennemer is een van de mooiste voorbeeld daarvan in Europa. Je kunt de zee dan wel niet zien van hieruit, het stijlvolle, zeer traditionele clubhuis zal u zeker bekoren. De baan, ontworpen door Harry Colt in 1920, is in 1985 met negen holes uitgebreid, maar het gedeelte waar dit gebeurde had minder natuurlijke aanleg daarvoor. De hoogte-verschillen zijn beperkt (met wat blinde slagen), al zal menige bal uiteindelijk na wat stuiteren en rollen op een interessante plaats tot rust komen. Laat de afwezigheid van water en de schaarste aan bomen (enkele vliegdennen) u niet overmoedig maken. De bunkers zijn talrijk en goed geplaatst, de struiken ontbreken niet. Als u ze weet te ontlopen, kunt u een goede score neerzetten. Op voorwaarde dat de wind niet te hard waait, maar dit spreekt vanzelf op dit type baan.

If Holland is a flat country, then here are her mountains. High dunes, wind and scant vegetation are the unmistakable features of a links course, of which Kennemer is one of the finest examples in Europe. You don't really see the sea, but you will appreciate the stylish and very traditional clubhouse. Designed by Harry Colt in 1920, the original course was supplemented with an additional 9 holes in 1985, but the natural terrain has not quite worked as well for the newer layout. The course is moderately hilly (with a few blind shots), enough for slightly wayward shots to kick, roll and end up in some pretty interesting positions. Don't feel too confident about the absence of water and the scarcity of trees; there are loads of bunkers, all well placed, and there is no shortage of prickly gorse, either. Keep out of them and you might hope to sign for a good score, providing the wind doesn't blow too hard. On this type of course, that goes without saying. An absolute must.

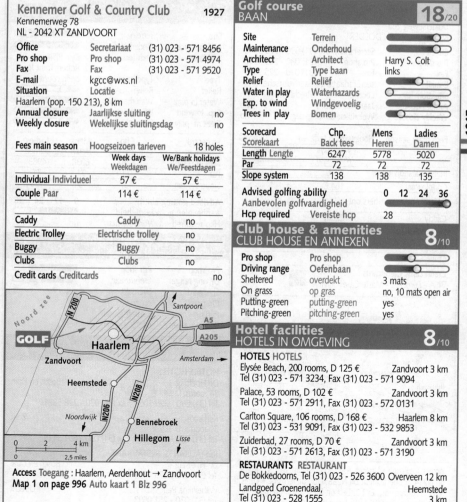

Kennemer Golf & Country Club — 1927

Kennemerweg 78
NL - 2042 XT ZANDVOORT

Office	Secretariaat	(31) 023 - 571 8456
Pro shop	Pro shop	(31) 023 - 571 4974
Fax	Fax	(31) 023 - 571 9520
E-mail	kgcc@wxs.nl	
Situation	Locatie	

Haarlem (pop. 150 213), 8 km

Annual closure	Jaarlijkse sluiting	no
Weekly closure	Wekelijkse sluitingsdag	no

Fees main season Hoogseizoen tarieven	18 holes	
	Week days Weekdagen	**We/Bank holidays** We/Feestdagen
Individual Individueel	57 €	57 €
Couple Paar	114 €	114 €

Caddy	Caddy	no
Electric Trolley	Electrische trolley	no
Buggy	Buggy	no
Clubs	Clubs	no
Credit cards	Creditcards	no

Noord zee · N 200 · Santpoort · A5 · A205 · GOLF · Haarlem · Zandvoort · Amsterdam → · Heemstede · N208 · N206 · Noordwijk · Bennebroek · Hillegom · Lisse · 0 2 4 km · 0 2,5 miles

Access Toegang : Haarlem, Aerdenhout → Zandvoort
Map 1 on page 996 Auto kaart 1 Blz 996

Golf course BAAN — 18/20

Site	Terrein	
Maintenance	Onderhoud	
Architect	Architect	Harry S. Colt
Type	Type baan	links
Relief	Reliëf	
Water in play	Waterhazards	
Exp. to wind	Windgevoelig	
Trees in play	Bomen	

Scorecard Scorekaart	**Chp.** Back tees	**Mens** Heren	**Ladies** Damen
Length Lengte	6247	5778	5020
Par	72	72	72
Slope system	138	138	135

Advised golfing ability Aanbevolen golfvaardigheid: 0 12 24 36
Hcp required Vereiste hcp: 28

Club house & amenities CLUB HOUSE EN ANNEXEN — 8/10

Pro shop	Pro shop	
Driving range	Oefenbaan	
Sheltered	overdekt	3 mats
On grass	op gras	no, 10 mats open air
Putting-green	putting-green	yes
Pitching-green	pitching-green	yes

Hotel facilities HOTELS IN OMGEVING — 8/10

HOTELS HOTELS

Elysée Beach, 200 rooms, D 125 € — Zandvoort 3 km
Tel (31) 023 - 571 3234, Fax (31) 023 - 571 9094

Palace, 53 rooms, D 102 € — Zandvoort 3 km
Tel (31) 023 - 571 2911, Fax (31) 023 - 572 0131

Carlton Square, 106 rooms, D 168 € — Haarlem 8 km
Tel (31) 023 - 531 9091, Fax (31) 023 - 532 9853

Zuiderbad, 27 rooms, D 70 € — Zandvoort 3 km
Tel (31) 023 - 571 2613, Fax (31) 023 - 571 3190

RESTAURANTS RESTAURANT

De Bokkedoorns, Tel (31) 023 - 526 3600 — Overveen 12 km
Landgoed Groenendaal, Tel (31) 023 - 528 1555 — Heemstede 3 km

LAGE VUURSCHE

17	7	7

Van het begin af aan was het duidelijk dat deze baan, die op initiatief van enkele vermogende golfers tot stand is gekomen, een bijzondere toevoeging aan de Nederlandse golfcollectie moest worden. En dat is gelukt ook. De onmiskenbare Amerikaanse hand van de beide architecten is zichtbaar in de ruime opzet, de grote greens, de brede waterpartijen en de afwisseling in problemen waar de speler mee geconfronteerd wordt. De aandacht mag geen moment verslappen, want als de opvallende hindernissen ontweken worden zijn er altijd nog wel wat sluwe heuveltjes of geniepige bunkertjes die de score kunnen bederven. Als straks de beplanting in dit opvallend open terrein volgroeid is, zal de uitdaging nog groter zijn. Gelukkig wacht aan het eind een zeer compleet, zij het wat kil clubhuis.

Right from the beginning it was clear that this project, an initiative of several well-to-do very private course locals, was meant to be a special feature among the compilation of Dutch courses. And so it is. They have asked this design to Robert Trent Jones Jr and one of the forthcoming stars of golf courses architecture, Kyle Phillips, who has already designed the much praised Kingsbarns, south of St Andrews. In Lage Vuursche, the unmistaken American identity of the two architects is visible in the spacious lay-out, the large greens, the wide waterhazards and the variation of problems the players are faced with. Concentration should never weaken, since some cunningly placed hillocks and treacherous bunkers can easily ruin the score. Later, when the trees and bushes in this remarkably open terrain will have matured, the challenge will be even bigger. Luckily there is a well-equipped, albeit somewhat bleak, clubhouse waiting for you.

Golfsociëteit de Lage Vuursche — 2001

Dolderseweg 262
NL - 3734 BS DEN DOLDER

Office	Secretariaat	(31) 030 - 225 9510
Pro shop	Pro shop	(31) 030 - 225 9510
Fax	Fax	(31) 030 - 225 9515
E-mail	secretariaat@golflagevuursche.nl	
Situation	Locatie	Utrecht, 15 km
Annual closure	Jaarlijkse sluiting	no
Weekly closure	Wekelijkse sluitingsdag	no

Fees main season Hoogseizoen tarieven	Week days Weekdagen	We/Bank holidays We/Feestdagen
		18 holes
Individual Individueel	82 €	*
Couple Paar	164 €	*

* Weekends: members only

Caddy	Caddy	no
Electric Trolley	Electrische trolley	no
Buggy	Buggy	no
Clubs	Clubs	no

Credit cards Creditcards
VISA - Eurocard - MasterCard - AMEX

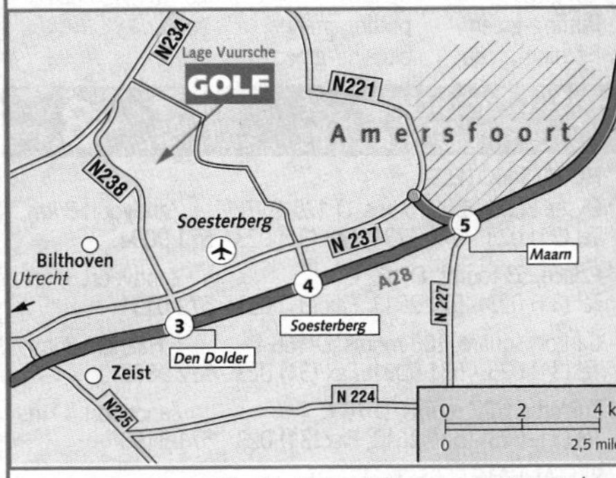

Access Toegang : • Utrecht, A27 → Hilversum. Exit 32. Right on N234 → Soest. Right on N238. Golf on left side.• Utrecht A28 → Amersfoort. Exit 3. Left on N238. Golf on right side.
Map 1 on page 996 Auto kaart 1 Blz 996

Golf course BAAN — 17/20

Site	Terrein	
Maintenance	Onderhoud	
Architect	Architect	Kyle Phillips Robert Trent Jones
Type	Type baan	open country
Relief	Reliëf	
Water in play	Waterhazards	
Exp. to wind	Windgevoelig	
Trees in play	Bomen	

Scorecard Scorekaart	Chp. Back tees	Mens Heren	Ladies Damen
Length Lengte	6287	6038	4983
Par	71	71	71
Slope system	137	134	128

Advised golfing ability Aanbevolen golfvaardigheid — 0 12 24 36

Hcp required Vereiste hcp — no

Club house & amenities CLUB HOUSE EN ANNEXEN — 7/10

Pro shop	Pro shop	
Driving range	Oefenbaan	
Sheltered	overdekt	yes
On grass	op gras	no
Putting-green	putting-green	yes
Pitching-green	pitching-green	yes

Hotel facilities HOTELS IN OMGEVING — 7/10

HOTELS HOTELS

De Hoefslag — Bosch en Duin
34 rooms, D 147 €
Tel (31) 030 - 225 1051, Fax (31) 030 - 228 5821

Kerkebosch — Zeist
30 rooms, D 107 €
Tel (31) 030 - 691 4734, Fax (31) 030 - 691 3114

RESTAURANTS RESTAURANT

De Hoefslag — Bosch en Duin
Tel (31) 030 - 225 1051

Wilhelmina Park — Utrecht
Tel (31) 030 - 251 0693

LAUSWOLT

14 | 6 | 7

Opnieuw een golfbaan die in twee fasen tot stand is gekomen, maar waar de samenwerking Pennink-Steel, twee ontwerpers met eenzelfde achtergrond, een vrij consistent en gelijkmatig resultaat heeft opgeleverd. Vooral omdat de meeste holes in een bosgebied liggen, met nadruk op eenheid van stijl. Zoals altijd kunnen de bomen het leven zuur maken voor zwierige spelers. Je moet echt recht slaan en je niet teveel om de lengte bekommeren (zeker niet van de medaltees), wat de meeste spelers als muziek in de oren zal klinken. Er zijn maar weinig fairway-bunkers en die er zijn leveren niet al te veel problemen op. Ook bij de greens liggen niet veel bunkers, zodat de meeste greens met een stuiterend schot gehaald kunnen worden. De greens zelf zijn middelgroot, redelijk gevormd en makkelijk te lezen. Zoals je in dit waterrijke gebied mag verwachten komt water regelmatig in het spel, soms onverwachts, zelfs een beetje stiekem. Het gelijknamige hotel voegt extra allure aan de baan toe.

Yet another course built in two parts, but the partnership between Pennink and Steel, two designers of the same culture, has produced a rather consistent and even result, especially since the majority of holes are laid out in a forest to accentuate unity of style. But as always, trees also make life complicated for wayward players. You have to play straight here and not necessarily look for length all the time (not from the front tees, anyway), which is probably good news for most players. There are few fairway bunkers, and the ones there are don't add much to the overall difficulty. Green-side bunkers are scarce, too, meaning that most greens can be approached with bump and run shots. The greens themselves are mid-sized, moderately contoured and easy to read. As you might expect in a province with so many lakes, water comes into play, sometimes surprisingly and even sneakily. The hotel on site simply adds to the course's overall appeal.

Golf en Country Club Lauswolt — 1966

Van Harinxmaweg 8a
NL - 9244 CJ BEESTERZWAAG

Office	Secretariaat	(31) 0512 - 383 590
Pro shop	Pro shop	(31) 0512 - 383 869
Fax	Fax	(31) 0512 - 383 739
Web	—	
Situation	Locatie	Drachten, 5 km
Groningen (pop. 170 535), 40 km		
Annual closure	Jaarlijkse sluiting	no
Weekly closure	Wekelijkse sluitingsdag	no

Fees main season Hoogseizoen tarieven	**Week days** Weekdagen	**We/Bank holidays** We/Feestdagen
		full day
Individual Individueel	50 €	68 €
Couple Paar	100 €	136 €

Caddy	Caddy	no
Electric Trolley	Electrische trolley	no
Buggy	Buggy	no
Clubs	Clubs	9 €
Credit cards	Creditcards	

VISA - Eurocard - MasterCard - DC - AMEX

Access Toegang : A7 Groningen-Drachten, Exit 28 → Beetsterzwaag
Map 1 on page 996 Auto kaart 1 Blz 996

Golf course BAAN — 14/20

Site	Terrein	
Maintenance	Onderhoud	
Architect	Architect	Frank Pennink Donald Steel
Type	Type baan	forest
Relief	Reliëf	
Water in play	Waterhazards	
Exp. to wind	Windgevoelig	
Trees in play	Bomen	

Scorecard Scorekaart	**Chp.** Back tees	**Mens** Heren	**Ladies** Damen
Length Lengte	6146	5898	4962
Par	72	72	72
Slope system	131	127	121

Advised golfing ability Aanbevolen golfvaardigheid: **0 12 24 36**
Hcp required Vereiste hcp: 36

Club house & amenities CLUB HOUSE EN ANNEXEN — 6/10

Pro shop	Pro shop	
Driving range	Oefenbaan	
Sheltered	overdekt	4 mats
On grass	op gras	no, 10 mats open air
Putting-green	putting-green	yes
Pitching-green	pitching-green	yes

Hotel facilities HOTELS IN OMGEVING — 7/10

HOTELS HOTELS

Landgoed Lauswolt — on site
58 rooms, D 134 €
Tel (31) 0512 - 381 245, Fax (31) 0512 - 381 496

Het Witte Huis, 8 rooms, D 43 € — Beetsterzwaag
Tel (31) 0512 - 382 222, Fax (31) 0512 - 382 307 — 1 km

Hotel Drachten, 48 rooms, D 79 € — Drachten
Tel (31) 0512 - 520 705, Fax (31) 0512 - 523 232 — 5 km

RESTAURANTS RESTAURANT

Landgoed Lauswolt, Tel (31) 0512 - 381 245 — on site

De Wilgenhoeve, Tel (31) 0512 - 512 510 — Drachten 5 km

NOORDWIJK

18 | 7 | 8

De derde parel in de trilogie van Nederlandse linksbanen. Met magnifiek uitzicht over de duinen en de bollenvelden in het binnenland. Een klassieke lay-out, waarbij alleen natuurlijke elementen in het spel komen. Met alle moeilijkheden van het golfspel in de duinen, zoals potbunkers, blinde slagen en de wind. Slechts vijf holes liggen in bebost terrein. Ook hier kennen de fairways maar weinig vlakke stukken, dus is een goede techniek nodig voor elke slag. En om de bal laag te houden als het waait. De meeste greens worden omringd door rough of heuveltjes, zonder al te veel bunkers, maar denk niet dat scoren gemakkelijk is. Andere interessante elementen zijn de dichte struiken in de rough, een enkel poeltje en de renovatie van het clubhuis. Een uitdagende baan, die tot de beste van Europa gerekend kan worden (bij voorkeur spelen op een werkdag).

The third absolute gem in the magnificent trilogy of Dutch links, one that offers some magnificent views over the dunes and inland, covered with fields of flowers in the Spring. The layout is a classic, bringing into play only natural elements and the difficulties of golfing amidst sand dunes, including pot bunkers, blind shots and exposure to the wind. Only five holes are laid out over woody terrain. Again, there are few flat lies, so good technique is needed to shape the shot and to hit low balls when the wind blows. As most of the greens are surrounded by rough or rolling mounds, there aren't too many bunkers, but don't ever think scoring is easy. Other interesting features are the thick bushes in the middle of the rough, a single water hazard and the welcome renovation of the clubhouse. A challenging layout that has to be rated amongst the front-running courses in Europe (choose a week-day to play here).

1020

Noordwijkse Golfclub

Randweg 25
NL - 2204 AL NOORDWIJK

Office	Secretariaat	(31) 0252 - 373 763
Pro shop	Pro shop	(31) 0252 - 373 763
Fax	Fax	(31) 0252 - 370 044
E-mail	noordwijkse.gc@worldonline.nl	
Situation	Locatie	Leiden, 15 km
Annual closure	Jaarlijkse sluiting	no
Weekly closure	Wekelijkse sluitingsdag	no

Fees main season Hoogseizoen tarieven	18 holes	
	Week days Weekdagen	**We/Bank holidays** We/Feestdagen
Individual Individueel	64 €	*
Couple Paar	128 €	*

* Weekends: members only

Caddy	Caddy	no
Electric Trolley	Electrische trolley	no
Buggy	Buggy	yes
Clubs	Clubs	no

Credit cards Creditcards
VISA - Eurocard - DC - Pinpas

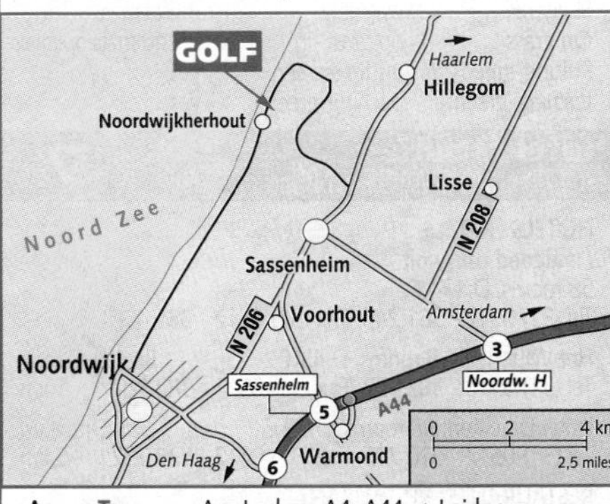

Access Toegang : Amsterdam, A4, A44 → Leiden. Exit 3 → Noordwijk aan Zee. 6 km → Nordwijkerhout. 1 km → Zee
Map 1 on page 996 Auto kaart 1 Blz 996

Golf course BAAN — 18/20

Site	Terrein	
Maintenance	Onderhoud	
Architect	Architect	Frank Pennink
Type	Type baan	links
Relief	Reliëf	
Water in play	Waterhazards	
Exp. to wind	Windgevoelig	
Trees in play	Bomen	

Scorecard Scorekaart	**Chp.** Back tees	**Mens** Heren	**Ladies** Damen
Length Lengte	6242	5879	5024
Par	72	72	72
Slope system	140	131	123

Advised golfing ability Aanbevolen golfvaardigheid — 0 12 24 36
Hcp required Vereiste hcp 28

Club house & amenities CLUB HOUSE EN ANNEXEN — 7/10

Pro shop	Pro shop	
Driving range	Oefenbaan	
Sheltered	overdekt	5 mats
On grass	op gras	no, 3 mats open air
Putting-green	putting-green	yes
Pitching-green	pitching-green	yes

Hotel facilities HOTELS IN OMGEVING — 8/10

HOTELS HOTELS

Huis ter Duin — Noordwijk 6 km
238 rooms, D 216 €
Tel (31) 071 - 361 9220, Fax (31) 071 - 361 9401

Hotel Alexander, 62 rooms, D 88 € — Noordwijk 6 km
Tel (31) 071 - 361 8900, Fax (31) 071 - 361 7882

De Witte Raaf, 35 rooms, D 52 € — Noordwijk 1 km
Tel (31) 0252 - 375 984, Fax (31) 0252 - 377 578

RESTAURANTS RESTAURANT

Cleyburg, Tel (31) 071 - 364 8448 — Noordwijk-Binnen 8 km

De Palmentuin, Tel (31) 071 - 361 9340 — Noordwijk 6 km

NUNSPEET North/East

15	5	6

Temidden van oude bospercelen zijn drie lussen van elk negen holes aangelegd. Het levert een aantrekkelijke, maar ook vrij smalle golfbaan op. Misschien is het terrein net iets te klein voor 27 holes en zou een 18-holesbaan meer op zijn plaats zijn geweest. Hoewel, als je geen probleem hebt met holes die soms wat kunstmatig aandoen, blijft er een 'spannende' baan over. Vooral de 'North'-baan, waar op de zesde hole een zandverstuiving voor een soort superbunker zorgt. De 'North' en 'East' baan eindigen beide op een grote dubbelgreen. Het clubhuis en de oefenfaciliteiten zijn groot genoeg om meerdere groepen te hulsvesten. Wel vreemd: in de kleedkamers zijn golfschoenen uit den boze. Dus altijd schone sokken meenemen !

Three loops of 9 holes have each been cut out of the existing woodland, making a pretty but somewhat narrow layout. Maybe the total area was just too small for 27 holes and a full-size 18-holer with an additional par-3 course would have been more appropriate. Yet if you accept that some holes are a little artificial, what is left is still an attractive layout, especially the North course, where the 6th hole features a huge natural sandtrap in the form of a drifting dune. Both the North and East courses finish on a large twin green. The clubhouse and practice facilities are good enough to handle groups easily, the only strange phenomenon here being the fact that golf shoes are not allowed in the locker-rooms.

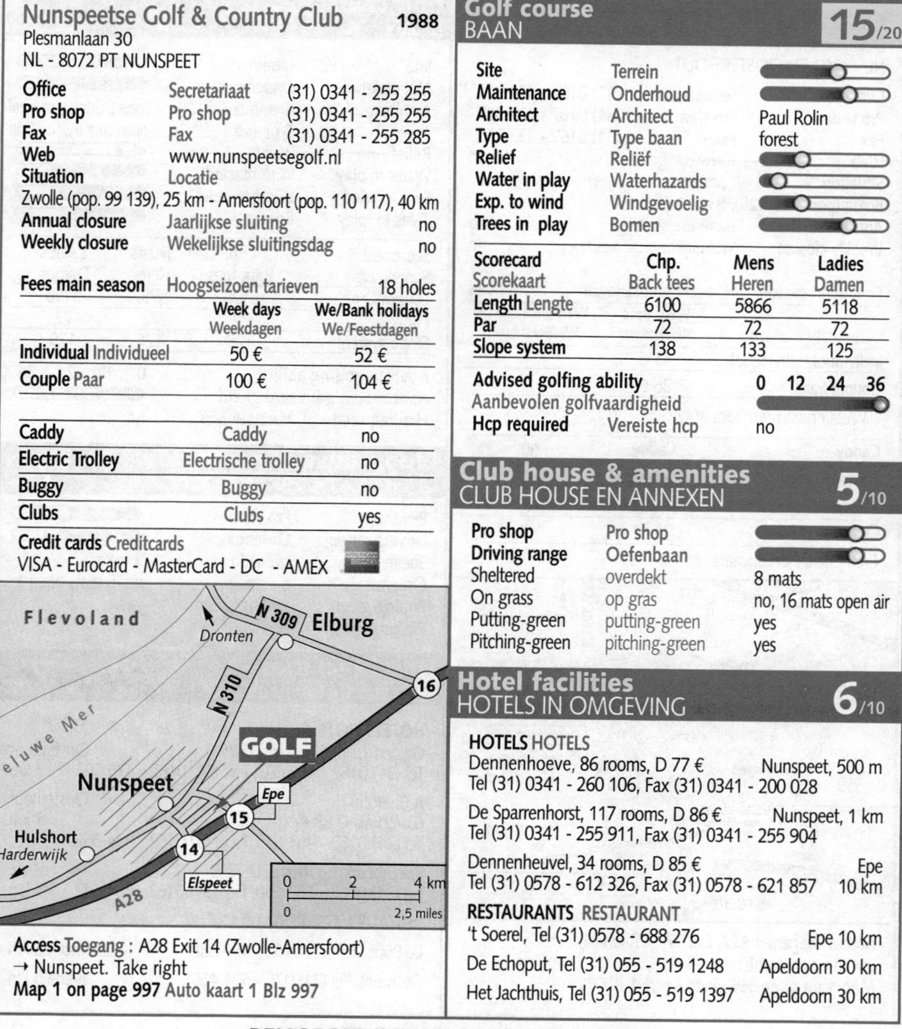

Nunspeetse Golf & Country Club 1988
Plesmanlaan 30
NL - 8072 PT NUNSPEET

Office	Secretariaat	(31) 0341 - 255 255
Pro shop	Pro shop	(31) 0341 - 255 255
Fax	Fax	(31) 0341 - 255 285
Web	www.nunspeetsegolf.nl	
Situation	Locatie	

Zwolle (pop. 99 139), 25 km - Amersfoort (pop. 110 117), 40 km

Annual closure	Jaarlijkse sluiting	no
Weekly closure	Wekelijkse sluitingsdag	no

Fees main season Hoogseizoen tarieven — 18 holes

	Week days / Weekdagen	We/Bank holidays / We/Feestdagen
Individual Individueel	50 €	52 €
Couple Paar	100 €	104 €

Caddy	Caddy	no
Electric Trolley	Electrische trolley	no
Buggy	Buggy	no
Clubs	Clubs	yes

Credit cards Creditcards
VISA - Eurocard - MasterCard - DC - AMEX

Access Toegang : A28 Exit 14 (Zwolle-Amersfoort) → Nunspeet. Take right
Map 1 on page 997 Auto kaart 1 Blz 997

Golf course / BAAN — 15/20

Site	Terrein	
Maintenance	Onderhoud	
Architect	Architect	Paul Rolin
Type	Type baan	forest
Relief	Reliëf	
Water in play	Waterhazards	
Exp. to wind	Windgevoelig	
Trees in play	Bomen	

Scorecard Scorekaart	Chp. Back tees	Mens Heren	Ladies Damen
Length Lengte	6100	5866	5118
Par	72	72	72
Slope system	138	133	125

Advised golfing ability Aanbevolen golfvaardigheid: 0 12 24 36
Hcp required Vereiste hcp: no

Club house & amenities / CLUB HOUSE EN ANNEXEN — 5/10

Pro shop	Pro shop	
Driving range	Oefenbaan	
Sheltered	overdekt	8 mats
On grass	op gras	no, 16 mats open air
Putting-green	putting-green	yes
Pitching-green	pitching-green	yes

Hotel facilities / HOTELS IN OMGEVING — 6/10

HOTELS HOTELS

Dennenhoeve, 86 rooms, D 77 € — Nunspeet, 500 m
Tel (31) 0341 - 260 106, Fax (31) 0341 - 200 028

De Sparrenhorst, 117 rooms, D 86 € — Nunspeet, 1 km
Tel (31) 0341 - 255 911, Fax (31) 0341 - 255 904

Dennenheuvel, 34 rooms, D 85 € — Epe 10 km
Tel (31) 0578 - 612 326, Fax (31) 0578 - 621 857

RESTAURANTS RESTAURANT

't Soerel, Tel (31) 0578 - 688 276 — Epe 10 km
De Echoput, Tel (31) 055 - 519 1248 — Apeldoorn 30 km
Het Jachthuis, Tel (31) 055 - 519 1397 — Apeldoorn 30 km

OOSTERHOUT

15 | 7 | 7

Helaas is een deel van het aangrenzende industrieterrein zichtbaar en is de autoweg continu hoorbaar. Voor het overige waant u zich hier temidden van het buitenleven (weilanden, graanvelden, koeien) op een baan die veel aandacht voor ecologie heeft. Zo wordt de rough lang gehouden om de knaagdieren te huisvesten, die op hun beurt roofvogels aantrekken. Ondanks de relatief jonge leeftijd oogt de baan vrij volwassen. Een paar losse bomen en struiken zijn in het ontwerp opgenomen en vormen zo hindernissen, net als waterpartijen, talloze bunkers en de wind, die altijd aanwezig lijkt. Vier vijvertjes komen in het spel op acht holes, waarbij ze op de 5e en 15e recht voor de green liggen. Twee fraaie par-3 holes, die vooral onervaren spelers ontzag zullen inboezemen. Behalve een paar blinde bunkers heeft de baan een eerlijk karakter. Uitgezonderd misschien de 16e hole, een controversiële dogleg.

Unfortunately, a number of buildings from the nearby industrial estate can still be seen and the noise from the road is never-ending. Otherwise, you are in the country here (meadows, fields of wheat and cows) and the club pays very special attention to the environment. Hence a rough that is left to grow rather tall, attracting rodents, falcons and eagles. Despite its tender age, this course is remarkably mature. A few isolated trees or copses are fully integrated into the course and form one of the difficulties, along with the water hazards, numerous bunkers and the wind, which is always a frequent feature. Four small lakes come into play on eight holes, forming frontal hazards on the 5th and 15th holes, two fine par 3s which could be a real handful for inexperienced players. Despite a few hidden hazards, the course is forthright in style, except the 16th, a very controversial dog-leg.

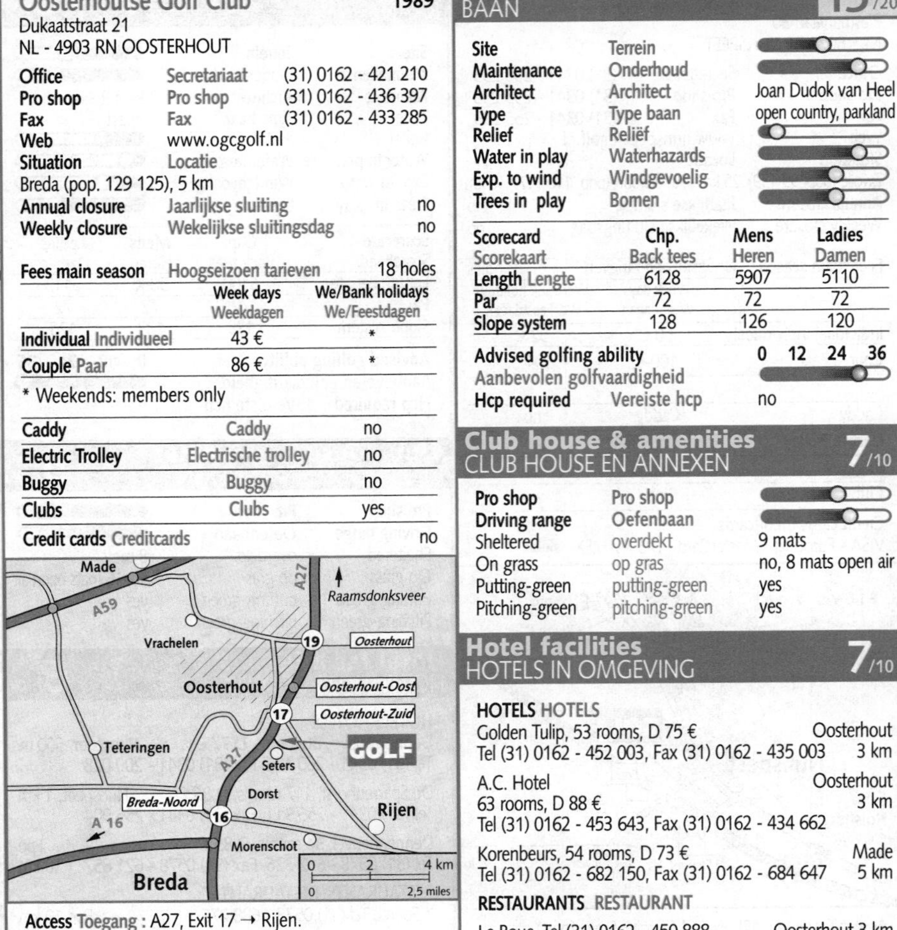

Oosterhoutse Golf Club — 1989

Dukaatstraat 21
NL - 4903 RN OOSTERHOUT

Office	Secretariaat	(31) 0162 - 421 210
Pro shop	Pro shop	(31) 0162 - 436 397
Fax	Fax	(31) 0162 - 433 285
Web	www.ogcgolf.nl	
Situation	Locatie	

Breda (pop. 129 125), 5 km

Annual closure	Jaarlijkse sluiting	no
Weekly closure	Wekelijkse sluitingsdag	no

Fees main season Hoogseizoen tarieven	18 holes	
	Week days Weekdagen	We/Bank holidays We/Feestdagen
Individual Individueel	43 €	*
Couple Paar	86 €	*

* Weekends: members only

Caddy	Caddy	no
Electric Trolley	Electrische trolley	no
Buggy	Buggy	no
Clubs	Clubs	yes
Credit cards	Creditcards	no

Access Toegang : A27, Exit 17 → Rijen.
200 m, turn right. → Golf
Map 1 on page 996 Auto kaart 1 Blz 996

Golf course BAAN — 15/20

Site	Terrein	
Maintenance	Onderhoud	
Architect	Architect	Joan Dudok van Heel
Type	Type baan	open country, parkland
Relief	Reliëf	
Water in play	Waterhazards	
Exp. to wind	Windgevoelig	
Trees in play	Bomen	

Scorecard Scorekaart	Chp. Back tees	Mens Heren	Ladies Damen
Length Lengte	6128	5907	5110
Par	72	72	72
Slope system	128	126	120

Advised golfing ability Aanbevolen golfvaardigheid — 0 12 24 36
Hcp required Vereiste hcp — no

Club house & amenities CLUB HOUSE EN ANNEXEN — 7/10

Pro shop	Pro shop	
Driving range	Oefenbaan	
Sheltered	overdekt	9 mats
On grass	op gras	no, 8 mats open air
Putting-green	putting-green	yes
Pitching-green	pitching-green	yes

Hotel facilities HOTELS IN OMGEVING — 7/10

HOTELS HOTELS

Golden Tulip, 53 rooms, D 75 € — Oosterhout
Tel (31) 0162 - 452 003, Fax (31) 0162 - 435 003 — 3 km

A.C. Hotel — Oosterhout
63 rooms, D 88 € — 3 km
Tel (31) 0162 - 453 643, Fax (31) 0162 - 434 662

Korenbeurs, 54 rooms, D 73 € — Made
Tel (31) 0162 - 682 150, Fax (31) 0162 - 684 647 — 5 km

RESTAURANTS RESTAURANT

Le Bouc, Tel (31) 0162 - 450 888 — Oosterhout 3 km

De Arent, Tel (31) 076 - 514 4601 — Breda 5 km

RIJK VAN NIJMEGEN Nijmeegse Baan

14	6	5

Deze baan was een van der eerste commerciële projecten in Nederland en als zodanig zeer succesvol. Oorspronkelijk lagen er twee kortere 9-holesbanen en een 18-holes wedstrijdbaan. De 9-holesbanen zijn samengevoegd en uitgebreid tot een volwaardige 18-holesbaan, de Groesbeekse Baan. Nog steeds wat korter, maar ook veel heuvelachtiger dan de andere, de Nijmeegse Baan. Hoewel de vele bosjes die tussen de holes zijn geplant wat bescherming bieden, is de wind een factor om terdege rekening mee te houden. Net als met de vele, soms van de tee niet-zichtbare bunkers. Er zijn meerder holes met blinde slagen naar de green. Alles bij elkaar een prettige baan in een golvend landschap, dat in Nederland niet veel voorkomt.

This course was one of the early commercial golf projects in the Netherlands and a rather successful one, too. It originally consisted of one 18-hole course and two short 9-holers, but the latter have been merged into a second 18-hole course (Groesbeekse Baan). It is a little shorter but also much more hilly than its senior companion, the Nijmeegse Baan. Although the many bushes planted between the holes seem to offer some protection from the wind, it is still a factor to consider. As are the many bunkers, some of which are not easily visible from the tees. There are also several holes with blind shots to the greens. Altogether, this is a pleasant course in rolling countryside not often seen in the Netherlands, with excellent clubhouse and practice facilities.

Golfbaan Rijk van Nijmegen — 1987

Postweg 17
NL - 6561 KJ GROESBEEK

Office	Secretariaat	(31) 024 - 397 6644
Pro shop	Pro shop	(31) 024 - 397 6644
Fax	Fax	(31) 024 - 397 6942
Web		www.golfbaanhetrijkvannijmegen.nl
Situation	Locatie	Nijmegen (pop. 147 000), 5 km
Annual closure	Jaarlijkse sluiting	no
Weekly closure	Wekelijkse sluitingsdag	no

Fees main season / Hoogseizoen tarieven	18 holes	
	Week days / Weekdagen	We/Bank holidays / We/Feestdagen
Individual Individueel	39 €	43 €
Couple Paar	78 €	86 €
Caddy / Caddy	no	
Electric Trolley / Electrische trolley	no	
Buggy / Buggy	18 €	
Clubs / Clubs	5 €	

Credit cards Creditcards
VISA - Eurocard - MasterCard - DC - AMEX

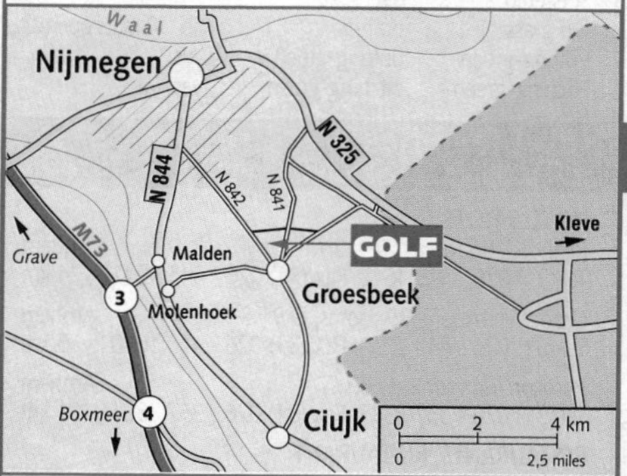

Access Toegang : Nijmegen: A73, Exit 3 → Groesbeek → Nijmegen
Map 1 on page 997 Auto kaart 1 Blz 997

Golf course — BAAN — 14/20

Site	Terrein	
Maintenance	Onderhoud	
Architect	Architect	Paul Rolin
Type	Type baan	parkland
Relief	Reliëf	
Water in play	Waterhazards	
Exp. to wind	Windgevoelig	
Trees in play	Bomen	

Scorecard / Scorekaart	Chp. / Back tees	Mens / Heren	Ladies / Damen
Length Lengte	6076	6010	5307
Par	72	72	72
Slope system	127	126	121

Advised golfing ability / Aanbevolen golfvaardigheid: 0 12 24 36
Hcp required / Vereiste hcp: no

Club house & amenities — CLUB HOUSE EN ANNEXEN — 6/10

Pro shop	Pro shop	
Driving range	Oefenbaan	
Sheltered	overdekt	24 mats
On grass	op gras	no, 9 mats open air
Putting-green	putting-green	yes
Pitching-green	pitching-green	yes

Hotel facilities — HOTELS IN OMGEVING — 5/10

HOTELS HOTELS

Hotel Erica, 59 rooms, D 73 € — Berg en Dal
Tel (31) 024 - 684 3514, Fax (31) 024 - 684 3613 — 2 km

Hotel Val Monte, 103 rooms, D 39 € — Berg en Dal
Tel (31) 024 - 684 2000, Fax (31) 024 - 684 3353 — 2 km

Jachtslot Mookerheide, 20 rooms, D 73 € — Molenhoek
Tel (31) 024 - 358 3035, Fax (31) 024 - 358 4355 — 6 km

RESTAURANTS RESTAURANT

Jachslot Mookerheide, Tel (31) 024 - 358 3035 — Molenhoek
Chalet Brakenstein, Tel (31) 024 - 355 3949 — Nijmegen 5 km
Claudius, Tel (31) 024 - 322 1456 — Nijmegen 5 km

ROSENDAEL

15 | 7 | 7

De enige zwakke schakel hier is de rumoerige nabijheid van twee autowegen, hoewel die niet bestonden aan het eind van de vorige eeuw toen deze baan tussen bos, heide en doornenstruiken werd aangelegd. Dit zijn de oudste holes in Nederland en de eerste negen volgen nog het originele ontwerp. In de loop der tijden zijn ingrijpende veranderingen aangebracht, hoewel het oorspronkelijke plan van Del Court van Krimpen onaangetast is gebleven. We vermoeden dat Harry Colt iets met de latere wijzigingen te maken heeft gehad. Het zou niet verbazen, gegeven de positionering van de hazards en het natuurlijk karakter van de baan, die in licht heuvelachtig terrein ligt. De tweede negen holes zijn in 1977 gereedgekomen in een stijl die aansluit op de eerste negen. Let ook eens op de grappige holes, zoals de 13e, een korte dogleg met een hoger liggende tee en green. En alle par-3 holes, echte juweeltjes. Rosendaal is zonder twijfel een van Neerlands beste banen.

The only weak link here is the noisy proximity of two motorways, although they didn't exist at the turn of the century when this course was created through forest, heather and gorse. This was Holland's very first course, and the front nine are the original layout. Significant changes have been made, although the original design of Del Court van Krimpen remains unspoiled. We suspect that Harry Colt had something to do with these changes, it wouldn't be surprising given the layout of hazards and the natural character of the course over slightly hilly terrain. The back nine were completed in 1977 in a style consistent with the front nine. Make a note of some amusing holes here, like the 13th, a short dog-leg with elevated tee and green, and all the par 3, pure gems. Rosendael is unquestionably one of Holland's best inland courses.

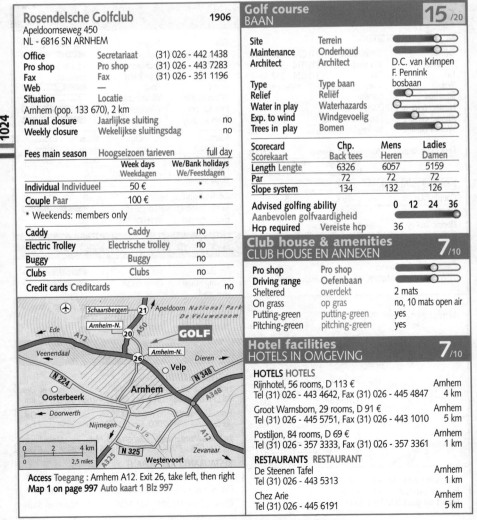

Rosendelsche Golfclub — 1906

Apeldoornseweg 450
NL - 6816 SN ARNHEM

Office	Secretariaat	(31) 026 - 442 1438
Pro shop	Pro shop	(31) 026 - 443 7283
Fax	Fax	(31) 026 - 351 1196
Web	—	
Situation	Locatie	

Arnhem (pop. 133 670), 2 km

Annual closure	Jaarlijkse sluiting	no
Weekly closure	Wekelijkse sluitingsdag	no

1024

Fees main season Hoogseizoen tarieven		full day
	Week days Weekdagen	We/Bank holidays We/Feestdagen
Individual Individueel	50 €	*
Couple Paar	100 €	*

* Weekends: members only

Caddy	Caddy	no
Electric Trolley	Electrische trolley	no
Buggy	Buggy	no
Clubs	Clubs	no
Credit cards Creditcards		no

Schaarsbergen
21
Apeldoorn National Park De Veluwezoom
Arnheim-N.
20
A50
Ede
A12
GOLF
Veenendaal
26
Arnheim-N.
Dieren
Velp
N 224
N 348
Oosterbeerk
Arnhem
A348
Doorwerth
Nijmegen
Rijn
A12
0 2 4 km
0 2,5 miles
N 325
Zevanaar
A325
Westervoort

Access Toegang : Arnhem A12. Exit 26, take left, then right
Map 1 on page 997 Auto kaart 1 Blz 997

Golf course BAAN — 15/20

Site	Terrein	
Maintenance	Onderhoud	
Architect	Architect	D.C. van Krimpen F. Pennink
Type	Type baan	bosbaan
Relief	Reliëf	
Water in play	Waterhazards	
Exp. to wind	Windgevoelig	
Trees in play	Bomen	

Scorecard Scorekaart	Chp. Back tees	Mens Heren	Ladies Damen
Length Lengte	6326	6057	5159
Par	72	72	72
Slope system	134	132	126

Advised golfing ability / Aanbevolen golfvaardigheid: 0 12 24 36
Hcp required / Vereiste hcp: 36

Club house & amenities CLUB HOUSE EN ANNEXEN — 7/10

Pro shop	Pro shop	
Driving range	Oefenbaan	
Sheltered	overdekt	2 mats
On grass	op gras	no, 10 mats open air
Putting-green	putting-green	yes
Pitching-green	pitching-green	yes

Hotel facilities HOTELS IN OMGEVING — 7/10

HOTELS HOTELS

Rijnhotel, 56 rooms, D 113 € — Arnhem
Tel (31) 026 - 443 4642, Fax (31) 026 - 445 4847 — 4 km

Groot Warnsborn, 29 rooms, D 91 € — Arnhem
Tel (31) 026 - 445 5751, Fax (31) 026 - 443 1010 — 5 km

Postiljon, 84 rooms, D 69 € — Arnhem
Tel (31) 026 - 357 3333, Fax (31) 026 - 357 3361 — 1 km

RESTAURANTS RESTAURANT

De Steenen Tafel — Arnhem
Tel (31) 026 - 443 5313 — 1 km

Chez Arie — Arnhem
Tel (31) 026 - 445 6191 — 5 km

SINT NICOLAASGA

15	7	5

Er is maar weinig reliëf in Friesland, de provincie van de wijde horizon en telkens wisselende luchten. In dit land van meren en weilanden vormen koeien en paarden een deel van het landschap. Er liggen maar weinig golfbanen, maar dit is een van de beste, heel fraai opgenomen in de omgeving. Een vlakke baan, niet erg lang, met brede fairways en weinig bomen, maar des te meer struiken om u dwars te zitten. Long-hitters kunnen zich laten gaan, maar moeten wel rekening houden met de wind, die het leven aardig zuur kan maken. Hetzelfde geldt voor de waterhazards (vijvertjes en sloten) die op zo'n twaalf holes in het spel komen. Deze nog vrij nieuwe baan is snel gerijpt en biedt veel variatie, zowel visueel (er is een hoop grond verplaatst) als golftechnisch. Een minpunt zijn de lange afstanden tussen de holes. Heel bijzonder is de klokkenstoel op het kerkhofje, aan drie zijden door de baan ingesloten.

There is little relief to speak of in the Frise, a region of endless horizons and changing skies. In this land of lakes, pastureland and crops, cows and horses are all part of the landscape. Golf courses are few and far between here, but this is one of the best, blending in very nicely with the surrounding countryside. Very flat, not very long but with wide fairways, it has few trees to bother you but quite a few bushes. Long-hitters will let rip, but will still have to watch out for the wind, which can make life very difficult. The same goes for the water hazards (ponds and ditches), in play on about a dozen holes. This recent course has quickly matured and has considerable variety to it, both visually (a lot of earth was moved) and technically. The one minor flaw are the long walks between holes, and the one peculiarity the little cemetery in front of the clubhouse, overlooked by a bell-tower and surrounded on three sides by the course.

Burggolf Sint Nicolaasga — 1990

Legemeersterweg 18
NL - 8527 DS LEGEMEER

Office	Secretariaat	(31) 0513 - 499 466
Pro shop	Pro shop	(31) 0513 - 499 466
Fax	Fax	(31) 0513 - 499 091
E-mail		vegilinbosschen@club.tip.nl
Situation	Locatie	
Heerenveen (pop. 38 936), 15 km		
Annual closure	Jaarlijkse sluiting	no
Weekly closure	Wekelijkse sluitingsdag	no

Fees main season Hoogseizoen tarieven	18 holes	
	Week days Weekdagen	**We/Bank holidays** We/Feestdagen
Individual Individueel	36 €	41 €
Couple Paar	72 €	82 €
Caddy Caddy		no
Electric Trolley Electrische trolley		no
Buggy Buggy		18 €
Clubs Clubs		9 €

Credit cards Creditcards
VISA - Eurocard - MasterCard - DC - Pinpas - AMEX

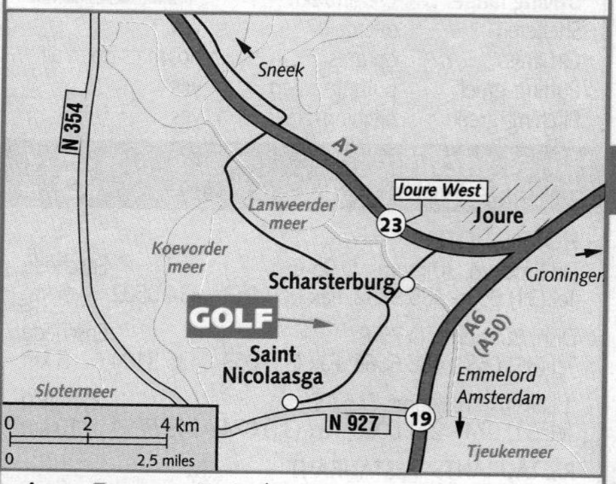

Access Toegang : Amsterdam A6 → Groningen/Leeuwarden.
Exit 19 → Woudsend. 3.5 km → Golf
Map 1 on page 996 Auto kaart 1 Blz 996

Golf course — BAAN — 15/20

Site	Terrein	
Maintenance	Onderhoud	
Architect	Architect	Paul Rolin, Alan Rijks
Type	Type baan	polder, open country
Relief	Reliëf	
Water in play	Waterhazards	
Exp. to wind	Windgevoelig	
Trees in play	Bomen	

Scorecard Scorekaart	**Chp.** Back tees	**Mens** Heren	**Ladies** Damen
Length Lengte	6038	5756	4993
Par	72	72	72
Slope system	135	132	131

Advised golfing ability Aanbevolen golfvaardigheid: 0 12 24 36
Hcp required Vereiste hcp: no

Club house & amenities — CLUB HOUSE EN ANNEXEN — 7/10

Pro shop	Pro shop	
Driving range	Oefenbaan	
Sheltered	overdekt	10 mats
On grass	op gras	no, 15 mats open air
Putting-green	putting-green	yes
Pitching-green	pitching-green	yes

Hotel facilities — HOTELS IN OMGEVING — 5/10

HOTELS HOTELS

Hotel Legemeer, 14 rooms, D 84 € — Legemeer
Tel (31) 0513 - 432 999, Fax (31) 0513 - 432 876

Lauswolt, 58 rooms, D 134 € — Beetsterzwaag
Tel (31) 0527 - 291 833, Fax (31) 0527 - 291 836 — 35 km

Postiljon, 55 rooms, D 59 € — Heerenveen
Tel (31) 0513 - 618 618, Fax (31) 0513 - 629 100 — 15 km

RESTAURANTS RESTAURANT

Kaatje bij de Sluis — Blokzijl
Tel (31) 0527 - 291 833 — 20 km

Sir Sebastian, Tel (31) 0513 - 650 408 — Heerenveen 15 km

SYBROOK

15 | 6 | 6

Deze baan ligt buiten de traditionele toeristische routes, in het groene land van Twente, dichtbij Duitsland. Veel water, weilanden, dichte bossen en grote boerderijen, waarvan de architectuur kennelijk de inspiratie vormde toen het clubhuis met binnenplaats werd ontworpen. Sybrook is een van de weinige nieuwe banen die in bosgebied mochten worden aangelegd. Bossen waarin nog volop wild voorkomt. Die ziet u dan ook regelmatig in de vroege ochtend of avond. Er zijn wat waterhazards, maar niet overdreven veel. De aantrekkingskracht van deze baan zit in een aantal doorkijkjes en de bloeiende rhododendrons. Het is geen ideale baan voor onstuimige spelers, want er wordt om voorzichtigheid en precisie gevraagd. Ondanks de jonge leeftijd, maakt de baan een volwassen indruk. Het is een lange baan, dus voor de meeste spelers zijn de backtees taboe.

This is a course off the traditional tourist track in the very green region of Twente, close to Germany. Water abounds, as do pasture-land, thick forest and large farms, whose architecture obviously inspired that of the Clubhouse, built with an inner courtyard. Sybrook is one of the few new courses laid out in a forest, which is still home to all sorts of wild animals. You will see a lot of furry creatures at dawn or in the early evening. Several small water hazards come into play, but never excessively so. The appeal of this course is all the greater for a number of views over the countryside and the flowering rhododendrons. Sybrook is not the ideal course for the reckless player, as it demands care, a little thought and considerable accuracy. Despite its infancy, there is a clear impression of maturity. This is a long course, so we would advise the front tees for most players.

1026

Golf & Countryclub 't Sybrook — 1994

Veendijk 100
NL - 7525 PZ ENSCHEDE

Office	Secretariaat	(31) 0541 - 530 331
Pro shop	Pro shop	(31) 0541 - 530 331
Fax	Fax	(31) 0541 - 531 690
Web	—	
Situation	Locatie	Hengelo, 10 km

Enschede (pop. 147 624), 5 km

Annual closure	Jaarlijkse sluiting	no
Weekly closure	Wekelijkse sluitingsdag	no

Fees main season Hoogseizoen tarieven — 18 holes

	Week days Weekdagen	We/Bank holidays We/Feestdagen
Individual Individueel	43 €	43 €
Couple Paar	86 €	86 €
Caddy	Caddy	no
Electric Trolley	Electrische trolley	no
Buggy	Buggy	no
Clubs	Clubs	no

Credit cards Creditcards
VISA - Eurocard - MasterCard - AMEX

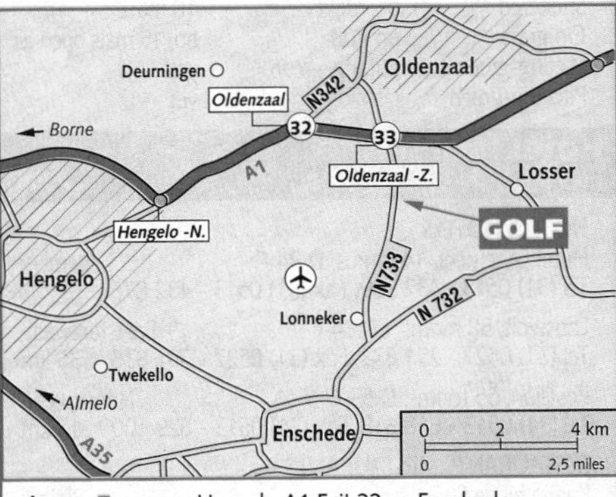

Access Toegang : Hengelo A1 Exit 33 → Enschede. 2,5 km, take left
Map 1 on page 997 Auto kaart 1 Blz 997

Golf course BAAN — 15/20

Site	Terrein	
Maintenance	Onderhoud	
Architect	Architect	Alan Rijks Paul Rolin
Type	Type baan	forest
Relief	Reliëf	
Water in play	Waterhazards	
Exp. to wind	Windgevoelig	
Trees in play	Bomen	

Scorecard Scorekaart	Chp. Back tees	Mens Heren	Ladies Damen
Length Lengte	6242	5898	4994
Par	72	72	72
Slope system	133	129	123

Advised golfing ability Aanbevolen golfvaardigheid — 0 12 24 36
Hcp required Vereiste hcp — no

Club house & amenities CLUB HOUSE EN ANNEXEN — 6/10

Pro shop	Pro shop	
Driving range	Oefenbaan	
Sheltered	overdekt	yes
On grass	op gras	no, mats open air
Putting-green	putting-green	yes
Pitching-green	pitching-green	yes

Hotel facilities HOTELS IN OMGEVING — 6/10

HOTELS HOTELS

De Broeierd, 30 rooms, D 95 € — Enschede 5 km
Tel (31) 053 - 435 9882, Fax (31) 053 - 434 0502

Dish, 80 rooms, D 75 € — Enschede 5 km
Tel (31) 053 - 486 6666, Fax (31) 053 - 435 3104

't Lansink, 18 rooms, D 57 € — Hengelo 10 km
Tel (31) 074 - 291 0066, Fax (31) 074 - 243 5891

RESTAURANTS RESTAURANT

't Koesthuis — Enschede 5 km
Tel (31) 053 - 432 866

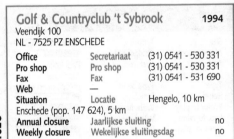

Mondriaan, Tel (31) 074 - 291 5321 — Hengelo 10 km

TOXANDRIA

14 | 7 | 6

Een ontwerp van John S.F. Morrison, die werd geholpen door Harry Colt en Sir Guy Campbell. De baan is in de loop der tijd aangepast en recent met twee holes uitgebreid. Zo midden in een bos laat de baan een indruk van rust achter, als je het lawaai van de weg en de nabij gelegen vliegbasis even wegdenkt. In grote lijnen is het een echte Britse baan, zonder veel verrassingen, met natuurlijk de bomen als belangrijkste hindernis (er zijn veel doglegs). Vooral vanaf de backtees kan de baan soms erg nauw ogen. De ruwweg twintig natuurlijk aandoende fairway-bunkers spelen een belangrijke rol door hun strategische ligging. De greens zijn middelgroot, goed ontworpen, goed bewaakt en over het algemeen open genoeg om allerlei soorten approaches toe te staan. Aardigheidje: de 150-meter markers bestaan uit nestkastjes in de bomen.

Designed by John S.F. Morrison, who worked with Harry Colt and Sir Guy Campbell, this course has been altered and recently lengthened with two new holes. Laid out in a forest, it exudes an impression of tranquillity, if you can forget the slight traffic noise and the planes from a nearby air base. The general style is rather British and offers no great surprises, while the main difficulties are, naturally, the trees (there are a lot of dog-legs), especially from the back-tees from where the fairways at times look despairingly narrow. The twenty or so very natural-looking fairway bunkers also play an important role through their strategic positioning. The greens are mid-size, slightly contoured, neatly designed, well-guarded and, by and large, open enough to allow all types of approach shots. Interestingly, the 150 yard-to-green markers are nests placed in the trees.

Noord-Brabantsche Golfclub Toxandria — 1928

Veenstraat 89
NL - 5124 NC MOLENSCHOT

Office	Secretariaat	(31) 0161 - 411 200
Pro shop	Pro shop	(31) 0161 - 411 200
Fax	Fax	(31) 0161 - 411 715
Web	www.toxandria.nl	
Situation	Locatie	

Breda (pop. 129 125), 5 km

Annual closure	Jaarlijkse sluiting	no
Weekly closure	Wekelijkse sluitingsdag	no

Fees main season Hoogseizoen tarieven	**Week days** Weekdagen	**We/Bank holidays** We/Feestdagen
		18 holes
Individual Individueel	50 €	59 €
Couple Paar	100 €	118 €
Caddy Caddy	no	
Electric Trolley Electrische trolley	no	
Buggy Buggy	no	
Clubs Clubs	no	
Credit cards Creditcards		no

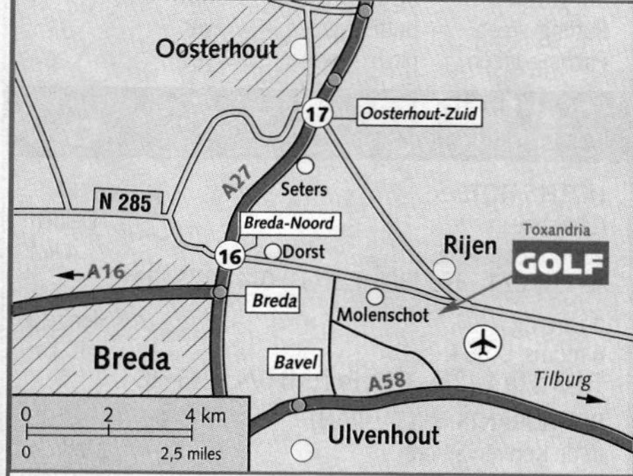

Access Toegang : A27 Utrecht-Breda Exit 16.
N263 → Rijen. 4 km → Molenschot
Map 1 on page 996 Auto kaart 1 Blz 996

Golf course BAAN — 14/20

Site	Terrein	
Maintenance	Onderhoud	
Architect	Architect	J. Morrison
Type	Type baan	forest
Relief	Reliëf	
Water in play	Waterhazards	
Exp. to wind	Windgevoelig	
Trees in play	Bomen	

Scorecard Scorekaart	**Chp.** Back tees	**Mens** Heren	**Ladies** Damen
Length Lengte	6140	5974	5188
Par	72	72	72
Slope system	137	135	129

Advised golfing ability Aanbevolen golfvaardigheid: 0 12 24 36

Hcp required Vereiste hcp: no

Club house & amenities CLUB HOUSE EN ANNEXEN — 7/10

Pro shop	Pro shop	
Driving range	Oefenbaan	
Sheltered	overdekt	8 mats
On grass	op gras	no, mats open air
Putting-green	putting-green	yes
Pitching-green	pitching-green	yes

Hotel facilities HOTELS IN OMGEVING — 6/10

HOTELS HOTELS

De Herbergh, 44 rooms, D 68 € — Rijen 2 km
Tel (31) 0161 - 224 318, Fax (31) 0161 - 222 327

Motel Gilze-Rijen, 134 rooms, D 50 € — Rijen 2 km
Tel (31) 0161 - 454 951, Fax (31) 0161 - 452 171

Mercure Hotel, 40 rooms, D 109 € — Breda 5 km
Tel (31) 0161 - 522 0200, Fax (31) 0161 - 521 4967

RESTAURANTS RESTAURANT

La Grille d'Or — Breda 5 km
Tel (31) 0161 - 520 4333

Mirabelle — Breda 5 km
Tel (31) 0161 - 565 6650

TWENTE

15 | 7 | 6

Tientallen jaren bracht de Twentsche Golfclub door op een kleine, maar fijne 9-holesbaan, ingeklemd tussen de Hengelo en Enschede. Die baan ligt er nog steeds, maar de club is verhuisd naar een ruimere "outfit" in de bossen ten westen van de dubbelstad. Het decor van de baan wordt gevormd door oude bossen, met daartussen opvallend veel open ruimtes (van nature) en opvallend veel water (aangelegd) in de vorm van vijf vijvers. Soms hebben die alleen een decoratieve functie, maar op negen holes komt het water ook echt in het spel. Naast de bomen en het water is de lengte een factor om rekening mee te houden. Vooral op de tweede negen, met drie par-4 holes rond de 400 meter. Het nieuwe clubhuis heeft door het hoge rode pannendak het karakter van een Twentsche boerderij.

For dozens of years the Twentsche Golfclub was based at a short but pretty 9-hole course, stuck in between Hengelo and Enschede. That original course is still open, but the club moved to a larger outfit in the woods west of the Twin-cities. The stage there is set by old forests, with a remarkable amount of open space (natural) and an equally remarkable amount of water (artificial) in the form of five ponds. Often the water only serves as decoration but on nine holes it actually comes into play. Apart from the water and the trees, length is a factor to reckon with, especially on the back-nine, with three par-4 holes around 440 yards. The newly-built clubhouse resembles a traditional local farmhouse thanks to its bright red tiled roof.

Twentsche Golf Club — 1997

Almelosestraat 17
NL - 7495 TG AMBT-DELDEN

Office	Secretariaat	(31) 074 - 384 1167
Pro shop	Pro shop	(31) 074 - 384 1054
Fax	Fax	(31) 074 - 384 1067
Web	—	
Situation	Locatie	

Hengelo (pop. 75 000), 10 km

Annual closure	Jaarlijkse sluiting	no
Weekly closure	Wekelijkse sluitingsdag	no

Fees main season Hoogseizoen tarieven	18 holes	
	Week days Weekdagen	**We/Bank holidays** We/Feestdagen
Individual Individueel	43 €	50 €
Couple Paar	86 €	100 €

Caddy	Caddy	no
Electric Trolley	Electrische trolley	no
Buggy	Buggy	no
Clubs	Clubs	yes
Credit cards	Creditcards	no

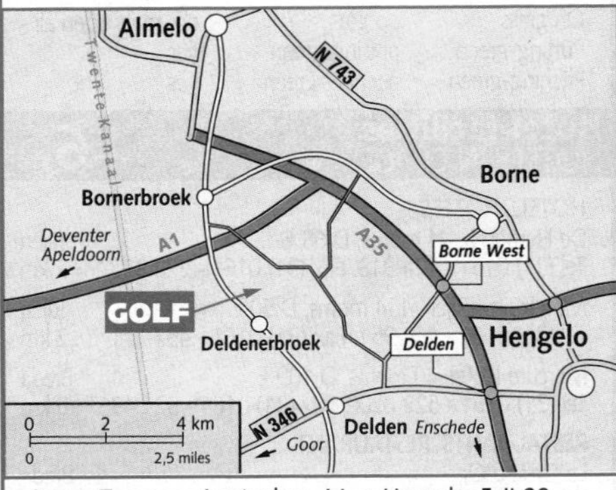

Access Toegang : Amsterdam, A1 → Hengelo, Exit 28, N347, then N346 → Delden, then → Bornebroek.
Map 1 on page 997 Auto kaart 1 Blz 997

Golf course — BAAN — 15/20

Site	Terrein	
Maintenance	Onderhoud	
Architect	Architect	Tom MacAuley
Type	Type baan	forest, parkland
Relief	Reliëf	
Water in play	Waterhazards	
Exp. to wind	Windgevoelig	
Trees in play	Bomen	

Scorecard Scorekaart	**Chp.** Back tees	**Mens** Heren	**Ladies** Damen
Length Lengte	6296	6178	5241
Par	72	72	72
Slope system	125	124	119

Advised golfing ability 0 12 24 36
Aanbevolen golfvaardigheid
Hcp required Vereiste hcp — certificate

Club house & amenities — CLUB HOUSE EN ANNEXEN — 7/10

Pro shop	Pro shop	
Driving range	Oefenbaan	
Sheltered	overdekt	7 mats
On grass	op gras	no
Putting-green	putting-green	yes
Pitching-green	pitching-green	yes

Hotel facilities — HOTELS IN OMGEVING — 6/10

HOTELS HOTELS

Carelshaven, — Delden 4 km
20 rooms, D 75 €
Tel (31) 074 - 376 1305, Fax (31) 074 - 376 1291

't Lansing, — Hengelo 10 km
6 rooms, D 66 €
Tel (31) 074 - 291 0066, Fax (31) 074 - 243 5891

RESTAURANTS RESTAURANT

In de Kop'ren Smorre — Markelo 10 km
Tel (31) 0547 - 361 344

In den Drost van Twenthe — Delden 3 km
Tel (31) 074 - 376 4055

WOUWSE PLANTAGE

15	7	6

De oorspronkelijk aangelegde holes liggen in bebost terrein, waar bomen natuurlijk de belangrijkste hindernis vormen. Zeker op de vier dog-legs en de lange smalle 6e, nu 15e hole. Zo ook op de daaropvolgende schitterende par-3, waar de bomen voor de green weinig ruimte voor fouten laten. Later werden negen nieuwe holes aangelegd, op vroegere landbouwgrond, met vier kleine vijvertjes en een paar sloten, maar ook met bredere fairways. Oude en nieuwe holes zijn door elkaar gemengd, wat variatie in het spel, maar ook behoorlijke afstanden tussen de holes heeft opgeleverd. Een nadeel is dat je tegen de tijd dat je aan de 'oude' greens gewend bent, overstapt naar de nieuwe en omgekeerd. Dat maakt het spel niet eenvoudiger, maar misschien hebben alleen de wat betere spelers hier last van.

The front nine were laid out in woody terrain and trees naturally form the main difficulty, especially on the four dog-legs and the long, narrow 15th. Likewise, on the 16th, a beautiful par 3, the trees in front of the green leave little room for error. They then created nine new holes, over much more open farming land, with four small water hazards and a few ditches, but with much wider fairways. The old and new holes have been intermingled, thus varying the pleasure but sometimes leaving considerable distances between green and next tee. Another obvious drawback is that by the time you get accustomed to the grass and greens on the old holes, you are back to the new ones, and vice versa. This does not make scoring easy, and it just might be that better players are more affected by this subtle difference than their less experienced counterparts.

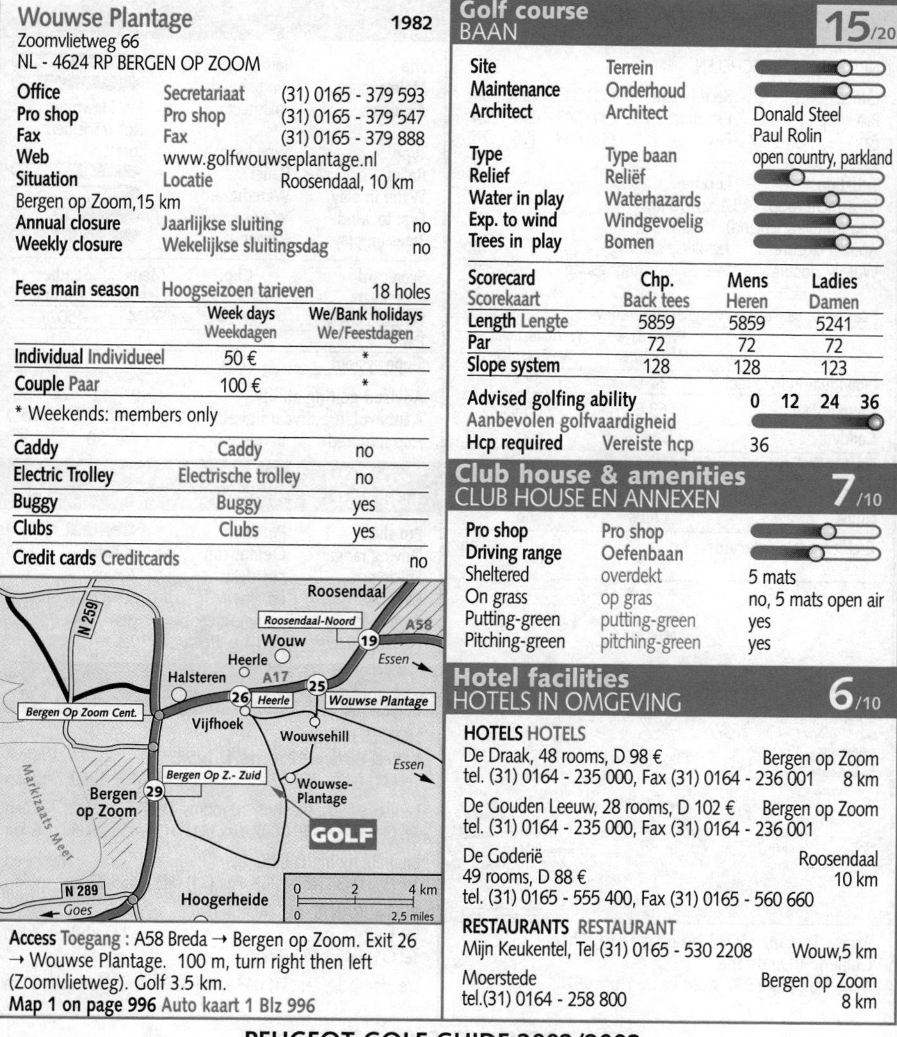

Wouwse Plantage 1982
Zoomvlietweg 66
NL - 4624 RP BERGEN OP ZOOM

Office	Secretariaat	(31) 0165 - 379 593
Pro shop	Pro shop	(31) 0165 - 379 547
Fax	Fax	(31) 0165 - 379 888
Web	www.golfwouwseplantage.nl	
Situation	Locatie	Roosendaal, 10 km
Bergen op Zoom,15 km		
Annual closure	Jaarlijkse sluiting	no
Weekly closure	Wekelijkse sluitingsdag	no

Fees main season Hoogseizoen tarieven	18 holes	
	Week days Weekdagen	We/Bank holidays We/Feestdagen
Individual Individueel	50 €	*
Couple Paar	100 €	*

* Weekends: members only

Caddy	Caddy	no
Electric Trolley	Electrische trolley	no
Buggy	Buggy	yes
Clubs	Clubs	yes
Credit cards Creditcards		no

Access Toegang : A58 Breda → Bergen op Zoom. Exit 26 → Wouwse Plantage. 100 m, turn right then left (Zoomvlietweg). Golf 3.5 km.
Map 1 on page 996 Auto kaart 1 Blz 996

Golf course BAAN 15/20

Site	Terrein	
Maintenance	Onderhoud	
Architect	Architect	Donald Steel Paul Rolin
Type	Type baan	open country, parkland
Relief	Reliëf	
Water in play	Waterhazards	
Exp. to wind	Windgevoelig	
Trees in play	Bomen	

Scorecard Scorekaart	**Chp.** Back tees	**Mens** Heren	**Ladies** Damen
Length Lengte	5859	5859	5241
Par	72	72	72
Slope system	128	128	123

Advised golfing ability Aanbevolen golfvaardigheid — 0 12 24 36
Hcp required Vereiste hcp 36

Club house & amenities CLUB HOUSE EN ANNEXEN 7/10

Pro shop	Pro shop	
Driving range	Oefenbaan	
Sheltered	overdekt	5 mats
On grass	op gras	no, 5 mats open air
Putting-green	putting-green	yes
Pitching-green	pitching-green	yes

Hotel facilities HOTELS IN OMGEVING 6/10

HOTELS HOTELS
De Draak, 48 rooms, D 98 € — Bergen op Zoom
tel. (31) 0164 - 235 000, Fax (31) 0164 - 236 001 — 8 km
De Gouden Leeuw, 28 rooms, D 102 € — Bergen op Zoom
tel. (31) 0164 - 235 000, Fax (31) 0164 - 236 001
De Goderië — Roosendaal
49 rooms, D 88 € — 10 km
tel. (31) 0165 - 555 400, Fax (31) 0165 - 560 660

RESTAURANTS RESTAURANT
Mijn Keukentel, Tel (31) 0165 - 530 2208 — Wouw,5 km
Moerstede — Bergen op Zoom
tel.(31) 0164 - 258 800 — 8 km

ZUID LIMBURGSE

14	7	8

We zitten hier dicht bij Aken, een van de belangrijkste Duitse steden, waarvan de historische waarde, sinds de grootse plannen van Karel de Grote, nooit in twijfel is getrokken. Dit gebied is ook het hoogste van Nederland... iets onder de 300 meter (elk land heeft zijn bergen, Moeder Natuur bepaalt hoe hoog ze zijn!). De baan werd aangelegd als een 9-holes baan en werd uitgebreid tot 18 holes in 1990. De 'oude' holes lopen door een bos, terwijl acht van de 'nieuwe' holes in een open landschap liggen met sterke hoogteverschillen en prachtige vergezichten. Al met al is de baan goed te bespelen, voor iedereen. Om je handicap te spelen moet je wel de bomen op de eerste negen zien te ontlopen en op de twee negen vooral nauwkeurige teeshots afleveren. Afgedwaalde ballen komen snel op onplezierige plaatsen terecht, op sterk glooiende hellingen.

we are very close to Aachen, one of the great German cities whose historical importance, since the great European designs of Charlemagne, has never been questioned. This lovely region is also one of the highest in the Netherlands...a little below 300 metres (each country has its natural mountains, mother nature decides how high!). The course here began as a 9-holer and was extended to 18 holes in 1980. The first holes wind their way through a forest, while 8 of the last 9 are in open countryside with sharp differences in level and some beautiful views. All in all, the course is easily walkable, for everyone. Playing to your handicap demands avoidance of the trees on the way out and carefully placed drives on the way in. Wayward shots can leave your ball in some very tricky positions, with steeply sloping lies.

Zuid Limburgse Golf & Countryclub 1956

Dalbissenweg 22
NL - 6281 NC MECHELEN

Office	Secretariaat	(31) 043 - 455 1254
Pro shop	Pro shop	(31) 043 - 455 1254
Fax	Fax	(31) 043 - 455 1576
Web	—	
Situation	Locatie	

Maastricht (pop. 118 102), 18 km
Aachen (Deutschland), 15 km

Annual closure	Jaarlijkse sluiting	no
Weekly closure	Wekelijkse sluitingsdag	no

Fees main season Hoogseizoen tarieven		full day
	Week days Weekdagen	**We/Bank holidays** We/Feestdagen
Individual Individueel	34 €	43 €
Couple Paar	68 €	86 €
Caddy	Caddy	no
Electric Trolley	Electrische trolley	no
Buggy	Buggy	yes
Clubs	Clubs	no
Credit cards Creditcards		no

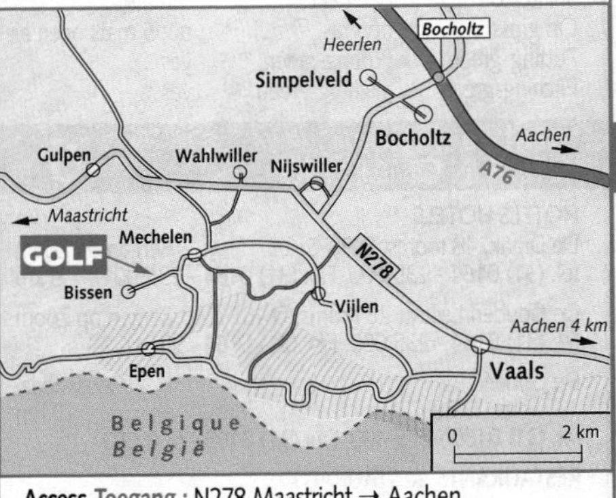

Access Toegang : N278 Maastricht → Aachen.
Gulpen → Landsrade.
Map 1 on page 997 Auto kaart 1 Blz 997

Golf course BAAN 14/20

Site	Terrein	
Maintenance	Onderhoud	
Architect	Architect	FW Hawtree Rolin/Snelders
Type	Type baan	forest
Relief	Reliëf	
Water in play	Waterhazards	
Exp. to wind	Windgevoelig	
Trees in play	Bomen	

Scorecard Scorekaart	**Chp.** Back tees	**Mens** Heren	**Ladies** Damen
Length Lengte	5924	5924	5071
Par	71	71	71
Slope system	125	125	126

Advised golfing ability 0 12 24 36
Aanbevolen golfvaardigheid
Hcp required Vereiste hcp We: 30

Club house & amenities CLUB HOUSE EN ANNEXEN 7/10

Pro shop	Pro shop	
Driving range	Oefenbaan	
Sheltered	overdekt	2 mats
On grass	op gras	no, 8 mats open air
Putting-green	putting-green	yes
Pitching-green	pitching-green	yes

Hotel facilities HOTELS IN OMGEVING 8/10

HOTELS HOTELS

Kasteel Wittem, 12 rooms, D 125 € — Wittem
Tel (31) 043 - 450 1208, Fax (31) 043 - 450 1260 — 12 km

Landgoed Schoutenhof, 10 rooms, D 57 € — Epen
Tel (31) 043 - 455 2002, Fax (31) 043 - 455 2605 — 8 km

Brull, 32 rooms, D 68 € — Mechelen
Tel (31) 043 - 455 1263, Fax (31) 043 - 455 2300 — 4 km

RESTAURANTS RESTAURANT

De Leuf — Ubachsberg 4 km
Tel (31) 045 - 575 0226

De Bloasbalg, Tel (31) 043 - 451 1364 — Wahlwiller 5 km

Norway

Larvik

Norway
Norge

They say that skiing is as important to the Norwegians as cycling is to the Danes, a logical assumption when snow covers the whole country for a good part of the year. Despite this, the west coast can be surprisingly mild thanks to the warming influence of the Gulf Stream. You can play golf between April and October from Bergen to Oslo, and for 55,000 Norwegians, golf clubs are the summer version of ski poles. As in all northern countries, golf here is a sporting activity like any other and golfing snobbery is never as blatant in Norway as it can be in other countries of Europe. Naturally, the 90 courses (28 eighteen-holers) are not all as well manicured as Augusta, but they are very quickly groomed into good condition once winter is over. Opening dates depend entirely on the thawing frost and snow.

Det hevdes at skigåing er like viktig for nordmenn som sykling er det for danskene. En logisk antagelse med tanke på at landet er dekket med snø en stor del av året. Til tross for dette kan det være overraskende mildt på vestkysten – takket været Golfstrømmens innflytelse. Fra Oslo til Bergen kan du spille golf i perioden april til oktober, og for 70.000 nordmenn er golfkøllene en slags sommerutgave av skistavene. Som i alle de nordiske landene er golf en sportsaktivitet på lik linje med de fleste andre idretter. Golf er heller ikke så snobbete som den kan oppleves i andre europeiske land. Naturligvis er ikke alle de 90 banene (28 av dem er 18 hulls) i så god stand og velstelt som Augusta, men så fort vinteren har tatt farvel fremstår banene i bra stand. Sesongåpning på den enkelte bane avhenger mye av våren og hvor raskt snø og frost slipper taket.

Map No 1
Kort 1
km
0 10 20
Meland
Stavanger
MICHELIN
HORDALAND
ROGALAND
AUST-AGDER
VEST-AGDER
BERGEN
STAVANGER
Kristiansand
Egersund
Flekkefjord
Sandnes
Sola
Haugesund
Voss
Odda
Mandal
Lindås
Leirvåg
Duesund
Knarvik
Askøy
Kleppestø
Osterøya
Vaksdal
Dale
Stamnes
Tyssebotn
Samnanger
Tysse
Norheimsund
Øystese
Ålvik
Kvanndal
Utne
Strandebarm
Jondal
Tørvikbygd
Eikelandsosen
Vengjaneset
Hatvik
Osøyro
Krokeide
Telavåg
Hjellestad
Klokkarvik
Steinsland
Krossfjorden
Huftarøy
Halhjem
Bjørnafjorden
Storebø
Husavik
Våge
Gjermundshavn
Ænes
Løfallstrand
Rosendal
Tysnesøy
Sandvikvåg
Fitjar
Hodnanes
Jektevik
Stord
Hardangerfjorden
Rubbestadneset
Bømlo
Sagvåg
Leirvik
Sunde
Husnes
Utåker
Siggjarvåg
Mosterhamn
Skånevik
Utbjoa
Langevåg
Førde
Ølen
Etne
Buavåg
Sandeid
Vikedal
Haraldshaugen
Avaldsnes
Akrehamn
Karmøy
Kopervik
Tysvær
Nedstrand
Førresvik
Bokn
Boknafjorden
Skudeneshavn
Åres
Mortavika
Finnøy
Judaberg
Rennesøy
Vikevåg
Kvitsøy
Randaberg
Tau
Jørpeland
Prekestolen
Hommersåk
Oanes
Forsand
Lysefjorden
Lauvvik
Oltedal
Dirdal
Kleppe
Ålgård
Bryne
Nærbø
Jæren
Varhaug
Vigrestad
Brusand
Sirevåg
Hellvik
Vikeså
Bjerkreim
Dalane
Moi
Hauge
Åna Sira
Sira
Kvinesdal
Feda
Apta
Listafjorden
Vestbygda
Farsund
Lyngdal
Alleen
Høllen
Lindesnes
Vigeland
Søgne
Nodeland
Skålevik
Hamre
Lillesand
Birkeland
Vennesla
Mosby
Konsmo
Hægebostad
Eiken
Åseral
Tonstad
Risnes
Sirdalen
Sirdalsvatn
Kvinesdal
Svartevatn
Evje
Byglandsfjord
Bygland
Byglandsfj.
Iveland
Setesdal
Otra
Valle
Bykle
Bykleheiene
Hovden
Haukeligrend
Vinje
Edland
Rauland
Totak
Åmot
Eidsborg
Dalen
Fyresdal
Fyresvatn
Rosskrepp fjorden
Svartevatn
Lyseheiene
Setesdalsheiene
Suldalsvatn
Suldal
Sand
Sauda
Ryfylke
Vindsvik
Nesvik
Tøtlandsvik
Hjelmeland
Jelsa
Røldal
Haukelifjell
Hardangervidda
Hårteigen
Tyssedal
Folgefonna
Lofthus
Kinsarvik
Sørfjorden
Brimnes
Eidfjord
Eidfjorden
Vøringsfossen
Fossli
Bruravik
Granvin
Ulvik
Hardangerjøkulen
1862
1691
Stølsheimen
Fresvikbreen
1660
Gudvangen
Undredal
Aurland
Flåm
Lærdalsøyri
Hallingskarvet
Dølemo
Ryfylke
1034

Sorknes
Øyer
Follebu
Fåberg
Nordseter
Sjusjøen
Birkebeiner-Løypa
Jørstadmoen
Lillehammer
Rena
Vigrom
Brøttum
Ormtjernkampen
Hurum
Hegge
Øye
Grindaheim
Valdres
Lomen
Leira
Fagernes
Hemsedal
Aurdal
Begna
Reinli
Bagn
Dokka
Biri
Stein
Moelv
Brumunddal
Redalen
Ringsaker
Stavsjø
Hamar
Løten
Gjøvik
Raufoss
Kapp
Stange
Hovet
Hol
Torpo
Ål
Gol
Geilo
Nesbyen
Hallingdal
Hedal
Nes
Holmen
Skreia
Mjøsa
Espa
Dagali
Tunhovdfjorden
BUSKERUD
Flå
Krøderen
Sperillen
Randsfjorden
Brandbu
Jaren
Hurdal
Uvdal
Rødberg
Norefjell
Gran
Sand
Nore
Numedal
Sokna
Eidsvoll
Dal
Noresund
Jevnaker
Nannestad
Tinn
Austbygd
Hønefoss
Gardermoen
Jessheim
Nes
Prestfoss
Tyristrand
Rollag
Nittedal
Hauger
Ask
Kongsvinger
Årnes
Rjukan
Tyrifjord
Bønsnes
Kløfta
Gausta 1883
Tinnsjø
Vikersund
Åmot
OSLO
Flesberg
Frogner
Glomma
Lillestrøm
Oslo
Sylling
Fetsund
Blefjell
AKERSHUS
Tinnoset
Bolkesjø
Drammen
Nesoddtangen
Bjørkelangen
Losby
1035
Hjartdal
Sauland
Hokksund
Heddal
Kongsberg
Mjøndalen
Løken
TELEMARK
Åros
Ski
Hemnes
Lifjell
Skollenborg
Eiker
Seljord
Notodden
Svelvik
Drøbak
Skjønhaug
Eidsfoss
Sande
Tofte
Vestby
Skrim
Askim
Kviteseid
Bø
Holmestrand
Hvittingfoss
Mysen
Gvarv
Akerhaugen
Våler
Horten
Svarstad
Lunde
Borre
Ørje
Norsjø
MOSS
VESTFOLD
Ulefoss
Vansjø
Rakkestad
Andebu
Rygge
SKIEN
Siljan
Åsgårdstrand
ØSTFOLD
Tønsberg
Råde
Ise
Stokke
Porsgrunn
Sarpsborg
Sandefjord
Skjeberg
Herre
Årøysund
Drangedal
Langangen
Fredrikstad
Brevik
Tjøme
Larvik
Halden
Langesund
Hvaler
Nevlunghavn
Stavern
Kragerø
Jomfruland
Strömstad
Bengtsfors
Søndeled
Skee
Larvik
Ed
Koster
Øysang
Risør
Arendal
Tvedestrand
Hirtshals
Frederikshavn
Kiel-København
Bäckefors
Eydehavn
Grebbestad
Tanumshede
Vitlycke
Högsäter
Arendal
Fjällbacka
MICHELIN
d'après carte n° 985 - 10ème édition - 2002.
Autorisation n° 0102062.

Classification

CLASSIFICATION OF COURSES
RANGERING AV BANENE

This classification gives priority consideration to the score awarded to the actual course.

Denne rangeringen er basert på poeng er gitt den aktuelle banen.

Courses score / Rangering av banene — Page / Side

17	8	6	Larvik	1040
16	6	5	Borre	1038
16	8	6	Losby	1041
16	7	4	Meland	1042
16	6	7	Stavanger	1045
15	7	5	Arendal	1037
15	7	9	Oslo	1043
15	6	4	Sorknes	1044
14	6	6	Tyrifjord	1046
13	7	6	Hauger	1039

Classification

HOTEL FACILITIES
RANGERING AV HOTELL FASILITETER

15	7	**9**	Oslo	1043
16	6	**7**	Stavanger	1045
13	7	**6**	Hauger	1039
17	8	**6**	Larvik	1040
16	8	**6**	Losby	1041
14	6	**6**	Tyrifjord	1046
15	7	**5**	Arendal	1037
16	6	**5**	Borre	1038
16	7	**4**	Meland	1042
15	6	**4**	Sorknes	1044

TYPE OF COURSE
BANETYPE

Forest
Meland 1042, Sorknes 1044

Hilly Tyrifjord 1046

Inland Arendal 1037

Llinks Larvik 1040

Mountain Crans-sur-Sierre 1276

Open Country
Borre 1038, Hauger 1039,
Larvik 1040, Losby 1041

Parkland
Oslo 1043, Stavanger 1045, Tyrifjord 1046

ARENDAL

15 | 7 | 5

Arendal blir ofte kalt Nordens Venezia på grunn av de mange kanalene som rant gjennom byen. De fleste av disse har forsvunnet i dag, men stort antall trebygninger og hus bekrefter fremdeles hvor betydningsfullt disse kanalene var for Arendal. Denne golfbanen er ytterligere et argument som tjener byens livskraft, bygd i 1991 uten hjelp fra noen golfbanearkitekter. For en gang skyld har denne form for vågestykke blitt en suksess. Den er mye bakker (du bør være i god fysisk form) og enkelte vanskeligheter ser man ikke før de dukker opp. Får man imidlertid kontroll på vanskelighetene viser banen seg å være en meget god utfordring. Det er ikke en lang bane, men den er utmerket balansert og greenene er vel designet på måte som kan gjøre det vanskelig å spille til sitt handicap. Mens de første ni hullene er heller åpne, så medfører trær og vannhindre at det må utvises forsiktighet på hjemturens ni siste hull. Det er en stor fordel å ha spilt banen tidligere, og det gjelder å merke seg at klubbhuset er åpent rundt på grunn av skisesongen.

Arendal used to be called the Venice of the North on account of the very many canals that ran through the town. Most of these have disappeared today, but a good number of wooden buildings and houses still testify to the former importance of Arendal. This golf course is further argument in favour of the town's vitality, built in 1991 without the services of a golf architect. For once, this sort of venture has been successful. It is rather hilly (you need to be in good shape physically) and some of the difficulties are hidden from view, but once under control, it proves to be a very good challenge. This is not a long course but it is nicely balanced and the greens are designed well enough to make playing to your handicap a sometimes awkward proposition. In addition, while the front 9 are rather open, the trees and water hazards on the way home call for extreme caution. Well worth getting to know, and note that the club-house stays open all year for the skiing season.

Arendal og Omegn Golfklubb — 1991

Nes Verk
N - 4900 TVEDESTRAND

Office	Kontor	(47) 371 990 30
Pro shop	Pro shop	(47) 371 990 30
Fax	Fax	(47) 371 602 11
Web	www.arendalgk.no	
Situation	Beliggenhet	Arendal, 20 km
Annual closure	Årlig stenging	1/11→30/4
Weekly closure	Ukentlig stenging	no

Fees main season Tariffer i høysesongen	18 holes	
	Week days Ukedager	**We/Bank holidays** Week-end/Frydag
Individual Individuell	NKr 280	NKr 330
Couple Par	NKr 560	NKr 660

Juniors: – 50%

Caddy	Caddy	no
Electric Trolley	Elektrisk vogn	yes
Buggy	Golfbil	yes
Clubs	Køller	yes

Credit cards Kredittkort
VISA - Eurocard - MasterCard - DC - AMEX

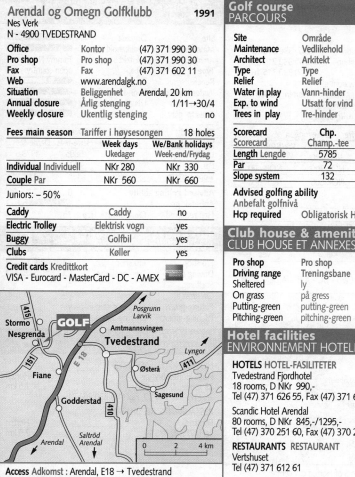

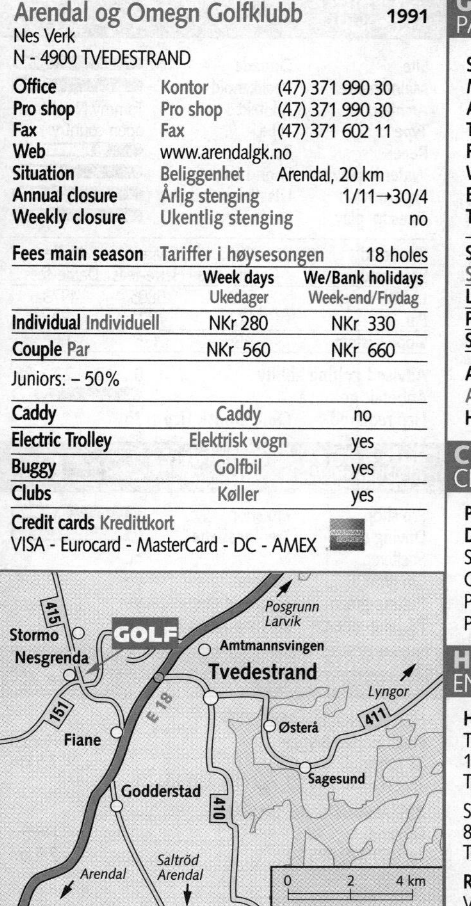

Access Adkomst : Arendal, E18 → Tvedestrand
Exit "Fjanesvingen". Golf 2 km from E18 on 112
Map 1 on page 1035 Kort 1 på side: 1035

Golf course — PARCOURS — 15/20

Site	Område	
Maintenance	Vedlikehold	
Architect	Arkitekt	Unknown
Type	Type	inland
Relief	Relief	
Water in play	Vann-hinder	
Exp. to wind	Utsatt for vind	
Trees in play	Tre-hinder	

Scorecard Scorecard	**Chp.** Champ.-tee	**Mens** Herre-tees	**Ladies** Dame-tees
Length Lengde	5785	5528	4683
Par	72	72	72
Slope system	132	132	132

Advised golfing ability 0 12 24 36
Anbefalt golfnivå
Hcp required Obligatorisk Hcp 36

Club house & amenities — CLUB HOUSE ET ANNEXES — 7/10

Pro shop	Pro shop	
Driving range	Treningsbane	
Sheltered	ly	yes
On grass	på gress	yes (Summer)
Putting-green	putting-green	yes
Pitching-green	pitching-green	yes

Hotel facilities — ENVIRONNEMENT HOTELIER — 5/10

HOTELS HOTEL-FASILITETER

Tvedestrand Fjordhotel — Tvedestrand 10 km
18 rooms, D NKr 990,-
Tel (47) 371 626 55, Fax (47) 371 626 18

Scandic Hotel Arendal — Arendal 20 km
80 rooms, D NKr 845,-/1295,-
Tel (47) 370 251 60, Fax (47) 370 267 07

RESTAURANTS RESTAURANT

Vertshuset — Tvedestrand 10 km
Tel (47) 371 612 61

BORRE

16 | 6 | 5

Folk som assosierer Norge med fjorder vil bli overrasket over de mange små buktene med fiskelandsbyer som ligger sørvest for Oslo. Før du tar dem i nærmere øyesyn er det verdt å gjøre et stopp ved Borre, like ved Horten. Banen ble anlagt rundt den noble herregården Semb. Deler av banen ligger på et tidligere jordbruksområde mens de øvrige hullene snor seg igjennom et skoglandskap. Tommy Nordström har gjort denne banen til en av de beste i landet. En bane som gir utfordringer for de gode spillerne, men som samtidig tar vare på de med høyt handicap. Den er vakkert bygd, men man likevel klart å gi den et naturlig utseende. Den avslører mange slags vanskeligheter og utfordringer, og du vil snarlig beklage din manglende evne til å slå ballene kontrollert i de forskjellige retningene. Banen er ikke spesielt preget av bakker og den er lett å gå rundt. Banen preges av ypperlige greener og med et meget hyggelig miljø. På Borre opplever man en golfrunde som helst ikke vil ta slutt. Så derfor, hvorfor ikke komme tilbake ved en senere anledning?

People who associate Norway with fjords will be surprised by the little coves and fishing villages lying to the south-west of Oslo. Before you see them for yourselves, stop off and play a round at Borre, close to Horten. The course was laid out around the noble mansion of Semb, partly over an old farm and partly over more woodland landscape. Tommy Nordstrom has made this into one of the country's best courses, one that is both challenging for the better golfer and well suited to higher-handicappers. Well landscaped but still with a crisp natural look, it clearly reveals difficulties of every kind and soon has you regretting your inability to bend the ball deliberately in either direction. The course is not too hilly and easily walkable, and with well-guarded, excellent greens and a very pleasant environment, this is one round of golf you will be sorry to finish. But there again, who is to stop you from coming back for more?

Barre Golfklubb — 1991

Semb Hovedgård
N - 3186 HORTEN

Office	Kontor	(47) 330 715 15
Pro shop	Pro shop	(47) 330 715 15
Fax	Fax	(47) 330 715 16
Web	www.borregk.no	
Situation	Beliggenhet	Horten, 2,5 km
Annual closure	Årlig stenging	1/11→31/3
Weekly closure	Ukentlig stenging	no

Fees main season Tariffer i høysesongen	Full day	
	Week days Ukedager	**We/Bank holidays** Week-end/Frydag
Individual Individuell	NOK 300	NOK 400
Couple Par	NOK 600	NOK 800

Juniors: – 50%

Caddy	Caddy	no
Electric Trolley	Elektrisk vogn	no
Buggy	Golfbil	yes
Clubs	Køller	yes

Credit cards Kredittkort
VISA - Eurocard - MasterCard - DC - JCB - AMEX

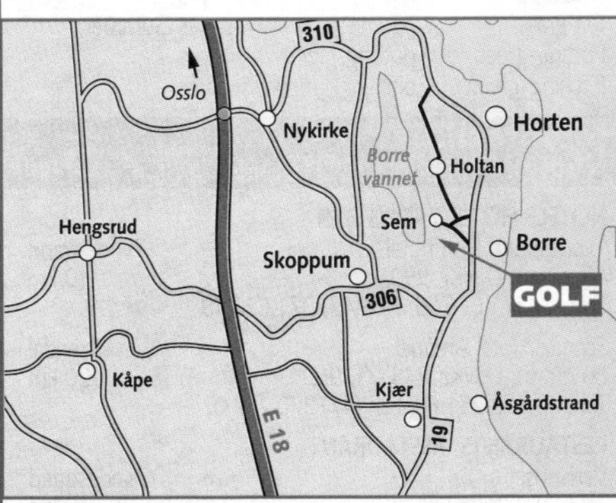

Access Adkomst : 2,5 km S of Horten city centre
Map 1 on page 1035 Kort 1 på side: 1035

Golf course PARCOURS — 16/20

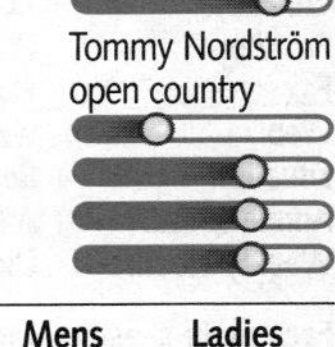

Site	Område	
Maintenance	Vedlikehold	
Architect	Arkitekt	Tommy Nordström
Type	Type	open country
Relief	Relief	
Water in play	Vann-hinder	
Exp. to wind	Utsatt for vind	
Trees in play	Tre-hinder	

Scorecard Scorecard	**Chp.** Champ.-tee	**Mens** Herre-tees	**Ladies** Dame-tees
Length Lengde	5805	5805	4973
Par	72	72	72
Slope system	135	135	135

Advised golfing ability Anbefalt golfnivå — 0 12 24 36
Hcp required Obligatorisk Hcp 35

Club house & amenities CLUB HOUSE ET ANNEXES — 6/10

Pro shop	Pro shop	
Driving range	Treningsbane	
Sheltered	ly	no
On grass	på gress	yes
Putting-green	putting-green	yes
Pitching-green	pitching-green	yes

Hotel facilities ENVIRONNEMENT HOTELIER — 5/10

HOTELS HOTEL-FASILITETER
Hotel Horten Brygge — Horten 2,5 km
23 rooms, D NKr 650,-
Tel (47) 330 204 20, Fax (47) 330 204 21

RESTAURANTS RESTAURANT
Fishland — Horten 2,5 km
Tel (47) 330 488 10

HAUGER

13 | 7 | 6

Spørsmålet er om Hauger en god mesterskapsbane? Det er utvilsomt en fysisk test å spille 18 hull. Seniorer og mindre veltrente golfere kanskje har mer igjen av å tilbringe noen timer i det fantastiske klubbhuset som tidligere var en forpakterbolig og betrakte det bakre landskapet som omgir banen. Etter å ha spilt banen vil man for alltid huske greenene. De er meget raske og ondulerte. Under disse forholdene vil du kanskje spille til ditt handicap, men det skal godt gjøres å senke det. Enkelte av hullene pærer preg av en linksbane med en meget lang og tøff rough. Andre hull minner mer om en park- og innlandsbane. Sagt med andre ord: Du trenger å mestre de fleste type slag og det er viktig å slå rett. Om du ikke tenker for mye på scoren er Hauger en utrolig bra bane hvis man ønsker å lære seg å spille på alle typer baner. For å være ærlig vil vi dessverre ikke anbefale banen for spillere med høyere enn handicap 15, eller kanskje 18. Med litt mer "normale" greener ville Hauger utvilsomt vært en mesterskapsbane.

The question is: is this course a good championship test? It is certainly a demanding physical test, where seniors and the less athletic golfer might do better to wait in the superb farmhouse used as a club-house and admire the beautiful scenery. This is also a memorable course for the greens, all very slick and sometimes with contours that some might consider a little over the top. Under these conditions, you might just about play to your handicap but you will be hard pushed to lower it. Some of the holes have a distinctive links flavour with very tough, tall rough, others are more like inland or parkland holes. In other words, you will need the full panoply of shots and have to hit it straight. If you don't pay too much attention to your score, Hauger is an excellent course for learning and sustaining an all-round game. We wouldn't honestly recommend this to players with a handicap higher than 15 or maybe 18, which is a pity. With more reasonable greens, it really would have been a good championship test.

Hauger Golfklubb — **1996**
Ramstadvn. 18
N - 1480 SLATTUM

Office	Kontor	(47) 670 737 70
Pro shop	Pro shop	(47) 670 784 00
Fax	Fax	(47) 670 737 77
Web	www.hauger-golfklubb.no	
Situation	Beliggenhet	

Lillestrøm, 10 km - Oslo (pop. 458 500), 20 km

Annual closure	Årlig stenging	1/11→30/4
Weekly closure	Ukentlig stenging	no

Fees main season Tariffer i høysesongen	18 holes	
	Week days Ukedager	**We/Bank holidays** Week-end/Frydag
Individual Individuell	NKr 375	NKr 450
Couple Par	NKr 750	NKr 900

Juniors: NKr 190

Caddy	Caddy	no
Electric Trolley	Elektrisk vogn	NKr 150 /18 holes
Buggy	Golfbil	no
Clubs	Køller	NKr 350 /18 holes

Credit cards Kredittkort
VISA - Eurocard - MasterCard - DC

Jaren
Nannestad
Hamar
Frogner
Skedsmokorset
Slattum
Solberg
4
E 6
120
Hvam
22
22
Kjeller
GOLF
Skjetten
Lillestrøm
Strømmen
Fetsund
Oslo
0 2 4 km

Access Adkomst : Oslo, E6 North. Left on Rv.122 by Olavsgaard Hotel. 1 km → Golf
Map 1 on page 1035 Kort 1 på side: 1035

Golf course PARCOURS — 13/20

Site	Område	
Maintenance	Vedlikehold	
Architect	Arkitekt	Jeremy Turner
Type	Type	open country
Relief	Relief	
Water in play	Vann-hinder	
Exp. to wind	Utsatt for vind	
Trees in play	Tre-hinder	

Scorecard Scorecard	**Chp.** Champ.-tee	**Mens** Herre-tees	**Ladies** Dame-tees
Length Lengde	6393	5974	4987
Par	72	72	72
Slope system	133	133	133

Advised golfing ability Anbefalt golfnivå — 0 12 24 36

Hcp required Obligatorisk Hcp — 28 Men/32 Ladies

Club house & amenities CLUB HOUSE ET ANNEXES — 7/10

Pro shop	Pro shop	
Driving range	Treningsbane	
Sheltered	ly	yes
On grass	på gress	yes (Summer)
Putting-green	putting-green	yes
Pitching-green	pitching-green	yes

Hotel facilities ENVIRONNEMENT HOTELIER — 6/10

HOTELS HOTEL-FASILITETER

Quality Olavsgaard Hotel — Skjetten 2,5 km
162 rooms, D NKr 890,-/1395,-
Tel (47) 638 477 00, Fax (47) 638 476 00

Grand Hotel — Oslo 20 km
281 rooms, D NKr 300,-
Tel (47) 224 293 90, Fax (47) 224 212 25

RESTAURANTS RESTAURANT

Quality Olavsgaard — Skjetten 2,5 km
Tel (47) 638 477 00

Bagatelle, Tel (47) 224 463 97 — Oslo 20 km

Spiesestedet Feinschmecker Tel (47) 224 417 77 — Oslo

LARVIK

17 | 8 | 6

Du vil for alltid huske denne banen som en stor vakker park med til dels en fantastisk utsikt over sjøen. Banen ligger like ved Fritzøe Gård med noen minneverdige arkitektoniske innslag som erindrer deg om å være på en linksbane. Her gjelder det å holde seg unna roughen. Den er både lang og saftig, og kan gi deg traumatiske opplevelser i forsøk på å komme ut på fairway igjen - hvis du i det hele tatt finner ballen. Dette til tross, både fairwayene og den korte roughen er brede nok for de fleste spillerne. Problemet er kanskje størst for de som virkelig vil slå langt og kan komme ut av kurs. Det er visselig ikke arkitekt Jan Sederholms stil å straffe for hardt de som hører hjemme blant middels- og høyhandicapere. Det eneste skjønnhetsfeilen ved banen er at den er for flat og hullene for i de fleste tilfeller den samme utforming. Heldigvis har vanskelighetene på banen en forskjellig og særegen karakter. Larvik er udiskutabelt en av de beste banene i Norge, og det vil være synd om man ikke får spilt banen hvis man en sjelden gang er i landet.

You may well remember this as a big, beautiful park with some great views over the sea, and as a course close to Fritzsøe Gård with some memorable architectural features reminiscent of a links course. So first off, be careful to avoid the tall rough, from where escape can be traumatic, if ever you find your ball. However, the fairways and short rough are still wide enough for most players, except the really big hitters who might stray a little too much off-course. It is certainly not the usual style of architect Jan Sederholm to punish too severely the slightly wayward shots from mid- to high-handicappers. The only slight blemish is the overall flatness of the course, creating a certain sameness on most holes. Fortunately the difficulties are more distinctive. Larvik is unquestionably one of the country's finest courses and it would be a pity not to play it if you come to Norway only on rare occasions.

1040

Larvik Golfklubb — 1994

Fritzsøe Gård
N - 3267 LARVIK

Office	Kontor	(47) 331 401 40
Pro shop	Pro shop	(47) 331 406 80
Fax	Fax	(47) 331 401 49
Web	www.larvikgolf.no	
Situation	Beliggenhet	Larvik, 3 km
Annual closure	Årlig stenging	1/12→31/3
Weekly closure	Ukentlig stenging	no

Fees main season Tariffer i høysesongen — 18 holes

	Week days Ukedager	We/Bank holidays Week-end/Frydag
Individual Individuell	NKr 300	NKr 400
Couple Par	NKr 600	NKr 800

Juniors: – 50%

Caddy	Caddy	no
Electric Trolley	Elektrisk vogn	no
Buggy	Golfbil	yes
Clubs	Køller	yes

Credit cards Kredittkort
VISA - Eurocard - MasterCard - AMEX

Tönsberg
Porsgrunn
Farris
E18
40
Sandefjord
303
Tjölling
Fritzoehus
Langesund
302
Larvik
GOLF
Tanum
Larviksfjorden
301
Stavern
0 2 4 km

Access Adkomst : Oslo, E18 → Skien/Kristiansand. Rv.301 to Stavern. 3km, right → Fritzsøe Gård.
Map 1 on page 1035 Kort 1 på side: 1035

Golf course PARCOURS — 17/20

Site	Område	
Maintenance	Vedlikehold	
Architect	Arkitekt	Jan Sederholm
Type	Type	links, open country
Relief	Relief	
Water in play	Vann-hinder	
Exp. to wind	Utsatt for vind	
Trees in play	Tre-hinder	

Scorecard Scorecard	Chp. Champ.-tee	Mens Herre-tees	Ladies Dame-tees
Length Lengde	6235	5848	5093
Par	72	72	72
Slope system	130	130	122

Advised golfing ability Anbefalt golfnivå — 0 12 24 36

Hcp required Obligatorisk Hcp 35

Club house & amenities CLUB HOUSE ET ANNEXES — 8/10

Pro shop	Pro shop	
Driving range	Treningsbane	
Sheltered	ly	yes
On grass	på gress	yes
Putting-green	putting-green	yes
Pitching-green	pitching-green	yes

Hotel facilities ENVIRONNEMENT HOTELIER — 6/10

HOTELS HOTEL-FASILITETER

Quality Grand Hotel Farris — Larvik 3 km
88 rooms, D NKr 950,-/1220,-
Tel (47) 331 878 00, Fax (47) 331 870 45

RESTAURANTS RESTAURANT

Skipperstua — Stavern 3 km
Tel (47) 331 992 15

LOSBY

16 | 8 | 6

Med vakker beliggenhet, og hotell allerede på plass, virker det som at alt er tilrettelagt for en lysende fremtid for Losby. Banen er plassert i et åpent landskap, hvor Peter Nordwall har lagt ut flere vannhindere, som ofte kommer inn i spillet. Greenene er godt beskyttet, og krever ferdigheter i presisjonsgolf. Innspillene må stemme både i retning og lengde. Da banen kan väre litt vanskelig , anbefaler vi spillere med 24 eller höyere i handikap å heller spille matchgolf enn slaggolf. Banen er lang, velplanert og lett å gå. Den oppleves som en bane for fremtidige turneringer.

On a very pleasant site close to Oslo, Losby seems to be all the more destined for a bright future in that it already boasts an on-site hotel. The course has been laid out over very open land with pleasant trees, where Peter Nordwall has produced a number of water hazards that often come into play. In particular, the greens are very well guarded and call for some serious skills in target golf, starting with accurate approach shots in terms of both distance and direction. As the course is rather difficult for players with a handicap of 24 or higher, our advice to the lesser player would be to opt for the rather less depressing match-play formula. Being rather long, well landscaped and easy to walk, Losby is equally remarkable for some rather disconcerting greens, which help promise a fine future of championship golf for the course as a whole.

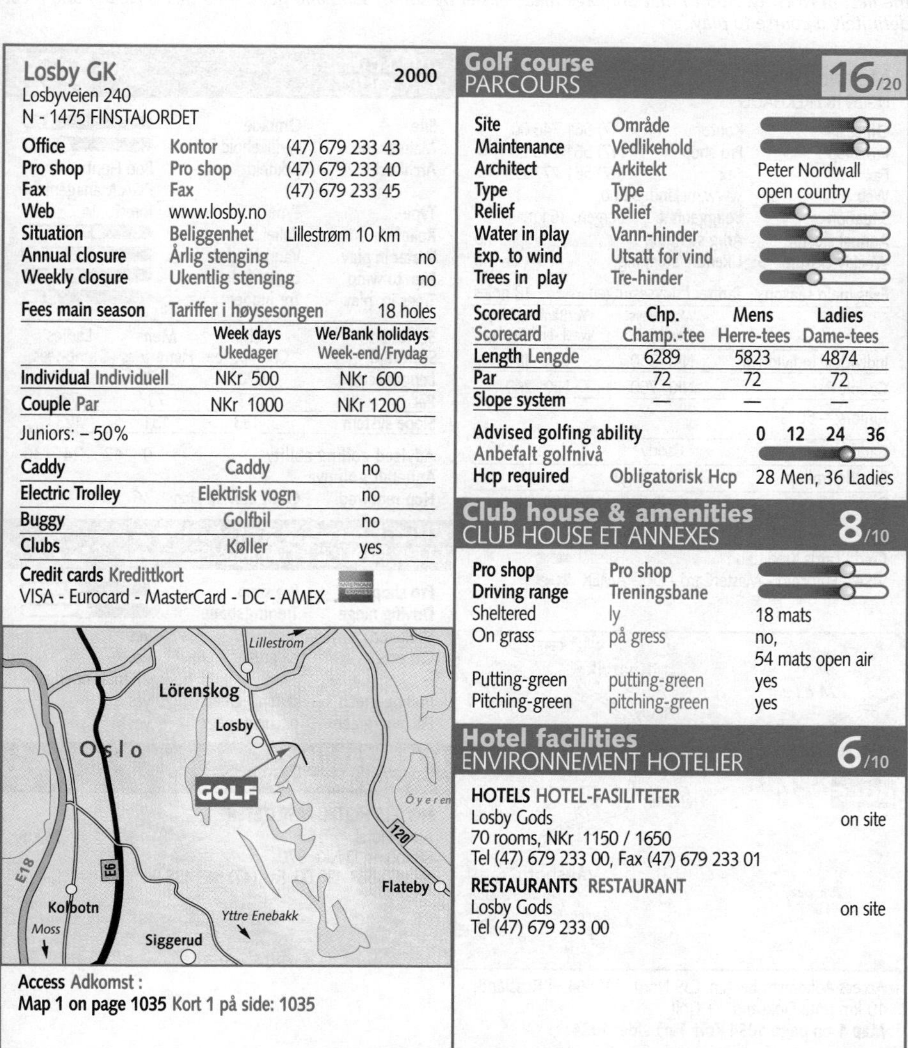

Losby GK — 2000

Losbyveien 240
N - 1475 FINSTAJORDET

Office	Kontor	(47) 679 233 43
Pro shop	Pro shop	(47) 679 233 40
Fax	Fax	(47) 679 233 45
Web	www.losby.no	
Situation	Beliggenhet	Lillestrøm 10 km
Annual closure	Årlig stenging	no
Weekly closure	Ukentlig stenging	no

Fees main season / Tariffer i høysesongen	Week days / Ukedager	We/Bank holidays / Week-end/Frydag
		18 holes
Individual Individuell	NKr 500	NKr 600
Couple Par	NKr 1000	NKr 1200

Juniors: – 50%

Caddy	Caddy	no
Electric Trolley	Elektrisk vogn	no
Buggy	Golfbil	no
Clubs	Køller	yes

Credit cards Kredittkort
VISA - Eurocard - MasterCard - DC - AMEX

Access Adkomst :
Map 1 on page 1035 Kort 1 på side: 1035

Golf course PARCOURS — 16/20

Site	Område	
Maintenance	Vedlikehold	
Architect	Arkitekt	Peter Nordwall
Type	Type	open country
Relief	Relief	
Water in play	Vann-hinder	
Exp. to wind	Utsatt for vind	
Trees in play	Tre-hinder	

Scorecard / Scorecard	Chp. / Champ.-tee	Mens / Herre-tees	Ladies / Dame-tees
Length Lengde	6289	5823	4874
Par	72	72	72
Slope system	—	—	—

Advised golfing ability / Anbefalt golfnivå: 0 12 24 36

Hcp required — Obligatorisk Hcp — 28 Men, 36 Ladies

Club house & amenities CLUB HOUSE ET ANNEXES — 8/10

Pro shop	Pro shop	
Driving range	Treningsbane	
Sheltered	ly	18 mats
On grass	på gress	no, 54 mats open air
Putting-green	putting-green	yes
Pitching-green	pitching-green	yes

Hotel facilities ENVIRONNEMENT HOTELIER — 6/10

HOTELS HOTEL-FASILITETER
Losby Gods — on site
70 rooms, NKr 1150 / 1650
Tel (47) 679 233 00, Fax (47) 679 233 01

RESTAURANTS RESTAURANT
Losby Gods — on site
Tel (47) 679 233 00

MELAND

16 | 7 | 4

På dette stedet får man inntrykk av å väre i paradisets siste hjörne. Hadde det ikke värt for at banen er såpass god, kunne man fort ha glemt selve spillet, for istedet å beundre utsikten over det skiftende fjordlandskepet. Banen, som ligger vakkert mellom skog og steisröys, reflekterer en utmerket forståelse for spillet golf. Her er det nok den mere erfarene golferen som vil trives best, da evnen til å skifte mellom presisjonsgolf og engelsk linksgolf er helt nödvendig. Det finnes vanskeligheter som ikke er synlige ved förste öyekast, Så det kan väre en god ide å gå en treningsrunde. Dette er en ung bane, og den trenger litt tid til å sette seg. Men den er, med sine store velplanerte greener, allerede blandt de beste i Norge. Legg til den gode dreneringen, som kommer av at jorden består av sand og torv, og dette er absolutt en bane verdt å spille.

This is not the world's end, simply a site where the impression is of being in one of the last corners of paradise on earth. From most tees, the ever-changing views over the fjord might almost keep you from playing, if the course was not so good. The layout of the greens and fairways, which wind their way through forest dotted with flush rocks and today's obligatory water hazards, reflects an excellent knowledge of the game of golf. The more experienced players will enjoy this course the most, having to mix target golf with a number of British style bump 'n run shots. Not all the difficulties are clearly visible, though, so a practice round or a little reconnoitring might be a good idea. From the back tees, Meland is championship golf. It is a young course that needs to mature, but the often large and well-designed greens already figure amongst the best in Norway. Add to that drainage made easier by soil of sand and peat, then this is clearly and most definitely a course to play..

Meland GK — 1999

N - 5918 FREKHAUG

Office	Kontor	(47) 561 746 00
Pro shop	Pro shop	(47) 561 746 20
Fax	Fax	(47) 561 777 22
Web	www.melandgolf.no	
Situation	Beliggenhet	Bergen, 36 km
Annual closure	Årlig stenging	no
Weekly closure	Ukentlig stenging	no

Fees main season / Tariffer i høysesongen	Week days / Ukedager	We/Bank holidays / Week-end/Frydag
18 holes		
Individual Individuell	NKr 350	NKr 380
Couple Par	NKr 700	NKr 760

Juniors: – 50%

Caddy	Caddy	no
Electric Trolley	Elektrisk vogn	no
Buggy	Golfbil	NKr 250 /18 holes
Clubs	Køller 1/2 série	50 F/jour

Credit cards Kredittkort
VISA - Eurocard - MasterCard - DC - AMEX

Knarvik · E39 · Meland · Flatøy · Osterfjorden · Fløksand · 564 · Osterøy · GOLF · Herdlafjorden · Frekhaug · E39 · Vågsbotn · Askøy · Oslo · Bergen

Access Adkomst : Bergen, E39 North, RV 564 → Rossland, 10 km until Floksand, → Golf

Map 1 on page 1034 Kort 1 på side: 1034

Golf course — PARCOURS — 16/20

Site	Område	
Maintenance	Vedlikehold	
Architect	Arkitekt	Bob Hunt, PGA Management
Type	Type	forest
Relief	Relief	
Water in play	Vann-hinder	
Exp. to wind	Utsatt for vind	
Trees in play	Tre-hinder	

Scorecard / Scorecard	Chp. / Champ.-tee	Mens / Herre-tees	Ladies / Dame-tees
Length Lengde	6203	5979	5257
Par	73	73	73
Slope system	133	131	123

Advised golfing ability Anbefalt golfnivå — 0 12 24 36

Hcp required Obligatorisk Hcp 36

Club house & amenities — CLUB HOUSE ET ANNEXES — 7/10

Pro shop	Pro shop	
Driving range	Treningsbane	
Sheltered	ly	yes
On grass	på gress	no, 27 mats open air
Putting-green	putting-green	yes
Pitching-green	pitching-green	yes

Hotel facilities — ENVIRONNEMENT HOTELIER — 4/10

HOTELS HOTEL-FASILITETER

Alver Hotel — 18 km
88 rooms, D NKr 970
Tel (47) 563 438 00, Fax (47) 563 438 90

OSLO

15 | 7 | 9

I denne meget hyggelige by gjelder det å ta turen om Ibsen museet, Nasjonalgalleriet og Edvard Munch museet for deretter å besøke Bygdøy og Viking museet. Ditt neste stopp blir 18 hulls banen på Bogstad, bare fire kilometer fra sentrum av landets hovedstad. Banen ble anlagt i 1925 og har opp gjennom årene gjennom en stadig utvikling. Den er lokalisert ved Bogstadvannet som ligger i et typisk norsk skoglandskap med fin utsikt til Holmenkollen og den berømte hoppbakken. Banen er omgitt av mye trær, men de er der mest som dekorasjon og utgjør sjelden noe fare for selve spillet unntatt for å skape noen få dog-leg hull. Vannet er ute av spill med unntak av hull 16, et meget vakkert par 3 hull over Bogstadvannet. Ellers er problemene godt spredt rundt om på banen og hullene kan oppfattes som meget forskjellige, alt fra de mest stressede til de mest avslappende. Greenene er store og til dels ondulerte. Derfor vil majoriteten av de som spiller her komme trygt rundt de 18 hullene uten altfor store problemer.

In this very pleasant city, make it along to the Ibsen Museum, the National Gallery (Najonalgalleriet) and the Edvard Münch museum, then visit the Bigdøy peninsula to see the Viking boat museum. Your next stop will be the 18-hole Oslo golf course, opened in 1925 but recently restyled. It is located on the edge of Lake Bogstad in a typically Norwegian forest setting with some fine views over the hills of Holmenkollen. There are a lot of trees on the course, but more for decoration than to provide any real danger, or to create a few dog-leg holes. Water keeps nicely out of the way except on the 16th, a pretty par 3 over a lake. Otherwise, the trouble is well spread around the course with some very different holes alternating stress and relaxation. The greens are on the large side and sometimes elevated and well-guarded, but the majority of players shouldn't have too much trouble getting home safely. This is the one big Oslo golf club, so you are best advised to play here during the week.

Oslo Golfklubb — 1925

Bogstad, Ankerveien 127
N - 0757 OSLO

Office	Kontor	(47) 225 105 65
Pro shop	Pro shop	(47) 225 054 92
Fax	Fax	(47) 225 105 61
Web	www.oslogk.no	
Situation	Beliggenhet	Oslo city centre, 8 km
Annual closure	Årlig stenging	1/11→30/4
Weekly closure	Ukentlig stenging	no

Fees main season Tariffer i høysesongen	18 holes	
	Week days Ukedager	**We/Bank holidays** Week-end/Frydag
Individual Individuell	NKr 350	NKr 400
Couple Par	NKr 700	NKr 800

Juniors: – 50%

Caddy	Caddy	no
Electric Trolley	Elektrisk vogn	no
Buggy	Golfbil	no
Clubs	Køller	NKr 100 /18 holes

Credit cards Kredittkort
VISA - Eurocard - MasterCard - DC - AMEX

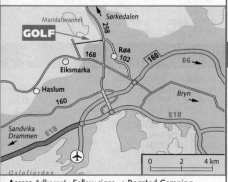

Access Adkomst : Follow signs → Bogstad Camping.
10 mn drive from centre of town
Map 1 on page 1035 Kort 1 på side: 1035

Golf course — PARCOURS — 15/20

Site	Område	
Maintenance	Vedlikehold	
Architect	Arkitekt	Unknown
Type	Type	parkland
Relief	Relief	
Water in play	Vann-hinder	
Exp. to wind	Utsatt for vind	
Trees in play	Tre-hinder	

Scorecard Scorecard	**Chp.** Champ.-tee	**Mens** Herre-tees	**Ladies** Dame-tees
Length Lengde	6144	5789	4994
Par	72	72	72
Slope system	135	132	124

Advised golfing ability Anbefalt golfnivå — 0 12 24 36
Hcp required Obligatorisk Hcp — 20 Men/28 Ladies

Club house & amenities — CLUB HOUSE ET ANNEXES — 7/10

Pro shop	Pro shop	
Driving range	Treningsbane	
Sheltered	ly	yes
On grass	på gress	no
Putting-green	putting-green	yes
Pitching-green	pitching-green	yes

Hotel facilities — ENVIRONNEMENT HOTELIER — 9/10

HOTELS HOTEL-FASILITETER

Holmenkollen Park Hotel — Oslo 3 km
221 rooms, D NKr 1045,-/1645,-
Tel (47) 229 220 00, Fax (47) 221 461 92

Clarion Royal Christiania — Oslo 7 km
378 rooms, D NKr 1495,-
Tel (47) 231 080 00, Fax (47) 231 080 80

Gyldenløve, 168 rooms, D NKr 810,- — Oslo 6 km
Tel (47) 226 010 90, Fax (47) 226 033 90

RESTAURANTS RESTAURANT

Frogneseteren, Tel (47) 221 408 90 — Oslo 5 km
Le Canard, Tel (47) 225 434 00 — Oslo 7 km

SORKNES

15 | 6 | 4

Når villgjessene flyr er ikke Lillehammer så langt unna, men det tar minst en time med bil for å komme til den nærmest byen Hamar. Storstedet Rena blir delt av Norges lengste elv Glomma. En av sideelvene heter Skynna som renner tvers gjennom golfbanen og utgjør en av de store hindringene. Den andre store hindringen er furuskogen. Banen ble lagt ut av J. Søgaard tidlig på 1990-tallet. På slutten av runden vil du huske greenen på hull 18 som er formet som et hjerte. Imidlertid handler banen om mer enn bare den fancy trimmingen av nevnte green. For det første, til tross for plasseringen utenfor allfarvei i bunn på en avsidesliggende dal så er det totalt sett en bra bane. For det andre, vedlikeholdet er bra og det er i seg selv en prestasjon når man tar klimaet i betraktning. Og til slutt, den generelle balansen i layout er fantastisk med en blanding av vanskelige og lette hull. Du vil huske banen for de mange forskjellige slagene som trengs for å komme rundt og det gjelder spesielt tre tøffe hull, inkludert det 17 (par 3 med vann). Vel verdt å vite, selv om det ikke er noen enkel sak å komme hit.

As the wild-goose flies, Lillehammer is not so far away, but it takes at least an hour by car to reach the first large town of Hamar... Rena is crossed by the longest river in Norway, the Glomma, into which flows the Skynna, which also crosses this course and forms one of the major hazards. The other is the pine forest through which the course was laid out by J. Søgaard in the early 1990s. Over the closing stages you will remember the 18th green, a heart-shaped affair, but Sorknes has more to be said for it than that sort of fancy trimming. Firstly, despite its out-of-the-way location at the bottom of a remote valley, it is a good course overall. Secondly, maintenance is good, no mean feat in a climate that is anything but tropical, and finally the general balance of the layout is excellent, with easier and tougher holes evenly arranged. The variety of shots you will need to play makes this a course to remember with three tough holes, including the 17th, a par 3 with water. Well worth knowing, even if getting here is no easy matter.

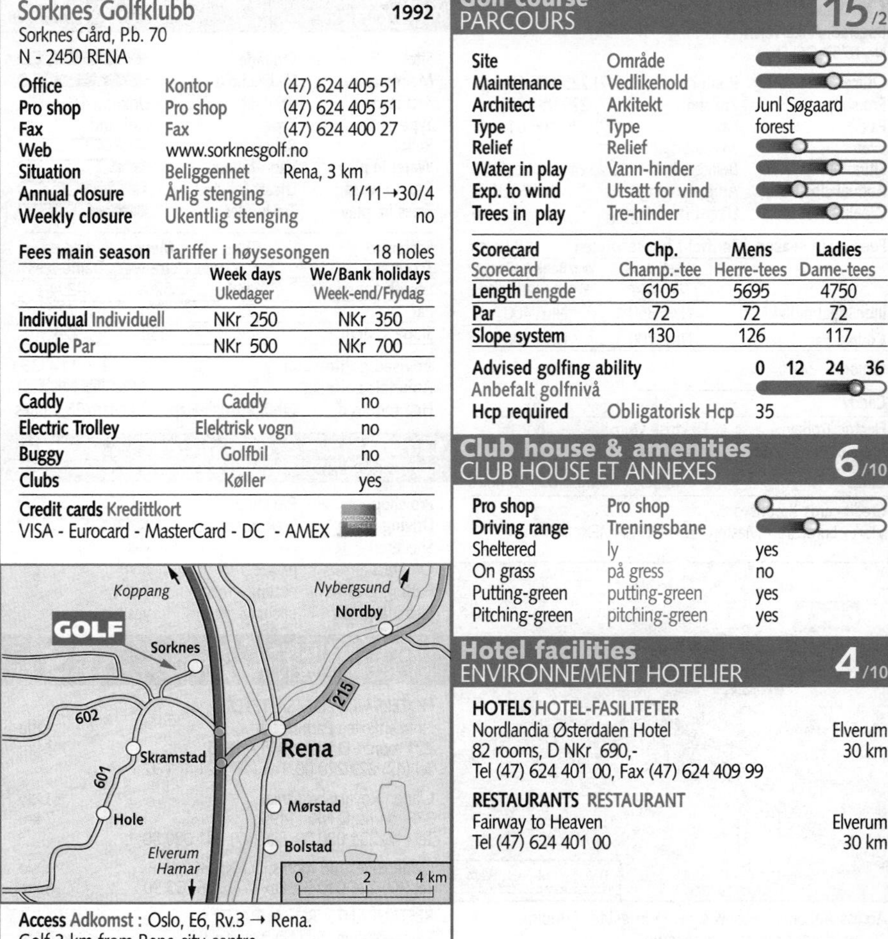

Sorknes Golfklubb — 1992

Sorknes Gård, P.b. 70
N - 2450 RENA

Office	Kontor	(47) 624 405 51
Pro shop	Pro shop	(47) 624 405 51
Fax	Fax	(47) 624 400 27
Web	www.sorknesgolf.no	
Situation	Beliggenhet	Rena, 3 km
Annual closure	Årlig stenging	1/11→30/4
Weekly closure	Ukentlig stenging	no

Fees main season Tariffer i høysesongen — 18 holes

	Week days / Ukedager	We/Bank holidays / Week-end/Frydag
Individual Individuell	NKr 250	NKr 350
Couple Par	NKr 500	NKr 700

Caddy	Caddy	no
Electric Trolley	Elektrisk vogn	no
Buggy	Golfbil	no
Clubs	Køller	yes

Credit cards Kredittkort
VISA - Eurocard - MasterCard - DC - AMEX

Access Adkomst : Oslo, E6, Rv.3 → Rena.
Golf 3 km from Rena city centre.
Map 1 on page 1035 Kort 1 på side: 1035

Golf course / PARCOURS — 15/20

Site	Område	
Maintenance	Vedlikehold	
Architect	Arkitekt	Junl Søgaard
Type	Type	forest
Relief	Relief	
Water in play	Vann-hinder	
Exp. to wind	Utsatt for vind	
Trees in play	Tre-hinder	

Scorecard / Scorecard	Chp. / Champ.-tee	Mens / Herre-tees	Ladies / Dame-tees
Length Lengde	6105	5695	4750
Par	72	72	72
Slope system	130	126	117

Advised golfing ability Anbefalt golfnivå — 0 12 24 36

Hcp required Obligatorisk Hcp 35

Club house & amenities / CLUB HOUSE ET ANNEXES — 6/10

Pro shop	Pro shop	
Driving range	Treningsbane	
Sheltered	ly	yes
On grass	på gress	no
Putting-green	putting-green	yes
Pitching-green	pitching-green	yes

Hotel facilities / ENVIRONNEMENT HOTELIER — 4/10

HOTELS HOTEL-FASILITETER
Nordlandia Østerdalen Hotel — Elverum 30 km
82 rooms, D NKr 690,-
Tel (47) 624 401 00, Fax (47) 624 409 99

RESTAURANTS RESTAURANT
Fairway to Heaven — Elverum 30 km
Tel (47) 624 401 00

STAVANGER

16 | 6 | 7

Den tidligere havnen for sardinfiske er nå senter for oljeproduksjonen i Nordsjøen, men byen er fremdeles like sjarmerende som tidligere år. Stavanger er også byen hvor man kan innlede reisen langs den vakre Vestlandskysten. Norge slik du ser det postkortene. Golfbanen, som ligger ved bredden Stokkavannet, ble anlagt midt i blant et kupert, men ikke urimelig bakkete landskap med fjell, trær, busker og myrer. Baneskaperne har klart å skape en naturskjønn og attraktivt ramme på og rundt banen som inneholder vanskeligheter av alle slag. Den har fått et meget godt rykte på seg fra de beste norske golfspillerne til tross for at lengden er forholdsvis kort. Banen er først og fremst for gode tekniske spillere. Du være nøyaktig og du må hele tiden skifte taktikk avhengig av tidligere slag. Derfor det gjelder det hele tide å gjøre riktig køllevalg. Hvis du vil ha en god score, prøv å utforske banen liten på forhånd. Hull 1, for eksempel, har et blind utslag med driven og et blindt innspill på greenen. Sagt på en annen måte, hvis du bruker 95 slag oftere enn du vanligvis gjør så må du begynne å spille taktisk for å komme rundt banen og ha glede av det.

This former sardine fishing port is now the North Sea oil production centre but is still as charming as ever. It is also the starting point for visiting the wonderful Fjord coast, the Norway you see on postcards. The present course, on the shores of Lake Stokka, was laid out amidst rolling but not unduly hilly countryside of rocks, trees, bushes and marshes, creating a picturesque and attractive setting, and difficulties of all sorts. It has acquired an excellent reputation with top Norwegian players, despite relatively short yardage, as this is a course for the golfing technician. You have to be accurate, be able to change tactics depending on the previous shot and be spot-on when choosing the right club to play. If you are set on carding a good score, try a little reconnoitring beforehand. Hole number one, for example, has a blind drive and a blind green to boot. With this said, if you break 95 more often than not, in theory you have what it takes to get around the course and enjoy it.

Stavanger Golfklubb — 1956

Longebakke 45
N - 4042 HAFRSFJORD

Office	Kontor	(47) 515 570 25
Pro shop	Pro shop	(47) 515 554 31
Fax	Fax	(47) 515 573 11
Web	www.sgk.no	
Situation	Beliggenhet	Stavanger, 5 km
Annual closure	Årlig stenging	1/12→31/3
Weekly closure	Ukentlig stenging	no

Fees main season / Tariffer i høysesongen	18 holes	
	Week days / Ukedager	We/Bank holidays / Week-end/Frydag
Individual Individuell	NKr 300	NKr 300
Couple Par	NKr 600	NKr 600

Caddy	Caddy	no
Electric Trolley	Elektrisk vogn	no
Buggy	Golfbil	no
Clubs	Køller	yes

Credit cards Kredittkort
VISA - Eurocard - MasterCard - DC - JCB - AMEX

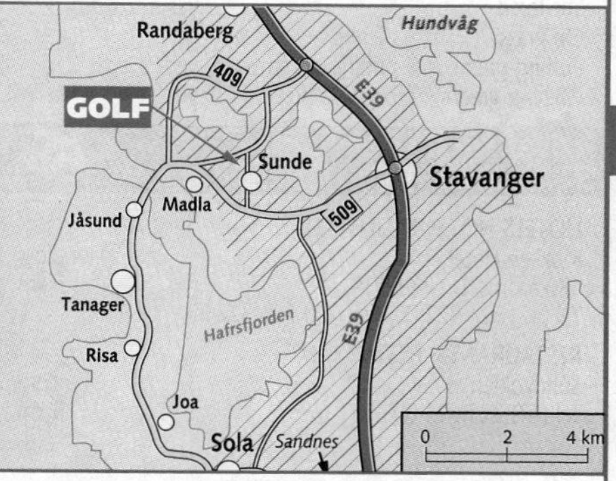

Access Adkomst : Stavanger Rv 510 to Madla. 300 m Rv 509
Map 1 on page 1034 Kort 1 på side: 1034

Golf course / PARCOURS — 16/20

Site	Område	
Maintenance	Vedlikehold	
Architect	Arkitekt	Fred Smith
Type	Type	parkland
Relief	Relief	
Water in play	Vann-hinder	
Exp. to wind	Utsatt for vind	
Trees in play	Tre-hinder	

Scorecard / Scorecard	Chp. / Champ.-tee	Mens / Herre-tees	Ladies / Dame-tees
Length Lengde	5494	5494	4863
Par	71	71	71
Slope system	128	128	128

Advised golfing ability / Anbefalt golfnivå: 0 12 24 36
Hcp required — Obligatorisk Hcp: 36 (We 28/36)

Club house & amenities / CLUB HOUSE ET ANNEXES — 6/10

Pro shop	Pro shop	
Driving range	Treningsbane	
Sheltered	ly	no
On grass	på gress	no
Putting-green	putting-green	yes
Pitching-green	pitching-green	yes

Hotel facilities / ENVIRONNEMENT HOTELIER — 7/10

HOTELS HOTEL-FASILITETER

Radisson SAS Atlantic Hotel — Stavanger 5 km
352 rooms, D NKr 750,-/1495,-
Tel (47) 517 600 05, Fax (47) 517 600 01

Rica Park Hotel — Stavanger 5 km
59 rooms, D NKr 895,-/1325,-
Tel (47) 517 005 00, Fax (47) 517 004 00

RESTAURANTS RESTAURANT

Bevaremegvel — Stavanger 5 km
Tel (47) 518 438 60

TYRIFJORD

14 | 6 | 6

35 kilometer utenfor Oslo finner du en bane som for alltid vil gi deg gode minner selv om scoren ble ødelagt etter å ha spilt en runde. Fredfullt plassert på en øy med god utsikt over Tyrifjorden. Her oppleves en storartet panoramautsikt som du bare får lyst til å nye resten av dagen, særlig hvis legger og føtter verker etter ansluttet spill. God fysisk form er så absolutt en fordel her. Du bør også være i golfmessig god form for å få en god score på denne banen som er designet av Jan Sederholm og Tor Eia. Hvert hull har sin egen personlighet. Et stort antall blinde slag og greener gjør at man har noe å kappes med og det er så absolutt en fordel å spille med et medlem på den første runden. Han eller hun vil kunne fortelle deg hvor noen av de usynlige fellene og hindringene gjemmer seg. Riktignok påvirker farene deg mer psykisk enn det de i virkelighet er. Det er to hull som må tåle mye kritikk og det gjelder hullene 14 og 18. Her bør noe gjøres. Det er så absolutt en fordel å være kjentmann på banen. Og det er godt å kjenne til banen.

At 35 km from Oslo, here is a course to leave you with sweet memories, even if you did mess up your card. Located peacefully on an island overlooking the Tyrifjorden, it provides a magnificent panorama that you could spend the whole day admiring, especially if your legs are not up to the walk and climb. Fitness is a distinct advantage here. Your game has to be in pretty good shape, too, to play this course designed by Jan Sederholm and Tor Eia with good landscaping sense. Each hole has its own personality, but with a number of blind shots and greens to cope with, we would suggest playing with a club member the first time out. He or she will tell you where the sometimes invisible traps and hazards lie, even though the danger is more psychological than real. The only real criticism would concern holes 14 and 18, which leave a lot to be desired. Otherwise, if you can forget about the landscape, which will necessarily affect your judgment, this course is worth getting to know. You won't find many others in the region!

Tyrifjord Golfklubb — 1996

Postbox 91
N - 3529 RØYSE

Office	Kontor	(47) 321 613 30
Pro shop	Pro shop	(47) 321 613 62
Fax	Fax	(47) 321 613 40
Web	www.tyrifjord-golfklubb.no	
Situation	Beliggenhet	
Oslo (pop. 458 500), 35 km		
Annual closure	Årlig stenging	1/11→30/4
Weekly closure	Ukentlig stenging	no

Fees main season Tariffer i høysesongen	18 holes	
	Week days Ukedager	**We/Bank holidays** Week-end/Frydag
Individual Individuell	NKr 300	NKr 350
Couple Par	NKr 600	NKr 700

Juniors: – 50%

Caddy	Caddy	no
Electric Trolley	Elektrisk vogn	no
Buggy	Golfbil	no
Clubs	Køller	no

Credit cards Kredittkort
VISA - Eurocard - MasterCard - DC - AMEX

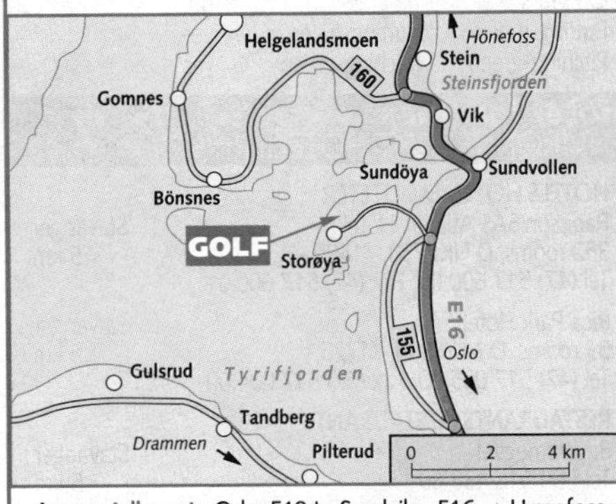

Access Adkomst : Oslo, E18 to Sandvika, E16 → Hønefoss. Golf on Storøya
Map 1 on page 1035 Kort 1 på side: 1035

Golf course — PARCOURS — 14/20

Site	Område	
Maintenance	Vedlikehold	
Architect	Arkitekt	Jan Sederholm Tor Eia
Type	Type	hilly, parkland
Relief	Relief	
Water in play	Vann-hinder	
Exp. to wind	Utsatt for vind	
Trees in play	Tre-hinder	

Scorecard Scorecard	**Chp.** Champ.-tee	**Mens** Herre-tees	**Ladies** Dame-tees
Length Lengde	5747	5747	4960
Par	72	72	72
Slope system	136	136	126

Advised golfing ability Anbefalt golfnivå — 0 12 24 36
Hcp required Obligatorisk Hcp 36

Club house & amenities — CLUB HOUSE ET ANNEXES — 6/10

Pro shop	Pro shop	
Driving range	Treningsbane	
Sheltered	ly	yes
On grass	på gress	no
Putting-green	putting-green	yes
Pitching-green	pitching-green	yes

Hotel facilities — ENVIRONNEMENT HOTELIER — 6/10

HOTELS HOTEL-FASILITETER
Klokken Hotel — Hønefoss 5 km
130 rooms, D NKr 990,-
Tel (47) 321 322 00, Fax (47) 321 327 93

RESTAURANTS RESTAURANT
Sundvolden Hotel — Tyrifjord 5 km
Tel (47) 321 621 00

EUROPE'S TOP 1000 GOLF COURSES

Portugal

São Lourenço

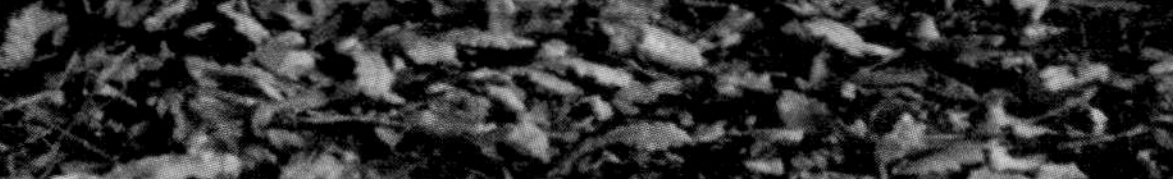

Portugal

With a privileged climate, Portugal has long been a winter refuge for tourists from northern Europe, and especially for golfers. The country has only 7,500 players and around 45 eighteen-hole courses. All are open to the public, but they do tend to get crowded on week-ends with club members, especially in the Lisbon area. It is, therefore, always preferable to book a tee-off time, especially in the Algarve in the south of the country, where visitors abound from Autumn to Spring. Summer is also a pleasant time to play, with a cooling sea breeze to ease the heat.

Com um clima privilegiado, Portugal é desde há muito tempo um refúgio de inverno para os turistas do Norte da Europa e em particular golfistas. O País conta com cerca de 7 500 golfistas e 45 percursos de 18 buracos. Todos estão abertos ao público, mas aos fins de semana congestionam-se um pouco com os sócios dos Clubes, sobretudo na regiäó de Lisboa.
Assim, é sempre melhor reservar, os tempos de saída, nomeadamente na região do Algarve, ao sul de Portugal, onde os visitantes são em grande número, do Outono à Primavera. O Verão é contudo uma época agradável, onde uma suave brisa maritimal, atenua o calor.

Map No 1
Mapa na página 1
km
0 10 20
VIGO
Ourense
Orense
Baiona
Cabo Silleiro
A Ramallosa
Gondomar
Porriño
Ponteareas
Mondariz
Ribadavia
Outomuro
A Cañiza
Cortegada
Salvaterra de Miño
As Neves
Río Miño
São Gregório
Melgaço
Celanova
A Merca
Tui
Arrabal
Tomiño
Valença do Minho
Monção
Sto Pedro da Torre
Castro Laboreiro
Bande
A Garda
Sta Tecla
Vila Nova de Cerveira
Rubiães
Parades de Coura
Parque nacional
Sa da Peneda
Bgem do Alto Lindoso
Mugueimes
Moledo do Minho
Caminha
Vila Praia de Âncora
Arcos de Valdevez
Lindoso
Fondevila
Ponte de Lima
Bravães
Ponte da Barca
Sa do Gerês
Montalegre
Viana do Castelo
MINHO
Darque
Terras de Bouro
Peneda-Gerês
Gerês
Paradela
Caldelas
Vila Verde
Bouro
Amares
Vieira do Minho
Venda Nova
Salto
Esposende
Barcelos
Ofir
Braga
Mte Sameiro
Bom Jesus
Pinheiro
Povoa de Lanhoso
Sa da Cabreira
Caldelas (Taipas)
Guimarães
Cabeceiras
Arco de Baúlhe
Rates
Póvoa de Varzim
Vila do Conde
Vila Nova de Famalicão
Trofa
Penha
Fafe
Sto Tirso
Caldas de Vizela
Felgueiras
Celorico
Mondim
Vila Pouca de
DOURO
Lousada
Vila Real
Amarante
Maia
Matosinhos
Paços de Ferreira
Paredes
PORTO
Valongo
Penatiel
Marco de Canaveses
Sa do Marão
Vila Nova de Gaia
Gondomar
Paço de Sousa
Baião
Mesão Frio
Peso da
Sta Marta de Penaguião
Valadares
Avintes
Entre-os-Rios
Sande
R. Tâmega
Miramar
Espinho
Castelo de Paiva
Cinfães
Oliveira do Douro
Resende
Lamego
Esmoriz
Tarouca
Sta Maria da Feira
S. João da Madeira
Arouca
Sa do Montemuro
S. João de Tarouca
Moimenta da Beira
Furadouro
Ovar
Vale de Cambra
Castro Daire
Rio Paiva
Chãs de Arada
Vila Nova de Paiva
Torreira
Murtosa
Estarreja
Sever do Vouga
BEIRA
S. Pedro do Sul
Aguiar da
Rio Vouga
Ria de Aveiro
S. Jacinto
Aveiro
Albergaria-a-Velha
Oliveira de Frades
Vouzela
Montebelo
Praia da Barra
Ílhavo
Águeda
Sátão
Viseu
Penalva do Castelo
Vagos
Caramulo
Sa do Caramulo
Campo de Beisteros
Mangualde
Praia de Mira
Mamarrosa
Oliveira do Bairro
Anadia
Tondela
Canas de Senhorim
Nelas
Mira
Curia
Rio Dão
Mondego
Mealhada
Luso
Sta Comba Dão
Carregal do Sal
Seia
Praia de Tocha
Cantanhede
Tocha
Mortágua
Buçaco
Pampilhosa
Oliveira do Hospital
Manteigas
Arazede
LITORAL
Tábua
S. Romão
Torre
Loriga
Unhais da Serra
Rio Alva
Montemor-o-Velho
Penacova
Buarcos
Figueira da Foz
Villa Nova de Poiares
Arganil
SERRA
COIMBRA
MICHELIN

Castro Caldelas
Alto del Couso
A Rúa
Puente de Domingo Flórez
Montes
Sta Colomba de Somoza
Maceda
Alto del Rodicio
Puebla de Trives
Freixido
Casoio
Baños de Molgas
Manzaneda
1778
O Bolo
E. de Prada
2185
Teleno
Manzaneda
A Veiga
Seixo
1707
Embalse de Bao
Peña Trevinca
2124
Encinedo
Vilar de Barrio
Alto de Covelo
1052
Viana do Bolo
Truchas
Embalse de Las Portas
E. de S. Sebastián
Sierra de la Cabrera
S. Martín de Castañeda
Castrocontrigo
Laza
Lago de Sanabria
Ribadelago
Peña Nofre
1291
A Gudiña
Pillo de la Canda
Puebla de Sanabria
Justel
Galende
Espadañedo
Alto de Estivadas
Alto de Fumaces
Alto do Cañizo
1085
1262
Palacios de Sanabria
Verín
850
A Mezquita
Padornelo
Pedralba
Ungilde
Monbuey
Moimenta
Corraes
1276
E. de Cernadilla
E. de Valparaiso
Calabor
Portelo
Sa de la Culebra
Peña Mira
1238
Villardeciervos
Feces
Parque natural de Montesinho
Ferreras de Abajo
Vila Verde da Raia
Vinhais
Figueruela de Arriba
Pto de Sazad
Chaves
Bragança
Milhão
S. Vicente de la Cabeza
Rebordelo
Rio Tuella
Penhas Juntas
Quintanilha
S. Vitero
Vidago
Trabazos
Torre de D. Chama
1318
Sa de Nogueira
Rio Sabor
Alcañices
Sta Comba de Rossas
Valpaços
Sta Luz
910
Carrazedo de Montenegro
1147
Padrela
Montes
Fonfría
Izeda
Vimioso
Macedo de Cavaleiros
Mirandela
Murça
999
Morais
Rio Duero
Ricobayo
Miranda do Douro
Bornes
Sa de Bornes
983
Trintade
Bgem de Picote
Sendim
Alijó
Vila Flor
Mogadouro
Alfândega da Fé
Bermillo de Sayago
Fermoselle
785
Rio Tua
Pinhão
Carrazeda de Ansiães
Bgem da Bemposta
883
Fonte Longa
Rio Sabor
Embalse de Almendra
885
Sa. do Mogadouro
Torre de Moncorvo
Lagoaça
Villarino
Almeida
S. João da Pesqueira
Masueco
Trabanca
Carviçais
Vila Nova de Foz Côa
Embalse de Aldeadávia
Freixo de Espada à Cinta
Villaseco de los Reyes
Penedono
Barruecopardo
Embalse de Saucelle
Barca de Alva
Mêda
La Fregeneda
Vitigudino
Villar de Peralonso
Sernancelhe
Hinojosa de Duero
Alta
Lumbrales
Rio Côa
Figueira de Castelo Rodrigo
Sando
977
Marofa
El Cubo de Don Sancho
Villavieja de Yeltes
826
Berzosa
S. Felices de los Gallegos
Trancoso
Rio Huebra
Vila Franca das Naves
Pinhel
La Fuente de S. Esteban
fin 2003
Almeida
Martín de Yeltes
Freixedas
Celorico da Beira
Castillejo de Martín Viejo
Sancti Spíritus
Cabrillas
Vecinos
Rio Yeltes
1283
Vilar Formoso
Tamames
Arrifana
Vale de Estrela
Guarda
Fuentes de Oñoro
Ciudad Rodrigo
Cerdeira
El Bodón
Pega
Rio Côa
Aldeia da Ponte
Fuenteguinaldo
Belmonte
La Alberguería de Argañán
Sabugal
Caria
Sto Estêvão
1051
MICHELIN
d'après cartes n° 940 - 5ème édition - 2002 et
n° 990 - 23ème édition - 2002. Autorisation n° 0102062.

Map No 2
Mapa na página 2
km
0 10 20
Praia d'el Rey
Golden Eagle
Quinta da Beloura
Penha Longa
Belas
Oitavos
Quinta da Marinha
Aroeira
Quinta do Peru
Troia
MICHELIN
Praia de Mira
Mira
Mamarrosa
Oliveira do Bairro
Anadia
Curia
Mealhada
Luso
Buçaco
Pampilhos
Praia de Tocha
Tocha
Cantanhede
Arazede
Cabo Mondego
Buarcos
Figueira da Foz
Montemor-o-Velho
Penacova
COIMBRA
Rio Mondego
Condeixa-a-Nova
Miranda do Corvo
Soure
Louriçal
Degracias
Penela
Pedrógão
Praia da Vieira
Vieira
Monte Redondo
Monte Real
Pombal
Sicó
Ansião
Pontão
Figueiró dos Vinhos
S. Pedro de Moel
Pinhal de Leiria
Marinha Grande
Leiria
Martingança
Batalha
Alvaiázere
Barqueiro
Cernache de Bonjardim
Nazaré
Cruz da Légua
Porto de Mós
Ourém
Fátima
Ferreira do Zêzere
Rio Zêzere
S. Martinho do Porto
Alcobaça
Alfeizerão
Mira de Aire
Tomar
Bgem do Castelo de Bode
Foz del Arelho
Ilha Berlenga
Cabo Carvoeiro
Baleal
Peniche
Caldas da Rainha
Óbidos
Serra de Aire
Sa dos Candeeiros
Torres Novas
Sardoal
Constância
Alcanena
Alcanede
Entroncamento
Almourol
Abrantes
Atouguia da Baleia
Rio Maior
Golegã
Vila Nova da Barquinha
Tramagal
Rossio
Lourinhã
Bombarral
Cadaval
Chamusca
Alcanhões
Bemposta
Praia de Sta Cruz
Cercal
Sa de Montejunto
Santarém
Alpiarça
Almeirim
Chouto
Torres Vedras
Aldeia Gavinha
Cartaxo
Avèiras de Cima
Azambuja
Alenquer
Sobral de Mte Agraço
Muge
Rio Tejo
Ericeira
Sapataria
Arruda dos Vinhos
Carregado
Salvaterra de Magos
São José da Lamarosa
Montargil
Bgem de Montargil
Malveira
Bucelas
Vila Franca de Xira
Benavente
Rio Sorraia
Cabo da Roca
Colares
Sintra
Loures
Alverca do Ribatejo
Porto Alto
Coruche
Couço
Ribª da Raia
Amadora
Sacavém
Sto Estêvão
Mora
Queluz
LISBOA
Ribª de Divor
Pavia
Cabo Raso
Cascais
Estoril
Oeiras
Alcochete
Montijo
Brotas
Trafaria
Almada
Barreiro
Canha
Lavre
Seixal
Moita
Taipadas
Coina
Pinhal Novo
Cruzamento de Pegões
Arraiolos
Vendas Novas
Palmela
Vila Nogueira de Azeitão
Setúbal
Marateca
Montemor-o-Novo
Santana
Sa da Arrábida
Portinho
Península de Tróia
Sesimbra
Santiago do Escoural
S. Cristóvão
Rio Sado
ESTREMADURA
RIBATEJO
ALTO
PORTO

1052

Tondela
Canas de Senhorim
Nelas
Mondego
Carregal do Sal
Oliveira do Hospital
Tábua
Seia
Gouveia
ESTRELA
Manteigas
Valhelhas
Vale de Estrela
Guarda
Arrifana
Vilar Formoso
Fuentes de Oñoro
Castillejo de Martín Viejo
Cerdeira
Pega
Aldeia da Ponte
Fuenteguinaldo
S. Romão
Loriga
Torre
Penhas da Saude
Belmonte
Sabugal
La Alberguería de Argañán
Arganil
SERRA
DA
S. Pedro de Açor
Unhais da Serra
Teixoso
Caria
Sto Estêvão
Covilhã
Tortosendo
Paúl
Rio Zêzere
Rio Ceira
Góis
Fundão
Silvares
Meimoa
Penamacor
Valverde del Fresno
Navasfrías
Sa de Malcata
Mezas
Acebo
Gata
Hoyos
Perales del Puerto
Cilleros
Pampilhosa da Serra
Sa da Gardunha
Vale de Prazeres
Alpedrinha
S. Vicente da Beira
Orvalho
Foz Giraldo
Cambas
Medelim
Monsanto
Moraleja
Rio Erges
Termas de Monfortinho
Oleiros
Sa de Alvelos
Salgueiro do Campo
Alcains
Escalos de Cima
Idanha a Nova
Alcafozes
Casillas
BEIRA
BAIXA
Sarzedas
Sobreira Formosa
Castelo Branco
Ladoeiro
Zebreira
Zarza la Mayor
Segura
Ceclavín
Acehuche
Piedras Albas
Rio Ocreza
Bgem de Cedillo
Malpica do T.
Rosmaninhal
Alcántara
Embalse de Alcántara
Garrovillas
Vila Velha de Ródão
Fratel
Cedillo
Herrera de Alcántara
RÍO TAJO
Montalvão
Santiago de Alcántara
Rio Sever
Brozas
Navas del Madroño
Gavião
RIO TEJO
Nisa
Arez
Bgem da Póvoda
Membrío
Tolosa
Alpalhão
Castelo de Vide
Marvão
Valencia de Alcántara
Salorino
Herreruela
Arroyo de la Luz
Casar de Cáceres
Mte da Pedra
Flor da Rosa
Crato
Portalegre
Parque Natural de São Mamede
Sa de S. Mamede
S. Vicente de Alcántara
Torrico de S. Pedro
Aliseda
Malpartida de Cáceres
Ponte de Sor
Alter do Chão
Rio Salor
Sa de S. Pedro
Pto del
PORTUGAL
Avis
Cabeço de Vide
La Codosera
Alburquerque
Puebla de Obando
Fronteira
Arronches
Pto de los Conejeros
Villar del Rey
Pto del Zángano
Monforte
La Roca de la Sierra
Casa Branca
Sousel
Sta Eulália
Bgem do Caia
Campo Maior
La Nava de Santiago
Veiros
Vila Fernando
Vimieiro
Estremoz
Elvas
Badajoz
Montijo
Talavera la Real
Puebla de la Calzada
Lobón
Évoramonte
Borba
Vila-Boim
Vila Viçosa
Juromenha
Azaruja
Arroyo de S. Serván
Torremegía
Corte de Peleas
Alandroal
La Albuera
S. Miguel de Machede
Redondo
Olivenza
Valverde de Leganés
Solana de los Barros
Terena
Guadiana
Évora
Aceuchal
MICHELIN
1053

Map No 3
Mapa na página 3

km
0 10 20

Aroeira
Quinta do Peru
Troia
Palmares
Penina
Vale da Pinta
Salgados
Vila Sol
Pinheiros Altos
Vale do Lobo
S. Lourenço
Vilamoura
Quinta do Lago Ria Formosa

LISBOA
Sacavém
Alcochete
Montijo
Almada
Barreiro
Seixal
Coina
Moita
Pinhal Novo
Palmela
Vila Nogueira de Azeitão
Setúbal
Santana
Sª da Arrábida
Sesimbra
Cabo Espichel
Portinho
Península de Tróia
Rio Sado
Sto Estêvão
Canha
Taipadas
Cruzamento de Pegões
Vendas Novas
Marateca
Montemor-o-Novo
Lavre
Mora
Brotas
Arraiolos
Santiago do Escoural
S. Cristóvão
Bgem de Pego do Altar
Comporta
Alcácer do Sal
Alcáçovas
Casa Branca
Torrão
Alvito
Melides
Grândola
Costa de Sto André
Vila Nova de Sto André
Santiago do Cacém
Sines
Cabo de Sines
Azinheira dos Barros
Sta Margarida do Sado
Odivelas
Bgem de Odivelas
Ferreira do Alentejo
Beringel
Abela
Ermidas-Aldeia
Alvalade
S. Domingos
Ervidel
Bgem do Roxo
Tanganheira
Bgem de Campilhas
Cercal
Aljustrel
Albernoa
Vila Nova de Milfontes
Sta Luzia
Bgem de Monte da Rocha
Vale de Açor
S. Martinho das Amoreiras
Garvão
Castro Verde
Alcaria
Odemira
Ourique
Rio Mira
Sta Clara-a-Velha
Bgem de Sta Clara
S. Teotónio
Sabóia
Odeceixe
Santana da Serra
Almodôvar
Nave Redonda
S. Marcos da Serra
Sª do Mú
Aljezur
Monchique
Sª de Monchique
Alfambra
Ameixial
Carrapateira
S. Bartolomeu de Messines
Porto de Lagos
Silves
Barranco Velho
Vila do Bispo
Alvor
Portimão
Algoz
Alcantarilha
Parderne
Boliqueime
Loulé
Cabo de São Vicente
Sagres
Lagos
Praia da Rocha
Lagoa
Carvoeiro
Armação de Pêra
Ferreiras
Albufeira
Quarteira
Almansil
S. Brás de Alportel
Estói
Faro
Olhão
Ponta de Sagres
Cabo de Sta Maria
Parque natural
ALENTEJO
ALGARVE

1054

MICHELIN

Casa Branca
Sousel
Sta Eulália
Bgem do Caia
Campo Maior
La Roca de la Sierra
La Nava de Santiago
Veiros
Vila Fernando
Vimieiro
Estremoz
Elvas
Badajoz
Montijo
Talavera la Real
Puebla de la Calzada
Évoramonte
Borba
Vila-Boim
Vila Viçosa
Juromenha
Azaruja
Alandroal
Lobón
Arroyo de S. Serván
Corte de Peleas
Torremegía
S. Miguel de Machede
Redondo
Olivenza
La Albuera
Valverde de Leganés
Solana de los Barros
Évora
Terena
GUADIANA
Almendral
Aceuchal
Sta Marta
Villalba de los Barros
Montoito
Cheles
Alconchel
Salvatierra de los Barros
S. Manços
Monsaraz
Barcarrota
Feria
Fuente del Maestre
Reguengos de Monsaraz
Higuera de Vargas
Los Santos de Maimona
São Marcos do Campo
Mourão
S. Leonardo
Villanueva del Fresno
Burguillos del Cerro
Zafra
Portel
Valle de Matamoros
Zahinos
Jerez de los Caballeros
Granja
Pto de Sto Domingo
Vidigueira
Alqueva
Oliva de la Frontera
Bgem d'Alqueva (en Construção)
Amareleja
Valencia del Ventoso
Pedrógão
Moura
Pto de la Granja
S. Cristóbal
Safara
Fregenal de la Sierra
Barrancos
Encinasola
Higuera la Real
Segura de León
Brinches
Pias
Cumbres Mayores
Sobral da Adiça
Fuentes de León
Serpa
Rosal de la Frontera
Aroche
Arroyomolinos de León
Vila Nova de São Bento
Vila Verde de Ficalho
Cañaveral de León
Galaroza
Cortegana
Jabugo
Aracena
Embalse de Aracena
Cabezo Gordo
Almonaster la Real
Sta Olalla del Cala
Sta Bárbara
S. Telmo
Sa de Aracena
Paymogo
Higuera de la Sierra
Zufre
Mina de S. Domingos
Cabezas Rubias
El Cerro de Andévalo
Puebla de Guzmán
Minas de Riotinto
Nerva
Zalamea
1055
ILHA DA MADEIRA
Ponta do Tristão
Porto Moniz
Santa
Achadas da Cruz
Ribeira da Janela
Ponta de São Jorge
Arco de São Jorge
São Jorge
Seixal
Ponta Delgada
Boa Ventura
Santana
Ponta do Pargo
São Vicente
Ponta do Clérigo
Remal
Ruivo do Paúl
Pico Ruivo
Faial
Madeira
Ginjas
Rosário
São Roque
Porto da Cruz
Fajã da Ovelha
Rabaçal
Parque Natural
Paúl do Mar
Prazeres
Boca da Encumeada
Portela
Estreito da Calheta
Arieiro
Jardim do Mar
Ribeiro Frio
Prainha
Arco da Calheta
Caniçal
Pta de São Lourenço
Calheta
Serra de Água
Curral das Freiras
Eira do Serrado
Poiso
Sto António da Serra
Machico
Madalena do Mar
Canhas
Água de Pena
Estreito de Câmara de Lobos
Camacha
Ponta do Sol
Monte
Santa Cruz
Campanário
Ribeira Brava
Gaula
Cabo Girão
Câmara de Lobos
Caniço
São Martinho
São Gonçalo
Ponta do Garajau
Ponta da Cruz
FUNCHAL
MICHELIN
30 000

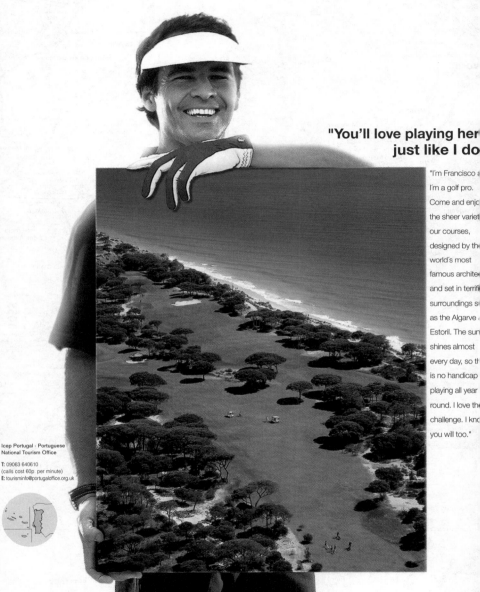

Classification

CLASSIFICATION OF COURSES
CLASSIFICAÇÃO DOS PERCURSOS

This classification gives priority consideration to the score awarded to the actual course.

Courses score / Nota do percurso				Page / Página
17	6	5	Praia d'El Rey	1069
17	6	8	S. Lourenço	1075
16	6	8	Penha Longa	1066
16	7	8	Quinta do Lago *B/C*	1072
16	7	5	Santo da Serra	1077
16	6	5	Troia	1078
16	7	7	Vilamoura I *(Old Course)*	1082
15	7	7	Oitavos	1064
15	6	7	Vale do Lobo *Royal Golf Course*	1080
14	6	6	Aroeira *Aroeira I*	1059
14	6	6	Aroeira *Aroeira II*	1060
14	8	5	Belas	1061
14	5	4	Golden Eagle	1062
14	7	8	Penina	1067
14	7	7	Pinheiros Altos	1068
14	8	7	Quinta da Beloura	1070
14	7	7	Quinta da Marinha	1071
14	7	8	Quinta do Lago *Ria Formosa*	1073
14	7	5	Quinta do Peru	1074
14	6	6	Vale da Pinta	1079
14	7	7	Vila Sol	1081
14	7	7	Vilamoura III *(Laguna)*	1083
14	7	7	Vilamoura *Millenium*	1084
13	5	5	Montebelo	1063
13	7	5	Palmares	1065
13	6	6	Salgados	1076

1057

Classification

HOTELS FACILITIES
CLASSIFICAÇÃO DO ENVOLVIMENTO HOTELEIRO

16	6	**8**	Penha Longa	1066
14	7	**8**	Penina	1067
16	7	**8**	Quinta do Lago *B/C*	1072
14	7	**8**	Quinta do Lago *Ria Formosa*	1073
17	6	**8**	S. Lourenço	1075
15	7	**7**	Oitavos	1064
14	7	**7**	Pinheiros Altos	1068
14	8	**7**	Quinta da Beloura	1070
14	7	**7**	Quinta da Marinha	1071
15	6	**7**	Vale do Lobo *Royal Golf Course*	1080
14	7	**7**	Vila Sol	1081
16	7	**7**	Vilamoura I *(Old Course)*	1082
14	7	**7**	Vilamoura III *(Laguna)*	1083
14	7	**7**	Vilamoura *Millenium*	1084
14	6	**6**	Aroeira *Aroeira I*	1059
14	6	**6**	Aroeira *Aroeira II*	1060
13	6	**6**	Salgados	1076
14	6	**6**	Vale da Pinta	1079
14	8	**5**	Belas	1061
13	5	**5**	Montebelo	1063
13	7	**5**	Palmares	1065
17	6	**5**	Praia d'El Rey	1069
14	7	**5**	Quinta do Peru	1074
16	7	**5**	Santo da Serra	1077
16	6	**5**	Troia	1078
14	5	**4**	Golden Eagle	1062

RECOMMENDED GOLFING STAY
ESTADIA DE GOLF RECOMENDADA

Aroeira *Aroeira I*	14	6	6	1059	S. Lourenço	17	6	8	1075
Aroeira *Aroeira II*	14	6	6	1060	Troia	16	6	5	1078
Oitavos	15	7	7	1064	Vale do Lobo *Royal Golf Course*	15	6	7	1080
Penha Longa	16	6	8	1066	Vilamoura *Vilamoura I (Old Course)*	16	7	7	1082
Quinta da Marinha	14	7	7	1071	Vilamoura *Vilamoura III (Laguna)*	14	7	7	1083
Quinta do Lago *B/C*	16	7	8	1072	Vilamoura *Millenium*	14	7	7	1084
Quinta do Lago *Ria Formosa*	14	7	8	1073					

RECOMMENDED GOLFING HOLIDAYS
FÉRIAS RECOMENDADAS

Algarve: Palmares 1065, Penina 1067, Salgados 1076, Vale da Pinta 1079, Pinheiros Altos 1068, Quinta do Lago 1072 / 1073, S. Lourenço 1075, Vale do Lobo 1080, Vila Sol 1081, Vilamoura 1082/1083/ 1084.

Lisboa/Cascais: Praia d'El Rey 1069, Quinta da Marinha 1071, Oitavos 1064, Penha Longa, 1066, Troia 1078, Aroeira 1059/1060...

Madeira: Santo da Serra, 1077

TYPE OF COURSE
TIPOS DE PERCURSOS

Forest

Aroeira 1059/1060, Pinheiros Altos 1068, Quinta da Marinha 1071, Quinta do Lago *B/C* 1072, Quinta do Lago *Ria Formosa* 1073, Quinta do Peru 1074, S. Lourenço 1075, Vale do Lobo *Royal Golf Course* 1080, Vila Sol 1081, Vilamoura (Old Course *Millenium*) 1082/1084.

Hilly

Belas 1061, Montebelo 1063, Santo da Serra 1077

Inland

Golden Eagle 1062, Montebelo 1063, Palmares 1065, Vale da Pinta 1079.

Links

Praia d'El Rey 1069, Troia 1078 .

Mountain

Penha Longa 1066, Santo da Serra 1077

Open country

Belas 1061, Penina 1067, Oitavos 1064, Pinheiros Altos 1068. Vilamoura III (Laguna) 1083.

Seaside course

Oitavos 1064, Palmares 1065, Praia d'El Rey 1069, S. Lourenço 1075, Salgados 1076, Troia 1078, Vale do Lobo*Royal Golf Course* 1080.

Residential

Penha Longa 1066, Quinta da Beloura 1070 Quinta da Marinha 1071, Quinta do Lago *B/C Ria Formosa* 1072/1073, Quinta do Peru 1074 Vale da Pinta 1079 Vila Sol 1081.

AROEIRA Aroeira I

14 | 6 | 6

A primeira impressão é a de um ambiente muito agradável entre pinheiros e flores silvestres, habitat natural de diversos tipos de aves. Sem interferir com esse quadro o arquitecto Frank Pennink realizou um percurso de uma grande franqueza, e com um traçado muito simples, onde os obstáculos (a excepção das árvores) raramente sao perigosos. Os jogadores médios e os prin-cipiantes sentem-se logo à vontade neste percurso amigável, onde se caminha fácilmente e onde os "rough" não são muito penalizantes. Os melhores jogadores, no entanto, podem achá-lo um pouco monotono para jogar muitas vezes, uma vez que lhe faltam verdadeiros desafios, com a excepção do 11, redesenhado por Robert Trent Jones. Em contrapartida a Aroeira é um local ideal para se jogar uma partida em família ou para uma partida entre amigos.

The first impression is one of a very pleasant setting of pine-trees and wild flowers, and the natural habitat for numerous birds. Without spoiling the scenery, architect Frank Penninck has laid out a clear and candid course of rather simple design, where the hazards are seldom too dangerous (except the trees). High-handicappers and beginners will feel immediately at home on this friendly and easily-walkable course, where the rough and undergrowth could never be called penalising. The better players might possibly find it boring to play regularly, given the absence of real challenge. Only the 11th hole, redesigned by Robert Trent Jones, stands out from a pretty colourless picture. By contrast, Aroeira is the ideal spot for a round with all the family and for giving less experienced players welcome practice.

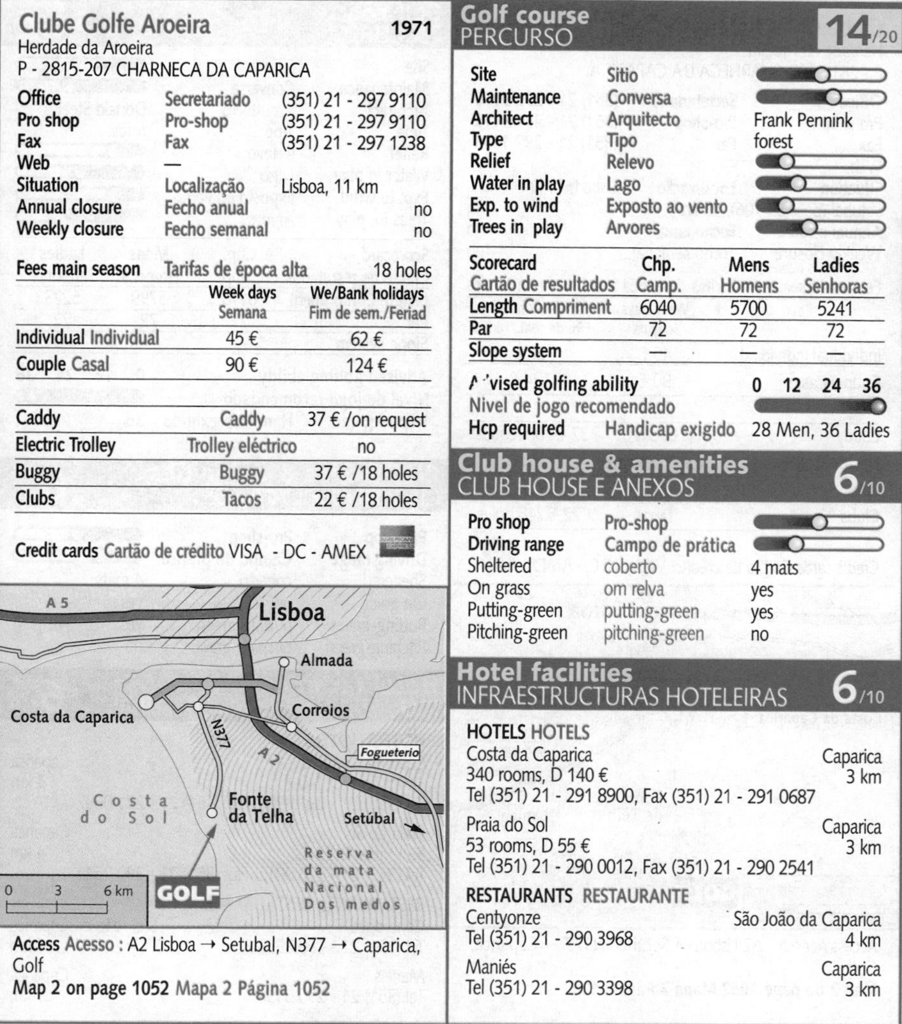

Clube Golfe Aroeira — 1971

Herdade da Aroeira
P - 2815-207 CHARNECA DA CAPARICA

Office	Secretariado	(351) 21 - 297 9110
Pro shop	Pro-shop	(351) 21 - 297 9110
Fax	Fax	(351) 21 - 297 1238
Web	—	
Situation	Localização	Lisboa, 11 km
Annual closure	Fecho anual	no
Weekly closure	Fecho semanal	no

Fees main season Tarifas de época alta	18 holes	
	Week days Semana	We/Bank holidays Fim de sem./Feriad
Individual Individual	45 €	62 €
Couple Casal	90 €	124 €

Caddy	Caddy	37 € /on request
Electric Trolley	Trolley eléctrico	no
Buggy	Buggy	37 € /18 holes
Clubs	Tacos	22 € /18 holes

Credit cards Cartão de crédito VISA - DC - AMEX

Access Acesso : A2 Lisboa → Setubal, N377 → Caparica, Golf

Map 2 on page 1052 Mapa 2 Página 1052

Golf course PERCURSO — 14/20

Site	Sitio	
Maintenance	Conversa	
Architect	Arquitecto	Frank Pennink
Type	Tipo	forest
Relief	Relevo	
Water in play	Lago	
Exp. to wind	Exposto ao vento	
Trees in play	Arvores	

Scorecard Cartão de resultados	Chp. Camp.	Mens Homens	Ladies Senhoras
Length Compriment	6040	5700	5241
Par	72	72	72
Slope system	—	—	—

Advised golfing ability / Nivel de jogo recomendado: 0 12 24 36

Hcp required Handicap exigido: 28 Men, 36 Ladies

Club house & amenities CLUB HOUSE E ANEXOS — 6/10

Pro shop	Pro-shop	
Driving range	Campo de prática	
Sheltered	coberto	4 mats
On grass	om relva	yes
Putting-green	putting-green	yes
Pitching-green	pitching-green	no

Hotel facilities INFRAESTRUCTURAS HOTELEIRAS — 6/10

HOTELS HOTELS

Costa da Caparica — Caparica 3 km
340 rooms, D 140 €
Tel (351) 21 - 291 8900, Fax (351) 21 - 291 0687

Praia do Sol — Caparica 3 km
53 rooms, D 55 €
Tel (351) 21 - 290 0012, Fax (351) 21 - 290 2541

RESTAURANTS RESTAURANTE

Centyonze — São João da Caparica 4 km
Tel (351) 21 - 290 3968

Maniés — Caparica 3 km
Tel (351) 21 - 290 3398

AROEIRA Aroeira II

14 | 6 | 6

O primeiro percurso, com assinatura Pennink já data de uma trintena de anos. Hei-lo completado por uns segundos 18 buracos cujo traçado foi confiado a Donald Steel. A longa tradição britânica continua portanto. Mas o pinhal dá-lhe um carácter meridional iniludível. Reencontramos com prazer a sobriedade de Steel num puro estilo "Inland". Ele juntou-lhe alguns buracos muito mais americanizados, nomeadamente pela inclusão de alguns obstáculos de água que dão um aspecto um pouco artificial ao desenho ou se se preferir uma certa falta de unidade visual. O local é bastante plano, sendo animado por leves movimentos de terras que definem bem os diferentes buracos. Os Par 4 são de dimensões razoáveis e s´o 18 ultrapassa os 400m. Os Par 5 permitem, praticamente que todos os jogadores "compridos" possam arriscar o ataque aos "Greens" em duas pancadas. Os outros jogadores, poderão sonhar em conseguir os mesmos resultados por outros meios, sendo aqui a precisão mais importante do que a distância. Trata-se de uma boa realização para todos os níveis de jogo, com o senão da presença de uma urbanização demasiado evidente ao longo dos "Fairways".

The first course was already thirty years old, so the time was right to add a second 18-hole layout, designed this time by Donald Steel. So the long British tradition continues, although the pine forest adds a definite southern Mediterranean touch. The sobriety of Donald Steel is always a pleasant feature with his pure inland style, but here he has added three much more American holes with the introduction of water hazards which give the layout a slightly artificial feel. Or, if you will, a certain lack of visual unity. The site is rather flat but marked by slight shifts in terrain which help to clearly define each hole. The par 4s are reasonable in length with only the 18th longer than 400 metres (440 yards), while the par 5s invite virtually all big-hitters to go for the green in two. The rest of us can card the same results in a different way, as accuracy here is often more important than length off the tee. A good course for golfers of all levels, the one regret being the very visible real estate programmes alongside the fairways.

Clube Golfe Aroeira — 2000

Herdade da Aroeira
P - 2815-207 CHARNECA DA CAPARICA

Office	Secretariado	(351) 21 - 297 9110
Pro shop	Pro-shop	(351) 21 - 297 9110
Fax	Fax	(351) 21 - 297 1238
Web	—	
Situation	Localização	Lisboa, 11 km

Setubal (pop. 89 106), 48 km

Annual closure	Fecho anual	no
Weekly closure	Fecho semanal	no

Fees main season Tarifas de época alta	18 holes	
	Week days Semana	We/Bank holidays Fim de sem./Feriad
Individual Individual	45 €	62 €
Couple Casal	90 €	124 €

Caddy	Caddy	37 € /on request
Electric Trolley	Trolley eléctrico	no
Buggy	Buggy	37 € /18 holes
Clubs	Tacos	22 € /18 holes

Credit cards Cartão de crédito VISA - DC - AMEX

Access Acesso : A2 Lisboa → Setubal, N377 → Caparica, Golf
Map 2 on page 1052 Mapa 2 Página 1052

Golf course PERCURSO — 14/20

Site	Sitio	
Maintenance	Conversa	
Architect	Arquitecto	Donald Steel
Type	Tipo	forest
Relief	Relevo	
Water in play	Lago	
Exp. to wind	Exposto ao vento	
Trees in play	Arvores	

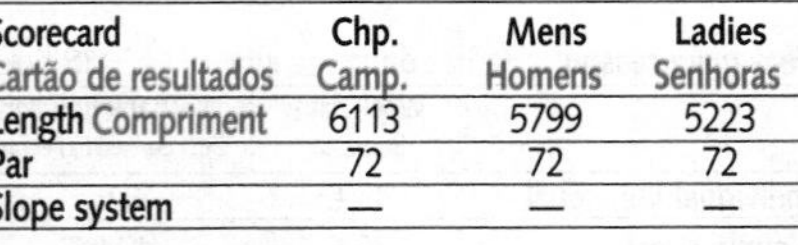

Scorecard Cartão de resultados	Chp. Camp.	Mens Homens	Ladies Senhoras
Length Compriment	6113	5799	5223
Par	72	72	72
Slope system	—	—	—

Advised golfing ability 0 12 24 36
Nivel de jogo recomendado
Hcp required Handicap exigido 36

Club house & amenities CLUB HOUSE E ANEXOS — 6/10

Pro shop	Pro-shop	
Driving range	Campo de prática	
Sheltered	coberto	4 mats
On grass	om relva	yes
Putting-green	putting-green	yes
Pitching-green	pitching-green	no

Hotel facilities INFRAESTRUCTURAS HOTELEIRAS — 6/10

HOTELS HOTELS

Costa da Caparica — Caparica 3 km
340 rooms, D 140 €
Tel (351) 21 - 291 8900, Fax (351) 21 - 291 0687

Praia do Sol — Caparica 4 km
53 rooms, D 55 €
Tel (351) 21 - 290 0012, Fax (351) 21 - 290 2541

RESTAURANTS RESTAURANTE

Centyonze — São João da Caparica 4 km
Tel (351) 21 - 290 3968

Maniés — Caparica 3 km
Tel (351) 21 - 290 3398

BELAS

14 | 8 | 5

Situada numa das grandes regiões golfisticas de Portugal, Belas está próxima de Lisboa, mas tanbêm do Palácio de Queluz, uma espêcie de pequeno Versailles, com laivos de «rococo», alternando os quartos íntimos com as salas de aparato, tudo rodeado de magníficos jardins... Não se encontrará em Belas um gosto tão ostentivo na decoração. A essência de um percurso de golf não reside verdadeiramente no luxo nem na simetria dos jardins â francesa. O Arquitecto moldou o seu traçado num terreno bastante aberto e muito acidentado onde temos o direito de preferir jogar com um "buggy" (pode dizer que é por causa do Sol). Devido a certos aspectos visuais e técnicos, pelo tipo de jogo que é necessário desenvolver, Belas pode lembrar Pevero ou Is Molas. Em todo o caso é pêlos seus desafíos que representa um bom futuro percurso de campeonato, ao ponto que os "handicaps" mais elevados terão sem duvida alguma dificuldade em retirar um enorme prazer em jogá-lo.

Located in one of Portugal's top golfing regions, Belas is close to Lisbon and also to the Castle of Queluz, a sort of smaller form of Versailles with a touch of rococo and alternating small chambers and huge state rooms, all surrounded by superb gardens. You won't find such an ostentatious taste for decoration at Belas, as the essence of a golf course is neither sheer luxury nor the symmetry of French style gardens. The architect has laid out this course over rather open, rolling terrain where you have every right to prefer playing with a buggy (say it is because of the sun). Through certain visual and technical aspects and through the type of game you need to produce, Belas is reminiscent of Pevero or Is Molas. In any case, given the challenges here, this is a future excellent championship course, even to the extent of it not always being too much fun for high-handicappers. The course unwinds smoothly with a neat balance of all forms of hazard.

Belas Clube de Campo — 1997

Casal de Carregueira
P - 2605-199 BELAS

Office	Secretariado	(351) 21 - 962 6640
Pro shop	Pro-shop	(351) 21 - 962 6640
Fax	Fax	(351) 21 - 962 6641
Web	www.belas-clube-de-campo.pt	
Situation	Localização	Lisboa, 18 km
Annual closure	Fecho anual	no
Weekly closure	Fecho semanal	no

Fees main season Tarifas de época alta		18 holes
	Week days Semana	**We/Bank holidays** Fim de sem./Feriad
Individual Individual	63 €	73 €
Couple Casal	126 €	146 €

Members of Portuguese Clubs: – 50%

Caddy	Caddy	no
Electric Trolley	Trolley eléctrico	no
Buggy	Buggy	35 € /18 holes
Clubs	Tacos	25 € /18 holes

Credit cards Cartão de crédito
VISA - Eurocard - DC - AMEX

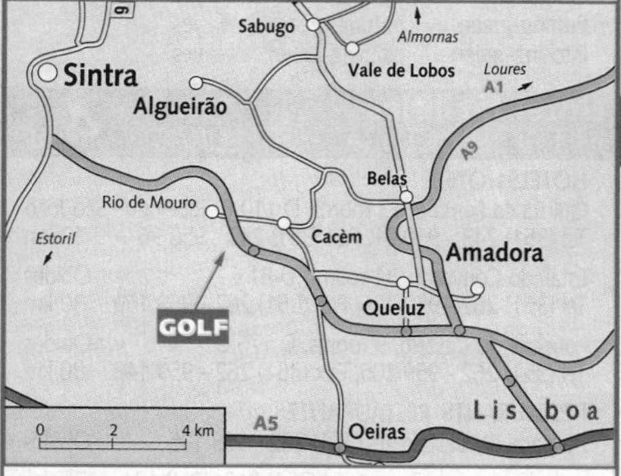

Access Acesso : Lisboa, N 117 → Sintra/Queluz and Belas. Follow signs to Golf.
Map 2 on page 1052 Mapa 2 Página 1052

Golf course PERCURSO — 14/20

Site	Sitio	
Maintenance	Conversa	
Architect	Arquitecto	Rocky Roquemore
Type	Tipo	open country, hilly
Relief	Relevo	
Water in play	Lago	
Exp. to wind	Exposto ao vento	
Trees in play	Arvores	

Scorecard Cartão de resultados	**Chp.** Camp.	**Mens** Homens	**Ladies** Senhoras
Length Compriment	6380	6065	4995
Par	72	72	72
Slope system	—	—	—

Advised golfing ability Nivel de jogo recomendado — 0 12 24 36
Hcp required Handicap exigido — 28 Men/36 Ladies

Club house & amenities CLUB HOUSE E ANEXOS — 8/10

Pro shop	Pro-shop	
Driving range	Campo de prática	
Sheltered	coberto	no
On grass	om relva	yes
Putting-green	putting-green	yes
Pitching-green	pitching-green	yes

Hotel facilities INFRAESTRUCTURAS HOTELEIRAS — 5/10

HOTELS HOTELS

Pousada D. Maria I. — Queluz 6 km
24 rooms, D 190 €
Tel (351) 21 - 435 6158, Fax (351) 21 - 435 6189

Palacio de Seteais — Sintra 12 km
29 rooms, D 249 €
Tel (351) 21 - 923 3200, Fax (351) 21 - 923 4277

RESTAURANTS RESTAURANTE

Cozinha Velha — Queluz 6 km
Tel (351) 21 - 435 6158

Tacho Real, Tel (351) 21 - 923 5277 — Sintra 12 km

Cantinho de São Pedro Tel (351) 21 - 923 0267 — Sintra

GOLDEN EAGLE

14 | 5 | 4

Este percurso recente, oferece uma boa ocasiào para ir ver Obidos, uma linda cidade tanto medieval como renascentista, dominada pôr um castelo onde está instalada a Pousada. Não é mesmo ao lado do golf, mas julgamos que um jogador não tem dificuldade de fazer meia hora de automóvel pois não? Com o dever cultural cumprido e com a consciência tranquila ela poderá consagrar-se ao percurso. De passagem lamentar-se-à que não se tenha dado ao campo um nome português, mesmo sendo os britânicos uma boa parte do contingente de turistas de golf em Portugal. Numa bonita paisagem campestre com uma ondulação agradável, Rocky Roquemore apresentou um bom "test" de golf, muito franco, com alguns greens muito bem protegidos, mas com as dificuldades sempre visíveis e sem golpes cegos apesar do relevo. O seu comprimento é muito respeitável mas as saídas da frente encurtam-no em 450 metros, o que encantará aqueles que regressam sempre enfadados com a sua procura de distância.

This course is a good opportunity to go and see Obidos, a very pretty medieval and renaissance town overlooked by a castle which houses the Pousada, a hotel and restaurant comparable to the Spanish Paradors. This is not quite alongside the golf course, but a half-hour ride for a golfer is nothing, surely. With a clear conscience after your shot of culture, it's time to think about golfing. Firstly, what a pity they chose an English rather than Portuguese name for the course, even though the Brits form a big proportion of the golf-trotting tourists coming to Portugal. In a pretty country landscape with pleasant rolling valleys, Rocky Roquemore has produced a good and very candid test of golf with some very well defended greens, visible difficulties and no blind shots, despite the topology. Yardage is very respectable, but the front tees shorten the course by 450 metres, a joy and relief for golfers who strive for distance but actually get very little.

Golden Eagle Golf Club — 1994

Quinta do Brinçal - Apartado 219
P - 2040-998 RIO MAIOR

Office	Secretariado	(351) 243 - 908 148
Pro shop	Pro-shop	(351) 243 - 908 148
Fax	Fax	(351) 243 - 908 149
Web	—	
Situation	Localização	

Lisboa (pop. 662 782), 59 km

Annual closure	Fecho anual	no
Weekly closure	Fecho semanal	no

Fees main season / Tarifas de época alta	Week days / Semana	We/Bank holidays / Fim de sem./Feriad
18 holes		
Individual Individual	37 €	47 €
Couple Casal	74 €	94 €

Juniors: 15 € / 20 € (Weekends)

Caddy	Caddy	12 €
Electric Trolley	Trolley eléctrico	no
Buggy	Buggy	27 € /18 holes
Clubs	Tacos	no

Credit cards Cartão de crédito
VISA - Eurocard - DC - AMEX

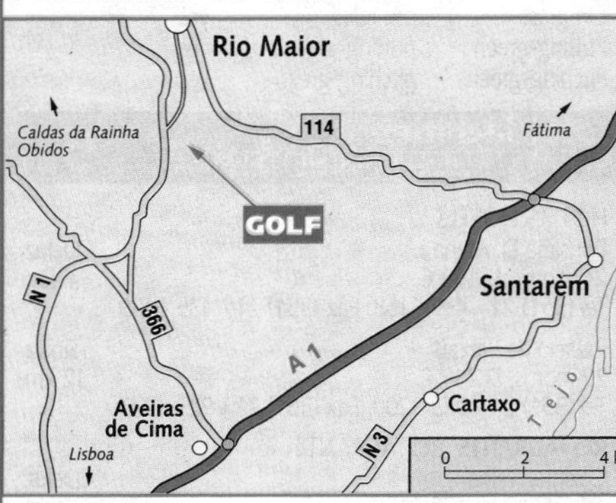

Access Acesso : Lisboa, A1. Km 46 in Avéiras, → Rio Maior. Quebradas, → Golf.

Map 2 on page 1052 Mapa 2 Página 1052

Golf course / PERCURSO — 14/20

Site	Sitio	
Maintenance	Conversa	
Architect	Arquitecto	Rocky Roquemore
Type	Tipo	inland
Relief	Relevo	
Water in play	Lago	
Exp. to wind	Exposto ao vento	
Trees in play	Arvores	

Scorecard / Cartão de resultados	Chp. / Camp.	Mens / Homens	Ladies / Senhoras
Length Compriment	6203	5744	5018
Par	72	72	72
Slope system	—	—	—

Advised golfing ability / Nivel de jogo recomendado: 0 12 24 36

Hcp required / Handicap exigido: 28 Men/36 Ladies

Club house & amenities / CLUB HOUSE E ANEXOS — 5/10

Pro shop	Pro-shop	
Driving range	Campo de prática	
Sheltered	coberto	no
On grass	om relva	yes
Putting-green	putting-green	yes
Pitching-green	pitching-green	yes

Hotel facilities / INFRAESTRUCTURAS HOTELEIRAS — 4/10

HOTELS HOTELS

Quinta da Ferraria, 13 rooms, D 110 € — Ribeira de São João
Tel (351) 243 - 950 01, Fax (351) 243 - 956 96 — 12 km

Estal. do Convento, 31 rooms, D 81 € — Obidos
Tel (351) 262 - 959 216, Fax (351) 262 - 959 159 — 30 km

Pousada do Castelo, 9 rooms, D 176 € — Obidos
Tel (351) 262 - 959 105, Fax (351) 262 - 959 148 — 30 km

RESTAURANTS RESTAURANTE

Pousada do Castelo Tel (351) 262 - 959 105 — Obidos

A Ilustre Casa de Ramiro Tel (351) 262 - 959 194 — Obidos

Cantinho da Serra — Alto da Serra
Tel (351) 243 - 995 166 — 6 km

MONTEBELO

13 | 5 | 5

Não é só o Algarve ou os arredores de Lisboa que contam no panorama golfistico de Portugal. Nem só o mar e as praias. Essa é a razão por que devemos dar um lugar especial a este percurso nas proximidades de Vizeu, no Portugal profundo, donde se avistam panoramas soberbos das montanhas vizinhas, especialmente o mais alto pico do país (a Serra da Estrela) com os seus cumes cobertos de neve no Inverno. Este percurso, bastante acidentado, onde no entanto se pode caminhar, pode considerar-se uma espécie de Crans-sur-Sierre português e em que os declives e as ladeiras constituem a principais dificuldades, ainda que esporadicamente apareçam obstáculos de água a interferir com o jogo. O "picante" são algumas pancadas "cegas". No entanto todos os "Greens" são bem visíveis mas recomenda-se que se jogue aqui algumas vezes para se poder estabelecer uma estratégia eficaz. Os autores do projecto, Mark Stilwell e Malcolm Kenyon não serão dos arquitectos mais conhecidos mas fizeram aqui um bom trabalho. É de apreciar aqui a tranquilidade local, onde – coisa rara em Portugal – nenhum núcleo de habitações vem perturbar o prazer do golf.

There is more to golf in Portugal than just the Algarve and the outskirts of Lisbon. Or the sea and beaches, for that matter. This is why we have reserved a special slot for this course close to Viseu in deepest Portugal, a site that offers some superb vistas over the surrounding mountains, particularly the Serra da Estrela, the country's highest peak which is snow-capped in winter. The course is rather hilly (but walkable) and is a sort of Portuguese version of Switzerland's Crans-sur-Sierre, where the main difficulties are slopes and steep topography. Water comes into play on only a few holes and a few blind shots also add a little spice to the round. Although all the greens are visible, you are best advised to play a few rounds here to fix some sort of game strategy. The course's designers, Mark Stilwell and Malcolm Kenyon, are hardly the world's most famous architects but they have done a great job here. The course is all the more enjoyable for the site's tranquillity: not a single condo in sight, something of a rarity in Portugal these days.

Golfe Montebelo — 2000

P - 3510-643 FARMINHAO-VISEU

Office	Secretariado	(351) 232 - 856 464
Pro shop	Pro-shop	(351) 232 - 856 464
Fax	Fax	(351) 232 - 856 401
Web	golfemontebelo	
Situation	Localização	
Viseu (pop. 23 672), 10 km		
Annual closure	Fecho anual	no
Weekly closure	Fecho semanal	no

Fees main season Tarifas de época alta	Week days Semana	We/Bank holidays Fim de sem./Feriad
		18 holes
Individual Individual	25 €	40 €
Couple Casal	50 €	80 €
Juniors: – 50%		

Caddy	Caddy	15 € /on request
Electric Trolley	Trolley eléctrico	no
Buggy	Buggy	30 € /18 holes
Clubs	Tacos	12 € /18 holes

Credit cards Cartão de crédito
VISA - Eurocard - MasterCard - DC - AMEX

Aveiro
IP5
14
13
Viseu
Torredeita
Boa Aldeia
N337-1
Farminhão
N337
GOLF
IP3
S. Miguel do Outeiro
Coimbra
Parada de Gonta
0 2 4 km

Access Acesso : Porto A1 South → Aveiro. Exit 16, then IP 5 to Viseu

Map 1 on page 1050 Mapa 1 Página 1050

Golf course — PERCURSO — 13/20

Site	Sitio	
Maintenance	Conversa	
Architect	Arquitecto	Mark Stilwell Malcolm Kenyon
Type	Tipo	inland, hilly
Relief	Relevo	
Water in play	Lago	
Exp. to wind	Exposto ao vento	
Trees in play	Arvores	

Scorecard Cartão de resultados	Chp. Camp.	Mens Homens	Ladies Senhoras
Length Compriment	6317	5718	5134
Par	72	72	72
Slope system	—	—	—

Advised golfing ability Nivel de jogo recomendado — 0 12 24 36

Hcp required Handicap exigido no

Club house & amenities — CLUB HOUSE E ANEXOS — 5/10

Pro shop	Pro-shop	
Driving range	Campo de prática	
Sheltered	coberto	yes
On grass	om relva	yes
Putting-green	putting-green	yes
Pitching-green	pitching-green	yes

Hotel facilities — INFRAESTRUCTURAS HOTELEIRAS — 5/10

HOTELS HOTELS

Hotel Montebelo, 116 rooms, D 90 € — Viseu
Tel (351) 232 - 420 000, Fax (351) 232 - 415 400 — 12 km

Casa de Terreiro, 5 rooms, D 65 € — S. Miguel Outeiro
Tel (351) 232 - 951 127, Fax (351) 232 - 951 127 — 3 km

Hotel Grao Vasco, 111 rooms, D 80 € — Viseu
Tel (351) 232 - 423 511, Fax (351) 232 - 426 444 — 12 km

RESTAURANTS RESTAURANTE

O Cortigo, Tel (351) 232 - 423 853 — Viseu 12 km

Muralha da Se, Tel (351) 232 - 437 777 — Viseu 12 km

Os Antonios, Tel (351) 232 - 949 515 — Nelas 15 km

OITAVOS

15 | 7 | 7

Trata-se de um novo percurso, na costa, junto de Cascais na antiga Quinta da Marinha, vizinho de outro já existente, propriedade de outra empresa. Também aqui se optou por arquitectos americanos. Depois de haver na zona um Trent Jones é Arthur Hills que foi encarregue do desenho deste percurso. Deve tratar-se de uma das suas primeiras realizações, senão a primeira, na Europa. A localização é muito interessante, muito próxima do Mar mas com belas vistas da Serra. Está bastante exposto ao vento o que vai complicar a tarefa dos jogadores. Porem, havendo bastante paralelismo no desenho, todo o vento contra passa a ser a favor sem que haja muita subtilidade. O terreno arenoso, as ondulações próprias do terreno bem como a sobriedade do desenho de Hills conferem ao local um carácter menos americano do que se poderia imaginar. Só algumas depressões fazem figura de obstáculos de água. Os jogadores pouco experimentados ou mesmo médios terão certamente dificuldade em fazerem aqui bons resultados, ou mesmo em ultrapassar as subtilezas do desenho. Aconselha-se que joguem preferencialmente em "Match Play" o que será menos mortal para os seus "Ego".

This new course located at Quinta da Marinha is a neighbour to the other well-known course that belongs to another company. Here too, they went for an American architect. After Robert Trent Jones, Arthur Hills was assigned with the layout, and this must be one of his first courses in Europe, if not the first. It is an interesting site, very close to the sea but with some pleasant views of the mountains behind. It is also rather exposed to the wind, but as the holes often run up and down, any headwind will always become a tailwind with very few subtle changes of direction. The sandy soil, measured slopes and general sobriety of Hills' design give the course a slightly less American character than one might have imagined, with only a few ditches serving as water hazards. Inexperienced or average players will almost certainly find this tough-going, so match-play should be the order of the day to avoid too many bruised egos.

Oitavos Golfe — 2001

Casa da Quinta, 25 - Qta da Marinha
P - 2750-15 CASCAIS

Office	Secretariado	(351) 21 - 486 0000
Pro shop	Pro-shop	(351) 21 - 486 0000
Fax	Fax	(351) 21 - 486 9233
Web	www.quinta-da-marinha.pt	
Situation	Localização	

Lisboa (pop. 662 782), 26 km - Cascais (pop. 29 882), 6 km

Annual closure	Fecho anual	no
Weekly closure	Fecho semanal	no

Fees main season Tarifas de época alta	18 holes	
	Week days Semana	**We/Bank holidays** Fim de sem./Feriad
Individual Individual	90 €	150 €
Couple Casal	180 €	300 €

Caddy	Caddy	no
Electric Trolley	Trolley eléctrico	10 € /18 holes
Buggy	Buggy	25 € /18 holes
Clubs	Tacos	20 € /18 holes

Credit cards Cartão de crédito VISA - AMEX

Access Acesso : Lisboa A5 → Cascais, N 247 → Praia do Guincho, Golf just after Quinta da Marinha.
Map 2 on page 1052 Mapa 2 Página 1052

Golf course — PERCURSO — 15/20

Site	Sitio	
Maintenance	Conversa	
Architect	Arquitecto	Arthur Hills
Type	Tipo	seaside course, open country
Relief	Relevo	
Water in play	Lago	
Exp. to wind	Exposto ao vento	
Trees in play	Arvores	

Scorecard Cartão de resultados	**Chp.** Camp.	**Mens** Homens	**Ladies** Senhoras
Length Compriment	6379	5947	4573
Par	71	71	71
Slope system	—	—	—

Advised golfing ability 0 12 24 36
Nivel de jogo recomendado
Hcp required Handicap exigido 36

Club house & amenities — CLUB HOUSE E ANEXOS — 7/10

Pro shop	Pro-shop	
Driving range	Campo de prática	
Sheltered	coberto	no
On grass	om relva	yes
Putting-green	putting-green	yes
Pitching-green	pitching-green	yes

Hotel facilities — INFRAESTRUCTURAS HOTELEIRAS — 7/10

HOTELS HOTELS

Fortaleza do Guincho — Praia do Guincho 3 km
29 rooms, D 254 €
Tel (351) 21 - 487 0491, Fax (351) 21 - 487 0431

Casa da Pergola, 10 rooms, D 100 € — Cascais 4 km
Tel (351) 21 - 482 0040, Fax (351) 21 - 483 4791

Estalagem Senhora da Guia, 39 rooms, D 120 € — Cascais 4 km
Tel (351) 01 - 487 92 39, Fax (351) 01 - 486 92 27

RESTAURANTS RESTAURANTE

Casa Velha, Tel (351) 21 - 483 2586 — Cascais 4 km

Visconde da Luz, Tel (351) 21 - 484 7410 — Cascais 4 km

PALMARES

13 | 7 | 5

Como muitos dos percursos portugueses foi desenhado por Frank Pennink a partir de dois espaços diferentes: cinco buracos sáo à beira mar, com uma arquitectura que faz lembrar um "links", os outros desenvolvem-se entre pinheiros, muito mais acidentados e com magníficas vistas sobre o Atlântico. Os buracos de borda de água constituem o encanto e o interesse principal deste percurso que para alem disso tem um desenho muito simples. Alguns "drives" podem causar problemas mas os golfistas de todos os níveis não encontrarão muitas dificuldades para além das criadas pelo seu proprio jogo. Os "greens" são muito simples, bastante pequenos e pouco defendidos. Nesta bela paisagem seria de mau gosto estragar o prazer! Se este percurso não dá para maravilhar, não deixa de ser muito agradável para se passar uma tarde em família ou com um grupo de amigos aínda que de níveis diferentes.

Like many courses in Portugal, Palmares was designed by Frank Pennink using two different sorts of space: five holes run along the seashore in true links style, the others are laid out amidst a much hillier pine forest with some magnificent views over the Atlantic. The seaboard holes give the course its basic charm and appeal, as otherwise the design is fairly simple. Some tee-shots can cause problems, but apart from those arising from your own game, there are no real difficulties here, whatever your playing ability. The greens are very simple, smallish and wide open. In such pretty countryside, it would have been in very poor taste to make life too difficult. This course might not be over-exciting, but it is great fun to play with the family or friends, whatever their ability.

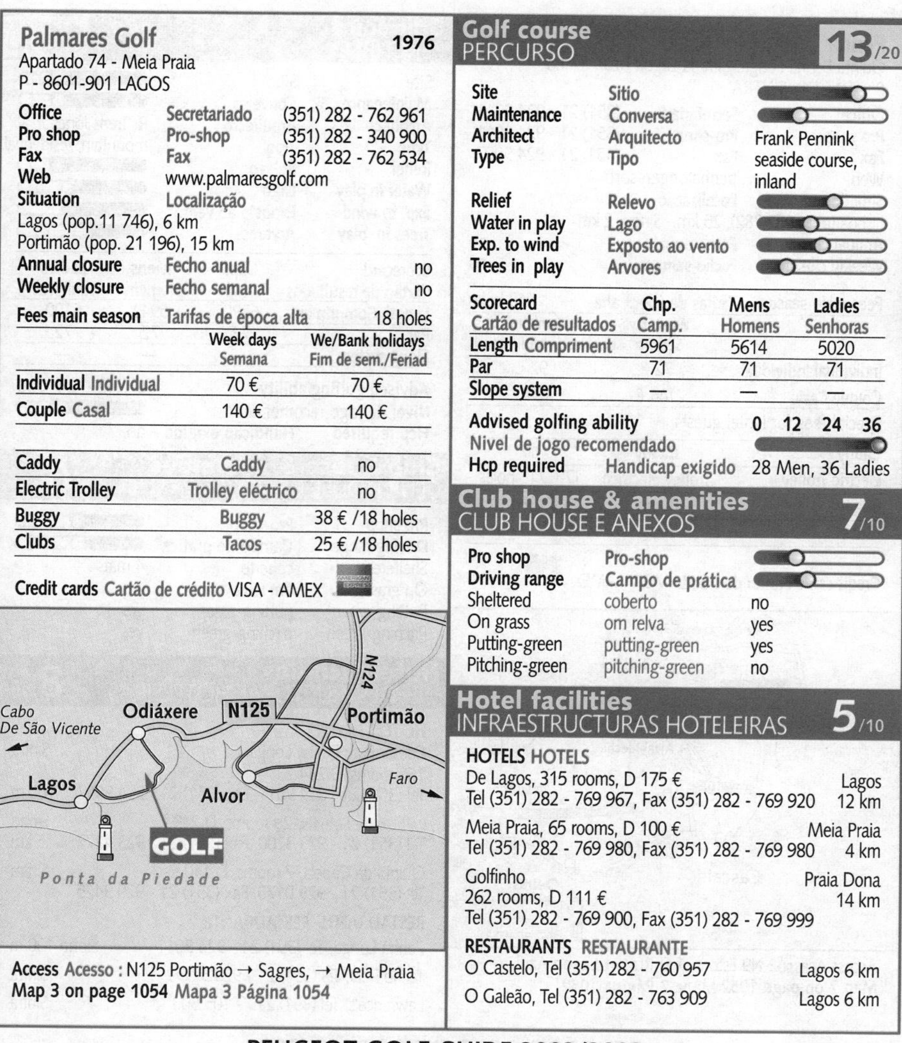

Palmares Golf — **1976**
Apartado 74 - Meia Praia
P - 8601-901 LAGOS

Office	Secretariado	(351) 282 - 762 961
Pro shop	Pro-shop	(351) 282 - 340 900
Fax	Fax	(351) 282 - 762 534
Web	www.palmaresgolf.com	
Situation	Localização	

Lagos (pop.11 746), 6 km
Portimão (pop. 21 196), 15 km

Annual closure	Fecho anual	no
Weekly closure	Fecho semanal	no

Fees main season Tarifas de época alta		18 holes
	Week days Semana	**We/Bank holidays** Fim de sem./Feriad
Individual Individual	70 €	70 €
Couple Casal	140 €	140 €

Caddy	Caddy	no
Electric Trolley	Trolley eléctrico	no
Buggy	Buggy	38 € /18 holes
Clubs	Tacos	25 € /18 holes

Credit cards Cartão de crédito VISA - AMEX

Access Acesso : N125 Portimão → Sagres, → Meia Praia
Map 3 on page 1054 Mapa 3 Página 1054

Golf course — PERCURSO — 13/20

Site	Sitio	
Maintenance	Conversa	
Architect	Arquitecto	Frank Pennink
Type	Tipo	seaside course, inland
Relief	Relevo	
Water in play	Lago	
Exp. to wind	Exposto ao vento	
Trees in play	Arvores	

Scorecard Cartão de resultados	**Chp.** Camp.	**Mens** Homens	**Ladies** Senhoras
Length Compriment	5961	5614	5020
Par	71	71	71
Slope system	—	—	—

Advised golfing ability Nivel de jogo recomendado — 0 12 24 36
Hcp required Handicap exigido — 28 Men, 36 Ladies

Club house & amenities — CLUB HOUSE E ANEXOS — 7/10

Pro shop	Pro-shop	
Driving range	Campo de prática	
Sheltered	coberto	no
On grass	om relva	yes
Putting-green	putting-green	yes
Pitching-green	pitching-green	no

Hotel facilities — INFRAESTRUCTURAS HOTELEIRAS — 5/10

HOTELS HOTELS

De Lagos, 315 rooms, D 175 € — Lagos 12 km
Tel (351) 282 - 769 967, Fax (351) 282 - 769 920

Meia Praia, 65 rooms, D 100 € — Meia Praia 4 km
Tel (351) 282 - 769 980, Fax (351) 282 - 769 980

Golfinho — Praia Dona 14 km
262 rooms, D 111 €
Tel (351) 282 - 769 900, Fax (351) 282 - 769 999

RESTAURANTS RESTAURANTE

O Castelo, Tel (351) 282 - 760 957 — Lagos 6 km
O Galeão, Tel (351) 282 - 763 909 — Lagos 6 km

PENHA LONGA

16 | 6 | 8

Localizado num belo local histórico, semeado de vestigios do passado, é um dos bons exitos dos ultimos anos. O desenho de Robert Trent Jones Junior é muito imaginativo e seduzirá primeiramente os bons jogadores que deverão saber ultrapassar com habilidade os numerosos obstáculos que se lhes deparam, para alem do terreno acidentado que oferece, porem, belas vistas do mar e da serra. O comprimento do percurso e a sua variedade exigem um jogo muito complete desde as saídas até aos "greens" de boa dimensao e bem modelados. Os jogadores menos habilitados podera escolher as saidas mais avançadas para retirar ao jogo um máximo de prazer. E certo que as dificuldades subsistem, mas se não derem demasiada importância ao "score" terão muitas ocasiões de exercer a sua destrêsa, ou mesmo de progredir sobre um percurso exigente depois de terem feito a mão nalgum percurso, mais facil, da região. A manutenção é geralmente muito bom.

In a beautiful historical site, dotted with vestiges from the past, this is one of the best courses in recent years. The very imaginative design of Robert Trent Jones Jnr. will firstly appeal to very good players, who will need all their skills to negotiate the numerous hazards and the steep hills, which offer some beautiful views over the sea and mountain. The length and variety of the course demand a good, all-round game from tee to green, most of the latter being large and well contoured. Lesser players will play from the front tees to really enjoy themselves. The difficulties are still there, of course, but if they don't pay too much attention to dropped strokes, average golfers will have many opportunities to exercise their skills and even make progress on a demanding course. This is a good test after getting warmed up on some of the easier courses in the region. Upkeep is generally good.

Penha Longa Golf Club 1994

Quinta Penha Longa, Estrada Lagoa Azul - Linho
P - 2714-511 SINTRA

Office	Secretariado	(351) 21 - 924 9011
Pro shop	Pro-shop	(351) 21 - 924 9011
Fax	Fax	(351) 21 - 924 9007
Web	penhalongaresort	
Situation	Localização	

Lisboa (pop. 662 782), 25 km - Sintra, 2 km

Annual closure	Fecho anual	no
Weekly closure	Fecho semanal	no

Fees main season Tarifas de época alta	Week days Semana	We/Bank holidays Fim de sem./Feriad
		18 holes
Individual Individual	72 €	92 €
Couple Casal	144 €	184 €

Special fees for Hotel guests

Caddy	Caddy	no
Electric Trolley	Trolley eléctrico	17 € /18 holes
Buggy	Buggy	35 € /18 holes
Clubs	Tacos	18 € /18 holes

Credit cards Cartão de crédito VISA - AMEX

Access Acesso : N9 Estoril → Sintra, → Lagon Azul
Map 2 on page 1052 Mapa 2 Página 1052

Golf course PERCURSO 16/20

Site	Sitio	
Maintenance	Conversa	
Architect	Arquitecto	R. Trent Jones Jr
Type	Tipo	mountain, residential
Relief	Relevo	
Water in play	Lago	
Exp. to wind	Exposto ao vento	
Trees in play	Arvores	

Scorecard Cartão de resultados	**Chp.** Camp.	**Mens** Homens	**Ladies** Senhoras
Length Compriment	6290	5942	5100
Par	72	72	72
Slope system	—	—	—

Advised golfing ability 0 12 24 36
Nivel de jogo recomendado
Hcp required Handicap exigido no

Club house & amenities CLUB HOUSE E ANEXOS 6/10

Pro shop	Pro-shop	
Driving range	Campo de prática	
Sheltered	coberto	4 mats
On grass	om relva	yes
Putting-green	putting-green	yes
Pitching-green	pitching-green	yes

Hotel facilities INFRAESTRUCTURAS HOTELEIRAS 8/10

HOTELS HOTELS

Caesar Park Penha Longa, 160 rooms, D 244 € — Sintra
Tel (351) 21 - 924 9011, Fax (351) 21 - 924 9007 — 100 m

Palacio de Seteais, 29 rooms, D 249 € — Sintra
Tel (351) 21 - 923 3200, Fax (351) 21 - 923 4277 — 5 km

Quinta da Capela, 7 rooms, D 140 € — Sintra
Tel (351) 21 - 929 0170, Fax (351) 21 - 929 3425

RESTAURANTS RESTAURANTE

Penha Longa, Tel (351) 21 - 924 9011 — Sintra 100 m
Tacho Real, Tel (351) 21 - 923 5277 — Sintra
Lawrence's, Tel (351) 219 - 105 500 — Sintra

PENINA

14	7	8

Tendo estado fechado para obras durante alguns meses, o primeiro Campo de Golfe do Algarve em termos de antiguade, sofreu alguns melhoramentos mas sem grandes moficações. Continua um percurso longo e difícil dos "Tees" de campeonato, tornando-se mais acessivel dos "Tees" normais. Bastante plano e tendo algumas árvores a dificultar as pancadas não chegam no entanto a ser perigosas. O seu traçado salienta-se por um bom número de "bunkers" com bom desenho mas sem nada de especial a assinalar. A sua colocação sugere um estilo britânico que se torna evidente se nos lembrarmos que foi desenhado por Henry Cotton. A Penina pode por vezes lembrar "Carnoustie" sem no entanto se poder considerar um verdadeiro "links" o que aumentaria ainda a sua dificuldade. Se conseguirmos bater longe e direito, a bola estará sempre em boa posição. Os greens, bastante grandes e razoavelmente planos não causam problemas - embora haja necessidade de os atingir... De salientar os 4 par 5 da 2a volta. A sua situação e o equipamento hoteleiro da Penina fazem dele um destino de sucesso.

The Algarve's very first course has in recent years been given a fresh look, but with no notable changes. It is still long and tough from the back tees, but mellows the further forward you go. Very flat and covered with a variety of trees which, although in play, are none too dangerous, this layout is marked by the huge number of bunkers, correctly designed but with no real personality. Their positioning testifies to an obvious British style, knowing that the course was in fact designed by Henry Cotton. Besides, Penina is a little reminiscent of Carnoustie in some ways, but without the links features, which would only increase the difficulty here. If you can drive long and straight, you will always find your ball in a good position. The greens, which are pretty large and generally flat, pose no real problem, the trouble is reaching them. A noticeable feature are the four par 5s on the back nine. An excellent destination.

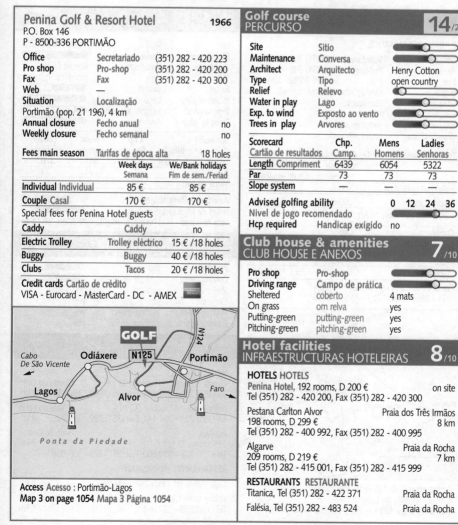

Penina Golf & Resort Hotel — 1966

P.O. Box 146
P - 8500-336 PORTIMÃO

Office	Secretariado	(351) 282 - 420 223
Pro shop	Pro-shop	(351) 282 - 420 200
Fax	Fax	(351) 282 - 420 300
Web	—	
Situation	Localização	
Portimão (pop. 21 196), 4 km		
Annual closure	Fecho anual	no
Weekly closure	Fecho semanal	no

Fees main season Tarifas de época alta		18 holes
	Week days Semana	**We/Bank holidays** Fim de sem./Feriad
Individual Individual	85 €	85 €
Couple Casal	170 €	170 €

Special fees for Penina Hotel guests

Caddy	Caddy	no
Electric Trolley	Trolley eléctrico	15 € /18 holes
Buggy	Buggy	40 € /18 holes
Clubs	Tacos	20 € /18 holes

Credit cards Cartão de crédito
VISA - Eurocard - MasterCard - DC - AMEX

Access Acesso : Portimão-Lagos
Map 3 on page 1054 Mapa 3 Página 1054

Golf course — PERCURSO — 14/20

Site	Sitio	
Maintenance	Conversa	
Architect	Arquitecto	Henry Cotton
Type	Tipo	open country
Relief	Relevo	
Water in play	Lago	
Exp. to wind	Exposto ao vento	
Trees in play	Arvores	

Scorecard Cartão de resultados	**Chp.** Camp.	**Mens** Homens	**Ladies** Senhoras
Length Compriment	6439	6054	5322
Par	73	73	73
Slope system	—	—	—

Advised golfing ability — 0 12 24 36
Nivel de jogo recomendado

Hcp required Handicap exigido no

Club house & amenities — CLUB HOUSE E ANEXOS — 7/10

Pro shop	Pro-shop	
Driving range	Campo de prática	
Sheltered	coberto	4 mats
On grass	om relva	yes
Putting-green	putting-green	yes
Pitching-green	pitching-green	yes

Hotel facilities — INFRAESTRUCTURAS HOTELEIRAS — 8/10

HOTELS HOTELS

Penina Hotel, 192 rooms, D 200 € — on site
Tel (351) 282 - 420 200, Fax (351) 282 - 420 300

Pestana Carlton Alvor — Praia dos Três Irmãos
198 rooms, D 299 € — 8 km
Tel (351) 282 - 400 992, Fax (351) 282 - 400 995

Algarve — Praia da Rocha
209 rooms, D 219 € — 7 km
Tel (351) 282 - 415 001, Fax (351) 282 - 415 999

RESTAURANTS RESTAURANTE

Titanica, Tel (351) 282 - 422 371 — Praia da Rocha

Falésia, Tel (351) 282 - 483 524 — Praia da Rocha

PINHEIROS ALTOS

14 | 7 | 7

Os dois 9 buracos são muito diferentes. Os primeiros, muito acidentados e cansativos, desenvolvem-se entre pinheiros, sempre em jogo. Os segundos são planos, com àgua, practicamente em todos os buracos. Esta falta de unidade pode explicar-se pela intervenção de McEvoy a Howard Swan sobre o desenho original de Ronald Fream. O ritmo de jogo pode ser prejudicado para os jogadores que se deixem perturbar pelo ambiente circundante. A qualidade e o desenho dos "greens", alguns dificeis de lêr, é um dos pontos positivos, para mais por estarem bem defendidos, o que torna os "aproches" muito interessantes. Não e um percurso para se jogar todos os dias, mas merece algumas vistas muito atentas, desde que se jogue das saídas de trás e se esteja em boa forma física. Muito próximo do parque natural da Ria Formosa este golf dispõe de muito boas instalações de treino, nomeadamente para o jogo curto.

The two 9-hole courses are very different. The front nine, hilly and tiring, are laid out in a pine forest, where trees come very much into play. The back nine are flatter, with water on virtually every hole. This lack of unity might be explained by the work made by McEvoy and Howard Swan on Ronald Fream's original design, and it might upset players who are over-attentive to surroundings. Otherwise, the excellence and design of the greens, some of which are tricky to read, are very positive points, all the more so in that their defence makes for some very interesting approach shots. This is not a course you would play every day, but it does deserve some careful visiting, providing you and your game are fit enough for the back-tees. Close to the Ria Formosa Nature Park, the course boasts excellent practice facilities, particularly for the short game.

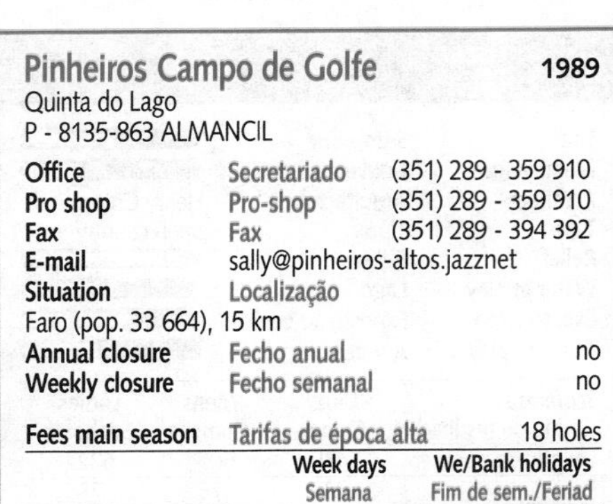

Pinheiros Campo de Golfe **1989**
Quinta do Lago
P - 8135-863 ALMANCIL

Office	Secretariado	(351) 289 - 359 910
Pro shop	Pro-shop	(351) 289 - 359 910
Fax	Fax	(351) 289 - 394 392
E-mail	sally@pinheiros-altos.jazznet	
Situation	Localização	
Faro (pop. 33 664), 15 km		
Annual closure	Fecho anual	no
Weekly closure	Fecho semanal	no

Fees main season Tarifas de época alta	18 holes	
	Week days Semana	**We/Bank holidays** Fim de sem./Feriad
Individual Individual	100 €	100 €
Couple Casal	200 €	200 €

– 20% for members of Algarve golf clubs.

Caddy	Caddy	no
Electric Trolley	Trolley eléctrico	no
Buggy	Buggy	no
Clubs	Tacos	25 € /18 holes

Credit cards Cartão de crédito
VISA - MasterCard - DC - AMEX

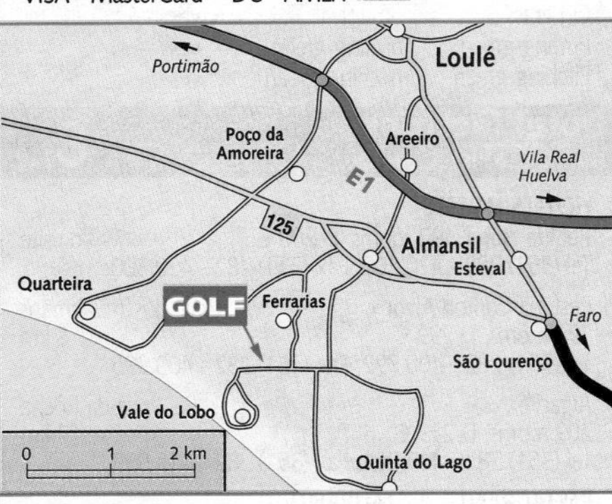

Access Acesso : N 125 Faro → Portimão.
Almansil → Vale do Lobo
Map 3 on page 1054 Mapa 3 Página 1054

Golf course PERCURSO — 14/20

Site	Sitio	
Maintenance	Conversa	
Architect	Arquitecto	Ronald Fream
Type	Tipo	forest, open country
Relief	Relevo	
Water in play	Lago	
Exp. to wind	Exposto ao vento	
Trees in play	Arvores	

Scorecard Cartão de resultados	**Chp.** Camp.	**Mens** Homens	**Ladies** Senhoras
Length Compriment	6057	5614	4762
Par	71	71	71
Slope system	—	—	—

Advised golfing ability 0 12 24 36
Nivel de jogo recomendado

Hcp required Handicap exigido 28 Men, 36 Ladies

Club house & amenities CLUB HOUSE E ANEXOS — 7/10

Pro shop	Pro-shop	
Driving range	Campo de prática	
Sheltered	coberto	no
On grass	om relva	yes
Putting-green	putting-green	yes
Pitching-green	pitching-green	yes

Hotel facilities INFRAESTRUCTURAS HOTELEIRAS — 7/10

HOTELS HOTELS

Quinta do Lago, 141 rooms, D 175 € — Quinta do Lago
Tel (351) 289 - 396 666, Fax (351) 289 - 396 393 — 3 km

Dona Filipa, 147 rooms, D 224 € — Vale do Lobo
Tel (351) 289 - 394 141, Fax (351) 289 - 394 288 — 8 km

Ria Park — Vale do Garrão
175 rooms, D 195 € — 3 km
Tel (351) 289 - 359 800, Fax (351) 289 - 359 888

RESTAURANTS RESTAURANTE

Casa Velha, Tel (351) 289 - 394 983 — 2 km

Bobby Jones Club — Vilar do Golf
Tel (351) 289 - 394 695 — 1 km

PRAIA D'EL REY

17 | 6 | 5

Durante muito tempo braço direito de Robert Trent Jones, Cabell Robinson impos-se como um arquitecto imaginativo e muito conhecedor a todos os niveis do golf. Praia D'El Rey é disso a demonstração. Com uma bela localização à beira mar rodeado de pinheiros, por vezes espectaculares, este percurso tem muitos aspectos em que se assemelha a um Links tradicional, obrigando a bem trabalhar a bola. Quando o vento sopra, porem raramente tão violentamente como na Escócia ou Irlanda, isto acrescenta um condimento especial a u prato de grande qualidade. A despeito da sua juventude, Praia d'El Rey promete vir a ser um dos grandes percursos da península Ibérica. Tem ainda a vantagem de permitir tanto partidas de golf de alto nível como jornadas agradáveis em família.

For many years Robert Trent Jones' right-hand man, Cabell Robinson has become established as an imaginative designer and excellent connoisseur of golf played at all levels. Praia d'El Rey is further demonstration of his expertise. Set on a very beautiful and often spectacular sea-side site enhanced with pine-trees on some holes, the course has many facets of a traditional links with the need to work the ball all ways. And while the wind is kinder than in Scotland or Ireland, it can often add a little spice to what is already a savoury dish. Although still in infancy, Praia d'El Rey promises to emerge as one of the great courses on the Iberian peninsula, with the extra pleasure of allowing rounds of golf for highly skilled players and enjoyable days with the family.

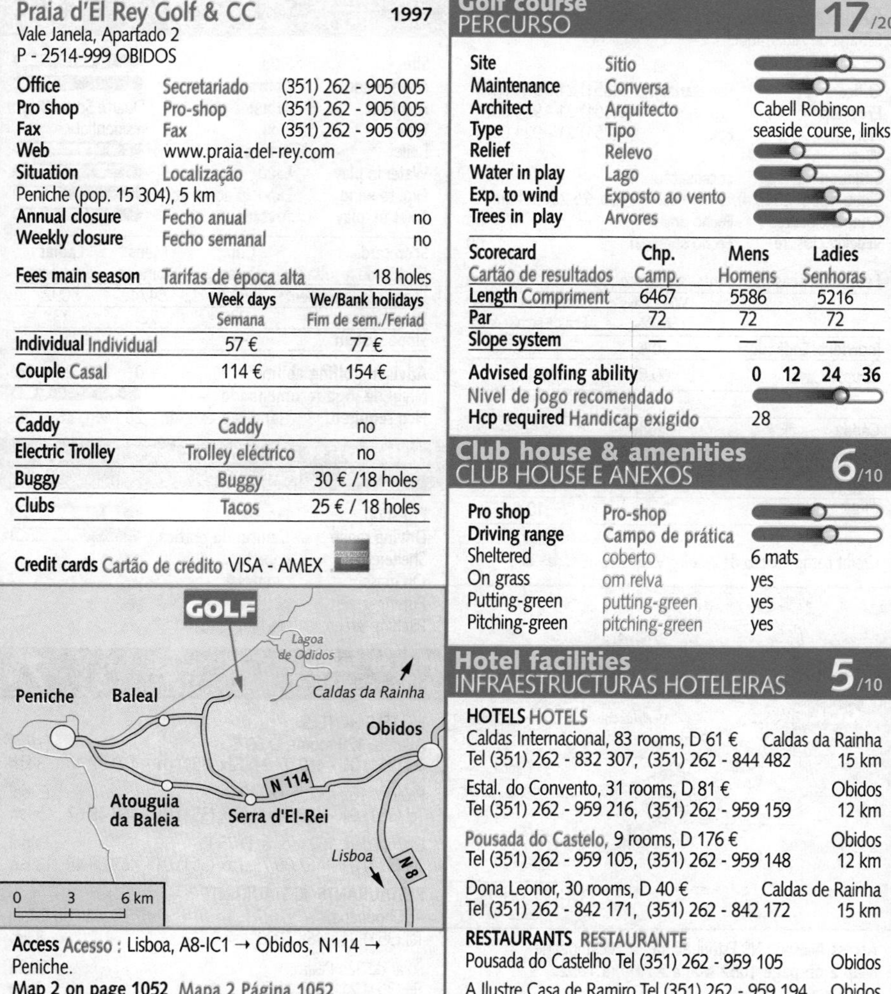

Praia d'El Rey Golf & CC 1997
Vale Janela, Apartado 2
P - 2514-999 OBIDOS

Office	Secretariado	(351) 262 - 905 005
Pro shop	Pro-shop	(351) 262 - 905 005
Fax	Fax	(351) 262 - 905 009
Web	www.praia-del-rey.com	
Situation	Localização	
Peniche (pop. 15 304), 5 km		
Annual closure	Fecho anual	no
Weekly closure	Fecho semanal	no

Fees main season Tarifas de época alta	Week days Semana	18 holes We/Bank holidays Fim de sem./Feriad
Individual Individual	57 €	77 €
Couple Casal	114 €	154 €

Caddy	Caddy	no
Electric Trolley	Trolley eléctrico	no
Buggy	Buggy	30 € /18 holes
Clubs	Tacos	25 € / 18 holes

Credit cards Cartão de crédito VISA - AMEX

Access Acesso : Lisboa, A8-IC1 → Obidos, N114 → Peniche.
Map 2 on page 1052 Mapa 2 Página 1052

Golf course / PERCURSO — 17/20

Site	Sitio	
Maintenance	Conversa	
Architect	Arquitecto	Cabell Robinson
Type	Tipo	seaside course, links
Relief	Relevo	
Water in play	Lago	
Exp. to wind	Exposto ao vento	
Trees in play	Arvores	

Scorecard Cartão de resultados	Chp. Camp.	Mens Homens	Ladies Senhoras
Length Compriment	6467	5586	5216
Par	72	72	72
Slope system	—	—	—

Advised golfing ability Nivel de jogo recomendado: 0 12 24 36
Hcp required Handicap exigido: 28

Club house & amenities / CLUB HOUSE E ANEXOS — 6/10

Pro shop	Pro-shop	
Driving range	Campo de prática	
Sheltered	coberto	6 mats
On grass	om relva	yes
Putting-green	putting-green	yes
Pitching-green	pitching-green	yes

Hotel facilities / INFRAESTRUCTURAS HOTELEIRAS — 5/10

HOTELS HOTELS

Caldas Internacional, 83 rooms, D 61 € — Caldas da Rainha
Tel (351) 262 - 832 307, (351) 262 - 844 482 — 15 km

Estal. do Convento, 31 rooms, D 81 € — Obidos
Tel (351) 262 - 959 216, (351) 262 - 959 159 — 12 km

Pousada do Castelo, 9 rooms, D 176 € — Obidos
Tel (351) 262 - 959 105, (351) 262 - 959 148 — 12 km

Dona Leonor, 30 rooms, D 40 € — Caldas de Rainha
Tel (351) 262 - 842 171, (351) 262 - 842 172 — 15 km

RESTAURANTS RESTAURANTE

Pousada do Castelho Tel (351) 262 - 959 105 — Obidos
A Ilustre Casa de Ramiro Tel (351) 262 - 959 194 — Obidos

QUINTA DA BELOURA

14 | 8 | 7

Desenhado por Duarte Sotto Mayor, secundo a concepção de Rocky Roquemore é o mais recente percurso desta região. O envolvimento imobiliário deverá vir a ser gradualmente escondido pela plantação de pinheiros, carvalhos, palmeiras etc, o que permitirá de melhor defenir os "fairways". Os obstáculos de agua e os "bunkers" estão pouco em jogo, à excepção de alguns lagos perigosos, principalmente nos últimos buracos. Porem, todas as dificuldades estão bem à vista, nada é aqui uma fonte de surpresas, nem mesmo os "greens" bem desenhados e fáceis de lêr. Percebe-se que não hoyuve aqui à intenção de fazer um percurso de campeonato nem para os jogadores muito compridos nem para os mestres do jogo curto que não vão encontrar motivos para saciar as suas emoções. Tem de jogar-se bastante direito mas os jogadores de nível médio ou mesmo os principiantes conseguirão fazer.

This is the region's newest course, designed by Duarte Sottomayor and Rocky Roquemore. The surrounding property development should gradually be blotted out by a plantation programme of new pine, oak and/or palm trees, also designed to outline the fairways. The sand and water hazards are seldom in play, with the exception of a few dangerous lakes, especially over the last holes. But all the difficulties here are clear to see with no surprises, not even on the greens, which are rather well designed and easy to read. Visibly, no-one was aiming to build a course for tournaments, big-hitters or short-game wizards, who will probably find this lay-out a little low on excitement. The key is to play straight, and then high-handicappers and even beginners can card an honourable score.

Quinta da Beloura Golf Club — 1994

Estrada de Albarraque
P - 2710 SINTRA

Office	Secretariado	(351) 21 - 924 0021
Pro shop	Pro-shop	(351) 21 - 924 0021
Fax	Fax	(351) 21 - 924 0061
Web	—	
Situation	Localização	

Sintra, (pop. 20 574), 3 km - Estoril (pop. 25 230), 4 km

Annual closure	Fecho anual	no
Weekly closure	Fecho semanal	no

Fees main season Tarifas de época alta	18 holes	
	Week days Semana	**We/Bank holidays** Fim de sem./Feriad
Individual Individual	30 €	42 €
Couple Casal	60 €	84 €

Caddy	Caddy	no
Electric Trolley	Trolley eléctrico	no
Buggy	Buggy	27 €
Clubs	Tacos	10 €

Credit cards Cartão de crédito VISA - AMEX

Serra de Sintra
Sintra
GOLF
Alcabideche
N 249
Estoril
10
9
Lisboa →
A 5
N6
Cascais
Oeiras
Costa do Estoril
0 2 4 km

Access Acesso : N9 Estoril-Sintra, → Alcabideche
Map 2 on page 1052 Mapa 2 Página 1052

Golf course — PERCURSO — 14/20

Site	Sitio	
Maintenance	Conversa	
Architect	Arquitecto	Duarte Sotto Mayor
Type	Tipo	residential
Relief	Relevo	
Water in play	Lago	
Exp. to wind	Exposto ao vento	
Trees in play	Arvores	

Scorecard Cartão de resultados	**Chp.** Camp.	**Mens** Homens	**Ladies** Senhoras
Length Compriment	5917	5474	5092
Par	72	72	73
Slope system	—	—	—

Advised golfing ability Nivel de jogo recomendado — 0 12 24 36
Hcp required Handicap exigido — 28 Men, 36 Ladies

Club house & amenities — CLUB HOUSE E ANEXOS — 8/10

Pro shop	Pro-shop	
Driving range	Campo de prática	
Sheltered	coberto	no
On grass	om relva	yes
Putting-green	putting-green	yes
Pitching-green	pitching-green	yes

Hotel facilities — INFRAESTRUCTURAS HOTELEIRAS — 7/10

HOTELS HOTELS

Atlantis, 129 rooms, D 60 € — Estoril
Tel (351) 01 - 469 07 21, Fax (351) 01 - 469 07 40 — 3 km

Palacio, 162 rooms, D 140 € — Estoril
Tel (351) 01 - 468 04 00, Fax (351) 01 - 468 48 67 — 15 km

Estoril Eden, 162 rooms, D 75 € — Estoril
Tel (351) 01 - 467 05 73, Fax (351) 01 - 467 08 48 — 18 km

RESTAURANTS RESTAURANTE

A. Choupana, — S. Joán do Estoril
Tel (351) 21 - 468 3099 — 8 km

Solar de São Pedro — Sintra
Tel (351) 21 - 923 1860 — 3 km

QUINTA DA MARINHA

14	7	7

Embora situado numa imensa zona de pinhal, este percurso merecia que lhe tivessem concecido um pouco mais de espaço para permitor a Robert Trent Jones de dar averdadeira medida do seu talento. O seu desenho é de muito boa qualidade, mas para conseguir um par 71, teve de criar 5 pares 5 para contrabalançar os 6 pares 3 (entre os quais os belos 5 e 14) o que provoca um ritmo de jogo pouco habitual. Aqueles que conhecem o estilo do arquitecto não ficam surprendidos mas terão a impressão que já jogaram aqueles buracos noutro lugar qualquer. Isto não retira muito ao prazer do jogo e do local, donde se pode apreciar algumas lindas vistas do mar, nomeadamente n° 13, o buraco modêlo do percurso. As dificuldades são numerosas, equilibradas e bem visiveis, permitindo jogar o percurso desde a primeira vez sem temer armadilhas escondidas. Em contrapardida náo fica muito por descobrir se o percurso fôr jogado frequentemente. Por pouco, tinha-se obtido um exito total.

Although sited in a huge pine estate, this course would have deserved a little more space to enable Trent Jones to fully express his many talents. This is certainly an excellent layout, but to achieve a par 71, he had to create five par 5s to offset the six par 3s (including the pretty 5th and 14th holes). Hence a rather unusually balanced course. Those of you who know the designer's style will not be surprised, but you will get the impression of having already played some of these holes before. But don't let that detract from the pleasure of golfing on a site that offers some beautiful views over the sea, notably from the 13th, the course's signature hole. Difficulties are manifold but visible, so new-comers need have no fear of hidden hazards. In contrast, you will soon get to the bottom of everything the course has to offer if you play here often. This looks very much like a missed opportunity to create a great golf course.

Clube Golfe Quinta da Marinha

Quinta da Marinha, Casa 36
P - 2750 CASCAIS

Office	Secretariado	(351) 21 - 486 0180
Pro shop	Pro-shop	(351) 21 - 486 0180
Fax	Fax	(351) 21 - 486 9488
Web	www.quinta-da-marinha.com	
Situation	Localização	

Cascais (pop. 29 882), 6 km - Lisboa (pop. 662 782), 26 km

Annual closure	Fecho anual	no
Weekly closure	Fecho semanal	no

Fees main season Tarifas de época alta	Week days Semana	We/Bank holidays Fim de sem./Feriad
		18 holes
Individual Individual	60 €	75 €
Couple Casal	120 €	150 €

Special fees for juniors and Portuguese clubs members

Caddy	Caddy	40 € /on request
Electric Trolley	Trolley eléctrico	20 € /18 holes
Buggy	Buggy	33 € /18 holes
Clubs	Tacos	45 € /18 holes

Credit cards Cartão de crédito VISA - AMEX

Access Acesso : Lisboa A5, → Cascais, N 247 → Praia do Guincho
Map 2 on page 1052 Mapa 2 Página 1052

Golf course PERCURSO 14/20

Site	Sitio	
Maintenance	Conversa	
Architect	Arquitecto	Robert Trent Jones
Type	Tipo	forest, residential
Relief	Relevo	
Water in play	Lago	
Exp. to wind	Exposto ao vento	
Trees in play	Arvores	

Scorecard Cartão de resultados	**Chp.** Camp.	**Mens** Homens	**Ladies** Senhoras
Length Compriment	6014	5606	5081
Par	71	71	71
Slope system	—	—	—

Advised golfing ability Nivel de jogo recomendado: 0 12 24 36

Hcp required Handicap exigido no

Club house & amenities CLUB HOUSE E ANEXOS 7/10

Pro shop	Pro-shop	
Driving range	Campo de prática	
Sheltered	coberto	no
On grass	om relva	yes
Putting-green	putting-green	yes
Pitching-green	pitching-green	no

Hotel facilities INFRAESTRUCTURAS HOTELEIRAS 7/10

HOTELS HOTELS

Estoril Sol, 298 rooms, D 200 € — Cascais 3 km
Tel (351) 21 - 483 9000, Fax (351) 21 - 483 2280

Atlantic Gardens, 150 rooms, D 165 € — Cascais 8 km
Tel (351) 21 - 483 3737, Fax (351) 21 - 483 5226

Cidadela, 110 rooms, D 125 € — Cascais 9 km
Tel (351) 21 - 482 7600, Fax (351) 21 - 486 7226

Quinta da Marinha, 182 rooms, D 150 € — Cascais 5
Tel (351) 21 - 486 0100, Fax (351) 21 - 486 9488

RESTAURANTS RESTAURANTE

Fortaleza do Guincho, Tel (351) 21 - 487 0491 — Cascais 3 km

Porto de Santa Maria — Praia do Guincho
Tel (351) 21 - 487 0240 — 3 km

QUINTA DO LAGO B/C

16 | 7 | 8

A despeito da qualidade dos outros grupos de 9 buracos, a combinaçao dos percursos B e C é a mais satisfatória e a que foi mais utilizada nas grandes competições. O seu comprimento não deve assustar. E razoável a partir das saídas normais. A largura dos "fairways" e o equilibrio do comprimento dos buracos, torna o percurso acessivel a todos os jogadores com alguma experiência. Para mais, anatureza arenosa do terreno permite não so andar com prazer, mas tambem fazer roalr muito a bola. Os obstáculos de àgua entram em jogo em alguns buracos mas a principal dificuldade são os pinheiros que sobresaiem de outros tipos de vegetação. Pelo seu equilibrio, este percurso permite um jogo confortável sem criar problemas inuteis aos golfistas em férias. A Quinta do Lago conquistou uma bela reputação, seria merecida se a manutenção fosse sempre impecável.

Despite the excellence of the two other 9-hole courses, the B & C combination is the most satisfying and the most widely used for top tournaments. The yardage is nothing to be afraid of and is reasonable from the normal tees. And the width of the fairways and nicely balanced length of holes make this a course playable by any golfer with some experience. What's more, the sandy sub-soil makes it a pleasure to walk and gives balls a lot of extra roll. Water hazards are in play only on a few holes, and the main difficulties are the pine-trees looming over the heather, and the broom. A nicely balanced course for a relaxed round of golf, and one that doesn't create needless problems for golfers on holiday. Quinta do Lago has acquired a great reputation, which would be deserved if upkeep were immaculate all the time.

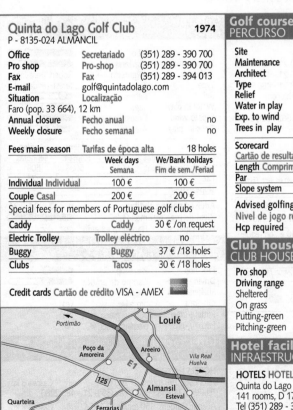

Quinta do Lago Golf Club — 1974

P - 8135-024 ALMANCIL

Office	Secretariado	(351) 289 - 390 700
Pro shop	Pro-shop	(351) 289 - 390 700
Fax	Fax	(351) 289 - 394 013
E-mail	golf@quintadolago.com	
Situation	Localização	
Faro (pop. 33 664), 12 km		
Annual closure	Fecho anual	no
Weekly closure	Fecho semanal	no

Fees main season Tarifas de época alta	18 holes	
	Week days Semana	**We/Bank holidays** Fim de sem./Feriad
Individual Individual	100 €	100 €
Couple Casal	200 €	200 €
Special fees for members of Portuguese golf clubs		

Caddy	Caddy	30 € /on request
Electric Trolley	Trolley eléctrico	no
Buggy	Buggy	37 € /18 holes
Clubs	Tacos	30 € /18 holes

Credit cards Cartão de crédito VISA - AMEX

Access Acesso : N 125 Faro → Portimão, Almancil → Quinta do Lago
Map 3 on page 1054 Mapa 3 Página 1054

Golf course PERCURSO — 16/20

Site	Sitio	
Maintenance	Conversa	
Architect	Arquitecto	William Mitchell
Type	Tipo	forest, residential
Relief	Relevo	
Water in play	Lago	
Exp. to wind	Exposto ao vento	
Trees in play	Arvores	

Scorecard Cartão de resultados	**Chp.** Camp.	**Mens** Homens	**Ladies** Senhoras
Length Compriment	6488	5870	5192
Par	72	72	72
Slope system	—	—	—

Advised golfing ability 0 12 24 36
Nivel de jogo recomendado
Hcp required Handicap exigido 28 Men, 36 Ladies

Club house & amenities CLUB HOUSE E ANEXOS — 7/10

Pro shop	Pro-shop	
Driving range	Campo de prática	
Sheltered	coberto	no
On grass	om relva	no (25 mats)
Putting-green	putting-green	yes
Pitching-green	pitching-green	yes

Hotel facilities INFRAESTRUCTURAS HOTELEIRAS — 8/10

HOTELS HOTELS

Quinta do Lago — Quinta do Lago 3 km
141 rooms, D 175 €
Tel (351) 289 - 396 666, Fax (351) 289 - 396 393

Dona Filipa, 147 rooms, D 224 € — Vale do Lobo
Tel (351) 289 - 394 141, Fax (351) 289 - 394 288 — 6 km

RESTAURANTS RESTAURANTE

Casa Velha, Tel (351) 289 - 394 983 — Quinta do Lago 3 km

São Gabriel, Tel (351) 289 - 394 521 — Almancil5 km

Henrique Leis — Vale Formoso (Loulé)
Tel (351) 289 - 393 438 — 10 km

Casa dos Pinheiros, Tel (351) 289 - 394 832 — Almancil 5 km

QUINTA DO LAGO Ria Formosa 14 | 7 | 8

Sob o nome de Ria Formosa reuniram-se os percursos A e D da Quinta do Lago, desenhados por dois arquitectos diferentes, William Mitchell e Rocky Roquemore. Resulta num certo desequilibrio visual e golfístico, uma vez que as personalidades dos dois signatários é forçosamente diferente. Este "defeito" contribui, porem, para da muita variedade aos 18 buracos que são, pelo menos, identicos no ponto de vista da vegetação. A estrategia é bastante simples, os "greens" são desenhados com gosto, o desenho geral é bastante imaginativo com uma estética principalmente americana, principalmente pela integração de vários lagos, sobretudo aos primeiros 9 buracos. Em relação ao outro percurso do complexo é aínda mais adequado a todos os níveis de jogo, quer se trate de jogar para o seu próprio resultado ou numa competição. Se juntarmos a este vasto complexo o belo e mítico percurso do São Lourenço confirma-se a necessidade de uma visita.

The A & D courses of Quinta do Lago, collectively called Ria Formosa, were designed by two different architects, William Mitchell and Joseph Lee. The result is a slight feeling of visual and golfing imbalance created by two necessarily different personalities and styles. In fact, this "flaw" actually adds a lot of variety to the 18-hole layout, where the vegetation at least is the same. Game strategy is simple to see, the greens have been tastefully designed and the general layout is rather imaginative and mainly American in style with the presence of several lakes, especially on the front nine. Compared to the other course on the same site, the A & D combination is even better suited to all levels, whichever way you play. Add to this huge golf resort the fabulous neighbouring course of San Lorenzo, then a long visit is called for.

Quinta do Lago Golf Club — 1977

P - 8135-024 ALMANCIL

Office	Secretariado	(351) 289 - 390 700
Pro shop	Pro-shop	(351) 289 - 390 700
Fax	Fax	(351) 289 - 394 013
E-mail	golf@quintadolago.com	
Situation	Localização	
Faro (pop. 33 664), 12 km		
Annual closure	Fecho anual	no
Weekly closure	Fecho semanal	no

Fees main season Tarifas de época alta	Week days Semana	We/Bank holidays Fim de sem./Feriad
		18 holes
Individual Individual	85 €	85 €
Couple Casal	170 €	170 €

Special fees for members of Portuguese golf clubs

Caddy	Caddy	30 € /on request
Electric Trolley	Trolley eléctrico	no
Buggy	Buggy	37 € /18 holes
Clubs	Tacos	30 € /18 holes

Credit cards Cartão de crédito VISA - AMEX

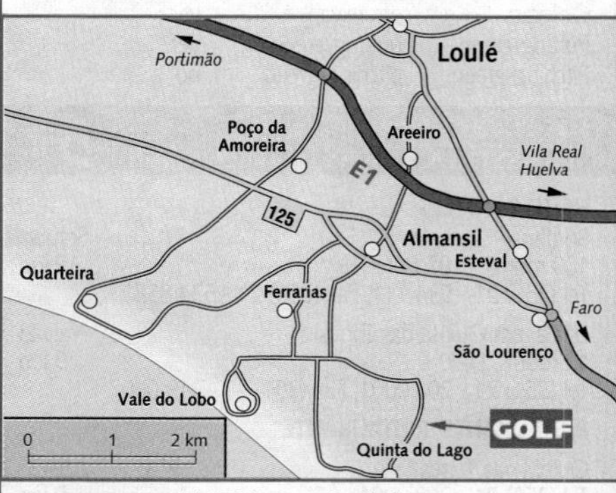

Access Acesso : N 125 Faro → Portimão, Almancil → Quinta do Lago
Map 3 on page 1054 Mapa 3 Página 1054

Golf course PERCURSO — 14/20

Site	Sitio	
Maintenance	Conversa	
Architect	Arquitecto	William Mitchell Rocky Roquemore
Type	Tipo	forest, residential
Relief	Relevo	
Water in play	Lago	
Exp. to wind	Exposto ao vento	
Trees in play	Arvores	

Scorecard Cartão de resultados	Chp. Camp.	Mens Homens	Ladies Senhoras
Length Compriment	6205	5804	5031
Par	72	72	72
Slope system	—	—	—

Advised golfing ability Nivel de jogo recomendado — 0 12 24 36

Hcp required Handicap exigido 28 Men, 36 Ladies

Club house & amenities CLUB HOUSE E ANEXOS — 7/10

Pro shop	Pro-shop	
Driving range	Campo de prática	
Sheltered	coberto	no
On grass	om relva	no (25 mats)
Putting-green	putting-green	yes
Pitching-green	pitching-green	yes

Hotel facilities INFRAESTRUCTURAS HOTELEIRAS — 8/10

HOTELS HOTELS

Quinta do Lago, 141 rooms, D 175 € — Quinta do Lago
Tel (351) 289 - 396 666, Fax (351) 289 - 396 393 — 3 km

Dona Filipa, 147 rooms, D 224 € — Vale do Lobo
Tel (351) 289 - 394 141, Fax (351) 289 - 394 288 — 6 km

RESTAURANTS RESTAURANTE

Casa Velha, Tel (351) 289 - 394 983 Quinta do Lago 3 km

São Gabriel, Tel (351) 289 - 394 521 — Almancil5 km

Henrique Leis — Vale Formoso (Loulé)
Tel (351) 289 - 393 438 — 10 km

Casa dos Pinheiros, Tel (351) 289 - 394 832 Almancil 5 km

QUINTA DO PERU

14 | 7 | 5

A visão de algumas realizações imobiliarias é largamente compensada pelos belas paisagens. Esta agradável impressão é confirmada pela qualidade do percurso, muito recente mas já em boa condição. Com aos excepções de 2 pares 3, compridos e bem protegidos por lagos, este desenho de Rocky Roquemore adapta-se muito bem a todo o tipo de jogadores se não escolherem as saídas mais longas. O sentimento dominante é o de um percurso bem equilibrado e de uma grande franquesa com os obstáculos bem visiveis. As dificuldades são bastante numerosas para evitar o aborrecimento sem no entanto se tornar opressivo, tendo "greens" bem desenhados. Construido no meio de um agradável pinhal, com um relêvo moderato está evidentemente destinado a dar prazer e os melhores jogadores tirarão dele o melhor partido a partir das saídas de trás. A qualidade das instalações de treino permitem que se passe uma agradável jornada.

The sight of several property development projects is compensated by some beautiful landscapes, and this pleasant impression is confirmed by the excellence of the course, a very recent layout but one that is already in good condition. With the exception of two par 3s, both long and tightly defended by water, this Rocky Roquemore design is well suited to players of all abilities if they avoid the back-tees. The overall feeling is one of a nicely balanced and candid course, where hazards are clearly there to be seen. Although evenly spaced to give golfers room to breathe, there are enough difficulties to keep you on your toes, and the greens are interesting. Laid out in a flattish and pleasant pine forest, this course is obviously designed for fun, and the better players will be better off playing from the back. The standard of practice facilities makes this a good day's golfing.

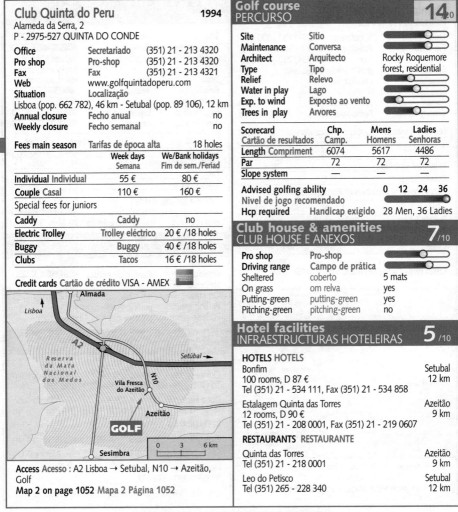

Club Quinta do Peru — 1994

Alameda da Serra, 2
P - 2975-527 QUINTA DO CONDE

Office	Secretariado	(351) 21 - 213 4320
Pro shop	Pro-shop	(351) 21 - 213 4320
Fax	Fax	(351) 21 - 213 4321
Web	www.golfquintadoperu.com	
Situation	Localização	

Lisboa (pop. 662 782), 46 km - Setubal (pop. 89 106), 12 km

Annual closure	Fecho anual	no
Weekly closure	Fecho semanal	no

Fees main season Tarifas de época alta	18 holes	
	Week days Semana	We/Bank holidays Fim de sem./Feriad
Individual Individual	55 €	80 €
Couple Casal	110 €	160 €

Special fees for juniors

Caddy	Caddy	no
Electric Trolley	Trolley eléctrico	20 € /18 holes
Buggy	Buggy	40 € /18 holes
Clubs	Tacos	16 € /18 holes

Credit cards Cartão de crédito VISA - AMEX

Almada
Lisboa
A2
Reserva da Mata Nacional dos Medos
Setúbal
N10
Vila Fresca do Azeitão
Azeitão
GOLF
Sesimbra
0 3 6 km

Access Acesso : A2 Lisboa → Setubal, N10 → Azeitão, Golf

Map 2 on page 1052 Mapa 2 Página 1052

Golf course PERCURSO — 14/20

Site	Sitio	
Maintenance	Conversa	
Architect	Arquitecto	Rocky Roquemore
Type	Tipo	forest, residential
Relief	Relevo	
Water in play	Lago	
Exp. to wind	Exposto ao vento	
Trees in play	Arvores	

Scorecard Cartão de resultados	Chp. Camp.	Mens Homens	Ladies Senhoras
Length Compriment	6074	5617	4486
Par	72	72	72
Slope system	—	—	—

Advised golfing ability Nivel de jogo recomendado — 0 12 24 36

Hcp required Handicap exigido — 28 Men, 36 Ladies

Club house & amenities CLUB HOUSE E ANEXOS — 7/10

Pro shop	Pro-shop	
Driving range	Campo de prática	
Sheltered	coberto	5 mats
On grass	om relva	yes
Putting-green	putting-green	yes
Pitching-green	pitching-green	no

Hotel facilities INFRAESTRUCTURAS HOTELEIRAS — 5/10

HOTELS HOTELS

Bonfim — Setubal 12 km
100 rooms, D 87 €
Tel (351) 21 - 534 111, Fax (351) 21 - 534 858

Estalagem Quinta das Torres — Azeitão 9 km
12 rooms, D 90 €
Tel (351) 21 - 208 0001, Fax (351) 21 - 219 0607

RESTAURANTS RESTAURANTE

Quinta das Torres — Azeitão 9 km
Tel (351) 21 - 218 0001

Leo do Petisco — Setubal 12 km
Tel (351) 265 - 228 340

S. LOURENÇO

17 | 6 | 8

E incontestávelmente o N° 1 de Portugal, pelo seu traçado pelo seu ambiente e pela sua manutenção. Num belo local rodeado de casas de grande qualidade, Joseph Lee demonstrou uma grande imaginação e uma preocupação de espectaculo visual e golfístico. Aqui é necessário não só utilizar todos os ferros do saco, mas tambem utilizá-los de forma diferente tão importante se torna a colocação das pancadas para se conseguir um bom resultado. Há um encontro de todas as dificuldades: arevores, "bunkers", lagos e largos braços da Ria Formosa. A tranquilidade e a beleza da paisagem incitam a dar o melhor de si próprio e a responder aos desafios técnicos postos pelo arquitecto. E certo que os jogadores inexperientes terão dificuldades, mas para aqueles que tem um handicap razoável será o culminar de uma viagem golfistica. Quanto aos jogadores de bom nível, terão aqui um máximo de prazer ao tentarem enfrentar este percurso.

This is unquestionably Portugal's top course for its design and setting (upkeep is sometimes questionable). Given a very beautiful site, dotted by some equally attractive villas, Joseph Lee employed heaps of imagination and considerable concern for golf as a visual spectacle. Here, you not only use every club in your bag, you also use clubs in different ways. That's how important positioning the ball can be for a good score. The course has every difficulty in the book: trees, fairway bunkers, lakes and a large arm of the Ria Formosa. The tranquillity and beauty of the landscape prompt the golfer to play above himself and meet the technical challenges laid down by the designer. Inexperienced players will have problems, sure, but with a decent handicap, a day spent here can be the perfect climax to a golfing holiday. The better players will have fun trying to tame a course such as this.

S. Lourenço Golf Club — 1988

Le Merdien D. Filipa, Vale do Lobo
P - 8135-901 ALMANCIL

Office	Secretariado	(351) 289 - 396 522
Pro shop	Pro-shop	(351) 289 - 396 522
Fax	Fax	(351) 289 - 396 908
Web	—	
Situation	Localização	
Faro (pop.33 664), 15 km		
Annual closure	Fecho anual	no
Weekly closure	Fecho semanal	no

Fees main season	Tarifas de época alta	18 holes
	Week days Semana	We/Bank holidays Fim de sem./Feriad
Individual Individual	125 €	125 €
Couple Casal	250 €	250 €

Caddy	Caddy	no
Electric Trolley	Trolley eléctrico	17 € /18 holes
Buggy	Buggy	45 € /18 holes
Clubs	Tacos	30 € /18 holes

Credit cards Cartão de crédito VISA - AMEX

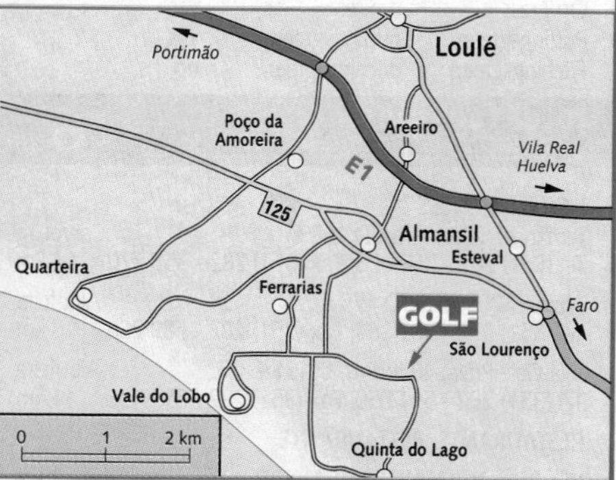

Access Acesso : N125 Faro → Portimão, Almancil → Quinta do Lago
Map 3 on page 1054 Mapa 3 Página 1054

Golf course PERCURSO — 17/20

Site	Sitio	
Maintenance	Conversa	
Architect	Arquitecto	Joseph Lee
Type	Tipo	seaside course, forest
Relief	Relevo	
Water in play	Lago	
Exp. to wind	Exposto ao vento	
Trees in play	Arvores	

Scorecard Cartão de resultados	Chp. Camp.	Mens Homens	Ladies Senhoras
Length Compriment	6238	5837	5171
Par	72	72	72
Slope system	—	—	—

Advised golfing ability — 0 12 24 36
Nivel de jogo recomendado
Hcp required — Handicap exigido — 28 Men, 36 Ladies

Club house & amenities CLUB HOUSE E ANEXOS — 6/10

Pro shop	Pro-shop	
Driving range	Campo de prática	
Sheltered	coberto	no
On grass	om relva	yes
Putting-green	putting-green	yes
Pitching-green	pitching-green	no

Hotel facilities INFRAESTRUCTURAS HOTELEIRAS — 8/10

HOTELS HOTELS

Quinta do Lago, 141 rooms, D 175 € — Quinta do Lago
Tel (351) 289 - 396 666, Fax (351) 289 - 396 393 — 2 km

Dona Filipa, 147 rooms, D 224 € — Vale do Lobo
Tel (351) 289 - 394 141, Fax (351) 289 - 394 288 — 3 km

RESTAURANTS RESTAURANTE

Casa Velha, Tel (351) 289 - 394 983 — Quinta do Lago 3 km

São Gabriel, Tel (351) 289 - 394 521 — Almancil 5 km

Henrique Leis — Vale Formoso (Loulé)
Tel (351) 289 - 393 438 — 5 km

Casa dos Pinheiros — Almancil
Tel (351) 289 - 394 832 — 4 km

SALGADOS

13 | 6 | 6

Aqueles que não gostam de àgua, arriscam-se a passar aqui um mau bocado, uma vez que está presente em jogo em todos os buracos mas é o prêço a pagar para ter uma paisagem marinha muito agradável e desnuda. O comprimento do percurso não é deshumano (tem de se utilizar muitas vezes ferros curtos) e os jogadores direitos estarão à vontade bem como aqueles que controlam bem a bola: a colocação das pancadas de saída é muito importante para se estar bem posicionado para atacar os "greens" bem defendidos. São bastante planos sem terem um desenho escepcional, sendo para alem disso fáceis de lêr. Como a maior parte dos percursos de Portugal este traçado de Pedro de Vasconcellos (revisto por Robert Muir Graves) é acessivel a todos os jogadores. Não podem esperar cumprir fácilmente os seus handicaps mas encontrarão multiplas ocasiões para se habituarem à presença da àgua, muitas vezes intimidatórias para os amadores.

Golfers who are allergic to water might have a tough time here, as just about every hole has its water hazard. This is the price you pay for a very pleasant and bare marine landscape. The course is very reasonable in length (the second shot is often a short iron) and straight-hitters and flighters of the ball will feel at home. Placing the tee-shot is more important than usual to get a better angle at the very well defended greens, which are rather flat, easy to read and pleasantly designed. Like the majority of courses in Portugal, this Pedro de Vasconcelos layout (restyled by Robert Muir Graves) is playable for golfers of all abilities. They won't find it easy to play to their handicap, but they will find numerous opportunities to get used to the sort of water hazard that often intimidates the average golfer.

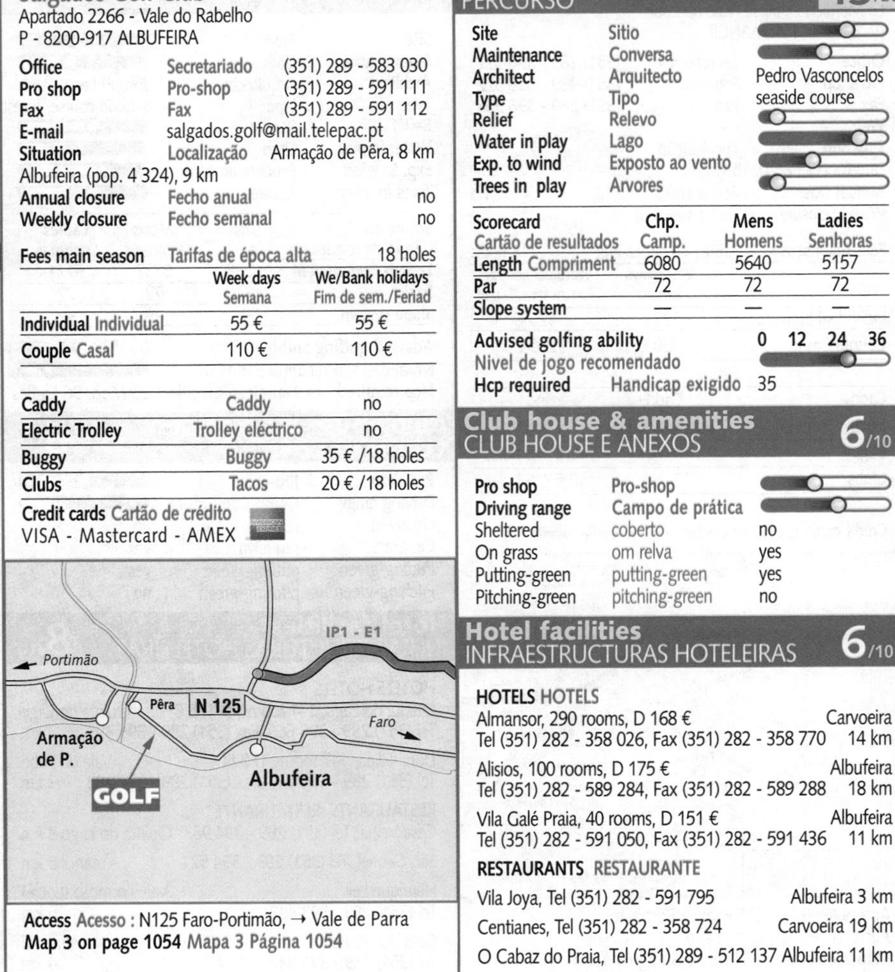

Salgados Golf Club — 1995

Apartado 2266 - Vale do Rabelho
P - 8200-917 ALBUFEIRA

Office	Secretariado	(351) 289 - 583 030
Pro shop	Pro-shop	(351) 289 - 591 111
Fax	Fax	(351) 289 - 591 112
E-mail	salgados.golf@mail.telepac.pt	
Situation	Localização	Armação de Pêra, 8 km

Albufeira (pop. 4 324), 9 km

Annual closure	Fecho anual	no
Weekly closure	Fecho semanal	no

Fees main season Tarifas de época alta	18 holes	
	Week days Semana	**We/Bank holidays** Fim de sem./Feriad
Individual Individual	55 €	55 €
Couple Casal	110 €	110 €

Caddy	Caddy	no
Electric Trolley	Trolley eléctrico	no
Buggy	Buggy	35 € /18 holes
Clubs	Tacos	20 € /18 holes

Credit cards Cartão de crédito
VISA - Mastercard - AMEX

Access Acesso : N125 Faro-Portimão, → Vale de Parra
Map 3 on page 1054 Mapa 3 Página 1054

Golf course PERCURSO — 13/20

Site	Sitio	
Maintenance	Conversa	
Architect	Arquitecto	Pedro Vasconcelos
Type	Tipo	seaside course
Relief	Relevo	
Water in play	Lago	
Exp. to wind	Exposto ao vento	
Trees in play	Arvores	

Scorecard Cartão de resultados	**Chp.** Camp.	**Mens** Homens	**Ladies** Senhoras
Length Compriment	6080	5640	5157
Par	72	72	72
Slope system	—	—	—

Advised golfing ability Nivel de jogo recomendado — 0 12 24 36
Hcp required Handicap exigido 35

Club house & amenities CLUB HOUSE E ANEXOS — 6/10

Pro shop	Pro-shop	
Driving range	Campo de prática	
Sheltered	coberto	no
On grass	om relva	yes
Putting-green	putting-green	yes
Pitching-green	pitching-green	no

Hotel facilities INFRAESTRUCTURAS HOTELEIRAS — 6/10

HOTELS HOTELS

Almansor, 290 rooms, D 168 € — Carvoeira
Tel (351) 282 - 358 026, Fax (351) 282 - 358 770 — 14 km

Alisios, 100 rooms, D 175 € — Albufeira
Tel (351) 282 - 589 284, Fax (351) 282 - 589 288 — 18 km

Vila Galé Praia, 40 rooms, D 151 € — Albufeira
Tel (351) 282 - 591 050, Fax (351) 282 - 591 436 — 11 km

RESTAURANTS RESTAURANTE

Vila Joya, Tel (351) 282 - 591 795 — Albufeira 3 km

Centianes, Tel (351) 282 - 358 724 — Carvoeira 19 km

O Cabaz do Praia, Tel (351) 289 - 512 137 Albufeira 11 km

SANTO DA SERRA 16 7 5

A várias centenas de metros de altitude, este percurso oferece panorámicas de uma beleza fántastica, sobre a Ilha da Madeira e o Oceano Atlântico. E um dos percursos mais extraordinários da Europa. O inconveniente da sua situação, em média montanha, é a de que se torna bastante cansativo par jogar a pé, mas a beleza do espectáculo, nomeadamente nos buracos 12 e 13, valem alguns esforços. O Arquitecto Robert Trent Jones jogou com delícia e imaginação sobre um terreno extraordinário e propõe aos jogadores de todos os níveis desafios apaixonantes. Estes terão que estudar bem a estratégia a seguir em cada buraco sem se distraírem demasiado com a paisagem. As dificuldades são múltiplas mas sempre bem visíveis, com uma vegetação muito rica, "roughs" bastante densos, "bunkers" muito em jogo, "greens" bem trabalhados mas tendo um único obstáculo de água. Em contrapardida o seu comprimento mantém-se razoável... se não houver vento. Aconselha-se jogar em "match-play", é um percurso muito divertido.

At several hundred metres above sea-level, this course primarily offers a fantastically beautiful panorama over the island of Madeira and the Atlantic ocean. The drawback of being half-way up a mountain is the toll it takes on your feet and legs. But the beauty of the site, especially on the 12th and 13th holes is well worth the effort. Designer Robert Trent Jones used a lot of fun and imagination over this remarkable terrain and offers some exciting challenges to players of all abilities, who will need to consider carefully their strategy on each hole, without being distracted by the scenery. The difficulties are many and varied, but always there to be seen: lush vegetation, pretty thick rough, omnipresent bunkers, well-designed greens but just the one water hazard. In contrast, yardage is reasonable... as long as the wind doesn't blow. Try it in match-play, it's great fun. A new 9 hole-course has just been opened on the west side of this course.

Clube de Golf Santo da Serra 1991

Casais Proximos
P - 9200-152 SANTO ANTONIO DA SERRA

Office	Secretariado	(351) 291 - 552 356
Pro shop	Pro-shop	(351) 291 - 552 356
Fax	Fax	(351) 291 - 552 367
Web	www.santodaserragolf.com	
Situation	Localização	

Machico (pop. 2 142), 6 km - Funchal (pop. 99 244), 26 km

Annual closure	Fecho anual	no
Weekly closure	Fecho semanal	no

Fees main season	Tarifas de época alta	18 holes
	Week days Semana	**We/Bank holidays** Fim de sem./Feriad
Individual Individual	50 €	50 €
Couple Casal	100 €	100 €
Caddy	Caddy	no
Electric Trolley	Trolley eléctrico	no
Buggy	Buggy	35 € /18 holes
Clubs	Tacos	25 € /18 holes

Credit cards Cartão de crédito VISA - DC - AMEX

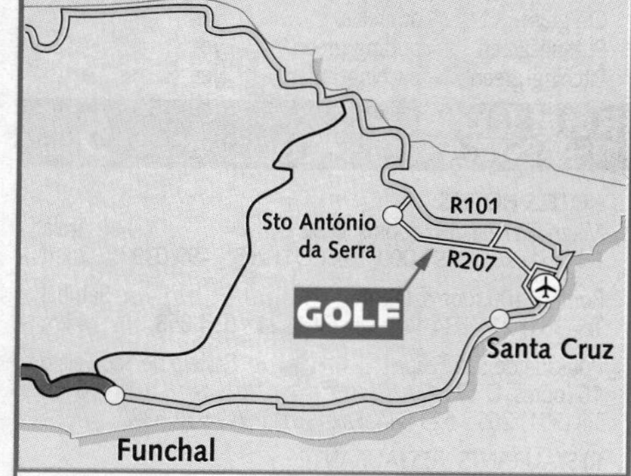

Access Acesso : E 101 Funchal → Machico.
N 675 → Sto da Serra
Map 3 on page 1055 Mapa 3 Página 1055

Golf course PERCURSO 16/20

Site	Sitio	
Maintenance	Conversa	
Architect	Arquitecto	Robert Trent Jones
Type	Tipo	mountain, hilly
Relief	Relevo	
Water in play	Lago	
Exp. to wind	Exposto ao vento	
Trees in play	Arvores	

Scorecard Cartão de resultados	**Chp.** Camp.	**Mens** Homens	**Ladies** Senhoras
Length Compriment	6039	5496	4511
Par	72	72	72
Slope system	—	—	—

Advised golfing ability 0 12 24 36
Nivel de jogo recomendado
Hcp required Handicap exigido 36

Club house & amenities CLUB HOUSE E ANEXOS 7/10

Pro shop	Pro-shop	
Driving range	Campo de prática	
Sheltered	coberto	no
On grass	om relva	yes
Putting-green	putting-green	yes
Pitching-green	pitching-green	yes

Hotel facilities INFRAESTRUCTURAS HOTELEIRAS 5/10

HOTELS HOTELS

Reids, 158 rooms, D 374 € — Funchal
Tel (351) 291 - 763 001, Fax (351) 291 - 717 177 — 21 km

Cliff Bay Resort, 197 rooms, D 384 € — Funchal
Tel (351) 291 - 707 700, Fax (351) 291 - 762 525 — 21 km

Madeira Carlton, 374 rooms, D 205 € — Funchal
Tel (351) 291 - 231 031, Fax (351) 291 - 227 284 — 21 km

RESTAURANTS RESTAURANTE

Casa Velha — Funchal
Tel (351) 291 - 225 749 — 21 km

Quinta Palmeira — Funchal
Tel (351) 291 - 221 814 — 21 km

TROIA

16 | 6 | 5

Foi durente muito tempo o melhor percurso de Portugal. Mas uma manutenção muito irregular e mediocre, reduziram bastante o seu prestígio. E pena porque a intelligência estratégica de Robert Trent Jones foi magistral. Localizado numa peninsula à beira mar, êle interpretou a tradição dos "links" com a presença constante da areia bem como um envolvimento de pinheiros e plantas silvestres especificas da região. O percurso parece por vezes mais estreito do que é na realidade mas os obstáculos são bem visiveis e estão bem colocados, come por exemplo alguns "bunkers" profundos: defendem vigorosamente "greens" geralmente bastante pequenos e bem modelados. Troia é um grande desafio para os bons jugadores mas tambem é umteste apaixonante para os outros: é sempre muito instrutivo jogar num grande percurso de golf, num quadro atraente e natural.

For many year this was the best course in Portugal, but inadequate and inconsistent upkeep has considerably dulled its prestige. It was a pity, because the strategic intelligence deployed by designer Robert Trent Jones is brilliant, but things are going better. Over a seaboard peninsula, he has given his own interpretation of the links tradition with ubiquitous sand and a setting of maritime pines and wild plants, both typical of this region. The course often looks tighter than it actually is, but the hazards are clear to see and well located, particularly several deep bunkers. They provide stern defence for greens that are generally rather small and well-contoured. Troia is a great challenge for the better player and an exciting test for the rest. There is always something to learn from playing a great golf course in a natural and attractive setting.

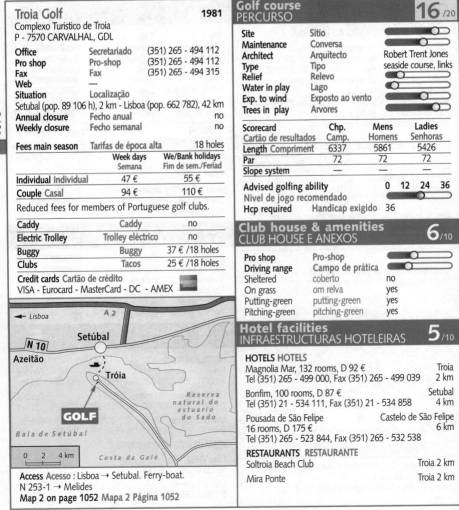

Troia Golf — 1981

Complexo Turistico de Troia
P - 7570 CARVALHAL, GDL

Office	Secretariado	(351) 265 - 494 112
Pro shop	Pro-shop	(351) 265 - 494 112
Fax	Fax	(351) 265 - 494 315
Web	—	
Situation	Localização	

Setubal (pop. 89 106 h), 2 km - Lisboa (pop. 662 782), 42 km

Annual closure	Fecho anual	no
Weekly closure	Fecho semanal	no

Fees main season Tarifas de época alta — 18 holes

	Week days / Semana	We/Bank holidays / Fim de sem./Feriad
Individual Individual	47 €	55 €
Couple Casal	94 €	110 €

Reduced fees for members of Portuguese golf clubs.

Caddy	Caddy	no
Electric Trolley	Trolley eléctrico	no
Buggy	Buggy	37 € /18 holes
Clubs	Tacos	25 € /18 holes

Credit cards Cartão de crédito
VISA - Eurocard - MasterCard - DC - AMEX

Lisboa
A 2
Setúbal
N 10
Azeitão
Tróia
GOLF
Reserva natural do estuario do Sado
Baia de Setúbal
Costa da Galé
0 2 4 km

Access Acesso : Lisboa → Setubal. Ferry-boat.
N 253-1 → Melides
Map 2 on page 1052 Mapa 2 Página 1052

Golf course — PERCURSO — 16/20

Site	Sitio	
Maintenance	Conversa	
Architect	Arquitecto	Robert Trent Jones
Type	Tipo	seaside course, links
Relief	Relevo	
Water in play	Lago	
Exp. to wind	Exposto ao vento	
Trees in play	Arvores	

Scorecard Cartão de resultados	**Chp.** Camp.	**Mens** Homens	**Ladies** Senhoras
Length Compriment	6337	5861	5426
Par	72	72	72
Slope system	—	—	—

Advised golfing ability Nivel de jogo recomendado — 0 12 24 36
Hcp required Handicap exigido 36

Club house & amenities — CLUB HOUSE E ANEXOS — 6/10

Pro shop	Pro-shop	
Driving range	Campo de prática	
Sheltered	coberto	no
On grass	om relva	yes
Putting-green	putting-green	yes
Pitching-green	pitching-green	yes

Hotel facilities — INFRAESTRUCTURAS HOTELEIRAS — 5/10

HOTELS HOTELS

Magnolia Mar, 132 rooms, D 92 € — Troia
Tel (351) 265 - 499 000, Fax (351) 265 - 499 039 — 2 km

Bonfim, 100 rooms, D 87 € — Setubal
Tel (351) 21 - 534 111, Fax (351) 21 - 534 858 — 4 km

Pousada de São Felipe — Castelo de São Felipe
16 rooms, D 175 € — 6 km
Tel (351) 265 - 523 844, Fax (351) 265 - 532 538

RESTAURANTS RESTAURANTE

Soltroia Beach Club — Troia 2 km
Mira Ponte — Troia 2 km

VALE DA PINTA

14 | 6 | 6

Muito ondulado, mas não deixa de ser fácil para jogar a pé.. Este percurso foi desenhado pelo Americano Ronald Fream. Os que conhencem o seu estilo poderão julgar que ele aqui não foi tão exigente para os golfistas como em outros locais. Visivelmente manteve o espirito de que são sobretudo turistas de nível de jogo médio que visitam a região. Para mais, quis preservar a natureza do terreno e portanto não abusou dos obstáculos de água. Os "greens" são bastante profundos e requerem uma boa precisão nos "approaches" mas estão razoavelmente defendidos, o que acentua a impressão "amigável" do percurso. As sáidas múltiplas permitem adaptá-lo a todos os níveis de jogo e a distrairse sem ter a sensação de ser um percurso fácil de mais. Os melhores jogadores ficam "aguados". Durante o passeio, poder-se-ão admirar belas oliveiras, algumas com mais de 700 anos; existe um exemplar que se calcula que tenha 1200 anos: se ele pudesse contar-nos a sua vida!

A little hilly but nonetheless easily walkable, this course was designed by Ronald Fream. Those of you who know his style might consider that he has been less demanding here than elsewhere, and visibly he bore in mind the fact that the region is visited primarily by mid-to-high handicappers on holiday. He also set out to preserve the natural look of the terrain and did not overdo the water hazards. The greens are rather deep and call for accurate approach shots, but they are reasonably defended, a fact that underlines the friendly feeling you get with this course. The many different tee-areas adapt the course easily to all players, who can enjoy themselves without feeling that the course is too easy, but the best might want more than this. In passing, a word of admiration for the beautiful olive-trees, some of which are over 700 years old. One is even 1200 years old: its life-story would make interesting reading!.

Vale da Pinta — **1992**

Apartado 1011
P - 8400-908 CARVOEIRO

Office	Secretariado	(351) 282 - 340 900
Pro shop	Pro-shop	(351) 282 - 340 900
Fax	Fax	(351) 282 - 340 901
Web	www.pestanagolf.com	
Situation	Localização	

Carvoeiro, 13 km - Faro (pop. 33 664), 42 km

Annual closure	Fecho anual	no
Weekly closure	Fecho semanal	no

Fees main season Tarifas de época alta	18 holes	
	Week days Semana	**We/Bank holidays** Fim de sem./Feriad
Individual Individual	70 €	70 €
Couple Casal	140 €	140 €
Juniors: – 50%		
Caddy	Caddy	no
Electric Trolley	Trolley eléctrico	no
Buggy	Buggy	35 € /18 holes
Clubs	Tacos	22 € /18 holes

Credit cards Cartão de crédito VISA - AMEX - DC

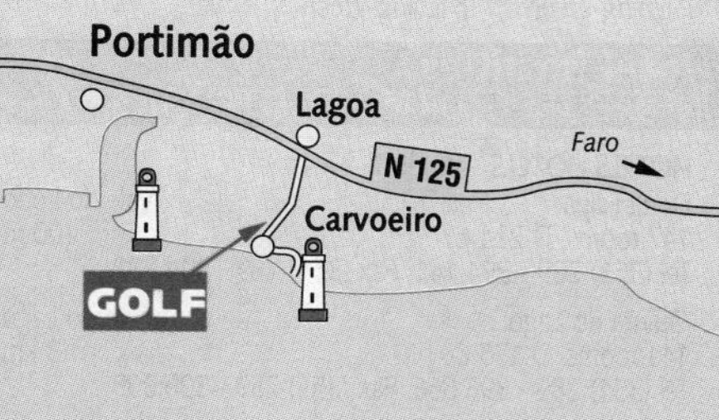

Access Acesso : N125 Lagos-Faro. Lagoa → Carvoeiro
Map 3 on page 1054 Mapa 3 Página 1054

Golf course PERCURSO — 14/20

Site	Sitio	
Maintenance	Conversa	
Architect	Arquitecto	Ronald Fream
Type	Tipo	inland, residential
Relief	Relevo	
Water in play	Lago	
Exp. to wind	Exposto ao vento	
Trees in play	Arvores	

Scorecard Cartão de resultados	**Chp.** Camp.	**Mens** Homens	**Ladies** Senhoras
Length Compriment	5861	5382	4528
Par	71	71	71
Slope system	—	—	—

Advised golfing ability Nivel de jogo recomendado — 0 12 24 36

Hcp required Handicap exigido — 28 Men, 36 Ladies

Club house & amenities CLUB HOUSE E ANEXOS — 6/10

Pro shop	Pro-shop	
Driving range	Campo de prática	
Sheltered	coberto	6 mats
On grass	om relva	yes
Putting-green	putting-green	yes
Pitching-green	pitching-green	yes

Hotel facilities INFRAESTRUCTURAS HOTELEIRAS — 6/10

HOTELS HOTELS

Almansor, 290 rooms, D 168 € — Carvoeira 3 km
Tel (351) 282 - 358 026, Fax (351) 282 - 358 770

Alisios, 100 rooms, D 175 € — Albufeira 13 km
Tel (351) 282 - 589 284, Fax (351) 282 - 589 288

Vila Galé Praia, 40 rooms, D 151 € — Albufeira 13 km
Tel (351) 282 - 591 050, Fax (351) 282 - 591 436

RESTAURANTS RESTAURANTE

Vila Joya, Tel (351) 282 - 591 795 — Albufeira 3 km

Centianes, Tel (351) 282 - 358 724 — Carvoeira13 km

O Cabaz do Praia, Tel (351) 289 - 512 137 — Albufeira

VALE DO LOBO Royal Golf Course

15 | 6 | 7

Era um dos mais famosos percursos de Portugal, sobretudo devido a um dos seus buracos (agora é o 16) que se jogar por cima de uma serie de três falésias. Os restantes 26 buracos não estavam à mesma altura. Acrescentando-lhe 9 buracos novos e alguns melhoramentos, eis que surge o percurso "Royal", fruto do trabalho realizado com um intervalo de 30 anos entre Henry Cotton e Rocky Roquemore. Os restantes 18 buracos passaram a chamar-se "Ocean Course". No "Royal" nota-se que os estilos dos dois arquitectos se fundem harmoniosamente, numa espécie de cásamento entre a estética e os estilos de jogo americano e britânico. Há que felicitar Roquemore por ter evitado com inteligência as rupturas visuais brutais, embora cada buraco tenha a personalidade suficiente para ser memorizado. Vale do Lobo propõe-se agora um excelente teste de golf, acrescido do facto de ser um lindo percurso, arborizado por milhares de pinheiros, oliveiras, figueiras, larangeiras que invadem frequentemente a linha de jogo.

This used to be one of Portugal's most famous courses, especially for one of the holes here (now the 16th) played over three rows of cliffs. The other 26 holes unfortunately were not always up to standard. Today, with nine new holes and a little rejuvenation, here is the "Royal" course, the work of Henry Cotton and Rocky Roquemore with a 30 year interval in between. The other 18 holes are now the "Ocean" course. On the Royal, the styles of the two architects blend together perfectly, sort of dovetailing the visual appeal and styles of American and British courses. Roquemore must be congratulated for having cleverly avoided any clashes in overall visual harmony, even though each hole has enough personality to stick in the memory. Vale do Lobo now offers an excellent test of golf in addition to being a very pretty course covered with thousands of pine, olive, fig and orange trees which come into play. A must.

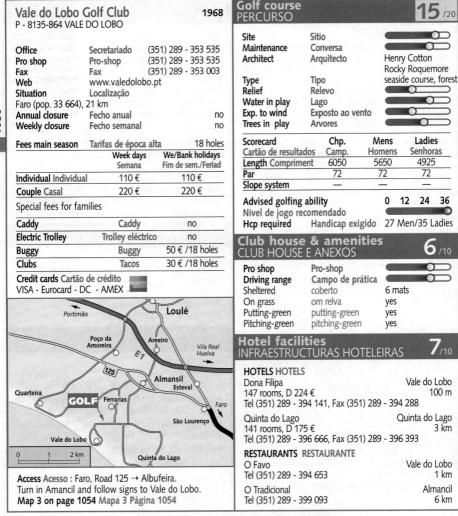

Vale do Lobo Golf Club — 1968

P - 8135-864 VALE DO LOBO

Office	Secretariado	(351) 289 - 353 535
Pro shop	Pro-shop	(351) 289 - 353 535
Fax	Fax	(351) 289 - 353 003
Web	www.valedolobo.pt	
Situation	Localização	
Faro (pop. 33 664), 21 km		
Annual closure	Fecho anual	no
Weekly closure	Fecho semanal	no

Fees main season Tarifas de época alta	18 holes	
	Week days Semana	**We/Bank holidays** Fim de sem./Feriad
Individual Individual	110 €	110 €
Couple Casal	220 €	220 €
Special fees for families		

Caddy	Caddy	no
Electric Trolley	Trolley eléctrico	no
Buggy	Buggy	50 € /18 holes
Clubs	Tacos	30 € /18 holes

Credit cards Cartão de crédito
VISA - Eurocard - DC - AMEX

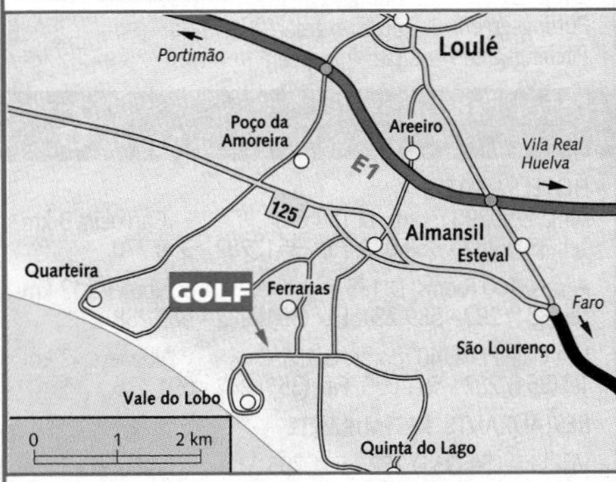

Access Acesso : Faro, Road 125 → Albufeira.
Turn in Amancil and follow signs to Vale do Lobo.
Map 3 on page 1054 Mapa 3 Página 1054

Golf course — PERCURSO — 15/20

Site	Sitio	
Maintenance	Conversa	
Architect	Arquitecto	Henry Cotton Rocky Roquemore
Type	Tipo	seaside course, forest
Relief	Relevo	
Water in play	Lago	
Exp. to wind	Exposto ao vento	
Trees in play	Arvores	

Scorecard Cartão de resultados	**Chp.** Camp.	**Mens** Homens	**Ladies** Senhoras
Length Compriment	6050	5650	4925
Par	72	72	72
Slope system	—	—	—

Advised golfing ability — 0 12 24 36
Nivel de jogo recomendado

Hcp required Handicap exigido — 27 Men/35 Ladies

Club house & amenities — CLUB HOUSE E ANEXOS — 6/10

Pro shop	Pro-shop	
Driving range	Campo de prática	
Sheltered	coberto	6 mats
On grass	om relva	yes
Putting-green	putting-green	yes
Pitching-green	pitching-green	yes

Hotel facilities — INFRAESTRUCTURAS HOTELEIRAS — 7/10

HOTELS HOTELS

Dona Filipa — Vale do Lobo
147 rooms, D 224 € — 100 m
Tel (351) 289 - 394 141, Fax (351) 289 - 394 288

Quinta do Lago — Quinta do Lago
141 rooms, D 175 € — 3 km
Tel (351) 289 - 396 666, Fax (351) 289 - 396 393

RESTAURANTS RESTAURANTE

O Favo — Vale do Lobo
Tel (351) 289 - 394 653 — 1 km

O Tradicional — Almancil
Tel (351) 289 - 399 093 — 6 km

VILA SOL

14 | 7 | 7

Criado em 1991 numa zona de pinhal com alguns sobreiros bem como algumas figueiras a amendoeiras. Vila Sol foi desenhada po Donald Steel que não procurou em renegar o seu espírito britânico. Renunciou a quaisquer movimentos de terra espectaculares, conservando o lado natural do terreno. Pode lastimar-se que não tenha um traçado mais original, mas não dixa de ser um percurso bem adaptado a uma grande variedade de jogadores embora os primeiros buracos sejam um pouco difíceis para amadores. Podem tranquilizar-se, o seguimento é mas tranquilo. Bastante estreito, o percurso pode causar problemas aos jogadores imprecisos. Deverão jogar com cuidado para evitar as árvores e salvar o seu par. Com excepção do "green" do 11, os outros são bastante visiveis pouco defendidos, planos a de dimensão média. Com muito boa manutenção este percurso não é uma obra prima, mas merece o desvio.

Created in 1991 over an estate of pine, cork-oak, fig and almond trees, Vila Sol was laid out by Donald Steel, who worked in a distinctly British style. Preferring to keep the terrain's natural look, there was no spectacular earth-moving. This is an arguable point, as we would have liked a more personal layout. As it is, the course is very honest and playable by all golfers, even though the first holes are a tough test for the average hacker. They can relax, though, because the course tends to ease off later on. This is a rather tight course which can cause problems to wayward hitters. Getting out of the trees to save par requires some well-flighted recovery shots. With the exception of the 11th hole, all the greens are visible, relatively undefended, rather flat and medium-sized. A well upkept course, hardly a masterpiece but well worth the trip.

Golf de Vila Sol — 1991

Alto do Semino. Est. Nacional 396, km 24,8
P - 8125-305 QUARTEIRA

Office	Secretariado	(351) 289 - 300 505
Pro shop	Pro-shop	(351) 289 - 300 505
Fax	Fax	(351) 289 - 316 499
E-mail	golfreservation@vilasol.pt	
Situation	Localização	

Quarteira (pop.8 905), 3 km - Faro (pop. 33 664), 18 km

Annual closure	Fecho anual	no
Weekly closure	Fecho semanal	no

Fees main season Tarifas de época alta	18 holes	
	Week days Semana	**We/Bank holidays** Fim de sem./Feriad
Individual Individual	90 €	90 €
Couple Casal	180 €	180 €

– 50% for members of Portuguese golf clubs

Caddy	Caddy	no
Electric Trolley	Trolley eléctrico	15 € /18 holes
Buggy	Buggy	40 € /18 holes
Clubs	Tacos	20 € /18 holes

Credit cards Cartão de crédito VISA - AMEX

GOLF
Lagoa de Odidos
Peniche
Baleal
Caldas da Rainha
Obidos
N 114
Atouguia da Baleia
Serra d'El-Rei
Lisboa
N8
0 3 6 km

Access Acesso : N1, N125 → Faro, N 396 → Quarteira
Map 3 on page 1054 Mapa 3 Página 1054

Golf course PERCURSO — 14/20

Site	Sitio	
Maintenance	Conversa	
Architect	Arquitecto	Donald Steel
Type	Tipo	forest, residential
Relief	Relevo	
Water in play	Lago	
Exp. to wind	Exposto ao vento	
Trees in play	Arvores	

Scorecard Cartão de resultados	**Chp.** Camp.	**Mens** Homens	**Ladies** Senhoras
Length Compriment	6335	5975	5406
Par	72	72	72
Slope system	—	—	—

Advised golfing ability Nivel de jogo recomendado: 0 12 24 36
Hcp required Handicap exigido: 28 Men, 36 Ladies

Club house & amenities CLUB HOUSE E ANEXOS — 7/10

Pro shop	Pro-shop	
Driving range	Campo de prática	
Sheltered	coberto	no
On grass	om relva	yes
Putting-green	putting-green	yes
Pitching-green	pitching-green	yes

Hotel facilities INFRAESTRUCTURAS HOTELEIRAS — 7/10

HOTELS HOTELS

Marinotel, 378 rooms, D 274 € — Vilamoura
Tel (351) 289 - 389 988, Fax (351) 289 - 389 869 — 3 km

Atlantis, 310 rooms, D 197 € — Vilamoura
Tel (351) 289 - 389 977, Fax (351) 289 - 389 962 — 4 km

Ampalius, 357 rooms, D 187 € — Vilamoura
Tel (351) 289 - 388 008, Fax (351) 289 - 380 911 — 4 km

Dom Pedro Golf, 101 rooms, D 190 € — Vilamoura
Tel (351) 289 - 300 700, Fax (351) 289 - 300 701 — 2 km

RESTAURANTS RESTAURANTE

Al Garb (Atlantis), Tel (351) 289 - 389 974 Vilamoura 4 km

Gril Sirius, Tel (351) 289 - 389 988 Vilamoura 3 km

VILAMOURA I (Old Course)

16 | 7 | 7

Construídos entre 1973 e 1990, o complexo de quarto percursos de Vilamoura foi-se pouco a pouco modernizando. O primeiro, Vilamoura I, continua a ser o mais interessante e a sua renovação, em particular, dos greens, acrescenta ao prazer da sua reabertura. O arquitecto Frank Pennink soube preservar a naturalidade de uma paisagem magnífica, servida de uma bela vegetação. O seu percurso lembra muitas vezes a arquitectura dos golfes britânicos de interior, com a vantagem do clima. Embora tenha um par 73, é suficientemente longo para perturbar os jogadores imprecisos, pois as arvores estão muito em jogo. Os pares 3 tambén não são fáceis. E um persurso para técnicistas, expertos na arte de trabalhar a bola, mas os cinco pares 5 podem salvar os resultados de outro modo ameaçados. Um excelente test bem rejuvenescido.

Built between 1973 and 1990, the four-course complex at Vilamoura has gradually been modernised. The oldest, Vilamoura 1, is still the most interesting and its restyling, especially the greens, has made its re-opening all the more enjoyable. Designer Frank Pennink has successfully preserved the natural look of magnificent landscape and vegetation. The layout is often reminiscent of some of the great British parkland courses, with the climate as an added benefit. Although a par 73, it is long enough to upset wayward hitters as the trees are very much in play. The par 3s are no walk-over, either, making this a course for the technically-minded golfer who excels in working the ball. But rest assured, the par 5s can save a card that the other holes might have condemned to the litter-bin. An excellent test of golf, now looking wonderfully younger.

VILAMOURA GOLF CLUB 1969

P - 8125-507 VILAMOURA

Office	Secretariado	(351) 289 - 310 330
Pro shop	Pro-shop	(351) 289 - 301 166
Fax	Fax	(351) 289 - 310 349
Web	www.vilamoura.net	
Situation	Localização	

Quarteira (pop. 8 905), 3 km - Faro, (pop. 33 664), 20 km

Annual closure	Fecho anual	no
Weekly closure	Fecho semanal	no

Fees main season Tarifas de época alta	Week days Semana	We/Bank holidays Fim de sem./Feriad
		18 holes
Individual Individual	100 €	100 €
Couple Casal	200 €	200 €

Juniors: 50 €

Caddy	Caddy	no
Electric Trolley	Trolley eléctrico	12 € /18 holes
Buggy	Buggy	45 € /18 holes
Clubs	Tacos	37 € /18 holes

Credit cards Cartão de crédito VISA - AMEX

Loulé
← Portimão
E1 - IP1
N 396
Faro
N 125
Vilamoura
GOLF
Quarteira
Quinta do Lago
0 2 4 km

Access Acesso : N125 Lagos-Faro. → Vilamoura
Map 3 on page 1054 Mapa 3 Página 1054

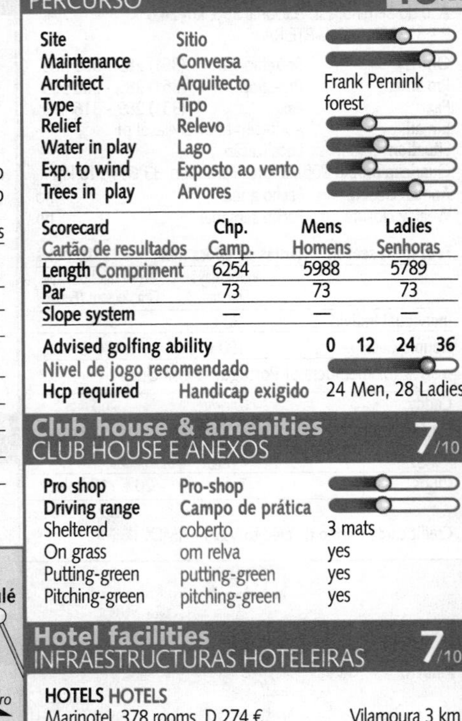

Golf course PERCURSO 16/20

Site	Sitio	
Maintenance	Conversa	
Architect	Arquitecto	Frank Pennink
Type	Tipo	forest
Relief	Relevo	
Water in play	Lago	
Exp. to wind	Exposto ao vento	
Trees in play	Arvores	

Scorecard Cartão de resultados	Chp. Camp.	Mens Homens	Ladies Senhoras
Length Compriment	6254	5988	5789
Par	73	73	73
Slope system	—	—	—

Advised golfing ability Nivel de jogo recomendado 0 12 24 36
Hcp required Handicap exigido 24 Men, 28 Ladies

Club house & amenities CLUB HOUSE E ANEXOS 7/10

Pro shop	Pro-shop	
Driving range	Campo de prática	
Sheltered	coberto	3 mats
On grass	om relva	yes
Putting-green	putting-green	yes
Pitching-green	pitching-green	yes

Hotel facilities INFRAESTRUCTURAS HOTELEIRAS 7/10

HOTELS HOTELS

Marinotel, 378 rooms, D 274 € Vilamoura 3 km
Tel (351) 289 - 389 988, Fax (351) 289 - 389 869

Atlantis, 310 rooms, D 197 € Vilamoura 4 km
Tel (351) 289 - 389 977, Fax (351) 289 - 389 962

Ampalius, 357 rooms, D 187 € Vilamoura 4 km
Tel (351) 289 - 388 008, Fax (351) 289 - 380 911

Dom Pedro Golf, 101 rooms, D 190 € Vilamoura
Tel (351) 289 - 300 700, Fax (351) 289 - 300 701

RESTAURANTS RESTAURANTE

Al Garb (Atlantis), Tel (351) 289 - 389 974 Vilamoura 4 km

Gril Sirius, Tel (351) 289 - 389 988 Vilamoura 3 km

VILAMOURA III (Laguna) 14 7 7

Em comparação com Vilamoura II, este percurso tem uma estética e uma paisagem muito diferente. De facto, é constituido por 3 grupos de 9 buracos que se combinam (Pinhal, Lago, Marina) próximo do mar. O desenho é do arquitecto Joseph Lee (e Rocky Roquemore) um dos grandes representantes da "Escola da Florida", come se nota sobretudo nos percursos Lago e Marina que são, alias, os mais interessantes. Como o seu nome indica a água está muito presente: em cerca de metade dos buracos. Mas o aspecto natural do terreno foi mantido. Os jogadores com distância podem exprimir-se ai melhor do que nos outros percursos do complexo, visto terem "fairways" mais largos e o arvoredo ser menos ameaçador, mesmo que visualmente seja mais intimidante do que o é na realidade. Vilamoura III é, apesar de tudo, mais difícil para fazer resultado: é o mais divertido para "match-play". Os greens têm um desenho interessante mas há que cuidar da manutenção, aliás como no resto do complexo que é uma verdadeira fábrica de golfe.

In a different style and landscape as the two others, this course consists in fact of three combinable 9-holers (Pinhal, Lago and Marina), close to the Atlantic. It was designed by Joseph Lee (and Rocky Roquemore), one of the great representatives of the Florida school, as is clear to see on the "Lago" and "Marina" course, the most interesting of the three, as it happens. As their name suggests, water is in great supply on about half the holes, but the terrain's natural look has been preserved. Big-hitters can hit more freely than on the other courses in this resort, as the fairways are wider and the trees less threatening. Even though it looks more intimidating than it plays, making a good score can be hard going, so match-play is often more fun. The greens are interestingly designed, but upkeep needs watching here and throughout the resort, where golf is non-stop production-business.

VILAMOURA GOLF CLUB 1990

P - 8125-507 VILAMOURA

Office	Secretariado	(351) 289 - 310 330
Pro shop	Pro-shop	(351) 289 - 301 166
Fax	Fax	(351) 289 - 310 349
Web	www.vilamoura.net	
Situation	Localização	

Quarteira (pop. 8 905), 3 km - Faro, (pop. 33 664), 20 km

Annual closure	Fecho anual	no
Weekly closure	Fecho semanal	no

Fees main season Tarifas de época alta	18 holes	
	Week days / Semana	We/Bank holidays / Fim de sem./Feriad
Individual Individual	50 €	50 €
Couple Casal	100 €	100 €

Caddy	Caddy	no
Electric Trolley	Trolley eléctrico	12 € /18 holes
Buggy	Buggy	45 € /18 holes
Clubs	Tacos	37 € /18 holes

Credit cards Cartão de crédito VISA - AMEX

Access Acesso : N125 Lagos-Faro. → Vilamoura
Map 3 on page 1054 Mapa 3 Página 1054

Golf course PERCURSO 14/20

Site	Sitio	
Maintenance	Conversa	
Architect	Arquitecto	Joseph Lee, Rocky Roquemore
Type	Tipo	open country
Relief	Relevo	
Water in play	Lago	
Exp. to wind	Exposto ao vento	
Trees in play	Arvores	

Scorecard Cartão de resultados	Chp. Camp.	Mens Homens	Ladies Senhoras
Length Compriment	6130	5760	4900
Par	72	72	72
Slope system	—	—	—

Advised golfing ability Nivel de jogo recomendado — 0 12 24 36

Club house & amenities CLUB HOUSE E ANEXOS 7/10

Pro shop	Pro-shop	
Driving range	Campo de prática	
Sheltered	coberto	3 mats
On grass	om relva	yes
Putting-green	putting-green	yes
Pitching-green	pitching-green	yes

Hotel facilities INFRAESTRUCTURAS HOTELEIRAS 7/10

HOTELS HOTELS

Marinotel, 378 rooms, D 274 € — Vilamoura 3 km
Tel (351) 289 - 389 988, Fax (351) 289 - 389 869

Atlantis, 310 rooms, D 197 € — Vilamoura 4 km
Tel (351) 289 - 389 977, Fax (351) 289 - 389 962

Ampalius, 357 rooms, D 187 € — Vilamoura 4 km
Tel (351) 289 - 388 008, Fax (351) 289 - 380 911

Dom Pedro Golf, 101 rooms, D 190 € — Vilamoura
Tel (351) 289 - 300 700, Fax (351) 289 - 300 701

RESTAURANTS RESTAURANTE

Al Garb (Atlantis), Tel (351) 289 - 389 974 Vilamoura 4 km

Gril Sirius, Tel (351) 289 - 389 988 Vilamoura 3 km

VILAMOURA Millenium

14 | 7 | 7

Junto do " Old Course", já remodelado, do " Pinhal " e do " Laguna ", restavam a Vilamoura (essa verdadeira fábrica de Golfe do Algarve) 9 buracos. Acabam de ser levado a 18 buracos com a adição de mais 9 desenhados por Martin Hawtree e tomou o nome de " Milenium " para o que não necessita ser-se um Einstein para inventar um tal nome. Os arredores do campo não se sentirão lesados, uma vez que os pinheiros são uma parte importante parte do "decor" e o ambiente é bastante similar. Nota-se que se encarregou o arquitecto de realizar um percurso para turistas de todos os níveis, para que possam jogar rapidamente, sem terem de procurar demasiadas bolas, mas encontrando sempre alguma pimenta no jogo... As dificuldades são aqui reais mas nunca impossíveis de suplantar. A construção foi bem executada e com o tempo as condições deverão ainda melhorar. Bastante repousante para jogar e bastante natural visualmente, mistura um pouco os estilos, o que é natural, uma vez que parte dos primeiros 9 buracos já existiam. Por vezes teria sido desejável um pouco mais de imaginação ou loucura, mas pelo menos não houve erros!

Alongside the already restyled Old Course, the "Pinhal" and the "Laguna" courses, there remained a 9-hole layout in Vilamoura, the golf factory of the Algarve. It has just been extended to 18 holes by Martin Hawtree and christened "Millennium" (how long did it take them to think that one up, we wonder). Regulars here will feel at home on this course, with pine trees forming a large part of the scenery in a similar sort of environment as the other courses. Visibly the architect was charged with designing a course for tourists of all abilities so that they could play quickly without too much time spent looking for lost balls, with a little spice added here and there. The difficulties are real enough but never impossible to get around. The course has been well built and should improve with time. A rather natural-looking and relaxing course to play, it mixes up different styles, which is only logical when you start with an existing 9-hole layout. We might have wished for a little more imagination or folly but at least there are no glaring errors.

VILAMOURA GOLF CLUB 2000

P - 8125-507 VILAMOURA

Office	Secretariado	(351) 289 - 310 330
Pro shop	Pro-shop	(351) 289 - 301 166
Fax	Fax	(351) 289 - 310 349
Web	www.vilamoura.net	
Situation	Localização	

Quarteira (pop. 8 905), 3 km - Faro, (pop. 33 664), 20 km

Annual closure	Fecho anual	no
Weekly closure	Fecho semanal	no

Fees main season Tarifas de época alta	18 holes	
	Week days Semana	We/Bank holidays Fim de sem./Feriad
Individual Individual	90 €	90 €
Couple Casal	180 €	180 €

Caddy	Caddy	no
Electric Trolley	Trolley eléctrico	12 € /18 holes
Buggy	Buggy	45 € /18 holes
Clubs	Tacos	37 € /18 holes

Credit cards Cartão de crédito VISA - AMEX 

Access Acesso : N125 Lagos-Faro. → Vilamoura
Map 3 on page 1054 Mapa 3 Página 1054

Golf course PERCURSO 14/20

Site	Sitio	
Maintenance	Conversa	
Architect	Arquitecto	Martin Hawtree
Type	Tipo	forest
Relief	Relevo	
Water in play	Lago	
Exp. to wind	Exposto ao vento	
Trees in play	Arvores	

Scorecard Cartão de resultados	Chp. Camp.	Mens Homens	Ladies Senhoras
Length Compriment	5784	5496	4767
Par	72	72	72
Slope system	—	—	—

Advised golfing ability Nivel de jogo recomendado 0 12 24 36

Hcp required Handicap exigido 36

Club house & amenities CLUB HOUSE E ANEXOS 7/10

Pro shop	Pro-shop	
Driving range	Campo de prática	
Sheltered	coberto	3 mats
On grass	om relva	yes
Putting-green	putting-green	yes
Pitching-green	pitching-green	yes

Hotel facilities INFRAESTRUCTURAS HOTELEIRAS 7/10

HOTELS HOTELS

Marinotel, 378 rooms, D 274 € Vilamoura 3 km
Tel (351) 289 - 389 988, Fax (351) 289 - 389 869

Atlantis, 310 rooms, D 197 € Vilamoura 4 km
Tel (351) 289 - 389 977, Fax (351) 289 - 389 962

Ampalius, 357 rooms, D 187 € Vilamoura 4 km
Tel (351) 289 - 388 008, Fax (351) 289 - 380 911

Dom Pedro Golf, 101 rooms, D 190 € Vilamoura
Tel (351) 289 - 300 700, Fax (351) 289 - 300 701

RESTAURANTS RESTAURANTE

Al Garb (Atlantis), Tel (351) 289 - 389 974 Vilamoura 4 km

Gril Sirius, Tel (351) 289 - 389 988 Vilamoura 3 km

EUROPE'S TOP 1000 GOLF COURSES

Spain

Valderrama

No es sólo un coche

PEUGEOT 206 COUPE Y CABRIO

La verdadera belleza es única. Pero hay excepciones que confirman la regla. La verdadera belleza es única.

www.peugeot.es 902 366 24 7 Peugeot Directo

Spain
España

H Spain boasts around 200,000 golfers, 165 eighteen-hole courses and more than 80 nine-hole layouts. Helped by an extremely pleasant climate and attractive geographic location, Spain is one of Europe's leading tourist destinations, where regions such as the Costa Del Sol, the Balearic Islands, the Costa Brava and the Canaries have very much to offer when it comes to great golf. To appeal to today's golfer, they can and do put forward arguments such as the excellence and variety of facilities, which combine golf and tourism, plus standards of service for customers.

The tradition of golf in Spain dates back to over a century and has helped to produce some outstanding professional players and amateur golfers who have won all the top international honours. But since golf is not exactly the most "popularised" sport in Spain, the country is only now beginning to build public and municipal courses to rank with the traditional private clubs which are generally to be found around the country's major cities.

As a general rule, club members have full priority and green fees are high enough to be prohibitive. Excepting the truly commercial courses, it is preferable to carry a letter of introduction from your own club and proof of handicap.

España cuenta con 200.000 jugadores federados, 165 campos de 18 hoyos, 80 campos de 9 hoyos y casi 50 campos cortos (de pares 3 y pitch & putt, variedad de fuerte implantación en los últimos años). Especialmente por su clima benévolo y por su situación geográfica, España es uno de los principales destinos del turismo de golf en Europa, con ofertas bien conocidas en la Costa del Sol de Málaga, en Mallorca, en la Costa Brava y en las islas Canarias. Hay que celebrar, precisamente, que la industria turístico-golfística española está añadiendo valores de calidad en su oferta de instalaciones y servicio a sus clientes.

España también tiene una tradición centenaria en el deporte del golf que ha producido y produce extraordinarios campeones profesionales así como jugadores amateur ganadores de los principales títulos internacionales. Y como el golf todavía no es un deporte popular aquí, existe una clara tendencia a construir y equipar campos municipales y públicos como alternativa a los clubs privados históricos que se encuentran, generalmente, junto a las grandes ciudades.

Por regla general los socios y abonados de clubs y campos gozan de ciertos privilegios horarios para sus salidas y algunos green-fees tienen un precio disuasorio porque la afluencia de jugadores locales no deja espacio para los forasteros. Siempre es recomendable presentarse en los campos que se visitan con una carta del club habitual del jugador que certifique su handicap.

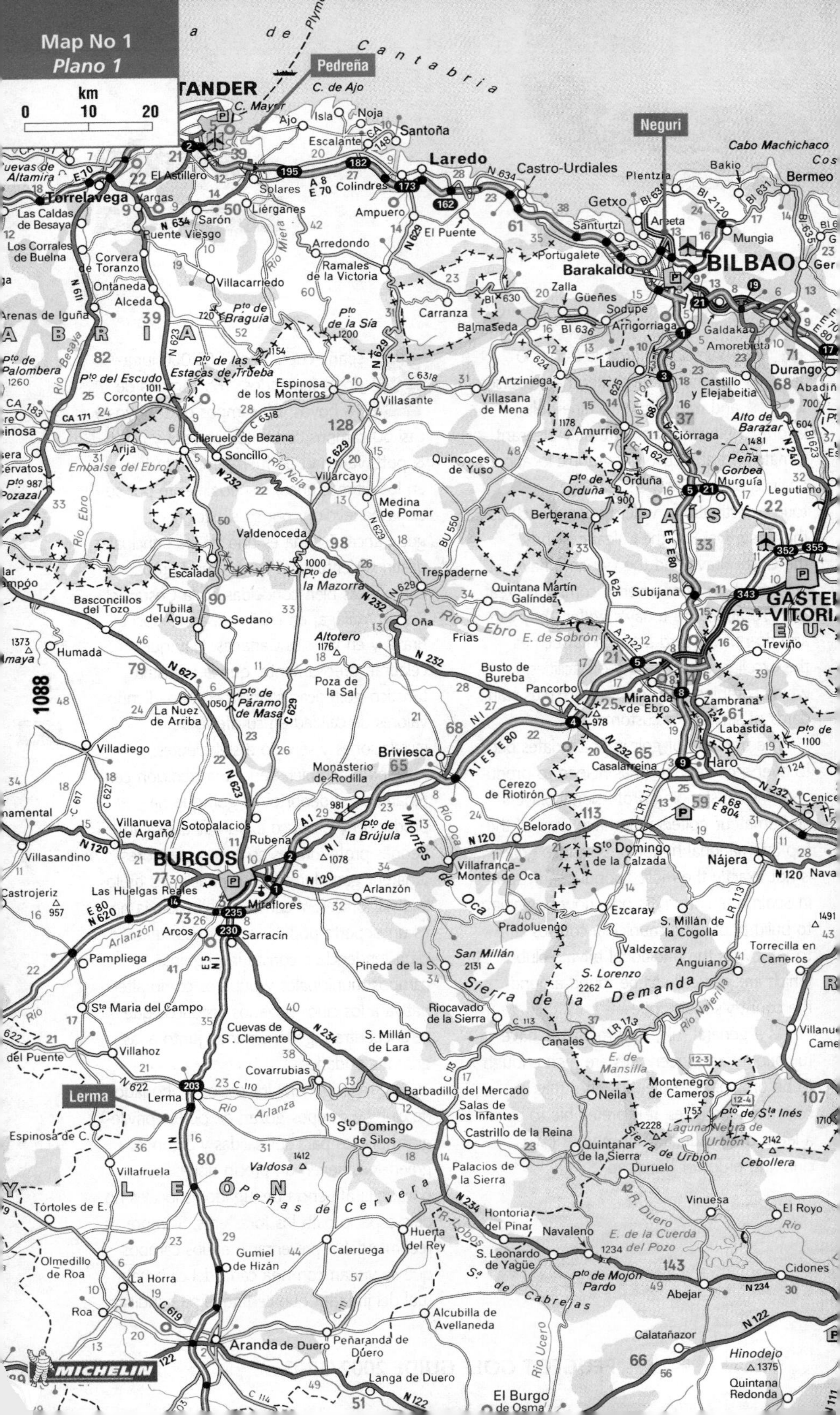
Map No 1
Plano 1
km
0 10 20
Pedreña
Neguri
Lerma
Mar Cantábrica
Plymouth
SANTANDER
C. Mayor
C. de Ajo
Ajo
Isla
Noja
Santoña
Escalante
Laredo
Castro-Urdiales
Cabo Machichaco
Bakio
Bermeo
Plentzia
Getxo
Areeta
Mungia
Santurtzi
Portugalete
Barakaldo
BILBAO
Galdakao
Amorebieta
Durango
Abadiño
Torrelavega
El Astillero
Vargas
Solares
Colindres
Ampuero
Liérganes
Las Caldas de Besaya
Los Corrales de Buelna
Puente Viesgo
Sarón
Corvera de Toranzo
Ontaneda
Alceda
Arenas de Iguña
Villacarriedo
Arredondo
Ramales de la Victoria
El Puente
Carranza
Zalla
Güeñes
Sodupe
Balmaseda
Arrigorriaga
Laudio
Artziniega
Villasana de Mena
Castillo y Elejabeitia
Alto de Barazar
Amurrio
Orduña
Ciórraga
Peña Gorbea
Murguía
Legutiano
Pto de Braguía
Pto de la Sía
Pto de las Estacas de Trueba
Pto de Palombera
Pto del Escudo
Corconte
Espinosa de los Monteros
Villasante
Reinosa
Arija
Embalse del Ebro
Cilleruelo de Bezana
Soncillo
Río Nela
Quincoces de Yuso
Pto de Orduña
Berberana
Villarcayo
Medina de Pomar
Pto de Pozazal
Valdenoceda
Pto de la Mazorra
Trespaderne
Quintana Martín Galíndez
Subijana
GASTEIZ VITORIA
PAÍS VASCO
Escalada
Basconcillos del Tozo
Tubilla del Agua
Sedano
Oña
Frías
Río Ebro
E. de Sobrón
Humada
Altotero
Poza de la Sal
Busto de Bureba
Pancorbo
Miranda de Ebro
Treviño
Zambrana
Labastida
Haro
Casalarreina
La Nuez de Arriba
Pto de Páramo de Masa
Villadiego
Briviesca
Monasterio de Rodilla
Cerezo de Riotirón
Belorado
Sto Domingo de la Calzada
Nájera
Villanueva de Argaño
Sotopalacios
Rubena
Pto de la Brújula
Montes de Oca
Villafranca-Montes de Oca
Villasandino
BURGOS
Castrojeriz
Las Huelgas Reales
Miraflores
Arlanzón
Ezcaray
S. Millán de la Cogolla
Arcos
Sarracín
Pradoluengo
Pampliega
Pineda de la S.
San Millán
Valdezcaray
Anguiano
Torrecilla en Cameros
S. Lorenzo
Sierra de la Demanda
Sta María del Campo
Cuevas de S. Clemente
Riocavado de la Sierra
Canales
Río Najerilla
Villahoz
S. Millán de Lara
E. de Mansilla
Covarrubias
Barbadillo del Mercado
Neila
Montenegro de Cameros
Lerma
Río Arlanza
Salas de los Infantes
Pto de Sta Inés
Espinosa de C.
Sto Domingo de Silos
Castrillo de la Reina
Laguna Negra de Urbión
Quintanar de la Sierra
Sierra de Urbión
Cebollera
Villafruela
Valdosa
Palacios de la Sierra
Duruelo
LEÓN
Peñas de Cervera
Tórtoles de E.
Hontoria del Pinar
Vinuesa
El Royo
R. Duero
E. de la Cuerda del Pozo
Huerta del Rey
Navaleno
Caleruega
S. Leonardo de Yagüe
Olmedillo de Roa
Gumiel de Hizán
Pto de Mojón Pardo
Abejar
Cidones
La Horra
Sa de Cabrejas
Roa
Alcubilla de Avellaneda
Aranda de Duero
Peñaranda de Duero
Calatañazor
Hinodejo
Langa de Duero
El Burgo de Osma
Quintana Redonda
Río Ucero
MICHELIN

Seignosse (F)
Hossegor (F)
Chiberta (F)
Biarritz-le-Phare (F)
Makila Golf Club (F)
San Sebastian
Chantaco (F)
Arcangues (F)
Ulzama
Castillo de Gorraiz
BIARRITZ
Bayonne
Dax
Soustons
Hossegor
Capbreton
Tarnos
Boucau
Anglet
Bidart
St Jean-de-Luz
Hendaye
Hondarribia
DONOSTIA / S. SEBASTIÁN
Pasaia
Irun
Behobia
Oiartzun
Hernani
Zarautz
Zumaia
Deba
Ondarroa
Lekeitio
Markina-Xemein
Eibar
Elgóibar
Azkoitia
Azpeitia
Zestoa
Lasarte
Andoain
Villabona
Tolosa
Ordizia
Beasain
Zumárraga
Bergara
Arrasate / Mondragon
Oñati
Santuario de S. Ignacio de Loyola
Leitza
Lekunberri
Betelu
Altsasu
Etxarri-Aranatz
Irurtzun
Olazti (Burunda)
Salvatierra
Pto de Etxegarate
Pto de Urbasa
Sierra de Urbasa
IRUÑA/ PAMPLONA
Oricáin
Egüés
Noáin
Lizarra/ Estella
Puente la Reina
Campanas
Artajona
Tafalla
Olite
Larraga
Allo
Lerín
Sesma
Lodosa
Mendavia
Los Arcos
Torres del Rio
Viana
Logroño
Acedo
Sta Cruz
Andosilla
Falces
Peralta
Carcastillo
Caparroso
Marcilla
Villafranca
Milagro
Calahorra
S. Adrián
El Villar de Arnedo
Rincón de Soto
Arnedo
Arnedillo
Autol
Aldeanueva de Ebro
Alfaro
Castejón
Valtierra
Arguedas
Corella
Cintruénigo
Fitero
Tudela
Murchante
Cascante
Fustiñana
Buñuel
Cortes
Tarazona
Borja
Ainzón
Veruela
Tabuenca
Ágreda
Olvega
Matalebreras
Almenar
Villarroya
Gravalos
Cornago
Cervera del Río Alhama
Valverde de Cervera
S. Pedro Manrique
Pto de Oncala
Magaña
Castilruiz
Almajano
Pto del Madero
Sa del Moncayo
Ayedo
Elizondo
Doneztebe
Velate
Bera
Ainhoa
Espelette
Cambo-les-Bains
Ustaritz
Hasparren
Guéthary
Ascain
St Pée
la Rhune
Bidache
la Bastide-Clairence
Grtes d'Isturits et d'Oxocelhaya
St Palais
Peyrehorade
St Vincent-de-Tyrosse
St Martin-de-Seignanx
Erratzu
St Etienne-de-Baïgorry
St Jean-Pied-de-Port
Valcarlos
Urepel
Pto Ibañeta
Orreaga
Auritz
Aribe
Ochagavía
Escároz
Isaba
Roncal
Agoitz
E. de Itoiz
Navascués
Burgui
Lumbier
Leyre
Yesa
Sangüesa
Embalse de Yesa
Sos del Rey Católico
Mauléon-Licharre
Tardets-Sorholus
Pic d'Orhy
Pico d'Orhi
Pto de Larrau
Alto Laza
La Oliva
Uncastillo
Sádaba
Asin
Luna
Valareña
Ejea de los Caballeros
Erla
Piedratajada
Las Pedrosas
Castejón de Valdejasa
Loma Negra
Tauste
Mallén
N A V A R R A
P Y R É N
1089
MICHELIN
d'après carte n° 990 - 23ème édition - 2002.
Autorisation n° 0102062.

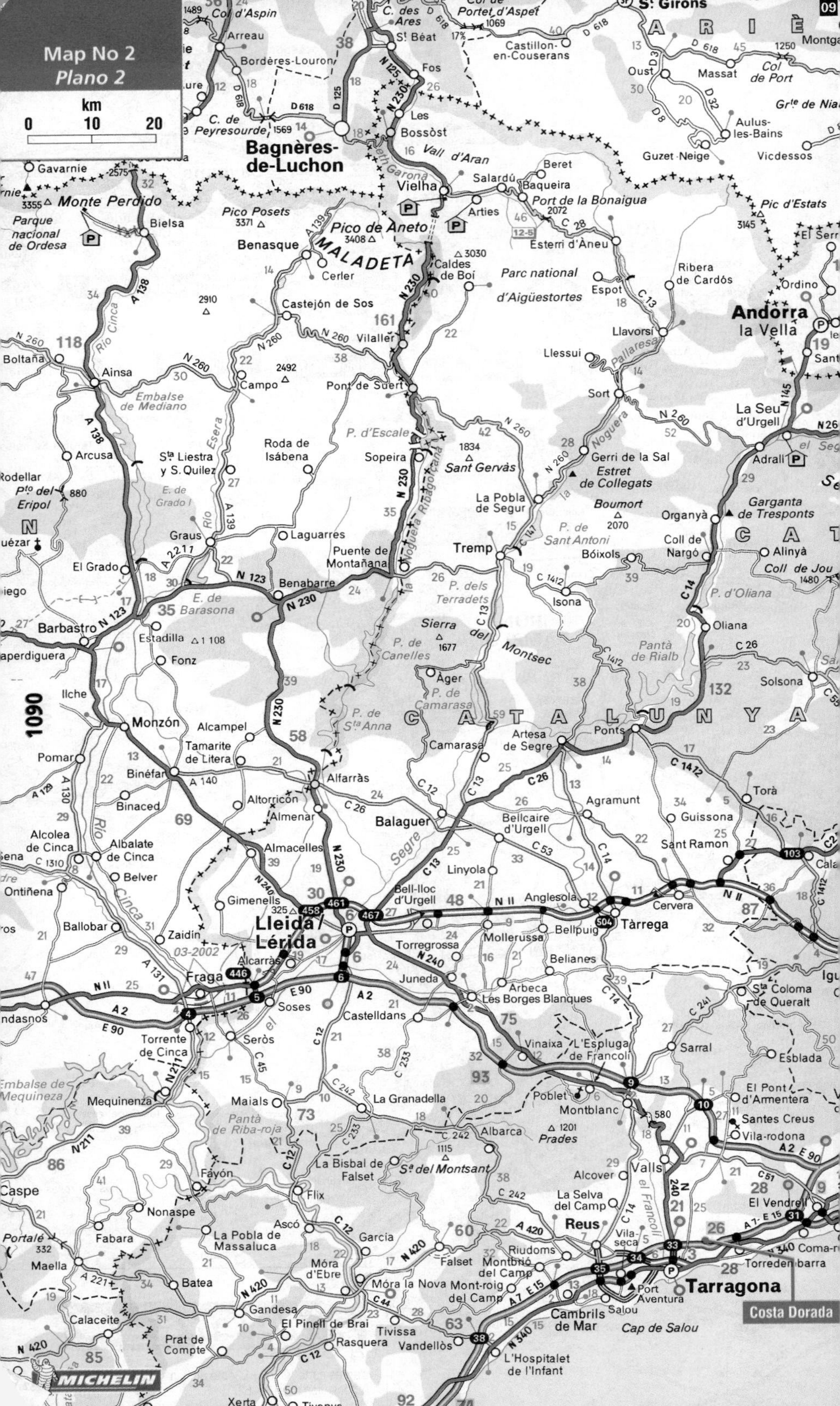
Map No 2
Plano 2
km
0 10 20
09
Michelin
Bagnères-de-Luchon
Col d'Aspin
Arreau
Bordères-Louron
C. de Peyresourde
C. des Ares
Col de Portet d'Aspet
St Girons
Castillon-en-Couserans
Ariège
Massat
Col de Port
Oust
Aulus-les-Bains
Guzet Neige
Vicdessos
St Béat
Fos
Les Bossòst
Vall d'Aran
Vielha
Salardú
Beret
Baqueira
Port de la Bonaigua
Arties
Esterri d'Àneu
Pic d'Estats
Gavarnie
Monte Perdido
Parque nacional de Ordesa
Bielsa
Pico Posets
Pico de Aneto
Maladeta
Benasque
Cerler
Caldes de Boí
Parc national d'Aigüestortes
Espot
Ribera de Cardós
Ordino
Andorra la Vella
Llavorsí
Llessui
Castejón de Sos
Vilaller
Boltaña
Ainsa
Embalse de Mediano
Campo
Pont de Suert
Sort
La Seu d'Urgell
Adrall
Arcusa
Sta Liestra y S. Quilez
Roda de Isábena
P. d'Escale
Sopeira
Sant Gervàs
Gerri de la Sal
Estret de Collegats
Rodellar
Pto del Eripol
E. de Grado I
La Pobla de Segur
Boumort
Organyà
Garganta de Tresponts
Graus
Laguarres
Puente de Montañana
Tremp
P. de Sant Antoni
Coll de Nargó
Alinyà
Coll de Jou
Bóixols
El Grado
Benabarre
P. dels Terradets
Isona
P. d'Oliana
Oliana
E. de Barasona
Barbastro
Estadilla
Sierra del Montsec
P. de Canelles
Pantà de Rialb
Fonz
Àger
P. de Camarasa
Solsona
Ilche
Monzón
Alcampel
P. de Sta Anna
Catalunya
Camarasa
Artesa de Segre
Ponts
Tamarite de Litera
Pomar
Binéfar
Alfarràs
Torà
Binaced
Altorricón
Almenar
Balaguer
Agramunt
Guissona
Alcolea de Cinca
Albalate de Cinca
Almacelles
Bellcaire d'Urgell
Sant Ramon
Belver
Linyola
Ontiñena
Gimenells
Bell-lloc d'Urgell
Anglesola
Cervera
Ballobar
Lleida/Lérida
Mollerussa
Bellpuig
Tàrrega
Zaidín
Torregrossa
Belianes
Alcarràs
Fraga
Juneda
Arbeca
Sta Coloma de Queralt
Soses
Les Borges Blanques
Castelldans
Torrente de Cinca
Seròs
Vinaixa
L'Espluga de Francolí
Sarral
Esblada
Embalse de Mequinenza
Mequinenza
Maials
La Granadella
Poblet
Montblanc
El Pont d'Armentera
Santes Creus
Vila-rodona
Pantà de Riba-roja
Albarca
Prades
Caspe
Fayón
La Bisbal de Falset
Sa del Montsant
Alcover
Valls
Flix
La Selva del Camp
El Vendrell
Nonaspe
Ascó
Reus
Fabara
La Pobla de Massaluca
Garcia
Vila-seca
Coma-ruga
Maella
Móra d'Ebre
Falset
Riudoms
Montbrió del Camp
Torredembarra
Batea
Móra la Nova
Mont-roig del Camp
Port Aventura
Tarragona
Gandesa
Salou
Costa Dorada
Calaceite
El Pinell de Brai
Tivissa
Cambrils de Mar
Cap de Salou
Prat de Compte
Rasquera
Vandellòs
L'Hospitalet de l'Infant
Xerta
Tivenys

PERPIGNAN
BARCELONA
PYRÉNÉES-ORIENTALES
CATALUÑA
Fontanals
Cerdaña
Peralada
Torremirona
Pals
Empordà
Osona Montanya
PGA de Catalunya
Golf d'Aro (Mas Nou)
Costa Brava
Masia Bach
San Cugat
El Prat
Quillan
Couiza
Mouthoumet
Chalabre
Lavelanet
Rennes-les-Bs
Tuchan
Salses-le-Chau
Port-Leucate
Port-Barcarès
Rivesaltes
St Laurent-de-la-Salanque
Axat
St-Paul-de-Fenouillet
Belcaire
Col de Chioula
Ax-les-Thermes
Quérigut
Latour-de-France
Estagel
Sournia
Millas
Ille-s-Têt
Canet-Plage
St Cyprien-Plage
Molitg-les-Bains
C. de Jau
Prades
Vinça
Thuir
Elne
Argelès
Collioure
Port-Vendres
Banyuls
Cerbère
Portbou
Pas de la Casa
Pic Carlit
C. de Puymorens
Font-Romeu
Col de la Quillane
Olette
Vernet-les-Bs
Pic du Canigou
St Martin
Mont-Louis
Saillagouse
Llivia
Puigcerdà
Bourg-Madame
Bellver de Cerdanya
Céret
le Boulou
le Perthus
Amélie-les-Bs-Palalda
Arles
la Preste
Prats-de-Mollo
Roc de France
Roc de Frausa
La Jonquera
Capmany
El Port de Llançà
Llançà
Núria
Setcases
Col d'Ares
Pto de Ares
Puigmal
Collada de Toses
Queralbs
Super-Molina
La Molina
Ribes de Freser
Camprodon
Sant Joan de les Abadesses
Sant Pau de Seguries
Figueres/Figueras
S. Pere de Roda
Cadaqués
Roses
Castelló d'Empúries
Golf de Roses
Baga
La Pobla de Lillet
Gombrèn
Castellfollit de la Roca
Ripoll
Collado de Coubet
Olot
Besalú
Bàscara
Empúries
L'Escala
Vilada
Les Llosses
Puigsacalm
Berga
Sant Agustí de Lluçanes
Sant Quirze de Besora
Sta Pau
Sant Esteve d'en Bas
Banyoles
Viladamat
L'Estartit
Gironella
Sant Boi de Lluçanès
Manlleu
P. de Susqueda
Amer
Girona/Gerona
La Bisbal d'Empordà
Parlavà
Torroella de Montgrí
Pals
Prats de Lluçanes
Sant Hipòlit de Voltregà
Olost
P. de Sau
Puig-reig
Vilanova de Sau
Anglès
Cassà de la Selva
Palafrugell
Aigua Blava
Navàs
Vic
Sant Hilari Sacalm
Calonge
Calella de Palafrugell
Balsareny
Tona
Viladrau
Sta Coloma de Farners
Caldes de Malavella
Llagostera
Palamós
Sant Antoni de C.
Platja d'Aro
Sallent
Artés
Moià
Sa de Montseny
Arbúcies
Sils
Vidreres
S' Agaró
S. Feliu de Guíxols
Centelles
Hostalric
Manresa
Castellterçol
Montseny
Breda
El Figaro
Sant Quirze Safaja
Sant Celoni
Tossa de Mar
Lloret de Mar
La Garriga
Tordera
Sta Susanna
Blanes
Monistrol
Caldes de Montbui
Cardedeu
Malgrat de Mar
Castellar del Vallès
Pineda de Mar
Granollers
Sant Andreu de Llavaneres
Calella
Sant Pol de Mar
Terrassa/Tarrasa
Sabadell
Esparreguera
La Roca
Argentona
Canet de Mar
Arenys de Mar
Olesa
Mataró
Martorell
Rubí
S. Cugat
Premià de Mar
El Masnou
Sadurní Anoia
Molins de Rei
Badalona
Begues
Gavà
El Prat de Llobregat
Genova
Garraf
Castelldefels
Sitges
Vilanova i la Geltrú
Dorada
MICHELIN

1091

Map No 3
Plano 3
km
0 10 20
1092
VALLADOLID
MADRID
Segovia
Ávila
El Escorial
Aranjuez
Lerma
La Herreria
La Moraleja
Club de Campo
La Dehesa
RSHE Club de Campo
Jarama R.A.C.E.
Olivar de la Hinojosa
Puerto de Hierro
CASTILLA Y LEÓN
ESPAÑA
COMUNIDAD DE MADRID
SIERRA DE GUADARRAMA
GREDOS
Peñas de Cervera
Palencia
Magaz
Baltanás
Espinosa de C.
Villafruela
Baños de Cerrato
Dueñas
Cevico de la Torre
Valoria la Buena
Esguevillas de E.
Fombellida
Tórtoles de E.
Olmedillo de Roa
La Horra
Roa
Gumiel de Hizán
Caleruega
Villafuerte
Cabezón
Villanubla
Zaratán
Simancas
Tordesillas
Laguna de Duero
Tudela de Duero
Quintanilla de Onésimo
Peñafiel
Fuentecén
Aranda de Duero
Peñaranda de Duero
Valdosa
Boecillo
Valdestillas
Montemayor de Pililla
Portillo
Cogeces del Monte
Campaspero
Sacramenia
Honrubia de la Cuesta
Maderuelo
Mojados
La Seca
S. Miguel del Arroyo
Olombrada
Fuentidueña
Rubio
Iscar
Cuéllar
Pedrajas de S. Esteban
Olmedo
Hontalbilla
Boceguillas
Samboal
Cantalejo
Sepúlveda
Riaza
Ataquines
Coca
Navas de Oro
Navalmanzano
Aguilafuente
Cerezo de Abajo
La Pinilla
Lobo
S. Cristóbal de la Vega
Nava de la Asunción
Carbonero el Mayor
Turégano
Pedraza de la Sierra
Prádena
Puerto de Somosierra
Arévalo
Montuenga
Sta María la Real de Nieva
La Salceda
Pto de Navafría
Buitrago del Lozoya
E. de El Villar
Adanero
Sanchidrián
Sangarcia
Abades
Torrecaballeros
San Ildefonso-la Granja
Lozoyuela
E. de El Atazar
Hernansancho
Labajos
Madrona
Rascafría
El Paular
Peñalara
Pto de la Morcuera
La Cabrera
Velayos
Mingorria
Villacastín
Pto de Navacerrada
Miraflores de la Sierra
Torrelaguna
Cercedilla
Navacerrada
Viñuelas
El Espinar
S. Rafael
Pto de Guadarrama
Guadarrama
Manzanares el Real
Colmenar Viejo
El Casar de Talamanca
Valdihuela
Las Navas del Marqués
Valle de los Caídos
Collado-Villalba
Navalperal de P.
Galapagar
Torrelodones
Pto de Paramera
Alcobendas
Cobeña
Barraco
El Hoyo de Pinares
Robledo de Chavela
Las Rozas
El Pardo
Barajas
Burgohondo
Cebreros
Valdemorillo
Navaluenga
El Tiemblo
E. de Burguillo
Aravaca
Brunete
Torrejón de Ardoz
Vicálvaro
Loeches
Piedralaves
Casavieja
La Adrada
S. Martin de Valdeiglesias
Chapinería
Villaviciosa de Odón
Sotillo de la Adrada
Cadalso de los Vidrios
Villa del Prado
Aldea del Fresno
Navalcarnero
Móstoles
Leganés
Getafe
Arganda
Méntrida
Almorox
Fuenlabrada
Parla
Griñón
Navamorcuende
Escalona
Valmojado
Pinto
S. Martin de la Vega
El Real de S. Vicente
Torrejón de la Calzada
Morata de Tajuña
Sta Cruz del Retamar
Valdemoro
Ciempozuelos
Illescas
Seseña
Camarena
Chinchón
Maqueda
Yuncos
Esquivias
Colmenar de Oreja
Fuensalida
Sta Olalla
Torrijos
Añover de Tajo
Ocaña
Noblejas
Villarrubia de Santiago
Talavera de la Reina
Río Pisuerga
Río Esgueva
Río Duero
Río Duratón
Río Cega
Río Eresma
Río Alberche
Río Tiétar
Río Jarama
Río Guadarrama
MICHELIN

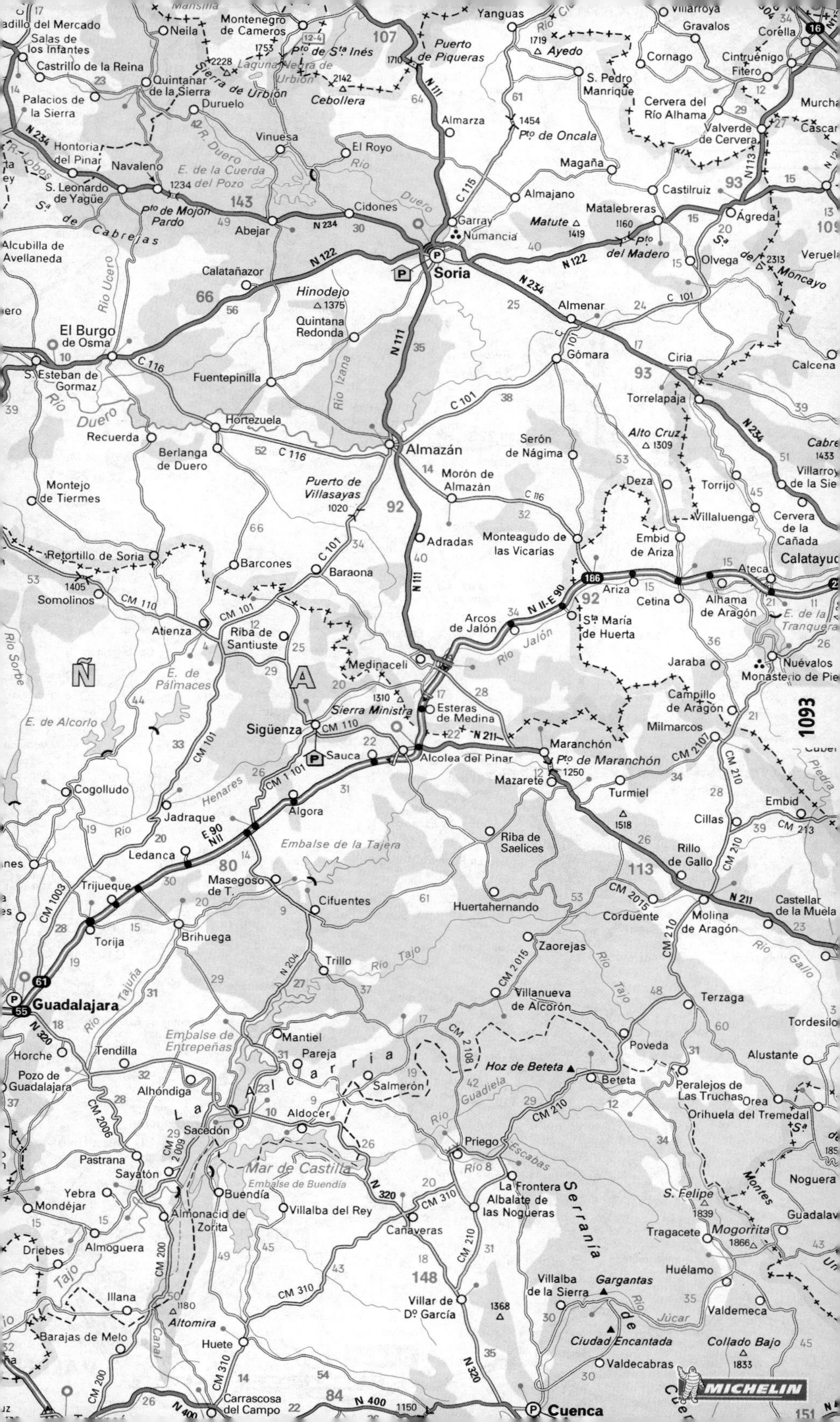

Mansilla
adillo del Mercado
Salas de los Infantes
Castrillo de la Reina
Palacios de la Sierra
Neila
Montenegro de Cameros
Quintanar de la Sierra
Duruelo
Sierra de Urbión
Laguna Negra de Urbión
2228
1753
Pto de Sta Inés
107
2142
Cebollera
Yanguas
Puerto de Piqueras
1710
N 111
Ayedo
1719
Villarroya
Gravalos
Cornago
Corella
Cintruénigo
Fitero
S. Pedro Manrique
Cervera del Río Alhama
Valverde de Cervera
Murcha
Cascar
16
N 234
Hontoria del Pinar
Navaleno
S. Leonardo de Yagüe
Sa de Cabrejas
1234
Pto de Mojón Pardo
143
R. Duero
E. de la Cuerda del Pozo
Vinuesa
El Royo
Río Duero
Almarza
1454
Pto de Oncala
Magaña
Almajano
C 115
Garray
Numancia
Matute
1419
Matalebreras
1160
Pto del Madero
Castilruiz
93
Ágreda
N 113
Sa de Moncayo
2313
Olvega
Veruela
Abejar
Cidones
N 234
Alcubilla de Avellaneda
Río Ucero
N 122
Calatañazor
Soria
N 122
N 234
66
Hinodejo
1375
Quintana Redonda
Almenar
C 101
El Burgo de Osma
S. Esteban de Gormaz
C 116
Fuentepinilla
N 111
Río Izana
Gómara
Ciria
Calcena
93
Torrelapaja
Río Duero
Recuerda
Hortezuela
Berlanga de Duero
C 116
C 101
Almazán
Serón de Nágima
Alto Cruz
1309
N 234
Cabre
1433
Villarroy de la Sie
Montejo de Tiermes
Puerto de Villasayas
1020
92
Morón de Almazán
C 116
Deza
Torrijo
Cervera de la Cañada
Villaluenga
Adradas
Monteagudo de las Vicarías
Embid de Ariza
Retortillo de Soria
1405
Somolinos
Barcones
C 101
Baraona
186
Ariza
Cetina
Ateca
Calatayud
Alhama de Aragón
E. de la Tranquera
CM 110
CM 101
Atienza
Riba de Santiuste
Arcos de Jalón
N II-E 90
Sta María de Huerta
Río Jalón
Río Sorbe
Ñ
E. de Pálmaces
A
Medinaceli
Jaraba
Nuévalos
Monasterio de Pie
1093
E. de Alcorlo
1310
Sierra Ministra
Esteras de Medina
Campillo de Aragón
Sigüenza
CM 110
N 211
Milmarcos
CM 101
Sauca
Alcolea del Pinar
Maranchón
Pto de Maranchón
CM 2107
Piedra
1250
Mazarete
Turmiel
CM 210
Cogolludo
Río Henares
CM 1 101
Algora
1518
Embid
CM 213
Jadraque
Riba de Saelices
Cillas
Río
E 90 NII
Embalse de la Tajera
Ledanca
80
Rillo de Gallo
113
Trijueque
Masegoso de T.
Cifuentes
Huertahernando
CM 2015
Castellar de la Muela
N 211
CM 1003
Torija
Brihuega
Corduente
Molina de Aragón
Zaorejas
Río Gallo
Río Tajuña
N 204
Trillo
Río Tajo
Río Tajo
CM 2015
CM 210
61
55
Guadalajara
N 320
Villanueva de Alcorón
Terzaga
Tordesilo
Embalse de Entrepeñas
Mantiel
Poveda
Tendilla
Horche
Pareja
CM 2108
Alustante
La Alcarria
Hoz de Beteta
Pozo de Guadalajara
Alhóndiga
Salmerón
Beteta
Peralejos de Las Truchas
Orea
CM 2006
Sacedón
Aldocer
Río Guadiela
CM 210
Orihuela del Tremedal
Sa
CM 2009
Priego
Río Escabas
Pastrana
Sayatón
Mar de Castilla
Embalse de Buendía
Río
N 320
La Frontera
Noguera
Yebra
Buendía
Villalba del Rey
CM 310
Albalate de las Nogueras
Serranía
S. Felipe
1839
Montes
Mondéjar
Almonacid de Zorita
Cañaveras
CM 210
Tragacete
Mogorrita
1866
Guadalav
Driebes
Almoguera
Tajo
CM 200
148
Huélamo
Villalba de la Sierra
Gargantas
Illana
1180
Altomira
CM 310
Villar de Do García
1368
Río Júcar
Valdemeca
Barajas de Melo
Canal
Huete
Ciudad Encantada
Collado Bajo
1833
Valdecabras
CM 310
CM 200
N 320
84
N 400
1150
Carrascosa del Campo
N 400
Cuenca
MICHELIN
151

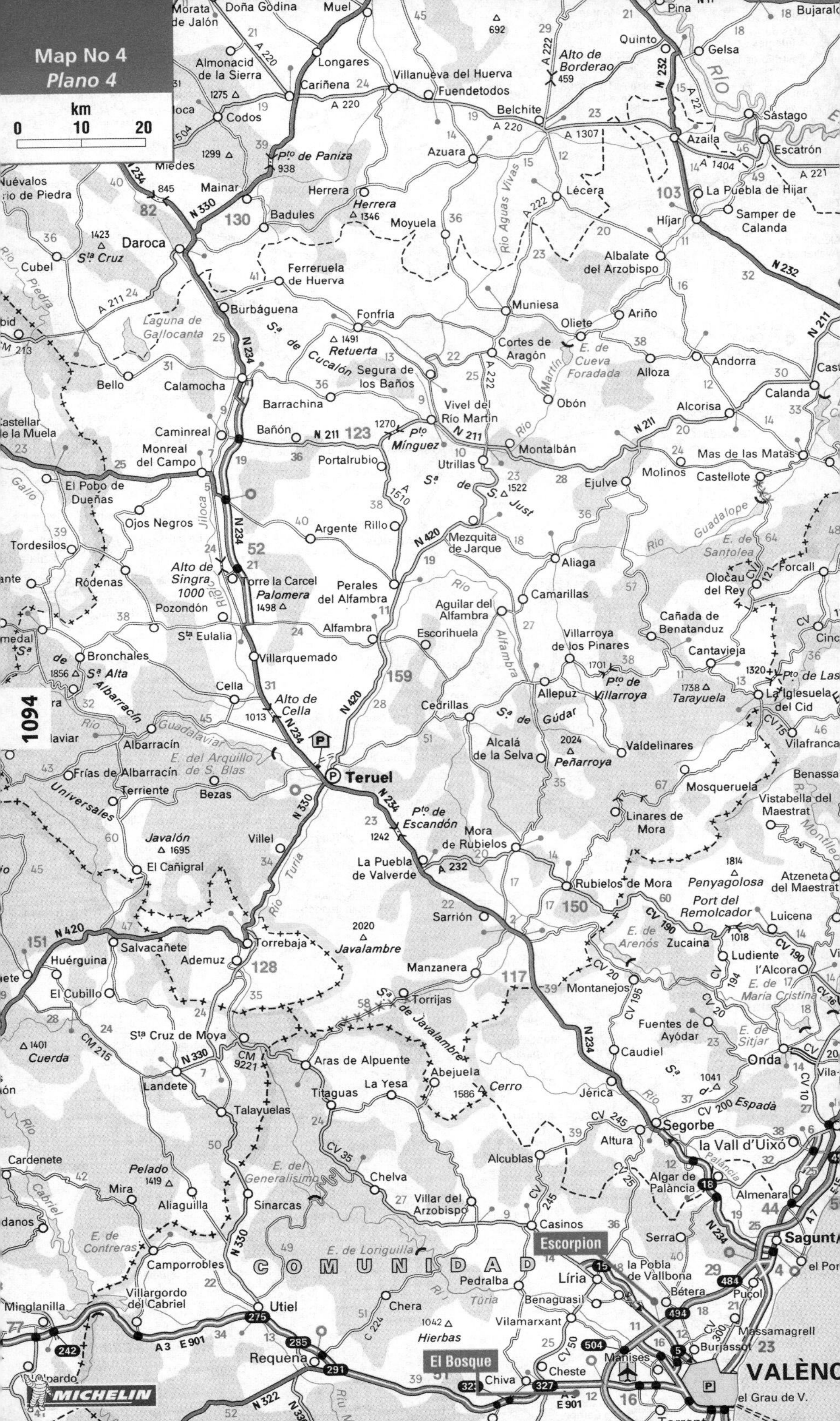

Map No 4
Plano 4
km
0 10 20
Morata de Jalón
Doña Godina
Muel
Almonacid de la Sierra
Longares
Cariñena
Villanueva del Huerva
Fuendetodos
Codos
Belchite
Alto de Borderao
Pina
Quinto
Gelsa
Sástago
Azaila
Escatrón
Río Ebro
Pto de Paniza
Azuara
Mainar
Herrera
Herrera
Lécera
La Puebla de Hijar
Samper de Calanda
Híjar
Nuévalos
rio de Piedra
Badules
Moyuela
Daroca
Sta Cruz
Cubel
Ferreruela de Huerva
Albalate del Arzobispo
Río Aguas Vivas
Burbáguena
Laguna de Gallocanta
Muniesa
Ariño
Fonfría
Oliete
Retuerta
Sa de Cucalón
Cortes de Aragón
E. de Cueva Foradada
Alloza
Andorra
Segura de los Baños
Bello
Calamocha
Barrachina
Obón
Calanda
Vivel del Río Martín
Alcorisa
Castellar de la Muela
Caminreal
Bañón
Pto Mínguez
Río Martín
Montalbán
Mas de las Matas
Monreal del Campo
Portalrubio
Utrillas
Molinos
Castellote
El Pobo de Dueñas
Sa de S. Just
Ejulve
Ojos Negros
Argente
Rillo
Mezquita de Jarque
Río Guadalope
Tordesilos
E. de Santolea
Alto de Singra
Torre la Carcel
Aliaga
Forcall
Rodenas
Palomera
Perales del Alfambra
Olocau del Rey
Pozondón
Camarillas
Aguilar del Alfambra
Río Alfambra
Cañada de Benatanduz
Sta Eulalia
Alfambra
Escorihuela
Villarroya de los Pinares
Cantavieja
Bronchales
Villarquemado
Pto de Villarroya
Pto de Las
Sa Alta de Albarracín
Tarayuela
La Iglesuela del Cid
Cella
Alto de Cella
Allepuz
1094
Cedrillas
Sa de Gúdar
Albarracín
Río Guadalaviar
Alcalá de la Selva
Peñarroya
Valdelinares
Vilafranca
E. del Arquillo de S. Blas
Frías de Albarracín
Teruel
Terriente
Bezas
Mosqueruela
Benassal
Sa Universales
Pto de Escandón
Linares de Mora
Vistabella del Maestrat
Villel
Javalón
Mora de Rubielos
Río Montlleó
La Puebla de Valverde
El Cañigral
Río Turia
Rubielos de Mora
Penyagolosa
Atzeneta del Maestrat
Sarrión
Port del Remolcador
Luicena
Javalambre
Torrebaja
E. de Arenós
Zucaina
Ludiente
Salvacañete
Ademuz
Huérguina
Manzanera
l'Alcora
E. de Maria Cristina
El Cubillo
Torrijas
Montanejos
Sa de Javalambre
Sta Cruz de Moya
Fuentes de Ayódar
E. de Sitjar
Cuerda
Aras de Alpuente
Caudiel
Onda
Landete
Abejuela
Cerro
Titaguas
La Yesa
Jérica
Sa d' Espadà
Talayuelas
Segorbe
Altura
la Vall d'Uixó
Cardenete
E. del Generalisimo
Alcublas
Algar de Palància
Río Palància
Pelado
Mira
Chelva
Almenara
Aliaguilla
Sinarcas
Villar del Arzobispo
Sagunt
Casinos
Serra
E. de Contreras
Escorpion
E. de Loriguilla
Camporrobles
COMUNIDAD
La Pobla de Vallbona
el Port
Pedralba
Llíria
Bétera
Puçol
Villargordo del Cabriel
Benaguasil
Minglanilla
Utiel
Chera
Río Túria
Vilamarxant
Massamagrell
Hierbas
Burjassot
Requena
El Bosque
Cheste
Manises
Chiva
VALÈNCIA
el Grau de V.
Torrent
MICHELIN
N 234
N 330
N 211
N 420
N 232
A 220
A 222
A 1307
A 1404
A 221
A 211
A 232
CV 190
CV 20
CV 195
CV 245
CV 25
CV 200
CV 35
CV 15
C 224
CM 215
CM 9221
A 3
E 901
A 7
N 322

GOLF

MICHELIN

Map No 5
Plano 5
km
0 10 20
1096
TOLEDO
Ciudad Real
Aranjuez
Puertollano
Valdepeñas
Manzanares
Daimiel
Consuegra
Madridejos
Ocaña
Argandа
Getafe
Leganés
Fuenlabrada
Parla
Pinto
Valdemoro
Ciempozuelos
Illescas
Seseña
Esquivias
Yuncos
Chinchón
Colmenar de Oreja
Morata de Tajuña
Perales
S. Martín de la Vega
Navalcarnero
Méntrida
Almorox
Griñón
Torrejón de la Calzada
Valmojado
Sta Cruz del Retamar
Camarena
Fuensalida
Sta Olalla
Torrijos
Cebolla
La Pueblanueva
El Carpio de Tajo
Escalonilla
La Puebla de Montalbán
Bargas
Añover de Tajo
Mocejón
Villasequilla de Yepes
Yepes
Noblejas
Villarrubia de Santiago
Dosbarrios
Villatobas
La Guardia
Huerta de Valdecarábanos
Villanueva de Bogas
Lillo
El Romeral
Tembleque
Villacañas
La Villa de Don Fadrique
Quero
Villafranca de los Caballeros
Camuñas
Herencia
Alcázar de S. Juan
Puerto Lápice
Villarta de S. Juan
Arenas de S. Juan
Villarrubia de los Ojos
Urda
Mora
Orgaz
Los Yébenes
Almonacid de Toledo
Sonseca
Layos
Polán
Gálvez
Cuerva
Menasalbas
Las Ventas con Peña Aguilera
Navahermosa
Los Navalmorales
S. Martín de Montalbán
Navalucillos
Embalse de Castrejón
E. de Guajaraz
Río Tajo
Río Guadarrama
Río Algodor
MONTES DE TOLEDO
Corral de Cantos
Retuerta del Bullaque
El Molinillo
E. de Torre de Abraham
Horcajo de los Montes
Machero
Alcoba
El Robledo
Los Cortijos
Calderina
Fuente el Fresno
Malagón
Porzuna
Fernancaballero
Pto de la Peralosa
Arroba de los Montes
Piedrabuena
Luciana
Saceruela
E. de El Vicario
CASTILLA
Carrión de Calatrava
Torralba de Calatrava
Miguelturra
Pozuelo de Calatrava
Almagro
Bolaños de Calatrava
Membrilla
La Solana
Villanueva de Franco
S. Carlos del Valle
Moral de Calatrava
Argamasilla de Alba
Río Guadiana
Río Azuer
Abenójar
Caracuel
Argamasilla de Calatrava
Almodóvar del Campo
Aldea del Rey
Calzada de Calatrava
Convento de Calatrava
E. Vega del Jabalón
Río Jabalón
Río Valdeazogues
Brazatortas
Villanueva de S. Carlos
Atalaya de la Calzada
Mestanza
Sta Cruz de Mudela
Torrenueva
E. de la Cabezuela
Judio
Pto de Niefla
E. de Montoro
Pto de Valderrepisa
Viso del Marqués
Almuradiel
Castellar de Santiago
Solana del Pino
Bañuela
Sa Madrona
S. Lorenzo de Calatrava
Estrella
Fuencaliente
Conquista
Villanueva de Córdoba
Azuel
Cardeña
Sa de Cardeña
Río de las Yeguas
Sa de Andújar
E. del Jándula
Río Jándula
El Centenillo
Sta Elena
Desfiladero de Despeñaperros
La Carolina
Río Guarrizas
Río Guadalén
E. de Guadalén
Santisteban del Puerto
N 401
N 403
N 400
N 301
N 420
N 430
N IV E 5
CM 400
CM 401
CM 412
CM 4111
CM 4110
CM 4112
CM 413
CM 410
CM 3000
CM 3107
A 420
A 301
MICHELIN

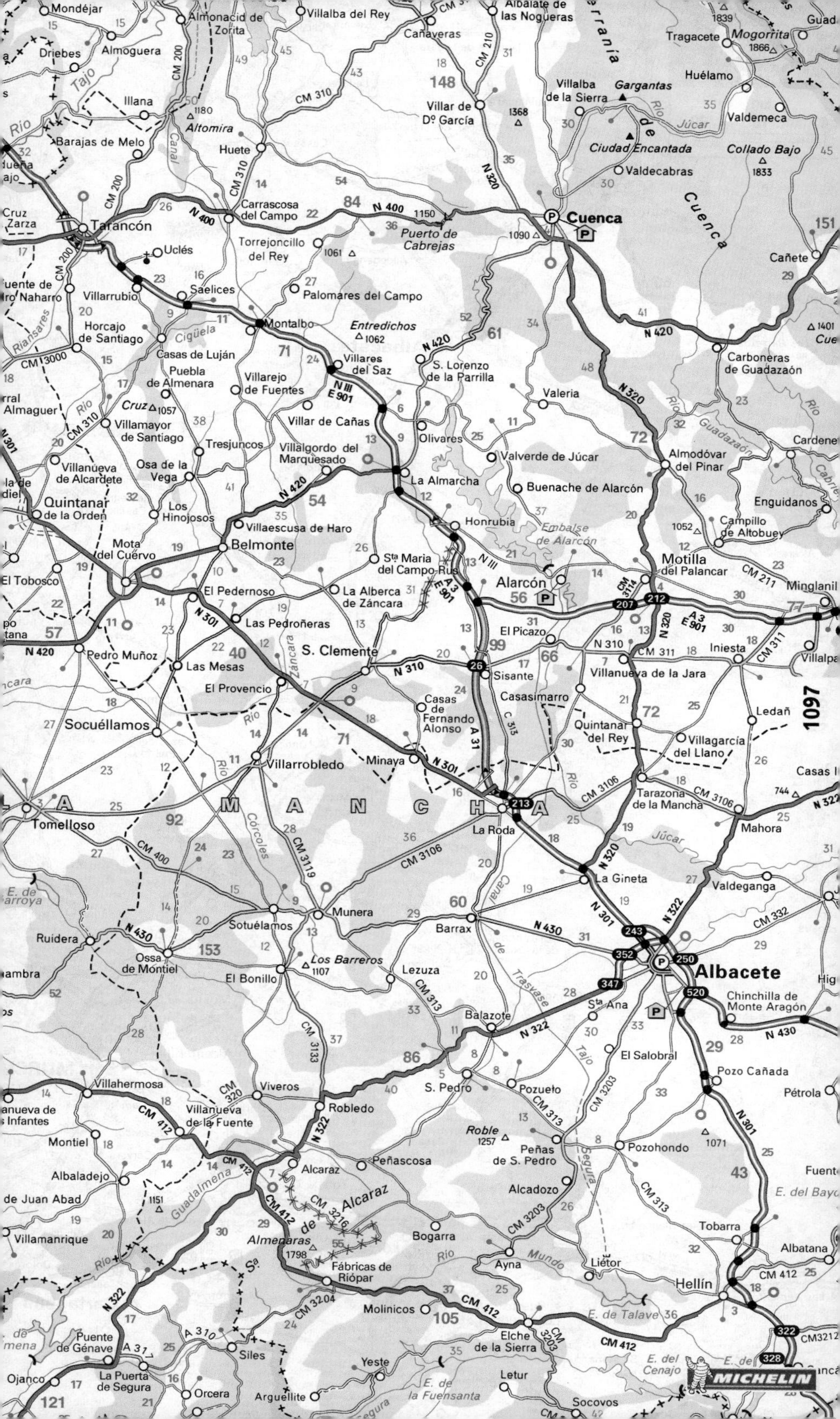

Mondéjar
Almonacid de Zorita
Villalba del Rey
Albalate de las Nogueras
Serranía de Cuenca
Tragacete
Mogorrita
Guad
Driebes
Almoguera
Cañaveras
Tajo
Illana
Huélamo
Villalba de la Sierra
Gargantas
Villar de Dº García
Valdemeca
Altomira
Río Júcar
Barajas de Melo
Huete
Ciudad Encantada
Collado Bajo
Valdecabras
Carrascosa del Campo
Tarancón
Cruz Zarza
Cuenca
Puerto de Cabrejas
Torrejoncillo del Rey
Uclés
Cañete
Fuente de Pedro Naharro
Villarrubio
Saelices
Palomares del Campo
Entredichos
Horcajo de Santiago
Montalbo
Casas de Luján
Villares del Saz
S. Lorenzo de la Parrilla
Carboneras de Guadazaón
Puebla de Almenara
Villarejo de Fuentes
Valeria
Almaguer
Cruz
Villar de Cañas
Villamayor de Santiago
Olivares
Cardenete
Tresjuncos
Villalgordo del Marquesado
Valverde de Júcar
Almodóvar del Pinar
Villanueva de Alcardete
Osa de la Vega
La Almarcha
Buenache de Alarcón
Enguidanos
Quintanar de la Orden
Los Hinojosos
Honrubia
Campillo de Altobuey
Villaescusa de Haro
Embalse de Alarcón
Mota del Cuervo
Belmonte
Sta María del Campo Rus
Motilla del Palancar
El Toboso
Alarcón
Minglanilla
El Pedernoso
La Alberca de Záncara
Las Pedroñeras
El Picazo
Iniesta
Pedro Muñoz
S. Clemente
Villanueva de la Jara
Villalpa
Las Mesas
Sisante
El Provencio
Casas de Fernando Alonso
Casasimarro
Ledaña
Socuéllamos
Quintanar del Rey
Villagarcía del Llano
Villarrobledo
Minaya
Casas I
Tarazona de la Mancha
Tomelloso
La Mancha
La Roda
Mahora
Júcar
Córcoles
Munera
La Gineta
Valdeganga
E. de Peñarroya
Ruidera
Sotuélamos
Barrax
Ossa de Montiel
El Bonillo
Los Barreros
Lezuza
Albacete
Hig
Chinchilla de Monte Aragón
Sta Ana
Balazote
El Salobral
Canal de Trasvase Tajo Segura
Villahermosa
Viveros
S. Pedro
Pozo Cañada
Pozuelo
Pétrola
Villanueva de los Infantes
Villanueva de la Fuente
Robledo
Montiel
Roble
Pozohondo
Peñas de S. Pedro
Albaladejo
Alcaraz
Peñascosa
Fuente
Guadalmena
Alcadozo
E. del Bayco
Torre de Juan Abad
Sierra de Alcaraz
Villamanrique
Bogarra
Tobarra
Almenaras
Albatana
Río Mundo
Ayna
Liétor
Fábricas de Riópar
Hellín
Molinicos
E. de Talave
Elche de la Sierra
Puente de Génave
Siles
Yeste
E. del Cenajo
Ojanco
La Puerta de Segura
Orcera
Letur
E. de la Fuensanta
Arguellite
Segura
Socovos
MICHELIN
1097

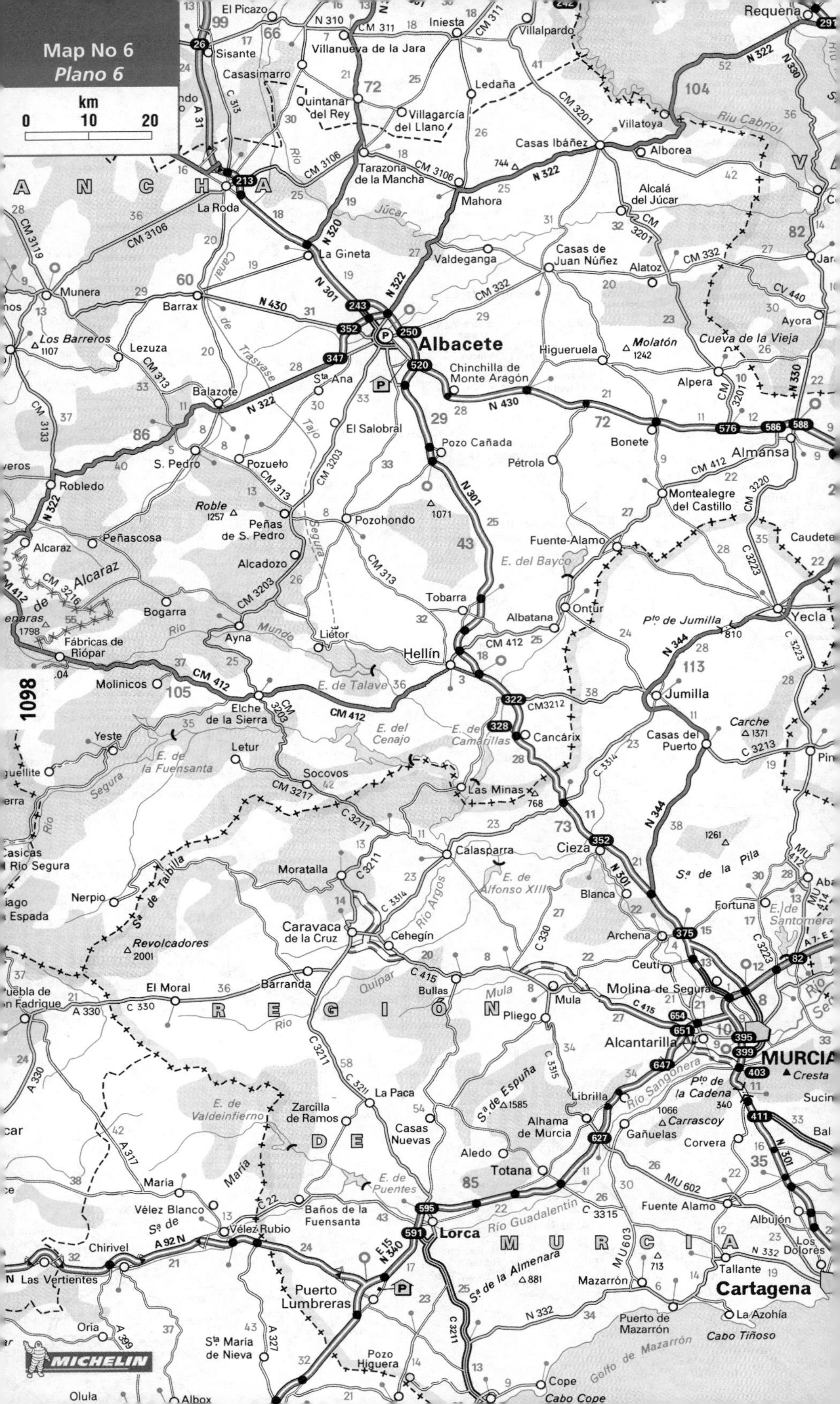
Map No 6
Plano 6
km
0 10 20
1098
MICHELIN
El Picazo
Sisante
Casasimarro
Villanueva de la Jara
Iniesta
Villalpardo
Requena
Quintanar del Rey
Villagarcía del Llano
Ledaña
Villatoya
Casas Ibáñez
Alborea
Tarazona de la Mancha
Mahora
La Roda
Alcalá del Júcar
La Gineta
Valdeganga
Casas de Juan Núñez
Alatoz
Munera
Barrax
Albacete
Chinchilla de Monte Aragón
Higueruela
Molatón
Los Barreros
Lezuza
Sta Ana
Alpera
Balazote
El Salobral
Pozo Cañada
Bonete
Almansa
S. Pedro
Pozuelo
Pétrola
Robledo
Roble
Peñas de S. Pedro
Pozohondo
Montealegre del Castillo
Alcaraz
Peñascosa
Alcadozo
Fuente-Alamo
Caudete
E. del Bayco
Bogarra
Tobarra
Albatana
Ontur
Yecla
Pto de Jumilla
Ayna
Fábricas de Riópar
Liétor
Hellín
Molinicos
Elche de la Sierra
E. de Talave
Jumilla
Yeste
E. del Cenajo
E. de Camarillas
Cancárix
Casas del Puerto
Carche
E. de la Fuensanta
Letur
Socovos
Las Minas
Calasparra
Cieza
Moratalla
E. de Alfonso XIII
Blanca
Sa de la Pila
Fortuna
Nerpio
Sa de Taibilla
Revolcadores
Caravaca de la Cruz
Cehegín
Archena
Ceutí
Molina de Segura
El Moral
Barranda
Bullas
Mula
Pliego
Alcantarilla
MURCIA
Cresta
REGIÓN DE MURCIA
Río Segura
Río Mundo
Río Júcar
Riu Cabriol
Río Argos
Río Quípar
Río Mula
Río Sangonera
Río Guadalentín
Canal de Trasvase Tajo Segura
Sa de Alcaraz
La Paca
Zarcilla de Ramos
E. de Valdeinfierno
Sa de Espuña
Alhama de Murcia
Librilla
Pto de la Cadena
Carrascoy
Gañuelas
Corvera
Casas Nuevas
Aledo
Totana
E. de Puentes
Baños de la Fuensanta
María
Vélez Blanco
Sa de María
Vélez Rubio
Chirivel
Las Vertientes
Lorca
Fuente Alamo
Albujón
Los Dolores
Tallante
Cartagena
Puerto Lumbreras
Sa de la Almenara
Mazarrón
Puerto de Mazarrón
La Azohía
Cabo Tiñoso
Golfo de Mazarrón
Oria
Sta María de Nieva
Pozo Higuera
Cope
Cabo Cope
Olula
Albox
Puebla de Don Fadrique
Casicas del Río Segura
Santiago de la Espada
E. de Santomera
Sucina
Ayora
Cueva de la Vieja
Jarafuel

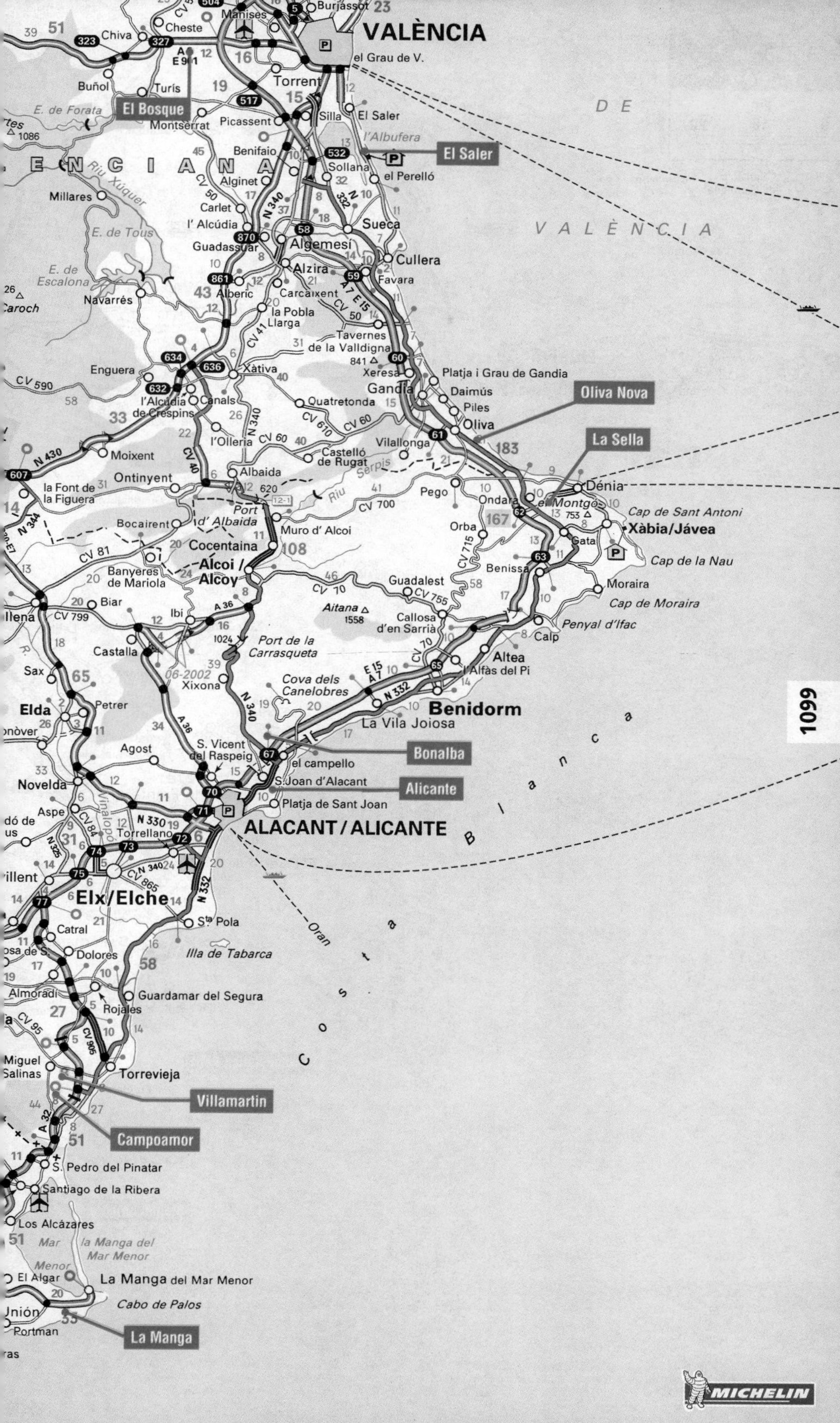

VALÈNCIA
Burjassot
Manises
Cheste
Chiva
Buñol
Turís
El Bosque
el Grau de V.
Torrent
Silla
El Saler
Picassent
Montserrat
E. de Forata
l'Albufera
Benifaio
Sollana
El Saler
el Perelló
Alginet
Millares
Riu Xúquer
Carlet
l' Alcúdia
Guadassuar
Sueca
Algemesí
E. de Tous
Alzira
Cullera
Favara
E. de Escalona
Alberic
Carcaixent
Navarrés
la Pobla Llarga
Tavernes de la Valldigna
Xeresa
Enguera
Xàtiva
Canals
l'Alcúdia de Crespins
Quatretonda
Gandia
Platja i Grau de Gandia
Daimús
Piles
Oliva
Oliva Nova
l'Olleria
Vilallonga
La Sella
Moixent
Castelló de Rugat
Riu Serpis
Ontinyent
Albaida
la Font de la Figuera
Pego
Ondara
Dénia
el Montgó
Cap de Sant Antoni
Xàbia/Jávea
Port d' Albaida
Muro d' Alcoi
Orba
Gata
Bocairent
Cocentaina
Alcoi / Alcoy
Benissa
Cap de la Nau
Banyeres de Mariola
Guadalest
Moraira
Cap de Moraira
Biar
Ibi
Aitana 1558
Callosa d'en Sarrià
Penyal d'Ifac
Calp
Castalla
Port de la Carrasqueta
Altea
l'Alfàs del Pi
Sax
Xixona
Cova dels Canelobres
Elda
Petrer
Benidorm
La Vila Joiosa
Agost
S. Vicent del Raspeig
Bonalba
el campello
Novelda
S.Joan d'Alacant
Alicante
Aspe
Platja de Sant Joan
ALACANT / ALICANTE
Torrellano
Elx/Elche
Costa Blanca
Catral
Sta Pola
Oran
Dolores
Illa de Tabarca
Almoradí
Guardamar del Segura
Rojales
Miguel Salinas
Torrevieja
Villamartin
Campoamor
S. Pedro del Pinatar
Santiago de la Ribera
Los Alcázares
Mar Menor
la Manga del Mar Menor
El Algar
La Manga del Mar Menor
Cabo de Palos
Portman
La Manga
MICHELIN

Map No 7
Plano 7
km
0 10 20
Cabezas Rubias
El Cerro de Andévalo
Minas de Riotinto
Nerva
Zalamea la Real
Calañas
Tharsis
Alosno
El Madroño
El Castillo de las Guardas
Valverde del Camino
Alcoutim
Sanlúcar de Guadiana
Villanueva de los Castillejos
E. de Sancho
Río Odiel
S. Silvestre de Guzmán
S. Bartolomé de la Torre
E. del Piedras
Gibraleón
Beas
Trigueros
Río Tinto
La Palma del Condado
Aznalcóllar
Gerena
Castilleja del Campo
Sanlúcar la Mayor
Las Pajanosas
Villablanca
Lepe
Cartaya
Huelva
Niebla
S. Juan del Puerto
Moguer
Bonares
Bollullos del Condado
Rociana del Condado
Palos de la Frontera
La Rábida
El Rompido
Ayamonte
Isla Cristina
La Antilla
Vila Real de Sto António
Punta Umbría
Islantilla
Almonte
Pilas
Aznalcázar
Bollullos de la M.
La Puebla del Río
Villamanrique de la Condesa
Colinas
Zaudin
El Rocío
Mazagón
Villafranco del Guadalquivir
GOLFO DE CÁDIZ
Torre de la Higuera
Matalascañas
Parque nacional de Doñana
Isla Mayor
RIO GUADALQUIVIR
RIO GUADIANA
Lebrija
Trebujena
El Cuervo
Sanlúcar de Barrameda
Chipiona
Montecastillo
Jerez de la Frontera
Rota
El Puerto de Sta María
Bahía de Cádiz
El Portal
CÁDIZ
Puerto Real
S. Fernando
Islas Canarias
Costa de la Luz
Chiclana de la Frontera
Sancti Petri
Novo Sancti Petri
Naveros
Conil de la Frontera
Vejer de la Frontera
Cabo de Trafalgar
Barbate
Monteenmedio
MICHELIN

Sevilla
Pineda
Guadalhorce
La Quinta
Lauro Golf
Los Arqueros
Alhaurin
Las Brisas
Los Naranjos
La Zagaleta
Monte Mayor
Aloha
Torrequebrada
Mijas
La Duquesa
Estepona
Guadalmina
La Cala
Malaga
San Roque
Sotogrande
Marbella
Valderrama
Almenara
Alcaideza
SEVILLA
CÓRDOBA
Écija
Carmona
Utrera
Osuna
Marchena
Morón de la Frontera
Antequera
Ronda
Marbella
Estepona
Fuengirola
Algeciras
Gibraltar
La Línea de la Concepción
Tarifa
Ceuta
Puente Genil
Dos Hermanas
Alcalá de Guadaira
RÍO GUADALQUIVIR
ECHO DE GIBRALTAR
MICHELIN

Map No 8
Plano 8
km
0 10 20
GRANADA
Jaén
Málaga
Úbeda
Baeza
Linares
Bailén
Andújar
Motril
MICHELIN

Villamanrique
Almenaras
1798
Fábricas de Riópar
Bogarra
Ayna
Río Mundo
Liétor
Tobarra
Albatana
Hellín
CM 412
CM 3203
CM 3204
CM 3216
CM 3217
Molinicos
105
Elche de la Sierra
E. de Talave
N 322
E. de Jalmena
Puente de Génave
A 310
A 317
Siles
Yeste
E. del Cenajo
E. de Camarillas
Letur
Del Ojanco
121
La Puerta de Segura
Orcera
Arguellite
E. de la Fuensanta
Río Segura
Socovos
Las Minas
768
A 314
Beas de Segura
Cortijos Nuevos
Segura de la Sierra
1809
Yelmo
C 3211
Guadalquivir
Garganta
Hornos
Casicas del Río Segura
Calasparra
E. de Alfonso XIII
Blanquilla
1830
Sa de Cazorla
Sierra de Segura
Pontones
Santiago de la Espada
Nerpio
Sa de Taibilla
Moratalla
Caravaca de la Cruz
Cehegín
Río Argos
C 3314
E. del Tranco
1964
Revolcadores
2001
Pto de las Palomas
1290
Sa de Castril
La Losa
Sa de la Sagra
2381
Puebla de Don Fadrique
El Moral
Barranda
C 330
A 330
Bullas
C 415
Quípar
Mula
Pliego
R E G I Ó N
E. de S. Clemente
E. de la Bolera
A 326
Castril
Huéscar
E. de Valdeinfierno
Zarcilla de Ramos
La Paca
Casas Nuevas
Sa de España
1585
Alhama de Murcia
C 3315
D E
Pozo Alcón
Castilléjar
Galera
Orce
María
Aledo
Totana
85
E. del Negratín
Cortes de Baza
Vélez Blanco
E. de Puentes
Baños de la Fuensanta
Lorca
Río Guadalentín
Benamaurel
Sa de María
Vélez Rubio
C 22
Cúllar Baza
Chirivel
A 92 N
Las Vertientes
137
E 15
N 340
Puerto Lumbreras
M
1103
A 315
Zújar
Baza
Caniles
A 334
Oria
A 399
Lúcar
1722
Sta María de Nieva
A 327
Pozo Higuera
N 332
Sa de la A
Sta Bárbara
2271
Sierra de Baza
Tíjola
Serón
Purchena
Olula del Río
Macael
Cantoria
Albox
Huércal-Overa
Pulpí
Águilas
S. Juan de los Terreros
Cuevas del Almanzora
A 332
Los Lobos
Villaricos
Tetica
2080
Sierra de los Filabres
A 349
C 3325
Albánchez
Río Almanzora
2168
Calar Alto
Tahal
Antas
Vera
Fiñana
Escúllar
Uleila del Campo
Lubrín
Los Gallardos
Garrucha
102
Doña María Ocaña
Abla
Gérgal
Turre
Mojácar
A 370-N340A
Sorbas
Ohanes
Alboloduy
N 324
C 3326
Canjáyar
Tabernas
127
Lucainena de las Torres
Río Ardarax
Illar
Alhamilla
1387
N 341
Carboneras
Gádor
Alhama de Almería
A 348
Morrón
2236
Sierra de Gádor
Níjar
Benahadux
La Mesa Roldán
128
S. Isidro
Parque natural
ALMERÍA
Dalías
Las Negras
129
Cabo de Gata-Níjar
El Ejido
Aguadulce
El Alquián
Benahadux
Pta de la Polacra
Punta del Río
Roquetas de Mar
Cabo de Gata
S. José
Almerimar
Golfo de Almería
Cabo de Gata
Melilla
Almerimar
S o l
MICHELIN

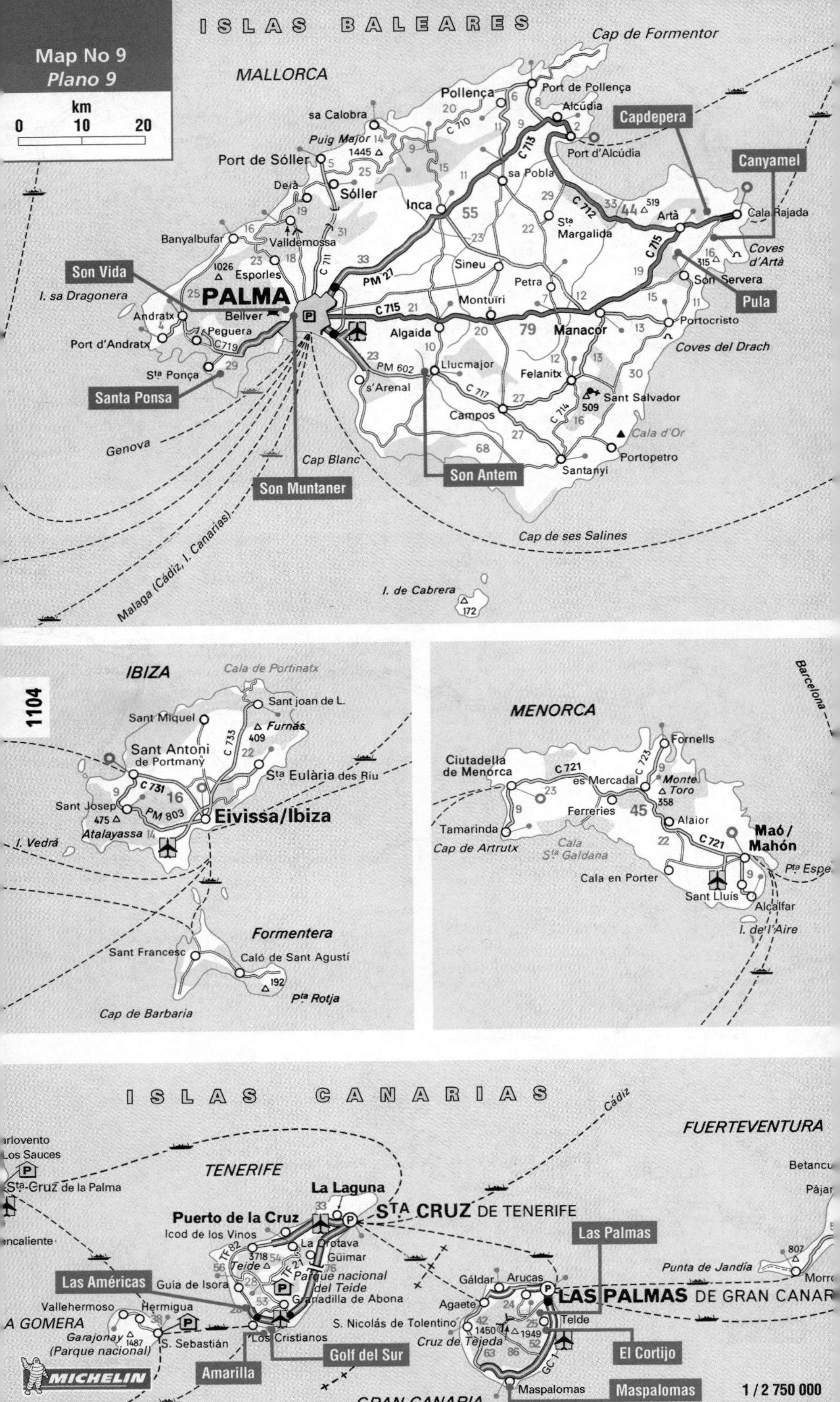
Map No 9
Plano 9
km
0 10 20
ISLAS BALEARES
MALLORCA
Cap de Formentor
Pollença
Port de Pollença
Alcúdia
Port d'Alcúdia
Capdepera
Canyamel
sa Calobra
Puig Major
1445
Port de Sóller
Sóller
Deià
Inca
sa Pobla
Cala Rajada
Artà
Sta Margalida
Coves d'Artà
Banyalbufar
Valldemossa
Son Vida
Esporles
1026
I. sa Dragonera
PALMA
Bellver
Andratx
Peguera
Port d'Andratx
Sta Ponça
Santa Ponsa
Sineu
Petra
Montuïri
Son Servera
Pula
Algaida
Manacor
Portocristo
Coves del Drach
Llucmajor
s'Arenal
Felanitx
Sant Salvador
509
Campos
Cala d'Or
Portopetro
Santanyí
Genova
Cap Blanc
Son Muntaner
Son Antem
Cap de ses Salines
Malaga (Cádiz, I. Canarias)
I. de Cabrera
172
C 710
C 713
C 712
C 715
C 711
PM 27
C 719
PM 602
C 717
C 714
IBIZA
Cala de Portinatx
Sant joan de L.
Sant Miquel
Furnás
409
Sant Antoni de Portmany
C 733
Sta Eulària des Riu
C 731
PM 803
Sant Josep
475
Atalayassa
Eivissa/Ibiza
I. Vedrá
Formentera
Sant Francesc
Caló de Sant Agustí
192
Pta Rotja
Cap de Barbaria
MENORCA
Barcelona
Fornells
Ciutadella de Menorca
C 721
C 723
es Mercadal
Monte Toro
358
Ferreries
Alaior
Tamarinda
Cap de Artrutx
Cala Sta Galdana
Maó / Mahón
Pta Espe
Cala en Porter
Sant Lluís
Alcalfar
I. de l'Aire
ISLAS CANARIAS
Cádiz
FUERTEVENTURA
arlovento
Los Sauces
Sta Cruz de la Palma
TENERIFE
La Laguna
Puerto de la Cruz
STA CRUZ DE TENERIFE
Icod de los Vinos
La Orotava
Güimar
3718
Teide
Parque nacional del Teide
Las Américas
Guía de Isora
Granadilla de Abona
Vallehermoso
Hermigua
A GOMERA
Garajonay (Parque nacional)
1487
S. Sebastián
Los Cristianos
Golf del Sur
Amarilla
encaliente
Betancu
Pájar
Punta de Jandía
807
Morro
Las Palmas
Gáldar
Arucas
Agaete
LAS PALMAS DE GRAN CANAR
Telde
S. Nicolás de Tolentino
1450
1949
Cruz de Tejeda
El Cortijo
Maspalomas
GRAN CANARIA
MICHELIN
1 / 2 750 000

CLASSIFICATION OF COURSES
CLASIFICACION DE LOS RECORRIDOS

This classification gives priority consideration to the score awarded to the actual course.

Esta clasificacíon da prioridad a la nota atribuida al recorrido.

Course score / Nota del recorrido				Page / Página
19	8	6	Valderrama	1198
18	7	6	El Saler	1128
18	8	7	Las Brisas	1154
18	7	7	PGA de Catalunya	1179
18	8	9	Puerta de Hierro *Abajo*	1181
18	7	6	Real Sociedad Club de Campo	1184
18	8	7	Sotogrand	1194
17	7	8	Aloha	1113
17	7	7	Castillo de Gorraiz	1120
17	5	8	El Cortijo	1126
17	7	6	El Prat *Verde*	1127
17	7	6	Emporda	1129
17	6	5	Fontanals	1132
17	8	6	La Cala *Norte*	1140
17	7	4	Lerma	1157
17	8	8	Montecastillo	1168
17	7	7	Neguri	1170
17	8	8	San Roque	1185
17	7	8	Sevilla	1189
16	8	7	Bonmont	1116
16	8	8	Club de Campo	1122
16	7	4	El Bosque	1125
16	7	8	Golf del Sur	1134
16	8	8	Islantilla	1138
16	8	6	La Cala *Sur*	1141
16	7	8	La Moraleja *La Moraleja 2*	1149
16	7	7	La Zagaleta	1152
16	7	8	Las Américas	1153
16	7	7	Los Naranjos	1159
16	7	8	Maspalomas	1163
16	7	6	Mediterraneo	1164
16	6	7	Mijas *Los Lagos*	1165
16	8	7	Monteenmedio	1169
16	7	7	Novo Sancti Petri	1171
16	7	6	Pals	1175
16	8	9	Puerta de Hierro *Arriba*	1182
16	8	8	Son Antem *Oeste*	1191
16	8	9	Son Muntaner	1192
16	6	6	Ulzama	1197
16	7	6	Villamartin	1199
16	7	6	Zaudin	1200
15	8	8	Alicant	1110
15	7	7	Amarilla	1114
15	6	6	Canyamel	1118
15	7	6	Capdepera	1119
15	3	7	Golf d'Aro (Mas Nou)	1133
15	6	6	La Herreria	1144
15	7	7	La Manga *Norte*	1145
15	7	7	La Manga *Sur*	1147
15	7	8	La Moraleja *La Moraleja 1*	1148
15	6	5	La Sella	1151
15	7	8	Marbella	1161
15	7	6	Masia Bach	1162
15	6	5	Pedreña	1177
15	7	8	Peralada	1178
15	7	9	Pineda	1180
15	8	8	Son Antem *Este*	1190
14	6	7	Alcaidesa	1108
14	7	5	Alhaurin	1109
14	7	7	Almerimar	1112
14	6	6	Bonalba	1115
14	6	6	Campoamor	1117
14	7	7	Cerdaña	1121
14	7	7	Costa Brava	1123
14	7	6	Estepona	1131
14	6	5	Granada	1135
14	7	6	Guadalhorc	1136
14	7	7	Guadalmina *Sur*	1137
14	7	4	La Dehesa	1142
14	7	7	La Manga *Oeste*	1146
14	8	8	La Quinta	1150
14	8	8	Las Palmas	1155
14	7	7	Lauro	1156
14	6	7	Los Arqueros	1158
14	6	7	Oliva Nova	1172

Classification

GOLF COURSES / CLASIFICACION DE LOS RECORRIDOS

14	7	4	Osona Montanya	1174
14	6	4	Panoramica	1176
14	6	6	San Sebastián	1186
14	6	7	Son Vida	1193
14	7	7	Torrequebrada	1196
13	8	8	Almenara	1111
13	6	6	Costa Dorada	1124
13	8	4	Escorpion	1130
13	7	6	Jarama R.A.C.E.	1139
13	7	6	La Duquesa	1143
13	4	6	Málaga	1160
13	6	7	Mijas *Los Olivos*	1166
13	5	5	Monte Mayor	1167
13	7	8	Olivar de la Hinojosa	1173
13	6	5	Pula	1183
13	6	5	Sant Cugat	1187
13	6	7	Santa Ponsa	1188
13	7	7	Torremirona	1195

RECOMMENDED GOLFING STAY
ESTANCIA DE GOLF RECOMENDADA

Club de Campo	16	8	8	1122
Emporda	17	7	6	1129
Islantilla	16	8	8	1138
La Cala *Norte*	17	8	6	1140
La Cala *Sur*	16	8	6	1141
La Dehesa	14	7	4	1142
La Manga *Norte*	15	7	7	1145
La Manga *Oeste*	14	7	7	1146
La Manga *Sur*	15	7	7	1147
Mijas *Los Lagos*	16	6	7	1165
Mijas *Los Olivos*	13	6	7	1166
Montecastillo	17	8	8	1168
San Roque	17	8	8	1185
Son Antem *Este*	15	8	8	1190
Son Antem *Oeste*	16	8	8	1191
Son Muntaner	16	8	9	1192
Son Vida	14	6	7	1193

RECOMMENDED GOLFING HOLIDAYS
VACACIONES RECOMENDADAS

Aloha	17	7	8	1113
Bonmont	16	8	7	1116
Canyamel	15	6	6	1118
Capdepera	15	7	6	1119
Costa Dorada	13	6	6	1124
El Bosque	16	7	4	1125
El Saler	18	7	6	1128
Islantilla	16	8	8	1138
La Cala *Norte*	17	8	6	1140
La Cala Sur	16	8	6	1141
La Manga *Norte/Oeste/Sur*				1145
La Sella	15	6	5	1151
Las Brisas	18	8	7	1154
Las Palmas	14	8	8	1155
Marbella	15	7	8	1161
Maspalomas	16	7	8	1163
Mediterraneo	16	7	6	1164
Mijas *Los Lagos/Los Olivos*				1165
Novo Sancti Petri	16	7	7	1171
Pals	16	7	6	1175
Pula	13	6	5	1183
Santa Ponsa	13	6	7	1188
Son Antem *Este/Oeste*	15	8	8	1190
Torrequebrada	14	7	7	1196

TYPE OF COURSE
TIPO DE RECORRIDOS

Forest
Almenara 1111, Islantilla 1138, Club de Campo 1122, Emporda 1129, La Herreria 1144, Lerma 1157, Maspalomas 1163, Neguri 1170 Osona Montanya 1174, Pals 1175, Panoramica 1176, Pedreña 1177, PGA de Catalunya 1179, Real Sociedad Club de Campo 1184, San Sebastián 1186, Ulzama 1197.

Hilly
Bonalba 1115, Campoamor 1117, Capdepera 1119, Cerdaña 1121, Costa Brava 1123 Costa Dorada 1124, Guadalhorce 1136, La Duquesa 1143, La Herreria 1144, La Manga *Norte* 1145, La Quinta 1150 La Sella 1151, La Zagaleta 1152 Los Arqueros 1158, Marbella 1161, Mijas *Los Olivos* 1166, Osona Montanya 1174, Real Sociedad Club de Campo 1184, San Roque 1185, San Sebastián 1186, Sant Cugat 1187, Villamartin 1199, Torrequebrada 1196.

Inland
Almenara 1111, Oliva Nova 1172, Son Antem *Este / Oeste* 1190/1191, Torremirona 1195.

Links
El Saler 1128.

Mountain
Alhaurin 1109, Canyamel 1118, Estepona 1131, Golf d'Aro (Mas Nou) 1133, La Cala *Norte* 1140, La Cala *Sur* 1141, Los Arqueros 1158 Masia Bach 1162, Monte Mayor 1167.

Country
Bonalba 1115, Canyamel 1118, Capdepera 1119, El Bosque 1125 Escorpion 1130, Jarama R.A.C.E. 1139 La Dehesa 1142, La Manga *Oeste - Sur* 1146/1147 La Moraleja *La Moraleja 1 & 2* 1148/1149 La Sella 1151, Lauro 1156, Lerma 1157, Mediterraneo 1164, Mijas *Los Lagos - Los Olivos* 1165/1166, Montecastillo 1168, Pula 1183, Sevilla 1189, Villamartin 1199, Zaudin 1200.

Open Country
Bonmont 1116, Emporda 1129, Fontanals 1132, Granada 1135, Guadalhorce 1136, La Duquesa 1143 Olivar de la Hinojosa 1173, Peralada 1178, Santa Ponsa 1188.

Parkland
Alicant 1110, Aloha 1113, Amarilla 1114 Castillo de Gorraiz 1120, El Cortijo 1126, Golf d'Aro (Mas Nou) 1133, Golf del Sur 1134, Guadalmina *Sur* 1137, Las Américas 1153, Las Brisas 1154, Las Palmas 1155, Los Naranjos 1159, Monteenmedio 1169, Oliva Nova 1172, PGA de Catalunya 1179, Pineda 1180, Puerta de Hierro *Abajo / Arriba* 1181/1182, San Roque 1185, Son Muntaner 1192, Son Vida 1193, Sotogrande 1194, Torremirona 1195, Valderrama 1198

Residential
Aloha 1113, Bonmont 1116, Campoamor 1117, Castillo de Gorraiz 1120, Costa Brava 1123, El Bosque 1125, La Manga *Norte / Sur* 1145/1147, La Quinta 1150, La Zagaleta 1152, Las Brisas 1154, Los Naranjos 1159, Panoramica 1176 Sant Cugat 1187, Santa Ponsa 1188, Son Vida 1193, Zaudin 1200.

Seaside course
Alcaidesa 1108, Almerimar 1112, El Prat *Verde* 1127, Guadalmina *Sur* 1137 Islantilla 1138, Málaga 1160 Novo Sancti Petri 1171 Pedreña 1177, Sotogrande 1194.

ALCAIDESA

14 | 6 | 7

Las obras del 99 han resultado muy eficaces y el campo ha ganado en su calidad de mantenimiento en una zona de fuerte desarrollo del golf, donde efectivamente se juega con uno de los mayores alicientes de este deporte como es la brisa marina. Ahora el campo responde a la espectacularidad de sus vistas sobre el Mediterráneo y la enorme Roca de Gibraltar que domina gran parte del recorrido. El campo se ha bautizado como links porque está junto al mar y hay que saber jugar con viento, pero la naturaleza del suelo, el diseño y la preparación de las zonas de caída de la bola son beignos y cómodos para que jugadores de cualquier edad y handicap puedan disfrutar de un buen día de golf, sin prescindir del reto de saber dirigir la bola. Los greenes no son inmensos ni excesivamente complicados pero para hacer una buena tarjeta o ganar un partido hay que afinar en el juego corto y pegar recto.

The work carried out in 1999 has apparently worked wonders for the maintenance of this fast-developing golf club. It is great fun playing here when there is a little sea breeze in the air. Right now, the course is even more in keeping with the spectacular vista over the Mediterranean sea and the massive rock of Gibraltar, which dominates a large part of the course. Alcaidesa has been called a links because it is situated along the coastline and because you need to know how to handle the wind. However, the type of soil, layout and breadth of the landing areas are well suited to players of all ages and abilities who are looking for a good day's golfing without having to bend the ball one way or the other. The greens are neither oversized nor too complicated, but to card a good score or win your bet, you will need to hit it straight and have a sharp short game.

Alcaidesa Links Golf Course — 1991

Ctra. Nacional, Km 124,6
E - 11315 LA LINEA

Office	Secretaria	(34) 956 - 791 040
Pro shop	Pro-shop	(34) 956 - 791 042
Fax	Fax	(34) 956 - 791 041
Web	www.alcaidesa.com	
Situation	Situación	Gibraltar, 10 km
Algeciras (pop. 101 556), 15 km		
Annual closure	Cierre anual	no
Weekly closure	Cierre semanal	no
Fees main season	Precios tempor. alta	18 holes

	Week days Semana	We/Bank holidays Fin de sem./fiestas
Individual Individual	60 €	60 €
Couple Pareja	120 €	120 €

Caddy	Caddy	no
Electric Trolley	Carro eléctrico	no
Buggy	Coche	33 € /18 holes
Clubs	Palos	15 € / 18 holes

Credit cards Tarjetas de crédito
VISA - MasterCard - DC - AMEX

Access Acceso : Marbella → Estepona, Sotogrande → Cadiz, Golf on the left (km 124,6)
Map 7 on page 1101 Plano 7 Página 1101

Golf course RECORRIDO — 14/20

Site	Emplazamiento	
Maintenance	Mantenimiento	
Architect	Arquitecto	P. Alliss, Clive Clark
Type	Tipo	seaside course
Relief	Relieve	
Water in play	Agua	
Exp. to wind	Exp. al viento	
Trees in play	Arboles	

Scorecard Tarjeta	Chp. Campeonato	Mens Caballeros	Ladies Damas
Length Longitud	6158	5459	4586
Par	72	72	72
Slope system	—	—	—

Advised golfing ability Nivel de juego aconsejado: 0 12 24 36
Hcp required Handicap exigido: 28 Men., 36 Ladies

Club house & amenities CLUB HOUSE Y DEPENDENCIAS — 6/10

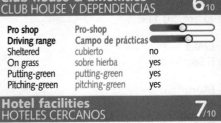

Pro shop	Pro-shop	
Driving range	Campo de prácticas	
Sheltered	cubierto	no
On grass	sobre hierba	yes
Putting-green	putting-green	yes
Pitching-green	pitching-green	yes

Hotel facilities HOTELES CERCANOS — 7/10

HOTELS HOTELES

Almenara, 150 rooms, D 192 € — San Roque
Tel (34) 956 - 582 000, Fax (34) 956 - 582 001 — 5 km

San Roque, 50 rooms, D 210 € — San Roque
Tel (34) 956 - 613 030, Fax (34) 956 - 613 012 — 2 km

Royal Golf, 52 rooms, D 116 € — Sotogrande
Tel (34) 956 - 796 263, Fax (34) 956 - 785 159 — 4 km

RESTAURANTS RESTAURANTE

Los Remos, Tel (34) 956 - 698 412 — San Roque 5 km
Pedro, Tel (34) 956 - 698 453 — San Roque
Vicente, Tel (34) 956 790 212 — Sotogrande 7 km

ALHAURIN

14 | 7 | 5

Al lado de Mijas, este ambicioso proyecto, aún no acabado, es prometedor, sobre todo teniendo en cuenta que la firma de Ballesteros es una excelente publicidad. En un magnífico entorno, con vistas espectaculares hacia la montaña, ha diseñado un recorrido bastante accidentado (a veces demasiado), que exige un juego preciso, aunque sólo sea para evitar algunos barrancos,e incluso el rough, a menudo en la línea de juego y muy ösalvaje. Favorece a aquellos que juegan en "fade", por lo que los jugadores con tendencia al "slice" no se sentirán muy perjudicados. Un buen número de tees de salida permite adaptar el recorrido a todos los niveles de juego, pero los jugadores con poca experiencia tendrán problemas. Los obstáculos de agua dan a veces un aspecto americano a este diseño que a pesar de todo está en armonía con el paisaje. Hay que tener muy en cuenta el recorrido anejo de 18 hoyos reservado a los "junior" , ... y a los padres si los niños les invitan!

Next door to Mijas, this ambitious and still incomplete resort promises a great deal, all the more so in that the label of Ballesteros is a commercial argument of the highest order. In a magnificent setting with spectacular views over mountains, Seve has designed a very, and sometimes too, hilly course, which demands precision golf, if only to avoid a number of precipices or even the rough, a frequent hazard and growing wild. It is a course for players who fade the ball, allowing the amateur slice more leeway than they might usually find. The many different tees make this a course for all levels, but inexperienced players will have problems. Water hazards sometimes give the layout a very American style, although the general character blends harmoniously with the setting. Worthy of note is the adjoining 18-hole course reserved for juniors, and their parents if invited by the kids!

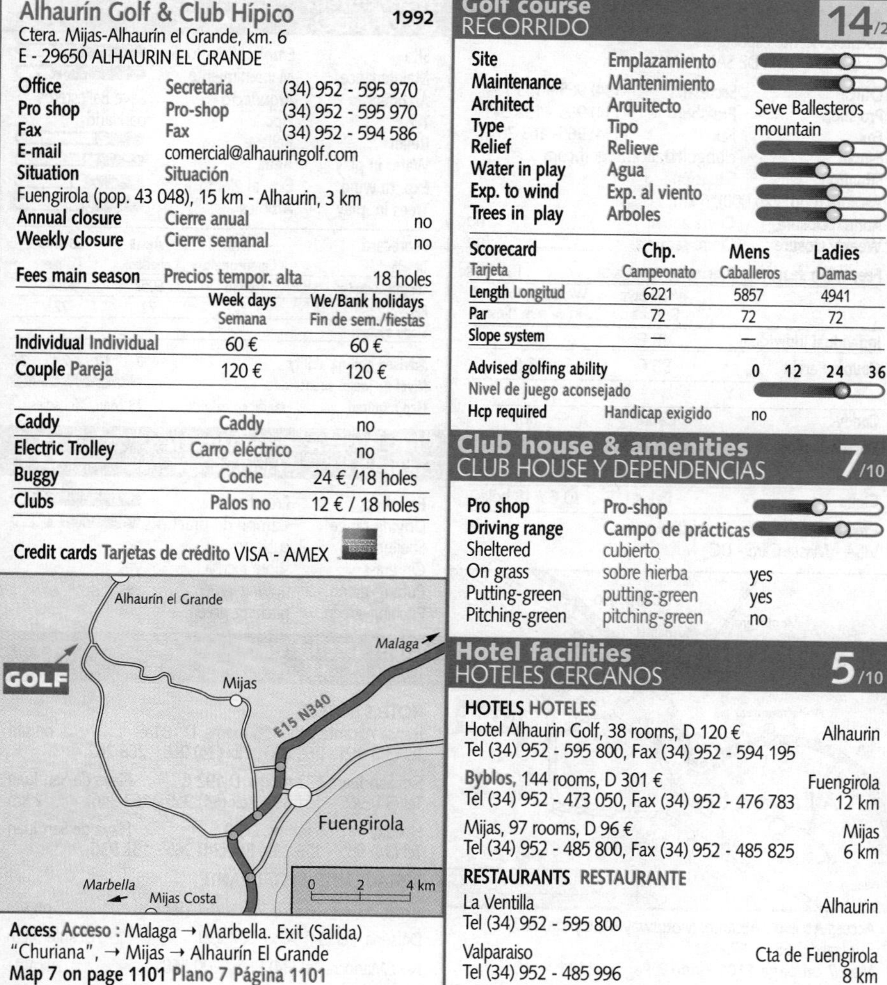

Alhaurín Golf & Club Hípico 1992
Ctera. Mijas-Alhaurín el Grande, km. 6
E - 29650 ALHAURIN EL GRANDE

Office	Secretaria	(34) 952 - 595 970
Pro shop	Pro-shop	(34) 952 - 595 970
Fax	Fax	(34) 952 - 594 586
E-mail	comercial@alhauringolf.com	
Situation	Situación	

Fuengirola (pop. 43 048), 15 km - Alhaurin, 3 km

Annual closure	Cierre anual	no
Weekly closure	Cierre semanal	no

Fees main season Precios tempor. alta	Week days Semana	We/Bank holidays Fin de sem./fiestas
		18 holes
Individual Individual	60 €	60 €
Couple Pareja	120 €	120 €

Caddy	Caddy	no
Electric Trolley	Carro eléctrico	no
Buggy	Coche	24 € /18 holes
Clubs	Palos no	12 € / 18 holes

Credit cards Tarjetas de crédito VISA - AMEX

Access Acceso : Malaga → Marbella. Exit (Salida) "Churiana", → Mijas → Alhaurín El Grande
Map 7 on page 1101 Plano 7 Página 1101

Golf course RECORRIDO 14/20

Site	Emplazamiento	
Maintenance	Mantenimiento	
Architect	Arquitecto	Seve Ballesteros
Type	Tipo	mountain
Relief	Relieve	
Water in play	Agua	
Exp. to wind	Exp. al viento	
Trees in play	Arboles	

Scorecard Tarjeta	Chp. Campeonato	Mens Caballeros	Ladies Damas
Length Longitud	6221	5857	4941
Par	72	72	72
Slope system	—	—	—

Advised golfing ability Nivel de juego aconsejado: 0 12 24 36
Hcp required Handicap exigido: no

Club house & amenities CLUB HOUSE Y DEPENDENCIAS 7/10

Pro shop	Pro-shop	
Driving range	Campo de prácticas	
Sheltered	cubierto	
On grass	sobre hierba	yes
Putting-green	putting-green	yes
Pitching-green	pitching-green	no

Hotel facilities HOTELES CERCANOS 5/10

HOTELS HOTELES

Hotel Alhaurin Golf, 38 rooms, D 120 € — Alhaurin
Tel (34) 952 - 595 800, Fax (34) 952 - 594 195

Byblos, 144 rooms, D 301 € — Fuengirola 12 km
Tel (34) 952 - 473 050, Fax (34) 952 - 476 783

Mijas, 97 rooms, D 96 € — Mijas 6 km
Tel (34) 952 - 485 800, Fax (34) 952 - 485 825

RESTAURANTS RESTAURANTE

La Ventilla — Alhaurin
Tel (34) 952 - 595 800

Valparaiso — Cta de Fuengirola 8 km
Tel (34) 952 - 485 996

ALICANTE

15 | 8 | 8

Alicante golf nace en una zona de actividad turística muy intensa con el doble objetivo de atender a una población de residentes y a la alta demanda que se produce en períodos de vacaciones. En este contexto, este campo se distingue por una esmerada puesta a punto del concepto deportivo y del de servicios. El campo está muy bien acabado, incluso desde el punto de vista estético, a pesar de que varios de los últimos hoyos (existe el proyecto de ampliar el campo hacia otra zona no tan urbanizada) son inmensas avenidas verdes entre bloques de apartamentos, que se compensan con calles generosamente amplias. Esta sensación de amplitud permite atacar los hoyos largos con un buen margen de confianza, especialmente necesaria para jugar unos greenes muy interesantes. Nótese el terreno en reparación permanente 50 metros delante del 15 (par 5): las ruinas de una casa romana del siglo II.

The golf course of Alicante has made room for itself in a very busy tourist area with the twin objective of satisfying local golfers and of meeting extra demand during the holiday periods. In this setting, the course stands out for its excellence both as a polished sports resort and for the services on offer. It certainly is very well designed, particularly in terms of visual appeal and the diversity of the finishing holes. And there are plans to extend the course in a less built-up area, which is good news since some of the wide-open fairways here are lined with condos. This impression of space means you can go for the wider holes with added confidence, a considerable asset for hitting some interestingly contoured and well-protected greens. For the record, the ground under repair on the 15th hole houses the ruins of an ancient Roman villa dating from the 2nd century.

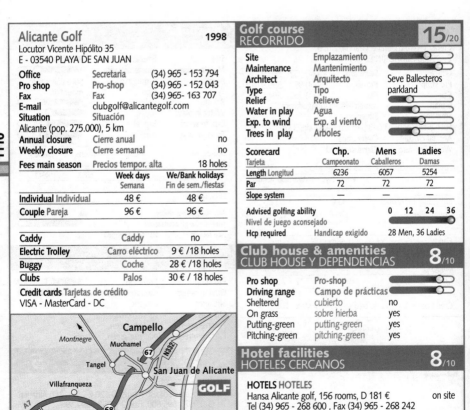

Alicante Golf — 1998

Locutor Vicente Hipólito 35
E - 03540 PLAYA DE SAN JUAN

Office	Secretaria	(34) 965 - 153 794
Pro shop	Pro-shop	(34) 965 - 152 043
Fax	Fax	(34) 965- 163 707
E-mail	clubgolf@alicantegolf.com	
Situation	Situación	

Alicante (pop. 275.000), 5 km

Annual closure	Cierre anual	no
Weekly closure	Cierre semanal	no

Fees main season Precios tempor. alta	Week days Semana	We/Bank holidays Fin de sem./fiestas
		18 holes
Individual Individual	48 €	48 €
Couple Pareja	96 €	96 €

Caddy	Caddy	no
Electric Trolley	Carro eléctrico	9 € /18 holes
Buggy	Coche	28 € /18 holes
Clubs	Palos	30 € / 18 holes

Credit cards Tarjetas de crédito
VISA - MasterCard - DC

Campello
Montnegre
Muchamel
Tangel
San Juan de Alicante
Villafranqueza
GOLF
A7
67
68
N332
Playa de San Juan
Alicante
0 2 4 km

Access Acceso : Alicante, Motorway (Autopista) A-7, Exit (salida) 68 → "Playas"
Map 7 on page 1101 Plano 7 Página 1101

Golf course RECORRIDO — 15/20

Site	Emplazamiento	
Maintenance	Mantenimiento	
Architect	Arquitecto	Seve Ballesteros
Type	Tipo	parkland
Relief	Relieve	
Water in play	Agua	
Exp. to wind	Exp. al viento	
Trees in play	Arboles	

Scorecard Tarjeta	Chp. Campeonato	Mens Caballeros	Ladies Damas
Length Longitud	6236	6057	5254
Par	72	72	72
Slope system	—	—	—

Advised golfing ability Nivel de juego aconsejado: 0 12 24 36
Hcp required Handicap exigido: 28 Men, 36 Ladies

Club house & amenities CLUB HOUSE Y DEPENDENCIAS — 8/10

Pro shop	Pro-shop	
Driving range	Campo de prácticas	
Sheltered	cubierto	no
On grass	sobre hierba	yes
Putting-green	putting-green	yes
Pitching-green	pitching-green	yes

Hotel facilities HOTELES CERCANOS — 8/10

HOTELS HOTELES

Hansa Alicante golf, 156 rooms, D 181 € — on site
Tel (34) 965 - 268 600 , Fax (34) 965 - 268 242

Sidi San Juan, 172 rooms, D 192 € — Playa de San Juan 2 km
Tel (34) 965 - 161 300, Fax (34) 965 - 163 346

Holiday Inn, 66 rooms, D 90 € — Playa de San Juan
Tel (34) 965 - 156 185, Fax (34) 965 - 153 936

RESTAURANTS RESTAURANTE

Alicante Golf ,Tel (34) 965 - 153 794 — on site
Dársena, Tel (34) 965 - 207 399 — Alicante 5 km
Nou Manolin, Tel (34) 965 - 200 368 — Alicante

ALMENARA

13 | 8 | 8

La Inmobiliaria Sotogrande, que hace varios años vendió el campo "de abajo" (el primero de la zona) a los socios, ha decidido ahora desarrollar el negocio del turismo de golf. Almenara es la primera realidad de un complejo en el que están previstos dos campos de golf y dos hoteles, que se halla sobre el campo de Valderrama y linda con el de San Roque. Este campo, abierto en la primavera de 1999, está construido en un terreno de fuerte desnivel y el diseño de Dave Thomas le añade dificultad, con calles estrechas y sus típicos bunkers de calle de altos taludes que castigan todas las bolas que no estén perfectamente dirigidas. No es un campo largo y por causa de los peligros que flanquean y cruzan las calles es recomendable dejar el driver en la bolsa en muchos hoyos del recorrido. La construcción es buena, el mantenimiento está muy cuidado y los greenes, no especialmente grandes pero con interesantes movimientos, son excelentes. No es obligatorio jugar en coche, pero pocas piernas resistirán hacerlo a pie.

The Sotogrande Real Estate Company, which firstly sold the "lower" terrain (the first) to members of the Sotogrande golf club, has decided to extend its activities to golf tourism. Almenara is the first complex which has provided for golf courses and hotels, located between the Valderrama and San Roque courses. The Almenara course, opened in the Spring of 1999, has been built over very hilly terrain and the Dave Thomas layout adds even more difficulties with narrow fairways and typical, high-lipped fairway bunkers, which catch anything hit off-target. This is not a wide course and what with the danger lurking alongside or across the fairways you are often better off leaving the driver in the bag. A well built course where maintenance is good and the greens - never very large but interestingly contoured - are excellent. You don't have to play with a buggy, but if you don't you sure will need sturdy legs.

Almenara Golf Hotel — 1999

Avenida Almenara s/n.
E - 11310 SOTOGRANDE

Office	Secretaria	(34) 956 - 790 300
Pro shop	Pro-shop	(34) 956 - 582 000
Fax	Fax	(34) 956 - 791 041
E-mail	almenara.golf@nh-hoteles.es	
Situation	Situación	Estepona, 30 km

Algeciras (pop. 101 556), 30 km

Annual closure	Cierre anual	no
Weekly closure	Cierre semanal	no

Fees main season Precios tempor. alta	18 holes	
	Week days Semana	**We/Bank holidays** Fin de sem./fiestas
Individual Individual	60 €	60 €
Couple Pareja	120 €	120 €

Caddy	Caddy	no
Electric Trolley	Carro eléctrico	6 € /18 holes
Buggy	Coche	36 € /18 holes
Clubs	Palos	24 € / 18 holes

Credit cards Tarjetas de crédito
VISA - Eurocard - MasterCard - AMEX

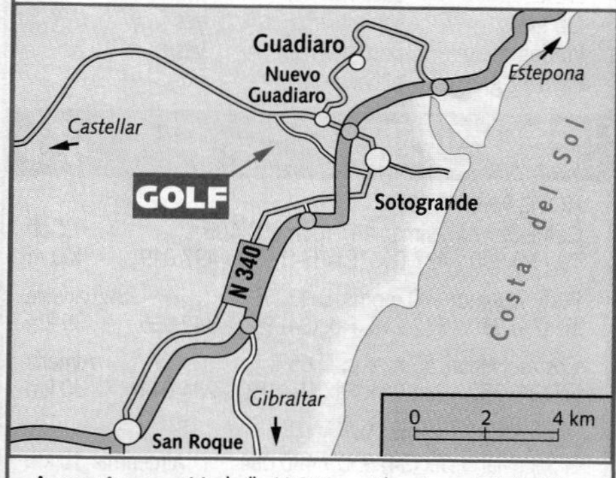

Access Acceso : Marbella N-340 → Algeciras. Exit (salida 127). → Valderrama, Sotogrande Alto.
Map 7 on page 1101 Plano 7 Página 1101

Golf course RECORRIDO — 13/20

Site	Emplazamiento	
Maintenance	Mantenimiento	
Architect	Arquitecto	Dave Thomas
Type	Tipo	inland, forest
Relief	Relieve	
Water in play	Agua	
Exp. to wind	Exp. al viento	
Trees in play	Arboles	

Scorecard Tarjeta	**Chp.** Campeonato	**Mens** Caballeros	**Ladies** Damas
Length Longitud	6168	5726	4783
Par	72	72	72
Slope system	—	—	—

Advised golfing ability Nivel de juego aconsejado — 0 12 24 36
Hcp required Handicap exigido — 28 Men/36 Ladies

Club house & amenities CLUB HOUSE Y DEPENDENCIAS — 8/10

Pro shop	Pro-shop	
Driving range	Campo de prácticas	
Sheltered	cubierto	no
On grass	sobre hierba	yes
Putting-green	putting-green	yes
Pitching-green	pitching-green	yes

Hotel facilities HOTELES CERCANOS — 8/10

HOTELS HOTELES

Hotel Almenara, 150 rooms, D 192 € — San Roque o
Tel (34) 956 - 582 000, Fax (34) 956 - 582 001

Royal Golf, 52 rooms, D 116 € — Sotogrande 4 km
Tel (34) 956 - 796 263, Fax (34) 956 - 785 159

Club Maritimo, 39 rooms, D 168 € — Sotogrande 5 km
Tel (34) 956 - 790 200, Fax (34) 956 - 790 377

RESTAURANTS RESTAURANTE

Los Remos — San Roque 10 km
Tel (34) 956 - 698 412

Vicente, Tel (34) 956 790 212 — Sotogrande 5 km

Clau en el Don Benito, Tel (34) 956 782 342 — San Roque

ALMERIMAR

14 | 7 | 7

Situado en un zona urbanizada con toda clase de distracciones, colaboraron en su diseño Ron Kirby y Gary Player. Tiene una vegetación rica que, en contraste con el fondo de montañas áridas, da la impresión de un oasis. Ha sido comprado por una sociedad japonesa con la intención de transformar este complejo en uno de los grandes centros turísticos del sur de Europa. Sus calles anchas, sus bunkers grandes y sus amplios obstáculos de agua en la línea de juego en una media docena de hoyos, dan a este recorrido un incontestable estilo de inspiración americana. Su longitud puede parecer importante desde cualquiera de los tees de salida, pero las bolas por lo general ruedan bastante. El punto álgido del recorrido se encuentra en el hoyo 12, un par 3, más bien largo, con el green en medio de una isla y que intimidará a muchos jugadores !

Located in a built-up area where there are all sorts of leisure facilities, this course was designed at a period when Ron Kirby and Gary Player were working together. Lush vegetation affords a pleasant, oasis-style contrast with the arid mountains in the background. The course has been taken over by a Japanese group, which is keen to transform the complex into one of the biggest tourist resorts in southern Europe. With wide fairways, large bunkers and huge water hazards in play on half a dozen holes, the course is unquestionably American in style. It may seem a little long, whichever tee you use, but the ball generally rolls a long way here. The highlight of the course is the 12th hole, a rather long par 3 with an island green. A daunting prospect for many a player.

Golf Almerimar S.L. — 1976

Urb. Almerimar
E - 04700 EL EJIDO - ALMERIA

Office Secretaria (34) 950 - 497 454
Pro shop Pro-shop (34) 950 - 497 050
Fax Fax (34) 950 - 497 233
E-mail golfalmerimar@a2000.es
Situation Situación
El Ejido (pop. 41 700), 10 km
Almería (pop. 159 587), 32 km
Annual closure Cierre anual — no
Weekly closure Cierre semanal — no

Fees main season Precios tempor. alta	18 holes	
	Week days Semana	**We/Bank holidays** Fin de sem./fiestas
Individual Individual	45 €	45 €
Couple Pareja	90 €	90 €

Caddy	Caddy	on request
Electric Trolley	Carro eléctrico	no
Buggy	Coche	25 € /18 holes
Clubs	Palos	15 € / 18 holes

Credit cards Tarjetas de crédito
VISA - MasterCard - AMEX

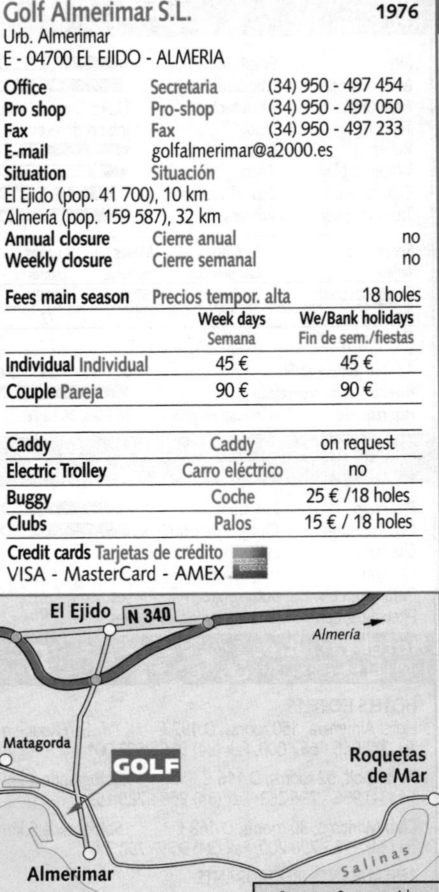

Access Acceso : Almería N340 → El Ejido, Almerimar
Map 8 on page 1103 Plano 8 Página 1103

Golf course RECORRIDO — 14/20

Site	Emplazamiento	
Maintenance	Mantenimiento	
Architect	Arquitecto	Gary Player Ron Kirby
Type	Tipo	seaside course
Relief	Relieve	
Water in play	Agua	
Exp. to wind	Exp. al viento	
Trees in play	Arboles	

Scorecard Tarjeta	**Chp.** Campeonato	**Mens** Caballeros	**Ladies** Damas
Length Longitud	5981	5892	5101
Par	72	72	72
Slope system	—	—	—

Advised golfing ability Nivel de juego aconsejado — 0 12 24 36
Hcp required Handicap exigido — 28 Men, 36 Ladies

Club house & amenities CLUB HOUSE Y DEPENDENCIAS — 7/10

Pro shop	Pro-shop	
Driving range	Campo de prácticas	
Sheltered	cubierto	no
On grass	sobre hierba	yes
Putting-green	putting-green	yes
Pitching-green	pitching-green	no

Hotel facilities HOTELES CERCANOS — 7/10

HOTELS HOTELES

Golf Hotel Almerimar, 147 rooms, D 105 € — Golf
Tel (34) 950 - 497 050, Fax (34) 950 - 497 019 — 400 m

Porto Magno, 400 rooms, D 132 € — Aguadulce
Tel (34) 950 - 342 216, Fax (34) 950 - 342 965 — 35 km

Costasol Hotel, 55 rooms, D 65 € — Almería
Tel (34) 950 - 234 011, Fax (34) 950 - 234 011 — 30 km

RESTAURANTS RESTAURANTE

El Segoviano, Tel (34) 950 - 480 084 — Almerimar 10 km

El Bello Rincón — Ctra de Almería
Tel (34) 950 - 238 427 — 25 km

ALOHA

17 | 7 | 8

Ya desde su apertura sedujo este recorrido diseñado por Javier Arana y las recientes obras efectuadas lo han mejorado aún más. Aquí es primordial la precisión de los golpes, sobre todo los de salida: Aloha no es un recorrido muy largo, pero sí a veces estrecho y accidentado. Los árboles son a menudo peligrosos, ciertos greens son ciegos, otros en alto, pero que ruedan siempre bien. Por tanto hay que permanecer constantemente atento, sobre todo para pegar a la bola con efecto en cualquier dirección. Con su original diseño, este recorrido deja una impresión de gran armonía e inteligente utilización golfística del terreno, sobre todo en tres hoyos de gran calidad: el 1, el 12 y el 18. Algunas inclinaciones naturales del campo pueden ser peligrosas, al igual que muchos obstáculos de agua, sobre todo a la vuelta. Agradable y bien decorado, Aloha es una excelente test de golf y un lugar donde no se cansa uno de jugar.

This course, designed by Javier Arana, was an attractive proposition from the first day it opened, and recent work has helped to improve the overall layout. It is important here to place your shots carefully, especially off the tee. Aloha is not a very long course, but it is sometimes tight and hilly; the trees are often dangerous and a number of greens are blind, multi-tiered and very fast. You have to keep your wits about you all the time, especially when trying to work the ball in all directions. Although an original layout, Aloha leaves an impression of harmony and intelligent use of terrain from a golfing point of view, especially on holes 1, 12 and 18, all three excellent. A number of natural banks can cause problems, as can several water hazards, particularly on the back nine. Pleasant to play and well laid out, Aloha is an excellent test of golf which is always a pleasure to play.

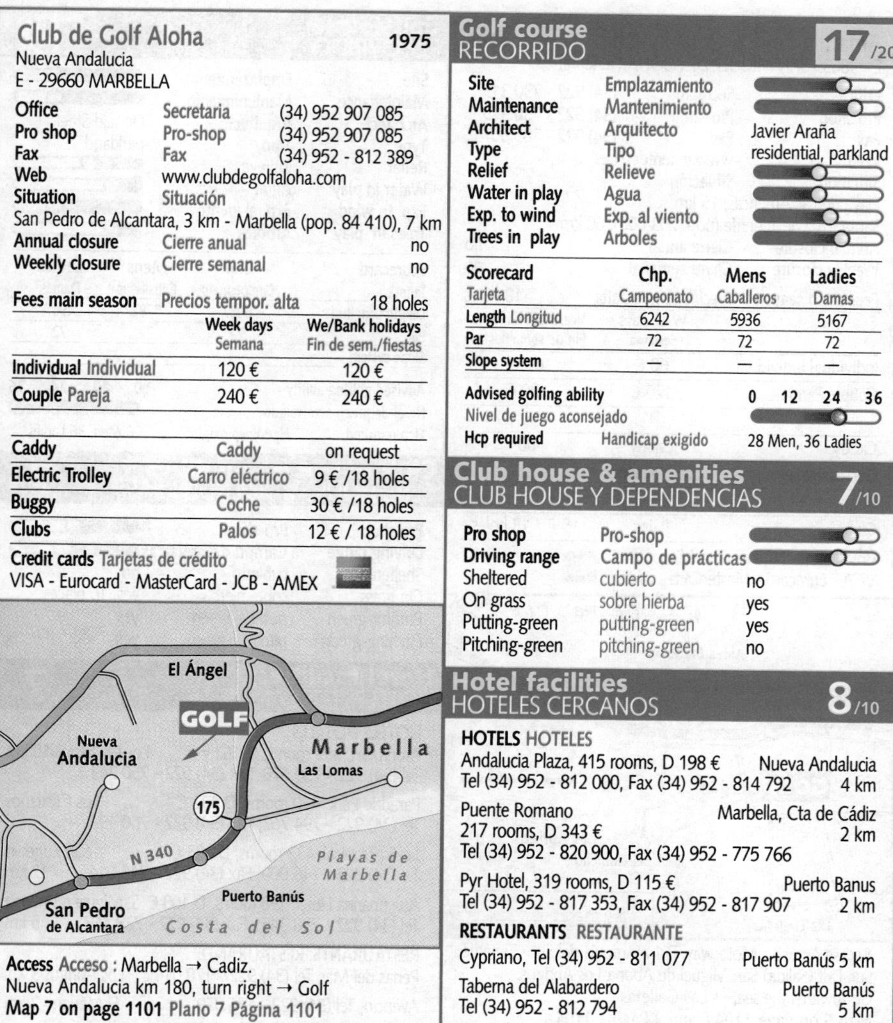

Club de Golf Aloha — 1975

Nueva Andalucia
E - 29660 MARBELLA

Office	Secretaria	(34) 952 907 085
Pro shop	Pro-shop	(34) 952 907 085
Fax	Fax	(34) 952 - 812 389
Web	www.clubdegolfaloha.com	
Situation	Situación	

San Pedro de Alcantara, 3 km - Marbella (pop. 84 410), 7 km

Annual closure	Cierre anual	no
Weekly closure	Cierre semanal	no

Fees main season Precios tempor. alta	Week days Semana	We/Bank holidays Fin de sem./fiestas
		18 holes
Individual Individual	120 €	120 €
Couple Pareja	240 €	240 €

Caddy	Caddy	on request
Electric Trolley	Carro eléctrico	9 € /18 holes
Buggy	Coche	30 € /18 holes
Clubs	Palos	12 € / 18 holes

Credit cards Tarjetas de crédito
VISA - Eurocard - MasterCard - JCB - AMEX

Access Acceso : Marbella → Cadiz.
Nueva Andalucia km 180, turn right → Golf
Map 7 on page 1101 Plano 7 Página 1101

Golf course RECORRIDO — 17/20

Site	Emplazamiento	
Maintenance	Mantenimiento	
Architect	Arquitecto	Javier Araña
Type	Tipo	residential, parkland
Relief	Relieve	
Water in play	Agua	
Exp. to wind	Exp. al viento	
Trees in play	Arboles	

Scorecard Tarjeta	Chp. Campeonato	Mens Caballeros	Ladies Damas
Length Longitud	6242	5936	5167
Par	72	72	72
Slope system	—	—	—

Advised golfing ability Nivel de juego aconsejado: 0 12 24 36
Hcp required Handicap exigido: 28 Men, 36 Ladies

Club house & amenities CLUB HOUSE Y DEPENDENCIAS — 7/10

Pro shop	Pro-shop	
Driving range	Campo de prácticas	
Sheltered	cubierto	no
On grass	sobre hierba	yes
Putting-green	putting-green	yes
Pitching-green	pitching-green	no

Hotel facilities HOTELES CERCANOS — 8/10

HOTELS HOTELES

Andalucia Plaza, 415 rooms, D 198 € — Nueva Andalucia
Tel (34) 952 - 812 000, Fax (34) 952 - 814 792 — 4 km

Puente Romano — Marbella, Cta de Cádiz
217 rooms, D 343 € — 2 km
Tel (34) 952 - 820 900, Fax (34) 952 - 775 766

Pyr Hotel, 319 rooms, D 115 € — Puerto Banus
Tel (34) 952 - 817 353, Fax (34) 952 - 817 907 — 2 km

RESTAURANTS RESTAURANTE

Cypriano, Tel (34) 952 - 811 077 — Puerto Banús 5 km

Taberna del Alabardero — Puerto Banús
Tel (34) 952 - 812 794 — 5 km

AMARILLA

15 | 7 | 7

Este es un buen campo de vacaciones. Está en un plano descendente hacia el mar por lo cual algunos hoyos disfrutan de unas vistas espléndidas dominando el Atlántico y otros hoyos lo sortean audazmente. El 5 es un par 3 de 115 metros que se conoce como Pebble Beach porque hay que tirar sobre un acantilado. El 6, en cambio, es un par 4 de 331 metros, en subida, de espaldas al mar, que domina el Teide, el volcán dormido y nevado en invierno que preside el panorama desde le centro de la isla. No es un campo difícil ni especialmente largo, suele soplar una brisa marina que refresca y motiva al buen jugador a desplegar los recursos de su juego con viento. Unas recientes obras de mantenimiento han mejorado sensiblemente el estado general del campo. El pitch & putt es recomendable por su esmerado ciudado y decoración.

Here is an excellent holiday course. It is located on a slope stretching down to the sea and offers some holes with splendid views over the Atlantic and others a little less spectacular but just as interesting and daring. Hole N°5 for example is a par 3 of 115 metres, reminiscent of Pebble Beach because you have to hit the tee-shot over a cliff. By contrast, the 6th is an uphill 331-metre par 4, turning away from the sea, overlooked by the Teide, a dormant volcano whose winter snows enhance the panorama in the middle of the island. Amarilla is not an impossible course, nor is it particularly long, and there is often a stiff sea breeze which refreshes and encourages golfers who know how to cope with wind. Recent maintenance work has significantly improved the condition of the course, and the pitch 'n putt layout is highly recommended for its manicured appearance and decoration.

Amarilla Golf & Country Club — 1989

E - 38639 SAN MIGUEL DE ABONA (Tenerife)

Office	Secretaria	(34) 922 - 730 319
Pro shop	Pro-shop	(34) 922 - 730 319
Fax	Fax	(34) 922 - 785 557
Web	www.tenerifegolf.es	
Situation	Situación	

Playa de Las Americas, 15 km
Santa Cruz de Tenerife (pop. 203 000), 60 km

Annual closure	Cierre anual	no
Weekly closure	Cierre semanal	no

Fees main season Precios tempor. alta	**Week days** Semana	**We/Bank holidays** Fin de sem./fiestas
		18 holes
Individual Individual	60 €	60 €
Couple Pareja	120 €	120 €

Caddy	Caddy	no
Electric Trolley	Carro eléctrico	no
Buggy	Coche	30 € /18 holes
Clubs	Palos	15 € / 18 holes

Credit cards Tarjetas de crédito
VISA - Eurocard - MasterCard - AMEX

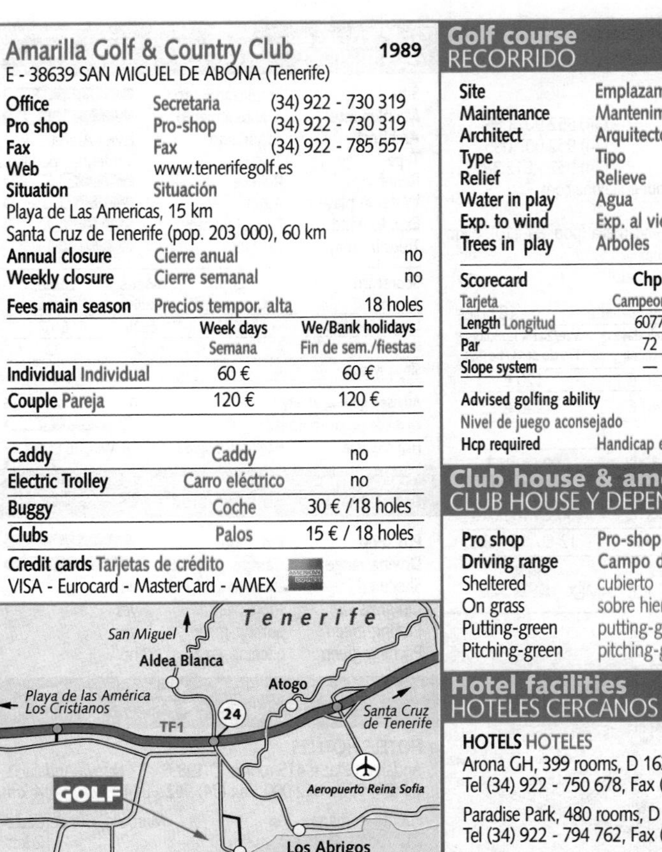

Access Acceso : Motorway TF1 / Autovia del Sur - Tenerife Sur. Exit (Salida) San Miguel de Abona-Los Abrigos. Go towards the sea, → Las Galletas

Map 9 on page 1104 Plano 9 Página 1104

Golf course RECORRIDO — 15/20

Site	Emplazamiento	
Maintenance	Mantenimiento	
Architect	Arquitecto	Donald Steel
Type	Tipo	parkland
Relief	Relieve	
Water in play	Agua	
Exp. to wind	Exp. al viento	
Trees in play	Arboles	

Scorecard Tarjeta	**Chp.** Campeonato	**Mens** Caballeros	**Ladies** Damas
Length Longitud	6077	5782	4967
Par	72	72	72
Slope system	—	—	—

Advised golfing ability Nivel de juego aconsejado: 0 12 24 36

Hcp required Handicap exigido: 28 Men, 36 Ladies

Club house & amenities CLUB HOUSE Y DEPENDENCIAS — 7/10

Pro shop	Pro-shop	
Driving range	Campo de prácticas	
Sheltered	cubierto	no
On grass	sobre hierba	yes, 15 places
Putting-green	putting-green	yes
Pitching-green	pitching-green	yes

Hotel facilities HOTELES CERCANOS — 7/10

HOTELS HOTELES

Arona GH, 399 rooms, D 162 € — Los Cristianos 10 km
Tel (34) 922 - 750 678, Fax (34) 922 - 750 243

Paradise Park, 480 rooms, D 132 € — Los Cristianos
Tel (34) 922 - 794 762, Fax (34) 922 - 750 193

Jardin Tropical, 432 rooms, D 285 € — San Eugenio 17 km
Tel (34) 922 - 746 000, Fax (34) 922 - 746 014

Augamarina Hotel, 198 rooms, D 100 € — S. Miguel de Abona 5 km
Tel (34) 922 - 738 345 , Fax (34) 922 - 738 417

RESTAURANTS RESTAURANTE

Perlas del Mar, Tel (34) 922 - 170 014 — Los Abrigos 3 km

Avencio, Tel (34) 922 - 176 079 — El Médano 2 km

BONALBA

14 | 6 | 6

Confirma la clase de Ramón Espinosa. Bonalba a pesar de su corta existencia es un recorrido que hay que conocer. La diversidad de los hoyos y la variedad de golpes que hay que jugar constituye un desafío para los más técnicos que tendrán que evitar numerosos laguitos, en línea de juego en una buena mitad del recorrido, que aparecen después de los primeros hoyos que sirven de precalentamiento. Pero no hay que dejarse impresionar por esas dificultades: con tees de salida adelantados, resultará divertido para cualquier jugador. Sólo los buenos pegadores escogerán las salidas de atrás, donde la longitud y colocación de los obstáculos dan al recorrido su verdadera fisionomía. No obstante, para emitir un juicio más definitivo hay que esperar que la vegetación se desarrolle: se han plantado 3.000 árboles, especialmente palmeras. Pero ya desde ahora es un recorrido que merece la pena conocer.

This is definitely a Ramon Espinosa layout which, despite its tender years, is a course worth knowing. The variety between holes and shots makes this a good challenge for technicans, who like the rest have to negotiate a number of small lakes, in play on half the holes, especially at the beginning. Thereafter the going gets a little easier. But don't be put off by the water; if they play from the front tees, players of all abilities can get along together here. Only the big-hitters will prefer the back-tees, where the length of the layout and position of hazards give the course its true physionomy. To really judge, though, we'll wait until the plants and trees start to grow. Some 3,000 were planted, especially palm trees, but this is already a course well worth knowing about.

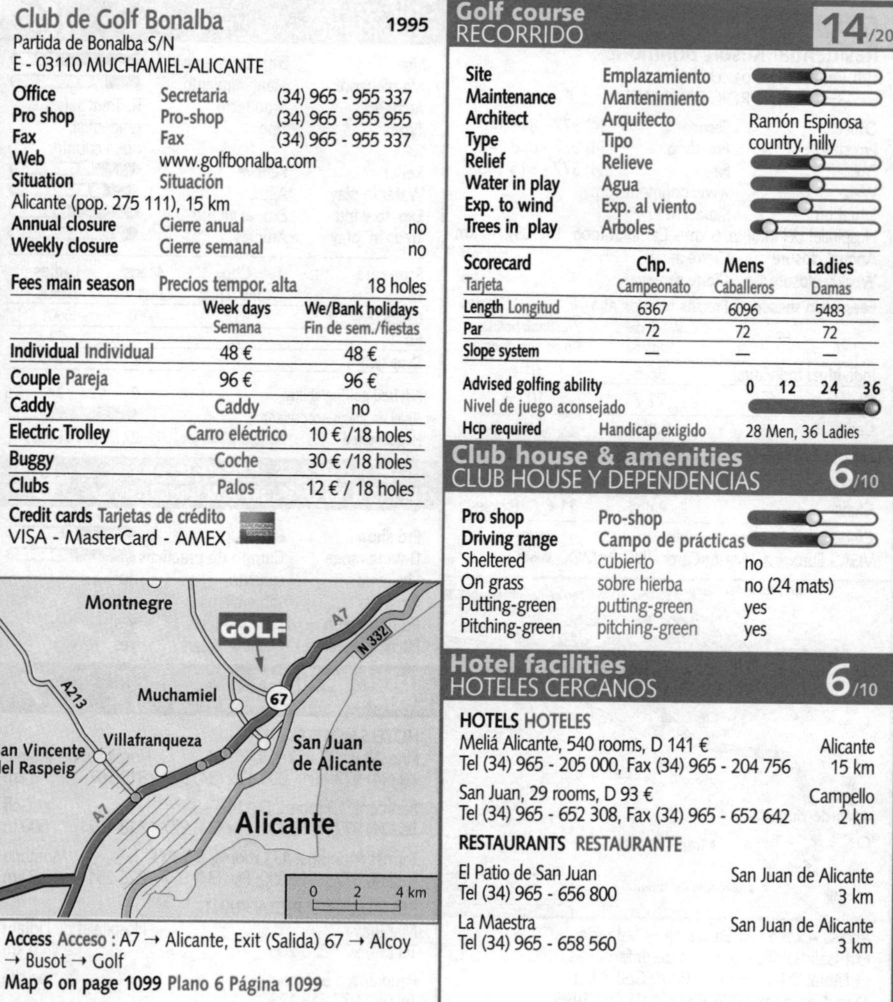

Club de Golf Bonalba 1995

Partida de Bonalba S/N
E - 03110 MUCHAMIEL-ALICANTE

Office	Secretaria	(34) 965 - 955 337
Pro shop	Pro-shop	(34) 965 - 955 955
Fax	Fax	(34) 965 - 955 337
Web	www.golfbonalba.com	
Situation	Situación	
Alicante (pop. 275 111), 15 km		
Annual closure	Cierre anual	no
Weekly closure	Cierre semanal	no

Fees main season Precios tempor. alta	Week days Semana	We/Bank holidays Fin de sem./fiestas
		18 holes
Individual Individual	48 €	48 €
Couple Pareja	96 €	96 €
Caddy Caddy		no
Electric Trolley Carro eléctrico		10 € /18 holes
Buggy Coche		30 € /18 holes
Clubs Palos		12 € / 18 holes

Credit cards Tarjetas de crédito
VISA - MasterCard - AMEX

Access Acceso : A7 → Alicante, Exit (Salida) 67 → Alcoy → Busot → Golf
Map 6 on page 1099 Plano 6 Página 1099

Golf course RECORRIDO 14/20

Site	Emplazamiento	
Maintenance	Mantenimiento	
Architect	Arquitecto	Ramón Espinosa
Type	Tipo	country, hilly
Relief	Relieve	
Water in play	Agua	
Exp. to wind	Exp. al viento	
Trees in play	Arboles	

Scorecard Tarjeta	**Chp.** Campeonato	**Mens** Caballeros	**Ladies** Damas
Length Longitud	6367	6096	5483
Par	72	72	72
Slope system	—	—	—

Advised golfing ability Nivel de juego aconsejado 0 12 24 36
Hcp required Handicap exigido 28 Men, 36 Ladies

Club house & amenities CLUB HOUSE Y DEPENDENCIAS 6/10

Pro shop	Pro-shop	
Driving range	Campo de prácticas	
Sheltered	cubierto	no
On grass	sobre hierba	no (24 mats)
Putting-green	putting-green	yes
Pitching-green	pitching-green	yes

Hotel facilities HOTELES CERCANOS 6/10

HOTELS HOTELES

Meliá Alicante, 540 rooms, D 141 € — Alicante 15 km
Tel (34) 965 - 205 000, Fax (34) 965 - 204 756

San Juan, 29 rooms, D 93 € — Campello 2 km
Tel (34) 965 - 652 308, Fax (34) 965 - 652 642

RESTAURANTS RESTAURANTE

El Patio de San Juan — San Juan de Alicante 3 km
Tel (34) 965 - 656 800

La Maestra — San Juan de Alicante 3 km
Tel (34) 965 - 658 560

BONMONT

16 | 8 | 7

Robert Trent Jones Jr, siguiendo la tradición de su padre, ha creado un diseño muy estratégico en el que constantemente hay que calcular los riesgos antes de jugar. Lo ha construido con un refinamiento estético muy personal, removiendo grandes cantidades de tierra, tarea indispensable para poder jugar en un terreno tan rocoso. El terreno es muy accidentado: tiene profundos barrancos, riachuelos y lagos, bunkers grandes magistralmente colocados, como es norma de la casa Trent Jones, y greenes muy interesantes y provocadores. Con estos elementos y distancias razonables parece evidente que estamos hablando de algo excepcional, y lo es, pero el gran problema de Bonmont es el habitual viento dominante muy fuerte, que distorsiona totalmente las distancias y el diseño. Ojalá acierte el visitante a jugar un día de calma; al menos, de brisa.

In the family tradition, Robert Trent Jones Jnr. has designed a highly strategic layout, where risks constantly need calculating before each shot. He has modeled space in his very own tasteful and stylish way, but also with impressive contouring of the land. And this was necessary for this rocky terrain to be at all playable. The terrain is uneven and hilly: watch out for some deep ravines, ditches and lakes, strategically well-located bunkering and (as usual with Trent Jones), a number of very tricky and deceptive greens. When you consider the above plus the course's very respectable yardage, it is obvious that this is no ordinary layout. The greatest problem playing Bonmont is the prevailing wind, which is often very gusty and completely changes all notion of distance and evaluation of the layout. First time out, try and play in calm weather or in no worse than a light breeze.

Golf Hotel & Residential Resort Bonmont — 1990

Urb. Terres Noves parcela 84
E - 43300 MONT-ROIG DEL CAMP

Office	Secretaria	(34) 977 - 818 140
Pro shop	Pro-shop	(34) 977 - 818 140
Fax	Fax	(34) 977 - 818 146
Web	www.bonmont.com	
Situation	Situación	

Hospitalet del Infante, 6 km - Cambrils (pop. 14 903), 15 km

Annual closure	Cierre anual	no
Weekly closure	Cierre semanal	no
Fees main season	Precios tempor. alta	18 holes

	Week days Semana	We/Bank holidays Fin de sem./fiestas
Individual Individual	36 €	51 €
Couple Pareja	72 €	102 €
Caddy Caddy		no
Electric Trolley Carro eléctrico		9 € /18 holes
Buggy Coche		33 € /18 holes
Clubs Palos		21 € / 18 holes

Credit cards Tarjetas de crédito
VISA - Eurocard - MasterCard - DC - AMEX

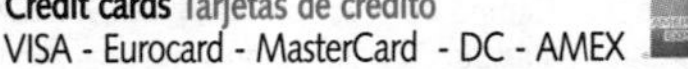

Access Acceso : A7 Barcelona → Valencia, Exit (salida) 38. Hospitalet del Infante → Mora, 2 km → Mont Roig, Golf 4 km
Map 4 on page 1095 Plano 4 Página 1095

Golf course RECORRIDO — 16/20

Site	Emplazamiento	
Maintenance	Mantenimiento	
Architect	Arquitecto	R. Trent Jones Jr
Type	Tipo	residential, open country
Relief	Relieve	
Water in play	Agua	
Exp. to wind	Exp. al viento	
Trees in play	Arboles	

Scorecard Tarjeta	Chp. Campeonato	Mens Caballeros	Ladies Damas
Length Longitud	6371	6050	5501
Par	72	72	72
Slope system	—	—	—

Advised golfing ability Nivel de juego aconsejado — 0 12 24 36

Hcp required Handicap exigido — 27 Men, 36 Ladies

Club house & amenities CLUB HOUSE Y DEPENDENCIAS — 8/10

Pro shop	Pro-shop	
Driving range	Campo de prácticas	
Sheltered	cubierto	no
On grass	sobre hierba	yes
Putting-green	putting-green	yes
Pitching-green	pitching-green	yes

Hotel facilities HOTELES CERCANOS — 7/10

HOTELS HOTELES

Pino Alto, 137 rooms, D 111 € — Hospitalet del Infante
Tel (34) 977 - 811 000, Fax (34) 977 - 810 907 — 6 km

Bonmont, 19 rooms, D 114 € — Golf
Tel (34) 977 - 818 129, Fax (34) 977 - 818 102 — 500 m

Termes Montbrio, 133 rooms, D 230 € — Montbrio
Tel (34) 977 - 814 000, Fax (34) 977 - 826 251 — 8 km

RESTAURANTS RESTAURANTE

Mar Brava — Hospitalet de l'Infant
Tel (34) 977 820 206 — 5 km

Panorámico Bonmont — on site
Tel (34) 977 818 129

CAMPOAMOR

14 | 6 | 6

La belleza del lugar anuncia una agradable jornada en medio de un paisaje con poco arbolado en el que predomina la vegetación de monte. Es un recorrido no muy accidentado con una longitud que gustará a los pegadores que podrán intentar llegar a green en dos pares 4 muy cortos (el 11 y el 13) y ganar puntos en los pares 5. El diseño de Sanz y García no denota una gran imaginación ya que lo que han intentado ante todo es agradar a todos los jugadores, logrando un recorrido muy funcional. Con greens correctos y poco protegidos se pueden obtener buenos resultados que agradarán a los jugadores. Bien es verdad que se pueden encontrar en la región recorridos más difíciles, pero Campoamor es un buen test para afinar su juego sin demasiadas dificultades. Un verdadero recorrido para las vacaciones.

A very pretty site heralds a pleasant day's golfing in rather open countryside, where the garrigue shrub is the main and most attractive form of vegetation. The course is not hilly, and the length will appeal to big-hitters, who can try and reach two very short par 4s (the 11th and 13th) from the tee and pick up points on the par 5s. The Sanz and Garcia layout has nothing exceptionally imaginative about it, but their aim was to appeal to players, so the course's functional side is a positive point. The greens are good but have few bunkers, and the opportunities are there to card a good score, always a welcome treat for the wounded ego. You can certainly find more challenging courses than this in the region, but Campoamor is a great place to sharpen up your game without too many mishaps. A real holiday course.

Real Club de Golf Campoamor — 1989

Ctra de Torrevieja a Cartagena, km 9
E - 03192 DEHESA DE CAMPOAMOR - ORIHUELA

Office	Secretaria	(34) 965 - 321 366
Pro shop	Pro-shop	(34) 965 - 321 366
Fax	Fax	(34) 965 - 320 506
E-mail	rcgcampoamor@oriolnet.com	
Situation	Situación	

Alicante (pop. 275 111), 57 km - Torrevieja, 8 km

Annual closure	Cierre anual	no
Weekly closure	Cierre semanal	no

Fees main season Precios tempor. alta	**Week days** Semana	**We/Bank holidays** Fin de sem./fiestas
18 holes		
Individual Individual	42 €	42 €
Couple Pareja	84 €	84 €

Caddy	Caddy	no
Electric Trolley	Carro eléctrico	no
Buggy	Coche	27 € /18 holes
Clubs	Palos	9 € / 18 holes
Credit cards	Tarjetas de crédito	no

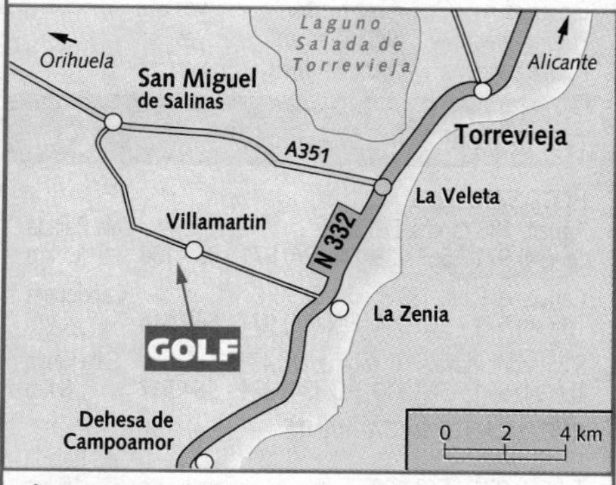

Access Acceso : N332 Torrevieja → Dehesa de Campoamor, Cabo Roig, Km 48 → Golf
Map 6 on page 1099 Plano 6 Página 1099

Golf course — RECORRIDO — 14/20

Site	Emplazamiento	
Maintenance	Mantenimiento	
Architect	Arquitecto	Gregorio Sanz Carmelo Garcia
Type	Tipo	hilly, residential
Relief	Relieve	
Water in play	Agua	
Exp. to wind	Exp. al viento	
Trees in play	Arboles	

Scorecard Tarjeta	**Chp.** Campeonato	**Mens** Caballeros	**Ladies** Damas
Length Longitud	6203	6056	5094
Par	72	72	72
Slope system	—	—	—

Advised golfing ability Nivel de juego aconsejado: 0 12 24 36
Hcp required Handicap exigido: 28 Men, 36 Ladies

Club house & amenities — CLUB HOUSE Y DEPENDENCIAS — 6/10

Pro shop	Pro-shop	
Driving range	Campo de prácticas	
Sheltered	cubierto	no
On grass	sobre hierba	yes
Putting-green	putting-green	yes
Pitching-green	pitching-green	yes

Hotel facilities — HOTELES CERCANOS — 6/10

HOTELS HOTELES

Torrejoven, 105 rooms, D 79 € Tel (34) 965 - 707 145, Fax (34) 965 - 715 315	Torrevieja 4 km
Orihuela Costa, 15 rooms, D 84 € Tel (34) 966 - 760 800, Fax (34) 966 - 761 326	La Zenia 8 km
Meridional, 52 rooms, D 111 € Tel (34) 965 - 728 340, Fax (34) 965 - 728 306	Guardamar del Segura 20 km

RESTAURANTS RESTAURANTE

Cabo Roig Tel (34) 966 - 760 290	Torrevieja 8 km
Morales Tel (34) 966 - 721 293	Los Montesinos

CANYAMEL

15 | 6 | 6

Emplazado dentro de un paisaje típico de la montaña mallorquina, es un éxito de José Gancedo el haber conseguido realizar algunos hoyos espectaculares en la parte más accidentada (los nueve hoyos de la ida). Se ha preservado la naturaleza, así como algunas tapias e incluso una antigua granja que delimita el ángulo del dog-leg del hoyo 9. Al igual que en otros golfs de la isla hay que reflexionar antes de atacar, logrando muchas veces mejores resultados si se juega la seguridad y se sabe evitar las dificultades. Mejor es preservar sus fuerzas para atacar unos greens a menudo en alto, con escalones y bien protegidos. Su longitud es razonable y hay que juagarlo varias veces para mejor apreciar la progresión de los resultados. No se aburre uno. Un campo que merece plenamente la excursión a un extremo de la isla.

In a typical setting of Majorcan countryside and mountains, Canyamel is a pretty little number designed by José Gancedo. The hillier part of the course (the front 9) includes some quite spectacular holes. The land's natural beauty has been preserved, together with some low walls and even an old farmhouse marking the corner of the dog-leg on hole N° 9. As with many other courses on the island, this is not a layout to attack without thinking first. Playing safe often gives better results. If you keep out of trouble, the going is easier and you can save your strength (important here) to negotiate some tricky approach shots to elevated, multi-tiered and well-defended greens. Very human in length, Canyamel is a course you want to play several times, not to understand it (it has little to hide) but to enjoy getting your score down. Good fun all the way. A course which is well worth a visit to this remote part of the island.

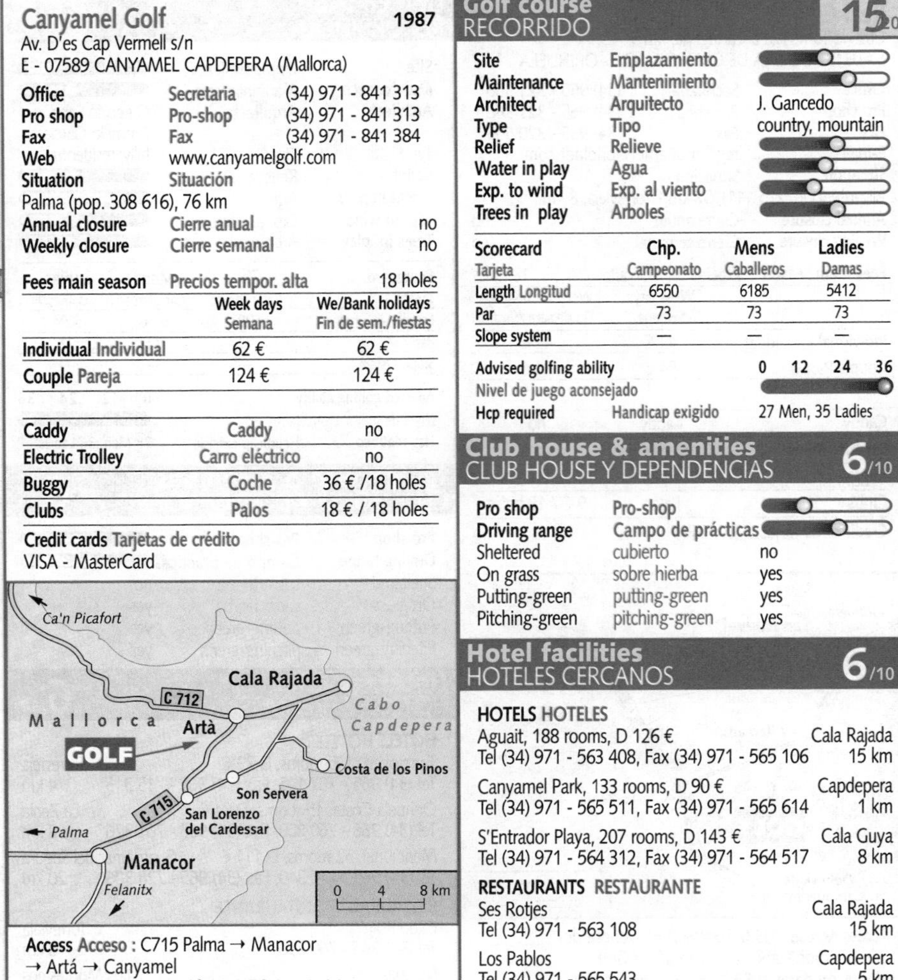

Canyamel Golf — 1987

Av. D'es Cap Vermell s/n
E - 07589 CANYAMEL CAPDEPERA (Mallorca)

Office	Secretaria	(34) 971 - 841 313
Pro shop	Pro-shop	(34) 971 - 841 313
Fax	Fax	(34) 971 - 841 384
Web	www.canyamelgolf.com	
Situation	Situación	

Palma (pop. 308 616), 76 km

Annual closure	Cierre anual	no
Weekly closure	Cierre semanal	no

Fees main season Precios tempor. alta	Week days Semana	We/Bank holidays Fin de sem./fiestas
	18 holes	
Individual Individual	62 €	62 €
Couple Pareja	124 €	124 €

Caddy	Caddy	no
Electric Trolley	Carro eléctrico	no
Buggy	Coche	36 € /18 holes
Clubs	Palos	18 € / 18 holes

Credit cards Tarjetas de crédito
VISA - MasterCard

Access Acceso : C715 Palma → Manacor → Artá → Canyamel
Map 9 on page 1104 Plano 9 Página 1104

Golf course RECORRIDO — 15/20

Site	Emplazamiento	
Maintenance	Mantenimiento	
Architect	Arquitecto	J. Gancedo
Type	Tipo	country, mountain
Relief	Relieve	
Water in play	Agua	
Exp. to wind	Exp. al viento	
Trees in play	Arboles	

Scorecard Tarjeta	Chp. Campeonato	Mens Caballeros	Ladies Damas
Length Longitud	6550	6185	5412
Par	73	73	73
Slope system	—	—	—

Advised golfing ability Nivel de juego aconsejado: 0 12 24 36
Hcp required Handicap exigido: 27 Men, 35 Ladies

Club house & amenities CLUB HOUSE Y DEPENDENCIAS — 6/10

Pro shop	Pro-shop	
Driving range	Campo de prácticas	
Sheltered	cubierto	no
On grass	sobre hierba	yes
Putting-green	putting-green	yes
Pitching-green	pitching-green	yes

Hotel facilities HOTELES CERCANOS — 6/10

HOTELS HOTELES

Aguait, 188 rooms, D 126 € — Cala Rajada
Tel (34) 971 - 563 408, Fax (34) 971 - 565 106 — 15 km

Canyamel Park, 133 rooms, D 90 € — Capdepera
Tel (34) 971 - 565 511, Fax (34) 971 - 565 614 — 1 km

S'Entrador Playa, 207 rooms, D 143 € — Cala Guya
Tel (34) 971 - 564 312, Fax (34) 971 - 564 517 — 8 km

RESTAURANTS RESTAURANTE

Ses Rotjes — Cala Rajada
Tel (34) 971 - 563 108 — 15 km

Los Pablos — Capdepera
Tel (34) 971 - 565 543 — 5 km

CAPDEPERA

15 | 7 | 6

Es una obra de Dan Maples que ha trabajado mucho en Carolina del Norte y en Florida. De hecho los seis lagos le dan un aire de estilo americano sin desfigurar el paisaje natural. Desde las salidas de atrás es un excelente recorrido de competición que se puede "dulcificar" escogiendo tees de salida más avanzados, logrando así que las calles parezcan menos estrechas. Tiene muchos bunkers y bosques de los que es difícil salir. Hay que saber manejar bien todos los palos, sin olvidar el pat en unos greens bastante grandes y con ondulaciones nada fáciles de apreciar. Si a la belleza de algunas vistas hacia la montaña añadimos la calidad de los cuidados de mantenimiento, comprenderemos mejor por qué Capdepera se sitúa entre los mejores recorridos de Mallorca.

This is one of the few courses in Europe designed by Dan Maples, who has worked extensively in North Carolina and Florida. The American style is evident with the six artificial lakes, which in no way upset the natural look of the landscape and terrain. This is an excellent tournament course from the back-tees and one which gradually mellows as you move further forward. From the front, the course doesn't look as tight, and the many bunkers and tough undergrowth seem less harrowing. You will need every club in the bag, not forgetting the putter on greens which are on the large side, well-shaped and not always easy to read. Add to this some pretty viewpoints over the mountains and good general upkeep and you will understand why we consider this to be a class golf course, one of the very best in Majorca.

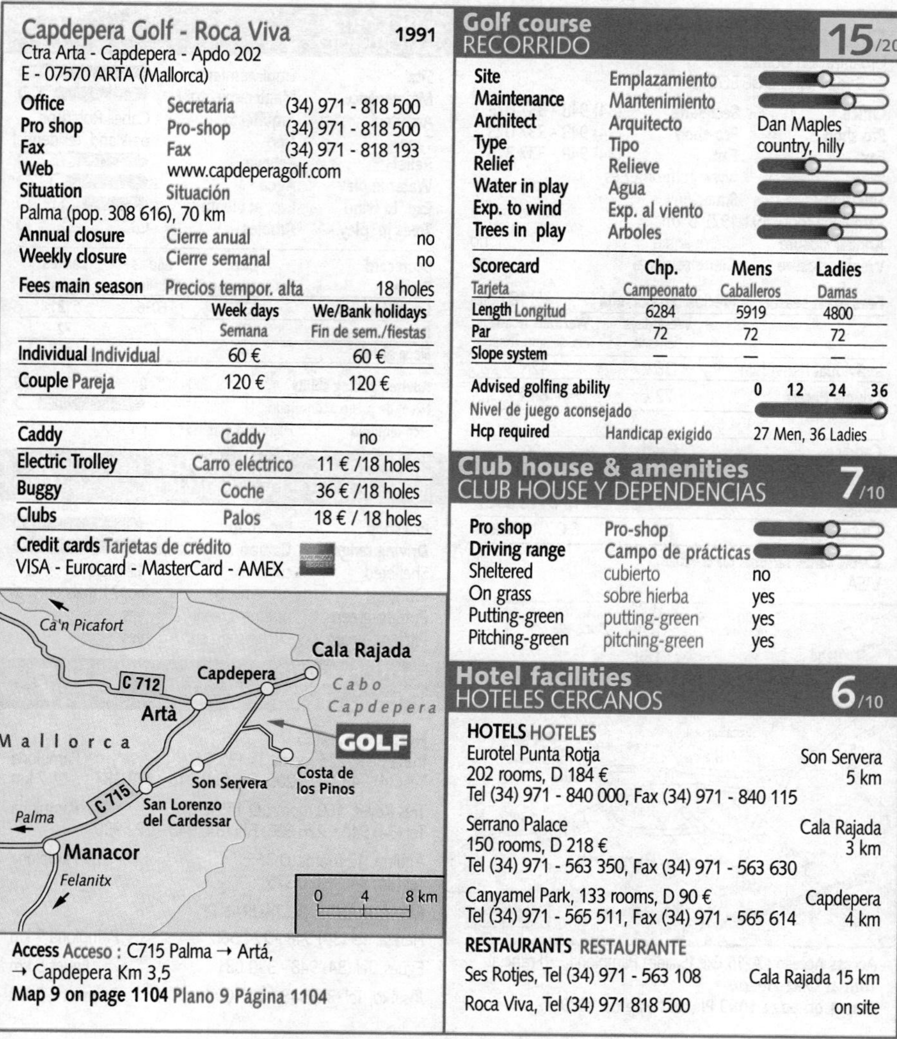

Capdepera Golf - Roca Viva 1991
Ctra Arta - Capdepera - Apdo 202
E - 07570 ARTA (Mallorca)

Office	Secretaria	(34) 971 - 818 500
Pro shop	Pro-shop	(34) 971 - 818 500
Fax	Fax	(34) 971 - 818 193
Web	www.capdeperagolf.com	
Situation	Situación	
Palma (pop. 308 616), 70 km		
Annual closure	Cierre anual	no
Weekly closure	Cierre semanal	no

Fees main season Precios tempor. alta	**Week days** Semana	**We/Bank holidays** Fin de sem./fiestas
		18 holes
Individual Individual	60 €	60 €
Couple Pareja	120 €	120 €

Caddy	Caddy	no
Electric Trolley	Carro eléctrico	11 € /18 holes
Buggy	Coche	36 € /18 holes
Clubs	Palos	18 € / 18 holes

Credit cards Tarjetas de crédito
VISA - Eurocard - MasterCard - AMEX

Access Acceso : C715 Palma → Artá,
→ Capdepera Km 3,5
Map 9 on page 1104 Plano 9 Página 1104

Golf course RECORRIDO — 15/20

Site	Emplazamiento	
Maintenance	Mantenimiento	
Architect	Arquitecto	Dan Maples
Type	Tipo	country, hilly
Relief	Relieve	
Water in play	Agua	
Exp. to wind	Exp. al viento	
Trees in play	Arboles	

Scorecard Tarjeta	**Chp.** Campeonato	**Mens** Caballeros	**Ladies** Damas
Length Longitud	6284	5919	4800
Par	72	72	72
Slope system	—	—	—

Advised golfing ability Nivel de juego aconsejado: 0 12 24 36
Hcp required Handicap exigido: 27 Men, 36 Ladies

Club house & amenities CLUB HOUSE Y DEPENDENCIAS — 7/10

Pro shop	Pro-shop	
Driving range	Campo de prácticas	
Sheltered	cubierto	no
On grass	sobre hierba	yes
Putting-green	putting-green	yes
Pitching-green	pitching-green	yes

Hotel facilities HOTELES CERCANOS — 6/10

HOTELS HOTELES

Eurotel Punta Rotja — Son Servera 5 km
202 rooms, D 184 €
Tel (34) 971 - 840 000, Fax (34) 971 - 840 115

Serrano Palace — Cala Rajada 3 km
150 rooms, D 218 €
Tel (34) 971 - 563 350, Fax (34) 971 - 563 630

Canyamel Park, 133 rooms, D 90 € — Capdepera 4 km
Tel (34) 971 - 565 511, Fax (34) 971 - 565 614

RESTAURANTS RESTAURANTE

Ses Rotjes, Tel (34) 971 - 563 108 — Cala Rajada 15 km
Roca Viva, Tel (34) 971 818 500 — on site

CASTILLO DE GORRAIZ | 17 | 7 | 7

No había muchos golfs en la región de Pamplona y teniendo en cuenta que el de Ulzama ha sido ampliado a 18 hoyos muy recientemente, la creación de Castillo de Gorraiz ha sido muy bien acogida. Las instalaciones son muy completas con un amplísimo campo de prácticas, tenis y piscina. Su creador es Cabell Robinson, autor también de La Cala en la Costa del Sol y de soberbios recorridos en Marruecos (el del Rey en Agadir y el sorprendente Amelkis de Marrakech). Ha sabido aprovechar el terreno reservando una parte a residencias entre las que serpentean las calles anchas y muy abiertas. Los tees de salida son elevados dominando los hoyos. No siempre es necesario utilizar el drive ya que al peligro de roughs densos recomienda la prudencia si no se tiene mucha precisión. Tres grandes obstáculos de agua se encuentran el la línea de juego, lo que obliga a bien calcular tanto la distancia como la precisión de los golpes. Un golf bien logrado.

Given that the region of Pamplona is not too well off for golf courses and that Ulzama has only recently been upgraded to a full 18-holer, the advent of Castillo de Gorraiz was most welcome. Facilities are excellent, with a huge driving range, tennis courts and a pool. The course is the work of Cabell Robinson, who designed La Cala on the Costa del Sol and some superb courses in Morocco (including the King's Course in Agadir and the astonishing Amelkis in Marrakesh). Here he has worked wonders with the terrain, a part of which is reserved for villas through which the wide and very open fairways wind their way around the course. The tee-boxes are elevated so you are looking down on the holes, and you don't always have to use the driver; danger from the thick rough calls for care if accuracy is not your forte. At the other end of the fairway, the huge, roundly-contoured greens give you the opportunity to show your putting skills. Three large water hazards are also in play, so length as well as accuracy is at a premium. A very fine course.

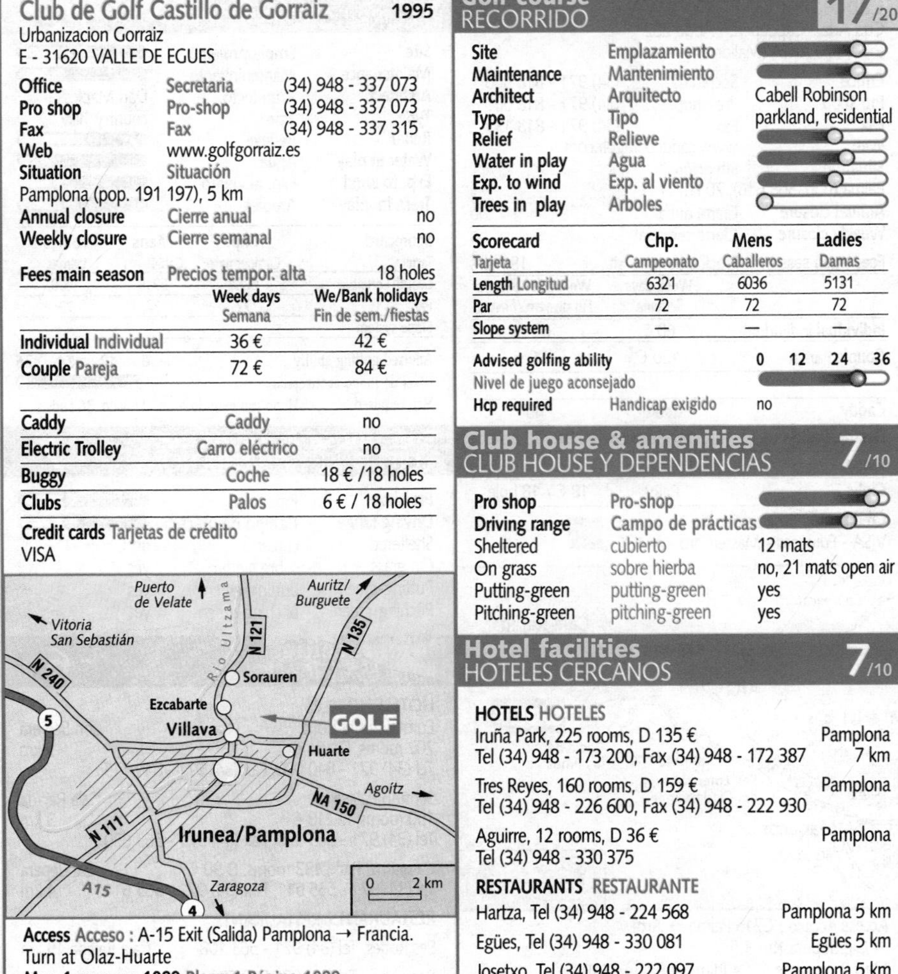

Club de Golf Castillo de Gorraiz — 1995

Urbanizacion Gorraiz
E - 31620 VALLE DE EGUES

Office	Secretaria	(34) 948 - 337 073
Pro shop	Pro-shop	(34) 948 - 337 073
Fax	Fax	(34) 948 - 337 315
Web	www.golfgorraiz.es	
Situation	Situación	
Pamplona (pop. 191 197), 5 km		
Annual closure	Cierre anual	no
Weekly closure	Cierre semanal	no

Fees main season Precios tempor. alta	Week days Semana	We/Bank holidays Fin de sem./fiestas
		18 holes
Individual Individual	36 €	42 €
Couple Pareja	72 €	84 €

Caddy	Caddy	no
Electric Trolley	Carro eléctrico	no
Buggy	Coche	18 € /18 holes
Clubs	Palos	6 € / 18 holes

Credit cards Tarjetas de crédito
VISA

Access Acceso : A-15 Exit (Salida) Pamplona → Francia. Turn at Olaz-Huarte
Map 1 on page 1089 Plano 1 Página 1089

Golf course RECORRIDO — 17/20

Site	Emplazamiento	
Maintenance	Mantenimiento	
Architect	Arquitecto	Cabell Robinson
Type	Tipo	parkland, residential
Relief	Relieve	
Water in play	Agua	
Exp. to wind	Exp. al viento	
Trees in play	Arboles	

Scorecard Tarjeta	Chp. Campeonato	Mens Caballeros	Ladies Damas
Length Longitud	6321	6036	5131
Par	72	72	72
Slope system	—	—	—

Advised golfing ability 0 12 24 36
Nivel de juego aconsejado
Hcp required Handicap exigido no

Club house & amenities CLUB HOUSE Y DEPENDENCIAS — 7/10

Pro shop	Pro-shop	
Driving range	Campo de prácticas	
Sheltered	cubierto	12 mats
On grass	sobre hierba	no, 21 mats open air
Putting-green	putting-green	yes
Pitching-green	pitching-green	yes

Hotel facilities HOTELES CERCANOS — 7/10

HOTELS HOTELES

Iruña Park, 225 rooms, D 135 € — Pamplona 7 km
Tel (34) 948 - 173 200, Fax (34) 948 - 172 387

Tres Reyes, 160 rooms, D 159 € — Pamplona
Tel (34) 948 - 226 600, Fax (34) 948 - 222 930

Aguirre, 12 rooms, D 36 € — Pamplona
Tel (34) 948 - 330 375

RESTAURANTS RESTAURANTE

Hartza, Tel (34) 948 - 224 568 — Pamplona 5 km
Egües, Tel (34) 948 - 330 081 — Egües 5 km
Josetxo, Tel (34) 948 - 222 097 — Pamplona 5 km

CERDAÑA

14	7	7

Situado en plena naturaleza, este recorrido es algo más que un simple paseo. Era de esperar dada la fama de Javier Arana, cuyos diseños dejan siempre de lado lo que es trivial y son testimonio de un gran conocimiento del golf. Ha sabido adaptarse a un terreno en el que las desnivelaciones ya eran suficientes para no añadir más dificultades. Las calles son claras, sin trampas, lo esencial del juego se desarrolla en las llegadas a green, donde es necesario evitar árboles y algunos bunkers peligrosos. No muy largo, a veces estrecho, este recorrido exige precisión, favorece el placer del golf entre jugadores de diferente nivel o en familia. Tan robusto y natural como siempre, aparece en esta edición con cambios en las notas: la del campo ha mejorado por el buen mantenimiento que está teniendo los últimos años, consiguiendo incluso greenes de calidad; la de la casa-club baja porque se ha quedado reducida a caddy master y vestuarios porque se quemó el chalet, ya en reconstrucción, aunque su actividad hotelera continúa en los apartamentos anexos. En agosto de 2000 se abrieron otros 9 hoyos, par 36, muy interesantes, de una belleza escénica notable.

Located out in the country, this course is more than just a pleasant walk. And this is only to be expected from Javier Arana, whose layouts are always out of the ordinary and reveal considerable golfing intelligence. He has played a lot with the terrain and the marked differences in relief in order not to add too many hazards. With the fairways free of traps, the key to playing the course is around the greens, avoiding the trees and the few dangerous bunkers. Not particularly long and sometimes tight, this course places emphasis on accuracy and provides shared golfing pleasure among players of different levels or with the family. Without having relinquished any of its tough, natural appearance, this course deserves a better score. Maintenance has been much improved in recent years, particularly the excellence of the greens. At the time of printing, the club-house was being refurbished and space was limited, but hotel accommodation is still available in the neighbouring buildings. In addition, 9 interesting and cleverly landscaped new holes were opened in August 2000.

Real Club de Golf de Cerdaña — 1929

Apartat de correus 63
E - 17520 PUIGCERDA

Office	Secretaria	(34) 972 - 141 408
Pro shop	Pro-shop	(34) 972 - 141 040
Fax	Fax	(34) 972 - 881 338
Web	—	
Situation	Situación	

Puigcerdà (pop. 6 414), 1 km - Barcelona (pop. 1 681 132), 150 km

Annual closure	Cierre anual	no
Weekly closure	Cierre semanal	no

Fees main season Precios tempor. alta	Week days Semana	We/Bank holidays Fin de sem./fiestas
18 holes		
Individual Individual	30 €	48 €
Couple Pareja	60 €	96 €

Caddy	Caddy	no
Electric Trolley	Carro eléctrico	6 € /18 holes
Buggy	Coche	30 € /18 holes
Clubs	Palos	6 € / 18 holes

Credit cards Tarjetas de crédito
VISA - Eurocard - MasterCard - AMEX

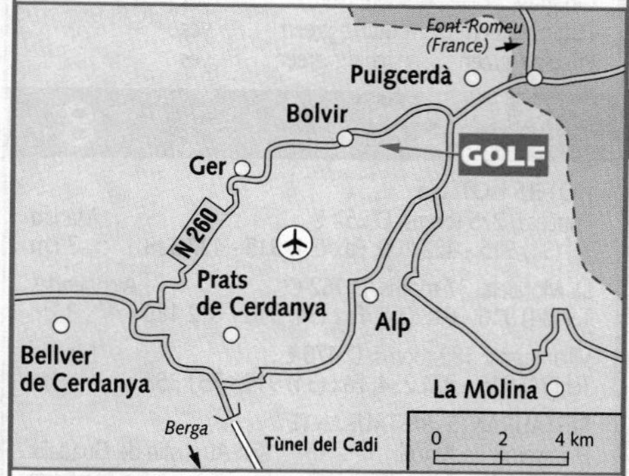

Access Acceso : Barcelona A18 → Manresa → "Tunel del Cadi y Puigcerda"

Map 2 on page 1091 Plano 2 Página 1091

Golf course RECORRIDO — 14/20

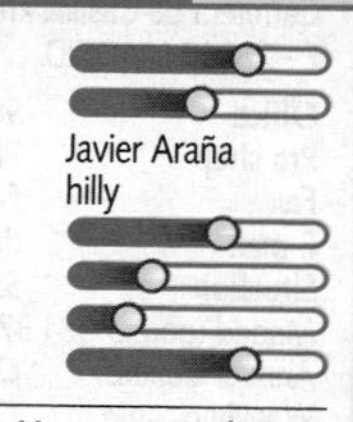

Site	Emplazamiento	
Maintenance	Mantenimiento	
Architect	Arquitecto	Javier Araña
Type	Tipo	hilly
Relief	Relieve	
Water in play	Agua	
Exp. to wind	Exp. al viento	
Trees in play	Arboles	

Scorecard Tarjeta	Chp. Campeonato	Mens Caballeros	Ladies Damas
Length Longitud	5886	5726	5015
Par	71	71	71
Slope system	—	—	—

Advised golfing ability Nivel de juego aconsejado: 0 12 24 36

Hcp required Handicap exigido: 27 Men, 36 Ladies

Club house & amenities CLUB HOUSE Y DEPENDENCIAS — 7/10

Pro shop	Pro-shop	
Driving range	Campo de prácticas	
Sheltered	cubierto	7 mats
On grass	sobre hierba	yes
Putting-green	putting-green	yes
Pitching-green	pitching-green	yes

Hotel facilities HOTELES CERCANOS — 7/10

HOTELS HOTELES

Torre del Remei, 11 rooms, D 276 € — Bolvir de Cerdaña
Tel (34) 972 - 140 182, Fax (34) 972 - 140 449 — 1 km

Chalet del Golf, 11 rooms, D 81 € — Puigcerda
Tel (34) 972 - 880 950, Fax (34) 972 - 880 966 — 500 m

Park Hotel, 54 rooms, D 78 € — Puigcerdá
Tel (34) 972 - 880 750, Fax (34) 972 - 880 754 — 3 km

RESTAURANTS RESTAURANTE

Torre del Remei — Bolvir de Cerdaña
Tel (34) 972 - 140 182 — 1 km

La Tieta — Puigcerda
Tel (34) 972 - 880 156 — 2 km

CLUB DE CAMPO

16	8	8

Una vez más, Javier Arana demuestra aquí estar entre los mejores arquitéctos del siglo. Es una pena que no haya expresado su talento fuera de las fronteras españolas. A la vez exigente por su longitud así como por la precisión que requiere, éste campo nos proporciona un placer siempre renovado. De mediano relieve, no se deja descubrir tan facilmente y hacen falta muchas veces para llegar a entender todas sus sutilezas. Los árboles y los bunkers de recorrido constituyen sus principales dificultades, y le damos las gracias a Arana de no haber creado demasiados problemas en los accesos a los greenes. Ultimamente Manuel Piñero ha remodelado el campo y se ha construído un nuevo recorrido de pares 3. Hay que decir que el índice de ocupación del campo es altísimo ya que el Club de Campo es uno de los más grandes de España. Aconsejamos por tanto a los visitantes de evitar los fines de semana.

Here again, Javier Arana gives a further demonstration of why he will go down as one of the century's greatest architects. What a shame his great talent is not on show outside his home country. Demanding both in length and accuracy, this course, located just outside Madrid, is a real joy to play everytime. Averagely hilly (but easy to walk), the course is not easy to discover and needs several rounds to grasp the subtler points. The trees and fairway bunkers are the main difficulties, and we should be grateful to Arana for not having created too many difficulties when approaching the greens. Manuel Piñero has recently reshaped the course and designed a new par-3 layout. It should also be said that the course is very busy in what is certainly Spain's biggest golf club. So follow our advice and avoid week-ends.

Club de Campo Villa de Madrid — 1932

Carretera de Castilla km 2
E - 28040 MADRID

Office	Secretaria	(34) 915 - 502 010
Pro shop	Pro-shop	(34) 915 - 502 010
Fax	Fax	(34) 915 - 502 023
E-mail	deportes.ccvm@retemail.es	
Situation	Situación	

Madrid (pop. 3 084 373), 1 km

Annual closure	Cierre anual	no
Weekly closure	Cierre semanal	no
Fees main season	Precios tempor. alta	18 holes

	Week days Semana	We/Bank holidays Fin de sem./fiestas
Individual Individual	32 € *	77 € *
Couple Pareja	64 € *	154 € *

Access to the club (Acceso al Club): 11 € (weekdays), 23 € (We)

Caddy	Caddy	no
Electric Trolley	Carro eléctrico	8 € /18 holes
Buggy	Coche	26 € /18 holes
Clubs	Palos	17 € / 18 holes
Credit cards Tarjetas de crédito		no

Access Acceso : Madrid, Carretera de Castilla → Segovia
Map 3 on page 1092 Plano 3 Página 1092

Golf course RECORRIDO — 16/20

Site	Emplazamiento	
Maintenance	Mantenimiento	
Architect	Arquitecto	Javier Arana
Type	Tipo	forest
Relief	Relieve	
Water in play	Agua	
Exp. to wind	Exp. al viento	
Trees in play	Arboles	

Scorecard Tarjeta	**Chp.** Campeonato	**Mens** Caballeros	**Ladies** Damas
Length Longitud	6335	6094	5169
Par	72	72	72
Slope system	—	—	—

Advised golfing ability Nivel de juego aconsejado — 0 12 24 36

Hcp required Handicap exigido — 28 Men, 36 Ladies

Club house & amenities CLUB HOUSE Y DEPENDENCIAS — 8/10

Pro shop	Pro-shop	
Driving range	Campo de prácticas	
Sheltered	cubierto	112 mats
On grass	sobre hierba	yes
Putting-green	putting-green	yes
Pitching-green	pitching-green	yes

Hotel facilities HOTELES CERCANOS — 8/10

HOTELS HOTELES

Princesa, 275 rooms, D 252 € — Madrid 3 km
Tel (34) 915 - 422 100, Fax (34) 915 - 427 328

La Moraleja, 37 rooms, D 162 € — Alcobendas 3 km
Tel (34) 916 - 618 055, Fax (34) 916 - 612 188

Villamagna, 182 rooms, D 475 € — Madrid 4 km
Tel (34) 915 - 871 234, Fax (34) 915 - 751 358

RESTAURANTS RESTAURANTE

El Caserón de Araceli — San Augustin de Guadalix 6 km
Tel (34) 918 - 418 531

Zalacain, Tel (34) 915 - 614 840 — Madrid 5 km

La Trainera, Tel (34) 915 - 760 575 — Madrid

COSTA BRAVA

14 | 7 | 7

El gabinete del arquitecto Hamilton Stutt no es de los más conocidos, pero aquí ha construido un recorrido simpático, sin dificultades infranqueables permitiendo que jugadores de todos los niveles y edades pasen un día agradable. El relieve es mesurado, las pendientes suaves, alternando hoyos anchos y estrechos rodeados de pinos a menudo en la línea de juego y alcornoques, lo que obliga a pegar con efecto a la bola para contornearlos, pasar por arriba... o por debajo.Los greens están bien protegidos, correctamente diseñados y la mayor parte de las veces se puede aprochar haciendo rodar la bola. Sólo hay un hoyo ciego, reflejando así la filosofía del recorrido: el golf es para todo el mundo y si hay recorridos exigentes también tiene que haber otros para los golfistas de nivel medio. Este forma parte de esa categoría, pero los buenos jugadores tampoco se aburrirán.

Hamilton Stutt is not the most famous name in golf course design, but here they have produced a pleasant course without insuperable difficulties on which players of all levels and all ages can spend an enjoyable day. The ground relief is moderate, with a few gentle slopes and alternating wide and tight fairways edged by pine and oak trees that are often very much in play. The player will often have to work the ball to get around them, put the ball over the top... or keep low below the branches. The greens are well defended and correctly designed, but most of them can be approached with chip shots. Only one green is blind, which reflects the thinking behind the whole course, namely golf is for everyone, and while there are demanding courses, there should also be courses for average players. This is one such course, but even the best players will have fun.

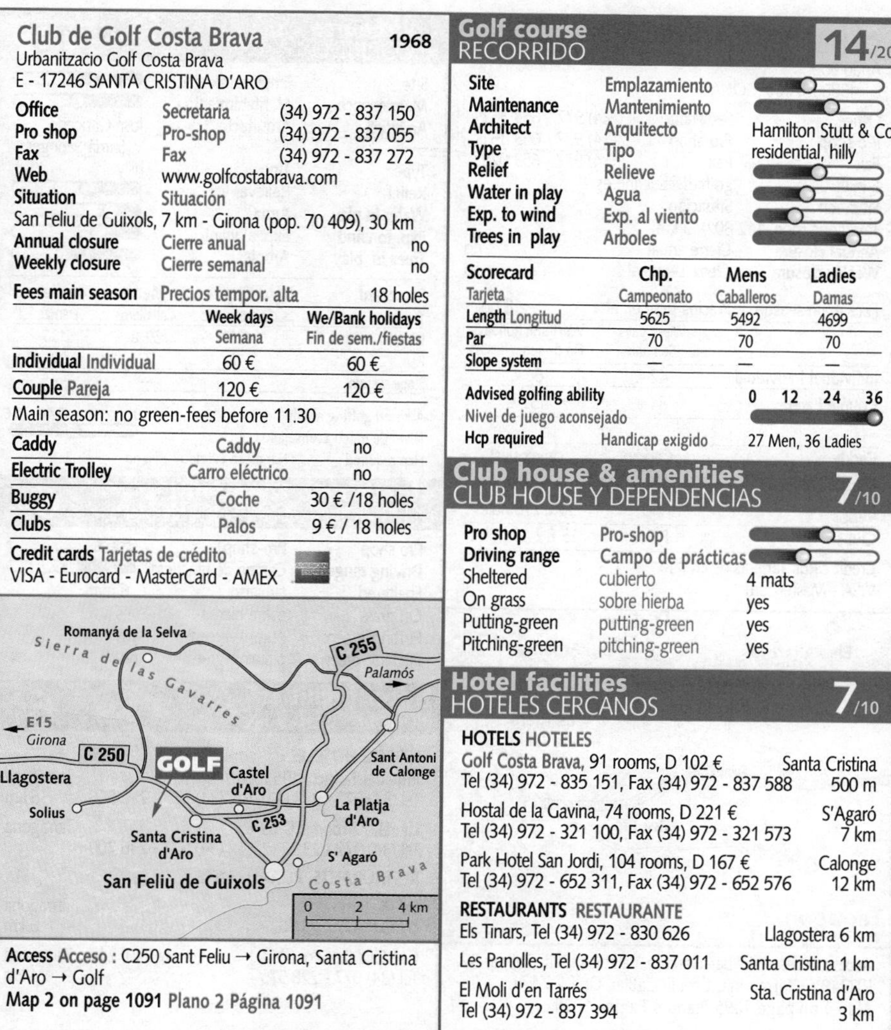

Club de Golf Costa Brava **1968**
Urbanitzacio Golf Costa Brava
E - 17246 SANTA CRISTINA D'ARO

Office	Secretaria	(34) 972 - 837 150
Pro shop	Pro-shop	(34) 972 - 837 055
Fax	Fax	(34) 972 - 837 272
Web	www.golfcostabrava.com	
Situation	Situación	

San Feliu de Guixols, 7 km - Girona (pop. 70 409), 30 km

Annual closure	Cierre anual	no
Weekly closure	Cierre semanal	no

Fees main season Precios tempor. alta	**Week days** Semana	**We/Bank holidays** Fin de sem./fiestas
		18 holes
Individual Individual	60 €	60 €
Couple Pareja	120 €	120 €

Main season: no green-fees before 11.30

Caddy	Caddy	no
Electric Trolley	Carro eléctrico	no
Buggy	Coche	30 € /18 holes
Clubs	Palos	9 € / 18 holes

Credit cards Tarjetas de crédito
VISA - Eurocard - MasterCard - AMEX

Access Acceso : C250 Sant Feliu → Girona, Santa Cristina d'Aro → Golf
Map 2 on page 1091 Plano 2 Página 1091

Golf course RECORRIDO — 14/20

Site	Emplazamiento	
Maintenance	Mantenimiento	
Architect	Arquitecto	Hamilton Stutt & Co
Type	Tipo	residential, hilly
Relief	Relieve	
Water in play	Agua	
Exp. to wind	Exp. al viento	
Trees in play	Arboles	

Scorecard Tarjeta	**Chp.** Campeonato	**Mens** Caballeros	**Ladies** Damas
Length Longitud	5625	5492	4699
Par	70	70	70
Slope system	—	—	—

Advised golfing ability Nivel de juego aconsejado: 0 12 24 36
Hcp required Handicap exigido: 27 Men, 36 Ladies

Club house & amenities CLUB HOUSE Y DEPENDENCIAS — 7/10

Pro shop	Pro-shop	
Driving range	Campo de prácticas	
Sheltered	cubierto	4 mats
On grass	sobre hierba	yes
Putting-green	putting-green	yes
Pitching-green	pitching-green	yes

Hotel facilities HOTELES CERCANOS — 7/10

HOTELS HOTELES

Golf Costa Brava, 91 rooms, D 102 € — Santa Cristina
Tel (34) 972 - 835 151, Fax (34) 972 - 837 588 — 500 m

Hostal de la Gavina, 74 rooms, D 221 € — S'Agaró
Tel (34) 972 - 321 100, Fax (34) 972 - 321 573 — 7 km

Park Hotel San Jordi, 104 rooms, D 167 € — Calonge
Tel (34) 972 - 652 311, Fax (34) 972 - 652 576 — 12 km

RESTAURANTS RESTAURANTE

Els Tinars, Tel (34) 972 - 830 626 — Llagostera 6 km

Les Panolles, Tel (34) 972 - 837 011 — Santa Cristina 1 km

El Moli d'en Tarrés — Sta. Cristina d'Aro
Tel (34) 972 - 837 394 — 3 km

COSTA DORADA 13 6 6

El lugar es agradable y descansado. A pesar de que el recorrido se sitúa muy a menudo en la falda de la ladera y es muy ondulado, no se necesita alquilar un coche. Las calles con hierba bien tupida sostienen bien la bola, los greens la aguantan bien, sólo algunos olivos aislados o agrupados pueden perturbar la trayectoria de juego: no es un recorrido de gran dificultad y gustará a la mayoría de los jugadores. El recorrido no ofrece emociones fuertes, aunque la vuelta, a partir del 12, es más técnica que la ida, especialmente en los dos pares 5 (el 13 y el 16). Sin embargo, los arquitectos podrían haber tenido un poco más de imaginación colocando dificultades en lugares más amenazadores. En la familia de golfs gratos y agradables para todos los niveles de juego, Costa Dorada ocupa un buen lugar.

The site is pleasant and relaxing after reaching the course set in a little palm grove. Although much of Costa Dorada is laid out on the side of a hill with rolling fairways, it is easily walkable. The lushly-grassed fairways carry the ball well and the greens pitch well, too. Only a few isolated or bunches of olive trees can get in the way of your ball, so this is not too complicated a course to get around. Most players will like its honest style, but they shouldn't expect too much in the way of excitement, even though from the 12th hole onwards the course becomes more technical, especially the two par 5s (especially holes 13 and 16). We might have expected a little more imagination from the architects, with hazards perhaps located in a more threatening manner. But in the family of pleasant and encouraging courses for all levels of play, Costa Dorada is a front-runner.

Club de Golf Costa Dorada Tarragona 1982

Apdo 600
E - 43080 TARRAGONA

Office	Secretaria	(34) 977 - 653 361
Pro shop	Pro-shop	(34) 977 - 653 361
Fax	Fax	(34) 977 - 653 028
E-mail	golfcdt@teleline.es	
Situation	Situación	

Tarragona (pop. 112 802), 5 km

Annual closure	Cierre anual	no
Weekly closure	Cierre semanal	no

Fees main season Precios tempor. alta	Week days Semana	We/Bank holidays Fin de sem./fiestas
		18 holes
Individual Individual	42 €	66 €
Couple Pareja	84 €	132 €

Caddy	Caddy	on request
Electric Trolley	Carro eléctrico	6 € /18 holes
Buggy	Coche	30 € /18 holes
Clubs	Palos	15 € / 18 holes

Credit cards Tarjetas de crédito
VISA - MasterCard

Access Acceso : A7 Barcelona → Valencia, Exit (Salida) 32, RN340 → Tarragona, Ctra El Catllar, Golf 2,7 km.
Map 4 on page 1095 Plano 4 Página 1095

Golf course RECORRIDO 13/20

Site	Emplazamiento	
Maintenance	Mantenimiento	
Architect	Arquitecto	José Gancedo V. Sardá Saenger
Type	Tipo	hilly
Relief	Relieve	
Water in play	Agua	
Exp. to wind	Exp. al viento	
Trees in play	Arboles	

Scorecard Tarjeta	Chp. Campeonato	Mens Caballeros	Ladies Damas
Length Longitud	6223	5978	5136
Par	72	72	72
Slope system	—	—	—

Advised golfing ability 0 12 24 36
Nivel de juego aconsejado
Hcp required Handicap exigido no

Club house & amenities CLUB HOUSE Y DEPENDENCIAS 6/10

Pro shop	Pro-shop	
Driving range	Campo de prácticas	
Sheltered	cubierto	6 mats
On grass	sobre hierba	yes
Putting-green	putting-green	yes
Pitching-green	pitching-green	no

Hotel facilities HOTELES CERCANOS 6/10

HOTELS HOTELES
Imperial Tarraco, 155 rooms, D 102 € — Tarragona 6 km
Tel (34) 977 - 233 040, Fax (34) 977 - 216 566

Lauria, 72 rooms, D 63 € — Tarragona
Tel (34) 977 - 236 712, Fax (34) 977 - 236 700

RESTAURANTS RESTAURANTE
Sol Ric — Tarragona 6 km
Tel (34) 977 - 232 032

Can Sala (Les Fonts) — N 240, 2 km, Tarragona 4 km
Tel (34) 977 - 228 575

EL BOSQUE

16	7	4

La buena calidad del conjunto inmobiliario no sólo no molesta a los jugadores sino que se adapta muy bien al estilo americano del recorrido. Si añadimos que más vale alquilar un coche, uno podría creerse en Estados Unidos. El Bosque figura entre los buenos éxitos de Robert Trent Jones en España. El relieve es importante, se juega a menudo en pendiente y felizmente la estrategia de juego es clara ya que si los obstáculos son bien visibles, no dejan de ser peligrosos. La primera vez uno se siente acosado (para obtener un buen resultado) por una serie de greens ciegos que requieren trayectorias altas. No hay que dudar tirar a bandera puesto que los greens aguantan bien la bola. Los hoyos están bien integrados en el paisaje cuyo disño y dificultades son variados, sobre todo cuatro excelentes dog-legs. Hay que hacer mención especial de los pares 3.

The surrounding real estate is a stylish programme and won't bother the players, especially since the properties fit in very well with what is a very American-style course. Add to that the definite advantage of playing with a buggy and you might think you actually were on American soil. El Bosque is one of the great success-stories of Robert Trent Jones in Spain. It is hilly, you are often faced with a sloping lie, but the game strategy is pretty clear. And that's lucky, because although the hazards are visible, they are very dangerous. First time out, players looking for a good score will have trouble only with a series of blind greens which demand high approach shots. Go for the pin, too, because these greens pitch well. The holes blend in well with the landscape, and the design and difficulties vary considerably. In particular there are four beautiful dog-legs. A special mention should go to the quality of the par 3s.

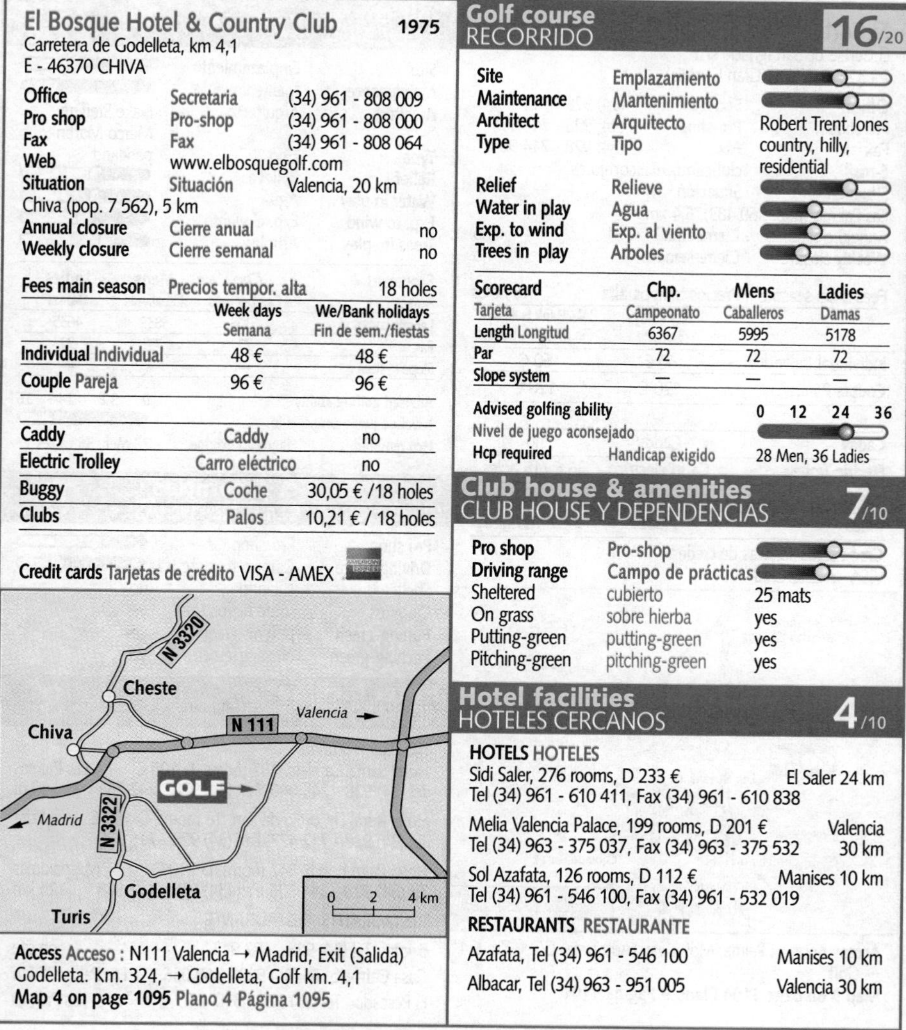

El Bosque Hotel & Country Club 1975

Carretera de Godelleta, km 4,1
E - 46370 CHIVA

Office	Secretaria	(34) 961 - 808 009
Pro shop	Pro-shop	(34) 961 - 808 000
Fax	Fax	(34) 961 - 808 064
Web	www.elbosquegolf.com	
Situation	Situación	Valencia, 20 km
Chiva (pop. 7 562), 5 km		
Annual closure	Cierre anual	no
Weekly closure	Cierre semanal	no

Fees main season Precios tempor. alta		18 holes
	Week days Semana	**We/Bank holidays** Fin de sem./fiestas
Individual Individual	48 €	48 €
Couple Pareja	96 €	96 €

Caddy	Caddy	no
Electric Trolley	Carro eléctrico	no
Buggy	Coche	30,05 € /18 holes
Clubs	Palos	10,21 € / 18 holes

Credit cards Tarjetas de crédito VISA - AMEX

Access Acceso : N111 Valencia → Madrid, Exit (Salida) Godelleta. Km. 324, → Godelleta, Golf km. 4,1
Map 4 on page 1095 Plano 4 Página 1095

Golf course RECORRIDO 16/20

Site	Emplazamiento	
Maintenance	Mantenimiento	
Architect	Arquitecto	Robert Trent Jones
Type	Tipo	country, hilly, residential
Relief	Relieve	
Water in play	Agua	
Exp. to wind	Exp. al viento	
Trees in play	Arboles	

Scorecard Tarjeta	**Chp.** Campeonato	**Mens** Caballeros	**Ladies** Damas
Length Longitud	6367	5995	5178
Par	72	72	72
Slope system	—	—	—

Advised golfing ability Nivel de juego aconsejado: 0 12 24 36
Hcp required Handicap exigido: 28 Men, 36 Ladies

Club house & amenities CLUB HOUSE Y DEPENDENCIAS 7/10

Pro shop	Pro-shop	
Driving range	Campo de prácticas	
Sheltered	cubierto	25 mats
On grass	sobre hierba	yes
Putting-green	putting-green	yes
Pitching-green	pitching-green	yes

Hotel facilities HOTELES CERCANOS 4/10

HOTELS HOTELES

Sidi Saler, 276 rooms, D 233 € — El Saler 24 km
Tel (34) 961 - 610 411, Fax (34) 961 - 610 838

Melia Valencia Palace, 199 rooms, D 201 € — Valencia 30 km
Tel (34) 963 - 375 037, Fax (34) 963 - 375 532

Sol Azafata, 126 rooms, D 112 € — Manises 10 km
Tel (34) 961 - 546 100, Fax (34) 961 - 532 019

RESTAURANTS RESTAURANTE

Azafata, Tel (34) 961 - 546 100 — Manises 10 km

Albacar, Tel (34) 963 - 951 005 — Valencia 30 km

EL CORTIJO

17 | 5 | 8

Blake Sterling, que fue jefe del equipo de Pete Dye, ha construido con Marco Martin un gran campo (en España decimos ìcampazoî) en una finca que había sido una platanera. Los primeros nueve recuerdan algo a un links, con todas las salvedades del mundo porque estamos rodeados de palmeras y lagos paradisíacos que entrarán øfatalmente? en juego en la otra parte del campo. Largas distancias, cambiantes casi siempre por los vientos atlánticos. Greenes rápidos que piden mucho estudio y mucha estrategia y un diseño que obliga a pensar los golpes con varias opciones posibles. El campo está en un complejo deportivo y turístico (tenis, padel, hípica, restaurantes, hotel, etc) todavía por finalizar - la casa-club todavía es provisional- que comprende un campo corto (pitch & putt) de excepcional calidad y bellleza comparable a la de tan magnífico recorrido.

Blake Sterling, formerly project manager with Pete Dye, teamed up with Marco Martin to design this great and highly ambitious course spread over an old banana plantation. The front nine have very much the feel of a links course, with all the sand in the world piled up and surrounded by palm trees and paradisiacal lakes that you will always find in play over the back nine. The holes are on the long side and never quite the same, depending on the wind blowing in from the Atlantic. The greens are slick and call for some very careful forethought and a good sense of strategy, simply because their design always leaves you with several options. This fine course has taken up residence in a sports and tourist resort offering tennis, paddle tennis, horse-riding, restaurants and a hotel. For the time being, the club-house is a temporary affair, but this is more than made up for by a truly excellent pitch 'n putt layout equal in quality to the full course.

El Cortijo Club de Campo — 1999

El Cortijo de San Ignacio s/n
E - 35218 TELDE (Gran Canaria)

Office	Secretaria	(34) 928 - 711 111
Pro shop	Pro-shop	(34) 928 - 711 111
Fax	Fax	(34) 928 - 714 905
E-mail	clubcampo@elcortijo.es	
Situation	Situación	

Las Palmas (pop. 360 483), 6,4 km

Annual closure	Cierre anual	no
Weekly closure	Cierre semanal	no

Fees main season Precios tempor. alta		18 holes
	Week days Semana	**We/Bank holidays** Fin de sem./fiestas
Individual Individual	60 €	60 €
Couple Pareja	120 €	120 €

Caddy	Caddy	no
Electric Trolley	Carro eléctrico	36 € /18 holes
Buggy	Coche	30 € /18 holes
Clubs	Palos	9 € / 18 holes

Credit cards Tarjetas de crédito
VISA - MasterCard

Access Acceso : Palma, Motorway (Autopista) GC 1. Km 6,4 → Golf
Map 9 on page 1104 Plano 9 Página 1104

Golf course RECORRIDO — 17/20

Site	Emplazamiento	
Maintenance	Mantenimiento	
Architect	Arquitecto	Blake Sterling Marco Martìn
Type	Tipo	parkland
Relief	Relieve	
Water in play	Agua	
Exp. to wind	Exp. al viento	
Trees in play	Arboles	

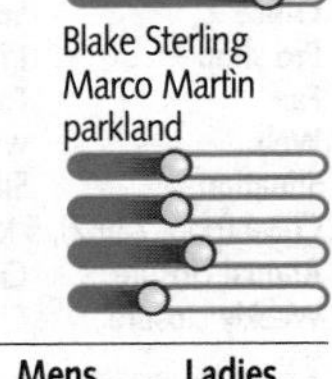

Scorecard Tarjeta	**Chp.** Campeonato	**Mens** Caballeros	**Ladies** Damas
Length Longitud	6308	5833	4635
Par	72	72	72
Slope system	—	—	—

Advised golfing ability 0 12 24 36
Nivel de juego aconsejado

Hcp required Handicap exigido 28 Men, 36 Ladies

Club house & amenities CLUB HOUSE Y DEPENDENCIAS — 5/10

Pro shop	Pro-shop	
Driving range	Campo de prácticas	
Sheltered	cubierto	no
On grass	sobre hierba	yes
Putting-green	putting-green	yes
Pitching-green	pitching-green	yes

Hotel facilities HOTELES CERCANOS — 8/10

HOTELS HOTELES

Hotel Santa Catalina, 187 rooms, D 108 € — Las Palmas
Tel (34) 928 - 243 040, Fax (34) 928 - 242 764 — 5 km

Hotel Rural El Cortijo de San, 18 rooms, D 108 € — on site
Tel (34) 928 - 712 427, Fax (34) 928 - 715 029

Hotel Palm Beach, 347 rooms, D 210 € — Maspalomas
Tel (34) 928 - 141 806, Fax (34) 928 - 141 808 — 25 km

RESTAURANTS RESTAURANTE

5 Jotas, Tel (34) 928 - 682 943 — on site
Casa Carmelo, Tel (34) 928 - 469 056 — Las Palmas 5 km
El Pescador, Tel (34) 928 - 330 432 — Las Palmas

EL PRAT Verde

17	7	6

Con toda razón, uno de los recorridos más famosos de España. Llano y al borde del mar, despliega algunos de sus hoyos entre pinos, aunque la mayor parte, por haberse secado, han desaparecido del resto del recorrido. En cambio algunas palmeras pueden complicar la vida y trayectoria de los jugadores. Sin que su arquitectura sea la de los tradicionales links, sin embargo presenta un aspecto típicamente briánico, tal vez una forma de homenaje por parte del arquitecto Javier Arana. Si los bunkers son numerosos tanto en calle como alrededor de los greens, en general no están en la línea de juego, lo que permite escoger entre aprochar por alto o hacer rodar la bola y cambiar de juego en función del viento. Los roughs, difíciles a causa de la hierba bermuda, sí que están en la línea de juego. Muy equilibrado, sin artificios, este grande de España pertenece a la mejor nobleza. La ampliación del aeropuerto de Barcelona sobre estos terrenos cierra ya prácticamente el recorrido amarillo, mientras el club inicia la construcción de otros 36 hoyos, obra de Greg Norman, al otro lado de la ciudad.

One of Spain's most famous courses, and quite rightly so. Flat and by the sea, the first holes wind their way through the pines, but on the rest of the course most of the trees have disappeared because of disease. In contrast, certain palm trees can make life difficult for off-line shots. Without having the typical architecture of a links course, it offers traditional British character, perhaps as a form of tribute from the architect Javier Arana. While bunkers are plentiful on the fairways and around the greens, they are not generally in the line of fire, thus allowing players to choose between pitching and chipping onto the greens, and to vary their play depending on the wind. The rough, however, is very much to the fore, and the Bermuda grass can be a tough proposition. Well-balanced and totally honest, this great little Spanish number is of the very best vintage. Future development work for the airport has led to the closure of the Amarillo course and could result in a complete change of location for the club as a whole. The project is also of 36 holes, designed by Greg Norman.

Real Club de Golf "El Prat" — 1954

Ap. de Correus 10
E - 08820 EL PRAT DE LLOBREGAT

Office	Secretaria	(34) 933 - 790 278
Pro shop	Pro-shop	(34) 933 - 790 278
Fax	Fax	(34) 933 - 795 102
E-mail	rcgpe@rcgep	
Situation	Situación	Barcelona, 10 km
Annual closure	Cierre anual	no
Weekly closure	Cierre semanal	no

Fees main season Precios tempor. alta	18 holes	
	Week days Semana	**We/Bank holidays** Fin de sem./fiestas
Individual Individual	80 € *	160 € *
Couple Pareja	160 € *	320 € *

* Only 30 visitors each weekday / 10 visitors each day during weekends

Caddy	Caddy	36 € /18 holes
Electric Trolley	Carro eléctrico	4 € /18 holes
Buggy	Coche	24 € /18 holes
Clubs	Palos	18 € / 18 holes

Credit cards Tarjetas de crédito VISA - MasterCard

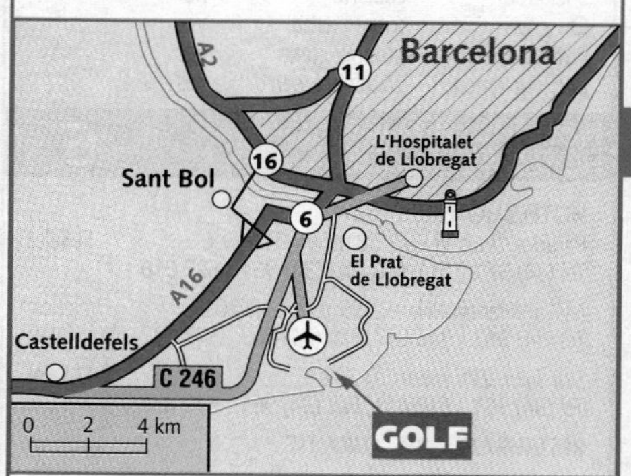

Access Acceso : C246 → Sitges → El Prat de Llobregat, El Prat, Golf 1 km
Map 2 on page 1091 Plano 2 Página 1091

Golf course RECORRIDO — 17/20

Site	Emplazamiento	
Maintenance	Mantenimiento	
Architect	Arquitecto	Javier Araña
Type	Tipo	seaside course
Relief	Relieve	
Water in play	Agua	
Exp. to wind	Exp. al viento	
Trees in play	Arboles	

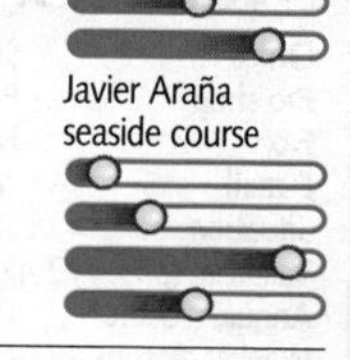

Scorecard Tarjeta	**Chp.** Campeonato	**Mens** Caballeros	**Ladies** Damas
Length Longitud	6224	5947	5124
Par	73	73	73
Slope system	—	—	—

Advised golfing ability Nivel de juego aconsejado — 0 12 24 36
Hcp required Handicap exigido — 28 Men, 36 Ladies

Club house & amenities CLUB HOUSE Y DEPENDENCIAS — 7/10

Pro shop	Pro-shop	
Driving range	Campo de prácticas	
Sheltered	cubierto	8 mats
On grass	sobre hierba	yes
Putting-green	putting-green	yes
Pitching-green	pitching-green	yes

Hotel facilities HOTELES CERCANOS — 6/10

HOTELS HOTELES

Alfa Aeropuerto, 99 rooms, D 143 € — Mercabarna 5 km
Tel (34) 933 - 362 564, Fax (34) 933 - 355 592

Rallye, 107 rooms, D 126 € — Barcelona 10 km
Tel (34) 933 - 399 050, Fax (34) 934 - 110 790

Barcelona Plaza Hotel, 357 rooms, D 228 € — Barcelona
Tel (34) 934 - 262 600, Fax (34) 934 - 262 351

RESTAURANTS RESTAURANTE

Casa Alcaide, Tel (34) 933 - 791 012 — El Prat 1 km
Gran Mercat (Hotel Alfa), Tel (34) 933 - 362 564 — Mercabarna 5 km
Via Veneto, Tel (34) 932 - 007 244 — Barcelona 10 km
Neichel, Tel (34) 932 - 038 408 — Barcelona

EL SALER

18 | 7 | 6

El placer de saborear uno de los mejores recorridos de Europa sólo puede verse alterado por un cuidado mediano. Los hoyos de links (del 5 al 9 y del 16 al 18) pueden compararse a los mejores recorridos del Reino Unido a los que el gran arquitecto Javier Arana ha rendido homenaje. Los demás hoyos presentan la misma estética y sólo el bosque les da un aspecto diferente. Hay muchos greens y obstáculos ciegos, lo que es característico en este tipo de recorridos que se amoldan a las dunas. Los greens son inmensos con caídas y ondulaciones difíciles. Por supuesto, jugar aquí su handicap es problemático, hay que dominar todos los golpes de golf, sobre todo con viento, y es casi una alegría perder ante tal recorrido. Incluso en neto será muy difícil igualar la proeza de Bernhard Langer, que lográ aquí un 62 el último día del Open de España en 1984...

Only rather average standards of upkeep might spoil the joys of savouring one of Europe's best courses. The links holes (5 to 9 and 16 to 18) bear comparison with the best courses in the UK, to which architect Javier Arana has paid tribute here. The other holes are equally attractive, but run through a forest. There are a lot of blind greens and hazards here, but this is typical of this kind of course which hugs the dunes. The greens are often huge and the slopes hard to read. Naturally, playing to your handicap on a course of this standard can pose problems, as it takes every shot in the book, especially when the wind is up. But losing to a course like this is almost a pleasure. Even with a net score, you will be hard put to equal the achievement of Bernhard Langer, who carded a 62 here in the last round of the 1984 Spanish Open...

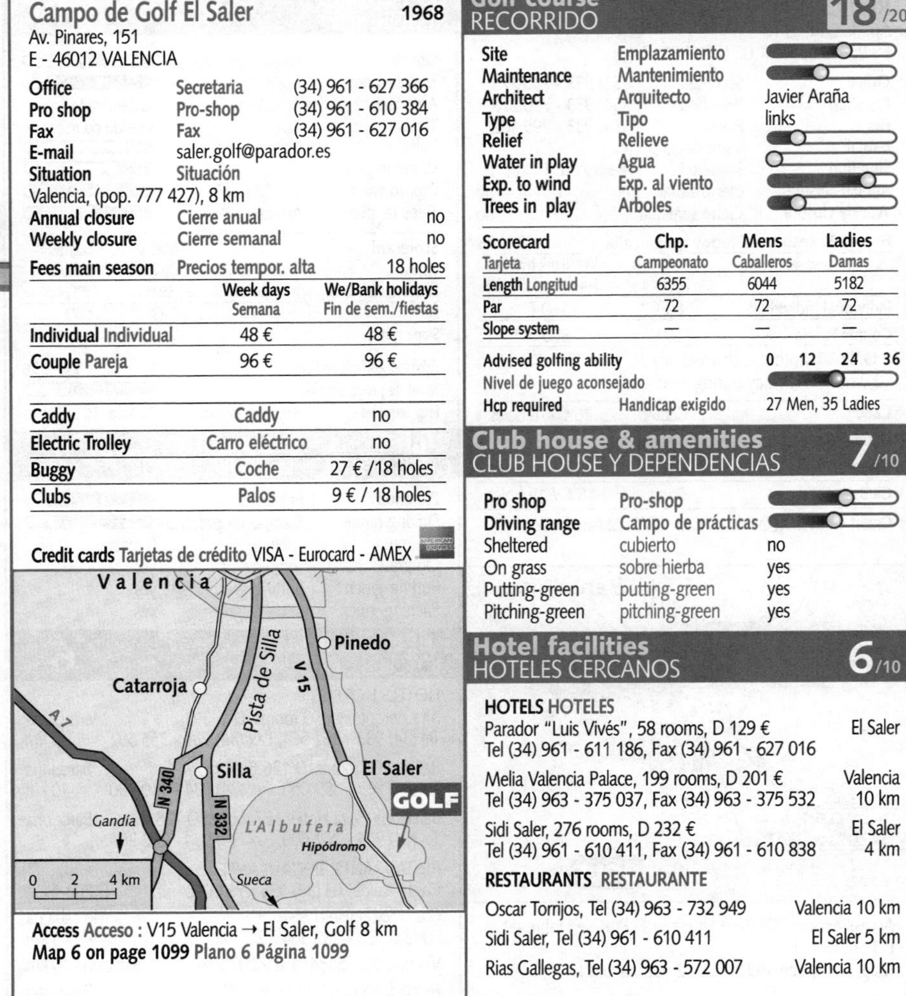

Campo de Golf El Saler — 1968

Av. Pinares, 151
E - 46012 VALENCIA

Office	Secretaria	(34) 961 - 627 366
Pro shop	Pro-shop	(34) 961 - 610 384
Fax	Fax	(34) 961 - 627 016
E-mail	saler.golf@parador.es	
Situation	Situación	
Valencia, (pop. 777 427), 8 km		
Annual closure	Cierre anual	no
Weekly closure	Cierre semanal	no

Fees main season Precios tempor. alta	**Week days** Semana	**We/Bank holidays** Fin de sem./fiestas
		18 holes
Individual Individual	48 €	48 €
Couple Pareja	96 €	96 €

Caddy	Caddy	no
Electric Trolley	Carro eléctrico	no
Buggy	Coche	27 € /18 holes
Clubs	Palos	9 € / 18 holes

Credit cards Tarjetas de crédito VISA - Eurocard - AMEX

Access Acceso : V15 Valencia → El Saler, Golf 8 km
Map 6 on page 1099 Plano 6 Página 1099

Golf course RECORRIDO — 18/20

Site	Emplazamiento	
Maintenance	Mantenimiento	
Architect	Arquitecto	Javier Araña
Type	Tipo	links
Relief	Relieve	
Water in play	Agua	
Exp. to wind	Exp. al viento	
Trees in play	Arboles	

Scorecard Tarjeta	**Chp.** Campeonato	**Mens** Caballeros	**Ladies** Damas
Length Longitud	6355	6044	5182
Par	72	72	72
Slope system	—	—	—

Advised golfing ability Nivel de juego aconsejado — 0 12 24 36

Hcp required Handicap exigido — 27 Men, 35 Ladies

Club house & amenities CLUB HOUSE Y DEPENDENCIAS — 7/10

Pro shop	Pro-shop	
Driving range	Campo de prácticas	
Sheltered	cubierto	no
On grass	sobre hierba	yes
Putting-green	putting-green	yes
Pitching-green	pitching-green	yes

Hotel facilities HOTELES CERCANOS — 6/10

HOTELS HOTELES

Parador "Luis Vivés", 58 rooms, D 129 € — El Saler
Tel (34) 961 - 611 186, Fax (34) 961 - 627 016

Melia Valencia Palace, 199 rooms, D 201 € — Valencia 10 km
Tel (34) 963 - 375 037, Fax (34) 963 - 375 532

Sidi Saler, 276 rooms, D 232 € — El Saler 4 km
Tel (34) 961 - 610 411, Fax (34) 961 - 610 838

RESTAURANTS RESTAURANTE

Oscar Torrijos, Tel (34) 963 - 732 949 — Valencia 10 km
Sidi Saler, Tel (34) 961 - 610 411 — El Saler 5 km
Rias Gallegas, Tel (34) 963 - 572 007 — Valencia 10 km

EMPORDÀ 17 7 6

Empordá tendrá en el futuro 36 hoyos. 18 hoyos ya han alcanzado su madurez (se han abierto otros 9). Los admiradores de von Hagge no se sorprenderán del diseño característico de montículos que separan las calles, sobre todo en los hoyos sin árboles. Fuera de calle, los roughs están cortados a diferentes alturas hasta convertirse en hierbas altas en los montículos. Esta preparación refinada se confirma con unos greens de excelente calidad, bien diseñados y a menudo muy largos, lo que complica la elección del palo en función de la colocación de las banderas. Si se tiene en cuenta los numerosos tees de salida, la longitud del recorrido puede variar al infinito. Espectacular y muy bien concebido, jugar aquí es apasionante y se ha convertido en uno de los grandes recorridos de Cataluña

Eventually, Emporda will feature 36 holes. A new and beautiful club-house has been built. 18 holes have reached maturity (and 9 others are open and very interesting too). Admirers of von Hagge will not be surprised by this layout, with mounds separating fairways, particularly on the holes without trees. Off the fairway there are two levels of rough before the high grass on the mounds. The same refined preparation is to be found on the excellent greens, which are well designed and often very long, another factor to complicate club selection according to pin positions. When looking at the very many tees, the length of this course can vary enormously. A spectacular, very well "crafted" and exciting course to play, whatever your level, this is already one of the great courses in Catalonia.

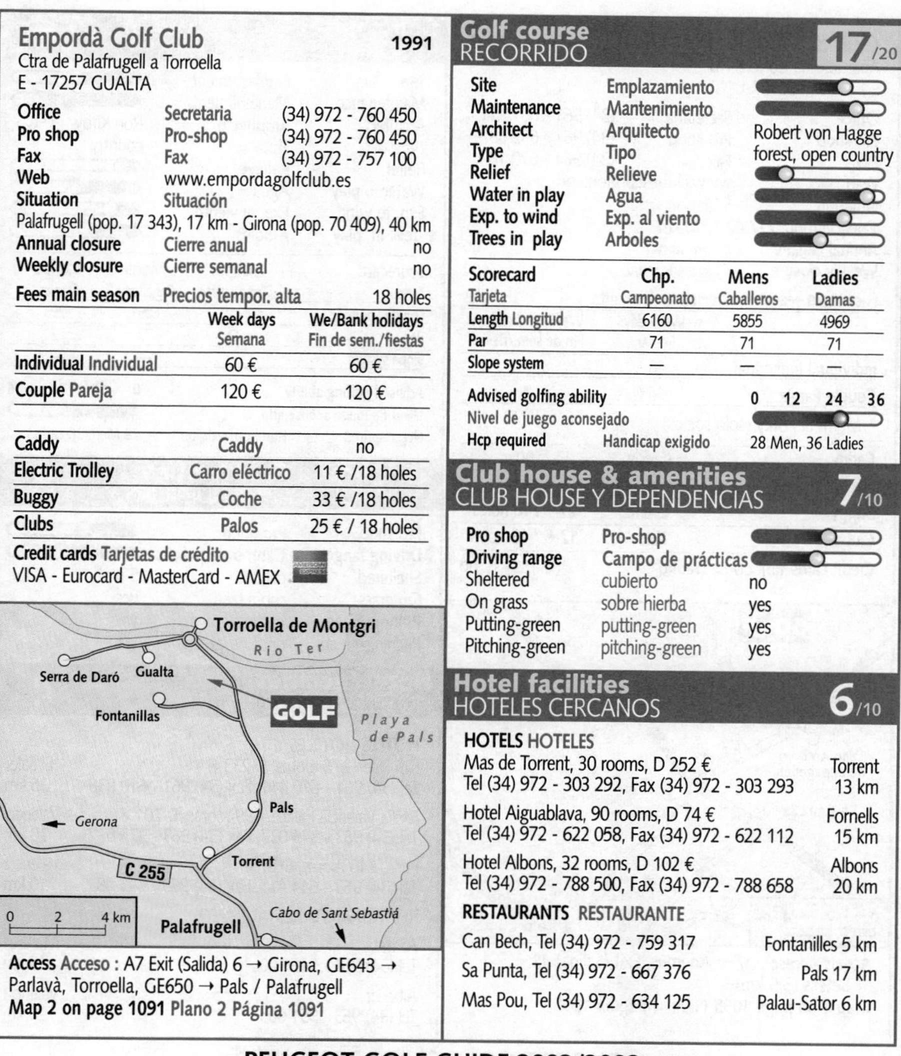

Empordà Golf Club 1991

Ctra de Palafrugell a Torroella
E - 17257 GUALTA

Office	Secretaria	(34) 972 - 760 450
Pro shop	Pro-shop	(34) 972 - 760 450
Fax	Fax	(34) 972 - 757 100
Web	www.empordagolfclub.es	
Situation	Situación	

Palafrugell (pop. 17 343), 17 km - Girona (pop. 70 409), 40 km

Annual closure	Cierre anual	no
Weekly closure	Cierre semanal	no

Fees main season Precios tempor. alta	Week days Semana	We/Bank holidays Fin de sem./fiestas
		18 holes
Individual Individual	60 €	60 €
Couple Pareja	120 €	120 €

Caddy	Caddy	no
Electric Trolley	Carro eléctrico	11 € /18 holes
Buggy	Coche	33 € /18 holes
Clubs	Palos	25 € / 18 holes

Credit cards Tarjetas de crédito
VISA - Eurocard - MasterCard - AMEX

Access Acceso : A7 Exit (Salida) 6 → Girona, GE643 → Parlavà, Torroella, GE650 → Pals / Palafrugell
Map 2 on page 1091 Plano 2 Página 1091

Golf course RECORRIDO 17/20

Site	Emplazamiento	
Maintenance	Mantenimiento	
Architect	Arquitecto	Robert von Hagge
Type	Tipo	forest, open country
Relief	Relieve	
Water in play	Agua	
Exp. to wind	Exp. al viento	
Trees in play	Arboles	

Scorecard Tarjeta	Chp. Campeonato	Mens Caballeros	Ladies Damas
Length Longitud	6160	5855	4969
Par	71	71	71
Slope system	—	—	—

Advised golfing ability 0 12 24 36
Nivel de juego aconsejado
Hcp required Handicap exigido 28 Men, 36 Ladies

Club house & amenities CLUB HOUSE Y DEPENDENCIAS 7/10

Pro shop	Pro-shop	
Driving range	Campo de prácticas	
Sheltered	cubierto	no
On grass	sobre hierba	yes
Putting-green	putting-green	yes
Pitching-green	pitching-green	yes

Hotel facilities HOTELES CERCANOS 6/10

HOTELS HOTELES

Mas de Torrent, 30 rooms, D 252 € Tel (34) 972 - 303 292, Fax (34) 972 - 303 293	Torrent 13 km
Hotel Aiguablava, 90 rooms, D 74 € Tel (34) 972 - 622 058, Fax (34) 972 - 622 112	Fornells 15 km
Hotel Albons, 32 rooms, D 102 € Tel (34) 972 - 788 500, Fax (34) 972 - 788 658	Albons 20 km

RESTAURANTS RESTAURANTE

Can Bech, Tel (34) 972 - 759 317	Fontanilles 5 km
Sa Punta, Tel (34) 972 - 667 376	Pals 17 km
Mas Pou, Tel (34) 972 - 634 125	Palau-Sator 6 km

ESCORPION

13 | 8 | 4

Construido en un antiguo naranjal, Escorpión ofrece una vegetación compuesta de naranjos y también de palmeras y algarrobos. Se puede jugar fácilmente sin coche. Sus excelentes cuidados realzan el interés de un diseño sencillo y no excepcional. Si bien hay que deplorar la semejanza repetitiva de los pares 4 (en dog-leg), debe resaltarse al menos la calidad técnica de los pares 5 y de los pares 3. No obstante, no se puede decir que este recorrido sea muy difícil por lo que se puede jugar fácilmente en familia o entre amigos de diferentes niveles de juego. Los greens son buenos, bien diseñados y los ante-green poco protegidos: se pueden atacar haciendo rodar la bola. Hay agua en la línea de juego de ocho hoyos, sin que ésto pueda asustar al jugador con cierta precisión. Finalmente, hay que resaltar la calidad y belleza del conjunto que alberga el club-house, muy bien restaurado.

Built in a former orange orchard, Escorpion naturally has a lot of orange trees, together with palm trees and carobs. It is easily walkable and the excellent maintenance work enhances the appeal of what is an honest, but never exceptional, layout. The repetitive style of the par 4s (all dog-legs) is a pity, but the par 3s and 5s are high standard, technical holes. With that said, no-one would consider this to be a tough course, and it is fun to play with the family or friends. The greens are grassy and well-designed, and the few frontal and green-side hazards mean you can often roll the ball onto the putting surface. Water is in play on eight of the holes, but should not unduly scare the more accurate players. One last item is the club house, whose splendid buildings have been beautifully renovated.

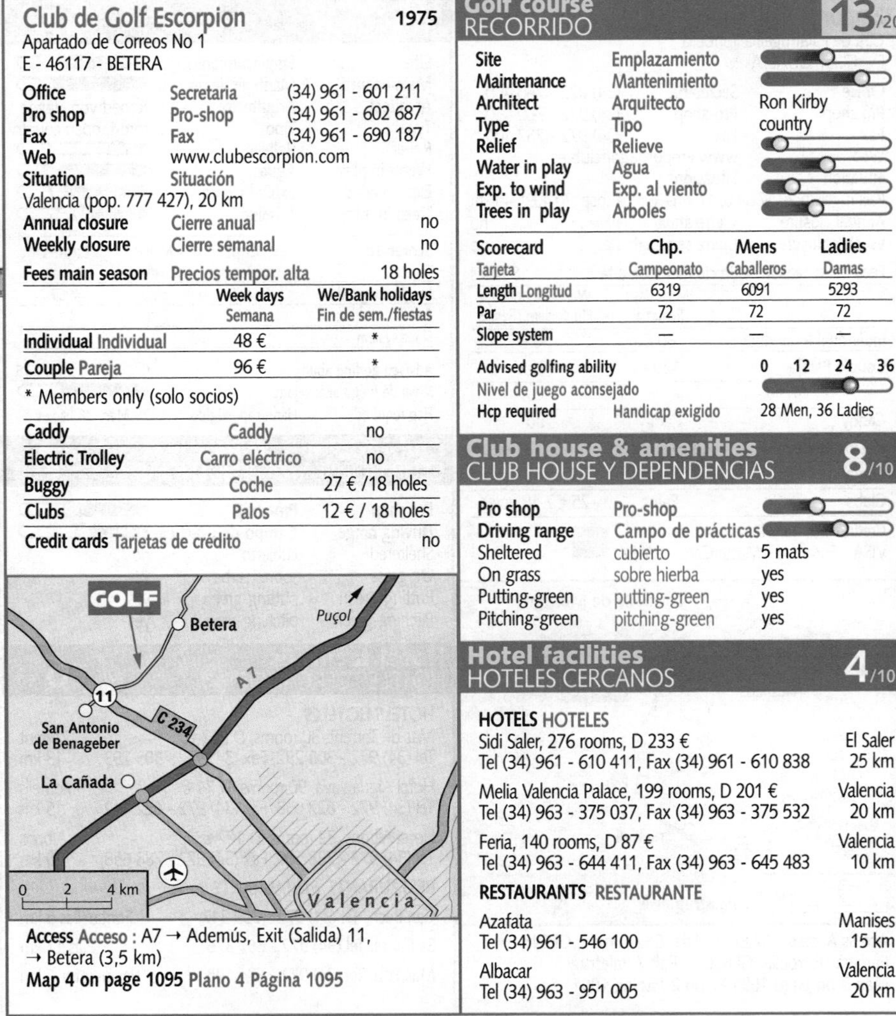

Club de Golf Escorpion — 1975

Apartado de Correos No 1
E - 46117 - BETERA

Office	Secretaria	(34) 961 - 601 211
Pro shop	Pro-shop	(34) 961 - 602 687
Fax	Fax	(34) 961 - 690 187
Web	www.clubescorpion.com	
Situation	Situación	

Valencia (pop. 777 427), 20 km

Annual closure	Cierre anual	no
Weekly closure	Cierre semanal	no

Fees main season Precios tempor. alta	Week days Semana	We/Bank holidays Fin de sem./fiestas
18 holes		
Individual Individual	48 €	*
Couple Pareja	96 €	*

* Members only (solo socios)

Caddy	Caddy	no
Electric Trolley	Carro eléctrico	no
Buggy	Coche	27 € /18 holes
Clubs	Palos	12 € / 18 holes
Credit cards	Tarjetas de crédito	no

Access Acceso : A7 → Ademús, Exit (Salida) 11, → Betera (3,5 km)
Map 4 on page 1095 Plano 4 Página 1095

Golf course RECORRIDO — 13/20

Site	Emplazamiento	
Maintenance	Mantenimiento	
Architect	Arquitecto	Ron Kirby
Type	Tipo	country
Relief	Relieve	
Water in play	Agua	
Exp. to wind	Exp. al viento	
Trees in play	Arboles	

Scorecard Tarjeta	**Chp.** Campeonato	**Mens** Caballeros	**Ladies** Damas
Length Longitud	6319	6091	5293
Par	72	72	72
Slope system	—	—	—

Advised golfing ability Nivel de juego aconsejado — 0 12 24 36
Hcp required Handicap exigido — 28 Men, 36 Ladies

Club house & amenities CLUB HOUSE Y DEPENDENCIAS — 8/10

Pro shop	Pro-shop	
Driving range	Campo de prácticas	
Sheltered	cubierto	5 mats
On grass	sobre hierba	yes
Putting-green	putting-green	yes
Pitching-green	pitching-green	yes

Hotel facilities HOTELES CERCANOS — 4/10

HOTELS HOTELES

Sidi Saler, 276 rooms, D 233 € Tel (34) 961 - 610 411, Fax (34) 961 - 610 838	El Saler 25 km
Melia Valencia Palace, 199 rooms, D 201 € Tel (34) 963 - 375 037, Fax (34) 963 - 375 532	Valencia 20 km
Feria, 140 rooms, D 87 € Tel (34) 963 - 644 411, Fax (34) 963 - 645 483	Valencia 10 km

RESTAURANTS RESTAURANTE

Azafata Tel (34) 961 - 546 100	Manises 15 km
Albacar Tel (34) 963 - 951 005	Valencia 20 km

ESTEPONA

14 | 7 | 6

Es de esperar que este paisaje de montaña no quede alterado por los proyectos de construcción inmobiliaria, que el recorrido conserve un aspecto natural, en contraste con los grandes recorridos ajardinados, y que la flora y fauna salvajes conserven sus hábitos y su medio ambiente. En una buena mitad del recorrido hay muchas subidas y bajadas por lo que se aconseja alquilar un coche. El arquitecto José Luis López, con inteligencia y buen sentido de golf, ha sabido transformar este terreno difícil. Los greens está¿n bien diseñados,son de buena calidad e interesantes de jugar. Por lo que respecta a las dificultades, hay que evaluar con mucha precisión las ondulaciones del terreno para escoger el buen palo, evitar los roughs poco acogedores. No hay que dejarse impresionar por el hoyo 3, ni por el muy largo par cinco llamado "la pista de esquí", ni tampoco por los lagos del hoyo 10. Si se quiere cambiar del ambiente "chic" de los recorridos de la costa, Estepona es un buen destino.

Hopefully, this mountain landscape will not be spoilt by real estate projects, the course will retain its natural appearance, in contrast with larger, more manicured courses, and the wild flora and fauna will carry on living and growing the way they are. A good half of the course is very hilly, so a buggy is more than recommended. Architect José-Luis Lopez has shaped this difficult terrain intelligently and with a good golfing mind. The well-designed and good quality greens are interesting to play. The course's difficulties involve more often than not assessing the changes in relief to choose the right clubs, avoiding the most unwelcome rough, and not being overwhelmed by the third hole, a very long par 5 called the "ski trail", or by the lakes around the tenth. Estepona is a handy address to make a change from the posher world of the coastal courses.

Estepona Golf

Apdo Correos 532
E - 29680 ESTEPONA

Office	Secretaria	(34) 952 - 113 081
Pro shop	Pro-shop	(34) 952 - 113 081
Fax	Fax	(34) 952 - 113 080
Web	www.esteponagolf.com	
Situation	Situación	

Gibraltar (pop. 28 339), 40 km -Estepona (pop. 36 307), 10 km

Annual closure	Cierre anual	no
Weekly closure	Cierre semanal	no

Fees main season Precios tempor. alta	18 holes	
	Week days Semana	**We/Bank holidays** Fin de sem./fiestas
Individual Individual	48 €	48 €
Couple Pareja	96 €	96 €
Caddy Caddy		no
Electric Trolley Carro eléctrico		no
Buggy Coche		30 € /18 holes
Clubs Palos		15 € / 18 holes

Credit cards Tarjetas de crédito
VISA

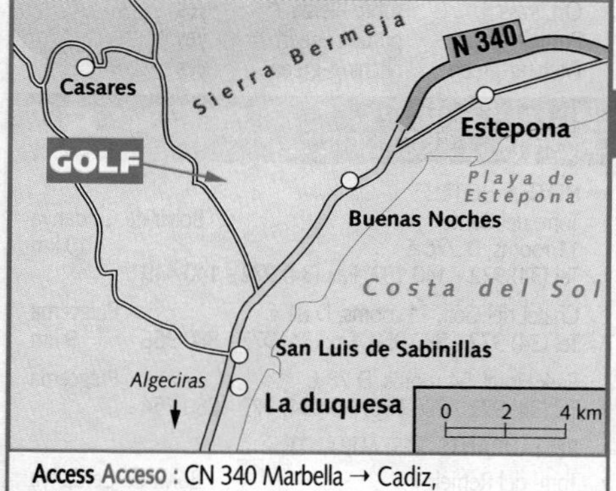

Access Acceso : CN 340 Marbella → Cadiz, Estepona km 150
Map 7 on page 1101 Plano 7 Página 1101

Golf course RECORRIDO — 14/20

Site	Emplazamiento	
Maintenance	Mantenimiento	
Architect	Arquitecto	José Luis Lopez
Type	Tipo	mountain
Relief	Relieve	
Water in play	Agua	
Exp. to wind	Exp. al viento	
Trees in play	Arboles	

Scorecard Tarjeta	**Chp.** Campeonato	**Mens** Caballeros	**Ladies** Damas
Length Longitud	6001	5610	5137
Par	72	72	72
Slope system	—	—	—

Advised golfing ability Nivel de juego aconsejado: 0 12 24 36
Hcp required Handicap exigido: 28 Men, 36 Ladies

Club house & amenities CLUB HOUSE Y DEPENDENCIAS — 7/10

Pro shop	Pro-shop	
Driving range	Campo de prácticas	
Sheltered	cubierto	no
On grass	sobre hierba	yes
Putting-green	putting-green	yes
Pitching-green	pitching-green	no

Hotel facilities HOTELES CERCANOS — 6/10

HOTELS HOTELES

Kempinski, 150 rooms, D 291 € Tel (34) 952 - 809 500, Fax (34) 952 - 809 550	Estepona 7 km
Las Dunas, 75 rooms, D 246 € Tel (34) 952 - 794 345, Fax (34) 952 - 794 825	Estepona 15 km
El Paraiso, 182 rooms, D 184 € Tel (34) 952 - 883 000, Fax (34) 952 - 882 019	Estepona 8 km

RESTAURANTS RESTAURANTE

De Medici, Tel (34) 952 - 884 687	Estepona
El Rocio, Tel (34) 952 - 800 046	Estepona
Casa de mi Azuela, Tel (34) 952 - 791 967	Estepona

FONTANALS 17 6 5

Fontanals se sitúa en primera línea entre los golfs de la Costa Brava. Rodeado de montañas, aunque llano, con algunas ondulaciones, es un test de primer orden con multitud de obstáculos, encontrándose los más peligrosos en los hoyos más cortos. Numerosos bunkers de calle y de green, con contornos muy elaborados (un poco al estilo de Trent Jones), ponen a prueba el sentido táctico y la virtuosidad del jugador, sin que la suerte intervenga para nada en un buen resultado. Se ha cuidado mucho la estética con muretes o guijarros delimitando los obstáculos de agua. Por momentos impresionante y siempre espectacular, este recorrido de Ramón Espinosa es largo , propicio a los buenos pegadores y en general a los jugadores con experiencia y con un buen juego corto. Difícilmente se le encontrarán defectos a esta obra maestra.

The Fontanals course is already at the forefront of courses along the Costa Brava. Surrounded by mountains but flat with only a few rolling fairways, this is a test of golf of the highest order with a multitude of hazards, the most dangerous of which are reserved for the short holes. Countless fairway and green-side bunkers, all carefully shaped (a little in the style of Trent Jones), are a great test for the tactical mind and virtuosity of any player, and luck plays no role in a good score. Very special care has been given to the visual side, with the water hazards neatly lined with low walls or pebbles. Often impressive and sometimes quite spectacular, this course by Ramon Espinosa is long and can be recommended to long-hitters and in general to experienced players with a sharp short game. They will be hard pushed to find any faults in this superb achievement.

Golf Fontanals de Cerdanya — 1994

E - 17538 SORIGUEROLA,
FONTANALS DE CERDANYA

Office	Secretaria	(34) 972 - 144 374
Pro shop	Pro-shop	(34) 972 - 144 374
Fax	Fax	(34) 972 - 890 856
E-mail	golffontanals@ctv.es	
Situation	Situación	

Puigcerdà (pop. 6 414), 12 km

Annual closure	Cierre anual	no
Weekly closure	Cierre semanal	no

restaurant closed on tuesdays

1132

Fees main season Precios tempor. alta	Week days Semana	We/Bank holidays Fin de sem./fiestas (18 holes)
Individual Individual	36 €	96 €
Couple Pareja	72 €	192 €
Caddy Caddy		no
Electric Trolley Carro eléctrico		9 € /18 holes
Buggy Coche		30 € /18 holes
Clubs Palos		6 € / 18 holes

Credit cards Tarjetas de crédito
VISA - Eurocard - MasterCard

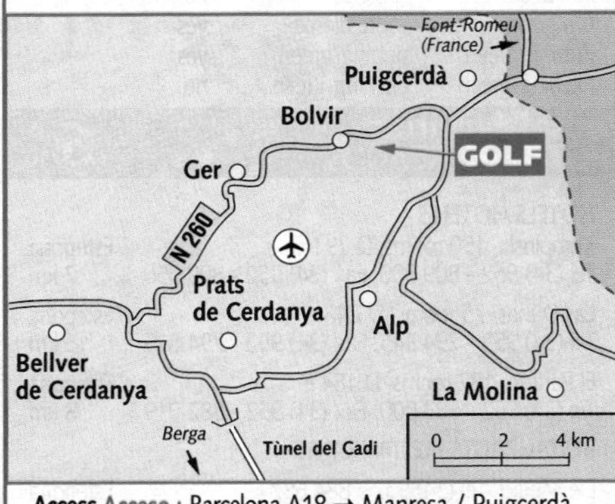

Access Acceso : Barcelona A18 → Manresa / Puigcerdà. Manresa E9 → Puigcerdà, Alp → Golf on left hand side
Map 2 on page 1091 Plano 2 Página 1091

Golf course — RECORRIDO — 17/20

Site	Emplazamiento	
Maintenance	Mantenimiento	
Architect	Arquitecto	Ramón Espinosa
Type	Tipo	open country
Relief	Relieve	
Water in play	Agua	
Exp. to wind	Exp. al viento	
Trees in play	Arboles	

Scorecard Tarjeta	**Chp.** Campeonato	**Mens** Caballeros	**Ladies** Damas
Length Longitud	6454	6159	5256
Par	72	72	72
Slope system	—	—	—

Advised golfing ability Nivel de juego aconsejado — 0 12 24 36
Hcp required Handicap exigido — 28 Men, 36 Ladies

Club house & amenities — CLUB HOUSE Y DEPENDENCIAS — 6/10

Pro shop	Pro-shop	
Driving range	Campo de prácticas	
Sheltered	cubierto	14 mats
On grass	sobre hierba	yes
Putting-green	putting-green	yes
Pitching-green	pitching-green	yes

Hotel facilities — HOTELES CERCANOS — 5/10

HOTELS HOTELES

Torre del Remei — Bolvir de Cerdanya
11 rooms, D 276 € — 10 km
Tel (34) 972 - 140 182, Fax (34) 972 - 140 449

Chalet del Golf, 11 rooms, D 81 € — Puigcerda
Tel (34) 972 - 880 950, Fax (34) 972 - 880 966 — 9 km

Park Hotel, 54 rooms, D 78 € — Puigcerdá
Tel (34) 972 - 880 750, Fax (34) 972 - 880 754

RESTAURANTS RESTAURANTE

Torre del Remei — Bolvir de Cerdanya
Tel (34) 972 - 140 182 — 10 km

La Vila, Tel (34) 972 - 140 804 — Puigcerdà 8 km

GOLF D'ARO (MAS NOU) 15 3 7

Encaramado en la cima de una pequeña montaña, como un mirador dominando la geografía espectacular de la Costa Brava -mar y pinos-, es un campo impresionante en la mayoría de sus hoyos. Ramón Espinosa pensó más en los buenos jugadores que los altos de handicap, los cuales tienen que asustarse ante los profundos barrancos que flanquean una docena de hoyos y están llenos de matorrales (una regla local los considera igual que obstáculos de agua). Más vale no relajar la concentración y es mejor la precisión que la distancia. Es preferible evitar los días de viento. Antes de pensar en el resultado más vale reconocer el terreno una o dos veces, aunque sólo sea para identificar los sitios peligros os, calcular las distancias y... cuántas bolas conviene llevar en la bolsa. Nada fácil, pero interesante en un escenario realmente espectacular. Tras atravesar una temporada de importantes problemas, el campo ha vuelto al buen estado que merece su diseño. Pero no hay casa club sino solamente unos servicios mínimos de atención al cliente, aunque tiene un amplio campo de prácticas.

Perched on the summit of a little mountain, like a watchtower overlooking the spectacular scenery of the Costa Brava - all sea and pines -, this is an impressively spacious course, at least for most of the holes. Ramon Espinosa obviously had the good golfer in mind more than the high-handicapper, who might not be too impressed by some fearsomely deep ravines filled with dense bushes lining about a dozen holes. Luckily, a local rule considers these to be water hazards. Focus is the key word here, with accuracy taking priority over distance. When the wind really blows, you might be best advised to stay in the club-house. You would also be wise to reconnoitre the course a few times before thinking about a good score, locating the danger spots and taking account of distance and the number of balls you might need. Nothing is easy but everything is interesting in this truly spectacular setting. Despite ongoing cash problems, this club has preserved the excellent standards of maintenance it deserves. Club-house facilities are now at a bare minimum but the driving range is as extensive as ever.

Club Golf d'Aro- Mas Nou 1990

Urb. Mas Nou s/n - Apartado Correo 429
E - 17250 PLATJA D'ARO

Office	Secretaria	(34) 972 - 826 900
Pro shop	Pro-shop	(34) 972 - 816 727
Fax	Fax	(34) 972 - 826 906
Web	www.golfspain.com	
Situation	Situación	

Platja d'Aro (pop. 4 785), 4 km
Sant Feliu de Guixols (pop.16 088 h), 10 km

Annual closure	Cierre anual	no
Weekly closure	Cierre semanal	no

Fees main season	Precios tempor. alta	18 holes
	Week days Semana	**We/Bank holidays** Fin de sem./fiestas
Individual Individual	54 €	54 €
Couple Pareja	108 €	108 €
Caddy Caddy		no
Electric Trolley Carro eléctrico		12 € /18 holes
Buggy Coche		30 € /18 holes
Clubs Palos		12 € / 18 holes

Credit cards Tarjetas de crédito
VISA - Eurocard - MasterCard - AMEX

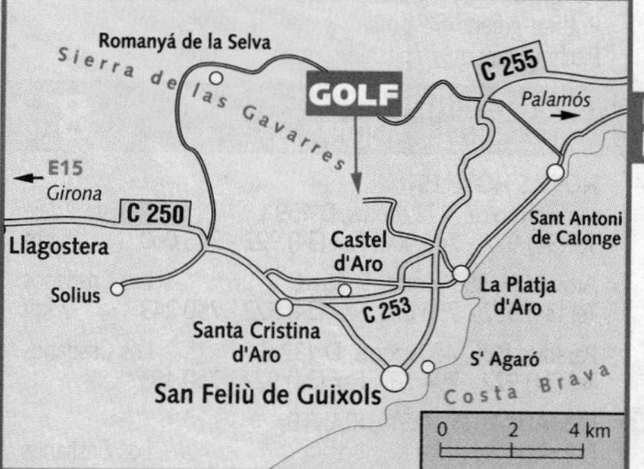

Access Acceso : Barcelona, A2. Exit (Salida) 9. Platja d'Aro, turn right → Urban. Mas Nou
Map 2 on page 1091 Plano 2 Página 1091

Golf course RECORRIDO 15/20

Site	Emplazamiento	
Maintenance	Mantenimiento	
Architect	Arquitecto	Ramón Espinosa
Type	Tipo	mountain, parkland
Relief	Relieve	
Water in play	Agua	
Exp. to wind	Exp. al viento	
Trees in play	Arboles	

Scorecard Tarjeta	**Chp.** Campeonato	**Mens** Caballeros	**Ladies** Damas
Length Longitud	6218	6004	5031
Par	72	72	72
Slope system	—	—	—

Advised golfing ability 0 12 24 36
Nivel de juego aconsejado
Hcp required Handicap exigido 36

Club house & amenities CLUB HOUSE Y DEPENDENCIAS 3/10

Pro shop	Pro-shop	
Driving range	Campo de prácticas	
Sheltered	cubierto	10 mats
On grass	sobre hierba	yes
Putting-green	putting-green	yes
Pitching-green	pitching-green	yes

Hotel facilities HOTELES CERCANOS 7/10

HOTELS HOTELES

Park Hotel San Jordi, 104 rooms, D 167 € — Calonge 4 km
Tel (34) 972 - 652 311, Fax (34) 972 - 652 576

Golf Costa Brava — Santa Cristina 10 km
91 rooms, D 102 €
Tel (34) 972 - 835 151, Fax (34) 972 - 837 588

Platjapark, 200 rooms, D 115 € — Platja d'Aro 4 km
Tel (34) 972 - 816 805, Fax (34) 972 - 816 803

RESTAURANTS RESTAURANTE

Las Panolles, Tel (34) 972 - 837 011 — Platja d'Aro 8 km
Carles Camos-Big Rock, Tel (34) 972 - 818 012 — Platja d'Aro
Arabi, Tel (34) 972 - 816 376 — Platja d'Aro

GOLF DEL SUR

16 | 7 | 8

Este es un campo con tres recorridos de 9 hoyos que se pueden combinar entre sí. El recorrido principal consiste en jugar los campos Sur y Norte. Recientes obras de acondicionamiento han mejorado mucho el estado del campo. Sus hoyos más famosos son el 2 del Sur, un par 3 de 193 metros cuyo green es una isla verde rodeada de bunker de arena negra propia de la zona, y el hoyo 4 del recorrido Norte, un par 4 de 289 metros impresionante porque sube de espaldas al mar junto a un formidable barranco. Es un recorrido muy variado en el que Pepe Gancedo hace sus peculiares guiños al jugador, bien poniéndole ante un golpe original, bien reclamándole un approach de buen tacto. Las referencias y la decoración del campo se fundamentan en la flora autóctona que, además de alegrar los ojos, enmarca al jugador en el hoyo.

This course comprises 3 combinable nine-holers, but the reference course is certainly the South and North played together. Recent development work has done much to improve the general condition of the course, where perhaps the most remarkable hole is N°2 on the South layout, a par 3 of 193 metres, where the green is a sort of green island amidst bunkers full of the region's black sand. Almost as impressive is hole N°4 on the North course, a great par 4 of just 289 metres, where the terraced steps up the fairway towards the sea present a tremendous barrier. This is a very varied layout where Pepe Gancedo had players very much in mind, asking them to carefully place their shots before thinking about doing anything too original, and calling for a sharp short game. The decoration is the island's natural flora which not only is a sight to behold but also comes into play.

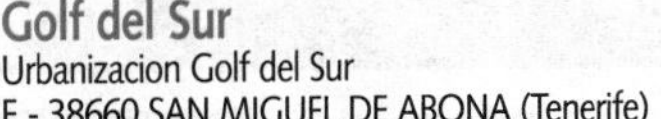

Golf del Sur — 1989

Urbanizacion Golf del Sur
E - 38660 SAN MIGUEL DE ABONA (Tenerife)

Office	Secretaria	(34) 922 - 738 170
Pro shop	Pro-shop	(34) 922 - 738 170
Fax	Fax	(34) 922 - 738 272
Web	www.golfdelsur.net	
Situation	Situación	

Santa Cruz de Tenerife (pop. 203 000), 75 km
Playa de Las Americas, 15 km

Annual closure	Cierre anual	no
Weekly closure	Cierre semanal	no
Fees main season	Precios tempor. alta	18 holes

	Week days Semana	We/Bank holidays Fin de sem./fiestas
Individual Individual	62 €	62 €
Couple Pareja	124 €	124 €
Caddy	Caddy	no
Electric Trolley	Carro eléctrico	9 € /18 holes
Buggy	Coche	30 € /18 holes
Clubs	Palos	15 € /18 holes

Credit cards Tarjetas de crédito
VISA - MasterCard - AMEX

Access Acceso : Motorway TF1 / Autovia del Sur, Exit (Salida) 24 (Km 62.5), → Los Abrigos.
First right to Urbanización Golf del Sur
Map 9 on page 1104 Plano 9 Página 1104

Golf course — RECORRIDO — 16/20

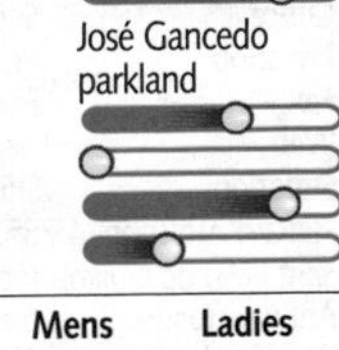

Site	Emplazamiento	
Maintenance	Mantenimiento	
Architect	Arquitecto	José Gancedo
Type	Tipo	parkland
Relief	Relieve	
Water in play	Agua	
Exp. to wind	Exp. al viento	
Trees in play	Arboles	

Scorecard Tarjeta	Chp. Campeonato	Mens Caballeros	Ladies Damas
Length Longitud	5870	5578	4829
Par	72	72	72
Slope system	—	—	—

Advised golfing ability Nivel de juego aconsejado — 0 12 24 36
Hcp required Handicap exigido — 28 Men, 36 Ladies

Club house & amenities — CLUB HOUSE Y DEPENDENCIAS — 7/10

Pro shop	Pro-shop	
Driving range	Campo de prácticas	
Sheltered	cubierto	no
On grass	sobre hierba	yes, 20 places
Putting-green	putting-green	yes
Pitching-green	pitching-green	yes

Hotel facilities — HOTELES CERCANOS — 8/10

HOTELS HOTELES

Jardin Tropical, 421 rooms, D 159 € — Costa Adeje
Tel (34) 922 - 746 000, Fax (34) 922 - 746 060 — 15 km

Arona GH, 399 rooms, D 162 € — Los Cristianos
Tel (34) 922 - 750 678, Fax (34) 922 - 750 243 — 7 km

Paradise Park, 480 rooms, D 132 € — Los Cristianos
Tel (34) 922 - 794 762, Fax (34) 922 - 750 193

RESTAURANTS RESTAURANTE

El Rincón del Arroz — Los Cristianos
Tel (34) 922 - 797 370 — 7 km

El Jable, Tel (34) 922 - 390 698 — San Isidro 7 km

Avencio, Tel (34) 922 - 176 079 — El Médano 2 km

GRANADA

14 | 6 | 5

A noventa minutos de la costa, este recorrido no sólo ofrece una buena oportunidad de jugar al golf cuando se va a visitar la soberbia ciudad de Granada, sino que merece la pena por si mismo. Está situado en altura frente a Sierra Nevada, pero sin demasiadas cuestas, su longitud es razonable, salvo en los pares 3 y en los demás hoyos (sobre todo a la vuelta) si se sale de atrás. Las dificultades están colocadas de manera estratégica y peligrosa si no se tiene mucha precisión, especialmente los temibles obsáculos de agua entre los hoyos 15 y 17. Los greens están bien diseñados, son bastante grandes, bien protegidos, con sutiles ondulaciones. En este tipo de recorrido con dificultades bien repartidas, no hay que dudar en atacar en cuanto la ocasión se presente. Se aconsejará jugar con golfistas de mismo nivel para apreciar mejor los desafíos tácticos, pero es un recorrido muy agradable para todo tipo de jugadores.

This course, 90 minutes inland, not only provides a great opportunity to play golf when visiting the superb city of Granada, it is also well worth playing. At altitude, it stands opposite the Sierra Nevada, although the layout is rather flat and the length reasonable, except the par 3s and if you choose to play from the back tees (especially on the back nine). Hazards are strategically placed and often dangerous for wayward shots, especially the formidable water hazards between the 15th and 17th holes. The greens are well-designed, rather large and well defended with tricky slopes. This is a type of course where the difficulties are evenly spread, inviting players to attack whenever the opportunity arises. We recommend playing here with golfers of your own level in order to better appreciate the tactical challenges, but the course is a pleasant day's golfing for everyone.

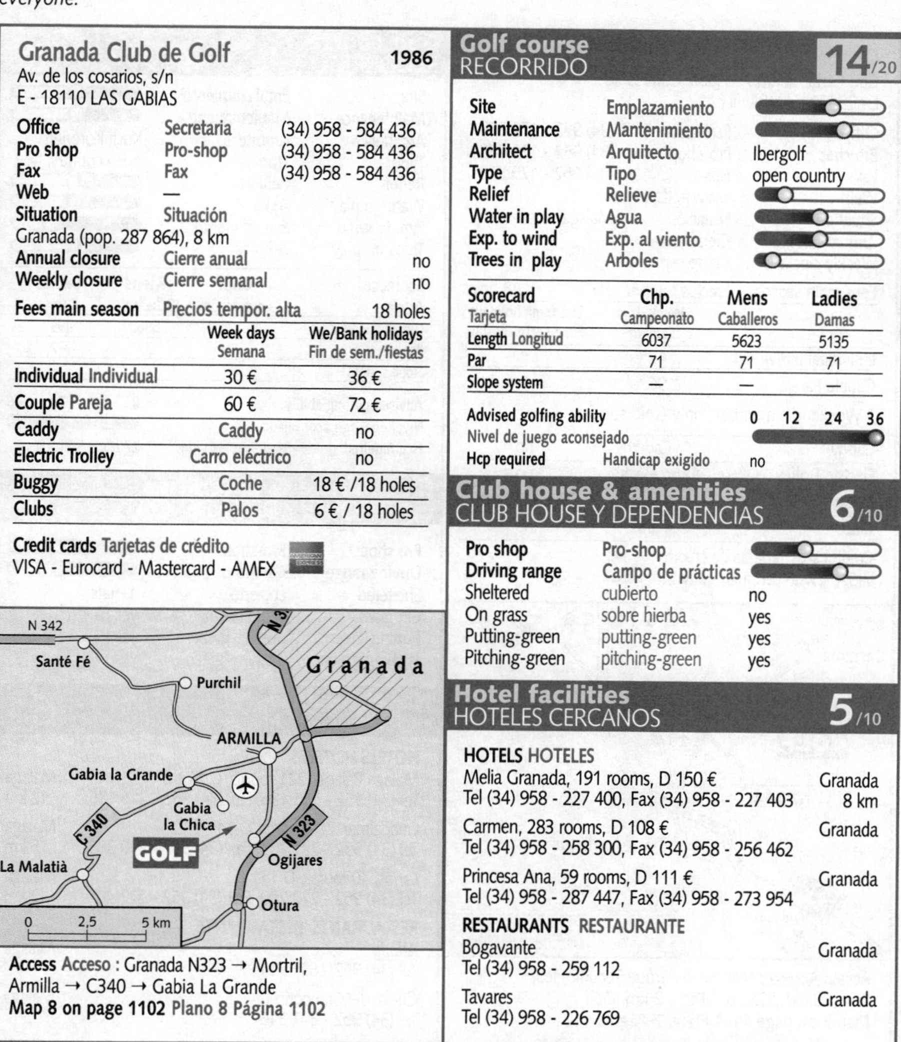

Granada Club de Golf — 1986

Av. de los cosarios, s/n
E - 18110 LAS GABIAS

Office	Secretaria	(34) 958 - 584 436
Pro shop	Pro-shop	(34) 958 - 584 436
Fax	Fax	(34) 958 - 584 436
Web	—	
Situation	Situación	
Granada (pop. 287 864), 8 km		
Annual closure	Cierre anual	no
Weekly closure	Cierre semanal	no

Fees main season Precios tempor. alta	Week days Semana	We/Bank holidays Fin de sem./fiestas
18 holes		
Individual Individual	30 €	36 €
Couple Pareja	60 €	72 €
Caddy Caddy	no	
Electric Trolley Carro eléctrico	no	
Buggy Coche	18 € /18 holes	
Clubs Palos	6 € / 18 holes	

Credit cards Tarjetas de crédito
VISA - Eurocard - Mastercard - AMEX

Access Acceso : Granada N323 → Mortril, Armilla → C340 → Gabia La Grande
Map 8 on page 1102 Plano 8 Página 1102

Golf course RECORRIDO — 14/20

Site	Emplazamiento	
Maintenance	Mantenimiento	
Architect	Arquitecto	Ibergolf
Type	Tipo	open country
Relief	Relieve	
Water in play	Agua	
Exp. to wind	Exp. al viento	
Trees in play	Arboles	

Scorecard Tarjeta	Chp. Campeonato	Mens Caballeros	Ladies Damas
Length Longitud	6037	5623	5135
Par	71	71	71
Slope system	—	—	—

Advised golfing ability Nivel de juego aconsejado: 0 12 24 36
Hcp required Handicap exigido: no

Club house & amenities CLUB HOUSE Y DEPENDENCIAS — 6/10

Pro shop	Pro-shop	
Driving range	Campo de prácticas	
Sheltered	cubierto	no
On grass	sobre hierba	yes
Putting-green	putting-green	yes
Pitching-green	pitching-green	yes

Hotel facilities HOTELES CERCANOS — 5/10

HOTELS HOTELES

Melia Granada, 191 rooms, D 150 € — Granada 8 km
Tel (34) 958 - 227 400, Fax (34) 958 - 227 403

Carmen, 283 rooms, D 108 € — Granada
Tel (34) 958 - 258 300, Fax (34) 958 - 256 462

Princesa Ana, 59 rooms, D 111 € — Granada
Tel (34) 958 - 287 447, Fax (34) 958 - 273 954

RESTAURANTS RESTAURANTE

Bogavante — Granada
Tel (34) 958 - 259 112

Tavares — Granada
Tel (34) 958 - 226 769

GUADALHORCE

14 | 7 | 6

En la campiña al oeste de Málaga, este recorrido diseñado por el finlandés Kosti Kuronen presenta dos caras: los nueve primeros hoyos son bastante clásicos, los nueve últimos más imaginativos con greens en alto, calles y lagos bien cuidados. Los greens son de excelente calidad, a veces dobles (6 y 8, 12 y 16), rápidos y bien protegidos, y aguantan bien la bola. El conjunto no es que sea excepcional, pero es muy agradable y divertido el jugar todas las fórmulas de golf, tanto con jugadores de mismo nivel como de niveles muy diferentes. Sobre todo reserva sus dificultades a los mejores, respondiendo exactamente a la definición de un buen campo de golf, y el hecho de que no sea necesario alquilar un coche hace que sea muy placentero el jugar en familia. Algunas trampas estratégicas le dan un cierto encanto e incitan a jugarlo varias veces.

In the countryside to the west of Malaga, this course, designed by Finnish architect Kosti Kuronen, offers two different faces. The front nine are classical holes, while the back nine are more imaginative with elevated greens, lakes and well laid out fairways. The greens are excellent, sometimes double (6 and 8, 12 and 16), fast and well-defended, but they pitch well. This is probably not an exceptional course, but it is very pleasant and fun to play with players of your own standard or with anyone, for that matter. In fact, the difficulties of Guadalhorce, as with any good course, are reserved for the better players, and being easily playable on foot it is great fun to play with all the family. A few strategic traps add a little spice to the round and make you want to come back and play it again.

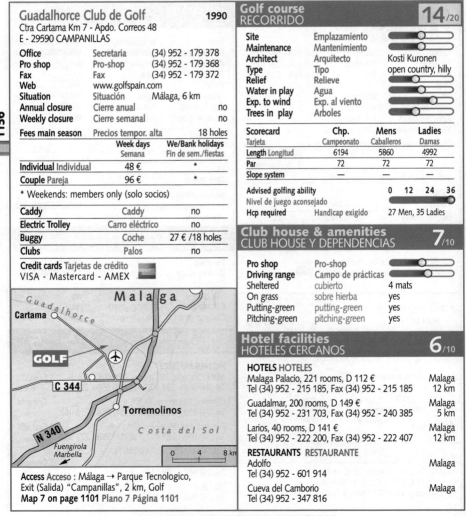

Guadalhorce Club de Golf — 1990

Ctra Cartama Km 7 - Apdo. Correos 48
E - 29590 CAMPANILLAS

Office	Secretaria	(34) 952 - 179 378
Pro shop	Pro-shop	(34) 952 - 179 368
Fax	Fax	(34) 952 - 179 372
Web	www.golfspain.com	
Situation	Situación	Málaga, 6 km
Annual closure	Cierre anual	no
Weekly closure	Cierre semanal	no

Fees main season Precios tempor. alta		18 holes
	Week days Semana	We/Bank holidays Fin de sem./fiestas
Individual Individual	48 €	*
Couple Pareja	96 €	*

* Weekends: members only (solo socios)

Caddy	Caddy	no
Electric Trolley	Carro eléctrico	no
Buggy	Coche	27 € /18 holes
Clubs	Palos	no

Credit cards Tarjetas de crédito
VISA - Mastercard - AMEX

Malaga
Guadalhorce
Cartama
GOLF
C 344
Torremolinos
N 340
Costa del Sol
Fuengirola
Marbella
0 4 8 km

Access Acceso : Málaga → Parque Tecnologico, Exit (Salida) "Campanillas", 2 km, Golf
Map 7 on page 1101 Plano 7 Página 1101

Golf course RECORRIDO — 14/20

Site	Emplazamiento	
Maintenance	Mantenimiento	
Architect	Arquitecto	Kosti Kuronen
Type	Tipo	open country, hilly
Relief	Relieve	
Water in play	Agua	
Exp. to wind	Exp. al viento	
Trees in play	Arboles	

Scorecard Tarjeta	Chp. Campeonato	Mens Caballeros	Ladies Damas
Length Longitud	6194	5860	4992
Par	72	72	72
Slope system	—	—	—

Advised golfing ability / Nivel de juego aconsejado: 0 12 24 36
Hcp required — Handicap exigido — 27 Men, 35 Ladies

Club house & amenities CLUB HOUSE Y DEPENDENCIAS — 7/10

Pro shop	Pro-shop	
Driving range	Campo de prácticas	
Sheltered	cubierto	4 mats
On grass	sobre hierba	yes
Putting-green	putting-green	yes
Pitching-green	pitching-green	yes

Hotel facilities HOTELES CERCANOS — 6/10

HOTELS HOTELES

Malaga Palacio, 221 rooms, D 112 € — Malaga
Tel (34) 952 - 215 185, Fax (34) 952 - 215 185 — 12 km

Guadalmar, 200 rooms, D 149 € — Malaga
Tel (34) 952 - 231 703, Fax (34) 952 - 240 385 — 5 km

Larios, 40 rooms, D 141 € — Malaga
Tel (34) 952 - 222 200, Fax (34) 952 - 222 407 — 12 km

RESTAURANTS RESTAURANTE

Adolfo — Malaga
Tel (34) 952 - 601 914

Cueva del Camborio — Malaga
Tel (34) 952 - 347 816

GUADALMINA Sur

14 | 7 | 7

Es el segundo recorrido creado en la Costa del Sol, diseñado por el legendario Javier Arana. Mucho más llano que el "Norte", sin embargo sus calles son más anchas, con árboles a menudo en la línea de juego. Al tener pocas carreteras que lo atraviesen, se juega más tranquilamente, al menos en los hoyos que dan al mar. Más difícil de lo que parece, sobre todo con viento, no se siúa entre los más exigentes de la costa, máxime teniendo en cuenta que sus dificultades son perfectamente visibles y la estrategia de juego evidente. Un riachuelo está en la línea de juego en varios hoyos, pero no es demasiado peligroso. La ida tiene algunos hoyos bastante largos, mientras que a la vuelta hay algunos bastante cortos, especialmente pares 4 cortitos en los que los bienvenidos birdies pueden aliviar la tarjeta , pares 3 de buena calidad (sobre todo el 11) y dos pares 5 de los que en uno al menos (el 17) se puede llegar en dos golpes. Hay que conocerlo.

This is the second course opened on the Costa del Sol designed by the legendary Javier Arana. Much flatter than the "Norte", it also has wider fairways and more trees, which often get in the way. There are fewer roads around, so it is a quieter course, at least for the holes facing the sea. Harder than it looks, especially when the wind is up, it is not the most challenging course on this coast, especially since the hazards are perfectly visible and playing strategy rather obvious. A small river comes into play on several holes but is rarely too dangerous. The front nine include some rather long holes, while the inward half has a number of shortish holes, notably the short part 4s, where a few welcome birdies can do your score-card a world of good, enjoyable par 3s (especially the 11th) and two par 5s, of which at least one (the 17th) is reachable in two. Worth knowing.

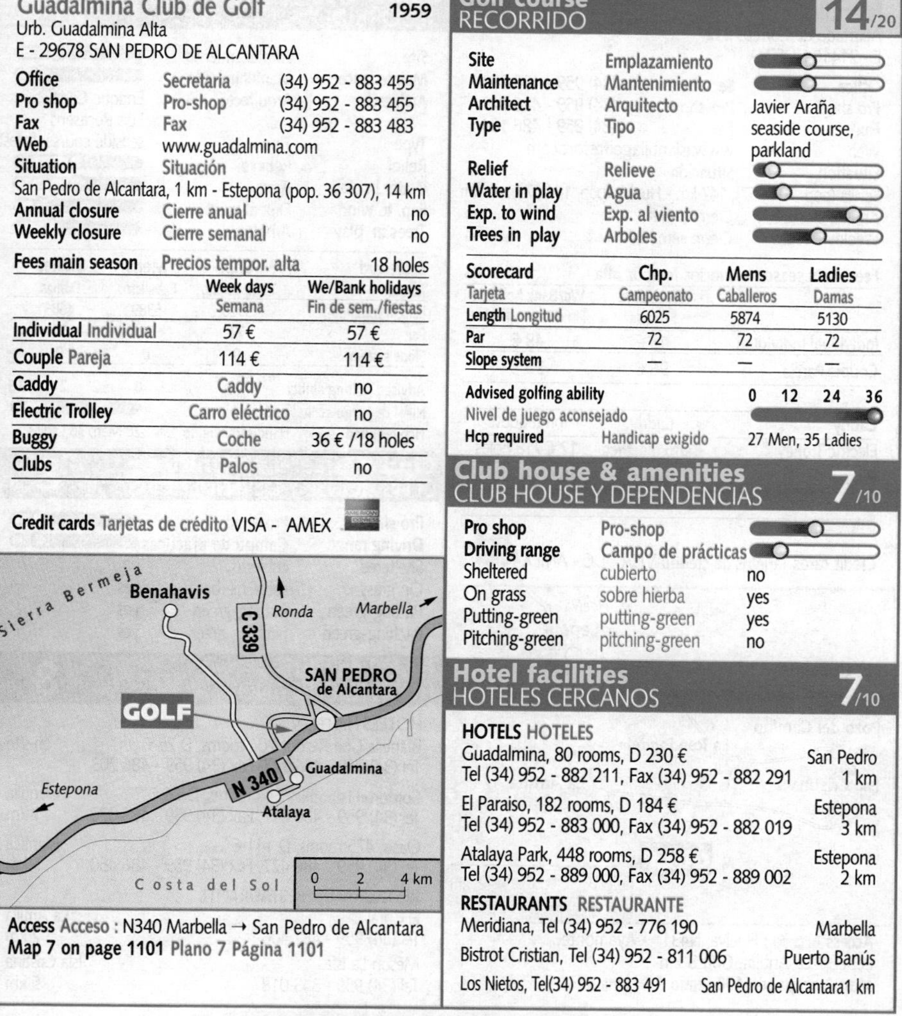

Guadalmina Club de Golf — 1959

Urb. Guadalmina Alta
E - 29678 SAN PEDRO DE ALCANTARA

Office	Secretaria	(34) 952 - 883 455
Pro shop	Pro-shop	(34) 952 - 883 455
Fax	Fax	(34) 952 - 883 483
Web	www.guadalmina.com	
Situation	Situación	

San Pedro de Alcantara, 1 km - Estepona (pop. 36 307), 14 km

Annual closure	Cierre anual	no
Weekly closure	Cierre semanal	no

Fees main season Precios tempor. alta	18 holes	
	Week days Semana	**We/Bank holidays** Fin de sem./fiestas
Individual Individual	57 €	57 €
Couple Pareja	114 €	114 €
Caddy Caddy	no	
Electric Trolley Carro eléctrico	no	
Buggy Coche	36 € /18 holes	
Clubs Palos	no	

Credit cards Tarjetas de crédito VISA - AMEX

Access Acceso : N340 Marbella → San Pedro de Alcantara
Map 7 on page 1101 Plano 7 Página 1101

Golf course RECORRIDO — 14/20

Site	Emplazamiento	
Maintenance	Mantenimiento	
Architect	Arquitecto	Javier Araña
Type	Tipo	seaside course, parkland
Relief	Relieve	
Water in play	Agua	
Exp. to wind	Exp. al viento	
Trees in play	Arboles	

Scorecard Tarjeta	**Chp.** Campeonato	**Mens** Caballeros	**Ladies** Damas
Length Longitud	6025	5874	5130
Par	72	72	72
Slope system	—	—	—

Advised golfing ability Nivel de juego aconsejado: 0 12 24 36
Hcp required Handicap exigido: 27 Men, 35 Ladies

Club house & amenities CLUB HOUSE Y DEPENDENCIAS — 7/10

Pro shop	Pro-shop	
Driving range	Campo de prácticas	
Sheltered	cubierto	no
On grass	sobre hierba	yes
Putting-green	putting-green	yes
Pitching-green	pitching-green	no

Hotel facilities HOTELES CERCANOS — 7/10

HOTELS HOTELES

Guadalmina, 80 rooms, D 230 € Tel (34) 952 - 882 211, Fax (34) 952 - 882 291	San Pedro 1 km
El Paraiso, 182 rooms, D 184 € Tel (34) 952 - 883 000, Fax (34) 952 - 882 019	Estepona 3 km
Atalaya Park, 448 rooms, D 258 € Tel (34) 952 - 889 000, Fax (34) 952 - 889 002	Estepona 2 km

RESTAURANTS RESTAURANTE

Meridiana, Tel (34) 952 - 776 190	Marbella
Bistrot Cristian, Tel (34) 952 - 811 006	Puerto Banús
Los Nietos, Tel(34) 952 - 883 491	San Pedro de Alcantara1 km

ISLANTILLA

16 | 8 | 8

Con 27 hoyos y un bonito club-house de estilo andaluz, el conjunto de este ambicioso proyecto domina el Atlántico. Los magníficos árboles de este inmenso parque han sido preservados y constituyen una de las dificultades con bosquecitos que penalizan. Adeñás de los numerosos bunkers bien diseñados y de un cierto número de obstáculos de agua, greens ondulados y a menudo en alto hacen muy técnico un recorrido generalmente utilizado como el principal 18 hoyos. Raramente existen trampas escondidas y se puede afrontar sin miedo. La anchura de las calles pueden dar la impresión de que es un recorrido fácil, pero es una impresión ilusoria, sobre todo desde las salidas de atrás. Si al gusto de jugar se añade el placer de la vista (especialmente el Océano en el 12), Islantilla es una de las buenas sorpresas de estos últimos años y merece la pena conocerlo.

The 27 holes and attractive Andalusian style clubhouse of this ambitious complex overlook the Atlantic Ocean. The fine trees in this huge park have been spared and form some of the difficulties along with penalising undergrowth. In addition to the well-designed bunkers and a number of water hazards, the well-contoured and often elevated greens (some are blind) help make the 18 holes generally used as the main course a rather technical layout. But since the traps are rarely concealed, there is not a great deal to be afraid of. The wide fairways perhaps give the impression of a course that is easy to score on, but this is only an impression, especially when playing from the back tees. If you combine the pleasure of playing and the surrounding view (notably over the ocean on hole N° 12), Islantilla is one of the nicest surprises in recent years and well worth the trip.

1138

Islantilla **1991**
Apartado de Correos 212
E - 21410 HUELVA

Office	Secretaria	(34) 959 - 486 039
Pro shop	Pro-shop	(34) 959 - 486 049
Fax	Fax	(34) 959 - 486 104
Web	www.islantillagolfresort.com	
Situation	Situación	

Sevilla (pop. 704 857), 147 km - Huelva (pop. 144 579), 40 km

Annual closure	Cierre anual	no
Weekly closure	Cierre semanal	no

Fees main season Precios tempor. alta		18 holes
	Week days Semana	We/Bank holidays Fin de sem./fiestas
Individual Individual	48 €	48 €
Couple Pareja	96 €	96 €

Caddy	Caddy	on request
Electric Trolley	Carro eléctrico	12 € /18 holes
Buggy	Coche	36 € /18 holes
Clubs	Palos	18 € / 18 holes

Credit cards Tarjetas de crédito VISA - DC - AMEX

Huelva
Lepe
El Empalme
Pozo del Camino
La Rendondela
Isla Cristina
La Antilla
GOLF
0 2,5 5 km

Access Acceso : Huelva, N431 → Ayamonte, Lepe → La Antilla, Golf 3 km
Map 7 on page 1100 Plano 7 Página 1100

Golf course RECORRIDO 16/20

Site	Emplazamiento	
Maintenance	Mantenimiento	
Architect	Arquitecto	Enrique Canales Luis Recasens
Type	Tipo	seaside course, forest
Relief	Relieve	
Water in play	Agua	
Exp. to wind	Exp. al viento	
Trees in play	Arboles	

Scorecard Tarjeta	Chp. Campeonato	Mens Caballeros	Ladies Damas
Length Longitud	5926	5389	4686
Par	72	72	72
Slope system	0	0	0

Advised golfing ability Nivel de juego aconsejado 0 12 24 36
Hcp required Handicap exigido 28 Men, 36 Ladies

Club house & amenities CLUB HOUSE Y DEPENDENCIAS 8/10

Pro shop	Pro-shop	
Driving range	Campo de prácticas	
Sheltered	cubierto	no
On grass	sobre hierba	yes
Putting-green	putting-green	yes
Pitching-green	pitching-green	yes

Hotel facilities HOTELES CERCANOS 8/10

HOTELS HOTELES

Islantilla Golf Resort, 204 rooms, D 75 € — on site
Tel (34) 959 - 486 377, Fax (34) 959 - 486 203

Confortel Islantilla, 344 rooms, D 76 € — Islantilla 1 km
Tel (34) 959 - 486 017, Fax (34) 959 - 486 070

Oasis, 475 rooms, D 141 € — Islantilla 5 km
Tel (34) 959 - 486 422, Fax (34) 959 - 486 450

RESTAURANTS RESTAURANTE

El Coral — La Antilla 2 km
Tel (34) 959 - 481 406

Meson La Isla — Isla Cristina 5 km
Tel (34) 959 - 343 018

JARAMA R.A.C.E.

13	7	6

El interesante diseño de Arana se ve desgraciadamente alterado por el paso de los años y por una tierra demasiado vieja que provoca problemas de drenaje en tiempo humedo, problemas que sin embargo el Real Automovil Club de España están tratando remediar. Bien situado, con magníficas vistas, sería un sitio muy tranquilo para jugar si la proximidad del circuito automovilístico no trajese a veces problemas sonoros. Sería una pena sin embargo no aceptar una visita al campo ya que si requiere una cierta longitud (¡sobre todo desde atrás!), es lo suficientemente amplio para permitir cualquier error de dirección muy frecuentes con el driver. Cierto es que los árboles y los bunkers de recorrido constituyen sus principales defensas, pero serán sobre todo los tiros a green que proporcionarán a los jugadores imprecisos los principales problemas. Será más por la precisión que por la longitud que podremos aspirar a jugar nuestro handicap.

Javier Arana's interesting design has unfortunately been badly affected by aging terrain and a few drainage problems in wet weather. We are told that the Royal Automobile Club of Spain (the course's owner) envisage remedying this very shortly. Well located with some wonderful views, this would be a very quiet place to play if it weren't for the racing track close-by (going by the same name of Jarama), which can be noisy at times. It would, though, be a shame to turn down a visit here, because while the course demands length off the tee (especially from the back), it is wide enough to forgive the all too frequent sliced or hooked drive. Although the trees and fairway bunkers form a solid wall of defence, the biggest problems here for wayward hitters are approach shots to greens. Accuracy more than length is called for if you want to hope to play to your handicap.

Club Jarama R.A.C.E. — 1967

Carretera de Madrid Burgos km 28,100
E - 28700 S.S. DE LOS REYES

Office	Secretaria	(34) 916 - 570 011
Pro shop	Pro-shop	(34) 916 - 570 011
Fax	Fax	(34) 916 - 570 462
Web	www.golfspain.com	
Situation	Situación	

Madrid (pop. 3 084 673), 28 km

Annual closure	Cierre anual	no
Weekly closure	Cierre semanal	no

Fees main season Precios tempor. alta	Week days Semana	We/Bank holidays Fin de sem./fiestas
		18 holes
Individual Individual	51 €	51 €
Couple Pareja	102 €	102 €

Members' guests only (Visitantes sólo si son invitados de socio)

Caddy	Caddy	no
Electric Trolley	Carro eléctrico	4 € /18 holes
Buggy	Coche	24 € /18 holes
Clubs	Palos	no
Credit cards Tarjetas de crédito		no

Access Acceso : Carretera Madrid → Burgos, Km 28,100
Map 3 on page 1092 Plano 3 Página 1092

Golf course RECORRIDO — 13/20

Site	Emplazamiento	
Maintenance	Mantenimiento	
Architect	Arquitecto	Javier Arana
Type	Tipo	country
Relief	Relieve	
Water in play	Agua	
Exp. to wind	Exp. al viento	
Trees in play	Arboles	

Scorecard Tarjeta	**Chp.** Campeonato	**Mens** Caballeros	**Ladies** Damas
Length Longitud	6497	6070	5109
Par	72	72	72
Slope system	—	—	—

Advised golfing ability Nivel de juego aconsejado — 0 12 24 36
Hcp required Handicap exigido — 28 Men, 36 Ladies

Club house & amenities CLUB HOUSE Y DEPENDENCIAS — 7/10

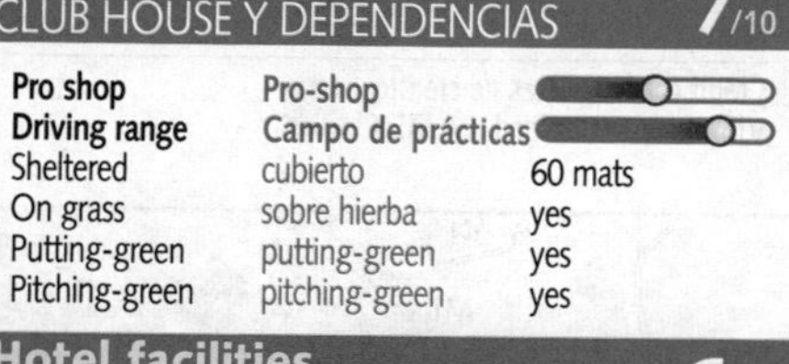

Pro shop	Pro-shop	
Driving range	Campo de prácticas	
Sheltered	cubierto	60 mats
On grass	sobre hierba	yes
Putting-green	putting-green	yes
Pitching-green	pitching-green	yes

Hotel facilities HOTELES CERCANOS — 6/10

HOTELS HOTELES

Chamartin, 360 rooms, D 150 € — Madrid 20 km
Tel (34) 913 - 344 900, Fax (34) 917 - 330 214

Melia Castilla, 900 rooms, D 230 € — Madrid
Tel (34) 915 - 675 000, Fax (34) 915 - 675 051

La Moraleja, 37 rooms, D 162 € — Alcobendas 15 km
Tel (34) 916 - 618 055, Fax (34) 916 - 612 188

RESTAURANTS RESTAURANTE

Mesón Tejas Verde — S.S. de Los Reyes 10 km
Tel (34) 916 - 527 307

Vicente, Tel (34) 916 - 513 171 — S.S. de Los Reyes

Izamar, Tel (34) 916 - 543 893 — S.S. de Los Reyes

1139

LA CALA Norte

17 | 8 | 6

Es un verdadero éxito el haber podido alojar dos recorridos en una región tan montañosa..., ¡ se necesita estar en excelente condición física para prescindir de un coche! . El "Norte" ofrece buenas ocasiones de utilizar el drive, pero en general es tan importante colocar la bola y los roughs tan peligrosos (matorrales), que la madera 3 es más que suficiente. Las ondulaciones del recorrido y las impresiones ópticas exigen reflexión tanto en cada golpe como en la elección del palo, por lo que se aconseja ñás bien a jugadores ya experimentados. Sólo después de haberlo jugado una o dos veces se puede intentar obtener un buen resultado, pero es un recorrido para jugar sobre todo en match-play, apasionante por el diseño de las caídas de los greens, generalmente protegidos por grandes y profundos bunkers. Pequeño consuelo en caso de decepción: sólo hay agua en dos hoyos y la vista panorámica sobre esta región salvaje es magnífica.

Accommodating two courses into such a moutainous region is something of an exploit, but you need to be pretty fit to refuse a buggy. The "Norte" offers some fine opportunities to take the driver out of the bag, but as a general rule, positioning the ball is so important and the rough so dangerous (scrub) that the 3-wood (or long-iron) will suffice. The general relief of this course and the optical illusions call for careful consideration when choosing the club before every shot, which is why we recommend it for experienced players. After one or two reconnaissance rounds they might think about scoring, but this is a course made for match-play, an exciting format on these contoured greens which are generally well-defended by large, deep bunkers. A minor compensation in the event of wayward shot-making is the thought that water only comes into play on two holes and the vista over this wild region is magnificent.

La Cala Resort — 1990

La Cala de Mijas
E - 29647 MIJAS COSTA

Office	Secretaria	(34) 952 - 669 033
Pro shop	Pro-shop	(34) 952 - 669 000
Fax	Fax	(34) 952 - 669 039
Web	www.lacala.com	
Situation	Situación	

Marbella (pop. 84 410), 20 km - Mijas (pop. 32 835), 10 km

Annual closure	Cierre anual	no
Weekly closure	Cierre semanal	no

Fees main season Precios tempor. alta	Week days Semana	We/Bank holidays Fin de sem./fiestas
18 holes		
Individual Individual	57 €	57 €
Couple Pareja	114 €	114 €

Caddy	Caddy	no
Electric Trolley	Carro eléctrico	no
Buggy	Coche	30, € /18 holes
Clubs	Palos	18 € / 18 holes

Credit cards Tarjetas de crédito
VISA - MasterCard - AMEX

Access Acceso : Málaga, N340 → Fuengirola, Cala de Mijas → Golf
Map 7 on page 1101 Plano 7 Página 1101

Golf course RECORRIDO — 17/20

Site	Emplazamiento	
Maintenance	Mantenimiento	
Architect	Arquitecto	Cabell Robinson
Type	Tipo	mountain
Relief	Relieve	
Water in play	Agua	
Exp. to wind	Exp. al viento	
Trees in play	Arboles	

Scorecard Tarjeta	**Chp.** Campeonato	**Mens** Caballeros	**Ladies** Damas
Length Longitud	6187	5782	4759
Par	72	73	73
Slope system	—	—	—

Advised golfing ability Nivel de juego aconsejado: 0 12 24 36
Hcp required Handicap exigido: 28 Men, 36 Ladies

Club house & amenities CLUB HOUSE Y DEPENDENCIAS — 8/10

Pro shop	Pro-shop	
Driving range	Campo de prácticas	
Sheltered	cubierto	no
On grass	sobre hierba	yes
Putting-green	putting-green	yes
Pitching-green	pitching-green	yes

Hotel facilities HOTELES CERCANOS — 6/10

HOTELS HOTELES

La Cala Resort, 83 rooms, D 287 € — on site
Tel (34) 952 - 669 000, Fax (34) 952 - 669 039

Byblos, 144 rooms, D 301 € — Fuengirola 6 km
Tel (34) 952 - 473 050, Fax (34) 952 - 476 783

Mijas, 97 rooms, D 97 € — Mijas 20 km
Tel (34) 952 - 485 800, Fax (34) 952 - 485 825

RESTAURANTS RESTAURANTE

El Olivar — Mijas 20 km
Tel (34) 952 - 486 196

El Tomate — Fuengirola 6 km
Tel (34) 952 - 473 599

LA CALA Sur

16 | 8 | 6

Preferir uno u otro de los dos recorridos de La Cala es una cuestión de gusto. El "Sur" da la impresión de ser un poco más corto, o en todo caso que perdona más lo errores. También aquí los desniveles son engañosos y no hay que fiarse de la longitud teórica de los hoyos. Los drive aterrizan a menudo en zonas en alto y una vegetación densa forma una buena parte de los roughs. Algunas pendientes pronunciadas alrededor de los greens exigen un buen juego corto y mucha intuición. Al igual que en el "Norte", poco importa el resultado cuando se juega por primera vez y para mantener intacto el placer de jugar hay que aceptar las cosas como vienen y con un cierto sentido del humor. Si es mejor que los principiantes se abstengan y prefieran las excelentes instalaciones del campo de prácticas, los jugadores más aguerridos alquilarán un coche para saborear una jornada apasionante.

Preference for one or the other of La Cala courses is a matter of taste. The "Sur" gives the impression of being a little less long, or in any case of being more forgiving for mis-hit shots. Here, too, the terrain's physical contours are misleading and not too much faith should be put in the theoretical lengths of holes. The drive often lands on plateaus which players should not stray too far from, as a large part of rough here is dense vegetation. A number of steep slopes around the greens call for a sharp short game and loads of intuition. As with the "Norte", the score is of little consequence when playing the course for the first time. To really enjoy yourself, take things as they come and never lose your sense of humour. While beginners should refrain from playing the course and stick to the excellent practice facilities, the more proficient players can hop in a buggy and soak up an exciting day's golf.

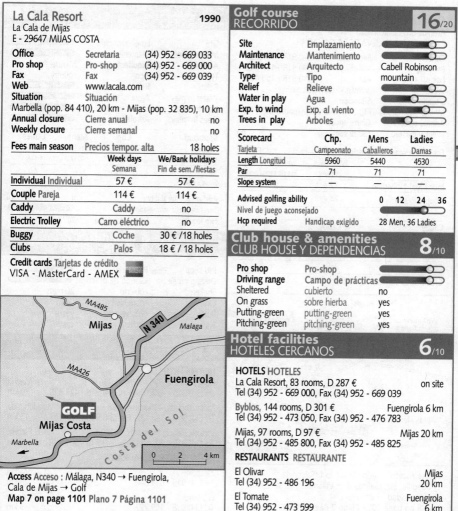

La Cala Resort — **1990**
La Cala de Mijas
E - 29647 MIJAS COSTA

Office	Secretaria	(34) 952 - 669 033
Pro shop	Pro-shop	(34) 952 - 669 000
Fax	Fax	(34) 952 - 669 039
Web	www.lacala.com	
Situation	Situación	

Marbella (pop. 84 410), 20 km - Mijas (pop. 32 835), 10 km

Annual closure	Cierre anual	no
Weekly closure	Cierre semanal	no

Fees main season Precios tempor. alta	18 holes	
	Week days Semana	**We/Bank holidays** Fin de sem./fiestas
Individual Individual	57 €	57 €
Couple Pareja	114 €	114 €
Caddy Caddy	no	
Electric Trolley Carro eléctrico	no	
Buggy Coche	30 € /18 holes	
Clubs Palos	18 € / 18 holes	

Credit cards Tarjetas de crédito
VISA - MasterCard - AMEX

Access Acceso : Málaga, N340 → Fuengirola, Cala de Mijas → Golf
Map 7 on page 1101 Plano 7 Página 1101

Golf course RECORRIDO — 16/20

Site	Emplazamiento	
Maintenance	Mantenimiento	
Architect	Arquitecto	Cabell Robinson
Type	Tipo	mountain
Relief	Relieve	
Water in play	Agua	
Exp. to wind	Exp. al viento	
Trees in play	Arboles	

Scorecard Tarjeta	**Chp.** Campeonato	**Mens** Caballeros	**Ladies** Damas
Length Longitud	5960	5440	4530
Par	71	71	71
Slope system	—	—	—

Advised golfing ability Nivel de juego aconsejado: 0 12 24 36
Hcp required Handicap exigido: 28 Men, 36 Ladies

Club house & amenities CLUB HOUSE Y DEPENDENCIAS — 8/10

Pro shop	Pro-shop	
Driving range	Campo de prácticas	
Sheltered	cubierto	no
On grass	sobre hierba	yes
Putting-green	putting-green	yes
Pitching-green	pitching-green	yes

Hotel facilities HOTELES CERCANOS — 6/10

HOTELS HOTELES

La Cala Resort, 83 rooms, D 287 € — on site
Tel (34) 952 - 669 000, Fax (34) 952 - 669 039

Byblos, 144 rooms, D 301 € — Fuengirola 6 km
Tel (34) 952 - 473 050, Fax (34) 952 - 476 783

Mijas, 97 rooms, D 97 € — Mijas 20 km
Tel (34) 952 - 485 800, Fax (34) 952 - 485 825

RESTAURANTS RESTAURANTE

El Olivar — Mijas 20 km
Tel (34) 952 - 486 196

El Tomate — Fuengirola 6 km
Tel (34) 952 - 473 599

LA DEHESA

14 | 7 | 4

El recorrido de La Dehesa forma parte de un gran complejo concebido para el ocio familiar, siendo igual de agradable para el golfista como para el no golfista, éste último se ve reducido demasiadas veces a ser un mero acompañante durante las vacaciones de golf. Las instalaciones de entrenamiento les permitirá incluso iniciarse en la práctica del golf. A la hora de diseñar el campo, Manuel Piñero pensó en todos los jugadores: es un campo competitivo, pero existen siempre soluciones para salirse de los peligros que encierra. Estos son numerosos durante los 18 hoyos, pero están los suficientemente a la vista para poder decidir rápidamente atacar a ser prudente. Los greenes son suficientemente amplios, bien defendidos, pero agradables de atacar y de jugar. Los espacios muy abiertos, el respeto del entorno existente y las magníficas vistas de la Sierra Madrileña dan al lugar una gran belleza.

The La Dehesa course is part of a large resort designed for family recreation, an equally pleasant spot for golfers and non-golfers alike. On a golfing day, the latter are often left having to accompany their playing partners, but not so here. What's more, the practice facilities might even entice them into having a swing themselves. In designing this course, Manuel Pinero spared a thought for everyone: it is a competitive layout, but there are always solutions for getting around the main difficulties. There is indeed a lot of danger, well spread over the 18 holes, but hazards are visible enough for anyone to decide quickly whether to "go for it" or "lay up". Wide open space, the respect for existing natural beauty and some magnificent views over the Madrid Sierra make this a wonderful spot for golf.

Golf La Dehesa — 1992

Avenida de la Universidad S/N
E - 28691 VILLANUEVA DE LA CAÑADA

Office	Secretaria	(34) 918 - 157 022
Pro shop	Pro-shop	(34) 918 - 157 022
Fax	Fax	(34) 918 - 155 468
Web	www.golfladehesa.com	
Situation	Situación	

Madrid (pop. 3 084 673), 28 km - Brunete (pop. 2 505), 5 km

Annual closure	Cierre anual	no
Weekly closure	Cierre semanal	no

Fees main season Precios tempor. alta	Week days Semana	We/Bank holidays Fin de sem./fiestas
		18 holes
Individual Individual	37 €	97 €
Couple Pareja	74 €	194 €

Caddy	Caddy	no
Electric Trolley	Carro eléctrico	6 € /18 holes
Buggy	Coche	24 € /18 holes
Clubs	Palos	no
Credit cards	Tarjetas de crédito	no

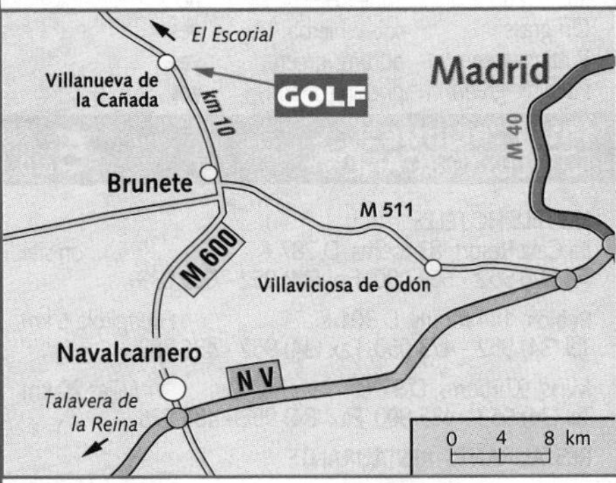

Access Acceso : Madrid M4O, Exit (Salida) 41 → Boadilla. Exit (Salida) 8 → Villanueva de la Cañada → Universidad → Brunete

Map 3 on page 1092 Plano 3 Página 1092

Golf course — RECORRIDO — 14/20

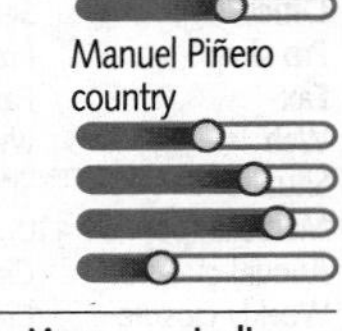

Site	Emplazamiento	
Maintenance	Mantenimiento	
Architect	Arquitecto	Manuel Piñero
Type	Tipo	country
Relief	Relieve	
Water in play	Agua	
Exp. to wind	Exp. al viento	
Trees in play	Arboles	

Scorecard Tarjeta	**Chp.** Campeonato	**Mens** Caballeros	**Ladies** Damas
Length Longitud	6444	6037	5146
Par	72	72	72
Slope system	—	—	—

Advised golfing ability / Nivel de juego aconsejado: 0 12 24 36

Hcp required Handicap exigido: 28 Men, 36 Ladies

Club house & amenities — CLUB HOUSE Y DEPENDENCIAS — 7/10

Pro shop	Pro-shop	
Driving range	Campo de prácticas	
Sheltered	cubierto	20 mats
On grass	sobre hierba	yes
Putting-green	putting-green	yes
Pitching-green	pitching-green	yes

Hotel facilities — HOTELES CERCANOS — 4/10

HOTELS HOTELES

Husa Princesa, 275 rooms, D 236 € — Madrid 30 km
Tel (34) 915 - 422 100, Fax (34) 915 - 427 328

Majadahonda, 41 rooms, D 98 € — Majadahonda 15 km
Tel (34) 916 - 382 122, Fax (34) 916 - 382 157

Victoria Palace, 90 rooms, D 120 € — El Escorial 1 km
Tel (34) 918 - 901 511, Fax (34) 918 - 901 248

RESTAURANTS RESTAURANTE

Zalacain — Madrid 28 km
Tel (34) 915 - 614 840

El Vivero — Brunete 5 km
Tel (34) 918 - 159 222

LA DUQUESA

13 | 7 | 6

Rodeando la colina de El Hacho, verdadero balcón sobre el mar con una magnífica vista sobre Gibraltar, La Duquesa es uno de los múltiples recorridos de Robert Trent Jones en el sur de España. Pero no es el más difícil: los greens están a menudo en alto y algunas veces son ciegos, no con excesivas caídas, hay numerosos bunkers de los que no es difícil salir, las calles a menudo inclinadas pero no con excesivo peligro. Los roughs son tupidos, aunque bien alejados de la calle, los obstáculos de agua poco numerosos (dos lagos), este recorrido permite jugar con toda la familia sin que ningún jugador se sienta "desplazado". A pesar de las numerosas cuestas no es necesario un coche. Gozarán de una cierta ventaja los jugadores con precisión, pero también los buenos pegadores tendrán ocasión de expresarse. La nota baja que damos a este campo es para no defraudar a los fans de RTJ. Es verdad que estamos jugando un Trent Jones, pero el terreno y la realización le han ayudado poco a expresar su arte de hacer campos de golf.

Running right around the El Hacho hill, which provides a balcony over the Mediterranean and a fine view of Gibraltar, La Duquesa is one of a number of courses designed by Robert Trent Jones in the south of Spain. But it is not the most difficult: the greens are often elevated and sometimes blind, but only gently contoured. There are loads of bunkers but they are not too difficult to escape from, the fairways sometimes have a sideways slope, but this is nothing too dangerous. With thick but generally distant rough and only a few water hazards (two lakes), this is a course for all the family without any one player feeling left behind. Despite the slopes, the course is easily playable on foot. Precision play is rewarded but the long-hitters also have good opportunity to swing the driver. For a Robert Trent Jones course, the score may seem a little low. Of course you will always want to play a Trent Jones layout, but the nature of the terrain here seems to have cramped the architect's style and creativity.

Golf & Country Club La Duquesa — 1987

Urb. El Hacho - km. 143,5
E - 29691 MANILVA

Office	Secretaria	(34) 952 - 890 425
Pro shop	Pro-shop	(34) 952 - 890 725
Fax	Fax	(34) 952 - 890 425
Web	www.golfspain.com	
Situation	Situación	

Estepona (pop. 36 307), 15 km - Gibraltar (pop. 28 339), 30 km

Annual closure	Cierre anual	no
Weekly closure	Cierre semanal	no

Fees main season Precios tempor. alta	**Week days** Semana	**We/Bank holidays** Fin de sem./fiestas
		18 holes
Individual Individual	48 €	48 €
Couple Pareja	96 €	96 €

Caddy	Caddy	no
Electric Trolley	Carro eléctrico	no
Buggy	Coche	30 € /18 holes
Clubs	Palos	12 € / 18 holes

Credit cards Tarjetas de crédito
VISA - Eurocard - MasterCard - AMEX

N 340
Estepona
Playa de Estepona
Manilva
San Luis de Sabinillas
La Duquesa
Costa del Sol
Algeciras
GOLF
0 2 4 km

Access Acceso : Estepona N340 → Cadiz, Manilva, Golf
Map 7 on page 1101 Plano 7 Página 1101

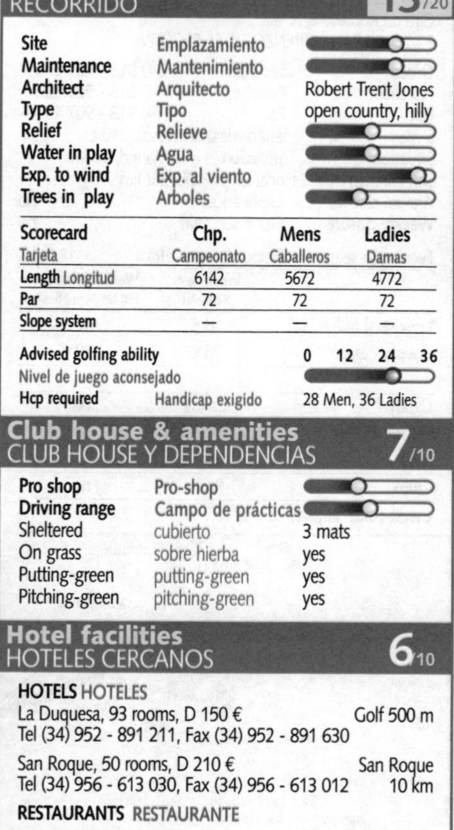

Golf course RECORRIDO — 13/20

Site	Emplazamiento	
Maintenance	Mantenimiento	
Architect	Arquitecto	Robert Trent Jones
Type	Tipo	open country, hilly
Relief	Relieve	
Water in play	Agua	
Exp. to wind	Exp. al viento	
Trees in play	Arboles	

Scorecard Tarjeta	**Chp.** Campeonato	**Mens** Caballeros	**Ladies** Damas
Length Longitud	6142	5672	4772
Par	72	72	72
Slope system	—	—	—

Advised golfing ability Nivel de juego aconsejado: 0 12 24 36
Hcp required Handicap exigido: 28 Men, 36 Ladies

Club house & amenities CLUB HOUSE Y DEPENDENCIAS — 7/10

Pro shop	Pro-shop	
Driving range	Campo de prácticas	
Sheltered	cubierto	3 mats
On grass	sobre hierba	yes
Putting-green	putting-green	yes
Pitching-green	pitching-green	yes

Hotel facilities HOTELES CERCANOS — 6/10

HOTELS HOTELES

La Duquesa, 93 rooms, D 150 € — Golf 500 m
Tel (34) 952 - 891 211, Fax (34) 952 - 891 630

San Roque, 50 rooms, D 210 € — San Roque 10 km
Tel (34) 956 - 613 030, Fax (34) 956 - 613 012

RESTAURANTS RESTAURANTE

Meson del Castillo — Manilva 2 km
Tel (34) 952 - 890 766

Macues — Manilva 2 km
Tel (34) 952 - 890 339

LA HERRERIA

15 | 6 | 6

Es muy raro poder jugar a proximidad de monumentos históricos como el Monasterio de San Lorenzo del Escorial que domina el recorrido. La Herreria es tan espectacular como las vistas que proporciona. En el diseño de Antonio Lucena Gómez los peligros vienen de los árboles y los bunkers, que defienden al mismo las caídas de drive como los greenes, bastante lisos pero a la vez bien moldeados. Estas dificultades no son nunca infranquables sea cual sea el nivel del jugador ya que son muy visibles para permitir adoptar una estrategia que nos permita eludir las malas sorpresas. Si el 2 es un par 5 muy complicado, las vistas panorámicas de los hoyos 12, 13 y 14 permiten reposar el espíritu antes de abordar el hoyo 18, uno de los mejores pares 4 de España... La reciente remodelación de los nueve primeros es el signo del buen mantenimiento que se merece un buen campo a los pies de un gran monumento.

It is rare indeed to be able to swing a club so close to historical landmarks such as the Monasterio de San Lorenzo de El Escorial, which overlooks this course. La Herreria is also one of the truly public courses in the Madrid area, even though private courses are beginning to open up to visitors. The site is as spectacular as the vistas from the course, designed by Antonio Lucena Gomez. The main hazards are the trees and bunkers, guarding both the drive landing zone and the greens, the latter being flat but well shaped. These difficulties are never impossible to negociate, whatever your level of proficiency, and are visible enough to adopt a strategy to avoid unpleasant surprises. While the second hole is a rather complicated par 5, the scenic views from the 12th, 13th and 14 th holes are enough to calm frayed nerves before attacking the 18th, one of the best par 4s in Spain. The recent reshaping of the front nine has underlined a concern to protect the excellence of this course, which lies at the foot of the magnificent landmark el Escorial.

La Herreria Club de Golf — 1968

Ctra de Robledo S/N
E - 28200 SAN LORENZO DE EL ESCORIAL

Office	Secretaria	(34) 918 - 905 111
Pro shop	Pro-shop	(34) 918 - 908 326
Fax	Fax	(34) 918 - 907 154
E-mail	laherreria@clientes.fujitsu.es	
Situation	Situación	Madrid, 57 km

San Lorenzo de El Escorial (pop. 8 704), 2 km

Annual closure	Cierre anual	no
Weekly closure	Cierre semanal	no

Fees main season Precios tempor. alta		18 holes
	Week days Semana	**We/Bank holidays** Fin de sem./fiestas
Individual Individual	48 €	60 €
Couple Pareja	96 €	120 €

Caddy	Caddy	no
Electric Trolley	Carro eléctrico	8 € /18 holes
Buggy	Coche	33 € /18 holes
Clubs	Palos	no
Credit cards	Tarjetas de crédito	no

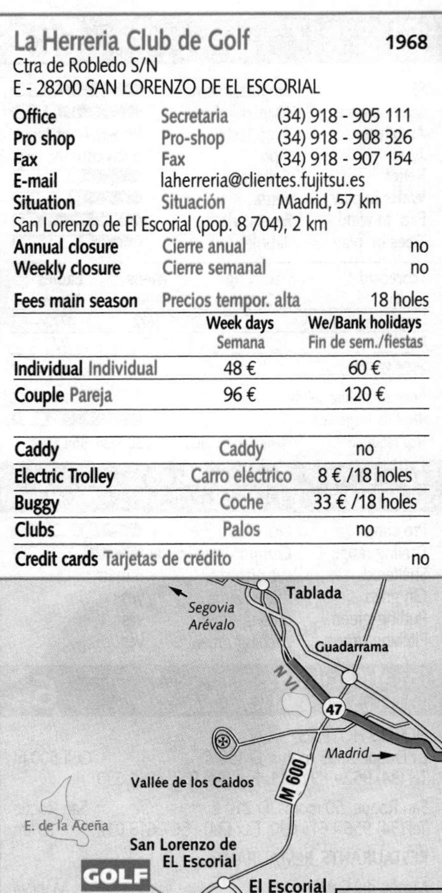

Access Acceso : Madrid A6 → Segovia. Exit (Salida) El Escorial, M600 → San Lorenzo de El Escorial. → Robledo de Chavela, Golf on the left

Map 3 on page 1092 Plano 3 Página 1092

Golf course RECORRIDO — 15/20

Site	Emplazamiento	
Maintenance	Mantenimiento	
Architect	Arquitecto	Ant. Lucena Gomez
Type	Tipo	forest, hilly
Relief	Relieve	
Water in play	Agua	
Exp. to wind	Exp. al viento	
Trees in play	Arboles	

Scorecard Tarjeta	**Chp.** Campeonato	**Mens** Caballeros	**Ladies** Damas
Length Longitud	6050	6050	5121
Par	72	72	72
Slope system	—	—	—

Advised golfing ability Nivel de juego aconsejado: 0 12 24 36

Hcp required Handicap exigido: 28 Men, 36 Ladies

Club house & amenities CLUB HOUSE Y DEPENDENCIAS — 6/10

Pro shop	Pro-shop	
Driving range	Campo de prácticas	
Sheltered	cubierto	no
On grass	sobre hierba	yes
Putting-green	putting-green	yes
Pitching-green	pitching-green	no

Hotel facilities HOTELES CERCANOS — 6/10

HOTELS HOTELES

Victoria Palace, 90 rooms, D 120 € — San Lorenzo 2 km
Tel (34) 918 - 901 511, Fax (34) 918 - 901 248

Cristina, 90 rooms, D 120 € — San Lorenzo
Tel (34) 918 - 901 961, Fax (34) 918 - 901 204

Miranda Suizo, 52 rooms, D 78 € — San Lorenzo
Tel (34) 918 - 904 711, Fax (34) 918 - 904 352

RESTAURANTS RESTAURANTE

Charolés — San Lorenzo
Tel (34) 918 - 905 975

Parilla Principe — San Lorenzo
Tel (34) 918 - 901 611

LA MANGA Norte

15 | 7 | 7

Mucha gente lo prefiere a pesar de ser más corto que el "Sur". No se trata de una oposición sino de subrayar la diversidad de los dos recorridos y permitir pasar de uno a otro según se esté más o menos en forma. El "Norte", aunque mucho más corto, no se le puede considerar como un recorrido fácil ya que exige mucha precisión. Tan bien cuidado como su vecino, la longitud de los hoyos es muy variada y con un poco de intuición no es muy difícil evitar las trampas. Los greens no son muy grandes y están poco protegidos, lo que evita la presión a los los jugadores con poca experiencia. El paisaje es agradable, pero mejor evitarlo en los días de mucho calor en pleno verano. La Manga es una "fábrica" de golf, y aunque hay muchas distracciones deportivas, sin embargo los amantes de cultura y turismo pueden quedar un poco defraudados.

Although much shorter than its "South" sister, the "North" does have its supporters. We won't set out to compare the two, only to emphasise the variety they offer, allowing players to switch from one to the other depending on their game. Although much less long, the "North" can still be a handful because of the emphasis on precision. Generally as well upkept as its neighbour, the course offers considerable variety in the length of holes, but with a little intuition, you can get around the traps. The greens are not huge and not well defended, so they take some of the pressure off inexperienced players. The landscape is pleasant, but the course could hardly be recommended at the height of summer. La Manga is a golfing mega-centre, and while there are many other sports and leisure activities in the area, non-golfing lovers of culture and sightseeing might soon wish they were somewhere else.

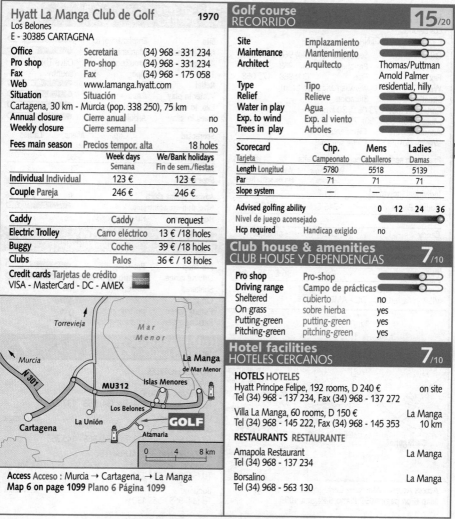

Hyatt La Manga Club de Golf — 1970

Los Belones
E - 30385 CARTAGENA

Office	Secretaria	(34) 968 - 331 234
Pro shop	Pro-shop	(34) 968 - 331 234
Fax	Fax	(34) 968 - 175 058
Web	www.lamanga.hyatt.com	
Situation	Situación	

Cartagena, 30 km - Murcia (pop. 338 250), 75 km

Annual closure	Cierre anual	no
Weekly closure	Cierre semanal	no

Fees main season Precios tempor. alta	18 holes	
	Week days Semana	**We/Bank holidays** Fin de sem./fiestas
Individual Individual	123 €	123 €
Couple Pareja	246 €	246 €

Caddy	Caddy	on request
Electric Trolley	Carro eléctrico	13 € /18 holes
Buggy	Coche	39 € /18 holes
Clubs	Palos	36 € / 18 holes

Credit cards Tarjetas de crédito
VISA - MasterCard - DC - AMEX

Torrevieja
Mar Menor
Murcia
N 301
MU312
La Manga de Mar Menor
Islas Menores
Los Belones
La Unión
Cartagena
GOLF
Atamaria
0 4 8 km

Access Acceso : Murcia → Cartagena, → La Manga
Map 6 on page 1099 Plano 6 Página 1099

Golf course RECORRIDO — 15/20

Site	Emplazamiento	
Maintenance	Mantenimiento	
Architect	Arquitecto	Thomas/Puttman Arnold Palmer
Type	Tipo	residential, hilly
Relief	Relieve	
Water in play	Agua	
Exp. to wind	Exp. al viento	
Trees in play	Arboles	

Scorecard Tarjeta	**Chp.** Campeonato	**Mens** Caballeros	**Ladies** Damas
Length Longitud	5780	5518	5139
Par	71	71	71
Slope system	—	—	—

Advised golfing ability Nivel de juego aconsejado: 0 12 24 36
Hcp required Handicap exigido: no

Club house & amenities CLUB HOUSE Y DEPENDENCIAS — 7/10

Pro shop	Pro-shop	
Driving range	Campo de prácticas	
Sheltered	cubierto	no
On grass	sobre hierba	yes
Putting-green	putting-green	yes
Pitching-green	pitching-green	yes

Hotel facilities HOTELES CERCANOS — 7/10

HOTELS HOTELES

Hyatt Principe Felipe, 192 rooms, D 240 € — on site
Tel (34) 968 - 137 234, Fax (34) 968 - 137 272

Villa La Manga, 60 rooms, D 150 € — La Manga 10 km
Tel (34) 968 - 145 222, Fax (34) 968 - 145 353

RESTAURANTS RESTAURANTE

Amapola Restaurant — La Manga
Tel (34) 968 - 137 234

Borsalino — La Manga
Tel (34) 968 - 563 130

LA MANGA Oeste

14 | 7 | 7

En el complejo golfístico de la Manga, la apertura de un tercer recorrido de 18 hoyos era esperada desde hacía ya mucho tiempo. De hecho se trata de los 9 hoyos existentes desde 1970, rejuvenecidos y completados por Dave Thomas. Los que conocen su trabajo en San Roque encontrarán aquí muchos de los aspectos visuales - sobre todo en la forma de los bunkers - del campo gaditano aunque el conjunto no pretenda igualar ese éxito. La limitacíon del espacio ha influido en ello, lo que ha motivado que el arquitécto haya preferido hacer un campo más corto pero a la voz más técnico. Los nueve últimos hoyos son muy acidentados, más que los primeros, pero caminar por ellos no es complicado. Arboles y arbustos han sido habilmente colocados así como tres lagos. Los pares 3 son bastante largos, y si los pegadores pueden aspirar a tocar los pares 5 de dos, también pueden aspirar al birdie en algunos pares 4 muy cortos. Un tanto difícil para los jugadores poco experimentados, este recorrido es muy divertido para los buenos jugadores.

The opening of a third 18-hole course at La Manga golf resort had been awaited for some time. It is in fact an extension of an existing 9-holer built in 1970, rejuvenated and completed by Dave Thomas. If you know his course at San Roque, you will recognise several of the same visual aspects here, notably in the shape of the bunkers, but the course as a whole is not quite in the same class. There was less space to play with, so the architect preferred to create a rather short, but nonetheless very technical layout. The back 9 are a little hillier than the rest of the course, although walking is never an ordeal. Trees and thickets have been cleverly brought into play, as have three lakes. The par 3s are on the long side, and while long-hitters will attempt to reach the par 5s in two, they can also hope for the elusive birdie on some very short par 4s. A course that is a little difficult for learners, but great fun for the better players.

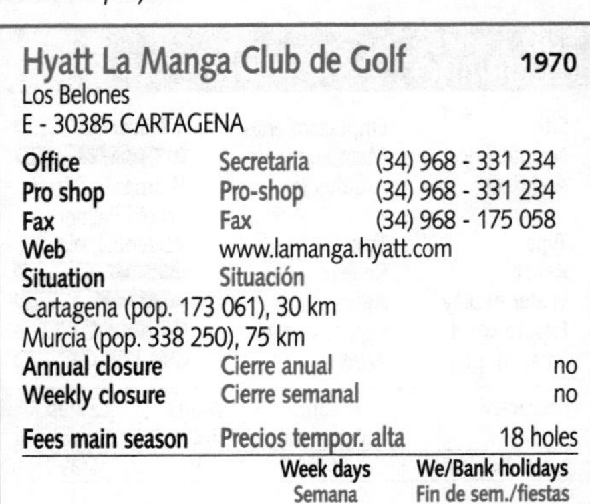

Hyatt La Manga Club de Golf — 1970

Los Belones
E - 30385 CARTAGENA

Office	Secretaria	(34) 968 - 331 234
Pro shop	Pro-shop	(34) 968 - 331 234
Fax	Fax	(34) 968 - 175 058
Web	www.lamanga.hyatt.com	
Situation	Situación	

Cartagena (pop. 173 061), 30 km
Murcia (pop. 338 250), 75 km

Annual closure	Cierre anual	no
Weekly closure	Cierre semanal	no

Fees main season Precios tempor. alta — 18 holes

	Week days Semana	We/Bank holidays Fin de sem./fiestas
Individual Individual	123 €	123 €
Couple Pareja	246 €	246 €

Caddy	Caddy	on request
Electric Trolley	Carro eléctrico	13 € /18 holes
Buggy	Coche	39 € /18 holes
Clubs	Palos	36 € / 18 holes

Credit cards Tarjetas de crédito
VISA - MasterCard - DC - AMEX

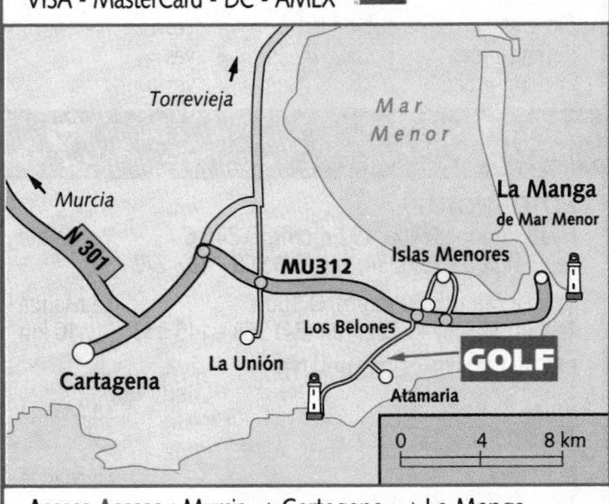

Access Acceso : Murcia → Cartagena, → La Manga
Map 6 on page 1099 Plano 6 Página 1099

Golf course RECORRIDO — 14/20

Site	Emplazamiento	
Maintenance	Mantenimiento	
Architect	Arquitecto	Dave Thomas
Type	Tipo	country
Relief	Relieve	
Water in play	Agua	
Exp. to wind	Exp. al viento	
Trees in play	Arboles	

Scorecard Tarjeta	Chp. Campeonato	Mens Caballeros	Ladies Damas
Length Longitud	5971	5680	4922
Par	73	73	73
Slope system	—	—	—

Advised golfing ability Nivel de juego aconsejado — 0 12 24 36

Hcp required Handicap exigido — no

Club house & amenities CLUB HOUSE Y DEPENDENCIAS — 7/10

Pro shop	Pro-shop	
Driving range	Campo de prácticas	
Sheltered	cubierto	no
On grass	sobre hierba	yes
Putting-green	putting-green	yes
Pitching-green	pitching-green	yes

Hotel facilities HOTELES CERCANOS — 7/10

HOTELS HOTELES

Hyatt Principe Felipe, — on site
192 rooms, D 240 €
Tel (34) 968 - 137 234, Fax (34) 968 - 137 272

Villa La Manga — La Manga 10 km
60 rooms, D 150 €
Tel (34) 968 - 145 222, Fax (34) 968 - 145 353

RESTAURANTS RESTAURANTE

Amapola Restaurant — La Manga
Tel (34) 968 - 137 234

Borsalino — La Manga
Tel (34) 968 - 563 130

LA MANGA Sur

15 | 7 | 7

El complejo de La Manga es desde hace mucho tiempo uno de los más famosos de España con construcciones immobiliarias que no todos apreciarán. El recorrido "Sur" es el más largo y sin duda el más franco, aunque sea necesario juagarlo varias veces para impregnarse de sus sutilezas. Arnold Palmer ha modificado, con gran acierto, el diseño original mejorando su aspecto visual y acentuando una estética de carácter americano, aunque bien es verdad que hubiera podido diseñar mejor tanto los bunkers como los greens. Hay muchos obstáculos de agua pequeños, especialmente en el 17 y el 18. La longitud de este recorrido es un excelente test: si logra jugar su handicap querrá decir que posee un juego muy completo. Sin que sea una obra maestra y teniendo en cuenta el lugar, es un recorrido que no se debe ignorar.

La Manga has long been one of Spain's most famous resorts and a site for real estate property development that is not to everyone's taste. The "South" course is the longest and certainly the most open, even though you need several rounds to understand the more subtle sides to it. Arnold Palmer made a few welcome visual changes to the original layout, emphasising the American style design, but the great man's restyling was unable to hide the fact that the bunkers and greens could have been redesigned better. The course is dotted with little water hazards, especially on the 17th and 18th holes. The length of the course makes it a good test, and if you play to your handicap, you will have shown good all-round skills and versatility. This is not your actual masterpiece, but the facilities on site make this a course not to be missed.

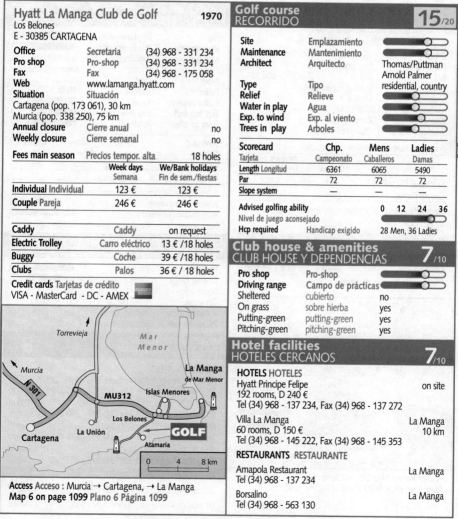

Hyatt La Manga Club de Golf — 1970

Los Belones
E - 30385 CARTAGENA

Office	Secretaria	(34) 968 - 331 234
Pro shop	Pro-shop	(34) 968 - 331 234
Fax	Fax	(34) 968 - 175 058
Web	www.lamanga.hyatt.com	
Situation	Situación	

Cartagena (pop. 173 061), 30 km
Murcia (pop. 338 250), 75 km

Annual closure	Cierre anual	no
Weekly closure	Cierre semanal	no

Fees main season Precios tempor. alta		18 holes
	Week days Semana	**We/Bank holidays** Fin de sem./fiestas
Individual Individual	123 €	123 €
Couple Pareja	246 €	246 €

Caddy	Caddy	on request
Electric Trolley	Carro eléctrico	13 € /18 holes
Buggy	Coche	39 € /18 holes
Clubs	Palos	36 € / 18 holes

Credit cards Tarjetas de crédito
VISA - MasterCard - DC - AMEX

Torrevieja
Mar Menor
Murcia
N 301
La Manga de Mar Menor
MU312
Islas Menores
Los Belones
La Unión
Cartagena
GOLF
Atamaria
0 4 8 km

Access Acceso : Murcia → Cartagena, → La Manga
Map 6 on page 1099 Plano 6 Página 1099

Golf course RECORRIDO — 15/20

Site	Emplazamiento	
Maintenance	Mantenimiento	
Architect	Arquitecto	Thomas/Puttman Arnold Palmer
Type	Tipo	residential, country
Relief	Relieve	
Water in play	Agua	
Exp. to wind	Exp. al viento	
Trees in play	Arboles	

Scorecard Tarjeta	**Chp.** Campeonato	**Mens** Caballeros	**Ladies** Damas
Length Longitud	6361	6065	5490
Par	72	72	72
Slope system	—	—	—

Advised golfing ability 0 12 24 36
Nivel de juego aconsejado
Hcp required Handicap exigido — 28 Men, 36 Ladies

Club house & amenities CLUB HOUSE Y DEPENDENCIAS — 7/10

Pro shop	Pro-shop	
Driving range	Campo de prácticas	
Sheltered	cubierto	no
On grass	sobre hierba	yes
Putting-green	putting-green	yes
Pitching-green	pitching-green	yes

Hotel facilities HOTELES CERCANOS — 7/10

HOTELS HOTELES

Hyatt Principe Felipe — on site
192 rooms, D 240 €
Tel (34) 968 - 137 234, Fax (34) 968 - 137 272

Villa La Manga — La Manga 10 km
60 rooms, D 150 €
Tel (34) 968 - 145 222, Fax (34) 968 - 145 353

RESTAURANTS RESTAURANTE

Amapola Restaurant — La Manga
Tel (34) 968 - 137 234

Borsalino — La Manga
Tel (34) 968 - 563 130

LA MORALEJA La Moraleja 1

15 | 7 | 8

En la época de la construcción de éste campo (como de Muirfield Village en los Estados Unidos), Jack Nicklaus trabajada con Desmond Muirhead, uno de los arquitéctos más originales de éste siglo, y uno de los menos orientados sobre la longitud a cualquier precio. Si La Moraleja 1 es bastante corto, exige la máxima precisión si se quiere conseguir un buen resultado, sobre todo porque los greenes son bastante pequeños, muy ondulados, rápidos y muy bien defendidos. Si se les quiere atacar en buena posición, es importante colocar correctamente el drive, lo que no siempre es fácil, y mucha lucidez a la hora de seleccionar el palo: sobre los 4 pares 4 cortos será recomendable jugar un hierro de salida. Los pegadores impenitentes podrán intentar los más posible de los greenes, o atacar de dos los pares 5, sobre todo en match-play ya que los peligros son constantes. Un campo muy divertido sin ser por ello una obra maestra inolvidable.

When building this course (the same goes for Muirfield Village in the United States), Jack Nicklaus was working with Desmond Muirhead, one of the most original course designers of our day, and one who doesn't go for length at any price. While La Moraleja 1 is on the short side, it demands extreme accuracy for a good card, especially since the greens are only average in size, steeply contoured, quick and very well guarded. To be in the right position to make your approach, the drive has to be exactly in the right place, a feat that is not always so easy and one that demands clear-headed club selection. On the four very short par 4s, for example, you are best advised to use a long iron. Incorrigible big-hitters can attempt to get as close as possible to the green and also reach the par 5s in two, at least in match-play, the ideal formula given the profusion of dangerous hazards. A very amusing course, but hardly an unforgettable master-piece.

Golf La Moraleja — 1976

Paseo Marquesa Viuda de Aldana, 50
E - 28109 LA MORALEJA-MADRID

Office	Secretaria	(34) 916 - 500 700
Pro shop	Pro-shop	(34) 916 - 507 018
Fax	Fax	(34) 916 - 504 331
Web	www.golfspain.com	
Situation	Situación	

Madrid (pop. 3 084 673), 12 km

Annual closure	Cierre anual	no
Weekly closure	Cierre semanal	no

Fees main season Precios tempor. alta	Week days Semana	We/Bank holidays Fin de sem./fiestas
		18 holes
Individual Individual	48 €	120 €
Couple Pareja	96 €	240 €

member's guests only (solo invitados de socios)

Caddy	Caddy	no
Electric Trolley	Carro eléctrico	6 € /18 holes
Buggy	Coche	25 € /18 holes
Clubs	Palos	12 € / 18 holes
Credit cards	Tarjetas de crédito	no

Access Acceso : Madrid → Burgos
Map 3 on page 1092 Plano 3 Página 1092

Golf course RECORRIDO — 15/20

Site	Emplazamiento	
Maintenance	Mantenimiento	
Architect	Arquitecto	Jack Nicklaus, Desmond Muirhead
Type	Tipo	country
Relief	Relieve	
Water in play	Agua	
Exp. to wind	Exp. al viento	
Trees in play	Arboles	

Scorecard Tarjeta	**Chp.** Campeonato	**Mens** Caballeros	**Ladies** Damas
Length Longitud	5992	5706	4937
Par	72	72	72
Slope system	—	—	—

Advised golfing ability Nivel de juego aconsejado: 0 12 24 36
Hcp required Handicap exigido: member's guests only

Club house & amenities CLUB HOUSE Y DEPENDENCIAS — 7/10

Pro shop	Pro-shop	
Driving range	Campo de prácticas	
Sheltered	cubierto	no
On grass	sobre hierba	no (30 mats)
Putting-green	putting-green	yes
Pitching-green	pitching-green	no

Hotel facilities HOTELES CERCANOS — 8/10

HOTELS HOTELES

Novotel-Campo de las Naciones, 246 rooms, D 126 €
Tel (34) 917 - 211 818, Fax (34) 917 - 211 122 — 600 m

Sofitel, 179 rooms, D 246 € — 100 m
Tel (34) 917 - 210 070, Fax (34) 917 - 210 515

Melia Castilla, 900 rooms, D 230 € — Madrid
Tel (34) 915 - 675 000, Fax (34) 915 - 675 051 — 10 km

Aristos, 24 rooms, D 144 € — Madrid
Tel (34) 913 - 450 450, Fax (34) 913 - 451 023

RESTAURANTS RESTAURANTE

Zalacain, Tel (34) 915 - 614 840 — Madrid

Principe de Viana, Tel (34) 914 - 571 549 — Madrid

LA MORALEJA La Moraleja 2

16	7	8

Este segundo recorrido del gran club de La Moraleja ha sido diseñado por los arquitéctos asociados a Jack Nicklaus. Este no lo ha firmado, pero su influencia sobre sus colaboradores se deja sentir. Los greenes son de grand tamaño, y los tres putts no son raros, sobre todo si se está alejado de la bandera. Es entonces cuando las numerosas caídas y la rapidez de la superficie exigen una gran concentración en la lectura del green y mucho toque. Están bien protegidos por el agua, por árboles, por unos bunkers muy dibujados, sobre todo en el 9 y 18, cuando protegen éste doble green. La primera mitad es tal vez menos impresionante pero ello no significa ni mucho menos que se deba bajar la guardia. Hay que estar alerta los 18 hoyos puesto que las dificultades surgen cuando uno menos se lo espera. La estrategia de juego en función de la forma del momento juega pues un papel determinante. Tiene que conocerse aunque se deben evitar los fines de semana.

This second golf course on the Club La Moraleja was designed by architects associated with Jack Nicklaus, and although not carrying his signature, the great man evidently had some influence on his partners. The greens are huge and three-putts not an uncommon occurrence, especially if you are nowhere near the pin, as the numerous slopes and speed of the putting surfaces call for careful reading and a delicate touch. They are often well-guarded by water, sometimes by trees and by well-designed bunkers, especially on the 9th and 18th holes, which share a double green. The first half of the course is less intimidating, but that doesn't mean you can take things easy. Stay on your toes the whole time, because the difficulties here crop up when you least expect them. As a result, game strategy, depending on the shape of your game, plays a significant role. Well worth knowing, but avoid week-ends.

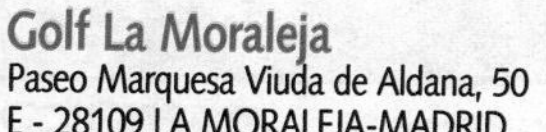

Golf La Moraleja

Paseo Marquesa Viuda de Aldana, 50
E - 28109 LA MORALEJA-MADRID

Office	Secretaria	(34) 916 - 500 700
Pro shop	Pro-shop	(34) 916 - 507 018
Fax	Fax	(34) 916 - 504 331
Web	www.golfspain.com	
Situation	Situación	
Madrid (pop. 3 084 673), 12 km		
Annual closure	Cierre anual	no
Weekly closure	Cierre semanal	no

Fees main season Precios tempor. alta		18 holes
	Week days Semana	**We/Bank holidays** Fin de sem./fiestas
Individual Individual	48 €	120 €
Couple Pareja	96 €	240 €
member's guests only (solo invitados de socios)		

Caddy	Caddy	no
Electric Trolley	Carro eléctrico	6 € /18 holes
Buggy	Coche	25 € /18 holes
Clubs	Palos	12 € / 18 holes
Credit cards Tarjetas de crédito		no

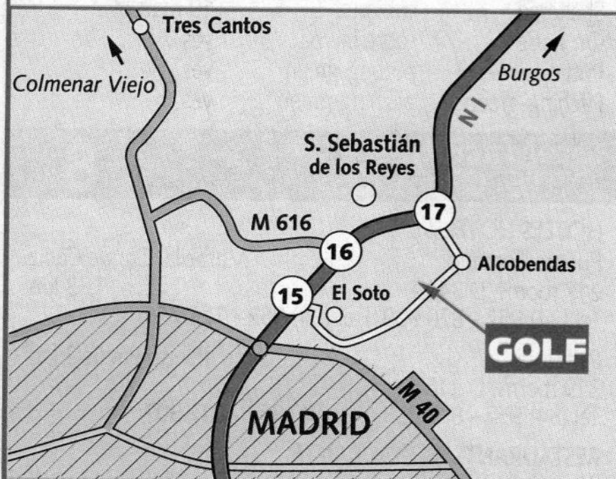

Access Acceso : Madrid → Burgos
Map 3 on page 1092 Plano 3 Página 1092

Golf course RECORRIDO 16/20

Site	Emplazamiento	
Maintenance	Mantenimiento	
Architect	Arquitecto	Golden Bear Design Associates
Type	Tipo	country
Relief	Relieve	
Water in play	Agua	
Exp. to wind	Exp. al viento	
Trees in play	Arboles	

Scorecard Tarjeta	**Chp.** Campeonato	**Mens** Caballeros	**Ladies** Damas
Length Longitud	6451	5888	5014
Par	72	72	72
Slope system	—	—	—

Advised golfing ability Nivel de juego aconsejado — 0 12 24 36
Hcp required Handicap exigido — member's guests only

Club house & amenities CLUB HOUSE Y DEPENDENCIAS 7/10

Pro shop	Pro-shop	
Driving range	Campo de prácticas	
Sheltered	cubierto	no
On grass	sobre hierba	no (30 mats)
Putting-green	putting-green	yes
Pitching-green	pitching-green	no

Hotel facilities HOTELES CERCANOS 8/10

HOTELS HOTELES

Novotel-Campo de las Naciones, 246 rooms, D 126 € Tel (34) 917 - 211 818, Fax (34) 917 - 211 122	600 m
Sofitel, 179 rooms, D 246 € Tel (34) 917 - 210 070, Fax (34) 917 - 210 515	100 m
Melia Castilla, 900 rooms, D 230 € Tel (34) 915 - 675 000, Fax (34) 915 - 675 051	Madrid 10 km
Aristos, 24 rooms, D 144 € Tel (34) 913 - 450 450, Fax (34) 913 - 451 023	Madrid

RESTAURANTS RESTAURANTE

Zalacain, Tel (34) 915 - 614 840	Madrid
El Olivo, Tel (34) 913 - 591 535	Madrid

LA QUINTA

14 | 8 | 8

Dos grandes campeones, Antonio Garrido y Manuel Piñero, han diseñado uno de los recorridos más técnicos de la región , con un total de 27 hoyos, siendo la combinación de "San Pedro" y de "Guadaiza" la más larga. Como las distancias no son excesivas, los jugadores precisos se encontrarán más agusto que los pegadores a pesar de que las zonas de caída del drive sean anchas y los tees de salida a menudo en alto. Hay dificultades de todas clases : árboles, bunkers de green, ríos y lagos no siempre a la vista. El relieve es bastante accidentado, sin que sea exagerado, lo que complica la apreciación de los aproches: conviene tirar a bandera para evitar los putts largos ya que las caídas de green son difíciles de apreciar. No todo el mundo apreciará el entorno inmobiliario (cosa inevitable en la región) escondido parcialmente por la vegetación de este gran jardín.

Two top champions, Antonio Garrido and Manuel Pinero, designed this, one of the region's most technical golf courses comprising 27 holes. The "San Pedro" and "Guadaiza" together form the longest 18-hole combination. Not being over-long, accurate players will probably feel more at home than the big hitters, even though the landing areas for drives are pretty wide and the tees often elevated. There are all kinds of hazards here, from trees to green-side bunkers to rivers and lakes, and they are not always very visible. This is pretty hilly terrain, a factor which complicates the approach shot. It is also important to go for the pin to avoid over-long putts, as the greens are tricky to read. The property development surroundings are not to everyone's liking but are unavoidable in this part of the world and are partly concealed by the trees.

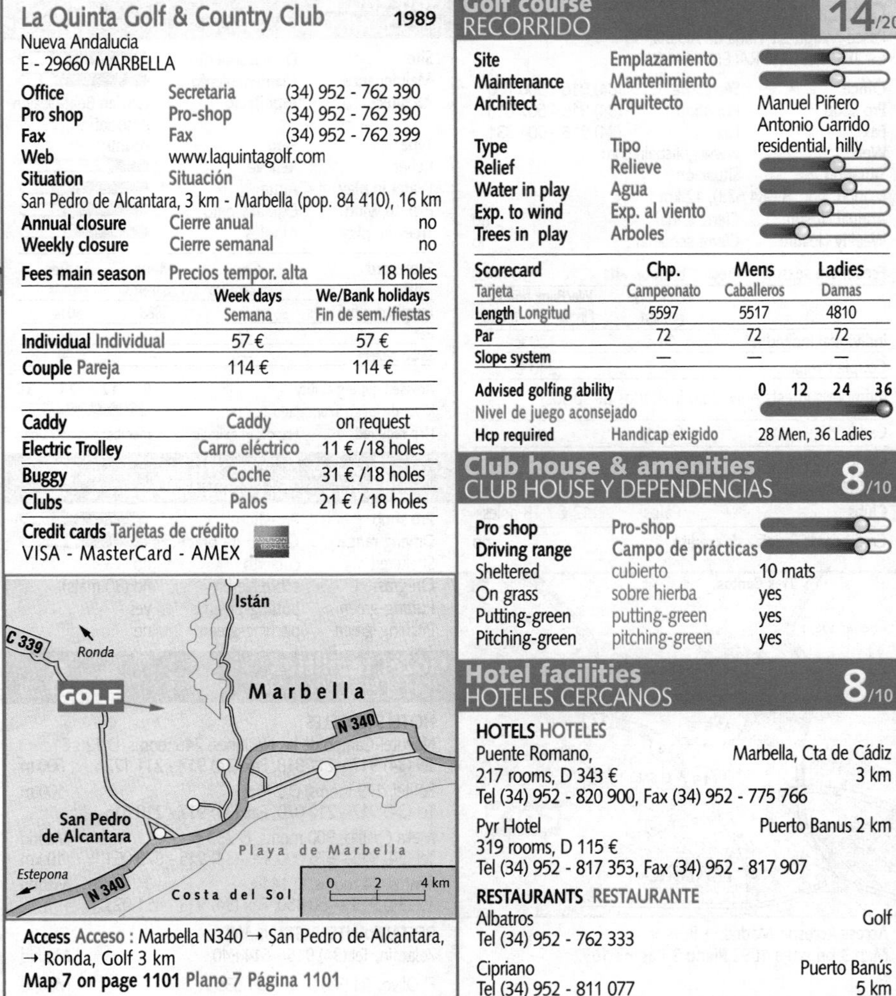

La Quinta Golf & Country Club 1989

Nueva Andalucia
E - 29660 MARBELLA

Office	Secretaria	(34) 952 - 762 390
Pro shop	Pro-shop	(34) 952 - 762 390
Fax	Fax	(34) 952 - 762 399
Web	www.laquintagolf.com	
Situation	Situación	

San Pedro de Alcantara, 3 km - Marbella (pop. 84 410), 16 km

Annual closure	Cierre anual	no
Weekly closure	Cierre semanal	no

Fees main season Precios tempor. alta	**Week days** Semana	**We/Bank holidays** Fin de sem./fiestas
		18 holes
Individual Individual	57 €	57 €
Couple Pareja	114 €	114 €

Caddy	Caddy	on request
Electric Trolley	Carro eléctrico	11 € /18 holes
Buggy	Coche	31 € /18 holes
Clubs	Palos	21 € / 18 holes

Credit cards Tarjetas de crédito
VISA - MasterCard - AMEX

Access Acceso : Marbella N340 → San Pedro de Alcantara, → Ronda, Golf 3 km
Map 7 on page 1101 Plano 7 Página 1101

Golf course RECORRIDO 14/20

Site	Emplazamiento	
Maintenance	Mantenimiento	
Architect	Arquitecto	Manuel Piñero Antonio Garrido
Type	Tipo	residential, hilly
Relief	Relieve	
Water in play	Agua	
Exp. to wind	Exp. al viento	
Trees in play	Arboles	

Scorecard Tarjeta	**Chp.** Campeonato	**Mens** Caballeros	**Ladies** Damas
Length Longitud	5597	5517	4810
Par	72	72	72
Slope system	—	—	—

Advised golfing ability Nivel de juego aconsejado — 0 12 24 36

Hcp required Handicap exigido — 28 Men, 36 Ladies

Club house & amenities CLUB HOUSE Y DEPENDENCIAS 8/10

Pro shop	Pro-shop	
Driving range	Campo de prácticas	
Sheltered	cubierto	10 mats
On grass	sobre hierba	yes
Putting-green	putting-green	yes
Pitching-green	pitching-green	yes

Hotel facilities HOTELES CERCANOS 8/10

HOTELS HOTELES

Puente Romano, — Marbella, Cta de Cádiz 3 km
217 rooms, D 343 €
Tel (34) 952 - 820 900, Fax (34) 952 - 775 766

Pyr Hotel — Puerto Banus 2 km
319 rooms, D 115 €
Tel (34) 952 - 817 353, Fax (34) 952 - 817 907

RESTAURANTS RESTAURANTE

Albatros — Golf
Tel (34) 952 - 762 333

Cipriano — Puerto Banús 5 km
Tel (34) 952 - 811 077

LA SELLA

15 | 6 | 5

Situado en la falda de una montaña no es un recorrido excesivamente cansado, pero en pleno verano es mejor alquilar un coche. De longitud moderada, si se domina con maestría todos los palos se puede lograr un buen resultado. Pinos, naranjos, olivos y almendros le dan un cierto colorido y suponen muchos problemas para jugadores sin precisión. Con una arquitectura bastante personal, La Sella demuestra que sus creadores conocían muy bien toda la gama de jugadores, adaptando las dificulta¨des a los diferentes tees de salida. Efectivamente, Juan de la Cuadra lo diseñó con la experta ayuda de José María Olazabal. Si se falla la llegada a green, habrá que emplear toda la virtuosidad del campeón español para salvar el par.... La Sella es uno de los buenos golfs de la región.

Although laid out on the side of a mountain, the course can be walked, although a buggy is advisable in mid-summer to get a bit of air. La Sella is not too long, but if all your clubs are in good working order, a good score should not be beyond you. The pine, orange, olive and almond trees bring a touch of colour and relief, and sometimes a number of problems for wayward hitters. A very personal design, La Sella shows how much the architects knew about players of all ability, as difficulties are geared to the different tees. Not surprisingly, the course was laid out by Juan de la Cuadra, expertly assisted by José-Maria Olazabal. If you miss the greens, you will need some of the Spanish champion's virtuosity to save par. La Sella is a good address in the region.

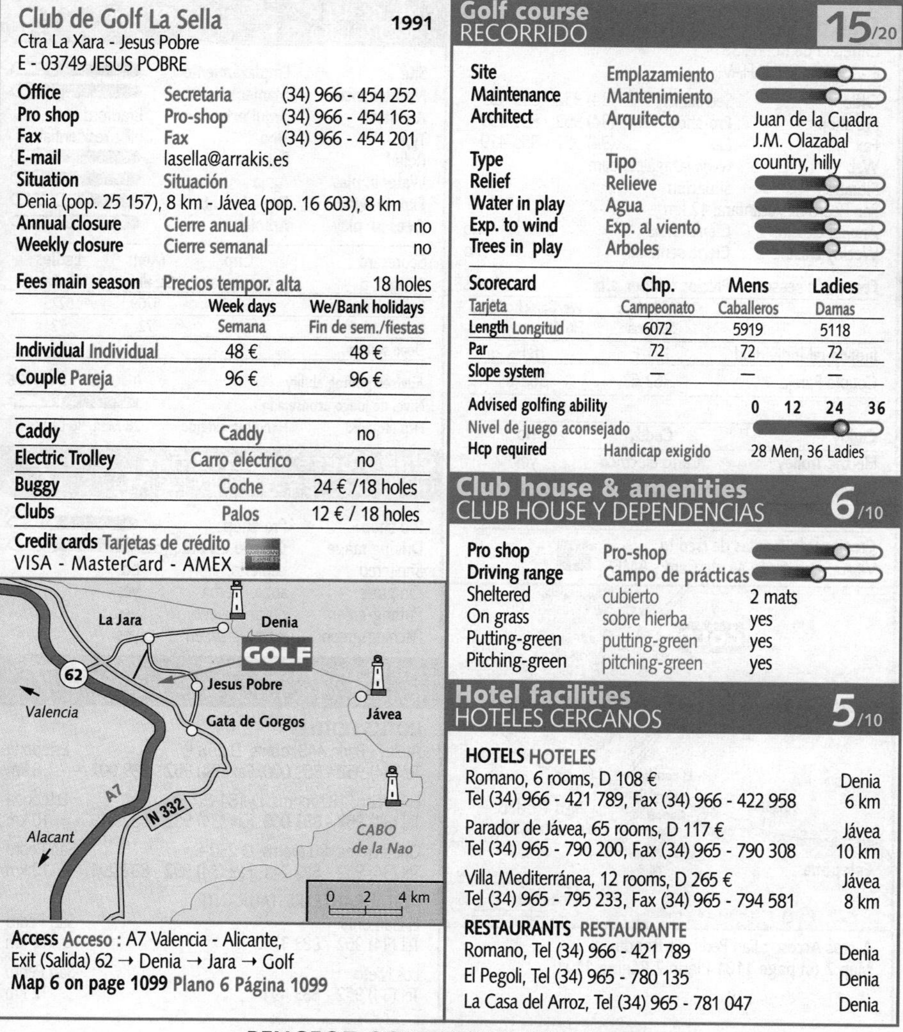

Club de Golf La Sella — **1991**
Ctra La Xara - Jesus Pobre
E - 03749 JESUS POBRE

Office	Secretaria	(34) 966 - 454 252
Pro shop	Pro-shop	(34) 966 - 454 163
Fax	Fax	(34) 966 - 454 201
E-mail	lasella@arrakis.es	
Situation	Situación	

Denia (pop. 25 157), 8 km - Jávea (pop. 16 603), 8 km

Annual closure	Cierre anual	no
Weekly closure	Cierre semanal	no

Fees main season Precios tempor. alta	**Week days** Semana	**We/Bank holidays** Fin de sem./fiestas
	18 holes	
Individual Individual	48 €	48 €
Couple Pareja	96 €	96 €

Caddy	Caddy	no
Electric Trolley	Carro eléctrico	no
Buggy	Coche	24 € /18 holes
Clubs	Palos	12 € / 18 holes

Credit cards Tarjetas de crédito
VISA - MasterCard - AMEX

Access Acceso : A7 Valencia - Alicante,
Exit (Salida) 62 → Denia → Jara → Golf
Map 6 on page 1099 Plano 6 Página 1099

Golf course RECORRIDO — 15/20

Site	Emplazamiento	
Maintenance	Mantenimiento	
Architect	Arquitecto	Juan de la Cuadra J.M. Olazabal
Type	Tipo	country, hilly
Relief	Relieve	
Water in play	Agua	
Exp. to wind	Exp. al viento	
Trees in play	Arboles	

Scorecard Tarjeta	**Chp.** Campeonato	**Mens** Caballeros	**Ladies** Damas
Length Longitud	6072	5919	5118
Par	72	72	72
Slope system	—	—	—

Advised golfing ability Nivel de juego aconsejado — 0 12 24 36
Hcp required Handicap exigido — 28 Men, 36 Ladies

Club house & amenities CLUB HOUSE Y DEPENDENCIAS — 6/10

Pro shop	Pro-shop	
Driving range	Campo de prácticas	
Sheltered	cubierto	2 mats
On grass	sobre hierba	yes
Putting-green	putting-green	yes
Pitching-green	pitching-green	yes

Hotel facilities HOTELES CERCANOS — 5/10

HOTELS HOTELES

Romano, 6 rooms, D 108 € Tel (34) 966 - 421 789, Fax (34) 966 - 422 958	Denia 6 km
Parador de Jávea, 65 rooms, D 117 € Tel (34) 965 - 790 200, Fax (34) 965 - 790 308	Jávea 10 km
Villa Mediterránea, 12 rooms, D 265 € Tel (34) 965 - 795 233, Fax (34) 965 - 794 581	Jávea 8 km

RESTAURANTS RESTAURANTE

Romano, Tel (34) 966 - 421 789	Denia
El Pegoli, Tel (34) 965 - 780 135	Denia
La Casa del Arroz, Tel (34) 965 - 781 047	Denia

LA ZAGALETA

16 | 7 | 7

Es un recorrido muy privado, merece la pena esforzarse en conocer algún socio para que le inviten a jugar. Es aconsejable coger un coche ya que los desnivelaciones son grandes: es casi un recorrido de montaña, situado a menos de diez kilómetros de la Costa del Sol. Hay que jugar sin miedo a perder bolas, evitar los barrancos y sobrevolar bastantes obstáculos de agua. No obstante, cualquier jugador (no los principiantes!) puede adaptarse al recorrido utilizando uno de los muchos tees de salida construidos por el arquitecto. La estética es bastante americana, un poco similar a ciertos recorridos de California del Sur. Las calles son bastante anchas, los greens muy amplios, con caídas y rápidos. El mantenimiento es de muy buena calidad, cosa no muy difícil de obtener dado el limitado número de jugadores.

A very private course but one which is worth the effort involved in getting to know members well enough to be invited. They will certainly recommend a buggy because there is some steep climbing to do on what is almost a mountain style course, less than 7 miles from the Costa del Sol. Here you should not be too afraid of losing balls, just make sure you avoid the ravines and lift the ball over the many water hazards. Despite these obvious pitfalls, players of all levels (but not beginners) can play here because there are so many different tee-boxes. The style is definitely American and rather similar to some of the courses in southern California. The fairways are wide and the greens large, often multi-tiered, slick and fast. An emphatic word, too, for the excellence of green-keeping, perhaps a task made easier when there are so few players out on the course.

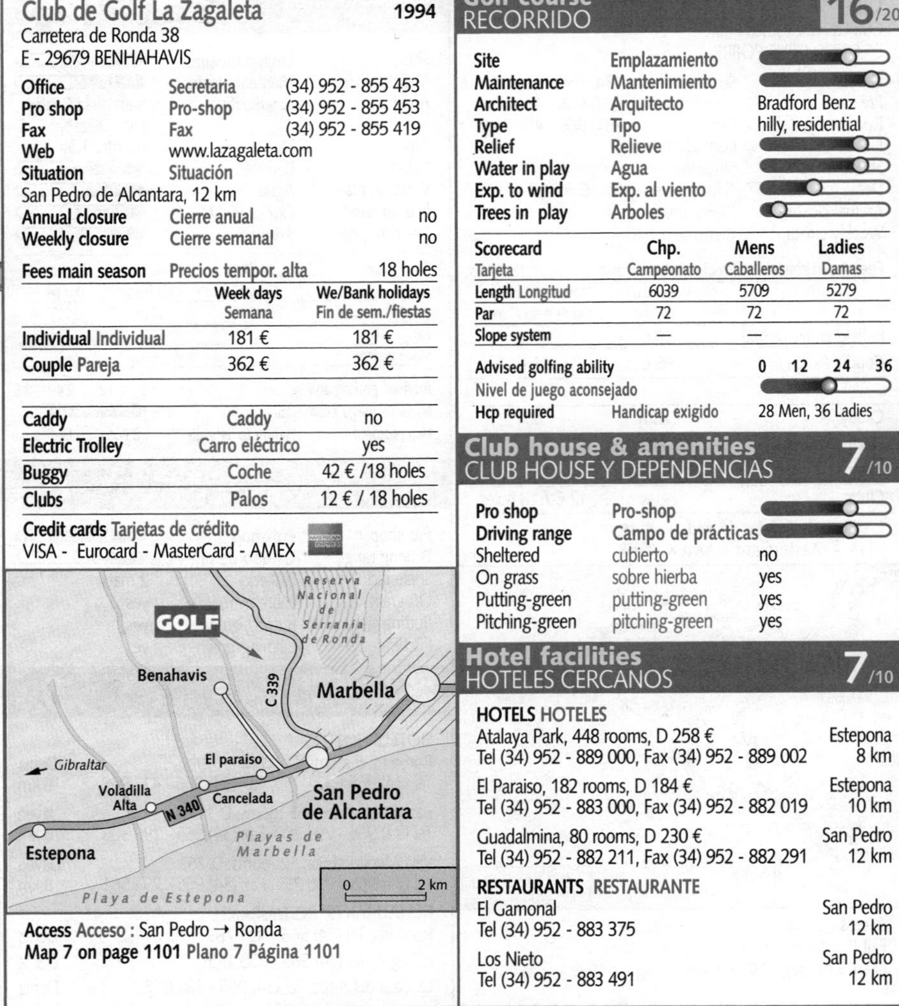

Club de Golf La Zagaleta — 1994

Carretera de Ronda 38
E - 29679 BENHAHAVIS

Office	Secretaria	(34) 952 - 855 453
Pro shop	Pro-shop	(34) 952 - 855 453
Fax	Fax	(34) 952 - 855 419
Web	www.lazagaleta.com	
Situation	Situación	
San Pedro de Alcantara, 12 km		
Annual closure	Cierre anual	no
Weekly closure	Cierre semanal	no

Fees main season Precios tempor. alta — 18 holes

	Week days Semana	We/Bank holidays Fin de sem./fiestas
Individual Individual	181 €	181 €
Couple Pareja	362 €	362 €

Caddy	Caddy	no
Electric Trolley	Carro eléctrico	yes
Buggy	Coche	42 € /18 holes
Clubs	Palos	12 € / 18 holes

Credit cards Tarjetas de crédito
VISA - Eurocard - MasterCard - AMEX

Access Acceso : San Pedro → Ronda
Map 7 on page 1101 Plano 7 Página 1101

Golf course RECORRIDO — 16/20

Site	Emplazamiento	
Maintenance	Mantenimiento	
Architect	Arquitecto	Bradford Benz
Type	Tipo	hilly, residential
Relief	Relieve	
Water in play	Agua	
Exp. to wind	Exp. al viento	
Trees in play	Arboles	

Scorecard Tarjeta	**Chp.** Campeonato	**Mens** Caballeros	**Ladies** Damas
Length Longitud	6039	5709	5279
Par	72	72	72
Slope system	—	—	—

Advised golfing ability Nivel de juego aconsejado — 0 12 24 36

Hcp required Handicap exigido — 28 Men, 36 Ladies

Club house & amenities CLUB HOUSE Y DEPENDENCIAS — 7/10

Pro shop	Pro-shop	
Driving range	Campo de prácticas	
Sheltered	cubierto	no
On grass	sobre hierba	yes
Putting-green	putting-green	yes
Pitching-green	pitching-green	yes

Hotel facilities HOTELES CERCANOS — 7/10

HOTELS HOTELES

Atalaya Park, 448 rooms, D 258 € Tel (34) 952 - 889 000, Fax (34) 952 - 889 002	Estepona 8 km
El Paraiso, 182 rooms, D 184 € Tel (34) 952 - 883 000, Fax (34) 952 - 882 019	Estepona 10 km
Guadalmina, 80 rooms, D 230 € Tel (34) 952 - 882 211, Fax (34) 952 - 882 291	San Pedro 12 km

RESTAURANTS RESTAURANTE

El Gamonal Tel (34) 952 - 883 375	San Pedro 12 km
Los Nieto Tel (34) 952 - 883 491	San Pedro 12 km

LAS AMÉRICAS

16 | 7 | 8

Es el más "urbano" de los campos del sur de Tenerife, en un oasis verde del formidable complejo hotelero y residencial Playa de Las Américas-Costa Adeje. Pero el ladrillo -y las últimas grúas- de los alrededores guarda prudente distancia y a ello colabora un diseño abierto con múltiples referencias -palmeras y agua, sobre todo- que ocupan la atención del jugador. No es un campo largo -en el 4 y en el 14 los pegadores tirarán a green- pero hay que tener cuidado con los fuera límites, el agua, los bunkers bien colocados y los greenes, muy francos, que son grandes, rápidos y movidos y, por lo tanto, hay que jugarlos con respeto. Habitualmente sopla una brisa que refresca la temperatura y altera un poco el vuelo de la bola. El mantenimiento del campo merece un aplauso especial.

This is the most residential of all the courses on the south coast of Tenerife, lying in the lush oasis of the huge hotel and residential resort of la Playa de las Americas Costa Adeje. Turn your eyes away from the bricks and last few cranes that surround the course and take a close look at a layout that has much to be said for it, especially the palm trees and water hazards that should keep you busy for some time. This is not a very long course (the longer-hitters can try and drive the green on holes 4 and 14), but watch out for OB, the water and some well-placed bunkers close to the greens. The putting surfaces are true, large and slick, so treat them with respect. To cool the summer heat, there is often a refreshing little breeze blowing here, and it can easily have an influence on where your ball ends up, so again, care is called for. A special mention should go to the excellent standard of maintenance and green-keeping.

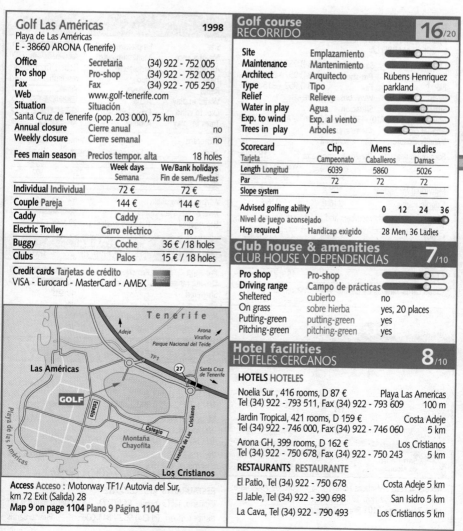

Golf Las Américas — 1998

Playa de Las Américas
E - 38660 ARONA (Tenerife)

Office	Secretaria	(34) 922 - 752 005
Pro shop	Pro-shop	(34) 922 - 752 005
Fax	Fax	(34) 922 - 705 250
Web	www.golf-tenerife.com	
Situation	Situación	

Santa Cruz de Tenerife (pop. 203 000), 75 km

Annual closure	Cierre anual	no
Weekly closure	Cierre semanal	no

Fees main season Precios tempor. alta		18 holes
	Week days Semana	**We/Bank holidays** Fin de sem./fiestas
Individual Individual	72 €	72 €
Couple Pareja	144 €	144 €
Caddy	Caddy	no
Electric Trolley	Carro eléctrico	no
Buggy	Coche	36 € /18 holes
Clubs	Palos	15 € / 18 holes

Credit cards Tarjetas de crédito
VISA - Eurocard - MasterCard - AMEX

Access Acceso : Motorway TF1/ Autovia del Sur, km 72 Exit (Salida) 28
Map 9 on page 1104 Plano 9 Página 1104

Golf course RECORRIDO — 16/20

Site	Emplazamiento	
Maintenance	Mantenimiento	
Architect	Arquitecto	Rubens Henriquez
Type	Tipo	parkland
Relief	Relieve	
Water in play	Agua	
Exp. to wind	Exp. al viento	
Trees in play	Arboles	

Scorecard Tarjeta	**Chp.** Campeonato	**Mens** Caballeros	**Ladies** Damas
Length Longitud	6039	5860	5026
Par	72	72	72
Slope system	—	—	—

Advised golfing ability Nivel de juego aconsejado: 0 12 24 36
Hcp required Handicap exigido: 28 Men, 36 Ladies

Club house & amenities CLUB HOUSE Y DEPENDENCIAS — 7/10

Pro shop	Pro-shop	
Driving range	Campo de prácticas	
Sheltered	cubierto	no
On grass	sobre hierba	yes, 20 places
Putting-green	putting-green	yes
Pitching-green	pitching-green	yes

Hotel facilities HOTELES CERCANOS — 8/10

HOTELS HOTELES

Noelia Sur , 416 rooms, D 87 € — Playa Las Americas
Tel (34) 922 - 793 511, Fax (34) 922 - 793 609 — 100 m

Jardin Tropical, 421 rooms, D 159 € — Costa Adeje
Tel (34) 922 - 746 000, Fax (34) 922 - 746 060 — 5 km

Arona GH, 399 rooms, D 162 € — Los Cristianos
Tel (34) 922 - 750 678, Fax (34) 922 - 750 243 — 5 km

RESTAURANTS RESTAURANTE

El Patio, Tel (34) 922 - 750 678 — Costa Adeje 5 km
El Jable, Tel (34) 922 - 390 698 — San Isidro 5 km
La Cava, Tel (34) 922 - 790 493 — Los Cristianos 5 km

LAS BRISAS

18 | 7 | 7

Uno de los grandes recorridos de la Costa del Sol, aunque conservando una dimensión humana por el gran número de tees de salida que permiten que los jugadores de nivel medio puedan evolucionar sin miedo. Rodeado de bonitos chalés, el terreno es poco accidentado, y numerosos greens en alto complican los aproches. Numerosos bunkers y obsáculos de agua (en la línea de juego en 12 hoyos) protegen los greens. Aquí es necesario poseer un juego preciso y muy completo (hoyos estrechos alternan con otros más anchos), se debe tirar a bandera y saber dar toda clase de golpes para obtener un buen resultado. Ya en el green queda todavía mucho por hacer ya que no es fácil calcular las caídas. Es apasionante jugar en este golf tanto en stroke-play como en match-play, es el más divertido de todos los "monumentos" de la región, aunque sólo sea por su seducción visual añadida a la calidad del desafío.

One of the really great courses on the Costa del Sol but one that has kept a very human dimension through the number of tees, allowing players of average standard to play the course without feeling terrorised. Surrounded by beautiful villas, the terrain is pretty even but the many elevated greens make approach shots a tricky business. The greens are well protected by the many bunkers and water hazards (affecting 12 holes in all). Las Brisas calls for accurate, comprehensive golf (tight holes alternate with wider fairways) and the ability to play most shots in order to card a good score. The emphasis here is on American-style target golf. Although once on the greens, you are still far from home and dry, because none of them are easy to read. An exciting course for stroke-play and match-play, this is the most amusing of the region's golfing landmarks, if only for the view which adds to the amazing challenge of golf.

Real Club de Golf Las Brisas — 1968

Apartado 147 - Nueva Andalucia
E - 29660 MARBELLA

Office	Secretaria	(34) 952 - 813 021
Pro shop	Pro-shop	(34) 952 - 813 021
Fax	Fax	(34) 952 - 815 518
Web	www.brisasgolf.com	
Situation	Situación	

Marbella (pop. 84 410), 15 km - San Pedro de Alcantara, 6 km

Annual closure	Cierre anual	no
Weekly closure	Cierre semanal	no
Fees main season	Precios tempor. alta	18 holes

	Week days Semana	We/Bank holidays Fin de sem./fiestas
Individual Individual	108 €	108 €
Couple Pareja	216 €	216 €

Main season: mostly members and guests, ask before coming

Caddy	Caddy	27 € /18 holes
Electric Trolley	Carro eléctrico	12 € /18 holes
Buggy	Coche	36 € /18 holes
Clubs	Palos	15 € / 18 holes

Credit cards Tarjetas de crédito VISA - MasterCard

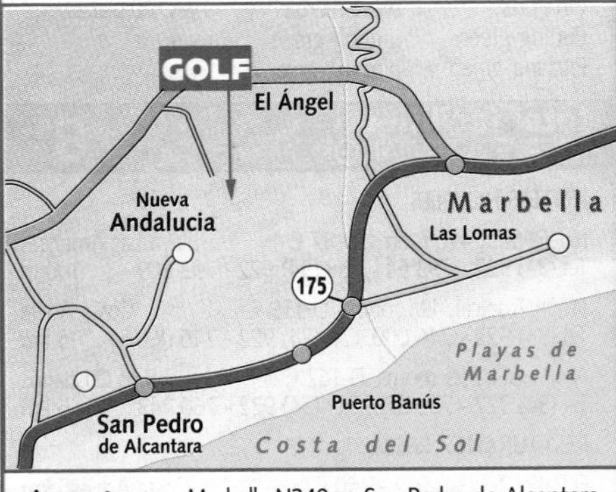

Access Acceso : Marbella N340 → San Pedro de Alcantara, Nueva Andalucia (km 174), turn right → Golf
Map 7 on page 1101 Plano 7 Página 1101

Golf course RECORRIDO — 18/20

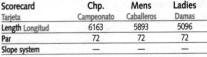

Site	Emplazamiento	
Maintenance	Mantenimiento	
Architect	Arquitecto	Robert Trent Jones
Type	Tipo	residential, parkland
Relief	Relieve	
Water in play	Agua	
Exp. to wind	Exp. al viento	
Trees in play	Arboles	

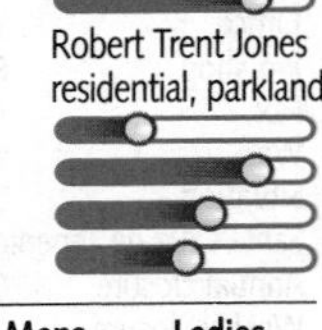

Scorecard Tarjeta	**Chp.** Campeonato	**Mens** Caballeros	**Ladies** Damas
Length Longitud	6163	5893	5096
Par	72	72	72
Slope system	—	—	—

Advised golfing ability 0 12 24 36
Nivel de juego aconsejado
Hcp required Handicap exigido 28 Men, 32 Ladies

Club house & amenities CLUB HOUSE Y DEPENDENCIAS — 7/10

Pro shop	Pro-shop	
Driving range	Campo de prácticas	
Sheltered	cubierto	4 mats
On grass	sobre hierba	yes
Putting-green	putting-green	yes
Pitching-green	pitching-green	yes

Hotel facilities HOTELES CERCANOS — 7/10

HOTELS HOTELES

Puente Romano — Marbella 4 km
217 rooms, D 343 €
Tel (34) 952 - 820 900, Fax (34) 952 - 775 766

Melia Don Pepe — Marbella 8 km
200 rooms, D 295 €
Tel (34) 952 - 770 300, Fax (34) 952 - 779 954

Pyr Hotel — Puerto Banus 13 km
319 rooms, D 115 €
Tel (34) 952 - 817 353, Fax (34) 952 - 817 907

RESTAURANTS RESTAURANTE

Cipriano, Tel (34) 952 - 811 077 — Puerto Banús 4 km
Bistrot Cristian, Tel (34) 952 - 811 006 — Puerto Banús

LAS PALMAS

14	8	8

Es el club más antiguo de España, fundado en 1891 en las afueras de Las Palmas. La expansión de la ciudad obligó a trasladarlo en 1956 y se asienta ahora en un paraje natural, llamado los Llanos de Bandama, a 14 kilómetros de la ciudad. El ambiente del club y su diseño natural mantienen la tradición inglesa de sus fundadores. El terreno es muy escarpado y la casa-club de estilo clásico, domina todo el recorrido y ofrece unas espléndidas vistas sobre las rocas volcánicas y barrancos que lo rodean. El campo no es de medidas largas, pero hay varios hoyos en subida que hay que tratar con el máximo respeto. Es preciso dominar el vuelo de la bola para mantener la bola en juego en un recorrido, que sin ser estrecho, incita al jugador a pensar cuál es el mejor sitio para colocar cada salida.

This is Spain's oldest golf club, whose course was originally laid out in the suburbs of Las Palmas de Gran Canaria. In 1956, as the city expanded, the club moved out into the country close to Llanos de Bandama, some 14 km from the city. The atmosphere in this club, just like the actual course, faithfully upholds the British tradition laid down by the club's founding members. The course is very hilly (but only a limited number of buggies are available) and the very classically styled club-house overlooks the whole course providing a magnificent scenic view of the surrounding volcanic rocks and ravines. The 18 holes (designed by MacKenzie Ross but restyled since) are not particularly wide and there are quite a few uphill holes that need to be negotiated very carefully. Accuracy is of the essence to keep the ball in play on a course where the tight fairways force the golfer to think long and hard about careful placing of the ball before each shot.

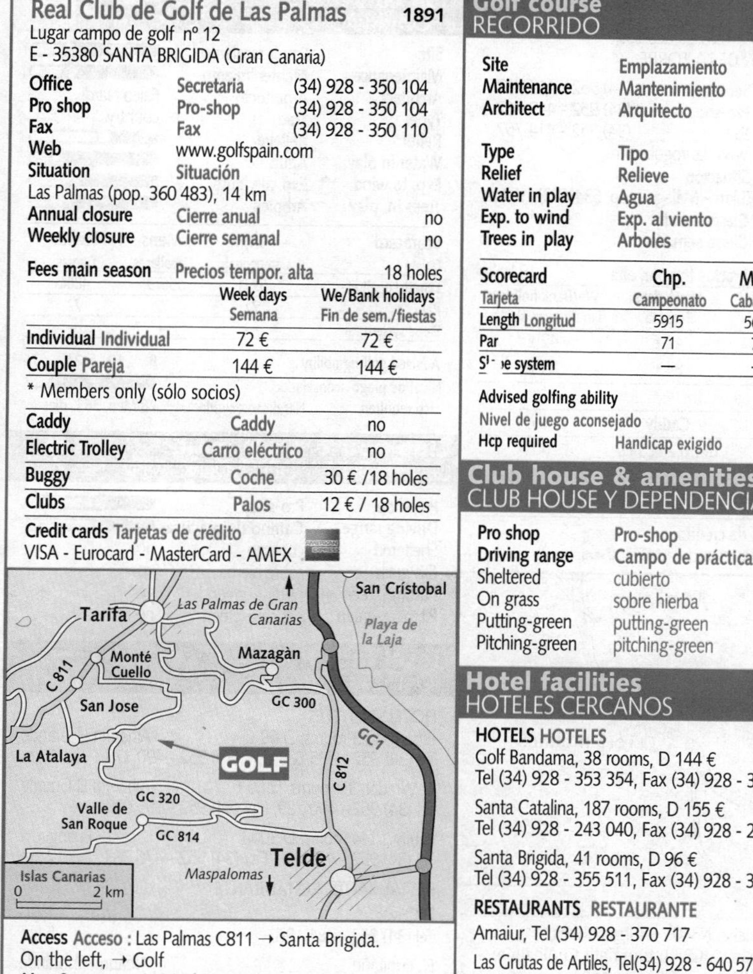

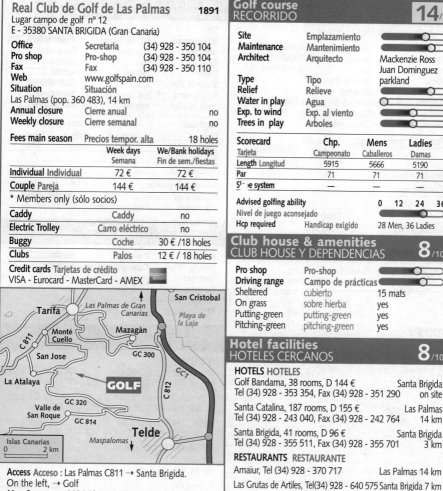

Real Club de Golf de Las Palmas — 1891

Lugar campo de golf nº 12
E - 35380 SANTA BRIGIDA (Gran Canaria)

Office	Secretaria	(34) 928 - 350 104
Pro shop	Pro-shop	(34) 928 - 350 104
Fax	Fax	(34) 928 - 350 110
Web	www.golfspain.com	
Situation	Situación	

Las Palmas (pop. 360 483), 14 km

Annual closure	Cierre anual	no
Weekly closure	Cierre semanal	no

Fees main season Precios tempor. alta	18 holes	
	Week days Semana	**We/Bank holidays** Fin de sem./fiestas
Individual Individual	72 €	72 €
Couple Pareja	144 €	144 €

* Members only (sólo socios)

Caddy	Caddy	no
Electric Trolley	Carro eléctrico	no
Buggy	Coche	30 € /18 holes
Clubs	Palos	12 € / 18 holes

Credit cards Tarjetas de crédito
VISA - Eurocard - MasterCard - AMEX

Access Acceso : Las Palmas C811 → Santa Brigida.
On the left, → Golf
Map 9 on page 1104 Plano 9 Página 1104

Golf course RECORRIDO — 14/20

Site	Emplazamiento	
Maintenance	Mantenimiento	
Architect	Arquitecto	Mackenzie Ross Juan Dominguez
Type	Tipo	parkland
Relief	Relieve	
Water in play	Agua	
Exp. to wind	Exp. al viento	
Trees in play	Arboles	

Scorecard Tarjeta	**Chp.** Campeonato	**Mens** Caballeros	**Ladies** Damas
Length Longitud	5915	5666	5190
Par	71	71	71
Slope system	—	—	—

Advised golfing ability Nivel de juego aconsejado — 0 12 24 36
Hcp required Handicap exigido — 28 Men, 36 Ladies

Club house & amenities CLUB HOUSE Y DEPENDENCIAS — 8/10

Pro shop	Pro-shop	
Driving range	Campo de prácticas	
Sheltered	cubierto	15 mats
On grass	sobre hierba	yes
Putting-green	putting-green	yes
Pitching-green	pitching-green	yes

Hotel facilities HOTELES CERCANOS — 8/10

HOTELS HOTELES

Golf Bandama, 38 rooms, D 144 € Tel (34) 928 - 353 354, Fax (34) 928 - 351 290	Santa Brigida on site
Santa Catalina, 187 rooms, D 155 € Tel (34) 928 - 243 040, Fax (34) 928 - 242 764	Las Palmas 14 km
Santa Brigida, 41 rooms, D 96 € Tel (34) 928 - 355 511, Fax (34) 928 - 355 701	Santa Brigida 3 km

RESTAURANTS RESTAURANTE

Amaiur, Tel (34) 928 - 370 717	Las Palmas 14 km
Las Grutas de Artiles, Tel(34) 928 - 640 575	Santa Brigida 7 km
El Novillo Precoz, Tel (34) 928 - 221 659	Las Palmas 14 km

LAURO

14	7	7

Al final de una carretera de montaña, está situado en un lugar muy tranquilo. Cada hoyo lleva el nombre de un célebre torero, pero no por eso se trata de un recorrido agresivo que exija dotes de combate. Al contrario, la belleza de los paisajes inspira calma y el recorrido en sí mismo es más bien acogedor, incluso para los jugadores con poca experiencia. Cantidad de olivos bordean la mayor parte de las calles y algunos obstáculos de agua están situados en plena línea de juego (hoyos 9,14,17 y 18) sin ser temibles. De razonable dificultad, prácticamente sin trampas escondidas (los obstáculos son perfectamente visibles), Lauro Golf es un recorrido muy noble y el sitio ideal para evaluar el nivel de su juego actual y sus propias posibilidades frente a jugadores de nivel equivalente. El campo ha mejorado en mantenimiento y estado y se ha ampliado con otros nueve hoyos.

This course is a quiet little place at the end of a mountain road. Each hole bears the name of a famous torero but the course itself is far from being aggressive and does not call for any real fighting virtues. On the contrary, the beautiful landscape inspires peace and quiet and the layout is a friendly one, even for inexperienced players. Numerous olive trees line most of the fairways and certain water hazards are very much to the fore (on the 9th, 14th, 17th and 18th holes) but never fearsome. Never too demanding with virtually no hidden traps (all hazards are clearly visible) and benign greens, Lauro Golf is a very honest layout and the ideal spot to assess your current game and potential and to measure up with players of similar ability. The better players can card flattering scores and do their ego a world of good. The course has shown a great improvement, both for maintenance and with the opening of nine new holes.

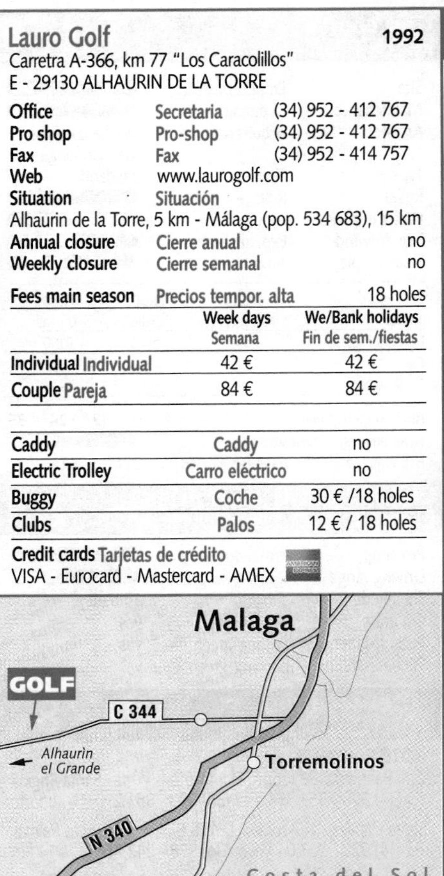

Lauro Golf **1992**
Carretra A-366, km 77 "Los Caracolillos"
E - 29130 ALHAURIN DE LA TORRE

Office	Secretaria	(34) 952 - 412 767
Pro shop	Pro-shop	(34) 952 - 412 767
Fax	Fax	(34) 952 - 414 757
Web	www.laurogolf.com	
Situation	Situación	

Alhaurin de la Torre, 5 km - Málaga (pop. 534 683), 15 km

Annual closure	Cierre anual	no
Weekly closure	Cierre semanal	no

Fees main season Precios tempor. alta		18 holes
	Week days Semana	**We/Bank holidays** Fin de sem./fiestas
Individual Individual	42 €	42 €
Couple Pareja	84 €	84 €

Caddy	Caddy	no
Electric Trolley	Carro eléctrico	no
Buggy	Coche	30 € /18 holes
Clubs	Palos	12 € / 18 holes

Credit cards Tarjetas de crédito
VISA - Eurocard - Mastercard - AMEX

Access Acceso : Málaga, N340 → Torremolinos,
Exit (salida) "Churiana", C344, turn right to Alhaurín
Map 7 on page 1101 Plano 7 Página 1101

Golf course RECORRIDO — 14/20

Site	Emplazamiento	
Maintenance	Mantenimiento	
Architect	Arquitecto	Falco Nardi
Type	Tipo	country
Relief	Relieve	
Water in play	Agua	
Exp. to wind	Exp. al viento	
Trees in play	Arboles	

Scorecard Tarjeta	**Chp.** Campeonato	**Mens** Caballeros	**Ladies** Damas
Length Longitud	5971	5679	4864
Par	72	72	72
Slope system	—	—	—

Advised golfing ability Nivel de juego aconsejado — 0 12 24 36
Hcp required Handicap exigido — 28 Men, 36 Ladies

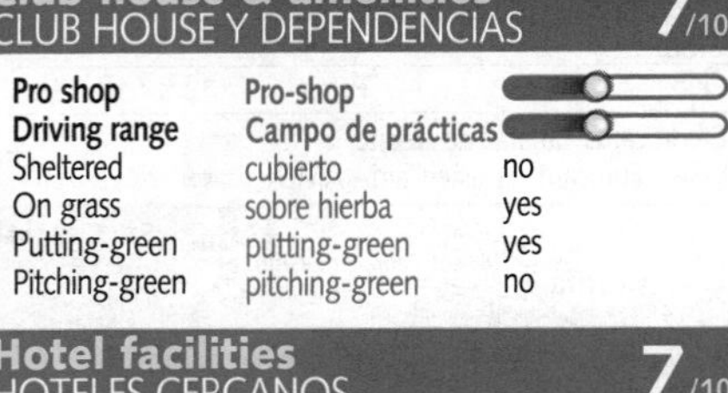

Club house & amenities CLUB HOUSE Y DEPENDENCIAS — 7/10

Pro shop	Pro-shop	
Driving range	Campo de prácticas	
Sheltered	cubierto	no
On grass	sobre hierba	yes
Putting-green	putting-green	yes
Pitching-green	pitching-green	no

Hotel facilities HOTELES CERCANOS — 7/10

HOTELS HOTELES
Brisamer, 23 rooms, D 68 € — Alhaurin El Grande
Tel (34) 952 - 595 683, Fax (34) 952 - 490 175 — 5 km

El Mirador, 34 rooms, D 60 € — Alhaurin El Grande
Tel (34) 952 - 490 789, Fax (34) 952 - 595 029

Byblos, 144 rooms, D 300 € — Fuengirola
Tel (34) 952 - 473 050, Fax (34) 952 - 476 783 — 12 km

RESTAURANTS RESTAURANTE
El Olivar, — Mijas
Tel (34) 952 - 486 196 — 5 km

El, Ermitaño — Alhaurin El Grande
Tel (34) 952 - 963 004

LERMA

17 | 7 | 4

Uno de los arquitéctos más originales de su época, José Gancedo, ha diseñado en un magnífico paraje un campo a la vez espectacular y lleno de encanto. Si se le puede considerar como difícil para los buenos jugadores, sobre todo desde las barras de atrás, se adapta sin embargo perfectamente a los jugadores todos los niveles. Tendrán aún más placer ya que no es imposible cumplir su handicap, siempre y cuando sean conscientes de sua limitaciones. El trazado exige una excelente estrategia y un buen dominio de la bola. Suele recompensar más al jugador técnico que coloca la bola que al pegador que puede encontrar dificultades con los árboles o los obstáculos de agua. Sin embargo en el 18 los pegadores tendrán la oportunidad de jugar a green por encima del lago, sobre todo si juegan en match-play, la fórmula ideal para descubrir el campo. Bien equilibrado en su desarrollo, con un buen diseño, Lerma pertenece sin duda a la categoría de campos "inteligentes".

José Gancedo, one of today's most original architects, has designed a spectacular and truly charming layout over a beautiful site. While considered tough for the better players, especially from the back-tees, it is nonetheless largely suitable for players of all abilities. They will find it all the more pleasing in that playing to their handicap is not impossible, as long as they know their limits. The course demands tight strategy and excellent ball control, and generally will reward the accurate technician more than the long-hitters, who may have problems with the trees and water. But on the 18th, they can try and hit the green over the lake, especially in match-play, the ideal format when discovering this course. Well-balanced and nicely-landscaped, Lerma is undoubtedly one of the more "intelligent" courses.

Club de Golf de Lerma — 1992

Autovía Madrid-Burgos Km 195,5
E - 09340 LERMA

Office	Secretaria	(34) 947 - 171 214
Pro shop	Pro-shop	(34) 947 - 171 214
Fax	Fax	(34) 947 - 171 216
E-mail	golflerma@csa.es	
Situation	Situación	

Burgos (pop. 169 111), 45 km - Lerma (pop. 2 417), 8 km

Annual closure	Cierre anual	no
Weekly closure	Cierre semanal	Monday (Lunes)

Fees main season Precios tempor. alta	18 holes	
	Week days Semana	**We/Bank holidays** Fin de sem./fiestas
Individual Individual	36 €	48 €
Couple Pareja	72 €	96 €

Caddy	Caddy	no
Electric Trolley	Carro eléctrico	9 € /18 holes
Buggy	Coche	30 € /18 holes
Clubs	Palos	12 € / 18 holes

Credit cards Tarjetas de crédito
VISA - MasterCard

Access Acceso : Madrid → Burgos, Km 195
Map 3 on page 1092 Plano 3 Página 1092

Golf course — RECORRIDO — 17/20

Site	Emplazamiento	
Maintenance	Mantenimiento	
Architect	Arquitecto	José Gancedo
Type	Tipo	country, forest
Relief	Relieve	
Water in play	Agua	
Exp. to wind	Exp. al viento	
Trees in play	Arboles	

Scorecard Tarjeta	**Chp.** Campeonato	**Mens** Caballeros	**Ladies** Damas
Length Longitud	6263	5905	5064
Par	72	72	72
Slope system	—	—	—

Advised golfing ability — 0 12 24 36
Nivel de juego aconsejado
Hcp required Handicap exigido — 28 Men, 36 Ladies

Club house & amenities — CLUB HOUSE Y DEPENDENCIAS — 7/10

Pro shop	Pro-shop	
Driving range	Campo de prácticas	
Sheltered	cubierto	8 mats
On grass	sobre hierba	yes
Putting-green	putting-green	yes
Pitching-green	pitching-green	yes

Hotel facilities — HOTELES CERCANOS — 4/10

HOTELS HOTELES

Alisa , 36 rooms, D 51 € Tel (34) 947 - 170 250, Fax (34) 947 - 171 160	Lerma 8 km
Arlanza, 40 rooms, D 579 € Tel (34) 947 - 406 441, Fax (34) 947 - 400 502	Covarrubias 22 km
Landa Palace, 42 rooms, D 168 € Tel (34) 947 - 206 343, Fax (34) 947 - 264 676	Burgos 42 km
Rey Chindasvinto, 14 rooms, D 51 € Tel (34) 947 - 406 560, Fax (34) 947 - 406 543	Covarrubias 22 km

RESTAURANTS RESTAURANTE

Lis 2, Tel (34) 947 - 170 126	Lerma 8 km
Casa Ojeda, Tel (34) 947 - 209 052	Burgos 45 km

LOS ARQUEROS

14	6	7

Desde los paisajes áridos de la carretera que sube a Ronda, da la impresión de ser un golf "extremado". En realidad no lo es, pero sus pronunciadas cuestas aconsejan utilizar un coche para jugar más fácilmente en este recorrido cuya construcción exigió enormes obras para nivelar el terreno. No es muy largo, estrecho en algunos sitios, los obstáculos son peligrosos y situados en la línea de juego, lo que incita a jugar con cierta prudencia. Teniendo en cuenta que el arquitecto es Seve Ballesteros, atraerá más bien a los jugadores de ataque que serán recompensados por sus golpes audaces, sobre todo los que juegan en "fade" o los especialistas de bolas altas cuyo objetivo son unos greens no inmensos, sin grandes trampas, que aguantan bien la bola y su trayectoria a la hora de patear. De gran imaginación y espectacular, se recomienda conocerlo antes de seguir camino hacia la bella ciudad de Ronda.

From the road and arid landscape leading to Ronda,, the impression is one of an extremely hilly golf course. This is not quite the case, but the steep slopes call for the use of a buggy to play a little more easily on a course whose construction demanded very considerable grading work. It is not very long, but sometimes tight, and the hazards are always in play and dangerously placed. The result can sometimes be an over-cautious approach when playing the course. Designed by Seve Ballesteros, Los Arqueros should appeal to attacking players and will reward bold strokes. This is particularly true for players who fade the ball or who are specialists of high shots aimed at the smallish greens, which have little in the way of traps, pitch well and putt true. Imaginative and sometimes quite spectacular, this course is to be recommended before getting back on the road and heading for the beautiful town of Ronda.

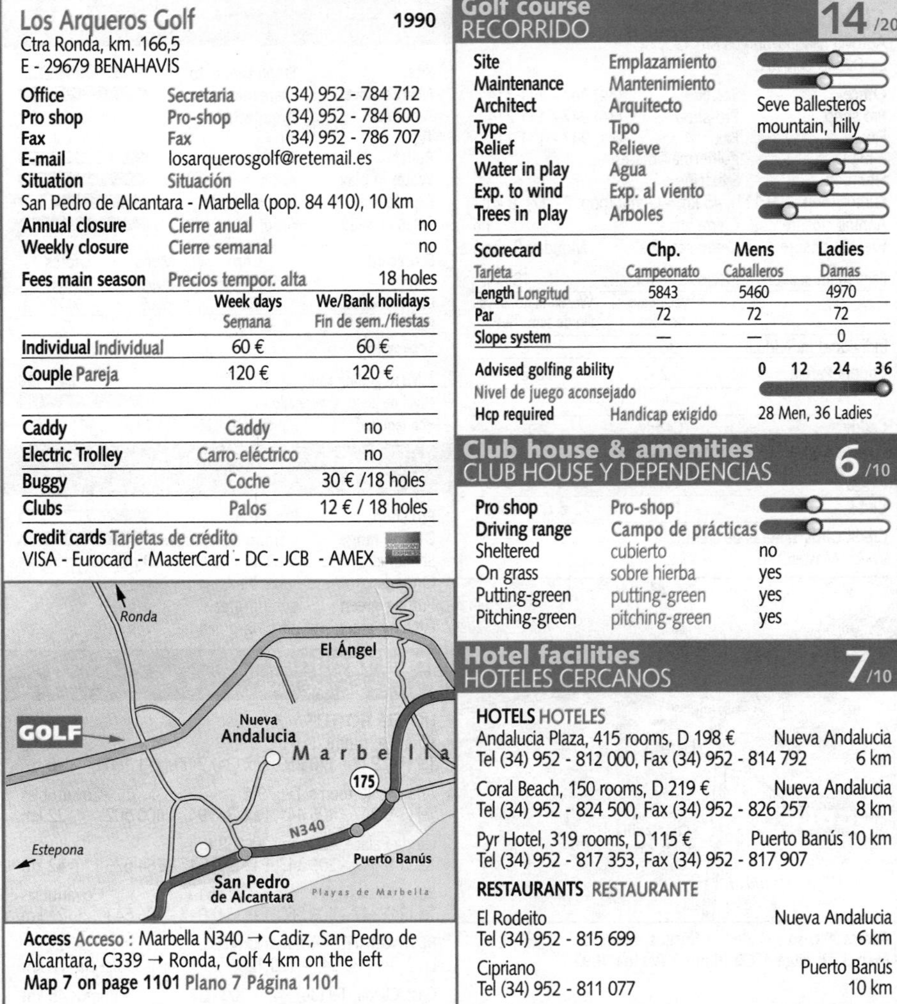

Los Arqueros Golf — 1990

Ctra Ronda, km. 166,5
E - 29679 BENAHAVIS

Office	Secretaria	(34) 952 - 784 712
Pro shop	Pro-shop	(34) 952 - 784 600
Fax	Fax	(34) 952 - 786 707
E-mail	losarquerosgolf@retemail.es	
Situation	Situación	

San Pedro de Alcantara - Marbella (pop. 84 410), 10 km

Annual closure	Cierre anual	no
Weekly closure	Cierre semanal	no

Fees main season Precios tempor. alta		18 holes
	Week days Semana	**We/Bank holidays** Fin de sem./fiestas
Individual Individual	60 €	60 €
Couple Pareja	120 €	120 €

Caddy	Caddy	no
Electric Trolley	Carro eléctrico	no
Buggy	Coche	30 € /18 holes
Clubs	Palos	12 € / 18 holes

Credit cards Tarjetas de crédito
VISA - Eurocard - MasterCard - DC - JCB - AMEX

Access Acceso : Marbella N340 → Cadiz, San Pedro de Alcantara, C339 → Ronda, Golf 4 km on the left
Map 7 on page 1101 Plano 7 Página 1101

Golf course RECORRIDO — 14/20

Site	Emplazamiento	
Maintenance	Mantenimiento	
Architect	Arquitecto	Seve Ballesteros
Type	Tipo	mountain, hilly
Relief	Relieve	
Water in play	Agua	
Exp. to wind	Exp. al viento	
Trees in play	Arboles	

Scorecard Tarjeta	**Chp.** Campeonato	**Mens** Caballeros	**Ladies** Damas
Length Longitud	5843	5460	4970
Par	72	72	72
Slope system	—	—	0

Advised golfing ability Nivel de juego aconsejado — 0 12 24 36

Hcp required Handicap exigido — 28 Men, 36 Ladies

Club house & amenities CLUB HOUSE Y DEPENDENCIAS — 6/10

Pro shop	Pro-shop	
Driving range	Campo de prácticas	
Sheltered	cubierto	no
On grass	sobre hierba	yes
Putting-green	putting-green	yes
Pitching-green	pitching-green	yes

Hotel facilities HOTELES CERCANOS — 7/10

HOTELS HOTELES

Andalucia Plaza, 415 rooms, D 198 € — Nueva Andalucia
Tel (34) 952 - 812 000, Fax (34) 952 - 814 792 — 6 km

Coral Beach, 150 rooms, D 219 € — Nueva Andalucia
Tel (34) 952 - 824 500, Fax (34) 952 - 826 257 — 8 km

Pyr Hotel, 319 rooms, D 115 € — Puerto Banús 10 km
Tel (34) 952 - 817 353, Fax (34) 952 - 817 907

RESTAURANTS RESTAURANTE

El Rodeito — Nueva Andalucia
Tel (34) 952 - 815 699 — 6 km

Cipriano — Puerto Banús
Tel (34) 952 - 811 077 — 10 km

LOS NARANJOS

16 | 7 | 7

En el corazón del "Valle del golf" en Nueva Andalucía, Los Naranjos, sin ser un monstruo, es uno de los más famosos diseños de Robert Trent Jones. Las mejoras en el mantenimiento del recorrido y la construcción de un nuevo club-house han contribuido a restaurar su gloria. Los nueve primeros hoyos, ligeramente accidentados, obligan a reflexionar tanto sobre la elección del palo como sobre la trayectoria de la bola. La vuelta es prácticamente llana, insinuándose entre naranjos, y más favorable a los pegadores que no dudarán en salir de atrás. Los jugadores más razonables encontrarán que este recorrido es ya bastante largo desde los tees de salida "normales". ¿Por qué sufrir si se puede evitar? En cada partido hallarán toda clase de situaciones diferentes de las que podrán gozar. Los greens están bien protegidos, son muy grandes y se ven bien las caídas.

At the heart of "Golf Valley" in Nueva Andalucia, "Los Naranjos" (meaning Orange Trees) is one of Robert Trent Jones' more famous designs but it is no monster. Considerably improved upkeep and the building of a new club house have helped restore its former glory. The front nine, on slightly broken terrain, require careful thought as much for the choice of club as for the trajectory of the ball. The back nine are virtually flat holes winding their way between the orange trees. They will appeal to long hitters who in every case won't think twice about playing the course from the back tees. More reasonable players will find the course long enough from the "normal" tees; after all, why suffer when you don't have to? All sorts of different situations arise every time you play here, so the course is sure-fire enjoyment every time. The greens are well-defended, often huge but never too difficult to read.

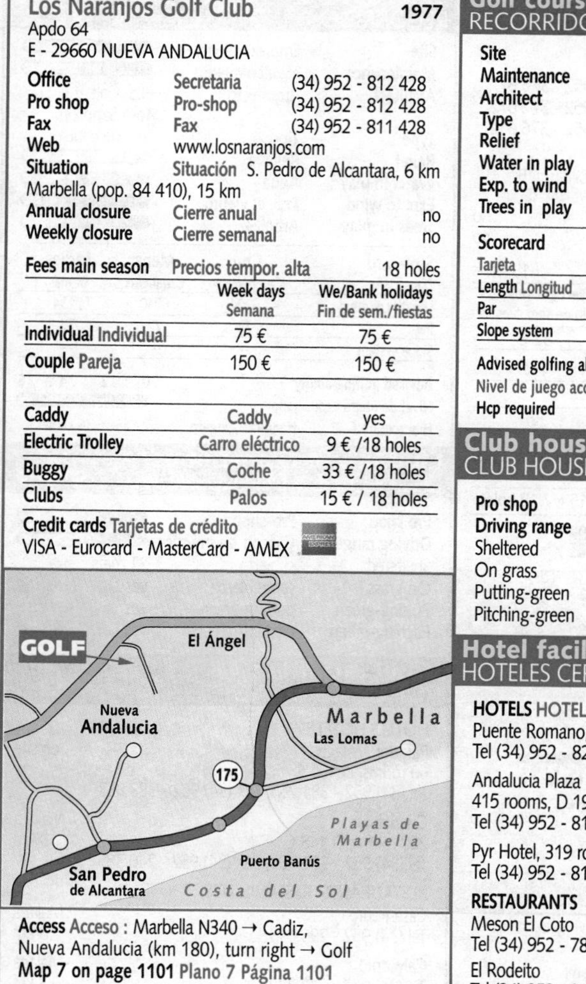

Los Naranjos Golf Club — 1977

Apdo 64
E - 29660 NUEVA ANDALUCIA

Office	Secretaria	(34) 952 - 812 428
Pro shop	Pro-shop	(34) 952 - 812 428
Fax	Fax	(34) 952 - 811 428
Web	www.losnaranjos.com	
Situation	Situación	S. Pedro de Alcantara, 6 km

Marbella (pop. 84 410), 15 km

Annual closure	Cierre anual	no
Weekly closure	Cierre semanal	no

Fees main season Precios tempor. alta	18 holes	
	Week days Semana	**We/Bank holidays** Fin de sem./fiestas
Individual Individual	75 €	75 €
Couple Pareja	150 €	150 €

Caddy	Caddy	yes
Electric Trolley	Carro eléctrico	9 € /18 holes
Buggy	Coche	33 € /18 holes
Clubs	Palos	15 € / 18 holes

Credit cards Tarjetas de crédito
VISA - Eurocard - MasterCard - AMEX

Access Acceso : Marbella N340 → Cadiz, Nueva Andalucia (km 180), turn right → Golf
Map 7 on page 1101 Plano 7 Página 1101

Golf course RECORRIDO — 16/20

Site	Emplazamiento	
Maintenance	Mantenimiento	
Architect	Arquitecto	Robert Trent Jones
Type	Tipo	parkland, residential
Relief	Relieve	
Water in play	Agua	
Exp. to wind	Exp. al viento	
Trees in play	Arboles	

Scorecard Tarjeta	**Chp.** Campeonato	**Mens** Caballeros	**Ladies** Damas
Length Longitud	6457	6038	5143
Par	72	72	72
Slope system	—	—	—

Advised golfing ability Nivel de juego aconsejado: 0 12 24 36
Hcp required Handicap exigido: 28 Men, 36 Ladies

Club house & amenities CLUB HOUSE Y DEPENDENCIAS — 7/10

Pro shop	Pro-shop	
Driving range	Campo de prácticas	
Sheltered	cubierto	no
On grass	sobre hierba	yes
Putting-green	putting-green	yes
Pitching-green	pitching-green	yes

Hotel facilities HOTELES CERCANOS — 7/10

HOTELS HOTELES

Puente Romano, 217 rooms, D 343 € — Marbella 5 km
Tel (34) 952 - 820 900, Fax (34) 952 - 775 766

Andalucia Plaza — Nueva Andalucia 1,5 km
415 rooms, D 198 €
Tel (34) 952 - 812 000, Fax (34) 952 - 814 792

Pyr Hotel, 319 rooms, D 115 € — Puerto Banús 4 km
Tel (34) 952 - 817 353, Fax (34) 952 - 817 907

RESTAURANTS RESTAURANTE

Meson El Coto — San Pedro → Ronda 7 km
Tel (34) 952 - 785 123

El Rodeito — Nueva Andalucia 6 km
Tel (34) 952 - 815 699

MÁLAGA

13 | 4 | 6

No solamente es el primer recorrido de golf abierto en la famosa Costa del Sol, sino también el primer campo propiedad y dirigido por la empresa estatal Paradores, rama hostelera del Turismo oficial. Paradores ha puesto interés en tener el campo en buenas condiciones y prolongar hasta las puertas de Málaga el turismo de golf que tiene su epicentro alrededor de Marbella. El campo es un monumento histórico construído por H.S. Colt y supervisado por Tom Simpson, que alterna el diseño de parque natural, entre árboles frondosos, con los hoyos al borde de la playa a los que solamente faltan las dunas para que sea un auténtico links. El lugar tiene un gran encanto natural y los primeros nueve hoyos son especialmente interesantes, con bunkers muy bien situados y una distribución de espacios que anima a emplear todos los recursos del buen juego corto.

This was not only the very first course on the Costa del Sol, it is now also the first course to be controlled and managed by the state enterprise Paradores, the hotel branch of Spanish Tourism. Paradores set out to keep the course in sufficiently good condition in order to prolong Marbella-based golf tourism down as far as Malaga. The course is a sort of historical monument designed by H.S. Colt under the supervision of Tom Simpson. The result is an alternating string of natural parkland holes, very thick trees and seaside holes where only the dunes are lacking for this to look like a real links course. The natural site has a lot of charm about it, especially the particularly interesting front nine. Bunkers are well located and space has been cleverly used to add spice to the back nine, where a tight short game comes in very handy.

1160

Real Club de Campo de Málaga — 1925

Apdo 324
E - 29080 MALAGA

Office	Secretaria	(34) 952 - 376 677
Pro shop	Pro-shop	(34) 952 - 372 072
Fax	Fax	(34) 952 - 376 612
Web	www.parador.es	
Situation	Situación	Málaga, 10 km

Torremolinos (pop. 35 309), 4 km

Annual closure	Cierre anual	no
Weekly closure	Cierre semanal	no

Fees main season Precios tempor. alta	18 holes	
	Week days Semana	**We/Bank holidays** Fin de sem./fiestas
Individual Individual	32 €	32 €
Couple Pareja	64 €	64 €

Caddy	Caddy	no
Electric Trolley	Carro eléctrico	no
Buggy	Coche	30 € /18 holes
Clubs	Palos	15 € / 18 holes

Credit cards Tarjetas de crédito
VISA - Eurocard - MasterCard - AMEX

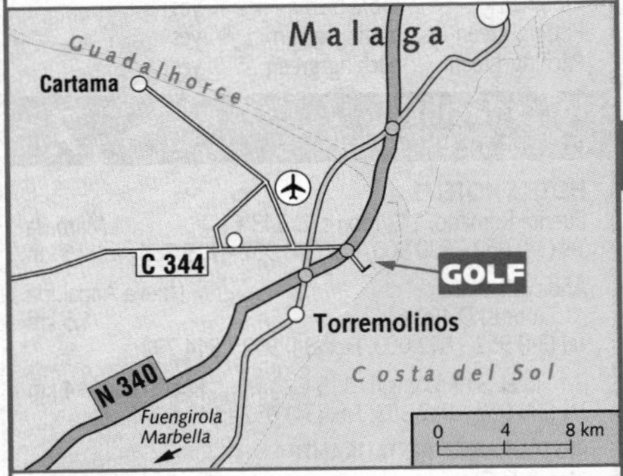

Access Acceso : Málaga → Torremolinos, on the left → Parador del Golf

Map 7 on page 1101 Plano 7 Página 1101

Golf course — RECORRIDO — 13/20

Site	Emplazamiento	
Maintenance	Mantenimiento	
Architect	Arquitecto	H.S. Colt, Tom Simpson
Type	Tipo	seaside course
Relief	Relieve	
Water in play	Agua	
Exp. to wind	Exp. al viento	
Trees in play	Arboles	

Scorecard Tarjeta	**Chp.** Campeonato	**Mens** Caballeros	**Ladies** Damas
Length Longitud	6204	6040	5134
Par	72	72	72
Slope system	—	—	—

Advised golfing ability Nivel de juego aconsejado — 0 12 24 36

Hcp required Handicap exigido — 27 Men, 36 Ladies

Club house & amenities — CLUB HOUSE Y DEPENDENCIAS — 4/10

Pro shop	Pro-shop	
Driving range	Campo de prácticas	
Sheltered	cubierto	21 mats
On grass	sobre hierba	yes
Putting-green	putting-green	yes
Pitching-green	pitching-green	yes

Hotel facilities — HOTELES CERCANOS — 6/10

HOTELS HOTELES

Parador Málaga — on site
60 rooms, D 105 €
Tel (34) 952 - 381 255, Fax (34) 952 - 388 963

Guadalmar — Malaga 3 km
200 rooms, D 148 €
Tel (34) 952 - 231 703, Fax (34) 952 - 240 385

RESTAURANTS RESTAURANTE

Casa Pedro — Málaga 3 km
Tel (34) 952 - 290 013

Calycanto — Málaga 3 km
Tel (34) 952 - 212 222

MARBELLA

15 | 7 | 8

Muy en cuesta, es mejor alquilar un coche y a pesar de las dificultades que ello implica habría que actualizarlo. La gran diversidad de hoyos y de golpes que hay que jugar es asombrosa, encontrando los famosos bunkers del arquitecto y algunos obstáculos de agua peligrosos que requieren un serio análisis de su buena forma de juego, antes de tomar una decisión entre el ataque o la prudencia. Teniendo en cuenta que los greenes tienen muchas caídas: hay que atacar resueltamente a bandera. No se trata ni mucho menos de un recorrido imposible, pero los jugadores sin handicap sufrirán más que los otros. Algunas hondonadas y sinuosidades del terreno son una seria amenaza para los drives en algunos hoyos. Bien es verdad que por momentos el maravilloso panorama sobre el mar puede servir de consuelo a ciertos desastres.

This is rather broken terrain, making walking a little difficult, but the demanding layout is very much back in the modern trend. The variety of holes and the shots they require is remarkable. There are, of course, the architect's hallmark bunkers and a number of dangerous water hazards, which call for serious analysis of current playing form before deciding whether to attack or lay up. All the more so in that the greens are well designed and definitely favour players who go for the pin. It is not an impossible course, far from it, but high-handicappers will suffer, especially with the few ravines and hollows that pose a serious threat to a number of tee-shots. The scenic views over the sea will more than compensate should disaster strike.

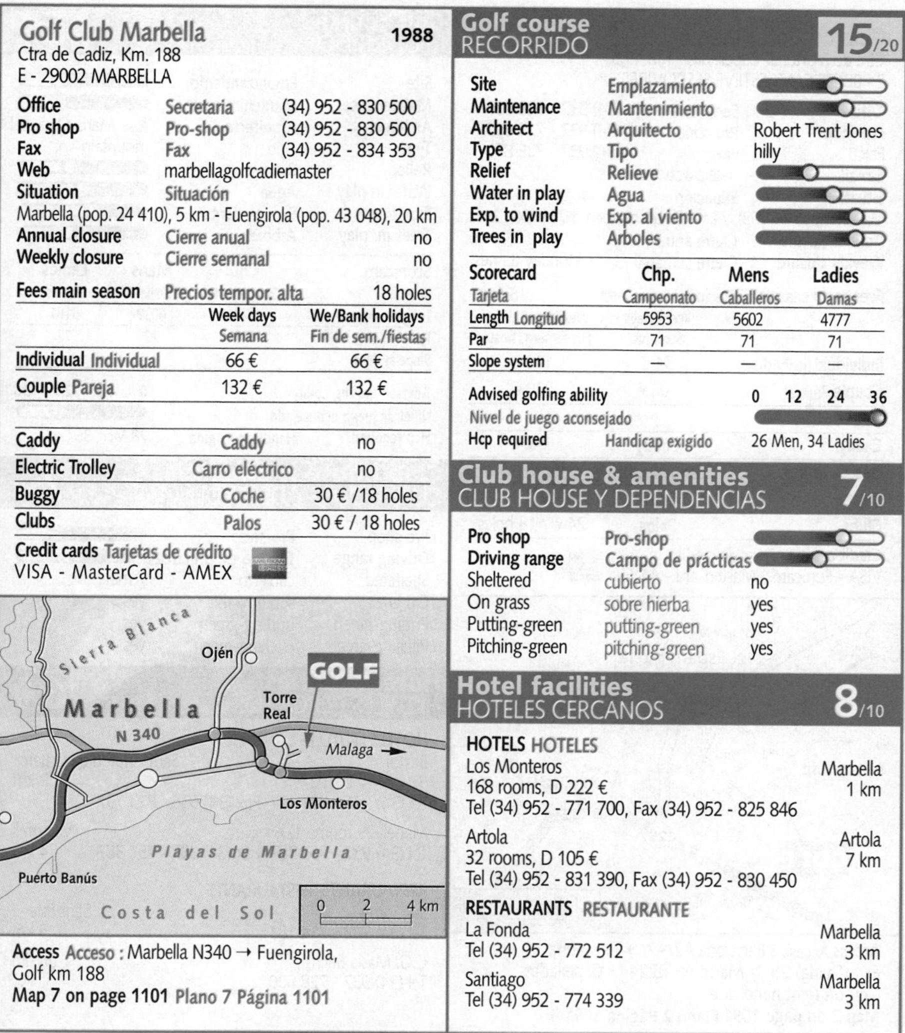

Golf Club Marbella — 1988

Ctra de Cadiz, Km. 188
E - 29002 MARBELLA

Office	Secretaria	(34) 952 - 830 500
Pro shop	Pro-shop	(34) 952 - 830 500
Fax	Fax	(34) 952 - 834 353
Web	marbellagolfcadiemaster	
Situation	Situación	

Marbella (pop. 24 410), 5 km - Fuengirola (pop. 43 048), 20 km

Annual closure	Cierre anual	no
Weekly closure	Cierre semanal	no
Fees main season	Precios tempor. alta	18 holes

	Week days / Semana	We/Bank holidays / Fin de sem./fiestas
Individual Individual	66 €	66 €
Couple Pareja	132 €	132 €

Caddy	Caddy	no
Electric Trolley	Carro eléctrico	no
Buggy	Coche	30 € /18 holes
Clubs	Palos	30 € / 18 holes

Credit cards Tarjetas de crédito
VISA - MasterCard - AMEX

Access Acceso : Marbella N340 → Fuengirola, Golf km 188
Map 7 on page 1101 Plano 7 Página 1101

Golf course / RECORRIDO — 15/20

Site	Emplazamiento	
Maintenance	Mantenimiento	
Architect	Arquitecto	Robert Trent Jones
Type	Tipo	hilly
Relief	Relieve	
Water in play	Agua	
Exp. to wind	Exp. al viento	
Trees in play	Arboles	

Scorecard Tarjeta	Chp. Campeonato	Mens Caballeros	Ladies Damas
Length Longitud	5953	5602	4777
Par	71	71	71
Slope system	—	—	—

Advised golfing ability Nivel de juego aconsejado: 0 12 24 36
Hcp required Handicap exigido: 26 Men, 34 Ladies

Club house & amenities / CLUB HOUSE Y DEPENDENCIAS — 7/10

Pro shop	Pro-shop	
Driving range	Campo de prácticas	
Sheltered	cubierto	no
On grass	sobre hierba	yes
Putting-green	putting-green	yes
Pitching-green	pitching-green	yes

Hotel facilities / HOTELES CERCANOS — 8/10

HOTELS HOTELES

Los Monteros — Marbella 1 km
168 rooms, D 222 €
Tel (34) 952 - 771 700, Fax (34) 952 - 825 846

Artola — Artola 7 km
32 rooms, D 105 €
Tel (34) 952 - 831 390, Fax (34) 952 - 830 450

RESTAURANTS RESTAURANTE

La Fonda — Marbella 3 km
Tel (34) 952 - 772 512

Santiago — Marbella 3 km
Tel (34) 952 - 774 339

MASIA BACH

15 | 7 | 6

Es mejor utilizar un coche sobre todo en los tramos accidentados de un hoyo a otro, a pesar de que el relieve del recorrido en sí mismo sea moderado. José María Olazábal ha sabido sacar provecho de un terreno a primera vista más bien quebrado y peligroso. El relieve impide muy a menudo ver los greens desde los tees de salida de los pares 4 y 5, pero los bunkers de calle indican la línea de juego y acogen las bolas imprecisas. Los pares 3, generalmente con hondanadas en medio, parecen peligrosos pero de longitud razonable. Los greens tienen muchas caídas, son o muy largos o muy anchos y aguantan bien la bola. Incluso cuando la posición de las banderas puede dificultar seriamente el juego ,sobre todo si se ha salido de atrás, Masia Bach es un recorrido menos peligroso de lo que generalmente piensan los jugadores si logran conservar su aplomo y una cierta precisión.

A buggy can come in handy here to cross the broken terrain between holes, but much of the course here is not too hilly. José Maria Olazabal has brought the best out of what, at first sight, looks to be much more rugged and dangerous terrain. Indeed, the relief often obscures any view of the greens from the tees on the par 4s and 5s, but the fairway bunkers show the line of play and often stop mishit balls in their tracks. Generally laid out with large hollows between tee and green, the par 3s look dangerous but their lengths are very reasonable. The greens are very undulating, sometimes very long or very wide, and pitch well. Even though the pin positions can sometimes seriously complicate play when driving from the back-tees, Masia Bach is a friendlier course for players of all levels than people might think. As long as they keep a cool head, and play straight.

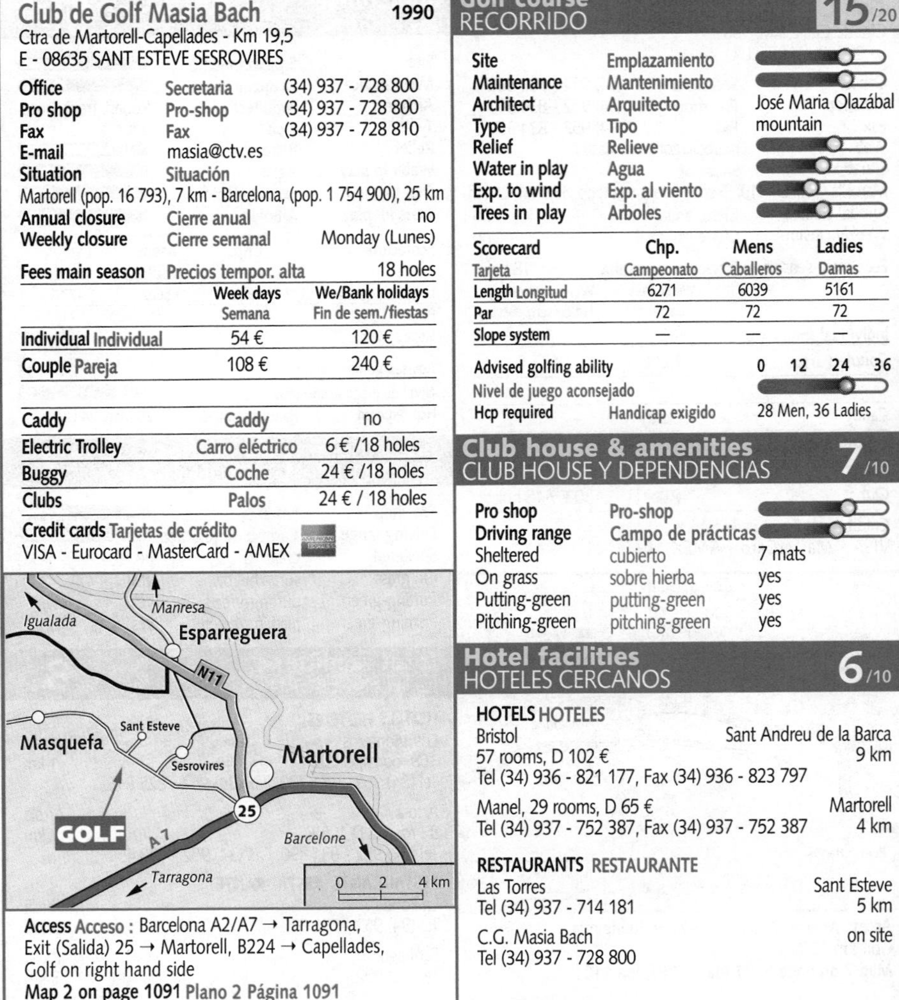

Club de Golf Masia Bach — 1990

Ctra de Martorell-Capellades - Km 19,5
E - 08635 SANT ESTEVE SESROVIRES

Office	Secretaria	(34) 937 - 728 800
Pro shop	Pro-shop	(34) 937 - 728 800
Fax	Fax	(34) 937 - 728 810
E-mail	masia@ctv.es	
Situation	Situación	

Martorell (pop. 16 793), 7 km - Barcelona, (pop. 1 754 900), 25 km

Annual closure	Cierre anual	no
Weekly closure	Cierre semanal	Monday (Lunes)

Fees main season Precios tempor. alta	18 holes	
	Week days Semana	**We/Bank holidays** Fin de sem./fiestas
Individual Individual	54 €	120 €
Couple Pareja	108 €	240 €

Caddy	Caddy	no
Electric Trolley	Carro eléctrico	6 € /18 holes
Buggy	Coche	24 € /18 holes
Clubs	Palos	24 € / 18 holes

Credit cards Tarjetas de crédito
VISA - Eurocard - MasterCard - AMEX

Access Acceso : Barcelona A2/A7 → Tarragona, Exit (Salida) 25 → Martorell, B224 → Capellades, Golf on right hand side
Map 2 on page 1091 Plano 2 Página 1091

Golf course — RECORRIDO — 15/20

Site	Emplazamiento	
Maintenance	Mantenimiento	
Architect	Arquitecto	José Maria Olazábal
Type	Tipo	mountain
Relief	Relieve	
Water in play	Agua	
Exp. to wind	Exp. al viento	
Trees in play	Arboles	

Scorecard Tarjeta	**Chp.** Campeonato	**Mens** Caballeros	**Ladies** Damas
Length Longitud	6271	6039	5161
Par	72	72	72
Slope system	—	—	—

Advised golfing ability Nivel de juego aconsejado: 0 12 24 36
Hcp required Handicap exigido: 28 Men, 36 Ladies

Club house & amenities — CLUB HOUSE Y DEPENDENCIAS — 7/10

Pro shop	Pro-shop	
Driving range	Campo de prácticas	
Sheltered	cubierto	7 mats
On grass	sobre hierba	yes
Putting-green	putting-green	yes
Pitching-green	pitching-green	yes

Hotel facilities — HOTELES CERCANOS — 6/10

HOTELS HOTELES

Bristol — Sant Andreu de la Barca
57 rooms, D 102 € — 9 km
Tel (34) 936 - 821 177, Fax (34) 936 - 823 797

Manel, 29 rooms, D 65 € — Martorell
Tel (34) 937 - 752 387, Fax (34) 937 - 752 387 — 4 km

RESTAURANTS RESTAURANTE

Las Torres — Sant Esteve
Tel (34) 937 - 714 181 — 5 km

C.G. Masia Bach — on site
Tel (34) 937 - 728 800

MASPALOMAS

16 | 7 | 8

Prácticamente en el borde del mar y cerca de la ciudad, Maspalomas fue construido en un terreno muy llano cerca de las dunas, lo que le da un aspecto de links que uno no se espera encontrar en la Isla de Gran Canaria. La paternidad de Mackenzie Ross (autor de la reconstrucción de Turnberry) ofrece la garantía de autenticidad de estilo. Aunque es un recorrido de competición muy exigente, sin embargo es un buen golf para ir de vacaciones. Es un par 73 de longitud razonable, pero con dificuldades enormes, que invita a los jugadores a proceder sin complejos y según sus posibilidades. No hay que dormirse ni extraviarse en las dunas, donde el rough es muy peligroso. Grandes bunkers con una arena de agradable color amarillo esperan las bolas poco precisas. La flora subtropical compuesta de palmeras, pinos canarios y marítimos, ibiscos, buganvillas, etc., confiere un color muy particular a este diseño bastante britanico...

Virtually by the sea and in town, Maspalomas was built on a very flat land. Its layout, close to sand-dunes, gives it a links style which you wouldn't expect to find on Grand Canary island, and the patronage of Mackenzie Ross (who re-designed Turnberry) provides a sure-fire guarantee of authenticity in terms of style. Although this is a rather challenging tournament course, it still makes for very good holiday golfing and so is very "functional" golfing facility in this part of the world. This is a par 73 of reasonable with no insurmountable difficulties, inviting players to "go for it" to the best of their ability. But they'll need to keep on their toes and not stray into the dunes where the rough can make a big dent in your card. Large bunkers filled with pretty yellow sand also wait the mis-hit ball (and others too). The sub-tropical vegetation of palm-trees, Canary pines, hibiscus-trees and bougainvillaea add special colour to this very British-style layout.

Club de Golf Maspalomas — 1968

Auda de Neckerman S/N
E - 35100 MASPALOMAS (Gran Canaria)

Office	Secretaria	(34) 928 - 762 581
Pro shop	Pro-shop	(34) 928 - 767 343
Fax	Fax	(34) 928 - 768 245
Web	www.maspalomasgolf.net	
Situation	Situación	

Las Palmas (pop. 360 483), 30 km

Annual closure	Cierre anual	no
Weekly closure	Cierre semanal	no

Fees main season Precios tempor. alta	18 holes	
	Week days Semana	**We/Bank holidays** Fin de sem./fiestas
Individual Individual	66 €	66 €
Couple Pareja	132 €	132 €

Caddy	Caddy	no
Electric Trolley	Carro eléctrico	no
Buggy	Coche	30 € /18 holes
Clubs	Palos	12 € / 18 holes

Credit cards Tarjetas de crédito
VISA - Eurocard - MasterCard

Access Acceso : Autopista Sur, → Maspalomas
Map 9 on page 1104 Plano 9 Página 1104

Golf course RECORRIDO — 16/20

Site	Emplazamiento	
Maintenance	Mantenimiento	
Architect	Arquitecto	Mackenzie Ross
Type	Tipo	forest
Relief	Relieve	
Water in play	Agua	
Exp. to wind	Exp. al viento	
Trees in play	Arboles	

Scorecard Tarjeta	**Chp.** Campeonato	**Mens** Caballeros	**Ladies** Damas
Length Longitud	6189	6037	5210
Par	73	73	73
Slope system	—	—	—

Advised golfing ability Nivel de juego aconsejado: 0 12 24 36
Hcp required Handicap exigido 30

Club house & amenities CLUB HOUSE Y DEPENDENCIAS — 7/10

Pro shop	Pro-shop	
Driving range	Campo de prácticas	
Sheltered	cubierto	12 mats
On grass	sobre hierba	yes
Putting-green	putting-green	yes
Pitching-green	pitching-green	yes

Hotel facilities HOTELES CERCANOS — 8/10

HOTELS HOTELES

Ifa-Faro, 183 rooms, D 209 € — Maspalomas 3 km
Tel (34) 928 - 142 214, Fax (34) 928 - 141 940

Palm Beach, 347 rooms, D 313 € — Maspalomas
Tel (34) 928 - 140 806, Fax (34) 928 - 141 808

Gran Hotel Meloneras — San Bartolomé 2,5 km
1137 rooms, D 120 €
Tel (34) 928 - 128 100, Fax (34) 928 - 128 122

RESTAURANTS RESTAURANTE

La Aquarela, Tel (34) 928 - 140 178 — Maspalomas
Amaiur, Tel (34) 928 - 761 414 — Maspalomas
Orangerie, Tel (34) 928 - 140 806 — Maspalomas 3 km

MEDITERRANEO

16 | 7 | 6

Este recorrido ha contribuido a la fama creciente de su arquitecto Ramón Espinosa. Es una joya depositada en un amplio valle, sus sutiles dificultades lo hacen más delicado de lo que a primera vista parece, sin por ello desalentar a los jugadores de nivel medio. Los bunkers de calle y de green están inteligentemente situados y bien visibles e indican la táctica de juego que hay que adoptar. Algunos árboles aislados obligan a pegar la bola con efecto y algunos lagos pequeñitos están en línea de juego en siete hoyos, completando una panoplia de dificultades muy variadas. Los greens, tan tupidos como las calles, son falsamente planos y desconcertantes si no se les examina con mucha atención. Inteligente y franco, es un recorrido para todo el mundo y se puede aconsejar tanto por su armonía como por su cuidadoso mantenimiento: se pasa una óptima jornada.

This course has done much to enhance the growing reputation of architect Ramon Espinosa. This is a gem of a course located in a wide valley, and the subtly placed hazards make it tougher than you might think at first sight, but not to the point of scaring off the lesser players. The fairway and green-side bunkers are cleverly located and visible enough to help your game tactics. A few isolated trees call for elaborate shots, moving the ball both ways, and small ponds are in play on seven holes, thus completing a highly varied panoply of hazards. The greens, as grassy as the fairways, are deceptively flat and disconcerting if not read carefully. An intelligent and honest course, this is a golfing arena for everyone. Being well-balanced and well-cared for, it is a course well worth recommending for spending a great day out.

Club de Campo Mediterraneo — 1978

Urbanización "La Coma" S/N
E - 12190 BORRIOL (CASTELLON DE LA PLANA)

Office	Secretaria	(34) 964 - 321 227
Pro shop	Pro-shop	(34) 964 - 321 653
Fax	Fax	(34) 964 - 321 653
Web	www.ccmediterraneo.com	
Situation	Situación	

Castellón de la Plana (pop. 138 489), 5 km

Annual closure	Cierre anual	no
Weekly closure	Cierre semanal	no

Fees main season / Precios tempor. alta	Week days / Semana	We/Bank holidays / Fin de sem./fiestas
		18 holes
Individual Individual	36 €	42 €
Couple Pareja	72 €	84 €

Caddy	Caddy	no
Electric Trolley	Carro eléctrico	9 € /18 holes
Buggy	Coche	21 € /18 holes
Clubs	Palos	9 € / 18 holes
Credit cards	Tarjetas de crédito	no

Access Acceso : A7 Barcelona-Valencia, Exit (Salida) 46 → Castellón Norte. 700 m on the right → "Club de Campo". Golf 2,5 km

Map 4 on page 1095 Plano 4 Página 1095

Golf course RECORRIDO — 16/20

Site	Emplazamiento	
Maintenance	Mantenimiento	
Architect	Arquitecto	Ramón Espinosa
Type	Tipo	country
Relief	Relieve	
Water in play	Agua	
Exp. to wind	Exp. al viento	
Trees in play	Arboles	

Scorecard / Tarjeta	Chp. / Campeonato	Mens / Caballeros	Ladies / Damas
Length Longitud	6239	6038	5266
Par	72	72	72
Slope system	—	—	—

Advised golfing ability / Nivel de juego aconsejado: 0 12 24 36

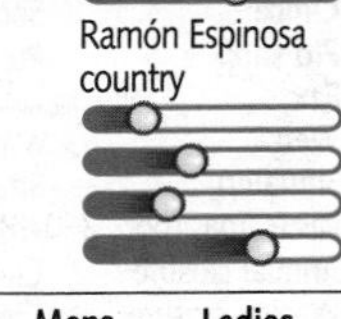

Hcp required — Handicap exigido — 28 Men, 36 Ladies

Club house & amenities CLUB HOUSE Y DEPENDENCIAS — 7/10

Pro shop	Pro-shop	
Driving range	Campo de prácticas	
Sheltered	cubierto	no
On grass	sobre hierba	yes
Putting-green	putting-green	yes
Pitching-green	pitching-green	yes

Hotel facilities HOTELES CERCANOS — 6/10

HOTELS HOTELES

Intur Castellón, 123 rooms, D 118 € — Castellón
Tel (34) 964 - 225 000, Fax (34) 964 - 232 606 — 5 km

Turcosa, 70 rooms, D 69 € — El Grao/Castellón
Tel (34) 964 - 283 600, Fax (34) 964 - 284 737 — 7 km

Mindoro, 103 rooms, D 96 € — Castellón
Tel (34) 964 - 222 300, Fax (34) 964 - 233 154 — 5 km

RESTAURANTS RESTAURANTE

Mare Nostrum — El Grao/Castellón
Tel (34) 964 - 282 929 — 7 km

Tasca del Puerto — El Grao/Castellón
Tel (34) 964 - 284 481 — 7 km

MIJAS Los Lagos

16 | 6 | 7

De los dos recorridos de Mijas, éste es para los "pegadores" y el que da mayor sensación de espacio. Bien es verdad que hay ocho lagos en la línea de juego en una decena de hoyos, pero las calles son anchas. Y menos mal, porque Los Lagos es muy largo, sin muchas cuestas, lo que permite jugarlo sin recurrir a un coche. Algo característico de Trent Jones es la disposición de los bunkers, no sólo para defender los greens, sino para dificultar la tarea de quienes intentan cortar en los dog-legs. Además, presenta una cierta variedad visual en hoyos que son muy semejantes entre sí. Los greens son extensos, con bastantes caídas, en muy buen estado, y su rapidez no impide que aguanten bien la bola: cosa muy importante ya que a menudo hay que aprochar con hierros largos. Que los jugadores medianos no se desanimen, pueden acortar el recorrido escogiendo tees de salida más adelantados.

Of the two courses at Mijas, this is the one for the big-hitters and for the greatest impression of open space. Sure, the eight lakes are very much to the fore on ten holes, but the fairways are wide. And so they should be, because "Los Lagos" is very long. But it is a pleasant course to play walking, as the terrain is relatively flat. Typical of Trent Jones, the bunkers are there not only to defend the greens but also to trap players who try and cut corners on the dog-legs. They also add a little variety to holes that are often very similar in style. The greens are huge, undulating and in good condition, and although fast they pitch well. This is important because approach shots often call for a long iron. Average players should not lose heart though, as they can shorten the course considerably by playing off the front-tees.

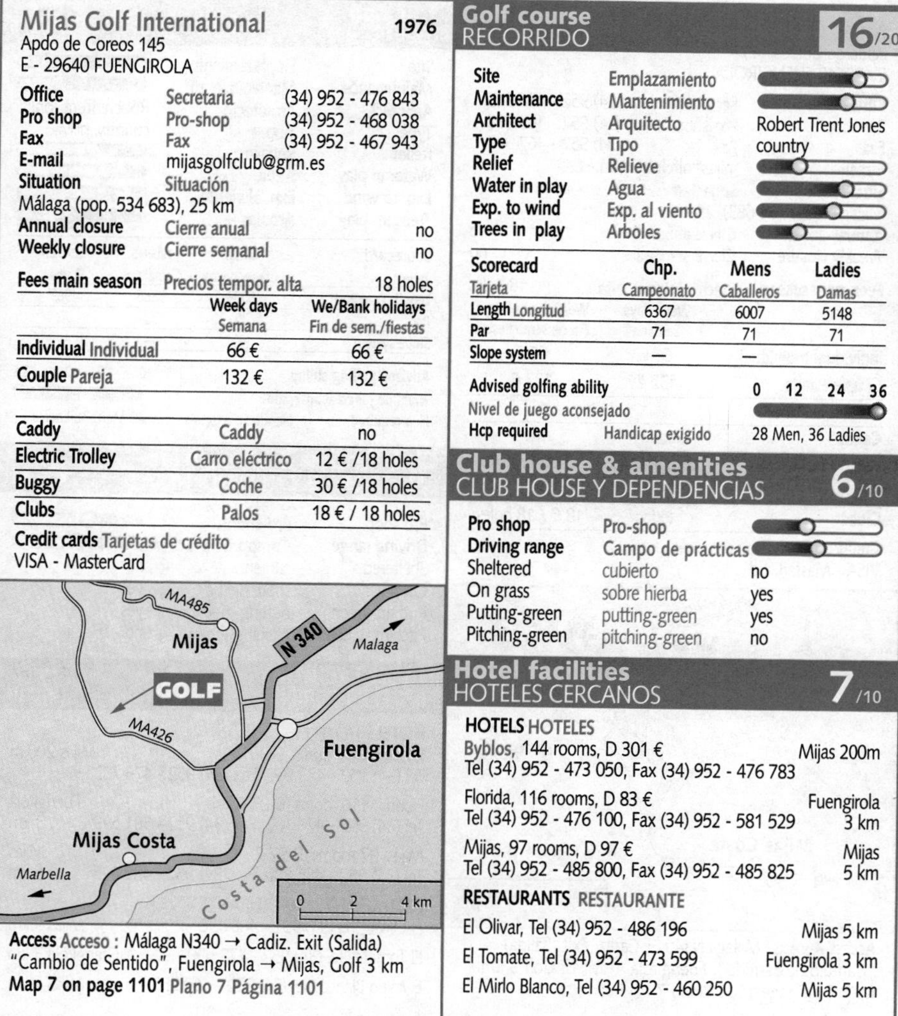

Mijas Golf International — 1976

Apdo de Coreos 145
E - 29640 FUENGIROLA

Office	Secretaria	(34) 952 - 476 843
Pro shop	Pro-shop	(34) 952 - 468 038
Fax	Fax	(34) 952 - 467 943
E-mail	mijasgolfclub@grm.es	
Situation	Situación	
Málaga (pop. 534 683), 25 km		
Annual closure	Cierre anual	no
Weekly closure	Cierre semanal	no

Fees main season Precios tempor. alta	18 holes	
	Week days Semana	**We/Bank holidays** Fin de sem./fiestas
Individual Individual	66 €	66 €
Couple Pareja	132 €	132 €

Caddy	Caddy	no
Electric Trolley	Carro eléctrico	12 € /18 holes
Buggy	Coche	30 € /18 holes
Clubs	Palos	18 € / 18 holes

Credit cards Tarjetas de crédito
VISA - MasterCard

Access Acceso : Málaga N340 → Cadiz. Exit (Salida) "Cambio de Sentido", Fuengirola → Mijas, Golf 3 km
Map 7 on page 1101 Plano 7 Página 1101

Golf course / RECORRIDO — 16/20

Site	Emplazamiento	
Maintenance	Mantenimiento	
Architect	Arquitecto	Robert Trent Jones
Type	Tipo	country
Relief	Relieve	
Water in play	Agua	
Exp. to wind	Exp. al viento	
Trees in play	Arboles	

Scorecard Tarjeta	**Chp.** Campeonato	**Mens** Caballeros	**Ladies** Damas
Length Longitud	6367	6007	5148
Par	71	71	71
Slope system	—	—	—

Advised golfing ability Nivel de juego aconsejado: 0 12 24 36
Hcp required Handicap exigido: 28 Men, 36 Ladies

Club house & amenities / CLUB HOUSE Y DEPENDENCIAS — 6/10

Pro shop	Pro-shop	
Driving range	Campo de prácticas	
Sheltered	cubierto	no
On grass	sobre hierba	yes
Putting-green	putting-green	yes
Pitching-green	pitching-green	no

Hotel facilities / HOTELES CERCANOS — 7/10

HOTELS HOTELES

Byblos, 144 rooms, D 301 € — Mijas 200m
Tel (34) 952 - 473 050, Fax (34) 952 - 476 783

Florida, 116 rooms, D 83 € — Fuengirola 3 km
Tel (34) 952 - 476 100, Fax (34) 952 - 581 529

Mijas, 97 rooms, D 97 € — Mijas 5 km
Tel (34) 952 - 485 800, Fax (34) 952 - 485 825

RESTAURANTS RESTAURANTE

El Olivar, Tel (34) 952 - 486 196 — Mijas 5 km
El Tomate, Tel (34) 952 - 473 599 — Fuengirola 3 km
El Mirlo Blanco, Tel (34) 952 - 460 250 — Mijas 5 km

MIJAS Los Olivos

13 | 6 | 7

De los dos recorridos de Mijas, Los Olivos conviene más a los jugadores de nivel medio. Por supuesto es estrecho, rodeado de numerosos olivos, algunos lagos pueden perturbar a los jugadores con poca técnica, su relieve es ligeramente más accidentado que el de "Los Lagos", pero encontrarán un trazado más a su medida y al alcance de sus posibilidades. Los greens son más pequeños, algunos ciegos, pero aguantan correctamente la bola y la progresión general del recorrido lo hace más divertido para jugar en familia cuando el resultado es menos importante que el placer. No es un recorrido para atacar y ciertamente no fue diseñado para ello. Da la impresión que Trent Jones quiso poner de relieve en Mijas dos facetas muy diferentes de su buen hacer. En todo caso, este conjunto permite que todos puedan escoger según su forma actual.

When choosing between the two courses at Mijas, average players are perhaps better off playing Los Olivos. The course is certainly tight and bordered by numerous olive trees, there are a few lakes to scare players with limited technique and the relief is in part much more broken than its sister course, Los Lagos. But the layout is probably much more within their scope and ability. The greens are smaller and some are blind, but they pitch pretty well and the general layout makes this course fun for playing with the family when scores are less important than having a good time. It is not a course for attacking players and visibly was not designed to be so. You get the impression that Trent Jones wanted to demonstrate two very different facets of his architectural know-how at Mijas. In any case, this golfing resort allows everyone to choose according to the shape of his or her game.

Mijas Golf International — 1976

Apdo de Coreos 145
E - 29640 FUENGIROLA

Office	Secretaria	(34) 952 - 476 843
Pro shop	Pro-shop	(34) 952 - 468 038
Fax	Fax	(34) 952 - 467 943
E-mail		mijasgolfclub@grm.es
Situation	Situación	

Málaga (pop. 534 683), 25 km

Annual closure	Cierre anual	no
Weekly closure	Cierre semanal	no

Fees main season Precios tempor. alta		18 holes
	Week days Semana	**We/Bank holidays** Fin de sem./fiestas
Individual Individual	66 €	66 €
Couple Pareja	132 €	132 €

Caddy	Caddy	no
Electric Trolley	Carro eléctrico	12 € /18 holes
Buggy	Coche	30 € /18 holes
Clubs	Palos	18 € / 18 holes

Credit cards Tarjetas de crédito
VISA - MasterCard

Access Acceso : Málaga N340 → Cadiz. Exit (Salida) "Cambio de Sentido", Fuengirola → Mijas, Golf 3 km
Map 7 on page 1101 Plano 7 Página 1101

Golf course RECORRIDO — 13/20

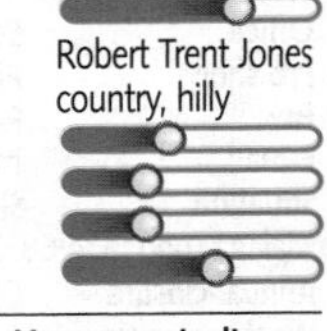

Site	Emplazamiento	
Maintenance	Mantenimiento	
Architect	Arquitecto	Robert Trent Jones
Type	Tipo	country, hilly
Relief	Relieve	
Water in play	Agua	
Exp. to wind	Exp. al viento	
Trees in play	Arboles	

Scorecard Tarjeta	**Chp.** Campeonato	**Mens** Caballeros	**Ladies** Damas
Length Longitud	6009	5866	4969
Par	72	72	72
Slope system	—	—	—

Advised golfing ability Nivel de juego aconsejado — 0 12 24 36
Hcp required Handicap exigido — 28 Men, 36 Ladies

Club house & amenities CLUB HOUSE Y DEPENDENCIAS — 6/10

Pro shop	Pro-shop	
Driving range	Campo de prácticas	
Sheltered	cubierto	no
On grass	sobre hierba	yes
Putting-green	putting-green	yes
Pitching-green	pitching-green	no

Hotel facilities HOTELES CERCANOS — 7/10

HOTELS HOTELES

Byblos, 144 rooms, D 301 € — Mijas 200 m
Tel (34) 952 - 473 050, Fax (34) 952 - 476 783

Florida, 116 rooms, D 83 € — Fuengirola 3 km
Tel (34) 952 - 476 100, Fax (34) 952 - 581 529

Mijas, 97 rooms, D 97 € — Mijas 5 km
Tel (34) 952 - 485 800, Fax (34) 952 - 485 825

RESTAURANTS RESTAURANTE

El Olivar, Tel (34) 952 - 486 196 — Mijas 5 km

El Tomate, Tel (34) 952 - 473 599 — Fuengirola 3 km

El Mirlo Blanco, Tel (34) 952 - 460 250 — Mijas 5 km

MONTE MAYOR

13 | 5 | 5

El golf más extravagante de toda la región y sin duda de España. Diseñado por Pepe Gancedo, este recorrido o gusta o se detesta. En plena montaña y muy expuesto al viento, reserva toda clase de sorpresas, hasta tal punto que algunos hoyos "normales" parecen insulsos. Sinuoso entre rocas, franqueando quebradas, bajando colinas, en medio de una vegetación salvaje y tupida, hay que conservar el dominio de sí mismo. Si se sale de calle, ¡o desgracia!. Pero las reglas locales son indulgentes: toda bola perdida se considera que reposa en un obstáculo de agua lateral. Uno se encuentra solo ante su propio juego como si estuviese al otro lado del mundo. Que el emblema del recorrido sea un toro no es mera casualidad: hay que luchar contra él, aguantar sus embistes, esquivar sus ataques. Se acaba agotado pero encantado de los magníficos paisajes. Un recorrido barroco, de gran inteligencia e imposible de ignorar.

The most extravagant course in the whole region and certainly in the whole of Spain. Designed by Pepe Gancedo, you either love it or hate it, with no middle ground. Right in the mountains and very exposed to the wind, it reserves every sort of surprise to the extent where certain "normal" holes look positively insipid. Winding its way through rocks, crossing gorges and running down hills amidst wild thick vegetation, the course calls for a cool head. Too bad if you miss the fairways. But the local rules are pretty lenient, as any lost ball is considered to be in a side water hazard. Here you are at the world's end, alone with your game of golf. It is no accident to see that the course's emblem is a bull; you have to fight it, stave off its charges and sidestep its attacks. You leave the 18th green exhausted but delighted with the magnificent landscapes. A baroque course of great intelligence, and one that is impossible to overlook.

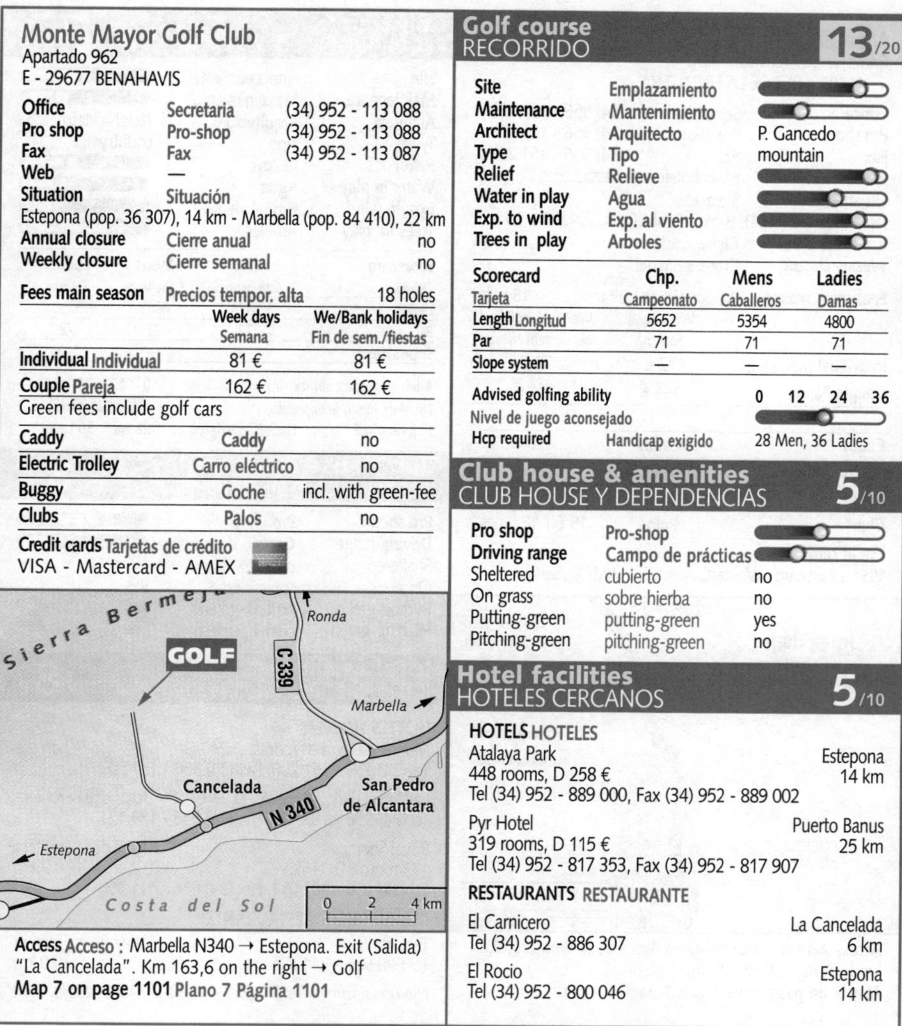

Monte Mayor Golf Club

Apartado 962
E - 29677 BENAHAVIS

Office	Secretaria	(34) 952 - 113 088
Pro shop	Pro-shop	(34) 952 - 113 088
Fax	Fax	(34) 952 - 113 087
Web	—	
Situation	Situación	

Estepona (pop. 36 307), 14 km - Marbella (pop. 84 410), 22 km

Annual closure	Cierre anual	no
Weekly closure	Cierre semanal	no

Fees main season	Precios tempor. alta	18 holes
	Week days Semana	**We/Bank holidays** Fin de sem./fiestas
Individual Individual	81 €	81 €
Couple Pareja	162 €	162 €

Green fees include golf cars

Caddy	Caddy	no
Electric Trolley	Carro eléctrico	no
Buggy	Coche	incl. with green-fee
Clubs	Palos	no

Credit cards Tarjetas de crédito
VISA - Mastercard - AMEX

Access Acceso : Marbella N340 → Estepona. Exit (Salida) "La Cancelada". Km 163,6 on the right → Golf
Map 7 on page 1101 Plano 7 Página 1101

Golf course RECORRIDO — 13/20

Site	Emplazamiento	
Maintenance	Mantenimiento	
Architect	Arquitecto	P. Gancedo
Type	Tipo	mountain
Relief	Relieve	
Water in play	Agua	
Exp. to wind	Exp. al viento	
Trees in play	Arboles	

Scorecard Tarjeta	**Chp.** Campeonato	**Mens** Caballeros	**Ladies** Damas
Length Longitud	5652	5354	4800
Par	71	71	71
Slope system	—	—	—

Advised golfing ability Nivel de juego aconsejado: 0 12 24 36
Hcp required Handicap exigido: 28 Men, 36 Ladies

Club house & amenities CLUB HOUSE Y DEPENDENCIAS — 5/10

Pro shop	Pro-shop	
Driving range	Campo de prácticas	
Sheltered	cubierto	no
On grass	sobre hierba	no
Putting-green	putting-green	yes
Pitching-green	pitching-green	no

Hotel facilities HOTELES CERCANOS — 5/10

HOTELS HOTELES

Atalaya Park — Estepona 14 km
448 rooms, D 258 €
Tel (34) 952 - 889 000, Fax (34) 952 - 889 002

Pyr Hotel — Puerto Banus 25 km
319 rooms, D 115 €
Tel (34) 952 - 817 353, Fax (34) 952 - 817 907

RESTAURANTS RESTAURANTE

El Carnicero — La Cancelada 6 km
Tel (34) 952 - 886 307

El Rocio — Estepona 14 km
Tel (34) 952 - 800 046

MONTECASTILLO

17 | 8 | 8

Era de esperar encontrarse un día con la firma de Jack Nicklaus en el sur de España. Ha sacado buen partido de un terreno moderadamente accidentado, y si los greens están frecuentemente en alto, no hay hoyos ciegos ni hoyos en subida, lo que confirma su filosofía de que: "hay que ver lo que hay que hacer". Prueba de ello el 18 con el tee de salida allá en alto. En realidad es un recorrido franco y difícil de lidiar, pero su dificultad general no impide el jugarlo en familia (salvo los principiantes), siempre y cuando cada uno se mantenga tranquilo y no se obsesione por el resultado. Todas las dificultades se concentran en la línea de juego (sobre todo los obstáculos de agua), y hay muchos fuera de límites. La variedad de situaciones incita a jugarlo varias veces para comprender mejor sus sutilezas. Espectacular y original (por la región), este recorrido no reniega el espíritu americano de su autor. Los que conocen sus otras realizaciones no quedarán sorprendidos.

It was only to be expected that one day Jack Nicklaus would leave his mark in southern Spain. He has extracted the best out of a moderately hilly terrain, and while the greens are frequently elevated, there are no blind or uphill holes, thus illustrating the great man's philosophy of: "you have to see what you have to do". Witness hole N° 18 with a very elevated tee. As a result, this is a very open but very tricky course to get around, but the general difficulty does not prevent this from being a course for all the family (but not beginners) as long as you keep cool and don't get obsessed with your score. All the hazards are very much in play, especially the water and even more so the out-of-bounds. The variety of situations will make you want to play Montecastillo several times to fully understand the more subtle sides to the course. Spectacular and original (for the region, that is), the course does not break with the American spirit of its designer. Players who know his other courses will not be surprised.

Montecastillo Hotel & Golf Resort — 1992

Carretera de Arcos, km. 9,6
E - 11406 JEREZ DE LA FRONTERA

Office	Secretaria	(34) 956 - 151 200
Pro shop	Pro-shop	(34) 956 - 151 200
Fax	Fax	(34) 956 - 151 209
Web	www.hotelmontecastillo.com	
Situation	Situación	

Jerez (pop. 184 364), 8 km - Sevilla (pop. 704 857), 70 km

Annual closure	Cierre anual	no
Weekly closure	Cierre semanal	no

Fees main season Precios tempor. alta		18 holes
	Week days / Semana	We/Bank holidays / Fin de sem./fiestas
Individual Individual	72 €	72 €
Couple Pareja	144 €	144 €

Caddy	Caddy	no
Electric Trolley	Carro eléctrico	no
Buggy	Coche	36 € /18 holes
Clubs	Palos	18 € / 18 holes

Credit cards Tarjetas de crédito
VISA - Eurocard - MasterCard - DC - AMEX

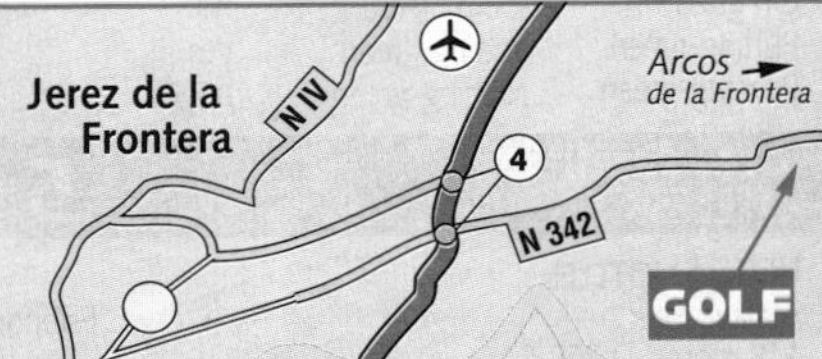

Access Acceso : Jerez, N342 → Arcos de la Frontera, 9,8 km turn right, Golf 1,5 km
Map 7 on page 1100 Plano 7 Página 1100

Golf course — RECORRIDO — 17/20

Site	Emplazamiento	
Maintenance	Mantenimiento	
Architect	Arquitecto	Jack Nicklaus
Type	Tipo	country
Relief	Relieve	
Water in play	Agua	
Exp. to wind	Exp. al viento	
Trees in play	Arboles	

Scorecard Tarjeta	Chp. Campeonato	Mens Caballeros	Ladies Damas
Length Longitud	6424	6043	5230
Par	72	72	72
Slope system	—	—	—

Advised golfing ability Nivel de juego aconsejado — 0 12 24 36
Hcp required Handicap exigido — 28 Men, 36 Ladies

Club house & amenities — CLUB HOUSE Y DEPENDENCIAS — 8/10

Pro shop	Pro-shop	
Driving range	Campo de prácticas	
Sheltered	cubierto	18 mats
On grass	sobre hierba	yes
Putting-green	putting-green	yes
Pitching-green	pitching-green	yes

Hotel facilities — HOTELES CERCANOS — 8/10

HOTELS HOTELES

Montecastillo, 120 rooms, D 240 € — on site
Tel (34) 956 - 151 200, Fax (34) 956 - 151 209

La Cueva Park, 58 rooms, D 93 € — Jerez de la Frontera
Tel (34) 956 - 189 120, Fax (34) 956 - 189 121

Royal Sherry — Jerez de la Frontera
173 rooms, D 116 € — 7 km
Tel (34) 956 - 303 011, Fax (34) 956 - 311 300

RESTAURANTS RESTAURANTE

Tendido 6 — Jerez de la Frontera
Tel (34) 956 - 344 835 — 10 km

Mesón La Cueva, Tel(34) 956 - 189 020 Montecastillo 1 km

MONTEENMEDIO

16	8	7

La Dehesa de Monteenmedio es un recorrido reciente de buena calidad en general, salido del pincel de Alejandro Maldonado y que creemos es, hasta ahora, su realización más prestigiosa. La región está cada día mejor equipada de golfs, y es cada vez más difícil encontrar terrenos entre Málaga, Marbella y Gibraltar. Las novedades van hacia el oeste. En este recorrido, por el momento no se aceptan más de 60 jugadores al día, distribuidos en partidas a veinte minutos de intervalo, lo que garantiza una gran comodidad de juego. Las calles y greens son anchos favoreciendo a los jugadores de tipo medio que son la mayor parte de los visitantes de la región. La mayor parte de las veces en los segundos golpes hacia los greens se pueden utilizar hierros medianos. Los pares 3 exigen mucha precisión. No obstante hay que permanecer vigilitantes y no atacar de cualquier manera, ya que la configuración natural del terreno ha sido preservada al igual que la vegetación, mientras que el agua es un elemento más bien decorativo que no dificulta el juego.

La Dehesa de Monteenmedio is a recent course of generally excellent standard thanks to the design skills of Alejandro Maldonado, from whom this is the most prestigious achievement to date as far as we know. This region is being given more and more courses as land becomes increasingly scarce between Malaga, Marbella and Gibraltar. The west is where it is all happening. For the time being this course admits only 60 players a day teeing off at 20 minutes intervals, so you are in for a relaxed round. The fairways and greens are wide, which is good news for the average players who form the core of green-feers visiting the region. Most of their approach shots will be medium-irons, and the par 3s call for an accurate tee-shot. However, they will need to be careful and not go for the greens in any old way, because the designer has kept the terrain's natural contours and vegetation. There is water but it is more decorative than really in play.

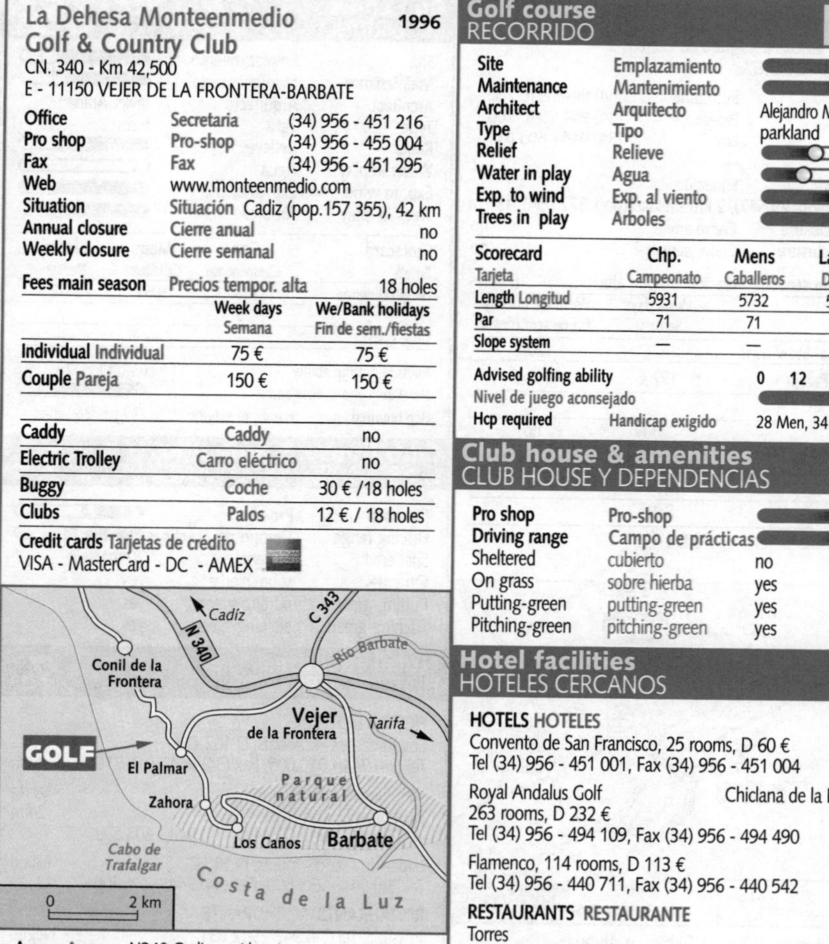

La Dehesa Monteenmedio Golf & Country Club — 1996

CN. 340 - Km 42,500
E - 11150 VEJER DE LA FRONTERA-BARBATE

Office	Secretaria	(34) 956 - 451 216
Pro shop	Pro-shop	(34) 956 - 455 004
Fax	Fax	(34) 956 - 451 295
Web	www.monteenmedio.com	
Situation	Situación	Cadiz (pop.157 355), 42 km
Annual closure	Cierre anual	no
Weekly closure	Cierre semanal	no

Fees main season Precios tempor. alta	Week days Semana	We/Bank holidays Fin de sem./fiestas
		18 holes
Individual Individual	75 €	75 €
Couple Pareja	150 €	150 €

Caddy	Caddy	no
Electric Trolley	Carro eléctrico	no
Buggy	Coche	30 € /18 holes
Clubs	Palos	12 € / 18 holes

Credit cards Tarjetas de crédito
VISA - MasterCard - DC - AMEX

Access Acceso : N340 Cadiz → Algeciras.
Map 7 on page 1101 Plano 7 Página 1101

Golf course RECORRIDO — 16/20

Site	Emplazamiento	
Maintenance	Mantenimiento	
Architect	Arquitecto	Alejandro Maldonado
Type	Tipo	parkland
Relief	Relieve	
Water in play	Agua	
Exp. to wind	Exp. al viento	
Trees in play	Arboles	

Scorecard Tarjeta	**Chp.** Campeonato	**Mens** Caballeros	**Ladies** Damas
Length Longitud	5931	5732	5782
Par	71	71	72
Slope system	—	—	—

Advised golfing ability Nivel de juego aconsejado — 0 12 24 36
Hcp required Handicap exigido — 28 Men, 34 Ladies

Club house & amenities CLUB HOUSE Y DEPENDENCIAS — 8/10

Pro shop	Pro-shop	
Driving range	Campo de prácticas	
Sheltered	cubierto	no
On grass	sobre hierba	yes
Putting-green	putting-green	yes
Pitching-green	pitching-green	yes

Hotel facilities HOTELES CERCANOS — 7/10

HOTELS HOTELES

Convento de San Francisco, 25 rooms, D 60 € — Vejer
Tel (34) 956 - 451 001, Fax (34) 956 - 451 004

Royal Andalus Golf — Chiclana de la Frontera
263 rooms, D 232 €
Tel (34) 956 - 494 109, Fax (34) 956 - 494 490

Flamenco, 114 rooms, D 113 € — Conil
Tel (34) 956 - 440 711, Fax (34) 956 - 440 542

RESTAURANTS RESTAURANTE

Torres — Barbate 5 km
Tel (34) 956 - 430 985

NEGURI

17 | 7 | 7

Junto a El Saler, El Prat o el Club de Campo, Neguri es uno de los grandes ejemplos del estilo de Javier Arana, a la vez humilde (en su respeto a la tradición), y muy personal (en su interpretación). Considerado como un club privado, abre sus puertas entre semana a los jugadores de fuera nunca muy numerosos ya que Bilbao no es un destino prioritario para el turismo. Campo para los entendidos, Neguri está en perfectos condiciones aunque la tierra éste demasiado cansada. A su trazado clásico y de una rara elegancia, pocos cambios han sido incorporados desde sus orígines aunque numerosos pinos hayan sido plantados para sustituir las especies desaparecidas en primera linea de calle. Ha sido una saludable iniciatitiva ya que reconstruirán, con el conjunto de bunkers, las principales dificultades de juego. Muy difícil desde las barras de atrás, Neguri es un poco más asequible desde las otras salidas, pero sus sutilezas exigen un cierto nivel de juego para poder ser apreciadas plenamente.

With El Saler, El Prat or Club de Campo, Neguri is one of the great examples of the Javier Arana style, at once humble (in his respect of tradition) and very personal (in his interpretation). Considered to be a private club, Neguri half-opens its doors to green-feers during the week, although visitors can hardly be accused of invading the course given that Bilbao is not yet a major tourist destination. A course for connoisseurs, Neguri is in good condition, although the soil seems to be growing a little weary. Few changes have been made to the original layout, a classic design of uncommon elegance, but a large number of pine-trees have been planted to replace the trees that have disappeared from the front-line of the fairway limits. This is a welcome initiative, because with the bunkers the trees form the course's main difficulties. Very tough from the back-tees, Neguri mellows slightly when playing further forward, but the course's subtleties require a certain standard of skill to be fully appreciated.

Real Sociedad de Golf de Neguri

Campo "La Galea", Aptdo de Correos 9
E - 48990 ALGORTA

Office	Secretaria	(34) 944 - 910 200
Pro shop	Pro-shop	(34) 944 - 910 200
Fax	Fax	(34) 944 - 605 611
Web	—	
Situation	Situación	

Algorta (pop. 79 517), 2 km - Bilbao (pop. 372 054), 13 km

Annual closure	Cierre anual	no
Weekly closure	Cierre semanal	no

Fees main season Precios tempor. alta	Week days Semana	We/Bank holidays Fin de sem./fiestas
18 holes		
Individual Individual	96 €	120 €
Couple Pareja	192 €	240 €

Caddy	Caddy	no
Electric Trolley	Carro eléctrico	5 € /18 holes
Buggy	Coche	no
Clubs	Palos	no

Credit cards Tarjetas de crédito
VISA

Access Acceso : Bilbao → Getxo, → Algorta
Map 1 on page 1088 Plano 1 Página 1088

Golf course RECORRIDO — 17/20

Site	Emplazamiento	
Maintenance	Mantenimiento	
Architect	Arquitecto	Javier Arana
Type	Tipo	forest
Relief	Relieve	
Water in play	Agua	
Exp. to wind	Exp. al viento	
Trees in play	Arboles	

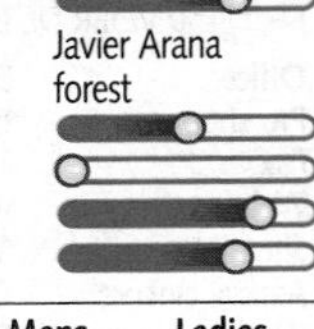

Scorecard Tarjeta	**Chp.** Campeonato	**Mens** Caballeros	**Ladies** Damas
Length Longitud	6280	6054	5112
Par	72	72	72
Slope system	—	—	—

Advised golfing ability Nivel de juego aconsejado: 0 12 24 36
Hcp required Handicap exigido: 28 Men, 36 Ladies

Club house & amenities CLUB HOUSE Y DEPENDENCIAS — 7/10

Pro shop	Pro-shop	
Driving range	Campo de prácticas	
Sheltered	cubierto	20 mats
On grass	sobre hierba	yes
Putting-green	putting-green	yes
Pitching-green	pitching-green	yes

Hotel facilities HOTELES CERCANOS — 7/10

HOTELS HOTELES

Los Tamarises, 42 rooms, D 102 € — Algorta 4 km
Tel (34) 944 - 910 005, Fax (34) 944 - 911 310

Igeretxe Agustín — Algorta 2 km
21 rooms, D 91 €
Tel (34) 944 - 910 009, Fax (34) 944 - 608 599

Lopez de Aro, 53 rooms, D 180 € — Bilbao 13 km
Tel (34) 944 - 235 500, Fax (34) 944 - 234 500

RESTAURANTS RESTAURANTE

Jolastoki, Tel (34) 949 - 912 031 — Neguri
Cubita, Tel (34) 944 - 911 700 — Algorta 2 km
Zortziko, Tel (34) 944 - 239 743 — Bilbao 13 km

NOVO SANCTI PETRI 16 7 7

Con 36 hoyos el campo responde a su alta ocupación. El diseño de Ballesteros es propio de un campo de vacaciones, sin excesivas complicaciones pero dispuesto a plantear diversas dificultades a jugadores de nivel medio, con obstáculos de agua en ciertas zonas, bunkers bien hechos aunque no intimidatorios y líneas de árboles que obligan a esmerarse en la precisión de los golpes de salida. Favorece a los jugadores que tienen facilidad para mover la bola de derecha a izquierda y los aproches hacia los amplios greenes han de hacerse por alto ya que están bien protegidos. El recorrido A es más variado, con hoyos muy abiertos, más expuesto a la brisa marina y con relieves moderados; mientras el recorrido B es más llano, generalmente entre pinos. Uno y otro, en definitva, tienen que dejar al jugador con el dulce sabor de boca de haber sabido superar el test de un gran campeón.

With 36 holes, this layout is just what any holidaying golfer is looking for. This Ballesteros design is just what the proverbial doctor ordered without any excessive complications but just a few headaches for the average player: water hazards here and there and a light scattering of well-placed bunkers to make sure you keep it straight off the tee. It all works in favour of golfers who can flight the ball from right to left and hit high approach shots to attack nicely-sized but well protected greens. Course A offers the most variety with a number of very open holes exposed to the sea breeze and only moderate slopes to contend with. Course B is flatter and winds its way through a pine forest. All in all, both courses give players the pleasant impression of having successfully sat the examination prepared by the great golfer who designed them.

Golf Novo Sancti Petri S.A. 1991

Urb. Novo Sancti Petri - Playa de la Barrosa
E - 11139 CHICLANA DE LA FRONTERA - CADIZ

Office Secretaria (34) 956 - 494 005
Pro shop Pro-shop (34) 956 -494 005-17
Fax Fax (34) 956 - 494 350
Web www.golf-novosancti.es
Situation Situación Jerez (pop. 184 364), 50 km
Chiclana de la Frontera (pop. 46 610), 11 km
Annual closure Cierre anual no
Weekly closure Cierre semanal no

Fees main season Precios tempor. alta	18 holes	
	Week days Semana	**We/Bank holidays** Fin de sem./fiestas
Individual Individual	51 €	51 €
Couple Pareja	102 €	102 €

Caddy	Caddy	30 € /18 holes
Electric Trolley	Carro eléctrico	12 € /18 holes
Buggy	Coche	30 € /18 holes
Clubs	Palos	18 € / 18 holes

Credit cards Tarjetas de crédito
VISA - Eurocard - MasterCard - DC - AMEX

Access Acceso : N340 Chiclana de la Frontera → Sancti Petri
Map 7 on page 1100 Plano 7 Página 1100

Golf course RECORRIDO 16/20

Site	Emplazamiento	
Maintenance	Mantenimiento	
Architect	Arquitecto	Seve Ballesteros
Type	Tipo	seaside course
Relief	Relieve	
Water in play	Agua	
Exp. to wind	Exp. al viento	
Trees in play	Arboles	

Scorecard Tarjeta	**Chp.** Campeonato	**Mens** Caballeros	**Ladies** Damas
Length Longitud	6510	6169	5337
Par	72	72	72
Slope system	—	—	—

Advised golfing ability 0 12 24 36
Nivel de juego aconsejado
Hcp required Handicap exigido 28 Men, 36 Ladies

Club house & amenities CLUB HOUSE Y DEPENDENCIAS 7/10

Pro shop	Pro-shop	
Driving range	Campo de prácticas	
Sheltered	cubierto	no
On grass	sobre hierba	yes
Putting-green	putting-green	yes
Pitching-green	pitching-green	yes

Hotel facilities HOTELES CERCANOS 7/10

HOTELS HOTELES
Royal Andalus Golf — Playa de la Barrosa 1
263 rooms, D 232 €
Tel (34) 956 - 494 109, Fax (34) 956 - 494 490

Tryp Costa Golf, 195 rooms, D 172 € — La Barrosa
Tel (34) 956 - 494 535, Fax (34) 956 - 494 626 — 10 km

Playa La Barrosa, 264 rooms, D 175 € — Playa de la Barrosa
Tel (34) 956 - 494 824, Fax (34) 956 - 494 860 — 500 m

RESTAURANTS RESTAURANTE
Novo Golf Gachito — Chiclana dela Frontera
Tel (34) 956 - 495 249 — 100 m

El Faro, Tel (34) 956 - 211 068 — Cádiz 25 km

OLIVA NOVA

14 | 6 | 7

Esta es una de las más recientes realizaciones de Severiano Ballesteros. En el extremo sur de la Costa Valenciana, lindando con la superturística y residencial costa de Alicante donde los campos de golf se multiplican para atender la demanda y preferencias de alemanes y centroeuropeos en general, Oliva Nova ofrece un campo completo por su cuidado mantenimiento y los diversos elementos del trazado que permiten jugar golpes muy variados. El agua es un elemento de riesgo que aparece constantemente, tanto señalando la referencia de dirección de los golpes de salida como enmarcando muchos greenes. Los greenes son delicados de atacar y de jugar, por sus caídas acusadas y porque varios de ellos están construídos en pendiente, en subida por la parte delantera y en bajada por el fondo. En un terreno llano próximo al mar, que disfruta por la tanto de la refrescante brisa marina, el recorrido necesita un tiempo para que la vegetación plantada adquiera envergadura.

This is one of the more recent designs by Severiano Ballesteros to the extreme south of the Costa Valenciana, where golf courses are mushrooming to attract customers from Northern Europe and especially Germany. Oliva Nova is a very complete and well-groomed course, where the layout calls for a whole variety of shots. Water is a risk element that is constantly around to attract shots hit slightly off the fairway or to guard any number of greens. The latter are difficult both to approach and to play, being sharply contoured and in many cases built on slopes, where the front part of the green slopes sideways and the rear section runs away. Close to the sea (the cooling sea-breeze is often much appreciated), this course calls for a little patience until the newly planted plants and trees start to really grow.

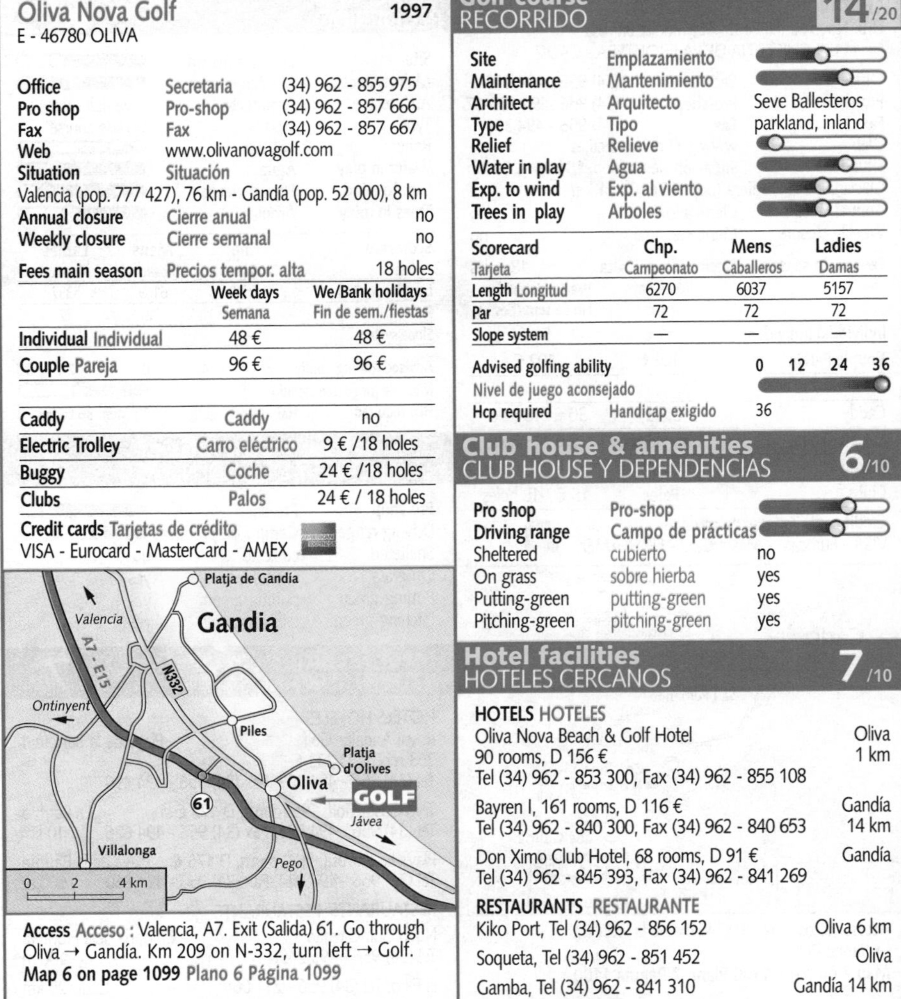

Oliva Nova Golf — 1997

E - 46780 OLIVA

Office	Secretaria	(34) 962 - 855 975
Pro shop	Pro-shop	(34) 962 - 857 666
Fax	Fax	(34) 962 - 857 667
Web	www.olivanovagolf.com	
Situation	Situación	

Valencia (pop. 777 427), 76 km - Gandía (pop. 52 000), 8 km

Annual closure	Cierre anual	no
Weekly closure	Cierre semanal	no

Fees main season Precios tempor. alta — 18 holes

	Week days Semana	We/Bank holidays Fin de sem./fiestas
Individual Individual	48 €	48 €
Couple Pareja	96 €	96 €

Caddy	Caddy	no
Electric Trolley	Carro eléctrico	9 € /18 holes
Buggy	Coche	24 € /18 holes
Clubs	Palos	24 € / 18 holes

Credit cards Tarjetas de crédito
VISA - Eurocard - MasterCard - AMEX

Access Acceso : Valencia, A7. Exit (Salida) 61. Go through Oliva → Gandía. Km 209 on N-332, turn left → Golf.
Map 6 on page 1099 Plano 6 Página 1099

Golf course RECORRIDO — 14/20

Site	Emplazamiento	
Maintenance	Mantenimiento	
Architect	Arquitecto	Seve Ballesteros
Type	Tipo	parkland, inland
Relief	Relieve	
Water in play	Agua	
Exp. to wind	Exp. al viento	
Trees in play	Arboles	

Scorecard Tarjeta	Chp. Campeonato	Mens Caballeros	Ladies Damas
Length Longitud	6270	6037	5157
Par	72	72	72
Slope system	—	—	—

Advised golfing ability Nivel de juego aconsejado — 0 12 24 36

Hcp required Handicap exigido — 36

Club house & amenities CLUB HOUSE Y DEPENDENCIAS — 6/10

Pro shop	Pro-shop	
Driving range	Campo de prácticas	
Sheltered	cubierto	no
On grass	sobre hierba	yes
Putting-green	putting-green	yes
Pitching-green	pitching-green	yes

Hotel facilities HOTELES CERCANOS — 7/10

HOTELS HOTELES

Oliva Nova Beach & Golf Hotel 90 rooms, D 156 € Tel (34) 962 - 853 300, Fax (34) 962 - 855 108	Oliva 1 km
Bayren I, 161 rooms, D 116 € Tel (34) 962 - 840 300, Fax (34) 962 - 840 653	Gandía 14 km
Don Ximo Club Hotel, 68 rooms, D 91 € Tel (34) 962 - 845 393, Fax (34) 962 - 841 269	Gandía

RESTAURANTS RESTAURANTE

Kiko Port, Tel (34) 962 - 856 152	Oliva 6 km
Soqueta, Tel (34) 962 - 851 452	Oliva
Gamba, Tel (34) 962 - 841 310	Gandía 14 km

OLIVAR DE LA HINOJOSA | 13 | 7 | 8

En España al igual que en numerosos páises, los jugadores profesionales sucumben a la tentación del diseño de campos, con suertes diversas. José Rivero no sólo se ha preocupado de sus colegas de alto nivel, ha pensado igualmente en todos los niveles, y éste recorrido (próximo al Campo de las Naciones y al aeropuerto) les convendrá perfectamente. Si un exceso de longitud y suficientemente amplio ofrece al debutante y al jugador experto la posibilidad de pasar una jornada agradable en un sitio esplendido. Sin embargo para conseguir un buen resultado, se necessitará saber jugar todo tipo de golpes, tener una estrategia de juego eficaz, y sacar a relucir sus dotes de buen pateador ya que si las ondulaciones son moderadas, algunas posiciones de banderas pueden ser peligrosas cuando nuestro tiro a green no ha sido muy preciso. Un mejor mantenimiento del rough y de las zonas de salida redundaría en beneficio del placer que procurá el campo.

In Spain as in many other countries, professional golfers fall for the lure of course design, with mixed results. José Rivero not only set out to satisfy his professional colleagues, he also spared many a thought for players of all abilities. This course (close to Campo de Las Naciones and the airport) will suit them just fine. Very wide without being agressively long, it allows beginners and experts alike to spend a great day on a pleasant site. To score well, though, you will need to play the full panoply of shots, decide upon and stick to an effective game strategy and putt your best, because while the greens are reasonably contoured, certain pin positions can be dangerous when the approach shot strays off target. Slightly tidier green-keeping, especially for the rough and around the teeboxes, could only enhance the pleasure of playing here.

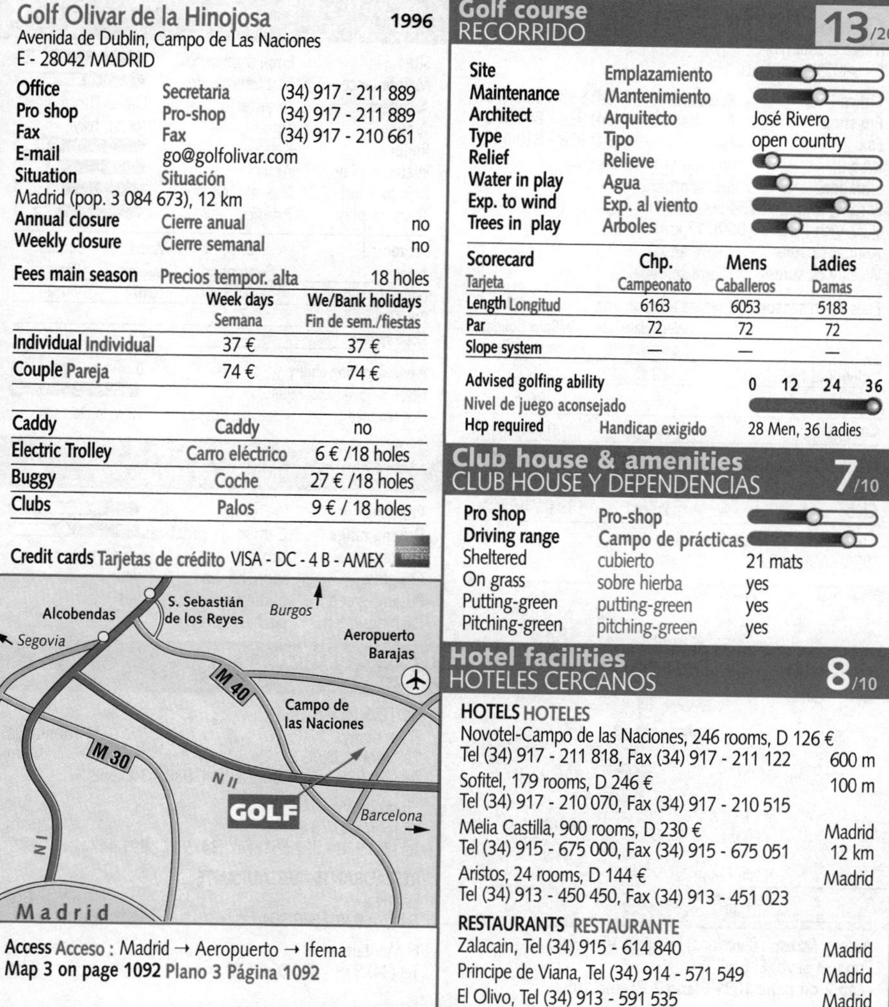

Golf Olivar de la Hinojosa — 1996

Avenida de Dublin, Campo de Las Naciones
E - 28042 MADRID

Office	Secretaria	(34) 917 - 211 889
Pro shop	Pro-shop	(34) 917 - 211 889
Fax	Fax	(34) 917 - 210 661
E-mail	go@golfolivar.com	
Situation	Situación	

Madrid (pop. 3 084 673), 12 km

Annual closure	Cierre anual	no
Weekly closure	Cierre semanal	no

Fees main season Precios tempor. alta	18 holes	
	Week days Semana	We/Bank holidays Fin de sem./fiestas
Individual Individual	37 €	37 €
Couple Pareja	74 €	74 €

Caddy	Caddy	no
Electric Trolley	Carro eléctrico	6 € /18 holes
Buggy	Coche	27 € /18 holes
Clubs	Palos	9 € / 18 holes

Credit cards Tarjetas de crédito VISA - DC - 4 B - AMEX

Access Acceso : Madrid → Aeropuerto → Ifema
Map 3 on page 1092 Plano 3 Página 1092

Golf course RECORRIDO — 13/20

Site	Emplazamiento	
Maintenance	Mantenimiento	
Architect	Arquitecto	José Rivero
Type	Tipo	open country
Relief	Relieve	
Water in play	Agua	
Exp. to wind	Exp. al viento	
Trees in play	Arboles	

Scorecard Tarjeta	Chp. Campeonato	Mens Caballeros	Ladies Damas
Length Longitud	6163	6053	5183
Par	72	72	72
Slope system	—	—	—

Advised golfing ability Nivel de juego aconsejado: 0 12 24 36
Hcp required Handicap exigido: 28 Men, 36 Ladies

Club house & amenities CLUB HOUSE Y DEPENDENCIAS — 7/10

Pro shop	Pro-shop	
Driving range	Campo de prácticas	
Sheltered	cubierto	21 mats
On grass	sobre hierba	yes
Putting-green	putting-green	yes
Pitching-green	pitching-green	yes

Hotel facilities HOTELES CERCANOS — 8/10

HOTELS HOTELES

Novotel-Campo de las Naciones, 246 rooms, D 126 € Tel (34) 917 - 211 818, Fax (34) 917 - 211 122	600 m
Sofitel, 179 rooms, D 246 € Tel (34) 917 - 210 070, Fax (34) 917 - 210 515	100 m
Melia Castilla, 900 rooms, D 230 € Tel (34) 915 - 675 000, Fax (34) 915 - 675 051	Madrid 12 km
Aristos, 24 rooms, D 144 € Tel (34) 913 - 450 450, Fax (34) 913 - 451 023	Madrid

RESTAURANTS RESTAURANTE

Zalacain, Tel (34) 915 - 614 840	Madrid
Principe de Viana, Tel (34) 914 - 571 549	Madrid
El Olivo, Tel (34) 913 - 591 535	Madrid

OSONA MONTANYA

14 | 7 | 4

Dave Thomas no ha querido añadir demasiadas dificultades técnicas a un recorrido bastante físico por sus cuestas. Naturalmente, hay árboles en la línea de juego, también algunos obstáculos de agua y aunque los bunkers de green están bastante alejados son poco visibles (están como hundidos) al igual que los bunkers de calle. Los greens tienen en general un declive bastante importante y pueden ser peligrosos cuando son rápidos. Todo ello hace que la estrategia de juego sea delicada cuando no se conoce el recorrido. Una vez conocido se pueden cortar los dog-legs con un buen drive, ya sea voleando los árboles o imprimiendo efecto a la bola. Agradable y variado merece la pena jugarlo varias veces, pero dada su situación en altura y en el interior, no se aconseja ir en invierno a no ser que se quiera contemplar el panorama de los Pirineos nevados desde la terraza del precioso club-house.

Dave Thomas did not want to add too many technical difficulties to an already hilly and physically quite demanding course. The trees are there, of course, together with a little water, but while the green-side bunkers are not too close to the greens, they are hard to see (they are sunk into dips). The same goes for the fairway bunkers. There is quite a lot of slope on the greens, which can be difficult when playing fast. All this makes for a tricky choice of game strategy when playing the course for the first time. When you know the course, long drivers can cut corners on the dog-legs either by hitting over the trees or by flighting the ball. Pleasant and varied, this pretty course is well worth a few visits, but the high-altitude location inland is not to be recommended in winter, except perhaps to gaze over the panorama of the snow-covered Pyrenees from the terrace of the very elegant club-house.

Club de Golf Osona Montanya — 1989

Masia el Estanyol
E - 08553 EL BRULL

Office	Secretaria	(34) 938 - 840 170
Pro shop	Pro-shop	(34) 938 - 840 170
Fax	Fax	(34) 938 - 840 407
Web	www.golfmontanya.com	
Situation	Situación	

Barcelona (pop. 1 754 900), 60 km
Vic / Vich (pop. 30 060), 17 km

Annual closure	Cierre anual	no
Weekly closure	Cierre semanal	no

Fees main season Precios tempor. alta — 18 holes

	Week days / Semana	We/Bank holidays / Fin de sem./fiestas
Individual Individual	48 €	48 €
Couple Pareja	96 €	96 €
Caddy Caddy		on request
Electric Trolley Carro eléctrico		9 € /18 holes
Buggy Coche		33 € /18 holes
Clubs Palos		183 € / 18 holes

Credit cards Tarjetas de crédito
VISA - MasterCard

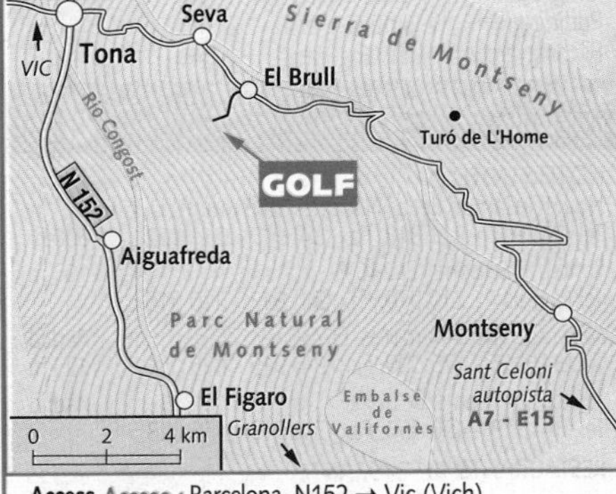

Access Acceso : Barcelona, N152 → Vic (Vich).
Tona → Seva, El Brull
Map 2 on page 1091 Plano 2 Página 1091

Golf course RECORRIDO — 14/20

Site	Emplazamiento	
Maintenance	Mantenimiento	
Architect	Arquitecto	David Thomas
Type	Tipo	forest, hilly
Relief	Relieve	
Water in play	Agua	
Exp. to wind	Exp. al viento	
Trees in play	Arboles	

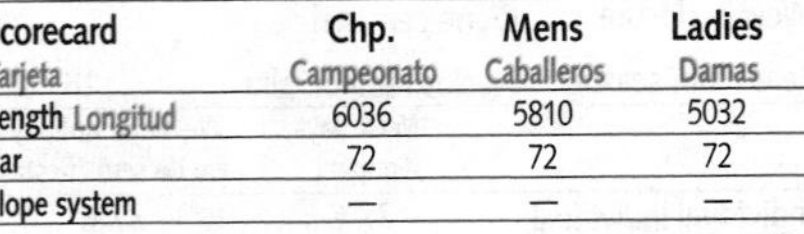

Scorecard Tarjeta	**Chp.** Campeonato	**Mens** Caballeros	**Ladies** Damas
Length Longitud	6036	5810	5032
Par	72	72	72
Slope system	—	—	—

Advised golfing ability Nivel de juego aconsejado — 0 12 24 36
Hcp required Handicap exigido — 28 Men, 36 Ladies

Club house & amenities CLUB HOUSE Y DEPENDENCIAS — 7/10

Pro shop	Pro-shop	
Driving range	Campo de prácticas	
Sheltered	cubierto	25 mats
On grass	sobre hierba	yes
Putting-green	putting-green	yes
Pitching-green	pitching-green	no

Hotel facilities HOTELES CERCANOS — 4/10

HOTELS HOTELES

El Montanya — Montanya 4 km
120 rooms, D 96 €
Tel (34) 938 - 840 606, Fax (34) 938 - 840 558

Ciutat de Vic — Vic 20 km
36 rooms, D 78 €
Tel (34) 938 - 892 551, Fax (34) 938 - 891 447

RESTAURANTS RESTAURANTE

Estanyol — Golf
Tel (34) 938 - 840 354

El Montanya — Montanya 4 km
Tel (34) 938 - 840 004

PALS

16 | 7 | 6

Pals no ha usurpado su reputación. Su situación entre pinos, su tranquilidad, su moderado relieve (algunos greens en alto), la flexibilidad entre diferentes tees de salida, lo convierten en un recorrido atractivo para todos los niveles. Su terreno arenoso aguanta bien la lluvia y ofrece una confortable alfombra a los jugadores. Su diseño clásico (FW Hawtree) pone esencialmente en línea de juego árboles y bunkers que protegen los greens. El bosque no sólo es denso, lo que obliga a pegar un buen drive para evitarlo y buenos golpes para salir de él, sino que además la envergadura de los pinos, en forma de sombrilla, estrecha las calles y alguna que otra vez la bola queda encaramada en las ramas. El arquitecto ha revalorizado este terreno ideal para construir un golf conservando su aspecto natural. Los greens son fáciles de apreciar pero no muy grandes.

The reputation of Pals is rightfully deserved. This is firstly a very appealing course for all levels, laid out in the quiet of pinetrees, with mainly smooth unbroken terrain (only a few elevated greens) and the flexibility afforded by several different tees. The sandy terrain also soaks up any rain very quickly and provides a very comfortable carpet for players to play on. The classic design (F.W. Hawtree) basically brings bunkers into play to defend the greens, and uses trees. The forest is not only pretty thick - requiring good drives to keep out, and very good recovery shots to get out, of the woods - but the span of these parasol pines tends to make the fairways narrower, and the branches sometimes even keep the balls! The architect has successfully developed this ideal terrain for building a golf course while preserving its natural character. The greens are comparatively easy to read and not very large.

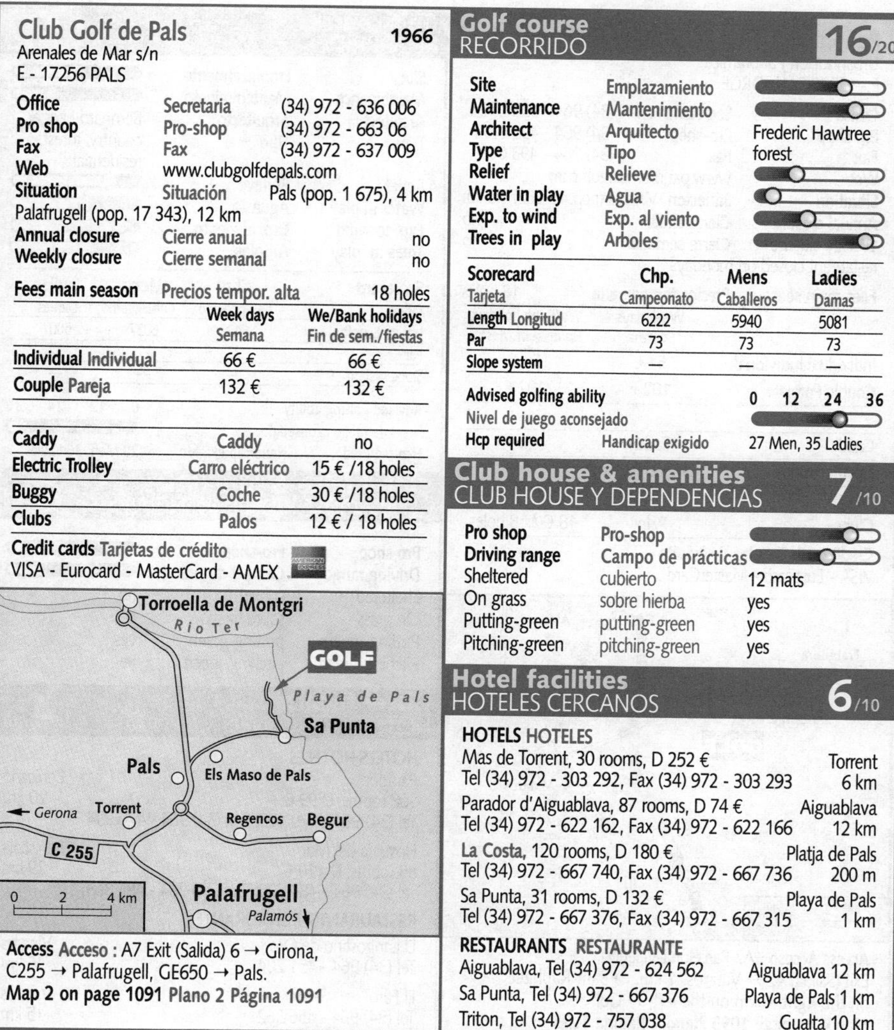

Club Golf de Pals — 1966

Arenales de Mar s/n
E - 17256 PALS

Office	Secretaría	(34) 972 - 636 006
Pro shop	Pro-shop	(34) 972 - 663 06
Fax	Fax	(34) 972 - 637 009
Web	www.clubgolfdepals.com	
Situation	Situación	Pals (pop. 1 675), 4 km

Palafrugell (pop. 17 343), 12 km

Annual closure	Cierre anual	no
Weekly closure	Cierre semanal	no

Fees main season Precios tempor. alta	18 holes	
	Week days Semana	**We/Bank holidays** Fin de sem./fiestas
Individual Individual	66 €	66 €
Couple Pareja	132 €	132 €

Caddy	Caddy	no
Electric Trolley	Carro eléctrico	15 € /18 holes
Buggy	Coche	30 € /18 holes
Clubs	Palos	12 € / 18 holes

Credit cards Tarjetas de crédito
VISA - Eurocard - MasterCard - AMEX

Access Acceso : A7 Exit (Salida) 6 → Girona, C255 → Palafrugell, GE650 → Pals.
Map 2 on page 1091 Plano 2 Página 1091

Golf course RECORRIDO — 16/20

Site	Emplazamiento	
Maintenance	Mantenimiento	
Architect	Arquitecto	Frederic Hawtree
Type	Tipo	forest
Relief	Relieve	
Water in play	Agua	
Exp. to wind	Exp. al viento	
Trees in play	Arboles	

Scorecard Tarjeta	**Chp.** Campeonato	**Mens** Caballeros	**Ladies** Damas
Length Longitud	6222	5940	5081
Par	73	73	73
Slope system	—	—	—

Advised golfing ability Nivel de juego aconsejado: 0 12 24 36
Hcp required Handicap exigido: 27 Men, 35 Ladies

Club house & amenities CLUB HOUSE Y DEPENDENCIAS — 7/10

Pro shop	Pro-shop	
Driving range	Campo de prácticas	
Sheltered	cubierto	12 mats
On grass	sobre hierba	yes
Putting-green	putting-green	yes
Pitching-green	pitching-green	yes

Hotel facilities HOTELES CERCANOS — 6/10

HOTELS HOTELES

Mas de Torrent, 30 rooms, D 252 € Tel (34) 972 - 303 292, Fax (34) 972 - 303 293	Torrent 6 km
Parador d'Aiguablava, 87 rooms, D 74 € Tel (34) 972 - 622 162, Fax (34) 972 - 622 166	Aiguablava 12 km
La Costa, 120 rooms, D 180 € Tel (34) 972 - 667 740, Fax (34) 972 - 667 736	Platja de Pals 200 m
Sa Punta, 31 rooms, D 132 € Tel (34) 972 - 667 376, Fax (34) 972 - 667 315	Playa de Pals 1 km

RESTAURANTS RESTAURANTE

Aiguablava, Tel (34) 972 - 624 562	Aiguablava 12 km
Sa Punta, Tel (34) 972 - 667 376	Playa de Pals 1 km
Triton, Tel (34) 972 - 757 038	Gualta 10 km

PANORAMICA

14 | 6 | 4

Panorámica es un campo joven, situado en un espacio relativamente llano, cómodo y agradable para el amateur medio. La primera vuelta tienes tres pares 3 y tres pares 5, sin demasiadas complicaciones, capaces de animar a muchos jugadores a realizar una buena vuelta. Hay varios tees de salida en alto que invitan a pegar drives fáciles y, desde las marcas medias, el campo no es excesivamente largo. También hay varios greenes en alto, sin visión para precisar el approach. El rough suele estar corado muy bajo y el estado general del mantenimiento del campo es excelente. Ello hace suponer que a este campo le favorecerá el paso del tiempo, por ejemplo, cuando crezcan los árboles que se han plantado y se asiente el entorno. En una zona de rica gastronomía mediterránea, pero sin tradición golfística, el campo todavía tiene una ocupación reducida. Con una casa-club confortable, sus servicios e instalaciones son típicos del campo de vacaciones.

Panoramica is still a young course over a relatively flat setting, enjoyable and playable by the average golfer. The outward nine include three par 3s and three par 5s without too many difficulties, and might prompt many of you to card a good score. All the tee-boxes are elevated, which will tempt a lot of players to use the driver, and from the forward tees the course is not too long. Likewise, the greens are more or less elevated so you don't always get a clear view of the approach you should be playing. The rough is not too long and overall green-keeping is of an excellent standard. This course will obviously improve with time, for example when the many young trees have grown to full maturity. In a region rich in Mediterranean gastronomy but not so well off for golf courses, Panoramica is not too busy just yet, although the comfortable clubhouse, facilities and services make this a typical vacation course.

Panoramica Golf & Country Club — 1995

Urbanización Panoramica
E - 12320 SAN JORGE

Office	Secretaria	(34) 964 - 493 072
Pro shop	Pro-shop	(34) 964 - 493 072
Fax	Fax	(34) 964 - 493 063
Web	www.panoramicagolf.com	
Situation	Situación	Vinaròs (pop. 19 202), 15 km
Annual closure	Cierre anual	no
Weekly closure	Cierre semanal	no

restaurant closed on mondays

Fees main season Precios tempor. alta	Week days Semana	We/Bank holidays Fin de sem./fiestas
18 holes		
Individual Individual	51 €	51 €
Couple Pareja	102 €	102 €

Caddy	Caddy	no
Electric Trolley	Carro eléctrico	no
Buggy	Coche	30 € /18 holes
Clubs	Palos	18 € / 18 holes

Credit cards Tarjetas de crédito
VISA - Eurocard - MasterCard

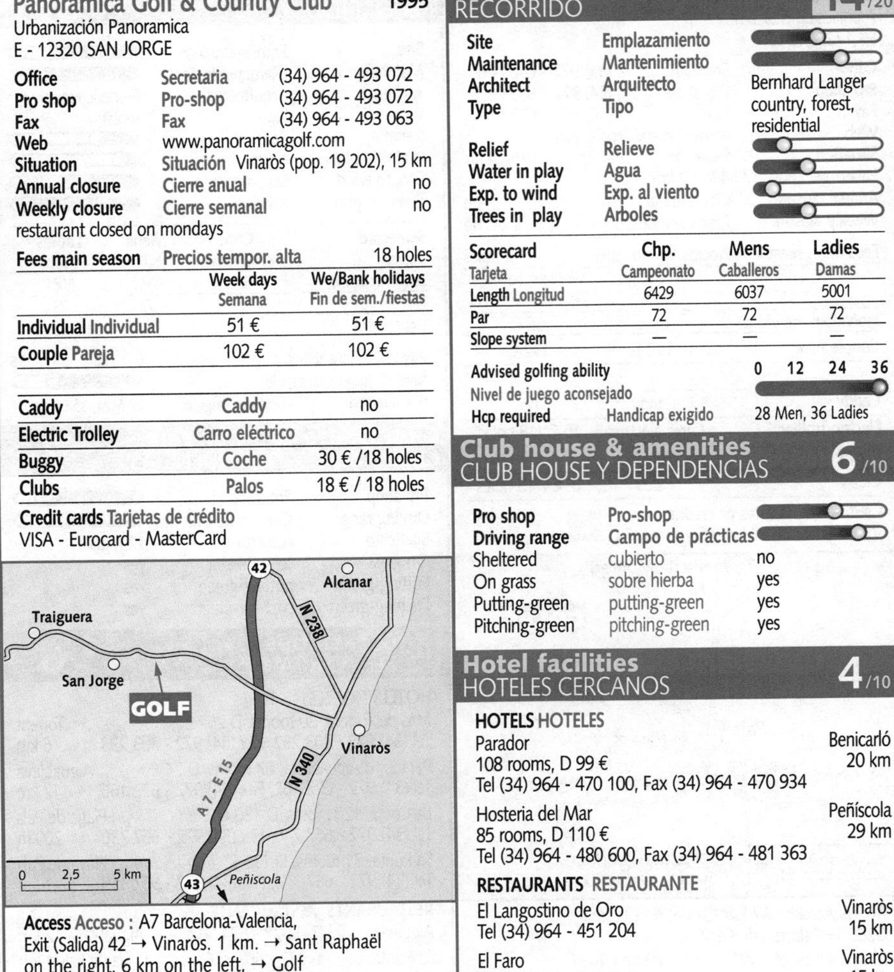

Access Acceso : A7 Barcelona-Valencia, Exit (Salida) 42 → Vinaròs. 1 km. → Sant Raphaël on the right. 6 km on the left, → Golf
Map 4 on page 1095 Plano 4 Página 1095

Golf course RECORRIDO — 14/20

Site	Emplazamiento	
Maintenance	Mantenimiento	
Architect	Arquitecto	Bernhard Langer
Type	Tipo	country, forest, residential
Relief	Relieve	
Water in play	Agua	
Exp. to wind	Exp. al viento	
Trees in play	Arboles	

Scorecard Tarjeta	Chp. Campeonato	Mens Caballeros	Ladies Damas
Length Longitud	6429	6037	5001
Par	72	72	72
Slope system	—	—	—

Advised golfing ability / Nivel de juego aconsejado: 0 12 24 36
Hcp required / Handicap exigido: 28 Men, 36 Ladies

Club house & amenities CLUB HOUSE Y DEPENDENCIAS — 6/10

Pro shop	Pro-shop	
Driving range	Campo de prácticas	
Sheltered	cubierto	no
On grass	sobre hierba	yes
Putting-green	putting-green	yes
Pitching-green	pitching-green	yes

Hotel facilities HOTELES CERCANOS — 4/10

HOTELS HOTELES

Parador — Benicarló 20 km
108 rooms, D 99 €
Tel (34) 964 - 470 100, Fax (34) 964 - 470 934

Hosteria del Mar — Peñiscola 29 km
85 rooms, D 110 €
Tel (34) 964 - 480 600, Fax (34) 964 - 481 363

RESTAURANTS RESTAURANTE

El Langostino de Oro — Vinaròs 15 km
Tel (34) 964 - 451 204

El Faro — Vinaròs 15 km
Tel (34) 964 - 456 362

PEDREÑA

15	6	5

En éste marco incomparable, con unas vistas magníficas, Severiano Ballesteros hizo su aprendizaje. Y cuando recorremos éste trazado muy británico (con todas las astucias estratégicas de su diseñador Harry Colt), cuando debemos negociar con los árboles, y muchas veces salirnos de ellos, entendemos que el campeón español haya acumulado todos los recursos para salirse de las situaciones más difíciles. Aquí hace falta pegar recto (lo que no es precisamente su fuerte). Bastante accidentado, con roughs a menudo muy densos, el campo tiene algunos greenes ciegos lo que complica todavía más sus aspectos técnicos que compensan ampliamente su falta de longitud. Sin embargo el jugador medio que sepa jugar recto se las arreglará muy bien, sobre todo en match-play, ya que es un campo perfecto para asumir riesgos. En cuanto a los mejores, deberán aplacar sus ansias y adaptar su técnica a la situación.

This impressive site, with some magnificent views, is where Severiano Ballesteros learnt his trade. When you play this classical layout (with all the strategic tricks of architect Harry Colt) and as you cope with all the trees and sometimes struggle to find your way out of them, you realise that the Spanish champion learnt his amazing art of recovery in very tough conditions indeed. Here, you have to drive straight (that was never Seve's forte). Rather hilly, with some often thick rough, this highly-reputed course includes a few blind greens, which complicate a still further the technical aspects of playing here and easily make up for the lack of yardage. With this said, average and straight players should get by just fine, especially in match-play, because this is the ideal terrain for taking risks. As for the wunderkinds, they'll just have to keep a check on their adrenaline flow and adjust their technique to matters at hand.

Real Golf de Pedreña

Apartado, 233
E - 39 080 SANTANDER

Office	Secretaria	(34) 942 - 500 001
Pro shop	Pro-shop	(34) 942 - 500 001
Fax	Fax	(34) 942 - 500 136
Web	www.realgolfdepedrena.com	
Situation	Situación	
Santander (pop. 196 218), 24 km		
Annual closure	Cierre anual	no
Weekly closure	Cierre semanal	no

Fees main season	Precios tempor. alta	18 holes
	Week days Semana	We/Bank holidays Fin de sem./fiestas
Individual Individual	60 €	60 €
Couple Pareja	120 €	120 €

Caddy	Caddy	no
Electric Trolley	Carro eléctrico	9 € /18 holes
Buggy	Coche	30 € /18 holes
Clubs	Palos	12 € / 18 holes
Credit cards Tarjetas de crédito		no

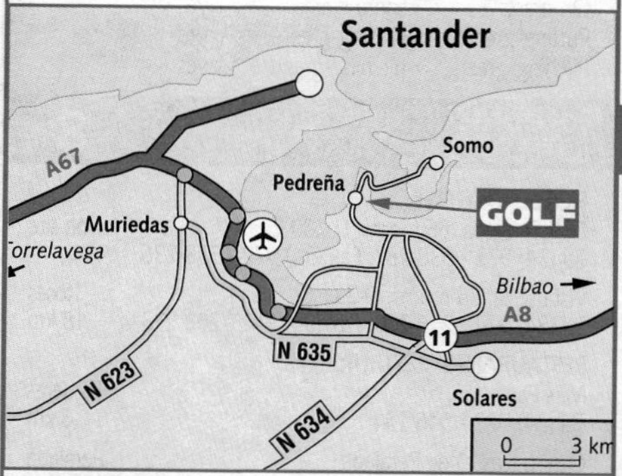

Access Acceso : Bilbao, N 634, N 635 → Santander.
Map 1 on page 1088 Plano 1 Página 1088

Golf course RECORRIDO 15/20

Site	Emplazamiento	
Maintenance	Mantenimiento	
Architect	Arquitecto	Harry S. Colt
Type	Tipo	seaside course, forest
Relief	Relieve	
Water in play	Agua	
Exp. to wind	Exp. al viento	
Trees in play	Arboles	

Scorecard Tarjeta	**Chp.** Campeonato	**Mens** Caballeros	**Ladies** Damas
Length Longitud	5764	5511	4764
Par	70	70	70
Slope system	—	—	—

Advised golfing ability 0 12 24 36
Nivel de juego aconsejado

Hcp required Handicap exigido 28 Men, 36 Ladies

Club house & amenities CLUB HOUSE Y DEPENDENCIAS 6/10

Pro shop	Pro-shop	
Driving range	Campo de prácticas	
Sheltered	cubierto	5 mats
On grass	sobre hierba	yes
Putting-green	putting-green	yes
Pitching-green	pitching-green	no

Hotel facilities HOTELES CERCANOS 5/10

HOTELS HOTELES

Real, 123 rooms, D 246 € Tel (34) 942 - 272 550, Fax (34) 942 - 274 573	Santander 24 km
NH Ciudad de Santander 60 rooms, D 138 € Tel (34) 942 - 227 965, Fax (34) 942 - 217 303	Santander
Sardinero, 108 rooms, D 116 € Tel (34) 942 - 271 100, Fax (34) 942 - 271 698	Santander

RESTAURANTS RESTAURANTE

La Sardina, Tel (34) 942 - 271 035	Santander
Mesón Segoviano, Tel (34) 942 - 311 010	Santander
Rhin, Tel (34) 942 - 273 034	Santander

PERALADA

15 | 7 | 8

Un recorrido táctico. En primer lugar hay que sobrepasar los bunkers, saber evitarlos o quedarse corto: en cada par 4, un bunker de calle acoge las caídas de drive entre 190 y 240 metros desde las salidas de atrás. Después y en cinco hoyos hay que decidir si se puede sobrepasar un río situado a unos treinta metros antes del green. Pero estas dificultades no menguan la franqueza de un recorrido en el que algunos dog-legs y varios fuera de límites ayudan a mantener la concentración. Poniendo empeño se puede jugar su handicap. En todo caso, es un recorrido agradable para jugar en familia dejando que cada uno escoja el tee de salida que más le convenga. Al igual que las calles y los greens (hay 8 con doble escalón), los roughs son densos, sembrados de olivos y es de desear que el proyecto de construcción de casas se lleve a cabo en los espacios vacíos entre algunos hoyos.

This is a tactical course. First of all you have to avoid the sand by either carrying the bunkers or laying up short. Because on each par 4, a fairway bunker lurks close to the drive landing zone, from 190 to 240 metres from the back-tees. Then, on five holes you have to decide whether to carry a widish river located about thirty metres in front of the greens. But these difficulties take absolutely nothing away from the course's openness, where a few gentle dog-legs and out-of-bounds help keep players focused. With a little concentration, you might even play to your handicap at Peralada. But at all events, this is a pleasant course for all the family where everyone can choose the tees that suit them best. Like the fairways and the greens (8 of which have two tiers), the thick rough is dotted with olive trees. Hopefully, the villas under development in the open spaces between certain holes will soon be finished.

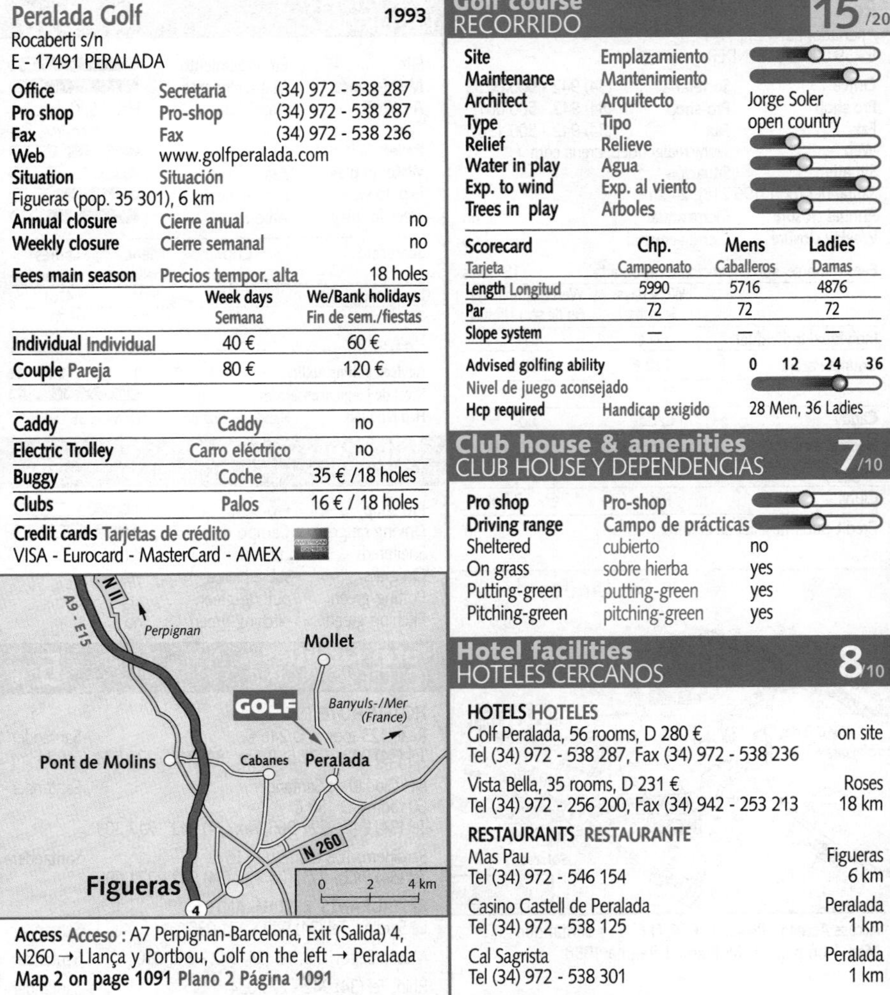

Peralada Golf — 1993
Rocaberti s/n
E - 17491 PERALADA

Office	Secretaria	(34) 972 - 538 287
Pro shop	Pro-shop	(34) 972 - 538 287
Fax	Fax	(34) 972 - 538 236
Web	www.golfperalada.com	
Situation	Situación	

Figueras (pop. 35 301), 6 km

Annual closure	Cierre anual	no
Weekly closure	Cierre semanal	no

Fees main season Precios tempor. alta		18 holes
	Week days Semana	**We/Bank holidays** Fin de sem./fiestas
Individual Individual	40 €	60 €
Couple Pareja	80 €	120 €

Caddy	Caddy	no
Electric Trolley	Carro eléctrico	no
Buggy	Coche	35 € /18 holes
Clubs	Palos	16 € / 18 holes

Credit cards Tarjetas de crédito
VISA - Eurocard - MasterCard - AMEX

Access Acceso : A7 Perpignan-Barcelona, Exit (Salida) 4, N260 → Llança y Portbou, Golf on the left → Peralada
Map 2 on page 1091 Plano 2 Página 1091

Golf course — RECORRIDO — 15/20

Site	Emplazamiento	
Maintenance	Mantenimiento	
Architect	Arquitecto	Jorge Soler
Type	Tipo	open country
Relief	Relieve	
Water in play	Agua	
Exp. to wind	Exp. al viento	
Trees in play	Arboles	

Scorecard Tarjeta	**Chp.** Campeonato	**Mens** Caballeros	**Ladies** Damas
Length Longitud	5990	5716	4876
Par	72	72	72
Slope system	—	—	—

Advised golfing ability Nivel de juego aconsejado — 0 12 24 36
Hcp required Handicap exigido — 28 Men, 36 Ladies

Club house & amenities — CLUB HOUSE Y DEPENDENCIAS — 7/10

Pro shop	Pro-shop	
Driving range	Campo de prácticas	
Sheltered	cubierto	no
On grass	sobre hierba	yes
Putting-green	putting-green	yes
Pitching-green	pitching-green	yes

Hotel facilities — HOTELES CERCANOS — 8/10

HOTELS HOTELES

Golf Peralada, 56 rooms, D 280 € — on site
Tel (34) 972 - 538 287, Fax (34) 972 - 538 236

Vista Bella, 35 rooms, D 231 € — Roses 18 km
Tel (34) 972 - 256 200, Fax (34) 942 - 253 213

RESTAURANTS RESTAURANTE

Mas Pau — Figueras 6 km
Tel (34) 972 - 546 154

Casino Castell de Peralada — Peralada 1 km
Tel (34) 972 - 538 125

Cal Sagrista — Peralada 1 km
Tel (34) 972 - 538 301

PGA DE CATALUNYA

18 | 7 | 7

La apertura en junio de 1999 del golf de Caldes de Malavella, pocos kilómetros al sur de Girona y dentro de la zona de influencia turística de la Costa Brava, enriquece sobremanera la oferta de buen golf en el noreste de España, donde hay playas y pinos hasta el borde del mar, tradición cultural y gastronómica, paisajes sugestivos y ágiles vías de comunicación. El recorrido es bello, bueno y exigente, con excelentes vistas que llegan hasta los Pirineos. Las calles son anchas y onduladas, abiertas en un frondoso bosque de pinos y alcornoques, pero el raf es implacable, y los dos grandes lagos, entre el 3 y el 5 y entre el 11 y el 13, añaden dimensión y vistas escénicas al campo. Los greenes, muy defendidos tanto por la distancia como por bunkers, agua y accidentes del terreno, tienen unas dimensiones espléndidas y gran movimiento para el disfrute del buen pateador. Los desniveles y las distancias de green a tee demandan una buena preparación física del jugador que, sin duda, verá gratamente compensado su esfuerzo ante la inteligencia del diseño que premia el buen golpe, la buena calidad de la construcción y el estado de este soberbio recorrido.

The opening of the Caldes de Malavella course has enhanced the bunch of great courses in this part of Spain, which boasts assets such as beaches and pine forests, a great tradition for culture and good food, superb landscapes and good communications. This course is at once good, beautiful and demanding, with some wonderful views over the Pyrenees. The fairways are wide and rolling, laid out in a forest thick with pine and cork-oak trees, but the rough is uncompromising and the two large lakes placed between the 3rd and 5th and the 11th and 13th holes add a scenic dimension to the whole layout. The greens, difficult to reach through sheer length and tightly guarded by sand-traps, water and sloping terrain, provide added interest for good putters. The hilly terrain and distance between green and tee-box are best suited to the fit golfer who, in return, will be rewarded for his or her effort by the intelligence of a layout which helps the best shots, and by the excellence that has gone into the building and maintaining of this very fine course.

PGA Golf de Catalunya — 1999

Apartado de correos 60 / Ctra N-II, Km 701
E - 17455 CALDES DE MALAVELLA

Office	Secretaria	(34) 972 - 472 577
Pro shop	Pro-shop	(34) 972 - 472 577
Fax	Fax	(34) 972 - 470 493
Web	www.pgacatalunya.com	
Situation	Situación	

Girona (pop. 71 000), 13 km

Annual closure	Cierre anual	no
Weekly closure	Cierre semanal	no

Fees main season Precios tempor. alta		18 holes
	Week days Semana	We/Bank holidays Fin de sem./fiestas
Individual Individual	60 €	60 €
Couple Pareja	120 €	120 €
Caddy	Caddy	no
Electric Trolley	Carro eléctrico	no
Buggy	Coche	30 € /18 holes
Clubs	Palos	15 € / 18 holes

Credit cards Tarjetas de crédito
VISA - Eurocard - MasterCard - AMEX

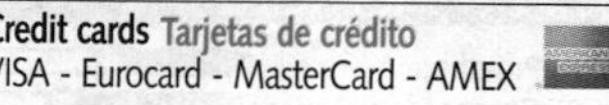

Access Acceso : Barcelona, A2 Exit (salida) 9. N2 → Girona. Golf after Km 701 point.
Map 2 on page 1091 Plano 2 Página 1091

Golf course RECORRIDO — 18/20

Site	Emplazamiento	
Maintenance	Mantenimiento	
Architect	Arquitecto	Neil Coles Angel Gallardo
Type	Tipo	parkland, forest
Relief	Relieve	
Water in play	Agua	
Exp. to wind	Exp. al viento	
Trees in play	Arboles	

Scorecard Tarjeta	**Chp.** Campeonato	**Mens** Caballeros	**Ladies** Damas
Length Longitud	6588	6226	5310
Par	72	72	72
Slope system	—	—	—

Advised golfing ability Nivel de juego aconsejado — 0 12 24 36

Hcp required Handicap exigido — 28 Men/36 Ladies

Club house & amenities CLUB HOUSE Y DEPENDENCIAS — 7/10

Pro shop	Pro-shop	
Driving range	Campo de prácticas	
Sheltered	cubierto	no
On grass	sobre hierba	yes (100 places)
Putting-green	putting-green	yes
Pitching-green	pitching-green	yes

Hotel facilities HOTELES CERCANOS — 7/10

HOTELS HOTELES

Balneario Vichy Catalan — Caldes de Malavella 5 km
82 rooms, D 126 €
Tel (34) 972 - 470 000, Fax (34) 972 - 472 299

Carlemany, 87 rooms, D 96 € — Girona 13 km
Tel (34) 972 - 211 212, Fax (34) 972 - 214 994

La Gavina, 74 rooms, D 221 € — S'Agaró 28 km
Tel (34) 972 - 321 100, Fax (34) 972 - 321 573

RESTAURANTS RESTAURANTE

Can Geli, Tel (34) 972 - 470 275 — Caldes de Malavella 1 km
Hostal de la Granota, Tel (34) 972 - 853 044 — Vidreras 6 km
Cal Ros, Tel (34) 972 - 217 379 — Girona 14 km

PINEDA

15 | 7 | 9

Se trata de un recorrido con todas las características de un Country Club, con actividades sociales y deportivas variadas (tenis, piscina, paddle) al lado de Sevilla, lo que le asegura una fuerte frecuentación. Esencialmente son los invitados de los socios quienes pueden jugar. Creado en 1939, el recorrido sólo tenía 9 hoyos, y ha habido que esperar hasta 1992 para verlo convertido en un 18 hoyos con una longitud respetable. Su estética es la de un verdadero parque con abundante vegetación, cosa bella y apreciable sobre todo en los veranos calurosos. Los hoyos están bien estructurados y el ritmo de juego es excelente. Hay que ser muy precisos en los segundos golpes ya que los greens no son muy grandes. En realidad es un recorridos muy formador que ha facilitado excelentes jugadores a los equipos nacionales españoles.

Pineda is part of a real country-club concept with a wide variety of social and sporting activities (tennis, swimming-pool, paddle-tennis) at the gates of Seville. This makes it a busy course and explains why the majority of visitors are member guests. Created in 1939, Pineda originally had only 9 holes and was extended to 18 holes and a very respectable yardage only in 1992. This is a park-style course with lush vegetation which most will find pretty welcome, particularly on hot summer afternoons. The holes are neatly proportioned and the layout well-balanced, but your approach shots must be accurate to hit the smallish greens. This is in fact a very instructive course, as it has provided many excellent players who have go on to play in the Spanish national teams.

Real Golf Club Pineda de Sevilla — 1939

Avda. Jerez, s/n
E - 41012 SEVILLA

Office	Secretaria	(34) 954 - 611 400
Pro shop	Pro-shop	(34) 954 - 611 400
Fax	Fax	(34) 954 - 617 704
Web	www.rcpineda.com	
Situation	Situación	Sevilla (pop. 70 4857), 3 km
Annual closure	Cierre anual	no
Weekly closure	Cierre semanal	no

Fees main season Precios tempor. alta	Week days Semana	We/Bank holidays Fin de sem./fiestas
18 holes		
Individual Individual	51 €	*
Couple Pareja	102 €	*

* Only with members (solo con socios)
8 visitors only each weekday

Caddy	Caddy	no
Electric Trolley	Carro eléctrico	no
Buggy	Coche	no
Clubs	Palos	no
Credit cards	Tarjetas de crédito	no

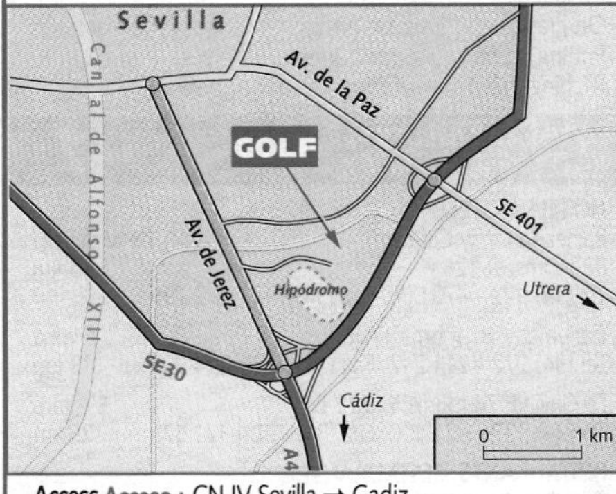

Access Acceso : CN IV Sevilla → Cadiz, in El Cortijo de Pineda
Map 7 on page 1101 Plano 7 Página 1101

Golf course RECORRIDO — 15/20

Site	Emplazamiento	
Maintenance	Mantenimiento	
Architect	Arquitecto	R.& F. M. Benjumea, Luis Recasens
Type	Tipo	parkland
Relief	Relieve	
Water in play	Agua	
Exp. to wind	Exp. al viento	
Trees in play	Arboles	

Scorecard Tarjeta	Chp. Campeonato	Mens Caballeros	Ladies Damas
Length Longitud	6147	6037	5077
Par	72	72	72
Slope system	—	—	—

Advised golfing ability Nivel de juego aconsejado: 0 12 24 36
Hcp required Handicap exigido: 28 Men, 36 Ladies

Club house & amenities CLUB HOUSE Y DEPENDENCIAS — 7/10

Pro shop	Pro-shop	
Driving range	Campo de prácticas	
Sheltered	cubierto	10 mats
On grass	sobre hierba	yes
Putting-green	putting-green	yes
Pitching-green	pitching-green	yes

Hotel facilities HOTELES CERCANOS — 9/10

HOTELS HOTELES

Melia Sevilla, 361 rooms, D 178 € Tel (34) 954 - 421 511, Fax (34) 954 - 422 977	Sevilla 5 km
Alfonso XIII, 127 rooms, D 355 € Tel (34) 954 - 917 000, Fax (34) 954 - 917 099	Sevilla 3 km
Gran Hotel Renacimiento 288 rooms, D 171 € Tel (34) 954 - 462 222, Fax (34) 954 - 460 428	Sevilla 4 km

RESTAURANTS RESTAURANTE

La Dorada, Tel (34) 954 - 921 066	Sevilla 4 km
La Albahaca, Tel (34) 954 - 220 714	Sevilla
El Espigon, Tel (34) 954 - 626 851	Sevilla

PUERTA DE HIERRO Abajo | 18 | 8 | 9

Las nuevas vías rápidas de la periferia de Madrid afectaron al viejo campo "de debajo" de Puerta de Hierro que nunca había conseguido hacerse famoso. Robert Trent Jones hijo recibió el encargo de recomponer estos otros 18 hoyos que el club necesita para sus dos mil jugadores activos y el resultado es un recorrido de considerable dificultad e innegable belleza. Encinas, pinos y monte bajo componen el marco de unas calles anchas que suben y bajan siguiendo el relieve del terreno. En la mayoría de los hoyos es preciso pegar largo y colocar el golpe de salida en el lugar preciso para poder atacar unos greenes amplísimos, bien defendidos por enormes bunkers, con acentuados movimientos y plataformas que obligan a medir muy bien los pats. Por todo ello hay que considerarlo un magnífico test para la más alta competición e incluso un campo muy interesante para jugarlo desde los tees alternativos.

The new expressways around the city of Madrid have had their effect on the old "lower" course of Puerta de Hierro, which has lost quite a bit of its fame and appeal. Robert Trent Jones Jnr. was assigned with redesigning the 18 holes of the second course that the club needed for its 2,000 active members. The result is this extremely difficult but very beautiful course, where oak-trees, pines and little mounds line fairways, which hug the natural contours of the terrain. On most of the holes you need to be long and place your shot with considerable precision in order to attack the huge greens. These are well guarded by vast sand-traps, are sharply contoured and sometimes multi-tiered to make putting a trickier business than usual. Nonetheless, Puerta de Hierro 2 is a magnificent test for the highest level tournaments and also a very interesting course for the lesser player hitting it from the front tees.

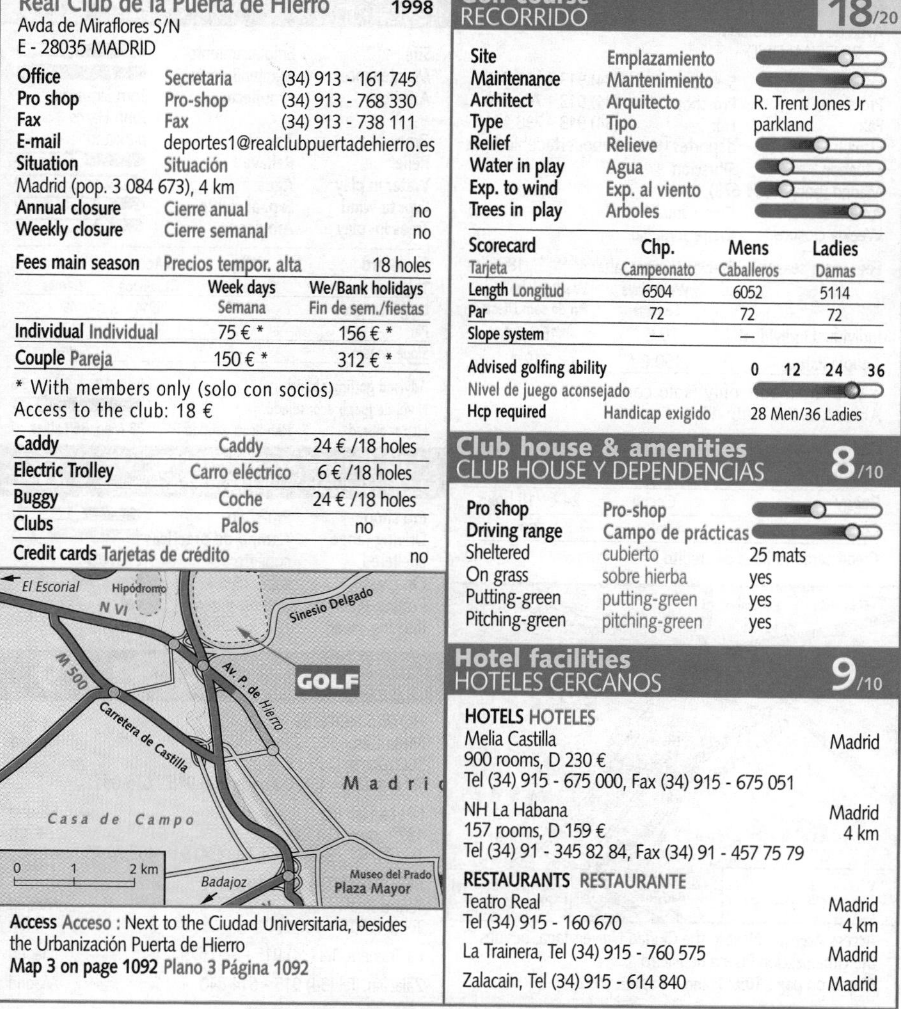

Real Club de la Puerta de Hierro 1998
Avda de Miraflores S/N
E - 28035 MADRID

Office	Secretaria	(34) 913 - 161 745
Pro shop	Pro-shop	(34) 913 - 768 330
Fax	Fax	(34) 913 - 738 111
E-mail	deportes1@realclubpuertadehierro.es	
Situation	Situación	

Madrid (pop. 3 084 673), 4 km

Annual closure	Cierre anual	no
Weekly closure	Cierre semanal	no

Fees main season Precios tempor. alta	18 holes	
	Week days Semana	**We/Bank holidays** Fin de sem./fiestas
Individual Individual	75 € *	156 € *
Couple Pareja	150 € *	312 € *

* With members only (solo con socios)
Access to the club: 18 €

Caddy	Caddy	24 € /18 holes
Electric Trolley	Carro eléctrico	6 € /18 holes
Buggy	Coche	24 € /18 holes
Clubs	Palos	no
Credit cards	Tarjetas de crédito	no

Access Acceso : Next to the Ciudad Universitaria, besides the Urbanización Puerta de Hierro
Map 3 on page 1092 Plano 3 Página 1092

Golf course RECORRIDO 18/20

Site	Emplazamiento	
Maintenance	Mantenimiento	
Architect	Arquitecto	R. Trent Jones Jr
Type	Tipo	parkland
Relief	Relieve	
Water in play	Agua	
Exp. to wind	Exp. al viento	
Trees in play	Arboles	

Scorecard Tarjeta	**Chp.** Campeonato	**Mens** Caballeros	**Ladies** Damas
Length Longitud	6504	6052	5114
Par	72	72	72
Slope system	—	—	—

Advised golfing ability / Nivel de juego aconsejado: 0 12 24 36
Hcp required Handicap exigido: 28 Men/36 Ladies

Club house & amenities CLUB HOUSE Y DEPENDENCIAS 8/10

Pro shop	Pro-shop	
Driving range	Campo de prácticas	
Sheltered	cubierto	25 mats
On grass	sobre hierba	yes
Putting-green	putting-green	yes
Pitching-green	pitching-green	yes

Hotel facilities HOTELES CERCANOS 9/10

HOTELS HOTELES

Melia Castilla — Madrid
900 rooms, D 230 €
Tel (34) 915 - 675 000, Fax (34) 915 - 675 051

NH La Habana — Madrid 4 km
157 rooms, D 159 €
Tel (34) 91 - 345 82 84, Fax (34) 91 - 457 75 79

RESTAURANTS RESTAURANTE

Teatro Real — Madrid 4 km
Tel (34) 915 - 160 670

La Trainera, Tel (34) 915 - 760 575 — Madrid

Zalacain, Tel (34) 915 - 614 840 — Madrid

PUERTA DE HIERRO Arriba | 16 | 8 | 9

Este recorrido, diseñado por Tom Simpson en 1904, fue remodelado en los años 70 y a lo largo de 2000/2001 se ha reformardo en profundidad con el principal objetivo de renovarlo y adaptarlo a las distancias del golf actual. Autores de estas reformas son Robert Trent Jones, Jr. y Kyle Philips. El nuevo campo ha contemplado las modernas distancias de vuelo y rodadura de la bola y vuelve a poner en juego los bunkers y otros obstáculos que siempre han hecho del viejo Puerta de Hierro –probablemente el club más selecto de España- un campo de precisión y estrategia. Ahora los greenes son más amplios, tienen diferentes planos, siguen siendo rápidos y reciben el abrazo envenado de esos bunkers "marca de la casa" Trent Jones.

Designed in 1904 by Tom Simpson, this course was remodelled in the 1970s and 2000 for a better. The skyline is one of hills and woods with constantly sloping landscape embracing the natural terrain. The greens are generally average in size, of excellent standard, fast and slick. A very good tournament course which is not over-wide, Puerta de Hierro calls for extreme accuracy if you want to card a good score. But even mid-handicappers will not find this too troublesome because you can always play safe on every hole. There are no water hazards, either, or other difficulties that force you to shape those delicate shots to make par or scrape a bogey. This prestigious club - you'll need to be invited to play here - also boasts a second 18-hole course rebuilt over a very American layout by Robert Trent Jones with an array of water hazards, re-opened in 1998.

1182

Real Club de la Puerta de Hierro — 1904

Avda de Miraflores S/N
E - 28035 MADRID

Office	Secretaria	(34) 913 - 161 745
Pro shop	Pro-shop	(34) 913 - 768 330
Fax	Fax	(34) 913 - 738 111
E-mail	deportes1@realclubpuertadehierro.es	
Situation	Situación	

Madrid (pop. 3 084 673), 4 km

Annual closure	Cierre anual	no
Weekly closure	Cierre semanal	no

Fees main season Precios tempor. alta	18 holes	
	Week days Semana	**We/Bank holidays** Fin de sem./fiestas
Individual Individual	75 € *	156 € *
Couple Pareja	150 € *	312 *

* With members only (solo con socios)
Access to the club: 18 €

Caddy	Caddy	24 € /18 holes
Electric Trolley	Carro eléctrico	6 € /18 holes
Buggy	Coche	24 € /18 holes
Clubs	Palos	no
Credit cards Tarjetas de crédito		no

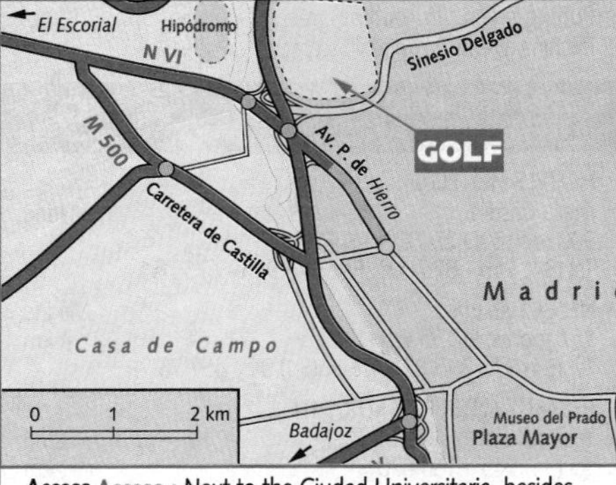

Access Acceso : Next to the Ciudad Universitaria, besides the Urbanización Puerta de Hierro
Map 3 on page 1092 Plano 3 Página 1092

Golf course RECORRIDO — 16/20

Site	Emplazamiento	
Maintenance	Mantenimiento	
Architect	Arquitecto	Tom Simpson John Harris
Type	Tipo	parkland
Relief	Relieve	
Water in play	Agua	
Exp. to wind	Exp. al viento	
Trees in play	Arboles	

Scorecard Tarjeta	**Chp.** Campeonato	**Mens** Caballeros	**Ladies** Damas
Length Longitud	6347	5914	4962
Par	72	72	72
Slope system	—	—	—

Advised golfing ability Nivel de juego aconsejado: 0 12 24 36
Hcp required Handicap exigido: 28 Men, 36 Ladies

Club house & amenities CLUB HOUSE Y DEPENDENCIAS — 8/10

Pro shop	Pro-shop	
Driving range	Campo de prácticas	
Sheltered	cubierto	25 mats
On grass	sobre hierba	yes
Putting-green	putting-green	yes
Pitching-green	pitching-green	yes

Hotel facilities HOTELES CERCANOS — 9/10

HOTELS HOTELES

Melia Castilla — Madrid
900 rooms, D 230 €
Tel (34) 915 - 675 000, Fax (34) 915 - 675 051

NH La Habana — Madrid 4 km
157 rooms, D 159 €
Tel (34) 91 - 345 82 84, Fax (34) 91 - 457 75 79

RESTAURANTS RESTAURANTE

Teatro Real — Madrid 4 km
Tel (34) 915 - 160 670

La Trainera, Tel (34) 915 - 760 575 — Madrid

Zalacain, Tel (34) 915 - 614 840 — Madrid

PULA

13 | 6 | 5

Inaugurado en 1995, es un recorrido prometedor, con espacios ya bien tupidos a pesar de su corta existencia. Dado su relieve no es necesario alquilar un coche. Los greens, bastante en alto, hay que atacarlos elevando bien la bola. La anchura de las calles da sensación de espacio, cosa que agradará a los pegadores, pero no hay que fiarse ya que algunos obstáculos no son muy visibles. El arquitecto Francisco López Segales no ha pretendido realizar cosas espectaculares sino que ha mantenido la tradición británica con inteligencia y buen gusto. Y en todo caso ha logrado un recorrido que hay que seguir de cerca con interés, bien adaptado a los diferentes niveles de juego y bien integrado en un paisaje que ofrece magníficas vistas panorámicas sobre el mar y la montaña.

Opened in 1995, Pula is a promising course with an already well-grassed and pleasant playing surface, despite its early age. Only slightly hilly, the course is easy to walk, but elevated greens call for controlled high approach shots. The width of the fairways gives a pleasant sensation of open space, and will appeal to big-hitters, although they should watch out for a number of hazards that are not always clearly visible. Designer Francisco Lopes Segales has not attempted any sort of exploit in style and has followed a British tradition with intelligence and good taste. At all events, he has succeeded in creating a course whose development deserves to be watched closely. It is well suited to players of all abilities, fits in beautifully with the landscape and offers fine panoramas over the sea and mountains.

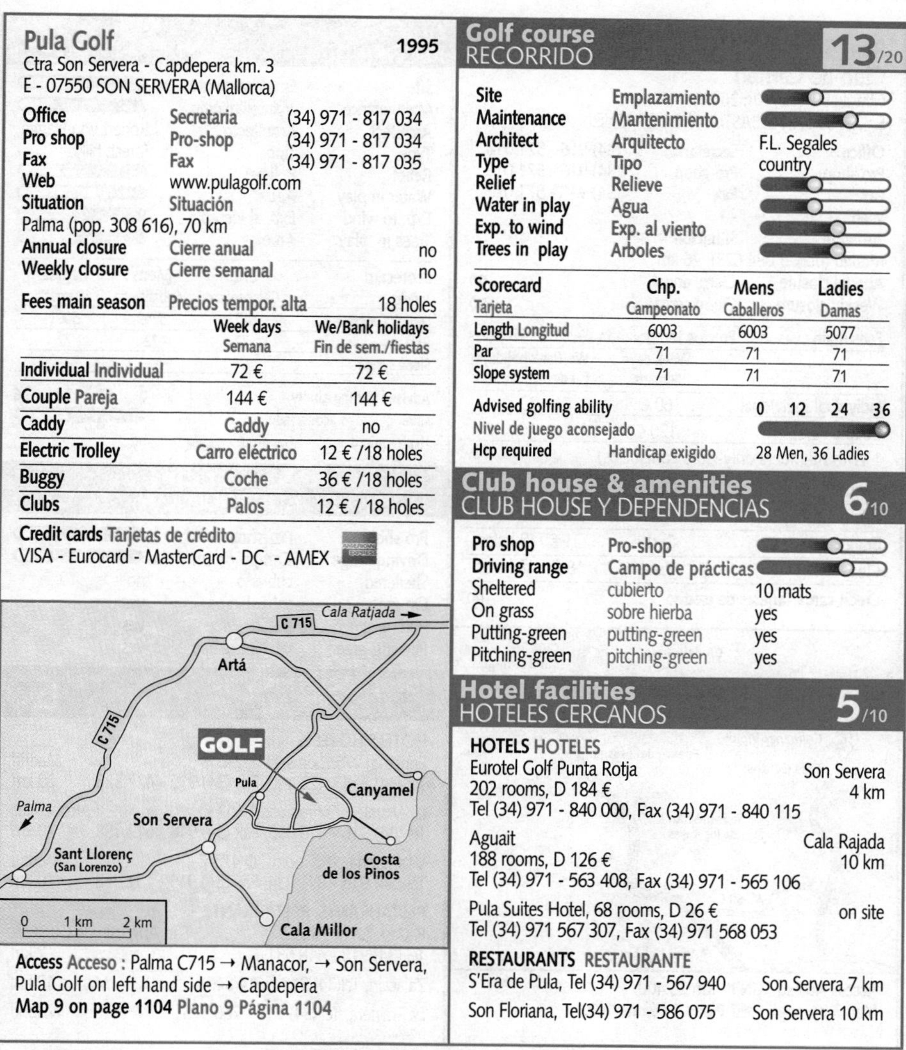

Pula Golf — **1995**

Ctra Son Servera - Capdepera km. 3
E - 07550 SON SERVERA (Mallorca)

Office	Secretaria	(34) 971 - 817 034
Pro shop	Pro-shop	(34) 971 - 817 034
Fax	Fax	(34) 971 - 817 035
Web	www.pulagolf.com	
Situation	Situación	
Palma (pop. 308 616), 70 km		
Annual closure	Cierre anual	no
Weekly closure	Cierre semanal	no

Fees main season Precios tempor. alta		18 holes
	Week days Semana	We/Bank holidays Fin de sem./fiestas
Individual Individual	72 €	72 €
Couple Pareja	144 €	144 €
Caddy	Caddy	no
Electric Trolley	Carro eléctrico	12 € /18 holes
Buggy	Coche	36 € /18 holes
Clubs	Palos	12 € / 18 holes

Credit cards Tarjetas de crédito
VISA - Eurocard - MasterCard - DC - AMEX

Access Acceso : Palma C715 → Manacor, → Son Servera, Pula Golf on left hand side → Capdepera
Map 9 on page 1104 Plano 9 Página 1104

Golf course RECORRIDO — 13/20

Site	Emplazamiento	
Maintenance	Mantenimiento	
Architect	Arquitecto	F.L. Segales
Type	Tipo	country
Relief	Relieve	
Water in play	Agua	
Exp. to wind	Exp. al viento	
Trees in play	Arboles	

Scorecard Tarjeta	Chp. Campeonato	Mens Caballeros	Ladies Damas
Length Longitud	6003	6003	5077
Par	71	71	71
Slope system	71	71	71

Advised golfing ability Nivel de juego aconsejado — 0 12 24 36
Hcp required Handicap exigido — 28 Men, 36 Ladies

Club house & amenities CLUB HOUSE Y DEPENDENCIAS — 6/10

Pro shop	Pro-shop	
Driving range	Campo de prácticas	
Sheltered	cubierto	10 mats
On grass	sobre hierba	yes
Putting-green	putting-green	yes
Pitching-green	pitching-green	yes

Hotel facilities HOTELES CERCANOS — 5/10

HOTELS HOTELES

Eurotel Golf Punta Rotja — Son Servera 4 km
202 rooms, D 184 €
Tel (34) 971 - 840 000, Fax (34) 971 - 840 115

Aguait — Cala Rajada 10 km
188 rooms, D 126 €
Tel (34) 971 - 563 408, Fax (34) 971 - 565 106

Pula Suites Hotel, 68 rooms, D 26 € — on site
Tel (34) 971 567 307, Fax (34) 971 568 053

RESTAURANTS RESTAURANTE

S'Era de Pula, Tel (34) 971 - 567 940 — Son Servera 7 km

Son Floriana, Tel(34) 971 - 586 075 — Son Servera 10 km

REAL SOCIEDAD CLUB DE CAMPO 18 | 7 | 6

Construido en una pequeña colina, en un terreno muy típico de los alrededores de Madrid, este nuevo recorrido de la Real Sociedad Hípica Española de Club de Campo ofrece una gran variedad de distancias y tipo de hoyos gracias a sus múltiples tees de salida. Nos encontramos con el afán de variedad de Robert von Hagge y su diseño bien característico: roughs espesos, calles muy cuidadas en superficie, greens amplios con múltiples desniveles, constituyendo un recorrido destinado más bien a los buenos jugadores. Pero también los jugadores inteligentes y sagaces técnicos sabrán salvar un buen resultado si son diestros en el juego corto. La ambición del club es clara: organizar grandes competiciones internacionales. Cercano al circuito del Jarama, el golf añade un nuevo elemento a una región bien servida en golfs de calidad (Jarama R.A.C.E., La Moraleja). El segundo recorrido de 18 hoyos de 6.121 metros, obra también de von Hagge, responde a las objetivos de diversificación del club.

Built on a little hill, typical of the type of terrain found around Madrid, the new course belonging to the Real Sociedad Hípica Española de Club de Campo offers an amazing combination of distances and types of hole thanks to the many different tee-boxes. This reflects the emphasis on variety which is the trademark of Robert von Hagge (who also designed Emporda). Other distinctive features are the thick rough, highly contoured fairways and huge, multi-tiered greens which generally tend to make this a course for good players. It is also intended for smart players and fine craftsmen who can save their card if their short game is on song. The club's ambition is clearly to host major international competitions. Close to the Jarama circuit, this layout is a new addition to a region already spoilt for excellent courses (Jarama R.A.C.E., La Moraleja). The second 18-hole course (6,121 m), also designed by Robert von Hagge, is a further reflection of this club's ambitions.

1184

Real Sociedad Hipica Española Club de Campo 1997

Ctra de Burgos - Km 26,400
E - 28709 SAN SEBASTIAN DE LOS REYES

Office	Secretaria	(34) 916 - 571 018
Pro shop	Pro-shop	(34) 916 - 571 018
Fax	Fax	(34) 916 - 571 022
Web	—	
Situation	Situación	

Madrid (pop. 3 084 673), 26 km

Annual closure	Cierre anual	no
Weekly closure	Cierre semanal	no

Fees main season Precios tempor. alta	18 holes	
	Week days Semana	**We/Bank holidays** Fin de sem./fiestas
Individual Individual	60 €	*
Couple Pareja	120 €	*

* With members only (solo con socios)

Caddy	Caddy	no
Electric Trolley	Carro eléctrico	4 € /18 holes
Buggy	Coche	21 € /18 holes
Clubs	Palos	18 € / 18 holes

Credit cards Tarjetas de crédito no

Access Acceso : CN I - Km 26,400
Map 3 on page 1092 Plano 3 Página 1092

Golf course RECORRIDO 18/20

Site	Emplazamiento	
Maintenance	Mantenimiento	
Architect	Arquitecto	Robert von Hagge
Type	Tipo	forest, hilly
Relief	Relieve	
Water in play	Agua	
Exp. to wind	Exp. al viento	
Trees in play	Arboles	

Scorecard Tarjeta	**Chp.** Campeonato	**Mens** Caballeros	**Ladies** Damas
Length Longitud	6121	5759	5001
Par	72	72	72
Slope system	—	—	—

Advised golfing ability Nivel de juego aconsejado 0 12 24 36
Hcp required Handicap exigido no

Club house & amenities CLUB HOUSE Y DEPENDENCIAS 7/10

Pro shop	Pro-shop	
Driving range	Campo de prácticas	
Sheltered	cubierto	no
On grass	sobre hierba	yes
Putting-green	putting-green	yes
Pitching-green	pitching-green	yes

Hotel facilities HOTELES CERCANOS 6/10

HOTELS HOTELES

Princesa, 275 rooms, D 252 € — Madrid
Tel (34) 915 - 422 100, Fax (34) 915 - 427 328 — 20 km

La Moraleja, 37 rooms, D 162 € — Alcobendas
Tel (34) 916 - 618 055, Fax (34) 916 - 612 188 — 20 km

Villamagna, 182 rooms, D 475 € — Madrid
Tel (34) 915 - 871 234, Fax (34) 915 - 751 358 — 10 km

RESTAURANTS RESTAURANTE

El Caserón de Araceli — San Augustin de Guadalix
Tel (34) 918 - 418 531 — 7 km

Zalacain, Tel(34) 915 - 614 840 — Madrid 10 km

La Trainera, Tel (34) 915 - 760 575 — Madrid

SAN ROQUE

17 | 8 | 8

San Roque gustará incluso a los que no les gustan los golfs inmobiliarios. En primer lugar porque las casas y residencias que lo rodean son magníficas, y en segundo lugar porque están apartadas del recorrido. No es necesario alquilar un coche y está bien protegido por los árboles, excepto un tramo expuesto al viento, entre el 13 y el 15, que bordea la colina. Muy largo saliendo desde atrás y con una ida muy estrecha, es más "humano" con los tees de salida adelantados para los jugadores con un handicap superior a 10. Exige ser un jugador completo, con mucho "feeling" para negociar los aproches a greens con muchas caídas y que están perfectamente protegidos, así como una gran finura en el juego corto. Si a ésto añadimos la calidad de las instalaciones y de su mantenimiento, comprenderemos que Tony Jacklin y Dave Thomas han diseñado uno de los grandes recorridos de la Costa. Unico reproche: su dificultad para los jugadores con poca experiencia (difícil para jugar en familia).

Golfers who don't like property development courses will love San Roque. Firstly because the villas and residences are magnificent, secondly because the course is some distance from them. The terrain is easy for walking and well protected by trees, except the 13th and 15th holes, laid out on the side of a hill and exposed to the wind. Very long off the back-tees, compounded by tight fairways on the front nine, the course is more "human" when played from the front-tees for players with handicaps in double figures. It demands an all-round game and a lot of feeling to negotiate the approach shots to greens that are very undulating and perfectly well-defended. A well-honed short game is also in order. Add to these compliments the quality of upkeep and of the facilities and you will understand how Tony Jacklin and Dave Thomas have designed one of the coast's great courses. One minor criticism would be the course's difficulty for inexperienced players (hard to play with all the family).

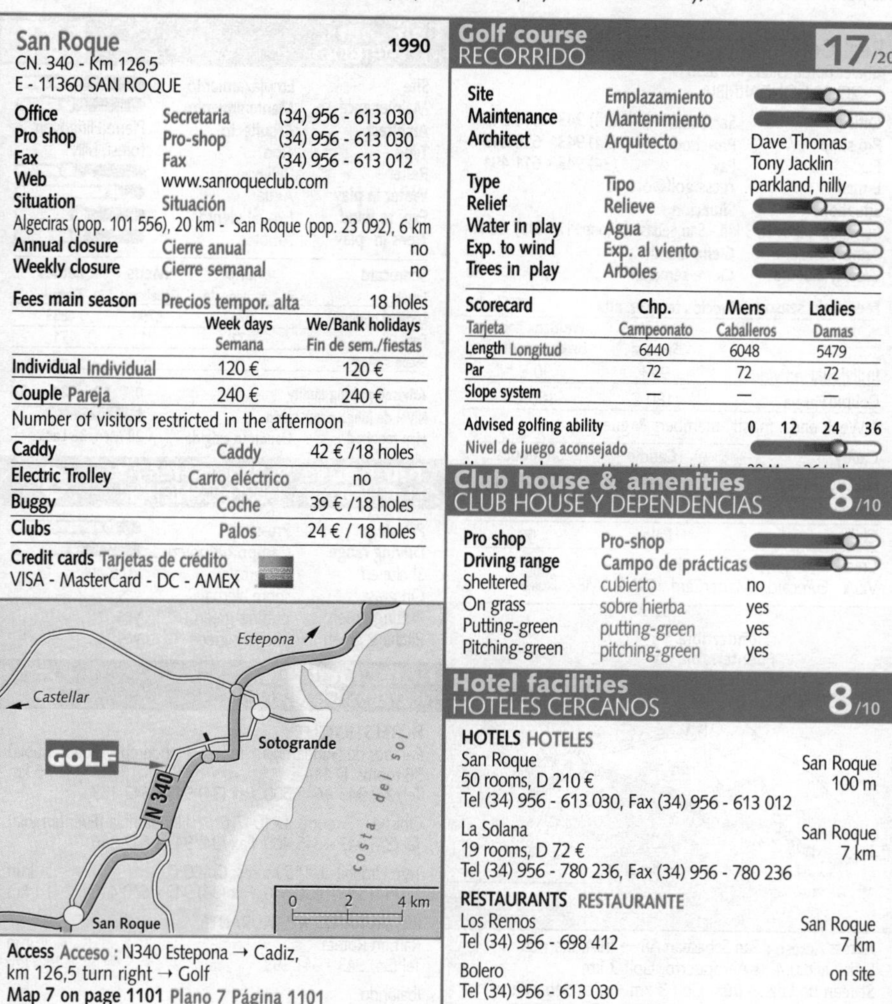

San Roque — 1990
CN. 340 - Km 126,5
E - 11360 SAN ROQUE

Office	Secretaria	(34) 956 - 613 030
Pro shop	Pro-shop	(34) 956 - 613 030
Fax	Fax	(34) 956 - 613 012
Web	www.sanroqueclub.com	
Situation	Situación	

Algeciras (pop. 101 556), 20 km - San Roque (pop. 23 092), 6 km

Annual closure	Cierre anual	no
Weekly closure	Cierre semanal	no

Fees main season Precios tempor. alta	Week days Semana	We/Bank holidays Fin de sem./fiestas
	18 holes	
Individual Individual	120 €	120 €
Couple Pareja	240 €	240 €

Number of visitors restricted in the afternoon

Caddy	Caddy	42 € /18 holes
Electric Trolley	Carro eléctrico	no
Buggy	Coche	39 € /18 holes
Clubs	Palos	24 € / 18 holes

Credit cards Tarjetas de crédito
VISA - MasterCard - DC - AMEX

Access Acceso : N340 Estepona → Cadiz, km 126,5 turn right → Golf
Map 7 on page 1101 Plano 7 Página 1101

Golf course RECORRIDO — 17/20

Site	Emplazamiento	
Maintenance	Mantenimiento	
Architect	Arquitecto	Dave Thomas, Tony Jacklin
Type	Tipo	parkland, hilly
Relief	Relieve	
Water in play	Agua	
Exp. to wind	Exp. al viento	
Trees in play	Arboles	

Scorecard Tarjeta	**Chp.** Campeonato	**Mens** Caballeros	**Ladies** Damas
Length Longitud	6440	6048	5479
Par	72	72	72
Slope system	—	—	—

Advised golfing ability 0 12 24 36
Nivel de juego aconsejado

Club house & amenities CLUB HOUSE Y DEPENDENCIAS — 8/10

Pro shop	Pro-shop	
Driving range	Campo de prácticas	
Sheltered	cubierto	no
On grass	sobre hierba	yes
Putting-green	putting-green	yes
Pitching-green	pitching-green	yes

Hotel facilities HOTELES CERCANOS — 8/10

HOTELS HOTELES

San Roque — San Roque 100 m
50 rooms, D 210 €
Tel (34) 956 - 613 030, Fax (34) 956 - 613 012

La Solana — San Roque 7 km
19 rooms, D 72 €
Tel (34) 956 - 780 236, Fax (34) 956 - 780 236

RESTAURANTS RESTAURANTE

Los Remos — San Roque 7 km
Tel (34) 956 - 698 412

Bolero — on site
Tel (34) 956 - 613 030

SAN SEBASTIÁN

14 | 6 | 6

Es la cuna y feudo del gran campeón español José Maria Olazábal, a quien se puede ver muy amenudo en el campo de práticas?. El recorrido fue diseñado por el profesional francés Pierre Hirigoyen en un terreno con muchas cuestas y con una media docena de hoyos en una planicie bastante húmeda con algunos obstáculos de agua. La dificuldad esencial, a parte de dejar la pelota en calle, radica en no ponerse nervioso ni desmoralizarse ante los muchos desniveles del terreno. Sin embargo, los obstáculos son visibles y se puede decir que es un recorrido claro con algunos greens en alto dando lugar a situaciones muy variadas alrededor de los mismos, lo que explica la virtuosidad adquirida por Olazábal. Es muy difícil jugar su handicap desde las salidas de atrás, a pesare de que no sea excesivamente largo, por lo que es mejor escoger salidas más avanzadas. No es un recorrido que guste a todos, pero posee un personalidad incontestable. Las montañas son realmente muy bonitas...

It is the home course and fief of the top Spanish champion Olazábal, who can often be seen on the driving range. The course was designed by the French pro Pierre Hirigoyen over very hilly terrain, although half a dozen holes are flattish, dampish and protected by a few hazards. The essential difficulty here, apart from keeping your ball in the fairway, is keeping cool head and not letting the steep slopes get the better of you. Luckily, the hazards are clearly in view and the course hides nothing, apart from a number of elevated greens. There is a variety of interesting situations around the greens, which might explain the virtuosity of Olazábal in this area, developed out on the course. A good score is a tough proposition from the back tees, but a distinct possibility when playing further forward. Not everyone loves this course, but it does have definite personality. And the mountains look beautiful.

Real Golf Club de San Sebastián — 1968

Chalet Borda Gain Apartado 6
E - 20280 HONDARRIBIA

Office	Secretaria	(34) 943 - 616 845
Pro shop	Pro-shop	(34) 943 - 616 845
Fax	Fax	(34) 943 - 611 491
E-mail	rgcss.golf@oto.cc	
Situation	Situación	

Irún (pop. 53 861), 3 km - San Sebastián (pop. 176 019), 18 km

Annual closure	Cierre anual	no
Weekly closure	Cierre semanal	no

Fees main season Precios tempor. alta	**Week days** Semana	**We/Bank holidays** Fin de sem./fiestas
	18 holes	
Individual Individual	90 €	90 € *
Couple Pareja	180 €	180 € *

* Week ends: mostly members & guests

Caddy	Caddy	on request
Electric Trolley	Carro eléctrico	7 € /18 holes
Buggy	Coche	25 € /18 holes
Clubs	Palos	no

Credit cards Tarjetas de crédito
VISA - Eurocard - MasterCard - DC - AMEX

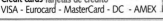

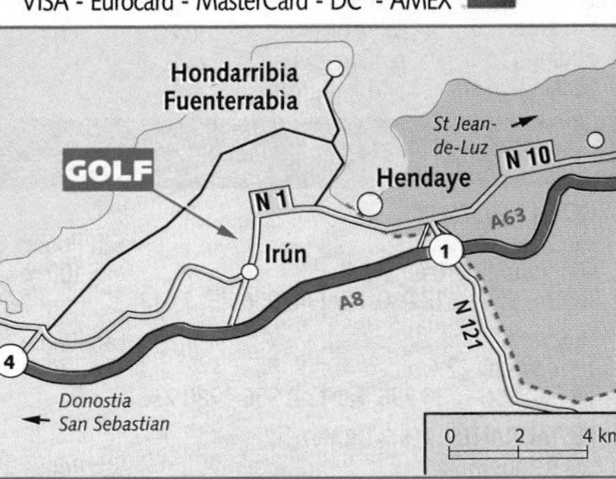

Access Acceso : San Sebastián A8 → Irún, Biarritz.
Exit (Salida) 4 → Aeropuerto, Golf 3 km
St Jean de Luz → Irún, Golf 3 km → San Sebastián
Map 1 on page 1088 Plano 1 Página 1088

Golf course RECORRIDO — 14/20

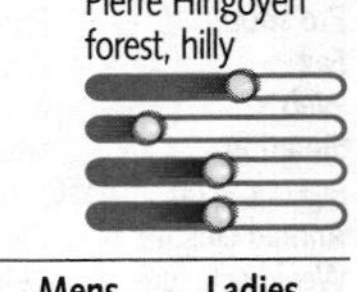

Site	Emplazamiento	
Maintenance	Mantenimiento	
Architect	Arquitecto	Pierre Hirigoyen
Type	Tipo	forest, hilly
Relief	Relieve	
Water in play	Agua	
Exp. to wind	Exp. al viento	
Trees in play	Arboles	

Scorecard Tarjeta	**Chp.** Campeonato	**Mens** Caballeros	**Ladies** Damas
Length Longitud	5962	5790	4883
Par	71	71	71
Slope system	—	—	—

Advised golfing ability 0 12 24 36
Nivel de juego aconsejado
Hcp required Handicap exigido 28 Men, 36 Ladies

Club house & amenities CLUB HOUSE Y DEPENDENCIAS — 6/10

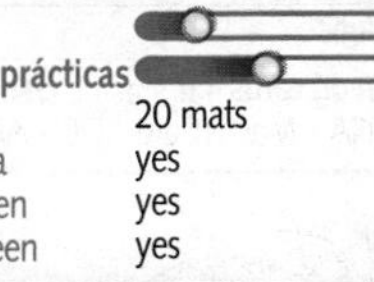

Pro shop	Pro-shop	
Driving range	Campo de prácticas	
Sheltered	cubierto	20 mats
On grass	sobre hierba	yes
Putting-green	putting-green	yes
Pitching-green	pitching-green	yes

Hotel facilities HOTELES CERCANOS — 6/10

HOTELS HOTELES

Parador de Hondarribia — Hondarribia (Fuenterrabia)
36 rooms, D 114 € — 5 km
Tel (34) 943 - 645 500, Fax (34) 943 - 642 153

Obispo, 17 rooms, D 1047 € — Hondarribia (Fuenterrabia)
Tel (34) 943 - 645 400, Fax (34) 943 - 642 386

Tryp Urdanibia, 115 rooms, D 100 € — Irún
Tel (34) 943 - 630 440, Fax (34) 943 - 630 410 — 1 km

RESTAURANTS RESTAURANTE

Ramón Roteta — Irún
Tel (34) 943 - 641 693 — 5 km

Ibaiondo — Irún
Tel (34) 943 - 632 888 — 1 km

SANT CUGAT

13 | 6 | 5

A pesar de ser un terreno accidentado, es tan fácil jugar caminando en Sant Cugat que sólo tiene un coche para alquilar. No es difícil lograr un buen resultado: las dificultades están a la vista, rara vez en la línea de juego, hasta tal punto que se puede aprochar a green haciendo rodar la bola (evitando sobrepasarlos). Algunos obstáculos de agua, algunos bunkers de green, árboles y bosque, son las mayores dificultades de este recorrido. Su escasa longitud permite no sólo jugar fácilmente su handicap sino que lo hace muy agradable para jugar en match-play: pueden caer muchos birdies. Los buenos jugadores se explayarán agusto y no dudarán en intentar llegar a green con el drive en ciertos pares 4. Los principiantes conseguirán sus primeros pares. Un golf para todos y de buena calidad.

Despite the broken terrain, San Cugat is easy to walk around, which is just as well as there is only one buggy. And it is not too difficult to shoot a good score, either. The hazards are clearly in view and seldom affect your game, to the extent that many greens can be approached with chip shots (but beware overshooting the green!). A few water hazards, certain green-side bunkers, trees and woods form the basic part of the course's difficulties. Being a short course, most players should play to their handicap without too much problem, and it is also fun for match-play, with birdies more common than usual. Very good players will have lots of fun and won't think twice about driving the green on a number of short par 4s, while beginners should easily find their feet. A good quality golf-course, for everyone to enjoy.

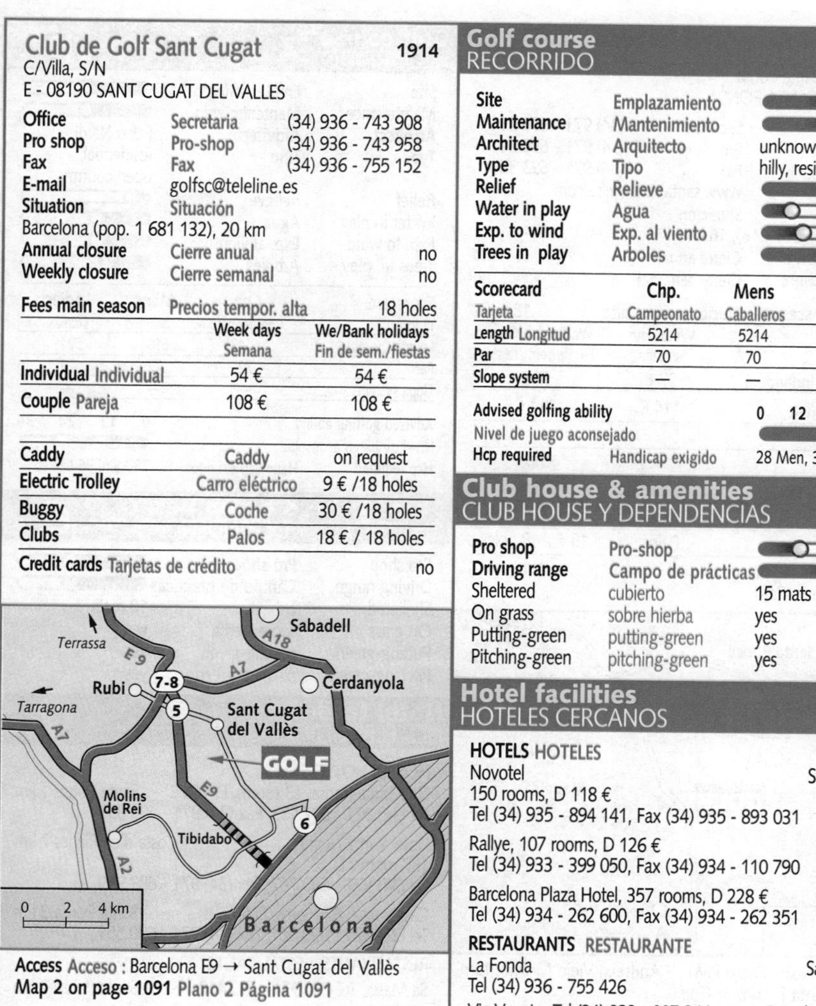

Club de Golf Sant Cugat — 1914

C/Villa, S/N
E - 08190 SANT CUGAT DEL VALLES

Office	Secretaria	(34) 936 - 743 908
Pro shop	Pro-shop	(34) 936 - 743 958
Fax	Fax	(34) 936 - 755 152
E-mail	golfsc@teleline.es	
Situation	Situación	
Barcelona (pop. 1 681 132), 20 km		
Annual closure	Cierre anual	no
Weekly closure	Cierre semanal	no

Fees main season / Precios tempor. alta	18 holes	
	Week days / Semana	We/Bank holidays / Fin de sem./fiestas
Individual Individual	54 €	54 €
Couple Pareja	108 €	108 €

Caddy	Caddy	on request
Electric Trolley	Carro eléctrico	9 € /18 holes
Buggy	Coche	30 € /18 holes
Clubs	Palos	18 € / 18 holes
Credit cards	Tarjetas de crédito	no

Access Acceso : Barcelona E9 → Sant Cugat del Vallès
Map 2 on page 1091 Plano 2 Página 1091

Golf course / RECORRIDO — 13/20

Site	Emplazamiento	
Maintenance	Mantenimiento	
Architect	Arquitecto	unknown
Type	Tipo	hilly, residential
Relief	Relieve	
Water in play	Agua	
Exp. to wind	Exp. al viento	
Trees in play	Arboles	

Scorecard / Tarjeta	Chp. / Campeonato	Mens / Caballeros	Ladies / Damas
Length Longitud	5214	5214	4578
Par	70	70	70
Slope system	—	—	—

Advised golfing ability / Nivel de juego aconsejado: 0 12 24 36

Hcp required / Handicap exigido: 28 Men, 36 Ladies

Club house & amenities / CLUB HOUSE Y DEPENDENCIAS — 6/10

Pro shop	Pro-shop	
Driving range	Campo de prácticas	
Sheltered	cubierto	15 mats
On grass	sobre hierba	yes
Putting-green	putting-green	yes
Pitching-green	pitching-green	yes

Hotel facilities / HOTELES CERCANOS — 5/10

HOTELS HOTELES

Novotel — Sant Cugat 2 km
150 rooms, D 118 €
Tel (34) 935 - 894 141, Fax (34) 935 - 893 031

Rallye, 107 rooms, D 126 € — Barcelona 20 km
Tel (34) 933 - 399 050, Fax (34) 934 - 110 790

Barcelona Plaza Hotel, 357 rooms, D 228 € — Barcelona
Tel (34) 934 - 262 600, Fax (34) 934 - 262 351

RESTAURANTS RESTAURANTE

La Fonda — Sant Cugat
Tel (34) 936 - 755 426

Via Veneto, Tel (34) 932 - 007 244 — Barcelona 20 km

SANTA PONSA

13 | 6 | 7

Con tres recorridos (de lo cuales uno es privado) y dos otros en proyecto, Santa Ponsa se está convirtiendo en un conjunto residencial imponente y difícil de ignorar cuando se está jugando: los jugadores no encontrarán ninguna intimidad. El diseño de Folco Nardi es sobrio, aunque convencional, sin inspiración excepcional y curiosamente más difícil con los tees de salida adelantados. La longitud puede intimidar a los jugadores de tipo medio y a las señoras: la primera vez es mucho más divertido jugar en match-play que intentar cumplir su handicap. Los greens, de una superficie normal, son más bien planos y protegidos sólo por los costados, lo que permite llegar haciendo rodar la bola...La mayor dificultad son los obstáculos de agua. Los cuidados de mantenimiento son correctos.

With three courses (one of which is private) and two others on the drawing board, Santa Ponsa is an impressive residential resort, a fact that can be hard to forget even when you are on the course. There is very little privacy. Folco Nardi's layout is discreet and rather conventional with nothing exceptional in terms of inspiration. Strangely, the course is harder to play from the front tees than from the back. Owing to the very little difference between tee-positions, the length of the course can be intimidating for high-handicappers and ladies. First time out, match-play will be much more fun than trying to play your handicap. The medium-sized greens are generally flat and are defended on the sides only, so you can roll (or top!) the ball onto the green. The main hazard is the water. Upkeep is good.

Golf Santa Ponsa — 1977

Urb. Golf Santa Ponsa
E - 07184 SANTA PONSA

Office	Secretaria	(34) 971 - 690 211
Pro shop	Pro-shop	(34) 971 - 690 211
Fax	Fax	(34) 971 - 693 364
Web	www.santaponsaimisa.com	
Situation	Situación	

Palma (pop. 308 616), 16 km

Annual closure	Cierre anual	no
Weekly closure	Cierre semanal	no

Fees main season Precios tempor. alta — 18 holes

	Week days Semana	We/Bank holidays Fin de sem./fiestas
Individual Individual	57 €	57 €
Couple Pareja	114 €	114 €

Caddy	Caddy	no
Electric Trolley	Carro eléctrico	no
Buggy	Coche	36 € /18 holes
Clubs	Palos	15 € / 18 holes

Credit cards Tarjetas de crédito
VISA - MasterCard

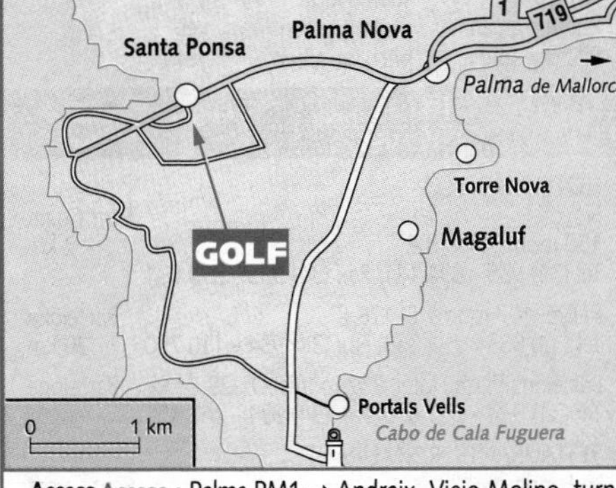

Access Acceso : Palma PM1 → Andraix, Viejo Molino, turn left → Santa Ponsa, → Golf
Map 9 on page 1104 Plano 9 Página 1104

Golf course RECORRIDO — 13/20

Site	Emplazamiento	
Maintenance	Mantenimiento	
Architect	Arquitecto	Falco Nardi
Type	Tipo	residential, open country
Relief	Relieve	
Water in play	Agua	
Exp. to wind	Exp. al viento	
Trees in play	Arboles	

Scorecard Tarjeta	**Chp.** Campeonato	**Mens** Caballeros	**Ladies** Damas
Length Longitud	6543	6106	5241
Par	72	72	72
Slope system	—	—	—

Advised golfing ability Nivel de juego aconsejado — 0 12 24 36
Hcp required Handicap exigido — 28 Men, 36 Ladies

Club house & amenities CLUB HOUSE Y DEPENDENCIAS — 6/10

Pro shop	Pro-shop	
Driving range	Campo de prácticas	
Sheltered	cubierto	10 mats
On grass	sobre hierba	yes
Putting-green	putting-green	yes
Pitching-green	pitching-green	yes

Hotel facilities HOTELES CERCANOS — 7/10

HOTELS HOTELES

Golf Santa Ponsa, 13 rooms, D 168 € — Santa Ponsa 1 km
Tel (34) 971 - 697 133, Fax (34) 971 - 694 853

Hotel Punta Negra — Costa d'en Blanes 7 km
137 rooms, D 204 €
Tel (34) 971 - 680 762, Fax (34) 971 - 683 919

Casablanca, 87 rooms, D 69 € — Santa Ponsa 3 km
Tel (34) 971 - 690 361, Fax (34) 971 - 690 551

RESTAURANTS RESTAURANTE

Sa Masia, Tel (34) 971 - 690 412 — Santa Ponsa 2 km

Samanthas, Tel (34) 971 - 700 000 — Palma 15 km

SEVILLA

17 | 7 | 8

Con una gran preocupación por los detalles y la estrategia, José María Olazábal ha "firmado" este recorrido. Al limitar la talla de los greens, ha querido favorecer el juego corto, uno de sus puntos fuertes. Al ser un malabarista con la bola, ha creado un recorrido que necesita dominar perfectamente todos los efectos y trayectorias (altas y bajas). Hay un gran número de bunkers y obstáculos de agua en la línea de juego, completados por 12.000 árboles y matorrales plantados para lograr un recorrido más complejo... y no sólo para protegerse del sol en verano. Equilibrado en su conjunto se adapta bien a los diferentes niveles de juego y se complica a medida que se retroceden los tees de salida. Franco y fácil de jugar sin coche, el Real Golf de Sevilla es una síntesis del estilo americano y de los links. Todo este conjunto de cualidades explican su éxito.

A course carrying the José-Maria Olazabal "label" where a lot of attention has gone into the finest detail and strategy. By restricting ther size of the greens, he has highlighted the short game, one of his own fortes. And because Olazabal is a worker of the ball, the course demands skills for every trajectory (high and low) and for fashioning the ball both ways. The course has a large number of bunkers and water hazards, all very much in play, and these will be completed by the 12,000 trees and bushes that have been planted to make the course a little trickier... and not only to provide shade from the sun in summer. This is a finely balanced layout that adapts easily to different levels of skill and becomes more complex from the back-tees. Open and easy to walk, the Real Golf de Seville is a sort of synthesis combining American and links style golf. Might this explain the course's success?

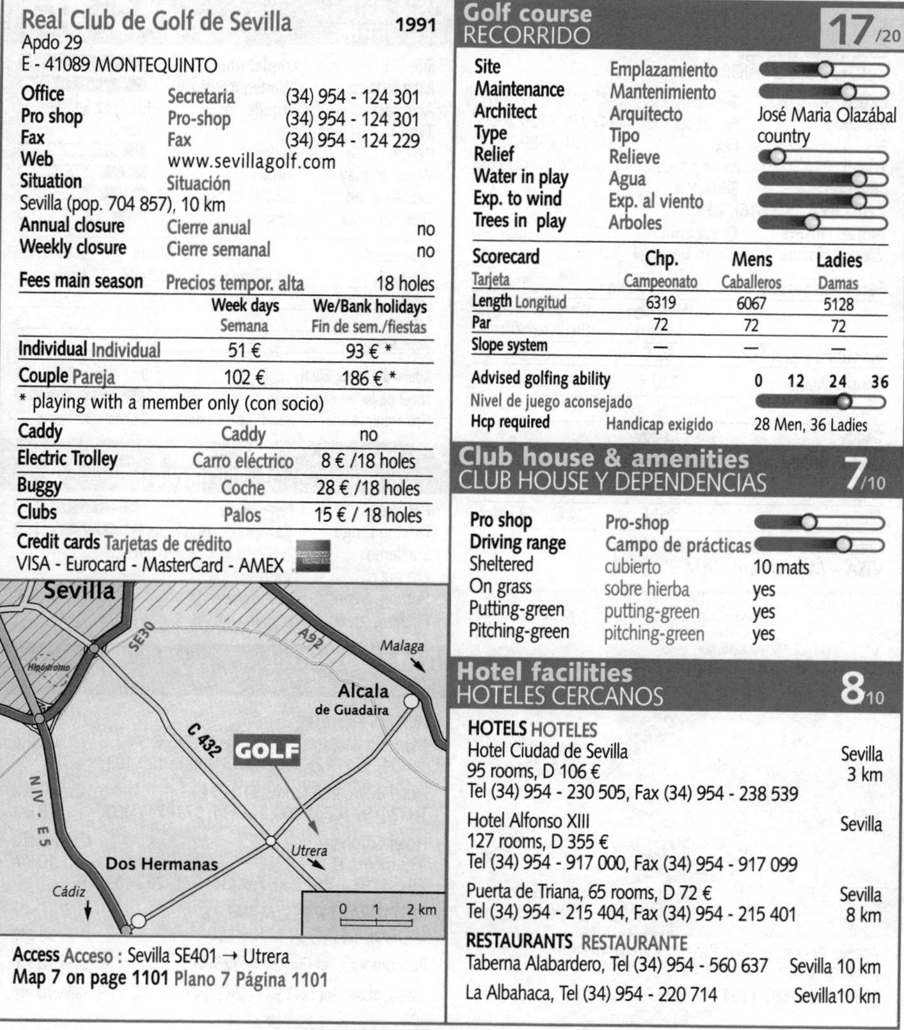

Real Club de Golf de Sevilla 1991
Apdo 29
E - 41089 MONTEQUINTO

Office	Secretaria	(34) 954 - 124 301
Pro shop	Pro-shop	(34) 954 - 124 301
Fax	Fax	(34) 954 - 124 229
Web	www.sevillagolf.com	
Situation	Situación	

Sevilla (pop. 704 857), 10 km

Annual closure	Cierre anual	no
Weekly closure	Cierre semanal	no

Fees main season Precios tempor. alta	**Week days** Semana	**We/Bank holidays** Fin de sem./fiestas
		18 holes
Individual Individual	51 €	93 € *
Couple Pareja	102 €	186 € *

* playing with a member only (con socio)

Caddy	Caddy	no
Electric Trolley	Carro eléctrico	8 € /18 holes
Buggy	Coche	28 € /18 holes
Clubs	Palos	15 € / 18 holes

Credit cards Tarjetas de crédito
VISA - Eurocard - MasterCard - AMEX

Access Acceso : Sevilla SE401 → Utrera
Map 7 on page 1101 Plano 7 Página 1101

Golf course RECORRIDO **17**/20

Site	Emplazamiento	
Maintenance	Mantenimiento	
Architect	Arquitecto	José Maria Olazábal
Type	Tipo	country
Relief	Relieve	
Water in play	Agua	
Exp. to wind	Exp. al viento	
Trees in play	Arboles	

Scorecard Tarjeta	**Chp.** Campeonato	**Mens** Caballeros	**Ladies** Damas
Length Longitud	6319	6067	5128
Par	72	72	72
Slope system	—	—	—

Advised golfing ability Nivel de juego aconsejado: 0 12 24 36
Hcp required Handicap exigido: 28 Men, 36 Ladies

Club house & amenities CLUB HOUSE Y DEPENDENCIAS **7**/10

Pro shop	Pro-shop	
Driving range	Campo de prácticas	
Sheltered	cubierto	10 mats
On grass	sobre hierba	yes
Putting-green	putting-green	yes
Pitching-green	pitching-green	yes

Hotel facilities HOTELES CERCANOS **8**/10

HOTELS HOTELES
Hotel Ciudad de Sevilla — Sevilla 3 km
95 rooms, D 106 €
Tel (34) 954 - 230 505, Fax (34) 954 - 238 539

Hotel Alfonso XIII — Sevilla
127 rooms, D 355 €
Tel (34) 954 - 917 000, Fax (34) 954 - 917 099

Puerta de Triana, 65 rooms, D 72 € — Sevilla 8 km
Tel (34) 954 - 215 404, Fax (34) 954 - 215 401

RESTAURANTS RESTAURANTE
Taberna Alabardero, Tel (34) 954 - 560 637 — Sevilla 10 km
La Albahaca, Tel (34) 954 - 220 714 — Sevilla10 km

SON ANTEM Este

15 | 8 | 8

El "viejo" Son Antem ha tenido siempre fama de tener "los mejores greenes de la isla", título que merece porque su diseñador es uno de los más reconocidos greenkeepers de España. El recorrido es totalmente llano, en un escenario de arboleda baja salpicado con lagos refrescantes a la vista que apenas entran en juego, que es agradable de andar porque además está tan alejado de las estridencias de las carreteras que s ólo se oyen perdices y pichones. Es un buen recorrido de vacaciones, cómodo y abierto para pasar un día tranquilo habiendo afinado a placer el toque del pat.

The "old" Son Antem is famed for having the best greens on these islands, as the designer is one of the most highly reputed green-keepers in Spain. The course is absolutely flat and located in a setting of low trees dotted with small lakes, each one as refreshing to look at as it is (or should be) easy to avoid. Additionally, this is also a very pleasant course to walk without having to put up with the noise of traffic, a definite asset on an island as busy as this. All you hear here is the singing of birds. So a great holiday course, convenient and pretty open for spending a quiet day while honing your skill at putting the ball in exactly the right place.

Son Antem Golf Resort & Spa — 1994

Carretera de Llucmajor
E - 07620 LLUCMAJOR (Mallorca)

Office	Secretaria	(34) 971 - 129 200
Pro shop	Pro-shop	(34) 971 - 129 200
Fax	Fax	(34) 971 - 129 202
E-mail	mhrs.pmigs.dir.of.golf@marriott.com	
Situation	Situación	

Palma (pop. 308 616), 20 km

Annual closure	Cierre anual	no
Weekly closure	Cierre semanal	no

Fees main season Precios tempor. alta	18 holes	
	Week days Semana	We/Bank holidays Fin de sem./fiestas
Individual Individual	60 €	60 €
Couple Pareja	120 €	120 €

Caddy	Caddy	no
Electric Trolley	Carro eléctrico	no
Buggy	Coche	36 € /18 holes
Clubs	Palos	24 € / 18 holes

Credit cards Tarjetas de crédito
VISA - MasterCard - AMEX

Access Acceso : Palma PM19 → Aeropuerto, → Llucmajor PM602, km 3,4 → Golf
Map 9 on page 1104 Plano 9 Página 1104

Golf course RECORRIDO — 15/20

Site	Emplazamiento	
Maintenance	Mantenimiento	
Architect	Arquitecto	F. López Segales
Type	Tipo	inland
Relief	Relieve	
Water in play	Agua	
Exp. to wind	Exp. al viento	
Trees in play	Arboles	

Scorecard Tarjeta	Chp. Campeonato	Mens Caballeros	Ladies Damas
Length Longitud	6393	6071	5043
Par	72	72	72
Slope system	—	—	—

Advised golfing ability Nivel de juego aconsejado — 0 12 24 36
Hcp required Handicap exigido — 27 Men, 35 Ladies

Club house & amenities CLUB HOUSE Y DEPENDENCIAS — 8/10

Pro shop	Pro-shop	
Driving range	Campo de prácticas	
Sheltered	cubierto	yes
On grass	sobre hierba	yes
Putting-green	putting-green	yes
Pitching-green	pitching-green	yes

Hotel facilities HOTELES CERCANOS — 8/10

HOTELS HOTELES

Mallorca Marriott, 215 rooms, D 215 € Tel (34) 971- 129 100, Fax (34) 971- 129 103	on site
Hotel Delta, 288 rooms, D 210 € Tel (34) 971- 741 000, Fax (34) 971- 741 000	Cala Blava 8 km
Hotel Garonda 133 rooms, D 103 € Tel (34) 971- 262 200, Fax (34) 971- 262 109	Can Pastilla 10 km

RESTAURANTS RESTAURANTE

El Olivar, Tel (34) 971- 129 100	on site
Binicomprat, Tel (34) 971- 125 411	Algaida 10 km
Caís Cotxer, Tel (34) 971- 262 049	Can Pastilla 10 km

SON ANTEM Oeste

16	8	8

Marriott ha hecho una fuerte inversión en su complejo de Son Antem hasta el punto de construir un segundo recorrido con las características de los campos de gama alta. Por metros, el recorrido Oeste es algo más corto que el este pero, sin embargo, aquí las exigencias de pegada con precisión son mayores porque las calles bordeadas de árboles se ven estrechas, porque tres lagos afectan directamente el juego de cinco hoyos y porque el campo tiene un moldeado que obliga a pensar los golpes y a estudiar "el buen fallo" para resolver la vuelta con èxito. Esta guía se ha elaborado antes de que el campo se abriera al juego, pero la trayectoria de Son Antem y del propietario justifican este voto de confianza.

Marriott has given a decisive boost to its Son Antem resort by building a second golf course that has all the features of an upmarket layout. It may well be shorter than the neighbouring Este course but it is much more demanding technically speaking and in terms of accuracy, not only because of the trees that line the fairways but also on account of three lakes which come directly into play on five holes. The course is also designed in such a way that golfers have to think about and plan their shots and work out the right tactics to negotiate the tighter holes. When we visited for this latest edition, the course was not yet open, but the reputation of the resort's proprietor and the very serious approach of the whole enterprise would seem to justify our vote of confidence.

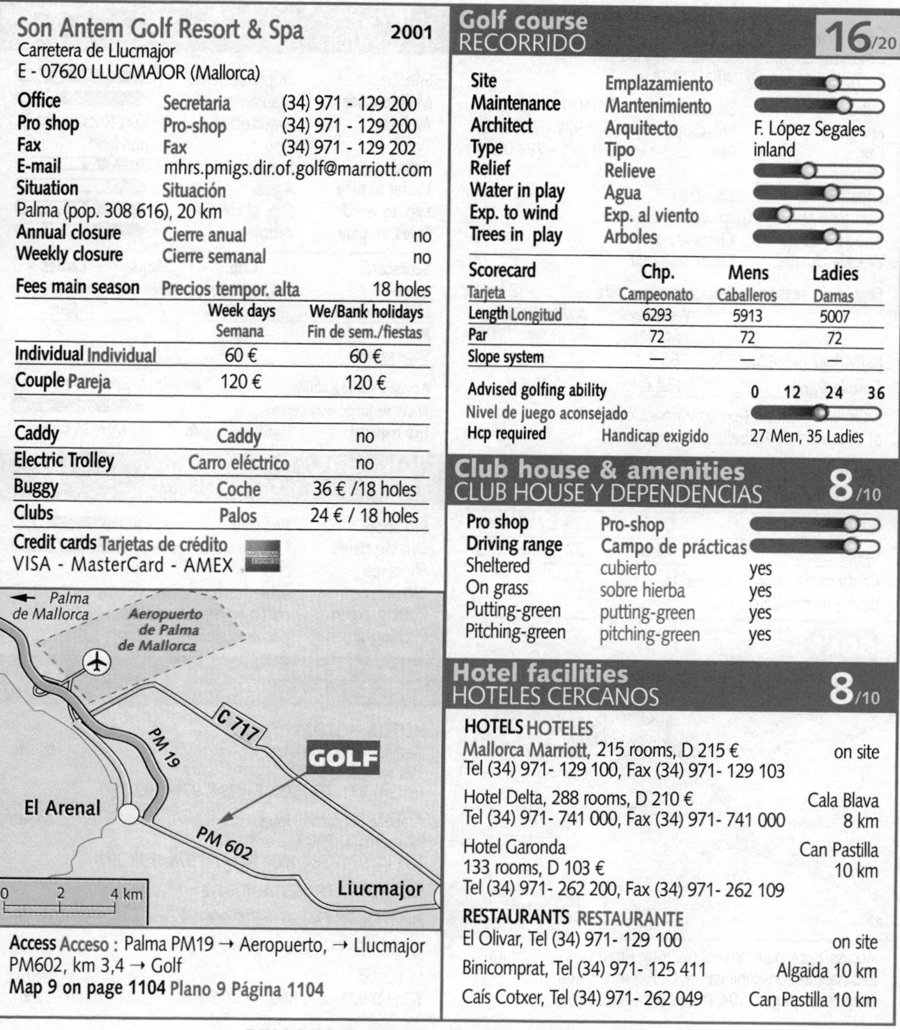

Son Antem Golf Resort & Spa — 2001

Carretera de Llucmajor
E - 07620 LLUCMAJOR (Mallorca)

Office	Secretaria	(34) 971 - 129 200
Pro shop	Pro-shop	(34) 971 - 129 200
Fax	Fax	(34) 971 - 129 202
E-mail		mhrs.pmigs.dir.of.golf@marriott.com
Situation	Situación	
Palma (pop. 308 616), 20 km		
Annual closure	Cierre anual	no
Weekly closure	Cierre semanal	no

Fees main season / Precios tempor. alta	Week days / Semana	We/Bank holidays / Fin de sem./fiestas
	18 holes	
Individual Individual	60 €	60 €
Couple Pareja	120 €	120 €

Caddy	Caddy	no
Electric Trolley	Carro eléctrico	no
Buggy	Coche	36 € /18 holes
Clubs	Palos	24 € / 18 holes

Credit cards Tarjetas de crédito
VISA - MasterCard - AMEX

Access Acceso : Palma PM19 → Aeropuerto, → Llucmajor PM602, km 3,4 → Golf
Map 9 on page 1104 Plano 9 Página 1104

Golf course RECORRIDO — 16/20

Site	Emplazamiento	
Maintenance	Mantenimiento	
Architect	Arquitecto	F. López Segales
Type	Tipo	inland
Relief	Relieve	
Water in play	Agua	
Exp. to wind	Exp. al viento	
Trees in play	Arboles	

Scorecard / Tarjeta	Chp. / Campeonato	Mens / Caballeros	Ladies / Damas
Length Longitud	6293	5913	5007
Par	72	72	72
Slope system	—	—	—

Advised golfing ability / Nivel de juego aconsejado: 0 12 24 36
Hcp required / Handicap exigido: 27 Men, 35 Ladies

Club house & amenities CLUB HOUSE Y DEPENDENCIAS — 8/10

Pro shop	Pro-shop	
Driving range	Campo de prácticas	
Sheltered	cubierto	yes
On grass	sobre hierba	yes
Putting-green	putting-green	yes
Pitching-green	pitching-green	yes

Hotel facilities HOTELES CERCANOS — 8/10

HOTELS HOTELES

Mallorca Marriott, 215 rooms, D 215 € — on site
Tel (34) 971- 129 100, Fax (34) 971- 129 103

Hotel Delta, 288 rooms, D 210 € — Cala Blava 8 km
Tel (34) 971- 741 000, Fax (34) 971- 741 000

Hotel Garonda, 133 rooms, D 103 € — Can Pastilla 10 km
Tel (34) 971- 262 200, Fax (34) 971- 262 109

RESTAURANTS RESTAURANTE

El Olivar, Tel (34) 971- 129 100 — on site
Binicomprat, Tel (34) 971- 125 411 — Algaida 10 km
Caís Cotxer, Tel (34) 971- 262 049 — Can Pastilla 10 km

SON MUNTANER

16 | 8 | 9

He aquí un campo comercial y sin embargo exclusivo: sólo pueden jugar las personas que estèn alojadas en los dos hoteles del parque Son Vida, ahora una exquisita ciudad de vacaciones con dos campos de golf, a 10 minutos del centro de Palma de Mallorca. Son Muntaner es un campo perfectamente integrado en su medio mediterráneo - almedros, algorrobos, pinos y olivos acompañan amablemente al jugador - ; es uno de aquellos campos en que no es difícil recordar cada hoyo despuès de haberlo jugado por primera vez, y donde se pueden jugar todos los palos de la bolsa; es de distancias cómodas pero tambièn tiene golpes muy exigentes en el 5 (un par 3 en subida de 205 metros) y en 15, que es el hoyo más largo del campo y tiene, bajo el tee, un majestuoso olivo milenario de 9 metros de cuerda.

This is a commercial golf course reserved exclusively for guests staying at the two hotels in the Son Vida park, a lovely holiday village with two golf courses lying just 10 minutes away from Palma. Son Muntaner has been designed to fit in perfectly with its Mediterranean environment and is lined with almond trees, carobs, pine and olive trees. This is one of those courses where you easily remember the holes after just a single round and where you will need every club in your bag. It is not excessively long but certain holes suddenly appear to be very challenging, like the 5th, an uphill par 3 stretching some 205 metres, then the 15th, the longest hole on the course. Before driving, look around and admire the age-old olive tree: the circumference of the trunk measures more than 9 metres.

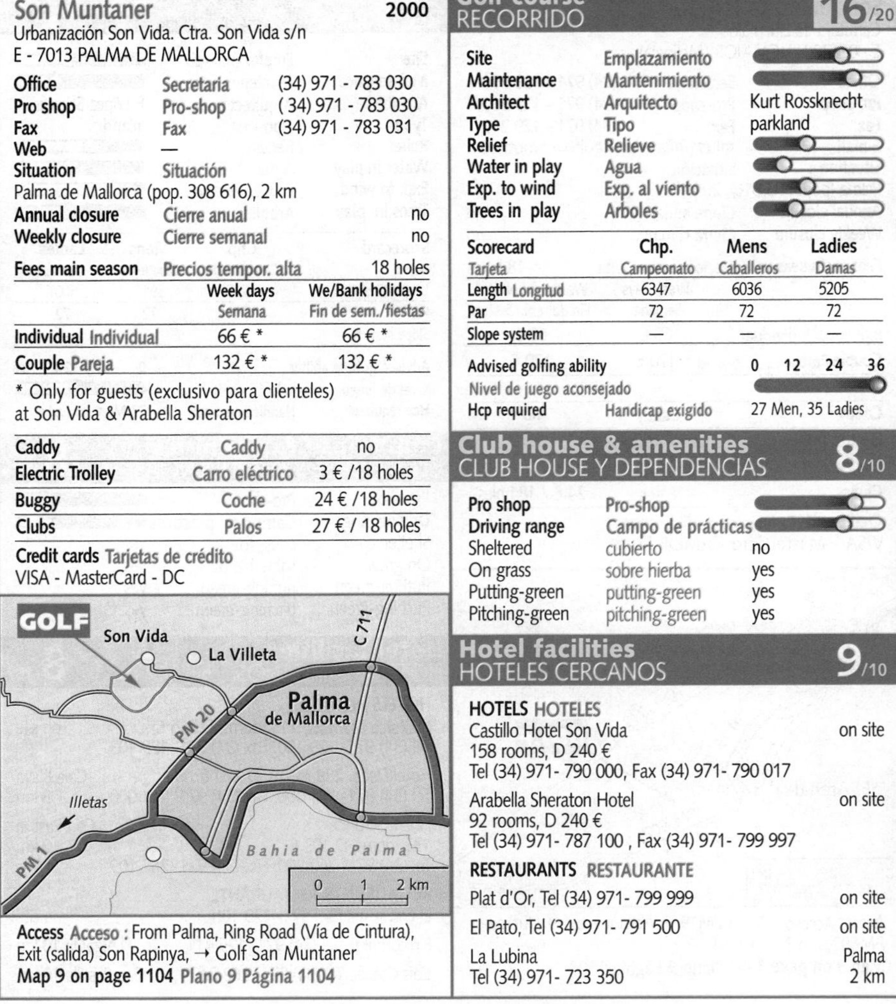

Son Muntaner — **2000**
Urbanización Son Vida. Ctra. Son Vida s/n
E - 7013 PALMA DE MALLORCA

Office	Secretaria	(34) 971 - 783 030
Pro shop	Pro-shop	(34) 971 - 783 030
Fax	Fax	(34) 971 - 783 031
Web	—	
Situation	Situación	

Palma de Mallorca (pop. 308 616), 2 km

Annual closure	Cierre anual	no
Weekly closure	Cierre semanal	no

Fees main season Precios tempor. alta	18 holes	
	Week days Semana	**We/Bank holidays** Fin de sem./fiestas
Individual Individual	66 € *	66 € *
Couple Pareja	132 € *	132 € *

* Only for guests (exclusivo para clienteles) at Son Vida & Arabella Sheraton

Caddy	Caddy	no
Electric Trolley	Carro eléctrico	3 € /18 holes
Buggy	Coche	24 € /18 holes
Clubs	Palos	27 € / 18 holes

Credit cards Tarjetas de crédito
VISA - MasterCard - DC

Access Acceso : From Palma, Ring Road (Vía de Cintura), Exit (salida) Son Rapinya, → Golf San Muntaner
Map 9 on page 1104 Plano 9 Página 1104

Golf course RECORRIDO — 16/20

Site	Emplazamiento	
Maintenance	Mantenimiento	
Architect	Arquitecto	Kurt Rossknecht
Type	Tipo	parkland
Relief	Relieve	
Water in play	Agua	
Exp. to wind	Exp. al viento	
Trees in play	Arboles	

Scorecard Tarjeta	**Chp.** Campeonato	**Mens** Caballeros	**Ladies** Damas
Length Longitud	6347	6036	5205
Par	72	72	72
Slope system	—	—	—

Advised golfing ability Nivel de juego aconsejado — 0 12 24 36
Hcp required Handicap exigido — 27 Men, 35 Ladies

Club house & amenities CLUB HOUSE Y DEPENDENCIAS — 8/10

Pro shop	Pro-shop	
Driving range	Campo de prácticas	
Sheltered	cubierto	no
On grass	sobre hierba	yes
Putting-green	putting-green	yes
Pitching-green	pitching-green	yes

Hotel facilities HOTELES CERCANOS — 9/10

HOTELS HOTELES

Castillo Hotel Son Vida — on site
158 rooms, D 240 €
Tel (34) 971- 790 000, Fax (34) 971- 790 017

Arabella Sheraton Hotel — on site
92 rooms, D 240 €
Tel (34) 971- 787 100 , Fax (34) 971- 799 997

RESTAURANTS RESTAURANTE

Plat d'Or, Tel (34) 971- 799 999 — on site

El Pato, Tel (34) 971- 791 500 — on site

La Lubina — Palma
Tel (34) 971- 723 350 — 2 km

SON VIDA

14 | 6 | 7

Sus numerosos dog-legs ofrecen la oportunidad de arriesgar para acortar aún más este recorrido cuyas principales dificultades son los bunkers (colocados a uno y otro lado de los greens), algún que otro obstáculo de agua (en el 16 y 18) y losárboles: pinos, palmeras, almendros.... Desde las salidas da la impresión de ser un recorrido estrecho y con sorpresas, pero las calles se ensanchan a la caída de los drives. FW Hawtree ha sabido sacar buen partido de un terreno ondulado sin querer mostrar excesivas pretensiones arquitectónicas. Los greens son redondos, sin fantasías, planos, no muy grandes y ligeramente en alto. A pesar del carácter residencial, Son Vida conserva un aspecto muy natural. La calidad de su mantenimiento y su equilibrio nos incitan a aconsejarlo a todos los jugadores, cualquiera que sea su handicap. El campo ha estado cerrado durante todo el año 2001 para realizar mejoras en el sistema de riego y drenajes, aprovechando para remodelar greenes y las calles de los cinco últimos hoyos, bajo la dirección del arquitecto Kurt Rossnecht, con lo cual ha quedado alargado en más de ochenta metros.

The very many dog-legs provide the opportunity to take risks and shorten this course still further. The main hazards are the bunkers (on either side of the green), a few rare water hazards (on the 16th and 18th holes) and the pine, palm and almond trees. The course often looks very tight from the tee, and this can cause surprise, but the fairways open out to reach a fair width at driving length. F.W. Hawtree has made good use of averagely hilly terrain but was obviously not attempting any real architectural exploit. In particular, the greens are round, fancy-free, flat, not very large and slightly elevated. Despite the residential side, Son Vida still has a very natural appearance to it, upkeep is good and the balanced layout makes this a course we would recommend to players of all abilities. The course was closed in 2001 to carry out watering and draining work and also to reshape the greens and fairways of the last five holes under the supervision of course architect Kurt Rossknecht. He lengthened the course by more than 80 metres.

Son Vida Golf S.A. — 1964

Urb./Son Vida s/n
E - 07013 PALMA DE MALLORCA

Office	Secretaria	(34) 971 - 791 210
Pro shop	Pro-shop	(34) 971 - 791 210
Fax	Fax	(34) 971 - 791 127
Web	www.sonvidagolf.com	
Situation	Situación	
Palma (pop. 308 616), 3 km		
Annual closure	Cierre anual	no
Weekly closure	Cierre semanal	no

Fees main season Precios tempor. alta	**Week days** Semana	**We/Bank holidays** Fin de sem./fiestas
		18 holes
Individual Individual	63 €	63 €
Couple Pareja	126 €	126 €

Caddy	Caddy	no
Electric Trolley	Carro eléctrico	no
Buggy	Coche	36 € /18 holes
Clubs	Palos	27 € / 18 holes

Credit cards Tarjetas de crédito
VISA - MasterCard

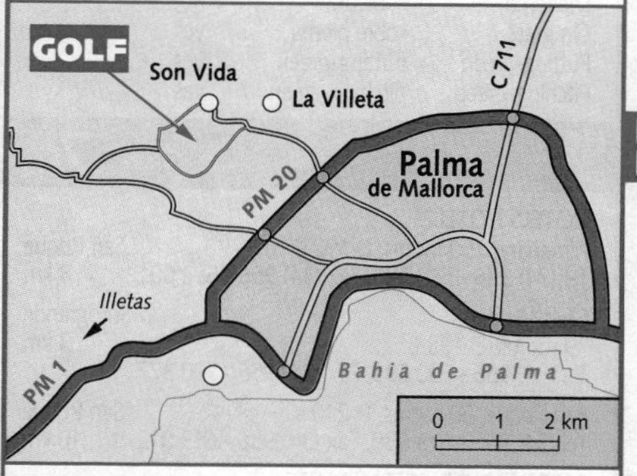

Access Acceso : From Palma, Ring Road (Vía de Cintura), Exit (salida) Son Rapinya, → Urban. Son Vida
Map 9 on page 1104 Plano 9 Página 1104

Golf course — RECORRIDO — 14/20

Site	Emplazamiento	
Maintenance	Mantenimiento	
Architect	Arquitecto	F.W. Hawtree
Type	Tipo	parkland, residential
Relief	Relieve	
Water in play	Agua	
Exp. to wind	Exp. al viento	
Trees in play	Arboles	

Scorecard Tarjeta	**Chp.** Campeonato	**Mens** Caballeros	**Ladies** Damas
Length Longitud	5820	5820	4990
Par	72	72	72
Slope system	—	—	—

Advised golfing ability — 0 12 24 36
Nivel de juego aconsejado
Hcp required — Handicap exigido — 28 Men, 36 Ladies

Club house & amenities — CLUB HOUSE Y DEPENDENCIAS — 6/10

Pro shop	Pro-shop	
Driving range	Campo de prácticas	
Sheltered	cubierto	10 mats
On grass	sobre hierba	yes
Putting-green	putting-green	yes
Pitching-green	pitching-green	yes

Hotel facilities — HOTELES CERCANOS — 7/10

HOTELS HOTELES

Arabella Sheraton Golf Hotel — on site
92 rooms, D 240 €
Tel (34) 971 - 787 100, Fax (34) 971 - 787 101

Castillo Hotel Son Vida — on site
158 rooms, D 240 €
Tel (34) 971- 790 000, Fax (34) 971- 790 017

Saratoga, 187 rooms, D 120 € — Palma 6 km
Tel (34) 971 - 727 240, Fax (34) 971 - 727 312

RESTAURANTS RESTAURANTE

El Pato, Tel (34) 971 - 791 500 — on site

Diplomatic, Tel (34) 971 - 726 482 — Palma 6 km

SOTOGRANDE

18 | 8 | 7

Abierto en 1964, es uno de los clubs con más solera de la Costa y uno de los mejores recorridos. La prioridad la tienen los socios, aunque se admiten visitantes (reservar de antemano). En un sitio muy tranquilo, rodeado de casas espléndidas, con variedad de árboles (pinos, olivos, alcornoques, eucaliptus y palmeras), es más duro de lo que uno quisiera y menos de lo que parece. Gracias en parte a la ausencia casi total de rough, lo que permite que los "pegadores" puedan expresarse con todas sus fuerzas sin más preocupación que la de evitar los numerosos obstáculos de agua concentrados sobre todo en los últimos hoyos. Los golfistas de diferentes niveles se deleitarán con esta armoniosa preparación del recorrido, a pesar de que los greens sean extensos, con muchas caídas y a menudo asesinen el resultado. Bien acompasado, con dificultades bien repartidas, Sotogrande es uno de los grandes ejemplos de la arquitectura de Trent Jones, y uno de los mejores recorridos de España, muchas veces eclipsado por su vecino Valderrama.

Opened in 1964, this is one of the coast's poshest golf clubs and also one of the best courses. Members have priority but it is open to visitors (book in advance). On a very quiet site, encircled by majestic houses and enhanced with numerous trees (pine, olive, oak, eucalyptus and palm trees), it is at once harder than you would like and easier than it looks. This is partly because of the virtual absence of rough, enabling long-hitters to open their shoulders with no worries other than avoiding the numerous water hazards, concentrated particularly over the last holes. But players of all levels will have fun with this friendly preparation, even though the greens are huge, very undulating and often murderous for the score card. Very well paced with difficulties evenly spread around the course, Sotogrande is one of the great examples of architecture à la Trent Jones and one of the best courses in Spain, a bit in the shadow of Valderrama.

Real Club de Golf Sotogrande — 1964

Paseo del Parque S/N
E - 11310 SOTOGRANDE

Office	Secretaria	(34) 956 - 785 012
Pro shop	Pro-shop	(34) 956 - 785 014
Fax	Fax	(34) 956 - 795 029
Web	www.golfsotogrande.com	
Situation	Situación	

Algeciras (pop. 101 556), 30 km - Estepona (pop. 36 307), 30 km

Annual closure	Cierre anual	no
Weekly closure	Cierre semanal	no

Fees main season Precios tempor. alta	18 holes	
	Week days Semana	**We/Bank holidays** Fin de sem./fiestas
Individual Individual	132 €	*
Couple Pareja	264 €	*

* Members only

Caddy	Caddy	36 € /18 holes
Electric Trolley	Carro eléctrico	6 € /18 holes
Buggy	Coche	30 € /18 holes
Clubs	Palos	18 € / 18 holes

Credit cards Tarjetas de crédito
VISA - MasterCard - AMEX

Estepona
Castellar
GOLF
Sotogrande
N 340
costa del sol
San Roque
0 2 4 km

Access Acceso : N340 Estepona → Cadiz. Sotogrande, Golf on the left
Map 7 on page 1101 Plano 7 Página 1101

Golf course RECORRIDO — 18/20

Site	Emplazamiento	
Maintenance	Mantenimiento	
Architect	Arquitecto	Robert Trent Jones
Type	Tipo	seaside course, parkland
Relief	Relieve	
Water in play	Agua	
Exp. to wind	Exp. al viento	
Trees in play	Arboles	

Scorecard Tarjeta	**Chp.** Campeonato	**Mens** Caballeros	**Ladies** Damas
Length Longitud	6224	5853	5077
Par	72	72	72
Slope system	—	—	—

Advised golfing ability — 0 12 24 36
Nivel de juego aconsejado
Hcp required Handicap exigido — 25 Men, 30 Ladies

Club house & amenities CLUB HOUSE Y DEPENDENCIAS — 8/10

Pro shop	Pro-shop	
Driving range	Campo de prácticas	
Sheltered	cubierto	no
On grass	sobre hierba	yes
Putting-green	putting-green	yes
Pitching-green	pitching-green	yes

Hotel facilities HOTELES CERCANOS — 7/10

HOTELS HOTELES

Almenara, 150 rooms, D 192 € — San Roque 8 km
Tel (34) 956 - 582 000, Fax (34) 956 - 582 001

Club Maritimo — Sotogrande 3 km
39 rooms, D 168 €
Tel (34) 956 - 790 200, Fax (34) 956 - 790 377

San Roque, 50 rooms, D 210 € — San Roque 10 km
Tel (34) 956 - 613 030, Fax (34) 956 - 613 012

RESTAURANTS RESTAURANTE

Los Remos, Tel (34) 956 - 698 412 — San Roque 15 km

Pedr, Tel (34) 956 - 698 453o — San Roque

TORREMIRONA

13	7	7

Este campo se halla en el centro de una planicie con unas vistas espléndidas sobre las estribaciones de los Pirineos que han recogido en sus cuadros famosos pintores locales. Le faltan unos cuantos años para que la vegetación plantada con él crezca y se asiente pero uno de los tesoros del emplazamiento es su luz y el colorido de la naturaleza que lo rodea. Es un campo cómodo de jugar, prácticamente llano. No es largo, aunque los pegadores podrán disfrutar en dos pares 4 exigentes, y permite jugar con cierta tranquilidad, aunque el recorrido sorprende gratamente de vez en cuando con tiros que merecen una gran concentración, como la salida del 10, un par 3 con agua a la izquierda, o la del 15, un par 3 con el green en alto. El campo, pues, es versátil porque los jugadores expertos pueden hallar en él ocasiones de plantearse el reto de dar el golpe precisamente indicado, y los jugadores de mayor handicap tienen muchas opciones para cubrir su recorrido sin excesivos riesgos. El hotel abierto recientemente junto al tee del 1 sugiere además que es un buen modelo de instalación para unas confortables vacaciones de golf.

This course lies at the centre of a plain giving some splendid views over the foothills of the Pyrenees, as illustrated by four famous local artists. Of course it will take years for the young plantation to grow and mature but the location of this layout already provides magnificent light and colours from the natural setting all around. This is a virtually flat and easy course to play. It is not wide, though, but big-hitters will enjoy two demanding par 4s in particular. It also has a few surprises in store when shots call for extra concentration, like at the 10th hole, a par 3 with water to the left, or the 15th, another par 3 with an elevated green. This is a versatile course in that skilled players have the chance to attack the pin if they play straight, while the higher-handicap golfer has a number of options open to him or her to get around the course without any excessive risk-taking. The hotel opened behind the first tee-box makes this a model resort for a pleasant stay and an enjoyable golf holiday.

Torremirona Golf Club — 1993

Ctra. N-260, Km 46
E - 17744 NAVATA

Office	Secretaria	(34) 972 - 553 737
Pro shop	Pro-shop	(34) 972 - 553 737
Fax	Fax	(34) 972 - 553 716
Web	www.torremirona.com	
Situation	Situación	

Figueras (pop. 35 301), 10 km

Annual closure	Cierre anual	no
Weekly closure	Cierre semanal	no

Fees main season Precios tempor. alta	**Week days** Semana	**We/Bank holidays** Fin de sem./fiestas
		18 holes
Individual Individual	53 € *	57 €
Couple Pareja	106 €	114 €

* Weekdays and Sunday

Caddy	Caddy	no
Electric Trolley	Carro eléctrico	12,02 € /18 holes
Buggy	Coche	36,06 € /18 holes
Clubs	Palos	21,03 € / 18 holes

Credit cards Tarjetas de crédito
VISA - Eurocard - MasterCard - AMEX

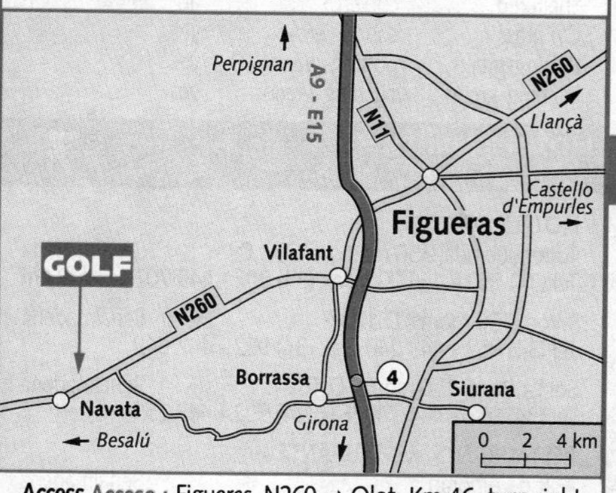

Access Acceso : Figueras, N260 → Olot, Km 46, turn right.
Map 2 on page 1091 Plano 2 Página 1091

Golf course — RECORRIDO — 13/20

Site	Emplazamiento	
Maintenance	Mantenimiento	
Architect	Arquitecto	Tecnoa Eugenio Aguado
Type	Tipo	parkland, inland
Relief	Relieve	
Water in play	Agua	
Exp. to wind	Exp. al viento	
Trees in play	Arboles	

Scorecard Tarjeta	**Chp.** Campeonato	**Mens** Caballeros	**Ladies** Damas
Length Longitud	6192	5949	5124
Par	72	72	72
Slope system	—	—	—

Advised golfing ability Nivel de juego aconsejado — 0 12 24 36
Hcp required Handicap exigido — 28 Men/36 Ladies

Club house & amenities — CLUB HOUSE Y DEPENDENCIAS — 7/10

Pro shop	Pro-shop	
Driving range	Campo de prácticas	
Sheltered	cubierto	no
On grass	sobre hierba	yes (25 places)
Putting-green	putting-green	yes
Pitching-green	pitching-green	yes

Hotel facilities — HOTELES CERCANOS — 7/10

HOTELS HOTELES

Torremirona, 49 rooms, D 162 € — on site
Tel (34) 972 - 566 700, Fax (34) 972 - 566 767

Mas Falgarona, 9 rooms, D 138 € — Avinyonet 5 km
Tel (34) 972 - 546 628, Fax (34) 972 - 547 071

Empordá, 42 rooms, D 100 € — Figueras 11 km
Tel (34) 972 - 500 562, Fax (34) 972 - 509 358

RESTAURANTS RESTAURANTE

El Canigo, Tel (34) 972 - 566 700 — Figueras 11 km
Mas Pau, Tel (34) 972 - 546 154 — Avinyonet 5 km
Durán, Tel (34) 972 - 501 250 — Figueras 10 km

TORREQUEBRADA

14	7	7

Fiel a su filosofía, Pepe Gancedo ha adaptado el recorrido a un terreno cuyo relieve hace que sea muy complejo y difícil el jugar sin coche. La calidad de los golpes de salida es de importancia capital: se puede perder todo de entrada con golpes demasiado desperdigados. No hay que dejarse engañar por su reducida distancia, ya que las múltiples dificultades hacen que hasta los golpes del juego corto sean delicados: árboles, bosque, rough, bunkers y obstáculos de agua se encuentran en la línea de juego. La belleza del panorama es de poco consuelo si se pierde el control de la bola. Al menos las primeras veces hay que jugar en match-play: de esta manera el recorrido es divertido (incluso en los hoyos ciegos) excepto para los jugadores con poca experiencia en quienes aumentará la presián cuando les vayan quedando pocas bolas...

True to his philosophy, Pepe Gancedo has adapted the course to the terrain, whose relief makes it difficult not only to walk but also to play. Here, the tee-shot is of prime importance. A wild drive and all may be lost. And don't be fooled by the short yardage because the numerous hazards make even the shortest irons a tricky business. Trees, woods, rough, bunkers and water are all very much to the fore, and the beauty of the scenery is scant consolation should you lose your grip and your game. For the first couple of rounds, you are better off in match-play, in which case the course can be great fun (even on the few blind holes) except for the less experienced players, who will feel the pressure even more when they start running out of balls...

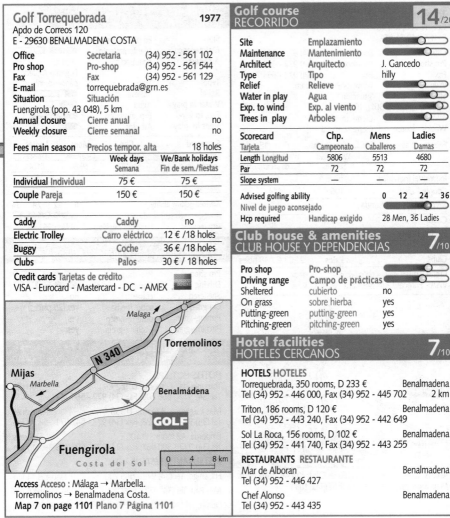

Golf Torrequebrada — 1977

Apdo de Correos 120
E - 29630 BENALMADENA COSTA

Office	Secretaria	(34) 952 - 561 102
Pro shop	Pro-shop	(34) 952 - 561 544
Fax	Fax	(34) 952 - 561 129
E-mail	torrequebrada@grn.es	
Situation	Situación	
Fuengirola (pop. 43 048), 5 km		
Annual closure	Cierre anual	no
Weekly closure	Cierre semanal	no

Fees main season Precios tempor. alta	18 holes	
	Week days Semana	**We/Bank holidays** Fin de sem./fiestas
Individual Individual	75 €	75 €
Couple Pareja	150 €	150 €

Caddy	Caddy	no
Electric Trolley	Carro eléctrico	12 € /18 holes
Buggy	Coche	36 € /18 holes
Clubs	Palos	30 € / 18 holes

Credit cards Tarjetas de crédito
VISA - Eurocard - Mastercard - DC - AMEX

Access Acceso : Málaga → Marbella.
Torremolinos → Benalmadena Costa.
Map 7 on page 1101 Plano 7 Página 1101

Golf course RECORRIDO — 14/20

Site	Emplazamiento	
Maintenance	Mantenimiento	
Architect	Arquitecto	J. Gancedo
Type	Tipo	hilly
Relief	Relieve	
Water in play	Agua	
Exp. to wind	Exp. al viento	
Trees in play	Arboles	

Scorecard Tarjeta	**Chp.** Campeonato	**Mens** Caballeros	**Ladies** Damas
Length Longitud	5806	5513	4680
Par	72	72	72
Slope system	—	—	—

Advised golfing ability Nivel de juego aconsejado — 0 12 24 36

Hcp required Handicap exigido — 28 Men, 36 Ladies

Club house & amenities CLUB HOUSE Y DEPENDENCIAS — 7/10

Pro shop	Pro-shop	
Driving range	Campo de prácticas	
Sheltered	cubierto	no
On grass	sobre hierba	yes
Putting-green	putting-green	yes
Pitching-green	pitching-green	yes

Hotel facilities HOTELES CERCANOS — 7/10

HOTELS HOTELES

Torrequebrada, 350 rooms, D 233 € — Benalmadena
Tel (34) 952 - 446 000, Fax (34) 952 - 445 702 — 2 km

Triton, 186 rooms, D 120 € — Benalmadena
Tel (34) 952 - 443 240, Fax (34) 952 - 442 649

Sol La Roca, 156 rooms, D 102 € — Benalmadena
Tel (34) 952 - 441 740, Fax (34) 952 - 443 255

RESTAURANTS RESTAURANTE

Mar de Alboran — Benalmadena
Tel (34) 952 - 446 427

Chef Alonso — Benalmadena
Tel (34) 952 - 443 435

ULZAMA

16 | 6 | 6

Creado en 1965, Ulzama se ha convertido en 18 hoyos en 1990. Situado a 500 metros de altura, discurre en un terreno bastante accidentado en el que los jugadores poco en forma acabarán agotados. La adaptación del recorrido al terreno es extraordinaria: se trata de una de las últimas obras del gran arquitecto Javier Arana. Toda la panorámica transcurre en medio de un inmenso bosque. Aunque las calles no son muy estrechas, el jugador que no logre mantener la bola bien recta será "recompensado" a la altura de sus errores. Es un recorrido natural, con un paisaje análogo al de un parque con unos greens de superficie media y bastante llanos. Felizmente no hay muchos bunkers ya que muchos golpes son ciegos. Hay que conocerlo antes para lograr un buen resultado. Para el jugador de tipo medio es un reccorido de longitud asequible en el que los pares 3 son bastante largos exceptuando el hoyo numero 2.

Opened in 1965, Ulzama was extended to 18 holes only in 1990. At over 1500 ft. above sea-level, it unfolds over hilly terrain where the less fit player will probably feel the strain. But the way the course has been adapted to the lie of the land is quite remarkable, hardly a surprise when you learn that this is one of the latest courses by the great designer Javier Arana. The major visual feature is basically its layout in a majestic oak forest. With this said, the fairways are never too tight, which doesn't mean to say that players who make a mess of their tee-shot and don't hit it straight won't be penalised accordingly. This course is a very natural-looking layout in landscape reminiscent of park-land with average-sized, rather flat greens. Bunkers are limited in number, which is probably a good thing given the number of blind shots, and you need to know the course well before any hope of shooting a good score. For the average player, this is a course of reachable length but the par 3s are on the long side (except hole N° 2)

Club de Golf Ulzama — 1965

E - 31799 GUERENDIAIN - VALLE DE ULZAMA

Office	Secretaria	(34) 948 - 305 162
Pro shop	Pro-shop	(34) 948 - 305 471
Fax	Fax	(34) 948 - 309 209
Web	www.golfspainfederacion.com	
Situation	Situación	
Pamplona (pop. 191 197), 22 km		
Annual closure	Cierre anual	no
Weekly closure	Cierre semanal	no

Fees main season / Precios tempor. alta	Week days / Semana	We/Bank holidays / Fin de sem./fiestas
		18 holes
Individual Individual	42 €	54 €
Couple Pareja	84 €	108 €

Only 20 visitors admitted per day (20 green-fees al día)

Caddy	Caddy	no
Electric Trolley	Carro eléctrico	5 € /18 holes
Buggy	Coche	24 € /18 holes
Clubs	Palos	6 € / 18 holes

Credit cards Tarjetas de crédito
VISA

Access Acceso : Pamplona, N-121 → Irun. Turn in Ostiz (km 15) → Lizaso (Valle Ulzama) after 6 km.
Map 1 on page 1089 Plano 1 Página 1089

Golf course — RECORRIDO — 16/20

Site	Emplazamiento	
Maintenance	Mantenimiento	
Architect	Arquitecto	Javier Arana F. Redon/J. Guiber
Type	Tipo	forest
Relief	Relieve	
Water in play	Agua	
Exp. to wind	Exp. al viento	
Trees in play	Arboles	

Scorecard / Tarjeta	Chp. / Campeonato	Mens / Caballeros	Ladies / Damas
Length Longitud	6232	6065	5154
Par	73	72	72
Slope system	—	—	—

Advised golfing ability / Nivel de juego aconsejado: 0 12 24 36
Hcp required / Handicap exigido: 28 Men, 36 Ladies

Club house & amenities — CLUB HOUSE Y DEPENDENCIAS — 6/10

Pro shop	Pro-shop	
Driving range	Campo de prácticas	
Sheltered	cubierto	no
On grass	sobre hierba	yes
Putting-green	putting-green	yes
Pitching-green	pitching-green	yes

Hotel facilities — HOTELES CERCANOS — 6/10

HOTELS HOTELES

Ventas Ulzama, 15 rooms, D 51 € — Puerto Belate
Tel (34) 948 - 305 138, Fax (34) 948 - 305 138 — 8 km

Lorentxo, 9 rooms, D 90 € — Olabe
Tel (34) 948 - 332 486, Fax (34) 948 - 332 679 — 10 km

Aguirre, 12 rooms, D 42 € — Oricain
Tel (34) 948 - 330 375 — 14 km

RESTAURANTS RESTAURANTE

Josetxo, Tel (34) 948 - 222 097 — Pamplona 21 km
La Chistera, Tel (34) 948 - 210 512 — Pamplona
Castillo de Javier, Tel (34) 948 - 221 894 — Pamplona

VALDERRAMA

19 | 8 | 6

No hay que perdérselo porque es un campo en condiciones de juego exquisitas, lo cual justifica la nota máxima que concede esta guía. Valderrama ha adquirido notoriedad internacional bajo la impulsión de su propietario Jaime Ortiz-Patiño, quien impuso no sólo modificaciones del recorrido original (sobre todo el 17) sino que ha exigido un mantenimiento del campo de excepcional calidad (hasta uno teme sacar chuletas). La dificultad estratégica del trazado, la omnipresencia de árboles, la dimensión de los bunkers y algunos obstáculos de agua, le obligan a uno a estudiar muy bien cada golpe. Las caídas de los greens aumentan aún más la presión. Es inútil esperar jugar su handicap, incluso a los grandes campeones les cuesta muchísimo jugar el par. Pero ante la calidad del desafío, le entran ganas a uno de seguir sus pasos y anticiparse a la "cumbre" de Valderrama cuando la "Ryder Cup 1997" enfrente a los equipos de Estados Unidos y de Europa. Es un golf privado donde se admiten visitantes previa reserva. No hay que perdérselo.

Valderrama has gained international fame through the energy of proprietor Jaime Ortiz-Patiño, who not only insisted on making changes to the original layout (notably to the 17th hole) but also demanded exceptional standards of course upkeep (you hardly dare take a divot!). But honestly, if the standards of maintenance here were not quite as excellent, this sometimes controversial course would certainly not be rated as high as it is... The strategic difficulty, omnipresent trees, the size of the bunkers and a few water hazards keep the player constantly on his wits for every stroke. And the pressure is made worse when it comes to reading the greens. Don't bother about playing to your handicap, as even the top champions find making par a tough enough task. But the quality of this challenge is enough to make anyone want to walk in footsteps of the professionals in anticipation of the 1997 "summit" at Valderrama, when the Ryder Cup is due to be staged here. This is a private course but is open to green-feers who book in advance. Not to be missed.

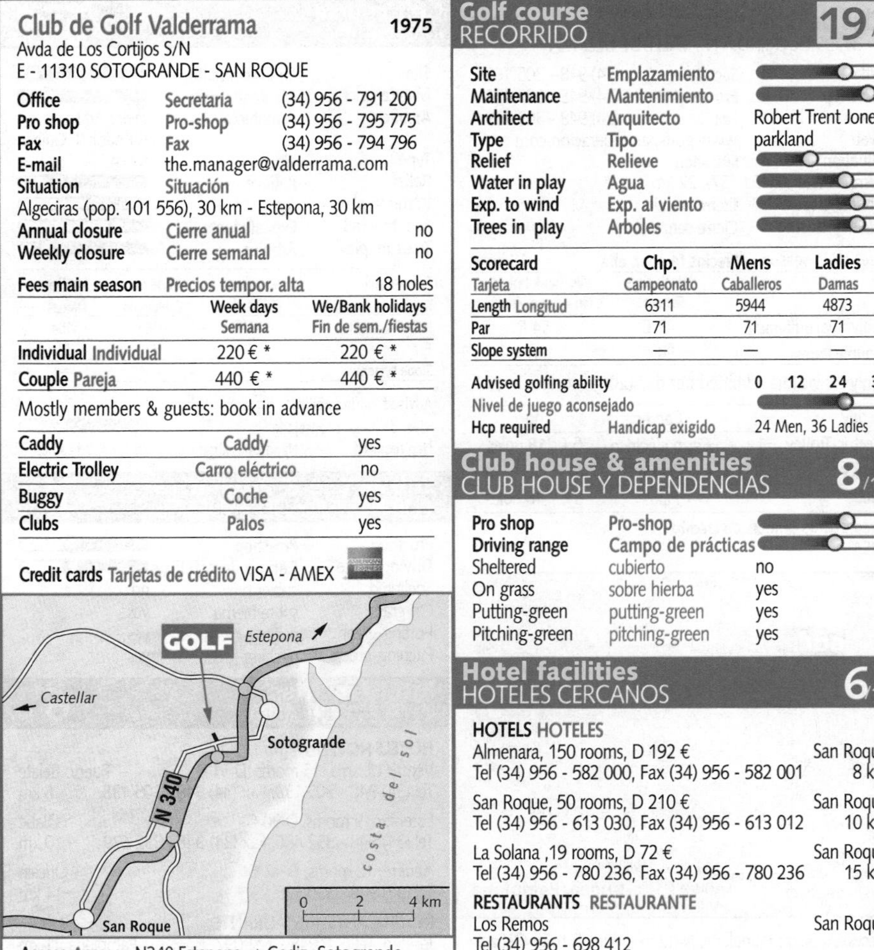

Club de Golf Valderrama — 1975

Avda de Los Cortijos S/N
E - 11310 SOTOGRANDE - SAN ROQUE

Office	Secretaría	(34) 956 - 791 200
Pro shop	Pro-shop	(34) 956 - 795 775
Fax	Fax	(34) 956 - 794 796
E-mail	the.manager@valderrama.com	
Situation	Situación	

Algeciras (pop. 101 556), 30 km - Estepona, 30 km

Annual closure	Cierre anual	no
Weekly closure	Cierre semanal	no

Fees main season Precios tempor. alta — 18 holes

	Week days / Semana	We/Bank holidays / Fin de sem./fiestas
Individual Individual	220 € *	220 € *
Couple Pareja	440 € *	440 € *

Mostly members & guests: book in advance

Caddy	Caddy	yes
Electric Trolley	Carro eléctrico	no
Buggy	Coche	yes
Clubs	Palos	yes

Credit cards Tarjetas de crédito VISA - AMEX

Access Acceso : N340 Estepona → Cadiz. Sotogrande, Golf on the right
Map 7 on page 1101 Plano 7 Página 1101

Golf course RECORRIDO — 19/20

Site	Emplazamiento	
Maintenance	Mantenimiento	
Architect	Arquitecto	Robert Trent Jones
Type	Tipo	parkland
Relief	Relieve	
Water in play	Agua	
Exp. to wind	Exp. al viento	
Trees in play	Arboles	

Scorecard Tarjeta	**Chp.** Campeonato	**Mens** Caballeros	**Ladies** Damas
Length Longitud	6311	5944	4873
Par	71	71	71
Slope system	—	—	—

Advised golfing ability Nivel de juego aconsejado — 0 12 24 36
Hcp required Handicap exigido — 24 Men, 36 Ladies

Club house & amenities CLUB HOUSE Y DEPENDENCIAS — 8/10

Pro shop	Pro-shop	
Driving range	Campo de prácticas	
Sheltered	cubierto	no
On grass	sobre hierba	yes
Putting-green	putting-green	yes
Pitching-green	pitching-green	yes

Hotel facilities HOTELES CERCANOS — 6/10

HOTELS HOTELES

Almenara, 150 rooms, D 192 € — San Roque
Tel (34) 956 - 582 000, Fax (34) 956 - 582 001 — 8 km

San Roque, 50 rooms, D 210 € — San Roque
Tel (34) 956 - 613 030, Fax (34) 956 - 613 012 — 10 km

La Solana ,19 rooms, D 72 € — San Roque
Tel (34) 956 - 780 236, Fax (34) 956 - 780 236 — 15 km

RESTAURANTS RESTAURANTE

Los Remos — San Roque
Tel (34) 956 - 698 412

Pedro — San Roque
Tel (34) 956 - 698 453

VILLAMARTIN

16 | 7 | 6

Aunque todavía no goza de fama internacional, merece la pena ir a Villamartín. Sin que sea un recorrido excesivamente largo, Paul Putman, con mucha imaginación, ha sabido adaptar su diseño al terreno, dándole gran personalidad: se aconseja que sólo los mejores elijan los tees de salida de atrás. Varios pares 4 más bien cortos permiten disfrutar un poquito. El agua, que tan poco gusta a los jugadores de tipo medio, se halla verdaderamente en línea de juego en tres hoyos (sobre todo en el 9), y preferirán admirar los árboles, raramente en línea de juego pero muy presentes. Los greens son de buen tamaño, con ligeras ondulaciones y aguantan bien la bola aún cuando el golpe no sea perfecto. Es un recorrido adaptable fácilmente para jugar en familia y con jugadores de niveles diferentes, y en general muy bien cuidado.

Although yet to forge a great international reputation, Villamartin is well worth going out of your way for. While not a terribly long course, the layout has personality and has been cleverly adopted to the terrain thanks to Paul Putman's keen imagination. In our opinion, the back-tees are for the best players only. A number of short par 4s are fun to play, and water is only really in play on three holes (especially the 9th). High-handicappers, who tend not to like water, can preferably admire the trees, which although rarely in play, are very much a part of the course. The greens are large, rolling and pitch well, even from slightly mishit shots. This is a most versatile and generally well-prepared course, easy to play with the family or with players of all different levels.

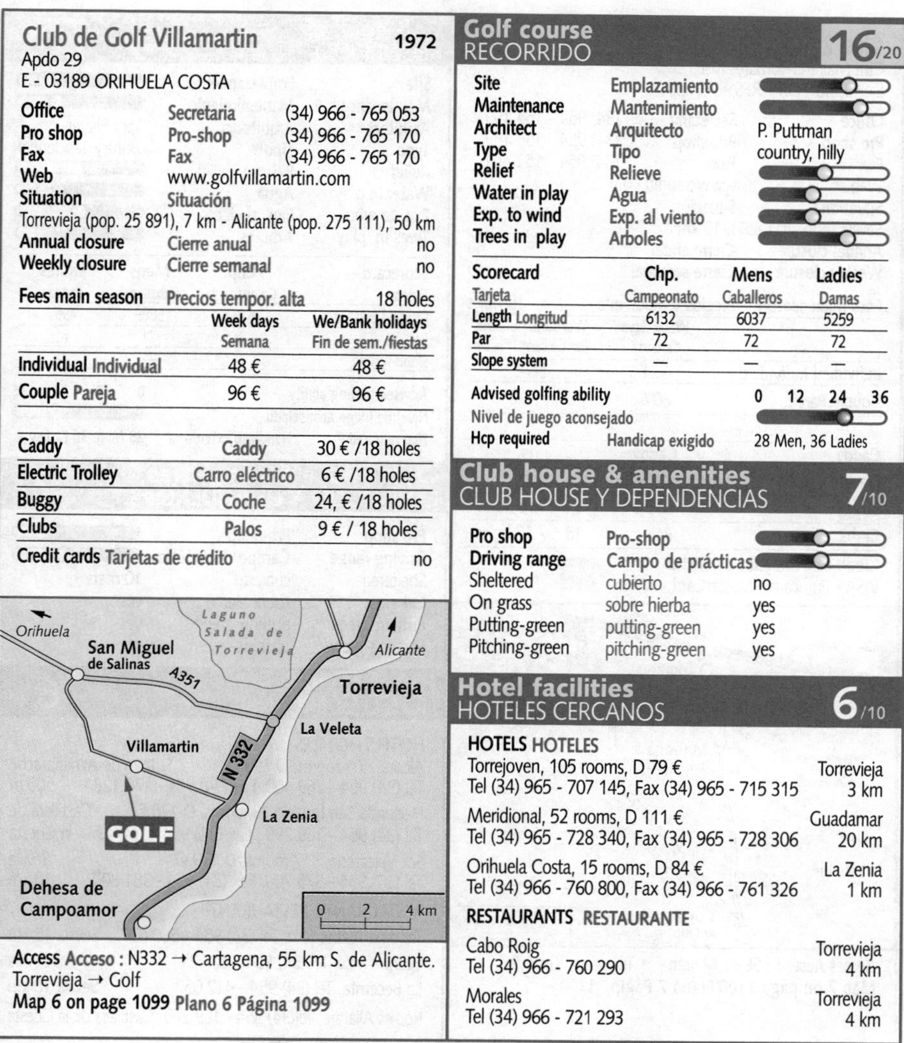

Club de Golf Villamartin — 1972

Apdo 29
E - 03189 ORIHUELA COSTA

Office	Secretaria	(34) 966 - 765 053
Pro shop	Pro-shop	(34) 966 - 765 170
Fax	Fax	(34) 966 - 765 170
Web	www.golfvillamartin.com	
Situation	Situación	

Torrevieja (pop. 25 891), 7 km - Alicante (pop. 275 111), 50 km

Annual closure	Cierre anual	no
Weekly closure	Cierre semanal	no

Fees main season Precios tempor. alta	Week days Semana	We/Bank holidays Fin de sem./fiestas
		18 holes
Individual Individual	48 €	48 €
Couple Pareja	96 €	96 €

Caddy	Caddy	30 € /18 holes
Electric Trolley	Carro eléctrico	6 € /18 holes
Buggy	Coche	24, € /18 holes
Clubs	Palos	9 € / 18 holes
Credit cards Tarjetas de crédito		no

Access Acceso : N332 → Cartagena, 55 km S. de Alicante. Torrevieja → Golf
Map 6 on page 1099 Plano 6 Página 1099

Golf course RECORRIDO — 16/20

Site	Emplazamiento	
Maintenance	Mantenimiento	
Architect	Arquitecto	P. Puttman
Type	Tipo	country, hilly
Relief	Relieve	
Water in play	Agua	
Exp. to wind	Exp. al viento	
Trees in play	Arboles	

Scorecard Tarjeta	Chp. Campeonato	Mens Caballeros	Ladies Damas
Length Longitud	6132	6037	5259
Par	72	72	72
Slope system	—	—	—

Advised golfing ability Nivel de juego aconsejado: 0 12 24 36
Hcp required Handicap exigido: 28 Men, 36 Ladies

Club house & amenities CLUB HOUSE Y DEPENDENCIAS — 7/10

Pro shop	Pro-shop	
Driving range	Campo de prácticas	
Sheltered	cubierto	no
On grass	sobre hierba	yes
Putting-green	putting-green	yes
Pitching-green	pitching-green	yes

Hotel facilities HOTELES CERCANOS — 6/10

HOTELS HOTELES

Torrejoven, 105 rooms, D 79 € — Torrevieja 3 km
Tel (34) 965 - 707 145, Fax (34) 965 - 715 315

Meridional, 52 rooms, D 111 € — Guadamar 20 km
Tel (34) 965 - 728 340, Fax (34) 965 - 728 306

Orihuela Costa, 15 rooms, D 84 € — La Zenia 1 km
Tel (34) 966 - 760 800, Fax (34) 966 - 761 326

RESTAURANTS RESTAURANTE

Cabo Roig — Torrevieja 4 km
Tel (34) 966 - 760 290

Morales — Torrevieja 4 km
Tel (34) 966 - 721 293

ZAUDIN

16 | 7 | 6

En veinte años, el arquitecto Gary Player ha evolucionado. Sus recorridos son más detallistas y las dificultades más variadas. Aparte de unos cuantos hoyos dispuestos en ida y vuelta y la distancia a veces larga de un hoyo a otro, Zaudín figura entre las buenas realizaciones del Sur de España. Palmeras, naranjos y grandes lagos hacen pensar en Florida, pero los olivos están tan presentes como en el panorama de Sevilla. Aquí, el drive de salida en los pares 4 y 5 no plantea grandes problemas pero los aproches son delicados (especialmente en 17 y 18). Una vez en el green, no hay malas sorpresas, no son inmensos ni tortuosos. La distancia razonable del recorrido y la calidad de las instalaciones hacen que sea una realización prometedora.

The architecture of Gary Player has evolved in 20 years: his courses are now much more intricate in the smaller details and offer a greater variety of difficulty. If we exclude the large number of holes running parallel up and down and the sometimes long walk between holes, Zaudin is one of the great golfing achievements in southern Spain. The palm trees, orange trees and large lakes are reminiscent of Florida, but olive groves are as present as the views over Seville. The tee-shots on the par 4s and par 5s pose no real danger but the approach shots are often tricky affairs (especially on the 17th and 18th holes). Once on the greens, there are no unpleasant surprises in store. They are not huge, but they are not too tortuous, either. The reasonable length of this course and the standard of facilities make this a most inviting location.

Club Zaudin Golf S.A. — 1993

Ctra Mairena-Tomares Km 1,5
E - 41940 TOMARES - SEVILLA

Office	Secretaria	(34) 954 - 154 159
Pro shop	Pro-shop	(34) 954 - 154 159
Fax	Fax	(34) 954 - 152 452
Web	www.zaudin.com	
Situation	Situación	

Sevilla (pop. 704 857), 10 km

Annual closure	Cierre anual	no
Weekly closure	Cierre semanal	no

Fees main season Precios tempor. alta	Week days Semana	We/Bank holidays Fin de sem./fiestas
	18 holes	
Individual Individual	40 €	56 €
Couple Pareja	80 €	112 €

Caddy	Caddy	no
Electric Trolley	Carro eléctrico	no
Buggy	Coche	26 € /18 holes
Clubs	Palos	13 € / 18 holes

Credit cards Tarjetas de crédito
VISA - Eurocard - MasterCard - AMEX

Access Acceso : SE 30 Mairena → Tomares, Km 1,5
Map 7 on page 1100 Plano 7 Página 1100

Golf course RECORRIDO — 16/20

Site	Emplazamiento	
Maintenance	Mantenimiento	
Architect	Arquitecto	Gary Player
Type	Tipo	country, residential
Relief	Relieve	
Water in play	Agua	
Exp. to wind	Exp. al viento	
Trees in play	Arboles	

Scorecard Tarjeta	**Chp.** Campeonato	**Mens** Caballeros	**Ladies** Damas
Length Longitud	6192	5869	4967
Par	71	71	71
Slope system	—	—	—

Advised golfing ability Nivel de juego aconsejado — 0 12 24 36
Hcp required Handicap exigido — 28 Men, 36 Ladies

Club house & amenities CLUB HOUSE Y DEPENDENCIAS — 7/10

Pro shop	Pro-shop	
Driving range	Campo de prácticas	
Sheltered	cubierto	10 mats
On grass	sobre hierba	yes
Putting-green	putting-green	yes
Pitching-green	pitching-green	no

Hotel facilities HOTELES CERCANOS — 6/10

HOTELS HOTELES

Alcora, 401 rooms, D 195 — S. Juan de Aznalfarache
Tel (34) 954 - 769 400, Fax (34) 954 - 170 128 — 500 m

Hacienda San Ignacio 18 rooms, D 120 € — Castillera de la Cuesta
Tel (34) 954 - 169 290 , Fax (34) 954 - 161 437

Sol Macarena, 317 rooms, D 139 € — Sevilla
Tel (34) 954 - 375 700, Fax (34) 954 - 381 803 — 10 km

RESTAURANTS RESTAURANTE

Taberna Alabardero, Tel (34) 954 - 560 637 — Sevilla 15 km
Egaña Oriza, Tel (34) 954 - 227 211 — Sevilla
La Becerrita, Tel (34) 954 - 412 057 — Sevilla 10 km
Robles Aljarafe, Tel(34) 954 - 169 260 — Castilleja de la Cuesta

EUROPE'S TOP 1000 GOLF COURSES

Sweden

Halmstad

Sweden
Sverige

From May to September, southern Europeans can easily play golf in Sweden over long periods of daylight which often allow at least two rounds a day. With more than 450,000 players for almost 300 eighteen-hole courses, Sweden is one of the leading golf countries on the continent of Europe. Thanks to golf being considered above all else as a sport like soccer, tennis or skiing, and thanks finally to intelligent organization and media exposure, Sweden has produced an amazing number of champion golfers. Amongst the men, Jesper Parnevik, Per-Ulrik Johansson and Jarmo Sandelin are just three out of a whole bunch of good players. And as Sweden cultivates equality in sport and elsewhere, the output of top women players is equally impressive, with star players such as Liselotte Neumann, Helen Alfredsson, Sophie Gustafson or the phenomenal Annika Sorenstam.

Från maj till september är dagarna långa och fyllda av dagsljus. Ofta är det möjligt att hinna med två rundor om dagen. Med mer än 450 000 golfare fördelade på över 300 banor är Sverige en av de ledande golfnationerna i Europa.. Utvecklingen beror naturligtvis mycket på det stöd som spelet åtnjuter och att golf betraktas som vilken sport som helst, i jämnhöjd med fotboll, tennis och skidåkning. Detta har inneburit att Sverige har fått fram en rad stora golfspelare: Jesper Parnevik, Per-Ulrik Johansson och Jarmo Sandelin är bara tre av många exempel. Och eftersom Sverige är ett jämlikt land, såväl inom idrottens värld som inom övriga områden, är antalet kvinnliga stjärnor lika imponerande! Tänk bara på Liselotte Neumann, Helen Alfredsson, Sophie Gustafson och den fenomenala Annika Sörenstam.

Map No 1
Karta 1
km
0 10 20
1204
Fjällbacka
Stenungsund
Göteborg
Kungsbacka
Forsgården
Skövde
Gränna
Jönköping
A 6
Värnamo
Falkenberg
Halmstad
Båstad
Torekov
Mölle
Ängelhom
Vasatorp
Asserbo (DK)
Simon's (DK)
Rungsted (DK)
Söderhåsen
Perstorp
Rya
Bosjökloster
Barsebäck
Landskrona
Eslöv
Kristianstad
Lunds Akademiska
København (DK)
Bokskogen
Flommens
Falsterbo
Ljunghusen
GÖTEBORG
JÖNKÖPING
KØBENHAVN
MALMÖ
VÄSTRA GÖTALANDS LÄN
HALLANDS LÄN
KATTEGAT
MICHELIN

Nyköping
Oxelösund
Bråviken
NORRKÖPING
Nävekvarn
Kolmården
Jönåker
Stigtomta
Krokek
Åby
Lindö
Runtuna
Trosa
Nynäshamn
Finspång
Motala
Borensberg
Ljungsbro
Kimstad
Göta Kanal
Vreta Kloster
Kaga
Vadstena
Skänninge
Malmslätt
Vikingstad
Linghem
Söderköping
LINKÖPING
Mantorp
Mjölby
Rök
Björsäter
ÖSTERGÖTLANDS LÄN
Åtvidaberg
Boxholm
Tranås
Valdemarsvik
Kisa
Överum
Gamleby
Västervik
Gdansk
Sommen
Aneby
Österbymo
Norra Kvill
Eksjö
Vimmerby
Ankarsrum
Mariannelund
Storebro
Hultsfred
Vetlanda
Sävsjö
Korsberga
Virserum
Kristdala
Fårbo
Oskarshamn
Byxelkrok
Böda
Blå Jungfrun
Löttorp
Fågelfors
Högsby
Emån
Åseda
KALMAR LÄN
Grönskåra
Rottne
Lenhovda
Mönsterås
Okno
Växjö
Bäckebo
Orrefors
Borgholm
Köpingsvik
Öland
Ekerum
Gärdslösa
Hovmantorp
Lessebo
Eriksmåle
Nybro
Lindsdal
Kalmar
Smedby
Färjestaden
Emmaboda
Gårdby
Tingsryd
Urshult
Karlevi
Resmo
Söderåkra
Mörbylånga
Stora Alvaret
Torsås
BLEKINGE LÄN
Rödeby
Grönhögen
Bräkne-Hoby
Kallinge
Karlskrona
Ronneby
Nättraby
Jämjö
Karlshamn
Björketorp
Gdynia
Visby
Klintehamn
Vamlingbo
1205
MICHELIN
d'après carte n° 985 - 10ème édition - 2002.
Autorisation n° 0102062.

Map No 2
Karta 2
km
0 10 20
Bro-Bålsta
Europeantour Club (Kungsängen)
Ullna
Täby
Österåker
Stockholm
Drottningholm
1/340 0
Karlstad
Örebro
Forsbacka
MICHELIN
Sigtuna
Märsta
Norrsunda
Rosersberg
Skånela
Markim
Orkesta
Lindholmen
Vada
Karby
Gröndal
Ormsta
Angarn
Löwenströmska-lasarettet
Hammarby
Upplands-Väsby
Frestaby
Vallentuna
Byle
Bällsta
Vallentunasjön
Ullnasjön
Västra Ryd
Bro
Brunna
Säbyholm
Tibble
Ed
Bollstanäs
Rotebro
Norrviken
Kungsängen
Björknäs
Bro fjarden
Kallhäll
Gorvaln
Edsberg
Ensta
Täby
Rydbo
Östra Ryd
Sollentuna
Edsviken
Enebyberg
Roslags-Nässby
Jakobsberg
Helenelund
Danderyd
St Värtan
Djursholm
Kungsberga
Vänthol men
Viksjö
Järfälla
Kista
Barkarby
Ulriksdal
Mörby
Stocksund
Bogesund
Hilleshög
Ricksättra
Spånga
Färentuna
Hässelby
Färingsö
Vällingby
Solvalla
Sundbyberg
Lidingö
Millesgården
Sånga
Svartsjö
Lambarfj.
Bromma
Solna
Haga
Brevik
Stenhamra
Ängby
Nockeby
Alvik
Östermalm
Värtan
STOCKHOLM
Skå
Lovö
Långholmen
Skansen
Essingen
Södermalm
Tureholm
Hammargården
Drottningholm
Nacka
Hägersten
Årsta
Fisksätra
Rastaborg
Ekerön
Älvnäs
Mälarhöjden
Saltsjöbaden
Närsta
Kaggeholm
Ekerö
Älvsjö
Enskede
Skärholmen
Segeltorp
Örby
Stureby
Skarpnäck
Sturehov
Högdalen
Älta
Vårby
Stuvsta
Hallunda
Fittja
Botkyrka
Farsta
Sköndal
Huddinge
Skrubba
Alby
Bornsjön
Magelungen
Trångsund
Salem
Skogås
Tullingesjön
Södertälje
Länna
Edane
Glava
Klässbol
Glafsfjorden
Deje
Molkom
Kil
Forshaga
Storfors
Nora
Lindesberg
Årjäng
Skåre
Karlstad
Vålberg
Fröv
Grums
Skoghall
Långeserud
Nysäter
Kristinehamn
Karlskoga
Glanshammar
Garphyttan
ÖREBRO
Degerfors
Säffle
Svartå
Bengtsfors
Åmål
Kumla
Pålsboda
Ed
Dals Långed
Hallsberg
Gullspång
Laxå
Skagern
Bäckefors
Vänern
Askersund
Sjötorp
Stjärnsund
Dalbosjön
Mellerud
Unden
Olshammar
Mariestad
Läckö
Töreboda
Tiveden
Tjällmo

Norrfjärden
Gnarp
Bergsjö
Harmånger
Strömsbruk
Ljusdal
Färila
Delsbo
Hälsingtuna
Malsta
Järvsö
Forsa
Hudiksvall
Iggesund
GÄVLEBORGS LÄN
Öjung
Mattsmyra
Vallsta
Arbrå
Enånger
Enhammarsfjärden
Edsbyn
Ovanåker
Tronö
Bollnäs
Alfta
Söderhamn
Sandarne
Ljusne
Kilafors
Skog
Hälsingeleden
Ljusnan
Bingsjö
Lingbo
Åmot
Norrsundet
Bergby
Ockelbo
Enviken
Svärdsjö
Lumsheden
Järbo
Gavlebukten
Gävle
Falun
Sandviken
Valbo
Storvik
Hofors
Skutskär
Lovstabukten
Älvkarleby
Vika
Storsjön
Långshyttan
Arsunda
Stora Skedvi
Skarplinge
Öregrundsgrepen
Mehedeby
Lövstabruk
Garpenberg
Söderfors
Tierp
Säter
Österfärnebo
Öregrund
Hedemora
Horndal
Gysinge
UPPSALA LÄN
Östhammar
Månkarbo
Österbybruk
Gimo
Avesta
Dalälven
Vendel
Söderbärke
Östervåla
Viksta
Grisslehamn
Norberg
Tensta
Salsta
Björklinge
Vattholma
Hallstavik
Bälinge
Rasbo
Väddö
Sala
Salbohed
Heby
Gåvsta
Virsbo
Edsbro
Skinnskatteberg
Uppsala
UPPSALA
VÄSTMANLANDS LÄN
Fjärdhundra
Sävja
Norrtälje
Örsundsbro
Skokloster
Rimbo
Kapellskär
Surahammar
Skultuna
Tillberga
Knivsta
Hallstahammar
Frösåker
Märsta
Arlanda
Ängsö
Kolsva
Enköping
Sigtuna
Norrsunda
STOCKHOLMS LÄN
Kolbäck
VÄSTERÅS
Bålsta
Upplands-Väsby
Köping
Ängsö
Vallentuna
Tidö
Bro
Åkersberga
Kungsör
Torshälla
Sollentuna
Täby
Österåker
Jäder
Arboga
Strängnäs
Lidingö
Skogstorp
Eskilstuna
Drottningholm
Tallinn
Helsinki
Fågelbro
Åkers styckebruk
Mariefred
Gripsholm
Sturehov
Boo
Alberga
Stora Sundby
Hjälmaren
STOCKHOLM
Tyresö
Turinge
Tumba
Nämndöfj.
SÖDERMANLANDS LÄN
Södertälje
Hälleforsnäs
Malmköping
Nykvarn
Jordbro
Stjärnhov
Vingåker
Flen
Järna
Väster-Haninge
Haninge
Klaipeda
Baven
Gnesta
Sorunda
Katrineholm
Vagnhärad
Tullgarn
Mysingen
Eriksberg
Bettna
Ösmo
Tisnaren
Runtuna
Nynäshamn
Yngaren
Trosa
Stigtomta
Jönåker
Kolmården
Nyköping
Åby
BOTTENHAVET
BOTTNISKA VIKEN
(GOLFE DE BOTTNIE)
1207
MICHELIN

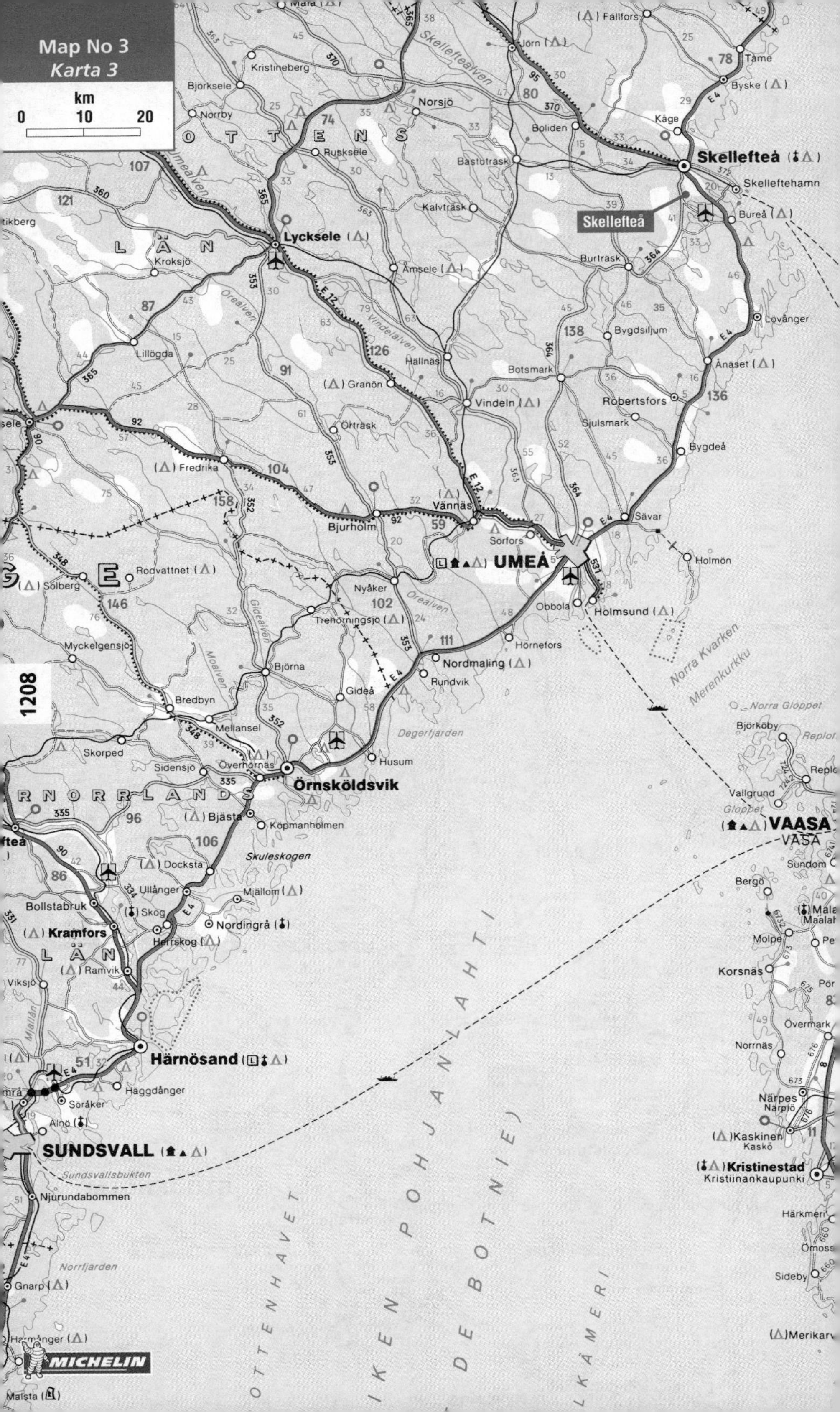

Map No 3
Karta 3
km
0 10 20
1208
Skellefteå
Skelleftehamn
Bureå
Fällfors
Tåme
Byske
Kåge
Jörn
Boliden
Bastuträsk
Kalvträsk
Burträsk
Lövånger
Bygdsiljum
Ånaset
Botsmark
Robertsfors
Sjulsmark
Bygdeå
Vindeln
Hällnäs
Åmsele
Norsjö
Kristineberg
Björksele
Norrby
Rusksele
Lycksele
Kroksjö
Lillögda
Granön
Örträsk
Fredrika
Bjurholm
Vännäs
Sörfors
UMEÅ
Sävar
Holmön
Obbola
Holmsund
Hörnefors
Nordmaling
Rundvik
Nyåker
Trehörningsjö
Björna
Gideå
Husum
Bredbyn
Mellansel
Skorped
Sidensjö
Överhörnäs
Örnsköldsvik
Bjästa
Köpmanholmen
Skuleskogen
Docksta
Ullånger
Mjällom
Nordingrå
Skog
Herrskog
Bollstabruk
Kramfors
Ramvik
Viksjö
Härnösand
Häggdånger
Söråker
Alnö
SUNDSVALL
Sundsvallsbukten
Njurundabommen
Norrfjärden
Gnarp
Harmånger
Malsta
Rodvattnet
Solberg
Myckelgensjö
Degerfjärden
Norra Kvarken
Merenkurkku
Norra Gloppet
Björköby
Replot
Vallgrund
Gloppet
VAASA
VASA
Sundom
Bergö
Maalahti
Molpe
Korsnäs
Övermark
Norrnäs
Närpes
Närpiö
Kaskinen
Kaskö
Kristinestad
Kristiinankaupunki
Härkmeri
Sideby
Skellefteälven
Umeälven
Vindelälven
Öreälven
Gideälven
Moälven
Mjällån
BOTTENHAVET
SELKÄMERI
MICHELIN

CLASSIFICATION OF COURSES
VI RANKAR BANORNA

This classification gives priority consideration to the score awarded to the actual course.

Rankingen syftar endast på golfbanan.

Course score Banans betyg				Page Sid
18	7	6	Barsebäck	1215
18	7	5	Falsterbo	1227
18	8	7	Halmstad	1236
18	7	7	Ljunghusen	1245
18	7	5	Örebro	1248
17	7	6	Bro-Bålsta	1220
17	7	6	European Tour Club (Kungsängen)	1224
17	7	7	Kristianstad	1242
17	5	7	Skövde	1253
17	7	8	Stenungsund	1255
17	8	6	Ullna	1260
16	7	6	Ängsö	1213
16	6	5	Åtvidaberg	1214
16	7	7	Båstad *Old Course*	1216
16	6	7	Bokskogen	1217
16	7	7	Bråviken	1219
16	9	5	Fågelbro	1225
16	7	7	Flommen	1229
16	7	4	Forsbacka	1230
16	7	5	Frösåker	1232
16	8	6	Haninge	1237
16	7	7	Jönköping	1238
16	7	5	Lunds Akademiska	1246
16	6	6	Österåker	1249
16	8	9	Stockholm	1256
16	7	7	Täby	1257
16	7	7	Vasatorp	1263
16	7	5	Visby	1265
15	6	6	Ängelholm	1212
15	7	6	Bosjökloster	1218
15	6	3	Fjällbacka	1228
15	6	7	Göteborg	1234
15	7	5	Gränna	1235
15	5	8	Kalmar	1239
15	6	6	Karlstad	1241
15	6	6	Kungsbacka	1243
15	9	7	Landskrona *Gul Bana*	1244
15	7	5	Mölle	1247
15	7	8	Rya	1251
15	7	5	Söderåsen	1254
15	7	5	Värnamo	1262
15	6	7	Växjö	1264
14	7	6	A 6	1211
14	9	6	Drottningholm	1221
14	7	7	Ekerum	1222
14	7	5	Eslöv	1223
14	7	7	Falkenberg	1226
14	6	7	Forsgården	1231
14	6	6	Gävle	1233
14	6	6	Karlshamn	1240
14	7	5	Perstorp	1250
14	6	5	Skellefteå	1252
14	7	7	Torekov	1258
14	6	7	Tranås	1259
13	6	6	Upsala	1261

RECOMMENDED GOLFING STAY
REKOMMENDERAD GOLFVISTELSE

Barsebäck	18	7	6	1215
Falsterbo	18	7	5	1227
Halmstad	18	8	7	1236
Haninge	16	8	6	1237
Kalmar	15	5	8	1239
Ljunghusen	18	7	7	1245
Örebro	18	7	5	1248
Skövde	17	5	7	1253

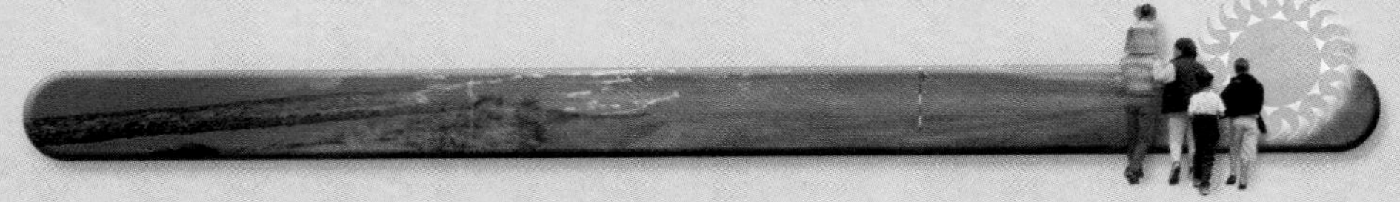

RECOMMENDED HOLIDAYS
REKOMMENDERAD SEMESTERORT

Båstad	16	7	7	1216	Kungsbacka	15	6	6	1243
Ekerum	14	7	7	1222	Ljunghusen	18	7	7	1245
Falsterbo	18	7	5	1227	Mölle	15	7	5	1247
Fjällbacka	15	6	3	1228	Rya	15	7	8	1251
Flommen	16	7	7	1229	Torekov	14	7	7	1258
Forsgården	14	6	7	1231					

TYPE OF COURSE
BANTYP

Forest
A6 1211, Åtvidaberg 1214, Bråviken 1219, European Tour Club (Kungsängen) 1224, Fågelbro 1225, Falkenberg 1226, Forsbacka 1230, Gävle 1233, Halmstad 1236, Haninge 1237, Karlshamn 1240, Karlstad 1241, Örebro 1248, Perstorp 1250, Skellefteå 1252, Söderåsen 1254, Tranås 1259, Upsala 1261, Värnamo 1262, Vasatorp 1263, Växjö 1264.

Forest
Ängsö 1213.

Links
Falsterbo 1227, Flommen 1229

Open Country
Ängsö 1213, Bosjökloster 1218, Bro-Bålsta1220, Fjällbacka 1228, Forsgården 1231, Gränna 1235, Kristianstad 1242, Stenungsund 1255, Torekov 1258.

Parkland
Ängelholm 1212, Barsebäck 1215, Båstad *Old Course* 1216, Bokskogen 1217, Bosjökloster 1218, Bråviken 1219, Bro-Bålsta 1220, Drottningholm 1221, Ekerum 1222, Eslöv 1223, Falkenberg 1226, Fjällbacka 1228, Forsbacka 1230, Frösåker 1232, Gävle 1233, Göteborg 1234, Gränna 1235, Halmstad 1236 Haninge 1237, Jönköping 1238, Kalmar 1239, Karlshamn 1240, Karlstad 1241, Kungsbacka 1243, Kristianstad 1242, Landskrona *Gul Bana* 1244, Lunds Akademiska 1246, Mölle 1247, Örebro 1248, Österåker 1249, Perstorp 1250, Skövde 1253, Rya 1251, Söderåsen 1254 Stenungsund 1255, Stockholm 1256, Täby 1257, Tranås 1259, Ullna 1260, Upsala 1261, Värnamo 1262, Vasatorp 1263, Växjö 1264, Visby 1265.

Seaside course
Barsebäck 1215, Falsterbo 1227, Flommen 1229, Frösåker 1232, Kungsbacka 1243, Landskrona 1244, Ljunghusen 1245, Rya 1251, Täby 1257, Torekov 1258, Visby 1265

Hilly
A 6 1211, European Tour Club (Kungsängen) 1224, Mölle 1247.

A 6

14 | 7 | 6

Tillsammans med Jönköping och Gränna är detta en av de bästa banorna på vackra Vätterns sydöstra sida. Fast från A 6 syns inte den 2 000 kvadratmeter stora och på sina ställen bråddjupa sjön (128 meter där det är som djupast). Om du är på väg norrut på E4 i det svindlande vackra landskapet rekommenderas ett besök på denna till namnet märkliga bana. Den är designad av Peter Nordwall, som här har ritat greener som ligger väl skyddade och som i varje fall för honom är förvånansvärt små. De är med andra ord inte alldeles lätta att träffa. Banan är relativt kuperad och bjuder på några ställen på en härlig utsikt. Detta innebär också att du under rundan kommer ställas inför några blinda slag, och dessutom skär en ravin in i spelet på flera hål och hotar att ställa till det för dig. Som på alla banor av den här typen krävs det några rundor innan du känner dig hemma. Försök att hålla huvudet kallt eller ännu bättre – lira en runda med en medlem som känner till alla problemen. Eller så struntar du helt enkelt i att föra scorekort! Vad du än väljer – på A 6 kommer du finna det svårt att gå på din handicap. Så därför gör det inte så mycket om du spelar med sämre spelare än du själv. Gå ut med hela familjen eller med vänner med högre handicap.

This is one of the best courses on the south-east side of the wonderful lake Vättern, some 2,000 sq. km of water reaching a depth of up to 128 metres. Before heading northward across the superb landscapes to be seen on the A4 motorway (speed limits vary between 90 and 100 km), this course going by the strange name A6 is well worth a round or two. It was designed by Peter Nordwall, who produced some well-guarded greens that are smaller than usual (for him) and so a little trickier to approach. The course is on the steep side, which gives a wild natural setting but also a number of blind shots and a dangerous ravine in play on several holes. As with every course like this, it is difficult to get a clear idea of game strategy first time out. To tackle it with as cool a head as possible, try to play a round with a member, do your own reconnoitring or simply forget about keeping score. Whatever, it will never be easy to play to your handicap here, so make the most of it and play with the family or friends who are not as good as you.

A 6 Golfklubb — 1989

Centralvägen
S - 553 05 JÖNKÖPING

Office	Sekretariat	(46) 036 - 308 130
Pro shop	Pro shop	(46) 036 - 719 105
Fax	Fax	(46) 036 - 308 140
E-mail	abgolf@swipnet.se	
Situation	Läge	Jönköpping, 3 km
Annual closure	Årlig stängning	no
Weekly closure	Daglig stängning	no

Fees main season Tariff hög säsong		Full day
	Week days Veckodag	**We/Bank holidays** Lör/Söndag/Helgdag
Individual Individuellt	SKr 250	SKr 250
Couple Par	SKr 420	SKr 420

Juniors: - 50%

Caddy	Caddie	no
Electric Trolley	El vagn	no
Buggy	Golfbil	no
Clubs	Klubbor	SKr 100 /18 holes

Credit cards Kredit kort VISA - AMEX

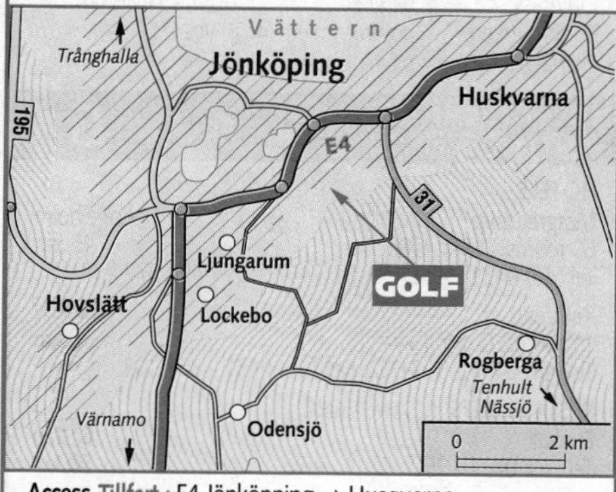

Access Tillfart : E4 Jönköpping → Husqvarna. → "Nya A 6".
Map 1 on page 1204 Karta 1 se sid: 1204

Golf course — BANA — 14/20

Site	Läge	
Maintenance	Underhåll	
Architect	Arkitekt	Peter Nordwall
Type	Karaktär	forest, hilly
Relief	Nivåskillnader	
Water in play	Vatten på spelfältet	
Exp. to wind	Vindutsatt	
Trees in play	Träd på spelfältet	

Scorecard Scorekort	**Chp.** Back tees	**Mens** Herrtee	**Ladies** Damtee
Length Längd	6268	5668	4881
Par	72	72	72
Slope system	0	135	132

Advised golfing ability Rekommenderad spelnivå — 0 12 24 36

Hcp required Hcp erfordrad 36

Club house & amenities — KLUBBHUS OCH OMGIVNING — 7/10

Pro shop	Pro shop	
Driving range	Träningsbana	
Sheltered	tåkt	no
On grass	på gräs	yes
Putting-green	putting-green	yes
Pitching-green	pitching-green	yes

Hotel facilities — HOTELL OMGIVNING — 6/10

HOTELS

Jönköppings Hotell & Konferens — Jönköpping on site
60 rooms, D SKr 900
Tel (46) 036 - 171 800, Fax (46) 036 - 171 835

Comfort Home Hotel Victoria — Jönköpping 5 km
90 rooms, D SKr 1000
Tel (46) 036 - 712 800, Fax (46) 036 - 715 050

RESTAURANTS RESTAURANG

Restaurang Borgmästaren — Jönköpping 3 km
Tel (46) 036 - 161 440

Restaurang Dragon — Jönköpping 3 km
Tel (46) 036 - 172 800

Krogen Svarta Börsen Tel (46) 036 - 712 222 — Jönköpping

ÄNGELHOLM

15 | 6 | 6

En charmig liten bana i den djupaste av skogar... hm, det låter som den första textraden i en sång, men det är också det absolut bästa sättet att beskriva Ängelholm på. Den långtslående kanske inte är så förtjust i alla träden, ty detta är en bana som kräver försiktighet och premierar spelstrategi mer än långa drives. En del slag, som inspelet över vattnet på nionde hålet, är minst sagt utmanande, men generellt sett är detta en bana som framför allt kräver tålamod och självkontroll. Golfare av alla skicklighetsgrader trivs här, och som familjebana är den utomordentlig. Det viktigaste är att slå rakt, men den som har en bra bollträff och kan slå höga slag in mot greenerna och få bollen att stanna snabbt har en stor fördel. Ännu bättre om du är så duktig att du kan skruva den åt bägge hållen. Greenerna är medelstora men på inget vis lätthanterliga. Eller för att göra en snabb sammanfattning: För att spela den här banan sitter man gärna i bilen en timme.

A pretty little course down in the woods. This could be the first line of a song, but actually it is the first and most obvious way to describe the charm of Ängelholm. The wilder-hitters might not take too kindly to all these trees, but the caution required here will force them to think in terms more of game strategy than long drives. Some shots, like over the water on the 9th hole, are a little intimidating, but generally speaking this course plays with an open hand and simply has to be addressed with patience and self-restraint. Golfers of all levels soon get to like it, especially when playing with the family, as this is a course that also teaches you how to play. To play straight, of course, but also to strike the ball solidly on a layout that calls for target golf, balls hit high which stop quickly. If you can work the ball both ways, then so much the better. The greens are average in size and well enough designed to make putting more than just a formality. Put simply, it is well worth driving 30 or 40 miles out of your way to play Ängelholm.

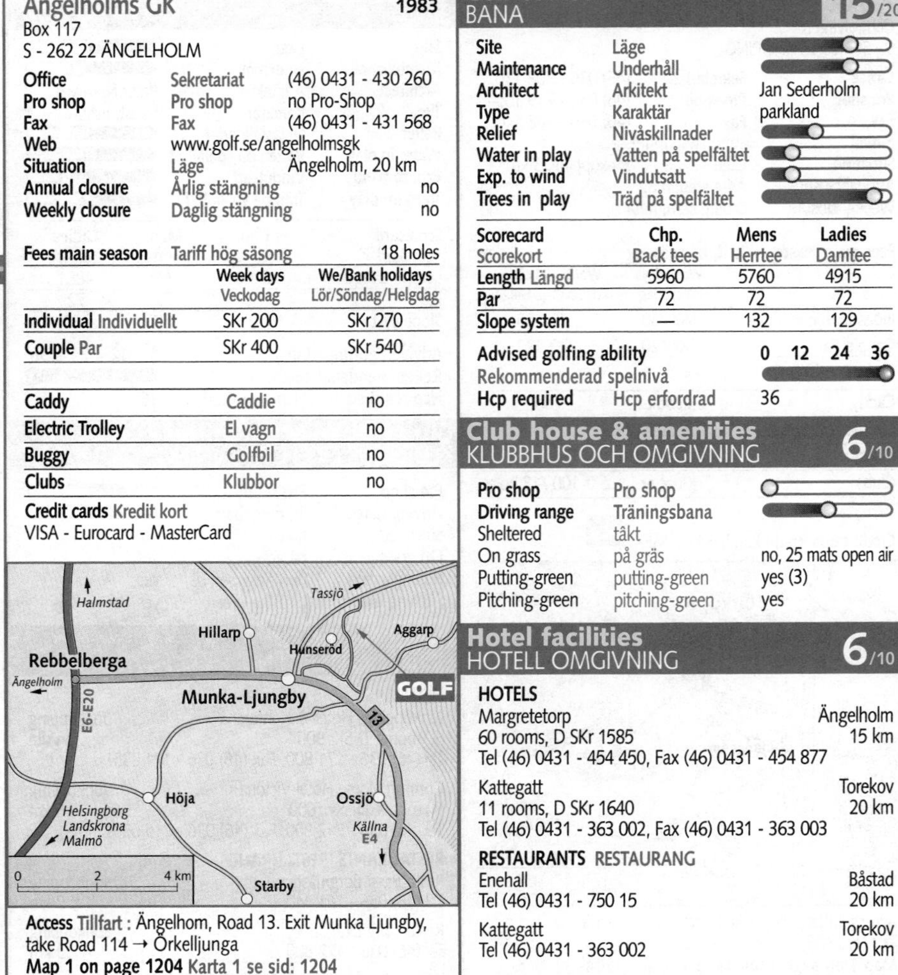

Angelholms GK — 1983

Box 117
S - 262 22 ÄNGELHOLM

Office	Sekretariat	(46) 0431 - 430 260
Pro shop	Pro shop	no Pro-Shop
Fax	Fax	(46) 0431 - 431 568
Web	www.golf.se/angelholmsgk	
Situation	Läge	Ängelholm, 20 km
Annual closure	Årlig stängning	no
Weekly closure	Daglig stängning	no

Fees main season Tariff hög säsong	Week days Veckodag	We/Bank holidays Lör/Söndag/Helgdag
	18 holes	
Individual Individuellt	SKr 200	SKr 270
Couple Par	SKr 400	SKr 540

Caddy	Caddie	no
Electric Trolley	El vagn	no
Buggy	Golfbil	no
Clubs	Klubbor	no

Credit cards Kredit kort
VISA - Eurocard - MasterCard

Access Tillfart : Ängelhom, Road 13. Exit Munka Ljungby, take Road 114 → Örkelljunga
Map 1 on page 1204 Karta 1 se sid: 1204

Golf course BANA — 15/20

Site	Läge	
Maintenance	Underhåll	
Architect	Arkitekt	Jan Sederholm
Type	Karaktär	parkland
Relief	Nivåskillnader	
Water in play	Vatten på spelfältet	
Exp. to wind	Vindutsatt	
Trees in play	Träd på spelfältet	

Scorecard Scorekort	Chp. Back tees	Mens Herrtee	Ladies Damtee
Length Längd	5960	5760	4915
Par	72	72	72
Slope system	—	132	129

Advised golfing ability Rekommenderad spelnivå — 0 12 24 36
Hcp required Hcp erfordrad 36

Club house & amenities KLUBBHUS OCH OMGIVNING — 6/10

Pro shop	Pro shop	
Driving range	Träningsbana	
Sheltered	täkt	
On grass	på gräs	no, 25 mats open air
Putting-green	putting-green	yes (3)
Pitching-green	pitching-green	yes

Hotel facilities HOTELL OMGIVNING — 6/10

HOTELS

Margretetorp — Ängelholm
60 rooms, D SKr 1585 — 15 km
Tel (46) 0431 - 454 450, Fax (46) 0431 - 454 877

Kattegatt — Torekov
11 rooms, D SKr 1640 — 20 km
Tel (46) 0431 - 363 002, Fax (46) 0431 - 363 003

RESTAURANTS RESTAURANG

Enehall — Båstad
Tel (46) 0431 - 750 15 — 20 km

Kattegatt — Torekov
Tel (46) 0431 - 363 002 — 20 km

ÄNGSÖ

16 | 7 | 6

En bana nära staden Västerås som helst ska besökas under den torra årstiden, blötan kan ställa till en del problem under våren. Sagt det, måste vi genast konstatera att närheten till Mälaren och landskapets skönhet nästan får dig att glömma bort själva spelet. Nivåskillnaderna är måttliga, men ett par upphöjda greener kan ge de svåraste flaggplaceringar. Men innan du har nått till greenen måste du handskas med resten av banan, med fairways som kan vara minst sagt lömska att träffa. På många hål frestas du att gena över doglegs, misslyckas du står det dig dyrt. Detta är en förrädisk bana eftersom den ser lite svårare ut än vad den egentligen är. Detta gäller från klubbtee, från backtee kan banan vara ett riktigt monster, och då finns det oftast bara ett sätt: långt och rakt. Och det är ju inget problem, eller hur? Ängsö är en härlig utmaning på en härlig plats. Kan man önska sig något mer?

Close to Västerås, this course has to be played in fine weather, as wetness can be a problem. However, the nearby magnificent lake Mälaren and surrounding countryside almost make you forget you are here to play golf. The topography of the terrain is never excessive, but a few elevated greens sometimes lead to blind pin positions. Before getting that far, you will find some of the fairways a little deceptive in terms of view and distance, where the temptation to cut corners can prove fatal. The lush vegetation and number of hazards call for extreme accuracy off the tee and even an ability to flight the ball. In reality, this is a deceptive course because it looks more difficult than it actually is, so keep a cool head and do not be over-influenced by what you see. This is valid, of course, when playing from the normal tees, as the back-tees can sometimes turn the course into a real monster, where the only solution is to hit it very long and very straight. The way we all do, right? A great challenge and a great site. Who could ask for more?

Ängsö GK — 1984

Björnövägen 2
S - 721 30 VÄSTERÅS

Office	Sekretariat	(46) 0171 - 441 041
Pro shop	Pro shop	(46) 0171 - 441 041
Fax	Fax	(46) 0171 - 441 049
Web	www.angsogolf.org	
Situation	Läge	Västerås, 20 km
Annual closure	Årlig stängning	no
Weekly closure	Daglig stängning	no

Fees main season Tariff hög säsong	18 holes	
	Week days Veckodag	**We/Bank holidays** Lör/Söndag/Helgdag
Individual Individuellt	SKr 220	SKr 300
Couple Par	SKr 440	SKr 600

Caddy	Caddie	no
Electric Trolley	El vagn	no
Buggy	Golfbil	SKr 150 /18 holes
Clubs	Klubbor	SKr 100 /18 holes

Credit cards Kredit kort
VISA - Eurocard - MasterCard

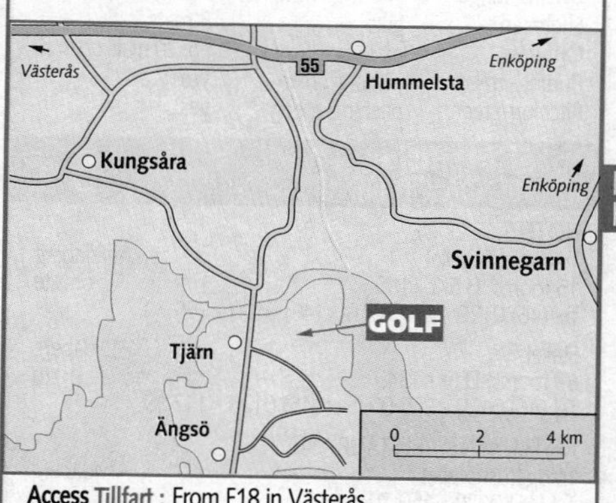

Access Tillfart : From E18 in Västerås, Exit Hällamotet. → Irsta. After 5 km, → Golf
Map 2 on page 1206 Karta 2 se sid: 1206

Golf course — BANA — 16/20

Site	Läge	
Maintenance	Underhåll	
Architect	Arkitekt	Åke Hultström
Type	Karaktär	forest, parkland, open country
Relief	Nivåskillnader	
Water in play	Vatten på spelfältet	
Exp. to wind	Vindutsatt	
Trees in play	Träd på spelfältet	

Scorecard Scorekort	**Chp.** Back tees	**Mens** Herrtee	**Ladies** Damtee
Length Längd	6327	5880	5029
Par	72	72	72
Slope system	—	130	126

Advised golfing ability Rekommenderad spelnivå — 0 12 24 36
Hcp required Hcp erfordrad — 30 Men, 36 Ladies

Club house & amenities — KLUBBHUS OCH OMGIVNING — 7/10

Pro shop	Pro shop	
Driving range	Träningsbana	
Sheltered	tåkt	no
On grass	på gräs	no, 15 mats open air
Putting-green	putting-green	yes
Pitching-green	pitching-green	yes

Hotel facilities — HOTELL OMGIVNING — 6/10

HOTELS

Hotell Arkad, 43 rooms, D SKr 1250 — Västerås 20 km
Tel (46) 021 - 120 480, Fax (46) 021 - 830 050

Radisson, 203 rooms, D SKr 1325 — Västerås 20 km
Tel (46) 021 - 101 010, Fax (46) 021 - 101 091

Stadshotellet, 137 rooms, D SKr 1245 — Västerås 20 km
Tel (46) 021 - 180 420, Fax (46) 021 - 102 810

RESTAURANTS RESTAURANG

Lemone — Västerås 20 km
Tel (46) 021 - 410 60 75

ÅTVIDABERG

16 | 6 | 5

Banan i Åtvidaberg smälter in i landskapet mellan skogar och sjöar. I ett land med mängder av vattendrag hittar du naturligtvis också vattenhinder på banan. Det finns dock inget konstgjort amerikanskt över dessa, utan de är naturliga och typiska för sin omgivning. Initialt kanske du tycker att detta är en lätt bana, men skenet bedrar och om du inte passar dig hamnar du lätt i problem. Här finns massor med skog och även enskilda träd kommer i spel (hål nummer 10 till exempel). Flera skarpa doglegs kräver att du är duktig på att manövrera bollen. Akta dig också för bunkrarna. Greenerna är mellanstora och ett par stycken är upphöjda. Allt som allt gör det att du behöver spela banan några gånger för att komma underfull med den. Hur som helst, en weekend på hotellet som ligger på banan är ett frestande förslag. Låt oss avsluta med att berömma det 11e hålet, en fantastisk par 5 som går utmed en sjö. Åtvidaberg är en charmerande upplevelse, och dessutom är man snart klara med ombyggnaden av banan som kommer att göra den ännu bättre. Renoveringen av banan är nu klar.

Typical of the surrounding countryside, the Åtvidaberg course is set amidst lakes and forests. In a land dotted with countless stretches of water, the water hazards here are very much Swedish style, not American. At first sight you might think this an easy course, but although playable by golfers of all abilities, it can also be dangerous. With the woods, a few isolated trees here and there (hole N° 10 for example), several dog-legs where skills in bending the ball will come in handy, a number of traps around the course, and average-sized and sometimes elevated greens, you will need to play several times to get to grips with this challenging layout. Anyway, a week-end's stay in the on-course hotel (with restaurant) will always be a tempting proposition. In a few words, special praise in order for the excellent 11th hole, a beautiful par 5 alongside a lake, the charm of the whole site and the renovation of the course, now completed.

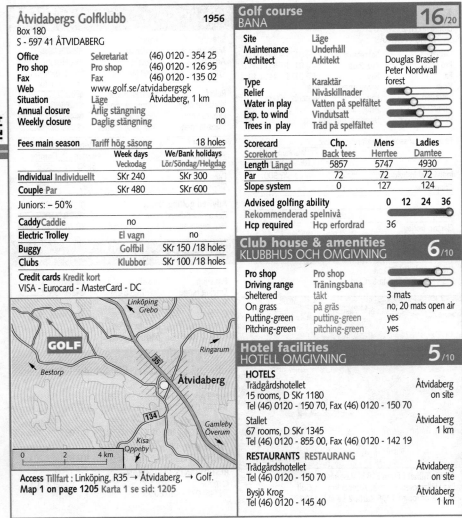

Åtvidabergs Golfklubb — 1956

Box 180
S - 597 41 ÅTVIDABERG

Office	Sekretariat	(46) 0120 - 354 25
Pro shop	Pro shop	(46) 0120 - 126 95
Fax	Fax	(46) 0120 - 135 02
Web	www.golf.se/atvidabergsgk	
Situation	Läge	Åtvidaberg, 1 km
Annual closure	Årlig stängning	no
Weekly closure	Daglig stängning	no

Fees main season Tariff hög säsong	18 holes	
	Week days Veckodag	**We/Bank holidays** Lör/Söndag/Helgdag
Individual Individuellt	SKr 240	SKr 300
Couple Par	SKr 480	SKr 600

Juniors: – 50%

Caddy Caddie	no	
Electric Trolley	El vagn	no
Buggy	Golfbil	SKr 150 /18 holes
Clubs	Klubbor	SKr 100 /18 holes

Credit cards Kredit kort
VISA - Eurocard - MasterCard - DC

Access Tillfart : Linköping, R35 → Åtvidaberg, → Golf.
Map 1 on page 1205 Karta 1 se sid: 1205

Golf course BANA — 16/20

Site	Läge	
Maintenance	Underhåll	
Architect	Arkitekt	Douglas Brasier, Peter Nordwall
Type	Karaktär	forest
Relief	Nivåskillnader	
Water in play	Vatten på spelfältet	
Exp. to wind	Vindutsatt	
Trees in play	Träd på spelfältet	

Scorecard Scorekort	**Chp.** Back tees	**Mens** Herrtee	**Ladies** Damtee
Length Längd	5857	5747	4930
Par	72	72	72
Slope system	0	127	124

Advised golfing ability Rekommenderad spelnivå — 0 12 24 36
Hcp required Hcp erfordrad — 36

Club house & amenities KLUBBHUS OCH OMGIVNING — 6/10

Pro shop	Pro shop	
Driving range	Träningsbana	
Sheltered	tåkt	3 mats
On grass	på gräs	no, 20 mats open air
Putting-green	putting-green	yes
Pitching-green	pitching-green	yes

Hotel facilities HOTELL OMGIVNING — 5/10

HOTELS

Trädgårdshotellet — Åtvidaberg on site
15 rooms, D SKr 1180
Tel (46) 0120 - 150 70, Fax (46) 0120 - 150 70

Stallet — Åtvidaberg 1 km
67 rooms, D SKr 1345
Tel (46) 0120 - 855 00, Fax (46) 0120 - 142 19

RESTAURANTS RESTAURANG

Trädgårdshotellet — Åtvidaberg on site
Tel (46) 0120 - 150 70

Bysjö Krog — Åtvidaberg 1 km
Tel (46) 0120 - 145 40

BARSEBÄCK

18	7	6

Från klubbhuset har du en fantastisk vy över Öresund som skiljer Sverige och Danmark åt. Träningsmöjligheterna är utomordentliga, och eftersom banan rankas som en av de bästa i Sverige är en runda här ett måste. Vid sidan av the "Old Course" finns här ytterligare en bana ritad av Donald Steele. De första hålen vindlar genom tät skog, vilket kräver raka utslag samt en förmåga att manövrera bollen och att du är duktig på att rädda dig ur svåra lägen. Därefter når banan fram till vattnet och i stället för precisionsgolf blir det nu viktigt att kunna slå låga slag för att undgå vinden (en måttlig bris är dock vanligare än en kuling). För spelare som hoppas på ett lågt resultat är Barsebäck alltid en utmaning. Om inte annat får du glädja dig åt den omväxlande rundan som layouten bjuder. Den här banan kan du spela gång på gång utan att tröttna på den. Banan tar emot Solheims Cup år 2004.

The Club house here gives a splendid view over the Öresund, a large stretch of the North Sea which separates Sweden and Denmark. Practice facilities are also first rate, and as the course rates as one of the best in Sweden, a round or two here is a must. This is the "Old Course", subsequently supplemented by another Donald Steel 18-hole layout, some holes of which were successfully used to form a composite course for the Scandinavian Masters one year. The first holes wind their way through thick but well-cleared woods, which require straight driving, an ability to bend the ball and skilled recovery shots. Then the course reaches the seaboard, where target golf has to give way to the ability to hit low, bump and run shots and take account of the always windy conditions (often a breeze rather than a gale). Although challenging for golfers looking for low scores, Barsebäck is still playable by the less skilled player, if only for experience in learning different styles of play. A superb course you can play over and over again and still get excited about. The Solheim Cup will be played here in 2004.

Barsebäck Golf & Country Club — 1969

S - 246 55 LÖDDEKÖPINGE

Office	Sekretariat	(46) 046 - 776 230
Pro shop	Pro shop	(46) 046 - 775 127
Fax	Fax	(46) 046 - 772 630
Web	www.golf.se/barsebackgcc	
Situation	Läge	Lund, 20 km
Annual closure	Årlig stängning	no
Weekly closure	Daglig stängning	no

Fees main season Tariff hög säsong	18 holes	
	Week days Veckodag	**We/Bank holidays** Lör/Söndag/Helgdag
Individual Individuellt	SKr 390	SKr 390
Couple Par	SKr 780	SKr 780

Juniors: – 50%

Caddy Caddie	no	
Electric Trolley	El vagn	SKr 150
Buggy	Golfbil	SKr 200 /18 holes
Clubs	Klubbor	SKr 150 /18 holes

Credit cards Kredit kort
VISA - Eurocard - MasterCard - DC - AMEX

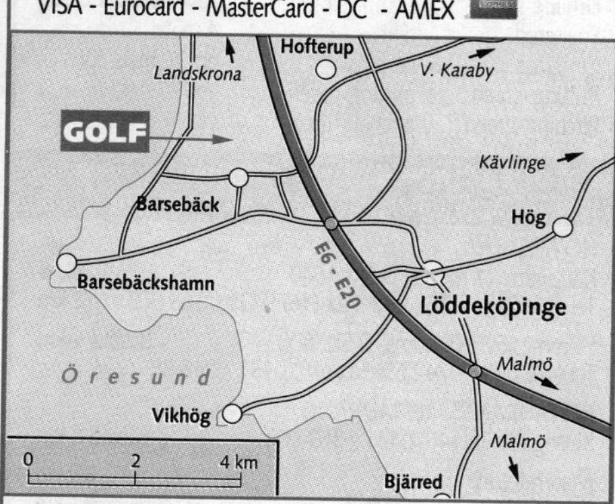

Access Tillfart : E6 Malmö-Helsingborg:
Exit Löddeköpinge. → Golfbana.
Map 1 on page 1204 Karta 1 se sid: 1204

Golf course — BANA — 18/20

Site	Läge	
Maintenance	Underhåll	
Architect	Arkitekt	Ture Bruce
Type	Karaktär	seaside course, parkland
Relief	Nivåskillnader	
Water in play	Vatten på spelfältet	
Exp. to wind	Vindutsatt	
Trees in play	Träd på spelfältet	

Scorecard Scorekort	**Chp.** Back tees	**Mens** Herrtee	**Ladies** Damtee
Length Längd	6250	5905	4950
Par	72	72	72
Slope system	—	119	116

Advised golfing ability 0 12 24 36
Rekommenderad spelnivå
Hcp required Hcp erfordrad 36

Club house & amenities — KLUBBHUS OCH OMGIVNING — 7/10

Pro shop	Pro shop	
Driving range	Träningsbana	
Sheltered	täkt	7 mats
On grass	på gräs	yes
Putting-green	putting-green	yes
Pitching-green	pitching-green	yes

Hotel facilities — HOTELL OMGIVNING — 6/10

HOTELS

Grand Hotell, 84 rooms, D SKr 1695 — Lund 20 km
Tel (46) 046 - 280 61 00, Fax (46) 046 - 280 61 50

Lundia, 97 rooms, D SKr 1550 — Lund 20 km
Tel (46) 046 - 280 65 00, Fax (46) 046 - 280 65 10

Järavallen, 40 rooms, D SKr 1500 — Barsebäck on site
Tel (46) 046 - 777 050, Fax (46) 046 - 775 898

RESTAURANTS RESTAURANG

Grand Hotell Tel (46) 046 - 280 61 00 — Lund 20 km
Bantorget Tel (46) 046 - 320 200 — Lund 20 km

1215

BÅSTAD Old Course

16	7	7

Båstad är en av Sveriges mest berömda semesterorter. Här spelar man tennis och golf, och njuter på de vackra sandstränderna. Banan designades på 30-talet av Hawtree och Taylor, och smälter på ett fint sätt in i landskapet. Den rankas regelbundet bland de 20 bästa i Sverige. Initialt finansierades den av Ludvig Nobel (Alfreds brorson) för att attrahera engelska affärsmän. Banan är belägen på en halvö och har ett gammalt och mycket charmigt klubbhus. Den är ordentligt kuperad, vilket ger dig många intressanta lägen under din vandring. Detta gör bara layouten ännu bättre. Medelhandicaparen kommer att lära sig mycket under rundans gång, han behöver dock inte oroa sig över att bli av med särskilt många bollar. Största svårigheten är de ofta starkt ondulerade greenerna som tenderar att vara mycket snabba. Är du inte vän med din putter kan det stå dig riktigt dyrt. Flera av greenerna är också upphöjda, vilket kräver höga slag in mot dem. Varje hål är minnesvärt skiljer sig från det föregående utan att harmonin störs.

The town of Båstad is one of Sweden's most famous seaside resorts, where tennis and golf are as much a part of the picture as the superb beaches. Designed in 1930 by Hawtree and Taylor, the natural-looking but well-landscaped "Old Course" is regularly ranked in the country's top 20 golf courses. It was financed by Ludvig Nobel (the nephew of Alfred) with the purpose of attracting British golfers. Located on a peninsula with a very old-style club-house, all 18 holes involve a lot of climbing and provide all sorts of situations from where that little white ball has to be hit. This makes the layout all the more interesting... and instructive for mid-handicappers, who shouldn't have too much trouble with lost balls. One of the main difficulties lies with the greens, which are steeply contoured and often very slick. An off-day with the putter can be an expensive business stroke-wise. More, as some of the putting surfaces are elevated, high approach shots are the order of the day. Each hole is different and memorable, but this does nothing to deter from the overall impression of harmony and the measured layout of difficulties.

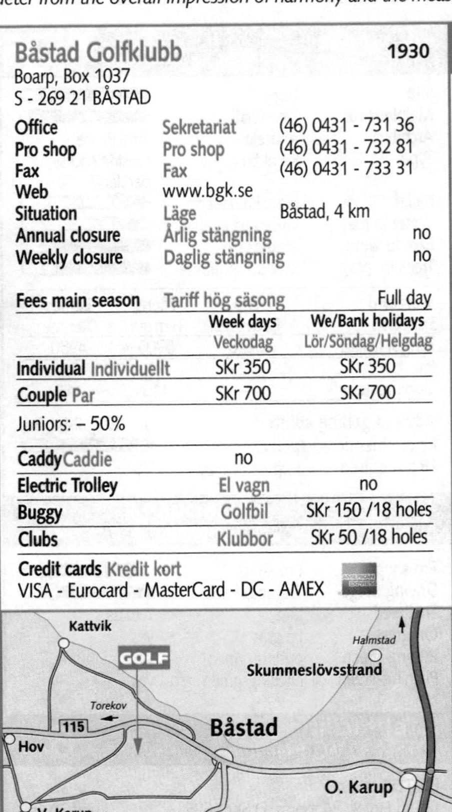

Båstad Golfklubb — 1930

Boarp, Box 1037
S - 269 21 BÅSTAD

Office	Sekretariat	(46) 0431 - 731 36
Pro shop	Pro shop	(46) 0431 - 732 81
Fax	Fax	(46) 0431 - 733 31
Web	www.bgk.se	
Situation	Läge	Båstad, 4 km
Annual closure	Årlig stängning	no
Weekly closure	Daglig stängning	no

Fees main season Tariff hög säsong		Full day
	Week days Veckodag	**We/Bank holidays** Lör/Söndag/Helgdag
Individual Individuellt	SKr 350	SKr 350
Couple Par	SKr 700	SKr 700

Juniors: – 50%

Caddy Caddie		no
Electric Trolley	El vagn	no
Buggy	Golfbil	SKr 150 /18 holes
Clubs	Klubbor	SKr 50 /18 holes

Credit cards Kredit kort
VISA - Eurocard - MasterCard - DC - AMEX

Access Tillfart : E6. Båstad → Torekov. → Golf.
Map 1 on page 1204 Karta 1 se sid: 1204

Golf course BANA — 16/20

Site	Läge	
Maintenance	Underhåll	
Architect	Arkitekt	Hawtree & Taylor
Type	Karaktär	parkland
Relief	Nivåskillnader	
Water in play	Vatten på spelfältet	
Exp. to wind	Vindutsatt	
Trees in play	Träd på spelfältet	

Scorecard Scorekort	**Chp.** Back tees	**Mens** Herrtee	**Ladies** Damtee
Length Längd	5632	5520	4787
Par	71	71	71
Slope system	121	121	118

Advised golfing ability Rekommenderad spelnivå — 0 12 24 36
Hcp required Hcp erfordrad — 36

Club house & amenities KLUBBHUS OCH OMGIVNING — 7/10

Pro shop	Pro shop	
Driving range	Träningsbana	
Sheltered	tåkt	4 mats
On grass	på gräs	no, 20 mats open air
Putting-green	putting-green	yes
Pitching-green	pitching-green	yes

Hotel facilities HOTELL OMGIVNING — 7/10

HOTELS

Kattegatt, 11 rooms, D SKr 1640 — Torekov 12 km
Tel (46) 0431 - 363 002, Fax (46) 0431 - 363 003

Hemmeslöv, 90 rooms, D SKr 800 — Båstad 4 km
Tel (46) 0431 - 742 65, Fax (46) 0431 - 748 88

RESTAURANTS RESTAURANG

Kattegatt, Tel (46) 0431 - 363 002 — Båstad 8 km

Margretetorp — Båstad 11 km
Tel (46) 0431 - 454 450

Enehall — Båstad 10 km
Tel (46) 0431 - 750 15

BOKSKOGEN

16 | 6 | 7

Den här banan arrangerade PLM Open under många år. Och inte undra på det! Banan är ett bra test, framför allt om du väljer att spela från backtee eller om du inte är så lång med drivern. Under sommaren är ruffarna tjocka och besvärliga, och fångar effektivt upp varje felriktat slag. Trots detta är vandringen mellan de höga bokarna så njutningsfylld att inte ens en liten vit boll kan förstöra din dag. Du behöver inte spela särskilt många rundor för att snabbt förstå att de flesta hinder ser du redan från tee. Banan är bredare än vad den verkar att vara. De största svårigheterna ligger i längden och några minst sagt knepiga greener. Allt detta gör Bokskogen till en bra värdemätare för hur du slår bollen. Även medelhandicapare kommer att ha stort utbyte av rundan om de inte förväntar sig underverk på scorekortet. Bokskogen ligger 20 kilometer från Malmö, och här finns förutom den nyss nämnda banan ytterligare en 18-hålare. Den senare är något kortare och mer lättspelad.

This course hosted the PLM Open for many a year and remains a very well maintained layout with no shortage of trouble if you play from the back tees or have a problem of length. In addition, the rough grows tall and thick in the summer and presents a serious threat to wayward shots. Despite this, the walk through a large forest of birch trees is so pleasant that even a little white ball can't really spoil your enjoyment. You don't need many rounds here to understand the layout, as all hazards are clearly visible, the course is wider than it looks and the main difficulty lies with reaching and successfully negotiating some pretty lively greens, which are often multi-tiered and elevated. All this makes Bokskogens a good yardstick for how well you are striking the ball, and a course playable by mid-handicappers if they don't go out looking for miracle scores. Some twenty kilometres from Malmö, this is a fine golfing complex with a second and somewhat shorter 18 hole course for your added enjoyment.

Bokskogens Golfklubb — 1964

Torrups Nygård
S - 230 40 BARA

Office	Sekretariat	(46) 040 - 406 900
Pro shop	Pro shop	(46) 040 - 481 153
Fax	Fax	(46) 040 - 406 929
Web	www.bokskogen.com	
Situation	Läge	Malmö, 20 km
Annual closure	Årlig stängning	no
Weekly closure	Daglig stängning	no

Fees main season Tariff hög säsong		18 holes
	Week days Veckodag	**We/Bank holidays** Lör/Söndag/Helgdag
Individual Individuellt	SKr 400	SKr 400
Couple Par	SKr 800	SKr 800

Juniors: - 50%

Caddy Caddie	no	
Electric Trolley	El vagn	no
Buggy	Golfbil	SKr 100 /18 holes
Clubs	Klubbor	SKr 150 /18 holes

Credit cards Kredit kort
VISA - Eurocard - MasterCard - DC - AMEX

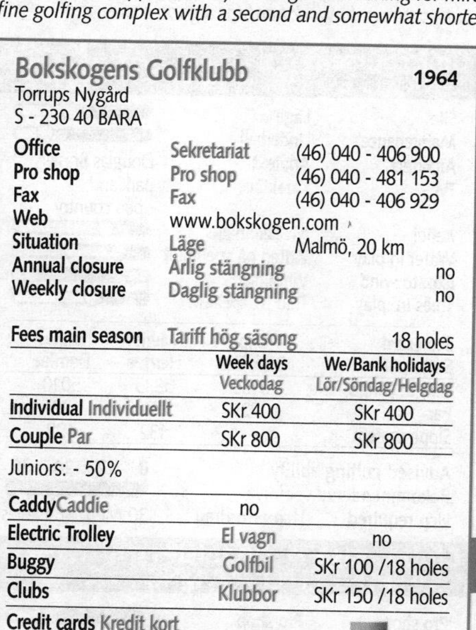

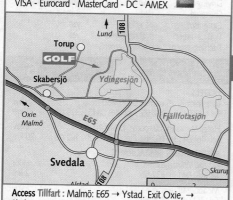

Access Tillfart : Malmö: E65 → Ystad. Exit Oxie, → Skabersjö, turn right at church, left at Torup, → Golf.
Map 1 on page 1204 Karta 1 se sid: 1204

Golf course — BANA — 16/20

Site	Läge	
Maintenance	Underhåll	
Architect	Arkitekt	Anders Amilon Jan Sederholm
Type	Karaktär	parkland
Relief	Nivåskillnader	
Water in play	Vatten på spelfältet	
Exp. to wind	Vindutsatt	
Trees in play	Träd på spelfältet	

Scorecard Scorekort	**Chp.** Back tees	**Mens** Herrtee	**Ladies** Damtee
Length Längd	6306	6006	5238
Par	72	72	72
Slope system	—	133	127

Advised golfing ability Rekommenderad spelnivå — 0 12 24 36
Hcp required Hcp erfordrad 36

Club house & amenities — KLUBBHUS OCH OMGIVNING — 6/10

Pro shop	Pro shop	
Driving range	Träningsbana	
Sheltered	tåkt	3 mats
On grass	på gräs	yes
Putting-green	putting-green	yes
Pitching-green	pitching-green	no

Hotel facilities — HOTELL OMGIVNING — 7/10

HOTELS

Mäster Johan, 69 rooms, D SKr 1695 — Malmö 20 km
Tel (46) 040 - 664 64 00, Fax (46) 040 - 664 64 01

Scandic Hotel Triangeln, 210 rooms, D SKr 1689 — Malmö
Tel (46) 040 - 693 47 00, Fax (46) 040 - 693 47 11

Savoy Hotel, 109 rooms, D SKr 1450 — Malmö 20 km
Tel (46) 040 - 702 30, Fax (46) 040 - 664 48 50

RESTAURANTS RESTAURANG

Johan P Saluhallen, Tel (46) 040 - 971 818 — Malmö
Årstiderna Tel (46) 040 - 230 910 — Malmö
Nyströms Gastronomi Tel (46) 040 - 305 303 — Malmö

BOSJÖKLOSTER

15 | 7 | 6

Douglas Brasier är en av de mest efterfrågade arkitekterna i Sverige, och med Bosjökloster fick han en riktig fullträff, en bana som är en utmaning för såväl den skicklige spelaren som höghandicaparen. Låt vara att vid första anblicken ser Bosjökloster rätt ordinär ut, men du får snart anledning att ändra dig. Från tee är banan ärlig, och kan du bara undvika ruffarna är den relativt bred. En gång i tiden var den till och med riktigt bred, men för varje år växer träden högre och fairways krymper. När vinden blåser gäller det att vara extra försiktig och tänka till lite extra över klubbvalen. Men svårigheterna tar inte slut där: Ju närmare green du kommer desto mer fantasi och känsla behöver du. Greenerna är inte bara knepiga att hitta rätt linje på, under sommaren är de även blixthala och då gäller det att slå inspelen med precision. Om du behöver förbättra ditt närspel är detta en bra plats att vässa det på. När du har fått nog av att nöta pitchar kan du alltid ta en paus och beundra den vackra Ringsjön. Detta är en bana för alla, men du behöver arbeta hårt för en bra score.

As an architect, Douglas Brasier is in great demand in Sweden and this course is one of his finest achievements. It is a great test for both good players and high-handicappers. Although at first sight this looks to be just an average course, you soon find yourself thinking otherwise. Off the tee it is an honest and open proposition, as long as you keep out of the rough. And although once very wide open, it has tended to become narrower as the trees have grown taller. When the wind starts to blow, you need to be extra careful and think long and hard over club selection. But it does not end there, as the closer you get to the greens, the more imagination and "feel" you need. The greens are not only tricky when putting, they are also very fast, especially in summer, and call for skilful short approach shots. If you need to sharpen up your short game, come and practice here. When you have had enough, take time out to admire lake Ringsjön down below. A course for everyone, but you have to work hard for a good score.

Bosjökloster GK — 1974

S - 234 95 HÖÖR

Office	Sekretariat	(46) 0413 - 258 96
Pro shop	Pro shop	(46) 0413 - 258 60
Fax	Fax	(46) 0413 - 258 95
Web	www.golf.se/bosjoklostersgk	
Situation	Läge	Höör, 5 km
Annual closure	Årlig stängning	no
Weekly closure	Daglig stängning	no

Fees main season Tariff hög säsong	Week days Veckodag	We/Bank holidays Lör/Söndag/Helgdag
	18 holes	
Individual Individuellt	SKr 200	SKr 240
Couple Par	SKr 400	SKr 480

Caddy	Caddie	no
Electric Trolley	El vagn	no
Buggy	Golfbil	SKr 200 /18 holes
Clubs	Klubbor	SKr 100 /18 holes

Credit cards Kredit kort VISA - Eurocard - MasterCard

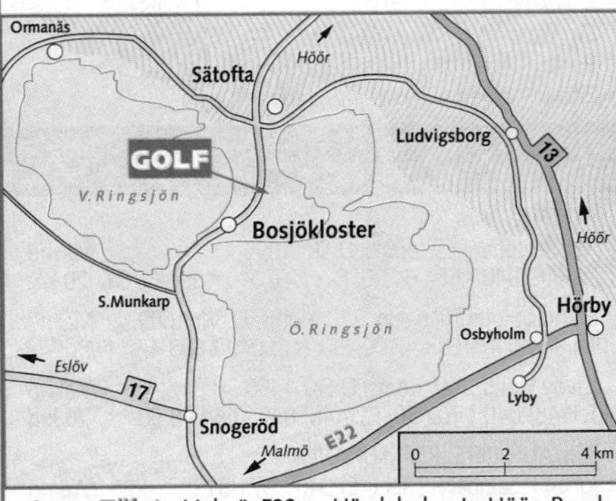

Access Tillfart : Malmö, E22 → Hässleholm. In Höör, Road 23 → Malmö, golf on left hand side

Map 1 on page 1204 Karta 1 se sid: 1204

Golf course BANA — 15/20

Site	Läge	
Maintenance	Underhåll	
Architect	Arkitekt	Douglas Brasier
Type	Karaktär	parkland, open country
Relief	Nivåskillnader	
Water in play	Vatten på spelfältet	
Exp. to wind	Vindutsatt	
Trees in play	Träd på spelfältet	

Scorecard Scorekort	Chp. Back tees	Mens Herrtee	Ladies Damtee
Length Längd	6135	5835	5010
Par	72	72	72
Slope system	—	132	128

Advised golfing ability / Rekommenderad spelnivå: 0 12 24 36

Hcp required / Hcp erfordrad: 30 Men, 36 Ladies

Club house & amenities KLUBBHUS OCH OMGIVNING — 7/10

Pro shop	Pro shop	
Driving range	Träningsbana	
Sheltered	täkt	2 mats
On grass	på gräs	yes
Putting-green	putting-green	yes
Pitching-green	pitching-green	yes

Hotel facilities HOTELL OMGIVNING — 6/10

HOTELS

Ringsjökrog, 15 rooms, D SKr 850 — Höör 2 km
Tel (46) 0413 - 332 55, Fax (46) 0413 - 335 03

Hotell Stensson, 80 rooms, D SKr 1095 — Eslöv 20 km
Tel (46) 0413 - 160 10, Fax (46) 0413 - 102 16

RESTAURANTS RESTAURANG

Ringsjö Wärdshus — Höör 2 km
Tel (46) 0413 - 332 55

Medborgarhuset — Eslöv 20 km
Tel (46) 0413 - 106 64

BRÅVIKEN

16 | 7 | 7

Det är ett nöje att bara köra upp till klubbhuset och restaurangen som ryms i familjen Mannheims gamla herrgård. Banan ligger utlagd på mark som har skapat en högst varierande upplevelse: öppna landskap, parklandskap och skog borgar för variation hela vägen. Trots topografin har arkitekten Björn Magnusson lyckats bygga en bana med väl synliga hinder från tee, vilket gör det enklare för golfaren att hitta den bästa strategin. Bråviken kan vid första anblicken verka vara ganska vänlig, men du måste hela tiden vara på din vakt: misstag bestraffas snabbt och hårt. Framför allt måste du vara försiktig med alla de taggiga buskar som växer runt greenerna. Om din boll hamnar där är den ospelbar, och i värsta fall förlorad. Detta om detta, förutom banan vill vi även påpeka att atmosfären är vänlig och avslappnad, vilket bör få alla golfare att känna sig som hemma. Bråviken är väl värd att besöka.

The pleasure starts with the drive up to the club-house and restaurant, both located in the former manor of Mannheim. The estate over which the course has been laid out results in very different styles of hole: wide open space, parkland or forest mean variety all the way. Despite the topology, architect Björn Magnusson succeeded in never concealing the hazards from every tee-box, thus making it easier to draw up the most effective game strategy possible. Bråvikens might appear very friendly at first sight, but watch out all the same: mistakes are quickly and severely punished. Be especially careful with the bramble bushes around the greens, where your ball will end up at best unplayable, at worst lost. What we can say is that the sanction is at least proportional to the mistake you make. Add to this the relaxed and friendly atmosphere here, and every golfer will feel confident about playing the course. Well worth getting to know.

Bråvikens Golfklubb — 1992

Manheims Säteri
S - 605 91 NORRKÖPING

Office	Sekretariat	(46) 011 - 340 041
Pro shop	Pro shop	(46) 011 - 340 091
Fax	Fax	(46) 034 - 340 045
Web	—	
Situation	Läge	Norrköping, 8 km
Annual closure	Årlig stängning	no
Weekly closure	Daglig stängning	no

Fees main season Tariff hög säsong	Week days Veckodag	We/Bank holidays Lör/Söndag/Helgdag
		18 holes
Individual Individuellt	SKr 260	SKr 340
Couple Par	SKr 520	SKr 680

Special fees for juniors

Caddy Caddie	no	
Electric Trolley	El vagn	no
Buggy	Golfbil	no
Clubs	Klubbor	SKr 100

Credit cards Kredit kort
VISA - Eurocard - MasterCard - JCB - AMEX

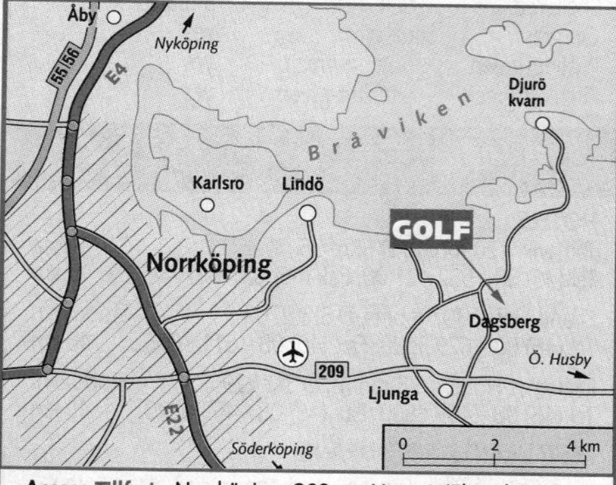

Access Tillfart : Norrköping, 209 → Airport (Flygplats). 881 → Djurön, → Golf
Map 1 on page 1205 Karta 1 se sid: 1205

Golf course — BANA — 16/20

Site	Läge	
Maintenance	Underhåll	
Architect	Arkitekt	Brian Magnusson
Type	Karaktär	forest, parkland
Relief	Nivåskillnader	
Water in play	Vatten på spelfältet	
Exp. to wind	Vindutsatt	
Trees in play	Träd på spelfältet	

Scorecard Scorekort	Chp. Back tees	Mens Herrtee	Ladies Damtee
Length Längd	6040	5635	5000
Par	72	72	72
Slope system	—	125	128

Advised golfing ability Rekommenderad spelnivå: 0 12 24 36
Hcp required Hcp erfordrad: no

Club house & amenities — KLUBBHUS OCH OMGIVNING — 7/10

Pro shop	Pro shop	
Driving range	Träningsbana	
Sheltered	tåkt	5 mats
On grass	på gräs	no, 15 mats open air
Putting-green	putting-green	yes
Pitching-green	pitching-green	yes

Hotel facilities — HOTELL OMGIVNING — 7/10

HOTELS

Mauritzbergs Slott — Vikbolandet 22 km
16 rooms, D SKr 2100
Tel (46) 0125 - 501 00, Fax (46) 0125 - 501 04

President Hotel — Norrköping 9 km
78 rooms, D SKr 1295
Tel (46) 011 - 129 520, Fax (46) 011 - 100 710

RESTAURANTS RESTAURANG

Guskelov, Tel (46) 011 - 134 400 — Norrköping 8 km
Bacchus, Tel (46) 011 - 100 740 — Norrköping 8 km
O'Leary's, Tel (46) 011 - 105 107 — Norrköping 8 km

BRO-BÅLSTA

17 | 7 | 6

Här är banan där Annika och Charlotta Sörenstam växte upp och lärde sig att spela, och med det i bakhuvudet förstår man varför bägge har blivit så duktiga med puttern. Om du kan putta här så kan du nämligen putta överallt! Peter Nordwall har designat greener med så skarpa konturer att en del är på gränsen till att vara orättvisa. De är också väldigt stora, så stora att bunkrar och vattenhinder knappast kommer i spel när du slår in mot dem. Från tee är det dock en helt annan historia, speciellt för de långtslående som kan råka i alla möjliga sorters svårigheter om utslaget blir snett. Med detta sagt kan vi konstatera att det är en mycket intelligent layout med väl synliga hinder från tee. Medelgolfaren, som inte slår så långt, kan sprida bollarna rätt rejält och ändå komma undan med det. Om vi dessutom tillägger att banan ligger i ett fantastiskt och böljande landskap så förstår du varför det utan vidare är värt att tillbringa en hel dag här.

This is where Anika and Charlotta Sorenstam learned their trade and it is no wonder that both are such good putters. If you can putt well here, you can putt well anywhere. These Peter Nordwall greens are very sharply contoured even to the extent of sometimes appearing almost unfair. They are also very large, even too large in relation to the type of shot you need to play. They are so big in fact that the bunkers and water hazards don't even come into play, although they definitely do for the tee-shot, particularly for the longer-hitters. With this said, the layout is plainly intelligent, hazards are clearly visible from the tee-box and strategy obvious enough. Moreover, the "average" player has all the room in the world to hit a bad shot and not really suffer the consequences. If we complete the picture by saying that the site is one of pleasantly rolling terrain and set in a beautiful natural setting, you will understand that this course is well worth a full day's golfing.

Bro-Bålsta Golfklubb — 1982

Ginnlögs väg
S - 197 91 BRO

Office	Sekretariat	(46) 08 - 582 413 00
Pro shop	Pro shop	(46) 08 - 582 413 05
Fax	Fax	(46) 08 - 582 400 06
Web	www.golf.se/brobalstagk	
Situation	Läge	Stockholm, 40 km
Annual closure	Årlig stängning	no
Weekly closure	Daglig stängning	no

Fees main season Tariff hög säsong	Full day	
	Week days Veckodag	**We/Bank holidays** Lör/Söndag/Helgdag
Individual Individuellt	SKr 330	SKr 380
Couple Par	SKr 660	SKr 760

Juniors: - 50%

Caddy	Caddie	no
Electric Trolley	El vagn	no
Buggy	Golfbil	no
Clubs	Klubbor	SKr 150 /18 holes

Credit cards Kredit kort
VISA - Eurocard - MasterCard

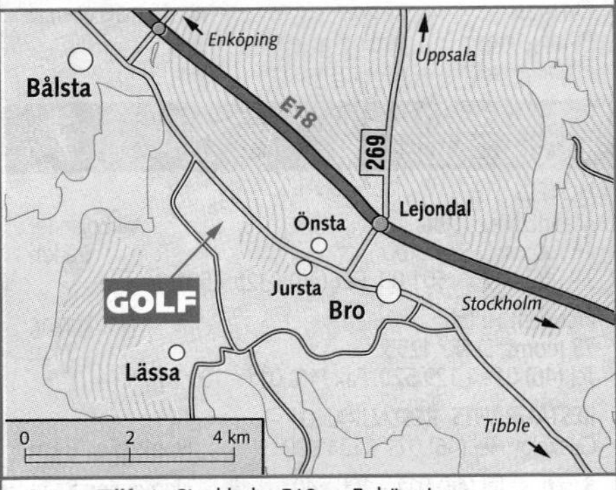

Access Tillfart : Stockholm E18 → Enköpping. Exit Bålsta. 1 km → Golf
Map 2 on page 1206 Karta 2 se sid: 1206

Golf course BANA — 17/20

Site	Läge	
Maintenance	Underhåll	
Architect	Arkitekt	Peter Nordwall
Type	Karaktär	parkland, open country
Relief	Nivåskillnader	
Water in play	Vatten på spelfältet	
Exp. to wind	Vindutsatt	
Trees in play	Träd på spelfältet	

Scorecard Scorekort	**Chp.** Back tees	**Mens** Herrtee	**Ladies** Damtee
Length Längd	6505	5890	5160
Par	73	73	73
Slope system	—	128	126

Advised golfing ability Rekommenderad spelnivå — 0 12 24 36
Hcp required Hcp erfordrad — 30 Men, 32 Ladies

Club house & amenities KLUBBHUS OCH OMGIVNING — 7/10

Pro shop	Pro shop	
Driving range	Träningsbana	
Sheltered	tåkt	3 mats
On grass	på gräs	yes
Putting-green	putting-green	yes
Pitching-green	pitching-green	yes

Hotel facilities HOTELL OMGIVNING — 6/10

HOTELS

Tamsvik, 120 rooms, D SKr 995 — Bålsta
Tel (46) 08 - 582 421 00, Fax (46) 08 - 582 425 29 — 5 km

Grand Hotel, 307 rooms, D SKr 2700 — Stockholm
Tel (46) 08 - 679 3500, Fax (46) 08 - 611 8606 — 40 km

Diplomat Hotel, 128 rooms, D SKr 2295 — Stockholm
Tel (46) 08 - 459 6800, Fax (46) 08 - 459 6820 — 40 km

RESTAURANTS RESTAURANG

Fredsgatan 12, Tel (46) 08 - 248 052 — Stockholm 40 km
Franska Matsalen, Tel (46) 08 - 679 3584 — Stockholm 40 km
Cliff Barnes, Tel (46) 08 - 318 070 — Stockholm 40 km

DROTTNINGHOLM 14 | 9 | 6

Drottningholms slott är arkitektoniskt en korsning mellan barock och neoklassisk stil, ett Versailles i miniatyr för en monarki som strävar mot enkelhet. På sommaren är teatern här en fantastisk plats för operauppsättningar. Kinaslottet och trädgårdarna är också värda ett besök. Det senare gäller även för banan, även om den knappast bjuder på några större överraskningar väl du har spelat några rundor här. Banan är en blandning av parkbanekaraktär och öppna landskap. Den är byggd av Sköld och Sundblom, och är en trevlig bekantskap för medelgolfaren och låghandicaparen. För den som hoppas på en riktigt bra score är Drottningholm en bra utmaning. Inte minst för att en missad fairway oftast innebär ett besök i den tjocka ruffen (framför allt på sommaren) eller i skogen. Vattenhinder kommer egentligen bara i spel på två av hålen, det femte och det 18e. Däremot är det viktigt att kunna skruva bollen från tee, framför allt på dogleg-hålen, om du inte vill ställas inför ett "blint" inspel.

Between the Baroque and the neo-classical, the castle of Drottningholm is a sort of unpretentious Château de Versailles for a monarchy that thrives on simplicity. In summer, the theatre here is a marvellous setting for operas, while the Chinese pavilion (Kina Slott) and the gardens are both well worth the visit. The same goes for the course here, even though after a few rounds you will find nothing to really surprise you. The site is a blend of parkland and wide open space, as Swedish as the layout of Sköld and Sundblom. This course is pleasant to play for mid- and low-handicappers and a real challenge for golfers looking to card a low score, as a missed fairway can be very costly, especially on account of the trees and tall rough (particularly in summer). The water hazards only really come into play on the 5 and 18th holes, while a number of tee-shots call for some bending of the ball, especially on the dog-leg holes (five of the par 4s), if you don't want to be left with a "blind" shot.

Drottningholms Golfklubb — 1959

PL 183
S - 178 93 DROTTNINGHOLM

Office	Sekretariat	(46) 08 - 759 0085
Pro shop	Pro shop	(46) 08 - 759 0314
Fax	Fax	(46) 08 - 759 0851
Web	www.golf.se/drottningholmsgk	
Situation	Läge	Stockholm, 25 km
Annual closure	Årlig stängning	no
Weekly closure	Daglig stängning	no

Fees main season Tariff hög säsong		Full day
	Week days Veckodag	**We/Bank holidays** Lör/Söndag/Helgdag
Individual Individuellt	SKr 350	SKr 400
Couple Par	SKr 700	SKr 800
Juniors: – 50%		

Caddy	Caddie	no
Electric Trolley	El vagn	no
Buggy	Golfbil	no
Clubs	Klubbor	SKr 300 /18 holes

Credit cards Kredit kort
VISA - Eurocard - MasterCard

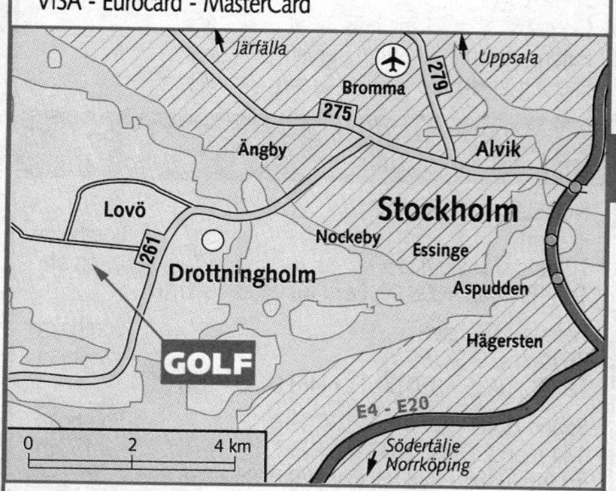

Access Tillfart : Stockholm, Drottningholmsvägen. → Slottet. Exit Lovö Kyrka. 300 m → Golf
Map 2 on page 1206 Karta 2 se sid: 1206

Golf course — BANA — 14/20

Site	Läge	
Maintenance	Underhåll	
Architect	Arkitekt	Rafael Sundblom Nils Sköld
Type	Karaktär	parkland
Relief	Nivåskillnader	
Water in play	Vatten på spelfältet	
Exp. to wind	Vindutsatt	
Trees in play	Träd på spelfältet	

Scorecard Scorekort	**Chp.** Back tees	**Mens** Herrtee	**Ladies** Damtee
Length Längd	6125	5745	5040
Par	71	71	71
Slope system	—	121	120

Advised golfing ability Rekommenderad spelnivå — 0 12 24 36
Hcp required Hcp erfordrad — 30 Men, 35 Ladies

Club house & amenities — KLUBBHUS OCH OMGIVNING — 9/10

Pro shop	Pro shop	
Driving range	Träningsbana	
Sheltered	tåkt	2 mats
On grass	på gräs	no, 25 mats open air
Putting-green	putting-green	yes
Pitching-green	pitching-green	yes

Hotel facilities — HOTELL OMGIVNING — 6/10

HOTELS

Grand Hotel, 307 rooms, D SKr 2700 — Stockholm 25 km
Tel (46) 08 - 679 3500, Fax (46) 08 - 611 8606

First Hotel Reisen, 144 rooms, D SKr 1895 — Stockholm 25 km
Tel (46) 08 - 223 260, Fax (46) 08 - 201 559

Diplomat Hotel, 128 rooms, D SKr 2295 — Stockholm 25 km
Tel (46) 08 - 459 6800, Fax (46) 08 - 459 6820

RESTAURANTS RESTAURANG

Fredsgatan 12 — Stockholm 25 km
Tel (46) 08 - 248 052

Franska Matsalen Tel (46) 08 - 679 3584 — Stockholm 25 km

Cliff Barnes Tel (46) 08 - 318 070 — Stockholm 25 km

EKERUM

14 | 7 | 7

Till Öland kommer man via den sex kilometer långa Ölandsbron. Här finns fyra golfbanor. Den bästa är Ekerum, en 27-hålsanläggning. Totalt är ön 12 mil lång, och består huvudsakligen av hedar där många intressanta växter och färglar går att finna. En vandring eller en cykeltur över Stora Alvaret (på den södra delen av ön) är en ljuvlig upplevelse. Hotellet på golfbanan är en bra utgångspunkt, framför allt för barnfamiljer. Att spela den här banan är också en upplevelse utöver det vanliga. Den sluttar ned mot havet, är lättpromenerad och inte alltför svår om du kan hålla dig borta från ruffen. Faktum är att varje gång du går ut här känns det som om du har en bra score på gång. Men att träffa greenerna på rätt antal slag är inte hela hemligheten. Greenerna är enorma, många av dem har platåer och är starkt ondulerade. Att hålla treputten borta är inte så lätt. Banans omgivningar höjer upplevelsen, för om vi ska vara ärlig är inte detta ett mästerverk, men du slösar definitivt inte bort din tid om du spelar här.

With 27 holes, this is the largest of the four courses on the Island of Öland, linked by a 4 mile bridge to the south-eastern coast of mainland Sweden. The island, some 80 miles long, partly consists of vast moor-land which is home to some very interesting plants and birds. A walk or bicycle ride over Stora Alvaret (the southern part of the island) is a wonderful experience and the golf course hotel is an excellent base-camp for family expeditions. Playing this course is something of an experience as well. It slopes down towards a stretch of sea, is easy to play walking and not too tough if you can keep out of some very thick rough. In fact, every time you play you feel you can card a very good score, but hitting the greens in regulation is simply not enough. The putting surfaces are huge, often multi-tiered and highly-contoured and very conducive to three-putting. Of course the quality of the landscape "enhances" what is probably not an outstanding course, but you aren't wasting your time playing here.

Ekerum Golfklubb & Resort — 1990

S - 387 92 BORGHOLM

Office	Sekretariat	(46) 0485 - 800 20
Pro shop	Pro shop	(46) 0485 - 808 77
Fax	Fax	(46) 0485 - 800 10
Web	—	
Situation	Läge	Kalmar, 27 km
Annual closure	Årlig stängning	no
Weekly closure	Daglig stängning	no

Fees main season / Tariff hög säsong	Week days / Veckodag	We/Bank holidays / Lör/Söndag/Helgdag
	Full day	
Individual Individuellt	SKr 190	SKr 190
Couple Par	SKr 380	SKr 380

Juniors: – 50%

Caddy	Caddie	no
Electric Trolley	El vagn	no
Buggy	Golfbil	SKr 200 /18 holes
Clubs	Klubbor	SKr 100 /18 holes

Credit cards Kredit kort
VISA - Eurocard - MasterCard - DC - AMEX

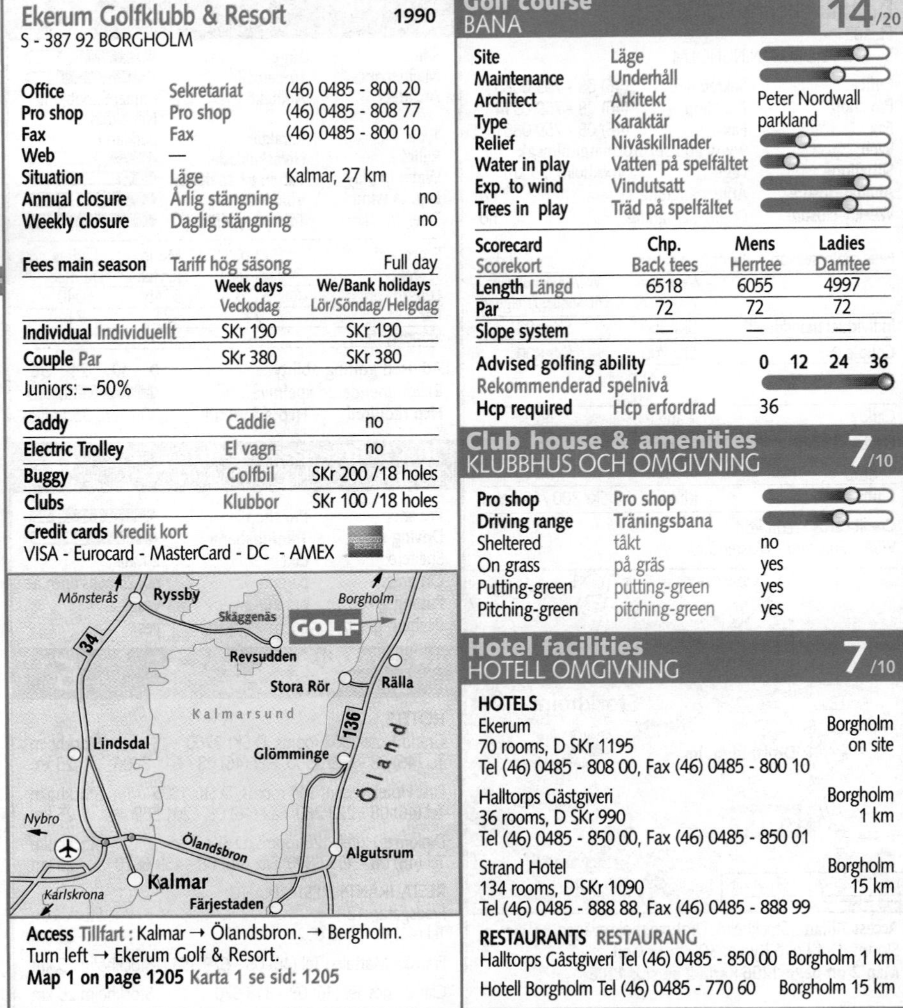

Access Tillfart : Kalmar → Ölandsbron. → Bergholm. Turn left → Ekerum Golf & Resort.
Map 1 on page 1205 Karta 1 se sid: 1205

Golf course BANA — 14/20

Site	Läge	
Maintenance	Underhåll	
Architect	Arkitekt	Peter Nordwall
Type	Karaktär	parkland
Relief	Nivåskillnader	
Water in play	Vatten på spelfältet	
Exp. to wind	Vindutsatt	
Trees in play	Träd på spelfältet	

Scorecard Scorekort	Chp. Back tees	Mens Herrtee	Ladies Damtee
Length Längd	6518	6055	4997
Par	72	72	72
Slope system	—	—	—

Advised golfing ability Rekommenderad spelnivå: 0 12 24 36
Hcp required Hcp erfordrad: 36

Club house & amenities KLUBBHUS OCH OMGIVNING — 7/10

Pro shop	Pro shop	
Driving range	Träningsbana	
Sheltered	täkt	no
On grass	på gräs	yes
Putting-green	putting-green	yes
Pitching-green	pitching-green	yes

Hotel facilities HOTELL OMGIVNING — 7/10

HOTELS

Ekerum — Borgholm on site
70 rooms, D SKr 1195
Tel (46) 0485 - 808 00, Fax (46) 0485 - 800 10

Halltorps Gästgiveri — Borgholm 1 km
36 rooms, D SKr 990
Tel (46) 0485 - 850 00, Fax (46) 0485 - 850 01

Strand Hotel — Borgholm 15 km
134 rooms, D SKr 1090
Tel (46) 0485 - 888 88, Fax (46) 0485 - 888 99

RESTAURANTS RESTAURANG

Halltorps Gästgiveri Tel (46) 0485 - 850 00 — Borgholm 1 km
Hotell Borgholm Tel (46) 0485 - 770 60 — Borgholm 15 km

ESLÖV

14 | 7 | 5

Detta är bondeland, och golfaren som kommer hit blir kanske inte sådär överdrivet imponerad vid första anblicken: Klubbhuset ligger mitt på ett öppet fält, men på sommaren är det betydligt charmigare när färgstarka jordbruksfält svarar för inramningen. Flera av hålen är ganska kuperade, vilket kan tyckas vara aningen ovanligt i Skåne. Banan byggdes i två etapper, de senare byggda hålen har något större greener och är inte fullt så förrädiska. Även om vi befinner oss långt från havet brukar vinden kunna blåsa rätt rejält, vilket torkar upp greenerna och gör dem hårda och snabba. Första nio är vidöppna och där får vinden fritt spelrum, medan andra nio bjuder på mer lä. De fyra sista hålen kan lätt förstöra ett scorekort, om det nu inte redan är förstört av bågra sneda slag. Den största faran är den tjocka ruffen. Sagt det kan vi konstatera att höghandicaparen kan ha riktigt kul här. Det finns nämligen inte alltför många vattenhinder att förlora bollen i, även om det kan vara nog så besvärligt att slå ur ruffen. En bana som ligger en bit från allfarsvägen men som definitivt är värd en runda eller två.

This is farming territory where there is nothing much to impress the golfer who comes here for the first time; the club-house is set out over wide open space but the colourful fields in summer add considerable charm. In addition, some of the holes are hilly, a rare phenomenon in Scania, and are a little reminiscent of the downs of Sussex or Kent in the UK. The 18-hole layout was built in two stages; the later holes have larger and slightly less treacherous greens than the others, but all the putting surfaces tend to get very dry and quick when the wind blows, even though we are relatively far from the seaboard. The wind actually blows all it likes over the wide open front nine, then swirls through the trees on the back nine. The last four holes can easily ruin any card that has not already been punished by inaccurate shot-making. The one thing your card won't survive, though, is the tall rough. With this said, high-handicap golfers will have fun, there is little water and so few opportunities to lose balls, even if playing them can sometimes be difficult. A course off the beaten track and well worth a round or two.

Eslövs Golfklubb — 1968

Box 150
S - 241 22 ESLÖV

Office	Sekretariat	(46) 0413 - 186 10
Pro shop	Pro shop	(46) 0413 - 162 13
Fax	Fax	(46) 0413 - 186 13
Web	www.golf.se/eslovsgk	
Situation	Läge	Eslöv, 13 km
Annual closure	Årlig stängning	no
Weekly closure	Daglig stängning	no

Fees main season / Tariff hög säsong	Week days / Veckodag	We/Bank holidays / Lör/Söndag/Helgdag
	Full day	
Individual / Individuellt	SKr 220	SKr 270
Couple / Par	SKr 440	SKr 540

Juniors: 100:-/130:-

Caddy	Caddie	no
Electric Trolley	El vagn	no
Buggy	Golfbil	no
Clubs	Klubbor	SKr 50 /18 holes

Credit cards Kredit kort VISA - Eurocard - MasterCard

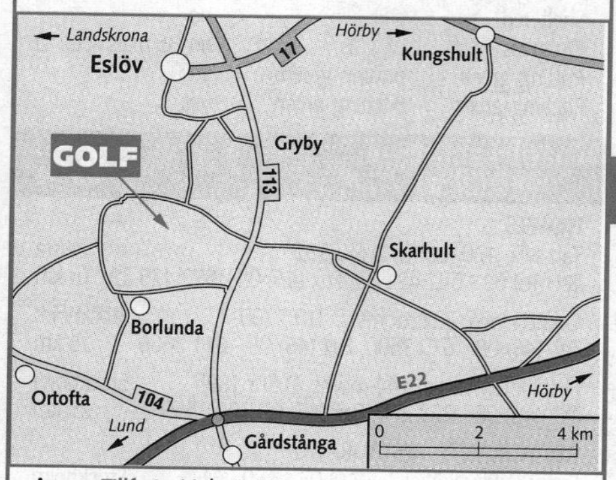

Access Tillfart : Malmö, E22 → Lund, Kristianstad. E113 → Eslöv. → "Ellinge".
Map 1 on page 1204 Karta 1 se sid: 1204

Golf course / BANA — 14/20

Site	Läge	
Maintenance	Underhåll	
Architect	Arkitekt	Ture Bruce
Type	Karaktär	parkland
Relief	Nivåskillnader	
Water in play	Vatten på spelfältet	
Exp. to wind	Vindutsatt	
Trees in play	Träd på spelfältet	

Scorecard / Scorekort	Chp. / Back tees	Mens / Herrtee	Ladies / Damtee
Length Längd	5825	5630	4845
Par	70	70	70
Slope system	—	125	122

Advised golfing ability / Rekommenderad spelnivå: 0 12 24 36

Hcp required / Hcp erfordrad: 36

Club house & amenities / KLUBBHUS OCH OMGIVNING — 7/10

Pro shop	Pro shop	
Driving range	Träningsbana	
Sheltered	tåkt	6 mats
On grass	på gräs	yes
Putting-green	putting-green	yes
Pitching-green	pitching-green	yes

Hotel facilities / HOTELL OMGIVNING — 5/10

HOTELS

Hotell Stensson — Eslöv 5 km
80 rooms, D SKr 1095
Tel (46) 0413 - 160 10, Fax (46) 0413 - 102 16

Hotell Villasjöhusen — Eslöv 3 km
6 rooms, D SKr 560
Tel (46) 0413 - 120 18, Fax (46) 0413 - 120 18

RESTAURANTS RESTAURANG

Medborgarhuset — Eslöv 5 km
Tel (46) 0413 - 106 64

Cupido, Tel (46) 0413 - 102 42 — Eslöv 5 km

EUROPEAN TOUR CLUB (KUNGSÄNGEN) 17 | 7 | 6

Den här anläggningen, som också kallas för Kungsängen, består av 36 hål – den kortare slingan heter Queen's Course och den längre slingan heter King's Course, som vi avhandlar här. King's Course designades av Anders Forsbrand och målsättningarna var två: Dels skulle det bli en mästerskapsbana, dels skulle den vara spelbar för oss amatörer som i slutändan betalar kalaset. Detta är en mycket lång bana, kuperad och väldigt tekniskt krävande. King's är knappast en bana för den med ett högt handicap eller som bara spelar golf för att få gå ut och gå i naturen. Å andra sidan, golfare som letar efter en utmaning som testar deras tålamod och förmåga att scora väl ska definitivt åka hit. Några av hålen är rent layout-mässigt mindre lyckade, andra är helt magnifika (exempelvis 18e). European Tour har investerat massor med pengar i banan. Så har också greenområdena snabbt förbättrats, och banan är kanske den bästa i Stockholm. Men ännu kommer det att ta ytterligare en liten tid innan banan är helt färdig och lever upp till alla högt ställda förväntningar.

This golf comprises two courses, of which the Queen's Course is on the short side, and the King's the one we are reviewing here. It was designed by Anders Forsbrand with a view to becoming a championship course, but it shouldn't be forgotten that week in, week out, it is we amateurs who play and pay. This very long layout is technically extremely demanding and very hilly: as there are neither carts nor caddies, it takes a fit golfer to enjoy playing here. Kings is definitely not to be recommended to people who think of golf as a purely leisure activity or to high-handicappers. On the other hand, golfers who look to test their patience and their ability to score well, work on their strategy or develop their technique must play this course. While they may dispute the golfing spirit of some holes, others are simply excellent (especially the 18th). It will take a while for this course to reach full maturity and see whether it lives up to its promises, but the European Tour invested a lot of money. The areas around the greens have improved over the last few years, and it may be the best course around Stockholm.

European Tour Club — 1992

Box 133
S - 196 21 KUNGSÄNGEN

Office	Sekretariat	(46) 08 - 584 507 30
Pro shop	Pro shop	(46) 08 - 584 507 31
Fax	Fax	(46) 08 - 584 710 02
Web	www.etc-sthlm.se	
Situation	Läge	Stockholm, 25 km
Annual closure	Årlig stängning	no
Weekly closure	Daglig stängning	no

Fees main season Tariff hög säsong		Full day
	Week days Veckodag	We/Bank holidays Lör/Söndag/Helgdag
Individual Individuellt	SKr 550	SKr 550
Couple Par	SKr 1100	SKr 1100

Juniors: - 50%

Caddy	Caddie	no
Electric Trolley	El vagn	no
Buggy	Golfbil	no
Clubs	Klubbor	SKr 250 /18 holes

Credit cards Kredit kort
VISA - Eurocard - MasterCard - DC - AMEX

Access Tillfart : Stockholm, E18 → Enköpping.
Exit Tibble/Brunna. → Golf
Map 2 on page 1206 Karta 2 se sid: 1206

Golf course BANA 17/20

Site	Läge	
Maintenance	Underhåll	
Architect	Arkitekt	Anders Forsbrand
Type	Karaktär	forest, hilly
Relief	Nivåskillnader	
Water in play	Vatten på spelfältet	
Exp. to wind	Vindutsatt	
Trees in play	Träd på spelfältet	

Scorecard Scorekort	Chp. Back tees	Mens Herrtee	Ladies Damtee
Length Längd	6248	5784	4827
Par	72	72	72
Slope system	—	133	127

Advised golfing ability Rekommenderad spelnivå — 0 12 24 36

Hcp required Hcp erfordrad — 36

Club house & amenities KLUBBHUS OCH OMGIVNING 7/10

Pro shop	Pro shop	
Driving range	Träningsbana	
Sheltered	tåkt	no
On grass	på gräs	no, 35 mats open air
Putting-green	putting-green	yes
Pitching-green	pitching-green	yes

Hotel facilities HOTELL OMGIVNING 6/10

HOTELS

Tamsvik, 120 rooms, D SKr 995 — Bålsta
Tel (46) 08 - 582 421 00, Fax (46) 08 - 582 425 29 — 15 km

Grand Hotel, 307 rooms, D SKr 2700 — Stockholm
Tel (46) 08 - 679 3500, Fax (46) 08 - 611 8606 — 25 km

First Hotel Reisen, 144 rooms, D SKr 1895 — Stockholm
Tel (46) 08 - 223 260, Fax (46) 08 - 201 559 — 25 km

RESTAURANTS RESTAURANG

Svenska Pizzaköket Tel (46) 08 - 150 061 — Stockholm

Ocean Tel (46) 08 - 652 4090 — Stockholm 25 km

Franska Matsalen Tel (46) 08 - 679 3584 — Stockholm 25 km

FÅGELBRO

16	9	5

För att komma hit åker du genom ytterområdena av Skärgården, denna fantastiska värld med över 20 000 öar och klippor och som sträcker sig hela 140 kilometer ut i Östersjön. Många stockholmare har sommarhus i närheten, och under högsäsong är därför trycket hårt på Fågelbro. Paradoxalt nog ser du aldrig havet från banan, vilket dock inte förtar intrycket av att detta är en härlig naturupplevelse. Designen är mycket amerikansk, vilket märks sista nio där vatten kommer i spel på hela sex av hålen. Första nio är helt annorlunda och har mycket mer av parkbanekaraktär. Fågelbro är inte lång men har du problem med dina utslag kommer du snart att hamna i svårigheter. Lyckligtvis behöver du inte använda drivern så ofta – följ ett gott råd och låt den stanna i bagen. Här finns knappast ett enda hål där du kan slappna av, vilket höghandicapare inte kommer att uppskatta. Å andra sidan kommer belöningen efter rundan i klubbhuset som är ett av Sveriges charmigaste. Framför allt måste greenerna nämnas, de är i utmärkt kondition redan tidigt på våren.

To get here from Stockholm, you have to drive between land and water along the edge of the Skärgården, an incredible archipelago of more than 20,000 islands and reefs stretching some 140 km into the Baltic Sea. This is the summer or week-end residence of many of the capital city's inhabitants and Fågelbro is one of the busiest courses. Paradoxically this is a wonderful natural setting where you never see the sea. The design is pure American, meaning that water is in play on six of the last nine holes, while the front nine are spread over what looks more like a huge park. Fågelbro is not long but will pose big problems on days when your driving is not up to scratch. Fortunately, the driver is seldom indispensable so keep it in your bag on this narrow course where the borderline between a good and bad score is slim indeed. There is not a single hole where you can relax, and high handicappers won't like that at all. There is however the reward of the club-house, one of the most charming of its kind in the whole of Sweden. A special consideration to the greens, in very good condition even in early Spring.

Fågelbro Golf & Country Club — 1991

Fågelbro Säteri
S - 139 60 VÄRMDÖ

Office	Sekretariat	(46) 08 - 571 418 00
Pro shop	Pro shop	(46) 08 - 571 418 00
Fax	Fax	(46) 08 - 571 406 71
E-mail	info@fagelbrogcc.golf.se	
Situation	Läge	Stockholm, 35 km
Annual closure	Årlig stängning	no
Weekly closure	Daglig stängning	no

Fees main season Tariff hög säsong	Week days Veckodag	We/Bank holidays Lör/Söndag/Helgdag
		full day
Individual Individuellt	SKr 500	SKr 600
Couple Par	SKr 1000	SKr 1200

Juniors: SKr 200 /SKr 250

Caddy	Caddie	no
Electric Trolley	El vagn	no
Buggy	Golfbil	SKr 250 /18 holes
Clubs	Klubbor	SKr 250 /18 holes

Credit cards Kredit kort
VISA - Eurocard - MasterCard - DC - AMEX

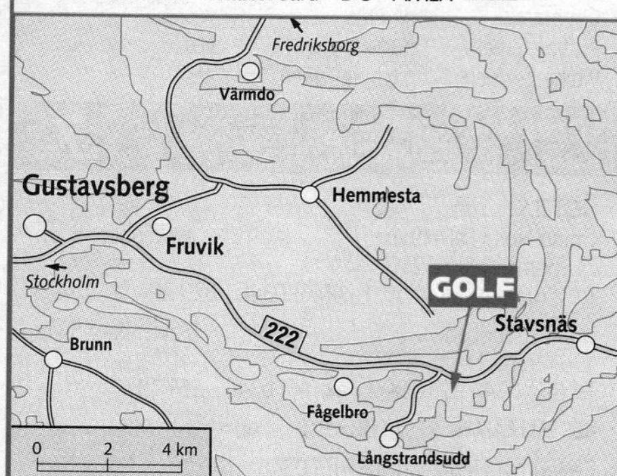

Access Tillfart : Stockholm, Väg 222 → Stavanäs/Djurö
Map 2 on page 1207 Karta 2 se sid: 1207

Golf course — BANA — 16/20

Site	Läge	
Maintenance	Underhåll	
Architect	Arkitekt	Björn Eriksson
Type	Karaktär	forest
Relief	Nivåskillnader	
Water in play	Vatten på spelfältet	
Exp. to wind	Vindutsatt	
Trees in play	Träd på spelfältet	

Scorecard Scorekort	Chp. Back tees	Mens Herrtee	Ladies Damtee
Length Längd	5974	5445	4535
Par	71	71	71
Slope system	—	130	124

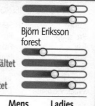

Advised golfing ability Rekommenderad spelnivå — 0 12 24 36
Hcp required Hcp erfordrad — 24 Men, 30 Ladies

Club house & amenities — KLUBBHUS OCH OMGIVNING — 9/10

Pro shop	Pro shop	
Driving range	Träningsbana	
Sheltered	täkt	2 mats
On grass	på gräs	no, 16 mats open air
Putting-green	putting-green	yes
Pitching-green	pitching-green	no

Hotel facilities — HOTELL OMGIVNING — 5/10

HOTELS

Fågelbrohus, 72 rooms, D SKr 1245 Tel (46) 08 - 571 401 00, Fax (46) 08 - 571 401 71	Golfklubb 100 m
Grand Hotel, 307 rooms, D SKr 2700 Tel (46) 08 - 679 3500, Fax (46) 08 - 611 8606	Stockholm 35 km
First Hotel Reisen 144 rooms, D SKr 1895 Tel (46) 08 - 223 260, Fax (46) 08 - 201 559	Stockholm 35 km

RESTAURANTS RESTAURANG

Fågelbro, Tel (46) 08 - 759 0750	Stockholm
Fredsgatan 12 Tel (46) 08 - 248 052	Stockholm
Franska Matsalen, Tel (46) 08 - 679 3584	Stockholm

FALKENBERG

14 | 7 | 7

I Falkenberg finner man många företag med keramik- och krukproduktion. Det är också en av de bästa städerna om man vill fånga en lax, vilket till och med går att göra i Ätran som rinner rakt igenom staden. Konstälskare får också sitt lystmäte tillfredsställt genom ett besök i kyrkan. Golfbanan ligger nära havet mitt i ett skogsparti, inte helt ovanligt i ett land där skogen är en nationell resurs. Banan smälter mjukt in i ett mjukt böljande landskap, där träden är mer dekorativa än riktigt farliga. Det samma gäller för bunkrarna, åarna och dammarna – de är i spel, men utgör inte någon överdriven hotbild. Därmed får man också en klar idé över filosofin bakom den här banan: Det är viktigt att bygga mästerskapsanläggningar för de bästa spelarna, men det är lika viktigt att konstruera banor för medelgolfaren. Detta är en bana som du som medlem kan spela gång på gång utan att tröttna. Som greenfee-spelare är det också möjligt att ta sig runt Falkenberg utan att behöva vara ett taktiskt snille.

Falkenberg is a production centre for ceramics and pottery and also one of the leading sites for salmon-fishing, even in the river Åtran which crosses the city. Art lovers will also enjoy the paintings in the church of Skt Laurentil. The golf course is laid out close to the sea in the middle of a forest, a contrast often found in a country where timber and its derivative are a major national resource. Yet this is not an oppressive course and some of the terrain is rather more like rolling landscape, where the trees are more decorative than truly dangerous. Likewise, the bunkers, rivers and ponds are in play but never excessively so, giving a general idea of the measured side to this course. It is important to build championship courses for the top players, but equally so to create layouts that can be played by the lesser golfer. This is the type of course where you can play as a member and never grow tired of it, or where you can come and play once or twice without having to do too much tactical thinking.

Falkenbergs Golfklubb — 1962

Golfvägen
S - 311 72 FALKENBERG

Office	Sekretariat	(46) 0346 - 502 87
Pro shop	Pro shop	(46) 0346 - 505 60
Fax	Fax	(46) 0346 - 509 97
E-mail	info@falkenbergsgk.se	
Situation	Läge	Falkenberg, 5 km
Annual closure	Årlig stängning	no
Weekly closure	Daglig stängning	no

Fees main season Tariff hög säsong		Full day
	Week days Veckodag	**We/Bank holidays** Lör/Söndag/Helgdag
Individual Individuellt	SKr 280	SKr 280
Couple Par	SKr 560	SKr 560
Juniors: – 50%		

Caddy	Caddie	no
Electric Trolley	El vagn	yes
Buggy	Golfbil	no
Clubs	Klubbor	yes
Credit cards	Kredit kort	

VISA - Eurocard - MasterCard - DC - JCB - AMEX

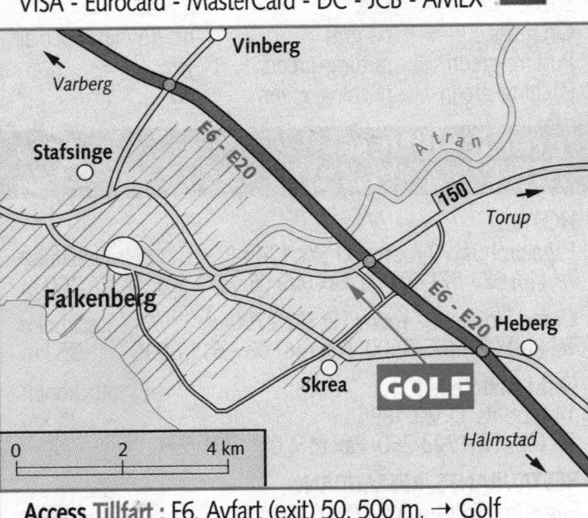

Access Tillfart : E6. Avfart (exit) 50. 500 m, → Golf
Map 1 on page 1204 Karta 1 se sid: 1204

Golf course BANA — 14/20

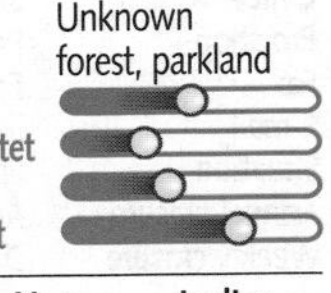

Site	Läge	
Maintenance	Underhåll	
Architect	Arkitekt	Unknown
Type	Karaktär	forest, parkland
Relief	Nivåskillnader	
Water in play	Vatten på spelfältet	
Exp. to wind	Vindutsatt	
Trees in play	Träd på spelfältet	

Scorecard Scorekort	**Chp.** Back tees	**Mens** Herrtee	**Ladies** Damtee
Length Längd	6125	5785	5084
Par	72	72	72
Slope system	—	136	127

Advised golfing ability Rekommenderad spelnivå — **0 12 24 36**

Hcp required Hcp erfordrad — 35

Club house & amenities KLUBBHUS OCH OMGIVNING — 7/10

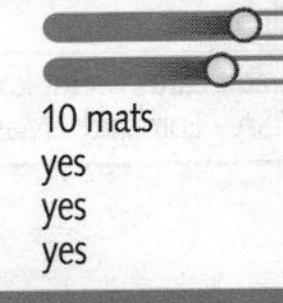

Pro shop	Pro shop	
Driving range	Träningsbana	
Sheltered	tåkt	10 mats
On grass	på gräs	yes
Putting-green	putting-green	yes
Pitching-green	pitching-green	yes

Hotel facilities HOTELL OMGIVNING — 7/10

HOTELS

Grand Hotel Falkenberg — Falkenberg 5 km
71 rooms, D SKr 1210
Tel (46) 0346 - 144 50, Fax (46) 0346 - 829 25

Hotel Strandbaden — Falkenberg 5 km
135 rooms, D SKr 1035
Tel (46) 0346 - 714 900, Fax (46) 0346 - 161 11

RESTAURANTS RESTAURANG

Restaurant Hertigenn, Tel (46) 0346 - 100 18 — Falkenberg

Laxbutiken, Tel (46) 0346 - 511 10 — Falkenberg

Harry's Restaurant och Pub — Falkenberg
Tel (46) 0346 - 100 77

FALSTERBO

18 | 7 | 5

Detta är en av få linksbanor utanför Storbritannien där det känns som om du befinner dig på Skottlands östkust. Banan är omgärdad av vatten på tre sidor, och framför allt på första nio hålen finns också ett antal dammar. Övriga problem är den tjocka ruffen och bunkrar som lurar antingen på sidorna eller mitt i fairway. Greenerna kan man ofta närma sig med låga rullslag. Blåser det inte är banan i det närmaste ofarlig. Men de dagar när det friskar i, och det gör det nästan alltid, måste du ha god bollkontroll och kreativa lösningar. Spelare med bra känsla blir belönade, framför allt när det kommer till att rädda par runt greenerna. Några få rader av träd i banans ytterområde avskärmar Falsterbo från resten av omgivningen, och en gammal fyr mitt i området är ett pittoreskt inslag i en miljö som annars saknar starka färger. Längre söderut än så här kommer du inte i Sverige, och på våren är det här platsen att se de första gässen och änderna. Några väljer till och med att stanna och bygga bo i detta golfparadis. Vi förstår varför! Vi börjar se stora förbättringar på och runt greenerna.

This is one of the pure links courses outside the British Isles, where you feel as if you are on the east coast of Scotland. Surrounded by water on three sides, there is also a number of ponds, particularly on the front nine. The other problems are basically the tall rough and bunkers, which lurk on either side and across the fairways, and beside greens which can often be reached with bump and run shots. Without wind, this course is almost tame. When the wind blows, which it mostly does, you need good ball control and constant creativity. Players with good hands and touch are rewarded, particularly when it comes to saving par around the greens. A few rows of trees on the outskirts isolate the course from its surroundings and an old lighthouse adds a touch of colour to a rather bleak landscape. This is the southernmost part of Sweden where you first see the ducks and geese flying back to herald the first days of spring. Some even stop to nest alongside this little golfer's paradise, and understandably so. We also start to see the beautiful result of the renovation of greens and surrounding areas.

Falsterbo Golfklubb — 1911

Fyrvägen
S - 239 40 FALSTERBO

Office	Sekretariat	(46) 040 - 470 078
Pro shop	Pro shop	(46) 040 - 475 252
Fax	Fax	(46) 040 - 472 722
Web	www.falsterbogk.com	
Situation	Läge	Malmö, 30 km
Annual closure	Årlig stängning	no
Weekly closure	Daglig stängning	no

Fees main season Tariff hög säsong		Full day
	Week days Veckodag	**We/Bank holidays** Lör/Söndag/Helgdag
Individual Individuellt	SKr 280	SKr 380
Couple Par	SKr 560	SKr 760

19/6 → 20/8: GF SKr 350 / Juniors: – 50%

Caddy	Caddie	no
Electric Trolley	El vagn	no
Buggy	Golfbil	no
Clubs	Klubbor	SKr 150 /18 holes

Credit cards Kredit kort
VISA - Eurocard - MasterCard - DC - AMEX

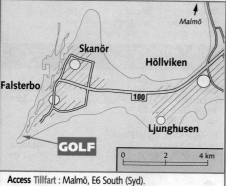

Access Tillfart : Malmö, E6 South (Syd).
→ Skanör/Falsterbo.
Map 1 on page 1204 Karta 1 se sid: 1204

Golf course — BANA — 18/20

Site	Läge	
Maintenance	Underhåll	
Architect	Arkitekt	Gunnar Bauer
Type	Karaktär	links, seaside course
Relief	Nivåskillnader	
Water in play	Vatten på spelfältet	
Exp. to wind	Vindutsatt	
Trees in play	Träd på spelfältet	

Scorecard Scorekort	**Chp.** Back tees	**Mens** Herrtee	**Ladies** Damtee
Length Längd	6065	5785	5040
Par	71	71	71
Slope system	—	125	123

Advised golfing ability Rekommenderad spelnivå — 0 12 24 36
Hcp required Hcp erfordrad — 32

1227

Club house & amenities — KLUBBHUS OCH OMGIVNING — 7/10

Pro shop	Pro shop	
Driving range	Träningsbana	
Sheltered	tåkt	no
On grass	på gräs	yes
Putting-green	putting-green	yes
Pitching-green	pitching-green	yes

Hotel facilities — HOTELL OMGIVNING — 5/10

HOTELS

Hotell Gässlingen — Skanör 5 km
13 rooms, D SKr 1300
Tel (46) 040 - 459 100, Fax (46) 040 - 359 113

Hotell Spelabäcken — Skanör 1 km
18 rooms, D SKr 850
Tel (46) 040 - 475 300, Fax (46) 040 - 473 242

RESTAURANTS RESTAURANG

Skänors Gästgiveri — Skanör 4 km
Tel (46) 040 - 475 690

Kaptensgården, Tel (46) 040 - 470 750 — Falsterbo 1 km

Vellinge Gästgiveri, Tel (46) 040 - 424 865 — Vellinge 7 km

FJÄLLBACKA

15 | 6 | 3

För inte så länge sedan tycktes det att Fjällbacka låg alldeles för långt bort från allfarsvägarna. Men platsen har sin berömmelse inte endast tack vare att Ingrid Bergman brukade åka hit på semestern: Detta är hummerns, krabbans och musslans huvudstad. Banan, som ritades av Erik Röös, öppnade 1967 och är resultatet av det arbete som visionären Harry Järund la ner. I dag är det en mycket välkänd bana belägen i ett ganska fantastiskt landskap, smala strängar av platt mark kantade av bergig terräng. Fairways vaktas på sina ställen av klippor, ungefär som på banorna i Arizona, enda skillnaden är att "öknen" här är grön och att en å rinner genom området och på flera ställen korsar banan. Fjällbaka är inte lång, men spelaren som kan manövrera bollen och då och då slå ett punchslag under vinden blir belönad därefter. Flera bunkrar har restaurerats och ett par vattenhinder har tillkommit som gör att banan spelas avsevärt längre. Trots att detta är en inlandsbana är känslan av seasidegolf stark, framför allt när man måste spela klassiska rullslag in mot greenerna.

Fjällbacka, long considered too far out of the way, owes its reputation not only to the fact that Ingrid Bergman used to come here in summer, but also to its status as one of the northern capitals of lobster, crab and oysters. This course was opened in 1967, promoted by a visionary named Harry Järund and designed by Erik Röös. Today, it has become a very well known course over a quite amazing site, a rocky region with patches of soil. The fairways are sort of guarded by the rocks, rather like on some of the courses in Arizona, the only difference being that the "desert" here is all green and crossed by a river that often comes into play. The course is not long, but players who can bend the ball, play knock-down shots or punch the ball will get their reward. With the renovation of several bunkers and the addition of new water hazards, this course will play a bit longer. Despite this being an inland course, there is still a seaside atmosphere, particularly when it comes to playing some good old bump and run shots to well-contoured greens.

Fjällbacka Golfklubb — 1967

PL 2005
S - 450 71 FJÄLLBACKA

Office	Sekretariat	(46) 0525 - 311 50
Pro shop	Pro shop	(46) 0525 - 315 60
Fax	Fax	(46) 0525 - 321 22
Web	www.fjallbacka.com/fjgk	
Situation	Läge	

Fjällbacka, 2 km - Göteborg, 120 km

1228

Annual closure	Årlig stängning	no
Weekly closure	Daglig stängning	no

Fees main season Tariff hög säsong	**Week days** Veckodag	**We/Bank holidays** Lör/Söndag/Helgdag
		18 holes
Individual Individuellt	SKr 300	SKr 300
Couple Par	SKr 600	SKr 600

Juniors: – 50%

Caddy	Caddie	no
Electric Trolley	El vagn	no
Buggy	Golfbil	SKr 150 /18 holes
Clubs	Klubbor	SKr 100 /18 holes

Credit cards Kredit kort VISA - Eurocard - MasterCard

Grebbestad
GOLF
Tanumshede
Uddevalla
E6
Ned Bräcke
Torsbo
Rabbalsheder
Fjällbacka
163
Hamburgsund
Kville
Dingle
E6
0 2 4 km

Access Tillfart : Göteborg E6. Dingle, R163 → Fjällbacka.
Golf 2 km north of Fjällbacka.
Map 1 on page 1204 Karta 1 se sid: 1204

Golf course BANA — 15/20

Site	Läge	
Maintenance	Underhåll	
Architect	Arkitekt	Erik Röös
Type	Karaktär	parkland, open country
Relief	Nivåskillnader	
Water in play	Vatten på spelfältet	
Exp. to wind	Vindutsatt	
Trees in play	Träd på spelfältet	

Scorecard Scorekort	**Chp.** Back tees	**Mens** Herrtee	**Ladies** Damtee
Length Längd	5935	5655	4985
Par	72	72	72
Slope system	—	128	126

Advised golfing ability Rekommenderad spelnivå — 0 12 24 36

Hcp required Hcp erfordrad 36

Club house & amenities KLUBBHUS OCH OMGIVNING — 6/10

Pro shop	Pro shop	
Driving range	Träningsbana	
Sheltered	tåkt	6 mats
On grass	på gräs	yes
Putting-green	putting-green	yes
Pitching-green	pitching-green	yes

Hotel facilities HOTELL OMGIVNING — 3/10

HOTELS

Stara Hottelet — Fjällbacka 2 km
22 rooms, D SKr 1160
Tel (46) 0525 - 310 03
Fax (46) 0525 - 310 93

RESTAURANTS RESTAURANG

Restaurant Klassen — Fjällbacka 2 km
Tel (46) 0525 - 310 03

FLOMMEN

16 | 7 | 7

Tillsammans med Falsterbo och Ljunghusen utgör Flommen en berömd trio, där Falsterbo, förstås, är den mest omtalade banan utanför Sverige. Vad gäller närheten till vatten så är det ett faktum som inte bara gör sig påmint för att Flommen ligger på en halvö – nix, här kommer vatten i spel på varje hål. Här finns inga träd, bara den eviga vinden, året om. För friluftsmänniskan är detta en mycket upphetsande bana, måhända lite mindre för golfaren som inte är i form eller som älskar att ströva i skogen. Hindrena syns tydligt från tee och är mycket farliga oavsett om vi talar om ruffen, bunkrarna eller vattnet (översvämningar kan vara ett problem). Några av greenerna är upphöjda, en del är svårlästa och kenpigaatt träffa. För matchspel är detta en idealisk bana eftersom ingenting kan tas för givet. Den modige har en fördel över den överdrivet försiktige. Om dina bollar tar slut får du ägna dig åt att tillsammans med alla fågelskådare studera det fantastiska naturlivet.

With Falsterbo and Ljunghusens, Flommens makes up a famous threesome of courses, the best known of which outside Sweden is Falsterbo. This sort of peninsula gives you all the more the impression of being surrounded by water in that the stuff comes into play on virtually every hole. There are no trees here, just wind all year, so an exciting course for sports lovers, a little less so for golfers who prefer a stroll through the forest or who are not on top of their game. The hazards are visible enough and effectively dangerous, whether rough, bunkers or, of course, water. And the greens are sometimes elevated (the terrain is subject to flooding on occasions), not always flat and difficult to approach. This is your ideal course for match-play, as here nothing is ever over: daring is sometimes more rewarding than extreme caution. If you run out of balls, take time off to explore a region where the wild-life is quite exceptional and attracts a good number of bird-watchers.

Flommens Golfklubb — 1935

Fädriften
S - 239 40 FALSTERBO

Office	Sekretariat	(46) 040 - 475 017
Pro shop	Pro shop	(46) 040 - 475 016
Fax	Fax	(46) 040 - 473 157
Web	www.flommensgk.com	
Situation	Läge	Malmö, 30 km
Annual closure	Årlig stängning	no
Weekly closure	Daglig stängning	no

Fees main season Tariff hög säsong		Full day
	Week days Veckodag	**We/Bank holidays** Lör/Söndag/Helgdag
Individual Individuellt	SKr 300	SKr 300
Couple Par	SKr 600	SKr 600

Juniors: – 50%

Caddy	Caddie	no
Electric Trolley	El vagn	no
Buggy	Golfbil	no
Clubs	Klubbor	no

Credit cards Kredit kort
VISA - Eurocard - MasterCard - AMEX

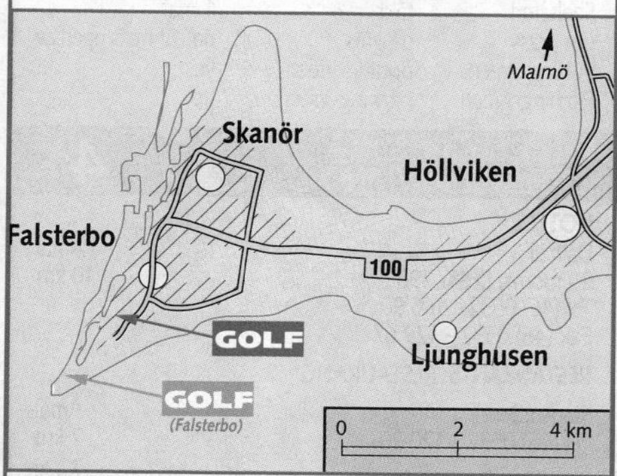

Access Tillfart : Malmö, E6 → Vellinge, → Skanör-Falsterbo, → Falsterbo. → Flommens Golfklubb.
Map 1 on page 1204 Karta 1 se sid: 1204

Golf course BANA — 16/20

Site	Läge	
Maintenance	Underhåll	
Architect	Arkitekt	Stig Bergendorff Stig Kristersson
Type	Karaktär	seaside course, links
Relief	Nivåskillnader	
Water in play	Vatten på spelfältet	
Exp. to wind	Vindutsatt	
Trees in play	Träd på spelfältet	

Scorecard Scorekort	**Chp.** Back tees	**Mens** Herrtee	**Ladies** Damtee
Length Längd	6035	5745	4955
Par	72	72	72
Slope system	—	123	124

Advised golfing ability Rekommenderad spelnivå — 0 12 24 36
Hcp required Hcp erfordrad 36

Club house & amenities KLUBBHUS OCH OMGIVNING — 7/10

Pro shop	Pro shop	
Driving range	Träningsbana	
Sheltered	tåkt	no
On grass	på gräs	yes
Putting-green	putting-green	yes
Pitching-green	pitching-green	yes

Hotel facilities HOTELL OMGIVNING — 7/10

HOTELS

Hotel Gässlingen — Skanör 4 km
13 rooms, D SKr 1300
Tel (46) 040 - 459 100, Fax (46) 040 - 359 113

Hotell Spelabäcken — Skanör 1 km
18 rooms, D SKr 850
Tel (46) 040 - 475 300, Fax (46) 040 - 473 242

RESTAURANTS RESTAURANG

Skänors Gästgiveri Tel (46) 040 - 475 690 — Skanör 10 km
Vellinge Gästgiveri, Tel (46) 040 - 424 865 — Vellinge 15 km
Kaptensgården Tel (46) 040 - 470 750 — Falsterbo 1 km

FORSBACKA

16 | 7 | 4

Många svenska banor är vackert infogade i naturen. Forsbacka är inget undantag. Banan ligger nära Åmål, en liten stad på Vätterns strand. Den är belägen i ett underbart landskap mellan sjöar och skog, ungefär som man föreställer sig ett svenskt vykort. Men eftersom den är ganska kuperad och här inte finns några golfbilar rekommenderar vi den endast till den som är i bra fysisk form och som inte är rädd för vatten, träd eller höga kullar. Som på de flesta kuperade banor vill man gärna veta vilka hinder som finns framför en, här finns dock inga gömda elakheter så länge du håller dig på fairway. De mest minnesvärda hålen är sjuan och nian, som bägge kräver långa slag och stor precision. Många golfare tycker att Forsbacka är en av Sveriges vackraste banor, andra kanske tycker att den är i väl förrädiska laget. Hur som helst, du måste spela här för att bilda dig en egen uppfattning.

Many Swedish courses are beautifully immersed in nature, and this is one of them. Forsbacka is close to Åmål, a small town on the shores of the Vänern, the largest lake in western Europe. The course offers a wonderful landscape of lakes and forests, rather like a postcard of Sweden, but being rather hilly and given the absence of carts we would recommend it only for golfers who are in good shape physically and for players for whom water, trees and slopes hold no fears. As with all hilly courses, we would like to see the hazards ahead, but here there are not really any hidden traps or unpleasant surprises in store. On this exciting course, perhaps the most memorable holes are from 7 to 9, where that hardest of combinations - length and accuracy - is a total and absolute necessity. For many golfers, Forsbacka is one of Sweden's most beautiful parkland courses, others might find it a little treacherous. Whatever, you will need to play it yourself to form your own opinion, which certainly won't be one of indifference.

Forsbacka Golfklubb — 1971

Box 136
S - 662 23 ÅMÅL

Office	Sekretariat	(46) 0532 - 430 55
Pro shop	Pro shop	(46) 0532 - 431 19
Fax	Fax	(46) 0532 - 431 16
E-mail		forsbackagolf@telia.com
Situation	Läge	Karlstad, 75 km
Annual closure	Årlig stängning	no
Weekly closure	Daglig stängning	no

Fees main season Tariff hög säsong	Full day	
	Week days Veckodag	**We/Bank holidays** Lör/Söndag/Helgdag
Individual Individuellt	SKr 220	SKr 300
Couple Par	SKr 440	SKr 600

Juniors: - 50 %

Caddy	Caddie	no
Electric Trolley	El vagn	no
Buggy	Golfbil	SKr 100 /18 holes
Clubs	Klubbor	SKr 90 /18 holes

Credit cards Kredit kort
VISA - Eurocard - MasterCard

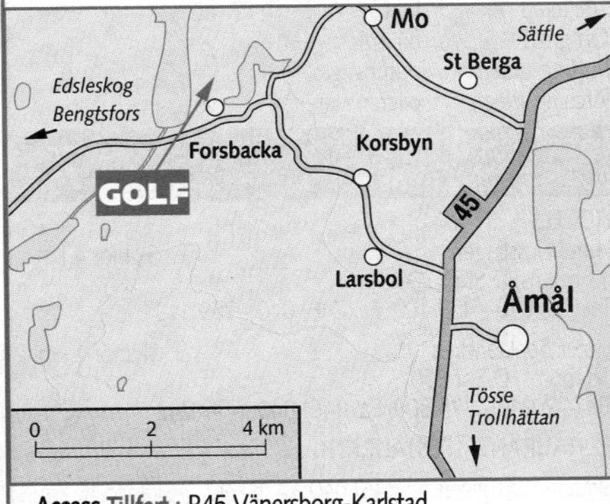

Access Tillfart : R45 Vänersborg-Karlstad.
Exit R164 → Bengtsfors. → Golf
Map 2 on page 1206 Karta 2 se sid: 1206

Golf course BANA — 16/20

Site	Läge	
Maintenance	Underhåll	
Architect	Arkitekt	Nils Sköld
Type	Karaktär	forest, parkland
Relief	Nivåskillnader	
Water in play	Vatten på spelfältet	
Exp. to wind	Vindutsatt	
Trees in play	Träd på spelfältet	

Scorecard Scorekort	**Chp.** Back tees	**Mens** Herrtee	**Ladies** Damtee
Length Längd	6040	5755	5050
Par	72	72	72
Slope system	—	133	133

Advised golfing ability Rekommenderad spelnivå — 0 12 24 36

Hcp required Hcp erfordrad 36

Club house & amenities KLUBBHUS OCH OMGIVNING — 7/10

Pro shop	Pro shop	
Driving range	Träningsbana	
Sheltered	tåkt	1 mat
On grass	på gräs	no, 12 mats open air
Putting-green	putting-green	yes
Pitching-green	pitching-green	no

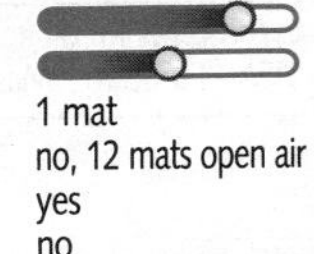

Hotel facilities HOTELL OMGIVNING — 4/10

HOTELS

Dalhall — Åmål 10 km
20 rooms, D SKr 790
Tel (46) 0532 - 166 90
Fax (46) 0532 - 129 67

RESTAURANTS RESTAURANG

Stadshotellet — Åmål 7 km
Tel (46) 0532 - 120 20

Barhörnan — Åmål 7 km
Tel (46) 0532 - 146 00

FORSGÅRDEN

14 | 6 | 7

Om du befinner dig söder om Göteborg är Kungsbacka med alla sina pastellfärgade hus ett givet stopp. Landskapet är platt och harmonierar med västskustens enorma, vita stränder som packas täta med människor på sommaren. Forsgården har 27 hål, varav en riktig 18-hålare. Omgärdad av hus och vägar är kanske inte detta den vanligaste eller mest upphetsande plats för en bana. Men väl ute på banan ser du tack vare naturens terräng ingenting av detta. Forsgården är en mästerskapsbana där hindrena ofta är mer i spel för låghandicaparen än för höghandicaparen. Landningsområdena för driven är smala, och det är lätt att hamna i såväl sand som vatten. Att attackera greenerna är inte heller särskilt lätt. De är väl skyddade av kullar, sluttningar och bunkrar. Att ha ett taktiskt sinne på Forsgården är ett stort plus, allt eftersom dina beslut kan betyda skillnaden mellan katastrof och succé. Bästa exemplet på detta är trean, en kort par 4, men nog så knepigt om du spelar det fel. Forsgården är ett bra test på din golf, även om den måhända kunde ha varit aningen charmigare.

The lovely little hamlet of Kungsbacka with its pastel-coloured houses is an essential stop-off when touring this region to the south of Göteborg, which is flat and lined with huge and very busy beaches during the summer. The Forsgården Golfklubb consists of 27 holes, including a real 18-hole course. Surrounded by houses and roads, this open space is hardly the most attractive or typical course around, but once out on the course you are isolated from the outside world by the terrain's natural relief. This is a championship course where the hazards affect more the play of low-handicappers than that of the 18-plus hacker, a logical state of affairs. So certain landing areas for the drive are threatened by sand or hazards, with water very definitely in play. Attacking the greens is never easy, either, as they are well guarded by mounds, slopes and other bunkers. Having a game strategy is essential here, as the decisions you take can result in a disastrous or successful round of golf. The best example is hole number 3, a short par 4, with all the usual risks involved. A good test of golf, even more so when the wind blows.

Forsgårdens Golfklubb — 1989

Gamla Forsvägen 1
S - 434 47 KUNGSBACKA

Office	Sekretariat	(46) 0300 - 566 354
Pro shop	Pro shop	(46) 0300 - 566 350
Fax	Fax	(46) 0300 - 566 351
Web	www.golf.se/forsgardensgk	
Situation	Läge	Göteborg, 27 km
Annual closure	Årlig stängning	no
Weekly closure	Daglig stängning	no

Fees main season Tariff hög säsong	**Week days** Veckodag	**We/Bank holidays** Lör/Söndag/Helgdag
		18 holes
Individual Individuellt	SKr 250	SKr 300
Couple Par	SKr 500	SKr 600

Juniors: – 50%

Caddy	Caddie	no
Electric Trolley	El vagn	no
Buggy	Golfbil	SKr 200 /18 holes
Clubs	Klubbor	SKr 180 /18 holes

Credit cards Kredit kort
VISA - Eurocard - MasterCard - DC - AMEX

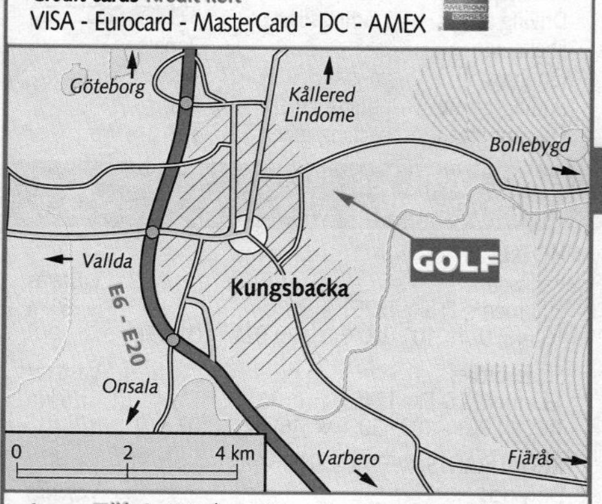

Access Tillfart : Göteborg E6 → Kungsbacka. → Fjäras
Map 1 on page 1204 Karta 1 se sid: 1204

Golf course — BANA — 14/20

Site	Läge	
Maintenance	Underhåll	
Architect	Arkitekt	Sune Linde
Type	Karaktär	open country
Relief	Nivåskillnader	
Water in play	Vatten på spelfältet	
Exp. to wind	Vindutsatt	
Trees in play	Träd på spelfältet	

Scorecard Scorekort	**Chp.** Back tees	**Mens** Herrtee	**Ladies** Damtee
Length Längd	6310	5755	4840
Par	72	72	72
Slope system	—	132	128

Advised golfing ability Rekommenderad spelnivå — 0 12 24 36

Hcp required Hcp erfordrad 36

Club house & amenities — KLUBBHUS OCH OMGIVNING — 6/10

Pro shop	Pro shop	
Driving range	Träningsbana	
Sheltered	tåkt	4 mats
On grass	på gräs	yes
Putting-green	putting-green	yes
Pitching-green	pitching-green	yes

Hotel facilities — HOTELL OMGIVNING — 7/10

HOTELS

Hotell Halland, 30 rooms, D SKr 1050 — Kungsbacka
Tel (46) 0300 - 775 30, Fax (46) 0300 - 162 25 — 3 km

Hotell Nattmössan, 20 rooms, D SKr 850 — Kungsbacka
Tel (46) 0300 - 775 30, Fax (46) 0300 - 162 25 — 5 km

Säröhus, 83 rooms, D SKr 1095 — Särö
Tel (46) 031 - 936 090, Fax (46) 031 - 936 185 — 12 km

RESTAURANTS RESTAURANG

Pio Pepe — Kungsbacka
Tel (46) 0300 - 199 04 — 3 km

Hotell Halland — Kungsbacka
Tel (46) 0300 - 775 30 — 3 km

FRÖSÅKER

16 | 7 | 5

En timme från Stockholm hittar du Frösåker. Letar du dig vidare till närbelägna Västerås finner du bland sevärheterna en sällsynt vacker kyrka och ett kvarter av gamla timmerhus. Även om detta är en relatiivt ny bana har den snabbt fått ett utomordentligt rykte. Inledningen är måhända lite tam, men sedan tar saker och ting fart och när du slutligen når 18e står du inför ett av Sveriges allra bästa hål. Hindrena på Frösåker kommer i alla former och harmonierar väl med landskapet i övrigt. Sista nio är betydligt mer utmanande än de första, och det är lätt att frestas att ta risker. Om du slår någorlunda rakt, förmår att hålla dig kall och har en hygglig teknik så har du alla möjligheter att komma in på ett bra resultat. För den som slår snett kan ruffen vålla stora problem, särskilt med tanke på att höga inspel med gott om bakskruv är ett måste på flera av hålen. En aning för svår för den inte fullt så erfarne golfaren, en njutning för alla andra.

An hour away from Stockholm, Frösåker is also very close to Västerås, where amongst other things you will find a very beautiful cathedral and an old district full of timber houses. Although very new, this course has quickly built up an excellent reputation. Before reaching the magnificent 18th, one of the finest holes in the whole country, you start off with a few rather indifferent holes. Then things start to get more exciting in a much more attractive park landscape, where hazards of all shapes and sizes are brought into play, clearly and with a sense of harmony. The back 9 are even more demanding than the outward half and you will be tempted to take risks. If you are a reasonably straight hitter, can keep a cool head and have the proper technique to work the ball, you will come through with flying colours. For the more wayward hitters, the rough can be more than a handful, especially since approach shots to the greens are not easy and call for high shots with a little spin if possible. A wee difficult for inexperienced players, a real pleasure for the better golfers.

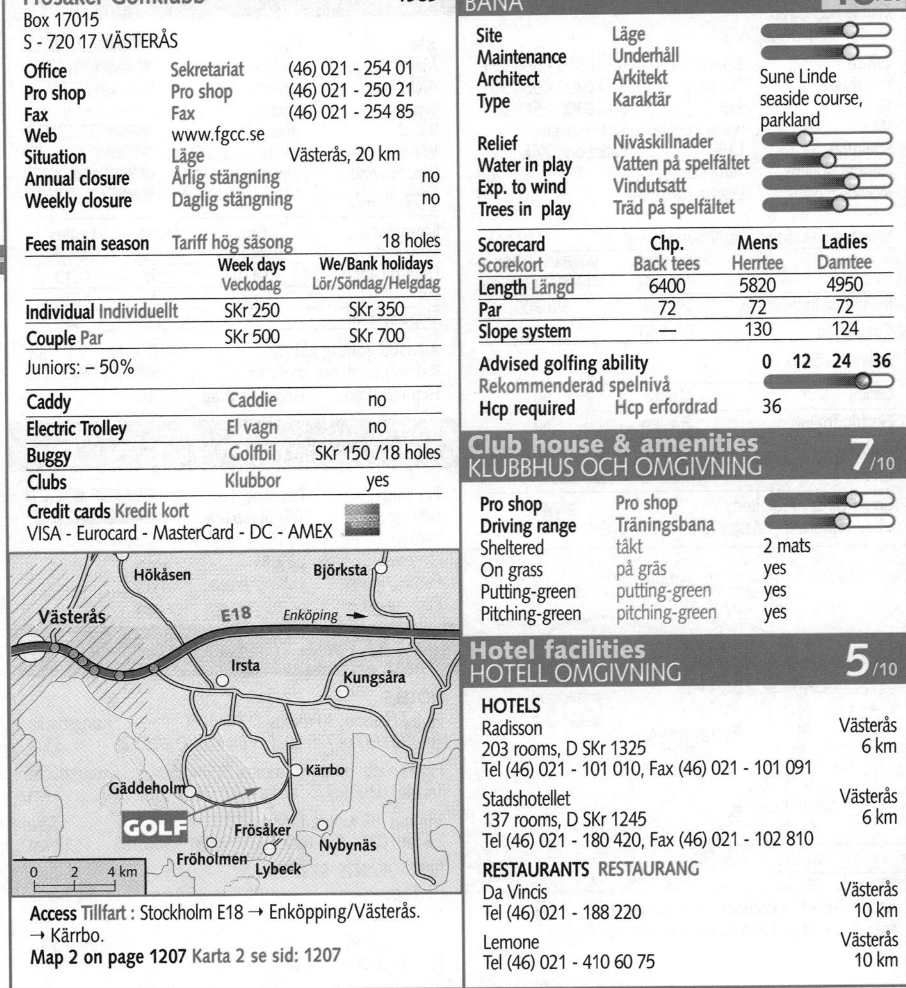

Frösåker Golfklubb — 1989

Box 17015
S - 720 17 VÄSTERÅS

Office	Sekretariat	(46) 021 - 254 01
Pro shop	Pro shop	(46) 021 - 250 21
Fax	Fax	(46) 021 - 254 85
Web	www.fgcc.se	
Situation	Läge	Västerås, 20 km
Annual closure	Årlig stängning	no
Weekly closure	Daglig stängning	no

Fees main season Tariff hög säsong	18 holes	
	Week days Veckodag	**We/Bank holidays** Lör/Söndag/Helgdag
Individual Individuellt	SKr 250	SKr 350
Couple Par	SKr 500	SKr 700

Juniors: – 50%

Caddy	Caddie	no
Electric Trolley	El vagn	no
Buggy	Golfbil	SKr 150 /18 holes
Clubs	Klubbor	yes

Credit cards Kredit kort
VISA - Eurocard - MasterCard - DC - AMEX

Access Tillfart : Stockholm E18 → Enköpping/Västerås. → Kärrbo.
Map 2 on page 1207 Karta 2 se sid: 1207

Golf course BANA — 16/20

Site	Läge	
Maintenance	Underhåll	
Architect	Arkitekt	Sune Linde
Type	Karaktär	seaside course, parkland
Relief	Nivåskillnader	
Water in play	Vatten på spelfältet	
Exp. to wind	Vindutsatt	
Trees in play	Träd på spelfältet	

Scorecard Scorekort	**Chp.** Back tees	**Mens** Herrtee	**Ladies** Damtee
Length Längd	6400	5820	4950
Par	72	72	72
Slope system	—	130	124

Advised golfing ability Rekommenderad spelnivå — 0 12 24 36
Hcp required Hcp erfordrad — 36

Club house & amenities KLUBBHUS OCH OMGIVNING — 7/10

Pro shop	Pro shop	
Driving range	Träningsbana	
Sheltered	tåkt	2 mats
On grass	på gräs	yes
Putting-green	putting-green	yes
Pitching-green	pitching-green	yes

Hotel facilities HOTELL OMGIVNING — 5/10

HOTELS

Radisson — Västerås 6 km
203 rooms, D SKr 1325
Tel (46) 021 - 101 010, Fax (46) 021 - 101 091

Stadshotellet — Västerås 6 km
137 rooms, D SKr 1245
Tel (46) 021 - 180 420, Fax (46) 021 - 102 810

RESTAURANTS RESTAURANG

Da Vincis — Västerås 10 km
Tel (46) 021 - 188 220

Lemone — Västerås 10 km
Tel (46) 021 - 410 60 75

GÄVLE

14	6	6

Här ligger två banor utlagda i en ganska flack terräng i ett skogs- och parklandskap. Arkitekterna Nils Sköld, Jan Sederholm och Björn Eriksson är välkända namn i Sverige. Framför allt är vattenhindren en ständig källa till oro, och ibland är de direkt farliga. Om du endast spelar Gävle en gång kanske du inte ser de mer subtila poängerna med layouten, och då är det väl tveksamt om det är värt att åka 20 mil för att spela här. Men banan är definitivt en av de bättre norr om Stockholm, och den förtjänar absolut mer än en snabbvisit. Så har du tagit dig över Dalälven, stanna till ett tag. Även om det bara är 10 mil till Stockholm så märker du på atmosfären att du har kommit en bit norrut i landet. Ett utflyktsmål vi absolut vill tipsa om är Storsjön, nära Sandviken och bara tio minuter bort med bil – en av de mest pittoreska vyer man kan hitta i den här regionen.

Two courses are laid out over a rather flat terrain in a combination of forest and parkland styles. Architects Nils Sköld, Jan Sederholm and Björn Eriksson are well known names in Sweden and with their new Avan layout, they designed a course where the risk factor is even greater than here on Gävle course. The water hazards in particular are a constant threat and sometimes downright dangerous. If you play this course once only, you will be hard pushed to understand the more subtle points of the layout. You probably would not travel 200 miles just to play here, but it really is one of the better courses to the north of Stockholm. It deserves more than a fleeting visit when you are in this region crossed by the Dalälven, one of the twisting rivers running down from the mountains that separate Sweden from Norway. There is indeed a very Nordic flavour to this part of the world, which lies about 100 kilometres from the Swedish capital. If you make it this far north, go and visit lake Storsjön, about a ten minute drive next to Sandviken, one of the most picturesque sights in this part of the country.

Gävle Golfklubb — 1949

Bönavägen 23
S - 805 95 GÄVLE

Office	Sekretariat	(46) 026 - 120 333
Pro shop	Pro shop	(46) 026 - 121 410
Fax	Fax	(46) 026 - 516 468
Web	www.gavlegolf.com	
Situation	Läge	Gävle, 3 km
Annual closure	Årlig stängning	no
Weekly closure	Daglig stängning	no

Fees main season Tariff hög säsong	Full day	
	Week days Veckodag	**We/Bank holidays** Lör/Söndag/Helgdag
Individual Individuellt	SKr 200	SKr 250
Couple Par	SKr 400	SKr 500

Juniors: – 50%

Caddy	Caddie	no
Electric Trolley	El vagn	no
Buggy	Golfbil	SKr 200 /18 holes
Clubs	Klubbor	SKr 100 /18 holes

Credit cards Kredit kort
VISA - Eurocard - MasterCard

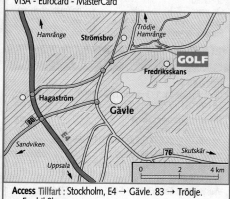

Access Tillfart : Stockholm, E4 → Gävle. 83 → Trödje. → FredrikSkans.

Map 2 on page 1207 Karta 2 se sid: 1207

Golf course — BANA — 14/20

Site	Läge	
Maintenance	Underhåll	
Architect	Arkitekt	Sköld, Sederholm Eriksson
Type	Karaktär	forest, parkland
Relief	Nivåskillnader	
Water in play	Vatten på spelfältet	
Exp. to wind	Vindutsatt	
Trees in play	Träd på spelfältet	

Scorecard Scorekort	**Chp.** Back tees	**Mens** Herrtee	**Ladies** Damtee
Length Längd	5915	5720	4875
Par	72	72	72
Slope system	—	117	127

Advised golfing ability Rekommenderad spelnivå: 0 12 24 36

Hcp required Hcp erfordrad: no

Club house & amenities — KLUBBHUS OCH OMGIVNING — 6/10

Pro shop	Pro shop	
Driving range	Träningsbana	
Sheltered	tåkt	no
On grass	på gräs	yes
Putting-green	putting-green	yes
Pitching-green	pitching-green	yes

Hotel facilities — HOTELL OMGIVNING — 6/10

HOTELS

Scandic Hotel — Gävle 5 km
200 rooms, D SKr 660
Tel (46) 026 - 188 060, Fax (46) 026 - 141 860

Hotell Winn — Gävle 7 km
200 rooms, D SKr 1000
Tel (46) 026 - 177 000, Fax (46) 026 - 647 009

RESTAURANTS RESTAURANG

Johanssons Köle, Tel (46) 026 - 100 734 — Gävle 3 km
Church Street Saloon, Tel (46) 026 - 126 211 — Gävle 3 km
Bali Garden, Tel (46) 026 - 124 322 — Gävle 3 km

GÖTEBORG

15 | 6 | 7

Detta är Sveriges äldsta bana, och få en starttid här på en helg är snudd på omöjligt. Den byggdes 1904, och träden som då planterades har nu hunnit växa sig stora och mäktiga vilket gör en del hål synnerligen knixiga. Här är du inte mycket hjälpt av råstyrka, betydligt bättre är att fokusera på precisionen. Men det ska du nog lyckas med eftersom banan är ganska kort och ligger i ett böljande landskap som inte är alltför fysiskt krävande. Dessutom är konditionen på banan nästan alltid i högklass, vilket gör att man gärna åker hit för att spela en vänskaplig match. Göteborg, eller i folkmun Hovås, kräver inte en gudabenådad talang, däremot ett hyggligt spel med fairwayträna och mellanjärnen samt de korta järnen. Det här är en perfekt bana att spela och ladda upp på inför tuffare uppgifter, eller som avslutning på en trevlig dag i staden, där vi rekommenderar ett besök i hamnen, centrum, Konstmuseumet eller Röhsska Museumet.

This is the oldest course in Sweden where playing on week-ends is nigh on impossible. It was designed in 1904, and some of the oldest holes are all the narrower and trickier today in that the trees have grown upwards and outwards since they were first planted. It is on these holes in particular that brute force is best left in the locker room and replaced by emphasis on accuracy. This should not be too much of a handicap, though, as the course is short and set out over rolling terrain, which you can walk quite easily, especially since the grass and green-keeping in general are excellent. Indeed, the condition of the greens and fairways makes the course even more pleasant to play and it can be great fun playing friendly matches here. Göteborg does not require any particular heaven-sent talent, just all-round skills for fairway woods and your medium and short irons. It is a good course to hone your game before squaring up to more demanding challenges or after a pleasant visit to a city where there is much to see, particularly the harbour, the city centre, the Konstmuseum and the Röhsska Museet (dedicated to decorative arts).

Göteborgs Golfklubb — 1904

Box 2056
S - 436 02 HOVÅS

Office	Sekretariat	(46) 031 - 282 444
Pro shop	Pro shop	(46) 031 - 286 159
Fax	Fax	(46) 031 - 685 333
E-mail	kansli@ggk.o.se	
Situation	Läge	Göteborg, 15 km
Annual closure	Årlig stängning	no
Weekly closure	Daglig stängning	no

Fees main season Tariff hög säsong		18 holes
	Week days Veckodag	**We/Bank holidays** Lör/Söndag/Helgdag
Individual Individuellt	SKr 350	SKr 400
Couple Par	SKr 700	SKr 800

Juniors: – 50%

Caddy	Caddie	no
Electric Trolley	El vagn	no
Buggy	Golfbil	no
Clubs	Klubbor	no

Credit cards Kredit kort
VISA - Mastercard - AMEX

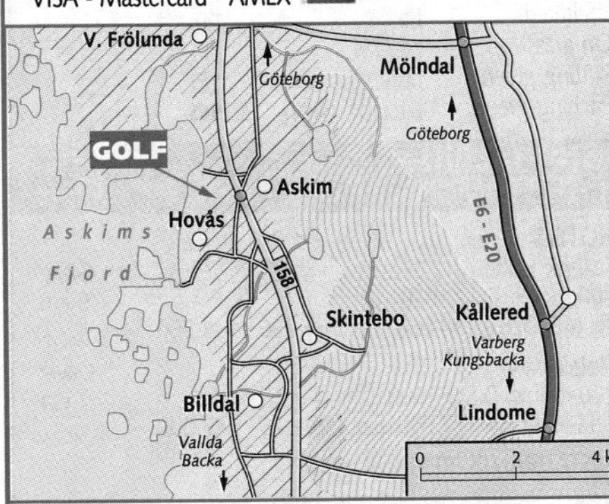

Access Tillfart : Göteborg, V 158 → Särö.
Map 1 on page 1204 Karta 1 se sid: 1204

Golf course BANA — 15/20

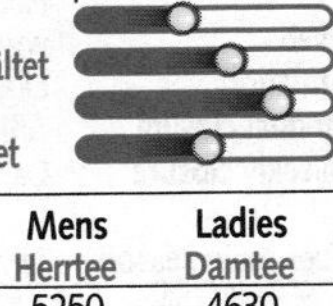

Site	Läge	
Maintenance	Underhåll	
Architect	Arkitekt	Andrew Person
Type	Karaktär	parkland
Relief	Nivåskillnader	
Water in play	Vatten på spelfältet	
Exp. to wind	Vindutsatt	
Trees in play	Träd på spelfältet	

Scorecard Scorekort	**Chp.** Back tees	**Mens** Herrtee	**Ladies** Damtee
Length Längd	5575	5250	4630
Par	70	70	70
Slope system	—	125	123

Advised golfing ability Rekommenderad spelnivå — 0 12 24 36
Hcp required Hcp erfordrad — 30

Club house & amenities KLUBBHUS OCH OMGIVNING — 6/10

Pro shop	Pro shop	
Driving range	Träningsbana	
Sheltered	tåkt	2 mats
On grass	på gräs	no (mats open air)
Putting-green	putting-green	yes
Pitching-green	pitching-green	no

Hotel facilities HOTELL OMGIVNING — 7/10

HOTELS

Quality Hotel 11, 133 rooms, D SKr 1350 — Göteborg
Tel (46) 031 - 779 11 11, Fax (46) 031 - 779 11 10 — 15 km

Sheraton Göteborgs Hotel — Göteborg
333 rooms, D SKr 2180 — 15 km
Tel (46) 031 - 806 000, Fax (46) 031 - 159 888

Victors, 35 rooms, D SKr 1250 — Göteborg
Tel (46) 031 - 174 180, Fax (46) 031 - 139 610 — 15 km

RESTAURANTS RESTAURANG

Westra Piren, Tel (46) 031 - 519 555 — Göteborg 15 km
Le Village, Tel (46) 031 - 242 003 — Göteborg 15 km
Fiskekrogen, Tel (46) 031 - 101 005 — Göteborg 15 km

GRÄNNA

15 | 7 | 5

Oavsett om du kommer norr eller söderifrån hamnar du på E 4 utmed Vätterns strand. Detta är tveklöst Sveriges vackraste väg.Inte heller lär du bli besviken på Gränna. Damer, äldre spelare och juniorer kan njuta fullt ut – här finns nämligen inga omöjliga hinder som inte går att slå över med utslaget. Vad gäller medelhandicapare så kommer de också att trivas eftersom de sällan når hindrena som är så strategiskt placerade att de endast bekymrar de bättre spelarna. Från utslagsplatserna är det generella intrycket att fairways är mycket smala. Men detta är faktiskt en synvilla och mer ett psykologiskt problem än ett reellt, vilket kanske kan förklara att den som spelar här för första gången ofta är överdrivet försiktig. På Gränna kan man tydligt se banarkitekten Peter Nordwalls signum: Stora greener! Normalt innebär detta att de även blir aningen försvarslösa, men eftersom de på Gränna är starkt kuperade kommer du att inse att den viktigaste klubban i bagen är din putter. Bortsett från tre-fyra rätt ordinära hål är Gränna absolut värd ett besök, så är givetvis också stan med sina färgglada hus, och glöm för all del inte bort att äta en polkagris.

You will love the trip down the E4 road alongside the Vättern, and Gränna will certainly not disappoint you either. Ladies, seniors, kids and beginners will love it here because there are none of those impossible carries from the tee. Mid-handicappers will be happy too, as the hazards out on the course are seldom in play for them, and the better players will be in their element, as the main hazards are reserved just for them. From the tee-boxes (generally elevated) you get the impression of the fairways here being very narrow. This is in fact an optical illusion and psychological trap, which explains why golfers playing here for the first time tend to be over-cautious. The course clearly carries the hallmarks of architect Peter Nordwall, i.e. very large greens, a feature that tends to blunt their defences, but as the contours are very pronounced, the putter once again will be the most important club in your bag. Excepting three or four very ordinary holes, Gränna really is worth a visit, as is the village of the same name to see the coloured houses and taste the local barley sugar called polkagrisar.

Gränna Golfklubb — 1989

Västanå Slott
S - 563 92 GRÄNNA

Office	Sekretariat	(46) 0390 - 100 30
Pro shop	Pro shop	(46) 0500 - 106 29
Fax	Fax	(46) 0500 - 100 34
E-mail	info.grannagk@telia.com	
Situation	Läge	Jönköping, 32 km
Annual closure	Årlig stängning	no
Weekly closure	Daglig stängning	no

Fees main season Tariff hög säsong	full day	
	Week days Veckodag	**We/Bank holidays** Lör/Söndag/Helgdag
Individual Individuellt	SKr 200	SKr 250
Couple Par	SKr 400	SKr 500

Juniors: SKr 100

Caddy	Caddie	no
Electric Trolley	El vagn	no
Buggy	Golfbil	SKr 150 /18 holes
Clubs	Klubbor	SKr 200 /18 holes

Credit cards Kredit kort
VISA - Eurocard - MasterCard - DC - AMEX

Access Tillfart : Gränna E4. 5 km Exit Gyllene Uttern. → Västanå Slott.
Map 1 on page 1204 Karta 1 se sid: 1204

Golf course — BANA — 15/20

Site	Läge	
Maintenance	Underhåll	
Architect	Arkitekt	Peter Nordwall
Type	Karaktär	parkland, open country
Relief	Nivåskillnader	
Water in play	Vatten på spelfältet	
Exp. to wind	Vindutsatt	
Trees in play	Träd på spelfältet	

Scorecard Scorekort	**Chp.** Back tees	**Mens** Herrtee	**Ladies** Damtee
Length Längd	5967	5515	4741
Par	72	72	72
Slope system	—	132	130

Advised golfing ability Rekommenderad spelnivå — 0 12 24 36
Hcp required Hcp erfordrad 36

Club house & amenities — KLUBBHUS OCH OMGIVNING — 7/10

Pro shop	Pro shop	
Driving range	Träningsbana	
Sheltered	tåkt	2 mats
On grass	på gräs	no, 16 mats open air
Putting-green	putting-green	yes
Pitching-green	pitching-green	yes

Hotel facilities — HOTELL OMGIVNING — 5/10

HOTELS

Västanå Slott, 20 rooms, D SKr 850 — on site
Tel (46) 0390 - 500 00, Fax (46) 0390 - 411 875

Stora Hotellet, 114 rooms, D SKr 1295 — Jönköping 32 km
Tel (46) 036 - 100 000, Fax (46) 036 - 719 320

John Bauer, 100 rooms, D SKr 1200 — Jönköping 32 km
Tel (46) 036 - 349 000, Fax (46) 036 - 719 320

RESTAURANTS RESTAURANG

Västanå Slott, Tel (46) 0390 - 107 00 — on site
Esters Restaurang, Tel (46) 036 - 349 000 — Jönköping 32 km
Trottoaren, Tel (46) 036 - 100 000 — Jönköping 32 km

HALMSTAD

18 | 8 | 7

Banan ligger vid Tylösand, vilket är den populäraste stranden i staden. I övrigt rekommenderar vi att du besöker Stortorget och Miniland – det senare är ett Sverige uppbyggt i miniatyr med 73 skalenliga modeller av välkända landmärken och personer hämtade från legender och sagor. Efter detta ska du absolut ta dig tid för en runda golf på en av Sveriges allra bästa banor – utlagd i en tät tallskog och även om du inte kan se havet kan du på många ställen höra och känna det. Varje hål är kantat av träd, och därför finns det heller inget behov för ruff. Träden ger dig känslan av att hålen är längre och smalare än vad de verkligen är, och resultatet blir ofta att du spelar alltför försiktigt. Ett antal fairwaybunkers är extra luriga (framför allt på tvåan), för att inte tala om ån som rinner genom banan, och som lätt ställer till med problem på 12e och 16e hålen. I matchspel kan vad som helst hända där! Lyckligtvis är många av hindrena utom räckhåll för höghandicaparen – därför är också Halmstad relativt sett tuffare för den bättre spelaren. Är du inspirerad blir du dock belönad! Förutom mästerskapsbanan finns ytterligare en underbart, utmanande 18-hålsbana på området. Halmstad är ett måste!

This course is at Tylösand, the most popular beach in Halmstad, where essential visiting includes the "Miniland" attraction, a miniature Sweden with reduced-scale models of the finest landmarks and characters from tales and legends of the country. Then move on an play one of the greatest courses in Sweden, laid out in a pine forest where you can always hear the sea without seeing it. Each hole is lined with trees, which are so dominant that there is no need for rough. They give the impression of long, narrow fairways and often result in the golfer playing too cautiously. A few fairway bunkers also lurk dangerously, as do a number of streams and ditches, like on the 12th and 16th holes. These can make all the difference in a match-play round. On the other hand, many of the hazards are out of reach for high-handicappers, meaning that Halmstad is a tough proposition for the better players, but one that rewards inspired play. With another shorter but beautiful and very challenging 18-hole course, Halmstad is a must.

Halmstad Golfklubb — 1938

Tylösand
S - 302 73 HALMSTAD

Office	Sekretariat	(46) 035 - 176 800
Pro shop	Pro shop	(46) 035 - 176 801
Fax	Fax	(46) 035 - 176 820
Web	www.hgk.se	
Situation	Läge	Halmstad, 9 km
Annual closure	Årlig stängning	no
Weekly closure	Daglig stängning	no

Fees main season Tariff hög säsong		18 holes
	Week days Veckodag	**We/Bank holidays** Lör/Söndag/Helgdag
Individual Individuellt	SKr 450	SKr 450
Couple Par	SKr 900	SKr 900

Special fees for juniors

Caddy	Caddie	no
Electric Trolley	El vagn	SKr 85 /18 holes
Buggy	Golfbil	no
Clubs	Klubbor	SKr 100 /18 holes

Credit cards Kredit kort
VISA - Eurocard - MasterCard - AMEX

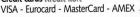

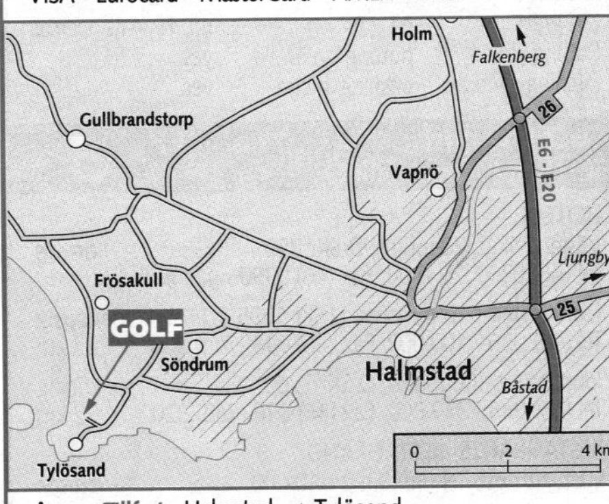

Access Tillfart : Halmstad, → Tylösand.
Map 1 on page 1204 Karta 1 se sid: 1204

Golf course — BANA — 18/20

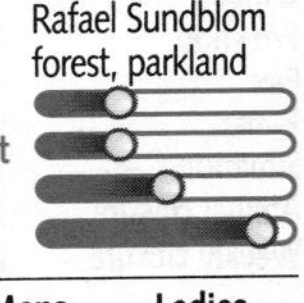

Site	Läge	
Maintenance	Underhåll	
Architect	Arkitekt	Rafael Sundblom
Type	Karaktär	forest, parkland
Relief	Nivåskillnader	
Water in play	Vatten på spelfältet	
Exp. to wind	Vindutsatt	
Trees in play	Träd på spelfältet	

Scorecard Scorekort	**Chp.** Back tees	**Mens** Herrtee	**Ladies** Damtee
Length Längd	6317	5955	5116
Par	72	72	72
Slope system	—	133	129

Advised golfing ability — 0 12 24 36
Rekommenderad spelnivå
Hcp required Hcp erfordrad — 28 Men, 36 Ladies

Club house & amenities — KLUBBHUS OCH OMGIVNING — 8/10

Pro shop	Pro shop	
Driving range	Träningsbana	
Sheltered	täkt	3 mats
On grass	på gräs	yes
Putting-green	putting-green	yes
Pitching-green	pitching-green	yes

Hotel facilities — HOTELL OMGIVNING — 7/10

HOTELS

Tylöhus, 230 rooms, D SKr 1300 Tel (46) 035 - 305 00, Fax (46) 035 - 324 39	Halmstad 0.5 km
Scandic Hotell, 129 rooms, D SKr 1387 Tel (46) 035 - 218 800, Fax (46) 035 - 148 956	Halmstad 9 km
Hotell Continental, 46 rooms, D SKr 1165 Tel (46) 035 - 176 300, Fax (46) 035 - 128 604	Halmstad 9 km

RESTAURANTS RESTAURANG

Pio & Company, Tel (46) 035 - 210 669	Halmstad 9 km
Mårtensson, Tel (46) 035 - 177 575	Halmstad 9 km
Klosterköket, Tel (46) 035 - 124 050	Halmstad 9 km

HANINGE

16 | 8 | 6

Strax söder om Stockholm ligger denna utomordentliga bana och med ett rykte om sig att vara en riktig mästerskapsanläggning. Detta ska dock inte avskräcka medelhandicaparen som kommer att ha en härlig runda framför sig, låt vara att han kanske inte blir alltför stolt över scoren. För det första: Klubbhuset är någonting alldeles extra, ett slott från 1400-talet. För det andra: Banan är en mix mellan öppna hål och parkbane-karaktär. Och eftersom vatten kommer i spel på sju av hålen så kan man verkligen säga att detta är en komplett bana. Långtslående kan sträcka ut ordentligt då fyra av par 5-hålen är möjliga att nå på två slag. Det kan behövas eftersom det är lätt att scoren drar iväg på par 4-hålen och par 3-hålen. Greenerna är mycket bra designade, ganska stora och kuperade och med riktigt besvärliga lutningar på några ställen. De är dessutom väl skyddade bakom bunkrar och kullar som gör det eftersträvansvärt med höga inspel. Arkitekten har lyckats bygga en behaglig bana som kräver all din skicklighet. Med en ny 9-hålsbana och en par 3-hålsbana samt utmärkta träningsmöjligheter är detta en suverän golfanläggning.

This excellent course has the reputation of being a fine championship test. This shouldn't deter mid-handicappers, who will have a lot of fun playing here, even though they might not be too proud of their card. Firstly, the clubhouse is a real picture, in an old 15th century castle. Then, the course itself mixes open holes with park-land and forest. And as water comes into play on seven holes, you could call this a complete course. Long-hitters can give it a real whack, probably reaching four of the par 5s in two and putting a few strokes in the bank in the process. They will need them on the par 3s and par 4s. The greens are well-designed, rather large and well contoured; some even have a number of very steep slopes. They are also well-guarded by bunkers and a series of mounds which call for high approach shots. The architect has succeeded in designing an enjoyable course, for which you will need all your skill and technique. A 9-hole course, a par 3 course and good practice facilities complete this great golfing complex.

Haninge Golfklubb — 1986

Årsta Slott
S - 136 91 HANINGE

Office	Sekretariat	(46) 08 - 500 328 58
Pro shop	Pro shop	(46) 08 - 500 328 55
Fax	Fax	(46) 08 - 500 328 51
Web	www.haningegk.se	
Situation	Läge	Stockholm, 30 km
Annual closure	Årlig stängning	no
Weekly closure	Daglig stängning	no

Fees main season Tariff hög säsong — Full day

	Week days / Veckodag	We/Bank holidays / Lör/Söndag/Helgdag
Individual Individuellt	SKr 360	SKr 420
Couple Par	SKr 720	SKr 840

Juniors: – 50%

Caddy	Caddie	no
Electric Trolley	El vagn	no
Buggy	Golfbil	no
Clubs	Klubbor	SKr 125 /18 holes

Credit cards Kredit kort
VISA - Eurocard - MasterCard

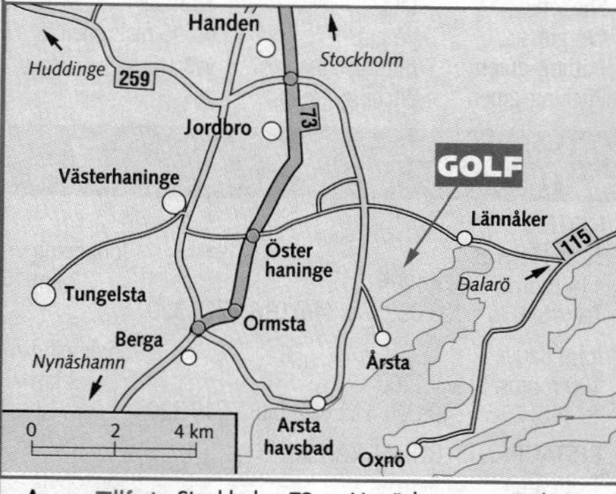

Access Tillfart : Stockholm, 73 → Nynäshamn. → Dalarö. → "Årsta Havsbad"
Map 2 on page 1207 Karta 2 se sid: 1207

Golf course — BANA — 16/20

Site	Läge	
Maintenance	Underhåll	
Architect	Arkitekt	Jan Sederholm
Type	Karaktär	forest, parkland
Relief	Nivåskillnader	
Water in play	Vatten på spelfältet	
Exp. to wind	Vindutsatt	
Trees in play	Träd på spelfältet	

Scorecard Scorekort	Chp. Back tees	Mens Herrtee	Ladies Damtee
Length Längd	6242	5874	5094
Par	73	73	73
Slope system	—	130	130

Advised golfing ability Rekommenderad spelnivå — 0 12 24 36

Hcp required Hcp erfordrad — 36

Club house & amenities — KLUBBHUS OCH OMGIVNING — 8/10

Pro shop	Pro shop	
Driving range	Träningsbana	
Sheltered	tåkt	2 mats
On grass	på gräs	yes
Putting-green	putting-green	yes (3)
Pitching-green	pitching-green	yes (2)

Hotel facilities — HOTELL OMGIVNING — 6/10

HOTELS

Grand Hotel, 307 rooms, D SKr 2700 — Stockholm 20 km
Tel (46) 08 - 679 3500, Fax (46) 08 - 611 8606

First Hotel Reisen, 144 rooms, D SKr 1895 — Stockholm 20 km
Tel (46) 08 - 223 260, Fax (46) 08 - 201 559

City Hotel Slöjdgatan — Stockholm 20 km
292 rooms, D SKr 1680
Tel (46) 08 - 723 72 00, Fax (46) 08 - 723 72 09

RESTAURANTS RESTAURANG

Paul and Norbert Tel (46) 08 - 661 72 36 — Stockholm
Franska Matsalen Tel (46) 08 - 679 3584 — Stockholm
Clas På Hörnet, Tel (46) 08 - 165 130 — Stockholm

JÖNKÖPING

16 | 7 | 7

Staden är en bra start för en resa runt Vättern, Sveriges näst största sjö, berömd för sitt kalla, klara och för all del stormiga vatten när vinden ligger på. Bara några minuter söder om staden ligger banan i en kuperad terräng med ett charmerande klubbhus i centrum. Den öppnades 1938 och är med dagens mått mätt ganska kort, och här kan faktiskt även vardagshackaren hoppas på att träffa parfyrorna på två slag. Problemet är att man sällan får ett rakt läge utan ständigt står i sluttningar. På så vis är Jönköping ingen lätt nöt att knäcka, framför allt som de flesta hinder finns runt de väldesignade och snabba greenerna. De spelare med bra teknik och ett smart huvud på axlarna har en stor fördel. Trevligt är också att alla spelare, oavsett skicklighet, kan spela med varandra och ha stort utbyte av rundan – vilket inte är så vanligt som man kanske tror. Jönköping är ett bra exempel på att längd faktiskt inte är allt.

This little town is the starting point for trips around the Vättern, Sweden's second largest lake known for its clear, cold and rough water when the wind blows. Just a few minutes to the south of the town, this 18-hole course is laid out over hilly terrain around a charming club house. Opened in 1938, today it might be considered very short, where even the average hacker can hope (repeat, hope) to hit the longest par 4s in two. But like everyone else, they won't often find flat lies from where to hit the next shot. In fact, Jönköpings is all the more dangerous because of its shortness; most of the difficulties lie on and around the greens, which are excellent and well-designed putting surfaces given unfailing protection by sand and other hazards. The wily technicians and players with brawn and brain in good working order will probably score better than the rest. Players of all abilities can happily play together, a fun factor that is less frequent than one might think. Jönköping is a fine example of a good course not necessarily having to be a long course.

Jönköpings Golfklubb — 1938

Kettilstorp
S - 556 27 JÖNKÖPING

Office	Sekretariat	(46) 036 - 765 67
Pro shop	Pro shop	(46) 036 - 763 90
Fax	Fax	(46) 036 - 765 11
Web	www.golf.se/jonkopingsgk	
Situation	Läge	Jönköping, 3 km
Annual closure	Årlig stängning	no
Weekly closure	Daglig stängning	no

1238

Fees main season Tariff hög säsong	Full day	
	Week days Veckodag	**We/Bank holidays** Lör/Söndag/Helgdag
Individual Individuellt	SKr 250	SKr 300
Couple Par	SKr 500	SKr 600

Juniors: – 50%

Caddy	Caddie	no
Electric Trolley	El vagn	no
Buggy	Golfbil	no
Clubs	Klubbor	SKr 100 /18 holes

Credit cards Kredit kort
VISA - Eurocard - MasterCard

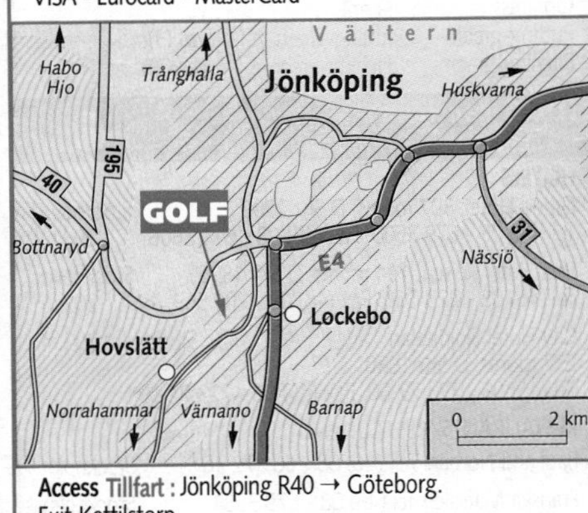

Access Tillfart : Jönköping R40 → Göteborg.
Exit Kettilstorp.
Map 1 on page 1204 Karta 1 se sid: 1204

Golf course — BANA — 16/20

Site	Läge	
Maintenance	Underhåll	
Architect	Arkitekt	F. Deyer
Type	Karaktär	parkland
Relief	Nivåskillnader	
Water in play	Vatten på spelfältet	
Exp. to wind	Vindutsatt	
Trees in play	Träd på spelfältet	

Scorecard Scorekort	**Chp.** Back tees	**Mens** Herrtee	**Ladies** Damtee
Length Längd	5564	5313	4717
Par	70	70	70
Slope system	—	123	123

Advised golfing ability Rekommenderad spelnivå — 0 12 24 36
Hcp required Hcp erfordrad — 30 Men, 30 Ladies

Club house & amenities — KLUBBHUS OCH OMGIVNING — 7/10

Pro shop	Pro shop	
Driving range	Träningsbana	
Sheltered	täkt	15 mats
On grass	på gräs	no, 15 mats open air
Putting-green	putting-green	yes
Pitching-green	pitching-green	yes

Hotel facilities — HOTELL OMGIVNING — 7/10

HOTELS

Stora Hotellet, — Jönköping 3 km
114 rooms, D SKr 1295
Tel (46) 036 - 100 000, Fax (46) 036 - 719 320

John Bauer, — Jönköping 3 km
100 rooms, D SKr 1200
Tel (46) 036 - 349 000, Fax (46) 036 - 719 320

RESTAURANTS RESTAURANG

Trottoaren — Jönköping 3 km
Tel (46) 036 - 100 000

Esters Restaurang — Jönköping 3 km
Tel (46) 036 - 349 000

KALMAR

15 | 5 | 8

Bron mellan Öland och Kalmar betyder numera att du kan spela Ekerum och Kalmar på samma dag, eller varför inte trycka in två rundor i Kalmar? Här finns nämligen två utmärkta banor. Mästerskapsbanan är resultatet av elva hål från den gamla banan, byggd 1947, och sju hål från den nya banan som öppnade 1992. Låt vara att många tyckte det var ett helgerån att blanda nytt och gammalt när så gjordes, men bortsett från några av de nya greenerna har det blivit en lyckad mix. Hålen smälter perfekt in i varandra. Från klubbbhuset tittar du ut över Östersjön, och på första hålet spelar du till och med över vattnet. Efter ettan får du vara beredd på att alla klubbor kommer i spel om du vill undvika hindrena, dit ett antal strategiskt placerade träd får räknas. På Kalmar gäller det att hålla sig borta från skogen. Av största betydelse är att tänka innan du slår och att använda dig av de resurser du har för dagen, en bra teknik skadar förstås inte heller. Eftersom de flesta hinder syns tydligt från tee får du leta efter en annan ursäkt för en misslyckad score!

The bridge between Öland and Kalmar now means you can play Ekerum and Kalmar in one summer's day, and maybe even squeeze in 36 holes in Kalmar. This championship course is in fact a mix of 11 holes from the old course, created in 1947, with seven holes from the new course opened in 1992. Some saw this as plain sacrilege, but you have to admit that the two go together well. Now, the holes blend into each other in a perfect match. The whole complex magnificently overlooks the Baltic and the first hole is in fact played over water. The rest of the programme calls for every club in your bag, if only to avoid the hazards, which include some very dangerous trees. Here more than usual, if you keep long and straight you will be literally out of the woods. Course management is vital using whatever resources you have on that particular day, and good golfing technique. As all the difficulties are clearly in view, you will have to find another excuse for a bad score.

Kalmar Golfklubb — 1947

Box 278
S - 391 23 KALMAR

Office	Sekretariat	(46) 0480 - 472 111
Pro shop	Pro shop	(46) 0480 - 472 049
Fax	Fax	(46) 0480 - 472 314
Web	www.golf.se/kalmargk	
Situation	Läge	Kalmar, 8 km
Annual closure	Årlig stängning	no
Weekly closure	Daglig stängning	no

Fees main season / Tariff hög säsong	Week days / Veckodag	We/Bank holidays / Lör/Söndag/Helgdag
	Full day	
Individual Individuellt	SKr 300	SKr 300
Couple Par	SKr 600	SKr 600

Special fees for juniors

Caddy	Caddie	no
Electric Trolley	El vagn	no
Buggy	Golfbil	SKr 150 /18 holes
Clubs	Klubbor	SKr 125 /18 holes

Credit cards Kredit kort
VISA - Eurocard - MasterCard - DC

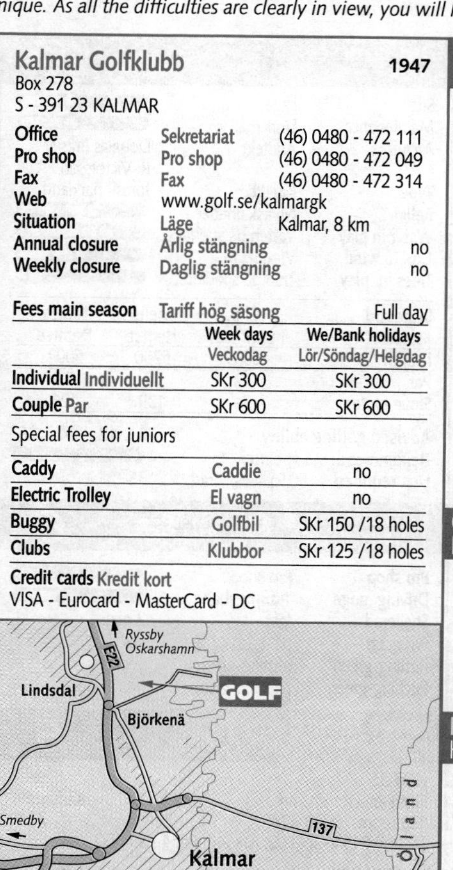

Access Tillfart : Kalmar E22 Exit Kalmar N/Lindsdal.
Map 1 on page 1205 Karta 1 se sid: 1205

Golf course BANA — 15/20

Site	Läge	
Maintenance	Underhåll	
Architect	Arkitekt	Sundblom/Gierdsjö Sköld/Sune Linde
Type	Karaktär	parkland
Relief	Nivåskillnader	
Water in play	Vatten på spelfältet	
Exp. to wind	Vindutsatt	
Trees in play	Träd på spelfältet	

Scorecard / Scorekort	Chp. / Back tees	Mens / Herrtee	Ladies / Damtee
Length Längd	6028	5685	4864
Par	72	72	72
Slope system	—	126	122

Advised golfing ability / Rekommenderad spelnivå: 0 12 24 36
Hcp required / Hcp erfordrad: 36

Club house & amenities KLUBBHUS OCH OMGIVNING — 5/10

Pro shop	Pro shop	
Driving range	Träningsbana	
Sheltered	tåkt	12 mats
On grass	på gräs	no, 7 mats open air
Putting-green	putting-green	yes
Pitching-green	pitching-green	yes

Hotel facilities HOTELL OMGIVNING — 8/10

HOTELS

Packhuset, 68 rooms, D SKr 1350 — Kalmar 8 km
Tel (46) 0480 - 570 00, Fax (46) 0480 - 866 42

Slottshotellet, 44 rooms, D SKr 1450 — Kalmar 8 km
Tel (46) 0480 - 882 60, Fax (46) 0480 - 882 66

Kalmarsund Hotell, 85 rooms, D SKr 1310 — Kalmar 8 km
Tel (46) 0480 - 181 00, Fax (46) 0480 - 411 337

RESTAURANTS RESTAURANG

Kalmar Hamnkrog, Tel (46) 0480 - 411 020 — Kalmar 8 km
Matisse, Tel (46) 0480 - 272 86 — Kalmar 8 km
Källaren Kronan, Tel (46) 0480 - 411 400 — Kalmar 8 km

KARLSHAMN

14 | 6 | 6

Detta är en historisk region, som har sett allt från en rysk ubåt stranda på klipporna till en 26 kilo tung lax fångas i Mörrum. Banan är utlagd genom tät skog där det inte finns några som helst flyktvägar att hoppas på. Hemligheten är att ignorera träden, för faktum är att fairways är bredare än vad de verkar. Hur som helst, det har sin charm att rädda sig ur skogen, och det är även möjligt då ett stort arbete har lagts ned på att rensa undervegetationen. Nåväl, för den mer klaustrofobiske och snedslående golfaren är kanske inte "charm" det rätta ordet. Han kommer att få det svårt att slappna av och njuta av spelet. Men det är heller ingen idé att vara överdrivet försiktig från tee eftersom detta bara leder till långa andraslag in mot greener som på sina ställen vaktas av djupa och rymningssäkra bunkrar. Greenerna har också sin historia: Många är upphöjda eller ligger precis intill sluttningar vilket kräver ett taktiskt sinne då det inte alltid går att rulla in bollen. Det sägs att efter en runda här så drömmer du i veckor om stora, vackra träd.

An historical region, where a Russian submarine once came to grief on the rocks just off the coast and where a 55 lb. salmon was caught, close to Mörrum, one of the great fishery centres that are so important to Swedish gastronomy. The golf course was laid out through a forest, from which there is no escaping on virtually every hole. The secret is to try to ignore it, as the fairways are wider than they look. And anyway, it's such fun hitting little recovery shots from out of the trees because the undergrowth has been thoroughly cleared. Fun might not be the word for the more claustrophobic golfer or wayward hitter, as they will find it hard to relax and really hit the ball here. Being over-careful off the tee will often lead to a very long second shot, which will have to avoid some deep and distinctly inescapable greenside bunkers. The greens, last but not least, are often elevated or at the bottom of a hill; this calls for careful thinking and often rules out the bump and run shot. They say that after playing here you spend the next few weeks dreaming about big beautiful trees.

Karlshamns Golfklubb — 1966

Box 188
S - 374 23 KARLSHAMN

Office	Sekretariat	(46) 0454 - 500 85
Pro shop	Pro shop	(46) 0454 - 541 41
Fax	Fax	(46) 0454 - 501 60
Web	www.golf.se/karlshamnsgk	
Situation	Läge	Karlshamn, 7 km
Annual closure	Årlig stängning	no
Weekly closure	Daglig stängning	no

Fees main season Tariff hög säsong		18 holes
	Week days Veckodag	**We/Bank holidays** Lör/Söndag/Helgdag
Individual Individuellt	SKr 220	SKr 250
Couple Par	SKr 440	SKr 500

Special fees for juniors

Caddy	Caddie	no
Electric Trolley	El vagn	no
Buggy	Golfbil	no
Clubs	Klubbor	SKr 150 /18 holes

Credit cards Kredit kort
VISA - Eurocard - MasterCard

Svängsta
126
29
Torarp
GOLF
Asarum
Mörrum
Ronneby
E22
Karlshamn
Pukavik
Elleholm
0 2 4 km

Access Tillfart : Karlshamn E22 → Kristianstad. Mörrum, R29. Golf north of Mörrum.
Map 1 on page 1205 Karta 1 se sid: 1205

Golf course — BANA — 14/20

Site	Läge	
Maintenance	Underhåll	
Architect	Arkitekt	Douglas Brasier R. Victorsson
Type	Karaktär	forest, parkland
Relief	Nivåskillnader	
Water in play	Vatten på spelfältet	
Exp. to wind	Vindutsatt	
Trees in play	Träd på spelfältet	

Scorecard Scorekort	**Chp.** Back tees	**Mens** Herrtee	**Ladies** Damtee
Length Längd	6039	5750	5002
Par	72	72	72
Slope system	—	139	126

Advised golfing ability 0 12 24 36
Rekommenderad spelnivå
Hcp required Hcp erfordrad 36

Club house & amenities — KLUBBHUS OCH OMGIVNING — 6/10

Pro shop	Pro shop	
Driving range	Träningsbana	
Sheltered	tåkt	2 mats
On grass	på gräs	yes
Putting-green	putting-green	yes
Pitching-green	pitching-green	no

Hotel facilities — HOTELL OMGIVNING — 6/10

HOTELS

First Hotel Karlshamn — Karlshamn 7 km
132 rooms, D SKr 1285
Tel (46) 0454 - 890 00, Fax (46) 0454 - 891 50

Scandic Hotel — Karlshamn 10 km
9 rooms, D SKr 1322
Tel (46) 0454 -166 60, Fax (46) 0454 - 186 66

RESTAURANTS RESTAURANG

Lord Nelson, Tel (46) 0454 - 845 35 — Karlshamn 7 km
Loch Ness, Tel (46) 0454 - 126 00 — Karlshamn 7 km
Gourmet Grön, Tel (46) 0454 - 164 40 — Karlshamn 7 km

KARLSTAD

15 | 6 | 6

Detta är i hjärtat av Värmland – ett landskap av skogar, forsar, sjöar, små bondgårdar och härliga måltider. Det var också hemvist för Selma Lagerlöf, författaren till Nils Holgerssons underbara resor, som är en underbar hyllning till Sverige. Lagerlöfs hus ligger mindre än en timmes resa från banan, som vindlar genom lummig skog och är en njutning för den som gillar vildmarksliv, något som kan skänka tröst åt den som olyckligtvis inte har någon av sina bästa dagar, vilket är lätt hänt här om man inte driver bollen bra från tee. Banan är mycket lång, och på vår och höst är den ofta blöt och tung. Då är många av par 4-hålen svåra att nå även för den bättre spelaren. Men Karlstad är inte bara skog, det finns också relativt öppna partier, vilket vi är tacksamma för. Flertalet av greenerna är dock väldigt svårlästa, och troligen är banan relativt sett svårare för låghandicaparen än för höghandicaparen som inte behöver träffa varje green på rätt antal slag. Om du kan låta bli att stressa upp dig över resultatet så får du en ljuvlig och avslappnad dag på en bana som på ett väldigt fint sätt smälter in i omgivningarna. Och varför inte ta en lektion av Henry Reis, Annika Sörenstams tränare...?

This is the capital of Värmland, a landscape of forests, streams, lakes, small farms and rich food (sausage, roast pork with oat mash). It is also the region of Selma Lagerlöf, the author of The Travels of Nils Holgersson, an ode to Sweden. Karlstad runs through a forest and is a real treat for lovers of wildlife, which can offer some solace and compensation for the disappointing score they might have to settle for here, unless they are hitting their driver really well. The course is very long, wet outside summer, and some of the par 4s are hard to reach, even for the better player. Yet its openness works in its favour, despite a number of greens that are difficult to read. In actual fact, the lower handicap golfer is more likely to suffer here than the lesser golfers, who can easily put up with not hitting greens in regulation. If you can keep your mind off worrying about carding a good score, you can relax, enjoy a great round. And take a lesson with the headpro, Henri Reis, Annika Sorenstam' teacher.

Karlstad Golfklubb — 1958

Höja 510
S - 655 92 KARLSTAD

Office	Sekretariat	(46) 054 - 86 6 353
Pro shop	Pro shop	(46) 054 - 866 270
Fax	Fax	(46) 054 - 866 478
Web	www.golf.se/karlstadgk	
Situation	Läge	Karlstad, 8 km
Annual closure	Årlig stängning	no
Weekly closure	Daglig stängning	no

Fees main season Tariff hög säsong	Week days Veckodag	We/Bank holidays Lör/Söndag/Helgdag (Full day)
Individual Individuellt	SKr 250	SKr 250
Couple Par	SKr 500	SKr 500

Juniors: – 50%

Caddy	Caddie	no
Electric Trolley	El vagn	no
Buggy	Golfbil	SKr 150 /18 holes
Clubs	Klubbor	SKr 150 /18 holes

Credit cards Kredit kort
VISA - Eurocard - MasterCard - DC

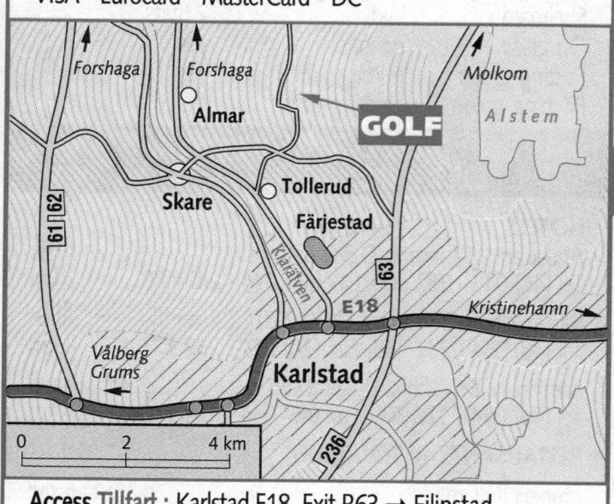

Access Tillfart : Karlstad E18. Exit R63 → Filipstad. 4 km → Golf
Map 2 on page 1206 Karta 2 se sid: 1206

Golf course — BANA — 15/20

Site	Läge	
Maintenance	Underhåll	
Architect	Arkitekt	Nils Sköld, Sune Linde
Type	Karaktär	forest, parkland
Relief	Nivåskillnader	
Water in play	Vatten på spelfältet	
Exp. to wind	Vindutsatt	
Trees in play	Träd på spelfältet	

Scorecard Scorekort	Chp. Back tees	Mens Herrtee	Ladies Damtee
Length Längd	6215	5985	5060
Par	72	72	72
Slope system	—	131	130

Advised golfing ability Rekommenderad spelnivå — 0 12 24 36
Hcp required Hcp erfordrad — 36

Club house & amenities — KLUBBHUS OCH OMGIVNING — 6/10

Pro shop	Pro shop	
Driving range	Träningsbana	
Sheltered	täkt	8 mats
On grass	på gräs	yes
Putting-green	putting-green	yes
Pitching-green	pitching-green	yes

Hotel facilities — HOTELL OMGIVNING — 6/10

HOTELS

Plaza Hotel — Karlstad 5 km
121 rooms, D SKr 1385
Tel (46) 054 - 100 200, Fax (46) 054 - 100 224

Stadshotellet — Karlstad 6 km
139 rooms, D SKr 1250
Tel (46) 054 - 293 000, Fax (46) 054 - 293 031

RESTAURANTS RESTAURANG

Tiffany — Karlstad 7 km
Tel (46) 054 - 153 388

Vivaldi — Karlstad 5 km
Tel (46) 054 - 100 200

KRISTIANSTAD

17 | 7 | 7

I Skåne känner du omedelbart impulserna från Danmark, vilket är rätt logiskt med tanke på hur länge landskapet tillhörde danskarna. Det var ju inte förrän i början av 1800-talet som Skåne en gång för alla blev svenskt och Sverige fick sin naturliga kustlinje. Detta är jordbruksland i ett långsamt böljande landskap, och den topografin återspeglar sig också i banan. Kristianstad ligger inte långt från havet – sandjorden och layouten påminner också om en linksbana, fast i själva verket befinner vi oss i ett parklandskap. Många greener närmar man sig bäst med låga rullslag, framför allt de dagar när vinden ligger på. Banan ändrar gång på gång karaktär, såväl visuellt som rent strategiskt. Ibland är den vänlig, ibland direkt fientlig. Nyckelhålen är 14-16 – massor med vatten kommer i spel och en otålig själ riskerar att bestraffas hårt. De här hindrena ska dock inte hindra höghandicaparen från att spela här. Banan genomgick för några år sedan en omfattande renovering, och utan tvekan till det bättre. Den är nu en av de konditionsmässigt bästa banorna i Sverige.

Scania (Skåne) is the Swedish south, where there is a definite Danish influence, a logical enough state of affairs when you realize that Denmark only granted Sweden its natural maritime frontier in the early 18th century. Here, we are in farming country in a landscape of gently rolling valleys, and this course reflects the same topology. Located not far from the sea, the sandy soil and layout are reminiscent of a links course, although in reality the setting is one large park. The grass is wonderful and many of the greens can be reached with low running shots, a considerable advantage given how windy it can be here. The course changes faces time and time again, both visually and strategically, now friendly, now distinctly hostile. The key holes are 14 through 16, spectacular numbers with a lot of water where impatience can cost you dearly. These difficulties, however, should not prevent the higher-handicap golfers from playing here and rubbing shoulders with the better players. The course has been restyled a few years ago, for the better. This is now one of the best kept courses in Sweden.

1242

Kristianstads Golfklubb — 1924

Box 41
S - 296 21 ÅHUS

Office	Sekretariat	(46) 044 - 247 656
Pro shop	Pro shop	(46) 044 - 247 429
Fax	Fax	(46) 044 - 247 635
Web	www.kristianstadsgk.com	
Situation	Läge	Kristianstad, 18 km
Annual closure	Årlig stängning	no
Weekly closure	Daglig stängning	no

Fees main season Tariff hög säsong	Full day	
	Week days Veckodag	**We/Bank holidays** Lör/Söndag/Helgdag
Individual Individuellt	SKr 280	SKr 280
Couple Par	SKr 560	SKr 560

Juniors: – 50 %

Caddy	Caddie	no
Electric Trolley	El vagn	no
Buggy	Golfbil	SKr 100 /18 holes
Clubs	Klubbor	SKr 100 /18 holes

Credit cards Kredit kort
VISA - Eurocard - MasterCard - DC - AMEX

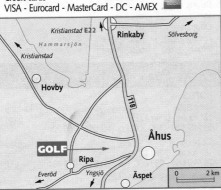

Kristianstad E22
Rinkaby
Sölvesborg
Hammarsjön
Kristianstad
Hovby
118
Åhus
GOLF
Ripa
Everöd
Yngsjö
Äspet
0 2 km

Access Tillfart : Malmö, E22 → Kristianstad. 118 → Åhus. Rondell i Åhus → Golf

Map 1 on page 1204 Karta 1 se sid: 1204

Golf course BANA — 17/20

Site	Läge	
Maintenance	Underhåll	
Architect	Arkitekt	Douglas Brasier Tommy Nordström
Type	Karaktär	parkland, open country
Relief	Nivåskillnader	
Water in play	Vatten på spelfältet	
Exp. to wind	Vindutsatt	
Trees in play	Träd på spelfältet	

Scorecard Scorekort	**Chp.** Back tees	**Mens** Herrtee	**Ladies** Damtee
Length Längd	6046	5675	4940
Par	71	71	71
Slope system	—	123	123

Advised golfing ability Rekommenderad spelnivå — 0 12 24 36

Hcp required Hcp erfordrad — 36

Club house & amenities KLUBBHUS OCH OMGIVNING — 7/10

Pro shop	Pro shop	
Driving range	Träningsbana	
Sheltered	täkt	2 mats
On grass	på gräs	yes
Putting-green	putting-green	yes
Pitching-green	pitching-green	yes

Hotel facilities HOTELL OMGIVNING — 7/10

HOTELS

Åhustrand, 57 rooms, D SKr 650 — Åhus
Tel (46) 044 - 289 300, Fax (46) 044 - 249 480 — 3 km

Kastanjelund, 24 rooms, D SKr 720 — Åhus
Tel (46) 044 - 232 533, Fax (46) 044 - 232 177 — 6 km

Kristian IV, 86 rooms, D SEK 1385 — Kristianstad
Tel (46) 044 - 126 300, Fax (46) 044 - 124 140 — 14 km

RESTAURANTS RESTAURANG

Kippers Källare — Kristianstad
Tel (46) 044 - 106 200 — 14 km

Kung Kristian — Kristianstad
Tel (46) 044 - 210 034 — 14 km

KUNGSBACKA

15 | 6 | 6

Banan öppnade 1974, arkitekten heter Frank Pennink, och det finns ingen som helst anledning varför du skulle spela dåligt här, inte med tanke på att här finns ett magnifikt övningsfält, tre puttinggreener och fyra pitchinggreener... Men, men – banan är en sällsynt tuff nöt att knäcka, Först och främst måste du lära dig att växla mellan olika typer av golf. Till en början spelar vi i ett parklandskap, sedan övergår det till golf med seasidekänsla och därefter golf i tät, ogenomtränglig skog. Den trånga avslutningen där vinden torkar upp greenerna och gör dem hårda är en alldeles egen historia, inte minst med tanke på hur svårt det är att få bollen att stanna kvar på det finklippta. Svårigheten ligger alltså i att ställa om från att ha försökt lura vinden med låga slag till att spela klassisk målgolf med höga slag. Detta är ett riktigt nervtest! Två nya bäckar gör det alls inte lättare. För höghandicaparen kan det bli lite väl mycket av det goda, om han nu inte förmår att ta det med jämnmod och inse att han ännu har mycket att lära. Har han den distansen kan han mycket väl spela Kungsbacka.

There is no reason why you should play badly here, after all there is a huge driving range, three putting greens and four pitching greens to practice on. No reason that is, except for the course itself. Firstly you have to adjust to some abrupt changes of surroundings, from parkland to seaboard to forest. You start off over wide open space and end up down a narrow strait where the wind can twist and turn, dry the greens and make those approach shots even tougher. From the roll-on shots by the sea you then have to change modes to target golf. For the nerves, nothing is simple here, especially since the last section of the course is the most demanding. This is a tough proposition for high-handicappers, who will be hard pushed to keep up with the better players, and two new creeks does not make it any easier, though. Yet if they can take it like a man and realize willingly that they still have much to learn, then there's no reason why they should not play a round or two here.

Kungsbacka Golfklubb — 1974

Hamra Gård 515
S - 429 44 SÄRÖ

Office	Sekretariat	(46) 031 - 936 171
Pro shop	Pro shop	(46) 031 - 936 279
Fax	Fax	(46) 031 - 935 085
Web	www.kbgk.org	
Situation	Läge	Göteborg, 25 km
Annual closure	Årlig stängning	no
Weekly closure	Daglig stängning	no

Fees main season Tariff hög säsong	**Week days** Veckodag	**We/Bank holidays** Lör/Söndag/Helgdag
		18 holes
Individual Individuellt	SKr 250	SKr 300
Couple Par	SKr 500	SKr 600

Juniors: – 50%

Caddy	Caddie	no
Electric Trolley	El vagn	no
Buggy	Golfbil	SKr 200 /18 holes
Clubs	Klubbor	SKr 150 /18 holes

Credit cards Kredit kort
VISA - Eurocard - MasterCard

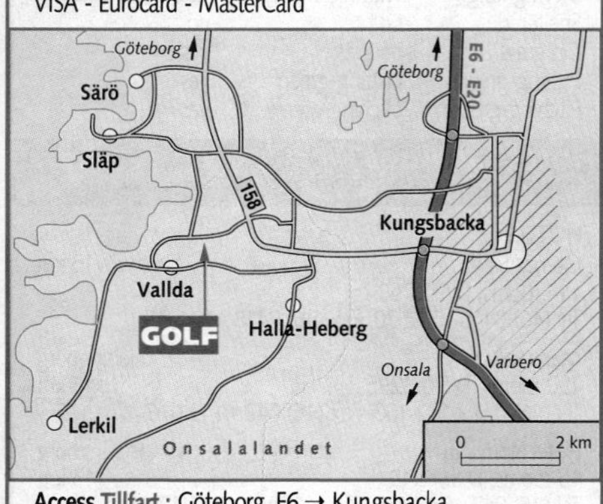

Access Tillfart : Göteborg, E6 → Kungsbacka. Exit 60 → Särö. 7 km → Golf
Map 1 on page 1204 Karta 1 se sid: 1204

Golf course — BANA — 15/20

Site	Läge	
Maintenance	Underhåll	
Architect	Arkitekt	Frank Pennink
Type	Karaktär	seaside course, parkland
Relief	Nivåskillnader	
Water in play	Vatten på spelfältet	
Exp. to wind	Vindutsatt	
Trees in play	Träd på spelfältet	

Scorecard Scorekort	**Chp.** Back tees	**Mens** Herrtee	**Ladies** Damtee
Length Längd	6096	5831	5030
Par	72	72	72
Slope system	—	137	136

Advised golfing ability Rekommenderad spelnivå — 0 12 24 36
Hcp required Hcp erfordrad 36

Club house & amenities — KLUBBHUS OCH OMGIVNING — 6/10

Pro shop	Pro shop	
Driving range	Träningsbana	
Sheltered	tåkt	8 mats
On grass	på gräs	no, 22 mats open air
Putting-green	putting-green	ja
Pitching-green	pitching-green	ja

Hotel facilities — HOTELL OMGIVNING — 6/10

HOTELS

Säröhus, 83 rooms, D SKr 1095 — Särö
Tel (46) 031 - 936 090, Fax (46) 031 - 936 185 — 4 km

Hotell Holland, 30 rooms, D SKr 1050 — Kungsbacka
Tel (46) 0300 - 775 30, Fax (46) 0300 - 162 25 — 12 km

Hotell Nattmösan, 20 rooms, D SKr 850 — Kungsbacka
Tel (46) 0300 - 775 30, Fax (46) 0300 - 162 25 — 10 km

RESTAURANTS RESTAURANG

Hotell Holland, Tel (46) 0300 - 775 30 — Kungsbacka 12 km
Pio Pepe, Tel (46) 0300 - 199 04 — Kungsbacka 11 km
Kliv in Kök & Bar, Tel (46) 0300 - 199 04 — Kungsbacka

LANDSKRONA Gul Bana

15 | 9 | 7

Ture Bruce och Åke Persson har designat ett antal banor tillsammans, inklusive Landskrona som är en av deras senare skapelser. Från det att du anländer så trivs du här, med klubbhuset, restaurangen och omklädningsrummen i den gamla gården. Här finns också ett golfmuseum. Mångfalden fortsätter ute på banan, som växlar mellan parklandskap och seaside och en härlig utsikt över Öresund. Men Landskrona är inte bara vacker, den är också en läcker bana att spela som från första till sista hålet överraskar dig. Den är inte så svår, men vinden kan göra det besvärligt och den är definitivt inte så kort som du först förleds att tro. Lyckligtvis är layouten ganska öppen, men du måste vara försiktig så du inte hamnar i någon av de många fairwaybunkrarna eller den tuffa ruffen som brukar dra till sig missriktade drives. För att ta dig runt banan måste du fatta vettiga beslut, framför allt runt greenen. Detta är en bana för alla, men den premierar den tänkande golfaren.

Ture Bruce and Åke Persson have designed any number of courses in Sweden, including this, one of their most recent achievements. Things look good the moment you arrive here, with the club-house, restaurant and locker-rooms laid out inside old farm-buildings. There is also a golf museum. This is all the diversity of golf, which as it happens continues out on the course with park-land and inland styles alternating with seaside landscapes and views over the Öresund. Yet Landskrona is not only great to look at, it is also great to play, with a course that grabs you and amazes throughout. It is not all that difficult, but the wind can make it tricky and suddenly seem not as short as you thought. Fortunately the layout is very open with hazards clear to see, but you will need to be especially careful to avoid the fairway bunkers and rough, which is tough enough for wayward drivers to spend most of the day there. On the technical side, you need an all-round game and be able to go for the right option, especially with your short game. A course for everyone, especially golfers who can keep a clear mind.

Landskrona GK — 1962

Erikstorp
S - 261 61 LANDSKRONA

Office	Sekretariat	(46) 0418 - 446 260
Pro shop	Pro shop	(46) 0418 - 159 75
Fax	Fax	(46) 0418 - 446 262
Web	www.golf.se/landskronagk	
Situation	Läge	Landskrona, 3 km
Annual closure	Årlig stängning	no
Weekly closure	Daglig stängning	no

Fees main season Tariff hög säsong	18 holes	
	Week days Veckodag	**We/Bank holidays** Lör/Söndag/Helgdag
Individual Individuellt	SKr 220	SKr 260
Couple Par	SKr 440	SKr 520

Caddy	Caddie	no
Electric Trolley	El vagn	no
Buggy	Golfbil	no
Clubs	Klubbor	no

Credit cards Kredit kort
VISA - Eurocard - MasterCard

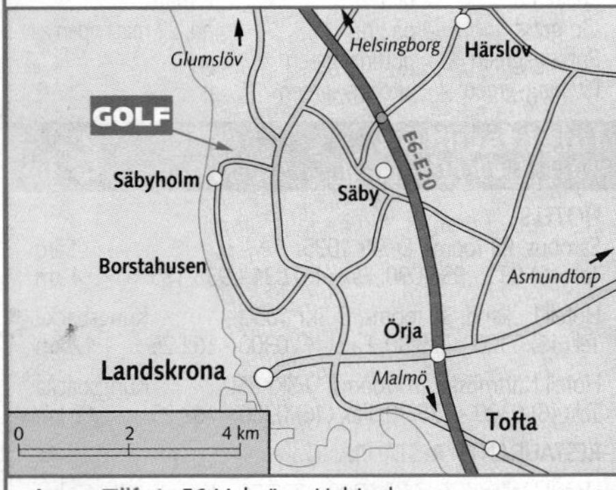

Access Tillfart : E6 Malmö → Helsingborg, Exit Landskrona N., → Borstahusen
Map 1 on page 1204 Karta 1 se sid: 1204

Golf course BANA — 15/20

Site	Läge	
Maintenance	Underhåll	
Architect	Arkitekt	Ture Bruce Åke Persson
Type	Karaktär	seaside course, parkland
Relief	Nivåskillnader	
Water in play	Vatten på spelfältet	
Exp. to wind	Vindutsatt	
Trees in play	Träd på spelfältet	

Scorecard Scorekort	**Chp.** Back tees	**Mens** Herrtee	**Ladies** Damtee
Length Längd	5730	5585	4850
Par	71	71	71
Slope system	—	123	123

Advised golfing ability Rekommenderad spelnivå — 0 12 24 36
Hcp required Hcp erfordrad 36

Club house & amenities KLUBBHUS OCH OMGIVNING — 9/10

Pro shop	Pro shop	
Driving range	Träningsbana	
Sheltered	tåkt	no
On grass	på gräs	yes
Putting-green	putting-green	yes
Pitching-green	pitching-green	yes

Hotel facilities HOTELL OMGIVNING — 7/10

HOTELS

Örenäs Slott, — Glumslöv 15 km
114 rooms, D SKr 750
Tel (46) 0418 - 702 30, Fax (46) 0418 - 731 81

Marina Plaza — Helsingborg 15 km
190 rooms, D SKr 1295
Tel (46) 042 - 192 100, Fax (46) 042 - 149 616

Hotel Nouveau — Helsingborg 15 km
15 rooms, D SKr 945
Tel (46) 042 - 347 420, Fax (46) 042 - 347 431

RESTAURANTS RESTAURANG

Oskar Trapp, Tel (46) 042 - 146 044 — Helsingborg 15 km

LJUNGHUSEN

18 | 7 | 7

Några tips innan du slår ut: När du begraver bollen i tjock ljung (vilket du kommer att göra), så försök att ta dig därifrån så fort som möjligt, även om detta innebär att du bara hackar bollen några meter till höger eller vänster. En annan sak: När du har en nedförsputt i medvind så behöver du...äsch, glöm det! För att scora väl på den här banan måste du ha stor fantasi och hela tiden befinna dig på rätt sida om flaggan. På den här typen av seaside-bana räcker det alltså inte med att ha tränat som en galning på övningsfältet. Här krävs andra kunskaper! Du måste kunna manövrera bollen åt bägge hållen. På sätt och vis är detta klassisk linksgolf, även om du inte kommer se några gigantiska sandklitter som du kan göra på Irland. Vad som däremot finns här är ljung – tjock och ogenomtränglig på sommaren. Därför verkar också fairways från utslagsplatserna vara löjligt smala. Men detta är faktiskt inte riktigt sant, och spelare av alla skicklighetsgrader verkligen ha ett fint utbyte av en runda här. I varje fall så länge som du är villig att eftertänksamt ta dig an varje slag, ett i taget. En del tycker till och med att banan är bättre än närbelägna Falsterbo.

When (not if) you bury your ball in the heather (and you will), get back into the fairway at all costs, even if it means hacking the ball just a couple of yards. When faced with a downhill putt with the wind behind you, well, forget it. To score well, you must be on the right side of the pin and show creativity from tee to green. On this kind of seaside course, the standard shots you learn at practice are not enough. You have to bend that ball in every direction. You won't find the spectacular sights of huge Irish-style dunes here, but you will be confronted with each and every feature of links play. With the addition of heather, you get the impression from the tee-box that the fairways are ridiculously narrow. This is not really true, as Ljunghusens is a course for golfers of all abilities, as long as they review their strategy at each shot. Your reward will be to contemplate with a positive eye this huge stretch of purple, yellow and green, which really comes to life in the summer twilight. Some consider this course even better than nearby Falsterbo.

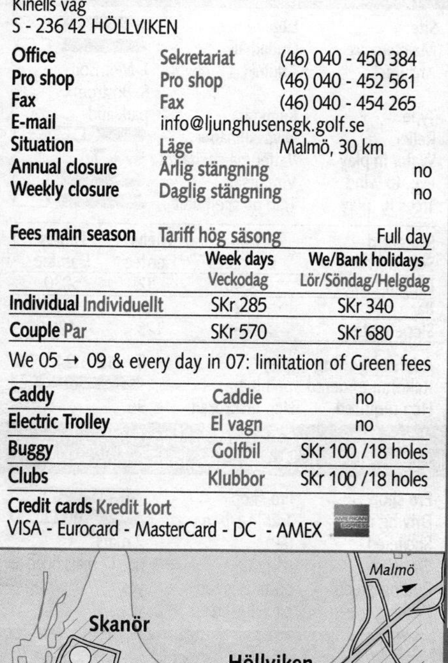

Ljunghusens Golfklubb — 1932

Kinells väg
S - 236 42 HÖLLVIKEN

Office	Sekretariat	(46) 040 - 450 384
Pro shop	Pro shop	(46) 040 - 452 561
Fax	Fax	(46) 040 - 454 265
E-mail	info@ljunghusensgk.golf.se	
Situation	Läge	Malmö, 30 km
Annual closure	Årlig stängning	no
Weekly closure	Daglig stängning	no

Fees main season Tariff hög säsong	Full day	
	Week days Veckodag	**We/Bank holidays** Lör/Söndag/Helgdag
Individual Individuellt	SKr 285	SKr 340
Couple Par	SKr 570	SKr 680

We 05 → 09 & every day in 07: limitation of Green fees

Caddy	Caddie	no
Electric Trolley	El vagn	no
Buggy	Golfbil	SKr 100 /18 holes
Clubs	Klubbor	SKr 100 /18 holes

Credit cards Kredit kort
VISA - Eurocard - MasterCard - DC - AMEX

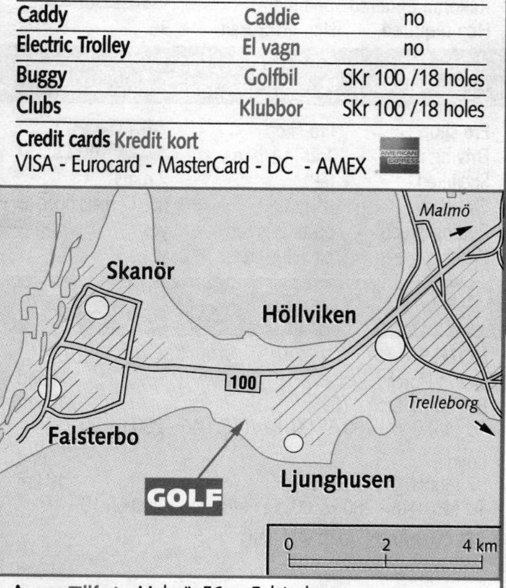

Access Tillfart : Malmö: E6 → Falsterbo.
Map 1 on page 1204 Karta 1 se sid: 1204

Golf course — BANA — 18/20

Site	Läge	
Maintenance	Underhåll	
Architect	Arkitekt	Douglas Brasier
Type	Karaktär	seaside course
Relief	Nivåskillnader	
Water in play	Vatten på spelfältet	
Exp. to wind	Vindutsatt	
Trees in play	Träd på spelfältet	

Scorecard Scorekort	**Chp.** Back tees	**Mens** Herrtee	**Ladies** Damtee
Length Längd	6115	5895	5120
Par	72	72	72
Slope system	—	131	131

Advised golfing ability 0 12 24 36
Rekommenderad spelnivå
Hcp required Hcp erfordrad 36

Club house & amenities — KLUBBHUS OCH OMGIVNING — 7/10

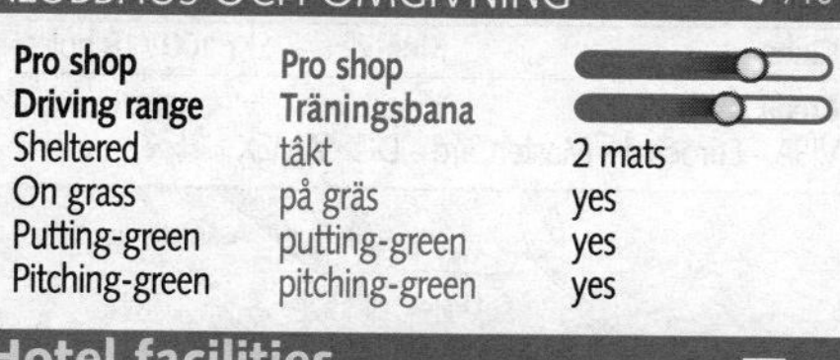

Pro shop	Pro shop	
Driving range	Träningsbana	
Sheltered	tåkt	2 mats
On grass	på gräs	yes
Putting-green	putting-green	yes
Pitching-green	pitching-green	yes

Hotel facilities — HOTELL OMGIVNING — 7/10

HOTELS

Hotell Gässlingen — Skanör 8 km
13 rooms, D SKr 1300
Tel (46) 040 - 459 100, Fax (46) 040 - 359 113

Hotell Spelabäcken — Skanör 6 km
18 rooms, D SKr 850
Tel (46) 040 - 475 300, Fax (46) 040 - 473 242

RESTAURANTS RESTAURANG

Skänors Gästgiveri — Skanör 10 km
Tel (46) 040 - 475 690

Vellinge Gästgiveri, Tel (46) 040 - 424 865 — Vellinge 15 km

Kaptensgården, Tel (46) 040 - 470 750 — Falsterbo 1 km

LUNDS AKADEMISKA

16 | 7 | 5

Lund är en härlig plats att besöka, bubblande av liv, vilket kanske inte är så konstigt med tanke på att det är Sveriges näst största universitetsstad. Ett av många utflyktsmål vi rekommenderar att besöka är den stora domkyrkan. Några kilometer österut frånn själva staden ligger i en nationalpark en bana ritad 1936 av Morrison, vars namn är förknippat med många av Europas bästa banor. Under sommaren växer ruffen tjock och vild, och straffar sneda drives obarmhärtigt. Första nio är som en vandring genom en lummig park. Andra nio ligger öppnare och är svårare. Helt logiskt kommer banans klimax i avslutningen. På hålen 16-18 förenar sig ruffen, vattnet och skogen i ett gemensamt försök att förstöra din score. Om du klarar detta så kan du spela var som helst! Alla älskar den här charmerande platsen, men det är troligen en utmaning som uppskattas mer av den bättre spelaren.

Lund is a very pleasant, bustling place and Sweden second's largest university city. Art-lovers should make a point of visiting the Romanesque cathedral and the astronomical clock with automatons. Several miles to the east lies a national park and a golf course designed in 1936 by Morrison, whose name is linked with many of the top courses in Europe. Here in summer, the rough grows high and thick and punishes wild driving unrelentlessly. The outward nine are like a walk through a huge tree-strewn park, the back nine are laid out over more open space, but are tougher to play. Quite logically the climax comes over the finishing holes, 16 through 18, where water, rough and trees join forces to ruin your card. If you can resist this treatment, you can play just about everywhere. Everyone loves this spot, it's so charming, but it is a challenge that is probably better appreciated and accepted by the more proficient players.

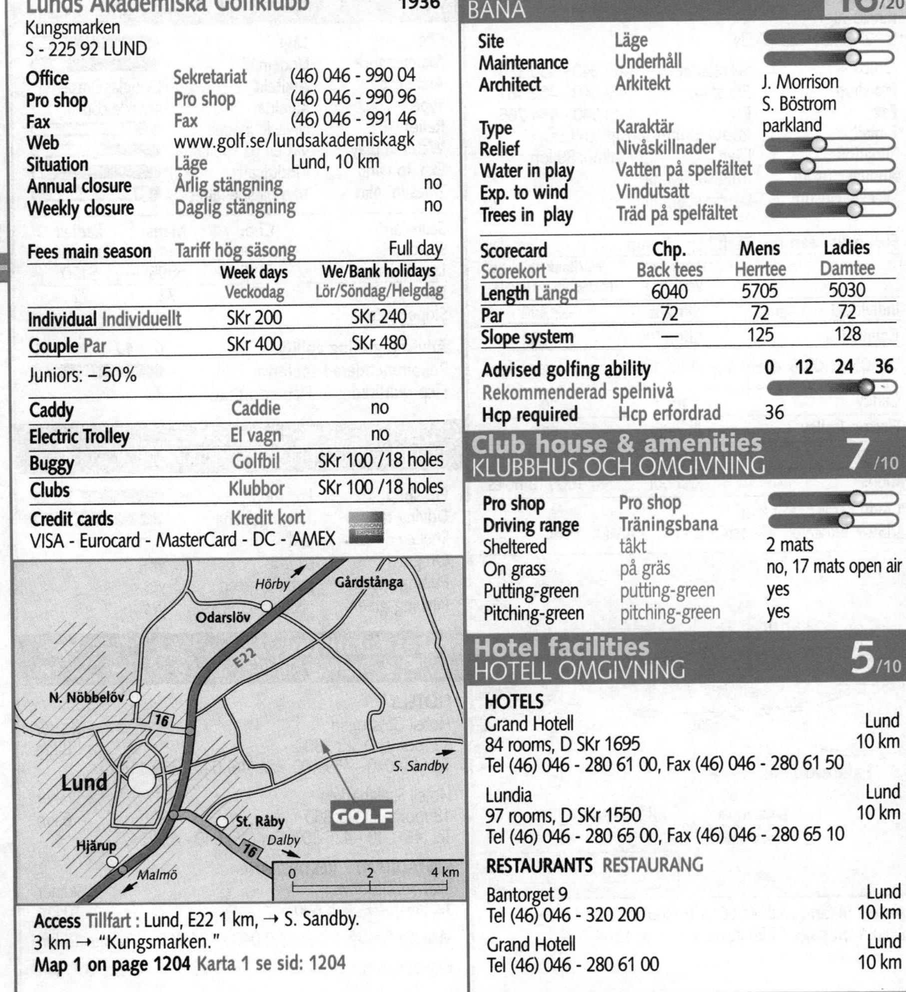

Lunds Akademiska Golfklubb — 1936

Kungsmarken
S - 225 92 LUND

Office	Sekretariat	(46) 046 - 990 04
Pro shop	Pro shop	(46) 046 - 990 96
Fax	Fax	(46) 046 - 991 46
Web		www.golf.se/lundsakademiskagk
Situation	Läge	Lund, 10 km
Annual closure	Årlig stängning	no
Weekly closure	Daglig stängning	no

Fees main season / Tariff hög säsong	Week days / Veckodag	We/Bank holidays / Lör/Söndag/Helgdag
	Full day	
Individual Individuellt	SKr 200	SKr 240
Couple Par	SKr 400	SKr 480

Juniors: – 50%

Caddy	Caddie	no
Electric Trolley	El vagn	no
Buggy	Golfbil	SKr 100 /18 holes
Clubs	Klubbor	SKr 100 /18 holes

Credit cards — Kredit kort
VISA - Eurocard - MasterCard - DC - AMEX

Access Tillfart : Lund, E22 1 km, → S. Sandby. 3 km → "Kungsmarken."
Map 1 on page 1204 Karta 1 se sid: 1204

Golf course — BANA — 16/20

Site	Läge	
Maintenance	Underhåll	
Architect	Arkitekt	J. Morrison, S. Böstrom
Type	Karaktär	parkland
Relief	Nivåskillnader	
Water in play	Vatten på spelfältet	
Exp. to wind	Vindutsatt	
Trees in play	Träd på spelfältet	

Scorecard / Scorekort	Chp. / Back tees	Mens / Herrtee	Ladies / Damtee
Length Längd	6040	5705	5030
Par	72	72	72
Slope system	—	125	128

Advised golfing ability / Rekommenderad spelnivå: 0 12 24 36
Hcp required / Hcp erfordrad: 36

Club house & amenities — KLUBBHUS OCH OMGIVNING — 7/10

Pro shop	Pro shop	
Driving range	Träningsbana	
Sheltered	tåkt	2 mats
On grass	på gräs	no, 17 mats open air
Putting-green	putting-green	yes
Pitching-green	pitching-green	yes

Hotel facilities — HOTELL OMGIVNING — 5/10

HOTELS

Grand Hotell — Lund 10 km
84 rooms, D SKr 1695
Tel (46) 046 - 280 61 00, Fax (46) 046 - 280 61 50

Lundia — Lund 10 km
97 rooms, D SKr 1550
Tel (46) 046 - 280 65 00, Fax (46) 046 - 280 65 10

RESTAURANTS RESTAURANG

Bantorget 9 — Lund 10 km
Tel (46) 046 - 320 200

Grand Hotell — Lund 10 km
Tel (46) 046 - 280 61 00

MÖLLE

15 | 7 | 5

Vägen upp till Kullaberg förbi Höganäs är med alla sina fiskeläger vacker som ett vykort. Detta är Sveriges keramik-centrum, och väl framme i Mölle kan du begrunda det faktum att du nu är på platsen där män och kvinnor för första gången fick sola och bada tillsammans. Golfbanan ligger högre upp i en nationalpark, och att den är belägen där förklarar också varför antalet bunkrar är begränsat på banan (endast elva stycken). Nåväl, de flesta greener är små, uppbyggda på platåer och ligger väl skyddade. Du behöver kunna slå höga inspel här, men många hål kräver också att du behärskar låga rullslag. Banan är kraftigt kuperad, vilket kan vara slitsamt (det finns inga golfbilar). Om du ska kunna klara dig runt här och träffa greenerna måste du ha ett brett register av olika typer av slag, framför allt med mellanjärnen och de korta järnen. Eftersom banan inte är särskilt lång kan du gott lämna drivern hemma. Layouten bör passa de flesta spelarkategorier, men vi varnar för vinden, den kan vara riktigt besvärlig.

The road along the Kullen peninsula is as pretty as a picture with fishing villages and the town of Höganäs, the centre of the Swedish ceramics and sandstone pottery industry on the way to Mölle, the first seaside resort in Sweden where men and women were able to bathe together. The golf course is higher up in a national park, a fact that limited the number of bunkers (11 green-side traps). No matter, many of the greens are small, elevated and well-guarded, but only one is really blind. You need to hit the ball high here, of course, but approach shots hit along the ground (deliberately) are often a better solution. Hilly enough to deter tired legs (there are no carts), Mölle requires all sorts of shots, especially with medium and short irons, to hit the greens. This is not really a long course and the driver can easily stay in the bag all day. Over a layout that is well suited to all playing abilities, the wind can be the most bothersome element to distract from the pleasure of playing here.

Mölle Golfklubb — 1944

Box 44
S - 260 42 MÖLLE

Office	Sekretariat	(46) 042 - 347 520
Pro shop	Pro shop	(46) 042 - 347 012
Fax	Fax	(46) 042 - 347 523
Web	www.mollegk.m.se	
Situation	Läge	Helsingborg, 30 km
Annual closure	Årlig stängning	no
Weekly closure	Daglig stängning	no

Fees main season Tariff hög säsong	Full day	
	Week days Veckodag	**We/Bank holidays** Lör/Söndag/Helgdag
Individual Individuellt	SKr 280	SKr 280
Couple Par	SKr 560	SKr 560

Juniors: –50%

Caddy	Caddie	no
Electric Trolley	El vagn	no
Buggy	Golfbil	SKr 100 /18 holes
Clubs	Klubbor	SKr 150 /18 holes

Credit cards Kredit kort
VISA - Eurocard - MasterCard

Access Tillfart : Helsingborg, R111 → Höganäs/Mölle. Mölle, → Kullens Fyr.
Map 1 on page 1204 Karta 1 se sid: 1204

Golf course BANA — 15/20

Site	Läge	
Maintenance	Underhåll	
Architect	Arkitekt	Ture Bruce
Type	Karaktär	parkland, hilly
Relief	Nivåskillnader	
Water in play	Vatten på spelfältet	
Exp. to wind	Vindutsatt	
Trees in play	Träd på spelfältet	

Scorecard Scorekort	**Chp.** Back tees	**Mens** Herrtee	**Ladies** Damtee
Length Längd	5467	5312	4627
Par	70	70	70
Slope system	—	131	125

Advised golfing ability Rekommenderad spelnivå — 0 12 24 36
Hcp required Hcp erfordrad — 32 Men, 36 Ladies

Club house & amenities KLUBBHUS OCH OMGIVNING — 7/10

Pro shop	Pro shop	
Driving range	Träningsbana	
Sheltered	tåkt	no
On grass	på gräs	yes
Putting-green	putting-green	yes
Pitching-green	pitching-green	yes

Hotel facilities HOTELL OMGIVNING — 5/10

HOTELS

Kullabergs Värdshus, 89 rooms, D SKr 1295 — Mölle on site
Tel (46) 042 - 185 390, Fax (46) 042 - 149 616

Hotel Nouveau, 15 rooms, D SKr 945 — Helsingborg 30 km
Tel (46) 042 - 347 420, Fax (46) 042 - 347 431

Marina Plaza, 190 rooms, D SKr 1295 — Helsingborg 30 km
Tel (46) 042 - 192 100, Fax (46) 042 - 149 616

RESTAURANTS RESTAURANG

Le Petit, Tel (46) 042 - 219 727 — Helsingborg 30 km
Oskar Trapp, Tel (46) 042 - 146 044 — Helsingborg 30 km
Gastro Tel (46) 042 - 243 470 — Helsingborg 30 km

ÖREBRO

18 | 7 | 5

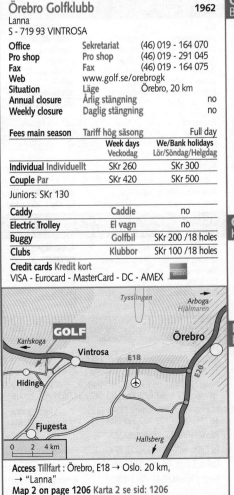

Trots att den inte är monsterlång räknas Örebro som en av de bästa banorna i Sverige. Det är en trevlig plats att besöka med ett charmigt klubbhus och ett övningsfält som är bland det bästa vi kan erbjuda här i landet. Pitch- och puttbanan är också en höjdare! När du väl har värmt upp kan du börja fundera över att attackera banrekordet som innehas av Joakim Haeggman och Pierre Fulke på 63 slag. Båda spelarna är kända för sin skicklighet med drivern, och det kommer du också behöva. Detta gäller framför allt för första nio där träden är mer i spel än på sista nio. Dessutom skadar det inte att vara utrustad med en stor portion tålamod och ta chanserna när de dyker upp. Du måste också vara smart när du attackerar greenerna, av vilka fler ligger på platåer. Örebro är en härlig utmaning där en sund teknik är att föredra framför muskler. Och du – tycker du det blir för svårt är det inte nödvändigt att spela från backtee.

Despite its "reasonable" length, Örebro is generally considered to be one of the very best courses in Sweden. It is a pleasant spot, the club-house very agreeable, the driving range is one of the best in the country (but not sheltered) and there is a pitch and putt course that is great fun. When nicely warmed up, you can start to think about getting out there and trying to beat the course record of 63 set by Joakim Haeggman and Pierre Fulke. Both players are straight drivers and you will need the same accuracy, at least on the front nine, where the forest poses more of a threat than on the inward nine. You need to be patient here and grasp the right opportunities provided by your own talent or any luck that comes your way. You also need to be smart to appreciate some of the approach shots to greens that are sometimes elevated but never oversized. Örebro is a mighty challenge but places emphasis more on technique than power, an asset for golfers who always look to their swing (or change of club) to hit the ball 20 yards further. To make things a little easier, players can always opt for the less awesome forward tees.

Örebro Golfklubb — 1962

Lanna
S - 719 93 VINTROSA

Office	Sekretariat	(46) 019 - 164 070
Pro shop	Pro shop	(46) 019 - 291 045
Fax	Fax	(46) 019 - 164 075
Web	www.golf.se/orebrogk	
Situation	Läge	Örebro, 20 km
Annual closure	Årlig stängning	no
Weekly closure	Daglig stängning	no

Fees main season Tariff hög säsong		Full day
	Week days Veckodag	**We/Bank holidays** Lör/Söndag/Helgdag
Individual Individuellt	SKr 260	SKr 300
Couple Par	SKr 420	SKr 500

Juniors: SKr 130

Caddy	Caddie	no
Electric Trolley	El vagn	no
Buggy	Golfbil	SKr 200 /18 holes
Clubs	Klubbor	SKr 100 /18 holes

Credit cards Kredit kort
VISA - Eurocard - MasterCard - DC - AMEX

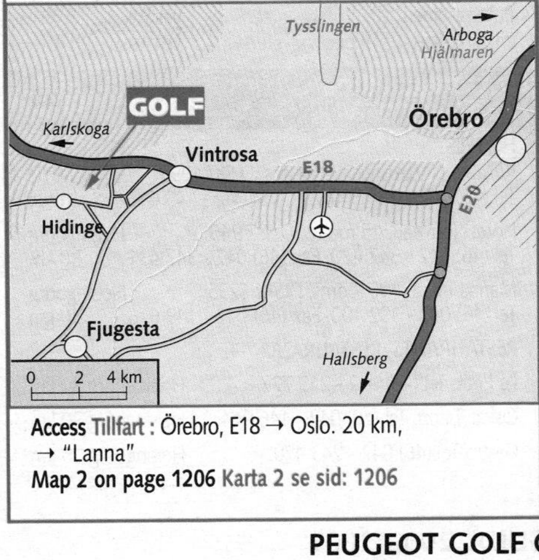

Access Tillfart : Örebro, E18 → Oslo. 20 km, → "Lanna"
Map 2 on page 1206 Karta 2 se sid: 1206

Golf course — BANA — 18/20

Site	Läge	
Maintenance	Underhåll	
Architect	Arkitekt	Flera
Type	Karaktär	forest, parkland
Relief	Nivåskillnader	
Water in play	Vatten på spelfältet	
Exp. to wind	Vindutsatt	
Trees in play	Träd på spelfältet	

Scorecard Scorekort	**Chp.** Back tees	**Mens** Herrtee	**Ladies** Damtee
Length Längd	6160	5860	5065
Par	71	71	71
Slope system	—	136	126

Advised golfing ability Rekommenderad spelnivå — 0 12 24 36
Hcp required Hcp erfordrad — 36

Club house & amenities — KLUBBHUS OCH OMGIVNING — 7/10

Pro shop	Pro shop	
Driving range	Träningsbana	
Sheltered	täkt	no
On grass	på gräs	yes
Putting-green	putting-green	yes
Pitching-green	pitching-green	yes

Hotel facilities — HOTELL OMGIVNING — 5/10

HOTELS

Golf Hotellet, 12 rooms, D SKr 380 Tel (46) 019 - 291 065, Fax (46) 019 - 291 055	Örebro on site
Stora Hotellet, 132 rooms, D SKr 1295 Tel (46) 019 - 156 900, Fax (46) 019 - 156 950	Örebro 20 km
Scandic Grand Hotel 220 rooms, D SKr 1398 Tel (46) 019 - 150 200, Fax (46) 019 - 185 814	Örebro 20 km

RESTAURANTS RESTAURANG

Slottohällaren, Tel (46) 019 - 156 900	Örebro 20 km
Babar, Tel (46) 019 - 101 900	Örebro 20 km
Tulins, Tel (46) 019 - 132 530	Örebro 20 km

ÖSTERÅKER

16 | 6 | 6

Det amerikanska sättet att bygga banor har haft ett stort inflytande i Europa. Allt fler banor byggs som är väldigt straffande i sin natur. Österåker är inget undantag från den här trenden som har sitt upphov i dagens nya teknologi som har gett oss järnklubbor som går allt högre och wedgar som får mer och mer loft. Många av greenerna vaktas av ett stort antal hinder, de är dessutom relativt hårda vilket gör att du måste slå höga pitch-slag mot dem för att få bollen att stanna. Om du har en lobbwedge – stoppa den i bagen! Du behöver dessutom långa, raka utslag – framför allt under sommaren då ruffen växer hög. En tuff utmaning, framför allt de första nio som är betydligt trixigare än andra nio som är längre men inte fullt så krävande. Om du har en dålig svingdag får du förlita dig på ditt närspel, men eftersom detta är något förunnat låghandicappare så kan spelare med högre handicap få det besvärligt. För att göra saken än mer problematisk så är vatten i spel på åtta av hålen. Av rundan kommer du framför allt att minnas de spektakulära par 3-hålen. Här har Europatouren för damer kommit på besök, och över de senaste åren har en rad tees och greener uppgraderats.

This course is no exception to the trend that today's equipment tends to favour, namely irons designed to hit higher balls, including very wide-angle wedges. A lot of the greens here are guarded at the front by a number of hazards, and as they are also pretty firm you have to hit high pitches and be able to stop the ball on the putting surface. If you have a lob-wedge, put it in your bag. Otherwise, what with the tall rough in summer, you need some straight driving as well, a tough proposition early in the day because the front nine are a good deal trickier than the back nine, which are longer but less demanding. If your swing is off-colour, your short game should help you out, but as this part of golf is not always the forte of high-handicappers, they could be in trouble. To top it all, some fearsome water is in play on eight holes. The holes to remember on this course are the spectacular par 3s. Over the last few years, quite a few of tees and greens have been remodeled, with the venue of the European Ladies Tour.

Österåkers Golfklubb — 1990

Hagby 1:1
S - 184 92 ÅKERSBERGA

Office	Sekretariat	(46) 08 - 540 851 90
Pro shop	Pro shop	(46) 08 - 540 684 49
Fax	Fax	(46) 08 - 540 668 32
Web	www.ostgk.se	
Situation	Läge	Stockholm, 20 km
Annual closure	Årlig stängning	no
Weekly closure	Daglig stängning	no

Fees main season Tariff hög säsong	Week days Veckodag	We/Bank holidays Lör/Söndag/Helgdag (Full day)
Individual Individuellt	SKr 320	SKr 380
Couple Par	SKr 640	SKr 760

Juniors: – 50%

Caddy	Caddie	no
Electric Trolley	El vagn	no
Buggy	Golfbil	no
Clubs	Klubbor	SKr 175 /18 holes

Credit cards Kredit kort
VISA - Eurocard - MasterCard - DC - AMEX

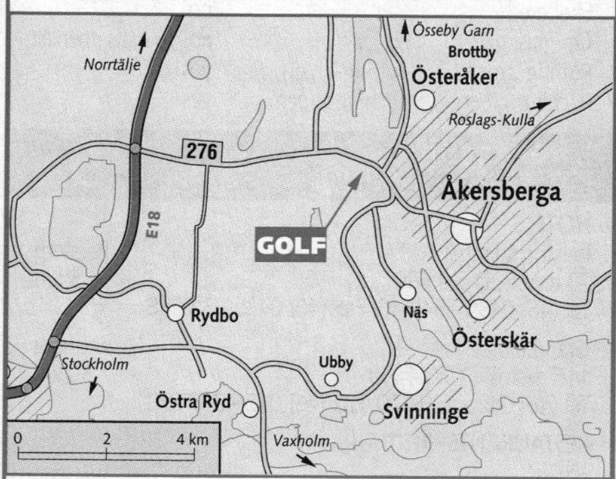

Access Tillfart : Stockholm, E18 → Norrtälje. → Åkersberga, → Waxholm
Map 2 on page 1206 Karta 2 se sid: 1206

Golf course — BANA — 16/20

Site	Läge	
Maintenance	Underhåll	
Architect	Arkitekt	Sven Tumba, Jan Sederholm
Type	Karaktär	parkland
Relief	Nivåskillnader	
Water in play	Vatten på spelfältet	
Exp. to wind	Vindutsatt	
Trees in play	Träd på spelfältet	

Scorecard Scorekort	Chp. Back tees	Mens Herrtee	Ladies Damtee
Length Längd	6145	5790	5010
Par	72	72	72
Slope system	—	137	133

Advised golfing ability Rekommenderad spelnivå — 0 12 24 36
Hcp required Hcp erfordrad — 29 Men, 34 Ladies

Club house & amenities — KLUBBHUS OCH OMGIVNING — 6/10

Pro shop	Pro shop	
Driving range	Träningsbana	
Sheltered	täkt	6 mats
On grass	på gräs	no, 30 mats open air
Putting-green	putting-green	yes
Pitching-green	pitching-green	yes

Hotel facilities — HOTELL OMGIVNING — 6/10

HOTELS
Silja Hotel Ariadne — Stockholm Värtahamnen 17 km
283 rooms, D SKr 1960
Tel (46) 08 - 665 78 00, Fax (46) 08 - 662 76 70

Lord Nelson, 31 rooms, D SKr 1890 — Stockholm 20 km
Tel (46) 08 - 232 390, Fax (46) 08 - 101 089

Victory, 45 rooms, D SKr 2390 — Stockholm 20 km
Tel (46) 08 - 143 090, Fax (46) 08 - 202 177

RESTAURANTS RESTAURANG
Eriks, Tel (46) 08 - 238 500 — Stockholm 20 km
Stallmästeregården, Tel (46) 08 - 610 13 00 — Stockholm
Den Gyldene Freden, (46) 08 - 249 760 — Stockholm

PERSTORP

14 | 7 | 5

I de norra delarna av Skåne kryper de vidsträckta öppna fälten in i de täta skogarna. Det är nästan onödigt att påpeka att precision är viktigt. Perstorp är smal, men ändå inte helt omöjlig, andraslagen in mot greenerna blir nämligen ofta relativt korta. Därför är det inte heller alltid nödvändigt att slå drive från tee. Greenerna är små och förrädiska, börjar du missa dem behöver du alla wedgar du någonsin kan få plats med i bagen. Långtslående kommer nog känna sig en smula frustrerade, men spelet behöver den här typen av banor som tvingar dig att hålla igen och som premierar den smarte golfaren. Topografin kan också ställa till en hel del bekymmer när det gäller klubbvalen. Perstorp är en utomordentlig bana på sommaren när det inte är så blött i terrängen. Förlägg familjemästerskapet hit!

Here we are in the north of the region of Skåne, where wide open spaces give way to deep forests. Needless to say, accuracy is of the essence, at least to keep your tee shot in play. A tight course, but not necessarily too oppressive, because the second shot is never very long and there really is no need for the driver. The greens are on the small side and treacherous to boot. They require some careful approach shots and all the wedges you can carry when you miss them. Big-hitters off the tee will probably feel a little frustrated, but golf needs this type of course for driver freaks to learn a little restraint and give the "technicians" the chance to get their own back. The topography of the course also calls for careful club selection. A good course in the summer when not too wet and the ideal site for the Year's Family Championships.

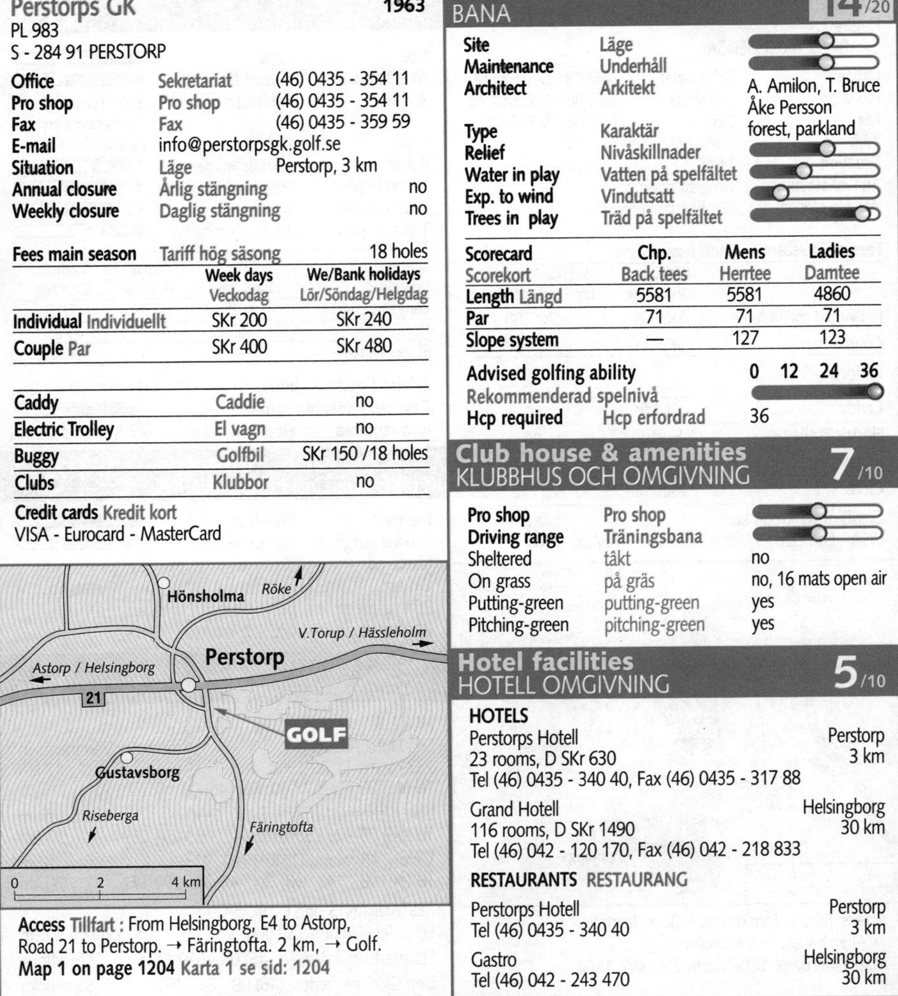

Perstorps GK — **1963**
PL 983
S - 284 91 PERSTORP

Office	Sekretariat	(46) 0435 - 354 11
Pro shop	Pro shop	(46) 0435 - 354 11
Fax	Fax	(46) 0435 - 359 59
E-mail	info@perstorpsgk.golf.se	
Situation	Läge	Perstorp, 3 km
Annual closure	Årlig stängning	no
Weekly closure	Daglig stängning	no

Fees main season Tariff hög säsong	Week days Veckodag	We/Bank holidays Lör/Söndag/Helgdag
	18 holes	
Individual Individuellt	SKr 200	SKr 240
Couple Par	SKr 400	SKr 480

Caddy	Caddie	no
Electric Trolley	El vagn	no
Buggy	Golfbil	SKr 150 /18 holes
Clubs	Klubbor	no

Credit cards Kredit kort
VISA - Eurocard - MasterCard

Access Tillfart : From Helsingborg, E4 to Astorp, Road 21 to Perstorp. → Färingtofta. 2 km, → Golf.
Map 1 on page 1204 Karta 1 se sid: 1204

Golf course BANA — 14/20

Site	Läge	
Maintenance	Underhåll	
Architect	Arkitekt	A. Amilon, T. Bruce Åke Persson
Type	Karaktär	forest, parkland
Relief	Nivåskillnader	
Water in play	Vatten på spelfältet	
Exp. to wind	Vindutsatt	
Trees in play	Träd på spelfältet	

Scorecard Scorekort	Chp. Back tees	Mens Herrtee	Ladies Damtee
Length Längd	5581	5581	4860
Par	71	71	71
Slope system	—	127	123

Advised golfing ability 0 12 24 36
Rekommenderad spelnivå
Hcp required Hcp erfordrad 36

Club house & amenities KLUBBHUS OCH OMGIVNING — 7/10

Pro shop	Pro shop	
Driving range	Träningsbana	
Sheltered	tåkt	no
On grass	på gräs	no, 16 mats open air
Putting-green	putting-green	yes
Pitching-green	pitching-green	yes

Hotel facilities HOTELL OMGIVNING — 5/10

HOTELS

Perstorps Hotell — Perstorp 3 km
23 rooms, D SKr 630
Tel (46) 0435 - 340 40, Fax (46) 0435 - 317 88

Grand Hotell — Helsingborg 30 km
116 rooms, D SKr 1490
Tel (46) 042 - 120 170, Fax (46) 042 - 218 833

RESTAURANTS RESTAURANG

Perstorps Hotell — Perstorp 3 km
Tel (46) 0435 - 340 40

Gastro — Helsingborg 30 km
Tel (46) 042 - 243 470

RYA

15 | 7 | 8

Även när bron mellan Malmö och Köpenhamn har byggts kommer man fortfarande kunna tura mellan Helsingborg och Helsingør, den kortaste vägen mellan Sverige och Danmark. Från Rya, strax söder om Helsingborg, ser man inte bara Öresund utan även Danmark på andra sidan sundet. Bortsett från fem ganska kuperade hål är resten av banan platt och varierar i stil mellan links och parkbanekaraktär. På några hål kommer träd i spel, annars är det vattenhinder som är de största hoten, framför allt på det fjärde och det åttonde, som kan vara svåra för höghandicaparen. Nåja, det åttonde hålet ställer till med problem för alla – ett vattenhinder skär igenom fairway precis framför greenen på detta par 5-hål som måste räknas vara ett av de bästa i hela landet. 16e är också minnesvärt – en par 3 med sundet och Danmark i bakgrunden. Efter rundan kan du ta med dig barnen till stranden (50 meter bort), men räkna inte med några Medelhavstemperaturer.

Even when the motorway-train link from Malmö to København is open, there will still be the ferry link between Helsingborg and Helsingør, the shortest way of getting from one country to the other. From the Rya course, to the south of Helsingborg, you can see not only the Öresund strait but also Denmark on the other side. Aside from five rather hilly holes, the rest of the course is flat with a style varying from links to parkland. Trees are in play only on a few holes, otherwise the hazards that are present are very dangerous, particularly on holes 4 and 8, where water will cause trouble for the high-handicap golfers. In fact, hole N° 8 will cause problems for everyone, with water crossing the fairway next to the green of this superb par 5, which has to rate as one of the finest holes in the whole country. The 16th, too, is a great hole, a short par 3 with the sea and Denmark in the background. At the end of your round, you can take the children to the beach (less than 60 yards away) and even go for a swim (but don't expect Mediterranean temperatures).

Rya Golfklubb — 1935

PL 5500
S - 255 92 HELSINGBORG

Office	**Sekretariat**	(46) 042 - 220 182
Pro shop	**Pro shop**	(46) 042 - 221 688
Fax	**Fax**	(46) 042 - 220 394
Web	www.rya-gk.com	
Situation	**Läge**	Helsingborg, 10 km
Annual closure	**Årlig stängning**	no
Weekly closure	**Daglig stängning**	no

Fees main season / **Tariff hög säsong**	Full day	
	Week days / **Veckodag**	**We/Bank holidays** / **Lör/Söndag/Helgdag**
Individual Individuellt	SKr 320	SKr 320
Couple Par	SKr 640	SKr 640
Juniors: SKr 150		

Caddy	**Caddie**	no
Electric Trolley	**El vagn**	no
Buggy	**Golfbil**	no
Clubs	**Klubbor**	SKr 100 /18 holes

Credit cards Kredit kort
VISA - Eurocard - MasterCard

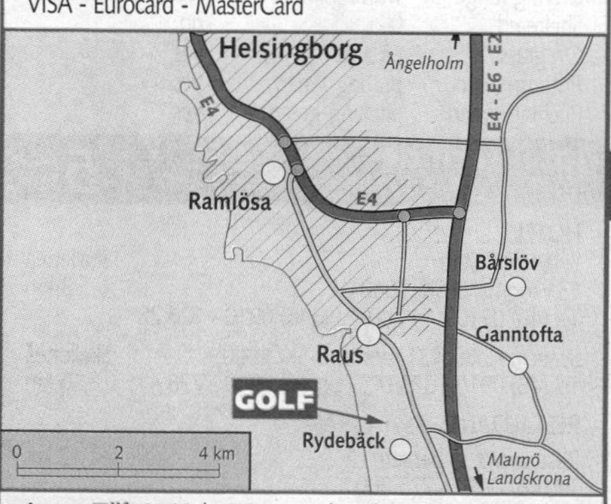

Access Tillfart : Malmö E6 → Helsingborg. → Rydebäck. → Golf
Map 1 on page 1204 Karta 1 se sid: 1204

Golf course BANA — 15/20

Site	**Läge**	
Maintenance	**Underhåll**	
Architect	**Arkitekt**	Rafael Sundblom
Type	**Karaktär**	seaside course, parkland
Relief	**Nivåskillnader**	
Water in play	**Vatten på spelfältet**	
Exp. to wind	**Vindutsatt**	
Trees in play	**Träd på spelfältet**	

Scorecard / **Scorekort**	**Chp.** / **Back tees**	**Mens** / **Herrtee**	**Ladies** / **Damtee**
Length Längd	5857	5558	4846
Par	71	71	71
Slope system	—	124	126

Advised golfing ability 0 12 24 36
Rekommenderad spelnivå
Hcp required **Hcp erfordrad** 32

Club house & amenities KLUBBHUS OCH OMGIVNING — 7/10

Pro shop	**Pro shop**	
Driving range	**Träningsbana**	
Sheltered	tåkt	yes
On grass	på gräs	yes
Putting-green	putting-green	yes
Pitching-green	pitching-green	yes

Hotel facilities HOTELL OMGIVNING — 8/10

HOTELS

Marina Plaza, 190 rooms, D SKr 1295 — Helsingborg
Tel (46) 042 - 192 100, Fax (46) 042 - 149 616 — 7 km

Hotell Nouveau, 89 rooms, D SKr 1145 — Helsingborg
Tel (46) 042 - 185 390, Fax (46) 042 - 140 885 — 7 km

Grand Hotell, 116 rooms, D SKr 1490 — Helsingborg
Tel (46) 042 - 120 170, Fax (46) 042 - 218 833 — 7 km

RESTAURANTS RESTAURANG

Le Petit, Tel (46) 042 - 219 727 — Helsingborg 7 km

Oskar Trapp, Tel (46) 042 - 146 044 — Helsingborg 7 km

Gastro, Tel (46) 042 - 243 470 — Helsingborg 7 km

SKELLEFTEÅ

14 | 6 | 5

Skellefteå ligger i ett ingenmansland mellan norr och söder i Sverige. Ändå finns polcirkeln på ett relativt nära avstånd, och här kan sommardagarna kännas oändliga. Om du är tillräckligt vältränad kan du spela flera banor om dagen och ändå hinna njuta av var och en av dem. Banan är ganska flack och från utslagsplatserna kan du se de flesta av hindren. Fairway kantas av träd, och dessa undviker du bäst genom en smula klokskap förenat med skicklighet: Spela försiktigt när du behöver det, slå en kontrollerad fade, och så vidare. Till sist besegrar sunt förnuft ren råstyrka. Fyra talangfulla arkitekter har byggt denna bana i omgångar mellan 1970-1995, vilket kan få en att tro att detta skulle ge en splittrad helhetsbild, men så är det inte. Skellefteå är utan vidare den bästa banan i den här regionen. För lite extra inspiration inför nästa runda rekommenderas ett besök i gamla stan.

This is not yet the great North, but it is not the south either; the Polar Circle is not so far away and summer days can seem endless. If you are fit enough, you will have the time to play several courses in a day and fully appreciate the difficulties of each one. From the tees on this relatively flat and tree-strewn terrain, you can see most of the hazards, which are most effectively avoided with a little skill and thought, i.e. playing short here, fading the ball there, and so forth. At the final count, using your head is more important than physical strength. Four talented architects helped to design this course between 1970 and 1995, which has still nonetheless retained a certain unity. All in all, this is a good and the most impressive course to be found in this part of Sweden. Spare a little time to see the old Parish village of Bonnstan, you might find a little extra inspiration for your next round.

1252

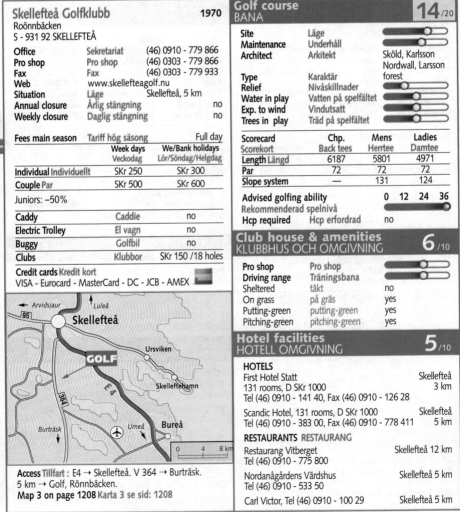

Skellefteå Golfklubb — 1970

Roönnbäcken
S - 931 92 SKELLEFTEÅ

Office	Sekretariat	(46) 0910 - 779 866
Pro shop	Pro shop	(46) 0303 - 779 866
Fax	Fax	(46) 0303 - 779 933
Web	www.skellefteagolf.nu	
Situation	Läge	Skellefteå, 5 km
Annual closure	Årlig stängning	no
Weekly closure	Daglig stängning	no

Fees main season Tariff hög säsong	Week days Veckodag	We/Bank holidays Lör/Söndag/Helgdag
		Full day
Individual Individuellt	SKr 250	SKr 300
Couple Par	SKr 500	SKr 600

Juniors: –50%

Caddy	Caddie	no
Electric Trolley	El vagn	no
Buggy	Golfbil	no
Clubs	Klubbor	SKr 150 /18 holes

Credit cards Kredit kort
VISA - Eurocard - MasterCard - DC - JCB - AMEX

Access Tillfart : E4 → Skellefteå. V 364 → Burträsk. 5 km → Golf, Rönnbäcken.
Map 3 on page 1208 Karta 3 se sid: 1208

Golf course BANA — 14/20

Site	Läge	
Maintenance	Underhåll	
Architect	Arkitekt	Sköld, Karlsson Nordwall, Larsson
Type	Karaktär	forest
Relief	Nivåskillnader	
Water in play	Vatten på spelfältet	
Exp. to wind	Vindutsatt	
Trees in play	Träd på spelfältet	

Scorecard Scorekort	Chp. Back tees	Mens Herrtee	Ladies Damtee
Length Längd	6187	5801	4971
Par	72	72	72
Slope system	—	131	124

Advised golfing ability Rekommenderad spelnivå: 0 12 24 36
Hcp required Hcp erfordrad: no

Club house & amenities KLUBBHUS OCH OMGIVNING — 6/10

Pro shop	Pro shop	
Driving range	Träningsbana	
Sheltered	tåkt	no
On grass	på gräs	yes
Putting-green	putting-green	yes
Pitching-green	pitching-green	yes

Hotel facilities HOTELL OMGIVNING — 5/10

HOTELS

First Hotel Statt — Skellefteå 3 km
131 rooms, D SKr 1000
Tel (46) 0910 - 141 40, Fax (46) 0910 - 126 28

Scandic Hotel, 131 rooms, D SKr 1000 — Skellefteå 5 km
Tel (46) 0910 - 383 00, Fax (46) 0910 - 778 411

RESTAURANTS RESTAURANG

Restaurang Vitberget — Skellefteå 12 km
Tel (46) 0910 - 775 800

Nordanågårdens Värdshus — Skellefteå 5 km
Tel (46) 0910 - 533 50

Carl Victor, Tel (46) 0910 - 100 29 — Skellefteå 5 km

SKÖVDE

17 | 5 | 7

Det här är en bra bas om man ska utforska områdena kring Sveriges två största sjöar, Vänern och Vättern. Besöka exempelvis Mariestad, där kan du ta en sväng runt den magnifika kyrkan eller bara strosa runt bland de vackra trähusen. Precis utanför Skövde hittar man golfbanan med det lilla, men charmiga klubbhuset byggt högst upp på en kulle, och för att ta sig dit krävs nästan lika mycket energi som att spela banan (alla med dålig kondition är härmed varnade). Genom att studera greenernas storlek förstår man snabbt vem som har designat banan: Peter Nordwall, förstås. Han har lagt ut en lång och svår bana, där bra bollträff är ett måste. På Skövde är allting stort, från utslagsplatserna till amerikansk-inspirerade fairways. För faktum är att de är bredare än vad de verkar vara vid första anblicken. Tur är det, för första gången ser du bara hinder – skog och tjock ruff. En av banans stora förtjänster är att den är så omväxlande, vilket verkligen kräver att du kan använda alla klubbor i bagen. Även höghandicapare kommer dock ha en kul dag på banan – även om den kanske blir lite längre än vanligt. Skövde har blivit vald till "Den bästa banan byggd på 1990-talet i Sverige".

This town is a base-camp to explore the two great Swedish lakes of Vättern and Vänern, on the shores of which you will find the little town of Mariestad and visit the cathedral and old wooden houses. Just outside the town, a charming but small club-house stands atop a hill which requires about as much stamina to reach as the course does to play (veterans be warned). The size of the greens are a good clue to who designed this course, none other than Peter Nordwall, who has laid out a long and difficult course, where the ball needs to be hit crisp and clean. Everything is big here, from the tee-boxes to the rather American style fairways. In fact, the holes are wider than you think and all you see are the hazards of trees and tall rough. One of the qualities of this course is the variety of holes and of the shots you need to play. High-handicappers will have fun working their way around this course, but it may take them a little longer than usual to get home safely. Skövde has been elected as "the best course built in the 90's in Sweden".

Skövde Golfklubb — 1991

Box 269
S - 541 26 SKÖVDE

Office	Sekretariat	(46) 0500 - 411 535
Pro shop	Pro shop	(46) 0500 - 412 537
Fax	Fax	(46) 0500 - 410 116
Web	www.skovdegk.nu	
Situation	Läge	Skövde, 5 km
Annual closure	Årlig stängning	no
Weekly closure	Daglig stängning	no

Fees main season Tariff hög säsong	**Week days** Veckodag	**We/Bank holidays** Lör/Söndag/Helgdag
		Full day
Individual Individuellt	SKr 240	SKr 240
Couple Par	SKr 480	SKr 480
Special fees for juniors		

Caddy	Caddie	no
Electric Trolley	El vagn	no
Buggy	Golfbil	no
Clubs	Klubbor	no

Credit cards Kredit kort
VISA - Eurocard - MasterCard - DC - AMEX

Lerdala
Mariestad
Töreboda
48
Skara
Skövde
Vämb
49
Tibro
GOLF
Skultorp
46
Falköping
0 2 4 km

Access Tillfart : Jönköping R47/48 → Skövde. R49 → Skara. Cementa/Rockwool, → Simsjön. Golf 2 km

Map 1 on page 1204 Karta 1 se sid: 1204

Golf course BANA — 17/20

Site	Läge	
Maintenance	Underhåll	
Architect	Arkitekt	Peter Nordwall
Type	Karaktär	parkland
Relief	Nivåskillnader	
Water in play	Vatten på spelfältet	
Exp. to wind	Vindutsatt	
Trees in play	Träd på spelfältet	

Scorecard Scorekort	**Chp.** Back tees	**Mens** Herrtee	**Ladies** Damtee
Length Längd	6215	5740	4885
Par	72	72	72
Slope system	—	130	124

Advised golfing ability Rekommenderad spelnivå — 0 12 24 36

Hcp required Hcp erfordrad — 36

1253

Club house & amenities KLUBBHUS OCH OMGIVNING — 5/10

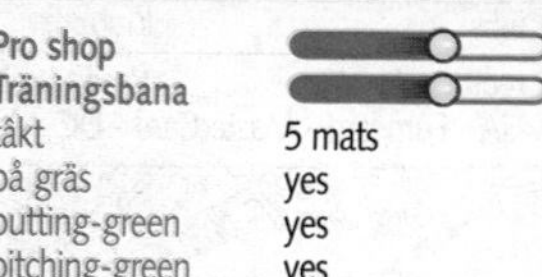

Pro shop	Pro shop	
Driving range	Träningsbana	
Sheltered	täkt	5 mats
On grass	på gräs	yes
Putting-green	putting-green	yes
Pitching-green	pitching-green	yes

Hotel facilities HOTELL OMGIVNING — 7/10

HOTELS

Billingehus, 240 rooms, D SKr 1350 Tel (46) 0500 - 445 700, Fax (46) 0500 - 483 880	Skövde 3 km
Billingen, 106 rooms, D SKr 1195 Tel (46) 0500 - 410 790, Fax (46) 0500 - 417 310	Skövde 4 km
Knista Hotel, 79 rooms, D SKr 1140 Tel (46) 0500 - 463 170, Fax (46) 0500 - 463 075	Skövde 10 km

RESTAURANTS RESTAURANG

Skafferiet, Tel (46) 0500 - 411 177	Skövde 5 km
Parnassen, Tel (46) 0500 - 411 912	Skövde 5 km
Orient Palace, Tel (46) 0500 - 489 883	Skövde 5 km

SÖDERÅSEN

15 | 7 | 5

Sista biten upp mot klubbhuset är magnifik med träd på bägge sidor. Detta är ett typiskt skånskt landskap, och tankarna går till dignande smörgåsbord med lax, sill, ål och mycket mer. Banan kan dock lätt trycka ned din positivism med all skog, tjock ruff och strategiskt utplacerade diken. Var kylig: Det viktigaste är att ha ett bra huvud och förmåga att anpassa sig när saker inte riktigt går som det är tänkt. Sedan skadar det förstås inte heller med en smula ödmjukhet! Om du tycker om att spela banor som utvecklar dig som golfare kommer du älska att spela här. Även höghandicapare klarar sig runt om de inte överskattar sin egen kapacitet, vill säga. Greenerna är relativt små, och ofta väldigt snabba. Många är upphöjda och kräver ett delikat närspel – särskilt många greenträffar på rätt antal slag kan du nämligen inte räkna med. Detta gäller framför allt på par 4-hålen som är tuffa att nå på två slag.

The drive to this course set amidst an ocean of trees is simply splendid, the same goes for the typical countryside of Skåne, the country's southernmost province, famous for its smörgåsbord, a sort of huge brunch based on fish (salmon, herring and eels in season) and meat (particularly duck and goose). A forest, tall rough and a few very well located ditches can easily wear down the optimism of any golfer here. The basic requirements are good game strategy, the ability to adapt when things don't go quite the way you planned (this does happen) and a certain degree of humility (as always). You will love playing here if you appreciate courses which help make you become a better golfer. High-handicappers, as long as they don't overestimate their playing ability, will get by without too much damage. The greens are rather small, frequently fast and slick, often elevated and always requiring a lot of touch to stop the ball when your approach has missed its target. Many holes stick in the mind, particularly the 2nd, a par 4 which is tough to reach in two shots and a good yardstick for gauging the shape of your game on any one particular day.

1254

Söderåsens Golfklubb — 1972

Box 41
S - 260 50 BILLESHOLM

Office	Sekretariat	(46) 042 - 733 37
Pro shop	Pro shop	(46) 042 - 724 45
Fax	Fax	(46) 042 - 739 63
Web	www.golf.se/soderasenskagk	
Situation	Läge	Helsingborg, 20 km
Annual closure	Årlig stängning	no
Weekly closure	Daglig stängning	no

Fees main season / Tariff hög säsong	Week days / Veckodag	We/Bank holidays / Lör/Söndag/Helgdag
	Full day	
Individual Individuellt	SKr 220	SKr 280
Couple Par	SKr 440	SKr 560

Juniors: – 50%

Caddy	Caddie	no
Electric Trolley	El vagn	no
Buggy	Golfbil	SKr 200 /18 holes
Clubs	Klubbor	SKr 100 /18 holes

Credit cards Kredit kort
VISA - Eurocard - MasterCard - DC - AMEX

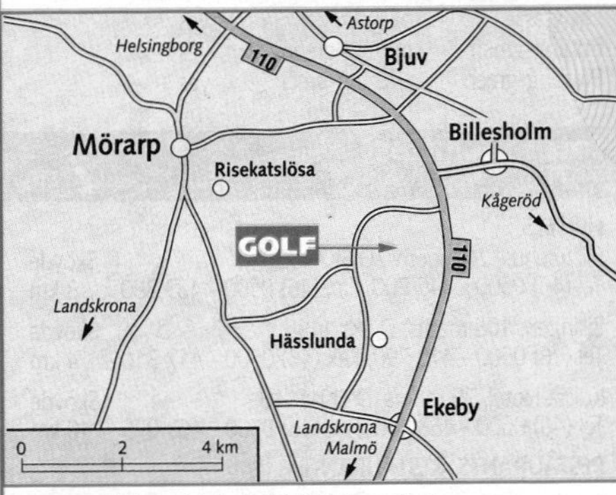

Access Tillfart : Malmö, E6. R110. → Golf
Map 1 on page 1204 Karta 1 se sid: 1204

Golf course BANA — 15/20

Site	Läge	
Maintenance	Underhåll	
Architect	Arkitekt	Ture Bruce
Type	Karaktär	forest, parkland
Relief	Nivåskillnader	
Water in play	Vatten på spelfältet	
Exp. to wind	Vindutsatt	
Trees in play	Träd på spelfältet	

Scorecard / Scorekort	Chp. / Back tees	Mens / Herrtee	Ladies / Damtee
Length Längd	6050	5657	4879
Par	71	71	71
Slope system	—	134	128

Advised golfing ability / Rekommenderad spelnivå: 0 12 24 36

Hcp required / Hcp erfordrad: 36

Club house & amenities KLUBBHUS OCH OMGIVNING — 7/10

Pro shop	Pro shop	
Driving range	Träningsbana	
Sheltered	tåkt	2 mats
On grass	på gräs	yes
Putting-green	putting-green	yes
Pitching-green	pitching-green	yes

Hotel facilities HOTELL OMGIVNING — 5/10

HOTELS

Marina Plaza, 190 rooms, D SKr 1295 — Helsingborg 20 km
Tel (46) 042 - 192 100, Fax (46) 042 - 149 616

Hotell Nouveau, 89 rooms, D SKr 1145 — Helsingborg 20 km
Tel (46) 042 - 185 390, Fax (46) 042 - 140 885

Grand Hotell — Helsingborg 20 km
116 rooms, D SKr 1490
Tel (46) 042 - 120 170, Fax (46) 042 - 218 833

RESTAURANTS RESTAURANG

Gastro, Tel (46) 042 - 243 470 — Helsingborg 20 km

Le Petit, Tel (46) 042 - 219 727 — Helsingborg 20 km

Oskar Trapp, Tel (46) 042 - 146 044 — Helsingborg 20 km

STENUNGSUND

17 | 7 | 8

Utsikten med alla fjordar och öar går inte av för hackor. Från banan kan du skymta havet, men i grunden är detta en inlandsbana. Peter Nordwall har ritat på sitt speciella sätt, med andra ord: allting är stort. Anråseå, som skär genom banan, har han dock inte lyckats förvandla till en ocean. Hur som helst, atmosfären är en skotsk seaside-känsla, och layouten fordrar att du kan slå flera typer av slag med hygglig bollträff. Banan är mycket ung, dock ska sägas att den verkar vara betydligt äldre. Skötseln är tipp-topp! Trots att banan är väldigt ung känns den mogen, framför allt beroende på det suveräna underhållningsarbete som banpersonalen svarar för. Dessutom är jordmånen utmärkt, vilket bidrar till att banan är i god kondition redan tidigt på våren. Detta är en riktig mästerskapsbana, vilket innebär att alla hinder finns åtminstone 200 meter från tee – höghandicapare kan därmed lugnt andas ut. Fast på greenerna kommer de att mötas av samma problem som de bättre spelarna – här är det känsla och fantasi som gäller.

From the Stenungsund course, you can make out the sea in the distance, although this is very much an inland course. Here again, Peter Nordwall has done everything in his own, oversized style, and while he has brought the Anräseå river into play, at least he was unable to transform it into an ocean. All the same, you still find a sort of Scottish seaside course atmosphere here, a layout which requires the full range of shots and some solid striking of the ball. Still very young, the course looks much older, especially thanks to maintenance and green-keeping. The great soil has something to do with it, and the course is in good condition from early spring. A real championship course indeed, but as all the hazards are at least 220 yards (200 metres) from the tee, mid- and high-handicappers can breathe easily. They will however be on an equal footing with the better players when tackling the huge greens, where touch and feel count for much more than long game technique.

Stenungsund Golfklubb — 1993

PL Lundby 7480
S - 444 93 STENUNGSUND

Office	Sekretariat	(46) 0303 - 778 470
Pro shop	Pro shop	(46) 0303 - 778 188
Fax	Fax	(46) 0303 - 778 350
Web	www.golf.se/stenungsundsgk	
Situation	Läge	Göteborg, 45 km
Annual closure	Årlig stängning	no
Weekly closure	Daglig stängning	no

Fees main season / Tariff hög säsong	Week days / Veckodag	We/Bank holidays / Lör/Söndag/Helgdag
18 holes		
Individual Individuellt	SKr 240	SKr 280
Couple Par	SKr 480	SKr 560

Juniors: – 50%

Caddy	Caddie	no
Electric Trolley	El vagn	no
Buggy	Golfbil	SKr 150 /18 holes
Clubs	Klubbor	SKr 100 /18 holes
Credit cards Kredit kort		no

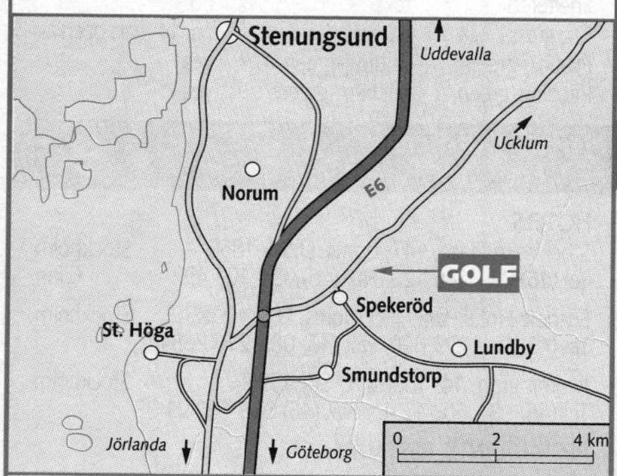

Access Tillfart : Göteborg, E6 → "Stora Höga-motet". → Ucklum. 1,5 km Golf
Map 1 on page 1204 Karta 1 se sid: 1204

Golf course BANA — 17/20

Site	Läge	
Maintenance	Underhåll	
Architect	Arkitekt	Peter Nordwall
Type	Karaktär	parkland, open country
Relief	Nivåskillnader	
Water in play	Vatten på spelfältet	
Exp. to wind	Vindutsatt	
Trees in play	Träd på spelfältet	

Scorecard / Scorekort	Chp. / Back tees	Mens / Herrtee	Ladies / Damtee
Length Längd	6238	5825	4936
Par	72	72	72
Slope system	—	131	128

Advised golfing ability / Rekommenderad spelnivå: 0 12 24 36

Hcp required / Hcp erfordrad: 36

Club house & amenities KLUBBHUS OCH OMGIVNING — 7/10

Pro shop	Pro shop	
Driving range	Träningsbana	
Sheltered	tåkt	no
On grass	på gräs	yes
Putting-green	putting-green	yes
Pitching-green	pitching-green	yes

Hotel facilities HOTELL OMGIVNING — 8/10

HOTELS

Stenungsbaden Yacht Club — Stenungsund 5 km
200 rooms, D SKr 1190
Tel (46) 0303 - 831 00, Fax (46) 0303 - 844 43

Solliden, 13 rooms, D SKr 945 — Stenungsund
Tel (46) 0303 - 698 70, Fax (46) 0303 - 870 00

Hotel Reis, 17 rooms, D SKr 595 — Stenungsund
Tel (46) 0303 - 770 011, Fax (46) 0303 - 824 72

RESTAURANTS RESTAURANG

Bara Kök och Bar, Tel (46) 0303 - 654 50 — Stenungsund
Sjökanten, Tel (46) 0303 - 770 040 — Stenungsund
Stenungsbaden, Tel (46) 0303 - 831 00 — Stenungsund

STOCKHOLM

16	8	9

Kevinge är huvudstadens stolthet med en medlemskö som nu är 50 år lång. Är du 20 år så se till att skriva upp dina ofödda barnbarn på listan! Layouten har en skotsk känsla, framför allt i hur bunkrarna har lagts ut. Detta är inget att förvånas över då såväl Morrison som Nicholson har varit inblandade i banbygget. Greenerna ligger väl skyddade bakom hinder, de är svåra att läsa, många har branta sluttningar och i en del fall ställs man dessutom inför ett blint inspel. De blinda slagen är dock ett mindre problem för de långtslående. Naturen är relativt kuperad, och med tanke på hur nära banan ligger staden är det förvånansvärt tyst och stilla. Träden ser inte bara till att dämpa oväsendet runt omkring de är dessutom en ständig oroskälla för oss golfare, inte minst på banans sex dogleg-hål. Om du ska göra en bra score här måste du ha ordning på spelet. Par år 69, och eftersom det finns få par 5-hål är birdiemöjligheterna begränsade. Banan är sällsynt charmig och oftast i excellent kondition. Se bara till att vara ute i god tid om du vill boka en starttid.

This is the great Stockholm course, where the membership waiting list has now reached fifty years! If you are 20, enrol your future grand-children now. The layout has a certain Scottish flavour to it, particularly in the way the bunkers are laid out. This is hardly surprising, as Morrison had a lot to do with the design, along with Nicholson; greens that are already tough to read, sharply contoured and sometimes blind are also very well guarded. The blind shots are perhaps less of a problem for long hitters, as the layout is rather hilly and strangely quiet for a city course. The trees dampen the surrounding noise but are also a major hazard, especially on the six dog-legs. To score here, you simply have to play very well, especially since being a par 69, there are few par 5s to bring that welcome birdie or two. A charming course in superb condition, situated in a splendid city, the Stockholms Golfklub is not easy to play, but if you have enough patience to secure a tee-off time, you will be well rewarded.

1256

Stockholms Kolfklubb — 1932

Kevingestrand 20
S - 182 57 DANDERYD

Office	Sekretariat	(46) 08 - 544 907 15
Pro shop	Pro shop	(46) 08 - 544 907 11
Fax	Fax	(46) 08 - 544 907 12
E-mail	info@stockholmsgk.golf.se	
Situation	Läge	Stockholm, 7 km
Annual closure	Årlig stängning	no
Weekly closure	Daglig stängning	no

Fees main season Tariff hög säsong		Full day
	Week days Veckodag	**We/Bank holidays** Lör/Söndag/Helgdag
Individual Individuellt	SKr 500	SKr 600
Couple Par	SKr 1000	SKr 1200

Juniors: – 50%

Caddy	Caddie	no
Electric Trolley	El vagn	no
Buggy	Golfbil	no
Clubs	Klubbor	SKr 200 /18 holes

Credit cards Kredit kort
VISA - Eurocard - MasterCard

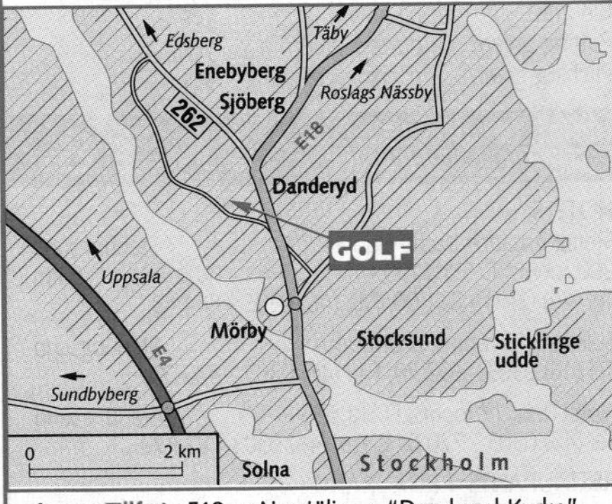

Access Tillfart : E18 → Norrtälje → "Danderyd Kyrka", 262 → Sollentuna, → Golf
Map 2 on page 1206 Karta 2 se sid: 1206

Golf course BANA — 16/20

Site	Läge	
Maintenance	Underhåll	
Architect	Arkitekt	John Morrison M. Nicholson
Type	Karaktär	parkland
Relief	Nivåskillnader	
Water in play	Vatten på spelfältet	
Exp. to wind	Vindutsatt	
Trees in play	Träd på spelfältet	

Scorecard Scorekort	**Chp.** Back tees	**Mens** Herrtee	**Ladies** Damtee
Length Längd	5437	5164	4552
Par	69	69	69
Slope system	—	121	122

Advised golfing ability Rekommenderad spelnivå — 0 12 24 36

Hcp required Hcp erfordrad — 30 Men, 36 Ladies

Club house & amenities KLUBBHUS OCH OMGIVNING — 8/10

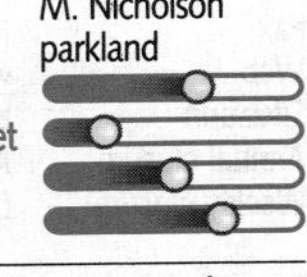

Pro shop	Pro shop	
Driving range	Träningsbana	
Sheltered	täkt	no
On grass	på gräs	no, 14 mats open air
Putting-green	putting-green	yes
Pitching-green	pitching-green	yes

Hotel facilities HOTELL OMGIVNING — 9/10

HOTELS

Stockholm Plaza, 147 rooms, D SKr 1850 — Stockholm 6 km
Tel (46) 08 - 145 120, Fax (46) 08 - 103 492

Scandic Hotel Park, 195 rooms, D SKr 2185 — Stockholm
Tel (46) 08 - 229 620, Fax (46) 08 - 216 268

Mornington, 141 rooms, D SKr 1595 — Stockholm
Tel (46) 08 - 663 12 40, Fax (46) 08 - 662 21 79

RESTAURANTS RESTAURANG

Videgård, Tel (46) 08 - 411 61 53 — Stockholm
Operakällaren, Tel (46) 08 - 676 58 00 — Stockholm 7 km
Wedholms Fisk, Tel (46) 08 - 611 78 74 — Stockholm 7 km

TÄBY

16 | 7 | 7

Klubbhuset ligger i en gammal herrgård i trä. Från verandan njuter du av dagens vedermödor och blickar ut över 18e greenen. När du tänker tillbaka på din runda kan du reflektera en stund över att det var här som Jesper Parnevik lärde sig spela golf. Då förstår man varför han blev den mästare som han är på att manövrera och kontrollera bollen. På Täby kommer nämligen alla klubbor i bagen till användning. Du kommer definitivt råka ut för några rejäla överraskningar. Banan ligger i ett kuperat skogsområde, och det är sällan som du får ett platt läge (vilket kan vara knepigt för höghandicaparen). På 14e kliver du plötsligt ut ur skogen och de fyra följande hålen ändrar banan karaktär. Nu är det seaside-golf som gäller! Fast havet heter här Vallentunasjön. På Täby, som på så många andra banor, är det viktigt att kunna skruva bollen från tee för att få ett så bra inspelsläge som möjligt (om du nu inte behärskar att slå bollen spikrakt, vilket är det svåraste slaget i golf). Om du bara har en dag över för golfspel så spela Ullna på förmiddagen och Täby på eftermiddagen.

The Club house is located in a former private mansion made from wood, where you can enjoy the end of the day on a veranda overlooking the 18th green. When looking back over your round, you might well remember that Jesper Parnevik learned his trade here. No wonder he became such a good worker of the ball. At Täby, you need every club in your bag and every shot in the book. Expect a few surprises too, as the holes are laid out in the middle of a forest over hilly terrain, meaning that you are hardly ever playing the ball from a flat lie (not easy for high-handicappers). Suddenly, when playing holes 14 through 17, you are in a whole change of scenery, similar to a seaside course except that here the course unwinds alongside lake Vallentunasjön. At Täby as elsewhere, astute placing of the drive is essential off the tee, fading and drawing the ball (unless you hit it perfectly straight, perhaps the hardest thing to do in golf). If you only have one day for golfing, play Ullna in the morning and Täby in the afternoon.

Täby Golfklubb — 1968

Skålhamra Gård
S - 187 70 TÄBY

Office	Sekretariat	(46) 08 - 510 234 22
Pro shop	Pro shop	(46) 08 - 510 233 36
Fax	Fax	(46) 08 - 510 234 41
Web	www.taby-gk.com	
Situation	Läge	Stockholm, 25 km
Annual closure	Årlig stängning	no
Weekly closure	Daglig stängning	no

Fees main season / Tariff hög säsong	Week days / Veckodag	We/Bank holidays / Lör/Söndag/Helgdag
		Full day
Individual Individuellt	SKr 400	SKr 450
Couple Par	SKr 800	SKr 900

Juniors: – 50%

Caddy	Caddie	no
Electric Trolley	El vagn	no
Buggy	Golfbil	SKr 250 /18 holes
Clubs	Klubbor	SKr 200 /18 holes

Credit cards Kredit kort
VISA - Eurocard - MasterCard

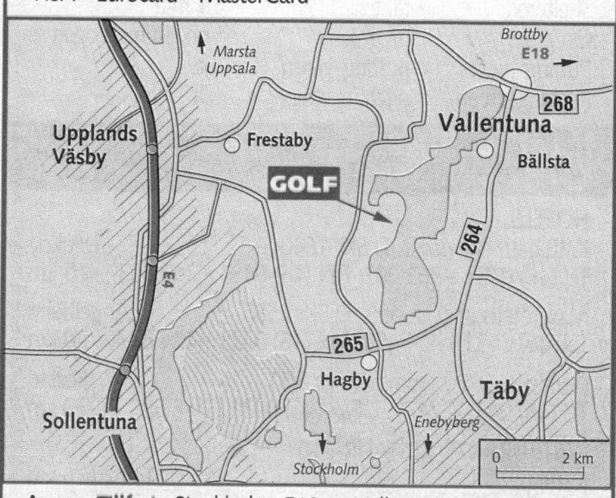

Access Tillfart : Stockholm, E18 → Vallentuna, "Danderyds Kyrka". 3 km → "Skålhamra 7"
Map 2 on page 1206 Karta 2 se sid: 1206

Golf course / BANA — 16/20

Site	Läge	
Maintenance	Underhåll	
Architect	Arkitekt	Nils Sköld
Type	Karaktär	seaside course, parkland
Relief	Nivåskillnader	
Water in play	Vatten på spelfältet	
Exp. to wind	Vindutsatt	
Trees in play	Träd på spelfältet	

Scorecard / Scorekort	Chp. / Back tees	Mens / Herrtee	Ladies / Damtee
Length Längd	6105	5812	5036
Par	72	72	72
Slope system	—	129	129

Advised golfing ability 0 12 24 36
Rekommenderad spelnivå
Hcp required Hcp erfordrad 36

Club house & amenities / KLUBBHUS OCH OMGIVNING — 7/10

Pro shop	Pro shop	
Driving range	Träningsbana	
Sheltered	tåkt	3 mats
On grass	på gräs	no, 24 mats open air
Putting-green	putting-green	yes
Pitching-green	pitching-green	yes

Hotel facilities / HOTELL OMGIVNING — 7/10

HOTELS

Radisson SAS Royal Park — Stockholm 20 km
184 rooms, D SKr 1900
Tel (46) 08 - 624 55 00, Fax (46) 08 - 858 566

Silja Hotel Ariadne — Stockholm 25 km
283 rooms, D SKr 1960
Tel (46) 08 - 665 78 00, Fax (46) 08 - 662 76 70

First Hotel Reisen — Stockholm 25 km
144 rooms, D SKr 1895
Tel (46) 08 - 223 260, Fax (46) 08 - 201 559

RESTAURANTS RESTAURANG

Edsbacka Krog, Tel (46) 08 - 850 815 — Sollentuna 15 km
Stallmästaregården, Tel (46) 08 - 610 13 00 — Stockholm

TOREKOV

14	7	7

Torekov ligger längst ute på Bjärehalvön, en halvö norr om Helsingborg. Banan öppnade redan 1925 men byggdes om i början av 90-talet av Nils Sköld. Vi kan tillägga att han lyckades väl. Klimatet och sandjorden gör det i princip möjligt att spela året om här. Banan är kort, men kräver bra drives eller långa järnslag från tee för att ge dig möjlighet att spela in mot greenerna med ett mellanjärn eller ett kort järn. Det är i varje fall vad du kan hoppas på de dagar det är vindstilla, vilket händer ungefär två gånger om året. De andra 363 dagarna får du plocka fram ditt skotska spel och studsa och rulla bollen upp på greener som ofta är hårda och snabba. Det finns definitivt bättre golfbanor än denna, men få har en större charm och ett sådant lugnt behagligt tempo. Några monsterhål finns inte så detta är en perfekt bana för hela familjen att åka till. Dessutom, har du bra bollträff finns möjligheten till en låg runda.

Even further afield than Båstad, Torekov is situated at the tip of Bjärehalvön, a peninsula to the north of Malmö and Helsingborg. The course here was opened in 1925, but it was significantly altered in the early 1990s by Nils Sköld, for the better we might add. The climate and largely sandy soil make this course playable virtually all year (a rare occurrence in Sweden). A very short layout, it calls for some excellent driving or long irons off the tee to end up with a short or medium iron going into the green, at least if the wind is quiet. This is the case about two days a year. For the other 363 days, you will have to call on all your Scottish flair when selecting the right club to play and master the bump and run shot to hit greens that are often firm and slick. There are certainly better courses than this, but few have greater charm and such an easy pace and tempo. There are few high-risk holes, so this is an ideal course for family holidays, where the pleasure of playing together counts for more than carding a reasonable score. At the same time, if you want to shoot a low score, you are of course very free to do so.

Torekovs Golfklubb — 1925

Box 81
S - 260 93 TOREKOV

Office	Sekretariat	(46) 0431 - 363 572
Pro shop	Pro shop	(46) 0431 - 364 121
Fax	Fax	(46) 0431 - 364 916
Web	www.togk.se	
Situation	Läge	Båstad, 15 km
Annual closure	Årlig stängning	no
Weekly closure	Daglig stängning	no

1258

Fees main season Tariff hög säsong	Week days Veckodag	We/Bank holidays Lör/Söndag/Helgdag
	Full day	
Individual Individuellt	SKr 280	SKr 280
Couple Par	SKr 560	SKr 560

Juniors: – 50%

Caddy	Caddie	no
Electric Trolley	El vagn	SKr 100 /18 holes
Buggy	Golfbil	SKr 150 /18 holes
Clubs	Klubbor	SKr 100 /18 holes

Credit cards Kredit kort
VISA - Eurocard - MasterCard - AMEX

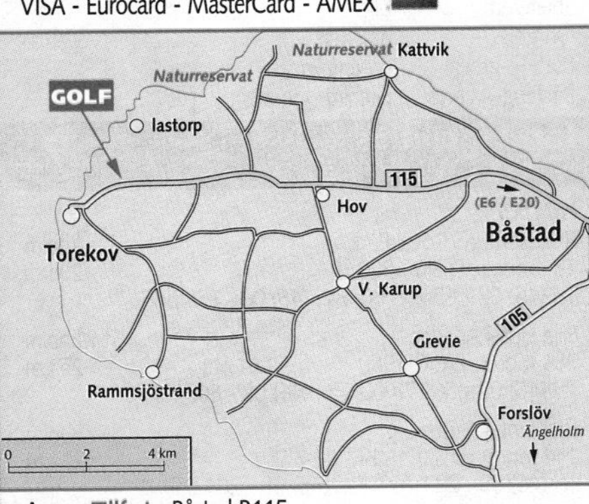

Access Tillfart : Båstad R115.
Map 1 on page 1204 Karta 1 se sid: 1204

Golf course BANA — 14/20

Site	Läge	
Maintenance	Underhåll	
Architect	Arkitekt	Nils Sköld
Type	Karaktär	seaside course, open country
Relief	Nivåskillnader	
Water in play	Vatten på spelfältet	
Exp. to wind	Vindutsatt	
Trees in play	Träd på spelfältet	

Scorecard Scorekort	Chp. Back tees	Mens Herrtee	Ladies Damtee
Length Längd	5707	5707	5027
Par	72	72	72
Slope system	—	130	126

Advised golfing ability Rekommenderad spelnivå — 0 12 24 36

Hcp required Hcp erfordrad — 36

Club house & amenities KLUBBHUS OCH OMGIVNING — 7/10

Pro shop	Pro shop	
Driving range	Träningsbana	
Sheltered	tåkt	1 mat
On grass	på gräs	no, 14 mats open air
Putting-green	putting-green	ja
Pitching-green	pitching-green	ja

Hotel facilities HOTELL OMGIVNING — 7/10

HOTELS

Kattegatt, 11 rooms, D SKr 1640 — Torekov 5 km
Tel (46) 0431 - 363 002, Fax (46) 0431 - 363 003

Margretetorp, 60 rooms, D SKr 1585 — Ängelholm 20 km
Tel (46) 0431 - 454 450, Fax (46) 0431 - 454 877

Hemmestör, 90 rooms, D SKr 800 — Båstad 20 km
Tel (46) 0431 - 742 65, Fax (46) 0431 - 748 88

RESTAURANTS RESTAURANG

Kattegatt — Torekov 5 km
Tel (46) 0431 - 363 002

Enehall, Tel (46) 0431 - 750 15 — Båstad 10 km

Margretetorp, Tel (46) 0431 - 454 450 — Båstad 20 km

TRANÅS

14	6	7

Staden ligger mitt i djupaste Småland, omgiven av skogar och mörkblåa sjöar – ett paradis för fotvandrare och sportfiskare. Banan står att finna österut nära sjön Sommen. Den är smal och slingrar sig fram mellan träden, men någon större längd från tee behövs inte utan en trätrea räcker ofta långt. Detta är ett smart sätt att undvika strategiskt utlagda fairwaybunkers som annars är som en magnet för bollen. Många doglegs gör också att den som verkligen kan manövrera bollen har julafton här. Redan på första hålet kan långtslående försöka nå greenen med utslaget, men frågan är om de känner sig bekväma på en smal bana som denna? Har de en bra dag med drivern kommer de dock ha att hamna väldigt nära greenen på några par 4-hål. Greenerna är för övrigt typiska för hur man byggde på 50-talet. De är små, mycket ondulerade och är svåra att stanna en boll på. Därför krävs mycket känsla i närspelet. Åk hit, om det så bara är för att uppleva charmen med den här platsen.

The town is situated in the middle of Småland, a region of forests and blue-steel lakes, a sort of paradise for hikers and anglers. The course lies to the east, very close to lake Sommen. It is a narrow layout amongst trees, but no great length is required off the tee and a 3-wood will often do very nicely. This is also a very reassuring club to hit in that the fairway bunkers seem to have a magnetic effect on mis-hit drives. More, the very many dog-legs ideally call for skill in bending the ball both ways, making this a home from home course for technicians and tacticians. Long-hitters can certainly go for the green as from hole number one, but generally speaking they won't feel quite as comfortable on this sort of course. With a good tee-shot, though, they will probably end up with a short iron into the greens, which are typically 1950s style: on the small side, very contoured and hard to stop the ball on. When you miss them you are left with some tricky pitch or chip shots. Worth knowing, if only for the charm of the site.

Tranås Golfklubb — 1952

Box 430
S - 573 25 TRANÅS

Office	Sekretariat	(46) 0140 - 311 661
Pro shop	Pro shop	(46) 0140 - 169 20
Fax	Fax	(46) 0140 - 161 61
Web	www.golf.se/tranasgk	
Situation	Läge	Jönköping, 78 km
Annual closure	Årlig stängning	no
Weekly closure	Daglig stängning	no

Fees main season Tariff hög säsong		Full day
	Week days Veckodag	**We/Bank holidays** Lör/Söndag/Helgdag
Individual Individuellt	SKr 220	SKr 260
Couple Par	SKr 440	SKr 520

Special fees for juniors

Caddy	Caddie	no
Electric Trolley	El vagn	no
Buggy	Golfbil	SKr 100 /18 holes
Clubs	Klubbor	SKr 100 /18 holes

Credit cards Kredit kort
VISA - Eurocard - MasterCard

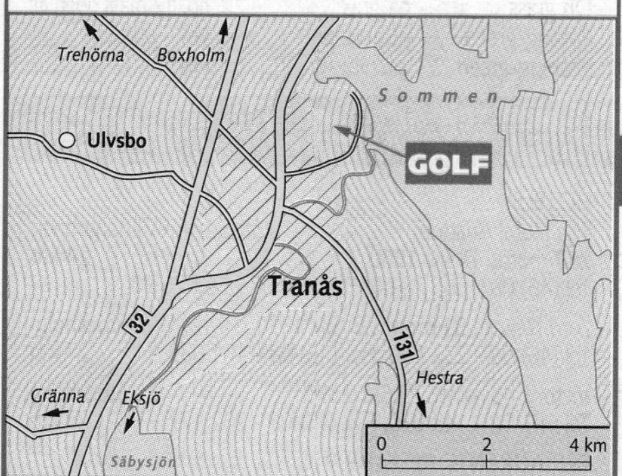

Access Tillfart : Jönköping E4 → Linköping. Gränna Exit R133 → Tranås, R32 → Tranås. 2 km N, → Golf
Map 1 on page 1205 Karta 1 se sid: 1205

Golf course — BANA — 14/20

Site	Läge	
Maintenance	Underhåll	
Architect	Arkitekt	Sundholm
Type	Karaktär	forest, parkland
Relief	Nivåskillnader	
Water in play	Vatten på spelfältet	
Exp. to wind	Vindutsatt	
Trees in play	Träd på spelfältet	

Scorecard Scorekort	**Chp.** Back tees	**Mens** Herrtee	**Ladies** Damtee
Length Längd	6014	5768	5022
Par	72	72	72
Slope system	—	128	128

Advised golfing ability Rekommenderad spelnivå — 0 12 24 36
Hcp required Hcp erfordrad 36

Club house & amenities — KLUBBHUS OCH OMGIVNING — 6/10

Pro shop	Pro shop	
Driving range	Träningsbana	
Sheltered	tåkt	1 mat
On grass	på gräs	no, 14 mats open air
Putting-green	putting-green	yes
Pitching-green	pitching-green	yes

Hotel facilities — HOTELL OMGIVNING — 7/10

HOTELS

Statt Hotell, 52 rooms, D SKr 970 — Tranås 5 km
Tel (46) 0140 - 566 00, Fax (46) 0140 - 561 51

Badhotellet — Tranås 5 km
57 rooms, D SKr 725
Tel (46) 0140 - 462 00, Fax (46) 0140 - 461 85

Hotell Åberg, 20 rooms, D SKr 740 — Tranås 3 km
Tel (46) 0140 - 130 80, Fax (46) 0140 - 562 02

RESTAURANTS RESTAURANG

Queens , Tel (46) 0140 - 539 99 — Tranås 3 km
Krogen, Tel (46) 0140 - 161 45 — Tranås 3 km

ULLNA

17 | 8 | 6

En dag på Ullna måste börja med att du står och filosoferar i klubbhusets värme och blickar ut över Ullnasjön och ser solen reflektera i vattnet. Det här kommer definitivt få dig i rätt sinnesstämning. Tredje hålet är en kort och oförglömlig par 3a med en ögreen. Faktum är att du finner vatten så gott som överallt, på tolv av hålen kommer vatten i spel. För att leverera en bra score här är det nödvändigt att du är i absolut toppform. Ullna är en väldigt ärlig bana som inte gömmer sina hinder – de syns tydligt från tee. Den är dessutom nästan helt platt, och sammantaget är den ett av de finaste exempel på "targetgolf" som finns i Sverige. De duktiga spelarna kommer säkert göra en eller annan birdie för att kompensera för oundvikliga bogeys. Sven Tumba, banarkitekten, har dock inte gjort livet lätt för höghandicaparen, som kommer att tvingas plocka upp bollen på många hål (om han har några kvar, vill säga). Ullna är spektakulär, konstgjord och välmanikyrerad, och en högst oförglömlig upplevelse. Och då inte bara för de 4 och de 17 hålen, som är bland de bästa som man kan finna i Sverige. Det här är en bana för konnässörer och skickliga spelare som kan slå bollen högt och med precision, vilket inte alltid är så lätt när vinden ligger på.

Contemplating the sun will certainly put you in the right frame of mind for your round because water is almost everywhere, coming into play on 12 holes. You will need to be on top of your game to card a good score. This is a very forthright course which clearly shows it hand in terms of hazards; it is also virtually flat and one of the finest examples of target golf in the whole of Sweden. All the same, while the best players should come through unscathed and find a few birdies to make up for the inevitable bogeys, architect Sven Tumba did not spare too many thoughts for the higher-handicappers, who will spend a lot of time picking up their balls (if they have any left). Spectacular, artificial and finely contoured, Ullna is a memorable course, and not only for holes 4 and 17, two of the finest in the country. It is a course for connoisseurs and skilled players who can hit high, accurate shots..

Ullna Golf & Country Club — 1981

Rosenkälla
S - 184 94 Åkersberga

Office	Sekretariat	(46) 08 - 514 412 30
Pro shop	Pro shop	(46) 08 - 514 412 30
Fax	Fax	(46) 08 - 510 260 68
Web	www.ullnagolf.se	
Situation	Läge	Stockholm, 27 km
Annual closure	Årlig stängning	no
Weekly closure	Daglig stängning	no

Fees main season Tariff hög säsong		Full day
	Week days Veckodag	**We/Bank holidays** Lör/Söndag/Helgdag
Individual Individuellt	SKr 600	SKr 600
Couple Par	SKr 1200	SKr 1200

Juniors: 160:-

Caddy	Caddie	no
Electric Trolley	El vagn	no
Buggy	Golfbil	SKr 250 /18 holes
Clubs	Klubbor	SKr 300 /18 holes

Credit cards Kredit kort
VISA - Eurocard - MasterCard - DC - AMEX

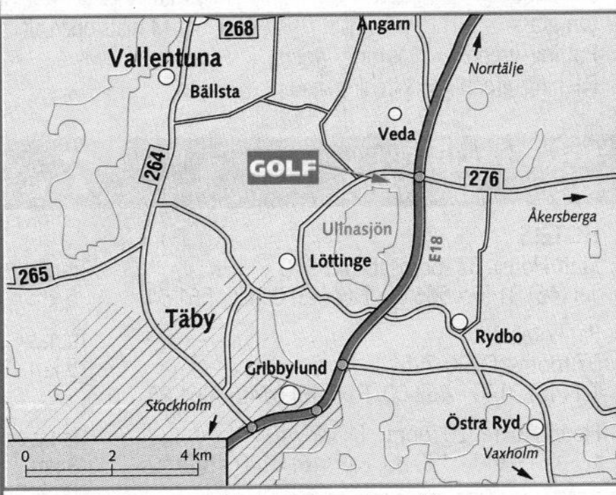

Access Tillfart : Stockholm, E 18 → Norrtälje.
→ Åkersberga, → Gribbylund, → Golf
Map 2 on page 1206 Karta 2 se sid: 1206

Golf course BANA — 17/20

Site	Läge	
Maintenance	Underhåll	
Architect	Arkitekt	Sven Tumba
Type	Karaktär	parkland
Relief	Nivåskillnader	
Water in play	Vatten på spelfältet	
Exp. to wind	Vindutsatt	
Trees in play	Träd på spelfältet	

Scorecard Scorekort	**Chp.** Back tees	**Mens** Herrtee	**Ladies** Damtee
Length Längd	6210	5750	4915
Par	72	72	72
Slope system	—	145	142

Advised golfing ability Rekommenderad spelnivå — 0 12 24 36
Hcp required Hcp erfordrad — 24 Men, 30 Ladies

Club house & amenities KLUBBHUS OCH OMGIVNING — 8/10

Pro shop	Pro shop	
Driving range	Träningsbana	
Sheltered	tåkt	25 mats
On grass	på gräs	no, 12 mats open air
Putting-green	putting-green	yes
Pitching-green	pitching-green	yes

Hotel facilities HOTELL OMGIVNING — 6/10

HOTELS

Silja Hotel Ariadne — Stockholm Värtahamnen
283 rooms, D SKr 1960 — 24 km
Tel (46) 08 - 665 78 00, Fax (46) 08 - 662 76 70

Lord Nelson, 31 rooms, D SKr 1890 — Stockholm
Tel (46) 08 - 232 390, Fax (46) 08 - 101 089 — 27 km

Victory, 45 rooms, D SKr 2390 — Stockholm
Tel (46) 08 - 143 090, Fax (46) 08 - 202 177 — 27 km

RESTAURANTS RESTAURANG

Eriks, Tel (46) 08 - 238 500 — Stockholm 27 km
Stallmästeregården, Tel (46) 08 - 610 13 00 — Stockholm
Den Gyldene Freden, Tel (46) 08 - 249 760 — Stockholm

UPSALA

13 | 6 | 6

Staden Uppsala är berömd för sin katerdral, sina museum och en historia som ofta har varit våldsam, såväl politiskt som intellektuellt. Uppsala är också hem för landets äldsta universitet. Fast något vilt studentliv kan vi knappast förknippa Upsala Golfklubb med, även om vi får allt fler yngre golfare i landet. Banan är ganska flack och växlar mellan parkbanekaraktär och skog, en typisk svensk landskapsbild med andra ord. Framför allt de långa par 4-hålen kräver väl träffade drives om du ska ha en möjlighet att nå greenerna på rätt antal slag. Hindernas variation och placering kräver att du håller huvudet kallt. Det här är en typisk inlandsbana, därmed inte sagt att det för jämnan är vindstilla. Vinden kan på den här banan spela en avgörande betydelse. Detta är en mästerskapsbana ofta använd för stora nationella tävlingar. Ytterligare en 18-hålsbana öppnade våren 2001 och anläggningen består nu av 36 hål.

The city of Uppsala is famous for its Gothic cathedral, museums and tangible vestiges of an eventful and oftentimes violent past history both intellectually and politically. It is home to the country's oldest university. The Upsala Golfklubb course lies well away from the hustle and bustle of young undergraduates, even though young golfers make up a large contingent of Swedish golfers. A rather flat layout in a landscape of parkland and forest frequently found in a country so attached to nature, the course calls for long drives on all the par 4s if you want to hit the greens in regulation. The standard, variety and location of hazards call for tight strategy, and for a course which, to all intents and purposes is an inland layout, the wind can play a major role and have a significant effect on scores. A serious course which is often used for nationwide tournaments. A second 18-hole course has opened during Spring 2001, we will consider it in the future when it will have matured.

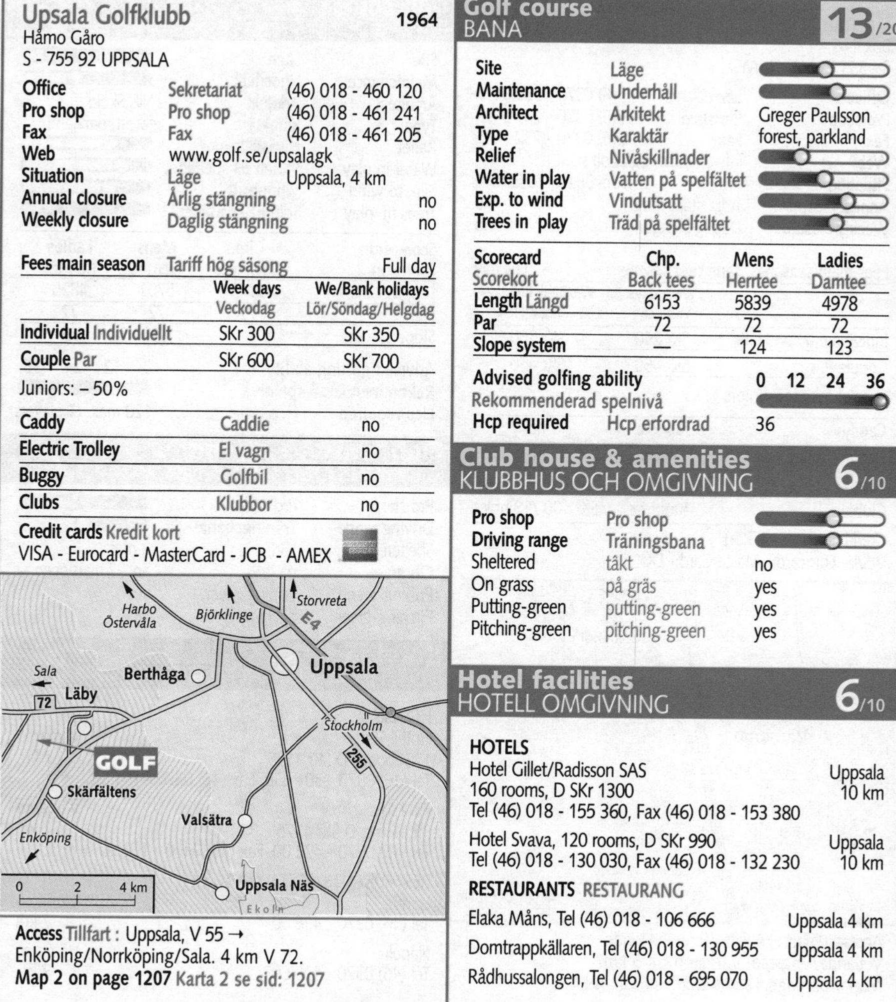

Upsala Golfklubb — 1964

Håmo Gåro
S - 755 92 UPPSALA

Office	Sekretariat	(46) 018 - 460 120
Pro shop	Pro shop	(46) 018 - 461 241
Fax	Fax	(46) 018 - 461 205
Web	www.golf.se/upsalagk	
Situation	Läge	Uppsala, 4 km
Annual closure	Årlig stängning	no
Weekly closure	Daglig stängning	no

Fees main season / Tariff hög säsong	Full day	
	Week days / Veckodag	We/Bank holidays / Lör/Söndag/Helgdag
Individual Individuellt	SKr 300	SKr 350
Couple Par	SKr 600	SKr 700

Juniors: – 50%

Caddy	Caddie	no
Electric Trolley	El vagn	no
Buggy	Golfbil	no
Clubs	Klubbor	no

Credit cards Kredit kort
VISA - Eurocard - MasterCard - JCB - AMEX

Access Tillfart : Uppsala, V 55 → Enköping/Norrköping/Sala. 4 km V 72.
Map 2 on page 1207 Karta 2 se sid: 1207

Golf course / BANA — 13/20

Site	Läge	
Maintenance	Underhåll	
Architect	Arkitekt	Greger Paulsson
Type	Karaktär	forest, parkland
Relief	Nivåskillnader	
Water in play	Vatten på spelfältet	
Exp. to wind	Vindutsatt	
Trees in play	Träd på spelfältet	

Scorecard / Scorekort	Chp. / Back tees	Mens / Herrtee	Ladies / Damtee
Length Längd	6153	5839	4978
Par	72	72	72
Slope system	—	124	123

Advised golfing ability / Rekommenderad spelnivå: 0 12 24 36
Hcp required / Hcp erfordrad: 36

Club house & amenities / KLUBBHUS OCH OMGIVNING — 6/10

Pro shop	Pro shop	
Driving range	Träningsbana	
Sheltered	tåkt	no
On grass	på gräs	yes
Putting-green	putting-green	yes
Pitching-green	pitching-green	yes

Hotel facilities / HOTELL OMGIVNING — 6/10

HOTELS

Hotel Gillet/Radisson SAS — Uppsala 10 km
160 rooms, D SKr 1300
Tel (46) 018 - 155 360, Fax (46) 018 - 153 380

Hotel Svava, 120 rooms, D SKr 990 — Uppsala 10 km
Tel (46) 018 - 130 030, Fax (46) 018 - 132 230

RESTAURANTS RESTAURANG

Elaka Måns, Tel (46) 018 - 106 666 — Uppsala 4 km
Domtrappkällaren, Tel (46) 018 - 130 955 — Uppsala 4 km
Rådhussalongen, Tel (46) 018 - 695 070 — Uppsala 4 km

VÄRNAMO

15 | 7 | 5

Tack vare E 4 ligger banan perfekt till för dig som färdas från Malmö till Stockholm, eller tvärtom. Ändå kan Värnamo, i en positiv mening, kännas som att komma till världens ände. Att släntra upp till klubbhuset en tidig morgon och titta ut över sjön Hindsen är en magisk upplevelse. Som så många andra svenska banor är Värnamo byggd på en romantisk, nästan teatralisk plats. Klarar du av par 3-hålen är du på väg mot en bra score. Fast den riktiga utmaningen finns i de något upphöjda greenerna som dessutom inte är alldeles lätta att läsa. Missar du en green skadar det inte om du har en vass lobbwedge i bagen. På Värnamo finns inga riktiga monsterhinder som avskräcker höghandicaparen, medan det för den bättre spelaren gäller att undvika skogen om han vill briljera inför släkt och vänner och visa vad han kan göra med en golfklubba. Såväl för män som kvinnor är denna halvsvåra bana definitivt att föredra framför att spela en riktig tuffing. Här vinner charmen!

A very reachable course, which is close to the motorway running across the country from south-west Malmö to Stockholm further north-east. But it is still far enough for the golfer to feel as if he were playing at the ends of the earth. Arriving early morning at the club house built on a small hill overlooking lake Hindsen is a magic experience. Like many Swedish courses, this has a romantic, theatrical setting, but that is only the beginning. It might be on the short side, but start off by getting the better of the par 3s and you can think about carding a good score. Here, the real challenge lies with the slightly elevated greens, which are sharply contoured and tough to read. You will also need a lot of touch. A missed green cries out for a lob-wedge, if you have one. There are no excessive hazards to deter the high-handicapper, while the better players will have to come to terms with the trees before showing friends and family what he or she can do with a golf club. Whether for men or ladies, this averagely difficult course offers more fun than any really tough challenge.

1262

Värnamo Golfklubb — 1962

Box 146
S - 331 21 VÄRNAMO

Office	Sekretariat	(46) 0370 - 239 91
Pro shop	Pro shop	(46) 0370 - 239 91
Fax	Fax	(46) 0370 - 232 16
Web	info@varnamogk.golf.se	
Situation	Läge	Jönköping, 70 km
Annual closure	Årlig stängning	no
Weekly closure	Daglig stängning	no

Fees main season Tariff hög säsong	Week days Veckodag	We/Bank holidays Lör/Söndag/Helgdag
		Full day
Individual Individuellt	SKr 250	SKr 250
Couple Par	SKr 450	SKr 450
Special fees for juniors		

Caddy	Caddie	no
Electric Trolley	El vagn	no
Buggy	Golfbil	SKr 200 /18 holes
Clubs	Klubbor	SKr 100 /18 holes

Credit cards Kredit kort
VISA - Eurocard - MasterCard - DC

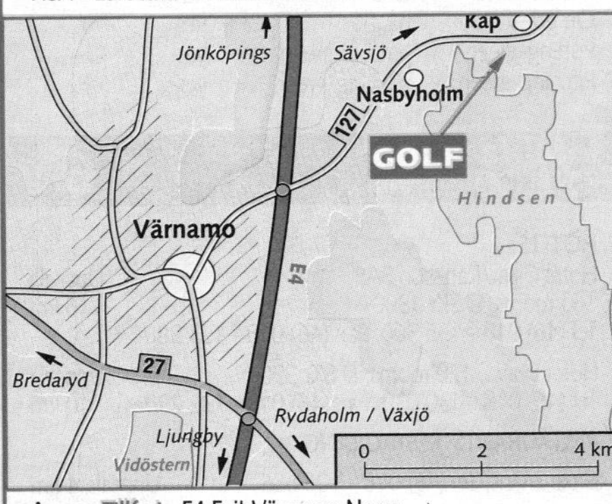

Access Tillfart : E4 Exit Värnamo Norra. → Vetlanda/Vrigstad. Värnamo GK 5 km.
Map 1 on page 1204 Karta 1 se sid: 1204

Golf course — BANA — 15/20

Site	Läge	
Maintenance	Underhåll	
Architect	Arkitekt	Nils Sköld
Type	Karaktär	forest, parkland
Relief	Nivåskillnader	
Water in play	Vatten på spelfältet	
Exp. to wind	Vindutsatt	
Trees in play	Träd på spelfältet	

Scorecard Scorekort	Chp. Back tees	Mens Herrtee	Ladies Damtee
Length Längd	5943	5701	4825
Par	72	72	72
Slope system	—	135	126

Advised golfing ability Rekommenderad spelnivå — 0 12 24 36
Hcp required Hcp erfordrad — 120 max. (4 players)

Club house & amenities — KLUBBHUS OCH OMGIVNING — 7/10

Pro shop	Pro shop	
Driving range	Träningsbana	
Sheltered	tåkt	2 mat
On grass	på gräs	no, 22 mats open air
Putting-green	putting-green	yes
Pitching-green	pitching-green	yes

Hotel facilities — HOTELL OMGIVNING — 5/10

HOTELS

Hotell Statt, — Värnamo 7 km
125 rooms, D SKr 1195
Tel (46) 0370 - 301 530, Fax (46) 0370 - 134 69

Tre Liljor, — Värnamo 7 km
39 rooms, D SKr 1275
Tel (46) 0370 - 473 00, Fax (46) 0370 - 168 90

RESTAURANTS RESTAURANG

Harrys — Värnamo 7 km
Tel (46) 0370 - 498 00

Napoli — Värnamo 7 km
Tel (46) 0370 - 120 60

VASATORP

16 | 7 | 7

Vasatorp är en av många utmärkta banor som ligger runt Helsingborg, en fantastisk stad för den historieintresserade – inte minst för att detta är skådeplatsen för många krigsbataljer mellan Sverige och Danmark genom århundradena. Knappt fem kilometer bort skymtar man Helsingør. Vasatorps golfbana gömmer inga obehagliga överraskningar: Slå rakt och håll dig på fairway, och du kommer att göra en bra score (svårare än så är inte golf). Trots den täta skogen är banan förhållandevis bred – även för Ballesteros, som när han vann SEO här spred sina drives både till höger och vänster. Om du ska ha en chans att nå på rätt antal slag och få bra inspelsvinklar måste du välja drivern från tee. Många greener är omgärdade av kullar, vilket ställer höga krav på dina inspel. Greenerna är relativt stora och kan bjuda på en stor variation vad gäller flaggplaceringarna, något som kan inverka högst påtagligt på ditt resultat. Här är det amerikansk målgolf som gäller – höga inspel är att föredra framför att rulla in bollen. För höghandicaparen är det bäst att spela här på sommaren då marken är torr och bollen rullar långt. Sagt det kan vi konstatera att Vasatorp kan bli ganska blöt, framför allt på våren. Den andra 18-hålsbanan som finns här måste också nämnas.

This course has no traps in store: hit it straight, keep in the fairway and you will card a good score (golf is that simple). Despite the trees, the whole complex is wide, enough so for Ballesteros to have won here even though he sprayed his drives left and right into the undergrowth. Quite simply, here you have to hit the driver if you want to reach the long holes in regulation and approach the greens from the right angle. A number of sandhills and mounds can complicate your approach shots. The greens are pretty huge, with many different pin positions that can seriously damage your card, especially since here you have to play target golf rather than bump and run shots. High-handicappers are best advised to play Vasatorps in summer, when the ground is dry and affords welcome roll for added length. With this said, this course can get rather wet, especially in the Spring. A last word for the excellent second 18-hole course here.

Vasatorps Golfklubb — **1973**
Box 13035
S - 250 13 HELSINGBORG

Office	Sekretariat	(46) 042 - 235 058
Pro shop	Pro shop	(46) 042 - 235 045
Fax	Fax	(46) 042 - 235 135
Web	www.golf.se/vasatorpsgk	
Situation	Läge	Helsingborg, 7 km
Annual closure	Årlig stängning	no
Weekly closure	Daglig stängning	no

Fees main season Tariff hög säsong		Full day
	Week days Veckodag	**We/Bank holidays** Lör/Söndag/Helgdag
Individual Individuellt	SKr 300	SKr 300
Couple Par	SKr 600	SKr 600

Juniors: – 50%

Caddy	Caddie	no
Electric Trolley	El vagn	SKr 50 /18 holes
Buggy	Golfbil	no
Clubs	Klubbor	SKr 150 /18 holes

Credit cards Kredit kort
VISA - Eurocard - MasterCard - DC - AMEX

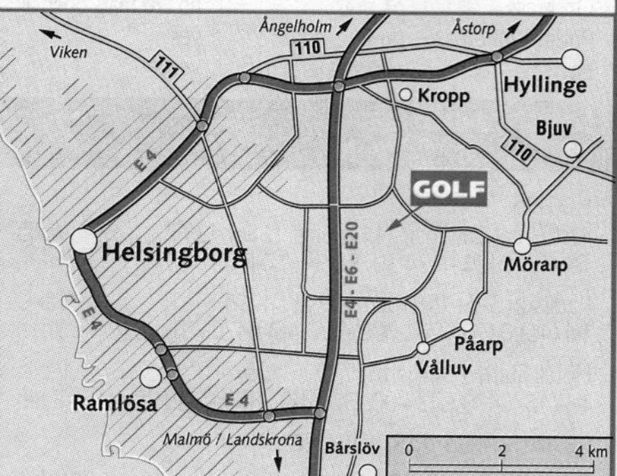

Access Tillfart : Kelsingborg, E4 West (Österut) → "Höganäsrondellen". → Råå. Turn left at traffic lights (Trafiklij, vä). 500 m → Kropp.
Map 1 on page 1204 Karta 1 se sid: 1204

Golf course BANA — 16/20

Site	Läge	
Maintenance	Underhåll	
Architect	Arkitekt	Ture Bruce
Type	Karaktär	forest, parkland
Relief	Nivåskillnader	
Water in play	Vatten på spelfältet	
Exp. to wind	Vindutsatt	
Trees in play	Träd på spelfältet	

Scorecard Scorekort	**Chp.** Back tees	**Mens** Herrtee	**Ladies** Damtee
Length Längd	6165	5895	5510
Par	72	72	72
Slope system	—	133	128

Advised golfing ability Rekommenderad spelnivå — 0 12 24 36
Hcp required Hcp erfordrad — 36

Club house & amenities KLUBBHUS OCH OMGIVNING — 7/10

Pro shop	Pro shop	
Driving range	Träningsbana	
Sheltered	tåkt	7 mats
On grass	på gräs	no, 30 mats open air
Putting-green	putting-green	yes
Pitching-green	pitching-green	yes

Hotel facilities HOTELL OMGIVNING — 7/10

HOTELS

Marina Plaza, 190 rooms, D SKr 1295 — Helsingborg
Tel (46) 042 - 192 100, Fax (46) 042 - 149 616 — 7 km

Hotell Nouveau, 89 rooms, D SKr 1145 — Helsingborg
Tel (46) 042 - 185 390, Fax (46) 042 - 140 885 — 7 km

Grand Hotell, 116 rooms, D SKr 1490 — Helsingborg
Tel (46) 042 - 120 170, Fax (46) 042 - 218 833 — 7 km

RESTAURANTS RESTAURANG

Oskar Trapp — Helsingborg
Tel (46) 042 - 146 044 — 7 km

Gastro — Helsingborg
Tel (46) 042 - 243 470 — 7 km

VÄXJÖ

15 | 6 | 7

Växjö golfbana designades 1961 av Douglas Brasier, en arkitekt som ligger bakom många kvalitetsbanor. Här finns massor med träd, på våren kan banan var ganska blöt och landar du i den tjocka ruffen kan du få många besvärliga lägen. Spelare med bra drives har en klar fördel här, förutsatt naturligtvis att de kan följa upp med precisa inspel mot de väl skyddade greenerna. Fast höghandicaparen kommer att uppskatta att det inte finns några riktigt besvärliga hinder precis framför utslagsplatserna. Men det ska också sägas – den här banan är inte lätt, inte för någon. Banans svårigheter är jämt fördelade över de 18 hålen, även om sluthålet bjuder på något alldeles extra. Här krävs en perfekt drive om du ska avsluta rundan på ett bra sätt. Växjö är betydligt bättre än genomsnittsbanan, layouten är av gammalt klassiskt snitt, men ändå med många fantasifulla inslag, exempelvis sjätte hålet, en par 5, där du har många alternativa spelmöjligheter att välja mellan.

At the famous nearby Kosta Boda factory, you will find everything to treat yourself to a fine trophy to reward your performance on this layout. Designed in 1961 by Douglas Brasier, an architect who has built many a quality course, Växjö is full of trees, is often wet in the spring and autumn, and has a very thick first layer of rough from where extracting your ball can be a difficult proposition. Good drivers have a clear advantage here, providing of course that they successfully pursue their route to medium-sized, well-guarded greens. The absence of hazards immediately in front of the tee-boxes will reassure the less experienced players, even though this course is easy for no-one. The difficulties are evenly spread around the course and come to a head on the 18th hole, where the drive has to be perfect to finish your round with some satisfaction. A course well above average, rather classical in style but with a zest of imagination here and there, like on the 6th hole, a par 5 where you can choose one of several options.

Växjö Golfklubb — 1961

Araby Herrgård Box 227
S - 351 05 VÄXJÖ

Office	Sekretariat	(46) 0470 - 215 15
Pro shop	Pro shop	no Proshop
Fax	Fax	(46) 042 - 215 57
Web	www.golf.se/vaxjogk	
Situation	Läge	Växjö, 10 km
Annual closure	Årlig stängning	no
Weekly closure	Daglig stängning	no

Fees main season Tariff hög säsong		Full day
	Week days Veckodag	We/Bank holidays Lör/Söndag/Helgdag
Individual Individuellt	SKr 250	SKr 250
Couple Par	SKr 500	SKr 500

Juniors: – 50%

Caddy	Caddie	no
Electric Trolley	El vagn	no
Buggy	Golfbil	SKr 200 /18 holes
Clubs	Klubbor	no

Credit cards Kredit kort
VISA - Eurocard - MasterCard

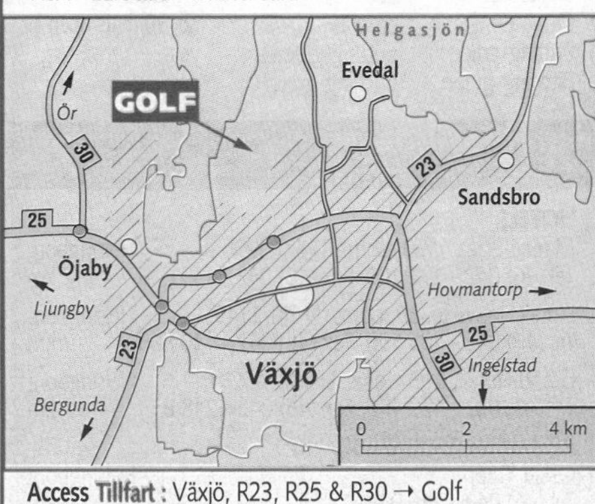

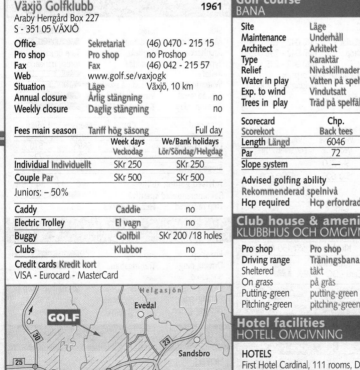

Access Tillfart : Växjö, R23, R25 & R30 → Golf
Map 1 on page 1204 Karta 1 se sid: 1204

Golf course BANA — 15/20

Site	Läge	
Maintenance	Underhåll	
Architect	Arkitekt	Douglas Brasier
Type	Karaktär	forest, parkland
Relief	Nivåskillnader	
Water in play	Vatten på spelfältet	
Exp. to wind	Vindutsatt	
Trees in play	Träd på spelfältet	

Scorecard Scorekort	Chp. Back tees	Mens Herrtee	Ladies Damtee
Length Längd	6046	5799	5059
Par	72	72	72
Slope system	—	134	125

Advised golfing ability Rekommenderad spelnivå: 0 12 24 36
Hcp required Hcp erfordrad: 36

Club house & amenities KLUBBHUS OCH OMGIVNING — 6/10

Pro shop	Pro shop	
Driving range	Träningsbana	
Sheltered	täkt	no
On grass	på gräs	no, 20 mats open air
Putting-green	putting-green	yes
Pitching-green	pitching-green	yes

Hotel facilities HOTELL OMGIVNING — 7/10

HOTELS

First Hotel Cardinal, 111 rooms, D SKr 1335 — Växjö 7 km
Tel (46) 0470 - 134 30, Fax (46) 0470 - 169 64

Radisson SAS, 158 rooms, D SKr 1295 — Växjö 7 km
Tel (46) 0470 - 701 000, Fax (46) 0470 - 701 010

Hotell Statt, 124 rooms, D SKr 1125 — Växjö 7 km
Tel (46) 0470 - 134 00, Fax (46) 0470 - 448 37

RESTAURANTS RESTAURANG

Spisen, Tel (46) 0470 - 123 00 — Växjö 7 km
Munhen, Tel (46) 0470 - 160 60 — Växjö 7 km
Teaterparken, Tel (46) 0470 - 399 00 — Växjö 7 km

VISBY

16 | 7 | 5

Bli inte skrämd av Gotlands geografiska läge! Klimatet är milt och på sommaren flockas turisterna här. Precis som handelsmännen gjorde under medeltiden. Faktum är att Visby har så många avtryck från den här perioden att UNESCO har satt staden på sin lista över kulturminnesmärkta platser. Kustlinjen är något alldeles extra, och nästan halva banan är också utlagd nära denna, resten av hålen vindlar fram i ett skogsparti. Det finns ingen hejd på alla hinder och det krävs att du inte släpper på koncentrationen. Även greenerna är lagom knepiga. De som byggdes 1959 är små och förrädiska, medan de som byggdes i början av 90-talet är större och mer kuperade. Som du kanske förstår är vinden här en avgörande faktor, något som du kommer att känna direkt på första hålet: Längs hela högersidan lurar vatten. För att ta dig till Gotland väntar en färjetur på 4–8 timmar (beroende på vilket bolag du åker med), så en bra idé är att stanna här i några dagar och spela banan flera gånger (samt niohålsbanan som ligger på området). Beställ "Dagens fisk" i restaurangen, njut av den och den magnifika utsikten.

Don't be put off by the very "Nordic" location of the isle of Gotland; for the region, the climate is very mild and the area is a very popular and famous holiday destination. In the Middle Ages, it was also a very busy trading centre, and the town of Visby has so many vestiges of this period that it is on the UNESCO world heritage list of historical sites. The coastline is equally impressive, where this course is laid out half beside the sea, half amidst trees. There is no shortage of hazards to keep you on your toes, and the greens, too, can cause their share of problems. Those built in 1959 are small and treacherous, the others, built in the 1990s, are larger and contoured. Obviously, the wind here is a decisive factor, as you will see and feel straightaway on hole number one. Here, your brushes with water begin down the right-hand side of the fairway. Getting here involves an four to eight-hour trip (depending if you go by ferry or the new catamaran), so a good idea is to stay for several days, play the course a number of times (this and the adjacent nine-hole layout), and enjoy your dinner with the fish of the day and a great view over the sea.

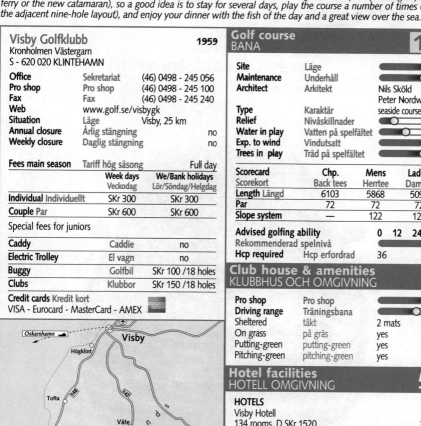

Visby Golfklubb — 1959

Kronholmen Västergarn
S - 620 020 KLINTEHAMN

Office	Sekretariat	(46) 0498 - 245 056
Pro shop	Pro shop	(46) 0498 - 245 100
Fax	Fax	(46) 0498 - 245 240
Web	www.golf.se/visbygk	
Situation	Läge	Visby, 25 km
Annual closure	Årlig stängning	no
Weekly closure	Daglig stängning	no

Fees main season Tariff hög säsong	Full day	
	Week days Veckodag	**We/Bank holidays** Lör/Söndag/Helgdag
Individual Individuellt	SKr 300	SKr 300
Couple Par	SKr 600	SKr 600

Special fees for juniors

Caddy	Caddie	no
Electric Trolley	El vagn	no
Buggy	Golfbil	SKr 100 /18 holes
Clubs	Klubbor	SKr 150 /18 holes

Credit cards Kredit kort
VISA - Eurocard - MasterCard - AMEX

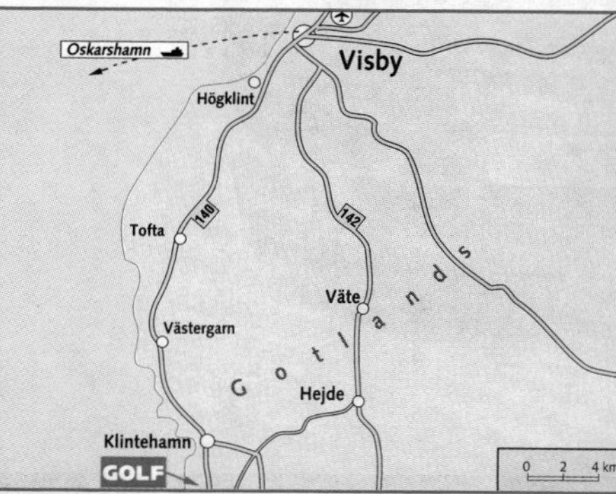

Access Tillfart : Stockholm, R79 → Nynäshamn. Ferry → Visby. R140 → Klintehamn. 25 km, → Golf
Map 1 on page 1205 Karta 1 se sid: 1205

Golf course — BANA — 16/20

Site	Läge	
Maintenance	Underhåll	
Architect	Arkitekt	Nils Sköld Peter Nordwall
Type	Karaktär	seaside course, parkland
Relief	Nivåskillnader	
Water in play	Vatten på spelfältet	
Exp. to wind	Vindutsatt	
Trees in play	Träd på spelfältet	

Scorecard Scorekort	**Chp.** Back tees	**Mens** Herrtee	**Ladies** Damtee
Length Längd	6103	5868	5094
Par	72	72	72
Slope system	—	122	121

Advised golfing ability Rekommenderad spelnivå — 0 12 24 36
Hcp required Hcp erfordrad — 36

Club house & amenities — KLUBBHUS OCH OMGIVNING — 7/10

Pro shop	Pro shop	
Driving range	Träningsbana	
Sheltered	tåkt	2 mats
On grass	på gräs	yes
Putting-green	putting-green	yes
Pitching-green	pitching-green	yes

Hotel facilities — HOTELL OMGIVNING — 5/10

HOTELS

Visby Hotell — Visby 30 km
134 rooms, D SKr 1520
Tel (46) 0498 - 204 000, Fax (46) 0498 - 211 320

Strand Hotell — Visby 30 km
110 rooms, D SKr 1325
Tel (46) 0498 - 258 800, Fax (46) 0498 - 258 811

RESTAURANTS RESTAURANG

Lindgården — Visby 30 km
Tel (46) 0498 - 218 700

Visby Hotell — Visby 30 km
Tel (46) 0498 - 204 000

EUROPE'S TOP 1000 GOLF COURSES

Switzerland

Domaine Impérial

Switzerland
Schweiz
Suisse
Svizzera

As in other European countries, the majority of courses featured here are private but open to the general public with a few restrictions or limited access on week-ends. The best idea is to make enquiries and book in advance, and remember that a letter of introduction from your own club is always a good idea. With 35,000 players and about fifty 18-hole courses, Switzerland is not a top golfing country, especially as certain environmental restrictions (more or less well-founded) have hampered development of the game, but the courses are very good and often set amidst some fabulous landscapes.

Comme dans les autres pays d'Europe, la majeure partie des golfs présentés ici sont privés, mais ouverts au public avec quelques restrictions ou difficultés d'accès en week-end. Il convient donc de s'informer et de réserver à l'avance, et une lettre d'introduction de votre club ne sera jamais inutile. Avec 35.000 joueurs, et une cinquantaine de 18 trous, la Suisse n'est pas un très grand pays golfique, certaines contraintes environnementales (plus ou moins fondées) entravent quelque peu son développement, mais ses parcours sont de qualité et souvent situés dans des paysages superbes.

Wie auch in anderen europäischen Ländern sind die meisten Golfplätze privat, aber der Öffentlichkeit unter gewissen Vorbehalten oder Einschränkungen an den Wochenenden zugänglich. Es ist daher empfehlenswert, sich vorgängig zu informieren oder zu reservieren, und ein Empfehlungsschreiben Ihres Clubs ist sicher immer nützlich. Mit ihren 35'000 Golfern und ungefähr 50 18-Loch-Bahnen zählt die Schweiz sicherlich nicht zu den bekannten Golfländern, aber dafür befinden sich die Golfplätze in einer landschaftlich reizvollen Umgebung.

CLASSIFICATION OF COURSES
CLASSEMENT DES PARCOURS
EINTEILUNG DER GOLFPLÄTZE

This classification gives priority consideration to the score awarded to the actual course.

Courses score / Note du parcours / Note für den Golfplatz				Page / Seite
18	8	6	Domaine Impérial	1277
17	7	8	Genève	1280
16	7	7	Lausanne	1283
16	8	7	Sempachersee	1291
15	7	6	Blumisberg	1274
15	6	6	Engadin	1278
15	7	6	Les Bois	1284
15	7	8	Lugano	1285
15	7	6	Zumikon	1293
14	7	8	Crans-sur-Sierre	1276
14	7	6	Gruyère (La)	1281
14	6	6	Interlaken	1282
14	7	7	Neuchâtel	1288
14	7	6	Schönenberg	1290
13	7	6	Bad Ragaz	1273
13	7	6	Breitenloo	1275
13	7	6	Ennetsee-Holzhäusern	1279
13	6	7	Luzern	1286
13	6	5	Montreux	1287
13	7	7	Niederbüren	1289
13	6	6	Wylihof	1292

TYPE OF COURSE
TYPE DE PARCOURS,
TYP DES GOLFPLATZES

Country
Engadin 1278, Domaine Impérial 1277, Gruyère (La) 1281, Schönenberg 1290.

Forest
Bad Ragaz 1273, Blumisberg 1274 Domaine Impérial 1277, Les Bois 1284, Luzern 1286, Sempachersee 1291.

hilly Luzern 1286.

Mountain Crans-sur-Sierre 1276

Open Country
Blumisberg 1274, Ennetsee-Holzhäusern 1279, Interlaken 1282, Sempachersee 1291, Wylihof 1292.

Parkland
Bad Ragaz 1273, Breitenloo 1275, Crans-sur-Sierre 1276, Engadin 1278, Genève 1280, Interlaken 1282, Lausanne 1283, Lugano 1285, Montreux 1287, Neuchâtel 1288, Niederbüren 1289, Zumikon 1293.

Map No 1
Carte 1
km
0 10 20
1270
Vesoul
Luxeuil
Lure
Belfort
Montbéliard
Héricourt
Thann
Cernay
Ensisheim
MULHOUSE
Altkirch
BASEL
St Louis
Delle
Porrentruy
Delémont
Laufen
Liestal
Moutier
Solothurn
Grenchen
Biel/
Bienne
BESANÇON
DOUBS
JURA
Ornans
Pontarlier
Morteau
le Locle
la Chaux-
de-Fonds
St. Imier
Neuchâtel
BERN
Fribourg
Payerne
Yverdon-les-Bains
Estavayer
Murten
Thun
Frutigen
Bulle
Gruyères
Romont
Moudon
VAUD
SUISSE
LAUSANNE
Ouchy
Morges
Vevey
Montreux
Aigle
Bex
Martigny
Sion
Crans
Montana
Gstaad
Saanen
Zweisimmen
Adelboden
Leukerbad
Évian
Thonon
LAC LÉMAN
Nyon
Rolle
GENÈVE
Annemasse
Bonneville
Cluses
Morzine
Avoriaz
Chamonix-
Mont-Blanc
T. d. M. Bianco
T. du Mont Blanc
MONTE BIANCO
MONT BLANC
St Gervais
Megève
Sallanches
la Clusaz
Thônes
ANNECY
Rumilly
HAUTE-SAVOIE
VAL
Champagnole
Morez
St Claude
Gex
Divonne
St Julien
Verbier
Orsières
C. d. Gran S. Bernardo
Col du Grd St Bernard
Traforo d. Gran S. Bernardo
Tunnel du Grd St Bernard

1271
Breitenloo
Niederbüren
Zurich Zumikon
Ennetsee-Holzhausern
Schönenberg
Sempachersee
Luzern
Interlaken-Unterseen
Patriziale Ascona
Lugano
Feldberg
Schluchsee
Bonndorf
Bernau-im Schwarzwald
St. Blasien
Schönau
Todtmoos
Stühlingen
Schaffhausen
Neuhausen
Singen
Überlingen
Salem
Bodman-Radolfzell
Birnau
Markdorf
Meersburg
Allensbach
Horn
Stein
Konstanz
Steckborn
Kreuzlingen
Immenstaad
Bodensee
Waldshut-Tiengen
Wehr
Bad Säckingen
Rheinfelden (Baden)
Zurzach
RHEIN
Laufenburg
Weinfelden
Romanshorn
Arbon
Frauenfeld
Bülach
Winterthur
Wängi
Bischofszell
Amriswil
Rorschach
Wil
St. Gallen
Brugg
Baden
Kloten
Teufen
Altstätten
Sissach
Gossau
Herisau
Aarau
Dietikon
Lenzburg
Pfäffikon
ZÜRICH
Olten
Wohlen
Uster
Wetzikon
Wattwil
Urnäsch
Appenzell
Säntis
2502
AARGAU
Wald
Rüti
Aarburg
Kulm
Horgen
Meilen
Wädenswil
Kaltbrunn
Unterwasser
Gams
Muri
Reinach
Rapperswil
Buchs
Langenthal
Hochdorf
Zug
Walensee
Walenstadt
Sursee
Einsiedeln
Näfels
Flums
Küssnacht
Arth
Sattel
Sargans
Ruswil
LUZERN
Rigi
Vitznau
Schwyz
Glarus
Bad Ragaz
Kriens
Weggis
Gersau
Bächistock
2914
Entlebuch
Stansstad
Brunnen
Seelisberg
Sumiswald
Pilatus
Beckenried
Linthal
Piz Sardona
3056
Langnau
Flüelen
Sarnen
Stans
Flims
Waldhaus
Reichenau
Flühli
Altdorf
Klausenpass
SCHWEIZ
GRA
UNTERWALDEN
Engelberg
URI
Lungern
Brünigpass
Titlis
3239
Ilanz
Brienz
Meiringen
Wassen
Vorderrhein
Disentis/Mustèr
Sustenpass
Oberalppass
2044
Thusis
Interlaken
Göschenen
SVIZZ
Hospental
Andermatt
Piz Medel
Grindelwald
Pso del Lucomagno
Hinterrhein
Splügen
Wengen
Lauterbrunnen
Grimselpass
Furkapass
Pso d. S. Gottardo
Olivone
Pso del S. Bernardino
Mürren
Finsteraarhorn
Airolo
Rheinwaldhorn
S. Bernardino
Jungfrau
Münster
Nufenenpass
Kandersteg
Aletschhorn
Mesocco
Lötschbergtunnel
Formazza
Peccia
Sonogno
Biasca
Goppenstein
Bignasco
TICINO
Brig
Visp
Baceno
Simplonpass
Locarno
Bellinzona
Gravedona
Grächen
Iselle
S. Maria Maggiore
Ascona
Brissago
St Niklaus
Bognanco
Domodossola
Cannobio
Menaggio
Saas-Fee
Villadossola
Cannero Riv.
LUGANO
Cadenabbia
Tremezzo
Täsch
Luino
Gandria
Zermatt
Mergozzo
Verbania-Pallanza
Ponte Tresa
Campione
M. Generoso
1703
MONTE ROSA
Anzola d'Ossola
Macugnaga
Baveno
Gravellona-Toce
Omegna
Nonio
Meina
Arona
Gressoney-la-Trinite
Alagna Valsesia
Champoluc
Varallo
Orta
S. Giulio
MICHELIN
d'après cartes n° 987 - 28ème édition, n° 988 - 25ème édition et n° 989 - 30ème édition - 2002. Autorisation n° 0102062.

Map No 2
Carte 2
km
0 10 20
Bodensee-Weissensberg (D)
Lindau-Bad Schachen (D)
Niederbüren
Bad Ragaz
Engadin Samedan
Lugano
"L'Albenza" Bergamo (I)
Villa d'Este (I)
Monticello (I)
MICHELIN
1272
Ravensburg
Kempten
Wangen
Isny
Roßhaupten
Meckenbeuren
Tettnang
Friedrichshafen
Langenargen
Lindau
Bregenz
Nesselwang
Füssen
Pfronten
Oberstaufen
Immenstadt
Sonthofen
Oberjoch-P.
Reutte
Hindelang
Tannheim
Weißenbach
Deutsche Alpenstraße
Romanshorn
Arbon
Amriswil
Rorschach
Bischofszell
Wil
St. Gallen
Gossau
Herisau
Teufen
Appenzell
Urnäsch
Wattwil
Säntis
2502
Lustenau
Dornbirn
Altstätten
Hohenems
Götzis
Rankweil
Feldkirch
Egg
Bizau
Schoppernau
Hochtannbergpaß
Baad
Kleinwalsertal
Riezlern
Hirschegg
Mittelberg
Fischen
Nebelhorn
2224
Oberstdorf
Elbigenalp
Holzgau
Steeg
Warth
Schröcken
Lech
Zürs
Flexenpaß
Klösterle
Arlbergpaß
Arlberg-Straßentunnel
St. Anton
Landeck
Parseierspitze
3036
Imst
Berwang
Fernpaß
VORARLBERG
Thüringen
Nenzing
Bludenz
Brand
Schruns
St. Gallenkirch
Gaschurn
Partenen
Gargellen
Lünersee
2964
Galtür
Ischgl
Trisanna
Serfaus
Ried
Pfunds
Nauders
Reschenpaß/
Pso di Resia
Bielerhöhe
2036
Piz Buin
3312
Silvrettagruppe
Gams
Unterwasser
Buchs
Vaduz
LIECHTENSTEIN
Walensee
Walenstadt
Flums
Sargans
Maienfeld
Glarus
Linthal
Piz Sardona
3056
Landquart
Schiers
Küblis
Klosters
Weissfluhgipfel
2844
Davos
Chur
Reichenau
Flims Waldhaus
Ilanz
GRAUBÜNDEN
Arosa
Lenzerheide
Valbella
Thusis
Tiefencastel
Savognin
Bergün/Bravuogn
Albulapass
2312
Piz Kesch
3418
Flüelapass
2383
Susch
Ardez
Scuol (Schuls)
Zernez
Martina
Ofenpass/Pass dal Fuorn
2149
Müstair
Tubre/Taufers i. M.
Malles Ven.
S. Valentino a
Zuoz
Samedan
Livigno
Pass Umbr
2502
Trafoi
Stilfserjoch
Pso d. Stelvio
2757
M. Cevedale
3769
Bormio
Sta Caterina Valfurva
Pso di Foscagno
2291
Pontresina
St-Moritz
Julierpass
2284
Silvaplana
Sils/Segl Maria
Maloja
1815
Piz Bernina
4049
Pso del Bernina
2330
Poschiavo
VIZZERA
Hinterrhein
Splügen
Splügenpass
2113
Pso dello Spluga
Pso del S. Bernardino
2065
S. Bernardino
Rheinwaldhorn
3402
Olivone
Medel
Cresta
Madesimo
Mesocco
Soglio
Castasegna
Chiavenna
Chiesa in Valmalenco
M. Disgrazia
3678
Biasca
Bellinzona
Bagni del Masino
Sondrio
Tresenda
Tirano
Edolo
Aprica
Grosio
Ponte di Legno
Pso di Gavia
2621
M. Adamello
3554
Gravedona
Colico
Morbegno
Alpi Orobie
Pzo di Coca
3052
Pso del Vivione
1828
Gerola Alta
Foppolo
Pso S. Marco
2554
Valbondione
Schilpario
Dezzo
Pso d. Presolana
1297
Breno
Pso di Croce Domini
1892
Bagolino
Menaggio
Bellano
Varenna
Bellagio
Cadenabbia
Tremezzo
LUGANO
Gandria
Campione
M. Generoso
1703
Morcote
Mendrisio
Barzio
Piazza Brembana
Clusone
Darfo-Boario Terme
Lovere
Pisogne
Collio
S. Pellegrino Terme
Gandino
Lecco
Calolziocorte
Cernobbio
Como
Chiasso
Varese
Erba
Oggiono
Selvino
Albino
Lago d'Iseo
Vestone
Idro
Gardone Val Trompia
Trescore Balneario
Sarnico
Iseo
Lumezzane
Odolo
Bergamo
Seriate
Cantu
Merate
Ponte
Olona
LOMBARDIA

BAD RAGAZ

13 | 7 | 6

Wie viele andere Schweizer Plätze stammt auch dieser Parcours aus der Feder Donald Harradines, einem begnadeten Architekten, der die Natur gekonnt in seine Arbeit einbezieht. Das Bergpanorama und die bewaldete Gegend verleihen Bad Ragaz einen besonderen Charme. Gestaltung und Platzcharakter bergen keine Überraschungen, aber der Golfcourse garantiert dank seinen wenig ausgeprägten Geländeformen und seiner vernünftigen Länge für Spielfreude. Zu bedauern wäre höchstens, dass der Fluss, der durch die Anlage führt, das Spiel etwas zu wenig beeinflusst. Die eher schmalen Fairways der ersten neun Loch verlangen präzise Bälle. Longhitter spielen ihre Trümpfe auf der zweiten Platzhälfte aus. In Bad Ragaz bietet sich die Chance für schmeichelhafte Scores. Warum nicht?

Like many Swiss courses, Bad Ragaz was designed by Donald Harradine, a generally academic architect who willingly lets nature keep the upper hand. Moreover, the setting for Bad Ragaz is a very pleasant site in a forest surrounded by mountains. The course itself has very little in the way of stylish surprises or outstanding personality, but it is pleasant to play for its flattish relief and very reasonable length. It is a pity that the river crossing the course was not brought into play in a more imaginative way. The front nine are rather tight and call for precision play, while the back nine give greater scope to the long-hitters. A round of golf here is perhaps the opportunity to sign for a flattering score, but why not, after all?

Bad Ragaz Golf Club — 1957

CH - 7310 BAD RAGAZ

Office	Sekretariat	(41) 081 - 303 37 17
Pro shop	Pro shop	(41) 081 - 303 37 15
Fax	Fax	(41) 081 - 303 37 27
Web	www.resortragaz.ch	
Situation	Lage	

Bad Ragaz (pop. 4 757) - Chur (pop. 30 800), 24 km

Annual closure	Jährliche Schliessung	8/12→18/1
Weekly closure	Wöchentliche Schliessung	no

Fees main season Preisliste hochsaison		Full day
	Week days Woche	**We/Bank holidays** We/Feiertag
Individual Individuell	CHF 120	CHF 120
Couple Ehepaar	CHF 240	CHF 240

ASG members: CHF 100

Caddy	Caddy	no
Electric Trolley	Elektrokarren	CHF 20 /18 holes
Buggy	Elektrischer Wagen	medical reasons
Clubs	Leihschläger	CHF 20 /18 holes

Credit cards Kreditkarten
VISA - Eurocard - MasterCard - DC - AMEX

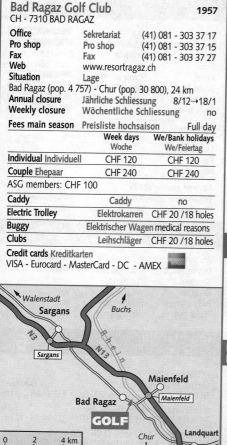

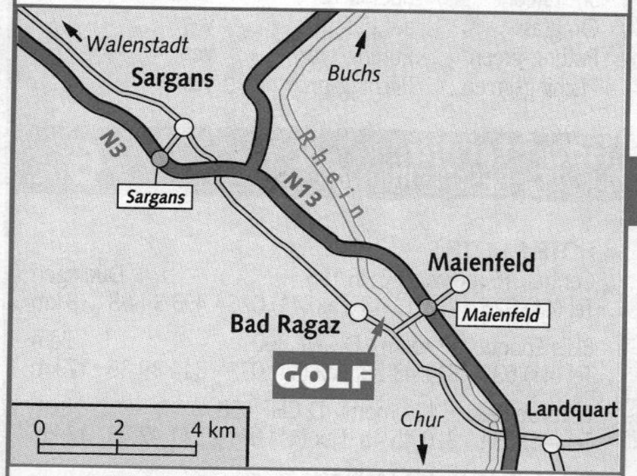

Access Zufahrt : Motorway (Autobahn) N 13 → Maienfeld → Bad Ragaz → Golf
Map 2 on page 1271 Karte 2 Seite 1271

Golf course PLATZ — 13/20

Site	Lage	
Maintenance	Instandhaltung	
Architect	Architekt	Donald Harradine
Type	Typ	forest, parkland
Relief	Begehbarkeit	
Water in play	Platz mit Wasser	
Exp. to wind	Wind ausgesetzt	
Trees in play	Platz mit Bäumen	

Scorecard Scorekarte	**Chp.** Chp.	**Mens** Herren	**Ladies** Damen
Length Länge	5700	5490	4860
Par	70	70	70
Slope system	119	117	115

Advised golfing ability Empfohlene Spielstärke — 0 12 24 36
Hcp required Min. Handicap — 30

Club house & amenities KLUBHAUS UND NEBENGEBÄUDE — 7/10

Pro shop	Pro shop	
Driving range	Übungsplatz	
Sheltered	überdacht	12 mats
On grass	auf Rasen	no, 12 mats open air
Putting-green	Putting-grün	yes
Pitching-green	Pitching-grün	yes

Hotel facilities HOTEL BESCHREIBUNG — 6/10

HOTELS HOTELS

Grand Hotel Hof Ragaz, 127 rooms, D CHF 535 — Bad Ragaz
Tel (41) 081 - 303 30 30, Fax (41) 081 - 303 30 33

Bristol, 27 rooms, D CHF 300 — Bad Ragaz
Tel (41) 081 - 303 77 77, Fax (41) 081 - 303 77 78

Schloss Ragaz, 58 rooms, D CHF 242 — Bad Ragaz
Tel (41) 081 - 302 23 55, Fax (41) 081 - 302 62 26

RESTAURANTS RESTAURANT

Aebtestube, Tel (41) 081 - 303 30 30 — Bad Ragaz

Löwen, Tel (41) 081 - 302 13 06 — Bad Ragaz

BLUMISBERG

15 | 7 | 6

Blumisberg - mit Aussicht auf den Jura und die Alpen - liegt in coupiertem Gelände mit stolzem Baumbestand (vor allem auf den ersten neun Loch). Die Anlage ist aber trotzdem zu Fuss zu bewältigen. Die Mehrheit der Holes bietet gut sichtbare Hindernisse, hauptsächlich Greenbunker. Die Greens sind von mittlerer Grösse, gut verteidigt, relativ wellig und einige Etagengreens eignen sich für interessante Fahnenpositionen. Schon mittlere Handicaps finden zu einem guten Spielrhythmus und geniessen die vernünftige Länge der Holes. Gute Golfer legen ihr Ballkönnen vor allem auf gewissen, schräg abfallenden Fairways in die Waagschale. Der Platz geniesst einen sehr guten Unterhalt.

With the Jura mountains on one side and the Alps on the other, Blumisberg is hilly and woody (especially the front nine), but walkable if you settle for just the 18 holes. Although a few holes require a little explanation, the vast majority hide nothing with clearly visible hazards, basically green-side bunkers. The greens are average in size, well-defended and sloping, with a number of two-tiered surfaces which make for some interesting pin positions. By and large, players can get a good rhythm going and the length of the course is reasonable enough to suit all players of decent ability. The best will be in their element here, working the ball both ways in order to card a good score. This is important, especially to handle some of the sloping fairways. Green-keeping and general upkeep are good.

Golf & Country Club Blumisberg — 1959

CH - 3184 WÜNNEWIL

Office	Sekretariat	(41) 026 - 496 34 38
Pro shop	Pro shop	(41) 026 - 496 17 27
Fax	Fax	(41) 026 - 496 35 23
Web	—	
Situation	Lage	

Freiburg (pop. 31 939), 17 km - Bern (123 254), 17 km

Annual closure	Jährliche Schliessung	15/11→15/3
Weekly closure	Wöchentliche Schliessung	no

Fees main season Preisliste hochsaison	Full day	
	Week days Woche	**We/Bank holidays** We/Feiertag
Individual Individuell	90 CHF	*
Couple Ehepaar	180 CHF	*

* We: only with members (nur in Mitgliederbegleitung)

Caddy	Caddy	no
Electric Trolley	Elektrokarren	CHF 20 /18 h.
Buggy	Elektrischer Wagen	CHF 50 /18 h.
Clubs	Leihschläger	CHF 25 /18 h.
Credit cards Kreditkarten		no

Access Zufahrt : Motorway (Autobahn) E 25 Freiburg-Bern → Flamat, 6 km → Freiburg. 4,5 km → Dietisberg. → Golf

Map 1 on page 1269 Karte 1 Seite 1269

Golf course — PLATZ — 15/20

Site	Lage	
Maintenance	Instandhaltung	
Architect	Architekt	B. von Limburger
Type	Typ	forest, open country
Relief	Begehbarkeit	
Water in play	Platz mit Wasser	
Exp. to wind	Wind ausgesetzt	
Trees in play	Platz mit Bäumen	

Scorecard Scorekarte	**Chp.** Chp.	**Mens** Herren	**Ladies** Damen
Length Länge	6011	5687	4977
Par	72	72	72
Slope system	129	127	125

Advised golfing ability Empfohlene Spielstärke — 0 12 24 36

Hcp required Min. Handicap 30

Club house & amenities — KLUBHAUS UND NEBENGEBÄUDE — 7/10

Pro shop	Pro shop	
Driving range	Übungsplatz	
Sheltered	überdacht	4 mats
On grass	auf Rasen	yes
Putting-green	Putting-grün	yes
Pitching-green	Pitching-grün	yes

Hotel facilities — HOTEL BESCREIBUNG — 6/10

HOTELS HOTELS

Central, 16 rooms, D CHF 188 — Düdingen
Tel (41) 026 - 493 13 48, Fax (41) 026 - 493 34 88 — 8 km

Belle Epoque, 17 rooms, D CHF 300 — Bern
Tel (41) 031 - 311 43 36, Fax (41) 031 - 311 39 36 — 17 km

Bellevue Palace, 124 rooms, D CHF 450 — Bern
Tel (41) 031 - 320 45 45, Fax (41) 031 - 311 47 43 — 17 km

RESTAURANTS RESTAURANT

Central, Tel (41) 026 - 493 13 48 — Düdingen 8 km

Le Moléson, Tel (41) 031 - 741 02 40 — Flamatt 8 km

BREITENLOO

13 | 7 | 6

Ein kleiner, bewaldeter Flecken auf dem Land mit Aussichten auf die umliegende Gegend. Donald Harradine hat diesen Platz (wie viele Schweizer Golfcourses) in britischem Stil in eine hügelige Landschaft gezeichnet. Das Gelände wird auf den zweiten neun Loch etwas flacher. Mit einigen Out of bounds und kleinen Wasserhindernissen sind die Schwierigkeiten nicht allzu zahlreich, aber der Ball muss auf den Fairways gut plaziert werden, um die Greens leicht angreifen zu können. Präzision im Umgang mit dem kleinen Ball kann sich als nützlich erweisen. In jedem Fall lässt sich dieser gut gepflegte Platz unter Golfern verschiedener Niveaus mit viel Spass spielen - vor allem im Sommer, wenn der Ball gut rollt.

A little patch of remote forest in the countryside, with wide spaces opening onto the surrounding region. Another Harradine course, Breitenloo has a clearly British style to it and is laid out over a gently hilly terrain (even though the back nine are flatter). Despite a number of out-of-bounds and small water hazards, the difficulties are few and far between, are evenly spread and clearly visible. Some of the greens need a carefully placed tee-shot for an easier second shot, and fading or drawing the ball can, as always, prove helpful. At all events, this well-cared for course is easily playable by all the family or with players of varying ability. All good fun, especially in summer when the ball rolls a lot.

Golf Club Breitenloo — 1966

Untere Zaüne 9
CH - 8001 ZÜRICH

Office	**Sekretariat**	(41) 01 - 836 40 80
Pro shop	**Pro shop**	(41) 01 - 836 40 80
Fax	**Fax**	(41) 01 - 837 10 85
Web	—	
Situation	**Lage**	
Zürich (pop. 336 821), 22 km		
Annual closure	**Jährliche Schliessung**	31/10→31/3
Weekly closure	**Wöchentliche Schliessung**	no

Fees main season Preisliste hochsaison	Week days Woche	We/Bank holidays We/Feiertag
	18 holes	
Individual Individuell	CHF 110	CHF 180 *
Couple Ehepaar	CHF 220	CHF 360 *

* We: with members only (nur in Mitgliederbegleitung)

Caddy	**Caddy**	on request
Electric Trolley	**Elektrokarren**	CHF 30 /18 holes
Buggy	**Elektrischer Wagen**	no
Clubs	**Leihschläger**	CHF 30 /full day
Credit cards	**Kreditkarten**	no

Access Zufahrt : Zürich-Kloten → Kloten → Bassersdorf → Birchwil-Oberwil, in Oberwil (Restaurant Linde) → Golf
Map 2 on page 1270 Karte 2 Seite 1270

Golf course PLATZ — 13/20

Site	**Lage**	
Maintenance	**Instandhaltung**	
Architect	**Architekt**	Donald Harradine
Type	**Typ**	parkland
Relief	**Begehbarkeit**	
Water in play	**Platz mit Wasser**	
Exp. to wind	**Wind ausgesetzt**	
Trees in play	**Platz mit Bäumen**	

Scorecard Scorekarte	Chp. Chp.	Mens Herren	Ladies Damen
Length Länge	6109	5734	5092
Par	72	72	72
Slope system	132	128	123

Advised golfing ability **Empfohlene Spielstärke** — 0 12 24 36
Hcp required **Min. Handicap** — 30

Club house & amenities KLUBHAUS UND NEBENGEBÄUDE — 7/10

Pro shop	**Pro shop**	
Driving range	**Übungsplatz**	
Sheltered	überdacht	6 mats
On grass	auf Rasen	yes
Putting-green	Putting-grün	yes
Pitching-green	Pitching-grün	yes

Hotel facilities HOTEL BESCHREIBUNG — 6/10

HOTELS HOTELS

Zum Bären, 14 rooms, D CHF 215 — Nürensdorf 4 km
Tel (41) 01 - 838 36 36, Fax (41) 01 - 836 36 46

Renaissance Hôtel, 204 rooms, D CHF 295 — Glattbrugg 14 km
Tel (41) 01 - 874 50 00, Fax (41) 01 - 874 50 01

Dolder Grand Hotel, 168 rooms, D CHF 600 — Zürich 22 km
Tel (41) 01 - 269 30 00, Fax (41) 01 - 269 30 01

RESTAURANTS RESTAURANT

Zum Bären, Tel (41) 01 - 838 36 36 — Nürensdorf 4 km

Sonnenberg ,Tel (41) 01 - 266 97 97 — Zürich 22 km

CRANS-SUR-SIERRE

14 | 7 | 8

C'est le plus célèbre parcours de Suisse, grâce aux efforts de son président Gaston Barras pour y accueillir depuis des années le European Masters professionnel. Il n'est jamais vraiment intimidant : ses obstacles sont bien visibles, modérément en jeu, la difficulté principale reste le choix de club en fonction des dénivellations. Assez accidenté, il est d'ailleurs fatigant à jouer à pied. La splendeur du panorama sur les Alpes (Cervin, Mont Blanc, Alpes bernoises) est parfois à couper le souffle, et console des petites désillusions golfiques. En altitude, les balles volant loin, quelques drives peuvent être flatteurs. Un bon parcours de vacances, avec un entretien fonction de la longueur de l'hiver. On attendait quelques remodelages de ce tracé: Seve Ballesteros a d'abord introduit des modifications au 15 et au 17, devenus plus esthétiques et délicats. D'autres modifications sont intervenues, avec l'allongement de plusieurs trous.

This is the most famous of Swiss courses thanks to the work put in by club chairman Gaston Barras to stage the European Masters here over the past few years. The course is never really intimidating, the hazards are clearly in view and not always directly in play. The main problem is the choice of club to offset the steep gradients. It is a hilly course which can be tiring to cover on foot. The beautiful scenery of the Alps (Cervin, Mont Blanc) is quite breath-taking and enough to make up for the mishaps that can so easily mess up your card. At altitude, the ball travels further and a number of drives will prove flattering. A good holiday course where green-keeping is depending on the weather. A little restyling work had been awaited here, and Seve Ballesteros has firstly made a few changes to the 15th and 17th holes, which are now more attractive and trickier. Other alterations have been added since, and the course lengthened.

1276

Golf Club de Crans-sur-Sierre — 1907

CH - 3953 CRANS-SUR-SIERRE

Office	Secrétariat	(41) 027 - 485 97 97
Pro shop	Pro-shop	(41) 027 - 485 97 97
Fax	Fax	(41) 027 - 481 97 98
Web	www.swissgolfnetwork.ch	
Situation	Situation	

Sierre (pop. 13 917), 15 km

Annual closure	Fermeture annuelle	31/10→30/4
Weekly closure	Fermeture hebdomadaire	no

Fees main season Tarifs haute saison		18 holes
	Week days Semaine	We/Bank holidays We/Férié
Individual Individuel	CHF 130	CHF 140
Couple Couple	CHF 260	CHF 280

ASG members: CHF 98 - CHF 105 (We)

Caddy	Caddy	on request
Electric Trolley	Chariot électrique	CHF 25 / 18 holes
Buggy	Voiturette	CHF 90 /18 holes
Clubs	Clubs	CHF 25 /full day

Credit cards Cartes de crédit
VISA - Eurocard - MasterCard - DC - AMEX

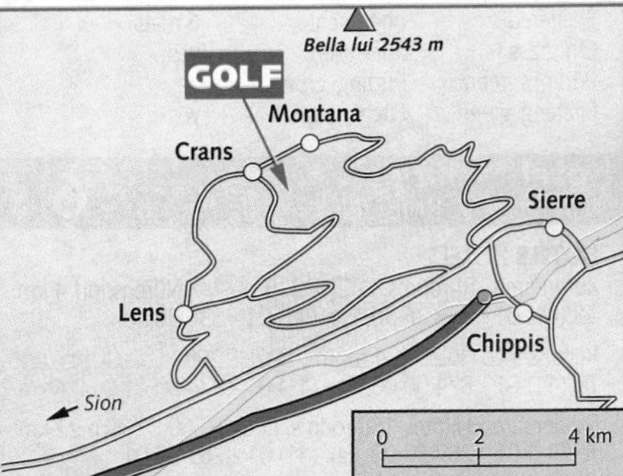

Access Accès : Lausanne → Montreux. In Sierre → Crans
Map 1 on page 1269 Carte 1 Page 1269

Golf course PARCOURS — 14/20

Site	Site	
Maintenance	Entretien	
Architect	Architecte	M. Nicholson Seve Ballesteros
Type	Type	mountain, parkland
Relief	Relief	
Water in play	Eau en jeu	
Exp. to wind	Exposé au vent	
Trees in play	Arbres en jeu	

Scorecard Carte de score	Chp. Chp.	Mens Mess.	Ladies Da.
Length Long.	6328	5917	5092
Par	72	72	72
Slope system	138	130	136

Advised golfing ability Niveau de jeu recommandé — 0 12 24 36
Hcp required Handicap exigé 36

Club house & amenities CLUB-HOUSE ET ANNEXES — 7/10

Pro shop	Pro-shop	
Driving range	Practice	
Sheltered	couvert	9 mats
On grass	sur herbe	yes
Putting-green	putting-green	yes
Pitching-green	pitching green	yes

Hotel facilities ENVIRONNEMENT HOTELIER — 8/10

HOTELS HÔTELS

Grand Hôtel du Golf, 72 rooms, D CHF 600 Crans-sur-Sierre
Tel (41) 027 - 485 42 42, Fax (41) 027 - 485 42 43

Alpina et Savoy, 44 rooms, D CHF 500 Crans-sur-Sierre
Tel (41) 027 - 485 09 00, Fax (41) 027 - 485 09 99

Alpha, 23 rooms, D CHF 280 Crans-sur-Sierre
Tel (41) 027 - 484 24 00, Fax (41) 027 - 484 24 10

RESTAURANTS RESTAURANT

Hostellerie du Pas de l'Ours Crans-sur-Sierre
Tel (41) 027 - 485 93 33

Cervin, Tel (41) 027 - 481 21 80 Vermala 4 km

La Côte, Tel (41) 027 - 455 13 51 Corin-de-la-Crête 13 km

DOMAINE IMPÉRIAL

18 | 8 | 6

Par son esthétique et la stratégie de jeu, ce parcours est le plus nettement américain des golfs suisses (c'est un Pete Dye !). En bordure du Lac Léman, avec de belles perspectives sur le Jura et les Alpes, il se joue sans fatigue physique, mais les fairways bien travaillés, les profonds bunkers, la diversité des obstacles (arbres , obstacles d'eau) et l'intelligence de leur placement en font un défi permanent, constamment renouvelé : on joue ici tous les clubs de son sac, et de multiples façons. On notera en particulier l'excellent rythme du parcours, la subtilité des par 3, de longueur pourtant fort raisonnable, et le modelage de greens très défendus, qu'il faut savoir "rater du bon côté". Techniquement impressionnant, il se laisse apprivoiser si l'on ajoute la réflexion à la maîtrise du jeu. L'entretien a bien progressé depuis quelques années, tous les détails sont soignés, et les greens sont souvent rapides. A la hauteur de l'architecte !

In style and game strategy, this is clearly the most American of all Swiss courses (designed by Pete Dye). On the banks of lake Geneva with fine views over the Jura mountains and the Alps, it is an easily walkable course, but the well-designed fairways, the deep bunkers, the variety of hazards (trees and water) and the intelligence deployed in placing them make this course a permanent challenge which will never lie down. You play every club in the bag, and in different ways. In particular, this is a good course for quick play with subtle but reasonably-lengthed par 3s and well-designed, well-defended greens which, if you are going to miss, should not be missed on the wrong side. Although technically very impressive, you can keep your head above water by playing with skill and brains. Green-keeping is much improved since a few years ; every detail is carefully tended and the greens are fast... matching the standard of the architect.

Domaine Impérial — 1987

Villa Prangins - CH - 1196 GLAND

Office	Secrétariat	(41) 022 - 999 06 00
Pro shop	Pro-shop	(41) 022 - 999 06 80
Fax	Fax	(41) 022 - 999 06 06
E-mail		golf_domaine_imperial@bluewin.ch
Situation	Situation	Nyon (pop. 15 666), 3 km
Annual closure	Fermeture annuelle	21/12→28/2
Weekly closure	Fermeture hebdomadaire	Monday(lundi)

Fees main season Tarifs haute saison	18 holes	
	Week days Semaine	**We/Bank holidays** We/Férié
Individual Individuel	CHF 150	*
Couple Couple	CHF 300	*

* We : members only (membres seulement)

Caddy	Caddy	on request
Electric Trolley	Chariot électrique	CHF 50
Buggy	Voiturette	medical reasons only
Clubs	Clubs	CHF 25 /18 holes

Credit cards Cartes de crédit
VISA - Eurocard - MasterCard - AMEX

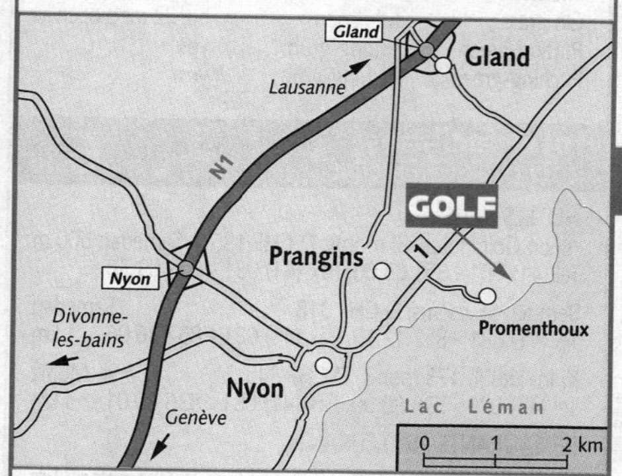

Access Accès : Genève-Lausanne → Gland, "Route Suisse" → Genève, 400 m on left hand side
Map 1 on page 1269 Carte 1 Page 1269

Golf course — PARCOURS — 18/20

Site	Site	
Maintenance	Entretien	
Architect	Architecte	Pete Dye
Type	Type	forest, country
Relief	Relief	
Water in play	Eau en jeu	
Exp. to wind	Exposé au vent	
Trees in play	Arbres en jeu	

Scorecard Carte de score	**Chp.** Chp.	**Mens** Mess.	**Ladies** Da.
Length Long.	6346	5913	5023
Par	72	72	72
Slope system	129	122	121

Advised golfing ability Niveau de jeu recommandé — 0 12 24 36
Hcp required Handicap exigé — 30

Club house & amenities — CLUB-HOUSE ET ANNEXES — 8/10

Pro shop	Pro-shop	
Driving range	Practice	
Sheltered	couvert	10 places
On grass	sur herbe	non
Putting-green	putting-green	oui
Pitching-green	pitching green	oui

Hotel facilities — ENVIRONNEMENT HOTELIER — 6/10

HOTELS HÔTELS

Hôtel de la Plage, 11 rooms, D CHF 125 — Gland
Tel (41) 022 - 364 10 35, Fax (41) 022 - 364 34 81 — 4 km

Beau Rivage, 46 rooms, D CHF 360 — Nyon
Tel (41) 022 - 365 41 41, Fax (41) 022 - 365 41 65 — 5 km

RESTAURANTS RESTAURANT

Restaurant du Golf — on site
Tel (41) 022 - 999 06 00

Café du Marché — Nyon
Tel (41) 022 - 362 35 00 — 5 km

1277

ENGADIN

15 | 6 | 6

Vor mehr als einem Jahrhundert entstanden, wurde dieser Platz mehrmals und von Mario Verdieri wesentlich verändert, hat aber dabei seinen britischen Touch nicht verloren. Der Kontrast zu den majestätischen Schneegipfeln rundum ist beeindruckend. Wasserläufe und kleine Seen sind die wesentlichen Hindernisse, aber die besten Spieler werden sich davon wenig beeindrucken lassen und richtig loslegen, da auch Bäume nicht zu stark ins Spielgeschehen eingreifen. Dieser sehr natürliche und angenehme Golfcourse würde mit der Neugestaltung gewisser Greens und einigen verteidigenden Hindernissen (man kann den Ball oft rollen lassen) anspruchsvoller werden. Doch er soll vor allem Vergnügen und gutes Scores ermöglichen und nicht Hochleistungen abverlangen.

Opened more than a century ago, this course has undergone many a facelift, essentially by Mario Verdieri, but has retained an evidently British flavour in contrast with the majestic setting of snow-capped mountains. Little lakes and rivers form the main hazards, but these should not over-concern the better players who have the chance here to open their shoulders, since the trees (a lot of very old larch trees) are never too much in play. This is a very natural and deliberately pleasing course which could be made more demanding by redesigning some of the greens and creating hazards to defend them more effectively (you can often chip and roll the ball from fairway to green). But as we said, it was designed more for fun and for producing flattering scores than for any great exploit on the part of the player.

Engadin Golf 1893

CH - 7503 SAMEDAN

Office	Sekretariat	(41) 081 - 851 04 66
Pro shop	Pro shop	(41) 081 - 851 04 60
Fax	Fax	(41) 081 - 851 04 67
E-mail	golfengadin@compunet.ch	
Situation	Lage	

St-Moritz (pop. 5 057), 5 km

Annual closure	Jährliche Schliessung	14/10→15/5
Weekly closure	Wöchentliche Schliessung	no

Fees main season Preisliste hochsaison	Week days Woche	We/Bank holidays We/Feiertag
		Full day
Individual Individuell	CHF 90	CHF 90
Couple Ehepaar	CHF 180	CHF 180

Caddy	Caddy	on request
Electric Trolley	Elektrokarren	no
Buggy	Elektrischer Wagen	medical reasons
Clubs	Leihschläger	CHF 30 /full day

Credit cards Kreditkarten
VISA - Eurocard - MasterCard - DC - AMEX

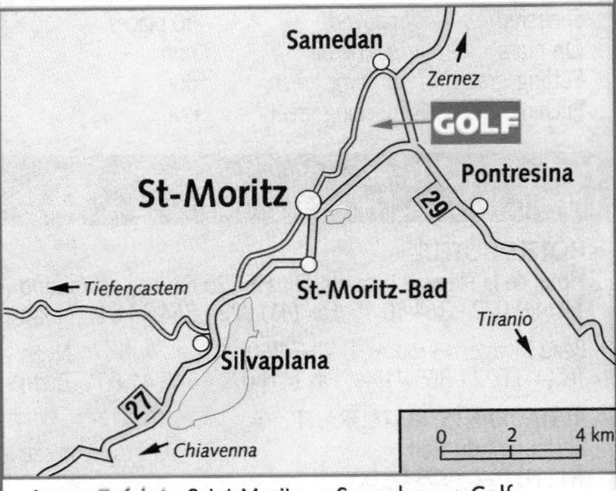

Access Zufahrt : Saint Moritz → Samedan, → Golf
Map 2 on page 1271 Karte 2 Seite 1271

Golf course PLATZ 15/20

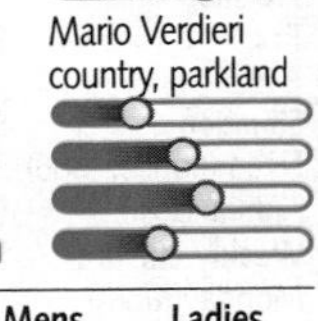

Site	Lage	
Maintenance	Instandhaltung	
Architect	Architekt	Mario Verdieri
Type	Typ	country, parkland
Relief	Begehbarkeit	
Water in play	Platz mit Wasser	
Exp. to wind	Wind ausgesetzt	
Trees in play	Platz mit Bäumen	

Scorecard Scorekarte	Chp. Chp.	Mens Herren	Ladies Damen
Length Länge	6217	5923	5106
Par	72	72	72
Slope system	134	130	133

Advised golfing ability Empfohlene Spielstärke 0 12 24 36
Hcp required Min. Handicap 30

Club house & amenities KLUBHAUS UND NEBENGEBÄUDE 6/10

Pro shop	Pro shop	
Driving range	Übungsplatz	
Sheltered	überdacht	no
On grass	auf Rasen	no, 22 mats open air
Putting-green	Putting-grün	yes
Pitching-green	Pitching-grün	yes

Hotel facilities HOTEL BESCHREIBUNG 6/10

HOTELS HOTELS

Alpen Golf Hotel, 40 rooms, D CHF 185 — Samedan 500 m
Tel (41) 081 - 851 03 00, Fax (41) 081 - 851 03 38

Bernina, 56 rooms, D CHF 318 — Samedan 1 km
Tel (41) 081 - 852 12 12, Fax (41) 081 - 852 36 06

Kulm Hotel, 173 rooms, D CHF 845 — St. Moritz 5 km
Tel (41) 081 - 836 80 00, Fax (41) 081 - 836 80 01

RESTAURANTS RESTAURANT

Jöhri's Talvo, Tel (41) 081 - 833 44 55 — Champfer 8 km

Jörimann's Refugium, — St. Moritz 5 km
Tel (41) 081 - 833 30 00

ENNETSEE-HOLZHÄUSERN 13 7 6

1995 war es soweit: der erste öffentliche Golfplatz der Schweiz wurde eröffnet. Er wurde in einer wenig schmeichelnden Industriezone erbaut, doch dieses Manko könnte mit einem soliden Bepflanzungsprogramm behoben werden. Mit dem Ziel, Golfer auszubilden und eine erschwingliche Alternative zu den Privatclubs zu bieten, wurden keine zusätzlichen golferischen Schwierigkeiten gesucht (kaum Wasserhindernisse im Spiel), was die besten Spieler enttäuschen mag. Es ist schade, dass die Greens und Bunkers nicht vielseitiger gestaltet wurden. Der sonst angenehm zu spielende Platz würde so mehr fürs Auge bieten und dem Stammspieler zu technisch vielseitigeren Herausforderungen verhelfen. Die Anlage offeriert nebst dem Golfplatz grossanglegte Trainingsmöglichkeiten.

This was at last Switzerland's first truly public golf course, opened in 1995. It has been laid out on an industrial site which is still a little unattractive but it could easily grow into something much better with a good plantation programme. The aim here is to coach golfers and offer an economical alternative to the private courses. As a result, there was no deliberate quest for difficulty (for example, there are very few water hazards in play), so the better players might feel disappointed. It is though a shame that the greens and bunkers weren't given more careful thought - they would have added a little more style and pleasure to a course which elsewhere makes for a pleasant round of golf - and that there is not more technical variety for the people who play here regularly. The whole complex also includes huge practice facilities.

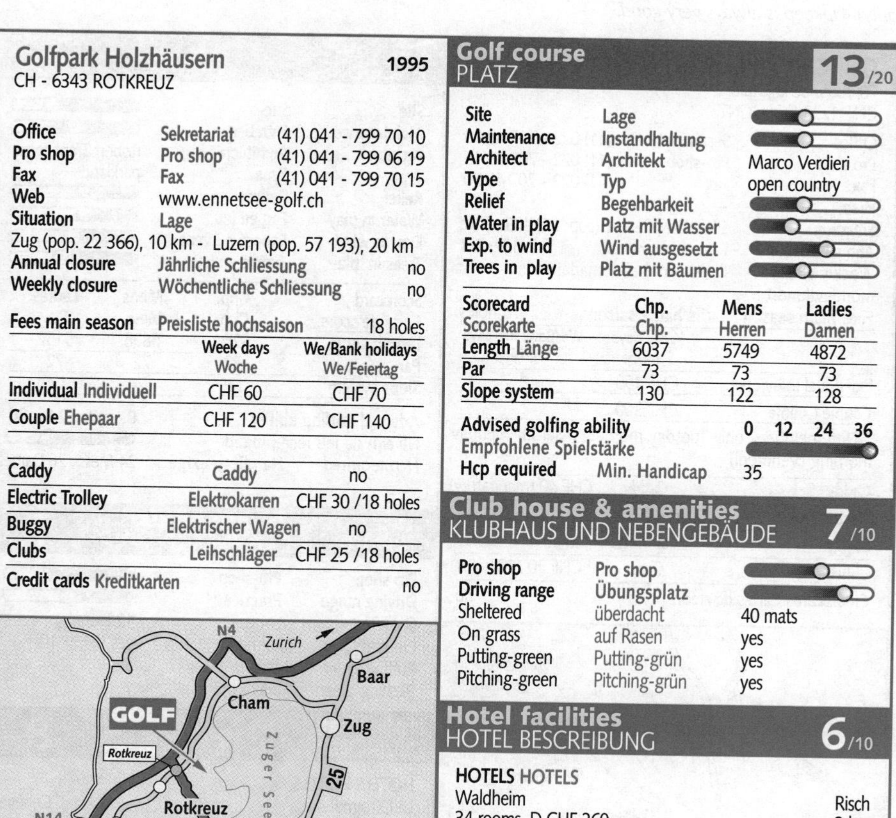

Golfpark Holzhäusern **1995**
CH - 6343 ROTKREUZ

Office	Sekretariat	(41) 041 - 799 70 10
Pro shop	Pro shop	(41) 041 - 799 06 19
Fax	Fax	(41) 041 - 799 70 15
Web	www.ennetsee-golf.ch	
Situation	Lage	

Zug (pop. 22 366), 10 km - Luzern (pop. 57 193), 20 km

Annual closure	Jährliche Schliessung	no
Weekly closure	Wöchentliche Schliessung	no

Fees main season Preisliste hochsaison	18 holes	
	Week days Woche	**We/Bank holidays** We/Feiertag
Individual Individuell	CHF 60	CHF 70
Couple Ehepaar	CHF 120	CHF 140

Caddy	Caddy	no
Electric Trolley	Elektrokarren	CHF 30 /18 holes
Buggy	Elektrischer Wagen	no
Clubs	Leihschläger	CHF 25 /18 holes
Credit cards	Kreditkarten	no

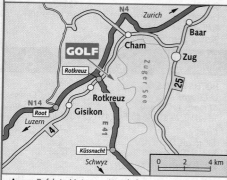

Access Zufahrt : Motorway (Autobahn) N4 or N14 → Rotkreuz → Industrie Ost → "Golfpark"
Map 2 on page 1270 Karte 2 Seite 1270

Golf course PLATZ 13/20

Site	Lage	
Maintenance	Instandhaltung	
Architect	Architekt	Marco Verdieri
Type	Typ	open country
Relief	Begehbarkeit	
Water in play	Platz mit Wasser	
Exp. to wind	Wind ausgesetzt	
Trees in play	Platz mit Bäumen	

Scorecard Scorekarte	**Chp.** Chp.	**Mens** Herren	**Ladies** Damen
Length Länge	6037	5749	4872
Par	73	73	73
Slope system	130	122	128

Advised golfing ability 0 12 24 36
Empfohlene Spielstärke
Hcp required Min. Handicap 35

Club house & amenities KLUBHAUS UND NEBENGEBÄUDE 7/10

Pro shop	Pro shop	
Driving range	Übungsplatz	
Sheltered	überdacht	40 mats
On grass	auf Rasen	yes
Putting-green	Putting-grün	yes
Pitching-green	Pitching-grün	yes

Hotel facilities HOTEL BESCREIBUNG 6/10

HOTELS HOTELS

Waldheim — Risch 2 km
34 rooms, D CHF 260
Tel (41) 041 - 799 70 70, Fax (41) 041 - 799 70 79

Parkhotel, — Zug 10 km
110 rooms, D CHF 400
Tel (41) 041 - 727 48 48, Fax (41) 041 - 727 48 49

RESTAURANTS RESTAURANT

Rathauskeller,Tel (41) 041 - 711 00 58	Zug 10 km
Hecht, Tel (41) 041 - 729 81 30	Zug 10 km
Raben, Tel (41) 041 - 780 13 12	Cham 4 km

"Cologny" reste un des parcours suisses les plus intéressants, et l'un des clubs les plus prestigieux. Nul n'en sera étonné : Robert Trent Jones en est l'auteur. Dans un site magnifique surplombant le Lac Léman, il a une fois de plus signé un dessin très imaginatif et d'une grande intelligence stratégique. La multiplicité des départs et des positions de drapeaux permet de l'adapter à tous les niveaux, même si les joueurs très moyens auront du mal à y scorer. Les greens sont vastes (un double green aux 9 et 18), très dessinés, ce qui rend essentielle une bonne maîtrise du petit jeu et du putting... même si l'on réussit à bien travailler la balle au grand jeu, notamment sur les nombreux dog-legs. Une consolation pour ceux dont le swing n'est pas exceptionnel : si certains arbres peuvent poser problème, il y a peu d'obstacles d'eau (8, 16 et 17). Un grand classique toujours bien entretenu.

One of the most fashionable golf clubs and one of the most interesting Swiss courses, and, surprise surprise, it was designed by a one Robert Trent Jones. In a magnificent setting overlooking Lake Geneva, Jones has once again come up with a very imaginative layout calling for considerable strategic intelligence. The many different tees and pin positions make this a course for players of all ability, even though your average hacker will find scoring a tough proposition. The greens are huge (the 9th and 18th have a double green) and well designed, thus calling for good putting skills and a sharp short game, even if your long game is on tune with the ball moving both ways, particularly on the very many dog-legs. There is one consolation for high-handicappers, namely that although a few trees may cause problems, there are few water hazards (on the 8th, 16th and 17th holes only). Upkeep is always very good.

Golf Club de Genève — 1972

70, route de la Capite
CH - 1233 COLOGNY

Office	Secrétariat	(41) 022 - 707 48 00
Pro shop	Pro-shop	(41) 022 - 707 48 15
Fax	Fax	(41) 022 - 707 48 20
Web	—	
Situation	Situation	Genève (pop. 172 486), 5 km
Annual closure	Fermeture annuelle	7/12→7/3
Weekly closure	Fermeture hebdomadaire	

monday(lundi)

Fees main season Tarifs haute saison — 18 holes

	Week days Semaine	We/Bank holidays We/Férié
Individual Individuel	CHF 150	*
Couple Couple	CHF 300	*

* Non members: only Tuesday morning (Mardi) → Friday morning (Vendredi)

Caddy	Caddy	CHF 40 (mandatory)
Electric Trolley	Chariot électrique	CHF 20
Buggy	Voiturette	medical reasons
Clubs	Clubs	CHF 20 /18 holes
Credit cards	Cartes de crédit	no

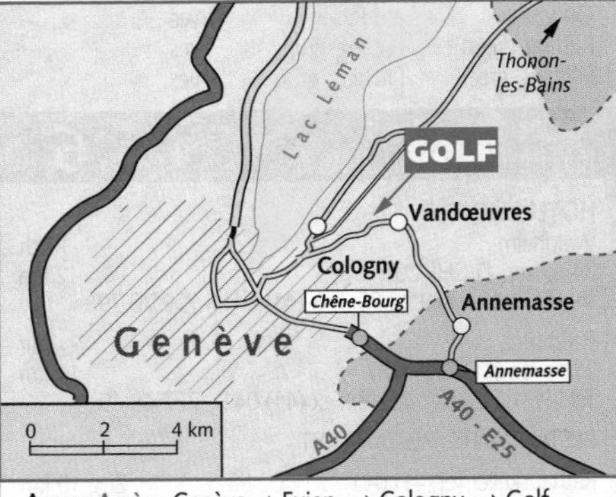

Access Accès : Genève → Evian, → Cologny, → Golf
Map 1 on page 1269 Carte 1 Page 1269

Golf course PARCOURS — 17/20

Site	Site	
Maintenance	Entretien	
Architect	Architecte	Robert Trent Jones
Type	Type	parkland
Relief	Relief	
Water in play	Eau en jeu	
Exp. to wind	Exposé au vent	
Trees in play	Arbres en jeu	

Scorecard Carte de score	Chp. Chp.	Mens Mess.	Ladies Da.
Length Long.	6250	5898	5152
Par	72	72	72
Slope system	125	124	125

Advised golfing ability Niveau de jeu recommandé — 0 12 24 36

Hcp required Handicap exigé — 24 Mess., 26 Dames

Club house & amenities CLUB-HOUSE ET ANNEXES — 7/10

Pro shop	Pro-shop	
Driving range	Practice	
Sheltered	couvert	12 mats
On grass	sur herbe	yes (04 → 10)
Putting-green	putting-green	yes
Pitching-green	pitching green	yes

Hotel facilities ENVIRONNEMENT HOTELIER — 8/10

HOTELS HÔTELS

La Cigogne — Genève 5 km
42 rooms, D CHF 440
Tel (41) 022 - 818 40 40, Fax (41) 022 - 818 40 50

Century — Genève
130 rooms, D CHF 420
Tel (41) 022 - 592 88 88, Fax (41) 022 - 592 88 78

RESTAURANTS RESTAURANT

Le Bistro de Cologny, Tel (41) 022 - 736 57 80 — Cologny 4 km
Auberge du Lion d'Or, Tel (41) 022 - 736 44 32 — Cologny
Le Béarn, Tel (41) 022 - 321 00 28 — Genève 6 km

GRUYÈRE (LA) | 14 | 7 | 6

Il n'est pas très habituel de conseiller des parcours courts, mais celui-ci, avec son par 68, est des plus amusants. Evidemment, les golfeurs du plus haut niveau n'y seront pas à l'aise, mais ils sont une minorité ! En premier lieu, Jeremy Pern a tiré un parti remarquable d'un terrain difficile à adapter au golf, et mis l'accent sur la précision, dans tous les secteurs du jeu. Qu'il s'agisse du drive, du second coup, des approches vers des greens très défendus ou du putting, cet aspect ludique est à la fois intéressant et formateur. Le parcours est assez physique, mais les fairways (étroits) sont assez plats, ce qui ne rend pas la marche trop ardue. L'imagination et l'intelligence de l'architecte en font une réussite, même s'il n'a pas eu l'espace pour s'exprimer pleinement. La qualité de l'entretien et la facilité relative pour y scorer en font une bonne adresse, relevée encore par un environnement magnifique au bord du lac de Gruyère.

It is not every day that we recommend short courses, but this one, a par 68, is most amusing. The most proficient golfers will obviously not feel too excited about it, but they are a minority anyway. Firstly, Jeremy Pern has done a remakable job with terrain that was difficult to harness for golf and has placed emphasis on precision in every department of the game. Whether for the drive, the second shot, approaches to very well-guarded greens or putting, this fun aspect is both interesting and educational. The course is pretty hilly, although the actual fairways are rather flat (and narrow), which means easy walking. The architect's imagination and intelligence have made this a class course, even though space was restricted. The standard of green-keeping and the relative ease of scoring make this a good address, enhanced by a magnificent setting on the banks of Lake Gruyère.

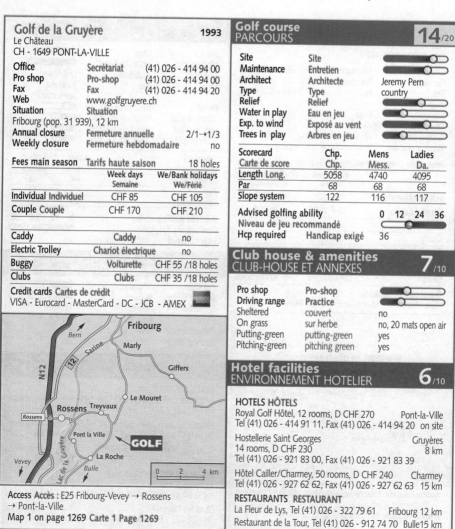

Golf de la Gruyère **1993**
Le Château
CH - 1649 PONT-LA-VILLE

Office	**Secrétariat**	(41) 026 - 414 94 00
Pro shop	**Pro-shop**	(41) 026 - 414 94 00
Fax	**Fax**	(41) 026 - 414 94 20
Web	www.golfgruyere.ch	
Situation	**Situation**	
Fribourg (pop. 31 939), 12 km		
Annual closure	**Fermeture annuelle**	2/1→1/3
Weekly closure	**Fermeture hebdomadaire**	no

Fees main season Tarifs haute saison		18 holes
	Week days Semaine	**We/Bank holidays** We/Férié
Individual Individuel	CHF 85	CHF 105
Couple Couple	CHF 170	CHF 210

Caddy	**Caddy**	no
Electric Trolley	**Chariot électrique**	no
Buggy	**Voiturette**	CHF 55 /18 holes
Clubs	**Clubs**	CHF 35 /18 holes

Credit cards Cartes de crédit
VISA - Eurocard - MasterCard - DC - JCB - AMEX

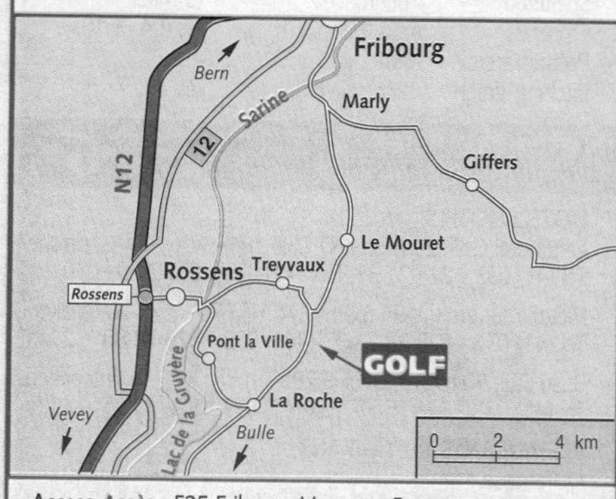

Access Accès : E25 Fribourg-Vevey → Rossens → Pont-la-Ville
Map 1 on page 1269 Carte 1 Page 1269

Golf course PARCOURS 14/20

Site	**Site**	
Maintenance	**Entretien**	
Architect	**Architecte**	Jeremy Pern
Type	**Type**	country
Relief	**Relief**	
Water in play	**Eau en jeu**	
Exp. to wind	**Exposé au vent**	
Trees in play	**Arbres en jeu**	

Scorecard Carte de score	**Chp.** Chp.	**Mens** Mess.	**Ladies** Da.
Length Long.	5058	4740	4095
Par	68	68	68
Slope system	122	116	117

Advised golfing ability / **Niveau de jeu recommandé**: 0 12 24 36
Hcp required **Handicap exigé** 36

Club house & amenities CLUB-HOUSE ET ANNEXES 7/10

Pro shop	**Pro-shop**	
Driving range	**Practice**	
Sheltered	couvert	no
On grass	sur herbe	no, 20 mats open air
Putting-green	putting-green	yes
Pitching-green	pitching green	yes

Hotel facilities ENVIRONNEMENT HOTELIER 6/10

HOTELS HÔTELS

Royal Golf Hôtel, 12 rooms, D CHF 270 — Pont-la-Ville
Tel (41) 026 - 414 91 11, Fax (41) 026 - 414 94 20 — on site

Hostellerie Saint Georges — Gruyères
14 rooms, D CHF 230 — 8 km
Tel (41) 026 - 921 83 00, Fax (41) 026 - 921 83 39

Hôtel Cailler/Charmey, 50 rooms, D CHF 240 — Charmey
Tel (41) 026 - 927 62 62, Fax (41) 026 - 927 62 63 — 15 km

RESTAURANTS RESTAURANT

La Fleur de Lys, Tel (41) 026 - 322 79 61 — Fribourg 12 km
Restaurant de la Tour, Tel (41) 026 - 912 74 70 — Bulle15 km

INTERLAKEN

14 | 6 | 6

Vom Thunerseeufer nur durch eine Naturschutzzone getrennt, bietet der Interlakner Golfplatz je nach Wasserstand des Sees und Regenmenge recht feuchte Bedingungen, doch er gibt ein gutes Beispiel für das Miteinander von Golf und Oekologie ab. Die recht flache Anlage steht in einem faszinierenden Kontrast zu den umliegenden Berner Alpengipfeln. Der Spielrhythmus ist ansprechend, doch die ersten fünf Loch können - bedingt durch ihre beträchtliche Länge - eine gute Scorekarte schon zu allem Anfang gefährden. Die gut und vielseitig gestalteten Greens bieten einige interessante Annäherungen. Moderate Schwierigkeiten bestimmen den Gesamteindruck dieses Golfcourses, der sich zur angenehmen Familienrunde eignet. Einige Fairways mögen vor allem aus Sicht des hintersten Abschlags schmal erscheinen. Einem Abschlag übrigens, den man bei Regen besser ignoriert.

Not far from Lake Thun, from which the course is separated by a protected natural expanse of land, this can be a very wet course when it rains but forms a good example of coexistence with ecological requirements. In contrast with the impressive mountain setting, the course is rather flat and can be played at a good pace, even though the first five holes are a tough proposition in terms of length and can spoil any hope of returning a good card. The greens are well cut out, rather varied and make for some interesting approach shots. The overriding impression is that of a course where difficulties have been kept to a reasonable minimum for a pleasant round of golf with all the family. With this said, some holes can look decidedly tight, especially from the back tees, which should be unashamedly forgotten whenever it rains.

Golf-Club Interlaken-Unterseen

Postfach 110
CH - 3800 INTERLAKEN

Office	Sekretariat	(41) 033 - 823 60 16
Pro shop	Pro shop	(41) 033 - 822 79 70
Fax	Fax	(41) 033 - 823 42 03
Web	—	
Situation	Lage	

Interlaken (pop. 5 056), 2 km

Annual closure	Jährliche Schliessung	15/11→31/3
Weekly closure	Wöchentliche Schliessung	no

1282

Fees main season Preisliste hochsaison — 18 holes

	Week days Woche	We/Bank holidays We/Feiertag
Individual Individuell	CHF 80	CHF 90
Couple Ehepaar	CHF 160	CHF 180

Caddy	Caddy	no
Electric Trolley	Elektrokarren	CHF 20 /18 holes
Buggy	Elektrischer Wagen	no
Clubs	Leihschläger	CHF 30 /18 holes

Credit cards Kreditkarten
VISA - Eurocard - MasterCard - AMEX

Access Zufahrt : Motorway (Autobahn) N8. Exit Unterseen → Thunersee, Golf
Map 2 on page 1270 Karte 2 Seite 1270

Golf course PLATZ — 14/20

Site	Lage	
Maintenance	Instandhaltung	
Architect	Architekt	Unknown
Type	Typ	parkland, open country
Relief	Begehbarkeit	
Water in play	Platz mit Wasser	
Exp. to wind	Wind ausgesetzt	
Trees in play	Platz mit Bäumen	

Scorecard Scorekarte	Chp. Chp.	Mens Herren	Ladies Damen
Length Länge	6270	5840	5183
Par	72	72	72
Slope system	126	125	123

Advised golfing ability Empfohlene Spielstärke — 0 12 24 36
Hcp required Min. Handicap — 30

Club house & amenities KLUBHAUS UND NEBENGEBÄUDE — 6/10

Pro shop	Pro shop	
Driving range	Übungsplatz	
Sheltered	überdacht	13 mats
On grass	auf Rasen	yes (04 → 10)
Putting-green	Putting-grün	yes
Pitching-green	Pitching-grün	yes

Hotel facilities HOTEL BESCREIBUNG — 6/10

HOTELS HOTELS

Landhotel Golf, 26 rooms, D CHF 184 — on site
Tel (41) 033 - 823 21 31, Fax (41) 033 - 823 21 91

Victoria Jungfrau, 184 rooms, D CHF 670 — Interlaken 2 km
Tel (41) 033 - 828 28 28, Fax (41) 033 - 828 28 80

Beau Site, 50 rooms, D CHF 285 — Interlaken 1 km
Tel (41) 033 - 826 75 75, Fax (41) 033 - 826 75 85

RESTAURANTS RESTAURANT

La Terrasse — Interlaken 2 km
Tel (41) 033 - 828 28 28

Stocker's Degusta — Interlaken
Tel (41) 033 - 822 00 29

LAUSANNE

16 | 7 | 7

Un parcours séduisant et tranquille à première vue, mais dont les nombreuses difficultés se révèlent peu à peu, dans ce site très boisé. Bien rythmé dans son enchaînement, il est souvent étroit, assez vallonné, mais sans vraiment de pièges cachés. Le remodelage des greens par Jeremy Pern a rajeuni ce parcours classique de façon spectaculaire, et oblige plus encore à penser avant de jouer, d'autant que les bunkers de green, également retravaillés, amènent à porter souvent la balle au lieu de la faire rouler. Les joueurs moyens, qui ont souvent du mal à le faire, auront intérêt à jouer des départs avancés. Très agréable à jouer en été quand le terrain est sec, il pouvait s'avérer plus difficile dans des conditions humides, le placement de la balle au drive devenant alors encore plus crucial, mais des travaux ont nettement amélioré cet aspect des choses, tout en maintenant le cachet du parcours. Une véritable réussite où les greens sont revenus en bonne condition.

At first view, an appealing and quiet golf course, but one where the numerous difficulties gradually emerge in a very woody site. With nicely paced continuity, the fairways are often tight and rather hilly, but with no real hidden traps. Recent restyling by architect Jeremy Pern has spectacularly rejuvenated this classic course which now requires more careful thought before each shot, especially since the green-side bunkers, which have also been redesigned, often call for a high lob shot instead of the easier chip into the green. Average players, who often have problems with this kind of approach, will be better off playing from the front tees. Very pleasant to play in summer when the terrain is dry, Lausanne can prove to be a tougher proposition in wet conditions, when placing the ball off the tee becomes even more crucial. However, work has been carried out and has distinctly improved this side of things without affecting the courses's cachet. A great success.

Golf Club de Lausanne — 1931

3, route du Golf
CH - 1000 Lausanne 25

Office	Secrétariat	(41) 021 - 784 84 84
Pro shop	Pro-shop	(41) 021 - 784 84 74
Fax	Fax	(41) 021 - 784 84 80
Web	golf.lausanne@bluewin.ch	
Situation	Situation	
Lausanne (pop. 114 161), 5 km		
Annual closure	Fermeture annuelle	15/12→15/3
Weekly closure	Fermeture hebdomadaire	no

Fees main season / Tarifs haute saison	18 holes	
	Week days / Semaine	We/Bank holidays / We/Férié
Individual Individuel	CHF 100	CHF 120
Couple Couple	CHF 200	CHF 240

Under 21: – 50%

Caddy	Caddy	on request
Electric Trolley	Chariot électrique	no
Buggy	Voiturette	CHF 80 /18 holes
Clubs	Clubs	CHF 25 /18 holes

Credit cards Cartes de crédit
VISA - MasterCard

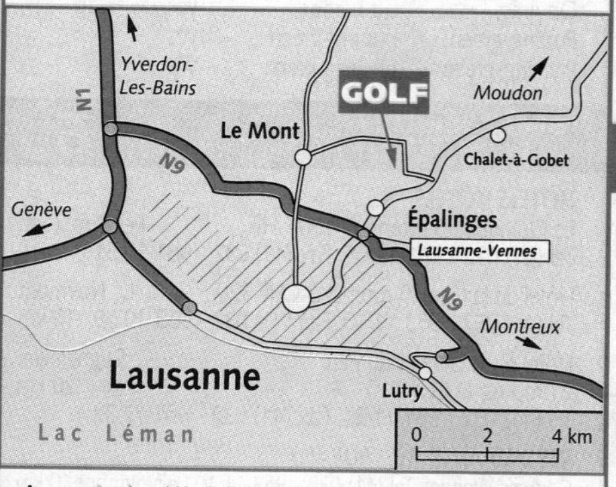

Access Accès : N9, Exit (sortie) Vennes → Epalinges. Chalet-à-Gobet, → Le Mont, Golf
Map 1 on page 1269 Carte 1 Page 1269

Golf course PARCOURS — 16/20

Site	Site	
Maintenance	Entretien	
Architect	Architecte	Narbel Jeremy Pern
Type	Type	parkland
Relief	Relief	
Water in play	Eau en jeu	
Exp. to wind	Exposé au vent	
Trees in play	Arbres en jeu	

Scorecard / Carte de score	Chp. / Chp.	Mens / Mess.	Ladies / Da.
Length Long.	6197	5793	5139
Par	72	72	72
Slope system	134	129	129

Advised golfing ability / Niveau de jeu recommandé: 0 12 24 36
Hcp required / Handicap exigé: 27

Club house & amenities CLUB-HOUSE ET ANNEXES — 7/10

Pro shop	Pro-shop	
Driving range	Practice	
Sheltered	couvert	4 mats
On grass	sur herbe	yes (05 → 10)
Putting-green	putting-green	yes
Pitching-green	pitching green	yes

Hotel facilities ENVIRONNEMENT HOTELIER — 7/10

HOTELS HÔTELS

Les Chevreuils, 30 rooms, D CHF 200 Vers-chez-les-Blancs
Tel (41) 021 - 784 20 21, Fax (41) 021 - 784 15 45 5 km

Beau Rivage Palace, 169 rooms, D CHF 490 Lausanne
Tel (41) 021 - 613 33 33, Fax (41) 021 - 613 33 34 6 km

Victoria, 51 rooms, D CHF 340 Lausanne
Tel (41) 021 - 342 02 02, Fax (41) 021 - 342 02 22

RESTAURANTS RESTAURANT

Hôtel de Ville (Rochat), Tel (41) 021 - 634 05 05 Crissier 10 km

La Grappe d'Or, Tel (41) 021 - 323 07 60 Lausanne

A la Pomme de Pin, Tel (41) 021 - 323 46 56 Lausanne

LES BOIS

15	7	6

Le Golf Club Les Bois se trouve au milieu de la région des Franches Montagnes, typique du Jura Suisse. Un vrai et superbe décor d'opérette. Le terrain est accidenté, mais acceptable sur le plan physique (chariot électrique ou voiturette pour les moins solides). Il a été construit en deux temps, mais la différence entre les greens commence à s'atténuer. Le parcours mélange les trous en forêt et les trous en espace plus ouvert, l'ensemble étant harmonieux et très bien équilibré. Certes, on ne voit pas tous les obstacles, et l'on ne peut concevoir une bonne stratégie de jeu avant d'avoir joué au moins trois fois, mais sachez au moins que ce parcours est aussi franc qu'on le devine, et qu'il n'est pas vraiment nécessaire de travailler la balle. En revanche, il faut savoir lire ces greens, pas du tout évidents. Pour finir, vous garderez en particulier le souvenir des trous 14 à 16 au milieu des sapins, qui peuvent déjà figurer parmi les plus beaux trous de Suisse. Un golf de très bon niveau, et jouable par tous.

The Golf Club Les Bois is located amidst the region of Franches Montagnes that is typical of the Swiss Jura mountains. A superb decor in true operetta style. The terrain is hilly but not over-demanding physically (think about an electric trolley or buggy for the less able). It was built in two phases, which is less evident now than two years ago. The course is a mixture of holes through a forest and holes in more open space, all harmoniously put together with clever balance. You definitely do not see all the hazards and effective game strategy is not possible before playing the course at least three times. Suffice it to say that this layout is as open and honest as you might guess and you don't really need to bend or flight the ball. What you do need to know is how to read the greens here, which are anything but straightforward. The holes you will remember are 14 through 16 in the middle of pine trees, which might rank as some of the finest holes of golf in the whole of Switzerland. A first rate course, playable by everyone.

Golf Club Les Bois — 1995

Les Murs, Case Postale 26
CH - 2336 LES BOIS

Office	Secrétariat	(41) 032 - 961 10 03
Pro shop	Pro-shop	(41) 032 - 961 19 44
Fax	Fax	(41) 032 - 961 10 17
Web	www.suissegolfnetwork.ch	
Situation	Situation	

La Chaux-de-Fonds (pop. 37 321), 12 km

Annual closure	Fermeture annuelle	1/11→1/4
Weekly closure	Fermeture hebdomadaire	no

Fees main season Tarifs haute saison	18 holes	
	Week days Semaine	**We/Bank holidays** We/Férié
Individual Individuel	CHF 80	CHF 90
Couple Couple	CHF 160	CHF 180
Caddy	Caddy	no
Electric Trolley	Chariot électrique	CHF 50 /18 holes
Buggy	Voiturette	CHF 50 /18 holes
Clubs	Clubs	CHF 30

Credit cards Cartes de crédit
VISA - Eurocard - MasterCard - DC - AMEX 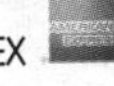

Access Accès : Genève, Lausanne, Bern : A1 → Neuchâtel. N20 → La Chaux-de-Fonds. Road 18 → Saignelégier.
Map 1 on page 1269 Carte 1 Page 1269

Golf course — PARCOURS — 15/20

Site	Site	
Maintenance	Entretien	
Architect	Architecte	Jeremy Pern
Type	Type	forest, country
Relief	Relief	
Water in play	Eau en jeu	
Exp. to wind	Exposé au vent	
Trees in play	Arbres en jeu	

Scorecard Carte de score	**Chp.** Chp.	**Mens** Mess.	**Ladies** Da.
Length Long.	6053	5650	4778
Par	72	72	72
Slope system	119	115	115

Advised golfing ability Niveau de jeu recommandé — 0 12 24 36
Hcp required Handicap exigé 35

Club house & amenities — CLUB HOUSE ET ANNEXES — 7/10

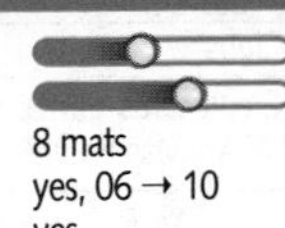

Pro shop	Pro-shop	
Driving range	Practice	
Sheltered	couvert	8 mats
On grass	sur herbe	yes, 06 → 10
Putting-green	putting-green	yes
Pitching-green	pitching green	yes

Hotel facilities — ENVIRONNEMENT HOTELIER — 6/10

HOTELS HÔTELS

Le Quinquet, 5 rooms, D 100 CHF — Les Bois 2 km
Tel (41) 032 - 961 12 06, Fax (41) 032 - 961 16 51

Hôtel de la Gare, 5 rooms, D CHF 320 — Le Noirmont 10 km
Tel (41) 032 - 953 11 10, Fax (41) 032 - 953 10 59

Hötel de la Gare et du Parc — Saignelégier 20 km
21 rooms, D CHF 210
Tel (41) 032 - 951 11 21, Fax (41) 032 - 951 12 32

RESTAURANTS RESTAURANT

Georges Wenger, Tel (41) 032 - 953 11 10 Le Noirmont 10 km

Hötel de la Gare et du Parc — Saignelégier 20 km
Tel (41) 032 - 951 11 21

LUGANO

15 | 7 | 8

Fondata nel 1925, il percorso é stato rimodellato succesivamente da Donald Harradine e Cabell Robinson che à aggiunto qualche laghetto al corso d'acqua esistente, ma non ha potuto allungarlo per la mancanza dello spazio. I green sono ben difesi, ció che puo ostacolare il desiderio di performance. Molto franco, non ha bisogno di essere giocate dieci volte per essere capito, la vegetazione attenua molto l'impressione di va e vieni suggeriti dal disegno, e obligga i giocatori d'un altro livello, dove possono rifarsi con la precisione, in quanto il percorso non é molto lungo. In un sito ed una piacevole regione, é un buon percorso di vacanze, la sua manutenzione deve essere migliorata per attribuirgli una nota migliore.

Opened in 1925, the course has been successively reshaped by Donald Harradine and recently by Cabell Robinson, who added several lakes to the existing river but were unable to lengthen the course owing to lack of space. Most of the greens are now remodeled and well defended, which may cut short any desire to go for the performance. You don't need to play this very honest course ten times to understand what it is about. The vegetation reduces the impression of up and down holes, suggested by the layout, and forces long-hitters to fade or draw the ball to get a good approach into the green. Good and not so good players can get along well together here, where lack of precision is offset by short yardage. In a pleasant setting and region, this is a good holiday course, but to get the best score, green-keeping and maintenance must be at the best level.

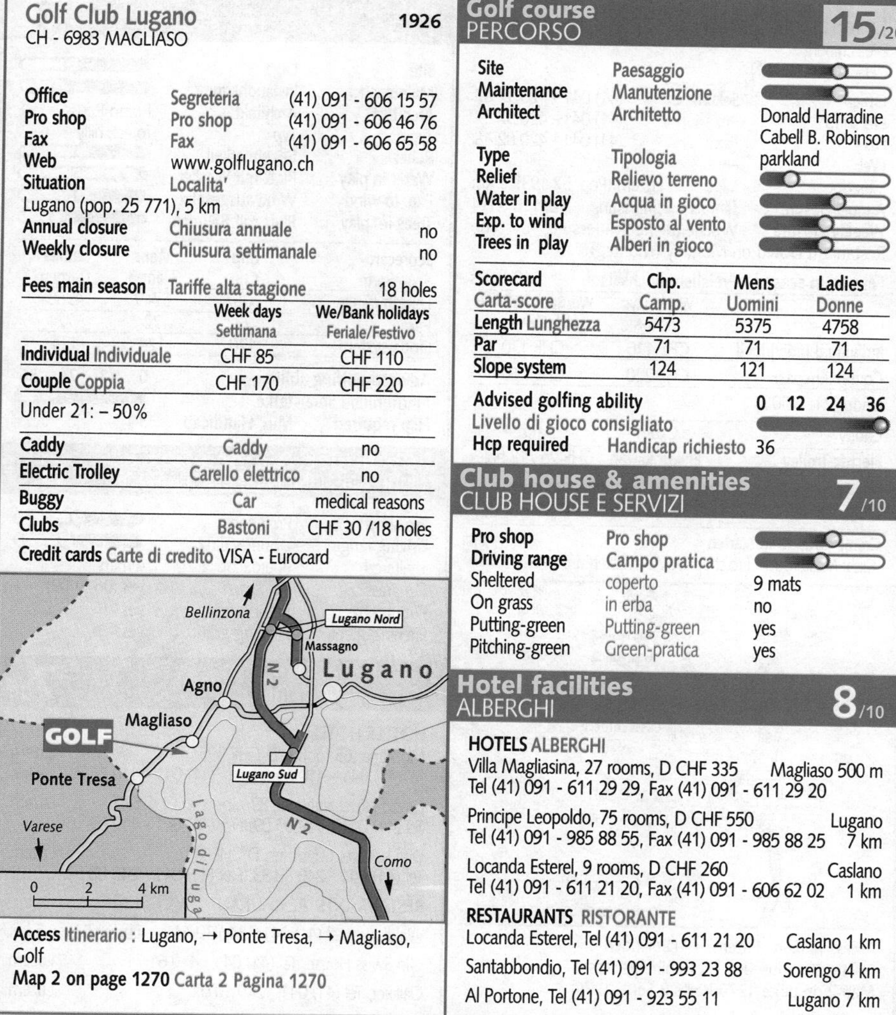

Golf Club Lugano — 1926

CH - 6983 MAGLIASO

Office	Segreteria	(41) 091 - 606 15 57
Pro shop	Pro shop	(41) 091 - 606 46 76
Fax	Fax	(41) 091 - 606 65 58
Web	www.golflugano.ch	
Situation	Localita'	

Lugano (pop. 25 771), 5 km

Annual closure	Chiusura annuale	no
Weekly closure	Chiusura settimanale	no

Fees main season Tariffe alta stagione		18 holes
	Week days Settimana	**We/Bank holidays** Feriale/Festivo
Individual Individuale	CHF 85	CHF 110
Couple Coppia	CHF 170	CHF 220

Under 21: – 50%

Caddy	Caddy	no
Electric Trolley	Carello elettrico	no
Buggy	Car	medical reasons
Clubs	Bastoni	CHF 30 /18 holes

Credit cards Carte di credito VISA - Eurocard

Access Itinerario : Lugano, → Ponte Tresa, → Magliaso, Golf

Map 2 on page 1270 Carta 2 Pagina 1270

Golf course PERCORSO — 15/20

Site	Paesaggio	
Maintenance	Manutenzione	
Architect	Architetto	Donald Harradine, Cabell B. Robinson
Type	Tipologia	parkland
Relief	Relievo terreno	
Water in play	Acqua in gioco	
Exp. to wind	Esposto al vento	
Trees in play	Alberi in gioco	

Scorecard Carta-score	**Chp.** Camp.	**Mens** Uomini	**Ladies** Donne
Length Lunghezza	5473	5375	4758
Par	71	71	71
Slope system	124	121	124

Advised golfing ability Livello di gioco consigliato — 0 12 24 36

Hcp required Handicap richiesto 36

Club house & amenities CLUB HOUSE E SERVIZI — 7/10

Pro shop	Pro shop	
Driving range	Campo pratica	
Sheltered	coperto	9 mats
On grass	in erba	no
Putting-green	Putting-green	yes
Pitching-green	Green-pratica	yes

Hotel facilities ALBERGHI — 8/10

HOTELS ALBERGHI

Villa Magliasina, 27 rooms, D CHF 335 — Magliaso 500 m
Tel (41) 091 - 611 29 29, Fax (41) 091 - 611 29 20

Principe Leopoldo, 75 rooms, D CHF 550 — Lugano 7 km
Tel (41) 091 - 985 88 55, Fax (41) 091 - 985 88 25

Locanda Esterel, 9 rooms, D CHF 260 — Caslano 1 km
Tel (41) 091 - 611 21 20, Fax (41) 091 - 606 62 02

RESTAURANTS RISTORANTE

Locanda Esterel, Tel (41) 091 - 611 21 20 — Caslano 1 km

Santabbondio, Tel (41) 091 - 993 23 88 — Sorengo 4 km

Al Portone, Tel (41) 091 - 923 55 11 — Lugano 7 km

LUZERN

13 | 6 | 7

1925 erbaut und seither mehrfach verändert, bietet dieser Golfcourse hübsche und abwechslungsreiche Aussichten auf den Vierwaldstättersee, auf Hügellandschaften und auf verschneite Berge. Bie betonten Geländeformen wurden geschickt einbezogen, denn die grossen Höhenunterschiede liegen meist zwischen den Holes. Doglegs sind wenige zu finden, aber die Bahnen sind oft schmal, verlangen gerade Schläge und den einen oder anderen Flirt mit Baümen. Bei nur einem Wasserhindernis haben gute Spieler Chancen auf tiefe Scores, obwohl Annäherungen auf oft tiefergelegene oder überhöhte Greens solide Schläge verlangen. Ein traditionelles Platzkonzept, dem aber die Schwierigkeiten eines modernen Courses nicht fehlen und die charmante Umgebung machen Luzern zum lohnenden Golfabstecher.

This course has been considerably restyled since its opening in 1925. There are a number of different pretty views over lake Lucerne, the hills and the snow-capped mountains. The terrain is steep and rather hilly but has been well utilised, as the steepest slopes are to be found primarily between holes. There are few doglegs, as most holes are often straight and require straight shots, skirting the trees. With a single water hazard, skilled players will doubtless find this an easy course to score on, even though care is called for when attacking the greens, which are rarely on the same level as the fairway (elevated or in a hollow). We liked the charm of the site and a certain idea of old-style golf courses, without the difficulties found on many modern courses.

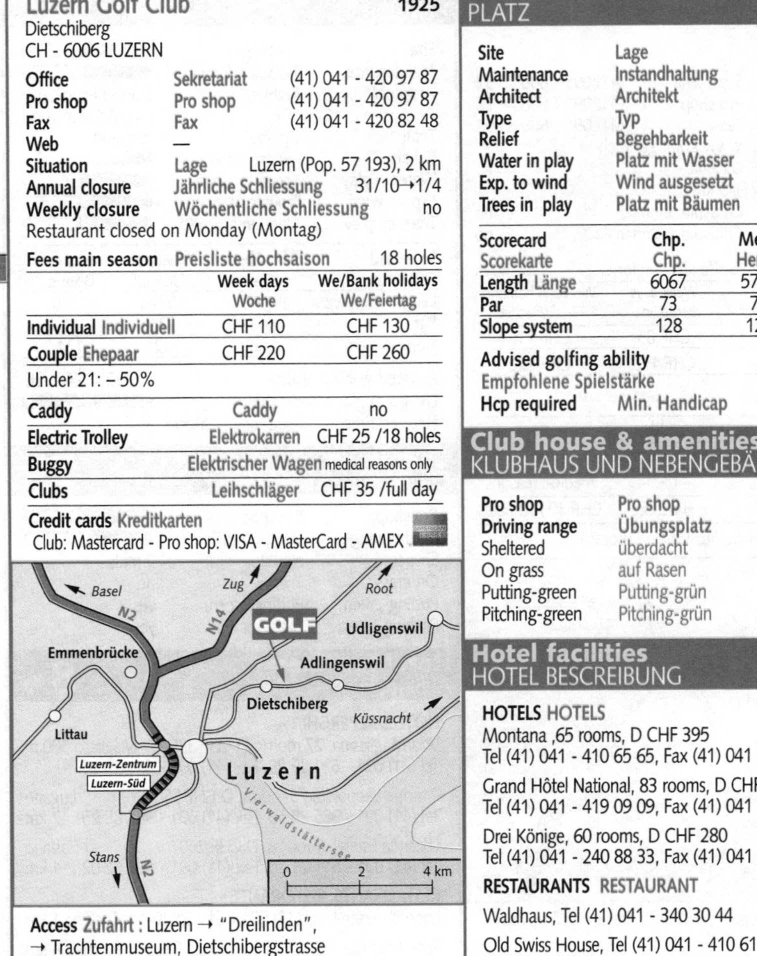

Luzern Golf Club 1925
Dietschiberg
CH - 6006 LUZERN

Office	Sekretariat	(41) 041 - 420 97 87
Pro shop	Pro shop	(41) 041 - 420 97 87
Fax	Fax	(41) 041 - 420 82 48
Web	—	
Situation	Lage	Luzern (Pop. 57 193), 2 km
Annual closure	Jährliche Schliessung	31/10→1/4
Weekly closure	Wöchentliche Schliessung	no

Restaurant closed on Monday (Montag)

Fees main season Preisliste hochsaison	Week days Woche	We/Bank holidays We/Feiertag
18 holes		
Individual Individuell	CHF 110	CHF 130
Couple Ehepaar	CHF 220	CHF 260
Under 21: – 50%		

Caddy	Caddy	no
Electric Trolley	Elektrokarren	CHF 25 /18 holes
Buggy	Elektrischer Wagen	medical reasons only
Clubs	Leihschläger	CHF 35 /full day

Credit cards Kreditkarten
Club: Mastercard - Pro shop: VISA - MasterCard - AMEX

Access Zufahrt : Luzern → "Dreilinden", → Trachtenmuseum, Dietschibergstrasse
Map 2 on page 1270 Karte 2 Seite 1270

Golf course PLATZ — 13/20

Site	Lage	
Maintenance	Instandhaltung	
Architect	Architekt	Ruzzo Reuss
Type	Typ	forest, hilly
Relief	Begehbarkeit	
Water in play	Platz mit Wasser	
Exp. to wind	Wind ausgesetzt	
Trees in play	Platz mit Bäumen	

Scorecard Scorekarte	Chp. Chp.	Mens Herren	Ladies Damen
Length Länge	6067	5749	4968
Par	73	72	72
Slope system	128	124	124

Advised golfing ability Empfohlene Spielstärke 0 12 24 36
Hcp required Min. Handicap 30

Club house & amenities KLUBHAUS UND NEBENGEBÄUDE — 6/10

Pro shop	Pro shop	
Driving range	Übungsplatz	
Sheltered	überdacht	4 mats
On grass	auf Rasen	yes (06 → 09)
Putting-green	Putting-grün	yes
Pitching-green	Pitching-grün	yes

Hotel facilities HOTEL BESCREIBUNG — 7/10

HOTELS HOTELS

Montana ,65 rooms, D CHF 395 — Luzern 2 km
Tel (41) 041 - 410 65 65, Fax (41) 041 - 410 66 76

Grand Hôtel National, 83 rooms, D CHF 570 — Luzern
Tel (41) 041 - 419 09 09, Fax (41) 041 - 419 09 10

Drei Könige, 60 rooms, D CHF 280 — Luzern
Tel (41) 041 - 240 88 33, Fax (41) 041 - 240 88 52

RESTAURANTS RESTAURANT

Waldhaus, Tel (41) 041 - 340 30 44 — Luzern/Horw 5 km

Old Swiss House, Tel (41) 041 - 410 61 71 — Luzern

Galliker, Tel (41) 041 - 240 10 02 — Luzern

MONTREUX

13 | 6 | 5

On pourrait souligner la beauté du panorama sur les Alpes , mais cette qualité est commune à la majorité des golfs de Suisse ! Elle contribue au moins à faire apprécier un parcours autrement sans originalité particulière, et sans obstacles d'eau. Eviter les arbres constitue le principal "challenge", car ils sont souvent en jeu, et rompent un peu la monotonie des trous, trop similaires de dessin pour frapper la mémoire. Les difficultés ne sont pas très grandes, ce qui peut réserver des parties plaisantes entre joueurs de niveau différent, mais les meilleurs resteront certainement sur leur faim. Les greens sont en meilleur état qu'autrefois. Si vous passez dans la région...

We could point to the beautiful scenery of the Alps, but such panoramas are common to the majority of Swiss courses. But it does help the player to enjoy a course which otherwise has no particular originality and no water hazards. The main challenge is to avoid the trees, which are often in play and break the monotony of holes which are too similar to really leave an indelible impression. The difficulties are not enormous, which can lead to pleasant rounds with friends of differing ability, but the better players will feel a touch of frustration. When we visited, the greens were in a much better condition than before, so if you are in the neighbourhood, it's worth a visit.

Golf Club Montreux

Route d'Evian
CH - 1860 AIGLE

Office	Secrétariat	(41) 024 - 466 46 16
Pro shop	Pro-shop	(41) 024 - 466 14 64
Fax	Fax	(41) 024 - 466 60 47
Web	—	
Situation	Situation	

Montreux (pop. 21 476), 25 km

Annual closure	Fermeture annuelle	no
Weekly closure	Fermeture hebdomadaire	no

Fees main season Tarifs haute saison		18 holes
	Week days Semaine	**We/Bank holidays** We/Férié
Individual Individuel	CHF 80	CHF 100
Couple Couple	CHF 160	CHF 200

Under 21: CHF 50 - CHF 60 (We)

Caddy	Caddy	no
Electric Trolley	Chariot électrique	no
Buggy	Voiturette	no
Clubs	Clubs	CHF 10 /18 holes

Credit cards Cartes de crédit
VISA - Eurocard - Mastercard - DC - AMEX

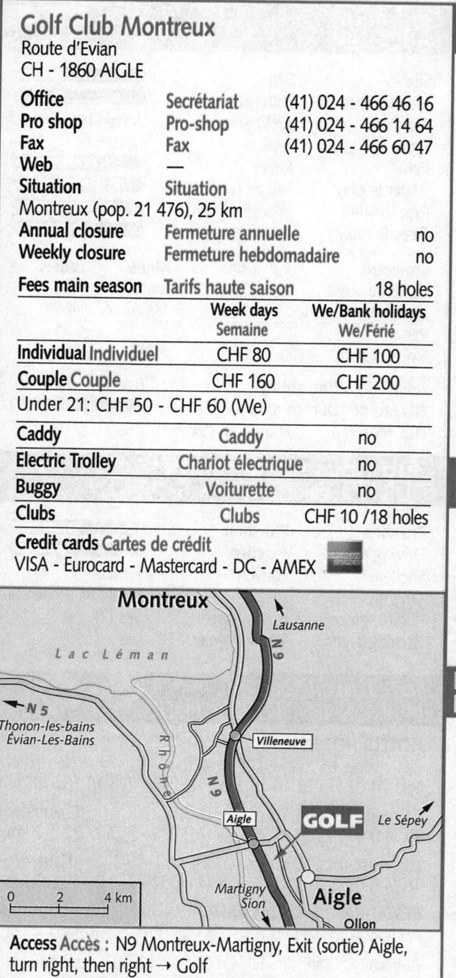

Access Accès : N9 Montreux-Martigny, Exit (sortie) Aigle, turn right, then right → Golf
Map 1 on page 1269 Carte 1 Page 1269

Golf course PARCOURS — 13/20

Site	Site	
Maintenance	Entretien	
Architect	Architecte	
Type	Type	parkland
Relief	Relief	
Water in play	Eau en jeu	
Exp. to wind	Exposé au vent	
Trees in play	Arbres en jeu	

Scorecard Carte de score	**Chp.** Chp.	**Mens** Mess.	**Ladies** Da.
Length Long.	6143	5782	5083
Par	72	72	72
Slope system	122	122	121

Advised golfing ability Niveau de jeu recommandé — 0 12 24 36
Hcp required Handicap exigé 36

Club house & amenities CLUB-HOUSE ET ANNEXES — 6/10

Pro shop	Pro-shop	
Driving range	Practice	
Sheltered	couvert	6 mats
On grass	sur herbe	yes
Putting-green	putting-green	yes
Pitching-green	pitching green	yes

Hotel facilities ENVIRONNEMENT HOTELIER — 5/10

HOTELS HÔTELS

Le Montreux Palace, 235 rooms, D CHF 560 — Montreux
Tel (41) 021 - 962 12 12, Fax (41) 021 - 962 17 17 — 25 km

Villa Toscane, 46 rooms, D CHF 290 — Montreux
Tel (41) 021 - 963 84 21, Fax (41) 021 - 963 84 26

Nord, 19 rooms, D CHF 300 — Aigle 20 km
Tel (41) 024 - 468 10 55, Fax (41) 024 - 468 10 56

RESTAURANTS RESTAURANT

Le Pont de Brent — Montreux-Brent
Tel (41) 021 - 964 52 30 — 30 km

L'Ermitage, Tel (41) 021 - 964 44 11 — Montreux 25 km

NEUCHÂTEL

14	7	7

Ce parcours accidenté, mais sans excès, a été dessiné dans une ancienne zone agricole au pied du Jura. L'absence d'arrosage automatique oblige à le déconseiller en temps de forte sécheresse, mais les précipitations naturelles permettent de le maintenir généralement en bon état. Les obstacles sont rarement très dangereux (quelques hors-limites), et la longueur raisonnable permet d'offrir pas mal d'occasions de birdie (ou de pars pour les joueurs moyens). Pas de pièges ici ni de complications artificielles : ce parcours a été coulé dans la nature, à l'intention évidente des familles, ou de ceux qui ne souhaitent pas trop se compliquer la vie sur un parcours (ils sont nombreux).

This is a hilly course laid out over a former farming region at the foot of the Jura mountains. There being no automatic sprinklers, it is not a course to be recommended during a drought, but natural rainfall generally tends to keep it in good condition. The hazards are rarely very dangerous (a few out-of-bounds) and the reasonable length can produce more than one opportunity to catch an elusive birdie (or the equally elusive par for lesser players). There are no traps or artificial complications here, as this course was cast in natural land, evidently intended for families or golfers who prefer not to make life any more complicated than it often can be on a golf course (and there are a lot of those).

Golf & Country Club Neuchâtel 1975

Hameau de Voëns
CH - 2072 SAINT-BLAISE

Office	Secrétariat	(41) 032 - 753 55 50
Pro shop	Pro-shop	(41) 032 - 753 70 84
Fax	Fax	(41) 032 - 753 29 40
E-mail	golf.ne@swissonline.ch	
Situation	Situation	

Neuchâtel (pop. 31 740), 5 km

Annual closure	Fermeture annuelle	15/11→15/3
Weekly closure	Fermeture hebdomadaire	no

Fees main season Tarifs haute saison	Week days Semaine	We/Bank holidays We/Férié (18 holes)
Individual Individuel	CHF 80	CHF 100
Couple Couple	CHF 160	CHF 200
Caddy Caddy		no
Electric Trolley Chariot électrique		no
Buggy Voiturette		medical reasons
Clubs Clubs		CHF 25 /18 holes

Credit cards Cartes de crédit
VISA - Eurocard - Mastercard - AMEX 

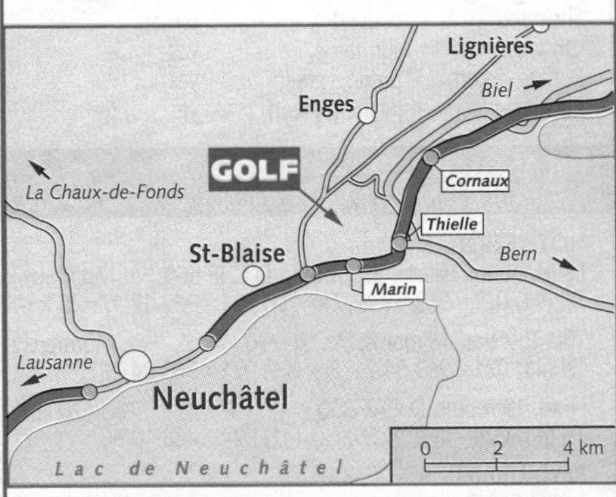

Access Accès : A1 Bâle-Payerne, Exit (sortie) Neuchâtel. In Kerzers → Neuchâtel to St Blaise, → Lignières. 3 km, Voëns, golf on the left.
Map 1 on page 1269 Carte 1 Page 1269

Golf course PARCOURS 14/20

Site	Site	
Maintenance	Entretien	
Architect	Architecte	Donald Harradine
Type	Type	parkland
Relief	Relief	
Water in play	Eau en jeu	
Exp. to wind	Exposé au vent	
Trees in play	Arbres en jeu	

Scorecard Carte de score	Chp. Chp.	Mens Mess.	Ladies Da.
Length Long.	5913	5605	4835
Par	71	71	71
Slope system	129	125	121

Advised golfing ability 0 12 24 36
Niveau de jeu recommandé
Hcp required Handicap exigé 36

Club house & amenities CLUB-HOUSE ET ANNEXES 7/10

Pro shop	Pro-shop	
Driving range	Practice	
Sheltered	couvert	8 mats
On grass	sur herbe	no, 12 mats open air
Putting-green	putting-green	yes (2)
Pitching-green	pitching green	yes

Hotel facilities ENVIRONNEMENT HOTELIER 7/10

HOTELS HÔTELS

Beaurivage, 65 rooms, D CHF 420 — Neuchâtel
Tel (41) 032 - 723 15 15, Fax (41) 032 - 723 16 16 — 9 km

Chaumont et Golf, 65 rooms, D CHF 230 — Chaumont
Tel (41) 032 - 754 21 75, Fax (41) 032 - 753 27 22 — 2 km

Les Vieux Toits, 10 rooms, D CHF 180 — Hauterive
Tel (41) 032 - 753 42 42, Fax (41) 032 - 753 24 52 — 2 km

RESTAURANTS RESTAURANT

Au Boccalino, Tel (41) 032 - 753 36 80 — Saint-Blaise 4 km
Auberge du Grand Pin, Tel (41) 032 - 731 77 07 — Peseux 12 km
Hôtel DuPeyrou, Tel (41) 032 - 725 11 83 — Neuchâtel 9 km

NIEDERBÜREN

13 | 7 | 7

Niederbüren, entworfen von dem allseits gefragten Donald Harradine, entrollt sich wie ein schmales Band vor den Augen des Spielers, ganz so wie der Old Course von St. Andrews. Nur, dass der Platz an dem Flüsschen Thun liegt und nicht am Meer. Einzig der Entwurf entspricht britischer Tradition, der Vergleich lässt sich nicht weiter ausdehnen. Es beginnt damit, dass der Wind hier längst nicht so häufig und so gewaltig weht. Weiterhin bilden die Bunker die haupsächliche Bedrohung der Fairways, jedoch veranlassen deren Profil und Schwierigkeitsgrad zu keinerlei Besorgnis. Die Bahnen sind von Tannen gesäumt, die an ein gerades Spiel appellieren und keinerlei Fehler zulassen, wie etwa die breiten Flächen der richtigen Links. Der Platz ist insgesamt nicht zu lang und die schwierigen Passagen sind gleichmässig verteilt. Es handelt sich um ein angenehmes Areal, ideal für die ganze Familie.

Laid out by the prolific designer Donald Harradine, Niederbüren is peculiar in that it unwinds in a narrow strip, like the Old Course at St Andrews, only alongside the river Thun and not the sea. Despite the British tradition here, the comparison ends there. Firstly the wind is less frequent and more clement, then the basic hazards emerge as bunkers, although their shape and difficulty are anything but fearsome. The fairways here are lined with fir-trees, which call for accuracy and do not leave the room for error you find on real links courses. The layout is moderate in length and difficulties are evenly spread around the course. A pleasant course for all the family.

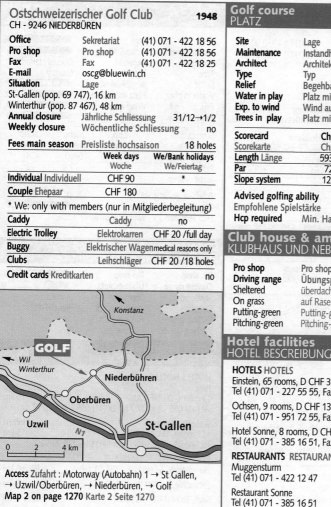

Ostschweizerischer Golf Club — 1948

CH - 9246 NIEDERBÜREN

Office	Sekretariat	(41) 071 - 422 18 56
Pro shop	Pro shop	(41) 071 - 422 18 56
Fax	Fax	(41) 071 - 422 18 25
E-mail	oscg@bluewin.ch	
Situation	Lage	

St-Gallen (pop. 69 747), 16 km
Winterthur (pop. 87 467), 48 km

Annual closure	Jährliche Schliessung	31/12→1/2
Weekly closure	Wöchentliche Schliessung	no

Fees main season Preisliste hochsaison	18 holes	
	Week days Woche	**We/Bank holidays** We/Feiertag
Individual Individuell	CHF 90	*
Couple Ehepaar	CHF 180	*

* We: only with members (nur in Mitgliederbegleitung)

Caddy	Caddy	no
Electric Trolley	Elektrokarren	CHF 20 /full day
Buggy	Elektrischer Wagen	medical reasons only
Clubs	Leihschläger	CHF 20 /18 holes
Credit cards Kreditkarten		no

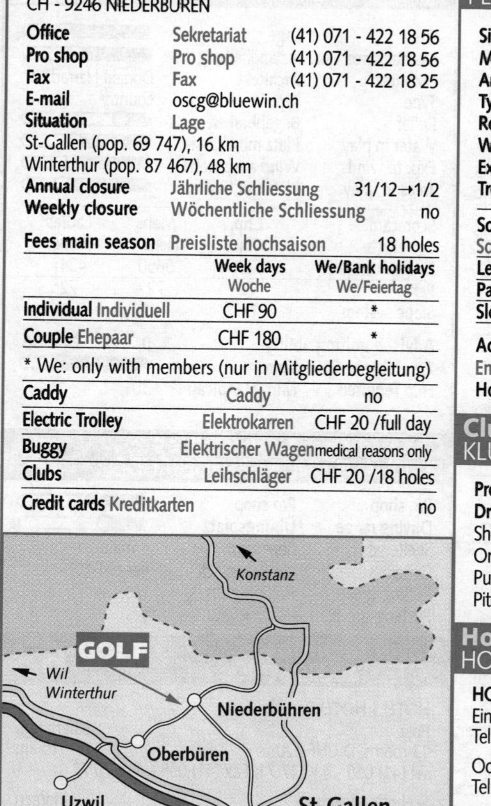

Access Zufahrt : Motorway (Autobahn) 1 → St Gallen, → Uzwil/Oberbüren, → Niederbüren, → Golf
Map 2 on page 1270 Karte 2 Seite 1270

Golf course — PLATZ — 13/20

Site	Lage	[rating bar]
Maintenance	Instandhaltung	[rating bar]
Architect	Architekt	Donald Harradine
Type	Typ	parkland
Relief	Begehbarkeit	[rating bar]
Water in play	Platz mit Wasser	[rating bar]
Exp. to wind	Wind ausgesetzt	[rating bar]
Trees in play	Platz mit Bäumen	[rating bar]

Scorecard Scorekarte	**Chp.** Chp.	**Mens** Herren	**Ladies** Damen
Length Länge	5930	5698	5040
Par	72	72	72
Slope system	128	124	119

Advised golfing ability Empfohlene Spielstärke — 0 12 24 36
Hcp required Min. Handicap 30

Club house & amenities — KLUBHAUS UND NEBENGEBÄUDE — 7/10

Pro shop	Pro shop	[rating bar]
Driving range	Übungsplatz	[rating bar]
Sheltered	überdacht	6 mats
On grass	auf Rasen	yes
Putting-green	Putting-grün	yes
Pitching-green	Pitching-grün	yes

Hotel facilities — HOTEL BESCREIBUNG — 7/10

HOTELS HOTELS

Einstein, 65 rooms, D CHF 350 — St. Gallen
Tel (41) 071 - 227 55 55, Fax (41) 071 - 227 55 77 — 16 km

Ochsen, 9 rooms, D CHF 135 — Niederuzwil
Tel (41) 071 - 951 72 55, Fax (41) 071 - 951 81 73 — 10 km

Hotel Sonne, 8 rooms, D CHF 150 — Gossau
Tel (41) 071 - 385 16 51, Fax (41) 071 - 385 90 22 — 12 km

RESTAURANTS RESTAURANT

Muggensturm — Bischofszell
Tel (41) 071 - 422 12 47 — 6 km

Restaurant Sonne — Gossau
Tel (41) 071 - 385 16 51 — 12 km

SCHÖNENBERG

14 | 7 | 6

Die Lage des Platzes auf einem schmalen Terrain entlang des Flüsschens Krebs erklärt die zahlreichen aber nicht allzu spielbestimmenden Out of bounds und auch den feuchten Torfboden. Von der hintersten Abschlägen gespielt, ist der Platz recht lang. Bäume, Bunkers und zahlreiche Wasserflächen scheuen entwichene Bälle nicht und machen die Aufgaben heikel. Die Strategie ist auf jedem Hole wichtig und macht das Spiel vielfältig und interessant. Auch ohne golfarchitektonische Sonderleistungen ist Schönenberg eine ausserordentliche Anlage und dank geschützten Zonen ein gutes Beispiel für das Nebeneinander von Golf und Natur.

A lay-out on a narrow strip of terrain along the river Krebs explains both the many out-of bounds (although not too many in play) and the wetness of the soil, which is basically peat. Reasonable from the normal tees, it gets much longer from the back-tees, especially since the bunkers and many water hazards easily collect balls hit off-target. Each hole requires a definite strategy, but this and especially the variety of holes make it a pleasant course to play. Without displaying any exceptional imagination on the part of the architect, Schönenberg is a very attractive course and again shows a good example of ecology and golf living easily side by side (several areas are natural trust land). This is always a thorny problem in Switzerland.

Golf & Country Club Schönenberg — 1968

CH - 8824 SCHÖNENBERG

Office	Sekretariat	(41) 01 - 788 90 40
Pro shop	Pro shop	(41) 01 - 788 90 55
Fax	Fax	(41) 01 - 788 90 45
Web	—	
Situation	Lage	

Zürich (pop. 336 821), 25 km

Annual closure	Jährliche Schliessung	15/11→20/3
Weekly closure	Wöchentliche Schliessung	no

Fees main season Preisliste hochsaison	18 holes	
	Week days Woche	**We/Bank holidays** We/Feiertag
Individual Individuell	CHF 110	*
Couple Ehepaar	CHF 220	*

* We: members only (nur Mitglieder)

Caddy	Caddy	no
Electric Trolley	Elektrokarren	CHF 20 /18 holes
Buggy	Elektrischer Wagen	no
Clubs	Leihschläger	yes

Credit cards Kreditkarten
VISA - Eurocard - Mastercard - AMEX

Access Zufahrt : Autobahn Zürich-Chur → Horgen oder Wädenswil, → Zug, Hirsel → Schönenberg, Golf 1,5 km.
Map 2 on page 1270 Karte 2 Seite 1270

Golf course PLATZ — 14/20

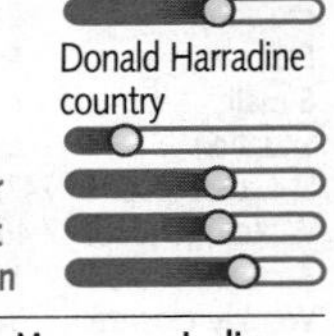

Site	Lage	
Maintenance	Instandhaltung	
Architect	Architekt	Donald Harradine
Type	Typ	country
Relief	Begehbarkeit	
Water in play	Platz mit Wasser	
Exp. to wind	Wind ausgesetzt	
Trees in play	Platz mit Bäumen	

Scorecard Scorekarte	**Chp.** Chp.	**Mens** Herren	**Ladies** Damen
Length Länge	6205	5650	4847
Par	72	72	72
Slope system	137	131	129

Advised golfing ability Empfohlene Spielstärke — 0 12 24 36
Hcp required Min. Handicap — 30

Club house & amenities KLUBHAUS UND NEBENGEBÄUDE — 7/10

Pro shop	Pro shop	
Driving range	Übungsplatz	
Sheltered	überdacht	4 mats
On grass	auf Rasen	yes (04-10)
Putting-green	Putting-grün	yes
Pitching-green	Pitching-grün	yes

Hotel facilities HOTEL BESCREIBUNG — 6/10

HOTELS HOTELS

Post — Biberbrugg 15 km
13 rooms, D CHF 120
Tel (41) 055 - 412 27 71, Fax (41) 055 - 412 70 72

Seehotel Meierhof — Horgen 5 km
113 rooms, D CHF 250
Tel (41) 01 - 728 91 91, Fax (41) 01 - 728 92 92

RESTAURANTS RESTAURANT

Zur Faktorei, Tel (41) 01 - 784 03 16 — Bäch 6 km
Eichmühle, Tel (41) 01 - 780 34 44 — Wädenswil 5 km
Seeli, Tel (41) 01 - 784 03 07 — Bäch 6 km

SEMPACHERSEE 16 8 7

Die Gegend ist eher flach, bietet aber dennoch eine wunderschöne Sicht auf dem Sempachersee und liegt in der Nähe eines der bekannten Schlachtfelder des Mittelalters. Bevor Sie diesen Platz spielen, tun Sie gut daran, ihn und seine Tücken zu studieren. Er bietet einiges an Schwierigkeiten, die man entweder umgehen oder mit einigem Risiko direkt angreifen kann. Oder man kann auch etwas überraschendes versuchen... Dabei stellt man fest, dass er gar nicht so ungastlich ist. Die Fairways sind angenehm breit, denn die Bäume müssen noch wachsen, bevor der Platz seinen definitiven Charakter seigen kann. Im Moment gilt es vor allem bei den Abschlägen auf das hohe Rough zu achten, und auch die zahlreichen Wasser können sich als beachtliche Hindernisse erweisen. Die Greens sind von mittlerer Grösse aber schön gezeichnet und je nach Fahnenposition kann der Schwierigkeitsgrad recht stark variert werden. In dieser wunderschönen Gegend wird der insgesamt unterhaltsam und intelligent angelegte Platz im Laufe der nächsten Jahre noch einiges an Qualität gewinnen.

The site is flat but provides an outstanding view over the Sempachersee, at about 1 kilometre from a famous battlefield. Battling is perhaps the right word when it comes to contending with these 18 holes, with careful study of your opponent's strengths required before going on the offensive. The course conceals some of its difficulties but you can get around them, or take risks and "take 'em by surprise". If you succeed, it won't be such a hostile proposition after all. The area is still nicely wide open and the trees will have to grow a bit before Sempachersee shows its true colours. For the time being, watch out for the tall rough, which threatens many a tee-shot, and several water hazards that are laid out in a rather classic, albeit effective style. Greens are average in size, well-designed and provide a good number of different pin positions to make the golfer's life a little more difficult. In a superb region, this amusing and intelligent course can only get better and better.

Golf Sempachersee — 1996

CH - 6024 HILDISRIEDEN

Office	Sekretariat	(41) 041 - 462 71 71
Pro shop	Pro shop	(41) 041 - 462 71 75
Fax	Fax	(41) 041 - 462 71 72
Web	www.golf-sempachersee.ch	
Situation	Lage	

Luzern (pop. 57 193), 20 km

Annual closure	Jährliche Schliessung	no
Weekly closure	Wöchentliche Schliessung	no

Fees main season / Preisliste hochsaison	18 holes	
	Week days / Woche	We/Bank holidays / We/Feiertag
Individual Individuell	CHF 80	*
Couple Ehepaar	CHF 160	*

* We: with members only (nur in Mitgliederbegleitung)

Caddy	Caddy	no
Electric Trolley	Elektrokarren	CHF 25 /18 holes
Buggy	Elektrischer Wagen	CHF 50 /18 holes
Clubs	Leihschläger	CHF 45 /full day

Credit cards Kreditkarten
VISA - Eurocard - AMEX

Rothbach, Schopfen, Beromünster, GOLF, Länkenhof, Basel, Eich, Hildisrieden, A2, Sempach, Sempacher See, Emmen Luzern, 0, 1, 2 km

Access Zufahrt : Luzern, N2 → Basel. → Sempach, Hildisrieden.
Map 2 on page 1270 Karte 2 Seite 1270

Golf course / PLATZ — 16/20

Site	Lage	
Maintenance	Instandhaltung	
Architect	Architekt	Kurt Rossknecht
Type	Typ	open country, forest
Relief	Begehbarkeit	
Water in play	Platz mit Wasser	
Exp. to wind	Wind ausgesetzt	
Trees in play	Platz mit Bäumen	

Scorecard / Scorekarte	Chp. / Chp.	Mens / Herren	Ladies / Damen
Length Länge	6180	5858	5153
Par	72	72	72
Slope system	127	122	125

Advised golfing ability / Empfohlene Spielstärke: 0 12 24 36
Hcp required / Min. Handicap: 30

Club house & amenities / KLUBHAUS UND NEBENGEBÄUDE — 8/10

Pro shop	Pro shop	
Driving range	Übungsplatz	
Sheltered	überdacht	10 mats
On grass	auf Rasen	yes
Putting-green	Putting-grün	yes
Pitching-green	Pitching-grün	yes

Hotel facilities / HOTEL BESCHREIBUNG — 7/10

HOTELS HOTELS

Vogelsang, 11 rooms, D CHF 195 — Eich
Tel (41) 041 - 462 66 66, Fax (41) 041 - 462 66 65 — 5 km

Château Gütsch, 31 rooms, D CHF 420 — Luzern
Tel (41) 041 - 249 41 00, Fax (41) 041 - 249 41 91 — 20 km

RESTAURANTS RESTAURANT

Herlisberg Wirtshaus — Herlisberg 10 km
Tel (41) 041 - 930 12 80

Vogelsang, Tel (41) 041 - 462 66 66 — Vogelsang 5 km

Marc Zimmermann, Tel (41) 041 - 249 41 41 — Luzern 20 km

Schlössli Utenberg, Tel (41) 041 - 420 00 22 — Luzern 16 km

WYLIHOF

13 | 6 | 6

Bedingt durch seine Länge und Wasserhindernisse auf sechs Holes ist dieser Platz vor allem von den hinteren Abschlägen schwierig zu meistern. Dies um so mehr, weil Steine und schlechtes Gras in den Roughs bei unserem Besuch dem Gesamtzustand noch abträglich waren. Die Anlage ist aber jung und muss noch bearbeitet werden. Die Umgebung am Ufer der Aare ist nicht von überragender Schönheit, bietet aber einige schöne Blicke auf den Jura. Architektonisch wurde gut gearbeitet, aber die geniale Gestaltung blieb aus. Der Ball kann meist rollenderweise auf die Greens gebracht werden, was Spieler beruhigt, die sich von den Wassergefahren beeindrucken lassen. Der Platz versteckt seine golferischen Tücken kaum und kann mit gesundem Selbstvertrauen angegangen werden. Auch schon beim erstem Mal.

Judging by length and the number of water hazards (on 6 holes), this is a tough course to play from the back-tees, especially since the state of upkeep was pretty rough when we visited, notably because of the stones and weeds in the rough. But this is still a young course and further work is still needed. On the banks of the Aar, the setting is hardly outstanding, despite a few pleasant views over the Jura mountains. The architecture has been given careful thought, but without any special flair for landscaping. Most of the time, players can chip the ball onto the green, which will reassure lesser players who are already under stress from the water hazards. At least the course does not have too many hidden traps, meaning that golfers can play here confidently, even the first time out.

Golf Club Wylihof — 1995

CH - 4708 LUTERBACH

Office	Sekretariat	(41) 032 - 682 28 28
Pro shop	Pro shop	(41) 032 - 682 28 28
Fax	Fax	(41) 032 - 682 65 17
Web	—	
Situation	Lage	

Solothurn (pop. 15 208), 8 km

Annual closure	Jährliche Schliessung	no
Weekly closure	Wöchentliche Schliessung	no

Fees main season Preisliste hochsaison		18 holes
	Week days Woche	**We/Bank holidays** We/Feiertag
Individual Individuell	CHF 90	CHF 90
Couple Ehepaar	CHF 180	CHF 180

* We: only with members (nur in Mitgliederbegleitung).

Caddy	Caddy	no
Electric Trolley	Elektrokarren	no
Buggy	Elektrischer Wagen	medical reasons
Clubs	Leihschläger	yes

Credit cards Kreditkarten
VISA - Eurocard - MasterCard

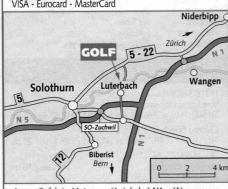

Access Zufahrt : Motorway (Autobahn) N1→ Wangen A/Aar, → Solothurn, → Koppingen, after bridge over Aar river (Aarbrücke), turn left → Golf

Map 1 on page 1269 Karte 1 Seite 1269

Golf course PLATZ — 13/20

Site	Lage	
Maintenance	Instandhaltung	
Architect	Architekt	Ruzzo Reuss
Type	Typ	open country
Relief	Begehbarkeit	
Water in play	Platz mit Wasser	
Exp. to wind	Wind ausgesetzt	
Trees in play	Platz mit Bäumen	

Scorecard Scorekarte	**Chp.** Chp.	**Mens** Herren	**Ladies** Damen
Length Länge	6584	6141	5286
Par	73	73	73
Slope system	137	129	130

Advised golfing ability Empfohlene Spielstärke — 0 12 24 36

Hcp required Min. Handicap 36

Club house & amenities KLUBHAUS UND NEBENGEBÄUDE — 6/10

Pro shop	Pro shop	
Driving range	Übungsplatz	
Sheltered	überdacht	16 mats
On grass	auf Rasen	yes
Putting-green	Putting-grün	yes
Pitching-green	Pitching-grün	yes

Hotel facilities HOTEL BESCREIBUNG — 6/10

HOTELS HOTELS

Krone, 42 rooms, D CHF 265 — Solothurn
Tel (41) 032 - 622 44 12, Fax (41) 032 - 622 37 24 — 10 km

Astoria, 40 rooms, D CHF 175 — Solothurn
Tel (41) 032 - 622 75 71, Fax (41) 032 - 623 68 57

Roter Turm, 35 rooms, D CHF 230 — Solothurn
Tel (41) 032 - 622 96 21, Fax (41) 032 - 622 98 65

RESTAURANTS RESTAURANT

Zum Alten Stephan — Solothurn
Tel (41) 032 - 622 11 09 — 10 km

Chutz, Tel (41) 032 - 622 34 71 — Langendorf 8 km

ZUMIKON 15 7 6

Die ersten neun Loch in Zumikon sind recht flach, aber sehr lang. Der Weg zurück ist mit einigen Schräglagen und Hängen wesentlich coupierter und kann Senioren Mühe bereiten. Dieser Nachteil wird aber durch kürzere Spielbahnen kompensiert. Die gut plazierten Hindernisse stören vor allem gute Golfer, beeinflussen aber das Spiel höherer Handicaps wenig. Zumikon ist ein guter Test des golferischen Könnens, lässt aber in seinem durchschnittlischen Design das gewisse Etwas an Originalität und den perfekten Unterhalt der Greens vermissen. Trotzdem langweilt sich hier niemand, und das ist für Golfer jedes Handicaps ein wichtiger Punkt.

The front nine at Zumikon are pretty flat but very long. The back nine are much hillier with a number of dangerous slopes in all directions, often a problem for senior players but one that is offset by the shorter length of holes. The hazards are generally well sited and tend to bother the better players more than the rest. Reassuring for the latter, at least. Zumikon is a very honourable test of golf, but we were sorry to see a little lack of originality and stamina in a very reasonable layout, and greens in a fair condition only, still putting this course a little way behind the best courses in Switzerland. However, there is never a dull moment here, and golfers of all levels will appreciate that.

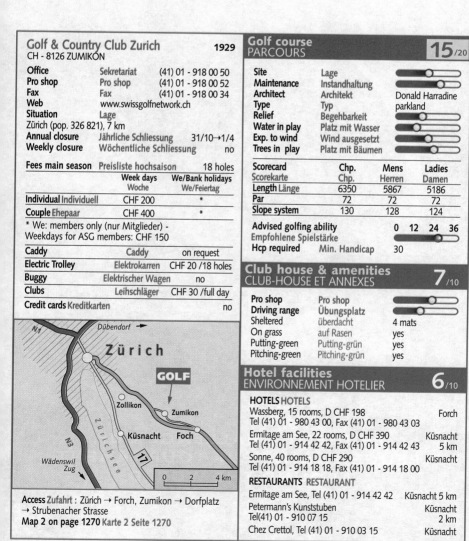

Golf & Country Club Zurich — 1929

CH - 8126 ZUMIKON

Office	Sekretariat	(41) 01 - 918 00 50
Pro shop	Pro shop	(41) 01 - 918 00 52
Fax	Fax	(41) 01 - 918 00 34
Web	www.swissgolfnetwork.ch	
Situation	Lage	Zürich (pop. 326 821), 7 km
Annual closure	Jährliche Schliessung	31/10→1/4
Weekly closure	Wöchentliche Schliessung	no

Fees main season Preisliste hochsaison	18 holes	
	Week days Woche	**We/Bank holidays** We/Feiertag
Individual Individuell	CHF 200	*
Couple Ehepaar	CHF 400	*

* We: members only (nur Mitglieder) - Weekdays for ASG members: CHF 150

Caddy	Caddy	on request
Electric Trolley	Elektrokarren	CHF 20 /18 holes
Buggy	Elektrischer Wagen	no
Clubs	Leihschläger	CHF 30 /full day
Credit cards	Kreditkarten	no

Access Zufahrt : Zürich → Forch, Zumikon → Dorfplatz → Strubenacher Strasse

Map 2 on page 1270 Karte 2 Seite 1270

Golf course — PARCOURS 15/20

Site	Lage	
Maintenance	Instandhaltung	
Architect	Architekt	Donald Harradine
Type	Typ	parkland
Relief	Begehbarkeit	
Water in play	Platz mit Wasser	
Exp. to wind	Wind ausgesetzt	
Trees in play	Platz mit Bäumen	

Scorecard Scorekarte	**Chp.** Chp.	**Mens** Herren	**Ladies** Damen
Length Länge	6350	5867	5186
Par	72	72	72
Slope system	130	128	124

Advised golfing ability Empfohlene Spielstärke — 0 12 24 36

Hcp required Min. Handicap — 30

Club house & amenities — CLUB-HOUSE ET ANNEXES 7/10

Pro shop	Pro shop	
Driving range	Übungsplatz	
Sheltered	überdacht	4 mats
On grass	auf Rasen	yes
Putting-green	Putting-grün	yes
Pitching-green	Pitching-grün	yes

Hotel facilities — ENVIRONNEMENT HOTELIER 6/10

HOTELS HOTELS

Wassberg, 15 rooms, D CHF 198 — Forch
Tel (41) 01 - 980 43 00, Fax (41) 01 - 980 43 03

Ermitage am See, 22 rooms, D CHF 390 — Küsnacht 5 km
Tel (41) 01 - 914 42 42, Fax (41) 01 - 914 42 43

Sonne, 40 rooms, D CHF 290 — Küsnacht
Tel (41) 01 - 914 18 18, Fax (41) 01 - 914 18 00

RESTAURANTS RESTAURANT

Ermitage am See, Tel (41) 01 - 914 42 42 — Küsnacht 5 km

Petermann's Kunststuben — Küsnacht 2 km
Tel(41) 01 - 910 07 15

Chez Crettol, Tel (41) 01 - 910 03 15 — Küsnacht

Other countries

Moscow

Other countries Czech Republic Slovenia Russia Turkey

Golf in Europe is broadening its frontiers eastwards and to the south. To the east, the Czech Republic has a golfing heritage rich enough to produce several excellent courses for more than 7,000 local players, and even Russia now has one superb 18-hole course. Slovenia has rejuvenated and even expanded the "old" course at Bled. Further south, golf is an important asset for tourism and courses are beginning to spring up, for the time being catering more to foreign golfers in search of sunnier climes than to local players. Turkey is one country which has systematically been building some good courses in the seaside areas of Antalya and Belek. In the years ahead, we can expect to see a big increase in the number of golf-playing countries and some first-rate courses, particularly in Greece.

En Europe, le golf élargit ses frontières et gagne vers l'Est et vers le sud. A l'est, la République Tchèque possède un passé golfique assez riche pour avoir plusieurs bons parcours et plus de 7.000 joueurs. Même la Russie possède aujourd'hui un superbe parcours de 18 trous. La Slovénie a rajeuni son « vieux » parcours de Bled et l'agrandit même. Plus au sud, le golf est un important atout pour le tourisme et les parcours commencent à sortir de terre, pour l'instant davantage destinés aux joueurs étrangers avides de soleil qu'aux joueurs locaux. La Turquie est l'un de ces pays à avoir systématiquement construit de bons parcours autour des importantes stations balnéaires de Belek et Antalya. Au cours des années à venir, on peut s'attendre à voir s'étendre encore le nombre de pays golfiques, et de parcours de qualité, en Grèce notamment.

PRAHA KARLSTEJN

15	6	7

There is no point in trying to describe the riches of Prague in a few lines, except to rate it amongst the "world's most beautiful cities" alongside Paris, Bruges, Florence or Venice... Simply treat yourself to a stop-off on the Plzen road (Plzen is a beer centre and a 1 hour drive) to play this course on the edge of the superb, tree-covered valley of Berounka, at the foot of Hrad Karlstejn, the castle built by emperor Charles IV and magnificently restored in the 19th century. This course has very quickly made a name for itself, appealing to golfers not only for the site but also for being a very intelligent layout. It is also very modern in its careful bunkering (huge fairway traps), the bringing into play of natural contours and the variety of holes. Water comes into play only a few holes, but the profile of the many dog-legs, one or two very elevated greens and the variety of shots you need to shape make this a rather tricky challenge that golfers will only start to master after several outings. The architects set out to achieve the eternal Trent Jones project of "easy bogey, tough birdie", and they succeeded. Even shooting par is no easy feat.

Il serait aussi vain de tenter de décrire les richesses de Prague, que d'autres. "plus belles villes du monde" comme Paris, Bruges, Florence ou Venise... Offrez-vous simplement une halte sur la route de Plzen, capitale de la bière (1 heure de route), pour jouer ce parcours au bord de la superbe vallée voisée de la Berounka, à l'ombre de Hrad Karlstejn, la château construit par l'empereur Charles IV et magnifiquement restauré au XIXè siècle. Ce golf s'est très vite bâti une réputation, il a séduit par son site, mais aussi son parcours très intelligent. Il est aussi très moderne par son bunkering soigné (vastes bunkers de fairway), la mise en jeu des reliefs, la variété des trous. L'eau n'est vraiment en jeu que sur quelques trous, mais le profil des nombreux doglegs, un ou deux- greens très en hauteur, la variété des coups à jouer en font un challenge assez délicat, que l'on ne maîtrise pas en une seule fois. Les architectes ont voulu réaliser l'éternel projet de Trent Jones "bogey facile, birdie difficile". Ils ont réussi : même le par n'est pas simple.

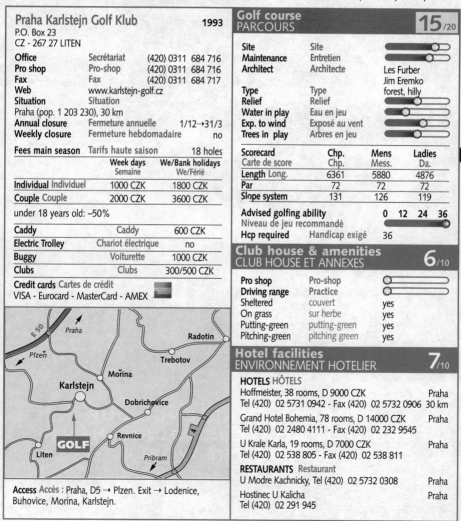

Praha Karlstejn Golf Klub 1993

P.O. Box 23
CZ - 267 27 LITEN

Office	Secrétariat	(420) 0311 684 716
Pro shop	Pro-shop	(420) 0311 684 716
Fax	Fax	(420) 0311 684 717
Web	www.karlstejn-golf.cz	
Situation	Situation	
Praha (pop. 1 203 230), 30 km		
Annual closure	Fermeture annuelle	1/12→31/3
Weekly closure	Fermeture hebdomadaire	no

Fees main season Tarifs haute saison		18 holes
	Week days Semaine	**We/Bank holidays** We/Férié
Individual Individuel	1000 CZK	1800 CZK
Couple Couple	2000 CZK	3600 CZK

under 18 years old: –50%

Caddy	Caddy	600 CZK
Electric Trolley	Chariot électrique	no
Buggy	Voiturette	1000 CZK
Clubs	Clubs	300/500 CZK

Credit cards Cartes de crédit
VISA - Eurocard - MasterCard - AMEX

Access Accès : Praha, D5 → Plzen. Exit → Lodenice, Buhovice, Morina, Karlstejn.

Golf course PARCOURS — 15/20

Site	Site	
Maintenance	Entretien	
Architect	Architecte	Les Furber, Jim Eremko
Type	Type	forest, hilly
Relief	Relief	
Water in play	Eau en jeu	
Exp. to wind	Exposé au vent	
Trees in play	Arbres en jeu	

Scorecard Carte de score	**Chp.** Chp.	**Mens** Mess.	**Ladies** Da.
Length Long.	6361	5880	4876
Par	72	72	72
Slope system	131	126	119

Advised golfing ability 0 12 24 36
Niveau de jeu recommandé

Hcp required Handicap exigé 36

Club house & amenities CLUB HOUSE ET ANNEXES — 6/10

Pro shop	Pro-shop	
Driving range	Practice	
Sheltered	couvert	yes
On grass	sur herbe	yes
Putting-green	putting-green	yes
Pitching-green	pitching green	yes

Hotel facilities ENVIRONNEMENT HOTELIER — 7/10

HOTELS HÔTELS

Hoffmeister, 38 rooms, D 9000 CZK — Praha
Tel (420) 02 5731 0942 - Fax (420) 02 5732 0906 — 30 km

Grand Hotel Bohemia, 78 rooms, D 14000 CZK — Praha
Tel (420) 02 2480 4111 - Fax (420) 02 232 9545

U Krale Karla, 19 rooms, D 7000 CZK — Praha
Tel (420) 02 538 805 - Fax (420) 02 538 811

RESTAURANTS Restaurant

U Modre Kachnicky, Tel (420) 02 5732 0308 — Praha

Hostinec U Kalicha — Praha
Tel (420) 02 291 945

BLED King's Course

15 | 7 | 8

If you are holidaying in the south of Austria or in north-eastern Italy, you are only a short drive away from the Bled golf course in Slovenia, in a mountainous region where the beauty of the landscape with a spectacular lake is second to none. The present 18-hole layout was designed in 1937 then restyled by Donald Harradine before being re-opened in 1972. But the real development is ongoing, with an additional 9-hole course now being upgraded to 18 holes. Although this is a mountainous region, the actual course is none too hilly and hazards are clearly visible on what is a classic layout. Many golfers will be reassured by the absence of water, but that doesn't mean you can hit it just anywhere, as thick trees line the fairways and from the back-tees yardage is more than respectable. Add to this a large and comfortable club-house sporting local architecture (with rooms) and very good hotels nearby, and you see why Bled is a pretty destination off the beaten track. The quality and appeal of the course are also a good reason for a visit here.

Wer im Süden von Österreich oder im Nordosten von Italien Urlaub macht, ist nur eine kurze Autofahrt von Bled in Slowenien entfernt. Der Platz liegt in einer der reizvollsten Alpenlandschaften Europas mit einem zauberhaften See. Der 18-Loch-Platz wurde 1937 erbaut und 1972 von Donald Harradine überarbeitet. Weitere neun Löcher, ebenfalls von Harradine, sind bereits fertiggestellt, und es bestehen Pläne für einen weiteren Ausbau der Anlage. Obwohl der Platz von herrlichen Bergen umgeben, ist der 18-Loch-Meisterschaftsplatz trotz einiger Höhenunterschiede, die den Reiz etlicher Löcher dieses klassischen Designs ausmachen, kein "Bergziegenplatz", sondern gut begehbar. Viele Golfer werden es schätzen, dass im Gegensatz zu den neuen neun Löcher auf dem alten Platz keine Wasserhindernisse lauern. Aber das bedeutet nicht, dass man hier nach Belieben streuen kann, da die Spielbahnen von dichtem Wald umgeben sind. Von den hinteren Meisterschaftsabschlägen weist der Platz eine ordentliche Länge auf. Das reizvolle Clubhaus mit etlichen Zimmern und einige vorzügliche Hotels machen Bled zu einem Geheimtip. Die Qualität und der Reiz des Platzes alleine sind allerdings auch allein eine Reise wert.

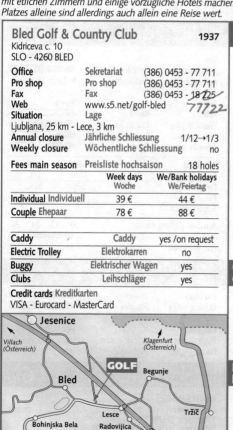

Bled Golf & Country Club — 1937

Kidriceva c. 10
SLO - 4260 BLED

Office	Sekretariat	(386) 0453 - 77 711
Pro shop	Pro shop	(386) 0453 - 77 711
Fax	Fax	(386) 0453 - 18 225
Web	www.s5.net/golf-bled	
Situation	Lage	

Ljubljana, 25 km - Lece, 3 km

Annual closure	Jährliche Schliessung	1/12→1/3
Weekly closure	Wöchentliche Schliessung	no

Fees main season Preisliste hochsaison		18 holes
	Week days Woche	**We/Bank holidays** We/Feiertag
Individual Individuell	39 €	44 €
Couple Ehepaar	78 €	88 €

Caddy	Caddy	yes /on request
Electric Trolley	Elektrokarren	no
Buggy	Elektrischer Wagen	yes
Clubs	Leihschläger	yes

Credit cards Kreditkarten
VISA - Eurocard - MasterCard

Access Zufahrt : Ljubljana → München/Salzburg
Map 2 on page 935 Karte 2 Seite 935

Golf course PARCOURS — 15/20

Site	Lage	
Maintenance	Instandhaltung	
Architect	Architekt	Donald Harradine (remodeled it)
Type	Typ	mountain, parkland
Relief	Begehbarkeit	
Water in play	Platz mit Wasser	
Exp. to wind	Wind ausgesetzt	
Trees in play	Platz mit Bäumen	

Scorecard Scorekarte	**Chp.** Chp.	**Mens** Herren	**Ladies** Damen
Length Länge	6339	5982	5403
Par	73	73	73
Slope system	—	—	—

Advised golfing ability Empfohlene Spielstärke — 0 12 24 36
Hcp required Min. Handicap — 36

Club house & amenities CLUB HOUSE ET ANNEXES — 7/10

Pro shop	Pro shop	
Driving range	Übungsplatz	
Sheltered	überdacht	12 mats
On grass	auf Rasen	yes
Putting-green	Putting-grün	yes (2)
Pitching-green	Pitching-grün	yes (3)

Hotel facilities ENVIRONNEMENT HOTELIER — 8/10

HOTELS HOTELS

Club House Hotel Bled, 13 rooms, D from DM 45 € — on site
Tel (386) 0453 - 78 300, Fax (386) 0453 - 78 327

Villa Bled, 30 rooms, D 160-360 € — Bled 5 km
Tel (386) 0457 - 91 500, Fax (386) 0457 - 41 320

Grand Hotel Toplice, 120 rooms, D 90-140 € — Bled 3 km
Tel (386) 0457 - 91 000, Fax (386) 0457 - 41 841

RESTAURANTS RESTAURANT

King's Club House, Tel (386) 0453 - 78 300 — on site
Villa Bled, Tel (386) 0457 - 91 500 — Bled 5 km
Gostilna Kunstelj, Tel (386) 0445 - 304 — Radovljica 5 km

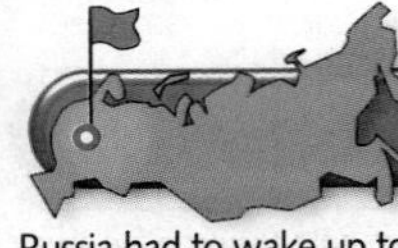

MOSCOW

17	7	6

Russia had to wake up to golf one day or another, and although for the time being the majority of golfers are Western businessmen or diplomats, it is surely only a matter of time before we see a Russian champion. At least they have a great course to play on. Built over a 120 hectare estate, this layout also boasts a hotel and modern houses that reminded us of the little dachas in Doctor Zhivago. This is a Trent Jones Jnr. course through and through, looking like a little corner of America. But failing a "Russian" style of golf architecture, the landscape of birch-trees and lakes adds considerable local colour. Actually, through its strategic intelligence, the loving care that went into every detail of the design, the layout and balance of course difficulties and for sheer golfing excellence, this course is a must. With a number of different tee-boxes, it is also playable by everyone. The standard of accommodation makes this a top-notch week-end golf-course, albeit not necessarily within the means of your average "Moujik" on the street.

La Russie devait bien s'éveiller un jour au golf... et même si pour l'instant les diplomates et businessmen occidentaux forment le gros des pratiquants ici, il y aura sans doute un jour de grands joueurs russes. Au moins ont-ils ici un grand parcours ! Construit à l'intérieur d'un domaine de 120 hectares, il s'accompagne d'un hôtel et de maisons modernes réminiscentes des "datchas" du Docteur Jivago. Ce parcours de Trent Jones Jr est en droite ligne de toutes ses créations, comme un petit coin d'Amérique. Néanmoins, à défaut d'une style "russe" d'architecture de golf, le paysage de bouleaux et de lacs est là pour donner la couleur locale. Par son intellignece stratégique, le soin apporté au dessin des moindres détails, la disposition et l'équilibre des difficultés, ce parcours est un "must", à la portée de tous (ou presque) par l'étagement des départs. La qualité du "réceptif" en fait un lieu de week-end de grande qualité... mais pas à la portée du "moujik" moyen.

Le Meridien Moscow Country Club — 1993

Nakhabino, Krasnogorsky District
MOSCOW REGION 143 430 RUSSIA

Office	Secrétariat	(7) 095 - 926 5911
Pro shop	Pro-shop	(7) 095 - 926 5910
Fax	Fax	(7) 095 - 926 5921
Web	www.mcc.co.ru	
Situation	Situation	Moscow, 15 km
Annual closure	Fermeture annuelle	no
Weekly closure	Fermeture hebdomadaire	monday

1302

Fees main season Tarifs haute saison	18 holes	
	Week days Semaine	**We/Bank holidays** We/Férié
Individual Individuel	US$ 75	US$ 100
Couple Couple	US$ 150	US$ 200

Caddy	Caddy	on request/US$ 17
Electric Trolley	Chariot électrique	no
Buggy	Voiturette	no
Clubs	Clubs	US$ 25

Credit cards Cartes de crédit
VISA - MasterCard - JCB - AMEX

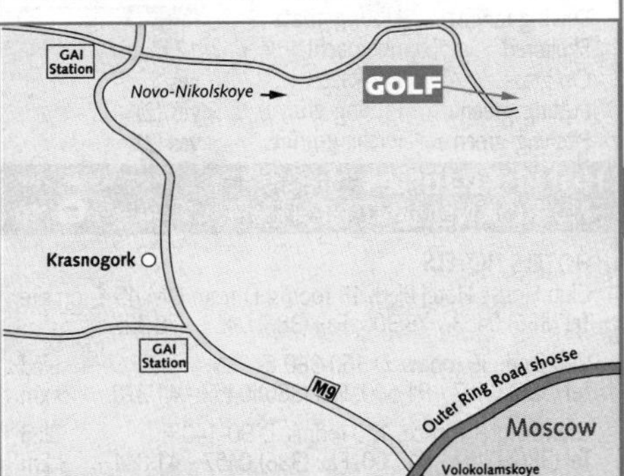

Access Accès : Moscow, Volokolamskoye Shosde. Gai Station, turn right → Krasnogorsk and Novo-Nikolskoye. Gai Station, right turn at sign "Moscow Country Club, 2.6 km"

Golf course PARCOURS — 17/20

Site	Site	
Maintenance	Entretien	
Architect	Architecte	R. Trent Jones Jr
Type	Type	forest
Relief	Relief	
Water in play	Eau en jeu	
Exp. to wind	Exposé au vent	
Trees in play	Arbres en jeu	

Scorecard Carte de score	**Chp.** Chp.	**Mens** Mess.	**Ladies** Da.
Length Long.	6390	5953	5248
Par	72	72	72
Slope system	0	0	0

Advised golfing ability 0 12 24 36
Niveau de jeu recommandé
Hcp required Handicap exigé 36

Club house & amenities CLUB HOUSE ET ANNEXES — 7/10

Pro shop	Pro-shop	
Driving range	Practice	
Sheltered	couvert	10 mats
On grass	sur herbe	yes
Putting-green	putting-green	yes
Pitching-green	pitching green	yes

Hotel facilities ENVIRONNEMENT HOTELIER — 6/10

HOTELS HÔTELS
Le Meridien — on site
130 rooms, D US$ 325
Tel (7) 095 - 926 5911, Fax (7) 095 - 926 5921

RESTAURANTS RESTAURANTS
Le Meridien — on site

GLORIA GOLF RESORT | 15 | 7 | 7

As everywhere else in this region where the climate is so pleasant, the Gloria course is rather flat and the very many trees (there are a lot of pines) bring some welcome shade when you hit your ball slightly off-target. There is little tall rough to speak of, so getting back on the "short stuff" is no real problem. Only slightly trickier are the one or two huge fairway bunkers, which are more in play for the mid-handicapper than they are for the better player. You might even find them a little too large, serving no purpose other than visual appeal or to clearly outline each hole. The green-side bunkers are no big hazard either, a reassuring thought when approaching the greens with bump and run shots... hit deliberately or otherwise. We couldn't help thinking that the design of Michel Gayon might have made more of this site, but the course is very pleasant to play during the holidays for players of all abilities. Here, visitors will find excellent practice facilities, a few practice holes, a beach hotel and beach to ensure a holiday without too much shade (see above!).

Comme dans toute cette région au climat très agréable, le parcours de Gloria est assez plat, et de nombreux arbres (beaucoup de pins) apportent des ombrages bienvenus... quand on égare un peu ses coups. Mais comme il y a peu de haut rough, on s'en dégage facilement. Sans doute plus que de quelques immenses bunkers, qui posent plus de problèmes aux joueurs moyens qu'aux joueurs expérimentés. On peut d'ailleurs les trouver un peu trop grands, sans nécessité autre qu'esthétique, ou pour bien délimiter les trous. Les bunkers de green ne sont pas très dangereux non plus, ce qui rassure quand on approche les greens en faisant rouler la balle... que ce soit volontaire ou non. On peut penser que l'architecte Michel Gayon aurait pu tirer encore meilleur parti d'un tel site à l'intention des meilleurs, mais ce parcours a voulu être très plaisant à jouer en vacances, pour tous les niveaux, qui trouveront ici de très bonnes installations d'entraînement, quelques trous d'apprentissage, l'hôtel sur place et la plage garantissant un séjour sans ombres.

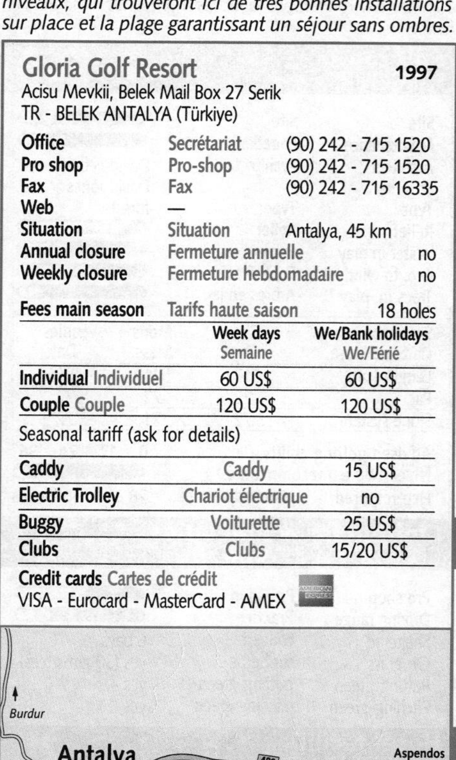

Gloria Golf Resort — 1997

Acisu Mevkii, Belek Mail Box 27 Serik
TR - BELEK ANTALYA (Türkiye)

Office	Secrétariat	(90) 242 - 715 1520
Pro shop	Pro-shop	(90) 242 - 715 1520
Fax	Fax	(90) 242 - 715 16335
Web	—	
Situation	Situation	Antalya, 45 km
Annual closure	Fermeture annuelle	no
Weekly closure	Fermeture hebdomadaire	no

Fees main season Tarifs haute saison — 18 holes

	Week days Semaine	We/Bank holidays We/Férié
Individual Individuel	60 US$	60 US$
Couple Couple	120 US$	120 US$

Seasonal tariff (ask for details)

Caddy	Caddy	15 US$
Electric Trolley	Chariot électrique	no
Buggy	Voiturette	25 US$
Clubs	Clubs	15/20 US$

Credit cards Cartes de crédit
VISA - Eurocard - MasterCard - AMEX

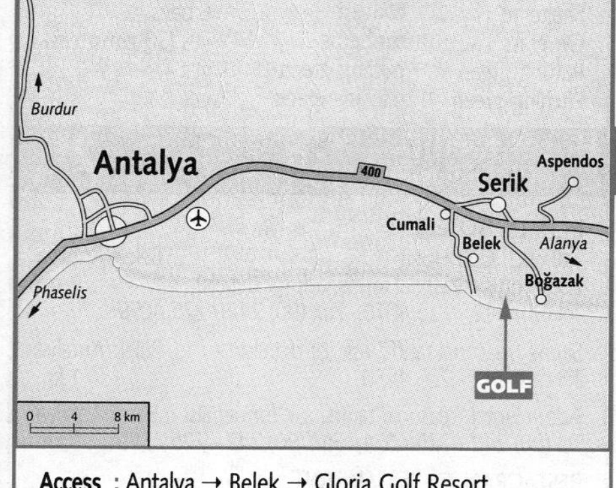

Access : Antalya → Belek → Gloria Golf Resort

Golf course — PARCOURS — 15/20

Site	Site	
Maintenance	Entretien	
Architect	Architecte	Michel Gayon
Type	Type	forest, parkland
Relief	Relief	
Water in play	Eau en jeu	
Exp. to wind	Exposé au vent	
Trees in play	Arbres en jeu	

Scorecard Carte de score	Chp. Chp.	Mens Mess.	Ladies Da.
Length Long.	6288	5900	5200
Par	72	72	72
Slope system	72	72	72

Advised golfing ability Niveau de jeu recommandé — 0 12 24 36
Hcp required Handicap exigé — 28 Men/36 Ladies

Club house & amenities — CLUB HOUSE ET ANNEXES — 7/10

Pro shop	Pro-shop	
Driving range	Practice	
Sheltered	couvert	24 mats
On grass	sur herbe	no
Putting-green	putting-green	yes
Pitching-green	pitching green	yes

Hotel facilities — ENVIRONNEMENT HOTELIER — 7/10

HOTELS HÔTELS
Gloria Golf Resort Hotel — Gloria Golf Resort on site
420 rooms, D from 92 US$
Tel (90) 242 - 715 1520,
Fax (90) 242 - 715 1525

RESTAURANTS RESTAURANT
4 restaurants — Gloria Golf Resort on site
Tel (90) 242 - 715 1520

NATIONAL GC

15 | 7 | 7

This is a highly promising course. The entranceway, gardens and club-house make this a very pleasant and relaxing site, before or after your round. The course was laid out by David Jones and David Feherty, one of the more colourful and interesting characters in today's world of professional golf. We might also have expected a little more "fantasy" from Feherty, but while the style is a clever blend of American and British features, the constraints involved in building a course that is playable for everyone might have dampened his enthusiasm in this respect. Although the course is perfectly playable and even fun for the less experienced or reasonable golfer (who should play from the yellow and red tees), it is still a tricky proposition for the low handicapper, as the fairways get very narrow when winding between trees. Hazards are well located but always in view, which is probably a good thing because strategy is important here and skills in bending the ball something of a necessity to avoid a few isolated and carefully positioned trees. In a superb setting (to a backdrop of snow-capped mountains), this is a course whose development is very good.

C'est un parcours très prometteur. L'entrée, les jardins et le Clubhouse en font un endroit très agréable et relaxant, avant ou après le parcours. Celui-ci a été dessiné par David Jones et David Feherty, l'un des personnages les plus colorés et les plus intéressants du golf professionnel d'aujourd'hui. On aurait d'ailleurs pu attendre un peu plus de "folie" de sa part, et si le style est un habile mélange de britannique et d'américain, les contraintes d'avoir à faire un parcours jouable pour tous ont peut être restreint ses élans. Si ce parcours est tout à fait jouable et même amusant pour les joueurs peu expérimentés ou raisonnables (ils partiront des départs jaune et rouge), il reste délicat pour les meilleurs joueurs, car il est souvent étroit quand il s'insinue (souvent) entre les arbres. Les obstacles sont bien placés, mais toujours visibles. Heureusement, car la stratégie est ici importante, et le travail de la balle n'est pas superflu, avec quelques arbres isolés très judicieusement placés. Dans un superbe environnement (avec les montagnes enneigées en arrière plan), c'est une réalisation dont l'évolution est excellente.

1304

National Golf Club — 1994

Belek Turizm Merkezi
TR - 07500 SERIK ANTALYA (Türkiye)

Office	Secrétariat	(90) 242 - 725 5401
Pro shop	Pro-shop	(90) 242 - 725 5401
Fax	Fax	(90) 242 - 725 5399
Web		—
Situation	Situation	Antalya, 35 km
Annual closure	Fermeture annuelle	no
Weekly closure	Fermeture hebdomadaire	no

Fees main season Tarifs haute saison	Week days Semaine	We/Bank holidays We/Férié
		18 holes
Individual Individuel	65 US$	65 US$
Couple Couple	130 US$	130 US$

US$ or Euros. Seasonal tariffs (ask for details).

Caddy	Caddy	on request
Electric Trolley	Chariot électrique	no
Buggy	Voiturette	25 US$
Clubs	Clubs	15/20 US$

Credit cards Cartes de crédit
VISA - Eurocard - MasterCard - AMEX

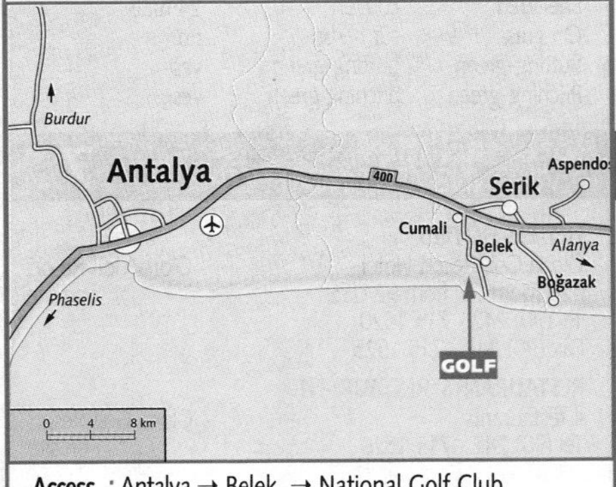

Access : Antalya → Belek. → National Golf Club

Golf course / PARCOURS — 15/20

Site	Site	
Maintenance	Entretien	
Architect	Architecte	David Feherty David Jones
Type	Type	forest
Relief	Relief	
Water in play	Eau en jeu	
Exp. to wind	Exposé au vent	
Trees in play	Arbres en jeu	

Scorecard Carte de score	Chp. Chp.	Mens Mess.	Ladies Da.
Length Long.	6172	5410	4886
Par	72	72	72
Slope system	72	71	72

Advised golfing ability — Niveau de jeu recommandé: 0 12 24 36

Hcp required — Handicap exigé: 28 Men/36 Ladies

Club house & amenities / CLUB HOUSE ET ANNEXES — 7/10

Pro shop	Pro-shop	
Driving range	Practice	
Sheltered	couvert	6 bays
On grass	sur herbe	yes (30 grass tees)
Putting-green	putting-green	yes
Pitching-green	pitching green	yes

Hotel facilities / ENVIRONNEMENT HOTELIER — 7/10

HOTELS HÔTELS

Tatbeach Golf Hotel — Belek/Antalya
260 rooms (seasonal tariffs, ask for details) — 2 km
Tel (90) 242 - 725 4076, Fax (90) 242 - 725 4099

Sirene (seasonal tariffs, ask for details) — Belek/Antalya
Tel (90) 242 - 725 4130 — 1 km

Adora Hotel (seasonal tariffs, ask for details) — Belek Antalya
Tel (90) 242 - 725 4051, Fax (90) 242 - 725 4359 — 1 km

RESTAURANTS RESTAURANT

In the Hotels — Belek Antalya

NOBILIS

17 | 8 | 6

There is every reason to consider this excellent course as the best of the better layouts in the region. When approaching the club-house, you will notice the very pleasant landscape, with holes laid out amidst a pine forest along the river Acisu. Off the tee, the course is relatively easy; the problems for birdie-hunting golfers begin with the second shot and concern the mid-handicapper a little less than the better players. The greens especially are very well defended, particularly by often deep but visible bunkers, which are well shaped in the tradition of architect Dave Thomas. The secret is simple: place your drive for an easier approach, and work on bending the ball, it will come in useful. You still have all the time and leisure to focus on your game though, as there is little hilly relief to speak of, there are no blind shots and only the greens are elevated. Water is not too much of a danger here and is rarely frontal (except on hole N° 10). If we also throw in the excellent driving range, it is clear that Nobilis has everything to become a great holiday destination, with villas of all shapes and sizes alongside holes N° 8 and 9.

On peut penser que la qualité de ce parcours le place en tête des bons golfs de la région. Dès l'arrivée au Club house, le paysage est très plaisant, les trous ayant été tracés au milieu d'une pinède le long de la rivière Acisu. C'est un parcours relativement facile à driver, les difficultés commencent ensuite pour les chasseurs de birdies, elles concernent moins les handicaps moyens. Les greens sont en particulier très bien gardés, notamment par des bunkers souvent profonds mais bien visibles, et bien modelés, dans la tradition de l'architecte Dave Thomas. Ainsi, il convient de bien placer les coups de départ pour faciliter l'angle d'approche, et savoir travailler la balle n'est pas un luxe. Mais on a tout le loisir de se concentrer sur le jeu, car les reliefs sont limités, il n'y a pas de coups aveugles, seuls les greens étant surélevés. L'eau n'est pas ici trop dangereuse et rarement frontale (sauf au 10). Si l'on ajoute un excellent practice, Nobilis a tout pour devenir une grande destination de vacances, avec les villas de toutes tailles à louer le long du 8 et du 9.

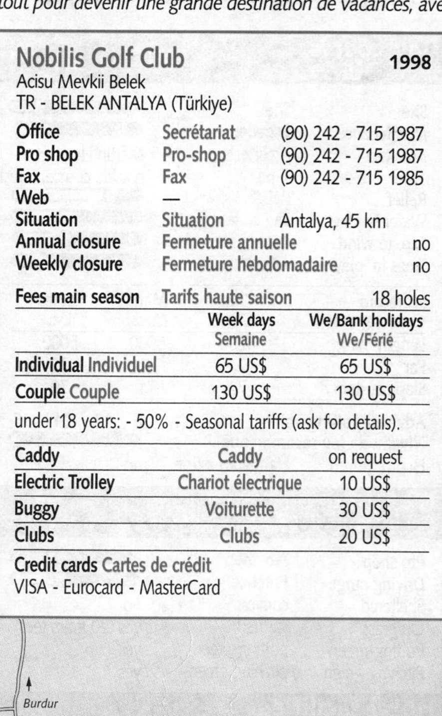

Nobilis Golf Club — 1998

Acisu Mevkii Belek
TR - BELEK ANTALYA (Türkiye)

Office	Secrétariat	(90) 242 - 715 1987
Pro shop	Pro-shop	(90) 242 - 715 1987
Fax	Fax	(90) 242 - 715 1985
Web	—	
Situation	Situation	Antalya, 45 km
Annual closure	Fermeture annuelle	no
Weekly closure	Fermeture hebdomadaire	no

Fees main season Tarifs haute saison		18 holes
	Week days Semaine	**We/Bank holidays** We/Férié
Individual Individuel	65 US$	65 US$
Couple Couple	130 US$	130 US$

under 18 years: - 50% - Seasonal tariffs (ask for details).

Caddy	Caddy	on request
Electric Trolley	Chariot électrique	10 US$
Buggy	Voiturette	30 US$
Clubs	Clubs	20 US$

Credit cards Cartes de crédit
VISA - Eurocard - MasterCard

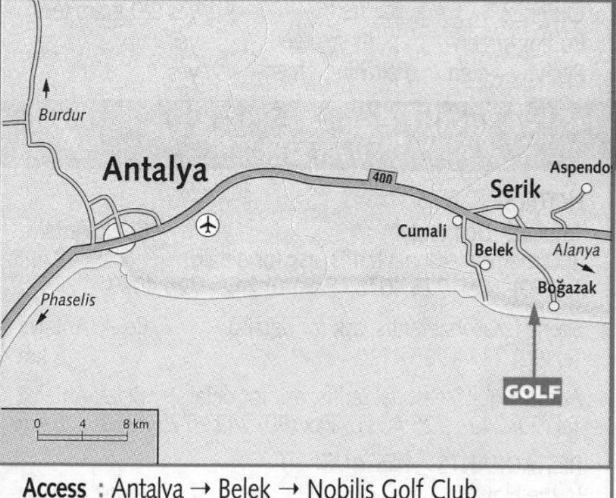

Access : Antalya → Belek → Nobilis Golf Club

Golf course PARCOURS — 17/20

Site	Site	
Maintenance	Entretien	
Architect	Architecte	Dave Thomas
Type	Type	forest, parkland
Relief	Relief	
Water in play	Eau en jeu	
Exp. to wind	Exposé au vent	
Trees in play	Arbres en jeu	

Scorecard Carte de score	**Chp.** Chp.	**Mens** Mess.	**Ladies** Da.
Length Long.	6312	5877	5103
Par	72	72	72
Slope system	72	72	72

Advised golfing ability Niveau de jeu recommandé — 0 12 24 36

Hcp required Handicap exigé — 28 Men/36 Ladies

Club house & amenities CLUB HOUSE ET ANNEXES — 8/10

Pro shop	Pro-shop	
Driving range	Practice	
Sheltered	couvert	no
On grass	sur herbe	yes
Putting-green	putting-green	yes
Pitching-green	pitching green	yes

Hotel facilities ENVIRONNEMENT HOTELIER — 6/10

HOTELS HÔTELS

Nobilis Villas — Nobilis Golf Club, on site
600 - 1500 US$ (week)
Tel (90) 242 - 715 1987, Fax (90) 242 - 715 1985

Gloria Golf Resort Hotel — Gloria Golf Resort, 5 km
420 rooms , D from 92 US$
Tel (90) 242 - 715 1520, Fax (90) 242 - 715 1525

RESTAURANTS RESTAURANT

Club house — Nobilis Golf Club, on site
Tel (90) 242 - 715 1987

4 restaurants — Gloria Golf Resort, 5 km
Tel (90) 242 - 715 1520

TAT GOLF BELEK

14	7	7

This 1996 course was designed by Martin Hawtree and is one of his best. It consists of three looping 9-hole layouts that are combinable any way and similar in length. The toughest have to be the Yellow and Red courses, where the water hazards lurk quite impressively. The style of course shifts to good effect between a links and parkland layout, but style is perhaps not the right word for the monumental club-house, which spoils the view over mountains and sea. The most significant hazard is the river Besgösz (and affluents thereof) which is in play on about half the holes. It should be said, though, that water looks more dangerous than it actually is, and the drive landing area are wide open targets. The relatively flat layout is landscaped with a lot of trees and some sometimes thick rough. Bunkers are few and far between but generally well located. Such a measured approach to bringing difficulties into play gives every hope of being able to play to one's handicap without too much trouble. Visibly, if the architect had been asked to produce a course that forgives those little mistakes made by golfers on holidays, then here we would have to say "mission accomplished".

Ouvert en 1996, ce parcours a été dessiné par Martin Hawtree, dont c'est l'une des meilleures réalisations. Il se compose de trois boucles de 27 trous combinables et de longueurs équivalentes, dont les plus difficiles sont le Yellow et le Red, où les obstacles d'eau peuvent impressionner. De fait, l'esthétique oscille entre le links et le parc, de manière assez heureuse. Plus que le monumental Club house, qui gâche la vue sur les montagnes et la mer. Le plus important obstacle est la rivière Besgösz (et ses affluents) qui viennent en jeu sur la moitié des trous. Cela dit, l'eau est plus présente au regard que vraiment dangereuse, et les zones d'arrivée de drive offrent de larges cibles. De nombreux arbres, un rough parfois épais viennent paysager cet ensemble relativement plat. Les bunkers ne sont pas très nombreux, mais généralement bien placés. Cette mesure dans la mise en jeu des difficultés permet d'espérer jouer son handicap sans trop de problèmes. Visiblement, si l'on a demandé à l'architecte de faire un parcours pardonnant les petites erreurs des golfeurs en vacances, la mission est accomplie.

TAT International Golf Belek — 1996

Tat Beach Golf Hotel - Üçkum Tepesi Mevkii P.K. 71
TR - BELEK ANTALYA (Türkiye)

Office	Secrétariat	(90) 242 - 725 5303
Pro shop	Pro-shop	(90) 242 - 725 5303
Fax	Fax	(90) 242 - 725 5299
Web	—	
Situation	Situation	Antalya, 38 km
Annual closure	Fermeture annuelle	no
Weekly closure	Fermeture hebdomadaire	no

1306

Fees main season Tarifs haute saison	18 holes	
	Week days Semaine	**We/Bank holidays** We/Férié
Individual Individuel	65 US$	65 US$
Couple Couple	130 US$	130 US$

Seasonal tariffs (ask for details)

Caddy	Caddy	no
Electric Trolley	Chariot électrique	no
Buggy	Voiturette	30 US$
Clubs	Clubs	15/20 US$

Credit cards Cartes de crédit
VISA - Eurocard - MasterCard - AMEX

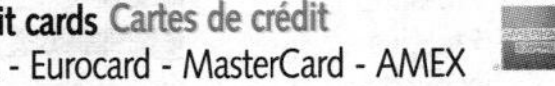

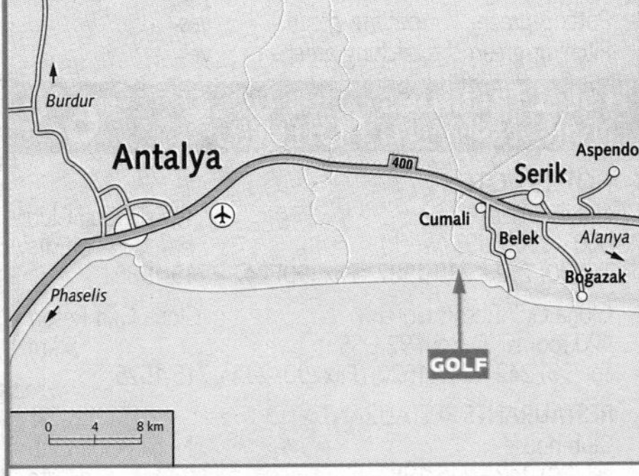

Access : Antalya → Belek → Tatbeach Golf Hotel

Golf course — PARCOURS — 14/20

Site	Site	
Maintenance	Entretien	
Architect	Architecte	Martin Hawtree
Type	Type	seaside course, forest
Relief	Relief	
Water in play	Eau en jeu	
Exp. to wind	Exposé au vent	
Trees in play	Arbres en jeu	

Scorecard Carte de score	**Chp.** Chp.	**Mens** Mess.	**Ladies** Da.
Length Long.	6200	5900	5000
Par	72	72	72
Slope system	72	71	70

Advised golfing ability — Niveau de jeu recommandé: 0 12 24 36
Hcp required — Handicap exigé: no

Club house & amenities — CLUB HOUSE ET ANNEXES — 7/10

Pro shop	Pro-shop	
Driving range	Practice	
Sheltered	couvert	no
On grass	sur herbe	yes (20 grass tees)
Putting-green	putting-green	yes
Pitching-green	pitching green	yes

Hotel facilities — ENVIRONNEMENT HOTELIER — 7/10

HOTELS HÔTELS

Tatbeach Golf Hotel — Belek/Antalya
260 rooms (seasonal tariffs, ask for details) — 8 km
Tel (90) 242 - 725 4076, Fax(90) 242 - 725 4099

Sirene (seasonal tariffs, ask for details) — Belek/Antalya
Tel (90) 242 - 725 4130 — 8 km

Adora Hotel (seasonal tariffs, ask for details) — Belek Antalya
Tel (90) 242 - 725 4051, Fax (90) 242 - 725 4359 — 6 km

RESTAURANTS RESTAURANT

In the Hotels — Belek Antalya

ALPHABETIC ORDER AND CLOSEST AIRPORTS
CLASSEMENT ALPHABÉTIQUE ET AÉROPORTS
ALPHABETISCHE EINTEILUNG UND FLUGHAFEN
I ALFABETISK ORDNING OCH NÄRMASTE FLYGPLATSER
CLASIFICACION ALFABETICA Y AEROPUERTOS
ORDINE ALFABETICO E AEROPORTI PIÙ VICINI

GOLF COURSE PARCOURS GOLFPLATZ GOLFBANER RECORRIDOS PERCORSO		CLASSIFICATIONS CLASSEMENT EINTEILUNGEN RANKINGEN LAS CLASIFICACIONES CLASSIFICA	✈	PAGE PAGE SEITE SIDE PÁGINA PAGINA
A				
A 6	S	14 7 6	Jönköpping, 8 km	1211
Abenberg	D	14 7 6	Nürnberg, 30 km	376
Aberdovey	W	17 7 7	Cardiff, 140 km	792
Ableiges	F	15 6 4	Charles-de-Gaulle, 48 km	207
Aboyne	Sc	14 6 6	Aberdeen, 45 km	690
Adare	IRL	15 6 7	Shannon, 20 km	828
Ailette (L')	F	15 6 5	Charles-de-Gaulle, 109 km	208
Aisses (Les)	F	16 5 4	Orly, 145 km	209
Aix-les-Bains	F	13 5 7	Chambéry, 13 km	210
Albarella	I	14 8 8	Venezia, 50 km	943
Albi	F	15 6 6	Albi, 4 km - Toulouse, 65 km	211
Alcaidesa	E	14 6 7	Gibraltar, 10 km	1108
Aldeburgh	Eng	13 6 7	Stansted, 140 km	512
Alhaurin	E	14 7 5	Malaga, 30 km	1109
Alicante	E	15 8 8	Alicante, 15 km	1110
Alloa	Sc	15 7 6	Edinburgh, 50 km	691
Almenara	E	13 8 8	Málaga, 100 km	1111
Almerimar	E	14 7 7	Almería, 48 km	1112
Aloha	E	17 7 8	Malaga, 60 km	1113
Alwoodley (The)	Eng	18 7 7	Leeds, 7 km	513
Alyth	Sc	14 6 6	Edinburgh, 96 km	692
Am Mondsee	A	16 7 7	Salzburg, 25 km	80
Amarilla	E	15 7 7	Tenerife, 4 km	1114
Ambrosiano	I	13 7 7	Milano, 75 km	944
Amirauté (L')	F	14 7 8		212
Amnéville	F	13 6 5	Metz-Nancy, 35 km	213
Amsterdam	N	15 7 7	Amsterdam Schiphol, 10 km	999
Anderstein	N	14 7 6	Amsterdam-Schiphol, 60 km	1000
Ängelholm	S	15 6 6	Malmö, 120 km	1212
Ängsö	S	16 7 6	Arlanda, 70 km	1213
Annonay-Gourdan	F	13 6 5	Lyon-Saint Exupéry, 90 km	214
Antognolla	I	15 8 7	Perugia, 30 km	945
Antwerp	B	16 7 7	Antwerpen, 15 km	97
Apremont	F	15 8 6	Charles de Gaulle, 34 km	215
Arcachon	F	13 6 6	Bordeaux, 66 km	216
Arcangues	F	14 7 8	Biarritz-Parme, 3 km	217
Ardglass	NIR	14 6 4	Belfast, 65 km	912
Arendal	Nw	15 7 5	Kristiansand, 80 km	1037
Aroeira	P	14 6 6	Lisboa, 11 km	1059
Aroeira	P	14 6 6	Lisboa, 11 km	1060
Arras	F	14 6 6	Charles-de-Gaulle, 150 km	218
Arzaga	I	15 9 8	Verona, 45 km	946
Ascona (Patriziale)	CH	15 7 7	Lugano, 40 km	999
Ashburnham	W	17 6 5	Cardiff, 90 km	793
Ashridge	Eng	16 7 6	Heathrow, 48 km	514
Asolo	I	13 7 7	Venezia, 66 km	947
Asserbo	Da	15 7 6	København, 70 km	126
Athlone	IRL	13 6 6	Dublin, 125 km	829
Åtvidaberg	S	16 6 5	Linköping, 35 km	1214
Augerville	F	13 6 4	Orly, 70 km	219
Augsburg	D	15 7 7	München, 90 km	377
Aura	Fi	13 5 5	Helsinki, 180 km	147
Ayr (Belleisle)	Sc	16 5 7	Glasgow, 55 km	693
B				
Baberton	Sc	14 6 8	Edinburgh, 8 km	694
Bad Abbach-Deutenhof	D	15 7 7	München, 90 km	378
Bad Bevensen	D	15 5 7	Hamburg, 100 km	379
Bad Griesbach	D	17 9 9	München, 180 km	380
Bad Liebenzell	D	14 7 7	Stuttgart, 40 km	382
Bad Ragaz	CH	13 7 6	Zürich-Kloten, 100 km	1273
Bad Wörishofen	D	14 6 6	München, 120 km	383
Baden	F	15 6 5	Lorient, 45 km	220
Badgemore Park	Eng	14 7 7	Heathrow, 48 km	515
Bâle-Hagenthal	F	15 7 7	Bâle-Mulhouse, 8 km	221
Ballater	Sc	15 6 7	Dyce, 35 km	695
Ballybunion	IRL	19 7 6	Shannon, 88 km	830/831
Ballykisteen	IRL	14 7 6	Shannon, 50 km Cork, 90 km	832
Ballyliffin	IRL	17 6 5	Belfast, 160 km	833/834
Bamberg	D	15 7 7	Nürnberg, 40 km	384
Banchory	Sc	14 7 7	Aberdeen, 32 km	696
Bangor	NIR	14 6 6	Belfast, 40 km	913
Barbaroux	F	17 7 6	Toulon-Hyères, 51 km	222
Barlassina	I	14 8 7	Milano, 35 km	948
Barsebäck	S	18 7 6	Malmö, 50 km	1215
Båstad	S	16 7 7	Halmstad, 30 km	1216
Bath	Eng	16 6 9	Bristol, 20 km	516
Batouwe	N	15 7 3	Amsterdam Schiphol, 80 km	1001
Baule (La)	F	15 7 8	Nantes, 60 km	223
Bearna	IRL	14 7 7	Galway, 20 km	835
Beau Desert	Eng	16 7 7	Birmingham, 30 km	517
Beaufort	IRL	13 6 7	Cork, 85 km	836

Belas	P	14 8 5	Lisboa, 15 km	1061
Belek (TAT Golf)	T	14 7 7	Antalya, 35 km	1306
Bélesbat	F	14 7 7	Orly, 40 km	224
Belle-Dune	F	16 6 5	Le Touquet, 25 km	225
Belmullet	IRL	15 5 3	Sligo, 115 km	837
Belvoir Park	NIR	15 5 6	Belfast, 12 km	914
Bercuit	B	13 7 7	Bruxelles (Brussel), 30 km	98
Bergamo - L'Albenza	I	16 7 7	Bergamo, 18 km	949
Bergisch Land	D	16 7 7	Düsseldorf, 20 km	385
Berkhamsted	Eng	16 7 6	Heathrow, 48 km	518
Berkshire (The)	Eng	17 8 7	Heathrow, 25 km	519/520
Berlin-Wannsee	D	16 8 9	Berlin, 40 km	386
Berwick-upon-Tweed	Eng	15 6 5	Newcastle, 60 km	521
Besançon	F	13 7 5	Bâle-Mulhouse, 170 km	226
Béthemont	F	13 6 5	Charles-de-Gaulle, 55 km	227
Beuerberg	D	17 7 6	München, 80 km	387
Biarritz-le-Phare	F	14 6 8	Biarritz-Parme, 3 km	228
Biblis Wattenheim	D	15 6 7	Frankfurt, 60 km	388
Biella - Le Betulle	I	18 7 8	Torino, 75 km	950
Bitburger Land	D	15 7 8	Luxembourg, 55 km	389
Bitche	F	14 6 5	Strasbourg, 80 km	229
Blackmoor	Eng	17 6 5	Heathrow, 65 km	522
Blainroe	IRL	13 6 6	Dublin, 65 km	838
Blairgowrie	Sc	18 8 6	Edinburgh, 90 km	697/698
Bled	SLO	15 7 8	Ljubljana, 25 km	1301
Blumisberg	Ch	15 7 6	Genève, 135 km, Zürich, 156 km	1274
Boat of Garten	Sc	14 6 7	Inverness, 45 km	699
Bodensee-Weissensberg	D	16 7 7	Zürich, 130 km München, 180 km	390
Bogogno	I	17 8 7	Milano, 33 km	951/952
Bokskogen	S	16 6 7	Malmö, 7 km	1217
Bologna	I	13 7 7	Bologna, 6 km	953
Bolton Old Links	Eng	15 5 7	Manchester, 25 km	523
Bonalba	E	14 6 6	Alicante, 15 km	1115
Bondues	F	16 7 6	Lille-Lesquin, 20 km	230/231
Bonmont	E	16 8 7	Barcelona, 140 km	1116
Bordes (Les)	F	19 8 6	Orly, 130 km	232
Borre	Nw	16 6 5	Oslo, 75 km	1038
Bosjökloster	S	15 7 6	Malmö, 70 km	1218
Boulie (La)	F	15 7 8	Orly, 20 km	233
Bowood (Cornwall)	Eng	16 7 6	Plymouth, 65 km	524
Bowood G&CC	Eng	17 6 6	Bristol, 50 km	525
Brampton	Eng	17 7 6	Glasgow, 160 km	526
Brancepeth Castle	Eng	14 6 5	Newcastle, 20 km	527
Braunschweig	D	14 6 7	Hannover, 75 km	391
Bråviken	S	16 7 7	Norrköping, 5 km	1219
Breitenloo	CH	13 7 6	Zürich-Kloten, 8 km	1275
Bresse (La)	F	16 7 5	Lyon-Saint Exupéry, 62 km	234
Brest Iroise	F	14 7 6	Brest, 20 km	235
Bretesche (La)	F	15 7 7	Nantes, 61 km	236
Brigode	F	14 7 6	Lille, 15 km	237
Bro-Bålsta	S	17 7 6	Stockholm, 35 km	1220
Broadstone	Eng	17 7 7	Bournemouth, 17 km	528
Broekpolder	N	15 7 6	Rotterdam, 15 km	1002
Brokenhurst Manor	Eng	15 6 6	Southampton, 16 km	529
Brora	Sc	15 7 7	Inverness, 92 km	700
Bruntsfield	Sc	15 8 9	Edinburgh, 10 km	701
Buchanan Castle	Sc	14 6 6	Glasgow, 33 km	702
Buckinghamshire	Eng	17 8 7	Heathrow, 16 km	530
Bude & North Cornwall	Eng	15 6 5	Exeter, 70 km	531
Bundoran	IRL	13 6 7	Sligo, 45 km Belfast, 176 km	839
Burnham & Berrow	Eng	18 7 6	Bristol, 38 km	532
Burntisland	Sc	14 6 6	Edinburgh, 27 km	703
Buxtehude	D	16 7 6	Hamburg, 60 km	392

C

Cairndhu	NIR	13 6 5	Belfast, 40 km	915
Caldy	Eng	17 7 7	Liverpool, 38 km	533
Callander	Sc	13 6 7	Glasgow, 65 km	704
Camberley Heath	Eng	16 6 6	Heathrow, 50 km	534
Came Down	Eng	15 5 6	Exeter, 53 km	535
Campoamor	E	14 6 6	Alicante, 50 km	1117
Cannes Mandelieu	F	14 7 8	Nice, 38 km	238
Cannes-Mougins	F	15 7 8	Nice, 18 km	239
Canyamel	E	15 6 6	Palma, 68 km	1118
Cap d'Agde	F	15 6 5	Béziers, 25 km	240
Capdepera	E	15 7 6	Palma, 62 km	1119
Carden Park	Eng	17 8 8	Manchester, 50 km	536
Cardiff	W	14 6 8	Cardiff, 16 km	794
Cardigan	W	15 6 5	Cardiff, 140 km	795
Cardross	Sc	14 6 5	Glasgow, 25 km	705
Carlisle	Eng	17 7 7	Glasgow, 160 km	537
Carlow	IRL	16 6 7	Dublin, 100 km	840
Carmarthen	W	15 7 4	Cardiff, 100 km	796
Carnegie Club (Skibo Castle)	Sc	15 9 7	Inverness, 76 km	706
Carnoustie	Sc	19 5 6	Edinburgh, 100 km	707/708
Castelconturbia	I	18 8 8	Milano, 30 km	954
Castelgandolfo	I	15 7 7	Roma Fiumicino, 53 km	955
Castello di Tolcinasco	I	14 8 7	Milano, 50 km	956
Castillo de Gorraiz	E	17 7 7	Pamplona, 8 km	1120
Castle	IRL	13 6 8	Dublin, 18 km	841
Castle Combe (Manor House)	Eng	15 8 7	Bristol, 45 km	593
Castlerock	NIR	16 6 6	Belfast, 80 km	916
Castletown	Eng	18 6 8	Ronaldsway, 4 km	538
Castletroy	IRL	13 6 6	Shannon, 18 km	842
Ceann Sibeal (Dingle Links)	IRL	15 5 4	Cork, 160 km	851
Celtic Manor	W	18 9 7	Cardiff, 30 km	797
Cély	F	15 7 6	Orly, 40 km	241
Cerdaña	E	14 7 7	Barcelona, 150 km	1121
Cervia	I	13 6 9	Bologna, 96 km	957
Chailly (Château de)	F	14 8 6	Dijon-Bourgogne, 66 km	242
Chambon-s-Lignon	F	14 5 7	Lyon-Saint Exupéry, 145 km	243
Chamonix	F	15 6 7	Genève-Cointrin, 80 km	244
Champ de Bataille	F	14 6 3	Rouen, 35 km	245
Chantaco	F	14 7 7	Biarritz-Parme, 15 km	246
Chantilly	F	18 7 6	Charles-de-Gaulle, 21 km	247
Charleville	IRL	13 4 6	Cork, 60 km	843
Charmeil	F	16 6 6	Grenoble, 15 km	248
Chart Hills	Eng	18 8 6	Gatwick, 50 km	539
Château de Preisch	F	15 7 6	Luxembourg, 20 km	249
Chaumont-en-Vexin	F	14 6 4	Roissy CdG, 60 km	250
Chesterfield	Eng	13 6 7	Manchester, 70 km	540
Cheverny	F	14 7 6	Tours-St-Symphorien, 70 km	251
Chiberta	F	16 6 8	Biarritz-Parme, 5 km	252
Citywest	IRL	13 6 8	Dublin, 20 km	844
Clandeboye	NIR	15 6 6	Belfast, 35 km	917
Clitheroe	Eng	17 7 7	Manchester, 60 km	541
Club de Campo	E	16 8 8	Madrid, 20 km	1122
Club zur Vahr (Garlstedt)	D	18 6 5	Bremen, 30 km	393
Cognac	F	13 7 5	Angoulème, 44 km	207
Collingtree Park	Eng	14 8 7	Luton, 45 km	542
Connemara	IRL	15 6 6	Galway, 100 km	845
Conwy	W	17 7 8	Manchester, 180 km	798

Golf	Country	Rating	Airport	Page
Cork GC	IRL	15 3 5	Cork, 10 km	846
Cosmopolitan	I	14 6 7	Pisa, 15 km	958
Costa Brava	E	14 7 7	Barcelona, 100 km	1123
Costa Dorada	E	13 6 6	Barcelona, 100 km	1124
County Louth	IRL	18 5 6	Dublin, 36 km	847
County Sligo	IRL	17 4 4	Sligo, 15 km	848
County Tipperary	IRL	15 7 5	Cork, 90 km Dublin, 156 km	849
Courson	F	16 7 3	Orly, 20 km	208/209
Courtown	IRL	14 5 5	Dublin, 105 km	850
Coxmoor	Eng	15 6 6	East Midlands, 40 km	543
Crail Balcomie Links	Sc	15 6 6	Edinburgh, 85 km	709
Crans-sur-Sierre	Ch	14 7 8	Sion, 25 km Genève, 200 km	1276
Crieff	Sc	15 7 7	Edinburgh, 70 km	710
Cromstrijen	N	16 8 5	Rotterdam, 35 km	1003
Cruden Bay	Sc	18 7 6	Aberdeen, 38 km	711
Cumberwell Park	Eng	17 7 7	Bristol, 40 km	544

D

Golf	Country	Rating	Airport	Page
Dalmahoy	Sc	17 8 8	Edinburgh, 5 km	712
Dartmouth	Eng	16 9 6	Plymouth, 60 km	545
Deauville (New Golf)	F	14 7 8	Charles-de-Gaulle, 220 km	256
De Pan	N	16 8 7	Amsterdam, 65 km	1004
Delamere Forest	Eng	15 6 7	Manchester, 40 km	546
Dellach	A	15 7 7	Graz, 130 km	81
Denham	Eng	15 7 7	Heathrow, 16 km	547
Dieppe-Pourville	F	14 6 5		210
Dinard	F	13 6 7	Rennes 75 km, Dinard 6 km	211
Dingle Links (Ceann Sibeal)	IRL	15 5 4	Cork, 160 km	851
Disneyland Paris	F	16 7 8	Orly, 40 km - C.de G, 28 km	212
Divonne	F	14 6 7	Genève-Cointrin, 15 km	213
Domaine Impérial	CH	18 8 6	Genève-Cointrin, 25 km	1277
Domont-Montmorency	F	13 7 4	Charles-de-Gaulle, 20 km	214
Domtal-Mommenheim	D	14 7 7	Frankfurt, 40 km	394
Donegal (Murvagh)	IRL	16 6 6	Belfast, 160 km Sligo, 45 km	852
Dooks	IRL	15 5 5	Cork, 115 km	853
Downfield	Sc	17 6 7	Edinburgh, 80 km	713
Dromoland Castle	IRL	14 7 8	Shannon, 15 km	854
Drottningholm	S	14 9 6	Stockholm, 75 km	1221
Druids Glen	IRL	16 9 7	Dublin, 40 km	855
Duddingston	Sc	15 7 9	Edinburgh, 12 km	714
Duff House Royal	Sc	15 6 6	Aberdeen, 75 km	715
Duke's Course St Andrews	Sc	16 7 8	Edinburgh, 80 km	716
Dumfries & County	Sc	15 7 5	Edinburgh/Glasgow, 115 km	717
Dunbar	Sc	16 5 6	Edinburgh, 48 km	718
Dundalk	IRL	15 6 6	Dublin, 80 km	856
Dunfermline	Sc	15 7 7	Edinburgh, 25 km	719
Düsseldorfer	D	15 7 7	Düsseldorf, 8 km	395

E

Golf	Country	Rating	Airport	Page
East Devon	Eng	16 6 7	Exeter, 10 km	548
East Renfrewshire	Sc	15 6 8	Glasgow, 20 km	720
East Sussex National	Eng	17 8 7	Gatwick, 35 km	549
Edzell	Sc	14 6 3	Aberdeen, 60 km	721
Efteling	N	16 8 5	Eindhoven, 40 km	1005
Eichenheim	A	17 8 8	München, 120 km	82
Eindhoven	N	18 8 6	Eindhoven, 12 km	1006
Ekerum	S	14 7 7	Kalmar, 27 km	1222
El Bosque	E	16 7 4	Valencia, 5 km	1125
El Cortijo	E	17 5 8	Las Palmas, 25 km	1126
El Prat	E	17 7 6	Barcelona, 7 km	1127
El Saler	E	18 7 6	Valencia, 16 km	1128
Elfrather Mühle	D	14 7 7	Düsseldorf, 30 km	396
Elgin	Sc	15 7 6	Aberdeen, 100 km	722
Elie	Sc	15 6 6	Edinburgh, 80 km	723
Elm Park	IRL	13 7 8	Dublin, 17 km	857
Emporda	E	17 7 6	Barcelona 120 km Perpignan, 90 km	1129
Engadin	Ch	15 6 6	Zürich, 225 km	1278
Ennetsee-Holzhäusern	Ch	13 7 6	Zürich-Kloten, 45 km	1279
Enniscrone	IRL	17 8 6	Sligo, 55 km	858
Esbjerg	Da	15 6 5	Billund, 70 km	127
Eschenried	D	14 7 7	München, 35 km	397
Escorpion	E	13 8 4	Valencia-Manises, 10 km	1130
Esery	F	15 7 5	Genève-Cointrin,16 km	215
Esker Hills	IRL	14 6 6	Dublin, 100 km	859
Eslöv	S	14 7 5	Malmö, 50 km	1223
Espoo	Fi	16 7 6	Helsinki, 25 km	148
Essener Oefte	D	15 8 7	Düsseldorf, 25 km	398
Estepona	E	14 7 6	Gibraltar, 40 km	1131
Estérel Latitudes	F	16 6 7	Nice, 60 km	216
Etiolles Les Cerfs	F	15 7 6	Orly, 15 km	217
Etretat	F	14 7 6	Le Havre-Octeville, 20 km	218
European (The)	IRL	18 5 6	Dublin, 90 km	860
European Tour Club (Kungsängen)	S	17 7 6	Stockholm, 30 km	1224
Evian	F	15 7 9	Genève-Cointrin, 52 km	219

F

Golf	Country	Rating	Airport	Page
Fågelbro	S	16 9 5	Stockholm, 75 km	1225
Fairhaven	Eng	17 7 8	Manchester, 100 km	550
Faithlegg	IRL	13 7 7	Cork, 135 km	861
Falkenberg	S	14 7 7	Göteborg, 115 km	1226
Falkenstein	D	18 6 7	Hamburg, 30 km	399
Falkirk Tryst	Sc	13 6 6	Edinburgh, 32 km	724
Falmouth	Eng	14 6 7	Exeter, 120 km	551
Falnuée	B	14 7 4	Charleroi, 25 km	99
Falsterbo	S	18 7 5	Malmö, 45 km	1227
Fanø	Da	15 4 7	Esbjerg, 10 km	128
Feldafing	D	16 7 6	München, 80 km	400
Felixstowe & Ferry	Eng	15 6 6	Stansted, 120 km	552
Ferndown	Eng	17 7 7	Bournemouth, 7 km	553
Feucherolles	F	15 7 5	Orly, 30 km	220
Filey	Eng	13 5 5	Leeds, 110 km	554
Firenze - Ugolino	I	13 8 9	Firenze, 16 km	959
Fjällbacka	S	15 6 3	Göteborg, 130 km	1228
Fleesensee	D	17 8 8	Berlin, 145 km	401
Flommen	S	16 7 7	Malmö, 45 km	1229
Fontainebleau	F	17 7 7	Orly, 40 km	221
Fontana	A	16 8 7	Wien, 45 km	83
Fontanals	E	17 6 5	Perpignan, 110 km	1132
Fontcaude	F	14 6 6	Montpellier- Fréjorgues, 15 km	222
Fontenailles	F	14 7 6	Orly, 55 km	223
Fontenelles (Les)	F	14 6 4	Nantes, 70 km	224
Forest of Arden	Eng	15 8 8	Birmingham, 6 km	555
Forest Pines	Eng	17 6 7	Humberside, 11 km	556
Forfar	Sc	14 6 6	Edinburgh, 120 km	725
Formby	Eng	18 7 7	Manchester, 80 km	557
Formby Hall	Eng	14 8 6	Manchester, 80 km	558
Forsbacka	S	16 7 4	Karlstad, 70 km	1230

Forsgården	S	14 6 7	Göteborg, 25 km	1231
Fortrose & Rosemarkie	Sc	16 6 5	Inverness, 40 km	726
Fota Island	IRL	16 7 6	Cork, 18 km	862
Franciacorta	I	14 7 8	Bergamo, 30 km	960
Frankfurter GC	D	17 7 8	Frankfurt, 5 km	402
Fränkische Schweiz	D	14 7 6	Nürnberg, 45 km	403
Frégate	F	15 7 7	Toulon Hyères, 50 km	225
Frilford Heath	Eng	14 7 7	Heathrow, 75 km	559
Frösåker	S	16 7 5	Stockholm, 80 km	1232
Fulford	Eng	17 7 8	Leeds, 35 km	560
Fürstlicher GC Bad Waldsee	D	17 7 8	Stuttgart, 140 km	404
Fürstliches Hofgut Kolnhausen	D	14 7 6	Frankfurt, 60 km	405

G

Gainsborough-Karsten Lakes	Eng	14 8 6	Humberside, 40 km	561
Galway Bay	IRL	14 7 6	Galway, 6 km	863
Galway GC	IRL	13 6 6	Galway, 12 km	864
Ganton	Eng	19 8 5	Leeds, 60 km	562
Gardagolf	I	15 8 8	Bergamo, 73 km	961
Garlenda	I	14 7 8	Genova, 75 km	962
Garlstedt (Club zur Vahr)	D	18 6 5	Bremen, 30 km	393
Garmisch-Partenkirchen	D	14 6 7	München, 110 km	406
Gävle	S	14 6 6	Stockholm, 140 km	1233
Gelpenberg	N	14 4 5	Eelde, 50 km	1007
Gendersteyn	N	15 7 7	Eindhoven, 10 km	1008
Genève	Ch	17 7 8	Genève-Cointrin, 10 km	1280
Glamorganshire	W	14 7 8	Cardiff, 13 km	799
Glasson	IRL	16 7 7	Dublin, 120 km	865
Glen	Sc	14 7 7	Edinburgh, 30 km	727
Glen of the Downs	IRL	13 6 7	Dublin, 40 km	866
Gleneagles	Sc	18 9 7	Edinburgh, 70 km	728/729/730
Gloria Golf Resort	T	15 7 7	Antalya, 42 km	1303
Goes	N	15 7 6	Rotterdam, 80 km	1009
Gog Magog	Eng	15 7 8	Stansted, 48 km	563
Golden Eagle	P	14 5 4	Lisboa, 55 km	1062
Golf d'Aro (Mas Nou)	E	15 3 7	Girona, 25 km	1133
Golf del Sur	E	16 7 8	Tenerife *Sur*, 2 km	1134
Golfresort Haugschlag-Waldviertel	A	16 8 6	Wien, 160 km	84
Golspie	Sc	14 5 4	Inverness, 90 km	731
Göteborg	S	15 6 7	Göteborg, 25 km	1234
Gouverneur (Le)	F	16 6 6	Lyon-S Exupéry, 40 km	226/227
Graafschap	N	15 7 6	Amsterdam-Schiphol, 110 km	1010
Granada	E	14 6 5	Granada, 15 km	1135
Grand Ducal de Luxembourg	L	13 6 7	Luxembourg, 1 km	117
Grande Bastide (La)	F	16 6 6	Nice, 26 km	228
Grande-Motte (La)	F	16 6 4	Montpellier, 10 km	229
Grange	IRL	16 5 8	Dublin, 20 km	867
Gränna	S	15 7 5	Jönköping, 40 km	1235
Grantown on Spey	Sc	14 6 7	Inverness, 56 km	732
Granville	F	14 4 4	Bréville, 4 km	230
Grasse	F	13 7 7	Nice, 37 km	9999
Greenore	IRL	14 6 5	Dublin, 104 km	868
Grenoble Bresson	F	17 7 6	Grenoble, 50 km	231
Grevelingenhout	N	14 7 4	Rotterdam, 65 km	1011
Gruyère (La)	CH	14 7 6	Genève, 120 km	1281
Guadalhorce	E	14 7 6	Málaga, 4 km	1136
Guadalmina	E	14 7 7	Málaga, 64 km	1137
Gujan-Mestras	F	15 7 6	Bordeaux-Mérignac, 50 km	232
Gullane	Sc	17 8 7	Edinburgh, 50 km	733
Gut Altentann	A	17 7 6	Salzburg, 17 km	85
Gut Grambek	D	16 7 6	Hamburg, 50 km	407
Gut Kaden	D	15 7 6	Hamburg, 20 km	408
Gut Lärchenhof	D	17 9 7	Köln-Bonn, 35 km	409
Gut Ludwigsberg	D	15 6 6	München, 70 km	410
Gut Thailing	D	16 7 5	München, 65 km	411
Gütersloh (Westfälischer GC)	D	17 7 7	Paderborn, 30 km	412

H

Haagsche	N	18 7 8	Amsterdam 45 km	1012
Hadley Wood	Eng	16 7 7	Heathrow, 48 km	564
Haggs Castle	Sc	15 7 9	Glasgow, 9 km	734
Hainaut	B	15 7 5	St-Ghislain, 10 km	100
Hallamshire	Eng	15 6 8	Leeds, 25 km	565
Halmstad	S	18 8 7	Göteborg, 160 km	1236
Hamburg-Ahrensburg	D	16 8 7	Hamburg, 20 km	413
Hanau-Wilhelmsbad	D	16 6 6	Frankfurt, 25 km	414
Haninge	S	16 8 6	Stockholm, 70 km	1237
Hankley Common	Eng	16 6 6	Heathrow, 50 km	566
Hannover	D	16 7 7	Hannover, 12 km	415
Hardelot	F	16 6 6	Lille, 153 km	233
Harrogate	Eng	15 7 7	Leeds Bradford, 25 km	567
Hauger	Nw	13 7 6	Oslo, 20 km	1039
Haut-Poitou	F	14 6 4	Poitiers-Biart, 25 km	234
Hawkstone Park	Eng	15 8 7	Manchester, 65 km	568
Hayling	Eng	16 7 7	Southampton, 45 km	569
Headfort	IRL	15 6 6	Dublin, 55 km	869
Hechingen-Hohenzollern	D	14 6 6	Stuttgart, 50 km	416
Heilbronn-Hohenlohe	D	14 7 8	Stuttgart, 80 km	417
Helsinki	Fi	16 7 8	Helsinki, 19 km	149
Henley	Eng	14 6 7	Heathrow, 48 km	570
Herkenbosch	N	16 7 6	Maastricht, 35 km	1013
Hermitage	IRL	15 6 8	Dublin, 10 km	870
Hertfordshire (The)	Eng	15 7 7	Heathrow, 55 km	571
Hever	Eng	14 8 8	Gatwick, 25 km	572
High Post	Eng	15 6 7	Heathrow, 130 km	573
Hillside	Eng	18 7 7	Manchester, 80 km	574
Hilversum	N	16 7 7	Amsterdam-Schiphol, 40 km	1014
Himmerland	Da	16 8 6	Aalborg, 50 km	129
Hindhead	Eng	16 7 6	Heathrow, 55 km	575
Hof Trages	D	15 7 5	Frankfurt, 45 km	418
Hoge Kleij	N	15 6 7	Amsterdam-Schiphol, 50 km	1015
Hohenpähl	D	15 7 6	München, 73 km	419
Hollinwell (Notts)	Eng	18 6 6	Birmingham, 69 km	604
Holstebro	Da	16 6 5	Århus, 100 km	130
Holyhead	W	16 7 5	Manchester, 220 km	800
Hossegor	F	16 6 6	Biarritz-Parme, 28 km	235
Houtrak	N	16 8 8	Amsterdam, 20 km	1016
Hoylake (Royal Liverpool)	Eng	18 8 7	Liverpool, 35 km	623
Hubbelrath	D	17 8 6	Düsseldorf, 18 km	420
Huddersfield (Fixby)	Eng	16 6 7	Leeds Bradford, 25 km	576
Hunstanton	Eng	17 7 6	Stansted, 150 km	577
Huntercombe	Eng	14 6 7	Heathrow, 65 km	578
Huntly	Sc	14 6 6	Aberdeen, 56 km	735
I Roveri	I	17 7 7	Torino, 7 km	963

I - J

Iffeldorf	D	16 7 6	München, 70 km	421
Ilkley	Eng	18 7 6	Leeds, 15 km	579
Im Chiemgau	D	15 7 6	München, 100 km	422
Interlaken	Ch	14 6 6	Bern, 59 km	1282
International Club du Lys	F	15 7 7	Charles-de-Gaulle, 25 km	236
Inverness	Sc	16 7 8	Glasgow, 256 km	736
Ipswich (Purdis Heath)	Eng	16 7 7	Stansted, 84 km	580
Is Arenas	I	17 2 6	Cagliari, 110 km	964
Is Molas	I	17 7 8	Cagliari, 35 km	965
Isernhagen	D	15 7 6	Hannover, 17 km	423
Islantilla	E	16 8 8	Faro (Portugal), 69 km	1138
Isle Adam (L')	F	16 7 4	Charles-de-Gaulle, 23 km	237
Isle of Purbeck	Eng	16 7 6	Bournemouth, 16 km	581
Jakobsberg	D	15 7 6	Frankfurt, 100 km	424
Jarama R.A.C.E.	E	13 7 6	Madrid, 20 km	1139
John O'Gaunt	Eng	16 7 6	Luton 28 km Heathrow, 65 km	582
Jönköping	S	16 7 7	Jönköping, 2 km	1238
Joyenval	F	16 8 7	Orly, 32 km	238/239

K

K Club	IRL	17 8 8	Dublin, 44 km	871
Kalmar	S	15 5 8	Kalmar, 5 km	1239
Karlovy Vary	Cz	15 7 6	Karlovy Vary, 1 km	1297
Karlshamn	S	14 6 6	Kristianstad, 60 km	1240
Karlstad	S	15 6 6	Karlstad, 6 km	1241
Keerbergen	B	14 7 6	Brussel (Bruxelles), 15 km	101
Kempferhof (Le)	F	18 8 6	Strasbourg-Entzheim, 14 km	240
Kennemer	N	18 8 8	Amsterdam-Schiphol, 20 km	1017
Kikuoka	L	16 7 7	Luxembourg, 10 km	118
Kilkea Castle	IRL	15 6 6	Dublin, 70 km	872
Kilkenny	IRL	13 7 6	Dublin, 110 km	873
Killarney	16	7 8	Cork, 105 km	874/875
Killorglin	IRL	14 6 5	Cork, 126 km	876
Kilmarnock (Barassie)	Sc	17 6 8	Glasgow, 50 km	737
Kingsbarns	Sc	19 8 6	Edinburgh, 80 km	738
Kingussie	Sc	15 4 5	Inverness, 70 km	739
Kirkistown Castle	NIR	15 6 5	Belfast, 55 km	918
Klagenfurt-Seltenheim	A	17 6 8	Klagenfurt, 3 km	86
Knock	NIR	15 7 6	Belfast, 21 km	919
København	Da	16 7 7	København, 30 km	131
Köln	D	17 6 7	Köln-Bonn, 25 km	425
Korsør	Da	14 4 6	Odense, 40 km	132
Krefelder	D	17 7 7	Düsseldorf, 30 km	426
Kristianstad	S	17 7 7	Malmö, 90 km	1242
Kungsängen European Tour Club	S	17 7 6	Stockholm, 30 km	1224
Kungsbacka	S	15 6 6	Göteborg, 30 km	1243

L

La Cala	E	17 8 6	Málaga, 35 km	1140/1141
La Dehesa	E	14 7 4	Madrid, 35 km	1142
La Duquesa	E	13 7 6	Gibraltar, 30 km	1143
La Herreria	E	15 6 6	Madrid, 60 km	1144
La Manga	E	15 7 7	Alicante, 110 km	1145/46/47
La Moraleja	E	16 7 8	Madrid, 15 km	1148/1149
La Moye	Eng	17 7 8	Jersey, 3 km	583
La Pinetina	I	13 7 8	Milano, 48 km	966
La Quinta	E	14 8 8	Málaga, 64 km	1150
La Sella	E	15 6 5	Valencia, 70 km	1151
La Zagaleta	E	16 7 7	Malaga, 65 km	1152
Lacanau	F	14 6 7	Bordeaux-Mérignac, 55 km	241
Ladybank	Sc	17 7 5	Edinburgh, 56 km	740
Lage Vuursche	N	17 7 7	Amsterdam, 65 km	1018
Lahinch	IRL	17 6 6	Shannon, 55 km	877
Lanark	Sc	16 6 5	Edinburgh, 48 km	741
Landskrona	S	15 9 7	Malmö, 45 km	1244
Langland Bay	W	15 7 7	Cardiff, 65 km	801
Largue (La)	F	15 7 4	Bâle-Mulhouse, 35 km	242
Larvik	Nw	17 8 6	Oslo, 120 km	1040
Las Américas	E	16 7 8	Tenerife, 15 km	1153
Las Brisas	E	18 8 7	Málaga, 60 km	1154
Las Palmas	E	14 8 8	Las Palmas, 20 km	1155
Læsø	Da	15 7 5	Aalborg, 100 km	133
Lauro	E	14 7 7	Málaga, 10 km	1156
Lausanne	CH	16 7 7	Genève-Cointrin, 60 km	1283
Lauswolt	N	14 6 7	Groningen-Eelde, 50 km	1019
Laval-Changé	F	14 7 5	Nantes, 100 km	243
Le Pavoniere	I	14 8 8	Firenze, 15 km	967
Le Prieuré	F	14 7 5	Roissy, 70 km	244
Le Querce	I	17 8 7	Roma, 95 km	968
Le Robinie	I	15 8 8	Milano, 9 km	969
Lee Valley	IRL	13 7 6	Cork, 14 km	878
Lerma	E	17 7 4	Madrid, 200 km	1157
Les Bois	CH	15 7 6	Genève, 140 km	1284
Letham Grange	Sc	15 7 5	Edinburgh, 110 km	742
Leven	Sc	16 6 6	Edinburgh, 56 km	743
Lichtenau-Weickershof	D	15 7 6	Nürnberg, 40 km	427
Lignano	I	14 7 7	Venezia, 108 km	970
Limburg	B	16 7 4	Brussel (Bruxelles), 75 km	102
Limère	F	17 6 5	Orly, 130 km	245
Limerick County	IRL	15 7 6	Shannon, 40 km	879
Lindau-Bad Schachen	D	15 7 8	Zürich, 130 km München,180 km	428
Linden Hall	Eng	17 8 6	Newcastle, 40 km	584
Lindenhof	D	14 8 8	Frankfurt, 16 km	429
Lindrick	Eng	17 6 6	Leeds/Bradford, 40 km	585
Liphook	Eng	16 7 6	Gatwick, 48 km	586
Lisburn	NIR	15 7 6	Belfast, 14 km	920
Little Aston	Eng	17 7 8	Birmingham, 25 km	587
Littlestone	Eng	14 6 5	Gatwick, 110 km	588
Ljunghusen	S	18 7 7	Malmö, 45 km	1245
Llandudno (Maesdu)	W	15 5 8	Manchester, 160 km	802
Llanymynech	W	14 6 4	Manchester, 120 km	803
Loch Lomond	Sc	18 8 6	Glasgow, 32 km	744
London Golf Club	Eng	15 9 7	Gatwick, 58 km	589
Longniddry	Sc	14 7 6	Edinburgh, 30 km	745
Los Arqueros	E	14 6 7	Málaga, 65 km	1158
Los Naranjos	E	16 7 7	Málaga, 62 km	1159
Losby	Nw	16 8 6	Oslo, 36 km	1041
Lothianburn	Sc	14 6 8	Edinburgh, 12 km	746
Lübeck-Travemünder	D	17 8 8	Hamburg, 90 km	430
Luffness New	Sc	16 5 6	Edinburgh, 30 km	747
Lugano	CH	15 7 8	Lugano (Agno), 2 km	1285
Lundin	Sc	16 6 7	Edinburgh, 55 km	748
Lunds Akademiska	S	16 7 5	Malmö, 25 km	1246
Lüneburger Heide	D	16 7 5	Hamburg, 70 km	431
Luttrellstown	IRL	15 7 7	Dublin, 10 km	880
Luxembourg (Grand Ducal)	L	13 6 7	Luxembourg, 1 km	117
Luzern	CH	13 6 7	Zürich, 70 km	1286
Lys Chantilly (International Club)	F	15 7 7	Charles-de-Gaulle, 25 km	236
Lytham Green Drive	Eng	15 7 8	Manchester, 100 km	590

M

Golf	Country	Rating	Closest airport	Page
Machrie	Sc	17 7 7	Islay Airport, 5 km	749
Machrihanish	Sc	18 6 4	Glasgow (+ ferry or air)	750
Main-Taunus	D	14 7 6	Frankfurt, 20 km	432
Maison Blanche	F	14 8 5	Genève-Cointrin, 10 km	246
Makila Golf Club	F	15 6 8	Biarritz-Parme, 4 km	247
Málaga	E	13 4 6	Málaga, 3 km	1160
Malahide	IRL	13 7 8	Dublin, 7 km	881
Malone	NIR	13 6 6	Belfast, 16 km	921
Manchester	Eng	16 7 7	Manchester, 20 km	591
Mannings Heath	Eng	14 8 6	Gatwick, 18 km	592
Manor House (Castle Combe)	Eng	15 8 7	Bristol, 45 km	593
Marbella	E	15 7 8	Málaga, 51 km	1161
Marco Simone	I	15 8 8	Roma, 73 km	971
Margara	I	13 7 7	Torino, 109 km	972
Mariánské Lázne	Cz	14 7 6	Praha, 160 km	1298
Märkischer Potsdam	D	14 7 6	Berlin, 45 km	433
Marriott St Pierre	W	16 8 7	Cardiff, 45 km	804
Masia Bach	E	15 7 6	Barcelona, 40 km	1162
Mas Nou (Golf d'Aro)	E	15 3 7	Girona, 25 km	1133
Maspalomas	E	16 7 8	Las Palmas, 30 km	1163
Massereene	NIR	14 5 6	Belfast, 7 km	922
Master	Fi	15 7 7	Helsinki, 25 km	150
Mazamet-La Barouge	F	13 5 4	Toulouse-Blagnac, 90 km	248
Mediterraneo	E	16 7 6	Valencia-Manises, 70 km	1164
Médoc	F	18 7 5	Bordeaux, 20 km	249/250
Meland	Nw	16 7 4	Bergen, 60 km	1042
Memmingen Gut Westerhart	D	14 6 6	München, 140	434
Mendip	Eng	15 5 7	Bristol, 30 km	594
Meon Valley	Eng	15 8 7	Southampton, 16 km	595
Mere	Eng	15 7 7	Manchester, 8 km	596
Mijas	E	16 6 7	Málaga, 20 km	1165/1166
Milano	I	16 9 8	Milano, 70 km	973
Mittelrheinischer	D	17 7 7	Frankfurt, 100 km	435
Modena	I	13 7 7	Bologna, 40 km	974
Moliets	F	17 6 5	Biarritz-Parme, 50 km	251
Molinetto	I	13 8 8	Milano, 50 km	975
Mölle	S	15 7 5	Malmö, 110 km	1247
Møn	Da	15 7 7	København, 120 km	134
Monifieth	Sc	17 7 7	Edinburgh, 96 km	751
Monkstown	IRL	15 6 7	Cork, 15 km	882
Mont-Garni	B	13 7 6	Bruxelles, 70 km	103
Monte Carlo (Mont Agel)	F	14 6 7	Nice, 20 km	252
Monte Mayor	E	13 5 5	Málaga, 65 km	1167
Montebelo	P	13 5 5	Porto, 130 km	1063
Montecastillo	E	17 8 8	Jerez, 7 km	1168
Montecchia	I	13 8 8	Venezia, 95 km	976
Monteenmedio	E	16 8 7	Jerez, 70 km	1169
Monticello	I	14 8 7	Milano, 30 km	977
Montpellier-Massane	F	16 7 5	Montpellier, 14 km	253
Montreux	CH	13 6 5	Genève-Cointrin, 85 km	1287
Montrose	Sc	17 5 6	Aberdeen, 72 km	752
Moor Allerton	Eng	15 6 7	Leeds Bradford, 15 km	597
Moor Park	Eng	17 8 7	Heathrow, 16 km	598
Moortown	Eng	18 7 7	Leeds, 10 km	599
Moray	Sc	17 5 5	Inverness, 60 km	753
Morfontaine	F	18 6 6	Charles-de-Gaulle, 25 km	254
Moscow	Ru	17 7 6	Moscow, 35 km	1302
Motzener See	D	17 8 6	Berlin, 45 km	436
Mount Juliet	IRL	18 9 8	Dublin, 136 km	883
Mount Wolseley	IRL	13 6 5	Dublin, 93 km	884
Muirfield	Sc	19 7 6	Edinburgh, 40 km	754
Mullingar	IRL	15 5 5	Dublin, 90 km	885
Mullion	Eng	15 5 5	Exeter, 160 km	600
München-Riedhof	D	16 7 7	München, 90 km	437
Münchner-Strasslach	D	15 6 7	München, 80 km	438
Murcar	Sc	15 6 6	Aberdeen, 12 km	755
Murhof (Steiermärkischer)	A	16 8 7	Graz, 20 km	88
Murrayshall	Sc	14 7 8	Edinburgh, 72 km	756
Murvagh (Donegal)	IRL	16 6 6	Belfast, 160 km Sligo, 45 km	852

N

Golf	Country	Rating	Closest airport	Page
Nahetal	D	14 8 6	Frankfurt, 90 km	439
Nairn	Sc	19 7 8	Inverness, 9 km	757
Nairn Dunbar	Sc	15 7 7	Inverness, 15 km	758
National	F	18 6 6	Orly, 32 km	255
National GC	T	15 7 7	Antalya, 32 km	1304
Nefyn & District	W	16 7 5	Manchester, 180 km	805
Neguri	E	17 7 7	Bilbao, 12 km	1170
Neuchâtel	CH	14 7 7	Genève-Cointrin, 125 km	1288
Neuhof	D	15 7 7	Frankfurt, 18 km	440
New Golf Deauville	F	14 7 8	Charles-de-Gaulle, 220 km	256
Newbury & Crookham	Eng	15 6 7	Heathrow, 80 km	601
Newport	W	15 6 7	Cardiff, 30 km	806
Newtonmore	Sc	14 5 5	Inverness, 72 km	759
Niederbüren	CH	13 7 7	Zürich-Kloten, 80 km	1289
Nîmes-Campagne	F	17 7 6	Nîmes-Garons, 2 km	257
Nobilis	T	17 8 6	Antalya, 42 km	1305
Noordwijk	N	18 7 8	Amsterdam Schiphol, 35 km	1020
Nordcenter	Fi	15 7 5	Helsinki,	151
North Berwick	Sc	18 7 8	Edinburgh, 50 km	760
North Foreland	Eng	13 7 7	Gatwick, 140 km	602
North Hants	Eng	17 7 6	Heathrow, 40 km	603
North Wales (Llandudno)	W	17 6 8	Manchester, 160 km	807
Northop Country Park	W	16 9 6	Manchester, 70 km	808
Notts (Hollinwell)	Eng	18 6 6	Birmingham, 69 km	604
Novo Sancti Petri	E	16 7 7	Jerez, 50 km	1171
Nunspeet	N	15 5 6	Amsterdam-Schiphol, 85 km	1021

O

Golf	Country	Rating	Closest airport	Page
Oberfranken	D	17 6 5	Nürnberg, 80 km	441
Oberschwaben Bad Waldsee	D	15 6 6	Stuttgart, 140 km	442
Oitavos	P	15 7 7	Lisboa, 30 km	1064
Old Head	IRL	16 7 7	Cork, 20 km	886
Olgiata	I	16 8 6	Roma Fiumicino, 25 km	978
Oliva Nova	E	14 6 7	Valencia, 76 km	1172
Olivar de la Hinojosa	E	13 7 8	Madrid, 1 km	1173
Omaha Beach	F	14 7 5	Caen, 40 km	258
Oostende	B	15 7 7	Brussel (Bruxelles), 115 km	104
Oosterhout	N	15 7 7	Amsterdam-Schiphol, 100 km	1022
Orchardleigh	Eng	16 7 7	Bristol, 32 km	605
Örebro	S	18 7 5	Örebro, 15 km	1248
Ormskirk	Eng	14 6 4	Manchester, 48 km	606
Öschberghof	D	15 7 7	Stuttgart, 100 km	443
Oslo	Nw	15 7 9	Oslo, 10 km	1043
Osona Montanya	E	14 7 4	Barcelona, 80 km	1174
Österåker	S	16 6 6	Stockholm, 40 km	1249
Oudenaarde	B	14 6 6	Brussel (Bruxelles), 85 km	105
Ozoir-la-Ferrière	F	13 7 5	Charles-de-Gaulle, 47 km	259

P - Q

Padova	I	14 8 8	Venezia, 40 km	979
Palingbeek	B	13 6 6	Lille, 60 km	106
Palmares	P	13 7 5	Faro, 75 km	1065
Pals	E	16 7 6	Barcelona, 120 km	1175
Panmure	Sc	17 6 5	Edinburgh, 100 km	761
Pannal	Eng	15 6 7	Leeds, 20 km	607
Panoramica	E	14 6 4	Valencia, 150 km	1176
Parco de' Medici	I	13 6 9	Roma Fiumicino, 15 km	980
Paris International	F	16 7 5	Charles-de-Gaulle, 15 km	260
Parkstone	Eng	16 7 8	Bournemouth, 12 km	608
Patriziale Ascona	CH	15 7 7	Lugano, 40 km	999
Patshull Park Hotel	Eng	13 8 8	Birmingham, 48 km	609
Pau	F	13 6 8	Pau-Pyrénées, 5 km	261
Pedreña	E	15 6 5	Santander, 7 km	1177
Penha Longa	P	16 6 8	Lisboa, 25 km	1066
Penina	P	14 7 8	Faro, 60 km	1067
Pennard	W	18 6 6	Cardiff, 50 km	809
Peralada	E	15 7 8	Perpignan (France), 60 km	1178
Perranporth	Eng	16 6 6	Plymouth, 80 km	610
Perstorp	S	14 7 5	Malmö, 70 km	1250
Pevero	I	17 8 8	Olbia, 30 km	981
PGA de Catalunya	E	18 7 7	Barcelona, 133 km	1179
Pickala	Fi	15 8 5	Helsinki, 60 km	152
Pineda	E	15 7 9	Sevilla, 15 km	1180
Pinheiros Altos	P	14 7 7	Faro, 12 km	1068
Pinnau	D	14 6 6	Hamburg, 25 km	444
Pitlochry	Sc	14 6 7	Edinburgh, 105 km	762
Pleasington	Eng	16 8 6	Manchester, 45 km	611
Pléneuf-Val-André	F	17 7 5	262	
Ploemeur Océan	F	15 7 6	Lorient Lann-Bihoué, 4 km	263
Poggio dei Medici	I	15 7 7	Firenze, 28 km	982
Pont Royal	F	16 6 5	Marseille-Marignane, 50 km	264
Porcelaine (La)	F	14 6 4	Limoges-Bellegarde, 15 km	265
Pornic	F	15 6 6	Nantes-Atlantique, 41 km	266
Portal	Eng	15 8 7	Manchester, 30 km	612
Porters Park	Eng	15 7 7	Heathrow, 30 km	613
Portmarnock	IRL	19 7 8	Dublin, 8 km	887
Portmarnock Links	IRL	17 7 8	Dublin, 8 km	888
Portpatrick (Dunskey)	Sc	15 6 7	Glasgow, 150 km	763
Portsalon	IRL	16 5 5	Belfast, 160 km	889
Portstewart	NIR	16 7 7	Belfast, 64 km	923
Powerscourt	IRL	15 7 7	Dublin, 20 km	890
Powfoot	Sc	16 6 4	Glasgow, 130 km	764
Praha Karlstejn	Cz	15 6 7	Praha, 50 km	1299
Praia d'El Rey	P	17 6 5	Lisboa, 75 km	1069
Prestbury	Eng	17 8 7	Manchester, 15 km	614
Prestwick	Sc	18 6 7	Glasgow, 55 km	765
Prestwick St Nicholas	Sc	16 6 7	Glasgow, 55 km	766
Prince de Provence (Vidauban)	F	19 8 7	Nice, 100 km	267
Prince's	Eng	14 6 4	Gatwick, 145 km	615
Puerta de Hierro	E	18 8 9	Madrid, 15 km	1181/1182
Pula	E	13 6 5	Palma, 63 km	1183
Punta Ala	I	14 6 8	Firenze, 140 km	983
Pyle & Kenfig	W	17 7 5	Cardiff, 25 km	810
Quinta da Beloura	P	14 8 7	Lisboa, 26 km	1070
Quinta da Marinha	P	14 7 7	Lisboa, 28 km	1071
Quinta do Lago	P	16 7 8	Faro, 10 km	1072/1073
Quinta do Peru	P	14 7 5	Lisboa, 46 km	1074

R

Rapallo	I	13 8 8	Genova, 59 km	984
Raray (Château de)	F	14 7 4	Roissy, 34 km	268
Rathsallagh	I	14 7 6	Dublin, 80 km	891
Ravenstein	B	17 8 7	Bruxelles, 12 km	107
Real Sociedad Club de Campo	E	18 7 6	Madrid, 20 km	1184
Rebetz	F	16 6 4	Charles-de-Gaulle, 67 km	269
Reichsstadt Bad Windsheim	D	14 6 7	Nürnberg, 50 km	445
Reichswald-Nürnberg	D	16 7 7	Nürnberg, 2 km	446
Reims-Champagne	F	13 7 6	Charles-de-Gaulle, 120 km	270
Rethmar	D	17 8 7	Hannover, 25 km	447
Rheine/Mesum	D	16 8 7	Münster/Osnabrück, 18 km	448
Rheinhessen	D	14 8 7	Frankfurt, 55 km	449
Rigenée	B	14 7 6	Bruxelles, 35 km	108
Rijk van Nijmegen	N	14 6 5	Eindhoven, 65 km	1023
Rimini	I	13 6 8	Rimini, 10 km	985
Ring of Kerry	IRL	15 7 7	Cork, 75 km	892
Rinkven	B	14 6 5	Antwerpen, 30 km	109
Riva dei Tessali	I	13 7 7	Bari, 128 km	986
Riviéra Golf Club	F	13 7 8	Nice Côte d'Azur, 32 km	271
Rochefort-Chisan	F	14 6 4	Orly, 35 km	272
Rolls of Monmouth	W	15 6 6	Cardiff, 65 km	811
Roma - Acquasanta	I	16 8 9	Roma, 30 km	987
Roncemay	F	15 7 7	Orly, 135 km	273
Rosapenna	IRL	16 7 6	Sligo, 150 k/Belfast, 160 km	893
Rosendael	N	15 7 7	Amsterdam, 90 km	1024
Ross-on-Wye	Eng	15 5 6	Birmingham, 95 km	616
Rosslare	IRL	13 5 6	Dublin, 160 km	894
Roxburghe (The)	Sc	15 7 7	Edinburgh, 90 km	767
Royal Aberdeen	Sc	18 7 8	Aberdeen, 10 km	768
Royal Ashdown Forest	Eng	14 7 6	Gatwick, 20 km	617
Royal Belfast	NIR	15 7 7	Belfast, 30 km	924
Royal Birkdale (The)	Eng	19 9 7	Manchester, 80 km	618
Royal Burgess	Sc	16 7 9	Edinburgh, 4 km	769
Royal Cinque Ports	Eng	17 6 5	Gatwick, 145 km	619
Royal County Down	NIR	19 6 7	Belfast, 48 km	925
Royal Cromer	Eng	15 7 6	Stansted, 120 km	620
Royal Dornoch	Sc	19 7 7	Inverness, 82 km	770
Royal Dublin	IRL	16 8 7	Dublin, 13 km	895
Royal Guernsey	Eng	16 7 7	Guernsey, 8 km	621
Royal Jersey	Eng	16 7 8	Jersey, 10 km	622
Royal Latem	B	15 8 6	Brussel, 65 km	110
Royal Liverpool (Hoylake)	Eng	18 8 7	Liverpool, 35 km	623
Royal Lytham & St Anne's	Eng	19 7 8	Manchester, 100 km	624
Royal Mid-Surrey	Eng	14 3 8	Heathrow, 17 km	625
Royal Mougins	F	17 8 8	Nice, 29 km	274
Royal Musselburgh	Sc	16 8 7	Edinburgh, 20 km	771
Royal North Devon (Westward Ho!)	Eng	18 6 6	Plymouth, 90 km	626
Royal Oak	Da	15 7 5	Billund, 60 km	135
Royal Porthcawl	W	19 7 6	Cardiff, 25 km	812
Royal Portrush	NIR	19 7 7	Belfast, 80 km	926/927
Royal St David's	W	18 6 5	Manchester, 120 km	813
Royal St George's	Eng	19 7 5	Gatwick, 145 km	627
Royal Troon	Sc	19 7 7	Glasgow, 50 km	772
Royal West Norfolk (Brancaster)	Eng	17 7 6	Stansted, 150 km	628
Royal Wimbledon	Eng	16 7 8	Heathrow, 40 km	629
Royal Winchester	Eng	15 6 8	Heathrow, 90 km	630
Royal Zoute	B	18 7 7	Brussel (Bruxelles), 108 km	111
Rudding Park	Eng	15 8 8	Leeds, 20 km	631
Rungsted	Da	17 7 7	København, 40	136
Rya	S	15 7 8	Malmö, 120 km	1251
Rye	Eng	18 6 6	London Gatwick, 60 km	632

S

Course	Country	Rating	Closest airport	Page
S. Lourenço	P	17 6 8	Faro, 12 km	1075
Sablé-Solesmes	F	16 7 4	Orly, 250 km	275
Saint Donat	F	16 7 8	Nice, 37 km	276
Saint-Cloud	F	14 8 7	Orly, 25 km	277
Saint-Endréol	F	15 7 4	Nice, 70 km	278
Saint-Germain	F	17 7 7	Orly, 30 km	279
Saint-Jean-de-Monts	F	16 6 5	Nantes, 68 km	280
Saint-Laurent	F	14 7 5	Lorient Lann-Bihoué, 40 km	281
Saint-Nom-la-Bretèche	F	17 8 8	Orly, 30 km	282/3
Saint-Thomas	F	14 7 5	Béziers-Vias, 15 km	284
Sainte-Baume (La)	F	14 7 6	Marseille-Marignane, 73 km	285
Sainte-Maxime	F	13 7 8	Toulon, 55 km	286
Salgados	P	13 6 6	Faro, 55 km	1076
Samsø	Da	15 4 7	Århus, 50 km	137
San Roque	E	17 8 8	Gibraltar, 15 km	1185
San Sebastián	E	14 6 6	Biarritz (France), 20 km	1186
Sand Moor	Eng	14 7 7	Leeds, 10 km	633
Sandiway	Eng	17 5 7	Manchester, 35 km	634
Sant Cugat	E	13 6 5	Barcelona, 35 km	1187
Santa Ponsa	E	13 6 7	Palma, 26 km	1188
Santo da Serra	P	16 7 5	Funchal, 6 km	1077
Sarfvik	Fi	16 8 7	Helsinki, 25 km	153
Sart-Tilman	B	16 7 7	Liège, 20 km	112
Saunton	Eng	18 7 6	Plymouth, 90 km	635
Savenay	F	14 5 4	Nantes-Atlantique, 40 km	287
Scharmützelsee	D	18 8 7	Berlin, 80 km	451
Schloss Braunfels	D	16 7 7	Frankfurt, 85 km	452
Schloss Ebreichsdorf	A	16 8 6	Wien, 15 km	87
Schloss Egmating	D	15 7 7	München, 55 km	453
Schloss Klingenburg	D	15 6 6	München, 150 km	454
Schloss Langenstein	D	16 8 7	Stuttgart, 150 km	455
Schloss Lüdersburg	D	15 7 6	Hamburg, 50 km	456
Schloss Myllendonk	D	16 7 7	Düsseldorf, 25 km	457
Schloss Nippenburg	D	17 8 6	Stuttgart, 35 km	458
Schloss Wilkendorf	D	17 7 5	Berlin, 50 km	459
Schönenberg	CH	14 7 6	Zürich-Kloten, 30 km	1290
Schwanhof	D	17 8 6	Nürnberg, 85 km	460
Scotscraig	Sc	16 6 6	Edinburgh, 95 km	773
Sct. Knuds	Da	14 5 6	Odense, 30 km	138
Seacroft	Eng	17 6 4	Humberside, 80 km	636
Seapoint	IRL	15 6 6	Dublin, 48 km	896
Seascale	Eng	18 5 4	Manchester, 200 km	637
Seaton Carew	Eng	17 7 5	Teesside, 20 km	638
Seddiner See	D	18 9 7	Berlin, 50 km	461
Seignosse	F	17 7 7	Biarritz-Parme, 39 km	288
Semlin am See	D	16 8 7	Berlin, 70 km	462
Sempachersee	Ch	16 8 7	Zürich, 120 km	1291
Senne	D	16 8 7	Paderborn, 43 km	463
Servanes	F	13 5 7	Marseille-Marignane, 57 km	289
Sevilla	E	17 7 8	Sevilla, 10 km	1189
Shanklin & Sandown	Eng	15 7 6	Southampton, 65 km	639
Shannon	IRL	13 6 6	Shannon, 1 km	897
Sherborne	Eng	15 6 7	Bristol, 45 km	640
Sheringham	Eng	15 7 6	Stansted, 120 km	641
Sherwood Forest	Eng	17 7 6	East Midlands, 40 km	642
Shiskine (Blackwaterfoot)	Sc	17 5 5	Glasgow	774
Silloth-on-Solway	Eng	18 7 4	Glasgow, 200 km	643
Simon's	Da	14 7 7	København, 40 km	139
Sint Nicolaasga	N	15 7 5	Amsterdam Schiphol, 120 km	1025
Skellefteå	S	14 6 5	Skellefteå, 10 km	1252
Skibo Castle (Carnegie Club)	Sc	15 9 7	Inverness, 76 km	706
Skövde	S	17 5 7	Jönköping, 90 km	1253
Slaley Hall	Eng	17 8 7	Newcastle, 35 km	644
Slieve Russell	IRL	15 8 6	Dublin, 128 km	898
Söderåsen	S	15 7 5	Malmö, 120 km	1254
Son Antem	E	16 8 8	Palma, 10 km	1190/1191
Son Muntaner	E	16 8 9	Palma, 15 km	1192
Son Vida	E	14 6 7	Palma, 15 km	1193
Sorknes	Nw	15 6 4	Oslo, 165 km	1044
Sotogrande	E	18 8 7	Málaga, 120 km	1194
Soufflenheim	F	16 7 4	Strasbourg, 50 km	290
Southerndown	W	16 7 7	Cardiff, 36 km	814
Southerness	Sc	18 6 5	Glasgow, 155 km	775
Southport & Ainsdale	Eng	17 7 7	Manchester, 80 km	645
Spa (Les Fagnes)	B	17 7 7	Liège, 25 km	113
Spérone	F	17 7 5	Figari, 27 km	291
Spiegelven	B	14 7 8	Maastricht, 25 km	114
St Andrews	Sc	18 8 8	Edinburgh, 80 km	776/779
St Enodoc	Eng	18 7 4	Plymouth, 80 km	646
St George's Hill	Eng	17 7 7	Heathrow, 28 km	647
St Helen's Bay	IRL	14 6 6	Dublin, 160 km	899
St Laurence	Fi	14 5 4	Helsinki, 70 km	154
St Margaret's	IRL	16 7 7	Dublin, 6 km	900
St Mellion	Eng	17 9 7	Plymouth, 16 km	648
St. Dionys	D	17 7 6	Hamburg, 60 km	464
St. Eurach	D	16 7 6	München, 70 km	465
St. Leon-Rot	D	16 9 7	Frankfurt, 100 km	466/67
Stavanger	Nw	16 6 7	Stavanger, 10 km	1045
Steiermärkischer Murhof	A	16 8 7	Graz, 20 km	88
Stenungsund	S	17 7 8	Göteborg, 65 km	1255
Stockholm	S	16 8 9	Stockholm, 33 km	1256
Stoke Poges	Eng	17 8 8	Heathrow, 24 km	649
Stolper Heide	D	16 7 5	Berlin, 10 km	468
Stoneham	Eng	15 7 8	Southampton, 4 km	650
Strasbourg Illkirch	F	13 7 6	Strasbourg, 12 km	292
Strathaven	Sc	15 7 6	Glasgow, 35 km	780
Stuttgarter Solitude	D	17 5 5	Stuttgart, 25 km	469
Sunningdale	Eng	18 8 8	Heathrow, 20 km	651/652
Swinley Forest	Eng	16 6 8	Heathrow, 20 km	653
Sybrook	N	15 6 6	Enschede Twente, 5 km	1026
Sylt	D	15 6 8	Westerland, 5 km	470

T U

Course	Country	Rating	Closest airport	Page
Täby	S	16 7 7	Stockholm, 30 km	1257
Tain	Sc	17 6 6	Inverness, 65 km	781
Talma	Fi	14 8 6	Helsinki,	155
Tandridge	Eng	14 7 6	Gatwick, 18 km	654
TAT Golf Belek	T	14 7 7	Antalya, 35 km	1306
Taulane	F	15 7 4	Nice, 75 km	293
Tawast	Fi	14 7 5	156	
Taymouth Castle	Sc	13 4 6	Edinburgh, 125 km	782
Tegernseer Bad Wiessee	D	14 7 8	München, 85 km	471
Tenby	W	18 7 6	Cardiff, 75 km	815
The Belfry	Eng	16 9 8	Birmingham, 15 km	655/656
The Island	IRL	15 7 7	Dublin, 8 km	901
Thetford	Eng	14 7 5	Stansted, 90 km	657
Thorndon Park	Eng	14 7 6	Stansted, 37 km	658
Thornhill	Sc	15 6 5	Edinburgh, Glasgow, 109 km	783
Thorpeness	Eng	14 7 7	Stansted, 145 km	659
Thurlestone	Eng	16 6 4	Plymouth, 50 km	660
Torekov	S	14 7 7	Halmstad, 30 km	1258
Torino - La Mandria	I	16 8 7	Torino, 7 km	988
Torremirona	E	13 7 7	Barcelona, 150 km	1195
Torrequebrada	E	14 7 7	Málaga, 15 km	1196
Toulouse Palmola	F	15 7 4	Toulouse-Blagnac, 40 km	294

Toulouse-Seilh	F	15 7 6	Toulouse-Blagnac, 8 km	295
Touquet (Le)	F	16 6 7	Lille-Lesquin, 151 km	296
Toxandria	N	14 7 6	Eindhoven, 40 km	1027
Tralee	IRL	18 7 6	Cork, 120 km	902
Tramore	IRL	13 7 6	Cork, 120 km	903
Tranås	S	14 6 7	Jönköping, 85 km	1259
Treudelberg	D	13 8 7	Hamburg, 6 km	472
Trevose	Eng	17 7 7	Plymouth, 80 km	661
Troia	P	16 6 5	Lisboa, 42 km	1078
Tulfarris	IRL	15 7 6	Dublin, 50 km	904
Tullamore	IRL	15 6 5	Dublin, 96 km	905
Turnberry	Sc	19 9 8	Glasgow, 80 km	784
Tutzing	D	15 7 6	München, 80 km	473
Twente	N	15 7 6	Enschede Twente, 15 km	1028
Tyrifjord	Nw	14 6 6	Oslo, 45 km	1046
Ullna	S	17 8 6	Stockholm, 40 km	1260
Ulzama	E	16 6 6	Pamplona, 28 km	1197
Upsala	S	13 6 6	Stockholm, 30 km	1261
Urslautal	A	15 7 7	Salzburg, 55 km	89

V

Val de Sorne	F	14 7 5	Lyon-Satolas, 134 km	297
Val Queven	F	15 6 5	Lorient Lann-Bihoué, 3 km	298
Valderrama	E	19 8 6	Málaga, 120 km	1198
Vale da Pinta	P	14 6 6	Faro, 42 km	1079
Vale do Lobo	P	15 6 7	Faro, 18 km	1080
Vale of Glamorgan	W	16 8 7	Cardiff, 30 km	816
Varese	I	14 8 7	Milano, 25 km	989
Värnamo	S	15 7 5	Jönköping, 70 km	1262
Vasatorp	S	16 7 7	Malmö, 85 km	1263
Vaucouleurs (La)	F	15 7 4	Orly, 71 km	299
Växjö	S	15 6 7	Växjö, 8 km	1264
Vejle	Da	15 7 7	Billund, 40 km	140
Venezia	I	16 7 9	Venezia, 13 km	990
Verona	I	13 7 8	Verona, 5 km	991
Vidauban (Prince de Provence)	F	19 8 7	Nice, 100 km	267
Vila Sol	P	14 7 7	Faro, 22 km	1081
Vilamoura	P	16 7 7	Faro, 22 km	1082/1083/1084
Villa D'Este	I	16 9 8	Milano, 37 km	992
Villamartin	E	16 7 6	Alicante, 50 km	1199
Villette d'Anthon	F	17 7 5	Lyon-Saint Exupéry, 12 km	300
Visby	S	16 7 5	Visby, 30 km	1265
Volcans (Les)	F	14 6 5	Clermont-Ferrand, 19 km	301

W-Z

Walddörfer	D	16 7 6	Hamburg, 20 km	474
Wallasey	Eng	17 7 7	Liverpool, 35 km	662
Walton Heath	Eng	18 7 7	Gatwick, 15 km	663/664
Wantzenau (La)	F	16 6 6	Strasbourg, 27 km	302
Warrenpoint	NIR	13 6 5	Belfast, 75 km	928
Warwickshire (The)	Eng	15 7 8	Birmingham, 30 km	665
Wasserburg Anholt	D	15 7 7	Düsseldorf, 80 km	475
Waterford	IRL	14 6 6	Cork, 130 km Dublin, 170 km	906
Waterford Castle	IRL	14 5 6	Cork, 130 km Dublin, 170 km	907
Waterloo	B	16 8 7	Bruxelles, 20 km	115/116
Waterville	IRL	17 6 7	Cork, 150 km	908
Wendlohe	D	16 7 6	Hamburg, 10 km	476
Wentworth	Eng	18 8 7	Heathrow, 20 km	666/667
West Berkshire	Eng	15 7 7	Heathrow, 80 km	668
West Byfleet	Eng	14 6 8	Heathrow, 20 km	669
West Cornwall	Eng	16 7 6	Plymouth, 120 km	670
Westfälischer GC (Gütersloh)	D	17 7 7	Paderborn, 30 km	412
West Hill	Eng	16 6 6	Heathrow, 44 km	671
West Kilbride	Sc	16 7 5	Glasgow, 50 km	786
West Lancashire	Eng	17 7 7	Manchester, 80 km	672
West Surrey	Eng	15 7 7	Gatwick, 15 km	673
West Sussex	Eng	18 7 6	Gatwick, 40 km	674
Western Gailes	Sc	17 5 7	Glasgow, 50 km	787
Westerwood	Sc	14 8 6	Glasgow, 32 km	788
Weston-Super-Mare	Eng	16 6 7	Bristol, 25 km	675
Westport	IRL	15 7 7	Knock, 50 km	909
Westward Ho! Royal North Devon	Eng	18 6 6	Plymouth, 90 km	626
Wheatley	Eng	14 6 6	Leeds Bradford, 40 km	676
Whitekirk	Sc	15 7 7	Edinburgh, 50 km	789
Whittington Heath	Eng	17 6 7	Birmingham, 20 km	677
Wilmslow	Eng	16 7 6	Manchester, 6 km	678
Wimereux	F	14 4 5	Lille-Lesquin, 143 km	303
Wittelsbacher	D	17 7 6	München, 80 km	477
Woburn	Eng	17 7 7	Heathrow, 70 km	679/680
Woking	Eng	16 6 6	Heathrow, 38 km	681
Woodbridge	Eng	14 7 7	Stansted, 120 km	682
Woodbrook	IRL	15 7 6	Dublin, 30 km	910
Woodbury Park	Eng	15 9 6	Exeter, 10 km	683
Woodenbridge	IRL	16 7 6	Dublin, 88 km	911
Woodhall Spa	Eng	18 7 8	Humberside, 70 km	684
Worplesdon	Eng	16 7 6	Heathrow, 39 km	685
Wouwse Plantage	N	15 7 6	Eindhoven, 70 km	1029
Wylihof	CH	13 6 6	Zurich-Kloten, 110 km	1292
Zaudin	E	16 7 6	Sevilla, 15 km	1200
Zell am See Kaprun	A	16 7 6	Salzburg, 100 km	90
Zuid Limburgse	N	14 7 8	Maastricht, 25 km	1030
Zumikon	CH	15 7 6	Zurich-Kloten, 30 km	1293

EXCHANGE CROSS RATES
TABLEAU DE CHANGE DES MONNAIES
TABELLE FÜR DIE WÄHRUNGSUMRECHNUNG

	BF	DKr	F	DM	IR£	L	Fl
Belgium (BF)	**100**	18.44	16.26	4.848	1.952	4800	5.483
Denmark (DKr)	54.24	**10**	8.820	2.630	1.059	2604	2.963
France (F)	61.50	11.34	**10**	2.982	1.201	2952	3.360
Germany (DM)	20.63	3.803	3.354	**1**	0.403	990.0	1.127
Ireland (IR£)	51.22	9.443	8.329	2.483	**1**	2459	2.798
Italy (L)	2.083	0.384	0.339	0.101	0.041	**100**	0.114
Netherlands (Fl)	18.31	3.375	2.977	0.888	0.357	878.6	**1**
Norway (NKr)	50.77	9.359	8.255	2.461	0.991	2437	2.773
Portugal (Esc)	20.12	3.710	3.272	0.976	0.393	965.8	1.099
Spain (Pts)	24.24	4.470	3.942	1.175	0.473	1164	1.324
Sweden (SKr)	42.43	7.823	6.900	2.057	0.828	2037	2.318
Switzerland (CHF)	27.19	5.013	4.422	1.318	0.531	1305	1.485
Un. Kingdom (£)	64.55	11.90	10.50	3.130	1.260	3099	3.527
Canada (C$)	28.56	5.265	4.644	1.385	0.558	1371	1.560
United States ($)	44.73	8.246	7.273	2.169	0.873	2147	2.443
Japan (¥)	36.86	6.795	5.093	1.787	0.720	1769	2.013
Euro (€)	40.34	7.437	6.560	1.956	0.788	1936	2.204

Danish Kroner, French Franc, Norwegian Kroner and Swedish Kroner x 10.
Belgian Franc, Yen, Escudo, Lira and Peseta x 100.

Source: Financial Times, October 12, 2001

TABELL FOR VAXELOMRAKNING
CAMBIO DE DIVISAS
CAMBIO VALUTA

NKr	Esc	Pts	SKr	CHF	£	C$	$	¥	€
19.70	497.0	412.5	23.57	3.678	1.549	3.502	2.236	271.3	2.479
10.68	269.5	223.7	12.78	1.995	0.840	1.899	1.213	147.2	1.345
12.11	305.6	253.7	14.49	2.262	0.953	2.154	1.375	166.9	1.525
4.063	102.5	85.07	4.861	0.759	0.320	0.722	0.461	55.96	0.511
10.09	254.6	211.3	12.07	1.884	0.793	1.794	1.145	139.80	1.270
0.410	10.35	8.593	0.491	0.077	0.032	0.073	0.047	5.653	0.052
3.606	90.97	75.50	4.314	0.673	0.284	0.641	0.409	49.67	0.454
10	252.3	209.4	11.96	1.867	0.786	1.778	1.135	137.7	1.258
3.964	**100**	82.99	4.742	0.740	0.312	0.705	0.450	54.59	0.499
4.776	120.5	**100**	5.714	0.892	0.376	0.849	0.542	65.78	0.601
8.358	210.9	175.0	**10**	1.560	0.657	1.1486	0.949	115.1	1.052
5.357	135.1	112.2	6.409	**1**	0.421	0.952	0.608	73.78	0.674
12.72	320.8	266.3	15.22	2.374	**1**	2.261	1.4430	175.2	1.600
5.625	141.9	117.8	6.730	1.050	0.442	**1**	0.638	77.48	0.708
6.811	222.3	184.5	10.54	1.645	0.693	1.568	**1**	121.4	1.109
7.260	183.2	152.0	8.685	1.355	0.571	1.291	0.824	**100**	0.914
7.946	200.5	166.4	9.507	1.484	0.625	1.413	0.902	109.5	**1**

AUSTRIA	1 € = 13,7603 ÖS	1 ÖS = 0,0726 €
FINLAND	1 € = 5,9457 FIM	1 FIM = 0,1682 €
LUXEMBURG	1 € = 40,3399 FLUX	1 FLUX = 0,0248 €

Industrie Graphique

Picture acknowledgments

D.R. Gut Altentann P.75

Play Golf P.91

D.R. Rungsted P.119

Seppo Konstig P.141

Les Bordes P.157

Wolfgang Scheffler P.351

Brian Morgan P.510/478

Jean-François Lefevre P687/478

Brian Morgan P790/478

Jean-François Lefevre P.817

Giorgio Gatti P.929

Haagsche D.R. P.119

Mårten Niléhn P 993

Jean-François Lefevre P.1047

Jean-François Lefevre P.1085

Mårten Niléhn P.1201

Golf Events. P.1267

Wolfgang Scheffler P. 1295

© Editions D & G MOTTE
281, route de Lavaux
Case Postale 288 - CH 1095 Lutry
Email : info@peugeotgolfguide.org

Despite every effort, a number of errors may have crept in here and there when entering our information; we apologize for any such errata and will be glad to hear from you in order to eliminate them from the next edition.

En dépit de nos efforts, certaines erreurs ont pu se glisser dans la saisie des informations recueillies. Nous prions nos lecteurs de nous en excuser et de nous en informer, afin de pouvoir les rectifier dans la prochaine édition.

General coordination for inspection teams: Denys LEMERY
Data base design & layout: François GARRY

Impression ACTIS Industrie Graphique